The Sporting News

BASEBALL REGISTER

1999 EDITION

Editors/Baseball Register
MARK BONAVITA
BRENDAN ROBERTS

Contributing Editor/Baseball Register
JOHN DUXBURY

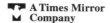

Efrem Zimbalist III, President and Chief Executive Officer, Times Mirror Magazines; **James H. Nuckols,** President, The Sporting News; **Francis X. Farrell,** Senior Vice President, Publisher; **John D. Rawlings,** Senior Vice President, Editorial Director; **John Kastberg,** Vice President, General Manager; **Kathy Kinkeade,** Vice President, Operations; **Steve Meyerhoff,** Executive Editor; **Joe Hoppel,** Senior Editor; **Ron Smith,** Senior Editor; **Craig Carter,** Statistical Editor; **Marilyn Kasal,** Production Director; **Terry Shea,** Database Analyst; **Michael Bruner,** Prepress Director; **Michael Behrens,** Art Director, Special Projects; **Christen Webster,** Macintosh Production Artist; **David Polmer and David Walton,** Editorial Assistants.

A Times Mirror
Company

Major league and minor league statistics compiled by STATS, Inc., Skokie, Ill.

Copyright ©1999 by The Sporting News, a division of Times Mirror Magazines, Inc., 10176 Corporate Square Drive, Suite 200, St. Louis, MO 63132-2924. All rights reserved. Printed in the U.S.A.

ISBN: 0-89204-605-8

10 9 8 7 6 5 4 3 2 1

CONTENTS

Players **4**

This section includes players who appeared in at least one major league game in 1998, other players who were listed on a 40-man major league roster as of January 20, 1999, and some top prospects.

Major league managers **629**

Hall of Fame additions **658**

This section includes the playing records of 1999 Hall of Fame inductees George Brett, Nolan Ryan and Robin Yount.

1998 major league statistical leaders **662**

EXPLANATION OF FOOTNOTES AND ABBREVIATIONS

Note for statistical comparisons: Player strikes forced the cancellation of games in the 1972 season (10 days missed), the 1981 season (50 days missed), the 1994 season (52 days missed) and the 1995 season (18 games missed).

Positions are listed in descending order of games played; because of limited space, pinch-hitter and pinch-runner are listed in the regular-season section only if a player did not play a defensive position.

*   Led league. For fielding statistics, the player led the league at the position shown.

•   Tied for league lead. For fielding statistics, the player tied for the league lead at the position shown.

†   Led league, but number indicated is total figure for two or more positions. Actual league-leading figure for a position is mentioned in "Statistical Notes" section.

‡   Tied for league lead, but number indicated is total figure for two or more positions. Actual league-tying figure for a position is mentioned in "Statistical Notes" section.

§   Led or tied for league lead, but total figure is divided between two different teams. Actual league-leading or league-tying figure is mentioned in "Statistical Notes" section.

■   Indicates a player's movement from one major league organization to another major league organization or to an independent minor league organization.

. . .   Statistic unavailable, inapplicable, unofficial or mathematically impossible to calculate.

—   Manager statistic inapplicable.

LEAGUES: A.A., Am. Assoc.—American Association. **A.L.**—American. **App., Appal.**—Appalachian. **Ar., Ariz.**—Arizona. **Cal., Calif.**—California. **Car., Caro.**—Carolina. **CRL**—Cocoa Rookie. **DSL**—Dominican Summer. **East.**—Eastern. **Evan.**—Evangeline. **Fla. St., Florida St.,** **FSL**—Florida State. **GCL**—Gulf Coast. **GSL**—Gulf States. **In.-Am.**—Inter-American. **Int'l.**—International. **J.P., Jap. Pac., Jp. Pac.**—Japan Pacific. **Jp. Cen., Jp. Cn.**—Japan Central. **Mex.**—Mexican. **Mex. Cen.**—Mexican Center. **Mid., Midw.**—Midwest. **Miss.-O.V.**—Mississippi-Ohio Valley. **N.C. St.**—North Carolina State. **N.L.**—National. **North.**—Northern. **N'west**—Northwest. **NYP, NY-Penn**—New York-Pennsylvania. **Pac. Coast, PCL**—Pacific Coast. **Pio.**—Pioneer. **S. Atl., SAL**—South Atlantic. **Soph.**—Sophomore. **Sou., South.**—Southern. **Taiw.**—Taiwan. **Tex.**—Texas. **W. Car., W. Caro.**—Western Carolinas.

TEAMS: Aguas.—Aguascalientes. **Alb./Colon.**—Albany/Colonie. **Ariz.**—Arizona. **Ariz. D-backs**—Arizona League Diamondbacks. **Belling.**—Bellingham. **Birm.**—Birmingham. **Brevard Co.**—Brevard County. **Cant./Akr.**—Canton/Akron. **Ced. Rap.**—Cedar Rapids. **Cent. Ore.**—Central Oregon. **Central Vall.**—Central Valley. **Char., Charl.**—Charleston. **Chatt.**—Chattanooga. **Chiba Lot.**—Chiba Lotte. **Ciu. Juarez**—Ciudad Juarez. **Colo. Spr., Colo. Springs**—Colorado Springs. **Day. Beach.**—Daytona Beach. **Dm., Dom.**—Dominican. **Dom. B. Jays**—Dominican Blue Jays. **Elizabeth.**—Elizabethton. **Estadio Quis.**—Estadio Quisqueya. **Eve.**—Everett. **Fort Lauder.**—Fort Lauderdale. **Fukuoka**—Fukuoka Daiei. **GC**—Gulf Coast. **GC Astros-Or.**—Gulf Coast Astros-Orange. **GC Royals-Bl.**—Gulf Coast Royals-Blue. **GC Whi. Sox**—Gulf Coast White Sox. **Grays Har.**—Grays Harbor. **Greens.**—Greensboro. **Greenw.**—Greenwood. **Guana.**—Guanajuato. **H.P.-Thomas.**—High Point-Thomasville. **Hunting.**—Huntington. **Jacksonv.**—Jacksonville. **Johns. City**—Johnson City. **Kane Co.**—Kane County. **Lake Charl.**—Lake Charles. **Matt.**—Mattoon. **M.C., Mex. City**—Mexico City. **Med. Hat**—Medicine Hat. **Monc.**—Monclova. **Niag. F., Niag. Falls**—Niagara Falls. **Okla. City**—Oklahoma City. **Pan. City**—Panama City. **Phoe.**—Phoenix. **Pomp. Beach**—Pompano Beach. **Pres. Lions**—President Lions. **Prin. Will., Prin. William**—Prince William. **Ral./Dur.**—Raleigh/Durham. **Rancho Cuca.**—Rancho Cucamonga. **Rocky Mount.**—Rocky Mountain. **Salt.**—Saltillo. **San. Dom., San. Domingo**—Santo Domingo. **San Bern.**—San Bernardino. **San Fran.**—San Francisco. **Schen.**—Schenectady. **Scran./W.B.**—Scranton/Wilkes-Barre. **S.C.**—South Carolina. **S.F. de Mac.**—San Francisco de Macoris. **San Luis Pot.**—San Luis Potosi. **S. Oregon**—Southern Oregon. **Spartan.**—Spartanburg. **St. Cath., St. Cathar.**—St. Catharines. **St. Peters.**—St. Petersburg. **States.**—Statesville. **Stock.**—Stockton. **T.-C.**—Tri-Cities. **Vanc.**—Vancouver. **Vent. Co.**—Ventura County. **W. Mich.**—West Michigan. **Win.-Salem, Winst.-Salem**—Winston-Salem. **Wis. Rap., Wis. Rapids**—Wisconsin Rapids. **W.P. Beach**—West Palm Beach. **W.Va.**—West Virginia. **Yuc.**—Yucatan.

STATISTICS: A—assists. **AB**—at-bats. **Avg.**—average. **BB**—bases on balls. **CG**—complete games. **E**—errors. **ER**—earned runs. **ERA**—earned-run average. **G**—games. **GIDP**—grounded into double plays. **GS**—games started. **H**—hits. **HR**—home runs. **IP**—innings pitched. **L**—losses. **Pct.**—winning percentage. **PO**—putouts. **Pos.**—position. **R**—runs. **RBI**—runs batted in. **SB**—stolen bases. **ShO**—shutouts. **SO**—strikeouts. **Sv.**—saves. **W**—wins. **2B**—doubles. **3B**—triples.

PLAYERS

ABBOTT, JEFF — OF — WHITE SOX

PERSONAL: Born August 17, 1972, in Atlanta. ... 6-2/190. ... Bats right, throws left. ... Full name: Jeffrey William Abbott.
HIGH SCHOOL: Dunwoody (Ga.).
COLLEGE: Kentucky.
TRANSACTIONS/CAREER NOTES: Selected by Chicago White Sox organization in 32nd round of free-agent draft (June 3, 1993); did not sign. ... Selected by White Sox organization in fourth round of free-agent draft (June 2, 1994).

Year Team (League)	Pos.	G	AB	R	H	2B	3B	HR	RBI	Avg.	BB	SO	SB	PO	A	E	Avg.
1994—Sarasota (Gulf Coast).	OF	4	15	4	7	1	0	1	3	.467	4	0	2	4	0	0	1.000
—Hickory (S. Atl.)	OF	63	224	47	88	16	6	6	48	.393	38	33	2	106	0	2	.981
1995—Prince Will. (Car.)	OF	70	264	41	92	16	0	4	47	.348	26	25	7	88	3	4	.958
—Birmingham (Sou.)	OF	55	197	25	63	11	1	3	28	.320	19	20	1	55	1	2	.966
1996—Nashville (A.A.)	OF	113	440	64	143	27	1	14	60	.325	32	50	12	186	5	2	.990
1997—Nashville (A.A.)	OF	118	465	*88	152	35	3	11	63	.327	41	52	12	237	6	0	*1.000
—Chicago (A.L.)	OF-DH	19	38	8	10	1	0	1	2	.263	0	6	0	15	0	0	1.000
1998—Chicago (A.L.)	OF-DH	89	244	33	68	14	1	12	41	.279	9	28	3	132	0	4	.971
Major league totals (2 years)		108	282	41	78	15	1	13	43	.277	9	34	3	147	0	4	.974

ABBOTT, JIM — P

PERSONAL: Born September 19, 1967, in Flint, Mich. ... 6-3/210. ... Throws left, bats left. ... Full name: James Anthony Abbott.
HIGH SCHOOL: Flint (Mich.) Central.
COLLEGE: Michigan.
TRANSACTIONS/CAREER NOTES: Selected by Toronto Blue Jays organization in 36th round of free-agent draft (June 3, 1985); did not sign. ... Selected by California Angels organization in first round (eighth pick overall) of free-agent draft (June 1, 1988). ... On disabled list (July 12-August 8, 1992). ... Traded to New York Yankees for 1B J.T. Snow, P Jerry Nielsen and P Russ Springer (December 6, 1992). ... On disabled list (June 10-25, 1993). ... Granted free agency (December 23, 1994). ... Signed by Chicago White Sox (April 8, 1995). ... Traded by White Sox with P Tim Fortugno to Angels for P Andrew Lorraine, P Bill Simas, P John Snyder and OF McKay Christensen (July 27, 1995). ... Granted free agency (October 31, 1995). ... Re-signed by Angels (January 9, 1996). ... Released by Angels (March 31, 1997). ... Signed by White Sox organization (May 27, 1998). ... Granted free agency (November 5, 1998).
HONORS: Named Golden Spikes Award winner by USA Baseball (1987). ... Named lefthanded pitcher on THE SPORTING NEWS college All-America team (1988). ... Named lefthanded pitcher on THE SPORTING NEWS A.L. All-Star team (1991).
STATISTICAL NOTES: Tied for A.L. lead with four balks in 1991. ... Pitched 4-0 no-hit victory against Cleveland (September 4, 1993).
MISCELLANEOUS: Member of 1988 U.S. Olympic baseball team.

Year Team (League)	W	L	Pct.	ERA	G	GS	CG	ShO	Sv.	IP	H	R	ER	BB	SO
1989—California (A.L.)	12	12	.500	3.92	29	29	4	2	0	181 1/3	190	95	79	74	115
1990—California (A.L.)	10	14	.417	4.51	33	33	4	1	0	211 2/3	*246	116	106	72	105
1991—California (A.L.)	18	11	.621	2.89	34	34	5	1	0	243	222	85	78	73	158
1992—California (A.L.)	7	15	.318	2.77	29	29	7	0	0	211	208	73	65	68	130
1993—New York (A.L.)■	11	14	.440	4.37	32	32	4	1	0	214	221	115	104	73	95
1994—New York (A.L.)	9	8	.529	4.55	24	24	2	0	0	160 1/3	167	88	81	64	90
1995—Chicago (A.L.)■	6	4	.600	3.36	17	17	3	0	0	112 1/3	116	50	42	35	45
—California (A.L.)■	5	4	.556	4.15	13	13	1	1	0	84 2/3	93	43	39	29	41
1996—California (A.L.)	2	*18	.100	7.48	27	23	1	0	0	142	171	128	118	78	58
—Vancouver (PCL)	0	2	.000	3.41	4	4	1	0	0	29	16	12	11	20	20
1997—						Out of organized baseball.									
1998—Hickory (S. Atl.)■	0	0	...	2.25	1	1	0	0	0	4	3	1	1	2	2
—Win.-Salem (Car.)	2	1	.667	5.40	4	4	0	0	0	21 2/3	17	13	13	7	13
—Birmingham (Southern)	2	3	.400	5.40	8	8	0	0	0	41 2/3	53	33	25	21	35
—Calgary (PCL)	2	2	.500	2.61	5	5	1	0	0	31	31	9	9	9	20
—Chicago (A.L.)	5	0	1.000	4.55	5	5	0	0	0	31 2/3	35	16	16	12	14
Major league totals (9 years)	85	100	.459	4.12	243	239	31	6	0	1592	1669	809	728	578	851

ABBOTT, KURT — IF — ROCKIES

PERSONAL: Born June 2, 1969, in Zanesville, Ohio. ... 6-0/198. ... Bats right, throws right. ... Full name: Kurt Thomas Abbott.
HIGH SCHOOL: Dixie Hollins (St. Petersburg, Fla.).
JUNIOR COLLEGE: St. Petersburg (Fla.) Junior College.
TRANSACTIONS/CAREER NOTES: Selected by Oakland Athletics organization in 15th round of free-agent draft (June 5, 1989). ... On Modesto disabled list (May 26-June 6, 1991). ... Traded by A's to Florida Marlins for OF Kerwin Moore (December 20, 1993). ... On Florida disabled list (April 19-May 6, 1995); included rehabilitation assignment to Charlotte (April 30-May 6). ... On Florida disabled list (May 6-21, 1996); included rehabilitation assignment to Charlotte (May 16-20). ... Traded by Marlins to A's for P Eric Ludwick (December 19, 1997). ... On Oakland disabled list (March 22-April 16, 1998); included rehabilitation assignment to Edmonton (April 7-16). ... Traded by A's to Colorado Rockies for a player to be named later and cash (June 9, 1998); A's acquired P Ara Petrosian to complete deal (June 16, 1998).
STATISTICAL NOTES: Led Arizona League shortstops with .922 fielding percentage in 1989. ... Led Southern League shortstops with 87 double plays in 1992. ... Career major league grand slams: 3.
MISCELLANEOUS: Holds Florida Marlins all-time record for most triples (19).

Year Team (League)	Pos.	G	AB	R	H	2B	3B	HR	RBI	Avg.	BB	SO	SB	PO	A	E	Avg.
1989—Arizona A's (Ariz.)	SS-2B-3B	36	155	27	42	5	3	0	25	.271	8	40	0	59	90	10	†.937
—S. Oregon (N'west)	SS	5	10	2	1	0	0	0	1	.100	0	3	1	6	7	1	.929
1990—Madison (Midwest)	SS-2B-3B	104	362	38	84	18	0	0	28	.232	47	74	21	180	268	40	.918
1991—Modesto (California)	SS	58	216	36	55	8	2	3	25	.255	29	55	6	78	130	9	.959
—Huntsville (Sou.)	SS	53	182	18	46	6	1	0	11	.253	17	39	6	89	164	13	.951

Year Team (League)	Pos.	G	AB	R	H	2B	3B	HR	RBI	Avg.	BB	SO	SB	PO	A	E	Avg.
						BATTING									**FIELDING**		
1992— Huntsville (Sou.)	SS	124	452	64	115	14	5	9	52	.254	31	75	16	196	342	29	*.949
— Tacoma (PCL)	SS	11	39	2	6	1	0	0	1	.154	4	9	1	21	32	4	.930
1993— Tacoma (PCL)	SS	133	480	75	153	36	11	12	79	.319	33	123	19	*210	367	30	.951
— Oakland (A.L.)	OF-SS-2B	20	61	11	15	1	0	3	9	.246	3	20	2	36	13	2	.961
1994— Florida (N.L.)■	SS	101	345	41	86	17	3	9	33	.249	16	98	3	162	260	15	.966
1995— Charlotte (Int'l)	SS	5	18	3	5	0	0	1	3	.278	1	3	1	5	15	2	.909
— Florida (N.L.)	SS	120	420	60	107	18	7	17	60	.255	36	110	4	149	290	19	.959
1996— Florida (N.L.)	SS-3B-2B	109	320	37	81	18	7	8	33	.253	22	99	3	123	205	12	.965
— Charlotte (Int'l)	SS-2B-3B	18	69	20	26	10	1	5	11	.377	7	18	2	31	60	2	.978
1997— Florida (N.L.) 2-O-S-3-DH		94	252	35	69	18	2	6	30	.274	14	68	3	126	136	8	.970
1998— Edmonton (PCL)■ ...	SS	7	25	5	10	2	0	2	4	.400	6	8	0	9	13	4	.846
— Oakland (A.L.) ...	S-O-DH-3	35	123	17	33	7	1	2	9	.268	10	34	2	46	70	11	.913
— Colorado (N.L.)■ O-2-S-3-DH		42	71	9	18	6	0	3	15	.254	2	19	0	32	24	1	.982
American League totals (2 years)		55	184	28	48	8	1	5	18	.261	13	54	4	82	83	13	.927
National League totals (5 years)		466	1408	182	361	77	19	43	171	.256	90	394	13	592	915	55	.965
Major league totals (6 years)		521	1592	210	409	85	20	48	189	.257	103	448	17	674	998	68	.961

DIVISION SERIES RECORD

Year Team (League)	Pos.	G	AB	R	H	2B	3B	HR	RBI	Avg.	BB	SO	SB	PO	A	E	Avg.
						BATTING									**FIELDING**		
1997— Florida (N.L.)	2B-PH	3	8	0	2	0	0	0	0	.250	0	0	0	3	6	0	1.000

CHAMPIONSHIP SERIES RECORD

Year Team (League)	Pos.	G	AB	R	H	2B	3B	HR	RBI	Avg.	BB	SO	SB	PO	A	E	Avg.
						BATTING									**FIELDING**		
1997— Florida (N.L.)	2B	2	8	0	3	1	0	0	0	.375	0	2	0	4	1	0	1.000

NOTES: Member of World Series championship team (1997).

WORLD SERIES RECORD

Year Team (League)	Pos.	G	AB	R	H	2B	3B	HR	RBI	Avg.	BB	SO	SB	PO	A	E	Avg.
						BATTING									**FIELDING**		
1997— Florida (N.L.)	DH-PH	3	3	0	0	0	0	0	0	.000	0	1	0	...	...	...	

ABBOTT, PAUL P

PERSONAL: Born September 15, 1967, in Van Nuys, Calif. ... 6-3/194. ... Throws right, bats right. ... Full name: Paul David Abbott.
HIGH SCHOOL: Sunny Hills (Fullerton, Calif.).
TRANSACTIONS/CAREER NOTES: Selected by Minnesota Twins organization in third round of free-agent draft (June 3, 1985). ... On Minnesota disabled list (March 28-June 5 and August 14-September 1, 1992). ... Released by Twins (March 2, 1993). ... Signed by Charlotte, Cleveland Indians organization (March 27, 1993). ... On Charlotte disabled list (April 8-May 6, 1993). ... Granted free agency (October 15, 1993). ... Signed by Omaha, Kansas City Royals organization (November 21, 1993). ... On disabled list (March 18-May 25 and June 16-30, 1994). ... Released by Omaha (June 30, 1994). ... Signed by Iowa, Chicago Cubs organization (March 17, 1995). ... Granted free agency (October 16, 1995). ... Signed by San Diego Padres organization (November 29, 1995). ... Granted free agency (October 15, 1996). ... Signed by Seattle Mariners organization (January 10, 1997). ... On Tacoma disabled list (May 23-July 14, 1997). ... On Orlando disabled list (April 2-August 21, 1998); included rehabilitation assignment to Arizona League Mariners (August 19-21). ... Released by Mariners (December 14, 1998).
STATISTICAL NOTES: Pitched 3-0 no-hit victory against Palm Springs (June 26, 1988, seven innings).

Year Team (League)	W	L	Pct.	ERA	G	GS	CG	ShO	Sv.	IP	H	R	ER	BB	SO
1985— Elizabethton (Appal.)	1	5	.167	6.94	10	10	1	0	0	35	33	32	27	32	34
1986— Kenosha (Midwest)	6	10	.375	4.50	25	15	1	0	0	98	102	62	49	73	73
1987— Kenosha (Midwest)	13	6	.684	3.65	26	25	1	0	0	145 1/3	102	76	59	103	138
1988— Visalia (California)	11	9	.550	4.18	28	•28	4	2	0	172 1/3	141	95	80	*143	*205
1989— Orlando (South.)	9	3	.750	4.37	17	17	1	0	0	90 2/3	71	48	44	48	102
1990— Portland (PCL)	5	14	.263	4.56	23	23	4	1	0	128 1/3	110	75	65	82	129
— Minnesota (A.L.)	0	5	.000	5.97	7	7	0	0	0	34 2/3	37	24	23	28	25
1991— Portland (PCL)	2	3	.400	3.89	8	8	1	1	0	44	36	19	19	28	40
— Minnesota (A.L.)	3	1	.750	4.75	15	3	0	0	0	47 1/3	38	27	25	36	43
1992— Portland (PCL)	4	1	.800	2.33	7	7	0	0	0	46 1/3	30	13	12	31	46
— Minnesota (A.L.)	0	0	...	3.27	6	0	0	0	0	11	12	4	4	5	13
1993— Cant./Akr. (Eastern)■	4	5	.444	4.06	13	12	1	0	0	75 1/3	72	34	34	28	86
— Cleveland (A.L.)	0	1	.000	6.38	5	5	0	0	0	18 1/3	19	15	13	11	7
— Charlotte (Int'l)	0	1	.000	6.63	4	4	0	0	0	19	25	16	14	7	12
1994— Omaha (Am. Assoc.)■	4	1	.800	4.87	15	10	0	0	0	57 1/3	57	32	31	45	48
1995— Iowa (Am. Assoc.)■	7	7	.500	3.67	46	11	0	0	0	115 1/3	104	50	47	64	*127
1996— Las Vegas (PCL)■	4	2	.667	4.18	28	0	0	0	7	28	27	14	13	12	37
1997— Tacoma (PCL)■	8	4	.667	4.13	17	14	3	0	0	93 2/3	80	48	43	29	117
— Ariz. Mariners (Ariz.)	0	0	...	0.93	3	3	0	0	0	9 2/3	0	2	1	7	13
1998— Ariz. Mariners (Ariz.)	0	0	...	0.00	1	0	0	0	0	3	1	0	0	1	6
— Tacoma (PCL)	1	0	1.000	1.20	3	3	0	0	0	15	9	2	2	5	20
— Seattle (A.L.)	3	1	.750	4.01	4	4	0	0	0	24 2/3	24	11	11	10	22
Major league totals (5 years)	6	8	.429	5.03	37	19	0	0	0	136	130	81	76	90	110

ABREU, BOB OF PHILLIES

PERSONAL: Born March 11, 1974, in Aragua, Venezuela. ... 6-0/186. ... Bats left, throws right. ... Full name: Bob Kelly Abreu. ... Name pronounced uh-BRAY-yew.
TRANSACTIONS/CAREER NOTES: Signed as non-drafted free agent by Houston Astros organization (August 21, 1990). ... On Houston disabled list (May 25-July 1, 1997); included rehabilitation assignments to Jackson (June 23-26) and New Orleans (June 27-July 1). ... Selected by Tampa Bay Devil Rays in first round (sixth pick overall) of expansion draft (November 18, 1997). ... Traded by Devil Rays to Philadelphia Phillies for SS Kevin Stocker (November 18, 1997).

STATISTICAL NOTES: Led Gulf Coast League outfielders with 11 assists in 1991. ... Led Texas League with .530 slugging percentage in 1994. ... Led Pacific Coast League outfielders with 18 assists in 1995. ... Led Pacific Coast League in caught stealing with 18 in 1996.

Year Team (League)	Pos.	G	AB	R	H	2B	3B	HR	RBI	Avg.	BB	SO	SB	PO	A	E	Avg.
1991— GC Astros (GCL)	OF-SS	56	183	21	55	7	3	0	20	.301	17	27	10	70	†13	5	.943
1992— Asheville (S. Atl.)	OF	135	480	81	140	21	4	8	48	.292	63	79	15	167	15	11	.943
1993— Osceola (Fla. St.)	OF	129	474	62	134	21	17	5	55	.283	51	90	10	179	18	8	.961
1994— Jackson (Texas)	OF	118	400	61	121	25	9	16	73	.303	42	81	12	113	3	4	.967
1995— Tucson (PCL)	OF-2B	114	415	72	126	24	*17	10	75	.304	67	120	16	207	†18	7	.970
1996— Tucson (PCL)	OF	132	484	86	138	14	*16	13	68	.285	83	111	24	202	15	7	.969
— Houston (N.L.)	OF	15	22	1	5	1	0	0	1	.227	2	3	0	6	0	0	1.000
1997— Houston (N.L.)	OF	59	188	22	47	10	2	3	26	.250	21	48	7	84	4	2	.978
— Jackson (Texas)	OF	3	12	2	2	1	0	0	0	.167	1	5	0	1	0	0	1.000
— New Orleans (A.A.)	OF	47	194	25	52	9	4	2	22	.268	21	49	7	99	4	1	.990
1998— Philadelphia (N.L.)■	OF	151	497	68	155	29	6	17	74	.312	84	133	19	272	17	8	.973
Major league totals (3 years)		225	707	91	207	40	8	20	101	.293	107	184	26	362	21	10	.975

DIVISION SERIES RECORD

Year Team (League)	Pos.	G	AB	R	H	2B	3B	HR	RBI	Avg.	BB	SO	SB	PO	A	E	Avg.
1997— Houston (N.L.)	PH	3	3	0	1	0	0	0	0	.333	0	2	1	...	...	...	...

ACEVEDO, JUAN · P · CARDINALS

PERSONAL: Born May 5, 1970, in Juarez, Mexico. ... 6-2/228. ... Throws right, bats right. ... Full name: Juan Carlos Acevedo. ... Name pronounced ah-sah-VAY-doh.
HIGH SCHOOL: Dundee-Crown (Carpentersville, Ill.).
JUNIOR COLLEGE: Parkland College (Ill.).
TRANSACTIONS/CAREER NOTES: Selected by Colorado Rockies organization in 14th round of free-agent draft (June 1, 1992). ... Traded by Rockies with P Arnold Gooch to New York Mets for P Bret Saberhagen and a player to be named later (July 31, 1995); Rockies acquired P David Swanson to complete deal (August 4, 1995). ... On New York disabled list (March 26-May 9, 1996); included rehabilitation assignment to Norfolk (April 10-May 9). ... Traded by Mets to St. Louis Cardinals for P Rigo Beltran (March 29, 1998). ... On St. Louis disabled list (July 18-August 16, 1998); included rehabilitation assignment to Memphis (August 6-16).
HONORS: Named Eastern League Pitcher of the Year (1994).
STATISTICAL NOTES: Tied for Eastern League lead with four balks in 1994. ... Tied for International League lead with four balks in 1997.

Year Team (League)	W	L	Pct.	ERA	G	GS	CG	ShO	Sv.	IP	H	R	ER	BB	SO
1992— Bend (Northwest)	0	0	...	13.50	1	0	0	0	0	2	4	3	3	1	3
— Visalia (California)	3	4	.429	5.43	12	12	1	0	0	$64\frac{2}{3}$	75	46	39	33	37
1993— Central Valley (Cal.)	9	8	.529	4.40	27	20	1	0	0	$118\frac{2}{3}$	119	68	58	58	107
1994— New Haven (East.)	*17	6	.739	*2.37	26	26	5	2	0	$174\frac{2}{3}$	142	56	46	38	161
1995— Colorado (N.L.)	4	6	.400	6.44	17	11	0	0	0	$65\frac{2}{3}$	82	53	47	20	40
— Colo. Springs (PCL)	1	1	.500	6.14	3	3	0	0	0	$14\frac{2}{3}$	18	11	10	7	7
— Norfolk (Int'l)■	0	0	...	0.00	2	2	0	0	0	3	0	0	0	1	2
1996— Norfolk (Int'l)	4	8	.333	5.96	19	19	2	1	0	$102\frac{2}{3}$	116	70	68	53	83
1997— Norfolk (Int'l)	6	6	.500	3.86	18	18	1	0	0	$116\frac{2}{3}$	111	55	50	34	99
— New York (N.L.)	3	1	.750	3.59	25	2	0	0	0	$47\frac{2}{3}$	52	24	19	22	33
1998— St. Louis (N.L.)■	8	3	.727	2.56	50	9	0	0	15	$98\frac{1}{3}$	83	30	28	29	56
— Memphis (Pacific Coast)	0	0	...	0.00	2	2	0	0	0	$8\frac{2}{3}$	5	0	0	1	6
Major league totals (3 years)	15	10	.600	4.00	92	22	0	0	15	$211\frac{2}{3}$	217	107	94	71	129

ADAMS, TERRY · P · CUBS

PERSONAL: Born March 6, 1973, in Mobile, Ala. ... 6-3/205. ... Throws right, bats right. ... Full name: Terry Wayne Adams.
HIGH SCHOOL: Montgomery (Semmes, Ala.).
TRANSACTIONS/CAREER NOTES: Selected by Chicago Cubs organization in fourth round of free-agent draft (June 3, 1991). ... On disabled list (June 21-September 21, 1993).

Year Team (League)	W	L	Pct.	ERA	G	GS	CG	ShO	Sv.	IP	H	R	ER	BB	SO
1991— Huntington (Appal.)	0	*9	.000	5.77	14	13	0	0	0	$57\frac{2}{3}$	67	*56	37	62	52
1992— Peoria (Midwest)	7	12	.368	4.41	25	25	3	1	0	157	144	95	77	86	96
1993— Daytona (Fla. St.)	3	5	.375	4.97	13	13	0	0	0	$70\frac{2}{3}$	78	47	39	43	35
1994— Daytona (Fla. St.)	9	10	.474	4.38	39	7	0	0	7	$84\frac{1}{3}$	87	47	41	46	64
1995— Orlando (South.)	2	3	.400	1.43	37	0	0	0	19	$37\frac{2}{3}$	23	9	6	16	26
— Iowa (Am. Assoc.)	0	0	...	0.00	7	0	0	0	5	$6\frac{1}{3}$	3	0	0	2	10
— Chicago (N.L.)	1	1	.500	6.50	18	0	0	0	1	18	22	15	13	10	15
1996— Chicago (N.L.)	3	6	.333	2.94	69	0	0	0	4	101	84	36	33	49	78
1997— Chicago (N.L.)	2	9	.182	4.62	74	0	0	0	18	74	91	43	38	40	64
1998— Chicago (N.L.)	7	7	.500	4.33	63	0	0	0	1	$72\frac{2}{3}$	72	39	35	41	73
— Iowa (Pacific Coast)	0	0	...	0.00	3	0	0	0	0	4	1	1	0	3	5
Major league totals (4 years)	13	23	.361	4.03	224	0	0	0	24	$265\frac{2}{3}$	269	133	119	140	230

ADAMSON, JOEL · P · RED SOX

PERSONAL: Born July 2, 1971, in Lakewood, Calif. ... 6-4/185. ... Throws left, bats left. ... Full name: Joel Lee Adamson.
HIGH SCHOOL: Artesia (Lakewood, Calif.).
JUNIOR COLLEGE: Cerritos College (Calif.).
TRANSACTIONS/CAREER NOTES: Selected by San Diego Padres organization in 31st round of free-agent draft (June 5, 1989); did not sign. ... Selected by Philadelphia Phillies organization in seventh round of free-agent draft (June 4, 1990). ... On Reading suspended list (June 1-8, 1992). ... Traded by Phillies organization with P Matt Whisenant to Florida Marlins for P Danny Jackson (November 17, 1992). ... On disabled

list (August 6-25, 1994 and June 8-July 23, 1995). ... Traded by Marlins to Milwaukee Brewers for a player to be named later (November 25, 1996); Marlins acquired P Ed Collins to complete deal (December 10, 1996). ... Selected by Arizona Diamondbacks in first round (15th pick overall) of expansion draft (November 18, 1997). ... On disabled list (April 27, 1998-remainder of season). ... Released by Diamondbacks (October 2, 1998). ... Signed by Oakland Athletics organization (December 11, 1998). ... Selected by Boston Red Sox from Athletics organization in Rule 5 major league draft (December 14, 1998).

Year	Team (League)	W	L	Pct.	ERA	G	GS	CG	ShO	Sv.	IP	H	R	ER	BB	SO
1990—	Princeton (Appalachian).....	2	5	.286	3.88	12	8	1	0	1	48 2/3	56	27	21	12	40
1991—	Spartanburg (SAL)............	4	4	.500	2.56	14	14	1	1	0	81	72	29	23	22	84
	— Clearwater (Fla. St.)..........	2	1	.667	3.03	5	5	0	0	0	29 2/3	28	12	10	7	20
1992—	Clearwater (Fla. St.)	5	6	.455	3.41	15	15	1	1	0	89 2/3	90	35	34	19	52
	— Reading (Eastern)	3	6	.333	4.27	10	10	2	0	0	59	68	36	28	13	35
1993—	High Desert (Calif.)■	5	5	.500	4.58	22	20	•6	*3	0	129 2/3	160	83	66	30	72
	— Edmonton (PCL)	1	2	.333	6.92	5	5	0	0	0	26	39	21	20	13	7
1994—	Portland (Eastern)	5	6	.455	4.34	33	11	2	2	7	91 1/3	95	51	44	32	59
1995—	Charlotte (Int'l)	8	4	.667	3.29	19	18	2	0	0	115	113	51	42	20	80
1996—	Charlotte (Int'l)	6	6	.500	3.78	44	8	0	0	3	97 2/3	108	48	41	28	84
	— Florida (N.L.)...................	0	0	. . .	7.36	9	0	0	0	0	11	18	9	9	7	7
1997—	Tucson (PCL)■.................	2	1	.667	4.36	6	6	0	0	0	33	38	16	16	8	24
	— Milwaukee (A.L.)	5	3	.625	3.54	30	6	0	0	0	76 1/3	78	36	30	19	56
1998—	Arizona (N.L.)■.................	0	3	.000	8.22	5	5	0	0	0	23	25	21	21	11	14
A.L. totals (1 year)......................		5	3	.625	3.54	30	6	0	0	0	76 1/3	78	36	30	19	56
N.L. totals (2 years)...................		0	3	.000	7.94	14	5	0	0	0	34	43	30	30	18	21
Major league totals (3 years)......		5	6	.455	4.89	44	11	0	0	0	110 1/3	121	66	60	37	77

AGBAYANI, BENNY   OF   METS

PERSONAL: Born December 28, 1971, in Honolulu, Hawaii. ... 6-0/225. ... Bats right, throws right. ... Full name: Benny Peter Agbayani Jr.
HIGH SCHOOL: St. Louis (Honolulu).
COLLEGE: Oregon Tech, then Hawaii Pacific.
TRANSACTIONS/CAREER NOTES: Selected by California Angels organization in 25th round of free-agent draft (June 1, 1992); did not sign. ... Selected by New York Mets organization in 30th round of free-agent draft (June 3, 1993). ... On Norfolk disabled list (May 10-June 6, 1998).
STATISTICAL NOTES: Tied for International League lead in caught stealing with 14 in 1997.

Year	Team (League)	Pos.	G	AB	R	H	2B	3B	HR	RBI	Avg.	BB	SO	SB	PO	A	E	Avg.
1993—	Pittsfield (NYP)	OF	51	167	26	42	6	3	2	22	.251	20	43	7	62	1	2	.969
1994—	St. Lucie (Fla. St.)	OF	119	411	72	115	13	5	5	63	.280	58	67	8	143	6	1	.993
1995—	Binghamton (East.)	OF	88	295	38	81	11	2	1	26	.275	39	51	12	100	3	3	.972
	— St. Lucie (Fla. St.)	OF	44	155	24	48	9	3	2	29	.310	26	27	8	37	1	2	.950
1996—	Binghamton (East.)	OF	21	53	7	9	1	0	2	8	.170	11	13	1	19	1	1	.952
	— Norfolk (Int'l)	OF-1B	99	331	43	92	13	9	7	56	.278	30	57	14	172	8	2	.989
1997—	Norfolk (Int'l)	OF	127	468	90	145	24	2	11	51	.310	67	106	29	207	12	5	.978
1998—	Norfolk (Int'l)	OF-1B	90	322	43	91	20	5	11	53	.283	50	58	16	151	4	4	.975
	— New York (N.L.)..........	OF	11	15	1	2	0	0	0	0	.133	1	5	0	6	0	0	1.000
Major league totals (1 year)			11	15	1	2	0	0	0	0	.133	1	5	0	6	0	0	1.000

AGUILERA, RICK   P   TWINS

PERSONAL: Born December 31, 1961, in San Gabriel, Calif. ... 6-5/203. ... Throws right, bats right. ... Full name: Richard Warren Aguilera. ... Name pronounced AG-yuh-LAIR-uh.
HIGH SCHOOL: Edgewood (West Covina, Calif.).
COLLEGE: Brigham Young.
TRANSACTIONS/CAREER NOTES: Selected by St. Louis Cardinals organization in 37th round of free-agent draft (June 3, 1980); did not sign. ... Selected by New York Mets organization in third round of free-agent draft (June 6, 1983). ... On New York disabled list (September 3-15, 1985). ... On New York disabled list (May 23-August 24, 1987); included rehabilitation assignment to Tidewater (August 10-24). ... On New York disabled list (April 19-June 19 and July 12-September 7, 1988); included rehabilitation assignments to St. Lucie (June 7-14) and Tidewater (June 15-19). ... Traded by Mets with P David West and three players to be named later to Minnesota Twins for P Frank Viola (July 31, 1989); Portland, Twins organization, acquired P Kevin Tapani and P Tim Drummond (August 1, 1989), and Twins acquired P Jack Savage to complete deal (October 16, 1989). ... Traded by Twins to Boston Red Sox for P Frank Rodriguez and a player to be named later (July 6, 1995); Twins acquired OF J.J. Johnson to complete deal (October 11, 1995). ... Granted free agency (October 31, 1995). ... Signed by Twins (December 11, 1995). ... On Minnesota disabled list (March 24-June 11 and September 7, 1996-remainder of season); included rehabilitation assignment to Fort Myers (May 31-June 11).
MISCELLANEOUS: Holds Minnesota Twins all-time records for most saves (248) and most games pitched (473). ... Made an out in only appearance as pinch hitter with New York (1989).

Year	Team (League)	W	L	Pct.	ERA	G	GS	CG	ShO	Sv.	IP	H	R	ER	BB	SO
1983—	Little Falls (NYP)	5	6	.455	3.72	16	15	4	•2	0	104	*109	55	43	26	84
1984—	Lynchburg (Carolina)	8	3	.727	2.34	13	13	6	•3	0	88 1/3	72	29	23	28	101
	— Jackson (Texas)	4	4	.500	4.57	11	11	2	1	0	67	68	37	34	19	71
1985—	Tidewater (Int'l)	6	4	.600	2.51	11	11	2	1	0	79	64	24	22	17	55
	— New York (N.L.)...............	10	7	.588	3.24	21	19	2	0	0	122 1/3	118	49	44	37	74
1986—	New York (N.L.).................	10	7	.588	3.88	28	20	2	0	0	141 2/3	145	70	61	36	104
1987—	New York (N.L.).................	11	3	.786	3.60	18	17	1	0	0	115	124	53	46	33	77
	— Tidewater (Int'l)	1	1	.500	0.69	3	3	0	0	0	13	8	2	1	1	10
1988—	New York (N.L.).................	0	4	.000	6.93	11	3	0	0	0	24 2/3	29	20	19	10	16
	— St. Lucie (Fla. St.)	0	0	. . .	1.29	2	2	0	0	0	7	8	1	1	1	5
	— Tidewater (Int'l)	0	0	. . .	1.50	1	1	0	0	0	6	6	1	1	1	4
1989—	New York (N.L.).................	6	6	.500	2.34	36	0	0	0	7	69 1/3	59	19	18	21	80
	— Minnesota (A.L.)■............	3	5	.375	3.21	11	11	3	0	0	75 2/3	71	32	27	17	57
1990—	Minnesota (A.L.)	5	3	.625	2.76	56	0	0	0	32	65 1/3	55	27	20	19	61
1991—	Minnesota (A.L.)	4	5	.444	2.35	63	0	0	0	42	69	44	20	18	30	61

Year Team (League)	W	L	Pct.	ERA	G	GS	CG	ShO	Sv.	IP	H	R	ER	BB	SO
1992— Minnesota (A.L.)	2	6	.250	2.84	64	0	0	0	41	66 2/3	60	28	21	17	52
1993— Minnesota (A.L.)	4	3	.571	3.11	65	0	0	0	34	72 1/3	60	25	25	14	59
1994— Minnesota (A.L.)	1	4	.200	3.63	44	0	0	0	23	44 2/3	57	23	18	10	46
1995— Minnesota (A.L.)	1	1	.500	2.52	22	0	0	0	12	25	20	7	7	6	29
— Boston (A.L.)■	2	2	.500	2.67	30	0	0	0	20	30 1/3	26	9	9	7	23
1996— Fort Myers (Fla. St.)■	2	0	1.000	3.75	2	2	0	0	0	12	13	5	5	1	12
— Minnesota (A.L.)	8	6	.571	5.42	19	19	2	0	0	111 1/3	124	69	67	27	83
1997— Minnesota (A.L.)	5	4	.556	3.82	61	0	0	0	26	68 1/3	65	29	29	22	68
1998— Minnesota (A.L.)	4	9	.308	4.24	68	0	0	0	38	74 1/3	75	35	35	15	57
A.L. totals (10 years)	39	48	.448	3.53	503	30	5	0	268	703	657	304	276	184	596
N.L. totals (5 years)	37	27	.578	3.58	114	59	5	0	7	473	475	211	188	137	351
Major league totals (14 years)	76	75	.503	3.55	617	89	10	0	275	1176	1132	515	464	321	947

DIVISION SERIES RECORD

Year Team (League)	W	L	Pct.	ERA	G	GS	CG	ShO	Sv.	IP	H	R	ER	BB	SO
1995— Boston (A.L.)	0	0	...	13.50	1	0	0	0	0	2/3	3	1	1	0	1

CHAMPIONSHIP SERIES RECORD

Year Team (League)	W	L	Pct.	ERA	G	GS	CG	ShO	Sv.	IP	H	R	ER	BB	SO
1986— New York (N.L.)	0	0	...	0.00	2	0	0	0	0	5	2	1	0	2	2
1988— New York (N.L.)	0	0	...	1.29	3	0	0	0	0	7	3	1	1	2	4
1991— Minnesota (A.L.)	0	0	...	0.00	3	0	0	0	3	3 1/3	1	0	0	0	3
Champ. series totals (3 years)	0	0	...	0.59	8	0	0	0	3	15 1/3	6	2	1	4	9

WORLD SERIES RECORD

NOTES: Flied out in only appearance as pinch hitter (1991). ... Member of World Series championship team (1986 and 1991).

Year Team (League)	W	L	Pct.	ERA	G	GS	CG	ShO	Sv.	IP	H	R	ER	BB	SO
1986— New York (N.L.)	1	0	1.000	12.00	2	0	0	0	0	3	8	4	4	1	4
1991— Minnesota (A.L.)	1	1	.500	1.80	4	0	0	0	2	5	6	1	1	1	3
World Series totals (2 years)	2	1	.667	5.63	6	0	0	0	2	8	14	5	5	2	7

ALL-STAR GAME RECORD

Year League	W	L	Pct.	ERA	GS	CG	ShO	Sv.	IP	H	R	ER	BB	SO
1991— American	0	0	...	0.00	0	0	0	0	1 1/3	2	0	0	0	3
1992— American	0	0	...	13.50	0	0	0	0	2/3	1	1	1	0	0
1993— American	0	0	...	0.00	0	0	0	0	1	2	0	0	0	2
All-Star totals (3 years)	0	0	...	3.00	0	0	0	0	3	5	1	1	0	5

ALDRED, SCOTT   P   DEVIL RAYS

PERSONAL: Born June 12, 1968, in Flint, Mich. ... 6-4/228. ... Throws left, bats left. ... Full name: Scott Phillip Aldred.

HIGH SCHOOL: Hill McCloy (Montrose, Mich.).

TRANSACTIONS/CAREER NOTES: Selected by Detroit Tigers organization in 16th round of free-agent draft (June 2, 1986). ... Selected by Colorado Rockies in first round (15th pick overall) of expansion draft (November 17, 1992). ... Claimed on waivers by Montreal Expos (April 29, 1993). ... On Montreal disabled list (May 15-September 11, 1993). ... Released by Expos (September 11, 1993). ... Missed entire 1994 season with injury. ... Signed by Detroit Tigers organization (February 19, 1995). ... Claimed on waivers by Minnesota Twins (May 28, 1996). ... On Salt Lake disabled list (August 7-September 19, 1997). ... Granted free agency (October 8, 1997). ... Signed by Tampa Bay Devil Rays (December 19, 1997).

Year Team (League)	W	L	Pct.	ERA	G	GS	CG	ShO	Sv.	IP	H	R	ER	BB	SO
1987— Fayetteville (S. Atl.)	4	9	.308	3.60	21	20	0	0	0	110	101	56	44	69	91
1988— Lakeland (Fla. St.)	8	7	.533	3.56	25	25	1	1	0	131 1/3	122	61	52	72	102
1989— London (Eastern)	10	6	.625	3.84	20	20	3	1	0	122	98	55	52	59	97
1990— Toledo (International)	6	15	.286	4.90	29	*29	2	0	0	158	145	93	86	81	133
— Detroit (A.L.)	1	2	.333	3.77	4	3	0	0	0	14 1/3	13	6	6	10	7
1991— Toledo (International)	8	8	.500	3.92	22	20	2	0	1	135 1/3	127	65	59	72	95
— Detroit (A.L.)	2	4	.333	5.18	11	11	1	0	0	57 1/3	58	37	33	30	35
1992— Detroit (A.L.)	3	8	.273	6.78	16	13	0	0	0	65	80	51	49	33	34
— Toledo (International)	4	6	.400	5.13	16	13	3	0	0	86	92	57	49	47	81
1993— Colorado (N.L.)■	0	0	...	10.80	5	0	0	0	0	6 2/3	10	10	8	9	5
— Montreal (N.L.)■	1	0	1.000	6.75	3	0	0	0	0	5 1/3	9	4	4	1	4
1994—							Did not play.								
1995— Lakeland (Fla. St.)■	4	2	.667	3.19	13	7	0	0	2	67 2/3	57	25	24	19	64
— Jacksonville (Southern)	1	0	1.000	0.00	2	2	0	0	0	12	9	0	0	1	11
1996— Detroit (A.L.)	0	4	.000	9.35	11	8	0	0	0	43 1/3	60	52	45	26	36
— Minnesota (A.L.)■	6	5	.545	5.09	25	17	0	0	0	122	134	73	69	42	75
1997— Minnesota (A.L.)	2	10	.167	7.68	17	15	0	0	0	77 1/3	102	66	66	28	33
— Salt Lake (PCL)	3	3	.500	7.03	7	7	0	0	0	39 2/3	56	39	31	16	23
1998— Durham (International)■	2	4	.333	5.35	7	7	0	0	0	35 1/3	44	26	21	14	19
— Tampa Bay (A.L.)	0	0	...	3.73	48	0	0	0	0	31 1/3	33	13	13	12	21
A.L. totals (6 years)	14	33	.298	6.16	132	67	1	0	0	410 2/3	480	298	281	181	241
N.L. totals (1 year)	1	0	1.000	9.00	8	0	0	0	0	12	19	14	12	10	9
Major league totals (7 years)	15	33	.313	6.24	140	67	1	0	0	422 2/3	499	312	293	191	250

ALEXANDER, MANNY   SS/2B   CUBS

PERSONAL: Born March 20, 1971, in San Pedro de Macoris, Dominican Republic. ... 5-10/180. ... Bats right, throws right. ... Full name: Manuel DeJesus Alexander.

TRANSACTIONS/CAREER NOTES: Signed as non-drafted free agent by Baltimore Orioles organization (February 4, 1988). ... On disabled list (April 26-July 23, 1990). ... On Rochester disabled list (May 9-19 and June 9-17, 1993). ... On Baltimore disabled list (March 25-May 2, 1995). ... Traded by Orioles with IF Scott McLain to New York Mets for P Hector Ramirez (March 22, 1997). ... On New York disabled list (June 13-July 19 and August 1-11, 1997). ... Traded by Mets to Chicago Cubs (August 14, 1997), as part of deal in which Mets traded OF Lance Johnson and two players to be named later to Cubs for OF Brian McRae, P Mel Rojas and P Turk Wendell (August 8, 1997); Mets traded P Mark Clark to Cubs to complete deal (August 11, 1997).

STATISTICAL NOTES: Led Appalachian League shortstops with 349 total chances in 1989. ... Led Carolina League shortstops with 651 total chances and 93 double plays in 1991.

Year Team (League)	Pos.	G	AB	R	H	2B	3B	HR	RBI	Avg.	BB	SO	SB	PO	A	E	Avg.
1988—						Dominican Summer League statistics unavailable.											
1989—Bluefield (Appal.)....	SS	65	*274	49	*85	13	2	2	34	.310	20	49	19	*140	177	*32	.908
1990—Wausau (Midwest).....	SS	44	152	16	27	3	1	0	11	.178	12	41	8	66	99	11	.938
1991—Hagerstown (East.).....	SS	3	9	3	3	1	0	0	2	.333	1	3	0	5	4	0	1.000
—Frederick (Carolina)....	SS	134	548	•81	*143	17	3	3	42	.261	44	68	47	*226	*393	32	*.951
1992—Hagerstown (East.)......	SS	127	499	69	129	23	8	2	41	.259	25	62	43	216	253	36	.929
—Rochester (Int'l)........	SS	6	24	3	7	1	0	0	3	.292	1	3	2	12	25	1	.974
—Baltimore (A.L.).........	SS	4	5	1	1	0	0	0	0	.200	0	3	0	3	3	0	1.000
1993—Rochester (Int'l)	SS	120	471	55	115	23	8	6	51	.244	22	60	19	184	335	18	*.966
—Baltimore (A.L.)..........	PR-DH	3	0	1	0	0	0	0	0	...	0	0	0	...	...	...	...
1994—Rochester (Int'l)........	SS-2B	111	426	63	106	23	6	6	39	.249	16	67	30	219	291	33	.939
1995—Baltimore (A.L.).........	2-S-3-DH	94	242	35	57	9	1	3	23	.236	20	30	11	139	170	10	.969
1996—Baltimore (A.L.).........S-2-3-O-DH-P		54	68	6	7	0	0	0	4	.103	3	27	3	26	47	5	.936
1997—New York (N.L.).........	2B-SS-3B	54	149	26	37	9	3	2	15	.248	9	38	11	59	130	4	.979
—St. Lucie (Fla. St.)	SS	1	4	0	1	0	0	0	0	.250	0	1	0	1	4	0	1.000
—Chicago (N.L.)■............	SS-2B	33	99	11	29	3	1	1	7	.293	8	16	2	38	91	7	.949
1998—Chicago (N.L.)............S-2-3-DH-O		108	264	34	60	10	1	5	25	.227	18	66	4	89	140	7	.970
American League totals (4 years)		155	315	43	65	9	1	3	27	.206	23	60	14	168	220	15	.963
National League totals (2 years)		195	512	71	126	22	5	8	47	.246	35	120	17	186	361	18	.968
Major league totals (6 years)		350	827	114	191	31	6	11	74	.231	58	180	31	354	581	33	.966

DIVISION SERIES RECORD

Year Team (League)	Pos.	G	AB	R	H	2B	3B	HR	RBI	Avg.	BB	SO	SB	PO	A	E	Avg.
1996—Baltimore (A.L.)..........	DH-PR	3	0	2	0	0	0	0	0	...	0	0	0	...	...	...	...
1998—Chicago (N.L.)............	SS-PH	2	5	0	0	0	0	0	0	.000	0	1	0	2	2	0	1.000
Division series totals (2 years)		5	5	2	0	0	0	0	0	.000	0	1	0	2	2	0	1.000

RECORD AS PITCHER

Year Team (League)	W	L	Pct.	ERA	G	GS	CG	ShO	Sv.	IP	H	R	ER	BB	SO
1996—Baltimore (A.L.)..................	0	0	...	67.50	1	0	0	0	0	2/3	1	5	5	4	0
Major league totals (1 year)........	0	0	...	67.50	1	0	0	0	0	2/3	1	5	5	4	0

ALFONSECA, ANTONIO   P   MARLINS

PERSONAL: Born April 16, 1972, in La Romana, Dominican Republic. ... 6-5/235. ... Throws right, bats right.
TRANSACTIONS/CAREER NOTES: Signed as non-drafted free agent by Montreal Expos organization (July 3, 1989). ... Selected by Edmonton, Florida Marlins organization, from Harrisburg, Expos organization in Rule 5 minor league draft (December 13, 1993). ... On disabled list (May 15-June 15, 1995 and July 12-September 3, 1996). ... On disabled list (May 14-31, 1998).

Year Team (League)	W	L	Pct.	ERA	G	GS	CG	ShO	Sv.	IP	H	R	ER	BB	SO
1990—DSL Expos (DSL)	3	5	.375	3.60	13	13	1	0	0	60	60	29	24	32	19
1991—GC Expos (GCL)	3	3	.500	3.88	11	10	0	0	0	51	46	33	22	25	38
1992—GC Expos (GCL)	3	4	.429	3.68	12	10	1	1	0	66	55	31	27	35	62
1993—Jamestown (NYP)	2	2	.500	6.15	15	4	0	0	1	33 2/3	31	26	23	22	29
1994—Kane County (Midwest)■...	6	5	.545	4.07	32	9	0	0	0	86 1/3	78	41	39	21	74
1995—Portland (Eastern)	9	3	.750	3.64	19	17	1	0	0	96 1/3	81	43	39	42	75
1996—Charlotte (Int'l)	4	4	.500	5.53	14	13	0	0	1	71 2/3	86	47	44	22	51
1997—Charlotte (Int'l)	7	2	.778	4.32	46	0	0	0	7	58 1/3	58	34	28	20	45
—Florida (N.L.)	1	3	.250	4.91	17	0	0	0	0	25 2/3	36	16	14	10	19
1998—Florida (N.L.)	4	6	.400	4.08	58	0	0	0	8	70 2/3	75	36	32	33	46
Major league totals (2 years)......	5	9	.357	4.30	75	0	0	0	8	96 1/3	111	52	46	43	65

DIVISION SERIES RECORD

Year Team (League)	W	L	Pct.	ERA	G	GS	CG	ShO	Sv.	IP	H	R	ER	BB	SO
1997—Florida (N.L.)							Did not play.								

CHAMPIONSHIP SERIES RECORD

Year Team (League)	W	L	Pct.	ERA	G	GS	CG	ShO	Sv.	IP	H	R	ER	BB	SO
1997—Florida (N.L.)							Did not play.								

WORLD SERIES RECORD

NOTES: Member of World Series championship team (1997).

Year Team (League)	W	L	Pct.	ERA	G	GS	CG	ShO	Sv.	IP	H	R	ER	BB	SO
1997—Florida (N.L.)	0	0	...	0.00	3	0	0	0	0	6 1/3	6	0	0	1	5

ALFONZO, EDGARDO   2B   METS

PERSONAL: Born November 8, 1973, in St. Teresa, Venezuela. ... 5-11/187. ... Bats right, throws right. ... Full name: Edgardo Antonio Alfonzo. ... Brother of Roberto Alfonzo, second baseman, New York Mets organization (1993-94).
HIGH SCHOOL: Cecilio Acosto (Venezuela).
TRANSACTIONS/CAREER NOTES: Signed as non-drafted free agent by New York Mets organization (February 19, 1991). ... On disabled list (August 11, 1995-remainder of season). ... On disabled list (May 4-19, 1998).
RECORDS: Shares single-game record for most doubles plays by second baseman—4 (1997).
STATISTICAL NOTES: Led New York-Pennsylvania League shortstops with 389 total chances and 39 double plays in 1992. ... Had 20-game hitting streak (June 10-July 10, 1997). ... Career major league grand slams: 1.

Year Team (League)	Pos.	G	AB	R	H	2B	3B	HR	RBI	Avg.	BB	SO	SB	PO	A	E	Avg.
1991—GC Mets (GCL)..........	2B-SS-3B	54	175	29	58	8	4	0	27	.331	34	12	6	99	108	9	.958
1992—St. Lucie (Fla. St.)	2B	4	5	0	0	0	0	0	0	.000	0	0	0	1	3	0	1.000
—Pittsfield (NYP)	SS	74	*298	44	*106	13	5	1	44	*.356	18	31	7	*126	*237	*26	.933

Year Team (League)	Pos.	G	AB	R	H	2B	3B	HR	RBI	Avg.	BB	SO	SB	PO	A	E	Avg.
1993—St. Lucie (Fla. St.)......	SS	128	494	75	145	18	3	11	86	.294	57	51	26	183	425	29	.954
1994—Binghamton (East.)....	SS-2B-1B	127	498	89	146	34	2	15	75	.293	64	55	14	206	408	27	.958
1995—New York (N.L.)........	3B-2B-SS	101	335	26	93	13	5	4	41	.278	12	37	1	81	171	7	.973
1996—New York (N.L.)........	2B-3B-SS	123	368	36	96	15	2	4	40	.261	25	56	2	146	246	11	.973
1997—New York (N.L.)........	3B-SS-2B	151	518	84	163	27	2	10	72	.315	63	56	11	98	290	12	.970
1998—New York (N.L.)........	3B-SS	144	557	94	155	28	2	17	78	.278	65	77	8	117	248	9	.976
Major league totals (4 years)		519	1778	240	507	83	11	35	231	.285	165	226	22	442	955	39	.973

ALICEA, LUIS — 2B — RANGERS

PERSONAL: Born July 29, 1965, in Santurce, Puerto Rico. ... 5-9/176. ... Bats both, throws right. ... Full name: Luis Rene Alicea. ... Brother of Ed Alicea, minor league infielder with Atlanta Braves (1988-93), Colorado Rockies (1993) and New York Mets (1995).. ... Name pronounced AH-la-SAY-uh.
HIGH SCHOOL: Liceo Castro (Rio Piedras, Puerto Rico).
COLLEGE: Florida State.
TRANSACTIONS/CAREER NOTES: Selected by St. Louis Cardinals organization in first round (23rd pick overall) of free-agent draft (June 2, 1986). ... On St. Petersburg disabled list (April 6-June 4, 1990). ... On Louisville disabled list (April 25-May 25, 1991). ... On St. Louis disabled list (June 1-July 6, 1992); included rehabilitation assignment to Louisville (July 2-6). ... Traded by Cardinals to Boston Red Sox for P Nate Minchey and OF Jeff McNeely (December 7, 1994). ... Claimed on waivers by Cardinals (March 19, 1996). ... Granted free agency (October 31, 1996). ... Signed by Anaheim Angels organization (January 20, 1997). ... Granted free agency (October 30, 1997). ... Signed by Texas Rangers (December 9, 1997).
HONORS: Named second baseman on THE SPORTING NEWS college All-America team (1986).
STATISTICAL NOTES: Switch-hit home runs in one game (July 28, 1995). ... Led A.L. second basemen with 699 total chances and 103 double plays in 1995. ... Career major league grand slams: 1.

Year Team (League)	Pos.	G	AB	R	H	2B	3B	HR	RBI	Avg.	BB	SO	SB	PO	A	E	Avg.
1986—Erie (N.Y.-Penn)..........	2B	47	163	40	46	6	1	3	18	.282	37	20	27	94	163	12	.955
—Arkansas (Texas)........	2B-SS	25	68	8	16	3	0	0	3	.235	5	11	0	39	63	4	.962
1987—Arkansas (Texas)........	2B	101	337	57	91	14	3	4	47	.270	49	28	13	184	251	11	*.975
—Louisville (A.A.)........	2B	29	105	18	32	10	2	2	20	.305	9	9	4	69	81	4	.974
1988—Louisville (A.A.)........	2B-SS-OF	49	191	21	53	11	6	1	21	.277	11	21	8	116	165	0	1.000
—St. Louis (N.L.)........	2B	93	297	20	63	10	4	1	24	.212	25	32	1	206	240	14	.970
1989—Louisville (A.A.)........	2B	124	412	53	102	20	3	8	48	.248	59	55	13	240	310	16	.972
1990—St. Petersburg (FSL)..	2B	29	95	14	22	1	4	0	12	.232	20	14	9	20	23	0	1.000
—Arkansas (Texas)........	2B	14	49	11	14	3	1	0	4	.286	7	8	2	24	34	4	.935
—Louisville (A.A.)........	3B	25	92	10	32	6	3	0	10	.348	5	12	0	14	39	6	.898
1991—Louisville (A.A.)........	2B	31	112	26	44	6	3	4	16	.393	14	8	5	68	95	5	.970
—St. Louis (N.L.)........	2B-3B-SS	56	68	5	13	3	0	0	0	.191	8	19	0	19	23	0	1.000
1992—Louisville (A.A.)........	2B-SS	20	71	11	20	8	0	0	6	.282	16	6	0	44	52	4	.960
—St. Louis (N.L.)........	2B-SS	85	265	26	65	9	11	2	32	.245	27	40	2	136	233	7	.981
1993—St. Louis (N.L.)........	2B-OF-3B	115	362	50	101	19	3	3	46	.279	47	54	11	210	281	11	.978
1994—St. Louis (N.L.)........	2B-OF	88	205	32	57	12	5	5	29	.278	30	38	4	126	149	4	.986
1995—Boston (A.L.)■..........	2B	132	419	64	113	20	3	6	44	.270	63	61	13	254	429	16	.977
1996—St. Louis (N.L.)■........	2B	129	380	54	98	26	3	5	42	.258	52	78	11	241	288	*24	.957
1997—Anaheim (A.L.)■........	2B-3B-DH	128	388	59	98	16	7	5	37	.253	69	65	22	223	287	12	.977
1998—Texas (A.L.)■............	2-3-DH-O	101	259	51	71	15	3	6	33	.274	37	40	4	97	143	9	.964
American League totals (3 years)		361	1066	174	282	51	13	17	114	.265	169	166	39	574	859	37	.975
National League totals (6 years)		566	1577	187	397	79	26	16	173	.252	189	261	29	938	1214	60	.973
Major league totals (9 years)		927	2643	361	679	130	39	33	287	.257	358	427	68	1512	2073	97	.974

DIVISION SERIES RECORD

Year Team (League)	Pos.	G	AB	R	H	2B	3B	HR	RBI	Avg.	BB	SO	SB	PO	A	E	Avg.
1995—Boston (A.L.)..............	2B	3	10	1	6	1	0	1	1	.600	2	2	1	6	11	1	.944
1996—St. Louis (N.L.)..........	2B	3	11	1	2	2	0	0	0	.182	1	4	0	2	5	1	.875
1998—Texas (A.L.)..............	PH-DH	1	1	0	0	0	0	0	0	.000	0	0	0	...	...	...	...
Division series totals (3 years)		7	22	2	8	3	0	1	1	.364	3	6	1	8	16	2	.923

CHAMPIONSHIP SERIES RECORD

Year Team (League)	Pos.	G	AB	R	H	2B	3B	HR	RBI	Avg.	BB	SO	SB	PO	A	E	Avg.
1996—St. Louis (N.L.).........	2B-PH	5	8	0	0	0	0	0	0	.000	2	1	0	5	7	1	.923

ALLEN, CHAD — OF — TWINS

PERSONAL: Born February 6, 1975, in Dallas. ... 6-1/195. ... Bats right, throws right. ... Full name: John Chad Allen.
HIGH SCHOOL: Duncanville (Texas).
COLLEGE: Texas A&M.
TRANSACTIONS/CAREER NOTES: Selected by Cincinnati Reds organization in 38th round of free-agent draft (June 3, 1993); did not sign. ... Selected by Minnesota Twins organization in fourth round of free-agent draft (June 4, 1996).
MISCELLANEOUS: Member of 1996 U.S. Olympic baseball team.

Year Team (League)	Pos.	G	AB	R	H	2B	3B	HR	RBI	Avg.	BB	SO	SB	PO	A	E	Avg.
1996—Fort Wayne (Midw.).....	OF	7	21	2	9	0	0	0	2	.429	3	2	1	4	1	0	1.000
1997—Fort Myers (FSL)........	OF	105	401	66	124	18	4	3	45	.309	40	51	27	206	10	5	.977
—New Britain (East.).....	OF	30	115	20	29	9	1	4	18	.252	9	21	2	35	1	1	.973
1998—New Britain (East.).....	OF	137	504	70	132	31	7	8	82	.262	51	78	21	185	11	4	.980

PERSONAL: Born January 11, 1972, in Anderson, Ind. ... 6-0/190. ... Bats right, throws right. ... Full name: Jermaine LaMont Allensworth.
HIGH SCHOOL: Madison Heights (Anderson, Ind.).
COLLEGE: Purdue.
TRANSACTIONS/CAREER NOTES: Selected by Pittsburgh Pirates organization in supplemental round ("sandwich pick" between first and second round, 34th pick overall) of free-agent draft (June 3, 1993); pick received as part of compensation for Houston Astros signing Type A free-agent P Doug Drabek. ... On Pittsburgh disabled list (May 16-June 22, 1997); included rehabilitation assignment to Calgary (June 18-22). ... Traded by Pirates to Kansas City Royals for P Manuel Bernal (June 27, 1998). ... Traded by Royals to New York Mets for a player to be named later (August 10, 1998); Royals received cash to complete deal (September 3, 1998).
STATISTICAL NOTES: Career major league grand slams: 1.

Year Team (League)	Pos.	G	AB	R	H	2B	3B	HR	RBI	Avg.	BB	SO	SB	PO	A	E	Avg.
1993— Welland (NYP)	OF	67	263	44	81	16	4	1	32	.308	24	38	18	140	2	3	.979
1994— Carolina (Southern)	OF	118	452	63	109	26	8	1	34	.241	39	79	16	245	5	6	.977
1995— Carolina (Southern)	OF	56	219	37	59	14	2	1	14	.269	25	34	13	131	3	2	.985
— Calgary (PCL)	OF	51	190	46	60	13	4	3	11	.316	13	30	13	90	2	1	.989
1996— Calgary (PCL)	OF	95	352	77	116	23	6	8	43	.330	39	61	25	196	4	6	.971
— Pittsburgh (N.L.)	OF	61	229	32	60	9	3	4	31	.262	23	50	11	139	4	3	.979
1997— Pittsburgh (N.L.)	OF	108	369	55	94	18	2	3	43	.255	44	79	14	189	5	4	.980
— Calgary (PCL)	OF	5	20	5	8	3	1	0	1	.400	2	4	1	8	0	0	1.000
1998— Pittsburgh (N.L.)	OF	69	233	30	72	13	3	3	24	.309	17	43	8	145	4	3	.980
— Kansas City (A.L.)■	OF	30	73	15	15	5	0	0	3	.205	9	17	7	54	0	1	.982
— New York (N.L.)■	OF	34	54	9	11	2	0	2	4	.204	2	16	0	22	0	0	1.000
American League totals (1 year)		30	73	15	15	5	0	0	3	.205	9	17	7	54	0	1	.982
National League totals (3 years)		272	885	126	237	42	8	12	102	.268	86	188	33	495	13	10	.981
Major league totals (3 years)		302	958	141	252	47	8	12	105	.263	95	205	40	549	13	11	.981

PERSONAL: Born December 20, 1976, in Richmond, Va. ... 6-3/190. ... Bats both, throws right. ... Full name: William Charles Alley.
HIGH SCHOOL: Palm Beach Lakes (West Palm Beach, Fla.).
TRANSACTIONS/CAREER NOTES: Selected by Baltimore Orioles organization in second round of free-agent draft (June 1, 1995).
STATISTICAL NOTES: Led Carolina League with 22 passed balls in 1998.

Year Team (League)	Pos.	G	AB	R	H	2B	3B	HR	RBI	Avg.	BB	SO	SB	PO	A	E	Avg.
1995— GC Orioles (GCL)	C	12	30	10	9	4	0	0	3	.300	11	4	0	61	6	2	.971
1996— Bluefield (Appal.)	C	24	67	7	13	4	0	0	4	.194	15	16	0	192	18	7	.968
1997— Delmarva (S. Atl.)	C	82	250	19	59	17	1	3	32	.236	34	45	7	503	79	12	.980
1998— Frederick (Carolina)	C	112	340	42	89	23	1	9	47	.262	60	60	0	604	83	10	.986

PERSONAL: Born October 26, 1972, in El Paso, Texas. ... 6-3/205. ... Throws left, bats left.
HIGH SCHOOL: Belair (El Paso, Texas).
JUNIOR COLLEGE: New Mexico Junior College.
TRANSACTIONS/CAREER NOTES: Selected by St. Louis Cardinals organization in 21st round of free-agent draft (June 3, 1993). ... On Madison disabled list (April 8, 1994-entire season). ... On Madison reserved list (November 4-December 14, 1994). ... On Memphis disabled list (July 10-21, 1998). ... Traded by Cardinals with P Braden Looper and SS Pablo Ozuna to Florida Marlins for SS Edgar Renteria (December 14, 1998).
STATISTICAL NOTES: Tied for Arizona League lead with 14 wild pitches in 1993.

Year Team (League)	W	L	Pct.	ERA	G	GS	CG	ShO	Sv.	IP	H	R	ER	BB	SO
1993— Ariz. Cardinals (Ariz.)	4	1	.800	3.21	20	4	0	0	0	42	38	19	15	14	56
— Johnson City (App.)	1	1	.500	4.15	3	3	0	0	0	4 1/3	6	2	2	3	4
1994—						Did not play.									
1995— Savannah (S. Atl.)	3	9	.250	3.92	20	20	0	0	0	108	108	62	47	40	72
1996— Peoria (Midwest)	8	6	.571	2.76	52	1	0	0	0	62	50	27	19	32	67
1997— Prince William (Caro.)	2	3	.400	1.67	•58	0	0	0	*36	64 2/3	38	18	12	32	83
1998— Arkansas (Texas)	4	1	.800	3.31	28	0	0	0	8	32 2/3	27	13	12	18	46
— Memphis (Pacific Coast)	3	1	.750	3.03	31	0	0	0	1	35 2/3	35	18	12	19	45

PERSONAL: Born November 6, 1973, in Santiago, Dominican Republic. ... 6-2/200. ... Throws right, bats right. ... Full name: Carlos Manuel Almanzar.
TRANSACTIONS/CAREER NOTES: Signed as non-drafted free agent by Toronto Blue Jays organization (December 10, 1990). ... On Knoxville disabled list (May 27-June 3, 1997). ... Traded by Blue Jays with P Woody Williams and OF Peter Tucci to San Diego Padres for P Joey Hamilton (December 13, 1998).

Year Team (League)	W	L	Pct.	ERA	G	GS	CG	ShO	Sv.	IP	H	R	ER	BB	SO
1991— Dom. B. Jays (DSL)	3	1	.750	2.83	6	6	1	0	0	35	36	17	11	11	20
1992— Dom. B. Jays (DSL)	10	0	1.000	2.01	13	11	2	1	1	67	45	26	15	31	60
1993— Dom. B. Jays (DSL)	5	2	.714	3.38	16	9	0	0	2	69 1/3	60	35	26	32	59
1994— Medicine Hat (Pioneer)	7	4	.636	2.87	14	14	0	0	0	84 2/3	82	38	27	19	77
1995— Knoxville (Southern)	3	12	.200	3.99	35	19	0	0	2	126 1/3	144	77	56	32	93
1996— Knoxville (Southern)	7	8	.467	4.85	54	0	0	0	0	94 2/3	106	58	51	33	105
1997— Knoxville (Southern)	1	1	.500	4.91	21	0	0	0	8	25 2/3	30	14	14	5	25
— Syracuse (Int'l)	5	1	.833	1.41	32	0	0	0	3	51	30	9	8	8	47
— Toronto (A.L.)	0	1	.000	2.70	4	0	0	0	0	3 1/3	1	1	1	1	4
1998— Toronto (A.L.)	2	2	.500	5.34	25	0	0	0	0	28 2/3	34	18	17	8	20
— Syracuse (Int'l)	3	6	.333	2.31	30	0	0	0	10	50 2/3	44	21	13	13	53
Major league totals (2 years)	2	3	.400	5.06	29	0	0	0	0	32	35	19	18	9	24

A

PERSONAL: Born February 5, 1968, in Ponce, Puerto Rico. ... 6-0/185. ... Bats both, throws right. ... Full name: Roberto Velazquez Alomar. ... Son of Sandy Alomar Sr., major league infielder with six teams (1964-78) and coach, San Diego Padres (1986-90); and brother of Sandy Alomar Jr., catcher, Cleveland Indians.

TRANSACTIONS/CAREER NOTES: Signed as non-drafted free agent by San Diego Padres organization (February 16, 1985). ... Traded by Padres with OF Joe Carter to Toronto Blue Jays for 1B Fred McGriff and SS Tony Fernandez (December 5, 1990). ... On suspended list (May 23-24, 1995). ... Granted free agency (October 30, 1995). ... Signed by Baltimore Orioles (December 21, 1995). ... On suspended list (April 1-7, 1997). ... On disabled list (July 30-August 26, 1997; and July 19-August 4, 1998). ... Granted free agency (October 26, 1998). ... Signed by Cleveland Indians (December 1, 1998).

RECORDS: Holds A.L. career record for most consecutive errorless games by second baseman—104 (June 21, 1994 through July 3, 1995). ... Holds A.L. single-season record for fewest double plays by second baseman (150 or more games)—66 (1992). ... Shares A.L. single-season records for most games with switch-hit home runs—2 (1996); and fewest errors by second baseman (150 or more games)—5 (1992).

HONORS: Won A.L. Gold Glove at second base (1991-96 and 1998). ... Named second baseman on THE SPORTING NEWS A.L. All-Star team (1992, 1996 and 1998). ... Named second baseman on THE SPORTING NEWS A.L. Silver Slugger team (1992 and 1996).

STATISTICAL NOTES: Led South Atlantic League second basemen with 35 errors in 1985. ... Led Texas League shortstops with 167 putouts and 34 errors in 1987. ... Led N.L. with 17 sacrifice hits in 1989. ... Led N.L. second basemen with 17 errors in 1990. ... Switch-hit home runs in one game four times (May 10, 1991; May 3, 1995; July 25 and August 14, 1996). ... Had 22-game hitting streak (May 12-June 8, 1996). ... Hit three home runs in one game (April 26, 1997). ... Career major league grand slams: 3.

Year	Team (League)	Pos.	G	AB	R	H	2B	3B	HR	RBI	Avg.	BB	SO	SB	PO	A	E	Avg.
1985—	Char., S.C. (S. Atl.)	2B-SS	*137	*546	89	160	14	3	0	54	.293	61	73	36	298	339	†36	.947
1986—	Reno (California)	2B	90	356	53	123	16	4	4	49	*.346	32	38	14	198	265	18	.963
1987—	Wichita (Texas)	SS-2B	130	536	88	171	41	4	12	68	.319	49	74	43	†188	309	†36	.932
1988—	Las Vegas (PCL)	2B	9	37	5	10	1	0	2	14	.270	1	4	3	22	29	1	.981
—	San Diego (N.L.)	2B	143	545	84	145	24	6	9	41	.266	47	83	24	319	459	16	.980
1989—	San Diego (N.L.)	2B	158	623	82	184	27	1	7	56	.295	53	76	42	341	472	*28	.967
1990—	San Diego (N.L.)	2B-SS	147	586	80	168	27	5	6	60	.287	48	72	24	316	404	†19	.974
1991—	Toronto (A.L.)■	2B	161	637	88	188	41	11	9	69	.295	57	86	53	333	447	15	.981
1992—	Toronto (A.L.)	2B-DH	152	571	105	177	27	8	8	76	.310	87	52	49	287	378	5	.993
1993—	Toronto (A.L.)	2B	153	589	109	192	35	6	17	93	.326	80	67	55	254	439	14	.980
1994—	Toronto (A.L.)	2B	107	392	78	120	25	4	8	38	.306	51	41	19	176	275	4	.991
1995—	Toronto (A.L.)	2B	130	517	71	155	24	7	13	66	.300	47	45	30	*272	267	4	*.993
1996—	Baltimore (A.L.)■	2B-DH	153	588	132	193	43	4	22	94	.328	90	65	17	279	445	11	.985
1997—	Baltimore (A.L.)	2B-DH	112	412	64	137	23	2	14	60	.333	40	43	9	202	301	6	.988
1998—	Baltimore (A.L.)	2B-DH	147	588	86	166	36	1	14	56	.282	59	70	18	251	*449	11	.985
American League totals (8 years)			1115	4294	733	1328	254	43	105	552	.309	511	469	250	2054	3001	70	.986
National League totals (3 years)			448	1754	246	497	78	12	22	157	.283	148	231	90	976	1335	63	.973
Major league totals (11 years)			1563	6048	979	1825	332	55	127	709	.302	659	700	340	3030	4336	133	.982

DIVISION SERIES RECORD

Year	Team (League)	Pos.	G	AB	R	H	2B	3B	HR	RBI	Avg.	BB	SO	SB	PO	A	E	Avg.
1996—	Baltimore (A.L.)	2B	4	17	2	5	0	0	1	4	.294	2	3	0	10	6	0	1.000
1997—	Baltimore (A.L.)	2B-PH	4	10	1	3	2	0	0	2	.300	1	1	0	3	6	0	1.000
Division series totals (2 years)			8	27	3	8	2	0	1	6	.296	3	4	0	13	12	0	1.000

CHAMPIONSHIP SERIES RECORD

RECORDS: Shares career record for most times grounded into double play—5.
NOTES: Named Most Valuable Player (1992).

Year	Team (League)	Pos.	G	AB	R	H	2B	3B	HR	RBI	Avg.	BB	SO	SB	PO	A	E	Avg.
1991—	Toronto (A.L.)	2B	5	19	3	9	0	0	0	4	.474	2	3	2	14	9	0	1.000
1992—	Toronto (A.L.)	2B	6	26	4	11	1	0	2	4	.423	2	1	5	16	15	0	1.000
1993—	Toronto (A.L.)	2B	6	24	3	7	1	0	0	4	.292	4	3	4	14	19	0	1.000
1996—	Baltimore (A.L.)	2B	5	23	2	5	2	0	0	1	.217	0	4	0	15	26	2	.953
1997—	Baltimore (A.L.)	2B	6	22	2	4	0	0	1	2	.182	7	3	0	10	17	2	.931
Championship series totals (5 years)			28	114	14	36	4	0	3	15	.316	15	14	11	69	86	4	.975

WORLD SERIES RECORD

RECORDS: Shares record for most at-bats in one inning—2 (October 20, 1993, eighth inning).
NOTES: Member of World Series championship team (1992 and 1993).

Year	Team (League)	Pos.	G	AB	R	H	2B	3B	HR	RBI	Avg.	BB	SO	SB	PO	A	E	Avg.
1992—	Toronto (A.L.)	2B	6	24	3	5	1	0	0	0	.208	3	3	3	5	12	0	1.000
1993—	Toronto (A.L.)	2B	6	25	5	12	2	1	0	6	.480	2	3	4	9	21	2	.938
World Series totals (2 years)			12	49	8	17	3	1	0	6	.347	5	6	7	14	33	2	.959

ALL-STAR GAME RECORD

RECORDS: Shares single-game record for most stolen bases—2 (July 14, 1992).
NOTES: Named Most Valuable Player (1998).

Year	League	Pos.	AB	R	H	2B	3B	HR	RBI	Avg.	BB	SO	SB	PO	A	E	Avg.
1990—	National	2B	1	0	0	0	0	0	0	.000	0	0	0	1	2	0	1.000
1991—	American	2B	4	0	0	0	0	0	0	.000	0	0	0	2	5	0	1.000
1992—	American	2B	3	1	1	0	0	0	0	.333	0	0	2	1	0	0	1.000
1993—	American	2B	3	1	1	0	0	1	1	.333	0	0	0	0	0	0	...
1994—	American	2B	3	1	1	0	0	0	0	.333	0	1	0	0	0	0	...
1995—	American	PR-2B	1	0	0	0	0	0	0	.000	0	0	1	0	0	0	...
1996—	American	2B	3	0	1	0	0	0	0	.333	0	0	0	0	3	0	1.000
1997—	American	2B	2	0	0	0	0	0	0	.000	0	1	0	1	5	0	1.000
1998—	American	2B	4	2	3	0	0	1	1	.750	1	0	1	3	2	0	1.000
All-Star Game totals (9 years)			24	5	7	0	0	2	2	.292	1	0	5	7	18	0	1.000

PERSONAL: Born June 18, 1966, in Salinas, Puerto Rico. ... 6-5/215. ... Bats right, throws right. ... Full name: Santos Velazquez Alomar Jr. ... Son of Sandy Alomar Sr., major league infielder with six teams (1964-78) and coach, San Diego Padres (1986-90); and brother of Roberto Alomar, second baseman, Cleveland Indians.

HIGH SCHOOL: Luis Munoz Rivera (Salinas, Puerto Rico).

TRANSACTIONS/CAREER NOTES: Signed as non-drafted free agent by San Diego Padres organization (October 21, 1983). ... Traded by Padres with OF Chris James and 3B Carlos Baerga to Cleveland Indians for OF Joe Carter (December 6, 1989). ... On Cleveland disabled list (May 15-June 17 and July 29, 1991-remainder of season); included rehabilitation assignments to Colorado Springs (June 8-17 and August 9-12). ... On disabled list (May 2-18, 1992). ... On suspended list (July 29-August 2, 1992). ... On Cleveland disabled list (May 1-August 7, 1993); included rehabilitation assignment to Charlotte, S.C. (July 22-August 7). ... On disabled list (April 24-May 11, 1994). ... On Cleveland disabled list (April 19-June 29, 1995); included rehabilitation assignment to Canton/Akron (June 22-29).

RECORDS: Shares major league single-game record for most doubles—4 (1997).

HONORS: Named Minor League co-Player of the Year by THE SPORTING NEWS (1988). ... Named Pacific Coast League Player of the Year (1988-89). ... Named Minor League Player of the Year by THE SPORTING NEWS (1989). ... Named A.L. Rookie Player of the Year by THE SPORTING NEWS (1990). ... Won A.L. Gold Glove at catcher (1990). ... Named A.L. Rookie of the Year by Baseball Writers' Association of America (1990).

STATISTICAL NOTES: Led Northwest League catchers with .985 fielding percentage and 421 putouts in 1984. ... Led Pacific Coast League catchers with 14 errors in 1988. ... Led Pacific Coast League catchers with 573 putouts in 1988 and 702 in 1989. ... Led Pacific Coast League catchers with 633 total chances in 1988 and 761 in 1989. ... Had 30-game hitting streak (May 25-July 6, 1997). ... Career major league grand slams: 2.

MISCELLANEOUS: Batted as switch hitter (1984-86).

								BATTING							FIELDING		
Year Team (League)	Pos.	G	AB	R	H	2B	3B	HR	RBI	Avg.	BB	SO	SB	PO	A	E	Avg.
1984—Spokane (N'west)	C-1B	59	219	13	47	5	0	0	21	.215	13	20	3	†465	51	8	†.985
1985—Char., S.C. (S. Atl.)	C-OF	100	352	38	73	7	0	3	43	.207	31	30	3	779	75	18	.979
1986—Beaumont (Texas)	C	100	346	36	83	15	1	4	27	.240	15	35	2	505	60	*18	.969
1987—Wichita (Texas)	C	103	375	50	115	19	1	8	65	.307	21	37	1	*606	50	*15	.978
1988—Las Vegas (PCL)	C-OF	93	337	59	100	9	5	16	71	.297	28	35	1	†574	46	†14	.978
—San Diego (N.L.)	PH	1	1	0	0	0	0	0	0	.000	0	1	0	...	...	...	...
1989—Las Vegas (PCL)	C-OF	131	*523	88	160	33	8	13	101	.306	42	58	3	†706	47	12	.984
—San Diego (N.L.)	C	7	19	1	4	1	0	1	6	.211	3	3	0	33	1	0	1.000
1990—Cleveland (A.L.)■	C	132	445	60	129	26	2	9	66	.290	25	46	4	686	46	*14	.981
1991—Cleveland (A.L.)	C-DH	51	184	10	40	9	0	0	7	.217	8	24	0	280	19	4	.987
—Colo. Springs (PCL)	C	12	35	5	14	2	0	1	10	.400	5	0	0	5	0	1	.833
1992—Cleveland (A.L.)	C-DH	89	299	22	75	16	0	2	26	.251	13	32	3	477	39	2	.996
1993—Cleveland (A.L.)	C	64	215	24	58	7	1	6	32	.270	11	28	3	342	25	6	.984
—Charlotte (Int'l)	C	12	44	8	16	5	0	1	8	.364	5	8	0	20	1	0	1.000
1994—Cleveland (A.L.)	C	80	292	44	84	15	1	14	43	.288	25	31	8	453	41	2	.996
1995—Cant./Akr. (Eastern)	C	6	15	3	6	1	0	0	1	.400	1	1	0	23	0	1	.958
—Cleveland (A.L.)	C	66	203	32	61	6	0	10	35	.300	7	26	3	364	22	2	.995
1996—Cleveland (A.L.)	C-1B	127	418	53	110	23	0	11	50	.263	19	42	1	724	48	9	.988
1997—Cleveland (A.L.)	C-DH	125	451	63	146	37	0	21	83	.324	19	48	0	743	40	*12	.985
1998—Cleveland (A.L.)	C-DH	117	409	45	96	26	2	6	44	.235	18	45	0	712	42	6	.992
American League totals (9 years)		851	2916	353	799	165	6	79	386	.274	145	322	22	4781	322	57	.989
National League totals (2 years)		8	20	1	4	1	0	1	6	.200	3	4	0	33	1	0	1.000
Major league totals (11 years)		859	2936	354	803	166	6	80	392	.274	148	326	22	4814	323	57	.989

DIVISION SERIES RECORD

								BATTING							FIELDING		
Year Team (League)	Pos.	G	AB	R	H	2B	3B	HR	RBI	Avg.	BB	SO	SB	PO	A	E	Avg.
1995—Cleveland (A.L.)	C	3	11	1	2	1	0	0	1	.182	0	1	0	22	1	0	1.000
1996—Cleveland (A.L.)	C	4	16	0	2	0	0	0	3	.125	0	2	0	40	4	1	.978
1997—Cleveland (A.L.)	C	5	19	4	6	1	0	2	5	.316	0	2	0	28	1	1	.967
1998—Cleveland (A.L.)	C	4	13	2	3	3	0	0	2	.231	1	4	0	29	0	1	.967
Division series totals (4 years)		16	59	7	13	5	0	2	11	.220	1	9	0	119	6	3	.977

CHAMPIONSHIP SERIES RECORD

								BATTING							FIELDING		
Year Team (League)	Pos.	G	AB	R	H	2B	3B	HR	RBI	Avg.	BB	SO	SB	PO	A	E	Avg.
1995—Cleveland (A.L.)	C	5	15	0	4	1	1	0	1	.267	1	1	0	30	3	1	.971
1997—Cleveland (A.L.)	C	6	24	3	3	0	0	1	4	.125	1	3	0	49	1	0	1.000
1998—Cleveland (A.L.)	C	5	16	1	1	0	0	0	0	.063	0	2	0	29	1	2	.938
Championship series totals (3 years)		16	55	4	8	1	1	1	5	.145	2	6	0	108	5	3	.974

WORLD SERIES RECORD

								BATTING							FIELDING		
Year Team (League)	Pos.	G	AB	R	H	2B	3B	HR	RBI	Avg.	BB	SO	SB	PO	A	E	Avg.
1995—Cleveland (A.L.)	C	5	15	0	3	2	0	0	1	.200	0	2	0	28	0	0	1.000
1997—Cleveland (A.L.)	C	7	30	5	11	1	0	2	10	.367	2	3	0	49	3	0	1.000
World Series totals (2 years)		12	45	5	14	3	0	2	11	.311	2	5	0	77	3	0	1.000

ALL-STAR GAME RECORD

NOTES: Named Most Valuable Player (1997).

							BATTING							FIELDING		
Year League	Pos.	AB	R	H	2B	3B	HR	RBI	Avg.	BB	SO	SB	PO	A	E	Avg.
1990—American	C	3	1	2	0	0	0	0	.667	0	0	0	3	0	0	1.000
1991—American	C	2	0	0	0	0	0	0	.000	0	0	0	2	0	0	1.000
1992—American	C	3	0	1	0	0	0	0	.333	0	0	0	3	0	0	1.000
1997—American	C	1	1	1	0	0	1	2	1.000	0	0	0	4	0	0	1.000
1998—American	C	1	0	1	0	0	0	1	1.000	0	0	0	5	0	0	1.000
All-Star Game totals (5 years)		10	2	5	0	0	1	3	.500	0	0	0	17	0	0	1.000

A

PERSONAL: Born July 3, 1966, in Atlanta. ... 6-3/195. ... Bats right, throws right. ... Full name: Moises Rojas Alou. ... Son of Felipe Alou, manager, Montreal Expos; nephew of Jesus Alou, major league outfielder with four teams (1963-75 and 1978-79); nephew of Matty Alou, major league outfielder with six teams (1960-74); and cousin of Mel Rojas, pitcher, Los Angeles Dodgers. ... Name pronounced moy-SEZZ ah-LOO.
HIGH SCHOOL: C.E.E. (Santo Domingo, Dominican Republic).
JUNIOR COLLEGE: Canada College (Calif.).
TRANSACTIONS/CAREER NOTES: Selected by Pittsburgh Pirates organization in first round (second pick overall) of free-agent draft (January 14, 1986). ... Traded by Pirates organization to Montreal Expos (August 16, 1990), completing deal in which Expos traded P Zane Smith to Pirates for P Scott Ruskin, SS Willie Greene and a player to be named later (August 8, 1990). ... On Montreal disabled list (March 19, 1991-entire season; July 7-27, 1992; September 18, 1993-remainder of season; August 18-September 5, 1995 and September 11, 1995-remainder of season). ... On disabled list (July 8-23, 1996). ... On suspended list (August 23-27, 1996). ... Granted free agency (December 7, 1996). ... Signed by Florida Marlins (December 12, 1996). ... Traded by Marlins to Houston Astros for P Oscar Henriquez, P Manuel Barrios and a player to be named later (November 11, 1997); Marlins acquired P Mark Johnson to complete deal (December 16, 1997).
HONORS: Named outfielder on THE SPORTING NEWS N.L. All-Star team (1994 and 1998). ... Named outfielder on THE SPORTING NEWS N.L. Silver Slugger team (1994 and 1998).
STATISTICAL NOTES: Led American Association outfielders with seven double plays in 1990. ... Career major league grand slams: 2.

Year	Team (League)	Pos.	G	AB	R	H	2B	3B	HR	RBI	Avg.	BB	SO	SB	PO	A	E	Avg.
1986—Watertown (NYP)		OF	69	254	30	60	9	*8	6	35	.236	22	72	14	134	6	7	.952
1987—Macon (S. Atl.)		OF	4	8	1	1	0	0	0	0	.125	2	4	0	6	0	0	1.000
—Watertown (NYP)		OF	39	117	20	25	6	2	4	8	.214	16	36	6	43	1	2	.957
1988—Augusta (S. Atl.)		OF	105	358	58	112	23	5	7	62	.313	51	84	24	220	10	9	.962
1989—Salem (Carolina)		OF	86	321	50	97	29	2	14	53	.302	35	69	12	166	12	10	.947
—Harrisburg (East.)		OF	54	205	36	60	5	2	3	19	.293	17	38	8	89	1	2	.978
1990—Harrisburg (East.)		OF	36	132	19	39	12	2	3	22	.295	16	21	7	93	2	1	.990
—Buffalo (A.A.)		OF	75	271	38	74	4	6	5	31	.273	30	43	9	169	10	8	.957
—Pittsburgh (N.L.)		OF	2	5	0	1	0	0	0	0	.200	0	0	0	3	0	0	1.000
—Indianapolis (A.A.)■ ..		OF	15	55	6	12	1	0	0	6	.218	3	7	4	27	2	0	1.000
—Montreal (N.L.)		OF	14	15	4	3	0	1	0	0	.200	0	3	0	6	1	0	1.000
1991—								Did not play.										
1992—Montreal (N.L.)		OF	115	341	53	96	28	2	9	56	.282	25	46	16	170	6	4	.978
1993—Montreal (N.L.)		OF	136	482	70	138	29	6	18	85	.286	38	53	17	254	11	4	.985
1994—Montreal (N.L.)		OF	107	422	81	143	31	5	22	78	.339	42	63	7	201	4	3	.986
1995—Montreal (N.L.)		OF	93	344	48	94	22	0	14	58	.273	29	56	4	147	5	3	.981
1996—Montreal (N.L.)		OF	143	540	87	152	28	2	21	96	.281	49	83	9	259	8	3	.989
1997—Florida (N.L.)■		OF	150	538	88	157	29	5	23	115	.292	70	85	9	248	4	3	.988
1998—Houston (N.L.)■		OF-DH	159	584	104	182	34	5	38	124	.312	84	87	11	232	11	5	.980
Major league totals (8 years)			919	3271	535	966	201	26	145	612	.295	337	476	73	1520	50	25	.984

DIVISION SERIES RECORD

Year	Team (League)	Pos.	G	AB	R	H	2B	3B	HR	RBI	Avg.	BB	SO	SB	PO	A	E	Avg.
1997—Florida (N.L.)		OF	3	14	1	3	1	0	0	1	.214	0	3	0	5	0	0	1.000
1998—Houston (N.L.)		OF	4	16	0	3	0	0	0	0	.188	0	2	0	4	0	0	1.000
Division series totals (2 years)			7	30	1	6	1	0	0	1	.200	0	5	0	9	0	0	1.000

CHAMPIONSHIP SERIES RECORD

Year	Team (League)	Pos.	G	AB	R	H	2B	3B	HR	RBI	Avg.	BB	SO	SB	PO	A	E	Avg.
1997—Florida (N.L.)		OF-PH	5	15	0	1	1	0	0	5	.067	1	3	0	3	0	0	1.000

WORLD SERIES RECORD

NOTES: Member of World Series championship team (1997).

Year	Team (League)	Pos.	G	AB	R	H	2B	3B	HR	RBI	Avg.	BB	SO	SB	PO	A	E	Avg.
1997—Florida (N.L.)		OF	7	28	6	9	2	0	3	9	.321	3	6	1	11	0	0	1.000

ALL-STAR GAME RECORD

Year	League	Pos.	AB	R	H	2B	3B	HR	RBI	Avg.	BB	SO	SB	PO	A	E	Avg.
1994—National	OF	1	0	1	1	0	0	1	1.000	0	0	0	0	0	0	...
1997—National	OF	2	0	1	0	0	0	0	.500	0	0	0	1	0	0	1.000
1998—National	OF	3	1	1	0	0	0	0	.333	0	2	0	0	0	0	...
All-Star Game totals (3 years)		6	1	3	1	0	0	1	.500	0	2	0	1	0	0	1.000

PERSONAL: Born March 6, 1974, in Navojoa, Sonora, Mexico. ... 6-1/205. ... Bats right, throws right. ... Full name: Gabriel De Jesus Alvarez.
HIGH SCHOOL: Bishop Amat (La Puente, Calif.).
COLLEGE: Southern California.
TRANSACTIONS/CAREER NOTES: Selected by San Diego Padres organization in second round of free-agent draft (June 1, 1995). ... Selected by Arizona Diamondbacks in first round (fifth pick overall) of expansion draft (November 18, 1997). ... Traded by Diamondbacks with 3B Joe Randa and P Matt Drews to Detroit Tigers for 3B Travis Fryman (November 18, 1997).
STATISTICAL NOTES: Led Southern League third basemen in errors with 32 in 1997. ... Led Southern League in grounding into double plays with 21 in 1997. ... Career major league grand slams: 1.

Year	Team (League)	Pos.	G	AB	R	H	2B	3B	HR	RBI	Avg.	BB	SO	SB	PO	A	E	Avg.
1995—Rancho Cuca. (Cal.) ...		SS-3B	59	212	41	73	17	2	6	36	.344	29	30	1	52	132	22	.893
—Memphis (Sou.)		2B-SS	2	9	0	5	1	0	0	4	.556	1	1	0	0	6	1	.857

Year Team (League)	Pos.	G	AB	R	H	2B	3B	HR	RBI	Avg.	BB	SO	SB	PO	A	E	Avg.
1996—Memphis (Sou.)	3B-SS	104	368	58	91	23	1	8	40	.247	64	87	2	62	161	31	.878
1997—Mobile (Southern)	3B-SS	114	427	71	128	28	2	14	78	.300	51	64	1	70	209	†33	.894
1998—Toledo (Int'l)■	3B	67	249	37	68	15	1	20	58	.273	30	60	3	38	142	15	.923
—Detroit (A.L.)	3B-DH	58	199	16	46	11	0	5	29	.231	18	65	1	38	93	19	.873
Major league totals (1 year)		58	199	16	46	11	0	5	29	.231	18	65	1	38	93	19	.873

ALVAREZ, WILSON   P   DEVIL RAYS

PERSONAL: Born March 24, 1970, in Maracaibo, Venezuela. ... 6-1/235. ... Throws left, bats left. ... Full name: Wilson Eduardo Alvarez.

TRANSACTIONS/CAREER NOTES: Signed as non-drafted free agent by Texas Rangers organization (September 23, 1986). ... Traded by Rangers with IF Scott Fletcher and OF Sammy Sosa to Chicago White Sox for OF Harold Baines and IF Fred Manrique (July 29, 1989). ... Traded by White Sox with P Danny Darwin and P Roberto Hernandez to San Francisco Giants for SS Michael Caruso, OF Brian Manning, P Lorenzo Barcelo, P Keith Foulke, P Bobby Howry and P Ken Vining (July 31, 1997). ... Granted free agency (November 1, 1997). ... Signed by Tampa Bay Devil Rays (December 3, 1997). ... On Tampa Bay disabled list (May 21-July 6, 1998); included rehabilitation assignments to Gulf Coast Devil Rays (June 26-29), St. Petersburg (June 30-July 4) and Durham (July 5-6).

RECORDS: Shares major league single-inning record for most strikeouts—4 (July 21, 1997, seventh inning).

STATISTICAL NOTES: Tied for Gulf Coast League lead with six home runs allowed in 1987. ... Pitched 7-0 no-hit victory for Chicago against Baltimore (August 11, 1991).

Year Team (League)	W	L	Pct.	ERA	G	GS	CG	ShO	Sv.	IP	H	R	ER	BB	SO
1987—Gastonia (S. Atl.)	1	5	.167	6.47	8	6	0	0	0	32	39	24	23	23	19
—GC Rangers (GCL)	2	5	.286	5.24	10	10	0	0	0	44 2/3	41	29	26	21	46
1988—Gastonia (S. Atl.)	4	11	.267	2.98	23	23	1	0	0	127	113	63	42	49	134
—Oklahoma City (A.A.)	1	1	.500	3.78	5	3	0	0	0	16 2/3	17	8	7	6	9
1989—Charlotte (Fla. St.)	7	4	.636	2.11	13	13	3	2	0	81	68	29	19	21	51
—Tulsa (Texas)	2	2	.500	2.06	7	7	1	1	0	48	40	14	11	16	29
—Texas (A.L.)	0	1	.000	...	1	1	0	0	0	0	3	3	3	2	0
—Birmingham (Southern)■	2	1	.667	3.03	6	6	0	0	0	35 2/3	32	12	12	16	18
1990—Birmingham (Southern)	5	1	.833	4.27	7	7	1	0	0	46 1/3	44	24	22	25	36
—Vancouver (PCL)	7	7	.500	6.00	17	15	1	0	0	75	91	54	50	51	35
1991—Birmingham (Southern)	10	6	.625	1.83	23	23	3	2	0	152 1/3	109	46	31	74	165
—Chicago (A.L.)	3	2	.600	3.51	10	9	2	1	0	56 1/3	47	26	22	29	32
1992—Chicago (A.L.)	5	3	.625	5.20	34	9	0	0	1	100 1/3	103	64	58	65	66
1993—Chicago (A.L.)	15	8	.652	2.95	31	31	1	1	0	207 2/3	168	78	68	*122	155
—Nashville (A.A.)	0	1	.000	2.84	1	1	0	0	0	6 1/3	7	7	2	2	8
1994—Chicago (A.L.)	12	8	.600	3.45	24	24	2	1	0	161 2/3	147	72	62	62	108
1995—Chicago (A.L.)	8	11	.421	4.32	29	29	3	0	0	175	171	96	84	93	118
1996—Chicago (A.L.)	15	10	.600	4.22	35	35	0	0	0	217 1/3	216	106	102	97	181
1997—Chicago (A.L.)	9	8	.529	3.03	22	22	2	1	0	145 2/3	126	61	49	55	110
—San Francisco (N.L.)■	4	3	.571	4.48	11	11	0	0	0	66 1/3	54	36	33	36	69
1998—Tampa Bay (A.L.)■	6	14	.300	4.73	25	25	0	0	0	142 2/3	130	78	75	68	107
—GC Devil Rays	0	0	...	0.00	1	1	0	0	0	3	2	0	0	1	4
—St. Petersburg (FSL)	0	1	.000	27.00	1	1	0	0	0	1 2/3	5	5	5	2	2
—Durham (International)	0	0	...	3.86	1	1	0	0	0	4 2/3	4	2	2	2	6
A.L. totals (9 years)	73	65	.529	3.90	211	185	10	4	1	1206 2/3	1111	584	523	593	877
N.L. totals (1 year)	4	3	.571	4.48	11	11	0	0	0	66 1/3	54	36	33	36	69
Major league totals (9 years)	77	68	.531	3.93	222	196	10	4	1	1273	1165	620	556	629	946

DIVISION SERIES RECORD

Year Team (League)	W	L	Pct.	ERA	G	GS	CG	ShO	Sv.	IP	H	R	ER	BB	SO
1997—San Francisco (N.L.)	0	1	.000	6.00	1	1	0	0	0	6	6	4	4	4	4

CHAMPIONSHIP SERIES RECORD

Year Team (League)	W	L	Pct.	ERA	G	GS	CG	ShO	Sv.	IP	H	R	ER	BB	SO
1993—Chicago (A.L.)	1	0	1.000	1.00	1	1	0	0	0	9	7	1	1	2	6

ALL-STAR GAME RECORD

Year League	W	L	Pct.	ERA	GS	CG	ShO	Sv.	IP	H	R	ER	BB	SO
1994—American	0	0	...	0.00	0	0	0	0	1	0	0	0	0	0

AMARAL, RICH   OF   ORIOLES

PERSONAL: Born April 1, 1962, in Visalia, Calif. ... 6-0/175. ... Bats right, throws right. ... Full name: Richard Louis Amaral. ... Name pronounced AM-ar-all.

HIGH SCHOOL: Estancia (Costa Mesa, Calif.).

JUNIOR COLLEGE: Orange Coast College (Calif.).

COLLEGE: UCLA.

TRANSACTIONS/CAREER NOTES: Selected by Chicago Cubs organization in second round of free-agent draft (June 6, 1983). ... Selected by Chicago White Sox organization from Cubs organization in Rule 5 minor league draft (December 6, 1988). ... Granted free agency (October 15, 1990). ... Signed by Seattle Mariners organization (November 25, 1990). ... On Seattle disabled list (May 29-July 17, 1991); included rehabilitation assignment to Calgary (July 11-17). ... On disabled list (August 1-16, 1993). ... On disabled list (March 28-April 14 and September 9, 1998-remainder of season). ... Granted free agency (October 26, 1998). ... Signed by Baltimore Orioles (December 21, 1998).

HONORS: Named second baseman on THE SPORTING NEWS college All-America team (1983).

STATISTICAL NOTES: Tied for New York-Pennsylvania League lead in double plays by second baseman with 39 in 1984. ... Tied for Carolina League lead in errors by second baseman with 25 in 1985. ... Led Pacific Coast League with .433 on-base percentage in 1991.

Year Team (League)	Pos.	G	AB	R	H	2B	3B	HR	RBI	Avg.	BB	SO	SB	PO	A	E	Avg.
1983—Geneva (NY-Penn)	2B-3B-SS	67	269	63	68	17	3	1	24	.253	45	47	22	135	205	14	.960
1984—Quad Cities (Mid.)	2B-SS	34	119	21	25	1	0	0	7	.210	24	29	12	62	73	6	.957

Year Team (League)	Pos.	G	AB	R	H	2B	3B	HR	RBI	Avg.	BB	SO	SB	PO	A	E	Avg.
1985—Win.-Salem (Car.)......	2B-3B	124	428	62	116	15	5	3	36	.271	59	68	26	228	318	‡27	.953
1986—Pittsfield (Eastern)......	2B	114	355	43	89	12	0	0	24	.251	39	65	25	228	266	14	.972
1987—Pittsfield (Eastern)......	2B-1B	104	315	45	80	8	5	0	28	.254	43	50	28	242	274	18	.966
1988—Pittsfield (Eastern)......	2-3-1-S-O	122	422	66	117	15	4	4	47	.277	56	53	54	288	262	19	.967
1989—Birmingham (Sou.)■	2B-SS-3B	122	432	*90	123	15	6	4	48	.285	88	66	57	198	256	23	.952
1990—Vancouver (PCL)......	S-3-2-0-1	130	462	87	139	*39	5	4	56	.301	88	68	20	154	260	15	.965
1991—Calgary (PCL)■	SS-2B	86	347	79	120	26	2	3	36	*.346	53	37	30	148	284	15	.966
— Seattle (A.L.)......	2-3-S-DH-1	14	16	2	1	0	0	0	0	.063	1	5	0	13	16	2	.935
1992—Calgary (PCL)......	SS-2B-OF	106	403	79	128	21	8	0	21	.318	67	69	*53	192	329	22	.959
— Seattle (A.L.)......	S-3-0-1-2	35	100	9	24	3	0	1	7	.240	5	16	4	33	68	3	.971
1993—Seattle (A.L.)......	2-3-S-DH-1	110	373	53	108	24	1	1	44	.290	33	54	19	180	270	10	.978
1994—Seattle (A.L.)......	2-0-S-DH-1	77	228	37	60	10	2	4	18	.263	24	28	5	107	118	15	.938
— Calgary (PCL)......	2B-OF	13	56	13	18	7	0	0	12	.321	4	6	2	28	35	3	.955
1995—Seattle (A.L.)......	OF-DH	90	238	45	67	14	2	2	19	.282	21	33	21	121	6	1	.992
1996—Seattle (A.L.)......	O-2-1-DH-3	118	312	69	91	11	3	1	29	.292	47	55	25	195	24	0	1.000
1997—Seattle (A.L.)......	O-1-2-DH-3-S	89	190	34	54	5	0	1	21	.284	10	34	12	103	29	3	.978
1998—Seattle (A.L.)......	O-2-1-DH-3	73	134	25	37	6	0	1	4	.276	13	24	11	90	14	0	1.000
Major league totals (8 years)		606	1591	274	442	73	8	11	142	.278	154	249	97	842	545	34	.976

DIVISION SERIES RECORD

Year Team (League)	Pos.	G	AB	R	H	2B	3B	HR	RBI	Avg.	BB	SO	SB	PO	A	E	Avg.
1995—Seattle (A.L.)								Did not play.									
1997—Seattle (A.L.)	1B-PH	2	4	2	2	0	0	0	0	.500	0	1	0	7	2	0	1.000

CHAMPIONSHIP SERIES RECORD

Year Team (League)	Pos.	G	AB	R	H	2B	3B	HR	RBI	Avg.	BB	SO	SB	PO	A	E	Avg.
1995—Seattle (A.L.)	PH	2	2	0	0	0	0	0	0	.000	0	1	0	...	...	...	...

AMARO, RUBEN   OF

PERSONAL: Born February 12, 1965, in Philadelphia. ... 5-10/187. ... Bats both, throws right. ... Son of Ruben Amaro Sr., infielder with four major league teams (1958 and 1960-69).
HIGH SCHOOL: William Penn Charter (Philadelphia).
COLLEGE: Stanford (degree in human biology, 1987).
TRANSACTIONS/CAREER NOTES: Selected by California Angels organization in 11th round of free-agent draft (June 2, 1987). ... Traded by Angels with P Kyle Abbott to Philadelphia Phillies for OF Von Hayes (December 8, 1991). ... On Scranton/Wilkes-Barre disabled list (April 26-May 7, 1993). ... Traded by Phillies to Cleveland Indians for P Heathcliff Slocumb (November 2, 1993). ... On Cleveland disabled list (July 29-September 1, 1995); included rehabilitation assignment to Buffalo (August 13-28). ... Released by Indians (November 9, 1995). ... Signed by Toronto Blue Jays organization (January 24, 1996). ... Released by Blue Jays organization (May 5, 1996). ... Signed by Phillies (May 6, 1996). ... Placed on voluntarily retired list (October 16, 1998); named assistant general manager by Phillies, effective at the end of 1998 season.
STATISTICAL NOTES: Led Northwest League in caught stealing with 11 in 1987. ... Tied for Texas League lead in being hit by pitch with nine in 1990.

Year Team (League)	Pos.	G	AB	R	H	2B	3B	HR	RBI	Avg.	BB	SO	SB	PO	A	E	Avg.
1987—Salem (Northwest)	0-3-1-S-2	71	241	51	68	7	3	3	41	.282	49	28	27	243	53	17	.946
1988—Palm Springs (Calif.)..	2-0-C-S	115	417	96	111	13	3	4	50	.266	105	61	42	258	188	18	.961
— Midland (Texas).........	2B	13	31	5	4	1	0	0	2	.129	4	5	4	14	30	1	.978
1989—Quad City (Midwest) ..	OF-2B	59	200	50	72	9	4	3	27	.360	45	25	20	94	34	4	.970
— Midland (Texas).........	OF	29	110	28	42	9	2	3	9	.382	10	19	7	34	2	2	.947
1990—Edmonton (PCL)........	OF	57	224	50	80	15	6	4	38	.357	29	23	8	97	8	0	1.000
— Edmonton (PCL)........	OF-1B	82	318	53	92	15	4	3	32	.289	40	43	32	161	5	2	.988
1991—Edmonton (PCL)	OF-2B-1B	121	472	*95	154	*42	6	3	42	.326	63	48	36	167	23	5	.974
— California (A.L.)........	OF-2B-DH	10	23	0	5	1	0	0	2	.217	3	3	0	9	6	1	.938
1992—Philadelphia (N.L.)■...	OF	126	374	43	82	15	6	7	34	.219	37	54	11	232	5	2	.992
— Scran./W.B. (Int'l).....	OF	18	68	8	20	4	1	1	10	.294	9	6	2	35	1	0	1.000
1993—Scran./W.B. (Int'l).......	OF-2B	101	412	76	120	30	5	9	37	.291	31	44	25	272	8	5	.982
— Philadelphia (N.L.)......	OF	25	48	7	16	2	2	1	6	.333	6	5	0	25	1	1	.963
1994—Charlotte (Int'l)■........	OF	43	181	39	58	12	4	3	17	.320	15	16	9	84	2	1	.989
— Cleveland (A.L.)........	OF-DH	26	23	5	5	1	0	2	5	.217	2	3	2	10	0	1	.909
1995—Cleveland (A.L.)........	OF-DH	28	60	5	12	3	0	1	7	.200	4	6	1	35	0	0	1.000
— Buffalo (A.A.)..........	OF	54	213	42	65	15	3	6	22	.305	18	29	6	102	2	1	.990
1996—Syracuse (Int'l)■........	OF	16	50	8	12	1	0	0	2	.240	10	11	6	23	2	0	1.000
— Philadelphia (N.L.)■ ..	OF-1B	61	117	14	37	10	0	2	15	.316	9	18	0	50	0	0	1.000
— Scran./W.B. (Int'l).......	OF-2B-3B	52	180	28	50	10	3	2	22	.278	14	29	7	110	9	1	.992
1997—Philadelphia (N.L.)......	OF-1B	117	175	18	41	6	1	2	21	.234	21	24	1	79	2	1	.988
1998—Philadelphia (N.L.)......	OF	92	107	7	20	5	0	1	10	.187	6	15	0	26	3	0	1.000
American League totals (3 years)		64	106	10	22	5	0	3	14	.208	9	12	3	54	6	2	.968
National League totals (5 years)		421	821	89	196	38	9	13	86	.239	79	116	12	412	11	4	.991
Major league totals (8 years)		485	927	99	218	43	9	16	100	.235	88	128	15	466	17	6	.988

CHAMPIONSHIP SERIES RECORD

Year Team (League)	Pos.	G	AB	R	H	2B	3B	HR	RBI	Avg.	BB	SO	SB	PO	A	E	Avg.
1995—Cleveland (A.L.)..........	PR-DH	3	1	1	0	0	0	0	0	.000	0	0	0	...	...	...	...

WORLD SERIES RECORD

Year Team (League)	Pos.	G	AB	R	H	2B	3B	HR	RBI	Avg.	BB	SO	SB	PO	A	E	Avg.
1995—Cleveland (A.L.)..........	PH-OF	2	2	0	0	0	0	0	0	.000	0	1	0	0	0	0	...

A

PERSONAL: Born November 1, 1974, in Evansville, Ind. ... 6-5/180. ... Throws right, bats right. ... Full name: John M. Ambrose.
HIGH SCHOOL: Evansville (Ind.) Memorial.
JUNIOR COLLEGE: John A. Logan College (III.).
TRANSACTIONS/CAREER NOTES: Selected by Chicago White Sox organization in second round of free-agent draft (June 3, 1994); pick received from Colorado Rockies as part of compensation for signing Type A free-agent OF Ellis Burks. ... On restricted list (April 9-September 6, 1996).
STATISTICAL NOTES: Tied for Carolina League lead with five balks in 1997.

Year Team (League)	W	L	Pct.	ERA	G	GS	CG	ShO	Sv.	IP	H	R	ER	BB	SO
1994— GC White Sox (GCL)	1	2	.333	3.66	11	10	0	0	0	46²/₃	34	21	19	24	43
— Hickory (S. Atl.)	1	1	.500	7.11	3	1	0	0	1	12²/₃	16	11	10	6	7
1995— Hickory (S. Atl.)	4	8	.333	3.95	14	14	0	0	0	73	65	41	32	35	49
— South Bend (Mid.)..............	1	1	.500	5.40	3	3	1	0	0	16²/₃	18	13	10	10	15
1996—							Did not play.								
1997— Win.-Salem (Car.)..............	8	13	.381	5.47	27	27	1	1	0	149²/₃	136	102	*91	*117	137
1998— Birmingham (Southern)	9	12	.429	5.18	31	22	0	0	0	140²/₃	156	90	81	69	103

PERSONAL: Born January 18, 1964, in Silver Spring, Md. ... 6-1/202. ... Bats left, throws left. ... Full name: Brady Kevin Anderson.
HIGH SCHOOL: Carlsbad (Calif.).
COLLEGE: UC Irvine.
TRANSACTIONS/CAREER NOTES: Selected by Boston Red Sox organization in 10th round of free-agent draft (June 3, 1985). ... Traded by Red Sox with P Curt Schilling to Baltimore Orioles for P Mike Boddicker (July 29, 1988). ... On Baltimore disabled list (June 8-July 20, 1990); included rehabilitation assignments to Hagerstown (July 5-12) and Frederick (July 13-17). ... On Baltimore disabled list (May 28-June 14, 1991) and June 23-July 8, 1993). ... Granted free agency (October 27, 1997). ... Re-signed by Orioles (December 7, 1997). ... On disabled list (April 20-May 8, 1998).
RECORDS: Holds major league single-season record for most home runs as leadoff batter—12 (1996).
STATISTICAL NOTES: Led A.L. outfielders with six double plays in 1992. ... Led A.L. in being hit by pitch with 22 in 1996 and 19 in 1997. ... Career major league grand slams: 2.

Year Team (League)	Pos.	G	AB	R	H	2B	3B	HR	RBI	Avg.	BB	SO	SB	PO	A	E	Avg.
1985— Elmira (N.Y.-Penn)......	OF	71	215	36	55	7	•6	5	21	.256	*67	32	13	119	5	3	.976
1986— Winter Haven (FSL)....	OF	126	417	86	133	19	11	12	87	.319	*107	47	44	280	5	1	*.997
1987— New Britain (East.)	OF	52	170	30	50	4	3	6	35	.294	45	24	7	127	2	2	.985
— Pawtucket (Int'l).........	OF	23	79	18	30	4	0	2	8	.380	16	8	2	48	1	0	1.000
1988— Boston (A.L.)............	OF	41	148	14	34	5	3	0	12	.230	15	35	4	87	3	1	.989
— Pawtucket (Int'l).........	OF	49	167	27	48	6	1	4	19	.287	26	33	8	115	4	2	.983
— Baltimore (A.L.)■.......	OF	53	177	17	35	8	1	1	9	.198	28	8	40	6	156	1	3	.981
1989— Baltimore (A.L.).........	OF-DH	94	266	44	55	12	2	4	16	.207	43	45	16	191	3	3	.985
— Rochester (Int'l)	OF	21	70	14	14	1	2	1	8	.200	12	13	2	1	0	0	1.000
1990— Baltimore (A.L.).........	OF-DH	89	234	24	54	5	2	3	24	.231	31	46	15	149	3	2	.987
— Hagerstown (East.)......	OF	9	34	8	13	0	2	1	5	.382	5	5	2	8	1	0	1.000
— Frederick (Carolina)....	OF	2	7	2	3	1	0	0	3	.429	1	1	0	1	0	0	1.000
1991— Baltimore (A.L.).........	OF-DH	113	256	40	59	12	3	2	27	.230	38	44	12	150	3	3	.981
— Rochester (Int'l)	OF	7	26	5	10	3	0	0	2	.385	7	4	4	19	1	0	1.000
1992— Baltimore (A.L.).........	OF	159	623	100	169	28	10	21	80	.271	98	98	53	382	10	8	.980
1993— Baltimore (A.L.).........	OF-DH	142	560	87	147	36	8	13	66	.263	82	99	24	296	7	2	.993
1994— Baltimore (A.L.).........	OF	111	453	78	119	25	5	12	48	.263	57	75	31	247	4	1	.996
1995— Baltimore (A.L.).........	OF	143	554	108	145	33	10	16	64	.262	87	111	26	268	1	3	.989
1996— Baltimore (A.L.).........	OF-DH	149	579	117	172	37	5	50	110	.297	76	106	21	341	10	3	.992
1997— Baltimore (A.L.).........	OF-DH	151	590	97	170	39	7	18	73	.288	84	105	18	276	2	3	.989
1998— Baltimore (A.L.).........	OF-DH	133	479	84	113	28	3	18	60	.236	75	78	21	269	1	4	.985
Major league totals (11 years)		1378	4919	810	1272	268	59	158	580	.259	694	882	247	2812	48	36	.988

DIVISION SERIES RECORD

NOTES: Hit home run in first at-bat (October 1, 1996).

Year Team (League)	Pos.	G	AB	R	H	2B	3B	HR	RBI	Avg.	BB	SO	SB	PO	A	E	Avg.
1996— Baltimore (A.L.).........	OF	4	17	3	5	0	0	2	4	.294	2	3	0	7	0	0	1.000
1997— Baltimore (A.L.).........	OF	4	17	3	6	1	0	1	4	.353	1	4	1	6	0	0	1.000
Division series totals (2 years)		8	34	6	11	1	0	3	8	.324	3	7	1	13	0	0	1.000

CHAMPIONSHIP SERIES RECORD

Year Team (League)	Pos.	G	AB	R	H	2B	3B	HR	RBI	Avg.	BB	SO	SB	PO	A	E	Avg.
1996— Baltimore (A.L.).........	OF	5	21	5	4	1	0	1	1	.190	3	5	0	8	0	0	1.000
1997— Baltimore (A.L.).........	OF	6	25	5	9	2	0	2	3	.360	4	4	2	13	0	1	.929
Championship series totals (2 years)		11	46	10	13	3	0	3	4	.283	7	9	2	21	0	1	.955

ALL-STAR GAME RECORD

Year League	Pos.	AB	R	H	2B	3B	HR	RBI	Avg.	BB	SO	SB	PO	A	E	Avg.
1992— American	OF	3	0	0	0	0	0	0	.000	0	0	0	1	0	0	1.000
1996— American	OF	2	0	0	0	0	0	0	.000	0	0	0	0	0	0	...
1997— American	OF	4	0	2	1	0	0	0	.500	0	0	0	1	0	0	1.000
All-Star Game totals (3 years)		9	0	2	1	0	0	0	.222	0	0	0	2	0	0	1.000

ANDERSON, BRIAN   P   DIAMONDBACKS

PERSONAL: Born April 26, 1972, in Geneva, Ohio. ... 6-1/190. ... Throws left, bats both. ... Full name: Brian James Anderson.
HIGH SCHOOL: Geneva (Ohio).
COLLEGE: Wright State.
TRANSACTIONS/CAREER NOTES: Selected by California Angels organization in first round (third pick overall) of free-agent draft (June 3, 1993). ... On California disabled list (May 7-June 7, 1994); included rehabilitation assignment to Lake Elsinore (May 27-June 7). ... On California disabled list (May 6-June 20, 1995); included rehabilitation assignment to Lake Elsinore (June 4-20). ... Traded by Angels to Cleveland Indians for P Jason Grimsley and P Pep Harris (February 15, 1996). ... On Cleveland disabled list (July 5-August 12, 1997); included rehabilitation assignment to Buffalo (August 3-13). ... Selected by Arizona Diamondbacks in first round (second pick overall) of expansion draft (November 18, 1997).
RECORDS: Shares major league single-inning record for most home runs allowed—4 (September 5, 1995, second inning).
HONORS: Named A.L. Rookie Pitcher of the Year by THE SPORTING NEWS (1994).
STATISTICAL NOTES: Tied for A.L. lead with five balks in 1994 and three in 1995. ... Tied for American Association lead with three balks in 1996. ... Led N.L. with six balks and tied for lead with 39 home runs allowed in 1998.
MISCELLANEOUS: Scored one run in three appearances as pinch runner (1998). ... Tied for Arizona Diamondbacks all-time record for most shutouts (1).

Year Team (League)	W	L	Pct.	ERA	G	GS	CG	ShO	Sv.	IP	H	R	ER	BB	SO
1993—Midland (Texas)	0	1	.000	3.38	2	2	0	0	0	10²/₃	16	5	4	0	9
—Vancouver (PCL)	0	1	.000	12.38	2	2	0	0	0	8	13	12	11	6	2
—California (A.L.)	0	0	...	3.97	4	1	0	0	0	11¹/₃	11	5	5	2	4
1994—California (A.L.)	7	5	.583	5.22	18	18	0	0	0	101²/₃	120	63	59	27	47
—Lake Elsinore (Calif.)	0	1	.000	3.00	2	2	0	0	0	12	6	4	4	0	9
1995—California (A.L.)	6	8	.429	5.87	18	17	1	0	0	99²/₃	110	66	65	30	45
—Lake Elsinore (Calif.)	1	1	.500	1.93	3	3	0	0	0	14	10	3	3	1	13
1996—Buffalo (A.A.)■	11	5	.688	3.59	19	19	2	0	0	128	125	57	51	28	85
—Cleveland (A.L.)	3	1	.750	4.91	10	9	0	0	0	51¹/₃	58	29	28	14	21
1997—Buffalo (A.A.)	7	1	.875	3.05	15	15	1	1	0	85²/₃	78	33	29	15	60
—Cleveland (A.L.)	4	2	.667	4.69	8	8	0	0	0	48	55	28	25	11	22
1998—Arizona (N.L.)■	12	13	.480	4.33	32	32	2	1	0	208	221	109	100	24	95
A.L. totals (5 years)	20	16	.556	5.25	58	53	1	0	0	312	354	191	182	84	139
N.L. totals (1 year)	12	13	.480	4.33	32	32	2	1	0	208	221	109	100	24	95
Major league totals (6 years)	32	29	.525	4.88	90	85	3	1	0	520	575	300	282	108	234

CHAMPIONSHIP SERIES RECORD

Year Team (League)	W	L	Pct.	ERA	G	GS	CG	ShO	Sv.	IP	H	R	ER	BB	SO
1997—Cleveland (A.L.)	1	0	1.000	1.42	3	0	0	0	0	6¹/₃	1	1	1	3	7

WORLD SERIES RECORD

Year Team (League)	W	L	Pct.	ERA	G	GS	CG	ShO	Sv.	IP	H	R	ER	BB	SO
1997—Cleveland (A.L.)	0	0	...	2.45	3	0	0	0	1	3²/₃	2	1	1	0	2

ANDERSON, GARRET   OF   ANGELS

PERSONAL: Born June 30, 1972, in Los Angeles. ... 6-3/215. ... Bats left, throws left. ... Full name: Garret Joseph Anderson.
HIGH SCHOOL: John F. Kennedy (Granada Hills, Calif.).
TRANSACTIONS/CAREER NOTES: Selected by California Angels organization in fourth round of free-agent draft (June 4, 1990). ... Angels franchise renamed Anaheim Angels for 1997 season.
HONORS: Named A.L. Rookie Player of the Year by THE SPORTING NEWS (1995).
STATISTICAL NOTES: Collected six hits in one game (September 27, 1996). ... Had 28-game hitting streak (June 28-July 31, 1998). ... Career major league grand slams: 3.

Year Team (League)	Pos.	G	AB	R	H	2B	3B	HR	RBI	Avg.	BB	SO	SB	PO	A	E	Avg.
1990—Ariz. Angels (Ariz.)	OF	32	127	5	27	2	0	0	14	.213	2	24	3	53	2	2	.965
—Boise (Northwest)	OF	25	83	11	21	3	1	1	8	.253	4	18	0	38	0	2	.950
1991—Quad City (Midwest)	OF	105	392	40	102	22	2	2	42	.260	20	89	5	158	7	10	.943
1992—Palm Springs (Calif.)	OF	81	322	46	104	15	2	1	62	.323	21	61	1	137	4	6	.959
—Midland (Texas)	OF	39	146	16	40	5	0	2	19	.274	9	30	2	62	6	1	.986
1993—Vancouver (PCL)	OF-1B	124	467	57	137	34	4	4	71	.293	31	95	3	198	13	2	.991
1994—Vancouver (PCL)	OF-1B	123	505	75	162	42	6	12	102	.321	28	93	3	196	10	2	.990
—California (A.L.)	OF	5	13	0	5	0	0	0	1	.385	0	2	0	10	0	0	1.000
1995—California (A.L.)	OF-DH	106	374	50	120	19	1	16	69	.321	19	65	6	213	7	5	.978
—Vancouver (PCL)	OF	14	61	9	19	7	0	0	12	.311	5	14	0	22	0	1	.957
1996—California (A.L.)	OF-DH	150	607	79	173	33	2	12	72	.285	27	84	1	316	5	7	.979
1997—Anaheim (A.L.)	OF-DH	154	624	76	189	36	3	8	92	.303	30	70	10	343	14	3	.992
1998—Anaheim (A.L.)	OF	156	622	62	183	41	7	15	79	.294	29	80	8	326	11	6	.983
Major league totals (5 years)		571	2240	267	670	129	13	51	313	.299	105	301	31	1208	37	21	.983

ANDERSON, JIMMY   P   PIRATES

PERSONAL: Born January 22, 1976, in Portsmouth, Va. ... 6-1/190. ... Throws left, bats left. ... Full name: James Drew Anderson Jr.
HIGH SCHOOL: Western Branch (Chesapeake, Va.).
TRANSACTIONS/CAREER NOTES: Selected by Pittsburgh Pirates organization in ninth round of free-agent draft (June 2, 1994). ... On disabled list (July 5-12, 1998).

Year Team (League)	W	L	Pct.	ERA	G	GS	CG	ShO	Sv.	IP	H	R	ER	BB	SO
1994—GC Pirates (GCL)	5	1	.833	1.60	10	10	0	0	0	56¹/₃	35	21	10	27	66
1995—Augusta (S. Atl.)	4	2	.667	1.53	14	14	0	0	0	76²/₃	51	15	13	31	75
—Lynchburg (Carolina)	1	5	.167	4.13	10	9	0	0	0	52¹/₃	56	29	24	21	32
1996—Lynchburg (Carolina)	5	3	.625	1.93	11	11	1	1	0	65¹/₃	51	25	14	21	56
—Carolina (Southern)	8	5	.615	3.34	17	16	0	0	0	97	92	40	36	44	79
1997—Carolina (Southern)	2	1	.667	1.46	4	4	0	0	0	24²/₃	16	6	4	9	23
—Calgary (PCL)	7	6	.538	5.68	21	21	0	0	0	103	124	78	65	64	71
1998—Nashville (Pacific Coast)	9	10	.474	5.02	35	17	0	0	0	123²/₃	144	87	69	72	63

ANDERSON, MARLON   2B   PHILLIES

PERSONAL: Born January 6, 1974, in Montgomery, Ala. ... 5-11/200. ... Bats left, throws right. ... Full name: Marlon Ordell Anderson.
HIGH SCHOOL: Prattville (Ala.).
COLLEGE: South Alabama.
TRANSACTIONS/CAREER NOTES: Selected by Philadelphia Phillies organization in second round of free-agent draft (June 1, 1995); choice received from St. Louis Cardinals as part of compensation for Cardinals signing Type A free-agent P Danny Jackson.
STATISTICAL NOTES: Led New York-Pennsylvania League second basemen with 398 total chances and 67 double plays in 1995. ... Led Eastern League with 748 total chances in 1997. ... Hit home run in first major league at-bat (September 8, 1998). ... Led International League second basemen with 681 total chances in 1998.

							BATTING								FIELDING		
Year	Team (League)	Pos.	G	AB	R	H	2B	3B	HR	RBI	Avg.	BB	SO	SB	PO	A	E	Avg.
1995—Batavia (NY-Penn)		2B	74	*312	52	92	13	4	3	40	.295	15	20	22	*153	*231	14	*.965
1996—Clearwater (FSL)		2B	60	257	37	70	10	3	2	22	.272	14	18	26	142	221	16	.958
—Reading (Eastern)		2B	75	314	38	86	14	3	3	28	.274	26	44	17	166	239	18	.957
1997—Reading (Eastern)		2B	137	*553	88	147	18	6	10	62	.266	42	77	27	*323	*396	*29	.961
1998—Scran./W.B. (Int'l)		2B	136	575	104	*176	32	*14	16	86	.306	28	77	24	262	391	*28	.959
—Philadelphia (N.L.)		2B	17	43	4	14	3	0	1	4	.326	1	6	2	14	30	1	.978
Major league totals (1 year)			17	43	4	14	3	0	1	4	.326	1	6	2	14	30	1	.978

ANDERSON, MATT   P   TIGERS

PERSONAL: Born August 17, 1976, in Louisville, Ky. ... 6-4/200. ... Throws right, bats right. ... Full name: Matthew Jason Anderson.
HIGH SCHOOL: St. Xavier (Louisville, Ky.).
COLLEGE: Rice.
TRANSACTIONS/CAREER NOTES: Selected by Detroit Tigers organization in first round (first pick overall) of free-agent draft (June 3, 1997).

Year	Team (League)	W	L	Pct.	ERA	G	GS	CG	ShO	Sv.	IP	H	R	ER	BB	SO
1998—Lakeland (Fla. St.)		1	0	1.000	0.69	17	0	0	0	3	26	18	4	2	8	34
—Jacksonville (Southern)		1	0	1.000	0.60	13	0	0	0	10	15	7	1	1	5	11
—Detroit (A.L.)		5	1	.833	3.27	42	0	0	0	0	44	38	16	16	31	44
Major league totals (1 year)		5	1	.833	3.27	42	0	0	0	0	44	38	16	16	31	44

ANDREWS, SHANE   3B   EXPOS

PERSONAL: Born August 28, 1971, in Dallas. ... 6-0/220. ... Bats right, throws right. ... Full name: Darrell Shane Andrews.
HIGH SCHOOL: Carlsbad (N.M.) Senior.
TRANSACTIONS/CAREER NOTES: Selected by Montreal Expos organization in first round (11th pick overall) of free-agent draft (June 4, 1990). ... On disabled list (August 3-11, 1993). ... On disabled list (May 1, 1997-remainder of season); included rehabilitation assignments to Ottawa (May 14-18) and West Palm Beach (July 26-August 10).
STATISTICAL NOTES: Led South Atlantic League third basemen with 98 putouts in 1992. ... Led International League third basemen with 436 total chances in 1994. ... Career major league grand slams: 3.

							BATTING								FIELDING		
Year	Team (League)	Pos.	G	AB	R	H	2B	3B	HR	RBI	Avg.	BB	SO	SB	PO	A	E	Avg.
1990—GC Expos (GCL)		3B	56	190	31	46	7	1	3	24	.242	29	46	11	42	105	17	.896
1991—Sumter (S. Atl.)		3B	105	356	46	74	16	7	11	49	.208	65	132	5	71	205	29	.905
1992—Albany (S. Atl.)		3B-1B	136	453	76	104	18	1	*25	87	.230	*107	*174	8	†125	212	26	.928
1993—Harrisburg (East.)		3B-SS	124	442	77	115	29	2	18	70	.260	64	118	10	74	217	23	.927
1994—Ottawa (Int'l)		3B	137	460	79	117	25	2	16	85	.254	80	126	6	84	*320	*32	.927
1995—Montreal (N.L.)		3B-1B	84	220	27	47	10	1	8	31	.214	17	68	1	182	97	7	.976
1996—Montreal (N.L.)		3B	127	375	43	85	15	2	19	64	.227	35	119	3	64	256	15	.955
1997—Montreal (N.L.)		3B	18	64	10	13	3	0	4	9	.203	3	20	0	11	40	6	.895
—Ottawa (Int'l)		3B	3	12	3	3	0	0	1	1	.250	1	0	0	2	4	0	1.000
—W.P. Beach (FSL)		3B	5	17	2	3	2	0	1	5	.176	2	7	0	2	9	1	.917
1998—Montreal (N.L.)		3B	150	492	48	117	30	1	25	69	.238	58	137	1	95	322	20	.954
Major league totals (4 years)			379	1151	128	262	58	4	56	173	.228	113	344	5	352	715	48	.957

ANDUJAR, LUIS   P   WHITE SOX

PERSONAL: Born November 22, 1972, in Bani, Dominican Republic. ... 6-2/215. ... Throws right, bats right. ... Full name: Luis Sanchez Andujar.
TRANSACTIONS/CAREER NOTES: Signed as non-drafted free agent by Chicago White Sox organization (February 25, 1991). ... On disabled list (July 8-18, 1992). ... On Birmingham disabled list (September 2, 1993-remainder of season; June 10-July 20 and August 9, 1994-remainder of season). ... Traded by White Sox with P Allen Halley to Toronto Blue Jays for P Tony Castillo and IF Domingo Cedeno (August 22, 1996). ... On Toronto disabled list (August 24-September 28, 1997). ... Granted free agency (October 6, 1997). ... Signed by Blue Jays organization (November 11, 1997). ... Released by Blue Jays (July 10, 1998). ... Signed by Chicago White Sox (July 13, 1998).
HONORS: Named Southern League Most Outstanding Pitcher (1995).
STATISTICAL NOTES: Pitched 1-0 no-hit victory for Birmingham against Memphis (August 8, 1995).

Year	Team (League)	W	L	Pct.	ERA	G	GS	CG	ShO	Sv.	IP	H	R	ER	BB	SO
1991—GC White Sox (GCL)		4	4	.500	2.45	10	10	1	•1	0	62 1/3	60	27	17	10	52
1992—South Bend (Mid.)		6	5	.545	2.92	32	15	1	1	3	120 1/3	109	49	39	47	91
1993—Sarasota (Florida State)		6	6	.500	1.99	18	11	2	0	0	86	67	26	19	28	76
—Birmingham (Southern)		5	0	1.000	1.82	6	6	0	0	0	39 2/3	31	9	8	18	48
1994—Birmingham (Southern)		3	7	.300	5.05	15	15	0	0	0	76 2/3	90	50	43	25	64
—GC White Sox (GCL)		1	0	1.000	0.00	2	0	0	0	0	6	3	1	0	1	6

Year Team (League)	W	L	Pct.	ERA	G	GS	CG	ShO	Sv.	IP	H	R	ER	BB	SO
1995—Birmingham (Southern)	14	8	.636	2.85	27	27	2	1	0	167 1/3	147	64	53	44	146
—Chicago (A.L.)	2	1	.667	3.26	5	5	0	0	0	30 1/3	26	12	11	14	9
1996—Nashville (A.A.)	1	4	.200	5.92	8	7	1	0	0	38	50	26	25	8	24
—W. Sox-Cards (GCL)	1	0	1.000	0.00	1	1	0	0	0	6	3	0	0	0	3
—Chicago (A.L.)	0	2	.000	8.22	5	5	0	0	0	23	32	22	21	15	6
—Syracuse (Int'l)■................	0	0	...	2.25	2	2	0	0	0	12	17	7	3	2	10
—Toronto (A.L.)	1	1	.500	5.02	3	2	0	0	0	14 1/3	14	8	8	1	5
1997—Toronto (A.L.)	0	6	.000	6.48	17	8	0	0	0	50	76	45	36	21	28
—Syracuse (Int'l)	1	6	.143	5.54	13	5	1	0	1	39	37	25	24	14	24
1998—Syracuse (Int'l)■...............	3	2	.600	2.12	20	0	0	0	8	34	23	9	8	6	24
—Toronto (A.L.)	0	0	...	9.53	5	0	0	0	0	5 2/3	12	6	6	2	1
—Calgary (PCL)■	3	3	.500	6.26	13	9	0	0	0	50 1/3	62	33	35	15	46
Major league totals (4 years)	3	10	.231	5.98	35	20	0	0	0	123 1/3	160	93	82	53	49

ANKIEL, RICK — P — CARDINALS

PERSONAL: Born July 19, 1979, in Fort Pierce, Fla. ... 6-1/210. ... Throws left, bats left. ... Full name: Richard Alexander Ankiel.
HIGH SCHOOL: Port St. Lucie (Fla.).
TRANSACTIONS/CAREER NOTES: Selected by St. Louis Cardinals organization in second round of free-agent draft (June 3, 1997).
HONORS: Named Carolina League Pitcher of the Year (1998).

Year Team (League)	W	L	Pct.	ERA	G	GS	CG	ShO	Sv.	IP	H	R	ER	BB	SO
1998—Peoria (Midwest)	3	0	1.000	2.06	7	7	0	0	0	35	15	8	8	12	41
—Prince William (Caro.)	9	6	.600	2.79	21	21	1	0	0	126	91	46	39	38	181

APPIER, KEVIN — P — ROYALS

PERSONAL: Born December 6, 1967, in Lancaster, Calif. ... 6-2/200. ... Throws right, bats right. ... Full name: Robert Kevin Appier. ... Name pronounced APE-ee-er.
HIGH SCHOOL: Antelope Valley (Lancaster, Calif.).
JUNIOR COLLEGE: Antelope Valley College (Calif.).
COLLEGE: Fresno State.
TRANSACTIONS/CAREER NOTES: Selected by Kansas City Royals organization in first round (ninth pick overall) of free-agent draft (June 2, 1987). ... On disabled list (July 26-August 12, 1995). ... On Kansas City disabled list (March 20-September 1, 1998); included rehabilitation assignments to Gulf Coast Royals (July 16-21), Lansing (July 22-26), Wichita (July 27-30) and Omaha (July 31-August 27).
RECORDS: Shares major league record for most strikeouts in one inning—4 (September 3, 1996, fourth inning).
HONORS: Named A.L. Rookie Pitcher of the Year by THE SPORTING NEWS (1990).
STATISTICAL NOTES: Pitched 4-0 one-hit, complete-game victory for Kansas City against Detroit (July 7, 1990). ... Pitched 1-0 one-hit, complete-game loss against Texas (July 27, 1993). ... Tied for A.L. lead with 14 wild pitches in 1997.
MISCELLANEOUS: Holds Kansas City Royals all-time record for most strikeouts (1,373).

Year Team (League)	W	L	Pct.	ERA	G	GS	CG	ShO	Sv.	IP	H	R	ER	BB	SO
1987—Eugene (Northwest)	5	2	.714	3.04	15	•15	0	0	0	77	81	43	26	29	72
1988—Baseball City (FSL)	10	9	.526	2.75	24	24	1	0	0	147 1/3	134	58	45	39	112
—Memphis (Sou.)	2	0	1.000	1.83	3	3	0	0	0	19 2/3	11	5	4	7	18
1989—Omaha (Am. Assoc.)	8	8	.500	3.95	22	22	3	2	0	139	141	70	61	42	109
—Kansas City (A.L.)	1	4	.200	9.14	6	5	0	0	0	21 2/3	34	22	22	12	10
1990—Omaha (Am. Assoc.)	2	0	1.000	1.50	3	3	0	0	0	18	15	3	3	3	17
—Kansas City (A.L.)	12	8	.600	2.76	32	24	3	3	0	185 2/3	179	67	57	54	127
1991—Kansas City (A.L.)	13	10	.565	3.42	34	31	6	3	0	207 2/3	205	97	79	61	158
1992—Kansas City (A.L.)	15	8	.652	2.46	30	30	3	0	0	208 1/3	167	59	57	68	150
1993—Kansas City (A.L.)	18	8	.692	*2.56	34	34	5	1	0	238 2/3	183	74	68	81	186
1994—Kansas City (A.L.)	7	6	.538	3.83	23	23	1	0	0	155	137	68	66	63	145
1995—Kansas City (A.L.)	15	10	.600	3.89	31	31	4	1	0	201 1/3	163	90	87	80	185
1996—Kansas City (A.L.)	14	11	.560	3.62	32	32	5	1	0	211 1/3	192	87	85	75	207
1997—Kansas City (A.L.)	9	13	.409	3.40	34	34	4	1	0	235 2/3	215	96	89	74	196
1998—GC Royals (GCL)	0	1	.000	2.70	1	1	0	0	0	3 1/3	3	3	1	1	2
—Lansing (Midwest)	0	0	...	2.25	1	1	0	0	0	4	4	1	1	0	5
—Wichita (Texas)	0	1	.000	6.00	1	1	0	0	0	6	8	4	4	2	1
—Omaha (Pacific Coast)	3	2	.600	7.03	6	6	0	0	0	32	41	25	25	12	22
—Kansas City (A.L.)	1	2	.333	7.80	3	3	0	0	0	15	21	13	13	5	9
Major league totals (10 years)	105	80	.568	3.34	259	247	31	10	0	1680 1/3	1496	673	623	573	1373

ALL-STAR GAME RECORD

Year League	W	L	Pct.	ERA	GS	CG	ShO	Sv.	IP	H	R	ER	BB	SO
1995—American	0	0	...	0.00	0	0	0	0	2	0	0	0	0	1

ARDOIN, DANNY — C — ATHLETICS

PERSONAL: Born July 8, 1974, in Mamou, La. ... 6-0/205. ... Bats right, throws right. ... Full name: Daniel Wayne Ardoin.
HIGH SCHOOL: Sacred Heart (Ville Platte, La.).
COLLEGE: McNeese State.
TRANSACTIONS/CAREER NOTES: Selected by Oakland Athletics organization in fifth round of free-agent draft (June 1, 1995). ... On disabled list (July 27-August 4, 1998).
STATISTICAL NOTES: Led Northwest League catchers with 477 total chances in 1995.

Year Team (League)	Pos.	G	AB	R	H	2B	3B	HR	RBI	Avg.	BB	SO	SB	PO	A	E	Avg.
1995— S. Oregon (N'west).....	C	58	175	28	41	9	1	2	23	.234	31	50	2	*402	*61	*14	.971
1996— Modesto (California) ..	C-3B-1B	91	317	55	83	13	3	6	34	.262	47	81	5	577	62	21	.968
1997— Visalia (California)......	C-1-3-O	43	145	16	34	7	1	3	19	.234	21	39	0	331	38	5	.987
— Huntsville (Sou.)........	C-3B	57	208	26	48	10	1	4	23	.231	17	38	2	302	45	10	.972
1998— Huntsville (Sou.)........	C-OF-1B	109	363	67	90	21	0	16	62	.248	62	87	8	560	87	12	.982

ARIAS, ALEX — IF — PHILLIES

PERSONAL: Born November 20, 1967, in New York. ... 6-3/197. ... Bats right, throws right. ... Full name: Alejandro Arias. ... Name pronounced air-REE-ahs.

HIGH SCHOOL: George Washington (New York).

TRANSACTIONS/CAREER NOTES: Selected by Chicago Cubs organization in third round of free-agent draft (June 2, 1987). ... Traded by Cubs with 3B Gary Scott to Florida Marlins for P Greg Hibbard (November 17, 1992). ... On disabled list (June 14-July 2, 1997). ... Released by Marlins (December 12, 1997). ... Signed by Philadelphia Phillies (December 26, 1997).

STATISTICAL NOTES: Led Midwest League shortstops with 655 total chances and 83 double plays in 1989. ... Led Southern League shortstops with 583 total chances and 81 double plays in 1991.

Year Team (League)	Pos.	G	AB	R	H	2B	3B	HR	RBI	Avg.	BB	SO	SB	PO	A	E	Avg.
1987— Wytheville (App.)........	SS-3B	61	233	41	69	7	0	0	24	.296	27	29	16	77	141	16	.932
1988— Char., W.Va. (SAL)....	SS-3B-2B	127	472	57	122	12	1	0	33	.258	54	44	41	184	396	32	.948
1989— Peoria (Midwest)........	SS	*136	506	74	140	10	*11	2	64	.277	49	67	31	*210	*408	37	.944
1990— Charlotte (Southern) ..	SS	119	419	55	103	16	3	4	38	.246	42	53	12	171	284	*42	.915
1991— Charlotte (Southern) ..	SS	134	488	69	134	26	0	4	47	.275	47	42	23	*203	*351	29	*.950
1992— Iowa (Am. Assoc.)......	SS-2B	106	409	52	114	23	3	5	40	.279	44	27	14	183	290	14	.971
— Chicago (N.L.)	SS	32	99	14	29	6	0	0	7	.293	11	13	0	43	74	4	.967
1993— Florida (N.L.)■..........	2B-3B-SS	96	249	27	67	5	1	2	20	.269	27	18	1	94	144	6	.975
1994— Florida (N.L.)	SS-3B	59	113	4	27	5	0	0	15	.239	9	19	0	37	51	2	.978
1995— Florida (N.L.)	SS-3B-2B	94	216	22	58	9	2	3	26	.269	22	20	1	57	127	9	.953
1996— Florida (N.L.)	3-S-1-2	100	224	27	62	11	2	3	26	.277	17	28	2	48	127	7	.962
1997— Florida (N.L.)	3B-SS	74	93	13	23	2	0	1	11	.247	12	12	0	26	38	2	.970
1998— Philadelphia (N.L.)■...	SS-3B-2B	56	133	17	39	8	0	1	16	.293	13	18	2	43	88	2	.985
Major league totals (7 years)		511	1127	124	305	46	5	10	121	.271	111	128	6	348	649	32	.969

DIVISION SERIES RECORD

Year Team (League)	Pos.	G	AB	R	H	2B	3B	HR	RBI	Avg.	BB	SO	SB	PO	A	E	Avg.
1997— Florida (N.L.)	PH	1	1	0	1	0	0	0	1	1.000	0	0	0	...	...	...	...

CHAMPIONSHIP SERIES RECORD

Year Team (League)	Pos.	G	AB	R	H	2B	3B	HR	RBI	Avg.	BB	SO	SB	PO	A	E	Avg.
1997— Florida (N.L.)	3B-PH	3	1	0	1	0	0	0	0	1.000	0	0	0	0	0	0	...

WORLD SERIES RECORD

NOTES: Member of World Series championship team (1997).

Year Team (League)	Pos.	G	AB	R	H	2B	3B	HR	RBI	Avg.	BB	SO	SB	PO	A	E	Avg.
1997— Florida (N.L.)	3B-PR	2	1	1	0	0	0	0	0	.000	0	0	0	0	0	0	...

ARIAS, GEORGE — 3B — PADRES

PERSONAL: Born March 12, 1972, in Tucson, Ariz. ... 5-11/190. ... Bats right, throws right. ... Full name: George Alberto Arias.

HIGH SCHOOL: Pueblo (Tucson, Ariz.).

JUNIOR COLLEGE: Pima Community College (Ariz.).

COLLEGE: Arizona.

TRANSACTIONS/CAREER NOTES: Selected by California Angels organization in seventh round of free-agent draft (June 3, 1993). ... Angels franchise renamed Anaheim Angels for 1997 season. ... Traded by Angels to San Diego Padres (August 19, 1997), completing deal in which Padres traded OF Rickey Henderson to Angels for P Ryan Hancock, P Stevenson Agosto and a player to be named later (August 13, 1997).

STATISTICAL NOTES: Led California League third basemen with 467 total chances and 27 double plays in 1994. ... Led Pacific Coast League third basemen with 99 putouts in 1997.

Year Team (League)	Pos.	G	AB	R	H	2B	3B	HR	RBI	Avg.	BB	SO	SB	PO	A	E	Avg.
1993— Cedar Rap. (Midw.)	3B-SS	74	253	31	55	13	3	9	41	.217	31	65	6	59	159	23	.905
1994— Lake Elsinore (Calif.) ..	3B	•134	514	89	144	28	3	23	80	.280	58	111	6	*122	*313	*32	.931
1995— Midland (Texas).........	3B-SS	134	520	91	145	19	10	30	104	.279	63	119	3	128	300	29	.937
1996— California (A.L.)	3B-DH	84	252	19	60	8	1	6	28	.238	16	50	2	50	190	10	.960
— Vancouver (PCL).......	3B	59	243	49	82	24	0	9	55	.337	20	38	2	50	135	6	.969
1997— Vancouver (PCL)	3B-SS	105	401	71	112	28	3	11	60	.279	39	51	3	96	213	14	.957
— Anaheim (A.L.)	DH-3B	3	6	1	2	0	0	0	1	.333	0	0	0	0	3	0	1.000
— Las Vegas (PCL)■	3B	10	30	4	10	4	1	1	5	.333	3	8	0	§6	15	2	.913
— San Diego (N.L.)	3B	11	22	2	5	1	0	0	2	.227	0	1	0	4	12	1	.941
1998— Las Vegas (PCL)	3B-1B	114	435	73	134	33	4	36	*119	.308	37	108	0	98	234	17	.951
— San Diego (N.L.)	3B-1B	20	36	4	7	1	1	1	4	.194	3	16	0	9	23	2	.941
American League totals (2 years)		87	258	20	62	8	1	6	29	.240	16	50	2	50	193	10	.960
National League totals (2 years)		31	58	6	12	2	1	1	6	.207	3	17	0	13	35	3	.941
Major league totals (3 years)		118	316	26	74	10	2	7	35	.234	19	67	2	63	228	13	.957

DIVISION SERIES RECORD

					BATTING										FIELDING		
Year	Team (League)	Pos.	G	AB	R	H	2B	3B	HR	RBI	Avg.	BB	SO	SB	PO	A	E	Avg.
1998— San Diego (N.L.)		PH	1	1	0	0	0	0	0	0	.000	0	1	0	...	...	...	...

CHAMPIONSHIP SERIES RECORD

					BATTING										FIELDING		
Year	Team (League)	Pos.	G	AB	R	H	2B	3B	HR	RBI	Avg.	BB	SO	SB	PO	A	E	Avg.
1998— San Diego (N.L.)									Did not play.									

WORLD SERIES RECORD

					BATTING										FIELDING		
Year	Team (League)	Pos.	G	AB	R	H	2B	3B	HR	RBI	Avg.	BB	SO	SB	PO	A	E	Avg.
1998— San Diego (N.L.)									Did not play.									

ARMAS JR., TONY   P   EXPOS

PERSONAL: Born April 29, 1978, in Puerto Piritu, Venezuela. ... 6-4/206. ... Throws right, bats right. ... Full name: Antonio Jose Armas Jr.. ... Son of Tony Armas, outfielder with four major league teams (1976-89).
TRANSACTIONS/CAREER NOTES: Signed as non-drafted free agent by New York Yankees organization (August 16, 1994). ... Traded by Yankees with a player to be named later to Boston Red Sox organization for C Mike Stanley and SS Randy Brown (August 13, 1997); Red Sox acquired P Jim Mecir to complete deal (September 29, 1997). ... Traded by Red Sox organization to Montreal Expos organization (November 18, 1997).

Year Team (League)	W	L	Pct.	ERA	G	GS	CG	ShO	Sv.	IP	H	R	ER	BB	SO
1995— GC Yankees (GCL).............	0	1	.000	0.64	5	4	0	0	0	14	12	9	1	6	13
1996— Oneonta (N.Y.-Penn)	1	1	.500	5.74	3	3	0	0	0	15²/₃	14	12	10	11	14
— GC Yankees (GCL).............	4	1	.800	3.15	8	7	0	0	1	45²/₃	41	18	16	13	45
1997—Greensboro (S. Atl.)	5	2	.714	1.05	9	9	2	1	0	51²/₃	36	13	6	13	64
—Tampa (Fla. St.).................	3	1	.750	3.33	9	9	0	0	0	46	43	23	17	16	26
—Sarasota (Florida State)■...	2	1	.667	6.62	3	3	0	0	0	17²/₃	18	13	13	12	9
1998—Jupiter (Florida State)■	12	8	.600	2.88	27	27	1	1	0	153¹/₃	140	63	49	59	136

ARROJO, ROLANDO   P   DEVIL RAYS

PERSONAL: Born July 18, 1968, in Havana, Cuba. ... 6-4/215. ... Throws right, bats right. ... Full name: Luis Rolando Arrojo.
TRANSACTIONS/CAREER NOTES: Signed as non-drafted free agent by Tampa Bay Devil Rays organization (April 21, 1997). ... On disabled list (September 21, 1998-remainder of season).
HONORS: Named A.L. Rookie Pitcher of the Year by THE SPORTING NEWS (1998).
STATISTICAL NOTES: Led A.L. with 19 hit batsmen in 1998.
MISCELLANEOUS: Member of Cuban national baseball team (1986-96). ... Holds Tampa Bay Devil Rays all-time records for lowest earned-run average (3.56), most wins (14), most innings pitched (202) and most shutouts (2). ... Tied for Tampa Bay Devil Rays all-time record for most complete games (2).

Year Team (League)	W	L	Pct.	ERA	G	GS	CG	ShO	Sv.	IP	H	R	ER	BB	SO
1997—St. Petersburg (FSL)	5	6	.455	3.43	16	16	4	1	0	89¹/₃	73	40	34	13	73
1998—Tampa Bay (A.L.)................	14	12	.538	3.56	32	32	2	2	0	202	195	84	80	65	152
Major league totals (1 year)........	14	12	.538	3.56	32	32	2	2	0	202	195	84	80	65	152

ALL-STAR GAME RECORD

Year League	W	L	Pct.	ERA	GS	CG	ShO	Sv.	IP	H	R	ER	BB	SO
1998— American	0	0	...	0.00	0	0	0	0	1	2	0	0	0	1

ASHBY, ANDY   P   PADRES

PERSONAL: Born July 11, 1967, in Kansas City, Mo. ... 6-5/190. ... Throws right, bats right. ... Full name: Andrew Jason Ashby.
HIGH SCHOOL: Park Hill (Kansas City, Mo.).
JUNIOR COLLEGE: Crowder College (Mo.).
TRANSACTIONS/CAREER NOTES: Signed as non-drafted free agent by Philadelphia Phillies organization (May 4, 1986). ... On Spartanburg disabled list (April 7-July 10, 1988). ... On Spartanburg disabled list (April 6-26, 1989). ... On Philadelphia disabled list (April 27-August 11, 1992); included rehabilitation assignments to Scranton/Wilkes-Barre (July 8-August 2 and August 6-10). ... Selected by Colorado Rockies in first round (25th pick overall) of expansion draft (November 17, 1992). ... Traded by Rockies to San Diego Padres (July 27, 1993), completing deal in which Padres traded P Bruce Hurst and P Greg W. Harris to Rockies for C Brad Ausmus, P Doug Bochtler and a player to be named later (July 26, 1993). ... On disabled list (June 6-22, June 29-July 15 and July 27-September 1, 1996; and May 20-June 15, 1997).
RECORDS: Shares major league record by striking out side on nine pitches (June 15, 1991, fourth inning).
MISCELLANEOUS: Had sacrifice hit in only appearance as pinch hitter (1996). ... Appeared in one game as pinch runner (1997).

Year Team (League)	W	L	Pct.	ERA	G	GS	CG	ShO	Sv.	IP	H	R	ER	BB	SO
1986— Bend (Northwest)	1	2	.333	4.95	16	6	0	0	2	60	56	40	33	34	45
1987—Spartanburg (SAL)	4	6	.400	5.60	13	13	1	0	0	64¹/₃	73	45	40	38	52
—Utica (N.Y.-Penn)................	3	7	.300	4.05	13	13	0	0	0	60	56	38	27	36	51
1988—Spartanburg (SAL)	1	1	.500	2.70	3	3	0	0	0	16²/₃	13	7	5	7	16
—Batavia (N.Y.-Penn)	3	1	.750	1.61	6	6	2	1	0	44²/₃	25	11	8	16	32
1989—Spartanburg (SAL)	5	9	.357	2.87	17	17	3	1	0	106²/₃	95	48	34	49	100
—Clearwater (Fla. St.)	1	4	.200	1.24	6	6	2	1	0	43²/₃	28	9	6	21	44
1990— Reading (Eastern)	10	7	.588	3.42	23	23	4	1	0	139²/₃	134	65	53	48	94
1991—Scran./W.B. (Int'l)..............	11	11	.500	3.46	26	26	•6	•3	0	161¹/₃	144	78	62	60	113
—Philadelphia (N.L.)..............	1	5	.167	6.00	8	8	0	0	0	42	41	28	28	19	26
1992—Philadelphia (N.L.)..............	1	3	.250	7.54	10	8	0	0	0	37	42	31	31	21	24
—Scran./W.B. (Int'l)..............	0	3	.000	3.00	7	7	1	0	0	33	23	13	11	14	18
1993—Colorado (N.L.)■..............	0	4	.000	8.50	20	9	0	0	1	54	89	54	51	32	33
—Colo. Springs (PCL)	4	2	.667	4.10	7	6	1	0	0	41²/₃	45	25	19	12	35
—San Diego (N.L.)■..............	3	6	.333	5.48	12	12	0	0	0	69	79	46	42	24	44
1994—San Diego (N.L.)..............	6	11	.353	3.40	24	24	4	0	0	164¹/₃	145	75	62	43	121

Year Team (League)	W	L	Pct.	ERA	G	GS	CG	ShO	Sv.	IP	H	R	ER	BB	SO
1995— San Diego (N.L.)	12	10	.545	2.94	31	•31	2	2	0	192 2/3	180	79	63	62	150
1996— San Diego (N.L.)	9	5	.643	3.23	24	24	1	0	0	150 2/3	147	60	54	34	85
1997— San Diego (N.L.)	9	11	.450	4.13	30	30	2	0	0	200 2/3	207	108	92	49	144
1998— San Diego (N.L.)	17	9	.654	3.34	33	33	5	1	0	226 2/3	223	90	84	58	151
Major league totals (8 years)	58	64	.475	4.01	192	179	14	3	1	1137	1153	571	507	342	778

DIVISION SERIES RECORD

Year Team (League)	W	L	Pct.	ERA	G	GS	CG	ShO	Sv.	IP	H	R	ER	BB	SO
1996— San Diego (N.L.)	0	0	...	6.75	1	1	0	0	0	5 1/3	7	4	4	1	5
1998— San Diego (N.L.)	0	0	...	6.75	1	1	0	0	0	4	6	3	3	1	4
Div. series totals (2 years)	0	0	...	6.75	2	2	0	0	0	9 1/3	13	7	7	2	9

CHAMPIONSHIP SERIES RECORD

Year Team (League)	W	L	Pct.	ERA	G	GS	CG	ShO	Sv.	IP	H	R	ER	BB	SO
1998— San Diego (N.L.)	0	0	...	2.08	2	2	0	0	0	13	14	3	3	2	5

WORLD SERIES RECORD

Year Team (League)	W	L	Pct.	ERA	G	GS	CG	ShO	Sv.	IP	H	R	ER	BB	SO
1998— San Diego (N.L.)	0	1	.000	13.50	1	1	0	0	0	2 2/3	10	7	4	1	1

ALL-STAR GAME RECORD

Year League	W	L	Pct.	ERA	GS	CG	ShO	Sv.	IP	H	R	ER	BB	SO
1998— National	0	0	...	9.00	0	0	0	0	1	1	1	1	1	0

ASHLEY, BILLY   OF   DEVIL RAYS

PERSONAL: Born July 11, 1970, in Taylor, Mich. ... 6-5/242. ... Bats right, throws right. ... Full name: Billy Manual Ashley.
HIGH SCHOOL: Belleville (Mich.).
TRANSACTIONS/CAREER NOTES: Selected by Los Angeles Dodgers organization in third round of free-agent draft (June 1, 1988). ... On disabled list (April 10-May 1, May 19-31 and June 8-July 8, 1991). ... On Albuquerque disabled list (May 1-16, 1994). ... On Los Angeles disabled list (April 21-May 13, 1996); included rehabilitation assignments to Albuquerque (April 30-May 1 and May 7-13). ... Released by Dodgers (March 29, 1998). ... Signed by Boston Red Sox organization (March 30, 1998). ... On Pawtucket disabled list (April 29-May 9, 1998). ... On Boston disabled list (September 11, 1998-remainder of season). ... Released by Red Sox (November 23, 1998). ... Signed by Tampa Bay Devil Rays organization (January 13, 1999).
HONORS: Named Pacific Coast League Most Valuable Player (1994).
STATISTICAL NOTES: Led Texas League with .534 slugging percentage in 1992. ... Led Pacific Coast League with .701 slugging percentage and tied for lead with seven intentional bases on balls received in 1994. ... Career major league grand slams: 1.

Year Team (League)	Pos.	G	AB	R	H	2B	3B	HR	RBI	Avg.	BB	SO	SB	PO	A	E	Avg.
1988— GC Dodgers (GCL)	OF	9	26	3	4	0	0	0	0	.154	1	9	1	8	2	0	1.000
1989— GC Dodgers (GCL)	OF	48	160	23	38	6	2	1	19	.238	19	42	16	50	3	5	.914
1990— Bakersfield (Calif.)	OF	99	331	48	72	13	1	9	40	.218	25	135	17	122	3	10	.926
1991— Vero Beach (FSL)	OF	61	206	18	52	11	2	7	42	.252	7	69	9	39	1	0	1.000
1992— San Antonio (Tex.)	OF-1B	101	380	60	106	23	1	*24	66	.279	16	111	13	129	9	3	.979
—Albuquerque (PCL)	OF	25	95	11	20	7	0	2	10	.211	6	42	1	39	1	2	.952
—Los Angeles (N.L.)	OF	29	95	6	21	5	0	2	6	.221	5	34	0	34	2	6	.857
1993— Albuquerque (PCL)	OF	125	482	88	143	31	4	26	*100	.297	35	*143	6	211	7	*11	.952
—Los Angeles (N.L.)	OF	14	37	0	9	0	0	0	0	.243	2	11	0	11	3	0	1.000
1994— Los Angeles (N.L.)	OF	2	6	0	2	1	0	0	0	.333	0	2	0	3	0	1	1.000
—Albuquerque (PCL)	OF	107	388	93	134	19	4	*37	105	.345	53	116	6	119	2	12	.910
1995— Los Angeles (N.L.)	OF	81	215	17	51	5	0	8	27	.237	25	88	0	102	2	3	.972
1996— Los Angeles (N.L.)	OF	71	110	18	22	2	1	9	25	.200	21	44	0	38	2	2	.952
—Albuquerque (PCL)	OF	7	23	6	8	1	0	1	9	.348	7	9	2	11	0	1	.917
1997— Los Angeles (N.L.)	OF	71	131	12	32	7	0	6	19	.244	8	46	0	39	2	4	.911
1998— Pawtucket (Int'l)■	1B-OF	63	218	40	59	12	0	14	51	.271	35	72	1	198	12	4	.981
—Boston (A.L.)	DH-1B-OF	13	24	3	7	3	0	3	7	.292	2	11	0	6	1	1	.875
American League totals (1 year)		13	24	3	7	3	0	3	7	.292	2	11	0	6	1	1	.875
National League totals (6 years)		268	594	53	137	20	1	25	77	.231	61	225	0	227	11	15	.941
Major league totals (7 years)		281	618	56	144	23	1	28	84	.233	63	236	0	233	12	16	.939

DIVISION SERIES RECORD

Year Team (League)	Pos.	G	AB	R	H	2B	3B	HR	RBI	Avg.	BB	SO	SB	PO	A	E	Avg.
1995— Los Angeles (N.L.)	PH	1	0	0	0	0	0	0	0	...	1	0	0	...	...	...	...
1996— Los Angeles (N.L.)	PH	2	2	0	0	0	0	0	0	.000	0	2	0	...	...	...	...
Division series totals (2 years)		3	2	0	0	0	0	0	0	.000	1	2	0	...	...	...	...

ASSENMACHER, PAUL   P   INDIANS

PERSONAL: Born December 10, 1960, in Allen Park, Mich. ... 6-3/210. ... Throws left, bats left. ... Full name: Paul Andre Assenmacher. ... Name pronounced AHSS-en-mahk-ur.
HIGH SCHOOL: Aquinas (Southgate, Mich.).
COLLEGE: Aquinas, Mich. (degree in business administration).
TRANSACTIONS/CAREER NOTES: Signed as non-drafted free agent by Atlanta Braves organization (July 10, 1983). ... On Atlanta disabled list (April 29-May 9, 1987 and August 10-25, 1988). ... Traded by Braves organization to Chicago Cubs for two players to be named later (August 24, 1989); Braves acquired C Kelly Mann and P Pat Gomez to complete deal (September 1, 1989). ... On disabled list (May 19-June 4, 1992). ... Traded by Cubs to New York Yankees as part of a three-way deal in which Yankees sent P John Habyan to Kansas City Royals and Royals sent OF Tuffy Rhodes to Cubs (July 30, 1993). ... Traded by Yankees to Chicago White Sox for P Brian Boehringer (March 21, 1994). ... Granted free agency (October 24, 1994). ... Signed by Cleveland Indians (April 10, 1995). ... Granted free agency (November 3, 1997). ... Re-signed by Indians (November 12, 1997).
RECORDS: Shares major league record for most strikeouts in one inning—4 (August 22, 1989, fifth inning).

Year Team (League)	W	L	Pct.	ERA	G	GS	CG	ShO	Sv.	IP	H	R	ER	BB	SO
1983— GC Braves (GCL)	1	0	1.000	2.21	10	3	1	1	2	36 2/3	35	14	9	4	44
1984— Durham (Carolina)	6	11	.353	4.28	26	24	3	1	0	147 1/3	153	78	70	52	147
1985— Durham (Carolina)	3	2	.600	3.29	14	0	0	0	1	38 1/3	38	16	14	13	36
— Greenville (Southern)	6	0	1.000	2.56	29	0	0	0	4	52 2/3	47	16	15	11	59
1986— Atlanta (N.L.)	7	3	.700	2.50	61	0	0	0	7	68 1/3	61	23	19	26	56
1987— Atlanta (N.L.)	1	1	.500	5.10	52	0	0	0	2	54 2/3	58	41	31	24	39
— Richmond (Int'l)	1	2	.333	3.65	4	4	0	0	0	24 2/3	30	11	10	8	21
1988— Atlanta (N.L.)	8	7	.533	3.06	64	0	0	0	5	79 1/3	72	28	27	32	71
1989— Atlanta (N.L.)	1	3	.250	3.59	49	0	0	0	0	57 2/3	55	26	23	16	64
— Chicago (N.L.)■	2	1	.667	5.21	14	0	0	0	0	19	19	11	11	12	15
1990— Chicago (N.L.)	7	2	.778	2.80	74	1	0	0	10	103	90	33	32	36	95
1991— Chicago (N.L.)	7	8	.467	3.24	75	0	0	0	15	102 2/3	85	41	37	31	117
1992— Chicago (N.L.)	4	4	.500	4.10	70	0	0	0	8	68	72	32	31	26	67
1993— Chicago (N.L.)	2	1	.667	3.49	46	0	0	0	0	38 2/3	44	15	15	13	34
— New York (A.L.)■	2	2	.500	3.12	26	0	0	0	0	17 1/3	10	6	6	9	11
1994— Chicago (A.L.)■	1	2	.333	3.55	44	0	0	0	1	33	26	13	13	13	29
1995— Cleveland (A.L.)■	6	2	.750	2.82	44	0	0	0	0	38 1/3	32	13	12	12	40
1996— Cleveland (A.L.)	4	2	.667	3.09	63	0	0	0	1	46 2/3	46	18	16	14	44
1997— Cleveland (A.L.)	5	0	1.000	2.94	75	0	0	0	4	49	43	17	16	15	53
1998— Cleveland (A.L.)	2	5	.286	3.26	69	0	0	0	3	47	54	22	17	19	43
A.L. totals (6 years)	20	13	.606	3.11	324	0	0	0	9	231 1/3	211	89	80	82	220
N.L. totals (8 years)	39	30	.565	3.44	505	1	0	0	47	591 1/3	556	250	226	216	558
Major league totals (13 years)	59	43	.578	3.35	829	1	0	0	56	822 2/3	767	339	306	298	778

DIVISION SERIES RECORD

RECORDS: Holds career record for most games by pitcher—13.

Year Team (League)	W	L	Pct.	ERA	G	GS	CG	ShO	Sv.	IP	H	R	ER	BB	SO
1995— Cleveland (A.L.)	0	0	...	0.00	3	0	0	0	0	1 2/3	0	0	0	0	3
1996— Cleveland (A.L.)	1	0	1.000	0.00	3	0	0	0	0	1 2/3	0	0	0	2	2
1997— Cleveland (A.L.)	0	0	...	5.40	4	0	0	0	0	3 1/3	2	2	2	2	2
1998— Cleveland (A.L.)	0	0	...	0.00	3	0	0	0	0	1	2	0	0	0	2
Div. series totals (4 years)	1	0	1.000	2.35	13	0	0	0	0	7 2/3	4	2	2	4	9

CHAMPIONSHIP SERIES RECORD

Year Team (League)	W	L	Pct.	ERA	G	GS	CG	ShO	Sv.	IP	H	R	ER	BB	SO
1989— Chicago (N.L.)	0	0	...	13.50	2	0	0	0	0	2/3	3	1	1	0	0
1995— Cleveland (A.L.)	0	0	...	0.00	3	0	0	0	0	1 1/3	0	0	0	1	2
1997— Cleveland (A.L.)	1	0	1.000	9.00	5	0	0	0	0	2	5	2	2	1	3
1998— Cleveland (A.L.)	0	0	...	0.00	3	0	0	0	0	2	0	0	0	0	3
Champ. series totals (4 years)	1	0	1.000	4.50	13	0	0	0	0	6	8	3	3	2	8

WORLD SERIES RECORD

Year Team (League)	W	L	Pct.	ERA	G	GS	CG	ShO	Sv.	IP	H	R	ER	BB	SO
1995— Cleveland (A.L.)	0	0	...	6.75	4	0	0	0	0	1 1/3	1	2	1	3	3
1997— Cleveland (A.L.)	0	0	...	0.00	5	0	0	0	0	4	5	0	0	0	6
World Series totals (2 years)	0	0	...	1.69	9	0	0	0	0	5 1/3	6	2	1	3	9

ASTACIO, PEDRO　　　　P　　　　ROCKIES

PERSONAL: Born November 28, 1969, in Hato Mayor, Dominican Republic. ... 6-2/208. ... Throws right, bats right. ... Full name: Pedro Julio Astacio. ... Name pronounced ah-STA-see-oh.
HIGH SCHOOL: Pilar Rondon (Dominican Republic).
TRANSACTIONS/CAREER NOTES: Signed as non-drafted free agent by Los Angeles Dodgers organization (November 21, 1987). ... On Albuquerque disabled list (April 26-May 21, 1992). ... Traded by Dodgers to Colorado Rockies for 2B Eric Young (August 19, 1997).
STATISTICAL NOTES: Led N.L. with nine balks in 1993. ... Led N.L. with 17 hit batsmen and tied for lead with 39 home runs allowed in 1998.

Year Team (League)	W	L	Pct.	ERA	G	GS	CG	ShO	Sv.	IP	H	R	ER	BB	SO
1989— GC Dodgers (GCL)	7	3	.700	3.17	12	12	1	•1	0	76 2/3	77	30	27	12	52
1990— Vero Beach (FSL)	1	5	.167	6.32	8	8	0	0	0	47	54	39	33	23	41
— Yakima (N'west)	2	0	1.000	1.74	3	3	0	0	0	20 2/3	9	8	4	4	22
— Bakersfield (California)	5	2	.714	2.77	10	7	1	0	0	52	46	22	16	15	34
1991— Vero Beach (FSL)	5	3	.625	1.67	9	9	3	1	0	59 1/3	44	19	11	8	45
— San Antonio (Tex.)	4	11	.267	4.78	19	19	2	1	0	113	142	67	60	39	62
1992— Albuquerque (PCL)	6	6	.500	5.47	24	15	1	0	0	98 2/3	115	68	60	44	66
— Los Angeles (N.L.)	5	5	.500	1.98	11	11	4	4	0	82	80	23	18	20	43
1993— Los Angeles (N.L.)	14	9	.609	3.57	31	31	3	2	0	186 1/3	165	80	74	68	122
1994— Los Angeles (N.L.)	6	8	.429	4.29	23	23	3	1	0	149	142	77	71	47	108
1995— Los Angeles (N.L.)	7	8	.467	4.24	48	11	1	1	0	104	103	53	49	29	80
1996— Los Angeles (N.L.)	9	8	.529	3.44	35	32	0	0	0	211 2/3	207	86	81	67	130
1997— Los Angeles (N.L.)	7	9	.438	4.10	26	24	2	1	0	153 2/3	151	75	70	47	115
— Colorado (N.L.)■	5	1	.833	4.25	7	7	0	0	0	48 2/3	49	23	23	14	51
1998— Colorado (N.L.)	13	14	.481	6.23	35	34	0	0	0	209 1/3	245	*160	*145	74	170
Major league totals (7 years)	66	62	.516	4.18	216	173	13	9	0	1144 2/3	1142	577	531	366	819

DIVISION SERIES RECORD

Year Team (League)	W	L	Pct.	ERA	G	GS	CG	ShO	Sv.	IP	H	R	ER	BB	SO
1995— Los Angeles (N.L.)	0	0	...	0.00	3	0	0	0	0	3 1/3	1	0	0	0	5
1996— Los Angeles (N.L.)	0	0	...	0.00	1	0	0	0	0	1 2/3	0	0	0	0	1
Div. series totals (2 years)	0	0	...	0.00	4	0	0	0	0	5	1	0	0	0	6

AURILIA, RICH   SS   GIANTS

PERSONAL: Born September 2, 1971, in Brooklyn, N.Y. ... 6-1/185. ... Bats right, throws right. ... Full name: Richard Santo Aurilia. ... Name pronounced uh-REEL-yuh.
HIGH SCHOOL: Xaverian (Brooklyn, N.Y.).
COLLEGE: St. John's.
TRANSACTIONS/CAREER NOTES: Selected by Texas Rangers organization in 24th round of free-agent draft (June 1, 1992). ... On disabled list (April 9-16, 1993). ... Traded by Rangers with IF/OF Desi Wilson to San Francisco Giants organization for P John Burkett (December 24, 1994). ... On San Francisco disabled list (September 24, 1996-remainder of season). ... On disabled list (July 4-20, 1998). ... Career major league grand slams: 1.

| | | | | | | | BATTING | | | | | | | | FIELDING | | |
Year Team (League)	Pos.	G	AB	R	H	2B	3B	HR	RBI	Avg.	BB	SO	SB	PO	A	E	Avg.
1992—Butte (Pioneer)..........	SS	59	202	37	68	11	3	3	30	.337	42	18	13	78	154	14	*.943
1993—Charlotte (Fla. St.)......	SS	122	440	80	136	16	5	5	56	.309	75	57	15	200	445	24	.964
1994—Tulsa (Texas).............	SS	129	458	67	107	18	6	12	57	.234	53	74	10	*237	374	24	*.962
1995—Shreveport (Texas)■..	SS	64	226	29	74	17	1	4	42	.327	27	26	10	122	237	14	.962
—Phoenix (PCL)	SS	71	258	42	72	12	0	5	34	.279	35	29	2	104	246	9	.975
—San Francisco (N.L.) ..	SS	9	19	4	9	3	0	2	4	.474	1	2	1	8	16	0	1.000
1996—Phoenix (PCL)...........	SS-2B	7	30	9	13	7	0	0	4	.433	2	3	1	10	25	1	.972
—San Francisco (N.L.) ..	SS-2B	105	318	27	76	7	1	3	26	.239	25	52	4	142	246	10	.975
1997—San Francisco (N.L.) ..	SS	46	102	16	28	8	0	5	19	.275	8	15	1	47	91	3	.979
—Phoenix (PCL).............	SS	8	34	9	10	2	0	1	5	.294	5	4	2	14	22	0	1.000
1998—San Francisco (N.L.) ..	SS	122	413	54	110	27	2	9	49	.266	31	62	3	154	313	10	.979
Major league totals (4 years)		282	852	101	223	45	3	19	98	.262	65	131	9	351	666	23	.978

AUSMUS, BRAD   C   TIGERS

PERSONAL: Born April 14, 1969, in New Haven, Conn. ... 5-11/195. ... Bats right, throws right. ... Full name: Bradley David Ausmus.
HIGH SCHOOL: Cheshire (Conn.).
COLLEGE: Dartmouth (degree in government).
TRANSACTIONS/CAREER NOTES: Selected by New York Yankees organization in 47th round of free-agent draft (June 2, 1987). ... Selected by Colorado Rockies in third round (54th pick overall) of expansion draft (November 17, 1992). ... Traded by Rockies with P Doug Bochtler and a player to be named later to San Diego Padres for P Bruce Hurst and P Greg W. Harris (July 26, 1993); Padres acquired P Andy Ashby to complete deal (July 27, 1993). ... Traded by Padres with SS Andujar Cedeno and P Russ Spear to Detroit Tigers for C John Flaherty and SS Chris Gomez (June 18, 1996). ... On Detroit suspended list (September 4-5, 1996). ... Traded by Tigers with P Jose Lima, P C.J. Nitkowski, P Trever Miller and IF Daryle Ward to Houston Astros for OF Brian L. Hunter, IF Orlando Miller, P Doug Brocail, P Todd Jones and cash (December 10, 1996). ... Traded by Astros with P C.J. Nitkowski to Tigers for C Paul Bako, P Dean Crow, P Brian Powell, P Mark Persails and 3B Carlos Villalobos (January 14, 1999).
STATISTICAL NOTES: Led Gulf Coast League catchers with 434 total chances in 1988. ... Led International League catchers with 666 putouts and 738 total chances in 1992. ... Led N.L. catchers with 683 putouts and 749 total chances in 1994. ... Led N.L. catchers with 14 double plays in 1995. ... Tied for N.L. lead in assists by catcher with 63 in 1995. ... Career major league grand slams: 1.

| | | | | | | | BATTING | | | | | | | | FIELDING | | |
Year Team (League)	Pos.	G	AB	R	H	2B	3B	HR	RBI	Avg.	BB	SO	SB	PO	A	E	Avg.
1988—Oneonta (NYP)	C	2	4	0	1	0	0	0	0	.250	0	2	0	0	0	0	...
—Sarasota (Fla. St.)	C	43	133	22	34	2	0	0	15	.256	11	25	5	*378	*47	9	.979
1989—Oneonta (NYP)	C-3B	52	165	29	43	6	0	1	18	.261	22	28	6	401	43	7	.984
1990—Prince Will. (Car.)	C	107	364	46	86	12	2	0	27	.236	32	73	2	662	84	5	*.993
1991—Prince Will. (Car.)	C	63	230	28	70	14	3	2	30	.304	24	37	17	419	54	5	.990
—Alb./Colon. (East.)	C	67	229	36	61	9	2	1	29	.266	27	36	14	470	56	4	.992
1992—Alb./Colon. (East.)	C	5	18	0	3	0	1	0	1	.167	2	3	2	30	2	1	.970
—Columbus (Int'l)	C-OF	111	364	48	88	14	3	2	35	.242	40	56	19	†666	63	9	.988
1993—Colo. Springs (PCL)■	C-OF	76	241	31	65	10	4	2	33	.270	27	41	10	393	57	6	.987
—San Diego (N.L.)■.....	C	49	160	18	41	8	1	5	12	.256	6	28	2	272	34	8	.975
1994—San Diego (N.L.)	C-1B	101	327	45	82	12	1	7	24	.251	30	63	5	†686	59	7	.991
1995—San Diego (N.L.)	C-1B	103	328	44	96	16	4	5	34	.293	31	56	16	656	†63	6	.992
1996—San Diego (N.L.)	C	50	149	16	27	4	0	1	13	.181	13	27	1	300	22	6	.982
—Detroit (A.L.)■	C	75	226	30	56	12	0	4	22	.248	26	45	3	452	35	4	.992
1997—Houston (N.L.)■	C	130	425	45	113	25	1	4	44	.266	38	78	14	807	73	7	.992
1998—Houston (N.L.)	C	128	412	62	111	10	4	6	45	.269	53	60	10	850	58	7	.992
American League totals (1 year)		75	226	30	56	12	0	4	22	.248	26	45	3	452	35	4	.992
National League totals (6 years)		561	1801	230	470	75	11	28	172	.261	171	312	48	3571	309	41	.990
Major league totals (6 years)		636	2027	260	526	87	11	32	194	.259	197	357	51	4023	344	45	.990

DIVISION SERIES RECORD

| | | | | | | | BATTING | | | | | | | | FIELDING | | |
Year Team (League)	Pos.	G	AB	R	H	2B	3B	HR	RBI	Avg.	BB	SO	SB	PO	A	E	Avg.
1997—Houston (N.L.)	C	2	5	1	2	1	0	0	2	.400	0	1	0	13	0	0	1.000
1998—Houston (N.L.)	C	4	9	0	2	0	0	0	0	.222	0	4	0	28	1	0	1.000
Division series totals (2 years)		6	14	1	4	1	0	0	2	.286	0	5	0	41	1	0	1.000

AVERY, STEVE   P   REDS

PERSONAL: Born April 14, 1970, in Trenton, Mich. ... 6-4/205. ... Throws left, bats left. ... Full name: Steven Thomas Avery. ... Son of Ken Avery, minor league pitcher (1962-63).
HIGH SCHOOL: John F. Kennedy (Taylor, Mich.).
TRANSACTIONS/CAREER NOTES: Selected by Atlanta Braves organization in first round (third pick overall) of free-agent draft (June 1, 1988). ... On Atlanta disabled list (July 13-September 2, 1996); included rehabilitation assignment to Greenville (August 12-18). ... On Boston disabled list (May 4-July 5, 1997); included rehabilitation assignments to Sarasota (June 12-25) and Gulf Coast Red Sox (June 25-July 5). ... Granted free agency (October 31, 1996). ... Signed by Boston Red Sox (January 22, 1997). ... Granted free agency (October 28, 1998). ... Signed by Cincinnati Reds (December 11, 1998).

HONORS: Named lefthanded pitcher on THE SPORTING NEWS N.L. All-Star team (1993).
MISCELLANEOUS: Received base on balls in only appearance as pinch hitter and appeared in one game as pinch runner (1991). ... Appeared in one game as pinch runner with Boston (1997). ... Scored two runs in five appearances as pinch runner with Boston (1998).

Year Team (League)	W	L	Pct.	ERA	G	GS	CG	ShO	Sv.	IP	H	R	ER	BB	SO
1988— Pulaski (Appalachian).........	7	1	.875	1.50	10	10	3	•2	0	66	38	16	11	19	80
1989— Durham (Carolina).............	6	4	.600	1.45	13	13	3	1	0	86²/₃	59	22	14	20	90
— Greenville (Southern)	6	3	.667	2.77	13	13	1	0	0	84¹/₃	68	32	26	34	75
1990— Richmond (Int'l).................	5	5	.500	3.39	13	13	3	0	0	82¹/₃	85	35	31	21	69
— Atlanta (N.L.)..................	3	11	.214	5.64	21	20	1	1	0	99	121	79	62	45	75
1991— Atlanta (N.L.)..................	18	8	.692	3.38	35	35	3	1	0	210¹/₃	189	89	79	65	137
1992— Atlanta (N.L.)..................	11	11	.500	3.20	35	•35	2	2	0	233²/₃	216	95	83	71	129
1993— Atlanta (N.L.)..................	18	6	.750	2.94	35	35	3	1	0	223¹/₃	216	81	73	43	125
1994— Atlanta (N.L.)..................	8	3	.727	4.04	24	24	1	0	0	151²/₃	127	71	68	55	122
1995— Atlanta (N.L.)..................	7	13	.350	4.67	29	29	3	1	0	173¹/₃	165	92	90	52	141
1996— Atlanta (N.L.)..................	7	10	.412	4.47	24	23	1	0	0	131	146	70	65	40	86
— Greenville (Southern)	0	0	...	0.00	1	1	0	0	0	²/₃	0	0	0	0	0
1997— Boston (A.L.)■.............	6	7	.462	6.42	22	18	0	0	0	96²/₃	127	76	69	49	51
— Sarasota (Florida State)......	0	0	...	0.00	1	1	0	0	0	3	2	0	0	1	3
— GC Red Sox (GCL)	0	0	...	1.50	1	1	0	0	0	6	5	3	1	0	8
— Pawtucket (Int'l)	1	0	1.000	0.00	1	1	0	0	0	5	1	0	0	3	1
1998— Boston (A.L.).................	10	7	.588	5.02	34	23	0	0	0	123²/₃	128	74	69	64	57
— Pawtucket (Int'l)	0	2	.000	5.56	3	3	0	0	0	11¹/₃	9	9	7	9	6
A.L. totals (2 years)	16	14	.533	5.64	56	41	0	0	0	220¹/₃	255	150	138	113	108
N.L. totals (7 years)	72	62	.537	3.83	203	201	14	6	0	1222¹/₃	1180	577	520	371	815
Major league totals (9 years)......	88	76	.537	4.10	259	242	14	6	0	1442²/₃	1435	727	658	484	923

DIVISION SERIES RECORD

Year Team (League)	W	L	Pct.	ERA	G	GS	CG	ShO	Sv.	IP	H	R	ER	BB	SO
1995— Atlanta (N.L.)......................	0	0	...	13.50	1	0	0	0	0	²/₃	1	1	1	0	1

CHAMPIONSHIP SERIES RECORD

RECORDS: Holds career record for most consecutive scoreless innings—22¹/₃ (1991-92). ... Holds single-series record for most consecutive scoreless innings—16¹/₃ (1991).
NOTES: Named Most Valuable Player (1991).

Year Team (League)	W	L	Pct.	ERA	G	GS	CG	ShO	Sv.	IP	H	R	ER	BB	SO
1991— Atlanta (N.L.)......................	2	0	1.000	0.00	2	2	0	0	0	16¹/₃	9	0	0	4	17
1992— Atlanta (N.L.)......................	1	1	.500	9.00	3	2	0	0	0	8	13	8	8	2	3
1993— Atlanta (N.L.)......................	0	0	...	2.77	2	2	0	0	0	13	9	5	4	6	10
1995— Atlanta (N.L.)......................	1	0	1.000	0.00	2	1	0	0	0	6	2	0	0	4	6
1996— Atlanta (N.L.)......................	0	0	...	0.00	2	0	0	0	0	2	2	0	0	1	1
Champ. series totals (5 years)	4	1	.800	2.38	11	7	0	0	0	45¹/₃	35	13	12	17	37

WORLD SERIES RECORD

NOTES: Member of World Series championship team (1995).

Year Team (League)	W	L	Pct.	ERA	G	GS	CG	ShO	Sv.	IP	H	R	ER	BB	SO
1991— Atlanta (N.L.)......................	0	0	...	3.46	2	2	0	0	0	13	10	6	5	1	8
1992— Atlanta (N.L.)......................	0	1	.000	3.75	2	2	0	0	0	12	11	5	5	3	11
1995— Atlanta (N.L.)......................	1	0	1.000	1.50	1	1	0	0	0	6	3	1	1	5	3
1996— Atlanta (N.L.)......................	0	1	.000	13.50	1	0	0	0	0	²/₃	1	2	1	4	0
World Series totals (4 years)	1	2	.333	3.41	6	5	0	0	0	31²/₃	25	14	12	13	22

ALL-STAR GAME RECORD

Year League	W	L	Pct.	ERA	GS	CG	ShO	Sv.	IP	H	R	ER	BB	SO
1993— National.................	0	0	...	0.00	0	0	0	0	1	1	3	0	1	1

AYALA, BOBBY   P   MARINERS

PERSONAL: Born July 8, 1969, in Ventura, Calif. ... 6-3/210. ... Throws right, bats right. ... Full name: Robert Joseph Ayala. ... Name pronounced eye-YAH-luh.
HIGH SCHOOL: Rio Mesa (Oxnard, Calif.).
TRANSACTIONS/CAREER NOTES: Signed as non-drafted free agent by Cincinnati Reds organization (June 27, 1988). ... Traded by Reds with C Dan Wilson to Seattle Mariners for P Erik Hanson and 2B Bret Boone (November 2, 1993). ... On Seattle disabled list (April 23-June 20, 1996); included rehabilitation assignments to Port City (June 6-8) and Tacoma (June 16-20).

Year Team (League)	W	L	Pct.	ERA	G	GS	CG	ShO	Sv.	IP	H	R	ER	BB	SO
1988— GC Reds (GCL).............	0	4	.000	3.82	20	0	0	0	3	33	34	23	14	12	24
1989— Greensboro (S. Atl.)..........	5	8	.385	4.10	22	19	1	0	0	105¹/₃	97	73	48	50	70
1990— Cedar Rapids (Midw.)	3	2	.600	3.38	18	7	3	1	1	53¹/₃	40	24	20	18	59
— Char., W.Va. (S. Atl.)	6	1	.857	2.43	21	4	2	1	2	74	48	23	20	21	73
1991— Chattanooga (Southern).....	3	1	.750	4.67	39	8	1	0	4	90²/₃	79	52	47	58	92
1992— Chattanooga (Southern).....	12	6	.667	3.54	27	27	3	3	0	162²/₃	152	75	64	58	154
— Cincinnati (N.L.).............	2	1	.667	4.34	5	5	0	0	0	29	33	15	14	13	23
1993— Indianapolis (A.A.).............	0	2	.000	5.67	5	5	0	0	0	27	36	19	17	12	19
— Cincinnati (N.L.).............	7	10	.412	5.60	43	9	0	0	3	98	106	72	61	45	65
1994— Seattle (A.L.)■................	4	3	.571	2.86	46	0	0	0	18	56²/₃	42	25	18	26	76
1995— Seattle (A.L.).................	6	5	.545	4.44	63	0	0	0	19	71	73	42	35	30	77
1996— Seattle (A.L.).................	6	3	.667	5.88	50	0	0	0	3	67¹/₃	65	45	44	25	61
— Port City (Southern)	0	0	...	0.00	2	1	0	0	0	1²/₃	0	0	0	1	2
— Tacoma (PCL)	0	0	...	0.00	1	1	0	0	0	1	0	0	0	1	1
1997— Seattle (A.L.).................	10	5	.667	3.82	71	0	0	0	8	96²/₃	91	45	41	41	92
1998— Seattle (A.L.).................	1	10	.091	7.29	62	0	0	0	8	75¹/₃	100	66	61	26	65
A.L. totals (5 years)	27	26	.509	4.88	292	0	0	0	56	367	371	223	199	148	374
N.L. totals (2 years)	9	11	.450	5.31	48	14	0	0	3	127	139	87	75	58	88
Major league totals (7 years)......	36	37	.493	4.99	340	14	0	0	59	494	510	310	274	206	462

DIVISION SERIES RECORD

Year Team (League)	W	L	Pct.	ERA	G	GS	CG	ShO	Sv.	IP	H	R	ER	BB	SO
1995— Seattle (A.L.)	0	0	...	54.00	2	0	0	0	0	$2/3$	6	4	4	1	0
1997— Seattle (A.L.)	0	0	...	40.50	1	0	0	0	0	$1 \, 1/3$	4	6	6	3	2
Div. series totals (2 years)	0	0	...	45.00	3	0	0	0	0	2	10	10	10	4	2

CHAMPIONSHIP SERIES RECORD

Year Team (League)	W	L	Pct.	ERA	G	GS	CG	ShO	Sv.	IP	H	R	ER	BB	SO
1995— Seattle (A.L.)	0	0	...	2.45	2	0	0	0	0	$3 \, 2/3$	3	1	1	3	3

AYBAR, MANNY   P   CARDINALS

A
B

PERSONAL: Born October 5, 1974, in Bani, Dominican Republic. ... 6-1/165. ... Throws right, bats right. ... Full name: Manuel Antonio Aybar.
TRANSACTIONS/CAREER NOTES: Signed as non-drafted free agent by St. Louis Cardinals organization (October 21, 1991). ... Name pronounced I-bar.

Year Team (League)	W	L	Pct.	ERA	G	GS	CG	ShO	Sv.	IP	H	R	ER	BB	SO
1992— Dom. Cardinals (DSL)	1	0	1.000	0.00	1	0	0	0	0	3	1	0	0	3	1
1993— Dom. Cardinals (DSL)	4	4	.500	3.15	13	11	1	0	0	$71 \, 1/3$	54	33	25	33	66
1994— Ariz. Cardinals (Ariz.)	6	1	.857	2.12	13	13	1	0	0	$72 \, 1/3$	69	25	17	9	79
1995— Savannah (S. Atl.)	3	8	.273	3.04	18	18	2	1	0	$112 \, 2/3$	82	46	38	36	99
— St. Petersburg (FSL)	2	5	.286	3.35	9	9	0	0	0	$48 \, 1/3$	42	27	18	16	43
1996— Arkansas (Texas)	8	6	.571	3.05	20	20	0	0	0	121	120	53	41	34	83
— Louisville (A.A.)	2	2	.500	3.23	5	5	0	0	0	$30 \, 2/3$	26	12	11	7	25
1997— Louisville (A.A.)	5	8	.385	3.48	22	22	3	•2	0	137	131	60	53	45	114
— St. Louis (N.L.)	2	4	.333	4.24	12	12	0	0	0	68	66	33	32	29	41
1998— St. Louis (N.L.)	6	6	.500	5.98	20	14	0	0	0	$81 \, 1/3$	90	58	54	42	57
— Memphis (Pacific Coast)	10	0	1.000	2.60	13	13	0	0	0	83	62	24	24	17	63
Major league totals (2 years)	8	10	.444	5.18	32	26	0	0	0	$149 \, 1/3$	156	91	86	71	98

RECORD AS POSITION PLAYER

Year Team (League)	Pos.	G	AB	R	H	2B	3B	HR	RBI	Avg.	BB	SO	SB	PO	A	E	Avg.
1992— Dom. Cardinals (DSL)	IF	55	153	18	31	5	0	1	11	.203	10	27	2	53	131	19	.906

BAERGA, CARLOS   2B

PERSONAL: Born November 4, 1968, in San Juan, Puerto Rico. ... 5-11/215. ... Bats both, throws right. ... Full name: Carlos Obed Ortiz Baerga. ... Name pronounced by-AIR-guh.
HIGH SCHOOL: Barbara Ann Rooshart (Rio Piedra, Puerto Rico).
TRANSACTIONS/CAREER NOTES: Signed as non-drafted free agent by San Diego Padres organization (November 4, 1985). ... Traded by Padres organization with C Sandy Alomar and OF Chris James to Cleveland Indians for OF Joe Carter (December 6, 1989). ... Traded to Indians with IF Alvaro Espinoza to New York Mets for IF Jose Vizcaino and IF Jeff Kent (July 29, 1996). ... Granted free agency (October 26, 1998).
RECORDS: Holds major league record for switch-hitting home runs in one inning (April 8, 1993, seventh inning). ... Shares major league single-inning record for most home runs—2 (April 8, 1993, seventh inning).
HONORS: Named second baseman on THE SPORTING NEWS A.L. All-Star team (1993 and 1995). ... Named second baseman on THE SPORTING NEWS A.L. Silver Slugger team (1993-94).
STATISTICAL NOTES: Led South Atlantic League second basemen with 29 errors in 1987. ... Led Texas League shortstops with 61 double plays in 1988. ... Led Texas League third basemen with 380 total chances in 1989. ... Led A.L. second basemen with 138 double plays in 1992. ... Led A.L. second basemen with 894 total chances in 1992 and 809 in 1993. ... Collected six hits in one game (April 11, 1992). ... Switch-hit home runs in one game (April 8, 1993). ... Hit three home runs in one game (June 17, 1993). ... Career major league grand slams: 1.

Year Team (League)	Pos.	G	AB	R	H	2B	3B	HR	RBI	Avg.	BB	SO	SB	PO	A	E	Avg.
1986— Char., S.C. (S. Atl.)	2B-SS	111	378	57	102	14	4	7	41	.270	26	60	6	202	245	27	.943
1987— Char., S.C. (S. Atl.)	2B-SS	134	515	83	157	23	•9	7	50	.305	38	107	26	253	341	†36	.943
1988— Wichita (Texas)	SS-2B	122	444	67	121	28	1	12	65	.273	31	83	4	221	325	33	.943
1989— Las Vegas (PCL)	3B	132	520	63	143	28	2	10	74	.275	30	98	6	*92	256	*32	.916
1990— Cleveland (A.L.)■	3B-SS-2B	108	312	46	81	17	2	7	47	.260	16	57	0	79	164	17	.935
— Colo. Springs (PCL)	3B	12	50	11	19	2	1	1	11	.380	5	4	1	18	31	4	.925
1991— Cleveland (A.L.)	3B-2B-SS	158	593	80	171	28	2	11	69	.288	48	74	3	217	421	27	.959
1992— Cleveland (A.L.)	2B-DH	161	657	92	205	32	1	20	105	.312	35	76	10	*400	*475	19	.979
1993— Cleveland (A.L.)	2B-DH	154	624	105	200	28	6	21	114	.321	34	68	15	*347	*445	17	.979
1994— Cleveland (A.L.)	2B-DH	103	442	81	139	32	2	19	80	.314	10	45	8	205	335	*15	.973
1995— Cleveland (A.L.)	2B-DH	135	557	87	175	28	2	15	90	.314	35	31	11	231	*444	19	.973
1996— Cleveland (A.L.)	2B	100	424	54	113	25	0	10	55	.267	16	25	1	191	308	15	.971
— New York (N.L.)■	1B-3B-2B	26	83	5	16	3	0	2	11	.193	5	2	0	103	12	4	.966
1997— New York (N.L.)	2B	133	467	53	131	25	1	9	52	.281	20	54	2	244	371	14	.978
1998— New York (N.L.)	2B	147	511	46	136	27	1	7	53	.266	24	55	0	289	340	9	.986
American League totals (7 years)		919	3609	545	1084	190	15	103	560	.300	194	376	48	1670	2592	129	.971
National League totals (3 years)		306	1061	104	283	55	2	18	116	.267	49	111	2	636	723	27	.981
Major league totals (9 years)		1225	4670	649	1367	245	17	121	676	.293	243	487	50	2306	3315	156	.973

DIVISION SERIES RECORD

Year Team (League)	Pos.	G	AB	R	H	2B	3B	HR	RBI	Avg.	BB	SO	SB	PO	A	E	Avg.
1995— Cleveland (A.L.)	2B	3	14	2	4	1	0	0	1	.286	0	1	0	8	5	1	.929

CHAMPIONSHIP SERIES RECORD

Year Team (League)	Pos.	G	AB	R	H	2B	3B	HR	RBI	Avg.	BB	SO	SB	PO	A	E	Avg.
1995— Cleveland (A.L.)	2B	6	25	3	10	0	0	1	4	.400	2	3	0	12	22	0	1.000

WORLD SERIES RECORD

					BATTING									FIELDING		
Year Team (League)	Pos.	G	AB	R	H	2B	3B	HR	RBI	Avg.	BB	SO	SB	PO	A	E	Avg.
1995— Cleveland (A.L.)..........	2B	6	26	1	5	2	0	0	4	.192	1	1	0	15	24	1	.975

ALL-STAR GAME RECORD

				BATTING									FIELDING		
Year League	Pos.	AB	R	H	2B	3B	HR	RBI	Avg.	BB	SO	SB	PO	A	E	Avg.
1992— American....................	2B	1	1	1	1	0	0	1	1.000	0	0	0	1	2	0	1.000
1993— American....................	2B	2	1	0	0	0	0	0	.000	0	1	0	0	1	0	1.000
1995— American....................	2B	3	1	3	1	0	0	0	1.000	0	0	0	1	2	0	1.000
All-Star Game totals (3 years)		6	3	4	2	0	0	1	.667	0	1	0	2	5	0	1.000

BAGWELL, JEFF   1B   ASTROS

PERSONAL: Born May 27, 1968, in Boston. ... 6-0/195. ... Bats right, throws right. ... Full name: Jeffrey Robert Bagwell.

HIGH SCHOOL: Xavier (Middletown, Conn.).

COLLEGE: Hartford.

TRANSACTIONS/CAREER NOTES: Selected by Boston Red Sox organization in fourth round of free-agent draft (June 5, 1989). ... Traded by Red Sox to Houston Astros for P Larry Andersen (August 31, 1990). ... On Houston disabled list (July 31-September 1, 1995); included rehabilitation assignment to Jackson (August 28-September 1). ... On disabled list (May 13-28, 1998).

RECORDS: Shares major league record for most home runs in one inning—2 (June 24, 1994, sixth inning). ... Shares major league single-game record for most doubles—4 (June 14, 1996).

HONORS: Named Eastern League Most Valuable Player (1990). ... Named N.L. Rookie Player of the Year by THE SPORTING NEWS (1991). ... Named N.L. Rookie of the Year by Baseball Writers' Association of America (1991). ... Named Major League Player of the Year by THE SPORTING NEWS (1994). ... Named first baseman on THE SPORTING NEWS N.L. All-Star team (1994, 1996 and 1997). ... Won N.L. Gold Glove at first base (1994). ... Named first baseman on THE SPORTING NEWS N.L. Silver Slugger team (1994 and 1997). ... Named N.L. Most Valuable Player by Baseball Writers' Association of America (1994).

STATISTICAL NOTES: Led Eastern League with 220 total bases and 12 intentional bases on balls received in 1990. ... Led N.L. in being hit by pitch with 13 in 1991. ... Led N.L. with 13 sacrifice flies in 1992. ... Hit three home runs in one game (June 24, 1994). ... Led N.L. with .750 slugging percentage in 1994. ... Led N.L. first basemen with 120 assists in 1994. ... Tied for N.L. lead in errors by first basemen with nine and double plays by first basemen with 94 in 1994. ... Career major league grand slams: 5.

MISCELLANEOUS: Holds Houston Astros all-time record for highest career batting average (.304).

					BATTING									FIELDING		
Year Team (League)	Pos.	G	AB	R	H	2B	3B	HR	RBI	Avg.	BB	SO	SB	PO	A	E	Avg.
1989— GC Red Sox (GCL)	3B-2B	5	19	3	6	1	0	0	3	.316	3	0	0	2	12	2	.875
—Winter Haven (FSL)....	3B-2B-1B	64	210	27	65	13	2	2	19	.310	22	25	1	53	109	12	.931
1990— New Britain (East.)	3B	136	481	63	*160	•34	7	4	61	.333	73	57	5	93	267	34	.914
1991— Houston (N.L.)■..........	1B	156	554	79	163	26	4	15	82	.294	75	116	7	1270	106	12	.991
1992— Houston (N.L.)	1B	•162	586	87	160	34	6	18	96	.273	84	97	10	1334	133	7	.995
1993— Houston (N.L.)	1B	142	535	76	171	37	4	20	88	.320	62	73	13	1200	113	9	.993
1994— Houston (N.L.)	1B-OF	110	400	*104	147	32	2	39	*116	.368	65	65	15	923	†121	‡9	.991
1995— Houston (N.L.)	1B	114	448	88	130	29	0	21	87	.290	79	102	12	1004	*129	7	.994
—Jackson (Texas)	1B	4	12	0	2	0	0	0	0	.167	3	2	0	24	6	0	1.000
1996— Houston (N.L.)	1B	*162	568	111	179	*48	2	31	120	.315	135	114	21	1336	*136	*16	.989
1997— Houston (N.L.)	1B-DH	*162	566	109	162	40	2	43	135	.286	127	122	31	1404	*137	11	.993
1998— Houston (N.L.)	1B	147	540	124	164	33	1	34	111	.304	109	90	19	1239	128	7	.995
Major league totals (8 years)		1155	4197	778	1276	279	21	221	835	.304	736	779	128	9710	1003	78	.993

DIVISION SERIES RECORD

					BATTING									FIELDING		
Year Team (League)	Pos.	G	AB	R	H	2B	3B	HR	RBI	Avg.	BB	SO	SB	PO	A	E	Avg.
1997— Houston (N.L.)	1B	3	12	0	1	0	0	0	0	.083	1	5	0	17	6	2	.920
1998— Houston (N.L.)	1B	4	14	0	2	0	0	0	4	.143	1	6	0	31	4	0	1.000
Division series totals (2 years)		7	26	0	3	0	0	0	4	.115	2	11	0	48	10	2	.967

ALL-STAR GAME RECORD

				BATTING									FIELDING		
Year League	Pos.	AB	R	H	2B	3B	HR	RBI	Avg.	BB	SO	SB	PO	A	E	Avg.
1994— National	PH-1B	4	1	2	0	0	0	0	.500	0	1	0	3	2	0	1.000
1996— National	1B	2	0	0	0	0	0	0	.000	0	1	0	5	0	0	1.000
1997— National	1B	3	0	0	0	0	0	0	.000	0	0	0	8	1	0	1.000
All-Star Game totals (3 years)		9	1	2	0	0	0	0	.222	0	2	0	16	3	0	1.000

BAILES, SCOTT   P

PERSONAL: Born December 18, 1962, in Chillicothe, Ohio. ... 6-2/171. ... Throws left, bats left. ... Full name: Scott Alan Bailes.

HIGH SCHOOL: Parkview (Springfield, Mo.).

JUNIOR COLLEGE: St. Louis Community College at Meramec.

COLLEGE: Southwest Missouri State.

TRANSACTIONS/CAREER NOTES: Selected by Texas Rangers organization in seventh round of free-agent draft (January 12, 1982); did not sign. ... Selected by Pittsburgh Pirates organization in secondary phase of free-agent draft (June 7, 1982). ... On disabled list (August 12, 1982-remainder of season). ... Traded by Pirates to Cleveland Indians organization (July 3, 1985), completing deal in which Indians traded SS Johnnie LeMaster to Pirates for a player to be named later (May 30, 1985). ... On disabled list (August 13-September 6, 1989). ... Traded by Indians to California Angels for IF Jeff Manto and P Colin Charland (January 9, 1990). ... On disabled list (June 30-July 15, 1991 and April 11-25, 1992). ... Released by Angels (October 15, 1992). ... Signed by Memphis, Kansas City Royals organization (February 26, 1993). ... Released by Memphis (April 3, 1993). ... Signed by Syracuse, Toronto Blue Jays organization (April 25, 1993). ... On voluntarily retired list (June 3, 1993-January 18, 1995). ... Released by Blue Jays (January 18, 1995). ... Signed by Rangers organization (December 16, 1996). ... Granted free agency (November 6, 1997). ... Re-signed by Rangers (December 7, 1997). ... On Texas disabled list (August 1-September 1, 1998); included rehabilitation assignments to Tulsa (August 13-20) and Oklahoma City (August 21-September 1). ... Granted free agency (October 30, 1998).

Year Team (League)	W	L	Pct.	ERA	G	GS	CG	ShO	Sv.	IP	H	R	ER	BB	SO
1982—Greenwood (S. Atl.)............	0	1	.000	7.24	3	1	1	0	0	13 2/3	17	12	11	6	8
1983—Alexandria (Caro.)	5	2	.714	3.36	52	1	0	0	7	75	67	38	28	45	101
1984—Nashua (Eastern)...............	6	8	.429	3.41	54	1	0	0	3	87	80	43	33	46	61
1985—Nashua (Eastern)...............	3	3	.500	2.83	30	0	0	0	8	47 2/3	44	22	15	20	42
—Waterbury (Eastern)■........	6	3	.667	2.62	13	11	3	1	1	79	78	36	23	23	53
1986—Cleveland (A.L.)...............	10	10	.500	4.95	62	10	0	0	7	112 2/3	123	70	62	43	60
1987—Cleveland (A.L.)...............	7	8	.467	4.64	39	17	0	0	6	120 1/3	145	75	62	47	65
1988—Cleveland (A.L.)...............	9	14	.391	4.90	37	21	5	2	0	145	149	89	79	46	53
1989—Cleveland (A.L.)...............	5	9	.357	4.28	34	11	0	0	0	113 2/3	116	57	54	29	47
1990—California (A.L.)■...........	2	0	1.000	6.37	27	0	0	0	0	35 1/3	46	30	25	20	16
—Edmonton (PCL)	0	1	.000	6.00	9	3	0	0	0	18	21	13	12	8	12
1991—California (A.L.)...............	1	2	.333	4.18	42	0	0	0	0	51 2/3	41	26	24	22	41
1992—California (A.L.)...............	3	1	.750	7.45	32	0	0	0	0	38 2/3	59	34	32	28	25
1993—Syracuse (Int'l)■..............	0	1	.000	2.21	19	0	0	0	2	20 1/3	19	10	5	3	22
1994—						Out of organized baseball.									
1995—						Out of organized baseball.									
1996—						Out of organized baseball.									
1997—Oklahoma City (A.A.)■......	2	3	.400	3.98	44	0	0	0	4	43	46	22	19	13	37
—Texas (A.L.)	1	0	1.000	2.86	24	0	0	0	0	22	18	9	7	10	14
1998—Texas (A.L.)	1	0	1.000	6.47	46	0	0	0	0	40 1/3	61	33	29	11	30
—Tulsa (Texas)	0	1	.000	10.80	2	0	0	0	1	1 2/3	4	2	2	0	4
—Oklahoma (Pacific Coast)...	0	0	. . .	0.00	1	0	0	0	0	1 1/3	2	0	0	0	2
Major league totals (9 years)......	**39**	**44**	**.470**	**4.95**	**343**	**59**	**5**	**2**	**13**	**679 2/3**	**758**	**423**	**374**	**256**	**351**

BAILEY, CORY — P — GIANTS

PERSONAL: Born January 24, 1971, in Herrin, Ill. ... 6-1/200. ... Throws right, bats right. ... Full name: Phillip Cory Bailey.
HIGH SCHOOL: Marion (Ill.).
COLLEGE: Southeastern Illinois.
TRANSACTIONS/CAREER NOTES: Selected by Boston Red Sox organization in 15th round of free-agent draft (June 3, 1991). ... Traded by Red Sox with 3B Scott Cooper and a player to be named later to St. Louis Cardinals for P Rheal Cormier and OF Mark Whiten (April 8, 1995). ... Traded by Cardinals to Texas Rangers for P David Chavarria and a player to be named later (December 16, 1996). ... Traded by Rangers to San Francisco Giants for P Chad Hartvigson (July 29, 1997).

Year Team (League)	W	L	Pct.	ERA	G	GS	CG	ShO	Sv.	IP	H	R	ER	BB	SO
1991—GC Red Sox (GCL)	0	0	. . .	0.00	1	0	0	0	1	2	2	1	0	1	1
—Elmira (N.Y.-Penn).............	2	4	.333	1.85	28	0	0	0	*15	39	19	10	8	12	54
1992—Lynchburg (Carolina)	5	7	.417	2.44	49	0	0	0	*23	66 1/3	43	20	18	30	87
1993—Pawtucket (Int'l)	4	5	.444	2.88	52	0	0	0	20	65 2/3	48	21	21	31	59
—Boston (A.L.)	0	1	.000	3.45	11	0	0	0	0	15 2/3	12	7	6	12	11
1994—Pawtucket (Int'l)	4	3	.571	3.23	53	0	0	0	19	61 1/3	44	25	22	38	52
—Boston (A.L.)	0	1	.000	12.46	5	0	0	0	0	4 1/3	10	6	6	3	4
1995—Louisville (A.A.)■.............	5	3	.625	4.55	55	0	0	0	*25	59 1/3	51	30	30	30	49
—St. Louis (N.L.)................	0	0	. . .	7.36	3	0	0	0	0	3 2/3	2	3	3	2	5
1996—St. Louis (N.L.)................	5	2	.714	3.00	51	0	0	0	0	57	57	21	19	30	38
—Louisville (A.A.)................	2	4	.333	5.82	22	0	0	0	1	34	29	22	22	20	27
1997—Oklahoma City (A.A.)■......	3	4	.429	3.40	42	0	0	0	15	50 1/3	49	20	19	23	38
—Phoenix (PCL)	4	0	1.000	1.56	13	0	0	0	3	17 1/3	16	4	3	6	14
—San Francisco (N.L.)	0	1	.000	8.38	7	0	0	0	0	9 2/3	15	9	9	4	5
1998—Fresno (Pacific Coast)	7	2	.778	2.47	57	0	0	0	10	94 2/3	79	31	26	18	76
—San Francisco (N.L.)	0	0	. . .	2.70	5	0	0	0	0	3 1/3	2	1	1	1	2
A.L. totals (2 years)	**0**	**2**	**.000**	**5.40**	**16**	**0**	**0**	**0**	**0**	**20**	**22**	**13**	**12**	**15**	**15**
N.L. totals (4 years)	**5**	**3**	**.625**	**3.91**	**66**	**0**	**0**	**0**	**0**	**73 2/3**	**76**	**34**	**32**	**37**	**50**
Major league totals (6 years)......	**5**	**5**	**.500**	**4.23**	**82**	**0**	**0**	**0**	**0**	**93 2/3**	**98**	**47**	**44**	**52**	**65**

BAINES, HAROLD — DH — ORIOLES

PERSONAL: Born March 15, 1959, in St. Michaels, Md. ... 6-2/195. ... Bats left, throws left. ... Full name: Harold Dougleas Baines.
HIGH SCHOOL: St. Michaels (Easton, Md.).
TRANSACTIONS/CAREER NOTES: Selected by Chicago White Sox organization in first round (first pick overall) of free-agent draft (June 7, 1977). ... On disabled list (April 7-May 8, 1987). ... Traded by White Sox with IF Fred Manrique to Texas Rangers for SS Scott Fletcher, OF Sammy Sosa and P Wilson Alvarez (July 29, 1989). ... Traded by Rangers to Oakland Athletics for two players to be named later (August 29, 1990). ... Rangers acquired P Joe Bitker and P Scott Chiamparino to complete deal (September 4, 1990). ... Granted free agency (October 27, 1992); accepted arbitration. ... Traded by A's to Baltimore Orioles for P Bobby Chouinard and P Allen Plaster (January 14, 1993). ... On Baltimore disabled list (May 5-27, 1993); included rehabilitation assignment to Bowie (May 25-27). ... Granted free agency (November 1, 1993). ... Re-signed by Orioles (December 2, 1993). ... Granted free agency (October 20, 1994). ... Re-signed by Orioles (December 23, 1994). ... Granted free agency (November 6, 1995). ... Signed by White Sox (December 11, 1995). ... Granted free agency (November 18, 1996). Re-signed by White Sox (January 10, 1997). ... Re-signed by White Sox (January 10, 1997). ... Traded by White Sox to Orioles for a player to be named later (July 29, 1997); White Sox acquired SS Juan Bautista to complete deal (August 18, 1997). ... Granted free agency (October 29, 1997). ... Re-signed by Orioles (December 19, 1997). ... On disabled list (July 11-August 4, 1998).
RECORDS: Shares major league single-game record for most plate appearances—12 (May 8, finished May 9, 1984, 25 innings). ... Shares A.L. record for longest errorless game by outfielder—25 innings (May 8, finished May 9, 1984). ... Shares A.L. single-game record for most innings by outfielder—25 (May 8, finished May 9, 1984).
HONORS: Named outfielder on THE SPORTING NEWS A.L. All-Star team (1985). ... Named designated hitter on THE SPORTING NEWS A.L. All-Star team (1988-89). ... Named designated hitter on THE SPORTING NEWS A.L. Silver Slugger team (1989).
STATISTICAL NOTES: Tied for American Association lead in double plays by outfielder with four in 1979. ... Hit three home runs in one game (July 7, 1982; September 17, 1984 and May 7, 1991). ... Led A.L. with 22 game-winning RBIs in 1983. ... Led A.L. with .541 slugging percentage in 1984. ... Career major league grand slams: 12.

B

Year Team (League)	Pos.	G	AB	R	H	2B	3B	HR	RBI	Avg.	BB	SO	SB	PO	A	E	Avg.
							BATTING								FIELDING		
1977—Appleton (Midwest)....	OF	69	222	37	58	11	2	5	29	.261	36	62	2	94	10	7	.937
1978—Knoxville (Southern)..	OF-1B	137	502	70	138	16	6	13	72	.275	43	91	3	291	22	13	.960
1979—Iowa (Am. Assoc.)......	OF	125	466	87	139	25	8	22	87	.298	33	80	5	222	•16	11	.956
1980—Chicago (A.L.).........	OF-DH	141	491	55	125	23	6	13	49	.255	19	65	2	229	6	9	.963
1981—Chicago (A.L.).........	OF-DH	82	280	42	80	11	7	10	41	.286	12	41	6	120	10	2	.985
1982—Chicago (A.L.).........	OF	161	608	89	165	29	8	25	105	.271	49	95	10	326	10	7	.980
1983—Chicago (A.L.).........	OF	156	596	76	167	33	2	20	99	.280	49	85	7	312	10	9	.973
1984—Chicago (A.L.).........	OF	147	569	72	173	28	10	29	94	.304	54	75	1	307	8	6	.981
1985—Chicago (A.L.).........	OF-DH	160	640	86	198	29	3	22	113	.309	42	89	1	318	8	2	.994
1986—Chicago (A.L.).........	OF-DH	145	570	72	169	29	2	21	88	.296	38	89	2	295	15	5	.984
1987—Chicago (A.L.).........	DH-OF	132	505	59	148	26	4	20	93	.293	46	82	0	13	0	0	1.000
1988—Chicago (A.L.).........	DH-OF	158	599	55	166	39	1	13	81	.277	67	109	0	14	1	2	.882
1989—Chicago (A.L.).........	DH-OF	70	333	55	107	20	1	13	56	.321	60	52	0	52	0	1	.981
—Texas (A.L.)■............	DH-OF	46	172	18	49	9	0	3	16	.285	13	27	0	2	0	1	.667
1990—Texas (A.L.)..........	DH	103	321	41	93	10	1	13	44	.290	47	63	0	...	...	...	...
—Oakland (A.L.)■........	DH-OF	32	94	11	25	5	0	3	21	.266	20	17	0	5	0	1	.833
1991—Oakland (A.L.).......	DH-OF	141	488	76	144	25	1	20	90	.295	72	67	0	11	1	1	.923
1992—Oakland (A.L.).......	DH-OF	140	478	58	121	18	0	16	76	.253	59	61	1	27	0	1	.964
1993—Baltimore (A.L.)■....	DH	118	416	64	130	22	0	20	78	.313	57	52	0	...	...	...	...
—Bowie (Eastern)..........	DH	2	6	0	0	0	0	0	0	.000	1	1	0	...	...	...	...
1994—Baltimore (A.L.)......	DH	94	326	44	96	12	1	16	54	.294	30	49	0	...	...	...	...
1995—Baltimore (A.L.)......	DH	127	385	60	115	19	1	24	63	.299	70	45	0	...	...	...	...
1996—Chicago (A.L.)■......	DH	143	495	80	154	29	0	22	95	.311	73	62	3	...	...	...	...
1997—Chicago (A.L.)■......	DH-OF	93	318	40	97	18	0	12	52	.305	41	47	0	0	0	0	...
—Baltimore (A.L.)■.......	DH	44	134	15	39	5	0	4	15	.291	14	15	0	...	...	...	...
1998—Baltimore (A.L.)......	DH	104	293	40	88	17	0	9	57	.300	32	40	0	...	...	...	...
Major league totals (19 years)		2537	9111	1208	2649	456	48	348	1480	.291	964	1327	33	2031	69	47	.978

NOTES: Hit home run in first at-bat (October 2, 1997).

DIVISION SERIES RECORD

Year Team (League)	Pos.	G	AB	R	H	2B	3B	HR	RBI	Avg.	BB	SO	SB	PO	A	E	Avg.
							BATTING								FIELDING		
1997—Baltimore (A.L.)..........	DH-PH	2	5	2	2	0	0	1	1	.400	1	0	0	...	...	...	...

CHAMPIONSHIP SERIES RECORD

Year Team (League)	Pos.	G	AB	R	H	2B	3B	HR	RBI	Avg.	BB	SO	SB	PO	A	E	Avg.
							BATTING								FIELDING		
1983—Chicago (A.L.)	OF	4	16	0	2	0	0	0	0	.125	1	3	0	5	1	0	1.000
1990—Oakland (A.L.)	DH	4	14	2	5	1	0	0	3	.357	2	1	1	...	...	...	...
1992—Oakland (A.L.)	DH	6	25	6	11	2	0	1	4	.440	0	3	0	...	...	...	...
1997—Baltimore (A.L.)	DH	6	17	1	6	0	0	1	2	.353	2	1	0	...	...	...	...
Championship series totals (4 years)		20	72	9	24	3	0	2	9	.333	5	8	1	5	1	0	1.000

WORLD SERIES RECORD

Year Team (League)	Pos.	G	AB	R	H	2B	3B	HR	RBI	Avg.	BB	SO	SB	PO	A	E	Avg.
							BATTING								FIELDING		
1990—Oakland (A.L.)	DH-PH	3	7	1	1	0	0	1	2	.143	1	2	0	...	...	...	...

ALL-STAR GAME RECORD

Year League	Pos.	AB	R	H	2B	3B	HR	RBI	Avg.	BB	SO	SB	PO	A	E	Avg.
							BATTING							FIELDING		
1985—American	PH	1	0	1	0	0	0	0	1.000	0	0	0	...	...	...	...
1986—American	PH	1	0	0	0	0	0	0	.000	0	0	0	...	...	...	...
1987—American	PH	1	0	0	0	0	0	0	.000	0	0	0	...	...	...	...
1989—American	DH	3	1	1	0	0	0	1	.333	0	1	0	...	...	...	...
1991—American	PH-DH	1	0	0	0	0	0	1	.000	0	0	0	...	...	...	...
All-Star Game totals (5 years)		7	1	2	0	0	0	2	.286	0	1	0	...	...	...	...

BAKO, PAUL   C   ASTROS

PERSONAL: Born June 20, 1972, in Lafayette, La. ... 6-2/205. ... Bats left, throws right. ... Full name: Gabor Paul Bako.

HIGH SCHOOL: Lafayette (La.).

COLLEGE: Southwestern Louisiana.

TRANSACTIONS/CAREER NOTES: Selected by Cincinnati Reds organization in fifth round of free-agent draft (June 3, 1993). ... Traded by Reds with P Donne Wall to Detroit Tigers for OF Melvin Nieves (November 11, 1997). ... Traded by Tigers with P Dean Crow, P Brian Powell, P Mark Persails and 3B Carlos Villalobos to Houston Astros for C Brad Ausmus and P C.J. Nitkowski (January 14, 1999).

STATISTICAL NOTES: Tied for Carolina League lead with 15 passed balls in 1995. ... Led Southern League catchers with 791 total chances in 1996. ... Tied for American Association lead in double plays with 10 and passed balls with nine by a catcher in 1997.

Year Team (League)	Pos.	G	AB	R	H	2B	3B	HR	RBI	Avg.	BB	SO	SB	PO	A	E	Avg.
							BATTING								FIELDING		
1993—Billings (Pioneer)........	C-1B	57	194	34	61	11	0	4	30	.314	22	37	5	323	45	6	.984
1994—Win.-Salem (Car.).......	C	90	289	29	59	9	1	3	26	.204	35	81	2	570	73	15	.977
1995—Win.-Salem (Car.).......	C	82	249	29	71	11	2	7	27	.285	42	66	3	478	49	6	.989
1996—Chattanooga (Sou.)	C	110	360	53	106	27	0	8	48	.294	48	93	1	*694	*84	13	.984
1997—Indianapolis (A.A.)......	C	104	321	34	78	14	1	8	43	.243	34	81	0	622	64	6	.991
1998—Toledo (Int'l)■..........	C	13	48	5	14	3	1	1	6	.292	1	13	0	75	5	1	.988
—Detroit (A.L.)............	C	96	305	23	83	12	1	3	30	.272	23	82	1	493	45	6	.989
Major league totals (1 year)		96	305	23	83	12	1	3	30	.272	23	82	1	493	45	6	.989

BALDWIN, JAMES   P   WHITE SOX

PERSONAL: Born July 15, 1971, in Southern Pines, N.C. ... 6-3/210. ... Throws right, bats right.
HIGH SCHOOL: Pinecrest (Southern Pines, N.C.).
TRANSACTIONS/CAREER NOTES: Selected by Chicago White Sox organization in fourth round of free-agent draft (June 4, 1990). ... On disabled list (August 3-19, 1994).
HONORS: Named A.L. Rookie Pitcher of the Year by THE SPORTING NEWS (1996).
STATISTICAL NOTES: Led American Association with 27 home runs allowed and tied for lead with three balks in 1995. ... Tied for American Association lead with three balks in 1995. ... Tied for A.L. lead with 14 wild pitches and three balks in 1997.

Year — Team (League)	W	L	Pct.	ERA	G	GS	CG	ShO	Sv.	IP	H	R	ER	BB	SO
1990— GC White Sox (GCL)	1	6	.143	4.10	9	7	0	0	0	37 1/3	32	29	17	18	32
1991— GC White Sox (GCL)	3	1	.750	2.12	6	6	0	0	0	34	16	8	8	16	48
— Utica (N.Y.-Penn)	1	4	.200	5.30	7	7	1	0	0	37 1/3	40	26	22	27	23
1992— South Bend (Mid.)	9	5	.643	2.42	21	21	1	1	0	137 2/3	118	53	37	45	137
— Sarasota (Florida State)	1	2	.333	2.87	6	6	1	0	0	37 2/3	31	13	12	7	39
1993— Birmingham (Southern)	8	5	.615	*2.25	17	17	•4	0	0	120	94	48	30	43	107
— Nashville (A.A.)	5	4	.556	2.61	10	10	1	0	0	69	43	21	20	36	61
1994— Nashville (A.A.)	12	6	.667	3.72	26	26	2	0	0	162	144	75	67	83	*156
1995— Chicago (A.L.)	0	1	.000	12.89	6	4	0	0	0	14 2/3	32	22	21	9	10
— Nashville (A.A.)	5	9	.357	5.85	18	18	0	0	0	95 1/3	120	76	62	44	89
1996— Nashville (A.A.)	1	1	.500	0.64	2	2	1	0	0	14	5	1	1	4	15
— Chicago (A.L.)	11	6	.647	4.42	28	28	0	0	0	169	168	88	83	57	127
1997— Chicago (A.L.)	12	•15	.444	5.27	32	32	1	0	0	200	205	128	117	83	140
1998— Chicago (A.L.)	13	6	.684	5.32	37	24	1	0	0	159	176	103	94	60	108
Major league totals (4 years)	36	28	.563	5.22	103	88	2	0	0	542 2/3	581	341	315	209	385

BALE, JOHN   P   BLUE JAYS

PERSONAL: Born May 22, 1974, in Cheverly, Md. ... 6-4/195. ... Throws left, bats left. ... Full name: John R. Bale.
HIGH SCHOOL: Crestview (Fla.).
JUNIOR COLLEGE: Jefferson Davis Community College (Ala.).
COLLEGE: Southern Mississippi.
TRANSACTIONS/CAREER NOTES: Selected by St. Louis Cardinals organization in 12th round of free-agent draft (June 2, 1994); did not sign. ... Selected by Toronto Blue Jays organization in fifth round of free-agent draft (June 4, 1996).

Year — Team (League)	W	L	Pct.	ERA	G	GS	CG	ShO	Sv.	IP	H	R	ER	BB	SO
1996— St. Catharines (NYP)	3	2	.600	4.86	8	8	0	0	0	33 1/3	39	21	18	11	35
1997— Hagerstown (S. Atl.)	7	7	.500	4.30	25	25	0	0	0	140 1/3	130	83	67	63	155
1998— Dunedin (Fla. St.)	4	5	.444	4.64	24	9	0	0	4	66	68	39	34	23	78
— Knoxville (Southern)	0	0	. . .	6.75	3	0	0	0	0	1 1/3	1	1	1	0	0

BALL, JEFF   IF   ATHLETICS

PERSONAL: Born April 17, 1969, in Merced, Calif. ... 5-10/185. ... Throws right, bats right. ... Full name: Jeffrey D. Ball.
HIGH SCHOOL: Atwater (Calif.).
COLLEGE: San Jose State.
TRANSACTIONS/CAREER NOTES: Selected by Houston Astros organization in 12th round of free-agent draft (June 4, 1990). ... Granted free agency (October 15, 1996). ... Signed by San Francisco Giants organization (November 25, 1996). ... Granted free agency (October 15, 1997). ... Re-signed by Giants organization (January 12, 1998). ... Granted free agency (December 21, 1998). ... Signed by Oakland Athletics organization (January 22, 1999).
STATISTICAL NOTES: Led Pacific League first basemen with .994 fielding percentage in 1998.

RECORD AS POSITION PLAYER

Year — Team (League)	Pos.	G	AB	R	H	2B	3B	HR	RBI	Avg.	BB	SO	SB	PO	A	E	Avg.
1990— Auburn (NY-Penn)	3B	70	263	40	76	18	1	5	38	.289	22	35	20	48	119	19	.898
1991— Osceola (Fla. St.)	3B-1B	118	392	53	96	15	3	5	51	.245	49	74	20	72	183	27	.904
1992— Jackson (Texas)	3B-1B-2B	93	278	27	53	13	2	5	24	.191	20	58	5	267	112	27	.933
1993— Quad City (Midwest)	0-1-3-2	112	389	69	114	28	2	14	76	.293	58	62	40	238	49	10	.966
1994— Jackson (Texas)	1-3-2-0	111	358	65	113	30	3	13	57	.316	34	74	9	339	114	10	.978
1995— Tucson (PCL)	3B-1B-OF	110	362	58	106	25	2	4	56	.293	25	66	11	310	109	8	.981
1996— Tucson (PCL)	1B-3B	116	429	64	139	31	2	19	73	.324	34	83	10	782	98	18	.980
1997— Phoenix (PCL)■	3B-1B-2B	126	470	90	151	38	3	18	103	.321	58	84	10	69	175	16	.938
1998— Fresno (PCL)	1B-3B-OF	124	456	81	135	29	0	21	80	.296	55	86	5	907	77	9	†.991
— San Francisco (N.L.)	1B	2	4	0	1	0	0	0	0	.250	0	0	0	10	0	0	1.000
Major league totals (1 year)		2	4	0	1	0	0	0	0	.250	0	0	0	10	0	0	1.000

BANKS, BRIAN   OF   BREWERS

PERSONAL: Born September 29, 1970, in Mesa, Ariz. ... 6-3/208. ... Bats both, throws right. ... Full name: Brian Glen Banks.
HIGH SCHOOL: Mountain View (Mesa, Ariz.).
COLLEGE: Brigham Young.
TRANSACTIONS/CAREER NOTES: Selected by Milwaukee Brewers organization in second round of free-agent draft (June 3, 1993); pick received as part of compensation for Seattle Mariners signing Type A free-agent P Chris Bosio.
STATISTICAL NOTES: Tied for Midwest League lead in double plays by outfielder with four in 1994. ... Career major league grand slams: 1.

Year Team (League)	Pos.	G	AB	R	H	2B	3B	HR	RBI	Avg.	BB	SO	SB	PO	A	E	Avg.
						BATTING									FIELDING		
1993— Helena (Pioneer)	OF	12	48	8	19	1	1	2	8	.396	11	8	1	25	0	1	.962
— Beloit (Midwest)	OF	38	147	21	36	5	1	4	19	.245	7	34	1	47	2	1	.980
1994— Beloit (Midwest)	OF-1B-3B	65	237	41	71	13	1	9	47	.300	29	40	11	123	5	2	.985
— Stockton (California) ..	OF	67	246	29	58	9	1	4	28	.236	38	46	3	108	5	4	.966
1995— El Paso (Texas)	OF-1B-3B	128	441	81	136	*39	10	12	78	.308	*81	113	9	245	11	10	.962
1996— New Orleans (A.A.)	OF-3B-C	137	487	71	132	29	7	16	64	.271	66	105	17	256	18	8	.972
— Milwaukee (A.L.)	OF-1B	4	7	2	4	2	0	1	2	.571	1	2	0	15	1	0	1.000
1997— Tucson (PCL)	OF-C	98	378	53	112	26	3	10	63	.296	35	83	7	194	13	3	.986
— Milwaukee (A.L.)	O-1-DH-3	28	68	9	14	1	0	1	8	.206	6	17	0	30	7	2	.949
1998— Louisville (Int'l)	O-C-1-3	85	299	58	87	18	1	21	66	.291	52	72	14	244	33	6	.979
— Milwaukee (N.L.)	C-1-3-O	24	24	3	7	2	0	1	5	.292	4	7	0	12	1	1	.929
American League totals (2 years)		32	75	11	18	3	0	2	10	.240	7	19	0	45	8	2	.964
National League totals (1 year)		24	24	3	7	2	0	1	5	.292	4	7	0	12	1	1	.929
Major league totals (3 years)		56	99	14	25	5	0	3	15	.253	11	26	0	57	9	3	.957

B

BANKS, WILLIE   P

PERSONAL: Born February 27, 1969, in Jersey City, N.J. ... 6-1/200. ... Throws right, bats right. ... Full name: Willie Anthony Banks.
HIGH SCHOOL: St. Anthony (Jersey City, N.J.).
TRANSACTIONS/CAREER NOTES: Selected by Minnesota Twins organization in first round (third pick overall) of free-agent draft (June 2, 1987). ... Traded by Twins to Chicago Cubs for P Dave Stevens and C Matt Walbeck (November 24, 1993). ... Traded by Cubs to Los Angeles Dodgers for P Dax Winslett (June 19, 1995). ... Claimed on waivers by Florida Marlins (August 10, 1995). ... Claimed on waivers by Philadelphia Phillies (October 4, 1995). ... Released by Phillies (March 8, 1996). ... Signed by New York Yankees organization (January 3, 1997). ... Traded by Yankees to Arizona Diamondbacks for P Scott Brow and P Joe Lisio (June 3, 1998). ... Granted free agency (December 21, 1998).
STATISTICAL NOTES: Led Appalachian League with 28 wild pitches and tied for lead with three balks in 1987. ... Pitched 1-0 no-hit victory for Visalia against Palm Springs (May 24, 1989). ... Led California League with 22 wild pitches in 1989. ... Tied for Pacific Coast League lead with 14 wild pitches in 1991. ... Tied for A.L. lead with five balks in 1993.
MISCELLANEOUS: Appeared in two games as pinch runner and struck out in only appearance as pinch hitter with Florida (1995).

Year Team (League)	W	L	Pct.	ERA	G	GS	CG	ShO	Sv.	IP	H	R	ER	BB	SO
1987— Elizabethton (Appal.)	1	8	.111	6.99	13	13	0	0	0	65 2/3	73	*71	*51	*62	71
1988— Kenosha (Midwest)	10	10	.500	3.72	24	24	0	0	0	125 2/3	109	73	52	*107	113
1989— Visalia (California)	12	9	.571	2.59	27	27	7	•4	0	174	122	70	50	85	*173
— Orlando (South.)	1	0	1.000	5.14	1	1	0	0	0	7	10	4	4	0	9
1990— Orlando (South.)	7	9	.438	3.93	28	28	1	0	0	162 2/3	161	93	71	98	114
1991— Portland (PCL)	9	8	.529	4.55	25	24	1	1	0	146 1/3	156	81	74	76	63
— Minnesota (A.L.)	1	1	.500	5.71	5	3	0	0	0	17 1/3	21	15	11	12	16
1992— Portland (PCL)	6	1	.857	1.92	11	11	2	1	0	75	62	20	16	34	41
— Minnesota (A.L.)	4	4	.500	5.70	16	12	0	0	0	71	80	46	45	37	37
1993— Minnesota (A.L.)	11	12	.478	4.04	31	30	0	0	0	171 1/3	186	91	77	78	138
1994— Chicago (N.L.)■...............	8	12	.400	5.40	23	23	1	1	0	138 1/3	139	88	83	56	91
1995— Chicago (N.L.)	0	1	.000	15.43	10	0	0	0	0	11 2/3	27	23	20	12	9
— Los Angeles (N.L.)■	0	2	.000	4.03	6	6	0	0	0	29	36	21	13	16	23
— Florida (N.L.)■	2	3	.400	4.32	9	9	0	0	0	50	43	27	24	30	30
1996—							Out of organized baseball.								
1997— Columbus (Int'l)■	14	5	.737	4.27	33	24	1	0	3	154	164	87	73	45	130
— New York (A.L.)	3	0	1.000	1.93	5	1	0	0	0	14	9	3	3	6	8
1998— New York (A.L.)	1	1	.500	10.05	9	0	0	0	0	14 1/3	20	16	16	12	8
— Arizona (N.L.)■	1	2	.333	3.09	33	0	0	0	1	43 2/3	34	21	15	25	32
A.L. totals (5 years)	20	18	.526	4.75	66	46	0	0	0	288	316	171	152	145	207
N.L. totals (3 years)	11	20	.355	5.12	81	38	1	1	1	272 2/3	279	180	155	139	185
Major league totals (7 years)	31	38	.449	4.93	147	84	1	1	1	560 2/3	595	351	307	284	392

BAPTIST, TRAVIS   P   TWINS

PERSONAL: Born September 30, 1971, in Forest Grove, Ore. ... 6-0/196. ... Throws left, bats left. ... Full name: Travis Steven Baptist.
HIGH SCHOOL: Hillsboro (Ore.).
TRANSACTIONS/CAREER NOTES: Selected by Toronto Blue Jays organization in 45th round of free-agent draft (June 4, 1990). ... On disabled list (April 17-June 1 and July 24, 1993-remainder of season). ... On disabled list (April 6-June 7, 1995). ... Selected by Minnesota Twins organization from Blue Jays organization in Rule 5 minor league draft (December 9, 1996).

Year Team (League)	W	L	Pct.	ERA	G	GS	CG	ShO	Sv.	IP	H	R	ER	BB	SO
1991— Medicine Hat (Pioneer)	4	4	.500	4.11	14	14	1	0	1	85 1/3	100	52	39	22	48
1992— Myrtle Beach (SAL)	11	2	.846	*1.45	19	19	2	1	0	118	81	24	19	22	97
1993— Knoxville (Southern)	1	3	.250	4.09	7	7	0	0	0	33	37	17	15	7	24
1994— Syracuse (Int'l)	8	8	.500	4.55	24	22	1	0	0	122 2/3	145	80	62	33	42
1995— Syracuse (Int'l)	3	4	.429	4.33	15	13	0	0	0	79	83	56	38	35	52
1996— Syracuse (Int'l)	7	6	.538	5.43	30	21	2	0	0	141	*187	91	85	46	77
1997— New Britain (East.)■	5	6	.455	3.41	36	3	0	0	0	60 2/3	49	27	23	26	50
— Salt Lake (PCL)	4	1	.800	2.08	7	6	1	1	0	47 2/3	47	16	11	9	28
1998— Salt Lake (PCL)	8	5	.615	3.12	21	21	1	0	0	135 2/3	128	53	47	41	98
— Minnesota (A.L.)	0	1	.000	5.67	13	0	0	0	0	27	34	18	17	11	11
Major league totals (1 year)	0	1	.000	5.67	13	0	0	0	0	27	34	18	17	11	11

BARBER, BRIAN   P   ROYALS

PERSONAL: Born March 4, 1973, in Hamilton, Ohio. ... 6-1/190. ... Throws right, bats right. ... Full name: Brian Scott Barber.
HIGH SCHOOL: Dr. Phillips (Orlando).

TRANSACTIONS/CAREER NOTES: Selected by St. Louis Cardinals organization in first round (22nd pick overall) of free-agent draft (June 3, 1991); pick received as part of compensation for New York Mets signing Type B free-agent OF Vince Coleman. ... On Louisville disabled list (April 21-May 14, 1994; May 21-June 15 and August 1-September 9, 1996). ... On Louisville suspended list (July 6-8, 1995). ... On St. Louis disabled list (March 23-May 29, 1997); including rehabilitation assignments to Prince William (May 2-7) and Arkansas (May 12-22). ... Granted free agency (December 21, 1997). ... Signed by Kansas City Royals organization (January 5, 1998).

Year Team (League)	W	L	Pct.	ERA	G	GS	CG	ShO	Sv.	IP	H	R	ER	BB	SO
1991— Johnson City (App.)	4	6	.400	5.40	14	13	0	0	0	73 1/3	62	48	44	38	84
1992— Springfield (Mid.)	3	4	.429	3.73	8	8	0	0	0	50 2/3	39	21	21	24	56
— St. Petersburg (FSL)	5	5	.500	3.26	19	19	1	0	0	113 1/3	99	51	41	46	102
1993— Arkansas (Texas)	9	8	.529	4.02	24	24	1	0	0	143 1/3	154	70	64	56	126
— Louisville (A.A.)	0	1	.000	4.76	1	1	0	0	0	5 2/3	4	3	3	4	5
1994— Louisville (A.A.)	4	7	.364	5.38	19	18	0	0	1	85 1/3	79	58	51	46	95
— Arkansas (Texas)	1	3	.250	3.25	6	6	0	0	0	36	31	15	13	16	54
1995— Louisville (A.A.)	6	5	.545	4.70	20	19	0	0	0	107 1/3	105	67	56	40	94
— St. Louis (N.L.)	2	1	.667	5.22	9	4	0	0	0	29 1/3	31	17	17	16	27
1996— Louisville (A.A.)	0	6	.000	5.62	11	11	1	0	0	49 2/3	49	37	31	26	33
— St. Louis (N.L.)	0	0	. . .	15.00	1	1	0	0	0	3	4	5	5	6	1
1997— Prince William (Caro.)	1	1	.500	4.09	2	2	0	0	0	11	10	5	5	5	13
— Arkansas (Texas)	0	1	.000	10.47	3	3	0	0	0	16 1/3	28	19	19	5	15
— Louisville (A.A.)	4	8	.333	6.90	18	18	0	0	0	92 2/3	93	80	71	44	74
1998— Omaha (Pacific Coast)■	8	4	.667	3.75	22	22	2	1	0	136 2/3	114	63	57	53	100
— Kansas City (A.L.)	2	4	.333	6.00	8	8	0	0	0	42	45	28	28	13	24
A.L. totals (1 year)	2	4	.333	6.00	8	8	0	0	0	42	45	28	28	13	24
N.L. totals (2 years)	2	1	.667	6.12	10	5	0	0	0	32 1/3	35	22	22	22	28
Major league totals (3 years)	4	5	.444	6.05	18	13	0	0	0	74 1/3	80	50	50	35	52

BARCELO, LORENZO   P   WHITE SOX

PERSONAL: Born September 10, 1977, in San Pedro de Macoris, Dominican Republic. ... 6-4/226. ... Throws right, bats right. ... Full name: Lorenzo A. Barcelo.
HIGH SCHOOL: Sanatonio (San Pedro de Macoris, Dominican Republic).
TRANSACTIONS/CAREER NOTES: Signed as non-drafted free agent by San Francisco Giants organization (May 23, 1994). ... Traded by Giants with SS Mike Caruso, OF Brian Manning, P Keith Foulke, P Bob Howry and P Ken Vining by Giants to Chicago White Sox for P Wilson Alvarez, P Danny Darwin and P Roberto Hernandez (July 31, 1997). ... On Birmingham disabled list (April 2, 1998-entire season); included rehabilitation assignment to Arizona League White Sox (June 29-July 9).
STATISTICAL NOTES: Led Midwest League with 16 home runs allowed in 1996.

Year Team (League)	W	L	Pct.	ERA	G	GS	CG	ShO	Sv.	IP	H	R	ER	BB	SO
1995— Bellingham (N'west)	3	2	.600	3.45	12	11	0	0	0	47	43	23	18	19	34
1996— Bellingham (N'west)	12	10	.545	3.54	26	26	1	0	0	152 2/3	138	70	60	46	139
1997— San Jose (California)	5	4	.556	3.94	16	16	1	1	0	89	91	45	39	30	89
— Shreveport (Texas)	2	0	1.000	4.02	5	5	0	0	0	31 1/3	30	19	14	8	20
— Birmingham (Southern)■ ..	2	1	.667	4.86	6	6	0	0	0	33 1/3	36	20	18	9	29
1998— Arizona White Sox (Ariz.) ...	0	1	.000	1.50	3	3	0	0	0	6	6	1	1	0	9

BARKER, GLEN   OF   ASTROS

PERSONAL: Born May 10, 1971, in Albany, N.Y. ... 5-10/180. ... Bats right, throws right. ... Full name: Glen F. Barker.
HIGH SCHOOL: Albany (N.Y.).
COLLEGE: The College of St. Rose (N.Y.).
TRANSACTIONS/CAREER NOTES: Selected by Detroit Tigers organization in 11th round of free-agent draft (June 3, 1993). ... Selected by Houston Astros from Tigers organization in Rule 5 major league draft (December 14, 1998).
STATISTICAL NOTES: Led Southern League outfielders in total chances with 323 in 1998.

Year Team (League)	Pos.	G	AB	R	H	2B	3B	HR	RBI	Avg.	BB	SO	SB	PO	A	E	Avg.
1993— Niagara Falls (NYP)	OF	72	253	49	55	11	4	5	23	.217	24	71	37	148	3	1	*.993
1994— Fayetteville (SAL)	OF	74	267	38	61	13	5	1	30	.228	33	79	41	144	6	3	.980
— Lakeland (Fla. St.)	OF	28	104	10	19	5	1	2	6	.183	4	34	5	71	4	2	.974
1995— Jacksonville (Sou.).....	OF	133	507	74	121	26	4	10	49	.239	33	*143	39	284	9	8	.973
1996— Jacksonville (Sou.)	OF	43	120	9	19	2	1	0	8	.158	8	36	6	91	2	2	.979
— Fayetteville (SAL)	OF	37	132	23	38	1	0	1	9	.288	16	34	20	91	3	1	.989
— Toledo (Int'l)..............	OF	24	80	13	20	2	1	0	2	.250	9	25	6	51	3	1	.982
1997— Toledo (Int'l).............	OF	21	47	9	9	1	0	1	3	.191	5	15	6	24	1	0	1.000
— Lakeland (Fla. St.)	OF	13	57	9	18	4	0	1	11	.316	4	17	7	34	0	0	1.000
— Jacksonville (Sou.).....	OF	69	257	47	72	8	4	6	29	.280	29	72	17	154	6	2	.988
1998— Jacksonville (Sou.).....	OF	110	453	95	127	29	6	6	54	.280	57	120	31	*307	16	0	*1.000

BARKER, KEVIN   1B   BREWERS

PERSONAL: Born July 26, 1975, in Bristol, Va. ... 6-3/205. ... Bats right, throws right. ... Full name: Kevin S. Barker.
HIGH SCHOOL: Virginia (Bristol, Va.).
COLLEGE: Virginia Tech.
TRANSACTIONS/CAREER NOTES: Selected by Milwaukee Brewers organization in third round of free-agent draft (June 4, 1996).

Year Team (League)	Pos.	G	AB	R	H	2B	3B	HR	RBI	Avg.	BB	SO	SB	PO	A	E	Avg.
1996— Ogden (Pioneer)	1B	71	281	61	89	19	4	9	56	.317	46	54	0	572	*44	11	.982
1997— El Paso (Texas)...........	1B	65	238	37	66	15	6	10	63	.277	28	40	3	455	30	9	.982
— Stockton (California) ..	1B	70	267	47	81	20	5	13	45	.303	25	60	4	476	31	6	.988
1998— El Paso (Texas)..........	1B	20	85	14	26	6	0	5	14	.306	3	21	2	198	16	1	.995
— Louisville (Int'l)	1B-OF	124	463	59	128	26	4	23	96	.276	36	97	2	957	*73	9	.991

BARKER, RICHIE   P   CUBS

PERSONAL: Born October 29, 1972, in Revere, Mass. ... 6-2/220. ... Throws right, bats right. ... Full name: Richard Frank Barker.
HIGH SCHOOL: Malden (Mass.).
JUNIOR COLLEGE: Quinsigamond Community College (Mass.).
TRANSACTIONS/CAREER NOTES: Selected by Chicago Cubs organization in 37th round of free-agent draft (June 2, 1994).

Year Team (League)	W	L	Pct.	ERA	G	GS	CG	ShO	Sv.	IP	H	R	ER	BB	SO
1994— Huntington (Appal.)	2	4	.333	5.95	17	0	0	0	0	39 1/3	36	35	26	25	22
1995— Rockford (Midwest)	2	0	1.000	3.71	32	0	0	0	1	43 2/3	45	20	18	20	23
1996— Daytona (Fla. St.)	4	0	1.000	5.67	17	0	0	0	0	27	34	23	17	18	14
— Rockford (Midwest)	1	1	.500	5.18	19	0	0	0	1	33	42	24	19	15	23
1997— Daytona (Fla. St.)	2	1	.667	3.35	29	1	0	0	1	51	49	27	19	15	38
— Orlando (South.)	0	1	.000	3.30	19	0	0	0	2	30	25	17	11	7	19
1998— West Tenn (Southern)	2	5	.286	2.68	•51	0	0	0	16	53 2/3	51	22	16	17	23
— Iowa (Pacific Coast)	3	1	.750	4.84	16	0	0	0	0	22 1/3	31	14	12	5	21

BARKLEY, BRIAN   P   RED SOX

PERSONAL: Born December 8, 1975, in Conroe, Texas. ... 6-2/180. ... Throws left, bats left. ... Full name: Brian Edward Barkley. ... Son of Jeff Barkley, pitcher with Cleveland Indians (1984-85); and grandson of W.S. Barkley, minor league infielder (1937-43).
HIGH SCHOOL: Midway (Hewitt, Texas).
JUNIOR COLLEGE: Okaloosa-Walton Community College (Fla.).
TRANSACTIONS/CAREER NOTES: Selected by Boston Red Sox organization in fifth round of free-agent draft (June 2, 1997).

Year Team (League)	W	L	Pct.	ERA	G	GS	CG	ShO	Sv.	IP	H	R	ER	BB	SO
1994— GC Red Sox (GCL)	0	1	.000	0.96	4	3	0	0	0	18 2/3	11	7	2	4	14
1995— Sarasota (Florida State)	8	10	.444	3.25	24	24	2	2	0	146 2/3	147	66	53	37	70
1996— Trenton (Eastern)	8	8	.500	5.72	22	21	0	0	0	119 2/3	126	79	76	56	89
1997— Trenton (Eastern)	12	9	.571	4.94	29	•29	4	0	1	178 2/3	*208	*113	*98	*79	121
1998— Pawtucket (Int'l)	7	9	.438	4.91	23	23	1	0	0	139 1/3	161	81	76	50	88
— Boston (A.L.)	0	0	...	9.82	6	0	0	0	0	11	16	13	12	9	2
Major league totals (1 year)	0	0	...	9.82	6	0	0	0	0	11	16	13	12	9	2

BARRETT, MICHAEL   3B/C   EXPOS

PERSONAL: Born October 22, 1976, in Atlanta, Ga. ... 6-0/195. ... Bats right, throws right. ... Full name: Michael P. Barrett.
HIGH SCHOOL: Pace Academy (Atlanta).
TRANSACTIONS/CAREER NOTES: Selected by Montreal Expos organization in first round (28th pick overall) of free-agent draft (June 1, 1995).

Year Team (League)	Pos.	G	AB	R	H	2B	3B	HR	RBI	Avg.	BB	SO	SB	PO	A	E	Avg.
1995— G.C. Expos (GCL)	SS-3B	50	183	22	57	13	4	0	19	.311	15	19	7	65	143	25	.893
— Vermont (NYP)	SS	3	10	0	1	0	0	0	1	.100	1	1	0	1	3	0	1.000
1996— Delmarva (S. Atl.)	C-3B	129	474	57	113	29	4	4	62	.238	18	42	5	607	74	15	.978
1997— W.P. Beach (FSL)	C	119	423	52	120	30	0	8	61	.284	36	49	7	629	78	13	.982
1998— Harrisburg (East.)	C-3B	120	453	78	145	32	2	19	87	.320	27	43	7	517	113	12	.981
— Montreal (N.L.)	C-3B	8	23	3	7	2	0	1	2	.304	3	6	0	22	9	3	.912
Major league totals (1 year)		8	23	3	7	2	0	1	2	.304	3	6	0	22	9	3	.912

BARRIOS, MANUEL   P   REDS

PERSONAL: Born September 21, 1974, in Cabecea, Panama. ... 6-0/185. ... Throws right, bats right. ... Full name: Manuel Antonio Barrios.
TRANSACTIONS/CAREER NOTES: Signed as non-drafted free agent by Houston Astros organization (March 2, 1993). ... On suspended list (September 4-8, 1996). ... Traded by Astros with P Oscar Henriquez and a player to be named later to Florida Marlins for OF Moises Alou (November 11, 1997). ... Traded by Marlins with OF Gary Sheffield, 3B Bobby Bonilla, C Charles Johnson and OF Jim Eisenreich to Los Angeles Dodgers for C Mike Piazza and 3B Todd Zeile (May 15, 1998). ... Claimed on waivers by Florida Marlins (August 10, 1998). ... Traded by Marlins to Cincinnati Reds for C Guillermo Garcia (December 2, 1998).

Year Team (League)	W	L	Pct.	ERA	G	GS	CG	ShO	Sv.	IP	H	R	ER	BB	SO
1993— Dom. Astros (DSL)	6	1	.857	4.64	13	12	2	0	0	77 2/3	77	57	40	23	59
1994— Quad City (Midwest)	0	6	.000	5.95	43	0	0	0	4	65	73	44	43	23	63
1995— Quad City (Midwest)	1	5	.167	2.25	50	0	0	0	23	52	44	16	13	17	55
1996— Jackson (Texas)	6	4	.600	2.37	60	0	0	0	23	68 1/3	60	29	18	29	69
1997— New Orleans (A.A.)	4	8	.333	3.27	57	0	0	0	0	82 2/3	70	32	30	34	77
— Houston (N.L.)	0	0	...	12.00	2	0	0	0	0	3	6	4	4	3	3
1998— Charlotte (Int'l)■	2	0	1.000	3.70	18	1	0	0	0	24 1/3	19	10	10	9	22
— Florida (N.L.)	0	0	...	3.38	2	0	0	0	0	2 2/3	4	1	1	2	1
— Albuquerque (PCL)■	1	3	.250	6.00	20	2	0	0	0	36	47	25	24	15	33
— Los Angeles (N.L.)	0	0	...	0.00	1	0	0	0	0	1	0	0	0	2	0
Major league totals (2 years)	0	0	...	6.75	5	0	0	0	0	6 2/3	10	5	5	7	4

BARRY, JEFF   OF   ROCKIES

PERSONAL: Born September 22, 1968, in Medford, Ore. ... 6-1/204. ... Bats both, throws right. ... Full name: Jeffrey Finis Barry.
HIGH SCHOOL: Medford (Ore.).
COLLEGE: San Diego State.
TRANSACTIONS/CAREER NOTES: Selected by Montreal Expos organization in fourth round of free-agent draft (June 4, 1990). ... On disabled list (September 5-20, 1991). ... Traded by Expos organization to New York Mets organization for P Blaine Beatty (December 9, 1991). ... On

St. Lucie disabled list (April 16-September 18, 1992). ... On disabled list (June 2-20, 1994). ... On suspended list (August 14-15, 1994). ... On Binghamton disabled list (August 26-September 5, 1995). ... Traded by Mets to San Diego Padres for P Pedro A. Martinez (December 15, 1995). ... Granted free agency (October 15, 1996). ... Signed by Colorado Rockies organization (January 8, 1997). ... Granted free agency (October 15, 1998). ... Re-signed by Rockies organization (December 18, 1998).
STATISTICAL NOTES: Tied for Eastern League lead with nine sacrifice flies in 1995. ... Tied for Pacific Coast League lead with three double plays by outfielder in 1998.

Year	Team (League)	Pos.	G	AB	R	H	2B	3B	HR	RBI	Avg.	BB	SO	SB	PO	A	E	Avg.
1990—	Jamestown (NYP)	OF	70	263	40	76	18	1	5	38	.289	22	35	20	88	8	5	.950
1991—	W.P. Beach (FSL).....	OF	116	437	48	92	16	3	4	31	.211	34	68	20	200	14	7	.968
1992—	St. Lucie (Fla. St.)■..	DH	3	9	0	3	2	0	0	1	.333	0	0	0	...	...	...	...
	—GC Mets (GCL)..........	DH	8	23	5	4	1	0	0	2	.174	6	2	2	...	...	...	...
1993—	St. Lucie (Fla. St.)	OF	114	420	68	108	17	5	4	50	.257	49	37	17	167	12	1	.994
1994—	Binghamton (East.)	OF	110	388	48	118	24	3	9	69	.304	35	62	10	144	6	5	.968
1995—	Norfolk (Int'l)	1B	12	41	3	9	2	0	0	6	.220	3	6	0	117	9	2	.984
	—Binghamton (East.)	OF-1B	80	290	49	78	17	6	11	53	.269	31	61	4	129	6	0	1.000
	—New York (N.L.).........	OF	15	15	2	2	1	0	0	0	.133	1	8	0	2	0	0	1.000
1996—	Memphis (Sou.)■......	3-0-1-2	91	226	29	55	7	0	3	25	.243	29	48	3	90	81	13	.929
	—Las Vegas (PCL)	OF	4	12	1	1	0	0	0	0	.083	3	0	0	12	0	1	.923
1997—	New York (East.)■...	OF-1B	40	146	21	32	4	0	5	12	.219	4	34	3	122	11	6	.957
	—Colo. Springs (PCL) ...	OF	81	273	46	82	13	3	13	70	.300	30	45	5	130	11	0	1.000
1998—	Colo. Springs (PCL) ..	O-3-P-1	100	349	55	91	19	6	8	55	.261	46	52	5	190	14	9	.958
	—Colorado (N.L.)	OF	15	34	4	6	1	0	0	2	.176	2	11	0	20	1	0	1.000
Major league totals (2 years)			30	49	6	8	2	0	0	2	.163	3	19	0	22	1	0	1.000

RECORD AS PITCHER

Year	Team (League)	W	L	Pct.	ERA	G	GS	CG	ShO	Sv.	IP	H	R	ER	BB	SO
1998—	Colo. Springs (PCL)	0	0	...	0.00	1	0	0	0	1	1	3	1	0	0	1

BARTEE, KIMERA — OF — TIGERS

PERSONAL: Born July 21, 1972, in Omaha, Neb. ... 6-0/190. ... Bats both, throws right. ... Full name: Kimera Anotchi Bartee.
HIGH SCHOOL: Central (Omaha, Neb.).
COLLEGE: Creighton.
TRANSACTIONS/CAREER NOTES: Selected by Baltimore Orioles organization in 14th round of free-agent draft (June 3, 1993). ... On Bowie disabled list (June 8-August 8, 1995). ... Traded by Orioles organization to Minnesota Twins organization (September 18, 1995), completing deal in which Orioles acquired P Scott Erickson from Twins for P Scott Klingenbeck and a player to be named later (July 7, 1995). ... Selected by Orioles from Twins organization in Rule 5 major league draft (December 4, 1995). ... Claimed on waivers by Detroit Tigers (March 13, 1996).
STATISTICAL NOTES: Led International League outfielders with 341 total chances in 1997.

Year	Team (League)	Pos.	G	AB	R	H	2B	3B	HR	RBI	Avg.	BB	SO	SB	PO	A	E	Avg.
1993—	Bluefield (Appal.)........	OF	66	264	59	65	15	2	4	37	.246	44	66	*27	124	5	4	.970
1994—	Frederick (Carolina)....	OF	130	514	97	150	22	4	10	57	.292	56	117	44	*304	7	6	.981
1995—	GC Orioles (GCL)......	OF	5	21	5	5	0	0	1	3	.238	3	2	1	15	0	0	1.000
	—Bowie (Eastern).........	OF	53	218	45	62	9	1	3	19	.284	23	45	22	155	4	6	.964
	—Rochester (Int'l)	OF	15	52	5	8	2	1	0	3	.154	0	16	0	37	2	0	1.000
1996—	Detroit (A.L.)■..........	OF-DH	110	217	32	55	6	1	1	14	.253	17	77	20	217	1	2	.991
1997—	Toledo (Int'l)............	OF	136	501	67	109	13	7	3	33	.218	52	*154	*33	*336	4	1	.997
	—Detroit (A.L.)	OF-DH	12	5	4	1	0	0	0	0	.200	2	2	3	3	0	0	1.000
1998—	Detroit (A.L.)	OF-DH	57	98	20	19	5	1	3	15	.194	6	35	9	51	3	2	.964
	—Toledo (Int'l).............	OF	51	215	24	53	10	0	2	13	.247	16	42	6	124	6	0	1.000
Major league totals (3 years)			179	320	56	75	11	2	4	29	.234	25	114	32	271	4	4	.986

BATES, FLETCHER — OF — MARLINS

PERSONAL: Born March 24, 1974, in Wilmington, N.C. ... 6-1/193. ... Bats both, throws right. ... Full name: Fletcher Shannon Bates.
HIGH SCHOOL: New Hanover (Wilmington, N.C.).
TRANSACTIONS/CAREER NOTES: Selected by New York Mets organization in fifth round of free-agent draft (June 3, 1993). ... Traded by Mets with P Scott Comer to Florida Marlins for P Dennis Cook (December 18, 1997).

Year	Team (League)	Pos.	G	AB	R	H	2B	3B	HR	RBI	Avg.	BB	SO	SB	PO	A	E	Avg.
1994—	GC Mets (GCL)..........	OF	52	183	23	39	5	3	5	29	.213	33	49	5	82	2	6	.933
	—St. Lucie (Fla. St.)	OF	7	24	2	6	1	1	1	4	.250	1	5	0	5	0	2	.714
1995—	Pittsfield (NYP)	OF	75	276	52	90	14	9	6	37	.326	41	72	17	119	6	12	.912
	—Binghamton (East.)	OF	2	8	1	0	0	0	0	0	.000	1	6	0	7	0	0	1.000
1996—	Capital City (SAL)......	OF	132	491	84	127	21	*13	15	72	.259	64	162	16	229	11	8	.968
1997—	St. Lucie (Fla. St.)	OF	70	253	49	76	19	11	11	38	.300	33	66	7	100	4	6	.945
	—Binghamton (East.)	OF	68	245	44	63	14	2	12	34	.257	26	71	9	96	7	4	.963
1998—	Portland (Eastern)■...	OF	•140	537	67	147	23	5	11	60	.274	46	118	19	266	9	11	.962

BATES, JASON — 2B/SS

PERSONAL: Born January 5, 1971, in Downey, Calif. ... 5-10/185. ... Bats both, throws right. ... Full name: Jason Charles Bates.
HIGH SCHOOL: Ezperanza (Anaheim, Calif.).
COLLEGE: Arizona.
TRANSACTIONS/CAREER NOTES: Selected by Colorado Rockies organization in seventh round of free-agent draft (June 1, 1992). ... On Colorado disabled list (April 20-May 14, 1998); included rehabilitation assignment to Colorado Springs (May 2-14, 1998). ... Released by Rockies (November 20, 1998).
STATISTICAL NOTES: Led Pacific Coast League shortstops with 87 double plays in 1994.

Year	Team (League)	Pos.	G	AB	R	H	2B	3B	HR	RBI	Avg.	BB	SO	SB	PO	A	E	Avg.
								BATTING								FIELDING		
1992—Bend (Northwest)......	SS	70	255	*57	73	10	3	6	31	.286	56	55	18	72	176	17	*.936
1993—Colo. Springs (PCL)...	SS-2B	122	449	76	120	21	2	13	62	.267	45	99	9	174	319	29	.944
1994—Colo. Springs (PCL)...	SS	125	458	68	131	19	5	10	76	.286	60	57	4	165	411	28	.954
1995—Colorado (N.L.)	2B-SS-3B	116	322	42	86	17	4	8	46	.267	42	70	3	170	255	5	.988
1996—Colorado (N.L.)	2B-SS-3B	88	160	19	33	8	1	1	9	.206	23	34	2	66	109	7	.962
1997—Colorado (N.L.)	2B-SS-3B	62	121	17	29	10	0	3	11	.240	15	27	0	44	68	3	.974
—Colo. Springs (PCL)...	SS-2B	35	135	21	32	6	1	3	18	.237	13	36	1	60	95	6	.963
1998—Colorado (N.L.)	2B-3B-SS	53	74	10	14	3	0	0	3	.189	8	21	0	15	27	2	.955
—Colo. Springs (PCL)...	SS-3B-2B	49	182	37	59	9	1	5	20	.324	17	31	1	47	80	10	.927
Major league totals (4 years)		319	677	88	162	38	5	12	69	.239	88	152	5	295	459	17	.978

DIVISION SERIES RECORD

Year	Team (League)	Pos.	G	AB	R	H	2B	3B	HR	RBI	Avg.	BB	SO	SB	PO	A	E	Avg.
								BATTING								FIELDING		
1995—Colorado (N.L.)	3B-PH-2B	4	4	0	1	0	0	0	0	.250	0	0	0	1	3	0	1.000

B

BATISTA, MIGUEL   P   EXPOS

PERSONAL: Born February 19, 1971, in Santo Domingo, Dominican Republic. ... 6-0/190. ... Throws right, bats right. ... Full name: Miguel Jerez Decartes Batista.

HIGH SCHOOL: Nuevo Horizondes (San Pedro de Macoris, Dominican Republic).

TRANSACTIONS/CAREER NOTES: Signed as non-drafted free agent by Montreal Expos organization (February 29, 1988). ... Selected by Pittsburgh Pirates organization from Expos organization in Rule 5 major league draft (December 9, 1991). ... Returned to Expos organization (April 23, 1992). ... On disabled list (April 14-30 and May 7, 1994-remainder of season). ... Released by Expos (November 18, 1994). ... Signed by Florida Marlins organization (December 9, 1994). ... Claimed on waivers by Chicago Cubs (December 17, 1996). ... Traded by Cubs to Expos for OF Henry Rodriguez (December 12, 1997).

Year	Team (League)	W	L	Pct.	ERA	G	GS	CG	ShO	Sv.	IP	H	R	ER	BB	SO
1988—																
1988—					Dominican Summer League statistics unavailable.											
1989—DSL Expos (DSL)	1	7	.125	4.24	13	11	0	0	0	68	56	46	32	50	60
1990—GC Expos (GCL)	4	3	.571	2.06	9	6	0	0	0	39 1/3	33	16	9	17	21
—Rockford (Midwest)	0	1	.000	8.76	3	2	0	0	0	12 1/3	16	13	12	5	7
1991—Rockford (Midwest)	11	5	.688	4.04	23	23	2	1	0	133 2/3	126	74	60	57	90
1992—Pittsburgh (N.L.)■	0	0	. . .	9.00	1	0	0	0	0	2	4	2	2	3	1
—W.P. Beach (FSL)■	7	7	.500	3.79	24	24	1	0	0	135 1/3	130	69	57	54	92
1993—Harrisburg (Eastern)	13	5	.722	4.34	26	26	0	0	0	141	139	79	68	86	91
1994—Harrisburg (Eastern)	0	1	.000	2.38	3	3	0	0	0	11 1/3	8	3	3	9	5
1995—Charlotte (Int'l)■	6	12	.333	4.80	34	18	0	0	0	116 1/3	118	79	62	60	58
1996—Charlotte (Int'l)	4	3	.571	5.38	47	2	0	0	4	77	93	57	46	39	56
—Florida (N.L.)	0	0	. . .	5.56	9	0	0	0	0	11 1/3	9	8	7	7	6
1997—Iowa (Am. Assoc.)■	9	4	.692	4.20	31	14	2	•2	0	122	117	60	57	38	95
—Chicago (N.L.)	0	5	.000	5.70	11	6	0	0	0	36 1/3	36	24	23	24	27
1998—Montreal (N.L.)■	3	5	.375	3.80	56	13	0	0	0	135	141	66	57	65	92
Major league totals (4 years)	3	10	.231	4.34	77	19	0	0	0	184 2/3	190	100	89	99	126

BATISTA, TONY   SS/2B   DIAMONDBACKS

PERSONAL: Born December 9, 1973, in Puerto Plata, Dominican Republic. ... 6-0/195. ... Bats right, throws right. ... Full name: Leocadio Francisco Batista.

TRANSACTIONS/CAREER NOTES: Signed as non-drafted free agent by Oakland Athletics organization (February 8, 1991). ... On Tacoma disabled list (July 29, 1993-remainder of season). ... On Oakland disabled list (August 27-September 12, 1997); included rehabilitation assignment to Edmonton (September 11-12). ... Selected by Arizona Diamondbacks in first round (27th pick overall) of expansion draft (November 18, 1997).

STATISTICAL NOTES: Led California League shortstops with .950 fielding percentage in 1994.

Year	Team (League)	Pos.	G	AB	R	H	2B	3B	HR	RBI	Avg.	BB	SO	SB	PO	A	E	Avg.
								BATTING								FIELDING		
1992—Arizona A's (Ariz.).......	2B-SS-OF	45	167	32	41	6	2	0	22	.246	15	29	1	67	124	8	.960
1993—Arizona A's (Ariz.).......	3B-2B-SS	24	104	21	34	6	2	2	17	.327	6	14	6	34	54	3	.967
—Tacoma (PCL)	OF	4	12	1	2	1	0	0	1	.167	1	4	0	6	9	0	1.000
1994—Modesto (California) ..	SS-2B	119	466	91	131	26	3	17	68	.281	54	108	7	182	372	30	†.949
1995—Huntsville (Sou.)	SS-2B	120	419	55	107	23	1	16	61	.255	29	98	7	168	371	29	.949
1996—Edmonton (PCL)	SS	57	205	33	66	17	4	8	40	.322	15	30	2	75	213	8	.973
—Oakland (A.L.)	2-3-DH-S	74	238	38	71	10	2	6	25	.298	19	49	7	96	191	5	.983
1997—Oakland (A.L.)	S-3-DH-2	68	188	22	38	10	1	4	18	.202	14	31	2	96	174	8	.971
—Edmonton (PCL)	SS	33	124	25	39	10	1	3	21	.315	17	18	2	40	78	6	.952
1998—Arizona (N.L.)■	2B-SS-3B	106	293	46	80	16	1	18	41	.273	18	52	1	123	205	6	.982
American League totals (2 years)		142	426	60	109	20	3	10	43	.256	33	80	9	192	365	13	.977
National League totals (1 year)		106	293	46	80	16	1	18	41	.273	18	52	1	123	205	6	.982
Major league totals (3 years)		248	719	106	189	36	4	28	84	.263	51	132	10	315	570	19	.979

BAUGHMAN, JUSTIN   2B   ANGELS

PERSONAL: Born August 1, 1974, in Mountain View, Calif. ... 5-11/180. ... Bats right, throws right. ... Full name: Justin Reis Baughman.

HIGH SCHOOL: Bellarmine Prep (San Jose, Calif.).

COLLEGE: Lewis & Clark (Ore.).

TRANSACTIONS/CAREER NOTES: Selected by California Angels organization in fifth round of free-agent draft (June 1, 1995). ... Angels franchise renamed Anaheim Angels for 1997 season.

STATISTICAL NOTES: Led Midwest League with 15 sacrifice hits in 1996. ... Led Midwest League shortstops with 595 total chances in 1996. ... Led California League shortstops with 674 total chances in 1997.

Year	Team (League)	Pos.	G	AB	R	H	2B	3B	HR	RBI	Avg.	BB	SO	SB	PO	A	E	Avg.
1995—	Boise (Northwest)	SS	58	215	26	50	4	3	1	20	.233	18	38	19	68	157	21	.915
1996—	Cedar Rap. (Midw.)	SS	127	464	78	115	17	8	5	48	.248	45	78	•50	*201	360	34	.943
1997—	Lake Elsinore (Calif.) ..	SS	134	478	71	131	14	3	2	48	.274	40	79	*68	*239	*403	32	.953
1998—	Vancouver (PCL)	2B-SS	54	222	35	66	10	4	0	15	.297	13	28	26	136	166	6	.981
—	Anaheim (A.L.)	2B-SS-DH	63	196	24	50	9	1	1	20	.255	6	36	10	106	155	8	.970
Major league totals (1 year)			63	196	24	50	9	1	1	20	.255	6	36	10	106	155	8	.970

BAUTISTA, DANNY — OF — BRAVES

PERSONAL: Born May 24, 1972, in Santo Domingo, Dominican Republic. ... 5-11/170. ... Bats right, throws right. ... Full name: Daniel Bautista. ... Stepson of Jesus de la Rosa, outfielder with Houston Astros (1974). ... Name pronounced bough-TEES-tuh.

TRANSACTIONS/CAREER NOTES: Signed as non-drafted free agent by Detroit Tigers organization (June 24, 1989). ... On disabled list (May 24-July 10, 1991). ... On Toledo disabled list (June 8-July 31, 1994). ... Traded by Tigers to Atlanta Braves for OF Anton French (May 31, 1996). ... On Atlanta disabled list (June 28, 1996-remainder of season). ... On Atlanta disabled list (March 23-April 23, 1997); included rehabilitation assignment to Richmond (April 18-23). ... On Atlanta disabled list (April 17-May 7 and August 25-September 17, 1998); included rehabilitation assignment to Greenville (May 5-7).

RECORDS: Shares major league single-game record for most strikeouts (nine inning game)—5 (May 28, 1995).

Year	Team (League)	Pos.	G	AB	R	H	2B	3B	HR	RBI	Avg.	BB	SO	SB	PO	A	E	Avg.
1989—	....						Dominican Summer League statistics unavailable.											
1990—	Bristol (Appal.)	OF	27	95	9	26	3	0	2	12	.274	8	21	2	43	2	0	1.000
1991—	Fayetteville (SAL)	OF	69	234	21	45	6	4	1	30	.192	21	65	7	137	6	4	.973
1992—	Fayetteville (SAL)	OF	121	453	59	122	22	0	5	52	.269	29	76	18	210	17	6	.974
1993—	London (Eastern)	OF	117	424	55	121	21	1	6	48	.285	32	69	28	256	13	3	.989
—	Detroit (A.L.)	OF-DH	17	61	6	19	3	0	1	9	.311	1	10	3	38	2	0	1.000
1994—	Detroit (A.L.)	OF-DH	31	99	12	23	4	1	4	15	.232	3	18	1	66	0	0	1.000
—	Toledo (Int'l)	OF	27	98	7	25	7	0	2	14	.255	6	23	2	54	1	1	.982
1995—	Detroit (A.L.)	OF	89	271	28	55	9	0	7	27	.203	12	68	4	164	3	2	.988
—	Toledo (Int'l)	OF	18	58	6	14	3	0	0	4	.241	1	10	1	32	1	2	.943
1996—	Detroit (A.L.)■	OF-DH	25	64	12	16	2	0	2	8	.250	9	15	1	38	0	1	.974
—	Atlanta (N.L.)■	OF	17	20	1	3	0	0	1	1	.150	2	5	0	10	0	0	1.000
1997—	Richmond (Int'l)	OF	46	170	28	48	10	3	2	28	.282	19	30	1	104	4	0	1.000
—	Atlanta (N.L.)	OF	64	103	14	25	3	2	3	9	.243	5	24	2	59	1	1	.984
1998—	Atlanta (N.L.)	OF-DH	82	144	17	36	11	0	3	17	.250	7	21	1	47	0	2	.959
—	Greenville (Southern) .	OF	2	6	1	2	0	0	1	2	.333	1	1	0	6	0	0	1.000
American League totals (4 years)			162	495	58	113	18	1	14	59	.228	25	111	9	306	5	3	.990
National League totals (3 years)			163	267	32	64	14	2	6	27	.240	14	50	3	116	1	3	.975
Major league totals (6 years)			325	762	90	177	32	3	20	86	.232	39	161	12	422	6	6	.986

DIVISION SERIES RECORD

Year	Team (League)	Pos.	G	AB	R	H	2B	3B	HR	RBI	Avg.	BB	SO	SB	PO	A	E	Avg.
1997—	Atlanta (N.L.)	OF	3	3	0	1	0	0	0	2	.333	0	1	0	0	0	0	...
1998—	Atlanta (N.L.)	OF	2	2	0	1	1	0	0	0	.500	0	0	0	2	0	0	1.000
Division series totals (2 years)			5	5	0	2	1	0	0	2	.400	0	1	0	2	0	0	1.000

CHAMPIONSHIP SERIES RECORD

Year	Team (League)	Pos.	G	AB	R	H	2B	3B	HR	RBI	Avg.	BB	SO	SB	PO	A	E	Avg.
1997—	Atlanta (N.L.)	OF	2	4	0	1	0	0	0	0	.250	0	0	0	4	0	0	1.000
1998—	Atlanta (N.L.)	PR-OF	5	5	0	0	0	0	0	0	.000	0	1	0	2	0	1	.667
Championship series totals (2 years)			7	9	0	1	0	0	0	0	.111	0	1	0	6	0	1	.857

BEAMON, TREY — OF

PERSONAL: Born February 11, 1974, in Dallas. ... 6-0/192. ... Bats left, throws right. ... Full name: Clifford Beamon.

HIGH SCHOOL: Warren Travis White (Dallas).

TRANSACTIONS/CAREER NOTES: Selected by Pittsburgh Pirates organization in second round of free-agent draft (June 1, 1992). ... Traded by Pirates with OF Angelo Encarnacion to San Diego Padres for OF Mark Smith and P Hal Garrett (March 29, 1997). ... Traded with P Tim Worrell to Detroit Tigers for P Dan Miceli, P Donne Wall and 3B Ryan Balfe (November 19, 1997). ... On Detroit disabled list (March 20-May 30, 1998); included rehabilitation assignment to Lakeland (May 11-13) and Toledo (May 14-30). ... Released by Tigers (December 11, 1998).

Year	Team (League)	Pos.	G	AB	R	H	2B	3B	HR	RBI	Avg.	BB	SO	SB	PO	A	E	Avg.
1992—	GC Pirates (GCL)	OF	13	39	9	12	1	0	1	6	.308	4	0	0	25	0	2	.926
—	Welland (NYP)	OF	19	69	15	20	5	0	3	9	.290	8	9	4	38	1	0	1.000
1993—	Augusta (S. Atl.).........	OF	104	373	64	101	18	6	0	45	.271	48	60	19	181	5	6	.969
1994—	Carolina (Southern)....	OF	112	434	69	140	18	9	5	47	*.323	33	53	24	170	11	10	.948
1995—	Calgary (PCL)............	OF	118	452	74	151	29	5	5	62	.334	39	55	18	201	14	9	.960
1996—	Calgary (PCL)............	OF	111	378	62	109	15	3	5	52	.288	55	63	16	161	7	13	.928
—	Pittsburgh (N.L.)	OF	24	51	7	11	2	0	0	6	.216	4	6	1	24	0	1	.960
1997—	Las Vegas (PCL)■	OF	90	329	64	108	19	4	5	49	.328	48	58	14	111	7	4	.967
—	San Diego (N.L.)	OF	43	65	5	18	3	0	0	7	.277	2	17	1	17	3	2	.909
1998—	Lakeland (Fla. St.)■...	OF	2	6	2	3	0	0	0	0	.500	3	0	0	2	0	0	1.000
—	Toledo (Int'l)	OF	56	207	31	49	6	0	3	18	.237	28	38	16	92	3	5	.950
—	Detroit (A.L.)	DH-OF	28	42	4	11	4	0	0	2	.262	5	13	1	7	0	0	1.000
American League totals (1 year)			28	42	4	11	4	0	0	2	.262	5	13	1	7	0	0	1.000
National League totals (2 years)			67	116	12	29	5	0	0	13	.250	6	23	2	41	3	3	.936
Major league totals (3 years)			95	158	16	40	9	0	0	15	.253	11	36	3	48	3	3	.944

PERSONAL: Born August 3, 1968, in Burbank, Calif. ... 6-1/235. ... Throws right, bats right. ... Full name: Rodney Roy Beck.
HIGH SCHOOL: Grant (Van Nuys, Calif.).
TRANSACTIONS/CAREER NOTES: Selected by Oakland Athletics organization in 13th round of free-agent draft (June 2, 1986). ... Traded by A's organization to San Francisco Giants organization for P Charlie Corbell (March 23, 1988). ... On disabled list (April 6-30, 1994). ... Granted free agency (October 27, 1997). ... Signed by Chicago Cubs (January 15, 1998).
MISCELLANEOUS: Holds San Francisco Giants franchise all-time record for most saves (199).

B

Year — Team (League)	W	L	Pct.	ERA	G	GS	CG	ShO	Sv.	IP	H	R	ER	BB	SO
1986— Medford (N'west)	1	3	.250	5.23	13	6	0	0	1	32 2/3	47	25	19	11	21
1987— Medford (N'west)	5	8	.385	5.18	17	12	2	0	0	92	106	74	53	26	69
1988— Clinton (Midwest)■	12	7	.632	3.00	28	23	5	1	0	177	177	68	59	27	123
1989— San Jose (California)	11	2	*.846	2.40	13	13	4	0	0	97 1/3	91	29	26	26	88
— Shreveport (Texas)	7	3	.700	3.55	16	14	4	1	0	99	108	45	39	16	74
1990— Shreveport (Texas)	10	3	.769	2.23	14	14	2	1	0	93	85	26	23	17	71
— Phoenix (PCL)	4	7	.364	4.93	12	12	2	0	0	76 2/3	100	51	42	18	43
1991— Phoenix (PCL)	4	3	.571	2.02	23	5	3	0	6	71 1/3	56	18	16	13	35
— San Francisco (N.L.)	1	1	.500	3.78	31	0	0	0	1	52 1/3	53	22	22	13	38
1992— San Francisco (N.L.)	3	3	.500	1.76	65	0	0	0	17	92	62	20	18	15	87
1993— San Francisco (N.L.)	3	1	.750	2.16	76	0	0	0	48	79 1/3	57	20	19	13	86
1994— San Francisco (N.L.)	2	4	.333	2.77	48	0	0	0	28	48 2/3	49	17	15	13	39
1995— San Francisco (N.L.)	5	6	.455	4.45	60	0	0	0	33	58 2/3	60	31	29	21	42
1996— San Francisco (N.L.)	0	9	.000	3.34	63	0	0	0	35	62	56	23	23	10	48
1997— San Francisco (N.L.)	7	4	.636	3.47	73	0	0	0	37	70	67	31	27	8	53
1998— Chicago (N.L.)■	3	4	.429	3.02	*81	0	0	0	51	80 1/3	86	33	27	20	81
Major league totals (8 years)	**24**	**32**	**.429**	**2.98**	**497**	**0**	**0**	**0**	**250**	**543 1/3**	**490**	**197**	**180**	**113**	**474**

DIVISION SERIES RECORD

Year — Team (League)	W	L	Pct.	ERA	G	GS	CG	ShO	Sv.	IP	H	R	ER	BB	SO
1997— San Francisco (N.L.)	0	0	...	0.00	1	0	0	0	0	1 1/3	1	0	0	0	1
1998— Chicago (N.L.)	0	0	...	16.20	1	0	0	0	0	1 2/3	5	3	3	2	1
Div. series totals (2 years)	**0**	**0**	**...**	**9.00**	**2**	**0**	**0**	**0**	**0**	**3**	**6**	**3**	**3**	**2**	**2**

ALL-STAR GAME RECORD

Year — League	W	L	Pct.	ERA	GS	CG	ShO	Sv.	IP	H	R	ER	BB	SO
1993— National	0	0	...	9.00	0	0	0	0	1	2	1	1	0	1
1994— National	0	0	...	0.00	0	0	0	0	1 2/3	1	0	0	0	1
1997— National							Did not play.							
All-Star totals (2 years)	**0**	**0**	**...**	**3.38**	**0**	**0**	**0**	**0**	**2 2/3**	**3**	**1**	**1**	**0**	**2**

PERSONAL: Born February 1, 1972, in Aurora, Ill. ... 5-10/193. ... Bats left, throws left. ... Full name: Richard Goodhard Becker.
HIGH SCHOOL: Aurora (Ill.) West.
TRANSACTIONS/CAREER NOTES: Selected by Minnesota Twins organization in third round of free-agent draft (June 4, 1990). ... On Minnesota disabled list (September 13, 1993-remainder of season and April 29-May 17, 1994). ... Traded by Twins to New York Mets for OF Alex Ochoa (December 12, 1997). ... Claimed on waivers by Baltimore Orioles (June 16, 1998). ... Released by Orioles (December 9, 1998). ... Signed by Milwaukee Brewers (January 11, 1999).
STATISTICAL NOTES: Led Appalachian League with .448 on-base percentage in 1990. ... Led Midwest League with 215 total bases in 1991. ... Led California League outfielders with 355 total chances in 1992. ... Led A.L. outfielders in double plays with five in 1995 and nine in 1996. ... Led A.L. outfielders with 412 total chances in 1996.

									BATTING							FIELDING		
Year — Team (League)	Pos.	G	AB	R	H	2B	3B	HR	RBI	Avg.	BB	SO	SB	PO	A	E	Avg.
1990— Elizabethton (App.)	OF	56	194	54	56	5	1	6	24	.289	*53	54	18	87	2	9	.908
1991— Kenosha (Midwest)	OF	130	494	100	132	*38	3	13	53	.267	72	108	19	270	19	11	.963
1992— Visalia (California)	OF	*136	506	*118	160	37	2	15	82	.316	*114	122	29	*332	17	6	.983
1993— Nashville (Southern)	OF	138	516	•93	148	25	7	15	66	.287	94	117	29	303	5	6	.981
— Minnesota (A.L.)	OF	3	7	3	2	2	0	0	0	.286	5	4	1	7	0	1	.875
1994— Minnesota (A.L.)	OF-DH	28	98	12	26	3	0	1	8	.265	13	25	6	87	2	1	.989
— Salt Lake (PCL)	OF	71	282	64	89	21	3	2	38	.316	40	56	7	189	8	3	.985
1995— Salt Lake (PCL)	OF	36	123	26	38	7	0	6	28	.309	26	24	6	108	5	1	.991
— Minnesota (A.L.)	OF	106	392	45	93	15	1	2	33	.237	34	95	8	275	12	4	.986
1996— Minnesota (A.L.)	OF	148	525	92	153	31	4	12	71	.291	68	118	19	*391	18	3	.993
1997— Minnesota (A.L.)	OF	132	443	61	117	22	3	10	45	.264	62	130	17	319	5	5	.985
1998— New York (N.L.)■	OF	49	100	15	19	4	2	3	10	.190	21	42	3	56	4	1	.984
— Baltimore (A.L.)■	OF-DH	79	113	22	23	1	0	3	11	.204	22	34	2	59	1	1	.984
American League totals (6 years)		496	1578	235	414	74	8	28	168	.262	204	406	53	1138	38	15	.987
National League totals (1 year)		49	100	15	19	4	2	3	10	.190	21	42	3	56	4	1	.984
Major league totals (6 years)		545	1678	250	433	78	10	31	178	.258	225	448	56	1194	42	16	.987

PERSONAL: Born January 20, 1972, in Oakland. ... 6-2/194. ... Throws left, bats left. ... Full name: Lucas Matthew Beech.
HIGH SCHOOL: Tom C. Clark (San Antonio).
JUNIOR COLLEGE: Navarro College (Texas).
COLLEGE: Houston.
TRANSACTIONS/CAREER NOTES: Selected by Philadelphia Phillies organization in seventh round of free-agent draft (June 2, 1994). ... On Philadelphia disabled list (May 9-25, 1997). ... On disabled list (August 10, 1998-remainder of season).

Year Team (League)	W	L	Pct.	ERA	G	GS	CG	ShO	Sv.	IP	H	R	ER	BB	SO
1994—Spartanburg (SAL)	4	4	.500	2.58	10	10	4	1	0	69 2/3	51	23	20	23	83
—Batavia (N.Y.-Penn)	2	1	.667	1.93	4	3	0	0	0	18 2/3	9	4	4	12	27
1995—Clearwater (Fla. St.)	9	4	.692	4.19	15	15	0	0	0	86	87	45	40	30	85
—Reading (Eastern)	2	4	.333	2.96	14	13	0	0	0	79	67	33	26	33	70
1996—Reading (Eastern)	11	6	.647	3.17	21	21	0	0	0	133 1/3	108	57	47	32	132
—Scran./W.B. (Int'l)	2	0	1.000	2.40	2	2	0	0	0	15	9	6	4	1	14
—Philadelphia (N.L.)	1	4	.200	6.97	8	8	0	0	0	41 1/3	49	32	32	11	33
1997—Clearwater (Fla. St.)	0	0	...	0.00	1	1	0	0	0	5 2/3	1	1	0	4	9
—Scran./W.B. (Int'l)	3	1	.750	5.70	5	5	1	0	0	30	24	20	19	10	38
—Philadelphia (N.L.)	4	9	.308	5.07	24	24	0	0	0	136 2/3	147	81	77	57	120
1998—Philadelphia (N.L.)	3	9	.250	5.15	21	21	0	0	0	117	126	78	67	63	113
Major league totals (3 years)	8	22	.267	5.37	53	53	0	0	0	295	322	191	176	131	266

BEIRNE, KEVIN — P — WHITE SOX B

PERSONAL: Born January 1, 1974, in Houston. ... 6-4/210. ... Throws right, bats left. ... Full name: Kevin P. Beirne. ... Son of Jim Beirne, wide receiver/tight end with Houston Oilers (1968-73, 1975 and 1976) and San Diego Chargers (1974).
HIGH SCHOOL: McCollough (The Woodlands, Texas).
COLLEGE: Texas A&M.
TRANSACTIONS/CAREER NOTES: Selected by Cincinnati Reds organization in 43rd round of free-agent draft (June 2, 1992); did not sign. ... Selected by Chicago White Sox organization in 11th round of free-agent draft (June 1, 1995).

Year Team (League)	W	L	Pct.	ERA	G	GS	CG	ShO	Sv.	IP	H	R	ER	BB	SO
1995—GC White Sox (GCL)	0	0	...	2.45	2	0	0	0	2	3 2/3	2	2	1	1	3
—Bristol (Appalachian)	1	0	1.000	0.00	9	0	0	0	2	9	4	0	0	4	12
—Hickory (S. Atl.)	0	0	...	4.50	3	0	0	0	1	4	7	2	2	0	4
1996—South Bend (Mid.)	4	11	.267	4.15	26	25	1	0	0	145 1/3	153	85	67	60	110
1997—Win.-Salem (Car.)	4	4	.500	3.05	13	13	1	0	0	82 2/3	66	38	28	28	75
—Birmingham (Southern)	6	4	.600	4.92	13	12	0	0	0	75	76	51	41	41	49
1998—Birmingham (Southern)	13	9	.591	3.44	26	26	2	1	0	167 1/3	142	77	64	87	153
—Calgary (PCL)	0	0	...	4.50	2	2	0	0	0	8	12	5	4	4	6

BELCHER, TIM — P — ANGELS

PERSONAL: Born October 19, 1961, in Sparta, Ohio. ... 6-3/225. ... Throws right, bats right. ... Full name: Timothy Wayne Belcher.
HIGH SCHOOL: Highland (Sparta, Ohio).
COLLEGE: Mt. Vernon (Ohio) Nazarene.
TRANSACTIONS/CAREER NOTES: Selected by Minnesota Twins organization in first round (first pick overall) of free-agent draft (June 6, 1983); did not sign. ... Selected by New York Yankees organization in secondary phase of free-agent draft (January 17, 1984); did not sign. ... Selected by Oakland Athletics organization in player compensation pool draft (February 8, 1984); A's received compensation for Baltimore Orioles signing Type A free-agent P Tom Underwood (February 7, 1984). ... On disabled list (April 10-May 4 and May 5-July 23, 1986). ... Traded by A's organization to Los Angeles Dodgers (September 3, 1987), completing deal in which Dodgers traded P Rick Honeycutt to A's for a player to be named later (August 29, 1987). ... On disabled list (August 17, 1990-remainder of season). ... Traded by Dodgers with P John Wetteland to Cincinnati Reds for OF Eric Davis and P Kip Gross (November 27, 1991). ... Traded by Reds to Chicago White Sox for P Johnny Ruffin and P Jeff Pierce (July 31, 1993). ... Granted free agency (October 26, 1993). ... Signed by Detroit Tigers (February 7, 1994). ... Granted free agency (October 20, 1994). ... Signed by Reds organization (May 3, 1995). ... Traded by Reds organization to Seattle Mariners for P Roger Salkeld (May 15, 1995). ... Granted free agency (October 31, 1995). ... Signed by Kansas City Royals (January 31, 1996). ... Granted free agency (October 26, 1998). ... Signed by Anaheim Angels (December 18, 1998).
HONORS: Named righthanded pitcher on THE SPORTING NEWS college All-America team (1983). ... Named N.L. Rookie Pitcher of the Year by THE SPORTING NEWS (1988).
STATISTICAL NOTES: Pitched 6-0 one-hit, complete-game victory against Pittsburgh (July 21, 1990). ... Pitched 4-0 one-hit, complete-game victory for Cincinnati against Atlanta (May 26, 1993). ... Led A.L. with 37 home runs allowed in 1998.

Year Team (League)	W	L	Pct.	ERA	G	GS	CG	ShO	Sv.	IP	H	R	ER	BB	SO
1984—Madison (Midwest)	9	4	.692	3.57	16	16	3	1	0	98 1/3	80	45	39	48	111
—Alb./Colon. (East.)	3	4	.429	3.33	10	10	2	0	0	54	37	30	20	41	40
1985—Huntsville (Southern)	11	10	.524	4.69	29	26	3	1	0	149 2/3	145	99	78	99	90
1986—Huntsville (Southern)	2	5	.286	6.57	9	9	0	0	0	37	50	28	27	22	25
1987—Tacoma (PCL)	9	11	.450	4.42	29	28	2	1	0	163	143	89	80	*133	136
—Los Angeles (N.L.)■	4	2	.667	2.38	6	5	0	0	0	34	30	11	9	7	23
1988—Los Angeles (N.L.)	12	6	.667	2.91	36	27	4	1	4	179 2/3	143	65	58	51	152
1989—Los Angeles (N.L.)	15	12	.556	2.82	39	30	•10	*8	1	230	182	81	72	80	200
1990—Los Angeles (N.L.)	9	9	.500	4.00	24	24	5	2	0	153	136	76	68	48	102
1991—Los Angeles (N.L.)	10	9	.526	2.62	33	33	2	1	0	209 1/3	189	76	61	75	156
1992—Cincinnati (N.L.)■	15	14	.517	3.91	35	34	2	1	0	227 2/3	201	*104	*99	80	149
1993—Cincinnati (N.L.)	9	6	.600	4.47	22	22	4	2	0	137	134	72	68	47	101
—Chicago (A.L.)■	3	5	.375	4.40	12	11	1	1	0	71 2/3	64	36	35	27	34
1994—Detroit (A.L.)■	7	*15	.318	5.89	25	•25	3	0	0	162	192	*124	106	78	76
1995—Indianapolis (A.A.)■	0	0	...	1.80	2	2	0	0	0	10	6	2	2	1	8
—Seattle (A.L.)■	10	12	.455	4.52	28	28	1	0	0	179 1/3	188	101	90	88	96
1996—Kansas City (A.L.)■	15	11	.577	3.92	35	35	4	1	0	238 2/3	262	117	104	68	113
1997—Kansas City (A.L.)	13	12	.520	5.02	32	32	3	1	0	213 1/3	242	128	119	70	113
1998—Kansas City (A.L.)	14	14	.500	4.27	34	34	2	0	0	234	247	127	111	73	130
A.L. totals (6 years)	62	69	.473	4.63	166	165	14	3	0	1099	1195	633	565	404	562
N.L. totals (7 years)	74	58	.561	3.34	195	175	27	15	5	1170 2/3	1015	485	435	388	883
Major league totals (12 years)	136	127	.517	3.97	361	340	41	18	5	2269 2/3	2210	1118	1000	792	1445

DIVISION SERIES RECORD

Year Team (League)	W	L	Pct.	ERA	G	GS	CG	ShO	Sv.	IP	H	R	ER	BB	SO
1995—Seattle (A.L.)	0	1	.000	6.23	2	0	0	0	0	4 1/3	4	3	3	5	0

CHAMPIONSHIP SERIES RECORD

Year	Team (League)	W	L	Pct.	ERA	G	GS	CG	ShO	Sv.	IP	H	R	ER	BB	SO
1988—	Los Angeles (N.L.)	2	0	1.000	4.11	2	2	0	0	0	15 1/3	12	7	7	4	16
1993—	Chicago (A.L.)	1	0	1.000	2.45	1	0	0	0	0	3 2/3	3	1	1	3	1
1995—	Seattle (A.L.)	0	1	.000	6.35	1	1	0	0	0	5 2/3	9	4	4	2	1
Champ. series totals (3 years)		3	1	.750	4.38	4	3	0	0	0	24 2/3	24	12	12	9	18

WORLD SERIES RECORD

NOTES: Member of World Series championship team (1988).

Year	Team (League)	W	L	Pct.	ERA	G	GS	CG	ShO	Sv.	IP	H	R	ER	BB	SO
1988—	Los Angeles (N.L.)	1	0	1.000	6.23	2	2	0	0	0	8 2/3	10	7	6	6	10

B

BELINDA, STAN   P   REDS

PERSONAL: Born August 6, 1966, in Huntingdon, Pa. ... 6-3/215. ... Throws right, bats right. ... Full name: Stanley Peter Belinda.
HIGH SCHOOL: State College (Pa.) Area.
JUNIOR COLLEGE: Allegany Community College (Md.).
TRANSACTIONS/CAREER NOTES: Selected by Pittsburgh Pirates organization in 10th round of free-agent draft (June 2, 1986). ... On Gulf Coast Pirates disabled list (June 21-30, 1986). ... Traded by Pirates to Kansas City Royals for P Jon Lieber and P Dan Miceli (July 31, 1993). ... Granted free agency (December 23, 1994). ... Signed by Boston Red Sox (April 9, 1995). ... On Boston disabled list (April 21-May 6, 1995); included rehabilitation assignment to Sarasota (May 4-5). ... On Boston disabled list (March 19-April 6, May 30-July 26 and August 20, 1996-remainder of season); included rehabilitation assignments to Sarasota (June 6-9) and Pawtucket (July 14-25). ... Granted free agency (October 14, 1996). ... Signed by Cincinnati Reds organization (December 21, 1996). ... On disabled list (June 3-July 9 and August 11, 1998-remainder of season).

Year	Team (League)	W	L	Pct.	ERA	G	GS	CG	ShO	Sv.	IP	H	R	ER	BB	SO
1986—	Watertown (NYP)	0	0	...	3.38	5	0	0	0	2	8	5	3	3	2	5
—	GC Pirates (GCL)	3	2	.600	2.66	17	0	0	0	7	20 1/3	23	12	6	2	17
1987—	Macon (S. Atl.)	6	4	.600	2.09	50	0	0	0	16	82	59	26	19	27	75
1988—	Salem (Carolina)	6	4	.600	2.76	53	0	0	0	14	71 2/3	54	33	22	32	63
1989—	Harrisburg (Eastern)	1	4	.200	2.33	32	0	0	0	13	38 2/3	32	13	10	25	33
—	Buffalo (A.A.)	2	2	.500	0.95	19	0	0	0	9	28 1/3	13	5	3	13	28
—	Pittsburgh (N.L.)	0	1	.000	6.10	8	0	0	0	0	10 1/3	13	8	7	2	10
1990—	Buffalo (A.A.)	3	1	.750	1.90	15	0	0	0	5	23 2/3	20	8	5	8	25
—	Pittsburgh (N.L.)	3	4	.429	3.55	55	0	0	0	8	58 1/3	48	23	23	29	55
1991—	Pittsburgh (N.L.)	7	5	.583	3.45	60	0	0	0	16	78 1/3	50	30	30	35	71
1992—	Pittsburgh (N.L.)	6	4	.600	3.15	59	0	0	0	18	71 1/3	58	26	25	29	57
1993—	Pittsburgh (N.L.)	3	1	.750	3.61	40	0	0	0	19	42 1/3	35	18	17	11	30
—	Kansas City (A.L.)■	1	1	.500	4.28	23	0	0	0	0	27 1/3	30	13	13	6	25
1994—	Kansas City (A.L.)	2	2	.500	5.14	37	0	0	0	1	49	47	36	28	24	37
1995—	Sarasota (Florida State)■.	0	0	...	4.50	1	1	0	0	0	2	2	1	1	0	2
—	Boston (A.L.)	8	1	.889	3.10	63	0	0	0	10	69 2/3	51	25	24	28	57
1996—	Boston (A.L.)	2	1	.667	6.59	31	0	0	0	1	28 2/3	31	22	21	20	18
—	Sarasota (Florida State)	0	1	.000	45.00	1	1	0	0	0	1	6	5	5	1	1
—	Pawtucket (Int'l)	1	0	1.000	0.00	6	0	0	0	1	7 2/3	2	2	0	2	7
1997—	Cincinnati (N.L.)■	1	5	.167	3.71	84	0	0	0	1	99 1/3	84	42	41	33	114
1998—	Cincinnati (N.L.)	4	8	.333	3.23	40	0	0	0	1	61 1/3	46	23	22	28	57
A.L. totals (4 years)		13	5	.722	4.43	154	0	0	0	13	174 2/3	159	96	86	78	137
N.L. totals (7 years)		24	28	.462	3.52	346	0	0	0	63	421 1/3	334	170	165	167	394
Major league totals (10 years)		37	33	.529	3.79	500	0	0	0	76	596	493	266	251	245	531

DIVISION SERIES RECORD

Year	Team (League)	W	L	Pct.	ERA	G	GS	CG	ShO	Sv.	IP	H	R	ER	BB	SO
1995—	Boston (A.L.)	0	0	...	0.00	1	0	0	0	0	1/3	0	0	0	0	0

CHAMPIONSHIP SERIES RECORD

Year	Team (League)	W	L	Pct.	ERA	G	GS	CG	ShO	Sv.	IP	H	R	ER	BB	SO
1990—	Pittsburgh (N.L.)	0	0	...	2.45	3	0	0	0	0	3 2/3	3	1	1	0	4
1991—	Pittsburgh (N.L.)	1	0	1.000	0.00	3	0	0	0	0	5	0	0	0	3	4
1992—	Pittsburgh (N.L.)	0	0	...	0.00	2	0	0	0	0	1 2/3	2	0	0	1	2
Champ. series totals (3 years)		1	0	1.000	0.87	8	0	0	0	0	10 1/3	5	1	1	4	10

BELL, DAVID   IF   MARINERS

PERSONAL: Born September 14, 1972, in Cincinnati. ... 5-10/175. ... Bats right, throws right. ... Full name: David Michael Bell. ... Son of Buddy Bell, major league third baseman with four teams (1972-89) and manager with Detroit Tigers (1996-98); brother of Mike Bell, infielder, New York Mets organization; and grandson of Gus Bell, major league outfielder with four teams (1950-64).
HIGH SCHOOL: Moeller (Cincinnati).
TRANSACTIONS/CAREER NOTES: Selected by Cleveland Indians organization in seventh round of free-agent draft (June 4, 1990). ... Traded by Indians with C Pepe McNeal and P Rick Heiserman to St. Louis Cardinals for P Ken Hill (July 27, 1995). ... On St. Louis disabled list (April 29-June 30, 1997); included rehabilitation assignments to Arkansas (June 10-19) and Louisville (June 20-26). ... Claimed on waivers by Indians (April 14, 1998). ... Traded by Indians to Seattle Mariners for 2B Joey Cora (August 31, 1998).
STATISTICAL NOTES: Led South Atlantic League in grounding into double plays with 22 in 1991. ... Led South Atlantic League third basemen with 389 total chances in 1991. ... Led Eastern League third basemen with 32 double plays in 1993. ... Led International League third basemen with .950 fielding percentage in 1994.

						BATTING								FIELDING		
Year	Team (League)	Pos.	G	AB	R	H	2B	3B	HR	RBI	Avg.	BB	SO	SB	PO	A	E	Avg.
1990—	GC Indians (GCL)	3B	30	111	18	29	5	1	0	13	.261	10	8	1	29	50	7	.919
—	Burlington (Appal.)	3B	12	42	4	7	1	1	0	2	.167	2	5	2	8	27	3	.921
1991—	Columbus (S. Atl.)	3B	136	491	47	113	24	1	5	63	.230	37	50	3	90	*268	31	.920
1992—	Kinston (Carolina)	3B	123	464	52	117	17	2	6	47	.252	54	66	2	83	264	20	.946

Year	Team (League)	Pos.	G	AB	R	H	2B	3B	HR	RBI	Avg.	BB	SO	SB	PO	A	E	Avg.
1993—Cant./Akr. (Eastern)	3B-2B-SS	129	483	69	141	20	2	9	60	.292	43	54	3	117	283	21	.950
1994—Charlotte (Int'l)	3B-SS-2B	134	481	66	141	17	4	18	88	.293	41	54	2	109	326	20	†.956
1995—Buffalo (A.A.)...............	3B-SS-2B	70	254	34	69	11	1	8	34	.272	22	37	0	46	172	11	.952
—Cleveland (A.L.)..........	3B	2	2	0	0	0	0	0	0	.000	0	0	0	0	2	0	1.000
—Louisville (A.A.)■........	2B	18	76	9	21	3	1	1	9	.276	2	10	4	39	54	1	.989
—St. Louis (N.L.)...........	2B-3B	39	144	13	36	7	2	2	19	.250	4	25	1	77	108	7	.964
1996—St. Louis (N.L.)...........	3B-2B-SS	62	145	12	31	6	0	1	9	.214	10	22	1	45	113	5	.969
—Louisville (A.A.)...........	2B-3B-SS	42	136	9	24	5	1	0	7	.176	7	15	1	66	114	5	.973
1997—St. Louis (N.L.)...........	3B-2B-SS	66	142	9	30	7	2	1	12	.211	10	28	1	55	95	8	.949
—Arkansas (Texas)........	3B	9	32	3	7	2	0	1	3	.219	2	2	1	3	15	1	.947
—Louisville (A.A.)...........	2B-3B-SS	6	22	3	5	0	0	1	4	.227	0	6	0	6	10	1	.941
1998—St. Louis (N.L.)...........	3B-2B	4	9	0	2	1	0	0	0	.222	0	3	0	1	4	0	1.000
—Cleveland (A.L.)..........	2-3-1-S	107	340	37	89	21	2	10	41	.262	22	54	0	201	306	9	.983
—Seattle (A.L.)■...........	2-1-3-0	21	80	11	26	8	0	0	8	.325	5	8	0	61	46	1	.991
American League totals (2 years)		130	422	48	115	29	2	10	49	.273	27	62	0	262	354	10	.984
National League totals (4 years)		171	440	34	99	21	4	4	40	.225	24	78	3	178	320	20	.961
Major league totals (4 years)		301	862	82	214	50	6	14	89	.248	51	140	3	440	674	30	.974

BELL, DEREK — OF — ASTROS

PERSONAL: Born December 11, 1968, in Tampa. ... 6-2/215. ... Bats right, throws right. ... Full name: Derek Nathaniel Bell.
HIGH SCHOOL: King (Tampa).
TRANSACTIONS/CAREER NOTES: Selected by Toronto Blue Jays organization in second round of free-agent draft (June 2, 1987). ... On Knoxville disabled list (July 30, 1988-remainder of season; June 13-21 and July 2-12, 1990). ... On Toronto disabled list (April 9-May 8, 1992); included rehabilitation assignment to Dunedin (April 27-May 4). ... Traded by Blue Jays with OF Stoney Briggs to San Diego Padres for OF Darrin Jackson (March 30, 1993). ... On suspended list (July 9-12, 1993 and July 9-17, 1994). ... Traded by Padres with OF Phil Plantier, P Pedro Martinez, P Doug Brocail, IF Craig Shipley and SS Ricky Gutierrez to Houston Astros for 3B Ken Caminiti, OF Steve Finley, SS Andujar Cedeno, 1B Robert Petagine, P Brian Williams and a player to be named later (December 28, 1994); Padres acquired P Sean Fesh to complete deal (May 1, 1995). ... On Houston disabled list (May 14-June 13, 1997); included rehabilitation assignment to New Orleans (June 6-13).
HONORS: Named International League Most Valuable Player (1991).
STATISTICAL NOTES: Led International League with 243 total bases in 1991. ... Led International League outfielders with seven double plays in 1991. ... Tied for N.L. lead with 10 sacrifice flies in 1998.

Year	Team (League)	Pos.	G	AB	R	H	2B	3B	HR	RBI	Avg.	BB	SO	SB	PO	A	E	Avg.
1987—St. Catharines (NYP) ..	OF	74	273	46	72	11	3	10	42	.264	18	60	12	126	6	2	.985
1988—Knoxville (Southern) ..	OF	14	52	5	13	3	1	0	4	.250	1	14	2	18	2	2	.909
1989—Knoxville (Southern) ..	OF	136	513	72	124	22	6	16	75	.242	26	92	15	216	12	9	.962
1990—Syracuse (Int'l)	OF	109	402	57	105	13	5	7	56	.261	23	75	21	220	9	5	.979
1991—Syracuse (Int'l)..........	OF	119	457	*89	*158	22	•12	13	*93	*.346	57	69	27	278	*15	*16	.948
—Toronto (A.L.).............	OF	18	28	5	4	0	0	0	1	.143	6	5	3	16	0	2	.889
1992—Toronto (A.L.)...........	OF-DH	61	161	23	39	6	3	2	15	.242	15	34	7	105	4	0	1.000
—Dunedin (Fla. St.)	OF	7	25	7	6	2	0	0	4	.240	4	4	3	13	0	2	.867
1993—San Diego (N.L.)■.....	OF-3B	150	542	73	142	19	1	21	72	.262	23	122	26	334	37	17	.956
1994—San Diego (N.L.)	OF	108	434	54	135	20	0	14	54	.311	29	88	24	247	3	10	.962
1995—Houston (N.L.)■........	OF	112	452	63	151	21	2	8	86	.334	33	71	27	201	10	8	.963
1996—Houston (N.L.)..........	OF	158	627	84	165	40	3	17	113	.263	40	123	29	283	16	7	.977
1997—Houston (N.L.)..........	OF-DH	129	493	67	136	29	3	15	71	.276	40	94	15	226	5	8	.967
—New Orleans (A.A.).....	OF	5	13	0	2	0	0	0	1	.154	1	1	1	10	0	0	1.000
1998—Houston (N.L.)..........	OF	156	630	111	198	41	2	22	108	.314	51	126	13	281	8	8	.973
American League totals (2 years)		79	189	28	43	6	3	2	16	.228	21	39	10	121	4	2	.984
National League totals (6 years)		813	3178	452	927	170	11	97	504	.292	216	624	134	1572	79	58	.966
Major league totals (8 years)		892	3367	480	970	176	14	99	520	.288	237	663	144	1693	83	60	.967

DIVISION SERIES RECORD

Year	Team (League)	Pos.	G	AB	R	H	2B	3B	HR	RBI	Avg.	BB	SO	SB	PO	A	E	Avg.
1997—Houston (N.L.)	OF	3	13	0	0	0	0	0	0	.000	0	3	0	3	0	0	1.000
1998—Houston (N.L.)	OF	4	16	1	2	0	0	1	1	.125	0	7	0	5	0	0	1.000
Division series totals (2 years)		7	29	1	2	0	0	1	1	.069	0	10	0	8	0	0	1.000

CHAMPIONSHIP SERIES RECORD

Year	Team (League)	Pos.	G	AB	R	H	2B	3B	HR	RBI	Avg.	BB	SO	SB	PO	A	E	Avg.
1992—Toronto (A.L.)...........	PR-OF	2	0	1	0	0	0	0	0	. . .	1	0	1	1	0	0	1.000

WORLD SERIES RECORD

NOTES: Member of World Series championship team (1992).

Year	Team (League)	Pos.	G	AB	R	H	2B	3B	HR	RBI	Avg.	BB	SO	SB	PO	A	E	Avg.
1992—Toronto (A.L.)...........	PH	2	1	1	0	0	0	0	0	.000	1	0	0	. . .		. . .	

BELL, JAY — 2B/SS — DIAMONDBACKS

PERSONAL: Born December 11, 1965, in Eglin AFB, Fla. ... 6-0/182. ... Bats right, throws right. ... Full name: Jay Stuart Bell.
HIGH SCHOOL: Tate (Gonzalez, Fla.).
TRANSACTIONS/CAREER NOTES: Selected by Minnesota Twins organization in first round (eighth pick overall) of free-agent draft (June 4, 1984). ... Traded by Twins with P Curt Wardle, OF Jim Weaver and a player to be named later to Cleveland Indians for P Bert Blyleven (August

1, 1985); Indians organization acquired P Rich Yett to complete deal (September 17, 1985). ... Traded by Indians to Pittsburgh Pirates for SS Felix Fermin (March 25, 1989). ... Traded by Pirates with 1B/3B Jeff King to Kansas City Royals for 3B Joe Randa, P Jeff Granger, P Jeff Martin and P Jeff Wallace (December 13, 1996). ... Granted free agency (November 4, 1997). ... Signed by Arizona Diamondbacks (November 17, 1997).

HONORS: Named shortstop on THE SPORTING NEWS N.L. All-Star team (1993). ... Won N.L. Gold Glove at shortstop (1993). ... Named shortstop on THE SPORTING NEWS N.L. Silver Slugger team (1993).

STATISTICAL NOTES: Led Appalachian League shortstops with 352 total chances and 43 double plays in 1984. ... Led California League shortstops with 84 double plays in 1985. ... Hit home run in first major league at-bat on first pitch (September 29, 1986). ... Led Eastern League shortstops with 613 total chances in 1986. ... Led American Association shortstops with 198 putouts, 322 assists, 30 errors and 550 total chances in 1987. ... Led N.L. with 39 sacrifice hits in 1990 and 30 in 1991. ... Had 22-game hitting streak (August 24-September 17, 1992). ... Led N.L. shortstops with 741 total chances in 1990, 754 in 1991, 816 in 1992, 794 in 1993 and 547 in 1994.. ... Led N.L. shortstops with 94 double plays in 1992. ... Career major league grand slams: 4.

							BATTING									FIELDING		
Year Team (League)	Pos.	G	AB	R	H	2B	3B	HR	RBI	Avg.	BB	SO	SB	PO	A	E	Avg.
1984— Elizabethton (App.).....	SS	66	245	43	54	12	1	6	30	.220	42	50	4	*109	*218	25	.929
1985— Visalia (California)......	SS	106	376	56	106	16	6	9	59	.282	41	73	10	176	330	53	.905
—Waterbury (Eastern)■	SS	29	114	13	34	11	2	1	14	.298	9	16	3	41	79	6	.952
1986— Waterbury (Eastern)...	SS	138	494	86	137	28	4	7	74	.277	87	65	10	197	*371	*45	.927
—Cleveland (A.L.).........	2B-DH	5	14	3	5	2	0	1	4	.357	2	3	0	1	6	2	.778
1987— Buffalo (A.A.)..........	SS-2B	110	362	71	94	15	4	17	60	.260	70	84	6	†201	†325	†30	.946
—Cleveland (A.L.).........	SS	38	125	14	27	9	1	2	13	.216	8	31	2	67	93	9	.947
1988— Cleveland (A.L.).........	SS-DH	73	211	23	46	5	1	2	21	.218	21	53	4	103	170	10	.965
—Colo. Springs (PCL)	SS	49	181	35	50	12	2	7	24	.276	26	27	3	87	171	18	.935
1989— Pittsburgh (N.L.)■	SS	78	271	33	70	13	3	2	27	.258	19	47	5	109	197	10	.968
—Buffalo (A.A.)........	SS-3B	86	298	49	85	15	3	10	54	.285	38	55	12	110	223	16	.954
1990— Pittsburgh (N.L.)	SS	159	583	93	148	28	7	7	52	.254	65	109	10	*260	459	22	.970
1991— Pittsburgh (N.L.)	SS	157	608	96	164	32	8	16	67	.270	52	99	10	239	*491	*24	.968
1992— Pittsburgh (N.L.)	SS	159	632	87	167	36	6	9	55	.264	55	103	7	*268	*526	22	.973
1993— Pittsburgh (N.L.)	SS	154	604	102	187	32	9	9	51	.310	77	122	16	*256	*527	11	*.986
1994— Pittsburgh (N.L.)	SS	110	424	68	117	35	4	9	45	.276	49	82	2	152	*380	15	.973
1995— Pittsburgh (N.L.)	SS-3B	138	530	79	139	28	4	13	55	.262	55	110	2	206	415	14	.978
1996— Pittsburgh (N.L.)	SS	151	527	65	132	29	3	13	71	.250	54	108	6	215	*478	10	*.986
1997— Kansas City (A.L.)■ ...	SS-3B	153	573	89	167	28	3	21	92	.291	71	101	10	229	450	10	.985
1998— Arizona (N.L.)■..........	SS-2B	155	549	79	138	29	5	20	67	.251	81	129	3	224	437	19	.972
American League totals (4 years)		269	923	129	245	44	5	26	130	.265	102	188	16	400	719	31	.973
National League totals (9 years)		1261	4728	702	1262	262	49	98	490	.267	507	909	61	1929	3910	147	.975
Major league totals (13 years)		1530	5651	831	1507	306	54	124	620	.267	609	1097	77	2329	4629	178	.975

CHAMPIONSHIP SERIES RECORD

RECORDS: Shares single-series record for most singles—9 (1991).

							BATTING									FIELDING		
Year Team (League)	Pos.	G	AB	R	H	2B	3B	HR	RBI	Avg.	BB	SO	SB	PO	A	E	Avg.
1990— Pittsburgh (N.L.)	SS	6	20	3	5	1	0	1	1	.250	4	3	0	4	22	1	.963
1991— Pittsburgh (N.L.)	SS	7	29	2	12	2	0	1	1	.414	0	10	0	13	19	1	.970
1992— Pittsburgh (N.L.)	SS	7	29	3	5	2	0	1	4	.172	3	4	0	6	8	1	.933
Championship series totals (3 years)		20	78	8	22	5	0	3	6	.282	7	17	0	23	49	3	.960

ALL-STAR GAME RECORD

					BATTING									FIELDING		
Year League	Pos.	AB	R	H	2B	3B	HR	RBI	Avg.	BB	SO	SB	PO	A	E	Avg.
1993— National......................	2B	1	0	0	0	0	0	0	.000	0	0	0	1	1	0	1.000

BELL, ROB   P   REDS

PERSONAL: Born January 17, 1977, in Newburgh, N.Y. ... 6-5/225. ... Throws right, bats right. ... Full name: Robert Allen Bell.
HIGH SCHOOL: Marlboro Central (N.Y.).
TRANSACTIONS/CAREER NOTES: Selected by Atlanta Braves organization in third round of free-agent draft (June 1, 1995). ... Traded by Braves with OF Michael Tucker and P Denny Neagle to Cincinnati Reds for 2B Bret Boone and P Mike Remlinger (November 10, 1998).

Year Team (League)	W	L	Pct.	ERA	G	GS	CG	ShO	Sv.	IP	H	R	ER	BB	SO
1995— GC Braves (GCL)	1	6	.143	6.88	10	8	0	0	0	34	38	29	26	14	33
1996— Eugene (Northwest)	5	6	.455	5.11	16	•16	0	0	0	81	89	49	46	29	74
1997— Macon (S. Atl.)...................	•14	7	.667	3.68	27	27	1	0	0	146 2/3	144	72	60	41	140
1998— Danville (Carolina)..............	7	9	.438	3.28	28	28	2	0	0	*178 1/3	169	79	65	46	*197

BELLE, ALBERT   OF   ORIOLES

PERSONAL: Born August 25, 1966, in Shreveport, La. ... 6-2/210. ... Bats right, throws right. ... Full name: Albert Jojuan Belle. ... Formerly known as Joey Belle.
HIGH SCHOOL: Huntington (Shreveport, La.).
COLLEGE: Louisiana State.
TRANSACTIONS/CAREER NOTES: Selected by Cleveland Indians organization in second round of free-agent draft (June 2, 1987). ... On suspended list (July 12-18, 1991; August 4-8, 1992; June 4-7, 1993; August 1-7, 1994; and June 21-22, 1996). ... Granted free agency (October 28, 1996). ... Signed by Chicago White Sox (November 19, 1996). ... Granted free agency (October 27, 1998). ... Signed by Baltimore Orioles (December 1, 1998).
RECORDS: Shares major league records for fewest double plays by outfielder (150 or more games)—0 (1996 and 1997); and most home runs in two consecutive games—5 (September 18 [2] and 19 [3], 1995). ... Shares A.L. single-season record for fewest errors by outfielder who led league in errors—8 (1993).
HONORS: Named outfielder on THE SPORTING NEWS A.L. All-Star team (1993-96 and 1998). ... Named outfielder on THE SPORTING NEWS A.L. Silver Slugger team (1993-96 and 1998). ... Named Major League Player of the Year by THE SPORTING NEWS (1995).

STATISTICAL NOTES: Hit three home runs in one game (September 4, 1992 and September 19, 1995). ... Led A.L. with 14 sacrifice flies in 1993. ... Led A.L. outfielders with seven double plays in 1993. ... Led A.L. in total bases with 294 in 1994 and 377 in 1995. ... Led A.L. with .690 slugging percentage in 1995. ... Led A.L. in grounding into double plays with 24 in 1995. ... Had 21-game hitting streak (April 27-May 21, 1996). ... Had 27-game hitting streak (May 3-June 1, 1997). ... Led A.L. in grounding into double plays with 26 in 1997. ... Led A.L. with 399 total bases, 15 sacrifice flies and .655 slugging percentage in 1998. ... Career major league grand slams: 11.
MISCELLANEOUS: Holds Cleveland Indians all-time record for most home runs (242).

Year	Team (League)	Pos.	G	AB	R	H	2B	3B	HR	RBI	Avg.	BB	SO	SB	PO	A	E	Avg.
1987—	Kinston (Carolina)	OF	10	37	5	12	2	0	3	9	.324	8	16	0	5	0	0	1.000
1988—	Kinston (Carolina)	OF	41	153	21	46	16	0	8	39	.301	18	45	2	43	5	5	.906
	— Waterloo (Midw.)	OF	9	28	2	7	1	0	1	2	.250	1	9	0	11	1	0	1.000
1989—	Cant./Akr. (Eastern)	OF	89	312	48	88	20	0	20	69	.282	32	82	8	136	4	3	.979
	— Cleveland (A.L.)	OF-DH	62	218	22	49	8	4	7	37	.225	12	55	2	92	3	2	.979
1990—	Cleveland (A.L.)...........	DH-OF	9	23	1	4	0	0	1	3	.174	1	6	0	0	0	0	...
	— Colo. Springs (PCL) ...	OF	24	96	16	33	3	1	5	19	.344	5	16	4	31	0	2	.939
	— Cant./Akr. (Eastern) ...	DH	9	32	4	8	1	0	0	3	.250	3	7	0	...	...	...	...
1991—	Cleveland (A.L.)..........	OF-DH	123	461	60	130	31	2	28	95	.282	25	99	3	170	8	•9	.952
	— Colo. Springs (PCL) ...	OF	16	61	9	20	3	2	2	16	.328	2	8	1	19	1	1	.952
1992—	Cleveland (A.L.)..........	DH-OF	153	585	81	152	23	1	34	112	.260	52	128	8	94	1	3	.969
1993—	Cleveland (A.L.)..........	OF-DH	159	594	93	172	36	3	38	*129	.290	76	96	23	338	16	5	.986
1994—	Cleveland (A.L.)..........	OF-DH	106	412	90	147	35	2	36	101	.357	58	71	9	205	8	6	.973
1995—	Cleveland (A.L.)..........	OF-DH	143	546	•121	173	•52	1	•50	•126	.317	73	80	5	304	7	6	.981
1996—	Cleveland (A.L.)..........	OF-DH	158	602	124	187	38	3	48	*148	.311	99	87	11	309	11	10	.970
1997—	Chicago (A.L.)■..........	OF-DH	161	634	90	174	45	1	30	116	.274	53	105	4	351	1	10	.972
1998—	Chicago (A.L.)..........	OF-DH	163	609	113	200	48	2	49	152	.328	81	84	6	316	11	8	.976
Major league totals (10 years)			1237	4684	795	1388	316	19	321	1019	.296	530	811	71	2179	66	59	.974

B

DIVISION SERIES RECORD

Year	Team (League)	Pos.	G	AB	R	H	2B	3B	HR	RBI	Avg.	BB	SO	SB	PO	A	E	Avg.
1995—	Cleveland (A.L.)..........	OF	3	11	3	3	1	0	1	3	.273	4	3	0	7	0	1	.875
1996—	Cleveland (A.L.)..........	OF	4	15	2	3	0	0	2	6	.200	4	2	1	11	1	0	1.000
Division series totals (2 years)			7	26	5	6	1	0	3	9	.231	8	5	1	18	1	1	.950

CHAMPIONSHIP SERIES RECORD

Year	Team (League)	Pos.	G	AB	R	H	2B	3B	HR	RBI	Avg.	BB	SO	SB	PO	A	E	Avg.
1995—	Cleveland (A.L.)..........	OF	5	18	1	4	1	0	1	1	.222	3	5	0	4	0	2	.667

WORLD SERIES RECORD

Year	Team (League)	Pos.	G	AB	R	H	2B	3B	HR	RBI	Avg.	BB	SO	SB	PO	A	E	Avg.
1995—	Cleveland (A.L.)..........	OF	6	17	4	4	0	0	2	4	.235	7	5	0	10	0	1	.909

ALL-STAR GAME RECORD

Year	League	Pos.	AB	R	H	2B	3B	HR	RBI	Avg.	BB	SO	SB	PO	A	E	Avg.
1993—	American	PH-DH	1	2	1	0	0	0	1	1.000	1	0	0	...	...	...	...
1994—	American	OF	2	0	0	0	0	0	0	.000	0	0	0	1	0	0	1.000
1995—	American	OF	3	0	0	0	0	0	0	.000	0	1	0	1	0	0	1.000
1996—	American	OF	4	0	0	0	0	0	0	.000	0	3	0	1	0	0	1.000
1997—	American....................							Did not play.									
All-Star Game totals (4 years)			10	2	1	0	0	0	1	.100	1	4	0	3	0	0	1.000

BELLHORN, MARK — 3B — ATHLETICS

PERSONAL: Born August 23, 1974, in Boston. ... 6-1/190. ... Bats both, throws right. ... Full name: Mark Christian Bellhorn.
HIGH SCHOOL: Oviedo (Fla.).
COLLEGE: Auburn.
TRANSACTIONS/CAREER NOTES: Selected by Oakland Athletics organization in second round of free agent draft (June 1, 1995).

Year	Team (League)	Pos.	G	AB	R	H	2B	3B	HR	RBI	Avg.	BB	SO	SB	PO	A	E	Avg.
1995—	Modesto (California) ..	SS	56	229	35	59	12	0	6	31	.258	27	52	5	94	172	21	.927
1996—	Huntsville (Sou.)	IF	131	468	84	117	24	5	10	71	.250	73	124	19	208	344	32	.945
1997—	Edmonton (PCL)	2B-SS-3B	70	241	54	79	18	3	11	46	.328	64	59	6	105	187	13	.957
	— Oakland (A.L.)	3-2-DH-S	68	224	33	51	9	1	6	19	.228	32	70	7	72	123	9	.956
1998—	Edmonton (PCL)	3-2-S-1	87	309	57	77	20	4	10	44	.249	62	90	6	95	205	11	.965
	— Oakland (A.L.)	3-DH-S-2	11	12	1	1	1	0	0	1	.083	3	4	2	3	7	0	1.000
Major league totals (2 years)			79	236	34	52	10	1	6	20	.220	35	74	9	75	130	9	.958

BELLIARD, RAFAEL — SS/2B

PERSONAL: Born October 24, 1961, in Pueblo Nuevo, Mao, Dominican Republic. ... 5-6/160. ... Bats right, throws right. ... Full name: Rafael Leonidas Matias Belliard. ... Name pronounced BELL-ee-ard.
TRANSACTIONS/CAREER NOTES: Signed as non-drafted free agent by Pittsburgh Pirates organization (July 10, 1980). ... On Buffalo disabled list (April 19-July 24, 1982). ... On Pittsburgh disabled list (June 28-August 28, 1984; July 28-August 12, 1986; August 27, 1987-remainder of season; and May 19-June 3, 1988). ... Granted free agency (November 5, 1990). ... Signed by Atlanta Braves (December 18, 1990). ... Granted free agency (October 25, 1994). ... Re-signed by Braves (December 28, 1994). ... Granted free agency (October 31, 1996). ... Re-signed by Braves (December 6, 1996). ... Granted free agency (October 29, 1997). ... Re-signed by Braves organization (December 5, 1997). ... On Atlanta disabled list (April 10, 1998-remainder of season); included rehabilitation assignment to Richmond (August 20-September 8). ... Granted free agency (October 23, 1998).

STATISTICAL NOTES: Led Carolina League with 12 sacrifice hits and tied for lead in caught stealing with 15 in 1981. ... Tied for Eastern League lead in double plays by shortstop with 69 in 1983. ... Led N.L. shortstops with .977 fielding percentage in 1988.

Year Team (League)	Pos.	G	AB	R	H	2B	3B	HR	RBI	Avg.	BB	SO	SB	PO	A	E	Avg.
									BATTING						FIELDING		
1980— GC Pirates (GCL)........	SS-2B-3B	12	42	6	9	1	0	0	2	.214	0	3	1	24	39	1	.984
—Shelby (S. Atl.)...........	SS	8	24	1	3	0	0	0	2	.125	1	3	0	10	27	5	.881
1981— Alexandria (Caro.)	SS	127	472	58	102	6	5	0	33	.216	26	92	42	•205	330	29	.949
1982— Buffalo (Eastern).........	SS	40	124	14	34	1	1	0	19	.274	8	16	6	56	87	5	.966
—Pittsburgh (N.L.)........	SS	9	2	3	1	0	0	0	0	.500	0	0	1	2	2	0	1.000
1983— Lynn (Eastern)............	SS-2B	127	431	63	113	13	2	2	37	.262	30	54	12	203	307	26	.951
—Pittsburgh (N.L.)........	SS	4	1	1	0	0	0	0	0	.000	0	1	0	1	3	0	1.000
1984— Pittsburgh (N.L.)........	SS-2B	20	22	3	5	0	0	0	0	.227	0	1	0	12	13	3	.893
1985— Pittsburgh (N.L.)........	SS	17	20	1	4	0	0	0	1	.200	0	5	0	13	23	2	.947
—Hawaii (PCL)	SS-2B	100	341	35	84	12	4	1	18	.246	4	49	9	172	289	5	.989
1986— Pittsburgh (N.L.)........	SS-2B	117	309	33	72	5	2	0	31	.233	26	54	12	147	317	12	.975
1987— Pittsburgh (N.L.)........	SS-2B	81	203	26	42	4	3	1	15	.207	20	25	5	113	191	6	.981
—Harrisburg (East.).......	SS	37	145	24	49	5	2	0	9	.338	6	16	7	59	115	7	.961
1988— Pittsburgh (N.L.)........	SS-2B	122	286	28	61	0	4	0	11	.213	26	47	7	134	261	9	†.978
1989— Pittsburgh (N.L.)........	SS-2B-3B	67	154	10	33	4	0	0	8	.214	8	22	5	71	138	3	.986
1990— Pittsburgh (N.L.)........	2B-SS-3B	47	54	10	11	3	0	0	6	.204	5	13	1	37	36	2	.973
1991— Atlanta (N.L.)■...........	SS	149	353	36	88	9	2	0	27	.249	22	63	3	168	361	18	.967
1992— Atlanta (N.L.).............	SS-2B	144	285	20	60	6	1	0	14	.211	14	43	0	152	291	14	.969
1993— Atlanta (N.L.).............	SS-2B	91	79	6	18	5	0	0	6	.228	4	13	0	53	99	1	.993
1994— Atlanta (N.L.).............	SS-2B	46	120	9	29	7	1	0	9	.242	2	29	0	45	86	1	.992
1995— Atlanta (N.L.).............	SS-2B	75	180	12	40	2	1	0	7	.222	6	28	2	74	181	1	.996
1996— Atlanta (N.L.).............	SS-2B	87	142	9	24	7	0	0	3	.169	2	22	3	65	150	5	.977
1997— Atlanta (N.L.).............	SS-2B	72	71	9	15	3	0	1	3	.211	1	17	0	37	69	1	.991
1998— Atlanta (N.L.).............	SS	7	20	1	5	0	0	0	1	.250	0	1	0	7	13	1	.952
—Richmond (Int'l).........	SS	13	43	6	6	0	0	1	2	.140	0	6	0	20	28	1	.980
Major league totals (17 years)		1155	2301	217	508	55	14	2	142	.221	136	384	39	1131	2234	79	.977

DIVISION SERIES RECORD

Year Team (League)	Pos.	G	AB	R	H	2B	3B	HR	RBI	Avg.	BB	SO	SB	PO	A	E	Avg.
									BATTING						FIELDING		
1995— Atlanta (N.L.).............	SS	4	5	1	0	0	0	0	0	.000	0	1	0	2	5	0	1.000
1996— Atlanta (N.L.).............	SS	3	0	0	0	0	0	0	0	. . .	0	0	0	0	0	0	. . .
1997— Atlanta (N.L.)										Did not play.							
Division series totals (2 years)		7	5	1	0	0	0	0	0	.000	0	1	0	2	5	0	1.000

CHAMPIONSHIP SERIES RECORD

Year Team (League)	Pos.	G	AB	R	H	2B	3B	HR	RBI	Avg.	BB	SO	SB	PO	A	E	Avg.
									BATTING						FIELDING		
1990— Pittsburgh (N.L.)........										Did not play.							
1991— Atlanta (N.L.).............	SS	7	19	0	4	0	0	0	1	.211	3	3	0	9	15	1	.960
1992— Atlanta (N.L.).............	SS-2B-PR	4	2	1	0	0	0	0	0	.000	1	0	0	2	3	0	1.000
1993— Atlanta (N.L.).............	PH-2-PR-S	2	1	1	0	0	0	0	0	.000	0	1	0	0	0	0	. . .
1995— Atlanta (N.L.).............	SS	4	11	1	3	0	0	0	0	.273	0	3	0	6	7	1	.929
1996— Atlanta (N.L.).............	2B-SS-PR	4	6	0	4	0	0	0	2	.667	0	0	0	2	5	0	1.000
1997— Atlanta (N.L.)										Did not play.							
Championship series totals (5 years)		21	39	3	11	0	0	0	3	.282	4	7	0	19	30	2	.961

WORLD SERIES RECORD

NOTES: Member of World Series championship team (1995).

Year Team (League)	Pos.	G	AB	R	H	2B	3B	HR	RBI	Avg.	BB	SO	SB	PO	A	E	Avg.
									BATTING						FIELDING		
1991— Atlanta (N.L.).............	SS	7	16	0	6	1	0	0	4	.375	1	2	0	8	21	0	1.000
1992— Atlanta (N.L.).............	SS-2B	4	4	0	0	0	0	0	0	.000	0	0	0	3	2	0	1.000
1995— Atlanta (N.L.).............	SS	6	16	0	0	0	0	0	1	.000	0	4	0	3	11	2	.875
1996— Atlanta (N.L.).............	SS-PR	4	0	0	0	0	0	0	0	. . .	0	0	0	0	3	0	1.000
World Series totals (4 years)		21	36	0	6	1	0	0	5	.167	1	6	0	14	37	2	.962

BELLIARD, RON   2B   BREWERS

PERSONAL: Born July 4, 1976, in Bronx, N.Y. ... 5-8/185. ... Bats right, throws right. ... Full name: Ronald Belliard. ... Name pronounced BELL-ee-ard.

HIGH SCHOOL: Central (Miami).

TRANSACTIONS/CAREER NOTES: Selected by Milwaukee Brewers organization in eighth round of free-agent draft (June 2, 1994).

STATISTICAL NOTES: Led Midwest League second basemen with 25 errors in 1995. ... Led Pacific Coast League second basemen with 229 putouts, 358 assists, 24 errors and 611 total chances and tied for league lead with 92 double plays in 1997. ... Led International League second basemen with 401 assists and 98 double plays in 1998.

Year Team (League)	Pos.	G	AB	R	H	2B	3B	HR	RBI	Avg.	BB	SO	SB	PO	A	E	Avg.
									BATTING						FIELDING		
1994— Ariz. Brewers (Ariz.) ...	2B-3B-SS	39	143	32	42	7	3	0	27	.294	14	25	7	54	119	12	.935
1995— Beloit (Midwest).........	2B-3B	130	461	76	137	28	5	13	76	.297	36	67	16	221	346	†26	.956
1996— El Paso (Texas)..........	2B	109	416	73	116	20	8	3	57	.279	60	51	26	246	314	16	.972
1997— Tucson (PCL)	2B-SS	118	443	80	125	35	4	4	55	.282	61	69	10	†233	†369	†26	.959
1998— Louisville (Int'l)	2B-SS	133	507	*114	163	36	7	14	73	.321	69	77	33	231	†408	14	.979
—Milwaukee (N.L.)........	2B	8	5	1	1	0	0	0	0	.200	0	0	0	0	0	0	. . .
Major league totals (1 year)		8	5	1	1	0	0	0	0	.200	0	0	0	0	0	0	. . .

BELTRAN, CARLOS · OF · ROYALS

PERSONAL: Born April 24, 1977, in Manati, Puerto Rico. ... 6-0/175. ... Bats both, throws right. ... Full name: Carlos Ivan Beltran.
HIGH SCHOOL: Fernando Callejas (Manati, Puerto Rico).
TRANSACTIONS/CAREER NOTES: Selected by Kansas City Royals organization in second round of free-agent draft (June 1, 1995).

Year Team (League)	Pos.	G	AB	R	H	2B	3B	HR	RBI	Avg.	BB	SO	SB	PO	A	E	Avg.
1995— GC Royals (GCL)	OF	52	180	29	50	9	0	0	23	.278	13	30	5	79	6	2	.977
1996— Lansing (Midwest)	OF	11	42	3	6	2	0	0	0	.143	1	11	1	28	2	2	.938
— Spokane (N'west)	OF	59	215	29	58	8	3	7	29	.270	31	65	10	99	6	7	.938
1997— Wilmington (Caro.)	OF	120	419	57	96	15	4	11	46	.229	46	96	17	236	7	8	.968
1998— Wilmington (Caro.)	OF	52	192	32	53	14	0	5	32	.276	25	39	11	109	4	2	.983
— Wichita (Texas)	OF	47	182	50	64	13	3	14	44	.352	23	30	7	93	2	4	.960
— Kansas City (A.L.)	OF	14	58	12	16	5	3	0	7	.276	3	12	3	44	0	1	.978
Major league totals (1 year)		14	58	12	16	5	3	0	7	.276	3	12	3	44	0	1	.978

B

BELTRAN, RIGO · P · METS

PERSONAL: Born November 13, 1969, in Tijuana, Mexico. ... 5-11/185. ... Throws left, bats left. ... Full name: Rigoberto Beltran.
HIGH SCHOOL: Point Lomas (San Diego).
COLLEGE: Wyoming.
TRANSACTIONS/CAREER NOTES: Selected by St. Louis Cardinals organization in 26th round of free-agent draft (June 3, 1991). ... Traded by Cardinals to New York Mets for P Juan Acevedo (March 29, 1998).
STATISTICAL NOTES: Led New York-Pennsylvania League with 12 balks in 1991. ... Led American Association with 18 wild pitches in 1994.

Year Team (League)	W	L	Pct.	ERA	G	GS	CG	ShO	Sv.	IP	H	R	ER	BB	SO
1991— Hamilton (NYP)	5	2	.714	2.63	21	4	0	0	0	48	41	17	14	19	69
1992— Savannah (S. Atl.)	6	1	.857	2.17	13	13	2	1	0	83	38	20	20	40	106
— St. Petersburg (FSL)	0	0	...	0.00	2	2	0	0	0	8	6	0	0	2	3
1993— Arkansas (Texas)	5	5	.500	3.25	18	16	0	0	0	$88^{2}/_{3}$	74	39	32	38	82
1994— Arkansas (Texas)	4	0	1.000	0.64	4	4	1	1	0	28	12	2	2	3	21
— Louisville (A.A.)	11	11	.500	5.07	23	23	1	0	0	$138^{1}/_{3}$	147	82	78	68	87
1995— Louisville (A.A.)	8	9	.471	5.21	24	24	0	0	0	$129^{2}/_{3}$	156	81	75	34	92
1996— Louisville (A.A.)	8	6	.571	4.35	38	16	3	1	0	$130^{1}/_{3}$	132	67	63	24	132
1997— Louisville (A.A.)	5	2	.714	2.32	9	8	1	0	0	$54^{1}/_{3}$	45	17	14	21	46
— St. Louis (N.L.)	1	2	.333	3.48	35	4	0	0	1	$54^{1}/_{3}$	47	25	21	17	50
1998— Norfolk (Int'l)■	6	5	.545	4.29	36	11	0	0	1	$94^{1}/_{3}$	104	51	45	40	98
— New York (N.L.)	0	0	...	3.38	7	0	0	0	0	8	6	3	3	4	5
Major league totals (2 years)	1	2	.333	3.47	42	4	0	0	1	$62^{1}/_{3}$	53	28	24	21	55

BELTRE, ADRIAN · 3B · DODGERS

PERSONAL: Born April 7, 1978, in Santo Domingo, Dominican Republic. ... 5-11/170. ... Bats right, throws right. ... Name pronounced bell-TREE.
HIGH SCHOOL: Liceo Maximo Gomez (Santo Domingo, Dominican Republic).
TRANSACTIONS/CAREER NOTES: Signed as non-drafted free agent by Los Angeles Dodgers (July 7, 1994). ... On San Bernardino disabled list (June 25-July 2, 1996). ... On Albuquerque disabled list (April 23-May 1 and May 12-19, 1998).
HONORS: Named Florida State League Most Valuable Player (1997).
STATISTICAL NOTES: Led Florida State League with .561 slugging percentage and 12 intentional bases on balls in 1997. ... Led Florida State League third basemen with 26 double plays in 1997.

Year Team (League)	Pos.	G	AB	R	H	2B	3B	HR	RBI	Avg.	BB	SO	SB	PO	A	E	Avg.
1995— Dom. Dodgers (DSL)	3B	62	218	56	67	15	3	8	40	.307	54	26	2	187	31	19	.920
1996— Savannah (S. Atl.)	3B-2B	68	244	48	75	14	3	16	59	.307	35	46	4	55	143	19	.912
— San Bern. (Calif.)	3B	63	238	40	62	13	1	10	40	.261	19	44	3	32	110	7	.953
1997— Vero Beach (FSL)	3B-OF	123	435	95	138	24	2	*26	*104	.317	67	66	25	83	231	37	.895
1998— San Antonio (Tex.)	3B	64	246	49	79	21	2	13	56	.321	39	37	20	41	130	17	.910
— Los Angeles (N.L.)	3B-SS	77	195	18	42	9	0	7	22	.215	14	37	3	32	131	13	.926
Major league totals (1 year)		77	195	18	42	9	0	7	22	.215	14	37	3	32	131	13	.926

BENARD, MARVIN · OF · GIANTS

PERSONAL: Born January 20, 1970, in Bluefields, Nicaragua. ... 5-9/185. ... Bats left, throws left. ... Full name: Marvin Larry Benard.
HIGH SCHOOL: Bell (Bell Gardens, Calif.).
JUNIOR COLLEGE: Los Angeles Harbor College.
COLLEGE: Lewis-Clark State (Idaho).
TRANSACTIONS/CAREER NOTES: Selected by Philadelphia Phillies organization in 20th round of free-agent draft (June 4, 1990); did not sign. ... Selected by San Francisco Giants organization in 50th round of free-agent draft (June 1, 1992). ... On disabled list (April 17-28, 1993).
STATISTICAL NOTES: Tied for Texas League lead in grounding into double plays with 15 in 1994. ... Led Texas League outfielders with five double plays in 1994.

Year Team (League)	Pos.	G	AB	R	H	2B	3B	HR	RBI	Avg.	BB	SO	SB	PO	A	E	Avg.
1992— Everett (N'west)	OF	64	161	31	38	10	2	1	17	.236	24	39	17	90	8	3	.970
1993— Clinton (Midwest)	OF	112	349	84	105	14	2	5	50	.301	56	66	42	179	10	5	.974
1994— Shreveport (Texas)	OF	125	454	66	143	32	3	4	48	.315	31	58	24	259	17	*12	.958

Year Team (League)	Pos.	G	AB	R	H	2B	3B	HR	RBI	Avg.	BB	SO	SB	PO	A	E	Avg.
						BATTING									FIELDING		
1995—Phoenix (PCL)...........	OF	111	378	70	115	14	6	6	32	.304	50	66	10	183	5	8	.959
—San Francisco (N.L.)..	OF	13	34	5	13	2	0	1	4	.382	1	7	1	19	0	1	1.000
1996—Phoenix (PCL)...........	OF	4	19	2	7	0	0	0	4	.368	2	2	1	10	0	0	1.000
—San Francisco (N.L.)..	OF	135	488	89	121	17	4	5	27	.248	59	84	25	309	7	5	.984
1997—San Francisco (N.L.)..	OF-DH	84	114	13	26	4	0	1	13	.228	13	29	3	27	2	1	.967
—Phoenix (PCL)...........	OF	17	60	14	20	5	0	0	5	.333	11	9	4	26	2	1	.966
1998—San Francisco (N.L.)..	OF-DH	121	286	41	92	21	1	3	36	.322	34	39	11	109	1	2	.982
Major league totals (4 years)		353	922	148	252	44	5	10	80	.273	107	159	40	464	10	8	.983

DIVISION SERIES RECORD

Year Team (League)	Pos.	G	AB	R	H	2B	3B	HR	RBI	Avg.	BB	SO	SB	PO	A	E	Avg.
						BATTING									FIELDING		
1997—San Francisco (N.L.)..	PH	2	2	0	0	0	0	0	0	.000	0	1	0	...	...	...	...

BENES, ALAN — P — CARDINALS

PERSONAL: Born January 21, 1972, in Evansville, Ind. ... 6-5/215. ... Throws right, bats right. ... Full name: Alan Paul Benes. ... Brother of Andy Benes, pitcher, Arizona Diamondbacks; and brother of Adam Benes, pitcher, St. Louis Cardinals organization. ... Name pronounced BEN-ess.
HIGH SCHOOL: Lake Forest (Ill.).
COLLEGE: Creighton.
TRANSACTIONS/CAREER NOTES: Selected by San Diego Padres organization in 49th round of free-agent draft (June 4, 1990); did not sign. ... Selected by St. Louis Cardinals organization in first round (16th pick overall) of free-agent draft (June 3, 1993). ... On Louisville disabled list (May 3-August 9, 1995). ... On disabled list (July 31, 1998-remainder of season and March 22, 1998-entire season).
HONORS: Named N.L. Rookie Pitcher of the Year by THE SPORTING NEWS (1996).

Year Team (League)	W	L	Pct.	ERA	G	GS	CG	ShO	Sv.	IP	H	R	ER	BB	SO
1993—Glens Falls (NYP)	0	4	.000	3.65	7	7	0	0	0	37	39	20	15	14	29
1994—Savannah (S. Atl.)	2	0	1.000	1.48	4	4	0	0	0	24 1/3	21	5	4	7	24
—St. Petersburg (FSL)	7	1	.875	1.61	11	11	0	0	0	78 1/3	55	18	14	15	69
—Arkansas (Texas)	7	2	.778	2.98	13	13	1	0	0	87 2/3	58	38	29	26	75
—Louisville (A.A.)	1	0	1.000	2.93	2	2	1	0	0	15 1/3	10	5	5	4	16
1995—Louisville (A.A.)	4	2	.667	2.41	11	11	2	1	0	56	37	16	15	14	54
—St. Louis (N.L.)	1	2	.333	8.44	3	3	0	0	0	16	24	15	15	4	20
1996—St. Louis (N.L.)	13	10	.565	4.90	34	32	3	1	0	191	192	120	104	87	131
1997—St. Louis (N.L.)	9	9	.500	2.89	23	23	2	0	0	161 2/3	128	60	52	68	160
1998—St. Louis (N.L.)							Did not play.								
Major league totals (3 years)	23	21	.523	4.17	60	58	5	1	0	368 2/3	344	195	171	159	311

CHAMPIONSHIP SERIES RECORD

Year Team (League)	W	L	Pct.	ERA	G	GS	CG	ShO	Sv.	IP	H	R	ER	BB	SO
1996—St. Louis (N.L.)	0	1	.000	2.84	2	1	0	0	0	6 1/3	3	2	2	3	5

BENES, ANDY — P — DIAMONDBACKS

PERSONAL: Born August 20, 1967, in Evansville, Ind. ... 6-6/245. ... Throws right, bats right. ... Full name: Andrew Charles Benes. ... Brother of Alan Benes, pitcher, St. Louis Cardinals; and brother of Adam Benes, pitcher, Cardinals organization. ... Name pronounced BEN-ess.
HIGH SCHOOL: Central (Evansville, Ind.).
COLLEGE: Evansville.
TRANSACTIONS/CAREER NOTES: Selected by San Diego Padres organization in first round (first pick overall) of free-agent draft (June 1, 1988). ... On suspended list (September 28, 1993-remainder of season). ... Traded by Padres with a player to be named later to Seattle Mariners for P Ron Villone and OF Marc Newfield (July 31, 1995); Mariners acquired P Greg Keagle to complete deal (September 16, 1995). ... Granted free agency (October 31, 1995). ... Signed by St. Louis Cardinals (December 23, 1995). ... On disabled list (March 23-April 28, 1997); included rehabilitation assignments to Prince William (April 11), Louisville (April 16) and Arkansas (April 22). ... Granted free agency (October 29, 1997). ... Signed by Arizona Diamondbacks (February 3, 1998).
RECORDS: Holds major league single-season record for fewest hits allowed for leader in most hits allowed—230 (1992).
HONORS: Named N.L. Rookie Pitcher of the Year by THE SPORTING NEWS (1989). ... Named Texas League Pitcher of the Year (1989).
STATISTICAL NOTES: Tied for N.L. lead with five balks in 1990. ... Pitched 7-0 one-hit, complete-game victory against New York (July 3, 1994).
MISCELLANEOUS: Holds San Diego Padres all-time record for most strikeouts (1,036). ... Member of 1988 U.S. Olympic baseball team (1988). ... Made an out in only appearance as pinch hitter (1998). ... Holds Arizona Diamondbacks all-time record for most wins (14), most innings pitched (231 1/3) and most strikeouts (164).

Year Team (League)	W	L	Pct.	ERA	G	GS	CG	ShO	Sv.	IP	H	R	ER	BB	SO
1989—Wichita (Texas)	8	4	.667	2.16	16	16	5	*3	0	108 1/3	79	32	26	39	115
—Las Vegas (PCL)	2	1	.667	8.10	5	5	0	0	0	26 2/3	41	29	24	12	29
—San Diego (N.L.)	6	3	.667	3.51	10	10	0	0	0	66 2/3	51	28	26	31	66
1990—San Diego (N.L.)	10	11	.476	3.60	32	31	2	0	0	192 1/3	177	87	77	69	140
1991—San Diego (N.L.)	15	11	.577	3.03	33	33	4	1	0	223	194	76	75	59	167
1992—San Diego (N.L.)	13	14	.481	3.35	34	34	2	2	0	231 1/3	*230	90	86	61	169
1993—San Diego (N.L.)	15	15	.500	3.78	34	34	4	2	0	230 2/3	200	111	97	86	179
1994—San Diego (N.L.)	6	*14	.300	3.86	25	25	2	2	0	172 1/3	155	82	74	51	*189
1995—San Diego (N.L.)	4	7	.364	4.17	19	19	1	1	0	118 2/3	121	65	55	45	126
—Seattle (A.L.)■	7	2	.778	5.86	12	12	0	0	0	63	72	42	41	33	45
1996—St. Louis (N.L.)	18	10	.643	3.83	36	34	3	1	1	230 1/3	215	107	98	77	160
1997—Prince William (Caro.)	0	0	...	0.00	1	1	0	0	0	5	3	1	0	1	9
—Louisville (A.A.)	0	0	...	1.80	1	1	0	0	0	5	3	1	1	1	5
—Arkansas (Texas)	1	0	1.000	1.29	1	1	0	0	0	7	2	1	1	2	6
—St. Louis (N.L.)	10	7	.588	3.10	26	26	0	0	0	177	149	64	61	61	175
1998—Arizona (N.L.)■	14	13	.519	3.97	34	34	1	0	0	231 1/3	221	111	102	74	164
A.L. totals (1 year)	7	2	.778	5.86	12	12	0	0	0	63	72	42	41	33	45
N.L. totals (10 years)	111	105	.514	3.61	283	280	19	9	1	1873 2/3	1713	821	751	614	1535
Major league totals (10 years)	118	107	.524	3.68	295	292	19	9	1	1936 2/3	1785	863	792	647	1580

DIVISION SERIES RECORD

Year Team (League)	W	L	Pct.	ERA	G	GS	CG	ShO	Sv.	IP	H	R	ER	BB	SO
1995— Seattle (A.L.)	0	0	...	5.40	2	2	0	0	0	11⅔	10	7	7	9	8
1996— St. Louis (N.L.)	0	0	...	5.14	1	1	0	0	0	7	6	4	4	1	9
Div. series totals (2 years)	0	0	...	5.30	3	3	0	0	0	18⅔	16	11	11	10	17

CHAMPIONSHIP SERIES RECORD

RECORDS: Shares N.L. single-series record for most hits allowed—19 (1996).

Year Team (League)	W	L	Pct.	ERA	G	GS	CG	ShO	Sv.	IP	H	R	ER	BB	SO
1995— Seattle (A.L.)	0	1	.000	23.14	1	1	0	0	0	2⅓	6	6	6	2	3
1996— St. Louis (N.L.)	0	0	...	5.28	3	2	0	0	0	15⅓	19	9	9	3	9
Champ. series totals (2 years)	0	1	.000	7.64	4	3	0	0	0	17⅔	25	15	15	5	12

ALL-STAR GAME RECORD

Year League	W	L	Pct.	ERA	GS	CG	ShO	Sv.	IP	H	R	ER	BB	SO
1993— National	0	0	...	4.50	0	0	0	0	2	2	1	1	0	2

BENITEZ, ARMANDO — P — METS

PERSONAL: Born November 3, 1972, in Ramon Santana, Dominican Republic. ... 6-4/225. ... Throws right, bats right.
TRANSACTIONS/CAREER NOTES: Signed as non-drafted free agent by Baltimore Orioles organization (April 1, 1990). ... On Baltimore disabled list (April 20-August 26, 1996); included rehabilitation assignments to Bowie (May 17-19) and Gulf Coast Orioles (August 13-26). ... On suspended list (May 20-28, 1998). ... Traded by Orioles to New York Mets for C Charles Johnson (December 1, 1998).

Year Team (League)	W	L	Pct.	ERA	G	GS	CG	ShO	Sv.	IP	H	R	ER	BB	SO
1990—															
				Dominican Summer League statistics unavailable.											
1991— GC Orioles (GCL)	3	2	.600	2.72	14	3	0	0	0	36⅓	35	16	11	11	33
1992— Bluefield (Appalachian)	1	2	.333	4.31	25	0	0	0	5	31⅓	35	31	15	23	37
1993— Albany (S. Atl.)	5	1	.833	1.52	40	0	0	0	14	53⅓	31	10	9	19	83
— Frederick (Carolina)	3	0	1.000	0.66	12	0	0	0	4	13⅔	7	1	1	4	29
1994— Bowie (Eastern)	8	4	.667	3.14	53	0	0	0	16	71⅔	41	29	25	39	106
— Baltimore (A.L.)	0	0	...	0.90	3	0	0	0	0	10	8	1	1	4	14
1995— Baltimore (A.L.)	1	5	.167	5.66	44	0	0	0	2	47⅔	37	33	30	37	56
— Rochester (Int'l)	2	2	.500	1.25	17	0	0	0	8	21⅔	10	4	3	7	37
1996— Baltimore (A.L.)	1	0	1.000	3.77	18	0	0	0	4	14⅓	7	6	6	6	20
— GC Orioles (GCL)	1	0	1.000	0.00	1	0	0	0	0	2	1	0	0	0	5
— Bowie (Eastern)	0	0	...	4.50	4	4	0	0	0	6	7	3	3	0	8
— Rochester (Int'l)	0	0	...	2.25	2	0	0	0	0	4	3	1	1	1	5
1997— Baltimore (A.L.)	4	5	.444	2.45	71	0	0	0	9	73⅓	49	22	20	43	106
1998— Baltimore (A.L.)	5	6	.455	3.82	71	0	0	0	22	68⅓	48	29	29	39	87
Major league totals (5 years)	11	16	.407	3.62	207	0	0	0	37	213⅔	149	91	86	129	283

DIVISION SERIES RECORD

Year Team (League)	W	L	Pct.	ERA	G	GS	CG	ShO	Sv.	IP	H	R	ER	BB	SO
1996— Baltimore (A.L.)	2	0	1.000	2.25	3	0	0	0	0	4	1	1	1	2	6
1997— Baltimore (A.L.)	0	0	...	3.00	3	0	0	0	0	3	3	1	1	2	4
Div. series totals (2 years)	2	0	1.000	2.57	6	0	0	0	0	7	4	2	2	4	10

CHAMPIONSHIP SERIES RECORD

Year Team (League)	W	L	Pct.	ERA	G	GS	CG	ShO	Sv.	IP	H	R	ER	BB	SO
1996— Baltimore (A.L.)	0	0	...	7.71	3	0	0	0	1	2⅓	3	2	2	4	2
1997— Baltimore (A.L.)	0	2	.000	12.00	4	0	0	0	0	3	3	4	4	4	6
Champ. series totals (2 years)	0	2	.000	10.13	7	0	0	0	1	5⅓	6	6	6	8	8

BENITEZ, YAMIL — OF — DIAMONDBACKS

PERSONAL: Born May 10, 1972, in San Juan, Puerto Rico. ... 6-2/195. ... Bats right, throws right. ... Full name: Yamil Antonio Benitez. ... Name pronounced ja-MEEL.
TRANSACTIONS/CAREER NOTES: Signed as non-drafted free agent by Montreal Expos organization (October 26, 1989). ... Traded by Expos to Kansas City Royals for P Melvin Bunch (January 28, 1997). ... Selected by Arizona Diamondbacks in first round (19th pick overall) of expansion draft (November 18, 1997).
STATISTICAL NOTES: Career major league grand slams: 1.

Year Team (League)	Pos.	G	AB	R	H	2B	3B	HR	RBI	Avg.	BB	SO	SB	PO	A	E	Avg.
							BATTING								FIELDING		
1990— GC Expos (GCL)	OF	22	83	6	19	1	0	1	5	.229	8	18	0	38	2	1	.976
1991— GC Expos (GCL)	OF	54	197	20	47	9	5	5	38	.239	12	55	10	85	2	3	.967
1992— Albany (S. Atl.)	OF	23	79	6	13	3	2	1	6	.165	5	49	0	30	0	1	.968
— Jamestown (NYP)	OF	44	162	24	44	6	6	3	23	.272	14	52	19	61	2	1	.984
1993— Burlington (Midw.)	OF	111	411	70	112	21	5	15	61	.273	29	99	18	167	4	10	.945
1994— Harrisburg (East.)	OF	126	475	58	123	18	4	17	91	.259	36	134	18	252	11	9	.967
1995— Ottawa (Int'l)	OF	127	474	66	123	24	6	18	69	.259	44	128	14	177	10	7	.964
— Montreal (N.L.)	OF	14	39	8	15	2	1	2	7	.385	1	7	0	18	1	1	.950
1996— Ottawa (Int'l)	OF	114	439	56	122	20	2	23	81	.278	28	120	11	197	14	7	.968
— Montreal (N.L.)	OF	11	12	0	2	0	0	0	2	.167	0	4	0	1	0	1	.500
1997— Omaha (A.A.)■	OF	92	329	61	97	14	1	21	71	.295	24	82	12	150	6	6	.963
— Kansas City (A.L.)	OF	53	191	22	51	7	1	8	21	.267	10	49	2	111	0	4	.965
1998— Arizona (N.L.)■	OF-DH	91	206	17	41	7	1	9	30	.199	14	46	2	101	4	3	.972
American League totals (1 year)		53	191	22	51	7	1	8	21	.267	10	49	2	111	0	4	.965
National League totals (3 years)		116	257	25	58	9	2	11	39	.226	15	57	2	120	5	5	.962
Major league totals (4 years)		169	448	47	109	16	3	19	60	.243	25	106	4	231	5	9	.963

PERSONAL: Born November 22, 1965, in Euclid, Ohio. ... 6-0/169. ... Bats right, throws right. ... Full name: Michael Paul Benjamin.
HIGH SCHOOL: Bellflower (Calif.).
JUNIOR COLLEGE: Cerritos College (Calif.).
COLLEGE: Arizona State.
TRANSACTIONS/CAREER NOTES: Selected by Minnesota Twins organization in seventh round of free-agent draft (January 9, 1985); did not sign. ... Selected by San Francisco Giants organization in third round of free-agent draft (June 2, 1987). ... On San Francisco disabled list (March 31-June 5, 1992); included rehabilitation assignment to Phoenix (April 20-May 10). ... On San Francisco disabled list (July 8-August 6, 1993); included rehabilitation assignment to San Jose (August 4-6). ... Traded by Giants to Philadelphia Phillies for P Jeff Juden and OF/1B Tommy Eason (October 6, 1995). ... On Philadelphia disabled list (March 23-April 26, 1996 and July 20, 1996-remainder of season); included rehabilitation assignments to Clearwater (April 8-17) and Scranton/Wilkes-Barre (April 21-26). ... Granted free agency (October 8, 1996). ... Signed by Boston Red Sox organization (January 31, 1997). ... Granted free agency (October 27, 1997). ... Re-signed by Red Sox (November 21, 1997). ... Granted free agency (October 26, 1998). ... Signed by Pittsburgh Pirates (November 17, 1998).
RECORDS: Holds modern major league record for most hits in three consecutive games—14 (June 11 [4], 13 [4] and 14 [6], 1995).
STATISTICAL NOTES: Led Pacific Coast League shortstops with 626 total chances in 1990. ... Collected six hits in one game (June 14, 1995).

							BATTING							FIELDING		
Year Team (League)	Pos.	G	AB	R	H	2B	3B	HR	RBI	Avg.	BB	SO	SB	PO	A	E	Avg.
1987— Fresno (California)......	SS	64	212	25	51	6	4	6	24	.241	24	71	6	89	188	21	.930
1988— Shreveport (Texas).....	SS	89	309	48	73	19	5	6	37	.236	22	63	14	134	248	11	.972
—Phoenix (PCL)...........	SS	37	106	13	18	4	1	0	6	.170	13	32	2	41	74	4	.966
1989— Phoenix (PCL)...........	SS-2B	113	363	44	94	17	6	3	36	.259	18	82	10	149	332	15	.970
—San Francisco (N.L.) ..	SS	14	6	6	1	0	0	0	0	.167	0	1	0	4	4	0	1.000
1990— Phoenix (PCL)...........	SS	118	419	61	105	21	7	5	39	.251	25	89	13	*216	*386	24	.962
—San Francisco (N.L.) ..	SS	22	56	7	12	3	1	2	3	.214	3	10	1	29	53	1	.988
1991— San Francisco (N.L.) ..	SS-3B	54	106	12	13	3	0	2	8	.123	7	26	3	64	123	3	.984
—Phoenix (PCL)...........	SS	64	226	34	46	13	2	6	31	.204	20	67	3	109	252	9	.976
1992— San Francisco (N.L.) ..	SS-3B	40	75	4	13	2	1	1	3	.173	4	15	1	34	71	1	.991
—Phoenix (PCL)...........	SS-2B	31	108	15	33	10	2	0	17	.306	3	18	4	51	92	2	.986
1993— San Francisco (N.L.) ..	SS-2B-3B	63	146	22	29	7	0	4	16	.199	9	23	0	74	133	5	.976
—San Jose (Calif.)........	SS-2B	2	8	1	0	0	0	0	0	.000	1	0	0	1	5	0	1.000
1994— San Francisco (N.L.) ..	SS-2B-3B	38	62	9	16	5	1	1	9	.258	5	16	5	33	70	3	.972
1995— San Francisco (N.L.) ..	3B-SS-2B	68	186	19	41	6	0	3	12	.220	8	51	11	51	121	4	.977
1996— Clearwater (FSL)■.....	SS	8	23	3	4	1	0	0	0	.174	3	4	1	9	20	2	.935
—Scran./W.B. (Int'l)......	SS	4	13	2	5	2	0	0	4	.385	3	0	0	3	12	0	1.000
—Philadelphia (N.L.)......	SS-2B	35	103	13	23	5	1	4	13	.223	12	21	3	38	87	6	.954
1997— Pawtucket (Int'l)■......	SS-3B-2B	33	105	12	26	4	1	4	12	.248	8	20	4	46	86	5	.964
—Boston (A.L.).............	3-S-2-1-DH-P	49	116	12	27	9	1	0	7	.233	4	27	2	50	81	6	.956
1998— Boston (A.L.).............	2-S-3-1-DH	124	349	46	95	23	0	4	39	.272	15	73	3	233	275	3	.994
American League totals (2 years)		173	465	58	122	32	1	4	46	.262	19	100	5	283	356	9	.986
National League totals (8 years)		334	740	92	148	31	4	17	64	.200	48	163	24	327	662	23	.977
Major league totals (10 years)		507	1205	150	270	63	5	21	110	.224	67	263	29	610	1018	32	.981

DIVISION SERIES RECORD

							BATTING							FIELDING		
Year Team (League)	Pos.	G	AB	R	H	2B	3B	HR	RBI	Avg.	BB	SO	SB	PO	A	E	Avg.
1998— Boston (A.L.).............	2B-1B	4	11	1	1	0	0	0	0	.091	1	3	0	13	9	0	1.000

RECORD AS PITCHER

Year Team (League)	W	L	Pct.	ERA	G	GS	CG	ShO	Sv.	IP	H	R	ER	BB	SO
1997— Boston (A.L.).....................	0	0	...	0.00	1	0	0	0	0	1	0	0	0	0	0

PERSONAL: Born April 17, 1972, in Waukegan, Ill. ... 6-0/190. ... Bats right, throws right. ... Full name: Gary David Bennett Jr.
HIGH SCHOOL: Waukegan East (Ill.).
TRANSACTIONS/CAREER NOTES: Selected by Philadelphia Phillies organization in 11th round of free-agent draft (June 4, 1990). ... On Clearwater disabled list (September 5-15, 1993). ... Granted free agency (October 8, 1996). ... Signed by Boston Red Sox organization (February 10, 1997). ... Granted free agency (October 15, 1997). ... Signed by Phillies organization (December 1, 1997).
STATISTICAL NOTES: Led Eastern League with 22 passed balls in 1994. ... Led Eastern League catchers with 13 double plays in 1995.

							BATTING							FIELDING		
Year Team (League)	Pos.	G	AB	R	H	2B	3B	HR	RBI	Avg.	BB	SO	SB	PO	A	E	Avg.
1990— Martinsville (App.)......	C	16	52	3	14	2	1	0	10	.269	4	15	0	80	3	3	.965
1991— Martinsville (App.)......	C	41	136	15	32	7	0	1	16	.235	17	26	0	291	34	2	.994
1992— Batavia (NY-Penn)......	C	47	146	22	30	2	0	0	12	.205	15	27	2	292	42	2	*.994
1993— Spartanburg (SAL)......	C	42	126	18	32	4	1	0	15	.254	12	22	0	199	35	2	.992
—Clearwater (FSL)	C	17	55	5	18	0	0	1	6	.327	3	10	0	70	12	0	1.000
1994— Clearwater (FSL)	C	19	55	6	13	3	0	0	10	.236	8	6	0	101	10	1	.991
—Reading (Eastern)	C	63	208	13	48	9	0	3	22	.231	14	26	0	376	64	2	.995
1995— Reading (Eastern)	C	86	271	27	64	11	0	4	40	.236	22	36	0	551	65	4	.994
—Scran./W.B. (Int'l).......	C	7	20	1	3	0	0	0	1	.150	2	2	0	38	4	0	1.000
—Philadelphia (N.L.)......	PH	1	1	0	0	0	0	0	0	.000	0	1	0	...	...	...	...
1996— Scran./W.B. (Int'l).......	C	91	286	37	71	15	1	8	37	.248	24	43	1	517	61	7	.988
—Philadelphia (N.L.)......	C	6	16	0	4	0	0	0	1	.250	2	6	0	35	5	0	1.000
1997— Pawtucket (Int'l)■.......	C-1B	71	224	16	48	7	1	4	22	.214	18	39	1	528	36	6	.986
1998— Scran./W.B. (Int'l)■.....	C-1B	86	282	33	72	18	0	10	40	.255	25	41	0	425	35	1	.998
—Philadelphia (N.L.)......	C	9	31	4	9	0	0	0	3	.290	5	5	0	50	2	0	1.000
Major league totals (3 years)		16	48	4	13	0	0	0	4	.271	7	12	0	85	7	0	1.000

BENNETT, JOEL   P   PHILLIES

PERSONAL: Born January 31, 1970, in Binghamton, N.Y. ... 6-1/160. ... Throws right, bats right. ... Full name: Joel Todd Bennett.
HIGH SCHOOL: Windsor (N.Y.) Central.
COLLEGE: East Stroudsburg (Pa.).
TRANSACTIONS/CAREER NOTES: Selected by Boston Red Sox organization in 21st round of free-agent draft (June 3, 1991). ... On disabled list (July 8-August 3, 1995). ... Released by Red Sox organization (May 6, 1996). ... Signed by Baltimore Orioles organization (July 27, 1996). ... Granted free agency (October 15, 1997). ... Re-signed by Orioles organization for 1998 season. ... Released by Orioles (July 24, 1998). ... Signed by Philadelphia Phillies organization (July 30, 1998). ... Granted free agency (October 15, 1998). ... Re-signed by Phillies organization (November 5, 1998).
STATISTICAL NOTES: Tied for Carolina League lead with six intentional bases on balls issued in 1993.

Year Team (League)	W	L	Pct.	ERA	G	GS	CG	ShO	Sv.	IP	H	R	ER	BB	SO
1991— GC Red Sox (GCL)	0	0	...	1.80	2	2	0	0	0	10	6	2	2	4	8
— Elmira (N.Y.-Penn)	5	3	.625	2.44	13	12	1	1	0	81	60	29	22	30	75
1992— Winter Haven (FSL)	7	11	.389	4.23	26	26	4	0	0	161 2/3	161	*86	*76	55	154
1993— Lynchburg (Carolina)	7	•12	.368	3.83	29	*29	3	1	0	*181	151	93	77	67	*221
1994— New Britain (Eastern)	11	7	.611	4.06	23	23	1	1	0	130 2/3	119	65	59	56	130
— Pawtucket (Int'l)	1	3	.250	6.86	4	4	0	0	0	21	19	16	16	12	24
1995— Pawtucket (Int'l)	2	4	.333	5.84	20	13	0	0	0	77	91	57	50	45	50
1996— Trenton (Eastern)	1	0	1.000	8.31	3	0	0	0	0	4 1/3	3	4	4	2	8
— Bowie (Eastern)■	2	3	.400	3.29	10	8	0	0	0	54 2/3	36	21	20	17	48
1997— Bowie (Eastern)	6	8	.429	3.18	44	10	0	0	4	113 1/3	89	45	40	40	146
1998— Rochester (Int'l)	10	0	1.000	3.64	18	15	1	0	0	101 1/3	99	46	41	37	99
— Baltimore (A.L.)	0	0	...	4.50	2	0	0	0	0	2	2	1	1	3	0
— Scran./W.B. (Int'l)■	1	2	.333	5.29	8	7	0	0	0	47 2/3	51	29	28	25	35
Major league totals (1 year)	0	0	...	4.50	2	0	0	0	0	2	2	1	1	3	0

BENNETT, SHAYNE   P   EXPOS

PERSONAL: Born April 10, 1972, in Adelaide, Australia. ... 6-5/220. ... Throws right, bats right. ... Full name: Shayne Anthony Bennett.
JUNIOR COLLEGE: DuPage (Ill.) Junior College.
TRANSACTIONS/CAREER NOTES: Selected by Boston Red Sox organization in 25th round of free-agent draft (June 2, 1993). ... Traded by Red Sox with P Rheal Cormier and 1B Ryan McGuire to Montreal Expos for SS Wil Cordero and P Bryan Eversgerd (January 10, 1996).

Year Team (League)	W	L	Pct.	ERA	G	GS	CG	ShO	Sv.	IP	H	R	ER	BB	SO
1993— GC Red Sox (GCL)	0	0	...	1.29	2	1	0	0	1	7	2	1	1	1	4
— Fort Lauderdale (FSL)	1	2	.333	1.72	23	0	0	0	6	31 1/3	26	8	6	11	23
1994— Sarasota (Florida State)	1	6	.143	4.47	15	8	0	0	3	48 1/3	46	31	24	27	28
1995— Sarasota (Florida State)	2	5	.286	2.56	52	0	0	0	24	59 2/3	50	23	17	21	69
— Trenton (Eastern)	0	1	.000	5.06	10	0	0	0	3	10 2/3	16	6	6	3	6
1996— Harrisburg (Eastern)■	8	8	.500	2.53	53	0	0	0	12	92 2/3	83	32	26	35	89
1997— Harrisburg (Eastern)	4	2	.667	4.40	23	1	0	0	2	47	47	28	23	20	38
— Ottawa (Int'l)	1	2	.333	1.57	25	0	0	0	14	34 1/3	23	8	6	21	29
— Montreal (N.L.)	0	1	.000	3.18	16	0	0	0	0	22 2/3	21	9	8	9	8
1998— Montreal (N.L.)	5	5	.500	5.50	62	0	0	0	1	91 2/3	97	61	56	45	59
Major league totals (2 years)	5	6	.455	5.04	78	0	0	0	1	114 1/3	118	70	64	54	67

BENSON, KRIS   P   PIRATES

PERSONAL: Born November 7, 1974, in Kennesaw, Ga. ... 6-4/190. ... Throws right, bats right. ... Full name: Kristen James Benson.
HIGH SCHOOL: Spayberry (Marietta, Ga.).
COLLEGE: Clemson.
TRANSACTIONS/CAREER NOTES: Selected by Pittsburgh Pirates organization in first round (first pick overall) of free-agent draft (June 2, 1996).
MISCELLANEOUS: Member of 1996 U.S. Olympic baseball team.

Year Team (League)	W	L	Pct.	ERA	G	GS	CG	ShO	Sv.	IP	H	R	ER	BB	SO
1997— Lynchburg (Carolina)	5	2	.714	2.58	10	10	0	0	0	59 1/3	49	20	17	13	72
— Carolina (Southern)	3	5	.375	4.98	14	14	0	0	0	68 2/3	81	49	38	32	66
1998— Nashville (Pacific Coast)	8	10	.444	5.37	28	28	1	1	0	156	162	102	93	50	129

BERE, JASON   P   REDS

PERSONAL: Born May 26, 1971, in Cambridge, Mass. ... 6-3/215. ... Throws right, bats right. ... Full name: Jason Phillip Bere. ... Name pronounced burr-AY.
HIGH SCHOOL: Wilmington (Mass.).
JUNIOR COLLEGE: Middlesex Community College (Mass.).
TRANSACTIONS/CAREER NOTES: Selected by Chicago White Sox organization in 36th round of free-agent draft (June 4, 1990). ... On Chicago disabled list (August 5-20, 1995); included rehabilitation assignment to South Bend (August 13-18). ... On Chicago disabled list (April 22-September 3 and September 14, 1996-remainder of season); included rehabilitation assignments to Nashville (May 14-19 and August 27-28), Gulf Coast White Sox (August 5-10), Hickory (August 10-16) and Birmingham (August 16-27). ... On Chicago disabled list (March 31-August 19, 1997); included rehabilitation assignments to Gulf Coast White Sox (July 2-7), Hickory (July 12), Birmingham (July 17-22) and Nashville (July 29-August 14). ... Released by White Sox (July 16, 1998). ... Signed by Cincinnati Reds organization (July 21, 1998).

Year Team (League)	W	L	Pct.	ERA	G	GS	CG	ShO	Sv.	IP	H	R	ER	BB	SO
1990— GC White Sox (GCL)	0	4	.000	2.37	16	2	0	0	1	38	26	19	10	19	41
1991— South Bend (Mid.)	9	12	.429	2.87	27	27	2	1	0	163	116	66	52	*100	158
1992— Sarasota (Florida State)	7	2	.778	2.41	18	18	1	1	0	116	84	35	31	34	106
— Birmingham (Southern)	4	4	.500	3.00	8	8	4	2	0	54	44	22	18	20	45
— Vancouver (PCL)	0	0	...	0.00	1	0	0	0	0	1	2	0	0	0	2
1993— Nashville (A.A.)	5	1	.833	2.37	8	8	0	0	0	49 1/3	36	19	13	25	52
— Chicago (A.L.)	12	5	.706	3.47	24	24	1	0	0	142 2/3	109	60	55	81	129

B

Year Team (League)	W	L	Pct.	ERA	G	GS	CG	ShO	Sv.	IP	H	R	ER	BB	SO
1994— Chicago (A.L.)	12	2	*.857	3.81	24	24	0	0	0	141²/₃	119	65	60	80	127
1995— Chicago (A.L.)	8	•15	.348	7.19	27	27	1	0	0	137²/₃	151	120	110	106	110
— Nashville (A.A.)	1	0	1.000	3.38	1	1	0	0	0	5¹/₃	6	2	2	2	7
1996— Chicago (A.L.)	0	1	.000	10.26	5	5	0	0	0	16²/₃	26	19	19	18	19
— Nashville (A.A.)	0	0	...	1.42	3	3	0	0	0	12²/₃	9	2	2	4	15
— GC White Sox (GCL)	0	1	.000	6.00	1	1	0	0	0	3	3	2	2	1	3
— Hickory (S. Atl.)	1	0	1.000	0.00	1	1	0	0	0	5	3	0	0	0	5
— Birmingham (Southern)	0	0	...	4.15	1	1	0	0	0	4¹/₃	4	2	2	4	5
1997— GC White Sox (GCL)	0	0	...	0.00	2	2	0	0	0	5	2	0	0	0	5
— Hickory (S. Atl.)	0	0	...	6.00	1	1	0	0	0	3	4	2	2	0	2
— Birmingham (Southern)	0	1	.000	7.71	2	2	0	0	0	7	8	7	6	2	7
— Nashville (A.A.)	1	1	.500	5.59	4	4	0	0	0	19¹/₃	23	13	12	7	13
— Chicago (A.L.)	4	2	.667	4.71	6	6	0	0	0	28²/₃	20	15	15	17	21
1998— Chicago (A.L.)	3	7	.300	6.45	18	15	2	0	0	83²/₃	98	71	60	58	53
— Cincinnati (N.L.)■	3	2	.600	4.12	9	7	0	0	0	43²/₃	39	20	20	20	31
A.L. totals (6 years)	39	32	.549	5.21	104	101	2	0	0	551	523	350	319	360	459
N.L. totals (1 year)	3	2	.600	4.12	9	7	0	0	0	43²/₃	39	20	20	20	31
Major league totals (6 years)......	42	34	.553	5.13	113	108	2	0	0	594²/₃	562	370	339	380	490

CHAMPIONSHIP SERIES RECORD

Year Team (League)	W	L	Pct.	ERA	G	GS	CG	ShO	Sv.	IP	H	R	ER	BB	SO
1993— Chicago (A.L.)	0	0	...	11.57	1	1	0	0	0	2¹/₃	5	3	3	2	3

ALL-STAR GAME RECORD

Year League	W	L	Pct.	ERA	GS	CG	ShO	Sv.	IP	H	R	ER	BB	SO
1994— American	0	1	.000	...	0	0	0	0	0	2	1	1	0	0

BERG, DAVE   IF   MARLINS

PERSONAL: Born September 3, 1970, in Roseville, Calif. ... 5-11/185. ... Bats right, throws right. ... Full name: David Scott Berg.
HIGH SCHOOL: Roseville (Calif.)
JUNIOR COLLEGE: Sacramento City College.
COLLEGE: Miami (Fla.).
TRANSACTIONS/CAREER NOTES: Selected by California Angels organization in 32nd round of free-agent draft (June 4, 1990); did not sign. ... Selected by Florida Marlins organization in 38th round of free-agent draft (June 3, 1993).
STATISTICAL NOTES: Led New York-Pennsylvania League third basemen with 158 assists in 1993. ... Led Midwest League third basemen with .948 fielding percentage in 1994.

							BATTING						FIELDING		
Year Team (League)	Pos.	G	AB	R	H	2B	3B	HR	RBI	Avg.	BB	SO	SB	PO	A	E	Avg.
1993— Elmira (N.Y.-Penn)......	3B-2B-OF	75	281	37	74	13	1	4	28	.263	34	37	7	55	†193	20	.925
1994— Kane County (Midw.)..	3B-2B	121	437	80	117	27	8	9	53	.268	54	80	8	73	236	17	†.948
1995— Brevard Co. (Fla. St.)..	SS-3B-2B	114	382	71	114	18	1	3	39	.298	68	61	9	157	348	26	.951
1996— Portland (Eastern)......	SS-3B	109	414	64	125	28	5	9	73	.302	42	60	17	143	358	26	.951
1997— Charlotte (Int'l)........	SS-2B-3B	117	424	76	125	26	6	9	47	.295	55	71	16	136	324	22	.954
1998— Florida (N.L.)	2B-3B-SS	81	182	18	57	11	0	2	21	.313	26	46	3	90	130	7	.969
Major league totals (1 year)		81	182	18	57	11	0	2	21	.313	26	46	3	90	130	7	.969

BERGMAN, SEAN   P   ASTROS

PERSONAL: Born April 11, 1970, in Joliet, Ill. ... 6-4/225. ... Throws right, bats right. ... Full name: Sean Frederick Bergman.
HIGH SCHOOL: Joliet (Ill.) Catholic.
COLLEGE: Southern Illinois-Carbondale.
TRANSACTIONS/CAREER NOTES: Selected by Detroit Tigers organization in fourth round of free-agent draft (June 3, 1991). ... On Detroit disabled list (June 26-July 17, 1995); included rehabilitation assignment to Toledo (July 10-17). ... Traded by Tigers with P Cade Gaspar and OF Todd Steverson to San Diego Padres for P Richie Lewis, OF Melvin Nieves and C Raul Casanova (March 22, 1996). ... Traded by Padres to Houston Astros for OF James Mouton (January 14, 1998).
MISCELLANEOUS: Fouled out in only appearance as pinch hitter and appeared in one game as pinch runner (1996).

Year Team (League)	W	L	Pct.	ERA	G	GS	CG	ShO	Sv.	IP	H	R	ER	BB	SO
1991— Niagara Falls (NYP)	5	7	.417	4.46	15	15	0	0	0	84²/₃	87	57	42	42	77
1992— Lakeland (Fla. St.)	5	2	.714	2.49	13	13	0	0	0	83	61	28	23	14	67
— London (Eastern)	4	7	.364	4.28	14	14	1	0	0	88¹/₃	85	52	42	45	59
1993— Toledo (International)	8	9	.471	4.38	19	19	3	0	0	117	124	62	57	53	91
— Detroit (A.L.)	1	4	.200	5.67	9	6	1	0	0	39²/₃	47	29	25	23	19
1994— Toledo (International)	11	8	.579	3.72	25	25	2	0	0	154²/₃	147	77	64	53	145
— Detroit (A.L.)	2	1	.667	5.60	3	3	0	0	0	17²/₃	22	11	11	7	12
1995— Detroit (A.L.)	7	10	.412	5.12	28	28	1	1	0	135¹/₃	169	95	77	67	86
— Toledo (International)	0	1	.000	6.00	1	1	0	0	0	3	4	2	2	0	4
1996— San Diego (N.L.)■	6	8	.429	4.37	41	14	0	0	0	113¹/₃	119	63	55	33	85
1997— San Diego (N.L.)	2	4	.333	6.09	44	9	0	0	0	99	126	72	67	38	74
1998— Houston (N.L.)■	12	9	.571	3.72	31	27	1	0	0	172	183	81	71	42	100
A.L. totals (3 years)	10	15	.400	5.28	40	37	2	1	0	192²/₃	238	135	113	97	117
N.L. totals (3 years)	20	21	.488	4.52	116	50	1	0	0	384¹/₃	428	216	193	113	259
Major league totals (6 years)......	30	36	.455	4.77	156	87	3	1	0	577	666	351	306	210	376

B

BERROA, GERONIMO   OF/DH   BLUE JAYS

PERSONAL: Born March 18, 1965, in Santo Domingo, Dominican Republic. ... 6-0/210. ... Bats right, throws right. ... Full name: Geronimo Emiliano Berroa. ... Name pronounced her-ON-i-mo bur-OH-uh.

TRANSACTIONS/CAREER NOTES: Signed as non-drafted free agent by Toronto Blue Jays organization (September 4, 1983). ... Selected by Atlanta Braves from Blue Jays organization in Rule 5 major league draft (December 5, 1988). ... Released by Braves (February 1, 1991). ... Signed by Calgary, Seattle Mariners organization (February 27, 1991). ... Contract sold by Mariners organization to Colorado Springs, Cleveland Indians organization (March 28, 1991). ... Granted free agency (October 15, 1991). ... Signed by Nashville, Cincinnati Reds organization (October 31, 1991). ... Released by Reds (November 20, 1992). ... Signed by Florida Marlins (December 9, 1992). ... Granted free agency (October 15, 1993). ... Signed by Oakland Athletics organization (January 20, 1994). ... On disabled list (August 2, 1994-remainder of season). ... Traded by A's to Baltimore Orioles for P Jimmy Haynes and a player to be named later (June 27, 1997); A's acquired P Mark Seaver to complete deal (September 2, 1997). ... Granted free agency (December 21, 1997). ... Signed by Cleveland Indians (January 29, 1998). ... On Cleveland disabled list (May 3-June 3, 1998). ... Traded by Indians to Detroit Tigers for P Tim Worrell and OF Dave Roberts (June 24, 1998). ... Granted free agency (October 23, 1998). ... Signed by Toronto Blue Jays organization (December 14, 1998).

RECORDS: Shares major league single-season record for most games with three home runs—2 (1996).

STATISTICAL NOTES: Led Southern League with 297 total bases in 1987. ... Led International League in being hit by pitch with 10 and tied for lead in sacrifice flies with eight in 1988. ... Led International League in grounding into double plays with 17 in 1990. ... Hit three home runs in one game (May 22 and August 12, 1996). ... Career major league grand slams: 2.

								BATTING							FIELDING		
Year	Team (League)	Pos.	G	AB	R	H	2B	3B	HR	RBI	Avg.	BB	SO	SB	PO	A	E	Avg.
1984— GC Jays (GCL)		OF-1B	62	235	31	59	16	1	3	34	.251	12	34	2	104	2	5	.955
1985— Kinston (Carolina)		OF	19	43	4	8	0	0	1	4	.186	4	10	0	13	1	1	.933
—Medicine Hat (Pio.)		OF	54	201	39	69	*22	2	6	45	.343	18	40	7	58	3	3	.953
—Florence (S. Atl.)		OF	19	66	7	21	2	0	3	20	.318	6	13	0	24	0	2	.923
1986— Ventura (Calif.)		OF	128	459	76	137	22	5	21	73	.298	38	92	12	194	9	14	.935
—Knoxville (Southern)		OF	1	4	0	0	0	0	0	0	.000	0	1	0	2	0	0	1.000
1987— Knoxville (Southern)		OF	134	523	87	150	33	3	36	108	.287	46	104	2	236	6	•15	.942
1988— Syracuse (Int'l)		OF	131	470	55	122	•29	1	8	64	.260	38	88	7	243	12	5	.981
1989— Atlanta (N.L.)■		OF	81	136	7	36	4	0	2	9	.265	7	32	0	67	1	2	.971
1990— Richmond (Int'l)		OF	135	499	56	134	17	2	12	80	.269	34	89	4	200	10	7	.968
—Atlanta (N.L.)		OF	7	4	0	0	0	0	0	0	.000	1	1	0	1	0	0	1.000
1991— Colo. Springs (PCL)■		OF	125	478	81	154	31	7	18	91	.322	35	88	2	151	14	5	.971
1992— Nashville (A.A.)■		OF	112	461	73	151	33	2	22	88	.328	32	69	8	194	16	5	.977
—Cincinnati (N.L.)		OF	13	15	2	4	1	0	0	0	.267	2	1	0	2	1	0	1.000
1993— Edmonton (PCL)■		OF-1B	90	327	64	107	33	4	16	68	.327	36	71	1	210	10	7	.969
—Florida (N.L.)		OF	14	34	3	4	1	0	0	0	.118	2	7	0	9	1	2	.833
1994— Oakland (A.L.)■		DH-OF-1B	96	340	55	104	18	2	13	65	.306	41	62	7	131	5	1	.993
1995— Oakland (A.L.)		DH-OF	141	546	87	152	22	3	22	88	.278	63	98	7	129	5	4	.971
1996— Oakland (A.L.)		DH-OF	153	586	101	170	32	1	36	106	.290	47	122	0	91	6	2	.980
1997— Oakland (A.L.)		OF-DH	73	261	40	81	12	0	16	42	.310	36	58	3	71	1	1	.986
—Baltimore (A.L.)■		DH-OF	83	300	48	78	13	0	10	48	.260	40	62	1	70	1	3	.959
1998— Cleveland (A.L.)■		OF-DH	20	65	6	13	3	1	0	3	.200	7	17	1	27	1	0	1.000
—Detroit (A.L.)■		DH-OF	52	126	17	30	4	1	1	10	.238	17	27	0	4	0	0	1.000
American League totals (5 years)			618	2224	354	628	104	8	98	362	.282	251	446	19	523	19	11	.980
National League totals (4 years)			115	189	12	44	6	0	2	9	.233	12	41	0	79	3	4	.953
Major league totals (9 years)			733	2413	366	672	110	8	100	371	.278	263	487	19	602	22	15	.977

DIVISION SERIES RECORD

								BATTING							FIELDING		
Year	Team (League)	Pos.	G	AB	R	H	2B	3B	HR	RBI	Avg.	BB	SO	SB	PO	A	E	Avg.
1997— Baltimore (A.L.)		DH-OF	4	13	4	5	1	0	2	2	.385	2	2	0	0	0	0	...

CHAMPIONSHIP SERIES RECORD

								BATTING							FIELDING		
Year	Team (League)	Pos.	G	AB	R	H	2B	3B	HR	RBI	Avg.	BB	SO	SB	PO	A	E	Avg.
1997— Baltimore (A.L.)		OF-DH	6	21	1	6	2	0	0	3	.286	0	3	0	9	0	0	1.000

BERRY, SEAN   3B   BREWERS

PERSONAL: Born March 22, 1966, in Santa Monica, Calif. ... 5-11/200. ... Bats right, throws right. ... Full name: Sean Robert Berry.

HIGH SCHOOL: West Torrance (Torrance, Calif.).

COLLEGE: UCLA.

TRANSACTIONS/CAREER NOTES: Selected by Boston Red Sox organization in fourth round of free-agent draft (June 4, 1984); did not sign. ... Selected by Kansas City Royals organization in secondary phase of free-agent draft (January 14, 1986). ... On disabled list (April 16-May 3, 1987). ... Traded by Royals with P Archie Corbin to Montreal Expos for P Bill Sampen and P Chris Haney (August 29, 1992). ... Traded by Expos to Houston Astros for P Dave Veres and C Raul Chavez (December 20, 1995). ... On Houston disabled list (April 7-22 and August 23-September 7, 1997); included rehabilitation assignment to New Orleans (April 18-22). ... Granted free agency (December 21, 1997). ... Re-signed by Astros (January 13, 1998). ... Granted free agency (October 26, 1998). ... Signed by Milwaukee Brewers (December 10, 1998).

STATISTICAL NOTES: Led Northwest League third basemen with 11 double plays in 1986. ... Career major league grand slams: 3.

								BATTING							FIELDING		
Year	Team (League)	Pos.	G	AB	R	H	2B	3B	HR	RBI	Avg.	BB	SO	SB	PO	A	E	Avg.
1986— Eugene (Northwest)		3B	65	238	53	76	20	2	5	44	.319	44	72	10	*63	96	21	.883
1987— Fort Myers (FSL)		3B	66	205	26	52	7	2	2	30	.254	46	65	5	39	101	23	.859
1988— Baseball City (FSL)		3B-SS-OF	94	304	34	71	6	4	4	30	.234	31	62	24	84	161	28	.897
1989— Baseball City (FSL)		3-0-2-S	116	399	67	106	19	7	4	44	.266	44	68	37	100	199	24	.926
1990— Memphis (Sou.)		3B	135	487	73	142	25	4	14	77	.292	44	89	18	79	238	27	.922
—Kansas City (A.L.)		3B	8	23	2	5	1	1	0	4	.217	2	5	0	7	10	1	.944
1991— Omaha (A.A.)		3B-SS-2B	103	368	62	97	21	9	11	54	.264	48	70	8	75	206	20	.934
—Kansas City (A.L.)		3B	31	60	5	8	3	0	0	1	.133	5	23	0	13	52	2	.970

Year Team (League)	Pos.	G	AB	R	H	2B	3B	HR	RBI	Avg.	BB	SO	SB	PO	A	E	Avg.
1992—Omaha (A.A.).............	3B	122	439	61	126	22	2	21	77	.287	39	87	6	86	239	21	*.939
—Montreal (N.L.)■......	3B	24	57	5	19	1	0	1	4	.333	1	11	2	10	19	4	.879
1993—Montreal (N.L.).........	3B	122	299	50	78	15	2	14	49	.261	41	70	12	66	153	15	.936
1994—Montreal (N.L.).........	3B	103	320	43	89	19	2	11	41	.278	32	50	14	66	147	14	.938
1995—Montreal (N.L.).........	3B-1B	103	314	38	100	22	1	14	55	.318	25	53	3	76	165	12	.953
1996—Houston (N.L.)■	3B	132	431	55	121	38	1	17	95	.281	23	58	12	67	194	22	.922
1997—New Orleans (A.A.)......	3B	3	9	1	3	0	0	0	0	.333	3	3	0	0	6	0	1.000
—Houston (N.L.)	3B-DH	96	301	37	77	24	1	8	43	.256	25	53	1	47	140	16	.921
1998—Houston (N.L.)	3B-DH	102	299	48	94	17	1	13	52	.314	31	50	3	55	150	10	.953
American League totals (2 years)		39	83	7	13	4	1	0	5	.157	7	28	0	20	62	3	.965
National League totals (7 years)		682	2021	276	578	136	8	78	339	.286	178	345	47	387	968	93	.936
Major league totals (9 years)		721	2104	283	591	140	9	78	344	.281	185	373	47	407	1030	96	.937

DIVISION SERIES RECORD

Year Team (League)	Pos.	G	AB	R	H	2B	3B	HR	RBI	Avg.	BB	SO	SB	PO	A	E	Avg.
1997—Houston (N.L.)..........	PH	1	1	0	0	0	0	0	0	.000	0	0	0	0	0	0	...
1998—Houston (N.L.)..........	3B	1	2	0	0	0	0	0	0	.000	0	1	0	0	2	1	.667
Division series totals (2 years)		2	3	0	0	0	0	0	0	.000	0	1	0	0	2	1	.667

BEVIL, BRIAN   P   ROYALS

PERSONAL: Born September 5, 1971, in Houston. ... 6-4/225. ... Throws right, bats right. ... Full name: Brian Scott Bevil.
HIGH SCHOOL: MacArthur (Houston).
JUNIOR COLLEGE: Angelina College (Texas).
TRANSACTIONS/CAREER NOTES: Selected by Kansas City Royals organization in 30th round of free-agent draft (June 4, 1990). ... On Memphis disabled list (July 24-1993-remainder of season). ... On Wichita temporarily inactive list (April 24-May 9, 1995). ... On Kansas City disabled list (June 24-August 28, 1998); included rehabilitation assignments to Gulf Coast Royals (July 16-23) and Omaha (July 24 and August 6-28). ... Granted free agency (December 21, 1998). ... Re-signed by Royals organization (December 21, 1998).

Year Team (League)	W	L	Pct.	ERA	G	GS	CG	ShO	Sv.	IP	H	R	ER	BB	SO
1991—GC Royals (GCL)	5	3	.625	1.93	13	12	2	0	0	65⅓	56	20	14	19	70
1992—Appleton (Midwest)............	9	7	.563	3.40	26	26	4	•2	0	156	129	67	59	63	168
1993—Wilmington (Caro.).............	7	1	.875	2.30	12	12	2	0	0	74⅓	46	21	19	23	61
—Memphis (Sou.)	3	3	.500	4.36	6	6	0	0	0	33	36	17	16	14	26
1994—Memphis (Sou.)	5	4	.556	3.51	17	17	0	0	0	100	75	42	39	40	78
1995—Wichita (Texas)	5	7	.417	5.84	15	15	0	0	0	74	85	51	48	35	57
—Omaha (Am. Assoc.)	1	3	.250	9.41	6	6	0	0	0	22	40	31	23	14	10
1996—Wichita (Texas)	9	2	•.818	2.02	13	13	2	0	0	75⅔	56	22	17	26	74
—Omaha (Am. Assoc.)	7	5	.583	4.12	12	12	0	0	0	67⅔	62	36	31	19	73
—Kansas City (A.L.)	1	0	1.000	5.73	3	1	0	0	0	11	9	7	7	5	7
1997—Wichita (Texas)	0	0	...	5.63	4	2	0	0	0	8	11	8	5	4	10
—Omaha (Am. Assoc.)	2	1	.667	4.38	26	3	0	0	1	39	34	22	19	22	47
—Kansas City (A.L.)	1	2	.333	6.61	18	0	0	0	1	16⅓	16	13	12	9	13
1998—Kansas City (A.L.)	3	1	.750	6.30	39	0	0	0	0	40	47	29	28	22	47
—GC Royals (GCL)	0	0	...	2.25	3	3	0	0	0	4	4	2	1	2	7
—Omaha (Pacific Coast)........	1	0	1.000	1.38	10	0	0	0	1	13	10	2	2	4	19
Major league totals (3 years)	5	3	.625	6.28	60	1	0	0	1	67⅓	72	49	47	36	67

BICHETTE, DANTE   OF   ROCKIES

PERSONAL: Born November 18, 1963, in West Palm Beach, Fla. ... 6-3/238. ... Bats right, throws right. ... Full name: Alphonse Dante Bichette. ... Name pronounced bih-SHETT.
HIGH SCHOOL: Jupiter (Fla.).
JUNIOR COLLEGE: Palm Beach Community College (Fla.).
TRANSACTIONS/CAREER NOTES: Selected by California Angels organization in 17th round of free-agent draft (June 4, 1984). ... Traded by Angels to Milwaukee Brewers for DH Dave Parker (March 14, 1991). ... Traded by Brewers to Colorado Rockies for OF Kevin Reimer (November 17, 1992).
HONORS: Named outfielder on THE SPORTING NEWS N.L. All-Star team (1995). ... Named outfielder on THE SPORTING NEWS N.L. Silver Slugger team (1995).
STATISTICAL NOTES: Led A.L. outfielders with seven double plays in 1991. ... Led N.L. outfielders with four double plays in 1994. ... Led N.L. with .620 slugging percentage and 359 total bases in 1995. ... Had 23-game hitting streak (May 22-June 18, 1995). ... Tied for N.L. lead with 10 sacrifice flies in 1996. ... Hit for the cycle (June 10, 1998). ... Tied for N.L. lead with six doubles plays by outfielder in 1998. ... Career major league grand slams: 6.
MISCELLANEOUS: Holds Colorado Rockies all-time records for most hits (1,101), most runs scored (561) and most runs batted in (693).

Year Team (League)	Pos.	G	AB	R	H	2B	3B	HR	RBI	Avg.	BB	SO	SB	PO	A	E	Avg.
1984—Salem (Northwest)	OF-1B-3B	64	250	27	58	9	2	4	30	.232	6	53	6	224	24	11	.958
1985—Quad Cities (Mid.) ...	1B-OF-C	137	547	58	145	28	4	11	78	.265	25	89	25	300	21	15	.955
1986—Palm Beach (Calif.)..	OF-3B	68	290	39	79	15	0	10	73	.272	21	53	2	78	68	11	.930
—Midland (Texas)	OF-3B	62	243	43	69	16	2	12	36	.284	18	50	3	131	30	11	.936
1987—Edmonton (PCL)	OF-3B	92	360	54	108	20	3	13	50	.300	26	68	3	169	21	9	.955
1988—Edmonton (PCL)	OF	132	509	64	136	29	•10	14	81	.267	25	78	7	218	*22	*15	.941
—California (A.L.)	OF	21	46	1	12	2	0	0	8	.261	0	7	0	44	2	1	.979
1989—California (A.L.)	OF-DH	48	138	13	29	7	0	3	15	.210	6	24	1	95	6	1	.990
—Edmonton (PCL)	OF	61	226	39	55	11	2	11	40	.243	24	39	4	92	9	1	.990
1990—California (A.L.)	OF	109	349	40	89	15	1	15	53	.255	16	79	5	183	12	7	.965
1991—Milwaukee (A.L.)■	OF-3B	134	445	53	106	18	3	15	59	.238	22	107	14	270	14	7	.976

Year	Team (League)	Pos.	G	AB	R	H	2B	3B	HR	RBI	Avg.	BB	SO	SB	PO	A	E	Avg.
1992— Milwaukee (A.L.)........		OF-DH	112	387	37	111	27	2	5	41	.287	16	74	18	188	6	2	.990
1993— Colorado (N.L.)■.......		OF	141	538	93	167	43	5	21	89	.310	28	99	14	308	14	9	.973
1994— Colorado (N.L.)		OF	*116	*484	74	147	33	2	27	95	.304	19	70	21	211	10	2	.991
1995— Colorado (N.L.)		OF	139	579	102	•197	38	2	*40	*128	.340	22	96	13	208	9	3	.986
1996— Colorado (N.L.)		OF	159	633	114	198	39	3	31	141	.313	45	105	31	255	5	9	.967
1997— Colorado (N.L.)		OF-DH	151	561	81	173	31	2	26	118	.308	30	90	6	225	4	3	.987
1998— Colorado (N.L.)		OF-DH	161	662	97	*219	48	2	22	122	.331	28	76	14	289	14	11	.965
American League totals (5 years)			424	1365	144	347	69	6	38	176	.254	60	291	40	780	40	18	.979
National League totals (6 years)			867	3457	561	1101	232	16	167	693	.318	172	536	99	1496	56	37	.977
Major league totals (11 years)			1291	4822	705	1448	301	22	205	869	.300	232	827	139	2276	96	55	.977

DIVISION SERIES RECORD

RECORDS: Shares N.L. career record for most doubles—3.

Year	Team (League)	Pos.	G	AB	R	H	2B	3B	HR	RBI	Avg.	BB	SO	SB	PO	A	E	Avg.
1995— Colorado (N.L.)		OF	4	17	6	10	3	0	1	3	.588	1	3	0	9	0	0	1.000

ALL-STAR GAME RECORD

Year	League	Pos.	AB	R	H	2B	3B	HR	RBI	Avg.	BB	SO	SB	PO	A	E	Avg.
1994— National......................		PH	1	0	1	0	0	0	0	1.000	0	0	0	...	...	...	...
1995— National......................		OF	1	0	0	0	0	0	0	.000	0	1	0	2	0	0	1.000
1996— National......................		OF	3	1	1	1	0	0	0	.333	0	1	0	0	0	0	...
1998— National......................		OF	2	0	0	0	0	0	0	.000	0	1	0	1	0	0	1.000
All-Star Game totals (4 years)			7	1	2	1	0	0	0	.286	0	3	0	3	0	0	1.000

BIESER, STEVEN — OF

PERSONAL: Born August 4, 1967, in Perryville, Mo. ... 5-10/170. ... Bats left, throws right. ... Full name: Steven Ray Bieser.
HIGH SCHOOL: St. Genevieve (Mo.)
JUNIOR COLLEGE: Jefferson College (Mo.), then Mineral Area Junior College (Mo.).
COLLEGE: Southeast Missouri State.
TRANSACTIONS/CAREER NOTES: Selected by Philadelphia Phillies organization in 32nd round of free-agent draft (June 5, 1989). ... Granted free agency (October 15, 1995). ... Signed by Ottawa, Montreal Expos organization (November 30, 1995). ... Granted free agency (October 15, 1996). ... Signed by New York Mets organization (November 21, 1996). ... Granted free agency (October 15, 1997). ... Signed by Pittsburgh Pirates organization (December 18, 1997). ... Granted free agency (September 29, 1998).
STATISTICAL NOTES: Led International League with 23 sacrifice hits in 1996.

Year	Team (League)	Pos.	G	AB	R	H	2B	3B	HR	RBI	Avg.	BB	SO	SB	PO	A	E	Avg.
1989— Batavia (NY-Penn)		OF-C	25	75	13	18	3	1	1	13	.240	12	20	2	104	8	2	.982
1990— Batavia (NY-Penn)		OF-3B	54	160	36	37	11	1	0	12	.231	26	28	13	83	7	1	.989
1991— Spartanburg (SAL)		O-C-1-3-S-P	60	168	25	41	6	0	0	13	.244	31	35	17	151	23	3	.983
1992— Clearwater (FSL)		C-OF-2B	73	203	33	58	6	5	0	10	.286	39	28	8	283	39	11	.967
—Reading (Eastern)		OF-C	33	139	20	38	5	4	0	8	.273	6	25	8	106	6	5	.957
1993— Reading (Eastern)		C-OF-P	53	170	21	53	6	3	1	19	.312	15	24	9	199	26	4	.983
—Scran./W.B. (Int'l)		OF-C-1B	26	83	3	21	4	0	0	4	.253	2	14	3	90	3	1	.989
1994— Scran./W.B. (Int'l)		O-C-3	93	228	42	61	13	1	0	15	.268	17	40	12	229	18	1	.996
1995— Scran./W.B. (Int'l)		C-OF-3B	95	245	37	66	12	6	1	33	.269	22	56	14	314	29	10	.972
1996— Ottawa (Int'l)■..........		O-C-2-P	123	382	63	123	24	4	1	32	.322	35	55	27	337	23	8	.978
1997— New York (N.L.)■.......		OF-C	47	69	16	17	3	0	0	4	.246	7	20	2	32	2	0	1.000
—Norfolk (Int'l)		O-2-C-3	41	122	6	20	5	0	0	4	.164	9	20	4	41	10	4	.927
1998— Nashville (PCL)■.......		C-OF-2B	82	206	30	53	11	4	1	24	.257	33	30	13	319	32	6	.983
—Pittsburgh (N.L.)		OF	13	11	2	3	1	0	0	1	.273	2	2	0	0	0	0	...
Major league totals (2 years)			60	80	18	20	4	0	0	5	.250	9	22	2	32	2	0	1.000

RECORD AS PITCHER

Year	Team (League)	W	L	Pct.	ERA	G	GS	CG	ShO	Sv.	IP	H	R	ER	BB	SO
1991— Spartanburg (SAL)	0	0	...	18.00	1	0	0	0	0	1	2	2	2	1	1
1993— Reading (Eastern)	0	0	...	0.00	1	0	0	0	0	1	0	0	0	1	1
1994— Scran./W.B. (Int'l)	0	0	...	0.00	1	0	0	0	0	$1/3$	0	0	0	0	0
1996— Ottawa (Int'l)■..................	0	0	...	18.00	1	0	0	0	0	1	3	4	2	3	1

BIGGIO, CRAIG — 2B — ASTROS

PERSONAL: Born December 14, 1965, in Smithtown, N.Y. ... 5-11/180. ... Bats right, throws right. ... Full name: Craig Alan Biggio. ... Name pronounced BEE-jee-oh.
HIGH SCHOOL: Kings Park (N.Y.).
COLLEGE: Seton Hall.
TRANSACTIONS/CAREER NOTES: Selected by Houston Astros organization in first round (22nd pick overall) of free-agent draft (June 2, 1987). ... Granted free agency (October 31, 1995). ... Re-signed by Astros (December 14, 1995).
HONORS: Named catcher on THE SPORTING NEWS college All-America team (1987). ... Named catcher on THE SPORTING NEWS N.L. Silver Slugger team (1989). ... Named second baseman on THE SPORTING NEWS N.L. All-Star team (1994-95 and 1997-98). ... Won N.L. Gold Glove at second base (1994-97). ... Named second baseman on THE SPORTING NEWS N.L. Silver Slugger team (1994-95 and 1997-98).
STATISTICAL NOTES: Led N.L. catchers with 889 putouts, 963 total chances and 13 passed balls in 1991. ... Led N.L. in being hit by pitch with 22 in 1995, 27 in 1996 and 34 in 1997. ... Led N.L. second basemen in total chances with 728 in 1995, 811 in 1996 and 863 in 1997. ... Career major league grand slams: 2.

Year Team (League)	Pos.	G	AB	R	H	2B	3B	HR	RBI	Avg.	BB	SO	SB	PO	A	E	Avg.
						BATTING									FIELDING		
1987—Asheville (S. Atl.)........	C-OF	64	216	59	81	17	2	9	49	.375	39	33	31	378	46	2	.995
1988—Tucson (PCL)........	C-OF	77	281	60	90	21	4	3	41	.320	40	39	19	318	33	6	.983
—Houston (N.L.)	C	50	123	14	26	6	1	3	5	.211	7	29	6	292	28	3	.991
1989—Houston (N.L.)	C-OF	134	443	64	114	21	2	13	60	.257	49	64	21	742	56	9	.989
1990—Houston (N.L.)	C-OF	150	555	53	153	24	2	4	42	.276	53	79	25	657	60	13	.982
1991—Houston (N.L.)	C-2B-OF	149	546	79	161	23	4	4	46	.295	53	71	19	†894	73	11	.989
1992—Houston (N.L.)	2B	•162	613	96	170	32	3	6	39	.277	94	95	38	*344	413	12	.984
1993—Houston (N.L.)	2B	155	610	98	175	41	5	21	64	.287	77	93	15	306	*447	14	.982
1994—Houston (N.L.)	2B	114	437	88	139	*44	5	6	56	.318	62	58	*39	•225	*338	7	.988
1995—Houston (N.L.)	2B	141	553	*123	167	30	2	22	77	.302	80	85	33	299	*419	10	.986
1996—Houston (N.L.)	2B	•162	605	113	174	24	4	15	75	.288	75	72	25	*361	*440	10	.988
1997—Houston (N.L.)	2B-DH	•162	619	*146	191	37	8	22	81	.309	84	107	47	*341	*504	18	.979
1998—Houston (N.L.)	2B-DH	160	646	123	210	*51	2	20	88	.325	64	113	50	318	431	15	.980
Major league totals (11 years)		1539	5750	997	1680	333	38	136	633	.292	698	866	318	4779	3209	122	.985

DIVISION SERIES RECORD

Year Team (League)	Pos.	G	AB	R	H	2B	3B	HR	RBI	Avg.	BB	SO	SB	PO	A	E	Avg.
						BATTING									FIELDING		
1997—Houston (N.L.)	2B	3	12	0	1	0	0	0	0	.083	1	0	0	4	8	1	.923
1998—Houston (N.L.)	2B	4	11	3	2	1	0	0	1	.182	4	4	0	9	10	1	.950
Division series totals (2 years)		7	23	3	3	1	0	0	1	.130	5	4	0	13	18	2	.939

ALL-STAR GAME RECORD

Year League	Pos.	AB	R	H	2B	3B	HR	RBI	Avg.	BB	SO	SB	PO	A	E	Avg.
					BATTING									FIELDING		
1991—National	C	1	0	0	0	0	0	0	.000	0	0	0	2	0	1	.667
1992—National	2B	2	0	0	0	0	0	0	.000	0	0	0	0	2	0	1.000
1994—National	2B	1	1	0	0	0	0	0	.000	0	0	0	2	1	0	1.000
1995—National	2B	2	1	1	0	0	1	1	.500	0	0	0	2	1	0	1.000
1996—National	2B	3	0	0	0	0	0	0	.000	0	1	0	1	1	0	1.000
1997—National	2B	3	0	0	0	0	0	0	.000	0	1	0	0	4	0	1.000
1998—National	2B	3	0	0	0	0	0	0	.000	0	3	0	2	4	0	1.000
All-Star Game totals (7 years)		15	2	1	0	0	1	2	.067	0	5	0	9	13	1	.957

BILLINGSLEY, BRENT   P   MARLINS

PERSONAL: Born April 19, 1975, in Downey, Calif. ... 6-2/200. ... Throws left, bats left. ... Full name: Brent Aaron Billingsley.
HIGH SCHOOL: Chino (Calif.).
COLLEGE: East Carolina, then Cal State Fullerton.
TRANSACTIONS/CAREER NOTES: Selected by Florida Marlins organization in fifth round of free-agent draft (June 2, 1996).
STATISTICAL NOTES: Tied for Eastern League lead with 24 home runs allowed in 1998.

Year Team (League)	W	L	Pct.	ERA	G	GS	CG	ShO	Sv.	IP	H	R	ER	BB	SO
1996—Utica (N.Y.-Penn)................	4	5	.444	4.01	15	•15	0	0	0	89²/₃	83	46	40	28	82
1997—Kane County (Midwest)......	14	7	.667	3.01	26	26	3	1	0	170²/₃	146	67	57	50	175
1998—Portland (Eastern).............	6	13	.316	3.74	28	28	0	0	0	171	172	90	71	70	*183

BLAIR, WILLIE   P   TIGERS

PERSONAL: Born December 18, 1965, in Paintsville, Ky. ... 6-1/185. ... Throws right, bats right. ... Full name: William Allen Blair.
HIGH SCHOOL: Johnson Central (Paintsville, Ky.).
COLLEGE: Morehead State.
TRANSACTIONS/CAREER NOTES: Selected by Toronto Blue Jays organization in 11th round of free-agent draft (June 2, 1986). ... Traded by Blue Jays to Cleveland Indians for P Alex Sanchez (November 6, 1990). ... Traded by Indians with C Eddie Taubensee to Houston Astros for OF Kenny Lofton and IF Dave Rohde (December 10, 1991). ... Selected by Colorado Rockies in first round (21st pick overall) of expansion draft (November 17, 1992). ... Granted free agency (December 20, 1994). ... Signed by Las Vegas, San Diego Padres organization (April 10, 1995). ... Re-signed by Padres (December 21, 1995). ... Re-signed by Padres (December 27, 1995). ... Traded by Padres with C Brian Johnson to Detroit Tigers for P Joey Eischen and P Cam Smith (December 17, 1996). ... On disabled list (May 5-June 3, 1997; included rehabilitation assignment to West Michigan (May 23-June 3). ... Granted free agency (October 27, 1997). ... Signed by Arizona Diamondbacks (December 6, 1997). ... Traded by Diamondbacks with C Jorge Fabregas and a player to be named later to New York Mets for OF Bernard Gilkey, P Nelson Figueroa and cash (July 31, 1998); Mets received cash to complete deal (September 3, 1998). ... Traded by Mets to Tigers for 3B/2B Joe Randa (December 4, 1998).
STATISTICAL NOTES: Combined with starter Pat Hentgen and Enrique Burgos in 2-1 no-hit victory for Dunedin against Osceola (May 10, 1988).

Year Team (League)	W	L	Pct.	ERA	G	GS	CG	ShO	Sv.	IP	H	R	ER	BB	SO
1986—St. Catharines (NYP).........	5	0	1.000	1.68	21	0	0	0	*12	53²/₃	32	10	10	20	55
1987—Dunedin (Fla. St.)	2	9	.182	4.43	50	0	0	0	13	85¹/₃	99	51	42	29	72
1988—Dunedin (Fla. St.)	2	0	1.000	2.70	4	0	0	0	0	6²/₃	5	2	2	4	5
—Knoxville (Southern)	5	5	.500	3.62	34	9	0	0	3	102	94	49	41	35	76
1989—Syracuse (Int'l)	5	6	.455	3.97	19	17	3	1	0	106²/₃	94	55	47	38	76
1990—Toronto (A.L.)	3	5	.375	4.06	27	6	0	0	0	68²/₃	66	33	31	28	43
—Syracuse (Int'l)	0	2	.000	4.74	3	3	1	0	0	19	20	13	10	8	6
1991—Colo. Springs (PCL)■......	9	6	.600	4.99	26	15	0	0	4	113²/₃	130	74	63	30	121
—Cleveland (A.L.)	2	3	.400	6.75	11	5	0	0	0	36	58	27	27	10	13
1992—Tucson (PCL)■.................	4	4	.500	2.39	21	2	1	0	2	52²/₃	50	20	14	12	35
—Houston (N.L.)	5	7	.417	4.00	29	8	0	0	0	78²/₃	74	47	35	25	48
1993—Colorado (N.L.)■..............	6	10	.375	4.75	46	18	0	0	0	146	184	90	77	42	84
1994—Colorado (N.L.)	0	5	.000	5.79	47	1	0	0	3	77²/₃	98	57	50	39	68

Year Team (League)	W	L	Pct.	ERA	G	GS	CG	ShO	Sv.	IP	H	R	ER	BB	SO
1995—San Diego (N.L.)■	7	5	.583	4.34	40	12	0	0	0	114	112	60	55	45	83
1996—San Diego (N.L.)	2	6	.250	4.60	60	0	0	0	1	88	80	52	45	29	67
1997—Detroit (A.L.)■■	16	8	.667	4.17	29	27	2	0	0	175	186	85	81	46	90
—West. Mich. (Mid.)	0	0	...	0.00	1	1	0	0	0	5	1	0	0	0	7
—Toledo (International)	0	0	...	0.00	1	1	0	0	0	7	1	1	0	2	4
1998—Arizona (N.L.)■	4	15	.211	5.34	23	23	0	0	0	146 2/3	165	91	87	51	71
—New York (N.L.)■	1	1	.500	3.14	11	2	0	0	0	28 2/3	23	10	10	10	21
A.L. totals (3 years)	21	16	.568	4.47	67	38	2	0	0	279 2/3	310	145	139	84	146
N.L. totals (6 years)	25	49	.338	4.75	256	64	1	0	4	679 2/3	736	407	359	241	442
Major league totals (9 years)	46	65	.414	4.67	323	102	3	0	4	959 1/3	1046	552	498	325	588

DIVISION SERIES RECORD

Year Team (League)	W	L	Pct.	ERA	G	GS	CG	ShO	Sv.	IP	H	R	ER	BB	SO
1996—San Diego (N.L.)	0	0	...	0.00	1	0	0	0	0	2	1	0	0	2	3

B

BLAKE, CASEY — 3B — BLUE JAYS

PERSONAL: Born August 23, 1973, in Des Moines, Iowa. ... 6-2/195. ... Bats right, throws right. ... Full name: William Casey Blake.
HIGH SCHOOL: Indianola (Iowa).
COLLEGE: Wichita State.
TRANSACTIONS/CAREER NOTES: Selected by Philadelphia Phillies organization in 11th round of free-agent draft (June 1, 1992); did not sign. ... Selected by New York Yankees organization in 45th round of free-agent draft (June 1, 1995); did not sign. ... Selected by Toronto Blue Jays organization in seventh round of free-agent draft (June 4, 1996).
STATISTICAL NOTES: Led Florida State League third basemen with 98 putouts and 39 errors in 1997.

Year Team (League)	Pos.	G	AB	R	H	2B	3B	HR	RBI	Avg.	BB	SO	SB	PO	A	E	Avg.
							BATTING								FIELDING		
1996—Hagerstown (SAL)......	3B-1B-OF	48	172	29	43	13	1	2	18	.250	11	40	5	33	83	12	.906
1997—Dunedin (Fla. St.)........	3B-SS	129	449	56	107	21	0	7	39	.238	48	91	19	†98	235	†39	.895
1998—Dunedin (Fla. St.)........	3B	88	340	62	119	28	3	11	65	*.350	30	81	9	64	183	16	.939
—Knoxville (Southern) ..	3B	45	172	41	64	15	4	7	38	.372	22	25	10	27	89	11	.913

BLAUSER, JEFF — SS — CUBS

PERSONAL: Born November 8, 1965, in Los Gatos, Calif. ... 6-1/190. ... Bats right, throws right. ... Full name: Jeffrey Michael Blauser. ... Name pronounced BLAU-zer.
HIGH SCHOOL: Placer (Sacramento).
COLLEGE: Sacramento City College.
TRANSACTIONS/CAREER NOTES: Selected by St. Louis Cardinals organization in first round (eighth pick overall) of free-agent draft (January 17, 1984); did not sign. ... Selected by Atlanta Braves organization in secondary phase of free-agent draft (June 4, 1984). ... On disabled list (May 14-30, 1990; May 2-20, 1994; and April 14-May 4 and July 16-September 1, 1996). ... Granted free agency (October 15, 1994). ... Re-signed by Braves (April 12, 1995). ... Granted free agency (November 2, 1997). ... Signed by Chicago Cubs (December 9, 1997). ... On disabled list (August 25-September 9, 1998).
HONORS: Named shortstop on THE SPORTING NEWS N.L. All-Star team (1997). ... Named shortstop on THE SPORTING NEWS N.L. Silver Slugger team (1997).
STATISTICAL NOTES: Led Carolina League shortstops with 506 total chances in 1986. ... Hit three home runs in one game (July 12, 1992). ... Led N.L. in being hit by pitch with 16 in 1993. ... Career major league grand slams: 4.

Year Team (League)	Pos.	G	AB	R	H	2B	3B	HR	RBI	Avg.	BB	SO	SB	PO	A	E	Avg.
							BATTING								FIELDING		
1984—Pulaski (Appalachian).	SS	62	217	41	54	6	1	3	24	.249	38	47	14	61	162	24	.903
1985—Sumter (S. Atl.).........	SS	125	422	74	99	19	0	5	49	.235	82	94	36	150	306	35	.929
1986—Durham (Carolina)......	SS	123	447	94	128	27	3	13	52	.286	81	92	36	167	*314	25	*.951
1987—Richmond (Int'l).........	SS-2B	33	113	11	20	1	0	1	12	.177	11	24	3	56	106	9	.947
—Atlanta (N.L.).............	SS	51	165	11	40	6	3	2	15	.242	18	34	7	65	166	9	.963
—Greenville (Southern) .	SS	72	265	35	66	13	3	4	32	.249	34	49	5	101	225	8	.976
1988—Richmond (Int'l).........	SS	69	271	40	77	19	1	5	23	.284	19	53	6	93	156	15	.943
—Atlanta (N.L.).............	2B-SS	18	67	7	16	3	1	2	7	.239	2	11	0	35	59	4	.959
1989—Atlanta (N.L.).............	3-2-S-O	142	456	63	123	24	2	12	46	.270	38	101	5	137	254	21	.949
1990—Atlanta (N.L.).............	S-2-3-O	115	386	46	104	24	3	8	39	.269	35	70	3	169	288	16	.966
1991—Atlanta (N.L.).............	SS-2B-3B	129	352	49	91	14	3	11	54	.259	54	59	5	136	219	17	.954
1992—Atlanta (N.L.).............	SS-2B-3B	123	343	61	90	19	3	14	46	.262	46	82	5	119	225	14	.961
1993—Atlanta (N.L.).............	SS	161	597	110	182	29	2	15	73	.305	85	109	16	189	426	19	.970
1994—Atlanta (N.L.).............	SS	96	380	56	98	21	4	6	45	.258	38	64	1	126	290	13	.970
1995—Atlanta (N.L.).............	SS	115	431	60	91	16	2	12	31	.211	57	107	8	151	337	15	.970
1996—Atlanta (N.L.).............	SS	83	265	48	65	14	1	10	35	.245	40	54	6	83	206	23	.926
1997—Atlanta (N.L.).............	SS-DH	151	519	90	160	31	4	17	70	.308	70	101	5	204	372	16	.973
1998—Chicago (N.L.)■.........	SS	119	361	49	79	11	3	4	26	.219	60	93	2	129	255	14	.965
Major league totals (12 years)		1303	4322	650	1139	212	31	113	487	.264	543	885	63	1543	3097	181	.962

DIVISION SERIES RECORD

Year Team (League)	Pos.	G	AB	R	H	2B	3B	HR	RBI	Avg.	BB	SO	SB	PO	A	E	Avg.
							BATTING								FIELDING		
1995—Atlanta (N.L.).............	SS	3	6	0	0	0	0	0	0	.000	1	3	0	5	11	1	.941
1996—Atlanta (N.L.).............	SS	3	9	0	1	00	0	0	0	.111	1	3	0	0	7	0	1.000
1997—Atlanta (N.L.).............	SS	3	10	2	3	0	0	1	4	.300	2	2	0	2	10	0	1.000
1998—Chicago (N.L.)...........	PH	2	2	0	0	0	0	0	0	.000	0	1	0	...	...	...	...
Division series totals (4 years)		11	27	2	4	0	0	1	4	.148	4	9	0	7	28	1	.972

CHAMPIONSHIP SERIES RECORD

RECORDS: Holds N.L. career record for most runs scored—18. ... Shares single-series record for most times hit by pitch—2 (1996).

Year Team (League)	Pos.	G	AB	R	H	2B	3B	HR	RBI	Avg.	BB	SO	SB	PO	A	E	Avg.
1991— Atlanta (N.L.)..............	SS-PH	2	2	0	0	0	0	0	0	.000	0	0	0	0	1	1	.500
1992— Atlanta (N.L.)..............	SS	7	24	3	5	0	1	1	4	.208	3	2	0	7	15	2	.917
1993— Atlanta (N.L.)..............	SS	6	25	5	7	1	0	2	4	.280	4	7	0	6	14	0	1.000
1995— Atlanta (N.L.)..............	SS	1	4	0	0	0	0	0	0	.000	1	2	0	4	6	0	1.000
1996— Atlanta (N.L.)..............	SS	7	17	5	3	0	1	0	2	.176	6	6	0	5	9	1	.933
1997— Atlanta (N.L.)..............	SS	6	20	5	6	0	0	1	1	.300	3	6	0	6	19	1	.962
Championship series totals (6 years)		29	92	18	21	1	2	4	11	.228	17	23	0	28	64	5	.948

WORLD SERIES RECORD

NOTES: Member of World Series championship team (1995); inactive.

Year Team (League)	Pos.	G	AB	R	H	2B	3B	HR	RBI	Avg.	BB	SO	SB	PO	A	E	Avg.
1991— Atlanta (N.L.)..............	SS-PH	5	6	0	1	0	0	0	0	.167	1	1	0	3	3	0	1.000
1992— Atlanta (N.L.)..............	SS	6	24	2	6	0	0	0	0	.250	1	9	2	7	22	0	1.000
1995— Atlanta (N.L.)..............						Did not play.											
1996— Atlanta (N.L.)..............	SS	6	18	2	3	1	0	0	1	.167	1	4	0	9	15	1	.960
World Series totals (3 years)		17	48	4	10	1	0	0	1	.208	3	14	2	19	40	1	.983

ALL-STAR GAME RECORD

Year League	Pos.	AB	R	H	2B	3B	HR	RBI	Avg.	BB	SO	SB	PO	A	E	Avg.
1993— National	SS	1	0	0	0	0	0	0	.000	0	1	0	1	2	1	.750
1997— National	SS	2	0	1	0	0	0	0	.500	0	0	0	1	1	0	1.000
All-Star Game totals (2 years)		3	0	1	0	0	0	0	.333	0	1	0	2	3	1	.833

BLOOD, DARIN — P — ORIOLES

PERSONAL: Born August 13, 1974, in Spokane, Wash. ... 6-2/180. ... Throws right, bats right. ... Full name: Darin C. Blood.
HIGH SCHOOL: Central Valley (Veradale, Wash.).
COLLEGE: Gonzaga.
TRANSACTIONS/CAREER NOTES: Selected by San Francisco Giants organization in third round of free-agent draft (June 1, 1995). ... Traded by Giants to Baltimore Orioles for OF/DH Joe Carter (July 24, 1998).
HONORS: Named California League Pitcher of the Year (1996).
STATISTICAL NOTES: Led California League with 26 wild pitches in 1996.

Year Team (League)	W	L	Pct.	ERA	G	GS	CG	ShO	Sv.	IP	H	R	ER	BB	SO
1995— Bellingham (N'west)..........	6	3	.667	2.54	14	13	0	0	0	74 1/3	63	26	21	32	78
1996— San Jose (California).........	*17	6	.739	*2.65	27	25	2	*2	0	170	140	59	50	71	*193
1997— Shreveport (Texas)............	8	10	.444	4.33	27	27	0	0	0	156	152	89	75	*83	90
1998— Fresno (Pacific Coast).......	4	5	.444	4.66	19	19	1	1	0	114	138	63	59	37	63
— Rochester (Int'l)■	3	2	.600	2.48	6	6	1	1	0	32 2/3	24	11	9	13	14

BLOWERS, MIKE — 3B/1B

PERSONAL: Born April 24, 1965, in Wurzburg, West Germany. ... 6-2/210. ... Bats right, throws right. ... Full name: Michael Roy Blowers.
HIGH SCHOOL: Bethel (Wash.).
JUNIOR COLLEGE: Tacoma (Wash.) Community College.
COLLEGE: Washington.
TRANSACTIONS/CAREER NOTES: Selected by Seattle Mariners organization in eighth round of free-agent draft (January 17, 1984); did not sign. ... Selected by San Francisco Giants organization in secondary phase of free-agent draft (June 4, 1984); did not sign. ... Selected by Baltimore Orioles organization in secondary phase of free-agent draft (January 9, 1985); did not sign. ... Selected by Montreal Expos organization in 10th round of free-agent draft (June 2, 1986). ... Traded by Expos to New York Yankees (August 31, 1989), completing deal in which Yankees traded P John Candelaria to Expos for a player to be named later (August 29, 1989). ... Traded by Yankees to Mariners for a player to be named later and cash (May 17, 1991); Yankees acquired P Jim Blueberg to complete deal (June 22, 1991). ... Traded by Mariners to Los Angeles Dodgers for 2B Miguel Cairo and 3B Willis Otanez (November 29, 1995). ... On disabled list (July 18, 1996-remainder of season). ... Granted free agency (October 15, 1996). ... Signed by Mariners organization (January 24, 1997). ... Granted free agency (October 28, 1997). ... Signed by Oakland Athletics (December 16, 1997). ... Granted free agency (October 23, 1998).
RECORDS: Shares major league single-month record for most grand slams—3 (August 1995). ... Shares A.L. single-game record for most errors by third baseman—4 (May 3, 1990).
STATISTICAL NOTES: Led Florida State League third basemen with .944 fielding percentage and 27 double plays in 1987. ... Led Southern League third basemen with 125 putouts and 27 double plays in 1988. ... Led American Association third basemen with .930 fielding percentage in 1989. ... Hit for the cycle (May 18, 1998). ... Career major league grand slams: 7.

Year Team (League)	Pos.	G	AB	R	H	2B	3B	HR	RBI	Avg.	BB	SO	SB	PO	A	E	Avg.
1986— Jamestown (NYP)	SS-3B	32	95	13	24	9	2	1	6	.253	17	18	3	48	73	16	.883
— GC Expos (GCL)	SS	31	115	14	25	3	1	2	17	.217	15	25	2	50	84	15	.899
1987— W.P. Beach (FSL)......	3B-SS-1B	136	491	68	124	30	3	16	71	.253	48	118	4	75	239	18	†.946
1988— Jacksonville (Sou.)....	3B-SS-2B	137	460	58	115	20	6	15	60	.250	68	114	6	†125	241	34	.915
1989— Indianapolis (A.A.).....	3B-SS	131	461	49	123	29	6	14	56	.267	41	109	3	91	214	23	†.930
— New York (A.L.)■..........	3B	13	38	2	10	0	0	0	3	.263	3	13	0	9	14	4	.852
1990— New York (A.L.)......	3B-DH	48	144	16	27	4	0	5	21	.188	12	50	1	26	63	10	.899
— Columbus (Int'l)..........	3B-1B-2B	62	230	30	78	20	6	6	50	.339	29	40	3	64	89	8	.950
1991— New York (A.L.)......	3B	15	35	3	7	0	0	1	1	.200	4	3	0	4	16	3	.870
— Calgary (PCL)■..........	3B-SS-1B	90	329	56	95	20	2	9	59	.289	40	74	3	56	163	19	.920
1992— Calgary (PCL)............	3B-1B-OF	83	300	56	95	28	2	9	67	.317	50	64	2	99	87	5	.974
— Seattle (A.L.)............	3B-1B	31	73	7	14	3	0	1	2	.192	6	20	0	28	44	1	.986

Year	Team (League)	Pos.	G	AB	R	H	2B	3B	HR	RBI	Avg.	BB	SO	SB	PO	A	E	Avg.
1993—	Seattle (A.L.)	3-DH-O-1-C	127	379	55	106	23	3	15	57	.280	44	98	1	70	225	15	.952
1994—	Seattle (A.L.)	3-1-DH-O	85	270	37	78	13	0	9	49	.289	25	60	2	142	109	9	.965
1995—	Seattle (A.L.)	3B-1B-OF	134	439	59	113	24	1	23	96	.257	53	128	2	116	174	16	.948
1996—	Los Angeles (N.L.)■..	3B-1B-SS	92	317	31	84	19	2	6	38	.265	37	77	0	76	122	9	.957
1997—	Seattle (A.L.)■	1-3-O-DH	68	150	22	44	5	0	5	20	.293	21	33	0	271	35	4	.987
1998—	Oakland (A.L.)■	3B-1B-DH	129	409	56	97	24	2	11	71	.237	39	116	1	113	174	19	.938
	American League totals (9 years)		650	1937	257	496	96	6	70	320	.256	207	521	7	779	854	81	.953
	National League totals (1 year)		92	317	31	84	19	2	6	38	.265	37	77	0	76	122	9	.957
	Major league totals (10 years)		742	2254	288	580	115	8	76	358	.257	244	598	7	855	976	90	.953

DIVISION SERIES RECORD

Year	Team (League)	Pos.	G	AB	R	H	2B	3B	HR	RBI	Avg.	BB	SO	SB	PO	A	E	Avg.
1995—	Seattle (A.L.)	3B-1B	5	18	0	3	0	0	0	1	.167	3	7	0	2	6	0	1.000
1997—	Seattle (A.L.)	3B	3	5	0	1	0	0	0	0	.200	0	3	0	1	2	0	1.000
	Division series totals (2 years)		8	23	0	4	0	0	0	1	.174	3	10	0	3	8	0	1.000

CHAMPIONSHIP SERIES RECORD

NOTES: Hit home run in first at-bat (October 10, 1995).

Year	Team (League)	Pos.	G	AB	R	H	2B	3B	HR	RBI	Avg.	BB	SO	SB	PO	A	E	Avg.
1995—	Seattle (A.L.)	3B	6	18	1	4	0	0	1	2	.222	0	4	0	5	9	0	1.000

B

BLUMA, JAIME   P   ROYALS

PERSONAL: Born May 18, 1972, in Beaufort, S.C. ... 5-11/195. ... Throws right, bats right. ... Full name: James Andrew Bluma.
HIGH SCHOOL: Owasso (Okla.).
COLLEGE: Wichita State.
TRANSACTIONS/CAREER NOTES: Selected by Kansas City Royals organization in third round of free-agent draft (June 2, 1994). ... On disabled list (March 28, 1997-entire season). ... Granted free agency (December 21, 1998). ... Re-signed by Royals organization (December 21, 1998).

Year	Team (League)	W	L	Pct.	ERA	G	GS	CG	ShO	Sv.	IP	H	R	ER	BB	SO
1994—	Eugene (Northwest)	2	1	.667	0.99	26	0	0	0	12	36 1/3	19	5	4	6	35
	Wilmington (Caro.).............	4	0	1.000	0.93	7	0	0	0	2	9 2/3	7	2	1	0	5
1995—	Wichita (Texas)	4	3	.571	3.09	42	0	0	0	22	55 1/3	38	19	19	9	31
	Omaha (Am. Assoc.)	0	0	. . .	3.04	18	0	0	0	4	23 2/3	21	13	8	14	12
1996—	Omaha (Am. Assoc.)	1	2	.333	3.12	52	0	0	0	25	57 2/3	57	22	20	20	40
	Kansas City (A.L.)	0	0	. . .	3.60	17	0	0	0	5	20	18	9	8	4	14
1997—									Did not play.							
1998—	Omaha (Pacific Coast)........	0	1	.000	6.28	14	0	0	0	2	14 1/3	19	13	10	7	8
	Wichita (Texas)	1	2	.333	5.37	39	0	0	0	0	62	67	49	37	35	38
	Major league totals (1 year)........	0	0	. . .	3.60	17	0	0	0	5	20	18	9	8	4	14

BOCACHICA, HIRAM   OF   DODGERS

PERSONAL: Born March 4, 1976, in Ponce, Puerto Rico. ... 5-11/165. ... Bats right, throws right. ... Full name: Hiram Colon Bocachica.
HIGH SCHOOL: Rexville (Bayamon, Puerto Rico).
TRANSACTIONS/CAREER NOTES: Selected by Montreal Expos organization in first round (21st pick overall) of free-agent draft (June 2, 1994). ... On West Palm Beach disabled list (May 16-July 12, 1996). ... On Harrisburg suspended list (June 15-18, 1997). ... On Harrisburg disabled list (June 18-25, 1997). ... Traded by Expos with P Carlos Perez and SS Mark Grudzielanek to Los Angeles Dodgers for 2B Wilton Guerrero, P Ted Lilly, OF Peter Bergeron and 1B Jonathan Tucker (July 31, 1998).
STATISTICAL NOTES: Led South Atlantic League shortstops with 58 errors in 1995.

Year	Team (League)	Pos.	G	AB	R	H	2B	3B	HR	RBI	Avg.	BB	SO	SB	PO	A	E	Avg.
1994—	GC Expos (GCL)	SS	43	168	31	47	9	0	5	16	.280	15	42	11	72	126	*23	.896
1995—	Albany (S. Atl.)	SS-2B	96	380	65	108	20	10	2	30	.284	52	78	47	165	265	†58	.881
1996—	W.P. Beach (FSL).........	SS	71	267	50	90	17	5	2	26	.337	34	47	21	37	83	24	.833
	G.C. Expos (GCL)	DH	9	32	11	8	3	0	0	2	.250	5	3	2	. . .	. . .	. . .	. . .
1997—	Harrisburg (East.).......	SS-2B	119	443	82	123	19	3	11	35	.278	41	98	29	135	186	32	.909
1998—	Harrisburg (East.).......	OF	80	296	39	78	18	4	4	27	.264	21	61	20	171	4	10	.946
	Ottawa (Int'l)	OF	12	41	5	8	3	1	0	5	.195	6	14	2	23	1	0	1.000
	Albuquerque (PCL)■..	OF	26	101	16	24	7	1	4	16	.238	13	24	5	80	2	2	.976

BOCHTLER, DOUG   P

PERSONAL: Born July 5, 1970, in West Palm Beach, Fla. ... 6-3/200. ... Throws right, bats right. ... Full name: Douglas Eugene Bochtler. ... Name pronounced BOCK-ler.
HIGH SCHOOL: John I. Leonard (Lake Worth, Fla.).
JUNIOR COLLEGE: Indian River Community College (Fla.).
TRANSACTIONS/CAREER NOTES: Selected by Montreal Expos organization in ninth round of free-agent draft (June 5, 1989). ... On disabled list (June 18-September 6, 1992). ... Selected by Colorado Rockies in second round (32nd pick overall) of expansion draft (November 17, 1992). ... On Colorado Springs disabled list (April 18-26, 1993). ... Traded by Rockies with C Brad Ausmus and a player to be named later to San Diego Padres for P Bruce Hurst and P Greg W. Harris (July 26, 1993); Padres acquired P Andy Ashby to complete deal (July 27, 1993). On disabled list (June 16-24 and August 24, 1994-remainder of season). ... On disabled list (July 2-17, 1997). ... Traded by Padres with IF Jorge Velandia to Oakland Athletics for P Don Wengert and IF David Newhan (November 26, 1997). ... Traded by A's to Detroit Tigers for cash (March 25, 1998). ... Claimed on waivers by Los Angeles Dodgers (October 6, 1998). ... Released by Dodgers (January 11, 1999).

Year—Team (League)	W	L	Pct.	ERA	G	GS	CG	ShO	Sv.	IP	H	R	ER	BB	SO
1989— GC Expos (GCL)	2	2	.500	3.21	9	9	1	0	0	47 2/3	46	22	17	20	45
1990— Rockford (Midwest)	9	12	.429	3.50	25	25	1	1	0	139	142	82	54	54	109
1991— W.P. Beach (FSL)	•12	9	.571	2.92	26	24	7	2	0	160 1/3	148	63	52	55	109
1992— Harrisburg (Eastern)	6	5	.545	2.32	13	13	2	1	0	77 2/3	50	25	20	36	89
1993— Colo. Springs (PCL)■	1	4	.200	6.93	12	11	0	0	0	50 2/3	71	41	39	26	38
— Central Valley (Cal.)	3	1	.750	3.40	8	8	0	0	0	47 2/3	40	23	18	28	43
— Las Vegas (PCL)■	0	5	.000	5.22	7	7	1	0	0	39 2/3	52	26	23	11	30
1994— Las Vegas (PCL)	3	7	.300	5.20	22	20	2	1	0	100 1/3	116	67	58	48	86
1995— Las Vegas (PCL)	2	3	.400	4.25	18	2	0	0	1	36	31	18	17	26	32
— San Diego (N.L.)	4	4	.500	3.57	34	0	0	0	1	45 1/3	38	18	18	19	45
1996— San Diego (N.L.)	2	4	.333	3.02	63	0	0	0	3	65 2/3	45	25	22	39	68
1997— San Diego (N.L.)	3	6	.333	4.77	54	0	0	0	2	60 1/3	51	35	32	50	46
1998— Detroit (A.L.)■	0	2	.000	6.15	51	0	0	0	0	67 1/3	73	48	46	42	45
A.L. totals (1 year)	0	2	.000	6.15	51	0	0	0	0	67 1/3	73	48	46	42	45
N.L. totals (3 years)	9	14	.391	3.78	151	0	0	0	6	171 1/3	134	78	72	108	159
Major league totals (4 years)	9	16	.360	4.45	202	0	0	0	6	238 2/3	207	126	118	150	204

DIVISION SERIES RECORD

Year—Team (League)	W	L	Pct.	ERA	G	GS	CG	ShO	Sv.	IP	H	R	ER	BB	SO
1996— San Diego (N.L.)	0	1	.000	27.00	1	0	0	0	0	1/3	0	1	1	3	0

BOEHRINGER, BRIAN   P   PADRES

PERSONAL: Born January 8, 1970, in St. Louis. ... 6-2/190. ... Throws right, bats both. ... Full name: Brian Edward Boehringer. ... Name pronounced BO-ring-er.
HIGH SCHOOL: Northwest (House Springs, Mo.).
JUNIOR COLLEGE: St. Louis Community College at Meramec.
COLLEGE: UNLV.
TRANSACTIONS/CAREER NOTES: Selected by Houston Astros organization in 10th round of free-agent draft (June 4, 1990); did not sign. ... Selected by Chicago White Sox organization in fourth round of free-agent draft (June 3, 1991). ... On Utica disabled list (June 29-August 25, 1991). ... On disabled list (June 24-August 25, 1992). ... Traded by White Sox organization to New York Yankees for P Paul Assenmacher (March 21, 1994). ... Placed on New York disabled list (May 27-August 19, 1997); included rehabilitation assignments to Gulf Coast Yankees (August 10-12) and Tampa (August 13-19). ... Selected by Tampa Bay Devil Rays in second round (30th pick overall) of expansion draft (November 18, 1997). ... Traded by Devil Rays with SS Andy Sheets to San Diego Padres for C John Flaherty (November 18, 1997).
STATISTICAL NOTES: Tied for Eastern League lead with four balks in 1994. ... Led International League with 11 hit batsmen in 1996.

Year—Team (League)	W	L	Pct.	ERA	G	GS	CG	ShO	Sv.	IP	H	R	ER	BB	SO
1991— GC White Sox (GCL)	1	1	.500	6.57	5	1	0	0	0	12 1/3	14	9	9	5	10
— Utica (N.Y.-Penn)	1	1	.500	2.37	4	4	0	0	0	19	14	8	5	8	19
1992— South Bend (Mid.)	6	7	.462	4.38	15	15	2	0	0	86 1/3	87	52	42	40	59
1993— Sarasota (Florida State)	10	4	.714	2.80	18	17	3	0	0	119	103	47	37	51	92
— Birmingham (Southern)	2	1	.667	3.54	7	7	1	0	0	40 2/3	41	20	16	14	29
1994— Alb./Colon. (East.)■	10	11	.476	3.62	27	27	5	1	0	171 2/3	165	85	69	57	145
1995— New York (A.L.)	0	3	.000	13.75	7	3	0	0	0	17 2/3	24	27	27	22	10
— Columbus (Int'l)	8	6	.571	2.77	17	17	3	0	0	104	101	39	32	31	58
1996— Columbus (Int'l)	11	7	.611	4.00	25	25	3	1	0	153	155	79	68	56	132
— New York (A.L.)	2	4	.333	5.44	15	3	0	0	0	46 1/3	46	28	28	21	37
1997— New York (A.L.)	3	2	.600	2.63	34	0	0	0	0	48	39	16	14	32	53
— GC Yankees (GCL)	0	0	. . .	0.00	1	1	0	0	0	2	1	0	0	0	2
— Tampa (Fla. St.)	0	1	.000	5.00	3	3	0	0	0	9	9	5	5	5	8
1998— San Diego (N.L.)■	5	2	.714	4.36	56	1	0	0	0	76 1/3	75	38	37	45	67
A.L. totals (3 years)	5	9	.357	5.54	56	6	0	0	0	112	109	71	69	75	100
N.L. totals (1 year)	5	2	.714	4.36	56	1	0	0	0	76 1/3	75	38	37	45	67
Major league totals (4 years)	10	11	.476	5.07	112	7	0	0	0	188 1/3	184	109	106	120	167

DIVISION SERIES RECORD

Year—Team (League)	W	L	Pct.	ERA	G	GS	CG	ShO	Sv.	IP	H	R	ER	BB	SO
1996— New York (A.L.)	1	0	1.000	6.75	2	0	0	0	0	1 1/3	3	2	1	2	0
1997— New York (A.L.)	0	0	. . .	0.00	1	0	0	0	0	1 2/3	1	0	0	1	2
1998— San Diego (N.L.)								Did not play.							
Div. series totals (2 years)	1	0	1.000	3.00	3	0	0	0	0	3	4	2	1	3	2

CHAMPIONSHIP SERIES RECORD

Year—Team (League)	W	L	Pct.	ERA	G	GS	CG	ShO	Sv.	IP	H	R	ER	BB	SO
1998— San Diego (N.L.)	0	0	. . .	0.00	3	0	0	0	0	3	3	0	0	1	1

WORLD SERIES RECORD

NOTES: Member of World Series championship team (1996).

Year—Team (League)	W	L	Pct.	ERA	G	GS	CG	ShO	Sv.	IP	H	R	ER	BB	SO
1996— New York (A.L.)	0	0	. . .	5.40	2	0	0	0	0	5	5	5	3	0	5
1998— San Diego (N.L.)	0	0	. . .	9.00	2	0	0	0	0	2	4	2	2	2	3
World Series totals (2 years)	0	0	. . .	6.43	4	0	0	0	0	7	9	7	5	2	8

BOGAR, TIM   IF   ASTROS

PERSONAL: Born October 28, 1966, in Indianapolis. ... 6-2/198. ... Bats right, throws right. ... Full name: Timothy Paul Bogar.
HIGH SCHOOL: Buffalo Grove (Ill.).
COLLEGE: Eastern Illinois.
TRANSACTIONS/CAREER NOTES: Selected by New York Mets organization in eighth round of free-agent draft (June 2, 1987). ... On disabled list (June 14, 1990-remainder of season). ... On disabled list (August 16-September 1, 1993). ... On New York disabled list (May 6-June 9, 1994); included rehabilitation assignment to Norfolk (June 4-9). ... Traded by Mets to Houston Astros for IF Luis Lopez (March 31, 1997). ... On disabled list (September 5, 1997-remainder of season). ... Granted free agency (October 23, 1998). ... Re-signed by Astros (December 7, 1998).
MISCELLANEOUS: Played all nine positions in one game for Tidewater (September 4, 1991).

Year	Team (League)	Pos.	G	AB	R	H	2B	3B	HR	RBI	Avg.	BB	SO	SB	PO	A	E	Avg.
1987—Little Falls (NYP).......	SS-2B	58	205	31	48	9	0	0	23	.234	18	39	2	79	194	24	.919
1988—Columbia (S. Atl.).......	2B-SS	45	142	19	40	4	2	3	21	.282	22	29	5	89	120	8	.963
—St. Lucie (Fla. St.)......	2B-SS-3B	76	236	34	65	7	1	2	30	.275	34	57	9	141	214	19	.949
1989—Jackson (Texas)........	SS	112	406	44	108	13	5	4	45	.266	41	57	8	185	351	29	.949
1990—Tidewater (Int'l).........	SS	33	117	10	19	2	0	0	4	.162	8	22	1	57	89	10	.936
1991—Williamsport (East.) ...	3-2-1-S	63	243	33	61	12	2	2	25	.251	20	44	13	100	137	8	.967
—Tidewater (Int'l).....S-2-3-C-1-O-P		65	218	23	56	11	0	1	23	.257	20	35	1	111	183	11	.964
1992—Tidewater (Int'l).........	2-S-3-P-1	129	481	54	134	32	1	5	38	.279	14	65	7	211	327	15	.973
1993—New York (N.L.).........	SS-3B-2B	78	205	19	50	13	0	3	25	.244	14	29	0	105	217	9	.973
1994—New York (N.L.).........	3-1-S-2-O	50	52	5	8	0	0	2	5	.154	4	11	1	77	38	1	.991
—Norfolk (Int'l)...........	3B-2B	5	19	0	2	0	0		1	.105	1	4	0	5	11	0	1.000
1995—New York (N.L.).........	S-3-1-2-O	78	145	17	42	7	0	1	21	.290	9	25	1	82	100	6	.968
1996—New York (N.L.).........	1-3-S-2	91	89	17	19	4	0	0	6	.213	8	20	1	104	61	1	.994
1997—Houston (N.L.)■.......	SS-3B-1B	97	241	30	60	14	4	4	30	.249	24	42	4	110	229	6	.983
1998—Houston (N.L.).........	S-2-3-DH	79	156	12	24	4	1	1	8	.154	9	36	2	63	147	3	.986
Major league totals (6 years)		473	888	100	203	42	5	11	95	.229	68	163	9	541	792	26	.981

RECORD AS PITCHER

Year	Team (League)	W	L	Pct.	ERA	G	GS	CG	ShO	Sv.	IP	H	R	ER	BB	SO
1991—Tidewater (Int'l)................	0	0	...	27.00	1	0	0	0	0	1/3	0	1	1	0	1
1992—Tidewater (Int'l)................	0	0	...	12.00	3	0	0	0	0	3	4	4	4	3	1

BOGGS, WADE — 3B — DEVIL RAYS

B

PERSONAL: Born June 15, 1958, in Omaha, Neb. ... 6-2/197. ... Bats left, throws right. ... Full name: Wade Anthony Boggs.

HIGH SCHOOL: H.B. Plant (Tampa).

JUNIOR COLLEGE: Hillsborough Community College (Fla.).

TRANSACTIONS/CAREER NOTES: Selected by Boston Red Sox organization in seventh round of free-agent draft (June 8, 1976). ... On disabled list (April 20-May 2, 1979). ... Granted free agency (October 26, 1992). ... Signed by New York Yankees (December 15, 1992). ... Granted free agency (November 11, 1995). ... Re-signed by Yankees (December 5, 1995). ... Granted free agency (November 1, 1997). ... Signed by Tampa Bay Devil Rays (December 9, 1997). ... On disabled list (April 18-May 8, 1998).

RECORDS: Shares major league single-season records for most games with at least one hit—135 (1985); fewest chances accepted by third baseman (150 or more games)—349 (1990); and fewest double plays by third baseman (150 or more games)—17 (1988). ... Holds A.L. records for most consecutive seasons with 200 or more hits—7 (1983-89); and most seasons and consecutive seasons leading league in intentional bases on balls received—6 (1987-92). ... Holds A.L. single-season record for most singles—187 (1985). ... Holds A.L. rookie-season record for highest batting average (100 or more games)—.349 (1982). ... Shares A.L. single-season record for fewest putouts by third baseman for leader—121 (1986); and fewest double plays by third baseman (150 or more games)—17 (1988).

HONORS: Named third baseman on THE SPORTING NEWS A.L. All-Star team (1983, 1985-88, 1991 and 1994). ... Named third baseman on THE SPORTING NEWS A.L. Silver Slugger team (1983, 1986-89, 1991 and 1993-94). ... Won A.L. Gold Glove at third base (1994-95).

STATISTICAL NOTES: Led Eastern League third basemen with .953 fielding percentage in 1979. ... Led International League with .3353 batting average in 1981. ... Led A.L with .449 on-base percentage in 1983, .450 in 1985, .453 in 1986, .461 in 1987, .476 in 1988 and .430 in 1989. ... Led A.L. third basemen with 30 double plays in 1984, 37 in 1987, 29 in 1989 and 29 in 1993. ... Had 28-game hitting streak (June 24-July 26, 1985). ... Led A.L. third basemen with 486 total chances in 1985. ... Had 20-game hitting streak (August 29-September 18, 1986). ... Had 25-game hitting streak (May 28-June 24, 1987). ... Led A.L. with 19 intentional bases on balls received in 1987, 1989, 1990 and 1992, with 25 in 1991 and tied for lead with 18 in 1988. ... Led A.L. in grounding into double plays with 23 in 1988. ... Led A.L. third basemen with .981 fielding percentage in 1995. ... Career major league grand slams: 4.

Year	Team (League)	Pos.	G	AB	R	H	2B	3B	HR	RBI	Avg.	BB	SO	SB	PO	A	E	Avg.
1976—Elmira (N.Y.-Penn.)......	3B	57	179	29	47	6	0	0	15	.263	29	15	2	36	75	16	.874
1977—Win.-Salem (Car.)......	3B-2B-SS	117	422	67	140	13	1	2	55	.332	65	22	8	145	223	27	.932
1978—Bristol (Eastern)........	3-S-2-O	109	354	63	110	14	2	1	32	.311	53	25	1	62	107	7	.960
1979—Bristol (Eastern)........	3B-SS-2B	113	406	56	132	17	2	0	41	.325	66	21	11	94	213	15	†.953
1980—Pawtucket (Int'l)........	3B-1B	129	418	51	128	21	0	1	45	.306	64	25	3	108	156	12	.957
1981—Pawtucket (Int'l)........	3B-1B	137	498	67	*167	*41	3	5	60	*.335	89	41	4	359	238	26	.958
1982—Boston (A.L.)...........	1-3-DH-O	104	338	51	118	14	1	5	44	.349	35	21	1	489	168	8	.988
1983—Boston (A.L.)...........	3B	153	582	100	210	44	7	5	74	*.361	92	36	3	118	368	*27	.947
1984—Boston (A.L.)...........	3B	158	625	109	203	31	4	6	55	.325	89	44	3	141	330	•20	.959
1985—Boston (A.L.)...........	3B	161	653	107	*240	42	3	8	78	*.368	96	61	2	134	335	17	.965
1986—Boston (A.L.)...........	3B	149	580	107	207	47	2	8	71	*.357	*105	44	0	*121	267	19	.953
1987—Boston (A.L.)...........	3B-1B-DH	147	551	108	200	40	6	24	89	*.363	105	48	1	112	277	14	.965
1988—Boston (A.L.)...........	3B-DH	155	584	*128	214	*45	6	5	58	*.366	*125	34	2	*122	250	11	.971
1989—Boston (A.L.)...........	3B-DH	156	621	•113	205	*51	7	3	54	.330	107	51	2	*123	264	17	.958
1990—Boston (A.L.)...........	3B-DH	155	619	89	187	44	5	6	63	.302	87	68	0	108	241	20	.946
1991—Boston (A.L.)...........	3B	144	546	93	181	42	2	8	51	.332	89	32	1	89	276	12	.968
1992—Boston (A.L.)...........	3B-DH	143	514	62	133	22	4	7	50	.259	74	31	1	70	229	15	.952
1993—New York (A.L.)■.......	3B-DH	143	560	83	169	26	1	2	59	.302	74	49	0	75	*311	12	*.970
1994—New York (A.L.)........	3B-1B	97	366	61	125	19	1	11	55	.342	61	29	2	66	218	10	.966
1995—New York (A.L.)........	3B-1B	126	460	76	149	22	4	5	63	.324	74	50	1	114	198	5	†.984
1996—New York (A.L.)........	3B-DH	132	501	80	156	29	2	2	41	.311	67	32	1	62	201	7	.974
1997—New York (A.L.)........	3B-DH-P	104	353	55	103	23	1	4	28	.292	48	38	0	42	140	4	.978
1998—Tampa Bay (A.L.)■......	3B-DH	123	435	51	122	23	4	7	52	.280	46	54	3	52	131	5	.973
Major league totals (17 years)		2350	8888	1473	2922	564	60	116	985	.329	1374	722	23	2038	4204	223	.966

DIVISION SERIES RECORD

Year	Team (League)	Pos.	G	AB	R	H	2B	3B	HR	RBI	Avg.	BB	SO	SB	PO	A	E	Avg.
1995—New York (A.L.).........	3B	4	19	4	5	2	0	1	3	.263	3	5	0	4	8	0	1.000
1996—New York (A.L.).........	3B	3	12	0	1	1	0	0	0	.083	0	2	0	2	1	0	1.000
1997—New York (A.L.).........	3B-PH	3	7	1	3	0	0	0	2	.429	0	0	0	0	1	0	1.000
Division series totals (3 years)		10	38	5	9	3	0	1	5	.237	3	7	0	6	10	0	1.000

CHAMPIONSHIP SERIES RECORD

RECORDS: Shares single-series record for most sacrifice flies—2 (1988).

Year Team (League)	Pos.	G	AB	R	H	2B	3B	HR	RBI	Avg.	BB	SO	SB	PO	A	E	Avg.
1986— Boston (A.L.).............	3B	7	30	3	7	1	1	0	2	.233	4	1	0	7	13	2	.909
1988— Boston (A.L.).............	3B	4	13	2	5	0	0	0	3	.385	3	4	0	6	6	0	1.000
1990— Boston (A.L.).............	3B	4	16	1	7	1	0	1	1	.438	0	3	0	6	10	0	1.000
1996— New York (A.L.).........	3B	3	15	1	2	0	0	0	0	.133	1	3	0	2	11	0	1.000
Championship series totals (4 years)		18	74	7	21	2	1	1	6	.284	8	11	0	21	40	2	.968

WORLD SERIES RECORD

NOTES: Member of World Series championship team (1996).

Year Team (League)	Pos.	G	AB	R	H	2B	3B	HR	RBI	Avg.	BB	SO	SB	PO	A	E	Avg.
1986— Boston (A.L.).............	3B	7	31	3	9	3	0	0	3	.290	4	2	0	4	15	0	1.000
1996— New York (A.L.).........	3B-PH	4	11	0	3	1	0	0	2	.273	1	0	0	0	0	0	...
World Series totals (2 years)		11	42	3	12	4	0	0	5	.286	5	2	0	4	15	0	1.000

ALL-STAR GAME RECORD

Year League	Pos.	AB	R	H	2B	3B	HR	RBI	Avg.	BB	SO	SB	PO	A	E	Avg.
1985— American	3B	0	0	0	0	0	0	0	...	1	0	0	0	0	0	...
1986— American	3B	3	0	1	0	0	0	0	.333	1	0	0	0	1	0	1.000
1987— American	3B	3	0	0	0	0	0	0	.000	0	0	0	0	3	0	1.000
1988— American	3B	3	0	1	0	0	0	0	.333	0	0	0	0	1	0	1.000
1989— American	3B	3	1	1	0	0	1	1	.333	0	0	0	1	1	0	1.000
1990— American	3B	2	0	2	0	0	0	0	1.000	1	0	0	0	4	0	1.000
1991— American	3B	2	1	1	0	0	0	0	.500	1	0	0	1	2	0	1.000
1992— American	3B	3	1	1	0	0	0	0	.333	0	1	0	1	0	0	1.000
1993— American	3B	1	0	0	0	0	0	0	.000	1	0	0	0	0	0	1.000
1994— American	3B	3	1	1	0	0	0	0	.333	0	2	0	0	2	0	1.000
1995— American	3B	2	0	1	0	0	0	0	.500	0	0	0	0	1	0	1.000
1996— American	3B	3	0	0	0	0	0	0	.000	0	0	0	1	2	0	1.000
All-Star Game totals (12 years)		28	4	9	0	0	1	1	.321	5	3	0	5	17	0	1.000

RECORD AS PITCHER

Year Team (League)	W	L	Pct.	ERA	G	GS	CG	ShO	Sv.	IP	H	R	ER	BB	SO
1997— New York (A.L.).................	0	0	...	0.00	1	0	0	0	0	1	0	0	0	1	1

BOHANON, BRIAN   P   ROCKIES

PERSONAL: Born August 1, 1968, in Denton, Texas. ... 6-2/240. ... Throws left, bats left. ... Full name: Brian Edward Bohanon Jr.

HIGH SCHOOL: North Shore (Houston).

TRANSACTIONS/CAREER NOTES: Selected by Texas Rangers organization in first round (19th pick overall) of free-agent draft (June 2, 1987). ... On disabled list (April 17, 1988-remainder of season). ... On Charlotte disabled list (April 7-May 2, 1989). ... On Texas disabled list (April 7-July 1, 1991); included rehabilitation assignments to Charlotte (June 1-10), Tulsa (June 10-23) and Oklahoma City (June 23-30). ... On Texas disabled list (April 28-May 13, 1992). ... On Texas disabled list (June 9-30, 1993); included rehabilitation assignment to Oklahoma City (June 21-30). ... Granted free agency (December 23, 1994). ... Signed by Detroit Tigers organization (March 6, 1995). ... Released by Tigers (October 13, 1995). ... Signed by Toronto Blue Jays organization (February 20, 1996). ... Granted free agency (October 3, 1996). ... Signed by New York Mets organization (December 18, 1996). ... Traded by Mets to Los Angeles Dodgers for P Greg McMichael and cash (July 10, 1998). ... Granted free agency (October 27, 1998). ... Signed by Colorado Rockies (November 9, 1998).

MISCELLANEOUS: Singled and struck out once in two appearances as pinch hitter (1997).

Year Team (League)	W	L	Pct.	ERA	G	GS	CG	ShO	Sv.	IP	H	R	ER	BB	SO
1987— GC Rangers (GCL).............	0	2	.000	4.71	5	4	0	0	0	21	15	13	11	5	21
1988— Charlotte (Fla. St.)..............	0	1	.000	5.40	2	2	0	0	0	6²/₃	6	4	4	5	9
1989— Charlotte (Fla. St.)..............	0	3	.000	1.81	11	7	0	0	1	54²/₃	40	16	11	20	33
— Tulsa (Texas)	5	0	1.000	2.20	11	11	1	1	0	73²/₃	59	20	18	27	44
1990— Texas (A.L.)	0	3	.000	6.62	11	6	0	0	0	34	40	30	25	18	15
— Oklahoma City (A.A.)........	1	2	.333	3.66	14	4	0	0	1	32	35	16	13	8	22
1991— Charlotte (Fla. St.)	1	0	1.000	3.86	2	2	0	0	0	11²/₃	6	5	5	4	7
— Tulsa (Texas)	0	1	.000	2.31	2	2	0	0	0	11²/₃	9	8	3	11	6
— Oklahoma City (A.A.)........	0	4	.000	2.91	7	7	0	0	0	46¹/₃	49	19	15	15	37
— Texas (A.L.)	4	3	.571	4.84	11	11	1	0	0	61¹/₃	66	35	33	23	34
1992— Oklahoma City (A.A.)........	4	2	.667	2.73	9	9	3	0	0	56	53	21	17	15	24
— Texas (A.L.)	1	1	.500	6.31	18	7	0	0	0	45²/₃	57	38	32	25	29
— Tulsa (Texas)	2	1	.667	1.27	6	6	1	0	0	28¹/₃	25	7	4	9	25
1993— Texas (A.L.)	4	4	.500	4.76	36	8	0	0	0	92²/₃	107	54	49	46	45
— Oklahoma City (A.A.)........	0	1	.000	6.43	2	2	0	0	0	7	7	6	5	3	7
1994— Oklahoma City (A.A.)........	5	10	.333	4.12	15	15	2	1	0	98¹/₃	106	56	45	33	88
— Texas (A.L.)	2	2	.500	7.23	11	5	0	0	0	37¹/₃	51	31	30	8	26
1995— Detroit (A.L.)■..................	1	1	.500	5.54	52	10	0	0	1	105²/₃	121	68	65	41	63
1996— Toronto (A.L.)■................	0	1	.000	7.77	20	0	0	0	1	22	27	19	19	19	17
— Syracuse (Int'l).................	4	3	.571	3.86	31	0	0	0	0	58¹/₃	56	29	25	17	38
1997— Norfolk (Int'l)■.................	9	3	.750	2.63	15	14	4	2	0	96	88	37	28	32	84
— New York (N.L.)................	6	4	.600	3.82	19	14	0	0	0	94¹/₃	95	49	40	34	66
1998— New York (N.L.)................	2	4	.333	3.15	25	4	0	0	0	54¹/₃	47	21	19	21	39
— Los Angeles (N.L.)■.........	5	7	.417	2.40	14	14	2	0	0	97¹/₃	74	35	26	36	72
A.L. totals (7 years)	12	15	.444	5.71	159	47	1	0	2	398²/₃	469	275	253	180	229
N.L. totals (2 years)	13	15	.464	3.11	58	32	2	0	0	246	216	105	85	91	177
Major league totals (9 years)......	25	30	.455	4.72	217	79	3	0	2	644²/₃	685	380	338	271	406

BOLICK, FRANK   3B/1B

PERSONAL: Born June 28, 1966, in Ashland, Pa. ... 5-10/175. ... Bats both, throws right. ... Full name: Frank Charles Bolick. ... Son of Frank Bolick, minor league pitcher (1966-77).

HIGH SCHOOL: Mt. Carmel (Pa.).

COLLEGE: Georgia Tech.

TRANSACTIONS/CAREER NOTES: Selected by Montreal Expos organization in 23rd round of free-agent draft (June 3, 1985); did not sign. ... Selected by Milwaukee Brewers organization in ninth round of free-agent draft (June 2, 1987). ... Traded by Brewers organization to Seattle Mariners organization for OF Mickey Brantley (June 6, 1990). ... Traded by Mariners with a player to be named later to Montreal Expos for P Dave Wainhouse and P Kevin Foster (November 20, 1992); Expos organization acquired C Miah Bradbury to complete deal (December 8, 1992). ... Granted free agency (October 15, 1993). ... Signed by Buffalo, Pittsburgh Pirates organization (November 27, 1993). ... Released by Buffalo, Pirates organization (May 17, 1994). ... Signed by New Haven, Colorado Rockies organization (June 3, 1994). ... Released by Rockies organization (May 15, 1995). ... Signed by Lubbock of Texas-Louisiana League (May 19, 1995). ... Signed by Buffalo, Cleveland Indians organization (August 1, 1995). ... Granted free agency (October 16, 1995). ... Signed by Boston Red Sox organization (February 27, 1996). ... Released by Red Sox (July 28, 1996). ... Signed by Lubbock of Texas-Louisiana League (July 1996). ... Granted free agency (October 15, 1997). ... Signed by Anaheim Angels organization (December 4, 1997). ... Suspended one game by American League (June 5, 1998) to be served in 1999 season. ... Granted free agency (October 15, 1998).

HONORS: Named California League Most Valuable Player (1990).

STATISTICAL NOTES: Led California League with 102 RBIs in 1990. ... Tied for California League lead with 13 sacrifice flies in 1990.

Year Team (League)	Pos.	G	AB	R	H	2B	3B	HR	RBI	Avg.	BB	SO	SB	PO	A	E	Avg.
1987—Helena (Pioneer)	3B	52	156	41	39	8	1	10	28	.250	41	44	4	5	13	1	.947
1988—Beloit (Midwest)	3B	55	180	28	41	14	1	2	16	.228	43	49	3	38	81	14	.895
—Ariz. Brewers (Ariz.)	3B	23	80	20	30	9	3	1	20	.375	22	8	1	23	55	4	.951
—Helena (Pioneer)	3B	40	131	35	39	10	1	10	38	.298	32	31	5	28	65	10	.903
1989—Beloit (Midwest)	3B-1B-OF	88	299	44	90	23	0	9	41	.301	47	52	9	47	108	15	.912
1990—Stockton (California)	3B-1B	50	164	39	51	9	1	8	36	.311	38	33	5	69	71	13	.915
—San Bern. (Calif.)■	3B	78	277	61	92	24	4	10	§66	.332	53	53	3	45	138	7	.963
1991—Jacksonville (Sou.)	3B-SS	136	468	69	119	19	0	16	73	.254	*84	115	5	88	256	17	.953
1992—Jacksonville (Sou.)	3B-1B	63	224	32	60	9	0	13	42	.268	42	38	1	51	126	5	.973
—Calgary (PCL)	3B	78	274	35	79	18	6	14	54	.288	39	52	4	36	121	14	.918
1993—Montreal (N.L.)■	1B-3B	95	213	25	45	13	0	4	24	.211	23	37	1	338	63	8	.980
—Ottawa (Int'l)	3B	2	8	0	1	0	0	0	0	.125	0	0	0	0	4	0	1.000
1994—Buffalo (A.A.)■	3B	35	95	18	25	6	0	2	8	.263	27	29	0	4	10	0	1.000
—New Haven (East.)■	1B-3B	85	301	53	76	13	0	21	63	.252	41	57	2	608	51	4	.994
1995—Colo. Springs (PCL)■	3B-1B	23	68	8	16	3	1	2	7	.235	8	14	0	20	27	3	.940
—Lubbock (Texas-La.)■	3-P-C-1-S	59	214	42	76	17	1	7	56	.355	46	33	1	46	112	12	.929
—Buffalo (A.A.)■	3B-1B-SS	20	65	11	16	6	0	3	10	.246	3	13	0	17	25	2	.955
1996—Lubbock (Texas-La.)	3B-1B	33	125	22	47	15	1	6	35	.376	19	14	0	47	67	4	.966
1997—Midland (Texas)■	3B	28	97	26	32	5	1	8	27	.330	26	18	0	6	28	5	.872
—Vancouver (PCL)	1B-3B-2B	102	362	61	110	27	4	16	66	.304	46	70	4	225	70	1	.997
1998—Anaheim (A.L.)■	DH-3-1-O	21	45	3	7	2	0	1	2	.156	11	8	0	9	7	0	1.000
—Vancouver (PCL)	3B-OF-1B	75	269	40	71	10	2	13	29	.264	28	47	0	82	79	8	.953
American League totals (1 year)		21	45	3	7	2	0	1	2	.156	11	8	0	9	7	0	1.000
National League totals (1 year)		95	213	25	45	13	0	4	24	.211	23	37	1	338	63	8	.980
Major league totals (2 years)		116	258	28	52	15	0	5	26	.202	34	45	1	347	70	8	.981

RECORD AS PITCHER

Year Team (League)	W	L	Pct.	ERA	G	GS	CG	ShO	Sv.	IP	H	R	ER	BB	SO
1995—Lubbock (Texas-La.)■	0	0	...	0.00	1	0	0	0	0	1	0	0	0	1	0

BONDS, BARRY   OF   GIANTS

PERSONAL: Born July 24, 1964, in Riverside, Calif. ... 6-2/210. ... Bats left, throws left. ... Full name: Barry Lamar Bonds. ... Son of Bobby Bonds, major league outfielder with eight teams (1968-81); and coach with Cleveland Indians (1984-87) and San Francisco Giants (1993-1996).

HIGH SCHOOL: Serra (San Mateo, Calif.).

COLLEGE: Arizona State.

TRANSACTIONS/CAREER NOTES: Selected by San Francisco Giants organization in second round of free-agent draft (June 7, 1982); did not sign. ... Selected by Pittsburgh Pirates organization in first round (sixth pick overall) of free-agent draft (June 3, 1985). ... On disabled list (June 15-July 4, 1992). ... Granted free agency (October 26, 1992). ... Signed by Giants (December 8, 1992). ... On suspended list (August 14-16, 1998).

RECORDS: Holds major league record for most seasons and consecutive seasons leading league in intentional bases on balls received—7 (1992-98). ... Shares major league single-season record for fewest assists by outfielder who led league in assists—14 (1990). ... Holds N.L. career record for most consecutive years leading league in bases on balls—4 (1994-97). ... Shares major league record for fewest double plays by outfielder (150 or more games)—0 (1997 and 1998). ... Shares N.L. single-season record for most consecutive times reached base safely—15 (August 31 [1], September 1 [5], 2 [4], 4 [5], 1998 [5 singles, 2 doubles, 2 home runs, 6 bases on balls]. ... Shares N.L. single-season record for fewest assists by outfielder (150 or more games)—2 (1993).

HONORS: Named outfielder on THE SPORTING NEWS college All-America team (1985). ... Named Major League Player of the Year by THE SPORTING NEWS (1990). ... Named N.L. Player of the Year by THE SPORTING NEWS (1990-91). ... Named outfielder on THE SPORTING NEWS N.L. All-Star team (1990-94 and 1996-97). ... Won N.L. Gold Glove as outfielder (1990-94 and 1996-97). ... Named outfielder on THE SPORTING NEWS N.L. Silver Slugger team (1990-94, 1996 and 1997). ... Named N.L. Most Valuable Player by Baseball Writers' Association of America (1990 and 1992-93).

STATISTICAL NOTES: Led N.L. with .565 slugging percentage in 1990, .624 in 1992 and .677 in 1993. ... Led N.L. with 32 intentional bases on balls received in 1992, 43 in 1993, 18 in 1994, 22 in 1995, 30 in 1996, 34 in 1997 and 29 in 1998. ... Led N.L. with .456 on-base percentage in 1992, .458 in 1993 and .431 in 1995. ... Led N.L. with 365 total bases in 1993. ... Hit three home runs in one game (August 2, 1994). ... Career major league grand slams: 8.

Year Team (League)	Pos.	G	AB	R	H	2B	3B	HR	RBI	Avg.	BB	SO	SB	PO	A	E	Avg.
							BATTING								**FIELDING**		
1985— Prince Will. (Car.)......	OF	71	254	49	76	16	4	13	37	.299	37	52	15	202	4	5	.976
1986— Hawaii (PCL)	OF	44	148	30	46	7	2	7	37	.311	33	31	16	109	4	2	.983
— Pittsburgh (N.L.)	OF	113	413	72	92	26	3	16	48	.223	65	102	36	280	9	5	.983
1987— Pittsburgh (N.L.)	OF	150	551	99	144	34	9	25	59	.261	54	88	32	330	15	5	.986
1988— Pittsburgh (N.L.)	OF	144	538	97	152	30	5	24	58	.283	72	82	17	292	5	6	.980
1989— Pittsburgh (N.L.)	OF	159	580	96	144	34	6	19	58	.248	93	93	32	365	14	6	.984
1990— Pittsburgh (N.L.)	OF	151	519	104	156	32	3	33	114	.301	93	83	52	338	•14	6	.983
1991— Pittsburgh (N.L.)	OF	153	510	95	149	28	5	25	116	.292	107	73	43	321	13	3	.991
1992— Pittsburgh (N.L.)	OF	140	473	*109	147	36	5	34	103	.311	*127	69	39	310	4	3	.991
1993— San Fran. (N.L.)■......	OF	159	539	129	181	38	4	*46	*123	.336	126	79	29	310	7	5	.984
1994— San Francisco (N.L.) ..	OF	112	391	89	122	18	1	37	81	.312	*74	43	29	198	10	3	.986
1995— San Francisco (N.L.) ..	OF	•144	506	109	149	30	7	33	104	.294	*120	83	31	279	12	6	.980
1996— San Francisco (N.L.) ..	OF	158	517	122	159	27	3	42	129	.308	*151	76	40	286	10	6	.980
1997— San Francisco (N.L.) ..	OF	159	532	123	155	26	5	40	101	.291	*145	87	37	289	10	5	.984
1998— San Francisco (N.L.) ..	OF	156	552	120	167	44	7	37	122	.303	130	92	28	301	2	5	.984
Major league totals (13 years)		1898	6621	1364	1917	403	63	411	1216	.290	1357	1050	445	3899	125	64	.984

DIVISION SERIES RECORD

Year Team (League)	Pos.	G	AB	R	H	2B	3B	HR	RBI	Avg.	BB	SO	SB	PO	A	E	Avg.
							BATTING								**FIELDING**		
1997— San Francisco (N.L.) ..	OF	3	12	0	3	2	0	0	2	.250	0	3	1	6	0	0	1.000

CHAMPIONSHIP SERIES RECORD

RECORDS: Shares single-inning record for most hits—2 (October 13, 1992, second inning).

Year Team (League)	Pos.	G	AB	R	H	2B	3B	HR	RBI	Avg.	BB	SO	SB	PO	A	E	Avg.
							BATTING								**FIELDING**		
1990— Pittsburgh (N.L.)	OF	6	18	4	3	0	0	0	1	.167	6	5	2	13	0	0	1.000
1991— Pittsburgh (N.L.)	OF	7	27	1	4	1	0	0	0	.148	2	4	3	14	1	1	.938
1992— Pittsburgh (N.L.)	OF	7	23	5	6	1	0	1	2	.261	6	4	1	17	0	0	1.000
Championship series totals (3 years)		20	68	10	13	2	0	1	3	.191	14	13	6	44	1	1	.978

ALL-STAR GAME RECORD

Year League	Pos.	AB	R	H	2B	3B	HR	RBI	Avg.	BB	SO	SB	PO	A	E	Avg.
						BATTING								**FIELDING**		
1990— National	OF	1	0	0	0	0	0	0	.000	1	0	0	2	0	0	1.000
1992— National	OF	3	1	1	1	0	0	0	.333	0	0	0	2	0	0	1.000
1993— National	OF	3	2	2	2	0	0	0	.667	0	0	0	1	0	0	1.000
1994— National	OF	3	0	0	0	0	0	0	.000	0	2	0	1	0	0	1.000
1995— National	OF	3	0	0	0	0	0	0	.000	0	1	0	0	0	0	...
1996— National	OF	3	0	1	0	0	0	0	.333	0	0	0	2	0	0	1.000
1997— National	OF	2	0	0	0	0	0	0	.000	1	1	1	2	0	0	1.000
1998— National	OF	2	1	1	0	0	1	3	.500	1	0	0	1	0	0	1.000
All-Star Game totals (8 years)		20	4	5	3	0	1	4	.250	3	4	1	11	0	0	1.000

BONES, RICKY P ORIOLES

PERSONAL: Born April 7, 1969, in Salinas, Puerto Rico. ... 6-0/202. ... Throws right, bats right. ... Full name: Ricardo Bones. ... Name pronounced BO-nuss.

HIGH SCHOOL: Guayama (Puerto Rico).

TRANSACTIONS/CAREER NOTES: Signed as non-drafted free agent by San Diego Padres organization (May 13, 1986). ... Traded by Padres with SS Jose Valentin and OF Matt Mieske to Milwaukee Brewers for 3B Gary Sheffield and P Geoff Kellogg (March 27, 1992). ... Traded by Brewers with a player to be named later to New York Yankees as compensation for injured status of OF/IF Pat Listach (August 29, 1996); Yankees acquired IF Gabby Martinez to complete deal (November 5, 1996). ... Granted free agency (October 25, 1996). ... Traded by Yankees to Cincinnati Reds (December 10, 1996). ... Released by Reds (May 6, 1997). ... Signed by Brewers organization (May 12, 1997). ... Traded by Brewers to Kansas City Royals organization for cash (June 26, 1997). ... Granted free agency (November 5, 1997). ... Signed by Minnesota Twins organization (January 6, 1998). ... Released by Twins (May 22, 1998). ... Signed by Royals organization (May 26, 1998). ... Granted free agency (October 29, 1998). ... Signed by Baltimore Orioles (December 21, 1998).

STATISTICAL NOTES: Led Texas League with 22 home runs allowed in 1989.

MISCELLANEOUS: Appeared in one game as outfielder with no chances (1993). ... Appeared in one game as pinch runner with Kansas City (1997).

Year Team (League)	W	L	Pct.	ERA	G	GS	CG	ShO	Sv.	IP	H	R	ER	BB	SO
1986— Spokane (N'west)	1	3	.250	5.59	18	9	0	0	0	58	63	44	36	29	46
1987— Charleston, S.C. (S. Atl.)	12	5	.706	3.65	26	26	4	1	0	170 1/3	*183	81	69	45	130
1988— Riverside (California)..........	15	6	.714	3.64	25	25	5	2	0	175 1/3	162	80	71	64	129
1989— Wichita (Texas)	10	9	.526	5.74	24	24	2	0	0	136 1/3	162	103	87	47	88
1990— Wichita (Texas)	6	4	.600	3.48	21	21	2	1	0	137	138	66	53	45	96
— Las Vegas (PCL)	2	1	.667	3.47	5	5	0	0	0	36 1/3	45	17	14	10	25
1991— Las Vegas (PCL)	8	6	.571	4.22	23	23	1	0	0	136 1/3	155	90	64	43	95
— San Diego (N.L.)	4	6	.400	4.83	11	11	0	0	0	54	57	33	29	18	31
1992— Milwaukee (A.L.)■	9	10	.474	4.57	31	28	0	0	0	163 1/3	169	90	83	48	65
1993— Milwaukee (A.L.)	11	11	.500	4.86	32	31	3	0	0	203 2/3	222	122	110	63	63
1994— Milwaukee (A.L.)	10	9	.526	3.43	24	24	4	1	0	170 2/3	166	76	65	45	57
1995— Milwaukee (A.L.)	10	12	.455	4.63	32	31	4	0	0	200 1/3	218	108	103	83	77
1996— Milwaukee (A.L.)	7	14	.333	5.83	32	23	0	0	0	145	170	104	94	62	59
— New York (A.L.)■	0	0	...	14.14	4	1	0	0	0	7	14	11	11	6	4
1997— Cincinnati (N.L.)■	0	1	.000	10.19	9	2	0	0	0	17 2/3	31	22	20	11	8
— Tucson (PCL)■	5	0	1.000	2.79	8	7	0	0	0	42	40	18	13	8	22
— Kansas City (A.L.)■	4	7	.364	5.97	21	11	1	0	0	78 1/3	102	59	52	25	36

Year Team (League)	W	L	Pct.	ERA	G	GS	CG	ShO	Sv.	IP	H	R	ER	BB	SO
1998—Salt Lake (PCL)■	5	1	.833	3.42	8	8	0	0	0	47⅓	41	20	18	19	41
—Omaha (Pacific Coast)■ .	1	2	.333	8.59	3	3	0	0	0	14⅔	19	16	14	10	8
—Kansas City (A.L.) .	2	2	.500	3.04	32	0	0	0	1	53⅓	49	18	18	24	38
A.L. totals (7 years)	53	65	.449	4.72	208	149	11	1	1	1021⅔	1110	588	536	356	399
N.L. totals (2 years)	4	7	.364	6.15	20	13	0	0	0	71⅔	88	55	49	29	39
Major league totals (8 years)	57	72	.442	4.82	228	162	11	1	1	1093⅓	1198	643	585	385	438

ALL-STAR GAME RECORD

Year League	W	L	Pct.	ERA	GS	CG	ShO	Sv.	IP	H	R	ER	BB	SO
1994— American				Did not play.										

BONILLA, BOBBY — OF/3B — METS

PERSONAL: Born February 23, 1963, in New York. ... 6-4/240. ... Bats both, throws right. ... Full name: Roberto Martin Antonio Bonilla. ... Name pronounced bo-NEE-yah.

HIGH SCHOOL: Lehman (Bronx, N.Y.).

COLLEGE: New York Technical College.

TRANSACTIONS/CAREER NOTES: Signed as non-drafted free agent by Pittsburgh Pirates organization (July 11, 1981). ... On Pittsburgh disabled list (March 25-July 19, 1985). ... Selected by Chicago White Sox from Pirates organization in Rule 5 major league draft (December 10, 1985). ... Traded by White Sox to Pittsburgh Pirates for P Jose DeLeon (July 23, 1986). ... Granted free agency (October 28, 1991). ... Signed by New York Mets (December 2, 1991). ... On suspended list (July 27-28, 1992). ... On disabled list (August 3-19, 1992). ... Traded by Mets with a player to be named later to Baltimore Orioles for OF Alex Ochoa and OF Damon Buford (July 28, 1995); Orioles acquired P Jimmy Williams to complete deal (August 17, 1995). ... Granted free agency (November 18, 1996). ... Signed by Florida Marlins (November 22, 1996). ... Traded by Marlins with OF Gary Sheffield, C Charles Johnson, OF Jim Eisenreich and P Manuel Barrios to Los Angeles Dodgers for C Mike Piazza and 3B Todd Zeile (May 15, 1998). ... On Florida disabled list (March 22-April 12, 1998). ... On Los Angeles disabled list (June 18-July 3 and July 15-August 5, 1998). ... Traded by Dodgers to Mets for P Mel Rojas (November 11, 1998).

RECORDS: Holds N.L. career record for most home runs by switch-hitter—233. ... Shares major league record for most doubles in one inning—2 (July 21, 1995, eighth inning). ... Shares A.L. single-season record for most sacrifice flies—17 (1996).

HONORS: Named third baseman on THE SPORTING NEWS N.L. All-Star team (1988). ... Named third baseman on THE SPORTING NEWS N.L. Silver Slugger team (1988). ... Named outfielder on THE SPORTING NEWS N.L. All-Star team (1990-91). ... Named outfielder on THE SPORTING NEWS N.L. Silver Slugger team (1990-91).

STATISTICAL NOTES: Led Eastern League outfielders with 15 errors in 1984. ... Switch-hit home runs in one game six times (July 3, 1987; April 6, 1988; April 23 and June 10, 1993; May 4, 1994; and May 12, 1995). ... Led N.L. third basemen with 489 total chances in 1988. ... Led N.L. third basemen with 35 errors in 1989. ... Led N.L. third basemen with 31 double plays in 1989. ... Led N.L. with 15 sacrifice flies in 1990. ... Had 20-game hitting streak (September 10-October 1, 1995). ... Led A.L. with 17 sacrifice flies in 1996. ... Career major league grand slams: 8.

							BATTING							FIELDING			
Year Team (League)	Pos.	G	AB	R	H	2B	3B	HR	RBI	Avg.	BB	SO	SB	PO	A	E	Avg.
1981—GC Pirates (GCL)........	1B-C-3B	22	69	6	15	5	0	0	7	.217	7	17	2	124	23	5	.967
1982—GC Pirates (GCL)........	1B	47	167	20	38	3	0	5	26	.228	11	20	2	318	36	*14	.962
1983—Alexandria (Caro.)	OF-1B	•136	504	88	129	19	7	11	59	.256	78	105	28	259	12	15	.948
1984—Nashua (Eastern)........	OF-1B	136	484	74	128	19	5	11	71	.264	49	89	15	312	8	†15	.955
1985—Prince Will. (Car.)	1B-3B	39	130	15	34	4	1	3	11	.262	16	29	1	180	9	2	.990
1986—Chicago (A.L.)■........	OF-1B	75	234	27	63	10	2	2	26	.269	33	49	4	361	22	2	.995
—Pittsburgh (N.L.)■........	OF-1B-3B	63	192	28	46	6	2	1	17	.240	29	39	4	90	16	3	.972
1987—Pittsburgh (N.L.)........	3B-OF-1B	141	466	58	140	33	3	15	77	.300	39	64	3	142	139	16	.946
1988—Pittsburgh (N.L.)........	3B	159	584	87	160	32	7	24	100	.274	85	82	3	121	*336	*32	.935
1989—Pittsburgh (N.L.)........	3B-1B-OF	•163	616	96	173	37	10	24	86	.281	76	93	8	190	334	†35	.937
1990—Pittsburgh (N.L.)........	OF-3B-1B	160	625	112	175	39	7	32	120	.280	45	103	4	315	35	15	.959
1991—Pittsburgh (N.L.)........	OF-3B-1B	157	577	102	174	*44	6	18	100	.302	90	67	2	247	144	15	.963
1992—New York (N.L.)■......	OF-1B	128	438	62	109	23	0	19	70	.249	66	73	4	277	9	4	.986
1993—New York (N.L.)........	OF-3B-1B	139	502	81	133	21	3	34	87	.265	72	96	3	238	112	17	.954
1994—New York (N.L.)........	3B	108	403	60	117	24	1	20	67	.290	55	101	4	78	215	*18	.942
1995—New York (N.L.)........	3B-OF-1B	80	317	49	103	25	4	18	53	.325	31	48	0	164	80	14	.946
—Baltimore (A.L.)■........	OF-3B	61	237	47	79	12	4	10	46	.333	23	31	0	80	48	5	.962
1996—Baltimore (A.L.).........	O-DH-1-3	159	595	107	171	27	5	28	116	.287	75	85	1	214	12	6	.974
1997—Florida (N.L.)■........	3B-DH-1B	153	562	77	167	39	3	17	96	.297	73	94	6	107	225	22	.938
1998—Florida (N.L.)........	3B	28	97	11	27	5	0	4	15	.278	12	22	0	18	41	5	.922
—Los Angeles (N.L.)■...	3B-OF	72	236	28	56	6	1	7	30	.237	29	37	1	56	84	13	.915
American League totals (3 years)		295	1066	181	313	49	11	40	188	.294	131	165	5	655	82	13	.983
National League totals (12 years)		1551	5615	851	1580	334	47	233	918	.281	702	919	39	2043	1770	209	.948
Major league totals (13 years)		1846	6681	1032	1893	383	58	273	1106	.283	833	1084	44	2698	1852	222	.953

DIVISION SERIES RECORD

							BATTING							FIELDING			
Year Team (League)	Pos.	G	AB	R	H	2B	3B	HR	RBI	Avg.	BB	SO	SB	PO	A	E	Avg.
1996—Baltimore (A.L.).........	OF	4	15	4	3	0	0	2	5	.200	4	6	0	9	0	1	.900
1997—Florida (N.L.).............	3B	3	12	1	4	0	0	1	3	.333	2	1	0	3	5	0	1.000
Division series totals (2 years)		7	27	5	7	0	0	3	8	.259	6	7	0	12	5	1	.944

CHAMPIONSHIP SERIES RECORD

RECORDS: Shares single-game record for most strikeouts—4 (October 10, 1996).

							BATTING							FIELDING			
Year Team (League)	Pos.	G	AB	R	H	2B	3B	HR	RBI	Avg.	BB	SO	SB	PO	A	E	Avg.
1990—Pittsburgh (N.L.)	OF-3B	6	21	0	4	1	0	0	1	.190	3	1	0	4	5	1	.900
1991—Pittsburgh (N.L.)	OF	7	23	2	7	2	0	0	1	.304	6	2	0	12	1	0	1.000
1996—Baltimore (A.L.)	OF	5	20	1	1	0	0	1	2	.050	1	4	0	11	0	0	1.000
1997—Florida (N.L.)	3B	6	23	3	6	1	0	0	4	.261	1	6	0	5	13	0	1.000
Championship series totals (4 years)		24	87	6	18	4	0	1	8	.207	11	13	0	32	19	1	.981

WORLD SERIES RECORD

NOTES: Member of World Series championship team (1997).

Year Team (League)	Pos.	G	AB	R	H	2B	3B	HR	RBI	Avg.	BB	SO	SB	PO	A	E	Avg.
1997— Florida (N.L.)	3B	7	29	5	6	1	0	1	3	.207	3	5	0	3	20	2	.920

ALL-STAR GAME RECORD

Year League	Pos.	AB	R	H	2B	3B	HR	RBI	Avg.	BB	SO	SB	PO	A	E	Avg.
1988— National	3B	4	0	0	0	0	0	0	.000	0	0	0	0	2	0	1.000
1989— National	PH-DH	2	0	2	0	0	0	0	1.000	0	0	0	...	...	...	...
1990— National	1B	1	0	0	0	0	0	0	.000	0	0	0	1	0	0	1.000
1991— National	DH	4	0	2	0	0	0	1	.500	0	1	0	...	...	...	...
1993— National	OF	1	0	1	0	0	0	0	1.000	0	0	0	2	0	0	1.000
1995— National	3B	1	0	0	0	0	0	0	.000	0	1	0	0	0	0	...
All-Star Game totals (6 years)		13	0	5	0	0	0	1	.385	0	2	0	3	2	0	1.000

BOONE, AARON   3B   REDS

PERSONAL: Born March 9, 1973, in La Mesa, Calif. ... 6-2/200. ... Bats right, throws right. ... Full name: Aaron John Boone. ... Son of Bob Boone, special assistant to the general manager, Cincinnati Reds and catcher with three major league teams (1972-90); brother of Bret Boone, second baseman, Atlanta Braves; grandson of Ray Boone, major league infielder with six teams (1948-60); and nephew of Rodney Boone, minor league catcher/outfielder (1972-75).

HIGH SCHOOL: Villa Park (Calif.).

COLLEGE: Southern California.

TRANSACTIONS/CAREER NOTES: Selected by California Angels organization in 43rd round of free-agent draft (June 3, 1991); did not sign. ... Selected by Cincinnati Reds organization in third round of free-agent draft (June 2, 1994).

STATISTICAL NOTES: Led Pioneer League third basemen with 46 putouts, 156 assists, 220 total chances and 13 double plays in 1994. ... Led Southern League third basemen with 101 putouts, 347 total chances and 28 double plays in 1996. ... Led American Association third basemen with 76 putouts, 241 assists, 336 total chances and 27 double plays in 1997.

Year Team (League)	Pos.	G	AB	R	H	2B	3B	HR	RBI	Avg.	BB	SO	SB	PO	A	E	Avg.
1994— Billings (Pioneer)	3B-1B	67	256	48	70	15	5	7	55	.273	36	35	6	†60	†158	18	.924
1995— Chattanooga (Sou.)	3B	23	66	6	15	3	0	0	3	.227	5	12	2	14	28	6	.875
— Win.-Salem (Car.)	3B	108	395	61	103	19	1	14	50	.261	43	77	11	59	*272	21	*.940
1996— Chattanooga (Sou.)	3B-SS	136	*548	86	158	*44	7	17	95	.288	38	77	21	†123	257	22	.945
1997— Indianapolis (A.A.)	3B-SS-2B	131	476	79	138	30	4	22	75	.290	40	81	12	†112	†269	24	.941
— Cincinnati (N.L.)	3B-2B	16	49	5	12	1	0	0	5	.245	2	5	1	11	22	3	.917
1998— Cincinnati (N.L.)	3B-2B-SS	58	181	24	51	13	2	2	28	.282	15	36	6	37	97	8	.944
— Indianapolis (Int'l)	3B-2B-SS	87	332	56	80	18	1	7	38	.241	31	71	17	72	243	19	.943
Major league totals (2 years)		74	230	29	63	14	2	2	33	.274	17	41	7	48	119	11	.938

BOONE, BRET   2B   BRAVES

PERSONAL: Born April 6, 1969, in El Cajon, Calif. ... 5-10/180. ... Bats right, throws right. ... Full name: Bret Robert Boone. ... Son of Bob Boone, special assistant to the general manager, Cincinnati Reds and catcher with three major league teams (1972-90); brother of Aaron Boone, third baseman, Cincinnati Reds; grandson of Ray Boone, major league infielder with six teams (1948-60); and nephew of Rodney Boone, minor league catcher/outfielder (1972-75).

HIGH SCHOOL: El Dorado (Yorba Linda, Calif.).

COLLEGE: Southern California.

TRANSACTIONS/CAREER NOTES: Selected by Minnesota Twins organization in 28th round of free-agent draft (June 2, 1987); did not sign. ... Selected by Seattle Mariners organization in fifth round of free-agent draft (June 4, 1990). ... Traded by Mariners with P Erik Hanson to Cincinnati Reds for P Bobby Ayala and C Dan Wilson (November 2, 1993). ... On disabled list (April 1-16, 1996). ... Traded by Reds with P Mike Remlinger to Atlanta Braves for P Denny Neagle, OF Michael Tucker and P Rob Bell (November 10, 1998).

RECORDS: Holds major league single-season record for highest fielding percentage by second baseman (100 or more games)—.997 (1997).

HONORS: Won N.L. Gold Glove at second base (1998).

STATISTICAL NOTES: Tied for Southern League lead in grounding into double plays with 21 in 1991. ... Led Southern League second basemen with 288 putouts in 1991. ... Led Pacific Coast League second basemen with 90 double plays in 1992. ... Led N.L. second basemen with 106 double plays in 1995. ... Hit three home runs in one game (September 31, 1998). ... Career major league grand slams: 1.

Year Team (League)	Pos.	G	AB	R	H	2B	3B	HR	RBI	Avg.	BB	SO	SB	PO	A	E	Avg.
1990— Peninsula (Caro.)	2B	74	255	42	68	13	2	8	38	.267	47	57	5	154	216	19	.951
1991— Jacksonville (Sou.)	2B-3B	*139	475	64	121	18	1	19	75	.255	72	123	9	†300	369	21	.970
1992— Calgary (PCL)	2B-SS	118	439	73	138	26	5	13	73	.314	60	88	17	268	366	10	.984
— Seattle (A.L.)	2B-3B	33	129	15	25	4	0	4	15	.194	4	34	1	72	96	6	.966
1993— Calgary (PCL)	2B	71	274	48	91	18	3	8	56	.332	28	58	3	146	180	8	.976
— Seattle (A.L.)	2B-DH	76	271	31	68	12	2	12	38	.251	17	52	2	140	177	3	.991
1994— Cincinnati (N.L.)■	2B-3B	108	381	59	122	25	2	12	68	.320	24	74	3	191	269	12	.975
1995— Cincinnati (N.L.)	2B	138	513	63	137	34	2	15	68	.267	41	84	5	*311	362	4	*.994
1996— Cincinnati (N.L.)	2B	142	520	56	121	21	3	12	69	.233	31	100	3	315	381	6	*.991
1997— Cincinnati (N.L.)	2B	139	443	40	99	25	1	7	46	.223	45	101	5	271	334	2	*.997
— Indianapolis (A.A.)	2B	3	7	1	2	1	0	0	1	.286	2	2	1	6	10	0	1.000
1998— Cincinnati (N.L.)	2B	157	583	76	155	38	1	24	95	.266	48	104	6	329	416	9	.988
American League totals (2 years)		109	400	46	93	16	2	16	53	.233	21	86	3	212	273	9	.982
National League totals (5 years)		684	2440	294	634	143	9	70	346	.260	189	463	22	1417	1762	33	.990
Major league totals (7 years)		793	2840	340	727	159	11	86	399	.256	210	549	25	1629	2035	42	.989

DIVISION SERIES RECORD

Year Team (League)	Pos.	G	AB	R	H	2B	3B	HR	RBI	Avg.	BB	SO	SB	PO	A	E	Avg.
1995— Cincinnati (N.L.)	2B	3	10	4	3	1	0	1	1	.300	1	3	1	7	5	0	1.000

CHAMPIONSHIP SERIES RECORD

						BATTING								FIELDING		
Year	Team (League)	Pos.	G	AB	R	H	2B	3B	HR	RBI	Avg.	BB	SO	SB	PO	A	E	Avg.
1995— Cincinnati (N.L.)		2B	4	14	1	3	0	0	0	0	.214	1	2	0	9	13	0	1.000

ALL-STAR GAME RECORD

					BATTING								FIELDING		
Year	League	Pos.	AB	R	H	2B	3B	HR	RBI	Avg.	BB	SO	SB	PO	A	E	Avg.
1998— National								Did not play.									

BOOTY, JOSH   3B

PERSONAL: Born April 29, 1975, in Starksville, Miss. ... 6-3/220. ... Bats right, throws right. ... Full name: Joshua Gibson Booty.

HIGH SCHOOL: Evangel Christian Academy (Shreveport, La.).

COLLEGE: Louisiana State.

B

TRANSACTIONS/CAREER NOTES: Selected by Florida Marlins organization in first round (fifth pick overall) of free-agent draft (June 2, 1994). ... On Kane County suspended list (May 10-13, 1995). ... On Kane County disabled list (May 17-June 12, 1995). ... On Charlotte disabled list (June 10-21, 1998). ... Placed on voluntarily retired list (January 22, 1999).

STATISTICAL NOTES: Led Eastern League third basemen with 361 total chances and 38 double plays in 1997.

							BATTING							FIELDING		
Year	Team (League)	Pos.	G	AB	R	H	2B	3B	HR	RBI	Avg.	BB	SO	SB	PO	A	E	Avg.
1994— GC Marlins (GCL)		IF	10	36	5	8	0	0	1	2	.222	5	8	1	13	32	6	.882
— Elmira (N.Y.-Penn)......		SS	4	16	1	4	1	0	0	1	.250	0	4	0	11	8	1	.950
1995— Kane County (Midw.)..		3B	31	109	6	11	2	0	1	6	.101	11	45	1	23	71	9	.913
— Elmira (N.Y.-Penn)......		3B	74	287	33	63	18	1	6	37	.220	19	85	4	56	173	26	.898
1996— Kane County (Midw.)..		3B	128	475	62	98	25	1	21	87	.206	46	*195	2	62	252	28	.918
— Florida (N.L.).............		3B	2	2	1	1	0	0	0	0	.500	0	1	0	0	0	0	...
1997— Portland (Eastern)		3B	122	448	42	94	19	2	20	69	.210	27	166	2	*75	*262	24	.934
— Florida (N.L.)..............		3B	4	5	2	3	0	0	0	1	.600	1	1	0	1	5	1	.857
1998— Florida (N.L.)..............		3B	7	19	0	3	1	0	0	3	.158	3	8	0	4	11	3	.833
— Charlotte (Int'l)..........		3B	38	127	9	18	3	0	3	11	.142	7	44	0	20	94	10	.919
— Portland (Eastern)		3B	71	247	28	50	8	3	10	39	.202	20	74	1	43	159	15	.931
Major league totals (3 years)			13	26	3	7	1	0	0	4	.269	4	9	0	5	16	4	.840

BORBON, PEDRO   P   DODGERS

PERSONAL: Born November 15, 1967, in Mao, Dominican Republic. ... 6-1/205. ... Throws left, bats left. ... Full name: Pedro Felix Borbon Jr. ... Son of Pedro Borbon, major league pitcher with four teams (1969-80). ... Name pronounced bor-BONE.

HIGH SCHOOL: DeWitt Clinton (Bronx, N.Y.).

JUNIOR COLLEGE: Ranger (Texas) Junior College.

TRANSACTIONS/CAREER NOTES: Selected by Milwaukee Brewers organization in 35th round of free-agent draft (June 3, 1985); did not sign. ... Selected by Los Angeles Dodgers organization in secondary phase of free-agent draft (January 14, 1986); did not sign. ... Signed as non-drafted free agent by Chicago White Sox organization (June 4, 1988). ... Released by White Sox organization (April 1, 1989). ... Signed by Atlanta Braves organization (August 25, 1989). ... On disabled list (April 8-26 and August 23, 1996-remainder of season); included rehabilitation assignment to Greenville (April 23-26). ... On disabled list (March 30, 1997-entire season). ... On Atlanta disabled list (March 29, 1998-entire season); included rehabilitation assignments to Macon (June 4-7), Greenville (June 9-July 5 and July 9-14) and Richmond (July 16-August 31 and September 1-8). ... Granted free agency (October 1, 1998). ... Signed by Dodgers (January 6, 1999).

STATISTICAL NOTES: Led Gulf Coast League with 14 balks in 1988.

Year	Team (League)	W	L	Pct.	ERA	G	GS	CG	ShO	Sv.	IP	H	R	ER	BB	SO
1988— GC White Sox (GCL)		5	3	.625	2.41	16	11	1	1	1	74 2/3	52	28	20	17	67
1989—								Did not play.								
1990— Burlington (Midw.)■............		11	3	.786	1.47	14	14	6	2	0	97 2/3	73	25	16	23	76
— Durham (Carolina).............		4	5	.444	5.43	11	11	0	0	0	61 1/3	73	40	37	16	37
1991— Durham (Carolina).............		4	3	.571	2.27	37	6	1	0	5	91	85	40	23	35	79
— Greenville (Southern)		0	1	.000	2.79	4	4	0	0	0	29	23	12	9	10	22
1992— Greenville (Southern)		8	2	.800	3.06	39	10	0	0	3	94	73	36	32	42	79
— Atlanta (N.L.)......................		0	1	.000	6.75	2	0	0	0	0	1 1/3	2	1	1	1	1
1993— Richmond (Int'l)................		5	5	.500	4.23	52	0	0	0	1	76 2/3	71	40	36	42	95
— Atlanta (N.L.)......................		0	0	...	21.60	3	0	0	0	0	1 2/3	3	4	4	3	2
1994— Richmond (Int'l)................		3	4	.429	2.79	59	0	0	0	4	80 2/3	66	29	25	41	82
1995— Atlanta (N.L.)....................		2	2	.500	3.09	41	0	0	0	2	32	29	12	11	17	33
1996— Atlanta (N.L.)....................		3	0	1.000	2.75	43	0	0	0	1	36	26	12	11	7	31
— Greenville (Southern)		0	0	...	0.00	1	0	0	0	0	1	0	0	0	0	0
1997— Atlanta (N.L.)....................								Did not play.								
1998— Macon (S. Atl.).................		0	0	...	9.00	3	0	0	0	0	3	4	3	3	1	3
— Greenville (Southern)		0	2	.000	4.74	16	0	0	0	0	19	21	14	10	14	10
— Richmond (Int'l)................		0	1	.000	5.70	20	0	0	0	0	23 2/3	29	17	15	8	15
Major league totals (4 years)		5	3	.625	3.42	89	0	0	0	3	71	60	29	27	28	67

DIVISION SERIES RECORD

Year	Team (League)	W	L	Pct.	ERA	G	GS	CG	ShO	Sv.	IP	H	R	ER	BB	SO
1995— Atlanta (N.L.).....................		0	0	...	0.00	1	0	0	0	0	1	1	0	0	0	3

WORLD SERIES RECORD

NOTES: Member of World Series championship team (1995).

Year	Team (League)	W	L	Pct.	ERA	G	GS	CG	ShO	Sv.	IP	H	R	ER	BB	SO
1995— Atlanta (N.L.).....................		0	0	...	0.00	1	0	0	0	1	1	0	0	0	0	2

PERSONAL: Born May 14, 1963, in Columbus, Ohio. ... 6-2/200. ... Bats right, throws right. ... Full name: Patrick Lance Borders. ... Brother of Todd Borders, minor league catcher (1988).

HIGH SCHOOL: Lake Wales (Fla.).

TRANSACTIONS/CAREER NOTES: Selected by Toronto Blue Jays organization in sixth round of free-agent draft (June 7, 1982). ... On Toronto disabled list (July 5-August 19, 1988); included rehabilitation assignment to Syracuse (July 30-August 19). ... Granted free agency (October 21, 1994). ... Signed by Kansas City Royals (April 10, 1995). ... Traded by Royals to Houston Astros for a player to be named later (August 12, 1995); Royals acquired P Rick Huisman to complete deal (August 17, 1995). ... On Houston suspended list (September 8-14, 1995). ... Granted free agency (November 6, 1995). ... Signed by St. Louis Cardinals organization (January 10, 1996). ... Traded by Cardinals to California Angels for P Ben VanRyn (June 15, 1996). ... Traded by Angels to Chicago White Sox for P Robert Ellis (July 27, 1996). ... Granted free agency (November 8, 1996). ... Signed by Cleveland Indians organization (December 13, 1996). ... Granted free agency (November 7, 1997). ... Re-signed by Indians organization (December 17, 1997). ... Granted free agency (November 3, 1998).

STATISTICAL NOTES: Tied for Southern League lead with 16 passed balls in 1987. ... Led A.L. catchers with 880 total chances in 1992 and 962 in 1993. ... Led A.L. with nine passed balls in 1994. ... Career major league grand slams: 1.

Year Team (League)	Pos.	G	AB	R	H	2B	3B	HR	RBI	Avg.	BB	SO	SB	PO	A	E	Avg.
1982—Medicine Hat (Pio.)	3B	61	217	30	66	12	2	5	33	.304	24	52	1	23	96	*25	.826
1983—Florence (S. Atl.)	3B	131	457	62	125	31	4	5	54	.274	46	116	4	70	233	*41	.881
1984—Florence (S. Atl.)	1B-3B-OF	131	467	69	129	32	5	12	85	.276	56	109	3	650	77	25	.967
1985—Kinston (Carolina)	1B	127	460	43	120	16	1	10	60	.261	45	116	6	854	42	*20	.978
1986—Florence (S. Atl.)	C-OF	16	40	8	15	7	0	3	9	.375	2	9	0	22	1	0	1.000
— Knoxville (Southern) ..	C-1B	12	34	3	12	1	0	2	5	.353	1	6	0	45	5	3	.943
— Kinston (Carolina)	C-1B-OF	49	174	24	57	10	0	6	26	.328	10	42	0	211	26	7	.971
1987—Dunedin (Fla. St.)	1B	3	11	0	4	0	0	0	1	.364	0	3	0	21	1	0	1.000
— Knoxville (Southern) ..	C-3B	94	349	44	102	14	1	11	51	.292	20	56	2	432	49	12	.976
1988—Toronto (A.L.)..........	C-DH-2-3	56	154	15	42	6	3	5	21	.273	3	24	0	205	19	7	.970
— Syracuse (Int'l)	C	35	120	11	29	8	0	3	14	.242	16	22	0	202	17	2	.991
1989—Toronto (A.L.)..........	C-DH	94	241	22	62	11	1	3	29	.257	11	45	2	261	27	6	.980
1990—Toronto (A.L.)..........	C-DH	125	346	36	99	24	2	15	49	.286	18	57	0	515	46	4	.993
1991—Toronto (A.L.)..........	C	105	291	22	71	17	0	5	36	.244	11	45	0	505	48	4	.993
1992—Toronto (A.L.)..........	C	138	480	47	116	26	2	13	53	.242	33	75	1	784	*88	8	.991
1993—Toronto (A.L.)..........	C	138	488	38	124	30	0	9	55	.254	20	66	2	869	*80	*13	.986
1994—Toronto (A.L.)..........	C	85	295	24	73	13	1	3	26	.247	15	50	1	583	*60	8	.988
1995—Kansas City (A.L.)■...	C-DH	52	143	14	33	8	1	4	13	.231	7	22	0	182	18	0	1.000
— Houston (N.L.)■......	C	11	35	1	4	0	0	0	0	.114	2	7	0	70	5	1	.987
1996—St. Louis (N.L.)■......	C-1B	26	69	3	22	3	0	0	4	.319	1	14	0	117	9	3	.977
— California (A.L.)■......	C	19	57	6	13	3	0	2	8	.228	3	11	0	111	14	2	.984
— Chicago (A.L.)■......	C-DH	31	94	6	26	1	0	3	6	.277	5	18	0	144	16	3	.982
1997—Cleveland (A.L.)■......	C	55	159	17	47	7	1	4	15	.296	9	27	0	312	19	0	1.000
1998—Cleveland (A.L.)	C-3B	54	160	12	38	6	0	0	6	.238	10	40	0	283	20	8	.974
American League totals (11 years)		952	2908	259	744	152	11	66	317	.256	145	480	6	4754	455	63	.988
National League totals (2 years)		37	104	4	26	3	0	0	4	.250	3	21	0	187	14	4	.980
Major league totals (11 years)		989	3012	263	770	155	11	66	321	.256	148	501	6	4941	469	67	.988

CHAMPIONSHIP SERIES RECORD

Year Team (League)	Pos.	G	AB	R	H	2B	3B	HR	RBI	Avg.	BB	SO	SB	PO	A	E	Avg.
1989— Toronto (A.L.).............	PH-C	1	1	0	1	0	0	0	1	1.000	0	0	0	1	0	0	1.000
1991— Toronto (A.L.).............	C	5	19	0	5	1	0	0	2	.263	0	0	0	38	4	2	.955
1992— Toronto (A.L.).............	C	6	22	3	7	0	0	1	3	.318	1	1	0	38	3	1	.976
1993— Toronto (A.L.).............	C	6	24	1	6	1	0	0	3	.250	0	6	1	41	4	0	1.000
Championship series totals (4 years)		18	66	4	19	2	0	1	9	.288	1	7	1	118	11	3	.977

WORLD SERIES RECORD

NOTES: Named Most Valuable Player (1992). ... Member of World Series championship team (1992 and 1993).

Year Team (League)	Pos.	G	AB	R	H	2B	3B	HR	RBI	Avg.	BB	SO	SB	PO	A	E	Avg.
1992— Toronto (A.L.).............	C	6	20	2	9	3	0	1	3	.450	2	1	0	48	5	1	.981
1993— Toronto (A.L.).............	C	6	23	2	7	0	0	0	1	.304	2	1	0	50	2	1	.981
World Series totals (2 years)		12	43	4	16	3	0	1	4	.372	4	2	0	98	7	2	.981

PERSONAL: Born July 21, 1965, in Marquette, Mich. ... 5-11/175. ... Bats right, throws right. ... Full name: Michael Todd Bordick.

HIGH SCHOOL: Hampden (Maine) Academy.

COLLEGE: Maine.

TRANSACTIONS/CAREER NOTES: Signed as non-drafted free agent by Oakland Athletics organization (July 10, 1986). ... On Tacoma disabled list (April 14-May 13, 1991). ... On Oakland disabled list (May 8-27, 1995); included rehabilitation assignment to Modesto (May 23-26). ... Granted free agency (December 7, 1996). ... Signed by Baltimore Orioles (December 13, 1996).

STATISTICAL NOTES: Led Pacific Coast League shortstops with .972 fielding percentage and 82 double plays in 1990. ... Led A.L. shortstops with 280 putouts and tied for lead with 108 double plays in 1993. ... Led A.L. with 15 sacrifice hits in 1998. ... Career major league grand slams: 1.

Year Team (League)	Pos.	G	AB	R	H	2B	3B	HR	RBI	Avg.	BB	SO	SB	PO	A	E	Avg.
1986— Medford (N'west)	SS	46	187	30	48	3	1	0	19	.257	40	21	6	68	143	18	.921
1987— Modesto (California) ..	SS	133	497	73	133	17	0	3	75	.268	87	92	8	216	305	17	*.968
1988— Huntsville (Sou.)	2B-SS-3B	132	481	48	130	13	2	0	28	.270	87	50	7	260	406	24	.965

Year	Team (League)	Pos.	G	AB	R	H	2B	3B	HR	RBI	Avg.	BB	SO	SB	PO	A	E	Avg.
								BATTING								**FIELDING**		
1989—Tacoma (PCL)	2B-SS-3B	136	487	55	117	17	1	1	43	.240	58	51	4	261	431	33	.954
1990—Oakland (A.L.)	3B-SS-2B	25	14	0	1	0	0	0	0	.071	1	4	0	9	8	0	1.000
—Tacoma (PCL)	SS-2B	111	348	49	79	16	1	2	30	.227	46	40	3	210	366	16	†.973
1991—Tacoma (PCL)	SS	26	81	15	22	4	1	2	14	.272	17	10	0	35	79	3	.974
—Oakland (A.L.)	SS-2B-3B	90	235	21	56	5	1	0	21	.238	14	37	3	146	213	11	.970
1992—Oakland (A.L.)	2B-SS	154	504	62	151	19	4	3	48	.300	40	59	12	311	449	16	.979
1993—Oakland (A.L.)	SS-2B	159	546	60	136	21	2	3	48	.249	60	58	10	†285	420	13	.982
1994—Oakland (A.L.)	SS-2B	114	391	38	99	18	4	2	37	.253	38	44	7	187	320	14	.973
1995—Oakland (A.L.)	SS-DH	126	428	46	113	13	0	8	44	.264	35	48	11	*245	338	10	.983
—Modesto (California) ..	SS	1	2	0	0	0	0	0	0	.000	0	0	0	2	1	0	1.000
1996—Oakland (A.L.)	SS	155	525	46	126	18	4	5	54	.240	52	59	5	265	*476	16	.979
1997—Baltimore (A.L.)■........	SS	153	509	55	120	19	1	7	46	.236	33	66	0	224	424	13	.980
1998—Baltimore (A.L.)........	SS	151	465	59	121	29	1	13	51	.260	39	65	6	236	*446	7	.990
Major league totals (9 years)		1127	3617	387	923	142	17	41	349	.255	312	440	54	1908	3094	100	.980

DIVISION SERIES RECORD

Year	Team (League)	Pos.	G	AB	R	H	2B	3B	HR	RBI	Avg.	BB	SO	SB	PO	A	E	Avg.
								BATTING								**FIELDING**		
1997—Baltimore (A.L.).........	SS	4	10	4	4	1	0	0	4	.400	4	2	0	4	15	0	1.000

CHAMPIONSHIP SERIES RECORD

Year	Team (League)	Pos.	G	AB	R	H	2B	3B	HR	RBI	Avg.	BB	SO	SB	PO	A	E	Avg.
								BATTING								**FIELDING**		
1992—Oakland (A.L.)	SS-2B	6	19	1	1	0	0	0	0	.053	1	2	1	15	14	0	1.000
1997—Baltimore (A.L.).........	SS	6	19	0	3	1	0	0	2	.158	0	6	0	5	14	0	1.000
Championship series totals (2 years)		12	38	1	4	1	0	0	2	.105	1	8	1	20	28	0	1.000

WORLD SERIES RECORD

Year	Team (League)	Pos.	G	AB	R	H	2B	3B	HR	RBI	Avg.	BB	SO	SB	PO	A	E	Avg.
								BATTING								**FIELDING**		
1990—Oakland (A.L.)	SS-PR	3	0	0	0	0	0	0	0	...	0	0	0	0	2	0	1.000

BORKOWSKI, DAVID   P   TIGERS

PERSONAL: Born February 7, 1977, in Detroit. ... 6-1/200. ... Throws right, bats right. ... Full name: David Richard Borkowski.
HIGH SCHOOL: Sterling Heights (Mich.).
TRANSACTIONS/CAREER NOTES: Selected by Detroit Tigers organization in 11th round of free-agent draft (June 1, 1995).
STATISTICAL NOTES: Pitched 6-0 no-hit victory against Kane County (April 20, 1997). ... Led Southern League with 25 home runs allowed in 1998.

Year	Team (League)	W	L	Pct.	ERA	G	GS	CG	ShO	Sv.	IP	H	R	ER	BB	SO
1995—Gulf Coast Tigers (GCL)	3	2	.600	2.96	10	10	1	0	0	51 2/3	45	24	17	8	36
—Lakeland (Fla. St.)	1	0	1.000	0.00	1	1	0	0	0	5	2	0	0	1	3
1996—Fayetteville (S. Atl.)	10	10	.500	3.33	27	27	5	0	0	178 1/3	158	85	66	54	117
1997—West. Mich. (Mid.)	•15	3	•.833	3.46	25	25	4	2	0	164	143	79	63	31	104
1998—Jacksonville (Southern)......	*16	7	.696	4.63	28	28	3	1	0	178 2/3	204	99	92	54	97

BORLAND, TOBY   P

PERSONAL: Born May 29, 1969, in Ruston, La. ... 6-6/193. ... Throws right, bats right. ... Full name: Toby Shawn Borland.
HIGH SCHOOL: Quitman (La.).
TRANSACTIONS/CAREER NOTES: Selected by Philadelphia Phillies organization in 27th round of free-agent draft (June 2, 1987). ... On Philadelphia disabled list (June 14-July 8, 1995); included rehabilitation assignment to Scranton/Wilkes-Barre (June 22-July 8). ... Traded by Phillies with P Ricardo Jordan to New York Mets for 1B Rico Brogna (November 27, 1996). ... Traded by Mets to Boston Red Sox for P Rick Trlicek (May 12, 1997). ... Granted free agency (October 15, 1997). ... Signed by Cincinnati Reds organization (November 27, 1997). ... Released by Reds (March 5, 1998). ... Signed by Philadelphia Phillies organization (March 6, 1998). ... Released by Phillies (July 6, 1998). ... Signed by Florida Marlins organization (July 14, 1998). ... Granted free agency (October 15, 1998).
STATISTICAL NOTES: Tied for Eastern League lead with three balks in 1991. ... Pitched one inning, combining with starter Craig Holman (two innings), Gregory Brown (two innings) and Ricky Bottalico (two innings) in seven-inning 2-0 no-hit victory for Reading against New Britain (September 4, 1993, first game).

Year	Team (League)	W	L	Pct.	ERA	G	GS	CG	ShO	Sv.	IP	H	R	ER	BB	SO
1988—Martinsville (App.)	2	3	.400	4.04	34	0	0	0	*12	49	42	26	22	29	43
1989—Spartanburg (SAL)	4	5	.444	2.97	47	0	0	0	9	66 2/3	62	29	22	35	48
1990—Clearwater (Fla. St.)	1	2	.333	2.26	44	0	0	0	5	59 2/3	44	21	15	35	44
—Reading (Eastern)	4	1	.800	1.44	14	0	0	0	0	25	16	6	4	11	26
1991—Reading (Eastern)	8	3	.727	2.70	*59	0	0	0	•24	76 2/3	68	31	23	56	72
1992—Scran./W.B. (Int'l).............	0	1	.000	7.24	27	0	0	0	1	27 1/3	25	23	22	26	25
—Reading (Eastern)	2	4	.333	3.43	32	0	0	0	5	42	39	23	16	32	45
1993—Reading (Eastern)	2	2	.500	2.52	44	0	0	0	13	53 2/3	38	17	15	20	74
—Scran./W.B. (Int'l).............	2	4	.333	5.76	26	0	0	0	1	29 2/3	31	20	19	20	26
1994—Scran./W.B. (Int'l).............	4	1	.800	1.68	27	1	0	0	4	53 2/3	36	12	10	21	61
—Philadelphia (N.L.).............	1	0	1.000	2.36	24	0	0	0	1	34 1/3	31	10	9	14	26
1995—Philadelphia (N.L.).............	1	3	.250	3.77	50	0	0	0	6	74	81	37	31	37	59
—Scran./W.B. (Int'l).............	0	0	...	0.00	8	0	0	0	0	11 1/3	5	0	0	6	15
1996—Philadelphia (N.L.).............	7	3	.700	4.07	69	0	0	0	0	90 2/3	83	51	41	43	76
1997—New York (N.L.)■.............	0	1	.000	6.08	13	0	0	0	1	13 1/3	11	9	9	14	7
—Boston (A.L.)■.................	0	0	...	13.50	3	0	0	0	0	3 1/3	6	5	5	7	1
—Pawtucket (Int'l)	2	0	1.000	3.99	28	2	0	0	2	47 1/3	50	22	21	25	46

Year	Team (League)	W	L	Pct.	ERA	G	GS	CG	ShO	Sv.	IP	H	R	ER	BB	SO
1998—	Reading (Eastern)■	1	3	.250	9.64	8	0	0	0	3	9 1/3	18	12	10	5	13
	— Scran./W.B. (Int'l)	0	2	.000	5.68	13	0	0	0	5	12 2/3	14	8	8	3	15
	— Philadelphia (N.L.)	0	0	...	5.00	6	0	0	0	0	9	8	5	5	5	9
	— Charlotte (Int'l)■	3	0	1.000	2.70	19	0	0	0	1	36 2/3	33	12	11	21	26
A.L. totals (1 year)		0	0	...	13.50	3	0	0	0	0	3 1/3	6	5	5	7	1
N.L. totals (5 years)		9	7	.563	3.86	162	0	0	0	0	221 1/3	214	112	95	113	177
Major league totals (5 years)		9	7	.563	4.01	165	0	0	0	8	224 2/3	220	117	100	120	178

BOROWSKI, JOE　　　　　　　　P　　　　　　　　BREWERS

PERSONAL: Born May 4, 1971, in Bayonne, N.J. ... 6-2/225. ... Throws right, bats right. ... Full name: Joseph Thomas Borowski.
HIGH SCHOOL: Marist (Bayonne, N.J.).
COLLEGE: Rutgers.
TRANSACTIONS/CAREER NOTES: Selected by Chicago White Sox organization in 32nd round of free-agent draft (June 5, 1989). ... Traded by White Sox organization to Baltimore Orioles organization for IF Pete Rose Jr. (March 21, 1991). ... Traded by Orioles with P Rachaad Stewart to Atlanta Braves for P Kent Mercker (December 17, 1995). ... Claimed on waivers by New York Yankees (September 15, 1997). ... On New York disabled list (August 24-September 8, 1998). ... Claimed on waivers by Milwaukee Brewers (December 4, 1998).

Year	Team (League)	W	L	Pct.	ERA	G	GS	CG	ShO	Sv.	IP	H	R	ER	BB	SO
1990—	GC White Sox (GCL)	2	•8	.200	5.58	12	11	0	0	0	61 1/3	74	*47	*38	25	67
1991—	Kane County (Midwest)■	7	2	.778	2.56	49	0	0	0	13	81	60	26	23	43	76
1992—	Frederick (Carolina)	5	6	.455	3.70	48	0	0	0	10	80 1/3	71	40	33	50	85
1993—	Frederick (Carolina)	1	1	.500	3.61	42	2	0	0	11	62 1/3	61	30	25	37	70
	— Bowie (Eastern)	3	0	1.000	0.00	9	0	0	0	0	17 2/3	11	0	0	11	17
1994—	Bowie (Eastern)	3	4	.429	1.91	49	0	0	0	14	66	52	14	14	28	73
1995—	Rochester (Int'l)	1	3	.250	4.04	28	0	0	0	6	35 2/3	32	16	16	18	32
	— Bowie (Eastern)	2	2	.500	3.92	16	0	0	0	7	20 2/3	16	9	9	7	32
	— Baltimore (A.L.)	0	0	...	1.23	6	0	0	0	0	7 1/3	5	1	1	4	3
1996—	Richmond (Int'l)■	1	5	.167	3.71	34	0	0	0	7	53 1/3	42	25	22	30	40
	— Atlanta (N.L.)	2	4	.333	4.85	22	0	0	0	0	26	33	15	14	13	15
1997—	Atlanta (N.L.)	2	2	.500	3.75	20	0	0	0	0	24	27	11	10	16	6
	— Richmond (Int'l)	1	2	.333	3.58	21	0	0	0	2	37 2/3	32	16	15	19	34
	— New York (A.L.)■	0	1	.000	9.00	1	0	0	0	0	2	2	2	2	4	2
1998—	Columbus (Int'l)	3	3	.500	2.93	45	0	0	0	4	73 2/3	66	25	24	39	67
	— New York (A.L.)	1	0	1.000	6.52	8	0	0	0	0	9 2/3	11	7	7	4	7
A.L. totals (3 years)		1	1	.500	4.74	15	0	0	0	0	19	18	10	10	12	12
N.L. totals (2 years)		4	6	.400	4.32	42	0	0	0	0	50	60	26	24	29	21
Major league totals (4 years)		5	7	.417	4.43	57	0	0	0	0	69	78	36	34	41	33

BOSKIE, SHAWN　　　　　　　　P

PERSONAL: Born March 28, 1967, in Hawthorne, Nev. ... 6-3/200. ... Throws right, bats right. ... Full name: Shawn Kealoha Boskie. ... Name pronounced BAH-skee.
HIGH SCHOOL: Reno (Nev.).
JUNIOR COLLEGE: Modesto (Calif.) Junior College.
TRANSACTIONS/CAREER NOTES: Selected by Chicago Cubs organization in first round (10th pick overall) of free-agent draft (January 14, 1986). ... On Chicago disabled list (August 5-September 26, 1990). ... On Chicago disabled list (July 27-September 1, 1992); included rehabilitation assignment to Iowa (August 24-September 1). ... On suspended list (August 31-September 3, 1993). ... Granted free agency (December 20, 1993). ... Re-signed by Cubs (December 22, 1993). ... Traded by Cubs to Philadelphia Phillies for P Kevin Foster (April 12, 1994). ... Traded by Phillies to Seattle Mariners for a player to be named later (July 21, 1994); Phillies acquired 1B Fred McNair to complete deal (September 7, 1994). ... On Seattle disabled list (July 31, 1994-remainder of season). ... Released by Mariners (November 18, 1994). ... Signed by Vancouver, California Angels organization (March 6, 1995). ... On California disabled list (July 6, 1995-remainder of season); included rehabilitation assignments to Lake Elsinore (August 10-24) and Vancouver (August 24-September 1). ... Granted free agency (December 21, 1995). ... Re-signed by Angels organization (January 29, 1996). ... Granted free agency (October 31, 1996). ... Signed by Baltimore Orioles (December 16, 1996). ... On disabled list (August 16-September 1, 1997). ... Granted free agency (October 29, 1997). ... Signed by Montreal Expos organization (February 3, 1998). ... On Ottawa disabled list (July 22, 1998-remainder of season). ... Granted free agency (October 15, 1998).
STATISTICAL NOTES: Led Appalachian League with 15 wild pitches in 1986. ... Led Carolina League with 17 hit batsmen in 1988. ... Led Southern League with 19 hit batsmen in 1989. ... Tied for A.L. lead with 40 home runs allowed in 1996. ... Tied for A.L. lead with 13 hit batsmen in 1996.
MISCELLANEOUS: Appeared in one game as pinch runner and made an out in only appearance as pinch hitter with Chicago (1991). ... Appeared in one game as pinch runner with Philadelphia (1994). ... Appeared in one game as pinch runner (1997).

Year	Team (League)	W	L	Pct.	ERA	G	GS	CG	ShO	Sv.	IP	H	R	ER	BB	SO
1986—	Wytheville (Appal.)	4	4	.500	5.33	14	12	1	0	0	54	42	41	32	57	40
1987—	Peoria (Midwest)	9	11	.450	4.35	26	25	1	0	0	149	149	91	72	56	100
1988—	Win.-Salem (Car.)	12	7	.632	3.39	27	27	4	2	0	186	176	83	70	89	164
1989—	Charlotte (Southern)	11	8	.579	4.38	28	28	5	0	0	181	*196	105	88	84	*164
1990—	Iowa (Am. Assoc.)	4	2	.667	3.18	8	8	1	0	0	51	46	22	18	21	51
	— Chicago (N.L.)	5	6	.455	3.69	15	15	1	0	0	97 2/3	99	42	40	31	49
1991—	Chicago (N.L.)	4	9	.308	5.23	28	20	0	0	0	129	150	78	75	52	62
	— Iowa (Am. Assoc.)	2	2	.500	3.57	7	6	2	0	0	45 1/3	43	19	18	11	29
1992—	Chicago (N.L.)	5	11	.313	5.01	23	18	0	0	0	91 2/3	96	55	51	36	39
	— Iowa (Am. Assoc.)	0	0	...	3.68	2	2	0	0	0	7 1/3	8	4	3	3	3
1993—	Chicago (N.L.)	5	3	.625	3.43	39	2	0	0	0	65 2/3	63	30	25	21	39
	— Iowa (Am. Assoc.)	6	1	.857	4.27	11	11	1	0	0	71 2/3	70	35	34	21	35
1994—	Chicago (N.L.)	0	0	...	0.00	2	0	0	0	0	3 2/3	3	0	0	2	3
	— Philadelphia (N.L.)■	4	6	.400	5.23	18	14	1	0	0	84 1/3	85	56	49	29	59
	— Seattle (A.L.)■	0	1	.000	6.75	2	1	0	0	0	2 2/3	4	2	2	1	0

Year	Team (League)	W	L	Pct.	ERA	G	GS	CG	ShO	Sv.	IP	H	R	ER	BB	SO
1995—	California (A.L.)■...............	7	7	.500	5.64	20	20	1	0	0	111²/₃	127	73	70	25	51
	— Lake Elsinore (Calif.)..........	0	0	...	4.09	3	3	0	0	0	11	15	7	5	4	8
	— Vancouver (PCL)..............	1	0	1.000	3.00	1	1	0	0	0	6	4	2	2	4	1
1996—	California (A.L.).................	12	11	.522	5.32	37	28	1	0	0	189¹/₃	226	126	112	67	133
1997—	Baltimore (A.L.)■..............	6	6	.500	6.43	28	9	0	0	1	77	95	57	55	26	50
1998—	Ottawa (Int'l)■..................	5	7	.417	4.55	13	13	0	0	0	87	100	48	44	21	51
	— Montreal (N.L.)..................	1	3	.250	9.17	5	5	0	0	0	17²/₃	34	21	18	4	10
A.L. totals (4 years)		25	25	.500	5.65	87	58	2	0	1	380²/₃	452	258	239	119	234
N.L. totals (6 years)		24	38	.387	4.74	130	74	2	0	0	489²/₃	530	282	258	173	260
Major league totals (9 years)		49	63	.438	5.14	217	132	4	0	1	870¹/₃	982	540	497	292	494

BOTTALICO, RICKY — P — CARDINALS

B

PERSONAL: Born August 26, 1969, in New Britain, Conn. ... 6-1/217. ... Throws right, bats left. ... Full name: Richard Paul Bottalico. ... Name pronounced ba-TAL-e-koh.

HIGH SCHOOL: South Catholic (Hartford, Conn.).

COLLEGE: Florida Southern, then Central Connecticut State.

TRANSACTIONS/CAREER NOTES: Signed as non-drafted free agent by Philadelphia Phillies organization (July 21, 1991). ... On Philadelphia disabled list (April 24-July 1, 1998); included rehabilitation assignment to Scranton/Wilkes-Barre (June 6-July 1). ... On suspended list (August 25-28, 1998). ... Traded by Phillies with P Garrett Stephenson to St. Louis Cardinals for OF Ron Gant, P Jeff Brantley and P Cliff Politte (November 19, 1998).

STATISTICAL NOTES: Pitched two innings, combining with starter Craig Holman (two innings), Gregory Brown (two innings) and Toby Borland (one inning) in seven-inning, 2-0 no-hit victory for Reading against New Britain (September 4, 1993, first game).

Year	Team (League)	W	L	Pct.	ERA	G	GS	CG	ShO	Sv.	IP	H	R	ER	BB	SO
1991—	Martinsville (App.)..............	3	2	.600	4.09	7	6	2	•1	0	33	32	20	15	13	38
	— Spartanburg (SAL)	2	0	1.000	0.00	2	2	0	0	0	15	4	0	0	2	11
1992—	Spartanburg (SAL)	5	10	.333	2.41	42	11	1	0	13	119²/₃	94	41	32	56	118
1993—	Clearwater (Fla. St.)	1	0	1.000	2.75	13	0	0	0	4	19²/₃	19	6	6	5	19
	— Reading (Eastern)	3	3	.500	2.25	49	0	0	0	20	72	63	22	18	26	65
1994—	Scran./W.B. (Int'l)...............	3	1	.750	8.87	19	0	0	0	3	22¹/₃	32	27	22	22	22
	— Reading (Eastern)	2	2	.500	2.53	38	0	0	0	22	42²/₃	29	13	12	10	51
	— Philadelphia (N.L.)............	0	0	...	0.00	3	0	0	0	0	3	3	0	0	1	3
1995—	Philadelphia (N.L.).............	5	3	.625	2.46	62	0	0	0	1	87²/₃	50	25	24	42	87
1996—	Philadelphia (N.L.).............	4	5	.444	3.19	61	0	0	0	34	67²/₃	47	24	24	23	74
1997—	Philadelphia (N.L.).............	2	5	.286	3.65	69	0	0	0	34	74	68	31	30	42	89
1998—	Philadelphia (N.L.).............	1	5	.167	6.44	39	0	0	0	6	43¹/₃	54	31	31	25	27
	— Scran./W.B. (Int'l).............	0	1	.000	2.92	10	5	0	0	1	12¹/₃	8	4	4	9	4
Major league totals (5 years)		12	18	.400	3.56	234	0	0	0	75	275²/₃	222	111	109	133	280

ALL-STAR GAME RECORD

Year	League	W	L	Pct.	ERA	GS	CG	ShO	Sv.	IP	H	R	ER	BB	SO
1996—	National	0	0	...	0.00	0	0	0	0	1	0	0	0	0	1

BOTTENFIELD, KENT — P — CARDINALS

PERSONAL: Born November 14, 1968, in Portland, Ore. ... 6-3/240. ... Throws right, bats right. ... Full name: Kent Dennis Bottenfield. ... Twin brother of Keven Bottenfield, minor league catcher/infielder (1986-87).

HIGH SCHOOL: James Madison (Portland, Ore.).

TRANSACTIONS/CAREER NOTES: Selected by Montreal Expos organization in fourth round of free-agent draft (June 2, 1986). ... Traded by Expos to Colorado Rockies for P Butch Henry (July 16, 1993). ... On Colorado disabled list (March 25-May 9, 1994); included rehabilitation assignment to Colorado Springs (April 10-May 9). ... Traded to Phoenix, San Francisco Giants organization (June 29, 1994). ... Released by Giants (November 8, 1994). ... Signed by Toledo, Detroit Tigers organization (April 3, 1995). ... Granted free agency (October 16, 1995). ... Signed by Iowa, Chicago Cubs organization (March 9, 1996). ... Granted free agency (December 21, 1997). ... Signed by St. Louis Cardinals (January 8, 1998).

Year	Team (League)	W	L	Pct.	ERA	G	GS	CG	ShO	Sv.	IP	H	R	ER	BB	SO
1986—	GC Expos (GCL)	5	6	.455	3.27	13	13	2	0	0	74¹/₃	73	•42	27	30	41
1987—	Burlington (Midw.)	9	13	.409	4.53	27	27	6	3	0	161	175	98	81	42	103
1988—	W.P. Beach (FSL).............	10	8	.556	3.33	27	27	9	4	0	181	165	80	67	47	120
1989—	Jacksonville (Southern)......	3	*17	.150	5.26	25	25	1	0	0	138²/₃	137	101	81	73	91
1990—	Jacksonville (Southern)......	12	10	.545	3.41	29	28	2	1	0	169	158	72	64	67	121
1991—	Indianapolis (A.A.)............	8	15	.348	4.06	29	27	•5	2	0	166¹/₃	155	97	75	61	108
1992—	Indianapolis (A.A.)............	•12	8	.600	3.43	25	23	3	1	0	152¹/₃	139	64	58	58	111
	— Montreal (N.L.)■..............	1	2	.333	2.23	10	4	0	0	1	32¹/₃	26	9	8	11	14
1993—	Montreal (N.L.)■..............	2	5	.286	4.12	23	11	0	0	0	83	93	49	38	33	33
	— Colorado (N.L.)■..............	3	5	.375	6.10	14	14	1	0	0	76²/₃	86	53	52	38	30
1994—	Colo. Springs (PCL)■..........	1	2	.333	4.94	5	4	1	0	0	31	35	19	17	11	17
	— Colorado (N.L.)..............	3	1	.750	5.84	15	1	0	0	1	24²/₃	28	16	16	10	15
	— Phoenix (PCL)■..............	2	1	.667	2.57	8	5	1	1	0	35	30	13	10	11	11
	— San Francisco (N.L.)	0	0	...	10.80	1	0	0	0	0	1²/₃	5	2	2	0	0
1995—	Toledo (International)■........	5	11	.313	4.54	27	19	2	1	1	136²/₃	148	80	69	55	68
1996—	Iowa (Am. Assoc.)■............	1	2	.333	2.19	28	0	0	0	18	24²/₃	19	9	6	8	14
	— Chicago (N.L.)..............	3	5	.375	2.63	48	0	0	0	1	61²/₃	59	25	18	19	33
1997—	Chicago (N.L.)..............	2	3	.400	3.86	64	0	0	0	2	84	82	39	36	35	74
1998—	St. Louis (N.L.)■..............	4	6	.400	4.44	44	17	0	0	4	133²/₃	128	72	66	57	98
Major league totals (6 years)		18	27	.400	4.27	219	47	1	0	9	497²/₃	507	265	236	203	297

BOURNIGAL, RAFAEL   IF   PIRATES

PERSONAL: Born May 12, 1966, in Azua, Dominican Republic. ... 5-11/176. ... Bats right, throws right. ... Full name: Rafael Antonio Bournigal.
HIGH SCHOOL: Domay (Dominican Republic).
JUNIOR COLLEGE: Canada College (Calif.).
COLLEGE: Florida State.
TRANSACTIONS/CAREER NOTES: Selected by Texas Rangers organization in 11th round of free-agent draft (January 9, 1985); did not sign. ... Selected by Baltimore Orioles organization in 10th round of free-agent draft (January 14, 1986); did not sign. ... Selected by Los Angeles Dodgers organization in 19th round of free-agent draft (June 2, 1987). ... On Albuquerque temporarily inactive list (April 22-30, 1994). ... Traded by Dodgers organization to Montreal Expos organization for P John Foster (June 9, 1995). ... On Ottawa disabled list (June 26-July 22, 1995). ... Granted free agency (October 16, 1995). ... Signed by Edmonton, Oakland Athletics organization (January 22, 1996). ... On disabled list (July 1-31, 1997); included rehabilitation assignment to Modesto (July 21-31). ... Released by Athletics (December 14, 1998). ... Signed by Pittsburgh Pirates organization (December 22, 1998).
STATISTICAL NOTES: Led Northwest League shortstops with .953 fielding percentage in 1988. ... Led Pacific Coast League shortstops with 636 total chances and 97 double plays in 1993.
MISCELLANEOUS: Served as player/coach with Vero Beach (1991).

Year — Team (League)	Pos.	G	AB	R	H	2B	3B	HR	RBI	Avg.	BB	SO	SB	PO	A	E	Avg.
1987— Great Falls (Pio.)	2B-SS	30	82	5	12	4	0	0	4	.146	3	7	0	49	47	4	.960
1988— Salem (Northwest)	SS-2B-3B	70	275	54	86	10	1	0	25	.313	38	32	11	76	179	12	†.955
1989— Vero Beach (FSL)	2B-SS	132	484	74	128	11	1	1	37	.264	33	21	18	219	378	15	.975
1990— San Antonio (Tex.)	SS-2B-3B	69	194	20	41	4	2	0	14	.211	8	25	2	99	136	6	.975
1991— Vero Beach (FSL)	SS-3B	20	66	6	16	2	0	0	3	.242	1	3	2	29	56	1	.988
— San Antonio (Tex.)	3B-SS-2B	16	65	6	21	2	0	0	9	.323	2	7	2	28	43	0	1.000
— Albuquerque (PCL).....	SS-2B-3B	66	215	34	63	5	5	0	29	.293	14	13	4	100	188	9	.970
1992— Albuquerque (PCL).....	SS	122	395	47	128	18	1	0	34	.324	22	7	5	*201	369	9	*.984
— Los Angeles (N.L.)	SS	10	20	1	3	1	0	0	0	.150	1	2	0	12	17	1	.967
1993— Albuquerque (PCL).....	SS	134	465	75	129	25	4	4	55	.277	29	18	3	196	*427	13	*.980
— Los Angeles (N.L.)	SS-2B	8	18	0	9	1	0	0	3	.500	0	2	0	5	14	0	1.000
1994— Albuquerque (PCL).....	SS	61	208	29	69	8	0	1	22	.332	9	9	2	66	209	4	.986
— Los Angeles (N.L.)	SS	40	116	2	26	3	1	0	11	.224	9	5	0	56	95	3	.981
1995— Albuquerque (PCL).....	SS	15	31	2	4	1	0	0	1	.129	1	2	0	7	32	2	.951
— Ottawa (Int'l)■..........	SS-2B-3B	19	54	2	11	4	0	0	6	.204	2	4	0	15	51	1	.985
— Harrisburg (East.).......	SS	29	95	12	21	3	1	0	7	.221	11	8	1	27	64	3	.968
1996— Oakland (A.L.)■.........	2B-SS	88	252	33	61	14	2	0	18	.242	16	19	4	128	208	2	.994
1997— Oakland (A.L.).........	SS-2B	79	222	29	62	9	0	1	20	.279	16	19	2	100	199	6	.980
— Modesto (California) ..	SS	7	21	0	5	1	0	0	2	.238	3	2	0	5	7	0	1.000
1998— Oakland (A.L.)	2B-SS-DH	85	209	23	47	11	0	1	19	.225	10	11	6	109	170	0	1.000
American League totals (3 years)		**252**	**683**	**85**	**170**	**34**	**2**	**2**	**57**	**.249**	**42**	**49**	**12**	**337**	**577**	**8**	**.991**
National League totals (3 years)		**58**	**154**	**3**	**38**	**5**	**1**	**0**	**14**	**.247**	**10**	**9**	**0**	**73**	**126**	**4**	**.980**
Major league totals (6 years)		**310**	**837**	**88**	**208**	**39**	**3**	**2**	**71**	**.249**	**52**	**58**	**12**	**410**	**703**	**12**	**.989**

BOWIE, MICAH   P   BRAVES

PERSONAL: Born November 10, 1974, in Humble, Texas. ... 6-4/185. ... Throws left, bats left. ... Full name: Micah Andrew Bowie.
HIGH SCHOOL: Kingwood (Texas).
TRANSACTIONS/CAREER NOTES: Signed as non-drafted free agent by Atlanta Braves organization (July 15, 1993). ... On Durham disabled list (July 4, 1996-remainder of season).

Year — Team (League)	W	L	Pct.	ERA	G	GS	CG	ShO	Sv.	IP	H	R	ER	BB	SO
1994— GC Braves (GCL)	0	3	.000	3.03	6	5	0	0	0	29²/₃	27	14	10	5	35
— Danville (Appalachian)........	3	1	.750	3.58	7	5	0	0	0	32²/₃	28	16	13	13	38
1995— Macon (S. Atl.)..............	4	1	.800	2.28	5	5	0	0	0	27²/₃	9	8	7	11	36
— Durham (Carolina)..............	4	11	.267	3.66	23	13	0	0	0	66¹/₃	55	29	27	33	65
1996— Durham (Carolina)..............	3	6	.333	3.66	14	13	0	0	0	66¹/₃	55	29	27	33	65
1997— Durham (Carolina)..............	2	2	.500	3.66	9	6	0	0	0	39¹/₃	29	16	16	27	44
— Greenville (Southern)	3	2	.600	3.50	8	7	0	0	0	43²/₃	34	19	17	26	41
1998— Greenville (Southern)	11	6	.647	3.48	30	•29	1	0	0	163	132	73	63	64	160

BOYD, JASON   P   DIAMONDBACKS

PERSONAL: Born February 23, 1973, in St. Clair, Ill. ... 6-3/170. ... Throws right, bats right. ... Full name: Jason Pernell Boyd.
HIGH SCHOOL: Edwardsville (Ill.).
JUNIOR COLLEGE: John A. Logan College (Ill.).
TRANSACTIONS/CAREER NOTES: Selected by Philadelphia Phillies organization in eighth round of free-agent draft (June 2, 1994). ... Selected by Arizona Diamondbacks in first round (23rd pick overall) of expansion draft (November 18, 1997). ... On disabled list (May 22, 1998-remainder of season).

Year — Team (League)	W	L	Pct.	ERA	G	GS	CG	ShO	Sv.	IP	H	R	ER	BB	SO
1994— Martinsville (App.)..............	3	7	.300	4.17	14	13	1	0	0	69	65	46	32	32	45
1995— Piedmont (S. Atl.)	6	8	.429	3.58	26	24	0	0	0	151	151	77	60	44	129
1996— Clearwater (Fla. St.)	11	8	.579	3.90	26	26	2	0	0	161²/₃	160	75	70	49	120
1997— Reading (Eastern)	10	6	.625	4.82	48	7	0	0	0	115²/₃	113	65	62	64	98
1998— Tucson (PCL)■	2	2	.500	6.23	15	0	0	0	0	21²/₃	28	22	15	14	13

BRADFORD, CHAD   P   WHITE SOX

PERSONAL: Born September 14, 1974, in Jackson, Miss. ... 6-5/205. ... Throws right, bats right. ... Full name: Chadwick L. Bradford.
HIGH SCHOOL: Byram (Jackson, Miss.).
JUNIOR COLLEGE: Hinds Community College (Miss.).
COLLEGE: Southern Mississippi.

TRANSACTIONS/CAREER NOTES: Selected by Chicago White Sox organization in 13th round of free-agent draft (June 4, 1996).

Year	Team (League)	W	L	Pct.	ERA	G	GS	CG	ShO	Sv.	IP	H	R	ER	BB	SO
1996—	Hickory (S. Atl.)	0	2	.000	0.90	28	0	0	0	18	30	21	7	3	7	27
1997—	Win.-Salem (Car.)	3	7	.300	3.95	46	0	0	0	15	$54\frac{2}{3}$	51	30	24	25	43
1998—	Birmingham (Southern)	1	1	.500	2.60	10	0	0	0	1	$17\frac{1}{3}$	13	6	5	8	14
	—Calgary (PCL)	4	1	.800	1.94	29	0	0	0	0	51	50	12	11	11	27
	—Chicago (A.L.)	2	1	.667	3.23	29	0	0	0	1	$30\frac{2}{3}$	27	16	11	7	11
Major league totals (1 year)		2	1	.667	3.23	29	0	0	0	1	$30\frac{2}{3}$	27	16	11	7	11

BRADLEY, RYAN — P — YANKEES

B

PERSONAL: Born October 26, 1975, in Covina, Calif. ... 6-4/226. ... Throws right, bats right. ... Full name: Ryan James Bradley.
HIGH SCHOOL: Ayala (Chino, Calif.).
COLLEGE: Arizona State.
TRANSACTIONS/CAREER NOTES: Selected by Kansas City Royals in 14th round of free-agent draft (June 2, 1994); did not sign. ... Selected by New York Yankees organization in supplemental round ("sandwich" pick between first and second round; 40th pick overall) of free-agent draft (June 3, 1997); pick received as compensation for Texas Rangers signing Type A free-agent P John Wetteland.
STATISTICAL NOTES: Pitched 8-0 no-hit victory for Tampa against Lakeland (June 22, 1998).

Year	Team (League)	W	L	Pct.	ERA	G	GS	CG	ShO	Sv.	IP	H	R	ER	BB	SO
1997—	Oneonta (N.Y.-Penn)	3	1	.750	1.35	14	0	0	0	1	$26\frac{2}{3}$	22	5	4	5	22
1998—	Tampa (Fla. St.)	7	4	.636	2.38	32	11	1	1	7	$94\frac{2}{3}$	59	29	25	30	112
	—Norwich (Eastern)	2	0	1.000	1.44	3	3	1	1	0	25	8	4	4	8	25
	—Columbus (Int'l)	0	1	.000	6.19	3	3	0	0	0	16	15	13	11	13	12
	—New York (A.L.)	2	1	.667	5.68	5	1	0	0	0	$12\frac{2}{3}$	12	9	8	9	13
Major league totals (1 year)		2	1	.667	5.68	5	1	0	0	0	$12\frac{2}{3}$	12	9	8	9	13

BRAGG, DARREN — OF — CARDINALS

PERSONAL: Born September 7, 1969, in Waterbury, Conn. ... 5-9/180. ... Bats left, throws right. ... Full name: Darren William Bragg.
HIGH SCHOOL: Taft (Watertown, Conn.).
COLLEGE: Georgia Tech.
TRANSACTIONS/CAREER NOTES: Selected by Seattle Mariners organization in 22nd round of free-agent draft (June 30, 1991). ... Traded by Mariners to Boston Red Sox for P Jamie Moyer (July 30, 1996). ... Granted free agency (December 21, 1998). ... Signed by St. Louis Cardinals (January 12, 1999).
STATISTICAL NOTES: Led Carolina League in caught stealing with 19 in 1992. ... Led Pacific Coast League outfielders with 344 total chances and five double plays in 1994. ... Career major league grand slams: 2.

Year	Team (League)	Pos.	G	AB	R	H	2B	3B	HR	RBI	Avg.	BB	SO	SB	PO	A	E	Avg.
							BATTING								FIELDING			
1991—	Peninsula (Caro.)	OF-2B	69	237	42	53	14	0	3	29	.224	66	72	21	167	9	4	.978
1992—	Peninsula (Caro.)	OF	135	428	*83	117	29	5	9	58	.273	*105	76	44	262	11	4	.986
1993—	Jacksonville (Sou.)	OF-P	131	451	74	119	26	3	11	46	.264	81	82	19	306	14	10	.970
1994—	Calgary (PCL)	OF	126	500	112	175	33	6	17	85	.350	68	72	28	317	20	7	.980
	—Seattle (A.L.)	DH-OF	8	19	4	3	1	0	0	2	.158	2	5	0	1	0	0	1.000
1995—	Seattle (A.L.)	OF-DH	52	145	20	34	5	1	3	12	.234	18	37	9	83	7	1	.989
	—Tacoma (PCL)	OF	53	212	24	65	13	3	4	31	.307	23	39	10	115	7	4	.968
1996—	Seattle (A.L.)	OF	69	195	36	53	12	1	7	25	.272	33	35	8	118	7	1	.992
	—Tacoma (PCL)	OF	20	71	17	20	8	0	3	8	.282	14	14	1	32	2	0	1.000
	—Boston (A.L.)■	OF	58	222	38	56	14	1	3	22	.252	36	39	6	136	5	2	.986
1997—	Boston (A.L.)	OF-3B	153	513	65	132	35	2	9	57	.257	61	102	10	364	11	5	.987
1998—	Boston (A.L.)	OF-DH	129	409	51	114	29	3	8	57	.279	42	99	5	218	6	1	*.996
Major league totals (5 years)			469	1503	214	392	96	8	30	175	.261	192	317	38	920	36	10	.990

DIVISION SERIES RECORD

Year	Team (League)	Pos.	G	AB	R	H	2B	3B	HR	RBI	Avg.	BB	SO	SB	PO	A	E	Avg.
							BATTING								FIELDING			
1998—	Boston (A.L.)	OF	3	12	0	1	0	0	0	0	.083	0	5	0	4	0	0	1.000

RECORD AS PITCHER

Year	Team (League)	W	L	Pct.	ERA	G	GS	CG	ShO	Sv.	IP	H	R	ER	BB	SO
1993—	Jacksonville (Southern)	0	0	...	9.00	1	0	0	0	0	1	3	1	1	0	0

BRAMMER, J.D. — P — INDIANS

PERSONAL: Born January 30, 1975, in West Logan, W.Va. ... 6-4/235. ... Throws right, bats right. ... Full name: John D. Brammer.
HIGH SCHOOL: Logan (W.Va.).
COLLEGE: Stanford.
TRANSACTIONS/CAREER NOTES: Selected by Cleveland Indians organization in fourth round of free-agent draft (June 4, 1996). ... On Kinston disabled list (May 20-July 15, 1998).

Year	Team (League)	W	L	Pct.	ERA	G	GS	CG	ShO	Sv.	IP	H	R	ER	BB	SO
1996—	Watertown (NYP)	5	0	1.000	3.55	17	0	0	0	1	38	27	22	15	28	49
1997—	Columbia (S. Atl.)	6	10	.375	7.02	28	23	0	0	1	$116\frac{2}{3}$	132	102	*91	50	105
1998—	Kinston (Carolina)	3	2	.600	1.33	15	0	0	0	2	27	15	6	4	8	33
	—Akron (Eastern)	1	0	1.000	5.23	11	0	0	0	3	$20\frac{2}{3}$	21	12	12	10	23

BRANSON, JEFF — IF — REDS

PERSONAL: Born January 26, 1967, in Waynesboro, Miss. ... 6-0/180. ... Bats left, throws right. ... Full name: Jeffery Glenn Branson.
HIGH SCHOOL: Southern Choctaw (Silas, Ala.).
COLLEGE: Livingston (Ala.) University.

TRANSACTIONS/CAREER NOTES: Selected by Cincinnati Reds organization in second round of free-agent draft (June 1, 1988). ... Traded by Reds with P John Smiley to Cleveland Indians for P Danny Graves, P Jim Crowell, P Scott Winchester and IF Damian Jackson (July 31, 1997). ... On Cleveland disabled list (August 2-September 1, 1998); included rehabilitation assignment to Buffalo (August 21-September 1). ... Granted free agency (October 23, 1998). ... Signed by Reds organization (November 17, 1998).

MISCELLANEOUS: Member of 1988 U.S. Olympic baseball team.

								BATTING							FIELDING		
Year	Team (League)	Pos.	G	AB	R	H	2B	3B	HR	RBI	Avg.	BB	SO	SB	PO	A	E	Avg.
1989—	Cedar Rap. (Midw.)	SS	127	469	70	132	28	1	10	68	.281	41	90	5	172	394	33	.945
1990—	Cedar Rap. (Midw.)	SS	62	239	37	60	13	4	6	24	.251	24	44	11	96	152	7	.973
	—Chattanooga (Sou.)	2B-SS	63	233	19	49	9	1	2	29	.210	13	48	3	122	151	13	.955
1991—	Chattanooga (Sou.)	SS-2B	88	304	35	80	13	3	2	28	.263	31	51	3	126	212	12	.966
	—Nashville (A.A.)	SS-2B-OF	43	145	10	35	4	1	0	11	.241	8	31	5	61	93	8	.951
1992—	Nashville (A.A.)	S-3-2-O	36	123	18	40	6	3	4	12	.325	9	19	0	59	76	5	.964
	—Cincinnati (N.L.)	2B-3B-SS	72	115	12	34	7	1	0	15	.296	5	16	0	46	63	7	.940
1993—	Cincinnati (N.L.)	S-2-3-1	125	381	40	92	15	1	3	22	.241	19	73	4	185	260	11	.976
1994—	Cincinnati (N.L.)	2-3-S-1	58	109	18	31	4	1	6	16	.284	5	16	0	39	52	1	.989
1995—	Cincinnati (N.L.)	3-S-2-1	122	331	43	86	18	2	12	45	.260	44	69	2	84	245	9	.973
1996—	Cincinnati (N.L.)	3B-SS-2B	129	311	34	76	16	4	9	37	.244	31	67	2	97	201	14	.955
1997—	Indianapolis (A.A.).....	SS-3B	15	57	7	12	3	0	1	4	.211	6	10	0	18	32	1	.980
	—Cincinnati (N.L.)	3B-2B-SS	65	98	9	15	3	1	1	5	.153	7	23	1	35	56	4	.958
	—Cleveland (A.L.)■......	2-3-S-DH	29	72	5	19	4	0	2	7	.264	7	17	0	23	60	1	.988
1998—	Cincinnati (N.L.)	2-3-1-S	63	100	6	20	4	1	1	9	.200	3	21	0	49	55	5	.954
	—Buffalo (Int'l)	3B-2B	12	46	5	12	4	1	0	2	.261	5	9	0	20	29	0	1.000
American League totals (2 years)			92	172	11	39	8	1	3	16	.227	10	38	0	72	115	6	.969
National League totals (6 years)			571	1345	156	334	63	10	31	140	.248	111	264	9	486	877	46	.967
Major league totals (7 years)			663	1517	167	373	71	11	34	156	.246	121	302	9	558	992	52	.968

DIVISION SERIES RECORD

								BATTING							FIELDING		
Year	Team (League)	Pos.	G	AB	R	H	2B	3B	HR	RBI	Avg.	BB	SO	SB	PO	A	E	Avg.
1995—	Cincinnati (N.L.)	3B	3	7	0	2	1	0	0	2	.286	2	0	0	1	8	0	1.000
1998—	Cleveland (A.L.)								Did not play.									

CHAMPIONSHIP SERIES RECORD

								BATTING							FIELDING		
Year	Team (League)	Pos.	G	AB	R	H	2B	3B	HR	RBI	Avg.	BB	SO	SB	PO	A	E	Avg.
1995—	Cincinnati (N.L.)	3B-PH	4	9	2	1	1	0	0	0	.111	0	2	1	1	3	0	1.000
1997—	Cleveland (A.L.)..........	DH	1	2	0	0	0	0	0	0	.000	0	2	0	...	...	...	...
1998—	Cleveland (A.L.)..........	PH	1	1	0	0	0	0	0	0	.000	0	0	0	...	...	...	...
Championship series totals (3 years)			6	12	2	1	1	0	0	0	.083	0	4	1	1	3	0	1.000

WORLD SERIES RECORD

								BATTING							FIELDING		
Year	Team (League)	Pos.	G	AB	R	H	2B	3B	HR	RBI	Avg.	BB	SO	SB	PO	A	E	Avg.
1997—	Cleveland (A.L.)..........	PH	1	1	0	0	0	0	0	0	.000	0	1	0	...	...	...	...

BRANTLEY, JEFF   P   PHILLIES

PERSONAL: Born September 5, 1963, in Florence, Ala. ... 5-10/190. ... Throws right, bats right. ... Full name: Jeffrey Hoke Brantley.

HIGH SCHOOL: W.A. Berry (Florence, Ala.).

COLLEGE: Mississippi State.

TRANSACTIONS/CAREER NOTES: Selected by Montreal Expos organization in 13th round of free-agent draft (June 4, 1984); did not sign. ... Selected by San Francisco Giants organization in sixth round of free-agent draft (June 3, 1985). ... Granted free agency (December 20, 1993). ... Signed by Cincinnati Reds (January 4, 1994). ... Granted free agency (October 17, 1994). ... Re-signed by Reds (October 28, 1994). ... On disabled list (March 19-April 6, 1996). ... On disabled list (March 27-April 15 and May 20, 1997-remainder of season). ... Traded by Reds to St. Louis Cardinals for 1B Dmitri Young (November 10, 1997). ... On St. Louis disabled list (March 23-April 9, 1998); included rehabilitation assignment to Arkansas (April 5-9). ... Traded by Cardinals with OF Ron Gant and P Cliff Politte to Philadelphia Phillies for P Ricky Bottalico and P Garrett Stephenson (November 19, 1998).

STATISTICAL NOTES: Tied for Pacific Coast League lead with 11 hit batsmen in 1987.

MISCELLANEOUS: Appeared in one game as pinch runner with San Francisco (1989).

Year	Team (League)	W	L	Pct.	ERA	G	GS	CG	ShO	Sv.	IP	H	R	ER	BB	SO
1985—	Fresno (California).............	8	2	.800	3.33	14	13	3	0	0	94²/₃	83	39	35	37	85
1986—	Shreveport (Texas)	8	10	.444	3.48	26	26	•8	3	0	165²/₃	139	78	64	68	125
1987—	Shreveport (Texas)	0	1	.000	3.09	2	2	0	0	0	11²/₃	12	7	4	4	7
	—Phoenix (PCL)...................	6	11	.353	4.65	29	28	2	0	0	170¹/₃	187	110	88	82	111
1988—	Phoenix (PCL)...................	9	5	.643	4.33	27	19	1	0	0	122²/₃	130	65	59	39	83
	—San Francisco (N.L.)	0	1	.000	5.66	9	1	0	0	1	20²/₃	22	13	13	6	11
1989—	San Francisco (N.L.)	7	1	.875	4.07	59	1	0	0	0	97¹/₃	101	50	44	37	69
	—Phoenix (PCL)...................	1	1	.500	1.26	7	0	0	0	3	14¹/₃	6	2	2	6	20
1990—	San Francisco (N.L.)	5	3	.625	1.56	55	0	0	0	19	86²/₃	77	18	15	33	61
1991—	San Francisco (N.L.)	5	2	.714	2.45	67	0	0	0	15	95¹/₃	78	27	26	52	81
1992—	San Francisco (N.L.)	7	7	.500	2.95	56	4	0	0	7	91²/₃	67	32	30	45	86
1993—	San Francisco (N.L.)	5	6	.455	4.28	53	12	0	0	0	113²/₃	112	60	54	46	76
1994—	Cincinnati (N.L.)■.............	6	6	.500	2.48	50	0	0	0	15	65¹/₃	46	20	18	28	63
1995—	Cincinnati (N.L.).............	3	2	.600	2.82	56	0	0	0	28	70¹/₃	53	22	22	20	62
1996—	Cincinnati (N.L.).............	1	2	.333	2.41	66	0	0	0	•44	71	54	21	19	28	76
1997—	Cincinnati (N.L.).............	1	1	.500	3.86	13	0	0	0	1	11²/₃	9	5	5	7	16
1998—	Arkansas (Texas)■.............	0	0	...	0.00	2	0	0	0	0	1²/₃	0	0	0	1	3
	—St. Louis (N.L.).................	0	5	.000	4.44	48	0	0	0	14	50²/₃	40	26	25	18	48
Major league totals (11 years)....		40	36	.526	3.15	532	18	0	0	144	774¹/₃	659	294	271	320	649

DIVISION SERIES RECORD

Year	Team (League)	W	L	Pct.	ERA	G	GS	CG	ShO	Sv.	IP	H	R	ER	BB	SO
1995—	Cincinnati (N.L.)	0	0	...	6.00	3	0	0	0	1	3	5	2	2	0	2

CHAMPIONSHIP SERIES RECORD

Year	Team (League)	W	L	Pct.	ERA	G	GS	CG	ShO	Sv.	IP	H	R	ER	BB	SO
1989—	San Francisco (N.L.)	0	0	...	0.00	3	0	0	0	0	5	1	0	0	2	3
1995—	Cincinnati (N.L.)	0	0	...	0.00	2	0	0	0	0	2 2/3	0	0	0	2	1
Champ. series totals (2 years)		0	0	...	0.00	5	0	0	0	0	7 2/3	1	0	0	4	4

WORLD SERIES RECORD

Year	Team (League)	W	L	Pct.	ERA	G	GS	CG	ShO	Sv.	IP	H	R	ER	BB	SO
1989—	San Francisco (N.L.)	0	0	...	4.15	3	0	0	0	0	4 1/3	5	2	2	3	1

ALL-STAR GAME RECORD

Year	League	W	L	Pct.	ERA	GS	CG	ShO	Sv.	IP	H	R	ER	BB	SO
1990—	National	0	1	.000	54.00	0	0	0	0	1/3	2	2	2	0	0

BRANYAN, RUSSELL — 3B — INDIANS

PERSONAL: Born December 19, 1975, in Warner Robins, Ga. ... 6-3/195. ... Bats left, throws right. ... Full name: Russell Oles Branyan.
HIGH SCHOOL: Stratford Academy (Warner Robins, Ga.).
TRANSACTIONS/CAREER NOTES: Selected by Cleveland Indians organization in seventh round of free-agent draft (June 2, 1994). ... On Akron disabled list (April 23-May 11 and May 16-August 15, 1998).
HONORS: Named Appalachian League Most Valuable Player (1996).
STATISTICAL NOTES: Led Appalachian League with .575 slugging percentage in 1996. ... Led Appalachian League third basemen with 24 double plays in 1996.

							BATTING							FIELDING		
Year	Team (League)	Pos.	G	AB	R	H	2B	3B	HR	RBI	Avg.	BB	SO	SB	PO	A	E	Avg.
1994—	Burlington (Appal.).....	3B	55	171	21	36	10	0	5	13	.211	25	64	4	32	88	21	.851
1995—	Columbus (S. Atl.)......	3B	76	277	46	71	8	6	19	55	.256	27	120	1	34	120	26	.856
1996—	Columbus (S. Atl.)......	3B	130	482	102	129	20	4	*40	*106	.268	62	166	7	82	256	44	.885
1997—	Kinston (Carolina)	3B	83	297	59	86	26	2	27	75	.290	52	94	3	64	118	21	.897
—	Akron (Eastern).........	3B	41	137	26	32	4	0	12	30	.234	28	56	0	31	98	11	.921
1998—	Akron (Eastern).........	3B	43	163	35	48	11	3	16	46	.294	35	58	1	24	72	7	.932
—	Cleveland (A.L.).........	3B	1	4	0	0	0	0	0	0	.000	0	2	0	1	0	0	1.000
Major league totals (1 year)			1	4	0	0	0	0	0	0	.000	0	2	0	1	0	0	1.000

BREDE, BRENT — OF/1B

PERSONAL: Born September 13, 1971, in New Baden, Ill. ... 6-4/208. ... Bats left, throws left. ... Full name: Brent David Brede. ... Name pronounced BREE-de.
HIGH SCHOOL: Wesclin (Trenton, Ill.).
TRANSACTIONS/CAREER NOTES: Selected by Minnesota Twins organization in fifth round of free-agent draft (June 4, 1990). ... Selected by Arizona Diamondbacks in first round (25th pick overall) of expansion draft (November 18, 1997). ... Released by Diamondbacks (November 6, 1998). ... Signed by Chiba Lotte of the Japan Pacific League (November 6, 1998).
STATISTICAL NOTES: Led Appalachian League outfielders with 123 putouts and 1.000 fielding percentage in 1991. ... Tied for Eastern League lead in double plays by outfielder with 10 in 1995. ... Led Pacific Coast League with .446 on-base percentage in 1996.

							BATTING							FIELDING		
Year	Team (League)	Pos.	G	AB	R	H	2B	3B	HR	RBI	Avg.	BB	SO	SB	PO	A	E	Avg.
1990—	Elizabethton (App.).....	OF	46	143	39	35	5	0	0	14	.245	30	30	14	63	3	2	.971
1991—	Kenosha (Midwest)	OF	53	156	12	30	3	2	0	10	.192	16	31	4	79	3	1	.988
—	Elizabethton (App.).....	OF-1B	*68	253	24	61	13	0	3	36	.241	30	48	13	†159	4	0	†1.000
1992—	Kenosha (Midwest)	OF-1B-3B	110	363	44	88	15	0	0	29	.242	53	77	10	236	19	7	.973
1993—	Fort Myers (FSL)	OF-1B	53	182	27	60	10	1	0	27	.330	32	19	8	83	7	3	.968
1994—	Fort Myers (FSL)	OF-1B	116	419	49	110	21	4	2	45	.263	63	60	18	210	10	5	.978
1995—	New Britain (East.)	OF-1B	134	449	71	123	28	2	3	39	.274	69	82	14	307	19	‡10	.970
1996—	Salt Lake (PCL)	OF-1B	132	483	102	168	38	8	11	86	.348	87	87	14	404	24	7	.984
—	Minnesota (A.L.)	OF	10	20	2	6	0	1	0	2	.300	1	5	0	12	1	0	1.000
1997—	Salt Lake (PCL)	OF-1B	84	328	82	116	27	4	9	76	.354	47	62	4	445	27	7	.985
—	Minnesota (A.L.)	OF-1B-DH	61	190	25	52	11	1	3	21	.274	21	38	7	188	9	4	.980
1998—	Arizona (N.L.)■..........	OF-1B-DH	98	212	23	48	9	3	2	17	.226	24	43	1	136	7	4	.973
—	Tucson (PCL)	OF-1B	29	96	16	30	8	1	2	16	.313	21	20	2	57	7	1	.985
American League totals (2 years)			71	210	27	58	11	2	3	23	.276	22	43	7	200	10	4	.981
National League totals (1 year)			98	212	23	48	9	3	2	17	.226	24	43	1	136	7	4	.973
Major league totals (3 years)			169	422	50	106	20	5	5	40	.251	46	86	8	336	17	8	.978

BRESTER, JASON — P — ROCKIES

PERSONAL: Born December 7, 1976, in Lincoln, Neb. ... 6-3/190. ... Throws left, bats left. ... Full name: Jason Scott Brester.
HIGH SCHOOL: Burlington-Edison (Burlington, Wash.).
TRANSACTIONS/CAREER NOTES: Selected by San Francisco Giants organization in second round of free-agent draft (June 1, 1992). ... On Shreveport disabled list (April 2-May 4, 1998). ... Traded by Giants to Colorado Rockies (August 17, 1998), completing deal in which Rockies traded OF Ellis Burks to Giants for OF Darryl Hamilton, P Jim Stoops and a player to be named later (July 31, 1998).

Year	Team (League)	W	L	Pct.	ERA	G	GS	CG	ShO	Sv.	IP	H	R	ER	BB	SO
1995—	Bellingham (N'west)..........	1	0	1.000	4.13	8	6	0	0	0	24	23	11	11	12	17
1996—	Burlington (Midw.)..........	10	9	.526	3.96	27	27	0	0	0	157	139	78	69	64	143
1997—	San Jose (California)	9	9	.500	4.24	26	26	0	0	0	142 1/3	164	80	67	52	172
1998—	Shreveport (Texas)............	2	8	.200	3.82	19	19	0	0	0	113	117	58	48	44	79
—	New Haven (East.)■..........	2	0	1.000	1.59	5	4	0	0	0	22 2/3	22	7	4	7	15

BREWER, BILLY　　　　　　　　　　P

PERSONAL: Born April 15, 1968, in Fort Worth, Texas. ... 6-1/197. ... Throws left, bats left. ... Full name: William Robert Brewer.
HIGH SCHOOL: Spring Hill (Longview, Texas).
COLLEGE: Dallas Baptist.
TRANSACTIONS/CAREER NOTES: Selected by Cleveland Indians organization in 26th round of free-agent draft (June 5, 1989); did not sign. ... Selected by Montreal Expos organization in 28th round of free-agent draft (June 4, 1990). ... On disabled list (April 12-June 11, 1991). ... Selected by Kansas City Royals from Expos organization in Rule 5 major league draft (December 7, 1992). ... Traded by Royals to Los Angeles Dodgers for SS Jose Offerman (December 17, 1995). ... Traded by Dodgers to New York Yankees for P Mike Judd (June 22, 1996). ... Granted free agency (December 20, 1996). ... Signed by Cincinnati Reds organization (December 21, 1996). ... Released by Reds (March 10, 1997). ... Signed by Oakland Athletics organization (March 18, 1997). ... On Oakland disabled list (April 6-28, 1997); included rehabilitation assignments to Visalia (April 21-24) and Edmonton (April 25-28). ... Released by A's (May 22, 1997). ... Signed by Philadelphia Phillies organization (May 27, 1997). ... On Philadelphia disabled list (August 18, 1997-remainder of season). ... Released by Phillies (October 10, 1997). ... Re-signed by Phillies organization (December 15, 1997). ... On disabled list (April 9, 1998-remainder of season). ... Granted free agency (October 15, 1998).

Year Team (League)	W	L	Pct.	ERA	G	GS	CG	ShO	Sv.	IP	H	R	ER	BB	SO
1990— Jamestown (NYP)	2	2	.500	2.93	11	2	0	0	1	27 2/3	23	10	9	13	37
1991— Rockford (Midwest)	3	3	.500	1.98	29	0	0	0	5	41	32	12	9	25	43
1992— W.P. Beach (FSL)	2	2	.500	1.73	28	0	0	0	8	36 1/3	27	10	7	14	37
— Harrisburg (Eastern)	2	0	1.000	5.01	20	0	0	0	0	23 1/3	25	15	13	18	18
1993— Kansas City (A.L.)■	2	2	.500	3.46	46	0	0	0	0	39	31	16	15	20	28
1994— Kansas City (A.L.)	4	1	.800	2.56	50	0	0	0	3	38 2/3	28	11	11	16	25
1995— Kansas City (A.L.)	2	4	.333	5.56	48	0	0	0	0	45 1/3	54	28	28	20	31
— Springfield (Mid.)	0	0	...	0.00	1	0	0	0	1	2	2	1	0	1	2
— Omaha (Am. Assoc.)	0	0	...	0.00	6	0	0	0	0	7	1	0	0	7	5
1996— Albuquerque (PCL)	2	2	.500	3.13	31	0	0	0	2	31 2/3	28	13	11	22	33
— New York (A.L.)■	1	0	1.000	9.53	4	0	0	0	0	5 2/3	7	6	6	8	8
— Columbus (Int'l)	0	2	.000	7.20	13	4	0	0	0	25	27	21	20	19	27
1997— Oakland (A.L.)■	0	0	...	13.50	3	0	0	0	0	2	4	3	3	2	1
— Visalia (California)	0	0	...	0.00	2	2	0	0	0	3	1	1	0	4	5
— Edmonton (PCL)	0	0	...	5.63	7	1	0	0	1	8	8	5	5	6	11
— Scran./W.B. (Int'l)■	2	1	.667	3.00	11	0	0	0	1	9	10	7	3	5	9
— Philadelphia (N.L.)	1	2	.333	3.27	25	0	0	0	0	22	15	8	8	11	16
1998— Philadelphia (N.L.)	0	1	.000	108.00	2	0	0	0	0	1/3	3	4	4	2	0
A.L. totals (5 years)	9	7	.563	4.34	151	0	0	0	3	130 2/3	124	64	63	66	93
N.L. totals (2 years)	1	3	.250	4.84	27	0	0	0	0	22 1/3	18	12	12	13	16
Major league totals (6 years)	10	10	.500	4.41	178	0	0	0	3	153	142	76	75	79	109

BROCAIL, DOUG　　　　　　　　P　　　　　　　　TIGERS

PERSONAL: Born May 16, 1967, in Clearfield, Pa. ... 6-5/235. ... Throws right, bats left. ... Full name: Douglas Keith Brocail.
HIGH SCHOOL: Lamar (Colo.).
JUNIOR COLLEGE: Lamar (Colo.) Community College.
TRANSACTIONS/CAREER NOTES: Selected by San Diego Padres organization in first round (12th pick overall) of free-agent draft (January 14, 1986). ... On Las Vegas disabled list (May 5-12, 1993). ... On San Diego disabled list (April 2-June 28, 1994); included rehabilitation assignments to Wichita (May 26-June 3) and Las Vegas (June 3-23). ... Traded by Padres with P Phil Plantier, OF Derek Bell, P Pedro Martinez, IF Craig Shipley and SS Ricky Gutierrez to Houston Astros for 3B Ken Caminiti, OF Steve Finley, SS Andujar Cedeno, 1B Robert Petagine, P Brian Williams and a player to be named later (December 28, 1994); Padres acquired P Sean Fesh to complete deal (May 1, 1995). ... On Houston disabled list (May 11-August 15, 1996); included rehabilitation assignments to Jackson (May 27-June 4) and Tucson (July 29-August 15). ... Traded by Astros with OF Brian L. Hunter, IF Orlando Miller, P Todd Jones and cash to Detroit Tigers for C Brad Ausmus, P Jose Lima, P C.J. Nitkowski, P Trever Miller and IF Daryle Ward (December 10, 1996). ... On suspended list (June 10-13, 1998). ... On disabled list (August 9-24, 1998).
MISCELLANEOUS: Appeared in six games as pinch runner with San Diego (1993). ... Appeared in two games as pinch runner with San Diego (1994). ... Appeared in one game as pinch runner with Houston (1995). ... Appeared in two games as pinch runner with Houston (1996).

Year Team (League)	W	L	Pct.	ERA	G	GS	CG	ShO	Sv.	IP	H	R	ER	BB	SO
1986— Spokane (N'west)	5	4	.556	3.81	16	•15	0	0	0	85	85	52	36	53	77
1987— Charleston, S.C. (S. Atl.)	2	6	.250	4.09	19	18	0	0	0	92 1/3	94	51	42	28	68
1988— Charleston, S.C. (S. Atl.)	8	6	.571	2.69	22	13	5	0	2	107	107	40	32	25	107
1989— Wichita (Texas)	5	9	.357	5.21	23	22	1	1	0	134 2/3	158	88	78	50	95
1990— Wichita (Texas)	2	2	.500	4.33	12	9	0	0	0	52	53	30	25	24	27
1991— Wichita (Texas)	10	7	.588	3.87	34	16	3	•3	6	146 1/3	147	77	63	43	108
1992— Las Vegas (PCL)	10	10	.500	3.97	29	25	4	0	0	172 1/3	187	82	76	63	103
— San Diego (N.L.)	0	0	...	6.43	3	3	0	0	0	14	17	10	10	5	15
1993— Las Vegas (PCL)	4	2	.667	3.68	10	8	0	0	1	51 1/3	51	26	21	14	32
— San Diego (N.L.)	4	13	.235	4.56	24	24	0	0	0	128 1/3	143	75	65	42	70
1994— Wichita (Texas)	0	0	...	0.00	2	0	0	0	0	4	3	1	0	1	2
— Las Vegas (PCL)	0	0	...	7.11	7	3	0	0	0	12 2/3	21	12	10	2	8
— San Diego (N.L.)	0	0	...	5.82	12	0	0	0	0	17	21	13	11	5	11
1995— Houston (N.L.)■	6	4	.600	4.19	36	7	0	0	1	77 1/3	87	40	36	22	39
— Tucson (PCL)	1	0	1.000	3.86	3	3	0	0	0	16 1/3	18	9	7	4	16
1996— Houston (N.L.)	1	5	.167	4.58	23	4	0	0	0	53	58	31	27	23	34
— Jackson (Texas)	0	0	...	0.00	2	2	0	0	0	4	1	0	0	1	5
— Tucson (PCL)	0	1	.000	7.36	5	1	0	0	0	7 1/3	12	6	6	1	4
1997— Detroit (A.L.)■	3	4	.429	3.23	61	4	0	0	2	78	74	31	28	36	60
1998— Detroit (A.L.)	5	2	.714	2.73	60	0	0	0	0	62 2/3	47	23	19	18	55
A.L. totals (2 years)	8	6	.571	3.01	121	4	0	0	2	140 2/3	121	54	47	54	115
N.L. totals (5 years)	11	22	.333	4.63	98	38	0	0	1	289 2/3	326	169	149	97	169
Major league totals (7 years)	19	28	.404	4.10	219	42	0	0	3	430 1/3	447	223	196	151	284

BROCK, CHRIS   P   GIANTS

PERSONAL: Born February 5, 1970, in Orlando. ... 6-0/185. ... Throws right, bats right. ... Full name: Terrence Christopher Brock.
HIGH SCHOOL: Lyman (Longwood, Fla.).
COLLEGE: Florida State.
TRANSACTIONS/CAREER NOTES: Selected by Atlanta Braves organization in 12th round of free-agent draft (June 1, 1992). ... On disabled list (July 26, 1995-remainder of season). ... Granted free agency (October 15, 1997). ... Signed by San Francisco Giants organization (December 20, 1997).

Year Team (League)	W	L	Pct.	ERA	G	GS	CG	ShO	Sv.	IP	H	R	ER	BB	SO
1992— Idaho Falls (Pioneer)	6	4	.600	2.31	15	15	1	0	0	78	61	27	20	48	72
1993— Macon (S. Atl.)	7	5	.583	2.70	14	14	1	0	0	80	61	37	24	33	92
— Durham (Carolina)..............	5	2	.714	2.51	12	12	1	0	0	79	63	28	22	35	67
1994— Greenville (Southern)	7	6	.538	3.74	25	23	2	2	0	137 1/3	128	68	57	47	94
1995— Richmond (Int'l)	2	8	.200	5.40	22	9	0	0	0	60	68	37	36	27	43
1996— Richmond (Int'l)	10	11	.476	4.67	26	25	3	0	0	150 1/3	137	95	78	61	112
1997— Richmond (Int'l)	10	6	.625	3.34	20	19	0	0	0	118 2/3	97	50	44	51	83
— Atlanta (N.L.)......................	0	0	...	5.58	7	6	0	0	0	30 2/3	34	23	19	19	16
1998— Fresno (Pacific Coast)■.....	11	3	.786	3.29	17	17	2	0	0	115	111	47	42	33	112
— San Francisco (N.L.)	0	0	...	3.90	13	0	0	0	0	27 2/3	31	13	12	7	19
Major league totals (2 years)......	**0**	**0**	**...**	**4.78**	**20**	**6**	**0**	**0**	**0**	**58 1/3**	**65**	**36**	**31**	**26**	**35**

B

BROCK, TARRIK   OF   MARINERS

PERSONAL: Born December 25, 1973, in Goleta, Calif. ... 6-3/170. ... Bats left, throws left. ... Full name: Tarrik Jumaan Brock.
HIGH SCHOOL: Hawthorne (Calif.).
TRANSACTIONS/CAREER NOTES: Selected by Detroit Tigers organization in second round of free-agent draft (June 3, 1991). ... Selected by Seattle Mariners organization from Tigers organization in Rule 5 minor league draft (December 9, 1996).

Year Team (League)	Pos.	G	AB	R	H	2B	3B	HR	RBI	Avg.	BB	SO	SB	PO	A	E	Avg.
1991— Bristol (Appal.)	OF	55	177	26	47	7	3	1	13	.266	22	42	14	49	0	6	.891
1992— Fayetteville (SAL)	OF	100	271	35	59	5	4	0	17	.218	31	69	15	160	9	4	.977
1993— Fayetteville (SAL)	OF	116	427	60	92	8	4	3	47	.215	54	108	25	178	12	10	.950
1994— Lakeland (Fla. St.)	OF	86	331	43	77	17	14	2	32	.233	38	89	15	168	7	3	.983
— Trenton (Eastern)	OF	34	115	12	16	1	4	2	11	.139	13	43	3	52	0	1	.981
1995— Toledo (Int'l)	OF	9	31	4	6	1	0	0	0	.194	2	17	2	12	1	1	.929
— Jacksonville (Sou.).....	OF	9	26	4	3	0	0	0	2	.115	3	14	2	12	1	1	.929
— Lakeland (Fla. St.)	OF	28	91	12	19	3	0	0	5	.209	12	32	5	56	1	2	.966
— Visalia (California)	OF	45	138	21	31	5	2	1	15	.225	17	52	11	90	4	5	.949
1996— Lakeland (Fla. St.)	OF	53	212	42	59	11	4	5	27	.278	17	61	9	89	5	3	.969
— Jacksonville (Sou.).....	OF	37	102	14	13	2	0	0	6	.127	10	36	3	48	5	4	.930
— Fayetteville (SAL)	OF	32	119	21	35	5	2	1	11	.294	14	31	4	49	1	2	.962
1997— Lancaster (Calif.)■.....	OF	132	402	88	108	21	12	7	47	.269	78	106	40	225	11	5	.979
1998— Orlando (South.)	OF	111	372	76	103	28	7	15	65	.277	59	110	17	173	11	2	.989
— Tacoma (PCL)	OF	24	94	14	23	2	3	1	14	.245	9	28	5	59	1	0	1.000

BROGNA, RICO   1B   PHILLIES

PERSONAL: Born April 18, 1970, in Turners Falls, Mass. ... 6-2/205. ... Bats left, throws left. ... Full name: Rico Joseph Brogna. ... Name pronounced BRONE-yah.
HIGH SCHOOL: Watertown (Conn.).
TRANSACTIONS/CAREER NOTES: Selected by Detroit Tigers organization in first round (26th pick overall) of free-agent draft (June 1, 1988). ... On Toledo disabled list (May 25-June 2, 1991). ... Traded by Tigers to New York Mets for 1B Alan Zinter (March 31, 1994). ... On disabled list (June 20, 1996-remainder of season). ... Traded by Mets to Philadelphia Phillies for P Ricardo Jordan and P Toby Borland (November 27, 1996).
STATISTICAL NOTES: Led Eastern League first basemen with 1,261 total chances and 117 double plays in 1990. ... Tied for N.L. lead with 10 sacrifice flies in 1998. ... Career major league grand slams: 2.

Year Team (League)	Pos.	G	AB	R	H	2B	3B	HR	RBI	Avg.	BB	SO	SB	PO	A	E	Avg.
1988— Bristol (Appal.)	1B-OF	60	209	37	53	11	2	7	33	.254	25	42	3	319	26	6	.983
1989— Lakeland (Fla. St.)	1B	128	459	47	108	20	7	5	51	.235	38	82	2	1098	83	13	.989
1990— London (Eastern)	1B	137	488	70	128	21	3	*21	•77	.262	50	100	1	*1155	*93	13	.990
1991— Toledo (Int'l)	1B	41	132	13	29	6	1	2	13	.220	4	26	2	311	37	5	.986
— London (Eastern)	1B-OF	77	293	40	80	13	1	13	51	.273	25	59	0	368	46	6	.986
1992— Toledo (Int'l).............	1B	121	387	45	101	19	4	10	58	.261	31	85	1	896	76	9	.991
— Detroit (A.L.)	1B-DH	9	26	3	5	1	0	1	3	.192	3	5	0	48	6	1	.982
1993— Toledo (Int'l).............	1B	129	483	55	132	30	3	11	59	.273	31	94	7	937	97	8	.992
1994— Norfolk (Int'l)■	1B	67	258	33	63	14	5	12	37	.244	15	62	1	583	47	3	.995
— New York (N.L.).........	1B	39	131	16	46	11	2	7	20	.351	6	29	1	307	28	1	.997
1995— New York (N.L.).........	1B	134	495	72	143	27	2	22	76	.289	39	111	0	1111	93	3	*.998
1996— New York (N.L.).........	1B	55	188	18	48	10	1	7	30	.255	19	50	0	440	31	2	.996
1997— Philadelphia (N.L.)■ ..	1B	148	543	68	137	36	1	20	81	.252	33	116	12	1053	119	7	.994
1998— Philadelphia (N.L.).....	1B	153	565	77	150	36	3	20	104	.265	49	125	7	1238	141	5	.996
American League totals (1 year)		9	26	3	5	1	0	1	3	.192	3	5	0	48	6	1	.982
National League totals (5 years)		529	1922	251	524	120	9	76	311	.273	146	431	20	4149	412	18	.996
Major league totals (6 years)		538	1948	254	529	121	9	77	314	.272	149	436	20	4197	418	19	.996

BROHAWN, TROY   P   DIAMONDBACKS

PERSONAL: Born January 14, 1973, in Cambridge, Md. ... 6-1/190. ... Throws left, bats left. ... Full name: Michael Troy Brohawn.
HIGH SCHOOL: Cambridge South Dorchester (Cambridge, Md.).
COLLEGE: Nebraska.
TRANSACTIONS/CAREER NOTES: Selected by San Francisco Giants organization in fourth round of free-agent draft (June 2, 1994). ... Traded by Giants to Arizona Diamondbacks (December 21, 1998), completing trade in which Diamondbacks traded P Felix Rodriguez to Giants for future considerations (December 8, 1998).

Year Team (League)	W	L	Pct.	ERA	G	GS	CG	ShO	Sv.	IP	H	R	ER	BB	SO
1994—San Jose (California)	0	2	.000	7.02	4	4	0	0	0	16 2/3	27	15	13	5	13
1995—San Jose (California)	7	3	.700	1.65	11	10	0	0	0	65 1/3	45	14	12	20	57
1996—Shreveport (Texas)	9	10	.474	4.60	28	28	0	0	0	156 2/3	163	99	80	49	82
1997—Shreveport (Texas)	13	5	.722	*2.56	26	26	1	•1	0	169	148	57	48	64	98
1998—Fresno (Pacific Coast)	10	8	.556	5.25	30	19	0	0	0	121 2/3	144	75	71	36	87

BROSIUS, SCOTT   3B   YANKEES

PERSONAL: Born August 15, 1966, in Hillsboro, Ore. ... 6-1/202. ... Bats right, throws right. ... Full name: Scott David Brosius. ... Name pronounced BRO-shus.
HIGH SCHOOL: Rex Putnam (Milwaukie, Ore.).
COLLEGE: Linfield College (Ore.).
TRANSACTIONS/CAREER NOTES: Selected by Oakland Athletics organization in 20th round of free-agent draft (June 2, 1987). ... On Tacoma disabled list (April 17-May 29, 1991). ... On Oakland disabled list (April 18-May 12, 1992); included rehabilitation assignment to Tacoma (May 6-12). ... On Oakland disabled list (July 13-August 3, 1992); included rehabilitation assignment to Tacoma (July 27-August 3). ... On Tacoma disabled list (July 28-August 5, 1993). ... On disabled list (June 8-26, 1994). ... On Oakland disabled list (May 5-June 25, 1996); included rehabilitation assignment to Edmonton (June 22-25). ... On Oakland disabled list (August 7-29, 1997); included rehabilitation assignment to Modesto (August 27-29). ... Traded by A's to New York Yankees (November 18, 1997), completing deal in which Yankees traded P Kenny Rogers and cash to A's for a player to be named later (November 7, 1997). ... Granted free agency (October 27, 1998). ... Re-signed by Yankees (November 9, 1998).
HONORS: Named third baseman on THE SPORTING NEWS A.L. All-Star team (1998).
STATISTICAL NOTES: Led Northwest League with seven sacrifice flies in 1987. ... Led Southern League with 274 total bases in 1990. ... Tied for Pacific Coast League lead in double plays by third baseman with 24 in 1992. ... Career major league grand slams: 1.

							BATTING								FIELDING		
Year Team (League)	Pos.	G	AB	R	H	2B	3B	HR	RBI	Avg.	BB	SO	SB	PO	A	E	Avg.
1987—Medford (N'west)	3-S-2-1-P	65	255	34	73	18	1	3	49	.286	26	36	5	123	148	38	.877
1988—Madison (Midwest)	S-3-0-1	132	504	82	153	28	2	9	58	.304	56	67	13	151	305	61	.882
1989—Huntsville (Sou.)	2-3-S-1	128	461	68	125	22	2	7	60	.271	58	62	4	225	316	34	.941
1990—Huntsville (Sou.)	SS-2B-3B	•142	547	94	*162	*39	2	23	88	.296	81	81	12	253	419	41	.942
—Tacoma (PCL)	2B	3	7	2	1	0	1	0	0	.143	1	3	0	3	5	0	1.000
1991—Tacoma (PCL)	3B-SS-2B	65	245	28	70	16	3	8	31	.286	18	29	4	49	168	14	.939
—Oakland (A.L.)	2-0-3-DH	36	68	9	16	5	0	2	4	.235	3	11	3	31	16	0	1.000
1992—Oakland (A.L.)	0-3-1-DH-S	38	87	13	19	2	0	4	13	.218	3	13	3	68	15	1	.988
—Tacoma (PCL)	3B-OF	63	236	29	56	13	0	9	31	.237	23	44	8	50	167	10	.956
1993—Oakland (A.L.)	0-1-3-S-DH	70	213	26	53	10	1	6	25	.249	14	37	6	173	29	2	.990
—Tacoma (PCL)	3-0-2-1-S	56	209	38	62	13	2	8	41	.297	21	50	8	101	109	13	.942
1994—Oakland (A.L.)	3B-OF-1B	96	324	31	77	14	1	14	49	.238	24	57	2	82	157	13	.948
1995—Oakland (A.L.)	3-0-1-2-S-DH	123	389	69	102	19	2	17	46	.262	41	67	4	208	121	15	.956
1996—Oakland (A.L.)	3B-1B-OF	114	428	73	130	25	0	22	71	.304	59	85	7	128	234	10	.973
—Edmonton (PCL)	3B	3	8	5	5	1	0	0	0	.625	3	1	0	0	4	2	.667
1997—Oakland (A.L.)	3B-SS-OF	129	479	59	97	20	1	11	41	.203	34	102	9	142	246	10	.975
—Modesto (California)	3B	2	3	1	1	0	0	0	1	.333	1	0	0	1	1	1	.667
1998—New York (A.L.)■	3B-1B-OF	152	530	86	159	34	0	19	98	.300	52	97	11	114	294	22	.949
Major league totals (8 years)		758	2518	366	653	129	5	95	347	.259	230	469	45	946	1112	73	.966

DIVISION SERIES RECORD

							BATTING								FIELDING		
Year Team (League)	Pos.	G	AB	R	H	2B	3B	HR	RBI	Avg.	BB	SO	SB	PO	A	E	Avg.
1998—New York (A.L.)	3B	3	10	1	4	0	0	1	3	.400	0	3	0	2	6	0	1.000

CHAMPIONSHIP SERIES RECORD

							BATTING								FIELDING		
Year Team (League)	Pos.	G	AB	R	H	2B	3B	HR	RBI	Avg.	BB	SO	SB	PO	A	E	Avg.
1998—New York (A.L.)	3B	6	20	2	6	1	0	1	6	.300	4	4	0	4	10	1	.933

WORLD SERIES RECORD

RECORDS: Shares record for most home runs in two consecutive innings—2 (October 20, 1998, seventh and eighth innings). ... Shares single-inning record for most at-bats—2 (October 17, 1998).
NOTES: Named Most Valuable Player (1998). ... Member of World Series championship team (1998).

							BATTING								FIELDING		
Year Team (League)	Pos.	G	AB	R	H	2B	3B	HR	RBI	Avg.	BB	SO	SB	PO	A	E	Avg.
1998—New York (A.L.)	3B	4	17	3	8	0	0	2	6	.471	0	4	0	3	6	0	1.000

ALL-STAR GAME RECORD

						BATTING								FIELDING		
Year League	Pos.	AB	R	H	2B	3B	HR	RBI	Avg.	BB	SO	SB	PO	A	E	Avg.
1998—American	3B	2	1	1	0	0	0	0	.500	0	1	1	0	0	1	.000

RECORD AS PITCHER

Year Team (League)	W	L	Pct.	ERA	G	GS	CG	ShO	Sv.	IP	H	R	ER	BB	SO
1987—Medford (N'west)	0	0	...	0.00	1	0	0	0	0	2	0	0	0	0	1

PERSONAL: Born March 17, 1969, in Butte, Mont. ... 6-3/200. ... Throws right, bats right. ... Full name: Scott John Brow. ... Name pronounced BRAUH.
HIGH SCHOOL: Hillsboro (Ore.).
COLLEGE: Washington.
TRANSACTIONS/CAREER NOTES: Selected by Toronto Blue Jays organization in seventh round of free-agent draft (June 4, 1990). ... On disabled list (April 20-July 31, 1995). ... Claimed on waivers by Atlanta Braves (September 30, 1996). ... Granted free agency (October 15, 1997). ... Signed by Arizona Diamondbacks organization (December 18, 1997). ... Traded by Diamondbacks with P Joe Lisio to New York Yankees organization for P Willie Banks (June 3, 1998). ... Granted free agency (October 15, 1998).

Year — Team (League)	W	L	Pct.	ERA	G	GS	CG	ShO	Sv.	IP	H	R	ER	BB	SO
1990—St. Catharines (NYP)	3	1	.750	2.27	9	7	0	0	0	39²/₃	34	18	10	11	39
1991—Dunedin (Fla. St.)	3	7	.300	4.78	15	12	0	0	0	69²/₃	73	50	37	28	31
1992—Dunedin (Fla. St.)	14	2	.875	2.43	25	25	3	1	0	*170²/₃	143	53	46	44	107
1993—Knoxville (Southern)	1	2	.333	3.32	3	3	1	0	0	19	13	8	7	9	12
—Toronto (A.L.)	1	1	.500	6.00	6	3	0	0	0	18	19	15	12	10	7
—Syracuse (Int'l)	6	8	.429	4.38	20	19	2	0	0	121¹/₃	119	63	59	37	64
1994—Toronto (A.L.)	0	3	.000	5.90	18	0	0	0	2	29	34	27	19	19	15
—Syracuse (Int'l)	5	3	.625	4.31	14	13	1	1	0	79¹/₃	77	45	38	38	30
1995—Syracuse (Int'l)	1	5	.167	9.00	11	5	0	0	0	31	52	39	31	18	14
1996—Syracuse (Int'l)	5	4	.556	4.93	18	11	0	0	0	76²/₃	84	49	42	26	52
—Toronto (A.L.)	1	0	1.000	5.59	18	1	0	0	0	38²/₃	45	25	24	25	23
1997—Richmond (Int'l)■	5	9	.357	4.45	61	1	0	0	18	83	89	48	41	35	62
1998—Arizona (N.L.)■	1	0	1.000	7.17	17	0	0	0	0	21¹/₃	22	17	17	14	13
—Columbus (Int'l)■	3	2	.600	5.46	30	3	0	0	0	59¹/₃	74	42	36	26	35
A.L. totals (3 years)	2	4	.333	5.78	42	4	0	0	2	85²/₃	98	67	55	54	45
N.L. totals (1 year)	1	0	1.000	7.17	17	0	0	0	0	21¹/₃	22	17	17	14	13
Major league totals (4 years)	3	4	.429	6.06	59	4	0	0	2	107	120	84	72	68	58

B

PERSONAL: Born February 7, 1974, in McComb, Miss. ... 6-0/185. ... Bats both, throws right. ... Full name: Adrian Demond Brown.
HIGH SCHOOL: McComb (Miss.).
TRANSACTIONS/CAREER NOTES: Selected by Pittsburgh Pirates organization in 48th round of free-agent draft (June 1, 1992).

Year — Team (League)	Pos.	G	AB	R	H	2B	3B	HR	RBI	Avg.	BB	SO	SB	PO	A	E	Avg.
1992—GC Pirates (GCL)	OF-1B	39	121	11	31	2	2	0	12	.256	0	12	8	60	4	1	.985
1993—Lethbridge (Pioneer)	OF	69	282	47	75	12	9	3	27	.266	17	34	22	119	4	1	*.992
1994—Augusta (S. Atl.)	OF	79	308	41	80	17	1	1	18	.260	14	38	19	121	6	2	.984
1995—Lynchburg (Caro.)	OF	54	215	30	52	5	2	1	14	.242	12	20	11	110	6	2	.983
—Augusta (S. Atl.)	OF	76	287	64	86	15	4	4	31	.300	33	23	25	124	8	7	.950
1996—Lynchburg (Caro.)	OF	52	215	39	69	9	3	4	25	.321	14	24	18	99	4	2	.981
—Carolina (Southern)	OF	84	341	48	101	11	3	3	25	.296	25	40	27	185	5	2	.990
1997—Carolina (Southern)	OF	37	145	29	44	4	4	2	15	.303	18	12	9	63	2	3	.956
—Pittsburgh (N.L.)	OF	48	147	17	28	6	0	1	10	.190	13	18	8	74	3	1	.987
—Calgary (PCL)	OF	62	248	53	79	10	1	1	19	.319	27	38	20	130	3	1	.993
1998—Nashville (PCL)	OF	85	311	58	90	12	5	3	27	.289	28	38	25	204	7	5	.977
—Pittsburgh (N.L.)	OF	41	152	20	43	4	1	0	5	.283	9	18	4	83	3	2	.977
Major league totals (2 years)		89	299	37	71	10	1	1	15	.237	22	36	12	157	6	3	.982

PERSONAL: Born June 22, 1971, in Porterville, Calif. ... 6-3/205. ... Bats left, throws left. ... Full name: Brant Michael Brown.
HIGH SCHOOL: Monache (Porterville, Calif.).
COLLEGE: Fresno State.
TRANSACTIONS/CAREER NOTES: Selected by Chicago Cubs organization in third round of free-agent draft (June 1, 1992). ... On Daytona disabled list (April 10-25, 1993). ... On Iowa disabled list (July 22-August 11, 1996). ... On Chicago disabled list (June 26-July 25, 1998); included rehabilitation assignment to Iowa (July 22-25). ... Traded by Cubs to Pittsburgh Pirates for P Jon Lieber (December 14, 1998).
STATISTICAL NOTES: Hit three home runs in one game (June 18, 1998).

Year — Team (League)	Pos.	G	AB	R	H	2B	3B	HR	RBI	Avg.	BB	SO	SB	PO	A	E	Avg.
1992—Peoria (Midwest)	1B	70	248	28	68	14	0	3	27	.274	24	49	3	582	39	6	.990
1993—Daytona (Fla. St.)	1B	75	266	26	91	8	7	3	33	.342	11	38	8	643	55	5	.993
—Orlando (South.)	1B	28	111	17	35	11	3	4	23	.315	6	19	2	237	27	3	.989
1994—Orlando (South.)	1B-OF	127	470	54	127	30	6	5	37	.270	37	86	11	1031	80	12	.989
1995—Orlando (South.)	1B-OF	121	446	67	121	27	4	6	53	.271	39	77	8	931	92	10	.990
1996—Iowa (Am. Assoc.)	1B	94	342	48	104	25	3	10	43	.304	19	65	6	762	66	8	.990
—Chicago (N.L.)	1B	29	69	11	21	1	0	5	9	.304	2	17	3	126	17	0	1.000
1997—Chicago (N.L.)	OF-1B	46	137	15	32	7	1	5	15	.234	7	28	2	121	7	2	.985
—Iowa (Am. Assoc.)	OF-1B	71	256	50	77	19	3	16	51	.301	31	44	6	202	13	4	.982
1998—Chicago (N.L.)	OF-1B	124	347	56	101	17	7	14	48	.291	30	95	4	212	3	7	.968
—Iowa (Pacific Coast)	OF-1B	3	11	1	4	0	0	0	0	.364	0	6	0	5	0	0	1.000
Major league totals (3 years)		199	553	82	154	25	8	24	72	.278	39	140	9	459	27	9	.982

DIVISION SERIES RECORD

Year — Team (League)	Pos.	G	AB	R	H	2B	3B	HR	RBI	Avg.	BB	SO	SB	PO	A	E	Avg.
1998—Chicago (N.L.)	PH	1	1	0	0	0	0	0	0	.000	0	0	0	...	...	...	...

BROWN, DERMAL　　　　　　　OF　　　　　　　ROYALS

PERSONAL: Born March 27, 1978, in Bronx, N.Y. ... 5-11/210. ... Bats left, throws right. ... Full name: Dermal Bram Brown.
HIGH SCHOOL: Marlboro (N.Y.) Central.
TRANSACTIONS/CAREER NOTES: Selected by Kansas City Royals organization in first round (14th pick overall) of free-agent draft (June 2, 1996).
HONORS: Named Northwest League Most Valuable Player in 1997.
STATISTICAL NOTES: Led Northwest League with 168 total bases and .564 slugging percentage in 1997. ... Tied for Carolina League lead with five intentional bases on balls in 1998.

								BATTING						FIELDING			
Year　Team (League)	Pos.	G	AB	R	H	2B	3B	HR	RBI	Avg.	BB	SO	SB	PO	A	E	Avg.
1996— GC Royals (GCL)	DH	7	20	1	1	1	0	0	1	.050	0	6	0	...	...	...	...
1997— Spokane (N'west)	OF	73	298	67	97	20	6	13	*73	.326	38	65	17	80	2	7	.921
1998— Wilmington (Caro.)......	OF	128	442	64	114	30	2	10	58	.258	53	115	26	124	5	13	.908
— Kansas City (A.L.)	DH-OF	5	3	2	0	0	0	0	0	.000	0	1	0	1	0	0	1.000
Major league totals (1 year)		**5**	**3**	**2**	**0**	**0**	**0**	**0**	**0**	**.000**	**0**	**1**	**0**	**1**	**0**	**0**	**1.000**

BROWN, EMIL　　　　　　　OF　　　　　　　PIRATES

PERSONAL: Born December 29, 1974, in Chicago. ... 6-2/192. ... Bats right, throws right. ... Full name: Emil Quincy Brown.
HIGH SCHOOL: Harlan (Chicago).
JUNIOR COLLEGE: Indian River Community College (Fla.).
TRANSACTIONS/CAREER NOTES: Selected by Oakland Athletics organization in sixth round of free-agent draft (June 2, 1994). ... On Modesto disabled list (April 10-July 1, 1996). ... On Modesto suspended list (August 29-September 2, 1996). ... Selected by Pittsburgh Pirates organization from A's organization in Rule 5 major league draft (December 9, 1996).
STATISTICAL NOTES: Led Midwest League outfielders with four double plays in 1995.

								BATTING						FIELDING			
Year　Team (League)	Pos.	G	AB	R	H	2B	3B	HR	RBI	Avg.	BB	SO	SB	PO	A	E	Avg.
1994— Arizona A's (Ariz.).......	OF	32	86	13	19	1	1	3	12	.221	13	12	5	43	3	1	.979
1995— W. Mich. (Mid.)	OF	124	459	63	115	17	3	3	67	.251	52	77	35	165	12	8	.957
1996— Modesto (California) ..	OF	57	211	50	64	10	1	10	47	.303	32	51	13	97	5	4	.962
— Scottsdale (Ariz.).......	OF	4	15	5	4	3	0	0	2	.267	3	2	1	3	1	0	1.000
1997— Pittsburgh (N.L.)■.....	OF	66	95	16	17	2	1	2	6	.179	10	32	5	53	2	3	.948
1998— Carolina (Southern)....	OF	123	466	89	154	31	2	14	67	.330	50	71	24	199	10	6	.972
— Pittsburgh (N.L.)	OF	13	39	2	10	1	0	0	3	.256	1	11	0	21	2	0	1.000
Major league totals (2 years)		**79**	**134**	**18**	**27**	**3**	**1**	**2**	**9**	**.201**	**11**	**43**	**5**	**74**	**4**	**3**	**.963**

BROWN, KEVIN　　　　　　　P　　　　　　　DODGERS

PERSONAL: Born March 14, 1965, in McIntyre, Ga. ... 6-4/200. ... Throws right, bats right. ... Full name: James Kevin Brown.
HIGH SCHOOL: Wilkinson County (Irwinton, Ga.).
COLLEGE: Georgia Tech.
TRANSACTIONS/CAREER NOTES: Selected by Texas Rangers organization in first round (fourth pick overall) of free-agent draft (June 2, 1986). ... On disabled list (August 14-29, 1990 and March 27-April 11, 1993). ... Granted free agency (October 15, 1994). ... Signed by Baltimore Orioles (April 9, 1995). ... On disabled list (June 23-July 17, 1995). ... Granted free agency (November 3, 1995). ... Signed by Florida Marlins (December 22, 1995). ... On disabled list (May 13-28, 1996). ... Traded by Marlins to San Diego Padres for P Rafael Medina, P Steve Hoff and 1B Derrek Lee (December 15, 1997). ... Granted free agency (October 26, 1998). ... Signed by Los Angeles Dodgers (December 12, 1998).
HONORS: Named righthanded pitcher on THE SPORTING NEWS college All-America team (1986). ... Named N.L. Pitcher of the Year by THE SPORTING NEWS (1998). ... Named righthanded pitcher on THE SPORTING NEWS N.L. All-Star team (1998).
STATISTICAL NOTES: Tied for A.L. lead with 13 hit batsmen in 1991. ... Tied for N.L. lead with 16 hit batsmen in 1996. ... Pitched 9-0 no-hit victory against San Francisco (June 10, 1997). ... Pitched 5-1 one-hit, complete-game victory against Los Angeles (July 16, 1997). ... Led N.L. with 14 hit batsmen in 1997. ... Pitched 4-0 one-hit, complete-game victory against Milwaukee (August 16, 1998).
MISCELLANEOUS: Made an out in only appearance as pinch hitter (1990). ... Appeared in one game as pinch runner (1993). ... Appeared in two games as pinch runner (1996). ... Holds Florida Marlins all-time records for most shutouts (5) and most complete games (11).

Year　Team (League)	W	L	Pct.	ERA	G	GS	CG	ShO	Sv.	IP	H	R	ER	BB	SO
1986— GC Rangers (GCL)............	0	0	...	6.00	3	0	0	0	0	6	7	4	4	2	1
— Tulsa (Texas)	0	0	...	4.50	3	2	0	0	0	10	9	7	5	5	10
— Texas (A.L.)	1	0	1.000	3.60	1	1	0	0	0	5	6	2	2	0	4
1987— Tulsa (Texas)	1	4	.200	7.29	8	8	0	0	0	42	53	36	34	18	26
— Oklahoma City (A.A.).........	0	5	.000	10.73	5	5	0	0	0	24 1/3	32	32	29	17	9
— Charlotte (Fla. St.)............	0	2	.000	2.72	6	6	1	0	0	36 1/3	33	14	11	17	21
1988— Tulsa (Texas)	12	10	.545	3.51	26	26	5	0	0	174 1/3	174	94	68	61	118
— Texas (A.L.)	1	1	.500	4.24	4	4	1	0	0	23 1/3	33	15	11	8	12
1989— Texas (A.L.)	12	9	.571	3.35	28	28	7	0	0	191	167	81	71	70	104
1990— Texas (A.L.)	12	10	.545	3.60	26	26	6	2	0	180	175	84	72	60	88
1991— Texas (A.L.)	9	12	.429	4.40	33	33	0	0	0	210 2/3	233	116	103	90	96
1992— Texas (A.L.)	•21	11	.656	3.32	35	35	11	0	0	*265 2/3	*262	117	98	76	173
1993— Texas (A.L.)	15	12	.556	3.59	34	34	12	3	0	233	228	105	93	74	142
1994— Texas (A.L.)	7	9	.438	4.82	26	•25	3	0	0	170	*218	109	91	50	123
1995— Baltimore (A.L.)■.............	10	9	.526	3.60	26	26	3	1	0	172 1/3	155	73	69	48	117
1996— Florida (N.L.)■...............	17	11	.607	*1.89	32	32	5	*3	0	233	187	60	49	33	159
1997— Florida (N.L.)	16	8	.667	2.69	33	33	6	2	0	237 1/3	214	77	71	66	205
1998— San Diego (N.L.)■	18	7	.720	2.38	36	•35	7	3	0	257	225	77	68	49	257
A.L. totals (9 years)	**88**	**73**	**.547**	**3.78**	**213**	**212**	**43**	**7**	**0**	**1451**	**1477**	**702**	**610**	**476**	**859**
N.L. totals (3 years)	**51**	**26**	**.662**	**2.33**	**101**	**100**	**18**	**8**	**0**	**727 1/3**	**626**	**214**	**188**	**148**	**621**
Major league totals (12 years)	**139**	**99**	**.584**	**3.30**	**314**	**312**	**61**	**15**	**0**	**2178 1/3**	**2103**	**916**	**798**	**624**	**1480**

B

DIVISION SERIES RECORD

RECORDS: Holds career record for most hit batsmen—3.

Year Team (League)	W	L	Pct.	ERA	G	GS	CG	ShO	Sv.	IP	H	R	ER	BB	SO
1997—Florida (N.L.)	0	0	...	1.29	1	1	0	0	0	7	4	1	1	0	5
1998—San Diego (N.L.)	1	0	1.000	0.61	2	2	0	0	0	14 2/3	5	1	1	7	21
Div. series totals (2 years)	1	0	1.000	0.83	3	3	0	0	0	21 2/3	9	2	2	7	26

CHAMPIONSHIP SERIES RECORD

RECORDS: Shares single-game record for most hits allowed—11 (October 14, 1997).

Year Team (League)	W	L	Pct.	ERA	G	GS	CG	ShO	Sv.	IP	H	R	ER	BB	SO
1997—Florida (N.L.)	2	0	1.000	4.20	2	2	1	0	0	15	16	7	7	5	11
1998—San Diego (N.L.)	1	1	.500	2.61	2	1	1	1	0	10 1/3	5	3	3	4	12
Champ. series totals (2 years)	3	1	.750	3.55	4	3	2	1	0	25 1/3	21	10	10	9	23

WORLD SERIES RECORD

NOTES: Member of World Series championship team (1997).

Year Team (League)	W	L	Pct.	ERA	G	GS	CG	ShO	Sv.	IP	H	R	ER	BB	SO
1997—Florida (N.L.)	0	2	.000	8.18	2	2	0	0	0	11	15	10	10	5	6
1998—San Diego (N.L.)	0	1	.000	4.40	2	2	0	0	0	14 1/3	14	7	7	6	13
World Series totals (2 years)	0	3	.000	6.04	4	4	0	0	0	25 1/3	29	17	17	11	19

ALL-STAR GAME RECORD

Year League	W	L	Pct.	ERA	GS	CG	ShO	Sv.	IP	H	R	ER	BB	SO
1992—American	1	0	1.000	0.00	1	0	0	0	1	0	0	0	0	1
1996—National	0	0	...	0.00	0	0	0	0	0	0	0	0	0	0
1997—National	0	0	...	0.00	0	0	0	0	1	1	0	0	0	0
1998—National	0	0	...	0.00	0	0	0	0	2/3	0	0	0	0	1
All-Star totals (4 years)	1	0	1.000	0.00	1	0	0	0	3 2/3	1	0	0	0	2

B

BROWN, KEVIN   C   BLUE JAYS

PERSONAL: Born April 21, 1973, in Valparaiso, Ind. ... 6-2/215. ... Bats right, throws right. ... Full name: Kevin Lee Brown.
HIGH SCHOOL: Pike Central (Petersburg, Ind.).
COLLEGE: Southern Indiana.
TRANSACTIONS/CAREER NOTES: Selected by Texas Rangers organization in second round of free-agent draft (June 2, 1994). ... Traded by Rangers to Toronto Blue Jays for P Tim Crabtree (March 14, 1998). ... On Toronto disabled list (June 13-30, 1998); included rehabilitation assignment to Syracuse (June 28-30).
STATISTICAL NOTES: Led American Association catchers with .991 fielding percentage and tied for the league lead in double plays with 10 in 1997.

							BATTING								FIELDING		
Year Team (League)	Pos.	G	AB	R	H	2B	3B	HR	RBI	Avg.	BB	SO	SB	PO	A	E	Avg.
1994—Hudson Valley (NYP)	C	68	233	33	57	*19	1	6	32	.245	23	•86	0	316	34	7	.980
1995—Charlotte (Fla. St.)	C-1B	107	355	48	94	25	1	11	57	.265	50	96	2	535	60	9	.985
— Okla. City (A.A.)	C	3	10	1	4	1	0	0	0	.400	2	4	0	6	0	2	.750
1996—Tulsa (Texas)	C-1B	128	460	77	121	27	1	26	86	.263	73	*150	0	594	69	13	.981
— Texas (A.L.)	C-DH	3	4	1	0	0	0	0	1	.000	2	2	0	11	1	0	1.000
1997—Okla. City (A.A.)	C-1B	116	403	56	97	18	2	19	50	.241	38	111	2	640	62	5	†.993
— Texas (A.L.)	C	4	5	1	2	0	0	1	1	.400	0	0	0	9	0	1	.900
1998—Toronto (A.L.)■	C	52	110	17	29	7	1	2	15	.264	9	31	0	261	19	2	.993
— Syracuse (Int'l)	C	2	8	2	5	2	0	0	0	.625	0	2	0	7	1	0	1.000
Major league totals (3 years)		59	119	19	31	7	1	3	17	.261	11	33	0	281	20	3	.990

BROWN, ROOSEVELT   OF   CUBS

PERSONAL: Born August 3, 1975, in Vicksburg, Miss. ... 5-11/195. ... Bats left, throws right. ... Full name: Roosevelt Lawayne Brown.
HIGH SCHOOL: Vicksburg (Miss.).
TRANSACTIONS/CAREER NOTES: Selected by Atlanta Braves organization in 20th round of free-agent draft (June 3, 1993). ... Traded by Braves organization to Florida Marlins organization for 3B Terry Pendleton (August 13, 1996). ... Selected by Chicago Cubs organization from Marlins organization in Rule 5 minor league draft (December 15, 1997).

							BATTING								FIELDING		
Year Team (League)	Pos.	G	AB	R	H	2B	3B	HR	RBI	Avg.	BB	SO	SB	PO	A	E	Avg.
1993—GC Braves (GCL)	OF	26	80	4	9	1	2	0	5	.113	2	9	2	18	4	4	.846
1994—Idaho Falls (Pio.)	OF	48	160	28	53	8	1	3	22	.331	17	15	8	63	3	1	.985
1995—Eugene (Northwest)	OF	57	165	28	51	12	4	7	32	.309	13	30	6	45	3	8	.857
1996—Macon (S. Atl.)	OF	113	413	61	115	27	0	19	64	.278	33	60	21	154	6	12	.930
— Kane Co. (Midw.)■	OF	11	40	1	6	2	0	0	3	.150	1	10	0	13	1	1	.933
1997—Kane County (Midw.)	OF	61	211	29	50	7	1	4	30	.237	22	52	5	75	5	6	.930
— Brevard Co. (Fla. St.)	OF	33	114	8	28	7	1	1	12	.246	7	31	0	44	5	1	.980
1998—Daytona (Fla. St.)■	OF	68	244	49	84	15	5	9	43	.344	23	46	3	106	4	2	.982
— West Tenn (Southern)	OF	42	160	20	42	11	0	6	24	.263	13	30	3	61	4	3	.956
— Iowa (Pacific Coast)	DH	1	3	0	1	1	0	0	2	.333	0	0	0				...

BROWNSON, MARK   P   ROCKIES

PERSONAL: Born June 17, 1975, in Lake Worth, Fla. ... 6-2/185. ... Throws right, bats left. ... Full name: Mark Phillip Brownson.
HIGH SCHOOL: Wellington (West Palm Beach, Fla.).
JUNIOR COLLEGE: Palm Beach Community College (Fla.).

TRANSACTIONS/CAREER NOTES: Selected by Colorado Rockies organization in 30th round of free-agent draft (June 3, 1993). ... On Colorado Springs disabled list (August 11-September 8, 1998).
STATISTICAL NOTES: Led Eastern league with 14 hit batsmen in 1997. ... Pitched shutout in first major league game (July 21, 1998).

Year Team (League)	W	L	Pct.	ERA	G	GS	CG	ShO	Sv.	IP	H	R	ER	BB	SO
1994—Ariz. Rockies (Ariz.)...........	4	1	.800	1.66	19	4	0	0	3	54 1/3	48	18	10	6	72
1995—Asheville (S. Atl.)...........	6	7	.462	4.01	23	12	0	0	1	98 2/3	106	52	44	29	94
1996—New Haven (East.)...............	8	13	.381	3.50	37	19	1	0	3	144	141	73	56	43	155
—Salem (Carolina)	2	1	.667	4.02	9	1	0	0	1	15 2/3	16	8	7	10	9
1997—New Haven (East.).............	10	9	.526	4.19	29	29	2	0	0	184 2/3	172	101	86	55	170
1998—Colo. Springs (PCL)........	6	8	.429	5.34	21	21	3	0	0	124 2/3	131	85	74	37	82
—Colorado (N.L.)	1	0	1.000	4.73	2	2	1	1	0	13 1/3	16	7	7	2	8
Major league totals (1 year)........	1	0	1.000	4.73	2	2	1	1	0	13 1/3	16	7	7	2	8

B

BRUCE, MO   IF   METS

PERSONAL: Born May 1, 1975, in Kansas City, Mo. ... 5-10/190. ... Bats right, throws right. ... Full name: Maurice DeWayne Bruce.
HIGH SCHOOL: Southeast (Kansas City, Mo.).
JUNIOR COLLEGE: Connors State College (Okla.).
TRANSACTIONS/CAREER NOTES: Signed as non-drafted free agent by New York Mets organization (September 11, 1995).
STATISTICAL NOTES: Led South Atlantic League third basemen with 83 putouts and 24 double plays in 1998.

Year Team (League)	Pos.	G	AB	R	H	2B	3B	HR	RBI	Avg.	BB	SO	SB	PO	A	E	Avg.
								BATTING							FIELDING		
1996—Kingsport (Appal.)......	2B	11	38	5	7	0	1	0	4	.184	0	7	2	14	21	3	.921
—GC Mets (GCL)..........	3B-2B-SS	31	123	16	35	6	3	0	9	.285	4	15	6	44	77	5	.960
1997—Kingsport (Appal.)......	OF-2B-1B	34	128	35	47	8	3	3	21	.367	16	20	14	55	16	3	.959
—Pittsfield (NYP)	2B-SS-OF	29	115	26	40	7	3	4	14	.348	11	23	12	74	76	12	.926
1998—Columbia (S. Atl.)......	3B-2B-SS	126	516	81	*176	24	4	15	74	*.341	41	107	45	†94	245	21	.942

BRUNSON, WILL   P   TIGERS

PERSONAL: Born March 20, 1970, in Irving, Texas. ... 6-6/185. ... Throws left, bats left. ... Full name: William Donald Brunson.
HIGH SCHOOL: DeSoto (Texas).
COLLEGE: Southwest Texas State.
TRANSACTIONS/CAREER NOTES: Selected by Cincinnati Reds organization in 21st round of free-agent draft (June 1, 1992). ... Traded by Reds to Los Angeles Dodgers organization for P Ben VanRyn (December 16, 1994). ... Claimed on waivers by Detroit Tigers (September 6, 1998).

Year Team (League)	W	L	Pct.	ERA	G	GS	CG	ShO	Sv.	IP	H	R	ER	BB	SO
1992—Princeton (Appalachian).....	5	5	.500	3.59	13	13	0	0	0	72 2/3	66	34	29	28	48
1993—Char., W.Va. (S. Atl.)	5	6	.455	3.93	37	15	0	0	0	123 2/3	119	68	54	50	103
1994—Win.-Salem (Car.)..........	12	7	.632	3.98	30	22	3	0	0	165	161	83	73	58	129
1995—San Bernardino (Calif.)■..	10	0	1.000	2.05	13	13	0	0	0	83 1/3	68	24	19	21	70
—San Antonio (Tex.)	4	5	.444	4.95	14	14	0	0	0	80	105	46	44	22	44
1996—San Antonio (Tex.)..........	3	1	.750	2.14	11	5	0	0	0	42	32	13	10	15	38
—Albuquerque (PCL).............	3	4	.429	4.47	9	9	1	0	0	54 1/3	53	29	27	23	47
1997—Albuquerque (PCL)..........	1	1	.500	6.49	27	0	0	0	0	26 1/3	39	19	19	10	25
—San Antonio (Tex.)	5	5	.500	3.47	17	11	2	•1	0	72 2/3	68	30	28	13	71
1998—Albuquerque (PCL)..........	5	8	.385	4.65	34	15	1	0	2	120	135	69	62	40	100
—Los Angeles (N.L.)	0	1	.000	11.57	2	0	0	0	0	2 1/3	3	3	3	2	1
—Detroit (A.L.)■	0	0	. . .	0.00	8	0	0	0	0	3	2	0	0	1	1
A.L. totals (1 year)....................	0	0	. . .	0.00	8	0	0	0	0	3	2	0	0	1	1
N.L. totals (1 year)....................	0	1	.000	11.57	2	0	0	0	0	2 1/3	3	3	3	2	1
Major league totals (1 year)........	0	1	.000	5.06	10	0	0	0	0	5 1/3	5	3	3	3	2

BRUSKE, JIM   P   YANKEES

PERSONAL: Born October 7, 1964, in East St. Louis, Ill. ... 6-1/185. ... Throws right, bats right. ... Full name: James Scott Bruske. ... Name pronounced BREW-ski.
HIGH SCHOOL: Palmdale (Calif.).
JUNIOR COLLEGE: Antelope Valley (Calif.).
COLLEGE: Loyola Marymount.
TRANSACTIONS/CAREER NOTES: Selected by San Diego Padres organization in seventh round of free-agent draft (January 9, 1985); did not sign. ... Selected by Seattle Mariners organization in third round of secondary phase of free-agent draft (June 3, 1985); did not sign. ... Selected by Cleveland Indians organization in first round (sixth player selected) of secondary phase of free-agent draft (June 2, 1986). ... On Canton-Akron disabled list (May 8-25, 1991). ... On Colorado Springs disabled list (May 7-June 9, 1992). ... Released by Indians organization (June 9, 1992). ... Signed by Houston Astros organization (June 22, 1992). ... On disabled list (May 7-30 and June 9-October 12, 1994). ... Granted free agency (October 15, 1994). ... Signed by Los Angeles Dodgers organization (January 18, 1995). ... On Albuquerque disabled list (May 3-11, 1995). ... Granted free agency (October 16, 1995). ... Re-signed by Dodgers organization (November 12, 1995). ... On Albuquerque disabled list (May 25-June 20, 1996). ... Granted free agency (October 15, 1996). ... Signed by Padres (December 3, 1996). ... On disabled list (August 6-25, 1997). ... Claimed on waivers by Dodgers (October 6, 1997). ... Traded by Dodgers to San Diego Padres for P Widd Workman (July 23, 1998). ... Traded by Padres with P Brad Kaufman to New York Yankees for OF Shea Morenz and P Ray Ricken (August 23, 1998).
MISCELLANEOUS: Played outfield only (1986-88). ... Struck out in only appearance as pinch hitter with San Diego (1997).

Year Team (League)	W	L	Pct.	ERA	G	GS	CG	ShO	Sv.	IP	H	R	ER	BB	SO
1986—Batavia (N.Y.-Penn)	0	0	. . .	18.00	1	0	0	0	0	1	1	2	2	3	3
1989—Cant./Akr. (Eastern)	0	0	. . .	13.50	2	0	0	0	0	2	3	3	3	2	1
1990—Cant./Akr. (Eastern)	9	3	.750	3.28	32	13	3	2	0	118	118	53	43	42	62
1991—Cant./Akr. (Eastern)	5	2	.714	3.47	17	11	0	0	1	80 1/3	73	36	31	27	35
—Colo. Springs (PCL)	4	1	1.000	2.45	7	1	0	0	0	25 2/3	19	9	7	8	13
1992—Colo. Springs (PCL)	2	0	1.000	4.58	7	0	0	0	10	17 2/3	24	11	9	6	8
—Jackson (Texas)■	4	3	.571	2.63	13	9	1	0	0	61 2/3	54	23	18	14	48

Year Team (League)	W	L	Pct.	ERA	G	GS	CG	ShO	Sv.	IP	H	R	ER	BB	SO
1993— Jackson (Texas)	9	5	.643	2.31	15	15	1	0	0	97 1/3	86	34	25	22	83
— Tucson (PCL)	4	2	.667	3.78	12	9	0	0	1	66 2/3	77	36	28	18	42
1994— Tucson (PCL)	3	1	.750	4.15	7	7	0	0	0	39	47	22	18	8	25
1995— Los Angeles (N.L.)■	0	0	...	4.50	9	0	0	0	1	10	12	7	5	4	5
— Albuquerque (PCL)	7	5	.583	4.11	43	6	0	0	4	114	128	54	52	41	99
1996— Albuquerque (PCL)	5	2	.714	4.06	36	0	0	0	4	62	63	34	28	21	51
— Los Angeles (N.L.)	0	0	...	5.68	11	0	0	0	0	12 2/3	17	8	8	3	12
1997— Las Vegas (PCL)■	5	4	.556	4.90	16	9	0	0	0	68	73	41	37	22	67
— San Diego (N.L.)	4	1	.800	3.63	28	0	0	0	0	44 2/3	37	22	18	25	32
1998— Las Vegas (N.L.)■	3	0	1.000	3.48	35	0	0	0	1	44	47	18	17	19	31
— San Diego (N.L.)■	0	0	...	3.86	4	0	0	0	0	7	10	4	3	4	4
— Las Vegas (PCL)	0	1	.000	6.00	5	0	0	0	1	6	8	4	4	1	2
— Columbus (Int'l)	0	0	...	1.17	4	0	0	0	1	7 2/3	7	1	1	2	9
— New York (A.L.)	1	0	1.000	3.00	3	1	0	0	0	9	9	3	3	1	3
A.L. totals (1 year)	1	0	1.000	3.00	3	1	0	0	0	9	9	3	3	1	3
N.L. totals (4 years)	7	1	.875	3.88	87	0	0	0	2	118 1/3	123	59	51	55	84
Major league totals (4 years)	8	1	.889	3.82	90	1	0	0	2	127 1/3	132	62	54	56	87

B

RECORD AS POSITION PLAYER

Year Team (League)	Pos.	G	AB	R	H	2B	3B	HR	RBI	Avg.	BB	SO	SB	PO	A	E	Avg.
1986— Batavia (NY-Penn)	OF-P	56	181	23	44	2	2	3	14	.243	21	50	7	85	4	5	.947
1987— Kinston (Carolina)	OF	123	439	62	102	16	3	7	61	.232	65	118	17	188	7	10	.951
1988— Williamsport (East.)	OF	135	443	49	105	12	3	1	44	.237	45	*138	16	238	11	4	.984
1989— Kinston (Carolina)	OF	63	217	29	63	12	1	5	36	.290	34	44	13	114	2	2	.983
— Cant./Akr. (Eastern)	OF-P-SS	51	134	17	32	5	0	1	7	.239	19	28	3	75	4	0	1.000

BUCHANAN, BRIAN   OF   TWINS

PERSONAL: Born July 21, 1973, in Miami. ... 6-4/220. ... Bats right, throws right. ... Full name: Brian James Buchanan.
HIGH SCHOOL: Fairfax (Va.).
COLLEGE: Virginia.
TRANSACTIONS/CAREER NOTES: Selected by New York Yankees organization in first round (24th pick overall) of free-agent draft (June 2, 1994). ... On disabled list (April 29, 1995-remainder of season). ... Traded by Yankees with P Eric Milton, P Danny Mota, SS Cristian Guzman and cash to Minnesota Twins for 2B Chuck Knoblauch (February 6, 1998).
STATISTICAL NOTES: Tied for Pacific Coast League lead with three double plays by outfielder in 1998.

Year Team (League)	Pos.	G	AB	R	H	2B	3B	HR	RBI	Avg.	BB	SO	SB	PO	A	E	Avg.
1994— Oneonta (NYP)	OF	50	177	28	40	9	2	4	26	.226	24	53	5	87	2	0	1.000
1995— Greensboro (S. Atl.)	OF	23	96	19	29	3	0	3	12	.302	9	17	7	31	1	1	.970
1996— Tampa (Fla. St.)	OF	131	526	65	137	22	4	10	58	.260	37	108	23	178	11	6	.969
1997— Norwich (Eastern)	OF	116	470	75	145	25	2	10	69	.309	32	85	11	192	11	8	.962
— Columbus (Int'l)	OF	18	61	8	17	1	0	4	7	.279	4	11	2	17	1	1	.947
1998— Salt Lake (PCL)■	OF	133	500	74	139	29	3	17	82	.278	36	90	14	244	6	8	.969

BUDDIE, MIKE   P   YANKEES

PERSONAL: Born December 12, 1970, in Berea, Ohio. ... 6-3/210. ... Throws right, bats right. ... Full name: Michael J. Buddie.
HIGH SCHOOL: St. Ignatius (Cleveland).
COLLEGE: Wake Forest.
TRANSACTIONS/CAREER NOTES: Selected by New York Yankees organization in fourth round of free-agent draft (June 1, 1992).

Year Team (League)	W	L	Pct.	ERA	G	GS	CG	ShO	Sv.	IP	H	R	ER	BB	SO
1992— Oneonta (N.Y.-Penn)	1	4	.200	3.88	13	13	1	0	0	67 1/3	69	36	29	34	87
1993— Greensboro (S. Atl.)	13	10	.565	4.87	27	26	0	0	0	155 1/3	138	104	84	89	143
1994— Tampa (Fla. St.)	12	5	.706	4.01	25	24	2	0	0	150 1/3	143	75	67	66	113
1995— Norwich (Eastern)	10	12	.455	4.81	29	27	2	0	1	149 2/3	155	*102	80	81	106
1996— Norwich (Eastern)	7	•12	.368	4.45	29	26	4	0	0	159 2/3	176	101	79	71	103
1997— Norwich (Eastern)	0	0	...	0.00	1	0	0	0	0	1	0	0	0	0	3
— Columbus (Int'l)	6	6	.500	2.64	53	0	0	0	13	75	85	24	22	25	67
1998— New York (A.L.)	4	1	.800	5.62	24	2	0	0	0	41 2/3	46	29	26	13	20
— Columbus (Int'l)	5	0	1.000	2.74	26	0	0	0	4	42 2/3	35	15	13	15	30
Major league totals (1 year)	4	1	.800	5.62	24	2	0	0	0	41 2/3	46	29	26	13	20

BUFORD, DAMON   OF   RED SOX

PERSONAL: Born June 12, 1970, in Baltimore. ... 5-10/170. ... Bats right, throws right. ... Full name: Damon Jackson Buford. ... Son of Don Buford, outfielder with Chicago White Sox (1963-67) and Baltimore Orioles (1968-72); and brother of Don Buford Jr., minor league infielder (1987-89).
HIGH SCHOOL: Birmingham (Calif.).
COLLEGE: Southern California.
TRANSACTIONS/CAREER NOTES: Selected by Baltimore Orioles organization in 10th round of free-agent draft (June 4, 1990). ... Traded by Orioles with OF Alex Ochoa to New York Mets for 3B/OF Bobby Bonilla and a player to be named later (July 28, 1995); Orioles acquired P Jimmy Williams to complete deal (August 17, 1995). ... Traded by Mets to Texas Rangers for OF Terrell Lowery (January 25, 1996). ... Traded by Rangers with C Jim Leyritz to Boston Red Sox for P Aaron Sele, P Mark Brandenburg and C Bill Haselman (November 6, 1997). ... On disabled list (May 18-June 3 and August 27-September 11, 1998).
STATISTICAL NOTES: Led Eastern League outfielders with 279 total chances in 1992. ... Led International League outfielders with 347 total chances in 1994. ... Career major league grand slams: 2.

Year	Team (League)	Pos.	G	AB	R	H	2B	3B	HR	RBI	Avg.	BB	SO	SB	PO	A	E	Avg.
1990—	Wausau (Midwest)	OF	41	160	31	48	7	2	1	14	.300	21	32	15	89	2	2	.978
1991—	Frederick (Carolina)....	OF	133	505	71	138	25	6	8	54	.273	51	92	50	293	7	5	.984
1992—	Hagerstown (East.).....	OF	101	373	53	89	17	3	1	30	.239	42	62	41	*264	13	2	.993
	— Rochester (Int'l)	OF	45	155	29	44	10	2	1	12	.284	14	23	23	100	1	3	.971
1993—	Rochester (Int'l)	OF	27	116	24	33	6	1	1	4	.284	7	16	10	73	3	3	.962
	— Baltimore (A.L.)..........	OF-DH	53	79	18	18	5	0	2	9	.228	9	19	2	61	2	1	.984
1994—	Baltimore (A.L.).........	DH-OF	4	2	2	1	0	0	0	0	.500	0	1	0	0	0	0	...
	— Rochester (Int'l)	OF	111	452	*89	122	21	4	16	66	.270	35	81	31	*339	4	4	.988
1995—	Baltimore (A.L.)	OF	24	32	6	2	0	0	0	2	.063	6	7	3	40	0	0	1.000
	— Rochester (Int'l)	OF	46	188	40	58	12	3	4	18	.309	17	26	17	115	2	2	.983
	— New York (N.L.)■	OF	44	136	24	32	5	0	4	12	.235	19	28	7	67	2	2	.972
1996—	Texas (A.L.)■..............	OF-DH	90	145	30	41	9	0	6	20	.283	15	34	8	93	3	0	1.000
1997—	Texas (A.L.)..............	OF-DH	122	366	49	82	18	0	8	39	.224	30	83	18	282	7	3	.990
1998—	Boston (A.L.)■..........	O-DH-2-3	86	216	37	61	14	4	10	42	.282	22	43	5	134	4	0	1.000
	American League totals (6 years)		379	840	142	205	46	4	26	112	.244	82	187	36	610	16	4	.994
	National League totals (1 year)		44	136	24	32	5	0	4	12	.235	19	28	7	67	2	2	.972
	Major league totals (6 years)		423	976	166	237	51	4	30	124	.243	101	215	43	677	18	6	.991

DIVISION SERIES RECORD

Year	Team (League)	Pos.	G	AB	R	H	2B	3B	HR	RBI	Avg.	BB	SO	SB	PO	A	E	Avg.
1996—	Texas (A.L.)	PR	2	0	0	0	0	0	0	0	...	0	0	0	...	0	0	...
1998—	Boston (A.L.).............PR-O-PH-DH		3	1	2	0	0	0	0	0	.000	0	0	0	1	0	0	1.000
	Division series totals (2 years)		5	1	2	0	0	0	0	0	.000	0	0	0	1	0	0	1.000

BUHNER, JAY   1B/OF   MARINERS

PERSONAL: Born August 13, 1964, in Louisville, Ky. ... 6-3/215. ... Bats right, throws right. ... Full name: Jay Campbell Buhner. ... Brother of Shawn Buhner, infielder, Mariners organization. ... Name pronounced BYOO-ner.

HIGH SCHOOL: Clear Creek (League City, Texas).

JUNIOR COLLEGE: McLennan Community College (Texas).

TRANSACTIONS/CAREER NOTES: Selected by Atlanta Braves organization in ninth round of free-agent draft (June 6, 1983); did not sign. ... Selected by Pittsburgh Pirates organization in secondary phase of free-agent draft (January 17, 1984). ... Traded by Pirates organization with IF Dale Berra and P Alfonso Pulido to New York Yankees for OF Steve Kemp, IF Tim Foli and cash (December 20, 1984). ... On disabled list (April 11-July 28, 1986). ... Traded by Yankees with P Rich Balabon and a player to be named later to Seattle Mariners for DH Ken Phelps (July 21, 1988); Mariners acquired P Troy Evers to complete deal (October 12, 1988). ... On Seattle disabled list (June 29-August 19, 1989); included rehabilitation assignment to Calgary (August 16-19). ... On Seattle disabled list (March 31-June 1, 1990); included rehabilitation assignment to Calgary (May 18-June 1). ... On Seattle disabled list (June 17-August 23, 1990). ... Granted free agency (October 28, 1994). ... Re-signed by Mariners (December 21, 1994). ... On disabled list (June 6-22, 1995). ... On Seattle disabled list (April 7-June 11 and September 8, 1998-remainder of season); included rehabilitation assignment to Tacoma (June 9-11).

RECORDS: Shares major league records for most strikeouts in two consecutive nine-inning games—8 (August 23-24, 1990); and most strikeouts in three consecutive games—10 (August 23-25, 1990).

HONORS: Won A.L. Gold Glove as outfielder (1996).

STATISTICAL NOTES: Tied for International League lead in double plays by outfielder with six in 1987. ... Hit for the cycle (June 23, 1993). ... Career major league grand slams: 7.

Year	Team (League)	Pos.	G	AB	R	H	2B	3B	HR	RBI	Avg.	BB	SO	SB	PO	A	E	Avg.
1984—	Watertown (NYP)	OF	65	229	43	74	16	3	9	•58	.323	42	58	3	106	8	1	.991
1985—	Fort Laud. (FSL)■.......	OF	117	409	65	121	18	10	11	76	.296	65	76	6	235	12	7	.972
1986—	Fort Laud. (FSL)........	OF	36	139	24	42	9	1	7	31	.302	15	30	1	84	7	3	.968
1987—	Columbus (Int'l)	OF	134	502	83	140	23	1	*31	85	.279	55	124	4	275	*20	6	.980
	— New York (A.L.)........	OF	7	22	0	5	2	0	0	1	.227	1	6	0	11	1	0	1.000
1988—	Columbus (Int'l)	OF	38	129	26	33	5	0	8	18	.256	19	33	1	83	3	1	.989
	— New York (A.L.)........	OF	25	69	8	13	0	0	3	13	.188	3	25	0	52	2	2	.964
	— Seattle (A.L.)■........	OF	60	192	28	43	13	1	10	25	.224	25	68	1	134	7	1	.993
1989—	Calgary (PCL)........	OF	56	196	43	61	12	1	11	45	.311	44	56	4	97	8	2	.981
	— Seattle (A.L.)........	OF	58	204	27	56	15	1	9	33	.275	19	55	1	106	6	4	.966
1990—	Calgary (PCL)........	OF	13	34	6	7	1	0	2	5	.206	7	11	0	14	1	0	1.000
	— Seattle (A.L.)........	OF-DH	51	163	16	45	12	0	7	33	.276	17	50	2	55	1	2	.966
1991—	Seattle (A.L.)........	OF	137	406	64	99	14	4	27	77	.244	53	117	0	244	15	5	.981
1992—	Seattle (A.L.)........	OF	152	543	69	132	16	3	25	79	.243	71	146	0	314	14	2	.994
1993—	Seattle (A.L.)........	OF-DH	158	563	91	153	28	3	27	98	.272	100	144	2	263	8	6	.978
1994—	Seattle (A.L.)........	OF-DH	101	358	74	100	23	4	21	68	.279	66	63	0	178	11	2	.990
1995—	Seattle (A.L.)........	OF-DH	126	470	86	123	23	0	40	121	.262	60	120	0	180	5	5	.989
1996—	Seattle (A.L.)........	OF-DH	150	564	107	153	29	0	44	138	.271	84	*159	0	251	9	3	.989
1997—	Seattle (A.L.)........	OF-DH	157	540	104	131	18	2	40	109	.243	119	*175	0	295	5	1	*.997
1998—	Seattle (A.L.)........	OF-DH	72	244	33	59	7	1	15	45	.242	38	71	0	127	5	2	.985
	— Tacoma (PCL)........	OF	2	4	2	2	2	0	0	2	.500	2	2	0	0	0	0	...
	Major league totals (12 years)		1254	4338	707	1112	200	19	268	840	.256	656	1199	6	2210	89	32	.986

DIVISION SERIES RECORD

Year	Team (League)	Pos.	G	AB	R	H	2B	3B	HR	RBI	Avg.	BB	SO	SB	PO	A	E	Avg.
1995—	Seattle (A.L.)	OF	5	24	2	11	1	0	1	3	.458	2	4	0	11	1	0	1.000
1997—	Seattle (A.L.)	OF	4	13	2	3	0	0	2	2	.231	3	6	0	5	1	0	1.000
	Division series totals (2 years)		9	37	4	14	1	0	3	5	.378	5	10	0	16	2	0	1.000

CHAMPIONSHIP SERIES RECORD

RECORDS: Shares A.L. single-series records for most home runs—3 (1995); and most strikeouts—8 (1995).

Year Team (League)	Pos.	G	AB	R	H	2B	3B	HR	RBI	Avg.	BB	SO	SB	PO	A	E	Avg.
1995— Seattle (A.L.)	OF	6	23	5	7	2	0	3	5	.304	2	8	0	15	0	1	.938

ALL-STAR GAME RECORD

Year League	Pos.	AB	R	H	2B	3B	HR	RBI	Avg.	BB	SO	SB	PO	A	E	Avg.
1996— American	OF	2	0	0	0	0	0	0	.000	0	0	0	1	0	0	1.000

BULLINGER, JIM — P

PERSONAL: Born August 21, 1965, in New Orleans. ... 6-2/190. ... Throws right, bats right. ... Full name: James Eric Bullinger. ... Name pronounced BULL-in-jer. ... Brother of Kirk Bullinger, pitcher, Boston Red Sox organization.
HIGH SCHOOL: Archbishop Rummel (Metairie, La.).
COLLEGE: New Orleans.
TRANSACTIONS/CAREER NOTES: Selected by Chicago Cubs organization in ninth round of free-agent draft (June 2, 1986). ... On Iowa disabled list (August 5-21, 1993). ... On Chicago disabled list (May 21-June 22, 1995); included rehabilitation assignment to Orlando (June 13-18). ... Granted free agency (December 20, 1996). ... Signed by Montreal Expos (January 16, 1997). ... Granted free agency (October 6, 1997). ... Signed by Chicago White Sox organization (January 9, 1998). ... Traded by White Sox to Seattle Mariners for P Marty Weymouth (March 26, 1998). ... On Tacoma disabled list (August 2, 1998-remainder of season). ... Granted free agency (October 15, 1998).
STATISTICAL NOTES: Led Carolina League shortstops with 92 double plays in 1987. ... Hit home run in first major league at-bat (June 8, 1992, first game). ... Pitched 3-1 one-hit, complete-game victory for Chicago against San Francisco (August 30, 1992).
MISCELLANEOUS: Played shortstop only (1986-88). ... Struck out in only appearance as pinch hitter with Chicago (1995). ... Appeared in one game as pinch runner (1996).

Year Team (League)	W	L	Pct.	ERA	G	GS	CG	ShO	Sv.	IP	H	R	ER	BB	SO
1989— Charlotte (Southern)	0	0	...	0.00	2	0	0	0	0	3	3	0	0	3	5
1990— Win.-Salem (Car.)..............	7	6	.538	3.70	14	13	3	0	0	90	81	43	37	46	85
—Charlotte (Southern)	3	4	.429	5.11	9	9	0	0	0	44	42	30	25	18	33
1991— Iowa (Am. Assoc.)..............	3	4	.429	5.40	8	8	0	0	0	46 2/3	47	32	28	23	30
—Charlotte (Southern)	9	9	.500	3.53	20	20	•8	0	0	142 2/3	132	62	56	61	128
1992— Iowa (Am. Assoc.)..............	1	2	.333	2.45	20	0	0	0	14	22	17	6	6	12	15
—Chicago (N.L.)	2	8	.200	4.66	39	9	1	0	7	85	72	49	44	54	36
1993— Iowa (Am. Assoc.)..............	4	6	.400	3.42	49	3	0	0	20	73 2/3	64	29	28	43	74
—Chicago (N.L.)	1	0	1.000	4.32	15	0	0	0	1	16 2/3	18	9	8	9	10
1994— Chicago (N.L.)	6	2	.750	3.60	33	10	1	0	2	100	87	43	40	34	72
1995— Chicago (N.L.)	12	8	.600	4.14	24	24	1	1	0	150	152	80	69	65	93
—Orlando (South.)	0	0	...	0.00	1	1	0	0	0	4	3	0	0	1	2
1996— Chicago (N.L.)	6	10	.375	6.54	37	20	1	1	1	129 1/3	144	101	94	68	90
1997— Montreal (N.L.)■..............	7	12	.368	5.56	36	25	2	2	0	155 1/3	165	106	96	74	87
1998— Seattle (A.L.)■..............	0	1	.000	15.88	2	1	0	0	0	5 2/3	13	10	10	2	4
—Tacoma (PCL)	8	7	.533	5.05	20	16	0	0	0	101 2/3	106	64	57	58	73
A.L. totals (1 year)	0	1	.000	15.88	2	1	0	0	0	5 2/3	13	10	10	2	4
N.L. totals (6 years)..................	34	40	.459	4.96	184	88	6	4	11	636 1/3	638	388	351	304	388
Major league totals (7 years)......	34	41	.453	5.06	186	89	6	4	11	642	651	398	361	306	392

RECORD AS POSITION PLAYER

Year Team (League)	Pos.	G	AB	R	H	2B	3B	HR	RBI	Avg.	BB	SO	SB	PO	A	E	Avg.
1986— Geneva (NY-Penn)......	SS	*78	248	35	61	•16	1	3	33	.246	*48	50	7	104	207	26	.923
1987— Win.-Salem (Car.)......	SS	129	437	58	112	12	3	9	48	.256	50	79	3	210	383	28	.955
1988— Pittsfield (Eastern)......	SS	88	242	21	41	6	1	3	33	.169	25	53	1	129	256	21	.948
—Win.-Salem (Car.)......	SS	32	104	13	20	4	2	1	11	.192	13	26	4	49	80	11	.921
1989— Charlotte (Southern) ..	SS-3B	124	320	34	69	13	1	3	28	.216	39	56	3	188	281	26	.947

BULLINGER, KIRK — P — RED SOX

PERSONAL: Born October 28, 1969, in New Orleans. ... 6-2/170. ... Throws right, bats right. ... Full name: Kirk Matthew Bullinger. ... Name pronounced BULL-in-jer. ... Brother of Jim Bullinger, pitcher with Chicago Cubs (1992-96), Montreal Expos (1997) and Seattle Mariners (1998).
HIGH SCHOOL: Archbishop Rummel (Metaire, La.).
COLLEGE: Southeastern Louisiana.
TRANSACTIONS/CAREER NOTES: Selected by St. Louis Cardinals in 32nd round of free-agent draft (June 1, 1992). ... Traded by Cardinals organization with OF DaRond Stovall and P Bryan Eversgerd to Montreal Expos organization for P Ken Hill (April 5, 1995). ... On Ottawa disabled list (April 9-July 3, 1998). ... Granted free agency (October 15, 1998). ... Signed by Boston Red Sox organization (December 14, 1998).

Year Team (League)	W	L	Pct.	ERA	G	GS	CG	ShO	Sv.	IP	H	R	ER	BB	SO
1992— Hamilton (NYP).............	2	2	.500	1.11	35	0	0	0	2	48 2/3	24	7	6	15	61
1993— Springfield (Mid.).............	1	3	.250	2.28	50	0	0	0	*33	51 1/3	26	19	13	21	72
1994— St. Petersburg (FSL)	2	0	1.000	1.17	39	0	0	0	6	53 2/3	37	16	7	20	50
1995— Harrisburg (Eastern)■	5	3	.625	2.42	56	0	0	0	7	67	61	22	18	25	42
1996— Ottawa (Int'l)	2	1	.667	3.52	10	0	0	0	0	15 1/3	10	6	6	9	9
—Harrisburg (Eastern)	3	4	.429	1.97	47	0	0	0	22	45 2/3	46	16	10	18	29
1997— Harrisburg (Eastern)	3	0	1.000	2.67	21	0	0	0	6	27	22	9	8	6	21
—W.P. Beach (FSL)..............	2	0	1.000	0.00	2	0	0	0	0	3 2/3	3	0	0	0	7
—Ottawa (Int'l)	3	4	.429	1.71	22	0	0	0	5	31 2/3	17	7	6	10	15
1998— Jupiter (Florida State)	0	0	...	5.40	8	0	0	0	0	10	9	7	6	2	12
—Ottawa (Int'l)	0	0	...	1.06	13	0	0	0	3	17	16	2	2	6	7
—Montreal (N.L.)...................	1	0	1.000	9.00	8	0	0	0	0	7	14	8	7	0	2
Major league totals (1 year)........	1	0	1.000	9.00	8	0	0	0	0	7	14	8	7	0	2

BURBA, DAVE   P   INDIANS

PERSONAL: Born July 7, 1966, in Dayton, Ohio. ... 6-4/240. ... Throws right, bats right. ... Full name: David Allen Burba. ... Nephew of Ray Hathaway, pitcher with Brooklyn Dodgers (1945).
HIGH SCHOOL: Kenton Ridge (Springfield, Ohio).
COLLEGE: Ohio State.
TRANSACTIONS/CAREER NOTES: Selected by Seattle Mariners organization in second round of free-agent draft (June 2, 1987). ... Traded by Mariners with P Bill Swift and P Mike Jackson to San Francisco Giants for OF Kevin Mitchell and P Mike Remlinger (December 11, 1991). ... Traded by Giants with OF Darren Lewis and P Mark Portugal to Cincinnati Reds for OF Deion Sanders, P John Roper, P Ricky Pickett, P Scott Service and IF Dave McCarty (July 21, 1995). ... On disabled list (August 7-27, 1997). ... Traded by Reds to Cleveland Indians for 1B Sean Casey (March 30, 1998).

Year Team (League)	W	L	Pct.	ERA	G	GS	CG	ShO	Sv.	IP	H	R	ER	BB	SO
1987— Bellingham (N'west)..........	3	1	.750	1.93	5	5	0	0	0	23⅓	20	10	5	3	24
— Salinas (Calif.)...................	1	6	.143	4.61	9	9	0	0	0	54⅔	53	31	28	29	46
1988—San Bernardino (Calif.).......	5	7	.417	2.68	20	20	0	0	0	114	106	41	34	54	102
1989—Williamsport (Eastern)	11	7	.611	3.16	25	25	5	1	0	156⅔	138	69	55	55	89
1990—Calgary (PCL)....................	10	6	.625	4.67	31	18	1	0	2	113⅔	124	64	59	45	47
— Seattle (A.L.)	0	0	...	4.50	6	0	0	0	0	8	8	6	4	2	4
1991—Calgary (PCL)....................	6	4	.600	3.53	23	9	0	0	4	71⅓	82	35	28	27	42
— Seattle (A.L.)	2	2	.500	3.68	22	2	0	0	1	36⅔	34	16	15	14	16
1992—San Francisco (N.L.)■.......	2	7	.222	4.97	23	11	0	0	0	70⅔	80	43	39	31	47
— Phoenix (PCL).....................	5	5	.500	4.72	13	13	0	0	0	74⅓	86	40	39	24	44
1993—San Francisco (N.L.)..........	10	3	.769	4.25	54	5	0	0	0	95⅓	95	49	45	37	88
1994—San Francisco (N.L.)..........	3	6	.333	4.38	57	0	0	0	0	74	59	39	36	45	84
1995—San Francisco (N.L.)..........	4	2	.667	4.98	37	0	0	0	0	43⅓	38	26	24	25	46
— Cincinnati (N.L.)■.............	6	2	.750	3.27	15	9	1	1	0	63⅓	52	24	23	26	50
1996—Cincinnati (N.L.).................	11	13	.458	3.83	34	33	0	0	0	195	179	96	83	97	148
1997—Cincinnati (N.L.).................	11	10	.524	4.73	30	27	2	0	0	160	157	88	84	73	131
1998—Cleveland (A.L.)■..........	15	10	.600	4.11	32	31	0	0	0	203⅔	210	100	93	69	132
A.L. totals (3 years)......	17	12	.586	4.06	60	33	0	0	1	248⅓	252	122	112	85	152
N.L. totals (6 years).....	47	43	.522	4.28	250	85	3	1	0	701⅔	660	365	334	334	594
Major league totals (9 years)......	64	55	.538	4.23	310	118	3	1	1	950	912	487	446	419	746

DIVISION SERIES RECORD

Year Team (League)	W	L	Pct.	ERA	G	GS	CG	ShO	Sv.	IP	H	R	ER	BB	SO
1995— Cincinnati (N.L.).................	1	0	1.000	0.00	1	0	0	0	0	1	2	0	0	1	0
1998— Cleveland (A.L.).................	1	0	1.000	5.06	1	0	0	0	0	5⅓	4	3	3	2	4
Div. series totals (2 years)	2	0	1.000	4.26	2	0	0	0	0	6⅓	6	3	3	3	4

CHAMPIONSHIP SERIES RECORD

Year Team (League)	W	L	Pct.	ERA	G	GS	CG	ShO	Sv.	IP	H	R	ER	BB	SO
1995— Cincinnati (N.L.).................	0	0	...	0.00	2	0	0	0	0	3⅔	3	0	0	4	0
1998— Cleveland (A.L.).................	1	0	1.000	3.00	3	0	0	0	0	6	3	4	2	5	8
Champ. series totals (2 years)	1	0	1.000	1.86	5	0	0	0	0	9⅔	6	4	2	9	8

BURGER, ROB   P   PHILLIES

PERSONAL: Born March 25, 1976, in Lancaster, Pa. ... 6-1/175. ... Throws right, bats right. ... Full name: Robert Paul Burger.
HIGH SCHOOL: Lampeter (Pa.)-Strasburg.
TRANSACTIONS/CAREER NOTES: Selected by Philadelphia Phillies organization in 10th round of free-agent draft (June 2, 1994). ... On disabled list (April 6-July 20, 1995).
STATISTICAL NOTES: Pitched 1-0 no-hit victory against Augusta (April 30, 1996).

Year Team (League)	W	L	Pct.	ERA	G	GS	CG	ShO	Sv.	IP	H	R	ER	BB	SO
1994—Martinsville (App.)..............	1	1	.500	5.68	7	5	0	0	0	19	20	13	12	8	30
1995—Martinsville (App.)..............	2	4	.333	4.65	9	9	0	0	0	40⅓	47	25	21	23	54
1996—Piedmont (S. Atl.)	10	12	.455	3.38	27	26	2	2	0	160	129	74	60	61	171
1997—Clearwater (Fla. St.)	11	9	.550	3.59	28	27	1	1	0	160⅔	131	79	64	*93	*154
1998—Reading (Eastern)	3	11	.214	6.03	33	19	1	0	0	115	119	88	77	69	102

BURKETT, JOHN   P   RANGERS

PERSONAL: Born November 28, 1964, in New Brighton, Pa. ... 6-3/215. ... Throws right, bats right. ... Full name: John David Burkett. ... Name pronounced bur-KETT.
HIGH SCHOOL: Beaver (Pa.).
TRANSACTIONS/CAREER NOTES: Selected by San Francisco Giants organization in sixth round of free-agent draft (June 6, 1983). ... Traded by Giants to Texas Rangers for IF Rich Aurilia and OF Desi Wilson (December 22, 1994). ... Granted free agency (April 7, 1995). ... Signed by Florida Marlins (April 9, 1995). ... Traded by Marlins to Texas Rangers for P Ryan Dempster and a player to be named later (August 8, 1996); Marlins acquired P Rick Helling to complete deal (September 3, 1996). ... On Texas disabled list (August 6-31, 1997); included rehabilitation assignment to Oklahoma City (August 26).
STATISTICAL NOTES: Led N.L. 10 hit batsmen in 1991.
MISCELLANEOUS: Had sacrifice hit in only appearance as pinch hitter (1995).

Year Team (League)	W	L	Pct.	ERA	G	GS	CG	ShO	Sv.	IP	H	R	ER	BB	SO
1983—Great Falls (Pio.)	2	6	.250	6.26	13	9	0	0	0	50⅓	73	44	35	30	38
1984—Clinton (Midwest)...............	7	6	.538	4.33	20	20	2	0	0	126⅔	128	81	61	38	83
1985—Fresno (California).............	7	4	.636	2.87	20	20	1	1	0	109⅔	98	43	35	46	72
1986—Fresno (California).............	0	3	.000	5.47	4	4	0	0	0	24⅔	34	19	15	8	14
— Shreveport (Texas)	10	6	.625	2.66	22	21	4	2	0	128⅔	99	46	38	42	73
1987—Shreveport (Texas)	•14	8	.636	3.34	27	27	6	1	0	*177⅔	181	75	66	53	126
— San Francisco (N.L.)	0	0	...	4.50	3	0	0	0	0	6	7	4	3	3	5

Year Team (League)	W	L	Pct.	ERA	G	GS	CG	ShO	Sv.	IP	H	R	ER	BB	SO
1988— Phoenix (PCL)....................	5	11	.313	5.21	21	21	0	0	0	114	141	79	66	49	74
— Shreveport (Texas)............	5	1	.833	2.13	7	7	2	1	0	50²/₃	33	15	12	18	34
1989— Phoenix (PCL)....................	10	11	.476	5.05	28	•28	2	1	0	167²/₃	197	111	94	59	105
1990— Phoenix (PCL)....................	2	1	.667	2.74	3	3	2	1	0	23	18	8	7	3	9
— San Francisco (N.L.)	14	7	.667	3.79	33	32	2	0	1	204	201	92	86	61	118
1991— San Francisco (N.L.)	12	11	.522	4.18	36	34	3	1	0	206²/₃	223	103	96	60	131
1992— San Francisco (N.L.)	13	9	.591	3.84	32	32	3	1	0	189²/₃	194	96	81	45	107
1993— San Francisco (N.L.)	•22	7	.759	3.65	34	34	2	1	0	231²/₃	224	100	94	40	145
1994— San Francisco (N.L.)	6	8	.429	3.62	25	25	0	0	0	159¹/₃	176	72	64	36	85
1995— Florida (N.L.)■.................	14	14	.500	4.30	30	30	4	0	0	188¹/₃	208	95	90	57	126
1996— Florida (N.L.)	6	10	.375	4.32	24	24	1	0	0	154	154	84	74	42	108
— Texas (A.L.)■...................	5	2	.714	4.06	10	10	1	1	0	68²/₃	75	33	31	16	47
1997— Texas (A.L.)	9	12	.429	4.56	30	30	2	0	0	189¹/₃	240	106	96	30	139
— Oklahoma City (A.A.).........	1	0	1.000	3.60	1	1	0	0	0	5	6	2	2	2	3
1998— Texas (A.L.)	9	13	.409	5.68	32	32	0	0	0	195	230	131	*123	46	131
A.L. totals (3 years)	23	27	.460	4.97	72	72	3	1	0	453	545	270	250	92	317
N.L. totals (8 years)	87	66	.569	3.95	217	211	15	3	1	1339²/₃	1387	646	588	344	825
Major league totals (10 years)....	110	93	.542	4.21	289	283	18	4	1	1792²/₃	1932	916	838	436	1142

DIVISION SERIES RECORD

Year Team (League)	W	L	Pct.	ERA	G	GS	CG	ShO	Sv.	IP	H	R	ER	BB	SO
1996— Texas (A.L.)	1	0	1.000	2.00	1	1	1	0	0	9	10	2	2	1	7

ALL-STAR GAME RECORD

Year League	W	L	Pct.	ERA	GS	CG	ShO	Sv.	IP	H	R	ER	BB	SO
1993— National	0	1	.000	40.50	0	0	0	0	²/₃	4	3	3	0	1

BURKS, ELLIS   OF   GIANTS

PERSONAL: Born September 11, 1964, in Vicksburg, Miss. ... 6-2/205. ... Bats right, throws right. ... Full name: Ellis Rena Burks.
HIGH SCHOOL: Everman (Texas).
JUNIOR COLLEGE: Ranger (Texas) Junior College.
TRANSACTIONS/CAREER NOTES: Selected by Boston Red Sox organization in first round (20th pick overall) of free-agent draft (January 11, 1983). ... On disabled list (March 26-April 12, 1988). ... On Boston disabled list (June 15-August 1, 1989); included rehabilitation assignment to Pawtucket (July 26-August 1). ... On disabled list (June 25, 1992-remainder of season). ... Granted free agency (December 19, 1992). ... Signed by Chicago White Sox (January 4, 1993). ... Granted free agency (October 27, 1993). ... Signed by Colorado Rockies (November 30, 1993). ... On Colorado disabled list (May 18-July 31, 1994); included rehabilitation assignment to Colorado Springs (July 18-20). ... On Colorado disabled list (April 17-May 5, 1995); included rehabilitation assignment to Colorado Springs (April 25-May 5). ... On disabled list (June 28-July 29, 1997). ... Traded by Rockies to San Francisco Giants for OF Darryl Hamilton, P James Stoops and a player to be named later (July 31, 1998); Rockies acquired P Jason Brester to complete deal (August 17, 1998). ... Granted free agency (November 2, 1998). ... Re-signed by Giants (November 13, 1998).
RECORDS: Shares major league single-inning record for most home runs—2 (August 27, 1990, fourth inning).
HONORS: Named outfielder on THE SPORTING NEWS A.L. All-Star team (1990). ... Named outfielder on THE SPORTING NEWS A.L. Silver Slugger team (1990). ... Won A.L. Gold Glove as outfielder (1990). ... Named outfielder on THE SPORTING NEWS N.L. All-Star team (1996). ... Named outfielder on THE SPORTING NEWS N.L. Silver Slugger team (1996).
STATISTICAL NOTES: Tied for Florida State League lead in double plays by outfielder with six in 1984. ... Led N.L. with 392 total bases and .639 slugging percentage in 1996. ... Career major league grand slams: 9.

							BATTING						FIELDING			
Year Team (League)	Pos.	G	AB	R	H	2B	3B	HR	RBI	Avg.	BB	SO	SB	PO	A	E	Avg.
1983— Elmira (N.Y.-Penn)......	OF	53	174	30	42	9	0	2	23	.241	17	43	9	89	5	2	.979
1984— Winter Haven (FSL)....	OF	112	375	52	96	15	4	6	43	.256	42	68	29	196	12	5	.977
1985— New Britain (East.)	OF	133	476	66	121	25	7	10	61	.254	42	85	17	306	9	8	.975
1986— New Britain (East.)	OF	124	462	70	126	20	3	14	55	.273	44	75	31	318	5	5	.985
1987— Pawtucket (Int'l)	OF	11	40	11	9	3	1	3	6	.225	7	7	1	25	0	0	1.000
— Boston (A.L.)	OF-DH	133	558	94	152	30	2	20	59	.272	41	98	27	320	15	4	.988
1988— Boston (A.L.)	OF-DH	144	540	93	159	37	5	18	92	.294	62	89	25	370	9	9	.977
1989— Boston (A.L.)	OF-DH	97	399	73	121	19	6	12	61	.303	36	52	21	245	7	6	.977
— Pawtucket (Int'l)	OF	5	21	4	3	1	0	0	0	.143	2	3	0	16	0	0	1.000
1990— Boston (A.L.)	OF-DH	152	588	89	174	33	8	21	89	.296	48	82	9	324	7	2	.994
1991— Boston (A.L.)	OF-DH	130	474	56	119	33	3	14	56	.251	39	81	6	283	2	2	.993
1992— Boston (A.L.)	OF-DH	66	235	35	60	8	3	8	30	.255	25	48	5	120	3	2	.984
1993— Chicago (A.L.)■........	OF	146	499	75	137	24	4	17	74	.275	60	97	6	313	6	6	.982
1994— Colorado (N.L.)■.......	OF	42	149	33	48	8	3	13	24	.322	16	39	3	79	2	3	.964
— Colo. Springs (PCL) ...	OF	2	8	4	4	1	0	1	2	.500	2	1	0	5	0	0	1.000
1995— Colo. Springs (PCL) ...	OF	8	29	9	9	2	1	2	6	.310	4	8	0	16	0	0	1.000
— Colorado (N.L.)	OF	103	278	41	74	10	6	14	49	.266	39	72	7	158	3	5	.970
1996— Colorado (N.L.)	OF	156	613	*142	211	45	8	40	128	.344	61	114	32	279	6	5	.983
1997— Colorado (N.L.)	OF	119	424	91	123	19	2	32	82	.290	47	75	7	207	6	4	.982
1998— Colorado (N.L.)	OF	100	357	54	102	22	5	16	54	.286	39	80	3	187	5	5	.975
— San Fran. (N.L.)■.......	OF	42	147	22	45	6	1	5	22	.306	19	31	8	89	1	1	.989
American League totals (7 years)		868	3293	515	922	184	31	110	461	.280	311	547	99	1975	49	31	.985
National League totals (5 years)		562	1968	383	603	110	25	120	359	.306	221	411	60	999	23	23	.978
Major league totals (12 years)		1430	5261	898	1525	294	56	230	820	.290	532	958	159	2974	72	54	.983

DIVISION SERIES RECORD

							BATTING						FIELDING			
Year Team (League)	Pos.	G	AB	R	H	2B	3B	HR	RBI	Avg.	BB	SO	SB	PO	A	E	Avg.
1995— Colorado (N.L.)	OF	2	6	1	2	1	0	0	2	.333	0	1	0	4	0	1	.800

CHAMPIONSHIP SERIES RECORD

Year Team (League)	Pos.	G	AB	R	H	2B	3B	HR	RBI	Avg.	BB	SO	SB	PO	A	E	Avg.
1988— Boston (A.L.).............	OF	4	17	2	4	1	0	0	1	.235	0	3	0	10	0	0	1.000
1990— Boston (A.L.).............	OF	4	15	1	4	2	0	0	0	.267	1	1	1	9	1	0	1.000
1993— Chicago (A.L.)............	OF	6	23	4	7	1	0	1	3	.304	3	5	0	15	0	0	1.000
Championship series totals (3 years)		**14**	**55**	**7**	**15**	**4**	**0**	**1**	**4**	**.273**	**4**	**9**	**1**	**34**	**1**	**0**	**1.000**

ALL-STAR GAME RECORD

NOTES: Named to A.L. All-Star team for 1990 game; replaced by Brook Jacoby due to injury.

Year League	Pos.	AB	R	H	2B	3B	HR	RBI	Avg.	BB	SO	SB	PO	A	E	Avg.
1990— American....................							Selected, did not play—injured.									
1996— National.....................	OF	2	0	1	0	1	0	0	.500	0	1	0	1	0	0	1.000

B

BURNETT, A.J.   P   MARLINS

PERSONAL: Born January 3, 1977, in North Little Rock, Ark. ... 6-5/205. ... Throws right, bats right. ... Full name: Allen James Burnett.
HIGH SCHOOL: Central Arkansas Christian (North Little Rock, Ark.).
TRANSACTIONS/CAREER NOTES: Selected by New York Mets organization in eighth round of free-agent draft (June 1, 1995). ... Traded by Mets with P Jesus Sanchez and OF Robert Stratton to Florida Marlins for P Al Leiter and 2B Ralph Milliard (February 6, 1998).
STATISTICAL NOTES: Tied for Appalachian League lead in wild pitches with 16 in 1996.

Year Team (League)	W	L	Pct.	ERA	G	GS	CG	ShO	Sv.	IP	H	R	ER	BB	SO
1995— GC Mets (GCL).................	2	3	.400	4.28	9	8	1	0	0	33²/₃	27	16	16	23	26
1996— Kingsport (Appalachian).....	4	0	1.000	3.88	12	12	0	0	0	58	31	26	25	54	68
1997— GC Mets (GCL).................	0	1	.000	3.18	3	2	0	0	0	11¹/₃	8	8	4	8	15
— Pittsfield (NYP)	3	1	.750	4.70	20	9	0	0	0	44	28	26	23	35	48
1998— Kane County (Midwest)......	10	4	.714	1.97	20	20	0	0	0	119	74	27	26	45	186

BURNITZ, JEROMY   OF   BREWERS

PERSONAL: Born April 15, 1969, in Westminster, Calif. ... 6-0/216. ... Bats left, throws right. ... Full name: Jeromy Neal Burnitz.
HIGH SCHOOL: Conroe (Texas).
COLLEGE: Oklahoma State.
TRANSACTIONS/CAREER NOTES: Selected by Milwaukee Brewers organization in 24th round of free-agent draft (June 2, 1987); did not sign. ... Selected by New York Mets organization in first round (17th pick overall) of free-agent draft (June 4, 1990). ... On disabled list (August 23-September 18, 1992). ... On Norfolk suspended list (August 11-13, 1994). ... Traded by Mets with P Joe Roa to Cleveland Indians for P Paul Byrd, P Jerry DiPoto, P Dave Mlicki and a player to be named later (November 18, 1994); Mets acquired 2B Jesus Azuaje to complete deal (December 6, 1994). ... Traded by Indians to Milwaukee Brewers for 3B/1B Kevin Seitzer (August 31, 1996).
RECORDS: Shares A.L. record for most home runs by pinch hitter in consecutive at-bats—2 (August 2 and 3, 1997).
STATISTICAL NOTES: Led New York-Pennsylvania League with .444 on-base percentage and tied for lead with six intentional bases on balls received in 1990. ... Led American Association with .503 slugging percentage in 1995. ... Led American Association with eight intentional bases on balls received in 1995. ... Career major league grand slams: 4.

Year Team (League)	Pos.	G	AB	R	H	2B	3B	HR	RBI	Avg.	BB	SO	SB	PO	A	E	Avg.
1990— Pittsfield (NYP)	OF	51	173	37	52	6	5	6	22	.301	45	39	12	79	2	0	1.000
— St. Lucie (Fla. St.)	OF	11	32	6	5	1	0	0	3	.156	7	12	1	18	1	0	1.000
1991— Williamsport (East.) ...	OF	135	457	80	103	16	•10	*31	*85	.225	*104	127	31	237	13	•11	.958
1992— Tidewater (Int'l)........	OF	121	445	56	108	21	3	8	40	.243	33	84	30	222	11	8	.967
1993— Norfolk (Int'l)	OF	65	255	33	58	15	3	8	44	.227	25	53	10	133	9	1	.993
— New York (N.L.).........	OF	86	263	49	64	10	6	13	38	.243	38	66	3	165	6	4	.977
1994— New York (N.L.)........	OF	45	143	26	34	4	0	3	15	.238	23	45	1	63	1	2	.970
— Norfolk (Int'l)	OF	85	314	58	75	15	5	14	49	.239	49	82	18	170	13	4	.979
1995— Buffalo (A.A.)■.......	OF	128	443	72	126	26	7	19	*85	.284	50	83	13	241	12	5	.981
— Cleveland (A.L.)........	OF-DH	9	7	4	4	1	0	0	0	.571	0	0	0	10	0	0	1.000
1996— Cleveland (A.L.)........	OF-DH	71	128	30	36	10	0	7	26	.281	25	34	2	44	0	0	1.000
— Milwaukee (A.L.)■.....	OF	23	72	8	17	4	0	2	14	.236	8	16	2	38	1	1	.975
1997— Milwaukee (A.L.)	OF	153	494	85	139	37	8	27	85	.281	75	111	20	256	13	7	.975
1998— Milwaukee (N.L.)	OF	161	609	92	160	28	1	38	125	.263	70	158	7	306	10	9	.972
American League totals (3 years)		**256**	**701**	**127**	**196**	**52**	**8**	**36**	**125**	**.280**	**108**	**158**	**24**	**348**	**14**	**8**	**.978**
National League totals (3 years)		**292**	**1015**	**167**	**258**	**42**	**7**	**54**	**178**	**.254**	**131**	**269**	**11**	**534**	**17**	**15**	**.973**
Major league totals (6 years)		**548**	**1716**	**294**	**454**	**94**	**15**	**90**	**303**	**.265**	**239**	**427**	**35**	**882**	**31**	**23**	**.975**

BURRELL, PAT   1B   PHILLIES

PERSONAL: Born October 10, 1976, in Eureka Springs, Ark. ... 6-4/225. ... Bats right, throws right. ... Name pronounced BURL.
HIGH SCHOOL: Bellarmine Prep (San Jose, Calif.).
COLLEGE: Miami (Fla.).
TRANSACTIONS/CAREER NOTES: Selected by Boston Red Sox organization in 43rd round of free-agent draft (June 1, 1995); did not sign. ... Selected by Philadelphia Phillies organization in first round (first pick overall) of free-agent draft (June 2, 1998).

Year Team (League)	Pos.	G	AB	R	H	2B	3B	HR	RBI	Avg.	BB	SO	SB	PO	A	E	Avg.
1998— Clearwater (FSL)	1B	37	132	29	40	7	1	7	30	.303	27	22	2	202	13	1	.995

BUSBY, MIKE   P   CARDINALS

PERSONAL: Born December 27, 1972, in Lomita, Calif. ... 6-4/210. ... Throws right, bats right. ... Full name: Michael James Busby.
HIGH SCHOOL: Banning (Wilmington, Calif.).
TRANSACTIONS/CAREER NOTES: Selected by St. Louis Cardinals organization in 14th round of free-agent draft (June 3, 1991). ... On Louisville disabled list (April 17-24, June 16-26, July 3-9, 1996 and April 3-June 10, 1997). ... On St. Louis disabled list (May 25-September 4, 1998); included rehabilitation assignment to Memphis (August 17-September 4).

Year Team (League)	W	L	Pct.	ERA	G	GS	CG	ShO	Sv.	IP	H	R	ER	BB	SO
1991— Ariz. Cardinals (Ariz.)	4	3	.571	3.51	11	11	0	0	0	59	67	35	23	29	71
1992— Savannah (S. Atl.)	4	•13	.235	3.67	28	•28	1	0	0	149²/₃	145	96	61	67	84
1993— Savannah (S. Atl.)	12	2	.857	2.44	23	21	1	1	0	143²/₃	116	49	39	31	125
1994— St. Petersburg (FSL)	6	•13	.316	4.45	26	26	1	0	0	151²/₃	166	82	75	49	89
1995— Arkansas (Texas)	7	6	.538	3.29	20	20	1	0	0	134	125	63	49	35	95
— Louisville (A.A.)	2	2	.500	3.29	6	6	1	0	0	38¹/₃	28	18	14	11	26
1996— St. Louis (N.L.)	0	1	.000	18.00	1	1	0	0	0	4	9	13	8	4	4
— Louisville (A.A.)	2	5	.286	6.38	14	14	0	0	0	72	89	57	51	44	53
1997— Louisville (A.A.)	4	8	.333	4.61	15	14	1	1	0	93²/₃	95	49	48	30	65
— St. Louis (N.L.)	0	2	.000	8.79	3	3	0	0	0	14¹/₃	24	14	14	4	6
1998— St. Louis (N.L.)	5	2	.714	4.50	26	2	0	0	0	46	45	23	23	15	33
— Memphis (Pacific Coast)	0	0	. . .	3.38	7	2	0	0	0	8	5	3	3	2	5
Major league totals (3 years)	5	5	.500	6.30	30	6	0	0	0	64¹/₃	78	50	45	23	43

BUSH, HOMER   2B   YANKEES

PERSONAL: Born November 12, 1972, in East St. Louis, Ill. ... 5-10/180. ... Bats right, throws right. ... Full name: Homer Giles Bush.
HIGH SCHOOL: East St. Louis (Ill.).
COLLEGE: Southern Illinois-Edwardsville.
TRANSACTIONS/CAREER NOTES: Selected by San Diego Padres organization in seventh round of free-agent draft (June 3, 1991). ... On Rancho Cucamonga disabled list (April 27-May 4 and May 9-26, 1994). ... On disabled list (May 20, 1996-remainder of season). ... Traded by Padres with rights to P Hideki Irabu, OF Gordon Amerson and player to be named later to New York Yankees for OF Ruben Rivera, P Rafael Medina and cash (April 22, 1997); Yankees acquired OF Vernon Maxwell to complete deal (June 9, 1997).

Year Team (League)	Pos.	G	AB	R	H	2B	3B	HR	RBI	Avg.	BB	SO	SB	PO	A	E	Avg.
1991— Ariz. Padres (Ariz.)	3B	32	127	16	41	3	2	0	16	.323	4	33	11	25	60	10	.895
1992— Char., S.C. (S. Atl.)	2B	108	367	37	86	10	5	0	18	.234	13	85	14	199	287	*34	.935
1993— Waterloo (Midw.)	2B	130	472	63	*152	19	3	5	51	.322	19	87	39	215	289	38	.930
1994— Rancho Cuca. (Cal.)	2B	39	161	37	54	10	3	0	16	.335	9	29	9	69	102	7	.961
— Wichita (Texas)	2B	59	245	35	73	11	4	3	14	.298	10	39	20	101	135	8	.967
1995— Memphis (Sou.)	2B	108	432	53	121	12	5	5	37	.280	15	83	34	235	268	16	.969
1996— Las Vegas (PCL)	2B	32	116	24	42	11	1	2	3	.362	3	33	3	67	88	5	.969
1997— Las Vegas (PCL)	2B	38	155	25	43	10	1	3	14	.277	7	40	5	73	103	4	.978
— Columbus (Int'l)■	2B	74	275	36	68	10	3	2	26	.247	25	56	12	153	253	9	.978
— New York (A.L.)	2B-DH	10	11	2	4	0	0	0	3	.364	0	0	0	8	13	2	.913
1998— New York (A.L.)	2-DH-3-S	45	71	17	27	3	0	1	5	.380	5	19	6	38	38	2	.974
Major league totals (2 years)		55	82	19	31	3	0	1	8	.378	5	19	6	46	51	4	.960

DIVISION SERIES RECORD

Year Team (League)	Pos.	G	AB	R	H	2B	3B	HR	RBI	Avg.	BB	SO	SB	PO	A	E	Avg.
1998— New York (A.L.)	PR-DH	1	0	0	0	0	0	0	0	. . .	0	0	1	. . .	. . .	. . .	. . .

CHAMPIONSHIP SERIES RECORD

Year Team (League)	Pos.	G	AB	R	H	2B	3B	HR	RBI	Avg.	BB	SO	SB	PO	A	E	Avg.
1998— New York (A.L.)	PR-DH	2	0	1	0	0	0	0	0	. . .	0	0	1	. . .	. . .	. . .	. . .

WORLD SERIES RECORD

NOTES: Member of World Series championship team (1998).

Year Team (League)	Pos.	G	AB	R	H	2B	3B	HR	RBI	Avg.	BB	SO	SB	PO	A	E	Avg.
1998— New York (A.L.)	PR-DH	2	0	0	0	0	0	0	0	. . .	0	0	0	. . .	. . .	. . .	. . .

BUTLER, ADAM   P   BRAVES

PERSONAL: Born August 17, 1973, in Fairfax, Va. ... 6-2/225. ... Throws left, bats left. ... Full name: Adam Christopher Butler.
HIGH SCHOOL: Lake Braddock (Burke, Va.).
COLLEGE: William & Mary.
TRANSACTIONS/CAREER NOTES: Signed as non-drafted free agent by Atlanta Braves organization (June 29, 1995).

Year Team (League)	W	L	Pct.	ERA	G	GS	CG	ShO	Sv.	IP	H	R	ER	BB	SO
1995— Eugene (Northwest)	4	1	.800	2.49	23	0	0	0	8	25¹/₃	15	9	7	12	50
1996— Macon (S. Atl.)	0	0	.000	1.23	12	0	0	0	8	14²/₃	5	3	2	3	23
— Durham (Carolina)	0	0	. . .	0.00	9	0	0	0	5	11	2	0	0	7	14
— Greenville (Southern)	1	4	.200	5.09	38	0	0	0	17	35¹/₃	36	22	20	16	31
1997— Greenville (Southern)	5	1	.833	2.57	46	0	0	0	22	49	40	16	14	15	56
1998— Atlanta (N.L.)	0	1	.000	10.80	8	0	0	0	0	5	5	7	6	6	7
— Richmond (Int'l)	3	7	.300	3.60	48	4	0	0	14	100	96	41	40	28	92
Major league totals (1 year)	0	1	.000	10.80	8	0	0	0	0	5	5	7	6	6	7

BUTLER, RICH   OF   DEVIL RAYS

PERSONAL: Born May 1, 1973, in Toronto. ... 6-1/205. ... Bats left, throws right. ... Full name: Richard Dwight Butler. ... Brother of Rob Butler, outfielder with Toronto Blue Jays (1993-94) and Philadelphia Phillies (1997).
HIGH SCHOOL: East York Collegiate (Toronto).
TRANSACTIONS/CAREER NOTES: Signed as non-drafted free agent by Toronto Blue Jays organization (September 24, 1990). ... On disabled list (April 4-August 17, 1996). ... Selected by Tampa Bay Devil Rays in first round (10th pick overall) of expansion draft (November 18, 1997). ... On Tampa Bay disabled list (May 10-June 16, 1998); included rehabilitation assignment to Durham (June 3-15).
STATISTICAL NOTES: Led International League with 281 total bases in 1997.

Year Team (League)	Pos.	G	AB	R	H	2B	3B	HR	RBI	Avg.	BB	SO	SB	PO	A	E	Avg.
1991— GC Jays (GCL)	OF	59	213	30	56	•6	7	0	13	.263	17	45	10	104	2	1	*.991
1992— Myrtle Beach (SAL)	OF	130	441	43	100	14	1	2	43	.227	37	90	11	186	4	8	.960
1993— Knoxville (Southern)	OF	6	21	3	2	0	1	0	0	.095	3	5	0	11	0	0	1.000
— Dunedin (Fla. St.)	OF	110	444	68	136	19	8	11	65	.306	48	64	11	157	7	2	.988
1994— Knoxville (Southern)	OF	53	192	29	56	7	4	3	22	.292	19	31	7	96	0	3	.970
— Syracuse (Int'l)	OF	94	302	34	73	6	2	3	27	.242	22	66	8	219	4	3	.987
1995— Syracuse (Int'l)	OF	69	199	20	32	4	2	2	14	.161	9	45	2	101	9	4	.965
— Knoxville (Southern)	OF	58	217	27	58	12	3	4	33	.267	25	41	11	106	5	3	.974
1996— Dunedin (Fla. St.)	DH	10	28	1	2	0	0	0	0	.071	5	9	4	...	...	...	...
1997— Syracuse (Int'l)	OF	•137	*537	*93	*161	30	9	24	87	.300	60	107	20	236	8	8	.968
— Toronto (A.L.)	OF	7	14	3	4	1	0	0	2	.286	2	3	0	5	0	0	1.000
1998—Tampa Bay (A.L.)■	OF	72	217	25	49	3	3	7	20	.226	15	37	4	113	4	0	1.000
— Durham (Int'l)	OF	38	145	28	43	8	0	8	35	.297	22	24	6	60	1	3	.953
Major league totals (2 years)		79	231	28	53	4	3	7	22	.229	17	40	4	118	4	0	1.000

BYRD, PAUL   P   PHILLIES

PERSONAL: Born December 3, 1970, in Louisville, Ky. ... 6-1/185. ... Throws right, bats right. ... Full name: Paul Gregory Byrd.
HIGH SCHOOL: St. Xavier (Louisville, Ky.).
COLLEGE: Louisiana State.
TRANSACTIONS/CAREER NOTES: Selected by Cincinnati Reds organization in 13th round of free-agent draft (June 1, 1988); did not sign. ... Selected by Cleveland Indians organization in fourth round of free-agent draft (June 3, 1991). ... On disabled list (August 12, 1992-remainder of season). ... On disabled list (May 23-July 24, 1993). ... Traded by Indians organization with P Dave Mlicki, P Jerry DiPoto and a player to be named later to New York Mets organization for OF Jeromy Burnitz and P Joe Roa (November 18, 1994); Mets acquired 2B Jesus Azuaje to complete deal (December 6, 1994). ... On Norfolk disabled list (June 1-19, 1995). ... On New York disabled list (March 22-June 9, 1996); included rehabilitation assignment to Norfolk (May 27-June 9). ... Traded by Mets with a player to be named later to Atlanta Braves for P Greg McMichael (November 25, 1996); Braves acquired P Andy Zwirchitz to complete deal (May 25, 1997). ... On Richmond disabled list (June 3-July 2, 1998). ... Claimed on waivers by Philadelphia Phillies (August 14, 1998).
STATISTICAL NOTES: Led Carolina League with seven balks in 1991.

Year Team (League)	W	L	Pct.	ERA	G	GS	CG	ShO	Sv.	IP	H	R	ER	BB	SO
1991— Kinston (Carolina)	4	3	.571	3.16	14	11	0	0	0	62 2/3	40	27	22	36	62
1992— Cant./Akr. (Eastern)	14	6	.700	3.01	24	24	4	0	0	152 1/3	122	68	51	75	118
1993— Charlotte (Int'l)	7	4	.636	3.89	14	14	1	1	0	81	80	43	35	30	54
— Cant./Akr. (Eastern)	0	0	...	3.60	2	1	0	0	0	10	7	4	4	3	8
1994— Cant./Akr. (Eastern)	5	9	.357	3.81	21	20	4	1	0	139 1/3	135	70	59	52	106
— Charlotte (Fla. St.)	2	2	.500	3.93	9	4	0	0	1	36 2/3	33	19	16	11	15
1995— Norfolk (Int'l)■	3	5	.375	2.79	22	10	1	0	6	87	71	29	27	21	61
— New York (N.L.)	2	0	1.000	2.05	17	0	0	0	0	22	18	6	5	7	26
1996—New York (N.L.)	1	2	.333	4.24	38	0	0	0	0	46 2/3	48	22	22	21	31
— Norfolk (Int'l)	2	0	1.000	3.52	5	0	0	0	1	7 2/3	4	3	3	4	8
1997—Atlanta (N.L.)■	4	4	.500	5.26	31	4	0	0	0	53	47	34	31	28	37
— Richmond (Int'l)	2	1	.667	3.18	3	3	0	0	0	17	14	6	6	1	14
1998— Richmond (Int'l)	5	5	.500	3.69	17	17	2	0	0	102 1/3	92	44	42	36	84
— Atlanta (N.L.)	0	0	...	13.50	1	0	0	0	0	2	4	3	3	1	1
— Philadelphia (N.L.)■	5	2	.714	2.29	8	8	2	1	0	55	41	16	14	17	38
Major league totals (4 years)	12	8	.600	3.78	95	12	2	1	0	178 2/3	158	81	75	74	133

BYRDAK, TIM   P   ROYALS

PERSONAL: Born October 31, 1973, in Oak Lawn, Ill. ... 5-11/160. ... Throws left, bats left. ... Full name: Timothy Christopher Byrdak. ... Name pronounced BIRD-ek.
HIGH SCHOOL: Oak Forest (Ill.).
JUNIOR COLLEGE: South Suburban College (Ill.).
COLLEGE: Rice.
TRANSACTIONS/CAREER NOTES: Selected by Kansas City Royals organization in fifth round of free-agent draft (June 2, 1994). ... On disabled list (June 27-August 19, 1996). ... On Omaha disabled list (April 3-June 9, 1997).

Year Team (League)	W	L	Pct.	ERA	G	GS	CG	ShO	Sv.	IP	H	R	ER	BB	SO
1994— Eugene (Northwest)	4	5	.444	3.07	15	15	0	0	0	73 1/3	60	33	25	20	77
1995— Wilmington (Caro.)	11	5	.688	2.16	27	26	0	0	0	166 1/3	118	46	40	45	127
1996— Wichita (Texas)	5	7	.417	6.91	15	15	0	0	0	84 2/3	112	73	65	44	47
1997— Wilmington (Caro.)	4	3	.571	3.51	22	2	0	0	3	41	34	17	16	12	47
1998— Wichita (Texas)	3	5	.375	4.15	34	0	0	0	2	52	58	29	24	28	37
— Omaha (Pacific Coast)	2	1	.667	2.45	26	0	0	0	1	36 2/3	31	13	10	20	32
— Kansas City (A.L.)	0	0	...	5.40	3	0	0	0	0	1 2/3	5	1	1	0	1
Major league totals (1 year)	0	0	...	5.40	3	0	0	0	0	1 2/3	5	1	1	0	1

CABRERA, JOLBERT　　　　　　　IF　　　　　　　INDIANS

PERSONAL: Born December 8, 1972, in Cartagena, Colombia. ... 6-0/177. ... Bats right, throws right. ... Full name: Jolbert Alexis Cabrera. ... Brother of Orlando Cabrera, shortstop, Montreal Expos.
HIGH SCHOOL: Confenalco (Cartagena, Colombia).
TRANSACTIONS/CAREER NOTES: Signed as non-drafted free agent by Montreal Expos organization (July 3, 1990). ... Granted free agency (October 17, 1997). ... Signed by Cleveland Indians organization (January 19, 1998).
STATISTICAL NOTES: Led International League in caught stealing with 15 in 1998.

Year Team (League)	Pos.	G	AB	R	H	2B	3B	HR	RBI	Avg.	BB	SO	SB	PO	A	E	Avg.
1990— Dom. Expos (DSL)	SS	29	115	31	36	3	2	0	12	.313	14	10	14				...
1991— Sumter (S. Atl.)	SS	101	324	33	66	4	0	1	20	.204	19	62	10	141	256	28	.934
1992— Albany (S. Atl.)	SS	118	377	44	86	9	2	0	23	.228	34	77	22	169	277	35	.927
1993— Burlington (Midw.)	SS	128	507	62	129	24	2	0	38	.254	39	93	31	•173	300	*36	.929
1994— W.P. Beach (FSL)	SS	83	266	32	54	4	0	0	13	.203	14	48	7	136	228	26	.933
— San Bern. (Calif.)	SS	30	109	14	27	5	1	0	11	.248	14	24	2	51	82	7	.950
— Harrisburg (East.)	SS	3	2	0	0	0	0	0	0	.000	0	1	0	0	1	0	1.000
1995— W.P. Beach (FSL)	SS-2B-3B	103	357	62	102	23	2	1	25	.286	38	61	19	148	294	29	.938
— Harrisburg (East.)	SS	9	35	4	10	2	0	0	1	.286	1	3	3	11	18	2	.935
1996— Harrisburg (East.)	SS-OF-3B	107	354	40	85	18	2	3	29	.240	23	63	10	179	306	25	.951
1997— Harrisburg (East.)	2B-SS-OF	48	171	28	43	9	0	2	11	.251	28	28	5	98	76	9	.951
— Ottawa (Int'l)	3-2-S-O	68	191	28	54	10	4	0	12	.283	11	31	15	51	127	7	.962
1998— Cleveland (A.L.)■	SS	1	2	0	0	0	0	0	0	.000	0	1	0	2	2	0	1.000
— Buffalo (Int'l)	SS-OF-2B	129	494	94	157	24	1	10	45	.318	68	71	25	235	352	27	.956
Major league totals (1 year)		1	2	0	0	0	0	0	0	.000	0	1	0	2	2	0	1.000

CABRERA, JOSE　　　　　　　P　　　　　　　ASTROS

PERSONAL: Born March 24, 1972, in Santiago, Dominican Republic. ... 6-0/160. ... Throws right, bats right. ... Full name: Jose Alberto Cabrera.
TRANSACTIONS/CAREER NOTES: Signed as non-drafted free agent by Cleveland Indians organization (October 12, 1990). ... On disabled list (May 11-28, 1993). ... On Canton disabled list (April 25-May 24, 1995). ... On Buffalo disabled list (April 4-13 and 17-25, 1997). ... Traded by Indians to Houston Astros organization for P Alvin Morman (May 10, 1997). ... On Houston disabled list (April 5, 1998-remainder of season); included rehabilitation assignment to New Orleans (July 4-20).

Year Team (League)	W	L	Pct.	ERA	G	GS	CG	ShO	Sv.	IP	H	R	ER	BB	SO
1991— DSL Indians (DSL)	6	4	.600	3.07	16	12	1	0	0	73 1/3	64	32	25	17	40
1992— Burlington (Appalachian)....	•8	3	.727	1.75	13	13	1	0	0	92 1/3	74	27	18	18	79
1993— Columbus (S. Atl.)	11	6	.647	2.67	26	26	1	0	0	155 1/3	122	54	46	53	105
1994— Kinston (Carolina)	4	13	.235	4.44	24	24	0	0	0	133 2/3	134	84	66	43	110
1995— Cant./Akr. (Eastern)	1	1	.500	1.02	4	3	0	0	0	17 2/3	7	2	2	8	19
— Bakersfield (California)	2	2	.500	3.92	7	7	0	0	0	41 1/3	40	25	18	21	52
1996— Cant./Akr. (Eastern)	4	3	.571	5.63	15	7	0	0	0	62 1/3	78	45	39	17	40
1997— Buffalo (A.A.)	3	0	1.000	1.20	5	0	0	0	0	15	8	2	2	7	11
— New Orleans (A.A.)	2	2	.500	2.54	31	0	0	0	0	46	31	13	13	13	48
— Houston (N.L.)	0	0	...	1.17	12	0	0	0	0	15 1/3	6	2	2	6	18
1998— Houston (N.L.)	0	0	...	8.31	3	0	0	0	0	4 1/3	7	4	4	1	1
— New Orleans (PCL)	0	0	...	5.40	5	0	0	0	1	5	2	3	3	1	6
Major league totals (2 years)	0	0	...	2.75	15	0	0	0	0	19 2/3	13	6	6	7	19

CABRERA, ORLANDO　　　　　　　SS　　　　　　　EXPOS

PERSONAL: Born November 2, 1974, in Cartagena, Columbia. ... 5-10/175. ... Bats right, throws right. ... Full name: Orlando Luis Cabrera. ... Brother of Jolbert Cabrera, infielder, Cleveland Indians organization.
TRANSACTIONS/CAREER NOTES: Signed as non-drafted free agent by Montreal Expos organization (June 1, 1993).

Year Team (League)	Pos.	G	AB	R	H	2B	3B	HR	RBI	Avg.	BB	SO	SB	PO	A	E	Avg.
1993— Dom. Expos (DSL)	IF	38	122	24	42	6	1	1	17	.344	18	11	14	86	76	3	.982
1994— GC Expos (GCL)	2B-SS-OF	22	73	13	23	4	1	0	11	.315	5	8	6	22	42	4	.941
1995— Vermont (NYP)	2B-SS	65	248	37	70	12	5	3	33	.282	16	28	15	135	189	17	.950
1996— Delmarva (S. Atl.)	SS-2B	134	512	86	129	28	4	14	65	.252	54	63	51	205	344	27	.953
1997— W.P. Beach (FSL)	SS-2B	69	279	56	77	19	2	5	26	.276	27	33	32	92	162	20	.927
— Harrisburg (East.)	SS-2B	35	133	34	41	13	2	5	20	.308	15	18	7	57	83	5	.966
— Ottawa (Int'l)	SS-2B	31	122	17	32	5	2	2	14	.262	7	16	8	45	94	3	.979
— Montreal (N.L.)	SS-2B	16	18	4	4	0	0	0	2	.222	1	3	1	11	15	1	.963
1998— Ottawa (Int'l)	SS-2B	66	272	31	63	9	4	0	26	.232	28	27	19	122	190	12	.963
— Montreal (N.L.)	SS-2B	79	261	44	73	16	5	3	22	.280	18	27	6	122	196	7	.978
Major league totals (2 years)		95	279	48	77	16	5	3	24	.276	19	30	7	133	211	8	.977

CADARET, GREG　　　　　　　P　　　　　　　DODGERS

PERSONAL: Born February 27, 1962, in Detroit. ... 6-3/230. ... Throws left, bats left. ... Full name: Gregory James Cadaret. ... Name pronounced CAD-uh-ray.
HIGH SCHOOL: Central Montacalm (Stanton, Mich.).
COLLEGE: Grand Valley State (Mich.).

C

TRANSACTIONS/CAREER NOTES: Selected by Oakland Athletics organization in 11th round of free-agent draft (June 6, 1983). ... Traded by A's organization with P Eric Plunk and OF Luis Polonia to New York Yankees for OF Rickey Henderson (June 21, 1989). ... Contract sold by Yankees to Cincinnati Reds (November 6, 1992). ... Released by Reds (July 26, 1993). ... Signed by Kansas City Royals (July 30, 1993). ... Granted free agency (October 25, 1993). ... Signed by Toronto Blue Jays organization (December 21, 1993). ... Released by Blue Jays (June 9, 1994). ... Signed by Detroit Tigers (June 17, 1994). ... Granted free agency (October 21, 1994). ... Signed by Edmonton, A's organization (April 8, 1995). ... Released by A's organization (April 24, 1995). ... Signed by Louisville, St. Louis Cardinals organization (May 2, 1995). ... On Louisville suspended list (May 21-23, 1995). ... Released by Louisville, Cardinals organization (June 6, 1995). ... Signed by Las Vegas, San Diego Padres organization (June 30, 1995). ... Granted free agency (October 16, 1995). ... Signed by Pittsburgh Pirates organization (January 8, 1996). ... Released by Pirates (May 2, 1996). ... Signed by Cleveland Indians organization (May 14, 1996). ... Granted free agency (October 15, 1996). ... Re-signed by Indians organization (January 31, 1997). ... Released by Indians (July 3, 1997). ... Signed by Anaheim Angels organization (July 10, 1997). ... Granted free agency (October 9, 1997). ... Re-signed by Angels organization (December 4, 1997). ... Released by Angels (August 20, 1998). ... Claimed on waivers by Texas Rangers (August 26, 1998). ... Granted free agency (October 28, 1998). ... Signed by Los Angeles Dodgers (January 12, 1999).

Year Team (League)	W	L	Pct.	ERA	G	GS	CG	ShO	Sv.	IP	H	R	ER	BB	SO
1983— Medford (N'west)	7	3	.700	4.36	12	11	1	1	0	64	73	36	31	36	51
1984— Modesto (California)	13	8	.619	3.05	26	26	6	2	0	171 1/3	162	79	58	82	138
1985— Huntsville (Southern)	3	7	.300	6.12	17	17	0	0	0	82 1/3	96	61	56	57	60
— Modesto (California)	3	9	.250	5.87	12	12	1	1	0	61 1/3	59	50	40	54	43
1986— Huntsville (Southern)	12	5	.706	5.41	28	28	1	0	0	141 1/3	166	106	85	98	113
1987— Huntsville (Southern)	5	2	.714	2.90	24	0	0	0	9	40 1/3	31	16	13	20	48
— Tacoma (PCL)	1	2	.333	3.46	7	0	0	0	1	13	5	6	5	13	12
— Oakland (A.L.)	6	2	.750	4.54	29	0	0	0	0	39 2/3	37	22	20	24	30
1988— Oakland (A.L.)	5	2	.714	2.89	58	0	0	0	3	71 2/3	60	26	23	36	64
1989— Oakland (A.L.)	0	0	. . .	2.28	26	0	0	0	0	27 2/3	21	9	7	19	14
— New York (A.L.)■	5	5	.500	4.58	20	13	3	1	0	92 1/3	109	53	47	38	66
1990— New York (A.L.)	5	4	.556	4.15	54	6	0	0	3	121 1/3	120	62	56	64	80
1991— New York (A.L.)	8	6	.571	3.62	68	5	0	0	3	121 2/3	110	52	49	59	105
1992— New York (A.L.)	4	8	.333	4.25	46	11	1	1	1	103 2/3	104	53	49	74	73
1993— Cincinnati (N.L.)■	2	1	.667	4.96	34	0	0	0	1	32 2/3	40	19	18	23	23
— Kansas City (A.L.)■	1	1	.500	2.93	13	0	0	0	0	15 1/3	14	5	5	7	2
1994— Toronto (A.L.)	0	1	.000	5.85	21	0	0	0	0	20	24	15	13	17	15
— Detroit (A.L.)■	1	0	1.000	3.60	17	0	0	0	2	20	17	9	8	16	14
1995— Louisville (A.A.)■	1	0	1.000	3.09	12	0	0	0	0	11 2/3	14	4	4	1	7
— Las Vegas (PCL)■	3	5	.375	5.88	28	4	0	0	0	52	56	40	34	22	52
1996— Calgary (PCL)■	0	3	.000	7.30	9	0	0	0	0	12 1/3	20	18	10	12	10
— Buffalo (A.A.)■	1	5	.167	3.66	32	3	0	0	2	64	59	28	26	29	44
1997— Buffalo (A.A.)	2	2	.500	4.86	29	1	0	0	4	50	46	31	27	35	49
— Vancouver (PCL)■	0	1	.000	3.14	9	0	0	0	3	14 1/3	11	5	5	4	16
— Anaheim (A.L.)	0	0	. . .	3.29	15	0	0	0	0	13 2/3	11	5	5	8	11
1998— Vancouver (PCL)	2	1	.667	0.00	9	0	0	0	1	10	4	2	0	3	12
— Anaheim (A.L.)	1	2	.333	4.14	39	0	0	0	1	37	38	17	17	15	37
— Texas (A.L.)■	0	0	. . .	4.70	11	0	0	0	0	7 2/3	11	4	4	3	5
A.L. totals (10 years)	36	31	.537	3.94	417	35	4	2	13	691 2/3	676	332	303	380	516
N.L. totals (1 year)	2	1	.667	4.96	34	0	0	0	1	32 2/3	40	19	18	23	23
Major league totals (10 years)	38	32	.543	3.99	451	35	4	2	14	724 1/3	716	351	321	403	539

CHAMPIONSHIP SERIES RECORD

Year Team (League)	W	L	Pct.	ERA	G	GS	CG	ShO	Sv.	IP	H	R	ER	BB	SO
1988— Oakland (A.L.)	0	0	. . .	27.00	1	0	0	0	0	1/3	1	1	1	0	0

WORLD SERIES RECORD

Year Team (League)	W	L	Pct.	ERA	G	GS	CG	ShO	Sv.	IP	H	R	ER	BB	SO
1988— Oakland (A.L.)	0	0	. . .	0.00	3	0	0	0	0	2	2	0	0	0	3

CAIRO, MIGUEL   2B   DEVIL RAYS

PERSONAL: Born May 4, 1974, in Anaco, Venezuela. ... 6-1/180. ... Bats right, throws right. ... Full name: Miguel Jesus Cairo.
HIGH SCHOOL: Escuela Anaco (Anaco, Venezuela).
TRANSACTIONS/CAREER NOTES: Signed as non-drafted free agent by Los Angeles Dodgers organization (September 20, 1990). ... Traded by Dodgers with 3B Willis Otanez to Seattle Mariners for 3B Mike Blowers (November 29, 1995). ... Traded by Mariners with P Bill Risley to Toronto Blue Jays for P Edwin Hurtado and P Paul Menhart (December 18, 1995). ... Traded by Blue Jays to Chicago Cubs for P Jason Stevenson (November 20, 1996). ... Selected by Tampa Bay Devil Rays in first round (eighth pick overall) of expansion draft (November 18, 1997).
STATISTICAL NOTES: Led California League in caught stealing with 23 in 1994. ... Led International League second basemen with 64 double plays in 1996. ... Led American Association in caught stealing with 15 in 1997.

Year Team (League)	Pos.	G	AB	R	H	2B	3B	HR	RBI	Avg.	BB	SO	SB	PO	A	E	Avg.
1991— Dom. Dodgers (DSL)	IF	57	203	16	45	5	1	0	17	.222	0	17	8	. . .	. . .	. . .	. . .
1992— Vero Beach (FSL)	2B-3B	36	125	7	28	0	0	0	7	.224	11	12	5	69	76	10	.935
— GC Dodgers (GCL)	SS-3B	21	76	10	23	5	2	0	9	.303	2	6	1	26	56	4	.953
1993— Vero Beach (FSL)	2B-SS-3B	90	346	50	109	10	1	1	23	.315	28	22	23	172	244	18	.959
1994— Bakersfield (Calif.)	2B-SS	133	533	76	155	23	4	2	48	.291	34	37	44	268	376	28	.958
1995— San Antonio (Tex.)	2B-SS	107	435	53	121	20	1	1	41	.278	26	31	33	210	316	23	.958
1996— Syracuse (Int'l)■	2B-3B-SS	120	465	71	129	14	4	3	48	.277	26	44	27	193	295	23	.955
— Toronto (A.L.)	2B	9	27	5	6	2	0	0	1	.222	2	9	0	22	18	0	1.000
1997— Iowa (Am. Assoc.)■	2B-SS	135	*569	82	159	35	4	5	46	.279	24	54	*40	248	386	20	.969
— Chicago (N.L.)	2B-SS	16	29	7	7	1	0	0	1	.241	2	3	0	16	18	0	1.000
1998— Tampa Bay (A.L.)	2B-DH	150	515	49	138	26	5	5	46	.268	24	44	19	278	429	16	.978
American League totals (2 years)		159	542	54	144	28	5	5	47	.266	26	53	19	300	447	16	.979
National League totals (1 year)		16	29	7	7	1	0	0	1	.241	2	3	0	16	18	0	1.000
Major league totals (3 years)		175	571	61	151	29	5	5	48	.264	28	56	19	316	465	16	.980

CAMERON, MIKE — OF — REDS

PERSONAL: Born January 8, 1973, in LaGrange, Ga. ... 6-2/190. ... Bats right, throws right. ... Full name: Michael Terrance Cameron.
HIGH SCHOOL: LaGrange (Ga.).
TRANSACTIONS/CAREER NOTES: Selected by Chicago White Sox organization in 18th round of free-agent draft (June 3, 1991). ... Traded by White Sox to Cincinnati Reds for 1B/3B Paul Konerko (November 11, 1998).
STATISTICAL NOTES: Tied for Carolina League lead in double plays by outfielder with four in 1994. ... Led Southern League with .600 slugging percentage and tied for lead in caught stealing with 15 in 1996. ... Led Southern League outfielders with 264 total chances in 1996.

								BATTING							FIELDING		
Year	Team (League)	Pos.	G	AB	R	H	2B	3B	HR	RBI	Avg.	BB	SO	SB	PO	A	E	Avg.
1991— GC Whi. Sox (GCL)		OF	44	136	20	30	3	0	0	11	.221	17	29	13	55	3	3	.951
1992— Utica (N.Y.-Penn)........		OF	26	87	15	24	1	4	2	12	.276	11	26	3	60	3	0	1.000
—South Bend (Mid.)........		OF	35	114	19	26	8	1	1	9	.228	10	37	2	67	0	3	.957
1993— South Bend (Mid.)......		OF	122	411	52	98	14	5	0	30	.238	27	101	19	248	13	4	.985
1994— Prince Will. (Car.).......		OF	131	468	86	116	15	*17	6	48	.248	60	101	22	275	10	6	.979
1995— Birmingham (Sou.).....		OF	107	350	64	87	20	5	11	60	.249	54	104	21	250	7	4	.985
—Chicago (A.L.)...........		OF	28	38	4	7	2	0	1	2	.184	3	15	0	33	1	0	1.000
1996— Birmingham (Sou.).....		OF-DH	123	473	*120	142	34	12	28	77	.300	71	117	*39	*249	8	7	.973
—Chicago (A.L.)...........		OF-DH	11	11	1	1	0	0	0	0	.091	1	3	0	7	0	0	1.000
1997— Nashville (A.A.)		OF	30	120	21	33	7	3	6	17	.275	18	31	4	63	3	1	.985
—Chicago (A.L.)...........		OF-DH	116	379	63	98	18	3	14	55	.259	55	105	23	334	5	5	.985
1998— Chicago (A.L.)...........		OF	141	396	53	83	16	5	8	43	.210	37	101	27	313	6	4	.988
Major league totals (4 years)			296	824	121	189	36	8	23	100	.229	96	224	50	687	12	9	.987

CAMINITI, KEN — 3B — ASTROS

PERSONAL: Born April 21, 1963, in Hanford, Calif. ... 6-0/200. ... Bats both, throws right. ... Full name: Kenneth Gene Caminiti. ... Name pronounced CAM-uh-NET-ee.
HIGH SCHOOL: Leigh (San Jose, Calif.).
COLLEGE: San Jose State.
TRANSACTIONS/CAREER NOTES: Selected by Houston Astros organization in third round of free-agent draft (June 4, 1984). ... On disabled list (April 19-May 11, 1992). ... Traded by Astros with OF Steve Finley, SS Andujar Cedeno, 1B Robert Petagine, P Brian Williams and a player to be named later to San Diego Padres for OF Phil Plantier, OF Derek Bell, P Pedro Martinez, P Doug Brocail, IF Craig Shipley and SS Ricky Gutierrez (December 28, 1994); Padres acquired P Sean Fesh to complete deal (May 1, 1995). ... On disabled list (May 12-27, 1997; and May 2-23, 1998). ... Granted free agency (October 23, 1998). ... Signed by Astros (November 17, 1998).
RECORDS: Holds major league single-season record for most games with switch-hit home runs—4 (1996). ... Holds major league record for most consecutive games with switch-hit home runs—2 (September 16-17, 1995). ... Shares major league single-season record for most runs batted in by switch hitter—130 (1996). ... Holds N.L. single-season record for highest slugging average by switch hitter—.621 (1996); and most games with switch-hit home runs—6 (1996). ... Holds N.L. career record for most games with switch-hit home runs—9. ... Holds N.L. record for most home runs by switch hitter in two consecutive seasons—66 (1995-96 and 1996-97).
HONORS: Named third baseman on THE SPORTING NEWS college All-America team (1984). ... Won N.L. Gold Glove at third base (1995-97). ... Named third baseman on THE SPORTING NEWS N.L. All-Star team (1996). ... Named third baseman on THE SPORTING NEWS N.L. Silver Slugger team (1996). ... Named N.L. Most Valuable Player by Baseball Writers' Association of America (1996).
STATISTICAL NOTES: Led Southern League third basemen with 34 double plays in 1986. ... Led Pacific Coast League third basemen with 382 total chances and 25 double plays in 1988. ... Switch-hit home runs in one game nine times (July 3, 1994; September 16, September 17 and September 19, 1995; August 1, August 21, August 28 and September 11, 1996; and July 12, 1998). ... Led N.L. third basemen with 424 total chances and 28 double plays in 1995. ... Tied for N.L. lead with 10 sacrifice flies in 1996. ... Hit three home runs in one game (July 12, 1998). ... Career major league grand slams: 4.

								BATTING							FIELDING		
Year	Team (League)	Pos.	G	AB	R	H	2B	3B	HR	RBI	Avg.	BB	SO	SB	PO	A	E	Avg.
1985— Osceola (Fla. St.)........		3B	126	468	83	133	26	9	4	73	.284	51	54	14	53	193	20	.925
1986— Columbus (Southern).		3B	137	513	82	154	29	3	12	81	.300	56	79	5	105	*299	33	.924
1987— Columbus (Southern).		3B	95	375	66	122	25	2	15	69	.325	25	58	11	55	205	21	.925
—Houston (N.L.)		3B	63	203	10	50	7	1	3	23	.246	12	44	0	50	98	8	.949
1988— Tucson (PCL)		3B	109	416	54	113	24	7	5	66	.272	29	54	13	*105	*250	27	.929
—Houston (N.L.)		3B	30	83	5	15	2	0	1	7	.181	5	18	0	12	43	3	.948
1989— Houston (N.L.)		3B	161	585	71	149	31	3	10	72	.255	51	93	4	126	335	22	.954
1990— Houston (N.L.)		3B	153	541	52	131	20	2	4	51	.242	48	97	9	118	243	21	.945
1991— Houston (N.L.)		3B	152	574	65	145	30	3	13	80	.253	46	85	4	129	293	23	.948
1992— Houston (N.L.)		3B	135	506	68	149	31	2	13	62	.294	44	68	10	102	210	11	.966
1993— Houston (N.L.)		3B	143	543	75	142	31	0	13	75	.262	49	88	8	123	264	24	.942
1994— Houston (N.L.)		3B	111	406	63	115	28	2	18	75	.283	43	71	4	79	200	9	.969
1995— San Diego (N.L.)■...		3B	143	526	74	159	33	0	26	94	.302	69	94	12	102	*295	*27	.936
1996— San Diego (N.L.)		3B	146	546	109	178	37	2	40	130	.326	78	99	11	103	310	20	.954
1997— San Diego (N.L.)		3B	137	486	92	141	28	0	26	90	.290	80	118	11	90	291	24	.941
1998— San Diego (N.L.)		3B	131	452	87	114	29	0	29	82	.252	71	108	6	77	207	*21	.931
Major league totals (12 years)			1505	5451	771	1488	307	15	196	841	.273	596	983	79	1111	2789	213	.948

DIVISION SERIES RECORD

RECORDS: Shares single-game record for most home runs—2 (October 5, 1996).

								BATTING							FIELDING		
Year	Team (League)	Pos.	G	AB	R	H	2B	3B	HR	RBI	Avg.	BB	SO	SB	PO	A	E	Avg.
1996— San Diego (N.L.)		3B	3	10	3	3	0	0	3	3	.300	3	5	0	0	5	3	.625
1998— San Diego (N.L.)		3B	4	14	2	2	0	0	0	0	.143	1	3	0	2	5	1	.875
Division series totals (2 years)			7	24	5	5	0	0	3	3	.208	4	8	0	2	10	4	.750

RECORDS: Shares single-game record for most bases on balls received—4 (October 8, 1998).

Year Team (League)	Pos.	G	AB	R	H	2B	3B	HR	RBI	Avg.	BB	SO	SB	PO	A	E	Avg.
								BATTING						FIELDING			
1998— San Diego (N.L.)	3B	6	22	3	6	0	0	2	4	.273	5	4	0	5	10	0	1.000

WORLD SERIES RECORD

Year Team (League)	Pos.	G	AB	R	H	2B	3B	HR	RBI	Avg.	BB	SO	SB	PO	A	E	Avg.
								BATTING						FIELDING			
1998— San Diego (N.L.)	3B	4	14	1	2	1	0	0	1	.143	2	7	0	2	2	2	.667

ALL-STAR GAME RECORD

Year League	Pos.	AB	R	H	2B	3B	HR	RBI	Avg.	BB	SO	SB	PO	A	E	Avg.
							BATTING						FIELDING			
1994— National	3B	1	0	0	0	0	0	0	.000	0	0	0	0	0	0	...
1996— National	3B	2	1	1	0	0	1	1	.500	0	1	0	0	0	1	.000
1997— National	3B	2	0	0	0	0	0	0	.000	0	0	0	0	0	0	...
All-Star Game totals (3 years)		**5**	**1**	**1**	**0**	**0**	**1**	**1**	**.200**	**0**	**1**	**0**	**0**	**0**	**1**	**.000**

CANDIOTTI, TOM   P   ATHLETICS

C

PERSONAL: Born August 31, 1957, in Walnut Creek, Calif. ... 6-2/221. ... Throws right, bats right. ... Full name: Thomas Caesar Candiotti. ... Name pronounced KAN-dee-AH-tee.

HIGH SCHOOL: Concord (Calif.).

COLLEGE: St. Mary's, Calif. (degree in business administration, 1979).

TRANSACTIONS/CAREER NOTES: Signed as non-drafted free agent by Victoria, independent (July 17, 1979). ... Released by Victoria (January 4, 1980). ... Signed by Fort Myers, Kansas City Royals organization (January 5, 1980). ... On Jacksonville disabled list (June 7-26, 1980). ... Selected by Vancouver, Milwaukee Brewers organization, from Royals organization in Rule 5 minor league draft (December 9, 1980). ... On disabled list (April 10-May 12, 1981 and April 13, 1982-remainder of season). ... On Vancouver disabled list (May 30-June 15, 1984). ... On Milwaukee disabled list (August 2-September 1, 1984); included rehabilitation assignment to Beloit (August 24-31). ... Granted free agency (October 15, 1985). ... Signed by Cleveland Indians (December 12, 1985). ... On disabled list (August 4-19, 1988; July 2-17, 1989; and May 7-22, 1990). ... Traded by Indians with OF Turner Ward to Toronto Blue Jays for P Denis Boucher, OF Glenallen Hill, OF Mark Whiten and a player to be named later (June 27, 1991); Indians acquired cash instead of player to complete deal (October 15, 1991). ... Granted free agency (November 7, 1991). ... Signed by Los Angeles Dodgers (December 3, 1991). ... On disabled list (August 9-24, 1992). ... Granted free agency (November 3, 1995). ... Re-signed by Dodgers (December 15, 1995). ... On Los Angeles disabled list (July 20-August 13, 1996); included rehabilitation assignment to San Bernardino (August 7-13). ... Granted free agency (October 28, 1997). ... Signed by Oakland Athletics (December 9, 1997).

RECORDS: Shares modern N.L. record for most hit batsmen in nine-inning game—4 (September 13, 1997). ... Shares major league record for most hit batsmen in one inning—3 (September 13, 1997, first inning).

STATISTICAL NOTES: Pitched 2-0 one-hit, complete-game victory against New York (August 3, 1987).

Year Team (League)	W	L	Pct.	ERA	G	GS	CG	ShO	Sv.	IP	H	R	ER	BB	SO
1979— Victoria (N'west)	5	1	.833	2.44	12	9	3	0	1	70	63	23	19	16	66
1980— Fort Myers (Fla. St.)■........	3	2	.600	2.25	7	5	3	0	0	44	32	16	11	9	31
—Jacksonville (Southern)......	7	8	.467	2.77	17	17	8	2	0	117	98	45	36	40	93
1981— El Paso (Texas)■	7	6	.538	2.80	21	14	6	1	0	119	137	51	37	27	68
1982—							Did not play.								
1983— El Paso (Texas)..............	1	0	1.000	2.92	7	0	0	0	2	24²/₃	23	10	8	7	18
—Vancouver (PCL)	6	4	.600	2.81	15	14	5	2	0	99¹/₃	87	35	31	16	61
—Milwaukee (A.L.)	4	4	.500	3.23	10	8	2	1	0	55²/₃	62	21	20	16	21
1984— Vancouver (PCL)	8	4	.667	2.89	15	15	4	0	0	96²/₃	96	36	31	22	53
—Milwaukee (A.L.)	2	2	.500	5.29	8	6	0	0	0	32¹/₃	38	21	19	10	23
—Beloit (Midwest)...............	0	1	.000	2.70	2	2	0	0	0	10	12	5	3	5	12
1985— El Paso (Texas)..............	1	0	1.000	2.76	4	4	2	1	0	29¹/₃	29	11	9	7	16
—Vancouver (PCL)	9	13	.409	3.94	24	24	0	0	0	150²/₃	178	83	66	36	97
1986— Cleveland (A.L.)■.............	16	12	.571	3.57	36	34	*17	3	0	252¹/₃	234	112	100	106	167
1987— Cleveland (A.L.).............	7	18	.280	4.78	32	32	7	2	0	201²/₃	193	132	107	93	111
1988— Cleveland (A.L.).............	14	8	.636	3.28	31	31	11	1	0	216²/₃	225	86	79	53	137
1989— Cleveland (A.L.).............	13	10	.565	3.10	31	31	4	0	0	206	188	80	71	55	124
1990— Cleveland (A.L.).............	15	11	.577	3.65	31	29	3	1	0	202	207	92	82	55	128
1991— Cleveland (A.L.).............	7	6	.538	2.24	15	15	3	0	0	108¹/₃	88	35	27	28	86
—Toronto (A.L.)■...............	6	7	.462	2.98	19	19	3	0	0	129²/₃	114	47	43	45	81
1992— Los Angeles (N.L.)■.........	11	•15	.423	3.00	32	30	6	2	0	203²/₃	177	78	68	63	152
1993— Los Angeles (N.L.).........	8	10	.444	3.12	33	32	2	0	0	213²/₃	192	86	74	71	155
1994— Los Angeles (N.L.).........	7	7	.500	4.12	23	22	5	0	0	153	149	77	70	54	102
1995— Los Angeles (N.L.).........	7	14	.333	3.50	30	30	1	1	0	190¹/₃	187	93	74	58	141
1996— Los Angeles (N.L.).........	9	11	.450	4.49	28	27	1	0	0	152¹/₃	172	91	76	43	79
—San Bernardino (Calif.)......	0	1	.000	5.00	2	2	0	0	0	9	11	6	5	4	10
1997— Los Angeles (N.L.).........	10	7	.588	3.60	41	18	0	0	3	135	128	60	54	40	89
1998— Oakland (A.L.)■.............	11	•16	.407	4.84	33	33	3	0	0	201	222	124	108	63	98
A.L. totals (9 years)	**95**	**94**	**.503**	**3.68**	**246**	**238**	**53**	**8**	**0**	**1605²/₃**	**1571**	**750**	**656**	**524**	**976**
N.L. totals (6 years)	**52**	**64**	**.448**	**3.57**	**187**	**159**	**15**	**3**	**0**	**1048**	**1005**	**485**	**416**	**329**	**718**
Major league totals (15 years)	**147**	**158**	**.482**	**3.64**	**433**	**397**	**68**	**11**	**0**	**2653²/₃**	**2576**	**1235**	**1072**	**853**	**1694**

DIVISION SERIES RECORD

Year Team (League)	W	L	Pct.	ERA	G	GS	CG	ShO	Sv.	IP	H	R	ER	BB	SO
1996— Los Angeles (N.L.)	0	0	...	0.00	1	0	0	0	0	2	0	0	0	0	1

CHAMPIONSHIP SERIES RECORD

Year Team (League)	W	L	Pct.	ERA	G	GS	CG	ShO	Sv.	IP	H	R	ER	BB	SO
1991— Toronto (A.L.)....................	0	1	.000	8.22	2	2	0	0	0	7²/₃	17	9	7	2	5

PERSONAL: Born March 10, 1963, in Brooklyn, N.Y. ... 5-8/160. ... Bats both, throws left. ... Full name: John Anthony Cangelosi. ... Name pronounced KAN-juh-LO-see.

HIGH SCHOOL: Miami Springs (Fla.) Senior.

JUNIOR COLLEGE: Miami-Dade (North) Community College.

TRANSACTIONS/CAREER NOTES: Selected by Chicago White Sox organization in fourth round of free-agent draft (January 12, 1982). ... Loaned by White Sox organization with IF Manny Salinas to Mexico City Reds of Mexican League (March 4-June 1, 1985) as part of deal in which IF Nelson Barrera was purchased by White Sox. ... Traded by White Sox to Pittsburgh Pirates (March 30, 1987), completing deal in which Pirates traded P Jim Winn to White Sox for a player to be named later (March 27, 1987). ... On Pittsburgh disabled list (June 6-27, 1988); included rehabilitation assignment to Buffalo (June 20-27). ... Granted free agency (December 20, 1990). ... Signed by Vancouver, White Sox organization (April 7, 1991). ... Traded by White Sox organization to Milwaukee Brewers for SS Esteban Beltre (May 23, 1991). ... Granted free agency (October 15, 1991). ... Signed by Texas Rangers organization (November 7, 1991). ... Released by Rangers (July 19, 1992). ... Signed by Toledo, Detroit Tigers organization (July 28, 1992). ... Granted free agency (October 15, 1992). ... Re-signed by Toledo, Tigers organization (February 8, 1993). ... On disabled list (April 8-May 4, 1993). ... Granted free agency (October 15, 1993). ... Signed by New York Mets organization (November 17, 1993). ... On suspended list (June 15-18, 1994). ... Released by Mets (July 8, 1994). ... Signed by Tucson, Houston Astros organization (March 23, 1995). ... Granted free agency (November 2, 1995). ... Re-signed by Astros organization (December 7, 1995). ... On suspended list (August 16-19, 1996). ... Granted free agency (November 18, 1996). ... Signed by Florida Marlins (November 26, 1996). ... Granted free agency (September 29, 1998).

STATISTICAL NOTES: Led Midwest League in caught stealing with 35 in 1983. ... Led International League in caught stealing with 18 in 1993.

Year Team (League)	Pos.	G	AB	R	H	2B	3B	HR	RBI	Avg.	BB	SO	SB	PO	A	E	Avg.
1982—Niagara Falls (NYP)	OF	•76	277	60	80	15	4	5	38	.289	•56	51	45	118	5	4	.969
1983—Appleton (Midwest)....	OF	128	439	87	124	12	4	1	48	.282	99	81	*87	262	10	6	.978
1984—Glens Falls (East.)	OF	138	464	91	133	17	1	1	38	.287	*101	66	65	310	11	11	.967
1985—M.C. Reds (Mex.)	OF	61	201	46	71	9	4	1	30	.353	50	19	17	127	7	6	.957
—Chicago (A.L.)	OF-DH	5	2	2	0	0	0	0	0	.000	0	1	0	1	0	0	1.000
—Buffalo (A.A.)	OF	78	244	34	58	8	5	1	21	.238	46	32	14	148	9	2	.987
1986—Chicago (A.L.)	OF-DH	137	438	65	103	16	3	2	32	.235	71	61	50	276	7	9	.969
1987—Pittsburgh (N.L.)■......	OF	104	182	44	50	8	3	4	18	.275	46	33	21	74	3	3	.963
1988—Pittsburgh (N.L.)	OF-P	75	118	18	30	4	1	0	8	.254	17	16	9	52	0	2	.963
—Buffalo (A.A.)	OF	37	145	23	48	6	0	0	10	.331	19	19	14	89	3	0	1.000
1989—Pittsburgh (N.L.)	OF	112	160	18	35	4	2	0	9	.219	35	20	11	71	1	2	.973
1990—Pittsburgh (N.L.)	OF	58	76	13	15	2	0	0	1	.197	11	12	7	24	0	0	1.000
—Buffalo (A.A.)	OF	24	89	17	31	2	2	0	7	.348	12	8	5	49	0	1	.980
1991—Vancouver (PCL)■......	OF	30	102	15	25	1	0	0	10	.245	11	8	9	39	2	3	.932
—Denver (A.A.)■	OF-1B-P	83	303	69	89	8	3	3	25	.294	59	29	26	118	10	3	.977
1992—Texas (A.L.)■	OF-DH	73	85	12	16	2	0	1	6	.188	18	16	6	76	4	3	.964
—Toledo (Int'l)■	OF	27	74	9	20	3	0	0	6	.270	7	13	11	48	1	0	1.000
1993—Toledo (Int'l)	OF-P	113	439	73	128	23	4	6	42	.292	56	59	39	252	5	7	.973
1994—New York (N.L.)■	OF	62	111	14	28	4	0	4	4	.252	19	20	5	64	5	0	1.000
1995—Tucson (PCL)■	OF	30	106	18	39	4	1	0	9	.368	19	11	11	67	2	1	.986
—Houston (N.L.)	OF-P	90	201	46	64	5	2	2	18	.318	48	42	21	92	4	5	.950
1996—Houston (N.L.)	OF	108	262	49	69	11	4	1	16	.263	44	41	17	113	5	3	.975
1997—Florida (N.L.)■	OF-P	103	192	28	47	8	0	1	12	.245	19	33	5	84	1	0	1.000
1998—Florida (N.L.)	OF-DH	104	171	19	43	8	0	1	10	.251	30	23	2	62	1	2	.969
American League totals (3 years)		215	525	79	119	18	3	3	38	.227	89	78	56	353	11	12	.968
National League totals (9 years)		816	1473	249	381	54	12	9	96	.259	269	240	98	636	20	17	.975
Major league totals (12 years)		1031	1998	328	500	72	15	12	134	.250	358	318	154	989	31	29	.972

DIVISION SERIES RECORD

Year Team (League)	Pos.	G	AB	R	H	2B	3B	HR	RBI	Avg.	BB	SO	SB	PO	A	E	Avg.
1997—Florida (N.L.)	PH	1	1	0	0	0	0	0	0	.000	0	0	0	...	...	...	...

CHAMPIONSHIP SERIES RECORD

Year Team (League)	Pos.	G	AB	R	H	2B	3B	HR	RBI	Avg.	BB	SO	SB	PO	A	E	Avg.
1997—Florida (N.L.)	PH-OF	3	5	0	1	0	0	0	0	.200	1	0	0	2	0	0	1.000

WORLD SERIES RECORD

NOTES: Member of World Series championship team (1997).

Year Team (League)	Pos.	G	AB	R	H	2B	3B	HR	RBI	Avg.	BB	SO	SB	PO	A	E	Avg.
1997—Florida (N.L.)	PH	3	3	0	1	0	0	0	0	.333	0	2	0	...	...	...	...

RECORD AS PITCHER

Year Team (League)	W	L	Pct.	ERA	G	GS	CG	ShO	Sv.	IP	H	R	ER	BB	SO
1988—Pittsburgh (N.L.)	0	0	...	0.00	1	0	0	0	0	2	1	0	0	0	0
1991—Denver (Am. Assoc.)■	0	0	...	2.45	2	0	0	0	0	3 2/3	3	1	1	2	1
1993—Toledo (International)	0	0	...	81.00	1	0	0	0	0	2/3	7	6	6	1	0
1995—Houston (N.L.)	0	0	...	0.00	1	0	0	0	0	1	0	0	0	1	0
1997—Florida (N.L.)■	0	0	...	0.00	1	0	0	0	0	1	0	0	0	1	0
Major league totals (3 years)	0	0	...	0.00	3	0	0	0	0	4	1	0	0	2	0

CANIZARO, JAY   IF   GIANTS

PERSONAL: Born July 4, 1973, in Beaumont, Texas. ... 5-9/178. ... Bats right, throws right. ... Full name: Jason Kyle Canizaro.

HIGH SCHOOL: West Orange-Stark (Orange, Texas).

JUNIOR COLLEGE: Blinn College (Texas).

COLLEGE: Oklahoma State.
TRANSACTIONS/CAREER NOTES: Selected by San Francisco Giants organization in fourth round of free-agent draft (June 3, 1993).
STATISTICAL NOTES: Led Arizona League second basemen with 33 double plays in 1993. ... Led Texas League second basemen with 19 errors in 1995. ... Career major league grand slams: 1.

Year Team (League)	Pos.	G	AB	R	H	2B	3B	HR	RBI	Avg.	BB	SO	SB	PO	A	E	Avg.
1993—Ariz. Giants (Ariz.)......	2B-SS	49	180	34	47	10	•6	3	*41	.261	22	40	12	102	106	10	.954
1994—San Jose (Calif.).........	2-S-3-O	126	464	77	117	16	2	15	69	.252	46	98	12	262	362	30	.954
1995—Shreveport (Texas).....	2B-SS	126	440	83	129	25	7	12	60	.293	58	98	16	254	333	†23	.962
1996—Phoenix (PCL)..........	2B-SS-3B	102	363	50	95	21	2	7	64	.262	46	77	14	194	308	14	.973
—San Francisco (N.L.)..	2B-SS	43	120	11	24	4	1	2	8	.200	9	38	0	64	91	6	.963
1997—Phoenix (PCL)...........	2B-3B	23	81	12	16	7	0	2	12	.198	9	24	2	32	46	2	.975
—Shreveport (Texas).....	2B-SS-3B	50	176	36	45	9	0	11	38	.256	26	44	2	80	124	6	.971
1998—Shreveport (Texas).....	2B	83	281	47	63	7	1	12	32	.224	53	46	5	145	255	10	.976
—Fresno (Pacific Coast)	2B-OF-SS	45	106	23	24	6	2	6	14	.226	17	23	0	49	64	2	.983
Major league totals (1 year)		43	120	11	24	4	1	2	8	.200	9	38	0	64	91	6	.963

CANSECO, JOSE — OF/DH — DEVIL RAYS

PERSONAL: Born July 2, 1964, in Havana, Cuba. ... 6-4/240. ... Bats right, throws right. ... Identical twin brother of Ozzie Canseco, outfielder with Oakland Athletics (1990) and St. Louis Cardinals (1992). ... Name pronounced can-SAY-co.
HIGH SCHOOL: Miami Coral Park Senior.
TRANSACTIONS/CAREER NOTES: Selected by Oakland Athletics organization in 15th round of free-agent draft (June 7, 1982). ... On Huntsville disabled list (May 14-June 3, 1985). ... On Oakland disabled list (March 23-July 13, 1989); included rehabilitation assignments to Huntsville (May 6 and June 28-July 13). ... On disabled list (June 8-23, 1990 and July 1-16, 1992). ... Traded by A's to Texas Rangers for OF Ruben Sierra, P Jeff Russell, P Bobby Witt and cash (August 31, 1992). ... On disabled list (June 24, 1993-remainder of season). ... Traded by Rangers to Boston Red Sox for OF Otis Nixon and 3B Luis Ortiz (December 9, 1994). ... On Boston disabled list (May 15-June 20, 1995); included rehabilitation assignment to Pawtucket (June 18-20). ... Granted free agency (October 30, 1995). ... Re-signed by Red Sox (December 6, 1995). ... On Boston disabled list (April 24-May 9 and July 26-September 17, 1996); included rehabilitation assignment to Pawtucket (May 7-9). ... Traded by Red Sox to A's for P John Wasdin and cash (January 27, 1997). ... On disabled list (August 1-20 and August 27, 1997-remainder of season). ... Granted free agency (October 31, 1997). ... Signed by Toronto Blue Jays (February 4, 1998). ... Granted free agency (October 22, 1998). ... Signed by Tampa Bay Devil Rays (December 11, 1998).
RECORDS: Shares major league record for most strikeouts in two consecutive games—8 (July 14 [3] and 16 [5], 1997). ... Shares major league single-game record for most strikeouts (nine-inning game)—5 (July 16, 1997); and most strikeouts in two consecutive games—8 (July 14 [3] and 16 [5], 1997). ... Shares major league single-season record for most consecutive bases on balls received—7 (August 4-5, 1992).
HONORS: Named Minor League Player of the Year by THE SPORTING NEWS (1985). ... Named Southern League Most Valuable Player (1985). ... Named A.L. Rookie Player of the Year by THE SPORTING NEWS (1986). ... Named A.L. Rookie of the Year by Baseball Writers' Association of America (1986). ... Named A.L. Player of the Year by THE SPORTING NEWS (1988). ... Named outfielder on THE SPORTING NEWS A.L. All-Star team (1988 and 1990-91). ... Named outfielder on THE SPORTING NEWS A.L. Silver Slugger team (1988 and 1990-91). ... Named A.L. Most Valuable Player by Baseball Writers' Association of America (1988). ... Named A.L. Comeback Player of the Year by THE SPORTING NEWS (1994). ... Named designated hitter on THE SPORTING NEWS A.L. Silver Slugger team (1998).
STATISTICAL NOTES: Led California League outfielders with eight double plays in 1984. ... Hit three home runs in one game (July 3, 1988 and June 13, 1994). ... Led A.L. with .569 slugging percentage in 1988. ... Led A.L. in grounding into double plays with 20 in 1994. ... Career major league grand slams: 6.

Year Team (League)	Pos.	G	AB	R	H	2B	3B	HR	RBI	Avg.	BB	SO	SB	PO	A	E	Avg.
1982—Miami (Fla. St.).........	3B	6	9	0	1	0	0	0	0	.111	1	3	0	3	1	1	.800
—Idaho Falls (Pio.)......	3B-OF	28	57	13	15	3	0	2	7	.263	9	13	3	6	17	3	.885
1983—Madison (Midwest).....	OF	34	88	8	14	4	0	3	10	.159	10	36	2	23	2	1	.962
—Medford (N'west)......	OF	59	197	34	53	15	2	11	40	.269	30	*78	6	46	5	5	.911
1984—Modesto (California) ..	OF	116	410	61	113	21	2	15	73	.276	74	127	10	216	17	9	.963
1985—Huntsville (Sou.)........	OF	58	211	47	67	10	2	25	80	.318	30	55	6	117	9	7	.947
—Tacoma (PCL)	OF	60	233	41	81	16	1	11	47	.348	40	66	5	81	7	2	.978
—Oakland (A.L.)	OF	29	96	16	29	3	0	5	13	.302	4	31	1	56	2	3	.951
1986—Oakland (A.L.)...........	OF-DH	157	600	85	144	29	1	33	117	.240	65	175	15	319	4	•14	.958
1987—Oakland (A.L.)...........	OF-DH	159	630	81	162	35	3	31	113	.257	50	157	15	263	12	7	.975
1988—Oakland (A.L.)...........	OF-DH	158	610	120	187	34	0	*42	*124	.307	78	128	40	304	11	7	.978
1989—Huntsville (Sou.)	OF	9	29	2	6	0	0	0	3	.207	5	11	1	9	0	0	1.000
—Oakland (A.L.)	OF-DH	65	227	40	61	9	1	17	57	.269	23	69	6	119	5	3	.976
1990—Oakland (A.L.)...........	OF-DH	131	481	83	132	14	2	37	101	.274	72	158	19	182	7	1	.995
1991—Oakland (A.L.)...........	OF-DH	154	572	115	152	32	1	•44	122	.266	78	152	26	245	5	•9	.965
1992—Oakland (A.L.)...........	OF-DH	97	366	66	90	11	0	22	72	.246	48	104	5	163	5	2	.988
—Texas (A.L.)■	OF-DH	22	73	8	17	4	0	4	15	.233	15	24	1	32	0	1	.970
1993—Texas (A.L.).............	OF-DH-P	60	231	30	59	14	1	10	46	.255	16	62	6	94	4	3	.970
1994—Texas (A.L.).............	DH	111	429	88	121	19	2	31	90	.282	69	114	15	...	...	...	...
1995—Boston (A.L.)■...........	DH-OF	102	396	64	121	25	1	24	81	.306	42	93	4	1	0	0	1.000
—Pawtucket (Int'l)........	DH	2	6	1	1	0	0	0	1	.167	1	5	0	...	...	...	...
1996—Boston (A.L.)...........	DH-OF	96	360	68	104	22	1	28	82	.289	63	82	3	17	1	0	1.000
—Pawtucket (Int'l)........	DH	2	5	0	1	0	0	0	0	.200	0	3	0	...	...	...	...
1997—Oakland (A.L.)■.........	DH-OF	108	388	56	91	19	0	23	74	.235	51	122	8	74	0	5	.938
1998—Toronto (A.L.)■.........	DH-OF	151	583	98	138	26	0	46	107	.237	65	*159	29	117	4	5	.960
Major league totals (14 years)		1600	6042	1018	1608	296	13	397	1214	.266	739	1630	193	1986	62	60	.972

DIVISION SERIES RECORD

Year Team (League)	Pos.	G	AB	R	H	2B	3B	HR	RBI	Avg.	BB	SO	SB	PO	A	E	Avg.
1995—Boston (A.L.).............	DH-OF	3	13	0	0	0	0	0	0	.000	2	2	0	4	0	0	1.000

CHAMPIONSHIP SERIES RECORD

RECORDS: Shares A.L. single-series record for most home runs—3 (1988).

Year	Team (League)	Pos.	G	AB	R	H	2B	3B	HR	RBI	Avg.	BB	SO	SB	PO	A	E	Avg.
									BATTING							FIELDING		
1988— Oakland (A.L.)	OF	4	16	4	5	1	0	3	4	.313	1	2	1	6	0	0	1.000	
1989— Oakland (A.L.)	OF-PH	5	17	1	5	0	0	1	3	.294	3	7	0	6	1	1	.875	
1990— Oakland (A.L.)	OF	4	11	3	2	0	0	0	1	.182	5	5	2	14	0	0	1.000	
Championship series totals (3 years)		13	44	8	12	1	0	4	8	.273	9	14	3	26	1	1	.964	

WORLD SERIES RECORD

RECORDS: Shares single-game record for most grand slams—1 (October 15, 1988). ... Shares single-inning record for most runs batted in—4 (October 15, 1988, second inning).

NOTES: Hit home run in first at-bat (October 15, 1988). ... Member of World Series championship team (1989).

Year	Team (League)	Pos.	G	AB	R	H	2B	3B	HR	RBI	Avg.	BB	SO	SB	PO	A	E	Avg.
									BATTING							FIELDING		
1988— Oakland (A.L.)	OF	5	19	1	1	0	0	1	5	.053	2	4	1	8	0	0	1.000	
1989— Oakland (A.L.)	OF	4	14	5	5	0	0	1	3	.357	4	3	1	6	0	0	1.000	
1990— Oakland (A.L.)	OF-PH-DH	4	12	1	1	0	0	1	2	.083	2	3	0	4	0	0	1.000	
World Series totals (3 years)		13	45	7	7	0	0	3	10	.156	8	10	2	18	0	0	1.000	

ALL-STAR GAME RECORD

Year	League	Pos.	AB	R	H	2B	3B	HR	RBI	Avg.	BB	SO	SB	PO	A	E	Avg.
								BATTING							FIELDING		
1986— American							Did not play.										
1988— American	OF	4	0	0	0	0	0	0	.000	0	1	0	3	0	0	1.000
1989— American						Selected, did not play—injured.											
1990— American	OF	4	0	0	0	0	0	0	.000	1	1	1	1	0	0	1.000
1992— American						Selected, did not play—injured.											
All-Star Game totals (2 years)		8	0	0	0	0	0	0	.000	1	2	1	4	0	0	1.000

RECORD AS PITCHER

Year	Team (League)	W	L	Pct.	ERA	G	GS	CG	ShO	Sv.	IP	H	R	ER	BB	SO
1993— Texas (A.L.)	0	0	...	27.00	1	0	0	0	0	1	2	3	3	3	0	

CARLSON, DAN — P — DIAMONDBACKS

PERSONAL: Born January 26, 1970, in Portland, Ore. ... 6-0/200. ... Throws right, bats right. ... Full name: Daniel Scott Carlson.

HIGH SCHOOL: Reynolds (Troutdale, Ore.).

JUNIOR COLLEGE: Mt. Hood Community College (Ore.).

TRANSACTIONS/CAREER NOTES: Selected by San Francisco Giants organization in 33rd round of free-agent draft (June 5, 1989). ... On disabled list (May 14-21, 1995). ... On San Francisco disabled list (March 27-April 11, 1997); included rehabilitation assignment to Bakersfield (April 5-10). ... Selected by Tampa Bay Devil Rays in first round (28th pick overall) of expansion draft (November 18, 1997). ... On Durham disabled list (July 20-August 14, 1998). ... Granted free agency (October 15, 1998). ... Signed by Arizona Diamondbacks organization (December 17, 1998).

STATISTICAL NOTES: Tied for Texas League lead with 15 home runs allowed in 1992.

Year	Team (League)	W	L	Pct.	ERA	G	GS	CG	ShO	Sv.	IP	H	R	ER	BB	SO
1990— Everett (Northwest).............	2	6	.250	5.34	17	11	0	0	0	62 1/3	60	42	37	33	77	
1991— Clinton (Midwest).............	•16	7	.696	3.08	27	27	5	3	0	181 1/3	149	69	62	76	164	
1992— Shreveport (Texas).............	*15	9	.625	3.19	27	•27	4	1	0	*186	166	85	66	60	*157	
1993— Phoenix (PCL)...................	5	6	.455	6.56	13	12	0	0	0	70	79	54	51	32	48	
— Shreveport (Texas).............	7	4	.636	2.24	15	15	2	1	0	100 1/3	86	30	25	26	81	
1994— Phoenix (PCL)...................	*13	6	.684	4.64	31	22	0	0	1	151 1/3	173	80	78	55	117	
1995— Phoenix (PCL)...................	9	5	.643	4.27	23	22	2	0	0	132 2/3	138	67	63	66	93	
1996— Phoenix (PCL)...................	•13	6	.684	3.44	33	15	2	0	1	146 2/3	135	61	56	46	123	
— San Francisco (N.L.)	1	0	1.000	2.70	5	0	0	0	0	10	13	6	3	2	4	
1997— Bakersfield (California).......	0	0	...	0.00	2	2	0	0	0	6	3	0	0	1	7	
— Phoenix (PCL)...................	13	3	*.813	3.88	29	14	0	0	3	109	102	53	47	36	108	
— San Francisco (N.L.)	0	0	...	7.63	6	0	0	0	0	15 1/3	20	14	13	8	14	
1998— Tampa Bay (A.L.)■.............	0	0	...	7.64	10	0	0	0	0	17 2/3	25	15	15	8	16	
— Durham (International).........	3	5	.375	6.35	19	11	0	0	0	68	87	52	48	28	59	
A.L. totals (1 year)	0	0	...	7.64	10	0	0	0	0	17 2/3	25	15	15	8	16	
N.L. totals (2 years)	1	0	1.000	5.68	11	0	0	0	0	25 1/3	33	20	16	10	18	
Major league totals (3 years)......	1	0	1.000	6.49	21	0	0	0	0	43	58	35	31	18	34	

CARMONA, CESARIN — SS — PADRES

PERSONAL: Born December 20, 1976, in Paya Bani, Dominican Republic. ... 5-10/155. ... Bats both, throws right. ... Full name: Cesarin M. Carmona.

HIGH SCHOOL: Paya Bani (Dominican Republic).

TRANSACTIONS/CAREER NOTES: Signed as non-drafted free agent by San Diego Padres organization (November 6, 1993).

Year	Team (League)	Pos.	G	AB	R	H	2B	3B	HR	RBI	Avg.	BB	SO	SB	PO	A	E	Avg.
									BATTING							FIELDING		
1994— Ariz. Padres (Ariz.)	2B-SS	35	130	19	26	3	4	0	8	.200	18	57	17	48	95	14	.911	
— Rancho Cuca. (Cal.)	2B	3	2	0	0	0	0	0	0	.000	0	1	0	0	1	0	1.000	
1995— Ariz. Padres (Ariz.)	SS	15	51	7	13	2	2	1	4	.255	5	10	3	17	28	7	.865	
— Clinton (Midwest).......	2B	42	129	13	23	2	1	0	5	.178	15	35	10	50	78	10	.928	
1996— Clinton (Midwest).......	SS	104	315	38	62	7	2	2	21	.197	44	104	8	90	287	35	.915	
1997— Clinton (Midwest).......	SS	65	234	33	59	7	2	11	32	.252	14	69	18	90	205	33	.899	
1998— Rancho Cuca. (Cal.) ...	SS	105	368	48	96	12	9	2	45	.261	17	99	21	127	336	*41	.919	

CARMONA, RAFAEL   P   MARINERS

PERSONAL: Born October 2, 1972, in Rio Piedras, Puerto Rico. ... 6-2/185. ... Throws right, bats left.
HIGH SCHOOL: Juano Colon (Comerio, Puerto Rico).
JUNIOR COLLEGE: Indian Hills Community College (Iowa).
TRANSACTIONS/CAREER NOTES: Selected by Seattle Mariners organization in 13th round of free-agent draft (June 3, 1993). ... On Tacoma disabled list (April 30-June 8, 1997). ... On Seattle disabled list (March 22, 1998-entire season); included rehabilitation assignments to Lancaster (May 5-18) and Orlando (May 23-June 6).

Year Team (League)	W	L	Pct.	ERA	G	GS	CG	ShO	Sv.	IP	H	R	ER	BB	SO
1993— Bellingham (N'west)	2	3	.400	3.79	23	0	0	0	2	35 2/3	33	19	15	14	30
1994— Riverside (California)	8	2	.800	2.81	50	0	0	0	21	67 1/3	48	22	21	19	63
1995— Port City (Southern)	0	1	.000	1.80	15	0	0	0	4	15	11	5	3	3	17
— Seattle (A.L.)	2	4	.333	5.66	15	3	0	0	1	47 2/3	55	31	30	34	28
— Tacoma (PCL)	4	3	.571	5.06	8	8	1	1	0	48	52	29	27	19	37
1996— Tacoma (PCL)	0	0	. . .	1.42	4	1	0	0	0	6 1/3	5	1	1	5	9
— Seattle (A.L.)	8	3	.727	4.28	53	1	0	0	1	90 1/3	95	47	43	55	62
1997— Tacoma (PCL)	2	5	.286	3.79	32	5	0	0	4	59 1/3	52	31	25	35	56
— Seattle (A.L.)	0	0	. . .	3.18	4	0	0	0	0	5 2/3	3	3	2	2	6
1998— Lancaster (Calif.)	0	1	.000	6.23	4	4	0	0	0	13	12	10	9	5	11
— Orlando (South.)	0	3	.000	14.29	4	4	0	0	0	11 1/3	18	18	18	6	11
Major league totals (3 years)	10	7	.588	4.70	72	4	0	0	2	143 2/3	153	81	75	91	96

CARPENTER, CHRIS   P   BLUE JAYS

PERSONAL: Born April 27, 1975, in Exeter, N.H. ... 6-6/215. ... Throws right, bats right. ... Full name: Christopher John Carpenter.
HIGH SCHOOL: Trinity (Manchester, N.H.).
TRANSACTIONS/CAREER NOTES: Selected by Toronto Blue Jays organization in first round (15th pick overall) of free-agent draft (June 3, 1993).

Year Team (League)	W	L	Pct.	ERA	G	GS	CG	ShO	Sv.	IP	H	R	ER	BB	SO
1994— Medicine Hat (Pioneer)	6	3	.667	2.76	15	15	0	0	0	84 2/3	76	40	26	39	80
1995— Dunedin (Fla. St.)	3	5	.375	2.17	15	15	0	0	0	99 1/3	83	29	24	50	56
— Knoxville (Southern)	3	7	.300	5.18	12	12	0	0	0	64 1/3	71	47	37	31	53
1996— Knoxville (Southern)	7	9	.438	3.94	28	28	1	0	0	171 1/3	161	94	75	91	150
1997— Syracuse (Int'l)	4	9	.308	4.50	19	19	3	2	0	120	113	64	60	53	97
— Toronto (A.L.)	3	7	.300	5.09	14	13	1	1	0	81 1/3	108	55	46	37	55
1998— Toronto (A.L.)	12	7	.632	4.37	33	24	1	1	0	175	177	97	85	61	136
Major league totals (2 years)	15	14	.517	4.60	47	37	2	2	0	256 1/3	285	152	131	98	191

CARRASCO, HECTOR   P   TWINS

PERSONAL: Born October 22, 1969, in San Pedro de Macoris, Dominican Republic. ... 6-2/225. ... Throws right, bats right. ... Full name: Hector Pacheco Pipo Carrasco. ... Name pronounced kuh-ROSS-ko.
HIGH SCHOOL: Liceo Mattias Mella (San Pedro de Macoris, Dominican Republic).
TRANSACTIONS/CAREER NOTES: Signed as non-drafted free agent by New York Mets organization (March 20, 1988). ... Released by Mets organization (January 6, 1992). ... Signed by Houston Astros organization (January 21, 1992). ... Traded by Astros organization with P Brian Griffiths to Florida Marlins organization for P Tom Edens (November 17, 1992). ... Traded by Marlins to Cincinnati Reds (September 10, 1993), completing deal in which Reds traded P Chris Hammond to Marlins for 3B Gary Scott and a player to be named later (March 27, 1993). ... On disabled list (May 12-June 1, 1994). ... Traded by Reds with P Scott Service to Kansas City Royals for OF Jon Nunnally and IF/OF Chris Stynes (July 15, 1997). ... Selected by Arizona Diamondbacks in second round (49th pick overall) of expansion draft (November 18, 1997). ... Claimed on waivers by Minnesota Twins (April 3, 1998).

Year Team (League)	W	L	Pct.	ERA	G	GS	CG	ShO	Sv.	IP	H	R	ER	BB	SO
1988— GC Mets (GCL)	0	2	.000	4.17	14	2	0	0	0	36 2/3	37	29	17	13	21
1989— Kingsport (Appalachian)	1	6	.143	5.74	12	10	0	0	0	53 1/3	69	49	34	34	55
1990— Kingsport (Appalachian)	0	0	. . .	4.05	3	1	0	0	0	6 2/3	8	3	3	1	5
1991— Pittsfield (NYP)	0	1	.000	5.40	12	1	0	0	1	23 1/3	25	17	14	21	20
1992— Asheville (S. Atl.)■	5	5	.500	2.99	49	0	0	0	8	78 1/3	66	30	26	47	67
1993— Kane County (Midwest)■..	6	12	.333	4.11	28	*28	0	0	0	149	153	90	68	76	127
1994— Cincinnati (N.L.)■	5	6	.455	2.24	45	0	0	0	6	56 1/3	42	17	14	30	41
1995— Cincinnati (N.L.)	2	7	.222	4.12	64	0	0	0	5	87 1/3	86	45	40	46	64
1996— Cincinnati (N.L.)	4	3	.571	3.75	56	0	0	0	0	74 1/3	58	37	31	45	59
— Indianapolis (A.A.)	0	1	.000	2.14	13	2	0	0	0	21	18	7	5	13	17
1997— Indianapolis (A.A.)	0	0	. . .	6.23	3	0	0	0	1	4 1/3	5	3	3	3	4
— Cincinnati (N.L.)	1	2	.333	3.68	38	0	0	0	0	51 1/3	51	25	21	25	46
— Kansas City (A.L.)■	1	6	.143	5.45	28	0	0	0	0	34 2/3	29	21	21	16	30
1998— Minnesota (A.L.)■	4	2	.667	4.38	63	0	0	0	1	61 2/3	75	30	30	31	46
A.L. totals (2 years)	5	8	.385	4.76	91	0	0	0	1	96 1/3	104	51	51	47	76
N.L. totals (4 years)	12	18	.400	3.54	203	0	0	0	11	269 1/3	237	124	106	146	210
Major league totals (5 years)	17	26	.395	3.86	294	0	0	0	12	365 2/3	341	175	157	193	286

CHAMPIONSHIP SERIES RECORD

Year Team (League)	W	L	Pct.	ERA	G	GS	CG	ShO	Sv.	IP	H	R	ER	BB	SO
1995— Cincinnati (N.L.)	0	0	. . .	0.00	1	0	0	0	0	1 1/3	1	0	0	0	3

CARTER, JOE   OF

PERSONAL: Born March 7, 1960, in Oklahoma City. ... 6-3/215. ... Bats right, throws right. ... Full name: Joseph Chris Carter. ... Brother of Fred Carter, minor league outfielder (1985-88); and cousin of Chris Carter, defensive back, New England Patriots.
HIGH SCHOOL: Millwood (Oklahoma City).

COLLEGE: Wichita State.

TRANSACTIONS/CAREER NOTES: Selected by Chicago Cubs organization in first round (second pick overall) of free-agent draft (June 8, 1981). ... On disabled list (April 9-19, 1982). ... Traded by Cubs organization with OF Mel Hall, P Don Schulze and P Darryl Banks to Cleveland Indians for C Ron Hassey, P Rick Sutcliffe and P George Frazier (June 13, 1984). ... On Cleveland disabled list (July 2-17, 1984). ... Traded by Indians to San Diego Padres for C Sandy Alomar, OF Chris James and 3B Carlos Baerga (December 6, 1989). ... Traded by Padres with 2B Roberto Alomar to Toronto Blue Jays for 1B Fred McGriff and SS Tony Fernandez (December 5, 1990). ... Granted free agency (October 30, 1992). ... Re-signed by Blue Jays (December 7, 1992). ... Granted free agency (October 28, 1997). ... Signed by Baltimore Orioles (December 12, 1997). ... Traded by Orioles to San Francisco Giants for P Darin Blood (July 24, 1998). ... Granted free agency (November 5, 1998).

RECORDS: Shares major league records for most home runs in two consecutive games—5 (July 18 [2] and 19 [3], 1989). ... Shares major league single-season record for most games with three or more home runs—2 (1989). ... Shares major league record for most home runs in one inning—2 (October 3, 1993, second inning). ... Holds A.L. career record for most games with three or more home runs—5.

HONORS: Named outfielder on THE SPORTING NEWS college All-America team (1980-81). ... Named College Player of the Year by THE SPORTING NEWS (1981). ... Named outfielder on THE SPORTING NEWS A.L. All-Star team (1991-92). ... Named outfielder on THE SPORTING NEWS A.L. Silver Slugger team (1991-92).

STATISTICAL NOTES: Led American Association with 265 total bases in 1983. ... Had 21-game hitting streak (May 17-June 8, 1986). ... Hit three home runs in one game five times (August 29, 1986; May 28, 1987; June 24 and July 19, 1989; and August 23, 1993). ... Led A.L. first basemen with 12 errors in 1987. ... Led A.L. in being hit by pitch with 10 in 1991. ... Led A.L. with 13 sacrifice flies in 1992 and 1994. ... Career major league grand slams: 10.

MISCELLANEOUS: Holds Toronto Blue Jays all-time record for most home runs (203).

Year	Team (League)	Pos.	G	AB	R	H	2B	3B	HR	RBI	Avg.	BB	SO	SB	PO	A	E	Avg.
1981—	Midland (Texas)	OF	67	249	42	67	15	3	5	35	.269	8	30	12	100	10	4	.965
1982—	Midland (Texas)	OF	110	427	84	136	22	8	25	98	.319	26	51	15	182	6	5	.974
1983—	Iowa (Am. Assoc.)	OF	124	*522	82	160	27	6	22	83	.307	17	•103	40	204	9	12	.947
	—Chicago (N.L.)	OF	23	51	6	9	1	1	0	1	.176	0	21	1	26	0	0	1.000
1984—	Iowa (Am. Assoc.)	OF	61	248	45	77	12	7	14	67	.310	20	31	11	142	6	2	.987
	—Cleveland (A.L.)■	OF-1B	66	244	32	67	6	1	13	41	.275	11	48	2	169	11	6	.968
1985—	Cleveland (A.L.)	O-1-DH-2-3	143	489	64	128	27	0	15	59	.262	25	74	24	311	17	6	.982
1986—	Cleveland (A.L.)	OF-1B	162	663	108	200	36	9	29	*121	.302	32	95	29	800	55	10	.988
1987—	Cleveland (A.L.)	1B-OF-DH	149	588	83	155	27	2	32	106	.264	27	105	31	782	46	†17	.980
1988—	Cleveland (A.L.)	OF	157	621	85	168	36	6	27	98	.271	35	82	27	444	8	7	.985
1989—	Cleveland (A.L.)	OF-1B-DH	•162	•651	84	158	32	4	35	105	.243	39	112	13	443	20	9	.981
1990—	San Diego (N.L.)■	OF-1B	*162	*634	79	147	27	1	24	115	.232	48	93	22	492	16	11	.979
1991—	Toronto (A.L.)	OF-DH	•162	638	89	174	42	3	33	108	.273	49	112	20	283	13	8	.974
1992—	Toronto (A.L.)	OF-DH-1B	158	622	97	164	30	7	34	119	.264	36	109	12	284	13	9	.971
1993—	Toronto (A.L.)	OF-DH	155	603	92	153	33	5	33	121	.254	47	113	8	289	7	8	.974
1994—	Toronto (A.L.)	OF-DH	111	435	70	118	25	2	27	103	.271	33	64	11	205	4	2	.991
1995—	Toronto (A.L.)	OF-1B-DH	139	558	70	141	23	0	25	76	.253	37	87	12	316	12	7	.979
1996—	Toronto (A.L.)	OF-1B-DH	157	625	84	158	35	7	30	107	.253	44	106	7	416	23	9	.980
1997—	Toronto (A.L.)	DH-OF-1B	157	612	76	143	30	4	21	102	.234	40	105	8	429	23	4	.991
1998—	Baltimore (A.L.)■	OF-DH-1B	85	283	36	70	15	1	11	34	.247	18	48	3	99	5	4	.963
	—San Fran. (N.L.)■	OF-1B	41	105	15	31	7	0	7	29	.295	6	13	1	102	8	1	.991
American League totals (14 years)			1963	7632	1070	1997	397	51	365	1300	.262	473	1260	207	5270	257	106	.981
National League totals (3 years)			226	790	100	187	35	2	31	145	.237	54	127	24	620	24	12	.982
Major league totals (16 years)			2189	8422	1170	2184	432	53	396	1445	.259	527	1387	231	5890	281	118	.981

CHAMPIONSHIP SERIES RECORD

RECORDS: Shares A.L. single-game record for most at-bats—6 (October 11, 1992, 11 innings).

Year	Team (League)	Pos.	G	AB	R	H	2B	3B	HR	RBI	Avg.	BB	SO	SB	PO	A	E	Avg.
1991—	Toronto (A.L.)	OF-DH	5	19	3	5	2	0	1	4	.263	1	5	0	4	1	0	1.000
1992—	Toronto (A.L.)	OF-1B	6	26	2	5	0	0	1	3	.192	2	4	2	16	1	1	.944
1993—	Toronto (A.L.)	OF	6	27	2	7	0	0	0	2	.259	1	5	0	12	1	0	1.000
Championship series totals (3 years)			17	72	7	17	2	0	2	9	.236	4	14	2	32	3	1	.972

WORLD SERIES RECORD

RECORDS: Holds career record for most sacrifice flies—4. ... Holds single-series record for most sacrifice flies—3 (1993).

NOTES: Member of World Series championship team (1992 and 1993).

Year	Team (League)	Pos.	G	AB	R	H	2B	3B	HR	RBI	Avg.	BB	SO	SB	PO	A	E	Avg.
1992—	Toronto (A.L.)	OF-1B	6	22	2	6	2	0	2	3	.273	3	2	0	27	1	0	1.000
1993—	Toronto (A.L.)	OF	6	25	6	7	1	0	2	8	.280	0	4	0	13	0	2	.867
World Series totals (2 years)			12	47	8	13	3	0	4	11	.277	3	6	0	40	1	2	.953

ALL-STAR GAME RECORD

Year	League	Pos.	AB	R	H	2B	3B	HR	RBI	Avg.	BB	SO	SB	PO	A	E	Avg.
1991—	American	OF	1	1	1	0	0	0	0	1.000	1	0	0	1	0	0	1.000
1992—	American	OF	3	1	2	0	0	0	1	.667	0	0	0	1	0	0	1.000
1993—	American	OF	3	1	1	0	0	0	0	.333	0	1	0	1	0	0	1.000
1994—	American	OF	3	0	0	0	0	0	0	.000	0	0	0	1	0	0	1.000
1996—	American	OF	1	0	1	0	0	0	0	1.000	0	0	0	0	0	0	....
All-Star Game totals (5 years)			11	3	5	0	0	0	1	.455	1	1	0	4	0	0	1.000

CARUSO, MIKE   SS   WHITE SOX

PERSONAL: Born May 27, 1977, in Queens, N.Y. ... 6-0/172. ... Bats left, throws right. ... Full name: Michael J. Caruso.

HIGH SCHOOL: Stoneman Douglas (Parkland, Fla.).

TRANSACTIONS/CAREER NOTES: Selected by San Francisco Giants organization in second round of free-agent draft (June 2, 1996). ... Traded by Giants with P Keith Foulke, P Lorenzo Barcelo, P Bobby Howry, P Ken Vining and OF Brian Manning to Chicago White Sox for P Danny Darwin, P Wilson Alvarez and P Roberto Hernandez (July 31, 1997).

Year Team (League)	Pos.	G	AB	R	H	2B	3B	HR	RBI	Avg.	BB	SO	SB	PO	A	E	Avg.
1996—Bellingham (N'west)...	SS-3B	73	312	48	91	13	1	2	24	.292	16	23	24	107	231	40	.894
1997—San Jose (Calif.).........	SS	108	441	76	147	24	11	2	50	.333	38	19	11	168	300	33	.934
—Win.-Salem (Car.)■...	SS	28	119	12	27	3	2	0	14	.227	4	8	3	44	67	7	.941
1998—Chicago (A.L.).........	SS	133	523	81	160	17	6	5	55	.306	14	38	22	216	378	*35	.944
Major league totals (1 year)		133	523	81	160	17	6	5	55	.306	14	38	22	216	378	35	.944

CARVER, STEVE — OF — PHILLIES

PERSONAL: Born September 27, 1972, in Houston. ... 6-3/215. ... Bats left, throws right. ... Full name: Steven Grady Carver. ... Nephew of Mark Littell, pitcher with Kansas City Royals and St. Louis Cardinals (1973 and 1975-82).
HIGH SCHOOL: The Bollis School (Jacksonville).
COLLEGE: Stanford (degree in psychology).
TRANSACTIONS/CAREER NOTES: Selected by Boston Red Sox organization in 38th round of free-agent draft (June 3, 1991); did not sign. ... Selected by Philadelphia Phillies organization in fourth round of free-agent draft (June 1, 1995). ... On disabled list (May 5-16 and July 5-August 22, 1997).

Year Team (League)	Pos.	G	AB	R	H	2B	3B	HR	RBI	Avg.	BB	SO	SB	PO	A	E	Avg.
1995—Batavia (NY-Penn)	1B	56	217	35	66	13	2	7	31	.304	17	29	2	451	17	8	.983
1996—Clearwater (FSL)	1B-3B-OF	117	436	59	121	32	0	17	79	.278	52	89	1	670	94	18	.977
1997—Reading (Eastern)	OF	79	282	41	74	11	3	15	43	.262	36	69	2	116	0	7	.943
1998—Reading (Eastern)	1B-OF	127	458	63	119	17	0	21	88	.260	64	108	0	742	71	12	.985
—Scran./W.B. (Int'l)........	OF	8	23	3	7	2	0	1	4	.304	2	10	0	8	0	0	1.000

CASANOVA, RAUL — C — TIGERS

PERSONAL: Born August 23, 1972, in Humacao, Puerto Rico. ... 6-0/195. ... Bats both, throws right.
HIGH SCHOOL: Ponce (Puerto Rico).
TRANSACTIONS/CAREER NOTES: Selected by New York Mets organization in eighth round of free-agent draft (June 4, 1990). ... Traded by Mets organization to San Diego Padres organization (December 7, 1992), completing deal in which Padres traded SS Tony Fernandez to Mets for P Wally Whitehurst, OF D.J. Dozier and a player to be named later (October 26, 1992). ... Traded by Padres with P Richie Lewis and OF Melvin Nieves to Detroit Tigers for P Sean Bergman, P Cade Gaspar and OF Todd Steverson (March 22, 1996). ... On Toledo disabled list (May 3-14, 1996). ... On Detroit disabled list (June 19-August 13, 1996); included rehabilitation assignments to Jacksonville (July 31-August 9) and Toledo (August 9-13). ... On Detroit disabled list (April 25-May 28 and July 21, 1998-remainder of season); included rehabilitation assignments to Toledo (May 8-27 and July 30-August 3).
STATISTICAL NOTES: Switch-hit home runs in one game (June 6, 1996).

Year Team (League)	Pos.	G	AB	R	H	2B	3B	HR	RBI	Avg.	BB	SO	SB	PO	A	E	Avg.
1990—GC Mets (GCL)	C	23	65	4	5	0	0	0	1	.077	4	16	0	141	20	8	.953
1991—GC Mets (GCL)	C	32	111	19	27	4	2	0	9	.243	12	22	3	211	24	5	.979
—Kingsport (Appl.)	C	5	18	0	1	0	0	0	0	.056	1	10	0	35	4	1	.975
1992—Columbia (S. Atl.).......	C	5	18	2	3	0	0	0	1	.167	1	4	0	29	1	0	1.000
—Kingsport (Appl.).......	C	42	137	25	37	9	1	4	27	.270	26	25	3	286	34	6	.982
1993—Waterloo (Midw.)■......	C-3B	76	227	32	58	12	0	6	30	.256	21	46	0	361	50	10	.976
1994—Rancho Cuca. (Cal.) ...	C	123	471	83	*160	27	2	23	120	*.340	43	97	1	593	55	14	.979
1995—Memphis (Sou.)	C	89	306	42	83	18	0	12	44	.271	25	51	4	531	55	*12	.980
1996—Toledo (Int'l)■............	C	49	161	23	44	11	0	8	28	.273	20	24	0	234	15	2	.992
—Detroit (A.L.)	C-DH	25	85	6	16	1	0	4	9	.188	6	18	0	123	12	3	.978
—Jacksonville (Sou.).....	C	8	30	5	10	2	0	4	9	.333	2	7	0	21	1	0	1.000
1997—Toledo (Int'l)	C	12	41	1	8	0	0	1	3	.195	3	8	0	77	8	2	.977
—Detroit (A.L.)	C-DH	101	304	27	74	10	1	5	24	.243	26	48	1	543	38	9	.985
1998—Detroit (A.L.)	C	16	42	4	6	2	0	1	3	.143	5	10	0	81	6	3	.967
—Toledo (Int'l)..............	C	50	171	17	44	8	0	7	26	.257	22	28	0	295	35	9	.973
Major league totals (3 years)		142	431	37	96	13	1	10	36	.223	37	76	1	747	56	15	.982

CASEY, SEAN — 1B — REDS

PERSONAL: Born July 2, 1974, in Willingsboro, N.J. ... 6-4/225. ... Bats left, throws right. ... Full name: Sean Thomas Casey.
HIGH SCHOOL: Upper St. Clair (Pittsburgh).
COLLEGE: Richmond.
TRANSACTIONS/CAREER NOTES: Selected by Cleveland Indians organization in second round of free-agent draft (June 1, 1995). ... On disabled list (July 23-September 23, 1996). ... On Akron disabled list (April 4-June 8, 1997). ... Traded by Indians to Cincinnati Reds for P Dave Burba (March 30, 1998). ... On Cincinnati disabled list (April 2-May 5, 1998); included rehabilitation assignment to Indianapolis (April 30-May 5).
STATISTICAL NOTES: Led Carolina League with .544 slugging percentage in 1996.

Year Team (League)	Pos.	G	AB	R	H	2B	3B	HR	RBI	Avg.	BB	SO	SB	PO	A	E	Avg.
1995—Watertown (NYP)	1B	55	207	26	68	18	0	2	37	.329	18	21	3	510	24	8	.985
1996—Kinston (Carolina)	1B	92	344	62	114	31	3	12	57	*.331	36	47	1	632	15	6	.991
1997—Akron (Eastern)	1B	62	241	38	93	19	1	10	66	.386	28	34	0	405	22	5	.988
—Buffalo (A.A.).............	1B	20	72	12	26	7	0	5	18	.361	9	11	0	17	1	0	1.000
—Cleveland (A.L.)..........	DH-1B	6	10	1	2	0	0	0	1	.200	1	2	0	2	0	0	1.000
1998—Cincinnati (N.L.)■......	1B	96	302	44	82	21	1	7	52	.272	43	45	1	643	36	4	.994
—Indianapolis (Int'l)	1B	27	95	14	31	8	1	1	13	.326	14	10	0	205	10	2	.991
American League totals (1 year)		6	10	1	2	0	0	0	1	.200	1	2	0	2	0	0	1.000
National League totals (1 year)		96	302	44	82	21	1	7	52	.272	43	45	1	643	36	4	.994
Major league totals (2 years)		102	312	45	84	21	1	7	53	.269	44	47	1	645	36	4	.994

PERSONAL: Born October 28, 1965, in Lynwood, Calif. ... 6-0/175. ... Throws left, bats right. ... Full name: Lawrence Paul Casian. ... Name pronounced CASS-ee-un.
HIGH SCHOOL: Lakewood (Calif.).
COLLEGE: Oral Roberts, then Cal State Fullerton.
TRANSACTIONS/CAREER NOTES: Selected by Minnesota Twins organization in sixth round of free-agent draft (June 2, 1987). ... On Minnesota disabled list (April 14-May 28, 1993); included rehabilitation assignment to Portland (May 14-27). ... Claimed on waivers by Cleveland Indians (July 14, 1994). ... Released by Indians (November 4, 1994). ... Signed by Iowa, Cubs organization (December 12, 1994). ... On Chicago disabled list (June 14-August 1, 1995); included rehabilitation assignment to Iowa (July 13-August 1). ... On Chicago disabled list (April 21-May 6, 1997). ... Claimed on waivers by Kansas City Royals (May 27, 1997). ... Released by Royals (August 25, 1997). ... Signed by Chicago White Sox organization (January 13, 1998). ... Granted free agency (October 15, 1998). ... Signed by Tampa Bay Devil Rays organization (November 19, 1998).
STATISTICAL NOTES: Pitched two innings, combining with starter David West (six innings) and Greg Johnson (one inning) in 5-0 no-hit victory for Portland against Vancouver (June 7, 1992).

Year Team (League)	W	L	Pct.	ERA	G	GS	CG	ShO	Sv.	IP	H	R	ER	BB	SO
1987— Visalia (California)	10	3	.769	2.51	18	15	2	1	2	97	89	35	27	49	96
1988— Orlando (South.)	9	9	.500	2.95	27	26	4	1	0	174	165	72	57	62	104
— Portland (PCL)	0	1	.000	0.00	1	0	0	0	0	2⅔	5	3	0	0	2
1989— Portland (PCL)	7	12	.368	4.52	28	27	0	0	0	169⅓	201	97	85	63	65
1990— Portland (PCL)	9	9	.500	4.48	37	23	1	0	0	156⅔	171	90	78	59	89
— Minnesota (A.L.)	2	1	.667	3.22	5	3	0	0	0	22⅓	26	9	8	4	11
1991— Minnesota (A.L.)	0	0	...	7.36	15	0	0	0	0	18⅓	28	16	15	7	6
— Portland (PCL)	3	2	.600	3.46	34	6	0	0	1	52	51	25	20	16	24
1992— Portland (PCL)	4	0	1.000	2.32	58	0	0	0	11	62	54	16	16	13	43
— Minnesota (A.L.)	1	0	1.000	2.70	6	0	0	0	0	6⅔	7	2	2	1	2
1993— Minnesota (A.L.)	5	3	.625	3.02	54	0	0	0	1	56⅔	59	23	19	14	31
— Portland (PCL)	1	0	1.000	0.00	7	0	0	0	0	7⅔	9	0	0	2	2
1994— Minnesota (A.L.)	1	3	.250	7.08	33	0	0	0	1	40⅔	57	34	32	12	18
— Cleveland (A.L.)■	0	2	.000	8.64	7	0	0	0	0	8⅓	16	9	8	4	2
1995— Iowa (Am. Assoc.)■	0	0	...	2.13	13	0	0	0	1	12⅔	9	3	3	2	9
— Chicago (N.L.)	1	0	1.000	1.93	42	0	0	0	0	23⅓	23	6	5	15	11
1996— Chicago (N.L.)	1	1	.500	1.88	35	0	0	0	0	24	14	5	5	11	15
— Iowa (Am. Assoc.)	3	2	.600	1.71	24	4	0	0	1	47⅓	37	13	9	11	32
1997— Chicago (N.L.)	0	1	.000	7.45	12	0	0	0	0	9⅔	16	9	8	2	7
— Kansas City (A.L.)■	0	2	.000	5.06	32	0	0	0	0	26⅔	32	15	15	6	16
1998— Calgary (PCL)■	4	1	.800	3.63	43	0	0	0	4	52	53	22	21	16	44
— Chicago (A.L.)	0	0	...	11.25	4	0	0	0	0	4	8	5	5	1	6
A.L. totals (7 years)	9	11	.450	5.10	156	3	0	0	2	183⅔	233	113	104	49	92
N.L. totals (3 years)	2	2	.500	2.84	89	0	0	0	0	57	53	20	18	28	33
Major league totals (9 years)	11	13	.458	4.56	245	3	0	0	2	240⅔	286	133	122	77	125

C

PERSONAL: Born November 8, 1976, in San Pedro de Macoris, Dominican Republic. ... 5-11/175. ... Bats right, throws right. ... Full name: Carlos Rafael Casimiro.
TRANSACTIONS/CAREER NOTES: Signed as non-drafted free agent by Baltimore Orioles organization (April 15, 1994).

Year Team (League)	Pos.	G	AB	R	H	2B	3B	HR	RBI	Avg.	BB	SO	SB	PO	A	E	Avg.
1994— Dom. Orioles (DSL)	IF	41	157	27	30	6	1	3	22	.191	28	41	14	64	76	19	.881
1995— GC Orioles (GCL)	2B-SS	32	107	14	27	4	2	2	11	.252	10	22	1	48	81	13	.908
1996— Bluefield (Appal.)	2B-3B	62	239	51	66	16	0	10	33	.276	20	52	22	103	131	13	.947
1997— Delmarva (S. Atl.)	2B	122	457	54	111	21	8	9	51	.243	26	108	20	204	287	21	.959
1998— Frederick (Carolina)	2B-3B-SS	131	478	44	113	23	9	15	61	.236	25	98	10	243	352	23	.963

PERSONAL: Born July 4, 1967, in Oaxaca, Mexico. ... 6-1/205. ... Bats right, throws right. ... Full name: Vinicio Soria Castilla. ... Name pronounced kass-TEE-uh.
HIGH SCHOOL: Instituto Carlos Gracida (Oaxaca, Mexico).
TRANSACTIONS/CAREER NOTES: Signed as non-drafted free agent by Saltillo of Mexican League. ... Contract sold by Saltillo to Atlanta Braves organization (March 19, 1990). ... Selected by Colorado Rockies in second round (40th pick overall) of expansion draft (November 17, 1992). ... On disabled list (May 20-June 4, 1993).
RECORDS: Holds N.L. single-season record for most at-bats without a triple—629 (1996).
HONORS: Named third baseman on THE SPORTING NEWS N.L. All-Star team (1995 and 1997-98). ... Named third baseman on THE SPORTING NEWS N.L. Silver Slugger team (1995 and 1997-98).
STATISTICAL NOTES: Led International League shortstops with 550 total chances and 72 double plays in 1992. ... Led N.L. third basemen with 506 total chances and 43 double plays in 1996. ... Had 22-game hitting streak (August 9-September 1, 1997). ... Led N.L. third basemen with 41 double plays in 1997. ... Career major league grand slams: 2.

Year Team (League)	Pos.	G	AB	R	H	2B	3B	HR	RBI	Avg.	BB	SO	SB	PO	A	E	Avg.
1987— Saltillo (Mexican)	3B	13	27	0	5	2	0	0	1	.185	0	5	0	10	31	1	.976
1988— Salt.-Monc. (Mex.)	SS	50	124	22	30	2	2	5	18	.242	8	29	1	53	105	13	.924
1989— Saltillo (Mexican)■	SS-3B	128	462	70	142	25	13	10	58	.307	33	70	11	224	427	34	.950
1990— Sumter (S. Atl.)■	SS	93	339	47	91	15	2	9	53	.268	28	54	2	139	320	23	.952
— Greenville (Southern)	SS	46	170	20	40	5	1	4	16	.235	13	23	4	71	167	7	.971
1991— Greenville (Southern)	SS	66	259	34	70	17	3	7	44	.270	9	35	0	86	221	11	.965
— Richmond (Int'l)	SS	67	240	25	54	7	4	7	36	.225	14	32	1	93	208	12	.962
— Atlanta (N.L.)	SS	12	5	1	1	0	0	0	0	.200	0	2	0	6	6	0	1.000

Year	Team (League)	Pos.	G	AB	R	H	2B	3B	HR	RBI	Avg.	BB	SO	SB	PO	A	E	Avg.
							BATTING									FIELDING		
1992—Richmond (Int'l)	SS	127	449	49	113	29	1	7	44	.252	21	68	1	162	357	*31	.944
—Atlanta (N.L.)	SS-3B	9	16	1	4	1	0	0	1	.250	1	4	0	2	12	1	.933
1993—Colorado (N.L.)■	SS	105	337	36	86	9	7	9	30	.255	13	45	2	141	282	11	.975
1994—Colorado (N.L.)	S-2-3-1	52	130	16	43	11	1	3	18	.331	7	23	2	67	78	2	.986
—Colo. Springs (PCL)	3B-2B-SS	22	78	13	19	6	1	1	11	.244	7	11	0	20	60	3	.964
1995—Colorado (N.L.)	3B-SS	139	527	82	163	34	2	32	90	.309	30	87	2	86	264	15	.959
1996—Colorado (N.L.)	3B	160	629	97	191	34	0	40	113	.304	35	88	7	97	*389	20	.960
1997—Colorado (N.L.)	3B	159	612	94	186	25	2	40	113	.304	44	108	2	112	*323	21	.954
1998—Colorado (N.L.)	3B-SS	•162	645	108	206	28	4	46	144	.319	40	89	5	110	316	13	.970
Major league totals (8 years)		798	2901	435	880	142	16	170	509	.303	170	446	20	621	1670	83	.965

DIVISION SERIES RECORD

Year	Team (League)	Pos.	G	AB	R	H	2B	3B	HR	RBI	Avg.	BB	SO	SB	PO	A	E	Avg.
							BATTING									FIELDING		
1995—Colorado (N.L.)	3B	4	15	3	7	1	0	3	6	.467	0	1	0	3	13	1	.941

ALL-STAR GAME RECORD

Year	League	Pos.	AB	R	H	2B	3B	HR	RBI	Avg.	BB	SO	SB	PO	A	E	Avg.
						BATTING									FIELDING		
1995—National	3B	2	0	0	0	0	0	0	.000	0	1	0	0	0	0	...
1998—National	3B	2	0	0	0	0	0	0	.000	0	0	0	0	2	0	1.000
All-Star Game totals (2 years)		4	0	0	0	0	0	0	.000	0	1	0	0	2	0	1.000

C

CASTILLO, ALBERTO   C   CARDINALS

PERSONAL: Born February 10, 1970, in San Juan de la Maguana, Dominican Republic. ... 6-0/185. ... Bats right, throws right. ... Full name: Alberto Terrero Castillo.

HIGH SCHOOL: Mercedes Maria Mateo (Dominican Republic).

TRANSACTIONS/CAREER NOTES: Signed as non-drafted free agent by New York Mets organization (April 15, 1987). ... On disabled list (July 3, 1992-remainder of season and June 1-July 13, 1994). ... On suspended list (August 27-29, 1994). ... Granted free agency (October 15, 1998). ... Signed by Philadelphia Phillies organization (November 5, 1998). ... Selected by St. Louis Cardinals from Phillies organization in Rule 5 major league draft (December 14, 1998).

STATISTICAL NOTES: Led International League catchers with 827 total chances and nine double plays in 1996.

Year	Team (League)	Pos.	G	AB	R	H	2B	3B	HR	RBI	Avg.	BB	SO	SB	PO	A	E	Avg.
							BATTING									FIELDING		
1987—Kingsport (Appal.)	C	7	9	1	1	0	0	0	0	.111	5	3	1	21	4	0	1.000
1988—GC Mets (GCL)	C	22	68	7	18	4	0	0	10	.265	4	4	2	126	13	1	.993
—Kingsport (Appal.)	C	24	75	7	22	3	0	1	14	.293	15	14	0	161	18	5	.973
1989—Kingsport (Appal.)	C-1B	27	74	15	19	4	0	3	12	.257	11	14	2	140	19	1	.994
—Pittsfield (NYP)	C	34	123	13	29	8	0	1	13	.236	7	26	2	186	26	2	.991
—St. Lucie (Fla. St.)	...	1	0	0	0	0	0	0	0	...	0	0	0	0	0	0	...
1990—Columbia (S. Atl.)	C	30	103	8	24	4	3	1	14	.233	10	21	1	187	22	5	.977
—Pittsfield (NYP)	C-OF-1B	58	187	19	41	8	1	4	24	.219	26	35	3	378	61	9	.980
1991—Columbia (S. Atl.)	C	90	267	35	74	20	3	3	47	.277	43	44	6	*734	86	15	.982
1992—St. Lucie (Fla. St.)	C	60	162	11	33	6	0	3	17	.204	16	37	0	317	40	12	.967
1993—St. Lucie (Fla. St.)	C	105	333	37	86	21	0	5	42	.258	28	46	0	*604	80	12	.983
1994—Binghamton (East.)	C-1B	90	315	33	78	14	0	7	42	.248	41	46	1	643	54	6	.991
1995—Norfolk (Int'l)	C	69	217	23	58	13	1	4	31	.267	26	32	2	469	44	7	.987
—New York (N.L.)	C	13	29	2	3	0	0	0	0	.103	3	9	1	66	9	2	.974
1996—New York (N.L.)	C	6	11	1	4	0	0	0	0	.364	0	4	0	23	0	0	1.000
—Norfolk (Int'l)	C	113	341	34	71	12	1	11	39	.208	39	67	2	*747	*72	8	.990
1997—New York (N.L.)	C	35	59	3	12	1	0	0	7	.203	9	16	0	142	8	2	.987
—Norfolk (Int'l)	C-OF	34	83	4	18	1	0	1	8	.217	17	16	1	197	16	7	.968
1998—New York (N.L.)	C-DH	38	83	13	17	4	0	2	7	.205	9	17	0	193	15	2	.990
—Norfolk (Int'l)	C-OF	21	49	4	9	2	0	1	6	.184	11	12	0	110	6	1	.991
Major league totals (4 years)		92	182	19	36	5	0	2	14	.198	21	46	1	424	32	6	.987

CASTILLO, CARLOS   P   WHITE SOX

PERSONAL: Born April 21, 1975, in Boston. ... 6-2/250. ... Throws right, bats right.

HIGH SCHOOL: Southwest (Miami).

TRANSACTIONS/CAREER NOTES: Selected by Chicago White Sox organization in third round of free-agent draft (June 2, 1994).

STATISTICAL NOTES: Tied for A.L. lead with three balks in 1998.

Year	Team (League)	W	L	Pct.	ERA	G	GS	CG	ShO	Sv.	IP	H	R	ER	BB	SO
1994—GC White Sox (GCL)	4	3	.571	2.59	12	12	0	0	0	59	53	20	17	10	57
—Hickory (S. Atl.)	2	0	1.000	0.00	3	1	0	0	0	12	3	0	0	2	17
1995—Hickory (S. Atl.)	5	6	.455	3.73	14	12	2	0	1	$79\frac{2}{3}$	85	42	33	18	67
1996—South Bend (Mid.)	9	9	.500	4.05	20	19	•5	0	0	$133\frac{1}{3}$	131	74	60	29	128
—Prince William (Caro.)	2	4	.333	3.95	6	6	•4	0	0	$43\frac{1}{3}$	45	22	19	4	30
1997—Chicago (A.L.)	2	1	.667	4.48	37	2	0	0	1	$66\frac{1}{3}$	68	35	33	33	43
—Nashville (A.A.)	0	0	...	1.50	4	0	0	0	3	6	4	1	1	0	4
1998—Chicago (A.L.)	6	4	.600	5.11	54	2	0	0	0	$100\frac{1}{3}$	94	61	57	35	64
—Calgary (PCL)	1	1	.500	9.00	2	2	0	0	0	8	12	8	8	4	4
Major league totals (2 years)	8	5	.615	4.86	91	4	0	0	1	$166\frac{2}{3}$	162	96	90	68	107

CASTILLO, FRANK   P   DIAMONDBACKS

PERSONAL: Born April 1, 1969, in El Paso, Texas. ... 6-1/200. ... Throws right, bats right. ... Full name: Frank Anthony Castillo.
HIGH SCHOOL: Eastwood (El Paso, Texas).
TRANSACTIONS/CAREER NOTES: Selected by Chicago Cubs organization in sixth round of free-agent draft (June 2, 1987). ... On disabled list (April 1-July 23, 1988). ... On Iowa disabled list (April 12-June 6, 1991). ... On Chicago disabled list (August 11-27, 1991). ... On suspended list (September 20-24, 1993). ... On Chicago disabled list (March 20-May 12, 1994); included rehabilitation assignments to Daytona (April 24), Orlando (April 25-May 2) and Iowa (May 2-10). ... On Iowa disabled list (June 21-July 1, 1994). ... Traded by Cubs to Colorado Rockies for P Matt Pool (July 15, 1997). ... Granted free agency (October 30, 1997). ... Signed by Detroit Tigers (December 11, 1997). ... On Detroit disabled list (March 24-April 28, 1998); included rehabilitation assignment to Lakeland (April 18-28). ... Granted free agency (October 27, 1998). ... Signed by Arizona Diamondbacks organization (January 12, 1999).
HONORS: Named Appalachian League Player of the Year (1987).
STATISTICAL NOTES: Pitched 4-0 no-hit victory against Huntsville (July 13, 1990, first game). ... Pitched 7-0 one-hit, complete-game victory against St. Louis (September 25, 1995).

Year Team (League)	W	L	Pct.	ERA	G	GS	CG	ShO	Sv.	IP	H	R	ER	BB	SO
1987—Wytheville (Appal.)	*10	1	*.909	2.29	12	12	•5	0	0	90⅓	86	31	23	21	83
— Geneva (N.Y.-Penn)	1	0	1.000	0.00	1	1	0	0	0	6	3	1	0	1	6
1988— Peoria (Midwest)	6	1	.857	0.71	9	8	2	2	0	51	25	5	4	10	58
1989—Win.-Salem (Car.)	9	6	.600	2.51	18	18	8	1	0	129⅓	118	42	36	24	114
—Charlotte (Southern)	3	4	.429	3.84	10	10	4	0	0	68	73	35	29	12	43
1990—Charlotte (Southern)	6	6	.500	3.88	18	18	4	1	0	111⅓	113	54	48	27	112
1991—Iowa (Am. Assoc.)	3	1	.750	2.52	4	4	1	1	0	25	20	7	7	7	20
—Chicago (N.L.)	6	7	.462	4.35	18	18	4	0	0	111⅔	107	56	54	33	73
1992—Chicago (N.L.)	10	11	.476	3.46	33	33	0	0	0	205⅓	179	91	79	63	135
1993—Chicago (N.L.)	5	8	.385	4.84	29	25	2	0	0	141⅓	162	83	76	39	84
1994—Daytona (Fla. St.)	0	1	.000	4.50	1	1	0	0	0	4	7	3	2	0	1
—Orlando (South.)	1	0	1.000	1.29	1	1	0	0	0	7	4	2	1	1	2
—Iowa (Am. Assoc.)	4	2	.667	3.27	11	11	0	0	0	66	57	30	24	10	64
—Chicago (N.L.)	2	1	.667	4.30	4	4	1	0	0	23	25	13	11	5	19
1995—Chicago (N.L.)	11	10	.524	3.21	29	29	2	2	0	188	179	75	67	52	135
1996—Chicago (N.L.)	7	•16	.304	5.28	33	33	1	1	0	182⅓	209	112	107	46	139
1997—Chicago (N.L.)	6	9	.400	5.42	20	19	0	0	0	98	113	64	59	44	67
—Colorado (N.L.)■	6	3	.667	5.42	14	14	0	0	0	86⅓	107	57	52	25	59
1998—Lakeland (Fla. St.)■	1	0	1.000	0.00	1	1	0	0	0	5	2	0	0	0	4
—Detroit (A.L.)	3	9	.250	6.83	27	19	0	0	1	116	150	91	88	44	81
A.L. totals (1 year)	3	9	.250	6.83	27	19	0	0	1	116	150	91	88	44	81
N.L. totals (7 years)	53	65	.449	4.39	180	175	10	3	0	1036	1081	551	505	307	711
Major league totals (8 years)	56	74	.431	4.63	207	194	10	3	1	1152	1231	642	593	351	792

CASTILLO, LUIS   2B   MARLINS

PERSONAL: Born September 12, 1975, in San Pedro de Macoris, Dominican Republic. ... 5-11/175. ... Bats both, throws right. ... Full name: Luis Antonio Donato Castillo.
HIGH SCHOOL: Colegio San Benito Abad (San Pedro de Macoris, Dominican Republic).
TRANSACTIONS/CAREER NOTES: Signed as non-drafted free agent by Florida Marlins organization (August 19, 1992). ... On disabled list (July 20-September 11, 1995). ... On Florida disabled list (May 7-22, 1997).
STATISTICAL NOTES: Led Gulf Coast League in caught stealing with 12 in 1994. ... Led Gulf Coast League second basemen with 142 putouts, 318 total chances, 40 double plays and .972 fielding percentage in 1994. ... Led Eastern League in caught stealing with 28 in 1996. ... Led Eastern League second basemen with 557 total chances and 87 double plays in 1996. ... Led International League in caught stealing with 15 in 1998.

Year Team (League)	Pos.	G	AB	R	H	2B	3B	HR	RBI	Avg.	BB	SO	SB	PO	A	E	Avg.
1993—Dom. Marlins (DSL)	IF	69	266	48	75	7	1	4	31	.282	36	22	21	151	180	20	.943
1994—GC Marlins (GCL)	2B-SS	57	216	49	57	8	0	0	16	.264	37	36	31	†144	170	9	†.972
1995—Kane County (Midw.)	2B	89	340	71	111	4	4	0	23	.326	55	50	41	193	241	17	.962
1996—Portland (Eastern)	2B	109	420	83	133	15	7	1	35	.317	66	68	*51	217	*326	14	*.975
—Florida (N.L.)	2B	41	164	26	43	2	1	1	8	.262	14	46	17	99	118	3	.986
1997—Florida (N.L.)	2B	75	263	27	63	8	0	0	8	.240	27	53	16	129	177	9	.971
—Charlotte (Int'l)	2B	37	130	25	46	5	0	0	5	.354	16	22	8	66	97	5	.970
1998—Florida (N.L.)	2B	100	381	74	109	11	2	0	15	.286	75	68	41	232	281	16	.970
—Florida (N.L.)	2B	44	153	21	31	3	2	1	10	.203	22	33	3	117	113	7	.970
Major league totals (3 years)		160	580	74	137	13	3	2	26	.236	63	132	36	345	408	19	.975

CASTILLO, TONY   P

PERSONAL: Born March 1, 1963, in Lara, Venezuela. ... 5-10/190. ... Throws left, bats left. ... Full name: Antonio Jose Castillo.
TRANSACTIONS/CAREER NOTES: Signed as non-drafted free agent by Toronto Blue Jays organization (February 16, 1983). ... On disabled list (April 10, 1986-entire season). ... Traded by Blue Jays organization with a player to be named later to Atlanta Braves for P Jim Acker (August 24, 1989); Braves organization acquired C Francisco Cabrera to complete deal (August 24, 1989). ... Traded by Braves with a player to be named later to New York Mets for P Alejandro Pena (August 28, 1991); Mets acquired P Joe Roa to complete deal (August 29, 1991). ... Traded by Mets with OF Mark Carreon to Detroit Tigers for P Paul Gibson and P Randy Marshall (January 22, 1992). ... On disabled list (June 8-August 29, 1992). ... Granted free agency (October 15, 1992). ... Signed by Syracuse, Blue Jays organization (January 11, 1993). ... Traded by Blue Jays with IF Domingo Cedeno to Chicago White Sox for P Luis Andujar and P Allen Halley (August 22, 1996). ... Granted free agency (December 7, 1996). ... Re-signed by White Sox (December 11, 1996). ... On disabled list (May 13-27, 1997). ... Released by White Sox (June 21, 1998).

Year Team (League)	W	L	Pct.	ERA	G	GS	CG	ShO	Sv.	IP	H	R	ER	BB	SO
1983—GC Blue Jays (GCL)	0	0	...	3.00	1	0	0	0	1	3	3	1	1	0	4
1984—Florence (S. Atl.)	11	8	.579	3.41	25	24	4	1	0	137⅓	123	71	52	50	96
1985—Kinston (Carolina)	11	7	.611	1.90	36	12	0	0	3	127⅔	111	44	27	48	136

C

Year	Team (League)	W	L	Pct.	ERA	G	GS	CG	ShO	Sv.	IP	H	R	ER	BB	SO
1986—								Did not play.								
1987—	Dunedin (Fla. St.)	6	2	.750	3.36	39	0	0	0	6	69$^{2}/_{3}$	62	30	26	19	62
1988—	Dunedin (Fla. St.)	4	3	.571	1.48	30	0	0	0	12	42$^{2}/_{3}$	31	9	7	10	46
	— Knoxville (Southern)	1	0	1.000	0.00	5	0	0	0	2	8	2	0	0	1	11
	— Toronto (A.L.)	1	0	1.000	3.00	14	0	0	0	0	15	10	5	5	2	14
1989—	Toronto (A.L.)	1	1	.500	6.11	17	0	0	0	1	17$^{2}/_{3}$	23	14	12	10	10
	— Syracuse (Int'l)	1	3	.250	2.81	27	0	0	0	5	41$^{2}/_{3}$	33	15	13	15	37
	— Atlanta (N.L.)■	0	1	.000	4.82	12	0	0	0	0	9$^{1}/_{3}$	8	5	5	4	5
1990—	Atlanta (N.L.)	5	1	.833	4.23	52	3	0	0	1	76$^{2}/_{3}$	93	41	36	20	64
	— Richmond (Int'l)	3	1	.750	2.52	5	4	1	1	0	25	14	7	7	6	27
1991—	Richmond (Int'l)	5	6	.455	2.90	23	17	0	0	0	118	89	47	38	32	78
	— Atlanta (N.L.)	1	1	.500	7.27	7	0	0	0	0	8$^{2}/_{3}$	13	9	7	5	8
	— New York (N.L.)	1	0	1.000	1.90	10	3	0	0	0	23$^{2}/_{3}$	27	7	5	6	10
1992—	Toledo (International)■	2	3	.400	3.63	12	9	0	0	2	44$^{2}/_{3}$	48	23	18	14	24
1993—	Syracuse (Int'l)■	0	0	. . .	0.00	1	1	0	0	0	6	4	2	0	0	2
	— Toronto (A.L.)	3	2	.600	3.38	51	0	0	0	0	50$^{1}/_{3}$	44	19	19	22	28
1994—	Toronto (A.L.)	5	2	.714	2.51	41	0	0	0	1	68	66	22	19	28	43
1995—	Toronto (A.L.)	1	5	.167	3.22	55	0	0	0	13	72$^{2}/_{3}$	64	27	26	24	38
1996—	Toronto (A.L.)	2	3	.400	4.23	40	0	0	0	1	72$^{1}/_{3}$	72	38	34	20	48
	— Chicago (A.L.)■	3	1	.750	1.59	15	0	0	0	1	22$^{2}/_{3}$	23	7	4	4	9
1997—	Chicago (A.L.)	4	4	.500	4.91	64	0	0	0	4	62$^{1}/_{3}$	74	48	34	23	42
1998—	Chicago (A.L.)	1	2	.333	8.00	25	0	0	0	0	27	38	25	24	11	14
A.L. totals (8 years)		21	20	.512	3.90	322	0	0	0	21	408$^{1}/_{3}$	414	205	177	144	246
N.L. totals (3 years)		7	3	.700	4.03	81	6	0	0	1	118$^{1}/_{3}$	141	62	53	35	87
Major league totals (10 years)....		28	23	.549	3.93	403	6	0	0	22	526$^{2}/_{3}$	555	267	230	179	333

CHAMPIONSHIP SERIES RECORD

Year	Team (League)	W	L	Pct.	ERA	G	GS	CG	ShO	Sv.	IP	H	R	ER	BB	SO
1993—	Toronto (A.L.)	0	0	. . .	0.00	2	0	0	0	0	2	0	0	0	1	1

WORLD SERIES RECORD

NOTES: Member of World Series championship team (1993).

Year	Team (League)	W	L	Pct.	ERA	G	GS	CG	ShO	Sv.	IP	H	R	ER	BB	SO
1993—	Toronto (A.L.)	1	0	1.000	8.10	2	0	0	0	0	3$^{1}/_{3}$	6	3	3	3	1

CASTRO, JUAN   SS   DODGERS

PERSONAL: Born June 20, 1972, in Los Mochis, Mexico. ... 5-10/187. ... Bats right, throws right.
HIGH SCHOOL: CBTIS 43 (Los Mochis, Mexico).
TRANSACTIONS/CAREER NOTES: Signed as non-drafted free agent by Los Angeles Dodgers organization (June 13, 1991). ... On Los Angeles disabled list (June 5-August 1, 1997).
STATISTICAL NOTES: Tied for Texas League lead in double plays by shortstop with 82 in 1994.

						BATTING							FIELDING			
Year	Team (League)	Pos.	G	AB	R	H	2B	3B	HR	RBI	Avg.	BB	SO	SB	PO	A	E	Avg.
1991—	Great Falls (Pio.)	SS-2B	60	217	36	60	4	2	1	27	.276	33	31	7	90	155	21	.921
1992—	Bakersfield (Calif.)	SS	113	446	56	116	15	4	4	42	.260	37	64	14	180	309	38	.928
1993—	San Antonio (Tex.)	SS-2B	118	424	55	117	23	8	7	41	.276	30	40	12	169	314	28	.945
1994—	San Antonio (Tex.)	SS	123	445	55	128	25	4	4	44	.288	31	66	4	187	377	29	.951
1995—	Albuquerque (PCL)	SS-2B	104	341	51	91	18	4	3	43	.267	20	42	4	152	344	14	.973
	— Los Angeles (N.L.)	3B-SS	11	4	0	1	0	0	0	0	.250	1	1	0	3	7	0	1.000
1996—	Albuquerque (PCL)	3B-SS-2B	17	56	12	21	4	2	1	8	.375	6	7	1	17	33	2	.962
	— Los Angeles (N.L.)	S-3-2-O	70	132	16	26	5	3	0	5	.197	10	27	1	54	84	3	.979
1997—	Albuquerque (PCL)	SS-2B	27	101	11	31	5	2	2	11	.307	4	20	1	33	83	9	.928
	— Los Angeles (N.L.)	SS-2B-3B	40	75	3	11	3	1	0	4	.147	7	20	0	36	65	1	.990
1998—	Los Angeles (N.L.)	SS-2B-3B	89	220	25	43	7	0	2	14	.195	15	37	0	95	182	10	.965
Major league totals (4 years)			210	431	44	81	15	4	2	23	.188	33	85	1	188	338	14	.974

DIVISION SERIES RECORD

						BATTING							FIELDING			
Year	Team (League)	Pos.	G	AB	R	H	2B	3B	HR	RBI	Avg.	BB	SO	SB	PO	A	E	Avg.
1996—	Los Angeles (N.L.)	2B	2	5	0	1	1	0	0	1	.200	1	1	0	4	3	0	1.000

CASTRO, NELSON   SS   ANGELS

PERSONAL: Born June 4, 1976, in Monte Cristi, Dominican Republic. ... 5-10/190. ... Bats both, throws right. ... Full name: Nelson Daniel Castro.
TRANSACTIONS/CAREER NOTES: Signed as non-drafted free agent by California Angels organization (January 14, 1994). ... Angels franchise renamed Anaheim Angels for 1997 season.
STATISTICAL NOTES: Led Arizona League shortstops with 297 total chances and 32 double plays in 1997. ... Led Northwest League shortstops with 323 total chances in 1997. ... Led California League shortstops with 591 total chances and 71 double plays in 1998.

						BATTING							FIELDING			
Year	Team (League)	Pos.	G	AB	R	H	2B	3B	HR	RBI	Avg.	BB	SO	SB	PO	A	E	Avg.
1994—	....						Dominican Summer League statistics unavailable.										
1995—	Ariz. Angels (Ariz.)	SS	55	190	34	37	1	2	0	22	.195	27	50	15	*106	*173	18	.939
1996—	Boise (Northwest)	PH	1	0	0	0	0	0	0	0	.000	0	0	0	. . .	. . .	. . .	. . .
	— Ariz. Angels (Ariz.)	SS	53	222	31	38	4	3	3	14	.171	32	42	25	75	164	14	.945
1997—	Boise (Northwest)	SS	69	293	74	86	16	1	7	37	.294	38	53	26	80	218	25	*.923
1998—	Lake Elsinore (Calif.) ..	SS	131	470	73	110	16	7	4	41	.234	40	101	36	•185	*372	34	.942

CASTRO, RAMON   C   MARLINS

PERSONAL: Born March 1, 1976, in Vega Baja, Puerto Rico. ... 6-3/225. ... Bats right, throws right. ... Full name: Ramon A. Castro.
HIGH SCHOOL: Lino P. Rivera (Vega Baja, Puerto Rico).
TRANSACTIONS/CAREER NOTES: Selected by Houston Astros organization in first round (17th pick overall) of free-agent draft (June 2, 1994). ... On Jackson disabled list (April 27-May 15, 1998). ... Traded by Astros to Florida Marlins for P Jay Powell and C Scott Makarewicz (July 6, 1998).

							BATTING							FIELDING		
Year Team (League)	Pos.	G	AB	R	H	2B	3B	HR	RBI	Avg.	BB	SO	SB	PO	A	E	Avg.
1994— GC Astros (GCL)	C	37	123	17	34	7	0	3	14	.276	17	14	5	210	24	4	.983
1995— Kissimmee (Fla. St.)...	C	36	120	6	25	5	0	0	8	.208	6	21	0	184	18	7	.967
— Auburn (NY-Penn)......	C	63	224	40	67	17	0	9	49	.299	24	27	0	297	46	2	.994
1996— Quad City (Midwest) ..	C	96	314	38	78	15	0	7	43	.248	31	61	2	660	82	10	.987
1997— Kissimmee (Fla. St.)...	C	115	410	53	115	22	1	8	65	.280	53	73	1	630	88	6	*.992
1998— Jackson (Texas)	C	48	168	27	43	6	0	8	25	.256	13	31	0	329	40	10	.974
— Portland (Eastern)■...	C	31	88	9	22	3	0	3	11	.250	8	21	0	82	5	5	.946

CATALANOTTO, FRANK   2B   TIGERS

PERSONAL: Born April 27, 1974, in Smithtown, N.Y. ... 6-0/195. ... Bats left, throws right. ... Full name: Frank John Catalanotto.
HIGH SCHOOL: Smithtown (N.Y.) East.
TRANSACTIONS/CAREER NOTES: Selected by Detroit Tigers organization in 10th round of free-agent draft (June 1, 1992). ... Selected by Oakland Athletics from Tigers organization in Rule 5 major league draft (December 9, 1996). ... Returned to Tigers organization (March 21, 1997). ... On Toledo disabled list (June 18-25, 1998).
STATISTICAL NOTES: Led Southern League second basemen with 681 total chances and 95 double plays in 1995. ... Led Southern League second basemen with 689 total chances and 99 double plays in 1996. ... Led International League second basemen with .984 fielding percentage in 1997.

							BATTING							FIELDING		
Year Team (League)	Pos.	G	AB	R	H	2B	3B	HR	RBI	Avg.	BB	SO	SB	PO	A	E	Avg.
1992— Bristol (Appal.)	2B	21	50	6	10	2	0	0	4	.200	8	8	0	8	6	2	.875
1993— Bristol (Appal.)	2B	55	199	37	61	9	5	3	22	.307	15	19	3	96	128	10	.957
1994— Fayetteville (SAL)	2B	119	458	72	149	24	8	3	56	.325	37	54	4	244	304	15	.973
1995— Jacksonville (Sou.).....	2B	134	491	66	111	19	5	8	48	.226	49	56	13	252	*411	18	*.974
1996— Jacksonville (Sou.).....	2B	132	497	105	148	34	6	17	67	.298	74	69	15	246	*421	•22	.968
1997— Toledo (Int'l)...............	2B-3B-OF	134	500	75	150	32	3	16	68	.300	47	80	12	168	351	18	†.966
— Detroit (A.L.).............	2B-DH	13	26	2	8	2	0	0	3	.308	3	7	0	7	9	0	1.000
1998— Detroit (A.L.)	2-DH-1-3	89	213	23	60	13	2	6	25	.282	12	39	3	162	51	3	.986
— Toledo (Int'l).............	1B-2B	28	105	20	35	6	3	4	28	.333	14	21	0	131	43	2	.989
Major league totals (2 years)		102	239	25	68	15	2	6	28	.285	15	46	3	169	60	3	.987

CATHER, MIKE   P   BRAVES

PERSONAL: Born December 17, 1970, in San Diego. ... 6-2/195. ... Throws right, bats right. ... Full name: Michael Peter Cather.
HIGH SCHOOL: Folsom (Calif.).
COLLEGE: California.
TRANSACTIONS/CAREER NOTES: Selected by Texas Rangers organization in 41st round of free-agent draft (June 3, 1993). ... Released by Tulsa, Rangers organization (June 14, 1995). ... Signed by Winnipeg Goldeyes, Northern League (July 4, 1995). ... Granted free agency following 1995 season. ... Signed by Atlanta Braves organization (February 9, 1996). ... On disabled list (May 30-June 12, 1996). ... On Atlanta disabled list (August 31, 1998-remainder of season).

Year Team (League)	W	L	Pct.	ERA	G	GS	CG	ShO	Sv.	IP	H	R	ER	BB	SO
1993— GC Rangers (GCL).............	1	1	.500	1.76	25	0	0	0	4	30 2/3	20	7	6	9	30
1994— Charlotte (Fla. St.).............	8	6	.571	3.88	44	0	0	0	6	60 1/3	56	33	26	40	53
1995— Tulsa (Texas)	0	2	.000	3.32	18	0	0	0	0	21 2/3	20	11	8	7	15
— Winnipeg (North.)■.........	4	2	.667	1.45	45	0	0	0	8	31	18	6	5	12	35
1996— Greenville (Southern)■......	3	4	.429	3.70	53	0	0	0	5	87 2/3	89	42	36	29	61
1997— Greenville (Southern)	5	2	.714	4.34	22	0	0	0	1	37 1/3	37	18	18	7	29
— Richmond (Int'l)...............	0	0	...	1.73	13	0	0	0	3	26	17	6	5	9	22
— Atlanta (N.L.)...................	2	4	.333	2.39	35	0	0	0	0	37 2/3	23	12	10	19	29
1998— Atlanta (N.L.)...................	2	2	.500	3.92	36	0	0	0	0	41 1/3	39	21	18	12	33
— Richmond (Int'l)...............	0	1	.000	5.87	11	0	0	0	0	15 1/3	22	12	10	6	10
Major league totals (2 years)......	4	6	.400	3.19	71	0	0	0	0	79	62	33	28	31	62

DIVISION SERIES RECORD

Year Team (League)	W	L	Pct.	ERA	G	GS	CG	ShO	Sv.	IP	H	R	ER	BB	SO
1997— Atlanta (N.L.).....................	0	0	...	0.00	1	0	0	0	0	2	0	0	0	1	2

CHAMPIONSHIP SERIES RECORD

Year Team (League)	W	L	Pct.	ERA	G	GS	CG	ShO	Sv.	IP	H	R	ER	BB	SO
1997— Atlanta (N.L.).....................	0	0	...	0.00	4	0	0	0	0	2 2/3	3	0	0	0	3

CEDENO, DOMINGO   2B/SS   ATHLETICS

PERSONAL: Born November 4, 1968, in La Romana, Dominican Republic. ... 6-0/170. ... Bats both, throws right.
TRANSACTIONS/CAREER NOTES: Signed as non-drafted free agent by Toronto Blue Jays organization (August 4, 1987). ... On disabled list (April 22-May 28, 1991). ... Traded by Blue Jays with P Tony Castillo to Chicago White Sox for P Luis Andujar and P Allen Halley (August 22, 1996). ... Granted free agency (December 20, 1996). ... Signed by Texas Rangers organization (January 15, 1997). ... On Texas disabled list (April 8-May 15, 1997); included rehabilitation assignment to Tulsa (May 3-15). ... Released by Rangers (December 11, 1998). ... Signed by Oakland Athletics organization (December 23, 1998).
STATISTICAL NOTES: Led Florida State League shortstops with 633 total chances and 74 double plays in 1990. ... Led Southern League with 12 sacrifice hits in 1991.

Year	Team (League)	Pos.	G	AB	R	H	2B	3B	HR	RBI	Avg.	BB	SO	SB	PO	A	E	Avg.
											BATTING				FIELDING			
1988—	....					Dominican Summer League statistics unavailable.												
1989—	Myrtle Beach (SAL)....	SS	9	35	4	7	0	0	0	2	.200	3	12	1	12	20	7	.821
	— Dunedin (Fla. St.)......	SS	9	28	3	6	0	1	0	1	.214	3	10	0	9	21	1	.968
	— Medicine Hat (Pio.)	SS	53	194	28	45	6	4	1	20	.232	23	65	6	100	141	•25	.906
1990—	Dunedin (Fla. St.)......	SS	124	493	64	109	12	10	7	61	.221	48	127	10	*215	*382	36	.943
1991—	Knoxville (Southern) ..	SS	100	336	39	75	7	6	1	26	.223	29	81	11	140	272	24	.945
1992—	Knoxville (Southern) ..	2B-SS	106	337	31	76	7	7	2	21	.226	18	88	8	189	254	28	.941
	— Syracuse (Int'l)..........	2B-SS	18	57	4	11	4	0	0	5	.193	3	14	0	36	43	0	1.000
1993—	Syracuse (Int'l)..........	SS-2B	103	382	58	104	16	10	2	28	.272	33	67	15	150	242	21	.949
	— Toronto (A.L.)...........	SS-2B	15	46	5	8	0	0	0	7	.174	1	10	1	10	39	1	.980
1994—	Toronto (A.L.)...........	2-S-3-O	47	97	14	19	2	3	0	10	.196	10	31	1	40	64	8	.929
	— Syracuse (Int'l)..........	2B-OF-SS	22	80	11	23	5	1	1	9	.288	8	13	3	42	33	2	.974
1995—	Toronto (A.L.)...........	SS-2B-3B	51	161	18	38	6	1	4	14	.236	10	35	0	85	132	3	.986
1996—	Toronto (A.L.)...........	2B-3B-SS	77	282	44	79	10	2	2	17	.280	15	60	5	127	198	9	.973
	— Chicago (A.L.)■	2B-SS-DH	12	19	2	3	2	0	0	3	.158	0	4	1	6	4	1	.909
1997—	Texas (A.L.)■	2-S-3-DH	113	365	49	103	19	6	4	36	.282	27	77	3	146	259	17	.960
	— Tulsa (Texas)	SS	2	9	0	4	0	1	0	0	.444	0	3	0	3	9	1	.923
	— Okla. City (A.A.)........	2B	6	28	0	10	2	0	0	2	.357	0	6	0	13	20	0	1.000
1998—	Texas (A.L.)...........	SS-DH-2B	61	141	19	37	9	1	2	21	.262	10	32	2	41	79	6	.952
Major league totals (6 years)			376	1111	151	287	48	13	12	108	.258	73	249	13	455	775	45	.965

CEDENO, ROGER — OF — METS

PERSONAL: Born August 16, 1974, in Valencia, Venezuela. ... 6-1/205. ... Bats both, throws right. ... Full name: Roger Leandro Cedeno.

TRANSACTIONS/CAREER NOTES: Signed as non-drafted free agent by Los Angeles Dodgers organization (March 28, 1991). ... On disabled list (June 27-July 14, 1994). ... On Los Angeles disabled list (March 25-April 17 and August 25, 1997-remainder of season); included rehabilitation assignment to Albuquerque (April 17-21). ... On Los Angeles disabled list (March 22-April 24, 1998); included rehabilitation assignment to Vero Beach (April 16-24). ... Traded by Dodgers with C Charles Johnson to New York Mets for C Todd Hundley and P Arnold Gooch (December 1, 1998).

STATISTICAL NOTES: Tied for Pioneer League lead with three intentional bases on balls received in 1992. ... Led Texas League in caught stealing with 20 in 1993. ... Led Pacific Coast League in caught stealing with 18 in 1995.

Year	Team (League)	Pos.	G	AB	R	H	2B	3B	HR	RBI	Avg.	BB	SO	SB	PO	A	E	Avg.
											BATTING				FIELDING			
1991—	Dom. Dodgers (DSL) .	OF	58	209	25	50	1	1	0	7	.239	0	0	26	...	...	...	...
1992—	Great Falls (Pio.)	OF	69	256	60	81	6	5	2	27	.316	51	53	*40	113	6	8	.937
1993—	San Antonio (Tex.)	OF	122	465	70	134	12	8	4	30	.288	45	90	28	213	6	9	.961
	— Albuquerque (PCL)....	OF	6	18	1	4	1	1	0	4	.222	3	3	0	12	0	1	.923
1994—	Albuquerque (PCL)....	OF	104	383	84	123	18	5	4	49	.321	51	57	30	194	7	8	.962
1995—	Albuquerque (PCL)....	OF	99	367	67	112	19	9	2	44	.305	53	56	23	189	3	3	.985
	— Los Angeles (N.L.)	OF	40	42	4	10	2	0	0	3	.238	3	10	1	43	0	1	.977
1996—	Los Angeles (N.L.)	OF	86	211	26	52	11	1	2	18	.246	24	47	5	117	2	2	.983
	— Albuquerque (PCL).....	OF	33	125	16	28	2	3	1	10	.224	15	22	6	71	2	0	1.000
1997—	Los Angeles (N.L.)	OF	80	194	31	53	10	2	3	17	.273	25	44	9	148	1	2	.987
	— Albuquerque (PCL)....	OF	29	113	21	40	4	4	2	9	.354	22	16	5	53	1	2	.964
1998—	Los Angeles (N.L.)	OF	105	240	33	58	11	1	2	17	.242	27	57	8	86	4	2	.978
	— Vero Beach (FSL)	OF	6	21	5	9	0	1	1	6	.429	5	5	1	14	0	1	.933
Major league totals (4 years)			311	687	94	173	34	4	7	55	.252	79	158	23	394	7	7	.983

CHAPMAN, WALKER — P — WHITE SOX

PERSONAL: Born February 25, 1976, in Cumberland, Md. ... 6-3/201. ... Throws right, bats right. ... Full name: Jeffry Walker Chapman.

HIGH SCHOOL: Beall (Frostburg, Md.).

TRANSACTIONS/CAREER NOTES: Selected by Minnesota Twins organization in sixth round of free-agent draft (June 2, 1994). ... Selected by Chicago White Sox from Twins organization in Rule 5 major league draft (December 14, 1998).

Year	Team (League)	W	L	Pct.	ERA	G	GS	CG	ShO	Sv.	IP	H	R	ER	BB	SO
1994—	GC Twins (GCL)................	5	6	.455	2.56	13	13	0	0	0	70 1/3	64	34	20	27	42
1995—	Fort Wayne (Midw.)......	2	6	.250	6.24	14	11	0	0	1	53 1/3	59	41	37	36	31
	— Elizabethton (Appal.)..........	0	1	.000	5.63	4	1	0	0	0	8	9	6	5	1	7
1996—	Fort Wayne (Midw.)......	6	8	.429	4.73	19	18	1	0	0	97	107	61	51	41	61
1997—	Fort Myers (Fla. St.)......	6	5	.545	5.80	27	14	0	0	1	90	121	64	58	32	65
1998—	New Britain (East.)............	1	3	.250	3.86	23	2	0	0	0	49	47	22	21	18	38
	— Fort Myers (Fla. St.)	4	0	1.000	1.97	24	0	0	0	2	50 1/3	40	17	11	15	47

CHARLTON, NORM — P — DEVIL RAYS

PERSONAL: Born January 6, 1963, in Fort Polk, La. ... 6-3/205. ... Throws left, bats both. ... Full name: Norman Wood Charlton III.

HIGH SCHOOL: James Madison (San Antonio).

COLLEGE: Rice (degrees in political science, religion and physical education, 1986).

TRANSACTIONS/CAREER NOTES: Selected by Montreal Expos organization in supplemental round ("sandwich pick" between first and second round, 28th pick overall) of free-agent draft (June 4, 1984); pick received as compensation for San Francisco Giants signing Type B free-agent 2B Manny Trillo. ... Traded by Expos organization with a player to be named later to Cincinnati Reds for IF Wayne Krenchicki (March 31, 1986); Reds acquired 2B Tim Barker to complete deal (April 2, 1986). ... On Cincinnati disabled list (April 6-June 26, 1987); included rehabilitation assignment to Nashville (June 9-26). ... On disabled list (May 26-June 11 and June 17-July 19, 1991). ... On suspended list (September 29 and October 4-6, 1991). ... Traded by Reds to Seattle Mariners for OF Kevin Mitchell (November 17, 1992). ... On suspended list (July 9-16, 1993). ... On disabled list (July 21-August 5 and August 8, 1993-remainder of season). ... Granted free agency (November 18, 1993). ... Signed by Philadelphia Phillies organization (February 3, 1994). ... On disabled list (March 31, 1994-entire season). ... Granted free agency (October

28, 1994). ... Re-signed by Phillies organization (December 22, 1994). ... Released by Phillies (July 10, 1995). ... Signed by Mariners (July 14, 1995). ... Granted free agency (November 7, 1997). ... Signed by Baltimore Orioles organization (December 15, 1997). ... Released by Orioles (July 28, 1998). ... Signed by Atlanta Braves organization (August 5, 1998). ... Granted free agency (October 27, 1998). ... Signed by Tampa Bay Devil Rays organization (January 20, 1999).

STATISTICAL NOTES: Led American Association with 13 wild pitches in 1988.

MISCELLANEOUS: Appeared in one game as pinch runner (1990). ... Appeared in two games as pinch runner (1991).

Year	Team (League)	W	L	Pct.	ERA	G	GS	CG	ShO	Sv.	IP	H	R	ER	BB	SO
1984—	W.P. Beach (FSL)	1	4	.200	4.58	8	8	0	0	0	39 1/3	51	27	20	22	27
1985—	W.P. Beach (FSL)	7	10	.412	4.57	24	23	5	2	0	128	135	79	65	79	71
1986—	Vermont (Eastern)■	10	6	.625	2.83	22	22	6	1	0	136 2/3	109	55	43	74	96
1987—	Nashville (A.A.)	2	8	.200	4.30	18	17	3	1	0	98 1/3	97	57	47	44	74
1988—	Nashville (A.A.)	11	10	.524	3.02	27	27	8	1	0	182	149	69	61	56	*161
—	Cincinnati (N.L.)	4	5	.444	3.96	10	10	0	0	0	61 1/3	60	27	27	20	39
1989—	Cincinnati (N.L.)	8	3	.727	2.93	69	0	0	0	0	95 1/3	67	38	31	40	98
1990—	Cincinnati (N.L.)	12	9	.571	2.74	56	16	1	1	2	154 1/3	131	53	47	70	117
1991—	Cincinnati (N.L.)	3	5	.375	2.91	39	11	0	0	1	108 1/3	92	37	35	34	77
1992—	Cincinnati (N.L.)	4	2	.667	2.99	64	0	0	0	26	81 1/3	79	39	27	26	90
1993—	Seattle (A.L.)■	1	3	.250	2.34	34	0	0	0	18	34 2/3	22	12	9	17	48
1994—								Did not play.								
1995—	Philadelphia (N.L.)■	2	5	.286	7.36	25	0	0	0	0	22	23	19	18	15	12
—	Seattle (A.L.)■	2	1	.667	1.51	30	0	0	0	14	47 2/3	23	12	8	16	58
1996—	Seattle (A.L.)	4	7	.364	4.04	70	0	0	0	20	75 2/3	68	37	34	38	73
1997—	Seattle (A.L.)	3	8	.273	7.27	71	0	0	0	14	69 1/3	89	59	56	47	55
1998—	Baltimore (A.L.)■	2	1	.667	6.94	36	0	0	0	0	35	46	27	27	25	41
—	Richmond (Int'l)■	0	0	...	0.00	2	0	0	0	0	2	2	0	0	0	1
—	Atlanta (N.L.)	0	0	...	1.38	13	0	0	0	1	13	7	2	2	8	6
A.L. totals (5 years)		12	20	.375	4.60	241	0	0	0	66	262 1/3	248	147	134	143	275
N.L. totals (7 years)		33	29	.532	3.14	276	37	1	1	30	535 2/3	459	215	187	213	439
Major league totals (10 years)		45	49	.479	3.62	517	37	1	1	96	798	707	362	321	356	714

DIVISION SERIES RECORD

Year	Team (League)	W	L	Pct.	ERA	G	GS	CG	ShO	Sv.	IP	H	R	ER	BB	SO
1995—	Seattle (A.L.)	1	0	1.000	2.45	4	0	0	0	1	7 1/3	4	2	2	3	9
1997—	Seattle (A.L.)	0	0	...	0.00	2	0	0	0	0	2 1/3	2	0	0	0	1
Div. series totals (2 years)		1	0	1.000	1.86	6	0	0	0	1	9 2/3	6	2	2	3	10

CHAMPIONSHIP SERIES RECORD

Year	Team (League)	W	L	Pct.	ERA	G	GS	CG	ShO	Sv.	IP	H	R	ER	BB	SO
1990—	Cincinnati (N.L.)	1	1	.500	1.80	4	0	0	0	0	5	4	2	1	3	3
1995—	Seattle (A.L.)	1	0	1.000	0.00	3	0	0	0	1	6	1	0	0	1	5
Champ. series totals (2 years)		2	1	.667	0.82	7	0	0	0	1	11	5	2	1	4	8

WORLD SERIES RECORD

NOTES: Member of World Series championship team (1990).

Year	Team (League)	W	L	Pct.	ERA	G	GS	CG	ShO	Sv.	IP	H	R	ER	BB	SO
1990—	Cincinnati (N.L.)	0	0	...	0.00	2	0	0	0	0	1	1	0	0	0	0

ALL-STAR GAME RECORD

Year	League	W	L	Pct.	ERA	GS	CG	ShO	Sv.	IP	H	R	ER	BB	SO
1992—	National	0	0	...	0.00	0	0	0	0	1	0	0	0	0	1

C

CHAVEZ, ERIC 3B ATHLETICS

PERSONAL: Born December 7, 1977, in Los Angeles. ... 6-1/195. ... Bats left, throws right. ... Full name: Eric Cesar Chavez. ... Name pronounced SHAH-vez.

HIGH SCHOOL: Mount Carmel (San Diego).

TRANSACTIONS/CAREER NOTES: Selected by Oakland Athletics organization in first round (10th pick overall) of free-agent draft (June 2, 1996).

Year	Team (League)	Pos.	G	AB	R	H	2B	3B	HR	RBI	Avg.	BB	SO	SB	PO	A	E	Avg.
								BATTING							FIELDING			
1997—	Visalia (California)	3B	134	520	67	141	30	3	18	100	.271	37	91	13	84	268	*32	.917
1998—	Huntsville (Sou.)	3B	88	335	66	110	27	1	22	86	.328	42	61	12	54	146	14	.935
—	Edmonton (PCL)	3B	47	194	38	63	18	0	11	40	.325	12	32	2	34	66	7	.935
—	Oakland (A.L.)	3B	16	45	6	14	4	1	0	6	.311	3	5	1	11	21	0	1.000
Major league totals (1 year)			16	45	6	14	4	1	0	6	.311	3	5	1	11	21	0	1.000

CHAVEZ, RAUL C MARINERS

PERSONAL: Born March 18, 1973, in Valencia, Venezuela. ... 5-11/210. ... Bats right, throws right. ... Full name: Raul Alexander Chavez.

TRANSACTIONS/CAREER NOTES: Signed as non-drafted free agent by Houston Astros organization (January 10, 1990). ... Traded by Astros organization with P Dave Veres to Montreal Expos for 3B Sean Berry (December 20, 1995). ... Traded by Expos to Seattle Mariners for OF Robert Perez (May 8, 1998).

STATISTICAL NOTES: Tied for International League lead in double plays by catcher with nine in 1997. ... Led Pacific Coast League catchers with 12 double plays in 1998.

Year	Team (League)	Pos.	G	AB	R	H	2B	3B	HR	RBI	Avg.	BB	SO	SB	PO	A	E	Avg.
								BATTING							FIELDING			
1990—	GC Astros (GCL)	SS-2B-3B	48	155	23	50	8	1	0	23	.323	7	12	5	67	119	9	.954
1991—	Burlington (Midw.)	SS-3B	114	420	54	108	17	0	3	41	.257	25	65	1	144	293	41	.914
1992—	Asheville (S. Atl.)	C	95	348	37	99	22	1	2	40	.284	16	39	1	456	77	13	.976
1993—	Osceola (Fla. St.)	C	58	197	13	45	5	1	0	16	.228	8	19	1	303	62	5	.986

Year Team (League)	Pos.	G	AB	R	H	2B	3B	HR	RBI	Avg.	BB	SO	SB	PO	A	E	Avg.
1994— Jackson (Texas)	C	89	251	17	55	7	0	1	22	.219	17	41	1	*563	64	9	.986
1995— Tucson (PCL)	C	32	103	14	27	5	0	0	10	.262	8	13	0	203	39	5	.980
— Jackson (Texas)	C	58	188	16	54	8	0	4	25	.287	8	17	0	316	52	5	.987
1996— Ottawa (Int'l)■	C	60	198	15	49	10	0	2	24	.247	11	31	0	363	50	4	.990
— Montreal (N.L.)..........	C	4	5	1	1	0	0	0	0	.200	1	1	1	14	0	1	1.000
1997— Ottawa (Int'l)	C	92	310	31	76	17	0	4	46	.245	18	42	1	593	*77	*15	.978
— Montreal (N.L.)..........	C	13	26	0	7	0	0	0	2	.269	0	5	1	47	8	0	1.000
1998— Ottawa (Int'l)	C	11	31	2	7	0	0	0	1	.226	5	5	0	71	15	0	1.000
— Tacoma (PCL)■	C	76	233	27	52	6	0	4	34	.223	22	41	1	523	*70	6	.990
— Seattle (A.L.).	C	1	1	0	0	0	0	0	0	.000	0	0	0	3	0	0	1.000
American League totals (1 year)		1	1	0	0	0	0	0	0	.000	0	0	0	3	0	0	1.000
National League totals (2 years)		17	31	1	8	0	0	0	2	.258	1	6	2	61	8	1	1.000
Major league totals (3 years)		18	32	1	8	0	0	0	2	.250	1	6	2	64	8	0	1.000

CHECO, ROBINSON   P

PERSONAL: Born September 9, 1971, in Santo Domingo, Dominican Republic. ... 6-1/185. ... Throws right, bats right. ... Full name: Robinson Perez Checo. ... Name pronounced CHAY-co.

TRANSACTIONS/CAREER NOTES: Signed as non-drafted free agent by California Angels organization (January 22, 1989). ... Released by Angels (March 5, 1990). ... Played for Hiroshima Toyo Carp organization of Japan Central League (1995 and 1996), including minor league seasons in Japan Western League (1992 and 1993). ... Played in China (1994). ... Rights obtained by Boston Red Sox from Carp (December 4, 1996). ... Signed by Red Sox (December 6, 1996). ... On Boston disabled list (March 21-May 13, 1997). ... On Pawtucket disabled list (May 12-July 29, 1998). ... Granted free agency (December 21, 1998).

Year Team (League)	W	L	Pct.	ERA	G	GS	CG	ShO	Sv.	IP	H	R	ER	BB	SO
1989—					Dominican Summer League statistics unavailable.										
1995— Hiroshima (Jp. Cn.).....	15	8	.652	2.74	28	17	10	3		193²/₃	143	64	59	98	166
1996— Hiroshima (Jp. Cn.).....	4	1	.800	4.80	9	9	3	1	0	50²/₃	52	31	27	24	36
1997— Sarasota (Florida State)■...	1	4	.200	5.30	11	11	0	0	0	56	54	37	33	27	63
— Trenton (Eastern)	1	0	1.000	2.35	1	1	0	0	0	7²/₃	6	3	2	1	9
— Pawtucket (Int'l)	4	2	.667	3.42	9	9	2	1	0	55¹/₃	41	22	21	16	56
— Boston (A.L.)......................	1	1	.500	3.38	5	2	0	0	0	13¹/₃	12	5	5	3	14
1998— Pawtucket (Int'l)	6	2	.750	4.56	11	10	0	0	0	53¹/₃	48	30	27	26	46
— Boston (A.L.)......................	0	2	.000	9.39	2	2	0	0	0	7²/₃	11	8	8	5	5
— GC Red Sox (GCL)	1	0	1.000	3.00	3	3	0	0	0	9	9	5	3	0	13
— Sarasota (Florida State)......	0	1	.000	9.00	1	1	0	0	0	2	3	2	2	1	4
Major league totals (2 years)......	1	3	.250	5.57	7	4	0	0	0	21	23	13	13	8	19

CHEN, BRUCE   P   BRAVES

PERSONAL: Born June 19, 1977, in Panama City, Panama. ... 6-1/180. ... Throws left, bats both. ... Full name: Bruce Kastulo Chen.

HIGH SCHOOL: Instituto Panamericano (Panama).

TRANSACTIONS/CAREER NOTES: Signed as non-drafted free agent by Atlanta Braves organization (July 1, 1993).

HONORS: Named Southern League Most Outstanding Pitcher (1998).

Year Team (League)	W	L	Pct.	ERA	G	GS	CG	ShO	Sv.	IP	H	R	ER	BB	SO
1994— GC Braves (GCL)..............	1	4	.200	3.80	9	7	0	0	1	42²/₃	42	21	18	3	26
1995— Danville (Appalachian)........	4	4	.500	3.97	14	13	1	0	0	70¹/₃	78	42	31	19	56
1996— Eugene (Northwest)	4	1	.800	2.27	11	8	0	0	0	35²/₃	23	13	9	14	55
1997— Macon (S. Atl.).................	12	7	.632	3.51	28	28	1	1	0	146¹/₃	120	67	57	44	182
1998— Greenville (Southern)	13	7	.650	3.29	24	23	1	0	0	139¹/₃	106	57	51	48	164
— Richmond (Int'l)	2	1	.667	1.88	4	4	0	0	0	24	17	5	5	19	29
— Atlanta (N.L.)......................	2	0	1.000	3.98	4	4	0	0	0	20¹/₃	23	9	9	9	17
Major league totals (1 year)........	2	0	1.000	3.98	4	4	0	0	0	20¹/₃	23	9	9	9	17

CHO, JIN HO   P   RED SOX

PERSONAL: Born August 16, 1975, in Jun Ju City, Korea. ... 6-3/210. ... Throws right, bats right.

TRANSACTIONS/CAREER NOTES: Signed as non-drafted free agent by Boston Red Sox organization (March 30, 1998).

MISCELLANEOUS: Member of 1996 South Korean Olympic team.

Year Team (League)	W	L	Pct.	ERA	G	GS	CG	ShO	Sv.	IP	H	R	ER	BB	SO
1998— Sarasota (Florida State)......	3	1	.750	3.09	5	5	0	0	0	32	33	14	11	5	30
— Trenton (Eastern)	5	2	.714	2.19	13	13	1	1	0	74	59	21	18	19	62
— Boston (A.L.)......................	0	3	.000	8.20	4	4	0	0	0	18²/₃	28	17	17	3	15
Major league totals (1 year)........	0	3	.000	8.20	4	4	0	0	0	18²/₃	28	17	17	3	15

CHOUINARD, BOBBY   P   DIAMONDBACKS

PERSONAL: Born May 1, 1972, in Manilla, The Phillipines. ... 6-1/185. ... Throws right, bats right. ... Full name: Robert William Chouinard.

HIGH SCHOOL: Forest Grove (Ore.).

TRANSACTIONS/CAREER NOTES: Selected by Baltimore Orioles organization in fifth round of free-agent draft (June 4, 1990). ... Traded by Orioles with P Allen Plaster to Oakland Athletics organization for OF Harold Baines (January 14, 1993). ... Granted free agency (October 15, 1997). ... Signed by Milwaukee Brewers organization (October 31, 1997). ... Claimed on waivers by Arizona Diamondbacks (June 1, 1998). ... On Arizona disabled list (August 22-September 8, 1998); included rehabilitation assignment to Tucson (September 6-8).

Year Team (League)	W	L	Pct.	ERA	G	GS	CG	ShO	Sv.	IP	H	R	ER	BB	SO
1990— Bluefield (Appalachian)	2	5	.286	3.70	10	10	2	1	0	56	61	34	23	14	30
1991— Kane County (Midwest)......	2	4	.333	4.64	6	6	0	0	0	33	45	24	17	5	17
— Bluefield (Appalachian)	5	1	.833	3.48	6	6	0	0	0	33²/₃	44	19	13	11	31
1992— Kane County (Midwest)...	10	14	.417	*2.08	26	26	*9	•2	0	181²/₃	151	60	42	38	112
1993— Modesto (California)■	8	10	.444	4.26	24	24	1	0	0	145²/₃	154	75	69	56	82
1994— Modesto (California)	12	5	.706	2.59	29	20	0	0	3	145²/₃	147	53	42	32	74
1995— Huntsville (Southern)	14	8	.636	3.62	29	*29	1	1	0	166²/₃	155	81	67	50	106
1996—Edmonton (PCL)	10	2	.833	2.77	15	15	0	0	0	84¹/₃	70	32	26	24	45
— Oakland (A.L.)	4	2	.667	6.10	13	11	0	0	0	59	75	41	40	32	32
1997— Edmonton (PCL)	6	6	.500	6.03	25	21	1	0	0	100	129	80	67	26	58
1998—Louisville (Int'l)■	2	1	.667	4.93	7	7	0	0	0	42	52	31	23	15	33
— Milwaukee (N.L.)	0	0	...	3.00	1	0	0	0	0	3	5	1	1	0	1
— Tucson (PCL)■	0	0	...	4.26	4	0	0	0	1	6¹/₃	6	3	3	0	6
— Arizona (N.L.)...................	0	2	.000	4.23	26	2	0	0	0	38¹/₃	41	23	18	11	26
A.L. totals (1 year)	4	2	.667	6.10	13	11	0	0	0	59	75	41	40	32	32
N.L. totals (1 year)......................	0	2	.000	4.14	27	2	0	0	0	41¹/₃	46	24	19	11	27
Major league totals (2 years)......	4	4	.500	5.29	40	13	0	0	0	100¹/₃	121	65	59	43	59

CHRISTENSEN, McKAY   OF   WHITE SOX

C

PERSONAL: Born August 14, 1975, in Upland, Calif. ... 5-11/180. ... Bats left, throws left. ... Full name: McKay A. Christensen.
HIGH SCHOOL: Clovis West (Fresno, Calif.).
TRANSACTIONS/CAREER NOTES: Selected by California Angels organization in first round (sixth pick overall) of free-agent draft (June 2, 1994). ... Traded by Angels with P Andrew Lorraine, P Bill Simas and P John Snyder to Chicago White Sox for P Jim Abbott and P Tim Fortugno (July 27, 1995). ... On disabled list (April 10-28 and June 2-17, 1998).
STATISTICAL NOTES: Tied for Carolina League lead with three double plays by outfielder in 1998.

							BATTING							FIELDING		
Year Team (League)	Pos.	G	AB	R	H	2B	3B	HR	RBI	Avg.	BB	SO	SB	PO	A	E	Avg.
1996— GC Whi. Sox (GCL)	OF	35	133	17	35	7	5	1	16	.263	10	23	10	54	2	1	.982
— Hickory (S. Atl.)	OF	6	11	0	0	0	0	0	0	.000	1	4	0	4	0	0	1.000
1997— Hickory (S. Atl.)	OF	127	503	95	141	12	*12	5	47	.280	52	81	28	*280	5	9	.969
1998— Win.-Salem (Car.).......	OF	95	361	69	103	17	6	4	32	.285	53	54	20	199	6	4	.981

CHRISTENSON, RYAN   OF   ATHLETICS

PERSONAL: Born March 28, 1974, in Redlands, Calif. ... 5-11/175. ... Bats right, throws right. ... Full name: Ryan Alan Christenson.
HIGH SCHOOL: Apple Valley (Calif.).
COLLEGE: Pepperdine.
TRANSACTIONS/CAREER NOTES: Selected by Oakland Athletics organization in 10th round of free-agent draft (June 1, 1995).

							BATTING							FIELDING		
Year Team (League)	Pos.	G	AB	R	H	2B	3B	HR	RBI	Avg.	BB	SO	SB	PO	A	E	Avg.
1995— S. Oregon (N'west).....	OF	49	158	14	30	4	1	1	16	.190	22	33	5	84	3	2	.978
1996— S. Oregon (N'west).....	OF	36	136	31	39	11	0	5	21	.287	19	21	8	78	5	4	.954
— W. Mich. (Mid.)	OF-3B	33	122	21	38	2	2	2	18	.311	13	22	2	64	1	3	.956
1997— Visalia (California)......	OF	83	308	69	90	18	8	13	54	.292	70	72	20	164	4	3	.982
— Huntsville (Sou.)	OF	29	120	39	44	9	3	2	18	.367	24	23	5	81	1	1	.988
1998— Edmonton (PCL)	OF	16	49	12	14	2	2	2	5	.286	11	11	2	42	1	0	1.000
— Edmonton (PCL)	OF	22	88	17	23	6	1	1	7	.261	15	24	4	56	2	0	1.000
— Oakland (A.L.)	OF	117	370	56	95	22	2	5	40	.257	36	106	5	284	7	5	.983
Major league totals (1 year)		117	370	56	95	22	2	5	40	.257	36	106	5	284	7	5	.983

CHRISTIANSEN, JASON   P   PIRATES

PERSONAL: Born September 21, 1969, in Omaha, Neb. ... 6-5/242. ... Throws left, bats right. ... Full name: Jason Samuel Christiansen.
HIGH SCHOOL: Elkhorn (Neb.).
JUNIOR COLLEGE: Iowa Western College.
COLLEGE: Cameron (Okla.).
TRANSACTIONS/CAREER NOTES: Signed as non-drafted free agent by Pittsburgh Pirates organization (July 5, 1991). ... On Calgary disabled list (August 12-September 5, 1996). ... On Pittsburgh disabled list (March 31-June 19, 1997).

Year Team (League)	W	L	Pct.	ERA	G	GS	CG	ShO	Sv.	IP	H	R	ER	BB	SO
1991— GC Pirates (GCL)...............	1	0	1.000	0.00	6	0	0	0	0	8	4	0	0	1	8
— Welland (N.Y.-Penn)..........	0	1	.000	2.53	8	1	0	0	0	21¹/₃	15	9	6	12	17
1992— Augusta (S. Atl.)...............	1	0	1.000	1.80	10	0	0	0	2	20	12	4	4	8	21
— Salem (Carolina)..............	3	1	.750	3.24	38	0	0	0	2	50	47	20	18	22	59
1993— Salem (Carolina)..............	1	1	.500	3.15	57	0	0	0	4	71¹/₃	48	30	25	24	70
— Carolina (Southern)...........	0	0	...	0.00	2	0	0	0	0	2²/₃	3	0	0	1	2
1994— Carolina (Southern)...........	2	1	.667	2.09	28	0	0	0	2	38²/₃	30	10	9	14	43
— Buffalo (A.A.)................	3	1	.750	2.41	33	0	0	0	0	33²/₃	19	9	9	16	39
1995— Pittsburgh (N.L.)..............	1	3	.250	4.15	63	0	0	0	0	56¹/₃	49	28	26	34	53
1996— Calgary (PCL).................	1	0	1.000	3.27	2	2	0	0	0	11	9	4	4	1	10
— Pittsburgh (N.L.)............	3	3	.500	6.70	33	0	0	0	0	44¹/₃	56	34	33	19	38
1997— Pittsburgh (N.L.)............	3	0	1.000	2.94	39	0	0	0	0	33²/₃	37	11	11	17	37
— Carolina (Southern)..........	0	1	.000	4.20	8	1	0	0	1	15	17	7	7	5	25
1998— Pittsburgh (N.L.)	3	3	.500	2.51	60	0	0	0	6	64²/₃	51	22	18	27	71
Major league totals (4 years)......	10	9	.526	3.98	195	0	0	0	6	199	193	95	88	97	199

PERSONAL: Born October 6, 1966, in Rome, N.Y. ... 6-5/215. ... Bats right, throws right. ... Full name: Angelo Dominic Cianfrocco. ... Name pronounced AR-kee SEE-un-FROCK-oh.
HIGH SCHOOL: Rome (N.Y.) Free Academy.
JUNIOR COLLEGE: Onondaga Community College (N.Y.).
COLLEGE: Purdue.
TRANSACTIONS/CAREER NOTES: Selected by Pittsburgh Pirates organization in 11th round of free-agent draft (January 14, 1986); did not sign. ... Selected by Pirates organization in secondary phase of free-agent draft (June 2, 1986); did not sign. ... Selected by Montreal Expos organization in fifth round of free-agent draft (June 2, 1987). ... On disabled list (June 27, 1990-remainder of season). ... On Ottawa disabled list (June 3-10, 1993). ... Traded by Expos to San Diego Padres for P Tim Scott (June 23, 1993). ... Released by Padres (November 28, 1994). ... Re-signed by Padres organization (December 1, 1994). ... On disabled list (May 6-21 and July 7-23, 1996). ... On San Diego disabled list (May 21-June 19, 1998); included rehabilitation assignment to Las Vegas (May 31-June 9). ... Released by Padres (November 17, 1998).
STATISTICAL NOTES: Led Southern League third basemen with 37 errors in 1989. ... Led Eastern League in being hit by pitch with nine in 1991. ... Led Eastern League first basemen with 95 assists and 110 double plays in 1991. ... Career major league grand slams: 1.

Year Team (League)	Pos.	G	AB	R	H	2B	3B	HR	RBI	Avg.	BB	SO	SB	PO	A	E	Avg.
1987—Jamestown (NYP)	2B-SS-1B	70	251	28	62	8	4	2	27	.247	9	59	2	125	179	22	.933
1988—Rockford (Midwest)	3B	126	455	54	115	34	0	15	65	.253	26	99	6	94	240	29	*.920
1989—Jacksonville (Sou.)	3B-2B-1B	132	429	46	105	22	7	7	50	.245	37	126	3	99	221	†38	.894
1990—Jacksonville (Sou.)	1B-3B-OF	62	196	18	43	10	0	5	29	.219	12	45	0	244	54	7	.977
1991—Harrisburg (East.)	1B-OF	124	456	71	144	21	•10	9	77	.316	38	112	11	1023	†95	11	.990
1992—Montreal (N.L.)	1B-3B-OF	86	232	25	56	5	2	6	30	.241	11	66	3	387	66	8	.983
—Indianapolis (A.A.)	1B-3B-SS	15	59	12	18	3	0	4	16	.305	5	15	1	62	14	5	.938
1993—Montreal (N.L.)	1B	12	17	3	4	1	0	1	1	.235	0	5	0	45	2	0	1.000
—Ottawa (Int'l)	OF-1B-3B	50	188	21	56	14	2	4	27	.298	7	33	4	188	26	3	.986
—San Diego (N.L.)■	3B-1B	84	279	27	68	10	2	11	47	.244	17	64	2	198	95	10	.967
1994—San Diego (N.L.)	3B-1B-SS	59	146	9	32	8	0	4	13	.219	3	39	2	58	67	7	.947
—Las Vegas (PCL)	3B	32	112	11	34	11	1	1	21	.304	12	23	0	43	6	2	.961
1995—Las Vegas (PCL)	1-3-O-C	89	322	51	100	20	2	10	58	.311	16	61	5	412	100	17	.968
—San Diego (N.L.)	1-S-O-2-3	51	118	22	31	7	0	5	31	.263	11	28	0	111	50	3	.982
1996—San Diego (N.L.)	1-3-S-O-2-C	79	192	21	54	13	3	2	32	.281	8	56	1	195	51	3	.988
1997—San Diego (N.L.)	1-3-2-S-O	89	220	25	54	12	0	4	26	.245	25	80	7	262	116	7	.982
1998—San Diego (N.L.)	1-3-2-O	40	72	4	9	3	0	1	5	.125	5	22	1	103	26	3	.977
—Las Vegas (PCL)	3-1-O-C-2-S	38	127	15	36	8	1	6	16	.283	11	35	3	119	34	4	.975
Major league totals (7 years)		500	1276	136	308	59	7	34	185	.241	80	360	16	1359	473	41	.978

DIVISION SERIES RECORD

Year Team (League)	Pos.	G	AB	R	H	2B	3B	HR	RBI	Avg.	BB	SO	SB	PO	A	E	Avg.
1996—San Diego (N.L.)	1B	3	3	1	1	0	0	0	0	.333	0	1	0	8	2	0	1.000

CIRILLO, JEFF   3B   BREWERS

PERSONAL: Born September 23, 1969, in Pasadena, Calif. ... 6-0/195. ... Bats right, throws right. ... Full name: Jeffrey Howard Cirillo.
HIGH SCHOOL: Providence (Burbank, Calif.).
COLLEGE: Southern California.
TRANSACTIONS/CAREER NOTES: Selected by Chicago Cubs organization in 37th round of free-agent draft (June 2, 1987); did not sign. ... Selected by Milwaukee Brewers organization in 11th round of free-agent draft (June 3, 1991). ... On New Orleans disabled list (July 22-August 6, 1993).
RECORDS: Shares N.L. single-season record for most double plays by third baseman—45 (1998).
STATISTICAL NOTES: Led Pioneer League in grounding into double plays with 11 in 1991. ... Led Pioneer League third basemen with 60 putouts, 104 assists and 179 total chances in 1991. ... Tied for Midwest League lead with six intentional bases on balls received in 1992. ... Led A.L. third basemen with 463 total chances and 29 double plays in 1997. ... Led N.L. in grounding into double plays with 26 in 1998. ... Led N.L. third basemen with 340 assists and 45 double plays in 1998. ... Career major league grand slams: 1.

Year Team (League)	Pos.	G	AB	R	H	2B	3B	HR	RBI	Avg.	BB	SO	SB	PO	A	E	Avg.
1991—Helena (Pioneer)	3B-OF	•70	286	60	100	16	2	10	51	.350	31	28	3	†71	†104	15	.921
1992—Stockton (California)	3B	7	27	2	6	1	0	0	5	.222	2	0	0	7	10	0	1.000
—Beloit (Midwest)	3B-2B	126	444	65	135	27	3	9	71	.304	84	85	21	115	309	26	.942
1993—El Paso (Texas)	2B-3B	67	249	53	85	16	2	9	41	.341	26	37	2	83	142	9	.962
—New Orleans (A.A.)	3B-2B-SS	58	215	31	63	13	2	3	32	.293	29	33	2	46	145	5	.974
1994—New Orleans (A.A.)	3B-2B-SS	61	236	45	73	18	2	10	46	.309	28	39	4	67	139	8	.963
—Milwaukee (A.L.)	3B-2B	39	126	17	30	9	0	3	12	.238	11	16	0	23	60	3	.965
1995—Milwaukee (A.L.)	3-2-1-S	125	328	57	91	19	4	9	39	.277	47	42	7	113	230	15	.958
1996—Milwaukee (A.L.)	3-DH-1-2	158	566	101	184	46	5	15	83	.325	58	69	4	112	242	18	.952
1997—Milwaukee (A.L.)	3B-DH	154	580	74	167	46	2	10	82	.288	60	74	4	•126	*320	17	.963
1998—Milwaukee (N.L.)	3B-1B	156	604	97	194	31	1	14	68	.321	79	88	10	149	†353	11	.979
American League totals (4 years)		476	1600	249	472	120	11	37	216	.295	176	201	15	374	852	53	.959
National League totals (1 year)		156	604	97	194	31	1	14	68	.321	79	88	10	149	353	11	.979
Major league totals (5 years)		632	2204	346	666	151	12	51	284	.302	255	289	25	523	1205	64	.964

ALL-STAR GAME RECORD

Year League	Pos.	AB	R	H	2B	3B	HR	RBI	Avg.	BB	SO	SB	PO	A	E	Avg.
1997—American	3B	1	0	0	0	0	0	0	.000	0	1	0	0	0	0	...

PERSONAL: Born September 3, 1962, in Tupelo, Miss. ... 6-2/210. ... Bats left, throws right. ... Full name: David Earl Clark. ... Brother of Louis Clark, wide receiver with Seattle Seahawks (1987-92).
HIGH SCHOOL: Shannon (Miss.).
COLLEGE: Jackson State (degree in marketing and management).
TRANSACTIONS/CAREER NOTES: Selected by Cleveland Indians organization in first round (11th pick overall) of free-agent draft (June 6, 1983). ... Traded by Indians to Chicago Cubs for OF Mitch Webster (November 20, 1989). ... Released by Cubs (April 1, 1991). ... Signed by Omaha, Kansas City Royals organization (April 29, 1991). ... Released by Royals (December 20, 1991). ... Signed by Pittsburgh Pirates organization (January 29, 1992). ... On Buffalo disabled list (May 11-18, 1992). ... On disabled list (July 26-September 11, 1995). ... Traded by Pirates to Los Angeles Dodgers for P Carl South (August 31, 1996). ... Granted free agency (October 28, 1996). ... Signed by Cubs organization (January 29, 1997). ... Granted free agency (October 27, 1997). ... Signed by Houston Astros (November 24, 1997).
HONORS: Named outfielder on THE SPORTING NEWS college All-America team (1983).

								BATTING							FIELDING		
Year Team (League)	Pos.	G	AB	R	H	2B	3B	HR	RBI	Avg.	BB	SO	SB	PO	A	E	Avg.
1983—Waterloo (Midw.)	OF	58	159	20	44	8	1	4	20	.277	19	32	2	37	4	1	.976
1984—Waterloo (Midw.)	OF	110	363	74	112	16	3	15	63	.309	57	68	20	128	10	4	.972
—Buffalo (Eastern)	OF	17	56	12	10	1	0	3	10	.179	9	13	1	23	2	1	.962
1985—Waterbury (Eastern) ...	OF	132	463	75	140	24	7	12	64	.302	86	79	27	204	11	11	.951
1986—Maine (Int'l)	OF	106	355	56	99	17	2	19	58	.279	52	70	6	150	4	6	.963
—Cleveland (A.L.)	OF-DH	18	58	10	16	1	0	3	9	.276	7	11	1	26	0	0	1.000
1987—Buffalo (A.A.)	OF	108	420	83	143	22	3	30	80	.340	52	62	14	181	*22	6	.971
—Cleveland (A.L.)	OF-DH	29	87	11	18	5	0	3	12	.207	2	24	1	24	1	0	1.000
1988—Cleveland (A.L.)	DH-OF	63	156	11	41	4	1	3	18	.263	17	28	0	36	0	2	.947
—Colo. Springs (PCL) ...	OF	47	165	27	49	10	2	4	31	.297	27	37	4	85	6	3	.968
1989—Cleveland (A.L.)	DH-OF	102	253	21	60	12	0	8	29	.237	30	63	0	27	0	1	.964
1990—Chicago (N.L.)■........	OF	84	171	22	47	4	2	5	20	.275	8	40	7	60	2	0	1.000
1991—Omaha (A.A.)■	OF-1B	104	359	45	108	24	3	13	64	.301	30	53	6	264	11	4	.986
—Kansas City (A.L.)	OF-DH	11	10	1	2	0	0	0	1	.200	1	1	0	0	0	0	...
1992—Buffalo (A.A.)■	OF-1B	78	253	43	77	17	6	11	55	.304	34	51	6	171	6	6	.967
—Pittsburgh (N.L.)	OF	23	33	3	7	0	0	2	7	.212	6	8	0	10	0	0	1.000
1993—Pittsburgh (N.L.)	OF	110	277	43	75	11	2	11	46	.271	38	58	1	132	3	6	.957
1994—Pittsburgh (N.L.)	OF	86	223	37	66	11	1	10	46	.296	22	48	2	107	5	3	.974
1995—Pittsburgh (N.L.)	OF	77	196	30	55	6	0	4	24	.281	24	38	3	98	1	4	.961
1996—Pittsburgh (N.L.)	OF	92	211	28	58	12	2	8	35	.275	31	51	2	80	3	1	.988
—Los Angeles (N.L.)■..	OF	15	15	0	3	0	0	0	1	.200	3	2	0	0	0	0	...
1997—Chicago (N.L.)■........	OF-DH	102	143	19	43	8	0	5	32	.301	19	34	1	39	2	2	.953
1998—Houston (N.L.)■........	OF-DH	93	131	12	27	7	0	0	4	.206	14	45	1	22	1	3	.885
American League totals (5 years)		223	564	54	137	22	1	17	69	.243	57	127	2	113	1	3	.974
National League totals (8 years)		682	1400	194	381	59	7	45	215	.272	165	324	17	548	17	19	.967
Major league totals (13 years)		905	1964	248	518	81	8	62	284	.264	222	451	19	661	18	22	.969

DIVISION SERIES RECORD

								BATTING							FIELDING		
Year Team (League)	Pos.	G	AB	R	H	2B	3B	HR	RBI	Avg.	BB	SO	SB	PO	A	E	Avg.
1996—Los Angeles (N.L.)	PH	2	2	0	0	0	0	0	0	.000	0	2	0	...	...	...	...
1998—Houston (N.L.)	PH	2	0	0	0	0	0	0	0	...	2	0	0	...	...	...	...
Division series totals (2 years)		4	2	0	0	0	0	0	0	.000	2	2	0	...	...	...	...

PERSONAL: Born May 12, 1968, in Bath, Ill. ... 6-5/235. ... Throws right, bats right. ... Full name: Mark Willard Clark.
HIGH SCHOOL: Balyki (Bath, Ill.).
JUNIOR COLLEGE: Lincoln Land Community College (Ill.).
TRANSACTIONS/CAREER NOTES: Selected by St. Louis Cardinals organization in ninth round of free-agent draft (June 1, 1988). ... On Arkansas disabled list (April 12-May 8, 1991). ... Traded by Cardinals with SS Juan Andujar to Cleveland Indians for OF Mark Whiten (March 31, 1993). ... On Cleveland disabled list (July 17-September 9, 1993 and July 21, 1994-remainder of season). ... Traded by Indians to New York Mets for P Reid Cornelius and OF Ryan Thompson (March 31, 1996). ... Traded by Mets to Chicago Cubs (August 8, 1997), as part of deal in which Mets traded OF Lance Johnson and two players to be named later to Cubs for OF Brian McRae, P Mel Rojas and P Turk Wendell (August 11, 1997); Mets traded IF Manny Alexander to Cubs to complete deal (August 14). ... Granted free agency (October 28, 1998). ... Signed by Texas Rangers (December 10, 1998).

Year Team (League)	W	L	Pct.	ERA	G	GS	CG	ShO	Sv.	IP	H	R	ER	BB	SO
1988—Hamilton (NYP)	6	7	.462	3.05	15	15	2	0	0	94 1/3	88	39	32	32	60
1989—Savannah (S. Atl.)	•14	9	.609	2.44	27	27	4	2	0	173 2/3	143	61	47	52	132
1990—St. Petersburg (FSL)	3	2	.600	3.05	10	10	1	1	0	62	63	33	21	14	58
—Arkansas (Texas)	5	11	.313	3.82	19	19	*5	0	0	115 1/3	111	66	49	37	87
1991—Arkansas (Texas)	5	5	.500	4.00	15	15	4	1	0	92 1/3	99	50	41	30	76
—Louisville (A.A.)	3	2	.600	2.98	7	6	1	1	0	45 1/3	43	17	15	15	29
—St. Louis (N.L.)	1	1	.500	4.03	7	2	0	0	0	22 1/3	17	10	10	11	13
1992—Louisville (A.A.)	4	4	.500	2.80	9	9	4	*3	0	61	56	20	19	15	38
—St. Louis (N.L.)	3	10	.231	4.45	20	20	1	1	0	113 1/3	117	59	56	36	44
1993—Cleveland (A.L.)■	7	5	.583	4.28	26	15	1	0	0	109 1/3	119	55	52	25	57
—Charlotte (Int'l)	1	0	1.000	2.08	2	2	0	0	0	13	9	5	3	2	12
1994—Cleveland (A.L.)■	11	3	.786	3.82	20	20	4	1	0	127 1/3	133	61	54	40	60
1995—Cleveland (A.L.)	9	7	.563	5.27	22	21	0	0	0	124 2/3	143	77	73	42	68
—Buffalo (A.A.)	4	0	1.000	3.57	5	5	0	0	0	35 1/3	39	14	14	10	17
1996—New York (N.L.)■	14	11	.560	3.43	32	32	2	0	0	212 1/3	217	98	81	48	142

Year Team (League)	W	L	Pct.	ERA	G	GS	CG	ShO	Sv.	IP	H	R	ER	BB	SO
1997— New York (N.L.)	8	7	.533	4.25	23	22	1	0	0	142	158	74	67	47	72
— Chicago (N.L.)■	6	1	.857	2.86	9	9	2	0	0	63	55	22	20	12	51
1998— Chicago (N.L.)	9	14	.391	4.84	33	33	2	1	0	$213\frac{2}{3}$	236	116	115	48	161
A.L. totals (3 years)	27	15	.643	4.46	68	56	7	1	0	$361\frac{1}{3}$	395	193	179	107	185
N.L. totals (5 years)	41	44	.482	4.10	124	118	8	2	0	$766\frac{2}{3}$	800	379	349	202	483
Major league totals (8 years)	68	59	.535	4.21	192	174	15	3	0	1128	1195	572	528	309	668

DIVISION SERIES RECORD

Year Team (League)	W	L	Pct.	ERA	G	GS	CG	ShO	Sv.	IP	H	R	ER	BB	SO
1998— Chicago (N.L.)	0	1	.000	3.00	1	1	0	0	0	6	7	4	2	1	4

CLARK, TONY — 1B — TIGERS

PERSONAL: Born June 15, 1972, in Newton, Kan. ... 6-7/245. ... Bats both, throws right. ... Full name: Anthony Christopher Clark.
HIGH SCHOOL: Valhalla (El Cajon, Calif.), then Christian (El Cajon, Calif.).
COLLEGE: Arizona (did not play baseball), then San Diego State.
TRANSACTIONS/CAREER NOTES: Selected by Detroit Tigers organization in first round (second pick overall) of free-agent draft (June 4, 1990). ... On Niagara Falls temporarily inactive list (June 17, 1991-remainder of season and August 17, 1992-remainder of season). ... On disabled list (August 24, 1993-remainder of season).
RECORDS: Holds A.L. single-season record for most games with switch-hit home runs—3 (1998).
STATISTICAL NOTES: Switch-hit home runs in one game four times (April 5, 1997; and June 17, July 26 and August 1, 1998). ... Led A.L. first basemen with 1,533 total chances in 1997. ... Career major league grand slams: 1.

							— BATTING —						— FIELDING —		
Year Team (League)	Pos.	G	AB	R	H	2B	3B	HR	RBI	Avg.	BB	SO	SB	PO	A	E	Avg.
1990— Bristol (Appal.)	OF	25	73	2	12	2	0	1	8	.164	6	28	0	23	3	0	1.000
1991—								Did not play.									
1992— Niagara Falls (NYP)	OF	27	85	12	26	9	0	5	17	.306	9	34	1	18	1	0	1.000
1993— Lakeland (Fla. St.)	OF	36	117	14	31	4	1	1	22	.265	18	32	0	34	0	2	.944
1994— Trenton (Eastern)	1B	107	394	50	110	25	0	21	86	.279	40	113	0	505	48	•13	.977
— Toledo (Int'l)	1B	25	92	10	24	4	0	2	13	.261	12	25	2	144	12	0	1.000
1995— Toledo (Int'l)	1B	110	405	50	98	17	2	14	63	.242	52	*129	0	615	51	*13	.981
— Detroit (A.L.)	1B	27	101	10	24	5	1	3	11	.238	8	30	0	253	18	4	.985
1996— Toledo (Int'l)	1B	55	194	42	58	7	1	14	36	.299	31	58	1	400	28	3	.993
— Detroit (A.L.)	1B-DH	100	376	56	94	14	0	27	72	.250	29	127	0	766	54	6	.993
1997— Detroit (A.L.)	1B-DH	159	580	105	160	28	3	32	117	.276	93	144	1	*1423	100	10	.993
1998— Detroit (A.L.)	1B-DH	157	602	84	175	37	0	34	103	.291	63	128	3	1265	102	13	.991
Major league totals (4 years)		443	1659	255	453	84	4	96	303	.273	193	429	4	3707	274	33	.992

CLARK, WILL — 1B — ORIOLES

PERSONAL: Born March 13, 1964, in New Orleans. ... 6-1/200. ... Bats left, throws left. ... Full name: William Nuschler Clark Jr.
HIGH SCHOOL: Jesuit (New Orleans).
COLLEGE: Mississippi State.
TRANSACTIONS/CAREER NOTES: Selected by Kansas City Royals organization in fourth round of free-agent draft (June 7, 1982); did not sign. ... Selected by San Francisco Giants organization in first round (second pick overall) of free-agent draft (June 3, 1985). ... On San Francisco disabled list (June 4-July 24, 1986); included rehabilitation assignment to Phoenix (July 7-24). ... On disabled list (August 26-September 10, 1993). ... Granted free agency (October 25, 1993). ... Signed by Texas Rangers (November 22, 1993). ... On Texas disabled list (June 8-23, June 30-July 14 and July 17-August 4, 1996); included rehabilitation assignment to Tulsa (August 1-4). ... On disabled list (March 28-April 18 and August 25, 1997-remainder of season). ... Granted free agency (November 5, 1998). ... Signed by Baltimore Orioles (December 7, 1998).
HONORS: Named designated hitter on The Sporting News college All-America team (1984). ... Named Golden Spikes Award winner by USA Baseball (1985). ... Named first baseman on The Sporting News college All-America team (1985). ... Named first baseman on The Sporting News N.L. All-Star team (1988-89 and 1991). ... Named first baseman on The Sporting News N.L. Silver Slugger team (1989 and 1991). ... Won N.L. Gold Glove at first base (1991).
STATISTICAL NOTES: Led N.L. first basemen with 130 double plays in 1987, 126 in 1988, 118 in 1990, 115 in 1991 and 130 in 1992. ... Led N.L. with 27 intentional bases on balls received in 1988. ... Led N.L. first basemen with 1,608 total chances in 1988, 1,566 in 1989 and 1,587 in 1990. ... Led N.L. with .536 slugging percentage and tied for lead with 303 total bases in 1991. ... Led A.L. first basemen with 1,051 total chances in 1994. ... Had 16-game hitting streak (August 22-September 7, 1998). ... Career major league grand slams: 3.
MISCELLANEOUS: Member of 1984 U.S. Olympic baseball team. ... Hit home run in first minor league at-bat (June 21, 1985) and first major league at-bat (April 8, 1986); both were on first swing.

							— BATTING —						— FIELDING —		
Year Team (League)	Pos.	G	AB	R	H	2B	3B	HR	RBI	Avg.	BB	SO	SB	PO	A	E	Avg.
1985— Fresno (California)	1B-OF	65	217	41	67	14	0	10	48	.309	62	46	11	523	51	6	.990
1986— San Francisco (N.L.)	1B	111	408	66	117	27	2	11	41	.287	34	76	4	942	72	11	.989
— Phoenix (PCL)	DH	6	20	3	5	0	0	0	1	.250	4	2	1	...	...	...	...
1987— San Francisco (N.L.)	1B	150	529	89	163	29	5	35	91	.308	49	98	5	1253	103	13	.991
1988— San Francisco (N.L.)	1B	*162	575	102	162	31	6	29	*109	.282	*100	129	9	*1492	104	12	.993
1989— San Francisco (N.L.)	1B	159	588	•104	196	38	9	23	111	.333	74	103	8	*1445	111	10	.994
1990— San Francisco (N.L.)	1B	154	600	91	177	25	5	19	95	.295	62	97	8	*1456	119	12	.992
1991— San Francisco (N.L.)	1B	148	565	84	170	32	7	29	116	.301	51	91	4	1273	110	4	*.997
1992— San Francisco (N.L.)	1B	144	513	69	154	40	1	16	73	.300	73	82	12	1275	105	10	.993
1993— San Francisco (N.L.)	1B	132	491	82	139	27	2	14	73	.283	63	68	2	1078	88	14	.988
1994— Texas (A.L.)■	1B-DH	110	389	73	128	24	2	13	80	.329	71	59	5	*968	73	•10	.990
1995— Texas (A.L.)	1B-DH	123	454	85	137	27	3	16	92	.302	68	50	0	1076	88	7	.994
1996— Texas (A.L.)	1B	117	436	69	124	25	1	13	72	.284	64	67	2	956	73	4	.996
— Tulsa (Texas)	1B	3	9	3	2	0	0	0	0	.222	2	0	0	21	3	0	1.000
1997— Texas (A.L.)	1B-DH	110	393	56	128	29	1	12	51	.326	49	62	0	880	62	4	.996
1998— Texas (A.L.)	1B-DH	149	554	98	169	41	1	23	102	.305	72	97	1	1079	73	13	.989
American League totals (5 years)		609	2226	381	686	146	8	77	397	.308	324	335	8	4959	369	38	.993
National League totals (8 years)		1160	4269	687	1278	249	37	176	709	.299	506	744	52	10214	812	86	.992
Major league totals (13 years)		1769	6495	1068	1964	395	45	253	1106	.302	830	1079	60	15173	1181	124	.992

DIVISION SERIES RECORD

							BATTING								FIELDING		
Year	Team (League)	Pos.	G	AB	R	H	2B	3B	HR	RBI	Avg.	BB	SO	SB	PO	A	E	Avg.
1996— Texas (A.L.)		1B	4	16	1	2	0	0	0	0	.125	4	2	0	35	4	0	1.000
1998— Texas (A.L.)		1B	3	11	0	1	0	0	0	0	.091	1	2	0	21	2	0	1.000
Division series totals (2 years)			7	27	1	3	0	0	0	0	.111	5	4	0	56	6	0	1.000

CHAMPIONSHIP SERIES RECORD

RECORDS: Holds single-series record for most hits—13. ... Shares single-series record for most total bases—24 (1989). ... Holds single-game record for most runs batted in—6 (October 4, 1989). ... Shares single-game record for most runs—4; and most grand slams—1 (October 4, 1989). ... Shares single-inning record for most runs batted in—4 (October 4, 1989, fourth inning). ... Shares N.L. single-series record for most consecutive hits—5 (1989). ... Shares N.L. single-game record for most hits—4 (October 4, 1989).

NOTES: Named N.L. Championship Series Most Valuable Player (1989).

							BATTING								FIELDING		
Year	Team (League)	Pos.	G	AB	R	H	2B	3B	HR	RBI	Avg.	BB	SO	SB	PO	A	E	Avg.
1987— San Francisco (N.L.)		1B	7	25	3	9	2	0	1	3	.360	3	6	1	63	7	1	.986
1989— San Francisco (N.L.)		1B	5	20	8	13	3	1	2	8	.650	2	2	0	43	6	0	1.000
Championship series totals (2 years)			12	45	11	22	5	1	3	11	.489	5	8	1	106	13	1	.992

WORLD SERIES RECORD

							BATTING								FIELDING		
Year	Team (League)	Pos.	G	AB	R	H	2B	3B	HR	RBI	Avg.	BB	SO	SB	PO	A	E	Avg.
1989— San Francisco (N.L.)		1B	4	16	2	4	1	0	0	0	.250	1	3	0	40	2	0	1.000

ALL-STAR GAME RECORD

						BATTING								FIELDING		
Year	League	Pos.	AB	R	H	2B	3B	HR	RBI	Avg.	BB	SO	SB	PO	A	E	Avg.
1988— National		1B	2	0	0	0	0	0	0	.000	0	0	0	4	1	0	1.000
1989— National		1B	2	0	0	0	0	0	0	.000	0	1	0	5	0	0	1.000
1990— National		1B	3	0	1	0	0	0	0	.333	0	0	0	6	0	0	1.000
1991— National		1B	2	0	1	0	0	0	0	.500	1	0	0	2	0	0	1.000
1992— National		PH-1B	2	1	1	0	0	1	3	.500	0	1	0	1	0	0	1.000
1994— American		1B	2	0	2	0	0	0	0	1.000	0	0	1	7	0	0	1.000
All-Star Game totals (6 years)			13	1	5	0	0	1	3	.385	1	2	1	25	1	0	1.000

C

CLAYTON, ROYCE   SS   RANGERS

PERSONAL: Born January 2, 1970, in Burbank, Calif. ... 6-0/183. ... Bats right, throws right. ... Full name: Royce Spencer Clayton.

HIGH SCHOOL: St. Bernard (Playa del Rey, Calif.).

TRANSACTIONS/CAREER NOTES: Selected by San Francisco Giants organization in first round (15th pick overall) of free-agent draft (June 1, 1988); pick received as compensation for Cincinnati Reds signing Type B free-agent OF Eddie Milner. ... Traded by Giants with a player to be named later to St. Louis Cardinals for P Allen Watson, P Rich DeLucia and P Doug Creek (December 14, 1995); Cardinals acquired 2B Chris Wimmer to complete deal (January 16, 1996). ... On St. Louis disabled list (June 24-July 9, 1998). ... Traded by Cardinals with P Todd Stottlemyre to Texas Rangers for P Darren Oliver, 3B Fernando Tatis and a player to be named later (July 31, 1998); Cardinals acquired OF Mark Little to complete deal (August 9, 1998). ... Granted free agency (October 23, 1998). ... Re-signed by Rangers (December 2, 1998).

STATISTICAL NOTES: Led Texas League shortstops with 80 double plays in 1991. ... Led N.L. shortstops with 103 double plays in 1993. ... Led N.L. shortstops with 654 total chances in 1995.

							BATTING								FIELDING		
Year	Team (League)	Pos.	G	AB	R	H	2B	3B	HR	RBI	Avg.	BB	SO	SB	PO	A	E	Avg.
1988— Everett (N'west)		SS	60	212	35	55	4	0	3	29	.259	27	54	10	75	166	35	.873
1989— Clinton (Midwest)		SS	104	385	39	91	13	3	0	24	.236	39	101	28	182	332	31	.943
—San Jose (Calif.)		SS	28	92	5	11	2	0	0	4	.120	13	27	10	53	71	8	.939
1990— San Jose (Calif.)		SS	123	460	80	123	15	10	7	71	.267	68	98	33	*202	358	37	.938
1991— Shreveport (Texas)		SS	126	485	84	136	22	8	5	68	.280	61	104	36	174	379	29	.950
—San Francisco (N.L.)		SS	9	26	0	3	1	0	0	2	.115	1	6	0	16	6	3	.880
1992— San Francisco (N.L.)		SS-3B	98	321	31	72	7	4	4	24	.224	26	63	8	142	257	11	.973
—Phoenix (PCL)		SS	48	192	30	46	6	2	3	18	.240	17	25	15	81	150	7	.971
1993— San Francisco (N.L.)		SS	153	549	54	155	21	5	6	70	.282	38	91	11	251	449	27	.963
1994— San Francisco (N.L.)		SS	108	385	38	91	14	6	3	30	.236	30	74	23	177	330	14	.973
1995— San Francisco (N.L.)		SS	138	509	56	124	29	3	5	58	.244	38	109	24	*223	•411	20	.969
1996— St. Louis (N.L.)■		SS	129	491	64	136	20	4	6	35	.277	33	89	33	171	347	15	.972
1997— St. Louis (N.L.)		SS	154	576	75	153	39	5	9	61	.266	33	109	30	228	*452	19	.973
1998— St. Louis (N.L.)		SS	90	355	59	83	19	1	4	29	.234	40	51	19	140	286	13	.970
—Texas (A.L.)■		SS	52	186	30	53	12	1	5	24	.285	13	32	5	88	152	7	.972
American League totals (1 year)			52	186	30	53	12	1	5	24	.285	13	32	5	88	152	7	.972
National League totals (8 years)			879	3212	377	817	150	28	37	309	.254	239	592	148	1348	2538	122	.970
Major league totals (8 years)			931	3398	407	870	162	29	42	333	.256	252	624	153	1436	2690	129	.970

DIVISION SERIES RECORD

							BATTING								FIELDING		
Year	Team (League)	Pos.	G	AB	R	H	2B	3B	HR	RBI	Avg.	BB	SO	SB	PO	A	E	Avg.
1996— St. Louis (N.L.)		SS	2	6	1	2	0	0	0	0	.333	3	1	0	4	5	0	1.000
1998— Texas (A.L.)		SS	3	9	0	2	0	0	0	0	.222	0	4	0	5	8	1	.929
Division series totals (2 years)			5	15	1	4	0	0	0	0	.267	3	5	0	9	13	1	.957

CHAMPIONSHIP SERIES RECORD

							BATTING								FIELDING		
Year	Team (League)	Pos.	G	AB	R	H	2B	3B	HR	RBI	Avg.	BB	SO	SB	PO	A	E	Avg.
1996— St. Louis (N.L.)		SS	5	20	4	7	0	0	0	1	.350	1	4	1	5	16	2	.913

ALL-STAR GAME RECORD

						BATTING								FIELDING		
Year	League	Pos.	AB	R	H	2B	3B	HR	RBI	Avg.	BB	SO	SB	PO	A	E	Avg.
1997— National		SS	1	0	0	0	0	0	0	.000	0	1	0	0	1	0	1.000

PERSONAL: Born August 4, 1962, in Dayton, Ohio. ... 6-4/230. ... Throws right, bats right. ... Full name: William Roger Clemens.
HIGH SCHOOL: Spring Woods (Houston).
JUNIOR COLLEGE: San Jacinto (North) College (Texas).
COLLEGE: Texas.
TRANSACTIONS/CAREER NOTES: Selected by New York Mets organization in 12th round of free-agent draft (June 8, 1981); did not sign. ... Selected by Boston Red Sox organization in first round (19th pick overall) of free-agent draft (June 6, 1983). ... On disabled list (July 8-August 3 and August 21, 1985-remainder of season). ... On suspended list (April 26-May 3, 1991). ... On Boston disabled list (June 19-July 16, 1993); included rehabilitation assignment to Pawtucket (July 11-16). ... On Boston disabled list (April 16-June 2, 1995); included rehabilitation assignments to Sarasota (May 25-28) and Pawtucket (May 28-June 2). ... Granted free agency (November 5, 1996). ... Signed by Toronto Blue Jays (December 13, 1996).
RECORDS: Holds major league single-game record for most strikeouts (nine-inning game)—20 (April 29, 1986 and September 18, 1996). ... Shares major league record for most putouts by pitcher in one inning—3 (June 27, 1992, sixth inning). ... Shares A.L. record for most consecutive seasons with 200 or more strikeouts—7 (1986-92); most seasons with 200 or more strikeouts—10; and most consecutive seasons with 100 or more strikeouts—13 (1986-98). ... Shares A.L. single-game record for most consecutive strikeouts—8 (April 29, 1986).
HONORS: Named Major League Player of the Year by THE SPORTING NEWS (1986). ... Named A.L. Pitcher of the Year by THE SPORTING NEWS (1986, 1991, 1997 and 1998). ... Named righthanded pitcher on THE SPORTING NEWS A.L. All-Star team (1986-87, 1991 and 1997). ... Named A.L. Most Valuable Player by Baseball Writers' Association of America (1986). ... Named A.L. Cy Young Award winner by Baseball Writers' Association of America (1986, 1987, 1991, 1997 and 1998).
STATISTICAL NOTES: Struck out 15 batters in one game (August 21, 1984; July 9, 1988; August 15 and September 21, 1998). ... Struck out 20 batters in one game (April 29, 1986 and September 18, 1996). ... Struck out 16 batters in one game (May 9 and July 15, 1988 and July 12, 1997). ... Pitched 6-0 one-hit, complete-game victory against Cleveland (September 10, 1988). ... Led A.L. with 14 hit batsmen in 1995. ... Struck out 18 batters in one game (August 25, 1998).
MISCELLANEOUS: Singled in only appearance as pinch hitter (1996).

Year — Team (League)	W	L	Pct.	ERA	G	GS	CG	ShO	Sv.	IP	H	R	ER	BB	SO
1983— Winter Haven (FSL)............	3	1	.750	1.24	4	4	3	1	0	29	22	4	4	0	36
— New Britain (East.)............	4	1	.800	1.38	7	7	1	1	0	52	31	8	8	12	59
1984— Pawtucket (Int'l)................	2	3	.400	1.93	7	6	3	1	0	46 2/3	39	12	10	14	50
— Boston (A.L.)................	9	4	.692	4.32	21	20	5	1	0	133 1/3	146	67	64	29	126
1985— Boston (A.L.)................	7	5	.583	3.29	15	15	3	1	0	98 1/3	83	38	36	37	74
1986— Boston (A.L.)................	*24	4	*.857	*2.48	33	33	10	1	0	254	179	77	70	67	238
1987— Boston (A.L.)................	•20	9	.690	2.97	36	36	*18	*7	0	281 2/3	248	100	93	83	256
1988— Boston (A.L.)................	18	12	.600	2.93	35	35	•14	*8	0	264	217	93	86	62	*291
1989— Boston (A.L.)................	17	11	.607	3.13	35	35	8	3	0	253 1/3	215	101	88	93	230
1990— Boston (A.L.)................	21	6	.778	*1.93	31	31	7	•4	0	228 1/3	193	59	49	54	209
1991— Boston (A.L.)................	18	10	.643	*2.62	35	•35	13	*4	0	*271 1/3	219	93	79	65	*241
1992— Boston (A.L.)................	18	11	.621	*2.41	32	32	11	*5	0	246 2/3	203	80	66	62	208
1993— Boston (A.L.)................	11	14	.440	4.46	29	29	2	1	0	191 2/3	175	99	95	67	160
— Pawtucket (Int'l)............	0	0	. . .	0.00	1	1	0	0	0	3 2/3	1	0	0	4	8
1994— Boston (A.L.)................	9	7	.563	2.85	24	24	3	1	0	170 2/3	124	62	54	71	168
1995— Sarasota (Florida State)......	0	0	. . .	0.00	1	1	0	0	0	4	0	0	0	2	7
— Pawtucket (Int'l)............	0	0	. . .	0.00	1	1	0	0	0	5	1	0	0	3	5
— Boston (A.L.)................	10	5	.667	4.18	23	23	0	0	0	140	141	70	65	60	132
1996— Boston (A.L.)................	10	13	.435	3.63	34	34	6	2	0	242 2/3	216	106	98	106	*257
1997— Toronto (A.L.)■............	*21	7	.750	*2.05	34	34	•9	•3	0	•264	204	65	60	68	*292
1998— Toronto (A.L.)................	•20	6	.769	*2.65	33	33	5	3	0	234 2/3	169	78	69	88	*271
Major league totals (15 years)....	**233**	**124**	**.653**	**2.95**	**450**	**449**	**114**	**44**	**0**	**3274 2/3**	**2732**	**1188**	**1072**	**1012**	**3153**

DIVISION SERIES RECORD

Year — Team (League)	W	L	Pct.	ERA	G	GS	CG	ShO	Sv.	IP	H	R	ER	BB	SO
1995— Boston (A.L.).....................	0	0	. . .	3.86	1	1	0	0	0	7	5	3	3	1	5

CHAMPIONSHIP SERIES RECORD

RECORDS: Holds single-series record for most hits allowed—22 (1986). ... Shares single-series record for most earned runs allowed—11 (1986). ... Shares single-game records for most earned runs allowed—7 (October 7, 1986); and most consecutive strikeouts—4 (October 6, 1988). ... Holds A.L. single-series record for most innings pitched—22 2/3 (1986). ... Shares A.L. single-game record for most runs allowed—8 (October 7, 1986).

Year — Team (League)	W	L	Pct.	ERA	G	GS	CG	ShO	Sv.	IP	H	R	ER	BB	SO
1986— Boston (A.L.).....................	1	1	.500	4.37	3	3	0	0	0	22 2/3	22	12	11	7	17
1988— Boston (A.L.).....................	0	0	. . .	3.86	1	1	0	0	0	7	6	3	3	0	8
1990— Boston (A.L.).....................	0	1	.000	3.52	2	2	0	0	0	7 2/3	7	3	3	5	4
Champ. series totals (3 years)	**1**	**2**	**.333**	**4.10**	**6**	**6**	**0**	**0**	**0**	**37 1/3**	**35**	**18**	**17**	**12**	**29**

WORLD SERIES RECORD

Year — Team (League)	W	L	Pct.	ERA	G	GS	CG	ShO	Sv.	IP	H	R	ER	BB	SO
1986— Boston (A.L.).....................	0	0	. . .	3.18	2	2	0	0	0	11 1/3	9	5	4	6	11

NOTES: Named Most Valuable Player (1986).

ALL-STAR GAME RECORD

Year — League	W	L	Pct.	ERA	GS	CG	ShO	Sv.	IP	H	R	ER	BB	SO
1986— American	1	0	1.000	0.00	1	0	0	0	3	0	0	0	0	2
1988— American	0	0	. . .	0.00	0	0	0	0	1	0	0	0	0	1
1990— American							Did not play.							
1991— American	0	0	. . .	9.00	0	0	0	0	1	1	1	1	0	0
1992— American	0	0	. . .	0.00	0	0	0	0	1	0	0	0	0	0
1997— American	0	0	. . .	0.00	0	0	0	0	1	1	0	0	0	0
1998— American	0	0	. . .	18.00	0	0	0	0	1	2	2	2	1	1
All-Star totals (6 years)	**1**	**0**	**1.000**	**3.38**	**1**	**0**	**0**	**0**	**8**	**6**	**3**	**3**	**1**	**4**

CLEMENT, MATT — P — PADRES

PERSONAL: Born August 12, 1974, in McCandless Township, Pa. ... 6-3/180. ... Throws right, bats right. ... Full name: Matthew Paul Clement.
HIGH SCHOOL: Butler (Pa.).
TRANSACTIONS/CAREER NOTES: Selected by San Diego Padres organization in third round of free-agent draft (June 3, 1993).
STATISTICAL NOTES: Led Pacific Coast League with 30 hit batsmen in 1998.

Year Team (League)	W	L	Pct.	ERA	G	GS	CG	ShO	Sv.	IP	H	R	ER	BB	SO
1994— Peoria (Arizona)	•8	5	.615	4.43	13	13	0	0	0	67	65	38	33	17	76
— Spokane (N'west)	1	1	.500	6.14	2	2	0	0	0	$7^{1}/_{3}$	8	7	5	11	4
1995— Rancho Cuca. (Cal.)	3	4	.429	4.24	12	12	0	0	0	$57^{1}/_{3}$	61	37	27	49	33
1996— Clinton (Midwest)	8	3	.727	2.80	16	16	1	•1	0	$96^{1}/_{3}$	66	31	30	52	109
— Rancho Cuca. (Cal.)	4	5	.444	5.59	11	11	0	0	0	$56^{1}/_{3}$	61	40	35	26	75
1997— Rancho Cuca. (Cal.)	6	3	.667	1.60	14	14	2	1	0	101	74	30	18	31	109
— Mobile (Southern)	6	5	.545	2.56	13	13	1	1	0	88	83	37	25	32	92
1998— Las Vegas (PCL)	10	9	.526	3.98	27	27	1	0	0	$171^{2}/_{3}$	157	94	76	85	160
— San Diego (N.L.)	2	0	1.000	4.61	4	2	0	0	0	$13^{2}/_{3}$	15	8	7	7	13
Major league totals (1 year)	2	0	1.000	4.61	4	2	0	0	0	$13^{2}/_{3}$	15	8	7	7	13

CLEMENTE, EDGARD — OF — ROCKIES

PERSONAL: Born December 15, 1975, in Santurce, Puerto Rico. ... 5-11/188. ... Bats right, throws right. ... Full name: Edgard A. Velazquez Clemente. ... Nephew of Roberto Clemente, outfielder with Pittsburgh Pirates (1955-72) and member of Baseball Hall of Fame. ... Formerly known as Edgard Velazquez.
HIGH SCHOOL: Colegio Hostos (Guaynabo, Puerto Rico).
TRANSACTIONS/CAREER NOTES: Selected by Colorado Rockies organization in 10th round of free-agent draft (June 3, 1993).
STATISTICAL NOTES: Tied for South Atlantic League record in double plays by outfielder with five in 1994. ... Led Carolina League outfielders with 296 total chances in 1995. ... Led Pacific Coast League outfielders with five double plays in 1997. ... Tied for Pacific Coast League lead with three double plays by outfielder in 1998.

Year Team (League)	Pos.	G	AB	R	H	2B	3B	HR	RBI	Avg.	BB	SO	SB	PO	A	E	Avg.
1993— Ariz. Rockies (Ariz.)	OF	39	147	20	36	4	2	2	20	.245	16	35	7	70	3	6	.924
1994— Asheville (S. Atl.)	OF	119	447	50	106	22	3	11	39	.237	23	120	9	219	15	•12	.951
1995— Salem (Carolina)	OF	131	497	74	149	25	6	13	69	.300	40	102	7	273	•16	7	.976
1996— New Haven (East.)	OF	132	486	72	141	29	4	19	62	.290	53	114	6	215	9	5	.978
1997— Colo. Springs (PCL)	OF	120	438	70	123	24	10	17	73	.281	34	119	6	208	13	6	.974
1998— Colo. Springs (PCL)	OF	135	493	79	124	21	7	22	82	.252	40	117	5	262	8	9	.968
— Colorado (N.L.)	OF	11	17	2	6	0	1	0	2	.353	2	8	0	6	0	1	.857
Major league totals (1 year)		11	17	2	6	0	1	0	2	.353	2	8	0	6	0	1	.857

CLINE, PAT — C — CUBS

PERSONAL: Born October 9, 1974, in Bradenton, Fla. ... 6-3/225. ... Bats right, throws right. ... Full name: James Patrick Cline.
HIGH SCHOOL: Manatee (Bradenton, Fla.).
TRANSACTIONS/CAREER NOTES: Selected by Chicago Cubs organization in sixth round of free-agent draft (June 3, 1993). ... On Gulf Coast Cubs disabled list (June 20-27, 1994). ... On Huntington disabled list (July 20, 1994-remainder of season).
STATISTICAL NOTES: Led Appalachian League with 17 passed balls in 1993. ... Tied for Midwest League lead with 18 passed balls in 1995. ... Led Florida State League catchers with 783 total chances in 1996. ... Led Pacific Coast League catchers with 867 total chances and 18 passed balls in 1998.

Year Team (League)	Pos.	G	AB	R	H	2B	3B	HR	RBI	Avg.	BB	SO	SB	PO	A	E	Avg.
1993— Huntington (Appal.)	C	33	96	17	18	6	0	2	13	.188	17	28	0	174	10	5	.974
1994— GC Cubs (GCL)	C	3	3	0	0	0	0	0	0	.000	0	0	0	2	0	0	1.000
1995— Rockford (Midwest)	C	112	390	65	106	17	0	13	77	.272	58	93	6	549	64	17	.973
1996— Daytona (Fla. St.)	C	124	434	75	121	30	2	17	76	.279	54	79	10	*697	70	16	.980
1997— Orlando (South.)	C	78	271	39	69	19	0	7	37	.255	27	78	2	416	35	5	.989
— Iowa (Am. Assoc.)	C	27	95	6	21	2	0	3	10	.221	10	24	0	188	11	2	.990
1998— Iowa (Pacific Coast)	C-1B	122	424	52	119	22	2	13	60	.281	36	59	2	*806	50	11	.987

CLONTZ, BRAD — P — RED SOX

PERSONAL: Born April 25, 1971, in Stuart, Va. ... 6-1/195. ... Throws right, bats right. ... Full name: John Bradley Clontz.
HIGH SCHOOL: Patrick County (Stuart, Va.).
COLLEGE: Virginia Tech.
TRANSACTIONS/CAREER NOTES: Selected by Atlanta Braves organization in 10th round of free-agent draft (June 1, 1992). ... Released by Braves (March 30, 1998). ... Signed by Los Angeles Dodgers (April 9, 1998). ... Traded by Dodgers with P Hideo Nomo to New York Mets for P Dave Mlicki and P Greg McMichael (June 4, 1998). ... On New York disabled list (September 11, 1998-remainder of season). ... Granted free agency (October 15, 1998). ... Signed by Boston Red Sox organization (December 14, 1998).
HONORS: Named Southern League Outstanding Pitcher (1994).

Year Team (League)	W	L	Pct.	ERA	G	GS	CG	ShO	Sv.	IP	H	R	ER	BB	SO
1992— Pulaski (Appalachian)	0	0	...	1.59	4	0	0	0	1	$5^{2}/_{3}$	3	1	1	2	7
— Macon (S. Atl.)	2	1	.667	3.91	17	0	0	0	2	23	19	14	10	10	18
1993— Durham (Carolina)	1	7	.125	2.75	51	0	0	0	10	$75^{1}/_{3}$	69	32	23	26	79
1994— Greenville (Southern)	1	2	.333	1.20	39	0	0	0	*27	45	32	13	6	10	49
— Richmond (Int'l)	0	0	...	2.10	24	0	0	0	11	$25^{2}/_{3}$	19	6	6	9	21
1995— Atlanta (N.L.)	8	1	.889	3.65	59	0	0	0	4	69	71	29	28	22	55
1996— Atlanta (N.L.)	6	3	.667	5.69	*81	0	0	0	1	$80^{2}/_{3}$	78	53	51	33	49

Year Team (League)	W	L	Pct.	ERA	G	GS	CG	ShO	Sv.	IP	H	R	ER	BB	SO
1997— Atlanta (N.L.)	5	1	.833	3.75	51	0	0	0	1	48	52	24	20	18	42
— Richmond (Int'l)	0	0	...	0.00	16	0	0	0	6	22	10	1	0	2	24
1998— Los Angeles (N.L.)■	2	0	1.000	5.66	18	0	0	0	0	20 2/3	15	13	13	10	14
— Albuquerque (PCL)	1	2	.333	7.71	6	0	0	0	0	7	11	10	6	5	12
— New York (N.L.)■	0	0	...	9.00	2	0	0	0	0	3	4	3	3	2	2
— Norfolk (Int'l)	2	4	.333	3.43	28	0	0	0	0	42	43	26	16	16	49
Major league totals (4 years)	21	5	.808	4.68	211	0	0	0	6	221 1/3	220	122	115	85	162

DIVISION SERIES RECORD

Year Team (League)	W	L	Pct.	ERA	G	GS	CG	ShO	Sv.	IP	H	R	ER	BB	SO
1995— Atlanta (N.L.)	0	0	...	0.00	1	0	0	0	0	1 1/3	0	0	0	0	2
1996— Atlanta (N.L.)							Did not play.								
Div. series totals (1 years)	0	0	...	0.00	1	0	0	0	0	1 1/3	0	0	0	0	2

CHAMPIONSHIP SERIES RECORD

Year Team (League)	W	L	Pct.	ERA	G	GS	CG	ShO	Sv.	IP	H	R	ER	BB	SO
1995— Atlanta (N.L.)	0	0	...	0.00	1	0	0	0	0	1/3	1	0	0	0	0
1996— Atlanta (N.L.)	0	0	...	0.00	1	0	0	0	0	2/3	0	0	0	0	0
Champ. series totals (2 years)	0	0	...	0.00	2	0	0	0	0	1	1	0	0	0	0

WORLD SERIES RECORD

NOTES: Member of World Series championship team (1995).

Year Team (League)	W	L	Pct.	ERA	G	GS	CG	ShO	Sv.	IP	H	R	ER	BB	SO
1995— Atlanta (N.L.)	0	0	...	2.70	2	0	0	0	0	3 1/3	2	1	1	0	2
1996— Atlanta (N.L.)	0	0	...	0.00	3	0	0	0	0	1 2/3	1	0	0	2	2
World Series totals (2 years)	0	0	...	1.80	5	0	0	0	0	5	3	1	1	2	4

CLOUDE, KEN — P — MARINERS

PERSONAL: Born January 9, 1975, in Baltimore. ... 6-1/180. ... Throws right, bats right. ... Full name: Kenneth Brian Cloude.
HIGH SCHOOL: McDonogh (Owings Mills, Md.).
TRANSACTIONS/CAREER NOTES: Selected by Seattle Mariners organization in sixth round of free-agent draft (June 3, 1993).

Year Team (League)	W	L	Pct.	ERA	G	GS	CG	ShO	Sv.	IP	H	R	ER	BB	SO
1994— Ariz. Mariners (Ariz.)	3	4	.429	2.06	12	7	0	0	0	52 1/3	36	22	12	19	61
1995— Wis. Rap. (Midw.)	9	8	.529	3.24	25	25	4	0	0	161	137	64	58	63	140
1996— Lancaster (Calif.)	15	4	.789	4.22	28	28	1	0	0	168 1/3	167	94	79	60	161
1997— Memphis (Sou.)	11	7	.611	3.87	22	22	3	•2	0	132 2/3	131	62	57	48	124
— Seattle (A.L.)	4	2	.667	5.12	10	9	0	0	0	51	41	32	29	26	46
1998— Seattle (A.L.)	8	10	.444	6.37	30	30	0	0	0	155 1/3	187	116	110	80	114
— Tacoma (PCL)	0	1	.000	6.75	1	1	0	0	0	4	4	3	3	1	4
Major league totals (2 years)	12	12	.500	6.06	40	39	0	0	0	206 1/3	228	148	139	106	160

CLYBURN, DANNY — OF — ORIOLES

PERSONAL: Born April 6, 1974, in Lancaster, S.C. ... 6-0/220. ... Bats right, throws right.
HIGH SCHOOL: Lancaster (S.C.).
TRANSACTIONS/CAREER NOTES: Selected by Pittsburgh Pirates organization in second round of free-agent draft (June 1, 1992). ... On disabled list (April 7-17, 1994). ... Traded by Pirates organization to Cincinnati Reds organization for OF Jacob Brumfield (October 11, 1994). ... Traded by Reds organization with P Tony Nieto to Baltimore Orioles organization for P Brad Pennington (June 16, 1995). ... On Bowie disabled list (July 17-24, 1996). ... On Baltimore disabled list (March 19-June 16, 1998); included rehabilitation assignment to Rochester (May 28-June 15).

Year Team (League)	Pos.	G	AB	R	H	2B	3B	HR	RBI	Avg.	BB	SO	SB	PO	A	E	Avg.
1992— GC Pirates (GCL)	OF	39	149	26	51	9	0	4	25	.342	5	20	7	41	0	3	.932
1993— Augusta (S. Atl.)	OF	127	457	55	121	21	4	9	66	.265	37	97	5	156	9	7	.959
1994— Salem (Carolina)	OF	118	461	57	126	19	0	22	90	.273	20	96	4	135	6	12	.922
1995— Win.-Salem (Car.)■	OF	59	227	27	59	10	2	11	41	.260	13	59	2	66	6	4	.947
— Frederick (Carolina)■	OF	15	45	4	9	4	0	0	4	.200	4	18	1	13	0	1	.929
— High Desert (Calif.)	OF	45	160	20	45	3	1	12	37	.281	17	41	2	63	6	5	.932
1996— Bowie (Eastern)	OF	95	365	51	92	14	5	18	55	.252	17	88	4	103	4	12	.899
1997— Rochester (Int'l)	OF	•137	520	91	156	33	5	20	76	.300	53	107	14	241	5	*10	.961
— Baltimore (A.L.)	OF	2	3	0	0	0	0	0	0	.000	0	2	0	0	0	0	...
1998— Rochester (Int'l)	OF	84	322	58	92	21	1	14	54	.286	34	72	11	125	4	4	.970
— Baltimore (A.L.)	OF-DH	11	25	6	7	0	0	1	3	.280	1	10	0	11	0	0	1.000
Major league totals (2 years)		13	28	6	7	0	0	1	3	.250	1	12	0	11	0	0	1.000

COFFIE, IVANON — IF — ORIOLES

PERSONAL: Born May 16, 1977, in Curacao, Netherlands Antilles. ... 6-1/170. ... Bats left, throws right. ... Full name: Ivanon Angelino Coffie.
TRANSACTIONS/CAREER NOTES: Signed as non-drafted free agent by Baltimore Orioles organization (July 28, 1995).
STATISTICAL NOTES: Led Gulf Coast League shortstops with .941 fielding percentage in 1996.

Year Team (League)	Pos.	G	AB	R	H	2B	3B	HR	RBI	Avg.	BB	SO	SB	PO	A	E	Avg.
1996— GC Orioles (GCL)	SS-3B	56	193	29	42	8	4	0	20	.218	23	26	6	81	175	16	†.941
1997— Delmarva (S. Atl.)	SS-3B	90	305	41	84	14	5	3	48	.275	23	45	19	126	203	19	.945
1998— Frederick (Carolina)	3B-SS	130	473	62	121	19	2	16	75	.256	48	109	17	126	216	25	.932

COGGIN, DAVE   P   PHILLIES

PERSONAL: Born October 30, 1976, in Covina, Calif. ... 6-4/205. ... Throws right, bats right. ... Full name: David Raymond Coggin.
HIGH SCHOOL: Upland (Calif.).
TRANSACTIONS/CAREER NOTES: Selected by Philadelphia Phillies organization in supplemental round ("sandwich pick" between first and second round, 30th pick overall) of free-agent draft (June 1, 1995). ... On disabled list (April 20-May 26, 1998).
STATISTICAL NOTES: Led Florida State League with 24 wild pitches in 1997.

Year Team (League)	W	L	Pct.	ERA	G	GS	CG	ShO	Sv.	IP	H	R	ER	BB	SO
1995— Martinsville (App.)	5	3	.625	3.00	11	11	0	0	0	48	45	25	16	31	37
1996— Piedmont (South Atlantic)..	9	12	.429	4.31	28	•28	3	3	0	169¹/₃	156	87	*81	46	129
1997— Clearwater (Fla. St.)	11	8	.579	4.70	27	27	3	2	0	155	160	96	81	86	110
1998— Reading (Eastern)	4	8	.333	4.14	20	20	0	0	0	108²/₃	106	58	50	62	65

COLBRUNN, GREG   1B   DIAMONDBACKS

PERSONAL: Born July 26, 1969, in Fontana, Calif. ... 6-0/205. ... Bats right, throws right. ... Full name: Gregory Joseph Colbrunn.
HIGH SCHOOL: Fontana (Calif.).
TRANSACTIONS/CAREER NOTES: Selected by Montreal Expos organization in sixth round of free-agent draft (June 2, 1987). ... On disabled list (April 10, 1991-entire season). ... On Indianapolis disabled list (April 9-May 5, 1992). ... On Montreal disabled list (August 2-18, 1992); included rehabilitation assignment to Indianapolis (August 13-18). ... On Montreal disabled list (April 5-21, 1993); included rehabilitation assignment to West Palm Beach (April 9-20). ... On Montreal disabled list (July 12, 1993-remainder of season); included rehabilitation assignment to Ottawa (July 27-August 2). ... Claimed on waivers by Florida Marlins (October 7, 1993). ... On Florida disabled list (April 9-May 27, and July 15-30, 1994); included rehabilitation assignments to Brevard County (May 12-18 and July 28-30) and Edmonton (May 18-27). ... On disabled list (July 24-August 8, 1996). ... Granted free agency (December 20, 1996). ... Signed by Minnesota Twins organization (January 24, 1997). ... Traded by Twins to Atlanta Braves for a player to be named later (August 14, 1997); Twins acquired OF Marc Lewis to complete deal (October 1, 1997). ... Granted free agency (October 23, 1997). ... Signed by Colorado Rockies organization (December 23, 1997). ... Traded by Rockies to Braves for P David Cortes, P Mike Porzio and a player to be named later (July 30, 1998); Rockies acquired P Anthony Briggs to complete deal (September 9, 1998). ... Granted free agency (October 23, 1998). ... Signed by Arizona Diamondbacks (November 17, 1998).
STATISTICAL NOTES: Had 21-game hitting streak (May 31-June 23, 1996). ... Career major league grand slams: 2.

Year Team (League)	Pos.	G	AB	R	H	2B	3B	HR	RBI	Avg.	BB	SO	SB	PO	A	E	Avg.
1988— Rockford (Midwest) ...	C	115	417	55	111	18	2	7	46	.266	22	60	5	595	81	15	.978
1989— W.P. Beach (FSL)	C	59	228	20	54	8	0	0	25	.237	6	29	3	376	49	5	.988
— Jacksonville (Sou.)	C	55	178	21	49	11	1	3	18	.275	13	33	0	304	34	4	.988
1990— Jacksonville (Sou.)	C	125	458	57	138	29	1	13	76	.301	38	78	1	698	58	15	.981
1991—							Did not play.										
1992— Indianapolis (A.A.)	1B	57	216	32	66	19	1	11	48	.306	7	41	1	441	27	4	.992
— Montreal (N.L.)	1B	52	168	12	45	8	0	2	18	.268	6	34	3	363	29	3	.992
1993— W.P. Beach (FSL)	1B	8	31	6	12	2	1	1	5	.387	4	1	0	74	5	1	.988
— Montreal (N.L.)	1B	70	153	15	39	9	0	4	23	.255	6	33	4	372	27	2	.995
— Ottawa (Int'l)	1B	6	22	4	6	1	0	0	8	.273	1	2	1	50	1	0	1.000
1994— Florida (N.L.)■	1B	47	155	17	47	10	0	6	31	.303	9	27	1	304	26	4	.988
— Brevard County (FSL).	1B	7	11	3	6	2	0	1	2	.545	1	0	0	16	1	1	.944
— Edmonton (PCL)	1B	7	17	2	4	0	0	1	2	.235	0	1	0	28	1	1	.967
1995— Florida (N.L.)	1B	138	528	70	146	22	1	23	89	.277	22	69	11	1066	90	5	.996
1996— Florida (N.L.)	1B	141	511	60	146	26	2	16	69	.286	25	76	4	1169	101	6	.995
1997— Minnesota (A.L.)■	1B-DH	70	217	24	61	14	0	5	26	.281	8	38	1	475	35	6	.988
— Atlanta (N.L.)	1B-DH	28	54	3	15	3	0	2	9	.278	2	11	0	54	6	1	.984
1998— Colorado (N.L.)■	1-O-DH-C	62	122	12	38	8	2	2	13	.311	8	23	3	222	21	2	.992
— Atlanta (N.L.)■	1B-OF	28	44	6	13	3	0	1	10	.295	2	11	1	57	4	0	1.000
American League totals (1 year)		70	217	24	61	14	0	5	26	.281	8	38	1	475	35	6	.988
National League totals (7 years)		566	1735	195	489	89	5	56	262	.282	80	284	27	3607	304	23	.994
Major league totals (7 years)		636	1952	219	550	103	5	61	288	.282	88	322	28	4082	339	29	.993

DIVISION SERIES RECORD

Year Team (League)	Pos.	G	AB	R	H	2B	3B	HR	RBI	Avg.	BB	SO	SB	PO	A	E	Avg.
1997— Atlanta (N.L.)	PH	1	1	0	1	0	0	0	2	1.000	0	0	0	0	0	0	...
1998— Atlanta (N.L.)	PH	2	2	0	0	0	0	0	0	.000	0	0	0	...	...	...	...
Division series totals (2 years)		3	3	0	1	0	0	0	2	.333	0	0	0	0	0	0	...

CHAMPIONSHIP SERIES RECORD

Year Team (League)	Pos.	G	AB	R	H	2B	3B	HR	RBI	Avg.	BB	SO	SB	PO	A	E	Avg.
1997— Atlanta (N.L.)	PH	3	3	0	2	0	0	0	0	.667	0	0	0	0	0	0	...
1998— Atlanta (N.L.)	PH	6	6	0	2	0	0	0	0	.333	0	2	0	...	...	...	...
Championship series totals (2 years)		9	9	0	4	0	0	0	0	.444	0	2	0	0	0	0	...

COLEMAN, MICHAEL   OF   RED SOX

PERSONAL: Born August 16, 1975, in Nashville. ... 5-11/180. ... Bats right, throws right. ... Full name: Michael D. Coleman.
HIGH SCHOOL: Stratford (Nashville).
TRANSACTIONS/CAREER NOTES: Selected by Boston Red Sox organization in 18th round of free-agent draft (June 2, 1994). ... On Pawtucket disabled list (May 9-June 11, 1998).

Year Team (League)	Pos.	G	AB	R	H	2B	3B	HR	RBI	Avg.	BB	SO	SB	PO	A	E	Avg.
										BATTING					FIELDING		
1994— Fort Myers (GCL)	OF	25	95	15	26	6	1	3	15	.274	10	20	5	32	0	0	1.000
— Utica (N.Y.-Penn)	OF	23	65	16	11	2	0	1	3	.169	14	21	11	35	2	2	.949
1995— Michigan (Midwest) ...	OF	112	422	70	113	16	2	11	61	.268	40	93	29	251	5	5	.981
1996— Sarasota (Fla. St.)	OF	110	407	54	100	20	5	1	36	.246	38	86	24	261	9	2	*.993
1997— Trenton (Eastern)	OF	102	385	56	116	17	8	14	58	.301	41	89	20	259	6	5	.981
— Pawtucket (Int'l)	OF	28	113	27	36	9	2	7	19	.319	12	27	4	53	2	4	.932
— Boston (A.L.)	OF	8	24	2	4	1	0	0	2	.167	0	11	1	16	0	1	.941
1998— Pawtucket (Int'l)	OF	93	340	47	86	13	0	14	37	.253	27	92	12	173	9	4	.978
Major league totals (1 year)		8	24	2	4	1	0	0	2	.167	0	11	1	16	0	1	.941

COLLIER, LOU   IF   BREWERS

PERSONAL: Born August 21, 1973, in Chicago. ... 5-10/183. ... Bats right, throws right. ... Full name: Louis Keith Collier.
HIGH SCHOOL: Vocational (Chicago).
JUNIOR COLLEGE: Kishwaukee Junior College (Ill.), then Triton Community College (Ill.).
TRANSACTIONS/CAREER NOTES: Selected by Pittsburgh Pirates organization in 31st round of free-agent draft (June 1, 1992). ... On Pittsburgh disabled list (May 22-June 7, 1998); included rehabilitation assignment to Lynchburg (June 3-7). ... Claimed on waivers by Milwaukee Brewers (December 18, 1998).

Year Team (League)	Pos.	G	AB	R	H	2B	3B	HR	RBI	Avg.	BB	SO	SB	PO	A	E	Avg.
										BATTING					FIELDING		
1993— Welland (NYP)	SS	50	201	35	61	6	2	1	19	.303	12	31	8	74	138	27	.887
1994— Augusta (S. Atl.)	SS	85	318	48	89	17	4	7	40	.280	25	53	32	106	262	34	.915
— Salem (Carolina)	SS	43	158	25	42	4	1	6	16	.266	15	29	5	65	129	11	.946
1995— Lynchburg (Caro.)	SS	114	399	68	110	19	3	4	38	.276	51	60	31	156	361	35	.937
1996— Carolina (Southern)....	SS	119	443	76	124	20	3	3	49	.280	48	73	29	189	310	30	.943
1997— Calgary (PCL)	SS-2B	112	397	65	131	31	5	1	48	.330	37	47	12	187	315	34	.937
— Pittsburgh (N.L.)	SS	18	37	3	5	0	0	0	3	.135	1	11	1	9	36	0	1.000
1998— Pittsburgh (N.L.)	SS	110	334	30	82	13	6	2	34	.246	31	70	2	148	287	18	.960
— Lynchburg (Caro.)	SS	5	18	4	3	2	0	0	0	.167	2	0	2	5	16	4	.840
Major league totals (2 years)		128	371	33	87	13	6	2	37	.235	32	81	3	157	323	18	.964

COLON, BARTOLO   P   INDIANS

PERSONAL: Born May 24, 1975, in Altamira, Dominican Republic. ... 6-0/185. ... Throws right, bats right.
TRANSACTIONS/CAREER NOTES: Signed as non-drafted free agent by Cleveland Indians organization (June 26, 1993). ... On Canton/Akron disabled list (May 30-July 24, 1996).
HONORS: Named Carolina League Pitcher of the Year (1995).
STATISTICAL NOTES: Pitched 4-0 no-hit victory against New Orleans (June 20, 1997).

Year Team (League)	W	L	Pct.	ERA	G	GS	CG	ShO	Sv.	IP	H	R	ER	BB	SO
1993— Santiago (DSL)	6	1	.857	2.59	11	10	2	1	1	66	44	24	19	33	48
1994— Burlington (Appalachian)....	7	4	.636	3.14	12	12	0	0	0	66	46	32	23	44	84
1995— Kinston (Carolina)	13	3	*.813	1.96	21	21	0	0	0	128 2/3	91	31	28	39	*152
1996— Cant./Akr. (Eastern)	2	2	.500	1.74	13	12	0	0	0	62	44	17	12	25	56
— Buffalo (A.A.)	0	0	...	6.00	8	0	0	0	0	15	16	10	10	8	19
1997— Cleveland (A.L.)	4	7	.364	5.65	19	17	1	0	0	94	107	66	59	45	66
— Buffalo (A.A.)	7	1	.875	2.22	10	10	1	1	0	56 2/3	45	15	14	23	54
1998— Cleveland (A.L.)	14	9	.609	3.71	31	31	6	2	0	204	205	91	84	79	158
Major league totals (2 years)	18	16	.529	4.32	50	48	7	2	0	298	312	157	143	124	224

DIVISION SERIES RECORD

Year Team (League)	W	L	Pct.	ERA	G	GS	CG	ShO	Sv.	IP	H	R	ER	BB	SO
1998— Cleveland (A.L.)	0	0	...	1.59	1	1	0	0	0	5 2/3	5	1	1	4	3

CHAMPIONSHIP SERIES RECORD

Year Team (League)	W	L	Pct.	ERA	G	GS	CG	ShO	Sv.	IP	H	R	ER	BB	SO
1998— Cleveland (A.L.)	1	0	1.000	1.00	1	1	0	0	0	9	4	1	1	4	3

ALL-STAR GAME RECORD

Year League	W	L	Pct.	ERA	GS	CG	ShO	Sv.	IP	H	R	ER	BB	SO
1998— American	1	0	1.000	27.00	0	0	0	0	1	2	3	3	1	1

CONE, DAVID   P   YANKEES

PERSONAL: Born January 2, 1963, in Kansas City, Mo. ... 6-1/190. ... Throws right, bats left. ... Full name: David Brian Cone.
HIGH SCHOOL: Rockhurst (Kansas City, Mo.).
TRANSACTIONS/CAREER NOTES: Selected by Kansas City Royals organization in third round of free-agent draft (June 8, 1981). ... On disabled list (April 8, 1983-entire season). ... Traded by Royals with C Chris Jelic to New York Mets for C Ed Hearn, P Rick Anderson and P Mauro Gozzo (March 27, 1987). ... On New York disabled list (May 28-August 14, 1987); included rehabilitation assignment to Tidewater (July 30-August 14). ... Traded by Mets to Toronto Blue Jays for IF Jeff Kent and a player to be named later (August 27, 1992); Mets acquired OF Ryan Thompson to complete deal (September 1, 1992). ... Granted free agency (October 30, 1992). ... Signed by Royals (December 8, 1992). ... Traded by Royals to Blue Jays for P David Sinnes, IF Chris Stynes and IF Tony Medrano (April 6, 1995). ... Traded by Blue Jays to New York Yankees for P Marty Janzen, P Jason Jarvis and P Mike Gordon (July 28, 1995). ... Granted free agency (November 3, 1995). ... Re-signed by Yankees (December 21, 1995). ... On New York disabled list (May 3-September 2, 1996); included rehabilitation assignment to Norwich (August 21-September 1). ... On disabled list (August 18-September 20, 1997). ... Granted free agency (November 5, 1998). ... Re-signed by Yankees (November 11, 1998).
RECORDS: Shares major league record for striking out side on nine pitches (August 30, 1991, seventh inning).

HONORS: Named righthanded pitcher on THE SPORTING NEWS A.L. All-Star team (1994). ... Named A.L. Cy Young Award winner by Baseball Writers' Association of America (1994).

STATISTICAL NOTES: Led Southern League with 27 wild pitches in 1984. ... Pitched 6-0 one-hit, complete-game victory against San Diego (August 29, 1988). ... Tied for N.L. lead with 10 balks in 1988. ... Pitched 1-0 one-hit, complete-game victory against St. Louis (September 20, 1991). ... Struck out 19 batters in one game (October 6, 1991). ... Pitched 4-0 one-hit, complete-game victory against California (May 22, 1994). ... Led A.L. with 229 $^1/_3$ innings pitched in 1995. ... Struck out 16 batters in one game (June 23, 1997). ... Tied for A.L. lead with 14 wild pitches in 1997.

MISCELLANEOUS: Singled in only appearance as pinch hitter (1990).

Year	Team (League)	W	L	Pct.	ERA	G	GS	CG	ShO	Sv.	IP	H	R	ER	BB	SO
1981—	GC Royals-Bl. (GCL)..........	6	4	.600	2.55	14	12	0	0	0	67	52	24	19	33	45
1982—	Charleston, S.C. (S. Atl.)	9	2	.818	2.06	16	16	1	1	0	104 $^2/_3$	84	38	24	47	87
—	Fort Myers (Fla. St.)..........	7	1	.875	2.12	10	9	6	1	0	72 $^1/_3$	56	21	17	25	57
1983—	....								Did not play.							
1984—	Memphis (Sou.)	8	12	.400	4.28	29	29	9	1	0	178 $^2/_3$	162	103	85	114	110
1985—	Omaha (Am. Assoc.)..........	9	15	.375	4.65	28	27	5	1	0	158 $^2/_3$	157	90	82	*93	115
1986—	Omaha (Am. Assoc.)..........	8	4	.667	2.79	39	2	2	0	14	71	60	23	22	25	63
—	Kansas City (A.L.)	0	0	. . .	5.56	11	0	0	0	0	22 $^2/_3$	29	14	14	13	21
1987—	New York (N.L.)■	5	6	.455	3.71	21	13	1	0	1	99 $^1/_3$	87	46	41	44	68
—	Tidewater (Int'l)	0	1	.000	5.73	3	3	0	0	0	11	10	8	7	6	7
1988—	New York (N.L.).................	20	3	*.870	2.22	35	28	8	4	0	231 $^1/_3$	178	67	57	80	213
1989—	New York (N.L.).................	14	8	.636	3.52	34	33	7	2	0	219 $^2/_3$	183	92	86	74	190
1990—	New York (N.L.).................	14	10	.583	3.23	31	30	6	2	0	211 $^2/_3$	177	84	76	65	*233
1991—	New York (N.L.).................	14	14	.500	3.29	34	34	5	2	0	232 $^2/_3$	204	95	85	73	*241
1992—	New York (N.L.)■	13	7	.650	2.88	27	27	7	•5	0	196 $^2/_3$	162	75	63	*82	214
—	Toronto (A.L.)■	4	3	.571	2.55	8	7	0	0	0	53	39	16	15	29	47
1993—	Kansas City (A.L.)■	11	14	.440	3.33	34	34	6	1	0	254	205	102	94	114	191
1994—	Kansas City (A.L.)	16	5	.762	2.94	23	23	4	3	0	171 $^2/_3$	130	60	56	54	132
1995—	Toronto (A.L.)■	9	6	.600	3.38	17	17	5	2	0	130 $^1/_3$	113	53	49	41	102
—	New York (A.L.)■	9	2	.818	3.82	13	13	1	0	0	§99	82	42	42	47	89
1996—	New York (A.L.)	7	2	.778	2.88	11	11	1	0	0	72	50	25	23	34	71
—	Norwich (Eastern)	0	0	. . .	0.90	2	2	0	0	0	10	9	3	1	1	13
1997—	New York (A.L.)	12	6	.667	2.82	29	29	1	0	0	195	155	67	61	86	222
1998—	New York (A.L.)	•20	7	.741	3.55	31	31	3	0	0	207 $^2/_3$	186	89	82	59	209
	A.L. totals (8 years)	88	45	.662	3.26	177	165	21	6	0	1205 $^1/_3$	989	468	436	477	1084
	N.L. totals (6 years)	80	48	.625	3.08	182	165	34	15	1	1191 $^1/_3$	991	459	408	418	1159
	Major league totals (13 years)...	168	93	.644	3.17	359	330	55	21	1	2396 $^2/_3$	1980	927	844	895	2243

DIVISION SERIES RECORD

RECORDS: Shares career record for most runs allowed—20; most earned runs allowed—20; and most games started—5. ... Holds A.L. career record for most hits allowed—32. ... Shares A.L. career record for most games started—5.

Year	Team (League)	W	L	Pct.	ERA	G	GS	CG	ShO	Sv.	IP	H	R	ER	BB	SO
1995—	New York (A.L.).................	1	0	1.000	4.60	2	2	0	0	0	15 $^2/_3$	15	8	8	9	14
1996—	New York (A.L.).................	0	1	.000	9.00	2	1	0	0	0	6	8	6	6	2	8
1997—	New York (A.L.).................	0	0	. . .	16.20	1	1	0	0	0	3 $^1/_3$	7	6	6	2	2
1998—	New York (A.L.).................	1	0	1.000	0.00	1	1	0	0	0	5 $^2/_3$	2	0	0	1	6
	Div. series totals (4 years)	2	1	.667	5.87	6	5	0	0	0	30 $^2/_3$	32	20	20	14	30

CHAMPIONSHIP SERIES RECORD

Year	Team (League)	W	L	Pct.	ERA	G	GS	CG	ShO	Sv.	IP	H	R	ER	BB	SO
1988—	New York (N.L.).................	1	1	.500	4.50	3	2	1	0	0	12	10	6	6	5	9
1992—	Toronto (A.L.)...................	1	1	.500	3.00	2	2	0	0	0	12	11	7	4	5	9
1996—	New York (A.L.).................	0	0	. . .	3.00	1	1	0	0	0	6	5	2	2	5	5
1998—	New York (A.L.).................	1	0	1.000	4.15	2	2	0	0	0	13	12	6	6	6	13
	Champ. series totals (4 years)	3	2	.600	3.77	8	7	1	0	0	43	38	21	18	21	36

WORLD SERIES RECORD

NOTES: Member of World Series championship team (1992, 1996 and 1998).

Year	Team (League)	W	L	Pct.	ERA	G	GS	CG	ShO	Sv.	IP	H	R	ER	BB	SO
1992—	Toronto (A.L.)....................	0	0	. . .	3.48	2	2	0	0	0	10 $^1/_3$	9	5	4	8	8
1996—	New York (A.L.).................	1	0	1.000	1.50	1	1	0	0	0	6	4	1	1	4	3
1998—	New York (A.L.).................	0	0	. . .	3.00	1	1	0	0	0	6	2	3	2	3	4
	World Series totals (3 years)	1	0	1.000	2.82	4	4	0	0	0	22 $^1/_3$	15	9	7	15	15

ALL-STAR GAME RECORD

Year	League	W	L	Pct.	ERA	GS	CG	ShO	Sv.	IP	H	R	ER	BB	SO
1988—	National	0	0	. . .	0.00	0	0	0	0	1	0	0	0	0	1
1992—	National	0	0	. . .	0.00	0	0	0	0	1	0	0	0	1	1
1994—	American	0	0	. . .	13.50	0	0	0	0	2	4	3	3	0	3
1997—	American	0	0	. . .	0.00	0	0	0	0	1	0	0	0	2	0
	All-Star totals (4 years)	0	0	. . .	5.40	0	0	0	0	5	4	3	3	2	5

CONINE, JEFF   OF   ROYALS

PERSONAL: Born June 27, 1966, in Tacoma, Wash. ... 6-1/220. ... Bats right, throws right. ... Full name: Jeffrey Guy Conine.

HIGH SCHOOL: Eisenhower (Rialto, Calif.).

COLLEGE: UCLA.

TRANSACTIONS/CAREER NOTES: Selected by Kansas City Royals organization in 58th round of free-agent draft (June 2, 1987). ... On disabled list (June 28, 1991-remainder of season). ... Selected by Florida Marlins in first round (22nd pick overall) of expansion draft (November 17, 1992). ... Traded by Marlins to Royals for P Blaine Mull (November 20, 1997). ... On Kansas City disabled list (March 25-May 5, 1998). ... On Kansas City disabled list (July 27-August 19, 1998); included rehabilitation assignment to Omaha (August 17-19).

RECORDS: Shares major league rookie-season record for most games—162 (1993).

HONORS: Named Southern League Most Valuable Player (1990).

STATISTICAL NOTES: Led Southern League first basemen with 1,164 putouts, 95 assists, 22 errors, 1,281 total chances and 108 double plays in 1990. ... Led N.L. with 12 sacrifice flies in 1995. ... Career major league grand slams: 3.

MISCELLANEOUS: Holds Florida Marlins all-time records for most hits (737), most runs batted in (422), most doubles (122) and highest career batting average (.291).

							BATTING								FIELDING		
Year Team (League)	Pos.	G	AB	R	H	2B	3B	HR	RBI	Avg.	BB	SO	SB	PO	A	E	Avg.
1988—Baseball City (FSL).....	1B-3B	118	415	63	113	23	9	10	59	.272	46	77	26	661	51	22	.970
1989—Baseball City (FSL).....	1B	113	425	68	116	12	7	14	60	.273	40	91	32	830	65	18	.980
1990—Memphis (Sou.)..........	1B-3B	137	487	89	156	37	8	15	95	.320	94	88	21	†1164	†95	†22	.983
—Kansas City (A.L.)	1B	9	20	3	5	2	0	0	2	.250	2	5	0	39	4	1	.977
1991—Omaha (A.A.).............	1B-OF	51	171	23	44	9	1	3	15	.257	26	39	0	392	41	7	.984
1992—Omaha (A.A.).............	1B-OF	110	397	69	120	24	5	20	72	.302	54	67	4	845	60	6	.993
—Kansas City (A.L.)	OF-1B	28	91	10	23	5	2	0	9	.253	8	23	0	75	3	0	1.000
1993—Florida (N.L.)■..........	OF-1B	*162	595	75	174	24	3	12	79	.292	52	135	2	403	25	2	.995
1994—Florida (N.L.)............	OF-1B	115	451	60	144	27	6	18	82	.319	40	92	1	408	24	6	.986
1995—Florida (N.L.)............	OF-1B	133	483	72	146	26	2	25	105	.302	66	94	2	292	18	6	.981
1996—Florida (N.L.)............	OF-1B	157	597	84	175	32	2	26	95	.293	62	121	1	478	48	8	.985
1997—Florida (N.L.)............	1B-OF	151	405	46	98	13	1	17	61	.242	57	89	2	897	104	8	.992
1998—Kansas City (A.L.)■....	OF-1B-DH	93	309	30	79	26	0	8	43	.256	26	68	3	235	7	1	.996
—Omaha (PCL).............	OF	2	9	0	0	0	0	0	0	.000	0	3	0	2	0	0	1.000
American League totals (3 years)		130	420	43	107	33	2	8	54	.255	36	96	3	349	14	2	.995
National League totals (5 years)		718	2531	337	737	122	14	98	422	.291	277	531	8	2478	219	30	.989
Major league totals (8 years)		848	2951	380	844	155	16	106	476	.286	313	627	11	2827	233	32	.990

DIVISION SERIES RECORD

							BATTING								FIELDING		
Year Team (League)	Pos.	G	AB	R	H	2B	3B	HR	RBI	Avg.	BB	SO	SB	PO	A	E	Avg.
1997—Florida (N.L.)	1B	3	11	3	4	1	0	0	0	.364	1	0	0	24	3	1	.964

CHAMPIONSHIP SERIES RECORD

							BATTING								FIELDING		
Year Team (League)	Pos.	G	AB	R	H	2B	3B	HR	RBI	Avg.	BB	SO	SB	PO	A	E	Avg.
1997—Florida (N.L.)	1B	6	18	1	2	0	0	0	1	.111	1	4	0	34	5	0	1.000

WORLD SERIES RECORD

NOTES: Member of World Series championship team (1997).

							BATTING								FIELDING		
Year Team (League)	Pos.	G	AB	R	H	2B	3B	HR	RBI	Avg.	BB	SO	SB	PO	A	E	Avg.
1997—Florida (N.L.)	1B-PH	6	13	1	3	0	0	0	2	.231	0	0	0	30	2	0	1.000

ALL-STAR GAME RECORD

NOTES: Hit home run in first at-bat (July 11, 1995). ... Named Most Valuable Player (1995).

					BATTING							FIELDING		
Year League	Pos.	AB	R	H	2B	3B	HR	RBI	Avg.	BB	SO	SB	PO	A	E	Avg.
1994— National......................							Did not play.									
1995— National......................	PH	1	1	1	0	0	1	1	1.000	0	0	0	...	...	...	...

CONNELLY, STEVE P GIANTS

PERSONAL: Born April 27, 1974, in Long Beach, Calif. ... 6-4/210. ... Throws right, bats right. ... Full name: Steven Lee Connelly.
HIGH SCHOOL: Woodrow Wilson (Long Beach, Calif.).
COLLEGE: Oklahoma.
TRANSACTIONS/CAREER NOTES: Selected by Oakland Athletics organization in 24th round of free-agent draft (June 1, 1995). ... Claimed on waivers by Boston Red Sox (December 16, 1998). ... Claimed on waivers by San Francisco Giants (January 8, 1999).

Year Team (League)	W	L	Pct.	ERA	G	GS	CG	ShO	Sv.	IP	H	R	ER	BB	SO
1995—S. Oregon (N'west).............	2	4	.333	3.81	17	0	0	0	2	28 1/3	29	17	12	14	19
1996—Modesto (California)	4	7	.364	3.76	52	0	0	0	14	64 2/3	58	33	27	32	65
1997—Huntsville (Southern)	3	3	.500	3.75	43	0	0	0	7	69 2/3	74	33	29	20	49
1998—Edmonton (PCL)	6	0	1.000	3.79	55	0	0	0	13	76	64	34	32	24	62
—Oakland (A.L.)	0	0	...	1.93	3	0	0	0	0	4 2/3	10	1	1	4	1
Major league totals (1 year)........	0	0	...	1.93	3	0	0	0	0	4 2/3	10	1	1	4	1

CONTI, JASON OF DIAMONDBACKS

PERSONAL: Born January 27, 1975, in Pittsburgh. ... 5-11/180. ... Bats left, throws right. ... Full name: Stanley Jason Conti.
HIGH SCHOOL: Seneca Valley (Harmony, Pa.).
COLLEGE: Pittsburgh.
TRANSACTIONS/CAREER NOTES: Selected by Arizona Diamondbacks organization in 32nd round of free-agent draft (June 4, 1996). ... Loaned by Diamondbacks to Tulsa, Texas Rangers organization (April 1, 1998). ... Returned to Diamondbacks organization (September 14, 1998).
STATISTICAL NOTES: Tied for Midwest League lead in double plays by outfielder with six in 1997.

							BATTING								FIELDING		
Year Team (League)	Pos.	G	AB	R	H	2B	3B	HR	RBI	Avg.	BB	SO	SB	PO	A	E	Avg.
1996—Lethbridge (Pioneer) ..	OF	63	226	63	83	15	1	4	49	.367	30	29	30	80	5	4	.955
1997—South Bend (Mid.).......	OF	117	458	78	142	22	10	3	43	.310	45	99	30	240	13	5	.981
—High Desert (Calif.)......	OF	14	59	15	21	5	1	2	8	.356	10	12	1	27	2	5	.853
1998—Tulsa (Texas)■.........	OF	130	530	*125	167	31	12	15	67	.315	63	96	19	183	*20	5	.976

PERSONAL: Born October 4, 1962, in Lamarque, Texas. ... 6-3/190. ... Throws left, bats left. ... Full name: Dennis Bryan Cook.

HIGH SCHOOL: Dickinson (Texas).

JUNIOR COLLEGE: Angelina College (Texas).

COLLEGE: Texas.

TRANSACTIONS/CAREER NOTES: Selected by San Diego Padres organization in sixth round of free-agent draft (January 11, 1983); did not sign. ... Selected by San Francisco Giants organization in 18th round of free-agent draft (June 3, 1985). ... Traded by Giants with P Terry Mulholland and 3B Charlie Hayes to Philadelphia Phillies for P Steve Bedrosian and a player to be named later (June, 18, 1989); Giants organization acquired IF Rick Parker to complete deal (August 7, 1989). ... Traded by Phillies to Los Angeles Dodgers for C Darrin Fletcher (September 13, 1990). ... Traded by Dodgers with P Mike Christopher to Cleveland Indians for P Rudy Seanez (December 10, 1991). ... Granted free agency (October 15, 1993). ... Signed by Chicago White Sox organization (January 5, 1994). ... Claimed on waivers by Indians (October 17, 1994). ... Traded by Indians to Texas Rangers for SS Guillermo Mercedes (June 22, 1995). ... Granted free agency (October 29, 1996). ... Signed by Florida Marlins (December 10, 1996). ... On suspended list (July 4-5, 1997). ... Traded by Marlins to New York Mets for OF Fletcher Bates and P Scott Comer (December 18, 1997). ... Granted free agency (October 23, 1998). ... Re-signed by Mets (November 18, 1998).

HONORS: Named Texas League Pitcher of the Year (1987).

STATISTICAL NOTES: Led A.L. with five balks in 1992.

MISCELLANEOUS: Appeared in one game as pinch runner with Philadelphia (1989). ... Singled once and scored once in five games as pinch hitter and appeared in one game as pinch runner with Philadelphia (1990). ... Appeared in one game as pinch runner (1997). ... Singled twice, scored once and had an RBI in two games as pinch hitter (1997).

Year Team (League)	W	L	Pct.	ERA	G	GS	CG	ShO	Sv.	IP	H	R	ER	BB	SO
1985— Clinton (Midwest)	5	4	.556	3.36	13	13	1	0	0	83	73	35	31	27	40
1986— Fresno (California)	12	7	.632	3.97	27	25	2	1	1	170	141	92	75	100	*173
1987— Shreveport (Texas)	9	2	.818	2.13	16	16	1	1	0	105 2/3	94	32	25	20	98
— Phoenix (PCL)	2	5	.286	5.23	12	11	1	0	0	62	72	45	36	26	24
1988— Phoenix (PCL)	11	9	.550	3.88	26	25	5	1	0	141 1/3	138	73	61	51	110
— San Francisco (N.L.)	2	1	.667	2.86	4	4	1	1	0	22	9	8	7	11	13
1989— Phoenix (PCL)	7	4	.636	3.12	12	12	3	1	0	78	73	29	27	19	85
— San Francisco (N.L.)	1	0	1.000	1.80	2	2	1	0	0	15	13	3	3	5	9
— Philadelphia (N.L.)■	6	8	.429	3.99	21	16	1	1	0	106	97	56	47	33	58
1990— Philadelphia (N.L.)	8	3	.727	3.56	42	13	2	1	1	141 2/3	132	61	56	54	58
— Los Angeles (N.L.)■	1	1	.500	7.53	5	3	0	0	0	14 1/3	23	13	12	2	6
1991— Albuquerque (PCL)	7	3	.700	3.63	14	14	1	0	0	91 2/3	73	46	37	32	84
— Los Angeles (N.L.)	1	0	1.000	0.51	20	1	0	0	0	17 2/3	12	3	1	7	8
— San Antonio (Tex.)	1	3	.250	2.49	7	7	1	0	0	50 2/3	43	20	14	10	45
1992— Cleveland (A.L.)■■	5	7	.417	3.82	32	25	1	0	0	158	156	79	67	50	96
1993— Cleveland (A.L.)	5	5	.500	5.67	25	6	0	0	0	54	62	36	34	16	34
— Charlotte (Int'l)	3	2	.600	5.06	12	6	0	0	0	42 2/3	46	26	24	6	40
1994— Chicago (A.L.)■	3	1	.750	3.55	38	0	0	0	0	33	29	17	13	14	26
1995— Cleveland (A.L.)■	0	0	. . .	6.39	11	0	0	0	0	12 2/3	16	9	9	10	13
— Texas (A.L.)■	0	2	.000	4.00	35	1	0	0	2	45	47	23	20	16	40
1996— Texas (A.L.)	5	2	.714	4.09	60	0	0	0	0	70 1/3	53	34	32	35	64
1997— Florida (N.L.)■	1	2	.333	3.90	59	0	0	0	0	62 1/3	64	28	27	28	63
1998— New York (N.L.)■	8	4	.667	2.38	73	0	0	0	1	68	60	21	18	27	79
A.L. totals (5 years)	18	17	.514	4.22	201	32	1	0	2	373	363	198	175	141	273
N.L. totals (6 years)	28	19	.596	3.44	226	39	5	3	2	447	410	193	171	167	294
Major league totals (11 years)	46	36	.561	3.80	427	71	6	3	4	820	773	391	346	308	567

DIVISION SERIES RECORD

Year Team (League)	W	L	Pct.	ERA	G	GS	CG	ShO	Sv.	IP	H	R	ER	BB	SO
1996— Texas (A.L.)	0	0	. . .	0.00	2	0	0	0	0	1 1/3	0	0	0	1	0
1997— Florida (N.L.)	1	0	1.000	0.00	2	0	0	0	0	3	0	0	0	1	3
Div. series totals (2 years)	1	0	1.000	0.00	4	0	0	0	0	4 1/3	0	0	0	2	3

CHAMPIONSHIP SERIES RECORD

Year Team (League)	W	L	Pct.	ERA	G	GS	CG	ShO	Sv.	IP	H	R	ER	BB	SO
1997— Florida (N.L.)	0	0	. . .	0.00	2	0	0	0	0	2 1/3	0	0	0	0	2

WORLD SERIES RECORD

NOTES: Member of World Series championship team (1997).

Year Team (League)	W	L	Pct.	ERA	G	GS	CG	ShO	Sv.	IP	H	R	ER	BB	SO
1997— Florida (N.L.)	1	0	1.000	0.00	3	0	0	0	0	3 2/3	1	0	0	1	5

PERSONAL: Born August 6, 1975, in Staunton, Va. ... 6-2/195. ... Throws right, bats right. ... Full name: Derrick W. Cook.

HIGH SCHOOL: Robert E. Lee (Staunton, Va.).

COLLEGE: James Madison.

TRANSACTIONS/CAREER NOTES: Selected by Cleveland Indians organization in 10th round of free-agent draft (June 3, 1993); did not sign. ... Selected by Texas Rangers organization in second round of free-agent draft (June 4, 1996).

Year Team (League)	W	L	Pct.	ERA	G	GS	CG	ShO	Sv.	IP	H	R	ER	BB	SO
1996— GC Rangers (GCL)	2	1	.667	4.70	6	5	1	1	0	23	25	14	12	11	13
1997— Pulaski (Appalachian)	2	2	.500	3.74	6	6	0	0	0	33 2/3	32	15	14	12	32
— Charlotte (Fla. St.)	5	2	.714	2.30	8	8	2	0	0	58 2/3	54	21	15	15	35
1998— Charlotte (Fla. St.)	13	7	.650	3.66	26	26	1	1	0	167 1/3	170	81	68	64	111

COOKE, STEVE   P   DEVIL RAYS

PERSONAL: Born January 14, 1970, in Kauai, Hawaii. ... 6-6/240. ... Throws left, bats right. ... Full name: Stephen Montague Cooke.
HIGH SCHOOL: Tigard (Ore.).
COLLEGE: Southern Idaho.
TRANSACTIONS/CAREER NOTES: Selected by Philadelphia Phillies organization in 53rd round of free-agent draft (June 1, 1988); did not sign. ... Selected by Pittsburgh Pirates organization in 35th round of free-agent draft (June 5, 1989). ... On Buffalo disabled list (May 18-28, 1992). ... On Pittsburgh disabled list (April 16, 1995-entire season); included rehabilitation assignments to Augusta (July 18) and Carolina (July 24-26). ... On Pittsburgh disabled list (March 30-June 19, 1996); included rehabilitation assignment to Carolina (May 27-June 19). ... On Carolina disabled list (August 23-September 2, 1996). ... Granted free agency (October 29, 1996). ... Re-signed by Pirates (November 20, 1996). ... Released by Pirates (December 15, 1997). ... Signed by Cincinnati Reds (December 22, 1997). ... On Cincinnati disabled list (April 3-19 and April 20, 1998-remainder of season); included rehabilitation assignment to Indianapolis (August 16-28). ... Released by Reds (September 30, 1998). ... Signed by Tampa Bay Devil Rays organization (January 20, 1999).

Year Team (League)	W	L	Pct.	ERA	G	GS	CG	ShO	Sv.	IP	H	R	ER	BB	SO
1990— Welland (N.Y.-Penn)	2	3	.400	2.35	11	11	0	0	0	46	36	21	12	17	43
1991— Augusta (S. Atl.)	5	4	.556	2.82	11	11	1	0	0	60²/₃	50	28	19	35	52
— Salem (Carolina)	1	0	1.000	4.85	2	2	0	0	0	13	14	8	7	2	5
— Carolina (Southern)	0	0	...	2.84	3	9	1	1	0	12²/₃	9	4	4	7	18
1992— Carolina (Southern)	2	2	.500	3.00	6	6	0	0	0	36	31	13	12	12	38
— Buffalo (A.A.)	6	3	.667	3.75	13	13	0	0	0	74¹/₃	71	35	31	36	52
— Pittsburgh (N.L.)	2	0	1.000	3.52	11	0	0	0	1	23	22	9	9	4	10
1993— Pittsburgh (N.L.)	10	10	.500	3.89	32	32	3	1	0	210²/₃	207	101	91	59	132
1994— Pittsburgh (N.L.)	4	11	.267	5.02	25	23	2	0	0	134¹/₃	157	79	75	46	74
1995— Augusta (S. Atl.)	1	0	1.000	0.00	1	1	0	0	0	5	2	0	0	1	6
— Carolina (Southern)	0	0	...	7.20	1	1	0	0	0	5	5	4	4	5	4
1996— Carolina (Southern)	1	5	.167	4.36	12	12	0	0	0	53²/₃	56	34	26	26	45
— Pittsburgh (N.L.)	0	0	...	7.56	3	0	0	0	0	8¹/₃	11	7	7	5	7
1997— Pittsburgh (N.L.)	9	15	.375	4.30	32	32	0	0	0	167¹/₃	184	95	80	77	109
1998— Cincinnati (N.L.)■	1	0	1.000	1.50	1	1	0	0	0	6	4	1	1	0	3
— Indianapolis (Int'l)	0	1	.000	37.80	2	2	0	0	0	1²/₃	3	7	7	5	0
Major league totals (6 years)	26	36	.419	4.31	104	88	5	1	1	549²/₃	585	292	263	191	335

COOMER, RON   3B   TWINS

PERSONAL: Born November 18, 1966, in Chicago. ... 5-11/210. ... Bats right, throws right. ... Full name: Ronald Bryan Coomer.
HIGH SCHOOL: Lockport (Ill.) Township.
COLLEGE: Taft (Calif.) College.
TRANSACTIONS/CAREER NOTES: Selected by Oakland Athletics organization in 14th round of free-agent draft (June 2, 1987). ... Released by A's organization (August 1, 1990). ... Signed by Chicago White Sox organization (March 18, 1991). ... On disabled list (June 5-19, 1992). ... On Birmingham disabled list (June 12-21, 1993). ... Traded by White Sox organization to Los Angeles Dodgers organization for P Isidro Martinez (December 27, 1993). ... Traded by Dodgers with P Greg Hansell, P Jose Parra and a player to be named later to Minnesota Twins for P Kevin Tapani and P Mark Guthrie (July 31, 1995); Twins acquired OF Chris Latham to complete deal (October 30, 1995).
STATISTICAL NOTES: Led Southern League with eight sacrifice flies and tied for lead in grounding into double plays with 21 in 1991. ... Led Southern League third basemen with 94 putouts, 396 total chances, 24 double plays and tied for lead with 26 errors in 1991. ... Led Pacific Coast League with 293 total bases in 1994. ... Led Pacific Coast League third basemen with .952 fielding percentage, 399 total chances and 299 assists in 1994. ... Tied for A.L. lead in grounding into double plays with 22 in 1998. ... Career major league grand slams: 1.

Year Team (League)	Pos.	G	AB	R	H	2B	3B	HR	RBI	Avg.	BB	SO	SB	PO	A	E	Avg.
1987— Medford (N'west)	3B-1B	45	168	23	58	10	2	1	26	.345	19	22	1	54	78	11	.923
1988— Modesto (California)	3B-1B	131	495	67	138	23	2	17	85	.279	60	88	2	78	105	16	.920
1989— Madison (Midwest)	3B-1B	61	216	28	69	15	0	4	28	.319	30	34	0	67	64	6	.956
1990— Huntsville (Sou.)	2B-1B-3B	66	194	22	43	7	0	3	27	.222	21	40	3	200	100	11	.965
1991— Birmingham (Sou.)■ ..	3B-1B	137	505	*81	129	27	5	13	76	.255	59	78	0	†113	278	‡26	.938
1992— Vancouver (PCL)	3B	86	262	29	62	10	0	9	40	.237	16	36	3	49	115	13	.927
1993— Birmingham (Sou.)......	3B-1B	69	262	44	85	18	0	13	50	.324	15	43	1	43	106	11	.931
— Nashville (A.A.)	3B	59	211	34	66	19	0	13	51	.313	10	29	1	30	107	16	.895
1994— Albuquerque (PCL)■..	3B-2B	127	535	89	181	34	6	22	*123	.338	26	62	4	81	†299	19	†.952
1995— Albuquerque (PCL)	3B	85	323	54	104	23	2	16	76	.322	18	28	5	335	93	9	.979
— Minnesota (A.L.)■	1-3-DH-O	37	101	15	26	3	1	5	19	.257	9	11	0	138	32	2	.988
1996— Minnesota (A.L.)	1-O-3-DH	95	233	34	69	12	1	12	41	.296	17	24	3	275	42	4	.988
1997— Minnesota (A.L.)	3-1-DH-O	140	523	63	156	30	2	13	85	.298	22	91	4	123	223	11	.969
1998— Minnesota (A.L.)	3-1-DH-O	137	529	54	146	22	1	15	72	.276	18	72	2	428	150	6	.990
Major league totals (4 years)		409	1386	166	397	67	5	45	217	.286	66	198	9	964	447	23	.984

COPPINGER, ROCKY   P   ORIOLES

PERSONAL: Born March 19, 1974, in El Paso, Texas. ... 6-5/245. ... Throws right, bats right. ... Full name: John Thomas Coppinger. ... Name pronounced COP-in-jer.
HIGH SCHOOL: Coronado (El Paso, Texas).
JUNIOR COLLEGE: Hillsboro (Texas).
TRANSACTIONS/CAREER NOTES: Selected by Baltimore Orioles in 17th round of free-agent draft (June 3, 1993). ... On Baltimore disabled list (March 31-April 15 and May 10, 1997-remainder of season); included rehabilitation assignments to Rochester (May 14-22), Gulf Coast Orioles (July 1-12) and Bowie (July 17-27). ... On Bowie disabled list (April 10-May 24, 1998).

Year Team (League)	W	L	Pct.	ERA	G	GS	CG	ShO	Sv.	IP	H	R	ER	BB	SO
1994— Bluefield (Appalachian)	4	3	.571	2.45	14	13	0	0	0	73¹/₃	51	24	20	40	88
1995— Frederick (Carolina)	7	1	.875	1.57	11	11	2	1	0	68²/₃	46	16	12	24	91
— Bowie (Eastern)	6	2	.750	2.69	13	13	2	2	0	83²/₃	58	33	25	43	62
— Rochester (Int'l)	3	0	1.000	1.04	5	5	0	0	0	34²/₃	23	5	4	17	19

C

Year Team (League)	W	L	Pct.	ERA	G	GS	CG	ShO	Sv.	IP	H	R	ER	BB	SO
1996— Rochester (Int'l)	6	4	.600	4.19	12	12	0	0	0	73	65	36	34	39	81
— Baltimore (A.L.)	10	6	.625	5.18	23	22	0	0	0	125	126	76	72	60	104
1997— Baltimore (A.L.)	1	1	.500	6.30	5	4	0	0	0	20	21	14	14	16	22
— Rochester (Int'l)	1	2	.333	5.52	3	3	0	0	0	$14^2/_3$	16	10	9	11	9
— GC Orioles (GCL)	0	0	...	1.80	3	3	0	0	0	10	7	3	2	0	13
— Bowie (Eastern)	1	1	.500	4.80	3	3	0	0	0	15	15	9	8	3	15
1998— Bowie (Eastern)	2	2	.500	4.35	7	6	0	0	0	31	26	18	15	11	30
— Rochester (Int'l)	8	3	.727	3.50	14	13	1	0	0	$87^1/_3$	80	38	34	43	64
— Baltimore (A.L.)	0	0	...	5.17	6	1	0	0	0	$15^2/_3$	16	9	9	7	13
Major league totals (3 years)	11	7	.611	5.32	34	27	0	0	0	$160^2/_3$	163	99	95	83	139

CHAMPIONSHIP SERIES RECORD

Year Team (League)	W	L	Pct.	ERA	G	GS	CG	ShO	Sv.	IP	H	R	ER	BB	SO
1996— Baltimore (A.L.)	0	1	.000	8.44	1	1	0	0	0	$5^1/_3$	6	5	5	1	3

COQUILLETTE, TRACE   2B   EXPOS

PERSONAL: Born June 4, 1974, in Carmicheal, Calif. ... 6-0/185. ... Bats right, throws right. ... Full name: Trace Robert Coquillette. ... Name pronounced COE-kill-ette.
HIGH SCHOOL: Casa Roble (Orangevale, Calif.).
JUNIOR COLLEGE: Sacramento City College.
TRANSACTIONS/CAREER NOTES: Selected by Montreal Expos organization in 10th round of free-agent draft (June 3, 1993). ... On West Palm Beach disabled list (June 2-August 1, 1996).
STATISTICAL NOTES: Led New York-Pennsylvania League second basemen with 366 total chances in 1994.

							BATTING							FIELDING		
Year Team (League)	Pos.	G	AB	R	H	2B	3B	HR	RBI	Avg.	BB	SO	SB	PO	A	E	Avg.
1993— G.C. Expos (GCL)	2B	44	159	27	40	4	3	2	11	.252	37	28	16	80	123	•12	.944
— W.P. Beach (FSL)	2B	6	18	2	5	3	0	0	3	.278	2	5	0	8	16	1	.960
1994— Burlington (Midw.)	2B	5	17	2	3	1	0	0	0	.176	1	4	1	6	14	1	.952
— Vermont (NYP)	2B	70	252	54	77	11	5	9	52	.306	23	40	7	125	216	*25	.932
1995— Albany (S. Atl.)	2B	128	458	67	123	27	4	3	57	.269	64	91	17	252	292	14	.975
1996— G.C. Expos (GCL)	2B-3B	7	25	4	4	1	0	0	0	.160	4	6	1	16	16	1	.970
— W.P. Beach (FSL)	2B-3B	72	266	39	67	17	4	1	27	.252	27	72	9	100	142	22	.917
1997— Harrisburg (East.)	2B-3B	81	293	46	76	17	3	10	51	.259	25	40	9	116	169	16	.947
— W.P. Beach (FSL)	2B-3B-OF	53	188	34	60	18	2	8	33	.319	27	27	8	90	111	7	.966
1998— Harrisburg (East.)	2B-3B	49	187	40	62	10	0	9	23	.332	15	41	10	61	124	7	.964
— Ottawa (Int'l)	2B-3B-OF	74	252	30	64	14	0	7	40	.254	17	38	3	125	140	9	.967

CORA, ALEX   SS   DODGERS

PERSONAL: Born October 18, 1975, in Caguas, Puerto Rico. ... 6-0/180. ... Bats left, throws right. ... Full name: Jose Alexander Cora. ... Brother of Joey Cora, second baseman with four major league teams (1987-1998).
HIGH SCHOOL: Bautista (Caguas, Puerto Rico).
COLLEGE: Miami (Fla.).
TRANSACTIONS/CAREER NOTES: Selected by Los Angeles Dodgers organization in third round of free-agent draft (June 4, 1996).
STATISTICAL NOTES: Led Texas League shortstops with 629 total chances and 88 double plays in 1997.

							BATTING							FIELDING		
Year Team (League)	Pos.	G	AB	R	H	2B	3B	HR	RBI	Avg.	BB	SO	SB	PO	A	E	Avg.
1996— Vero Beach (FSL)	SS-OF	61	214	26	55	5	4	0	26	.257	12	36	5	86	164	16	.940
1997— San Antonio (Tex.)	SS	127	448	52	105	20	4	3	48	.234	25	60	12	*197	*412	20	*.968
1998— Albuquerque (PCL)	SS-2B	81	299	42	79	17	5	5	45	.264	15	38	10	126	270	18	.957
— Los Angeles (N.L.)	SS-2B	29	33	1	4	0	1	0	0	.121	2	8	0	26	29	2	.965
Major league totals (1 year)		29	33	1	4	0	1	0	0	.121	2	8	0	26	29	2	.965

CORA, JOEY   2B   BLUE JAYS

PERSONAL: Born May 14, 1965, in Caguas, Puerto Rico. ... 5-8/162. ... Bats both, throws right. ... Full name: Jose Manuel Cora. ... Brother of Alex Cora, shortstop, Los Angeles Dodgers.
HIGH SCHOOL: Bautista (Caguas, Puerto Rico).
COLLEGE: Vanderbilt.
TRANSACTIONS/CAREER NOTES: Selected by San Diego Padres organization in first round (23rd pick overall) of free-agent draft (June 3, 1985); pick received as compensation for New York Yankees signing free-agent P Ed Whitson. ... On disabled list (June 22-August 15, 1986). ... Traded by Padres with IF Kevin Garner and OF Warren Newson to Chicago White Sox for P Adam Peterson and P Steve Rosenberg (March 31, 1991). ... On Chicago disabled list (June 22-July 11, 1991); included rehabilitation assignment to South Bend (July 9-11). ... On Chicago disabled list (June 30-July 15, 1994); included rehabilitation assignment to South Bend (July 11-15). ... Granted free agency (December 23, 1994). ... Signed by Seattle Mariners (April 6, 1995). ... Granted free agency (November 6, 1997). ... Re-signed by Mariners (November 18, 1997). ... Traded by Mariners to Cleveland Indians for IF David Bell (August 31, 1998). ... Granted free agency (October 29, 1998). ... Signed by Toronto Blue Jays (January 18, 1999).
RECORDS: Holds major league single-season record for fewest chances accepted by second baseman (150 or more games)—553 (1998).
STATISTICAL NOTES: Led Pacific Coast League second basemen with 24 errors in 1988 and 1989. ... Led A.L. with 19 sacrifice hits in 1993. ... Led A.L. second basemen in errors with 19 in 1993, 22 in 1995 and 20 in 1998. ... Had 24-game hitting streak (May 2-29, 1997). ... Had 16-game hitting streak (March 31-April 17, 1998). ... Had 20-game hitting streak (August 15-September 4, 1998).

							BATTING							FIELDING		
Year Team (League)	Pos.	G	AB	R	H	2B	3B	HR	RBI	Avg.	BB	SO	SB	PO	A	E	Avg.
1985— Spokane (N'west)	2B	43	170	48	55	11	2	3	26	.324	27	24	13	92	123	9	.960
1986— Beaumont (Texas)	2B-SS	81	315	54	96	5	5	3	41	.305	47	29	24	217	267	19	.962

C

Year Team (League)	Pos.	G	AB	R	H	2B	3B	HR	RBI	Avg.	BB	SO	SB	PO	A	E	Avg.
1987— San Diego (N.L.)	2B-SS	77	241	23	57	7	2	0	13	.237	28	26	15	123	200	10	.970
— Las Vegas (PCL)	2B-SS	81	293	50	81	9	1	1	24	.276	62	39	12	186	249	9	.980
1988— Las Vegas (PCL)	2B-3B-OF	127	460	73	136	15	3	3	55	.296	44	19	31	285	346	†26	.960
1989— Las Vegas (PCL)	2B-SS	119	507	79	157	25	4	0	37	.310	42	31	*40	245	349	†27	.957
— San Diego (N.L.)	SS-3B-2B	12	19	5	6	1	0	0	1	.316	1	0	1	11	15	2	.929
1990— San Diego (N.L.)	SS-2B-C	51	100	12	27	3	0	0	2	.270	6	9	8	59	49	11	.908
— Las Vegas (PCL)	SS-2B	51	211	41	74	13	9	0	24	.351	29	16	15	125	148	14	.951
1991— Chicago (A.L.)■........	2B-SS-DH	100	228	37	55	2	3	0	18	.241	20	21	11	107	192	10	.968
— South Bend (Mid.)......	2B	1	5	1	1	0	0	0	0	.200	0	1	1	2	4	0	1.000
1992— Chicago (A.L.)	2-DH-S-3	68	122	27	30	7	1	0	9	.246	22	13	10	60	84	3	.980
1993— Chicago (A.L.)	2B-3B	153	579	95	155	15	13	4	51	.268	67	63	20	296	413	†19	.974
1994— Chicago (A.L.)	2B-DH	90	312	55	86	13	4	2	30	.276	38	32	8	162	195	8	.978
— South Bend (Mid.)......	2B	3	11	3	5	1	0	0	1	.455	2	1	1	4	8	1	.923
1995— Seattle (A.L.)■..........	2B-SS	120	427	64	127	19	2	3	39	.297	37	31	18	205	262	†23	.953
1996— Seattle (A.L.)	2B-3B	144	530	90	154	37	6	6	45	.291	35	32	5	296	314	13	.979
1997— Seattle (A.L.)	2B	149	574	105	172	40	4	11	54	.300	53	49	6	*307	310	17	.973
1998— Seattle (A.L.)	2B	131	519	95	147	23	6	6	26	.283	62	50	13	212	270	*19	.962
— Cleveland (A.L.)■........	2B	24	83	16	19	4	0	0	6	.229	11	9	2	31	40	*1	.986
American League totals (8 years)		979	3374	584	945	160	39	30	278	.280	345	300	93	1676	2080	113	.971
National League totals (3 years)		140	360	40	90	11	2	0	16	.250	35	35	24	193	264	23	.952
Major league totals (11 years)		1119	3734	624	1035	171	41	30	294	.277	380	335	117	1869	2344	136	.969

DIVISION SERIES RECORD

Year Team (League)	Pos.	G	AB	R	H	2B	3B	HR	RBI	Avg.	BB	SO	SB	PO	A	E	Avg.
1995— Seattle (A.L.)	2B	5	19	7	6	1	0	1	1	.316	3	0	1	10	12	1	.957
1997— Seattle (A.L.)	2B	4	17	1	3	0	0	0	0	.176	0	4	0	7	11	0	1.000
1998— Cleveland (A.L.).........	2B-PH	4	10	2	0	0	0	0	0	.000	3	2	0	6	12	0	1.000
Division series totals (3 years)		13	46	10	9	1	0	1	1	.196	6	6	1	23	35	1	.983

CHAMPIONSHIP SERIES RECORD

Year Team (League)	Pos.	G	AB	R	H	2B	3B	HR	RBI	Avg.	BB	SO	SB	PO	A	E	Avg.
1993— Chicago (A.L.)	2B	6	22	1	3	0	0	0	1	.136	3	6	0	18	20	3	.927
1995— Seattle (A.L.)	2B	6	23	3	4	1	0	0	0	.174	1	0	2	15	12	1	.964
1998— Cleveland (A.L.).........	2B	2	7	1	1	0	0	0	0	.143	0	1	0	2	6	0	1.000
Championship series totals (3 years)		14	52	5	8	1	0	0	1	.154	4	7	2	35	38	4	.948

ALL-STAR GAME RECORD

Year League	Pos.	AB	R	H	2B	3B	HR	RBI	Avg.	BB	SO	SB	PO	A	E	Avg.
1997— American	PR-2B	1	0	0	0	0	0	0	.000	0	0	0	0	1	0	1.000

CORDERO, FRANCISCO   P   TIGERS

PERSONAL: Born August 11, 1977, in Santo Domingo, Dominican Republic. ... 6-2/200. ... Throws right, bats right. ... Full name: Francisco Javier Cordero.

HIGH SCHOOL: Colegio Luz de Arroyo Hondo (Dominican Republic).

TRANSACTIONS/CAREER NOTES: Signed as non-drafted free agent by Detroit Tigers organization (June 18, 1994). ... On Jamestown disabled list (June 28, 1996-remainder of season). ... On disabled list (May 22-June 18 and June 26, 1998-remainder of season).

Year Team (League)	W	L	Pct.	ERA	G	GS	CG	ShO	Sv.	IP	H	R	ER	BB	SO
1994— Dom. Tigers (DSL)	4	3	.571	3.90	12	12	0	0	0	60	65	47	26	27	36
1995— Fayetteville (S. Atl.)	0	3	.000	6.30	4	4	0	0	0	20	26	16	14	12	19
— Jamestown (NYP)	4	7	.364	5.22	15	14	0	0	0	88	96	62	51	37	54
1996— Fayetteville (S. Atl.)	0	0	. . .	2.57	2	1	0	0	0	7	2	2	2	6	7
— Jamestown (NYP)	0	0	. . .	0.82	2	2	0	0	0	11	5	1	1	2	10
1997— West. Mich. (Mid.)	6	1	.857	0.99	50	0	0	0	*35	54 1/3	36	13	6	15	67
1998— Jacksonville (Southern)......	1	1	.500	4.86	17	0	0	0	8	16 2/3	19	12	9	9	18

CORDERO, WIL   1B

PERSONAL: Born October 3, 1971, in Mayaguez, Puerto Rico. ... 6-2/195. ... Bats right, throws right. ... Full name: Wilfredo Nieva Cordero. ... Name pronounced cor-DARE-oh.

HIGH SCHOOL: Centro de Servicios Education de Mayaguez (Puerto Rico).

TRANSACTIONS/CAREER NOTES: Signed as non-drafted free agent by Montreal Expos organization (May 24, 1988). ... On Indianapolis disabled list (August 1, 1991-remainder of season; and May 12-June 11 and July 7-20, 1992). ... Traded by Expos with P Bryan Eversgerd to Boston Red Sox for P Rheal Cormier, 1B Ryan McGuire and P Shayne Bennett (January 10, 1996). ... On Boston disabled list (May 21-August 12, 1996; included rehabilitation assignments to Gulf Coast Red Sox (July 23-27) and Pawtucket (July 27-August 6). ... Released by Red Sox (September 28, 1997). ... Signed by Chicago White Sox (March 23, 1998). ... Granted free agency (November 3, 1998).

HONORS: Named shortstop on THE SPORTING NEWS N.L. Silver Slugger team (1994).

STATISTICAL NOTES: Career major league grand slams: 2.

Year Team (League)	Pos.	G	AB	R	H	2B	3B	HR	RBI	Avg.	BB	SO	SB	PO	A	E	Avg.
1988— Jamestown (NYP)	SS	52	190	18	49	3	0	2	22	.258	15	44	3	82	159	31	.886
1989— W.P. Beach (FSL)........	SS	78	289	37	80	12	2	6	29	.277	33	58	2	121	224	29	.922
— Jacksonville (Sou.).....	SS	39	121	9	26	6	1	3	17	.215	12	33	1	62	93	7	.957
1990— Jacksonville (Sou.)......	SS	131	444	63	104	18	4	7	40	.234	56	122	9	179	349	41	.928
1991— Indianapolis (A.A.)......	SS	98	360	48	94	16	4	11	52	.261	26	89	9	157	287	27	.943

Year	Team (League)	Pos.	G	AB	R	H	2B	3B	HR	RBI	Avg.	BB	SO	SB	PO	A	E	Avg.
1992— Indianapolis (A.A.)......	SS	52	204	32	64	11	1	6	27	.314	24	54	6	75	146	12	.948
— Montreal (N.L.)..........	SS-2B	45	126	17	38	4	1	2	8	.302	9	31	0	51	92	8	.947
1993— Montreal (N.L.)..........	SS-3B	138	475	56	118	32	2	10	58	.248	34	60	12	163	373	36	.937
1994— Montreal (N.L.)..........	SS	110	415	65	122	30	3	15	63	.294	41	62	16	124	316	22	.952
1995— Montreal (N.L.)..........	SS-OF	131	514	64	147	35	2	10	49	.286	36	88	9	168	281	22	.953
1996— Boston (A.L.)■......	2B-DH-1B	59	198	29	57	14	0	3	37	.288	11	31	2	82	110	10	.950
— GC Red Sox (GCL)	2B	3	10	1	3	0	0	1	3	.300	0	2	0	1	1	0	1.000
— Pawtucket (Int'l)	2B	4	10	2	3	1	0	1	2	.300	2	3	0	2	6	0	1.000
1997— Boston (A.L.)............	OF-DH-2B	140	570	82	160	26	3	18	72	.281	31	122	1	248	11	2	.992
1998— Birmingham (Sou.)■.	1B	11	35	6	10	2	0	2	11	.286	7	3	0	81	9	1	.989
— Chicago (A.L.)	1B-OF	96	341	58	91	18	2	13	49	.267	22	66	2	713	66	7	.991
American League totals (3 years)		295	1109	169	308	58	5	34	158	.278	64	219	5	1043	187	19	.985
National League totals (4 years)		424	1530	202	425	101	8	37	178	.278	120	241	37	506	1062	88	.947
Major league totals (7 years)		719	2639	371	733	159	13	71	336	.278	184	460	42	1549	1249	107	.963

ALL-STAR GAME RECORD

Year	League	Pos.	AB	R	H	2B	3B	HR	RBI	Avg.	BB	SO	SB	PO	A	E	Avg.
1994— National	SS	2	0	0	0	0	0	0	.000	0	0	0	1	1	0	1.000

CORDOVA, FRANCISCO   P   PIRATES

C

PERSONAL: Born April 26, 1972, in Veracruz, Mexico. ... 6-1/191. ... Throws right, bats right.

TRANSACTIONS/CAREER NOTES: Signed as non-drafted free agent by Pittsburgh Pirates organization (January 18, 1996).

STATISTICAL NOTES: Pitched nine innings, combining with Ricardo Rincon (one inning) in 3-0 no-hit victory against Houston (July 12, 1997).

Year	Team (League)	W	L	Pct.	ERA	G	GS	CG	ShO	Sv.	IP	H	R	ER	BB	SO
1992— M.C. Red Devils (Mex.)	3	0	1.000	5.79	16	1	0	0	0	28	28	19	18	14	15
1993— M.C. Red Devils (Mex.)	9	2	.818	3.23	43	4	1	0	4	106	96	44	38	47	71
1994— M.C. Red Devils (Mex.)	15	4	.789	2.33	41	15	6	3	8	150 1/3	122	43	39	43	104
1995— M.C. Red Devils (Mex.)	13	0	*1.000	3.10	27	20	1	0	4	125	131	52	43	42	88
1996— Pittsburgh (N.L.)■	4	7	.364	4.09	59	6	0	0	12	99	103	49	45	20	95
1997— Pittsburgh (N.L.)	11	8	.579	3.63	29	29	2	2	0	178 2/3	175	80	72	49	121
1998— Pittsburgh (N.L.)	13	14	.481	3.31	33	33	3	2	0	220 1/3	204	91	81	69	157
Major league totals (3 years)	28	29	.491	3.58	121	68	5	4	12	498	482	220	198	138	373

CORDOVA, MARTY   OF   TWINS

PERSONAL: Born July 10, 1969, in Las Vegas. ... 6-0/206. ... Bats right, throws right. ... Full name: Martin Keevin Cordova.

HIGH SCHOOL: Bishop Gorman (Las Vegas).

JUNIOR COLLEGE: Orange Coast College (Calif.).

COLLEGE: UNLV.

TRANSACTIONS/CAREER NOTES: Selected by San Diego Padres organization in eighth round of free-agent draft (June 2, 1987); did not sign. ... Selected by Minnesota Twins organization in 10th round of free-agent draft (June 5, 1989). ... On disabled list (April 12-May 20, 1991 and April 7-May 11, 1994). ... On Minnesota disabled list (April 11-May 26, 1997); included rehabilitation assignment to Salt Lake (May 20-26). ... On disabled list (April 27-May 12, 1998).

HONORS: Named California League Most Valuable Player (1992). ... Named A.L. Rookie of the Year by Baseball Writers' Association of America (1995).

STATISTICAL NOTES: Led California League with 302 total bases and .589 slugging percentage and tied for lead in grounding into double plays with 20 in 1992. ... Had 23-game hitting streak (June 5-29, 1996).

Year	Team (League)	Pos.	G	AB	R	H	2B	3B	HR	RBI	Avg.	BB	SO	SB	PO	A	E	Avg.
1989— Elizabethton (App.)......	OF-3B	38	148	32	42	2	3	8	29	.284	14	29	2	6	9	4	.789
1990— Kenosha (Midwest)	OF	81	269	35	58	7	5	7	25	.216	28	73	6	87	5	5	.948
1991— Visalia (California)	OF	71	189	31	40	6	1	7	19	.212	17	46	2	58	2	5	.923
1992— Visalia (California)	OF	134	513	103	175	31	6	*28	*131	.341	76	99	13	173	10	3	.984
1993— Nashville (Southern) ..	OF	138	508	83	127	30	5	19	77	.250	64	*153	10	209	7	2	*.991
1994— Salt Lake (PCL)	OF	103	385	69	138	25	4	19	66	.358	39	63	17	187	13	8	.962
1995— Minnesota (A.L.)	OF	137	512	81	142	27	4	24	84	.277	52	111	20	345	12	5	.986
1996— Minnesota (A.L.)	OF	145	569	97	176	46	1	16	111	.309	53	96	11	328	9	3	.991
1997— Minnesota (A.L.)	OF-DH	103	378	44	93	18	4	15	51	.246	30	92	5	217	12	2	.991
— Salt Lake (PCL)	OF	6	24	5	9	4	0	1	4	.375	2	3	1	3	0	1	.750
1998— Minnesota (A.L.)	OF-DH	119	438	52	111	20	2	10	69	.253	50	103	3	257	5	6	.978
Major league totals (4 years)		504	1897	274	522	111	11	65	315	.275	185	402	39	1147	38	16	.987

COREY, BRYAN   P   TIGERS

PERSONAL: Born October 21, 1973, in Thousand Oaks, Calif. ... 6-0/170. ... Throws right, bats right. ... Full name: Bryan Scott Corey.

HIGH SCHOOL: Thousand Oaks (Calif.).

JUNIOR COLLEGE: Los Angeles Pierce Junior College.

TRANSACTIONS/CAREER NOTES: Selected by Detroit Tigers organization in 12th round of free-agent draft (June 3, 1993). ... Selected by Arizona Diamondbacks in third round (63rd pick overall) of expansion draft (November 18, 1997). ... Claimed on waivers by Tigers (December 4, 1998).

MISCELLANEOUS: Played infield (1993-94).

Year Team (League)	W	L	Pct.	ERA	G	GS	CG	ShO	Sv.	IP	H	R	ER	BB	SO
1995— Jamestown (NYP)	2	2	.500	3.86	29	0	0	0	10	28	21	14	12	12	41
1996— Fayetteville (S. Atl.)	6	4	.600	1.21	60	0	0	0	34	82	50	19	11	17	101
1997— Jacksonville (Southern)......	3	8	.273	4.76	52	0	0	0	9	68	74	42	36	21	37
1998— Tucson (PCL)■.................	4	6	.400	5.44	39	10	0	0	2	$87^{2}/_{3}$	116	61	53	24	50
— Arizona (N.L.)	0	0	. . .	9.00	3	0	0	0	0	4	6	4	4	2	1
Major league totals (1 year).......	0	0	. . .	9.00	3	0	0	0	0	4	6	4	4	2	1

RECORD AS POSITION PLAYER

Year Team (League)	Pos.	G	BATTING										FIELDING			
			AB	R	H	2B	3B	HR	RBI	Avg.	BB	SO	SB	PO	A	E	Avg.
1993— Bristol (Appal.)	SS-2B	39	95	14	10	3	0	0	3	.105	26	35	2	53	80	10	.930
1994— Jamestown (NYP)	2B-SS-3B	41	85	14	13	1	1	0	3	.153	13	27	2	38	64	10	.911

CORSI, JIM   P   RED SOX

C

PERSONAL: Born September 9, 1961, in Newton, Mass. ... 6-1/220. ... Throws right, bats right. ... Full name: James Bernard Corsi.
HIGH SCHOOL: Newton (Mass.) North.
COLLEGE: St. Leo (Fla.) College (bachelor of arts degree in management).
TRANSACTIONS/CAREER NOTES: Selected by New York Yankees organization in 25th round of free-agent draft (June 7, 1982). ... On Fort Lauderdale disabled list (April 8-May 11, 1983). ... Released by Yankees organization (April 3, 1984). ... Signed by Greensboro, Boston Red Sox organization (April 1, 1985). ... Released by Red Sox organization (January 31, 1986). ... Re-signed by Red Sox organization (April 5, 1986). ... Released by Red Sox organization (April 2, 1987). ... Signed by Modesto, Oakland Athletics organization (April 12, 1987). ... On Oakland disabled list (March 29, 1990-entire season); included rehabilitation assignment to Tacoma (June 29-July 25). ... Granted free agency (December 20, 1990). ... Signed by Tucson, Houston Astros organization (March 19, 1991). ... Released by Astros (November 18, 1991). ... Signed by Tacoma, A's organization (March 16, 1992). ... Selected by Florida Marlins in second round (49th pick overall) of expansion draft (November 17, 1992). ... On Florida disabled list (March 27-April 30 and July 6, 1993-remainder of season); included rehabilitation assignment to High Desert (April 20-30). ... Granted free agency (October 15, 1993). ... Re-signed by Marlins organization (January 24, 1994). ... On Brevard County disabled list (April 11-July 5, 1994). ... Granted free agency (October 15, 1994). ... Signed by Edmonton, A's organization (January 20, 1995). ... On Oakland disabled list (June 22-August 8, 1995). ... On Oakland disabled list (April 28-May 18, 1996); included rehabilitation assignment to Modesto (May 17-18). ... Granted free agency (November 4, 1996). ... Signed by Red Sox organization (February 3, 1997). ... On Boston disabled list (June 2-July 1, 1997); included rehabilitation assignment to Gulf Coast Red Sox (June 23-30). ... Granted free agency (October 28, 1997). ... Re-signed by Red Sox (December 3, 1997). ... On Boston disabled list (July 18-August 6, 1998); included rehabilitation assignment to Pawtucket (August 3-6).

Year Team (League)	W	L	Pct.	ERA	G	GS	CG	ShO	Sv.	IP	H	R	ER	BB	SO
1982— Oneonta (N.Y.-Penn)	0	0	. . .	10.80	1	0	0	0	0	$3^{1}/_{3}$	5	4	4	2	6
— Paintsville (Appal.)	0	2	.000	2.90	8	4	0	0	0	31	32	11	10	13	20
1983— Greensboro (S. Atl.)	2	2	.500	4.09	12	7	1	0	1	$50^{2}/_{3}$	59	37	23	33	37
— Oneonta (N.Y.-Penn)	3	6	.333	4.25	11	10	2	0	0	$59^{1}/_{3}$	76	38	28	21	47
1984—						Out of organized baseball.									
1985— Greensboro (S. Atl.)■	5	8	.385	4.23	41	2	1	0	9	$78^{2}/_{3}$	94	49	37	23	84
1986— New Britain (East.)	2	3	.400	2.28	29	0	0	0	3	$51^{1}/_{3}$	52	13	13	20	38
1987— Modesto (California)■	3	1	.750	3.60	19	0	0	0	6	30	23	16	12	10	45
— Huntsville (Southern)	8	1	.889	2.81	28	0	0	0	4	48	30	17	15	15	33
1988— Tacoma (PCL)	2	5	.286	2.75	50	0	0	0	16	59	60	25	18	23	48
— Oakland (A.L.)	0	1	.000	3.80	11	1	0	0	0	$21^{1}/_{3}$	20	10	9	6	10
1989— Tacoma (PCL)	2	3	.400	4.13	23	0	0	0	8	$28^{1}/_{3}$	40	17	13	9	23
— Oakland (A.L.)	1	2	.333	1.88	22	0	0	0	0	$38^{1}/_{3}$	26	8	8	10	21
1990— Tacoma (PCL)	0	0	. . .	1.50	5	0	0	0	0	6	9	2	1	1	3
1991— Tucson (PCL)■	0	0	. . .	0.00	2	0	0	0	0	3	2	0	0	0	4
— Houston (N.L.)	0	5	.000	3.71	47	0	0	0	0	$77^{2}/_{3}$	76	37	32	23	53
1992— Tacoma (PCL)■	0	0	. . .	1.23	26	0	0	0	12	$29^{1}/_{3}$	22	8	4	10	21
— Oakland (A.L.)	4	2	.667	1.43	32	0	0	0	0	44	44	12	7	18	19
1993— High Desert (Calif.)■	0	1	.000	3.00	3	3	0	0	0	9	11	3	3	2	6
— Florida (N.L.)	0	2	.000	6.64	15	0	0	0	0	$20^{1}/_{3}$	28	15	15	10	7
1994— Brevard County (FSL)........	0	1	.000	1.64	6	0	0	0	0	11	8	3	2	0	11
— Edmonton (PCL)	0	1	.000	4.50	15	0	0	0	0	22	29	15	11	10	15
1995— Edmonton (PCL)■	0	0	. . .	0.00	3	0	0	0	3	3	0	0	0	1	3
— Oakland (A.L.)	2	4	.333	2.20	38	0	0	0	2	45	31	14	11	26	26
1996— Oakland (A.L.)	6	0	1.000	4.03	56	0	0	0	3	$73^{2}/_{3}$	71	33	33	34	43
— Modesto (California)	0	0	. . .	0.00	1	1	0	0	0	1	0	0	0	0	2
1997— Boston (A.L.)■.................	5	3	.625	3.43	52	0	0	0	2	$57^{2}/_{3}$	56	26	22	21	40
— Pawtucket (Int'l)	0	0	. . .	0.00	2	0	0	0	1	$2^{1}/_{3}$	2	0	0	1	3
— GC Red Sox (GCL)	1	0	1.000	0.00	3	2	0	0	0	4	2	1	0	0	6
1998— Boston (A.L.)	3	2	.600	2.59	59	0	0	0	0	66	58	23	19	23	49
— Pawtucket (Int'l)..................	0	0	. . .	0.00	1	1	0	0	0	2	3	0	0	0	1
A.L. totals (7 years)	21	14	.600	2.84	270	1	0	0	7	346	306	126	109	138	208
N.L. totals (2 years)	0	7	.000	4.32	62	0	0	0	0	98	104	52	47	33	60
Major league totals (9 years)......	21	21	.500	3.16	332	1	0	0	7	444	410	178	156	171	268

DIVISION SERIES RECORD

Year Team (League)	W	L	Pct.	ERA	G	GS	CG	ShO	Sv.	IP	H	R	ER	BB	SO
1998— Boston (A.L.)	0	0	. . .	0.00	2	0	0	0	0	3	1	0	0	1	2

CHAMPIONSHIP SERIES RECORD

Year Team (League)	W	L	Pct.	ERA	G	GS	CG	ShO	Sv.	IP	H	R	ER	BB	SO
1992— Oakland (A.L.)	0	0	. . .	0.00	3	0	0	0	0	2	2	0	0	3	0

COUNSELL, CRAIG   2B   MARLINS

PERSONAL: Born August 21, 1970, in South Bend, Ind. ... 6-0/175. ... Bats left, throws right. ... Full name: Craig John Counsell. ... Son of John Counsell, outfielder, Minnesota Twins organization (1964-68).
HIGH SCHOOL: Whitefish Bay (Milwaukee).
COLLEGE: Notre Dame.
TRANSACTIONS/CAREER NOTES: Selected by Colorado Rockies organization in 11th round of free-agent draft (June 1, 1992). ... On disabled list (April 7-May 13, July 30-August 6 and August 7-27, 1994). ... On disabled list (May 1-July 15 and July 18-September 3, 1996). ... Traded by Rockies to Florida Marlins for P Mark Hutton (July 27, 1997). ... On disabled list (August 4, 1998-remainder of season).
STATISTICAL NOTES: Led California League shortstops with 621 total chances in 1993. ... Led Pacific Coast League shortstops with 598 total chances and 86 double plays in 1995. ... Career major league grand slams: 2.

							BATTING							FIELDING		
Year Team (League)	Pos.	G	AB	R	H	2B	3B	HR	RBI	Avg.	BB	SO	SB	PO	A	E	Avg.
1992— Bend (Northwest)	2B-SS	18	61	11	15	6	1	0	8	.246	9	10	1	23	36	2	.967
1993— Central Valley (Cal.)	SS	131	471	79	132	26	3	5	59	.280	95	68	14	*233	353	35	.944
1994— New Haven (East.)	SS-2B	83	300	47	84	20	1	5	37	.280	37	32	4	122	242	27	.931
1995— Colo. Springs (PCL)	SS	118	399	60	112	22	6	5	53	.281	34	47	10	182	386	30	.950
— Colorado (N.L.)	SS	3	1	0	0	0	0	0	0	.000	1	0	0	1	1	0	1.000
1996— Colo. Springs (PCL)	2B-3B-SS	25	75	17	18	3	0	2	10	.240	24	7	4	35	64	4	.961
1997— Colo. Springs (PCL)	2B-SS	96	376	77	126	31	6	5	63	.335	45	38	12	213	260	9	.981
— Colorado (N.L.)	PR	1	0	0	0	0	0	0	0	...	0	0	0	...	...	...	...
— Florida (N.L.)■	2B	51	164	20	49	9	2	1	16	.299	18	17	1	124	149	3	.989
1998— Florida (N.L.)	2B	107	335	43	84	19	5	4	40	.251	51	47	3	237	299	5	.991
Major league totals (3 years)		162	500	63	133	28	7	5	56	.266	70	64	4	362	449	8	.990

DIVISION SERIES RECORD

							BATTING							FIELDING		
Year Team (League)	Pos.	G	AB	R	H	2B	3B	HR	RBI	Avg.	BB	SO	SB	PO	A	E	Avg.
1997— Florida (N.L.)	2B	3	5	0	2	1	0	0	1	.400	1	0	0	5	2	1	.875

CHAMPIONSHIP SERIES RECORD

							BATTING							FIELDING		
Year Team (League)	Pos.	G	AB	R	H	2B	3B	HR	RBI	Avg.	BB	SO	SB	PO	A	E	Avg.
1997— Florida (N.L.)	2B-PH	5	14	0	6	0	0	0	2	.429	3	3	0	7	9	1	.941

WORLD SERIES RECORD

NOTES: Member of World Series championship team (1997).

							BATTING							FIELDING		
Year Team (League)	Pos.	G	AB	R	H	2B	3B	HR	RBI	Avg.	BB	SO	SB	PO	A	E	Avg.
1997— Florida (N.L.)	2B	7	22	4	4	1	0	0	2	.182	6	5	1	18	15	1	.971

CRABTREE, ROBBIE   P   GIANTS

PERSONAL: Born November 25, 1972, in La Mirada, Calif. ... 6-0/175. ... Throws right, bats right. ... Full name: Robert H. Crabtree.
HIGH SCHOOL: Savanna (Anaheim, Calif.).
JUNIOR COLLEGE: Cypress (Calif.) College.
COLLEGE: Cal State Northridge.
TRANSACTIONS/CAREER NOTES: Selected by San Francisco Giants organization in 21st round of free-agent draft (June 4, 1996).

Year Team (League)	W	L	Pct.	ERA	G	GS	CG	ShO	Sv.	IP	H	R	ER	BB	SO
1996— Bellingham (N'west)	3	3	.500	2.77	28	0	0	0	4	52	38	18	16	14	72
1997— Bakersfield (California)	7	7	.500	5.13	45	9	1	0	1	112 1/3	124	77	64	59	116
1998— San Jose (California)	6	1	.857	0.99	24	0	0	0	2	54 1/3	39	6	6	8	67
— Shreveport (Texas)	2	0	1.000	1.67	26	0	0	0	4	54	30	11	10	16	56
— Fresno (Pacific Coast)	0	0	...	11.57	3	1	0	0	0	4 2/3	8	7	6	2	10

CRABTREE, TIM   P   RANGERS

PERSONAL: Born October 13, 1969, in Jackson, Mich. ... 6-4/200. ... Throws right, bats right. ... Full name: Timothy Lyle Crabtree.
HIGH SCHOOL: Grass Lake (Mich.).
COLLEGE: Michigan State.
TRANSACTIONS/CAREER NOTES: Selected by Toronto Blue Jays organization in second round of free-agent draft (June 1, 1992). ... On disabled list (August 16-September 6, 1996). ... On Toronto disabled list (June 4-August 3, 1997); included rehabilitation assignments to St. Catherines (July 22-24) and Syracuse (July 27-August 4). ... Traded by Blue Jays to Texas Rangers for C Kevin Brown (March 14, 1998).

Year Team (League)	W	L	Pct.	ERA	G	GS	CG	ShO	Sv.	IP	H	R	ER	BB	SO
1992— St. Catharines (NYP)	6	3	.667	1.57	12	12	2	0	0	69	45	19	12	22	47
— Knoxville (Southern)	0	2	.000	0.95	3	3	1	0	0	19	14	8	2	4	13
1993— Knoxville (Southern)	9	14	.391	4.08	27	27	2	2	0	158 2/3	178	93	72	59	67
1994— Syracuse (Int'l)	2	6	.250	4.17	51	9	0	0	2	108	125	58	50	49	58
1995— Syracuse (Int'l)	0	2	.000	5.40	26	0	0	0	5	31 2/3	38	25	19	12	22
— Toronto (A.L.)	0	2	.000	3.09	31	0	0	0	0	32	30	16	11	13	21
1996— Toronto (A.L.)	5	3	.625	2.54	53	0	0	0	1	67 1/3	59	26	19	22	57
1997— Toronto (A.L.)	3	3	.500	7.08	37	0	0	0	2	40 2/3	65	32	32	17	26
— St. Catharines (NYP)	0	0	...	3.00	2	1	0	0	0	3	3	2	1	0	3
— Syracuse (Int'l)	0	0	...	9.82	3	0	0	0	1	3 2/3	7	4	4	1	3
1998— Texas (A.L.)■	6	1	.857	3.59	64	0	0	0	0	85 1/3	86	40	34	35	60
Major league totals (4 years)	14	9	.609	3.83	185	0	0	0	3	225 1/3	240	114	96	87	164

DIVISION SERIES RECORD

Year Team (League)	W	L	Pct.	ERA	G	GS	CG	ShO	Sv.	IP	H	R	ER	BB	SO
1998— Texas (A.L.)	0	0	...	0.00	2	0	0	0	0	4	1	0	0	0	2

C

CRADLE, RICKEY — OF — TIGERS

PERSONAL: Born June 20, 1973, in Norfolk, Va. ... 6-2/180. ... Bats right, throws right. ... Full name: Rickey Nelson Cradle.
HIGH SCHOOL: Cerritos (Calif.).
TRANSACTIONS/CAREER NOTES: Selected by Toronto Blue Jays organization in fifth round of free-agent draft (June 3, 1991). ... Granted free agency (October 17, 1997). ... Signed by Seattle Mariners organization (November 7, 1997). ... On Tacoma disabled list (August 19-September 1, 1998). ... On Seattle disabled list (September 1, 1998-remainder of season). ... Released by Mariners (October 9, 1998). ... Signed by Detroit Tigers organization (November 24, 1998).

							BATTING							FIELDING		
Year Team (League)	Pos.	G	AB	R	H	2B	3B	HR	RBI	Avg.	BB	SO	SB	PO	A	E	Avg.
1991— GC Jays (GCL)...........	OF	44	131	16	28	4	3	1	6	.214	24	37	4	87	2	2	.978
1992— Medicine Hat (Pio.)	OF	65	217	38	49	8	0	9	36	.226	42	69	16	129	5	3	.978
1993— Hagerstown (SAL).......	OF	129	441	72	112	26	4	13	62	.254	68	125	19	185	18	11	.949
1994— Dunedin (Fla. St.).......	OF	114	344	65	88	14	3	10	39	.256	59	87	20	157	9	5	.971
1995— Knoxville (Southern) ..	OF	41	117	17	21	5	1	4	13	.179	17	29	3	45	3	1	.980
— Dunedin (Fla. St.)	OF	50	178	33	49	10	3	7	27	.275	28	49	6	94	4	0	1.000
1996— Knoxville (Southern) ..	OF	92	333	59	94	23	2	12	47	.282	55	65	15	135	8	4	.973
— Syracuse (Int'l)...........	OF	40	130	22	26	5	3	8	22	.200	14	39	1	67	5	4	.947
1997— Syracuse (Int'l)...........	OF	11	25	4	3	0	0	1	3	.120	2	9	0	9	1	0	1.000
— Knoxville (Southern) ..	OF	84	257	50	55	16	1	10	34	.214	41	67	5	104	5	2	.982
1998— Tacoma (PCL)■	OF	82	297	53	86	25	1	12	53	.290	24	76	9	143	5	0	1.000
— Seattle (A.L.)	OF	5	7	0	1	0	0	0	2	.143	1	5	1	2	0	0	1.000
Major league totals (1 year)		5	7	0	1	0	0	0	2	.143	1	5	1	2	0	0	1.000

CREDE, JOE — 3B — CUBS

PERSONAL: Born April 26, 1978, in Jefferson City, Mo. ... 6-3/185. ... Bats right, throws right. ... Full name: Joseph Crede. ... Name pronounced cree-DEE.
HIGH SCHOOL: Fatima (Westphalia, Mo.).
TRANSACTIONS/CAREER NOTES: Selected by Chicago White Sox organization in fifth round of free-agent draft (June 2, 1996).
HONORS: Named Carolina League Player of the Year (1998).
STATISTICAL NOTES: Led Gulf Coast League third basemen with 175 total chances in 1996. ... Led Carolina League with 253 total bases and 11 sacrifice flies in 1998. ... Led Carolina League third basemen with 420 total chances in 1998.

							BATTING							FIELDING		
Year Team (League)	Pos.	G	AB	R	H	2B	3B	HR	RBI	Avg.	BB	SO	SB	PO	A	E	Avg.
1996— GC Whi. Sox (GCL)	3B	56	221	30	66	17	1	4	32	.299	9	41	1	*42	*108	*25	.857
1997— Hickory (S. Atl.)	3B	113	402	45	109	25	0	5	62	.271	24	83	3	84	232	33	.905
1998— Win.-Salem (Car.).......	3B	*137	492	•92	155	32	3	20	*88	*.315	53	98	9	*100	*290	*30	.929

CRESPO, FELIPE — OF/IF — BLUE JAYS

PERSONAL: Born March 5, 1973, in Rio Piedras, Puerto Rico. ... 5-11/200. ... Bats both, throws right. ... Full name: Felipe Javier Clauso Crespo.
HIGH SCHOOL: Notre Dame (Caguas, Puerto Rico).
TRANSACTIONS/CAREER NOTES: Selected by Toronto Blue Jays organization in third round of free-agent draft (June 4, 1990). ... On disabled list (May 26-July 2, 1995). ... On Toronto disabled list (April 1-24, 1996); included rehabilitation assignment to Dunedin (April 12-24).
STATISTICAL NOTES: Led Southern League third basemen with 127 putouts and 42 errors in 1994.

							BATTING							FIELDING		
Year Team (League)	Pos.	G	AB	R	H	2B	3B	HR	RBI	Avg.	BB	SO	SB	PO	A	E	Avg.
1991— Medicine Hat (Pio.)	2B	49	184	40	57	11	4	4	31	.310	25	31	6	*97	133	*23	.909
1992— Myrtle Beach (SAL)....	2B-3B	81	263	43	74	14	3	1	29	.281	58	38	7	161	149	22	.934
1993— Dunedin (Fla. St.)	2B	96	345	51	103	16	8	6	39	.299	47	40	18	198	269	25	.949
1994— Knoxville (Southern) ..	3B2-B	129	502	74	135	30	4	8	49	.269	57	95	20	†127	270	†42	.904
1995— Syracuse (Int'l)..........	2B	88	347	56	102	20	5	13	41	.294	41	56	12	160	220	*25	.938
1996— Dunedin (Fla. St.)	2B	9	34	3	11	1	0	2	6	.324	2	3	1	18	18	2	.947
— Toronto (A.L.)	2B-3B-1B	22	49	6	9	4	0	0	4	.184	12	13	1	34	38	1	.986
— Syracuse (Int'l)...........	2-0-3-1	98	355	53	100	25	0	8	58	.282	56	39	10	220	143	19	.950
1997— Toronto (A.L.)	3B-DH-2B	12	28	3	8	0	1	1	5	.286	2	4	0	9	9	1	.947
— Syracuse (Int'l)..........	0-2-1-3	80	290	53	75	12	0	12	26	.259	46	38	7	247	103	12	.967
1998— Toronto (A.L.)............	O-2-DH-3-1	66	130	11	34	8	1	1	15	.262	15	27	4	67	17	4	.955
Major league totals (3 years)		100	207	20	51	12	2	2	24	.246	29	44	5	110	64	6	.967

CRESSEND, JACK — P — RED SOX

PERSONAL: Born May 13, 1975, in New Orleans. ... 6-1/185. ... Throws right, bats right. ... Full name: John Baptiste Cressend III.
HIGH SCHOOL: Mandeville (La.).
COLLEGE: Tulane.
TRANSACTIONS/CAREER NOTES: Signed as non-drafted free agent by Boston Red Sox organization (July 24, 1996).

Year Team (League)	W	L	Pct.	ERA	G	GS	CG	ShO	Sv.	IP	H	R	ER	BB	SO
1996— Lowell (NY-Penn.)	3	2	.600	2.36	9	8	0	0	0	45 2/3	37	15	12	17	57
1997— Sarasota (Florida State)......	8	11	.421	3.80	28	25	2	1	0	165 2/3	163	98	70	56	149
1998— Trenton (Eastern)	10	11	.476	4.34	29	•29	1	1	0	149 1/3	168	86	72	55	130

CROMER, TRIPP — SS — DODGERS

PERSONAL: Born November 21, 1967, in Lake City, S.C. ... 6-2/166. ... Bats right, throws right. ... Full name: Roy Bunyan Cromer III. ... Son of Roy Cromer, former scout with St. Louis Cardinals and minor league pitcher/second baseman (1960-63); brother of Brandon Cromer, minor league infielder (1992-98); brother of D.T. Cromer, first baseman/outfielder, Cincinnati Reds organization; and brother of Burke Cromer, pitcher, Atlanta Braves organization (1992-93).

HIGH SCHOOL: Lake City (S.C.).

COLLEGE: South Carolina.

TRANSACTIONS/CAREER NOTES: Selected by St. Louis Cardinals organization in third round of free-agent draft (June 5, 1989). ... On Arkansas disabled list (May 14-26, 1992). ... On Louisville disabled list (April 30-May 28 and July 5-August 3, 1993). ... On disabled list (May 20-27, 1996). ... Claimed on waivers by Los Angeles Dodgers (October 10, 1996). ... On disabled list (July 31, 1997-remainder of season). ... On Los Angeles disabled list (March 12-July 17 and July 31-September 1, 1998); included rehabilitation assignment to Albuquerque (June 16-26 and July 9-17) and San Bernardino (August 27-September 1).

Year Team (League)	Pos.	G	AB	R	H	2B	3B	HR	RBI	Avg.	BB	SO	SB	PO	A	E	Avg.
1989— Hamilton (NYP)	SS	35	137	18	36	6	3	0	6	.263	17	30	4	66	85	11	.932
1990— St. Peters. (FSL)	SS	121	408	53	88	12	5	5	38	.216	46	78	7	202	334	32	.944
1991— St. Peters. (FSL)	SS	43	137	11	28	3	1	0	10	.204	9	17	0	79	134	3	.986
— Arkansas (Texas)	SS	73	227	28	52	12	1	1	18	.229	15	37	0	117	198	10	.969
1992— Arkansas (Texas)	SS	110	339	30	81	16	6	7	29	.239	22	82	4	135	315	18	*.962
— Louisville (A.A.)	SS	6	25	5	5	1	1	1	7	.200	1	6	0	13	20	0	1.000
1993— Louisville (A.A.)	SS	85	309	39	85	8	4	11	33	.275	15	60	1	123	253	12	.969
— St. Louis (N.L.)	SS	10	23	1	2	0	0	0	0	.087	1	6	0	13	18	3	.912
1994— Louisville (A.A.)	SS	124	419	53	115	23	9	9	50	.274	33	85	5	165	370	12	*.978
— St. Louis (N.L.)	SS	2	0	1	0	0	0	0	0	...	0	0	0	0	0	1	.000
1995— St. Louis (N.L.)	SS-2B	105	345	36	78	19	0	5	18	.226	14	66	0	126	292	17	.961
1996— Louisville (A.A.)	SS-2B	80	244	28	55	4	4	4	25	.225	22	47	3	124	238	5	.986
1997— Albuquerque (PCL)■	2B-SS	43	140	25	45	8	6	5	24	.321	14	34	4	65	106	6	.966
— Los Angeles (N.L.)	2B-SS-3B	28	86	8	25	3	0	4	20	.291	6	16	0	47	61	3	.973
1998— Albuquerque (PCL)	SS	12	30	3	10	1	0	2	5	.333	1	5	0	3	17	1	.952
— Los Angeles (N.L.)	PH	6	6	1	1	0	0	1	1	.167	0	2	0	0	0	0	...
— San Bern. (Calif.)	2B	4	15	3	6	1	0	2	6	.400	0	2	0	2	8	0	1.000
Major league totals (5 years)		151	460	47	106	22	0	10	39	.230	21	90	0	186	371	24	.959

CROUSHORE, RICK — P — CARDINALS

PERSONAL: Born August 7, 1970, in Lakehurst, N.J. ... 6-4/210. ... Throws right, bats right. ... Full name: Richard Steven Croushore.

HIGH SCHOOL: Mount Vernon (Texas).

JUNIOR COLLEGE: Hutchinson (Kan.) Community College.

COLLEGE: James Madison.

TRANSACTIONS/CAREER NOTES: Signed as non-drafted free agent by St. Louis Cardinals organization (June 12, 1993). ... On disabled list (April 6-June 19, 1995).

Year Team (League)	W	L	Pct.	ERA	G	GS	CG	ShO	Sv.	IP	H	R	ER	BB	SO
1993— Glens Falls (NYP)	4	1	.800	3.05	31	0	0	0	1	41 1/3	38	16	14	22	36
1994— Madison (Midwest)	6	6	.500	4.10	•62	0	0	0	0	94 1/3	90	49	43	46	103
1995— St. Petersburg (FSL)	6	4	.600	3.51	12	11	0	0	0	59	44	25	23	32	57
1996— Arkansas (Texas)	5	10	.333	4.92	34	17	2	0	3	108	113	75	59	51	85
1997— Arkansas (Texas)	7	5	.583	4.18	17	16	1	0	0	92 2/3	111	52	43	37	67
— Louisville (A.A.)	1	2	.333	2.47	14	6	0	0	1	43 2/3	37	14	12	13	41
1998— Memphis (Pacific Coast)	0	3	.000	4.71	23	0	0	0	2	28 2/3	21	16	15	9	40
— St. Louis (N.L.)	0	3	.000	4.97	41	0	0	0	8	54 1/3	44	31	30	29	47
Major league totals (1 year)	0	3	.000	4.97	41	0	0	0	8	54 1/3	44	31	30	29	47

CROW, DEAN — P — ASTROS

PERSONAL: Born August 21, 1972, in Garland, Texas. ... 6-4/215. ... Throws right, bats left. ... Full name: Paul Dean Crow Jr.

HIGH SCHOOL: Stratford (Texas).

JUNIOR COLLEGE: San Jacinto College (Texas).

COLLEGE: Miami of Ohio, then Baylor.

TRANSACTIONS/CAREER NOTES: Selected by Seattle Mariners organization in 10th round of free-agent draft (June 3, 1993). ... On disabled list (June 15-26 and July 18, 1994-remainder of season). ... Traded by Mariners with P Scott Sanders and 3B Carlos Villalobos to Detroit Tigers for P Omar Olivares and P Felipe Lira (July 18, 1997). ... Traded by Tigers with C Paul Bako, P Brian Powell, P Mark Persails and 3B Carlos Villalobos to Houston Astros for C Brad Ausmus and P C.J. Nitkowski (January 14, 1999).

Year Team (League)	W	L	Pct.	ERA	G	GS	CG	ShO	Sv.	IP	H	R	ER	BB	SO
1993— Bellingham (N'west)	5	3	.625	1.89	25	0	0	0	4	47 2/3	31	14	10	21	38
1994— Appleton (Midwest)	2	4	.333	7.04	16	0	0	0	2	15 1/3	25	15	12	7	11
1995— Riverside (California)	3	4	.429	2.63	51	0	0	0	22	61 2/3	54	21	18	13	46
1996— Port City (Southern)	2	3	.400	3.04	60	0	0	0	26	68	64	35	23	20	43
1997— Tacoma (PCL)	4	2	.667	4.78	33	0	0	0	7	43 1/3	56	25	23	19	36
— Toledo (International)■	3	0	1.000	7.85	18	0	0	0	2	18 1/3	26	16	16	10	10
1998— Toledo (International)	2	0	1.000	1.48	24	0	0	0	10	24 1/3	21	8	4	3	12
— Detroit (A.L.)	2	2	.500	3.94	32	0	0	0	0	45 2/3	55	22	20	16	18
Major league totals (1 year)	2	2	.500	3.94	32	0	0	0	0	45 2/3	55	22	20	16	18

C

CROWELL, JIM   P   REDS

PERSONAL: Born May 14, 1974, in Minneapolis. ... 6-3/230. ... Throws left, bats right. ... Full name: James Everett Crowell.
HIGH SCHOOL: Valparaiso (Ind.).
COLLEGE: Indianapolis.
TRANSACTIONS/CAREER NOTES: Signed as non-drafted free agent by Cleveland Indians organization (June 17, 1995). ... Traded by Indians with P Danny Graves, P Scott Winchester and IF Damian Jackson to Cincinnati Reds for P John Smiley and IF Jeff Branson (July 31, 1997). ... On Chattanooga disabled list (April 27-August 10, 1998).

Year Team (League)	W	L	Pct.	ERA	G	GS	CG	ShO	Sv.	IP	H	R	ER	BB	SO
1995— Watertown (NYP)	5	2	.714	2.86	12	9	0	0	0	56 2/3	50	22	18	27	48
1996— Columbus (S. Atl.)	7	10	.412	4.14	28	•28	3	0	0	165 1/3	163	89	76	69	104
1997— Kinston (Carolina)	9	4	.692	2.37	17	17	0	0	0	114	96	41	30	26	94
— Akron (Eastern)	1	0	1.000	4.50	3	3	0	0	0	18	13	12	9	11	7
— Chattanooga (Southern)■	2	1	.667	2.84	3	3	0	0	0	19	19	6	6	5	14
— Indianapolis (A.A.)	1	1	.500	2.75	3	3	1	1	0	19 2/3	19	7	6	8	6
— Cincinnati (N.L.)	0	1	.000	9.95	2	1	0	0	0	6 1/3	12	7	7	5	3
1998— Chattanooga (Southern)	0	4	.000	8.51	5	5	0	0	0	24 1/3	38	27	23	17	10
— Char., W.Va. (S. Atl.)	0	4	.000	13.20	5	5	0	0	0	15	28	23	22	9	9
— Indianapolis (International)	0	0	...	6.75	1	1	0	0	0	4	7	3	3	0	2
Major league totals (1 year)	0	1	.000	9.95	2	1	0	0	0	6 1/3	12	7	7	5	3

CRUZ, DEIVI   SS   TIGERS

PERSONAL: Born November 6, 1975, in Bani, Dominican Republic. ... 6-0/184. ... Bats right, throws right. ... Full name: Deivi Garcia Cruz.
HIGH SCHOOL: Liceo Aliro Paulino Nizao (Dominican Republic).
TRANSACTIONS/CAREER NOTES: Signed as non-drafted free agent by San Francisco Giants (April 23, 1993). ... Selected by Los Angeles Dodgers organization from Giants organization in Rule 5 major league draft (December 9, 1996). ... Traded by Dodgers with OF Juan Hernaiz to Detroit Tigers for 2B Marcus Berblinger (December 9, 1996). ... On Detroit disabled list (March 20-April 27, 1998); included rehabilitation assignments to Lakeland (April 21-23) and Toledo (April 24-27).
STATISTICAL NOTES: Led Northwest League third basemen with 47 putouts and .941 fielding percentage in 1995. ... Led Midwest League shortstops with 427 assists and .980 fielding percentage in 1996. ... Career major league grand slams: 1.

Year Team (League)	Pos.	G	AB	R	H	2B	3B	HR	RBI	Avg.	BB	SO	SB	PO	A	E	Avg.
1993— Ariz. Giants (Ariz.)	3B-SS-1B	28	82	8	28	3	0	0	15	.341	4	5	3	17	52	2	.972
1994— Ariz. Giants (Ariz.)	SS-3B	18	53	10	16	8	0	0	5	.302	5	3	0	11	37	1	.980
1995— Burlington (Midw.)	2B-3B-SS	16	58	2	8	1	0	1	9	.138	4	7	1	20	42	2	.969
— Bellingham (N'west)	3B-2B	62	223	32	66	17	0	3	28	.296	19	21	6	†55	124	10	†.947
1996— Burlington (Midw.)	SS-3B	127	517	72	152	27	2	9	64	.294	35	49	12	159	†444	13	†.979
1997— Detroit (A.L.)■	SS	147	436	35	105	26	0	2	40	.241	14	55	3	192	420	13	.979
1998— Lakeland (Fla. St.)	SS	2	9	0	0	0	0	0	1	.000	0	1	0	1	2	0	1.000
— Toledo (Int'l)	SS	2	9	1	1	1	0	0	2	.111	2	3	0	2	7	0	1.000
— Detroit (A.L.)	SS	135	454	52	118	22	3	5	45	.260	13	55	3	196	445	11	.983
Major league totals (2 years)		282	890	87	223	48	3	7	85	.251	27	110	6	388	865	24	.981

CRUZ, JACOB   OF   INDIANS

PERSONAL: Born January 28, 1973, in Oxnard, Calif. ... 6-0/179. ... Bats left, throws left.
HIGH SCHOOL: Channel Islands (Oxnard, Calif.).
COLLEGE: Arizona State.
TRANSACTIONS/CAREER NOTES: Selected by California Angels organization in 45th round of free-agent draft (June 3, 1991); did not sign. ... Selected by San Francisco Giants organization in supplemental round ("sandwich pick" between first and second round; 32nd pick overall) of free-agent draft (June 2, 1994); pick received as part of compensation for Texas Rangers signing Type A free agent 1B Will Clark. ... Traded by Giants with P Steve Reed to Cleveland Indians for P Jose Mesa, IF Shawon Dunston and P Alvin Morman (July 24, 1998).
STATISTICAL NOTES: Led Pacific Coast League with 11 sacrifice flies in 1996. ... Led Pacific Coast League with .434 on-base percentage and tied for league lead with nine intentional bases on balls in 1997.

Year Team (League)	Pos.	G	AB	R	H	2B	3B	HR	RBI	Avg.	BB	SO	SB	PO	A	E	Avg.
1994— San Jose (Calif.)	OF	31	118	14	29	7	0	0	12	.246	9	22	0	42	2	2	.957
1995— Shreveport (Texas)	OF	127	458	88	136	33	1	13	77	.297	57	72	9	235	16	1	*.996
1996— Phoenix (PCL)	OF	121	435	60	124	26	4	7	75	.285	62	77	5	249	11	3	.989
— San Francisco (N.L.)	OF	33	70	10	18	3	0	3	10	.234	12	24	0	41	1	1	.977
1997— Phoenix (PCL)	OF	127	493	97	178	*45	3	12	95	*.361	64	64	18	239	*16	8	.970
— San Francisco (N.L.)	OF	16	25	3	4	1	0	0	3	.160	3	4	0	12	2	1	.933
1998— Fresno (Pacific Coast)	OF	89	342	60	102	17	3	18	62	.298	46	57	12	152	5	6	.963
— San Francisco (N.L.)	PH	3	3	0	0	0	0	0	0	.000	0	2	0	0	0	0	...
— Buffalo (Int'l)■	OF	43	169	32	56	8	2	13	36	.331	13	26	2	70	5	4	.949
— Cleveland (A.L.)	PH	1	1	0	0	0	0	0	0	.000	0	1	0	0	0	0	...
American League totals (1 year)		1	1	0	0	0	0	0	0	.000	0	1	0	0	0	0	...
National League totals (3 years)		52	105	13	22	4	0	3	13	.210	15	30	0	53	3	2	.966
Major league totals (3 years)		53	106	13	22	4	0	3	13	.208	15	31	0	53	3	2	.966

CRUZ JR., JOSE   OF   BLUE JAYS

PERSONAL: Born April 19, 1974, in Arroyo, Puerto Rico. ... 6-0/195. ... Bats both, throws right. ... Son of Jose Cruz Sr., outfielder with St. Louis Cardinals (1970-1974), Houston Astros (1975-1987) and New York Yankees (1988); nephew of Hector Cruz, major league

outfielder/third baseman with four teams (1973, 1975-1982); and nephew of Tommy Cruz, outfielder with St. Louis Cardinals (1973), Chicago White Sox (1977) and Nippon Ham Fighters of Japan League (1980-1985).
HIGH SCHOOL: Bellaire (Houston).
COLLEGE: Rice.
TRANSACTIONS/CAREER NOTES: Selected by Atlanta Braves organization in 15th round of free-agent draft (June 1, 1992); did not sign. ... Selected by Seattle Mariners organization in first round (third pick overall) of free-agent draft (June 1, 1995). ... Traded by Mariners to Toronto Blue Jays for P Mike Timlin and P Paul Spoljaric (July 31, 1997).
STATISTICAL NOTES: Switch-hit home runs in one game (August 24, 1997). ... Had 18-game hitting streak (August 5-24, 1998).

Year Team (League)	Pos.	G	AB	R	H	2B	3B	HR	RBI	Avg.	BB	SO	SB	PO	A	E	Avg.
1995— Everett (N'west)..........	OF	3	11	6	5	0	0	0	2	.455	3	3	1	7	0	0	1.000
— Riverside (Calif.)........	OF	35	144	34	37	7	1	7	29	.257	24	50	3	70	4	3	.961
1996— Lancaster (Calif.)........	OF	53	203	38	66	17	1	6	43	.325	39	33	7	62	7	1	.986
— Port City (Southern)...	OF	47	181	39	51	10	2	3	31	.282	27	38	5	90	6	1	.990
— Tacoma (PCL)	OF	22	76	15	18	1	2	6	15	.237	18	12	1	36	4	0	1.000
1997— Tacoma (PCL)	OF	50	190	33	51	16	2	6	30	.268	34	44	3	70	3	0	1.000
— Seattle (A.L.)	OF	49	183	28	49	12	1	12	34	.268	13	45	1	83	1	3	.966
— Toronto (A.L.)■..........	OF	55	212	31	49	7	0	14	34	.231	28	72	6	98	3	2	.981
1998— Toronto (A.L.)...........	OF	105	352	55	89	14	3	11	42	.253	57	99	11	247	7	4	.984
— Syracuse (Int'l)..........	OF	40	141	29	42	14	1	7	23	.298	32	32	8	99	7	1	.991
Major league totals (2 years)		209	747	114	187	33	4	37	110	.250	98	216	18	428	11	9	.980

CUMMINGS, JOHN   P   ROYALS   C

PERSONAL: Born May 10, 1969, in Torrance, Calif. ... 6-3/205. ... Throws left, bats left. ... Full name: John Russell Cummings.
HIGH SCHOOL: Canyon (Anaheim, Calif.).
COLLEGE: Southern California.
TRANSACTIONS/CAREER NOTES: Selected by New York Yankees organization in 32nd round of free-agent draft (June 1, 1988); did not sign. ... Selected by Seattle Mariners organization in eighth round of free-agent draft (June 4, 1990). ... On Calgary disabled list (August 1-8, 1993). ... On Seattle disabled list (May 11-28, 1994); included rehabilitation assignment to Appleton (May 23-26). ... Claimed on waivers by Los Angeles Dodgers (May 25, 1995). ... Traded by Dodgers with P Joey Eischen to Detroit Tigers for OF Chad Curtis (July 31, 1996). ... Granted free agency (October 15, 1997). ... Signed by Cleveland Indians organization (January 8, 1998). ... On Buffalo disabled list (May 5-20, 1998). ... Released by Indians (July 2, 1998). ... Signed by Boston Red Sox organization (July 19, 1998). ... Granted free agency (October 15, 1998). ... Signed by Kansas City Royals organization (December 17, 1998).
HONORS: Named Carolina League Pitcher of the Year (1992).

Year Team (League)	W	L	Pct.	ERA	G	GS	CG	ShO	Sv.	IP	H	R	ER	BB	SO
1990— Bellingham (N'west)..........	1	1	.500	2.12	6	6	0	0	0	34	25	11	8	9	39
— San Bernardino (Calif.)......	2	4	.333	4.20	7	7	1	0	0	40 2/3	47	27	19	20	30
1991— San Bernardino (Calif.)........	4	10	.286	4.06	29	20	0	0	1	124	129	79	56	61	120
1992— Peninsula (Caro.)	*16	6	.727	2.57	27	27	4	1	0	168 1/3	149	71	48	63	*144
1993— Seattle (A.L.)...................	0	6	.000	6.02	10	8	1	0	0	46 1/3	59	34	31	16	19
— Jacksonville (Southern)......	2	2	.500	3.15	7	7	1	0	0	45 2/3	50	24	16	9	35
— Calgary (PCL)	3	4	.429	4.13	11	10	0	0	0	65 1/3	69	40	30	21	42
1994— Seattle (A.L.)...................	2	4	.333	5.63	17	8	0	0	0	64	66	43	40	37	33
— Appleton (Midwest)..........	0	0	. . .	3.00	1	1	0	0	0	3	2	1	1	0	6
— Calgary (PCL)	1	0	1.000	1.50	1	1	0	0	0	6	3	1	1	2	4
— Riverside (California)........	0	1	.000	6.75	1	1	0	0	0	2 2/3	5	2	2	1	2
1995— Seattle (A.L.)...................	0	0	. . .	11.81	4	0	0	0	0	5 1/3	8	8	7	7	4
— Tacoma (PCL)	0	1	.000	7.71	1	1	0	0	0	2 1/3	6	4	2	3	3
— San Antonio (Tex.)■........	0	2	.000	3.95	6	5	0	0	0	27 1/3	28	13	12	7	13
— Los Angeles (N.L.)...........	3	1	.750	3.00	35	0	0	0	0	39	38	16	13	10	21
1996— Los Angeles (N.L.)...........	0	1	.000	6.75	4	0	0	0	0	5 1/3	12	7	4	2	5
— Albuquerque (PCL)............	2	6	.250	4.14	27	9	0	0	2	78 1/3	91	47	36	28	49
— Detroit (A.L.)■.................	3	3	.500	5.12	21	0	0	0	0	31 2/3	36	20	18	20	24
1997— Detroit (A.L.).................	2	0	1.000	5.47	19	0	0	0	0	24 2/3	32	22	15	14	8
— Toledo (International)........	2	1	.667	2.76	19	0	0	0	0	16 1/3	13	6	5	6	7
1998— Buffalo (Int'l)■................	0	1	.000	5.79	21	0	0	0	0	18 2/3	25	15	12	4	15
— Pawtucket (Int'l)■...........	0	5	.000	6.16	10	8	0	0	0	38	46	28	26	12	17
A.L. totals (5 years)	7	13	.350	5.81	71	16	1	0	0	172	201	127	111	94	88
N.L. totals (2 years)	3	2	.600	3.45	39	0	0	0	0	44 1/3	50	23	17	12	26
Major league totals (5 years)......	10	15	.400	5.33	110	16	1	0	0	216 1/3	251	150	128	106	114

DIVISION SERIES RECORD

Year Team (League)	W	L	Pct.	ERA	G	GS	CG	ShO	Sv.	IP	H	R	ER	BB	SO
1995— Los Angeles (N.L.)	0	0	. . .	20.25	2	0	0	0	0	1 1/3	3	3	3	2	3

CUMMINGS, MIDRE   OF   RED SOX

PERSONAL: Born October 14, 1971, in St. Croix, Virgin Islands. ... 6-0/190. ... Bats left, throws right. ... Full name: Midre Almeric Cummings.
HIGH SCHOOL: Miami Edison Senior.
TRANSACTIONS/CAREER NOTES: Selected by Minnesota Twins organization in supplemental round ("sandwich pick" between first and second round, 29th pick overall) of free-agent draft (June 4, 1990); pick received as part of compensation for Boston Red Sox signing Type A free-agent P Jeff Reardon. ... Traded by Twins organization with P Denny Neagle to Pittsburgh Pirates organization for P John Smiley (March 17, 1992). ... On Buffalo disabled list (April 24-June 6, 1994). ... On Calgary disabled list (June 17-July 1, 1995). ... Claimed on waivers by Philadelphia Phillies (July 8, 1997). ... Released by Phillies (February 24, 1998). ... Signed by Cincinnati Reds organization (February 27, 1998). ... Claimed on waivers by Boston Red Sox (March 19, 1998). ... On disabled list (July 29-September 7, 1998).
MISCELLANEOUS: Batted as switch-hitter (1990-92).

Year Team (League)	Pos.	G	AB	R	H	2B	3B	HR	RBI	Avg.	BB	SO	SB	PO	A	E	Avg.
1990— GC Twins (GCL).........	OF	47	177	28	56	3	4	5	28	.316	13	32	14	73	2	6	.926
1991— Kenosha (Midwest)	OF	106	382	59	123	20	4	4	54	*.322	22	66	28	166	6	•13	.930
1992— Salem (Carolina)■...	OF	113	420	55	128	20	5	14	75	.305	35	67	23	151	10	6	.964
1993— Carolina (Southern)....	OF	63	237	33	70	17	2	6	26	.295	14	23	5	99	7	4	.964
—Buffalo (A.A.)............	OF	60	232	36	64	12	1	9	21	.276	22	45	5	90	1	2	.978
—Pittsburgh (N.L.).......	OF	13	36	5	4	1	0	0	3	.111	4	9	0	21	0	0	1.000
1994— Buffalo (A.A.)............	OF	49	183	23	57	12	4	2	22	.311	13	26	5	117	2	0	1.000
—Pittsburgh (N.L.).......	OF	24	86	11	21	4	0	1	12	.244	4	18	0	49	1	2	.962
1995— Pittsburgh (N.L.).......	OF	59	152	13	37	7	1	2	15	.243	13	30	1	79	2	1	.988
—Calgary (PCL)............	OF	45	159	19	44	9	1	1	16	.277	6	27	1	96	4	6	.943
1996— Calgary (PCL)............	OF	97	368	60	112	24	3	8	55	.304	21	60	6	176	9	5	.974
—Pittsburgh (N.L.).......	OF	24	85	11	19	3	1	3	7	.224	0	16	0	49	0	1	.980
1997— Pittsburgh (N.L.).......	OF	52	106	11	20	6	2	3	8	.189	8	26	0	37	1	0	1.000
—Philadelphia (N.L.)■ ..	OF	63	208	24	63	16	4	1	23	.303	23	30	2	113	1	1	.991
1998— Boston (A.L.)■...........	DH-OF	67	120	20	34	8	0	5	15	.283	17	19	3	16	0	1	.941
American League totals (1 year)		67	120	20	34	8	0	5	15	.283	17	19	3	16	0	1	.941
National League totals (5 years)		235	673	75	164	37	8	10	68	.244	52	129	3	348	5	5	.986
Major league totals (6 years)		302	793	95	198	45	8	15	83	.250	69	148	6	364	5	6	.984

DIVISION SERIES RECORD

Year Team (League)	Pos.	G	AB	R	H	2B	3B	HR	RBI	Avg.	BB	SO	SB	PO	A	E	Avg.
1998— Boston (A.L.)..............	PH	3	3	0	0	0	0	0	0	.000	0	0	0	...	...	...	...

CUNNANE, WILL P PADRES

PERSONAL: Born April 24, 1974, in Suffern, N.Y. ... 6-2/175. ... Throws right, bats right. ... Full name: William Joseph Cunnane.
HIGH SCHOOL: Clarkstown North (New City, N.Y.).
TRANSACTIONS/CAREER NOTES: Signed as non-drafted free agent by Florida Marlins organization (August 18, 1992). ... On Portland disabled list (August 7-23, 1996). ... Selected by San Diego Padres organization from Marlins organization in Rule 5 major league draft (December 9, 1996). ... On San Diego disabled list (March 29-June 21, 1998); included rehabilitation assignment to Las Vegas (June 9-21).
MISCELLANEOUS: Appeared in one game as pinch runner (1997).

Year Team (League)	W	L	Pct.	ERA	G	GS	CG	ShO	Sv.	IP	H	R	ER	BB	SO
1993— GC Marlins (GCL)...............	3	3	.500	2.70	16	9	0	0	2	66$^{2}/_{3}$	75	32	20	8	64
1994— Kane County (Midwest)......	11	3	.786	*1.43	32	16	5	*4	1	138$^{2}/_{3}$	110	27	22	23	106
1995— Portland (Eastern).............	9	2	*.818	3.67	21	21	1	1	0	117$^{2}/_{3}$	120	48	48	34	83
1996— Portland (Eastern).............	10	12	.455	3.74	25	25	4	0	0	151$^{2}/_{3}$	156	73	63	30	101
1997— San Diego (N.L.)■	6	3	.667	5.81	54	8	0	0	0	91$^{1}/_{3}$	114	69	59	49	79
1998— Las Vegas (PCL)	1	2	.333	5.25	33	0	0	0	4	36	45	26	21	19	30
—San Diego (N.L.)	0	0	...	6.00	3	0	0	0	0	3	4	2	2	1	1
Major league totals (2 years)......	6	3	.667	5.82	57	8	0	0	0	94$^{1}/_{3}$	118	71	61	50	80

CURTIS, CHAD OF YANKEES

PERSONAL: Born November 6, 1968, in Marion, Ind. ... 5-10/185. ... Bats right, throws right. ... Full name: Chad David Curtis.
HIGH SCHOOL: Benson (Ariz.) Union.
JUNIOR COLLEGE: Yavapai College (Ariz.), then Cochise County Community College (Ariz.).
COLLEGE: Grand Canyon (Ariz.).
TRANSACTIONS/CAREER NOTES: Selected by California Angels organization in 45th round of free-agent draft (June 5, 1989). ... On disabled list (June 5-20, 1991). ... On suspended list (June 8-12, 1993). ... Traded by Angels to Detroit Tigers for OF/3B Tony Phillips (April 12, 1995). ... Traded by Tigers to Los Angeles Dodgers for P Joey Eischen and P John Cummings (July 31, 1996). ... Granted free agency (October 15, 1996). ... Signed by Cleveland Indians (December 18, 1996). ... On Cleveland disabled list (May 14-June 9, 1997). ... Traded by Indians to New York Yankees for P David Weathers (June 9, 1997); on disabled list when acquired by Yankees and activated on June 11.
STATISTICAL NOTES: Led Midwest League with 223 total bases in 1990. ... Tied for A.L. lead in caught stealing with 24 in 1993. ... Led A.L. outfielders with 448 total chances and tied for lead with nine errors in 1993. ... Led A.L. outfielders with 345 total chances in 1994. ... Career major league grand slams: 1.

Year Team (League)	Pos.	G	AB	R	H	2B	3B	HR	RBI	Avg.	BB	SO	SB	PO	A	E	Avg.
1989— Ariz. Angels (Ariz.)	2B-OF	32	122	30	37	4	4	3	20	.303	14	20	17	62	58	6	.952
—Quad City (Midwest) ..	OF	23	78	7	19	3	0	2	11	.244	6	17	7	34	1	1	.972
1990— Quad City (Midwest) ..	2B-OF	135	*492	87	*151	28	1	14	65	.307	57	76	64	216	221	26	.944
1991— Edmonton (PCL)	3B-2B-OF	115	431	81	136	28	7	9	61	.316	51	56	46	124	220	25	.932
1992— California (A.L.)...........	OF-DH	139	441	59	114	16	2	10	46	.259	51	71	43	250	*16	6	.978
1993— California (A.L.)...........	OF-2B	152	583	94	166	25	3	6	59	.285	70	89	48	426	13	‡9	.980
1994— California (A.L.)...........	OF	114	453	67	116	23	4	11	50	.256	37	69	25	*332	9	4	.988
1995— Detroit (A.L.)■...........	OF	144	586	96	157	29	3	21	67	.268	70	93	27	362	5	3	.992
1996— Detroit (A.L.)............	OF	104	400	65	105	20	1	10	37	.263	53	73	16	243	6	9	.965
—Los Angeles (N.L.)■ ..	OF	43	104	20	22	5	0	2	9	.212	17	15	2	62	2	1	.985
1997— Cleveland (A.L.)■.......	OF	22	29	8	6	1	0	3	5	.207	7	10	0	20	0	1	1.000
—Akron (Eastern)	OF	4	18	5	7	1	0	3	6	.389	0	3	0	5	2	0	1.000
—New York (A.L.)■.......	OF	93	320	51	93	21	1	12	50	.291	36	49	12	168	6	4	.978
1998— New York (A.L.).........	OF-DH	151	456	79	111	21	1	10	56	.243	75	80	21	306	8	5	.984
American League totals (7 years)		919	3268	519	868	156	15	83	370	.266	399	534	192	2107	63	40	.982
National League totals (1 year)		43	104	20	22	5	0	2	9	.212	17	15	2	62	2	1	.985
Major league totals (7 years)		962	3372	539	890	161	15	85	379	.264	416	549	194	2169	65	41	.982

DIVISION SERIES RECORD

				BATTING											FIELDING		
Year Team (League)	Pos.	G	AB	R	H	2B	3B	HR	RBI	Avg.	BB	SO	SB	PO	A	E	Avg.
1996— Los Angeles (N.L.)	OF	1	2	0	0	0	0	0	0	.000	1	1	0	2	0	0	1.000
1997— New York (A.L.)..........	OF-PR	4	6	0	1	0	0	0	0	.167	3	1	0	4	0	0	1.000
1998— New York (A.L.)..........	OF	3	3	1	2	1	0	0	0	.667	1	1	1	3	0	0	1.000
Division series totals (3 years)		8	11	1	3	1	0	0	0	.273	5	3	1	9	0	0	1.000

CHAMPIONSHIP SERIES RECORD

				BATTING											FIELDING		
Year Team (League)	Pos.	G	AB	R	H	2B	3B	HR	RBI	Avg.	BB	SO	SB	PO	A	E	Avg.
1998— New York (A.L.)..........	OF	2	4	0	0	0	0	0	0	.000	1	2	0	1	0	0	1.000

WORLD SERIES RECORD

NOTES: Member of World Series championship team (1998).

				BATTING											FIELDING		
Year Team (League)	Pos.	G	AB	R	H	2B	3B	HR	RBI	Avg.	BB	SO	SB	PO	A	E	Avg.
1998— New York (A.L.)					Did not play.												

CUYLER, MILT   OF   RANGERS

PERSONAL: Born October 7, 1968, in Macon, Ga. ... 5-10/185. ... Bats both, throws right. ... Full name: Milton Cuyler Jr. ... Name pronounced KY-ler.

HIGH SCHOOL: Southwest Macon (Macon, Ga.).

TRANSACTIONS/CAREER NOTES: Selected by Detroit Tigers organization in second round of free-agent draft (June 2, 1986). ... On disabled list (July 26, 1992-remainder of season and August 9, 1993-remainder of season). ... On Detroit disabled list (May 26-July 25, 1994); included rehabilitation assignment to Toledo (July 8-25). ... On Toledo disabled list (July 1-16, 1995). ... Released by Tigers (November 30, 1995). ... Signed by Boston Red Sox organization (December 21, 1995). ... On disabled list (June 13, 1996-remainder of season). ... Granted free agency (October 10, 1996). ... Signed by Montreal Expos organization (December 26, 1996). ... Released by Expos (March 13, 1997). ... Signed by Nashua Pride, Atlantic League (April 27, 1998). ... Contract purchased by Texas Rangers (September 5, 1998). ... Granted free agency (October 15, 1998). ... Re-signed by Rangers organization (October 23, 1998).

STATISTICAL NOTES: Led South Atlantic League with 17 sacrifice hits in 1987. ... Led Florida State League in caught stealing with 25 in 1988. ... Led Eastern League outfielders with 293 total chances in 1989. ... Led International League in caught stealing with 14 in 1990. ... Career major league grand slams: 2.

				BATTING											FIELDING		
Year Team (League)	Pos.	G	AB	R	H	2B	3B	HR	RBI	Avg.	BB	SO	SB	PO	A	E	Avg.
1986— Bristol (Appal.)	OF	45	174	24	40	3	5	1	11	.230	15	35	12	97	0	4	.960
1987— Fayetteville (SAL)	OF	94	366	65	107	8	4	2	34	.292	34	78	27	237	13	7	.973
1988— Lakeland (Fla. St.)	OF	132	483	*100	143	11	3	2	32	.296	71	83	50	257	8	4	.985
1989— Toledo (Int'l)	OF	24	83	4	14	3	2	0	6	.169	8	27	4	48	3	2	.962
— London (Eastern)	OF	98	366	69	96	8	7	7	34	.262	47	74	32	*272	13	8	.973
1990— Toledo (Int'l)	OF	124	461	77	119	11	8	2	42	.258	60	77	*52	290	4	7	.977
— Detroit (A.L.)	OF	19	51	8	13	3	1	0	8	.255	5	10	1	38	2	1	.976
1991— Detroit (A.L.)	OF	154	475	77	122	15	7	3	33	.257	52	92	41	411	7	6	.986
1992— Detroit (A.L.)	OF	89	291	39	70	11	1	3	28	.241	10	62	8	232	4	4	.983
1993— Detroit (A.L.)	OF	82	249	46	53	11	7	0	19	.213	19	53	13	211	2	7	.968
1994— Detroit (A.L.)	OF	48	116	20	28	3	1	1	11	.241	13	21	5	78	1	2	.975
— Toledo (Int'l)	OF	15	64	8	22	4	1	0	2	.344	3	11	4	33	0	3	.917
1995— Detroit (A.L.)	OF-DH	41	88	15	18	1	4	0	5	.205	8	16	2	50	2	4	.929
— Toledo (Int'l)	OF	54	203	33	62	10	4	6	28	.305	20	40	6	95	1	4	.960
1996— Boston (A.L.)■..........	OF-DH	50	110	19	22	1	2	2	12	.200	13	19	7	104	0	3	.972
1997—					Out of organized baseball.												
1998— Nashua (Atlantic)■	OF	73	249	62	77	18	6	6	33	.309	39	42	21	125	4	2	.985
— Oklahoma (PCL)■......	OF	2	6	0	0	0	0	0	0	.000	2	4	0	3	0	0	1.000
— Texas (A.L.)	DH-OF	7	6	3	3	2	0	1	3	.500	1	0	0	5	0	0	1.000
Major league totals (8 years)		490	1386	227	329	47	23	10	119	.237	121	273	77	1129	18	27	.977

DAAL, OMAR   P   DIAMONDBACKS

PERSONAL: Born March 1, 1972, in Maracaibo, Venezuela. ... 6-3/185. ... Throws left, bats left. ... Full name: Omar Jose Cordaro Daal.

HIGH SCHOOL: Valencia (Venezuela) Superior.

TRANSACTIONS/CAREER NOTES: Signed as non-drafted free agent by Los Angeles Dodgers organization (August 24, 1990). ... Traded by Dodgers to Montreal Expos for P Rick Clelland (December 14, 1995). ... Claimed on waivers by Toronto Blue Jays (July 25, 1997). ... Selected by Arizona Diamondbacks in second round (31st pick overall) of expansion draft (November 18, 1997). ... On Arizona disabled list (June 22-July 11, 1998); included rehabilitation assignment to Tucson (July 9-11).

MISCELLANEOUS: Holds Arizona Diamondbacks all-time records for lowest earned-run average (2.88); and most complete games (3). ... Tied for Arizona Diamondbacks all-time record for shutouts (1).

Year Team (League)	W	L	Pct.	ERA	G	GS	CG	ShO	Sv.	IP	H	R	ER	BB	SO
1990— Dom. Dodgers (DSL)	3	6	.333	1.18	17	13	6	0	2	$91^2/_3$	61	29	12	29	91
1991— Dom. Dodgers (DSL)	7	2	.778	1.16	13	13	0	0	0	93	30	17	12	32	81
1992— Albuquerque (PCL)............	0	2	.000	7.84	12	0	0	0	0	$10^1/_3$	14	9	9	11	9
— San Antonio (Tex.)	2	6	.250	5.02	35	5	0	0	5	$57^1/_3$	60	39	32	33	52
1993— Albuquerque (PCL)............	1	1	.500	3.38	6	0	0	0	2	$5^1/_3$	5	2	2	3	2
— Los Angeles (N.L.)	2	3	.400	5.09	47	0	0	0	0	$35^1/_3$	36	20	20	21	19
1994— Albuquerque (PCL)............	4	2	.667	5.19	11	5	0	0	1	$34^2/_3$	38	20	20	16	28
— Los Angeles (N.L.)	0	0	. . .	3.29	24	0	0	0	0	$13^2/_3$	12	5	5	5	9

C
D

Year	Team (League)	W	L	Pct.	ERA	G	GS	CG	ShO	Sv.	IP	H	R	ER	BB	SO
1995—	Albuquerque (PCL).............	2	3	.400	4.05	17	9	0	0	1	53 1/3	56	28	24	26	46
	— Los Angeles (N.L.)............	4	0	1.000	7.20	28	0	0	0	0	20	29	16	16	15	11
1996—	Montreal (N.L.)■..............	4	5	.444	4.02	64	6	0	0	0	87 1/3	74	40	39	37	82
1997—	Montreal (N.L.)..................	1	2	.333	9.79	33	0	0	0	1	30 1/3	48	35	33	15	16
	— Ottawa (Int'l)...................	0	1	.000	5.63	2	2	0	0	0	8	10	6	5	1	9
	— Toronto (A.L.)■................	1	1	.500	4.00	9	3	0	0	0	27	34	13	12	6	28
	— Syracuse (Int'l)...............	3	0	1.000	0.53	5	5	1	1	0	33 2/3	18	2	2	10	29
1998—	Arizona (N.L.)■...............	8	12	.400	2.88	33	23	3	1	0	162 2/3	146	60	52	51	132
	— Tucson (PCL)	0	0	. . .	3.00	1	1	0	0	0	3	3	2	1	1	4
A.L. totals (1 year)		1	1	.500	4.00	9	3	0	0	0	27	34	13	12	6	28
N.L. totals (6 years)		19	22	.463	4.25	229	29	3	1	1	349 1/3	345	176	165	144	269
Major league totals (6 years)......		20	23	.465	4.23	238	32	3	1	1	376 1/3	379	189	177	150	297

DALE, CARL   P   ATHLETICS

PERSONAL: Born December 7, 1972, in Indianapolis. ... 6-2/215. ... Throws right, bats right. ... Full name: James Carl Dale.
HIGH SCHOOL: Cookeville (Tenn.).
COLLEGE: Winthrop (S.C.).
TRANSACTIONS/CAREER NOTES: Selected by St. Louis Cardinals organization in second round of free-agent draft (June 2, 1994). ... Traded by Cardinals with OF Allen Battle, P Bret Wagner and P Jay Witasick to Oakland Athletics for P Todd Stottlemyre (January 6, 1996). ... On temporarily inactive list (June 12-19, 1996). ... On Huntsville disabled list (April 29-June 24, 1998).

Year	Team (League)	W	L	Pct.	ERA	G	GS	CG	ShO	Sv.	IP	H	R	ER	BB	SO
1994—	New Jersey (NYP)	2	7	.222	4.56	15	•15	0	0	0	73	79	44	37	38	75
1995—	Peoria (Midwest)	9	9	.500	2.94	24	24	2	1	0	143 2/3	124	66	47	62	104
1996—	Modesto (California)■.....	8	2	.800	4.28	26	24	0	0	0	128 1/3	124	79	61	72	102
1997—	Huntsville (Southern)	6	4	.600	5.38	20	16	0	0	0	85 1/3	95	61	51	43	57
1998—	Huntsville (Southern)	1	1	.500	4.61	3	3	0	0	0	13 2/3	13	7	7	8	10
	— Modesto (California)	1	2	.333	2.37	3	3	0	0	0	19	15	6	5	2	14
	— Edmonton (PCL)	5	3	.625	4.08	11	11	1	1	0	64	64	31	29	26	41

D

DALESANDRO, MARK   C/3B   BLUE JAYS

PERSONAL: Born May 14, 1968, in Chicago. ... 6-0/195. ... Bats right, throws right. ... Full name: Mark Anthony Dalesandro. ... Name pronounced DEE-uh-SAN-droh.
HIGH SCHOOL: St. Ignatius College Prep School (Chicago).
COLLEGE: Illinois.
TRANSACTIONS/CAREER NOTES: Selected by California Angels organization in 18th round of free-agent draft (June 4, 1990). ... Released by Angels (February 6, 1996). ... Signed by New York Yankees organization (February 12, 1996). ... Released by Yankees (April 4, 1996). ... Re-signed by Columbus, Yankees organization (May 3, 1996). ... Granted free agency (October 15, 1996). ... Signed by Chicago Cubs organization (December 23, 1996). ... On disabled list (April 27-May 4, 1997). ... Granted free agency (October 17, 1997). ... Signed by Toronto Blue Jays organization (December 2, 1997).
STATISTICAL NOTES: Tied for California League lead in grounding into double plays with 20 in 1992.

Year	Team (League)	Pos.	G	AB	R	H	2B	3B	HR	RBI	Avg.	BB	SO	SB	PO	A	E	Avg.
							BATTING								FIELDING			
1990—	Boise (Northwest)	OF-3B-1B	55	224	35	75	10	2	6	44	.335	18	42	6	37	23	6	.909
1991—	Quad City (Midwest) ..	3B-1B	125	487	63	133	17	8	5	69	.273	34	58	1	198	186	25	.939
1992—	Palm Springs (Calif.)...	1B-3B	126	492	72	146	30	3	7	92	.297	33	50	6	594	114	15	.979
1993—	Palm Springs (Calif.)..	C-1B	46	176	22	43	5	3	1	25	.244	15	20	3	271	42	7	.978
	— Midland (Texas).........	3B-C-1B	57	235	33	69	9	0	2	36	.294	8	30	1	137	60	12	.943
	— Vancouver (PCL)	3B	26	107	16	32	8	1	2	15	.299	6	13	1	19	59	7	.918
1994—	Vancouver (PCL)	3-C-1-O	51	199	29	63	9	1	1	31	.317	7	19	1	153	71	11	.953
	— California (A.L.).........	C-3B-OF	19	25	5	5	1	0	1	2	.200	2	4	0	19	5	1	.960
1995—	California (A.L.).........	C-DH-O	11	10	1	1	1	0	0	0	.100	0	2	0	11	0	0	1.000
	— Vancouver (PCL)	O-3-C-1	34	123	16	41	13	1	1	18	.333	6	12	2	56	8	2	.970
1996—	Columbus (Int'l)■.....	3-C-O-2	78	255	34	72	29	4	2	38	.282	17	31	2	128	75	10	.953
1997—	Iowa (Am. Assoc.)■..	C-3-1-O	115	405	48	106	14	0	8	48	.262	33	51	0	467	90	4	.993
1998—	Toronto (A.L.)■........	C-3-1-O	32	67	8	20	5	0	2	14	.299	1	6	0	76	9	2	.977
	— Syracuse (Int'l)..........	3B-C-OF	45	164	25	44	9	1	10	30	.268	12	20	1	60	16	3	.962
Major league totals (3 years)			62	102	14	26	7	0	3	16	.255	3	12	0	106	14	3	.976

D'AMICO, JEFF   P   BREWERS

PERSONAL: Born December 27, 1975, in St. Petersburg, Fla. ... 6-7/250. ... Throws right, bats right. ... Full name: Jeffrey Charles D'Amico.
HIGH SCHOOL: Northeast (St. Petersburg, Fla.).
TRANSACTIONS/CAREER NOTES: Selected by Milwaukee Brewers organization in first round (23rd pick overall) of free-agent draft (June 3, 1993). ... On disabled list (June 24, 1994-entire season). ... On Milwaukee disabled list (July 28-September 2, 1997; and January 14, 1998-entire season).

Year	Team (League)	W	L	Pct.	ERA	G	GS	CG	ShO	Sv.	IP	H	R	ER	BB	SO
1994—							Did not play.									
1995—	Beloit (Midwest)	13	3	*.813	2.39	21	20	3	1	0	132	102	40	35	31	119
1996—	El Paso (Texas).................	5	4	.556	3.19	13	13	3	0	0	96	89	42	34	13	76
	— Milwaukee (A.L.)	6	6	.500	5.44	17	17	0	0	0	86	88	53	52	31	53
1997—	Milwaukee (A.L.)	9	7	.563	4.71	23	23	1	1	0	135 2/3	139	81	71	43	94
	— Beloit (Midwest)	0	0	. . .	0.00	1	1	0	0	0	3	0	0	0	1	7
1998—	Milwaukee (A.L.)						Did not play.									
Major league totals (2 years)......		15	13	.536	4.99	40	40	1	1	0	221 2/3	227	134	123	74	147

D'AMICO, JEFF   P   ATHLETICS

PERSONAL: Born November 9, 1974, in Inglewood, Calif. ... 6-3/195. ... Throws right, bats right. ... Full name: Jeffrey Michael D'Amico.
HIGH SCHOOL: Redmond (Wash.).
TRANSACTIONS/CAREER NOTES: Selected by Oakland Athletics organization in second round of free-agent draft (June 3, 1993). ... On West Michigan disabled list (April 22-September 19, 1994). ... On Huntsville disabled list (June 25-July 10, 1998).
STATISTICAL NOTES: Led Southern League with five balks in 1998.
MISCELLANEOUS: Played infield only (1993-95).

Year Team (League)	W	L	Pct.	ERA	G	GS	CG	ShO	Sv.	IP	H	R	ER	BB	SO
1996— Modesto (California)	0	0	...	18.00	1	0	0	0	0	1	3	3	2	1	0
—Arizona A's (Arizona)	3	0	1.000	1.42	8	0	0	0	0	19	14	3	3	2	15
1997— Modesto (California)	7	3	.700	3.80	20	13	0	0	1	97	115	57	41	34	89
—Edmonton (PCL)	1	2	.333	8.22	10	7	0	0	1	30 2/3	42	29	28	6	19
1998— Huntsville (Southern)	5	5	.500	7.67	24	8	0	0	0	61	77	57	52	34	46
—Arizona A's (Arizona)	0	0	...	3.86	4	1	0	0	0	9 1/3	6	4	4	1	8

RECORD AS POSITION PLAYER

Year Team (League)	Pos.	G	AB	R	H	2B	3B	HR	RBI	Avg.	BB	SO	SB	PO	A	E	Avg.
1993— S. Oregon (N'west)	SS-3B	33	114	12	30	9	0	3	15	.263	9	25	2	43	67	14	.887
1994— W. Mich. (Mid.)	SS	9	36	5	10	3	0	0	3	.278	4	7	2	14	25	1	.975
1995— W. Mich. (Mid.)	SS-3B	125	434	56	98	24	1	7	55	.226	56	94	8	120	304	37	.920
1996— Modesto (California)	3-2-S-P	47	172	28	46	7	1	4	21	.267	19	31	3	36	101	19	.878

DAMON, JOHNNY   OF   ROYALS

PERSONAL: Born November 5, 1973, in Fort Riley, Kan. ... 6-2/190. ... Bats left, throws left. ... Full name: Johnny David Damon.
HIGH SCHOOL: Dr. Phillips (Orlando).
TRANSACTIONS/CAREER NOTES: Selected by Kansas City Royals organization in supplemental round ("sandwich pick" between first and second round, 35th pick overall) of free-agent draft (June 1, 1992); pick received as part of compensation for San Diego Padres signing Type A free-agent IF Kurt Stillwell. ... On suspended list (September 5-7, 1997).
HONORS: Named Texas League Player of the Year (1995).
STATISTICAL NOTES: Led Gulf Coast League with 109 total bases in 1992. ... Led Midwest League outfielders with five double plays in 1993. ... Led Texas League with .434 on-base percentage in 1995. ... Led Texas League with .534 slugging percentage in 1995. ... Led Texas League with 13 intentional bases on balls received in 1995. ... Career major league grand slams: 2.

Year Team (League)	Pos.	G	AB	R	H	2B	3B	HR	RBI	Avg.	BB	SO	SB	PO	A	E	Avg.
1992— GC Royals (GCL)	OF	50	192	*58	67	12	*9	4	24	*.349	31	21	33	77	7	1	.988
—Baseball City (FSL)	OF	1	1	0	0	0	0	0	0	.000	0	0	0	0	0	0	...
1993— Rockford (Midwest)	OF	127	511	82	148	25	*13	5	50	.290	52	83	59	240	14	6	.977
1994— Wilmington (Caro.)	OF	119	472	96	149	25	13	6	75	.316	62	55	44	273	9	3	.989
1995— Wichita (Texas)	OF	111	423	83	145	15	9	16	54	.343	67	35	26	296	11	5	.984
—Kansas City (A.L.)	OF	47	188	32	53	11	5	3	23	.282	12	22	7	110	0	1	.991
1996— Kansas City (A.L.)	OF-DH	145	517	61	140	22	5	6	50	.271	31	64	25	350	5	6	.983
1997— Kansas City (A.L.)	OF-DH	146	472	70	130	12	8	8	48	.275	42	70	16	322	5	4	.988
1998— Kansas City (A.L.)	OF	161	642	104	178	30	10	18	66	.277	58	84	26	372	10	4	.990
Major league totals (4 years)		499	1819	267	501	75	28	35	187	.275	143	240	74	1154	20	15	.987

DARENSBOURG, VIC   P   MARLINS

PERSONAL: Born November 13, 1970, in Los Angeles. ... 5-10/165. ... Throws left, bats left. ... Full name: Victor Anthony Darensbourg.
HIGH SCHOOL: Westchester (Los Angeles).
COLLEGE: Lewis and Clark (Ore.).
TRANSACTIONS/CAREER NOTES: Signed as non-drafted free agent by Florida Marlins organization (June 11, 1992). ... On disabled list entire 1995 season. ... On Portland disabled list (April 4-15, 1996). ... On Charlotte disabled list (April 25-June 21 and July 29-September 6, 1997).

Year Team (League)	W	L	Pct.	ERA	G	GS	CG	ShO	Sv.	IP	H	R	ER	BB	SO
1992— GC Marlins (GCL)	2	1	.667	0.64	8	4	0	0	2	42	28	5	3	11	37
1993— Kane County (Midwest)	9	1	.900	2.14	46	0	0	0	16	71 1/3	58	17	17	28	89
—High Desert (Calif.)	0	0	...	0.00	1	0	0	0	0	1	0	0	0	0	1
1994— Portland (Eastern)	10	7	.588	3.81	35	21	1	1	4	149	146	76	63	60	103
1995—							Did not play.								
1996— Brevard County (FSL)	0	0	...	0.00	2	0	0	0	0	3	1	0	0	1	5
—Brevard County (FSL)	0	0	...	0.00	2	0	0	0	0	3	1	0	0	1	5
—Charlotte (Int'l)	1	5	.167	3.69	47	0	0	0	7	63 1/3	61	30	26	32	66
1997— Charlotte (Int'l)	4	2	.667	4.38	27	0	0	0	2	24 2/3	22	12	12	15	21
1998— Florida (N.L.)	0	7	.000	3.68	59	0	0	0	1	71	52	29	29	30	74
Major league totals (1 year)	0	7	.000	3.68	59	0	0	0	1	71	52	29	29	30	74

DARR, MIKE   OF   PADRES

PERSONAL: Born March 21, 1976, in Corona, Calif. ... 6-3/205. ... Bats left, throws right. ... Full name: Michael Curtis Darr.
HIGH SCHOOL: Corona (Calif.).
TRANSACTIONS/CAREER NOTES: Selected by Detroit Tigers organization in second round of free-agent draft (June 2, 1994). ... On disabled list (April 4-May 28, 1996). ... Traded by Tigers with P Mike Skrmetta to San Diego Padres for 2B Jody Reed (March 22, 1997).

Year— Team (League)	Pos.	G	AB	R	H	2B	3B	HR	RBI	Avg.	BB	SO	SB	PO	A	E	Avg.
1994— Bristol (Appal.)	OF	44	149	23	41	6	0	1	18	.275	23	22	4	59	4	4	.940
1995— Fayetteville (SAL)	OF	112	395	58	114	21	2	5	66	.289	58	88	5	123	15	9	.939
1996— Lakeland (Fla. St.)	OF	85	311	26	77	14	7	0	38	.248	28	64	7	128	8	3	.978
1997— Rancho Cuca. (Cal.)■	OF	134	521	104	179	32	11	15	94	.344	57	90	23	176	12	8	.959
1998— Mobile (Southern)	OF	132	523	105	162	41	4	6	90	.310	62	79	28	261	13	6	.979

DARWIN, DANNY   P

PERSONAL: Born October 25, 1955, in Bonham, Texas. ... 6-3/202. ... Throws right, bats right. ... Full name: Daniel Wayne Darwin. ... Brother of Jeff Darwin, pitcher with Seattle Mariners (1994), Chicago White Sox (1996-97) and San Francisco Giants (1997-98).

HIGH SCHOOL: Bonham (Texas).

COLLEGE: Grayson County (Texas) College.

TRANSACTIONS/CAREER NOTES: Signed as non-drafted free agent by Texas Rangers organization (May 10, 1976). ... On disabled list (April 25-May 4 and May 22-June 11, 1977; June 5-26, 1980; March 25-April 10 and August 9-September 1, 1983). ... Traded by Rangers with a player to be named later to Milwaukee Brewers as part of a six-player, four-team deal in which Kansas City Royals acquired C Jim Sundberg from Brewers, Rangers acquired C Don Slaught from Royals, New York Mets organization acquired P Frank Wills from Royals and Brewers organization acquired P Tim Leary from Mets (January 18, 1985); Brewers organization acquired C Bill Hance from Rangers to complete deal (January 30, 1985). ... Granted free agency (November 12, 1985). ... Re-signed by Brewers (December 22, 1985). ... Traded by Brewers organization to Houston Astros for P Don August and a player to be named later (August 15, 1986); Brewers organization acquired P Mark Knudson to complete deal (August 21, 1986). ... Granted free agency (November 9, 1987). ... Re-signed by Astros (January 8, 1988). ... Granted free agency (December 7, 1990). ... Signed by Boston Red Sox (December 19, 1990). ... On disabled list (April 23-May 22 and July 5, 1991-remainder of season; and June 16, 1994-remainder of season). ... Granted free agency (October 21, 1994). ... Signed by Toronto Blue Jays (April 10, 1995). ... Released by Blue Jays (July 18, 1995). ... Signed by Oklahoma City, Rangers organization (July 31, 1995). ... Granted free agency (November 11, 1995). ... Signed by Carolina, Pittsburgh Pirates organization (February 4, 1996). ... Traded by Pirates to Astros for P Rich Loiselle (July 23, 1996). ... On Houston suspended list (August 16-21, 1996). ... Granted free agency (November 6, 1996). ... Signed by Chicago White Sox organization (February 7, 1997). ... Traded by White Sox with P Wilson Alvarez and P Roberto Hernandez to San Francisco Giants for SS Michael Caruso, OF Brian Manning, P Lorenzo Barcelo, P Keith Foulke, P Bobby Howry and P Ken Vining (July 31, 1997). ... Granted free agency (October 30, 1997). ... Re-signed by Giants (December 6, 1997). ... Granted free agency (November 3, 1998).

STATISTICAL NOTES: Tied for Western Carolinas League lead with five balks in 1976. ... Tied for Texas League lead with eight hit batsmen in 1977. ... Pitched 5-0 one-hit, complete-game victory against Boston (April 29, 1981). ... Pitched 4-1 one-hit, complete-game victory against Minnesota (August 19, 1985). ... Tied for A.L. lead with 34 home runs allowed in 1985. ... Pitched 5-0 one-hit, complete-game victory against Chicago (August 18, 1993).

MISCELLANEOUS: Appeared in four games as pinch runner (1990).

Year— Team (League)	W	L	Pct.	ERA	G	GS	CG	ShO	Sv.	IP	H	R	ER	BB	SO
1976— Asheville (W. Caro.)	6	3	.667	3.62	16	16	6	1	0	102	96	54	41	48	76
1977— Tulsa (Texas)	13	4	.765	2.51	23	23	6	•4	0	154	130	53	43	72	129
1978— Tucson (PCL)	8	9	.471	6.26	23	23	4	0	0	125	147	100	87	83	126
—Texas (A.L.)	1	0	1.000	4.00	3	1	0	0	0	9	11	4	4	1	8
1979— Tucson (PCL)	6	6	.500	3.60	13	13	4	1	0	95	89	43	38	42	65
—Texas (A.L.)	4	4	.500	4.04	20	6	1	0	0	78	50	36	35	30	58
1980— Texas (A.L.)	13	4	.765	2.62	53	2	0	0	8	110	98	37	32	50	104
1981— Texas (A.L.)	9	9	.500	3.64	22	22	6	2	0	146	115	67	59	57	98
1982— Texas (A.L.)	10	8	.556	3.44	56	1	0	0	7	89	95	38	34	37	61
1983— Texas (A.L.)	8	13	.381	3.49	28	26	9	2	0	183	175	86	71	62	92
1984— Texas (A.L.)	8	12	.400	3.94	35	32	5	2	0	223²/₃	249	110	98	54	123
1985— Milwaukee (A.L.)■	8	18	.308	3.80	39	29	11	1	2	217²/₃	212	112	92	65	125
1986— Milwaukee (A.L.)	6	8	.429	3.52	27	14	5	1	0	130¹/₃	120	62	51	35	80
—Houston (N.L.)	5	2	.714	2.32	12	8	1	0	0	54¹/₃	50	19	14	9	40
1987— Houston (N.L.)	9	10	.474	3.59	33	30	3	1	0	195²/₃	184	87	78	69	134
1988— Houston (N.L.)	8	13	.381	3.84	44	20	3	0	3	192	189	86	82	48	129
1989— Houston (N.L.)	11	4	.733	2.36	68	0	0	0	7	122	92	34	32	33	104
1990— Houston (N.L.)	11	4	.733	*2.21	48	17	3	0	2	162²/₃	136	42	40	31	109
1991— Boston (A.L.)■	3	6	.333	5.16	12	12	0	0	0	68	71	39	39	15	42
1992— Boston (A.L.)	9	9	.500	3.96	51	15	2	0	3	161¹/₃	159	76	71	53	124
1993— Boston (A.L.)	15	11	.577	3.26	34	34	2	1	0	229¹/₃	196	93	83	49	130
1994— Boston (A.L.)	7	5	.583	6.30	13	13	0	0	0	75²/₃	101	54	53	24	54
1995— Toronto (A.L.)■	1	8	.111	7.62	13	11	1	0	0	65	91	60	55	24	36
—Oklahoma City (A.A.)■	0	0	. . .	0.00	1	1	0	0	0	3	1	0	0	0	4
—Texas (A.L.)	2	2	.500	7.15	7	4	0	0	0	34	40	27	27	7	22
1996— Pittsburgh (N.L.)■	7	9	.438	3.02	19	19	0	0	0	122¹/₃	117	48	41	16	69
—Houston (N.L.)■	3	2	.600	5.95	15	6	0	0	0	42¹/₃	43	31	28	11	27
1997— Chicago (A.L.)■	4	8	.333	4.13	21	17	1	0	0	113¹/₃	130	60	52	31	62
—San Francisco (N.L.)■	1	3	.250	4.91	10	7	0	0	0	44	51	26	24	14	30
1998— San Francisco (N.L.)	8	10	.444	5.51	33	25	0	0	0	148²/₃	176	97	91	49	81
A.L. totals (15 years)	108	125	.464	3.98	434	239	43	9	20	1933¹/₃	1913	961	856	594	1219
N.L. totals (8 years)	63	57	.525	3.57	282	132	10	1	12	1084	1038	470	430	280	723
Major league totals (21 years)	171	182	.484	3.84	716	371	53	10	32	3017¹/₃	2951	1431	1286	874	1942

DAUBACH, BRIAN   1B   RED SOX

PERSONAL: Born February 11, 1972, in Belleville, Ill. ... 6-1/201. ... Bats left, throws right. ... Full name: Brian Michael Daubach.

HIGH SCHOOL: Belleville (Ill.) West.

TRANSACTIONS/CAREER NOTES: Selected by New York Mets organization in 17th round of free-agent draft (June 4, 1990). ... Granted free agency (October 15, 1996). ... Signed by Florida Marlins organization (November 7, 1996). ... Granted free agency (October 17, 1997). ... Re-signed by Marlins organization (January 6, 1998). ... Released by Marlins (November 19, 1998). ... Signed by Boston Red Sox organization (December 18, 1998).

STATISTICAL NOTES: Tied for Appalachian League lead in intentional bases on balls received with five in 1991. ... Led Appalachian League first basemen with 623 total chances and 41 double plays in 1991. ... Tied for Florida State League lead in double plays by first basemen with 127 in 1994. ... Led Eastern League first basemen with 111 double plays and .992 fielding percentage and tied for lead with 98 assists in 1995. ... Led Eastern League first basemen with 115 assists in 1996. ... Led International League with 10 sacrifice flies in 1997. ... Led International League with 315 total bases, .634 slugging percentage and nine intentional bases on balls received and tied for lead in being hit by pitch with 15 in 1998.

Year Team (League)	Pos.	G	AB	R	H	2B	3B	HR	RBI	Avg.	BB	SO	SB	PO	A	E	Avg.
1990—GC Mets (GCL)	1B	45	152	26	41	8	4	1	19	.270	22	41	2	274	16	7	.976
1991—Kingsport (Appal.)	1B	65	218	30	53	9	1	7	42	.243	33	64	1	*562	*52	9	.986
1992—Pittsfield (NYP)	1B	72	260	26	63	15	2	2	40	.242	30	61	4	609	•44	12	.982
1993—Capital City (SAL)	1B-OF	102	379	50	106	19	3	7	72	.280	52	84	6	393	43	5	.989
1994—St. Lucie (Fla. St.)	1B	129	450	52	123	30	2	6	74	.273	58	120	14	1172	*115	12	.991
1995—Binghamton (East.)	1B-3B	135	469	61	115	25	2	10	72	.245	51	104	6	1137	98	10	†.992
—Norfolk (Int'l)	1B	2	7	0	0	0	0	0	0	.000	1	0	0	21	3	0	1.000
1996—Binghamton (East.)	1B-3B	122	436	80	129	24	1	22	76	.296	74	103	7	1108	†115	11	.991
—Norfolk (Int'l)	1B	17	54	7	11	2	0	0	6	.204	6	14	1	72	3	0	1.000
1997—Charlotte (Int'l)■	1B	136	461	66	128	40	2	21	93	.278	65	126	1	870	62	8	.991
1998—Charlotte (Int'l)	OF-1B	140	497	102	157	*45	4	*35	*124	.316	80	114	9	362	28	3	.992
—Florida (N.L.)	1B	10	15	0	3	1	0	0	3	.200	1	5	0	23	1	0	1.000
Major league totals (1 year)		10	15	0	3	1	0	0	3	.200	1	5	0	23	1	0	1.000

DAVEY, TOM   P   BLUE JAYS

PERSONAL: Born September 11, 1973, in Garden City, Mich. ... 6-7/215. ... Throws right, bats right. ... Full name: Thomas Joseph Davey.
HIGH SCHOOL: Plymouth Salem (Canton, Mich.).
JUNIOR COLLEGE: Henry Ford Community College (Mich.).
TRANSACTIONS/CAREER NOTES: Selected by Toronto Blue Jays organization in fifth round of free-agent draft (June 2, 1994). ... Selected by Baltimore Orioles organization from Blue Jays organization in Rule 5 major league draft (December 9, 1996). ... Returned to Blue Jays organization (March 20, 1997).

Year Team (League)	W	L	Pct.	ERA	G	GS	CG	ShO	Sv.	IP	H	R	ER	BB	SO
1994—Medicine Hat (Pioneer)	2	•8	.200	5.12	14	14	0	0	0	65	76	59	37	*59	35
1995—St. Catharines (NYP)	4	3	.571	3.32	7	7	0	0	0	38	27	19	14	21	29
—Hagerstown (S. Atl.)	4	1	.800	3.38	8	8	0	0	0	37 1/3	29	23	14	31	25
1996—Hagerstown (S. Atl.)	10	9	.526	3.87	26	26	2	1	0	155 2/3	132	76	67	91	98
1997—Dunedin (Fla. St.)	1	3	.250	4.31	7	6	0	0	0	39 2/3	44	21	19	15	36
—Knoxville (Southern)	6	7	.462	5.83	20	16	0	0	0	92 2/3	108	65	60	50	72
1998—Knoxville (Southern)	5	3	.625	3.87	48	9	0	0	16	76 2/3	70	35	33	52	78

DAVIDSON, CLEATUS   2B/SS   TWINS

PERSONAL: Born November 1, 1976, in Bartow, Fla. ... 5-10/170. ... Bats both, throws right. ... Full name: Cleatus Lavon Davidson.
HIGH SCHOOL: Lake Wales (Fla.).
TRANSACTIONS/CAREER NOTES: Selected by Minnesota Twins organization in second round of free-agent draft (June 2, 1994).
STATISTICAL NOTES: Led Appalachian League shortstops with 33 double plays and 335 total chances in 1996. ... Led Midwest League second basemen with 271 putouts, 405 assists, 696 total chances and 98 double plays in 1997. ... Led Florida State League with 13 sacrifice hits in 1998. ... Led Florida State League second basemen with 320 putouts, 403 assists, 748 total chances and 98 double plays in 1998.

Year Team (League)	Pos.	G	AB	R	H	2B	3B	HR	RBI	Avg.	BB	SO	SB	PO	A	E	Avg.
1994—GC Twins (GCL)	SS-OF	24	85	8	15	1	0	0	5	.176	9	19	3	15	65	11	.879
1995—GC Twins (GCL)	SS-2B	21	75	11	15	2	1	0	5	.200	10	17	8	38	74	7	.941
—Elizabethton (App.)	SS	39	152	27	45	6	2	3	27	.296	11	31	10	54	113	22	.884
1996—Fort Wayne (Midw.)	SS	59	203	20	36	8	3	0	30	.177	23	45	2	86	185	24	.919
—Elizabethton (App.)	SS	95	248	•53	71	10	6	6	31	.286	39	45	17	*100	*200	*35	.896
1997—Fort Wayne (Midw.)	2B-OF	124	478	80	122	16	8	6	52	.255	52	100	39	†272	†405	20	.971
1998—Fort Myers (FSL)	2B-SS	130	527	97	127	12	7	2	45	.241	45	99	44	†325	†417	27	.965

DAVIS, BEN   C   PADRES

PERSONAL: Born March 10, 1977, in Chester, Pa. ... 6-4/205. ... Bats both, throws right. ... Full name: Matthew Benjamin Davis.
HIGH SCHOOL: Malvern (Pa.) Prep.
TRANSACTIONS/CAREER NOTES: Selected by San Diego Padres organization in first round (second pick overall) of free-agent draft (June 3, 1995).
STATISTICAL NOTES: Led Southern League catchers with 1,002 total chances in 1998.

Year Team (League)	Pos.	G	AB	R	H	2B	3B	HR	RBI	Avg.	BB	SO	SB	PO	A	E	Avg.
1995—Idaho Falls (Pio.)	C	52	197	36	55	8	3	5	46	.279	17	36	0	*362	44	6	.985
1996—Rancho Cuca. (Cal.)	C	98	353	35	71	10	1	6	41	.201	31	89	1	642	51	9	.987
1997—Rancho Cuca. (Cal.)	C-1B	122	474	67	132	30	1	17	76	.278	28	107	3	993	103	14	.987
1998—Mobile (Southern)	C	116	433	65	124	29	2	14	75	.286	42	60	4	*920	76	6	.994
—San Diego (N.L.)	C	1	1	0	0	0	0	0	0	.000	0	0	0	2	0	0	1.000
Major league totals (1 year)		1	1	0	0	0	0	0	0	.000	0	0	0	2	0	0	1.000

D

PERSONAL: Born January 17, 1960, in Kingston, Jamaica. ... 6-3/240. ... Bats both, throws right. ... Full name: Charles Theodore Davis.

HIGH SCHOOL: Dorsey (Los Angeles).

TRANSACTIONS/CAREER NOTES: Selected by San Francisco Giants organization in 11th round of free-agent draft (June 7, 1977). ... On Phoenix disabled list (August 19-28, 1981). ... Granted free agency (November 9, 1987). ... Signed by California Angels (December 1, 1987). ... On disabled list (July 17-August 9, 1990). ... Granted free agency (December 7, 1990). ... Signed by Minnesota Twins (January 29, 1991). ... Granted free agency (November 3, 1992). ... Signed by Angels (December 11, 1992). ... On disabled list (June 20-July 18, 1995). ... Traded by Angels to Kansas City Royals for P Mark Gubicza and P Mike Bovee (October 28, 1996). ... On disabled list (March 23-April 14, 1997). ... Granted free agency (October 29, 1997). ... Signed by New York Yankees (December 10, 1997). ... On New York disabled list (April 3-August 17, 1998); included rehabilitation assignment to Norwich (July 30-August 10) and Columbus (August 11-17).

STATISTICAL NOTES: Switch-hit home runs in one game 10 times (June 5, 1983; June 27 and September 15, 1987; July 30, 1988; July 1, 1989; October 2, 1992; May 11 and July 30, 1994; August 21, 1996 and June 7, 1997). ... Tied for A.L. lead with 10 sacrifice flies in 1988. ... Career major league grand slams: 7.

MISCELLANEOUS: Original nickname was Chili Bowl, which was prompted by a friend who saw Davis after he received a haircut in the sixth grade. The nickname was later shortened to Chili.

Year Team (League)	Pos.	G	AB	R	H	2B	3B	HR	RBI	Avg.	BB	SO	SB	PO	A	E	Avg.
1978—Cedar Rap. (Midw.)	C-OF	124	424	63	119	18	5	16	73	.281	36	103	15	365	45	25	.943
1979—Fresno (California)......	OF-C	134	490	91	132	24	5	21	95	.269	80	91	30	339	43	20	.950
1980—Shreveport (Texas).....	OF-C	129	442	50	130	30	4	12	67	.294	52	94	19	184	20	12	.944
1981—San Francisco (N.L.) ..	OF	8	15	1	2	0	0	0	0	.133	1	2	2	7	0	0	1.000
—Phoenix (PCL)...........	OF	88	334	76	117	16	6	19	75	.350	46	54	40	175	7	6	.968
1982—San Francisco (N.L.) ..	OF	154	641	86	167	27	6	19	76	.261	45	115	24	404	•16	12	.972
1983—San Francisco (N.L.) ..	OF	137	486	54	113	21	2	11	59	.233	55	108	10	357	7	9	.976
—Phoenix (PCL)...........	OF	10	44	12	13	2	0	2	9	.295	4	6	5	15	0	2	.882
1984—San Francisco (N.L.) ..	OF	137	499	87	157	21	6	21	81	.315	42	74	12	292	9	9	.971
1985—San Francisco (N.L.) ..	OF	136	481	53	130	25	2	13	56	.270	62	74	15	279	10	6	.980
1986—San Francisco (N.L.) ..	OF	153	526	71	146	28	3	13	70	.278	84	96	16	303	9	•9	.972
1987—San Francisco (N.L.) ..	OF	149	500	80	125	22	1	24	76	.250	72	109	16	265	6	7	.975
1988—California (A.L.)■.......	OF-DH	158	600	81	161	29	3	21	93	.268	56	118	9	299	10	*19	.942
1989—California (A.L.).........	OF-DH	154	560	81	152	24	1	22	90	.271	61	109	3	270	5	6	.979
1990—California (A.L.).........	DH-OF	113	412	58	109	17	1	12	58	.265	61	89	1	77	5	3	.965
1991—Minnesota (A.L.)■	DH	153	534	84	148	34	1	29	93	.277	95	117	5	2	0	0	1.000
1992—Minnesota (A.L.)	DH-OF-1B	138	444	63	128	27	2	12	66	.288	73	76	4	6	0	0	1.000
1993—California (A.L.)■.......	DH-P	153	573	74	139	32	0	27	112	.243	71	135	4	0	0	0	...
1994—California (A.L.).........	DH-OF	108	392	72	122	18	1	26	84	.311	69	84	3	5	0	0	1.000
1995—California (A.L.).........	DH	119	424	81	135	23	0	20	86	.318	89	79	3	...	...	...	...
1996—California (A.L.).........	DH	145	530	73	155	24	0	28	95	.292	86	99	5	...	...	...	...
1997—Kansas City (A.L.)■....	DH	140	477	71	133	20	0	30	90	.279	85	96	6	...	...	...	...
1998—New York (A.L.)■.......	DH	35	103	11	30	7	0	3	9	.291	14	18	0	...	...	...	...
—Norwich (Eastern)......	DH	11	37	2	9	3	0	1	5	.243	9	7	0	...	...	...	...
—Columbus (Int'l)........	DH	6	22	4	8	1	0	0	3	.364	4	3	0	...	...	...	...
American League totals (11 years)		1416	5049	749	1412	255	9	230	876	.280	760	1020	43	659	20	28	.960
National League totals (7 years)		874	3148	432	840	144	20	101	418	.267	361	578	95	1907	57	52	.974
Major league totals (18 years)		2290	8197	1181	2252	399	29	331	1294	.275	1121	1598	138	2566	77	80	.971

DIVISION SERIES RECORD

Year Team (League)	Pos.	G	AB	R	H	2B	3B	HR	RBI	Avg.	BB	SO	SB	PO	A	E	Avg.
1998—New York (A.L.).........	DH	2	6	0	1	0	0	0	0	.167	0	2	0	...	...	...	...

CHAMPIONSHIP SERIES RECORD

RECORDS: Shares A.L. single-series record for most strikeouts—8 (1991).

Year Team (League)	Pos.	G	AB	R	H	2B	3B	HR	RBI	Avg.	BB	SO	SB	PO	A	E	Avg.
1987—San Francisco (N.L.) ..	OF	6	20	2	3	1	0	0	0	.150	1	4	0	11	1	1	.923
1991—Minnesota (A.L.)	DH	5	17	3	5	2	0	0	2	.294	5	8	1	...	...	...	...
1998—New York (A.L.).........	PH-DH	5	14	2	4	1	0	1	5	.286	2	3	0	...	...	...	...
Championship series totals (3 years)		16	51	7	12	4	0	1	7	.235	8	15	1	11	1	1	.923

WORLD SERIES RECORD

NOTES: Member of World Series championship team (1991 and 1998).

Year Team (League)	Pos.	G	AB	R	H	2B	3B	HR	RBI	Avg.	BB	SO	SB	PO	A	E	Avg.
1991—Minnesota (A.L.)	DH-PH-OF	6	18	4	4	0	0	2	4	.222	2	3	0	1	0	0	1.000
1998—New York (A.L.).........	DH-PH	3	7	3	2	0	0	0	2	.286	3	2	0	...	...	...	...
World Series totals (2 years)		9	25	7	6	0	0	2	6	.240	5	5	0	1	0	0	1.000

ALL-STAR GAME RECORD

Year League	Pos.	AB	R	H	2B	3B	HR	RBI	Avg.	BB	SO	SB	PO	A	E	Avg.
1984—National	PH	1	0	0	0	0	0	0	.000	0	0	0	...	...	...	...
1986—National	OF	1	0	0	0	0	0	0	.000	0	1	0	0	0	0	...
1994—American	PH	1	0	0	0	0	0	0	.000	0	0	0	...	...	...	...
All-Star Game totals (3 years)		3	0	0	0	0	0	0	.000	0	1	0	0	0	0	...

RECORD AS PITCHER

Year Team (League)	W	L	Pct.	ERA	G	GS	CG	ShO	Sv.	IP	H	R	ER	BB	SO
1993—California (A.L.)■..............	0	0	...	0.00	1	0	0	0	0	2	0	0	0	0	0

DAVIS, DOUG   P   RANGERS

PERSONAL: Born September 21, 1975, in Sacramento. ... 6-3/185. ... Throws left, bats right. ... Full name: Douglas P. Davis.
JUNIOR COLLEGE: City College of San Francisco.
TRANSACTIONS/CAREER NOTES: Selected by Texas Rangers organization in 10th round of free-agent draft (June 4, 1996).

Year Team (League)	W	L	Pct.	ERA	G	GS	CG	ShO	Sv.	IP	H	R	ER	BB	SO
1996—GC Rangers (GCL)	3	1	.750	1.90	8	7	0	0	0	42 2/3	28	13	9	26	49
1997—GC Rangers (GCL)	3	1	.750	1.71	4	4	0	0	0	21	14	5	4	15	27
—Charlotte (Fla. St.)	5	3	.625	3.10	9	8	1	0	0	49 1/3	29	19	17	33	52
1998—Charlotte (Fla. St.)	11	7	.611	3.24	27	27	1	1	0	155 1/3	129	69	56	74	*173

DAVIS, ERIC   OF   CARDINALS

PERSONAL: Born May 29, 1962, in Los Angeles. ... 6-3/185. ... Bats right, throws right. ... Full name: Eric Keith Davis.
HIGH SCHOOL: Fremont (Los Angeles).
TRANSACTIONS/CAREER NOTES: Selected by Cincinnati Reds organization in eighth round of free-agent draft (June 3, 1980). ... On Cincinnati disabled list (August 16-September 1, 1984; May 3-18, 1989; April 25-May 19, 1990; June 12-27 and July 31-August 26, 1991). ... Traded by Reds with P Kip Gross to Los Angeles Dodgers for P Tim Belcher and P John Wetteland (November 27, 1991). ... On disabled list (May 23-June 19 and August 2-25, 1992). ... Granted free agency (November 3, 1992). ... Re-signed by Dodgers (December 1, 1992). ... Traded by Dodgers to Detroit Tigers for a player to be named later (August 31, 1993); Dodgers acquired P John DeSilva to complete deal (September 7, 1993). ... Granted free agency (October 28, 1993). ... Re-signed by Tigers (November 1, 1993). ... On disabled list (May 23-July 19 and July 27, 1994-remainder of season). ... Granted free agency (October 20, 1994). ... On retired list (October 20, 1994-January 2, 1996). ... Signed by Reds organization (January 2, 1996). ... On disabled list (May 26-June 10, 1996). ... Granted free agency (October 28, 1996). ... Signed by Baltimore Orioles (December 19, 1996). ... On disabled list (May 26-September 15, 1997). ... Granted free agency (October 27, 1998). ... Signed by St. Louis Cardinals (November 19, 1998).
RECORDS: Holds major league career record for highest stolen-base percentage (300 or more attempts)—.851. ... Shares major league record for most grand slams in two consecutive games—2 (May 4 and 5, 1996); and most strikeouts in two consecutive games—9 (April 24 [4] and 25 [5], 1987, 21 innings). ... Shares major league single-month record for most grand slams—3 (May 1987). ... Holds N.L. career record for highest stolen-base percentage (300 or more attempts)—.861. ... Shares major league record for most grand slams in two consecutive games—2 (August 13 and 14, 1991).
HONORS: Named outfielder on THE SPORTING NEWS N.L. All-Star team (1987 and 1989). ... Named outfielder on THE SPORTING NEWS N.L. Silver Slugger team (1987 and 1989). ... Won N.L. Gold Glove as outfielder (1987-89). ... Named N.L. Comeback Player of the Year by THE SPORTING NEWS (1996).
STATISTICAL NOTES: Hit three home runs in one game (September 10, 1986 and May 3, 1987). ... Led N.L. outfielders with 394 total chances in 1987. ... Led N.L. with 21 game-winning RBIs in 1988. ... Hit for the cycle (June 2, 1989). ... Had 30-game hitting streak (July 12-August 15, 1998). ... Career major league grand slams: 10.

Year Team (League)	Pos.	G	AB	R	H	2B	3B	HR	RBI	Avg.	BB	SO	SB	PO	A	E	Avg.
1980—Eugene (Northwest)	SS-2B-OF	33	73	12	16	1	0	1	11	.219	14	26	10	29	36	11	.855
1981—Eugene (Northwest)	OF	62	214	*67	69	10	4	11	39	.322	57	59	*40	94	11	4	.963
1982—Cedar Rap. (Midw.)	OF	111	434	80	120	20	5	15	56	.276	51	103	53	239	9	9	.965
1983—Waterbury (Eastern)	OF	89	293	56	85	13	1	15	43	.290	65	75	39	214	8	2	.991
—Indianapolis (A.A.)	OF	19	77	18	23	4	0	7	19	.299	8	22	9	61	1	1	.984
1984—Wichita (A.A.)	OF	52	194	42	61	9	5	14	34	.314	25	55	27	110	5	5	.958
—Cincinnati (N.L.)	OF	57	174	33	39	10	1	10	30	.224	24	48	10	125	4	1	.992
1985—Cincinnati (N.L.)	OF	56	122	26	30	3	3	8	18	.246	7	39	16	75	3	1	.987
—Denver (A.A.)	OF	64	206	48	57	10	2	15	38	.277	29	67	35	94	5	3	.971
1986—Cincinnati (N.L.)	OF	132	415	97	115	15	3	27	71	.277	68	100	80	274	2	7	.975
1987—Cincinnati (N.L.)	OF	129	474	120	139	23	4	37	100	.293	84	134	50	*380	10	4	.990
1988—Cincinnati (N.L.)	OF	135	472	81	129	18	3	26	93	.273	65	124	35	300	2	6	.981
1989—Cincinnati (N.L.)	OF	131	462	74	130	14	2	34	101	.281	68	116	21	298	2	5	.984
1990—Cincinnati (N.L.)	OF	127	453	84	118	26	2	24	86	.260	60	100	21	257	11	2	.993
1991—Cincinnati (N.L.)	OF	89	285	39	67	10	0	11	33	.235	48	92	14	190	5	3	.985
1992—Los Angeles (N.L.)■	OF	76	267	21	61	8	1	5	32	.228	36	71	19	123	0	5	.961
1993—Los Angeles (N.L.)	OF	108	376	57	88	17	0	14	53	.234	41	88	33	221	7	2	.991
—Detroit (A.L.)■	OF-DH	23	75	14	19	1	1	6	15	.253	14	18	2	52	0	1	.981
1994—Detroit (A.L.)	OF	37	120	19	22	4	0	3	13	.183	18	45	5	85	1	1	.989
1995—						Did not play—retired.											
1996—Cincinnati (N.L.)■	OF-1B	129	415	81	119	20	0	26	83	.287	70	121	23	279	3	3	.989
1997—Baltimore (A.L.)■	OF-DH	42	158	29	48	11	0	8	25	.304	14	47	6	39	0	1	.975
1998—Baltimore (A.L.)	OF-DH	131	452	81	148	29	1	28	89	.327	44	108	7	119	4	1	.992
American League totals (4 years)		233	805	143	237	45	2	45	142	.294	90	218	20	295	5	4	.987
National League totals (11 years)		1169	3915	713	1035	164	19	222	700	.264	571	1033	322	2522	49	39	.985
Major league totals (14 years)		1402	4720	856	1272	209	21	267	842	.269	661	1251	342	2817	54	43	.985

DIVISION SERIES RECORD

Year Team (League)	Pos.	G	AB	R	H	2B	3B	HR	RBI	Avg.	BB	SO	SB	PO	A	E	Avg.
1997—Baltimore (A.L.)	OF	3	9	0	2	0	0	0	2	.222	0	5	0	1	0	0	1.000

CHAMPIONSHIP SERIES RECORD

Year Team (League)	Pos.	G	AB	R	H	2B	3B	HR	RBI	Avg.	BB	SO	SB	PO	A	E	Avg.
1990—Cincinnati (N.L.)	OF	6	23	2	4	1	0	0	2	.174	1	9	0	12	1	0	1.000
1997—Baltimore (A.L.)	OF-DH	6	13	1	2	0	0	1	1	.154	1	3	0	3	0	0	1.000
Championship series totals (2 years)		12	36	3	6	1	0	1	3	.167	2	12	0	15	1	0	1.000

D

WORLD SERIES RECORD

NOTES: Hit home run in first at-bat (October 16, 1990). ... Member of World Series championship team (1990).

							BATTING									FIELDING		
Year	Team (League)	Pos.	G	AB	R	H	2B	3B	HR	RBI	Avg.	BB	SO	SB	PO	A	E	Avg.
1990— Cincinnati (N.L.)		OF	4	14	3	4	0	0	1	5	.286	0	0	0	4	0	0	1.000

ALL-STAR GAME RECORD

						BATTING								FIELDING		
Year	League	Pos.	AB	R	H	2B	3B	HR	RBI	Avg.	BB	SO	SB	PO	A	E	Avg.
1987— National		OF	3	0	0	0	0	0	0	.000	0	1	0	1	0	0	1.000
1989— National		OF	2	0	0	0	0	0	0	.000	1	0	1	1	0	0	1.000
All-Star Game totals (2 years)			5	0	0	0	0	0	0	.000	1	1	1	2	0	0	1.000

DAVIS, RUSS   3B   MARINERS

PERSONAL: Born September 13, 1969, in Birmingham, Ala. ... 6-0/195. ... Bats right, throws right. ... Full name: Russell Stewart Davis.
HIGH SCHOOL: Hueytown (Ala.).
JUNIOR COLLEGE: Shelton State Junior College (Ala.).
TRANSACTIONS/CAREER NOTES: Selected by New York Yankees organization in 29th round of free-agent draft (June 1, 1988). ... On disabled list (July 13-August 1, 1993). ... On Columbus disabled list (April 7-15 and August 26, 1994-remainder of season). ... Traded by Yankees with P Sterling Hitchcock to Seattle Mariners for 1B Tino Martinez, P Jeff Nelson and P Jim Mecir (December 7, 1995). ... On disabled list (June 8, 1996-remainder of season and August 25-September 26, 1997).
HONORS: Named Eastern League Most Valuable Player (1992).
STATISTICAL NOTES: Tied for New York-Pennsylvania League lead with 11 double plays by third baseman in 1989. ... Led Carolina League third basemen with 336 total chances and 18 double plays in 1990. ... Tied for Eastern League lead with .917 fielding percentage, 83 putouts, 205 assists, 26 errors and 314 total chances by third basemen in 1991. ... Led Eastern League with 237 total bases and .483 slugging percentage in 1992. ... Led International League third basemen with 25 errors in 1993. ... Led A.L. third basemen with 32 errors in 1998.

							BATTING								FIELDING		
Year	Team (League)	Pos.	G	AB	R	H	2B	3B	HR	RBI	Avg.	BB	SO	SB	PO	A	E	Avg.
1988— GC Yankees (GCL)		2B-3B	58	213	33	49	11	3	2	30	.230	16	39	6	64	105	15	.918
1989— Fort Laud. (FSL)		3B-2B	48	147	8	27	5	1	2	22	.184	11	38	3	32	72	17	.860
— Oneonta (NYP)		3B	65	236	33	68	7	5	7	42	.288	19	44	3	27	87	17	.870
1990— Prince Will. (Car.)		3B	137	510	55	127	*37	3	16	71	.249	37	136	3	*68	*244	24	.929
1991— Alb./Colon. (East.)		3B-2B	135	473	57	103	23	3	8	58	.218	50	102	3	‡83	‡206	‡26	‡.917
1992— Alb./Colon. (East.)		3B	132	491	77	140	23	4	22	71	.285	49	93	3	78	185	23	.920
1993— Columbus (Int'l)		3B-SS	113	424	63	108	24	1	26	83	.255	40	118	1	85	245	†26	.927
1994— Columbus (Int'l)		3B-1B	117	416	76	115	30	2	25	69	.276	62	93	3	86	250	23	.936
— New York (A.L.)		3B	4	14	0	2	0	0	0	1	.143	0	4	0	2	6	0	1.000
1995— Columbus (Int'l)		3B-1B	20	76	12	19	4	1	2	15	.250	17	23	0	17	31	7	.873
— New York (A.L.)		3B-DH-1B	40	98	14	27	5	2	2	12	.276	10	26	0	16	45	2	.968
1996— Seattle (A.L.)■		3B	51	167	24	39	9	0	5	18	.234	17	50	2	31	67	7	.933
1997— Seattle (A.L.)		3B-DH	119	420	57	114	29	1	20	63	.271	27	100	6	56	219	18	.939
1998— Seattle (A.L.)		3B-OF	141	502	68	130	30	1	20	82	.259	34	134	4	56	254	†34	.901
Major league totals (5 years)			355	1201	163	312	73	4	47	176	.260	88	314	12	161	591	61	.925

DIVISION SERIES RECORD

							BATTING								FIELDING		
Year	Team (League)	Pos.	G	AB	R	H	2B	3B	HR	RBI	Avg.	BB	SO	SB	PO	A	E	Avg.
1995— New York (A.L.)		3B	2	5	0	1	0	0	0	0	.200	0	2	0	0	1	0	1.000

DE LA ROSA, MAXIMO   P   MARINERS

PERSONAL: Born July 12, 1971, in Villa Mella, Dominican Republic. ... 5-11/170. ... Throws right, bats right.
HIGH SCHOOL: Ramon Mella (Villa Mella, Dominican Republic).
TRANSACTIONS/CAREER NOTES: Signed as non-drafted free agent by Cleveland Indians organization (February 24, 1990). ... Claimed on waivers by Seattle Mariners (February 26, 1998).
MISCELLANEOUS: Played outfield (1990-92).

Year	Team (League)	W	L	Pct.	ERA	G	GS	CG	ShO	Sv.	IP	H	R	ER	BB	SO
1993— Burlington (Appalachian)....		7	2	.778	3.77	14	•14	2	1	0	76 1/3	53	38	32	37	69
1994— Kinston (Carolina)		0	11	.000	5.04	13	13	0	0	0	69 2/3	82	56	39	38	53
— Columbus (S. Atl.)		4	2	.667	3.35	14	14	0	0	0	75 1/3	49	33	28	38	71
1995— Kinston (Carolina)		5	2	.714	2.19	43	0	0	0	8	61 2/3	46	23	15	37	61
— Cant./Akr. (Eastern)		0	0	. . .	54.00	1	0	0	0	0	1/3	1	2	2	1	0
1996— Cant./Akr. (Eastern)		11	5	.688	3.91	40	15	0	0	3	119 2/3	104	60	52	81	109
1997— Buffalo (A.A.)		2	2	.500	6.49	15	4	0	0	0	43	43	34	31	33	31
— Akron (Eastern)		4	9	.308	4.44	17	13	5	0	0	97 1/3	112	63	48	32	70
1998— Tacoma (PCL)■		2	1	.667	3.38	9	0	0	0	0	10 2/3	6	4	4	8	4
— Orlando (South.)		6	4	.600	3.03	42	0	0	0	8	62 1/3	47	23	21	24	51

RECORD AS POSITION PLAYER

							BATTING								FIELDING		
Year	Team (League)	Pos.	G	AB	R	H	2B	3B	HR	RBI	Avg.	BB	SO	SB	PO	A	E	Avg.
1990— Dom. Inds. (DSL)		OF	61	225	51	63	14	1	1	31	.280	36	24	15	. . .	. . .	. . .	. . .
1991— Dom. Inds. (DSL)		OF	60	219	43	67	8	2	4	36	.306	28	23	15	. . .	. . .	. . .	. . .
1992— Burlington (Appal.)		OF	62	222	27	54	5	1	1	30	.243	24	52	4	100	3	4	.963

D

DE LOS SANTOS, LUIS P YANKEES

PERSONAL: Born November 1, 1977, in Santo Domingo, Dominican Republic. ... 6-2/187. ... Throws right, bats right.
TRANSACTIONS/CAREER NOTES: Signed as non-drafted free agent by New York Yankees organization (February 11, 1995). ... On Norwich disabled list (April 23-May 22, 1998).
STATISTICAL NOTES: Pitched 4-0 no-hit victory against Batavia (July 28, 1996).

Year Team (League)	W	L	Pct.	ERA	G	GS	CG	ShO	Sv.	IP	H	R	ER	BB	SO
1995— Tampa (Fla. St.)	0	0	...	0.00	2	0	0	0	0	5	5	2	0	2	6
1996— Oneonta (N.Y.-Penn)	4	4	.500	3.72	10	10	3	2	0	58	44	28	24	21	62
— Greensboro (S. Atl.)	4	1	.800	4.83	7	6	0	0	0	31 2/3	39	17	17	11	21
1997— Greensboro (S. Atl.)	5	6	.455	3.05	14	14	1	0	0	88 2/3	91	45	30	13	62
— Tampa (Fla. St.)	5	0	1.000	2.34	10	10	0	0	0	61 2/3	49	19	16	8	39
— Norwich (Eastern)	1	1	.500	2.52	4	4	0	0	0	25	23	9	7	7	15
1998— Norwich (Eastern)	2	6	.250	4.90	13	13	2	0	0	79	97	49	43	23	51
— Tampa (Fla. St.)	4	2	.667	4.19	10	10	1	0	0	66 2/3	69	40	31	11	33

DE LOS SANTOS, VALERIO P BREWERS

PERSONAL: Born October 6, 1975, in Las Matas, Dominican Republic. ... 6-2/186. ... Throws left, bats left. ... Full name: Valerio Lorenzo De Los Santos.
TRANSACTIONS/CAREER NOTES: Signed as non-drafted free agent by Milwaukee Brewers organization (January 26, 1993). ... On El Paso disabled list (April 27-May 4, 1998).

Year Team (League)	W	L	Pct.	ERA	G	GS	CG	ShO	Sv.	IP	H	R	ER	BB	SO
1993— Dom. Dodgers (DSL)	1	7	.125	6.50	19	6	1	0	0	63 2/3	91	57	46	37	39
1994— Dom. Dodgers (DSL)	7	6	.538	3.69	17	•16	1	1	0	90 1/3	90	52	37	35	50
1995— Ariz. Brewers (Ariz.)	4	6	.400	2.20	14	12	0	0	0	82	81	34	20	12	57
1996— Beloit (Midwest)	10	8	.556	3.55	33	23	5	1	4	164 2/3	164	83	65	59	137
1997— El Paso (Texas)	6	10	.375	5.75	26	16	1	0	2	114 1/3	146	83	73	38	61
1998— El Paso (Texas)	6	2	.750	3.92	42	4	0	0	10	66 2/3	81	34	29	25	62
— Milwaukee (N.L.)	0	0	...	2.91	13	0	0	0	0	21 2/3	11	7	7	2	18
— Louisville (Int'l)	0	0	...	3.60	5	0	0	0	0	5	4	2	2	0	0
Major league totals (1 year)	0	0	...	2.91	13	0	0	0	0	21 2/3	11	7	7	2	18

DeHART, RICK P EXPOS

PERSONAL: Born March 21, 1970, in Topeka, Kan. ... 6-1/190. ... Throws left, bats left. ... Full name: Richard Allen DeHart.
HIGH SCHOOL: Seaman (Topeka, Kan.).
COLLEGE: Washburn.
TRANSACTIONS/CAREER NOTES: Signed as non-drafted free agent by Montreal Expos organization (March 24, 1992).

Year Team (League)	W	L	Pct.	ERA	G	GS	CG	ShO	Sv.	IP	H	R	ER	BB	SO
1992— Albany (S. Atl.)	9	6	.600	2.46	38	10	1	1	3	117	91	42	32	40	133
1993— San Bernardino (Calif.)	4	3	.571	3.04	9	9	0	0	0	53 1/3	56	26	18	25	44
— Harrisburg (Eastern)	2	4	.333	7.68	12	7	0	0	0	34	45	31	29	19	18
— W.P. Beach (FSL)	1	3	.250	3.00	7	7	1	1	0	42	42	14	14	17	33
1994— W.P. Beach (FSL)	9	7	.563	3.37	30	20	3	2	0	136 1/3	132	61	51	34	68
1995— Harrisburg (Eastern)	6	7	.462	4.84	35	12	0	0	1	93	94	62	50	39	64
1996— Harrisburg (Eastern)	1	2	.333	2.68	30	2	0	0	1	43 2/3	46	19	13	19	30
1997— Ottawa (Int'l)	0	4	.000	4.00	43	0	0	0	2	63	60	33	28	22	57
— Montreal (N.L.)	2	1	.667	5.52	23	0	0	0	0	29 1/3	33	21	18	14	29
1998— Ottawa (Int'l)	7	1	.875	3.23	38	0	0	0	4	53	46	19	19	17	48
— Montreal (N.L.)	0	0	...	4.82	26	0	0	0	1	28	34	22	15	13	14
Major league totals (2 years)	2	1	.667	5.18	49	0	0	0	1	57 1/3	67	43	33	27	43

DeJEAN, MIKE P ROCKIES

PERSONAL: Born September 28, 1970, in Baton Rouge, La. ... 6-2/212. ... Throws right, bats right. ... Full name: Michael Dwain DeJean.
HIGH SCHOOL: Walker (La.).
JUNIOR COLLEGE: Mississippi Delta Community College.
COLLEGE: Livingston (La.).
TRANSACTIONS/CAREER NOTES: Selected by New York Yankees organization in 24th round of free-agent draft (June 1, 1992). ... On disabled list (June 4-July 21 and July 26, 1993-remainder of season). ... Traded by Yankees with a player to be named later to Colorado Rockies for C Joe Girardi (November 20, 1995); Rockies acquired P Steve Shoemaker to complete deal (December 6, 1995). ... On Colorado disabled list (July 18-August 8, 1997); included rehabilitation assignment to New Haven (July 30-August 8). ... On disabled list (September 2, 1998-remainder of season).

Year Team (League)	W	L	Pct.	ERA	G	GS	CG	ShO	Sv.	IP	H	R	ER	BB	SO
1992— Oneonta (N.Y.-Penn)	0	0	...	0.44	20	0	0	0	16	20 2/3	12	3	1	3	20
1993— Greensboro (S. Atl.)	2	3	.400	5.00	20	0	0	0	9	18	22	12	10	8	16
1994— Tampa (Fla. St.)	0	2	.000	2.38	34	0	0	0	16	34	39	15	9	13	22
— Albany (Eastern)	0	2	.000	4.38	16	0	0	0	4	24 2/3	22	14	12	15	13
1995— Norwich (Eastern)	5	5	.500	2.99	59	0	0	0	20	78 1/3	58	29	26	34	57
1996— Colo. Springs (PCL)■	0	2	.000	5.13	30	0	0	0	1	40 1/3	52	24	23	21	31
— New Haven (East.)	0	0	...	3.22	16	0	0	0	11	22 1/3	20	9	8	8	12
1997— Colo. Springs (PCL)	0	1	.000	5.40	10	0	0	0	4	10	17	6	6	7	9
— Colorado (N.L.)	5	0	1.000	3.99	55	0	0	0	2	67 2/3	74	34	30	24	38
— New Haven (East.)	0	1	.000	6.00	2	0	0	0	0	3	3	2	2	2	2
1998— Colorado (N.L.)	3	1	.750	3.03	59	1	0	0	2	74 1/3	78	29	25	24	27
Major league totals (2 years)	8	1	.889	3.49	114	1	0	0	4	142	152	63	55	48	65

DeLUCIA, RICH — P — ANGELS

PERSONAL: Born October 7, 1964, in Reading, Pa. ... 6-0/190. ... Throws right, bats right. ... Full name: Richard Anthony DeLucia. ... Name pronounced duh-LOO-sha.
HIGH SCHOOL: Wyomissing (Pa.) Area.
COLLEGE: Tennessee.
TRANSACTIONS/CAREER NOTES: Selected by Toronto Blue Jays organization in 15th round of free-agent draft (June 3, 1985); did not sign. ... Selected by Seattle Mariners organization in sixth round of free-agent draft (June 2, 1986). ... On disabled list (April 10, 1987-remainder of season). ... On disabled list (May 31-July 2 and July 7, 1989-remainder of season). ... On Seattle disabled list (August 5-September 1, 1992); included rehabilitation assignment to Calgary (August 26-31). ... On Seattle disabled list (June 28-July 22, 1993); included rehabilitation assignment to Calgary (July 16-22). ... Released by Mariners (March 29, 1994). ... Signed by Cincinnati Reds organization (April 2, 1994). ... Granted free agency (October 15, 1994). ... Signed by Rochester, Baltimore Orioles organization (November 17, 1994). ... Selected by St. Louis Cardinals from Orioles organization in Rule 5 major league draft (December 5, 1994). ... Traded by Cardinals with P Allen Watson and P Doug Creek to San Francisco Giants for SS Royce Clayton and a player to be named later (December 14, 1995); Cardinals acquired 2B Chris Wimmer to complete deal (January 16, 1996). ... On San Francisco disabled list (March 25-May 2 and July 27-August 23, 1996); included rehabilitation assignments to San Jose (April 25-May 2 and August 18-23). ... Traded by Giants to Anaheim Angels for a player to be named later (April 14, 1997); Giants acquired P Travis Thurmond to complete deal (May 22, 1997). ... On Anaheim disabled list (July 15-September 2, 1997). ... Granted free agency (October 31, 1997). ... Re-signed by Angels (December 7, 1997). ... On suspended list (June 15-16, 1998).
STATISTICAL NOTES: Pitched seven-inning, 1-0 no-hit victory against Everett (July 17, 1986). ... Led A.L. with 31 home runs allowed in 1991.

Year Team (League)	W	L	Pct.	ERA	G	GS	CG	ShO	Sv.	IP	H	R	ER	BB	SO
1986— Bellingham (N'west)	8	2	.800	*1.70	13	11	1	•1	0	74	44	20	14	24	69
1987— Salinas (Calif.)	0	0	...	9.00	1	0	0	0	0	1	2	1	1	0	1
1988— San Bernardino (Calif.)	7	8	.467	3.10	22	22	0	0	0	127 2/3	110	57	44	59	118
1989— Williamsport (Eastern)	3	4	.429	3.79	10	10	0	0	0	54 2/3	59	28	23	13	41
1990— San Bernardino (Calif.)	4	1	.800	2.05	5	5	1	0	0	30 2/3	19	9	7	3	35
— Williamsport (Eastern)	6	6	.500	2.11	18	18	2	1	0	115	92	30	27	30	76
— Calgary (PCL)	2	2	.500	3.62	5	5	1	0	0	32 1/3	30	17	13	12	23
— Seattle (A.L.)	1	2	.333	2.00	5	5	1	0	0	36	30	9	8	9	20
1991— Seattle (A.L.)	12	13	.480	5.09	32	31	0	0	0	182	176	107	103	78	98
1992— Seattle (A.L.)	3	6	.333	5.49	30	11	0	0	1	83 2/3	100	55	51	35	66
— Calgary (PCL)	4	2	.667	2.45	8	5	2	1	1	40 1/3	32	11	11	14	38
1993— Seattle (A.L.)	3	6	.333	4.64	30	1	0	0	0	42 2/3	46	24	22	23	48
— Calgary (PCL)	1	5	.167	5.73	8	7	0	0	1	44	45	30	28	20	38
1994— Indianapolis (A.A.)■	5	1	.833	2.30	36	0	0	0	19	43	22	12	11	24	52
— Cincinnati (N.L.)	0	0	...	4.22	8	0	0	0	0	10 2/3	9	6	5	5	15
1995— St. Louis (N.L.)■	8	7	.533	3.39	56	1	0	0	0	82 1/3	63	38	31	36	76
1996— San Jose (California)■	0	0	...	2.45	5	4	0	0	0	7 1/3	5	2	2	3	11
— San Francisco (N.L.)	3	6	.333	5.84	56	0	0	0	0	61 2/3	62	44	40	31	55
1997— San Francisco (N.L.)	0	0	...	10.80	3	0	0	0	0	1 2/3	6	3	2	0	2
— Anaheim (A.L.)■	6	4	.600	3.61	33	0	0	0	3	42 1/3	29	18	17	27	42
1998— Anaheim (A.L.)	2	6	.250	4.27	61	0	0	0	3	71 2/3	56	36	34	46	73
A.L. totals (6 years)	27	37	.422	4.61	191	48	1	0	7	458 1/3	437	249	235	218	347
N.L. totals (4 years)	11	13	.458	4.49	123	1	0	0	0	156 1/3	140	91	78	72	148
Major league totals (9 years)	38	50	.432	4.58	314	49	1	0	7	614 2/3	577	340	313	290	495

DeROSA, MARK — SS — BRAVES

PERSONAL: Born February 2, 1975, in Passaic, N.J. ... 6-1/190. ... Bats right, throws right. ... Full name: Mark Thomas DeRosa.
HIGH SCHOOL: Bergen Catholic (Oradell, N.J.).
JUNIOR COLLEGE: Pennsylvania.
TRANSACTIONS/CAREER NOTES: Selected by Atlanta Braves organization in seventh round of free-agent draft (June 4, 1996).

Year Team (League)	Pos.	G	AB	R	H	2B	3B	HR	RBI	Avg.	BB	SO	SB	PO	A	E	Avg.
1996— Eugene (Northwest)	SS	70	255	43	66	13	1	2	28	.259	38	48	3	82	196	24	.921
1997— Durham (Carolina)	SS	92	346	51	93	11	3	8	37	.269	25	73	6	136	245	21	.948
1998— Greenville (Southern)	SS	125	461	67	123	26	2	8	49	.267	60	57	7	195	338	20	*.964
— Atlanta (N.L.)	SS	5	3	2	1	0	0	0	0	.333	0	1	0	1	1	0	1.000
Major league totals (1 year)		5	3	2	1	0	0	0	0	.333	0	1	0	1	1	0	1.000

DeSHIELDS, DELINO — 2B — ORIOLES

PERSONAL: Born January 15, 1969, in Seaford, Del. ... 6-1/175. ... Bats left, throws right. ... Full name: Delino Lamont DeShields. ... Name pronounced duh-LINE-oh.
HIGH SCHOOL: Seaford (Del.).
COLLEGE: Villanova.
TRANSACTIONS/CAREER NOTES: Selected by Montreal Expos organization in first round (12th pick overall) of free-agent draft (June 2, 1987). ... On disabled list (June 16-July 12, 1990 and August 12-September 11, 1993). ... Traded by Expos to Los Angeles Dodgers for P Pedro J. Martinez (November 19, 1993). ... On disabled list (May 26-June 20, 1994). ... Granted free agency (October 29, 1996). ... Signed by St. Louis Cardinals (November 20, 1996). ... On St. Louis disabled list (July 5-August 10, 1998); included rehabilitation assignment to Arkansas (August 5-10). ... Granted free agency (October 23, 1998). ... Signed by Baltimore Orioles (December 7, 1998).
RECORDS: Shares modern N.L. record for most hits in first major league game—4 (April 9, 1990). ... Shares major league single-game record for most strikeouts (nine-inning game)—5 (September 17, 1991, second game).
STATISTICAL NOTES: Led Gulf Coast League shortstops with 22 errors in 1987. ... Had 21-game hitting streak (June 28-July 21, 1993). ... Had 18-game hitting streak (May 30-June 20, 1998). ... Career major league grand slams: 1.

									BATTING						FIELDING			
Year	Team (League)	Pos.	G	AB	R	H	2B	3B	HR	RBI	Avg.	BB	SO	SB	PO	A	E	Avg.
1987—GC Expos (GCL)		SS-3B	31	111	17	24	5	2	1	4	.216	21	30	16	47	90	†22	.862
—Jamestown (NYP)		SS	34	96	16	21	1	2	1	5	.219	24	28	14	25	57	21	.796
1988—Rockford (Midwest) ...		SS	129	460	97	116	26	6	12	46	.252	95	110	59	173	344	42	.925
1989—Jacksonville (Sou.)....		SS	93	307	55	83	10	6	3	35	.270	76	80	37	127	218	34	.910
—Indianapolis (A.A.)........		SS	47	181	29	47	8	4	2	14	.260	16	53	16	73	101	13	.930
1990—Montreal (N.L.).........		2B	129	499	69	144	28	6	4	45	.289	66	96	42	236	371	12	.981
1991—Montreal (N.L.).........		2B	151	563	83	134	15	4	10	51	.238	95	*151	56	285	405	*27	.962
1992—Montreal (N.L.).........		2B	135	530	82	155	19	8	7	56	.292	54	108	46	251	360	15	.976
1993—Montreal (N.L.)..........		2B	123	481	75	142	17	7	2	29	.295	72	64	43	243	381	11	.983
1994—Los Angeles (N.L.)■..		2B-SS	89	320	51	80	11	3	2	33	.250	54	53	27	156	282	7	.984
1995—Los Angeles (N.L.)		2B	127	425	66	109	18	3	8	37	.256	63	83	39	204	330	•11	.980
1996—Los Angeles (N.L.)......		2B	154	581	75	130	12	8	5	41	.224	53	124	48	274	400	17	.975
1997—St. Louis (N.L.)■		2B	150	572	92	169	26	*14	11	58	.295	55	72	55	272	398	19	.972
1998—St. Louis (N.L.)..........		2B-1B	117	420	74	122	21	8	7	44	.290	56	61	26	247	273	9	.983
—Arkansas (Texas)........		2B	4	13	1	2	0	0	0	0	.154	2	6	0	6	5	0	1.000
Major league totals (9 years)			1175	4391	667	1185	167	61	56	394	.270	568	812	382	2168	3200	128	.977

DIVISION SERIES RECORD

									BATTING						FIELDING			
Year	Team (League)	Pos.	G	AB	R	H	2B	3B	HR	RBI	Avg.	BB	SO	SB	PO	A	E	Avg.
1995—Los Angeles (N.L.)		2B	3	12	1	3	0	0	0	0	.250	1	3	0	8	7	0	1.000
1996—Los Angeles (N.L.)		2B	2	4	0	0	0	0	0	0	.000	0	1	0	3	2	0	1.000
Division series totals (2 years)			5	16	1	3	0	0	0	0	.188	1	4	0	11	9	0	1.000

DeWITT, MATT — P — CARDINALS

PERSONAL: Born September 4, 1977, in San Bernardino, Calif. ... 6-4/220. ... Throws right, bats right. ... Full name: Matthew B. DeWitt.
HIGH SCHOOL: Valley (Las Vegas).
TRANSACTIONS/CAREER NOTES: Selected by St. Louis Cardinals organization in 10th round of free-agent draft (June 1, 1995).
STATISTICAL NOTES: Led Appalachian League pitchers with 17 home runs allowed in 1996.

Year	Team (League)	W	L	Pct.	ERA	G	GS	CG	ShO	Sv.	IP	H	R	ER	BB	SO
1995—Johnson City (App.)		2	6	.250	7.04	13	12	0	0	0	62 2/3	84	56	*49	32	45
1996—Johnson City (App.)		5	5	.500	5.42	14	*14	0	0	0	*79 2/3	66	53	48	26	58
1997—Peoria (Midwest)...............		9	9	.500	4.09	27	•27	1	0	0	158 1/3	152	84	72	57	121
1998—Prince William (Caro.)........		6	9	.400	3.64	24	24	1	0	0	148 1/3	132	65	60	18	118

D

DELGADO, CARLOS — 1B — BLUE JAYS

PERSONAL: Born June 25, 1972, in Aguadilla, Puerto Rico. ... 6-3/225. ... Bats left, throws right. ... Full name: Carlos Juan Delgado.
HIGH SCHOOL: Jose de Diego (Aguadilla, Puerto Rico).
TRANSACTIONS/CAREER NOTES: Signed as non-drafted free agent by Toronto Blue Jays organization (October 9, 1988). ... On Toronto disabled list (March 15-April 24, 1998); included rehabilitation assignment to Dunedin (April 17-19) and Syracuse (April 20-24).
HONORS: Named Florida State League Most Valuable Player (1992). ... Named Southern League Most Valuable Player (1993).
STATISTICAL NOTES: Led New York-Pennsylvania League catchers with 540 total chances and six double plays in 1990. ... Led South Atlantic League with 29 passed balls in 1991. ... Led Florida State League with 281 total bases, .579 slugging percentage, .402 on-base percentage and 11 intentional bases on balls received in 1992. ... Led Florida State League catchers with 784 total chances in 1992. ... Led Southern League with .524 slugging percentage, .430 on-base percentage and 18 intentional bases on balls received in 1993. ... Led Southern League catchers with 800 total chances in 1993. ... Led International League with .610 slugging percentage in 1995. ... Led International League with seven intentional bases on balls received in 1995. ... Had 19-game hitting streak (May 21-June 9, 1998). ... Hit three home runs in one game (August 4, 1998). ... Career major league grand slams: 5.

									BATTING						FIELDING			
Year	Team (League)	Pos.	G	AB	R	H	2B	3B	HR	RBI	Avg.	BB	SO	SB	PO	A	E	Avg.
1989—St. Catharines (NYP)..		C	31	89	9	16	5	0	0	11	.180	23	39	0	63	13	2	.974
1990—St. Catharines (NYP)..		C	67	228	30	64	13	0	6	39	.281	35	65	2	*471	*62	7	.987
1991—Myrtle Beach (SAL)....		C	132	441	72	126	18	2	18	70	.286	75	97	9	679	*100	19	.976
—Syracuse (Int'l)............		C	1	3	0	0	0	0	0	0	.000	0	2	0	5	0	0	1.000
1992—Dunedin (Fla. St.).......		C	133	485	83	*157	•30	2	*30	*100	.324	59	91	2	*684	89	11	.986
1993—Knoxville (Southern) ..		C	140	468	91	142	28	0	*25	*102	.303	*102	98	10	*683	*103	*14	.983
—Toronto (A.L.)............		DH-C	2	1	0	0	0	0	0	0	.000	1	0	0	2	0	0	1.000
1994—Toronto (A.L.)...........		OF-C	43	130	17	28	2	0	9	24	.215	25	46	1	56	2	2	.967
—Syracuse (Int'l)............		C-1B	85	307	52	98	11	0	19	58	.319	42	58	1	235	25	7	.974
1995—Toronto (A.L.)...........		OF-DH-1B	37	91	7	15	3	0	3	11	.165	6	26	0	54	2	0	1.000
—Syracuse (Int'l)............		1B-OF	91	333	59	106	23	4	22	74	.318	45	78	0	724	49	4	.995
1996—Toronto (A.L.)...........		DH-1B	138	488	68	132	28	2	25	92	.270	58	139	0	221	13	4	.983
1997—Toronto (A.L.)...........		1B-DH	153	519	79	136	42	3	30	91	.262	64	133	0	962	67	12	.988
1998—Dunedin (Fla. St.).......		1B	4	16	4	5	1	0	2	7	.313	2	4	0	13	0	0	1.000
—Syracuse (Int'l)............		1B	2	7	4	4	2	0	1	6	.571	2	0	0	2	2	0	1.000
—Toronto (A.L.)............		1B-DH	142	530	94	155	43	1	38	115	.292	73	139	3	1165	87	10	.992
Major league totals (6 years)			515	1759	265	466	118	6	105	333	.265	227	483	4	2460	171	28	.989

DELGADO, WILSON — SS — GIANTS

PERSONAL: Born July 15, 1975, in San Cristobal, Dominican Republic. ... 5-11/160. ... Bats both, throws right. ... Full name: Wilson Duran Delgado.
TRANSACTIONS/CAREER NOTES: Signed as non-drafted free agent by Seattle Mariners organization (October 29, 1992). ... Traded by Mariners with P Shawn Estes to San Francisco Giants for P Salomon Torres (May 21, 1995).
STATISTICAL NOTES: Led Pacific Coast League shortstops with 197 putouts, 547 total chances and 86 double plays in 1997.

Year Team (League)	Pos.	G	AB	R	H	2B	3B	HR	RBI	Avg.	BB	SO	SB	PO	A	E	Avg.
1993— Dom. Mariners (DSL).	IF	60	171	19	50	8	0	0	26	.292	34	25	5	96	148	16	.938
1994— Ariz. Mariners (Ariz.)..	SS-2B	39	149	30	56	5	4	0	10	*.376	15	24	13	58	114	10	.945
1995— Wis. Rap. (Mid.)........	SS	19	70	13	17	3	0	0	7	.243	3	15	3	29	65	6	.940
— Burlington (Midw.)■..	SS	93	365	52	113	20	3	5	37	.310	32	57	9	127	285	19	.956
1996— San Jose (Calif.)..........	SS	121	462	59	124	19	6	2	54	.268	48	89	8	192	343	24	.957
— Phoenix (PCL)...........	SS	12	43	1	6	0	0	0	1	.140	3	7	0	30	47	2	.975
— San Francisco (N.L.) ..	SS	6	22	3	8	0	0	0	2	.364	1	5	1	12	12	1	.960
1997— San Francisco (N.L.) ..	2B-SS	8	7	1	1	1	0	0	0	.143	0	2	0	2	3	0	1.000
— Phoenix (PCL)...........	SS-2B	119	416	47	120	22	4	9	59	.288	24	70	9	208	347	18	.969
1998— Fresno (PCL).............	SS	127	512	87	142	22	2	12	63	.277	52	92	9	205	373	23	.962
— San Francisco (N.L.) ..	SS	10	12	1	2	1	0	0	1	.167	1	3	0	3	6	0	1.000
Major league totals (3 years)		24	41	5	11	2	0	0	3	.268	2	10	1	17	21	1	.974

DELLUCCI, DAVID — OF — DIAMONDBACKS

PERSONAL: Born October 31, 1973, in Baton Rouge, La. ... 5-10/180. ... Bats left, throws left. ... Full name: David Michael Dellucci. ... Name pronounced duh-LOO-chee.
HIGH SCHOOL: Catholic (Baton Rouge, La.).
COLLEGE: Mississippi.
TRANSACTIONS/CAREER NOTES: Selected by Baltimore Orioles organization in 10th round of free agent draft (June 1, 1995). ... Selected by Arizona Diamondbacks in second round (45th pick overall) of expansion draft (November 18, 1997).
MISCELLANEOUS: Holds Arizona Diamondbacks all-time record for most triples (12).

Year Team (League)	Pos.	G	AB	R	H	2B	3B	HR	RBI	Avg.	BB	SO	SB	PO	A	E	Avg.
1995— Frederick (Carolina)....	OF	28	96	16	27	3	0	1	10	.281	12	10	1	26	2	1	.966
— Bluefield (Appal.)........	OF	20	69	11	23	5	1	2	12	.333	6	7	3	11	0	2	.846
1996— Frederick (Carolina)....	OF	59	185	33	60	11	1	4	28	.324	38	34	5	100	4	3	.972
— Bowie (Eastern)..........	OF	66	251	27	73	14	1	2	33	.291	28	56	2	134	5	3	.979
1997— Bowie (Eastern)..........	OF	107	385	71	126	29	3	20	55	.327	58	69	11	162	2	1	.994
— Baltimore (A.L.)..........	OF-DH	17	27	3	6	1	0	1	3	.222	4	7	0	20	1	0	1.000
1998— Tucson (PCL)■..........	OF	17	72	17	22	4	3	1	11	.306	5	8	4	38	0	0	1.000
— Arizona (N.L.).............	OF	124	416	43	108	19	*12	5	51	.260	33	103	3	230	3	3	.987
American League totals (1 year)		17	27	3	6	1	0	1	3	.222	4	7	0	20	1	0	1.000
National League totals (1 year)		124	416	43	108	19	12	5	51	.260	33	103	3	230	3	3	.987
Major league totals (2 years)		141	443	46	114	20	12	6	54	.257	37	110	3	250	4	3	.988

DEMPSTER, RYAN — P — MARLINS

PERSONAL: Born May 3, 1977, in Sachelt, B.C. ... 6-1/201. ... Throws right, bats right. ... Full name: Ryan Scott Dempster.
HIGH SCHOOL: Elphinstone (Gibsons, B.C.).
TRANSACTIONS/CAREER NOTES: Selected by Texas Rangers organization in third round of free-agent draft (June 1, 1995). ... Traded by Rangers with a player to be named later to Florida Marlins organization for P John Burkett (August 8, 1996); Marlins acquired P Rick Helling to complete deal (September 3, 1996).

Year Team (League)	W	L	Pct.	ERA	G	GS	CG	ShO	Sv.	IP	H	R	ER	BB	SO
1995— GC Rangers (GCL)..............	3	1	.750	2.36	8	6	1	0	0	34 1/3	34	21	9	17	37
— Hudson Valley (NYP).........	1	0	1.000	3.18	1	1	0	0	0	5 2/3	7	2	2	1	6
1996— Charleston, S.C. (SAL).......	7	11	.389	3.30	23	23	2	0	0	144 1/3	120	71	53	58	141
— Kane County (Midwest)......	2	1	.667	2.73	4	4	1	1	0	26 1/3	18	10	8	18	16
1997— Brevard County (FSL).......	10	9	.526	4.90	28	26	2	1	0	165 1/3	190	100	*90	46	131
1998— Portland (Eastern)...........	4	3	.571	3.22	7	7	0	0	0	44 2/3	34	20	16	15	33
— Florida (N.L.)....................	1	5	.167	7.08	14	11	0	0	0	54 2/3	72	47	43	38	35
— Charlotte (Int'l)................	3	1	.750	3.27	5	5	1	0	0	33	33	14	12	12	24
Major league totals (1 year)........	1	5	.167	7.08	14	11	0	0	0	54 2/3	72	47	43	38	35

DESSENS, ELMER — P — PIRATES

PERSONAL: Born January 13, 1972, in Hermosillo, Mexico. ... 6-0/187. ... Throws right, bats right. ... Full name: Elmer Dessens Jusaino. ... Name pronounced DAH-cenz.
HIGH SCHOOL: Carrera Technica (Hermosillo, Mexico).
TRANSACTIONS/CAREER NOTES: Signed as non-drafted free agent by Pittsburgh Pirates organization (January 27, 1993). ... Loaned by Pirates organization to Mexico City Red Devils of Mexican League for 1993 and 1994 seasons; returned to Pirates organization for 1995 season. ... Loaned by Pirates organization to Red Devils (May 7, 1996). ... Returned to Pirates organization (June 21, 1996). ... On Pittsburgh disabled list (July 31-September 10, 1996); included rehabilitation assignment to Carolina (August 16-September 10). ... Loaned by Pirates to Red Devils (March 27, 1997). ... Returned to Pirates (September 5, 1997). ... On Pittsburgh disabled list (April 8-24, 1998); included rehabilitation assignment to Nashville (April 21-24).

Year Team (League)	W	L	Pct.	ERA	G	GS	CG	ShO	Sv.	IP	H	R	ER	BB	SO
1993— M.C. Red Devils (Mex.)......	3	1	.750	2.35	14	0	0	0	2	30 2/3	31	8	8	5	16
1994— M.C. Red Devils (Mex.)......	11	4	.733	2.04	37	15	4	1	3	127 2/3	121	37	29	32	51
1995— Carolina (Southern)■........	*15	8	.652	*2.49	27	27	1	0	0	152	170	62	42	21	68
1996— Calgary (PCL)....................	2	2	.500	3.15	6	6	0	0	0	34 1/3	40	14	12	15	15
— M.C. Red Devils (Mex.)■...	7	0	1.000	1.26	7	7	1	0	0	50	44	12	7	10	17
— Pittsburgh (N.L.)■...........	0	2	.000	8.28	15	3	0	0	0	25	40	23	23	4	13
— Carolina (Southern)........	0	1	.000	5.40	5	1	0	0	0	11 2/3	15	8	7	4	7
1997— M.C. Red Devils (Mex.)■...	•16	5	.762	3.56	26	25	3	1	0	159 1/3	156	73	63	51	61
— Pittsburgh (N.L.)■...........	0	0	. . .	0.00	3	0	0	0	0	3 1/3	2	0	0	0	2
1998— Pittsburgh (N.L.)■...........	2	6	.250	5.67	43	5	0	0	0	74 2/3	90	50	47	25	43
— Nashville (Pacific Coast) ..	3	1	.750	3.30	6	6	0	0	0	30	32	12	11	6	13
Major league totals (3 years).......	2	8	.200	6.12	61	8	0	0	0	103	132	73	70	29	58

D

PERSONAL: Born April 10, 1963, in Casper, Wyo. ... 6-0/195. ... Bats right, throws right. ... Full name: Michael Devereaux. ... Name pronounced DEH-ver-oh.
HIGH SCHOOL: Kelly Walsh (Casper, Wyo.).
JUNIOR COLLEGE: Mesa (Ariz.) Community College.
COLLEGE: Arizona State (bachelor of arts degree in finance).
TRANSACTIONS/CAREER NOTES: Selected by Cleveland Indians organization in 26th round of free-agent draft (June 4, 1984); did not sign. ... Selected by Los Angeles Dodgers organization in fifth round of free-agent draft (June 3, 1985). ... Traded by Dodgers to Baltimore Orioles for P Mike Morgan (March 12, 1989). ... On Baltimore disabled list (May 17-June 15, 1990); included rehabilitation assignments to Frederick (June 9-10) and Hagerstown (June 11-15). ... On Baltimore disabled list (May 3-27, 1993); included rehabilitation assignment to Bowie (May 25-27). ... On disabled list (June 16-July 1, 1994). ... Granted free agency (October 21, 1994). ... Signed by Chicago White Sox (April 8, 1995). ... Traded by White Sox to Atlanta Braves for OF Andre King (August 25, 1995). ... Granted free agency (November 3, 1995). ... Signed by Orioles (January 11, 1996). ... Granted free agency (October 29, 1996). ... Signed by Texas Rangers (January 6, 1997). ... Released by Rangers (June 12, 1997). ... Signed by Dodgers organization (January 16, 1998). ... Released by Dodgers (May 6, 1998). ... Signed by San Diego Padres organization (June 9, 1998). ... On Las Vegas disabled list (July 27-August 7, 1998).
HONORS: Named outfielder on THE SPORTING NEWS A.L. All-Star team (1992).
STATISTICAL NOTES: Led Pioneer League with 152 total bases in 1985. ... Led Texas League with 11 sacrifice flies in 1987. ... Led Texas League outfielders with 349 total chances in 1987. ... Career major league grand slams: 3.

							BATTING								FIELDING		
Year	Team (League)	Pos.	G	AB	R	H	2B	3B	HR	RBI	Avg.	BB	SO	SB	PO	A	E	Avg.
1985—	Great Falls (Pio.)	OF	•70	*289	*73	*103	17	10	4	*67	.356	32	29	*40	100	4	5	.954
1986—	San Antonio (Tex.)	OF	115	431	69	130	22	2	10	53	.302	58	47	31	292	13	4	.987
1987—	San Antonio (Tex.)	OF	*135	*562	90	169	28	9	26	91	.301	48	65	33	*339	7	3	*.991
—	Albuquerque (PCL).....	OF	3	11	2	3	1	0	1	1	.273	0	2	1	4	1	0	1.000
—	Los Angeles (N.L.)	OF	19	54	7	12	3	0	0	4	.222	3	10	3	21	1	0	1.000
1988—	Albuquerque (PCL)....	OF	109	423	88	144	26	4	13	76	.340	44	46	33	211	5	7	.969
—	Los Angeles (N.L.)	OF	30	43	4	5	1	0	0	2	.116	2	10	0	29	0	0	1.000
1989—	Baltimore (A.L.)■......	OF-DH	122	391	55	104	14	3	8	46	.266	36	60	22	288	1	5	.983
1990—	Baltimore (A.L.).........	OF-DH	108	367	48	88	18	1	12	49	.240	28	48	13	281	4	5	.983
—	Frederick (Carolina)..	OF	2	8	3	4	0	0	1	3	.500	1	2	1	4	2	0	1.000
—	Hagerstown (East.).....	OF	4	20	4	5	3	0	0	3	.250	0	1	0	13	0	1	.929
1991—	Baltimore (A.L.).........	OF	149	608	82	158	27	10	19	59	.260	47	115	16	399	10	3	.993
1992—	Baltimore (A.L.).........	OF	156	653	76	180	29	11	24	107	.276	44	94	10	431	5	5	.989
1993—	Baltimore (A.L.).........	OF	131	527	72	132	31	3	14	75	.250	43	99	3	311	8	4	.988
—	Bowie (Eastern)..........	OF	2	7	1	2	1	0	0	2	.286	0	2	0	5	0	0	1.000
1994—	Baltimore (A.L.).........	OF-DH	85	301	35	61	8	2	9	33	.203	22	72	1	203	3	1	.995
1995—	Chicago (A.L.)■.........	OF	92	333	48	102	21	1	10	55	.306	25	51	6	187	4	3	.985
—	Atlanta (N.L.)............	OF	29	55	7	14	3	0	1	8	.255	2	11	2	41	0	0	1.000
1996—	Baltimore (A.L.)■.......	OF-DH	127	323	49	74	11	2	8	34	.229	34	53	8	170	7	3	.983
1997—	Texas (A.L.)■...........	OF	29	72	8	15	3	0	0	7	.208	7	10	1	40	0	0	1.000
1998—	Los Angeles (N.L.)■..	OF	9	13	0	4	1	0	0	1	.308	3	2	0	9	1	0	1.000
—	Las Vegas (PCL)■.....	OF	34	120	19	32	10	1	2	12	.267	9	13	1	47	2	1	.980
American League totals (9 years)			999	3575	473	914	162	33	104	465	.256	286	602	80	2310	42	29	.988
National League totals (4 years)			87	165	18	35	8	0	1	15	.212	10	33	5	100	2	0	1.000
Major league totals (12 years)			1086	3740	491	949	170	33	105	480	.254	296	635	85	2410	44	29	.988

DIVISION SERIES RECORD

							BATTING								FIELDING		
Year	Team (League)	Pos.	G	AB	R	H	2B	3B	HR	RBI	Avg.	BB	SO	SB	PO	A	E	Avg.
1995—	Atlanta (N.L.).............	OF-PH	4	5	1	1	0	0	0	0	.200	0	0	0	2	0	0	1.000
1996—	Baltimore (A.L.)..........	OF-PR	4	1	0	0	0	0	0	0	.000	0	0	0	2	0	0	1.000
Division series totals (2 years)			8	6	1	1	0	0	0	0	.167	0	0	0	4	0	0	1.000

NOTES: Named Most Valuable Player (1995).

CHAMPIONSHIP SERIES RECORD

							BATTING								FIELDING		
Year	Team (League)	Pos.	G	AB	R	H	2B	3B	HR	RBI	Avg.	BB	SO	SB	PO	A	E	Avg.
1995—	Atlanta (N.L.).............	OF	4	13	2	4	1	0	1	5	.308	1	2	0	2	0	0	1.000
1996—	Baltimore (A.L.).........	OF	3	2	0	0	0	0	0	0	.000	0	1	0	1	0	0	1.000
Championship series totals (2 years)			7	15	2	4	1	0	1	5	.267	1	3	0	3	0	0	1.000

WORLD SERIES RECORD

NOTES: Member of World Series championship team (1995).

							BATTING								FIELDING		
Year	Team (League)	Pos.	G	AB	R	H	2B	3B	HR	RBI	Avg.	BB	SO	SB	PO	A	E	Avg.
1995—	Atlanta (N.L.).............	OF-PH-DH	5	4	0	1	0	0	0	1	.250	2	1	0	0	0	1	.000

PERSONAL: Born October 5, 1968, in Brooklyn, N.Y. ... 5-11/180. ... Bats both, throws right. ... Full name: Alexis Diaz. ... Son of Mario Caballero Diaz, minor league infielder (1959-64).
HIGH SCHOOL: Manuel Mendez Licihea (Puerto Rico).
TRANSACTIONS/CAREER NOTES: Signed as non-drafted free agent by New York Mets organization (August 24, 1986). ... Traded by Mets with OF Darren Reed to Montreal Expos for OF Terrel Hansen and P David Sommer (April 2, 1991). ... On suspended list (August 30, 1991-remainder of season). ... Traded by Expos organization to Milwaukee Brewers organization for IF George Canale (October 15, 1991). ... On Milwaukee disabled list (May 3-August 30, 1993); included rehabilitation assignment to New Orleans (August 13-30). ... Granted free agency (December 20, 1993). ... Re-signed by Brewers (December 21, 1993). ... On disabled list (July 31, 1994-remainder of season). ... Claimed on waivers by Seattle Mariners (October 14, 1994). ... On Seattle disabled list (June 5-August 4 and August 12-September 2, 1996); included rehabilitation

D

assignments to Tacoma (July 15-August 4 and August 31-September 2). ... Granted free agency (October 8, 1996). ... Signed by Mets organization (November 19, 1996). ... Released by Norfolk, Mets organization (April 13, 1997). ... Signed by Texas Rangers organization (April 16, 1997). ... Granted free agency (October 15, 1997). ... Signed by San Francisco Giants organization (January 21, 1998). ... On Fresno disabled list (July 24-September 14, 1998). ... Released by Giants (September 14, 1998). ... Signed by Houston Astros organization (January 21, 1999).

Year	Team (League)	Pos.	G	AB	R	H	2B	3B	HR	RBI	Avg.	BB	SO	SB	PO	A	E	Avg.
1987—Kingsport (Appal.)......		SS	54	212	29	56	9	1	0	13	.264	16	31	*34	67	126	18	.915
—Little Falls (NYP).......		SS	12	47	7	16	4	1	0	8	.340	2	3	2	13	22	4	.897
1988—Columbia (S. Atl.).......		SS	123	481	82	126	14	*11	0	37	.262	21	49	28	175	299	*72	.868
—St. Lucie (Fla. St.)		SS	3	6	2	0	0	0	0	1	.000	0	4	0	3	3	3	.667
1989—St. Lucie (Fla. St.)........		SS-OF	102	416	54	106	11	10	1	33	.255	20	38	43	151	244	28	.934
—Jackson (Texas)........		2B	23	95	11	26	5	1	2	9	.274	3	11	3	25	65	3	.968
1990—Tidewater (Int'l)........		OF-2B-SS	124	437	55	112	15	2	1	36	.256	30	39	23	196	101	11	.964
1991—Indianapolis (A.A.)■..		O-S-3-2	108	370	48	90	14	4	1	21	.243	27	46	17	207	45	8	.969
1992—Denver (A.A.)■........		OF-2B-SS	106	455	67	122	17	4	1	41	.268	24	36	42	240	43	7	.976
—Milwaukee (A.L.)......		OF-DH	22	9	5	1	0	0	0	1	.111	0	0	3	10	0	0	1.000
1993—Milwaukee (A.L.)......		OF-DH	32	69	9	22	2	0	0	1	.319	0	12	5	46	1	1	.979
—New Orleans (A.A.)......		OF	16	55	8	16	2	0	0	5	.291	3	6	7	38	1	0	1.000
1994—Milwaukee (A.L.)......		OF-2B-DH	79	187	17	47	5	7	1	17	.251	10	19	5	138	11	2	.987
1995—Seattle (A.L.)■........		OF	103	270	44	67	14	0	3	27	.248	13	27	18	145	4	2	.987
—Tacoma (PCL)		OF	10	40	3	10	1	0	0	4	.250	2	5	1	15	1	0	1.000
1996—Seattle (A.L.)........		OF-DH	38	79	11	19	2	0	1	5	.241	2	8	6	55	1	1	.982
—Tacoma (PCL)		OF-3B	44	176	19	43	5	0	0	7	.244	7	20	5	76	5	2	.976
1997—Norfolk (Int'l)■.........		OF	7	26	0	2	1	0	0	1	.077	2	3	0	10	2	1	.923
—Okla. City (A.A.)■......		O-2-P-S	114	426	65	122	25	2	12	49	.286	33	53	26	180	52	10	.959
—Texas (A.L.)........		OF-1B-2B	28	90	8	20	4	0	2	12	.222	5	13	1	54	3	1	.983
1998—San Fran. (N.L.)■.......		OF	34	62	5	8	2	0	0	5	.129	0	15	1	28	2	0	1.000
—Fresno (PCL)		OF	11	39	2	7	0	0	0	2	.179	2	5	1	8	1	2	.818
American League totals (6 years)			302	704	94	176	27	7	7	63	.250	30	79	38	448	20	7	.985
National League totals (1 year)			34	62	5	8	2	0	0	5	.129	0	15	1	28	2	0	1.000
Major league totals (7 years)			336	766	99	184	29	7	7	68	.240	30	94	39	476	22	7	.986

DIVISION SERIES RECORD

Year	Team (League)	Pos.	G	AB	R	H	2B	3B	HR	RBI	Avg.	BB	SO	SB	PO	A	E	Avg.
1995—Seattle (A.L.)		OF-PH	2	3	0	1	0	0	0	0	.333	1	1	0	1	1	0	1.000

CHAMPIONSHIP SERIES RECORD

Year	Team (League)	Pos.	G	AB	R	H	2B	3B	HR	RBI	Avg.	BB	SO	SB	PO	A	E	Avg.
1995—Seattle (A.L.)		PH-OF	4	7	0	3	1	0	0	0	.429	1	1	0	1	0	0	1.000

RECORD AS PITCHER

Year	Team (League)	W	L	Pct.	ERA	G	GS	CG	ShO	Sv.	IP	H	R	ER	BB	SO
1997—Oklahoma City (A.A.)■.......		0	0	...	0.00	1	0	0	0	0	1	1	0	0	3	1

DIAZ, EDWIN · 2B · DIAMONDBACKS

PERSONAL: Born January 15, 1975, in Vega Alta, Puerto Rico. ... 5-11/170. ... Bats right, throws right.
HIGH SCHOOL: Maestro Ladi (Puerto Rico).
TRANSACTIONS/CAREER NOTES: Selected by Texas Rangers organization in second round of free-agent draft (June 3, 1993); pick received as compensation for Chicago Cubs signing Type A free-agent P Jose Guzman. ... Selected by Arizona Diamondbacks in first round (11th pick overall) of expansion draft (November 18, 1997).

Year	Team (League)	Pos.	G	AB	R	H	2B	3B	HR	RBI	Avg.	BB	SO	SB	PO	A	E	Avg.
1993—GC Rangers (GCL)......		2B	43	154	27	47	10	5	1	23	.305	19	21	12	78	100	6	.967
1994—Char., S.C. (S. Atl.).....		2B-SS	122	443	52	109	22	7	11	60	.246	22	107	11	204	303	31	.942
1995—Charlotte (Fla. St.)....		2B-SS	115	450	48	128	26	5	8	56	.284	33	94	8	213	277	16	.968
1996—Tulsa (Texas)		2B	121	500	70	132	33	6	16	65	.264	25	122	8	238	322	19	.967
1997—Okla. City (A.A.)		2B	20	73	6	8	3	1	1	4	.110	2	27	1	37	48	6	.934
—Tulsa (Texas)		2B	105	440	65	121	31	1	15	46	.275	33	102	6	170	312	*19	.962
1998—Arizona (N.L.)■........		2B	3	7	0	0	0	0	0	0	.000	0	2	0	7	8	1	.938
—Tucson (PCL)		2B-3B-SS	131	510	61	134	31	*12	2	49	.263	27	105	9	247	342	28	.955
Major league totals (1 year)			3	7	0	0	0	0	0	0	.000	0	2	0	7	8	1	.938

DIAZ, EINAR · C · INDIANS

PERSONAL: Born December 28, 1972, in Chiniqui, Panama. ... 5-10/165. ... Bats right, throws right. ... Full name: Einar Antonio Diaz.
TRANSACTIONS/CAREER NOTES: Signed as non-drafted free agent by Cleveland Indians organization (October 5, 1990).
STATISTICAL NOTES: Led Appalachian League third basemen with 125 assists and .959 fielding percentage in 1992. ... Led Appalachian League catchers with 54 assists and nine errors in 1993. ... Led South Atlantic League in grounding into double plays with 18 in 1994. ... Led South Atlantic League catchers with 966 total chances, 845 putouts, 112 assists and tied for lead with eight double plays in 1994. ... Led Carolina League catchers with 107 assists and .992 fielding percentage in 1995. ... Led Eastern League catchers with 15 errors in 1996. ... Led American Association catchers with 18 errors in 1997. ... Led International League catchers with 873 total chances in 1998.

Year	Team (League)	Pos.	G	AB	R	H	2B	3B	HR	RBI	Avg.	BB	SO	SB	PO	A	E	Avg.
1991—Dom. Inds. (DSL).......		...	62	239	35	67	6	3	1	29	.280	14	5	10	...	...	...	...
1992—Burlington (Appal.).....		3B-SS	52	178	19	37	3	0	1	14	.208	20	9	2	27	†137	7	†.959

Year Team (League)	Pos.	G	AB	R	H	2B	3B	HR	RBI	Avg.	BB	SO	SB	PO	A	E	Avg.
						BATTING								FIELDING			
1993— Burlington (Appal.).....	C-3B	60	231	40	69	15	3	5	33	.299	8	7	7	315	†55	†10	.974
— Columbus (S. Atl.)......	C	1	5	0	0	0	0	0	0	.000	0	1	0	3	1	0	1.000
1994— Columbus (S. Atl.)......	C-3B	120	491	67	137	23	2	16	71	.279	17	34	4	†848	†134	9	.991
1995— Kinston (Carolina)......	C-3B	104	373	46	98	21	0	6	43	.263	12	29	3	676	†111	7	†.991
1996— Cant./Akr. (Eastern) ...	C-3B	104	395	47	111	26	2	3	35	.281	12	22	3	765	88	†15	.983
— Cleveland (A.L.)..........	C	4	1	0	0	0	0	0	0	.000	0	0	0	4	0	0	1.000
1997— Buffalo (A.A.).............	C-3B	109	336	40	86	18	2	3	31	.256	18	34	2	653	67	†19	.974
— Cleveland (A.L.)..........	C	5	7	1	1	1	0	0	1	.143	0	2	0	18	3	1	.955
1998— Cleveland (A.L.)..........	C	17	48	8	11	1	0	2	9	.229	3	2	0	101	9	3	.973
— Buffalo (Int'l)	C	115	415	62	130	21	3	8	63	.313	21	33	3	*791	*70	*12	.986
Major league totals (3 years)		26	56	9	12	2	0	2	10	.214	3	4	0	123	12	4	.971

DIVISION SERIES RECORD

Year Team (League)	Pos.	G	AB	R	H	2B	3B	HR	RBI	Avg.	BB	SO	SB	PO	A	E	Avg.
						BATTING								FIELDING			
1998— Cleveland (A.L.)							Did not play.										

CHAMPIONSHIP SERIES RECORD

Year Team (League)	Pos.	G	AB	R	H	2B	3B	HR	RBI	Avg.	BB	SO	SB	PO	A	E	Avg.
						BATTING								FIELDING			
1998— Cleveland (A.L.)..........	C	4	4	0	0	0	0	0	0	.000	0	1	0	13	3	0	1.000

DICKSON, JASON   P   ANGELS

PERSONAL: Born March 30, 1973, in London, Ont. ... 6-0/202. ... Throws right, bats left. ... Full name: Jason Royce Dickson.

HIGH SCHOOL: James M. Hill (Chatham, N.B.).

JUNIOR COLLEGE: Northeastern Oklahoma A&M.

TRANSACTIONS/CAREER NOTES: Selected by California Angels organization in sixth round of free-agent draft (June 2, 1994). ... Angels franchise renamed Anaheim Angels for 1997 season.

HONORS: Named A.L. Rookie Pitcher of the Year by The Sporting News (1997).

Year Team (League)	W	L	Pct.	ERA	G	GS	CG	ShO	Sv.	IP	H	R	ER	BB	SO
1994— Boise (Northwest)	3	1	.750	3.86	9	7	0	0	1	44 1/3	40	22	19	18	37
1995— Cedar Rapids (Midw.)	14	6	.700	2.86	25	25	*9	1	0	173	151	71	55	45	134
1996— Midland (Texas)	5	2	.714	3.58	8	8	3	1	0	55 1/3	55	27	22	10	40
— Vancouver (PCL)	7	11	.389	3.80	18	18	*7	0	0	130 1/3	134	73	55	40	70
— California (A.L.)	1	4	.200	4.57	7	7	0	0	0	43 1/3	52	22	22	18	20
1997— Anaheim (A.L.)	13	9	.591	4.29	33	32	2	1	0	203 2/3	236	111	97	56	115
1998— Anaheim (A.L.)	10	10	.500	6.05	27	18	0	0	0	122	147	89	82	41	61
— Vancouver (PCL)	2	1	.667	1.78	4	4	4	0	0	25 1/3	26	5	5	4	18
Major league totals (3 years)	24	23	.511	4.90	67	57	2	1	0	369	435	222	201	115	196

ALL-STAR GAME RECORD

Year League	W	L	Pct.	ERA	GS	CG	ShO	Sv.	IP	H	R	ER	BB	SO
1997— American............................						Did not play.								

DIFELICE, MIKE   C   DEVIL RAYS

PERSONAL: Born May 28, 1969, in Philadelphia. ... 6-2/205. ... Bats right, throws right. ... Full name: Michael William Difelice. ... Name pronounced DEE-fah-lease.

HIGH SCHOOL: Bearden (Knoxville, Tenn.).

COLLEGE: Tennessee.

TRANSACTIONS/CAREER NOTES: Selected by St. Louis Cardinals organization in 11th round of free-agent draft (June 3, 1991). ... Selected by Tampa Bay Devil Rays in first round (20th pick overall) of expansion draft (November 18, 1997).

RECORDS: Shares major league single-season record for fewest double plays by catcher for leader—8 (1998).

STATISTICAL NOTES: Tied for N.L. lead in passed balls with 12 in 1997. ... Tied for A.L. lead in double plays by catcher with eight in 1998.

Year Team (League)	Pos.	G	AB	R	H	2B	3B	HR	RBI	Avg.	BB	SO	SB	PO	A	E	Avg.
						BATTING								FIELDING			
1991— Hamilton (NYP).........	C	43	157	10	33	5	0	4	15	.210	9	40	1	297	40	9	.974
1992— Hamilton (NYP).........	C-1B	18	58	11	20	3	0	2	9	.345	4	7	2	135	19	5	.969
— St. Peters. (FSL).........	C	17	53	0	12	3	0	0	4	.226	3	11	0	73	11	2	.977
1993— Springfield (Midw.)	C	8	20	5	7	1	0	0	3	.350	2	3	0	52	9	0	1.000
— St. Peters. (FSL).........	C	30	97	5	22	2	0	0	8	.227	11	13	1	165	23	7	.964
1994— Arkansas (Texas)........	C	71	200	19	50	11	2	2	15	.250	12	48	0	419	40	6	.987
1995— Arkansas (Texas)........	C	62	176	14	47	10	1	1	24	.267	23	29	1	327	48	6	.984
— Louisville (A.A.)	C	21	63	8	17	4	0	0	3	.270	5	11	1	111	10	2	.984
1996— Louisville (A.A.).........	C	79	246	25	70	13	0	9	33	.285	20	43	0	455	48	8	.984
— St. Louis (N.L.)...........	C	4	7	0	2	1	0	0	2	.286	0	1	0	15	1	0	1.000
1997— Arkansas (Texas)........	C	1	3	0	1	1	0	0	0	.333	1	0	0	6	2	0	1.000
— St. Louis (N.L.)...........	C-1B	93	260	16	62	10	1	4	30	.238	19	61	1	587	64	6	.991
— Louisville (A.A.).........	C	1	4	1	1	0	0	1	1	.250	0	1	0	3	1	0	1.000
1998— Tampa Bay (A.L.)■.....	C	84	248	17	57	12	3	3	23	.230	15	56	0	483	52	4	.993
American League totals (1 year)		84	248	17	57	12	3	3	23	.230	15	56	0	483	52	4	.993
National League totals (2 years)		97	267	16	64	11	1	4	32	.240	19	62	1	602	65	6	.991
Major league totals (3 years)		181	515	33	121	23	4	7	55	.235	34	118	1	1085	117	10	.992

DIPOTO, JERRY   P   ROCKIES

PERSONAL: Born May 24, 1968, in Jersey City, N.J. ... 6-2/205. ... Throws right, bats right. ... Full name: Gerard Peter Dipoto III.
HIGH SCHOOL: Toms River (N.J.).
COLLEGE: Virginia Commonwealth.
TRANSACTIONS/CAREER NOTES: Selected by Cleveland Indians organization in third round of free-agent draft (June 5, 1989). ... On Cleveland disabled list (March 25-June 12, 1994); included rehabilitation assignment to Charlotte (May 10-June 8). ... Traded by Indians with P Paul Byrd, P Dave Mlicki and a player to be named later to New York Mets for OF Jeromy Burnitz and P Joe Roa (November 18, 1994); Mets acquired 2B Jesus Azuaje to complete deal (December 6, 1994). ... Traded by Mets to Colorado Rockies for P Armando Reynoso (November 27, 1996).
STATISTICAL NOTES: Led Eastern League with 15 wild pitches and tied for lead with three balks in 1991.

Year Team (League)	W	L	Pct.	ERA	G	GS	CG	ShO	Sv.	IP	H	R	ER	BB	SO
1989— Watertown (NYP)	6	5	.545	3.61	14	14	1	0	0	87 1/3	75	42	35	39	98
1990— Kinston (Carolina)	11	4	.733	3.78	24	24	1	0	0	145 1/3	129	75	61	77	143
— Cant./Akr. (Eastern)	1	0	1.000	2.57	3	2	0	0	0	14	11	5	4	4	12
1991— Cant./Akr. (Eastern)	6	11	.353	3.81	28	26	2	0	0	156	143	83	66	74	97
1992— Colo. Springs (PCL)	9	9	.500	4.94	50	9	0	0	2	122	148	78	67	66	62
1993— Charlotte (Int'l)	6	3	.667	1.93	34	0	0	0	12	46 2/3	34	10	10	13	44
— Cleveland (A.L.)	4	4	.500	2.40	46	0	0	0	11	56 1/3	57	21	15	30	41
1994— Charlotte (Int'l)	3	2	.600	3.15	25	2	0	0	9	34 1/3	37	13	12	12	26
— Cleveland (A.L.)	0	0	. . .	8.04	7	0	0	0	0	15 2/3	26	14	14	10	9
1995— New York (N.L.)■	4	6	.400	3.78	58	0	0	0	2	78 2/3	77	41	33	29	49
1996— New York (N.L.)	7	2	.778	4.19	57	0	0	0	0	77 1/3	91	44	36	45	52
1997— Colorado (N.L.)■	5	3	.625	4.70	74	0	0	0	16	95 2/3	108	56	50	33	74
1998— Colorado (N.L.)	3	4	.429	3.53	68	0	0	0	19	71 1/3	61	31	28	25	49
A.L. totals (2 years)	4	4	.500	3.63	53	0	0	0	11	72	83	35	29	40	50
N.L. totals (4 years)	19	15	.559	4.10	257	0	0	0	37	323	337	172	147	132	224
Major league totals (6 years)	23	19	.548	4.01	310	0	0	0	48	395	420	207	176	172	274

DiSARCINA, GARY   SS   ANGELS

PERSONAL: Born November 19, 1967, in Malden, Mass. ... 6-2/205. ... Bats right, throws right. ... Full name: Gary Thomas DiSarcina. ... Brother of Glenn DiSarcina, shortstop, Chicago White Sox organization (1991-96). ... Name pronounced DEE-sar-SEE-na.
HIGH SCHOOL: Billerica (Mass.) Memorial.
COLLEGE: Massachusetts.
TRANSACTIONS/CAREER NOTES: Selected by California Angels organization in sixth round of free-agent draft (June 1, 1988). ... On disabled list (August 27, 1993-remainder of season and August 4-September 17, 1995). ... Angels franchise renamed Anaheim Angels for 1997 season.
RECORDS: Holds A.L. single-season record for fewest putouts by shortstop (150 or more games)—212 (1996).
STATISTICAL NOTES: Led Pacific Coast League shortstops with .968 fielding percentage and 419 assists in 1991. ... Led A.L. shortstops with 761 total chances in 1992. ... Led A.L. shortstops with 103 double plays in 1998.

Year Team (League)	Pos.	G	AB	R	H	2B	3B	HR	RBI	Avg.	BB	SO	SB	PO	A	E	Avg.
1988— Bend (Northwest)	SS	71	295	40	90	11	•5	2	39	.305	27	34	7	104	*237	27	.927
1989— Midland (Texas)	SS	126	441	65	126	18	7	4	54	.286	24	54	11	206	*411	30	.954
— California (A.L.)	SS	2	0	0	0	0	0	0	0	. . .	0	0	0	0	0	0	. . .
1990— Edmonton (PCL)	SS	97	330	46	70	12	2	4	37	.212	25	46	5	165	289	24	.950
— California (A.L.)	SS-2B	18	57	8	8	1	1	0	0	.140	3	10	1	17	57	4	.949
1991— Edmonton (PCL)	SS-2B	119	390	61	121	21	4	4	58	.310	29	32	16	191	†425	20	†.969
— California (A.L.)	SS-2B-3B	18	57	5	12	2	0	0	3	.211	3	4	0	29	45	4	.949
1992— California (A.L.)	SS	157	518	48	128	19	0	3	42	.247	20	50	9	250	*486	•25	.967
1993— California (A.L.)	SS	126	416	44	99	20	1	3	45	.238	15	38	5	193	362	14	.975
1994— California (A.L.)	SS	112	389	53	101	14	2	3	33	.260	18	28	3	159	*358	9	.983
1995— California (A.L.)	SS	99	362	61	111	28	6	5	41	.307	20	25	7	146	275	6	.986
1996— California (A.L.)	SS	150	536	62	137	26	4	5	48	.256	21	36	2	212	460	20	.971
1997— Anaheim (A.L.)	SS	154	549	52	135	28	2	4	47	.246	17	29	7	227	421	15	.977
1998— Anaheim (A.L.)	SS	157	551	73	158	39	3	3	56	.287	21	51	11	253	437	14	.980
Major league totals (10 years)		993	3435	406	889	177	19	26	315	.259	138	271	45	1486	2901	111	.975

ALL-STAR GAME RECORD

Year League	Pos.	AB	R	H	2B	3B	HR	RBI	Avg.	BB	SO	SB	PO	A	E	Avg.
1995— American	PR-SS	1	0	0	0	0	0	0	.000	0	0	0	0	0	0	. . .

DODD, ROBERT   P   PHILLIES

PERSONAL: Born March 14, 1973, in Kansas City, Kan. ... 6-3/195. ... Throws left, bats left. ... Full name: Robert Wayne Dodd.
HIGH SCHOOL: Plano (Texas).
JUNIOR COLLEGE: McLennan Community College (Texas).
COLLEGE: Florida.
TRANSACTIONS/CAREER NOTES: Selected by Philadelphia Phillies organization in 14th round of free-agent draft (June 2, 1994). ... On Scranton/Wilkes-Barre disabled list (July 6, 1996-remainder of season).

Year Team (League)	W	L	Pct.	ERA	G	GS	CG	ShO	Sv.	IP	H	R	ER	BB	SO
1994— Batavia (N.Y.-Penn)	2	4	.333	2.25	14	7	0	0	1	52	42	16	13	14	44
1995— Clearwater (Fla. St.)	8	7	.533	3.16	26	26	0	0	0	151	144	64	53	58	110
— Reading (Eastern)	0	0	. . .	0.00	1	0	0	0	0	1 1/3	0	0	0	2	0
1996— Reading (Eastern)	2	3	.400	3.56	18	18	0	0	0	43	41	21	17	24	35
— Scran./W.B. (Int'l)	0	0	. . .	8.10	8	2	0	0	0	20	32	21	18	9	12
1997— Reading (Eastern)	9	4	.692	3.25	63	0	0	0	8	80 1/3	61	29	29	21	94
1998— Scran./W.B. (Int'l)	4	1	.800	3.24	42	0	0	0	6	41 2/3	37	15	15	19	41
— Philadelphia (N.L.)	1	0	1.000	7.20	4	0	0	0	0	5	7	6	4	1	4
Major league totals (1 year)	1	0	1.000	7.20	4	0	0	0	0	5	7	6	4	1	4

DOSTER, DAVE   IF   PHILLIES

PERSONAL: Born October 8, 1970, in Fort Wayne, Ind. ... 5-10/181. ... Bats right, throws right. ... Full name: David Eric Doster.
HIGH SCHOOL: New Haven (Ind.).
COLLEGE: Indiana State.
TRANSACTIONS/CAREER NOTES: Selected by Philadelphia Phillies organization in 27th round of free-agent draft (June 3, 1993).
STATISTICAL NOTES: Led Florida State League second basemen with 743 total chances and 115 double plays in 1994. ... Led Eastern League with 254 total bases in 1995. ... Led Eastern League second basemen with 420 assists, 693 total chances and 91 double plays in 1995. ... Led International League with 10 sacrifice flies in 1998. ... Led International League third basemen with 283 assists and 389 total chances in 1998.

Year Team (League)	Pos.	G	AB	R	H	2B	3B	HR	RBI	Avg.	BB	SO	SB	PO	A	E	Avg.
1993— Spartanburg (SAL)	2B	60	223	34	61	15	0	3	20	.274	25	36	1	111	205	13	.960
— Clearwater (FSL)	2B-3B	9	28	4	10	3	1	0	2	.357	2	2	2	16	29	5	.900
1994— Clearwater (FSL)	2B	131	480	76	135	*42	4	13	74	.281	54	71	12	*278	*445	20	.973
1995— Reading (Eastern)	2B-OF	139	*551	84	146	39	3	21	79	.265	51	61	11	261	†420	12	.983
1996— Scran./W.B. (Int'l).......	2B	88	322	37	83	20	0	7	48	.258	26	54	7	197	203	6	.985
— Philadelphia (N.L.).....	2B-3B	39	105	14	28	8	0	1	8	.267	7	21	0	52	57	3	.973
1997— Scran./W.B. (Int'l).......	2B-3B	108	410	70	129	32	2	16	79	.315	30	60	5	152	248	14	.966
1998— Scran./W.B. (Int'l).......	3B-2B-SS	*141	*579	79	160	38	4	16	84	.276	51	80	23	107	†312	20	.954
Major league totals (1 year)		39	105	14	28	8	0	1	8	.267	7	21	0	52	57	3	.973

DOTEL, OCTAVIO   P   METS

PERSONAL: Born November 25, 1975, in Santo Domingo, Dominican Republic. ... 6-0/175. ... Throws right, bats right. ... Full name: Octavio Eduardo Dotel. ... Brother of Angel Dotel, third baseman with Los Angeles Dodgers organization (1991-93).
HIGH SCHOOL: Liceo Eansino Afuera (Dominican Republic).
TRANSACTIONS/CAREER NOTES: Signed as non-drafted free agent by New York Mets organization (March 20, 1993). ... On disabled list (July 18-August 16, 1996). ... On Binghamton disabled list (June 3-24, 1997).

Year Team (League)	W	L	Pct.	ERA	G	GS	CG	ShO	Sv.	IP	H	R	ER	BB	SO
1993— Dominican Mets (DSL).......	6	2	.750	4.10		11	0	0	0	59 1/3	46	30	27	38	48
1994— Dominican Mets (DSL).......	5	0	1.000	4.32	15	14	1	0	0	81 1/3	84	53	39	31	95
1995— GC Mets (GCL)	•7	4	.636	2.18	13	12	2	0	0	*74 1/3	48	23	18	17	*86
— St. Lucie (Fla. St.)	1	0	1.000	5.63	3	0	0	0	0	8	10	5	5	4	9
1996— Columbia (S. Atl.).............	11	3	.786	3.59	22	19	0	0	0	115 1/3	89	49	46	49	142
1997— St. Lucie (Fla. St.)	5	2	.714	2.52	9	8	1	1	0	50	44	18	14	23	39
— Binghamton (Eastern)	3	4	.429	5.98	12	12	0	0	0	55 2/3	66	50	37	38	40
— GC Mets (GCL)	0	0	. . .	0.96	3	2	0	0	1	9 1/3	9	1	1	2	7
1998— Binghamton (Eastern)	4	2	.667	1.97	10	10	2	1	0	68 2/3	41	19	15	24	82
— Norfolk (Int'l)	8	6	.571	3.45	17	16	1	0	0	99	82	47	38	43	118

DOUGHERTY, JIM   P   PIRATES

PERSONAL: Born March 8, 1968, in Brentwood, N.Y. ... 6-0/210. ... Throws right, bats right. ... Full name: James E. Dougherty.
HIGH SCHOOL: Ross (Brentwood, N.Y.).
COLLEGE: North Carolina.
TRANSACTIONS/CAREER NOTES: Selected by Houston Astros organization in 26th round of free-agent draft (June 4, 1990). ... On disabled list (August 22, 1994-remainder of season). ... Granted free agency (October 15, 1997). ... Signed by Oakland Athletics organization (December 5, 1997). ... Granted free agency (October 15, 1998). ... Signed by Pittsburgh Pirates organization (December 22, 1998).

Year Team (League)	W	L	Pct.	ERA	G	GS	CG	ShO	Sv.	IP	H	R	ER	BB	SO
1991— Asheville (S. Atl.)............	3	1	.750	1.52	62	0	0	0	28	83	63	17	14	25	78
1992— Osceola (Florida St.).........	5	2	.714	1.56	57	0	0	0	31	81	66	21	14	22	77
1993— Jackson (Texas)	2	2	.500	1.87	52	0	0	0	*36	53	39	15	11	21	55
1994— Tucson (PCL)	5	4	.556	4.12	55	0	0	0	*21	59	70	32	27	30	49
1995— Houston (N.L.)	8	4	.667	4.92	56	0	0	0	0	67 2/3	76	37	37	25	49
— Tucson (PCL)	1	0	1.000	3.27	8	0	0	0	1	11	11	4	4	5	12
1996— Tucson (PCL)	4	3	.571	3.50	46	0	0	0	1	61 2/3	65	35	24	27	53
— Houston (N.L.)	0	2	.000	9.00	12	0	0	0	0	13	14	14	13	11	6
1997— Norfolk (Int'l)■	10	1	*.909	1.45	49	0	0	0	4	62	45	11	10	43	59
1998— Oakland (A.L.)■	0	2	.000	8.25	9	0	0	0	0	12	17	11	11	7	3
— Edmonton (PCL)	2	1	.667	3.75	45	0	0	0	6	57 2/3	57	24	24	33	45
A.L. totals (1 year)	0	2	.000	8.25	9	0	0	0	0	12	17	11	11	7	3
N.L. totals (2 years)	8	6	.571	5.58	68	0	0	0	0	80 2/3	90	51	50	36	55
Major league totals (3 years)	8	8	.500	5.92	77	0	0	0	0	92 2/3	107	62	61	43	58

DRABEK, DOUG   P

PERSONAL: Born July 25, 1962, in Victoria, Texas. ... 6-1/190. ... Throws right, bats right. ... Full name: Douglas Dean Drabek. ... Name pronounced DRAY-bek.
HIGH SCHOOL: St. Joseph (Victoria, Texas).
COLLEGE: Houston.
TRANSACTIONS/CAREER NOTES: Selected by Cleveland Indians organization in fourth round of free-agent draft (June 3, 1980); did not sign. ... Selected by Chicago White Sox organization in 11th round of free-agent draft (June 6, 1983). ... Traded by White Sox with P Kevin Hickey to New York Yankees organization (August 13, 1984), completing deal in which Yankees traded IF Roy Smalley to White Sox for two players to be named later (July 18, 1984). ... Traded by Yankees with P Brian Fisher and P Logan Easley to Pittsburgh Pirates for P Rick Rhoden, P Cecilio Guante and P Pat Clements (November 26, 1986). ... On disabled list (April 26-May 18, 1987). ... Granted free agency (October 26, 1992). ... Signed by Houston Astros (December 1, 1992). ... On suspended list (September 12-17, 1995). ... On disabled list (August 23-

D

September 8, 1996). ... Granted free agency (November 18, 1996). ... Signed by White Sox (January 14, 1997). ... Granted free agency (October 30, 1997). ... Signed by Baltimore Orioles (December 11, 1997). ... On Baltimore disabled list (August 8-September 1, 1998); included rehabilitation assignment to Bowie (August 25-September 1). ... Granted free agency (October 27, 1998).

RECORDS: Shares major league single-season record for fewest double plays by pitcher who led league in double plays—4 (1992).

HONORS: Named N.L. Pitcher of the Year by THE SPORTING NEWS (1990). ... Named righthanded pitcher on THE SPORTING NEWS N.L. All-Star team (1990). ... Named N.L. Cy Young Award winner by Baseball Writers' Association of America (1990).

STATISTICAL NOTES: Pitched 11-0 one-hit, complete-game victory against Philadelphia (August 3, 1990). ... Pitched 8-0 one-hit, complete-game victory against St. Louis (May 27, 1991).

MISCELLANEOUS: Appeared in five games as pinch runner (1989). ... Appeared in one game as pinch runner (1991). ... Made an out in only appearance as pinch hitter (1992). ... Appeared in one game as pinch runner (1994). ... Appeared in two games as pinch runner (1995). ... Appeared in two games as pinch runner (1996). ... Appeared in one game as pinch runner (1997).

Year Team (League)	W	L	Pct.	ERA	G	GS	CG	ShO	Sv.	IP	H	R	ER	BB	SO
1983— Niagara Falls (NYP)	6	7	.462	3.65	16	13	3	0	0	103²/₃	99	52	42	48	103
1984— Appleton (Midwest)	1	0	1.000	1.80	1	1	0	0	0	5	3	1	1	3	6
— Glens Falls (East.)	12	5	.706	2.24	19	17	7	3	0	124²/₃	90	34	31	44	75
— Nashville (Southern)■	1	2	.333	2.32	4	4	2	0	0	31	30	11	8	10	22
1985— Alb./Colon. (East.)	13	7	.650	2.99	26	26	9	2	0	*192²/₃	153	71	64	55	*153
1986— Columbus (Int'l)	1	4	.200	7.29	8	8	0	0	0	42	50	36	34	25	23
— New York (A.L.)	7	8	.467	4.10	27	21	0	0	0	131²/₃	126	64	60	50	76
1987— Pittsburgh (N.L.)■	11	12	.478	3.88	29	28	1	1	0	176¹/₃	165	86	76	46	120
1988— Pittsburgh (N.L.)	15	7	.682	3.08	33	32	3	1	0	219¹/₃	194	83	75	50	127
1989— Pittsburgh (N.L.)	14	12	.538	2.80	35	34	8	5	0	244¹/₃	215	83	76	69	123
1990— Pittsburgh (N.L.)	*22	6	.786	2.76	33	33	9	3	0	231¹/₃	190	78	71	56	131
1991— Pittsburgh (N.L.)	15	14	.517	3.07	35	35	5	2	0	234²/₃	245	92	80	62	142
1992— Pittsburgh (N.L.)	15	11	.577	2.77	34	34	10	4	0	256²/₃	218	84	79	54	177
1993— Houston (N.L.)■	9	*18	.333	3.79	34	34	7	2	0	237²/₃	242	108	100	60	123
1994— Houston (N.L.)	12	6	.667	2.84	23	23	6	2	0	164²/₃	132	58	52	45	121
1995— Houston (N.L.)	10	9	.526	4.77	31	*31	2	1	0	185	205	104	98	54	143
1996— Houston (N.L.)	7	9	.438	4.57	30	30	1	0	0	175¹/₃	208	102	89	60	137
1997— Chicago (A.L.)■	12	11	.522	5.74	31	31	0	0	0	169¹/₃	170	109	108	69	85
1998— Baltimore (A.L.)■	6	11	.353	7.29	23	21	1	0	0	108²/₃	138	90	88	29	55
— Bowie (Eastern)	0	0	...	0.00	1	1	0	0	0	5	0	0	0	0	3
A.L. totals (3 years)	25	30	.455	5.62	81	73	1	0	0	409²/₃	434	263	256	148	216
N.L. totals (10 years)	130	104	.556	3.37	317	314	52	21	0	2125¹/₃	2014	878	796	556	1378
Major league totals (13 years)	155	134	.536	3.73	398	387	53	21	0	2535	2448	1141	1052	704	1594

CHAMPIONSHIP SERIES RECORD

RECORDS: Holds single-series record for most games lost—3 (1992). ... Shares N.L. career record for most complete games pitched—2.

Year Team (League)	W	L	Pct.	ERA	G	GS	CG	ShO	Sv.	IP	H	R	ER	BB	SO
1990— Pittsburgh (N.L.)	1	1	.500	1.65	2	2	1	0	0	16¹/₃	12	4	3	3	13
1991— Pittsburgh (N.L.)	1	1	.500	0.60	2	2	1	0	0	15	10	1	1	5	10
1992— Pittsburgh (N.L.)	0	3	.000	3.71	3	3	0	0	0	17	18	11	7	6	10
Champ. series totals (3 years)	2	5	.286	2.05	7	7	2	0	0	48¹/₃	40	16	11	14	33

ALL-STAR GAME RECORD

Year League	W	L	Pct.	ERA	GS	CG	ShO	Sv.	IP	H	R	ER	BB	SO
1994— National	0	0	...	13.50	0	0	0	0	²/₃	4	3	1	0	1

DRANSFELDT, KELLY   SS   RANGERS

PERSONAL: Born April 16, 1975, in Joliet, Ill. ... 6-2/195. ... Bats right, throws right. ... Full name: Kelly D. Dransfeldt.

HIGH SCHOOL: Morris (Ill.).

COLLEGE: Michigan.

TRANSACTIONS/CAREER NOTES: Selected by Texas Rangers organization in fourth round of free-agent draft (June 4, 1996).

STATISTICAL NOTES: Led New York-Pennsylvania League shortstops with 391 total chances in 1996. ... Led Florida State League shortstops with 227 putouts and 85 double plays in 1997.

								BATTING							**FIELDING**		
Year Team (League)	Pos.	G	AB	R	H	2B	3B	HR	RBI	Avg.	BB	SO	SB	PO	A	E	Avg.
1996— Hudson Valley (NYP)	SS	75	284	42	67	17	1	7	29	.236	27	76	13	*117	*253	*21	.946
1997— Charlotte (Fla. St.)	SS-3B	135	466	64	106	20	7	6	58	.227	42	115	25	†227	369	36	.943
1998— Charlotte (Fla. St.)	SS	67	245	46	79	17	0	18	76	.322	29	67	7	100	205	19	.941
— Tulsa (Texas)	SS	58	226	43	57	15	4	9	36	.252	18	79	8	81	184	14	.950

DREIFORT, DARREN   P   DODGERS

PERSONAL: Born May 3, 1972, in Wichita, Kan. ... 6-2/211. ... Throws right, bats right. ... Full name: Darren John Dreifort. ... Name pronounced DRY-fert.

HIGH SCHOOL: Wichita (Kan.) Heights.

COLLEGE: Wichita State.

TRANSACTIONS/CAREER NOTES: Selected by New York Mets organization in 11th round of free-agent draft (June 4, 1990); did not sign. ... Selected by Los Angeles Dodgers organization in first round (second pick overall) of free-agent draft (June 3, 1993). ... On San Antonio disabled list (July 7-28, 1994). ... On Albuquerque disabled list (August 27, 1994-remainder of season). ... On Los Angeles disabled list (April 23, 1995-entire season). ... On Los Angeles disabled list (March 25-May 16, 1996); included rehabilitation assignment to Albuquerque (April 18-May 15). ... On disabled list (May 12-June 17, 1997).

HONORS: Named righthanded pitcher on THE SPORTING NEWS college All-America team (1992-93). ... Named Golden Spikes Award winner by USA Baseball (1993).

MISCELLANEOUS: Member of 1992 U.S. Olympic baseball team. ... Singled with an RBI in one game as pinch hitter with Los Angeles (1994). ... Made an out in only appearance as pinch hitter with Los Angeles (1996). ... Received a base on balls in only appearance as pinch hitter (1998).

Year—Team (League)	W	L	Pct.	ERA	G	GS	CG	ShO	Sv.	IP	H	R	ER	BB	SO
1994—Los Angeles (N.L.)	0	5	.000	6.21	27	0	0	0	6	29	45	21	20	15	22
—San Antonio (Tex.)	3	1	.750	2.80	8	8	0	0	0	35 1/3	36	14	11	13	32
—Albuquerque (PCL)............	1	0	1.000	5.68	1	1	0	0	0	6 1/3	8	4	4	3	3
1995—Los Angeles (N.L.)						Did not play.									
1996—Albuquerque (PCL)............	5	6	.455	4.17	18	18	0	0	0	86 1/3	88	49	40	52	75
—Los Angeles (N.L.)	1	4	.200	4.94	19	0	0	0	0	23 2/3	23	13	13	12	24
1997—Los Angeles (N.L.)	5	2	.714	2.86	48	0	0	0	4	63	45	21	20	34	63
—Albuquerque (PCL)............	0	0	. . .	1.59	2	2	0	0	0	5 2/3	2	1	1	1	3
1998—Los Angeles (N.L.)	8	12	.400	4.00	32	26	1	1	0	180	171	84	80	57	168
Major league totals (4 years)......	14	23	.378	4.05	126	26	1	1	10	295 2/3	284	139	133	118	277

DIVISION SERIES RECORD

Year—Team (League)	W	L	Pct.	ERA	G	GS	CG	ShO	Sv.	IP	H	R	ER	BB	SO
1996—Los Angeles (N.L.)	0	0	. . .	0.00	1	0	0	0	0	2/3	0	0	0	0	0

DREW, J.D.　　　　OF　　　　CARDINALS

PERSONAL: Born November 20, 1975, in Valdosta, Ga. ... 6-1/195. ... Bats left, throws right. ... Full name: David Jonathan Drew. ... Brother of Tim Drew, pitcher, Cleveland Indians organization.

HIGH SCHOOL: Lowndes County (Hahira, Ga.).

COLLEGE: Florida State.

TRANSACTIONS/CAREER NOTES: Selected by San Francisco Giants organization in 20th round of free-agent draft (June 2, 1994); did not sign. ... Selected by Philadelphia Phillies organization in first round (second pick overall) of free-agent draft (June 3, 1997); did not sign. ... Selected by St. Louis Cardinals organization in first round (fifth pick overall) of free-agent draft (June 2, 1998). ... On Arkansas disabled list (July 21-August 6, 1998).

HONORS: Named Golden Spikes Award winner by USA Baseball (1997). ... Named college Player of the Year by THE SPORTING NEWS (1997). ... Named outfielder on THE SPORTING NEWS college All-America team (1997).

							BATTING							FIELDING		
Year—Team (League)	Pos.	G	AB	R	H	2B	3B	HR	RBI	Avg.	BB	SO	SB	PO	A	E	Avg.
1997—St. Paul (Northern).....	OF	44	170	51	58	6	1	18	50	.341	30	40	5	. . .	. . .	. . .	. . .
1998—St. Paul (Northern).....	OF	30	114	27	44	11	2	9	33	.386	21	32	8	. . .	. . .	. . .	. . .
—Arkansas (Texas)■.....	OF	19	67	18	22	3	1	5	11	.328	13	15	2	46	2	1	.980
—Memphis (PCL).....	OF	26	79	15	25	8	1	2	13	.316	22	18	1	54	3	2	.966
—St. Louis (N.L.)..........	OF	14	36	9	15	3	1	5	13	.417	4	10	0	19	1	0	1.000
Major league totals (1 year)		14	36	9	15	3	1	5	13	.417	4	10	0	19	1	0	1.000

DREWS, MATT　　　　P　　　　TIGERS

PERSONAL: Born August 29, 1974, in Sarasota, Fla. ... 6-8/230. ... Throws right, bats right. ... Full name: Matthew Ross Drews. ... Grandson of Karl Drews, pitcher with four major league baseball teams (1946-49 and 1951-54).

HIGH SCHOOL: Sarasota (Fla.).

TRANSACTIONS/CAREER NOTES: Selected by New York Yankees organization in first round (13th pick overall) of free-agent draft (June 3, 1993). ... Traded by Yankees with OF Ruben Sierra to Detroit Tigers for 1B/DH Cecil Fielder (July 31, 1996). ... Selected by Arizona Diamondbacks in second round (39th pick overall) of expansion draft (November 18, 1997). ... Traded by Diamondbacks with 3B Joe Randa and 3B Gabe Alvarez to Tigers for 3B Travis Fryman (November 18, 1997).

STATISTICAL NOTES: Led Southern League with 16 hit batsmen in 1997. ... Led International League with 16 hit batsmen in 1998.

Year—Team (League)	W	L	Pct.	ERA	G	GS	CG	ShO	Sv.	IP	H	R	ER	BB	SO
1994—Oneonta (N.Y.-Penn)	7	6	.538	2.10	14	14	1	0	0	90	76	31	21	19	69
1995—Tampa (Fla. St.)................	*15	7	.682	2.27	28	*28	3	0	0	182	142	73	46	58	140
1996—Columbus (Int'l)	0	4	.000	8.41	7	7	0	0	0	20 1/3	18	27	19	27	7
—Tampa (Fla. St.)................	0	3	.000	7.13	4	4	0	0	0	17 2/3	26	20	14	12	12
—Norwich (Eastern)	1	3	.250	4.50	9	9	0	0	0	46	40	26	23	33	37
—Jacksonville (Southern)■ ..	0	4	.000	4.35	6	6	1	0	0	31	26	18	15	19	40
1997—Jacksonville (Southern)......	8	11	.421	5.49	24	24	4	1	0	144 1/3	160	109	88	50	85
—Toledo (International).........	0	2	.000	6.60	3	3	0	0	0	15	14	11	11	14	7
1998—Toledo (International).........	5	17	.227	6.57	27	27	1	0	0	149 1/3	175	120	109	78	86

DRUMRIGHT, MIKE　　　　P　　　　TIGERS

PERSONAL: Born April 19, 1974, in Salina, Kan. ... 6-4/210. ... Throws right, bats left. ... Full name: Michael Robert Drumright.

HIGH SCHOOL: Valley Center (Kan.).

COLLEGE: Wichita State.

TRANSACTIONS/CAREER NOTES: Selected by Baltimore Orioles organization in 45th round of free-agent draft (June 1, 1992); did not sign. ... Selected by Detroit Tigers organization in first round (11th pick overall) of free-agent draft (June 1, 1995).

STATISTICAL NOTES: Led Southern League with six balks in 1996. ... Tied for International League lead with four balks in 1997.

Year—Team (League)	W	L	Pct.	ERA	G	GS	CG	ShO	Sv.	IP	H	R	ER	BB	SO
1995—Lakeland (Fla. St.)	1	1	.500	4.29	5	5	0	0	0	21	19	11	10	9	19
—Jacksonville (Southern)......	0	1	.000	3.69	5	5	0	0	0	31 2/3	30	13	13	15	34
1996—Jacksonville (Southern)......	6	4	.600	3.97	18	18	1	1	0	99 2/3	80	51	44	48	109
1997—Jacksonville (Southern)......	1	1	.500	1.57	5	5	0	0	0	28 2/3	16	7	5	13	24
—Toledo (International)	5	10	.333	5.06	23	23	0	0	0	133 1/3	134	78	75	•91	115
1998—Toledo (International)........	4	*19	.174	6.95	29	27	1	0	0	154	188	*130	*119	*94	91

PERSONAL: Born May 24, 1965, in Toronto. ... 6-2/180. ... Bats left, throws right. ... Full name: Robert Thomas Ducey.
HIGH SCHOOL: Glenview Park (Toronto).
JUNIOR COLLEGE: Seminole Community College (Fla.).
TRANSACTIONS/CAREER NOTES: Signed as non-drafted free agent by Toronto Blue Jays organization (May 16, 1984). ... On Toronto disabled list (June 9-September 2, 1989); included rehabilitation assignments to Syracuse (July 5-14 and August 24-September 2). ... Traded by Blue Jays with C Greg Myers to California Angels for P Mark Eichhorn (July 30, 1992). ... Released by Angels (November 19, 1992). ... Signed by Texas Rangers organization (December 18, 1992). ... On Oklahoma City disabled list (April 21-May 16, 1993). ... Released by Rangers (October 14, 1994). ... Signed by Nippon Ham Fighters of Japan Pacific League prior to 1995 season. ... Signed by Seattle Mariners organization (January 22, 1997). ... On Seattle disabled list (August 3-21, 1997). ... On Seattle disabled list (March 27-April 20, 1998). ... Granted free agency (December 21, 1998). ... Signed by Philadelphia Phillies (December 22, 1998).
STATISTICAL NOTES: Tied for Southern League lead in double plays by outfielder with six in 1986. ... Tied for International League lead in double plays by outfielder with four in 1990.

Year Team (League)	Pos.	G	AB	R	H	2B	3B	HR	RBI	Avg.	BB	SO	SB	PO	A	E	Avg.
1984—Medicine Hat (Pio.)	OF-1B	63	235	49	71	10	3	12	49	.302	41	61	13	185	11	6	.970
1985—Florence (S. Atl.)	OF-1B	134	529	78	133	22	2	13	86	.251	49	103	12	228	8	9	.963
1986—Ventura (Calif.) ..	OF-1B	47	178	36	60	11	3	12	38	.337	21	24	17	97	3	2	.980
—Knoxville (Southern) ..	OF	88	344	49	106	22	3	11	58	.308	29	59	7	186	10	6	.970
1987—Syracuse (Int'l)	OF	100	359	62	102	14	•10	10	60	.284	61	89	8	171	13	6	.968
—Toronto (A.L.)............	OF-DH	34	48	12	9	1	0	1	6	.188	8	10	2	31	0	0	1.000
1988—Syracuse (Int'l)	OF	90	317	40	81	14	4	7	42	.256	43	81	7	233	6	4	.984
—Toronto (A.L.)............	OF-DH	27	54	15	17	4	1	0	6	.315	5	7	1	35	1	0	1.000
1989—Toronto (A.L.)............	OF-DH	41	76	5	16	4	0	0	7	.211	9	25	2	56	3	0	1.000
—Syracuse (Int'l)..........	OF	10	29	0	3	0	1	0	3	.103	10	13	0	14	0	1	.933
1990—Syracuse (Int'l)..........	OF	127	438	53	117	32	7	7	47	.267	60	87	13	262	13	13	.955
—Toronto (A.L.)............	OF	19	53	7	16	5	0	0	7	.302	7	15	1	37	0	0	1.000
1991—Syracuse (Int'l)..........	OF	72	266	53	78	10	3	8	40	.293	51	58	5	120	1	0	1.000
—Toronto (A.L.)............	OF-DH	39	68	8	16	2	2	1	4	.235	6	26	2	32	1	4	.892
1992—Toronto (A.L.)............	OF-DH	23	21	3	1	1	0	0	0	.048	0	10	0	11	0	0	1.000
—California (A.L.)■......	OF-DH	31	59	4	14	3	0	0	2	.237	5	12	2	32	2	2	.944
1993—Okla. City (A.A.)■......	OF	105	389	68	118	17	•10	17	56	.303	46	97	17	244	8	7	.973
—Texas (A.L.).............	OF	27	85	15	24	6	3	2	9	.282	10	17	2	51	1	0	1.000
1994—Okla. City (A.A.)..........	OF	115	403	69	108	27	9	17	65	.268	75	91	9	221	9	4	.983
—Texas (A.L.).............	OF	11	29	1	5	1	0	0	1	.172	2	1	0	15	0	2	.882
1995—Nippon (Jap. Pac.)■..	...	117	425	61	106	19	4	25	61	.249	54	103	7	...	...	...	...
1996—Nippon (Jap. Pac.)	...	120	427	68	105	17	5	26	59	.246	86	90	3	...	...	...	...
1997—Tacoma (PCL)■	OF	23	74	8	24	8	0	0	11	.324	8	15	0	44	3	3	.940
—Seattle (A.L.)	OF	76	143	25	41	15	2	5	10	.287	6	31	3	66	3	1	.986
1998—Seattle (A.L.)	OF	97	217	30	52	18	2	5	23	.240	23	61	4	127	4	4	.970
Major league totals (10 years)		425	853	125	211	60	10	14	75	.247	81	215	19	493	15	13	.975

DIVISION SERIES RECORD

Year Team (League)	Pos.	G	AB	R	H	2B	3B	HR	RBI	Avg.	BB	SO	SB	PO	A	E	Avg.
1997—Seattle (A.L.)	PH-OF	2	4	0	2	0	0	0	1	.500	0	0	0	0	0	0	...

CHAMPIONSHIP SERIES RECORD

Year Team (League)	Pos.	G	AB	R	H	2B	3B	HR	RBI	Avg.	BB	SO	SB	PO	A	E	Avg.
1989—Toronto (A.L.)								Did not play.									
1991—Toronto (A.L.).............	PR-OF	1	1	0	0	0	0	0	0	.000	0	0	0	0	0	0	...

D

DUNCAN, CARLOS   IF   PHILLIES

PERSONAL: Born June 30, 1977, in San Pedro de Macoris, Dominican Republic. ... 6-1/185. ... Bats right, throws right. ... Full name: Jan Carlos Duncan. ... Brother of Mariano Duncan, infielder, New York Mets organization.
TRANSACTIONS/CAREER NOTES: Signed as non-drafted free agent by Philadelphia Phillies organization (November 12, 1994).

Year Team (League)	Pos.	G	AB	R	H	2B	3B	HR	RBI	Avg.	BB	SO	SB	PO	A	E	Avg.
1995—Dom. Phillies (DSL) ...	3B	51	182	27	42	7	4	0	25	.231	20	44	8	96	28	11	.919
1996—Dom. Phillies (DSL) ...	...	61	227	44	59	8	1	7	35	.260	20	51	23	...	...	...	...
1997—Martinsville (App.)......	SS	54	204	38	53	8	4	13	33	.260	14	62	11	74	157	29	.888
1998—Piedmont (S. Atl.)	3B-SS	32	111	20	22	3	2	3	12	.198	15	47	8	22	81	17	.858
—Batavia (NY-Penn)	3B	71	276	55	73	23	4	5	43	.264	29	101	13	41	159	24	.893

DUNCAN, COURTNEY   P   CUBS

PERSONAL: Born October 9, 1974, in Mobile, Ala. ... 6-0/180. ... Throws right, bats left. ... Full name: Courtney Demond Duncan.
HIGH SCHOOL: Daphne (Ala.).
COLLEGE: Grambling State.
TRANSACTIONS/CAREER NOTES: Selected by Chicago Cubs organization in 20th round of free-agent draft (June 2, 1996).

Year Team (League)	W	L	Pct.	ERA	G	GS	CG	ShO	Sv.	IP	H	R	ER	BB	SO
1996—Williamsport (NYP)	*11	1	*.917	2.19	15	•15	1	0	0	90 1/3	58	28	22	34	91
1997—Daytona (Fla. St.)	8	4	.667	*1.63	19	19	1	0	0	121 2/3	90	35	22	35	120
—Orlando (South.)	2	2	.500	3.40	8	8	0	0	0	45	37	28	17	29	45
1998—West Tenn (Southern)	7	9	.438	4.26	29	•29	0	0	0	162 2/3	141	89	77	*108	157

DUNSTON, SHAWON   SS

PERSONAL: Born March 21, 1963, in Brooklyn, N.Y. ... 6-1/180. ... Bats right, throws right. ... Full name: Shawon Donnell Dunston.
HIGH SCHOOL: Thomas Jefferson (Brooklyn, N.Y.).
TRANSACTIONS/CAREER NOTES: Selected by Chicago Cubs organization in first round (first pick overall) of free-agent draft (June 7, 1982). ... On disabled list (May 31-June 10, 1983). ... On Chicago disabled list (June 16-August 21, 1987); included rehabilitation assignment to Iowa (August 14-21). ... On disabled list (May 5, 1992-remainder of season and March 27-September 1, 1993). ... On suspended list (September 8-12, 1995). ... Granted free agency (October 31, 1995). ... Signed by San Francisco Giants (January 9, 1996). ... On disabled list (April 24-May 13 and August 5-October 1, 1996). ... Granted free agency (November 18, 1996). ... Signed by Cubs (December 7, 1996). ... On Chicago disabled list (June 9-24, 1997). ... Traded by Cubs to Pittsburgh Pirates for a player to be named later (August 31, 1997). ... Granted free agency (October 28, 1997). ... Signed by Cleveland Indians (February 16, 1998). ... Traded by Indians with P Jose Mesa and P Alvin Morman to Giants for P Steve Reed and OF Jacob Cruz (July 23, 1998). ... Granted free agency (October 23, 1998).
RECORDS: Shares modern major league single-game record for most triples—3 (July 28, 1990).
HONORS: Named shortstop on THE SPORTING NEWS N.L. All-Star team (1989).
STATISTICAL NOTES: Led N.L. shortstops with 817 total chances and tied for lead in double plays with 96 in 1986. ... Career major league grand slams: 2.

						BATTING								FIELDING		
Year Team (League)	Pos.	G	AB	R	H	2B	3B	HR	RBI	Avg.	BB	SO	SB	PO	A	E	Avg.
1982— GC Cubs (GCL)..........	SS-3B	53	190	27	61	11	0	2	28	.321	11	22	32	61	129	24	.888
1983— Quad Cities (Mid.)......	SS	117	455	65	141	17	8	4	62	.310	7	51	58	172	326	47	.914
1984— Midland (Texas).........	SS	73	298	44	98	13	3	3	34	.329	11	38	11	164	203	32	.920
— Iowa (Am. Assoc.)......	SS	61	210	25	49	11	1	7	27	.233	4	40	9	90	165	26	.907
1985— Chicago (N.L.).........	SS	74	250	40	65	12	4	4	18	.260	19	42	11	144	248	17	.958
— Iowa (Am. Assoc.)......	SS	73	272	24	73	9	6	2	28	.268	5	48	17	138	176	12	.963
1986— Chicago (N.L.).........	SS	150	581	66	145	36	3	17	68	.250	21	114	13	*320	*465	*32	.961
1987— Chicago (N.L.).........	SS	95	346	40	85	18	3	5	22	.246	10	68	12	160	271	14	.969
— Iowa (Am. Assoc.)......	SS	5	19	1	8	1	0	0	2	.421	0	3	1	6	12	1	.947
1988— Chicago (N.L.)■........	SS	155	575	69	143	23	6	9	56	.249	16	108	30	*257	455	20	.973
1989— Chicago (N.L.).........	SS	138	471	52	131	20	6	9	60	.278	30	86	19	213	379	17	.972
1990— Chicago (N.L.).........	SS	146	545	73	143	22	8	17	66	.262	15	87	25	255	392	20	.970
1991— Chicago (N.L.).........	SS	142	492	59	128	22	7	12	50	.260	23	64	21	*261	383	21	.968
1992— Chicago (N.L.).........	SS	18	73	8	23	3	1	0	2	.315	3	13	2	28	42	1	.986
1993— Chicago (N.L.).........	SS	7	10	3	4	2	0	0	2	.400	0	1	0	5	0	0	1.000
1994— Chicago (N.L.).........	SS	88	331	38	92	19	0	11	35	.278	16	48	3	121	218	12	.966
1995— Chicago (N.L.).........	SS	127	477	58	141	30	6	14	69	.296	10	75	10	187	336	17	.969
1996— San Fran. (N.L.)■......	SS	82	287	27	86	12	2	5	25	.300	13	40	8	116	217	15	.957
1997— Chicago (N.L.)■........	SS-OF	114	419	57	119	18	4	9	41	.284	8	64	29	179	227	12	.971
— Pittsburgh (N.L.)■......	SS	18	71	14	28	4	1	5	16	.394	0	11	3	28	55	3	.965
1998— Cleveland (A.L.)■.......	2-S-O-DH	62	156	26	37	11	3	3	12	.237	6	18	9	63	76	4	.972
— San Fran. (N.L.)■......	SS-OF-2B	36	51	10	9	2	0	3	8	.176	0	10	0	20	5	2	.926
American League totals (1 year)		62	156	26	37	11	3	3	12	.237	6	18	9	63	76	4	.972
National League totals (14 years)		1390	4979	614	1342	243	51	120	538	.270	184	831	186	2294	3693	203	.967
Major league totals (14 years)		1452	5135	640	1379	254	54	123	550	.269	190	849	195	2357	3769	207	.967

CHAMPIONSHIP SERIES RECORD

						BATTING								FIELDING		
Year Team (League)	Pos.	G	AB	R	H	2B	3B	HR	RBI	Avg.	BB	SO	SB	PO	A	E	Avg.
1989— Chicago (N.L.)............	SS	5	19	2	6	0	0	0	0	.316	1	1	1	10	14	1	.960

ALL-STAR GAME RECORD

					BATTING								FIELDING		
Year League	Pos.	AB	R	H	2B	3B	HR	RBI	Avg.	BB	SO	SB	PO	A	E	Avg.
1988— National.....................							Did not play.									
1990— National.....................	SS	2	0	0	0	0	0	0	.000	0	0	0	0	0	0	...

DUNWOODY, TODD   OF   MARLINS

PERSONAL: Born April 11, 1975, in Lafayette, Ind. ... 6-1/195. ... Bats left, throws left. ... Full name: Todd Franklin Dunwoody.
HIGH SCHOOL: West Lafayette (Ind.) Harrison.
TRANSACTIONS/CAREER NOTES: Selected by Florida Marlins organization in seventh round of free-agent draft (June 3, 1993). ... On Charlotte disabled list (April 11-18, 1998).
STATISTICAL NOTES: Led Eastern League with 267 total bases in 1996.

						BATTING								FIELDING		
Year Team (League)	Pos.	G	AB	R	H	2B	3B	HR	RBI	Avg.	BB	SO	SB	PO	A	E	Avg.
1993— GC Marlins (GCL).......	OF	31	109	13	21	2	2	0	7	.193	7	28	5	45	1	1	.979
1994— GC Marlins (GCL).......	OF	46	169	32	44	6	6	1	25	.260	21	28	11	91	1	1	.989
— Kane County (Midw.)..	OF	15	45	7	5	0	0	1	1	.111	5	17	1	21	2	0	1.000
1995— Kane County (Midw.)..	OF	132	494	89	140	20	8	14	89	.283	52	105	39	284	6	5	.983
1996— Portland (Eastern)......	OF	138	*552	88	153	30	6	24	93	.277	45	*149	24	254	2	1	*.996
1997— Charlotte (Int'l)...........	OF	107	401	74	105	16	7	23	62	.262	39	129	25	231	5	2	.992
— Florida (N.L.)...........	OF	19	50	7	13	2	2	2	7	.260	7	21	2	26	0	2	.929
1998— Charlotte (Int'l)..........	OF	28	102	20	31	6	3	6	22	.304	12	28	4	76	2	1	.987
— Florida (N.L.)...........	OF	116	434	53	109	27	7	5	28	.251	21	113	5	273	9	3	.989
Major league totals (2 years)		135	484	60	122	29	9	7	35	.252	28	134	7	299	9	5	.984

DURAN, ROBERTO P EXPOS

PERSONAL: Born March 6, 1973, in Moca, Dominican Republic. ... 6-0/205. ... Throws left, bats left. ... Full name: Roberto Alejandro Duran.
HIGH SCHOOL: Liceo Domingo Fantino (Moca, Dominican Republic).
TRANSACTIONS/CAREER NOTES: Signed as non-drafted free agent by Los Angeles Dodgers organization (February 10, 1990). ... On disabled list (May 8, 1991-remainder of season). ... Claimed on waivers by Toronto Blue Jays (March 14, 1996). ... Traded by Blue Jays to Detroit Tigers for OF Anton French (December 11, 1996). ... On Detroit disabled list (May 29, 1998-remainder of season); included rehabilitation assignments to Toledo (June 5-June 16) and Lakeland (August 14-September 12). ... Claimed on waivers by Montreal Expos (January 7, 1999).

Year Team (League)	W	L	Pct.	ERA	G	GS	CG	ShO	Sv.	IP	H	R	ER	BB	SO
1990— Dom. Dodgers (DSL)	0	2	.000	13.27	9	8	0	0	0	19 2/3	18	31	29	36	23
1991— Dom. Dodgers (DSL)	1	1	.500	3.18	3	3	0	0	0	11 1/3	8	8	4	8	22
1992— Vero Beach (FSL)	0	0	...	9.00	2	1	0	0	0	5	6	5	5	4	5
— GC Dodgers (GCL)	4	3	.571	2.79	9	8	0	0	0	38 2/3	22	17	12	31	57
1993— Vero Beach (FSL)	1	1	.500	3.72	8	0	0	0	0	9 2/3	10	4	4	8	9
— Yakima (N'west)	2	2	.500	6.98	20	3	0	0	0	40	37	34	31	42	50
1994— Bakersfield (California)	6	5	.545	4.82	42	4	0	0	10	65 1/3	61	43	35	48	86
1995— Vero Beach (FSL)	7	4	.636	3.38	23	22	0	0	0	101 1/3	82	42	38	70	114
1996— Knoxville (Southern)■	4	6	.400	5.13	19	16	0	0	0	80 2/3	72	52	46	61	74
— Dunedin (Fla. St.)	3	1	.750	1.12	8	8	1	1	0	48 1/3	31	9	6	19	54
1997— Jacksonville (Southern)■	4	2	.667	2.37	50	0	0	0	16	60 2/3	41	19	16	39	95
— Detroit (A.L.)	0	0	...	7.59	13	0	0	0	0	10 2/3	7	9	9	15	11
1998— Detroit (A.L.)	0	1	.000	5.87	18	0	0	0	0	15 1/3	9	10	10	17	12
— Toledo (International)	0	0	...	27.00	1	0	0	0	0	2/3	1	2	2	2	1
— Lakeland (Fla. St.)	0	0	...	4.15	8	0	0	0	0	8 2/3	4	5	4	13	9
Major league totals (2 years)	0	1	.000	6.58	31	0	0	0	0	26	16	19	19	32	23

DURHAM, RAY 2B WHITE SOX

PERSONAL: Born November 30, 1971, in Charlotte. ... 5-8/170. ... Bats both, throws right.
HIGH SCHOOL: Harding (Charlotte).
TRANSACTIONS/CAREER NOTES: Selected by Chicago White Sox organization in fifth round of free-agent draft (June 4, 1990). ... On Utica suspended list (April 1-May 22, 1992). ... On Sarasota disabled list (June 16-July 9, 1992).
RECORDS: Holds major league single-season record for fewest putouts by second baseman (150 or more games)—236 (1996).
STATISTICAL NOTES: Led Southern League in caught stealing with 25 in 1993. ... Led Southern League second basemen with 541 total chances in 1993. ... Led American Association with 261 total bases in 1994. ... Led American Association second basemen with 701 total chances and 92 double plays in 1994. ... Led A.L. second basemen with 738 total chances and 128 double plays in 1998. ... Career major league grand slams: 2.

							BATTING							FIELDING			
Year Team (League)	Pos.	G	AB	R	H	2B	3B	HR	RBI	Avg.	BB	SO	SB	PO	A	E	Avg.
1990— GC Whi. Sox (GCL)	2B-SS	35	116	18	32	3	3	0	13	.276	15	36	23	61	85	15	.907
1991— Utica (N.Y.-Penn)	2B	39	142	29	36	2	7	0	17	.254	25	44	12	54	101	12	.928
— GC Whi. Sox (GCL)	2B	6	23	3	7	1	0	0	4	.304	3	5	5	18	15	0	1.000
1992— Sarasota (Fla. St.)	2B	57	202	37	55	6	3	0	7	.272	32	36	28	66	107	10	.945
— GC Whi. Sox (GCL)	2B	5	13	3	7	2	0	0	2	.538	3	1	1	4	3	0	1.000
1993— Birmingham (Sou.)	2B	137	528	83	143	22	*10	3	37	.271	42	100	39	227	284	*30	.945
1994— Nashville (A.A.)	2B	133	527	89	156	33	*12	16	66	.296	46	91	34	*254	*429	*19	*.973
1995— Chicago (A.L.)	2B-DH	125	471	68	121	27	6	7	51	.257	31	83	18	245	298	15	.973
1996— Chicago (A.L.)	2B-DH	156	557	79	153	33	5	10	65	.275	58	95	30	236	423	11	.984
1997— Chicago (A.L.)	2B-DH	155	634	106	172	27	5	11	53	.271	61	96	33	270	395	*18	.974
1998— Chicago (A.L.)	2B	158	635	126	181	35	8	19	67	.285	73	105	36	282	438	18	.976
Major league totals (4 years)		594	2297	379	627	122	24	47	236	.273	223	379	117	1033	1554	62	.977

ALL-STAR GAME RECORD

						BATTING						FIELDING		
Year League	Pos.	AB	R	H	2B	3B	HR	RBI	Avg.	BB	SO	SB	PO	A	E	Avg.
1998— American	2B	1	1	1	0	0	0	1	1.000	0	0	0	0	0	0	...

DUVALL, MIKE P DEVIL RAYS

PERSONAL: Born October 11, 1974, in Warrenton, Va. ... 6-0/185. ... Throws left, bats right. ... Full name: Michael Alan Duvall.
HIGH SCHOOL: Fauquier (Warrenton, Va.).
JUNIOR COLLEGE: Potomac State College (W.Va.).
TRANSACTIONS/CAREER NOTES: Selected by Florida Marlins organization in 19th round of free-agent draft (June 1, 1995). ... Selected by Tampa Bay Devil Rays in second round (32nd pick overall) of expansion draft (November 18, 1997). ... On Durham disabled list (April 9-May 13, 1998).

Year Team (League)	W	L	Pct.	ERA	G	GS	CG	ShO	Sv.	IP	H	R	ER	BB	SO
1995— GC Marlins (GCL)	5	0	1.000	2.22	16	1	0	0	1	28 1/3	15	8	7	12	34
1996— Kane County (Midwest)	4	1	.800	2.06	41	0	0	0	8	48	43	20	11	21	46
1997— Brevard County (FSL)	1	0	1.000	0.73	11	0	0	0	6	12 1/3	7	1	1	3	9
— Portland (Eastern)	4	6	.400	1.84	45	0	0	0	18	68 1/3	63	20	14	20	49
1998— St. Petersburg (FSL)■	0	0	...	2.70	2	0	0	0	0	3 1/3	4	1	1	2	3
— Durham (International)	5	1	.625	3.22	32	9	1	0	0	72 2/3	74	31	26	32	55
— Tampa Bay (A.L.)	0	0	...	6.75	3	0	0	0	0	4	4	3	3	2	1
Major league totals (1 year)	0	0	...	6.75	3	0	0	0	0	4	4	3	3	2	1

PERSONAL: Born January 28, 1974, in Vacaville, Calif. ... 6-4/210. ... Bats right, throws right. ... Full name: Jermaine Trevell Dye.
HIGH SCHOOL: Will C. Wood (Vacaville, Calif.).
JUNIOR COLLEGE: Cosumnes River (Calif.) College.
TRANSACTIONS/CAREER NOTES: Selected by Atlanta Braves organization in 17th round of free-agent draft (June 3, 1993). ... On disabled list (July 13-August 9, 1995). ... Traded by Braves with P Jamie Walker to Kansas City Royals for OF Michael Tucker and IF Keith Lockhart (March 27, 1997). ... On Kansas City disabled list (April 17-May 3, 1997); included rehabilitation assignment to Omaha (May 1-3). ... On Kansas City disabled list (July 10-August 13, 1997); included rehabilitation assignment to Omaha (July 27-August 13). ... On Kansas City disabled list (March 23-May 8 and September 1, 1998-remainder of season); included rehabilitation assignment to Omaha (April 21-May 8).
STATISTICAL NOTES: Led South Atlantic League outfielders with six double plays in 1994. ... Career major league grand slams: 1.
MISCELLANEOUS: Hit home run in first major league at-bat (May 17, 1996).

						— BATTING —									— FIELDING —		
Year	Team (League)	Pos.	G	AB	R	H	2B	3B	HR	RBI	Avg.	BB	SO	SB	PO	A	E	Avg.
1993—	GC Braves (GCL)	OF-3B	31	124	17	43	14	0	0	27	.347	5	13	5	46	9	3	.948
	—Danville (Appal.)	OF	25	94	6	26	6	1	2	12	.277	8	10	19	51	1	2	.963
1994—	Macon (S. Atl.)	OF	135	506	73	151	*41	1	15	98	.298	33	82	19	263	*22	9	.969
1995—	Greenville (Sou.)	OF	104	403	50	115	26	4	15	71	.285	27	74	4	234	*22	5	.981
1996—	Richmond (Int'l)	OF	36	142	25	33	7	1	6	19	.232	5	25	3	83	2	4	.955
	—Atlanta (N.L.)	OF	98	292	32	82	16	0	12	37	.281	8	67	1	150	2	8	.950
1997—	Kansas City (A.L.)■	OF	75	263	26	62	14	0	7	22	.236	17	51	2	164	7	6	.966
	—Omaha (A.A.)	OF	39	144	21	44	6	0	10	25	.306	9	25	0	41	2	0	1.000
1998—	Omaha (PCL)	OF-1B	41	157	29	47	6	0	12	35	.299	19	29	7	119	4	1	.992
	—Kansas City (A.L.)	OF	60	214	24	50	5	1	5	23	.234	11	46	2	152	4	2	.987
American League totals (2 years)			135	477	50	112	19	1	12	45	.235	28	97	4	316	11	8	.976
National League totals (1 year)			98	292	32	82	16	0	12	37	.281	8	67	1	150	2	8	.950
Major league totals (3 years)			233	769	82	194	35	1	24	82	.252	36	164	5	466	13	16	.968

DIVISION SERIES RECORD

						— BATTING —									— FIELDING —		
Year	Team (League)	Pos.	G	AB	R	H	2B	3B	HR	RBI	Avg.	BB	SO	SB	PO	A	E	Avg.
1996—	Atlanta (N.L.)	OF	3	11	1	2	0	0	1	1	.182	0	6	1	11	1	0	1.000

CHAMPIONSHIP SERIES RECORD
RECORDS: Shares N.L. single-game record for most at-bats—6 (October 14, 1996).

						— BATTING —									— FIELDING —		
Year	Team (League)	Pos.	G	AB	R	H	2B	3B	HR	RBI	Avg.	BB	SO	SB	PO	A	E	Avg.
1996—	Atlanta (N.L.)	OF	7	28	2	6	1	0	0	4	.214	1	7	0	14	0	0	1.000

WORLD SERIES RECORD

						— BATTING —									— FIELDING —		
Year	Team (League)	Pos.	G	AB	R	H	2B	3B	HR	RBI	Avg.	BB	SO	SB	PO	A	E	Avg.
1996—	Atlanta (N.L.)	OF	5	17	0	2	0	0	0	1	.118	1	1	0	15	0	1	.938

D
E

PERSONAL: Born September 27, 1974, in Paradera, Aruba. ... 6-0/160. ... Throws left, bats left. ... Full name: Radhames Alviro Dykhoff. ... Name pronounced RAD-ham-es DIKE-off.
TRANSACTIONS/CAREER NOTES: Signed as non-drafted free agent by Baltimore Orioles organization (January 6, 1993).

Year	Team (League)	W	L	Pct.	ERA	G	GS	CG	ShO	Sv.	IP	H	R	ER	BB	SO
1993—	GC Orioles (GCL)	1	2	.333	3.40	14	3	0	0	1	45	37	22	17	11	29
1994—	GC Orioles (GCL)	3	6	.333	3.33	12	12	1	0	0	73	69	34	27	17	67
1995—	High Desert (Calif.)	1	5	.167	5.02	34	2	0	0	3	80 2/3	95	68	45	44	88
1996—	Frederick (Carolina)	2	6	.250	5.66	33	0	0	0	3	62	77	45	39	22	75
1997—	Bowie (Eastern)	0	0	...	8.31	7	0	0	0	0	8 2/3	10	9	8	7	7
	—Delmarva (S. Atl.)	0	0	...	0.00	1	0	0	0	1	3	3	0	0	0	3
	—Frederick (Carolina)	3	3	.500	2.42	31	0	0	0	5	67	48	19	18	52	98
1998—	Bowie (Eastern)	3	7	.300	4.71	38	8	0	0	1	93 2/3	83	51	49	52	98
	—Baltimore (A.L.)	0	0	...	18.00	1	0	0	0	0	1	2	2	2	1	1
Major league totals (1 year)		0	0	...	18.00	1	0	0	0	0	1	2	2	2	1	1

PERSONAL: Born November 11, 1969, in New York. ... 5-11/185. ... Bats right, throws right. ... Full name: Jacinto Damion Easley.
HIGH SCHOOL: Lakewood (Calif.).
JUNIOR COLLEGE: Long Beach (Calif.) City College.
COLLEGE: Long Beach State.
TRANSACTIONS/CAREER NOTES: Selected by California Angels organization in 30th round of free-agent draft (June 1, 1988). ... On disabled list (June 19-July 4 and July 28, 1993-remainder of season; and May 30-June 17, 1994). ... On California disabled list (April 1-May 10, 1996); included rehabilitation assignments to Vancouver (April 30-May 3) and Midland (May 6-9). ... Traded by Angels to Detroit Tigers for P Greg Gohr (July 31, 1996).
RECORDS: Holds major league single-season record for fewest putouts by second baseman for leader—285 (1998).
HONORS: Named second baseman on THE SPORTING NEWS A.L. Silver Slugger team (1998).
STATISTICAL NOTES: Led A.L. second basemen with 285 putouts and .985 fielding percentage in 1998. ... Had 19-game hitting streaks (May 10-30 and July 3-23, 1998). ... Career major league grand slams: 1.

Year	Team (League)	Pos.	G	AB	R	H	2B	3B	HR	RBI	Avg.	BB	SO	SB	PO	A	E	Avg.
1989— Bend (Northwest)......		2B	36	131	34	39	5	1	4	21	.298	25	21	9	49	89	22	.863
1990— Quad City (Midwest) ..		SS	103	365	59	100	19	3	10	56	.274	41	60	25	136	206	41	.893
1991— Midland (Texas).........		SS	127	452	73	115	24	5	6	57	.254	58	67	23	186	388	*47	.924
1992— Edmonton (PCL)		SS-3B	108	429	61	124	18	3	3	44	.289	31	44	26	152	342	30	.943
— California (A.L.)		3B-SS	47	151	14	39	5	0	1	12	.258	8	26	9	30	102	5	.964
1993— California (A.L.).........		2B-3B-DH	73	230	33	72	13	2	2	22	.313	28	35	6	111	157	6	.978
1994— California (A.L.).........		3B-2B	88	316	41	68	16	1	6	30	.215	29	48	4	122	179	7	.977
1995— California (A.L.).........		2B-SS	114	357	35	77	14	2	4	35	.216	32	47	5	186	276	10	.979
1996— Vancouver (PCL)		SS-2B-3B	12	48	13	15	2	1	2	8	.313	9	6	4	20	26	2	.958
— Midland (Texas)		3B-SS	4	14	1	6	2	0	0	2	.429	0	0	1	5	12	1	.944
— California (A.L.).........S-2-3-DH-O			28	45	4	7	1	0	2	7	.156	6	12	0	23	39	3	.954
— Detroit (A.L.)■		2-S-3-DH	21	67	10	23	1	0	2	10	.343	4	13	3	22	47	3	.958
1997— Detroit (A.L.)		2B-SS-DH	151	527	97	139	37	3	22	72	.264	68	102	28	244	405	12	.982
1998— Detroit (A.L.)		2B-SS-DH	153	594	84	161	38	2	27	100	.271	39	112	15	†312	480	12	†.985
Major league totals (7 years)			675	2287	318	586	125	10	66	288	.256	214	395	70	1050	1685	58	.979

ALL-STAR GAME RECORD

Year	League	Pos.	AB	R	H	2B	3B	HR	RBI	Avg.	BB	SO	SB	PO	A	E	Avg.
1998— American		PH	1	1	1	0	0	0	0	1.000	0	0	0	...	...	...	...

EBERT, DERRIN   P   BRAVES

PERSONAL: Born August 21, 1976, in Anaheim, Calif. ... 6-3/200. ... Throws left, bats right. ... Full name: Derrin Lee Ebert.
HIGH SCHOOL: Hesperia (Calif.).
JUNIOR COLLEGE: Victor Valley Community College (Calif.).
COLLEGE: Cal State Fullerton.
TRANSACTIONS/CAREER NOTES: Selected by Atlanta Braves organization in 18th round of free-agent draft (June 2, 1994).
STATISTICAL NOTES: Pitched 6-0 no-hit victory against Gulf Coast Marlins, seven innings (August 12, 1994).

Year	Team (League)	W	L	Pct.	ERA	G	GS	CG	ShO	Sv.	IP	H	R	ER	BB	SO
1994— GC Braves (GCL)		1	3	.250	2.93	10	7	1	1	0	43	40	18	14	8	25
1995— Macon (S. Atl.)..................		*14	5	.737	3.31	28	28	0	0	0	*182	*184	87	67	46	124
1996— Durham (Carolina).............		12	9	.571	4.00	27	27	2	0	0	166 1/3	189	102	74	37	99
1997— Greenville (Southern)		11	8	.579	4.10	27	25	0	0	0	175 2/3	191	95	80	48	101
1998— Richmond (Int'l).................		9	9	.500	4.51	29	29	0	0	0	163 2/3	195	94	82	49	88

ECHEVARRIA, ANGEL   OF   ROCKIES

E

PERSONAL: Born May 25, 1971, in Bridgeport, Conn. ... 6-3/226. ... Bats right, throws right. ... Full name: Angel Santos Echevarria.
HIGH SCHOOL: Bassick (Bridgeport, Conn.).
COLLEGE: Rutgers.
TRANSACTIONS/CAREER NOTES: Selected by Colorado Rockies organization in 17th round of free-agent draft (June 1, 1992). ... On Colorado disabled list (April 29-June 4 and July 29-August 16, 1997).

Year	Team (League)	Pos.	G	AB	R	H	2B	3B	HR	RBI	Avg.	BB	SO	SB	PO	A	E	Avg.
1992— Bend (Northwest).......		OF	57	205	24	46	4	1	5	30	.224	19	54	8	65	7	0	1.000
1993— Central Valley (Cal.)....		OF	104	358	45	97	16	2	6	52	.271	44	74	6	141	8	6	.961
1994— Central Valley (Cal.)....		OF	50	192	25	58	8	1	6	35	.302	9	25	2	52	3	1	.982
— New Haven (East.)......		OF	58	205	25	52	6	0	6	32	.254	15	46	2	91	5	2	.980
1995— New Haven (East.)......		OF	124	453	78	136	30	1	21	*100	.300	56	93	8	202	*20	5	.978
1996— Colo. Springs (PCL) ...		OF	110	415	67	140	19	2	16	74	.337	38	81	4	168	8	4	.978
— Colorado (N.L.)		OF	26	21	2	6	0	0	0	6	.286	2	5	0	1	0	0	1.000
1997— Colo. Springs (PCL) ...		OF-1B	77	295	59	95	24	0	13	80	.322	28	47	6	135	9	1	.993
— Colorado (N.L.)		OF	15	20	4	5	2	0	0	0	.250	2	5	0	4	1	0	1.000
1998— Colo. Springs (PCL) ...		1B-OF	85	301	50	98	21	2	15	60	.326	14	47	0	408	28	7	.984
— Colorado (N.L.)		1B-OF	19	29	7	11	3	0	1	9	.379	2	3	0	23	2	0	1.000
Major league totals (3 years)			60	70	13	22	5	0	1	15	.314	6	13	0	28	3	0	1.000

ECKERSLEY, DENNIS   P

PERSONAL: Born October 3, 1954, in Oakland. ... 6-2/195. ... Throws right, bats right. ... Full name: Dennis Lee Eckersley.
HIGH SCHOOL: Washington (Fremont, Calif.).
TRANSACTIONS/CAREER NOTES: Selected by Cleveland Indians organization in third round of free-agent draft (June 6, 1972). ... Traded by Indians with C Fred Kendall to Boston Red Sox for P Rick Wise, P Mike Paxton, 3B Ted Cox and C Bo Diaz (March 30, 1978). ... Traded by Red Sox with OF Mike Brumley to Chicago Cubs for 1B/OF Bill Buckner (May 25, 1984). ... Granted free agency (November 8, 1984). ... Re-signed by Cubs (November 28, 1984). ... On disabled list (August 11-September 7, 1985). ... Traded by Cubs with IF Dan Rohn to Oakland Athletics for OF Dave Wilder, IF Brian Guinn and P Mark Leonette (April 3, 1987). ... On disabled list (May 13-July 13, 1989). ... Granted free agency (October 25, 1994). ... Re-signed by A's (April 3, 1995). ... Traded by A's to St. Louis Cardinals for P Steve Montgomery (February 13, 1996). ... On disabled list (May 19-June 13, 1996). ... Granted free agency (October 29, 1997). ... Signed by Red Sox (December 9, 1997). ... On Boston disabled list (June 1-July 24, 1998; included rehabilitation assignment to Pawtucket (July 18-24). ... Granted free agency (November 3, 1998). ... Announced retirement (December 10, 1998).
RECORDS: Holds major league career record for most games pitched—1,071. ... Holds A.L. career records for most saves—324; most games pitched—869; and most consecutive errorless games by pitcher—470 (May 1, 1987 through May 4, 1995).
HONORS: Named A.L. Rookie Pitcher of the Year by THE SPORTING NEWS (1975). ... Named A.L. Fireman of the Year by THE SPORTING NEWS (1988 and 1992). ... Named A.L. co-Fireman of the Year by THE SPORTING NEWS (1991). ... Named A.L. Most Valuable Player by Baseball Writers' Association of America (1992). ... Named A.L. Cy Young Award winner by Baseball Writers' Association of America (1992).

STATISTICAL NOTES: Led Texas League with 10 hit batsmen in 1974. ... Pitched 1-0 no-hit victory against California (May 30, 1977). ... Pitched 2-0 one-hit, complete-game victory against Milwaukee (August 12, 1977, first game). ... Led A.L. with 30 home runs allowed in 1978. ... Pitched 3-1 one-hit, complete-game victory against Toronto (September 26, 1980).

MISCELLANEOUS: Holds Oakland Athletics all-time records for lowest earned run average (2.74), most games pitched (525) and most saves (320).

Year Team (League)	W	L	Pct.	ERA	G	GS	CG	ShO	Sv.	IP	H	R	ER	BB	SO
1972— Reno (California)	5	5	.500	4.80	12	12	3	1	0	75	87	46	40	33	56
1973— Reno (California)	12	8	.600	3.65	31	*31	11	•5	0	202	182	97	82	91	218
1974— San Antonio (Tex.)	•14	3	*.824	3.40	23	23	10	2	0	167	141	66	63	60	*163
1975— Cleveland (A.L.)	13	7	.650	2.60	34	24	6	2	2	187	147	61	54	90	152
1976— Cleveland (A.L.)	13	12	.520	3.44	36	30	9	3	1	199	155	82	76	78	200
1977— Cleveland (A.L.)	14	13	.519	3.53	33	33	12	3	0	247	214	100	97	54	191
1978— Boston (A.L.)■	20	8	.714	2.99	35	35	16	3	0	268	258	99	89	71	162
1979— Boston (A.L.)	17	10	.630	2.99	33	33	17	2	0	247	234	89	82	59	150
1980— Boston (A.L.)	12	14	.462	4.27	30	30	8	0	0	198	188	101	94	44	121
1981— Boston (A.L.)	9	8	.529	4.27	23	23	8	2	0	154	160	82	73	35	79
1982— Boston (A.L.)	13	13	.500	3.73	33	33	11	3	0	224 1/3	228	101	93	43	127
1983— Boston (A.L.)	9	13	.409	5.61	28	28	2	0	0	176 1/3	223	119	110	39	77
1984— Boston (A.L.)	4	4	.500	5.01	9	9	2	0	0	64 2/3	71	38	36	13	33
— Chicago (N.L.)■	10	8	.556	3.03	24	24	2	0	0	160 1/3	152	59	54	36	81
1985— Chicago (N.L.)	11	7	.611	3.08	25	25	6	2	0	169 1/3	145	61	58	19	117
1986— Chicago (N.L.)	6	11	.353	4.57	33	32	1	0	0	201	226	109	102	43	137
1987— Oakland (A.L.)■	6	8	.429	3.03	54	2	0	0	16	115 2/3	99	41	39	17	113
1988— Oakland (A.L.)	4	2	.667	2.35	60	0	0	0	45	72 2/3	52	20	19	11	70
1989— Oakland (A.L.)	4	0	1.000	1.56	51	0	0	0	33	57 2/3	32	10	10	3	55
1990— Oakland (A.L.)	4	2	.667	0.61	63	0	0	0	48	73 1/3	41	9	5	4	73
1991— Oakland (A.L.)	5	4	.556	2.96	67	0	0	0	43	76	60	26	25	9	87
1992— Oakland (A.L.)	7	1	.875	1.91	69	0	0	0	*51	80	62	17	17	11	93
1993— Oakland (A.L.)	2	4	.333	4.16	64	0	0	0	36	67	67	32	31	13	80
1994— Oakland (A.L.)	5	4	.556	4.26	45	0	0	0	19	44 1/3	49	26	21	13	47
1995— Oakland (A.L.)	4	6	.400	4.83	52	0	0	0	29	50 1/3	53	29	27	11	40
1996— St. Louis (N.L.)■	0	6	.000	3.30	63	0	0	0	30	60	65	26	22	6	49
1997— St. Louis (N.L.)	1	5	.167	3.91	57	0	0	0	36	53	49	24	23	8	45
1998— Boston (A.L.)■	4	1	.800	4.76	50	0	0	0	1	39 2/3	46	21	21	8	22
— Pawtucket (Int'l)	0	0	...	4.50	2	0	0	0	0	2	2	1	1	0	2
A.L. totals (20 years)	169	134	.558	3.47	869	280	91	18	324	2642	2439	1103	1019	626	1972
N.L. totals (5 years)	28	37	.431	3.62	202	81	9	2	66	643 2/3	637	279	259	112	429
Major league totals (24 years)	197	171	.535	3.50	1071	361	100	20	390	3285 2/3	3076	1382	1278	738	2401

DIVISION SERIES RECORD

Year Team (League)	W	L	Pct.	ERA	G	GS	CG	ShO	Sv.	IP	H	R	ER	BB	SO
1996— St. Louis (N.L.)	0	0	...	0.00	3	0	0	0	3	3 2/3	3	0	0	0	2
1998— Boston (A.L.)	0	0	...	9.00	1	0	0	0	0	1	1	1	1	0	1
Div. series totals (2 years)	0	0	...	1.93	4	0	0	0	3	4 2/3	4	1	1	0	3

RECORDS: Holds career record for most saves—11. ... Holds single-series record for most saves—4 (1988). ... Holds A.L. career record for most saves—10. ... Shares A.L. career records for most games pitched—14; and most games as relief pitcher—14.

NOTES: Named A.L. Championship Series Most Valuable Player (1988).

CHAMPIONSHIP SERIES RECORD

Year Team (League)	W	L	Pct.	ERA	G	GS	CG	ShO	Sv.	IP	H	R	ER	BB	SO
1984— Chicago (N.L.)	0	1	.000	8.44	1	1	0	0	0	5 1/3	9	5	5	0	0
1988— Oakland (A.L.)	0	0	...	0.00	4	0	0	0	4	6	1	0	0	2	5
1989— Oakland (A.L.)	0	0	...	1.59	4	0	0	0	3	5 2/3	4	1	1	0	2
1990— Oakland (A.L.)	0	0	...	0.00	3	0	0	0	2	3 1/3	2	0	0	0	3
1992— Oakland (A.L.)	0	0	...	6.00	3	0	0	0	1	3	8	2	2	0	2
1996— St. Louis (N.L.)	1	0	1.000	0.00	3	0	0	0	1	3 1/3	2	0	0	0	4
Champ. series totals (6 years)	1	1	.500	2.70	18	1	0	0	11	26 2/3	26	8	8	2	16

NOTES: Member of World Series championship team (1989).

WORLD SERIES RECORD

Year Team (League)	W	L	Pct.	ERA	G	GS	CG	ShO	Sv.	IP	H	R	ER	BB	SO
1988— Oakland (A.L.)	0	1	.000	10.80	2	0	0	0	0	1 2/3	2	2	2	1	2
1989— Oakland (A.L.)	0	0	...	0.00	2	0	0	0	1	1 2/3	0	0	0	0	0
1990— Oakland (A.L.)	0	1	.000	6.75	2	0	0	0	0	1 1/3	3	1	1	0	1
World Series totals (3 years)	0	2	.000	5.79	6	0	0	0	1	4 2/3	5	3	3	1	3

ALL-STAR GAME RECORD

Year League	W	L	Pct.	ERA	GS	CG	ShO	Sv.	IP	H	R	ER	BB	SO
1977— American	0	0	...	0.00	0	0	0	0	2	0	0	0	0	1
1982— American	0	1	.000	9.00	1	0	0	0	3	2	3	3	2	1
1988— American	0	0	...	0.00	0	0	0	0	1	0	0	0	0	1
1990— American	0	0	...	0.00	0	0	0	1	1	1	0	0	0	1
1991— American	0	0	...	0.00	0	0	0	1	1	0	0	0	0	1
1992— American	0	0	...	0.00	0	0	0	0	2/3	3	2	0	0	2
All-Star totals (6 years)	0	1	.000	3.12	1	0	0	3	8 2/3	6	5	3	2	7

EDMONDS, JIM   OF   ANGELS

PERSONAL: Born June 27, 1970, in Fullerton, Calif. ... 6-1/218. ... Bats left, throws left. ... Full name: James Patrick Edmonds.

HIGH SCHOOL: Diamond Bar (Calif.).

TRANSACTIONS/CAREER NOTES: Selected by California Angels organization in seventh round of free-agent draft (June 1, 1988). ... On disabled list (June 19-September 2, 1989; April 10-May 7 and May 23, 1991-remainder of season). ... On Vancouver disabled list (June 29-July 19, 1993). ... On California disabled list (May 26-June 10 and June 12-July 18, 1996); included rehabilitation assignment to Lake Elsinore (July 13-18). ... Angels franchise renamed Anaheim Angels for 1997 season. ... On disabled list (August 1-16, 1997).

HONORS: Named outfielder on The Sporting News A.L. All-Star team (1995). ... Won A.L. Gold Glove as outfielder (1997-98).
STATISTICAL NOTES: Had 23-game hitting streak (June 4-29, 1995). ... Career major league grand slams: 1.

Year	Team (League)	Pos.	G	AB	R	H	2B	3B	HR	RBI	Avg.	BB	SO	SB	PO	A	E	Avg.
1988—	Bend (Northwest)	OF	35	122	23	27	4	0	0	13	.221	20	44	4	59	1	1	.984
1989—	Quad City (Midwest)	OF	31	92	11	24	4	0	1	4	.261	7	34	1	47	2	3	.942
1990—	Palm Springs (Calif.)	OF	91	314	36	92	18	6	3	56	.293	27	75	5	199	9	10	.954
1991—	Palm Springs (Calif.)	OF-1B-P	60	187	28	55	15	1	2	27	.294	40	57	2	97	6	0	1.000
1992—	Midland (Texas)	OF	70	246	42	77	15	2	8	32	.313	41	83	3	139	6	5	.967
—	Edmonton (PCL)	OF	50	194	37	58	15	2	6	36	.299	14	55	3	79	5	1	.988
1993—	Vancouver (PCL)	OF	95	356	59	112	28	4	9	74	.315	41	81	6	167	4	3	.983
—	California (A.L.)	OF	18	61	5	15	4	1	0	4	.246	2	16	0	47	4	1	.981
1994—	California (A.L.)	OF-1B	94	289	35	79	13	1	5	37	.273	30	72	4	301	20	3	.991
1995—	California (A.L.)	OF	141	558	120	162	30	4	33	107	.290	51	130	1	401	8	1	.998
1996—	California (A.L.)	OF-DH	114	431	73	131	28	3	27	66	.304	46	101	4	280	6	1	.997
—	Lake Elsinore (Calif.)	OF	5	15	4	6	2	0	1	4	.400	1	1	0	5	0	0	1.000
1997—	Anaheim (A.L.)	OF-1B-DH	133	502	82	146	27	0	26	80	.291	60	80	5	395	16	5	.988
1998—	Anaheim (A.L.)	OF	154	599	115	184	42	1	25	91	.307	57	114	7	392	10	5	.988
Major league totals (6 years)			654	2440	430	717	144	10	116	385	.294	246	513	21	1816	64	16	.992

ALL-STAR GAME RECORD

Year	League	Pos.	AB	R	H	2B	3B	HR	RBI	Avg.	BB	SO	SB	PO	A	E	Avg.
1995—	American	PH-OF	1	0	0	0	0	0	0	.000	0	1	0	0	0	0	...

RECORD AS PITCHER

Year	Team (League)	W	L	Pct.	ERA	G	GS	CG	ShO	Sv.	IP	H	R	ER	BB	SO
1991—	Palm Springs (Calif.)	0	0	...	0.00	1	0	0	0	0	2	1	0	0	3	2

EDMONDSON, BRIAN   P   MARLINS

PERSONAL: Born January 29, 1973, in Fontana, Calif. ... 6-2/175. ... Throws right, bats right. ... Full name: Brian Christopher Edmondson.
HIGH SCHOOL: Norte Vista (Riverside, Calif.).
TRANSACTIONS/CAREER NOTES: Selected by Detroit Tigers organization in third round of free-agent draft (June 3, 1991); pick received as part of compensation for Milwaukee Brewers signing Type B free-agent P Edwin Nunez. ... Claimed on waivers by New York Mets (April 24, 1995). ... Selected by Atlanta Braves from Mets organization in Rule 5 major league draft (December 15, 1997). ... Claimed on waivers by Florida Marlins (June 4, 1998).
STATISTICAL NOTES: Tied for Appalachian League lead with seven home runs allowed in 1991.

Year	Team (League)	W	L	Pct.	ERA	G	GS	CG	ShO	Sv.	IP	H	R	ER	BB	SO
1991—	Bristol (Appalachian)	4	4	.500	4.57	12	12	1	0	0	69	72	38	35	23	42
1992—	Fayetteville (S. Atl.)	10	6	.625	3.36	28	27	3	1	0	155 1/3	145	69	58	67	125
1993—	Lakeland (Fla. St.)	8	5	.615	2.99	19	19	1	0	0	114 1/3	115	44	38	43	64
—	London (Eastern)	0	4	.000	6.26	5	5	1	0	0	23	30	23	16	13	17
1994—	Trenton (Eastern)	11	9	.550	4.56	26	26	2	0	0	162	171	89	82	61	90
1995—	Binghamton (Eastern)■	7	11	.389	4.76	23	22	2	1	0	134 1/3	150	82	71	59	69
1996—	Binghamton (Eastern)	6	6	.500	4.25	39	13	1	0	0	114 1/3	130	69	54	38	83
1997—	Binghamton (Eastern)	2	0	1.000	1.23	14	0	0	0	3	22	14	4	3	7	18
—	Norfolk (Int'l)	4	3	.571	2.90	31	4	0	0	1	68 1/3	62	27	22	37	65
1998—	Atlanta (N.L.)■	0	1	.000	4.32	10	0	0	0	0	16 2/3	14	10	8	8	8
—	Florida (N.L.)■	4	3	.571	3.79	43	0	0	0	0	59 1/3	62	28	25	29	32
Major league totals (1 year)		4	4	.500	3.91	53	0	0	0	0	76	76	38	33	37	40

EDSELL, GEOFF   P   ANGELS

PERSONAL: Born December 10, 1971, in Butler, Pa. ... 6-2/194. ... Throws right, bats right. ... Full name: Geoffrey Scott Edsell.
HIGH SCHOOL: Montoursville (Pa.).
COLLEGE: Old Dominion.
TRANSACTIONS/CAREER NOTES: Selected by Minnesota Twins organization in 33rd round of free-agent draft (June 4, 1990); did not sign. ... Selected by California Angels organization in sixth round of free-agent draft (June 3, 1993). ... On Midland suspended list (June 5-7, 1996). ... Angels franchise renamed Anaheim Angels for 1997 season.
STATISTICAL NOTES: Tied for Pacific Coast League lead with 12 hit batsmen in 1997.

Year	Team (League)	W	L	Pct.	ERA	G	GS	CG	ShO	Sv.	IP	H	R	ER	BB	SO
1993—	Boise (Northwest)	4	3	.571	6.89	13	13	1	0	0	64	64	52	49	40	63
1994—	Cedar Rapids (Midw.)	11	5	.688	3.02	17	17	4	1	0	125 1/3	109	54	42	65	84
—	Lake Elsinore (Calif.)	2	2	.500	4.05	9	7	0	0	0	40	38	21	18	24	26
1995—	Lake Elsinore (Calif.)	8	12	.400	3.67	23	22	1	1	0	139 2/3	127	81	57	67	134
—	Midland (Texas)	2	3	.400	5.91	5	5	1	0	0	32	39	26	21	16	19
1996—	Midland (Texas)	5	5	.500	4.70	14	14	0	0	0	88	84	53	46	47	60
—	Vancouver (PCL)	4	6	.400	3.43	15	15	3	•2	0	105	93	45	40	45	48
1997—	Vancouver (PCL)	14	11	.560	5.15	30	*29	*6	1	0	*183 1/3	196	121	105	*96	95
1998—	Vancouver (PCL)	4	8	.333	4.17	56	0	0	0	4	69	63	45	32	33	64

EILAND, DAVE   P

PERSONAL: Born July 5, 1966, in Dade City, Fla. ... 6-3/210. ... Throws right, bats right. ... Full name: David William Eiland. ... Name pronounced EYE-land.
HIGH SCHOOL: Zephyrhills (Fla.).
COLLEGE: South Florida, then Florida.

TRANSACTIONS/CAREER NOTES: Selected by New York Yankees organization in seventh round of free-agent draft (June 2, 1987). ... On New York disabled list (May 28-July 12, 1991); included rehabilitation assignment to Columbus (June 16-July 12). ... Released by Yankees (January 19, 1992). ... Signed by San Diego Padres organization (January 27, 1992). ... On San Diego disabled list (May 4-June 26, 1992); included rehabilitation assignment to Las Vegas (May 27-June 25). ... On San Diego disabled list (July 5-August 26, 1992); included rehabilitation assignment to Las Vegas (July 28-August 26). ... Granted free agency (December 7, 1992). ... Signed by Wichita, Padres organization (February 28, 1993). ... Granted free agency (May 27, 1993). ... Signed by Cleveland Indians organization (May 29, 1993). ... Traded by Indians organization to Texas Rangers organization for P Gerald Alexander and P Allan Anderson (August 4, 1993). ... Granted free agency (October 15, 1993). ... Signed by Yankees organization (March 12, 1994). ... Granted free agency (October 3, 1995). ... Signed by St. Louis Cardinals organization (December 6, 1995). ... On Louisville temporarily inactive list (April 10-18, 1996). ... On Louisville disabled list (May 14-22 and June 3-15, 1996). ... Released by Cardinals (June 15, 1996). ... Signed by Yankees organization (June 18, 1996). ... Granted free agency (October 15, 1996). ... Re-signed by Yankees organization (December 23, 1996). ... On Columbus disabled list (May 14-25, 1997). ... Granted free agency (October 15, 1997). ... Signed by Tampa Bay Devil Rays (December 19, 1997). ... Granted free agency (October 15, 1998).

HONORS: Named International League Most Valuable Pitcher (1990).

STATISTICAL NOTES: Hit home run in first major league at-bat (April 10, 1992).

Year	Team (League)	W	L	Pct.	ERA	G	GS	CG	ShO	Sv.	IP	H	R	ER	BB	SO
1987—	Oneonta (N.Y.-Penn)	4	0	1.000	1.84	5	5	0	0	0	29 1/3	20	6	6	3	16
	Fort Lauderdale (FSL)	5	3	.625	1.88	8	8	4	1	0	62 1/3	57	17	13	8	28
1988—	Alb./Colon. (East.)	9	5	.643	2.56	18	18	•7	2	0	119 1/3	95	39	34	22	66
	Columbus (Int'l)	1	1	.500	2.59	4	4	0	0	0	24 1/3	25	8	7	6	13
	New York (A.L.)	0	0	. . .	6.39	3	3	0	0	0	12 2/3	15	9	9	4	7
1989—	Columbus (Int'l)	9	4	.692	3.76	18	18	2	0	0	103	107	47	43	21	45
	New York (A.L.)	1	3	.250	5.77	6	6	0	0	0	34 1/3	44	25	22	13	11
1990—	Columbus (Int'l)	*16	5	.762	2.87	27	26	*11	•3	0	175 1/3	155	63	56	32	96
	New York (A.L.)	2	1	.667	3.56	5	5	0	0	0	30 1/3	31	14	12	5	16
1991—	New York (A.L.)	2	5	.286	5.33	18	13	0	0	0	72 2/3	87	51	43	23	18
	Columbus (Int'l)	6	1	.857	2.40	9	9	2	0	0	60	54	22	16	7	18
1992—	San Diego (N.L.)■	0	2	.000	5.67	7	7	0	0	0	27	33	21	17	5	10
	Las Vegas (PCL)	4	5	.444	5.23	14	14	0	0	0	63 2/3	78	43	37	11	31
1993—	San Diego (N.L.)	0	3	.000	5.21	10	9	0	0	0	48 1/3	58	33	28	17	14
	Charlotte (Int'l)■	1	3	.250	5.30	8	8	0	0	0	35 2/3	42	22	21	12	13
	Oklahoma City (A.A.)■	3	1	.750	4.29	7	7	1	0	0	35 2/3	39	18	17	9	15
1994—	Columbus (Int'l)	9	6	.600	3.58	26	26	0	0	0	140 2/3	141	72	56	33	84
1995—	Columbus (Int'l)	8	7	.533	3.14	19	18	1	1	0	109	109	44	38	22	62
	New York (A.L.)	1	1	.500	6.30	4	1	0	0	0	10	16	10	7	3	6
1996—	Louisville (A.A.)■	0	1	.000	5.55	8	6	0	0	0	24 1/3	27	17	15	8	17
	Columbus (Int'l)■	8	4	.667	2.92	15	15	3	0	0	92 1/3	77	37	30	13	76
1997—	Columbus (Int'l)	4	2	.667	6.64	13	11	0	0	0	62 1/3	80	47	46	14	43
	GC Yankees (GCL)	0	1	.000	9.00	2	1	0	0	0	7	12	8	7	0	5
	Tampa (Fla. St.)	1	0	1.000	3.75	3	3	0	0	0	12	11	5	5	0	11
1998—	Durham (International)■	13	5	.722	2.99	28	28	2	1	0	171 2/3	177	70	57	27	112
	Tampa Bay (A.L.)	0	1	.000	20.25	1	1	0	0	0	2 2/3	6	6	6	3	1
A.L. totals (6 years)		6	11	.353	5.48	37	29	0	0	0	162 2/3	199	115	99	51	59
N.L. totals (2 years)		0	5	.000	5.38	17	16	0	0	0	75 1/3	91	54	45	22	24
Major league totals (8 years)		6	16	.273	5.45	54	45	0	0	0	238	290	169	144	73	83

EINERTSON, CHIEF   P   YANKEES

PERSONAL: Born September 4, 1972, in Rhinelander, Wis. ... 6-2/190. ... Throws right, bats right. ... Full name: Darrell Lee Einertson.
HIGH SCHOOL: Urbandale (Iowa).
JUNIOR COLLEGE: Indian Hills Community College (Iowa).
COLLEGE: Cameron, then Iowa Wesleyan.
TRANSACTIONS/CAREER NOTES: Selected by New York Yankees organization in 11th round of free-agent draft (June 1, 1995). ... On Norwich disabled list (May 22-August 31, 1998). ... On New York disabled list (August 31, 1998-remainder of season).

Year	Team (League)	W	L	Pct.	ERA	G	GS	CG	ShO	Sv.	IP	H	R	ER	BB	SO
1995—	Oneonta (N.Y.-Penn)	0	4	.000	1.88	25	0	0	0	0	38 1/3	32	20	8	15	35
1996—	Greensboro (S. Atl.)	3	9	.250	2.70	48	0	0	0	0	70	69	29	21	19	48
1997—	Tampa (Fla. St.)	5	4	.556	2.15	45	0	0	0	6	71	63	24	17	19	55
1998—	Norwich (Eastern)	3	1	.750	1.02	17	0	0	0	0	35 1/3	23	7	4	10	33

EISENREICH, JIM   OF

PERSONAL: Born April 18, 1959, in St. Cloud, Minn. ... 5-11/195. ... Bats left, throws left. ... Full name: James Michael Eisenreich. ... Name pronounced EYES-en-rike.
HIGH SCHOOL: Technical (St. Cloud, Minn.).
COLLEGE: St. Cloud (Minn.) State.
TRANSACTIONS/CAREER NOTES: Selected by Minnesota Twins organization in 16th round of free-agent draft (June 3, 1980). ... On disabled list (May 6-28 and June 18-September 1, 1982). ... On disabled list (April 7, 1983); then transferred to voluntarily retired list (May 27, 1983-remainder of season). ... On disabled list (April 26-May 18, 1984). ... On voluntarily retired list (June 4, 1984-September 29, 1986). ... Claimed on waivers by Kansas City Royals (October 2, 1986). ... On Kansas City disabled list (August 25-September 9, 1987 and July 22-August 6, 1989). ... Granted free agency (October 30, 1991). ... Re-signed by Royals (January 31, 1992). ... On disabled list (August 12-September 7, 1992). ... Granted free agency (October 30, 1992). ... Signed by Philadelphia Phillies (January 20, 1993). ... Granted free agency (October 29, 1993). ... Re-signed by Phillies (November 24, 1993). ... Re-signed by Phillies (November 1, 1995). ... Re-signed by Phillies (December 7, 1995). ... Granted free agency (November 18, 1996). ... Signed by Florida Marlins (December 3, 1996). ... Traded by Marlins with OF Gary Sheffield, 3B Bobby Bonilla, C Charles Johnson and P Manuel Barrios to Los Angeles Dodgers for C Mike Piazza and 3B Todd Zeile (May 15, 1998). ... Granted free agency (October 27, 1998).
HONORS: Named Appalachian League co-Player of the Year (1980).
STATISTICAL NOTES: Career major league grand slams: 3.

Year	Team (League)	Pos.	G	AB	R	H	2B	3B	HR	RBI	Avg.	BB	SO	SB	PO	A	E	Avg.
1980—	Elizabethton (App.).....	OF	67	258	47	77	12	•4	3	41	.298	35	32	12	151	7	3	.981
—	Wis. Rap. (Mid.).........	DH	5	16	4	7	0	0	0	5	.438	1	0	1	...	...	...	...
1981—	Wis. Rap. (Mid.)........	OF	*134	489	101	•152	*27	0	23	99	.311	84	70	9	*295	17	9	.972
1982—	Minnesota (A.L.)	OF	34	99	10	30	6	0	2	9	.303	11	13	0	72	0	2	.973
1983—	Minnesota (A.L.)	OF	2	7	1	2	1	0	0	0	.286	1	1	0	6	1	0	1.000
1984—	Minnesota (A.L.)	OF-DH	12	32	1	7	1	0	0	3	.219	2	4	2	5	0	0	1.000
1985—	....					Out of organized baseball.												
1986—	....					Out of organized baseball.												
1987—	Memphis (Sou.)■......	DH	70	275	60	105	36	•10	11	57	.382	47	44	13	...	...	...	...
—	Kansas City (A.L.)	DH	44	105	10	25	8	2	4	21	.238	7	13	1	...	...	...	...
1988—	Kansas City (A.L.)	OF-DH	82	202	26	44	8	1	1	19	.218	6	31	9	109	0	4	.965
—	Omaha (A.A.)..............	OF	36	142	28	41	8	3	4	14	.289	9	20	9	73	1	1	.987
1989—	Kansas City (A.L.)	OF-DH	134	475	64	139	33	7	9	59	.293	37	44	27	273	4	3	.989
1990—	Kansas City (A.L.)	OF-DH	142	496	61	139	29	7	5	51	.280	42	51	12	261	6	1	*.996
1991—	Kansas City (A.L.)	OF-1-DH	135	375	47	113	22	3	2	47	.301	20	35	5	243	12	5	.981
1992—	Kansas City (A.L.)	OF-DH	113	353	31	95	13	3	2	28	.269	24	36	11	180	1	1	.995
1993—	Philadelphia (N.L.)■ ..	OF-1-B	153	362	51	115	17	4	7	54	.318	26	36	5	223	6	1	.996
1994—	Philadelphia (N.L.)......	OF	104	290	42	87	15	4	4	43	.300	33	31	6	179	4	2	.989
1995—	Philadelphia (N.L.)......	OF	129	377	46	119	22	2	10	55	.316	38	44	10	205	2	0	*1.000
1996—	Philadelphia (N.L.)......	OF	113	338	45	122	24	3	3	41	.361	31	32	11	167	3	4	.977
1997—	Florida (N.L.)■...........	OF-1-B-DH	120	293	36	82	19	1	2	34	.280	30	28	0	211	13	2	.991
1998—	Florida (N.L.)..............	1B-OF	30	64	9	16	1	0	1	7	.250	4	14	2	62	2	2	.970
—	Los Angeles (N.L.)■ ..	OF-1-B-DH	75	127	12	25	2	2	0	6	.197	12	22	4	53	3	1	.982
American League totals (9 years)			698	2144	251	594	121	23	25	237	.277	150	228	67	1149	24	16	.987
National League totals (6 years)			724	1851	241	566	100	16	27	240	.306	174	207	38	1100	33	12	.990
Major league totals (15 years)			1422	3995	492	1160	221	39	52	477	.290	324	435	105	2249	57	28	.988

DIVISION SERIES RECORD

Year	Team (League)	Pos.	G	AB	R	H	2B	3B	HR	RBI	Avg.	BB	SO	SB	PO	A	E	Avg.
1997—	Florida (N.L.).............	PH	2	0	0	0	0	0	0	0	...	2	0	0	...	...	...	...

CHAMPIONSHIP SERIES RECORD

Year	Team (League)	Pos.	G	AB	R	H	2B	3B	HR	RBI	Avg.	BB	SO	SB	PO	A	E	Avg.
1993—	Philadelphia (N.L.)......	OF-PH	6	15	0	2	1	0	0	1	.133	0	2	0	6	0	0	1.000
1997—	Florida (N.L.)	OF	1	3	0	0	0	0	0	0	.000	0	0	0	2	0	0	1.000
Championship series totals (2 years)			7	18	0	2	1	0	0	1	.111	0	2	0	8	0	0	1.000

WORLD SERIES RECORD

NOTES: Member of World Series championship team (1997).

Year	Team (League)	Pos.	G	AB	R	H	2B	3B	HR	RBI	Avg.	BB	SO	SB	PO	A	E	Avg.
1993—	Philadelphia (N.L.)......	OF	6	26	3	6	0	0	1	7	.231	2	4	0	18	0	0	1.000
1997—	Florida (N.L.)	PH-DH-1B	5	8	1	4	0	0	1	3	.500	3	1	0	3	1	0	1.000
World Series totals (2 years)			11	34	4	10	0	0	2	10	.294	5	5	0	21	1	0	1.000

E

ELARTON, SCOTT   P   ASTROS

PERSONAL: Born February 23, 1976, in Lamar, Colo. ... 6-7/240. ... Throws right, bats right. ... Full name: Vincent Scott Elarton.
HIGH SCHOOL: Lamar (Colo.).
TRANSACTIONS/CAREER NOTES: Selected by Houston Astros organization in first round (25th pick overall) of free-agent draft (June 2, 1994).

Year	Team (League)	W	L	Pct.	ERA	G	GS	CG	ShO	Sv.	IP	H	R	ER	BB	SO
1994—	GC Astros (GCL)	4	0	1.000	0.00	5	5	0	0	0	28	9	0	0	5	28
—	Quad City (Midwest)	4	1	.800	3.29	9	9	0	0	0	54²/₃	42	23	20	18	42
1995—	Quad City (Midwest)	13	7	.650	4.45	26	26	0	0	0	149²/₃	149	86	74	71	112
1996—	Kissimmee (Florida State)..	12	7	.632	2.92	27	27	3	1	0	172¹/₃	154	67	56	54	130
1997—	Jackson (Texas)	7	4	.636	3.24	20	20	2	0	0	133¹/₃	103	57	48	47	141
—	New Orleans (A.A.)............	4	4	.500	5.33	9	9	0	0	0	54	51	36	32	17	50
1998—	New Orleans (PCL)............	9	4	.692	4.01	14	14	2	1	0	92	71	42	41	41	100
—	Houston (N.L.)	2	1	.667	3.32	28	2	0	0	2	57	40	21	21	20	56
Major league totals (1 year)........		2	1	.667	3.32	28	2	0	0	2	57	40	21	21	20	56

DIVISION SERIES RECORD

Year	Team (League)	W	L	Pct.	ERA	G	GS	CG	ShO	Sv.	IP	H	R	ER	BB	SO
1998—	Houston (N.L.)	0	1	.000	4.50	1	0	0	0	0	2	1	1	1	1	3

ELDRED, CAL   P   BREWERS

PERSONAL: Born November 24, 1967, in Cedar Rapids, Iowa. ... 6-4/233. ... Throws right, bats right. ... Full name: Calvin John Eldred.
HIGH SCHOOL: Urbana (Iowa) Community.
COLLEGE: Iowa.
TRANSACTIONS/CAREER NOTES: Selected by Milwaukee Brewers organization in first round (17th pick overall) of free-agent draft (June 5, 1989). ... On disabled list (May 15, 1995-remainder of season). ... On Milwaukee disabled list (March 29-July 14, 1996); included rehabilitation assignment to New Orleans (June 10-July 9). ... On disabled list (July 26, 1998-remainder of season).
HONORS: Named A.L. Rookie Pitcher of the Year by THE SPORTING NEWS (1992).
STATISTICAL NOTES: Led American Association with 12 hit batsmen in 1991.
MISCELLANEOUS: Appeared in one game as pinch runner (1998).

Year	Team (League)	W	L	Pct.	ERA	G	GS	CG	ShO	Sv.	IP	H	R	ER	BB	SO
1989—	Beloit (Midwest)	2	1	.667	2.30	5	5	0	0	0	31 1/3	23	10	8	11	32
1990—	Stockton (California)	4	2	.667	1.62	7	7	3	1	0	50	31	12	9	19	75
—	El Paso (Texas)	5	4	.556	4.49	19	19	0	0	0	110 1/3	126	61	55	47	93
1991—	Denver (Am. Assoc.)	13	9	.591	3.75	29	*29	3	1	0	*185	161	82	77	84	*168
—	Milwaukee (A.L.)	2	0	1.000	4.50	3	3	0	0	0	16	20	9	8	6	10
1992—	Denver (Am. Assoc.)	10	6	.625	3.00	19	19	4	1	0	141	122	49	47	42	99
—	Milwaukee (A.L.)	11	2	.846	1.79	14	14	2	1	0	100 1/3	76	21	20	23	62
1993—	Milwaukee (A.L.)	16	16	.500	4.01	36	•36	8	1	0	*258	232	120	115	91	180
1994—	Milwaukee (A.L.)	11	11	.500	4.68	25	•25	6	0	0	179	158	96	93	84	98
1995—	Milwaukee (A.L.)	1	1	.500	3.42	4	4	0	0	0	23 2/3	24	10	9	10	18
1996—	New Orleans (A.A.)	2	2	.500	3.34	6	6	0	0	0	32 1/3	24	12	12	17	30
—	Milwaukee (A.L.)	4	4	.500	4.46	15	15	0	0	0	84 2/3	82	43	42	38	50
1997—	Milwaukee (A.L.)	13	•15	.464	4.99	34	34	1	1	0	202	207	118	112	89	122
1998—	Milwaukee (N.L.)	4	8	.333	4.80	23	23	0	0	0	133	157	82	71	61	86
A.L. totals (7 years)		58	49	.542	4.16	131	131	17	3	0	863 2/3	799	417	399	341	540
N.L. totals (1 year)		4	8	.333	4.80	23	23	0	0	0	133	157	82	71	61	86
Major league totals (8 years)		62	57	.521	4.24	154	154	17	3	0	996 2/3	956	499	470	402	626

ELSTER, KEVIN   SS

PERSONAL: Born August 3, 1964, in San Pedro, Calif. ... 6-2/205. ... Bats right, throws right. ... Full name: Kevin Daniel Elster.

HIGH SCHOOL: Marina (Huntington Beach, Calif.).

JUNIOR COLLEGE: Golden West College (Calif.).

TRANSACTIONS/CAREER NOTES: Selected by New York Mets organization in second round of free-agent draft (January 17, 1984). ... On Jackson disabled list (August 11, 1985-remainder of season). ... On disabled list (August 4, 1990-remainder of season; May 6-21, 1991; and April 13, 1992-remainder of season). ... Granted free agency (December 19, 1992). ... Signed by Los Angeles Dodgers organization (January 12, 1993). ... On Albuquerque disabled list (April 8-May 2, 1993). ... Released by Dodgers (May 17, 1993). ... Signed by Florida Marlins organization (May 22, 1993). ... Released by Marlins organization (June 4, 1993). ... Signed by San Diego Padres organization (December 17, 1993). ... Released by Padres organization (March 21, 1994). ... Signed by New York Yankees organization (May 1, 1994). ... On Columbus temporarily inactive list (May 1-June 1, 1994). ... On New York disabled list (July 7, 1994-remainder of season); included rehabilitation assignment to Albany (August 1-20). ... Released by Yankees (June 8, 1995). ... Signed by Kansas City Royals organization (June 29, 1995). ... Released by Royals organization (July 3, 1995). ... Signed by Philadelphia Phillies organization (July 7, 1995). ... Granted free agency (October 5, 1995). ... Signed by Texas Rangers organization (January 16, 1996). ... Granted free agency (October 31, 1996). ... Signed by Pittsburgh Pirates (December 20, 1996). ... On disabled list (May 17, 1997-remainder of season). ... Granted free agency (October 28, 1997). ... Signed by Rangers (December 8, 1997). ... On Texas disabled list (June 2-17, 1998). ... Released by Rangers (July 31, 1998).

RECORDS: Holds major league single-season record for fewest putouts by shortstop who led league in putouts—235 (1989). ... Holds N.L. career record for most consecutive errorless games by shortstop—88 (July 20, 1988 through May 8, 1989).

HONORS: Named A.L. Comeback Player of the Year by THE SPORTING NEWS (1996).

STATISTICAL NOTES: Led New York-Pennsylvania League shortstops with 358 total chances and 45 double plays in 1984. ... Led Texas League shortstops with 589 total chances and 83 double plays in 1986. ... Career major league grand slams: 2.

						BATTING								FIELDING			
Year	Team (League)	Pos.	G	AB	R	H	2B	3B	HR	RBI	Avg.	BB	SO	SB	PO	A	E	Avg.
1984—	Little Falls (NYP)	SS	71	257	35	66	7	3	3	35	.257	35	41	13	*128	214	16	*.955
1985—	Lynchburg (Caro.)	SS	59	224	41	66	9	0	7	26	.295	33	21	8	82	195	16	.945
—	Jackson (Texas)	SS	59	214	30	55	13	0	2	22	.257	19	29	2	107	220	10	.970
1986—	Jackson (Texas)	SS	127	435	69	117	19	3	2	52	.269	61	46	6	*196	*365	28	*.952
—	New York (N.L.)	SS	19	30	3	5	1	0	0	0	.167	3	8	0	16	35	2	.962
1987—	Tidewater (Int'l)	SS	134	*549	83	*170	33	7	8	74	.310	35	62	7	219	419	21	.968
—	New York (N.L.)	SS	5	10	1	4	2	0	0	1	.400	0	1	0	4	6	1	.909
1988—	New York (N.L.)	SS	149	406	41	87	11	1	9	37	.214	35	47	2	196	345	13	.977
1989—	New York (N.L.)	SS	151	458	52	106	25	2	10	55	.231	34	77	4	*235	374	15	.976
1990—	New York (N.L.)	SS	92	314	36	65	20	1	9	45	.207	30	54	2	159	251	17	.960
1991—	New York (N.L.)	SS	115	348	33	84	16	2	6	36	.241	40	53	2	149	299	14	.970
1992—	New York (N.L.)	SS	6	18	0	4	0	0	0	0	.222	0	2	0	8	10	0	1.000
1993—	San Antonio (Tex.)■	SS	10	39	5	11	2	1	0	7	.282	4	4	0	14	31	4	.918
1994—	Tampa (Fla. St.)■	2B-3B	3	11	2	2	1	0	0	2	.182	2	2	0	4	7	1	.917
—	Alb./Colon. (East.)	SS-3B-2B	41	135	19	33	7	0	2	21	.244	21	16	2	64	112	7	.962
—	New York (A.L.)	SS	7	20	0	0	0	0	0	0	.000	1	6	0	5	27	0	1.000
1995—	New York (A.L.)	SS-2B	10	17	1	2	1	0	0	0	.118	1	5	0	10	14	0	1.000
—	Omaha (A.A.)■	SS	11	42	5	10	4	0	0	6	.238	5	8	0	22	30	0	1.000
—	Scran./W.B. (Int'l)■	SS	5	17	2	5	3	0	0	2	.294	2	3	0	6	12	1	.947
—	Philadelphia (N.L.)	SS-1B-3B	26	53	10	11	4	1	1	9	.208	7	14	0	37	38	1	.987
1996—	Texas (A.L.)■	SS	157	515	79	130	32	2	24	99	.252	52	138	4	*285	441	14	.981
1997—	Pittsburgh (N.L.)■	SS	39	138	14	31	6	2	7	25	.225	21	39	0	54	123	1	.994
1998—	Texas (A.L.)■	SS	84	297	33	69	10	1	8	37	.232	33	66	0	107	257	9	.976
American League totals (4 years)			258	849	113	201	43	3	32	136	.237	87	215	4	407	739	23	.980
National League totals (9 years)			602	1775	190	397	85	9	42	208	.224	170	295	10	858	1481	64	.973
Major league totals (12 years)			860	2624	303	598	128	12	74	344	.228	257	510	14	1265	2220	87	.976

DIVISION SERIES RECORD

						BATTING								FIELDING			
Year	Team (League)	Pos.	G	AB	R	H	2B	3B	HR	RBI	Avg.	BB	SO	SB	PO	A	E	Avg.
1996—	Texas (A.L.)	SS	4	12	2	4	2	0	0	0	.333	3	2	1	6	7	1	.929

CHAMPIONSHIP SERIES RECORD

						BATTING								FIELDING			
Year	Team (League)	Pos.	G	AB	R	H	2B	3B	HR	RBI	Avg.	BB	SO	SB	PO	A	E	Avg.
1986—	New York (N.L.)	SS-PR	4	3	0	0	0	0	0	0	.000	0	1	0	2	3	0	1.000
1988—	New York (N.L.)	SS-PR	5	8	1	2	1	0	0	1	.250	3	0	0	7	7	2	.875
Championship series totals (2 years)			9	11	1	2	1	0	0	1	.182	3	1	0	9	10	2	.905

E

NOTES: Member of World Series championship team (1986).

Year Team (League)	Pos.	G	AB	R	H	2B	3B	HR	RBI	Avg.	BB	SO	SB	PO	A	E	Avg.
							BATTING								FIELDING		
1986— New York (N.L.)..........	SS	1	1	0	0	0	0	0	0	.000	0	0	0	3	3	1	.857

EMBREE, ALAN   P   GIANTS

PERSONAL: Born January 23, 1970, in Vancouver, Wash. ... 6-2/190. ... Throws left, bats left. ... Full name: Alan Duane Embree.
HIGH SCHOOL: Prairie (Vancouver, Wash.).
TRANSACTIONS/CAREER NOTES: Selected by Cleveland Indians organization in fifth round of free-agent draft (June 5, 1989). ... On Cleveland disabled list (April 1-June 2 and June 2, 1993-remainder of season); included rehabilitation assignment to Canton/Akron (June 2-15). ... On Cleveland disabled list (August 1-September 7, 1996); included rehabilitation assignment to Buffalo (August 6-September 4). ... Traded by Indians with OF Kenny Lofton to Atlanta Braves for OF Marquis Grissom and OF Dave Justice (March 25, 1997). ... Traded by Braves to Arizona Diamondbacks for P Russ Springer (June 23, 1998). ... Traded by Diamondbacks to San Francisco Giants for OF Dante Powell (November 10, 1998).

Year Team (League)	W	L	Pct.	ERA	G	GS	CG	ShO	Sv.	IP	H	R	ER	BB	SO
1990— Burlington (Appalachian)....	4	4	.500	2.64	15	•15	0	0	0	81²/₃	87	36	24	30	58
1991— Columbus (S. Atl.)............	10	8	.556	3.59	27	26	3	1	0	155¹/₃	126	80	62	77	137
1992— Kinston (Carolina)	10	5	.667	3.30	15	15	1	0	0	101	89	48	37	32	115
— Cant./Akr. (Eastern)	7	2	.778	2.28	12	12	0	0	0	79	61	24	20	28	56
— Cleveland (A.L.)................	0	2	.000	7.00	4	4	0	0	0	18	19	14	14	8	12
1993— Cant./Akr. (Eastern)	0	0	...	3.38	1	1	0	0	0	5¹/₃	3	2	2	3	4
1994— Cant./Akr. (Eastern)	9	•16	.360	5.50	30	27	2	1	0	157	183	106	96	64	81
1995— Buffalo (A.A.)................	3	4	.429	0.89	30	0	0	0	5	40²/₃	31	10	4	19	56
— Cleveland (A.L.)................	3	2	.600	5.11	23	0	0	0	1	24²/₃	23	16	14	16	23
1996— Cleveland (A.L.)................	1	1	.500	6.39	24	0	0	0	0	31	30	26	22	21	33
— Buffalo (A.A.)................	4	1	.800	3.93	20	0	0	0	5	34¹/₃	26	16	15	14	46
1997— Atlanta (N.L.)■..........	3	1	.750	2.54	66	0	0	0	0	46	36	13	13	20	45
1998— Atlanta (N.L.)............	1	0	1.000	4.34	20	0	0	0	0	18²/₃	23	14	9	10	19
— Arizona (N.L.)■............	3	2	.600	4.11	35	0	0	0	1	35	33	18	16	13	24
A.L. totals (3 years)	4	5	.444	6.11	51	4	0	0	1	73²/₃	72	56	50	45	68
N.L. totals (2 years)	7	3	.700	3.43	121	0	0	0	1	99²/₃	92	45	38	43	88
Major league totals (5 years)......	11	8	.579	4.57	172	4	0	0	2	173¹/₃	164	101	88	88	156

DIVISION SERIES RECORD

Year Team (League)	W	L	Pct.	ERA	G	GS	CG	ShO	Sv.	IP	H	R	ER	BB	SO
1996— Cleveland (A.L.)..................	0	0	...	9.00	3	0	0	0	0	1	0	1	1	0	1

CHAMPIONSHIP SERIES RECORD

Year Team (League)	W	L	Pct.	ERA	G	GS	CG	ShO	Sv.	IP	H	R	ER	BB	SO
1995— Cleveland (A.L.)..................	0	0	...	0.00	1	0	0	0	0	¹/₃	0	0	0	0	1
1997— Atlanta (N.L.)..................	0	0	...	0.00	1	0	0	0	0	1	0	0	0	1	1
Champ. series totals (2 years)	0	0	...	0.00	2	0	0	0	0	1¹/₃	0	0	0	1	2

WORLD SERIES RECORD

Year Team (League)	W	L	Pct.	ERA	G	GS	CG	ShO	Sv.	IP	H	R	ER	BB	SO
1995— Cleveland (A.L.)..................	0	0	...	2.70	4	0	0	0	0	3¹/₃	2	1	1	2	2

ENCARNACION, JUAN   OF   TIGERS

PERSONAL: Born March 8, 1976, in Las Matas de Faran, Dominican Republic. ... 6-3/187. ... Bats right, throws right. ... Full name: Juan DeDios Encarnacion. ... Name pronounced en-car-nah-CION.
HIGH SCHOOL: Liceo Mercedes Maria Mateo (Las Matas de Faran, Dominican Republic).
TRANSACTIONS/CAREER NOTES: Signed as non-drafted free agent by Detroit Tigers organization (December 27, 1992). ... On Detroit disabled list (March 20-April 29, 1998); included rehabilitation assignment to Lakeland (April 24-29).
STATISTICAL NOTES: Led Southern League in being hit by pitch with 12 in 1997. ... Tied for International League lead in double plays by outfielder with three in 1998.

Year Team (League)	Pos.	G	AB	R	H	2B	3B	HR	RBI	Avg.	BB	SO	SB	PO	A	E	Avg.
							BATTING								FIELDING		
1993— Dom. Tigers (DSL)	OF	72	251	36	63	13	4	13	49	.251	15	65	6	110	13	17	.879
1994— Bristol (Appal.)...........	OF	54	197	16	49	7	1	4	31	.249	13	54	9	83	*9	3	.968
— Fayetteville (SAL)	OF	24	83	6	16	1	1	4	4	.193	8	36	1	22	1	2	.920
— Lakeland (Fla. St.)........	OF	3	6	1	2	0	0	0	0	.333	0	3	0	0	0	0	...
1995— Fayetteville (SAL)	OF	124	457	62	129	31	7	16	72	.282	30	113	30	143	10	7	.956
1996— Lakeland (Fla. St.)	OF	131	499	54	120	31	2	15	58	.240	24	104	11	233	12	6	.976
1997— Jacksonville (Sou.).....	OF	131	493	91	159	31	4	26	90	.323	43	86	17	208	12	3	.987
— Detroit (A.L.).............	OF	11	33	3	7	1	1	1	5	.212	3	12	3	22	0	0	1.000
1998— Lakeland (Fla. St.)	OF	4	16	4	4	0	1	0	4	.250	2	4	4	7	1	0	1.000
— Toledo (Int'l).............	OF	92	356	55	102	17	3	8	41	.287	29	85	24	168	10	5	.973
— Detroit (A.L.).............	OF-DH	40	164	30	54	9	4	7	21	.329	7	31	7	60	4	1	.985
Major league totals (2 years)		51	197	33	61	10	5	8	26	.310	10	43	10	82	4	1	.989

ENCARNACION, MARIO   OF   ATHLETICS

PERSONAL: Born September 24, 1977, in Bani, Dominican Republic. ... 6-2/187. ... Bats right, throws right. ... Full name: Mario Gonzalez Encarnacion.
TRANSACTIONS/CAREER NOTES: Signed as non-drafted free agent by Oakland Athletics organization (July 11, 1994).

E

Year	Team (League)	Pos.	G	AB	R	H	2B	3B	HR	RBI	Avg.	BB	SO	SB	PO	A	E	Avg.
								BATTING								FIELDING		
1995—Dom. Athletics (DSL) .		OF	64	229	56	79	11	5	8	44	.345	40	36	17	112	9	7	.945
1996—W. Mich. (Mid.)		OF	118	401	55	92	14	3	7	43	.229	49	131	23	192	13	11	.949
1997—Modesto (California) ..		OF	111	364	70	108	17	9	18	78	.297	42	121	14	145	7	12	.927
1998—Huntsville (Sou.)		OF	110	357	70	97	15	2	15	61	.272	60	123	11	181	8	6	.969

ERDOS, TODD — P — YANKEES

PERSONAL: Born November 21, 1973, in Washington, Pa. ... 6-1/190. ... Throws right, bats right. ... Full name: Todd Michael Erdos. ... Name pronounced er-DOHS.
HIGH SCHOOL: Meadville (Pa.).
TRANSACTIONS/CAREER NOTES: Selected by San Diego Padres organization in ninth round of free-agent draft (June 1, 1992). ... On Arizona Padres disabled list (June 4-September 16, 1994). ... Selected by Arizona Diamondbacks in second round (41st pick overall) of expansion draft (November 18, 1997). ... Traded by Diamondbacks with P Marty Janzen to New York Yankees for IF Andy Fox (March 8, 1998). ... On Columbus disabled list (July 24, 1998-remainder of season).
STATISTICAL NOTES: Led Northwest League with 13 home runs allowed in 1993.

Year	Team (League)	W	L	Pct.	ERA	G	GS	CG	ShO	Sv.	IP	H	R	ER	BB	SO
1992—Ariz. Padres (Ariz.)		3	4	.429	2.65	12	9	1	0	0	57 2/3	36	28	17	18	61
—Spokane (N'west)		1	0	1.000	0.69	2	2	0	0	0	13	9	2	1	5	11
1993—Spokane (N'west)		5	6	.455	3.19	16	15	0	0	0	90 1/3	73	39	32	•53	64
—Waterloo (Midw.)		1	9	.100	8.31	11	11	0	0	0	47 2/3	64	51	44	31	27
1994—								Did not play.								
1995—Idaho Falls (Pioneer)		5	3	.625	3.48	32	0	0	0	0	41 1/3	34	19	16	30	48
1996—Rancho Cuca. (Cal.)		3	3	.500	3.74	55	0	0	0	17	67 1/3	63	33	28	37	82
1997—Mobile (Southern)		1	4	.200	3.36	55	0	0	0	27	59	45	22	22	22	49
—San Diego (N.L.)		2	0	1.000	5.27	11	0	0	0	0	13 2/3	17	9	8	4	13
1998—Columbus (Int'l)■		3	2	.600	4.62	39	0	0	0	16	48 2/3	52	27	25	20	50
—New York (A.L.)		0	0	...	9.00	2	0	0	0	0	2	5	2	2	1	0
A.L. totals (1 year)		0	0	...	9.00	2	0	0	0	0	2	5	2	2	1	0
N.L. totals (1 year)		2	0	1.000	5.27	11	0	0	0	0	13 2/3	17	9	8	4	13
Major league totals (2 years)		2	0	1.000	5.74	13	0	0	0	0	15 2/3	22	11	10	5	13

ERICKSON, SCOTT — P — ORIOLES

E

PERSONAL: Born February 2, 1968, in Long Beach, Calif. ... 6-4/230. ... Throws right, bats right. ... Full name: Scott Gavin Erickson.
HIGH SCHOOL: Homestead (Cupertino, Calif.).
JUNIOR COLLEGE: San Jose City College.
COLLEGE: Arizona.
TRANSACTIONS/CAREER NOTES: Selected by New York Mets organization in 36th round of free-agent draft (June 2, 1986); did not sign. ... Selected by Houston Astros organization in 34th round of free-agent draft (June 2, 1987); did not sign. ... Selected by Toronto Blue Jays organization in 44th round of free-agent draft (June 1, 1988); did not sign. ... Selected by Minnesota Twins organization in fourth round of free-agent draft (June 5, 1989). ... On disabled list (June 30-July 15, 1991; April 3-18, 1993 and May 15-31, 1994). ... Traded by Twins to Baltimore Orioles for P Scott Klingenbeck and a player to be named later (July 7, 1995); Twins acquired OF Kimera Bartee to complete deal (September 18, 1995).
RECORDS: Holds A.L. single-season record for fewest innings pitched for league leader—251 1/3 (1998).
STATISTICAL NOTES: Pitched 5-0 one-hit, complete-game victory against Boston (July 24, 1992, first game). ... Pitched 6-0 no-hit victory against Milwaukee (April 27, 1994). ... Tied for A.L. lead with nine hit batsmen in 1994.

Year	Team (League)	W	L	Pct.	ERA	G	GS	CG	ShO	Sv.	IP	H	R	ER	BB	SO
1989—Visalia (California)		3	4	.429	2.97	12	12	2	0	0	78 2/3	79	29	26	22	59
1990—Orlando (South.)		8	3	.727	3.03	15	15	3	1	0	101	75	38	34	24	69
—Minnesota (A.L.)		8	4	.667	2.87	19	17	1	0	0	113	108	49	36	51	53
1991—Minnesota (A.L.)		•20	8	.714	3.18	32	32	5	3	0	204	189	80	72	71	108
1992—Minnesota (A.L.)		13	12	.520	3.40	32	32	5	3	0	212	197	86	80	83	101
1993—Minnesota (A.L.)		8	*19	.296	5.19	34	34	1	0	0	218 2/3	*266	*138	126	71	116
1994—Minnesota (A.L.)		8	11	.421	5.44	23	23	2	1	0	144	173	95	87	59	104
1995—Minnesota (A.L.)		4	6	.400	5.95	15	15	0	0	0	87 2/3	102	61	58	32	45
—Baltimore (A.L.)■		9	4	.692	3.89	17	16	7	2	0	108 2/3	111	47	47	35	61
1996—Baltimore (A.L.)		13	12	.520	5.02	34	34	6	0	0	222 1/3	262	137	124	66	100
1997—Baltimore (A.L.)		16	7	.696	3.69	34	34	3	2	0	221 2/3	218	100	91	61	131
1998—Baltimore (A.L.)		16	13	.552	4.01	36	*36	*11	2	0	*251 1/3	*284	125	112	69	186
Major league totals (9 years)		115	96	.545	4.20	276	272	41	13	0	1783 1/3	1910	918	833	598	1005

DIVISION SERIES RECORD

Year	Team (League)	W	L	Pct.	ERA	G	GS	CG	ShO	Sv.	IP	H	R	ER	BB	SO
1996—Baltimore (A.L.)		0	0	...	4.05	1	1	0	0	0	6 2/3	6	3	3	2	6
1997—Baltimore (A.L.)		1	0	1.000	4.05	1	1	0	0	0	6 2/3	7	3	3	2	6
Div. series totals (2 years)		1	0	1.000	4.05	2	2	0	0	0	13 1/3	13	6	6	4	12

CHAMPIONSHIP SERIES RECORD

RECORDS: Shares A.L. record for most runs allowed in one inning—6 (October 13, 1996, third inning). ... Holds record for most home runs allowed in one inning—3 (October 13, 1996, third inning).

Year	Team (League)	W	L	Pct.	ERA	G	GS	CG	ShO	Sv.	IP	H	R	ER	BB	SO
1991—Minnesota (A.L.)		0	0	...	4.50	1	1	0	0	0	4	3	2	2	5	2
1996—Baltimore (A.L.)		0	1	.000	2.38	2	2	0	0	0	11 1/3	14	9	3	4	8
1997—Baltimore (A.L.)		1	0	1.000	4.26	2	2	0	0	0	12 2/3	15	7	6	1	6
Champ. series totals (3 years)		1	1	.500	3.54	5	5	0	0	0	28	32	18	11	10	16

WORLD SERIES RECORD

NOTES: Member of World Series championship team (1991).

Year	Team (League)	W	L	Pct.	ERA	G	GS	CG	ShO	Sv.	IP	H	R	ER	BB	SO
1991—Minnesota (A.L.)		0	0	...	5.06	2	2	0	0	0	10 2/3	10	7	6	4	5

ERSTAD, DARIN   OF   ANGELS

PERSONAL: Born June 4, 1974, in Jamestown, N.D. ... 6-2/210. ... Bats left, throws left. ... Full name: Darin Charles Erstad.
HIGH SCHOOL: Jamestown (N.D.).
COLLEGE: Nebraska.
TRANSACTIONS/CAREER NOTES: Selected by New York Mets organization in 13th round of free-agent draft (June 1, 1992); did not sign. ... Selected by California Angels organization in first round (first pick overall) of free-agent draft (June 1, 1995). ... Angels franchise renamed Anaheim Angels for 1997 season. ... On disabled list (August 4-19, 1998).
STATISTICAL NOTES: Had 15-game hitting streak (April 1-18, 1998). ... Career major league grand slams: 1.

							BATTING								FIELDING		
Year	Team (League)	Pos.	G	AB	R	H	2B	3B	HR	RBI	Avg.	BB	SO	SB	PO	A	E	Avg.
1995—	Ariz. Angels (Ariz.)	OF	4	18	2	10	1	0	0	1	.556	1	1	1	3	0	0	1.000
	— Lake Elsinore (Calif.)..	OF	25	113	24	41	7	2	5	24	.363	6	22	3	65	2	1	.985
1996—	Vancouver (PCL)........	OF-1B	85	351	63	107	22	5	6	41	.305	44	53	11	184	10	1	.995
	— California (A.L.)........	OF	57	208	34	59	5	1	4	20	.284	17	29	3	121	2	3	.976
1997—	Anaheim (A.L.)	1B-DH-OF	139	539	99	161	34	4	16	77	.299	51	86	23	1003	64	11	.990
1998—	Anaheim (A.L.)	OF-1B-DH	133	537	84	159	39	3	19	82	.296	43	77	20	580	43	3	.995
	Major league totals (3 years)		329	1284	217	379	78	8	39	179	.295	111	192	46	1704	109	17	.991

ALL-STAR GAME RECORD

					BATTING								FIELDING		
Year	League	Pos.	AB	R	H	2B	3B	HR	RBI	Avg.	BB	SO	SB	PO	A	E	Avg.
1998—	American	OF	2	1	0	0	0	0	0	.000	0	0	0	3	0	0	1.000

ESCOBAR, KELVIM   P   BLUE JAYS

PERSONAL: Born April 11, 1976, in La Guaria, Venezuela. ... 6-1/195. ... Throws right, bats right. ... Full name: Kelvim Jose Bolivar Escobar.
TRANSACTIONS/CAREER NOTES: Signed as non-drafted free agent by Toronto Blue Jays organization (July 9, 1992). ... On Toronto disabled list (April 16-May 6, 1998); included rehabilitation assignment to Syracuse (May 2-6).

Year	Team (League)	W	L	Pct.	ERA	G	GS	CG	ShO	Sv.	IP	H	R	ER	BB	SO
1993—	Dom. B. Jays (DSL)	2	1	.667	4.13	8	7	0	0	0	32²/₃	34	17	15	25	31
1994—	GC Blue Jays (GCL)	4	4	.500	2.35	11	10	1	0	1	65	56	23	17	18	64
1995—	Dom. B. Jays (DSL)	0	1	.000	1.72	3	2	0	0	0	15²/₃	14	3	3	5	20
	— Medicine Hat (Pioneer)	3	3	.500	5.71	14	14	1	•1	0	69¹/₃	66	47	44	33	75
1996—	Dunedin (Fla. St.)	9	5	.643	2.69	18	18	1	0	0	110¹/₃	101	44	33	33	113
	— Knoxville (Southern)	3	4	.429	5.33	10	10	0	0	0	54	61	36	32	24	44
1997—	Knoxville (Southern)	2	1	.667	3.70	5	5	1	0	0	24¹/₃	20	13	10	16	31
	— Dunedin (Fla. St.)	0	1	.000	3.75	3	2	0	0	0	12	16	9	5	3	16
	— Toronto (A.L.)....................	3	2	.600	2.90	27	0	0	0	14	31	28	12	10	19	36
1998—	Toronto (A.L.)...................	7	3	.700	3.73	22	10	0	0	0	79²/₃	72	37	33	35	72
	— Syracuse (Int'l)...................	2	2	.500	3.77	13	10	0	0	1	59²/₃	51	26	25	24	64
	Major league totals (2 years)	10	5	.667	3.50	49	10	0	0	14	110²/₃	100	49	43	54	108

ESPADA, JOSUE   IF   TWINS

PERSONAL: Born August 30, 1975, in Santurce, Puerto Rico. ... 5-10/175. ... Bats right, throws right.
TRANSACTIONS/CAREER NOTES: Selected by Oakland Athletics in second round of 1996 draft (June 2, 1996). ... On disabled list (April 18-May 23 and June 11-July 17, 1998). ... Selected by Minnesota Twins from Athletics organization in Rule 5 major league draft (December 14, 1998).

							BATTING								FIELDING		
Year	Team (League)	Pos.	G	AB	R	H	2B	3B	HR	RBI	Avg.	BB	SO	SB	PO	A	E	Avg.
1996—	S. Oregon (N'west).....	SS	15	54	7	12	1	0	1	5	.222	5	10	0	19	29	2	.960
	— W. Mich. (Mid.)	SS	23	74	9	20	2	0	0	4	.270	13	11	3	19	56	6	.926
1997—	Visalia (California)	SS	118	445	90	122	7	3	3	39	.274	72	69	46	196	346	32	.944
1998—	Huntsville (Sou.)	SS	51	161	29	41	7	1	1	22	.255	27	15	7	57	116	9	.951

ESPINAL, JOSE   P   TWINS

PERSONAL: Born August 31, 1976, in Santo Domingo, Dominican Republic. ... 6-1/185. ... Throws right, bats right. ... Full name: Jose Ramon Espinal (Feliz).
HIGH SCHOOL: Pedro Hernandez (Santo Domingo, Dominican Republic).
TRANSACTIONS/CAREER NOTES: Signed as non-drafted free agent by Chicago Cubs organization (March 31, 1994). ... Claimed on waivers by Minnesota Twins (December 18, 1998).

Year	Team (League)	W	L	Pct.	ERA	G	GS	CG	ShO	Sv.	IP	H	R	ER	BB	SO
1994—	Dom. Cubs (DSL)..............	1	4	.200	4.63	6	6	0	0	0	23¹/₃	23	19	12	13	25
1995—	GC Cubs (GCL)..................	3	2	.600	1.75	13	5	0	0	1	36	29	20	7	10	27
1996—	GC Cubs (GCL).................	4	1	.800	2.21	11	7	0	0	0	61	46	20	15	18	54
1997—	Rockford (Midwest)	10	10	.500	4.92	24	24	1	0	0	120²/₃	147	83	66	41	107
1998—	Daytona (Fla. St.)	10	10	.500	4.73	28	22	0	0	0	144²/₃	165	95	76	50	117

ESTALELLA, BOBBY   C   PHILLIES

PERSONAL: Born August 23, 1974, in Hialeah, Fla. ... 6-1/210. ... Bats right, throws right. ... Full name: Robert M. Estalella. ... Grandson of Bobby Estalella, outfielder with Washington Senators (1935-36, 1939 and 1942), St. Louis Browns (1941), and Philadelphia Athletics (1943-1945 and 1949).

E

HIGH SCHOOL: Cooper City (Fla.).
JUNIOR COLLEGE: Miami-Dade (South) Community College.
TRANSACTIONS/CAREER NOTES: Selected by Philadelphia Phillies organization in 23rd round of free-agent draft (June 1, 1992).
STATISTICAL NOTES: Tied for South Atlantic League lead in double plays by catcher with eight in 1994. ... Led Florida State League catchers with 864 total chances in 1995. ... Led International League with 928 total chances and tied for league lead in double plays by catcher with nine in 1997. ... Hit three home runs in one game (September 4, 1997). ... Career major league grand slams: 1.

Year Team (League)	Pos.	G	AB	R	H	2B	3B	HR	RBI	Avg.	BB	SO	SB	PO	A	E	Avg.
1993— Martinsville (App.)......	C	35	122	14	36	11	0	3	19	.295	14	24	0	210	25	6	.975
—Clearwater (FSL).......	C	11	35	4	8	0	0	0	4	.229	2	3	0	47	8	0	1.000
1994— Spartanburg (SAL).....	C	86	299	34	65	19	1	9	41	.217	31	85	0	592	87	10	.985
—Clearwater (FSL).......	C	13	46	3	12	1	0	2	9	.261	3	17	0	92	5	1	.990
1995— Clearwater (FSL).......	C	117	404	61	105	24	1	15	58	.260	56	76	0	*771	82	11	.987
—Reading (Eastern)......	C	10	34	5	8	1	0	2	9	.235	4	7	0	60	9	1	.986
1996— Reading (Eastern)......	C	111	365	48	89	14	2	23	72	.244	67	104	2	775	84	14	.984
—Scran./W.B. (Int'l)......	C	11	36	7	9	3	0	3	8	.250	5	10	0	55	6	2	.968
—Philadelphia (N.L.)......	C	7	17	5	6	0	0	2	4	.353	1	6	1	24	1	0	1.000
1997— Scran./W.B. (Int'l)......	C	123	433	63	101	32	0	16	65	.233	56	109	3	*844	71	13	.986
—Philadelphia (N.L.)......	C	13	29	9	10	1	0	4	9	.345	7	7	0	49	3	0	1.000
1998— Scran./W.B. (Int'l)......	C	76	242	49	68	14	1	17	49	.281	66	49	0	469	25	5	.990
—Philadelphia (N.L.)......	C	47	165	16	31	6	1	8	20	.188	13	49	0	321	12	4	.988
Major league totals (3 years)		67	211	30	47	7	1	14	33	.223	21	62	1	394	16	4	.990

ESTES, SHAWN   P   GIANTS

PERSONAL: Born February 18, 1973, in San Francisco. ... 6-2/192. ... Throws left, bats right. ... Full name: Aaron Shawn Estes.
HIGH SCHOOL: Douglas (Minden, Nev.).
TRANSACTIONS/CAREER NOTES: Selected by Seattle Mariners organization in first round (11th pick overall) of free-agent draft (June 3, 1991). ... On disabled list (August 19, 1993-remainder of season). ... On Appleton disabled list (April 8-July 19 and July 25-August 15, 1994). ... Traded by Mariners with IF Wilson Delgado to San Francisco Giants for P Salomon Torres (May 21, 1995). ... On disabled list (March 23-April 6, 1997). ... On San Francisco disabled list (July 11-September 4, 1998); included rehabilitation assignments to Bakersfield (August 26-29) and Fresno (August 30-September 4).
MISCELLANEOUS: Appeared in four games as pinch runner with San Francisco (1996). ... Appeared in four games as pinch runner (1997). ... Scored two runs in two games as pinch runner with San Francisco (1998).

Year Team (League)	W	L	Pct.	ERA	G	GS	CG	ShO	Sv.	IP	H	R	ER	BB	SO
1991— Bellingham (N'west)..........	1	3	.250	6.88	9	9	0	0	0	34	27	33	26	55	35
1992— Bellingham (N'west)..........	3	3	.500	4.32	15	15	0	0	0	77	84	55	37	45	77
1993— Appleton (Midwest)...........	5	9	.357	7.24	19	18	0	0	0	83 1/3	108	85	67	52	65
1994— Appleton (Midwest)...........	0	2	.000	4.58	5	4	0	0	0	19 2/3	19	13	10	17	28
—Ariz. Mariners (Ariz.)........	0	3	.000	3.15	5	5	0	0	0	20	16	9	7	6	31
1995— Wis. Rap. (Midw.)..........	0	0	...	0.90	2	2	0	0	0	10	5	1	1	5	11
—Burlington (Midw.)■.........	0	0	...	4.11	4	4	0	0	0	15 1/3	13	8	7	12	22
—San Jose (California)........	5	2	.714	2.17	9	8	0	0	0	49 2/3	32	13	12	17	61
—Shreveport (Texas).........	2	0	1.000	2.01	4	4	0	0	0	22 1/3	14	5	5	10	18
—San Francisco (N.L.)	0	3	.000	6.75	3	3	0	0	0	17 1/3	16	14	13	5	14
1996— Phoenix (PCL).............	9	3	.750	3.43	18	18	0	0	0	110 1/3	92	43	42	38	95
—San Francisco (N.L.)	3	5	.375	3.60	11	11	0	0	0	70	63	30	28	39	60
1997— San Francisco (N.L.)	19	5	.792	3.18	32	32	3	2	0	201	162	80	71	*100	181
1998— San Francisco (N.L.)	7	12	.368	5.06	25	25	1	1	0	149 1/3	150	89	84	80	136
—Bakersfield (California).......	0	0	...	0.00	1	1	0	0	0	4 1/3	3	0	0	1	5
—Fresno (Pacific Coast)........	1	0	1.000	1.80	1	1	0	0	0	5	3	1	1	3	6
Major league totals (4 years)......	29	25	.537	4.03	71	71	4	3	0	437 2/3	391	213	196	224	391

DIVISION SERIES RECORD

Year Team (League)	W	L	Pct.	ERA	G	GS	CG	ShO	Sv.	IP	H	R	ER	BB	SO
1997— San Francisco (N.L.)	0	0	...	15.00	1	1	0	0	0	3	5	5	5	4	3

ALL-STAR GAME RECORD

Year League	W	L	Pct.	ERA	GS	CG	ShO	Sv.	IP	H	R	ER	BB	SO
1997— National................	0	1	.000	18.00	0	0	0	0	1	1	2	2	1	1

ESTRADA, HORACIO   P   BREWERS

PERSONAL: Born October 19, 1975, in San Joaquin, Venezuela. ... 6-0/160. ... Throws left, bats left. ... Full name: Horacio Jimene Estrada.
HIGH SCHOOL: Domingo Segado (San Joaquin, Venezuela).
TRANSACTIONS/CAREER NOTES: Signed as non-drafted free agent by Milwaukee Brewers organization (July 3, 1992). ... On Louisville disabled list (May 28, 1998-remainder of season).

Year Team (League)	W	L	Pct.	ERA	G	GS	CG	ShO	Sv.	IP	H	R	ER	BB	SO
1993— Dom. Brewers (DSL)..........	1	2	.333	4.41	22	3	0	0	0	51	39	33	25	37	60
1994— Dom. Brewers (DSL)..........	3	4	.429	2.67	26	2	0	0	7	60 2/3	41	27	18	46	52
1995— Ariz. Brewers (Ariz.)..........	0	1	.000	3.71	8	1	0	0	2	17	13	9	7	8	21
—Helena (Pioneer).............	1	2	.333	5.40	13	0	0	0	0	30	27	21	18	24	30
1996— Beloit (Midwest)..............	2	1	.667	1.23	17	0	0	0	1	29 1/3	21	8	4	11	34
—Stockton (California)	1	3	.250	4.59	29	0	0	0	3	51	43	29	26	21	62
1997— El Paso (Texas).................	8	10	.444	4.74	29	23	1	0	1	153 2/3	174	93	81	70	127
1998— El Paso (Texas).................	5	0	1.000	4.53	8	8	0	0	0	49 2/3	50	27	25	21	37
—Louisville (Int'l)	0	0	...	3.00	2	2	0	0	0	12	10	4	4	5	4

ESTRELLA, LEO — P — BLUE JAYS

PERSONAL: Born February 20, 1975, in Puerto Plata, Dominican Republic. ... 6-1/175. ... Throws right, bats right. ... Full name: Leoncio Estrella.

HIGH SCHOOL: Liceo Padre Las Casas (Puerto Plata, Dominican Republic).

TRANSACTIONS/CAREER NOTES: Signed as non-drafted free agent by New York Mets organization (October 12, 1993). ... On Capital City disabled list (April 10-24, 1998). ... Traded by Mets organization to Toronto Blue Jays organization for IF/OF Tony Phillips (July 31, 1998).

Year — Team (League)	W	L	Pct.	ERA	G	GS	CG	ShO	Sv.	IP	H	R	ER	BB	SO
1994— Dominican Mets (DSL)	5	0	1.000	3.47	30	0	0	0	3	36 1/3	33	28	14	32	20
1995— Dominican Mets (DSL)	2	4	.333	5.44	12	8	0	0	0	43	61	37	26	13	32
1996— Kingsport (Appalachian)	6	3	.667	3.88	15	7	1	0	0	58	54	32	25	24	52
1997— Pittsfield (NYP)	7	6	.538	3.03	15	15	0	0	0	92	91	48	31	27	55
1998— Columbia (S. Atl.)	10	8	.556	3.93	20	20	3	0	0	119	120	66	52	23	97
— Hagerstown (S. Atl.)■	1	3	.250	4.50	5	5	0	0	0	30	34	19	15	13	27

EUSEBIO, TONY — C — ASTROS

PERSONAL: Born April 27, 1967, in San Jose de Los Llames, Dominican Republic. ... 6-2/210. ... Bats right, throws right. ... Full name: Raul Antonio Eusebio. ... Name pronounced you-SAY-bee-o.

HIGH SCHOOL: San Rafael (Dominican Republic).

TRANSACTIONS/CAREER NOTES: Signed as non-drafted free agent by Houston Astros organization (May 30, 1985). ... On disabled list (August 5, 1990-remainder of season; April 16-23, 1992; and August 24, 1993-remainder of season). ... On Houston disabled list (May 8-June 17 and June 22-August 7, 1996); included rehabilitation assignments to Tucson (June 10-17 and July 29-August 7).

STATISTICAL NOTES: Tied for Southern League lead in double plays by catcher with eight in 1989. ... Led Texas League catchers with .9963 fielding percentage and 12 double plays in 1992. ... Career major league grand slams: 2.

Year — Team (League)	Pos.	G	AB	R	H	2B	3B	HR	RBI	Avg.	BB	SO	SB	PO	A	E	Avg.
1985— GC Astros (GCL)	C	1	1	0	0	0	0	0	0	.000	0	0	0	4	0	0	1.000
1985—					Dominican Summer League statistics unavailable.												
1986—					Dominican Summer League statistics unavailable.												
1987— GC Astros (GCL)	C-1B	42	125	26	26	1	2	1	15	.208	18	19	8	204	24	4	.983
1988— Osceola (Fla. St.)	C-OF	118	392	45	96	6	3	0	40	.245	40	69	19	611	66	8	.988
1989— Columbus (Southern)	C	65	203	20	38	6	1	0	18	.187	38	47	7	355	46	7	.983
— Osceola (Fla. St.)	C	52	175	22	50	6	3	0	30	.286	19	27	5	290	40	5	.985
1990— Columbus (Southern)	C	92	318	36	90	18	0	4	37	.283	21	80	6	558	69	4	*.994
1991— Jackson (Texas)	C	66	222	27	58	8	3	2	31	.261	25	54	3	424	48	7	.985
— Tucson (PCL)	C	5	20	5	8	1	0	0	2	.400	3	3	1	40	1	0	1.000
— Houston (N.L.)	C	10	19	4	2	1	0	0	0	.105	6	8	0	49	4	1	.981
1992— Jackson (Texas)	C	94	339	33	104	9	3	5	44	.307	25	58	1	493	51	2	*.996
1993— Tucson (PCL)	C	78	281	39	91	20	1	1	43	.324	22	40	1	450	46	3	.994
1994— Houston (N.L.)	C	55	159	18	47	9	1	5	30	.296	8	33	0	263	24	2	.993
1995— Houston (N.L.)	C	113	368	46	110	21	1	6	58	.299	31	59	0	645	49	5	.993
1996— Houston (N.L.)	C	58	152	15	41	7	2	1	19	.270	18	20	0	255	24	1	.996
— Tucson (PCL)	C	15	53	8	22	4	0	0	14	.415	2	7	0	45	1	0	1.000
1997— Houston (N.L.)	C	60	164	12	45	2	0	1	18	.274	19	27	0	297	16	4	.987
1998— Houston (N.L.)	C	66	182	13	46	6	1	1	36	.253	18	31	1	352	19	3	.992
Major league totals (6 years)		362	1044	108	291	46	5	14	161	.279	100	178	1	1861	136	16	.992

DIVISION SERIES RECORD

Year — Team (League)	Pos.	G	AB	R	H	2B	3B	HR	RBI	Avg.	BB	SO	SB	PO	A	E	Avg.
1997— Houston (N.L.)	C	1	3	1	2	0	0	0	0	.667	0	1	1	6	1	0	1.000
1998— Houston (N.L.)	C	1	3	0	1	1	0	0	0	.333	0	2	0	6	0	0	1.000
Division series totals (2 years)		2	6	1	3	1	0	0	0	.500	0	3	1	12	1	0	1.000

EVANS, BART — P — ROYALS

PERSONAL: Born December 30, 1970, in Springfield, Mo. ... 6-2/210. ... Throws right, bats right. ... Full name: Bart Steven Evans.

HIGH SCHOOL: Mansfield (Mo.).

COLLEGE: Southwest Missouri State.

TRANSACTIONS/CAREER NOTES: Selected by Kansas City Royals organization in ninth round of free-agent draft (June 1, 1992). ... On disabled list (June 17, 1993-remainder of season). ... On Wichita temporarily inactive list (April 24-May 10, 1995). ... On disabled list (June 14-September 19, 1996). ... On Kansas City disabled list (August 28, 1998-remainder of season).

HONORS: Named Southern League Pitcher of the Year (1994).

Year — Team (League)	W	L	Pct.	ERA	G	GS	CG	ShO	Sv.	IP	H	R	ER	BB	SO
1992— Eugene (Northwest)	1	1	.500	6.23	13	1	0	0	0	26	17	20	18	31	39
1993— Rockford (Midwest)	10	4	.714	4.36	27	16	0	0	0	99	95	52	48	60	120
1994— Wilmington (Caro.)	10	3	.769	2.98	26	26	0	0	0	145	107	53	48	61	145
1995— Wichita (Texas)	0	4	.000	10.48	7	7	0	0	0	22 1/3	22	28	26	45	13
— Wilmington (Caro.)	4	1	.800	2.89	16	6	0	0	2	46 2/3	30	21	15	44	47
1996— Wichita (Texas)	1	2	.333	11.84	9	7	0	0	0	24 1/3	31	38	32	36	16
1997— Wilmington (Caro.)	0	1	.000	6.53	16	2	0	0	0	20 2/3	22	18	15	15	22
— Wichita (Texas)	1	2	.333	4.59	32	0	0	0	6	33 1/3	45	20	17	8	28
1998— Omaha (Pacific Coast)	3	1	.750	2.53	49	0	0	0	27	57	50	18	16	22	54
— Kansas City (A.L.)	0	0	. . .	2.00	8	0	0	0	0	9	7	3	2	0	7
Major league totals (1 year)	0	0	. . .	2.00	8	0	0	0	0	9	7	3	2	0	7

E

EVANS, TOM 3B BLUE JAYS

PERSONAL: Born July 9, 1974, in Kirkland, Wash. ... 6-1/200. ... Bats right, throws right. ... Full name: Thomas John Evans.
HIGH SCHOOL: Juanita (Kirkland, Wash.).
TRANSACTIONS/CAREER NOTES: Selected by Toronto Blue Jays organization in fourth round of free-agent draft (June 1, 1992). ... On disabled list (April 7-May 17, 1994). ... On Toronto disabled list (September 14-28, 1997). ... On Syracuse disabled list (July 29-August 11, 1998).
STATISTICAL NOTES: Led Florida State League third basemen with 435 total chances in 1995. ... Led Southern League with .453 on-base percentage in 1996. ... Led International league third basemen with 337 total chances and 27 double plays in 1997.

Year Team (League)	Pos.	G	AB	R	H	2B	3B	HR	RBI	Avg.	BB	SO	SB	PO	A	E	Avg.
1992— Medicine Hat (Pio.)	3B	52	166	17	36	3	0	1	21	.217	33	29	4	53	115	20	.894
1993— Hagerstown (SAL)......	3B-1B-SS	119	389	47	100	25	1	7	54	.257	53	92	9	92	181	27	.910
1994— Hagerstown (SAL)......	3B	95	322	52	88	16	2	13	48	.273	51	80	2	60	196	36	.877
1995— Dunedin (Fla. St.)	3B	130	444	63	124	29	3	9	66	.279	51	80	7	*92	*309	34	.922
1996— Knoxville (Southern) ..	3B-1B	120	394	87	111	27	1	17	65	.282	*115	113	4	52	146	12	.943
1997— Dunedin (Fla. St.)	3B	15	42	8	11	2	0	2	4	.262	11	10	0	6	12	2	.900
— Syracuse (Int'l)............	3B	107	376	60	99	17	1	15	65	.263	53	104	1	*83	*242	12	*.964
— Toronto (A.L.).............	3B	12	38	7	11	2	0	1	2	.289	2	10	0	9	24	3	.917
1998— Syracuse (Int'l)..........	3B	109	400	57	120	32	1	15	55	.300	50	74	11	89	208	14	.955
— Toronto (A.L.).............	3B	7	10	0	0	0	0	0	0	.000	1	2	0	5	3	1	.889
Major league totals (2 years)		19	48	7	11	2	0	1	2	.229	3	12	0	14	27	4	.911

EVERETT, CARL OF ASTROS

PERSONAL: Born June 3, 1971, in Tampa. ... 6-0/190. ... Bats both, throws right. ... Full name: Carl Edward Everett.
HIGH SCHOOL: Hillsborough (Tampa).
TRANSACTIONS/CAREER NOTES: Selected by New York Yankees organization in first round (10th pick overall) of free-agent draft (June 4, 1990). ... On Fort Lauderdale disabled list (July 7-August 15, 1992). ... Selected by Florida Marlins in second round (27th pick overall) of expansion draft (November 17, 1992). ... On High Desert disabled list (April 8-13, 1993). ... On Florida disabled list (July 23-August 10, 1994). ... On Edmonton suspended list (August 29, 1994-remainder of season). ... Traded by Marlins to New York Mets for 2B Quilvio Veras (November 29, 1994). ... On disabled list (April 12-27, 1996). ... Traded by Mets to Houston Astros for P John Hudek (December 22, 1997).
STATISTICAL NOTES: Led South Atlantic League in being hit by pitch with 23 in 1991. ... Switch-hit home runs in one game twice (April 20, 1997, first game; and April 24, 1998). ... Career major league grand slams: 3.

Year Team (League)	Pos.	G	AB	R	H	2B	3B	HR	RBI	Avg.	BB	SO	SB	PO	A	E	Avg.
1990— GC Yankees (GCL)......	OF	48	185	28	48	8	5	1	14	.259	15	38	15	64	5	5	.932
1991— Greensboro (S. Atl.) ...	OF	123	468	96	127	18	0	4	40	.271	57	122	28	250	14	7	.974
1992— Fort Laud. (FSL)........	OF	46	183	30	42	8	2	2	9	.230	12	40	11	111	5	3	.975
— Prince Will. (Car.)........	OF	6	22	7	7	0	0	4	9	.318	5	7	1	12	1	0	1.000
1993— High Desert (Calif.)■ .	OF	59	253	48	73	12	6	10	52	.289	22	73	24	124	6	2	.985
— Florida (N.L.).............	OF	11	19	0	2	0	0	0	0	.105	1	9	1	6	0	1	.857
— Edmonton (PCL)	OF	35	136	28	42	13	4	6	16	.309	19	45	12	69	12	2	.976
1994— Edmonton (PCL)	OF	78	321	63	108	17	2	11	47	.336	19	65	16	167	11	2	.989
— Florida (N.L.).............	OF	16	51	7	11	1	0	2	6	.216	3	15	4	28	2	0	1.000
1995— New York (N.L.)■.......	OF	79	289	48	75	13	1	12	54	.260	39	67	2	148	9	3	.981
— Norfolk (Int'l)............	OF-SS	67	260	52	78	16	4	6	35	.300	20	47	12	133	7	0	1.000
1996— New York (N.L.).........	OF	101	192	29	46	8	1	1	16	.240	21	53	6	96	4	7	.935
1997— New York (N.L.).........	OF	142	443	58	110	28	3	14	57	.248	32	102	17	226	8	7	.971
1998— Houston (N.L.)■........	OF	133	467	72	138	34	4	15	76	.296	44	102	14	296	12	4	.987
Major league totals (6 years)		482	1461	214	382	84	9	44	209	.261	140	348	44	800	35	22	.974

DIVISION SERIES RECORD

Year Team (League)	Pos.	G	AB	R	H	2B	3B	HR	RBI	Avg.	BB	SO	SB	PO	A	E	Avg.
1998— Houston (N.L.)	OF-PH	4	13	1	2	0	0	0	0	.154	0	4	0	8	0	0	1.000

EVERSGERD, BRYAN P CARDINALS

PERSONAL: Born February 11, 1969, in Centralia, Ill. ... 6-1/190. ... Throws left, bats right. ... Full name: Bryan David Eversgerd. ... Brother of Randy Eversgerd, pitcher, Toronto Blue Jays organization.
HIGH SCHOOL: Carlyle (Ill.).
JUNIOR COLLEGE: Kaskaskia Community College (Ill.).
TRANSACTIONS/CAREER NOTES: Signed as non-drafted free agent by St. Louis Cardinals organization (June 14, 1989). ... Traded by Cardinals with P Kirk Bullinger and OF DaRond Stovall to Montreal Expos for P Ken Hill (April 5, 1995). ... Traded by Expos with SS Wil Cordero to Boston Red Sox for P Rheal Cormier, 1B Ryan McGuire and P Shayne Bennett (January 10, 1996). ... Traded by Red Sox organization to Texas Rangers organization for a player to be named later (April 18, 1996); Red Sox acquired OF Rudy Pemberton to complete deal (April 24, 1996). ... Granted free agency (October 15, 1996). ... Signed by San Diego Padres organization (December 2, 1996). ... Released by Padres (March 22, 1997). ... Signed by Texas Rangers organization (May 1, 1997). ... Granted free agency (October 27, 1997). ... Signed by St. Louis Cardinals organization (January 22, 1998).

Year Team (League)	W	L	Pct.	ERA	G	GS	CG	ShO	Sv.	IP	H	R	ER	BB	SO
1989— Johnson City (App.)	2	3	.400	3.64	16	1	0	0	0	29 2/3	30	16	12	12	19
1990— Springfield (Mid.)	6	8	.429	4.14	20	15	2	0	0	104 1/3	123	60	48	26	55
1991— Savannah (S. Atl.)	1	5	.167	3.47	72	0	0	0	1	93 1/3	71	43	36	34	97
1992— St. Petersburg (FSL)	3	2	.600	2.68	57	1	0	0	0	74	65	25	22	25	57
— Arkansas (Texas)...............	0	1	1.000	6.75	6	0	0	0	0	5 1/3	7	4	4	2	4
1993— Arkansas (Texas)	4	4	.500	2.18	*62	0	0	0	0	66	60	24	16	19	68
1994— Louisville (A.A.)	1	1	.500	4.50	9	0	0	0	0	12	11	7	6	8	8
— St. Louis (N.L.)	2	3	.400	4.52	40	1	0	0	0	67 2/3	75	36	34	20	47
1995— Montreal (N.L.)■..............	0	0	. . .	5.14	25	0	0	0	0	21	22	13	12	9	8
— Ottawa (Int'l)	6	2	.750	2.38	38	0	0	0	2	53	49	21	14	26	45

Year Team (League)	W	L	Pct.	ERA	G	GS	CG	ShO	Sv.	IP	H	R	ER	BB	SO
1996—Trenton (Eastern)■	1	0	1.000	2.57	4	0	0	0	0	7	6	2	2	4	2
—Oklahoma City (A.A.)■	3	3	.500	2.74	38	5	0	0	4	65⅔	57	21	20	14	60
1997—Oklahoma City (A.A.)	1	3	.250	4.24	26	7	0	0	0	76⅓	91	48	36	24	43
—Texas (A.L.)	0	2	.000	20.25	3	0	0	0	0	1⅓	5	3	3	3	2
1998—Memphis (Pacific Coast)■	2	5	.286	3.34	49	0	0	0	0	56⅔	51	25	21	20	50
—St. Louis (N.L.)	0	0	...	9.00	8	0	0	0	0	6	9	7	6	2	4
A.L. totals (1 year)	0	2	.000	20.25	3	0	0	0	0	1⅓	5	3	3	3	2
N.L. totals (3 years)	2	3	.400	4.94	73	1	0	0	0	94⅔	106	56	52	31	59
Major league totals (4 years)	2	5	.286	5.16	76	1	0	0	0	96	111	59	55	34	61

EYRE, SCOTT   P   WHITE SOX

PERSONAL: Born May 30, 1972, in Inglewood, Calif. ... 6-1/190. ... Throws left, bats left. ... Full name: Scott Alan Eyre.
HIGH SCHOOL: Cyprus (Magna, Utah).
JUNIOR COLLEGE: College of Southern Idaho.
TRANSACTIONS/CAREER NOTES: Selected by Texas Rangers organization in ninth round of free-agent draft (June 3, 1991). ... Traded by Rangers organization to Chicago White Sox organization for SS Esteban Beltre (March 28, 1994). ... On disabled list (April 8-27, 1994). ... On Prince William disabled list (April 6-September 7, 1995).
HONORS: Named Southern League Most Outstanding Pitcher (1997).

Year Team (League)	W	L	Pct.	ERA	G	GS	CG	ShO	Sv.	IP	H	R	ER	BB	SO
1992—Butte (Pioneer)	7	3	.700	2.90	15	14	2	1	0	80⅔	71	30	26	39	94
1993—Charleston, S.C. (S. Atl.)	11	7	.611	3.45	26	26	0	0	0	143⅔	115	74	55	59	154
1994—South Bend (Mid.)■	8	4	.667	3.47	19	18	2	0	0	111⅔	108	56	43	37	111
1995—GC White Sox (GCL)	0	2	.000	2.30	9	9	0	0	0	27⅓	16	7	7	12	40
1996—Birmingham (Southern)	12	7	.632	4.38	27	27	0	0	0	158½	170	90	77	79	137
1997—Birmingham (Southern)	•13	5	.722	3.84	22	22	0	0	0	126⅔	110	61	54	55	127
—Chicago (A.L.)	4	4	.500	5.04	11	11	0	0	0	60⅔	62	36	34	31	36
1998—Chicago (A.L.)	3	8	.273	5.38	33	17	0	0	0	107	114	78	64	64	73
Major league totals (2 years)	7	12	.368	5.26	44	28	0	0	0	167⅔	176	114	98	95	109

FABREGAS, JORGE   C   MARLINS

PERSONAL: Born March 13, 1970, in Miami. ... 6-3/215. ... Bats left, throws right. ... Name pronounced FAB-ruh-gas.
HIGH SCHOOL: Christopher Columbus (Miami).
COLLEGE: Miami (Fla.).
TRANSACTIONS/CAREER NOTES: Selected by Cleveland Indians organization in 11th round of free-agent draft (June 1, 1988); did not sign. ... Selected by California Angels organization in supplemental round ("sandwich pick" between first and second round, 34th pick overall) of free-agent draft (June 3, 1991); pick received as part of compensation for Minnesota Twins signing Type A free-agent OF/DH Chili Davis. ... On disabled list (April 12-May 4 and July 28-September 5, 1992). ... Angels franchise renamed Anaheim Angels for 1997 season. ... Traded by Angels with P Chuck McElroy to Chicago White Sox for OF Tony Phillips and C Chad Kreuter (May 18, 1997). ... Selected by Arizona Diamondbacks in first round (seventh pick overall) of expansion draft (November 18, 1997). ... On Arizona disabled list (May 31-June 30, 1998); included rehabilitation assignment to Tucson (June 22-30). ... Traded by Diamondbacks with P Willie Blair and a player to be named later to New York Mets for OF Bernard Gilkey, P Nelson Figueroa and cash (July 31, 1998). ... Traded by Mets to Florida Marlins for P Oscar Henriquez (November 20, 1998).
STATISTICAL NOTES: Led Texas League with 17 passed balls in 1993.

Year Team (League)	Pos.	G	AB	R	H	2B	3B	HR	RBI	Avg.	BB	SO	SB	PO	A	E	Avg.
1992—Palm Springs (Calif.)	C	70	258	35	73	13	0	0	40	.283	30	27	0	436	63	*17	.967
1993—Midland (Texas)	C	113	409	63	118	26	3	6	56	.289	31	60	1	620	99	•11	.985
—Vancouver (PCL)	C	4	13	1	3	1	0	0	1	.231	1	3	0	30	3	0	1.000
1994—Vancouver (PCL)	C	66	211	17	47	6	1	1	24	.223	12	25	1	365	41	4	.990
—California (A.L.)	C	43	127	12	36	3	0	0	16	.283	7	18	2	217	16	3	.987
1995—California (A.L.)	C	73	227	24	56	10	0	1	22	.247	17	28	0	391	36	6	.986
—Vancouver (PCL)	C	21	73	9	18	3	0	4	10	.247	9	12	0	112	12	4	.969
1996—California (A.L.)	C-DH	90	254	18	73	6	0	2	26	.287	17	27	0	502	46	6	.989
—Vancouver (PCL)	C-1B	10	37	4	11	3	0	0	5	.297	4	4	0	27	2	0	1.000
1997—Anaheim (A.L.)	C	21	38	2	3	1	0	0	3	.079	3	3	0	81	5	1	.989
—Chicago (A.L.)■	C-1B	100	322	31	90	10	1	7	48	.280	11	43	1	520	46	7	.988
1998—Arizona (N.L.)■	C	50	151	8	30	4	0	1	15	.199	13	26	0	228	30	1	.996
—Tucson (PCL)	C	6	20	2	5	1	0	0	3	.250	3	1	0	28	3	0	1.000
—New York (N.L.)■	C	20	32	3	6	0	0	1	5	.188	1	6	0	62	6	2	.971
American League totals (4 years)		327	968	87	258	30	1	10	115	.267	55	119	3	1711	149	23	.988
National League totals (1 year)		70	183	11	36	4	0	2	20	.197	14	32	0	290	36	3	.991
Major league totals (5 years)		397	1151	98	294	34	1	12	135	.255	69	151	3	2001	185	26	.988

FARNSWORTH, KYLE   P   CUBS

PERSONAL: Born April 14, 1976, in Wichita, Kan. ... 6-4/205. ... Throws right, bats both. ... Full name: Kyle Lynn Farnsworth.
HIGH SCHOOL: Milton (Alpharetta, Ga.).
JUNIOR COLLEGE: Abraham Baldwin College (Ga.).
TRANSACTIONS/CAREER NOTES: Selected by Chicago Cubs organization in 47th round of free-agent draft (June 2, 1994).

Year Team (League)	W	L	Pct.	ERA	G	GS	CG	ShO	Sv.	IP	H	R	ER	BB	SO
1995—GC Cubs (GCL)	3	2	.600	0.87	16	0	0	0	1	31	22	8	3	11	18
1996—Rockford (Midwest)	9	6	.600	3.70	20	20	1	0	0	112	122	62	46	35	82
1997—Daytona (Fla. St.)	10	10	.500	4.09	27	27	2	0	0	156⅓	178	91	71	47	105
1998—West Tenn (Southern)	8	2	.800	2.77	13	13	0	0	0	81⅓	70	32	25	21	73
—Iowa (Pacific Coast)	5	9	.357	6.93	18	18	0	0	0	102⅔	129	88	79	36	79

E
F

FASANO, SAL   C   ROYALS

PERSONAL: Born August 10, 1971, in Chicago. ... 6-2/220. ... Bats right, throws right. ... Full name: Salvatore Frank Fasano.
HIGH SCHOOL: Hoffman Estates (Ill.).
COLLEGE: Evansville.
TRANSACTIONS/CAREER NOTES: Selected by Kansas City Royals organization in 37th round of free-agent draft (June 3, 1993). ... On Kansas City disabled list (April 20-May 9 and August 30, 1998-remainder of season); included rehabilitation assignment to Omaha (May 5-9).
STATISTICAL NOTES: Led Northwest League catchers with seven double plays in 1993.

							BATTING								FIELDING		
Year Team (League)	Pos.	G	AB	R	H	2B	3B	HR	RBI	Avg.	BB	SO	SB	PO	A	E	Avg.
1993— Eugene (Northwest) ...	C	49	176	25	47	11	1	10	36	.267	19	49	4	276	38	1	.997
1994— Rockford (Midwest) ...	C-1B	97	345	61	97	16	1	25	81	.281	33	66	8	527	86	12	.981
— Wilmington (Caro.).....	C-1B	23	90	15	29	7	0	7	32	.322	13	24	0	80	9	4	.957
1995— Wilmington (Caro.).....	C-1B	23	88	12	20	2	1	2	7	.227	5	16	0	132	12	0	1.000
— Wichita (Texas)	C-1B	87	317	60	92	19	2	20	66	.290	27	61	3	589	64	14	.979
1996— Kansas City (A.L.)	C	51	143	20	29	2	0	6	19	.203	14	25	1	291	14	5	.984
— Omaha (A.A.)..............	C-1B-3B	29	104	12	24	4	0	4	15	.231	6	21	0	198	21	4	.982
1997— Omaha (A.A.).............	C	49	152	17	25	7	0	4	14	.164	12	53	0	296	34	4	.988
— Kansas City (A.L.)	C-DH	13	38	4	8	2	0	1	1	.211	1	12	0	53	3	1	.982
— Wichita (Texas)	C-1B	40	131	27	31	5	0	13	27	.237	20	35	0	232	21	4	.984
1998— Kansas City (A.L.)	C-1B-3B	74	216	21	49	10	0	8	31	.227	10	56	1	437	25	2	.996
— Omaha (Pacific Coast)	C	4	14	1	3	1	0	1	2	.214	1	4	0	26	1	0	1.000
Major league totals (3 years)		**138**	**397**	**45**	**86**	**14**	**0**	**15**	**51**	**.217**	**25**	**93**	**2**	**781**	**42**	**8**	**.990**

FASSERO, JEFF   P   MARINERS

PERSONAL: Born January 5, 1963, in Springfield, Ill. ... 6-1/195. ... Throws left, bats left. ... Full name: Jeffrey Joseph Fassero. ... Name pronounced fuh-SAIR-oh.
HIGH SCHOOL: Griffin (Springfield, Ill.).
JUNIOR COLLEGE: Lincoln Land Community College (Ill.).
COLLEGE: Mississippi.
TRANSACTIONS/CAREER NOTES: Selected by St. Louis Cardinals organization in 22nd round of free-agent draft (June 4, 1984). ... Selected by Chicago White Sox organization from Cardinals organization in Rule 5 minor league draft (December 5, 1989). ... Released by White Sox organization (April 3, 1990). ... Signed by Cleveland Indians organization (April 9, 1990). ... Granted free agency (October 15, 1990). ... Signed by Indianapolis, Montreal Expos organization (January 3, 1991). ... On disabled list (July 24-August 11, 1994). ... Traded by Expos with P Alex Pacheco to Seattle Mariners for C Chris Widger, P Trey Moore and P Matt Wagner (October 29, 1996). ... On disabled list (March 22-April 12, 1998).
STATISTICAL NOTES: Pitched 5-0 no-hit victory for Arkansas against Jackson (June 12, 1989).

Year Team (League)	W	L	Pct.	ERA	G	GS	CG	ShO	Sv.	IP	H	R	ER	BB	SO
1984— Johnson City (App.)	4	7	.364	4.59	13	11	2	0	1	66 2/3	65	42	34	39	59
1985— Springfield (Mid.)..............	4	8	.333	4.01	29	15	1	0	1	119	125	78	53	45	65
1986— St. Petersburg (FSL)	13	7	.650	2.45	26	•26	6	1	0	*176	156	63	48	56	112
1987— Arkansas (Texas)	10	7	.588	4.10	28	27	2	1	0	151 1/3	168	90	69	67	118
1988— Arkansas (Texas)	5	5	.500	3.58	70	1	0	0	17	78	97	48	31	41	72
1989— Louisville (A.A.)................	3	10	.231	5.22	22	19	0	0	0	112	136	79	65	47	73
— Arkansas (Texas)	4	1	.800	1.64	6	6	2	1	0	44	32	11	8	12	38
1990— Cant./Akr. (Eastern)■	5	4	.556	2.80	*61	0	0	0	6	64 1/3	66	24	20	24	61
1991— Indianapolis (A.A.)■	3	0	1.000	1.47	18	0	0	0	4	18 1/3	11	3	3	7	12
— Montreal (N.L.)..................	2	5	.286	2.44	51	0	0	0	8	55 1/3	39	17	15	17	42
1992— Montreal (N.L.)..................	8	7	.533	2.84	70	0	0	0	1	85 2/3	81	35	27	34	63
1993— Montreal (N.L.)..................	12	5	.706	2.29	56	15	1	0	1	149 2/3	119	50	38	54	140
1994— Montreal (N.L.)..................	8	6	.571	2.99	21	21	1	0	0	138 2/3	119	54	46	40	119
1995— Montreal (N.L.)..................	13	14	.481	4.33	30	30	1	0	0	189	207	102	91	74	164
1996— Montreal (N.L.)..................	15	11	.577	3.30	34	34	5	1	0	231 2/3	217	95	85	55	222
1997— Seattle (A.L.)■	16	9	.640	3.61	35	•35	2	1	0	234 1/3	226	108	94	84	189
1998— Seattle (A.L.).................	13	12	.520	3.97	32	32	7	0	0	224 2/3	223	115	99	66	176
A.L. totals (2 years)	**29**	**21**	**.580**	**3.78**	**67**	**67**	**9**	**1**	**0**	**459**	**449**	**223**	**193**	**150**	**365**
N.L. totals (6 years)	**58**	**48**	**.547**	**3.20**	**262**	**100**	**8**	**1**	**10**	**850**	**782**	**353**	**302**	**274**	**750**
Major league totals (8 years)	**87**	**69**	**.558**	**3.40**	**329**	**167**	**17**	**2**	**10**	**1309**	**1231**	**576**	**495**	**424**	**1115**

DIVISION SERIES RECORD

Year Team (League)	W	L	Pct.	ERA	G	GS	CG	ShO	Sv.	IP	H	R	ER	BB	SO
1997— Seattle (A.L.)	1	0	1.000	1.13	1	1	0	0	0	8	3	1	1	4	3

FEBLES, CARLOS   2B   ROYALS

PERSONAL: Born May 24, 1976, in El Seybo, Dominican Republic. ... 5-11/170. ... Bats right, throws right. ... Full name: Carlos Manuel Febles.
HIGH SCHOOL: Sagrado Corazon de Jesus (Dominican Republic).
TRANSACTIONS/CAREER NOTES: Signed as non-drafted free agent by Kansas City Royals (November 2, 1993).
STATISTICAL NOTES: Led Gulf Coast League second basemen with 230 total chances and 39 double plays in 1995. ... Led Carolina League with 590 total chances and 85 double plays in 1997. ... Led Texas League with .441 on-base percentage in 1998.

							BATTING								FIELDING		
Year Team (League)	Pos.	G	AB	R	H	2B	3B	HR	RBI	Avg.	BB	SO	SB	PO	A	E	Avg.
1994— Dom. Royals (DSL)	2B	56	184	38	61	9	3	2	37	.332	38	27	12	113	113	16	.934
1995— GC Royals (GCL)	2B	54	188	40	53	13	5	3	20	.282	26	30	16	*117	101	12	.948
1996— Lansing (Midwest)	2B-SS	102	363	84	107	23	5	5	43	.295	66	64	30	206	292	19	.963
1997— Wilmington (Caro.).....	2B	122	438	78	104	27	6	3	29	.237	51	95	49	212	*355	*23	.961
1998— Wichita (Texas)	2B	126	432	110	141	28	9	14	52	.326	80	70	*51	248	334	19	.968
— Kansas City (A.L.)	2B	11	25	5	10	1	2	0	2	.400	4	7	2	16	18	0	1.000
Major league totals (1 year)		**11**	**25**	**5**	**10**	**1**	**2**	**0**	**2**	**.400**	**4**	**7**	**2**	**16**	**18**	**0**	**1.000**

F

PERSONAL: Born April 27, 1977, in Azua, Dominican Republic. ... 6-1/195. ... Bats right, throws right.
HIGH SCHOOL: Augustine de Chequer (Dominican Republic).
TRANSACTIONS/CAREER NOTES: Signed as non-drafted free agent by San Francisco Giants organization (February 7, 1994).
STATISTICAL NOTES: Led California League third basemen with 457 total chances and 39 double plays in 1997. ... Led Texas League third basemen with 21 double plays in 1998.

							BATTING							FIELDING		
Year Team (League)	Pos.	G	AB	R	H	2B	3B	HR	RBI	Avg.	BB	SO	SB	PO	A	E	Avg.
1994— Ariz. Giants (Ariz.)	3B	38	119	7	23	0	0	0	3	.193	2	20	2	19	82	5	.953
1995— Bellingham (N'west) ...	3B-1B	43	113	14	31	2	1	0	16	.274	7	33	1	30	37	2	.971
1996— Bellingham (N'west) ...	3B-1B	93	321	36	85	12	2	5	36	.265	18	65	5	66	186	17	.937
1997— Bakersfield (Calif.)	3B	135	515	59	140	25	4	14	56	.272	23	90	5	*112	*322	23	*.950
1998— Shreveport (Texas)	3B	100	364	39	96	23	2	12	50	.264	9	62	0	*71	204	22	*.926
— Fresno (Pacific Coast)	3B	3	7	1	3	1	0	1	3	.429	1	0	0	0	2	0	1.000

PERSONAL: Born November 26, 1974, in Mound Bayou, Miss. ... 5-9/175. ... Bats left, throws left. ... Full name: Anthony Laray Felston.
HIGH SCHOOL: Leland (Miss.).
COLLEGE: Mississippi.
TRANSACTIONS/CAREER NOTES: Selected by Minnesota Twins organization in 34th round of free-agent draft (June 4, 1996). ... On disabled list (July 1-24, 1997).

							BATTING							FIELDING		
Year Team (League)	Pos.	G	AB	R	H	2B	3B	HR	RBI	Avg.	BB	SO	SB	PO	A	E	Avg.
1996— GC Twins (GCL)	OF	2	4	2	2	0	0	0	0	.500	2	0	0	1	0	0	1.000
— Fort Wayne (Midw.)	OF	62	201	53	63	4	1	0	18	.313	43	36	22	117	6	0	1.000
1997— Fort Wayne (Midw.)	OF	94	338	63	94	10	2	2	29	.278	55	53	45	143	5	4	.974
1998— Fort Myers (FSL)	OF	114	427	74	119	8	0	0	43	.279	83	65	*86	233	8	7	.972
— New Britain (East.)	OF	12	45	5	10	2	0	0	5	.222	6	10	2	21	0	2	.913

PERSONAL: Born August 13, 1969, in Miami Beach, Fla. ... 6-1/225. ... Throws right, bats right. ... Full name: Alexander Fernandez.
HIGH SCHOOL: Pace (Miami).
JUNIOR COLLEGE: Miami-Dade (South) Community College.
COLLEGE: Miami (Fla.).
TRANSACTIONS/CAREER NOTES: Selected by Milwaukee Brewers organization in first round (24th pick overall) of free-agent draft (June 1, 1988); did not sign. ... Selected by Chicago White Sox organization in first round (fourth pick overall) of free-agent draft (June 4, 1990). ... Granted free agency (December 7, 1996). ... Signed by Florida Marlins (December 9, 1996). ... On disabled list (March 21, 1998-entire season).
HONORS: Named Golden Spikes Award winner by USA Baseball (1990).
STATISTICAL NOTES: Pitched 7-0 one-hit, complete-game victory for Chicago against Milwaukee (May 4, 1992). ... Pitched 1-0 one-hit, complete-game victory against Chicago (April 10, 1997).
MISCELLANEOUS: Had a sacrifice hit in only appearance as pinch hitter (1997).

Year Team (League)	W	L	Pct.	ERA	G	GS	CG	ShO	Sv.	IP	H	R	ER	BB	SO
1990— GC White Sox (GCL)	1	0	1.000	3.60	2	2	0	0	0	10	11	4	4	1	16
— Sarasota (Florida State)......	1	1	.500	1.84	2	2	0	0	0	14²/₃	8	4	3	3	23
— Birmingham (Southern)	3	0	1.000	1.08	4	4	0	0	0	25	20	7	3	6	27
— Chicago (A.L.)	5	5	.500	3.80	13	13	3	0	0	87²/₃	89	40	37	34	61
1991— Chicago (A.L.)	9	13	.409	4.51	34	32	2	0	0	191²/₃	186	100	96	88	145
1992— Chicago (A.L.)	8	11	.421	4.27	29	29	4	2	0	187²/₃	199	100	89	50	95
— Vancouver (PCL)	2	1	.667	0.94	4	3	2	1	0	28²/₃	15	8	3	6	27
1993— Chicago (A.L.)	18	9	.667	3.13	34	34	3	1	0	247¹/₃	221	95	86	67	169
1994— Chicago (A.L.)	11	7	.611	3.86	24	24	4	3	0	170¹/₃	163	83	73	50	122
1995— Chicago (A.L.)	12	8	.600	3.80	30	30	5	2	0	203²/₃	200	98	86	65	159
1996— Chicago (A.L.)	16	10	.615	3.45	35	35	6	1	0	258	248	110	99	72	200
1997— Florida (N.L.) ■	17	12	.586	3.59	32	32	5	1	0	220²/₃	193	93	88	69	183
1998— Florida (N.L.)							Did not play.								
A.L. totals (7 years)	79	63	.556	3.78	199	197	27	9	0	1346¹/₃	1306	626	566	426	951
N.L. totals (1 year)	17	12	.586	3.59	32	32	5	1	0	220²/₃	193	93	88	69	183
Major league totals (8 years)	96	75	.561	3.76	231	229	32	10	0	1567	1499	719	654	495	1134

DIVISION SERIES RECORD

Year Team (League)	W	L	Pct.	ERA	G	GS	CG	ShO	Sv.	IP	H	R	ER	BB	SO
1997— Florida (N.L.)	1	0	1.000	2.57	1	1	0	0	0	7	7	2	2	0	5

CHAMPIONSHIP SERIES RECORD

Year Team (League)	W	L	Pct.	ERA	G	GS	CG	ShO	Sv.	IP	H	R	ER	BB	SO
1993— Chicago (A.L.)	0	2	.000	1.80	2	2	0	0	0	15	15	6	3	6	10
1997— Florida (N.L.)	0	1	.000	16.88	1	1	0	0	0	2²/₃	6	5	5	1	3
Champ. series totals (2 years)	0	3	.000	4.08	3	3	0	0	0	17²/₃	21	11	8	7	13

WORLD SERIES RECORD

NOTES: Member of World Series championship team (1997); inactive due to injury.

Year Team (League)	W	L	Pct.	ERA	G	GS	CG	ShO	Sv.	IP	H	R	ER	BB	SO
1997— Florida (N.L.)							Did not play.								

F

FERNANDEZ, JOSE 3B EXPOS

PERSONAL: Born November 2, 1974, in La Vega, Dominican Republic. ... 6-0/220. ... Bats left, throws right. ... Full name: Jose Mayobanex Fernandez.
HIGH SCHOOL: Instituto Evangelico (Santo Domingo, Dominican Republic).
COLLEGE: Universidad Madre y Maestra (Santiago, Dominican Republic).
TRANSACTIONS/CAREER NOTES: Signed as non-drafted free agent by Montreal Expos organization (March 2, 1993). ... On Ottawa disabled list (September 1, 1998-remainder of season).

							BATTING								FIELDING		
Year	Team (League)	Pos.	G	AB	R	H	2B	3B	HR	RBI	Avg.	BB	SO	SB	PO	A	E	Avg.
1993—Dom. Expos (DSL)		IF	65	251	40	80	8	1	10	49	.319	32	23	2	103	223	25	.929
1994—G.C. Expos (GCL)		3B-1B	45	172	27	40	8	0	5	23	.233	14	35	11	87	77	9	.948
1995—Vermont (NYP)..........		3B	66	270	38	74	6	7	4	41	.274	13	51	29	48	157	21	.907
1996—Delmarva (S. Atl.).......		3B	126	421	72	115	23	6	12	70	.273	50	76	23	*102	239	35	.907
1997—Harrisburg (East.).......		3B-1B	29	96	10	22	3	1	4	11	.229	11	28	2	41	31	6	.923
—W.P. Beach (FSL).......		3B-1B	97	350	49	108	21	3	9	58	.309	37	76	22	89	193	15	.949
1998—Harrisburg (East.).......		3B-1B	104	369	59	109	27	1	17	58	.295	36	73	16	119	167	22	.929

FERNANDEZ, OSVALDO P

PERSONAL: Born November 4, 1968, in Holguin, Cuba. ... 6-2/193. ... Throws right, bats right.
HIGH SCHOOL: Universidad de Holguin (Holguin, Cuba).
TRANSACTIONS/CAREER NOTES: Signed as non-drafted free agent by San Francisco Giants organization (January 16, 1996). ... On disabled list (May 20-June 19 and June 26-September 28, 1997); included rehabilitation assignment to Phoenix (June 11-20). ... On disabled list (March 22, 1998-entire season). ... Granted free agency (December 21, 1998).
MISCELLANEOUS: Appeared in three games as pinch runner (1996). ... Appeared in one game as pinch runner with San Francisco (1997).

Year Team (League)	W	L	Pct.	ERA	G	GS	CG	ShO	Sv.	IP	H	R	ER	BB	SO
1996—San Francisco (N.L.)	7	13	.350	4.61	30	28	2	0	0	171 2/3	193	95	88	57	106
1997—San Francisco (N.L.)	3	4	.429	4.95	11	11	0	0	0	56 1/3	74	39	31	15	31
—Phoenix (PCL)	0	0	. . .	3.00	2	2	0	0	0	12	10	5	4	3	4
1998—San Francisco (N.L.)						Did not play.									
Major league totals (2 years)......	**10**	**17**	**.370**	**4.70**	**41**	**39**	**2**	**0**	**0**	**228**	**267**	**134**	**119**	**72**	**137**

FERNANDEZ, TONY IF BLUE JAYS

PERSONAL: Born June 30, 1962, in San Pedro de Macoris, Dominican Republic. ... 6-2/195. ... Bats both, throws right. ... Full name: Octavio Antonio Castro Fernandez.
HIGH SCHOOL: Gasto Fernando de Ligne (San Pedro de Macoris, Dominican Republic).
TRANSACTIONS/CAREER NOTES: Signed as non-drafted free agent by Toronto Blue Jays organization (April 24, 1979). ... On Syracuse disabled list (August 10-27, 1981). ... On disabled list (April 8-May 2, 1989). ... Traded by Blue Jays with 1B Fred McGriff to San Diego Padres for OF Joe Carter and 2B Roberto Alomar (December 5, 1990). ... Traded by Padres to New York Mets for P Wally Whitehurst, OF D.J. Dozier and a player to be named later (October 26, 1992); Padres acquired C Raul Casanova from Mets to complete deal (December 7, 1992). ... Traded by Mets to Blue Jays for OF Darrin Jackson (June 11, 1993). ... Granted free agency (November 3, 1993). ... Signed by Cincinnati Reds organization (March 8, 1994). ... Granted free agency (October 13, 1994). ... Signed by New York Yankees (December 15, 1994). ... On disabled list (May 21-June 8, 1995). ... On disabled list (March 24, 1996-remainder of season). ... Granted free agency (November 18, 1996). ... Signed by Cleveland Indians (December 28, 1996). ... Granted free agency (October 30, 1997). ... Signed by Blue Jays (December 8, 1997).
RECORDS: Shares major league record for most times caught stealing in one inning—2 (June 26, 1992, fifth inning). ... Holds A.L. career record for highest fielding percentage by shortstop (1,000 or more games)—.982. ... Holds A.L. single-season record for most games by shortstop—163 (1986). ... Shares A.L. single-season record for most games by switch hitter—163 (1986).
HONORS: Named shortstop on THE SPORTING NEWS A.L. All-Star team (1986). ... Won A.L. Gold Glove at shortstop (1986-89).
STATISTICAL NOTES: Led International League shortstops with 87 double plays in 1983. ... Led A.L. shortstops with 791 total chances in 1985 and 786 in 1990. ... Led N.L. third basemen with .991 fielding percentage in 1994. ... Hit for the cycle (September 3, 1995, 10 innings). ... Career major league grand slams: 2.
MISCELLANEOUS: Holds Toronto Blue Jays franchise all-time record for most triples (72), hits (1,406) and doubles (246).

							BATTING								FIELDING		
Year	Team (League)	Pos.	G	AB	R	H	2B	3B	HR	RBI	Avg.	BB	SO	SB	PO	A	E	Avg.
1980—Kinston (Carolina)		SS	62	187	28	52	6	2	0	12	.278	28	17	7	93	205	28	.914
1981—Kinston (Carolina)		SS	75	280	57	89	10	6	1	13	.318	49	20	15	121	227	19	.948
—Syracuse (Int'l)..........		SS	31	115	13	32	6	2	1	9	.278	7	15	9	69	80	3	.980
1982—Syracuse (Int'l)..........		SS	134	523	78	158	21	6	4	56	.302	42	31	22	*246	364	23	*.964
1983—Syracuse (Int'l)..........		SS	117	437	65	131	18	6	5	38	.300	57	27	35	*211	361	26	.957
—Toronto (A.L.).............		SS-DH	15	34	5	9	1	1	0	2	.265	2	2	0	16	17	0	1.000
1984—Syracuse (Int'l)..........		SS	26	94	12	24	1	0	0	6	.255	13	9	1	46	72	5	.959
—Toronto (A.L.).............		SS-3B-DH	88	233	29	63	5	3	3	19	.270	17	15	5	119	195	9	.972
1985—Toronto (A.L.).............		SS	161	564	71	163	31	10	2	51	.289	43	41	13	283	*478	15	.981
1986—Toronto (A.L.).............		SS	*163	*687	91	213	33	9	10	65	.310	27	52	25	*294	445	13	*.983
1987—Toronto (A.L.).............		SS	146	578	90	186	29	8	5	67	.322	51	48	32	*270	396	14	.979
1988—Toronto (A.L.).............		SS	154	648	76	186	41	4	5	70	.287	45	65	15	247	470	14	.981
1989—Toronto (A.L.).............		SS	140	573	64	147	25	9	11	64	.257	29	51	22	260	475	6	*.992
1990—Toronto (A.L.).............		SS	161	635	84	175	27	*17	4	66	.276	71	70	26	*297	*480	9	.989
1991—San Diego (N.L.)■		SS	145	558	81	152	27	5	4	38	.272	55	74	23	247	440	20	.972
1992—San Diego (N.L.)		SS	155	622	84	171	32	4	4	37	.275	56	62	20	240	405	11	.983
1993—New York (N.L.)■		SS	48	173	20	39	5	2	1	14	.225	25	19	6	83	150	6	.975
—Toronto (A.L.)■...........		SS	94	353	45	108	18	9	4	50	.306	31	26	15	196	260	7	.985
1994—Cincinnati (N.L.)■		3B-SS-2B	104	366	50	102	18	6	8	50	.279	44	40	12	67	195	4	†.985

F

Year	Team (League)	Pos.	G	AB	R	H	2B	3B	HR	RBI	Avg.	BB	SO	SB	PO	A	E	Avg.
1995—	New York (A.L.)■.......	SS-2B	108	384	57	94	20	2	5	45	.245	42	40	6	148	283	10	.977
1996—	....						Did not play.											
1997—	Cleveland (A.L.)■.......	2B-SS-DH	120	409	55	117	21	1	11	44	.286	22	47	6	219	322	11	.980
1998—	Toronto (A.L.)■.......	2B-3B-DH	138	486	71	156	36	2	9	72	.321	45	53	13	160	295	13	.972
American League totals (12 years)			1488	5584	738	1617	287	75	69	615	.290	425	510	178	2509	4116	136	.980
National League totals (4 years)			452	1719	235	464	82	17	17	139	.270	180	195	61	637	1190	41	.978
Major league totals (15 years)			1940	7303	973	2081	369	92	86	754	.285	605	705	239	3146	5306	177	.979

DIVISION SERIES RECORD

Year	Team (League)	Pos.	G	AB	R	H	2B	3B	HR	RBI	Avg.	BB	SO	SB	PO	A	E	Avg.
1995—	New York (A.L.).........	SS	5	21	0	5	2	0	0	0	.238	2	2	0	9	15	0	1.000
1997—	Cleveland (A.L.).........	2B-PH	4	11	0	2	1	0	0	4	.182	0	0	0	8	9	0	1.000
Division series totals (2 years)			9	32	0	7	3	0	0	4	.219	2	2	0	17	24	0	1.000

CHAMPIONSHIP SERIES RECORD

Year	Team (League)	Pos.	G	AB	R	H	2B	3B	HR	RBI	Avg.	BB	SO	SB	PO	A	E	Avg.
1985—	Toronto (A.L.)............	SS	7	24	2	8	2	0	0	2	.333	1	2	0	11	15	2	.929
1989—	Toronto (A.L.)............	SS	5	20	6	7	3	0	0	1	.350	1	2	5	9	15	0	1.000
1993—	Toronto (A.L.)............	SS	6	22	1	7	0	0	0	1	.318	2	4	0	12	8	0	1.000
1997—	Cleveland (A.L.).........	2B-PH	5	14	1	5	1	0	1	2	.357	1	2	0	9	10	1	.950
Championship series totals (4 years)			23	80	10	27	6	0	1	6	.338	5	10	5	41	48	3	.967

NOTES: Member of World Series championship team (1993).

WORLD SERIES RECORD

Year	Team (League)	Pos.	G	AB	R	H	2B	3B	HR	RBI	Avg.	BB	SO	SB	PO	A	E	Avg.
1993—	Toronto (A.L.)............	SS	6	21	2	7	1	0	0	9	.333	3	3	0	11	8	0	1.000
1997—	Cleveland (A.L.).........	2B-PH	5	17	1	8	1	0	0	4	.471	0	1	0	9	14	2	.920
World Series totals (2 years)			11	38	3	15	2	0	0	13	.395	3	4	0	20	22	2	.955

ALL-STAR GAME RECORD

Year	League	Pos.	AB	R	H	2B	3B	HR	RBI	Avg.	BB	SO	SB	PO	A	E	Avg.
1986—	American..................	SS	0	0	0	0	0	0	0	. . .	0	0	0	0	0	0	. . .
1987—	American..................	SS	2	0	0	0	0	0	0	.000	0	0	0	1	3	0	1.000
1989—	American..................	PR-SS	1	0	0	0	0	0	0	.000	0	0	0	2	2	0	1.000
1992—	National..................	SS	2	1	1	0	0	0	0	.500	0	0	0	3	0	0	1.000
All-Star Game totals (4 years)			5	1	1	0	0	0	0	.200	0	0	0	6	5	0	1.000

FETTERS, MIKE   P

PERSONAL: Born December 19, 1964, in Van Nuys, Calif. ... 6-4/226. ... Throws right, bats right. ... Full name: Michael Lee Fetters.
HIGH SCHOOL: Iolani (Honolulu, Hawaii).
COLLEGE: Pepperdine.
TRANSACTIONS/CAREER NOTES: Selected by Los Angeles Dodgers organization in 22nd round of free-agent draft (June 6, 1983); did not sign. ... Selected by California Angels organization in supplemental round ("sandwich pick" between first and second round, 27th pick overall) of free-agent draft (June 2, 1986); pick received as compensation for Baltimore Orioles signing Type A free-agent OF/IF Juan Beniquez. ... Traded by Angels with P Glenn Carter to Milwaukee Brewers for P Chuck Crim (December 10, 1991). ... On disabled list (May 3-19, 1992 and May 25-June 9, 1995). ... On Milwaukee disabled list (April 4-May 5, 1997); included rehabilitation assignment to Tucson (April 30-May 5). ... Traded by Brewers with P Ben McDonald and P Ron Villone to Cleveland Indians for OF Marquis Grissom and P Jeff Juden (December 8, 1997). ... Traded by Indians to Oakland Athletics for P Steve Karsay (December 8, 1997). ... On Oakland disabled list (April 6-26, 1998). ... Traded by A's to Anaheim Angels for a player to be named later and cash (August 10, 1998). ... Granted free agency (October 26, 1998).

Year	Team (League)	W	L	Pct.	ERA	G	GS	CG	ShO	Sv.	IP	H	R	ER	BB	SO
1986—	Salem (Northwest)............	4	2	.667	3.38	12	12	1	0	0	72	60	39	27	51	72
1987—	Palm Springs (Calif.)........	9	7	.563	3.57	19	19	2	0	0	116	106	62	46	73	105
1988—	Midland (Texas)............	8	8	.500	5.92	20	20	2	0	0	114	116	78	75	67	101
—Edmonton (PCL)............		2	0	1.000	1.93	2	2	1	0	0	14	8	3	3	10	11
1989—	Edmonton (PCL)............	12	8	.600	3.80	26	26	•6	2	0	168	160	80	71	72	*144
—California (A.L.)............		0	0	. . .	8.10	1	0	0	0	0	3 1/3	5	4	3	1	4
1990—	Edmonton (PCL)............	1	1	.500	0.99	5	5	1	1	0	27 1/3	22	9	3	13	26
—California (A.L.)............		1	1	.500	4.12	26	2	0	0	1	67 2/3	77	33	31	20	35
1991—	Edmonton (PCL)............	2	7	.222	4.87	11	11	1	0	0	61	65	39	33	26	43
—California (A.L.)............		2	5	.286	4.84	19	4	0	0	0	44 2/3	53	29	24	28	43
1992—	Milwaukee (A.L.)■............	5	1	.833	1.87	50	0	0	0	2	62 2/3	38	15	13	24	43
1993—	Milwaukee (A.L.)............	3	3	.500	3.34	45	0	0	0	0	59 1/3	59	29	22	22	23
1994—	Milwaukee (A.L.)............	1	4	.200	2.54	42	0	0	0	17	46	41	16	13	27	31
1995—	Milwaukee (A.L.)............	0	3	.000	3.38	40	0	0	0	22	34 2/3	40	16	13	20	33
1996—	Milwaukee (A.L.)............	3	3	.500	3.38	61	0	0	0	32	61 1/3	65	28	23	26	53
1997—	Milwaukee (A.L.)............	1	5	.167	3.45	51	0	0	0	6	70 1/3	62	30	27	33	62
—Tucson (PCL)............		0	0	. . .	10.80	2	0	0	0	0	1 2/3	1	2	2	1	0
1998—	Oakland (A.L.)■............	1	6	.143	3.99	44	0	0	0	5	47 1/3	48	26	21	21	34
—Anaheim (A.L.)■............		1	2	.333	5.56	12	0	0	0	0	11 1/3	14	8	7	4	9
Major league totals (10 years)....		18	33	.353	3.49	395	6	0	0	85	508 2/3	502	234	197	226	351

FICK, ROB   C/1B   TIGERS

PERSONAL: Born March 15, 1974, in Torrance, Calif. ... 6-1/189. ... Bats left, throws right. ... Full name: Robert Charles John Fick. ... Brother of Chris Fick, former outfielder/first baseman in St. Louis Cardinals and Arizona Diamondacks organizations; and brother of Chuck Fick, St. Louis Cardinals scout and former catcher in Montreal Expos and Oakland Athletics organization.
HIGH SCHOOL: Newbury Park (Calif.).
JUNIOR COLLEGE: Ventura (Calif.) College.
COLLEGE: Cal State Northridge.
TRANSACTIONS/CAREER NOTES: Selected by Oakland Athletics organization in 45th round of free-agent draft (June 1, 1992); did not sign. ... Selected by Detroit Tigers organization in 43rd round of free-agent draft (June 1, 1995); did not sign. ... Selected by Tigers organization in fifth round of free-agent draft (June 4, 1996).
HONORS: Named Midwest League Most Valuable Player (1997).
STATISTICAL NOTES: Led Midwest League with 262 total bases and .566 slugging percentage in 1997.

							BATTING							FIELDING		
Year Team (League)	Pos.	G	AB	R	H	2B	3B	HR	RBI	Avg.	BB	SO	SB	PO	A	E	Avg.
1996— Jamestown (NYP)	C	43	133	18	33	6	0	1	14	.248	12	25	3	155	13	3	.982
1997— W. Michigan (Midw.)..	1B-C-3B	122	463	100	*158	*50	3	16	90	*.341	75	74	0	1043	68	12	.989
1998— Jacksonville (Sou.).....	C-1B-OF	130	515	101	164	47	6	18	114	.318	71	83	8	540	45	9	.985
— Detroit (A.L.)	C-DH-1B	7	22	6	8	1	0	3	7	.364	2	7	1	27	1	1	.966
Major league totals (1 year)		7	22	6	8	1	0	3	7	.364	2	7	1	27	1	1	.966

FIELDER, CECIL   DH/1B

PERSONAL: Born September 21, 1963, in Los Angeles. ... 6-3/261. ... Bats right, throws right. ... Full name: Cecil Grant Fielder.
HIGH SCHOOL: Nogales (La Puente, Calif.).
COLLEGE: UNLV.
TRANSACTIONS/CAREER NOTES: Selected by Baltimore Orioles organization in 31st round of free-agent draft (June 8, 1981); did not sign. ... Selected by Kansas City Royals organization in secondary phase of free-agent draft (June 7, 1982). ... Traded by Royals organization to Toronto Blue Jays organization for OF Leon Roberts (February 4, 1983). ... Contract sold by Blue Jays to Hanshin Tigers of Japan Central League (December 22, 1988). ... Signed as free agent by Detroit Tigers (January 15, 1990). ... Traded by Tigers to New York Yankees for OF Ruben Sierra and P Matt Drews (July 31, 1996). ... On disabled list (July 16-September 16, 1997). ... Granted free agency (October 27, 1997). ... Signed by Anaheim Angels (December 19, 1997). ... Released by Angels (August 10, 1998). ... Signed by Cleveland Indians (August 13, 1998). ... Released by Indians (September 18, 1998).
RECORDS: Shares major league career record for most times hitting three or more consecutive home runs in a game—3. ... Shares major league records for most consecutive years leading league in runs batted in—3 (1990-92); and most years without a stolen base (150 games or more per year)—4. ... Shares major league single-season record for most games with three home runs—2 (1990).
HONORS: Named A.L. Player of the Year by THE SPORTING NEWS (1990). ... Named first baseman on THE SPORTING NEWS A.L. All-Star team (1990-91). ... Named first baseman on THE SPORTING NEWS A.L. Silver Slugger team (1990-91).
STATISTICAL NOTES: Led Pioneer League with 176 total bases and in being hit by pitch with eight in 1982. ... Led A.L. with 339 total bases and .592 slugging percentage in 1990. ... Led A.L. first basemen with 137 double plays in 1990. ... Hit three home runs in one game (May 6 and June 6, 1990; and April 16, 1996). ... Career major league grand slams: 11.

							BATTING							FIELDING		
Year Team (League)	Pos.	G	AB	R	H	2B	3B	HR	RBI	Avg.	BB	SO	SB	PO	A	E	Avg.
1982— Butte (Pioneer)..........	1B	69	273	73	88	*28	0	*20	68	.322	37	62	3	247	18	4	.985
1983— Florence (S. Atl.)■.....	1B	140	500	81	156	28	2	16	94	.312	58	90	2	957	64	16	.985
1984— Kinston (Carolina)	1B	61	222	42	63	12	1	19	49	.284	28	44	2	533	24	9	.984
— Knoxville (Southern) ..	1B	64	236	33	60	12	2	9	44	.254	22	48	0	173	10	4	.979
1985— Knoxville (Southern) ..	1B	96	361	52	106	26	2	18	81	.294	45	83	0	444	26	6	.987
— Toronto (A.L.)............	1B	30	74	6	23	4	0	4	16	.311	6	16	0	171	17	4	.979
1986— Toronto (A.L.)............	DH-1-3-O	34	83	7	13	2	0	4	13	.157	6	27	0	37	4	1	.976
— Syracuse (Int'l).........	OF-1B	88	325	47	91	13	3	18	68	.280	32	91	0	117	5	1	.992
1987— Toronto (A.L.)............	DH-1B-3B	82	175	30	47	7	1	14	32	.269	20	48	0	98	6	0	1.000
1988— Toronto (A.L.)............	DH-1-3-2	74	174	24	40	6	1	9	23	.230	14	53	0	101	12	1	.991
1989— Hanshin (Jp. Cn.)■......	...	106	384	60	116	11	0	38	81	.302	67	107	0	...	...	...	...
1990— Detroit (A.L.)■........	1B-DH	159	573	104	159	25	1	*51	*132	.277	90	*182	0	1190	111	14	.989
1991— Detroit (A.L.)............	1B-DH	•162	624	102	163	25	0	•44	*133	.261	78	151	0	1055	83	8	.993
1992— Detroit (A.L.)............	1B-DH	155	594	80	145	22	0	35	*124	.244	73	151	0	957	92	10	.991
1993— Detroit (A.L.)............	1B-DH	154	573	80	153	23	0	30	117	.267	90	125	0	971	78	10	.991
1994— Detroit (A.L.)............	1B-DH	109	425	67	110	16	2	28	90	.259	50	110	0	887	*108	7	.993
1995— Detroit (A.L.)............	1B-DH	136	494	70	120	18	1	31	82	.243	75	116	0	631	73	5	.993
1996— Detroit (A.L.)............	1B-DH	107	391	55	97	12	0	26	80	.248	63	91	2	589	59	7	.989
— New York (A.L.)■......	DH-1B	53	200	30	52	8	0	13	37	.260	24	48	0	74	4	0	1.000
1997— New York (A.L.)..........	DH-1B	98	361	40	94	15	0	13	61	.260	51	87	0	59	6	0	1.000
1998— Anaheim (A.L.)■........	1B-DH	103	381	48	92	16	1	17	68	.241	52	98	0	550	39	2	.997
— Cleveland (A.L.)■......	DH-1B	14	35	1	5	1	0	0	0	.143	1	13	0	12	2	1	.933
Major league totals (13 years)		1470	5157	744	1313	200	7	319	1008	.255	693	1316	2	7382	694	70	.991

DIVISION SERIES RECORD

							BATTING							FIELDING		
Year Team (League)	Pos.	G	AB	R	H	2B	3B	HR	RBI	Avg.	BB	SO	SB	PO	A	E	Avg.
1996— New York (A.L.)..........	DH	3	11	2	4	0	0	1	4	.364	1	2	0	...	...	...	...
1997— New York (A.L.)..........	DH	2	8	0	1	0	0	0	1	.125	0	3	0	...	...	...	...
Division series totals (2 years)		5	19	2	5	0	0	1	5	.263	1	5	0	...	...	...	...

CHAMPIONSHIP SERIES RECORD

							BATTING							FIELDING		
Year Team (League)	Pos.	G	AB	R	H	2B	3B	HR	RBI	Avg.	BB	SO	SB	PO	A	E	Avg.
1985— Toronto (A.L.)............	PH	3	3	0	1	1	0	0	0	.333	0	0	0	...	...	...	...
1996— New York (A.L.)..........	DH	5	18	3	3	0	0	2	8	.167	5	5	0	...	...	...	...
Championship series totals (2 years)		8	21	3	4	1	0	2	8	.190	5	5	0	...	...	...	...

F

WORLD SERIES RECORD

NOTES: Member of World Series championship team (1996).

									BATTING						FIELDING		
Year Team (League)	Pos.	G	AB	R	H	2B	3B	HR	RBI	Avg.	BB	SO	SB	PO	A	E	Avg.
1996— New York (A.L.)..........	DH-1B	6	23	1	9	2	0	0	2	.391	2	2	0	21	5	0	1.000

ALL-STAR GAME RECORD

							BATTING						FIELDING		
Year League	Pos.	AB	R	H	2B	3B	HR	RBI	Avg.	BB	SO	SB	PO	A	E	Avg.
1990— American....................	PH-1B	1	0	0	0	0	0	0	.000	0	0	0	3	1	0	1.000
1991— American....................	1B	3	0	0	0	0	0	0	.000	0	1	0	6	2	0	1.000
1993— American....................	1B	1	0	0	0	0	0	0	.000	0	0	0	4	0	0	1.000
All-Star Game totals (3 years)		5	0	0	0	0	0	0	.000	0	1	0	13	3	0	1.000

FIGGA, MIKE   C   YANKEES

PERSONAL: Born July 31, 1970, in Tampa. ... 6-0/200. ... Bats right, throws right. ... Full name: Michael Anthony Figga.
HIGH SCHOOL: Plant (Tampa).
JUNIOR COLLEGE: Central Florida Community College.
TRANSACTIONS/CAREER NOTES: Selected by New York Yankees organization in 44th round of free-agent draft (June 5, 1989). ... On disabled list (August 31, 1996-remainder of season). ... On Columbus disabled list (July 29-August 12, 1998).
STATISTICAL NOTES: Led Gulf Coast League catchers with 296 total chances in 1990. ... Led International League catchers with 15 double plays in 1998.

									BATTING						FIELDING		
Year Team (League)	Pos.	G	AB	R	H	2B	3B	HR	RBI	Avg.	BB	SO	SB	PO	A	E	Avg.
1990— GC Yankees (GCL)......	C	40	123	19	35	1	1	2	18	.285	17	33	4	*270	19	7	.976
1991— Prince Will. (Car.).......	C	55	174	15	34	6	0	3	17	.195	19	51	2	278	33	5	.984
1992— Fort Laud. (FSL).........	C	80	249	12	44	13	0	1	15	.177	13	78	3	568	71	12	.982
— Prince Will. (Car.).......	C	3	10	0	2	1	0	0	0	.200	2	3	1	27	1	0	1.000
1993— San Bern. (Calif.)........	C	83	308	48	82	17	1	25	71	.266	17	84	2	491	70	12	.979
— Alb./Colon. (East.)......	C	6	22	3	5	0	0	0	2	.227	2	9	1	31	2	1	.971
1994— Tampa (Fla. St.).........	C	111	420	48	116	17	5	15	75	.276	22	94	3	703	79	10	.987
— Alb./Colon. (East.)......	C	1	2	1	1	1	0	0	0	.500	0	1	0	5	0	0	1.000
1995— Norwich (Eastern)......	C	109	399	59	108	22	4	13	61	.271	43	90	1	640	92	11	.985
— Columbus (Int'l).........	C	8	25	2	7	1	0	1	3	.280	3	5	0	29	4	0	1.000
1996— Columbus (Int'l).........	C	4	11	3	3	1	0	0	0	.273	1	3	0	17	2	0	1.000
1997— Columbus (Int'l).........	C	110	390	48	95	14	4	12	54	.244	18	104	3	706	62	11	.986
— New York (A.L.)..........	DH-C	2	4	0	0	0	0	0	0	.000	0	3	0	6	0	0	1.000
1998— Columbus (Int'l).........	C-1B	123	461	57	129	30	3	26	95	.280	35	109	2	733	63	10	.988
— New York (A.L.)..........	C	1	4	1	1	0	0	0	0	.250	0	1	0	3	1	0	1.000
Major league totals (2 years)		3	8	1	1	0	0	0	0	.125	0	4	0	9	1	0	1.000

FIGUEROA, NELSON   P   DIAMONDBACKS

PERSONAL: Born May 18, 1974, in Brooklyn, N.Y. ... 6-1/155. ... Throws right, bats both. ... Full name: Nelson Walter Figueroa Jr.
HIGH SCHOOL: Abraham Lincoln (Brooklyn, N.Y.).
COLLEGE: Brandeis (Mass.).
TRANSACTIONS/CAREER NOTES: Selected by New York Mets organization in 30th round of free-agent draft (June 1, 1995). ... Traded by Mets with OF Bernard Gilkey and cash to Arizona Diamondbacks for P Willie Blair, C Jorge Fabregas and a player to be named later (July 31, 1998).
HONORS: Named South Atlantic League Most Outstanding Pitcher (1996).

Year Team (League)	W	L	Pct.	ERA	G	GS	CG	ShO	Sv.	IP	H	R	ER	BB	SO
1995— Kingsport (Appalachian).....	7	3	.700	3.07	12	12	2	*2	0	76 1/3	57	31	26	22	79
1996— Columbia (S. Atl.)............	14	7	.667	*2.04	26	25	*8	4	0	*185 1/3	119	55	42	58	*200
1997— Binghamton (Eastern)	5	11	.313	4.34	33	22	0	0	0	143	137	76	69	68	116
1998— Binghamton (Eastern)	12	3	.800	4.66	21	21	3	2	0	123 2/3	133	73	64	44	116
— Tucson (PCL)■	2	2	.500	3.70	7	7	0	0	0	41 1/3	46	22	17	16	29

FINLEY, CHUCK   P   ANGELS

PERSONAL: Born November 26, 1962, in Monroe, La. ... 6-6/226. ... Throws left, bats left. ... Full name: Charles Edward Finley.
HIGH SCHOOL: West Monroe (La.).
COLLEGE: Northeast Louisiana.
TRANSACTIONS/CAREER NOTES: Selected by California Angels organization in 15th round of free-agent draft (June 4, 1984); did not sign. ... Selected by Angels organization in secondary phase of free-agent draft (January 9, 1985). ... On disabled list (August 22-September 15, 1989 and April 6-22, 1992). ... Granted free agency (November 7, 1995). ... Re-signed by Angels (January 4, 1996). ... Angels franchise renamed Anaheim Angels for 1997 season. ... On Anaheim disabled list (March 23-April 15 and August 20, 1997-remainder of season); included rehabilitation assignment to Lake Elsinore (April 5-10).
HONORS: Named lefthanded pitcher on THE SPORTING NEWS A.L. All-Star team (1989-90).
STATISTICAL NOTES: Pitched 5-0 one-hit, complete-game victory against Boston (May 26, 1989). ... Struck out 15 batters in one game (June 24, 1989 and May 23, 1995). ... Led A.L. with 17 wild pitches in 1996.
MISCELLANEOUS: Holds Anaheim Angels franchise all-time records for most wins (153), innings pitched (2,461 2/3) and games pitched (403).

Year Team (League)	W	L	Pct.	ERA	G	GS	CG	ShO	Sv.	IP	H	R	ER	BB	SO
1985— Salem (Northwest)	3	1	.750	4.66	18	0	0	0	5	29	34	21	15	10	32
1986— Quad Cities (Midw.)............	1	0	1.000	0.00	10	0	0	0	6	12	4	0	0	3	16
— California (A.L.)..................	3	1	.750	3.30	25	0	0	0	0	46 1/3	40	17	17	23	37

F

Year	Team (League)	W	L	Pct.	ERA	G	GS	CG	ShO	Sv.	IP	H	R	ER	BB	SO
1987—	California (A.L.)	2	7	.222	4.67	35	3	0	0	0	90 2/3	102	54	47	43	63
1988—	California (A.L.)	9	15	.375	4.17	31	31	2	0	0	194 1/3	191	95	90	82	111
1989—	California (A.L.)	16	9	.640	2.57	29	29	9	1	0	199 2/3	171	64	57	82	156
1990—	California (A.L.)	18	9	.667	2.40	32	32	7	2	0	236	210	77	63	81	177
1991—	California (A.L.)	18	9	.667	3.80	34	34	4	2	0	227 1/3	205	102	96	101	171
1992—	California (A.L.)	7	12	.368	3.96	31	31	4	1	0	204 1/3	212	99	90	98	124
1993—	California (A.L.)	16	14	.533	3.15	35	35	*13	2	0	251 1/3	243	108	88	82	187
1994—	California (A.L.)	10	10	.500	4.32	25	•25	7	2	0	*183 1/3	178	95	88	71	148
1995—	California (A.L.)	15	12	.556	4.21	32	32	2	1	0	203	192	106	95	93	195
1996—	California (A.L.)	15	16	.484	4.16	35	35	4	1	0	238	241	124	110	94	215
1997—	Lake Elsinore (Calif.)	0	0	. . .	2.00	2	2	0	0	0	9	5	3	2	4	12
—	Anaheim (A.L.)	13	6	.684	4.23	25	25	3	1	0	164	152	79	77	65	155
1998—	Anaheim (A.L.)	11	9	.550	3.39	34	34	1	1	0	223 1/3	210	97	84	109	212
	Major league totals (13 years)	153	129	.543	3.66	403	346	56	14	0	2461 2/3	2347	1117	1002	1024	1951

CHAMPIONSHIP SERIES RECORD

Year	Team (League)	W	L	Pct.	ERA	G	GS	CG	ShO	Sv.	IP	H	R	ER	BB	SO
1986—	California (A.L.)	0	0	. . .	0.00	3	0	0	0	0	2	1	0	0	0	1

ALL-STAR GAME RECORD

Year	League	W	L	Pct.	ERA	GS	CG	ShO	Sv.	IP	H	R	ER	BB	SO
1989—	American							Did not play.							
1990—	American	0	0	. . .	0.00	0	0	0	0	1	0	0	0	1	1
1995—	American							Did not play.							
1996—	American	0	0	. . .	4.50	0	0	0	0	2	3	1	1	0	4
	All-Star totals (2 years)	0	0	. . .	3.00	0	0	0	0	3	3	1	1	1	5

FINLEY, STEVE   OF   DIAMONDBACKS

PERSONAL: Born March 12, 1965, in Union City, Tenn. ... 6-2/180. ... Bats left, throws left. ... Full name: Steven Allen Finley.

HIGH SCHOOL: Paducah (Ky.) Tilghman.

COLLEGE: Southern Illinois (degree in physiology).

TRANSACTIONS/CAREER NOTES: Selected by Atlanta Braves organization in 11th round of free-agent draft (June 2, 1986); did not sign. ... Selected by Baltimore Orioles organization in 13th round of free-agent draft (June 2, 1987). ... On Baltimore disabled list (April 4-22, 1989). ... On Baltimore disabled list (July 29-September 1, 1989); included rehabilitation assignment to Hagerstown (August 21-23). ... Traded by Orioles with P Pete Harnisch and P Curt Schilling to Houston Astros for 1B Glenn Davis (January 10, 1991). ... On disabled list (April 25-May 14, 1993). ... On Houston disabled list (June 13-July 3, 1994); included rehabilitation assignment to Jackson (June 28-July 3). ... Traded by Astros with 3B Ken Caminiti, SS Andujar Cedeno, 1B Roberto Petagine, P Brian Williams and a player to be named later to San Diego Padres for OF Phil Plantier, OF Derek Bell, P Pedro Martinez, P Doug Brocail, IF Craig Shipley and SS Ricky Gutierrez (December 28, 1994); Padres acquired P Sean Fesh to complete deal (May 1, 1995). ... On San Diego disabled list (April 20-May 6, 1997); included rehabilitation assignment by Padres to Rancho Cucamonga (April 25-May 6). ... Granted free agency (October 26, 1998). ... Signed by Arizona Diamondbacks (December 8, 1998).

RECORDS: Shares major league single-season record for most games with three home runs—2 (1997).

HONORS: Won N.L. Gold Glove as outfielder (1995-96).

STATISTICAL NOTES: Led International League outfielders with 315 total chances in 1988. ... Had 21-game hitting streak (June 20-July 14, 1996). ... Hit three home runs in one game (May 19 and June 23, 1997). ... Tied for N.L. lead with six double plays by outfielder in 1998. ... Career major league grand slams: 6.

Year	Team (League)	Pos.	G	AB	R	H	2B	3B	HR	RBI	Avg.	BB	SO	SB	PO	A	E	Avg.
1987—	Newark (NY-Penn)	OF	54	222	40	65	13	2	3	33	.293	22	24	26	122	7	4	.970
—	Hagerstown (Car.)	OF	15	65	9	22	3	2	1	5	.338	1	6	7	32	3	0	1.000
1988—	Hagerstown (Car.)	OF	8	28	2	6	2	0	0	3	.214	4	3	4	17	0	0	1.000
—	Charlotte (Southern)	OF	10	40	7	12	4	2	1	6	.300	4	3	2	14	0	0	1.000
—	Rochester (Int'l)	OF	120	456	61	*143	19	7	5	54	*.314	28	55	20	*289	14	*12	.962
1989—	Baltimore (A.L.)	OF-DH	81	217	35	54	5	2	2	25	.249	15	30	17	144	1	2	.986
—	Rochester (Int'l)	OF	7	25	2	4	0	0	0	2	.160	1	5	3	17	2	0	1.000
—	Hagerstown (East.)	OF	11	48	11	20	3	1	0	7	.417	4	3	4	35	2	3	.925
1990—	Baltimore (A.L.)	OF-DH	142	464	46	119	16	4	3	37	.256	32	53	22	298	4	7	.977
1991—	Houston (N.L.)■	OF	159	596	84	170	28	10	8	54	.285	42	65	34	323	13	5	.985
1992—	Houston (N.L.)	OF	•162	607	84	177	29	13	5	55	.292	58	63	44	417	8	3	.993
1993—	Houston (N.L.)	OF	142	545	69	145	15	*13	8	44	.266	28	65	19	329	12	4	.988
1994—	Houston (N.L.)	OF	94	373	64	103	16	5	11	33	.276	28	52	13	214	9	4	.982
—	Jackson (Texas)	OF	5	13	3	4	0	0	0	0	.308	4	0	1	6	0	0	1.000
1995—	San Diego (N.L.)■	OF	139	562	104	167	23	8	10	44	.297	59	62	36	291	8	7	.977
1996—	San Diego (N.L.)	OF	161	655	126	195	45	9	30	95	.298	56	87	22	385	7	7	.982
1997—	San Diego (N.L.)	OF	143	560	101	146	26	5	28	92	.261	43	92	15	338	10	4	.989
—	Rancho Cuca. (Cal.)	OF	4	14	3	4	0	0	2	3	.286	3	2	1	0	0	0	. . .
—	Mobile (Southern)	DH	1	4	1	2	0	0	1	2	.500	1	2	0	. . .	. . .	. . .	. . .
1998—	San Diego (N.L.)	OF	159	619	92	154	40	6	14	67	.249	45	103	12	351	12	7	.981
	American League totals (2 years)		223	681	81	173	21	6	5	62	.254	47	83	39	442	5	9	.980
	National League totals (8 years)		1159	4517	724	1257	222	69	114	484	.278	359	589	195	2648	79	41	.985
	Major league totals (10 years)		1382	5198	805	1430	243	75	119	546	.275	406	672	234	3090	84	50	.984

DIVISION SERIES RECORD

Year	Team (League)	Pos.	G	AB	R	H	2B	3B	HR	RBI	Avg.	BB	SO	SB	PO	A	E	Avg.
1996—	San Diego (N.L.)	OF	3	12	0	1	0	0	0	1	.083	0	4	1	10	0	0	1.000
1998—	San Diego (N.L.)	OF-PR	4	10	2	1	1	0	0	1	.100	1	4	0	6	0	0	1.000
	Division series totals (2 years)		7	22	2	2	1	0	0	2	.091	1	8	1	16	0	0	1.000

CHAMPIONSHIP SERIES RECORD

Year Team (League)	Pos.	G	AB	R	H	2B	3B	HR	RBI	Avg.	BB	SO	SB	PO	A	E	Avg.
1998— San Diego (N.L.)	OF	6	21	3	7	1	0	0	2	.333	6	2	1	15	0	0	1.000

WORLD SERIES RECORD

Year Team (League)	Pos.	G	AB	R	H	2B	3B	HR	RBI	Avg.	BB	SO	SB	PO	A	E	Avg.
1998— San Diego (N.L.)	OF	3	12	0	1	1	0	0	0	.083	0	2	1	9	1	0	1.000

ALL-STAR GAME RECORD

Year League	Pos.	AB	R	H	2B	3B	HR	RBI	Avg.	BB	SO	SB	PO	A	E	Avg.
1997— National	OF	1	0	0	0	0	0	0	.000	0	1	0	1	0	0	1.000

FLAHERTY, JOHN   C   DEVIL RAYS

PERSONAL: Born October 21, 1967, in New York. ... 6-1/200. ... Bats right, throws right. ... Full name: John Timothy Flaherty.

HIGH SCHOOL: St. Joseph's Regional (Montvale, N.J.).

COLLEGE: George Washington.

TRANSACTIONS/CAREER NOTES: Selected by Boston Red Sox organization in 25th round of free-agent draft (June 1, 1988). ... Traded by Red Sox to Detroit Tigers for C Rich Rowland (April 1, 1994). ... Traded by Tigers with SS Chris Gomez to San Diego Padres for C Brad Ausmus, SS Andujar Cedeno and P Russ Spear (June 18, 1996). ... Traded by Padres to Tampa Bay Devil Rays for P Brian Boehringer and IF Andy Sheets (November 18, 1997). ... On Tampa Bay disabled list (May 26-June 20, 1998); included rehabilitation assignment to Durham (June 14-20).

STATISTICAL NOTES: Tied for Florida State League lead with 19 passed balls in 1989. ... Had 27-game hitting streak (June 21-July 27, 1996). ... Career major league grand slams: 1.

Year Team (League)	Pos.	G	AB	R	H	2B	3B	HR	RBI	Avg.	BB	SO	SB	PO	A	E	Avg.
1988— Elmira (N.Y.-Penn)......	C	46	162	17	38	3	0	3	16	.235	12	23	2	235	39	7	.975
1989— Winter Haven (FSL)....	C-1B	95	334	31	87	14	2	4	28	.260	20	44	1	369	60	9	.979
1990— Pawtucket (Int'l)........	C-3B	99	317	35	72	18	0	4	32	.227	24	43	1	509	59	10	.983
— Lynchburg (Caro.)......	C	1	4	0	0	0	0	0	1	.000	0	1	0	3	2	0	1.000
1991— New Britain (East.)	C	67	225	27	65	9	0	3	18	.289	31	22	0	337	46	9	.977
— Pawtucket (Int'l)........	C	45	156	18	29	7	0	3	13	.186	15	14	0	270	18	•9	.970
1992— Boston (A.L.)	C	35	66	3	13	2	0	0	2	.197	3	7	0	102	7	2	.982
— Pawtucket (Int'l)........	C	31	104	11	26	3	0	0	7	.250	5	8	0	158	17	4	.978
1993— Pawtucket (Int'l)........	C	105	365	29	99	22	0	6	35	.271	26	41	0	626	78	10	.986
— Boston (A.L.)	C	13	25	3	3	2	0	0	2	.120	2	6	0	35	9	0	1.000
1994— Toledo (Int'l)■..........	C	44	151	20	39	10	2	7	17	.258	6	21	3	286	24	2	.994
— Detroit (A.L.)	C-DH	34	40	2	6	1	0	0	4	.150	1	11	0	78	9	0	1.000
1995— Detroit (A.L.)	C	112	354	39	86	22	1	11	40	.243	18	47	0	569	33	*11	.982
1996— Detroit (A.L.)	C	47	152	18	38	12	0	4	23	.250	8	25	1	243	13	5	.981
— San Diego (N.L.)■......	C	72	264	22	80	12	0	9	41	.303	9	36	2	471	29	5	.990
1997— San Diego (N.L.)	C	129	439	38	120	21	1	9	46	.273	33	62	4	753	65	11	.987
1998— Tampa Bay (A.L.)■......	C	91	304	21	63	11	0	3	24	.207	22	46	0	542	45	4	.993
— Durham (Int'l)	C	6	23	1	3	1	0	0	2	.130	1	5	0	23	4	0	1.000
American League totals (6 years)		332	941	86	209	50	1	18	95	.222	54	142	1	1569	116	22	.987
National League totals (2 years)		201	703	60	200	33	1	18	87	.284	42	98	6	1224	94	16	.988
Major league totals (7 years)		533	1644	146	409	83	2	36	182	.249	96	240	7	2793	210	38	.988

DIVISION SERIES RECORD

Year Team (League)	Pos.	G	AB	R	H	2B	3B	HR	RBI	Avg.	BB	SO	SB	PO	A	E	Avg.
1996— San Diego (N.L.)	C	2	4	0	0	0	0	0	0	.000	0	1	0	9	0	0	1.000

FLETCHER, DARRIN   C   BLUE JAYS

PERSONAL: Born October 3, 1966, in Elmhurst, Ill. ... 6-2/200. ... Bats left, throws right. ... Full name: Darrin Glen Fletcher. ... Son of Tom Fletcher, pitcher with Detroit Tigers (1962); and grandson of Glen Fletcher, minor league pitcher with Philadelphia Phillies organization (1938-1948).

HIGH SCHOOL: Oakwood (Ill.).

COLLEGE: Illinois.

TRANSACTIONS/CAREER NOTES: Selected by Los Angeles Dodgers organization in sixth round of free-agent draft (June 2, 1987). ... Traded by Dodgers to Philadelphia Phillies for P Dennis Cook (September 13, 1990). ... Traded by Phillies with cash to Montreal Expos for P Barry Jones (December 9, 1991). ... On Montreal disabled list (May 12-June 15, 1992); included rehabilitation assignment to Indianapolis (May 31-June 14). ... On disabled list (June 18-July 3, 1997). ... Granted free agency (October 27, 1997). ... Signed by Toronto Blue Jays (November 26, 1997). ... On disabled list (May 30-June 14, 1998).

STATISTICAL NOTES: Tied for Texas League lead in double plays by catcher with nine in 1988. ... Led Pacific Coast League catchers with 787 total chances in 1990. ... Led N.L. with 12 sacrifice flies in 1994. ... Career major league grand slams: 2.

Year Team (League)	Pos.	G	AB	R	H	2B	3B	HR	RBI	Avg.	BB	SO	SB	PO	A	E	Avg.
1987— Vero Beach (FSL)	C	43	124	13	33	7	0	0	15	.266	22	12	0	212	35	3	.988
1988— San Antonio (Tex.)	C	89	279	19	58	8	0	1	20	.208	17	42	2	529	64	5	*.992
1989— Albuquerque (PCL).....	C	100	315	34	86	16	1	5	44	.273	30	38	1	632	63	9	.987
— Los Angeles (N.L.)	C	5	8	1	4	0	0	1	2	.500	1	0	0	16	1	0	1.000
1990— Albuquerque (PCL).....	C	105	350	58	102	23	1	13	65	.291	40	37	1	*715	64	8	.990
— Los Angeles (N.L.)	C	2	1	0	0	0	0	0	0	.000	0	1	0	0	0	0	...
— Philadelphia (N.L.)■ ..	C	9	22	3	3	1	0	0	1	.136	1	5	0	30	3	0	1.000

Year Team (League)	Pos.	G	AB	R	H	2B	3B	HR	RBI	Avg.	BB	SO	SB	PO	A	E	Avg.
						BATTING									FIELDING		
1991—Scran./W.B. (Int'l)......	C-1B	90	306	39	87	13	1	8	50	.284	23	29	1	491	44	5	.991
—Philadelphia (N.L.)......	C	46	136	5	31	8	0	1	12	.228	5	15	0	242	22	2	.992
1992—Montreal (N.L.)■......	C	83	222	13	54	10	2	2	26	.243	14	28	0	360	33	2	.995
—Indianapolis (A.A.)......	C	13	51	2	13	2	0	1	9	.255	2	10	0	65	7	1	.986
1993—Montreal (N.L.)......	C	133	396	33	101	20	1	9	60	.255	34	40	0	620	41	8	.988
1994—Montreal (N.L.)......	C	94	285	28	74	18	1	10	57	.260	25	23	0	479	20	2	.996
1995—Montreal (N.L.)......	C	110	350	42	100	21	1	11	45	.286	32	23	0	613	44	4	.994
1996—Montreal (N.L.)......	C	127	394	41	105	22	0	12	57	.266	27	42	0	721	30	6	.992
1997—Montreal (N.L.)......	C	96	310	39	86	20	1	17	55	.277	17	35	1	606	26	4	.994
1998—Toronto (A.L.)■......	C-DH	124	407	37	115	23	1	9	52	.283	25	39	0	832	51	8	.991
American League totals (1 year)		124	407	37	115	23	1	9	52	.283	25	39	0	832	51	8	.991
National League totals (9 years)		705	2124	205	558	120	6	63	315	.263	156	212	1	3687	220	28	.993
Major league totals (10 years)		829	2531	242	673	143	7	72	367	.266	181	251	1	4519	271	36	.993

ALL-STAR GAME RECORD

Year League	Pos.	AB	R	H	2B	3B	HR	RBI	Avg.	BB	SO	SB	PO	A	E	Avg.
					BATTING								FIELDING		
1994—National......	C	0	0	0	0	0	0	0	...	0	0	0	3	0	0	1.000

FLORIE, BRYCE   P   TIGERS

PERSONAL: Born May 21, 1970, in Charleston, S.C. ... 5-11/192. ... Throws right, bats right. ... Full name: Bryce Bettencourt Florie.
HIGH SCHOOL: Hanahan (Charleston, S.C.).
COLLEGE: Trident Technical College (S.C.).
TRANSACTIONS/CAREER NOTES: Selected by San Diego Padres organization in fifth round of free-agent draft (June 1, 1988). ... Traded by Padres with P Ron Villone and OF Marc Newfield to Milwaukee Brewers for OF Greg Vaughn and a player to be named later (July 31, 1996); Padres acquired OF Gerald Parent to complete deal (September 16, 1996). ... On disabled list (August 31-September 8, 1997). ... Traded by Brewers with a player to be named later to Detroit Tigers for P Mike Myers, P Rick Greene and SS Santiago Perez (November 20, 1997). ... On Detroit disabled list (June 23-July 20, 1998); included rehabilitation assignment to Toledo (July 14-20).
STATISTICAL NOTES: Led Texas League with 25 wild pitches in 1993.

Year Team (League)	W	L	Pct.	ERA	G	GS	CG	ShO	Sv.	IP	H	R	ER	BB	SO
1988—Ariz. Padres (Ariz.)......	4	5	.444	7.98	11	6	0	0	0	38 1/3	52	44	34	22	29
1989—Spokane (N'west)......	4	5	.444	7.08	14	14	0	0	0	61	79	•66	48	40	50
—Charleston, S.C. (S. Atl.)......	1	7	.125	6.95	12	12	0	0	0	44	54	47	34	42	22
1990—Waterloo (Midw.)......	4	5	.444	4.39	14	14	1	0	0	65 2/3	60	37	32	37	38
1991—Waterloo (Midw.)......	7	6	.538	3.92	23	23	2	0	0	133	119	66	58	79	90
1992—High Desert (Calif.)......	9	7	.563	4.12	26	24	0	0	0	137 2/3	99	79	63	*114	106
—Charleston, S.C. (S. Atl.)......	0	1	.000	1.80	1	1	0	0	0	5	5	3	1	0	5
1993—Wichita (Texas)......	11	8	.579	3.96	27	•27	0	0	0	154 2/3	128	80	68	*100	133
1994—Las Vegas (PCL)......	2	5	.286	5.15	50	0	0	0	1	71 2/3	76	47	41	47	67
—San Diego (N.L.)......	0	0	...	0.96	9	0	0	0	0	9 1/3	8	1	1	3	8
1995—San Diego (N.L.)......	2	2	.500	3.01	47	0	0	0	1	68 2/3	49	30	23	38	68
1996—San Diego (N.L.)......	2	2	.500	4.01	39	0	0	0	0	49 1/3	45	24	22	27	51
—Milwaukee (A.L.)■......	0	1	.000	6.63	15	0	0	0	0	19	20	16	14	13	12
1997—Milwaukee (A.L.)......	4	4	.500	4.32	32	8	0	0	0	75	74	43	36	42	53
1998—Detroit (A.L.)■......	8	9	.471	4.80	42	16	0	0	0	133	141	80	71	59	97
—Toledo (International)......	0	0	...	0.00	1	1	0	0	0	4	0	0	0	0	3
A.L. totals (3 years)......	12	14	.462	4.80	89	24	0	0	0	227	235	139	121	114	162
N.L. totals (3 years)......	4	4	.500	3.25	95	0	0	0	1	127 1/3	102	55	46	68	127
Major league totals (5 years)......	16	18	.471	4.24	184	24	0	0	1	354 1/3	337	194	167	182	289

FLOYD, CLIFF   OF   MARLINS   F

PERSONAL: Born December 5, 1972, in Chicago. ... 6-4/235. ... Bats left, throws right. ... Full name: Cornelius Clifford Floyd.
HIGH SCHOOL: Thornwood (South Holland, Ill.).
TRANSACTIONS/CAREER NOTES: Selected by Montreal Expos organization in first round (14th pick overall) of free-agent draft (June 3, 1991). ... On disabled list (May 16-September 11, 1995). ... Traded by Expos to Florida Marlins for OF Joe Orsulak and P Dustin Hermanson (March 26, 1997). ... On disabled list (May 9-24 and June 21-September 1, 1997); included rehabilitation assignment to Charlotte (July 20-September 1).
HONORS: Named Minor League Player of the Year by THE SPORTING NEWS (1993). ... Named Eastern League Most Valuable Player (1993).
STATISTICAL NOTES: Led South Atlantic League with 261 total bases and nine intentional bases on balls received in 1992. ... Led Eastern League with .600 slugging percentage and 12 intentional bases on balls received in 1993.

Year Team (League)	Pos.	G	AB	R	H	2B	3B	HR	RBI	Avg.	BB	SO	SB	PO	A	E	Avg.
						BATTING									FIELDING		
1991—GC Expos (GCL)......	1B	56	214	35	56	9	3	6	30	.262	19	37	13	451	27	*15	.970
1992—Albany (S. Atl.)......	OF-1B	134	516	83	157	24	*16	16	*97	.304	45	75	32	423	29	17	.964
—W.P. Beach (FSL)......	OF	1	4	0	0	0	0	0	1	.000	0	1	0	2	0	0	1.000
1993—Harrisburg (East.)......	1B-OF	101	380	82	125	17	4	•26	*101	.329	54	71	31	564	27	19	.969
—Ottawa (Int'l)......	1B	32	125	12	30	2	2	2	18	.240	16	34	2	272	23	5	.983
—Montreal (N.L.)......	1B	10	31	3	7	0	0	1	2	.226	0	9	0	79	4	0	1.000
1994—Montreal (N.L.)......	1B-OF	100	334	43	94	19	4	4	41	.281	24	63	10	565	42	6	.990
1995—Montreal (N.L.)......	1B-OF	29	69	6	9	1	0	1	8	.130	7	22	3	146	12	3	.981
1996—Ottawa (Int'l)......	OF-3B	20	76	7	23	3	1	1	8	.303	7	20	2	38	1	2	.951
—Montreal (N.L.)......	OF-1B	117	227	29	55	15	4	6	26	.242	30	52	7	109	2	5	.957
1997—Florida (N.L.)......	OF-1B	61	137	23	32	9	1	6	19	.234	24	33	6	96	5	3	.971
—Charlotte (Int'l)......	OF-1B	39	131	27	48	10	0	9	33	.366	10	29	7	79	5	1	.988
1998—Florida (N.L.)......	OF-DH	153	588	85	166	45	3	22	90	.282	47	112	27	251	10	7	.974
Major league totals (6 years)		470	1386	189	363	89	12	40	186	.262	132	291	53	1246	75	24	.982

								BATTING						FIELDING		
Year Team (League)	Pos.	G	AB	R	H	2B	3B	HR	RBI	Avg.	BB	SO	SB	PO	A	E	Avg.
1997— Florida (N.L.)								Did not play.								

CHAMPIONSHIP SERIES RECORD

								BATTING						FIELDING		
Year Team (League)	Pos.	G	AB	R	H	2B	3B	HR	RBI	Avg.	BB	SO	SB	PO	A	E	Avg.
1997— Florida (N.L.)								Did not play.								

WORLD SERIES RECORD

NOTES: Member of World Series championship team (1997).

								BATTING						FIELDING		
Year Team (League)	Pos.	G	AB	R	H	2B	3B	HR	RBI	Avg.	BB	SO	SB	PO	A	E	Avg.
1997— Florida (N.L.)	PH-DH	4	2	1	0	0	0	0	0	.000	1	1	0	...	...	...	...

FONTENOT, JOE — P — MARLINS

PERSONAL: Born March 20, 1977, in Lafayette, La. ... 6-2/185. ... Throws right, bats right. ... Full name: Joseph D. Fontenot.
HIGH SCHOOL: Acadiana (Lafeytte, La.).
TRANSACTIONS/CAREER NOTES: Selected by San Francisco Giants organization in first round (16th pick overall) of free-agent draft (June 1, 1995). ... Traded by Giants with P Mike Villano and P Mick Pageler to Florida Marlins for P Robb Nen (November 18, 1997). ... On Florida disabled list (July 3, 1998-remainder of season); included rehabilitation assignment to Charlotte (July 28-August 1).
STATISTICAL NOTES: Led Texas League in hit batsmen with 12 in 1997.

Year Team (League)	W	L	Pct.	ERA	G	GS	CG	ShO	Sv.	IP	H	R	ER	BB	SO
1995— Bellingham (N'west)	0	3	.000	1.93	6	6	0	0	0	18 2/3	14	5	4	10	14
1996— San Jose (California)	9	4	.692	4.44	26	23	0	0	0	144	137	87	71	74	124
1997— Shreveport (Texas)	10	11	.476	5.53	26	26	1	0	0	151 1/3	171	105	93	65	103
1998— Portland (Eastern)■..........	3	1	.750	3.08	7	7	0	0	0	38	37	16	13	13	31
— Florida (N.L.)	0	7	.000	6.33	8	8	0	0	0	42 2/3	56	34	30	20	24
— Charlotte (Int'l)	0	1	.000	12.00	1	1	0	0	0	3	4	4	4	2	0
Major league totals (1 year)........	0	7	.000	6.33	8	8	0	0	0	42 2/3	56	34	30	20	24

FORBES, P.J. — 2B

PERSONAL: Born September 22, 1967, in Pittsburg, Kan. ... 5-10/160. ... Bats right, throws right. ... Full name: Patrick Joseph Forbes.
HIGH SCHOOL: St. Mary's Colgan (Pittsburg, Kan.).
COLLEGE: Wichita State.
TRANSACTIONS/CAREER NOTES: Selected by California Angels organization in 20th round of free-agent draft (June 4, 1990). ... On Vancouver disabled list (July 15-August 18, 1994). ... Granted free agency (October 15, 1996). ... Signed by Rochester, Baltimore Orioles organization (January 14, 1997). ... Granted free agency (October 15, 1997). ... Re-signed by Orioles (December 12, 1997). ... Released by Orioles (November 25, 1998).
STATISTICAL NOTES: Led Northwest League with eight sacrifice hits in 1990. ... Led Midwest League with 24 sacrifice hits in 1992. ... Led Texas League second basemen with 251 assists, 74 double plays and .970 fielding percentage in 1993. ... Led Pacific Coast League second basemen with .986 fielding percentage in 1995. ... Led Pacific Coast League second basemen with .986 fielding percentage in 1996.

Year Team (League)	Pos.	G	AB	R	H	2B	3B	HR	RBI	Avg.	BB	SO	SB	PO	A	E	Avg.
1990— Boise (Northwest)	2B	43	169	29	42	9	1	0	20	.249	23	22	11	93	109	8	.962
1991— Palm Springs (Calif.)..	2-O-1-S	94	349	45	93	14	2	2	26	.266	36	44	18	220	281	17	.967
1992— Quad City (Midwest) ..	2B-3B	105	376	53	106	16	5	2	46	.282	44	51	15	145	269	12	.972
1993— Midland (Texas)............	2B-1B	126	498	*90	159	23	2	15	64	.319	26	50	6	†260	372	19	†.971
— Vancouver (PCL)	2B	5	16	1	4	2	0	0	3	.250	0	3	0	15	13	0	1.000
1994— Ariz. Angels (Ariz.)	2B	2	6	1	0	0	0	0	0	.000	0	1	0	2	5	0	1.000
— Vancouver (PCL)	2B-SS-3B	90	318	39	91	21	2	1	40	.286	22	42	4	187	233	11	.974
1995— Vancouver (PCL)	2B-SS	109	369	47	101	22	3	1	52	.274	21	46	4	190	271	6	†.987
1996— Vancouver (PCL)	2-3-S-O	117	409	58	112	24	2	0	46	.274	42	44	4	235	308	9	†.984
1997— Rochester (Int'l)■........	2-3-S-O	116	434	67	118	22	2	8	54	.272	35	42	15	150	237	12	.970
1998— Rochester (Int'l)	2B-SS-3B	116	460	74	135	37	3	6	52	.293	36	54	10	207	305	7	.987
— Baltimore (A.L.).........	2B-3B-SS	9	10	0	1	0	0	0	2	.100	0	0	0	6	9	0	1.000
Major league totals (1 year)		9	10	0	1	0	0	0	2	.100	0	0	0	6	9	0	1.000

FORD, BEN — P — DIAMONDBACKS

PERSONAL: Born August 15, 1975, in Cedar Rapids, Iowa. ... 6-7/200. ... Throws right, bats right. ... Full name: Benjamin Cooper Ford.
HIGH SCHOOL: George Washington (Cedar Rapids, Iowa).
JUNIOR COLLEGE: Indian Hills Community College (Iowa).
TRANSACTIONS/CAREER NOTES: Selected by New York Yankees organization in 20th round of free-agent draft (June 2, 1994). ... Selected by Arizona Diamondbacks in first round (17th pick overall) of expansion draft (November 18, 1997).

Year Team (League)	W	L	Pct.	ERA	G	GS	CG	ShO	Sv.	IP	H	R	ER	BB	SO
1994— GC Yankees (GCL)............	2	2	.500	2.38	18	0	0	0	3	34	27	13	9	8	31
1995— Oneonta (N.Y.-Penn)	5	0	1.000	0.87	29	0	0	0	0	52	39	23	5	16	50
— Greensboro (S. Atl.)	0	0	...	5.14	7	0	0	0	0	7	4	4	4	5	8
1996— Greensboro (S. Atl.)	2	6	.250	4.26	43	0	0	0	2	82 1/3	75	48	39	33	84
1997— Tampa (Fla. St.)	4	0	1.000	1.93	32	0	0	0	18	37 1/3	27	8	8	14	37
— Norwich (Eastern)	4	3	.571	4.22	28	0	0	0	1	42 2/3	35	28	20	19	38
1998— Tucson (PCL)■	2	5	.286	4.35	48	0	0	0	13	68 1/3	68	41	33	33	63
— Arizona (N.L.)	0	0	...	9.90	8	0	0	0	0	10	13	12	11	3	5
Major league totals (1 year)........	0	0	...	9.90	8	0	0	0	0	10	13	12	11	3	5

FORDHAM, TOM   P   WHITE SOX

PERSONAL: Born February 20, 1974, in San Diego. ... 6-2/205. ... Throws left, bats left. ... Full name: Thomas James Fordham.
HIGH SCHOOL: Granite Hills (El Cajon, Calif.).
JUNIOR COLLEGE: Grossmont College (Calif.).
TRANSACTIONS/CAREER NOTES: Selected by Chicago White Sox organization in 11th round of free-agent draft (June 3, 1993).

Year	Team (League)	W	L	Pct.	ERA	G	GS	CG	ShO	Sv.	IP	H	R	ER	BB	SO
1993—	Sara. W. Sox (GCL)	1	1	.500	1.80	3	0	0	0	0	10	9	2	2	3	12
—	Sarasota (Florida State)	0	0	...	0.00	2	0	0	0	0	5	3	1	0	3	5
—	Hickory (S. Atl.)	4	3	.571	3.88	8	8	1	0	0	48²/₃	36	21	21	21	27
1994—	Hickory (S. Atl.)	10	5	.667	3.14	17	17	1	1	0	109	101	47	38	30	121
—	South Bend (Mid.)	4	4	.500	4.34	11	11	1	1	0	74²/₃	82	46	36	14	48
1995—	Prince William (Caro.)	9	0	1.000	2.04	13	13	1	1	0	84	66	20	19	35	78
—	Birmingham (Southern)	6	3	.667	3.38	14	14	2	1	0	82²/₃	79	35	31	28	61
1996—	Birmingham (Southern)	2	1	.667	2.65	6	6	0	0	0	37¹/₃	26	13	11	14	37
—	Nashville (A.A.)	10	8	.556	3.45	22	22	3	0	0	140²/₃	117	60	54	69	118
1997—	Nashville (A.A.)	6	7	.462	4.74	21	20	2	0	0	114	113	64	60	53	90
—	Chicago (A.L.)	0	1	.000	6.23	7	1	0	0	0	17¹/₃	17	13	12	10	10
1998—	Chicago (A.L.)	1	2	.333	6.75	29	5	0	0	0	48	51	36	36	42	23
—	Calgary (PCL)	4	2	.667	3.02	9	9	0	0	0	56²/₃	38	21	19	26	39
Major league totals (2 years)		1	3	.250	6.61	36	6	0	0	0	65¹/₃	68	49	48	52	33

FORDYCE, BROOK   C   REDS

PERSONAL: Born May 7, 1970, in New London, Conn. ... 6-0/190. ... Bats right, throws right. ... Full name: Brook Alexander Fordyce. ... Name pronounced FOR-dice.
HIGH SCHOOL: St. Bernard (Uncasville, Conn.).
TRANSACTIONS/CAREER NOTES: Selected by New York Mets organization in third round of free-agent draft (June 5, 1989). ... On disabled list (June 19-July 2 and July 18-August 30, 1994).... On suspended list (August 30-September 1, 1994). ... Claimed on waivers by Cleveland Indians (May 15, 1995). ... Granted free agency (October 16, 1995). ... Signed by Cincinnati Reds organization (December 7, 1995). ... On disabled list (July 16-August 5, 1997); included rehabilitation assignment to Indianapolis (July 21-August 5). ... On Cincinnati disabled list (July 13-August 12, 1998); included rehabilitation assignment to Indianapolis (August 4-12).
STATISTICAL NOTES: Led Appalachian League catchers with .991 fielding percentage in 1989. ... Led South Atlantic League in slugging percentage with .478 and tied for lead in grounding into double plays with 18 in 1990. ... Led South Atlantic League with 30 passed balls in 1990. ... Led Eastern League catchers with 795 total chances in 1992. ... Led International League catchers with 810 total chances and tied for lead in double plays by catcher with 11 in 1993.

							BATTING								FIELDING		
Year	Team (League)	Pos.	G	AB	R	H	2B	3B	HR	RBI	Avg.	BB	SO	SB	PO	A	E	Avg.
1989—	Kingsport (Appal.)	C-OF-3B	69	226	45	74	15	0	9	38	.327	30	26	10	311	28	4	†.988
1990—	Columbia (S. Atl.)	C	104	372	45	117	29	1	10	54	.315	39	42	4	574	63	15	.977
1991—	St. Lucie (Fla. St.)	C	115	406	42	97	19	3	7	55	.239	37	50	4	630	87	13	.982
1992—	Binghamton (East.)	C	118	425	59	118	30	0	11	61	.278	37	78	1	*713	*79	3	*.996
1993—	Norfolk (Int'l)	C	116	409	33	106	21	2	2	41	.259	26	62	2	*735	67	8	.990
1994—	Norfolk (Int'l)	C	66	229	26	60	13	3	3	32	.262	19	26	1	330	33	7	.981
1995—	New York (N.L.)	C	4	2	1	1	1	0	0	0	.500	1	0	0	0	0	0	...
—	Buffalo (A.A.)■	C-OF	58	176	18	44	13	0	0	9	.250	14	20	1	306	18	3	.991
1996—	Indianapolis (A.A.)■	C-1B	107	374	48	103	20	3	16	64	.275	25	56	2	620	49	4	*.994
—	Cincinnati (N.L.)	C	4	7	0	2	1	0	0	1	.286	3	1	0	18	0	0	1.000
1997—	Cincinnati (N.L.)	C-DH	47	96	7	20	5	0	1	8	.208	8	15	2	162	12	3	.983
—	Indianapolis (A.A.)	C	12	47	7	11	2	0	2	6	.234	5	6	1	73	8	0	1.000
1998—	Cincinnati (N.L.)	C	57	146	8	37	9	0	3	14	.253	11	28	0	288	20	7	.978
—	Indianapolis (Int'l)	C	6	24	4	6	1	0	2	3	.250	1	2	0	28	4	0	1.000
Major league totals (4 years)			112	251	16	60	16	0	4	23	.239	23	44	2	468	32	10	.980

FOSSAS, TONY   P   RANGERS

PERSONAL: Born September 23, 1957, in Havana, Cuba. ... 6-0/198. ... Throws left, bats left. ... Full name: Emilio Anthony Fossas.
HIGH SCHOOL: St. Mary's (Brookline, Mass.).
COLLEGE: South Florida.
TRANSACTIONS/CAREER NOTES: Selected by Minnesota Twins organization in ninth round of free-agent draft (June 6, 1978); did not sign. ... Selected by Texas Rangers organization in 12th round of free-agent draft (June 5, 1979). ... Released by Rangers organization (February 18, 1982). ... Signed by Chicago Cubs organization (March 11, 1982). ... Loaned by Cubs organization to Tabasco of Mexican League (March 15-April 7, 1982). ... Released by Cubs organization (April 7, 1982). ... Signed by Rangers organization (May 3, 1982). ... Granted free agency (October 15, 1985). ... Signed by California Angels organization (December 13, 1985). ... On disabled list (June 2, 1986-remainder of season). ... Granted free agency (October 15, 1987). ... Signed by Rangers organization (December 1, 1987). ... Granted free agency (October 15, 1988). ... Signed by Milwaukee Brewers organization (January 21, 1989). ... Released by Brewers organization (December 6, 1990). ... Signed by Boston Red Sox organization (January 23, 1991). ... Released by Red Sox (December 11, 1992). ... Re-signed by Red Sox organization (January 18, 1993). ... Granted free agency (December 20, 1993). ... Re-signed by Red Sox organization (January 20, 1994). ... Granted free agency (December 23, 1994). ... Signed by St. Louis Cardinals organization (April 11, 1995). ... Granted free agency (October 27, 1997). ... Signed by Seattle Mariners (December 16, 1997). ... Released by Mariners (June 10, 1998). ... Signed by Chicago Cubs organization (June 19, 1998). ... Released by Cubs (August 4, 1998). ... Signed by Rangers (August 19, 1998). ... Granted free agency (October 19, 1998). ... Re-signed by Rangers organization (January 7, 1999).

Year	Team (League)	W	L	Pct.	ERA	G	GS	CG	ShO	Sv.	IP	H	R	ER	BB	SO
1979—	GC Rangers (GCL)	6	3	.667	3.00	10	9	1	0	0	60	54	28	20	26	49
—	Tulsa (Texas)	1	1	.500	6.55	2	2	0	0	0	11	14	10	8	4	3
1980—	Asheville (S. Atl.)	8	2	.800	3.15	30	•27	8	2	2	*197	*187	84	69	69	140
1981—	Tulsa (Texas)	5	6	.455	4.16	38	12	1	1	2	106	113	65	49	44	57

Year	Team (League)	W	L	Pct.	ERA	G	GS	CG	ShO	Sv.	IP	H	R	ER	BB	SO
1982—	Tabasco (Mexican)■	0	3	.000	5.56	3	3	0	0	0	11⅓	15	14	7	10	6
	—Burlington (Midw.)■	8	9	.471	3.08	25	18	10	1	0	146⅓	121	63	50	33	115
1983—	Tulsa (Texas)	8	7	.533	4.20	24	16	6	1	0	133	123	77	62	46	103
	—Oklahoma City (A.A.)	1	2	.333	7.90	10	5	0	0	0	35⅓	55	33	31	12	23
1984—	Tulsa (Texas)	0	1	.000	4.50	4	0	0	0	2	10	12	5	5	3	7
	—Oklahoma City (A.A.)	5	9	.357	4.31	29	15	3	0	0	121	143	65	58	34	74
1985—	Oklahoma City (A.A.)	7	6	.538	4.75	30	13	2	0	0	110	121	65	58	36	49
1986—	Edmonton (PCL)■	3	3	.500	4.57	7	7	2	1	0	43⅓	53	23	22	12	15
1987—	Edmonton (PCL)	6	8	.429	4.99	40	15	1	0	0	117⅓	152	76	65	29	54
1988—	Oklahoma City (A.A.)■	3	0	1.000	2.84	52	0	0	0	4	66⅔	64	21	21	16	42
	—Texas (A.L.)	0	0	...	4.76	5	0	0	0	0	5⅔	11	3	3	2	0
1989—	Denver (Am. Assoc.)■	5	1	.833	2.04	24	1	0	0	0	35⅓	27	9	8	11	35
	—Milwaukee (A.L.)	2	2	.500	3.54	51	0	0	0	1	61	57	27	24	22	42
1990—	Milwaukee (A.L.)	2	3	.400	6.44	32	0	0	0	0	29⅓	44	23	21	10	24
	—Denver (Am. Assoc.)	5	2	.714	1.51	25	0	0	0	4	35⅔	29	8	6	10	45
1991—	Boston (A.L.)■	3	2	.600	3.47	64	0	0	0	1	57	49	27	22	28	29
1992—	Boston (A.L.)	1	2	.333	2.43	60	0	0	0	2	29⅔	31	9	8	14	19
1993—	Boston (A.L.)	1	1	.500	5.18	71	0	0	0	0	40	38	28	23	15	39
1994—	Boston (A.L.)	2	0	1.000	4.76	44	0	0	0	1	34	35	18	18	15	31
	—Pawtucket (Int'l)	2	0	1.000	0.00	11	0	0	0	0	9⅔	4	1	0	3	8
1995—	St. Louis (N.L.)■	3	0	1.000	1.47	58	0	0	0	0	36⅔	28	6	6	10	40
1996—	St. Louis (N.L.)	0	4	.000	2.68	65	0	0	0	2	47	43	19	14	21	36
1997—	St. Louis (N.L.)	2	7	.222	3.83	71	0	0	0	0	51⅔	62	32	22	26	41
1998—	Seattle (A.L.)■	0	3	.000	8.74	23	0	0	0	0	11⅓	19	11	11	6	10
	—Iowa (Pacific Coast)■	0	0	...	3.60	10	0	0	0	0	5	10	4	2	2	2
	—Chicago (N.L.)	0	0	...	9.00	8	0	0	0	0	4	8	4	4	6	6
	—Oklahoma (Pacific Coast)■	0	1	.000	5.40	4	0	0	0	0	6⅔	6	4	4	4	3
	—Texas (A.L.)	1	0	1.000	0.00	10	0	0	0	0	7⅓	3	0	0	4	7
A.L. totals (8 years)		12	13	.480	4.25	360	0	0	0	5	275⅓	287	146	130	116	201
N.L. totals (4 years)		5	11	.313	2.97	202	0	0	0	2	139⅓	141	61	46	63	123
Major league totals (11 years)		17	24	.415	3.82	562	0	0	0	7	414⅔	428	207	176	179	324

DIVISION SERIES RECORD

Year	Team (League)	W	L	Pct.	ERA	G	GS	CG	ShO	Sv.	IP	H	R	ER	BB	SO
1996—St. Louis (N.L.)								Did not play.								

CHAMPIONSHIP SERIES RECORD

Year	Team (League)	W	L	Pct.	ERA	G	GS	CG	ShO	Sv.	IP	H	R	ER	BB	SO
1996—St. Louis (N.L.)		0	0	...	2.08	5	0	0	0	0	4⅓	1	1	1	4	1

FOSTER, KEVIN   P   REDS

PERSONAL: Born January 13, 1969, in Evanston, Ill. ... 6-1/175. ... Throws right, bats right. ... Full name: Kevin Christopher Foster.
HIGH SCHOOL: Evanston (Ill.) Township.
COLLEGE: Kishwaukee College (Ill.).
TRANSACTIONS/CAREER NOTES: Selected by Montreal Expos organization in 29th round of free-agent draft (June 2, 1987). ... On Albany (Ga.) suspended list (April 9-May 6, 1992). ... Traded by Expos organization with P Dave Wainhouse to Seattle Mariners for IF Frank Bolick and a player to be named later (November 20, 1992); Expos organization acquired C Miah Bradbury to complete deal (December 8, 1992). ... Traded by Mariners to Philadelphia Phillies for P Bob Ayrault (June 12, 1993). ... Traded by Phillies to Chicago Cubs for P Shawn Boskie (April 12, 1994). ... On disabled list (August 17-September 1, 1997). ... On Chicago disabled list (March 22-June 9, 1998); included rehabilitation assignments to Daytona (May 23-27), West Tenn (May 28-June 3) and Iowa (June 4-9). ... Granted free agency (October 6, 1998). ... Signed by Cincinnati Reds organization (November 17, 1998).
STATISTICAL NOTES: Led N.L. with 32 home runs allowed in 1995.
MISCELLANEOUS: Played infield (1988-89). ... Appeared in three games as pinch runner (1995). ... Appeared in two games as pinch runner for Chicago (1996). ... Struck out three times and had a sacrifice hit in four appearances as pinch hitter (1997).

Year	Team (League)	W	L	Pct.	ERA	G	GS	CG	ShO	Sv.	IP	H	R	ER	BB	SO
1990—	GC Expos (GCL)	2	0	1.000	5.06	4	0	0	0	0	10⅔	9	6	6	6	11
	—Gate City (Pioneer)	1	7	.125	4.58	10	10	0	0	0	55	43	42	28	34	52
1991—	Sumter (S. Atl.)	10	4	.714	2.74	34	11	1	1	1	102	62	36	31	68	111
1992—	W.P. Beach (FSL)	7	2	.778	1.95	16	11	0	0	0	69⅓	45	19	15	31	66
1993—	Jacksonville (Southern)■	4	4	.500	3.97	12	12	1	1	0	65⅔	53	32	29	29	72
	—Scran./W.B. (Int'l)■	1	1	.500	3.93	17	9	1	0	0	71	63	32	31	29	59
	—Philadelphia (N.L.)	0	1	.000	14.85	2	1	0	0	0	6⅔	13	11	11	7	6
1994—	Reading (Eastern)	0	1	.000	6.00	1	1	0	0	0	6	7	4	4	1	3
	—Orlando (South.)■	1	0	1.000	0.95	3	3	1	1	0	19	8	2	2	2	21
	—Iowa (Am. Assoc.)	3	1	.750	4.28	6	6	1	0	0	33⅔	28	17	16	14	35
	—Chicago (N.L.)	3	4	.429	2.89	13	13	0	0	0	81	70	31	26	35	75
1995—	Chicago (N.L.)	12	11	.522	4.51	30	28	0	0	0	167⅔	149	90	84	65	146
1996—	Chicago (N.L.)	7	6	.538	6.21	17	16	1	0	0	87	98	63	60	35	53
	—Iowa (Am. Assoc.)	7	6	.538	4.30	18	18	3	1	0	115	106	56	55	46	87
1997—	Chicago (N.L.)	10	7	.588	4.61	26	25	1	0	0	146⅓	141	79	75	66	118
1998—	Daytona (Fla. St.)	0	0	...	10.13	3	0	0	0	0	2⅔	2	7	3	7	3
	—West Tenn (Southern)	1	0	1.000	2.25	2	0	0	0	0	4	5	1	1	1	5
	—Iowa (Pacific Coast)	5	6	.455	6.85	17	11	1	1	0	67	74	52	51	38	75
	—Chicago (N.L.)	0	0	...	16.20	3	0	0	0	0	3⅓	8	6	6	2	3
Major league totals (6 years)		32	29	.525	4.79	91	83	2	0	0	492	479	280	262	210	401

RECORD AS POSITION PLAYER

Year	Team (League)	Pos.	G	AB	R	H	2B	3B	HR	RBI	Avg.	BB	SO	SB	PO	A	E	Avg.
1988—	GC Expos (GCL)	3B-2B-SS	49	164	21	42	10	1	2	21	.256	21	33	16	38	92	18	.878
1989—	Rockford (Midwest)	3B-2B	44	117	9	19	3	2	1	15	.162	18	44	1	29	70	12	.892
1990—	W.P. Beach (FSL)	3B	3	6	0	1	0	1	0	2	.167	1	1	0	2	1	0	1.000

F

FOULKE, KEITH   P   WHITE SOX

PERSONAL: Born October 19, 1972, in San Diego. ... 6-0/195. ... Throws right, bats right. ... Full name: Keith Charles Foulke.
HIGH SCHOOL: Hargrove (Huffman, Texas).
JUNIOR COLLEGE: Galveston (Texas) College.
COLLEGE: Lewis-Clark State (Idaho).
TRANSACTIONS/CAREER NOTES: Selected by San Francisco Giants organization in ninth round of free-agent draft (June 2, 1994). ... Traded by Giants with SS Mike Caruso, OF Brian Manning, P Lorenzo Barcelo, P Bobby Howry and P Ken Vining to Chicago White Sox for P Wilson Alvarez, P Danny Darwin and P Roberto Hernandez (July 31, 1997). ... On disabled list (August 28, 1998-remainder of season).

Year Team (League)	W	L	Pct.	ERA	G	GS	CG	ShO	Sv.	IP	H	R	ER	BB	SO
1994—Everett (Northwest)	2	0	1.000	0.93	4	4	0	0	0	19 1/3	17	4	2	3	22
1995—San Jose (California)	13	6	.684	3.50	28	26	2	1	0	177 1/3	166	85	69	32	168
1996—Shreveport (Texas)	12	7	.632	*2.76	27	27	4	2	0	*182 2/3	149	61	56	35	129
1997—Phoenix (PCL)	5	4	.556	4.50	12	12	0	0	0	76	79	38	38	15	54
—San Francisco (N.L.)	1	5	.167	8.26	11	8	0	0	0	44 2/3	60	41	41	18	33
—Nashville (A.A.)■	0	0	...	5.79	1	1	0	0	0	4 2/3	8	3	3	0	4
—Chicago (A.L.)	3	0	1.000	3.45	16	0	0	0	3	28 2/3	28	11	11	5	21
1998—Chicago (A.L.)	3	2	.600	4.13	54	0	0	0	1	65 1/3	51	31	30	20	57
A.L. totals (2 years)	6	2	.750	3.93	70	0	0	0	4	94	79	42	41	25	78
N.L. totals (1 year)	1	5	.167	8.26	11	8	0	0	0	44 2/3	60	41	41	18	33
Major league totals (2 years)	7	7	.500	5.32	81	8	0	0	4	138 2/3	139	83	82	43	111

FOX, ANDY   OF/IF   DIAMONDBACKS

PERSONAL: Born January 12, 1971, in Sacramento. ... 6-4/205. ... Bats left, throws right. ... Full name: Andrew Junipero Fox.
HIGH SCHOOL: Christian Brothers (Sacramento).
TRANSACTIONS/CAREER NOTES: Selected by New York Yankees organization in second round of free-agent draft (June 5, 1989). ... On disabled list (June 11-21, 1991; April 9-22, 1992 and June 10-August 1, 1993). ... On Columbus disabled list (August 5-19, 1997). ... Traded by Yankees to Arizona Diamondbacks for P Marty Janzen and P Todd Erdos (March 8, 1998).
STATISTICAL NOTES: Led Carolina League third basemen with 96 putouts in 1992. ... Led Eastern League third basemen with 30 errors in 1994. ... Led International League third basemen with 22 double plays in 1995.

Year Team (League)	Pos.	G	AB	R	H	2B	3B	HR	RBI	Avg.	BB	SO	SB	PO	A	E	Avg.
1989—GC Yankees (GCL)	3B	40	141	26	35	9	2	3	25	.248	31	29	6	37	78	10	.920
1990—Greensboro (S. Atl.)	3B	134	455	68	99	19	4	9	55	.218	92	132	26	93	238	*45	.880
1991—Prince Will. (Car.)	3B	126	417	60	96	22	2	10	46	.230	81	104	15	85	247	*29	.920
1992—Prince Will. (Car.)	3B-SS	125	473	75	113	18	3	7	42	.239	54	81	28	†97	304	27	.937
1993—Alb./Colon. (East.)	3B	65	236	44	65	16	1	3	24	.275	32	54	12	59	150	19	.917
1994—Alb./Colon. (East.)	3B-SS-2B	121	472	75	105	20	3	11	43	.222	62	102	22	110	261	†34	.916
1995—Norwich (Eastern)	SS	44	175	23	36	3	5	5	17	.206	19	36	8	77	127	9	.958
—Columbus (Int'l)	3-S-O-2	82	302	61	105	16	6	9	37	.348	43	41	22	84	211	9	.970
1996—New York (A.L.)	2-3-S-DH-O	113	189	26	37	4	0	3	13	.196	20	28	11	96	158	12	.955
1997—Columbus (Int'l)	3-2-S-O	95	318	66	87	11	4	6	33	.274	54	64	28	111	218	14	.959
—New York (A.L.)	3-2-DH-S-O	22	31	13	7	1	0	0	1	.226	7	9	2	19	30	1	.980
1998—Arizona (N.L.)■	2-0-3-1	139	502	67	139	21	6	9	44	.277	43	97	14	307	175	8	.984
American League totals (2 years)		135	220	39	44	5	0	3	14	.200	27	37	13	115	188	13	.959
National League totals (1 year)		139	502	67	139	21	6	9	44	.277	43	97	14	307	175	8	.984
Major league totals (3 years)		274	722	106	183	26	6	12	58	.253	70	134	27	422	363	21	.974

DIVISION SERIES RECORD

Year Team (League)	Pos.	G	AB	R	H	2B	3B	HR	RBI	Avg.	BB	SO	SB	PO	A	E	Avg.
1996—New York (A.L.)	DH-PR	2	0	0	0	0	0	0	0	...	0	0	0	0	...	...	...
1997—New York (A.L.)	2B-PR	2	0	0	0	0	0	0	0	...	0	0	0	0	0	0	...
Division series totals (2 years)		4	0	0	0	0	0	0	0	...	0	0	0	0	0	0	...

CHAMPIONSHIP SERIES RECORD

Year Team (League)	Pos.	G	AB	R	H	2B	3B	HR	RBI	Avg.	BB	SO	SB	PO	A	E	Avg.
1996—New York (A.L.)	DH-PR	2	0	0	0	0	0	0	0	...	0	0	0	...	...	...	...

WORLD SERIES RECORD

NOTES: Member of World Series championship team (1996).

Year Team (League)	Pos.	G	AB	R	H	2B	3B	HR	RBI	Avg.	BB	SO	SB	PO	A	E	Avg.
1996—New York (A.L.)	2B-PR-3B	4	0	1	0	0	0	0	0	...	0	0	0	1	0	0	1.000

F

FOX, CHAD   P   BREWERS

PERSONAL: Born September 3, 1970, in Coronado, Calif. ... 6-3/194. ... Throws right, bats right. ... Full name: Chad Douglas Fox.
HIGH SCHOOL: Westfield (Houston).
JUNIOR COLLEGE: Blinn College (Texas).
COLLEGE: Tarleton State (Texas).
TRANSACTIONS/CAREER NOTES: Selected by Cincinnati Reds organization in 23rd round of free-agent draft (June 1, 1992). ... Traded by Reds organization with a player to be named later to Atlanta Braves for OF Mike Kelly (January 9, 1996); Braves acquired P Ray King to complete deal (June 11, 1996). ... On disabled list (July 16-September 3, 1996). ... Traded by Braves to Milwaukee Brewers for OF Gerald Williams (December 11, 1997). ... On Milwaukee disabled list (May 11-June 30, 1998); included rehabilitation assignment to Beloit (June 25-July 1).
STATISTICAL NOTES: Led Carolina League with 20 wild pitches in 1994.

Year Team (League)	W	L	Pct.	ERA	G	GS	CG	ShO	Sv.	IP	H	R	ER	BB	SO
1992— Princeton (Appalachian).....	4	2	.667	4.74	15	8	0	0	0	49 1/3	55	43	26	34	37
1993— Char., W.Va. (S. Atl.)	9	12	.429	5.37	27	26	0	0	0	135 2/3	138	100	81	97	81
1994— Win.-Salem (Car.)	12	5	.706	3.86	25	25	1	0	0	156 1/3	121	77	67	*94	137
1995— Chattanooga (Southern).....	4	5	.444	5.06	20	17	0	0	0	80	76	49	45	52	56
1996— Richmond (Int'l)■.............	3	10	.231	4.73	18	18	1	0	0	93 1/3	91	57	49	49	87
1997— Richmond (Int'l)	1	0	1.000	3.70	13	0	0	0	0	24 1/3	24	10	10	14	25
— Atlanta (N.L.)	0	1	.000	3.29	30	0	0	0	0	27 1/3	24	12	10	16	28
1998— Milwaukee (N.L.)■...........	1	4	.200	3.95	49	0	0	0	0	57	56	27	25	20	64
— Beloit (Midwest)................	0	1	.000	4.50	2	1	0	0	0	2	1	1	1	0	3
Major league totals (2 years)......	1	5	.167	3.74	79	0	0	0	0	84 1/3	80	39	35	36	92

FRANCO, JOHN — P — METS

PERSONAL: Born September 17, 1960, in Brooklyn, N.Y. ... 5-10/185. ... Throws left, bats left. ... Full name: John Anthony Franco.

HIGH SCHOOL: Lafayette (Brooklyn, N.Y.).

COLLEGE: St. John's.

TRANSACTIONS/CAREER NOTES: Selected by Los Angeles Dodgers organization in fifth round of free-agent draft (June 8, 1981). ... Traded by Dodgers organization with P Brett Wise to Cincinnati Reds organization for IF Rafael Landestoy (May 9, 1983). ... Traded by Reds with OF Don Brown to New York Mets for P Randy Myers and P Kip Gross (December 6, 1989). ... On disabled list (June 30-August 1 and August 26, 1992-remainder of season; April 17-May 7 and August 3-26, 1993). ... Granted free agency (October 18, 1994). ... Re-signed by Mets (April 5, 1995).

HONORS: Named N.L. Fireman of the Year by THE SPORTING NEWS (1988, 1990 and 1994).

MISCELLANEOUS: Holds Cincinnati Reds all-time record for most saves (148). ... Holds New York Mets all-time record for most saves (249) and most games pitched (439).

Year Team (League)	W	L	Pct.	ERA	G	GS	CG	ShO	Sv.	IP	H	R	ER	BB	SO
1981— Vero Beach (FSL)	7	4	.636	3.53	13	11	3	0	0	79	78	41	31	41	60
1982— Albuquerque (PCL).............	1	2	.333	7.24	5	5	0	0	0	27 1/3	41	22	22	15	24
— San Antonio (Tex.)	10	5	.667	4.96	17	17	3	0	0	105 1/3	137	70	58	46	76
1983— Albuquerque (PCL).............	0	0	. . .	5.40	11	0	0	0	0	15	10	11	9	11	8
— Indianapolis (A.A.)■	6	10	.375	4.85	23	18	2	0	2	115	148	69	62	42	54
1984— Wichita (Am. Assoc.)	1	0	1.000	5.79	6	0	0	0	0	9 1/3	8	6	6	4	11
— Cincinnati (N.L.)	6	2	.750	2.61	54	0	0	0	4	79 1/3	74	28	23	36	55
1985— Cincinnati (N.L.)	12	3	.800	2.18	67	0	0	0	12	99	83	27	24	40	61
1986— Cincinnati (N.L.)	6	6	.500	2.94	74	0	0	0	29	101	90	40	33	44	84
1987— Cincinnati (N.L.)	8	5	.615	2.52	68	0	0	0	32	82	76	26	23	27	61
1988— Cincinnati (N.L.)	6	6	.500	1.57	70	0	0	0	*39	86	60	18	15	27	46
1989— Cincinnati (N.L.)	4	8	.333	3.12	60	0	0	0	32	80 2/3	77	35	28	36	60
1990— New York (N.L.)■.............	5	3	.625	2.53	55	0	0	0	*33	67 2/3	66	22	19	21	56
1991— New York (N.L.)	5	9	.357	2.93	52	0	0	0	30	55 1/3	61	27	18	18	45
1992— New York (N.L.)	6	2	.750	1.64	31	0	0	0	15	33	24	6	6	11	20
1993— New York (N.L.)	4	3	.571	5.20	35	0	0	0	10	36 1/3	46	24	21	19	29
1994— New York (N.L.)■.............	1	4	.200	2.70	47	0	0	0	*30	50	47	20	15	19	42
1995— New York (N.L.)	5	3	.625	2.44	48	0	0	0	29	51 2/3	48	17	14	17	41
1996— New York (N.L.)	4	3	.571	1.83	51	0	0	0	28	54	54	15	11	21	48
1997— New York (N.L.)	5	3	.625	2.55	59	0	0	0	36	60	49	18	17	20	53
1998— New York (N.L.)	0	8	.000	3.62	61	0	0	0	38	64 2/3	66	28	26	29	59
Major league totals (15 years)....	77	68	.531	2.64	832	0	0	0	397	1000 2/3	921	351	293	385	760

ALL-STAR GAME RECORD

Year League	W	L	Pct.	ERA	GS	CG	ShO	Sv.	IP	H	R	ER	BB	SO
1986— National						Did not play.								
1987— National	0	0	. . .	0.00	0	0	0	0	2/3	0	0	0	0	0
1989— National						Did not play.								
1990— National	0	0	. . .	0.00	0	0	0	0	1	0	0	0	0	0
1991— National						Did not play.								
All-Star totals (2 years)	0	0	. . .	0.00	0	0	0	0	1 2/3	0	0	0	0	0

FRANCO, MATT — IF/OF — METS

PERSONAL: Born August 19, 1969, in Santa Monica, Calif. ... 6-1/210. ... Bats left, throws right. ... Full name: Matthew Neil Franco. ... Nephew of actor Kurt Russell.

HIGH SCHOOL: Westlake (Calif.).

TRANSACTIONS/CAREER NOTES: Selected by Chicago Cubs organization in seventh round of free-agent draft (June 2, 1987). ... On disabled list (May 6-13, 1994). ... Traded by Cubs to New York Mets organization for a player to be named later (April 8, 1996); Cubs acquired P Chris DeWitt to complete deal (June 11, 1996). ... On Norfolk disabled list (April 8-11, 1996). ... Granted free agency (October 15, 1996). ... Re-signed by Mets organization (November 21, 1996). ... On New York disabled list (June 29-July 14, 1998); included rehabilitation assignment to Norfolk (July 9-14).

STATISTICAL NOTES: Led Midwest League in grounding into double plays with 19 in 1990.

					BATTING									FIELDING		
Year Team (League)	Pos.	G	AB	R	H	2B	3B	HR	RBI	Avg.	BB	SO	SB	PO	A	E	Avg.
1987— Wytheville (App.)........	3B-1B-2B	62	202	25	50	10	1	1	21	.248	26	41	4	95	88	23	.888
1988— Wytheville (App.)........	3B-1B	20	79	14	31	9	1	0	16	.392	7	5	0	31	24	6	.902
— Geneva (NY-Penn)......	3B-1B	44	164	19	42	2	0	3	21	.256	19	13	2	190	43	14	.943
1989— Char., W.Va. (SAL)......	3-1-0-S	109	377	42	102	16	1	5	48	.271	57	40	2	113	189	22	.932
— Peoria (Midwest).......	3B	16	58	4	13	4	0	0	9	.224	5	5	0	11	32	6	.878
1990— Peoria (Midwest)........	1B-3B	123	443	52	125	*33	2	6	65	.282	43	39	4	810	75	18	.980
1991— Win.-Salem (Car.).......	1B-3B	104	307	44	66	12	1	4	41	.215	46	42	4	711	53	11	.986
1992— Charlotte (Southern) ..	3B-1B-OF	108	343	35	97	18	3	2	31	.283	26	46	3	248	69	13	.961
1993— Orlando (South.)	1B-3B	68	237	31	75	20	1	7	37	.316	29	30	3	444	40	4	.992

Year	Team (League)	Pos.	G	AB	R	H	2B	3B	HR	RBI	Avg.	BB	SO	SB	PO	A	E	Avg.
—	Iowa (Am. Assoc.)......	1-0-2-P	62	199	24	58	17	4	5	29	.291	16	30	4	450	39	2	.996
1994—	Iowa (Am. Assoc.)......	1B-3B-OF	128	437	63	121	32	4	11	71	.277	52	66	3	976	81	7	.993
1995—	Iowa (Am. Assoc.)......	3-1-P-C	121	455	51	128	28	5	6	58	.281	37	44	1	283	179	19	.960
—	Chicago (N.L.)............	2B-1B-3B	16	17	3	5	1	0	0	1	.294	0	4	0	2	2	0	1.000
1996—	Norfolk (Int'l)■........	3B-1B	133	508	74	*164	*40	2	7	81	.323	36	55	5	383	167	22	.962
—	New York (N.L.).........	3B-1B	14	31	3	6	1	0	1	2	.194	1	5	0	15	12	3	.900
1997—	Norfolk (Int'l)	OF-1B-3B	7	26	5	7	2	0	0	0	.269	2	2	0	13	4	0	1.000
—	New York (N.L.).........	3-1-DH-O	112	163	21	45	5	0	5	21	.276	13	23	1	61	52	4	.966
1998—	Norfolk (Int'l).........	3-0-1-DH	103	161	20	44	7	2	1	13	.273	23	26	0	84	23	1	.991
—	Norfolk (Int'l)	3B-OF-1B	5	19	2	7	1	0	0	1	.368	3	1	2	16	4	2	.909
Major league totals (4 years)			245	372	47	100	14	2	7	37	.269	37	58	1	162	89	8	.969

RECORD AS PITCHER

Year	Team (League)	W	L	Pct.	ERA	G	GS	CG	ShO	Sv.	IP	H	R	ER	BB	SO
1993—	Iowa (Am. Assoc.).............	0	0	...	36.00	1	0	0	0	0	1	5	4	4	1	1
1995—	Iowa (Am. Assoc.).............	0	0	...	0.00	1	0	0	0	0	1	1	0	0	1	1

FRANK, MIKE   OF   REDS

PERSONAL: Born January 14, 1975, in Pomona, Calif. ... 6-2/185. ... Bats left, throws left. ... Full name: Stephen Michael Frank.
HIGH SCHOOL: Escondido (Calif.).
COLLEGE: Santa Clara.
TRANSACTIONS/CAREER NOTES: Selected by Cincinnati Reds organization in seventh round of free-agent draft (June 3, 1997). ... On Cincinnati disabled list (July 27-August 25, 1998).
STATISTICAL NOTES: Tied for Pioneer League lead in intentional bases on balls received with five in 1997.

Year	Team (League)	Pos.	G	AB	R	H	2B	3B	HR	RBI	Avg.	BB	SO	SB	PO	A	E	Avg.
1997—	Billings (Pioneer)........	OF	69	266	62	100	22	6	10	62	.376	35	24	18	•118	*11	4	.970
1998—	Indianapolis (Int'l)......	OF	22	88	8	30	4	0	0	13	.341	7	9	1	44	2	1	.979
—	Cincinnati (N.L.).........	OF	28	89	14	20	6	0	0	7	.225	7	12	0	60	1	0	1.000
—	Chattanooga (Sou.)....	OF	58	231	43	75	12	4	12	43	.325	19	28	5	127	3	2	.985
Major league totals (1 year)			28	89	14	20	6	0	0	7	.225	7	12	0	60	1	0	1.000

FRASCATORE, JOHN   P   CARDINALS

PERSONAL: Born February 4, 1970, in Queens, N.Y. ... 6-1/210. ... Throws right, bats right. ... Full name: John Vincent Frascatore. ... Name pronounced FRASS-kuh-TOR-ee.
HIGH SCHOOL: Oceanside (N.Y.).
COLLEGE: C.W. Post (N.Y.).
TRANSACTIONS/CAREER NOTES: Selected by St. Louis Cardinals organization in 24th round of free-agent draft (June 3, 1991).
RECORDS: Shares N.L. record for most consecutive home runs allowed in one inning—3 (August 26, 1998, ninth inning).

Year	Team (League)	W	L	Pct.	ERA	G	GS	CG	ShO	Sv.	IP	H	R	ER	BB	SO
1991—	Hamilton (NYP).................	2	7	.222	9.20	30	1	0	0	1	30 1/3	44	38	31	22	18
1992—	Savannah (S. Atl.).............	5	7	.417	3.84	50	0	0	0	23	58 2/3	49	32	25	29	56
1993—	Springfield (Mid.)	7	12	.368	3.78	27	26	2	1	0	157 1/3	157	84	66	33	126
1994—	Arkansas (Texas)...............	7	3	.700	3.10	12	12	4	1	0	78 1/3	76	37	27	15	63
—	Louisville (A.A.)..............	8	3	.727	3.39	13	12	2	1	0	85	82	34	32	33	58
—	St. Louis (N.L.)..............	0	1	.000	16.20	1	1	0	0	0	3 1/3	7	6	6	2	2
1995—	Louisville (A.A.)..............	2	8	.200	3.95	28	10	1	0	5	82	89	54	36	34	55
—	St. Louis (N.L.)..............	1	1	.500	4.41	14	4	0	0	0	32 2/3	39	19	16	16	21
1996—	Louisville (A.A.)..............	6	13	.316	5.18	36	21	3	0	0	156 1/3	180	106	90	42	95
1997—	St. Louis (N.L.)..............	5	2	.714	2.48	59	0	0	0	0	80	74	25	22	33	58
1998—	St. Louis (N.L.)..............	3	4	.429	4.14	69	0	0	0	0	95 2/3	95	48	44	36	49
Major league totals (4 years)......		9	8	.529	3.74	143	5	0	0	0	211 2/3	215	98	88	87	130

FRAZIER, LOU   OF   PHILLIES

PERSONAL: Born January 26, 1965, in St. Louis. ... 6-2/175. ... Bats both, throws right. ... Full name: Arthur Louis Frazier.
HIGH SCHOOL: Jennings (Mo.).
JUNIOR COLLEGE: Scottsdale (Ariz.) Community College.
TRANSACTIONS/CAREER NOTES: Selected by Detroit Tigers organization in 10th round of free-agent draft (June 3, 1985); did not sign. ... Selected by Cleveland Indians organization in secondary phase of free-agent draft (January 14, 1986); did not sign. ... Selected by Houston Astros organization in secondary phase of free-agent draft (June 2, 1986). ... Traded by Astros organization to Detroit Tigers organization for IF Doug Strange (March 30, 1990). ... Granted free agency (October 15, 1992). ... Signed by Montreal Expos organization (December 8, 1992). ... Traded by Expos to Texas Rangers for a player to be named later (July 30, 1995); Expos acquired P Hector Fajardo to complete deal (August 5, 1995). ... On Oklahoma City disabled list (April 2-May 9, 1996). ... On Texas suspended list (September 1-4, 1996). ... Released by Rangers (December 5, 1996). ... Claimed on waivers by Seattle Mariners (December 13, 1996). ... Released by Mariners (March 28, 1997). ... Signed by Baltimore Orioles organization (April 8, 1997). ... Granted free agency (October 15, 1997). ... Signed by Chicago White Sox organization (January 13, 1998). ... Granted free agency (October 15, 1998). ... Signed by Philadelphia Phillies organization (November 9, 1998).
STATISTICAL NOTES: Led Eastern League in caught stealing with 23 in 1992.

Year	Team (League)	Pos.	G	AB	R	H	2B	3B	HR	RBI	Avg.	BB	SO	SB	PO	A	E	Avg.
1986—	GC Astros (GCL)	SS	51	178	39	51	7	2	1	23	.287	32	25	17	81	131	31	.872
1987—	Asheville (S. Atl.)........	SS	108	399	83	103	9	2	1	33	.258	68	89	75	172	297	48	.907
1988—	Osceola (Fla. St.)........	2-S-O-1	130	468	79	110	11	3	0	34	.235	90	104	*87	220	282	28	.947

F

Year	Team (League)	Pos.	G	AB	R	H	2B	3B	HR	RBI	Avg.	BB	SO	SB	PO	A	E	Avg.
1989—	Columbus (Southern).	2B-OF	135	460	65	106	10	1	4	31	.230	76	101	43	228	254	15	.970
1990—	London (Eastern)■	O-2-S-3	81	242	29	53	4	1	0	15	.219	27	52	20	123	68	15	.927
1991—	London (Eastern)	OF-2B	122	439	69	105	9	4	3	40	.239	77	87	42	210	36	12	.953
1992—	London (Eastern)	OF-2B	129	477	85	120	16	3	0	34	.252	*95	107	*58	255	12	10	.964
1993—	Montreal (N.L.)■........	OF-1B-2B	112	189	27	54	7	1	1	16	.286	16	24	17	98	9	2	.982
1994—	Montreal (N.L.)..........	OF-2B-1B	76	140	25	38	3	1	0	14	.271	18	23	20	61	4	1	.985
1995—	Montreal (N.L.)..........	OF-2B	35	63	6	12	2	0	0	3	.190	8	12	4	36	1	1	.974
—	Ottawa (Int'l)	OF	31	110	11	24	3	0	1	10	.218	13	20	10	73	3	2	.974
—	Texas (A.L.)■.............	OF-DH	49	99	19	21	2	0	0	8	.212	7	20	9	69	2	2	.973
1996—	Okla. City (A.A.)........	2B	58	208	28	51	8	3	3	16	.245	14	42	13	104	8	4	.966
—	Texas (A.L.)...........	OF-DH-2B	30	50	5	13	2	1	0	5	.260	8	10	4	31	3	2	.944
1997—	Bowie (Eastern)■.......	OF	25	103	20	24	4	2	0	8	.233	21	20	13	52	3	5	.917
—	Rochester (Int'l)	OF	84	302	40	75	12	4	2	39	.248	36	68	24	204	6	4	.981
1998—	Chicago (A.L.)■........	OF-DH	7	7	0	0	0	0	0	0	.000	2	6	4	5	0	0	1.000
—	Calgary (PCL)...........	OF	101	397	81	107	26	3	14	50	.270	57	84	*42	153	3	5	.969
American League totals (3 years)			86	156	24	34	4	1	0	13	.218	17	36	17	105	5	4	.965
National League totals (3 years)			223	392	58	104	12	2	1	33	.265	42	59	41	195	14	4	.981
Major league totals (5 years)			309	548	82	138	16	3	1	46	.252	59	95	58	300	19	8	.976

FREEL, RYAN   OF   BLUE JAYS

PERSONAL: Born March 8, 1976, in Jacksonville. ... 5-10/175. ... Bats right, throws right. ... Full name: Ryan Paul Freel.
HIGH SCHOOL: Englewood (Fla.).
JUNIOR COLLEGE: Tallahassee (Fla.) Community College.
TRANSACTIONS/CAREER NOTES: Selected by Toronto Blue Jays organization in 10th round of free-agent draft (June 1, 1995). ... On Dunedin disabled list (July 2-18 and July 23-30, 1997).

Year	Team (League)	Pos.	G	AB	R	H	2B	3B	HR	RBI	Avg.	BB	SO	SB	PO	A	E	Avg.
1995—	St. Catharines (NYP) ..	2B	65	243	30	68	10	5	3	29	.280	22	49	12	118	181	*19	.940
1996—	Knoxville (Southern) ..	OF-SS-2B	66	252	47	72	17	3	4	36	.286	33	32	18	127	35	3	.982
1997—	Knoxville (Southern) ..	SS	33	94	18	19	1	1	0	4	.202	19	13	5	44	92	13	.913
—	Dunedin (Fla. St.)	S-O-2-3	61	181	42	51	8	2	3	17	.282	46	28	24	88	93	18	.910
1998—	Knoxville (Southern) ..	OF-2B-SS	66	252	47	72	17	3	4	36	.286	33	32	18	127	35	3	.982
—	Syracuse (Int'l)..........	OF-2B	37	118	19	27	4	0	2	12	.229	26	16	9	57	19	3	.962

FRIAS, HANLEY   SS   DIAMONDBACKS

PERSONAL: Born December 5, 1973, in Villa Atiagracia, Dominican Republic. ... 6-0/165. ... Bats both, throws right. ... Full name: Hanley Acevedo Frias. ... Name pronounced FREE-us.
TRANSACTIONS/CAREER NOTES: Signed as non-drafted free agent by Texas Rangers organization (July 3, 1990). ... Selected by Arizona Diamondbacks in second round (51st pick overall) of expansion draft (November 18, 1997). ... On Arizona disabled list (March 20-July 14, 1998); included rehabilitation assignment to Tucson (June 9-July 8).
STATISTICAL NOTES: Tied for American Association lead in caught stealing with 15 in 1997. ... Led American Association shortstops with 623 total chances in 1997.

Year	Team (League)	Pos.	G	AB	R	H	2B	3B	HR	RBI	Avg.	BB	SO	SB	PO	A	E	Avg.
1991—	....					Dominican Summer League statistics unavailable.												
1992—	GC Rangers (GCL).......	2B-SS	58	205	37	50	9	2	0	28	.244	27	30	28	90	143	11	.955
1993—	Char., S.C. (S. Atl.).....	2-0-S-3	132	473	61	109	20	4	4	37	.230	40	108	27	211	249	25	.948
1994—	High Desert (Calif.).....	SS	124	452	70	115	17	6	3	59	.254	41	74	37	169	*404	37	.939
1995—	Charlotte (Fla. St.)......	SS	33	120	23	40	6	3	0	14	.333	15	11	8	45	106	11	.932
—	Tulsa (Texas)	SS	93	360	44	101	18	4	0	27	.281	45	53	14	137	301	24	.948
1996—	Tulsa (Texas)	SS	134	505	73	145	24	12	2	41	.287	30	73	9	197	*417	23	.964
1997—	Okla. City (A.A.).........	SS	132	484	64	128	17	4	5	46	.264	56	72	35	*176	*414	33	.947
—	Texas (A.L.)...............	SS-2B	14	26	4	5	1	0	0	1	.192	1	4	0	12	13	0	1.000
1998—	Tucson (PCL)■..........	SS-3B-2B	63	253	32	73	10	4	1	21	.289	24	41	16	92	172	12	.957
—	Arizona (N.L.)...........	2B-3B-SS	15	23	4	3	0	1	1	2	.130	0	5	0	9	10	0	1.000
American League totals (1 year)			14	26	4	5	1	0	0	1	.192	1	4	0	12	13	0	1.000
National League totals (1 year)			15	23	4	3	0	1	1	2	.130	0	5	0	9	10	0	1.000
Major league totals (2 years)			29	49	8	8	1	1	1	3	.163	1	9	0	21	23	0	1.000

FRYE, JEFF   2B   RED SOX

PERSONAL: Born August 31, 1966, in Oakland. ... 5-9/165. ... Bats right, throws right. ... Full name: Jeffrey Dustin Frye.
HIGH SCHOOL: Panama (Okla.).
JUNIOR COLLEGE: Carl Albert (Poteau, Okla.).
COLLEGE: Southeastern State (Durant, Okla.).
TRANSACTIONS/CAREER NOTES: Selected by Texas Rangers organization in 30th round of free-agent draft (June 1, 1988). ... On Texas disabled list (March 27, 1993-entire season; June 9-24, 1994; and June 3-18 and June 21-July 6, 1995). ... Granted free agency (December 21, 1995). ... Re-signed by Rangers organization (March 25, 1996). ... Released by Rangers organization (June 5, 1996). ... Signed by Boston Red Sox (June 5, 1996). ... On disabled list (March 13, 1998-entire season).
STATISTICAL NOTES: Led Pioneer League second basemen with 44 double plays in 1988. ... Tied for American Association lead in being hit by pitch with 11 in 1992.

F

Year	Team (League)	Pos.	G	AB	R	H	2B	3B	HR	RBI	Avg.	BB	SO	SB	PO	A	E	Avg.
1988—	Butte (Pioneer)...........	2B	54	185	47	53	7	1	0	14	.286	35	25	16	96	149	7	.972
1989—	Gastonia (S. Atl.)........	2B	125	464	85	145	26	3	1	40	*.313	72	53	33	242	340	14	*.977
1990—	Charlotte (Fla. St.)......	2B	131	503	77	137	16	7	0	50	.272	80	66	29	252	350	13	*.979
1991—	Tulsa (Texas)	2B	131	503	92	152	32	11	4	41	.302	71	60	15	262	322	*26	.957
1992—	Okla. City (A.A.)...........	2B	87	337	64	101	26	2	2	28	.300	51	39	11	212	248	7	.985
	—Texas (A.L.)	2B	67	199	24	51	9	1	1	12	.256	16	27	1	120	196	7	.978
1993—	....								Did not play.									
1994—	Okla. City (A.A.)...........	2B	17	68	7	19	3	0	1	5	.279	6	7	2	28	44	1	.986
	—Texas (A.L.)	2B-DH-3B	57	205	37	67	20	3	0	18	.327	29	23	6	90	136	4	.983
1995—	Texas (A.L.)	2B	90	313	38	87	15	2	4	29	.278	24	45	3	173	248	11	.975
1996—	Okla. City (A.A.)...........	2-S-O-3	49	181	25	43	10	0	1	18	.238	24	21	10	94	148	8	.968
	—Boston (A.L.)■...........	2-O-S-DH	105	419	74	120	27	2	4	41	.286	54	57	18	211	317	9	.983
1997—	Boston (A.L.)............2-3-O-DH-S-1127		404	56	126	36	2	3	51	.312	27	44	19	227	264	12	.976
1998—	Boston (A.L.)								Did not play.									
Major league totals (5 years)			446	1540	229	451	107	10	12	151	.293	150	196	47	821	1161	43	.979

FRYMAN, TRAVIS   3B   INDIANS

PERSONAL: Born March 25, 1969, in Lexington, Ky. ... 6-1/195. ... Bats right, throws right. ... Full name: David Travis Fryman.
HIGH SCHOOL: Tate (Gonzalez, Fla.).
TRANSACTIONS/CAREER NOTES: Selected by Detroit Tigers organization in supplemental round ("sandwich pick" between first and second round, 30th pick overall) of free-agent draft (June 2, 1987); pick received as compensation for Philadelphia Phillies signing Type A free-agent C Lance Parrish. ... Traded by Tigers to Arizona Diamondbacks for 3B Joe Randa, P Matt Drews and 3B Gabe Alvarez (November 18, 1997). ... Traded by Diamondbacks with P Tom Martin and cash to Cleveland Indians for 3B Matt Williams (December 1, 1997).
HONORS: Named shortstop on THE SPORTING NEWS A.L. All-Star team (1992). ... Named shortstop on THE SPORTING NEWS A.L. Silver Slugger team (1992). ... Named third baseman on THE SPORTING NEWS A.L. All-Star team (1993).
STATISTICAL NOTES: Led Appalachian League shortstops with 313 total chances in 1987. ... Hit for the cycle (July 28, 1993). ... Tied for A.L. lead with 13 sacrifice flies in 1994. ... Led A.L. third basemen with 313 total chances in 1994 and 337 in 1995. ... Led A.L. third basemen with 38 double plays in 1995. ... Led A.L. third basemen with 133 putouts and .979 fielding percentage in 1996. ... Career major league grand slams: 4.

Year	Team (League)	Pos.	G	AB	R	H	2B	3B	HR	RBI	Avg.	BB	SO	SB	PO	A	E	Avg.
1987—	Bristol (Appal.)	SS	67	248	25	58	9	0	2	20	.234	22	39	6	*103	187	•23	.927
1988—	Fayetteville (SAL)	SS-2B	123	411	44	96	17	4	0	47	.234	24	83	16	174	390	32	.946
1989—	London (Eastern)	SS	118	426	52	113	*30	1	9	56	.265	19	78	5	192	346	*27	.952
1990—	Toledo (Int'l)	SS	87	327	38	84	22	2	10	53	.257	17	59	4	128	277	26	.940
	—Detroit (A.L.)	3B-SS-DH	66	232	32	69	11	1	9	27	.297	17	51	3	47	145	14	.932
1991—	Detroit (A.L.)	3B-SS	149	557	65	144	36	3	21	91	.259	40	149	12	153	354	23	.957
1992—	Detroit (A.L.)	SS-3B	161	*659	87	175	31	4	20	96	.266	45	144	8	220	489	22	.970
1993—	Detroit (A.L.)	SS-3B-DH	151	607	98	182	37	5	22	97	.300	77	128	9	169	382	23	.960
1994—	Detroit (A.L.)	3B	114	*464	66	122	34	5	18	85	.263	45	*128	2	78	*221	14	.955
1995—	Detroit (A.L.)	3B	144	567	79	156	21	5	15	81	.275	63	100	4	107	*337	14	.969
1996—	Detroit (A.L.)	3B-SS	157	616	90	165	32	3	22	100	.268	57	118	4	149	†354	10	†.981
1997—	Detroit (A.L.)	3B	154	595	90	163	27	3	22	102	.274	46	113	16	•126	312	10	*.978
1998—	Cleveland (A.L.)■.......	3B-SS-DH	146	557	74	160	33	2	28	96	.287	44	125	10	101	242	13	.963
Major league totals (9 years)			1242	4854	681	1336	262	31	177	775	.275	434	1056	68	1150	2836	143	.965

DIVISION SERIES RECORD

Year	Team (League)	Pos.	G	AB	R	H	2B	3B	HR	RBI	Avg.	BB	SO	SB	PO	A	E	Avg.
1998—	Cleveland (A.L.)	3B	4	13	1	2	1	0	0	0	.154	3	4	1	5	8	0	1.000

CHAMPIONSHIP SERIES RECORD

Year	Team (League)	Pos.	G	AB	R	H	2B	3B	HR	RBI	Avg.	BB	SO	SB	PO	A	E	Avg.
1998—	Cleveland (A.L.)	3B	6	23	2	4	0	0	0	0	.174	1	5	1	1	7	1	.889

ALL-STAR GAME RECORD

Year	League	Pos.	AB	R	H	2B	3B	HR	RBI	Avg.	BB	SO	SB	PO	A	E	Avg.
1992—	American	SS	1	1	1	0	0	0	1	1.000	1	0	0	0	3	0	1.000
1993—	American	SS	1	0	0	0	0	0	0	.000	0	0	0	1	1	0	1.000
1994—	American	PH	1	0	0	0	0	0	0	.000	0	0	0	...	...	...	....
1996—	American	PH-3B	1	0	0	0	0	0	0	.000	0	1	0	0	1	0	1.000
All-Star Game totals (4 years)			4	1	1	0	0	0	1	.250	1	1	0	1	5	0	1.000

FUENTES, BRIAN   P   MARINERS

PERSONAL: Born August 9, 1975, in Merced, Calif. ... 6-4/220. ... Throws left, bats left. ... Full name: Brian Christopher Fuentes.
HIGH SCHOOL: Merced (Calif.).
JUNIOR COLLEGE: Merced (Calif.) Junior College.
TRANSACTIONS/CAREER NOTES: Selected by Seattle Mariners organization in 25th round of free-agent draft (June 1, 1995). ... On disabled list (April 2-20, 1998).

Year	Team (League)	W	L	Pct.	ERA	G	GS	CG	ShO	Sv.	IP	H	R	ER	BB	SO
1996—	Everett (Northwest)	0	1	.000	4.39	13	2	0	0	0	26 2/3	23	14	13	13	26
1997—	Wisconsin (Midwest)	6	7	.462	3.56	22	22	0	0	0	118 2/3	84	52	47	59	153
1998—	Lancaster (Calif.)...............	7	7	.500	4.17	24	22	0	0	0	118 2/3	121	73	55	81	137

FULLMER, BRAD   1B   EXPOS

PERSONAL: Born January 17, 1975, in Chatsworth, Calif. ... 6-1/220. ... Bats left, throws right. ... Full name: Bradley Ryan Fullmer.
HIGH SCHOOL: Montclair Prep (Van Nuys, Calif.).
TRANSACTIONS/CAREER NOTES: Selected by Montreal Expos organization in second round of free-agent draft (June 3, 1993). ... On disabled list (June 20, 1994-remainder of season).
STATISTICAL NOTES: Hit home run in first major league at-bat (September 2, 1997). ... Career major league grand slams: 1.

Year Team (League)	Pos.	G	AB	R	H	2B	3B	HR	RBI	Avg.	BB	SO	SB	PO	A	E	Avg.
1994—							Did not play.										
1995—Albany (S. Atl.)	3B-1B	123	468	69	•151	38	4	8	67	.323	36	33	10	269	66	30	.918
1996—W.P. Beach (FSL)	OF-1B	102	380	52	115	29	1	5	63	.303	32	43	4	197	10	7	.967
—Harrisburg (East.)	OF-1B	24	98	11	27	4	1	4	14	.276	3	8	0	43	1	2	.957
1997—Harrisburg (East.)	1B-OF	94	357	60	111	24	2	19	62	.311	30	25	6	538	41	6	.990
—Ottawa (Int'l)	1B-OF	24	91	13	27	7	0	3	17	.297	3	10	1	173	12	1	.995
—Montreal (N.L.)	1B-OF	19	40	4	12	2	0	3	8	.300	2	7	0	50	7	2	.966
1998—Montreal (N.L.)	1B	140	505	58	138	44	2	13	73	.273	39	70	6	1070	79	*17	.985
Major league totals (2 years)		159	545	62	150	46	2	16	81	.275	41	77	6	1120	86	19	.984

FUSSELL, CHRIS   P   ORIOLES

PERSONAL: Born May 19, 1976, in Oregon, Ohio. ... 6-2/185. ... Throws right, bats right. ... Full name: Christopher Wren Fussell.
HIGH SCHOOL: Clay (Ohio).
TRANSACTIONS/CAREER NOTES: Selected by Baltimore Orioles organization in ninth round of free-agent draft (June 2, 1994). ... On disabled list (July 13, 1996-remainder of season).

Year Team (League)	W	L	Pct.	ERA	G	GS	CG	ShO	Sv.	IP	H	R	ER	BB	SO
1994—GC Orioles (GCL)	2	3	.400	4.15	14	8	0	0	0	$56\frac{1}{3}$	53	30	26	24	65
1995—Bluefield (Appalachian)	9	1	.900	2.19	12	12	1	1	0	$65\frac{2}{3}$	37	18	16	32	98
1996—Frederick (Carolina)	5	2	.714	2.81	15	14	1	1	0	$86\frac{1}{3}$	71	36	27	44	94
1997—Bowie (Eastern)	1	8	.111	7.11	19	18	0	0	0	$82\frac{1}{3}$	102	71	65	58	71
—Frederick (Carolina)	3	3	.500	3.96	9	9	1	1	0	50	42	23	22	31	54
1998—Bowie (Eastern)	3	7	.300	4.26	18	18	0	0	0	93	87	54	44	52	84
—Rochester (Int'l)	5	2	.714	3.99	10	10	0	0	0	$58\frac{2}{3}$	50	30	26	28	51
—Baltimore (A.L.)	0	1	.000	8.38	3	2	0	0	0	$9\frac{2}{3}$	11	9	9	9	8
Major league totals (1 year)	0	1	.000	8.38	3	2	0	0	0	$9\frac{2}{3}$	11	9	9	9	8

GAETTI, GARY   3B   CUBS

PERSONAL: Born August 19, 1958, in Centralia, Ill. ... 6-0/205. ... Bats right, throws right. ... Full name: Gary Joseph Gaetti. ... Name pronounced guy-ETT-ee.
HIGH SCHOOL: Centralia (Ill.).
JUNIOR COLLEGE: Lake Land College (Ill.).
COLLEGE: Northwest Missouri State.
TRANSACTIONS/CAREER NOTES: Selected by St. Louis Cardinals organization in fourth round of free-agent draft (January 10, 1978); did not sign. ... Selected by Chicago White Sox organization in secondary phase of free-agent draft (June 6, 1978); did not sign. ... Selected by Minnesota Twins organization in secondary phase of free-agent draft (June 5, 1979). ... Granted free agency (November 9, 1987). ... Re-signed by Twins (January 7, 1988). ... On disabled list (August 21-September 5, 1988 and August 26-September 13, 1989). ... Granted free agency (December 7, 1990). ... Signed by California Angels (January 23, 1991). ... Released by Angels (June 3, 1993). ... Signed by Kansas City Royals (June 19, 1993). ... Granted free agency (October 25, 1993). ... Re-signed by Royals organization (December 16, 1993). ... On disabled list (July 5-20, 1994). ... Granted free agency (October 28, 1994). ... Re-signed by Royals organization (December 20, 1994). ... Granted free agency (November 3, 1995). ... Signed by Cardinals (December 18, 1995) ... On disabled list (April 28-May 14, 1996). ... Granted free agency (October 27, 1997). ... Re-signed by Cardinals (December 6, 1997). ... Released by Cardinals (August 14, 1998). ... Signed by Chicago Cubs (August 19, 1998). ... Granted free agency (October 23, 1998). ... Re-signed by Cubs (December 7, 1998).
RECORDS: Shares major league rookie-season record for most sacrifice flies—13 (1982).
HONORS: Won A.L. Gold Glove at third base (1986-89). ... Named third baseman on THE SPORTING NEWS A.L. Silver Slugger team (1995).
STATISTICAL NOTES: Tied for Appalachian League lead in errors by third baseman with 18 in 1979. ... Led Midwest League third basemen with 492 total chances and 35 double plays in 1980. ... Led Southern League third basemen with 122 putouts, 281 assists, 32 errors and 435 total chances in 1981. ... Hit home run in first major-league at-bat (September 20, 1981). ... Led A.L. with 13 sacrifice flies in 1982. ... Led A.L. third basemen with 131 putouts in 1983, 142 in 1984 and 146 in 1985. ... Led A.L. third basemen with 46 double plays in 1983, 36 in 1986 and 1990 and 39 in 1991. ... Led A.L. third basemen with 496 total chances in 1984, 473 in 1986, 438 in 1990 and 481 in 1991. ... Led A.L. third basemen with 334 assists in both 1984 and 1986 and 318 in 1990. ... Tied for A.L. lead in errors by third basemen with 20 in 1984. ... Led A.L. in grounding into double plays with 25 in 1987. ... Led A.L. third basemen with .982 fielding percentage in 1994. ... Led N.L. third basemen in fielding percentage with .978 in 1997 and .983 in 1998. ... Career major league grand slams: 9.

Year Team (League)	Pos.	G	AB	R	H	2B	3B	HR	RBI	Avg.	BB	SO	SB	PO	A	E	Avg.
1979—Elizabethton (App.)	3B-SS	66	230	50	59	15	2	14	42	.257	43	40	6	70	134	‡21	.907
1980—Wis. Rap. (Mid.)	3B	138	503	77	134	27	3	*22	82	.266	67	120	24	*94	*363	•35	.929
1981—Orlando (South.)	3B-1B	137	495	92	137	19	2	30	93	.277	58	105	15	†143	†282	†32	.930
—Minnesota (A.L.)	3B-DH	9	26	4	5	0	0	2	3	.192	0	6	0	5	17	0	1.000
1982—Minnesota (A.L.)	3B-SS-DH	145	508	59	117	25	4	25	84	.230	37	107	0	106	291	17	.959
1983—Minnesota (A.L.)	3B-SS-DH	157	584	81	143	30	3	21	78	.245	54	121	7	†131	361	17	.967
1984—Minnesota (A.L.)	3B-OF-SS	•162	588	55	154	29	4	5	65	.262	44	81	11	†163	†335	‡21	.960
1985—Minnesota (A.L.)	3-0-1-DH	160	560	71	138	31	0	20	63	.246	37	89	13	†162	316	18	.964
1986—Minnesota (A.L.)	3-S-O-2	157	596	91	171	34	1	34	108	.287	52	108	14	120	†335	21	.956
1987—Minnesota (A.L.)	3B-DH	154	584	95	150	36	2	31	109	.257	37	92	10	•134	261	11	.973
1988—Minnesota (A.L.)	3B-DH-SS	133	468	66	141	29	2	28	88	.301	36	85	7	105	191	7	.977
1989—Minnesota (A.L.)	3B-DH-1B	130	498	63	125	11	4	19	75	.251	25	87	6	115	253	10	.974

F

G

Year Team (League)	Pos.	G	AB	R	H	2B	3B	HR	RBI	Avg.	BB	SO	SB	PO	A	E	Avg.
1990— Minnesota (A.L.)	3B-SS	154	577	61	132	27	5	16	85	.229	36	101	6	125	†319	18	.961
1991— California (A.L.)■	3B	152	586	58	144	22	1	18	66	.246	33	104	5	111	*353	17	.965
1992— California (A.L.)	3B-1B-DH	130	456	41	103	13	2	12	48	.226	21	79	3	423	196	22	.966
1993— California (A.L.)	3B-1B-DH	20	50	3	9	2	0	0	4	.180	5	12	1	38	7	1	.978
— Kansas City (A.L.)■	3B-1B-DH	82	281	37	72	18	1	14	46	.256	16	75	0	147	146	6	.980
1994— Kansas City (A.L.)	3B-1B	90	327	53	94	15	3	12	57	.287	19	63	0	99	166	4	†.985
1995— Kansas City (A.L.)	3B-1B-DH	137	514	76	134	27	0	35	96	.261	47	91	3	182	228	16	.962
1996— St. Louis (N.L.)■	3B-1B	141	522	71	143	27	4	23	80	.274	35	97	2	148	231	10	.974
1997— St. Louis (N.L.)	3B-1B-P	148	502	63	126	24	1	17	69	.251	36	88	7	133	250	7	†.982
1998— St. Louis (N.L.)	3-1-P-2-O	91	306	39	81	23	1	11	43	.265	31	39	1	62	153	3	.986
— Chicago (N.L.)■	3B	37	128	21	41	11	0	8	27	.320	12	23	0	24	68	2	§.979
American League totals (15 years)		1972	7203	914	1832	349	32	292	1075	.254	499	1301	86	2166	3775	206	.966
National League totals (3 years)		417	1458	194	391	85	6	59	219	.268	114	247	10	367	702	22	.980
Major league totals (18 years)		2389	8661	1108	2223	434	38	351	1294	.257	613	1548	96	2533	4477	228	.968

DIVISION SERIES RECORD

Year Team (League)	Pos.	G	AB	R	H	2B	3B	HR	RBI	Avg.	BB	SO	SB	PO	A	E	Avg.
1996— St. Louis (N.L.)	3B	3	11	1	1	0	0	1	3	.091	0	3	0	1	3	0	1.000
1998— Chicago (N.L.)	3B	3	11	0	1	0	0	0	0	.091	0	4	0	2	6	1	.889
Division series totals (2 years)		6	22	1	2	0	0	1	3	.091	0	7	0	3	9	1	.923

CHAMPIONSHIP SERIES RECORD

RECORDS: Shares single-game record for most grand slams—1 (October 10, 1996). ... Shares single-inning record for most runs batted in—4 (October 10, 1996, seventh inning).

NOTES: Hit home run in first at-bat (October 7, 1987). ... Named Most Valuable Player (1987).

Year Team (League)	Pos.	G	AB	R	H	2B	3B	HR	RBI	Avg.	BB	SO	SB	PO	A	E	Avg.
1987— Minnesota (A.L.)	3B	5	20	5	6	1	0	2	5	.300	1	3	0	8	7	0	1.000
1996— St. Louis (N.L.)	3B	7	24	1	7	0	0	1	4	.292	1	5	0	4	12	0	1.000
Championship series totals (2 years)		12	44	6	13	1	0	3	9	.295	2	8	0	12	19	0	1.000

WORLD SERIES RECORD

RECORDS: Shares single-inning records for most at-bats—2; and most hits—2 (October 17, 1987, fourth inning).

NOTES: Member of World Series championship team (1987).

Year Team (League)	Pos.	G	AB	R	H	2B	3B	HR	RBI	Avg.	BB	SO	SB	PO	A	E	Avg.
1987— Minnesota (A.L.)	3B	7	27	4	7	2	1	1	4	.259	2	5	2	6	15	0	1.000

ALL-STAR GAME RECORD

Year League	Pos.	AB	R	H	2B	3B	HR	RBI	Avg.	BB	SO	SB	PO	A	E	Avg.
1988— American	PH	1	0	0	0	0	0	0	.000	0	0	0	...	...	...	...
1989— American	3B	1	0	0	0	0	0	0	.000	0	1	0	1	0	0	1.000
All-Star Game totals (2 years)		2	0	0	0	0	0	0	.000	0	1	0	1	0	0	1.000

RECORD AS PITCHER

Year Team (League)	W	L	Pct.	ERA	G	GS	CG	ShO	Sv.	IP	H	R	ER	BB	SO
1997— St. Louis (N.L.)	0	0	...	0.00	1	0	0	0	0	1/3	1	0	0	0	0
1998— St. Louis (N.L.)	0	0	...	0.00	1	0	0	0	0	1	2	0	0	0	0
Major league totals (2 years)	0	0	...	0.00	2	0	0	0	0	1 1/3	3	0	0	0	0

GAGNE, ERIC P DODGERS

PERSONAL: Born January 7, 1976, in Montreal. ... 6-2/195. ... Throws right, bats right. ... Full name: Eric Serge Gagne.

HIGH SCHOOL: Polyvalente Edouard Montpetit (Montreal).

TRANSACTIONS/CAREER NOTES: Signed as non-drafted free agent by Los Angeles Dodgers organization (July 26, 1995). ... On disabled list entire 1997 season.

Year Team (League)	W	L	Pct.	ERA	G	GS	CG	ShO	Sv.	IP	H	R	ER	BB	SO
1996— Savannah (S. Atl.)	7	6	.538	3.28	23	21	1	1	0	115 1/3	94	48	42	43	131
1997—							Did not play.								
1998— Vero Beach (FSL)	9	7	.563	3.74	25	25	3	1	0	139 2/3	118	69	58	48	144

GAILLARD, EDDIE P DEVIL RAYS

PERSONAL: Born August 13, 1970, in Camden, N.J. ... 6-1/200. ... Throws right, bats right. ... Full name: Julian Edward Gaillard III.

HIGH SCHOOL: Forest Hills (West Palm Beach, Fla.).

JUNIOR COLLEGE: Palm Beach Community College (Fla.).

COLLEGE: Florida Southern.

TRANSACTIONS/CAREER NOTES: Selected by Detroit Tigers organization in 13th round of free-agent draft (June 3, 1993). ... Claimed on waivers by Tampa Bay Devil Rays (April 2, 1998). ... On Tampa Bay disabled list (May 21-August 24, 1998); included rehabilitation assignments to Gulf Coast Devil Rays (June 20-22 and August 21-24), St. Petersburg (June 23-25), and Durham (June 26-July 10).

Year Team (League)	W	L	Pct.	ERA	G	GS	CG	ShO	Sv.	IP	H	R	ER	BB	SO
1993— Niagara Falls (NYP)	1	2	.333	3.68	3	3	0	0	0	14 2/3	15	6	6	4	12
— Fayetteville (S. Atl.)	5	2	.714	4.09	11	11	0	0	0	61 2/3	64	30	28	20	41
1994— Lakeland (Fla. St.)	6	1	.857	2.84	30	9	0	0	2	92	82	37	29	29	51
1995— Jacksonville (Southern)	0	1	.000	5.63	8	0	0	0	0	8	11	5	5	5	4
— Lakeland (Fla. St.)	2	4	.333	1.31	43	0	0	0	25	55	48	13	8	18	51

G

Year Team (League)	W	L	Pct.	ERA	G	GS	CG	ShO	Sv.	IP	H	R	ER	BB	SO
1996— Jacksonville (Southern)......	9	6	.600	3.38	56	0	0	0	1	88	82	40	33	50	76
1997— Toledo (International)........	1	4	.200	4.25	55	0	0	0	*28	53	52	27	25	24	54
— Detroit (A.L.)..................	1	0	1.000	5.31	16	0	0	0	1	20 1/3	16	12	12	10	12
1998— Tampa Bay (A.L.)■.............	0	0	...	5.87	6	0	0	0	0	7 2/3	4	5	5	3	5
— GC Devil Rays (GCL).........	0	0	...	0.00	2	2	0	0	0	4	0	0	0	1	5
— St. Petersburg (FSL)........	0	0	...	0.00	1	1	0	0	0	2	1	0	0	0	2
— Durham (International).......	2	0	1.000	7.65	18	0	0	0	0	20	27	18	17	11	21
Major league totals (2 years)......	1	0	1.000	5.46	22	0	0	0	1	28	20	17	17	13	17

GAJKOWSKI, STEVE   P   CUBS

PERSONAL: Born December 30, 1969, in Seattle. ... 6-2/185. ... Throws right, bats right. ... Full name: Stephen Robert Gajkowski.
HIGH SCHOOL: Newport (Bellevue, Wash.).
JUNIOR COLLEGE: Bellevue (Wash.) Community College.
TRANSACTIONS/CAREER NOTES: Selected by Cleveland Indians organization in 18th round of free-agent draft (June 4, 1990). ... Released by Indians (March 28, 1992). ... Signed by Chicago White Sox organization (May 7, 1992). ... Granted free agency (October 15, 1996). ... Signed by Seattle Mariners organization (November 25, 1996). ... Granted free agency (October 15, 1998). ... Signed by Chicago Cubs organization (November 13, 1998).

Year Team (League)	W	L	Pct.	ERA	G	GS	CG	ShO	Sv.	IP	H	R	ER	BB	SO
1990— Burlington (Appalachian)....	2	6	.250	4.10	14	10	1	0	0	63 2/3	74	34	29	23	44
1991— Columbus (S. Atl.)............	0	0	...	3.00	3	0	0	0	0	6	3	2	2	5	5
— Watertown (NYP)..............	3	3	.500	5.25	20	4	0	0	0	48	41	36	28	32	34
1992— Utica (N.Y.-Penn)■...........	3	2	.600	1.34	29	0	0	0	14	47	33	14	7	10	38
1993— Sarasota (Florida State)......	3	3	.500	2.07	43	0	0	0	15	69 2/3	52	21	16	17	46
— Birmingham (Southern)......	0	0	...	0.00	1	0	0	0	0	2 1/3	0	0	0	0	2
1994— Birmingham (Southern)......	11	4	.733	3.06	*58	0	0	0	8	82 1/3	78	35	28	26	44
1995— Nashville (A.A.)...............	0	1	.000	2.55	15	0	0	0	0	24 2/3	26	15	7	8	12
— Birmingham (Southern)......	4	4	.500	4.18	35	0	0	0	2	51 2/3	64	27	24	16	29
1996— Nashville (A.A.)..............	5	6	.455	3.94	49	8	0	0	2	107 1/3	113	61	47	41	47
1997— Tacoma (PCL)■.................	5	3	.625	3.87	44	3	0	0	2	93	100	43	40	24	48
1998— Tacoma (PCL)	3	3	.500	2.57	53	0	0	0	24	73 2/3	60	23	21	20	61
— Seattle (A.L.)	0	0	...	7.27	9	0	0	0	0	8 2/3	14	8	7	4	3
Major league totals (1 year)........	0	0	...	7.27	9	0	0	0	0	8 2/3	14	8	7	4	3

GALARRAGA, ANDRES   1B   BRAVES

PERSONAL: Born June 18, 1961, in Caracas, Venezuela. ... 6-3/235. ... Bats right, throws right. ... Full name: Andres Jose Galarraga. ... Name pronounced GAHL-ah-RAH-guh.
HIGH SCHOOL: Enrique Felmi (Caracas, Venezuela).
TRANSACTIONS/CAREER NOTES: Signed as non-drafted free agent by Montreal Expos organization (January 19, 1979). ... On disabled list (July 10-August 19 and August 20-September 4, 1986; and May 26-July 4, 1991). ... Traded by Expos to St. Louis Cardinals for P Ken Hill (November 25, 1991). ... On St. Louis disabled list (April 8-May 22, 1992; included rehabilitation assignment to Louisville (May 13-22). ... Granted free agency (October 27, 1992). ... Signed by Colorado Rockies (November 16, 1992). ... On disabled list (May 10-27 and July 25-August 21, 1993). ... Granted free agency (October 25, 1993). ... Re-signed by Rockies (December 6, 1993). ... On disabled list (July 29, 1994-remainder of season). ... On suspended list (August 3-5, 1997). ... Granted free agency (October 27, 1997). ... Signed by Atlanta Braves (November 20, 1997).
HONORS: Named Southern League Most Valuable Player (1984). ... Named first baseman on THE SPORTING NEWS N.L. Silver Slugger team (1988 and 1996). ... Won N.L. Gold Glove at first base (1989-90). ... Named N.L. Comeback Player of the Year by THE SPORTING NEWS (1993).
STATISTICAL NOTES: Led Southern League with 271 total bases, .508 slugging percentage and 10 intentional bases on balls received and tied for lead in being hit by pitch with nine in 1984. ... Led Southern League first basemen with 1,428 total chances and 130 double plays in 1984. ... Led N.L. in being hit by pitch with 10 in 1987 and tied for lead with 13 in 1989. ... Led N.L. with 329 total bases in 1988. ... Hit three home runs in one game (June 25, 1995). ... Collected six hits in one game (July 3, 1995). ... Led N.L. first basemen with 1,432 total chances and 129 double plays in 1995. ... Led N.L. first basemen with 1,528 putouts, 1,658 total chances and 154 double plays in 1996. ... Led N.L. first basemen with 1,590 total chances and 176 double plays in 1997. ... Had 15-game hitting streak (April 23-May 8, 1998). ... Career major league grand slams: 9.
MISCELLANEOUS: Holds Colorado Rockies all-time record for most home runs (172).

Year Team (League)	Pos.	G	AB	R	H	2B	3B	HR	RBI	Avg.	BB	SO	SB	PO	A	E	Avg.
						BATTING								FIELDING			
1979— W.P. Beach (FSL)........	1B	7	23	3	3	0	0	0	1	.130	2	11	0	2	1	0	1.000
— Calgary (Pioneer).......	1B-3B-C	42	112	14	24	3	1	4	16	.214	9	42	1	187	21	5	.977
1980— Calgary (Pioneer).......	1-3-C-O	59	190	27	50	11	4	4	22	.263	7	55	3	287	52	21	.942
1981— Jamestown (NYP).....	C-1-O-3	47	154	24	40	5	4	6	26	.260	15	44	0	154	15	0	1.000
1982— W.P. Beach (FSL)........	1B	105	338	39	95	20	2	14	51	.281	34	77	2	462	36	9	.982
1983— W.P. Beach (FSL)........	1B-OF-3B	104	401	55	116	18	3	10	66	.289	33	68	7	861	77	13	.986
1984— Jacksonville (Sou.).......	1B	143	533	81	154	28	4	27	87	.289	59	122	2	*1302	*110	16	.989
1985— Indianapolis (A.A.).......	1B-OF	121	439	*75	118	15	8	25	87	.269	45	103	3	930	63	14	.986
— Montreal (N.L.)...........	1B	24	75	9	14	1	0	2	4	.187	3	18	1	173	22	1	.995
1986— Montreal (N.L.)...........	1B	105	321	39	87	13	0	10	42	.271	30	79	6	805	40	4	.995
1987— Montreal (N.L.)...........	1B	147	551	72	168	40	3	13	90	.305	41	127	7	*1300	103	10	.993
1988— Montreal (N.L.)...........	1B	157	609	99	*184	*42	8	29	92	.302	39	*153	13	1464	103	10	.993
1989— Montreal (N.L.)...........	1B	152	572	76	147	30	1	23	85	.257	48	*158	12	1335	91	11	.992
1990— Montreal (N.L.)...........	1B	155	579	65	148	29	0	20	87	.256	40	*169	10	1300	94	10	.993
1991— Montreal (N.L.)...........	1B	107	375	34	82	13	2	9	33	.219	23	86	5	887	80	9	.991
1992— St. Louis (N.L.)■.........	1B	95	325	38	79	14	2	10	39	.243	11	69	5	777	62	8	.991
— Louisville (A.A.)	1B	11	34	3	6	0	1	2	3	.176	0	8	1	61	7	2	.971
1993— Colorado (N.L.)■.........	1B	120	470	71	174	35	4	22	98	*.370	24	73	2	1018	103	11	.990
1994— Colorado (N.L.)	1B	103	417	77	133	21	0	31	85	.319	19	93	8	953	65	8	.992

G

Year	Team (League)	Pos.	G	AB	R	H	2B	3B	HR	RBI	Avg.	BB	SO	SB	PO	A	E	Avg.
1995— Colorado (N.L.)	1B	143	554	89	155	29	3	31	106	.280	32	*146	12	*1299	120	*13	.991
1996— Colorado (N.L.)	1B-3B	159	626	119	190	39	3	*47	*150	.304	40	157	18	†1528	116	14	.992
1997— Colorado (N.L.)	1B	154	600	120	191	31	3	41	*140	.318	54	141	15	*1458	117	*15	.991
1998— Atlanta (N.L.)■..........	1B-DH	153	555	103	169	27	1	44	121	.305	63	146	7	1218	81	11	.992
Major league totals (14 years)		1774	6629	1011	1921	364	30	332	1172	.290	467	1615	121	15515	1197	140	.992

DIVISION SERIES RECORD

Year	Team (League)	Pos.	G	AB	R	H	2B	3B	HR	RBI	Avg.	BB	SO	SB	PO	A	E	Avg.
1995— Colorado (N.L.)	1B	4	18	1	5	1	0	0	2	.278	0	6	0	41	2	0	1.000
1998— Atlanta (N.L.)	1B	3	12	1	3	0	0	0	0	.250	1	3	0	5	0	0	1.000
Division series totals (2 years)		7	30	2	8	1	0	0	2	.267	1	9	0	46	2	0	1.000

CHAMPIONSHIP SERIES RECORD

RECORDS: Shares single-inning record for most runs batted in—4 (October 11, 1998, seventh inning).

Year	Team (League)	Pos.	G	AB	R	H	2B	3B	HR	RBI	Avg.	BB	SO	SB	PO	A	E	Avg.
1998— Atlanta (N.L.)	1B	6	21	1	2	0	0	1	4	.095	6	6	0	63	11	4	.949

ALL-STAR GAME RECORD

Year	League	Pos.	AB	R	H	2B	3B	HR	RBI	Avg.	BB	SO	SB	PO	A	E	Avg.
1988— National	1B	2	0	0	0	0	0	0	.000	0	1	0	6	0	0	1.000
1993— National	1B	1	0	0	0	0	0	0	.000	0	0	0	0	0	0	...
1997— National	PH-DH	1	0	0	0	0	0	0	.000	0	1	0	...	...	...	...
1998— National	1B	2	0	0	0	0	0	0	.000	0	0	0	7	0	0	1.000
All-Star Game totals (4 years)		6	0	0	0	0	0	0	.000	0	2	0	13	0	0	1.000

GALLAGHER, SHAWN   1B   RANGERS

PERSONAL: Born November 8, 1976, in Colorado Springs, Colo. ... 6-0/187. ... Bats right, throws right. ... Full name: Shawn Patrick Gallagher.
HIGH SCHOOL: New Hanover (Wilmington, N.C.).
TRANSACTIONS/CAREER NOTES: Selected by Texas Rangers organization in fifth round of free-agent draft (June 1, 1995).
HONORS: Named Florida State League Most Valuable Player (1998).
STATISTICAL NOTES: Led Gulf Coast League with 111 total bases in 1995. ... Led Appalachian League with .643 slugging percentage in 1997. ... Led Florida State League with 283 total bases in 1998.

Year	Team (League)	Pos.	G	AB	R	H	2B	3B	HR	RBI	Avg.	BB	SO	SB	PO	A	E	Avg.
1995— GC Rangers (GCL)......	1B	58	210	34	*71	13	3	7	40	.338	19	44	17	478	19	7	.986
— Hudson Valley (NYP)..	1B	5	20	1	3	2	0	0	4	.150	1	4	0	44	1	1	.978
1996— Char., S.C. (SAL)...	1B	88	303	29	68	11	4	7	32	.224	18	104	6	809	24	14	.983
— Hudson Valley (NYP)..	1B	44	176	15	48	10	2	4	29	.273	7	48	8	402	15	8	.981
1997— Charlotte (Fla. St.)...	1B	27	99	7	14	4	0	0	8	.141	5	35	0	232	10	4	.984
— Pulaski (Appalachian).	1B	50	199	41	64	13	3	15	52	.322	10	49	2	419	11	8	.982
1998— Charlotte (Fla. St.)......	1B	137	520	*111	160	*37	4	*26	*121	.308	66	116	18	1110	46	*19	.984

GALVEZ, RANDY   P   DODGERS

PERSONAL: Born July 26, 1978, in Guasave, Sinaloa, Mexico. ... 6-2/165. ... Throws right, bats right.
HIGH SCHOOL: Ignacia Arrayales de Castro (Mexico).
TRANSACTIONS/CAREER NOTES: Signed as non-drafted free agent by Los Angeles Dodgers organization (May 22, 1995). ... Loaned to Mexico City Red Devils of Mexican League for 1998 season.

Year	Team (League)	W	L	Pct.	ERA	G	GS	CG	ShO	Sv.	IP	H	R	ER	BB	SO
1995— Dom. Dodgers (DSL)	5	5	.500	4.27	32	0	0	0	2	$65\frac{1}{3}$	67	38	31	31	48
1996— Dom. Dodgers (DSL)	10	2	.833	2.53	13	12	0	0	0	$74\frac{2}{3}$	63	29	21	21	54
1997— Great Falls (Pio.)	3	1	.750	3.64	16	1	0	0	0	$29\frac{2}{3}$	29	14	12	10	29
1998— M.C. Red Devils (Mex.)■ ...	13	4	.765	3.60	24	24	3	0	0	150	158	71	60	52	83

GANT, RON   OF   PHILLIES

G

PERSONAL: Born March 2, 1965, in Victoria, Texas. ... 6-0/200. ... Bats right, throws right. ... Full name: Ronald Edwin Gant.
HIGH SCHOOL: Victoria (Texas).
TRANSACTIONS/CAREER NOTES: Selected by Atlanta Braves organization in fourth round of free-agent draft (June 6, 1983). ... On suspended list (July 31, 1991). ... Released by Braves (March 15, 1994). ... Signed by Cincinnati Reds (June 21, 1994). ... On Cincinnati disabled list (June 21, 1994-remainder of season). ... On suspended list (September 11-15, 1995). ... Granted free agency (October 30, 1995). ... Signed by St. Louis Cardinals (December 23, 1995). ... On disabled list (May 11-June 14, 1996). ... On disabled list (June 21-July 11, 1998). ... Traded by Cardinals with P Jeff Brantley and P Cliff Politte to Philadelphia Phillies for P Ricky Bottalico and P Garrett Stephenson (November 19, 1998).
HONORS: Named outfielder on THE SPORTING NEWS N.L. All-Star team (1991). ... Named outfielder on THE SPORTING NEWS N.L. Silver Slugger team (1991). ... Named N.L. Comeback Player of the Year by THE SPORTING NEWS (1995).
STATISTICAL NOTES: Led South Atlantic League second basemen with 75 double plays in 1984. ... Led Carolina League with 271 total bases in 1986. ... Led Southern League second basemen with 783 total chances and 108 double plays in 1987. ... Led N.L. second basemen with 26 errors in 1988. ... Career major league grand slams: 4.

Year	Team (League)	Pos.	G	AB	R	H	2B	3B	HR	RBI	Avg.	BB	SO	SB	PO	A	E	Avg.
1983— GC Braves (GCL)	SS	56	193	32	45	2	2	1	14	.233	41	34	4	68	134	22	.902
1984— Anderson (S. Atl.)	2B	105	359	44	85	14	6	3	38	.237	29	65	13	248	263	31	.943
1985— Sumter (S. Atl.)	2B-SS-OF	102	305	46	78	14	4	7	37	.256	33	59	19	160	200	10	.973
1986— Durham (Carolina)	2B	137	512	108	142	31	10	*26	102	.277	78	85	35	240	384	26	.960
1987— Greenville (Southern)	2B	140	527	78	130	27	3	14	82	.247	59	91	24	*328	*434	21	*.973
—Atlanta (N.L.)	2B	21	83	9	22	4	0	2	9	.265	1	11	4	45	59	3	.972
1988— Richmond (Int'l)	2B	12	45	3	14	2	2	0	4	.311	2	10	1	22	23	5	.900
—Atlanta (N.L.)	2B-3B	146	563	85	146	28	8	19	60	.259	46	118	19	316	417	†31	.959
1989— Atlanta (N.L.)	3B-OF	75	260	26	46	8	3	9	25	.177	20	63	9	70	103	17	.911
—Sumter (S. Atl.)	OF	12	39	13	15	4	1	1	5	.385	11	3	4	19	1	2	.909
—Richmond (Int'l)	OF-3B	63	225	42	59	13	2	11	27	.262	29	42	6	111	14	5	.962
1990— Atlanta (N.L.)	OF	152	575	107	174	34	3	32	84	.303	50	86	33	357	7	8	.978
1991— Atlanta (N.L.)	OF	154	561	101	141	35	3	32	105	.251	71	104	34	338	7	6	.983
1992— Atlanta (N.L.)	OF	153	544	74	141	22	6	17	80	.259	45	101	32	277	5	4	.986
1993— Atlanta (N.L.)	OF	157	606	113	166	27	4	36	117	.274	67	117	26	271	5	*11	.962
1994— Cincinnati (N.L.)■							Did not play.										
1995— Cincinnati (N.L.)	OF	119	410	79	113	19	4	29	88	.276	74	108	23	191	7	3	.985
1996— St. Louis (N.L.)■	OF	122	419	74	103	14	2	30	82	.246	73	98	13	216	4	5	.978
1997— St. Louis (N.L.)	OF-DH	139	502	68	115	21	4	17	62	.229	58	162	14	247	4	6	.977
1998— St. Louis (N.L.)	OF	121	383	60	92	17	1	26	67	.240	51	92	8	162	4	5	.971
Major league totals (11 years)		1359	4906	796	1259	229	38	249	779	.257	556	1060	215	2490	622	99	.969

DIVISION SERIES RECORD

Year	Team (League)	Pos.	G	AB	R	H	2B	3B	HR	RBI	Avg.	BB	SO	SB	PO	A	E	Avg.
1995— Cincinnati (N.L.)	OF	3	13	3	3	0	0	1	2	.231	0	3	0	8	1	0	1.000
1996— St. Louis (N.L.)	OF	3	10	3	4	1	0	1	4	.400	2	0	2	5	0	0	1.000
Division series totals (2 years)		6	23	6	7	1	0	2	6	.304	2	3	2	13	1	0	1.000

CHAMPIONSHIP SERIES RECORD

RECORDS: Shares single-game record for most grand slams—1 (October 7, 1992). ... Shares single-inning records for most runs batted in—4 (October 7, 1992, fifth inning); and most stolen bases—2 (October 10, 1991, third inning). ... Holds N.L. career record for most strikeouts—26. ... Holds N.L. single-series record for most stolen bases—7 (1991). ... Shares N.L. single-game record for most stolen bases—3 (October 10, 1991).

Year	Team (League)	Pos.	G	AB	R	H	2B	3B	HR	RBI	Avg.	BB	SO	SB	PO	A	E	Avg.
1991— Atlanta (N.L.)	OF	7	27	4	7	1	0	1	3	.259	2	4	7	15	2	0	1.000
1992— Atlanta (N.L.)	OF	7	22	5	4	0	0	2	6	.182	4	4	1	16	0	0	1.000
1993— Atlanta (N.L.)	OF	6	27	4	5	3	0	0	3	.185	2	9	0	10	1	1	.917
1995— Cincinnati (N.L.)	OF	4	16	1	3	0	0	0	1	.188	0	3	0	9	0	0	1.000
1996— St. Louis (N.L.)	OF	7	25	3	6	1	0	2	4	.240	2	6	0	12	0	0	1.000
Championship series totals (5 years)		31	117	17	25	5	0	5	17	.214	10	26	8	62	3	1	.985

WORLD SERIES RECORD

Year	Team (League)	Pos.	G	AB	R	H	2B	3B	HR	RBI	Avg.	BB	SO	SB	PO	A	E	Avg.
1991— Atlanta (N.L.)	OF	7	30	3	8	0	1	0	4	.267	2	3	1	19	0	0	1.000
1992— Atlanta (N.L.)	OF-PR-PH	4	8	2	1	1	0	0	0	.125	1	2	2	3	1	0	1.000
World Series totals (2 years)		11	38	5	9	1	1	0	4	.237	3	5	3	22	1	0	1.000

ALL-STAR GAME RECORD

Year	League	Pos.	AB	R	H	2B	3B	HR	RBI	Avg.	BB	SO	SB	PO	A	E	Avg.
1992— National	PH-OF	2	0	0	0	0	0	0	.000	0	0	0	1	0	0	1.000
1995— National	DH	2	0	0	0	0	0	0	.000	0	1	0	...	...	...	...
All-Star Game totals (2 years)		4	0	0	0	0	0	0	.000	0	1	0	1	0	0	1.000

GARCES, RICHARD   P

PERSONAL: Born May 18, 1971, in Maracay, Venezuela. ... 6-0/215. ... Throws right, bats right. ... Full name: Richard Aron Garces Jr. ... Name pronounced gar-SESS.

HIGH SCHOOL: Jose Felix Rivas (Maracay, Venezuela).

COLLEGE: Venezuela Universidad.

TRANSACTIONS/CAREER NOTES: Signed as non-drafted free agent by Minnesota Twins organization (December 29, 1987). ... On Portland suspended list (May 17-September 16, 1991). ... On Portland disabled list (July 28, 1991-remainder of season). ... Granted free agency (October 15, 1994). ... Signed by Iowa, Chicago Cubs organization (January 30, 1995). ... Claimed on waivers by Florida Marlins (August 9, 1995). ... Granted free agency (October 16, 1995). ... Signed by Boston Red Sox (April 25, 1996). ... On Boston disabled list (July 25-August 20 and August 24, 1996-remainder of season); included rehabilitation assignments to Pawtucket (August 9-20). ... On disabled list (March 27-April 27 and June 2-23, 1997); included rehabilitation assignment to Pawtucket (April 18-21, April 25-27 and June 12-23). ... On Boston disabled list (April 11-May 7, July 1-17 and August 3, 1998-remainder of season); included rehabilitation assignments to Pawtucket (April 21-May 7 and August 30-September 3) and Gulf Coast Red Sox (August 12-29). ... Released by Red Sox (November 23, 1998).

Year	Team (League)	W	L	Pct.	ERA	G	GS	CG	ShO	Sv.	IP	H	R	ER	BB	SO
1988— Elizabethton (Appal.)	5	4	.556	2.29	17	3	1	0	5	59	51	22	15	27	69
1989— Kenosha (Midwest)	9	10	.474	3.41	24	24	4	1	0	142 2/3	117	70	54	62	84
1990— Visalia (California)	2	2	.500	1.81	47	0	0	0	*28	54 2/3	33	14	11	16	75
—Orlando (South.)	2	1	.667	2.08	15	0	0	0	8	17 1/3	17	4	4	14	22
—Minnesota (A.L.)	0	0	...	1.59	5	0	0	0	2	5 2/3	4	2	1	4	1

G

Year Team (League)	W	L	Pct.	ERA	G	GS	CG	ShO	Sv.	IP	H	R	ER	BB	SO
1991— Portland (PCL)	0	1	.000	4.85	10	0	0	0	3	13	10	7	7	8	13
— Orlando (South.)	2	1	.667	3.31	10	0	0	0	0	16 1/3	12	6	6	14	17
1992— Orlando (South.)	3	3	.500	4.54	58	0	0	0	13	73 1/3	76	46	37	39	72
1993— Portland (PCL)	1	3	.250	8.33	35	7	0	0	0	54	70	55	50	64	48
— Minnesota (A.L.)	0	0	...	0.00	3	0	0	0	0	4	4	2	0	2	3
1994— Nashville (Southern)	4	5	.444	3.72	40	1	0	0	3	77 1/3	70	40	32	31	76
1995— Iowa (Am. Assoc.)■	0	2	.000	2.86	23	0	0	0	7	28 1/3	25	10	9	8	36
— Chicago (N.L.)	0	0	...	3.27	7	0	0	0	0	11	11	6	4	3	6
— Florida (N.L.)■	0	2	.000	5.40	11	0	0	0	0	13 1/3	14	9	8	8	16
1996— Pawtucket (Int'l)■	4	0	1.000	2.30	10	0	0	0	0	15 2/3	10	4	4	5	13
— Boston (A.L.)	3	2	.600	4.91	37	0	0	0	0	44	42	26	24	33	55
1997— Boston (A.L.)	0	1	.000	4.61	12	0	0	0	0	13 2/3	14	9	7	9	12
— Pawtucket (Int'l)	2	1	.667	1.45	26	0	0	0	5	31	24	5	5	13	42
1998— Boston (A.L.)	1	1	.500	3.33	30	0	0	0	1	46	36	19	17	27	34
— Pawtucket (Int'l)	0	1	.000	5.40	7	0	0	0	3	8 1/3	6	5	5	2	10
— GC Red Sox (GCL)	0	0	...	3.27	7	7	0	0	0	11	11	4	4	0	8
A.L. totals (5 years)	4	4	.500	3.89	87	0	0	0	3	113 1/3	100	58	49	75	105
N.L. totals (1 year)....................	0	2	.000	4.44	18	0	0	0	0	24 1/3	25	15	12	11	22
Major league totals (6 years)......	4	6	.400	3.99	105	0	0	0	3	137 2/3	125	73	61	86	127

GARCIA, AMAURY — 2B — MARLINS

PERSONAL: Born May 20, 1975, in Santo Domingo, Dominican Republic. ... 5-10/160. ... Bats right, throws right. ... Full name: Amaury Miguel Garcia.
HIGH SCHOOL: Colegio Discipulos de Jesus (Santo Domingo, Dominican Republic).
TRANSACTIONS/CAREER NOTES: Signed as non-drafted free agent by Florida Marlins organization (December 4, 1992).
STATISTICAL NOTES: Led Eastern League second basemen with 669 total chances in 1998.

Year Team (League)	Pos.	G	AB	R	H	2B	3B	HR	RBI	Avg.	BB	SO	SB	PO	A	E	Avg.
1993— Dom. Marlins (DSL) ...	IF	64	237	35	67	5	3	4	29	.283	31	41	9	129	112	19	.927
1994— GC Marlins (GCL).......	3B-2B-OF	58	208	46	65	9	3	0	25	.313	33	49	10	44	113	17	.902
1995— Kane County (Midw.)..	3B-2B	26	58	19	14	4	1	1	5	.241	18	12	5	11	31	13	.764
— Elmira (N.Y.-Penn)......	2B	62	231	40	63	7	3	0	17	.273	34	50	*41	128	178	18	.944
1996— Kane County (Midw.)..	2B	106	395	65	104	19	7	6	36	.263	62	84	37	219	286	19	.964
1997— Brevard Co. (Fla. St.)..	2B	124	479	77	138	30	2	7	44	.288	49	97	45	246	329	16	.973
1998— Portland (Eastern)	2B	137	544	79	147	19	6	13	62	.270	45	126	23	*287	355	*27	.960

GARCIA, APOSTOL — P — TIGERS

PERSONAL: Born August 3, 1976, in Las Matas de Faran, Dominican Republic. ... 6-0/155. ... Throws right, bats right.
HIGH SCHOOL: Liceo Mercedes Maria Mateo (Las Matas de Faran, Dominican Republic).
TRANSACTIONS/CAREER NOTES: Signed as non-drafted free agent by Detroit Tigers organization (December 6, 1992).
MISCELLANEOUS: Played infield (1993-96).

Year Team (League)	W	L	Pct.	ERA	G	GS	CG	ShO	Sv.	IP	H	R	ER	BB	SO
1997— West. Mich. (Mid.)	7	2	.778	3.02	33	5	0	0	1	65 2/3	48	26	22	31	52
1998— Lakeland (Fla. St.)	5	8	.385	5.43	34	16	1	0	1	119 1/3	155	89	72	52	56

RECORD AS POSITION PLAYER

Year Team (League)	Pos.	G	AB	R	H	2B	3B	HR	RBI	Avg.	BB	SO	SB	PO	A	E	Avg.
1993— Dom. Tigers (DSL)	OF-IF	65	150	24	29	2	0	0	6	.193	15	32	14	107	26	13	.911
1994— Bristol (Appal.)..........	SS-2B	47	130	20	20	3	0	0	8	.154	18	35	18	68	107	9	.951
— Lakeland (Fla. St.)	SS	6	15	0	4	0	0	0	0	.267	0	3	1	3	10	2	.867
1995— Jamestown (NYP)	SS-2B	60	200	25	47	8	3	0	21	.235	10	36	10	66	189	28	.901
1996— Fayetteville (SAL)	SS-2B	74	242	33	47	7	1	2	17	.194	21	77	12	105	181	30	.905

GARCIA, CARLOS — 2B

PERSONAL: Born October 15, 1967, in Tachira, Venezuela. ... 6-1/197. ... Bats right, throws right. ... Full name: Carlos Jesus Garcia.
HIGH SCHOOL: Bolivar (Venezuela).
TRANSACTIONS/CAREER NOTES: Signed as non-drafted free agent by Pittsburgh Pirates organization (January 9, 1987). ... On disabled list (July 28-August 14, 1995). ... On Pittsburgh disabled list (May 2-17 and July 22-August 27, 1996); included rehabilitation assignment to Calgary (August 23-25). ... Traded by Pirates with OF Orlando Merced and P Dan Plesac to Toronto Blue Jays for P Jose Silva, P Jose Pett, IF Brandon Cromer and three players to be named later (November 14, 1996); Pirates acquired P Mike Halperin, IF Abraham Nunez and C/OF Craig Wilson to complete deal (December 11, 1996). ... Granted free agency (December 21, 1997). ... Signed by Cleveland Indians (January 6, 1998). ... Released by Indians (March 25, 1998). ... Signed by Anaheim Angels (March 30, 1998). ... On Anaheim disabled list (May 13-June 13, 1998); included rehabilitation assignment to Vancouver (May 17-June 5). ... Granted free agency (September 29, 1998).
STATISTICAL NOTES: Led N.L. second basemen with 80 double plays in 1994. ... Had 21-game hitting streak (June 5-27, 1995).

Year Team (League)	Pos.	G	AB	R	H	2B	3B	HR	RBI	Avg.	BB	SO	SB	PO	A	E	Avg.
1987— Macon (S. Atl.)..........	SS	110	373	44	95	14	3	3	38	.255	23	80	20	161	262	42	.910
1988— Augusta (S. Atl.).........	SS	73	269	32	78	13	2	1	45	.290	22	46	11	138	207	29	.922
— Salem (Carolina)	SS	62	236	21	65	9	3	1	28	.275	10	32	8	131	151	24	.922
1989— Salem (Carolina)	SS	81	304	45	86	12	4	7	49	.283	18	51	19	137	262	32	.926
— Harrisburg (East.)........	SS	54	188	28	53	5	5	3	25	.282	8	36	6	84	131	7	.968
1990— Harrisburg (East.)........	SS	65	242	36	67	11	2	5	25	.277	16	36	12	101	209	14	.957
— Buffalo (A.A.).............	SS	63	197	23	52	10	0	5	18	.264	16	41	7	106	170	19	.936
— Pittsburgh (N.L.)	SS	4	4	1	2	0	0	0	0	.500	0	2	0	4	4	0	1.000

G

Year Team (League)	Pos.	G	AB	R	H	2B	3B	HR	RBI	Avg.	BB	SO	SB	PO	A	E	Avg.
1991— Buffalo (A.A.)...............	SS	53	463	62	123	21	6	7	60	.266	33	78	30	*212	332	*31	.946
— Pittsburgh (N.L.)........	SS-3B-2B	12	24	2	6	0	2	0	1	.250	1	8	0	11	18	1	.967
1992— Buffalo (A.A.)...............	SS-2B	113	426	73	129	28	9	13	70	.303	24	64	21	192	314	28	.948
— Pittsburgh (N.L.).......	2B-SS	22	39	4	8	1	0	0	4	.205	0	9	0	25	35	2	.968
1993— Pittsburgh (N.L.).......	2B-SS	141	546	77	147	25	5	12	47	.269	31	67	18	299	347	11	.983
1994— Pittsburgh (N.L.).......	2B	98	412	49	114	15	2	6	28	.277	16	67	18	•225	315	12	.978
1995— Pittsburgh (N.L.).......	2B-SS	104	367	41	108	24	2	6	50	.294	25	55	8	234	298	15	.973
1996— Pittsburgh (N.L.).......	2B-SS-3B	101	390	66	111	18	4	6	44	.285	23	58	16	160	284	11	.976
— Calgary (PCL).............	2B-SS	2	6	0	2	0	1	0	0	.333	0	0	0	3	5	0	1.000
1997— Toronto (A.L.)■.........	2B-SS-3B	103	350	29	77	18	2	3	23	.220	15	60	11	171	256	10	.977
1998— Anaheim (A.L.)■........	2B-SS-DH	19	35	4	5	1	0	0	5	.143	3	11	2	24	33	1	.983
— Vancouver (PCL)........	SS-2B	44	161	18	41	6	0	3	15	.255	8	22	2	78	103	10	.948
American League totals (2 years)		122	385	33	82	19	2	3	23	.213	18	71	13	195	289	11	.978
National League totals (7 years)		482	1782	240	496	83	15	30	174	.278	96	266	60	954	1301	52	.977
Major league totals (9 years)		604	2167	273	578	102	17	33	197	.267	114	337	73	1149	1590	63	.978

CHAMPIONSHIP SERIES RECORD

Year Team (League)	Pos.	G	AB	R	H	2B	3B	HR	RBI	Avg.	BB	SO	SB	PO	A	E	Avg.
1992— Pittsburgh (N.L.)	2B	1	1	0	0	0	0	0	0	.000	0	0	0	0	0	0	...

ALL-STAR GAME RECORD

Year League	Pos.	AB	R	H	2B	3B	HR	RBI	Avg.	BB	SO	SB	PO	A	E	Avg.
1994— National	2B	2	0	1	0	0	0	0	.500	0	0	0	0	1	0	1.000

GARCIA, FREDDY   3B   PIRATES

PERSONAL: Born August 1, 1972, in La Romana, Dominican Republic. ... 6-2/224. ... Bats right, throws right. ... Full name: Freddy Adrian Garcia.
TRANSACTIONS/CAREER NOTES: Signed as non-drafted free agent by Toronto Blue Jays organization (May 16, 1991). ... Selected by Pittsburgh Pirates from Blue Jays organization in Rule 5 major league draft (December 5, 1994).
STATISTICAL NOTES: Led Pioneer League third basemen with 267 total chances and tied for lead in double plays with 18 in 1993. ... Led New York-Pennsylvania League third basemen with 257 total chances and 18 double plays in 1994. ... Tied for Carolina League lead with 12 sacrifice flies in 1996. ... Led Carolina League third basemen with 29 double plays in 1996.

Year Team (League)	Pos.	G	AB	R	H	2B	3B	HR	RBI	Avg.	BB	SO	SB	PO	A	E	Avg.
1991— Villa Mella (DSL)........	IF	53	154	28	39	4	1	1	19	.253	39	36	8	...	...	...	...
1992— Blue Jays East (DSL)..	IF	70	249	56	73	13	2	12	62	.293	61	52	5	146	32	5	.973
1993— Medicine Hat (Pio.)....	3B	72	264	47	63	8	2	11	42	.239	31	71	4	*63	*175	•29	.891
1994— St. Catharines (NYP)..	3B	73	260	46	74	10	2	*13	40	.285	33	57	1	63	*169	25	.903
1995— Pittsburgh (N.L.).......	OF-3B	42	57	5	8	1	1	0	1	.140	8	17	0	19	15	1	.971
1996— Lynchburg (Caro.)......	3B	129	474	79	145	*39	3	•21	86	.306	44	86	4	96	285	*35	.916
1997— Calgary (PCL).............	3B	35	121	21	29	6	0	5	17	.240	9	20	0	18	53	12	.855
— Pittsburgh (N.L.)........	3B-1B	20	40	4	6	1	0	3	5	.150	2	17	0	21	9	3	.909
— Carolina (Southern)....	3B-1B	73	282	47	82	17	4	19	57	.291	18	56	0	93	155	22	.919
1998— Pittsburgh (N.L.).......	3B-1B	56	172	27	44	11	1	9	26	.256	18	45	0	53	104	8	.952
— Nashville (PCL)	3B-1B-OF	88	326	52	88	24	4	22	55	.270	25	89	0	185	153	19	.947
Major league totals (3 years)		118	269	36	58	13	2	12	32	.216	28	79	0	93	128	12	.948

GARCIA, FREDDY   P   MARINERS

PERSONAL: Born October 6, 1976, in Caracas, Venezuela. ... 6-4/235. ... Throws right, bats right.
TRANSACTIONS/CAREER NOTES: Signed as non-drafted free agent by Houston Astros organization (October 21, 1993). ... Traded by Astros with SS Carlos Guillen and a player to be named later to Seattle Mariners for P Randy Johnson (July 31, 1998); Mariners acquired P John Halama to complete deal (October 1, 1998).

Year Team (League)	W	L	Pct.	ERA	G	GS	CG	ShO	Sv.	IP	H	R	ER	BB	SO
1994— Dom. Astros (DSL).............	4	6	.400	5.29	16	15	0	0	0	85	80	61	50	38	68
1995— GC Astros (GCL)...............	6	3	.667	4.47	11	11	0	0	0	58 1/3	60	32	29	14	58
1996— Quad City (Midwest)	5	4	.556	3.12	13	13	0	0	0	60 2/3	57	27	21	27	50
1997— Kissimmee (Florida State)..	10	8	.556	2.56	27	27	5	2	0	179	165	63	51	49	131
1998— Jackson (Texas)...............	6	7	.462	3.24	19	19	2	0	0	119 1/3	94	48	43	58	115
— New Orleans (PCL).........	1	0	1.000	3.14	2	2	0	0	0	14 1/3	14	5	5	1	13
— Tacoma (PCL)■	3	1	.750	3.86	5	5	0	0	0	32 2/3	30	14	14	13	30

GARCIA, GUILLERMO   C/IF   MARLINS

PERSONAL: Born April 4, 1972, in Santiago, Dominican Republic. ... 6-3/215. ... Bats right, throws right. ... Full name: Guillermo Antonio Morel Garcia.
HIGH SCHOOL: Liceo Republica (Santiago, Dominican Republic).
TRANSACTIONS/CAREER NOTES: Signed as non-drafted free agent by New York Mets organization (November 20, 1989). ... Released by Mets (October 20, 1994). ... Signed by Cincinnati Reds organization (November 7, 1994). ... Traded by Reds to Florida Marlins for P Manuel Barrios (December 2, 1998).
STATISTICAL NOTES: Led South Atlantic League catchers with 36 passed balls in 1993. ... Led International League catchers with .990 fielding percentage in 1998.

G

Year Team (League)	Pos.	G	AB	R	H	2B	3B	HR	RBI	Avg.	BB	SO	SB	PO	A	E	Avg.
						BATTING									FIELDING		
1990— GC Mets (GCL)	2B-3B	42	136	9	25	1	2	0	6	.184	7	34	1	87	91	9	.952
1991— Kingsport (Appal.)	SS-P	14	33	9	8	1	1	0	2	.242	4	4	0	4	8	4	.750
— Pittsfield (NYP)	2B-SS	45	157	23	43	13	2	0	24	.274	15	38	4	120	120	5	.980
1992— Pittsfield (NYP)	2-C-1-S	73	272	36	54	11	1	2	26	.199	20	52	3	323	125	14	.970
1993— Capital City (SAL)	C-3B-2B	119	429	64	124	28	2	3	72	.289	49	60	10	650	115	19	.976
1994— St. Lucie (Fla. St.)	C-3-1-2	55	203	22	48	9	1	1	23	.236	13	24	0	244	53	3	.990
1995— Win.-Salem (Car.)■	C-1-3-S	78	245	26	58	10	2	3	29	.237	28	32	2	402	67	8	.983
1996— Indianapolis (A.A.)	C-2B-1B	16	47	4	12	2	0	0	0	.255	2	6	0	66	19	5	.944
— Chattanooga (Sou.)	C-2-1-3	60	203	25	64	12	0	6	36	.315	12	32	3	280	65	6	.983
1997— Chattanooga (Sou.)	C-2-1-S	20	74	11	21	1	1	4	19	.284	8	13	0	95	19	1	.991
— Indianapolis (A.A.)	C-2-3-1	55	151	16	36	2	0	10	20	.238	9	46	0	216	31	1	.996
1998— Indianapolis (Int'l)	C-1B-3B	93	334	48	85	20	0	19	60	.254	22	81	0	581	70	6	†.991
— Cincinnati (N.L.)	C	12	36	3	7	2	0	2	4	.194	2	13	0	74	6	1	.988
Major league totals (1 year)		12	36	3	7	2	0	2	4	.194	2	13	0	74	6	1	.988

RECORD AS PITCHER

Year Team (League)	W	L	Pct.	ERA	G	GS	CG	ShO	Sv.	IP	H	R	ER	BB	SO
1991— Kingsport (Appalachian)	0	0	...	0.00	2	0	0	0	0	2	1	0	0	0	3

GARCIA, JESSE — IF — ORIOLES

PERSONAL: Born September 24, 1973, in Corpus Christi, Texas. ... 5-10/155. ... Bats right, throws right. ... Full name: Jesus Jesse Garcia Jr.
HIGH SCHOOL: Robstown (Texas).
JUNIOR COLLEGE: Lee College (Texas).
TRANSACTIONS/CAREER NOTES: Selected by Baltimore Orioles organization in 26th round of free-agent draft (June 3, 1993). ... On disabled list (June 19, 1994-remainder of season). ... Granted free agency (December 21, 1998). ... Re-signed by Orioles organization (December 21, 1998).
STATISTICAL NOTES: Led California League with 20 sacrifice hits in 1996. ... Led California League second basemen with 263 putouts, 409 assists, .968 fielding percentage, 694 total chances and 81 double plays in 1996; tied for lead in errors with 22. ... Led Eastern League with 24 sacrifice hits in 1997. ... Led Eastern League second basemen with .985 fielding percentage in 1997.

Year Team (League)	Pos.	G	AB	R	H	2B	3B	HR	RBI	Avg.	BB	SO	SB	PO	A	E	Avg.
						BATTING									FIELDING		
1993— GC Orioles (GCL)	2B-SS-3B	48	156	20	37	4	0	0	16	.237	21	32	14	61	136	14	.934
1994—						Did not play.											
1995— Frederick (Carolina)	2B	124	365	52	82	11	3	3	27	.225	49	75	5	283	275	28	.952
1996— High Desert (Calif.)	2B-SS	137	459	94	122	21	5	10	66	.266	57	81	25	†263	†409	‡22	†.968
1997— Bowie (Eastern)	2B-SS-3B	*141	437	52	103	18	1	5	42	.236	38	71	7	290	377	13	†.981
1998— Bowie (Eastern)	2B-SS-OF	86	258	46	73	13	1	2	20	.283	34	37	12	133	196	9	.973
— Rochester (Int'l)	2B	44	160	20	47	6	4	0	18	.294	7	22	7	102	145	8	.969

GARCIA, KARIM — OF — TIGERS

PERSONAL: Born October 29, 1975, in Ciudad Obregon, Mexico. ... 6-0/172. ... Bats left, throws left. ... Full name: Gustavo Garcia.
HIGH SCHOOL: Preparatoria Abierta (Ciudad Obregon, Mexico).
TRANSACTIONS/CAREER NOTES: Signed as non-drafted free agent by Los Angeles Dodgers organization (July 16, 1992). ... On Los Angeles disabled list (September 1, 1997-remainder of season). ... Selected by Arizona Diamondbacks in first round (ninth pick overall) of expansion draft (November 18, 1997). ... Traded by Diamondbacks to Detroit Tigers for OF Luis Gonzalez (December 28, 1998).
HONORS: Named Minor League Player of the Year by THE SPORTING NEWS (1995).
STATISTICAL NOTES: Career major league grand slams: 1.

Year Team (League)	Pos.	G	AB	R	H	2B	3B	HR	RBI	Avg.	BB	SO	SB	PO	A	E	Avg.
						BATTING									FIELDING		
1993— Bakersfield (Calif.)	OF	123	460	61	111	20	9	19	54	.241	37	109	5	193	12	*13	.940
1994— Vero Beach (FSL)	OF	121	452	72	120	28	10	*21	84	.265	37	112	8	229	12	5	.980
1995— Albuquerque (PCL)	OF	124	474	88	151	26	10	20	•91	.319	38	102	12	185	7	*14	.932
— Los Angeles (N.L.)	OF	13	20	1	4	0	0	0	0	.200	0	4	0	5	2	0	1.000
1996— Albuquerque (PCL)	OF	84	327	54	97	17	10	13	58	.297	29	67	6	148	4	13	.921
— San Antonio (Tex.)	OF	35	129	21	32	6	1	5	22	.248	9	38	1	60	6	2	.971
— Los Angeles (N.L.)	OF	1	1	0	0	0	0	0	0	.000	0	1	0	0	0	0	...
1997— Albuquerque (PCL)	OF	71	262	53	80	17	6	20	66	.305	23	70	11	97	3	5	.952
— Los Angeles (N.L.)	OF	15	39	5	5	0	0	1	8	.128	6	14	0	13	0	0	1.000
1998— Arizona (N.L.)■	OF	113	333	39	74	10	8	9	43	.222	18	78	5	191	6	5	.975
— Tucson (PCL)	OF	27	106	21	33	4	2	10	27	.311	15	24	5	67	1	3	.958
Major league totals (4 years)		142	393	45	83	10	8	10	51	.211	24	97	5	209	8	5	.977

G

GARCIA, LUIS — IF — TIGERS

PERSONAL: Born May 20, 1975, in San Francisco De Macoris, Dominican Republic. ... 6-0/175. ... Bats right, throws right. ... Full name: Luis Rafael Garcia.
HIGH SCHOOL: Liceo Salome Urenna (Dominican Republic).
TRANSACTIONS/CAREER NOTES: Signed as non-drafted free agent Detroit Tigers organization (February 3, 1993).
STATISTICAL NOTES: Led Southern League shortstops with 676 total chances in 1996.

Year Team (League)	Pos.	G	AB	R	H	2B	3B	HR	RBI	Avg.	BB	SO	SB	PO	A	E	Avg.
1993— Bristol (Appal.)	2B-SS-3B	24	57	7	12	1	0	1	7	.211	3	11	3	33	55	5	.946
1994— Jamestown (NYP)	SS	67	239	21	47	8	2	1	19	.197	8	48	6	115	205	*27	.922
1995— Lakeland (Fla. St.)	SS-2B	102	361	39	101	10	4	2	35	.280	8	42	9	167	302	34	.932
—Jacksonville (Sou.)	SS-3B	17	47	6	13	0	0	0	5	.277	1	8	2	19	46	5	.929
1996— Jacksonville (Sou.)	SS	131	522	68	128	22	4	9	46	.245	12	90	15	*205	*435	*36	*.947
1997— Jacksonville (Sou.)	SS	126	456	55	122	19	1	5	48	.268	10	59	3	176	370	30	.948
1998— Toledo (Int'l)	SS-3B-2B	114	407	37	105	19	4	3	31	.258	8	59	3	158	292	23	.951

GARCIA, RAMON   P

PERSONAL: Born December 9, 1969, in Guanare, Venezuela. ... 6-2/200. ... Throws right, bats right. ... Full name: Ramon Antonio Garcia.
HIGH SCHOOL: Cesar Lizardo (Guanare, Venezuela).
TRANSACTIONS/CAREER NOTES: Signed as free agent by Chicago White Sox organization (June 30, 1987). ... On disabled list (May 28, 1993-remainder of season). ... Released by White Sox (September 15, 1993). ... Signed by Ottawa, Montreal Expos organization (February 11, 1995). ... Released by Ottawa (April 3, 1995). ... Signed by Milwaukee Brewers (April 3, 1996). ... Granted free agency (October 15, 1996). ... Re-signed by New Orleans, Brewers organization (November 4, 1996). ... Selected by Houston Astros from Brewers organization in Rule 5 major league draft (December 9, 1996). ... On disabled list (March 30, 1998-entire season). ... Granted free agency (December 21, 1998).
STATISTICAL NOTES: Pitched 2-0 no-hit victory against Sarasota (August 3, 1989). ... Led Florida State League with 10 home runs allowed in 1990.

Year Team (League)	W	L	Pct.	ERA	G	GS	CG	ShO	Sv.	IP	H	R	ER	BB	SO
1987— GC White Sox (GCL)	1	0	1.000	1.50	6	0	0	0	0	12	8	3	2	5	6
1988— GC White Sox (GCL)	2	1	.667	2.45	13	0	0	0	0	22	15	9	6	4	11
1989— GC White Sox (GCL)	6	4	.600	3.06	14	7	2	•1	0	53	34	21	18	17	52
1990— Sarasota (Florida State)	9	*14	.391	3.95	26	26	1	0	0	157 1/3	155	84	69	45	130
—Vancouver (PCL)	0	0	...	0.00	1	0	0	0	0	1	2	0	0	0	1
1991— Birmingham (Southern)	4	0	1.000	0.93	6	6	2	1	0	38 2/3	27	5	4	11	38
—Vancouver (PCL)	2	2	.500	4.05	4	4	0	0	0	26 2/3	24	13	12	7	17
—Chicago (A.L.)	4	4	.500	5.40	16	15	0	0	0	78 1/3	79	50	47	31	40
1992— Vancouver (PCL)	9	11	.450	3.71	28	•28	2	1	0	170	165	83	70	56	79
1993— Nashville (A.A.)	4	1	.800	4.01	7	7	1	1	0	42 2/3	45	22	19	11	25
1994—						Out of organized baseball.									
1995—						Out of organized baseball.									
1996— New Orleans (A.A.)■	2	1	.667	1.88	11	5	0	0	0	38 1/3	31	10	8	12	32
—Milwaukee (A.L.)	4	4	.500	6.66	37	2	0	0	4	75 2/3	84	58	56	21	40
1997— Houston (N.L.)■	9	8	.529	3.69	42	20	1	1	1	158 2/3	155	71	65	52	120
1998— Houston (N.L.)						Did not play.									
A.L. totals (2 years)	8	8	.500	6.02	53	17	0	0	4	154	163	108	103	52	80
N.L. totals (1 year)	9	8	.529	3.69	42	20	1	1	1	158 2/3	155	71	65	52	120
Major league totals (3 years)	17	16	.515	4.84	95	37	1	1	5	312 2/3	318	179	168	104	200

DIVISION SERIES RECORD

Year Team (League)	W	L	Pct.	ERA	G	GS	CG	ShO	Sv.	IP	H	R	ER	BB	SO
1997— Houston (N.L.)	0	0	...	0.00	2	0	0	0	0	1	1	2	0	1	1

GARCIAPARRA, NOMAR   SS   RED SOX

PERSONAL: Born July 23, 1973, in Whittier, Calif. ... 6-0/167. ... Bats right, throws right. ... Full name: Anthony Nomar Garciaparra.
HIGH SCHOOL: St. John Bosco (Bellflower, Calif.).
COLLEGE: Georgia Tech.
TRANSACTIONS/CAREER NOTES: Selected by Milwaukee Brewers organization in fifth round of free-agent draft (June 3, 1991); did not sign. ... Selected by Boston Red Sox organization in first round (12th pick overall) of free-agent draft (June 2, 1994). ... On Pawtucket disabled list (April 4-15 and April 19-July 11, 1996). ... On disabled list (May 9-28, 1998).
RECORDS: Holds A.L. rookie-season record for most consecutive games batted safely—30 (1997).
HONORS: Named A.L. Rookie Player of the Year by THE SPORTING NEWS (1997). ... Named shortstop on THE SPORTING NEWS A.L. All-Star team (1997). ... Named shortstop on THE SPORTING NEWS A.L. Silver Slugger team (1997). ... Named A.L. Rookie of the Year by Baseball Writers' Association of America (1997).
STATISTICAL NOTES: Led Eastern League shortstops with 624 total chances in 1994. ... Had 30-game hitting streak (July 26-August 29, 1997). ... Led A.L. shortstops in total chances with 720 and double plays with 113 in 1997. ... Had 16-game hitting streak (April 2-19, 1998). ... Had 24-game hitting streak (June 7-July 3, 1998). ... Career major league grand slams: 1.
MISCELLANEOUS: Member of 1992 U.S. Olympic baseball team.

Year Team (League)	Pos.	G	AB	R	H	2B	3B	HR	RBI	Avg.	BB	SO	SB	PO	A	E	Avg.
1994— Sarasota (Fla. St.)	SS	28	105	20	31	8	1	1	16	.295	10	6	5	42	72	3	.974
1995— Trenton (Eastern)	SS	125	513	77	137	20	8	8	47	.267	50	42	35	205	*396	23	.963
1996— Pawtucket (Int'l)	SS	43	172	40	59	15	2	16	46	.343	14	21	3	63	120	5	.973
—GC Red Sox (GCL)	SS	5	14	4	4	2	1	0	5	.286	1	0	0	7	12	1	.950
—Boston (A.L.)	SS-DH-2B	24	87	11	21	2	3	4	16	.241	4	14	5	37	51	1	.989
1997— Boston (A.L.)	SS	153	*684	122	*209	44	*11	30	98	.306	35	92	22	*249	450	21	.971
1998— Boston (A.L.)	SS	143	604	111	195	37	8	35	122	.323	33	62	12	228	402	25	.962
Major league totals (3 years)		320	1375	244	425	83	22	69	236	.309	72	168	39	514	903	47	.968

DIVISION SERIES RECORD
RECORDS: Holds single-series record for most runs batted in—11 (1998).

Year Team (League)	Pos.	G	AB	R	H	2B	3B	HR	RBI	Avg.	BB	SO	SB	PO	A	E	Avg.
1998— Boston (A.L.)	SS	4	15	4	5	1	0	3	11	.333	2	0	0	3	7	0	1.000

G

Year	League	Pos.	AB	R	H	2B	3B	BATTING HR	RBI	Avg.	BB	SO	SB	FIELDING PO	A	E	Avg.
1997—American		SS	1	0	0	0	0	0	0	.000	0	0	0	1	0	0	1.000

GARDNER, MARK   P   GIANTS

PERSONAL: Born March 1, 1962, in Los Angeles. ... 6-1/220. ... Throws right, bats right. ... Full name: Mark Allan Gardner.
HIGH SCHOOL: Clovis (Calif.).
JUNIOR COLLEGE: Fresno (Calif.) City College.
COLLEGE: Fresno State.
TRANSACTIONS/CAREER NOTES: Selected by California Angels organization in sixth round of free-agent draft (January 11, 1983); did not sign. ... Selected by Cleveland Indians organization in 17th round of free-agent draft (June 4, 1984); did not sign. ... Selected by Montreal Expos organization in eighth round of free-agent draft (June 3, 1985). ... On disabled list (September 20, 1990-remainder of season). ... On Montreal disabled list (April 2-May 14, 1991); included rehabilitation assignment to Indianapolis (April 11-May 8). ... Traded by Expos with P Doug Piatt to Kansas City Royals for C Tim Spehr and P Jeff Shaw (December 9, 1992). ... On Kansas City disabled list (July 7-August 27, 1993); included rehabilitation assignment to Omaha (July 28-August 26). ... Released by Royals (December 8, 1993). ... Signed by Edmonton, Florida Marlins organization (January 6, 1994). ... On Florida disabled list (June 8-26, 1994); included rehabilitation assignment to Brevard County (June 18-22). ... Granted free agency (February 17, 1995). ... Re-signed by Marlins (April 7, 1995). ... Granted free agency (October 16, 1995). ... Re-signed by Marlins organization (December 8, 1995). ... Granted free agency (March 28, 1996). ... Signed by San Francisco Giants (March 29, 1996). ... On San Francisco disabled list (July 3-21, 1996); included rehabilitation assignment to San Jose (July 17-21). ... Granted free agency (October 23, 1998). ... Re-signed by Giants (November 9, 1998).
RECORDS: Shares major league single-inning record for most hit batsmen—3 (August 15, 1992, first inning).
HONORS: Named American Association Pitcher of the Year (1989).
STATISTICAL NOTES: Led N.L. with nine hit batsmen in 1990. ... Pitched nine hitless innings against Los Angeles Dodgers, but gave up two hits in 10th inning and lost, 1-0, when reliever Jeff Fassero gave up game-winning hit in 10th (July 26, 1991).
MISCELLANEOUS: Struck out once in two games as pinch hitter for Montreal (1991). ... Had two sacrifice hits in three games as pinch hitter for San Francisco (1996).

Year Team (League)	W	L	Pct.	ERA	G	GS	CG	ShO	Sv.	IP	H	R	ER	BB	SO
1985—Jamestown (NYP)	0	0	. . .	2.77	3	3	0	0	0	13	9	4	4	4	16
—W.P. Beach (FSL)	5	4	.556	2.37	10	9	4	0	0	60 2/3	54	24	16	18	44
1986—Jacksonville (Southern)	10	11	.476	3.84	29	28	3	1	0	168 2/3	144	88	72	90	140
1987—Indianapolis (A.A.)	3	3	.500	5.67	9	9	0	0	0	46	48	32	29	28	41
—Jacksonville (Southern)	4	6	.400	4.19	17	17	1	0	0	101	101	50	47	42	78
1988—Jacksonville (Southern)	6	3	.667	1.60	15	15	4	2	0	112 1/3	72	24	20	36	130
—Indianapolis (A.A.)	4	2	.667	2.77	13	13	3	1	0	84 1/3	65	30	26	32	71
1989—Indianapolis (A.A.)	12	4	*.750	2.37	24	23	4	2	0	163 1/3	122	51	43	59	*175
—Montreal (N.L.)	0	3	.000	5.13	7	4	0	0	0	26 1/3	26	16	15	11	21
1990—Montreal (N.L.)	7	9	.438	3.42	27	26	3	3	0	152 2/3	129	62	58	61	135
1991—Indianapolis (A.A.)	2	0	1.000	3.48	6	6	0	0	0	31	26	13	12	16	38
—Montreal (N.L.)	9	11	.450	3.85	27	27	0	0	0	168 1/3	139	78	72	75	107
1992—Montreal (N.L.)	12	10	.545	4.36	33	30	0	0	0	179 2/3	179	91	87	60	132
1993—Kansas City (A.L.)■	4	6	.400	6.19	17	16	0	0	0	91 2/3	92	65	63	36	54
—Omaha (Am. Assoc.)	4	2	.667	2.79	8	8	1	0	0	48 1/3	34	17	15	19	41
1994—Florida (N.L.)■	4	4	.500	4.87	20	14	0	0	0	92 1/3	97	53	50	30	57
—Edmonton (PCL)	1	0	1.000	0.00	1	1	0	0	0	6	4	0	0	1	11
—Brevard County (FSL)	1	0	1.000	0.00	1	1	0	0	0	5	1	0	0	1	3
1995—Florida (N.L.)	5	5	.500	4.49	39	11	1	1	1	102 1/3	109	60	51	43	87
1996—San Francisco (N.L.)■	12	7	.632	4.42	30	28	4	1	0	179 1/3	200	105	88	57	145
—San Jose (California)	0	0	. . .	3.18	1	1	0	0	0	5 2/3	4	2	2	0	7
1997—San Francisco (N.L.)	12	9	.571	4.29	30	30	2	1	0	180 1/3	188	92	86	57	136
1998—San Francisco (N.L.)	13	6	.684	4.33	33	33	4	2	0	212	203	106	102	65	151
A.L. totals (1 year)	4	6	.400	6.19	17	16	0	0	0	91 2/3	92	65	63	36	54
N.L. totals (9 years)	74	64	.536	4.24	246	203	14	8	1	1293 1/3	1270	663	609	459	971
Major league totals (10 years)	78	70	.527	4.37	263	219	14	8	1	1385	1362	728	672	495	1025

GATES, BRENT   2B   TWINS

PERSONAL: Born March 14, 1970, in Grand Rapids, Mich. ... 6-1/190. ... Bats both, throws right. ... Full name: Brent Robert Gates.
HIGH SCHOOL: Grandville (Mich.).
COLLEGE: Minnesota.
TRANSACTIONS/CAREER NOTES: Selected by Oakland Athletics organization in first round (26th pick overall) of free-agent draft (June 3, 1991). ... On disabled list (April 10-May 5 and July 17, 1994-remainder of season). ... On disabled list (June 16, 1996-remainder of season). ... Released by A's (March 11, 1997). ... Signed by Seattle Mariners (March 16, 1997). ... Released by Mariners (December 15, 1997). ... Signed by Minnesota Twins organization (December 23, 1997). ... Granted free agency (September 30, 1998). ... Re-signed by Twins organization (December 15, 1998).
STATISTICAL NOTES: Led California League second basemen with 735 total chances and 105 double plays in 1992. ... Career major league grand slams: 1.

Year Team (League)	Pos.	G	AB	R	H	2B	3B	BATTING HR	RBI	Avg.	BB	SO	SB	FIELDING PO	A	E	Avg.
1991—S. Oregon (N'west)	SS-2B-3B	58	219	41	63	11	0	3	26	.288	30	33	8	77	177	15	.944
—Madison (Midwest)	SS-3B	4	12	4	4	2	0	0	1	.333	3	2	1	6	10	0	1.000
1992—Modesto (California)	2B	133	505	94	162	39	2	10	88	.321	85	60	9	*293	*420	•22	.970
1993—Huntsville (Sou.)	2B	12	45	7	15	4	0	1	11	.333	7	9	0	32	28	0	1.000
—Tacoma (PCL)	2B	12	44	7	15	7	0	1	4	.341	4	6	2	27	36	1	.984
—Oakland (A.L.)	2B	139	535	64	155	29	2	7	69	.290	56	75	7	281	431	14	.981
1994—Oakland (A.L.)	2B-1B	64	233	29	66	11	1	2	24	.283	21	32	3	113	159	8	.971

Year Team (League)	Pos.	G	AB	R	H	2B	3B	HR	RBI	Avg.	BB	SO	SB	PO	A	E	Avg.
1995— Oakland (A.L.)	2B-DH-1B	136	524	60	133	24	4	5	56	.254	46	84	3	241	428	12	.982
1996— Oakland (A.L.)	2B	64	247	26	65	19	2	2	30	.263	18	35	1	140	183	9	.973
1997— Seattle (A.L.)■......	3-2-S-DH-1-O	65	151	18	36	8	0	3	20	.238	14	21	0	26	82	5	.956
— Tacoma (PCL)	2B-SS	7	33	7	15	3	0	0	6	.455	4	2	0	10	12	4	.846
1998— Minnesota (A.L.)■	3-2-DH-1-S	107	333	31	83	15	0	3	42	.249	36	46	3	85	157	9	.964
Major league totals (6 years)		575	2023	228	538	106	9	22	241	.266	191	293	17	886	1440	57	.976

DIVISION SERIES RECORD

Year Team (League)	Pos.	G	AB	R	H	2B	3B	HR	RBI	Avg.	BB	SO	SB	PO	A	E	Avg.
1997— Seattle (A.L.)	3B-PH	2	4	0	0	0	0	0	0	.000	0	0	0	1	2	0	1.000

GIAMBI, JASON — 1B — ATHLETICS

PERSONAL: Born January 8, 1971, in West Covina, Calif. ... 6-3/235. ... Bats left, throws right. ... Full name: Jason Gilbert Giambi. ... Brother of Jeremy Giambi, outfielder, Kansas City Royals. ... Name pronounced GEE-om-bee.

HIGH SCHOOL: South Hills West (Covina, Calif.).

COLLEGE: Long Beach State.

TRANSACTIONS/CAREER NOTES: Selected by Milwaukee Brewers organization in 43rd round of free-agent draft (June 5, 1989); did not sign. ... Selected by Oakland Athletics organization in second round of free-agent draft (June 1, 1992). ... On disabled list (July 27-August 28, 1993). ... On Huntsville disabled list (April 7-14, 1994).

STATISTICAL NOTES: Had 25-game hitting streak (May 12-June 23, 1997). ... Had 17-game hitting streak (July 16-August 2, 1998). ... Had 16-game hitting streak (September 5-24, 1998). ... Career major league grand slams: 1.

MISCELLANEOUS: Member of 1992 U.S. Olympic baseball team.

Year Team (League)	Pos.	G	AB	R	H	2B	3B	HR	RBI	Avg.	BB	SO	SB	PO	A	E	Avg.
1992— S. Oregon (N'west).....	3B	13	41	9	13	3	0	3	13	.317	9	6	1	5	20	1	.962
1993— Modesto (California) ..	3B	89	313	72	91	16	2	12	60	.291	73	47	2	49	145	19	.911
1994— Huntsville (Sou.)	3B-1B	56	193	31	43	9	0	6	30	.223	27	31	0	111	77	11	.945
— Tacoma (PCL)	3B-SS	52	176	28	56	20	0	4	38	.318	25	32	1	39	110	8	.949
1995— Edmonton (PCL)	3B-1B	55	190	34	65	26	1	3	41	.342	34	26	0	38	98	9	.938
— Oakland (A.L.)	3B-1B-DH	54	176	27	45	7	0	6	25	.256	28	31	2	194	55	4	.984
1996— Oakland (A.L.)	1-0-3-DH	140	536	84	156	40	1	20	79	.291	51	95	0	478	117	11	.982
1997— Oakland (A.L.)	OF-1B-DH	142	519	66	152	41	2	20	81	.293	55	89	0	501	44	7	.987
1998— Oakland (A.L.)	1B-DH	153	562	92	166	28	0	27	110	.295	81	102	2	1255	73	*14	.990
Major league totals (4 years)		489	1793	269	519	116	3	73	295	.289	215	317	4	2428	289	36	.987

GIAMBI, JEREMY — OF — ROYALS

PERSONAL: Born September 30, 1974, in San Jose, Calif. ... 6-0/185. ... Bats left, throws left. ... Full name: Jeremy Dean Giambi. ... Brother of Jason Giambi, first baseman, Oakland Athletics.

HIGH SCHOOL: South Hills (West Covina, Calif.).

COLLEGE: Cal State Fullerton.

TRANSACTIONS/CAREER NOTES: Selected by Kansas City Royals organization in sixth round of free-agent draft (June 4, 1996). ... On Omaha disabled list (July 12-August 2, 1998).

HONORS: Led Northwest League with .440 on-base percentage in 1996. ... Led Pacific Coast League with .469 on-base percentage in 1998.

Year Team (League)	Pos.	G	AB	R	H	2B	3B	HR	RBI	Avg.	BB	SO	SB	PO	A	E	Avg.
1996— Spokane (N'west).......	OF	67	231	•58	63	17	0	6	39	.273	*61	32	22	97	3	*11	.901
1997— Lansing (Midwest)	OF	31	116	33	39	11	1	5	21	.336	23	16	5	30	2	0	1.000
— Wichita (Texas)	OF-1B	74	268	50	86	15	1	11	52	.321	44	47	4	117	2	3	.975
1998— Omaha (Pacific Coast)	OF-1B	96	325	68	121	21	2	20	66	*.372	57	64	8	113	8	3	.976
— Kansas City (A.L.)	OF-DH	18	58	6	13	4	0	2	8	.224	11	9	0	14	1	0	1.000
Major league totals (1 year)		18	58	6	13	4	0	2	8	.224	11	9	0	14	1	0	1.000

GIBBS, KEVIN — OF — DODGERS

G

PERSONAL: Born April 3, 1974, in Washington D.C. ... 6-2/185. ... Bats both, throws right. ... Full name: Kevin Casey Gibbs.

HIGH SCHOOL: St. John's (Washington, D.C.).

COLLEGE: Old Dominion.

TRANSACTIONS/CAREER NOTES: Selected by Los Angeles Dodgers in sixth round of free-agent draft (June 1, 1995). ... On disabled list (April 20-May 1 and July 19-26, 1997). ... On disabled list (April 10, 1998-remainder of season).

STATISTICAL NOTES: Tied for Florida State League lead in caught stealing with 19 in 1996. ... Tied for Florida State League lead in double plays by outfielder with four in 1996.

Year Team (League)	Pos.	G	AB	R	H	2B	3B	HR	RBI	Avg.	BB	SO	SB	PO	A	E	Avg.
1995— Vero Beach (FSL)	OF	7	20	1	5	1	0	0	2	.250	0	0	1	12	0	0	1.000
— San Bern. (Calif.)........	OF	5	13	1	3	1	0	0	0	.231	0	2	1	5	0	0	1.000
— Yakima (N'west)	OF	52	182	36	57	6	4	1	18	.313	36	46	*38	71	1	2	.973
1996— Vero Beach (FSL).....	OF	118	423	69	114	9	*11	0	33	.270	65	80	*60	252	11	4	.985
1997— San Antonio (Tex.)	OF	101	358	89	120	21	6	2	34	.335	72	48	49	215	2	4	.982
1998— Albuquerque (PCL).....	OF	2	8	1	1	0	0	0	1	.125	2	1	0	4	0	0	1.000

GIBSON, DERRICK   OF   ROCKIES

PERSONAL: Born February 5, 1975, in Winter Haven, Fla. ... 6-2/244. ... Bats right, throws right. ... Full name: Derrick Lamont Gibson.
HIGH SCHOOL: Haines City (Fla.).
TRANSACTIONS/CAREER NOTES: Selected by Colorado Rockies organization in 13th round of free-agent draft (June 3, 1993).
STATISTICAL NOTES: Tied for Pacific Coast League lead with three double plays by outfielder in 1998.

Year Team (League)	Pos.	G	AB	R	H	2B	3B	HR	RBI	Avg.	BB	SO	SB	PO	A	E	Avg.
1993— Ariz. Rockies (Ariz.)....	OF	34	119	13	18	2	2	0	10	.151	5	55	3	22	1	5	.821
1994— Bend (Northwest).......	OF	73	284	47	75	19	5	•12	57	.264	29	*102	14	82	*10	9	.911
1995— Asheville (S. Atl.)........	OF	135	506	91	148	16	10	•32	*115	.292	29	136	11	190	11	9	.957
1996— New Haven (East.)......	OF	122	449	58	115	21	4	15	62	.256	31	125	3	168	10	*13	.932
1997— New Haven (East.)......	OF	119	461	91	146	24	2	23	75	.317	36	100	20	188	8	*11	.947
— Colo. Springs (PCL) ...	OF	21	78	14	33	7	0	3	12	.423	5	9	0	30	0	1	.968
1998— Colo. Springs (PCL) ...	OF	126	497	84	145	20	3	14	81	.292	35	110	14	211	11	*13	.945
— Colorado (N.L.)	OF	7	21	4	9	1	0	0	2	.429	1	4	0	11	2	1	.929
Major league totals (1 year)		7	21	4	9	1	0	0	2	.429	1	4	0	11	2	1	.929

GILBERT, SHAWN   IF

PERSONAL: Born March 12, 1965, in Camden, N.J. ... 5-9/185. ... Bats right, throws right. ... Full name: Albert Shawn Gilbert Jr.
HIGH SCHOOL: Agua Fria Union (Avondale, Ariz.).
JUNIOR COLLEGE: Golden West College (Calif.).
COLLEGE: Arizona State, then Fresno State.
TRANSACTIONS/CAREER NOTES: Selected by Los Angeles Dodgers organization in 21st round of free-agent draft (June 6, 1983); did not sign. ... Selected by Cincinnati Reds organization in secondary phase of free-agent draft (January 9, 1985); did not sign. ... Selected by Minnesota Twins organization in secondary phase of free-agent draft (June 5, 1985); did not sign. ... Selected by Twins organization in 12th round of free-agent draft (June 2, 1987). ... Claimed on waivers by Chicago White Sox (November 12, 1992). ... Granted free agency (October 15, 1993). ... Signed by Scranton/Wilkes-Barre, Philadelphia Phillies organization (January 5, 1994). ... Granted free agency (October 16, 1995). ... Signed by New York Mets organization (January 30, 1996). ... On New York disabled list (June 16-30, 1997). ... Granted free agency (October 15, 1997). ... Re-signed by Mets organization (December 19, 1997). ... Traded by Mets organization with a player to be named later to St. Louis Cardinals organization for OF Wayne Kirby (June 10, 1998). ... Granted free agency (October 15, 1998).
STATISTICAL NOTES: Led Midwest League shortstops with 80 double plays in 1988. ... Led Southern League in caught stealing with 19 in 1991.

Year Team (League)	Pos.	G	AB	R	H	2B	3B	HR	RBI	Avg.	BB	SO	SB	PO	A	E	Avg.
1987— Visalia (California)	SS	82	272	39	61	5	0	5	27	.224	34	59	6	122	214	30	.918
1988— Visalia (California)	SS-2B	14	43	10	16	3	2	0	8	.372	10	7	1	18	34	10	.839
— Kenosha (Midwest)	SS	108	402	80	112	21	2	3	44	.279	63	61	49	151	325	41	.921
1989— Visalia (California)	SS	125	453	52	113	17	1	2	43	.249	54	70	42	204	382	39	.938
1990— Orlando (South.)	SS	123	433	68	110	18	2	4	44	.254	61	69	31	157	*361	41	.927
1991— Orlando (South.)	O-S-2-3	138	529	69	136	12	5	3	38	.257	53	71	*43	247	250	20	.961
1992— Portland (PCL)	S-O-2-3	138	444	60	109	17	2	3	52	.245	36	55	31	214	303	25	.954
1993— Nashville (A.A.)■........	3-O-S-2	104	278	28	63	17	2	0	17	.227	12	41	6	81	123	17	.923
1994— Scran./W.B. (Int'l)■......	SS-OF-2B	*141	*547	81	139	33	4	7	52	.254	66	86	20	215	275	27	.948
1995— Scran./W.B. (Int'l)......	SS-OF-3B	136	536	84	141	26	2	4	42	.263	64	102	16	213	361	28	.953
1996— Norfolk (Int'l)■..........	3-2-S-O	131	493	76	126	28	1	9	50	.256	46	97	17	174	312	25	.951
1997— Norfolk (Int'l)	S-O-2-3	78	288	53	76	13	1	8	33	.264	43	64	16	124	134	16	.942
— New York (N.L.)........	2-S-3-O	29	22	3	3	0	0	1	1	.136	1	8	1	11	8	1	.950
1998— Norfolk (Int'l)	O-S-3-2	39	133	21	36	8	0	2	12	.271	16	28	7	46	26	2	.973
— New York (N.L.)..........	3B	3	1	0	0	0	0	0	0	.000	0	1	0	0	0	0	...
— Memphis (PCL)■..........	3-0-2-S	62	216	37	58	15	2	7	32	.269	29	53	7	65	106	12	.934
— St. Louis (N.L.)..........	2B	4	2	0	1	0	0	0	0	.500	0	1	1	1	0	0	1.000
Major league totals (2 years)		36	27	4	4	0	0	1	1	.148	1	10	2	12	8	1	.952

GILES, BRIAN   OF   PIRATES

PERSONAL: Born January 20, 1971, in El Cajon, Calif. ... 5-11/200. ... Bats left, throws left. ... Full name: Brian Stephen Giles. ... Brother of Marcus Giles, second baseman, Atlanta Braves organization. ... Name pronounced JYLES.
HIGH SCHOOL: Granite Hills (El Cajon, Calif.).
TRANSACTIONS/CAREER NOTES: Selected by Cleveland Indians organization in 17th round of free-agent draft (June 5, 1989). ... On Canton/Akron disabled list (May 15-July 7, 1992). ... On Cleveland disabled list (June 1-July 7, 1998); included rehabilitation assignment to Buffalo (June 23-July 7). ... Traded by Indians to Pittsburgh Pirates for P Ricardo Rincon (November 18, 1998).
STATISTICAL NOTES: Led International League with 10 intentional bases on balls received in 1994. ... Led International League outfielders with five double plays in 1994. ... Career major league grand slams: 1.

G

Year Team (League)	Pos.	G	AB	R	H	2B	3B	HR	RBI	Avg.	BB	SO	SB	PO	A	E	Avg.
1989— Burlington (Appal.).....	OF	36	129	18	40	7	0	0	20	.310	11	19	6	52	3	1	.982
1990— Watertown (NYP)	OF	70	246	44	71	15	2	1	23	.289	48	23	11	108	8	1	.991
1991— Kinston (Carolina)	OF	125	394	71	122	14	0	4	47	.310	68	70	19	187	10	5	.975
1992— Cant./Akr. (Eastern) ...	OF	23	74	6	16	4	0	0	3	.216	10	10	3	45	0	0	1.000
— Kinston (Carolina)	OF	42	140	28	37	5	1	3	18	.264	30	21	3	74	5	1	.987
1993— Cant./Akr. (Eastern)	OF	123	425	64	139	17	6	6	64	.327	57	43	18	186	3	5	.974
1994— Charlotte (Int'l)..........	OF	128	434	74	136	18	3	16	58	.313	55	61	8	242	12	4	.984
1995— Buffalo (A.A.)............	OF	123	413	67	128	18	•8	15	67	.310	54	40	7	248	4	5	.981
— Cleveland (A.L.)..........	OF-DH	6	9	6	5	0	0	1	3	.556	0	1	0	2	1	0	1.000

Year Team (League)	Pos.	G	AB	R	H	2B	3B	HR	RBI	Avg.	BB	SO	SB	PO	A	E	Avg.
1996— Buffalo (A.A.)	OF	83	318	65	100	17	6	20	64	.314	42	29	1	132	5	2	.986
—Cleveland (A.L.)	DH-OF	51	121	26	43	14	1	5	27	.355	19	13	3	26	0	0	1.000
1997—Cleveland (A.L.)	OF-DH	130	377	62	101	15	3	17	61	.268	63	50	13	201	7	6	.972
1998—Cleveland (A.L.)	OF-DH	112	350	56	94	19	0	16	66	.269	73	75	10	213	7	5	.978
—Buffalo (Int'l)	OF	13	46	5	11	2	0	2	7	.239	6	8	0	18	0	1	.947
Major league totals (4 years)		299	857	150	243	48	4	39	157	.284	155	139	26	442	15	11	.976

DIVISION SERIES RECORD

Year Team (League)	Pos.	G	AB	R	H	2B	3B	HR	RBI	Avg.	BB	SO	SB	PO	A	E	Avg.
1996—Cleveland (A.L.)	PH	1	1	0	0	0	0	0	0	.000	0	1	0	...	...	...	...
1997—Cleveland (A.L.)	OF	3	7	0	1	0	0	0	0	.143	0	1	0	4	1	0	1.000
1998—Cleveland (A.L.)	OF-DH	3	10	1	2	1	0	0	0	.200	1	4	0	4	0	0	1.000
Division series totals (3 years)		7	18	1	3	1	0	0	0	.167	1	6	0	8	1	0	1.000

CHAMPIONSHIP SERIES RECORD

Year Team (League)	Pos.	G	AB	R	H	2B	3B	HR	RBI	Avg.	BB	SO	SB	PO	A	E	Avg.
1997—Cleveland (A.L.)	OF	6	16	1	3	3	0	0	0	.188	2	6	0	9	0	0	1.000
1998—Cleveland (A.L.)	OF-PH	4	12	0	1	0	0	0	0	.083	1	3	0	7	0	1	.875
Championship series totals (2 years)		10	28	1	4	3	0	0	0	.143	3	9	0	16	0	1	.941

WORLD SERIES RECORD

Year Team (League)	Pos.	G	AB	R	H	2B	3B	HR	RBI	Avg.	BB	SO	SB	PO	A	E	Avg.
1997—Cleveland (A.L.)	PH-OF	5	4	1	2	1	0	0	2	.500	4	1	0	2	0	0	1.000

GILKEY, BERNARD   OF   DIAMONDBACKS

PERSONAL: Born September 24, 1966, in St. Louis. ... 6-0/200. ... Bats right, throws right. ... Full name: Otis Bernard Gilkey.
HIGH SCHOOL: University City (Mo.).
TRANSACTIONS/CAREER NOTES: Signed as non-drafted free agent by St. Louis Cardinals organization (August 22, 1984). ... On disabled list (April 10-25, 1986 and May 29, 1987-remainder of season). ... On St. Louis disabled list (June 14-July 11, 1991 and April 29-May 14, 1993). ... On suspended list (July 8-9, 1994). ... Granted free agency (April 7, 1995). ... Re-signed by Cardinals (April 8, 1995). ... On St. Louis disabled list (June 28-July 17, 1995); included rehabilitation assignment to Louisville (July 15-17). ... Traded by Cardinals to New York Mets for P Eric Ludwick, P Erik Hiljus and OF Yudith Ozorio (January 22, 1996). ... On New York disabled list (April 27-May 12, 1998). ... Traded by Mets with P Nelson Figueroa and cash to Arizona Diamondbacks for P Willie Blair, C Jorge Fabregas and a player to be named later (July 31, 1998); Mets received cash to complete deal (September 3, 1998).
STATISTICAL NOTES: Led New York-Pennsylvania League outfielders with 185 total chances in 1985. ... Led Texas League in caught stealing with 22 in 1989. ... Led American Association in caught stealing with 33 in 1990. ... Led N.L. outfielders with 19 assists in 1993. ... Tied for N.L. lead in double plays by outfielder with four in 1995. ... Tied for N.L. lead with 12 sacrifice flies in 1997.

Year Team (League)	Pos.	G	AB	R	H	2B	3B	HR	RBI	Avg.	BB	SO	SB	PO	A	E	Avg.
1985—Erie (N.Y.-Penn)	OF	•77	*294	57	60	9	1	7	27	.204	55	57	34	*164	*13	*8	.957
1986—Savannah (S. Atl.)	OF	105	374	64	88	15	4	6	36	.235	84	57	32	220	7	5	.978
1987—Springfield (Midw.)	OF	46	162	30	37	5	0	0	9	.228	39	28	18	79	5	4	.955
1988—Springfield (Midw.)	OF	125	491	84	120	18	7	6	36	.244	65	54	54	165	10	6	.967
1989—Arkansas (Texas)	OF	131	500	*104	139	25	3	6	57	.278	70	54	*53	236	*22	9	.966
1990—Louisville (A.A.)	OF	132	499	83	147	26	8	3	46	.295	*75	49	45	236	18	•11	.958
—St. Louis (N.L.)	OF	18	64	11	19	5	2	1	3	.297	8	5	6	47	2	2	.961
1991—St. Louis (N.L.)	OF	81	268	28	58	7	2	5	20	.216	39	33	14	164	6	1	.994
—Louisville (A.A.)	OF	11	41	5	6	2	0	0	2	.146	6	10	1	33	1	0	1.000
1992—St. Louis (N.L.)	OF	131	384	56	116	19	4	7	43	.302	39	52	18	217	9	5	.978
1993—St. Louis (N.L.)	OF-1B	137	557	99	170	40	5	16	70	.305	56	66	15	251	†20	8	.971
1994—St. Louis (N.L.)	OF	105	380	52	96	22	1	6	45	.253	39	65	15	168	9	3	.983
1995—St. Louis (N.L.)	OF	121	480	73	143	33	4	17	69	.298	42	70	12	206	10	3	.986
—Louisville (A.A.)	OF	2	6	3	2	1	0	1	1	.333	1	0	0	2	0	0	1.000
1996—New York (N.L.)■	OF	153	571	108	181	44	3	30	117	.317	73	125	17	309	*18	6	.982
1997—New York (N.L.)	OF-DH	145	518	85	129	31	1	18	78	.249	70	111	7	251	*17	3	.989
1998—New York (N.L.)	OF	81	264	33	60	15	0	4	28	.227	32	66	5	121	9	1	.992
—Arizona (N.L.)■	OF	29	101	8	25	0	0	1	5	.248	11	14	4	49	3	1	.981
Major league totals (9 years)		1002	3587	553	997	216	22	105	478	.278	409	607	113	1783	103	33	.983

G

GIOVANOLA, ED   IF   PADRES

PERSONAL: Born March 4, 1969, in Los Gatos, Calif. ... 5-10/170. ... Bats left, throws right. ... Full name: Edward Thomas Giovanola.
HIGH SCHOOL: Bellarmine College Preparatory (San Jose, Calif.).
COLLEGE: Santa Clara.
TRANSACTIONS/CAREER NOTES: Selected by Atlanta Braves organization in seventh round of free-agent draft (June 4, 1990). ... On disabled list (May 29-June 5 and June 23-July 23, 1992). ... On Richmond disabled list (June 28-July 21, 1995). ... Claimed on waivers by San Diego Padres (October 13, 1997).
STATISTICAL NOTES: Led International League with .417 on-base percentage in 1995.

Year Team (League)	Pos.	G	AB	R	H	2B	3B	HR	RBI	Avg.	BB	SO	SB	PO	A	E	Avg.
1990—Idaho Falls (Pio.)	2B	25	98	25	38	6	0	0	13	.388	17	9	6	32	72	2	.981
—Sumter (S. Atl.)	2B	35	119	20	29	4	0	0	8	.244	34	17	8	61	125	3	.984
1991—Durham (Carolina)	3-S-2-O	101	299	50	76	9	0	6	27	.254	57	39	18	112	182	15	.951

Year	Team (League)	Pos.	G	AB	R	H	2B	3B	HR	RBI	Avg.	BB	SO	SB	PO	A	E	Avg.
1992—	Greenville (Southern) .	3B	75	270	39	72	5	0	5	30	.267	29	40	4	35	168	18	.919
1993—	Greenville (Southern) .	3B-2B	120	384	70	108	21	5	5	43	.281	84	49	6	94	281	14	.964
1994—	Greenville (Southern) .	3B	25	84	13	20	6	1	4	16	.238	10	12	2	20	41	2	.968
	— Richmond (Int'l)	3-S-2-O	98	344	48	97	16	2	6	30	.282	31	49	7	94	211	16	.950
1995—	Richmond (Int'l)	SS-3B	99	321	45	103	18	2	4	36	.321	55	37	8	125	286	15	.965
	— Atlanta (N.L.)	2B-3B-SS	13	14	2	1	0	0	0	0	.071	3	5	0	9	7	0	1.000
1996—	Richmond (Int'l)	S-2-3-O	62	210	29	62	15	1	3	16	.295	37	34	2	77	155	11	.955
	— Atlanta (N.L.)	3B-2B	43	82	10	19	2	0	0	7	.232	8	13	1	24	56	1	.988
1997—	Richmond (Int'l)	3B-SS-OF	116	395	65	115	23	5	2	46	.291	64	56	2	87	227	16	.952
	— Atlanta (N.L.)	3B-2B-SS	14	8	0	2	0	0	0	0	.250	2	1	0	0	6	0	1.000
1998—	San Diego (N.L.)■ .	3B-2B-SS	92	139	19	32	3	3	1	9	.230	22	22	1	56	122	3	.983
	— Las Vegas (PCL)	3B	4	15	4	5	0	0	0	1	.333	2	3	0	1	15	1	.941
Major league totals (4 years)			162	243	31	54	5	3	1	16	.222	35	41	2	89	191	4	.986

DIVISION SERIES RECORD

Year	Team (League)	Pos.	G	AB	R	H	2B	3B	HR	RBI	Avg.	BB	SO	SB	PO	A	E	Avg.
1998—	San Diego (N.L.)								Did not play.									

CHAMPIONSHIP SERIES RECORD

Year	Team (League)	Pos.	G	AB	R	H	2B	3B	HR	RBI	Avg.	BB	SO	SB	PO	A	E	Avg.
1998—	San Diego (N.L.)								Did not play.									

WORLD SERIES RECORD

Year	Team (League)	Pos.	G	AB	R	H	2B	3B	HR	RBI	Avg.	BB	SO	SB	PO	A	E	Avg.
1998—	San Diego (N.L.)								Did not play.									

GIPSON, CHARLES   OF/IF   MARINERS

PERSONAL: Born December 16, 1972, in Orange, Calif. ... 6-2/180. ... Bats right, throws right. ... Full name: Charles Wells Gipson Jr.
HIGH SCHOOL: Loara (Anaheim, Calif.).
JUNIOR COLLEGE: Cypress (Calif.) College.
TRANSACTIONS/CAREER NOTES: Selected by Seattle Mariners organization in 63rd round of free-agent draft (June 3, 1991). ... On disabled list (May 4-19, 1993).
STATISTICAL NOTES: Led Midwest League in being hit by pitch with 27 in 1993. ... Tied for Southern League lead in double plays by outfielder with four in 1995. ... Tied for Southern League lead in caught stealing with 15 in 1996.

Year	Team (League)	Pos.	G	AB	R	H	2B	3B	HR	RBI	Avg.	BB	SO	SB	PO	A	E	Avg.
1992—	Ariz. Mariners (Ariz.) ..	SS	39	124	30	29	2	0	0	14	.234	13	19	11	49	114	•23	.876
1993—	Appleton (Midwest)....	2B-OF-SS	109	348	53	89	13	1	0	20	.256	61	76	21	192	201	28	.933
1994—	Riverside (Calif.).........	OF	128	481	*102	141	12	3	1	41	.293	76	67	34	293	14	9	.972
1995—	Port City (Southern)...	OF-2B	112	391	36	87	11	2	0	29	.223	30	66	10	235	19	6	.977
1996—	Port City (Southern)...	OF-SS	119	407	54	109	12	3	1	30	.268	41	62	15	210	162	15	.961
1997—	Memphis (Sou.)	S-3-2-O	88	320	56	79	9	4	1	28	.247	34	71	31	143	211	23	.939
1998—	Seattle (A.L.)	OF-3B-DH	44	51	11	12	1	0	0	2	.235	5	9	2	40	5	2	.957
	— Tacoma (PCL)	O-S-2-3	75	278	39	67	16	2	0	11	.241	27	50	14	142	88	11	.954
Major league totals (1 year)			44	51	11	12	1	0	0	2	.235	5	9	2	40	5	2	.957

GIRARDI, JOE   C   YANKEES

PERSONAL: Born October 14, 1964, in Peoria, Ill. ... 5-11/200. ... Bats right, throws right. ... Full name: Joseph Elliott Girardi. ... Name pronounced jeh-RAR-dee.
HIGH SCHOOL: Spalding Institute (Peoria, Ill.).
COLLEGE: Northwestern (degree in industrial engineering, 1986).
TRANSACTIONS/CAREER NOTES: Selected by Chicago Cubs organization in fifth round of free-agent draft (June 2, 1986). ... On disabled list (August 27, 1986-remainder of season and August 7, 1988-remainder of season). ... On Chicago disabled list (April 17-August 6, 1991); included rehabilitation assignment to Iowa (July 23-August 6). ... Selected by Colorado Rockies in first round (19th pick overall) of expansion draft (November 17, 1992). ... On Colorado disabled list (June 5-August 11, 1993); included rehabilitation assignment to Colorado Springs (August 1-11). ... On disabled list (July 11-26, 1994). ... Traded by Rockies to New York Yankees for P Mike DeJean and a player to be named later (November 20, 1995); Rockies acquired P Steve Shoemaker to complete deal (December 6, 1995). ... Granted free agency (November 5, 1996). ... Re-signed by Yankees (December 3, 1996).
STATISTICAL NOTES: Led Carolina League catchers with 661 total chances and tied for lead with 17 passed balls in 1987. ... Led Eastern League catchers with .992 fielding percentage, 448 putouts, 76 assists and 528 total chances and tied for lead with five double plays in 1988. ... Tied for N.L. lead with 16 passed balls in 1990.

Year	Team (League)	Pos.	G	AB	R	H	2B	3B	HR	RBI	Avg.	BB	SO	SB	PO	A	E	Avg.
1986—	Peoria (Midwest)	C	68	230	36	71	13	1	3	28	.309	17	36	6	405	34	5	.989
1987—	Win.-Salem (Car.).......	C	99	364	51	102	9	8	8	46	.280	33	64	9	*569	*74	18	.973
1988—	Pittsfield (Eastern)......	C-OF	104	357	44	97	14	1	7	41	.272	29	51	7	†460	†76	6	†.989
1989—	Chicago (N.L.)	C	59	157	15	39	10	0	1	14	.248	11	26	2	332	28	7	.981
	— Iowa (Am. Assoc.)	C	32	110	12	27	4	2	2	11	.245	5	19	3	172	21	1	.995
1990—	Chicago (N.L.)	C	133	419	36	113	24	2	1	38	.270	17	50	8	653	61	11	.985
1991—	Chicago (N.L.)	C	21	47	3	9	2	0	0	6	.191	6	6	0	95	11	3	.972
	— Iowa (Am. Assoc.)	C	12	36	3	8	1	0	0	4	.222	4	8	2	62	5	3	.957

G

		BATTING												FIELDING			
Year Team (League)	Pos.	G	AB	R	H	2B	3B	HR	RBI	Avg.	BB	SO	SB	PO	A	E	Avg.
1992— Chicago (N.L.)	C	91	270	19	73	3	1	1	12	.270	19	38	0	369	51	4	.991
1993— Colorado (N.L.)■	C	86	310	35	90	14	5	3	31	.290	24	41	6	478	46	6	.989
— Colo. Springs (PCL) ...	C	8	31	6	15	1	1	1	6	.484	0	3	1	40	3	1	.977
1994— Colorado (N.L.)	C	93	330	47	91	9	4	4	34	.276	21	48	3	549	56	5	.992
1995— Colorado (N.L.)	C	125	462	63	121	17	2	8	55	.262	29	76	3	730	60	10	.988
1996— New York (A.L.)■......	C-DH	124	422	55	124	22	3	2	45	.294	30	55	13	803	46	3	.996
1997— New York (A.L.)	C	112	398	38	105	23	1	1	50	.264	26	53	2	829	55	5	.994
1998— New York (A.L.)	C	78	254	31	70	11	4	3	31	.276	14	38	2	541	38	3	.995
American League totals (3 years)		314	1074	124	299	56	8	6	126	.278	70	146	17	2173	139	11	.995
National League totals (7 years)		608	1995	218	536	79	14	18	190	.269	127	285	22	3206	313	46	.987
Major league totals (10 years)		922	3069	342	835	135	22	24	316	.272	197	431	39	5379	452	57	.990

DIVISION SERIES RECORD

		BATTING												FIELDING			
Year Team (League)	Pos.	G	AB	R	H	2B	3B	HR	RBI	Avg.	BB	SO	SB	PO	A	E	Avg.
1995— Colorado (N.L.)	C	4	16	0	2	0	0	0	0	.125	0	2	0	25	3	1	.966
1996— New York (A.L.)	C-PR	4	9	1	2	0	0	0	0	.222	4	1	0	28	1		1.000
1997— New York (A.L.)	C	5	15	2	2	0	0	0	0	.133	1	3	0	21	2	0	1.000
1998— New York (A.L.)	C	2	7	0	3	0	0	0	0	.429	0	1	0	19	1	0	1.000
Division series totals (4 years)		15	47	3	9	0	0	0	0	.191	5	7	0	93	7	1	.990

CHAMPIONSHIP SERIES RECORD

		BATTING												FIELDING			
Year Team (League)	Pos.	G	AB	R	H	2B	3B	HR	RBI	Avg.	BB	SO	SB	PO	A	E	Avg.
1989— Chicago (N.L.)	C	4	10	1	1	0	0	0	0	.100	1	2	0	20	0	0	1.000
1996— New York (A.L.)	C-PH	4	12	1	3	0	1	0	0	.250	1	3	0	22	0	0	1.000
1998— New York (A.L.)	C	3	8	2	2	0	0	0	0	.250	1	0	0	22	1	0	1.000
Championship series totals (3 years)		11	30	4	6	0	1	0	0	.200	3	5	0	64	1	0	1.000

WORLD SERIES RECORD

NOTES: Member of World Series championship team (1996 and 1998).

		BATTING												FIELDING			
Year Team (League)	Pos.	G	AB	R	H	2B	3B	HR	RBI	Avg.	BB	SO	SB	PO	A	E	Avg.
1996— New York (A.L.)	C	4	10	1	2	0	1	0	1	.200	1	2	0	23	4	0	1.000
1998— New York (A.L.)	C	2	6	0	0	0	0	0	0	.000	0	2	0	9	2	0	1.000
World Series totals (2 years)		6	16	1	2	0	1	0	1	.125	1	4	0	32	6	0	1.000

GIRON, ISABEL   P   BLUE JAYS

PERSONAL: Born November 17, 1977, in Villa Mella, Dominican Republic. ... 6-2/170. ... Throws right, bats right. ... Full name: Isabel Antonio Giron.
TRANSACTIONS/CAREER NOTES: Signed as non-drafted free agent by Toronto Blue Jays organization (August 10, 1994). ... On Knoxville disabled list (September 2-9, 1998).
MISCELLANEOUS: Played shortstop (1995).

Year Team (League)	W	L	Pct.	ERA	G	GS	CG	ShO	Sv.	IP	H	R	ER	BB	SO
1996— Dom. B. Jays (DSL)	6	1	.857	1.18	21	1	0	0	3	61	42	15	8	17	49
1997— Dom. B. Jays (DSL)	9	4	.692	1.64	14	14	4	3	0	99	64	24	18	19	109
1998— Hagerstown (S. Atl.)	10	9	.526	2.49	21	21	4	•3	0	126 1/3	110	57	35	27	129
— Knoxville (Southern)	1	1	.500	3.82	6	5	0	0	0	35 1/3	29	15	15	13	35

RECORD AS POSITION PLAYER

		BATTING												FIELDING			
Year Team (League)	Pos.	G	AB	R	H	2B	3B	HR	RBI	Avg.	BB	SO	SB	PO	A	E	Avg.
1995— Dom. B. Jays (DSL) ...	SS	36	120	14	30	4	1	2	13	.250	3	34	2	102	11	7	.942

GLANVILLE, DOUG   OF   PHILLIES

PERSONAL: Born August 25, 1970, in Hackensack, N.J. ... 6-2/180. ... Bats right, throws right. ... Full name: Douglas Metunwa Glanville.
HIGH SCHOOL: Teaneck (N.J.).
COLLEGE: Pennsylvania (degree in science and engineering).
TRANSACTIONS/CAREER NOTES: Selected by Chicago Cubs organization in first round (12th pick overall) of free-agent draft (June 3, 1991). ... Traded by Cubs to Philadelphia Phillies for 2B Mickey Morandini (December 23, 1997).
STATISTICAL NOTES: Led Carolina League outfielders with 312 total chances in 1992. ... Led Southern League in caught stealing with 20 in 1994. ... Led Southern League outfielders with 339 total chances in 1994. ... Had 18-game hitting streak (May 1-20, 1998). ... Had 17-game hitting streak (May 30-June 17, 1998).

		BATTING												FIELDING			
Year Team (League)	Pos.	G	AB	R	H	2B	3B	HR	RBI	Avg.	BB	SO	SB	PO	A	E	Avg.
1991— Geneva (NY-Penn)	OF	36	152	29	46	8	0	2	12	.303	11	25	17	77	4	0	1.000
1992— Win.-Salem (Car.)	OF	120	485	72	125	18	4	4	36	.258	40	78	32	*293	12	7	.978
1993— Daytona (Fla. St.)	OF	61	239	47	70	10	1	2	21	.293	28	24	18	123	11	7	.950
— Orlando (South.)	OF	73	296	42	78	14	4	9	40	.264	12	41	15	168	8	5	.972
1994— Orlando (South.)	OF	130	483	53	127	22	2	5	52	.263	24	49	26	*322	14	3	.991
1995— Iowa (Am. Assoc.)......	OF	112	419	48	113	16	2	4	37	.270	16	64	13	209	9	4	.982
1996— Iowa (Am. Assoc.)	OF	90	373	53	115	23	3	3	34	.308	12	35	15	217	6	3	.987
— Chicago (N.L.)	OF	49	83	10	20	5	1	1	10	.241	3	11	2	35	1	1	.973
1997— Chicago (N.L.)	OF	146	474	79	142	22	5	4	35	.300	24	46	19	247	12	3	.989
1998— Philadelphia (N.L.)■ ..	OF	158	*678	106	189	28	7	8	49	.279	42	89	23	360	14	2	.995
Major league totals (3 years)		353	1235	195	351	55	13	13	94	.284	69	146	44	642	27	6	.991

G

GLAUBER, KEITH   P   REDS

PERSONAL: Born January 18, 1972, in Brooklyn, N.Y. ... 6-2/190. ... Throws right, bats right. ... Full name: Keith H. Glauber.
HIGH SCHOOL: Marlboro (N.J.).
COLLEGE: Montclair (N.J.) State.
TRANSACTIONS/CAREER NOTES: Selected by St. Louis Cardinals organization in 42nd round of free-agent draft (June 2, 1994). ... Selected by Cincinnati Reds from Cardinals organization in Rule 5 major league draft (December 15, 1997). ... On Cincinnati disabled list (March 12-September 1, 1998); included rehabilitation assignments to Burlington (June 19-July 16), Chattanooga (August 1-10) and Indianapolis (August 10-September 1). ... Granted free agency (December 21, 1998). ... Re-signed by Reds (January 13, 1999).

Year	Team (League)	W	L	Pct.	ERA	G	GS	CG	ShO	Sv.	IP	H	R	ER	BB	SO
1994—	New Jersey (NYP)	4	6	.400	4.19	17	10	0	0	0	68 2/3	67	36	32	26	51
1995—	Savannah (S. Atl.)	2	1	.667	3.73	40	0	0	0	0	62 2/3	50	29	26	36	62
1996—	Peoria (Midwest)	3	3	.500	3.09	54	0	0	0	0	64	54	31	22	26	80
1997—	Arkansas (Texas)	5	7	.417	2.75	50	0	0	0	3	59	48	22	18	25	53
—	Louisville (A.A.)	1	3	.250	5.17	15	0	0	0	5	15 2/3	18	14	9	4	14
1998—	Burlington (Midw.)■	0	1	.000	3.86	7	1	0	0	0	14	13	9	6	6	13
—	Chattanooga (Southern)	1	1	.500	4.00	2	2	0	0	0	9	3	4	4	6	5
—	Indianapolis (Int'l)	1	3	.250	9.00	4	4	0	0	0	16	20	17	16	14	15
—	Cincinnati (N.L.)	0	0	...	2.35	3	0	0	0	0	7 2/3	6	2	2	1	4
Major league totals (1 year)		0	0	...	2.35	3	0	0	0	0	7 2/3	6	2	2	1	4

GLAUS, TROY   3B   ANGELS

PERSONAL: Born August 3, 1976, in Tarzana, Calif. ... 6-5/225. ... Bats right, throws right. ... Full name: Troy Edward Glaus. ... Name pronounced GLOSS.
HIGH SCHOOL: Carlsbad (Calif.).
COLLEGE: UCLA.
TRANSACTIONS/CAREER NOTES: Selected by San Diego Padres organization in second round of free-agent draft (June 2, 1994); did not sign. ... Selected by Anaheim Angels organization in first round (third pick overall) of free-agent draft (June 3, 1997).
MISCELLANEOUS: Member of 1996 U.S. Olympic baseball team.

Year	Team (League)	Pos.	G	AB	R	H	2B	3B	HR	RBI	Avg.	BB	SO	SB	PO	A	E	Avg.
1998—	Midland (Texas)	3B	50	188	51	58	11	2	19	51	.309	39	41	4	34	101	11	.925
—	Vancouver (PCL)	3B	59	219	33	67	16	0	16	42	.306	21	55	3	46	131	13	.932
—	Anaheim (A.L.)	3B	48	165	19	36	9	0	1	23	.218	15	51	1	27	85	7	.941
Major league totals (1 year)			48	165	19	36	9	0	1	23	.218	15	51	1	27	85	7	.941

GLAVINE, TOM   P   BRAVES

PERSONAL: Born March 25, 1966, in Concord, Mass. ... 6-1/185. ... Throws left, bats left. ... Full name: Thomas Michael Glavine. ... Brother of Mike Glavine, first baseman, Cleveland Indians organization. ... Name pronounced GLAV-in.
HIGH SCHOOL: Billerica (Mass.).
TRANSACTIONS/CAREER NOTES: Selected by Atlanta Braves organization in second round of free-agent draft (June 4, 1984).
HONORS: Named N.L. Pitcher of the Year by THE SPORTING NEWS (1991). ... Named lefthanded pitcher on THE SPORTING NEWS N.L. All-Star team (1991-92 and 1998). ... Named pitcher on THE SPORTING NEWS N.L. Silver Slugger team (1991, 1995, 1996 and 1998). ... Named N.L. Cy Young Award winner by Baseball Writers' Association of America (1991 and 1998).
STATISTICAL NOTES: Led Gulf Coast League with 12 wild pitches in 1984.
MISCELLANEOUS: Selected by Los Angeles Kings in fourth round (69th pick overall) of NHL entry draft (June 9, 1984). ... Appeared in eight games as pinch runner (1988). ... Appeared in one game as pinch runner (1989). ... Appeared in one game as pinch runner (1990). ... Received a base on balls and scored once in one game as pinch hitter and appeared in one game as pinch runner (1991). ... Singled and struck out in two appearances as pinch hitter (1992). ... Struck out in only appearance as pinch hitter (1994). ... Singled and struck out in three appearances as pinch hitter (1996).

Year	Team (League)	W	L	Pct.	ERA	G	GS	CG	ShO	Sv.	IP	H	R	ER	BB	SO
1984—	GC Braves (GCL)	2	3	.400	3.34	8	7	0	0	0	32 1/3	29	17	12	13	34
1985—	Sumter (S. Atl.)	9	6	.600	*2.35	26	26	2	1	0	168 2/3	114	58	44	73	174
1986—	Greenville (Southern)	11	6	.647	3.41	22	22	2	1	0	145 1/3	129	62	55	70	114
—	Richmond (Int'l)	1	5	.167	5.63	7	7	1	1	0	40	40	29	25	27	12
1987—	Richmond (Int'l)	6	12	.333	3.35	22	22	4	1	0	150 1/3	142	70	56	56	91
—	Atlanta (N.L.)	2	4	.333	5.54	9	9	0	0	0	50 1/3	55	34	31	33	20
1988—	Atlanta (N.L.)	7	*17	.292	4.56	34	34	1	0	0	195 1/3	201	111	99	63	84
1989—	Atlanta (N.L.)	14	8	.636	3.68	29	29	6	4	0	186	172	88	76	40	90
1990—	Atlanta (N.L.)	10	12	.455	4.28	33	33	1	0	0	214 2/3	232	111	102	78	129
1991—	Atlanta (N.L.)	•20	11	.645	2.55	34	34	•9	1	0	246 2/3	201	83	70	69	192
1992—	Atlanta (N.L.)	•20	8	.714	2.76	33	33	7	•5	0	225	197	81	69	70	129
1993—	Atlanta (N.L.)	•22	6	.786	3.20	36	•36	4	2	0	239 1/3	236	91	85	90	120
1994—	Atlanta (N.L.)	13	9	.591	3.97	25	25	2	0	0	165 1/3	173	76	73	70	140
1995—	Atlanta (N.L.)	16	7	.696	3.08	29	29	3	1	0	198 2/3	182	76	68	66	127
1996—	Atlanta (N.L.)	15	10	.600	2.98	36	*36	1	0	0	235 1/3	222	91	78	85	181
1997—	Atlanta (N.L.)	14	7	.667	2.96	33	33	5	2	0	240	197	86	79	79	152
1998—	Atlanta (N.L.)	*20	6	.769	2.47	33	33	4	3	0	229 1/3	202	67	63	74	157
Major league totals (12 years)		173	105	.622	3.31	364	364	43	18	0	2425 2/3	2270	995	893	817	1521

DIVISION SERIES RECORD
RECORDS: Holds N.L. career record for most bases on balls allowed—10.

G

Year Team (League)	W	L	Pct.	ERA	G	GS	CG	ShO	Sv.	IP	H	R	ER	BB	SO
1995— Atlanta (N.L.)	0	0	...	2.57	1	1	0	0	0	7	5	3	2	1	3
1996— Atlanta (N.L.)	1	0	1.000	1.35	1	1	0	0	0	6 2/3	5	1	1	3	7
1997— Atlanta (N.L.)	1	0	1.000	4.50	1	1	0	0	0	6	5	3	3	5	4
1998— Atlanta (N.L.)	0	0	...	1.29	1	1	0	0	0	7	3	1	1	1	8
Div. series totals (4 years)	2	0	1.000	2.36	4	4	0	0	0	26 2/3	18	8	7	10	22

CHAMPIONSHIP SERIES RECORD

RECORDS: Holds career record for most hit batsmen—5. ... Holds single-inning records for most runs allowed—8 (October 13, 1992, second inning); and most earned runs allowed—7 (October 13, 1992, second inning). ... Shares single-game record for most earned runs allowed—7 (October 13, 1992 and October 14, 1997). ... Holds career record for most earned runs allowed—32; and most hits allowed—74. ... Shares single-inning record for most hits allowed—6 (October 13, 1992, second inning). ... Shares career record for most games started—12. ... Shares N.L. career record for most series with one team—7 (Atlanta, 1991-93 and 1995-97). ... Shares N.L. single-series record for most hit batsmen—2 (1992).

NOTES: Received a base on balls in only appearance as pinch hitter (1998).

Year Team (League)	W	L	Pct.	ERA	G	GS	CG	ShO	Sv.	IP	H	R	ER	BB	SO
1991— Atlanta (N.L.)	0	2	.000	3.21	2	2	0	0	0	14	12	5	5	6	11
1992— Atlanta (N.L.)	0	2	.000	12.27	2	2	0	0	0	7 1/3	13	11	10	3	2
1993— Atlanta (N.L.)	1	0	1.000	2.57	1	1	0	0	0	7	6	2	2	0	5
1995— Atlanta (N.L.)	0	0	...	1.29	1	1	0	0	0	7	7	1	1	2	5
1996— Atlanta (N.L.)	1	1	.500	2.08	2	2	0	0	0	13	10	3	3	0	9
1997— Atlanta (N.L.)	1	1	.500	5.40	2	2	0	0	0	13 1/3	13	8	8	11	9
1998— Atlanta (N.L.)	0	2	...	2.31	2	2	0	0	0	11 2/3	13	6	3	9	8
Champ. series totals (7 years)	3	8	.273	3.93	12	12	0	0	0	73 1/3	74	36	32	31	49

WORLD SERIES RECORD

RECORDS: Shares single-inning records for most bases on balls allowed—4 (October 24, 1991, sixth inning); and most consecutive bases on balls allowed—3 (October 24, 1991, sixth inning).

NOTES: Named Most Valuable Player (1995). ... Member of World Series championship team (1995).

Year Team (League)	W	L	Pct.	ERA	G	GS	CG	ShO	Sv.	IP	H	R	ER	BB	SO
1991— Atlanta (N.L.)	1	1	.500	2.70	2	2	1	0	0	13 1/3	8	6	4	7	8
1992— Atlanta (N.L.)	1	1	.500	1.59	2	2	2	0	0	17	10	3	3	4	8
1995— Atlanta (N.L.)	2	0	1.000	1.29	2	2	0	0	0	14	4	2	2	6	11
1996— Atlanta (N.L.)	0	1	.000	1.29	1	1	0	0	0	7	4	2	1	3	8
World Series totals (4 years)	4	3	.571	1.75	7	7	3	0	0	51 1/3	26	13	10	20	35

ALL-STAR GAME RECORD

RECORDS: Holds single-game record for most hits allowed—9 (July 14, 1992). ... Holds single-inning record for most hits allowed—7 (July 14, 1992, first inning).

Year League	W	L	Pct.	ERA	GS	CG	ShO	Sv.	IP	H	R	ER	BB	SO
1991— National	0	0	...	0.00	1	0	0	0	2	1	0	0	1	3
1992— National	0	1	.000	27.00	1	0	0	0	1 2/3	9	5	5	0	2
1993— National							Did not play.							
1996— National	0	0	...	0.00	0	0	0	0	1	0	0	0	0	1
1997— National							Did not play.							
1998— National	0	0	...	27.00	0	0	0	0	1 1/3	5	4	4	3	0
All-Star totals (4 years)	0	1	.000	13.50	2	0	0	0	6	15	9	9	4	6

GLOVER, GARY   P   BLUE JAYS

PERSONAL: Born December 3, 1976, in Cleveland. ... 6-5/205. ... Throws right, bats right. ... Full name: John Gary Glover.
HIGH SCHOOL: Deland (Fla.).
TRANSACTIONS/CAREER NOTES: Selected by Toronto Blue Jays organization in 15th round of free-agent draft (June 2, 1994). ... On disabled list (August 10-September 8, 1994).

Year Team (League)	W	L	Pct.	ERA	G	GS	CG	ShO	Sv.	IP	H	R	ER	BB	SO
1994— GC Blue Jays (GCL)	0	0	...	47.25	2	0	0	0	0	1 1/3	4	8	7	4	2
1995— GC Blue Jays (GCL)	3	7	.300	4.91	12	10	2	0	0	62 1/3	62	48	34	26	46
1996— Medicine Hat (Pioneer)	3	*12	.200	7.75	15	•15	*2	0	0	83 2/3	*119	*94	72	29	54
1997— Hagerstown (S. Atl.)	6	*17	.261	3.73	28	28	3	0	0	173 2/3	165	94	72	58	155
1998— Knoxville (Southern)	0	5	.000	6.75	8	8	0	0	0	37 1/3	41	36	28	28	14
— Dunedin (Fla. St.)	7	6	.538	4.28	19	18	0	0	0	109 1/3	117	66	52	36	88

GLYNN, RYAN   P   RANGERS

PERSONAL: Born November 1, 1974, in Portsmouth, Va. ... 6-3/195. ... Throws right, bats right. ... Full name: Ryan David Glynn.
HIGH SCHOOL: Churchland (Portsmouth, Va.).
COLLEGE: Virginia Military Institute.
TRANSACTIONS/CAREER NOTES: Selected by Texas Rangers organization in fourth round of free-agent draft (June 1, 1995).

Year Team (League)	W	L	Pct.	ERA	G	GS	CG	ShO	Sv.	IP	H	R	ER	BB	SO
1995— Hudson Valley (NYP)	3	3	.500	4.70	9	8	0	0	0	44	56	27	23	16	21
1996— Charleston, S.C. (SAL)	8	7	.533	4.54	19	19	2	1	0	121	118	70	61	59	72
1997— Charlotte (Fla. St.)	8	7	.533	4.97	23	22	5	1	1	134	148	81	74	44	96
— Tulsa (Texas)	1	1	.500	3.38	3	3	0	0	0	21 1/3	21	9	8	10	18
1998— Tulsa (Texas)	9	6	.600	3.44	26	24	4	1	0	157	140	66	60	64	111

GOMES, WAYNE   P   PHILLIES

PERSONAL: Born January 15, 1973, in Hampton, Va. ... 6-2/226. ... Throws right, bats right. ... Full name: Wayne Maurice Gomes.
HIGH SCHOOL: Phoebus (Hampton, Va.).

COLLEGE: Old Dominion.
TRANSACTIONS/CAREER NOTES: Selected by Philadelphia Phillies organization in first round (fourth pick overall) of free-agent draft (June 3, 1993). ... On disabled list (May 12-June 23, 1995).
STATISTICAL NOTES: Led Florida State League with 27 wild pitches in 1994. ... Tied for Eastern League lead with six balks in 1995.

Year	Team (League)	W	L	Pct.	ERA	G	GS	CG	ShO	Sv.	IP	H	R	ER	BB	SO
1993—Batavia (N.Y.-Penn)		1	0	1.000	1.23	5	0	0	0	0	7 1/3	1	1	1	8	11
—Clearwater (Fla. St.)		0	0	...	1.17	9	0	0	0	4	7 2/3	4	1	1	9	13
1994—Clearwater (Fla. St.)		6	8	.429	4.74	23	21	1	1	0	104 1/3	85	63	55	82	102
1995—Reading (Eastern)		7	4	.636	3.96	22	22	1	1	0	104 2/3	89	54	46	70	102
1996—Reading (Eastern)		0	4	.000	4.48	*67	0	0	0	24	64 1/3	53	35	32	48	79
1997—Scran./W.B. (Int'l)		3	1	.750	2.37	26	0	0	0	7	38	31	11	10	24	36
—Philadelphia (N.L.)		5	1	.833	5.27	37	0	0	0	0	42 2/3	45	26	25	24	24
1998—Philadelphia (N.L.)		9	6	.600	4.24	71	0	0	0	1	93 1/3	94	48	44	35	86
Major league totals (2 years)......		**14**	**7**	**.667**	**4.57**	**108**	**0**	**0**	**0**	**1**	**136**	**139**	**74**	**69**	**59**	**110**

GOMEZ, CHRIS   SS   PADRES

PERSONAL: Born June 16, 1971, in Los Angeles, Calif. ... 6-1/195. ... Bats right, throws right. ... Full name: Christopher Cory Gomez.
HIGH SCHOOL: Lakewood (Calif.).
COLLEGE: Loyola-Marymount, then Long Beach State.
TRANSACTIONS/CAREER NOTES: Selected by California Angels organization in 37th round of free-agent draft (June 5, 1989); did not sign. ... Selected by Detroit Tigers organization in third round of free-agent draft (June 1, 1992). ... Traded by Tigers with C John Flaherty to San Diego Padres for C Brad Ausmus, SS Andujar Cedeno and P Russ Spear (June 18, 1996).

Year	Team (League)	Pos.	G	AB	R	H	2B	3B	HR	RBI	Avg.	BB	SO	SB	PO	A	E	Avg.
1992—London (Eastern)		SS	64	220	20	59	13	2	1	19	.268	20	34	1	100	174	14	.951
1993—Toledo (Int'l)		SS	87	277	29	68	12	2	0	20	.245	23	37	6	133	261	16	.961
—Detroit (A.L.)		SS-2B-DH	46	128	11	32	7	1	0	11	.250	9	17	2	69	118	5	.974
1994—Detroit (A.L.)		SS-2B	84	296	32	76	19	0	8	53	.257	33	64	5	140	210	8	.978
1995—Detroit (A.L.)		SS-2B-DH	123	431	49	96	20	2	11	50	.223	41	96	4	210	361	15	.974
1996—Detroit (A.L.)		SS	48	128	21	31	5	0	1	16	.242	18	20	1	77	114	6	.970
—San Diego (N.L.)■		SS	89	328	32	86	16	1	3	29	.262	39	64	2	124	261	13	.967
1997—San Diego (N.L.)		SS	150	522	62	132	19	2	5	54	.253	53	114	5	226	433	15	.978
1998—San Diego (N.L.)		SS	145	449	55	120	32	3	4	39	.267	51	87	1	180	397	12	*.980
American League totals (4 years)			301	983	113	235	51	3	20	130	.239	101	197	12	496	803	34	.974
National League totals (3 years)			384	1299	149	338	67	6	12	122	.260	143	265	8	530	1091	40	.976
Major league totals (6 years)			685	2282	262	573	118	9	32	252	.251	244	462	20	1026	1894	74	.975

DIVISION SERIES RECORD

Year	Team (League)	Pos.	G	AB	R	H	2B	3B	HR	RBI	Avg.	BB	SO	SB	PO	A	E	Avg.
1996—San Diego (N.L.)		SS	3	12	0	2	0	0	0	1	.167	0	4	0	8	5	0	1.000
1998—San Diego (N.L.)		SS	4	11	1	3	0	0	0	0	.273	4	1	0	6	9	1	.938
Division series totals (2 years)			7	23	1	5	0	0	0	1	.217	4	5	0	14	14	1	.966

CHAMPIONSHIP SERIES RECORD

Year	Team (League)	Pos.	G	AB	R	H	2B	3B	HR	RBI	Avg.	BB	SO	SB	PO	A	E	Avg.
1998—San Diego (N.L.)		SS	6	20	2	3	1	0	0	0	.150	2	5	0	5	14	1	.950

WORLD SERIES RECORD

Year	Team (League)	Pos.	G	AB	R	H	2B	3B	HR	RBI	Avg.	BB	SO	SB	PO	A	E	Avg.
1998—San Diego (N.L.)		SS	4	11	2	4	0	1	0	0	.364	1	1	0	5	9	0	1.000

GONZALEZ, ALEX   SS   BLUE JAYS

PERSONAL: Born April 8, 1973, in Miami. ... 6-0/200. ... Bats right, throws right. ... Full name: Alexander Scott Gonzalez.
HIGH SCHOOL: Miami Killian.
TRANSACTIONS/CAREER NOTES: Selected by Toronto Blue Jays organization in 14th round of free-agent draft (June 3, 1991). ... On Toronto disabled list (April 29-May 27, 1994); included rehabilitation assignment to Syracuse (May 14-27). ... On disabled list (August 13-September 14, 1997).
RECORDS: Shares major league single-game record for most strikeouts—6 (September 9, 1998, 13 innings). ... Shares A.L. record for most assists by shortstop (nine-inning game)—13 (1996).
STATISTICAL NOTES: Led Gulf Coast League shortstops with 247 total chances in 1991. ... Led Southern League with 253 total bases in 1993. ... Led Southern League shortstops with 682 total chances and 92 double plays in 1993. ... Led International League with 542 total chances in 1994. ... Led A.L. shortstops with 765 total chances and 122 double plays in 1996.

G

Year	Team (League)	Pos.	G	AB	R	H	2B	3B	HR	RBI	Avg.	BB	SO	SB	PO	A	E	Avg.
1991—GC Jays (GCL)...........		SS	53	191	29	40	5	4	0	10	.209	12	41	7	66	*160	21	.915
1992—Myrtle Beach (SAL)		SS	134	535	83	145	22	9	10	62	.271	38	119	26	*248	*406	48	.932
1993—Knoxville (S. Atl.)		SS	*142	561	*93	162	29	7	16	69	.289	39	110	38	*224	*428	30	*.956
1994—Toronto (A.L.)		SS	15	53	7	8	3	1	0	1	.151	4	17	3	18	49	6	.918
—Syracuse (Int'l)		SS	110	437	69	124	22	4	12	57	.284	53	92	23	*163	*348	*31	.943
1995—Toronto (A.L.).............		SS-3B-DH	111	367	51	89	19	4	10	42	.243	44	114	4	164	227	19	.954
1996—Toronto (A.L.)		SS	147	527	64	124	30	5	14	64	.235	45	127	16	279	465	21	.973
1997—Toronto (A.L.)		SS	126	426	46	102	23	2	12	35	.239	34	94	15	209	341	8	*.986
1998—Toronto (A.L.).............		SS	158	568	70	136	28	1	13	51	.239	28	121	21	259	427	17	.976
Major league totals (5 years)			557	1941	238	459	103	13	49	193	.236	155	473	59	929	1509	71	.972

GONZALEZ, ALEX — SS — MARLINS

PERSONAL: Born February 15, 1977, in Cagua, Venezuela. ... 6-0/170. ... Bats right, throws right. ... Full name: Alexander Gonzalez.
HIGH SCHOOL: Liceo Ramon Bastidas (Venezuela).
TRANSACTIONS/CAREER NOTES: Signed as non-drafted free agent by Florida Marlins organization (April 18, 1994). ... On Kane County disabled list (April 5-August 17, 1996). ... On Portland disabled list (September 7, 1996-remainder of season).

Year Team (League)	Pos.	G	AB	R	H	2B	3B	HR	RBI	Avg.	BB	SO	SB	PO	A	E	Avg.
1994—Dom. Marlins (DSL) ...	SS	54	239	30	54	7	3	3	31	.226	15	36	4	140	222	34	.914
1995—GC Marlins (GCL)	SS	53	187	30	55	7	4	2	30	.294	19	27	11	65	168	17	.932
— Brevard Co. (Fla. St.)..	SS	17	59	6	12	2	1	0	8	.203	1	14	1	26	51	8	.906
1996—Portland (Eastern)......	SS	11	34	4	8	0	1	0	1	.235	2	10	0	17	38	7	.887
— Kane County (Midw.)..	SS	4	10	2	2	0	0	0	0	.200	2	4	0	2	10	0	1.000
— GC Marlins (GCL).......	SS	10	41	6	16	3	0	0	6	.390	2	4	1	14	30	5	.898
1997—Portland (Eastern)......	SS	133	449	69	114	16	4	19	65	.254	27	83	4	192	423	*37	.943
1998—Charlotte (Int'l)............	SS	108	422	71	117	20	10	10	51	.277	28	80	4	161	322	20	.960
— Florida (N.L.).............	SS	25	86	11	13	2	0	3	7	.151	9	30	0	29	58	2	.978
Major league totals (1 year)		25	86	11	13	2	0	3	7	.151	9	30	0	29	58	2	.978

GONZALEZ, GABE — P — MARLINS

PERSONAL: Born May 24, 1972, in Long Beach, Calif. ... 6-1/160. ... Throws left, bats both. ... Full name: Gabriel Gonzalez.
HIGH SCHOOL: Wilson (Long Beach, Calif.).
COLLEGE: Long Beach State.
TRANSACTIONS/CAREER NOTES: Selected by Florida Marlins organization in the 16th round of free-agent draft (June 1, 1995).

Year Team (League)	W	L	Pct.	ERA	G	GS	CG	ShO	Sv.	IP	H	R	ER	BB	SO
1995— Kane County (Midwest)......	4	4	.500	2.28	32	0	0	0	1	43 1/3	32	18	11	14	41
1996— Charlotte (Int'l)..................	0	0	...	3.00	2	0	0	0	0	3	4	1	1	2	3
— Brevard County (FSL).........	1	9	.100	5.32	23	17	0	0	0	86 1/3	102	57	51	27	48
1997— Portland (Eastern).............	3	2	.600	2.11	29	0	0	0	3	42 2/3	43	12	10	5	28
— Charlotte (Int'l)..................	2	2	.500	2.74	37	1	0	0	3	42 2/3	38	15	13	14	24
1998— Florida (N.L.).....................	0	0	...	9.00	3	0	0	0	0	1	1	1	1	1	0
— Charlotte (Int'l)..................	3	9	.250	5.48	57	4	0	0	2	87	101	67	53	53	41
Major league totals (1 year)........	0	0	...	9.00	3	0	0	0	0	1	1	1	1	1	0

GONZALEZ, JEREMI — P — CUBS

PERSONAL: Born January 8, 1975, in Maracaibo, Venezuela. ... 6-2/210. ... Throws right, bats right. ... Full name: Geremis Segundo Acosta Gonzalez.
HIGH SCHOOL: Colegro La Chinita (Maracaibo, Venezuela).
TRANSACTIONS/CAREER NOTES: Signed as non-drafted free agent by Chicago Cubs organization (October 21, 1991). ... On disabled list (July 6-August 10, 1996). ... On disabled list (July 25, 1998-remainder of season).
STATISTICAL NOTES: Led Arizona League with 10 hit batsmen in 1992.
MISCELLANEOUS: Appeared in one game as pinch runner (1998).

Year Team (League)	W	L	Pct.	ERA	G	GS	CG	ShO	Sv.	IP	H	R	ER	BB	SO
1992— Arizona Cubs (Arizona)	0	5	.000	7.80	14	7	0	0	0	45	65	59	39	22	39
1993— Huntington (Appal.).............	3	9	.250	6.25	12	12	1	0	0	67 2/3	82	59	47	38	42
1994— Peoria (Midwest).................	1	7	.125	5.55	13	13	1	0	0	71 1/3	86	53	44	32	39
— Williamsport (NYP).............	4	6	.400	4.24	16	12	1	1	1	80 2/3	83	46	38	29	64
1995— Rockford (Midwest)	4	4	.500	5.10	12	12	1	0	0	65 1/3	63	43	37	28	36
— Daytona (Fla. St.)	5	1	.833	1.22	19	2	0	0	4	44 1/3	34	15	6	13	30
1996— Orlando (South.)	6	3	.667	3.34	17	14	0	0	0	97	95	39	36	28	85
1997— Iowa (Am. Assoc.)...............	2	2	.500	3.48	10	10	1	1	0	62	47	27	24	21	58
— Chicago (N.L.)...................	11	9	.550	4.25	23	23	1	1	0	144	126	73	68	69	93
1998— Chicago (N.L.).....................	7	7	.500	5.32	20	20	1	1	0	110	124	72	65	41	70
Major league totals (2 years)......	18	16	.529	4.71	43	43	2	2	0	254	250	145	133	110	163

GONZALEZ, JUAN — OF — RANGERS

PERSONAL: Born October 16, 1969, in Vega Baja, Puerto Rico. ... 6-3/220. ... Bats right, throws right. ... Full name: Juan Alberto Vazquez Gonzalez.
HIGH SCHOOL: Vega Baja (Puerto Rico).
TRANSACTIONS/CAREER NOTES: Signed as non-drafted free agent by Texas Rangers organization (May 30, 1986). ... On disabled list (April 27-June 17, 1988; March 30-April 26, 1991; April 16-June 1 and July 27-August 16, 1995; May 8-June 1, 1996; and March 24-May 2, 1997).
HONORS: Named American Association Most Valuable Player (1990). ... Named outfielder on THE SPORTING NEWS A.L. Silver Slugger team (1992-93 and 1996-98). ... Named outfielder on THE SPORTING NEWS A.L. All-Star team (1993, 1996 and 1998). ... Named A.L. Most Valuable Player by Baseball Writers' Association of America (1996 and 1998).
STATISTICAL NOTES: Led Texas League with 254 total bases in 1989. ... Led American Association with 252 total bases in 1990. ... Hit three home runs in one game (June 7, 1992 and August 28, 1993). ... Led A.L. with .632 slugging percentage in 1993. ... Had 21-game hitting streaks (June 25-July 19 and August 8-31, 1996). ... Had 20-game hitting streak (August 20-September 9, 1998). ... Career major league grand slams: 7.
MISCELLANEOUS: Holds Texas Rangers all-time records for most runs (677), most hits (1,238), most doubles (246), most home runs (301) and most runs batted in (947).

Year Team (League)	Pos.	G	AB	R	H	2B	3B	HR	RBI	Avg.	BB	SO	SB	PO	A	E	Avg.
						BATTING								FIELDING			
1986— GC Rangers (GCL)......	OF	60	*233	24	56	4	1	0	36	.240	21	57	7	89	6	•6	.941
1987— Gastonia (S. Atl.).......	OF	127	509	69	135	21	2	14	74	.265	30	92	9	234	10	12	.953
1988— Charlotte (Fla. St.)......	OF	77	277	25	71	14	3	8	43	.256	25	64	5	139	5	4	.973
1989— Tulsa (Texas).............	OF	133	502	73	147	30	7	21	85	.293	31	98	1	292	15	9	.972
— Texas (A.L.)...............	OF	24	60	6	9	3	0	1	7	.150	6	17	0	53	0	2	.964
1990— Okla. City (A.A.).........	OF	128	496	78	128	29	4	*29	*101	.258	32	109	2	220	7	8	.966
— Texas (A.L.)...............	OF-DH	25	90	11	26	7	1	4	12	.289	2	18	0	33	0	0	1.000
1991— Texas (A.L.)...............	OF-DH	142	545	78	144	34	1	27	102	.264	42	118	4	310	6	6	.981
1992— Texas (A.L.)...............	OF-DH	155	584	77	152	24	2	*43	109	.260	35	143	0	379	9	10	.975
1993— Texas (A.L.)...............	OF-DH	140	536	105	166	33	1	*46	118	.310	37	99	4	265	5	4	.985
1994— Texas (A.L.)...............	OF	107	422	57	116	18	4	19	85	.275	30	66	6	223	9	2	.991
1995— Texas (A.L.)...............	DH-OF	90	352	57	104	20	2	27	82	.295	17	66	0	6	1	0	1.000
1996— Texas (A.L.)...............	OF-DH	134	541	89	170	33	2	47	144	.314	45	82	2	163	6	2	.988
1997— Texas (A.L.)...............	DH-OF	133	533	87	158	24	3	42	131	.296	33	107	0	128	6	4	.971
1998— Texas (A.L.)...............	OF-DH	154	606	110	193	*50	2	45	*157	.318	46	126	2	213	8	4	.982
Major league totals (10 years)		1104	4269	677	1238	246	18	301	947	.290	293	842	18	1773	50	34	.982

DIVISION SERIES RECORD

RECORDS: Holds career record for highest slugging average (20 or more at-bats)—.857. ... Shares single-series record for most home runs— 5 (1996). ... Shares single-game record for most home runs—2 (October 2, 1996).
NOTES: Shares postseason single-series record for most home runs—5 (1996).

Year Team (League)	Pos.	G	AB	R	H	2B	3B	HR	RBI	Avg.	BB	SO	SB	PO	A	E	Avg.
						BATTING								FIELDING			
1996— Texas (A.L.)	OF	4	16	5	7	0	0	5	9	.438	4	2	0	8	0	0	1.000
1998— Texas (A.L.)	OF	3	12	1	1	1	0	0	0	.083	0	3	0	8	0	0	1.000
Division series totals (2 years)		7	28	6	8	1	0	5	9	.286	4	5	0	16	0	0	1.000

ALL-STAR GAME RECORD

Year League	Pos.	AB	R	H	2B	3B	HR	RBI	Avg.	BB	SO	SB	PO	A	E	Avg.
					BATTING								FIELDING			
1993— American	OF	1	0	0	0	0	0	0	.000	1	1	0	1	0	0	1.000
1998— American	OF	3	0	0	0	0	0	1	.000	0	1	0	0	0	0	...
All-Star Game totals (2 years)		4	0	0	0	0	0	1	.000	1	2	0	1	0	0	1.000

GONZALEZ, LARIEL   P   ROCKIES

PERSONAL: Born May 25, 1976, in San Cristobal, Dominican Republic. ... 6-4/228. ... Throws right, bats right. ... Full name: Lariel Alfonso Gonzalez.
TRANSACTIONS/CAREER NOTES: Signed as non-drafted free agent by Colorado Rockies organization (May 19, 1993).
STATISTICAL NOTES: Tied for Northwest League lead with five balks in 1995.

Year Team (League)	W	L	Pct.	ERA	G	GS	CG	ShO	Sv.	IP	H	R	ER	BB	SO
1993— DSL Rockies......................	0	4	.000	9.38	14	7	0	0	1	24	32	34	25	46	17
1994— Ariz. Rockies (Ariz.)............	3	2	.600	4.71	16	1	0	0	0	28 2/3	28	24	15	21	23
1995— Portland (Northwest)............	3	4	.429	4.06	15	11	0	0	2	57 2/3	44	31	26	43	48
1996— Asheville (S. Atl.)................	1	1	.500	3.60	35	0	0	0	4	45	37	21	18	37	53
1997— Salem (Carolina).................	5	0	1.000	2.53	44	0	0	0	8	57	42	19	16	23	79
1998— New Haven (East.)..............	0	4	.000	4.19	58	0	0	0	22	58	46	30	27	40	63
— Colorado (N.L.)	0	0	...	0.00	1	0	0	0	0	1	0	0	0	0	0
Major league totals (1 year)........	0	0	...	0.00	1	0	0	0	0	1	0	0	0	0	0

GONZALEZ, LUIS   OF   DIAMONDBACKS

PERSONAL: Born September 3, 1967, in Tampa. ... 6-2/190. ... Bats left, throws right. ... Full name: Luis Emilio Gonzalez.
HIGH SCHOOL: Jefferson (Tampa).
COLLEGE: South Alabama.
TRANSACTIONS/CAREER NOTES: Selected by Houston Astros organization in fourth round of free-agent draft (June 1, 1988). ... On disabled list (May 26-July 5, 1989 and August 29-September 13, 1991). ... On Houston disabled list (July 21-August 5, 1992). ... Traded by Astros with C Scott Servais to Chicago Cubs for C Rick Wilkins (June 28, 1995). ... Granted free agency (December 7, 1996). ... Signed by Astros (December 19, 1996). ... Granted free agency (October 28, 1997). ... Signed by Detroit Tigers (December 9, 1997). ... Traded by Tigers to Arizona Diamondbacks for OF Karim Garcia (December 28, 1998).
STATISTICAL NOTES: Tied for Southern League lead with 12 sacrifice flies and nine intentional bases on balls received in 1990. ... Led N.L. with 10 sacrifice flies in 1993. ... Had 23-game hitting streak (May 26-June 20, 1997). ... Career major league grand slams: 1.

G

Year Team (League)	Pos.	G	AB	R	H	2B	3B	HR	RBI	Avg.	BB	SO	SB	PO	A	E	Avg.
						BATTING								FIELDING			
1988— Asheville (S. Atl.)........	3B	31	115	13	29	7	1	2	14	.252	12	17	2	19	62	6	.931
— Auburn (NY-Penn)....	3B-SS-1B	39	157	32	49	10	3	5	27	.312	12	19	2	37	83	13	.902
1989— Osceola (Fla. St.)........	DH	86	287	46	82	16	7	6	38	.286	37	49	2	...	...	...	...
1990— Columbus (Southern)....	1B-3B	138	495	86	131	30	6	•24	89	.265	54	100	27	1039	88	23	.980
— Houston (N.L.)........	3B-1B	12	21	1	4	2	0	0	0	.190	2	5	0	22	10	0	1.000
1991— Houston (N.L.)...........	OF	137	473	51	120	28	9	13	69	.254	40	101	10	294	6	5	.984
1992— Houston (N.L.)...........	OF	122	387	40	94	19	3	10	55	.243	24	52	7	261	5	2	.993
— Tucson (PCL)	OF	13	44	11	19	4	2	1	9	.432	5	7	4	26	0	1	.963
1993— Houston (N.L.)	OF	154	540	82	162	34	3	15	72	.300	47	83	20	347	10	8	.978
1994— Houston (N.L.)	OF	112	392	57	107	29	4	8	67	.273	49	57	15	228	5	2	.991
1995— Houston (N.L.)	OF	56	209	35	54	10	4	6	35	.258	18	30	1	94	2	2	.980
— Chicago (N.L.)■........	OF	77	262	34	76	19	4	7	34	.290	39	33	5	172	5	4	.978

		BATTING												FIELDING		
Year Team (League)	Pos.	G	AB	R	H	2B	3B	HR	RBI	Avg.	BB	SO	SB	PO	A	E	Avg.
1996—Chicago (N.L.)	OF-1B	146	483	70	131	30	4	15	79	.271	61	49	9	244	7	3	.988
1997—Houston (N.L.)■	OF-1B	152	550	78	142	31	2	10	68	.258	71	67	10	266	10	5	.982
1998—Detroit (A.L.)■	OF-DH	154	547	84	146	35	5	23	71	.267	57	62	12	232	8	3	.988
American League totals (1 year)		154	547	84	146	35	5	23	71	.267	57	62	12	232	8	3	.988
National League totals (8 years)		968	3317	448	890	202	33	84	479	.268	351	477	77	1928	60	31	.985
Major league totals (9 years)		1122	3864	532	1036	237	38	107	550	.268	408	539	89	2160	68	34	.985

DIVISION SERIES RECORD

		BATTING												FIELDING		
Year Team (League)	Pos.	G	AB	R	H	2B	3B	HR	RBI	Avg.	BB	SO	SB	PO	A	E	Avg.
1997—Houston (N.L.)	OF	3	12	0	4	0	0	0	0	.333	0	1	0	13	1	1	.933

GOOCH, ARNOLD   P   DODGERS

PERSONAL: Born November 12, 1976, in Levittown, Pa. ... 6-2/210. ... Throws right, bats right. ... Full name: Arnold Walter Gooch.
HIGH SCHOOL: Neshaminy (Langhorne, Pa.).
TRANSACTIONS/CAREER NOTES: Selected by Colorado Rockies organization in ninth round of free-agent draft (June 3, 1994). ... Traded by Rockies to New York Mets for P Bret Saberhagen and a player to be named later (July 31, 1995); Rockies acquired P David Swanson to complete deal (August 4, 1995). ... On Binghamton disabled list (May 1-May 10, 1998). ... Traded by Mets with C Todd Hundley to Los Angeles Dodgers for C Charles Johnson and OF Roger Cedeno (December 1, 1998).

Year Team (League)	W	L	Pct.	ERA	G	GS	CG	ShO	Sv.	IP	H	R	ER	BB	SO
1994—Ariz. Rockies (Ariz.)	2	4	.333	2.64	15	9	0	0	0	58	45	28	17	16	66
1995—Asheville (S. Atl.)	5	8	.385	2.94	21	21	1	1	0	128²/₃	111	51	42	57	117
—Columbia (S. Atl.)■	2	3	.400	4.46	6	6	0	0	0	38¹/₃	39	25	19	15	34
1996—St. Lucie (Fla. St.)	12	12	.500	2.58	26	26	2	0	0	167²/₃	131	74	48	51	141
1997—Binghamton (Eastern)	10	•12	.455	5.09	27	27	4	1	0	161	179	106	91	76	98
1998—Binghamton (Eastern)	11	•14	.440	3.90	27	27	2	1	0	163²/₃	164	92	71	60	116

GOODEN, DWIGHT   P   INDIANS

PERSONAL: Born November 16, 1964, in Tampa. ... 6-3/210. ... Throws right, bats right. ... Full name: Dwight Eugene Gooden. ... Uncle of Gary Sheffield, outfielder, Los Angeles Dodgers.
HIGH SCHOOL: Hillsborough (Tampa).
TRANSACTIONS/CAREER NOTES: Selected by New York Mets organization in first round (fifth pick overall) of free-agent draft (June 7, 1982). ... On New York disabled list (April 1-June 5, 1987); included rehabilitation assignment to Tidewater (May 12-17 and May 21-June 1). ... On disabled list (July 2-September 2, 1989; August 24, 1991-remainder of season and July 18-August 8, 1992). ... On suspended list (September 2-7, 1993). ... On New York disabled list (April 22-June 9, 1994); included rehabilitation assignments to Norfolk (May 30-June 4) and Binghamton (June 4-9). ... On suspended list (June 28, 1994-remainder of season). ... Granted free agency (October 24, 1994). ... On suspended list (November 4, 1994-entire 1995 season). ... Signed by New York Yankees (February 20, 1996). ... On New York disabled list (April 11-June 15, 1997); included rehabilitation assignment to Norwich (May 18-June 2). ... Granted free agency (November 1, 1997). ... Signed by Cleveland Indians (December 8, 1997). ... On Cleveland disabled list (March 22-May 20, 1998); included rehabilitation assignment to Buffalo (May 3-20).
RECORDS: Holds major league rookie-season record for most strikeouts—276 (1984). ... Holds N.L. record for most strikeouts in three consecutive games—43 (September 7 [11], 12 [16] and 17 [16], 1984).
HONORS: Named Carolina League Pitcher of the Year (1983). ... Named N.L. Rookie Pitcher of the Year by THE SPORTING NEWS (1984). ... Named N.L. Rookie of the Year by Baseball Writers' Association of America (1984). ... Named N.L. Pitcher of the Year by THE SPORTING NEWS (1985). ... Named righthanded pitcher on THE SPORTING NEWS N.L. All-Star team (1985). ... Named N.L. Cy Young Award winner by Baseball Writers' Association of America (1985). ... Named pitcher on THE SPORTING NEWS N.L. Silver Slugger team (1992).
STATISTICAL NOTES: Pitched 10-0 one-hit, complete-game victory against Chicago (September 7, 1984). ... Struck out 16 batters in one game (September 12 and September 17, 1984; August 20, 1985). ... Tied for N.L. lead with seven balks in 1984. ... Struck out 15 batters in one game (May 11, 1990). ... Pitched 2-0 no-hit victory against Seattle (May 14, 1996).
MISCELLANEOUS: Appeared in one game as pinch runner (1990). ... Singled and made an out in two games as pinch hitter (1992). ... Tripled with an RBI in only appearance as pinch hitter (1993).

Year Team (League)	W	L	Pct.	ERA	G	GS	CG	ShO	Sv.	IP	H	R	ER	BB	SO
1982—Kingsport (Appalachian)	5	4	.556	2.47	9	9	4	2	0	65²/₃	53	34	18	25	66
—Little Falls (NYP)	0	1	.000	4.15	2	2	0	0	0	13	11	6	6	3	18
1983—Lynchburg (Carolina)	*19	4	.826	*2.50	27	27	10	*6	0	191	121	58	53	*112	*300
1984—New York (N.L.)	17	9	.654	2.60	31	31	7	3	0	218	161	72	63	73	*276
1985—New York (N.L.)	*24	4	.857	*1.53	35	35	*16	8	0	276²/₃	198	51	47	69	*268
1986—New York (N.L.)	17	6	.739	2.84	33	33	12	2	0	250	197	92	79	80	200
1987—Tidewater (Int'l)	3	0	1.000	2.05	4	4	1	0	0	22	20	7	5	9	24
—Lynchburg (Carolina)	0	0	. . .	0.00	1	1	0	0	0	4	2	0	0	2	3
—New York (N.L.)	15	7	.682	3.21	25	25	7	3	0	179²/₃	162	68	64	53	148
1988—New York (N.L.)	18	9	.667	3.19	34	34	10	3	0	248¹/₃	242	98	88	57	175
1989—New York (N.L.)	9	4	.692	2.89	19	17	0	0	1	118¹/₃	93	42	38	47	101
1990—New York (N.L.)	19	7	.731	3.83	34	34	2	1	0	232²/₃	229	106	99	70	223
1991—New York (N.L.)	13	7	.650	3.60	27	27	3	1	0	190	185	80	76	56	150
1992—New York (N.L.)	10	13	.435	3.67	31	31	3	0	0	206	197	93	84	70	145
1993—New York (N.L.)	12	15	.444	3.45	29	29	7	2	0	208²/₃	188	89	80	61	149
1994—New York (N.L.)	3	4	.429	6.31	7	7	0	0	0	41¹/₃	46	32	29	15	40
—Norfolk (Int'l)	0	0	. . .	0.00	1	1	0	0	0	3	0	0	0	1	4
—Binghamton (Eastern)	1	0	1.000	0.00	1	1	0	0	0	5	2	0	0	1	4
1995—						Out of organized baseball.									
1996—New York (A.L.)■	11	7	.611	5.01	29	29	1	1	0	170²/₃	169	101	95	88	126
1997—New York (A.L.)	9	5	.643	4.91	20	19	0	0	0	106¹/₃	116	61	58	53	66
—Norwich (Eastern)	3	0	1.000	3.00	3	3	0	0	0	18	13	6	6	5	14
—Columbus (Int'l)	1	1	.500	3.75	2	2	0	0	0	12	7	5	5	4	10

G

Year Team (League)	W	L	Pct.	ERA	G	GS	CG	ShO	Sv.	IP	H	R	ER	BB	SO
1998—Buffalo (Int'l)■	1	2	.333	9.00	4	4	0	0	0	16	23	16	16	7	18
—Cleveland (A.L.)	8	6	.571	3.76	23	23	0	0	0	134	135	56	56	51	83
A.L. totals (3 years)	28	18	.609	4.58	72	71	1	1	0	411	420	221	209	192	275
N.L. totals (11 years)	157	85	.649	3.10	305	303	67	23	1	2169 2/3	1898	823	747	651	1875
Major league totals (14 years)	185	103	.642	3.33	377	374	68	24	1	2580 2/3	2318	1044	956	843	2150

DIVISION SERIES RECORD

Year Team (League)	W	L	Pct.	ERA	G	GS	CG	ShO	Sv.	IP	H	R	ER	BB	SO
1997—New York (A.L.)	0	0	...	1.59	1	1	0	0	0	5 2/3	5	1	1	3	5
1998—Cleveland (A.L.)	0	0	...	54.00	1	1	0	0	0	1/3	1	2	2	2	1
Div. series totals (2 years)	0	0	...	4.50	2	2	0	0	0	6	6	3	3	5	6

CHAMPIONSHIP SERIES RECORD

RECORDS: Holds single-series record for most strikeouts—20 (1988). ... Shares N.L. single-game record for most innings pitched—10 (October 14, 1986).

Year Team (League)	W	L	Pct.	ERA	G	GS	CG	ShO	Sv.	IP	H	R	ER	BB	SO
1986—New York (N.L.)	0	1	.000	1.06	2	2	0	0	0	17	16	2	2	5	9
1988—New York (N.L.)	0	0	...	2.95	3	2	0	0	0	18 1/3	10	6	6	8	20
1998—Cleveland (A.L.)	0	1	.000	5.79	1	1	0	0	0	4 2/3	3	3	3	3	3
Champ. series totals (3 years)	0	2	.000	2.48	6	5	0	0	0	40	29	11	11	16	32

WORLD SERIES RECORD

NOTES: Member of World Series championship team (1986). ... Member of World Series championship team (1996); inactive.

Year Team (League)	W	L	Pct.	ERA	G	GS	CG	ShO	Sv.	IP	H	R	ER	BB	SO
1986—New York (N.L.)	0	2	.000	8.00	2	2	0	0	0	9	17	10	8	4	9

ALL-STAR GAME RECORD

RECORDS: Holds career record for most balks—2. ... Shares career record for most games lost—2.

Year League	W	L	Pct.	ERA	GS	CG	ShO	Sv.	IP	H	R	ER	BB	SO
1984—National	0	0	...	0.00	0	0	0	0	2	1	0	0	0	3
1985—National					Did not play.									
1986—National	0	1	.000	6.00	1	0	0	0	3	3	2	2	0	2
1988—National	0	1	.000	3.00	1	0	0	0	3	3	1	1	1	1
All-Star totals (3 years)	0	2	.000	3.38	2	0	0	0	8	7	3	3	1	6

GOODWIN, CURTIS   OF   ROCKIES

PERSONAL: Born September 30, 1972, in Oakland. ... 5-11/180. ... Bats left, throws left. ... Full name: Curtis LaMar Goodwin.

HIGH SCHOOL: San Leandro (Calif.).

TRANSACTIONS/CAREER NOTES: Selected by Baltimore Orioles organization in 12th round of free-agent draft (June 3, 1991). ... On Baltimore disabled list (August 20-September 4, 1995). ... Traded by Orioles with OF Trovin Valdez to Cincinnati Reds for P David Wells (December 26, 1995). ... Traded by Reds to Colorado Rockies for P Mark Hutton (December 10, 1997).

STATISTICAL NOTES: Led Midwest League outfielders with 327 total chances and seven double plays in 1992. ... Led Eastern League with 13 sacrifice hits in 1994. ... Led Eastern League outfielders with 323 total chances in 1994.

Year Team (League)	Pos.	G	AB	R	H	2B	3B	HR	RBI	Avg.	BB	SO	SB	PO	A	E	Avg.
1991—GC Orioles (GCL)	OF	48	151	32	39	5	0	0	9	.258	38	25	26	77	5	1	.988
1992—Kane County (Midw.)	OF	134	*542	85	153	7	5	1	42	.282	38	106	52	301	15	11	.966
1993—Frederick (Carolina)	OF	•138	*555	*98	•156	15	*10	2	42	.281	52	90	*61	271	9	7	.976
1994—Bowie (Eastern)	OF	*142	*597	*105	*171	18	8	2	37	.286	40	78	*59	*301	12	10	.969
1995—Rochester (Int'l)	OF	36	140	24	37	3	3	0	7	.264	12	15	17	81	1	3	.965
—Baltimore (A.L.)	OF-DH	87	289	40	76	11	3	1	24	.263	15	53	22	202	1	2	.990
1996—Indianapolis (A.A.)■	OF	91	337	57	88	19	4	2	30	.261	54	67	*40	172	4	4	.978
—Cincinnati (N.L.)	OF	49	136	20	31	3	0	0	5	.228	19	34	15	64	0	2	.970
1997—Indianapolis (A.A.)	OF	30	116	14	32	4	1	1	7	.276	15	20	11	57	2	0	1.000
—Cincinnati (N.L.)	OF	85	265	27	67	11	0	1	12	.253	24	53	22	159	3	0	1.000
1998—Colorado (N.L.)■	OF	119	159	27	39	7	0	1	6	.245	16	40	5	118	1	2	.983
American League totals (1 year)		87	289	40	76	11	3	1	24	.263	15	53	22	202	1	2	.990
National League totals (3 years)		253	560	74	137	21	0	2	23	.245	59	127	42	341	4	4	.989
Major league totals (4 years)		340	849	114	213	32	3	3	47	.251	74	180	64	543	5	6	.989

GOODWIN, TOM   OF   RANGERS

G

PERSONAL: Born July 27, 1968, in Fresno, Calif. ... 6-1/175. ... Bats left, throws right. ... Full name: Thomas Jones Goodwin.

HIGH SCHOOL: Central (Fresno, Calif.).

COLLEGE: Fresno State.

TRANSACTIONS/CAREER NOTES: Selected by Pittsburgh Pirates organization in sixth round of free-agent draft (June 2, 1986); did not sign. ... Selected by Los Angeles Dodgers organization in first round (22nd pick overall) of free-agent draft (June 5, 1989). ... Claimed on waivers by Kansas City Royals (January 6, 1994). ... Traded by Royals to Texas Rangers for 3B Dean Palmer (July 25, 1997).

HONORS: Named outfielder on THE SPORTING NEWS college All-America team (1989).

STATISTICAL NOTES: Tied for Pacific Coast League lead in caught stealing with 23 in 1991. ... Led American Association in caught stealing with 20 in 1994. ... Led A.L. in sacrifice hits with 14 in 1995 and 21 in 1996. ... Led A.L. in caught stealing with 22 in 1996 and 20 in 1998.

MISCELLANEOUS: Member of 1988 U.S. Olympic baseball team.

Year Team (League)	Pos.	G	AB	R	H	2B	3B	HR	RBI	Avg.	BB	SO	SB	PO	A	E	Avg.
1989—Great Falls (Pio.)	OF	63	240	*55	74	12	3	2	33	.308	28	30	*60	67	3	1	.986
1990—San Antonio (Tex.)	OF	102	428	76	119	15	4	0	28	.278	38	72	*60	264	7	3	*.989
—Bakersfield (Calif.)	OF	32	134	24	39	6	2	0	13	.291	11	22	22	55	2	0	1.000

Year	Team (League)	Pos.	G	AB	R	H	2B	3B	HR	RBI	Avg.	BB	SO	SB	PO	A	E	Avg.
							BATTING								FIELDING			
1991— Albuquerque (PCL).....		OF	132	509	84	139	19	4	1	45	.273	59	83	48	284	6	3	.990
— Los Angeles (N.L.).....		OF	16	7	3	1	0	0	0	0	.143	0	0	1	8	0	0	1.000
1992— Albuquerque (PCL).....		OF	82	319	48	96	10	4	2	28	.301	37	47	27	184	5	1	.995
— Los Angeles (N.L.).....		OF	57	73	15	17	1	1	0	3	.233	6	10	7	43	0	0	1.000
1993— Los Angeles (N.L.).....		OF	30	17	6	5	1	0	0	1	.294	1	4	1	8	0	0	1.000
— Albuquerque (PCL).....		OF	85	289	48	75	5	5	1	28	.260	30	51	21	145	1	2	.986
1994— Kansas City (A.L.)■..		DH-OF	2	2	0	0	0	0	0	0	.000	0	1	0	1	0	0	1.000
— Omaha (A.A.).............		OF	113	429	67	132	17	7	2	34	.308	23	60	*50	276	3	2	.993
1995— Kansas City (A.L.)		OF-DH	133	480	72	138	16	3	4	28	.288	38	72	50	292	6	3	.990
1996— Kansas City (A.L.)		OF-DH	143	524	80	148	14	4	1	35	.282	39	79	66	303	7	5	.984
1997— Kansas City (A.L.)		OF	97	367	51	100	13	4	2	22	.272	19	51	34	232	3	1	.996
— Texas (A.L.)■............		OF	53	207	39	49	13	2	0	17	.237	25	37	16	138	3	2	.986
1998— Texas (A.L.)		OF-DH	154	520	102	151	13	3	2	33	.290	73	90	38	370	5	3	.992
American League totals (5 years)			582	2100	344	586	69	16	9	135	.279	194	330	204	1336	24	14	.990
National League totals (3 years)			103	97	24	23	2	1	0	4	.237	7	14	9	59	0	0	1.000
Major league totals (8 years)			685	2197	368	609	71	17	9	139	.277	201	344	213	1395	24	14	.990

DIVISION SERIES RECORD

Year	Team (League)	Pos.	G	AB	R	H	2B	3B	HR	RBI	Avg.	BB	SO	SB	PO	A	E	Avg.
							BATTING								FIELDING			
1998— Texas (A.L.)		OF	2	4	0	1	0	0	0	0	.250	0	1	0	1	0	0	1.000

GORDON, TOM   P   RED SOX

PERSONAL: Born November 18, 1967, in Sebring, Fla. ... 5-9/180. ... Throws right, bats right. ... Full name: Thomas Gordon. ... Brother of Tony Gordon, minor league pitcher (1988-94).

HIGH SCHOOL: Avon Park (Fla.).

TRANSACTIONS/CAREER NOTES: Selected by Kansas City Royals organization in sixth round of free-agent draft (June 2, 1986). ... On disabled list (August 12-September 1, 1992 and May 8-24, 1995). ... Granted free agency (October 30, 1995). ... Signed by Boston Red Sox (December 21, 1995).

HONORS: Named A.L. Rookie Pitcher of the Year by THE SPORTING NEWS (1989). ... Named A.L. Fireman of the Year by THE SPORTING NEWS (1998).

STATISTICAL NOTES: Tied for Northwest League lead with four balks in 1987.

MISCELLANEOUS: Appeared in one game as pinch runner (1991). ... Appeared in one game as pinch runner (1995).

Year	Team (League)	W	L	Pct.	ERA	G	GS	CG	ShO	Sv.	IP	H	R	ER	BB	SO
1986— GC Royals (GCL)		3	1	.750	1.02	9	7	2	1	0	44	31	12	5	23	47
— Omaha (Am. Assoc.)..........		0	0	...	47.25	1	0	0	0	0	1 1/3	6	7	7	2	3
1987— Eugene (Northwest)		•9	0	•1.000	2.86	15	13	0	0	1	72 1/3	48	33	23	47	91
— Fort Myers (Fla. St.)		1	0	1.000	2.63	3	3	0	0	0	13 2/3	5	4	4	17	11
1988— Appleton (Midwest)		7	5	.583	2.06	17	17	5	1	0	118	69	30	27	43	*172
— Memphis (Sou.)		6	0	1.000	0.38	6	6	2	2	0	47 1/3	16	3	2	17	62
— Omaha (Am. Assoc.)		3	0	1.000	1.33	3	3	0	0	0	20 1/3	11	3	3	15	29
— Kansas City (A.L.)		0	2	.000	5.17	5	2	0	0	0	15 2/3	16	9	9	7	18
1989— Kansas City (A.L.)		17	9	.654	3.64	49	16	1	1	1	163	122	67	66	86	153
1990— Kansas City (A.L.)		12	11	.522	3.73	32	32	6	1	0	195 1/3	192	99	81	99	175
1991— Kansas City (A.L.)		9	14	.391	3.87	45	14	1	0	1	158	129	76	68	87	167
1992— Kansas City (A.L.)		6	10	.375	4.59	40	11	0	0	0	117 2/3	116	67	60	55	98
1993— Kansas City (A.L.)		12	6	.667	3.58	48	14	2	0	1	155 2/3	125	65	62	77	143
1994— Kansas City (A.L.)		11	7	.611	4.35	24	24	0	0	0	155 1/3	136	79	75	87	126
1995— Kansas City (A.L.)		12	12	.500	4.43	31	31	2	0	0	189	204	110	93	89	119
1996— Boston (A.L.)■............		12	9	.571	5.59	34	34	4	1	0	215 2/3	249	143	*134	105	171
1997— Boston (A.L.)		6	10	.375	3.74	42	25	2	1	0	182 2/3	155	85	76	78	159
1998— Boston (A.L.)		7	4	.636	2.72	73	0	0	0	*46	79 1/3	55	24	24	25	78
Major league totals (11 years)		104	94	.525	4.14	423	203	18	4	60	1627 1/3	1499	824	748	795	1407

DIVISION SERIES RECORD

Year	Team (League)	W	L	Pct.	ERA	G	GS	CG	ShO	Sv.	IP	H	R	ER	BB	SO
1998— Boston (A.L.)...................		0	1	.000	9.00	2	0	0	0	0	3	4	3	3	4	1

ALL-STAR GAME RECORD

Year	League	W	L	Pct.	ERA	GS	CG	ShO	Sv.	IP	H	R	ER	BB	SO
1998— American.........................		0	0	...	18.00	0	0	0	0	1	3	2	2	1	0

G GORECKI, RICK   P   DEVIL RAYS

PERSONAL: Born August 27, 1973, in Evergreen Park, Ill. ... 6-3/167. ... Throws right, bats right. ... Full name: Richard John Gorecki.

HIGH SCHOOL: Oak Forest (Ill.).

TRANSACTIONS/CAREER NOTES: Selected by Los Angeles Dodgers organization in 10th round of free-agent draft (June 3, 1991). ... On disabled list (May 27-June 3 and June 20-July 17, 1994). ... On Los Angeles disabled list (April 23, 1995-entire season); included rehabilitation assignments to Vero Beach (June 26-29 and July 9-August 3). ... On disabled list (March 25, 1996-entire season). ... Selected by Tampa Bay Devil Rays in second round (40th pick overall) of expansion draft (November 18, 1997). ... On Tampa Bay disabled list (April 18, 1998-remainder of season); included rehabilitation assignments to Gulf Coast Devil Rays (June 24-July 4) and St. Petersburg (July 5-20).

Year	Team (League)	W	L	Pct.	ERA	G	GS	CG	ShO	Sv.	IP	H	R	ER	BB	SO
1991— Great Falls (Pio.)		0	3	.000	4.41	13	10	0	0	0	51	44	34	25	27	56
1992— Bakersfield (California)		11	7	.611	4.05	25	24	0	0	0	129	122	68	58	90	115
1993— San Antonio (Tex.)		6	9	.400	3.35	26	26	0	0	0	156	136	76	58	62	118
1994— Albuquerque (PCL)		8	6	.571	5.07	22	21	0	0	0	103	119	65	58	60	73
1995— Vero Beach (FSL)		1	2	.333	0.67	6	5	0	0	0	27	19	6	2	9	24
1996—													Did not play.			

Year	Team (League)	W	L	Pct.	ERA	G	GS	CG	ShO	Sv.	IP	H	R	ER	BB	SO
1997—	San Bernardino (Calif.).......	2	3	.400	3.88	14	14	0	0	0	51	38	22	22	32	58
	—San Antonio (Tex.)	4	2	.667	1.39	7	7	0	0	0	45 1/3	26	8	7	15	33
	—Los Angeles (N.L.)	1	0	1.000	15.00	4	1	0	0	0	6	9	10	10	6	6
1998—	Tampa Bay (A.L.)■.............	1	2	.333	4.86	3	3	0	0	0	16 2/3	15	9	9	10	7
	—GC Devil Rays (GCL)	0	0	. . .	0.00	2	2	0	0	0	5	3	0	0	2	5
	—St. Petersburg (FSL)	0	0	. . .	0.00	1	1	0	0	0	4 2/3	4	0	0	1	7
A.L. totals (1 year)......................		1	2	.333	4.86	3	3	0	0	0	16 2/3	15	9	9	10	7
N.L. totals (1 year)......................		1	0	1.000	15.00	4	1	0	0	0	6	9	10	10	6	6
Major league totals (2 years)......		2	2	.500	7.54	7	4	0	0	0	22 2/3	24	19	19	16	13

GRACE, MARK   1B   CUBS

PERSONAL: Born June 28, 1964, in Winston-Salem, N.C. ... 6-2/200. ... Bats left, throws left. ... Full name: Mark Eugene Grace.
HIGH SCHOOL: Tustin (Calif.).
JUNIOR COLLEGE: Saddleback Community College (Calif.).
COLLEGE: San Diego State.
TRANSACTIONS/CAREER NOTES: Selected by Minnesota Twins organization in 15th round of free-agent draft (January 17, 1984); did not sign. ... Selected by Chicago Cubs organization in 24th round of free-agent draft (June 3, 1985). ... On disabled list (June 5-23, 1989). ... Granted free agency (October 15, 1994). ... Re-signed by Cubs (April 7, 1995). ... Granted free agency (November 3, 1995). ... Re-signed by Cubs (December 19, 1995). ... On disabled list (June 11-28, 1996 and April 4-19, 1997).
RECORDS: Holds major league single-season record for fewest double plays by first baseman (150 or more games)—82 (1998). ... Shares major league record for most assists by first baseman in one inning—3 (May 23, 1990, fourth inning). ... Holds N.L. single-season record for most assists by first baseman—180 (1990).
HONORS: Named Eastern League Most Valuable Player (1987). ... Named N.L. Rookie Player of the Year by THE SPORTING NEWS (1988). ... Won N.L. Gold Glove at first base (1992-93 and 1995-96).
STATISTICAL NOTES: Led Midwest League first basemen with 103 double plays in 1986. ... Led Eastern League with .545 slugging percentage in 1987. ... Led N.L. first basemen with 1,695 total chances in 1991, 1,725 in 1992 and 1,573 in 1993. ... Tied for N.L. lead in grounding into double plays with 25 in 1993. ... Led N.L. first basemen with 134 double plays in 1993. ... Hit for the cycle (May 9, 1993).

									BATTING						FIELDING		
Year	Team (League)	Pos.	G	AB	R	H	2B	3B	HR	RBI	Avg.	BB	SO	SB	PO	A	E	Avg.
1986—	Peoria (Midwest)........	1B-OF	126	465	81	159	30	4	15	95	*.342	60	28	6	1050	69	13	.989
1987—	Pittsfield (Eastern)......	1B	123	453	81	151	29	8	17	*101	.333	48	24	5	1054	*96	6	*.995
1988—	Iowa (Am. Assoc.)......	1B	21	67	11	17	4	0	0	14	.254	13	4	1	189	20	1	.995
	—Chicago (N.L.)	1B	134	486	65	144	23	4	7	57	.296	60	43	3	1182	87	•17	.987
1989—	Chicago (N.L.)	1B	142	510	74	160	28	3	13	79	.314	80	42	14	1230	126	6	.996
1990—	Chicago (N.L.)	1B	157	589	72	182	32	1	9	82	.309	59	54	15	1324	*180	12	.992
1991—	Chicago (N.L.)	1B	160	*619	87	169	28	5	8	58	.273	70	53	3	*1520	*167	8	.995
1992—	Chicago (N.L.)	1B	158	603	72	185	37	5	9	79	.307	72	36	6	*1580	*141	4	.998
1993—	Chicago (N.L.)	1B	155	594	86	193	39	4	14	98	.325	71	32	8	*1456	112	5	.997
1994—	Chicago (N.L.)	1B	106	403	55	120	23	3	6	44	.298	48	41	0	925	78	7	.993
1995—	Chicago (N.L.)	1B	143	552	97	180	*51	3	16	92	.326	65	46	6	1211	114	7	.995
1996—	Chicago (N.L.)	1B	142	547	88	181	39	1	9	75	.331	62	41	2	1259	107	4	.997
1997—	Chicago (N.L.)	1B	151	555	87	177	32	5	13	78	.319	88	45	2	1202	120	6	.995
1998—	Chicago (N.L.)	1B	158	595	92	184	39	3	17	89	.309	93	56	4	1279	122	8	.994
Major league totals (11 years)			1606	6053	875	1875	371	37	121	831	.310	768	489	63	14168	1354	84	.995

DIVISION SERIES RECORD

									BATTING						FIELDING		
Year	Team (League)	Pos.	G	AB	R	H	2B	3B	HR	RBI	Avg.	BB	SO	SB	PO	A	E	Avg.
1998—	Chicago (N.L.)	1B	3	12	0	1	0	0	0	1	.083	0	2	0	20	2	0	1.000

CHAMPIONSHIP SERIES RECORD

NOTES: Hit home run in first at-bat (October 4, 1989).

									BATTING						FIELDING		
Year	Team (League)	Pos.	G	AB	R	H	2B	3B	HR	RBI	Avg.	BB	SO	SB	PO	A	E	Avg.
1989—	Chicago (N.L.)	1B	5	17	3	11	3	1	1	8	.647	4	1	1	44	3	0	1.000

ALL-STAR GAME RECORD

								BATTING						FIELDING		
Year	League	Pos.	AB	R	H	2B	3B	HR	RBI	Avg.	BB	SO	SB	PO	A	E	Avg.
1993—	National	DH	3	0	0	0	0	0	0	.000	0	0	0	. . .	. . .	. . .	. . .
1995—	National	1B	0	0	0	0	0	0	0	. . .	0	0	0	1	0	0	1.000
1997—	National	1B	1	0	0	0	0	0	0	.000	0	0	0	1	0	0	1.000
All-Star Game totals (3 years)			4	0	0	0	0	0	0	.000	0	0	0	2	0	0	1.000

G

GRACE, MIKE   P   PHILLIES

PERSONAL: Born June 20, 1970, in Joliet, Ill. ... 6-4/219. ... Throws right, bats right. ... Full name: Michael James Grace.
HIGH SCHOOL: Joliet (Ill.) Catholic.
COLLEGE: Bradley.
TRANSACTIONS/CAREER NOTES: Selected by Philadelphia Phillies organization in 10th round of free-agent draft (June 3, 1991). ... On disabled list (April 9-June 8, July 8-20 and July 27, 1992-remainder of season; April 8, 1993-entire season; April 7-June 14, 1994; and June 3, 1996-remainder of season). ... On Philadelphia disabled list (March 27-June 25, 1997); included rehabilitation assignments to Reading (May 28-June 14) and Scranton/Wilkes-Barre (June 14-25).

Year	Team (League)	W	L	Pct.	ERA	G	GS	CG	ShO	Sv.	IP	H	R	ER	BB	SO
1991—	Batavia (N.Y.-Penn)	1	2	.333	1.39	6	6	0	0	0	32 1/3	20	9	5	14	36
	—Spartanburg (SAL)	3	1	.750	1.89	6	6	0	0	0	33 1/3	24	7	7	9	23

Year— Team (League)	W	L	Pct.	ERA	G	GS	CG	ShO	Sv.	IP	H	R	ER	BB	SO
1992— Spartanburg (SAL)	0	1	.000	4.94	6	6	0	0	0	27 1/3	25	16	15	8	21
1993—							Did not play.								
1994— Spartanburg (SAL)	5	5	.500	4.82	15	15	0	0	0	80 1/3	84	50	43	20	45
1995— Reading (Eastern)	13	6	.684	3.54	24	24	2	0	0	147 1/3	137	65	58	35	118
— Scran./W.B. (Int'l)	2	0	1.000	1.59	2	2	1	0	0	17	17	3	3	2	13
— Philadelphia (N.L.)	1	1	.500	3.18	2	2	0	0	0	11 1/3	10	4	4	4	7
1996— Philadelphia (N.L.)	7	2	.778	3.49	12	12	1	1	0	80	72	33	31	16	49
1997— Reading (Eastern)	1	3	.250	5.75	4	4	0	0	0	20 1/3	28	17	13	6	10
— Scran./W.B. (Int'l)	5	6	.455	4.56	12	12	4	0	0	75	84	43	38	27	55
— Philadelphia (N.L.)	3	2	.600	3.46	6	6	1	1	0	39	32	16	15	10	26
1998— Philadelphia (N.L.)	4	7	.364	5.48	21	15	0	0	0	90 1/3	116	61	55	30	46
— Scran./W.B. (Int'l)	3	6	.333	5.04	11	10	2	0	0	75	92	44	42	18	39
Major league totals (4 years)	15	12	.556	4.28	41	35	2	2	0	220 2/3	230	114	105	60	128

GRAFFANINO, TONY   2B   BRAVES

PERSONAL: Born June 6, 1972, in Amityville, N.Y. ... 6-1/195. ... Bats right, throws right. ... Full name: Anthony Joseph Graffanino. ... Name pronounced GRAF-uh-NEE-noh..
HIGH SCHOOL: East Islip (Islip Terrace, N.Y.).
TRANSACTIONS/CAREER NOTES: Selected by Atlanta Braves organization in 10th round of free-agent draft (June 4, 1990). ... On disabled list (July 3, 1995-remainder of season).
STATISTICAL NOTES: Led Pioneer League shortstops with 41 double plays in 1991. ... Led Carolina League second basemen with .968 fielding percentage in 1993. ... Led International League second basemen with 441 total chances in 1996.

							BATTING								FIELDING		
Year— Team (League)	Pos.	G	AB	R	H	2B	3B	HR	RBI	Avg.	BB	SO	SB	PO	A	E	Avg.
1990— Pulaski (Appalachian).	SS	42	131	23	27	5	1	0	11	.206	26	17	6	60	105	24	.873
1991— Idaho Falls (Pio.)	SS	66	274	53	95	16	4	4	56	.347	27	37	19	112	187	*29	.912
1992— Macon (S. Atl.)	2B	112	400	50	96	15	5	10	31	.240	50	84	9	178	239	17	.961
1993— Durham (Carolina)......	2B-SS	123	459	78	126	30	5	15	69	.275	45	78	24	186	263	15	†.968
1994— Greenville (Southern) .	2B	124	440	66	132	28	3	7	52	.300	50	53	29	254	326	14	.976
1995— Richmond (Int'l)	2B	50	179	20	34	6	0	4	17	.190	15	49	2	102	127	4	.983
1996— Richmond (Int'l)	2B	96	353	57	100	29	2	7	33	.283	34	72	11	*215	216	10	.977
— Atlanta (N.L.)	2B	22	46	7	8	1	1	0	2	.174	4	13	0	24	39	2	.969
1997— Atlanta (N.L.)..............	2-3-S-1	104	186	33	48	9	1	8	20	.258	26	46	6	90	180	5	.982
1998— Atlanta (N.L.)..............	2B-SS-3B	105	289	32	61	14	1	5	22	.211	24	68	1	139	227	11	.971
Major league totals (3 years)		231	521	72	117	24	3	13	44	.225	54	127	7	253	446	18	.975

DIVISION SERIES RECORD

							BATTING								FIELDING		
Year— Team (League)	Pos.	G	AB	R	H	2B	3B	HR	RBI	Avg.	BB	SO	SB	PO	A	E	Avg.
1997— Atlanta (N.L.)..............	2B	3	3	0	0	0	0	0	0	.000	2	1	0	1	6	0	1.000
1998— Atlanta (N.L.)..............	PH	1	0	0	0	0	0	0	0	...	0	0	0	...	...	...	...
Division series totals (2 years)		4	3	0	0	0	0	0	0	.000	2	1	0	1	6	0	1.000

CHAMPIONSHIP SERIES RECORD

							BATTING								FIELDING		
Year— Team (League)	Pos.	G	AB	R	H	2B	3B	HR	RBI	Avg.	BB	SO	SB	PO	A	E	Avg.
1997— Atlanta (N.L.)..............	2B	3	8	1	2	1	0	0	0	.250	0	3	0	4	2	0	1.000
1998— Atlanta (N.L.)..............	PH-2B	4	3	2	1	1	0	0	1	.333	2	1	0	2	5	0	1.000
Championship series totals (2 years)		7	11	3	3	2	0	0	1	.273	2	4	0	6	7	0	1.000

GRAVES, DANNY   P   REDS

PERSONAL: Born August 7, 1973, in Saigon, Vietnam. ... 5-11/185. ... Throws right, bats right. ... Full name: Daniel Peter Graves.
HIGH SCHOOL: Brandon (Fla.).
COLLEGE: Miami (Fla.).
TRANSACTIONS/CAREER NOTES: Selected by Cleveland Indians organization in fourth round of free-agent draft (June 2, 1994). ... Traded by Indians with P Jim Crowell, P Scott Winchester and IF Damian Jackson to Cincinnati Reds for P John Smiley and IF Jeff Branson (July 31, 1997).
MISCELLANEOUS: Injured knee during 1994 College World Series and did not play professional baseball during 1994 season.

Year— Team (League)	W	L	Pct.	ERA	G	GS	CG	ShO	Sv.	IP	H	R	ER	BB	SO
1995— Kinston (Carolina)	3	1	.750	0.82	38	0	0	0	21	44	30	11	4	12	46
— Cant./Akr. (Eastern)	1	0	1.000	0.00	17	0	0	0	10	23 1/3	10	1	0	2	11
— Buffalo (A.A.)	0	0	...	3.00	3	0	0	0	0	3	5	4	1	1	2
1996— Buffalo (A.A.)	4	3	.571	1.48	43	0	0	0	19	79	57	14	13	24	46
— Cleveland (A.L.)	2	0	1.000	4.55	15	0	0	0	0	29 2/3	29	18	15	10	22
1997— Buffalo (A.A.)	2	3	.400	4.19	19	3	0	0	2	43	45	21	20	11	21
— Cleveland (A.L.)	0	0	...	4.76	5	0	0	0	0	11 1/3	15	8	6	9	4
— Indianapolis (A.A.)■	1	0	1.000	3.09	11	0	0	0	5	11 2/3	7	4	4	5	5
— Cincinnati (N.L.)	0	0	...	6.14	10	0	0	0	0	14 2/3	26	14	10	11	7
1998— Indianapolis (Int'l)	1	0	1.000	1.93	13	0	0	0	0	14	15	3	3	3	11
— Cincinnati (N.L.)	2	1	.667	3.32	62	0	0	0	8	81 1/3	76	31	30	28	44
A.L. totals (2 years)	2	0	1.000	4.61	20	0	0	0	0	41	44	26	21	19	26
N.L. totals (2 years)	2	1	.667	3.75	72	0	0	0	8	96	102	45	40	39	51
Major league totals (3 years)	4	1	.800	4.01	92	0	0	0	8	137	146	71	61	58	77

G

GREBECK, CRAIG   IF   BLUE JAYS

PERSONAL: Born December 29, 1964, in Johnstown, Pa. ... 5-7/155. ... Bats right, throws right. ... Full name: Craig Allen Grebeck. ... Brother of Brian Grebeck, infielder with California Angels and Houston Astros organizations (1990-97). ... Name pronounced GRAY-bek.
HIGH SCHOOL: Lakewood (Calif.).
COLLEGE: Cal State Dominguez Hills.
TRANSACTIONS/CAREER NOTES: Signed as non-drafted free agent by Chicago White Sox organization (August 13, 1986). ... On disabled list (August 9, 1992-remainder of season). ... On Chicago disabled list (May 21-June 30, 1994); included rehabilitation assignment at Nashville (June 23-30). ... Granted free agency (December 21, 1995). ... Signed by Florida Marlins organization (December 22, 1995). ... On disabled list (July 4-August 13, 1996). ... Granted free agency (October 31, 1996). ... Signed by Anaheim Angels (December 6, 1996). ... Granted free agency (October 9, 1997). ... Signed by Toronto Blue Jays organization (November 27, 1997). ... On Toronto disabled list (April 20-May 5, 1998). ... Granted free agency (October 23, 1998). ... Re-signed by Blue Jays (October 27, 1998).
STATISTICAL NOTES: Led Southern League in grounding into double plays with 15 in 1989. ... Career major league grand slams: 1.

							BATTING							FIELDING		
Year	Team (League)	Pos.	G	AB	R	H	2B	3B	HR	RBI	Avg.	BB	SO	SB	PO	A	E	Avg.
1987— Peninsula (Caro.)	SS-3B	104	378	63	106	22	3	15	67	.280	37	62	3	137	278	16	.963
1988— Birmingham (Sou.)......	2B	133	450	57	126	21	1	9	53	.280	65	72	5	238	368	19	.970
1989— Birmingham (Sou.)......	SS-3B-2B	•143	•533	85	*153	25	4	5	80	.287	63	77	14	234	364	28	.955
1990— Chicago (A.L.)	3B-SS-2B	59	119	7	20	3	1	1	9	.168	8	24	0	36	98	3	.978
— Vancouver (PCL)	SS-3B-2B	12	41	8	8	0	0	1	3	.195	6	7	1	28	26	1	.982
1991— Chicago (A.L.)	3B-2B-SS	107	224	37	63	16	3	6	31	.281	38	40	1	104	183	10	.966
1992— Chicago (A.L.)	SS-3B-OF	88	287	24	77	21	2	3	35	.268	30	34	0	112	283	8	.980
1993— Chicago (A.L.)	SS-2B-3B	72	190	25	43	5	0	1	12	.226	26	26	1	91	185	5	.982
1994— Chicago (A.L.)	2B-SS-3B	35	97	17	30	5	0	0	5	.309	12	5	0	44	65	2	.982
— Nashville (A.A.)	SS	5	15	3	6	2	0	4	4	.400	1	2	0	5	12	1	.944
1995— Chicago (A.L.)	SS-3B-2B	53	154	19	40	12	0	1	18	.260	21	23	0	76	127	7	.967
1996— Florida (N.L.)■...........	2B-SS-3B	50	95	8	20	1	0	1	9	.211	4	14	0	67	66	2	.985
1997— Anaheim (A.L.)■.......2-S-3-O-DH	63	126	12	34	9	0	1	6	.270	18	11	0	68	88	2	.987
1998— Toronto (A.L.)■...........	2B-SS-3B	102	301	33	77	17	2	2	27	.256	29	42	2	151	269	11	.974
— Syracuse (Int'l)........	2B	1	3	0	1	0	0	0	0	.333	0	0	0	2	6	0	1.000
American League totals (8 years)		579	1498	174	384	88	8	15	143	.256	182	205	4	682	1298	48	.976
National League totals (1 year)		50	95	8	20	1	0	1	9	.211	4	14	0	67	66	2	.985
Major league totals (9 years)		629	1593	182	404	89	8	16	152	.254	186	219	4	749	1364	50	.977

CHAMPIONSHIP SERIES RECORD

							BATTING							FIELDING		
Year	Team (League)	Pos.	G	AB	R	H	2B	3B	HR	RBI	Avg.	BB	SO	SB	PO	A	E	Avg.
1993— Chicago (A.L.)	PH-3B	1	1	0	1	0	0	0	0	1.000	0	0	0	0	0	0	...

GREEN, CHAD   OF   BREWERS

PERSONAL: Born June 28, 1975, in Dunkirk, N.Y. ... 5-10/180. ... Bats right, throws right. ... Full name: Chad Elton Green.
HIGH SCHOOL: Mentor (Ohio).
COLLEGE: Kentucky.
TRANSACTIONS/CAREER NOTES: Selected by Kansas City Royals organization in ninth round of free-agent draft (June 3, 1993); did not sign. ... Selected by Milwaukee Brewers organization in first round (eighth pick overall) of free-agent draft (June 4, 1996). ... On Stockton disabled list (April 2-May 8 and June 24-July 18, 1998). ... On El Paso disabled list (July 27-August 10, 1998).
STATISTICAL NOTES: Led California League outfielders with 311 total chances in 1997.
MISCELLANEOUS: Member of 1996 U.S. Olympic baseball team.

							BATTING							FIELDING		
Year	Team (League)	Pos.	G	AB	R	H	2B	3B	HR	RBI	Avg.	BB	SO	SB	PO	A	E	Avg.
1996— Ogden (Pioneer)........	OF	21	81	22	29	4	1	3	8	.358	15	23	12	53	3	0	1.000
1997— Stockton (California) ..	OF	127	513	78	128	26	14	2	43	.250	37	138	37	*291	11	9	.971
1998— Stockton (California) ..	OF	40	151	30	52	13	2	0	17	.344	12	22	22	61	6	0	1.000
— El Paso (Texas)..........	PH	7	6	0	0	0	0	0	0	.000	1	3	0	...	...	...	...

GREEN, SHAWN   OF   BLUE JAYS

PERSONAL: Born November 10, 1972, in Des Plaines, Ill. ... 6-4/200. ... Bats left, throws left. ... Full name: Shawn David Green.
HIGH SCHOOL: Tustin (Calif.).
TRANSACTIONS/CAREER NOTES: Selected by Toronto Blue Jays organization in first round (16th pick overall) of free-agent draft (June 3, 1991); pick received as compensation for San Francisco Giants signing Type A free-agent P Bud Black. ... On disabled list (June 30-July 23, 1992). ... On Knoxville disabled list (June 11-July 24, 1993).
STATISTICAL NOTES: Tied for Florida State League lead with eight sacrifice flies in 1992. ... Career major league grand slams: 1.

G

							BATTING							FIELDING		
Year	Team (League)	Pos.	G	AB	R	H	2B	3B	HR	RBI	Avg.	BB	SO	SB	PO	A	E	Avg.
1992— Dunedin (Fla. St.)	OF	114	417	44	114	21	3	1	49	.273	28	66	22	182	3	5	.974
1993— Knoxville (Southern) ..	OF	99	360	40	102	14	2	4	34	.283	26	72	4	172	3	8	.956
— Toronto (A.L.)............	OF-DH	3	6	0	0	0	0	0	0	.000	0	1	0	1	0	0	1.000
1994— Syracuse (Int'l)...........	OF	109	433	82	149	27	3	13	61	*.344	40	54	19	220	5	1	*.996
— Toronto (A.L.)............	OF	14	33	1	3	1	0	0	1	.091	1	8	1	12	2	0	1.000
1995— Toronto (A.L.)............	OF	121	379	52	109	31	4	15	54	.288	20	68	1	207	9	6	.973
1996— Toronto (A.L.)............	OF-DH	132	422	52	118	32	3	11	45	.280	33	75	5	254	10	2	.992
1997— Toronto (A.L.)............	OF-DH	135	429	57	123	22	4	16	53	.287	36	99	14	173	6	3	.984
1998— Toronto (A.L.)............	OF	158	630	106	175	33	4	35	100	.278	50	142	35	311	14	7	.979
Major league totals (6 years)		563	1899	268	528	119	15	77	253	.278	140	393	56	958	41	18	.982

GREEN, TYLER   P   PHILLIES

PERSONAL: Born February 18, 1970, in Springfield, Ohio. ... 6-5/208. ... Throws right, bats right. ... Full name: Tyler Scott Green.
HIGH SCHOOL: Thomas Jefferson (Denver).
COLLEGE: Wichita State.
TRANSACTIONS/CAREER NOTES: Selected by Cincinnati Reds organization in third round of free-agent draft (June 1, 1988); did not sign. ... Selected by Philadelphia Phillies organization in first round (10th pick overall) of free-agent draft (June 3, 1991). ... On Clearwater disabled list (August 7, 1991-remainder of season). ... On Scranton/Wilkes-Barre disabled list (July 10, 1992-remainder of season and May 3-22, 1993). ... On disabled list (March 23, 1996-entire season). ... On Philadelphia disabled list (March 27-June 1, 1997); including rehabilitation assignment to Scranton/Wilkes-Barre (April 29-May 25). ... On disabled list (July 28-August 28, 1998).
STATISTICAL NOTES: Pitched 3-1 no-hit victory for Scranton/Wilkes-Barre against Ottawa (July 4, 1993, first game). ... Led International League with 12 hit batsmen in 1994.
MISCELLANEOUS: Appeared in one game as pinch runner (1995).

Year Team (League)	W	L	Pct.	ERA	G	GS	CG	ShO	Sv.	IP	H	R	ER	BB	SO
1991—Batavia (N.Y.-Penn)	1	0	1.000	1.20	3	3	0	0	0	15	7	2	2	6	19
—Clearwater (Fla. St.)	2	0	1.000	1.38	2	2	0	0	0	13	3	2	2	8	20
1992—Reading (Eastern)	6	3	.667	1.88	12	12	0	0	0	62 1/3	46	16	13	20	67
—Scran./W.B. (Int'l)	0	1	.000	6.10	2	2	0	0	0	10 1/3	7	7	7	12	15
1993—Philadelphia (N.L.)	0	0	. . .	7.36	3	2	0	0	0	7 1/3	16	9	6	5	7
—Scran./W.B. (Int'l)	6	10	.375	3.95	28	14	4	0	0	118 1/3	102	62	52	43	87
1994—Scran./W.B. (Int'l)	7	*16	.304	5.56	27	26	4	0	0	162	179	*110	*100	*77	95
1995—Philadelphia (N.L.)	8	9	.471	5.31	26	25	4	2	0	140 2/3	157	86	83	66	85
1996—							Did not play.								
1997—Scran./W.B. (Int'l)	4	8	.333	6.10	12	12	3	0	0	72 1/3	80	54	49	29	40
—Philadelphia (N.L.)	4	4	.500	4.93	14	14	0	0	0	76 2/3	72	50	42	45	58
1998—Philadelphia (N.L.)	6	12	.333	5.03	27	27	0	0	0	159 1/3	142	97	89	85	113
Major league totals (4 years)	18	25	.419	5.16	70	68	4	2	0	384	387	242	220	201	263

ALL-STAR GAME RECORD

Year League	W	L	Pct.	ERA	GS	CG	ShO	Sv.	IP	H	R	ER	BB	SO
1995—National	0	0	. . .	0.00	0	0	0	0	1	2	0	0	0	1

GREENE, CHARLIE   C   BREWERS

PERSONAL: Born January 23, 1971, in Miami. ... 6-2/190. ... Bats right, throws right. ... Full name: Charles Patrick Greene.
HIGH SCHOOL: Miami Killian.
JUNIOR COLLEGE: Miami-Dade (South) Community College.
TRANSACTIONS/CAREER NOTES: Selected by San Diego Padres organization in 19th round of free-agent draft (June 3, 1991). ... Selected by New York Mets organization from Padres organization in Rule 5 minor league draft (December 13, 1993). ... Claimed on waivers by Baltimore Orioles (September 11, 1997). ... Claimed on waivers by Milwaukee Brewers (December 5, 1998).
STATISTICAL NOTES: Tied for Midwest League lead in double plays by catcher with 11 in 1993.

Year Team (League)	Pos.	G	AB	R	H	2B	3B	HR	RBI	Avg.	BB	SO	SB	PO	A	E	Avg.
1991—Ariz. Padres (Ariz.)	C-1B-3B	49	183	27	52	15	1	5	38	.284	16	26	6	334	30	3	.992
1992—Char., S.C. (S. Atl.)	C-3B	98	298	22	55	9	1	1	24	.185	11	60	1	561	119	14	.980
1993—Waterloo (Midw.)	C-1-3-S	84	213	19	38	8	0	2	20	.178	13	33	0	460	96	16	.972
1994—St. Lucie (Fla. St.)■	C	69	224	23	57	4	0	0	21	.254	9	31	0	380	65	13	.972
—Binghamton (East.)	C	30	106	13	18	4	0	0	2	.170	6	18	0	190	30	3	.987
1995—Binghamton (East.)	C	100	346	26	82	13	0	2	34	.237	15	47	2	670	54	4	*.995
—Norfolk (Int'l)	C	27	88	6	17	3	0	0	4	.193	3	28	0	157	25	0	1.000
1996—Binghamton (East.)	C	100	336	35	82	17	0	2	27	.244	17	52	0	550	75	3	.995
—New York (N.L.)	C	2	1	0	0	0	0	0	0	.000	0	0	0	1	0	0	1.000
1997—Norfolk (Int'l)	C	76	238	27	49	7	0	8	28	.206	9	54	1	475	49	8	.985
—Baltimore (A.L.)■	C	5	2	0	0	0	0	0	1	.000	0	1	0	4	0	0	1.000
1998—Rochester (Int'l)	C	77	250	23	53	10	0	4	28	.212	9	54	1	517	55	7	.988
—Baltimore (A.L.)	C	13	21	1	4	1	0	0	0	.190	0	8	0	58	4	0	1.000
American League totals (2 years)		18	23	1	4	1	0	0	1	.174	0	9	0	62	4	0	1.000
National League totals (1 year)		2	1	0	0	0	0	0	0	.000	0	0	0	1	0	0	1.000
Major league totals (3 years)		20	24	1	4	1	0	0	1	.167	0	9	0	63	4	0	1.000

GREENE, TODD   C   ANGELS

PERSONAL: Born May 8, 1971, in Augusta, Ga. ... 5-10/208. ... Bats right, throws right. ... Full name: Todd Anthony Greene.
HIGH SCHOOL: Evans (Ga.).
COLLEGE: Georgia Southern.
TRANSACTIONS/CAREER NOTES: Selected by Atlanta Braves organization in 27th round of free-agent draft (June 5, 1989); did not sign. ... Selected by California Angels organization in 12th round of free-agent draft (June 3, 1993). ... On Vancouver disabled list (April 11-May 25, 1996). ... Angels franchise renamed Anaheim Angels for 1997 season. ... On Anaheim disabled list (August 20, 1997-remainder of season). ... On Anaheim disabled list (March 19-August 5, 1998); included rehabilitation assignments to Lake Elsinore (April 14-May 16, May 21 and May 27-31) and Vancouver (May 17-20, May 22-26, June 1-2 and July 17-August 5).
HONORS: Named California League Most Valuable Player (1994).
STATISTICAL NOTES: Led California League with 306 total bases, 12 intentional bases on balls received and .584 slugging percentage in 1994. ... Led California League catchers with 15 errors, 13 double plays and 44 passed balls in 1994.

Year Team (League)	Pos.	G	AB	R	H	2B	3B	HR	RBI	Avg.	BB	SO	SB	PO	A	E	Avg.
1993— Boise (Northwest)	OF	•76	*305	55	82	15	3	*15	*71	.269	34	44	4	136	4	3	.979
1994— Lake Elsinore (Calif.)..	C-OF-1B	133	524	98	158	*39	2	*35	*124	.302	64	96	10	624	90	†15	.979
1995— Midland (Texas)........	C-1B	82	318	59	104	19	1	26	57	.327	17	55	3	314	44	3	.992
— Vancouver (PCL)........	C	43	168	28	42	3	1	14	35	.250	11	36	1	175	17	1	.995
1996— Vancouver (PCL)........	C	60	223	27	68	18	0	5	33	.305	16	36	0	219	37	3	.988
— California (A.L.)........	C-DH	29	79	9	15	1	0	2	9	.190	4	11	2	119	19	0	1.000
1997— Anaheim (A.L.)..........	C-DH	34	124	24	36	6	0	9	24	.290	7	25	2	153	7	0	1.000
— Vancouver (PCL)........	C-1B-OF	64	260	51	92	22	0	25	75	.354	20	31	5	331	43	3	.992
1998— Lake Elsinore (Calif.)..	1B	12	44	9	10	2	0	1	6	.227	4	7	1	9	1	2	.833
— Vancouver (PCL)........	1B-C-OF	30	108	16	30	12	0	7	20	.278	12	17	1	97	7	1	.990
— Anaheim (A.L.)..........	OF-DH-1B	29	71	3	18	4	0	1	7	.254	2	20	0	28	1	0	1.000
Major league totals (3 years)		92	274	36	69	11	0	12	40	.252	13	56	4	300	27	0	1.000

GREENE, WILLIE — 3B/OF — BLUE JAYS

PERSONAL: Born September 23, 1971, in Milledgeville, Ga. ... 5-11/192. ... Bats left, throws right. ... Full name: Willie Louis Greene.

HIGH SCHOOL: Jones County (Gray, Ga.).

TRANSACTIONS/CAREER NOTES: Selected by Pittsburgh Pirates organization in first round (18th pick overall) of free-agent draft (June 5, 1989). ... Traded by Pirates organization with P Scott Ruskin and a player to be named later to Montreal Expos organization for P Zane Smith (August 8, 1990); Expos acquired OF Moises Alou to complete deal (August 16, 1990). ... Traded by Expos organization with OF Dave Martinez and P Scott Ruskin to Cincinnati Reds organization for P John Wetteland and P Bill Risley (December 11, 1991). ... On Cincinnati disabled list (August 21, 1993-remainder of season). ... On Indianapolis disabled list (June 7-19, 1995). ... On disabled list (June 27-July 12, 1996). ... Traded by Reds to Baltimore Orioles for OF Jeffrey Hammonds (August 10, 1998). ... Granted free agency (December 21, 1998). ... Signed by Toronto Blue Jays (January 18, 1999).

STATISTICAL NOTES: Led Florida State League third basemen with 31 errors in 1991. ... Led Southern League third basemen with 24 double plays in 1992. ... Led American Association third basemen with 23 errors in 1993. ... Hit three home runs in one game (September 24, 1996). ... Career major league grand slams: 3.

Year Team (League)	Pos.	G	AB	R	H	2B	3B	HR	RBI	Avg.	BB	SO	SB	PO	A	E	Avg.
1989— Princeton (Appal.)	SS	39	136	22	44	6	4	2	24	.324	9	29	4	33	69	19	.843
— GC Pirates (GCL)	SS	23	86	17	24	3	3	5	11	.279	9	6	4	25	49	3	.961
1990— Augusta (S. Atl.)........	SS-2B	86	291	59	75	12	4	11	47	.258	61	58	7	117	209	34	.906
— Salem (Carolina)	SS	17	60	9	11	1	1	3	9	.183	7	18	0	22	43	2	.970
— Rockford (Midwest)■	SS	11	35	4	14	3	0	0	2	.400	6	7	2	14	37	4	.927
1991— W.P. Beach (FSL)........	3B-SS	99	322	46	70	9	3	12	43	.217	50	93	10	72	184	†32	.889
1992— Cedar Rap. (Midw.)■.	3B	34	120	26	34	8	2	12	40	.283	18	27	3	13	60	8	.901
— Chattanooga (Sou.)	3B	96	349	47	97	19	2	15	66	.278	46	90	9	*77	174	14	*.947
— Cincinnati (N.L.)	3B	29	93	10	25	5	2	2	13	.269	10	23	0	15	40	3	.948
1993— Indianapolis (A.A.)......	3B-SS	98	341	62	91	19	0	22	58	.267	51	83	2	77	171	†23	.915
— Cincinnati (N.L.)	SS-3B	15	50	7	8	1	1	2	5	.160	2	19	0	19	37	1	.982
1994— Cincinnati (N.L.)	3B-OF	16	37	5	8	2	0	0	3	.216	6	14	0	2	21	1	.958
— Indianapolis (A.A.).....	3B-SS	114	435	77	124	24	1	23	80	.285	56	88	8	93	249	17	.953
1995— Cincinnati (N.L.)	3B	8	19	1	2	0	0	0	0	.105	3	7	0	1	13	0	1.000
— Indianapolis (A.A.).....	3B-SS-OF	91	325	57	79	12	2	19	45	.243	38	67	3	60	160	12	.948
1996— Cincinnati (N.L.)	3-O-1-S-2	115	287	48	70	5	5	19	63	.244	36	88	0	57	149	16	.928
1997— Cincinnati (N.L.)	3-O-1-S	151	495	62	125	22	1	26	91	.253	78	111	6	176	175	17	.954
1998— Cincinnati (N.L.)	3-O-S-DH	111	356	57	96	18	1	14	49	.270	56	80	6	92	132	13	.945
— Baltimore (A.L.)■........	OF-DH	24	40	8	6	1	0	1	5	.150	13	10	1	15	1	1	.941
American League totals (1 year)		24	40	8	6	1	0	1	5	.150	13	10	1	15	1	1	.941
National League totals (7 years)		445	1337	190	334	53	10	63	224	.250	191	342	12	362	567	51	.948
Major league totals (7 years)		469	1377	198	340	54	10	64	229	.247	204	352	13	377	568	52	.948

GREER, RUSTY — OF — RANGERS

PERSONAL: Born January 21, 1969, in Fort Rucker, Ala. ... 6-0/195. ... Bats left, throws left. ... Full name: Thurman Clyde Greer III.

HIGH SCHOOL: Albertville (Ala.).

COLLEGE: Montevallo (Ala.).

TRANSACTIONS/CAREER NOTES: Selected by Texas Rangers organization in 10th round of free-agent draft (June 4, 1990). ... On disabled list (July 31-August 22, 1992).

RECORDS: Shares major league record for fewest double plays by outfielder (150 or more games)—0 (1997 and 1998).

STATISTICAL NOTES: Led Florida State League with .395 on-base percentage in 1991. ... Career major league grand slams: 5.

G

Year Team (League)	Pos.	G	AB	R	H	2B	3B	HR	RBI	Avg.	BB	SO	SB	PO	A	E	Avg.
1990— Butte (Pioneer)	OF	62	226	48	78	12	6	10	50	.345	41	23	9	84	5	*8	.918
1991— Charlotte (Fla. St.)	OF-1B	111	388	62	114	25	1	5	48	.294	66	48	12	213	15	7	.970
— Tulsa (Texas)	OF	20	64	12	19	3	2	3	12	.297	17	6	2	34	0	0	1.000
1992— Tulsa (Texas)	1B-OF	106	359	47	96	22	4	5	37	.267	60	63	2	814	50	11	.987
1993— Tulsa (Texas)	1B	129	474	76	138	25	6	15	59	.291	53	79	10	1055	93	8	.993
— Okla. City (A.A.)..........	OF	8	27	6	6	2	0	1	4	.222	6	7	0	16	0	0	1.000
1994— Okla. City (A.A.)	OF-1B	31	111	18	35	12	1	3	13	.315	18	24	1	52	3	3	.948
— Texas (A.L.)	OF-1B	80	277	36	87	16	1	10	46	.314	46	46	0	216	4	6	.973
1995— Texas (A.L.)	OF-1B	131	417	58	113	21	2	13	61	.271	55	66	3	240	9	6	.976
1996— Texas (A.L.)	OF-DH-1B	139	542	96	180	41	6	18	100	.332	62	86	9	304	6	5	.984
1997— Texas (A.L.)	OF-DH	157	601	112	193	42	3	26	87	.321	83	87	9	318	9	*12	.965
1998— Texas (A.L.)	OF	155	598	107	183	31	5	16	108	.306	80	93	2	304	6	3	.990
Major league totals (5 years)		662	2435	409	756	151	17	83	402	.310	326	378	23	1382	34	32	.978

Year	Team (League)	Pos.	G	AB	R	H	2B	3B	HR	RBI	Avg.	BB	SO	SB	PO	A	E	Avg.
1996—	Texas (A.L.)	OF	4	16	2	2	0	0	0	0	.125	3	3	0	12	0	0	1.000
1998—	Texas (A.L.)	OF	3	11	0	1	0	0	0	0	.091	1	2	0	4	1	0	1.000
Division series totals (2 years)			7	27	2	3	0	0	0	0	.111	4	5	0	16	1	0	1.000

GREISINGER, SETH   P   TIGERS

PERSONAL: Born July 29, 1975, in Kansas City, Kan. ... 6-3/200. ... Throws right, bats right. ... Full name: Seth Adam Greisinger.
HIGH SCHOOL: McLean (Va.)
COLLEGE: Virginia.
TRANSACTIONS/CAREER NOTES: Selected by Cleveland Indians organization in seventh round of free-agent draft (June 3, 1993); did not sign. ... Selected by Detroit Tigers organization in first round (sixth pick overall) of free-agent draft (June 4, 1996).
STATISTICAL NOTES: Led Southern League in home runs allowed with 29 in 1997.
MISCELLANEOUS: Member of 1996 U.S. Olympic baseball team.

Year	Team (League)	W	L	Pct.	ERA	G	GS	CG	ShO	Sv.	IP	H	R	ER	BB	SO
1997—	Jacksonville (Southern) ...	10	6	.625	5.20	28	*28	1	0	0	159 1/3	194	103	92	53	105
1998—	Toledo (International)	3	4	.429	2.91	10	10	0	0	0	58 2/3	50	21	19	22	37
—	Detroit (A.L.)	6	9	.400	5.12	21	21	0	0	0	130	142	79	74	48	66
Major league totals (1 year)		6	9	.400	5.12	21	21	0	0	0	130	142	79	74	48	66

GRIEVE, BEN   OF   ATHLETICS

PERSONAL: Born May 4, 1976, in Arlington, Texas. ... 6-4/226. ... Bats left, throws right. ... Full name: Benjamin Grieve. ... Son of Tom Grieve, outfielder with four major league teams (1970-79). ... First father/son combination to be selected in the first round of free-agent draft.
HIGH SCHOOL: James W. Martin (Arlington, Texas).
TRANSACTIONS/CAREER NOTES: Selected by Oakland Athletics organization in first round (second overall pick) of free-agent draft (June 2, 1994).
RECORDS: Shares major league record for fewest double plays by outfielder (150 or more games)—0 (1998).
HONORS: Named Minor League Player of the Year by THE SPORTING NEWS (1997). ... Named Southern League Most Valuable Player (1997). ... Named A.L. Rookie Player of the Year by THE SPORTING NEWS (1998). ... Named A.L. Rookie of the Year by Baseball Writers' Association of America (1998).
STATISTICAL NOTES: Tied for Northwest League lead with seven intentional bases on balls received in 1994. ... Led Southern League with .455 on-base percentage in 1997.

Year	Team (League)	Pos.	G	AB	R	H	2B	3B	HR	RBI	Avg.	BB	SO	SB	PO	A	E	Avg.
1994—	S. Oregon (N'west)	OF	72	252	44	83	13	0	7	50	.329	51	48	2	133	8	6	.959
1995—	W. Mich. (Mid.)	OF	102	371	53	97	16	1	4	62	.261	60	75	11	125	6	8	.942
—	Modesto (California) ..	OF	28	107	17	28	5	0	2	14	.262	14	15	2	37	2	2	.951
1996—	Modesto (California) ..	OF	72	281	61	100	20	1	11	51	.356	38	52	8	104	5	5	.956
—	Huntsville (Sou.)	OF	63	232	34	55	8	1	8	32	.237	35	53	0	79	2	4	.953
1997—	Huntsville (Sou.)	OF	100	372	100	122	29	2	24	108	.328	81	75	5	193	6	•8	.961
—	Edmonton (PCL)	OF	27	108	27	46	11	1	7	28	.426	12	16	0	51	2	2	.964
—	Oakland (A.L.)	OF	24	93	12	29	6	0	3	24	.312	13	25	0	39	1	0	1.000
1998—	Oakland (A.L.)	OF-DH	155	583	94	168	41	2	18	89	.288	85	123	2	262	7	2	.993
Major league totals (2 years)			179	676	106	197	47	2	21	113	.291	98	148	2	301	8	2	.994

ALL-STAR GAME RECORD

Year	League	Pos.	AB	R	H	2B	3B	HR	RBI	Avg.	BB	SO	SB	PO	A	E	Avg.
1998—	American	PH	0	0	0	0	0	0	0	...	1	0	0	...	...	...	...

GRIFFEY JR., KEN   OF   MARINERS

PERSONAL: Born November 21, 1969, in Donora, Pa. ... 6-3/205. ... Bats left, throws left. ... Full name: George Kenneth Griffey Jr. ... Son of Ken Griffey Sr., hitting coach, Cincinnati Reds, and major league outfielder with four teams (1973-91); and brother of Craig Griffey, outfielder in Seattle Mariners and Cincinnati Reds organizations (1991-97).
HIGH SCHOOL: Moeller (Cincinnati).
TRANSACTIONS/CAREER NOTES: Selected by Seattle Mariners organization in first round (first pick overall) of free-agent draft (June 2, 1987). ... On San Bernardino disabled list (June 9-August 15, 1988). ... On disabled list (July 24-August 20, 1989; June 9-25, 1992; and June 20-July 13, 1996). ... On Seattle disabled list (May 27-August 15, 1995); included rehabilitation assignment to Tacoma (August 13-15).
RECORDS: Shares major league record for most consecutive games with one or more home runs—8 (July 20 through July 28, 1993).
HONORS: Won A.L. Gold Glove as outfielder (1990-98). ... Named outfielder on THE SPORTING NEWS A.L. All-Star team (1991, 1993-94 and 1996-98). ... Named outfielder on THE SPORTING NEWS A.L. Silver Slugger team (1991, 1993-94 and 1996-98). ... Named Major League Player of the Year by THE SPORTING NEWS (1997). ... Named A.L. Most Valuable Player by Baseball Writers' Association of America (1997).
STATISTICAL NOTES: Led A.L. outfielders with six double plays in 1989. ... Led A.L. with 359 total bases in 1993 and 393 in 1997. ... Hit three home runs in one game (May 24, 1996 and April 25, 1997). ... Led A.L. with 23 intentional bases on balls received in 1997. ... Led A.L. in slugging percentage with .646 in 1997. ... Led A.L. outfielders with 409 putouts and 425 total chances in 1998. ... Career major league grand slams: 10.
MISCELLANEOUS: Holds Seattle Mariners franchise all-time records for most runs (940), most hits (1,569), most home runs (350) and most runs batted in (1,018).

Year	Team (League)	Pos.	G	AB	R	H	2B	3B	HR	RBI	Avg.	BB	SO	SB	PO	A	E	Avg.
1987—	Bellingham (N'west) ...	OF	54	182	43	57	9	1	14	40	.313	44	42	13	117	4	1	*.992
1988—	San Bern. (Calif.)	OF	58	219	50	74	13	3	11	42	.338	34	39	32	145	3	2	.987
—	Vermont (Eastern)	OF	17	61	10	17	5	1	2	10	.279	5	12	4	40	2	1	.977

G

								BATTING								FIELDING		
Year	Team (League)	Pos.	G	AB	R	H	2B	3B	HR	RBI	Avg.	BB	SO	SB	PO	A	E	Avg.
1989—Seattle (A.L.)		OF-DH	127	455	61	120	23	0	16	61	.264	44	83	16	302	12	•10	.969
1990—Seattle (A.L.)		OF	155	597	91	179	28	7	22	80	.300	63	81	16	330	8	7	.980
1991—Seattle (A.L.)		OF-DH	154	548	76	179	42	1	22	100	.327	71	82	18	360	15	4	.989
1992—Seattle (A.L.)		OF-DH	142	565	83	174	39	4	27	103	.308	44	67	10	359	8	1	.997
1993—Seattle (A.L.)		OF-DH-1B	156	582	113	180	38	3	45	109	.309	96	91	17	317	8	3	.991
1994—Seattle (A.L.)		OF-DH	111	433	94	140	24	4	*40	90	.323	56	73	11	225	12	4	.983
1995—Seattle (A.L.)		OF-DH	72	260	52	67	7	0	17	42	.258	52	53	4	190	5	2	.990
—Tacoma (PCL)		DH	1	3	0	0	0	0	0	0	.000	0	1	0	...	...	...	...
1996—Seattle (A.L.)		OF-DH	140	545	125	165	26	2	49	140	.303	78	104	16	375	10	4	.990
1997—Seattle (A.L.)		OF-DH	157	608	*125	185	34	3	*56	*147	.304	76	121	15	388	9	6	.985
1998—Seattle (A.L.)		OF-DH-1B	161	633	120	180	33	3	*56	146	.284	76	121	20	†409	11	5	.988
Major league totals (10 years)			1375	5226	940	1569	294	27	350	1018	.300	656	876	143	3255	98	46	.986

DIVISION SERIES RECORD

RECORDS: Shares single-series record for most home runs—5 (1996). ... Shares single-game record for most home runs—2 (October 3, 1995).
NOTES: Shares postseason single-series record for most home runs—5 (1995).

								BATTING								FIELDING		
Year	Team (League)	Pos.	G	AB	R	H	2B	3B	HR	RBI	Avg.	BB	SO	SB	PO	A	E	Avg.
1995—Seattle (A.L.)		OF	5	23	9	9	0	0	5	7	.391	2	4	1	15	1	0	1.000
1997—Seattle (A.L.)		OF	4	15	0	2	0	0	0	2	.133	1	3	2	12	1	0	1.000
Division series totals (2 years)			9	38	9	11	0	0	5	9	.289	3	7	3	27	2	0	1.000

CHAMPIONSHIP SERIES RECORD

								BATTING								FIELDING		
Year	Team (League)	Pos.	G	AB	R	H	2B	3B	HR	RBI	Avg.	BB	SO	SB	PO	A	E	Avg.
1995—Seattle (A.L.)		OF	6	21	2	7	2	0	1	2	.333	4	4	2	13	0	1	.929

NOTES: Named Most Valuable Player (1992).

ALL-STAR GAME RECORD

							BATTING							FIELDING		
Year	League	Pos.	AB	R	H	2B	3B	HR	RBI	Avg.	BB	SO	SB	PO	A	E	Avg.
1990—American		OF	2	0	0	0	0	0	0	.000	1	0	0	2	0	0	1.000
1991—American		OF	3	0	2	0	0	0	0	.667	0	0	0	2	0	0	1.000
1992—American		OF	3	2	3	1	0	1	2	1.000	0	0	0	1	0	0	1.000
1993—American		OF	3	1	1	0	0	0	1	.333	0	1	0	2	0	0	1.000
1994—American		OF	3	0	2	1	0	0	1	.667	0	0	0	2	0	0	1.000
1995—American			Selected, did not play.													
1996—American			Selected, did not play.													
1997—American		OF	4	0	0	0	0	0	0	.000	0	2	0	0	0	0	...
1998—American		OF	3	1	2	0	0	0	1	.667	1	0	1	0	0	1	.000
All-Star Game totals (7 years)			21	4	10	2	0	1	5	.476	2	3	1	9	0	1	.900

GRISSOM, MARQUIS   OF   BREWERS

PERSONAL: Born April 17, 1967, in Atlanta. ... 5-11/188. ... Bats right, throws right. ... Full name: Marquis Deon Grissom. ... Brother of Antonio Grissom, outfielder in Philadelphia Phillies (1990 and 1991) and Montreal Expos organizations (1992-94). ... Name pronounced mar-KEESE.

HIGH SCHOOL: Lakeshore (College Park, Ga.).

COLLEGE: Florida A&M.

TRANSACTIONS/CAREER NOTES: Selected by Montreal Expos organization in third round of free-agent draft (June 1, 1988). ... On Montreal disabled list (May 29-June 30, 1990); included rehabilitation assignment to Indianapolis (June 25-30). ... Traded by Expos to Atlanta Braves for OF Roberto Kelly, OF Tony Tarasco and P Esteban Yan (April 6, 1995). ... Traded by Braves with OF Dave Justice to Cleveland Indians for OF Kenny Lofton and P Alan Embree (March 25, 1997). ... On disabled list (April 22-May 5, 1997). ... Traded by Indians with P Jeff Juden to Milwaukee Brewers for P Ben McDonald, P Mike Fetters and P Ron Villone (December 8, 1997).

HONORS: Won N.L. Gold Glove as outfielder (1993-96).

STATISTICAL NOTES: Led New York-Pennsylvania League with 146 total bases in 1988. ... Led N.L. outfielders with 333 total chances in 1994. ... Had 28-game hitting streak (July 25-August 24, 1996). ... Career major league grand slams: 3.

								BATTING								FIELDING		
Year	Team (League)	Pos.	G	AB	R	H	2B	3B	HR	RBI	Avg.	BB	SO	SB	PO	A	E	Avg.
1988—Jamestown (NYP)		OF	74	*291	*69	94	14	7	8	39	.323	35	39	23	123	•11	3	.978
1989—Jacksonville (Sou.).....		OF	78	278	43	83	15	4	3	31	.299	24	31	24	141	7	3	.980
—Indianapolis (A.A.)......		OF	49	187	28	52	10	4	2	21	.278	14	23	16	106	5	0	1.000
—Montreal (N.L.)............		OF	26	74	16	19	2	0	1	2	.257	12	21	1	32	1	2	.943
1990—Montreal (N.L.)............		OF	98	288	42	74	14	2	3	29	.257	27	40	22	165	5	2	.988
—Indianapolis (A.A.)......		OF	5	22	3	4	0	0	2	3	.182	0	5	1	16	0	0	1.000
1991—Montreal (N.L.)............		OF	148	558	73	149	23	9	6	39	.267	34	89	*76	350	•15	6	.984
1992—Montreal (N.L.)............		OF	159	*653	99	180	39	6	14	66	.276	42	81	*78	401	7	7	.983
1993—Montreal (N.L.)............		OF	157	630	104	188	27	2	19	95	.298	52	76	53	416	8	7	.984
1994—Montreal (N.L.)............		OF	110	475	96	137	25	4	11	45	.288	41	66	36	*321	7	5	.985
1995—Atlanta (N.L.)■............		OF	139	551	80	142	23	3	12	42	.258	47	61	29	309	9	2	.994
1996—Atlanta (N.L.).............		OF	158	671	106	207	32	10	23	74	.308	41	73	28	338	10	1	.997
1997—Cleveland (A.L.)■......		OF	144	558	74	146	27	6	12	66	.262	43	89	22	356	7	3	.992
1998—Milwaukee (N.L.)■.....		OF	142	542	57	147	28	1	10	60	.271	24	78	13	317	8	3	.991
American League totals (1 year)			144	558	74	146	27	6	12	66	.262	43	89	22	356	7	3	.992
National League totals (9 years)			1137	4442	673	1243	213	37	99	452	.280	320	585	336	2649	70	35	.987
Major league totals (10 years)			1281	5000	747	1389	240	43	111	518	.278	363	674	358	3005	77	38	.988

G

DIVISION SERIES RECORD

RECORDS: Holds single-game record for most hits—5 (October 7, 1995). ... Shares single-game record for most home runs—2 (October 4, 1995). ... Shares career record for most triples—1.

Year Team (League)	Pos.	G	AB	R	H	2B	3B	HR	RBI	Avg.	BB	SO	SB	PO	A	E	Avg.
1995— Atlanta (N.L.)..............	OF	4	21	5	11	2	0	3	4	.524	0	3	2	9	0	0	1.000
1996— Atlanta (N.L.)..............	OF	3	12	2	1	0	0	0	0	.083	1	2	1	4	0	1	.800
1997— Cleveland (A.L.).........	OF	5	17	3	4	0	1	0	0	.235	1	2	0	14	0	0	1.000
Division series totals (3 years)		12	50	10	16	2	1	3	4	.320	2	7	3	27	0	1	.964

CHAMPIONSHIP SERIES RECORD

RECORDS: Holds single-series record for most at-bats—35 (1996). ... Shares single-game record for most strikeouts—4 (October 11 [12 innings] and 15 [11 innings], 1997). ... Shares N.L. single-game record for most at-bats—6 (October 14 and 17, 1996).
NOTES: Named A.L. Championship Series Most Valuable Player (1997).

Year Team (League)	Pos.	G	AB	R	H	2B	3B	HR	RBI	Avg.	BB	SO	SB	PO	A	E	Avg.
1995—Atlanta (N.L.)..............	OF	4	19	2	5	0	1	0	0	.263	1	4	0	8	0	1	.889
1996—Atlanta (N.L.)..............	OF	7	35	7	10	1	0	1	3	.286	0	8	2	17	0	1	.944
1997—Cleveland (A.L.).........	OF	6	23	2	6	0	0	1	4	.261	1	9	3	13	1	0	1.000
Championship series totals (3 years)		17	77	11	21	1	1	2	7	.273	2	21	5	38	1	2	.951

WORLD SERIES RECORD

NOTES: Member of World Series championship team (1995).

Year Team (League)	Pos.	G	AB	R	H	2B	3B	HR	RBI	Avg.	BB	SO	SB	PO	A	E	Avg.
1995—Atlanta (N.L.)..............	OF	6	25	3	9	1	0	0	1	.360	1	3	3	13	0	0	1.000
1996—Atlanta (N.L.)..............	OF	6	27	4	12	2	1	0	5	.444	1	2	1	7	0	1	.875
1997—Cleveland (A.L.).........	OF	7	25	5	9	1	0	0	2	.360	4	4	0	19	0	1	.950
World Series totals (3 years)		19	77	12	30	4	1	0	8	.390	6	9	4	39	0	2	.951

ALL-STAR GAME RECORD

Year League	Pos.	AB	R	H	2B	3B	HR	RBI	Avg.	BB	SO	SB	PO	A	E	Avg.
1993—National......................	OF	3	0	0	0	0	0	0	.000	0	1	0	1	0	0	1.000
1994—National......................	OF	1	1	1	0	0	1	1	1.000	1	0	0	2	1	0	1.000
All-Star Game totals (2 years)		4	1	1	0	0	1	1	.250	1	1	0	3	1	0	1.000

GROOM, BUDDY   P   ATHLETICS

PERSONAL: Born July 10, 1965, in Dallas. ... 6-2/208. ... Throws left, bats left. ... Full name: Wedsel Gary Groom Jr.
HIGH SCHOOL: Red Oak (Texas).
COLLEGE: Mary Hardin-Baylor (Texas).
TRANSACTIONS/CAREER NOTES: Selected by Chicago White Sox organization in 12th round of free-agent draft (June 2, 1987). ... Selected by Detroit Tigers organization from White Sox organization in Rule 5 minor league draft (December 3, 1990). ... Traded by Tigers to Florida Marlins for a player to be named later (August 7, 1995); Tigers acquired P Mike Myers to complete deal (August 9, 1995). ... Granted free agency (October 16, 1995). ... Signed by Oakland Athletics organization (November 27, 1995).

Year Team (League)	W	L	Pct.	ERA	G	GS	CG	ShO	Sv.	IP	H	R	ER	BB	SO
1987—GC White Sox (GCL)	1	0	1.000	0.75	4	1	0	0	1	12	12	1	1	2	8
—Daytona Beach (FSL).........	7	2	.778	3.59	11	10	2	0	0	67 2/3	60	30	27	33	29
1988—Tampa (Fla. St.).........	13	10	.565	2.54	27	27	8	0	0	*195	181	69	55	51	118
1989—Birmingham (Southern)	13	8	.619	4.52	26	26	3	1	0	167 1/3	172	101	84	78	94
1990—Birmingham (Southern)	6	8	.429	5.07	20	20	0	0	0	115 1/3	135	81	65	48	66
1991—Toledo (International)■......	2	5	.286	4.32	24	6	0	0	1	75	75	39	36	25	49
—London (Eastern)	7	1	.875	3.48	11	7	0	0	0	51 2/3	51	20	20	12	39
1992—Toledo (International)	7	7	.500	2.80	16	16	1	0	0	109 1/3	102	41	34	23	71
—Detroit (A.L.)	0	5	.000	5.82	12	7	0	0	1	38 2/3	48	28	25	22	15
1993—Toledo (International)	9	3	.750	2.74	16	15	0	0	0	102	98	34	31	30	78
—Detroit (A.L.)	0	2	.000	6.14	19	3	0	0	0	36 2/3	48	25	25	13	15
1994—Toledo (International)	0	0	. . .	2.25	5	0	0	0	0	4	2	1	1	0	6
—Detroit (A.L.)	0	1	.000	3.94	40	0	0	0	1	32	31	14	14	13	27
1995—Detroit (A.L.)	1	3	.250	7.52	23	4	0	0	1	40 2/3	55	35	34	26	23
—Toledo (International)	2	3	.400	1.91	6	5	1	0	0	33	31	14	7	4	24
—Florida (N.L.)■..................	1	2	.333	7.20	14	0	0	0	0	15	26	12	12	6	12
1996—Oakland (A.L.)■..............	5	0	1.000	3.84	72	1	0	0	2	77 1/3	85	37	33	34	57
1997—Oakland (A.L.)...............	2	2	.500	5.15	78	0	0	0	3	64 2/3	75	38	37	24	45
1998—Oakland (A.L.)...............	3	1	.750	4.24	75	0	0	0	0	57 1/3	62	30	27	20	36
A.L. totals (7 years)	11	14	.440	5.05	319	15	0	0	8	347 1/3	404	207	195	152	218
N.L. totals (1 year)	1	2	.333	7.20	14	0	0	0	0	15	26	12	12	6	12
Major league totals (7 years)......	12	16	.429	5.14	333	15	0	0	8	362 1/3	430	219	207	158	230

GROSS, KIP   P   RED SOX

PERSONAL: Born August 24, 1964, in Scottsbluff, Neb. ... 6-2/194. ... Throws right, bats right. ... Full name: Kip Lee Gross.
HIGH SCHOOL: Gering (Neb.).
COLLEGE: Murray State, then Nebraska.
TRANSACTIONS/CAREER NOTES: Selected by St. Louis Cardinals organization in third round of free-agent draft (January 9, 1985); did not sign. ... Selected by New York Mets organization in fourth round of free-agent draft (June 2, 1986). ... Traded by Mets organization with P Randy Myers to Cincinnati Reds for P John Franco and OF Don Brown (December 6, 1989). ... Traded by Reds with OF Eric Davis to Los

Angeles Dodgers for P Tim Belcher and P John Wetteland (November 27, 1991). ... On Albuquerque disabled list (August 5-12, 1993). ... On Albuquerque temporarily inactive list (May 5-10, 1994). ... Released by Dodgers (May 10, 1994). ... Played for Nippon Ham Fighters of Japan Pacific League (1994-98). ... Signed by Boston Red Sox (January 5, 1999).

Year	Team (League)	W	L	Pct.	ERA	G	GS	CG	ShO	Sv.	IP	H	R	ER	BB	SO
1987—	Lynchburg (Carolina)	7	4	.636	2.72	16	15	2	0	0	89 1/3	92	37	27	22	39
1988—	St. Lucie (Fla. St.)	13	9	.591	2.62	28	27	7	3	0	178 1/3	153	72	52	53	124
1989—	Jackson (Texas)	6	5	.545	2.49	16	16	4	0	0	112	96	47	31	13	60
	— Tidewater (Int'l)	4	4	.500	3.97	12	12	0	0	0	70 1/3	72	33	31	17	39
1990—	Nashville (A.A.)■	12	7	.632	3.33	40	11	2	1	3	127	113	54	47	47	62
	— Cincinnati (N.L.)	0	0	...	4.26	5	0	0	0	0	6 1/3	6	3	3	2	3
1991—	Nashville (A.A.)	5	3	.625	2.08	14	6	1	1	0	47 2/3	39	13	11	16	28
	— Cincinnati (N.L.)	6	4	.600	3.47	29	9	1	0	0	85 2/3	93	43	33	40	40
1992—	Albuquerque (PCL)■	6	5	.545	3.51	31	14	2	0	8	107 2/3	96	48	42	36	58
	— Los Angeles (N.L.)	1	1	.500	4.18	16	1	0	0	0	23 2/3	32	14	11	10	14
1993—	Albuquerque (PCL)............	13	7	.650	4.05	59	7	0	0	13	124 1/3	115	58	56	41	96
	— Los Angeles (N.L.)	0	0	...	0.60	10	0	0	0	0	15	13	1	1	4	12
1994—	Albuquerque (PCL)............	1	1	.500	5.06	10	0	0	0	1	16	14	9	9	6	11
	— Nippon (Jap. Pac.)	6	12	.333	4.29	25	...	...	...	0	149	...	...	71	...	62
1995—	Nippon (Jap. Pac.)	16	13	.552	3.04	31	...	...	...	0	231	...	...	78	...	114
1996—	Nippon (Jap. Pac.)	17	9	.654	3.62	28	...	...	...	0	193 2/3	...	...	78	...	79
1997—	Nippon (Jap. Pac.)	13	11	.542	3.63	33	...	...	...	0	233 1/3	...	...	94	...	98
1998—	Nippon (Jap. Pac.)	3	4	.429	3.96	7	7	1	0	0	36 1/3	30	18	16	15	11
Major league totals (4 years)......		7	5	.583	3.31	60	10	1	0	0	130 2/3	144	61	48	56	69

GRUDZIELANEK, MARK   SS   DODGERS

PERSONAL: Born June 30, 1970, in Milwaukee. ... 6-1/185. ... Bats right, throws right. ... Full name: Mark James Grudzielanek. ... Name pronounced gress-UH-lawn-ick.
HIGH SCHOOL: J.M. Hanks (El Paso, Texas).
JUNIOR COLLEGE: Trinidad (Colo.) State Junior College.
TRANSACTIONS/CAREER NOTES: Selected by New York Mets organization in 17th round of free-agent draft (June 5, 1989); did not sign. ... Selected by Montreal Expos organization in 11th round of free-agent draft (June 3, 1991). ... On disabled list (July 13-August 9, 1993 and May 12-19, 1994). ... Traded by Expos with P Carlos Perez and OF Hiram Bocachica to Los Angeles Dodgers for 2B Wilton Guerrero, P Ted Lilly, OF Peter Bergeron and 1B Jonathan Tucker (July 31, 1998).
RECORDS: Holds major league single-season record for fewest chances accepted by shortstop who led league in chances accepted—683 (1997). ... Shares major league single-season record for fewest putouts by shortstop (150 or more games)—180 (1996).
HONORS: Named Eastern League Most Valuable Player (1994).
STATISTICAL NOTES: Led Eastern League shortstops with .959 fielding percentage in 1994. ... Led N.L. shortstops with 715 total chances and 99 double plays in 1997. ... Led N.L. shortstops with 33 errors in 1998.

							BATTING								FIELDING		
Year	Team (League)	Pos.	G	AB	R	H	2B	3B	HR	RBI	Avg.	BB	SO	SB	PO	A	E	Avg.
1991—	Jamestown (NYP)	SS	72	275	44	72	9	3	2	32	.262	18	43	14	112	206	23	.933
1992—	Rockford (Midwest) ...	SS	128	496	64	122	12	5	5	54	.246	22	59	25	173	290	41	.919
1993—	W.P. Beach (FSL).......	2-S-O-3	86	300	41	80	11	6	1	34	.267	14	42	17	105	135	13	.949
1994—	Harrisburg (East.).......	SS-3B	122	488	92	157	•37	3	11	66	.322	43	66	32	178	344	23	†.958
1995—	Montreal (N.L.)..........	SS-3B-2B	78	269	27	66	12	2	1	20	.245	14	47	8	94	198	10	.967
	— Ottawa (Int'l)	SS	49	181	26	54	9	1	1	22	.298	10	17	12	58	156	14	.939
1996—	Montreal (N.L.)..........	SS	153	657	99	201	34	4	6	49	.306	26	83	33	180	453	27	.959
1997—	Montreal (N.L.)..........	SS	156	*649	76	177	*54	3	4	51	.273	23	76	25	237	446	*32	.955
1998—	Montreal (N.L.)..........	SS	105	396	51	109	15	1	8	41	.275	21	50	11	152	283	23	.950
	— Los Angeles (N.L.)■ ..	SS	51	193	11	51	6	0	2	21	.264	5	23	7	78	172	§10	.962
Major league totals (4 years)			543	2164	264	604	121	10	21	182	.279	89	279	84	741	1552	102	.957

ALL-STAR GAME RECORD

						BATTING							FIELDING		
Year	League	Pos.	AB	R	H	2B	3B	HR	RBI	Avg.	BB	SO	SB	PO	A	E	Avg.
1996—	National	3B	1	0	0	0	0	0	0	.000	0	0	0	0	0	0	...

GRZANICH, MIKE   P   ASTROS

PERSONAL: Born August 24, 1972, in Canton, Ill. ... 6-1/180. ... Throws right, bats right. ... Full name: Michael Edward Grzanich.
HIGH SCHOOL: Lewistown (Ill.).
JUNIOR COLLEGE: Parkland College (Ill.).
TRANSACTIONS/CAREER NOTES: Selected by Houston Astros organization in 19th round of free-agent draft (June 1, 1992). ... On New Orleans disabled list (July 13-August 3, 1998).
STATISTICAL NOTES: Led New York-Pennsylvania League with 11 home runs allowed in 1993.

Year	Team (League)	W	L	Pct.	ERA	G	GS	CG	ShO	Sv.	IP	H	R	ER	BB	SO
1992—	GC Astros (GCL)	2	5	.286	4.54	17	17	0	0	3	33 2/3	38	21	17	14	29
1993—	Auburn (N.Y.-Penn)	5	•8	.385	4.82	16	14	•4	•1	0	93 1/3	106	*63	50	27	71
1994—	Quad City (Midwest)	11	7	.611	3.09	23	22	3	0	0	142 2/3	145	55	49	43	101
1995—	Jackson (Texas)	5	3	.625	2.74	50	0	0	0	8	65 2/3	55	22	20	38	44
1996—	Jackson (Texas)	5	4	.556	3.98	57	0	0	0	6	72 1/3	60	47	32	43	80
1997—	Jackson (Texas)	7	6	.538	4.96	38	13	0	0	12	101 2/3	114	68	56	46	73
1998—	New Orleans (PCL)............	1	2	.333	2.27	34	0	0	0	5	39 2/3	27	13	10	21	39
	— Houston (N.L.)	0	0	...	18.00	1	0	0	0	0	1	1	2	2	2	1
	— Kissimmee (Florida State) ..	1	1	.500	6.14	4	0	0	0	0	7 1/3	9	7	5	5	8
Major league totals (1 year)........		0	0	...	18.00	1	0	0	0	0	1	1	2	2	2	1

G

GUARDADO, EDDIE — P — TWINS

PERSONAL: Born October 2, 1970, in Stockton, Calif. ... 6-0/195. ... Throws left, bats right. ... Full name: Edward Adrian Guardado. ... Name pronounced gwar-DAH-doh.
HIGH SCHOOL: Franklin (Stockton, Calif.).
COLLEGE: San Joaquin Delta College (Calif.).
TRANSACTIONS/CAREER NOTES: Selected by Minnesota Twins organization in 21st round of free-agent draft (June 4, 1990).
STATISTICAL NOTES: Pitched 5-0 no-hit victory against Pulaski (August 26, 1991).

Year Team (League)	W	L	Pct.	ERA	G	GS	CG	ShO	Sv.	IP	H	R	ER	BB	SO
1991— Elizabethton (Appal.)	8	4	.667	1.86	14	13	3	•1	0	92	67	30	19	31	*106
1992— Kenosha (Midwest)	5	10	.333	4.37	18	18	2	1	0	101	106	57	49	30	103
— Visalia (California)	7	0	1.000	1.64	7	7	1	1	0	49 1/3	47	13	9	10	39
1993— Nashville (Southern)	4	0	1.000	1.24	10	10	2	2	0	65 1/3	53	10	9	10	57
— Minnesota (A.L.)	3	8	.273	6.18	19	16	0	0	0	94 2/3	123	68	65	36	46
1994— Salt Lake (PCL)	12	7	.632	4.83	24	24	2	0	0	151	171	90	81	51	87
— Minnesota (A.L.)	0	2	.000	8.47	4	4	0	0	0	17	26	16	16	4	8
1995— Minnesota (A.L.)	4	9	.308	5.12	51	5	0	0	2	91 1/3	99	54	52	45	71
1996— Minnesota (A.L.)	6	5	.545	5.25	•83	0	0	0	4	73 2/3	61	45	43	33	74
1997— Minnesota (A.L.)	0	4	.000	3.91	69	0	0	0	1	46	45	23	20	17	54
1998— Minnesota (A.L.)	3	1	.750	4.52	79	0	0	0	0	65 2/3	66	34	33	28	53
Major league totals (6 years)	16	29	.356	5.31	305	25	0	0	7	388 1/3	420	240	229	163	306

GUERRERO, VLADIMIR — OF — EXPOS

PERSONAL: Born February 9, 1976, in Nizao Bani, Dominican Republican ... 6-0/205. ... Bats right, throws right. ... Full name: Vladimir Alvino Guerrero. ... Brother of Wilton Guerrero, second baseman, Montreal Expos.
TRANSACTIONS/CAREER NOTES: Signed as non-drafted free agent by Montreal Expos organization (March 1, 1993). ... On disabled list (March 30-May 2, 1997); including rehabilitation assignment to West Palm Beach (April 29-May 2). ... On Montreal disabled list (June 5-21 and July 12-27, 1997); included rehabilitation assignment to West Palm Beach (April 29-May 2).
HONORS: Named Eastern League Most Valuable Player (1996). ... Named Minor League Player of the Year by THE SPORTING NEWS (1996).
STATISTICAL NOTES: Tied for South Atlantic League lead in double plays by outfielder with four in 1995. ... Led Eastern League with .438 on-base percentage and 13 intentional bases on balls received in 1996.

Year Team (League)	Pos.	G	AB	R	H	2B	3B	HR	RBI	Avg.	BB	SO	SB	PO	A	E	Avg.
						BATTING									FIELDING		
1993— Dom. Expos (DSL)	OF-IF-P	34	105	19	35	4	0	1	14	.333	8	13	4	75	7	5	.943
1994— Dom. Expos (DSL)	OF	25	92	34	39	11	0	12	35	.424	21	6	5	38	6	2	.957
— GC Expos (GCL)	OF	37	137	24	43	13	3	5	25	.314	11	18	0	64	9	1	.986
1995— Albany (S. Atl.)	OF	110	421	77	140	21	10	16	63	*.333	30	45	12	207	15	11	.953
1996— W.P. Beach (FSL)	OF	20	80	16	29	8	0	5	18	.363	3	10	2	28	5	3	.917
— Harrisburg (East.)	OF	118	417	84	150	32	8	19	78	*.360	51	42	17	184	13	8	.961
— Montreal (N.L.)	OF	9	27	2	5	0	0	1	1	.185	0	3	0	11	0	0	1.000
1997— W.P. Beach (FSL)	OF	3	10	0	4	2	0	0	2	.400	1	0	1	4	1	0	1.000
— Montreal (N.L.)	OF	90	325	44	98	22	2	11	40	.302	19	39	3	148	10	*12	.929
1998— Montreal (N.L.)	OF	159	623	108	202	37	7	38	109	.324	42	95	11	323	9	*17	.951
Major league totals (3 years)		258	975	154	305	59	9	50	150	.313	61	137	14	482	19	29	.945

RECORD AS PITCHER

Year Team (League)	W	L	Pct.	ERA	G	GS	CG	ShO	Sv.	IP	H	R	ER	BB	SO
1993— DSL Expos (DSL)	0	0	...	2.25	3	0	0	0	0	8	10	3	2	4	6

GUERRERO, WILTON — 2B — EXPOS

PERSONAL: Born October 24, 1974, in Don Gregorio, Dominican Republic. ... 6-0/175. ... Bats right, throws right. ... Brother of Vladimir Guerrero, outfielder, Montreal Expos.
HIGH SCHOOL: Escuela Primaria Don Gregorio (Dominican Republic).
TRANSACTIONS/CAREER NOTES: Signed as non-drafted free agent by Los Angeles Dodgers organization (October 8, 1991). ... On Albuquerque disabled list (June 26-July 5 and July 26-August 23, 1996). ... On suspended list (June 2-9, 1997). ... Traded by Dodgers with P Ted Lilly, OF Peter Bergeron and 1B Jonathan Tucker to Montreal Expos for P Carlos Perez, SS Mark Grudzielanek and OF Hiram Bocachica (July 31, 1998).
STATISTICAL NOTES: Led Florida State League in caught stealing with 20 in 1994. ... Led Texas League in caught stealing with 22 in 1995.

Year Team (League)	Pos.	G	AB	R	H	2B	3B	HR	RBI	Avg.	BB	SO	SB	PO	A	E	Avg.
						BATTING									FIELDING		
1992— Dom. Dodgers (DSL)	SS	61	225	52	87	7	4	0	38	.387	34	21	15	104	215	21	.938
1993— Great Falls (Pio.)	SS	66	256	44	76	5	1	0	21	.297	24	33	20	76	184	21	.925
— Dom. Dodgers (DSL)	SS	8	31	6	11	0	1	0	4	.355	4	3	2	15	18	1	.971
1994— Vero Beach (FSL)	SS	110	402	55	118	11	4	1	32	.294	29	71	23	111	292	17	.960
1995— San Antonio (Tex.)	SS	95	382	53	133	13	6	0	26	*.348	26	63	21	121	263	19	.953
— Albuquerque (PCL)	SS-OF	14	49	10	16	1	1	0	2	.327	1	7	2	13	39	9	.852
1996— Albuquerque (PCL)	2B-SS	98	425	79	146	17	12	2	38	.344	26	48	26	183	306	19	.963
— Los Angeles (N.L.)	OF	5	2	1	0	0	0	0	0	.000	0	2	0	0	0	0	...
1997— Los Angeles (N.L.)	2B-SS	111	357	39	104	10	9	4	32	.291	8	52	6	148	231	4	.990
— Albuquerque (PCL)	SS-2B	10	45	9	18	0	1	0	5	.400	2	3	3	16	38	5	.915
1998— Los Angeles (N.L.)	2B-SS-OF	64	180	21	51	4	3	0	7	.283	4	33	5	71	91	7	.959
— Albuquerque (PCL)	2B-OF	30	121	15	36	3	2	1	10	.298	9	12	11	55	49	1	.990
— Montreal (N.L.)■	2B	52	222	29	63	10	6	2	20	.284	10	30	3	103	130	6	.975
Major league totals (3 years)		232	761	90	218	24	18	6	59	.286	22	117	14	322	452	17	.979

G

GUEVARA, GIOMAR — 2B/SS — MARINERS

PERSONAL: Born October 23, 1972, in Miranda, Venezuela. ... 5-8/150. ... Bats both, throws right. ... Full name: Giomar Antonio Guevara.
TRANSACTIONS/CAREER NOTES: Signed as non-drafted free agent by Seattle Mariners organization (November 13, 1990). ... On disabled list (June 14-July 21, 1995). ... On Seattle disabled list (March 27-September 1, 1998); included rehabilitation assignments to Lancaster (July 18-August 10) and Orlando (August 14-September 1).

Year Team (League)	Pos.	G	AB	R	H	2B	3B	HR	RBI	Avg.	BB	SO	SB	PO	A	E	Avg.
1991—						Dominican Summer League statistics unavailable.											
1992— Dom. Dodgers (DSL) .	IF	45	163	30	51	13	4	1	24	.313	19	30	14	37	103	10	.933
1993— Bellingham (N'west)...	SS	62	211	31	48	8	3	1	23	.227	34	46	4	83	172	16	.941
1994— Appleton (Midwest)....	SS-2B	110	385	57	116	23	3	8	46	.301	42	77	9	171	270	23	.950
— Jacksonville (Sou.).....	SS	7	20	2	4	2	0	1	3	.200	2	9	0	12	25	3	.925
1995— Riverside (Calif.)........	SS	83	292	53	71	12	3	2	34	.243	30	71	7	123	231	27	.929
1996— Port City (Southern)...	SS-2B	119	414	60	110	18	2	2	41	.266	54	102	21	187	350	35	.939
1997— Tacoma (PCL)	2B-SS	54	176	29	43	5	1	2	13	.244	5	39	3	102	129	11	.955
— Memphis (Sou.)..........	SS	65	228	30	60	10	4	4	28	.263	20	42	5	80	217	13	.958
— Seattle (A.L.)	DH-2B-SS	5	4	0	0	0	0	0	0	.000	0	2	1	2	6	1	.889
1998— Lancaster (Calif.).......	2B-SS-3B	19	61	15	15	4	0	0	3	.246	14	20	1	28	58	2	.977
— Orlando (South.)........	SS-2B	14	45	13	15	5	1	0	6	.333	8	11	0	19	45	5	.928
— Seattle (A.L.)	2B-SS-DH	11	13	4	3	2	0	0	0	.231	4	4	0	8	13	0	1.000
Major league totals (2 years)		16	17	4	3	2	0	0	0	.176	4	6	1	10	19	1	.967

GUILLEN, CARLOS — 2B — MARINERS

PERSONAL: Born September 30, 1975, in Maracay, Venezuela. ... 6-1/180. ... Bats right, throws right. ... Full name: Carlos Alfonso Guillen.
TRANSACTIONS/CAREER NOTES: Signed as non-drafted free agent by Houston Astros organization (September 19, 1992). ... On disabled list (June 1-September 12, 1994). ... On disabled list (May 21-September 11, 1996). ... Traded by Astros with P Freddy Garcia and a player to be named later to Seattle Mariners for P Randy Johnson (July 31, 1998); Mariners acquired P John Halama to complete deal (October 1, 1998).

Year Team (League)	Pos.	G	AB	R	H	2B	3B	HR	RBI	Avg.	BB	SO	SB	PO	A	E	Avg.
1993— Dom. Astros (DSL).....	IF	18	56	12	14	4	2	0	8	.250	8	12	0	37	6	2	.956
1994—						Did not play.											
1995— Dom. Astros (DSL).....	DH	30	105	17	31	4	2	2	15	.295	9	17	17				...
1996— Quad City (Midwest) ..	SS	29	112	23	37	7	1	3	17	.330	16	25	13	47	71	9	.929
1997— Jackson (Texas)	SS	115	390	47	99	16	1	10	39	.254	38	78	6	169	313	35	.932
— New Orleans (A.A.)......	SS	3	13	3	4	1	0	0	0	.308	0	4	0	5	6	0	1.000
1998— New Orleans (PCL).....	SS	100	374	67	109	18	4	12	51	.291	31	61	3	145	287	26	.943
— Tacoma (PCL)■...........	2B	24	92	8	21	1	1	1	4	.228	9	17	1	49	63	2	.982
— Seattle (A.L.).............	2B	10	39	9	13	1	1	0	5	.333	3	9	2	15	29	0	1.000
Major league totals (1 year)		10	39	9	13	1	1	0	5	.333	3	9	2	15	29	0	1.000

GUILLEN, JOSE — OF — PIRATES

PERSONAL: Born May 17, 1976, in San Cristobal, Dominican Republic. ... 5-11/195. ... Bats right, throws right. ... Full name: Jose Manuel Guillen.
TRANSACTIONS/CAREER NOTES: Signed as non-drafted free agent by Pittsburgh Pirates organization (August 19, 1992).
HONORS: Named Carolina League Most Valuable Player (1996).
STATISTICAL NOTES: Led Carolina League with 263 total bases and grounding into double plays with 16 in 1996. ... Led Carolina League outfielders with six double plays in 1996. ... Career major league grand slams: 1.

Year Team (League)	Pos.	G	AB	R	H	2B	3B	HR	RBI	Avg.	BB	SO	SB	PO	A	E	Avg.
1993— Dom. Pirates (DSL)....	OF	63	234	39	53	3	4	11	41	.226	21	55	10	112	12	7	.947
1994— Bra. Pirates (GCL)	OF	30	110	17	29	4	1	4	11	.264	7	15	2	59	5	2	.970
1995— Erie (N.Y.-Penn).........	OF	66	258	41	81	17	1	*12	46	.314	10	44	1	107	10	13	.900
— Augusta (S. Atl.).........	OF	10	34	6	8	1	1	2	6	.235	2	9	0	5	0	0	1.000
1996— Lynchburg (Caro.)......	OF	136	*528	78	*170	30	0	•21	94	.322	20	73	24	224	16	*13	.949
1997— Pittsburgh (N.L.)	OF	143	498	58	133	20	5	14	70	.267	17	88	1	226	9	9	.963
1998— Pittsburgh (N.L.)	OF	153	573	60	153	38	2	14	84	.267	21	100	3	283	16	10	.968
Major league totals (2 years)		296	1071	118	286	58	7	28	154	.267	38	188	4	509	25	19	.966

GUILLEN, OZZIE — IF — BRAVES

G

PERSONAL: Born January 20, 1964, in Ocumare del Tuy, Miranda, Venezuela. ... 5-11/165. ... Bats left, throws right. ... Full name: Oswaldo Jose Barrios Guillen. ... Name pronounced GHEE-un.
TRANSACTIONS/CAREER NOTES: Signed as non-drafted free agent by San Diego Padres organization (December 17, 1980). ... Traded by Padres organization with P Tim Lollar, P Bill Long and 3B Luis Salazar to Chicago White Sox for P LaMarr Hoyt, P Kevin Kristan and P Todd Simmons (December 6, 1984). ... On disabled list (April 22, 1992-remainder of season). ... Granted free agency (October 31, 1997). ... Signed by Baltimore Orioles organization (January 29, 1998). ... Released by Orioles (May 1, 1998). ... Signed by Atlanta Braves (May 6, 1998). ... Granted free agency (November 2, 1998). ... Re-signed by Braves (December 2, 1998).
RECORDS: Holds major league single-season record for fewest bases on balls received (150 or more games)—10 (1996). ... Holds A.L. single-season record for fewest putouts by shortstop (150 or more games)—220 (1985).
HONORS: Named A.L. Rookie Player of the Year by THE SPORTING NEWS (1985). ... Named A.L. Rookie of the Year by Baseball Writers' Association of America (1985). ... Won A.L. Gold Glove at shortstop (1990).

STATISTICAL NOTES: Tied for California League lead with 14 sacrifice hits in 1982. ... Led Pacific Coast League shortstops with 362 assists and 549 total chances in 1984. ... Led A.L. shortstops with 760 total chances in 1987 and 863 in 1988. ... Led A.L. shortstops with 105 double plays in 1987. ... Career major league grand slams: 1.

MISCELLANEOUS: Batted as switch-hitter (1981-84).

Year Team (League)	Pos.	G	AB	R	H	2B	3B	HR	RBI	Avg.	BB	SO	SB	PO	A	E	Avg.
1981— GC Padres (GCL)	SS-2B	55	189	26	49	4	1	0	16	.259	13	24	8	105	135	15	.941
1982— Reno (California)	SS	130	528	*103	*183	33	1	2	54	.347	16	53	25	*240	399	41	.940
1983— Beaumont (Texas)	SS	114	427	62	126	20	4	2	48	.295	15	29	7	185	327	*38	.931
1984— Las Vegas (PCL)	SS-2B	122	463	81	137	26	6	5	53	.296	13	40	9	172	†364	17	.969
1985— Chicago (A.L.)■	SS	150	491	71	134	21	9	1	33	.273	12	36	7	220	382	12	*.980
1986— Chicago (A.L.)	SS-DH	159	547	58	137	19	4	2	47	.250	12	52	8	261	459	22	.970
1987— Chicago (A.L.)	SS	149	560	64	156	22	7	2	51	.279	22	52	25	266	475	19	.975
1988— Chicago (A.L.)	SS	156	566	58	148	16	7	0	39	.261	25	40	25	273	*570	20	.977
1989— Chicago (A.L.)	SS	155	597	63	151	20	8	1	54	.253	15	48	36	272	512	22	.973
1990— Chicago (A.L.)	SS	160	516	61	144	21	4	1	58	.279	26	37	13	252	474	17	.977
1991— Chicago (A.L.)	SS	154	524	52	143	20	3	3	49	.273	11	38	21	249	439	21	.970
1992— Chicago (A.L.)	SS	12	40	5	8	4	0	0	7	.200	1	5	1	20	39	0	1.000
1993— Chicago (A.L.)	SS	134	457	44	128	23	4	4	50	.280	10	41	5	189	361	16	.972
1994— Chicago (A.L.)	SS	100	365	46	105	9	5	1	39	.288	14	35	5	139	237	16	.959
1995— Chicago (A.L.)	SS-DH	122	415	50	103	20	3	1	41	.248	13	25	6	167	319	12	.976
1996— Chicago (A.L.)	SS-OF	150	499	62	131	24	8	4	45	.263	10	27	6	222	348	11	.981
1997— Chicago (A.L.)	SS	142	490	59	120	21	6	4	52	.245	22	24	5	207	348	15	.974
1998— Baltimore (A.L.)■	SS-3B	12	16	2	1	0	0	0	0	.063	1	2	0	3	11	1	.933
—Atlanta (N.L.)■	S-2-1-3	83	264	35	73	15	1	1	22	.277	24	25	1	97	166	6	.978
American League totals (14 years)		1755	6083	695	1609	240	68	24	565	.265	194	462	163	2740	4974	204	.974
National League totals (1 year)		83	264	35	73	15	1	1	22	.277	24	25	1	97	166	6	.978
Major league totals (14 years)		1838	6347	730	1682	255	69	25	587	.265	218	487	164	2837	5140	210	.974

DIVISION SERIES RECORD

Year Team (League)	Pos.	G	AB	R	H	2B	3B	HR	RBI	Avg.	BB	SO	SB	PO	A	E	Avg.
1998— Atlanta (N.L.)	PH	1	1	0	0	0	0	0	0	.000	0	0	0	...	...	...	...

CHAMPIONSHIP SERIES RECORD

Year Team (League)	Pos.	G	AB	R	H	2B	3B	HR	RBI	Avg.	BB	SO	SB	PO	A	E	Avg.
1993— Chicago (A.L.)	SS	6	22	4	6	1	0	0	2	.273	0	2	1	12	14	0	1.000
1998— Atlanta (N.L.)	PH-SS	4	12	1	5	0	0	0	1	.417	0	1	0	1	6	0	1.000
Championship series totals (2 years)		10	34	5	11	1	0	0	3	.324	0	3	1	13	20	0	1.000

ALL-STAR GAME RECORD

NOTES: Named to A.L. All-Star team; replaced by Kurt Stillwell due to injury (1988).

Year League	Pos.	AB	R	H	2B	3B	HR	RBI	Avg.	BB	SO	SB	PO	A	E	Avg.
1988— American							Selected, did not play.									
1990— American	SS	2	0	0	0	0	0	0	.000	0	0	0	0	2	0	1.000
1991— American	SS	0	0	0	0	0	0	0	...	0	0	0	1	0	0	1.000
All-Star Game totals (2 years)		2	0	0	0	0	0	0	.000	0	0	0	1	2	0	1.000

GUNDERSON, ERIC   P   RANGERS

PERSONAL: Born March 29, 1966, in Portland, Ore. ... 6-0/190. ... Throws left, bats right. ... Full name: Eric Andrew Gunderson.
HIGH SCHOOL: Aloha (Portland, Ore.).
COLLEGE: Portland State.
TRANSACTIONS/CAREER NOTES: Selected by San Francisco Giants organization in second round of free-agent draft (June 2, 1987). ... Released by Giants (March 31, 1992). ... Signed by Seattle Mariners organization (April 10, 1992). ... On Jacksonville disabled list (April 10-17, 1992). ... On Seattle suspended list (September 30-October 4, 1992). ... Released by Mariners (April 29, 1993). ... Signed by New York Mets organization (June 10, 1993). ... Granted free agency (October 15, 1993). ... Signed by San Diego Padres organization (December 24, 1993). ... Released by Las Vegas (April 2, 1994). ... Signed by Mets organization (May 5, 1994). ... Claimed on waivers by Mariners (August 4, 1995). ... Claimed on waivers by Boston Red Sox (August 10, 1995). ... Granted free agency (October 7, 1996). ... Signed by Texas Rangers organization (January 24, 1997). ... On disabled list (August 26-September 7, 1997).
STATISTICAL NOTES: Led California League with 17 hit batsmen in 1988.

Year Team (League)	W	L	Pct.	ERA	G	GS	CG	ShO	Sv.	IP	H	R	ER	BB	SO
1987— Everett (Northwest)	8	4	.667	2.46	15	•15	*5	•3	0	98²/₃	80	34	27	34	*99
1988— San Jose (California)	12	5	.706	2.65	20	20	5	•4	0	149¹/₃	131	56	44	52	151
—Shreveport (Texas)	1	2	.333	5.15	7	6	0	0	0	36²/₃	45	25	21	13	28
1989— Shreveport (Texas)	8	2	*.800	2.72	11	11	2	1	0	72²/₃	68	24	22	23	61
—Phoenix (PCL)	2	4	.333	5.04	14	14	2	1	0	85²/₃	93	51	48	36	56
1990— San Francisco (N.L.)	1	2	.333	5.49	7	4	0	0	0	19²/₃	24	14	12	11	14
—Phoenix (PCL)	5	7	.417	8.23	16	16	0	0	0	82	137	87	75	46	41
—Shreveport (Texas)	2	2	.500	3.25	8	8	1	1	0	52²/₃	51	24	19	17	44
1991— San Francisco (N.L.)	0	0	...	5.40	2	0	0	0	1	3¹/₃	6	4	2	1	2
—Phoenix (PCL)	7	6	.538	6.14	40	14	0	0	3	107	153	85	73	44	53
1992— Jacksonville (Southern)■	2	0	1.000	2.31	15	0	0	0	2	23¹/₃	18	10	6	7	23
—Calgary (PCL)	0	2	.000	6.02	27	1	0	0	5	52¹/₃	57	37	35	31	50
—Seattle (A.L.)	2	1	.667	8.68	9	0	0	0	0	9¹/₃	12	12	9	5	2
1993— Calgary (PCL)	0	1	.000	18.90	5	0	0	0	0	6²/₃	14	15	14	8	3
—Binghamton (Eastern)■	2	1	.667	5.24	20	1	0	0	1	22¹/₃	20	14	13	14	26
—Norfolk (Int'l)	3	2	.600	3.71	6	5	1	0	0	34	41	16	14	9	26
1994— St. Lucie (Fla. St.)	1	0	1.000	0.00	3	0	0	0	0	4²/₃	4	0	0	0	6

Year Team (League)	W	L	Pct.	ERA	G	GS	CG	ShO	Sv.	IP	H	R	ER	BB	SO
— Norfolk (Int'l)	3	1	.750	3.68	19	2	1	1	1	36 2/3	25	16	15	17	31
— New York (N.L.)................	0	0	...	0.00	14	0	0	0	0	9	5	0	0	4	4
1995— New York (N.L.)................	1	1	.500	3.70	30	0	0	0	0	24 1/3	25	10	10	8	19
— Boston (A.L.)■...............	2	1	.667	5.11	19	0	0	0	0	12 1/3	13	7	7	9	9
1996— Pawtucket (Int'l)	2	1	.667	3.48	26	1	0	0	2	33 2/3	38	15	13	9	34
— Boston (A.L.)	0	1	.000	8.31	28	0	0	0	0	17 1/3	21	17	16	8	7
1997— Texas (A.L.)■	2	1	.667	3.26	60	0	0	0	1	49 2/3	45	19	18	15	31
1998— Texas (A.L.)	0	3	.000	5.19	68	1	0	0	0	67 2/3	88	43	39	19	41
A.L. totals (5 years)	6	7	.462	5.12	184	1	0	0	1	156 1/3	179	98	89	56	90
N.L. totals (4 years)	2	3	.400	3.83	53	4	0	0	1	56 1/3	60	28	24	24	39
Major league totals (8 years)	8	10	.444	4.78	237	5	0	0	2	212 2/3	239	126	113	80	129

GUTHRIE, MARK P RED SOX

PERSONAL: Born September 22, 1965, in Buffalo. ... 6-4/211. ... Throws left, bats right. ... Full name: Mark Andrew Guthrie.
HIGH SCHOOL: Venice (Fla.).
COLLEGE: Louisiana State.
TRANSACTIONS/CAREER NOTES: Selected by St. Louis Cardinals organization in fourth round of free-agent draft (June 2, 1986); did not sign. ... Selected by Minnesota Twins organization in seventh round of free-agent draft (June 2, 1987). ... On disabled list (May 29, 1993-remainder of season). ... Traded by Twins with P Kevin Tapani to Los Angeles Dodgers for 1B/3B Ron Coomer, P Greg Hansell, P Jose Parra and a player to be named later (July 31, 1995); Twins acquired OF Chris Latham to complete deal (October 30, 1995). ... Granted free agency (October 29, 1996). ... Re-signed by Dodgers (November 6, 1996). ... Granted free agency (October 26, 1998). ... Signed by Boston Red Sox (December 19, 1998).
MISCELLANEOUS: Appeared in one game as pinch runner (1991).

Year Team (League)	W	L	Pct.	ERA	G	GS	CG	ShO	Sv.	IP	H	R	ER	BB	SO
1987— Visalia (California)	2	1	.667	4.50	4	1	0	0	0	12	10	7	6	5	9
1988— Visalia (California)	12	9	.571	3.31	25	25	4	1	0	171 1/3	169	81	63	86	182
1989— Orlando (Sou.)	8	3	.727	1.97	14	14	0	0	0	96	75	32	21	38	103
— Portland (PCL)	3	4	.429	3.65	7	7	1	0	0	44 1/3	45	21	18	16	35
— Minnesota (A.L.)	2	4	.333	4.55	13	8	0	0	0	57 1/3	66	32	29	21	38
1990— Minnesota (A.L.)	7	9	.438	3.79	24	21	3	1	0	144 2/3	154	65	61	39	101
— Portland (PCL)	1	3	.250	2.98	9	8	1	0	0	42 1/3	47	19	14	12	39
1991— Minnesota (A.L.)	7	5	.583	4.32	41	12	0	0	2	98	116	52	47	41	72
1992— Minnesota (A.L.)	2	3	.400	2.88	54	0	0	0	5	75	59	27	24	23	76
1993— Minnesota (A.L.)	2	1	.667	4.71	22	0	0	0	0	21	20	11	11	16	15
1994— Minnesota (A.L.)	4	2	.667	6.14	50	2	0	0	1	51 1/3	65	43	35	18	38
1995— Minnesota (A.L.)	5	3	.625	4.46	36	0	0	0	0	42 1/3	47	22	21	16	48
— Los Angeles (N.L.)■	0	2	.000	3.66	24	0	0	0	0	19 2/3	19	11	8	9	19
1996— Los Angeles (N.L.)	2	3	.400	2.22	66	0	0	0	1	73	65	21	18	22	56
1997— Los Angeles (N.L.)	1	4	.200	5.32	62	0	0	0	1	69 1/3	71	44	41	30	42
1998— Los Angeles (N.L.)	2	1	.667	3.50	53	0	0	0	0	54	56	26	21	24	45
A.L. totals (7 years)	29	27	.518	4.19	240	43	3	1	8	489 2/3	527	252	228	174	388
N.L. totals (4 years)	5	10	.333	3.67	205	0	0	0	2	216	211	102	88	85	162
Major league totals (10 years)	34	37	.479	4.03	445	43	3	1	10	705 2/3	738	354	316	259	550

DIVISION SERIES RECORD

Year Team (League)	W	L	Pct.	ERA	G	GS	CG	ShO	Sv.	IP	H	R	ER	BB	SO
1995— Los Angeles (N.L.)	0	0	...	6.75	3	0	0	0	0	1 1/3	2	1	1	1	1
1996— Los Angeles (N.L.)	0	0	...	0.00	1	0	0	0	0	1/3	0	0	0	1	1
Div. series totals (2 years)	0	0	...	5.40	4	0	0	0	0	1 2/3	2	1	1	2	2

CHAMPIONSHIP SERIES RECORD

Year Team (League)	W	L	Pct.	ERA	G	GS	CG	ShO	Sv.	IP	H	R	ER	BB	SO
1991— Minnesota (A.L.)	1	0	1.000	0.00	2	0	0	0	0	2 2/3	0	0	0	0	0

WORLD SERIES RECORD

NOTES: Member of World Series championship team (1991).

Year Team (League)	W	L	Pct.	ERA	G	GS	CG	ShO	Sv.	IP	H	R	ER	BB	SO
1991— Minnesota (A.L.)	0	1	.000	2.25	4	0	0	0	0	4	3	1	1	4	3

GUTIERREZ, RICKY SS ASTROS

G

PERSONAL: Born May 23, 1970, in Miami. ... 6-1/175. ... Bats right, throws right. ... Full name: Ricardo Gutierrez.
HIGH SCHOOL: American (Hialeah, Fla.).
TRANSACTIONS/CAREER NOTES: Selected by Baltimore Orioles organization in supplemental round ("sandwich pick" between first and second round, 28th pick overall) of free-agent draft (June 1, 1988); pick received as compensation for Orioles failing to sign 1987 No. 1 pick P Brad DuVall. ... Traded by Orioles to San Diego Padres (September 4, 1992), completing deal in which Padres traded P Craig Lefferts to Orioles for P Erik Schullstrom and a player to be named later (August 31, 1992). ... Traded by Padres with OF Phil Plantier, OF Derek Bell, P Pedro Martinez, P Doug Brocail and IF Craig Shipley to Houston Astros for 3B Ken Caminiti, OF Steve Finley, SS Andujar Cedeno, 1B Robert Petagine, P Brian Williams and a player to be named later (December 28, 1994); Padres acquired P Sean Fesh to complete deal (May 1, 1995). ... On disabled list (March 31-May 6, 1997); included rehabilitation assignment to New Orleans (April 29-May 6).
STATISTICAL NOTES: Led Appalachian League shortstops with 309 total chances in 1988.

						BATTING								FIELDING		
Year Team (League)	Pos.	G	AB	R	H	2B	3B	HR	RBI	Avg.	BB	SO	SB	PO	A	E	Avg.
1988— Bluefield (Appal.).......	SS	62	208	35	51	8	2	2	19	.245	44	40	5	*100	175	34	.890
1989— Frederick (Carolina)....	SS	127	456	48	106	16	2	3	41	.232	39	89	15	190	372	34	*.943
1990— Frederick (Carolina)....	SS	112	425	54	117	16	4	1	46	.275	38	59	12	192	286	26	.948
— Hagerstown (East.)......	SS	20	64	4	15	0	1	0	6	.234	3	8	2	31	36	4	.944

				BATTING										FIELDING			
Year Team (League)	Pos.	G	AB	R	H	2B	3B	HR	RBI	Avg.	BB	SO	SB	PO	A	E	Avg.
1991— Hagerstown (East.).....	SS	84	292	47	69	6	4	0	30	.236	57	52	11	158	196	22	.941
— Rochester (Int'l).........	SS-3B	49	157	23	48	5	3	0	15	.306	24	27	4	61	129	8	.960
1992— Rochester (Int'l).........	2B-SS	125	431	54	109	9	3	0	41	.253	53	77	14	251	283	15	.973
— Las Vegas (PCL)■..	SS	3	6	0	1	0	0	0	1	.167	1	3	0	1	8	0	1.000
1993— Las Vegas (PCL)	2B-SS	5	24	4	10	4	0	0	4	.417	0	4	4	11	14	2	.926
— San Diego (N.L.)	S-2-0-3	133	438	76	110	10	5	5	26	.251	50	97	4	194	305	14	.973
1994— San Diego (N.L.)	SS-2B	90	275	27	66	11	2	1	28	.240	32	54	2	93	202	22	.931
1995— Houston (N.L.)■........	SS-3B	52	156	22	43	6	0	0	12	.276	10	33	5	64	108	8	.956
— Tucson (PCL)	SS	64	236	46	71	12	4	1	26	.301	28	28	9	91	167	6	.977
1996— Houston (N.L.)	SS-3B-2B	89	218	28	62	8	1	1	15	.284	23	42	6	86	149	12	.951
1997— New Orleans (A.A.).....	SS	7	27	2	5	1	0	0	4	.185	2	4	0	12	21	1	.971
— Houston (N.L.)	SS-3B-2B	102	303	33	79	14	4	3	34	.261	21	50	5	104	191	8	.974
1998— Houston (N.L.)	SS	141	491	55	128	24	3	2	46	.261	54	84	13	215	404	15	.976
Major league totals (6 years)		607	1881	241	488	73	15	12	161	.259	190	360	35	756	1359	79	.964

DIVISION SERIES RECORD

				BATTING										FIELDING			
Year Team (League)	Pos.	G	AB	R	H	2B	3B	HR	RBI	Avg.	BB	SO	SB	PO	A	E	Avg.
1997— Houston (N.L.)	SS	3	8	0	1	0	0	0	0	.125	2	1	0	5	5	0	1.000
1998— Houston (N.L.)	SS	4	10	1	3	0	0	0	0	.300	3	7	1	7	13	0	1.000
Division series totals (2 years)		7	18	1	4	0	0	0	0	.222	5	8	1	12	18	0	1.000

GUZMAN, CRISTIAN   SS   TWINS

PERSONAL: Born March 21, 1978, in Santo Domingo, Dominican Republic. ... 6-0/150. ... Bats both, throws right.

TRANSACTIONS/CAREER NOTES: Signed as non-drafted free agent by New York Yankees organization (August 24, 1994). ... Traded by Yankees with P Eric Milton, P Danny Mota, OF Brian Buchanan and cash to Minnesota Twins for 2B Chuck Knoblauch (February 6, 1998).

STATISTICAL NOTES: Led South Atlantic League shortstops with 68 double plays in 1997. ... Led Eastern League with 17 sacrifice hits in 1998. ... Led Eastern League shortstops with 95 double plays in 1998.

				BATTING										FIELDING			
Year Team (League)	Pos.	G	AB	R	H	2B	3B	HR	RBI	Avg.	BB	SO	SB	PO	A	E	Avg.
1995— Dom. Yankees (DSL)..	. . .	46	160	24	43	6	5	3	20	.269	12	23	11	159	29	13	.882
1996— GC Yankees (GCL)......	SS	42	170	37	50	8	2	1	21	.294	10	31	7	55	106	20	.890
1997— Tampa (Fla. St.)	SS	4	14	4	4	0	0	0	1	.286	1	1	0	6	10	2	.889
— Greensboro (S. Atl.) ...	SS	124	495	68	135	21	4	4	52	.273	17	105	23	173	364	37	.936
1998— New Britain (East.)■ ..	SS	•140	566	68	157	29	5	1	40	.277	21	111	23	211	*426	*32	.952

GUZMAN, DOMINGO   P   PADRES

PERSONAL: Born April 5, 1975, in San Cristobal, Dominican Republic. ... 6-0/180. ... Throws right, bats right. ... Full name: Domingo Serrano Guzman.

TRANSACTIONS/CAREER NOTES: Signed as non-drafted free agent by San Diego Padres organization (June 15, 1993). ... On Clinton suspended list (May 15-18, 1997). ... On Rancho Cucamonga disabled list (April 2-May 26, 1998). ... On Mobile disabled list (August 7-27, 1998).

STATISTICAL NOTES: Pitched 6-0 no-hit victory vs. Butte (August 15, 1996).

Year Team (League)	W	L	Pct.	ERA	G	GS	CG	ShO	Sv.	IP	H	R	ER	BB	SO
1994— Ariz. Padres (Ariz.)	•8	4	.667	4.11	13	13	0	0	0	70	65	39	32	25	55
1995— Idaho Falls (Pioneer).........	2	1	.667	6.66	27	0	0	0	•11	25²/₃	25	22	19	25	33
1996— Idaho Falls (Pioneer).........	4	2	.667	4.13	15	10	1	•1	0	65¹/₃	52	41	30	29	75
— Clinton (Midwest).............	0	5	.000	12.63	6	5	0	0	0	20²/₃	32	33	29	19	18
1997— Clinton (Midwest).............	4	5	.444	3.19	12	12	5	0	0	79	66	36	28	25	91
— Rancho Cuca. (Cal.)	3	2	.600	5.45	6	6	0	0	0	38	42	23	23	16	39
1998— Rancho Cuca. (Cal.)	1	1	.500	3.74	4	4	0	0	0	21²/₃	22	11	9	6	16
— Mobile (Southern).............	5	2	.714	4.50	12	8	0	0	1	48	51	34	24	26	39

GUZMAN, JUAN   P   ORIOLES

PERSONAL: Born October 28, 1966, in Santo Domingo, Dominican Republic. ... 5-11/195. ... Throws right, bats right. ... Full name: Juan Andres Correa Guzman.

HIGH SCHOOL: Liceo Las Americas (Dominican Republic).

TRANSACTIONS/CAREER NOTES: Signed as non-drafted free agent by Los Angeles Dodgers organization (March 16, 1985). ... Traded by Dodgers to Toronto Blue Jays organization for IF Mike Sharperson (September 22, 1987). ... On Toronto disabled list (August 4-29, 1992); included rehabilitation assignment to Syracuse (August 24-25). ... On Toronto disabled list (May 16-June 5 and August 10-29, 1995); included rehabilitation assignment to Syracuse (August 25-26). ... On Toronto disabled list (May 23-June 7, 1996; May 29-June 26 and July 16-September 28, 1997). ... Traded by Blue Jays to Baltimore Orioles for P Nerio Rodriguez and OF Shannon Carter (July 31, 1998).

RECORDS: Holds A.L. single-season record for most wild pitches—26 (1993).

HONORS: Named A.L. Rookie Pitcher of the Year by THE SPORTING NEWS (1991).

STATISTICAL NOTES: Led Gulf Coast League with 15 wild pitches in 1985. ... Led Florida State League with 16 wild pitches in 1986. ... Led Southern League with 21 wild pitches in 1990. ... Led A.L. with 26 wild pitches in 1993 and tied for lead with 13 in 1994. ... Tied for A.L. lead with 16 losses in 1998.

Year Team (League)	W	L	Pct.	ERA	G	GS	CG	ShO	Sv.	IP	H	R	ER	BB	SO
1985— GC Dodgers (GCL)	5	1	.833	3.86	21	3	0	0	4	42	39	26	18	25	43
1986— Vero Beach (FSL)	10	9	.526	3.49	20	24	3	0	0	131¹/₃	114	69	51	90	96
1987— Bakersfield (California).......	5	6	.455	4.75	22	21	0	0	0	110	106	71	58	84	113

Year—Team (League)	W	L	Pct.	ERA	G	GS	CG	ShO	Sv.	IP	H	R	ER	BB	SO
1988— Knoxville (Southern)■	4	5	.444	2.36	46	2	0	0	6	84	52	29	22	61	90
1989— Syracuse (Int'l)	1	1	.500	3.98	14	0	0	0	0	20 1/3	13	9	9	30	28
— Knoxville (Southern)	1	4	.200	6.23	22	8	0	0	0	47 2/3	34	36	33	60	50
1990— Knoxville (Southern)	11	9	.550	4.24	37	21	2	0	1	157	145	84	74	80	138
1991— Syracuse (Int'l)	4	5	.444	4.03	12	11	0	0	0	67	46	39	30	42	67
— Toronto (A.L.)	10	3	.769	2.99	23	23	1	0	0	138 2/3	98	53	46	66	123
1992— Toronto (A.L.)	16	5	.762	2.64	28	28	1	0	0	180 2/3	135	56	53	72	165
— Syracuse (Int'l)	0	0	. . .	6.00	1	1	0	0	0	3	6	2	2	1	3
1993— Toronto (A.L.)	14	3	*.824	3.99	33	33	2	1	0	221	211	107	98	110	194
1994— Toronto (A.L.)	12	11	.522	5.68	25	•25	2	0	0	147 1/3	165	102	93	76	124
1995— Toronto (A.L.)	4	14	.222	6.32	24	24	3	0	0	135 1/3	151	101	95	73	94
— Syracuse (Int'l)	0	0	. . .	0.00	1	1	0	0	0	5	1	0	0	3	5
1996— Toronto (A.L.)	11	8	.579	*2.93	27	27	4	1	0	187 2/3	158	68	61	53	165
1997— Toronto (A.L.)	3	6	.333	4.95	13	13	0	0	0	60	48	42	33	31	52
— Dunedin (Fla. St.)	0	0	. . .	0.00	2	2	0	0	0	4	3	0	0	1	3
1998— Toronto (A.L.)	6	12	.333	4.41	22	22	2	0	0	145	133	83	71	65	113
— Baltimore (A.L.)■	4	§4	.500	4.23	11	11	0	0	0	66	60	34	31	33	55
Major league totals (8 years)	80	66	.548	4.08	206	206	15	2	0	1281 2/3	1159	646	581	579	1085

CHAMPIONSHIP SERIES RECORD

RECORDS: Shares single-inning record for most wild pitches—2 (October 5, 1993, first inning).

Year—Team (League)	W	L	Pct.	ERA	G	GS	CG	ShO	Sv.	IP	H	R	ER	BB	SO
1991— Toronto (A.L.)	1	0	1.000	3.18	1	1	0	0	0	5 2/3	4	2	2	4	2
1992— Toronto (A.L.)	2	0	1.000	2.08	2	2	0	0	0	13	12	3	3	5	11
1993— Toronto (A.L.)	2	0	1.000	2.08	2	2	0	0	0	13	8	4	3	9	9
Champ. series totals (3 years)	5	0	1.000	2.27	5	5	0	0	0	31 2/3	24	9	8	18	22

WORLD SERIES RECORD

NOTES: Member of World Series championship team (1992 and 1993).

Year—Team (League)	W	L	Pct.	ERA	G	GS	CG	ShO	Sv.	IP	H	R	ER	BB	SO
1992— Toronto (A.L.)	0	0	. . .	1.13	1	1	0	0	0	8	8	2	1	1	7
1993— Toronto (A.L.)	0	1	.000	3.75	2	2	0	0	0	12	10	6	5	8	12
World Series totals (2 years)	0	1	.000	2.70	3	3	0	0	0	20	18	8	6	9	19

ALL-STAR GAME RECORD

Year— League	W	L	Pct.	ERA	GS	CG	ShO	Sv.	IP	H	R	ER	BB	SO
1992— American	0	0	. . .	0.00	0	0	0	0	1	2	0	0	1	2

GWYNN, TONY OF PADRES

PERSONAL: Born May 9, 1960, in Los Angeles. ... 5-11/220. ... Bats left, throws left. ... Full name: Anthony Keith Gwynn. ... Brother of Chris Gwynn, outfielder with Los Angeles Dodgers (1987-1991 and 1994-95), Kansas City Royals (1992-93) and San Diego Padres (1996).

HIGH SCHOOL: Long Beach (Calif.) Polytechnic.

COLLEGE: San Diego State.

TRANSACTIONS/CAREER NOTES: Selected by San Diego Padres organization in third round of free-agent draft (June 8, 1981). ... On San Diego disabled list (August 26-September 10, 1982). ... On San Diego disabled list (March 26-June 21, 1983); included rehabilitation to Las Vegas (May 31-June 20). ... On disabled list (May 8-29, 1988; July 2-August 6, 1996; and August 13-September 1, 1998).

RECORDS: Holds N.L. career records for most years leading league in singles—7 (1984, 1986-87, 1989, 1994, 1995 and 1997); and most consecutive years batting .300 or over (50 or more games) since 1900—16. ... Holds N.L. single-season record for lowest batting average by leader—.313 (1988). ... Shares N.L. single-season record for most times collecting five or more hits in one game—4 (1993). ... Shares N.L. career record for most years leading league in batting average—8.

HONORS: Named Northwest League Most Valuable Player (1981). ... Named outfielder on THE SPORTING NEWS N.L. All-Star team (1984, 1986-87, 1989, 1994 and 1997). ... Named outfielder on THE SPORTING NEWS N.L. Silver Slugger team (1984, 1986-87, 1989, 1994-95 and 1997). ... Won N.L. Gold Glove as outfielder (1986-87 and 1989-91).

STATISTICAL NOTES: Had 25-game hitting streak (August 21-September 18, 1983). ... Led N.L. with .410 on-base percentage in 1984. ... Led N.L. outfielders with 360 total chances in 1986. ... Collected six hits in one game (August 4, 1993, 12 innings). ... Led N.L. in grounding into double plays with 20 in 1994. ... Had 20-game hitting streak (May 20-June 10, 1997). ... Tied for N.L. lead with 12 sacrifice flies in 1997. ... Career major league grand slams: 2.

MISCELLANEOUS: Holds San Diego Padres all-time records for most runs (1,302), most hits (2,928), most doubles (495), most triples (84), highest career batting average (.339), most runs batted in (1,042) and most stolen bases (311). ... Selected by San Diego Clippers in 10th round (210th pick overall) of 1981 NBA draft (June 9, 1981).

Year—Team (League)	Pos.	G	AB	R	H	2B	3B	HR	RBI	Avg.	BB	SO	SB	PO	A	E	Avg.
1981— Walla Walla (NWL)	OF	42	178	46	59	12	1	12	37	*.331	23	21	17	76	2	3	.963
— Amarillo (Texas)	OF	23	91	22	42	8	2	4	19	.462	5	7	5	41	1	0	1.000
1982— Hawaii (PCL)	OF	93	366	65	120	23	2	5	46	.328	18	18	14	208	11	4	.982
— San Diego (N.L.)	OF	54	190	33	55	12	2	1	17	.289	14	16	8	110	1	1	.991
1983— Las Vegas (PCL)	OF	17	73	15	25	6	0	0	7	.342	6	5	3	23	2	3	.893
— San Diego (N.L.)	OF	86	304	34	94	12	2	1	37	.309	23	21	7	163	9	1	.994
1984— San Diego (N.L.)	OF	158	606	88	*213	21	10	5	71	*.351	59	23	33	345	11	4	.989
1985— San Diego (N.L.)	OF	154	622	90	197	29	5	6	46	.317	45	33	14	337	14	4	.989
1986— San Diego (N.L.)	OF	160	*642	•107	*211	33	7	14	59	.329	52	35	37	*337	19	4	.989
1987— San Diego (N.L.)	OF	157	589	119	*218	36	13	7	54	*.370	82	35	56	298	13	6	.981
1988— San Diego (N.L.)	OF	133	521	64	163	22	5	7	70	*.313	51	40	26	264	8	5	.982
1989— San Diego (N.L.)	OF	158	604	82	*203	27	7	4	62	*.336	56	30	40	353	13	6	.984
1990— San Diego (N.L.)	OF	141	573	79	177	29	10	4	72	.309	44	23	17	327	11	5	.985
1991— San Diego (N.L.)	OF	134	530	69	168	27	11	4	62	.317	34	19	8	291	8	3	.990
1992— San Diego (N.L.)	OF	128	520	77	165	27	3	6	41	.317	46	16	3	270	9	5	.982
1993— San Diego (N.L.)	OF	122	489	70	175	41	3	7	59	.358	36	19	14	244	8	5	.981
1994— San Diego (N.L.)	OF	110	419	79	*165	35	1	12	64	*.394	48	19	5	191	6	3	.985
1995— San Diego (N.L.)	OF	135	535	82	•197	33	1	9	90	*.368	35	15	17	245	8	2	.992

G

Year—Team (League)	Pos.	G	AB	R	H	2B	3B	HR	RBI	Avg.	BB	SO	SB	PO	A	E	Avg.
1996—San Diego (N.L.)	OF	116	451	67	159	27	2	3	50	*.353	39	17	11	182	2	2	.989
1997—San Diego (N.L.)	OF-DH	149	592	97	*220	49	2	17	119	*.372	43	28	12	218	8	4	.983
1998—San Diego (N.L.)	OF-DH	127	461	65	148	35	0	16	69	.321	35	18	3	142	5	1	.993
Major league totals (17 years)		2222	8648	1302	2928	495	84	123	1042	.339	742	407	311	4317	153	61	.987

DIVISION SERIES RECORD

RECORDS: Shares N.L. career record for most doubles—3.

Year—Team (League)	Pos.	G	AB	R	H	2B	3B	HR	RBI	Avg.	BB	SO	SB	PO	A	E	Avg.
1996—San Diego (N.L.)	OF	3	13	0	4	1	0	0	1	.308	0	2	1	2	0	0	1.000
1998—San Diego (N.L.)	OF	4	15	1	3	2	0	0	2	.200	0	2	0	4	1	0	1.000
Division series totals (2 years)		7	28	1	7	3	0	0	3	.250	0	4	1	6	1	0	1.000

CHAMPIONSHIP SERIES RECORD

Year—Team (League)	Pos.	G	AB	R	H	2B	3B	HR	RBI	Avg.	BB	SO	SB	PO	A	E	Avg.
1984—San Diego (N.L.)	OF	5	19	6	7	3	0	0	3	.368	1	2	0	9	0	0	1.000
1998—San Diego (N.L.)	OF	6	26	1	6	1	0	0	2	.231	1	2	0	5	0	0	1.000
Championship series totals (2 years)		11	45	7	13	4	0	0	5	.289	2	4	0	14	0	0	1.000

WORLD SERIES RECORD

Year—Team (League)	Pos.	G	AB	R	H	2B	3B	HR	RBI	Avg.	BB	SO	SB	PO	A	E	Avg.
1984—San Diego (N.L.)	OF	5	19	1	5	0	0	0	0	.263	3	2	1	12	1	1	.929
1998—San Diego (N.L.)	OF	4	16	2	8	0	0	1	3	.500	1	0	0	6	0	0	1.000
World Series totals (2 years)		9	35	3	13	0	0	1	3	.371	4	2	1	18	1	1	.950

ALL-STAR GAME RECORD

RECORDS: Shares single-game record for most at-bats in nine-inning game—5 (July 12, 1994).
NOTES: Named to All-Star team for 1996 game; replaced by Henry Rodriguez due to injury.

Year—League	Pos.	AB	R	H	2B	3B	HR	RBI	Avg.	BB	SO	SB	PO	A	E	Avg.
1984—National	OF	3	0	1	0	0	0	0	.333	0	0	0	0	0	0	...
1985—National	OF	1	0	0	0	0	0	0	.000	0	0	0	1	0	0	1.000
1986—National	OF	3	0	0	0	0	0	0	.000	0	0	0	1	0	0	1.000
1987—National	PH	1	0	0	0	0	0	0	.000	0	0	0	...	...	...	...
1989—National	OF	2	1	1	0	0	0	0	.500	1	1	1	2	0	0	1.000
1990—National	PH	0	0	0	0	0	0	0	...	1	0	0	...	...	...	...
1991—National	OF	4	1	2	0	0	0	0	.500	0	0	0	6	0	0	1.000
1992—National	OF	2	0	0	0	0	0	0	.000	1	0	0	0	2	0	1.000
1993—National	OF	1	0	0	0	0	0	0	.000	0	0	0	0	0	0	...
1994—National	OF	5	2	2	1	0	0	2	.400	0	1	0	2	0	0	1.000
1995—National	OF	2	0	0	0	0	0	0	.000	0	0	0	1	0	0	1.000
1996—National							Selected, did not play.									
1997—National	DH	3	0	0	0	0	0	0	.000	0	0	0	0	0	0	...
1998—National	OF	2	0	1	0	0	0	2	.500	0	0	0	0	0	0	...
All-Star Game totals (13 years)		29	4	7	1	0	0	4	.241	3	1	1	13	2	0	1.000

HAAD, YAMID   C   PIRATES

PERSONAL: Born September 2, 1977, in Cartagena, Colombia. ... 6-2/204. ... Bats right, throws right. ... Full name: Yamid Salcedo Haad.
TRANSACTIONS/CAREER NOTES: Signed as non-drafted free agent by Pittsburgh Pirates organization (December 8, 1994).

Year—Team (League)	Pos.	G	AB	R	H	2B	3B	HR	RBI	Avg.	BB	SO	SB	PO	A	E	Avg.
1995—Dom. Pirates (DSL)....	C	36	118	17	30	1	0	0	8	.254	9	17	1	265	31	6	.980
1996—Dom. Pirates (DSL)....	C	56	205	29	66	9	0	5	28	.322	10	38	8	402	59	3	.994
1997—Erie (N.Y.-Penn).........	C	43	155	27	45	7	3	1	19	.290	7	27	3	267	30	3	.990
1998—Lynchburg (Caro.)......	C	88	299	32	76	8	2	5	34	.254	13	54	1	593	77	12	.982

HAAS, CHRIS   3B   CARDINALS

PERSONAL: Born October 15, 1976, in Paducah, Ky. ... 6-1/205. ... Bats left, throws right. ... Full name: Christopher M. Haas.
HIGH SCHOOL: St. Mary's (Paducah, Ky.).
TRANSACTIONS/CAREER NOTES: Selected by St. Louis Cardinals organization in supplemental round ("sandwich pick" between first and second round, 29th pick overall) of free-agent draft (June 1, 1995); pick received as part of compensation for Philadelphia Phillies signing Type A free-agent 1B Gregg Jefferies.
STATISTICAL NOTES: Led Appalachian League third basemen with 187 total chances in 1995.

Year—Team (League)	Pos.	G	AB	R	H	2B	3B	HR	RBI	Avg.	BB	SO	SB	PO	A	E	Avg.
1995—Johnson City (App.) ...	3B	•67	242	43	65	15	3	7	50	.269	*52	93	1	51	*116	20	.893
1996—Peoria (Midwest)........	3B	124	421	56	101	19	1	11	65	.240	64	169	3	75	241	42	.883
1997—Peoria (Midwest)........	3B	36	115	23	36	11	0	5	22	.313	22	38	3	16	52	6	.919
—Prince Will. (Car.).......	3B	100	361	58	86	10	2	14	54	.238	42	144	1	89	183	19	*.935
1998—Arkansas (Texas)........	3B-1B	132	445	75	122	27	4	20	83	.274	73	129	1	146	211	22	.942

G
H

HAIRSTON JR., JERRY   2B/SS   ORIOLES

PERSONAL: Born May 29, 1976, in Des Moines, Iowa. ... 5-10/170. ... Bats right, throws right. ... Full name: Jerry W. Hairston Jr. ... Grandson of Sam Hairston, catcher with Chicago White Sox (1951) and Cincinnati and Indianapolis of Negro American League (1945-49); son of Jerry Hairston, outfielder with Chicago White Sox (1973-77 and 1981-89) and Pittsburgh Pirates (1977); nephew of John Hairston, catcher/outfielder with Chicago Cubs (1969); and nephew of Sam Hairston Jr., former minor league player in Chicago White Sox organization (1966 and 1969).
HIGH SCHOOL: Naperville (Ill.) North.
COLLEGE: Southern Illinois-Carbondale.
TRANSACTIONS/CAREER NOTES: Selected by Baltimore Orioles organization in 11th round of free-agent draft (June 3, 1997).
STATISTICAL NOTES: Tied for Appalachian League lead in caught stealing with nine in 1997.

Year Team (League)	Pos.	G	AB	R	H	2B	3B	HR	RBI	Avg.	BB	SO	SB	PO	A	E	Avg.
1997— Bluefield (Appal.)........	SS	59	221	44	73	13	4	2	36	.330	21	29	13	84	174	14	*.949
1998— Frederick (Carolina)....	SS-2B	80	293	56	83	22	3	5	33	.283	28	32	13	116	281	24	.943
— Bowie (Eastern)..........	2B-SS	55	221	42	72	12	3	5	37	.326	20	25	6	109	135	5	.980
— Baltimore (A.L.).........	2B	6	7	2	0	0	0	0	0	.000	0	1	0	4	2	2	.750
Major league totals (1 year)		**6**	**7**	**2**	**0**	**0**	**0**	**0**	**0**	**.000**	**0**	**1**	**0**	**4**	**2**	**2**	**.750**

HALAMA, JOHN   P   MARINERS

PERSONAL: Born February 22, 1972, in Brooklyn, N.Y. ... 6-5/200. ... Throws left, bats left. ... Full name: John Thadeuz Halama. ... Name pronounced ha-LA-ma.
HIGH SCHOOL: Bishop Ford (Brooklyn, N.Y.).
COLLEGE: St. Francis (N.Y.).
TRANSACTIONS/CAREER NOTES: Selected by Houston Astros organization in 23rd round of free-agent draft (June 3, 1994). ... On New Orleans disabled list (July 2-August 6, 1998). ... Traded by Astros to Seattle Mariners (October 1, 1998); completing deal in which Mariners traded P Randy Johnson to Astros for SS Carlos Guillen, P Freddy Garcia and a player to be named later (July 31, 1998).

Year Team (League)	W	L	Pct.	ERA	G	GS	CG	ShO	Sv.	IP	H	R	ER	BB	SO
1994— Auburn (N.Y.-Penn)	4	1	.800	1.29	6	3	0	0	1	28	18	5	4	5	27
— Quad City (Midwest)	3	4	.429	4.56	9	9	1	1	0	51 1/3	63	31	26	18	37
1995— Quad City (Midwest)	1	2	.333	2.02	55	0	0	0	2	62 1/3	48	16	14	22	56
1996— Jackson (Texas)	9	10	.474	3.21	27	27	0	0	0	162 2/3	151	77	58	59	110
1997— New Orleans (A.A.)...........	13	3	*.813	2.58	26	24	1	0	0	171	150	57	49	32	126
1998— Houston (N.L.).................	1	1	.500	5.85	6	6	0	0	0	32 1/3	37	21	21	13	21
— New Orleans (PCL)............	12	3	.800	3.20	17	17	4	1	0	121	118	48	43	16	86
Major league totals (1 year)........	**1**	**1**	**.500**	**5.85**	**6**	**6**	**0**	**0**	**0**	**32 1/3**	**37**	**21**	**21**	**13**	**21**

HALL, DARREN   P   WHITE SOX

PERSONAL: Born July 14, 1964, in Marysville, Ohio. ... 6-3/207. ... Throws right, bats right. ... Full name: Michael Darren Hall.
HIGH SCHOOL: Nimitz (Irving, Texas).
COLLEGE: Dallas Baptist.
TRANSACTIONS/CAREER NOTES: Selected by Toronto Blue Jays organization in 28th round of free-agent draft (June 2, 1986). ... On disabled list (June 26, 1990-remainder of season; June 19-July 4 and July 24, 1995-remainder of season). ... Granted free agency (October 16, 1995). ... Signed by Los Angeles Dodgers (November 1, 1995). ... On Los Angeles disabled list (April 25-September 9, 1996); included rehabilitation assignment to Yakima (September 3-9). ... On Los Angeles disabled list (April 8-July 10 and August 14, 1998-remainder of season); included rehabilitation assignments to San Bernardino (June 13-15 and June 19-July 10) and San Antonio (June 16-18). ... Traded by Dodgers to Chicago White Sox for C Joe Sutton (January 12, 1999).
STATISTICAL NOTES: Tied for Pioneer League lead with 12 wild pitches in 1986.

Year Team (League)	W	L	Pct.	ERA	G	GS	CG	ShO	Sv.	IP	H	R	ER	BB	SO
1986— Medicine Hat (Pioneer)	5	7	.417	3.83	17	•16	1	1	0	89 1/3	91	64	38	47	60
1987— Myrtle Beach (SAL)	5	5	.500	3.51	41	0	0	0	6	66 2/3	57	31	26	28	68
1988— Dunedin (Fla. St.)	1	1	.500	1.93	4	0	0	0	1	9 1/3	6	2	2	5	15
— Knoxville (Southern)	3	2	.600	2.23	37	0	0	0	17	40 1/3	28	11	10	17	33
1989— Dunedin (Fla. St.)	1	4	.200	3.53	16	14	0	0	0	51	46	25	20	21	42
— Knoxville (Southern)	0	2	.000	3.66	13	0	0	0	1	19 2/3	21	12	8	10	10
1990— Knoxville (Southern)	3	5	.375	4.86	28	0	0	0	1	33 1/3	29	23	18	33	28
1991— Knoxville (Southern)	5	3	.625	2.60	42	0	0	0	2	69 1/3	56	23	20	27	78
1992— Syracuse (Int'l).................	4	6	.400	4.30	55	0	0	0	5	69	62	36	33	35	49
1993— Syracuse (Int'l).................	6	7	.462	5.33	60	0	0	0	13	79 1/3	75	51	47	31	68
1994— Syracuse (Int'l).................	1	0	1.000	1.59	6	0	0	0	3	5 2/3	5	2	1	2	7
— Toronto (A.L.)..................	2	3	.400	3.41	30	0	0	0	17	31 2/3	26	12	12	14	28
1995— Toronto (A.L.)..................	0	2	.000	4.41	17	0	0	0	3	16 1/3	21	9	8	9	11
1996— Los Angeles (N.L.)■	0	2	.000	6.00	9	0	0	0	0	12	13	9	8	5	12
— Yakima (N'west)	0	1	.000	3.00	2	2	0	0	0	3	5	2	1	0	4
1997— Los Angeles (N.L.)	3	2	.600	2.30	63	0	0	0	2	54 2/3	58	15	14	26	39
1998— Los Angeles (N.L.)	0	3	.000	10.32	11	0	0	0	0	11 1/3	17	14	13	5	8
— San Bernardino (Calif.).....	1	0	1.000	0.00	8	2	0	0	0	9 2/3	4	0	0	2	8
— San Antonio (Tex.)	0	0	. . .	10.80	2	2	0	0	0	1 2/3	1	2	2	1	2
A.L. totals (2 years)	**2**	**5**	**.286**	**3.75**	**47**	**0**	**0**	**0**	**20**	**48**	**47**	**21**	**20**	**23**	**39**
N.L. totals (3 years)	**3**	**7**	**.300**	**4.04**	**83**	**0**	**0**	**0**	**2**	**78**	**88**	**38**	**35**	**36**	**59**
Major league totals (5 years)	**5**	**12**	**.294**	**3.93**	**130**	**0**	**0**	**0**	**22**	**126**	**135**	**59**	**55**	**59**	**98**

HALLADAY, ROY   P   BLUE JAYS

PERSONAL: Born May 14, 1977, in Denver. ... 6-6/205. ... Throws right, bats right. ... Full name: Harry Leroy Halladay III.
HIGH SCHOOL: Arvada (Colo.) West.
TRANSACTIONS/CAREER NOTES: Selected by Toronto Blue Jays organization in first round (17th pick overall) of free-agent draft (June 1, 1995). ... On Syracuse disabled list (May 15-June 17, 1998).
STATISTICAL NOTES: Pitched 2-1 one-hit, complete-game victory against Detroit (September 27, 1998).

Year Team (League)	W	L	Pct.	ERA	G	GS	CG	ShO	Sv.	IP	H	R	ER	BB	SO
1995— GC Blue Jays (GCL)	3	5	.375	3.40	10	8	0	0	0	50 1/3	35	25	19	16	48
1996— Dunedin (Fla. St.)	15	7	.682	2.73	27	27	2	•2	0	164 2/3	158	55	50	46	109
1997— Knoxville (Southern)	2	3	.400	5.40	7	7	0	0	0	36 2/3	46	26	22	11	30
— Syracuse (Int'l)	7	10	.412	4.58	22	22	2	2	0	125 2/3	132	74	64	53	64
1998— Syracuse (Int'l)	9	5	.643	3.79	21	21	1	1	0	116 1/3	107	52	49	53	71
— Toronto (A.L.)	1	0	1.000	1.93	2	2	1	0	0	14	9	4	3	2	13
Major league totals (1 year)	1	0	1.000	1.93	2	2	1	0	0	14	9	4	3	2	13

HALTER, SHANE   SS   ROYALS

PERSONAL: Born November 8, 1969, in La Plata, Md. ... 6-0/180. ... Bats right, throws right. ... Full name: Shane David Halter.
HIGH SCHOOL: Hooks (Texas).
JUNIOR COLLEGE: Seminole (Okla.) Junior College.
COLLEGE: Texas.
TRANSACTIONS/CAREER NOTES: Selected by Cincinnati Reds organization in 16th round of free-agent draft (June 4, 1990); did not sign. ... Selected by Kansas City Royals organization in fifth round of free-agent draft (June 3, 1991).
STATISTICAL NOTES: Led Midwest League shortstops with 64 double plays in 1992. ... Led American Association with 19 sacrifice hits in 1995.

Year Team (League)	Pos.	G	AB	R	H	2B	3B	HR	RBI	Avg.	BB	SO	SB	PO	A	E	Avg.
1991— Eugene (Northwest)	SS	64	236	41	55	9	1	1	18	.233	49	60	12	*118	154	21	.928
1992— Appleton (Midwest)	SS	80	313	50	83	22	3	3	33	.265	41	54	21	150	227	16	.959
— Baseball City (FSL)	SS	44	117	11	28	1	0	1	14	.239	24	31	5	70	115	6	.969
1993— Wilmington (Caro.)	SS	54	211	44	63	8	5	5	32	.299	27	55	5	84	146	15	.939
— Memphis (Sou.)	SS	81	306	50	79	7	0	4	20	.258	30	74	4	142	229	16	.959
1994— Memphis (Sou.)	SS	129	494	61	111	23	1	6	35	.225	39	102	10	177	369	29	.950
1995— Omaha (A.A.)	SS-2B	124	392	42	90	19	3	8	39	.230	40	97	2	225	355	19	.968
1996— Omaha (A.A.)	O-3-S-2-P	93	299	43	77	24	0	3	33	.258	31	49	7	130	75	13	.940
— Charlotte (Int'l)	O-2-3-1	16	41	3	12	1	0	0	4	.293	2	8	0	15	10	1	.962
1997— Omaha (A.A.)	3-0-2-S	14	49	10	13	1	1	2	9	.265	6	10	0	22	14	2	.947
— Kansas City (A.L.)	O-2-3-S-DH	74	123	16	34	5	1	2	10	.276	10	28	4	63	40	1	.990
1998— Kansas City (A.L.)	S-O-3-2-P-1	86	204	17	45	12	0	2	13	.221	12	38	2	91	177	10	.964
— Omaha (PCL)	S-1-2-3-O	22	97	15	30	6	1	1	13	.309	6	15	4	64	46	3	.973
Major league totals (2 years)		160	327	33	79	17	1	4	23	.242	22	66	6	154	217	11	.971

RECORD AS PITCHER

Year Team (League)	W	L	Pct.	ERA	G	GS	CG	ShO	Sv.	IP	H	R	ER	BB	SO
1996— Omaha (Am. Assoc.)	0	0	...	9.00	1	0	0	0	0	1	2	1	1	1	0
1998— Kansas City (A.L.)	0	0	...	0.00	1	0	0	0	0	1	1	0	0	0	0
Major league totals (1 year)	0	0	...	0.00	1	0	0	0	0	1	1	0	0	0	0

HAMELIN, BOB   DH/1B

PERSONAL: Born November 29, 1967, in Elizabeth, N.J. ... 6-0/235. ... Bats left, throws left. ... Full name: Robert James Hamelin III.
HIGH SCHOOL: Irvine (Calif.).
JUNIOR COLLEGE: Rancho Santiago College (Calif.).
COLLEGE: UCLA.
TRANSACTIONS/CAREER NOTES: Selected by Kansas City Royals organization in second round of free-agent draft (June 1, 1988). ... On disabled list (June 25-July 2 and August 3, 1989-remainder of season; August 8, 1990-remainder of season; and May 27, 1991-remainder of season). ... On Omaha disabled list (April 9-June 10, 1992). ... On Kansas City disabled list (June 17-July 15, 1996); included rehabilitation assignment to Omaha (July 11-15). ... Released by Royals (March 26, 1997). ... Signed by Detroit Tigers organization (April 8, 1997). ... Granted free agency (December 21, 1997). ... Signed by Milwaukee Brewers organization (January 14, 1998). ... Released by Brewers (November 11, 1998).
RECORDS: Shares major league single-game record for most strikeouts (nine-inning game)—5 (May 24, 1995).
HONORS: Named A.L. Rookie Player of the Year by THE SPORTING NEWS (1994). ... Named A.L. Rookie of the Year by Baseball Writers' Association of America (1994).
STATISTICAL NOTES: Led Northwest League first basemen with 682 total chances in 1988. ... Led American Association first basemen with 1,205 total chances and 116 double plays in 1993.

Year Team (League)	Pos.	G	AB	R	H	2B	3B	HR	RBI	Avg.	BB	SO	SB	PO	A	E	Avg.
1988— Eugene (Northwest)	1B	70	235	42	70	19	1	*17	61	.298	56	67	9	*642	25	*15	.978
1989— Memphis (Sou.)	1B	68	211	45	62	12	5	16	47	.294	52	52	3	487	27	8	.985
1990— Omaha (A.A.)	1B	90	271	31	63	11	2	8	30	.232	62	78	2	396	32	4	.991
1991— Omaha (A.A.)	1B	37	127	13	24	3	1	4	19	.189	16	32	0	55	4	0	1.000
1992— Baseball City (FSL)	1B	11	44	7	12	0	1	1	6	.273	2	11	0	18	1	3	.864
— Memphis (Sou.)	1B	35	120	23	40	8	0	6	22	.333	26	17	0	173	9	2	.989
— Omaha (A.A.)	1B	27	95	9	19	3	1	5	15	.200	14	15	0	230	13	3	.988
1993— Omaha (A.A.)	1B	•137	479	77	124	19	3	29	84	.259	*82	94	8	*1104	*90	•11	.991
— Kansas City (A.L.)	1B	16	49	2	11	3	0	2	5	.224	6	15	0	129	9	2	.986
1994— Kansas City (A.L.)	DH-1B	101	312	64	88	25	1	24	65	.282	56	62	4	234	18	2	.992

H

Year	Team (League)	Pos.	G	AB	R	H	2B	3B	HR	RBI	Avg.	BB	SO	SB	PO	A	E	Avg.
1995—Kansas City (A.L.)	DH-1B	72	208	20	35	7	1	7	25	.168	26	56	0	66	9	0	1.000
—Omaha (A.A.)	1B	36	119	25	35	12	0	10	32	.294	31	34	2	157	19	6	.967
1996—Kansas City (A.L.)	DH-1B	89	239	31	61	14	1	9	40	.255	54	58	5	232	20	4	.984
—Omaha (A.A.)	1B	4	16	4	5	1	1	0	0	.313	1	4	1	37	1	0	1.000
1997—Toledo (Int'l)■..........	1B	27	91	14	22	7	0	6	24	.242	27	24	0	121	5	2	.984
—Detroit (A.L.)............	DH-1B	110	318	47	86	15	0	18	52	.270	48	72	2	29	1	0	1.000
1998—Milwaukee (N.L.)■.....	1B-DH	109	146	15	32	6	0	7	22	.219	16	30	0	230	7	2	.992
American League totals (5 years)		388	1126	164	281	64	3	60	187	.250	190	263	11	690	57	8	.989
National League totals (1 year)		109	146	15	32	6	0	7	22	.219	16	30	0	230	7	2	.992
Major league totals (6 years)		497	1272	179	313	70	3	67	209	.246	206	293	11	920	64	10	.990

HAMILTON, DARRYL   OF   ROCKIES

PERSONAL: Born December 3, 1964, in Baton Rouge, La. ... 6-1/192. ... Bats left, throws right. ... Full name: Darryl Quinn Hamilton.
HIGH SCHOOL: University (Baton Rouge, La.).
COLLEGE: Nicholls State (La.).
TRANSACTIONS/CAREER NOTES: Selected by Milwaukee Brewers organization in 11th round of free-agent draft (June 2, 1986). ... On disabled list (May 22-June 15, 1991; May 6-24, 1992; May 2-17, 1993; May 11-26 and June 10, 1994-remainder of season). ... Granted free agency (November 1, 1995). ... Signed by Texas Rangers (December 14, 1995). ... Granted free agency (November 18, 1996). ... Signed by San Francisco Giants (January 10, 1997). ... On San Francisco disabled list (April 18-May 8, 1997); included rehabilitation assignment to Phoenix (May 5-8, 1997). ... Traded by Giants with P James Stoops and a player to be named later to Colorado Rockies for OF Ellis Burks (July 31, 1998); Rockies acquired P Jason Brester to complete deal (August 17, 1998). ... Granted free agency (October 23, 1998). ... Re-signed by Rockies (November 9, 1998).
STATISTICAL NOTES: Led California League with nine intentional bases on balls received in 1987. ... Led N.L. outfielders with .997 fielding percentage in 1998. ... Career major league grand slams: 2.

Year	Team (League)	Pos.	G	AB	R	H	2B	3B	HR	RBI	Avg.	BB	SO	SB	PO	A	E	Avg.
1986—Helena (Pioneer)	OF	65	248	*72	•97	12	•6	0	35	*.391	51	18	34	132	9	0	*1.000
1987—Stockton (California) ..	OF	125	494	102	162	17	6	8	61	.328	74	59	42	221	8	1	*.996
1988—Denver (A.A.)	OF	72	277	55	90	11	4	0	32	.325	39	28	28	160	2	2	.988
—Milwaukee (A.L.)	OF-DH	44	103	14	19	4	0	1	11	.184	12	9	7	75	1	0	1.000
1989—Denver (A.A.)	OF	129	497	72	142	24	4	2	40	.286	42	58	20	263	11	0	*1.000
1990—Milwaukee (A.L.)	OF-DH	89	156	27	46	5	0	1	18	.295	9	12	10	120	1	1	.992
1991—Milwaukee (A.L.)	OF	122	405	64	126	15	6	1	57	.311	33	38	16	234	3	1	.996
1992—Milwaukee (A.L.)	OF	128	470	67	140	19	7	5	62	.298	45	42	41	279	10	0	*1.000
1993—Milwaukee (A.L.)	OF-DH	135	520	74	161	21	1	9	48	.310	45	62	21	340	10	3	.992
1994—Milwaukee (A.L.)	OF-DH	36	141	23	37	10	1	1	13	.262	15	17	3	60	2	0	1.000
1995—Milwaukee (A.L.)	OF-DH	112	398	54	108	20	6	5	44	.271	47	35	11	262	4	3	.989
1996—Texas (A.L.)■.............	OF	148	627	94	184	29	4	6	51	.293	54	66	15	387	2	0	•1.000
1997—San Fran. (N.L.)■.......	OF	125	460	78	124	23	3	5	43	.270	61	61	15	243	1	5	.980
—Phoenix (PCL).............	OF	3	14	1	4	1	0	1	2	.286	0	2	0	6	0	0	1.000
1998—San Francisco (N.L.) ..	OF	97	367	65	108	19	2	1	26	.294	59	53	9	194	4	0	*1.000
—Colorado (N.L.)■........	OF	51	194	30	65	9	1	5	25	.335	23	20	4	103	1	1	*.990
American League totals (8 years)		814	2820	417	821	123	25	29	304	.291	260	281	124	1757	33	8	.996
National League totals (2 years)		273	1021	173	297	51	6	11	94	.291	143	134	28	540	6	6	.989
Major league totals (10 years)		1087	3841	590	1118	174	31	40	398	.291	403	415	152	2297	39	14	.994

DIVISION SERIES RECORD

Year	Team (League)	Pos.	G	AB	R	H	2B	3B	HR	RBI	Avg.	BB	SO	SB	PO	A	E	Avg.
1996—Texas (A.L.)	OF	4	19	0	3	0	0	0	0	.158	0	2	0	16	1	0	1.000
1997—San Francisco (N.L.) ..	OF	2	5	1	0	0	0	0	0	.000	0	1	0	3	0	0	1.000
Division series totals (2 years)		6	24	1	3	0	0	0	0	.125	0	3	0	19	1	0	1.000

HAMILTON, JIMMY   P   INDIANS

PERSONAL: Born August 1, 1975, in Harrisonburg, Va. ... 6-3/190. ... Throws left, bats left. ... Full name: James A. Hamilton.
HIGH SCHOOL: Turner Ashby (Dayton, Va.).
COLLEGE: Ferrum (Va).
TRANSACTIONS/CAREER NOTES: Selected by Cleveland Indians organization in seventh round of free-agent draft (June 4, 1996).

Year	Team (League)	W	L	Pct.	ERA	G	GS	CG	ShO	Sv.	IP	H	R	ER	BB	SO
1996—Burlington (Appalachian)..		1	3	.250	4.00	10	10	0	0	0	45	45	22	20	16	50
1997—Columbus (S. Atl.).............		5	7	.417	4.46	22	22	0	0	0	123	123	68	61	66	137
1998—Kinston (Carolina)		4	6	.400	2.75	44	0	0	0	4	75 1/3	61	25	23	21	83

HAMILTON, JOEY   P   BLUE JAYS

PERSONAL: Born September 9, 1970, in Statesboro, Ga. ... 6-4/230. ... Throws right, bats right. ... Full name: Johns Joseph Hamilton.
HIGH SCHOOL: Statesboro (Ga.).
COLLEGE: Georgia Southern.
TRANSACTIONS/CAREER NOTES: Selected by Baltimore Orioles organization in 28th round of free-agent draft (June 1, 1988); did not sign. ... Selected by San Diego Padres organization in first round (eighth pick overall) of free-agent draft (June 3, 1991). ... On Rancho Cucamonga disabled list (April 5-20, 1993). ... On disabled list (April 24-May 17, 1997). ... Traded by Padres to Toronto Blue Jays for P Woody Williams, P Carlos Almanzar and OF Peter Tucci (December 13, 1998).
HONORS: Named righthanded pitcher on THE SPORTING NEWS college All-America second team (1990).
MISCELLANEOUS: Made an out in only appearance as pinch hitter (1998).

H

Year Team (League)	W	L	Pct.	ERA	G	GS	CG	ShO	Sv.	IP	H	R	ER	BB	SO
1992—Charleston, S.C. (S. Atl.)	2	2	.500	3.38	7	7	0	0	0	34 2/3	37	24	13	4	35
—High Desert (Calif.)	4	3	.571	2.74	9	8	0	0	0	49 1/3	46	20	15	18	43
—Wichita (Texas)	3	0	1.000	2.86	6	6	0	0	0	34 2/3	33	12	11	11	26
1993—Rancho Cuca. (Cal.)	1	0	1.000	4.09	2	2	0	0	0	11	11	5	5	2	6
—Wichita (Texas)	4	9	.308	3.97	15	15	0	0	0	90 2/3	101	55	40	36	20
—Las Vegas (PCL)	3	2	.600	4.40	8	8	0	0	0	47	49	25	23	22	33
1994—Las Vegas (PCL)	3	5	.375	2.73	9	9	1	1	0	59 1/3	69	25	18	22	32
—San Diego (N.L.)	9	6	.600	2.98	16	16	1	1	0	108 2/3	98	40	36	29	61
1995—San Diego (N.L.)	6	9	.400	3.08	31	30	2	2	0	204 1/3	189	89	70	56	123
1996—San Diego (N.L.)	15	9	.625	4.17	34	33	3	1	0	211 2/3	206	100	98	83	184
1997—San Diego (N.L.)	12	7	.632	4.25	31	29	1	0	0	192 2/3	199	100	91	69	124
1998—San Diego (N.L.)	13	13	.500	4.27	34	34	0	0	0	217 1/3	220	113	103	*106	147
Major league totals (5 years)	55	44	.556	3.83	146	142	7	4	0	934 2/3	912	442	398	343	639

DIVISION SERIES RECORD

Year Team (League)	W	L	Pct.	ERA	G	GS	CG	ShO	Sv.	IP	H	R	ER	BB	SO
1996—San Diego (N.L.)	0	1	.000	4.50	1	1	0	0	0	6	5	3	3	0	6
1998—San Diego (N.L.)	0	0	...	0.00	2	0	0	0	0	3 1/3	1	0	0	2	3
Div. series totals (2 years)	0	1	.000	2.89	3	1	0	0	0	9 1/3	6	3	3	2	9

CHAMPIONSHIP SERIES RECORD

Year Team (League)	W	L	Pct.	ERA	G	GS	CG	ShO	Sv.	IP	H	R	ER	BB	SO
1998—San Diego (N.L.)	0	1	.000	4.91	2	1	0	0	0	7 1/3	7	4	4	3	6

WORLD SERIES RECORD

Year Team (League)	W	L	Pct.	ERA	G	GS	CG	ShO	Sv.	IP	H	R	ER	BB	SO
1998—San Diego (N.L.)	0	0	...	0.00	1	0	0	0	0	1	0	0	0	1	1

HAMMOND, CHRIS — P

PERSONAL: Born January 21, 1966, in Atlanta. ... 6-1/195. ... Throws left, bats left. ... Full name: Christopher Andrew Hammond. ... Brother of Steve Hammond, outfielder with Kansas City Royals (1982).
HIGH SCHOOL: Vestavia Hills (Birmingham, Ala.).
JUNIOR COLLEGE: Gulf Coast Community College (Fla.).
COLLEGE: Alabama-Birmingham.
TRANSACTIONS/CAREER NOTES: Selected by Cincinnati Reds organization in sixth round of free-agent draft (January 14, 1986). ... On disabled list (July 27-September 1, 1991). ... Traded by Reds to Florida Marlins for 3B Gary Scott and a player to be named later (March 27, 1993); Reds acquired P Hector Carrasco to complete deal (September 10, 1993). ... On Florida disabled list (June 11-August 3, 1994); included rehabilitation assignments to Portland (June 24-25) and Brevard County (July 25-30). ... On Florida disabled list (April 16-May 13 and August 3-19, 1995); included rehabilitation assignments to Brevard County (May 4-9) and Charlotte (May 9-13). ... On Florida disabled list (June 9-July 14, 1996); included rehabilitation assignments to Brevard County (July 1-5) and Charlotte (July 5-14). ... Granted free agency (October 4, 1996). ... Signed by Boston Red Sox (December 17, 1996). ... On disabled list (June 30, 1997-remainder of season). ... Granted free agency (October 30, 1997). ... Signed by Kansas City Royals organization (January 12, 1998). ... Released by Royals (March 23, 1998). ... Signed by Marlins organization (March 27, 1998). ... Released by Marlins (June 2, 1998).
HONORS: Named American Association Pitcher of the Year (1990).
STATISTICAL NOTES: Career major league grand slams: 1.
MISCELLANEOUS: Appeared in two games as pinch runner (1992). ... Struck out in only appearance as pinch hitter (1993).

Year Team (League)	W	L	Pct.	ERA	G	GS	CG	ShO	Sv.	IP	H	R	ER	BB	SO
1986—GC Reds (GCL)	3	2	.600	2.81	7	7	1	0	0	41 2/3	27	21	13	17	53
—Tampa (Fla. St.)	0	2	.000	3.32	5	5	0	0	0	21 2/3	25	8	8	13	5
1987—Tampa (Fla. St.)	11	11	.500	3.55	25	24	6	0	0	170	174	81	67	60	126
1988—Chattanooga (Southern)	*16	5	.762	*1.72	26	26	4	2	0	182 2/3	127	48	35	77	127
1989—Nashville (A.A.)	11	7	.611	3.38	24	24	3	1	0	157 1/3	144	69	59	96	142
1990—Nashville (A.A.)	*15	1	*.938	*2.17	24	24	5	*3	0	149	118	43	36	63	*149
—Cincinnati (N.L.)	0	2	.000	6.35	3	3	0	0	0	11 1/3	13	9	8	12	4
1991—Cincinnati (N.L.)	7	7	.500	4.06	20	18	0	0	0	99 2/3	92	51	45	48	50
1992—Cincinnati (N.L.)	7	10	.412	4.21	28	26	0	0	0	147 1/3	149	75	69	55	79
1993—Florida (N.L.)■	11	12	.478	4.66	32	32	1	0	0	191	207	106	99	66	108
1994—Florida (N.L.)	4	4	.500	3.07	13	13	1	1	0	73 1/3	79	30	25	23	40
—Portland (Eastern)	0	0	...	0.00	1	1	0	0	0	2	0	0	0	0	2
—Brevard County (FSL)	0	0	...	1.23	2	2	0	0	0	7 1/3	4	3	1	3	5
1995—Brevard County (FSL)	0	0	...	0.00	1	1	0	0	0	4	3	1	0	0	4
—Charlotte (Int'l)	0	0	...	0.00	1	1	0	0	0	4	3	1	0	2	3
—Florida (N.L.)	9	6	.600	3.80	25	24	3	2	0	161	157	73	68	47	126
1996—Florida (N.L.)	5	8	.385	6.56	38	9	0	0	0	81	104	65	59	27	50
—Brevard County (FSL)	0	0	...	0.00	1	1	0	0	0	4	3	0	0	0	3
—Charlotte (Int'l)	1	0	1.000	7.20	1	1	0	0	0	5	5	4	4	0	3
1997—Boston (A.L.)■	3	4	.429	5.92	29	8	0	0	1	65 1/3	81	45	43	27	48
1998—Charlotte (Int'l)■	1	3	.250	4.82	5	5	0	0	0	28	35	17	15	14	22
—Florida (N.L.)	0	2	.000	6.59	3	3	0	0	0	13 2/3	20	11	10	8	8
A.L. totals (1 year)	3	4	.429	5.92	29	8	0	0	1	65 1/3	81	45	43	27	48
N.L. totals (8 years)	43	51	.457	4.43	162	128	5	3	0	778 1/3	821	420	383	286	465
Major league totals (9 years)	46	55	.455	4.54	191	136	5	3	1	843 2/3	902	465	426	313	513

H

HAMMONDS, JEFFREY — OF — REDS

PERSONAL: Born March 5, 1971, in Scotch Plains, N.J. ... 6-0/195. ... Bats right, throws right. ... Full name: Jeffrey Bryan Hammonds. ... Brother of Reggie Hammonds, outfielder with Pittsburgh Pirates organization (1984-86).
HIGH SCHOOL: Scotch Plains (N.J.)-Fanwood.
COLLEGE: Stanford.

TRANSACTIONS/CAREER NOTES: Selected by Toronto Blue Jays organization in ninth round of free-agent draft (June 5, 1989); did not sign. ... Selected by Baltimore Orioles organization in first round (fourth pick overall) of free-agent draft (June 1, 1992). ... On Hagerstown temporarily inactive list (August 6-September 14, 1992). ... On Rochester disabled list (May 17-28, 1993). ... On Baltimore disabled list (August 8-September 1 and September 28, 1993-remainder of season); included rehabilitation assignment to Bowie (August 28-September 1). ... On Baltimore disabled list (May 4-June 16, 1994; July 18-September 3, 1995; and August 17-September 22, 1996). ... On Baltimore disabled list (June 3-July 11, 1998); included rehabilitation assignment to Bowie (July 9-11). ... Traded by Orioles to Cincinnati Reds for 3B/OF Willie Greene (August 10, 1998).

HONORS: Named outfielder on The Sporting News college All-America team (1990 and 1992).

STATISTICAL NOTES: Career major league grand slams: 1.

MISCELLANEOUS: Member of 1992 U.S. Olympic baseball team.

Year Team (League)	Pos.	G	AB	R	H	2B	3B	HR	RBI	Avg.	BB	SO	SB	PO	A	E	Avg.
1993— Bowie (Eastern).........	OF	24	92	13	26	3	0	3	10	.283	9	18	4	48	2	0	1.000
— Rochester (Int'l)	OF	36	151	25	47	9	1	5	23	.311	5	27	6	72	1	0	1.000
— Baltimore (A.L.).........	OF-DH	33	105	10	32	8	0	3	19	.305	2	16	4	47	2	2	.961
1994— Baltimore (A.L.).........	OF	68	250	45	74	18	2	8	31	.296	17	39	5	147	5	6	.962
1995— Baltimore (A.L.).........	OF-DH	57	178	18	43	9	1	4	23	.242	9	30	4	88	1	1	.989
— Bowie (Eastern).........	OF	9	31	7	12	3	1	1	11	.387	10	7	3	12	0	1	.923
1996— Baltimore (A.L.).........	OF-DH	71	248	38	56	10	1	9	27	.226	23	53	3	145	3	3	.980
— Rochester (Int'l)	OF	34	125	24	34	4	2	3	19	.272	19	19	3	75	1	1	.987
1997— Baltimore (A.L.).........	OF-DH	118	397	71	105	19	3	21	55	.264	32	73	15	240	4	5	.980
1998— Baltimore (A.L.).........	OF-DH	63	171	36	46	12	1	6	28	.269	26	38	7	94	2	2	.980
— Bowie (Eastern).........	OF	3	6	4	2	0	0	0	0	.333	2	2	3	3	0	0	1.000
— Cincinnati (N.L.)■.....	OF	26	86	14	26	4	1	0	11	.302	13	18	1	64	3	1	.985
American League totals (6 years)		410	1349	218	356	76	8	51	183	.264	109	249	38	761	17	19	.976
National League totals (1 year)		26	86	14	26	4	1	0	11	.302	13	18	1	64	3	1	.985
Major league totals (6 years)		436	1435	232	382	80	9	51	194	.266	122	267	39	825	20	20	.977

DIVISION SERIES RECORD

Year Team (League)	Pos.	G	AB	R	H	2B	3B	HR	RBI	Avg.	BB	SO	SB	PO	A	E	Avg.
1997— Baltimore (A.L.).........	OF-PR	4	10	3	1	1	0	0	2	.100	2	2	1	8	1	0	1.000

CHAMPIONSHIP SERIES RECORD

Year Team (League)	Pos.	G	AB	R	H	2B	3B	HR	RBI	Avg.	BB	SO	SB	PO	A	E	Avg.
1997— Baltimore (A.L.).........	PH-OF-PR	5	3	0	0	0	0	0	0	.000	1	2	1	2	0	0	1.000

HAMPTON, MIKE   P   ASTROS

PERSONAL: Born September 9, 1972, in Brooksville, Fla. ... 5-10/180. ... Throws left, bats right. ... Full name: Michael William Hampton.

HIGH SCHOOL: Crystal River (Fla.).

TRANSACTIONS/CAREER NOTES: Selected by Seattle Mariners organization in sixth round of free-agent draft (June 4, 1990). ... Traded by Mariners with OF Mike Felder to Houston Astros for OF Eric Anthony (December 10, 1993). ... On disabled list (May 15-June 13, 1995; and June 16-July 4, 1998).

STATISTICAL NOTES: Led Arizona League with 10 wild pitches in 1990. ... Pitched 6-0 no-hit victory for San Bernardino against Visalia (May 31, 1991).

MISCELLANEOUS: Appeared in two games as pinch runner (1996).

Year Team (League)	W	L	Pct.	ERA	G	GS	CG	ShO	Sv.	IP	H	R	ER	BB	SO
1990— Ariz. Mariners (Ariz.).....	•7	2	.778	2.66	14	•13	0	0	0	64 1/3	52	32	19	40	59
1991— San Bernardino (Calif.).....	1	7	.125	5.25	18	15	1	1	0	73 2/3	71	58	43	47	57
— Bellingham (N'west).........	5	2	.714	1.58	9	9	0	0	0	57	32	15	10	26	65
1992— San Bernardino (Calif.).....	13	8	.619	3.12	25	25	6	•2	0	170	163	75	59	66	132
— Jacksonville (Southern).....	0	1	.000	4.35	2	2	1	0	0	10 1/3	13	5	5	1	6
1993— Seattle (A.L.)	1	3	.250	9.53	13	3	0	0	1	17	28	20	18	17	8
— Jacksonville (Southern).....	6	4	.600	3.71	15	14	1	0	0	87 1/3	71	43	36	33	84
1994— Houston (N.L.)■..............	2	1	.667	3.70	44	0	0	0	0	41 1/3	46	19	17	16	24
1995— Houston (N.L.)....................	9	8	.529	3.35	24	24	0	0	0	150 2/3	141	73	56	49	115
1996— Houston (N.L.)....................	10	10	.500	3.59	27	27	2	1	0	160 1/3	175	79	64	49	101
1997— Houston (N.L.)....................	15	10	.600	3.83	34	34	7	2	0	223	217	105	95	77	139
1998— Houston (N.L.)....................	11	7	.611	3.36	32	32	1	1	0	211 2/3	227	92	79	81	137
A.L. totals (1 year)	1	3	.250	9.53	13	3	0	0	1	17	28	20	18	17	8
N.L. totals (5 years)	47	36	.566	3.56	161	117	10	4	0	787	806	368	311	272	516
Major league totals (6 years)......	48	39	.552	3.68	174	120	10	4	1	804	834	388	329	289	524

DIVISION SERIES RECORD

Year Team (League)	W	L	Pct.	ERA	G	GS	CG	ShO	Sv.	IP	H	R	ER	BB	SO
1997— Houston (N.L.)	0	1	.000	11.57	1	1	0	0	0	4 2/3	2	6	6	8	2
1998— Houston (N.L.)	0	0	.000	1.50	1	1	0	0	0	6	2	1	1	1	2
Div. series totals (2 years)	1	1	.500	5.91	2	2	0	0	0	10 2/3	4	7	7	9	4

HANEY, CHRIS   P   DODGERS

PERSONAL: Born November 16, 1968, in Baltimore. ... 6-3/210. ... Throws left, bats left. ... Full name: Christopher Deane Haney. ... Son of Larry Haney, major league catcher with five teams (1966-70 and 1972-78); and coach, Milwaukee Brewers (1978-91).

HIGH SCHOOL: Orange County (Va.).

COLLEGE: UNC Charlotte.

TRANSACTIONS/CAREER NOTES: Selected by Milwaukee Brewers organization in 25th round of free-agent draft (June 2, 1987); did not sign. ... Selected by Montreal Expos organization in second round of free-agent draft (June 4, 1990). ... On Indianapolis disabled list (June 17-25,

1992). ... Traded by Expos with P Bill Sampen to Kansas City Royals for 3B Sean Berry and P Archie Corbin (August 29, 1992). ... On disabled list (July 13, 1995-remainder of season). ... On Kansas City disabled list (April 15-June 17 and June 27-September 3, 1997); included rehabilitation assignments to Omaha (May 31-June 13) and Wichita (August 25-29). ... On Kansas City disabled list (June 8-24, 1998); included rehabilitation assignment to Gulf Coast Royals (June 22). ... Traded by Royals to Chicago Cubs for cash (September 12, 1998). ... Granted free agency (October 27, 1998). ... Signed by Los Angeles Dodgers (January 6, 1999).

MISCELLANEOUS: Appeared in one game as pinch runner with Montreal (1992).

Year	Team (League)	W	L	Pct.	ERA	G	GS	CG	ShO	Sv.	IP	H	R	ER	BB	SO
1990—	Jamestown (NYP)	3	0	1.000	0.96	6	5	0	0	1	28	17	3	3	10	26
	— Rockford (Midwest)	2	4	.333	2.21	8	8	3	0	0	53	40	15	13	6	45
	— Jacksonville (Southern)	1	0	1.000	0.00	1	1	0	0	0	6	6	0	0	3	6
1991—	Harrisburg (Eastern)	5	3	.625	2.16	12	12	3	0	0	83 1/3	65	21	20	31	68
	— Montreal (N.L.)	3	7	.300	4.04	16	16	0	0	0	84 2/3	94	49	38	43	51
	— Indianapolis (A.A.)	1	1	.500	4.35	2	2	0	0	0	10 1/3	14	10	5	6	8
1992—	Montreal (N.L.)	2	3	.400	5.45	9	6	1	1	0	38	40	25	23	10	27
	— Indianapolis (A.A.)	5	2	.714	5.14	15	15	0	0	0	84	88	50	48	42	61
	— Kansas City (A.L.)■	2	3	.400	3.86	7	7	1	1	0	42	35	18	18	16	27
1993—	Omaha (Am. Assoc.)	6	1	.857	2.27	8	7	2	0	0	47 2/3	43	13	12	14	32
	— Kansas City (A.L.)	9	9	.500	6.02	23	23	1	1	0	124	141	87	83	53	65
1994—	Kansas City (A.L.)	2	2	.500	7.31	6	6	0	0	0	28 1/3	36	25	23	11	18
	— Omaha (Am. Assoc.)	8	7	.533	5.25	18	18	1	0	0	104 2/3	125	77	61	37	78
1995—	Kansas City (A.L.)	3	4	.429	3.65	16	13	1	0	0	81 1/3	78	35	33	33	31
1996—	Kansas City (A.L.)	10	14	.417	4.70	35	35	4	1	0	228	*267	136	119	51	115
1997—	Kansas City (A.L.)	1	2	.333	4.38	8	3	0	0	0	24 2/3	29	16	12	5	16
	— Omaha (Am. Assoc.)	1	0	1.000	3.79	4	3	0	0	0	19	16	12	8	6	7
	— Wichita (Texas)	0	1	.000	2.70	2	2	0	0	0	6 2/3	5	3	2	0	2
1998—	Kansas City (A.L.)	6	6	.500	7.03	33	12	0	0	0	97 1/3	125	78	76	36	51
	— GC Royals (GCL)	0	1	.000	0.00	1	1	0	0	0	2 1/3	2	2	0	0	1
	— Chicago (N.L.)■	0	0	. . .	7.20	5	0	0	0	0	5	3	4	4	1	4
A.L. totals (7 years)		33	40	.452	5.24	128	99	7	3	0	625 2/3	711	395	364	205	323
N.L. totals (3 years)		5	10	.333	4.58	30	22	1	1	0	127 2/3	137	78	65	54	82
Major league totals (8 years)		38	50	.432	5.13	158	121	8	4	0	753 1/3	848	473	429	259	405

HANEY, TODD   2B   METS

PERSONAL: Born July 30, 1965, in Galveston, Texas. ... 5-9/165. ... Bats right, throws right. ... Full name: Todd Michael Haney.

HIGH SCHOOL: Richfield (Waco, Texas).

JUNIOR COLLEGE: Panola Junior College (Texas).

COLLEGE: Texas.

TRANSACTIONS/CAREER NOTES: Selected by Seattle Mariners organization in 38th round of free-agent draft (June 2, 1987). ... Traded by Mariners organization to Detroit Tigers organization for P Dave Richards (January 21, 1991). ... Released by Tigers organization (April 4, 1991). ... Signed by Montreal Expos organization (April 7, 1991). ... On Indianapolis disabled list (April 12-July 16, 1992). ... Granted free agency (October 15, 1993). ... Signed by Chicago Cubs organization (December 14, 1993). ... Granted free agency (October 15, 1994). ... Re-signed by Cubs organization (January 9, 1995). ... Granted free agency (October 15, 1996). ... Signed by Mariners organization (December 12, 1996). ... On Tacoma disabled list (April 11-24, 1997). ... Traded by Mariners to Houston Astros organization for cash considerations (April 24, 1997). ... Granted free agency (October 15, 1997). ... Signed by New York Mets (December 6, 1997). ... On Norfolk disabled list (April 9-27, 1998). ... Granted free agency (October 15, 1998). ... Re-signed by Mets organization (December 14, 1998).

STATISTICAL NOTES: Led Midwest League second basemen with 29 double plays in 1988. ... Led American Association second basemen with .974 fielding percentage, 381 assists and 74 double plays in 1991.

Year	Team (League)	Pos.	G	AB	R	H	2B	3B	HR	RBI	Avg.	BB	SO	SB	PO	A	E	Avg.
1987—	Bellingham (N'west)	2B	66	252	57	64	11	2	5	27	.254	44	33	18	148	170	16	.952
1988—	Wausau (Midwest)	2B-SS	132	452	66	127	23	2	7	54	.281	56	54	35	282	318	30	.952
1989—	San Bern. (Calif.)	2B	25	107	10	27	5	0	0	7	.252	7	14	2	47	14	3	.953
	— Williamsport (East.)	2B	115	401	59	108	20	4	2	31	.269	49	43	13	213	313	*18	.967
1990—	Williamsport (East.)	2B	1	2	0	1	1	0	0	0	.500	1	0	0	1	1	0	1.000
	— Calgary (PCL)	2B	108	419	81	142	15	6	1	36	.339	37	38	16	206	292	15	.971
1991—	Indianapolis (A.A.)■	2B-SS	132	510	68	159	32	3	2	39	.312	47	49	12	232	†385	16	†.975
1992—	Indianapolis (A.A.)	2B	57	200	30	53	14	0	6	33	.265	37	34	1	113	161	7	.975
	— Montreal (N.L.)	2B	7	10	0	3	1	0	0	1	.300	0	0	0	2	6	0	1.000
1993—	Ottawa (Int'l)	2B-SS	136	506	69	147	30	4	3	46	.291	36	56	11	245	401	15	.977
1994—	Iowa (Am. Assoc.)■	2B-OF	83	305	48	89	22	1	3	35	.292	28	29	9	159	199	8	.978
	— Chicago (N.L.)	2B-3B	17	37	6	6	0	0	1	2	.162	3	3	2	20	28	1	.980
1995—	Iowa (Am. Assoc.)	2-S-3-O	90	326	38	102	20	2	4	30	.313	28	21	2	123	182	10	.968
	— Chicago (N.L.)	2B-3B	25	73	11	30	8	0	2	6	.411	7	11	0	34	61	2	.979
1996—	Chicago (N.L.)	2B-3B-SS	49	82	11	11	1	0	0	3	.134	7	15	1	32	65	3	.970
	— Iowa (Am. Assoc.)	2-3-S-P-O	66	240	20	59	13	0	2	19	.246	19	24	3	108	158	11	.960
1997—	Tacoma (PCL)■	3B-SS-OF	4	17	3	6	4	0	0	2	.353	2	2	0	5	9	0	1.000
	— New Orleans (A.A.)■	2B-3B	115	454	63	128	25	0	2	63	.282	43	50	5	213	260	5	*.990
1998—	St. Lucie (Fla. St.)■	2B	1	4	1	1	0	0	0	0	.250	0	0	0	3	2	0	1.000
	— Norfolk (Int'l)	3-S-O-2	117	440	84	152	33	4	3	51	*.345	55	44	11	126	182	16	.951
	— New York (N.L.)	2B-OF	3	3	0	0	0	0	0	0	.000	1	0	0	0	0	0	. . .
Major league totals (5 years)			101	205	28	50	10	0	3	12	.244	18	29	3	88	160	6	.976

RECORD AS PITCHER

Year	Team (League)	W	L	Pct.	ERA	G	GS	CG	ShO	Sv.	IP	H	R	ER	BB	SO
1996—	Iowa (Am. Assoc.)	0	0	. . .	0.00	1	0	0	0	0	1	2	0	0	0	0

H

PERSONAL: Born March 12, 1971, in Bellflower, Calif. ... 6-5/224. ... Throws right, bats right. ... Full name: Gregory Michael Hansell.
HIGH SCHOOL: John F. Kennedy (La Palma, Calif.).
TRANSACTIONS/CAREER NOTES: Selected by Boston Red Sox organization in 10th round of free-agent draft (June 5, 1989). ... Traded by Red Sox organization with OF Ed Perozo and a player to be named later to New York Mets organization for 1B Mike Marshall (July 27, 1990); Mets acquired C Paul Williams to complete deal (November 19, 1990). ... Traded by Mets organization with P Bob Ojeda to Los Angeles Dodgers organization for OF Hubie Brooks (December 15, 1990). ... On disabled list (June 19-July 8, 1993). ... Traded by Dodgers with 3B/1B Ron Coomer, P Jose Parra and a player to be named later to Minnesota Twins for P Kevin Tapani and P Mark Guthrie (July 31, 1995); Twins acquired OF Chris Latham to complete deal (October 30, 1995). ... Claimed on waivers by Boston Red Sox (October 11, 1996). ... Released by Red Sox (March 26, 1997). ... Signed by Milwaukee Brewers organization (March 31, 1997). ... Granted free agency (October 15, 1997). ... Signed by Arizona Diamondbacks organization (December 18, 1997). ... Released by Diamondbacks (March 25, 1998). ... Signed by Oakland Athletics organization (March 31, 1998). ... ... Traded by A's to Kansas City Royals (May 10, 1998), completing trade in which Royals traded C Mike Macfarlane to A's for a player to be named later (April 8, 1998). ... Granted free agency (October 15, 1998). ... Signed by San Francisco Giants (December 4, 1998).
STATISTICAL NOTES: Tied for Florida State League lead with 14 losses and 27 games started in 1990.

Year Team (League)	W	L	Pct.	ERA	G	GS	CG	ShO	Sv.	IP	H	R	ER	BB	SO
1989— GC Red Sox (GCL)	3	2	.600	2.53	10	8	0	0	2	57	51	23	16	23	44
1990— Winter Haven (FSL)	7	10	.412	3.59	21	21	2	1	0	115 1/3	95	63	46	64	79
—St. Lucie (Fla. St.)■	2	§4	.333	2.84	6	§6	0	0	0	38	34	22	12	15	16
1991— Bakersfield (California)■	14	5	.737	2.87	25	25	0	0	0	150 2/3	142	56	48	42	132
1992— San Antonio (Tex.)	6	4	.600	2.83	14	14	0	0	0	92 1/3	80	40	29	33	64
—Albuquerque (PCL)	1	5	.167	5.24	13	13	0	0	0	68 2/3	84	46	40	35	38
1993— Albuquerque (PCL)	5	10	.333	6.93	26	20	0	0	0	101 1/3	131	86	78	60	60
1994— Albuquerque (PCL)	10	2	*.833	2.99	47	6	0	0	8	123 1/3	109	44	41	31	101
1995— Los Angeles (N.L.)	0	1	.000	7.45	20	0	0	0	0	19 1/3	29	17	16	6	13
—Albuquerque (PCL)	1	1	.500	8.44	8	1	0	0	1	16	25	15	15	6	15
—Salt Lake (PCL)■	3	1	.750	5.01	7	5	0	0	0	32 1/3	39	20	18	4	17
1996— Minnesota (A.L.)	3	0	1.000	5.69	50	0	0	0	3	74 1/3	83	48	47	31	46
1997— Tucson (PCL)■	2	3	.400	4.64	40	9	0	0	2	87 1/3	99	52	45	27	76
—Milwaukee (A.L.)	0	0	...	9.64	3	0	0	0	0	4 2/3	5	5	5	1	5
1998— Edmonton (PCL)■	0	0	...	1.23	13	0	0	0	6	14 2/3	13	2	2	3	16
—Omaha (Pacific Coast)■	8	3	.727	3.00	46	0	0	0	7	69	63	25	23	15	59
A.L. totals (2 years)	3	0	1.000	5.92	53	0	0	0	3	79	88	53	52	32	51
N.L. totals (1 year)	0	1	.000	7.45	20	0	0	0	0	19 1/3	29	17	16	6	13
Major league totals (3 years)	3	1	.750	6.22	73	0	0	0	3	98 1/3	117	70	68	38	64

PERSONAL: Born November 24, 1968, in Long Beach, Calif. ... 6-0/195. ... Bats left, throws right. ... Full name: David Andrew Hansen.
HIGH SCHOOL: Rowland (Long Beach, Calif.).
TRANSACTIONS/CAREER NOTES: Selected by Los Angeles Dodgers organization in second round of free-agent draft (June 2, 1986). ... On disabled list (May 9-28, 1994). ... Granted free agency (November 27, 1996). ... Signed by Chicago Cubs organization (January 22, 1997). ... Granted free agency (October 27, 1997). ... Signed by Hanshin Tigers of Japan Central League (November 7, 1997). ... Signed by Dodgers (January 11, 1999).
STATISTICAL NOTES: Led California League third basemen with 45 errors in 1987. ... Led Florida State League with 210 total bases and tied for lead with nine sacrifice flies in 1988. ... Led Florida State League third basemen with 383 total chances and 24 double plays in 1988. ... Led Pacific Coast League third basemen with .926 fielding percentage, 254 assists, 349 total chances and 25 double plays in 1990. ... Career major league grand slams: 1.

Year Team (League)	Pos.	G	AB	R	H	2B	3B	HR	RBI	Avg.	BB	SO	SB	PO	A	E	Avg.
1986— Great Falls (Pio.)	O-3-C-2	61	204	39	61	7	3	1	36	.299	27	28	9	54	10	7	.901
1987— Bakersfield (Calif.)	3B-OF	132	432	68	113	22	1	3	38	.262	65	61	4	79	198	†45	.860
1988— Vero Beach (FSL)	3B	135	512	68	*149	•28	6	7	*81	.291	56	46	2	*102	*263	18	*.953
1989— San Antonio (Tex.)	3B	121	464	72	138	21	4	6	52	.297	50	44	3	*92	208	16	*.949
—Albuquerque (PCL)	3B	6	30	6	8	1	0	2	10	.267	2	3	0	3	8	3	.786
1990— Albuquerque (PCL)	3B-OF-SS	135	487	90	154	20	3	11	92	.316	*90	54	9	71	†255	26	†.926
—Los Angeles (N.L.)	3B	5	7	0	1	0	0	0	1	.143	0	0	0	0	1	1	.500
1991— Albuquerque (PCL)	3B-SS	68	254	42	77	11	1	5	40	.303	49	33	4	43	125	6	.966
—Los Angeles (N.L.)	3B-SS	53	56	3	15	4	0	1	5	.268	2	12	1	5	19	0	1.000
1992— Los Angeles (N.L.)	3B	132	341	30	73	11	0	6	22	.214	34	49	0	61	183	8	*.968
1993— Los Angeles (N.L.)	3B	84	105	13	38	3	0	4	30	.362	21	13	0	11	27	3	.927
1994— Los Angeles (N.L.)	3B	40	44	3	15	3	0	0	5	.341	5	5	0	0	6	1	.857
1995— Los Angeles (N.L.)	3B	100	181	19	52	10	0	1	14	.287	28	28	0	27	70	7	.933
1996— Los Angeles (N.L.)	3B-1B	80	104	7	23	1	0	0	6	.221	11	22	0	60	23	1	.988
1997— Chicago (N.L.)■	3B-1B-2B	90	151	19	47	8	2	3	21	.311	31	32	1	45	47	7	.929
1998— Hanshin (Jp.Cn.)■		121	400	42	101	13	1	11	55	.253	42	89	0	...	...	...	...
Major league totals (8 years)		584	989	94	264	40	2	15	104	.267	132	161	2	209	376	28	.954

DIVISION SERIES RECORD

Year Team (League)	Pos.	G	AB	R	H	2B	3B	HR	RBI	Avg.	BB	SO	SB	PO	A	E	Avg.
1995— Los Angeles (N.L.)	PH	3	3	0	2	0	0	0	0	.667	0	0	0	...	...	...	...
1996— Los Angeles (N.L.)	PH-3B	2	2	0	0	0	0	0	0	.000	0	0	0	1	0	0	1.000
Division series totals (2 years)		5	5	0	2	0	0	0	0	.400	0	0	0	1	0	0	1.000

HANSEN, JED — 2B — ROYALS

PERSONAL: Born August 19, 1972, in Tacoma, Wash. ... 6-1/195. ... Bats right, throws right. ... Full name: Jed Ramon Hansen.
HIGH SCHOOL: Capital (Olympia, Wash.).
COLLEGE: Stanford.
TRANSACTIONS/CAREER NOTES: Selected by Cleveland Indians organization in 21st round of free-agent draft (June 3, 1991); did not sign. ... Selected by Kansas City Royals organization in second round of free-agent draft (June 2, 1994).
STATISTICAL NOTES: Led Northwest League second basemen with 337 total chances in 1994. ... Tied for American Association lead in errors by second baseman with 17 in 1997.

							BATTING									FIELDING			
Year Team (League)	Pos.	G	AB	R	H	2B	3B	HR	RBI	Avg.	BB	SO	SB	PO	A	E	Avg.
1994— Eugene (Northwest) ...	2B	66	235	26	57	8	2	3	17	.243	24	56	6	*141	*189	7	*.979
1995— Springfield (Midw.)	2B	122	414	86	107	27	7	9	50	.258	78	73	44	220	*345	22	.963
1996— Wichita (Texas)	2B-OF	99	405	60	116	27	4	12	50	.286	29	72	14	196	276	10	.979
— Omaha (A.A.)	2B	29	99	14	23	4	0	3	9	.232	12	22	2	66	75	7	.953
1997— Omaha (A.A.)	2B-SS-3B	114	380	43	102	20	2	11	44	.268	32	78	8	205	323	‡23	.958
— Kansas City (A.L.)	2B	34	94	11	29	6	1	1	14	.309	13	29	3	56	77	1	.993
1998— Kansas City (A.L.)	2B	4	3	0	0	0	0	0	0	.000	0	3	0	1	0	0	1.000
— Omaha (Pacific Coast)	2B-SS-OF	127	417	63	116	19	7	16	56	.278	44	125	17	211	353	28	.953
Major league totals (2 years)		**38**	**97**	**11**	**29**	**6**	**1**	**1**	**14**	**.299**	**13**	**32**	**3**	**57**	**77**	**1**	**.993**

HANSON, ERIK — P — ROYALS

PERSONAL: Born May 18, 1965, in Kinnelon, N.J. ... 6-6/215. ... Throws right, bats right. ... Full name: Erik Brian Hanson.
HIGH SCHOOL: Peddie Prep (Highstown, N.J.).
COLLEGE: Wake Forest.
TRANSACTIONS/CAREER NOTES: Selected by Montreal Expos organization in seventh round of free-agent draft (June 6, 1983); did not sign. ... Selected by Seattle Mariners organization in second round of free-agent draft (June 2, 1986). ... On inactive list (June 12-August 18, 1986). ... On Seattle disabled list (May 25-August 4, 1989); included rehabilitation assignments to Calgary (June 14-22 and July 24-August 4). ... On Seattle disabled list (May 12-28 and May 29-June 22, 1991); included rehabilitation assignment to Calgary (June 16-20). ... On disabled list (August 23-September 12, 1992). ... Traded by Mariners with 2B Bret Boone to Cincinnati Reds for P Bobby Ayala and C Dan Wilson (November 2, 1993). ... On disabled list (August 9, 1994-remainder of season). ... Granted free agency (October 31, 1994). ... Signed by Boston Red Sox (April 11, 1995). ... Granted free agency (November 1, 1995). ... Signed by Toronto Blue Jays (December 22, 1995). ... On Toronto disabled list (March 24-April 17, 1997); included rehabilitation assignment to Dunedin (April 5-12). ... On Toronto disabled list (April 24-September 14, 1997). ... On Toronto disabled list (March 26-April 12, 1998); included rehabilitation assignment to Dunedin (April 9-10). ... Released by Blue Jays (June 16, 1998). ... Signed by Anaheim Angels organization (June 25, 1998). ... Granted free agency (October 15, 1998). ... Signed by Kansas City Royals organization (December 17, 1998).
STATISTICAL NOTES: Pitched 5-0 no-hit victory for Calgary against Las Vegas (August 21, 1988, second game).
MISCELLANEOUS: Scored once in two games as pinch runner; after pinch-running in one game, became designated hitter but made no plate appearance (1993).

Year Team (League)	W	L	Pct.	ERA	G	GS	CG	ShO	Sv.	IP	H	R	ER	BB	SO
1986— Chattanooga (Southern).....	0	0	. . .	3.86	3	2	0	0	0	9 1/3	10	4	4	4	11
1987— Chattanooga (Southern).....	8	10	.444	2.60	21	21	1	0	0	131 1/3	102	56	38	43	131
— Calgary (PCL)..................	1	3	.250	3.61	8	7	0	0	0	47 1/3	38	23	19	21	43
1988— Calgary (PCL)..................	12	7	.632	4.23	27	26	2	1	0	161 2/3	167	92	76	57	*154
— Seattle (A.L.)................	2	3	.400	3.24	6	6	0	0	0	41 2/3	35	17	15	12	36
1989— Seattle (A.L.)................	9	5	.643	3.18	17	17	1	0	0	113 1/3	103	44	40	32	75
— Calgary (PCL)..................	4	2	.667	6.87	8	8	1	0	0	38	51	30	29	11	37
1990— Seattle (A.L.)................	18	9	.667	3.24	33	33	5	1	0	236	205	88	85	68	211
1991— Seattle (A.L.)................	8	8	.500	3.81	27	27	2	1	0	174 2/3	182	82	74	56	143
— Calgary (PCL)..................	0	0	. . .	1.50	1	1	0	0	0	6	1	1	1	2	5
1992— Seattle (A.L.)................	8	*17	.320	4.82	31	30	6	1	0	186 2/3	209	110	100	57	112
1993— Seattle (A.L.)................	11	12	.478	3.47	31	30	7	0	0	215	215	91	83	60	163
1994— Cincinnati (N.L.)■.............	5	5	.500	4.11	22	21	0	0	0	122 2/3	137	60	56	23	101
1995— Boston (A.L.)■.............	15	5	.750	4.24	29	29	1	1	0	186 2/3	187	94	88	59	139
1996— Toronto (A.L.).............	13	17	.433	5.41	35	35	4	1	0	214 2/3	243	143	129	102	156
1997— Dunedin (Fla. St.).............	0	0	. . .	1.29	2	2	0	0	0	7	7	5	1	1	5
— Toronto (A.L.)................	0	0	. . .	7.80	3	2	0	0	0	15	15	13	13	6	18
1998— Dunedin (Fla. St.).............	0	0	. . .	2.25	1	1	0	0	0	4	4	1	1	2	5
— Toronto (A.L.)................	0	3	.000	6.24	11	8	0	0	0	49	73	34	34	29	21
— Vancouver (PCL)■.............	5	5	.500	4.50	14	14	2	1	0	82	82	43	41	36	60
A.L. totals (10 years)	**84**	**79**	**.515**	**4.15**	**223**	**217**	**26**	**5**	**0**	**1432 2/3**	**1467**	**716**	**661**	**481**	**1074**
N.L. totals (1 year)	**5**	**5**	**.500**	**4.11**	**22**	**21**	**0**	**0**	**0**	**122 2/3**	**137**	**60**	**56**	**23**	**101**
Major league totals (11 years)	**89**	**84**	**.514**	**4.15**	**245**	**238**	**26**	**5**	**0**	**1555 1/3**	**1604**	**776**	**717**	**504**	**1175**

DIVISION SERIES RECORD

Year Team (League)	W	L	Pct.	ERA	G	GS	CG	ShO	Sv.	IP	H	R	ER	BB	SO
1995— Boston (A.L.)..................	0	1	.000	4.50	1	1	1	0	0	8	4	4	4	4	5

ALL-STAR GAME RECORD

Year League	W	L	Pct.	ERA	GS	CG	ShO	Sv.	IP	H	R	ER	BB	SO
1995— American						Did not play.								

HARDTKE, JASON — 2B — REDS

PERSONAL: Born September 15, 1971, in Milwaukee. ... 5-10/175. ... Bats both, throws right. ... Full name: Jason Robert Hardtke. ... Name pronounced HART-kee.
HIGH SCHOOL: Leland (San Jose, Calif.).
TRANSACTIONS/CAREER NOTES: Selected by Cleveland Indians organization in third round of free-agent draft (June 4, 1990). ... Traded by Indians organization with a player to be named later to San Diego Padres organization for OF Thomas Howard (April 14, 1992); Padres

H

acquired C Christopher Maffett to complete deal (July 10, 1992). ... Selected by New York Mets organization from Padres organization in Rule 5 minor league draft (December 5, 1994). ... On Norfolk disabled list (July 1-30, 1996). ... Granted free agency (October 15, 1996). ... Resigned by Mets organization (November 21, 1996). ... Claimed on waivers by Chicago Cubs (October 15, 1997). ... Granted free agency (October 15, 1998). ... Signed by Cincinnati Reds organization (December 15, 1998).

STATISTICAL NOTES: Tied for Eastern League lead with nine sacrifice flies in 1995. ... Led International League with 516 total chances in 1997.

Year Team (League)	Pos.	G	AB	R	H	2B	3B	HR	RBI	Avg.	BB	SO	SB	PO	A	E	Avg.
1990— Burlington (Appal.).....	SS-2B	39	142	18	38	7	0	4	16	.268	23	19	11	36	118	9	.945
1991— Columbus (S. Atl.).....	SS-2B	139	534	•104	*155	26	8	12	81	.290	75	48	23	194	345	41	.929
1992— Waterloo (Midw.)■...	2B	110	411	75	125	27	4	8	47	.304	38	33	9	225	256	15	*.970
— High Desert (Calif.).....	DH	10	41	9	11	1	0	2	8	.268	4	4	1				. . .
1993— Rancho Cuca. (Cal.) ...	2B-3B-1B	130	*523	96	167	38	7	11	85	.319	61	54	7	248	337	23	.962
1994— Wichita (Texas)	3B-2B	75	255	26	60	15	1	5	29	.235	21	44	1	57	102	11	.935
— Rancho Cuca. (Cal.) ...	2B-3B	4	13	2	4	0	0	0	0	.308	3	2	0	9	7	0	1.000
1995— Norfolk (Int'l)■	2B	4	7	1	2	1	0	0	0	.286	2	0	1	5	2	0	1.000
— Binghamton (East.)	2B-3B	121	455	65	130	*42	4	4	52	.286	66	58	6	201	356	19	.967
1996— Binghamton (East.)	2B	35	137	23	36	11	0	3	16	.263	16	16	0	61	100	6	.964
— Norfolk (Int'l)............	2B	71	257	49	77	17	2	9	35	.300	29	29	4	149	175	5	.985
— New York (N.L.)..........	2B	19	57	3	11	5	0	0	6	.193	2	12	0	26	34	0	1.000
1997— Norfolk (Int'l)	2B	97	388	46	107	23	3	11	45	.276	40	54	3	187	*319	10	.981
— New York (N.L.)...........	2B-3B	30	56	9	15	2	0	2	8	.268	4	6	1	25	26	1	.981
— Binghamton (East.)	2B	6	26	3	10	2	0	1	4	.385	2	2	0	13	20	0	1.000
1998— Iowa (Pacific Coast)■	3B-2B	91	333	67	96	20	1	11	53	.288	35	46	7	68	144	12	.946
— Chicago (N.L.)	3B-DH-OF	18	21	2	5	0	0	2	2	.238	2	6	0	0	3	0	1.000
Major league totals (3 years)		67	134	14	31	7	0	2	16	.231	8	24	1	51	63	1	.991

HARNISCH, PETE   P   REDS

PERSONAL: Born September 23, 1966, in Commack, N.Y. ... 6-0/228. ... Throws right, bats right. ... Full name: Peter Thomas Harnisch.
HIGH SCHOOL: Commack (N.Y.).
COLLEGE: Fordham.
TRANSACTIONS/CAREER NOTES: Selected by Baltimore Orioles organization in supplemental round ("sandwich pick" between first and second round, 27th pick overall) of free-agent draft (June 2, 1987); pick received as compensation for Cleveland Indians signing Type A free-agent C Rick Dempsey. ... Traded by Orioles with P Curt Schilling and OF Steve Finley to Houston Astros for 1B Glenn Davis (January 10, 1991). ... On suspended list (July 7-9, 1992). ... On Houston disabled list (May 23-June 30, 1994); included rehabilitation assignment to Tucson (June 25-26). ... Traded by Astros to New York Mets for two players to be named later (November 28, 1994); Astros acquired P Andy Beckerman (December 6, 1994) and P Juan Castillo (April 12, 1995) to complete deal. ... Granted free agency (December 23, 1994). ... Re-signed by Mets (April 7, 1995). ... On disabled list (August 2, 1995-remainder of season). ... On New York disabled list (March 26-April 14, 1996); included rehabilitation assignment to St. Lucie (March 30-April 14). ... On New York suspended list (May 22-31, 1996). ... On New York disabled list (April 2-August 5, 1997); included rehabilitation assignments to Gulf Coast Mets (July 7-10), St. Lucie (July 11-19) and Norfolk (July 20-August 5). ... Traded by Mets to Milwaukee Brewers for OF Donny Moore (August 31, 1997). ... Granted free agency (October 27, 1997). ... Signed by Cincinnati Reds (January 21, 1998).
RECORDS: Shares major league record for striking out side on nine pitches (September 6, 1991, seventh inning). ... Shares N.L. record for most consecutive home runs allowed in one inning—4 (July 23, 1996, first inning).
STATISTICAL NOTES: Pitched 4-0 one-hit, complete-game victory against Chicago (July 10, 1993). ... Pitched 3-0 one-hit, complete-game victory against San Diego (September 17, 1993).
MISCELLANEOUS: Appeared in one game as pinch runner with Houston (1994). ... Appeared in one game as pinch runner with New York (1996).

Year Team (League)	W	L	Pct.	ERA	G	GS	CG	ShO	Sv.	IP	H	R	ER	BB	SO
1987— Bluefield (Appalachian)	3	1	.750	2.56	9	9	0	0	0	52 2/3	38	19	15	26	64
— Hagerstown (Caro.)...........	1	2	.333	2.25	4	4	0	0	0	20	17	7	5	14	18
1988— Charlotte (Southern)	7	6	.538	2.58	20	20	4	2	0	132 1/3	113	55	38	52	141
— Rochester (Int'l)	4	1	.800	2.16	7	7	3	2	0	58 1/3	44	16	14	14	43
— Baltimore (A.L.).................	0	2	.000	5.54	2	2	0	0	0	13	13	8	8	9	10
1989— Baltimore (A.L.).................	5	9	.357	4.62	18	17	2	0	0	103 1/3	97	55	53	64	70
— Rochester (Int'l)	5	5	.500	2.58	12	12	3	1	0	87 1/3	60	27	25	35	59
1990— Baltimore (A.L.).................	11	11	.500	4.34	31	31	3	0	0	188 2/3	189	96	91	86	122
1991— Houston (N.L.)■...............	12	9	.571	2.70	33	33	4	2	0	216 2/3	169	71	65	83	172
1992— Houston (N.L.)................	9	10	.474	3.70	34	34	0	0	0	206 2/3	182	92	85	64	164
1993— Houston (N.L.)................	16	9	.640	2.98	33	33	5	*4	0	217 2/3	171	84	72	79	185
1994— Houston (N.L.)................	8	5	.615	5.40	17	17	1	0	0	95	100	59	57	39	62
— Tucson (PCL)	0	0	. . .	0.00	1	1	0	0	0	5	2	0	0	1	1
1995— New York (N.L.)■.............	2	8	.200	3.68	18	18	0	0	0	110	111	55	45	24	82
1996— St. Lucie (Fla. St.)	1	0	1.000	2.77	2	2	0	0	0	13	11	4	4	0	12
— New York (N.L.)...............	8	12	.400	4.21	31	31	2	1	0	194 2/3	195	103	91	61	114
1997— GC Mets (GCL)................	0	0	. . .	12.00	1	1	0	0	0	3	7	4	4	0	5
— St. Lucie (Fla. St.)	1	0	1.000	3.00	2	2	0	0	0	12	5	5	4	4	7
— Norfolk (Int'l)	1	1	.500	5.40	3	3	0	0	0	16 2/3	16	12	10	10	16
— New York (N.L.)...............	0	1	.000	8.06	6	5	0	0	0	25 2/3	35	24	23	11	12
— Milwaukee (A.L.)■............	1	1	.500	5.14	4	3	0	0	0	14	13	9	8	12	10
1998— Cincinnati (N.L.)■............	14	7	.667	3.14	32	32	2	1	0	209	176	79	73	64	157
A.L. totals (4 years)	17	23	.425	4.51	55	53	5	0	0	319	312	168	160	171	212
N.L. totals (8 years)	69	61	.531	3.61	204	203	14	8	0	1275 1/3	1139	567	511	425	948
Major league totals (11 years)....	86	84	.506	3.79	259	256	19	8	0	1594 1/3	1451	735	671	596	1160

ALL-STAR GAME RECORD

Year League	W	L	Pct.	ERA	GS	CG	ShO	Sv.	IP	H	R	ER	BB	SO
1991— National	0	0	. . .	0.00	0	0	0	0	1	2	0	0	0	1

H

HARRIGER, DENNY   P

PERSONAL: Born July 21, 1969, in Kittanning, Pa. ... 5-11/185. ... Throws right, bats right. ... Full name: Dennis Scott Harriger.
HIGH SCHOOL: Ford City (Pa.).
TRANSACTIONS/CAREER NOTES: Selected by New York Mets organization in 18th round of free-agent draft (June 2, 1987). ... On St. Lucie disabled list (April 11-May 30, 1991). ... Granted free agency (October 15, 1993). ... Signed by San Diego Padres organization (November 9, 1993). ... Granted free agency (October 15, 1996). ... Signed by Detroit Tigers organization (November 25, 1996). ... Granted free agency (October 15, 1997). ... Re-signed by Tigers organization (December 8, 1997). ... Granted free agency (October 15, 1998).

Year Team (League)	W	L	Pct.	ERA	G	GS	CG	ShO	Sv.	IP	H	R	ER	BB	SO
1987— Kingsport (Appalachian).....	2	5	.286	4.33	12	7	0	0	0	43²/₃	43	31	21	22	24
1988— Kingsport (Appalachian).....	7	2	.778	2.14	13	13	2	1	0	92¹/₃	83	35	22	24	59
1989— Pittsfield (NYP)	2	0	1.000	1.71	3	3	1	1	0	21	20	4	4	0	17
— St. Lucie (Fla. St.)	5	3	.625	3.19	11	11	0	0	0	67²/₃	72	33	24	17	17
1990— St. Lucie (Fla. St.)	5	3	.625	3.52	27	7	1	0	2	71²/₃	73	36	28	20	47
1991— Columbia (S. Atl.)	2	0	1.000	0.00	2	2	1	1	0	11	5	0	0	2	13
— St. Lucie (Fla. St.)	6	1	.857	2.27	14	11	2	1	0	71¹/₃	67	20	18	12	37
1992— Binghamton (Eastern)	2	2	.500	3.80	11	0	0	0	0	21¹/₃	22	11	9	7	8
— St. Lucie (Fla. St.)	7	3	.700	2.24	27	10	0	0	3	88¹/₃	89	30	22	14	65
1993— Binghamton (Eastern)	13	10	.565	2.95	35	24	•4	*3	1	170²/₃	174	69	56	40	89
1994— Las Vegas (PCL)■	6	11	.353	5.95	30	25	3	0	0	157¹/₃	216	*122	104	44	87
1995— Las Vegas (PCL)	9	9	.500	4.07	29	•28	*7	*2	0	177	187	94	80	60	97
1996— Las Vegas (PCL)	10	7	.588	4.22	26	25	1	0	0	164¹/₃	183	91	77	51	102
1997— Toledo (International)■	11	8	.579	3.99	27	27	2	1	0	167	159	87	74	63	109
1998— Toledo (International)	5	12	.294	4.55	22	22	4	1	0	142¹/₃	151	78	72	48	87
— Detroit (A.L.)	0	3	.000	6.75	4	2	0	0	0	12	17	12	9	8	3
Major league totals (1 year).......	0	3	.000	6.75	4	2	0	0	0	12	17	12	9	8	3

HARRIGER, MARK   P   ANGELS

PERSONAL: Born April 29, 1975, in Inglewood, Calif. ... 6-2/196. ... Throws right, bats right.
HIGH SCHOOL: St. John Bosco (Bellflower, Calif.).
COLLEGE: San Diego State.
TRANSACTIONS/CAREER NOTES: Selected by California Angels organization in 18th round of free-agent draft (June 4, 1996). ... Angels franchise renamed Anaheim Angeles for 1997 season.

Year Team (League)	W	L	Pct.	ERA	G	GS	CG	ShO	Sv.	IP	H	R	ER	BB	SO
1996— Boise (Northwest)	0	0	. . .	8.31	7	0	0	0	0	4¹/₃	9	5	4	3	3
1997— Cedar Rapids (Midw.)	1	6	.143	7.82	12	11	1	1	0	50²/₃	70	50	44	33	50
— Boise (Northwest)	3	4	.429	7.94	13	12	0	0	0	51	51	52	45	36	42
1998— Cedar Rapids (Midw.)	8	4	.667	2.23	16	16	3	1	0	117	86	37	29	38	105
— Lake Elsinore (Calif.)	5	5	.500	4.09	13	12	3	1	0	81¹/₃	86	43	37	23	68

HARRIS, LENNY   OF/IF   ROCKIES

PERSONAL: Born October 28, 1964, in Miami. ... 5-10/220. ... Bats left, throws right. ... Full name: Leonard Anthony Harris.
HIGH SCHOOL: Jackson (Miami).
JUNIOR COLLEGE: Miami-Dade (North) Community College.
TRANSACTIONS/CAREER NOTES: Selected by Cincinnati Reds organization in fifth round of free-agent draft (June 6, 1983). ... Loaned by Reds organization to Glens Falls, Detroit Tigers organization (May 6-28, 1988). ... Traded by Reds with OF Kal Daniels to Los Angeles Dodgers for P Tim Leary and SS Mariano Duncan (July 18, 1989). ... Granted free agency (October 8, 1993). ... Signed by Reds (December 1, 1993). ... Granted free agency (October 31, 1996). ... Re-signed by Reds (November 13, 1996). ... Traded by Reds to New York Mets for P John Hudek (July 3, 1998). ... Granted free agency (October 27, 1998). ... Signed by Colorado Rockies (November 9, 1998).
STATISTICAL NOTES: Led Florida State League third basemen with 34 double plays in 1985. ... Led Eastern League third basemen with 116 putouts, 28 errors and 360 total chances in 1986. ... Led American Association in caught stealing with 22 in 1988. ... Led American Association second basemen with 23 errors in 1988. ... Career major league grand slams: 2.

Year Team (League)	Pos.	G	AB	R	H	2B	3B	HR	RBI	Avg.	BB	SO	SB	PO	A	E	Avg.
															FIELDING		
1983— Billings (Pioneer)........	3B	56	224	37	63	8	1	1	26	.281	13	35	7	34	95	22	.854
1984— Cedar Rap. (Midw.)	3B	132	468	52	115	15	3	6	53	.246	42	59	31	111	204	*34	.903
1985— Tampa (Fla. St.)	3B	132	499	66	129	11	8	3	51	.259	37	57	15	89	*277	*35	.913
1986— Vermont (Eastern)	3B-SS	119	450	68	114	17	2	10	52	.253	29	38	36	†119	220	†28	.924
1987— Nashville (A.A.)	SS-SS	120	403	45	100	12	3	2	31	.248	27	43	30	124	210	34	.908
1988— Nashville (A.A.)■	2B-SS-3B	107	422	46	117	20	2	0	35	.277	22	36	*45	203	247	†25	.947
— Glens Falls (East.)■	2B	17	65	9	22	5	1	1	7	.338	9	6	6	40	49	5	.947
— Cincinnati (N.L.)■	3B-2B	16	43	7	16	1	0	0	8	.372	5	4	4	14	33	1	.979
1989— Cincinnati (N.L.)	2B-SS-3B	61	188	17	42	4	0	2	11	.223	9	20	10	92	134	13	.946
— Nashville (A.A.)	2B	8	34	6	9	2	0	3	6	.265	0	5	0	23	20	0	1.000
— Los Angeles (N.L.)■ ..	O-2-3-S	54	147	19	37	6	1	1	15	.252	11	13	4	55	34	2	.978
1990— Los Angeles (N.L.)	3-2-O-S	137	431	61	131	16	4	2	29	.304	29	31	15	140	205	11	.969
1991— Los Angeles (N.L.)	3-2-S-O	145	429	59	123	16	1	3	38	.287	37	32	12	125	250	20	.949
1992— Los Angeles (N.L.)	2-3-O-S	135	347	28	94	11	0	0	30	.271	24	24	19	199	248	27	.943
1993— Los Angeles (N.L.)	2-3-S-O	107	160	20	38	6	1	2	11	.238	15	15	3	61	99	3	.982
1994— Cincinnati (N.L.)■	3-1-O-2	66	100	13	31	3	1	0	14	.310	5	13	7	27	29	6	.903
1995— Cincinnati (N.L.)	3-1-O-2	101	197	32	41	8	3	2	16	.208	14	20	10	147	68	4	.982
1996— Cincinnati (N.L.)	O-3-1-2	125	302	33	86	17	2	5	32	.285	21	31	14	199	66	6	.978
1997— Cincinnati (N.L.)	O-2-3-1	120	238	32	65	13	1	3	28	.273	18	18	4	120	57	3	.983
1998— Cincinnati (N.L.)	OF-DH-P	57	122	12	36	8	0	0	10	.295	8	9	1	37	2	3	.929
— New York (N.L.)■	O-3-2-1	75	168	18	39	7	0	6	17	.232	9	12	5	84	14	2	.980
Major league totals (11 years)		1199	2872	351	779	116	14	26	259	.271	205	242	108	1300	1239	101	.962

H

							BATTING							FIELDING		
Year	Team (League)	Pos.	G	AB	R	H	2B	3B	HR	RBI	Avg.	BB	SO	SB	PO	A	E	Avg.
1995— Cincinnati (N.L.)	PH	3	2	0	2	0	0	0	1	1.000	0	0	1	0	0	0	...

RECORD AS PITCHER

Year	Team (League)	W	L	Pct.	ERA	G	GS	CG	ShO	Sv.	IP	H	R	ER	BB	SO
1998— Cincinnati (N.L.)	0	0	...	0.00	1	0	0	0	0	1	0	0	0	0	1

HARRIS, PEP　　　　　　　　P　　　　　　　　ANGELS

PERSONAL: Born September 23, 1972, in Lancaster, S.C. ... 6-2/253. ... Throws right, bats right. ... Full name: Hernando Petrocelli Harris.
HIGH SCHOOL: Lancaster (S.C.).
TRANSACTIONS/CAREER NOTES: Selected by Cleveland Indians organization in seventh round of free-agent draft (June 3, 1991). ... On disabled list (June 4-15, 1992 and April 9-May 1, 1993). ... Traded by Indians with P Jason Grimsley to California Angels for P Brian Anderson (February 15, 1996). ... Angels franchise renamed Anaheim Angels for 1997 season. ... On Anaheim disabled list (March 19-April 18, 1998).

Year	Team (League)	W	L	Pct.	ERA	G	GS	CG	ShO	Sv.	IP	H	R	ER	BB	SO
1991— Burlington (Appalachian)....	4	3	.571	3.29	13	13	0	0	0	65 2/3	67	30	24	31	47
1992— Columbus (S. Atl.).............	7	4	.636	3.67	18	17	0	0	0	90 2/3	88	51	37	51	57
1993— Columbus (S. Atl.).............	7	8	.467	4.24	26	17	0	0	0	119	113	67	56	44	82
1994— Cant./Akr. (Eastern)	2	0	1.000	2.21	24	0	0	0	12	20 1/3	9	5	5	13	15
— Kinston (Carolina)	4	1	.800	1.93	27	0	0	0	8	32 2/3	21	14	7	16	37
1995— Cant./Akr. (Eastern)	6	3	.667	2.39	32	7	0	0	10	83	78	34	22	23	40
— Buffalo (A.A.)	2	1	.667	2.48	14	0	0	0	0	32 2/3	32	11	9	15	18
1996— Midland (Texas)■.............	2	2	.500	5.31	6	6	1	0	0	39	47	27	23	9	28
— Vancouver (PCL)■.............	9	3	.750	4.56	18	18	1	0	0	118 1/3	135	67	60	46	61
— California (A.L.)	2	0	1.000	3.90	11	3	0	0	0	32 1/3	31	16	14	17	20
1997— Anaheim (A.L.)	5	4	.556	3.62	61	0	0	0	0	79 2/3	82	33	32	38	56
1998— Lake Elsinore (Calif.)	0	1	.000	0.00	4	1	0	0	0	9 1/3	9	5	0	2	12
— Vancouver (PCL)	1	0	1.000	2.84	2	0	0	0	1	6 1/3	4	2	2	3	7
— Anaheim (A.L.)	3	1	.750	4.35	49	0	0	0	0	60	55	32	29	23	34
Major league totals (3 years)......	10	5	.667	3.92	121	3	0	0	0	172	168	81	75	78	110

HARRIS, REGGIE　　　　　　　P　　　　　　　ASTROS

PERSONAL: Born August 12, 1968, in Waynesboro, Va. ... 6-2/217. ... Throws right, bats right. ... Full name: Reginald Allen Harris. ... Cousin of Dell Curry, guard, Charlotte Hornets.
HIGH SCHOOL: Waynesboro (Va.).
TRANSACTIONS/CAREER NOTES: Selected by Boston Red Sox organization in first round (26th pick overall) of free-agent draft (June 2, 1987). ... Selected by Oakland Athletics from Red Sox organization in Rule 5 major league draft (December 4, 1989). ... On Oakland disabled list (March 29-July 3, 1990); included rehabilitation assignment to Huntsville (May 26-June 24). ... On Tacoma disabled list (June 17-August 4, 1991). ... Selected by Seattle Mariners from A's organization in Rule 5 major league draft (December 7, 1992). ... On Jacksonville disabled list (May 19-28, 1993). ... On Calgary temporarily inactive list (July 21-August 1, 1993). ... Granted free agency (October 15, 1993). ... Resigned by Mariners (November 11, 1993). ... Granted free agency (October 3, 1994). ... Signed by Omaha, Kansas City Royals organization (February 4, 1995). ... On disabled list (April 6-18, 1995). ... Released by Royals organization (April 25, 1995). ... Signed by Colorado Rockies organization (February 14, 1996). ... Released by Rockies (March 26, 1996). ... Signed by Boston Red Sox organization (May 7, 1996). ... On Trenton disabled list (June 12-24, 1996). ... Released by Red Sox (December 5, 1996). ... Signed by Philadelphia Phillies organization (December 23, 1996). ... On suspended list (August 29-September 1, 1997). ... Granted free agency (October 7, 1998). ... Signed by Houston Astros organization (January 9, 1998).
STATISTICAL NOTES: Led Pacific Coast League with 20 wild pitches in 1992.

Year	Team (League)	W	L	Pct.	ERA	G	GS	CG	ShO	Sv.	IP	H	R	ER	BB	SO
1987— Elmira (N.Y.-Penn).............	2	3	.400	5.01	9	8	1	1	0	46 2/3	50	29	26	22	25
1988— Lynchburg (Carolina)	1	8	.111	7.45	17	11	0	0	0	64	86	60	53	34	48
— Elmira (N.Y.-Penn).............	3	6	.333	5.30	10	10	0	0	0	54 1/3	56	37	32	28	46
1989— Winter Haven (FSL)	10	13	.435	3.99	29	26	1	0	0	153 1/3	144	81	68	77	85
1990— Huntsville (Southern)■......	0	2	.000	3.03	5	5	0	0	0	29 2/3	26	12	10	16	34
— Oakland (A.L.)	1	0	1.000	3.48	16	1	0	0	0	41 1/3	25	16	16	21	31
1991— Tacoma (PCL)	5	4	.556	4.99	16	15	0	0	0	83	83	55	46	58	72
— Oakland (A.L.)	0	0	...	12.00	2	0	0	0	0	3	5	4	4	3	2
1992— Tacoma (PCL)	6	*16	.273	5.71	29	•28	1	0	0	149 2/3	141	*108	*95	*117	111
1993— Jacksonville (Southern)■ ..	1	4	.200	4.78	9	8	0	0	0	37 2/3	33	24	20	22	30
— Calgary (PCL)	8	6	.571	5.20	17	15	1	0	0	88 1/3	74	55	51	61	75
1994— Calgary (PCL)	6	9	.400	8.12	20	18	0	0	0	98 2/3	137	99	89	51	73
1995— Omaha (Am. Assoc.)■.......	0	1	.000	18.00	2	0	0	0	0	2	5	4	4	1	2
1996— Trenton (Eastern)■..........	2	1	.667	1.46	33	0	0	0	17	37	17	6	6	19	43
— Boston (A.L.)	0	0	...	12.46	4	0	0	0	0	4 1/3	7	6	6	5	4
1997— Philadelphia (N.L.)■..........	1	3	.250	5.30	50	0	0	0	0	54 1/3	55	33	32	43	45
1998— New Orleans (PCL)■..........	2	3	.400	4.44	51	0	0	0	23	52 2/3	38	27	26	28	53
— Houston (N.L.)	0	0	...	6.00	6	0	0	0	0	6	6	4	4	2	2
A.L. totals (3 years)	1	0	1.000	4.81	22	1	0	0	0	48 2/3	37	26	26	29	37
N.L. totals (2 years)	1	3	.250	5.37	56	0	0	0	0	60 1/3	61	37	36	45	47
Major league totals (5 years)......	2	3	.400	5.12	78	1	0	0	0	109	98	63	62	74	84

HARTGRAVES, DEAN　　　　　　P　　　　　　PADRES

PERSONAL: Born August 12, 1966, in Bakersfield, Calif. ... 6-0/185. ... Throws left, bats right. ... Full name: Dean Charles Hartgraves.
HIGH SCHOOL: Crater (Central Point, Ore.).
JUNIOR COLLEGE: College of the Siskiyous (Calif.).
COLLEGE: Portland State.

H

TRANSACTIONS/CAREER NOTES: Selected by New York Mets organization in 12th round of free-agent draft (January 14, 1986); did not sign. ... Selected by Houston Astros organization in 20th round of free-agent draft (June 2, 1987). ... On disabled list (April 8-20 and July 12-September 20, 1993). ... Claimed on waivers by Atlanta Braves organization (July 25, 1996). ... Granted free agency (October 15, 1997). ... Signed by San Francisco Giants organization (January 12, 1998). ... Granted free agency (October 15, 1998). ... Signed by San Diego Padres organization (November 23, 1998).

STATISTICAL NOTES: Pitched 3-0 no-hit victory against Myrtle Beach (August 12, 1988, second game).

Year	Team (League)	W	L	Pct.	ERA	G	GS	CG	ShO	Sv.	IP	H	R	ER	BB	SO
1987—	Auburn (N.Y.-Penn)	0	5	.000	3.98	23	0	0	0	2	31 2/3	31	24	14	27	42
1988—	Asheville (S. Atl.)	5	9	.357	4.49	34	13	2	1	0	118 1/3	131	70	59	47	83
1989—	Asheville (S. Atl.)	5	8	.385	4.11	19	19	4	0	0	120 1/3	140	66	55	49	87
	— Osceola (Florida St.)	3	3	.500	2.95	7	6	1	1	0	39 2/3	36	20	13	12	21
1990—	Columbus (Southern)	8	8	.500	4.70	33	14	0	0	0	99 2/3	108	66	52	48	64
1991—	Jackson (Texas)	6	5	.545	2.68	19	9	3	0	0	74	60	25	22	25	44
	— Tucson (PCL)	3	0	1.000	3.09	16	3	1	1	0	43 2/3	47	17	15	20	18
1992—	Jackson (Texas)	9	6	.600	2.76	22	22	3	2	0	146 2/3	127	54	45	40	92
	— Tucson (PCL)	0	1	.000	24.75	5	1	0	0	0	8	26	24	22	9	6
1993—	Tucson (PCL)	1	6	.143	6.37	23	10	2	0	0	77 2/3	90	65	55	40	42
1994—	Tucson (PCL)	7	2	.778	5.07	47	4	0	0	3	97 2/3	106	64	55	36	54
1995—	Tucson (PCL)	3	2	.600	2.11	14	0	0	0	5	21 1/3	21	6	5	5	15
	— Houston (N.L.)	2	0	1.000	3.22	40	0	0	0	0	36 1/3	30	14	13	16	24
1996—	Tucson (PCL)	2	1	.667	1.89	18	0	0	0	4	19	17	6	4	8	13
	— Houston (N.L.)	0	0	...	5.21	19	0	0	0	0	19	18	11	11	16	16
	— Richmond (Int'l)■	0	0	...	2.08	4	0	0	0	0	8 2/3	4	2	2	2	8
	— Atlanta (N.L.)	1	0	1.000	4.34	20	0	0	0	0	18 2/3	16	10	9	7	14
1997—	Richmond (Int'l)	7	4	.636	4.48	50	0	0	0	3	72 1/3	76	38	36	39	56
1998—	Fresno (Pacific Coast)■	2	3	.400	3.97	38	1	0	0	3	70 1/3	67	35	31	19	64
	— San Francisco (N.L.)	0	0	...	9.53	5	0	0	0	0	5 2/3	10	7	6	4	4
Major league totals (3 years)		3	0	1.000	4.41	84	0	0	0	0	79 2/3	74	42	39	43	58

HASEGAWA, SHIGETOSHI   P   ANGELS

PERSONAL: Born August 1, 1968, in Kobe, Japan ... 5-11/171. ... Throws right, bats right. ... Name pronounced SHE-geh-TOE-she HAH-seh-GAH-wah.

COLLEGE: Ritsumeikan University (Kyoto, Japan).

TRANSACTIONS/CAREER NOTES: Played for Orix Blue Wave of Japan Pacific League (1991-96). ... Signed as free agent by Anaheim Angels (January 9, 1997).

Year	Team (League)	W	L	Pct.	ERA	G	GS	CG	ShO	Sv.	IP	H	R	ER	BB	SO
1991—	Orix (Jap. Pacific)	12	9	.571	3.55	28	25	11	3	1	185	184	76	73	50	111
1992—	Orix (Jap. Pacific)	6	8	.429	3.27	24	19	4	0	1	143 1/3	138	60	52	51	86
1993—	Orix (Jap. Pacific)	12	6	.667	2.71	23	22	9	3	0	159 2/3	146	61	48	48	86
1994—	Orix (Jap. Pacific)	11	9	.550	3.11	25	22	8	3	1	156 1/3	169	61	54	46	86
1995—	Orix (Jap. Pacific)	12	7	.632	2.89	24	23	9	4	0	171	167	62	55	51	91
1996—	Orix (Jap. Pacific)	4	6	.400	5.34	18	16	2	0	1	87 2/3	109	60	52	40	55
1997—	Anaheim (A.L.)■	3	7	.300	3.93	50	7	0	0	0	116 2/3	118	60	51	46	83
1998—	Anaheim (A.L.)	8	3	.727	3.14	61	0	0	0	5	97 1/3	86	37	34	32	73
Major league totals (2 years)		11	10	.524	3.57	111	7	0	0	5	214	204	97	85	78	156

HASELMAN, BILL   C   TIGERS

PERSONAL: Born May 25, 1966, in Long Branch, N.J. ... 6-3/223. ... Bats right, throws right. ... Full name: William Joseph Haselman.

HIGH SCHOOL: Saratoga (Calif.).

COLLEGE: UCLA.

TRANSACTIONS/CAREER NOTES: Selected by Texas Rangers organization in first round (23rd pick overall) of free-agent draft (June 2, 1987); pick received as compensation for New York Yankees signing Type A free-agent OF Gary Ward. ... On Oklahoma City disabled list (March 28-May 4, 1992). ... Claimed on waivers by Seattle Mariners (May 29, 1992). ... On suspended list (July 22-25, 1993). ... Granted free agency (October 15, 1994). ... Signed by Boston Red Sox (November 7, 1994). ... On disabled list (June 30-August 8, 1997); included rehabilitation assignment to Gulf Coast Red Sox (July 29-August 1) and Trenton (August 1-8). ... Traded by Red Sox with P Aaron Sele and P Mark Brandenburg to Rangers for C Jim Leyritz and OF Damon Buford (November 6, 1997). ... Granted free agency (October 23, 1998). ... Signed by Detroit Tigers (December 14, 1998).

RECORDS: Holds major league record for most chances accepted in consecutive nine-inning games—37 (April 29 and 30, 1996). ... Shares A.L. single-game record for most chances accepted by catcher (nine-inning game)—20 (September 18, 1996).

STATISTICAL NOTES: Led Texas League with 12 passed balls in 1989. ... Led Texas League catchers with 676 putouts, 90 assists, 20 errors, 786 total chances and 20 passed balls in 1990. ... Led American Association catchers with 673 putouts and 751 total chances in 1991. ... Tied for A.L. lead in passed balls with 17 in 1997. ... Career major league grand slams: 1.

Year	Team (League)	Pos.	G	AB	R	H	2B	3B	HR	RBI	Avg.	BB	SO	SB	PO	A	E	Avg.
1987—	Gastonia (S. Atl.)	C	61	235	35	72	13	1	8	33	.306	19	46	1	26	2	2	.933
1988—	Charlotte (Fla. St.)	C	122	453	56	111	17	2	10	54	.245	45	99	8	249	30	6	.979
1989—	Tulsa (Texas)	C	107	352	38	95	17	2	7	36	.270	40	88	5	508	63	9	.984
1990—	Tulsa (Texas)	C-1-0-3	120	430	68	137	39	2	18	80	.319	43	96	3	†722	†93	†20	.976
	— Texas (A.L.)	DH-C	7	13	0	2	0	0	0	3	.154	1	5	0	8	0	0	1.000
1991—	Okla. City (A.A.)	C-0-1-3	126	442	57	113	22	2	9	60	.256	61	89	10	†706	71	11	.986
1992—	Okla. City (A.A.)	OF-C	17	58	8	14	5	0	1	9	.241	13	12	1	45	7	3	.945
	— Calgary (PCL)■	C-OF	88	302	49	77	14	2	19	53	.255	41	89	3	227	23	6	.977
	— Seattle (A.L.)	C-OF	8	19	1	5	0	0	0	0	.263	0	7	0	19	2	0	1.000
1993—	Seattle (A.L.)	C-DH-OF	58	137	21	35	8	0	5	16	.255	12	19	2	236	17	2	.992
1994—	Seattle (A.L.)	C-DH-OF	38	83	11	16	7	1	1	8	.193	3	11	1	157	6	3	.982
	— Calgary (PCL)	C-1B	44	163	44	54	10	0	15	46	.331	30	33	1	219	16	5	.979
1995—	Boston (A.L.)■	C-DH-1-3	64	152	22	37	6	1	5	23	.243	17	30	0	259	16	3	.989

Year Team (League)	Pos.	G	AB	R	H	2B	3B	HR	RBI	Avg.	BB	SO	SB	PO	A	E	Avg.
						BATTING									FIELDING		
1996— Boston (A.L.).............	C-DH-1B	77	237	33	65	13	1	8	34	.274	19	52	4	507	33	3	.994
1997— Boston (A.L.).............	C	67	212	22	50	15	0	6	26	.236	15	44	0	373	40	7	.983
— GC Red Sox (GCL)	DH	4	16	2	2	0	0	0	1	.125	0	1	1	0	0	0	...
— Trenton (Eastern)	C	7	26	3	6	1	0	2	3	.231	2	2	0	30	2	0	1.000
1998— Texas (A.L.)■.............	C-DH	40	105	11	33	6	0	6	17	.314	3	17	0	176	8	1	.995
Major league totals (8 years)		359	958	121	243	55	3	31	127	.254	70	185	7	1735	122	19	.990

DIVISION SERIES RECORD

Year Team (League)	Pos.	G	AB	R	H	2B	3B	HR	RBI	Avg.	BB	SO	SB	PO	A	E	Avg.
						BATTING									FIELDING		
1995— Boston (A.L.).............	C	1	2	0	0	0	0	0	0	.000	0	0	0	6	0	0	1.000

HATCHER, CHRIS — OF — ROCKIES

PERSONAL: Born January 7, 1969, in Anaheim, Calif. ... 6-3/220. ... Bats right, throws right. ... Full name: Christopher Kenneth Hatcher.
HIGH SCHOOL: Thomas Jefferson (Council Bluffs, Iowa).
COLLEGE: Iowa.
TRANSACTIONS/CAREER NOTES: Selected by Houston Astros organization in third round of free-agent draft (June 4, 1990). ... On disabled list (June 8-July 15, 1992, June 3-July 1, 1993 and April 7-15, 1994). ... Granted free agency (October 15, 1996). ... Signed by Kansas City Royals organization (November 13, 1996). ... Granted free agency (October 15, 1997). ... Re-signed by Royals (February 1998). ... Granted free agency (October 15, 1998). ... Signed by Colorado Rockies organization (December 18, 1998).
HONORS: Named Pacific Coast League Most Valuable Player (1998).
STATISTICAL NOTES: Led Pacific Coast League first basemen with 15 errors in 1995. ... Led Pacific Coast League with 313 total bases in 1998.

Year Team (League)	Pos.	G	AB	R	H	2B	3B	HR	RBI	Avg.	BB	SO	SB	PO	A	E	Avg.
						BATTING									FIELDING		
1990— Auburn (NY-Penn)......	OF	72	259	37	64	10	0	9	45	.247	27	86	8	62	5	5	.931
1991— Burlington (Midw.)	OF	129	497	69	116	23	5	13	65	.233	46	*180	10	235	10	10	.961
1992— Osceola (Fla. St.)........	OF	97	367	49	103	19	6	17	68	.281	20	97	11	139	8	5	.967
1993— Jackson (Texas)	OF	101	367	45	95	15	3	15	64	.259	11	104	5	78	2	5	.941
1994— Tucson (PCL)	OF-1B	108	349	55	104	28	4	12	73	.298	19	90	5	150	3	5	.968
1995— Tucson (PCL)	1B-OF	94	290	59	83	19	2	14	50	.286	42	107	7	599	40	†15	.977
— Jackson (Texas)	OF-1B	11	39	5	12	1	0	1	3	.308	4	6	0	41	5	2	.958
1996— Jackson (Texas)	OF	41	156	29	48	9	1	13	36	.308	9	39	2	53	1	3	.947
— Tucson (PCL)	OF	95	348	53	105	21	4	18	61	.302	14	87	10	122	4	2	.984
1997— Wichita (Texas)■	OF	11	42	7	11	0	0	5	7	.262	4	16	1	9	0	1	.900
— Omaha (A.A.)	OF	68	222	34	51	9	0	11	24	.230	17	68	0	56	2	5	.921
1998— Omaha (PCL)..............	OF-1B-P	126	485	84	150	21	2	*46	106	.309	25	125	8	195	7	7	.967
— Kansas City (A.L.)	OF	8	15	0	1	0	0	0	1	.067	1	7	0	7	0	0	1.000
Major league totals (1 year)		8	15	0	1	0	0	0	1	.067	1	7	0	7	0	0	1.000

RECORD AS PITCHER

Year Team (League)	W	L	Pct.	ERA	G	GS	CG	ShO	Sv.	IP	H	R	ER	BB	SO
1998— Omaha (Pacific Coast)........	0	1	.000	9.00	1	0	0	0	0	1	1	1	1	3	0

HATTEBERG, SCOTT — C — RED SOX

PERSONAL: Born December 14, 1969, in Salem, Ore. ... 6-1/195. ... Bats left, throws right. ... Full name: Scott Allen Hatteberg. ... Name pronounced HAT-ee-berg.
HIGH SCHOOL: Eisenhower (Yakima, Wash.).
COLLEGE: Washington State.
TRANSACTIONS/CAREER NOTES: Selected by Philadelphia Phillies organization in 12th round of free-agent draft (June 1, 1988); did not sign. ... Selected by Boston Red Sox organization in supplemental round ("sandwich pick" between first and second round, 43rd pick overall) of free-agent draft (June 3, 1991); pick received as part of compensation for Kansas City signing Type A free-agent P Mike Boddicker. ... On disabled list (July 27-August 3, 1992).
STATISTICAL NOTES: Tied for A.L. lead in double plays by catcher with 13 and passed balls with 17 in 1997. ... Career major league grand slams: 1.

Year Team (League)	Pos.	G	AB	R	H	2B	3B	HR	RBI	Avg.	BB	SO	SB	PO	A	E	Avg.
						BATTING									FIELDING		
1991— Winter Haven (FSL)....	C	56	191	21	53	7	3	1	25	.277	22	22	1	261	35	5	.983
— Lynchburg (Caro.)	C	8	25	4	5	1	0	0	2	.200	7	6	0	35	2	0	1.000
1992— New Britain (East.)	C	103	297	28	69	13	2	1	30	.232	41	49	1	473	44	11	.979
1993— New Britain (East.)	C	68	227	35	63	10	2	7	28	.278	42	38	1	410	45	10	.978
— Pawtucket (Int'l)........	C	18	53	6	10	0	0	1	2	.189	6	12	0	131	4	5	.964
1994— New Britain (East.)	C	20	68	6	18	4	1	1	9	.265	7	9	0	125	14	1	.993
— Pawtucket (Int'l)........	C	78	238	26	56	14	0	7	19	.235	32	49	2	467	36	7	.986
1995— Pawtucket (Int'l)........	C	85	251	36	68	15	1	7	27	.271	40	39	2	446	45	•8	.984
— Boston (A.L.)............	C	2	2	1	1	0	0	0	0	.500	0	0	0	4	0	0	1.000
1996— Pawtucket (Int'l)........	C	90	287	52	77	16	0	12	49	.268	58	66	1	566	42	6	.990
— Boston (A.L.)............	C	10	11	3	2	1	0	0	0	.182	3	2	0	32	2	0	1.000
1997— Boston (A.L.)............	C-DH	114	350	46	97	23	1	10	44	.277	40	70	0	574	46	11	.983
1998— Boston (A.L.)............	C	112	359	46	99	23	1	12	43	.276	43	58	0	664	61	5	.993
Major league totals (4 years)		238	722	96	199	47	2	22	87	.276	86	130	0	1274	109	16	.989

DIVISION SERIES RECORD

Year Team (League)	Pos.	G	AB	R	H	2B	3B	HR	RBI	Avg.	BB	SO	SB	PO	A	E	Avg.
						BATTING									FIELDING		
1998— Boston (A.L.).............	C	3	9	0	1	0	0	0	0	.111	3	1	0	20	0	0	1.000

H

HAWKINS, LaTROY　　　　　P　　　　　TWINS

PERSONAL: Born December 21, 1972, in Gary, Ind. ... 6-5/202. ... Throws right, bats right.
HIGH SCHOOL: West Side (Gary, Ind.).
TRANSACTIONS/CAREER NOTES: Selected by Minnesota Twins organization in seventh round of free-agent draft (June 3, 1991).
STATISTICAL NOTES: Tied for A.L. lead with three balks in 1997.

Year　Team (League)	W	L	Pct.	ERA	G	GS	CG	ShO	Sv.	IP	H	R	ER	BB	SO
1991— GC Twins (GCL)	4	3	.571	4.75	11	11	0	0	0	55	62	34	29	26	47
1992— GC Twins (GCL)	3	2	.600	3.22	6	6	1	0	0	36 1/3	36	19	13	10	35
— Elizabethton (Appal.)	0	1	.000	3.38	5	5	1	0	0	26 2/3	21	12	10	11	36
1993— Fort Wayne (Midw.)	•15	5	.750	*2.06	26	23	4	•3	0	157 1/3	110	53	36	41	*179
1994— Fort Myers (Fla. St.)	4	0	1.000	2.33	6	6	1	1	0	38 2/3	32	10	10	6	36
— Nashville (Southern)	9	2	*.818	2.33	11	11	1	0	0	73 1/3	50	23	19	28	53
— Salt Lake (PCL)	5	4	.556	4.08	12	12	1	0	0	81 2/3	92	42	37	33	37
1995— Minnesota (A.L.)	2	3	.400	8.67	6	6	1	0	0	27	39	29	26	12	9
— Salt Lake (PCL)	9	7	.563	3.55	22	22	4	1	0	144 1/3	150	63	57	40	74
1996— Minnesota (A.L.)	1	1	.500	8.20	7	6	0	0	0	26 1/3	42	24	24	9	24
— Salt Lake (PCL)	9	8	.529	3.92	20	20	4	1	0	137 2/3	138	66	60	31	99
1997— Salt Lake (PCL)	9	4	.692	5.45	14	13	2	1	0	76	100	53	46	16	53
— Minnesota (A.L.)	6	12	.333	5.84	20	20	0	0	0	103 1/3	134	71	67	47	58
1998— Minnesota (A.L.)	7	14	.333	5.25	33	33	0	0	0	190 1/3	227	126	111	61	105
Major league totals (4 years)	16	30	.348	5.91	66	65	1	0	0	347	442	250	228	129	196

HAYES, CHARLIE　　　　　3B/1B　　　　　GIANTS

PERSONAL: Born May 29, 1965, in Hattiesburg, Miss. ... 6-0/220. ... Bats right, throws right. ... Full name: Charles Dewayne Hayes.
HIGH SCHOOL: Forrest County Agricultural (Brooklyn, Miss.).
TRANSACTIONS/CAREER NOTES: Selected by San Francisco Giants organization in fourth round of free-agent draft (June 6, 1983). ... On disabled list (July 20, 1983-remainder of season). ... Traded by Giants with P Dennis Cook and P Terry Mulholland to Philadelphia Phillies for P Steve Bedrosian and a player to be named later (June 18, 1989); Giants organization acquired IF Rick Parker to complete deal (August 7, 1989). ... Traded by Phillies to New York Yankees (February 19, 1992), completing deal in which Yankees traded P Darrin Chapin to Phillies for a player to be named later (January 8, 1992). ... Selected by Colorado Rockies in first round (third pick overall) of expansion draft (November 17, 1992). ... On suspended list (August 10-13, 1993). ... Granted free agency (December 23, 1994). ... Signed by Phillies (April 6, 1995). ... Granted free agency (November 2, 1995). ... Signed by Pittsburgh Pirates (December 28, 1995). ... Traded by Pirates to Yankees for a player to be named later (August 30, 1996); Pirates acquired P Chris Corn to complete deal (August 31, 1996). ... Traded by Yankees with cash to Giants for OF Chris Singleton and P Alberto Castillo (November 11, 1997).
STATISTICAL NOTES: Led Texas League third basemen with 27 double plays in 1986. ... Led Texas League third basemen with 334 total chances in 1987. ... Led Pacific Coast League in grounding into double plays with 19 in 1988. ... Led N.L. third basemen with 324 assists and tied for lead with 465 total chances in 1990. ... Tied for A.L. lead in double plays by third baseman with 29 in 1992. ... Tied for N.L. lead in grounding into double plays with 25 in 1993. ... Led N.L. in grounding into double plays with 23 in 1995. ... Career major league grand slams: 3.

Year　Team (League)	Pos.	G	AB	R	H	2B	3B	HR	RBI	Avg.	BB	SO	SB	PO	A	E	Avg.
						BATTING									FIELDING		
1983— Great Falls (Pio.)	3B-OF	34	111	9	29	4	2	0	9	.261	7	26	1	13	32	9	.833
1984— Clinton (Midwest)	3B	116	392	41	96	17	2	2	51	.245	34	110	4	68	216	28	.910
1985— Fresno (California)	3B	131	467	73	132	17	2	4	68	.283	56	95	7	*100	233	18	*.949
1986— Shreveport (Texas)	3B	121	434	52	107	23	2	5	45	.247	28	83	1	89	*259	25	.933
1987— Shreveport (Texas)	3B	128	487	66	148	33	3	14	75	.304	26	76	5	*100	*212	22	*.934
1988— Phoenix (PCL)	OF-3B	131	492	71	151	26	4	7	71	.307	34	91	4	206	100	23	.930
— San Francisco (N.L.)	OF-3B	7	11	0	1	0	0	0	0	.091	0	3	0	5	0	0	1.000
1989— Phoenix (PCL)	3-0-1-S-2	61	229	25	65	15	1	7	27	.284	15	48	5	76	76	8	.950
— San Francisco (N.L.)	3B	3	5	0	1	0	0	0	0	.200	0	1	0	2	1	0	1.000
— Scran./W.B. (Int'l)■	3B	7	27	4	11	3	1	1	3	.407	0	3	0	8	8	0	1.000
— Philadelphia (N.L.)	3B	84	299	26	77	15	1	8	43	.258	11	49	3	49	173	22	.910
1990— Philadelphia (N.L.)	3B-1B-2B	152	561	56	145	20	0	10	57	.258	28	91	4	151	†329	20	.960
1991— Philadelphia (N.L.)	3B-SS	142	460	34	106	23	1	12	53	.230	16	75	3	88	240	15	.956
1992— New York (A.L.)■	3B-1B	142	509	52	131	19	2	18	66	.257	28	100	3	125	249	13	.966
1993— Colorado (N.L.)■	3B-SS	157	573	89	175	*45	2	25	98	.305	43	82	11	123	292	20	.954
1994— Colorado (N.L.)	3B	113	423	46	122	23	4	10	50	.288	36	71	3	72	216	17	.944
1995— Philadelphia (N.L.)■	3B	141	529	58	146	30	3	11	85	.276	50	88	5	•104	264	14	.963
1996— Pittsburgh (N.L.)■	3B	128	459	51	114	21	2	10	62	.248	36	78	6	66	275	18	.950
— New York (A.L.)■	3B	20	67	7	19	3	0	2	13	.284	1	12	0	14	30	0	1.000
1997— New York (A.L.)	3B-2B	100	353	39	91	16	0	11	53	.258	40	66	3	67	169	13	.948
1998— San Fran. (N.L.)■	3B-1B-DH	111	329	39	94	8	0	12	62	.286	34	61	2	369	101	3	.994
American League totals (3 years)		262	929	98	241	38	2	31	132	.259	69	178	6	206	448	26	.962
National League totals (9 years)		1038	3649	399	981	185	13	98	510	.269	254	599	37	1029	1891	129	.958
Major league totals (11 years)		1300	4578	497	1222	223	15	129	642	.267	323	777	43	1235	2339	155	.958

DIVISION SERIES RECORD

Year　Team (League)	Pos.	G	AB	R	H	2B	3B	HR	RBI	Avg.	BB	SO	SB	PO	A	E	Avg.
						BATTING									FIELDING		
1996— New York (A.L.)	3B-DH	3	5	0	1	0	0	0	1	.200	0	0	0	1	3	0	1.000
1997— New York (A.L.)	3B-2B	5	15	0	5	0	0	0	1	.333	0	2	0	3	9	3	.800
Division series totals (2 years)		8	20	0	6	0	0	0	2	.300	0	2	0	4	12	3	.842

CHAMPIONSHIP SERIES RECORD

Year　Team (League)	Pos.	G	AB	R	H	2B	3B	HR	RBI	Avg.	BB	SO	SB	PO	A	E	Avg.
						BATTING									FIELDING		
1996— New York (A.L.)	PH-3B-DH	4	7	0	1	0	0	0	0	.143	2	2	0	0	3	0	1.000

NOTES: Member of World Series championship team (1996).

Year	Team (League)	Pos.	G	AB	R	H	2B	3B	HR	RBI	Avg.	BB	SO	SB	PO	A	E	Avg.
							BATTING									FIELDING		
1996—	New York (A.L.)	3B-PH-1B	4	16	2	3	0	0	0	1	.188	1	5	0	3	6	0	1.000

HAYNES, JIMMY   P   ATHLETICS

PERSONAL: Born September 5, 1972, in La Grange, Ga. ... 6-3/180. ... Throws right, bats right. ... Full name: Jimmy Wayne Haynes.
HIGH SCHOOL: Troup (La Grange, Ga.).
TRANSACTIONS/CAREER NOTES: Selected by Baltimore Orioles organization in seventh round of free-agent draft (June 3, 1991). ... Traded by Orioles with a player to be named later to Oakland Athletics for OF Geronimo Berroa (June 27, 1997); A's acquired P Mark Seaver to complete deal (September 2, 1997).

Year	Team (League)	W	L	Pct.	ERA	G	GS	CG	ShO	Sv.	IP	H	R	ER	BB	SO
1991—	GC Orioles (GCL)	3	2	.600	1.60	14	8	1	0	2	62	44	27	11	21	67
1992—	Kane County (Midwest)	7	11	.389	2.56	24	24	4	0	0	144	131	66	41	45	141
1993—	Frederick (Carolina)	12	8	.600	3.03	27	27	2	1	0	172 1/3	139	73	58	61	174
1994—	Bowie (Eastern)	13	8	.619	2.90	25	25	5	1	0	173 2/3	154	67	56	46	*177
	— Rochester (Int'l)	1	0	1.000	6.75	3	3	0	0	0	13 1/3	20	12	10	6	14
1995—	Rochester (Int'l)	•12	8	.600	3.29	26	25	3	1	0	167	162	77	61	49	*140
	— Baltimore (A.L.)	2	1	.667	2.25	4	3	0	0	0	24	11	6	6	12	22
1996—	Baltimore (A.L.)	3	6	.333	8.29	26	11	0	0	1	89	122	84	82	58	65
	— Rochester (Int'l)	1	1	.500	5.65	5	5	0	0	0	28 2/3	31	19	18	18	24
1997—	Rochester (Int'l)	5	4	.556	3.44	16	16	2	1	0	102	89	49	39	55	113
	— Edmonton (PCL)■	0	2	.000	4.85	5	5	0	0	0	29 2/3	36	22	16	11	24
	— Oakland (A.L.)	3	6	.333	4.42	13	13	0	0	0	73 1/3	74	38	36	40	65
1998—	Oakland (A.L.)	11	9	.550	5.09	33	33	1	1	0	194 1/3	229	124	110	88	134
Major league totals (4 years)		19	22	.463	5.53	76	60	1	1	1	380 2/3	436	252	234	198	286

HEATHCOTT, MIKE   P   WHITE SOX

PERSONAL: Born May 16, 1969, in Chicago. ... 6-3/180. ... Throws right, bats right. ... Full name: Michael Joseph Heathcott.
HIGH SCHOOL: Fenwick (Oak Park, Ill.).
COLLEGE: Creighton.
TRANSACTIONS/CAREER NOTES: Selected by Chicago White Sox organization in 13th round of free-agent draft (June 3, 1991). ... On disabled list (July 7, 1991-remainder of season). ... On disabled list (April 19-June 16, 1992). ... On disabled list (April 4-26, 1996). ... On Calgary disabled list (August 5-12, 1998).
STATISTICAL NOTES: Led Carolina League with 18 wild pitches in 1995.

Year	Team (League)	W	L	Pct.	ERA	G	GS	CG	ShO	Sv.	IP	H	R	ER	BB	SO
1991—	Utica (N.Y.-Penn)	3	1	.750	3.55	6	6	0	0	0	33	26	19	13	14	14
1992—	South Bend (Mid.)	9	5	.643	1.54	15	14	0	0	0	82	67	28	14	32	49
1993—	Sarasota (Florida State)	11	10	.524	3.61	26	26	6	1	0	179 1/3	174	90	72	62	83
1994—	Birmingham (Southern)	3	7	.300	5.79	17	17	0	0	0	98	126	71	63	44	44
	— Prince William (Caro.)	1	2	.333	3.98	9	8	1	0	0	43	51	28	19	23	27
1995—	Prince William (Caro.)	4	9	.308	4.67	27	14	1	0	3	88 2/3	96	56	46	36	68
1996—	Birmingham (Southern)	11	8	.579	4.02	23	23	1	0	0	147 2/3	138	72	66	55	108
1997—	Birmingham (Southern)	3	1	.750	1.83	30	1	0	0	7	59	50	20	12	25	47
	— Nashville (A.A.)	2	3	.400	7.33	17	0	0	0	0	27	39	23	22	12	23
1998—	Calgary (PCL)	9	6	.600	5.04	39	13	1	0	1	109	113	65	61	51	77
	— Chicago (A.L.)	0	0	. . .	3.00	1	0	0	0	0	3	2	1	1	1	3
Major league totals (1 year)		0	0	. . .	3.00	1	0	0	0	0	3	2	1	1	1	3

HEISERMAN, RICK   P   CARDINALS

PERSONAL: Born February 22, 1973, in Atlantic, Iowa. ... 6-7/225. ... Throws right, bats right. ... Full name: Richard Michael Heiserman.
HIGH SCHOOL: Millard South (Omaha, Neb.).
COLLEGE: Creighton.
TRANSACTIONS/CAREER NOTES: Selected by Cleveland Indians organization in third round of free-agent draft (June 2, 1994). ... Traded by Indians with C Pepe McNeal and IF David Bell to St. Louis Cardinals for P Ken Hill (July 27, 1995). ... On Memphis disabled list (June 11-20, 1998).

Year	Team (League)	W	L	Pct.	ERA	G	GS	CG	ShO	Sv.	IP	H	R	ER	BB	SO
1994—	Watertown (NYP)	1	0	1.000	2.31	7	0	0	0	0	11 2/3	6	3	3	5	6
1995—	Kinston (Carolina)	9	3	.750	3.74	19	19	1	0	0	113	97	55	47	42	86
	— St. Petersburg (FSL)■	2	3	.400	5.46	6	5	0	0	0	28	28	18	17	11	18
1996—	St. Petersburg (FSL)	10	8	.556	3.24	26	26	1	1	0	155 1/3	168	68	56	41	104
1997—	Arkansas (Texas)	5	8	.385	4.17	34	20	1	•1	4	131 2/3	151	73	61	36	90
	— Louisville (A.A.)	0	0	. . .	4.50	1	0	0	0	0	2	2	1	1	1	0
1998—	Arkansas (Texas)	0	3	.000	4.96	18	0	0	0	9	16 1/3	20	11	9	5	9
	— Memphis (Pacific Coast)	2	3	.400	4.02	40	0	0	0	6	40 1/3	54	21	18	14	28

HELLING, RICK   P   RANGERS

PERSONAL: Born December 15, 1970, in Devils Lake, N.D. ... 6-3/220. ... Throws right, bats right. ... Full name: Ricky Allen Helling.
HIGH SCHOOL: Lakota (Fargo, N.D.), then Shanley (N.D.).
JUNIOR COLLEGE: Kishwaukee College (Ill.).
COLLEGE: North Dakota, then Stanford.

H

TRANSACTIONS/CAREER NOTES: Selected by New York Mets organization in 50th round of free-agent draft (June 4, 1990); did not sign. ... Selected by Texas Rangers organization in first round (22nd pick overall) of free-agent draft (June 1, 1992). ... Traded by Rangers to Florida Marlins (September 3, 1996); completing deal in which Marlins traded P John Burkett to Rangers for P Ryan Dempster and a player to be named later (August 8, 1996). ... Traded by Marlins to Rangers for P Ed Vosberg (August 12, 1997).

STATISTICAL NOTES: Pitched 4-0 no-hit victory against Nashville (August 13, 1996).

MISCELLANEOUS: Member of 1992 U.S. Olympic baseball team.

Year	Team (League)	W	L	Pct.	ERA	G	GS	CG	ShO	Sv.	IP	H	R	ER	BB	SO
1992—	Charlotte (Fla. St.)............	1	1	.500	2.29	3	3	0	0	0	19²/₃	13	5	5	4	20
1993—	Tulsa (Texas).....................	12	8	.600	3.60	26	26	2	•2	0	177¹/₃	150	76	71	46	*188
—	Oklahoma City (A.A.)..........	1	1	.500	1.64	2	2	1	0	0	11	5	3	2	3	17
1994—	Texas (A.L.).......................	3	2	.600	5.88	9	9	1	1	0	52	62	34	34	18	25
—	Oklahoma City (A.A.)..........	4	12	.250	5.78	20	20	2	0	0	132¹/₃	153	93	85	43	85
1995—	Texas (A.L.).......................	0	2	.000	6.57	3	3	0	0	0	12¹/₃	17	11	9	8	5
—	Oklahoma City (A.A.)..........	4	8	.333	5.33	20	20	3	0	0	109²/₃	132	73	65	41	80
1996—	Oklahoma City (A.A.)..........	12	4	.750	2.96	23	22	2	1	0	140	124	54	46	38	157
—	Texas (A.L.).......................	1	2	.333	7.52	6	2	0	0	0	20¹/₃	23	17	17	9	16
—	Florida (N.L.)■...................	2	1	.667	1.95	5	4	0	0	0	27²/₃	14	6	6	7	26
1997—	Florida (N.L.).....................	2	6	.250	4.38	31	8	0	0	0	76	61	38	37	48	53
—	Texas (A.L.)■.....................	3	3	.500	4.58	10	8	0	0	0	55	47	29	28	21	46
1998—	Texas (A.L.).......................	•20	7	.741	4.41	33	33	4	2	0	216¹/₃	209	109	106	78	164
A.L. totals (5 years)		27	16	.628	4.90	61	55	5	3	0	356	358	200	194	134	256
N.L. totals (2 years)		4	7	.364	3.73	36	12	0	0	0	103²/₃	75	44	43	55	79
Major league totals (5 years)......		31	23	.574	4.64	97	67	5	3	0	459²/₃	433	244	237	189	335

DIVISION SERIES RECORD

Year	Team (League)	W	L	Pct.	ERA	G	GS	CG	ShO	Sv.	IP	H	R	ER	BB	SO
1998—	Texas (A.L.)	0	1	.000	4.50	1	1	0	0	0	6	8	3	3	1	9

HELMS, WES — 3B — BRAVES

PERSONAL: Born May 12, 1976, in Gastonia, N.C. ... 6-4/230. ... Bats right, throws right. ... Full name: Wesley Ray Helms.

HIGH SCHOOL: Ashbrook (Gastonia, N.C.).

TRANSACTIONS/CAREER NOTES: Selected by Atlanta Braves organization in 10th round of free-agent draft (June 2, 1994).

STATISTICAL NOTES: Led South Atlantic League third basemen with 25 double plays in 1995. ... Led International League third basemen with 24 double plays in 1998.

Year	Team (League)	Pos.	G	AB	R	H	2B	3B	HR	RBI	Avg.	BB	SO	SB	PO	A	E	Avg.
1994—GC Braves (GCL)		3B	56	184	22	49	15	1	4	29	.266	22	36	6	•47	93	20	.875
1995—Macon (S. Atl.)		3B	136	*539	89	149	32	1	11	85	.276	50	107	2	91	*269	40	.900
1996—Durham (Carolina)......		3B	67	258	40	83	19	2	13	54	.322	12	51	1	40	133	15	.920
—Greenville (Sou.)		3B	64	231	24	59	13	2	4	22	.255	13	48	2	50	96	12	.924
1997—Richmond (Int'l)		3B	32	110	11	21	4	0	3	15	.191	10	34	1	18	65	9	.902
—Greenville (Sou.)		3B	86	314	50	93	14	1	11	44	.296	33	50	3	60	147	11	.950
1998—Richmond (Int'l)		3B	125	451	56	124	27	1	13	75	.275	35	103	6	75	220	15	.952
—Atlanta (N.L.)..............		3B	7	13	2	4	1	0	1	2	.308	0	4	0	1	2	1	.750
Major league totals (1 year)			7	13	2	4	1	0	1	2	.308	0	4	0	1	2	1	.750

HELTON, TODD — 1B — ROCKIES

PERSONAL: Born August 20, 1973, in Knoxville, Tenn. ... 6-2/206. ... Bats left, throws left. ... Full name: Todd Lynn Helton.

HIGH SCHOOL: Knoxville (Tenn.) Central.

COLLEGE: Tennessee.

TRANSACTIONS/CAREER NOTES: Selected by San Diego Padres organization in second round of free-agent draft (June 1, 1992); did not sign. ... Selected by Colorado Rockies organization in first round (eighth pick overall) of free-agent draft (June 3, 1995). ... On New Haven disabled list (June 15-24, 1996).

HONORS: Named N.L. Rookie Player of the Year by THE SPORTING NEWS (1998).

STATISTICAL NOTES: Led N.L. first basemen with 156 double plays in 1998.

Year	Team (League)	Pos.	G	AB	R	H	2B	3B	HR	RBI	Avg.	BB	SO	SB	PO	A	E	Avg.
1995—Asheville (S. Atl.)........		1B	54	201	24	51	11	1	1	15	.254	25	32	1	388	21	4	.990
1996—New Haven (East.)......		1B	93	319	46	106	24	2	7	51	.332	51	37	2	788	61	5	.994
—Colo. Springs (PCL) ...		1B-OF	21	71	13	25	4	1	2	13	.352	11	12	0	144	17	2	.988
1997—Colo. Springs (PCL) ...		1B-OF	99	392	87	138	31	2	16	88	.352	61	68	3	622	64	9	.987
—Colorado (N.L.)		OF-1B	35	93	13	26	2	1	5	11	.280	8	11	0	84	12	0	1.000
1998—Colorado (N.L.)		1B	152	530	78	167	37	1	25	97	.315	53	54	3	1164	*146	7	.995
Major league totals (2 years)			187	623	91	193	39	2	30	108	.310	61	65	3	1248	158	7	.995

HEMPHILL, BRET — C — ANGELS

PERSONAL: Born December 17, 1971, in Santa Clara, Calif. ... 6-3/200. ... Bats both, throws right. ... Full name: Bret Ryan Hemphill.

HIGH SCHOOL: Cupertino (Calif.).

COLLEGE: Cal State Fullerton.

TRANSACTIONS/CAREER NOTES: Selected by Houston Astros organization in 29th round of free-agent draft (June 4, 1990); did not sign. ... Selected by California Angels in 14th round of free-agent draft (June 2, 1994). ... Angels franchise renamed Anaheim Angels for 1997 season. ... On disabled list (June 12-29, August 8, 1997-remainder of season and April 2-June 4, 1998).

STATISTICAL NOTES: Led Northwest League catchers with 534 putouts, 68 assists and 613 total chances and tied for lead in double plays with four in 1994. ... Led California League catchers with 989 total chances in 1996.

H

Year Team (League)	Pos.	G	AB	R	H	2B	3B	HR	RBI	Avg.	BB	SO	SB	PO	A	E	Avg.
1994— Boise (Northwest)	C-1B	71	252	44	74	16	1	3	36	.294	40	53	1	†548	†69	11	.982
1995— Cedar Rap. (Midw.)....	C	72	234	36	59	11	1	8	28	.252	21	54	0	429	69	4	.992
— Lake Elsinore (Calif.)..	C	45	146	12	29	7	0	1	17	.199	18	36	2	354	47	10	.976
1996— Lake Elsinore (Calif.)	C	108	399	64	105	21	3	17	64	.263	52	93	4	*879	*92	18	.982
1997— Midland (Texas)........	C	78	266	46	82	15	2	10	63	.308	47	56	0	425	48	7	.985
1998— Vancouver (PCL)	C	47	155	16	39	10	2	4	12	.252	12	33	0	226	15	3	.988

HENDERSON, RICKEY   OF   METS

PERSONAL: Born December 25, 1958, in Chicago. ... 5-10/190. ... Bats right, throws left. ... Full name: Rickey Henley Henderson.

HIGH SCHOOL: Technical (Oakland).

TRANSACTIONS/CAREER NOTES: Selected by Oakland Athletics organization in fourth round of free-agent draft (June 8, 1976). ... Traded by A's with P Bert Bradley and cash to New York Yankees for OF Stan Javier, P Jay Howell, P Jose Rijo, P Eric Plunk and P Tim Birtsas (December 5, 1984). ... On New York disabled list (March 30-April 22, 1985); included rehabilitation assignment to Fort Lauderdale (April 19-22). ... On disabled list (June 5-29 and July 26-September 1, 1987). ... Traded by Yankees to A's for P Greg Cadaret, P Eric Plunk and OF Luis Polonia (June 21, 1989). ... Granted free agency (November 13, 1989). ... Re-signed by A's (November 28, 1989). ... On disabled list (April 12-27, 1991; May 28-June 17 and June 30-July 16, 1992). ... Traded by A's to Toronto Blue Jays for P Steve Karsay and a player to be named later (July 31, 1993); A's acquired OF Jose Herrera to complete deal (August 6, 1993). ... Granted free agency (October 29, 1993). ... Signed by A's (December 17, 1993). ... On disabled list (May 11-27, 1994). ... Granted free agency (October 30, 1995). ... Signed by San Diego Padres (December 29, 1995). ... On San Diago disabled list (May 9-24, 1997). ... Traded by Padres to Anaheim Angels for P Ryan Hancock, P Stevenson Agosto and a player to be named later (August 13, 1997); Padres acquired 3B George Arias to complete deal (August 19, 1997). ... Granted free agency (October 27, 1997). ... Signed by A's (January 22, 1998). ... Granted free agency (October 26, 1998). ... Signed by New York Mets (December 13, 1998).

RECORDS: Holds major league career records for most stolen bases—1,297; and most home runs as leadoff batter—73. ... Holds major league single-season records for most stolen bases—130 (1982); and most times caught stealing—42 (1982). ... Holds major league record for most seasons leading league in stolen bases—12. ... Holds A.L. career records for most stolen bases—1,231; most home runs as lead-off batter—69; most times caught stealing—282. ... Holds A.L. records for most years with 50 or more stolen bases—12; and most consecutive years with 50 or more stolen bases—7 (1980-86). ... Shares A.L. single-season record for fewest times caught stealing (50 or more stolen bases)—8 (1993). ... Shares A.L. record for most stolen bases in two consecutive games—7 (July 3 [4], 15 innings, and 4 [3], 1983).

HONORS: Named outfielder on THE SPORTING NEWS A.L. All-Star team (1981, 1985 and 1990). ... Named outfielder on THE SPORTING NEWS A.L. Silver Slugger team (1981, 1985 and 1990). ... Won A.L. Gold Glove as outfielder (1981). ... Won THE SPORTING NEWS Silver Shoe Award (1982). ... Won THE SPORTING NEWS Golden Shoe Award (1983). ... Named A.L. Most Valuable Player by Baseball Writers' Association of America (1990).

STATISTICAL NOTES: Led California League in caught stealing with 22 in 1977. ... Led Eastern League in caught stealing with 28 in 1978. ... Led Eastern League outfielders with four double plays in 1978. ... Led A.L. in caught stealing with 26 in 1980, 22 in 1981, 42 in 1982, 19 in 1983 and tied for lead with 18 in 1986. ... Led A.L. outfielders with 341 total chances in 1981. ... Tied for A.L. lead in double plays by outfielder with five in 1988. ... Led A.L. with 77 stolen bases and 126 bases on balls in 1989. ... Tied for A.L. lead with 113 runs scored in 1989. ... Led A.L. with .439 on-base percentage in 1990. ... Career major league grand slams: 3.

MISCELLANEOUS: Holds Oakland Athletics franchise all-time record for most runs (1,270) and most stolen bases (867). ... Holds New York Yankees all-time record for most stolen bases (326).

Year Team (League)	Pos.	G	AB	R	H	2B	3B	HR	RBI	Avg.	BB	SO	SB	PO	A	E	Avg.
1976— Boise (Northwest)	OF	46	140	34	47	13	2	3	23	.336	33	32	29	99	3	*12	.895
1977— Modesto (Calif.)	OF	134	481	120	166	18	4	11	69	.345	104	67	*95	278	15	*20	.936
1978— Jersey City (East.)	OF	133	455	81	141	14	4	0	34	.310	83	67	*81	305	•15	7	.979
1979— Ogden (PCL)	OF	71	259	66	80	11	8	3	26	.309	53	41	44	149	6	6	.963
—Oakland (A.L.)	OF	89	351	49	96	13	3	1	26	.274	34	39	33	215	5	6	.973
1980—Oakland (A.L.)	OF-DH	158	591	111	179	22	4	9	53	.303	117	54	*100	407	15	7	.984
1981—Oakland (A.L.)	OF	108	423	*89	*135	18	7	6	35	.319	64	68	*56	*327	7	7	.979
1982—Oakland (A.L.)	OF-DH	149	536	119	143	24	4	10	51	.267	*116	94	*130	379	2	9	.977
1983—Oakland (A.L.)	OF-DH	145	513	105	150	25	7	9	48	.292	*103	80	*108	349	3	3	.992
1984—Oakland (A.L.)	OF	142	502	113	147	27	4	16	58	.293	86	81	*66	341	7	11	.969
1985—Fort Laud. (FSL)■......	OF	3	6	5	1	0	1	0	3	.167	5	2	1	6	0	0	1.000
—New York (A.L.)..........	OF-DH	143	547	*146	172	28	5	24	72	.314	99	65	*80	439	7	9	.980
1986—New York (A.L.)	OF-DH	153	608	*130	160	31	5	28	74	.263	89	81	*87	426	4	6	.986
1987—New York (A.L.)	OF-DH	95	358	78	104	17	3	17	37	.291	80	52	41	189	3	4	.980
1988—New York (A.L.)	OF-DH	140	554	118	169	30	2	6	50	.305	82	54	*93	320	7	12	.965
1989—New York (A.L.)	OF	65	235	41	58	13	1	3	22	.247	56	29	25	144	3	1	.993
—Oakland (A.L.)■	OF-DH	85	306	§72	90	13	2	9	35	.294	§70	39	§52	191	3	3	.985
1990—Oakland (A.L.)	OF-DH	136	489	*119	159	33	3	28	61	.325	97	60	*65	289	5	5	.983
1991—Oakland (A.L.)	OF-DH	134	470	105	126	17	1	18	57	.268	98	73	*58	249	10	8	.970
1992—Oakland (A.L.)	OF-DH	117	396	77	112	18	3	15	46	.283	95	56	48	231	9	4	.984
1993—Oakland (A.L.)	OF-DH	90	318	77	104	19	1	17	47	.327	85	46	31	182	5	5	.974
—Toronto (A.L.)■.........	OF	44	163	37	35	3	1	4	12	.215	35	19	22	76	1	2	.975
1994—Oakland (A.L.)■	OF-DH	87	296	66	77	13	0	6	20	.260	72	45	22	166	4	4	.977
1995—Oakland (A.L.)	OF-DH	112	407	67	122	31	1	9	54	.300	72	66	32	162	5	2	.988
1996—San Diego (N.L.)■	OF	148	465	110	112	17	2	9	29	.241	125	90	37	228	3	6	.975
1997—San Diego (N.L.)	OF	88	288	63	79	11	0	6	27	.274	71	62	29	160	4	7	.959
—Anaheim (A.L.)■......	DH-OF	32	115	21	21	3	0	2	7	.183	26	23	16	26	0	0	1.000
1998—Oakland (A.L.)■	OF	152	542	101	128	16	1	14	57	.236	*118	114	*66	327	3	4	.988
American League totals (19 years)		2376	8720	1841	2487	414	58	251	922	.285	1694	1238	1231	5435	114	112	.980
National League totals (2 years)		236	753	173	191	28	2	15	56	.254	196	152	66	388	7	13	.968
Major league totals (20 years)		2612	9473	2014	2678	442	60	266	978	.283	1890	1390	1297	5823	121	125	.979

DIVISION SERIES RECORD

Year Team (League)	Pos.	G	AB	R	H	2B	3B	HR	RBI	Avg.	BB	SO	SB	PO	A	E	Avg.
1981—Oakland (A.L.)	OF	3	11	3	2	0	0	0	0	.182	2	0	2	8	0	0	1.000
1996—San Diego (N.L.)	OF	3	12	2	4	0	0	1	1	.333	2	3	0	4	0	0	1.000
Division series totals (2 years)		6	23	5	6	0	0	1	1	.261	4	3	2	12	0	0	1.000

H

CHAMPIONSHIP SERIES RECORD

RECORDS: Holds career record of most stolen bases—16. ... Holds single-series record for most stolen bases—8 (1989). ... Holds single-game record for most stolen bases—4 (October 4, 1989). ... Shares single-inning records for most at-bats—2; most hits—2; most singles—2 (October 6, 1990, ninth inning); and most stolen bases—2 (October 4, 1989, fourth and seventh innings). ... Shares single-series record for most runs—8 (1989). ... Shares A.L. career record for most bases on balls received—17. ... Shares A.L. single-game record for most at-bats—6 (October 5, 1993).

NOTES: Named Most Valuable Player (1989).

Year Team (League)	Pos.	G	AB	R	H	2B	3B	HR	RBI	Avg.	BB	SO	SB	PO	A	E	Avg.
1981— Oakland (A.L.)	OF	3	11	0	4	2	1	0	1	.364	1	2	2	6	0	1	.857
1989— Oakland (A.L.)	OF	5	15	8	6	1	1	2	5	.400	7	0	8	13	0	1	.929
1990— Oakland (A.L.)	OF	4	17	1	5	0	0	0	3	.294	1	2	2	10	0	0	1.000
1992— Oakland (A.L.)	OF	6	23	5	6	0	0	0	1	.261	4	4	2	15	0	3	.833
1993— Toronto (A.L.)	OF	6	25	4	3	2	0	0	0	.120	4	5	2	9	0	1	.900
Championship series totals (5 years)		24	91	18	24	5	2	2	10	.264	17	13	16	53	0	6	.898

WORLD SERIES RECORD

RECORDS: Shares single-game record for most at-bats—6 (October 28, 1989).

NOTES: Member of World Series championship team (1989 and 1993).

Year Team (League)	Pos.	G	AB	R	H	2B	3B	HR	RBI	Avg.	BB	SO	SB	PO	A	E	Avg.
1989— Oakland (A.L.)	OF	4	19	4	9	1	2	1	3	.474	2	2	3	9	0	0	1.000
1990— Oakland (A.L.)	OF	4	15	2	5	2	0	1	1	.333	3	4	3	12	1	0	1.000
1993— Toronto (A.L.)	OF	6	22	6	5	2	0	0	2	.227	5	2	1	8	0	0	1.000
World Series totals (3 years)		14	56	12	19	5	2	2	6	.339	10	8	7	29	1	0	1.000

ALL-STAR GAME RECORD

RECORDS: Shares single-game record for most singles—3 (July 13, 1982).

Year League	Pos.	AB	R	H	2B	3B	HR	RBI	Avg.	BB	SO	SB	PO	A	E	Avg.
1980— American	OF	1	0	0	0	0	0	0	.000	0	1	0	0	0	0	...
1982— American	OF	4	1	3	0	0	0	0	.750	0	0	1	3	0	1	.750
1983— American	OF	1	0	0	0	0	0	1	.000	0	0	0	0	0	0	...
1984— American	OF	2	0	0	0	0	0	0	.000	0	0	0	0	0	0	...
1985— American	OF	3	1	1	0	0	0	0	.333	0	1	1	1	0	0	1.000
1986— American	OF	3	0	0	0	0	0	0	.000	0	1	0	2	0	0	1.000
1987— American	OF	3	0	1	0	0	0	0	.333	0	0	0	0	0	0	...
1988— American	OF	2	0	1	0	0	0	0	.500	1	0	0	1	0	0	1.000
1990— American	OF	3	0	0	0	0	0	0	.000	0	1	0	2	0	0	1.000
1991— American	OF	2	1	1	0	0	0	0	.500	0	0	0	0	0	0	...
All-Star Game totals (10 years)		24	3	7	0	0	0	1	.292	1	4	2	9	0	1	.900

HENDERSON, ROD — P — BREWERS

PERSONAL: Born March 11, 1971, in Greensburg, Ky. ... 6-4/195. ... Throws right, bats right. ... Full name: Rodney Wood Henderson.
HIGH SCHOOL: Glasgow (Ky.).
COLLEGE: Kentucky.
TRANSACTIONS/CAREER NOTES: Selected by Montreal Expos organization in second round of free-agent draft (June 1, 1992). ... On disabled list (June 19, 1992-remainder of season). ... On Montreal disabled list (July 18, 1995-remainder of season). ... On Ottawa disabled list (May 5-12, 1998). ... Released by Expos (May 12, 1998). ... Signed by Milwaukee Brewers organization (May 12, 1998).

Year Team (League)	W	L	Pct.	ERA	G	GS	CG	ShO	Sv.	IP	H	R	ER	BB	SO
1992— Jamestown (NYP)	0	0	...	6.00	1	1	0	0	0	3	2	3	2	5	2
1993— W.P. Beach (FSL)	12	7	.632	2.90	22	22	1	1	0	143	110	50	46	44	127
—Harrisburg (Eastern)	5	0	1.000	1.82	5	5	0	0	0	29 2/3	20	10	6	15	25
1994— Harrisburg (Eastern)	2	0	1.000	1.50	2	2	0	0	0	12	5	2	2	4	16
—Montreal (N.L.)	0	1	.000	9.45	3	2	0	0	0	6 2/3	9	9	7	7	3
—Ottawa (Int'l)	6	9	.400	4.62	23	21	0	0	1	122 2/3	123	67	63	67	100
1995— Harrisburg (Eastern)	3	6	.333	4.31	12	12	0	0	0	56 1/3	51	28	27	18	53
1996— Ottawa (Int'l)	4	11	.267	5.19	25	23	3	1	0	121 1/3	117	75	70	52	83
1997— Ottawa (Int'l)	5	9	.357	4.95	26	20	2	1	1	123 2/3	136	72	68	49	103
1998— Ottawa (Int'l)	0	1	.000	9.00	6	0	0	0	0	11	23	17	11	12	12
—Louisville (Int'l)■	11	5	.688	2.97	22	19	1	0	0	121 1/3	100	45	40	39	68
—Milwaukee (N.L.)	0	0	...	9.82	2	0	0	0	0	3 2/3	5	4	4	0	1
Major league totals (2 years)	0	1	.000	9.58	5	2	0	0	0	10 1/3	14	13	11	7	4

HENLEY, BOB — C — EXPOS

PERSONAL: Born January 30, 1973, in Mobile, Ala. ... 6-2/205. ... Bats right, throws right. ... Full name: Robert Clifton Henley.
HIGH SCHOOL: Mobile County (Grand Bay, Ala.).
JUNIOR COLLEGE: Okaloosa-Walton Community College (Fla.).
TRANSACTIONS/CAREER NOTES: Selected by Montreal Expos organization in 26th round of free-agent draft (June 13, 1991). ... On Gulf Coast Expos disabled list (June 18-August 31, 1992). ... On disabled list (July 20-30 and July 31, 1997-remainder of season). ... On Montreal disabled list (March 30-May 5, 1998); included rehabilitation assignment to Jupiter (April 21-May 5). ... On Ottawa disabled list (May 27-June 19, 1998).
STATISTICAL NOTES: Led South Atlantic League catchers with nine double plays in 1995. ... Tied for Eastern League lead with 11 double plays by catcher in 1996.

H

Year	Team (League)	Pos.	G	AB	R	H	2B	3B	HR	RBI	Avg.	BB	SO	SB	PO	A	E	Avg.
1992—	....								Did not play.									
1993—Jamestown (NYP)	......	C	60	206	25	53	10	4	7	29	.257	20	60	0	143	36	4	.978
1994—Burlington (Midw.)	.....	C-1B	98	346	72	104	20	1	20	67	.301	49	91	1	322	64	11	.972
1995—Albany (S. Atl.)	......	C	102	335	45	94	20	1	3	46	.281	83	57	1	684	*111	•14	.983
1996—Harrisburg (East.)	....	C	103	289	33	66	12	1	3	27	.228	70	78	1	565	*92	9	.986
1997—Harrisburg (East.)	....	C	79	280	41	85	19	0	12	49	.304	32	40	5	574	77	3	*.995
1998—Jupiter (Florida State)		C	13	50	10	17	3	0	2	14	.340	5	5	1	63	8	1	.986
—Ottawa (Int'l)	....	C	37	126	13	31	6	1	4	20	.246	12	34	1	176	22	2	.990
—Montreal (N.L.)	....	C	41	115	16	35	8	1	3	18	.304	11	26	3	189	14	1	.995
Major league totals (1 year)			41	115	16	35	8	1	3	18	.304	11	26	3	189	14	1	.995

HENRIQUEZ, OSCAR   P   METS

PERSONAL: Born January 28, 1974, in LaGuaira, Venezuela. ... 6-6/220. ... Throws right, bats right. ... Full name: Oscar Eduardo Henriquez.

TRANSACTIONS/CAREER NOTES: Signed as non-drafted free agent by Houston Astros organization (May 28, 1991). ... On disabled list (June 15, 1994-remainder of season). ... Traded by Astros with P Manuel Barrios and a player to be named later to Florida Marlins for OF Moises Alou (November 11, 1997). ... On Charlotte disabled list (July 14-31, 1998). ... Traded by Marlins to New York Mets for C Jorge Fabregas (November 20, 1998).

Year	Team (League)	W	L	Pct.	ERA	G	GS	CG	ShO	Sv.	IP	H	R	ER	BB	SO
1992—	....				Dominican League statistics unavailable.											
1993—Asheville (S. Atl.)	....	9	10	.474	4.44	27	26	2	1	0	150	154	95	74	70	117
1994—	....				Did not play.											
1995—Kissimmee (Florida State)	..	3	4	.429	5.04	20	0	0	0	1	44$\frac{2}{3}$	40	29	25	30	36
1996—Kissimmee (Florida State)	..	0	4	.000	3.97	37	0	0	0	15	34	28	18	15	29	40
1997—New Orleans (A.A.)	....	4	5	.444	2.80	*60	0	0	0	12	74	65	28	23	27	80
—Houston (N.L.)	....	0	1	.000	4.50	4	0	0	0	0	4	2	2	2	3	3
1998—Charlotte (Int'l)■	....	1	0	1.000	2.56	26	0	0	0	11	31$\frac{2}{3}$	29	12	9	12	37
—Florida (N.L.)	....	0	0	...	8.55	15	0	0	0	0	20	26	22	19	12	19
Major league totals (2 years)	......	0	1	.000	7.88	19	0	0	0	0	24	28	24	21	15	22

HENRY, BUTCH   P   MARINERS

PERSONAL: Born October 7, 1968, in El Paso, Texas. ... 6-1/205. ... Throws left, bats left. ... Full name: Floyd Bluford Henry III.

HIGH SCHOOL: Eastwood (El Paso, Texas).

TRANSACTIONS/CAREER NOTES: Selected by Cincinnati Reds organization in 15th round of free-agent draft (June 2, 1987). ... On disabled list (April 28, 1989-remainder of season). ... Traded by Reds with C Terry McGriff and P Keith Kaiser to Houston Astros (September 7, 1990), completing deal in which Astros traded 2B Bill Doran to Reds for three players to be named later (August 30, 1990). ... Selected by Colorado Rockies in second round (36th pick overall) of expansion draft (November 17, 1992). ... Traded by Rockies to Montreal Expos for P Kent Bottenfield (July 16, 1993). ... On disabled list (August 16, 1995-remainder of season). ... Claimed on waivers by Boston Red Sox (October 13, 1995). ... On disabled list (March 22, 1996-entire season). ... On Boston disabled list (May 5-June 23, 1997); included rehabilitation assignment to Sarasota (June 14-23). ... On Boston disabled list (March 14-April 14 and April 21, 1998-remainder of season); included rehabilitation assignment to Sarasota (April 8-10). ... Granted free agency (October 22, 1998). ... Signed by Seattle Mariners (December 15, 1998).

Year	Team (League)	W	L	Pct.	ERA	G	GS	CG	ShO	Sv.	IP	H	R	ER	BB	SO
1987—Billings (Pioneer)	....	4	0	1.000	4.63	9	5	0	0	0	35	37	21	18	12	38
1988—Cedar Rapids (Midw.)	....	16	2	*.889	2.26	27	27	1	1	0	187	144	59	47	56	163
1989—Chattanooga (Southern)	.....	1	3	.250	3.42	7	7	0	0	0	26$\frac{1}{3}$	22	12	10	12	19
1990—Chattanooga (Southern)	.....	8	8	.500	4.21	24	22	2	0	0	143$\frac{1}{3}$	151	74	67	58	95
1991—Tucson (PCL)■	....	10	11	.476	4.80	27	27	2	0	0	153$\frac{2}{3}$	192	92	82	42	97
1992—Houston (N.L.)	....	6	9	.400	4.02	28	28	2	1	0	165$\frac{2}{3}$	185	81	74	41	96
1993—Colorado (N.L.)■	....	2	8	.200	6.59	20	15	1	0	0	84$\frac{2}{3}$	117	66	62	24	39
—Montreal (N.L.)■	....	1	1	.500	3.93	10	1	0	0	0	18$\frac{1}{3}$	18	10	8	4	8
—Ottawa (Int'l)	....	3	1	.750	3.73	5	5	1	0	0	31$\frac{1}{3}$	34	15	13	1	25
1994—Ottawa (Int'l)	....	2	0	1.000	0.00	2	2	1	1	0	14	11	0	0	2	11
—Montreal (N.L.)	....	8	3	.727	2.43	24	15	0	0	1	107$\frac{1}{3}$	97	30	29	20	70
1995—Montreal (N.L.)	....	7	9	.438	2.84	21	21	1	1	0	126$\frac{2}{3}$	133	47	40	28	60
1996—Boston (A.L.)	....				Did not play.											
1997—Boston (A.L.)	....	7	3	.700	3.52	36	5	0	0	6	84$\frac{1}{3}$	89	36	33	19	51
—Sarasota (Florida State)	......	0	1	.000	5.40	2	2	0	0	0	8$\frac{1}{3}$	8	5	5	0	7
1998—Sarasota (Florida State)	......	0	1	.000	1.35	1	1	0	0	0	6$\frac{2}{3}$	4	2	1	0	5
—Boston (A.L.)	....	0	0	...	4.00	2	2	0	0	0	8	8	4	4	3	6
A.L. totals (2 years)	....	7	3	.700	3.57	38	7	0	0	6	93$\frac{1}{3}$	97	40	37	22	57
N.L. totals (4 years)	....	24	30	.444	3.81	103	80	4	2	1	502$\frac{2}{3}$	550	234	213	117	273
Major league totals (6 years)	......	31	33	.484	3.78	141	87	4	2	7	596	647	274	250	139	330

HENRY, DOUG   P   ASTROS

PERSONAL: Born December 10, 1963, in Sacramento. ... 6-4/205. ... Throws right, bats right. ... Full name: Richard Douglas Henry.

HIGH SCHOOL: Tennyson (Hayward, Calif.).

COLLEGE: Arizona State.

TRANSACTIONS/CAREER NOTES: Selected by New York Mets organization in 16th round of free-agent draft (June 7, 1982); did not sign. ... Selected by Milwaukee Brewers organization in eighth round of free-agent draft (June 3, 1985). ... On El Paso disabled list (April 5-June 5 and June 18-August 9, 1989). ... On Milwaukee disabled list (March 25-April 26, 1994); included rehabilitation assignments to El Paso (April 8-22) and New Orleans (April 22-26). ... Traded by Brewers to New York Mets for two players to be named later (November 30, 1994); Brewers

H

acquired C Javier Gonzales (December 6, 1994) and IF Fernando Vina (December 22, 1994) to complete deal. ... Released by Mets (November 25, 1996). ... Signed by San Francisco Giants (January 8, 1997). ... Granted free agency (October 27, 1997). ... Signed by Houston Astros (November 26, 1997).

STATISTICAL NOTES: Combined with Michael Ignasiak in 6-3 no-hit victory for Stockton against San Jose (April 15, 1990, first game).

Year	Team (League)	W	L	Pct.	ERA	G	GS	CG	ShO	Sv.	IP	H	R	ER	BB	SO
1986—	Beloit (Midwest)	7	8	.467	4.65	27	24	4	1	1	143 $1/3$	153	95	74	56	115
1987—	Beloit (Midwest)	8	9	.471	4.88	31	15	1	0	2	132 $2/3$	145	83	72	51	106
1988—	Stockton (California)	7	1	.875	1.78	23	1	1	0	7	70 $2/3$	46	19	14	31	71
—	El Paso (Texas)	4	0	1.000	3.15	14	3	3	1	0	45 $2/3$	33	16	16	19	50
1989—	Stockton (California)	0	1	.000	0.00	4	3	0	0	0	11	9	4	0	3	9
—	El Paso (Texas)	0	0	...	13.50	1	1	0	0	0	2	3	3	3	3	2
1990—	Stockton (California)	1	0	1.000	1.13	4	0	0	0	1	8	4	1	1	3	13
—	El Paso (Texas)	1	0	1.000	2.93	15	0	0	0	9	30 $2/3$	31	13	10	11	25
—	Denver (Am. Assoc.)	2	3	.400	4.44	27	0	0	0	8	50 $2/3$	46	26	25	27	54
1991—	Denver (Am. Assoc.)	3	2	.600	2.18	32	0	0	0	14	57 $2/3$	47	16	14	20	47
—	Milwaukee (A.L.)	2	1	.667	1.00	32	0	0	0	15	36	16	4	4	14	28
1992—	Milwaukee (A.L.)	1	4	.200	4.02	68	0	0	0	29	65	64	34	29	24	52
1993—	Milwaukee (A.L.)	4	4	.500	5.56	54	0	0	0	17	55	67	37	34	25	38
1994—	El Paso (Texas)	1	0	1.000	5.40	6	0	0	0	3	8 $1/3$	7	5	5	2	10
—	New Orleans (A.A.)	1	0	1.000	1.84	10	0	0	0	3	14 $2/3$	5	3	3	10	10
—	Milwaukee (A.L.)	2	3	.400	4.60	25	0	0	0	0	31 $1/3$	32	17	16	23	20
1995—	New York (N.L.)■	3	6	.333	2.96	51	0	0	0	4	67	48	23	22	25	62
1996—	New York (N.L.)	2	8	.200	4.68	58	0	0	0	9	75	82	48	39	36	58
1997—	San Francisco (N.L.)■	4	5	.444	4.71	75	0	0	0	3	70 $2/3$	70	45	37	41	69
1998—	Houston (N.L.)■	8	2	.800	3.04	59	0	0	0	2	71	55	25	24	35	59
A.L. totals (4 years)		9	12	.429	3.99	179	0	0	0	61	187 $1/3$	179	92	83	86	138
N.L. totals (4 years)		17	21	.447	3.87	243	0	0	0	18	283 $2/3$	255	141	122	137	248
Major league totals (8 years)		26	33	.441	3.92	422	0	0	0	79	471	434	233	205	223	386

DIVISION SERIES RECORD

Year	Team (League)	W	L	Pct.	ERA	G	GS	CG	ShO	Sv.	IP	H	R	ER	BB	SO
1997—	San Francisco (N.L.)	0	0	...	0.00	1	0	0	0	0	2	1	0	0	3	2
1998—	Houston (N.L.)	0	0	...	5.40	2	0	0	0	0	1 $2/3$	2	1	1	0	1
Div. series totals (2 years)		0	0	...	2.45	3	0	0	0	0	3 $2/3$	3	1	1	3	3

HENTGEN, PAT   P   BLUE JAYS

PERSONAL: Born November 13, 1968, in Detroit. ... 6-2/195. ... Throws right, bats right. ... Full name: Patrick George Hentgen. ... Name pronounced HENT-ghen.

HIGH SCHOOL: Fraser (Mich.).

TRANSACTIONS/CAREER NOTES: Selected by Toronto Blue Jays organization in fifth round of free-agent draft (June 2, 1986). ... On Toronto disabled list (August 13-September 29, 1992); included rehabilitation assignment to Syracuse (September 1-8).

HONORS: Named A.L. Pitcher of the Year by THE SPORTING NEWS (1996). ... Named righthanded pitcher on THE SPORTING NEWS A.L. All-Star team (1996). ... Named A.L. Cy Young Award winner by Baseball Writers' Association of America (1996).

STATISTICAL NOTES: Combined with relievers Willie Blair and Enrique Burgos in 2-1 no-hit victory against Osceola (May 10, 1988).

Year	Team (League)	W	L	Pct.	ERA	G	GS	CG	ShO	Sv.	IP	H	R	ER	BB	SO
1986—	St. Catharines (NYP)	0	4	.000	4.50	13	11	0	0	1	40	38	27	20	30	30
1987—	Myrtle Beach (SAL)	11	5	.688	2.35	32	*31	2	2	0	*188	145	62	49	60	131
1988—	Dunedin (Fla. St.)	3	12	.200	3.45	31	*30	0	0	0	151 $1/3$	139	80	58	65	125
1989—	Dunedin (Fla. St.)	9	8	.529	2.68	29	28	0	0	0	151 $1/3$	123	53	45	71	148
1990—	Knoxville (Southern)	9	5	.643	3.05	28	26	0	0	0	153 $1/3$	121	57	52	68	142
1991—	Syracuse (Int'l)	8	9	.471	4.47	31	•28	1	0	0	171	146	91	85	*90	*155
—	Toronto (A.L.)	0	0	...	2.45	3	1	0	0	0	7 $1/3$	5	2	2	3	3
1992—	Toronto (A.L.)	5	2	.714	5.36	28	2	0	0	0	50 $1/3$	49	30	30	32	39
—	Syracuse (Int'l)	1	2	.333	2.66	4	4	0	0	0	20 $1/3$	15	6	6	8	17
1993—	Toronto (A.L.)	19	9	.679	3.87	34	32	3	0	0	216 $1/3$	215	103	93	74	122
1994—	Toronto (A.L.)	13	8	.619	3.40	24	24	6	3	0	174 $2/3$	158	74	66	59	147
1995—	Toronto (A.L.)	10	14	.417	5.11	30	30	2	0	0	200 $2/3$	*236	*129	*114	90	135
1996—	Toronto (A.L.)	20	10	.667	3.22	35	35	*10	•3	0	*265 $2/3$	238	105	95	94	177
1997—	Toronto (A.L.)	15	10	.600	3.68	35	•35	•9	•3	0	•264	253	116	108	71	160
1998—	Toronto (A.L.)	12	11	.522	5.17	29	29	0	0	0	177 $2/3$	208	109	102	69	94
Major league totals (8 years)		94	64	.595	4.05	218	188	30	9	0	1356 $2/3$	1362	668	610	492	877

CHAMPIONSHIP SERIES RECORD

Year	Team (League)	W	L	Pct.	ERA	G	GS	CG	ShO	Sv.	IP	H	R	ER	BB	SO
1993—	Toronto (A.L.)	0	1	.000	18.00	1	1	0	0	0	3	9	6	6	2	3

WORLD SERIES RECORD

NOTES: Member of World Series championship team (1993).

Year	Team (League)	W	L	Pct.	ERA	G	GS	CG	ShO	Sv.	IP	H	R	ER	BB	SO
1993—	Toronto (A.L.)	1	0	1.000	1.50	1	1	0	0	0	6	5	1	1	3	6

ALL-STAR GAME RECORD

Year	League	W	L	Pct.	ERA	GS	CG	ShO	Sv.	IP	H	R	ER	BB	SO
1993—	American						Did not play.								
1994—	American	0	0	...	0.00	0	0	0	0	1	1	0	0	0	0
1997—	American	0	0	...	0.00	0	0	0	0	1	0	0	0	0	0
All-Star totals (2 years)		0	0	...	0.00	0	0	0	0	2	1	0	0	0	0

H

HEREDIA, FELIX   P   CUBS

PERSONAL: Born June 18, 1976, in Barahona, Dominican Republic. ... 6-0/180. ... Throws left, bats left.
HIGH SCHOOL: Escuela Dominical (Barahona, Dominican Republic).
TRANSACTIONS/CAREER NOTES: Signed as non-drafted free agent by Florida Marlins organization (November 22, 1992). ... Traded by Marlins with P Steve Hoff to Chicago Cubs for 3B Kevin Orie, P Todd Noel and P Justin Speier (July 31, 1998).

Year Team (League)	W	L	Pct.	ERA	G	GS	CG	ShO	Sv.	IP	H	R	ER	BB	SO
1993— GC Marlins (GCL)	5	1	.833	2.47	12	•12	0	0	0	62	50	18	17	11	53
1994— Kane County (Midwest)	4	5	.444	5.69	24	8	1	0	3	68	86	55	43	14	65
1995— Brevard County (FSL)	6	4	.600	3.57	34	8	0	0	1	95²/₃	101	52	38	36	76
1996— Portland (Eastern)	8	1	.889	1.50	55	0	0	0	5	60	48	11	10	15	42
— Florida (N.L.)	1	1	.500	4.32	21	0	0	0	0	16²/₃	21	8	8	10	10
1997— Florida (N.L.)	5	3	.625	4.29	56	0	0	0	0	56²/₃	53	30	27	30	54
1998— Florida (N.L.)	0	3	.000	5.49	41	2	0	0	2	41	38	30	25	32	38
— Chicago (N.L.)■	3	0	1.000	4.08	30	0	0	0	0	17²/₃	19	9	8	6	16
Major league totals (3 years)	9	7	.563	4.64	148	2	0	0	2	132	131	77	68	78	118

DIVISION SERIES RECORD

Year Team (League)	W	L	Pct.	ERA	G	GS	CG	ShO	Sv.	IP	H	R	ER	BB	SO
1997— Florida (N.L.)								Did not play.							
1998— Chicago (N.L.)	0	0	...	54.00	1	0	0	0	0	¹/₃	0	2	2	2	0

CHAMPIONSHIP SERIES RECORD

Year Team (League)	W	L	Pct.	ERA	G	GS	CG	ShO	Sv.	IP	H	R	ER	BB	SO
1997— Florida (N.L.)	0	0	...	5.40	2	0	0	0	0	3¹/₃	3	2	2	2	4

WORLD SERIES RECORD

NOTES: Member of World Series championship team (1997).

Year Team (League)	W	L	Pct.	ERA	G	GS	CG	ShO	Sv.	IP	H	R	ER	BB	SO
1997— Florida (N.L.)	0	0	...	0.00	4	0	0	0	0	5¹/₃	2	0	0	1	5

HEREDIA, GIL   P   ATHLETICS

PERSONAL: Born October 26, 1965, in Nogales, Ariz. ... 6-1/195. ... Throws right, bats right. ... Full name: Gilbert Heredia. ... Name pronounced err-AY-dee-uh.
HIGH SCHOOL: Nogales (Ariz.).
JUNIOR COLLEGE: Pima Community College (Ariz.).
COLLEGE: Arizona.
TRANSACTIONS/CAREER NOTES: Selected by Pittsburgh Pirates organization in first round (16th pick overall) of free-agent draft (January 17, 1984); did not sign. ... Selected by Baltimore Orioles organization in sixth round of free-agent draft (January 9, 1985); did not sign. ... Selected by San Francisco Giants organization in ninth round of free-agent draft (June 2, 1987). ... Loaned by Giants organization to San Luis Potosi of Mexican League (1989). ... Claimed on waivers by Montreal Expos (August 18, 1992). ... Granted free agency (December 21, 1995). ... Signed by Texas Rangers organization (January 5, 1996). ... Released by Rangers (November 13, 1996). ... Signed by Expos organization (January 13, 1997). ... Traded by Expos organization to Chicago Cubs organization for 2B Saul Bustos and OF David Jefferson (June 23, 1997). ... Granted free agency (October 15, 1997). ... Signed by Oakland Athletics organization (January 20, 1998).

Year Team (League)	W	L	Pct.	ERA	G	GS	CG	ShO	Sv.	IP	H	R	ER	BB	SO
1987— Everett (Northwest)	2	0	1.000	3.60	3	3	1	0	0	20	24	8	8	1	14
— Fresno (California)	5	3	.625	2.90	11	11	5	2	0	80²/₃	62	28	26	23	60
1988— San Jose (California)	13	12	.520	3.49	27	27	9	0	0	*206¹/₃	•216	107	80	46	121
1989— Shreveport (Texas)	1	0	1.000	2.55	7	2	1	0	0	24²/₃	28	10	7	4	8
— San Luis Potosi (Mex.)■	14	9	.609	2.99	24	24	15	3	0	180²/₃	183	73	60	35	125
1990— Phoenix (PCL)■	9	7	.563	4.10	29	19	0	0	1	147	159	81	67	37	75
1991— Phoenix (PCL)	9	11	.450	*2.82	33	15	•5	1	1	140¹/₃	155	60	44	28	75
— San Francisco (N.L.)	0	2	.000	3.82	7	4	0	0	0	33	27	14	14	7	13
1992— Phoenix (PCL)	5	5	.500	2.01	22	7	1	1	1	80²/₃	83	30	18	13	37
— San Francisco (N.L.)	2	3	.400	5.40	13	4	0	0	0	30	32	20	18	16	15
— Indianapolis (A.A.)■	2	0	1.000	1.02	3	3	0	0	0	17²/₃	18	2	2	3	10
— Montreal (N.L.)	0	0	...	1.84	7	1	0	0	0	14²/₃	12	3	3	4	7
1993— Ottawa (Int'l)	8	4	.667	2.98	16	16	1	0	0	102²/₃	97	46	34	26	66
— Montreal (N.L.)	4	2	.667	3.92	20	9	1	0	2	57¹/₃	66	28	25	14	40
1994— Montreal (N.L.)	6	3	.667	3.46	39	3	0	0	0	75¹/₃	85	34	29	13	62
1995— Montreal (N.L.)	5	6	.455	4.31	40	18	0	0	1	119	137	60	57	21	74
1996— Texas (A.L.)■	2	5	.286	5.89	44	0	0	0	1	73¹/₃	91	50	48	14	43
— Oklahoma City (A.A.)	0	0	...	1.86	6	0	0	0	0	9²/₃	11	3	2	0	4
1997— Ottawa (Int'l)■	0	4	.000	4.70	28	0	0	0	0	44	50	29	23	9	41
— Iowa (Am. Assoc.)■	4	2	.667	3.86	31	1	0	0	0	46²/₃	54	22	20	9	30
1998— Edmonton (PCL)■	10	8	.556	3.67	29	19	6	1	1	144²/₃	154	69	59	18	99
— Oakland (A.L.)	3	3	.500	2.74	8	6	0	0	0	42²/₃	43	14	13	3	27
A.L. totals (2 years)	5	8	.385	4.73	52	6	0	0	1	116	134	64	61	17	70
N.L. totals (5 years)	17	16	.515	3.99	126	39	1	0	3	329¹/₃	359	159	146	75	211
Major league totals (7 years)	22	24	.478	4.18	178	45	1	0	4	445¹/₃	493	223	207	92	281

HERMANSEN, CHAD   OF/IF   PIRATES

PERSONAL: Born September 10, 1977, in Salt Lake City. ... 6-2/185. ... Bats right, throws right. ... Full name: Chad B. Hermansen.
HIGH SCHOOL: Green Valley (Henderson, Nev.).
TRANSACTIONS/CAREER NOTES: Selected by Pittsburgh Pirates organization in first round (10th pick overall) of free-agent draft (June 1, 1995).
STATISTICAL NOTES: Tied for Southern League lead in errors by outfielder with eight in 1997.

H

Year Team (League)	Pos.	G	AB	R	H	2B	3B	HR	RBI	Avg.	BB	SO	SB	PO	A	E	Avg.
1995—Bra. Pirates (GCL)	SS	24	92	14	28	10	1	3	17	.304	9	19	0	20	56	10	.884
— Erie (N.Y.-Penn)	SS	44	165	30	45	8	3	6	25	.273	18	39	4	52	104	30	.839
1996—Augusta (S. Atl.)	SS	62	226	41	57	11	3	14	41	.252	38	65	11	71	135	25	.892
— Lynchburg (Caro.)	SS	66	251	40	69	11	3	10	46	.275	29	56	5	75	168	28	.897
1997—Carolina (Southern)....	OF-SS-2B	129	487	87	134	31	4	20	70	.275	69	*136	18	194	125	‡39	.891
1998—Nashville (PCL)	OF-2B	126	458	81	118	26	5	28	78	.258	50	152	21	208	21	14	.942

HERMANSON, DUSTIN   P   EXPOS

PERSONAL: Born December 21, 1972, in Springfield, Ohio. ... 6-0/205. ... Throws right, bats right. ... Full name: Dustin Michael Hermanson.
HIGH SCHOOL: Kenton Ridge (Springfield, Ohio).
COLLEGE: Kent.
TRANSACTIONS/CAREER NOTES: Selected by Pittsburgh Pirates organization in 39th round of free-agent draft (June 3, 1991); did not sign. ... Selected by San Diego Padres organization in first round (third pick overall) of free-agent draft (June 2, 1994). ... Traded by Padres to Florida Marlins for 2B Quilvio Veras (November 21, 1996). ... Traded by Marlins with OF Joe Orsulak to Montreal Expos for OF/1B Cliff Floyd (March 26, 1997). ... On disabled list (May 15-30, 1998).
STATISTICAL NOTES: Hit home run in first major league at-bat (April 16, 1997).

Year Team (League)	W	L	Pct.	ERA	G	GS	CG	ShO	Sv.	IP	H	R	ER	BB	SO
1994—Wichita (Texas)	1	0	1.000	0.43	16	0	0	0	8	21	13	1	1	6	30
— Las Vegas (PCL)	0	0	. . .	6.14	7	0	0	0	3	7 1/3	6	5	5	5	6
1995—Las Vegas (PCL)	0	1	.000	3.50	31	0	0	0	11	36	35	23	14	29	42
— San Diego (N.L.)	3	1	.750	6.82	26	0	0	0	0	31 2/3	35	26	24	22	19
1996—Las Vegas (PCL)	1	4	.200	3.13	42	0	0	0	21	46	41	20	16	27	54
— San Diego (N.L.)	1	0	1.000	8.56	8	0	0	0	0	13 2/3	18	15	13	4	11
1997—Montreal (N.L.)■...............	8	8	.500	3.69	32	28	1	1	0	158 1/3	134	68	65	66	136
1998—Montreal (N.L.)	14	11	.560	3.13	32	30	1	0	0	187	163	80	65	56	154
Major league totals (4 years)......	26	20	.565	3.85	98	58	2	1	0	390 2/3	350	189	167	148	320

HERNANDEZ, ALEX   OF   PIRATES

PERSONAL: Born May 28, 1977, in San Juan, Puerto Rico. ... 6-4/190. ... Bats left, throws left. ... Full name: Alexander Vargas Hernandez.
TRANSACTIONS/CAREER NOTES: Selected by Pittsburgh Pirates organization in fourth round of free-agent draft (June 1, 1995).

Year Team (League)	Pos.	G	AB	R	H	2B	3B	HR	RBI	Avg.	BB	SO	SB	PO	A	E	Avg.
1995—GC Pirates (GCL)........	OF-1B	49	186	24	50	5	3	1	17	.269	17	33	4	148	7	5	.969
1996—Erie (N.Y.-Penn).........	OF-1B	61	225	38	65	13	4	4	30	.289	20	47	7	305	19	7	.979
1997—Lynchburg (Caro.)	OF	131	520	75	151	37	4	5	68	.290	27	140	13	212	*15	9	.962
1998—Carolina (Southern)....	OF	115	452	62	117	22	7	8	48	.259	41	81	11	217	15	11	.955

HERNANDEZ, CARLOS A.   C   PADRES

PERSONAL: Born May 24, 1967, in San Felix, Bolivar, Venezuela. ... 5-11/215. ... Bats right, throws right. ... Full name: Carlos Alberto Hernandez.
HIGH SCHOOL: Escula Tecnica Industrial (San Felix, Bolivar, Venezuela).
TRANSACTIONS/CAREER NOTES: Signed as non-drafted free agent by Los Angeles Dodgers organization (October 10, 1984). ... On Albuquerque disabled list (May 27-June 20, 1990). ... On disabled list (April 4-22, 1994). ... On Los Angeles disabled list (May 17-June 14, 1996); included rehabilitation assignment to Albuquerque (June 5-14). ... Granted free agency (October 15, 1996). ... Signed by San Diego Padres organization (December 2, 1996). ... On San Diego disabled list (July 13-August 15, 1997); included rehabilitation assignments to Rancho Cucamonga (August 9-10) and Las Vegas (August 11-15). ... Granted free agency (October 31, 1997). ... Re-signed by Padres (November 12, 1997). ... Granted free agency (October 23, 1998). ... Re-signed by Padres (December 2, 1998).
STATISTICAL NOTES: Tied for Gulf Coast League lead in double plays by catcher with three in 1986. ... Led Texas League catchers with 737 total chances in 1989. ... Led Pacific Coast League catchers with 684 total chances in 1991.

Year Team (League)	Pos.	G	AB	R	H	2B	3B	HR	RBI	Avg.	BB	SO	SB	PO	A	E	Avg.
1985—GC Dodgers (GCL)	3B-1B	22	49	3	12	1	0	0	0	.245	3	8	0	48	16	2	.970
1986—GC Dodgers (GCL)	C-3B	57	205	19	64	7	0	1	31	.312	5	18	1	217	36	10	.962
1987—Bakersfield (Calif.)......	C	48	162	22	37	6	1	3	22	.228	14	23	8	181	26	8	.963
1988—Bakersfield (Calif.)......	C	92	333	37	103	15	2	5	52	.309	16	39	3	480	88	14	.976
— Albuquerque (PCL)......	C	3	8	0	1	0	0	0	1	.125	0	0	0	11	0	1	.917
1989—San Antonio (Tex.)	C	99	370	37	111	16	3	8	41	.300	12	46	2	*629	*90	*18	.976
— Albuquerque (PCL)......	C	4	14	1	3	0	0	0	1	.214	2	1	0	23	3	3	.897
1990—Albuquerque (PCL)......	C	52	143	11	45	8	1	0	16	.315	8	25	2	207	31	8	.967
— Los Angeles (N.L.)	C	10	20	2	4	1	0	0	1	.200	0	2	0	37	2	0	1.000
1991—Albuquerque (PCL)......	C	95	345	60	119	24	2	8	44	.345	24	36	5	*592	*77	*15	.978
— Los Angeles (N.L.)	C-3B	15	14	1	3	1	0	0	1	.214	0	5	1	24	4	1	.966
1992—Los Angeles (N.L.)	C	69	173	11	45	4	0	3	17	.260	11	21	0	295	37	7	.979
1993—Los Angeles (N.L.)	C	50	99	6	25	5	0	2	7	.253	2	11	0	181	15	7	.966
1994—Los Angeles (N.L.)	C	32	64	6	14	2	0	2	6	.219	1	14	0	104	13	0	1.000
1995—Los Angeles (N.L.)	C	45	94	3	14	1	0	2	8	.149	7	25	0	210	25	4	.983
1996—Los Angeles (N.L.)	C	13	14	1	4	0	0	0	0	.286	2	2	0	31	1	0	1.000
— Albuquerque (PCL)......	C-1B-3B	66	233	19	56	11	0	5	30	.240	11	49	5	331	38	9	.976
1997—San Diego (N.L.)■	C-1B	50	134	15	42	7	1	3	14	.313	3	27	0	239	29	3	.989
— Rancho Cuca. (Cal.)	C	1	4	0	1	0	0	0	0	.250	0	1	0	11	1	0	1.000
— Las Vegas (PCL)	C	3	10	1	4	0	0	1	5	.400	1	3	0	15	2	0	1.000
1998—San Diego (N.L.)	C-1B	129	390	34	102	15	0	9	52	.262	16	54	2	795	53	7	.992
Major league totals (9 years)		413	1002	79	253	36	1	21	106	.252	42	161	3	1916	179	29	.986

H

DIVISION SERIES RECORD

Year	Team (League)	Pos.	G	AB	R	H	2B	3B	HR	RBI	Avg.	BB	SO	SB	PO	A	E	Avg.
1998—	San Diego (N.L.)	C	4	12	0	5	0	0	0	0	.417	0	0		34	6	0	1.000

CHAMPIONSHIP SERIES RECORD

Year	Team (League)	Pos.	G	AB	R	H	2B	3B	HR	RBI	Avg.	BB	SO	SB	PO	A	E	Avg.
1998—	San Diego (N.L.)	C	6	18	2	6	1	0	0	0	.333	1	5	0	36	4	0	1.000

WORLD SERIES RECORD

Year	Team (League)	Pos.	G	AB	R	H	2B	3B	HR	RBI	Avg.	BB	SO	SB	PO	A	E	Avg.
1998—	San Diego (N.L.)	C-PH	4	10	0	2	0	0	0	0	.200	0	3	0	18	1	0	1.000

HERNANDEZ, CARLOS E. 2B ASTROS

PERSONAL: Born December 12, 1975, in Caracas, Venezuela. ... 5-9/175. ... Bats right, throws right. ... Full name: Carlos Eduardo Hernandez.
TRANSACTIONS/CAREER NOTES: Signed as non-drafted free agent by Houston Astros organization (July 2, 1992). ... On disabled list (August 1, 1997-remainder of season).
STATISTICAL NOTES: Tied for Midwest League lead in double plays by second baseman with 79 in 1996. ... Led Pacific Coast League second basemen with .983 fielding percentage in 1998.

Year	Team (League)	Pos.	G	AB	R	H	2B	3B	HR	RBI	Avg.	BB	SO	SB	PO	A	E	Avg.
1993—	Dom. Astros (DSL).....	IF	67	245	52	75	13	4	1	36	.306	27	29	36	181	134	21	.938
1994—	GC Astros (GCL)	2B-SS	51	192	45	62	10	1	0	23	.323	19	22	25	89	149	8	.967
1995—	Quad City (Midwest) ..	2B-SS	126	470	74	122	19	6	4	40	.260	39	68	*58	188	349	21	.962
1996—	Quad City (Midwest) ..	2B-SS	112	456	67	123	15	7	5	49	.270	27	71	41	238	336	19	.968
1997—	Jackson (Texas)	2B	91	363	62	106	12	1	4	33	.292	33	59	17	187	269	8	.983
1998—	New Orleans (PCL).....	2B-SS	134	494	64	147	23	2	1	54	.298	21	81	29	249	359	13	†.979

HERNANDEZ, ELVIN P CUBS

PERSONAL: Born August 20, 1977, in Ranchete, Dominican Republic. ... 6-1/195. ... Throws right, bats right. ... Full name: Elvin Radhames Hernandez.
TRANSACTIONS/CAREER NOTES: Signed as non-drafted free agent by Pittsburgh Pirates organization (June 29, 1993). ... On Carolina disabled list (July 18-August 10, 1997). ... Claimed on waivers by Minnesota Twins (October 15, 1998). ... Claimed on waivers by Chicago Cubs (November 19, 1998).

Year	Team (League)	W	L	Pct.	ERA	G	GS	CG	ShO	Sv.	IP	H	R	ER	BB	SO
1994—	DSL Pirates (DSL)..............	4	5	.444	2.70	11	10	2	0	0	70	62	28	21	13	68
1995—	Erie (N.Y.-Penn).................	6	1	.857	2.89	14	14	2	0	0	90 1/3	82	40	29	22	54
1996—	Augusta (S. Atl.)..............	*17	5	.773	3.14	27	27	2	1	0	157 2/3	140	60	55	16	171
1997—	Carolina (Southern)............	2	7	.222	5.73	17	17	0	0	0	92 2/3	104	67	59	26	66
—	Lynchburg (Carolina)	0	0	. . .	1.80	3	0	0	0	1	5	4	1	1	1	5
1998—	Carolina (Southern)............	3	6	.333	5.72	27	13	0	0	0	102 1/3	127	73	65	31	67

HERNANDEZ, JOSE IF CUBS

PERSONAL: Born July 14, 1969, in Vega Alta, Puerto Rico. ... 6-1/180. ... Bats right, throws right. ... Full name: Jose Antonio Hernandez.
HIGH SCHOOL: Maestro Ladi (Vega Alta, Puerto Rico).
COLLEGE: Interamerican University (Puerto Rico).
TRANSACTIONS/CAREER NOTES: Signed as non-drafted free agent by Texas Rangers organization (January 13, 1987). ... Claimed on waivers by Cleveland Indians (April 3, 1992). ... Traded by Indians to Chicago Cubs for P Heathcliff Slocumb (June 1, 1993).
STATISTICAL NOTES: Led Gulf Coast League third basemen with .950 fielding percentage, 47 putouts and 11 double plays in 1988. ... Led Florida State League shortstops with .959 fielding percentage in 1990. ... Career major league grand slams: 1.

Year	Team (League)	Pos.	G	AB	R	H	2B	3B	HR	RBI	Avg.	BB	SO	SB	PO	A	E	Avg.
1987—	GC Rangers (GCL)......	SS	24	52	5	9	1	1	0	2	.173	9	25	2	30	38	5	.932
1988—	GC Rangers (GCL)......	3-2-S-1-O	55	162	19	26	7	1	1	13	.160	12	36	4	†68	115	8	†.958
1989—	Gastonia (S. Atl.)......	3-S-2-O	91	215	35	47	7	6	1	16	.219	33	67	9	101	169	17	.941
1990—	Charlotte (Fla. St.).....	SS-OF	121	388	43	99	14	7	1	44	.255	50	122	11	192	372	25	†.958
1991—	Tulsa (Texas)..........	SS	91	301	36	72	17	4	1	20	.239	26	75	4	151	300	15	*.968
—	Okla. City (A.A.).........	SS	14	46	6	14	1	1	1	3	.304	4	10	0	32	43	3	.962
—	Texas (A.L.).............	SS-3B	45	98	8	18	2	1	0	4	.184	3	31	0	49	111	4	.976
1992—	Cant./Akr. (Eastern)■.	SS	130	404	56	103	16	4	3	46	.255	37	108	7	*226	320	*40	.932
—	Cleveland (A.L.).........	SS	3	4	0	0	0	0	0	0	.000	0	2	0	3	3	1	.857
1993—	Cant./Akr. (Eastern).....	SS-3B	45	150	19	30	6	0	2	17	.200	10	39	9	75	135	7	.968
—	Orlando (South.)■......	SS	71	263	42	80	8	3	8	33	.304	20	60	8	136	205	14	.961
—	Iowa (Am. Assoc.)......	SS	6	24	3	6	1	0	0	3	.250	0	2	0	14	26	1	.976
1994—	Chicago (N.L.)..........	3-S-2-O	56	132	18	32	2	3	1	9	.242	8	29	2	46	86	4	.971
1995—	Chicago (N.L.)..........	SS-2B-3B	93	245	37	60	11	4	13	40	.245	13	69	1	113	189	9	.971
1996—	Chicago (N.L.)..........	S-3-2-O	131	331	52	80	14	1	10	41	.242	24	97	4	148	248	20	.952
1997—	Chicago (N.L.)..........	3-S-2-O-DH-1	121	183	30	50	8	5	7	26	.273	14	42	2	79	91	8	.955
1998—	Chicago (N.L.)..........	3-O-S-1-2	149	488	76	124	23	7	23	75	.254	40	140	4	193	226	13	.970
American League totals (2 years)			48	102	8	18	2	1	0	4	.176	3	33	0	52	114	5	.971
National League totals (5 years)			550	1379	216	346	58	20	54	191	.251	99	377	13	579	840	54	.963
Major league totals (7 years)			598	1481	224	364	60	21	54	195	.246	102	410	13	631	954	59	.964

H

Year	Team (League)	Pos.	G	AB	R	H	2B	3B	HR	RBI	Avg.	BB	SO	SB	PO	A	E	Avg.
						BATTING										FIELDING		
1998—	Chicago (N.L.)...........	SS	2	7	1	2	0	0	0	0	.286	0	2	0	5	1	2	.750

HERNANDEZ, LIVAN — P — MARLINS

PERSONAL: Born February 20, 1975, in Villa Clara, Cuba. ... 6-2/225. ... Throws right, bats right. ... Full name: Eisler Hernandez. ... Brother of Orlando Hernandez, pitcher, New York Yankees.
TRANSACTIONS/CAREER NOTES: Signed as non-drafted free agent by Florida Marlins orgaization (January 13, 1996).
STATISTICAL NOTES: Led International League with four balks in 1996.
MISCELLANEOUS: Member of Cuban national baseball team (1994-95). ... Struck out once in two appearances as pinch hitter (1998).

Year	Team (League)	W	L	Pct.	ERA	G	GS	CG	ShO	Sv.	IP	H	R	ER	BB	SO
1996—	Charlotte (Int'l)..................	2	4	.333	5.14	10	10	0	0	0	49	61	32	28	34	45
—	Florida (N.L.)......................	0	0	. . .	0.00	1	0	0	0	0	3	3	0	0	2	2
1997—	Portland (Eastern).............	0	0	. . .	2.25	1	1	0	0	0	4	2	1	1	7	2
—	Charlotte (Int'l)..................	5	3	.625	3.98	14	14	0	0	0	81 1/3	76	39	36	38	58
—	Florida (N.L.)......................	9	3	.750	3.18	17	17	0	0	0	96 1/3	81	39	34	38	72
1998—	Florida (N.L.)......................	10	12	.455	4.72	33	33	9	0	0	234 1/3	*265	133	123	104	162
Major league totals (3 years)......		19	15	.559	4.23	51	50	9	0	0	333 2/3	349	172	157	144	236

DIVISION SERIES RECORD

Year	Team (League)	W	L	Pct.	ERA	G	GS	CG	ShO	Sv.	IP	H	R	ER	BB	SO
1997—	Florida (N.L.)......................	0	0	. . .	2.25	1	0	0	0	0	4	3	1	1	0	3

CHAMPIONSHIP SERIES RECORD

NOTES: Named N.L. Championship Series Most Valuable Player (1997).

Year	Team (League)	W	L	Pct.	ERA	G	GS	CG	ShO	Sv.	IP	H	R	ER	BB	SO
1997—	Florida (N.L.)......................	2	0	1.000	0.84	2	1	1	0	0	10 2/3	5	1	1	2	16

WORLD SERIES RECORD

NOTES: Named Most Valuable Player (1997). ... Member of World Series championship team (1997).

Year	Team (League)	W	L	Pct.	ERA	G	GS	CG	ShO	Sv.	IP	H	R	ER	BB	SO
1997—	Florida (N.L.)......................	2	0	1.000	5.27	2	2	0	0	0	13 2/3	15	9	8	10	7

HERNANDEZ, ORLANDO — P — YANKEES

PERSONAL: Born October 11, 1969, in Villa Clara, Cuba. ... 6-2/210. ... Throws right, bats right. ... Full name: Orlando P. Hernandez. ... Nickname: El Duque. ... Brother of Livan Hernandez, pitcher, Florida Marlins.
TRANSACTIONS/CAREER NOTES: Signed as non-drafted free agent by New York Yankees (March 23, 1998).

Year	Team (League)	W	L	Pct.	ERA	G	GS	CG	ShO	Sv.	IP	H	R	ER	BB	SO
1998—	Tampa (Fla. St.).................	1	1	.500	1.00	2	2	0	0	0	9	3	2	1	3	15
—	Columbus (Int'l)..................	6	0	1.000	3.83	7	7	0	0	0	42 1/3	41	19	18	17	59
—	New York (A.L.)..................	12	4	.750	3.13	21	21	3	1	0	141	113	53	49	52	131
Major league totals (1 year)........		12	4	.750	3.13	21	21	3	1	0	141	113	53	49	52	131

DIVISION SERIES RECORD

Year	Team (League)	W	L	Pct.	ERA	G	GS	CG	ShO	Sv.	IP	H	R	ER	BB	SO
1998—	New York (A.L.)..................							Did not play.								

CHAMPIONSHIP SERIES RECORD

Year	Team (League)	W	L	Pct.	ERA	G	GS	CG	ShO	Sv.	IP	H	R	ER	BB	SO
1998—	New York (A.L.)..................	1	0	1.000	0.00	1	1	0	0	0	7	3	0	0	2	6

WORLD SERIES RECORD

NOTES: Member of World Series championship team (1998).

Year	Team (League)	W	L	Pct.	ERA	G	GS	CG	ShO	Sv.	IP	H	R	ER	BB	SO
1998—	New York (A.L.)..................	1	0	1.000	1.29	1	1	0	0	0	7	6	1	1	3	7

HERNANDEZ, RAMON — C — ATHLETICS

PERSONAL: Born May 20, 1976, in Caracas, Venezuela. ... 6-0/203. ... Bats right, throws right. ... Full name: Ramon Jose Marin Hernandez.
TRANSACTIONS/CAREER NOTES: Signed as non-drafted free agent by Oakland Athletics organization (February 18, 1994).
HONORS: Named Arizona League Most Valuable Player (1995).
STATISTICAL NOTES: Led Arizona League catchers with a .982 fielding percentage in 1995. ... Led Midwest League catchers with 877 putouts and 981 total chances and tied for lead with 20 errors in 1996. ... Led California League with .427 on-base percentage in 1997. ... Led California League catchers with 16 errors in 1997. ... Led Southern League in being hit by pitch with 19 in 1998.

Year	Team (League)	Pos.	G	AB	R	H	2B	3B	HR	RBI	Avg.	BB	SO	SB	PO	A	E	Avg.
						BATTING										FIELDING		
1994—	Dom. Athletics (DSL) .	C	42	134	24	33	2	0	2	18	.246	18	10	1	182	28	2	.991
1995—	Arizona A's (Ariz.).......	C-1B-3B	48	143	37	52	9	6	4	37	.364	39	16	6	358	61	12	†.972
1996—	W. Mich. (Mid.).........	C-1B	123	447	62	114	26	2	12	68	.255	69	62	2	†917	85	‡20	.980
1997—	Visalia (California)......	C-1B	86	332	57	120	21	2	15	85	*.361	35	47	2	577	80	†16	.976
—	Huntsville (Sou.)	C-1B-3B	44	161	27	31	3	0	4	24	.193	18	23	0	274	27	1	.997
1998—	Huntsville (Sou.)	C-1B	127	479	83	142	24	1	15	98	.296	57	61	4	524	42	11	.981

H

PERSONAL: Born November 11, 1964, in Santurce, Puerto Rico. ... 6-4/235. ... Throws right, bats right. ... Full name: Roberto Manuel Hernandez.

HIGH SCHOOL: New Hampton (N.H.) Prep.

COLLEGE: South Carolina-Aiken.

TRANSACTIONS/CAREER NOTES: Selected by California Angels organization in first round (16th pick overall) of free-agent draft (June 2, 1986); pick received as compensation for Baltimore Orioles signing Type A free-agent OF/IF Juan Beniquez. ... On disabled list (May 6-21 and June 4-August 14, 1987). ... Traded by Angels with OF Mark Doran to Chicago White Sox organization for OF Mark Davis (August 2, 1989). ... On Vancouver disabled list (May 17-August 10, 1991). ... Traded by White Sox with P Wilson Alvarez and P Danny Darwin to San Francisco Giants for SS Mike Caruso, OF Brian Manning, P Lorenzo Barcelo, P Keith Foulke, P Bobby Howry and P Ken Vining (July 31, 1997). ... Granted free agency (October 30, 1997). ... Signed by Tampa Bay Devil Rays (November 18, 1997).

MISCELLANEOUS: Holds Tampa Bay Devil Rays all-time record for most saves (26).

Year	Team (League)	W	L	Pct.	ERA	G	GS	CG	ShO	Sv.	IP	H	R	ER	BB	SO
1986—	Salem (Northwest)	2	2	.500	4.58	10	10	0	0	0	55	57	37	28	42	38
1987—	Quad City (Midwest)	2	3	.400	6.86	7	6	0	0	1	21	24	21	16	12	21
1988—	Quad City (Midwest)	9	10	.474	3.17	24	24	6	1	0	164 $^2/_3$	157	70	58	48	114
	— Midland (Texas)	0	2	.000	6.57	3	3	0	0	0	12 $^1/_3$	16	13	9	8	7
1989—	Midland (Texas)	2	7	.222	6.89	12	12	0	0	0	64	94	57	49	30	42
	— Palm Springs (Calif.)	1	4	.200	4.64	7	7	0	0	0	42 $^2/_3$	49	27	22	16	33
	— South Bend (Mid.)■	1	1	.500	3.33	4	4	0	0	0	24 $^1/_3$	19	9	9	7	17
1990—	Birmingham (Southern)	8	5	.615	3.67	17	17	1	0	0	108	103	57	44	43	62
	— Vancouver (PCL)	3	5	.375	2.84	11	11	3	1	0	79 $^1/_3$	73	33	25	26	49
1991—	Birmingham (Southern)	2	1	.667	1.99	4	4	0	0	0	22 $^2/_3$	11	5	5	6	25
	— Vancouver (PCL)	4	1	.800	3.22	7	7	0	0	0	44 $^2/_3$	41	17	16	23	40
	— GC White Sox (GCL)	0	0	. . .	0.00	1	1	0	0	0	6	2	0	0	0	7
	— Chicago (A.L.)	1	0	1.000	7.80	9	3	0	0	0	15	18	15	13	7	6
1992—	Chicago (A.L.)	7	3	.700	1.65	43	0	0	0	12	71	45	15	13	20	68
	— Vancouver (PCL)	3	3	.500	2.61	9	0	0	0	2	20 $^2/_3$	13	9	6	11	23
1993—	Chicago (A.L.)	3	4	.429	2.29	70	0	0	0	38	78 $^2/_3$	66	21	20	20	71
1994—	Chicago (A.L.)	4	4	.500	4.91	45	0	0	0	14	47 $^2/_3$	44	29	26	19	50
1995—	Chicago (A.L.)	3	7	.300	3.92	60	0	0	0	32	59 $^2/_3$	63	30	26	28	84
1996—	Chicago (A.L.)	6	5	.545	1.91	72	0	0	0	38	84 $^2/_3$	65	21	18	38	85
1997—	Chicago (A.L.)	5	1	.833	2.44	46	0	0	0	27	48	38	15	13	24	47
	— San Francisco (N.L.)■	5	2	.714	2.48	28	0	0	0	4	32 $^2/_3$	29	9	9	14	35
1998—	Tampa Bay (A.L.)■	2	6	.250	4.04	67	0	0	0	26	71 $^1/_3$	55	33	32	41	55
A.L. totals (8 years)		31	30	.508	3.04	412	3	0	0	187	476	394	179	161	197	466
N.L. totals (1 year)		5	2	.714	2.48	28	0	0	0	4	32 $^2/_3$	29	9	9	14	35
Major league totals (8 years)		36	32	.529	3.01	440	3	0	0	191	508 $^2/_3$	423	188	170	211	501

DIVISION SERIES RECORD

Year	Team (League)	W	L	Pct.	ERA	G	GS	CG	ShO	Sv.	IP	H	R	ER	BB	SO
1997—	San Francisco (N.L.)	0	1	.000	20.25	3	0	0	0	0	1 $^1/_3$	5	3	3	3	1

CHAMPIONSHIP SERIES RECORD

Year	Team (League)	W	L	Pct.	ERA	G	GS	CG	ShO	Sv.	IP	H	R	ER	BB	SO
1993—	Chicago (A.L.)	0	0	. . .	0.00	4	0	0	0	1	4	4	0	0	0	1

ALL-STAR GAME RECORD

Year	League	W	L	Pct.	ERA	GS	CG	ShO	Sv.	IP	H	R	ER	BB	SO
1996—	American	0	0	. . .	0.00	0	0	0	0	1	1	0	0	0	0

HERNANDEZ, XAVIER   P   ORIOLES

PERSONAL: Born August 16, 1965, in Port Arthur, Texas. ... 6-2/195. ... Throws right, bats right. ... Full name: Francis Xavier Hernandez.

HIGH SCHOOL: Thomas Jefferson (Port Arthur, Texas).

COLLEGE: Southwestern Louisiana.

TRANSACTIONS/CAREER NOTES: Selected by Toronto Blue Jays organization in fourth round of free-agent draft (June 2, 1986). ... On disabled list (June 7-27, 1987). ... Selected by Houston Astros from Blue Jays organization in Rule 5 major league draft (December 4, 1989). ... On Houston disabled list (June 3-26, 1991); included rehabilitation assignment to Tucson (June 14-26). ... Traded by Astros to New York Yankees for P Domingo Jean and IF Andy Stankiewicz (November 27, 1993). ... On disabled list (July 27-August 11, 1994). ... Granted free agency (November 28, 1994). ... Signed by Cincinnati Reds (December 1, 1994). ... Released by Reds (April 17, 1996). ... Signed by Astros (April 24, 1996). ... Granted free agency (October 31, 1996). ... Signed by Texas Rangers (December 17, 1996). ... On disabled list (August 2, 1997-remainder of season). ... On Texas disabled list (March 22-May 5, 1998); included rehabilitation assignments to Tulsa (April 14-21) and Oklahoma (April 22-May 5). ... Granted free agency (October 28, 1998). ... Signed by Baltimore Orioles (December 17, 1998).

MISCELLANEOUS: Appeared in two games as pinch runner (1990).

Year	Team (League)	W	L	Pct.	ERA	G	GS	CG	ShO	Sv.	IP	H	R	ER	BB	SO
1986—	St. Catharines (NYP)	5	5	.500	2.67	13	10	1	1	0	70 $^2/_3$	55	27	21	16	69
1987—	St. Catharines (NYP)	3	3	.500	5.07	13	11	0	0	0	55	57	39	31	16	49
1988—	Myrtle Beach (SAL)	13	6	.684	2.55	23	22	2	2	0	148	116	52	42	28	111
	— Knoxville (Southern)	2	4	.333	2.90	11	11	2	0	0	68 $^1/_3$	73	32	22	15	33
1989—	Knoxville (Southern)	1	1	.500	4.13	4	4	1	0	0	24	25	11	11	11	17
	— Syracuse (Int'l)	5	6	.455	3.53	15	15	2	1	0	99 $^1/_3$	95	42	39	22	47
	— Toronto (A.L.)	1	0	1.000	4.76	7	0	0	0	0	22 $^2/_3$	25	15	12	8	7
1990—	Houston (N.L.)■	2	1	.667	4.62	34	1	0	0	0	62 $^1/_3$	60	34	32	24	24
1991—	Houston (N.L.)	2	7	.222	4.71	32	6	0	0	3	63	66	34	33	32	55
	— Tucson (PCL)	2	1	.667	2.75	16	3	0	0	4	36	35	16	11	9	34
1992—	Houston (N.L.)	9	1	.900	2.11	77	0	0	0	7	111	81	31	26	42	96
1993—	Houston (N.L.)	4	5	.444	2.61	72	0	0	0	9	96 $^2/_3$	75	37	28	28	101
1994—	New York (A.L.)■	4	4	.500	5.85	31	0	0	0	6	40	48	27	26	21	37
1995—	Cincinnati (N.L.)■	7	2	.778	4.60	59	0	0	0	3	90	95	47	46	31	84

H

Year— Team (League)	W	L	Pct.	ERA	G	GS	CG	ShO	Sv.	IP	H	R	ER	BB	SO
1996— Cincinnati (N.L.)	0	0	...	13.50	3	0	0	0	0	3 1/3	8	6	5	2	3
— Houston (N.L.)■	5	5	.500	4.22	58	0	0	0	6	74 2/3	69	39	35	26	78
1997— Texas (A.L.)■	0	4	.000	4.56	44	0	0	0	0	49 1/3	51	27	25	22	36
1998— Tulsa (Texas)	0	0	...	3.00	2	2	0	0	0	3	3	1	1	0	2
— Oklahoma (PCL)	0	0	...	1.35	5	0	0	0	0	6 2/3	5	1	1	1	9
— Texas (A.L.)	6	6	.500	3.57	46	0	0	0	1	58	43	27	23	30	41
A.L. totals (4 years)	11	14	.440	4.55	128	0	0	0	7	170	167	96	86	81	121
N.L. totals (6 years)	29	21	.580	3.68	335	7	0	0	28	501	454	228	205	185	441
Major league totals (10 years)	40	35	.533	3.90	463	7	0	0	35	671	621	324	291	266	562

CHAMPIONSHIP SERIES RECORD

Year— Team (League)	W	L	Pct.	ERA	G	GS	CG	ShO	Sv.	IP	H	R	ER	BB	SO
1995— Cincinnati (N.L.)	0	0	...	27.00	1	0	0	0	0	2/3	3	2	2	0	0

HERSHISER, OREL   P

PERSONAL: Born September 16, 1958, in Buffalo. ... 6-3/195. ... Throws right, bats right. ... Full name: Orel Leonard Hershiser IV. ... Brother of Gordie Hershiser, minor league pitcher (1987-88). ... Name pronounced her-SHY-zer.
HIGH SCHOOL: Cherry Hill (N.J.) East.
COLLEGE: Bowling Green State.
TRANSACTIONS/CAREER NOTES: Selected by Los Angeles Dodgers organization in 17th round of free-agent draft (June 5, 1979). ... On disabled list (April 27, 1990-remainder of season). ... On Los Angeles disabled list (March 31-May 29, 1991); included rehabilitation assignments to Bakersfield (May 8-13 and May 18-24), Albuquerque (May 13-18) and San Antonio (May 24-29). ... Granted free agency (November 1, 1991). ... Re-signed by Dodgers (December 3, 1991). ... Granted free agency (October 17, 1994). ... Signed by Cleveland Indians (April 8, 1995). ... On disabled list (June 22-July 7, 1995 and July 29-August 13, 1997). ... Granted free agency (October 29, 1997). ... Signed by San Francisco Giants (December 9, 1997). ... Granted free agency (November 2, 1998).
RECORDS: Holds major league single-season record for most consecutive scoreless innings—59 (August 30, sixth inning through September 28, 10th inning, 1988). ... Shares N.L. single-season record for fewest games lost by pitcher who led league in games lost—15 (1989 and 1992). ... Shares N.L. record for most shutouts in one month—5 (September 1988).
HONORS: Named Major League Player of the Year by THE SPORTING NEWS (1988). ... Named N.L. Pitcher of the Year by THE SPORTING NEWS (1988). ... Named righthanded pitcher on THE SPORTING NEWS N.L. All-Star team (1988). ... Won N.L. Gold Glove at pitcher (1988). ... Named N.L. Cy Young Award winner by Baseball Writers' Association of America (1988). ... Named pitcher on THE SPORTING NEWS N.L. Silver Slugger team (1993).
STATISTICAL NOTES: Pitched 2-0 one-hit, complete-game victory against San Diego (April 26, 1985). ... Pitched 6-0 one-hit, complete-game victory against Pittsburgh (July 23, 1985). ... Tied for N.L. lead with 19 sacrifice hits in 1988.
MISCELLANEOUS: Had sacrifice hit in only appearance as pinch hitter (1988). ... Singled once in two games as pinch hitter (1992). ... Started one game at third base but was replaced before first plate appearance and never played in field (1993).

Year— Team (League)	W	L	Pct.	ERA	G	GS	CG	ShO	Sv.	IP	H	R	ER	BB	SO
1979— Clinton (Midwest)	4	0	1.000	2.09	15	4	1	0	2	43	33	15	10	17	33
1980— San Antonio (Tex.)	5	9	.357	3.55	49	3	1	0	14	109	120	59	43	59	75
1981— San Antonio (Tex.)	7	6	.538	4.68	42	4	3	0	*15	102	94	54	53	50	95
1982— Albuquerque (PCL)	9	6	.600	3.71	47	7	2	0	4	123 2/3	121	73	51	63	93
1983— Albuquerque (PCL)	10	8	.556	4.09	49	10	6	0	16	134 1/3	132	73	61	57	95
— Los Angeles (N.L.)	0	0	...	3.38	8	0	0	0	1	8	7	6	3	6	5
1984— Los Angeles (N.L.)	11	8	.579	2.66	45	20	8	•4	2	189 2/3	160	65	56	50	150
1985— Los Angeles (N.L.)	19	3	*.864	2.03	36	34	9	5	0	239 2/3	179	72	54	68	157
1986— Los Angeles (N.L.)	14	14	.500	3.85	35	35	8	1	0	231 1/3	213	112	99	86	153
1987— Los Angeles (N.L.)	16	16	.500	3.06	37	35	10	1	1	*264 2/3	247	105	90	74	190
1988— Los Angeles (N.L.)	•23	8	.742	2.26	35	34	•15	*8	1	*267	208	73	67	73	178
1989— Los Angeles (N.L.)	15	•15	.500	2.31	35	33	8	4	0	*256 2/3	226	75	66	77	178
1990— Los Angeles (N.L.)	1	1	.500	4.26	4	4	0	0	0	25 1/3	26	12	12	4	16
1991— Bakersfield (California)	2	0	1.000	0.82	2	2	0	0	0	11	5	2	1	1	6
— Albuquerque (PCL)	0	0	...	0.00	1	1	0	0	0	5	5	0	0	0	5
— San Antonio (Tex.)	0	1	.000	2.57	1	1	0	0	0	7	11	3	2	1	5
— Los Angeles (N.L.)	7	2	.778	3.46	21	21	0	0	0	112	112	43	43	32	73
1992— Los Angeles (N.L.)	10	•15	.400	3.67	33	33	1	0	0	210 2/3	209	101	86	69	130
1993— Los Angeles (N.L.)	12	14	.462	3.59	33	33	5	1	0	215 2/3	201	106	86	72	141
1994— Los Angeles (N.L.)	6	6	.500	3.79	21	21	1	0	0	135 1/3	146	67	57	42	72
1995— Cleveland (A.L.)■	16	6	.727	3.87	26	26	1	1	0	167 1/3	151	76	72	51	111
1996— Cleveland (A.L.)	15	9	.625	4.24	33	33	1	0	0	206	238	115	97	58	125
1997— Cleveland (A.L.)	14	6	.700	4.47	32	32	1	0	0	195 1/3	199	105	97	69	107
1998— San Francisco (N.L.)■	11	10	.524	4.41	34	34	0	0	0	202	200	105	99	85	126
A.L. totals (3 years)	45	21	.682	4.21	91	91	3	1	0	568 2/3	588	296	266	178	343
N.L. totals (13 years)	145	112	.564	3.12	377	337	65	24	5	2358	2134	942	818	738	1569
Major league totals (16 years)	190	133	.588	3.33	468	428	68	25	5	2926 2/3	2722	1238	1084	916	1912

DIVISION SERIES RECORD

Year— Team (League)	W	L	Pct.	ERA	G	GS	CG	ShO	Sv.	IP	H	R	ER	BB	SO
1995— Cleveland (A.L.)	1	0	1.000	0.00	1	1	0	0	0	7 1/3	3	0	0	2	7
1996— Cleveland (A.L.)	0	0	...	5.40	1	1	0	0	0	5	7	4	3	3	3
1997— Cleveland (A.L.)	0	0	...	3.97	2	2	0	0	0	11 1/3	14	5	5	2	4
Div. series totals (3 years)	1	0	1.000	3.04	4	4	0	0	0	23 2/3	24	9	8	7	14

CHAMPIONSHIP SERIES RECORD

RECORDS: Holds single-series record for most innings pitched—24 2/3 (1988). ... Holds N.L. single-game record for most hit batsmen—2 (October 12, 1988). ... Shares N.L. career record for most complete games—2. ... Shares N.L. single-series record for most hit batsmen—2 (1988).
NOTES: Named N.L. Championship Series Most Valuable Player (1988). ... Named A.L. Championship Series Most Valuable Player (1995).

Year— Team (League)	W	L	Pct.	ERA	G	GS	CG	ShO	Sv.	IP	H	R	ER	BB	SO
1983— Los Angeles (N.L.)					Did not play.										
1985— Los Angeles (N.L.)	1	0	1.000	3.52	2	2	1	0	0	15 1/3	17	6	6	6	5

H

Year Team (League)	W	L	Pct.	ERA	G	GS	CG	ShO	Sv.	IP	H	R	ER	BB	SO
1988—Los Angeles (N.L.)	1	0	1.000	1.09	4	3	1	1	1	24 2/3	18	5	3	7	15
1995—Cleveland (A.L.)	2	0	1.000	1.29	2	2	0	0	0	14	9	3	2	3	15
1997—Cleveland (A.L.)	0	0	...	0.00	1	1	0	0	0	7	4	0	0	1	7
Champ. series totals (4 years)	4	0	1.000	1.62	9	8	2	1	1	61	48	14	11	17	42

WORLD SERIES RECORD

RECORDS: Shares single-game record for most earned runs allowed—7 (October 18, 1997).
NOTES: Named Most Valuable Player (1988). ... Member of World Series championship team (1988).

Year Team (League)	W	L	Pct.	ERA	G	GS	CG	ShO	Sv.	IP	H	R	ER	BB	SO
1988—Los Angeles (N.L.)	2	0	1.000	1.00	2	2	2	1	0	18	7	2	2	6	17
1995—Cleveland (A.L.)	1	1	.500	2.57	2	2	0	0	0	14	8	5	4	4	13
1997—Cleveland (A.L.)	0	2	.000	11.70	2	2	0	0	0	10	15	13	13	6	5
World Series totals (3 years)	3	3	.500	4.07	6	6	2	1	0	42	30	20	19	16	35

ALL-STAR GAME RECORD

Year League	W	L	Pct.	ERA	GS	CG	ShO	Sv.	IP	H	R	ER	BB	SO
1987—National	0	0	...	0.00	0	0	0	0	2	1	0	0	1	0
1988—National	0	0	...	0.00	0	0	0	0	1	0	0	0	0	0
1989—National							Did not play.							
All-Star totals (2 years)	0	0	...	0.00	0	0	0	0	3	1	0	0	1	0

HIDALGO, RICHARD — OF — ASTROS

PERSONAL: Born July 2, 1975, in Caracas, Venezuela. ... 6-3/190. ... Bats right, throws right. ... Full name: Richard Jose Hidalgo.
TRANSACTIONS/CAREER NOTES: Signed as non-drafted free agent by Houston Astros organization (July 2, 1991). ... On Houston disabled list (May 30-July 21, 1998); included rehabilitation assignment to New Orleans (July 11-21).
STATISTICAL NOTES: Led Texas League in grounding into double plays with 24 in 1996.

Year Team (League)	Pos.	G	AB	R	H	2B	3B	HR	RBI	Avg.	BB	SO	SB	PO	A	E	Avg.
1992—GC Astros (GCL)	OF	51	184	20	57	7	3	1	27	.310	13	27	14	67	6	0	1.000
1993—Asheville (S. Atl.)	OF	111	403	49	109	23	3	10	55	.270	30	76	21	197	*30	6	.974
1994—Quad City (Midwest)	OF	124	476	68	139	*47	6	12	76	.292	23	80	12	202	*23	11	.953
1995—Jackson (Texas)	OF	133	489	59	130	28	6	14	59	.266	32	76	8	238	14	5	.981
1996—Jackson (Texas)	OF	130	513	66	151	34	2	14	78	.294	29	55	11	302	14	6	.981
1997—New Orleans (A.A.)	OF	134	526	74	147	*37	5	11	78	.279	35	57	6	261	*15	9	.968
—Houston (N.L.)	OF	19	62	8	19	5	0	2	6	.306	4	18	1	28	0	0	1.000
1998—Houston (N.L.)	OF	74	211	31	64	15	0	7	35	.303	17	37	3	131	3	3	.978
—New Orleans (PCL)	OF	10	24	0	4	2	0	0	1	.167	3	2	0	17	0	0	1.000
Major league totals (2 years)		93	273	39	83	20	0	9	41	.304	21	55	4	159	3	3	.982

DIVISION SERIES RECORD

Year Team (League)	Pos.	G	AB	R	H	2B	3B	HR	RBI	Avg.	BB	SO	SB	PO	A	E	Avg.
1997—Houston (N.L.)	OF	2	5	1	0	0	0	0	0	.000	1	2	0	5	0	0	1.000
1998—Houston (N.L.)	OF	1	4	0	1	0	0	0	0	.250	0	1	0	1	0	0	1.000
Division series totals (2 years)		3	9	1	1	0	0	0	0	.111	1	3	0	6	0	0	1.000

HIGGINSON, BOBBY — OF — TIGERS

PERSONAL: Born August 18, 1970, in Philadelphia. ... 5-11/195. ... Bats left, throws right. ... Full name: Robert Leigh Higginson.
HIGH SCHOOL: Frankford (Philadelphia).
COLLEGE: Temple.
TRANSACTIONS/CAREER NOTES: Selected by Detroit Tigers organization in 12th round of free-agent draft (June 1, 1992). ... On Detroit disabled list (May 11-June 7, 1996); included rehabilitation assignment to Toledo (June 4-7). ... On disabled list (June 15-26, 1997). ... On suspended list (September 26, 1997).
RECORDS: Shares major league record for most consecutive home runs—4 (June 30 [3], July 1 [1], 1997).
STATISTICAL NOTES: Hit three home runs in one game (June 30, 1997). ... Tied for A.L. lead in double plays by outfielder with five in 1997. ... Career major league grand slams: 4.

Year Team (League)	Pos.	G	AB	R	H	2B	3B	HR	RBI	Avg.	BB	SO	SB	PO	A	E	Avg.
1992—Niagara Falls (NYP)	OF	70	232	35	68	17	4	2	37	.293	33	47	12	109	5	2	.983
1993—Lakeland (Fla. St.)	OF	61	223	42	67	11	7	3	25	.300	40	31	8	88	7	2	.979
—London (Eastern)	OF	63	224	25	69	15	4	4	35	.308	19	37	3	100	11	2	.982
1994—Toledo (Int'l)	OF	137	476	81	131	28	4	23	67	.275	46	99	16	282	10	8	.973
1995—Detroit (A.L.)	OF-DH	131	410	61	92	17	5	14	43	.224	62	107	6	247	*13	4	.985
1996—Detroit (A.L.)	OF-DH	130	440	75	141	35	0	26	81	.320	65	66	6	227	9	9	.963
—Toledo (Int'l)	OF	3	13	4	4	0	1	0	1	.308	3	0	0	3	0	0	1.000
1997—Detroit (A.L.)	OF-DH	146	546	94	163	30	5	27	101	.299	70	85	12	287	*20	9	.972
1998—Detroit (A.L.)	OF-DH	157	612	92	174	37	4	25	85	.284	63	101	3	303	18	6	.982
Major league totals (4 years)		564	2008	322	570	119	14	92	310	.284	260	359	27	1064	60	28	.976

HILL, GLENALLEN — OF — CUBS

PERSONAL: Born March 22, 1965, in Santa Cruz, Calif. ... 6-3/230. ... Bats right, throws right.
HIGH SCHOOL: Santa Cruz (Calif.).
TRANSACTIONS/CAREER NOTES: Selected by Toronto Blue Jays organization in ninth round of free-agent draft (June 6, 1983). ... On disabled list (July 6-21, 1990). ... Traded by Blue Jays with P Denis Boucher, OF Mark Whiten and a player to be named later to Cleveland Indians for

H

P Tom Candiotti and OF Turner Ward (June 27, 1991); Indians acquired cash instead of player to complete deal (October 15, 1991). ... On Cleveland disabled list (September 8, 1991-remainder of season). ... On Cleveland disabled list (April 23-May 22, 1992); included rehabilitation assignment to Canton/Akron (May 18-22). ... Traded by Indians to Chicago Cubs for OF Candy Maldonado (August 19, 1993). ... Granted free agency (October 27, 1993). ... Re-signed by Cubs (November 24, 1993). ... Granted free agency (April 7, 1995). ... Signed by San Francisco Giants (April 9, 1995). ... On San Francisco disabled list (May 27-August 5, 1996); included rehabilitation assignment to Phoenix (July 29-August 5). ... Granted free agency (October 29, 1997). ... Signed by Seattle Mariners organization (January 8, 1998). ... Claimed on waivers by Cubs (July 6, 1998). ... Granted free agency (October 23, 1998). ... Re-signed by Cubs (December 7, 1998).

STATISTICAL NOTES: Led Southern League with 287 total bases and tied for lead with 13 sacrifice flies in 1986. ... Led International League with 279 total bases and .578 slugging percentage in 1989. ... Career major league grand slams: 4.

Year Team (League)	Pos.	G	AB	R	H	2B	3B	HR	RBI	Avg.	BB	SO	SB	PO	A	E	Avg.
1983— Medicine Hat (Pio.)	OF	46	133	34	63	3	4	6	27	.474	17	49	4	63	3	6	.917
1984— Florence (S. Atl.)	OF	129	440	75	105	19	5	16	64	.239	63	*150	30	281	9	16	.948
1985— Kinston (Carolina)	OF	131	466	57	98	13	0	20	56	.210	57	*211	42	234	12	13	.950
1986— Knoxville (Southern) ..	OF	141	*570	87	159	23	6	*31	96	.279	39	*153	18	230	9	*21	.919
1987— Syracuse (Int'l)..........	OF	*137	536	65	126	25	6	16	77	.235	25	*152	22	176	10	10	.949
1988— Syracuse (Int'l)..........	OF	51	172	21	40	7	0	4	19	.233	15	59	7	101	2	1	.990
— Knoxville (Southern) ..	OF	79	269	37	71	13	2	12	38	.264	28	75	10	130	6	5	.965
1989— Syracuse (Int'l)..........	OF	125	483	*86	*155	31	*15	*21	72	.321	34	107	21	242	3	*7	.972
— Toronto (A.L.)............	OF-DH	19	52	4	15	0	0	1	7	.288	3	12	2	27	0	1	.964
1990— Toronto (A.L.)...........	OF-DH	84	260	47	60	11	3	12	32	.231	18	62	8	115	4	2	.983
1991— Toronto (A.L.)...........	DH-OF	35	99	14	25	5	2	3	11	.253	7	24	2	29	0	1	.967
— Cleveland (A.L.)■......	OF-DH	37	122	15	32	3	0	5	14	.262	16	30	4	89	0	2	.978
1992— Cleveland (A.L.)........	OF-DH	102	369	38	89	16	1	18	49	.241	20	73	9	126	5	6	.956
— Cant./Akr. (Eastern) ..	OF	3	9	1	1	1	0	0	1	.111	3	4	0	4	0	1	.800
1993— Cleveland (A.L.)........	OF-DH	66	174	19	39	7	2	5	25	.224	11	50	7	62	1	4	.940
— Chicago (N.L.)■.......	OF	31	87	14	30	7	0	10	22	.345	6	21	1	42	2	2	.957
1994— Chicago (N.L.).........	OF	89	269	48	80	12	1	10	38	.297	29	57	19	149	0	2	.987
1995— San Fran. (N.L.)■......	OF	132	497	71	131	29	4	24	86	.264	39	98	25	226	10	10	.959
1996— San Francisco (N.L.) ..	OF	98	379	56	106	26	0	19	67	.280	33	95	6	160	6	7	.960
— Phoenix (PCL)..........	OF	5	17	4	6	1	0	2	2	.353	0	3	1	8	0	0	1.000
1997— San Francisco (N.L.) ..	OF-DH	128	398	47	104	28	4	11	64	.261	19	87	7	158	2	9	.947
1998— Seattle (A.L.)■........	OF	74	259	37	75	20	2	12	33	.290	14	45	1	107	2	4	.965
— Chicago (N.L.)■.......	OF	48	131	26	46	5	0	8	23	.351	14	34	0	59	3	1	.984
American League totals (6 years)		417	1335	174	335	62	10	56	171	.251	89	296	33	555	12	20	.966
National League totals (6 years)		526	1761	262	497	107	9	82	300	.282	140	392	58	794	23	31	.963
Major league totals (10 years)		943	3096	436	832	169	19	138	471	.269	229	688	91	1349	35	51	.964

DIVISION SERIES RECORD

Year Team (League)	Pos.	G	AB	R	H	2B	3B	HR	RBI	Avg.	BB	SO	SB	PO	A	E	Avg.
1997— San Francisco (N.L.) ..	OF-PH	3	7	0	0	0	0	0	0	.000	2	2	0	2	0	0	1.000
1998— Chicago (N.L.)...........	OF	1	3	0	1	0	0	0	0	.333	1	2	1	3	0	0	1.000
Division series totals (2 years)		4	10	0	1	0	0	0	0	.100	3	4	1	5	0	0	1.000

HILL, KEN   P   ANGELS

PERSONAL: Born December 14, 1965, in Lynn, Mass. ... 6-2/214. ... Throws right, bats right. ... Full name: Kenneth Wade Hill.

HIGH SCHOOL: Classical (Lynn, Mass.).

COLLEGE: North Adams (Mass.) State.

TRANSACTIONS/CAREER NOTES: Signed as non-drafted free agent by Detroit Tigers organization (February 14, 1985). ... Traded by Tigers with a player to be named later to St. Louis Cardinals for C Mike Heath (August 10, 1986); Cardinals acquired 1B Mike Laga to complete deal (September 2, 1986). ... On St. Louis disabled list (March 26-May 9, 1988). ... On St. Louis disabled list (August 11-September 1, 1991); included rehabilitation assignment to Louisville (August 29-30). ... Traded by Cardinals to Montreal Expos for 1B Andres Galarraga (November 25, 1991). ... On Montreal disabled list (June 26-July 17, 1993); included rehabilitation assignment to Ottawa (July 12-15). ... Traded by Expos to Cardinals for P Brian Eversgerd, P Kirk Bullinger and OF Darond Stovall (April 5, 1995). ... Traded by Cardinals to Cleveland Indians for 3B/2B David Bell, P Rick Heiserman and C Pepe McNeal (July 27, 1995). ... Granted free agency (November 1, 1995). ... Signed by Texas Rangers (December 22, 1995). ... Traded by Rangers to Anaheim Angels for C Jim Leyritz and a player to be named later (July 29, 1997); Rangers acquired IF Rob Sasser to complete deal (October 31, 1997). ... On disabled list (May 1-24, 1997); included rehabilitation assignment to Tulsa (May 20-24). ... Granted free agency (November 7, 1997). ... Re-signed by Angels (November 15, 1997). ... On Anaheim disabled list (June 11-August 28, 1998); included rehabilitation assignments to Cedar Rapids (August 9-17) and Lake Elsinore (August 18-24).

RECORDS: Shares N.L. single-season record for fewest games lost by pitcher who led league in games lost—15 (1989).

STATISTICAL NOTES: Pitched 6-0 one-hit, complete-game victory against New York (June 8, 1992). ... Led N.L. with 16 sacrifice hits in 1994. ... Pitched 11-0 one-hit, complete-game victory against Detroit (May 3, 1996). ... Led A.L. with four balks in 1996. ... Led A.L. with 95 bases on balls in 1997.

MISCELLANEOUS: Made an out in only appearance as pinch hitter with Montreal (1993). ... Had sacrifice hit in only appearance as pinch hitter (1994).

Year Team (League)	W	L	Pct.	ERA	G	GS	CG	ShO	Sv.	IP	H	R	ER	BB	SO
1985— Gastonia (S. Atl.)...............	3	6	.333	4.96	15	12	0	0	0	69	60	51	38	57	48
1986— Gastonia (S. Atl.)...............	9	5	.643	2.79	22	16	1	0	0	122 2/3	95	51	38	80	86
— Glens Falls (East.)	0	1	.000	5.14	1	1	0	0	0	7	4	4	4	6	4
— Arkansas (Texas)■.............	1	2	.333	4.50	3	3	1	0	0	18	18	10	9	7	9
1987— Arkansas (Texas).............	3	5	.375	5.20	18	8	0	0	2	53 2/3	60	33	31	30	48
— St. Petersburg (FSL)	1	3	.250	4.17	18	4	0	0	2	41	38	19	19	17	32
1988— St. Louis (N.L.)...............	0	1	.000	5.14	4	1	0	0	0	14	16	9	8	6	6
— Arkansas (Texas)	9	9	.500	4.92	22	22	3	1	0	115 1/3	129	76	63	50	107
1989— Louisville (A.A.)...............	0	2	.000	3.50	3	3	0	0	0	18	13	8	7	10	18
— St. Louis (N.L.)...............	7	*15	.318	3.80	33	33	2	1	0	196 2/3	186	92	83	*99	112
1990— St. Louis (N.L.)...............	5	6	.455	5.49	17	14	1	0	0	78 2/3	79	49	48	33	58
— Louisville (A.A.)	6	1	.857	1.79	12	12	2	1	0	85 1/3	47	20	17	27	104
1991— St. Louis (N.L.)...............	11	10	.524	3.57	30	30	0	0	0	181 1/3	147	76	72	67	121
— Louisville (A.A.)...............	0	0	...	0.00	1	1	0	0	0	1	0	0	0	0	2

H

Year Team (League)	W	L	Pct.	ERA	G	GS	CG	ShO	Sv.	IP	H	R	ER	BB	SO
1992— Montreal (N.L.)■............	16	9	.640	2.68	33	33	3	3	0	218	187	76	65	75	150
1993— Montreal (N.L.)...............	9	7	.563	3.23	28	28	2	0	0	183²/₃	163	84	66	74	90
— Ottawa (Int'l)	0	0	. . .	0.00	1	1	0	0	0	4	1	0	0	1	0
1994— Montreal (N.L.)...............	•16	5	.762	3.32	23	23	2	1	0	154²/₃	145	61	57	44	85
1995— St. Louis (N.L.)■	6	7	.462	5.06	18	18	0	0	0	110¹/₃	125	71	62	45	50
— Cleveland (A.L.)■...........	4	1	.800	3.98	12	11	1	0	0	74²/₃	77	36	33	32	48
1996— Texas (A.L.)■...............	16	10	.615	3.63	35	35	7	•3	0	250²/₃	250	110	101	95	170
1997— Texas (A.L.)................	5	8	.385	5.19	19	19	0	0	0	111	129	69	64	56	68
— Tulsa (Texas)	0	0	. . .	0.00	1	1	0	0	0	5	2	0	0	1	3
— Anaheim (A.L.)■.............	4	4	.500	3.65	12	12	1	0	0	79	65	34	32	§39	38
1998— Anaheim (A.L.)...............	9	6	.600	4.98	19	19	0	0	0	103	123	60	57	47	57
— Cedar Rapids (Midw.)	0	0	. . .	1.23	2	2	0	0	0	7¹/₃	7	1	1	1	6
— Lake Elsinore (Calif.)	0	0	. . .	6.75	1	1	0	0	0	4	5	4	3	5	2
A.L. totals (4 years)	38	29	.567	4.18	97	96	9	3	0	618¹/₃	644	309	287	269	381
N.L. totals (8 years)	70	60	.538	3.65	186	180	10	5	0	1137¹/₃	1048	518	461	443	672
Major league totals (11 years)....	108	89	.548	3.83	283	276	19	8	0	1755²/₃	1692	827	748	712	1053

DIVISION SERIES RECORD

Year Team (League)	W	L	Pct.	ERA	G	GS	CG	ShO	Sv.	IP	H	R	ER	BB	SO
1995— Cleveland (A.L.).................	1	0	1.000	0.00	1	0	0	0	0	1¹/₃	1	0	0	0	2
1996— Texas (A.L.)	0	0	. . .	4.50	1	1	0	0	0	6	5	3	3	3	1
Div. series totals (2 years)	1	0	1.000	3.68	2	1	0	0	0	7¹/₃	6	3	3	3	3

CHAMPIONSHIP SERIES RECORD

Year Team (League)	W	L	Pct.	ERA	G	GS	CG	ShO	Sv.	IP	H	R	ER	BB	SO
1995— Cleveland (A.L.).................	1	0	1.000	0.00	1	1	0	0	0	7	5	0	0	3	6

WORLD SERIES RECORD

Year Team (League)	W	L	Pct.	ERA	G	GS	CG	ShO	Sv.	IP	H	R	ER	BB	SO
1995— Cleveland (A.L.).................	0	1	.000	4.26	2	1	0	0	0	6¹/₃	7	3	3	4	1

ALL-STAR GAME RECORD

Year League	W	L	Pct.	ERA	GS	CG	ShO	Sv.	IP	H	R	ER	BB	SO
1994— National	0	0	. . .	0.00	0	0	0	0	2	0	0	0	1	0

HILLENBRAND, SHEA   C   RED SOX

PERSONAL: Born July 27, 1975, in Mesa, Ariz. ... 6-1/190. ... Bats right, throws right. ... Full name: Shea Matthew Hillenbrand.
HIGH SCHOOL: Mountain View (Mesa, Ariz.).
JUNIOR COLLEGE: Mesa (Ariz.) Community College.
TRANSACTIONS/CAREER NOTES: Selected by Boston Red Sox organization in 10th round of free-agent draft (June 4, 1996).
STATISTICAL NOTES: Led Midwest League with 272 total bases and .546 slugging percentage in 1998. ... Led Midwest League with 20 passed balls in 1998. ... Led New York-Penn league first basemen with 17 errors in 1996.

Year Team (League)	Pos.	G	AB	R	H	2B	3B	HR	RBI	Avg.	BB	SO	SB	PO	A	E	Avg.
1996— Lowell (NY-Penn)	1B-3B	72	279	33	88	18	2	2	38	.315	18	32	4	427	31	†19	.960
1997— Michigan (Midwest)	1B-3B	64	224	28	65	13	3	3	39	.290	9	20	1	137	16	8	.950
— Sarasota (Fla. St.)	1B-3B	57	220	25	65	12	0	2	28	.295	7	29	9	198	53	20	.926
1998— Michigan (Midwest) ...	C-1B-3B	129	498	80	174	33	4	19	93	.349	19	49	13	700	64	14	.982

HINCH, A.J.   C   ATHLETICS

PERSONAL: Born May 15, 1974, in Waverly, Iowa. ... 6-1/205. ... Bats right, throws right. ... Full name: Andrew Jay Hinch.
HIGH SCHOOL: Midwest City (Okla.).
COLLEGE: Stanford.
TRANSACTIONS/CAREER NOTES: Selected by Chicago White Sox organization in second round of free-agent draft (June 2, 1992); did not sign. ... Selected by Minnesota Twins organization in third round of free-agent draft (June 1, 1995); did not sign. ... Selected by Oakland Athletics organization in third round of free-agent draft (June 4, 1996). ... On Modesto suspended list (June 7-9, 1997).
RECORDS: Shares major league single-season record for fewest double plays by catcher for leader—8 (1998).
STATISTICAL NOTES: Led California League catchers with .996 fielding percentage in 1997. ... Tied for A.L. lead in double plays by catcher with eight in 1998.
MISCELLANEOUS: Member of 1996 U.S. Olympic baseball team.

Year Team (League)	Pos.	G	AB	R	H	2B	3B	HR	RBI	Avg.	BB	SO	SB	PO	A	E	Avg.
1997— Modesto (California) ..	C-1B	95	333	70	103	25	3	20	73	.309	42	68	8	622	66	3	†.996
— Edmonton (PCL)	C-OF	39	125	23	47	7	0	4	24	.376	20	13	2	201	7	3	.986
1998— Oakland (A.L.)	C	120	337	34	78	10	0	9	35	.231	30	89	3	602	47	•9	.986
Major league totals (1 year)		120	337	34	78	10	0	9	35	.231	30	89	3	602	47	9	.986

HINCHLIFFE, BRETT   P   MARINERS

H

PERSONAL: Born July 21, 1974, in Detroit. ... 6-5/190. ... Throws right, bats right.
HIGH SCHOOL: Bishop Gallagher (Harper Woods, Mich.).
TRANSACTIONS/CAREER NOTES: Selected by Seattle Mariners organization in 16th round of free-agent draft (June 1, 1992).
STATISTICAL NOTES: Pitched 12-0 no-hit victory against Cedar Rapids (June 28, 1994).

Year Team (League)	W	L	Pct.	ERA	G	GS	CG	ShO	Sv.	IP	H	R	ER	BB	SO
1992—Ariz. Mariners (Ariz.)	5	4	.556	2.31	*24	0	0	0	3	35	42	17	9	9	26
1993—Ariz. Mariners (Ariz.)	0	4	.000	5.08	10	9	0	0	0	44 1/3	55	32	25	5	29
1994—Appleton (Midwest)	11	7	.611	3.21	27	27	3	1	0	173 2/3	140	79	62	50	160
1995—Riverside (California)	3	8	.273	6.61	15	15	0	0	0	77 2/3	110	69	57	35	68
1996—Lancaster (Calif.)	11	10	.524	4.24	27	26	0	0	0	163 1/3	179	105	77	64	146
1997—Memphis (Sou.)	10	10	.500	4.45	24	24	*5	1	0	145 2/3	159	81	72	45	107
1998—Lancaster (Calif.)	1	1	.500	1.59	3	3	0	0	0	17	8	5	3	5	26
—Tacoma (PCL)	10	8	.556	4.00	25	25	2	1	0	159 2/3	132	80	71	88	100

HITCHCOCK, STERLING   P   PADRES

PERSONAL: Born April 29, 1971, in Fayetteville, N.C. ... 6-1/192. ... Throws left, bats left. ... Full name: Sterling Alex Hitchcock.

HIGH SCHOOL: Armwood (Seffner, Fla.).

TRANSACTIONS/CAREER NOTES: Selected by New York Yankees organization in ninth round of free-agent draft (June 5, 1989). ... On disabled list (June 26-August 14, 1991). ... On Columbus disabled list (May 23-July 21, 1993). ... Traded by Yankees with 3B Russ Davis to Seattle Mariners for 1B Tino Martinez, P Jeff Nelson and P Jim Mecir (December 7, 1995). ... Traded by Mariners to San Diego Padres for P Scott Sanders (December 6, 1996). ... On disabled list (June 6-July 3, 1997).

STATISTICAL NOTES: Pitched 1-0 no-hit victory against Sumter (July 16, 1990). ... Struck out 15 batters in one game (August 29, 1998).

Year Team (League)	W	L	Pct.	ERA	G	GS	CG	ShO	Sv.	IP	H	R	ER	BB	SO
1989—GC Yankees (GCL)	*9	1	.900	1.64	13	•13	0	0	0	76 2/3	48	16	14	27	*98
1990—Greensboro (S. Atl.)	12	12	.500	2.91	27	27	6	*5	0	173 1/3	122	68	56	60	*171
1991—Prince William (Caro.)	7	7	.500	2.64	19	19	2	0	0	119 1/3	111	49	35	26	101
1992—Alb./Colon. (East.)	6	9	.400	2.58	24	24	2	0	0	146 2/3	116	51	42	42	*155
—New York (A.L.)	0	2	.000	8.31	3	3	0	0	0	13	23	12	12	6	6
1993—Columbus (Int'l)	3	5	.375	4.81	16	16	0	0	0	76 2/3	80	43	41	28	85
—New York (A.L.)	1	2	.333	4.65	6	6	0	0	0	31	32	18	16	14	26
1994—New York (A.L.)	4	1	.800	4.20	23	5	1	0	2	49 1/3	48	24	23	29	37
—Columbus (Int'l)	3	4	.429	4.32	10	9	1	0	0	50	53	30	24	18	47
—Alb./Colon. (East.)	1	0	1.000	1.80	1	1	0	0	0	5	4	1	1	0	7
1995—New York (A.L.)	11	10	.524	4.70	27	27	4	1	0	168 1/3	155	91	88	68	121
1996—Seattle (A.L.)■	13	9	.591	5.35	35	35	0	0	0	196 2/3	245	131	117	73	132
1997—San Diego (N.L.)■	10	11	.476	5.20	32	28	1	0	0	161	172	102	93	55	106
1998—San Diego (N.L.)	9	7	.563	3.93	39	27	2	1	1	176 1/3	169	83	77	48	158
A.L. totals (5 years)	29	24	.547	5.03	94	76	5	1	2	458 1/3	503	276	256	190	322
N.L. totals (2 years)	19	18	.514	4.54	71	55	3	1	1	337 1/3	341	185	170	103	264
Major league totals (7 years)	48	42	.533	4.82	165	131	8	2	3	795 2/3	844	461	426	293	586

DIVISION SERIES RECORD

Year Team (League)	W	L	Pct.	ERA	G	GS	CG	ShO	Sv.	IP	H	R	ER	BB	SO
1995—New York (A.L.)	0	0	. . .	5.40	2	0	0	0	0	1 2/3	2	2	1	2	1
1998—San Diego (N.L.)	1	0	1.000	1.50	1	1	0	0	0	6	3	1	1	0	11
Div. series totals (2 years)	1	0	1.000	2.35	3	1	0	0	0	7 2/3	5	3	2	2	12

CHAMPIONSHIP SERIES RECORD

RECORDS: Shares single-inning record for most wild pitches—2 (October 14, 1998, second inning).

NOTES: Named N.L. Championship Series Most Valuable Player (1998).

Year Team (League)	W	L	Pct.	ERA	G	GS	CG	ShO	Sv.	IP	H	R	ER	BB	SO
1998—San Diego (N.L.)	2	0	1.000	0.90	2	2	0	0	0	10	5	1	1	8	14

WORLD SERIES RECORD

Year Team (League)	W	L	Pct.	ERA	G	GS	CG	ShO	Sv.	IP	H	R	ER	BB	SO
1998—San Diego (N.L.)	0	0	.000	1.50	1	1	0	0	0	6	7	2	1	1	7

HOCKING, DENNY   SS   TWINS

PERSONAL: Born April 2, 1970, in Torrance, Calif. ... 5-10/189. ... Bats both, throws right. ... Full name: Dennis Lee Hocking.

HIGH SCHOOL: West Torrance (Calif.).

COLLEGE: El Camino College (Calif.).

TRANSACTIONS/CAREER NOTES: Selected by Minnesota Twins organization in 52nd round of free-agent draft (June 5, 1989). ... On Nashville disabled list (April 8-29, 1993). ... On Minnesota disabled list (March 22-April 30, May 30-June 29 and July 31-September 8, 1996); included rehabilitation assignments to Salt Lake (April 4-30, June 21-29 and August 24-September 8).

STATISTICAL NOTES: Led California League shortstops with 721 total chances in 1992. ... Led Pacific Coast League shortstops with .966 fielding percentage and 390 assists in 1995.

Year Team (League)	Pos.	G	AB	R	H	2B	3B	HR	RBI	Avg.	BB	SO	SB	PO	A	E	Avg.
1990—Elizabethton (App.)	SS-2B-3B	54	201	45	59	6	2	6	30	.294	40	26	14	77	179	20	.928
1991—Kenosha (Midwest)	SS	125	432	72	110	17	8	2	36	.255	77	69	22	193	308	42	.923
1992—Visalia (California)	SS	135	*550	117	*182	34	9	7	81	.331	72	77	38	214	*469	38	.947
1993—Nashville (Southern)	SS-2B	107	409	54	109	9	4	8	50	.267	34	66	15	144	300	30	.937
—Minnesota (A.L.)	SS-2B	15	36	7	5	1	0	0	0	.139	6	8	1	19	23	1	.977
1994—Salt Lake (PCL)	SS	112	394	61	110	14	6	5	57	.279	28	57	13	143	342	26	.949
—Minnesota (A.L.)	SS	11	31	3	10	3	0	0	2	.323	0	4	2	11	27	0	1.000
1995—Salt Lake (PCL)	SS-2B	117	397	51	112	24	2	8	75	.282	25	41	12	173	†393	20	†.966
—Minnesota (A.L.)	SS	9	25	4	5	0	2	0	3	.200	2	1	1	13	20	1	.971
1996—Minnesota (A.L.)	O-S-2-DH-1	49	127	16	25	6	0	1	10	.197	8	24	3	67	9	1	.987
—Salt Lake (PCL)	S-O-1-2-3	37	130	18	36	6	2	3	22	.277	10	17	2	51	69	3	.976
1997—Minnesota (A.L.)	S-3-O-2-DH-1	115	253	28	65	12	4	2	25	.257	18	51	3	124	146	4	.985
1998—Minnesota (A.L.)	2-S-O-3-DH-1	110	198	32	40	6	1	3	15	.202	16	44	2	118	102	4	.982
Major league totals (6 years)		309	670	90	150	28	7	6	55	.224	50	133	12	352	327	11	.984

H

PERSONAL: Born October 13, 1967, in Bellflower, Calif. ... 6-0/205. ... Throws right, bats right. ... Full name: Trevor William Hoffman. ... Brother of Glenn Hoffman, assistant coach, Los Angeles Dodgers; and major league infielder with Boston Red Sox (1980-87), Los Angeles Dodgers (1987) and California Angels (1989).
HIGH SCHOOL: Savanna (Anaheim, Calif.).
JUNIOR COLLEGE: Cypress (Calif.) College.
COLLEGE: Arizona.
TRANSACTIONS/CAREER NOTES: Selected by Cincinnati Reds organization in 11th round of free-agent draft (June 5, 1989). ... Selected by Florida Marlins in first round (eighth pick overall) of expansion draft (November 17, 1992). ... Traded by Marlins with P Jose Martinez and P Andres Berumen to San Diego Padres for 3B Gary Sheffield and P Rich Rodriguez (June 24, 1993).
RECORDS: Shares N.L. single-season record for most saves—53 (1998).
HONORS: Named N.L. Fireman of the Year by THE SPORTING NEWS (1996 and 1998).
MISCELLANEOUS: Played infield only (1989-90). ... Holds San Diego Padres all-time record for most saves (186).

Year Team (League)	W	L	Pct.	ERA	G	GS	CG	ShO	Sv.	IP	H	R	ER	BB	SO
1991— Cedar Rapids (Midw.)	1	1	.500	1.87	27	0	0	0	12	33²/₃	22	8	7	13	52
—Chattanooga (Southern)	1	0	1.000	1.93	14	0	0	0	8	14	10	4	3	7	23
1992—Chattanooga (Southern)	3	0	1.000	1.52	6	6	0	0	0	29²/₃	22	6	5	11	31
—Nashville (A.A.)	4	6	.400	4.27	42	5	0	0	6	65¹/₃	57	32	31	32	63
1993—Florida (N.L.)■	2	2	.500	3.28	28	0	0	0	2	35²/₃	24	13	13	19	26
—San Diego (N.L.)■	2	4	.333	4.31	39	0	0	0	3	54¹/₃	56	30	26	20	53
1994—San Diego (N.L.)	4	4	.500	2.57	47	0	0	0	20	56	39	16	16	20	68
1995—San Diego (N.L.)	7	4	.636	3.88	55	0	0	0	31	53¹/₃	48	25	23	14	52
1996—San Diego (N.L.)	9	5	.643	2.25	70	0	0	0	42	88	50	23	22	31	111
1997—San Diego (N.L.)	6	4	.600	2.66	70	0	0	0	37	81¹/₃	59	25	24	24	111
1998—San Diego (N.L.)	4	2	.667	1.48	66	0	0	0	*53	73	41	12	12	21	86
Major league totals (6 years)	34	25	.576	2.77	375	0	0	0	188	441²/₃	317	144	136	149	507

DIVISION SERIES RECORD

Year Team (League)	W	L	Pct.	ERA	G	GS	CG	ShO	Sv.	IP	H	R	ER	BB	SO
1996—San Diego (N.L.)	0	1	.000	10.80	2	0	0	0	0	1²/₃	3	2	2	1	2
1998—San Diego (N.L.)	0	0	...	0.00	4	0	0	0	2	3	3	1	0	1	4
Div. series totals (2 years)	0	1	.000	3.86	6	0	0	0	2	4²/₃	6	3	2	2	6

CHAMPIONSHIP SERIES RECORD

Year Team (League)	W	L	Pct.	ERA	G	GS	CG	ShO	Sv.	IP	H	R	ER	BB	SO
1998—San Diego (N.L.)	1	0	1.000	2.08	3	0	0	0	1	4¹/₃	2	1	1	2	7

WORLD SERIES RECORD

Year Team (League)	W	L	Pct.	ERA	G	GS	CG	ShO	Sv.	IP	H	R	ER	BB	SO
1998—San Diego (N.L.)	0	1	.000	9.00	1	0	0	0	0	2	2	2	2	1	0

ALL-STAR GAME RECORD

Year League	W	L	Pct.	ERA	GS	CG	ShO	Sv.	IP	H	R	ER	BB	SO
1998—National	0	0	...	9.00	0	0	0	0	1	1	1	1	0	1

RECORD AS POSITION PLAYER

Year Team (League)	Pos.	G	AB	R	H	2B	3B	HR	RBI	Avg.	BB	SO	SB	PO	A	E	Avg.
1989—Billings (Pioneer)	SS	61	201	22	50	5	0	1	20	.249	19	40	1	*116	140	•25	.911
1990—Char., W.Va. (SAL)	SS-3B	103	278	41	59	10	1	2	23	.212	38	53	3	114	209	30	.915

HOILES, CHRIS   C/1B   ORIOLES

PERSONAL: Born March 20, 1965, in Bowling Green, Ohio. ... 6-0/215. ... Bats right, throws right. ... Full name: Christopher Allen Hoiles.
HIGH SCHOOL: Elmwood (Wayne, Ohio).
COLLEGE: Eastern Michigan.
TRANSACTIONS/CAREER NOTES: Selected by Detroit Tigers organization in 19th round of free-agent draft (June 2, 1986). ... Traded by Tigers organization with P Cesar Mejia and P Robinson Garces to Baltimore Orioles (September 9, 1988), completing deal in which Orioles traded OF Fred Lynn to Tigers for three players to be named later (August 31, 1988). ... On Rochester disabled list (June 18-July 7, 1989). ... On Baltimore disabled list (June 22-August 18, 1992); included rehabilitation assignment to Hagerstown (August 11-18). ... On disabled list (August 3-24, 1993 and July 16-31, 1995). ... On Baltimore disabled list (June 17-July 18, 1997); included rehabilitation assignment to Bowie (July 15-18).
RECORDS: Shares major league single-game record for most grand slams—2 (August 14, 1998).
STATISTICAL NOTES: Led Appalachian League first basemen with .996 fielding percentage, 515 putouts and 551 total chances in 1986. ... Led Appalachian League with 143 total bases in 1986. ... Led Eastern League with .500 slugging percentage in 1988. ... Tied for Eastern League lead in double plays by catcher with five in 1988. ... Led A.L. catchers with .998 fielding percentage in 1991, 1.000 in 1997 and .995 in 1998. ... Led A.L. catchers with 658 total chances in 1994. ... Career major league grand slams: 8.

Year Team (League)	Pos.	G	AB	R	H	2B	3B	HR	RBI	Avg.	BB	SO	SB	PO	A	E	Avg.
1986—Bristol (Appal.)	1B-C	•68	253	42	81	*19	2	13	*57	.320	30	20	10	†563	38	4	†.993
1987—Glens Falls (East.)	C-1B-3B	108	380	47	105	12	0	13	53	.245	35	37	1	406	88	11	.978
1988—Glens Falls (East.)	C-1B	103	360	67	102	21	3	•17	73	.283	50	56	4	438	57	7	.986
—Toledo (Int'l)	C	22	69	4	11	1	0	2	6	.159	2	12	1	71	2	1	.986
1989—Rochester (Int'l)■	C-1B	96	322	41	79	19	1	10	51	.245	31	58	1	431	33	7	.985
—Baltimore (A.L.)	C-DH	6	9	0	1	1	0	0	0	.111	1	3	0	11	0	0	1.000
1990—Rochester (Int'l)	C-1B	74	247	52	86	20	1	18	56	.348	44	48	4	268	13	5	.983
—Baltimore (A.L.)	C-DH-1B	23	63	7	12	3	0	1	6	.190	5	12	0	62	6	0	1.000
1991—Baltimore (A.L.)	C-1B	107	341	36	83	15	0	11	31	.243	29	61	0	443	44	1	†.998
1992—Baltimore (A.L.)	C-DH	96	310	49	85	10	1	20	40	.274	55	60	0	500	31	3	.994
—Hagerstown (East.)	C	7	24	7	11	1	0	1	5	.458	2	5	0	16	5	0	1.000

H

Year Team (League)	Pos.	G	AB	R	H	2B	3B	HR	RBI	Avg.	BB	SO	SB	PO	A	E	Avg.
						BATTING								FIELDING			
1993— Baltimore (A.L.).........	C-DH	126	419	80	130	28	0	29	82	.310	69	94	1	696	64	5	.993
1994— Baltimore (A.L.).........	C	99	332	45	82	10	0	19	53	.247	63	73	2	*615	36	7	.989
1995— Baltimore (A.L.).........	C-DH	114	352	53	88	15	1	19	58	.250	67	80	1	659	33	3	*.996
1996— Baltimore (A.L.).........	C-1B	127	407	64	105	13	0	25	73	.258	57	97	0	777	42	7	.992
1997— Baltimore (A.L.).........	C-DH-1-3	99	320	45	83	15	0	12	49	.259	51	86	1	622	31	0	†1.000
— Bowie (Eastern).........	C	3	7	1	1	1	0	0	2	.143	3	2	0	12	0	0	1.000
1998— Baltimore (A.L.).........	C-DH-1B	97	267	36	70	12	0	15	56	.262	38	50	0	529	39	3	†.995
Major league totals (10 years)		894	2820	415	739	122	2	151	449	.262	435	616	5	4914	326	29	.994

DIVISION SERIES RECORD

Year Team (League)	Pos.	G	AB	R	H	2B	3B	HR	RBI	Avg.	BB	SO	SB	PO	A	E	Avg.
						BATTING								FIELDING			
1996— Baltimore (A.L.).........	C-PH	4	7	1	1	0	0	0	0	.143	4	3	0	14	3	0	1.000
1997— Baltimore (A.L.).........	C	3	7	1	1	0	0	1	1	.143	2	1	0	23	0	0	1.000
Division series totals (2 years)		7	14	2	2	0	0	1	1	.143	6	4	0	37	3	0	1.000

CHAMPIONSHIP SERIES RECORD

Year Team (League)	Pos.	G	AB	R	H	2B	3B	HR	RBI	Avg.	BB	SO	SB	PO	A	E	Avg.
						BATTING								FIELDING			
1996— Baltimore (A.L.).........	C-PH	4	12	1	2	0	0	1	2	.167	1	3	0	23	2	0	1.000
1997— Baltimore (A.L.).........	C	4	14	1	2	0	0	0	0	.143	2	5	0	47	2	0	1.000
Championship series totals (2 years)		8	26	2	4	0	0	1	2	.154	3	8	0	70	4	0	1.000

HOLBERT, RAY   SS   ROYALS

PERSONAL: Born September 25, 1970, in Torrance, Calif. ... 6-0/175. ... Bats right, throws right. ... Full name: Ray Arthur Holbert III. ... Brother of Aaron Holbert, shortstop, Tampa Bay Devil Rays organization.

HIGH SCHOOL: David Starr Jordan (Long Beach, Calif.).

TRANSACTIONS/CAREER NOTES: Selected by San Diego Padres organization in third round of free-agent draft (June 1, 1988). ... On disabled list (July 7-28, 1992). ... On San Diego disabled list (July 30, 1995-remainder of season). ... Traded by Padres to Houston Astros for P Pedro A. Martinez (October 10, 1995). ... Granted free agency (October 15, 1996). ... Signed by Detroit Tigers organization (December 15, 1996). ... Granted free agency (October 15, 1997). ... Signed by Atlanta Braves organization (January 13, 1998). ... Released by Braves (May 13, 1998). ... Signed by Montreal Expos organization (May 18, 1998). ... Granted free agency (October 15, 1998). ... Signed by Kansas City Royals organization (December 17, 1998).

STATISTICAL NOTES: Led Arizona League shortstops with .927 fielding percentage and 132 assists in 1988. ... Led Midwest League shortstops with 642 total chances and 75 double plays in 1990. ... Led Texas League with nine sacrifice flies in 1993. ... Led Pacific Coast League with 10 sacrifice hits in 1994. ... Led Pacific Coast League shortstops with 34 errors in 1994. ... Led International League shortstops with 183 putouts in 1997. ... Career major league grand slams: 1.

Year Team (League)	Pos.	G	AB	R	H	2B	3B	HR	RBI	Avg.	BB	SO	SB	PO	A	E	Avg.
						BATTING								FIELDING			
1988— Ariz. Padres (Ariz.).....	SS-3B	49	170	38	44	1	0	3	19	.259	38	32	20	59	†137	15	†.929
1989— Waterloo (Midw.).........	SS-3B	117	354	37	55	7	1	0	20	.155	41	99	13	205	303	32	.941
1990— Waterloo (Midw.).........	SS	133	411	51	84	10	1	3	39	.204	51	117	16	*233	*378	31	.952
1991— High Desert (Calif.).....	SS	122	386	76	102	14	2	4	51	.264	56	83	19	196	331	*37	.934
1992— Wichita (Texas)	SS	95	304	46	86	7	3	2	23	.283	42	68	26	150	217	17	.956
1993— Wichita (Texas)	SS	112	388	56	101	13	5	5	48	.260	54	87	30	155	267	30	.934
1994— Las Vegas (PCL)	SS-OF	118	426	68	128	21	5	8	52	.300	50	99	27	157	333	†34	.935
— San Diego (N.L.).........	SS	5	5	1	1	0	0	0	0	.200	0	4	0	0	0	0	...
1995— San Diego (N.L.).....	SS-2B-OF	63	73	11	13	2	1	2	5	.178	8	20	4	27	58	5	.944
— Las Vegas (PCL)	2B	9	26	3	3	1	0	0	3	.115	5	10	1	9	26	1	.972
1996— Tucson (PCL)■.........	SS	28	97	13	24	3	2	0	10	.247	7	19	4	37	65	9	.919
1997— Toledo (Int'l)■...........	SS-3B	109	372	43	90	18	7	7	37	.242	32	109	16	†187	302	25	.951
1998— Richmond (Int'l)■.......	SS	1	1	1	0	0	0	0	0	.000	2	1	0	2	3	1	.833
— Atlanta (N.L.).........	SS	8	15	2	2	0	0	0	1	.133	2	4	0	6	14	1	.952
— Ottawa (Int'l)■.........	SS-3B-2B	86	266	38	82	17	4	2	25	.308	29	66	10	133	207	11	.969
— Montreal (N.L.).........	2B	2	5	0	0	0	0	0	0	.000	0	1	0	2	3	0	1.000
Major league totals (3 years)		78	98	14	16	2	1	2	6	.163	10	29	4	35	75	6	.948

HOLDRIDGE, DAVID   P   MARINERS

PERSONAL: Born February 5, 1969, in Wayne, Mich. ... 6-3/190. ... Throws right, bats right. ... Full name: David Allen Holdridge.

HIGH SCHOOL: Ocean View (Huntington Beach, Calif.).

TRANSACTIONS/CAREER NOTES: Selected by California Angels organization in supplemental round ("sandwich pick" between first and second round, 31st pick overall) of free-agent draft (June 2, 1987); pick received as compensation for Oakland Athletics signing Type A free-agent DH/OF Reggie Jackson. ... Traded by Angels organization to Philadelphia Phillies organization for C Lance Parrish (October 3, 1988). ... On Reading disabled list (May 27-June 25, 1991). ... Selected by Angels from Phillies organization in Rule 5 minor league draft (December 9, 1991). ... Granted free agency (October 3, 1996). ... Signed by Seattle Mariners organization (December 13, 1996).

STATISTICAL NOTES: Tied for Florida State League lead with 11 home runs allowed in 1989. ... Tied for Eastern League lead with 13 home runs allowed in 1990. ... Led California League with 21 wild pitches in 1992.

Year Team (League)	W	L	Pct.	ERA	G	GS	CG	ShO	Sv.	IP	H	R	ER	BB	SO
1988— Quad City (Midwest)	6	12	.333	3.87	28	28	0	0	0	153²/₃	151	92	66	66	110
1989— Clearwater (Fla. St.)■.......	7	10	.412	5.71	24	24	3	0	0	132¹/₃	147	*100	*84	77	77
1990— Reading (Eastern)	8	12	.400	4.58	24	24	1	0	0	127²/₃	114	74	65	*79	78
1991— Reading (Eastern)	0	2	.000	5.47	7	7	0	0	0	26¹/₃	26	24	16	34	19
— Clearwater (Fla. St.)	0	0	...	7.56	15	0	0	0	1	25	34	23	21	21	23
1992— Palm Springs (Calif.)■.......	12	12	.500	4.25	28	27	3	•2	0	159	169	99	75	87	135

H

Year	Team (League)	W	L	Pct.	ERA	G	GS	CG	ShO	Sv.	IP	H	R	ER	BB	SO
1993—	Midland (Texas)..................	8	10	.444	6.08	27	•27	1	1	0	151	*202	*117	*102	55	123
1994—	Midland (Texas)..................	7	4	.636	3.93	38	2	0	0	2	66 1/3	66	33	29	23	59
	—Vancouver (PCL).............	0	0	...	5.14	4	0	0	0	0	7	12	7	4	4	4
1995—	Vancouver (PCL)..............	0	2	.000	4.61	11	0	0	0	1	13 2/3	18	10	7	7	13
	—Lake Elsinore (Calif.)..........	3	0	1.000	0.98	12	0	0	0	0	18 1/3	13	3	2	5	24
	—Midland (Texas)................	1	0	1.000	1.78	14	0	0	0	1	25 1/3	20	8	5	8	23
1996—	Vancouver (PCL)..............	2	1	.667	4.63	29	0	0	0	1	35	39	19	18	23	26
	—Lake Elsinore (Calif.)..........	0	0	...	2.08	12	0	0	0	6	13	11	3	3	2	21
1997—	Memphis (Sou.)■..............	0	3	.000	3.34	30	0	0	0	17	35	31	14	13	17	37
	—Tacoma (PCL)	1	1	.500	2.96	15	0	0	0	1	24 1/3	21	9	8	13	24
1998—	Tacoma (PCL)	7	5	.583	3.31	42	0	0	0	7	70 2/3	55	28	26	34	73
	—Seattle (A.L.)	0	0	...	4.05	7	0	0	0	0	6 2/3	6	3	3	4	6
Major league totals (1 year)........		0	0	...	4.05	7	0	0	0	0	6 2/3	6	3	3	4	6

HOLLANDSWORTH, TODD   OF   DODGERS

PERSONAL: Born April 20, 1973, in Dayton, Ohio. ... 6-2/215. ... Bats left, throws left. ... Full name: Todd Mathew Hollandsworth.
HIGH SCHOOL: Newport (Bellevue, Wash.).
TRANSACTIONS/CAREER NOTES: Selected by Los Angeles Dodgers organization in third round of free-agent draft (June 3, 1991); pick received as part of compensation for Kansas City Royals signing Type B free-agent OF/DH Kirk Gibson. ... On Los Angeles disabled list (May 3-July 7 and August 9-September 12, 1995); included rehabilitation assignments to San Bernardino (June 6-7) and Albuquerque (June 27-July 7). ... On Los Angeles disabled list (August 2-16 and August 17-September 6, 1997); included rehabilitation assigment to San Bernardino (August 15-17). ... On disabled list (June 5, 1998-remainder of season).
HONORS: Named N.L. Rookie of the Year by Baseball Writers' Association of America (1996).

Year	Team (League)	Pos.	G	AB	R	H	2B	3B	HR	RBI	Avg.	BB	SO	SB	PO	A	E	Avg.
							BATTING									FIELDING		
1991—	Yakima (N'west)	OF	56	203	34	48	5	1	8	33	.236	27	57	11	106	1	7	.939
1992—	Bakersfield (Calif.)	OF	119	430	70	111	23	5	13	58	.258	50	113	27	230	8	6	.975
1993—	San Antonio (Tex.)	OF	126	474	57	119	24	9	17	63	.251	29	101	24	246	13	12	.956
1994—	Albuquerque (PCL)	OF	132	505	80	144	31	5	19	91	.285	46	96	15	237	5	13	.949
1995—	Los Angeles (N.L.)	OF	41	103	16	24	2	0	5	13	.233	10	29	2	60	1	4	.938
	—San Bern. (Calif.)........	OF	1	2	0	1	0	0	0	0	.500	0	1	0	0	0	0	...
	—Albuquerque (PCL).....	OF	10	38	9	9	2	0	2	4	.237	6	8	1	19	3	0	1.000
1996—	Los Angeles (N.L.)	OF	149	478	64	139	26	4	12	59	.291	41	93	21	217	7	5	.978
1997—	Los Angeles (N.L.)	OF	106	296	39	73	20	2	4	31	.247	17	60	5	185	2	3	.984
	—Albuquerque (PCL).....	OF	13	56	13	24	4	3	1	14	.429	4	4	2	32	1	0	1.000
	—San Bern. (Calif.)........	OF	2	8	1	2	0	1	0	2	.250	1	2	0	2	1	0	1.000
1998—	Los Angeles (N.L.)	OF	55	175	23	47	6	4	3	20	.269	9	42	4	87	1	4	.957
Major league totals (4 years)			351	1052	142	283	54	10	24	123	.269	77	224	32	549	11	16	.972

DIVISION SERIES RECORD
RECORDS: Shares N.L. career record for most doubles—3.

Year	Team (League)	Pos.	G	AB	R	H	2B	3B	HR	RBI	Avg.	BB	SO	SB	PO	A	E	Avg.
							BATTING									FIELDING		
1995—	Los Angeles (N.L.)	OF-PH	2	2	0	0	0	0	0	0	.000	0	0	0	0	0	0	...
1996—	Los Angeles (N.L.)	OF	3	12	1	4	3	0	0	1	.333	0	3	0	4	0	0	1.000
Division series totals (2 years)			5	14	1	4	3	0	0	1	.286	0	3	0	4	0	0	1.000

HOLLINS, DAMON   OF   REDS

PERSONAL: Born June 12, 1974, in Fairfield, Calif. ... 5-11/180. ... Bats right, throws left. ... Full name: Damon Jamall Hollins.
HIGH SCHOOL: Vallejo (Calif.).
TRANSACTIONS/CAREER NOTES: Selected by Atlanta Braves organization in fourth round of free-agent draft (June 1, 1992). ... On disabled list (May 28-September 3, 1996). ... Traded by Braves to Los Angeles Dodgers for 2B Jose Pimentall (September 9, 1998). ... Released by Dodgers (November 22, 1998). ... Signed by Cincinnati Reds organization (December 15, 1998).
STATISTICAL NOTES: Led Southern League outfielders with 356 total chances in 1995.

Year	Team (League)	Pos.	G	AB	R	H	2B	3B	HR	RBI	Avg.	BB	SO	SB	PO	A	E	Avg.
							BATTING									FIELDING		
1992—	GC Braves (GCL)	OF	49	179	35	41	12	1	1	15	.229	30	22	15	83	6	1	.989
1993—	Danville (Appal.).........	OF	62	240	37	77	15	2	7	51	.321	19	30	10	95	*11	6	.946
1994—	Durham (Carolina)......	OF	131	485	76	131	28	0	23	88	.270	45	115	12	279	11	*13	.957
1995—	Greenville (Southern) .	OF	129	466	64	115	26	2	18	77	.247	44	120	6	*330	18	8	.978
1996—	Richmond (Int'l)	OF	42	146	16	29	9	0	0	8	.199	16	37	2	116	6	3	.976
1997—	Richmond (Int'l)........	OF	134	498	73	132	31	3	20	63	.265	45	84	7	319	14	8	.977
1998—	Richmond (Int'l)........	OF	119	436	61	115	26	3	13	48	.264	45	85	10	233	8	5	.980
	—Atlanta (N.L.)............	OF	3	6	0	1	0	0	0	0	.167	0	1	0	2	0	0	1.000
	—Los Angeles (N.L.)■..	OF	5	9	1	2	0	0	0	2	.222	0	2	0	5	0	0	1.000
Major league totals (1 year)			8	15	1	3	0	0	0	2	.200	0	3	0	7	0	0	1.000

HOLLINS, DAVE   3B/1B   ANGELS

PERSONAL: Born May 25, 1966, in Orchard Park, NY. ... 6-1/232. ... Bats both, throws right. ... Full name: David Michael Hollins.
HIGH SCHOOL: Orchard Park (N.Y.).
COLLEGE: South Carolina.
TRANSACTIONS/CAREER NOTES: Selected by San Diego Padres organization in sixth round of free-agent draft (June 2, 1987). ... Selected by Philadelphia Phillies from Padres organization in Rule 5 major league draft (December 4, 1989). ... On Philadelphia disabled list (August 16-

H

September 6, 1991); included rehabilitation assignment to Scranton/Wilkes-Barre (September 2-5). ... On suspended list (September 29-October 3, 1992). ... On disabled list (June 11-28, 1993). ... On Philadelphia disabled list (May 23-July 23 and July 25, 1994-remainder of season); included rehabilitation assignment to Scranton/Wilkes-Barre (July 16-23). ... On Philadelphia disabled list (June 12-27, 1995). ... Traded by Phillies to Boston Red Sox for OF Mark Whiten (July 24, 1995). ... On Boston disabled list (August 9, 1995-remainder of season). ... Granted free agency (December 21, 1995). ... Signed by Minnesota Twins (December 23, 1995). ... Traded by Twins to Seattle Mariners for a player to be named later (August 29, 1996); Twins acquired 1B David Arias to complete deal (September 13, 1996). ... Granted free agency (October 31, 1996). ... Signed by Anaheim Angels (November 20, 1996). ... On disabled list (August 10, 1998-remainder of season).

STATISTICAL NOTES: Led Northwest League with seven intentional bases on balls received in 1987. ... Led Northwest League third basemen with 241 total chances in 1987. ... Led Texas League with 10 sacrifice flies in 1989. ... Led N.L. in being hit by pitch with 19 in 1992. ... Led A.L. third basemen with 29 errors in 1997. ... Career major league grand slams: 3.

Year — Team (League)	Pos.	G	AB	R	H	2B	3B	HR	RBI	Avg.	BB	SO	SB	PO	A	E	Avg.
1987— Spokane (N'west)	3B	75	278	52	86	14	4	2	44	.309	53	36	20	*59	*167	15	*.938
1988— Riverside (Calif.)	3B-1B-SS	139	516	90	157	32	1	9	92	.304	82	67	13	102	248	29	.923
1989— Wichita (Texas)	3B	131	459	69	126	29	4	9	79	.275	63	88	8	77	209	25	.920
1990— Philadelphia (N.L.)■ ..	3B-1B	72	114	14	21	0	0	5	15	.184	10	28	0	27	37	4	.941
1991— Philadelphia (N.L.)	3B-1B	56	151	18	45	10	2	6	21	.298	17	26	1	67	62	8	.942
— Scran./W.B. (Int'l)	3B-1B	72	229	37	61	11	6	8	35	.266	43	43	4	67	105	10	.945
1992— Philadelphia (N.L.)	3B-1B	156	586	104	158	28	4	27	93	.270	76	110	9	120	253	18	.954
1993— Philadelphia (N.L.)	3B	143	543	104	148	30	4	18	93	.273	85	109	2	73	215	27	.914
1994— Philadelphia (N.L.)	3B-OF	44	162	28	36	7	1	4	26	.222	23	32	1	39	48	11	.888
— Scran./W.B. (Int'l)	OF	6	19	6	4	0	0	1	3	.211	5	4	0	12	1	2	.867
1995— Philadelphia (N.L.)	1B	65	205	46	47	12	2	7	25	.229	53	38	1	532	30	7	.988
— Boston (A.L.)	DH-OF	5	13	2	2	0	0	0	1	.154	4	7	0	3	0	0	1.000
1996— Minnesota (A.L.)■	3B-DH-SS	121	422	71	102	26	0	13	53	.242	71	102	6	81	206	15	.950
— Seattle (A.L.)■	3B-1B	28	94	17	33	3	0	3	25	.351	13	15	0	21	53	3	.961
1997— Anaheim (A.L.)	3B-1B	149	572	101	165	29	2	16	85	.288	62	124	16	208	249	†29	.940
1998— Anaheim (A.L.)	3B-1B-DH	101	363	60	88	16	2	11	39	.242	44	69	11	107	150	17	.938
American League totals (4 years)		404	1464	251	390	74	4	43	203	.266	194	317	33	420	658	64	.944
National League totals (6 years)		536	1761	314	455	87	13	67	273	.258	264	343	14	858	645	75	.952
Major league totals (9 years)		940	3225	565	845	161	17	110	476	.262	458	660	47	1278	1303	139	.949

CHAMPIONSHIP SERIES RECORD

Year — Team (League)	Pos.	G	AB	R	H	2B	3B	HR	RBI	Avg.	BB	SO	SB	PO	A	E	Avg.
1993— Philadelphia (N.L.)	3B	6	20	2	4	1	0	2	4	.200	5	4	1	5	4	0	1.000

WORLD SERIES RECORD

Year — Team (League)	Pos.	G	AB	R	H	2B	3B	HR	RBI	Avg.	BB	SO	SB	PO	A	E	Avg.
1993— Philadelphia (N.L.)	3B	6	23	5	6	1	0	0	2	.261	6	5	0	9	9	0	1.000

ALL-STAR GAME RECORD

Year — League	Pos.	AB	R	H	2B	3B	HR	RBI	Avg.	BB	SO	SB	PO	A	E	Avg.
1993— National	3B	1	0	1	1	0	0	0	1.000	0	0	0	1	0	0	1.000

HOLMES, DARREN   P   YANKEES

PERSONAL: Born April 25, 1966, in Asheville, N.C. ... 6-0/202. ... Throws right, bats right. ... Full name: Darren Lee Holmes.

HIGH SCHOOL: T.C. Roberson (Asheville, N.C.).

TRANSACTIONS/CAREER NOTES: Selected by Los Angeles Dodgers organization in 16th round of free-agent draft (June 4, 1984). ... On disabled list (June 5, 1986-remainder of season). ... Loaned by Dodgers organization to San Luis Potosi of the Mexican League (1988). ... Traded by Dodgers to Milwaukee Brewers for C Bert Heffernan (December 20, 1990). ... On Milwaukee disabled list (July 3-18, 1991); included rehabilitation assignment to Beloit (July 13-18). ... Selected by Colorado Rockies in first round (fifth pick overall) of expansion draft (November 17, 1992). ... On Colorado disabled list (May 30-June 24 and July 21-August 11, 1994); included rehabilitation assignments to Asheville (June 14-19) and Colorado Springs (June 20). ... On disabled list (April 30-May 15, 1997). ... Granted free agency (October 27, 1997). ... Signed by New York Yankees (December 22, 1997). ... On New York disabled list (July 30-September 4, 1998); included rehabilitation assignment to Tampa (August 31-September 4).

Year — Team (League)	W	L	Pct.	ERA	G	GS	CG	ShO	Sv.	IP	H	R	ER	BB	SO
1984— Great Falls (Pio.)	2	5	.286	6.65	18	6	1	0	0	44 2/3	53	41	33	30	29
1985— Vero Beach (FSL)	4	3	.571	3.11	33	0	0	0	2	63 2/3	57	31	22	35	46
1986— Vero Beach (FSL)	3	6	.333	2.92	11	10	0	0	0	64 2/3	55	30	21	39	59
1987— Vero Beach (FSL)	6	4	.600	4.52	19	19	1	0	0	99 2/3	111	60	50	53	46
1988— San Luis Potosi (Mex.)■	9	9	.500	4.64	23	23	7	1	0	139 2/3	151	88	72	92	110
— Albuquerque (PCL)■	0	1	.000	5.06	2	1	0	0	0	5 1/3	6	3	3	1	1
1989— San Antonio (Tex.)	5	8	.385	3.83	17	16	3	2	1	110 1/3	102	59	47	44	81
— Albuquerque (PCL)	1	4	.200	7.45	9	8	0	0	0	38 2/3	50	32	32	18	31
1990— Albuquerque (PCL)	12	2	*.857	3.11	56	0	0	0	13	92 2/3	78	34	32	39	99
— Los Angeles (N.L.)	0	1	.000	5.19	14	0	0	0	0	17 1/3	15	10	10	11	19
1991— Denver (Am. Assoc.)■	0	0	...	9.00	1	0	0	0	0	1	1	1	1	2	2
— Milwaukee (A.L.)	1	4	.200	4.72	40	0	0	0	3	76 1/3	90	43	40	27	59
— Beloit (Midwest)	0	0	...	0.00	2	0	0	0	2	2	0	0	0	0	3
1992— Denver (Am. Assoc.)	0	0	...	1.38	12	0	0	0	7	13	7	2	2	1	12
— Milwaukee (A.L.)	4	4	.500	2.55	41	0	0	0	6	42 1/3	35	12	12	11	31
1993— Colorado (N.L.)■	3	3	.500	4.05	62	0	0	0	25	66 2/3	56	31	30	20	60
— Colo. Springs (PCL)	1	0	1.000	0.00	3	2	0	0	0	8 2/3	1	0	0	1	9
1994— Colorado (N.L.)	0	3	.000	6.35	29	0	0	0	3	28 1/3	35	25	20	24	33
— Colo. Springs (PCL)	0	1	.000	8.22	4	2	0	0	0	7 2/3	11	7	7	3	12
— Asheville (S. Atl.)	0	0	...	0.00	2	1	0	0	0	3	1	0	0	1	4
1995— Colorado (N.L.)	6	1	.857	3.24	68	0	0	0	14	66 2/3	59	26	24	28	61
1996— Colorado (N.L.)	5	4	.556	3.97	62	0	0	0	1	77	78	41	34	28	73

H

Year Team (League)	W	L	Pct.	ERA	G	GS	CG	ShO	Sv.	IP	H	R	ER	BB	SO
1997— Colorado (N.L.)	9	2	.818	5.34	42	6	0	0	3	89 1/3	113	58	53	36	70
1998— New York (A.L.)■.............	0	3	.000	3.33	34	0	0	0	2	51 1/3	53	19	19	14	31
— Tampa (Fla. St.)	0	1	.000	4.50	2	1	0	0	0	2	4	2	1	0	6
A.L. totals (3 years)	5	11	.313	3.76	115	0	0	0	11	170	178	74	71	52	121
N.L. totals (6 years)	23	14	.622	4.46	277	6	0	0	46	345 1/3	356	191	171	147	316
Major league totals (9 years)......	28	25	.528	4.23	392	6	0	0	57	515 1/3	534	265	242	199	437

DIVISION SERIES RECORD

Year Team (League)	W	L	Pct.	ERA	G	GS	CG	ShO	Sv.	IP	H	R	ER	BB	SO
1995— Colorado (N.L.)	1	0	1.000	0.00	3	0	0	0	0	1 2/3	6	2	0	9	2
1998— New York (A.L.)							Did not play.								

CHAMPIONSHIP SERIES RECORD

Year Team (League)	W	L	Pct.	ERA	G	GS	CG	ShO	Sv.	IP	H	R	ER	BB	SO
1998— New York (A.L.)							Did not play.								

WORLD SERIES RECORD

NOTES: Member of World Series championship team (1998).

Year Team (League)	W	L	Pct.	ERA	G	GS	CG	ShO	Sv.	IP	H	R	ER	BB	SO
1998— New York (A.L.)							Did not play.								

HOLT, CHRIS   P   ASTROS

PERSONAL: Born September 18, 1971, in Dallas. ... 6-4/205. ... Throws right, bats right. ... Full name: Christopher Michael Holt.
HIGH SCHOOL: Skyline (Dallas).
JUNIOR COLLEGE: Navarro College (Texas).
TRANSACTIONS/CAREER NOTES: Selected by Houston Astros organization in third round of free-agent draft (June 1, 1992). ... On Houston disabled list (March 30, 1998-entire season); included rehabilitation assignment to Kissimmee (April 25-26).

Year Team (League)	W	L	Pct.	ERA	G	GS	CG	ShO	Sv.	IP	H	R	ER	BB	SO
1992— Auburn (N.Y.-Penn)	2	5	.286	4.45	14	14	0	0	0	83	75	48	41	24	81
1993— Quad City (Midwest)	11	10	.524	2.27	26	26	*10	•3	0	*186 1/3	162	70	47	54	176
1994— Jackson (Texas)	10	9	.526	3.45	26	25	5	•2	0	167	169	78	64	22	111
1995— Jackson (Texas)	2	2	.500	1.67	5	5	1	1	0	32 1/3	27	8	6	5	24
— Tucson (PCL)	5	8	.385	4.10	20	19	0	0	0	118 2/3	155	65	54	32	69
1996— Tucson (PCL)	9	6	.600	3.62	28	27	4	1	0	*186 1/3	208	87	75	38	137
— Houston (N.L.)	0	1	.000	5.79	4	0	0	0	0	4 2/3	5	3	3	3	0
1997— Houston (N.L.)	8	12	.400	3.52	33	32	0	0	0	209 2/3	211	98	82	61	95
1998— Kissimmee (Florida State) ..	0	1	.000	9.00	1	1	0	0	0	4	6	4	4	4	1
Major league totals (2 years)......	8	13	.381	3.57	37	32	0	0	0	214 1/3	216	101	85	64	95

HOLTZ, MIKE   P   ANGELS

PERSONAL: Born October 10, 1972, in Arlington, Va. ... 5-9/180. ... Throws left, bats left. ... Full name: Michael James Holtz.
HIGH SCHOOL: Central Cambria (Ebensburg, Pa.).
COLLEGE: Clemson.
TRANSACTIONS/CAREER NOTES: Selected by California Angels organization in 17th round of free-agent draft (June 2, 1994). ... Angels franchise renamed Anaheim Angels for 1997 season. ... On suspended list (June 18-20, 1998).

Year Team (League)	W	L	Pct.	ERA	G	GS	CG	ShO	Sv.	IP	H	R	ER	BB	SO
1994— Boise (Northwest)	0	0	...	0.51	22	0	0	0	11	35	22	4	2	11	59
1995— Lake Elsinore (Calif.)	4	4	.500	2.29	*56	0	0	0	3	82 2/3	70	26	21	23	101
1996— Midland (Texas)...............	1	2	.333	4.17	33	0	0	0	2	41	52	34	19	9	41
— California (A.L.)	3	3	.500	2.45	30	0	0	0	0	29 1/3	21	11	8	19	31
1997— Anaheim (A.L.)	3	4	.429	3.32	66	0	0	0	2	43 1/3	38	21	16	15	40
1998— Anaheim (A.L.)	2	2	.500	4.75	53	0	0	0	1	30 1/3	38	16	16	15	29
— Vancouver (PCL)	0	0	...	1.74	10	0	0	0	2	10 1/3	10	4	2	6	18
Major league totals (3 years)......	8	9	.471	3.50	149	0	0	0	3	103	97	48	40	49	100

HOLZEMER, MARK   P   ATHLETICS

PERSONAL: Born August 20, 1969, in Littleton, Colo. ... 6-0/165. ... Throws left, bats left. ... Full name: Mark Harold Holzemer. ... Name pronounced HOLE-zeh-mer.
HIGH SCHOOL: J.K. Mullen (Denver).
JUNIOR COLLEGE: Seminole (Okla.) Junior College.
TRANSACTIONS/CAREER NOTES: Selected by California Angels organization in fourth round of free-agent draft (June 2, 1987). ... On Midland disabled list (July 2-September 18, 1990; April 12-May 25 and June 7-26, 1991). ... On California disabled list (June 10-September 1, 1996); included rehabilitation assignment to Lake Elsinore (August 16-September 1). ... Granted free agency (October 15, 1996). ... Signed by Seattle Mariners organization (December 11, 1996). ... Granted free agency (October 16, 1997). ... Signed by Oakland Athletics organization (December 9, 1997).
STATISTICAL NOTES: Led Pacific Coast League with 15 wild pitches in 1994.

Year Team (League)	W	L	Pct.	ERA	G	GS	CG	ShO	Sv.	IP	H	R	ER	BB	SO
1988— Bend (Northwest)...............	4	6	.400	5.24	13	13	1	1	0	68 2/3	59	51	40	47	72
1989— Quad City (Midwest)	12	7	.632	3.36	25	25	3	1	0	139 1/3	122	68	52	64	131
1990— Midland (Texas)...............	1	7	.125	5.26	15	15	1	0	0	77	92	55	45	41	54
1991— Midland (Texas).................	0	0	...	1.42	2	2	0	0	0	6 1/3	3	2	1	5	7
— Palm Springs (Calif.)	0	4	.000	2.86	6	6	0	0	0	22	15	14	7	16	19
1992— Palm Springs (Calif.)	3	2	.600	3.00	5	5	2	0	0	30	23	10	10	13	32
— Midland (Texas).................	2	5	.286	3.83	7	7	2	0	0	44 2/3	45	22	19	13	36
— Edmonton (PCL)	5	7	.417	6.67	17	16	4	0	0	89	114	69	66	55	49

H

Year Team (League)	W	L	Pct.	ERA	G	GS	CG	ShO	Sv.	IP	H	R	ER	BB	SO
1993—Vancouver (PCL)	9	6	.600	4.82	24	23	2	0	0	145 2/3	158	94	78	70	80
—California (A.L.)	0	3	.000	8.87	5	4	0	0	0	23 1/3	34	24	23	13	10
1994—Vancouver (PCL)	5	10	.333	6.60	29	17	0	0	0	117 1/3	144	93	86	58	77
1995—Vancouver (PCL)	3	2	.600	2.47	28	4	0	0	2	54 2/3	45	18	15	24	35
—California (A.L.)	0	1	.000	5.40	12	0	0	0	0	8 1/3	11	6	5	7	5
1996—California (A.L.)	1	0	1.000	8.76	25	0	0	0	0	24 2/3	35	28	24	8	20
—Lake Elsinore (Calif.)	0	1	.000	2.38	9	3	0	0	0	11 1/3	10	3	3	4	10
1997—Tacoma (PCL)■	1	0	1.000	2.20	37	0	0	0	13	41	32	10	10	10	38
—Seattle (A.L.)	0	0	...	6.00	14	0	0	0	1	9	9	6	6	8	7
1998—Edmonton (PCL)■	1	1	.500	3.23	30	0	0	0	6	39	41	15	14	11	27
—Oakland (A.L.)	1	0	1.000	5.59	13	0	0	0	0	9 2/3	13	6	6	3	3
Major league totals (5 years)	2	4	.333	7.68	69	4	0	0	1	75	102	70	64	39	45

HOUSTON, TYLER   C   CUBS

PERSONAL: Born January 17, 1971, in Long Beach, Calif. ... 6-1/210. ... Bats left, throws right. ... Full name: Tyler Sam Houston.
HIGH SCHOOL: Valley (Las Vegas).
TRANSACTIONS/CAREER NOTES: Selected by Atlanta Braves organization in first round (second pick overall) of free-agent draft (June 5, 1989). ... On Greenville disabled list (June 25-July 5, 1993). ... Traded by Braves to Chicago Cubs for P Ismael Villegas (June 27, 1996). ... On disabled list (May 3-19, 1997); included rehabilitation assignment to Iowa (May 14-19, 1997). ... On Chicago disabled list (June 11-July 11, 1997); included rehabilitation assignment to Rockford (July 9-11). ... On suspended list (September 16, 1997). ... On disabled list (May 26-June 24, 1998).
STATISTICAL NOTES: Led Pioneer League with 14 passed balls in 1989.

Year Team (League)	Pos.	G	AB	R	H	2B	3B	HR	RBI	Avg.	BB	SO	SB	PO	A	E	Avg.
1989—Idaho Falls (Pio.)	C	50	176	30	43	11	0	4	24	.244	25	41	4	148	15	5	.970
1990—Sumter (S. Atl.)	C	117	442	58	93	14	3	13	56	.210	49	101	6	498	55	*18	.968
1991—Macon (S. Atl.)	C	107	351	41	81	16	3	8	47	.231	39	70	10	591	75	10	.985
1992—Durham (Carolina)	C-3B-1B	117	402	39	91	17	1	7	38	.226	20	89	5	493	65	15	.974
1993—Greenville (Southern)	C-OF	84	262	27	73	14	1	5	33	.279	13	50	5	410	34	9	.980
—Richmond (Int'l)	C	13	36	4	5	1	1	1	3	.139	1	8	0	69	2	3	.959
1994—Richmond (Int'l)	1B-C-OF	97	312	33	76	15	2	4	33	.244	16	44	3	619	54	7	.990
1995—Richmond (Int'l)	1-C-O-3	103	349	41	89	10	3	12	42	.255	18	62	3	579	69	11	.983
1996—Atlanta (N.L.)	1B-OF-3B	33	27	3	6	2	1	1	8	.222	1	9	0	16	1	0	1.000
—Chicago (N.L.)■	C-3-2-1	46	115	18	39	7	0	2	19	.339	8	18	3	139	25	3	.982
1997—Chicago (N.L.)	C-3-1-2-S	72	196	15	51	10	0	2	28	.260	9	35	1	280	37	5	.984
—Iowa (Am. Assoc.)	3B-C	6	23	0	5	2	0	0	4	.217	0	2	0	6	9	2	.882
—Rockford (Midwest)	C-3B	2	6	1	3	1	0	0	1	.500	0	0	0	5	0	0	1.000
1998—Chicago (N.L.)	C-3B-1B	95	255	26	65	7	1	9	33	.255	13	53	2	451	36	5	.990
Major league totals (3 years)		246	593	62	161	26	2	14	88	.272	31	115	6	886	99	13	.987

DIVISION SERIES RECORD

Year Team (League)	Pos.	G	AB	R	H	2B	3B	HR	RBI	Avg.	BB	SO	SB	PO	A	E	Avg.
1998—Chicago (N.L.)	C	3	6	1	1	0	0	1	1	.167	0	3	0	13	0	0	1.000

HOWARD, DAVID   IF/OF   CARDINALS

PERSONAL: Born February 26, 1967, in Sarasota, Fla. ... 6-0/175. ... Bats both, throws right. ... Full name: David Wayne Howard. ... Son of Bruce Howard, pitcher with Chicago White Sox (1963-67), Baltimore Orioles (1968) and Washington Senators (1968).
HIGH SCHOOL: Riverview (Sarasota, Fla.).
JUNIOR COLLEGE: Manatee Community College (Fla.).
TRANSACTIONS/CAREER NOTES: Selected by Kansas City Royals organization in 32nd round of free-agent draft (June 2, 1986). ... On disabled list (May 12-31 and July 23-August 9, 1989). ... On Kansas City disabled list (April 22-July 6, 1992); included rehabilitation assignments to Baseball City (June 16-20) and Omaha (June 20-July 5). ... On Kansas City disabled list (April 19-May 17, 1993); included rehabilitation assignment to Omaha (May 10-17). ... On Kansas City disabled list (June 7-August 10, 1993); included rehabilitation assignments to Omaha (July 15-23 and July 31-August 10). ... On disabled list (May 27-June 17, 1995; and August 14-September 1, 1997). ... On disabled list (August 14-September 1, 1997). ... Granted free agency (October 28, 1997). ... Signed by St. Louis Cardinals (December 4, 1997). ... On disabled list (May 24-June 8 and July 3, 1998-remainder of season).
STATISTICAL NOTES: Led A.L. shortstops with .982 fielding percentage in 1996.

Year Team (League)	Pos.	G	AB	R	H	2B	3B	HR	RBI	Avg.	BB	SO	SB	PO	A	E	Avg.
1987—Fort Myers (FSL)	SS	89	289	26	56	9	4	1	19	.194	30	68	11	123	273	28	.934
1988—Appleton (Midwest)	SS	110	368	48	82	9	4	1	22	.223	25	80	10	151	275	43	.908
1989—Baseball City (FSL)	S-O-3-2	83	267	36	63	7	3	3	30	.236	23	44	12	141	225	18	.953
1990—Memphis (Sou.)	SS-2B	116	384	41	96	10	4	5	44	.250	39	73	15	194	321	32	.941
1991—Omaha (A.A.)	SS-2B	14	41	2	5	0	0	0	2	.122	7	11	1	30	43	3	.961
—Kansas City (A.L.)	S-2-3-O-DH	94	236	20	51	7	0	1	17	.216	16	45	3	129	248	12	.969
1992—Kansas City (A.L.)	SS-OF	74	219	19	49	6	2	1	18	.224	15	43	3	124	204	8	.976
—Baseball City (FSL)	SS	3	9	3	4	1	0	0	0	.444	2	0	0	3	7	1	.909
—Omaha (A.A.)	SS	19	68	5	8	1	0	0	5	.118	3	8	1	25	52	8	.906
1993—Kansas City (A.L.)	2-S-3-O	15	24	5	8	0	1	0	2	.333	2	5	1	17	28	3	.938
—Omaha (A.A.)	SS	47	157	15	40	8	2	0	18	.255	7	20	3	76	137	8	.964
1994—Kansas City (A.L.)	3-S-2-DH-P-O	46	83	19	19	4	0	1	13	.229	11	23	3	27	79	1	.991
1995—Kansas City (A.L.)	2-S-O-DH-1	96	255	23	62	13	4	0	19	.243	24	41	6	167	195	29	.926
1996—Kansas City (A.L.)	S-2-1-DH-O	143	420	51	92	14	5	4	48	.219	40	74	5	210	411	11	†.983
1997—Kansas City (A.L.)	2-O-S-3-DH	80	162	24	39	8	1	1	13	.241	10	31	2	96	109	7	.967
1998—St. Louis (N.L.)■	2-S-3-O	46	102	15	25	1	1	2	12	.245	12	22	0	53	82	2	.985
American League totals (7 years)		547	1399	151	320	52	13	8	130	.229	118	262	23	770	1274	71	.966
National League totals (1 year)		46	102	15	25	1	1	2	12	.245	12	22	0	53	82	2	.985
Major league totals (8 years)		593	1501	166	345	53	14	10	142	.230	130	284	23	823	1356	73	.968

H

PERSONAL: Born December 11, 1964, in Middletown, Ohio. ... 6-2/205. ... Bats both, throws right. ... Full name: Thomas Sylvester Howard.
HIGH SCHOOL: Valley View (Germantown, Ohio).
COLLEGE: Ball State.
TRANSACTIONS/CAREER NOTES: Selected by San Diego Padres organization in first round (11th pick overall) of free-agent draft (June 2, 1986). ... On disabled list (June 5-July 17, 1989). ... Traded by Padres to Cleveland Indians for SS Jason Hardtke and a player to be named later (April 14, 1992); Padres acquired C Christopher Maffett to complete deal (July 10, 1992). ... Traded by Indians to Cincinnati Reds (August 20, 1993), completing deal in which Reds traded 1B Randy Milligan to Indians for a player to be named later (August 17, 1993). ... On Cincinnati disabled list (March 23-April 20, 1996); included rehabilitation assignments to Chattanooga (April 11-19) and Indianapolis (April 19-20). ... Released by Reds (November 18, 1996). ... Signed by Houston Astros (December 4, 1996). ... Granted free agency (October 28, 1997). ... Signed by Los Angeles Dodgers organization (January 7, 1998). ... Released by Dodgers (June 29, 1998).
HONORS: Named outfielder on THE SPORTING NEWS college All-America team (1986).

Year	Team (League)	Pos.	G	AB	R	H	2B	3B	HR	RBI	Avg.	BB	SO	SB	PO	A	E	Avg.
1986—	Spokane (N'west)	OF	13	55	16	23	3	3	2	17	.418	3	9	2	24	3	0	1.000
—	Reno (California)	OF	61	223	35	57	7	3	10	39	.256	34	49	10	104	5	6	.948
1987—	Wichita (Texas)	OF	113	401	72	133	27	4	14	60	.332	36	72	26	226	6	6	.975
1988—	Wichita (Texas)	OF	29	103	15	31	9	2	0	16	.301	13	14	6	51	2	2	.964
—	Las Vegas (PCL)	OF	44	167	29	42	9	1	0	15	.251	12	31	3	74	3	2	.975
1989—	Las Vegas (PCL)	OF	80	303	45	91	18	3	3	31	.300	30	56	22	178	7	2	.989
1990—	Las Vegas (PCL)	OF	89	341	58	112	26	8	5	51	.328	44	63	27	159	6	2	.988
—	San Diego (N.L.)	OF	20	44	4	12	2	0	0	0	.273	0	11	0	19	0	1	.950
1991—	San Diego (N.L.)	OF	106	281	30	70	12	3	4	22	.249	24	57	10	182	4	1	.995
—	Las Vegas (PCL)	OF	25	94	22	29	3	1	2	16	.309	10	16	11	54	2	2	.966
1992—	San Diego (N.L.)	PH	5	3	1	1	0	0	0	0	.333	0	0	0	...	...	...	...
—	Cleveland (A.L.)■	OF-DH	117	358	36	99	15	2	2	32	.277	17	60	15	185	5	2	.990
1993—	Cleveland (A.L.)■	OF-DH	74	178	26	42	7	0	3	23	.236	12	42	5	81	3	2	.977
—	Cincinnati (N.L.)■	OF	38	141	22	39	8	3	4	13	.277	12	21	5	73	4	1	.987
1994—	Cincinnati (N.L.)	OF	83	178	24	47	11	0	5	24	.264	10	30	4	80	2	3	.965
1995—	Cincinnati (N.L.)	OF	113	281	42	85	15	2	3	26	.302	20	37	17	127	2	2	.985
1996—	Cincinnati (N.L.)	OF	121	360	50	88	19	10	6	42	.244	17	51	6	160	7	3	.982
—	Chattanooga (Sou.)	OF	8	30	4	10	1	0	1	2	.333	2	7	1	8	0	0	1.000
—	Indianapolis (A.A.)	OF	1	6	2	2	0	0	1	2	.333	0	0	0	3	0	0	1.000
1997—	Houston (N.L.)■	OF	107	255	24	63	16	1	3	22	.247	26	48	1	107	5	0	1.000
1998—	Los Angeles (N.L.)■	OF-DH	47	76	9	14	4	0	2	4	.184	3	15	1	33	2	0	1.000
American League totals (2 years)			191	536	62	141	22	2	5	55	.263	29	102	20	266	8	4	.986
National League totals (9 years)			640	1619	206	419	87	19	27	153	.259	112	270	44	781	26	11	.987
Major league totals (9 years)			831	2155	268	560	109	21	32	208	.260	141	372	64	1047	34	15	.986

DIVISION SERIES RECORD

Year	Team (League)	Pos.	G	AB	R	H	2B	3B	HR	RBI	Avg.	BB	SO	SB	PO	A	E	Avg.
1995—	Cincinnati (N.L.)	OF	3	10	0	1	1	0	0	0	.100	0	2	0	5	0	0	1.000
1997—	Houston (N.L.)	PH	2	1	0	0	0	0	0	0	.000	1	1	0	0	0	0	...
Division series totals (2 years)			5	11	0	1	1	0	0	0	.091	1	3	0	5	0	0	1.000

CHAMPIONSHIP SERIES RECORD

Year	Team (League)	Pos.	G	AB	R	H	2B	3B	HR	RBI	Avg.	BB	SO	SB	PO	A	E	Avg.
1995—	Cincinnati (N.L.)	PH-OF	4	8	0	2	1	0	0	1	.250	2	0	0	2	0	0	1.000

PERSONAL: Born August 18, 1961, in Tucson, Ariz. ... 6-0/190. ... Bats left, throws right. ... Full name: Jack Robert Howell.
HIGH SCHOOL: Palo Verde (Tucson, Ariz.).
JUNIOR COLLEGE: Pima Community College (Ariz.).
COLLEGE: Arizona.
TRANSACTIONS/CAREER NOTES: Signed as non-drafted free agent by California Angels organization (August 6, 1983). ... On Edmonton disabled list (June 21-July 7, 1985). ... On California disabled list (May 23-June 9, 1990 and May 5-28, 1991). ... Traded by Angels to San Diego Padres for OF Shawn Abner (July 30, 1991). ... Granted free agency (October 28, 1991). ... Signed by Yakult Swallows of Japan Central League (December 8, 1991). ... Signed by Yomiuri Giants of Japan Central League (December 7, 1994). ... Signed by Angels organization (December 5, 1995). ... On California disabled list (June 16-July 19, 1996); included rehabilitation assignment to Lake Elsinore (July 13-19). ... Granted free agency (November 18, 1996). ... Re-signed by Angels organization (December 20, 1996). ... Angels franchise renamed Anaheim Angels for 1997 season. ... Granted free agency (October 30, 1997). ... Signed by Houston Astros (December 9, 1997). ... On disabled list (May 20, 1998-remainder of season).
STATISTICAL NOTES: Led California League third basemen with .943 fielding percentage, 259 assists, 368 total chances and 23 double plays in 1984. ... Led A.L. third basemen with .974 fielding percentage, 322 assists and 428 total chances in 1989. ... Career major league grand slams: 1.

Year	Team (League)	Pos.	G	AB	R	H	2B	3B	HR	RBI	Avg.	BB	SO	SB	PO	A	E	Avg.
1983—	Salem (Northwest)	3B-2B	21	76	23	30	2	5	3	12	.395	17	11	26	19	32	11	.823
1984—	Redwood (Calif.)	3B-1B	135	451	62	111	21	5	5	64	.246	44	95	12	96	†260	21	†.944
1985—	Edmonton (PCL)	3B-SS	79	284	55	106	22	3	13	48	.373	52	57	3	67	130	12	.943
—	California (A.L.)	3B	43	137	19	27	4	0	5	18	.197	16	33	1	33	75	8	.931
1986—	Edmonton (PCL)	3B	44	156	39	56	17	3	3	28	.359	38	29	1	28	84	8	.933
—	California (A.L.)	3B-DH-OF	63	151	26	41	14	2	4	21	.272	19	28	2	38	57	2	.979
1987—	California (A.L.)	OF-3B-2B	138	449	64	110	18	5	23	64	.245	57	118	4	185	95	7	.976
1988—	California (A.L.)	3B-OF	154	500	59	127	32	2	16	63	.254	46	130	2	97	249	17	.953

H

Year	Team (League)	Pos.	G	AB	R	H	2B	3B	HR	RBI	Avg.	BB	SO	SB	PO	A	E	Avg.
1989—California (A.L.)..........		3B-OF	144	474	56	108	19	4	20	52	.228	52	125	0	97	†322	11	†.974
1990—California (A.L.)..........		3B-SS-1B	105	316	35	72	19	1	8	33	.228	46	61	3	76	196	18	.938
—Edmonton (PCL)		3B-1B	20	75	14	25	7	1	2	15	.333	7	13	3	22	33	1	.982
1991—California (A.L.)		2-0-1-3-DH	32	81	11	17	2	0	2	7	.210	11	11	1	53	55	2	.982
—San Diego (N.L.)■...		3B	58	160	24	33	3	1	6	16	.206	18	33	0	33	98	2	.985
1992—Yakult (Jp. Cen.)■...		3B	113	387	67	128	21	1	*38	87	*.331	41	86	3	...	...	...	...
1993—Yakult (Jp. Cen.)		...	121	396	72	117	15	1	28	88	.295	86	83	3	...	...	...	...
1994—Yakult (Jp. Cen.).........		IF	105	363	54	91	14	0	20	56	.251	62	74	4	...	...	...	...
1995—Yomiuri (Jp. Cen.)■...		IF	66	219	35	61	10	0	14	41	.279	37	66	1	...	...	...	...
1996—California (A.L.)■......		3-DH-1-2	66	126	20	34	4	1	8	21	.270	10	30	0	28	44	9	.889
—Lake Elsinore (Calif.)..		3B	4	12	2	2	1	0	1	3	.167	3	4	0	3	8	1	.917
1997—Anaheim (A.L.).........		3B-DH-1B	77	174	25	45	7	0	14	34	.259	13	36	1	58	33	3	.968
1998—Houston (N.L.)■.......		1B-3B	24	38	4	11	5	0	1	7	.289	4	12	0	64	11	0	1.000
American League totals (9 years)			822	2408	315	581	119	15	100	313	.241	270	572	14	665	1126	77	.959
National League totals (2 years)			82	198	28	44	8	1	7	23	.222	22	45	0	97	109	2	.990
Major league totals (10 years)			904	2606	343	625	127	16	107	336	.240	292	617	14	762	1235	79	.962

CHAMPIONSHIP SERIES RECORD

Year	Team (League)	Pos.	G	AB	R	H	2B	3B	HR	RBI	Avg.	BB	SO	SB	PO	A	E	Avg.
1986—California (A.L.)..........		PH	2	1	0	0	0	0	0	0	.000	1	1	0	...	...	...	...

HOWRY, BOBBY   P   WHITE SOX

PERSONAL: Born August 4, 1973, in Phoenix. ... 6-5/215. ... Throws right, bats left. ... Full name: Bobby Dean Howry.
HIGH SCHOOL: Deer Valley (Phoenix).
JUNIOR COLLEGE: Yavapai College (Ariz.).
COLLEGE: McNeese State.
TRANSACTIONS/CAREER NOTES: Selected by San Francisco Giants organization in fifth round of free-agent draft (June 2, 1994). ... Traded by Giants with SS Mike Caruso, OF Brian Manning, P Keith Foulke, P Lorenzo Barcelo and P Ken Vining to Chicago White Sox for P Wilson Alvarez, P Danny Darwin and P Roberto Hernandez (July 31, 1997).

Year	Team (League)	W	L	Pct.	ERA	G	GS	CG	ShO	Sv.	IP	H	R	ER	BB	SO
1994—Everett (Northwest)......	0	4	.000	4.74	5	5	0	0	0	19	29	15	10	10	16
—Clinton (Midwest)..............	1	3	.250	4.20	9	8	0	0	0	49 1/3	61	29	23	16	22
1995—San Jose (California).........	12	10	.545	3.54	27	25	1	0	0	165 1/3	171	79	65	54	107
1996—Shreveport (Texas)............	12	10	.545	4.65	27	27	0	0	0	156 2/3	163	90	81	56	57
1997—Shreveport (Texas)............	6	3	.667	4.91	48	0	0	0	*22	55	58	35	30	21	43
—Birmingham (Southern)■..	0	0	...	2.84	12	0	0	0	0	12 2/3	16	4	4	3	3
1998—Calgary (PCL)....................	1	2	.333	3.41	23	0	0	0	5	31 2/3	25	12	12	10	22
—Chicago (A.L.)..................	0	3	.000	3.15	44	0	0	0	9	54 1/3	37	20	19	19	51
Major league totals (1 year)........	0	3	.000	3.15	44	0	0	0	9	54 1/3	37	20	19	19	51

HUBBARD, MIKE   C   RANGERS

PERSONAL: Born February 16, 1971, in Lynchburg, Va. ... 6-1/205. ... Bats right, throws right. ... Full name: Michael Wayne Hubbard.
HIGH SCHOOL: Amherst (Va.) County.
COLLEGE: James Madison.
TRANSACTIONS/CAREER NOTES: Selected by Chicago Cubs organization in eighth round of free-agent draft (June 1, 1992). ... Claimed on waivers by Montreal Expos (March 30, 1998). ... Granted free agency (September 29, 1998). ... Signed by Texas Rangers organization (December 2, 1998).

Year	Team (League)	Pos.	G	AB	R	H	2B	3B	HR	RBI	Avg.	BB	SO	SB	PO	A	E	Avg.
1992—Geneva (NY-Penn)......	C	50	183	25	44	4	4	3	25	.240	7	29	6	325	27	5	.986
1993—Daytona (Fla. St.).......	C-2B	68	245	25	72	10	3	1	20	.294	18	41	10	354	66	9	.979
1994—Orlando (South.)........	C-3B-1B	104	357	52	102	13	3	11	39	.286	29	58	7	498	78	12	.980
1995—Iowa (Am. Assoc.).......	C-3B	75	254	28	66	6	3	5	23	.260	26	60	6	447	34	9	.982
—Chicago (N.L.)...........	C	15	23	2	4	0	0	0	1	.174	2	2	0	33	0	1	.971
1996—Iowa (Am. Assoc.).......	C-3B-OF	67	232	38	68	12	0	7	33	.293	10	56	2	372	27	5	.988
—Chicago (N.L.)..........	C	21	38	1	4	0	0	1	4	.105	0	15	0	53	3	0	1.000
1997—Iowa (Am. Assoc.).......	C-OF	50	186	24	52	15	1	6	26	.280	11	23	2	310	22	2	.994
—Chicago (N.L.)..........	C-3B	29	64	4	13	0	0	1	2	.203	2	21	0	120	8	1	.992
1998—Montreal (N.L.)■........	C-2B	32	55	3	8	1	0	1	3	.145	0	17	0	83	4	0	1.000
—Ottawa (Int'l)............	C	20	70	9	16	5	0	0	8	.229	3	13	0	121	8	1	.992
Major league totals (4 years)		97	180	10	29	1	0	3	10	.161	4	55	0	289	15	2	.993

HUBBARD, TRENIDAD   OF   DODGERS

PERSONAL: Born May 11, 1966, in Chicago. ... 5-9/185. ... Bats right, throws right. ... Full name: Trenidad Aviel Hubbard. ... Cousin of Joe Cribbs, running back with Buffalo Bills (1980-83 and 1985).
HIGH SCHOOL: South Shore (Chicago).
COLLEGE: Southern (La.).
TRANSACTIONS/CAREER NOTES: Selected by Houston Astros organization in 12th round of free-agent draft (June 2, 1986). ... Granted free agency (October 15, 1992). ... Signed by Colorado Rockies organization (October 30, 1992). ... On disabled list (June 15-24, 1993). ... Granted free agency (October 15, 1993). ... Re-signed by Rockies organization (December 3, 1993). ... Granted free agency (October 15, 1994). ... Re-signed by Colorado Springs, Rockies organization (November 14, 1994). ... Claimed on waivers by San Francisco Giants (August 21, 1996). ... On San Francisco disabled list (September 13, 1996-remainder of season). ... Traded by Giants to Cleveland Indians for P Joe Roa (December 16, 1996), completing deal in which Indians traded IF Jeff Kent, IF Jose Vizcaino, P Julian Tavarez and a player to be named later

H

to Giants for 3B Matt Williams and a player to be named later (November 13, 1996). ... Granted free agency (October 8, 1997). ... Signed by Los Angeles Dodgers (December 3, 1997). ... On Los Angeles disabled list (May 14-June 22, 1998); included rehabilitation assignment to Albuquerque (June 9-22).

STATISTICAL NOTES: Led Texas League second basemen with 296 putouts, 653 total chances and 81 double plays in 1991. ... Tied for Pacific Coast League lead in caught stealing with 18 in 1993. ... Led Pacific Coast League with .416 on-base percentage in 1995.

MISCELLANEOUS: Batted lefthanded on occasion though not a switch hitter (1986-91).

Year	Team (League)	Pos.	G	AB	R	H	2B	3B	HR	RBI	Avg.	BB	SO	SB	PO	A	E	Avg.
1986—	Auburn (NY-Penn)......	2B-OF	70	242	42	75	12	1	1	32	.310	28	42	35	131	110	18	.931
1987—	Asheville (S. Atl.)........	2-O-C-3-P	101	284	39	67	8	1	1	35	.236	28	42	28	124	108	14	.943
1988—	Osceola (Fla. St.)........	2-C-O-3-1	130	446	68	116	15	11	3	65	.260	61	72	44	261	150	12	.972
1989—	Columbus (Sou.)........	2-C-O-3	104	348	55	92	7	8	3	37	.264	43	53	28	321	122	15	.967
	—Tucson (PCL)	OF-3B-C	21	50	3	11	2	0	0	2	.220	1	10	3	20	9	1	.967
1990—	Columbus (Sou.)........	2-O-C-3	95	335	39	84	14	4	4	35	.251	32	51	17	216	116	11	.968
	—Tucson (PCL)	2B-3B-C	12	27	5	6	2	2	0	2	.222	3	6	1	20	22	3	.933
1991—	Jackson (Texas)	2-O-1-P	126	455	78	135	21	3	2	41	.297	65	81	39	†299	338	21	.968
	—Tucson (PCL)	2B	2	4	0	0	0	0	0	0	.000	0	0	0	1	2	0	1.000
1992—	Tucson (PCL)	2B-3B	115	420	69	130	16	4	2	33	.310	45	68	34	238	353	18	.970
1993—	Colo. Springs (PCL)■	O-2-3-S	117	439	83	138	24	8	7	56	.314	47	57	33	208	29	6	.975
1994—	Colo. Springs (PCL) ...	OF	79	320	78	116	22	5	8	38	.363	44	40	28	183	5	7	.964
	—Colorado (N.L.)	OF	18	25	3	7	1	1	1	3	.280	3	4	0	4	0	0	1.000
1995—	Colo. Springs (PCL) ...	OF	123	480	*102	163	29	7	12	66	.340	61	59	*37	285	11	6	.980
	—Colorado (N.L.)	OF	24	58	13	18	4	0	3	9	.310	8	6	2	16	1	0	1.000
1996—	Colorado (N.L.)	OF	45	60	12	13	5	1	1	12	.217	9	22	2	32	0	0	1.000
	—Colo. Springs (PCL) ...	O-2-3-C	50	188	41	59	15	5	6	16	.314	28	14	6	89	55	4	.973
	—San Fran. (N.L.)■......	OF	10	29	3	6	0	1	1	2	.207	2	5	0	19	1	0	1.000
1997—	Buffalo (A.A.)■	OF-3B	103	375	71	117	22	1	16	60	.312	57	52	26	236	26	2	.992
	—Cleveland (A.L.).........	OF	7	12	3	3	1	0	0	0	.250	1	3	2	3	0	0	1.000
1998—	Los Angeles (N.L.)■ ..	OF-3B	94	208	29	62	9	1	7	18	.298	18	46	9	110	3	1	.991
	—Albuquerque (PCL).....	OF	11	30	6	9	0	0	3	5	.300	5	5	2	13	1	0	1.000
American League totals (1 year)			7	12	3	3	1	0	0	0	.250	1	3	2	3	0	0	1.000
National League totals (4 years)			191	380	60	106	19	4	13	44	.279	40	83	13	181	5	1	.995
Major league totals (5 years)			198	392	63	109	20	4	13	44	.278	41	86	15	184	5	1	.995

DIVISION SERIES RECORD

Year	Team (League)	Pos.	G	AB	R	H	2B	3B	HR	RBI	Avg.	BB	SO	SB	PO	A	E	Avg.
1995—	Colorado (N.L.)	PH	3	2	0	0	0	0	0	0	.000	0	0	0	...	...	...	...

RECORD AS PITCHER

Year	Team (League)	W	L	Pct.	ERA	G	GS	CG	ShO	Sv.	IP	H	R	ER	BB	SO
1987—	Asheville (S. Atl.)................	0	0	...	0.00	1	0	0	0	0	1	1	0	0	1	0
1991—	Jackson (Texas)	0	0	...	0.00	1	0	0	0	0	1	0	0	0	2	0

HUDEK, JOHN   P   REDS

PERSONAL: Born August 8, 1966, in Tampa. ... 6-1/205. ... Throws right, bats both. ... Full name: John Raymond Hudek. ... Name pronounced HOO-dek.

HIGH SCHOOL: H.B. Plant (Tampa).

COLLEGE: Florida Southern.

TRANSACTIONS/CAREER NOTES: Selected by Texas Rangers organization in 30th round of free-agent draft (June 3, 1985); did not sign. ... Selected by Chicago White Sox organization in 10th round of free-agent draft (June 1, 1988). ... Selected by Detroit Tigers from White Sox organization in Rule 5 minor league draft (December 7, 1992). ... On Toledo disabled list (April 8-28 and June 17-July 1, 1993). ... Claimed on waivers by Houston Astros (July 29, 1993). ... On disabled list (June 26, 1995-remainder of season). ... On Houston disabled list (March 22-July 15, 1996); included rehabilitation assignments to Kissimmee (June 21-30) and Tucson (June 30-July 15). ... Traded by Astros to New York Mets for OF Carl Everett (December 22, 1997). ... Traded by Mets to Cincinnati Reds for OF/IF Lenny Harris (July 3, 1998).

STATISTICAL NOTES: Combined with starter Jose Ventura and Chris Howard in 4-1 no-hit victory against Charlotte (April 18, 1991).

Year	Team (League)	W	L	Pct.	ERA	G	GS	CG	ShO	Sv.	IP	H	R	ER	BB	SO
1988—	South Bend (Mid.)..............	7	2	.778	1.98	26	0	0	0	8	54 2/3	45	19	12	21	35
1989—	Sarasota (Florida State)......	1	3	.250	1.67	27	0	0	0	15	43	22	10	8	13	39
	—Birmingham (Southern)	1	1	.500	4.24	18	0	0	0	11	17	14	8	8	9	10
1990—	Birmingham (Southern)	6	6	.500	4.58	42	10	0	0	4	92 1/3	84	59	47	52	67
1991—	Birmingham (Southern)	5	10	.333	3.84	51	0	0	0	13	65 2/3	58	39	28	28	49
1992—	Birmingham (Southern)	0	1	.000	2.31	5	0	0	0	1	11 2/3	9	4	3	11	9
	—Vancouver (PCL)	8	1	.889	3.16	39	3	1	1	2	85 1/3	69	36	30	45	61
1993—	Toledo (International)■......	1	3	.250	5.82	16	5	0	0	0	38 2/3	44	26	25	22	32
	—Tucson (PCL)■	3	1	.750	3.79	13	1	0	0	0	19	17	11	8	11	18
1994—	Tucson (PCL)	0	0	...	4.91	6	0	0	0	2	7 1/3	3	4	4	3	14
	—Houston (N.L.)	0	2	.000	2.97	42	0	0	0	16	39 1/3	24	14	13	18	39
1995—	Houston (N.L.)	2	2	.500	5.40	19	0	0	0	7	20	19	12	12	5	29
1996—	Kissimmee (Florida State)..	0	0	...	0.00	2	1	0	0	0	3	2	0	0	2	3
	—Tucson (PCL)	1	0	1.000	3.10	17	2	0	0	4	20 1/3	17	8	7	8	26
	—Houston (N.L.)	2	0	1.000	2.81	15	0	0	0	2	16	12	5	5	5	14
1997—	Houston (N.L.)	1	3	.250	5.98	40	0	0	0	0	40 2/3	38	27	27	33	36
	—New Orleans (A.A.)	0	0	...	0.44	19	0	0	0	7	20 2/3	3	1	1	3	26
1998—	New York (N.L.)■	1	4	.200	4.00	28	0	0	0	0	27	23	13	12	19	28
	—Cincinnati (N.L.)■..........	4	2	.667	2.43	30	0	0	0	0	37	27	14	10	28	40
Major league totals (5 years)......		10	13	.435	3.95	174	0	0	0	29	180	143	85	79	108	186

ALL-STAR GAME RECORD

Year	League	W	L	Pct.	ERA	GS	CG	ShO	Sv.	IP	H	R	ER	BB	SO
1994—	National	0	0	...	27.00	0	0	0	0	2/3	1	2	2	1	1

H

HUDLER, REX — OF/IF

PERSONAL: Born September 2, 1960, in Tempe, Ariz. ... 6-0/202. ... Bats right, throws right. ... Full name: Rex Allen Hudler.
HIGH SCHOOL: Bullard (Fresno, Calif.).
TRANSACTIONS/CAREER NOTES: Selected by New York Yankees organization in first round (18th pick overall) of free-agent draft (June 6, 1978); pick received as compensation for Chicago White Sox signing free-agent DH/OF Ron Blomberg. ... On Fort Lauderdale disabled list (May 18-31, 1979; May 10-June 15, 1980; and May 11-June 11, 1981). ... Traded by Yankees with P Rich Bordi to Baltimore Orioles for OF Gary Roenicke and a player to be named later (December 12, 1985); Yankees acquired OF Leo Hernandez to complete deal (December 16, 1985). ... On Baltimore disabled list (March 23-June 16, 1987); included rehabilitation assignment to Rochester (May 28-June 16). ... Granted free agency (October 15, 1987). ... Signed by Indianapolis, Montreal Expos organization (December 18, 1987). ... Traded by Expos to St. Louis Cardinals for P John Costello (April 23, 1990). ... On disabled list (May 7-June 29, 1992). ... Released by Cardinals (December 7, 1992). ... Signed by Yakult Swallows of Japan Central League (1993). ... Signed as free agent by San Francisco Giants organization (December 20, 1993). ... Released by Phoenix, Giants organization (March 22, 1994). ... Signed by California Angels (March 28, 1994). ... On disabled list (May 28-June 14, 1994). ... Granted free agency (October 18, 1994). ... Re-signed by Angels (December 6, 1994). ... Granted free agency (October 28, 1996). ... Signed by Philadelphia Phillies (November 21, 1996). ... On disabled list (April 12-May 6 and June 9-August 6, 1997); included rehabilitation assignments to Reading (April 25-28 and May 3-7), Clearwater (July 23-August 2) and Scranton/Wilkes-Barre (August 5-6). ... Released by Phillies (June 24, 1998). ... Signed by Cleveland Indians organization (July 2, 1998). ... Announced retirement (July 15, 1998).
STATISTICAL NOTES: Led International League second basemen with 95 double plays in 1984.

Year	Team (League)	Pos.	G	AB	R	H	2B	3B	HR	RBI	Avg.	BB	SO	SB	PO	A	E	Avg.
1978—	Oneonta (NYP)	SS	58	221	33	62	5	5	0	24	.281	21	29	16	123	21	22	.867
1979—	Fort Laud. (FSL)	S-3-2-O	116	414	37	104	14	1	1	25	.251	15	73	23	164	314	45	.914
1980—	Fort Laud. (FSL)	3-2-O-1	37	125	14	26	4	0	0	6	.208	2	25	2	55	71	5	.962
	—Greensboro (S. Atl.)	2B	20	75	7	17	3	1	2	9	.227	4	14	1	51	52	5	.954
1981—	Fort Laud. (FSL)	2-S-3-O	79	259	35	77	11	1	2	26	.297	13	31	6	104	238	19	.947
1982—	Nashville (Southern)	2B-SS-OF	89	299	27	71	14	1	0	24	.237	9	51	9	136	219	20	.947
	—Fort Laud. (FSL)	2B	9	32	2	8	1	0	1	6	.250	4	5	0	23	25	2	.960
1983—	Fort Laud. (FSL)	2B-SS	91	345	55	93	15	2	2	50	.270	26	44	30	195	245	15	.967
	—Columbus (Int'l)	2B-3B-SS	40	118	17	36	5	0	1	11	.305	6	25	1	55	95	4	.974
1984—	Columbus (Int'l)	2B	114	394	49	115	26	1	1	35	.292	16	61	11	266	348	16	.975
	—New York (A.L.)	2B	9	7	2	1	1	0	0	0	.143	1	5	0	4	7	0	1.000
1985—	Columbus (Int'l)	2-S-O-3-1	106	380	62	95	13	4	3	18	.250	17	51	29	192	234	17	.962
	—New York (A.L.)	2B-1B-SS	20	51	4	8	0	1	0	1	.157	1	9	0	42	51	2	.979
1986—	Rochester (Int'l)■	2-3-O-S	77	219	29	57	12	3	2	13	.260	16	32	12	135	191	15	.956
	—Baltimore (Int'l)	2B-3B	14	1	1	0	0	0	0	0	.000	0	0	1	2	3	1	.833
1987—	Rochester (Int'l)	OF-2B-SS	31	106	22	27	5	1	5	10	.255	2	15	9	51	15	2	.971
1988—	Indianapolis (A.A.)■	O-2-S-3	67	234	36	71	11	3	7	25	.303	10	35	14	102	96	4	.980
	—Montreal (N.L.)	2B-SS-OF	77	216	38	59	14	2	4	14	.273	10	34	29	116	168	10	.966
1989—	Montreal (N.L.)	2B-OF-SS	92	155	21	38	7	0	6	13	.245	6	23	15	59	59	7	.944
1990—	Montreal (N.L.)	PH	4	3	1	1	0	0	0	0	.333	0	1	0	0	0	0	...
	—St. Louis (N.L.)■	O-2-1-3-S	89	217	30	61	11	2	7	22	.281	12	31	18	158	42	5	.976
1991—	St. Louis (N.L.)	OF-1B-2B	101	207	21	47	10	2	1	15	.227	10	29	12	130	6	2	.986
1992—	St. Louis (N.L.)	2B-OF-1B	61	98	17	24	4	0	3	5	.245	2	23	2	44	39	3	.965
1993—	Yakult (Jp. Cen.)■	...	120	410	48	123	26	3	14	64	.300	32	77	1	...	...	...	...
1994—	California (A.L.)■	2-O-DH-3-1	56	124	17	37	8	0	8	20	.298	6	28	2	71	61	5	.964
1995—	California (A.L.)	2-O-DH-1	84	223	30	59	16	0	6	27	.265	10	48	13	122	115	4	.983
1996—	California (A.L.)	2-O-DH-1	92	302	60	94	20	3	16	40	.311	9	54	14	173	117	6	.980
1997—	Reading (Eastern)■	OF-2B	6	23	5	8	2	0	1	5	.348	1	2	0	4	1	0	1.000
	—Philadelphia (N.L.)	OF-2B	50	122	17	27	4	0	5	10	.221	6	28	1	61	10	3	.959
	—Clearwater (FSL)	OF-2B	9	34	8	11	2	1	3	6	.324	0	8	1	10	2	0	1.000
	—Scran./W.B. (Int'l)	2B	3	9	0	3	0	0	0	0	.333	0	0	1	5	0	0	1.000
1998—	Philadelphia (N.L.)	OF-1B	25	41	2	5	1	0	0	2	.122	4	12	0	27	1	0	1.000
	—Buffalo (Int'l)■	3-2-O-1	11	36	4	7	1	0	0	2	.194	4	10	0	16	11	3	.900
American League totals (6 years)			275	708	114	199	45	4	30	88	.281	27	144	30	414	354	18	.977
National League totals (7 years)			499	1059	147	262	51	6	26	81	.247	50	181	77	595	325	30	.968
Major league totals (13 years)			774	1767	261	461	96	10	56	169	.261	77	325	107	1009	679	48	.972

HUDSON, JOE — P — RANGERS

PERSONAL: Born September 29, 1970, in Philadelphia. ... 6-1/180. ... Throws right, bats right. ... Full name: Joseph Paul Hudson.
HIGH SCHOOL: Holy Cross (Delran, N.J.).
COLLEGE: West Virginia.
TRANSACTIONS/CAREER NOTES: Selected by Boston Red Sox organization in 27th round of free-agent draft (June 1, 1992). ... Traded by Red Sox to Milwaukee Brewers for IF Eddy Diaz (July 31, 1998). ... Released by Brewers (September 29, 1998). ... Signed by Texas Rangers organization (January 18, 1999).

Year	Team (League)	W	L	Pct.	ERA	G	GS	CG	ShO	Sv.	IP	H	R	ER	BB	SO
1992—	Elmira (N.Y.-Penn)	3	3	.500	4.38	19	7	0	0	0	72	76	46	35	33	38
1993—	Lynchburg (Carolina)	8	6	.571	4.06	49	1	0	0	0	84 1/3	97	49	38	38	62
1994—	Sarasota (Florida State)	3	1	.750	2.23	30	0	0	0	7	48 1/3	42	20	12	27	33
	—New Britain (East.)	5	3	.625	3.92	23	0	0	0	0	39	49	18	17	18	24
1995—	Trenton (Eastern)	0	1	.000	1.71	22	0	0	0	8	31 2/3	20	8	6	17	24
	—Boston (A.L.)	0	1	.000	4.11	39	0	0	0	1	46	53	21	21	23	29
1996—	Pawtucket (Int'l)	1	1	.500	3.51	25	0	0	0	5	33 1/3	29	19	13	21	18
	—Boston (A.L.)	3	5	.375	5.40	36	0	0	0	1	45	57	35	27	32	19
1997—	Pawtucket (Int'l)	2	1	.667	2.25	29	0	0	0	7	32	25	22	8	23	14
	—Boston (A.L.)	3	1	.750	3.53	26	0	0	0	0	35 2/3	39	16	14	14	14
1998—	Pawtucket (Int'l)	2	2	.500	4.53	46	0	0	0	10	47 2/3	57	32	24	23	32
	—Milwaukee (N.L.)■	0	0	...	162.00	1	0	0	0	0	1/3	2	6	6	4	0
	—Louisville (Int'l)	1	0	1.000	5.11	9	0	0	0	0	12 1/3	13	7	7	5	4
A.L. totals (3 years)		6	7	.462	4.41	101	0	0	0	2	126 2/3	149	72	62	69	62
N.L. totals (1 year)		0	0	...	162.00	1	0	0	0	0	1/3	2	6	6	4	0
Major league totals (4 years)		6	7	.462	4.82	102	0	0	0	2	127	151	78	68	73	62

H

Year	Team (League)	W	L	Pct.	ERA	G	GS	CG	ShO	Sv.	IP	H	R	ER	BB	SO
1995—	Boston (A.L.)	0	0	...	0.00	1	0	0	0	0	1	2	0	0	1	0

HUGHES, BOBBY   C   BREWERS

PERSONAL: Born March 10, 1971, in Burbank, Calif. ... 6-4/229. ... Bats right, throws right. ... Full name: Robert E. Hughes.
HIGH SCHOOL: Notre Dame (Sherman Oaks, Calif.).
COLLEGE: Loyola Marymount, then Southern California.
TRANSACTIONS/CAREER NOTES: Selected by Detroit Tigers organization in 47th round of free-agent draft (June 3, 1991); did not sign. ... Selected by Milwaukee Brewers organization in second round of free-agent draft (June 1, 1992). ... On disabled list (April 3-11 and May 4-20, 1997).
STATISTICAL NOTES: Led Midwest League catchers with 17 errors in 1993. ... Led Pacific Coast League catchers with 12 errors in 1997.

							BATTING								FIELDING		
Year	Team (League)	Pos.	G	AB	R	H	2B	3B	HR	RBI	Avg.	BB	SO	SB	PO	A	E	Avg.
1992—	Helena (Pioneer)	OF-C	11	40	5	7	1	1	0	6	.175	4	14	0	64	9	1	.986
1993—	Beloit (Midwest)	C-1B	98	321	42	89	11	3	17	56	.277	23	76	1	573	67	†18	.973
1994—	Stockton (California)	C-1B-3B	95	322	54	81	24	3	11	53	.252	33	83	2	517	63	8	.986
	—El Paso (Texas)	C	12	36	3	10	4	1	0	12	.278	5	7	0	52	8	1	.984
1995—	Stockton (California)	C-1B	52	179	22	42	9	2	8	31	.235	17	41	2	252	50	4	.987
	—El Paso (Texas)	C	51	173	11	46	12	0	7	27	.266	12	30	0	299	29	8	.976
1996—	New Orleans (A.A.)	C-1B-3B	37	125	11	25	5	0	4	15	.200	4	31	1	176	27	5	.976
	—El Paso (Texas)	C	67	237	43	72	18	1	15	39	.304	30	40	3	250	32	6	.979
1997—	Tucson (PCL)	C-3B	89	290	43	90	29	2	7	51	.310	24	46	0	455	48	†12	.977
1998—	Milwaukee (N.L.)	C-OF	85	218	28	50	7	2	9	29	.229	16	54	1	398	29	2	.995
Major league totals (1 year)			85	218	28	50	7	2	9	29	.229	16	54	1	398	29	2	.995

HUNDLEY, TODD   C   DODGERS

PERSONAL: Born May 27, 1969, in Martinsville, Va. ... 5-11/199. ... Bats both, throws right. ... Full name: Todd Randolph Hundley. ... Son of Randy Hundley, major league catcher with four teams (1964-77).
HIGH SCHOOL: William Fremd (Palatine, Ill.).
COLLEGE: William Rainey Harper College (Ill.).
TRANSACTIONS/CAREER NOTES: Selected by New York Mets organization in second round of free-agent draft (June 2, 1987); pick received as compensation for Baltimore Orioles signing Type B free-agent 3B/1B Ray Knight. ... On Tidewater disabled list (June 29-July 6, 1991). ... On disabled list (July 23, 1995-remainder of season). ... On New York disabled list (March 21-July 11 and August 28-September 12, 1998); included rehabilitation assignments to St. Lucie (June 24-July 6 and July 9), Gulf Coast Mets (July 7-8) and Norfolk (July 10-11 and August 31-September 8). ... Traded by Mets with P Arnold Gooch to Los Angeles Dodgers for C Charles Johnson and OF Roger Cedeno (December 1, 1998).
RECORDS: Holds major league single-season record for most home runs by catcher—41 (1996). ... Holds N.L. record for most home runs by switch hitter in two consecutive seasons—71. ... Holds N.L. single-season records for most home runs by switch hitter—41 (1996); and most strikeouts by switch hitter—146 (1996).
STATISTICAL NOTES: Led South Atlantic League in intentional bases on balls received with 10 and in grounding into double plays with 20 in 1989. ... Led South Atlantic League catchers with 826 putouts and 930 total chances in 1989. ... Tied for International League lead in errors by catcher with nine and double plays with 12 in 1991. ... Switch-hit home runs in one game five times (June 18, 1994; May 18; June 10, 1996; May 5 and July 20, 1997). ... Career major league grand slams: 4.

							BATTING								FIELDING		
Year	Team (League)	Pos.	G	AB	R	H	2B	3B	HR	RBI	Avg.	BB	SO	SB	PO	A	E	Avg.
1987—	Little Falls (NYP)	C	34	103	12	15	4	0	1	10	.146	12	27	0	181	25	7	.967
1988—	Little Falls (NYP)	C	52	176	23	33	8	0	2	18	.188	16	31	1	345	54	8	.980
	—St. Lucie (Fla. St.)	C	1	1	0	0	0	0	0	0	.000	2	1	0	4	0	1	.800
1989—	Columbia (S. Atl.)	C-OF	125	439	67	118	23	4	11	66	.269	54	67	6	†829	91	13	.986
1990—	Jackson (Texas)	C-3B	81	279	27	74	12	2	1	35	.265	34	44	5	474	63	9	.984
	—New York (N.L.)	C	36	67	8	14	6	0	0	2	.209	6	18	0	162	8	2	.988
1991—	Tidewater (Int'l)	C-1B	125	454	62	124	24	4	14	66	.273	51	95	1	585	63	‡9	.986
	—New York (N.L.)	C	21	60	5	8	0	1	1	7	.133	6	14	0	85	11	0	1.000
1992—	New York (N.L.)	C	123	358	32	75	17	0	7	32	.209	19	76	3	700	48	3	.996
1993—	New York (N.L.)	C	130	417	40	95	17	2	11	53	.228	23	62	1	592	63	8	.988
1994—	New York (N.L.)	C	91	291	45	69	10	1	16	42	.237	25	73	2	448	28	5	.990
1995—	New York (N.L.)	C	90	275	39	77	11	0	15	51	.280	42	64	1	488	29	7	.987
1996—	New York (N.L.)	C	153	540	85	140	32	1	41	112	.259	79	146	1	911	72	8	.992
1997—	New York (N.L.)	C-DH	132	417	78	114	21	2	30	86	.273	83	116	2	678	54	10	.987
1998—	St. Lucie (Fla. St.)	OF	12	42	4	9	2	0	1	6	.214	12	8	0	17	1	2	.900
	—GC Mets (GCL)	OF	1	2	0	0	0	0	0	0	.000	2	1	0	2	0	0	1.000
	—Norfolk (Int'l)	OF-C	10	30	9	13	1	0	4	15	.433	14	10	0	22	2	1	.960
	—New York (N.L.)	OF-C	53	124	8	20	4	0	3	12	.161	16	55	1	60	4	5	.928
Major league totals (9 years)			829	2549	340	612	118	7	124	397	.240	299	624	11	4124	317	48	.989

ALL-STAR GAME RECORD

						BATTING								FIELDING		
Year	League	Pos.	AB	R	H	2B	3B	HR	RBI	Avg.	BB	SO	SB	PO	A	E	Avg.
1996—	National	C	1	0	0	0	0	0	0	.000	0	0	0	1	0	0	1.000
1997—	National							Did not play.									
All-Star Game totals (1 year)			1	0	0	0	0	0	0	.000	0	0	0	1	0	0	1.000

H

PERSONAL: Born March 25, 1971, in Portland, Ore. ... 6-3/180. ... Bats right, throws right. ... Full name: Brian Lee Hunter.
HIGH SCHOOL: Fort Vancouver (Vancouver, Wash.).
TRANSACTIONS/CAREER NOTES: Selected by Houston Astros organization in second round of free-agent draft (June 5, 1989); pick received as part of compensation for Texas Rangers signing Type A free-agent P Nolan Ryan. ... On Houston disabled list (July 5-23, 1995); included rehabilitation assignment to Jackson (July 21-23). ... On Houston disabled list (June 29-July 27, 1996); included rehabilitation assignment to Tucson (July 23-27). ... Traded by Astros with IF Orlando Miller, P Doug Brocail, P Todd Jones and cash to Detroit Tigers for C Brad Ausmus, P Jose Lima, P C.J. Nitkowski, P Trever Miller and IF Daryle Ward (December 10, 1996).
RECORDS: Holds major league record for most at-bats with no hits in doubleheader (more than 18 innings)—13 (June 20, 1998, 26 innings). ... Shares major league single-season record for fewest double plays by outfielder (150 or more games)—0 (1997).
STATISTICAL NOTES: Tied for American Association lead with 249 total bases in 1997. ... Led A.L. in caught stealing with 18 in 1997. ... Led A.L. outfielders with 420 total chances in 1997. ... Career major league grand slams: 1.

Year	Team (League)	Pos.	G	AB	R	H	2B	3B	HR	RBI	Avg.	BB	SO	SB	PO	A	E	Avg.
1989—	GC Astros (GCL)	OF	51	206	15	35	2	0	0	13	.170	7	42	12	95	4	2	.980
1990—	Asheville (S. Atl.)	OF	127	444	84	111	14	6	0	16	.250	60	72	45	219	13	11	.955
1991—	Osceola (Fla. St.)	OF	118	392	51	94	15	3	1	30	.240	45	75	32	250	7	9	.966
1992—	Osceola (Fla. St.)	OF	131	489	62	146	18	9	1	62	.299	31	76	39	295	10	9	.971
1993—	Jackson (Texas)	OF	133	523	84	154	22	5	10	52	.294	34	85	*35	276	9	*14	.953
1994—	Tucson (PCL)	OF	128	513	*113	*191	28	9	10	51	*.372	52	52	*49	244	14	5	.981
	—Houston (N.L.)	OF	6	24	2	6	1	0	0	0	.250	1	6	2	14	1	1	.938
1995—	Tucson (PCL)	OF	38	155	28	51	5	1	1	16	.329	17	13	11	91	1	0	1.000
	—Houston (N.L.)	OF	78	321	52	97	14	5	2	28	.302	21	52	24	182	8	9	.955
	—Jackson (Texas)	OF	2	6	1	3	0	0	0	0	.500	1	0	0	5	0	0	1.000
1996—	Houston (N.L.)	OF	132	526	74	145	27	2	5	35	.276	17	92	35	279	11	•12	.960
	—Tucson (PCL)	OF	3	14	3	5	0	0	0	1	.357	0	2	3	8	0	0	1.000
1997—	Detroit (A.L.)■	OF	•162	658	112	177	29	7	4	45	.269	66	121	*74	*408	8	4	.990
1998—	Detroit (A.L.)	OF	142	595	67	151	29	3	4	36	.254	36	94	42	386	11	5	.988
American League totals (2 years)			304	1253	179	328	58	10	8	81	.262	102	215	116	794	19	9	.989
National League totals (3 years)			216	871	128	248	42	7	7	63	.285	39	150	61	475	20	22	.957
Major league totals (5 years)			520	2124	307	576	100	17	15	144	.271	141	365	177	1269	39	31	.977

PERSONAL: Born March 4, 1968, in El Toro, Calif. ... 6-0/225. ... Bats right, throws left. ... Full name: Brian Ronald Hunter.
HIGH SCHOOL: Paramount (Calif.).
JUNIOR COLLEGE: Cerritos College (Calif.).
TRANSACTIONS/CAREER NOTES: Selected by Atlanta Braves organization in eighth round of free-agent draft (June 2, 1987). ... On Atlanta disabled list (April 18-May 18, 1993). ... Traded by Braves to Pittsburgh Pirates for a player to be named later (November 17, 1993); Braves acquired SS Jose Delgado to complete deal (June 6, 1994). ... Traded by Pirates to Cincinnati Reds for a player to be named later (July 27, 1994); Pirates acquired OF Micah Franklin to complete deal (October 13, 1994). ... On Cincinnati disabled list (June 19-July 24 and August 14-September 1, 1995); included rehabilitation assignment to Indianapolis (August 22-31). ... Released by Reds (March 8, 1996). ... Signed by Seattle Mariners (May 4, 1996). ... Granted free agency (October 8, 1996). ... Signed by Reds organization (January 14, 1997). ... Granted free agency (October 15, 1997). ... Signed by St. Louis Cardinals (March 30, 1998). ... Released by Cardinals (August 2, 1998). ... Signed by Chicago White Sox organization (August 14, 1998). ... On Calgary disabled list (August 25-September 2, 1998). ... Granted free agency (October 15, 1998).
STATISTICAL NOTES: Led Appalachian League first basemen with 43 double plays in 1987. ... Led Midwest League first basemen with 21 errors in 1988. ... Tied for Southern League lead with nine sacrifice flies in 1989. ... Career major league grand slams: 2.

Year	Team (League)	Pos.	G	AB	R	H	2B	3B	HR	RBI	Avg.	BB	SO	SB	PO	A	E	Avg.
1987—	Pulaski (Appalachian)	1B-OF	65	251	38	58	10	2	8	30	.231	18	47	3	498	29	11	.980
1988—	Burlington (Midw.)	1B-OF	117	417	58	108	17	0	•22	71	.259	45	90	7	987	69	†22	.980
	—Durham (Carolina)	OF-1B	13	49	13	17	3	0	3	9	.347	7	8	2	52	6	0	1.000
1989—	Greenville (Southern)	OF-1B	124	451	57	114	19	2	19	82	.253	33	62	5	248	15	4	.985
1990—	Richmond (Int'l)	OF-1B	43	137	13	27	4	0	5	16	.197	18	37	2	126	5	3	.978
	—Greenville (Southern)	OF-1B	88	320	45	77	13	1	14	55	.241	43	62	6	189	19	8	.963
1991—	Richmond (Int'l)	OF	48	181	28	47	7	0	10	30	.260	11	24	3	121	4	4	.969
	—Atlanta (N.L.)	1B-OF	97	271	32	68	16	1	12	50	.251	17	48	0	624	46	8	.988
1992—	Atlanta (N.L.)	1B-OF	102	238	34	57	13	2	14	41	.239	21	50	1	542	50	4	.993
1993—	Atlanta (N.L.)	1B-OF	37	80	4	11	3	1	0	8	.138	2	15	0	168	13	1	.995
	—Richmond (Int'l)	1B-OF	30	99	16	24	7	0	6	26	.242	10	21	4	174	15	0	1.000
1994—	Pittsburgh (N.L.)■	1B-OF	76	233	28	53	15	1	11	47	.227	15	55	0	496	37	5	.991
	—Cincinnati (N.L.)■	OF-1B	9	23	6	7	1	0	4	10	.304	2	1	0	20	1	0	1.000
1995—	Cincinnati (N.L.)	1B-OF	40	79	9	17	6	0	1	9	.215	11	21	2	171	13	3	.984
	—Indianapolis (A.A.)	OF	9	36	7	13	5	0	4	11	.361	6	11	0	42	2	1	.978
1996—	Tacoma (PCL)	OF-1B	25	92	19	32	6	1	7	24	.348	9	11	1	45	5	1	.980
	—Seattle (A.L.)	1B-OF-DH	75	198	21	53	10	0	7	28	.268	15	43	0	280	10	5	.983
1997—	Indianapolis (A.A.)	OF	139	506	74	142	36	4	21	85	.281	42	76	9	734	56	9	.989
1998—	St. Louis (N.L.)■	OF-1B-DH	62	112	11	23	9	1	4	13	.205	7	23	1	66	3	3	.958
	—Calgary (PCL)■	OF-1B	11	31	1	3	1	0	0	6	.097	2	9	0	26	2	0	1.000
American League totals (1 year)			75	198	21	53	10	0	7	28	.268	15	43	0	280	10	5	.983
National League totals (6 years)			423	1036	124	236	63	6	46	178	.228	75	213	4	2087	163	24	.989
Major league totals (7 years)			498	1234	145	289	73	6	53	206	.234	90	256	4	2367	173	29	.989

H

Year Team (League)	Pos.	G	AB	R	H	2B	3B	HR	RBI	Avg.	BB	SO	SB	PO	A	E	Avg.
1991— Atlanta (N.L.)............	1B	5	18	2	6	2	0	1	4	.333	0	2	0	30	4	0	1.000
1992— Atlanta (N.L.)............	1B-PH	3	5	1	1	0	0	0	0	.200	0	1	0	7	0	0	1.000
Championship series totals (2 years)		8	23	3	7	2	0	1	4	.304	0	3	0	37	4	0	1.000

WORLD SERIES RECORD

Year Team (League)	Pos.	G	AB	R	H	2B	3B	HR	RBI	Avg.	BB	SO	SB	PO	A	E	Avg.
1991— Atlanta (N.L.)............	OF-1B-PH	7	21	2	4	1	0	1	3	.190	0	2	0	6	1	0	1.000
1992— Atlanta (N.L.)............	1B-PH-PR	4	5	0	1	0	0	0	2	.200	0	1	0	14	1	0	1.000
World Series totals (2 years)		11	26	2	5	1	0	1	5	.192	0	3	0	20	2	0	1.000

HUNTER, SCOTT — OF — METS

PERSONAL: Born December 17, 1975, in Philadelphia. ... 6-1/210. ... Bats right, throws right. ... Full name: Scott William Hunter.
HIGH SCHOOL: Northeast Philadelphia.
TRANSACTIONS/CAREER NOTES: Selected by Los Angeles Dodgers organization in fifth round of free-agent draft (June 3, 1993). ... Traded by Dodgers with OF Dwight Maness to New York Mets organization for OF Brett Butler (August 18, 1995). ... On disabled list (June 29, 1997-remainder of season).
STATISTICAL NOTES: Led Pioneer League third basemen with 33 errors in 1994. ... Tied for Eastern League lead with eight sacrifice flies in 1998.

Year Team (League)	Pos.	G	AB	R	H	2B	3B	HR	RBI	Avg.	BB	SO	SB	PO	A	E	Avg.
1994— Great Falls (Pio.)	3B-OF-SS	64	237	45	75	12	4	2	28	.316	25	40	17	38	113	†33	.821
1995— San Bern. (Calif.)	OF	113	379	68	108	19	3	11	59	.285	36	83	27	177	7	9	.953
— Columbia (S. Atl.)■...	OF	12	40	2	10	0	0	0	1	.250	2	13	2	21	1	1	.957
1996— St. Lucie (Fla. St.)	OF	127	475	71	122	19	1	2	38	.257	38	68	12	167	13	9	.952
1997— Binghamton (East.)	OF	80	289	45	74	12	2	10	31	.256	25	52	24	109	7	1	.991
1998— Binghamton (East.)	OF	130	487	80	153	25	3	14	65	.314	47	75	39	220	9	5	.979
— Norfolk (Int'l)	OF	7	21	2	3	0	0	0	3	.143	3	5	1	9	0	0	1.000

HUNTER, TORII — OF — TWINS

PERSONAL: Born July 18, 1975, in Pine Bluff, Ark. ... 6-2/201. ... Bats right, throws right. ... Full name: Torii Kedar Hunter. ... Name pronounced TORE-ee.
HIGH SCHOOL: Pine Bluff (Ark.).
TRANSACTIONS/CAREER NOTES: Selected by Minnesota Twins organization in first round (20th pick overall) of free-agent draft (June 3, 1993); pick recieved as part of compensation for Cincinnati Reds signing Type A free-agent P John Smiley. ... On New Britain disabled list (April 4-May 10, 1996). ... On Salt Lake disabled list (July 28-August 11, 1998).
STATISTICAL NOTES: Led Florida State League outfielders with seven double plays in 1995. ... Tied for Eastern League lead for double plays by an outfielder with four in 1997.

Year Team (League)	Pos.	G	AB	R	H	2B	3B	HR	RBI	Avg.	BB	SO	SB	PO	A	E	Avg.
1993— GC Twins (GCL)..........	OF	28	100	6	19	3	0	0	8	.190	4	23	4	50	1	•6	.895
1994— Fort Wayne (Midw.)....	OF	91	335	57	98	17	1	10	50	.293	25	80	8	224	12	7	.971
1995— Fort Myers (FSL)........	OF	113	391	64	96	15	2	7	36	.246	38	77	7	242	15	7	.973
1996— New Britain (East.)	OF	99	342	49	90	20	3	7	33	.263	28	60	7	207	11	4	.982
— Fort Myers (FSL)	OF	4	16	1	3	0	0	0	1	.188	2	5	1	9	0	0	1.000
1997— New Britain (East.)	OF	127	471	57	109	22	2	8	56	.231	47	94	8	252	7	7	.974
— Minnesota (A.L.)	PR	1	0	0	0	0	0	0	0	. . .	0	0	0	. . .	. . .	. . .	. . .
1998— New Britain (East.)	OF	82	308	42	87	24	3	6	32	.282	19	64	11	168	8	2	.989
— Minnesota (A.L.)	OF	6	17	0	4	1	0	0	2	.235	2	6	0	8	0	0	1.000
— Salt Lake (PCL)	OF	26	92	15	31	7	0	4	20	.337	1	13	2	55	1	2	.966
Major league totals (2 years)		7	17	0	4	1	0	0	2	.235	2	6	0	8	0	0	1.000

HUSKEY, BUTCH — OF/1B — MARINERS

PERSONAL: Born November 10, 1971, in Anadarko, Okla. ... 6-3/244. ... Bats right, throws right. ... Full name: Robert Leon Huskey.
HIGH SCHOOL: Eisenhower (Lawton, Okla.).
TRANSACTIONS/CAREER NOTES: Selected by New York Mets organization in seventh round of free-agent draft (June 5, 1989). ... On New York disabled list (August 3-September 1, 1998); included rehabilitation assignment to Norfolk (August 21-23). ... Traded by Mets to Seattle Mariners for P Lesli Brea (December 14, 1998).
HONORS: Named International League Most Valuable Player (1995).
STATISTICAL NOTES: Led Gulf Coast League third basemen with 50 putouts and 23 errors in 1989. ... Led Appalachian League third basemen with 217 total chances and tied for lead with 11 double plays in 1990. ... Led South Atlantic League with 256 total bases in 1991. ... Led South Atlantic League third basemen with 21 double plays in 1991. ... Led Florida State League third basemen with 456 total chances and 28 double plays in 1992. ... Led Eastern League third basemen with 101 putouts, 297 assists, 34 errors and 432 total chances in 1993. ... Led International League third basemen with 31 double plays in 1994. ... Had 20-game hitting streak (August 22-September 13, 1997).

Year Team (League)	Pos.	G	AB	R	H	2B	3B	HR	RBI	Avg.	BB	SO	SB	PO	A	E	Avg.
1989— GC Mets (GCL)...........	3B-1B	54	190	27	50	14	2	6	34	.263	14	36	4	†73	106	†23	.886
1990— Kingsport (Appal.)......	3B	*72	*279	39	75	13	0	14	53	.269	24	74	7	45	*150	•22	.899
1991— Columbia (S. Atl.).......	3B	134	492	88	141	27	5	*26	*99	.287	54	89	22	*102	218	31	.912
1992— St. Lucie (Fla. St.)	3B	134	493	65	125	17	1	18	75	.254	33	74	7	*108	*310	*38	.917

H

Year	Team (League)	Pos.	G	AB	R	H	2B	3B	HR	RBI	Avg.	BB	SO	SB	PO	A	E	Avg.
						BATTING										FIELDING		
1993—Binghamton (East.)		3B-SS	*139	*526	72	132	23	1	25	98	.251	48	102	11	†101	†297	†34	.921
—New York (N.L.)..........		3B	13	41	2	6	1	0	0	3	.146	1	13	0	9	27	3	.923
1994—Norfolk (Int'l)..........		3B	127	474	59	108	23	3	10	57	.228	37	88	16	*95	297	25	.940
1995—Norfolk (Int'l)..........		3B-OF-1B	109	394	66	112	18	1	*28	87	.284	39	88	8	248	132	13	.967
—New York (N.L.)..........		3B-OF	28	90	8	17	1	0	3	11	.189	10	16	1	16	60	6	.927
1996—New York (N.L.)..........		1B-OF-3B	118	414	43	115	16	2	15	60	.278	27	77	1	638	54	15	.979
1997—New York (N.L.)..........		O-1-3-DH	142	471	61	135	26	2	24	81	.287	25	84	8	377	38	15	.965
1998—New York (N.L.)..........		OF-DH	113	369	43	93	18	0	13	59	.252	26	66	7	166	8	4	.978
—Norfolk (Int'l)..........		DH	2	8	0	2	0	0	0	3	.250	0	1	0	0	0	0	...
Major league totals (5 years)			414	1385	157	366	62	4	55	214	.264	89	256	17	1206	187	43	.970

HUSON, JEFF   IF   ANGELS

PERSONAL: Born August 15, 1964, in Scottsdale, Ariz. ... 6-1/180. ... Bats left, throws right. ... Full name: Jeffrey Kent Huson. ... Name pronounced HYOO-son.

HIGH SCHOOL: Mingus Union (Cottonwood, Ariz.).

JUNIOR COLLEGE: Glendale (Ariz.) Community College.

COLLEGE: Wyoming.

TRANSACTIONS/CAREER NOTES: Signed as non-drafted free agent by Montreal Expos organization (August 18, 1985). ... Traded by Expos to Oklahoma City, Texas Rangers organization, for P Drew Hall (April 2, 1990). ... On Texas disabled list (August 8-31, 1991); included rehabilitation assignment to Oklahoma City (August 29-31). ... On Texas disabled list (March 27-May 27, June 5-July 15 and July 24-August 23, 1993); included rehabilitation assignment to Oklahoma City (May 24-27, July 10-15 and July 31-August 19). ... On Texas disabled list (March 25-June 6, 1994); included rehabilitation assignment to Oklahoma City (May 17-June 5). ... Released by Rangers (November 30, 1994). ... Signed by Rochester, Baltimore Orioles organization (December 31, 1994). ... On Baltimore disabled list (May 18-July 15, 1996); including rehabilitation assignment to Frederick (June 27-July 15). ... Released by Orioles (August 13, 1996). ... Signed by Colorado Springs, Colorado Rockies organization (August 19, 1996). ... Traded by Rockies to Milwaukee Brewers for a player to be named later (April 23, 1997). ... Granted free agency (October 28, 1997). ... Signed by Rockies organization (November 18, 1997). ... Selected by Seattle Mariners from Rockies organization in Rule 5 major league draft (December 15, 1997). ... Released by Mariners (July 8, 1998). ... Signed by Arizona Diamondbacks organization (August 7, 1998). ... Granted free agency (October 15, 1998). ... Signed by Anaheim Angels organization (November 18, 1998).

Year	Team (League)	Pos.	G	AB	R	H	2B	3B	HR	RBI	Avg.	BB	SO	SB	PO	A	E	Avg.
						BATTING										FIELDING		
1986—Burlington (Midw.).....		SS-3B-2B	133	457	85	132	19	1	16	72	.289	76	68	32	183	324	37	.932
—Jacksonville (Sou.).......		3B	1	4	0	0	0	0	0	0	.000	0	0	0	0	1	0	1.000
1987—W.P. Beach (FSL)........		SS-OF-2B	131	455	54	130	15	4	1	53	.286	50	30	33	234	347	34	.945
1988—Jacksonville (Sou.).......		S-2-O-3	128	471	72	117	18	1	0	34	.248	59	45	*56	217	285	26	.951
—Montreal (N.L.)...........		S-2-3-O	20	42	7	13	2	0	0	3	.310	4	3	2	18	41	4	.937
1989—Indianapolis (A.A.).......		SS-OF-2B	102	378	70	115	17	4	3	35	.304	50	26	30	172	214	17	.958
—Montreal (N.L.)...........		SS-2B-3B	32	74	1	12	5	0	0	2	.162	6	4	3	40	65	8	.929
1990—Texas (A.L.)■..........		SS-3B-2B	145	396	57	95	12	2	0	28	.240	46	54	12	183	304	19	.962
1991—Texas (A.L.)...........		SS-2B-3B	119	268	36	57	8	3	2	26	.213	39	32	8	143	269	15	.965
—Okla. City (A.A.).........		SS	2	6	0	3	1	0	0	2	.500	0	1	0	5	3	0	1.000
1992—Texas (A.L.)...........		S-2-O-DH	123	318	49	83	14	3	4	24	.261	41	43	18	178	250	9	.979
1993—Okla. City (A.A.).......		3-S-2-O	24	76	11	22	5	0	1	10	.289	13	10	1	39	52	3	.968
—Texas (A.L.)...........		S-2-DH-3	23	45	3	6	1	1	0	2	.133	0	10	0	25	42	6	.918
1994—Okla. City (A.A.).......		2-3-O-S	83	302	47	91	20	2	1	27	.301	30	32	18	140	165	7	.978
1995—Rochester (Int'l)■.......		SS-2B	60	223	28	56	9	0	3	21	.251	26	29	16	110	203	7	.978
—Baltimore (A.L.)........		3-2-DH-S	66	161	24	40	4	2	1	19	.248	15	20	5	59	89	1	.993
1996—Baltimore (A.L.)........		2B-3B-OF	17	28	5	9	1	0	0	2	.321	1	3	0	20	17	1	.974
—Rochester (Int'l).........		OF	2	8	0	2	0	0	0	1	.250	0	2	0	4	0	0	1.000
—Frederick (Carolina)....		OF	4	16	4	7	2	0	1	1	.438	2	0	0	6	0	0	1.000
—Bowie (Eastern)........		OF-3B	3	13	3	5	2	0	0	0	.385	1	0	4	4	4	0	1.000
—Colo. Springs (PCL)■		2B-SS	14	61	10	18	4	0	0	8	.295	3	1	6	36	42	1	.987
1997—Colo. Springs (PCL) ...		3B	9	20	3	7	3	0	1	5	.350	2	2	0	5	8	0	1.000
—Milwaukee (A.L.)■.......		2-1-O-DH-3	84	143	12	29	3	0	0	11	.203	5	15	3	109	52	1	.994
1998—Seattle (A.L.)■.......		2-3-1-DH-S-O	31	49	8	8	1	0	1	4	.163	5	6	1	31	14	2	.957
—Tucson (PCL)■		S-2-3-O	27	82	7	25	4	1	1	12	.305	5	14	0	39	54	6	.939
American League totals (8 years)			608	1408	194	327	44	11	8	116	.232	152	183	47	748	1037	54	.971
National League totals (2 years)			52	116	8	25	7	0	0	5	.216	10	9	5	58	106	12	.932
Major league totals (10 years)			660	1524	202	352	51	11	8	121	.231	162	192	52	806	1143	66	.967

HUTCHINS, NORM   OF   ANGELS

PERSONAL: Born November 20, 1975, in White Plains, N.Y. ... 5-11/200. ... Bats right, throws left. ... Full name: Norman Elliot Hutchins.

HIGH SCHOOL: Lincoln (N.Y.).

TRANSACTIONS/CAREER NOTES: Selected by California Angels organization in second round of free-agent draft (June 2, 1994). ... Angels franchise renamed Anaheim Angels for 1997 season. ... On Midland disabled list (May 15-June 28, 1998).

Year	Team (League)	Pos.	G	AB	R	H	2B	3B	HR	RBI	Avg.	BB	SO	SB	PO	A	E	Avg.
						BATTING										FIELDING		
1994—Mes. Roc./Cubs (Ar.)..		OF	43	136	8	26	4	1	0	7	.191	3	44	5	70	0	6	.921
1995—Mes. Roc./Cubs (Ar.)..		OF	14	59	9	16	1	1	0	7	.271	4	10	8	17	0	2	.895
—Boise (Northwest)		OF	45	176	34	44	6	2	2	11	.250	15	44	10	92	3	2	.979
1996—Cedar Rap. (Midw.) ...		OF	126	466	59	105	13	16	2	52	.225	28	110	22	*303	2	14	.956
1997—Lake Elsinore (Calif.) ..		OF	132	564	82	163	31	12	15	69	.289	23	147	39	266	9	•13	.955
1998—Midland (Texas)........		OF	89	394	74	123	20	10	10	50	.312	14	84	32	191	4	8	.961
—Vancouver (PCL)		OF	7	29	4	6	0	0	1	3	.207	2	9	1	12	0	0	1.000

H

HUTCHINSON, CHAD   P   CARDINALS

PERSONAL: Born February 21, 1977, in Del Mar, Calif. ... 6-5/230. ... Throws right, bats right. ... Son of Lloyd Hutchinson, outfielder in Philadelphia Phillies organization (1969-72).
HIGH SCHOOL: Torrey Pines (Encinitas, Calif.).
COLLEGE: Stanford.
TRANSACTIONS/CAREER NOTES: Selected by Atlanta Braves organization in first round (26th pick overall) of free-agent draft (June 1, 1995); did not sign. ... Selected by St. Louis Cardinals organization in second round of free-agent draft (June 2, 1998).

Year Team (League)	W	L	Pct.	ERA	G	GS	CG	ShO	Sv.	IP	H	R	ER	BB	SO
1998— New Jersey (NYP)	0	1	.000	3.52	3	3	0	0	0	15 1/3	15	7	6	4	20
— Prince William (Caro.)	2	0	1.000	2.79	5	5	0	0	0	29	20	12	9	11	31

HUTTON, MARK   P   DEVIL RAYS

PERSONAL: Born February 6, 1970, in South Adelaide, Australia. ... 6-6/240. ... Throws right, bats right. ... Full name: Mark Steven Hutton.
HIGH SCHOOL: Scotch College Private School (Adelaide, Australia).
TRANSACTIONS/CAREER NOTES: Signed as non-drafted free agent by New York Yankees organization (December 15, 1988). ... On Columbus disabled list (April 23-May 15, 1993). ... On Columbus temporarily inactive list (April 11-16, 1994). ... On Columbus disabled list (June 2-11, July 5-August 12, August 18-27 and August 28-September 4, 1994) ... On disabled list (June 8-26 and July 11, 1995-remainder of season). ... On New York disabled list (April 15-May 29, 1996); included rehabilitation assignments to Tampa (May 16-23) and Columbus (May 23-29). ... Traded by Yankees to Florida Marlins for P David Weathers (July 31, 1996). ... Traded by Marlins to Colorado Rockies for 2B Craig Counsell (July 27, 1997). ... Traded by Rockies to Cincinnati Reds for OF Curtis Goodwin (December 10, 1997). ... On Cincinnati disabled list (March 25-April 16 and May 22-June 9, 1998); included rehabilitation assignment to Indianapolis (May 25-June 9). ... On Indianapolis disabled list (August 24, 1998-remainder of season). ... Granted free agency (October 15, 1998). ... Signed by Tampa Bay Devil Rays organization (December 18, 1998).

Year Team (League)	W	L	Pct.	ERA	G	GS	CG	ShO	Sv.	IP	H	R	ER	BB	SO
1989— Oneonta (N.Y.-Penn)	6	2	.750	4.07	12	12	0	0	0	66 1/3	70	39	30	24	62
1990— Greensboro (S. Atl.)	1	10	.091	6.31	21	19	0	0	0	81 1/3	77	78	57	62	72
1991— Fort Lauderdale (FSL)	5	8	.385	2.45	24	24	3	0	0	147	98	54	40	65	117
— Columbus (Int'l)	1	0	1.000	1.50	1	1	0	0	0	6	3	2	1	5	5
1992— Alb./Colon. (East.)	13	7	.650	3.59	25	25	1	0	0	165 1/3	146	75	66	66	128
— Columbus (Int'l)	0	1	.000	5.40	1	0	0	0	0	5	7	4	3	2	4
1993— Columbus (Int'l)	10	4	.714	3.18	21	21	0	0	0	133	98	52	47	53	112
— New York (A.L.)	1	1	.500	5.73	7	4	0	0	0	22	24	17	14	17	12
1994— Columbus (Int'l)	2	5	.286	3.63	22	5	0	0	3	34 2/3	31	16	14	12	27
— New York (A.L.)	0	0	. . .	4.91	2	0	0	0	0	3 2/3	4	3	2	0	1
1995— Columbus (Int'l)	2	6	.250	8.43	11	11	0	0	0	52 1/3	64	51	49	24	23
1996— New York (A.L.)	0	2	.000	5.04	12	2	0	0	0	30 1/3	32	19	17	18	25
— Tampa (Fla. St.)	0	0	. . .	1.80	3	2	0	0	0	5	2	1	1	1	6
— Columbus (Int'l)	0	0	. . .	0.00	2	0	0	0	0	2	0	0	0	2	3
— Florida (N.L.)■	5	1	.833	3.67	13	9	0	0	0	56 1/3	47	23	23	18	31
1997— Florida (N.L.)	3	1	.750	3.78	32	0	0	0	0	47 2/3	50	24	20	19	29
— Colorado (N.L.)■	0	1	.000	7.11	8	1	0	0	0	12 2/3	22	10	10	7	10
1998— Cincinnati (N.L.)■	0	1	.000	7.41	10	2	0	0	0	17	24	14	14	17	3
— Indianapolis (Int'l)	4	6	.400	4.43	16	16	0	0	0	83 1/3	91	50	41	37	47
A.L. totals (3 years)	1	3	.250	5.30	21	6	0	0	0	56	60	39	33	35	38
N.L. totals (3 years)	8	4	.667	4.51	63	12	0	0	0	133 2/3	143	71	67	61	73
Major league totals (5 years)	9	7	.563	4.75	84	18	0	0	0	189 2/3	203	110	100	96	111

IAPOCE, ANTHONY   OF   BREWERS

PERSONAL: Born August 23, 1973, in Astoria, N.Y. ... 5-10/175. ... Bats both, throws left. ... Full name: Anthony Joseph Iapoce.
HIGH SCHOOL: Monsignor McClancy Memorial (East Elmhurst, N.Y.).
TRANSACTIONS/CAREER NOTES: Selected by Milwaukee Brewers organization in 33rd round of free-agent draft (June 2, 1994).
STATISTICAL NOTES: Led Arizona League outfielders with 102 total chances in 1994. ... Led Texas League in caught stealing with 20 in 1998. ... Led Texas League outfielders with 295 total chances in 1998.

						BATTING								FIELDING		
Year Team (League)	Pos.	G	AB	R	H	2B	3B	HR	RBI	Avg.	BB	SO	SB	PO	A	E	Avg.
1994— Ariz. Brewers (Ariz.)	OF	55	222	•37	55	7	2	0	25	.248	15	43	16	*90	9	3	.971
1995— Ariz. Brewers (Ariz.)	OF	3	3	2	1	0	0	0	0	.333	1	1	1	3	0	0	1.000
— Helena (Pioneer)	OF	39	146	43	44	7	0	0	13	.301	28	24	19	55	2	2	.966
1996— Beloit (Midwest)	OF	78	269	63	78	6	3	1	11	.290	44	54	23	126	5	2	.985
1997— Tucson (PCL)	OF	7	21	5	7	4	0	0	3	.333	1	4	0	18	0	0	1.000
— Stockton (California)	OF	99	387	48	103	13	4	1	27	.266	30	71	22	168	9	7	.962
1998— El Paso (Texas)	OF	133	*576	97	*181	23	6	2	53	.314	33	67	35	*279	8	8	.973

IBANEZ, RAUL   OF   MARINERS

PERSONAL: Born June 2, 1972, in Manhattan, N.Y. ... 6-2/200. ... Bats left, throws right. ... Full name: Raul Javier Ibanez.
HIGH SCHOOL: Sunset (Miami).
JUNIOR COLLEGE: Miami-Dade (South) Community College.
TRANSACTIONS/CAREER NOTES: Selected by Seattle Mariners organization in 36th round of free-agent draft (June 1, 1992). ... On disabled list (June 4-July 16, 1994). ... On Seattle disabled list (March 30-June 29, 1998); included rehabilitation assignment to Tacoma (May 30-June 28). ... On Tacoma disabled list (July 7-14, 1998).
STATISTICAL NOTES: Led California League with .612 slugging percentage in 1995. ... Led California League with 25 passed balls in 1995.

Year	Team (League)	Pos.	G	AB	R	H	2B	3B	HR	RBI	Avg.	BB	SO	SB	PO	A	E	Avg.
1992—Ariz. Mariners (Ariz.)..	1B-C-OF	33	120	25	37	8	2	1	16	.308	9	18	1	51	3	4	.931
1993—Appleton (Midwest)....	1B-C-OF	52	157	26	43	9	0	5	21	.274	24	31	0	98	2	2	.980
—Bellingham (N'west)...	C	43	134	16	38	5	2	0	15	.284	21	23	0	137	15	1	.993
1994—Appleton (Midwest)....	C-1B-OF	91	327	55	102	30	3	7	59	.312	32	37	10	304	28	10	.971
1995—Riverside (Calif.)........	C-1B	95	361	59	120	23	9	20	108	.332	41	49	4	465	54	12	.977
1996—Tacoma (PCL)	OF-1B	111	405	59	115	20	3	11	47	.284	44	56	7	201	12	11	.951
—Port City (Southern)...	OF-C-1B	19	76	12	28	8	1	1	13	.368	8	7	3	36	2	4	.905
—Seattle (A.L.)	DH	4	5	0	0	0	0	0	0	.000	0	1	0	0	0	0	...
1997—Tacoma (PCL)	OF	111	438	84	133	30	5	15	84	.304	32	75	7	192	12	5	.976
—Seattle (A.L.)	OF-DH	11	26	3	4	0	1	1	4	.154	0	6	0	9	0	0	1.000
1998—Tacoma (PCL)	OF	52	190	24	41	8	1	6	25	.216	24	47	1	78	2	1	.988
—Seattle (A.L.)	OF-1B-DH	37	98	12	25	7	1	2	12	.255	5	22	0	105	7	1	.991
Major league totals (3 years)		52	129	15	29	7	2	3	16	.225	5	29	0	114	7	1	.992

INCAVIGLIA, PETE   OF   DIAMONDBACKS

PERSONAL: Born April 2, 1964, in Pebble Beach, Calif. ... 6-1/230. ... Bats right, throws right. ... Full name: Peter Joseph Incaviglia. ... Son of Tom Incaviglia, minor league infielder (1948-55); and brother of Tony Incaviglia, minor league third baseman (1979-83).

HIGH SCHOOL: Monterey (Pebble Beach, Calif.).

COLLEGE: Oklahoma State.

TRANSACTIONS/CAREER NOTES: Selected by San Francisco Giants organization in 10th round of free-agent draft (June 7, 1982); did not sign. ... Selected by Montreal Expos organization in first round (eighth pick overall) of free-agent draft (June 3, 1985). ... Traded by Expos to Texas Rangers organization for P Bob Sebra and IF Jim Anderson (November 2, 1985). ... On disabled list (June 15-30, 1989). ... Released by Rangers (March 29, 1991). ... Signed by Detroit Tigers (April 7, 1991). ... On disabled list (June 13-July 5 and July 25-August 11, 1991). ... Granted free agency (October 31, 1991). ... Signed by Tucson, Houston Astros organization (January 27, 1992). ... Granted free agency (November 3, 1992). ... Signed by Philadelphia Phillies (December 8, 1992). ... Granted free agency (October 18, 1994). ... Signed by Chiba Lotte Marines of Japan Pacific League (December 28, 1994). ... Signed by Phillies organization (December 13, 1995). ... Traded by Phillies with 3B Todd Zeile to Baltimore Orioles for two players to be named later (August 29, 1996); Phillies acquired P Calvin Maduro and P Garrett Stephenson to complete deal (September 4, 1996). ... Granted free agency (October 31, 1996). ... Re-signed by Orioles (December 19, 1996). ... On Baltimore disabled list (March 31-April 17, 1997). ... Released by Orioles (July 14, 1997). ... Signed by New York Yankees organization (July 25, 1997). ... Released by Yankees (August 15, 1997). ... Signed by Tigers organization (January 29, 1998). ... Released by Tigers (April 23, 1998). ... Signed by Houston Astros organization (May 12, 1998). ... On Houston disabled list (August 25-September 9, 1998). ... Released by Astros (October 16, 1998). ... Signed by Arizona Diamondbacks organization (December 17, 1998).

RECORDS: Shares major league single-inning record for most doubles—2 (May 11, 1986, second game, fourth inning).

HONORS: Named designated hitter on THE SPORTING NEWS college All-America team (1985).

STATISTICAL NOTES: Career major league grand slams: 7.

Year	Team (League)	Pos.	G	AB	R	H	2B	3B	HR	RBI	Avg.	BB	SO	SB	PO	A	E	Avg.
1986—Texas (A.L.)	OF-DH	153	540	82	135	21	2	30	88	.250	55	*185	3	157	6	•14	.921
1987—Texas (A.L.)	OF-DH	139	509	85	138	26	4	27	80	.271	48	168	9	216	8	•13	.945
1988—Texas (A.L.)	OF-DH	116	418	59	104	19	3	22	54	.249	39	•153	6	172	12	2	.989
1989—Texas (A.L.)	OF-DH	133	453	48	107	27	4	21	81	.236	32	136	5	213	7	6	.973
1990—Texas (A.L.)	OF-DH	153	529	59	123	27	0	24	85	.233	45	146	3	290	12	8	.974
1991—Detroit (A.L.)■	OF-DH	97	337	38	72	12	1	11	38	.214	36	92	1	106	4	3	.973
1992—Houston (A.L.)	OF	113	349	31	93	22	1	11	44	.266	25	99	2	188	8	6	.970
1993—Philadelphia (N.L.)■..	OF	116	368	60	101	16	3	24	89	.274	21	82	1	164	4	5	.971
1994—Philadelphia (N.L.).....	OF	80	244	28	56	10	1	13	32	.230	16	71	1	90	2	2	.979
1995—Chiba Lot. (J.P.)■ ..	OF	...	243	25	44	5	0	10	31	.181	23	74	1	...	...	...	...
1996—Philadelphia (N.L.)■..	OF	99	269	33	63	7	2	16	42	.234	30	82	2	91	4	3	.969
—Baltimore (A.L.)■........	OF-DH	12	33	4	10	2	0	2	8	.303	0	7	0	9	1	0	1.000
1997—Baltimore (A.L.)	DH-OF	48	138	18	34	4	0	5	12	.246	11	43	0	20	0	1	.952
—Columbus (Int'l)■.......	OF	3	13	1	4	1	0	0	2	.308	0	4	0	7	1	0	1.000
—New York (A.L.)	DH	5	16	1	4	0	0	0	0	.250	0	3	0	...	...	...	...
1998—Detroit (A.L.)■.........	DH-OF	7	14	0	1	0	0	0	0	.071	1	6	0	0	0	0	...
—New Orleans (PCL)■..	OF	76	281	57	91	10	1	23	66	.324	34	63	11	62	1	3	.955
—Houston (N.L.)	OF	13	16	0	2	1	0	0	2	.125	1	4	0	3	0	0	1.000
American League totals (9 years)		863	2987	394	728	138	14	142	446	.244	267	939	27	1183	50	47	.963
National League totals (5 years)		421	1246	152	315	56	7	64	209	.253	93	338	6	536	18	16	.972
Major league totals (12 years)		1284	4233	546	1043	194	21	206	655	.246	360	1277	33	1719	68	63	.966

DIVISION SERIES RECORD

Year	Team (League)	Pos.	G	AB	R	H	2B	3B	HR	RBI	Avg.	BB	SO	SB	PO	A	E	Avg.
1996—Baltimore (A.L.)..........	OF-PR	2	5	1	1	0	0	0	0	.200	0	4	0	0	0	0	...
1998—Houston (N.L.)	PH	1	1	0	0	0	0	0	0	.000	0	1	0	...	...	...	...
Division series totals (2 years)		3	6	1	1	0	0	0	0	.167	0	5	0	0	0	0	...

CHAMPIONSHIP SERIES RECORD

Year	Team (League)	Pos.	G	AB	R	H	2B	3B	HR	RBI	Avg.	BB	SO	SB	PO	A	E	Avg.
1993—Philadelphia (N.L.)........	OF	3	12	2	2	0	0	1	1	.167	0	3	0	8	0	0	1.000
1996—Baltimore (A.L.)........	DH	1	2	1	1	0	0	0	0	.500	0	0	0	...	...	...	...
Championship series totals (2 years)		4	14	3	3	0	0	1	1	.214	0	3	0	8	0	0	1.000

WORLD SERIES RECORD

Year	Team (League)	Pos.	G	AB	R	H	2B	3B	HR	RBI	Avg.	BB	SO	SB	PO	A	E	Avg.
1993—Philadelphia (N.L.)......	OF-PH	4	8	0	1	0	0	0	1	.125	0	4	0	7	0	0	1.000

INGRAM, DARRON   OF   REDS

PERSONAL: Born June 7, 1976, in Lexington, Ky. ... 6-3/218. ... Bats right, throws right. ... Full name: Darron Scott Ingram.
HIGH SCHOOL: Bryan Station (Lexington, Ky.).
TRANSACTIONS/CAREER NOTES: Selected by Cincinnati Reds organization in 12th round of free-agent draft (June 2, 1994).

Year Team (League)	Pos.	G	AB	R	H	2B	3B	HR	RBI	Avg.	BB	SO	SB	PO	A	E	Avg.
1994—Princeton (Appal.)	OF-2B	46	131	13	26	5	1	2	11	.198	19	50	1	38	1	3	.929
1995—Princeton (Appal.)	OF	60	233	37	64	6	3	14	53	.275	11	78	3	98	2	5	.952
1996—Char., W.Va. (SAL)	OF	15	48	5	9	3	0	1	6	.188	8	19	0	4	0	0	1.000
—Billings (Pioneer)	OF	65	251	49	74	13	0	•17	56	.295	34	88	7	4	0	0	1.000
1997—Burlington (Midw.)	OF-1B	134	510	74	135	25	4	29	97	.265	46	195	8	340	18	8	.978
1998—Chattanooga (Sou.)	OF	125	466	62	108	21	9	17	65	.232	43	*169	4	203	5	3	.986

IRABU, HIDEKI   P   YANKEES

PERSONAL: Born May 5, 1969, in Hyogo, Japan. ... 6-4/240. ... Throws right, bats right.
TRANSACTIONS/CAREER NOTES: Rights acquired by San Diego Padres from Chiba Lotte Marines of Japan Pacific League (January 13, 1997). ... Rights traded by Padres with 2B Homer Bush, OF Gordon Amerson and a player to be named later to New York Yankees for OF Ruben Rivera, P Rafael Medina and cash (April 22, 1997); Padres traded OF Vernon Maxwell to Yankees to complete deal (June 9, 1997). ... Signed by Yankees (May 29, 1997).
STATISTICAL NOTES: Tied for A.L. lead with three balks in 1997.

Year Team (League)	W	L	Pct.	ERA	G	GS	CG	ShO	Sv.	IP	H	R	ER	BB	SO
1988—Lotte (Jap. Pac.)	2	5	.286	3.89	14	6	...	...	1	39 1/3	30	19	17	15	21
1989—Lotte (Jap. Pac.)	0	2	.000	3.53	33	2	...	...	9	51	37	20	20	27	50
1990—Lotte (Jap. Pac.)	8	5	.615	3.78	34	7	...	...	0	123 2/3	110	56	52	72	102
1991—Lotte (Jap. Pac.)	3	8	.273	6.88	24	14	...	...	0	100 2/3	110	78	77	70	78
1992—Chiba Lotte (Jp. Pac.)	0	5	.000	3.86	28	4	...	...	0	77	78	38	33	37	55
1993—Chiba Lotte (Jp. Pac.)	8	7	.533	3.10	32	8	...	...	1	142 1/3	125	59	49	58	160
1994—Chiba Lotte (Jp. Pac.)	*15	10	.600	3.04	27	20	...	...	0	207 1/3	170	77	70	94	239
1995—Chiba Lotte (Jp. Pac.)	11	11	.500	*2.53	28	18	...	...	0	203	158	70	57	72	239
1996—Chiba Lotte (Jp. Pac.)	12	6	.667	*2.40	23	20	3	...	0	157 1/3	108	57	42	59	167
1997—Tampa (Fla. St.)■	1	0	1.000	0.00	2	2	0	0	0	9	4	0	0	0	12
—Norwich (Eastern)	1	1	.500	4.50	2	2	0	0	0	10	13	5	5	0	9
—Columbus (Int'l)	2	0	1.000	1.67	4	4	1	1	0	27	19	7	5	5	28
—New York (A.L.)	5	4	.556	7.09	13	9	0	0	0	53 1/3	69	47	42	20	56
1998—New York (A.L.)	13	9	.591	4.06	29	28	2	1	0	173	148	79	78	76	126
Major league totals (2 years)	18	13	.581	4.77	42	37	2	1	0	226 1/3	217	126	120	96	182

DIVISION SERIES RECORD

Year Team (League)	W	L	Pct.	ERA	G	GS	CG	ShO	Sv.	IP	H	R	ER	BB	SO
1998—New York (A.L.)						Did not play.									

CHAMPIONSHIP SERIES RECORD

Year Team (League)	W	L	Pct.	ERA	G	GS	CG	ShO	Sv.	IP	H	R	ER	BB	SO
1998—New York (A.L.)						Did not play.									

WORLD SERIES RECORD

NOTES: Member of World Series championship team (1998).

Year Team (League)	W	L	Pct.	ERA	G	GS	CG	ShO	Sv.	IP	H	R	ER	BB	SO
1998—New York (A.L.)						Did not play.									

ISRINGHAUSEN, JASON   P   METS

PERSONAL: Born September 7, 1972, in Brighton, Ill. ... 6-3/196. ... Throws right, bats right. ... Full name: Jason Derik Isringhausen. ... Name pronounced IS-ring-how-zin.
HIGH SCHOOL: Southwestern (Brighton, Ill.).
JUNIOR COLLEGE: Lewis & Clark Community College (Ill.).
TRANSACTIONS/CAREER NOTES: Selected by New York Mets organization in 44th round of free-agent draft (June 3, 1991). ... On disabled list (August 13-September 1, 1996). ... On disabled list (March 24-August 27, 1997); included rehabilitation assignment to Norfolk (April 6-11 and August 22-27), Gulf Coast Mets (August 6-11) and St. Lucie (August 11-22). ... On disabled list (March 21, 1998-entire season).
HONORS: Named International League Most Valuable Pitcher (1995).

Year Team (League)	W	L	Pct.	ERA	G	GS	CG	ShO	Sv.	IP	H	R	ER	BB	SO
1992—GC Mets (GCL)	2	4	.333	4.34	6	6	0	0	0	29	26	19	14	17	25
—Kingsport (Appalachian)	4	1	.800	3.25	7	6	1	1	0	36	32	22	13	12	24
1993—Pittsfield (NYP)	7	4	.636	3.29	15	15	2	0	0	90 1/3	68	45	33	28	*104
1994—St. Lucie (Fla. St.)	6	4	.600	2.23	14	14	•6	•3	0	101	76	31	25	27	59
—Binghamton (Eastern)	5	4	.556	3.02	14	14	2	0	0	92 1/3	78	35	31	23	69
1995—Binghamton (Eastern)	2	1	.667	2.85	6	6	1	0	0	41	26	15	13	12	59
—Norfolk (Int'l)	9	1	*.900	1.55	12	12	3	*3	0	87	64	17	15	24	75
—New York (N.L.)	9	2	.818	2.81	14	14	1	0	0	93	88	29	29	31	55
1996—New York (N.L.)	6	14	.300	4.77	27	27	2	1	0	171 2/3	190	103	91	73	114
1997—Norfolk (Int'l)	0	2	.000	4.05	3	3	0	0	0	20	20	10	9	8	17
—GC Mets (GCL)	1	0	1.000	1.93	1	0	0	0	0	4 2/3	2	1	1	1	7
—St. Lucie (Fla. St.)	1	0	1.000	0.00	2	0	0	0	0	12	8	1	0	5	15
—New York (N.L.)	2	2	.500	7.58	6	6	0	0	0	29 2/3	40	27	25	22	25
1998—New York (N.L.)						Did not play.									
Major league totals (3 years)	17	18	.486	4.43	47	47	3	1	0	294 1/3	318	159	145	126	194

JACKSON, DAMIAN   SS   REDS

PERSONAL: Born August 16, 1973, in Los Angeles. ... 5-11/185. ... Bats right, throws right. ... Full name: Damian Jacques Jackson.
HIGH SCHOOL: Ygnacio Valley (Concord, Calif.).
JUNIOR COLLEGE: Laney (Calif.).
TRANSACTIONS/CAREER NOTES: Selected by Cleveland Indians organization in 44th round of free-agent draft (June 3, 1991). ... Traded by Indians with P Danny Graves, P Jim Crowell and P Scott Winchester to Cincinnati Reds for P John Smiley and IF Jeff Branson (July 31, 1997).
STATISTICAL NOTES: Led Appalachian League shortstops with 342 total chances and 45 double plays in 1992. ... Led Eastern League shortstops with 241 putouts, 446 assists, 54 errors, 741 total chances and 85 double plays in 1994. ... Led Eastern League in caught stealing with 22 in 1995. ... Tied for Eastern League lead in double plays by shortstop with 80 in 1995. ... Led American Association shortstops with 635 total chances and 84 double plays in 1996. ... Led International League shortstops with 227 putouts, 434 assists, 44 errors, 705 total chances and 101 double plays in 1998.

Year	Team (League)	Pos.	G	AB	R	H	2B	3B	HR	RBI	Avg.	BB	SO	SB	PO	A	E	Avg.
1992—	Burlington (Appal.)......	SS	62	226	32	56	12	1	0	23	.248	32	31	29	*102	*217	23	.933
1993—	Columbus (S. Atl.)......	SS	108	350	70	94	19	3	6	45	.269	41	61	26	191	324	52	.908
1994—	Cant./Akr. (Eastern)....	SS-OF	138	531	85	143	29	5	5	60	.269	60	121	37	†241	†446	†54	.927
1995—	Cant./Akr. (Eastern)....	SS	131	484	67	120	20	2	3	34	.248	65	103	40	*220	337	*36	.939
1996—	Buffalo (A.A.).............	SS	133	452	77	116	15	1	12	49	.257	48	78	24	*203	*403	29	.954
—	Cleveland (A.L.).........	P	5	10	2	3	2	0	0	1	.300	1	4	0	3	13	0	1.000
1997—	Buffalo (A.A.).............	SS-2B-OF	73	266	51	78	12	0	4	13	.293	37	45	20	128	246	23	.942
—	Cleveland (A.L.).........	SS-2B	8	9	2	1	0	0	0	0	.111	0	1	1	7	7	0	1.000
—	Indianapolis (A.A.)■..	2B-SS	19	71	12	19	6	1	0	7	.268	10	17	4	36	55	5	.948
—	Cincinnati (N.L.)........	SS-2B	12	27	6	6	2	1	1	2	.222	4	7	1	12	21	1	.971
1998—	Indianapolis (Int'l)......	SS-OF	131	517	102	135	36	10	6	49	.261	62	125	25	†230	†435	†44	.938
—	Cincinnati (N.L.)........	SS-OF	13	38	4	12	5	0	0	7	.316	6	4	2	20	21	1	.976
American League totals (2 years)			**13**	**19**	**4**	**4**	**2**	**0**	**0**	**1**	**.211**	**1**	**5**	**1**	**10**	**20**	**0**	**1.000**
National League totals (2 years)			**25**	**65**	**10**	**18**	**7**	**1**	**1**	**9**	**.277**	**10**	**11**	**3**	**32**	**42**	**2**	**.974**
Major league totals (3 years)			**38**	**84**	**14**	**22**	**9**	**1**	**1**	**10**	**.262**	**11**	**16**	**4**	**42**	**62**	**2**	**.981**

JACKSON, DARRIN   OF

PERSONAL: Born August 22, 1963, in Los Angeles. ... 6-0/191. ... Bats right, throws right. ... Full name: Darrin Jay Jackson.
HIGH SCHOOL: Culver City (Calif.).
TRANSACTIONS/CAREER NOTES: Selected by Chicago Cubs organization in second round of free-agent draft (June 8, 1981). ... Traded by Cubs with P Calvin Schiraldi and a player to be named later to San Diego Padres for OF Marvell Wynne and IF Luis Salazar (August 30, 1989); Padres acquired 1B Phil Stephenson to complete deal (September 5, 1989). ... Traded by Padres to Toronto Blue Jays for OF Derek Bell and OF Stoney Briggs (March 30, 1993). ... Traded by Blue Jays to New York Mets for SS Tony Fernandez (June 11, 1993). ... On New York disabled list (July 19-September 1, 1993). ... Granted free agency (December 20, 1993). ... Signed by Chicago White Sox organization (December 28, 1993). ... Granted free agency (October 15, 1994). ... Played with Seibu Lions of Japan Pacific League (1995-96). ... Signed by San Francisco Giants organization (December 20, 1996). ... Released by Giants (March 31, 1997). ... Signed by Minnesota Twins organization (April 24, 1997). ... Traded by Twins to Milwaukee Brewers for a player to be named later (August 30, 1997); Twins acquired P Mick Fieldbinder to complete deal (September 4, 1997). ... Granted free agency (October 27, 1997). ... Re-signed by Brewers (December 6, 1997). ... On disabled list (March 23-April 7, 1998). ... Granted free agency (October 22, 1998).
STATISTICAL NOTES: Led Gulf Coast League outfielders with 127 total chances in 1981. ... Tied for Texas League lead in double plays by outfielder with six in 1984. ... Tied for American Association lead in double plays by outfielder with six in 1987. ... Led N.L. in grounding into double plays with 21 in 1992. ... Led N.L. outfielders with 455 total chances and nine double plays in 1992. ... Career major league grand slams: 4.

Year	Team (League)	Pos.	G	AB	R	H	2B	3B	HR	RBI	Avg.	BB	SO	SB	PO	A	E	Avg.
1981—	GC Cubs (GCL)..........	OF	62	210	29	39	5	0	1	15	.186	28	53	18	*121	5	1	.992
1982—	Quad Cities (Mid.).......	OF	132	529	86	146	23	5	5	48	.276	47	106	58	266	9	8	.972
1983—	Salinas (Calif.)..........	OF	129	509	70	126	18	5	6	54	.248	38	111	36	237	15	13	.951
1984—	Midland (Texas)..........	OF	132	496	63	134	18	2	15	54	.270	49	102	13	286	*19	8	.974
1985—	Iowa (Am. Assoc.).......	OF	10	40	0	7	2	1	0	1	.175	3	10	1	19	0	0	1.000
—	Pittsfield (Eastern)......	OF	91	325	38	82	10	1	3	30	.252	34	64	8	221	5	0	1.000
—	Chicago (N.L.)...........	OF	5	11	0	1	0	0	0	0	.091	0	3	0	7	0	0	1.000
1986—	Pittsfield (Eastern)......	OF	137	•520	82	139	28	2	15	64	.267	43	115	42	320	*16	7	.980
1987—	Iowa (Am. Assoc.).......	OF	132	474	81	130	32	5	23	81	.274	26	110	13	290	15	6	.981
—	Chicago (N.L.)...........	OF	7	5	2	4	1	0	0	0	.800	0	0	0	1	0	0	1.000
1988—	Chicago (N.L.)...........	OF	100	188	29	50	11	3	6	20	.266	5	28	4	116	1	2	.983
1989—	Chicago (N.L.)...........	OF	45	83	7	19	4	0	1	8	.229	6	17	1	61	3	2	.970
—	Iowa (Am. Assoc.).......	OF	30	120	16	31	4	1	7	17	.258	7	22	4	66	12	0	1.000
—	San Diego (N.L.)■......	OF	25	87	10	18	3	0	3	12	.207	7	17	0	60	2	3	.954
1990—	San Diego (N.L.)........	OF	58	113	10	29	3	0	3	9	.257	5	24	3	63	1	1	.985
—	Las Vegas (PCL)	OF	29	98	14	27	4	0	5	15	.276	9	21	3	61	4	0	1.000
1991—	San Diego (N.L.)........	OF-P	122	359	51	94	12	1	21	49	.262	27	66	5	243	2	2	.992
1992—	San Diego (N.L.)........	OF	155	587	72	146	23	5	17	70	.249	26	106	14	436	*18	2	.996
1993—	Toronto (A.L.).............	OF	46	176	15	38	8	0	5	19	.216	8	53	0	86	2	1	.989
—	New York (N.L.)■.......	OF	31	87	4	17	1	0	1	7	.195	2	22	0	51	4	0	1.000
1994—	Chicago (A.L.)...........	OF	104	369	43	115	17	3	10	51	.312	27	56	7	223	2	1	.996
1995—	Seibu (Jp. Pac.)■........	...	128	506	66	146	28	3	20	68	.289	34	104	9	...	...	...	...
1996—	Seibu (Jp. Pac.)..........	...	126	489	42	130	21	3	19	64	.266	30	70	10	...	...	...	...
1997—	Salt Lake (PCL)■........	OF	19	80	14	24	3	3	1	12	.300	5	17	3	26	2	0	1.000
—	Minnesota (A.L.).........	OF	49	130	19	33	2	1	3	21	.254	4	21	2	93	4	1	.990
—	Milwaukee (A.L.)■......	OF	26	81	7	22	7	0	2	15	.272	2	10	2	55	2	0	1.000
1998—	Milwaukee (A.L.)........	OF-DH	114	204	20	49	13	1	4	20	.240	9	37	1	106	3	2	.982
American League totals (3 years)			**225**	**756**	**84**	**208**	**34**	**4**	**20**	**106**	**.275**	**41**	**140**	**11**	**457**	**10**	**3**	**.994**
National League totals (9 years)			**662**	**1724**	**205**	**427**	**71**	**10**	**56**	**195**	**.248**	**87**	**320**	**28**	**1144**	**34**	**14**	**.988**
Major league totals (11 years)			**887**	**2480**	**289**	**635**	**105**	**14**	**76**	**301**	**.256**	**128**	**460**	**39**	**1601**	**44**	**17**	**.990**

RECORD AS PITCHER

Year	Team (League)	W	L	Pct.	ERA	G	GS	CG	ShO	Sv.	IP	H	R	ER	BB	SO
1991—San Diego (N.L.)		0	0	...	9.00	1	0	0	0	0	2	3	2	2	2	0

JACKSON, MIKE   P   INDIANS

PERSONAL: Born December 22, 1964, in Houston. ... 6-2/225. ... Throws right, bats right. ... Full name: Michael Ray Jackson.
HIGH SCHOOL: Forest Brook (Houston).
JUNIOR COLLEGE: Hill Junior College (Texas).
TRANSACTIONS/CAREER NOTES: Selected by Philadelphia Phillies organization in 29th round of free-agent draft (June 6, 1983); did not sign. ... Selected by Phillies organization in secondary phase of free-agent draft (January 17, 1984). ... On Philadelphia disabled list (August 6-21, 1987). ... Traded by Phillies organization with OF Glenn Wilson and OF Dave Brundage to Seattle Mariners for OF Phil Bradley and P Tim Fortugno (December 9, 1987). ... Traded by Mariners with P Bill Swift and P Dave Burba to San Francisco Giants for OF Kevin Mitchell and P Mike Remlinger (December 11, 1991). ... On disabled list (July 24-August 9, 1993; June 17-July 2 and July 7, 1994-remainder of season). ... Granted free agency (October 17, 1994). ... Signed by Cincinnati Reds (April 8, 1995). ... On Cincinnati disabled list (April 20-June 5, 1995); included rehabilitation assignments to Chattanooga (May 21-30) and Indianapolis (May 30-June 5). ... Granted free agency (November 3, 1995). ... Signed by Mariners (February 2, 1996). ... Granted free agency (October 30, 1996). ... Signed by Cleveland Indians (December 12, 1996).
STATISTICAL NOTES: Led Carolina League with seven balks in 1985. ... Tied for N.L. lead with eight balks in 1987. ... Tied for A.L. lead with three balks in 1998.

Year	Team (League)	W	L	Pct.	ERA	G	GS	CG	ShO	Sv.	IP	H	R	ER	BB	SO
1984—Spartanburg (SAL)		7	2	.778	2.68	14	0	0	0	0	80 2/3	53	35	24	50	77
1985—Peninsula (Caro.)		7	9	.438	4.60	31	18	0	0	1	125 1/3	127	71	64	53	96
1986—Reading (Eastern)		2	3	.400	1.66	30	0	0	0	6	43 1/3	25	9	8	22	42
—Portland (PCL)		3	1	.750	3.18	17	0	0	0	3	22 2/3	18	8	8	13	23
—Philadelphia (N.L.)............		0	0	...	3.38	9	0	0	0	0	13 1/3	12	5	5	4	3
1987—Philadelphia (N.L.)............		3	10	.231	4.20	55	7	0	0	1	109 1/3	88	55	51	56	93
—Maine (International).........		1	0	1.000	0.82	2	2	0	0	0	11	9	2	1	5	13
1988—Seattle (A.L.)■		6	5	.545	2.63	62	0	0	0	4	99 1/3	74	37	29	43	76
1989—Seattle (A.L.)		4	6	.400	3.17	65	0	0	0	7	99 1/3	81	43	35	54	94
1990—Seattle (A.L.)		5	7	.417	4.54	63	0	0	0	3	77 1/3	64	42	39	44	69
1991—Seattle (A.L.)		7	7	.500	3.25	72	0	0	0	14	88 2/3	64	35	32	34	74
1992—San Francisco (N.L.)■		6	6	.500	3.73	67	0	0	0	2	82	76	35	34	33	80
1993—San Francisco (N.L.)		6	6	.500	3.03	*81	0	0	0	1	77 1/3	58	28	26	24	70
1994—San Francisco (N.L.)		3	2	.600	1.49	36	0	0	0	4	42 1/3	23	8	7	11	51
1995—Chattanooga (Southern)■..		0	0	...	0.00	3	2	0	0	0	3	2	0	0	0	2
—Indianapolis (A.A.)............		0	0	...	0.00	2	1	0	0	0	2	0	0	0	0	1
—Cincinnati (N.L.)..............		6	1	.857	2.39	40	0	0	0	2	49	38	13	13	19	41
1996—Seattle (A.L.)■		1	1	.500	3.63	73	0	0	0	6	72	61	32	29	24	70
1997—Cleveland (A.L.)■		2	5	.286	3.24	71	0	0	0	15	75	59	33	27	29	74
1998—Cleveland (A.L.)		1	1	.500	1.55	69	0	0	0	40	64	43	11	11	13	55
A.L. totals (7 years)		26	32	.448	3.16	475	0	0	0	89	575 2/3	446	233	202	241	512
N.L. totals (6 years)		24	25	.490	3.28	288	7	0	0	10	373 1/3	295	144	136	147	338
Major league totals (13 years)		50	57	.467	3.21	763	7	0	0	99	949	741	377	338	388	850

DIVISION SERIES RECORD

NOTES: Shares A.L. career record for most saves—3.

Year	Team (League)	W	L	Pct.	ERA	G	GS	CG	ShO	Sv.	IP	H	R	ER	BB	SO
1995—Cincinnati (N.L.)		0	0	...	0.00	3	0	0	0	0	3 2/3	4	0	0	0	1
1997—Cleveland (A.L.)		1	0	1.000	0.00	4	0	0	0	0	4 1/3	3	0	0	1	5
1998—Cleveland (A.L.)		0	0	...	4.50	3	0	0	0	3	4	3	2	2	1	1
Div. series totals (3 years)		1	0	1.000	1.50	10	0	0	0	3	12	10	2	2	2	7

CHAMPIONSHIP SERIES RECORD

Year	Team (League)	W	L	Pct.	ERA	G	GS	CG	ShO	Sv.	IP	H	R	ER	BB	SO
1995—Cincinnati (N.L.)		0	1	.000	23.14	3	0	0	0	0	2 1/3	5	6	6	4	1
1997—Cleveland (A.L.)		0	0	...	0.00	5	0	0	0	0	4 1/3	1	0	0	1	7
1998—Cleveland (A.L.)		0	0	...	0.00	1	0	0	0	1	1	0	0	0	0	2
Champ. series totals (3 years)		0	1	.000	7.04	9	0	0	0	1	7 2/3	6	6	6	5	10

WORLD SERIES RECORD

Year	Team (League)	W	L	Pct.	ERA	G	GS	CG	ShO	Sv.	IP	H	R	ER	BB	SO
1997—Cleveland (A.L.)		0	0	...	1.93	4	0	0	0	0	4 2/3	5	1	1	3	4

JACKSON, RYAN   1B/OF   MARLINS

PERSONAL: Born November 11, 1971, in Sarasota, Fla. ... 6-3/185. ... Bats left, throws left. ... Full name: Ryan Dewitte Jackson.
HIGH SCHOOL: Cardinal Mooney (Sarasota, Fla.).
COLLEGE: Duke.
TRANSACTIONS/CAREER NOTES: Selected by Florida Marlins organization in seventh round of free-agent draft (June 2, 1994). ... On Kane County disabled list (April 5-August 1, 1996). ... On Portland disabled list (August 1-26, 1996).
STATISTICAL NOTES: Career major league grand slams: 1.

Year	Team (League)	Pos.	G	AB	R	H	2B	3B	HR	RBI	Avg.	BB	SO	SB	PO	A	E	Avg.
								BATTING								**FIELDING**		
1994—Elmira (N.Y.-Penn)......		OF-1B	72	276	46	80	18	1	6	41	.290	22	40	4	176	15	7	.965
1995—Kane County (Midw.)...		OF-1B	132	471	78	138	*39	6	10	82	.293	67	74	13	571	32	7	.989
1996—Brevard Co. (Fla. St.)..		1B	6	26	4	8	2	0	1	4	.308	1	7	1	28	2	2	.938
—GC Marlins (GCL).......		1B-OF	8	26	5	9	0	0	0	7	.346	1	3	2	35	3	0	1.000
1997—Portland (Eastern)......		OF-1B	134	491	87	153	28	4	26	98	.312	51	85	2	227	9	5	.979
1998—Florida (N.L.)		1B-OF-DH	111	260	26	65	15	1	5	31	.250	20	73	1	341	21	10	.973
—Charlotte (Int'l)		1B-OF	13	50	5	19	4	0	2	11	.380	4	14	2	57	6	0	1.000
Major league totals (1 year)			111	260	26	65	15	1	5	31	.250	20	73	1	341	21	10	.973

JACOB, RUSSELL   P   DIAMONDBACKS

PERSONAL: Born January 2, 1975, in Bartow, Fla. ... 6-6/225. ... Throws right, bats right.
HIGH SCHOOL: Winter Haven (Fla.).
TRANSACTIONS/CAREER NOTES: Selected by Seattle Mariners organization in 23rd round of free-agent draft (June 3, 1993). ... On disabled list (May 30-July 6, 1996). ... Selected by Arizona Diamondbacks from Mariners organization in Rule 5 major league draft (December 15, 1997).

Year	Team (League)	W	L	Pct.	ERA	G	GS	CG	ShO	Sv.	IP	H	R	ER	BB	SO
1994—	Peoria (Arizona)	0	0	...	2.70	8	2	0	0	0	13 1/3	9	4	4	5	12
1995—	Peoria (Arizona)	6	2	.750	2.88	12	11	0	0	0	56 1/3	47	29	18	31	54
1996—	Wisconsin (Midwest)	4	4	.500	5.27	24	10	0	0	2	68 1/3	67	48	40	53	63
1997—	Wisconsin (Midwest)	4	2	.667	4.44	21	9	0	0	1	77	62	41	38	58	76
1998—	High Desert (Calif.)■	3	2	.600	4.41	31	7	0	0	1	67 1/3	78	42	33	26	64

JACOBS, DWAYNE   P   WHITE SOX

PERSONAL: Born July 17, 1976, in Jacksonville. ... 6-10/225. ... Throws right, bats right. ... Full name: Dwayne Allen Jacobs.
HIGH SCHOOL: First Coast (Jacksonville).
TRANSACTIONS/CAREER NOTES: Selected by Atlanta Braves organization in 24th round of free-agent draft (June 2, 1994). ... On restricted list (June 12, 1995-remainder of season). ... On disabled list (April 22-May 11, 1996). ... Claimed on waivers by Chicago White Sox (November 19, 1998).
STATISTICAL NOTES: Led Carolina League with 19 wild pitches in 1998.

Year	Team (League)	W	L	Pct.	ERA	G	GS	CG	ShO	Sv.	IP	H	R	ER	BB	SO
1994—	GC Braves (GCL)	1	2	.333	8.16	12	1	0	0	0	28 2/3	35	29	26	19	14
1995—									Did not play.							
1996—	Macon (S. Atl.)	2	7	.222	6.80	26	15	0	0	0	82	85	82	62	76	76
1997—	Durham (Carolina)	4	8	.333	5.01	25	24	1	1	0	116 2/3	112	78	65	85	115
1998—	Danville (Carolina)	5	10	.333	4.99	31	19	0	0	0	110	92	71	61	*89	112

JACOME, JASON   P

PERSONAL: Born November 24, 1970, in Tulsa, Okla. ... 6-1/185. ... Throws left, bats left. ... Full name: Jason James Jacome. ... Name pronounced HOCK-ah-me.
HIGH SCHOOL: Rincon (Tucson, Ariz.).
JUNIOR COLLEGE: Pima Community College (Ariz.).
TRANSACTIONS/CAREER NOTES: Selected by New York Mets organization in 12th round of free-agent draft (June 3, 1991). ... On Norfolk disabled list (June 5-16 and June 17-July 21, 1995). ... Traded by Mets with P Allen McDill to Kansas City Royals for P Derek Wallace and a player to be named later (July 21, 1995); Mets acquired P John Carter to complete deal (November 16, 1995). ... Claimed on waivers by Cleveland Indians (May 8, 1997). ... On Buffalo disabled list (April 9-21 and May 23-June 6, 1998). ... Released by Indians (November 3, 1998).

Year	Team (League)	W	L	Pct.	ERA	G	GS	CG	ShO	Sv.	IP	H	R	ER	BB	SO
1991—	Kingsport (Appalachian)	5	4	.556	1.63	12	7	3	•1	2	55 1/3	35	18	10	13	48
1992—	Columbia (S. Atl.)	4	1	.800	1.03	8	8	1	0	0	52 2/3	40	7	6	15	49
	— St. Lucie (Fla. St.)	6	7	.462	2.83	17	17	5	1	0	114 1/3	98	45	36	30	66
1993—	St. Lucie (Fla. St.)	6	3	.667	3.08	14	14	2	2	0	99 1/3	106	37	34	23	66
	— Binghamton (Eastern)	8	4	.667	3.21	14	14	0	0	0	87	85	36	31	38	56
1994—	Norfolk (Int'l)	8	6	.571	2.84	19	19	4	1	0	126 2/3	138	57	40	42	80
	— New York (N.L.)	4	3	.571	2.67	8	8	1	1	0	54	54	17	16	17	30
1995—	New York (N.L.)	0	4	.000	10.29	5	5	0	0	0	21	33	24	24	15	11
	— Norfolk (Int'l)	2	4	.333	3.92	8	8	0	0	0	43 2/3	40	21	19	13	31
	— Kansas City (A.L.)■	4	6	.400	5.36	15	14	1	0	0	84	101	52	50	21	39
1996—	Kansas City (A.L.)	0	4	.000	4.72	49	2	0	0	1	47 2/3	67	27	25	22	32
1997—	Kansas City (A.L.)	0	0	...	9.45	7	0	0	0	0	6 2/3	13	7	7	5	3
	— Cleveland (A.L.)■	2	0	1.000	5.27	21	4	0	0	0	42 2/3	45	26	25	15	24
	— Buffalo (A.A.)	3	1	.750	3.16	7	7	1	0	0	37	41	14	13	10	23
1998—	Buffalo (Int'l)	14	2	*.875	3.26	24	24	2	0	0	154 2/3	161	62	56	38	109
	— Cleveland (A.L.)	0	1	.000	14.40	1	1	0	0	0	5	10	8	8	3	2
A.L. totals (4 years)		6	11	.353	5.56	93	21	1	0	1	186	236	120	115	66	100
N.L. totals (2 years)		4	7	.364	4.80	13	13	1	1	0	75	87	41	40	32	41
Major league totals (5 years)		10	18	.357	5.34	106	34	2	1	1	261	323	161	155	98	141

JAHA, JOHN   1B

PERSONAL: Born May 27, 1966, in Portland, Ore. ... 6-1/224. ... Bats right, throws right. ... Full name: John Emil Jaha. ... Name pronounced JAH-ha.
HIGH SCHOOL: David Douglas (Portland, Ore.).
TRANSACTIONS/CAREER NOTES: Selected by Milwaukee Brewers organization in 14th round of free-agent draft (June 4, 1984). ... On disabled list (April 6-August 1, 1990 and May 21-June 6, 1995). ... On Milwaukee disabled list (June 24-July 27, 1995); included rehabilitation assignments to Beloit (July 16-20) and New Orleans (July 20-27). ... On disabled list (June 3, 1997-remainder of season). ... On Milwaukee disabled list (April 23-June 7 and August 16-September 1, 1998); included rehabilitation assignment to Beloit (June 4-8). ... Granted free agency (October 26, 1998).
HONORS: Named Texas League Most Valuable Player (1991).
STATISTICAL NOTES: Led Northwest League with 144 total bases and tied for lead with four intentional bases on balls received in 1986. ... Led Texas League with 301 total bases, .619 slugging percentage and .438 on-base percentage in 1991. ... Led Texas League first basemen with 81 assists in 1991. ... Career major league grand slams: 5.

Year	Team (League)	Pos.	G	AB	R	H	2B	3B	HR	RBI	Avg.	BB	SO	SB	PO	A	E	Avg.
1985—	Helena (Pioneer)	3B	24	68	13	18	3	0	2	14	.265	14	23	4	9	32	1	.976
1986—	Tri-Cities (NWL)	1B-3B	•73	258	65	82	13	2	*15	67	.318	*70	75	9	352	101	18	.962
1987—	Beloit (Midwest)	3B-1B-SS	122	376	68	101	22	0	7	47	.269	102	86	10	493	113	18	.971
1988—	Stockton (California)	1B	99	302	58	77	14	6	8	54	.255	69	85	10	793	60	5	*.994
1989—	Stockton (California)..	1B-3B	140	479	83	140	26	5	25	91	.292	*112	115	8	1081	62	8	.993
1990—	Stockton (California)..	DH	26	84	12	22	5	0	4	19	.262	18	25	0	...	...	...	...
1991—	El Paso (Texas)	1B-3B	130	486	*121	167	38	3	*30	*134	.344	78	101	12	883	†87	10	.990
1992—	Denver (A.A.)	1B	79	274	61	88	18	2	18	69	.321	50	60	6	654	50	7	.990
—	Milwaukee (A.L.)	1B-DH-OF	47	133	17	30	3	1	2	10	.226	12	30	10	286	22	0	1.000
1993—	Milwaukee (A.L.)	1B-3B-2B	153	515	78	136	21	0	19	70	.264	51	109	13	1187	128	10	.992
1994—	Milwaukee (A.L.)	1B-DH	84	291	45	70	14	0	12	39	.241	32	75	3	660	47	8	.989
—	New Orleans (A.A.)	1B	18	62	8	25	7	1	2	16	.403	12	8	2	122	14	1	.993
1995—	Milwaukee (A.L.)	1B-DH	88	316	59	99	20	2	20	65	.313	36	66	2	649	60	2	.997
—	Beloit (Midwest)	DH	1	4	1	0	0	0	0	0	.000	0	1	0	...	...	...	...
—	New Orleans (A.A.)	1B	3	10	2	4	1	0	1	3	.400	2	1	0	9	2	0	1.000
1996—	Milwaukee (A.L.)	1B-DH	148	543	108	163	28	1	34	118	.300	85	118	3	676	58	6	.992
1997—	Milwaukee (A.L.)	1B-DH	46	162	25	40	7	0	11	26	.247	25	40	1	220	14	2	.992
1998—	Milwaukee (N.L.)	1B-DH	73	216	29	45	6	1	7	38	.208	49	66	1	441	23	3	.994
—	Beloit (Midwest)	DH	2	4	1	0	0	0	0	0	.000	2	2	0	...	...	...	...
American League totals (6 years)			566	1960	332	538	93	4	98	328	.274	241	438	32	3678	329	28	.993
National League totals (1 year)			73	216	29	45	6	1	7	38	.208	49	66	1	441	23	3	.994
Major league totals (7 years)			639	2176	361	583	99	5	105	366	.268	290	504	33	4119	352	31	.993

JAMES, MIKE   P   ANGELS

PERSONAL: Born August 15, 1967, in Fort Walton Beach, Fla. ... 6-3/205. ... Throws right, bats right. ... Full name: Michael Elmo James.
HIGH SCHOOL: Fort Walton Beach (Fla.).
JUNIOR COLLEGE: Lurleen B. Wallace State Junior College (Ala.).
TRANSACTIONS/CAREER NOTES: Selected by Los Angeles Dodgers organization in 43rd round of free-agent draft (June 2, 1987). ... On Albuquerque disabled list (July 12-August 26, 1992). ... On Vero Beach disabled list (July 2-9, 1993). ... Traded by Dodgers to California Angels for OF Reggie Williams (October 26, 1993). ... On California disabled list (May 11-June 1, 1995); included rehabilitation assignment to Lake Elsinore (May 25-June 1). ... Angels franchise renamed Anaheim Angels for 1997 season. ... On disabled list (July 3-27, 1997 and May 5, 1998-remainder of season).

Year	Team (League)	W	L	Pct.	ERA	G	GS	CG	ShO	Sv.	IP	H	R	ER	BB	SO
1988—	Great Falls (Pio.)	7	1	*.875	3.76	14	12	0	0	0	67	61	36	28	41	59
1989—	Bakersfield (California)	11	8	.579	3.78	27	27	1	1	0	159 2/3	144	82	67	78	127
1990—	San Antonio (Tex.)	11	4	.733	3.32	26	26	3	0	0	157	144	73	58	78	97
1991—	Albuquerque (PCL)	1	3	.250	6.60	13	8	0	0	0	45	51	36	33	30	39
—	San Antonio (Tex.)	9	5	.643	4.53	15	15	2	1	0	89 1/3	88	54	45	51	74
1992—	Albuquerque (PCL)	2	1	.667	5.59	18	6	0	0	1	46 2/3	55	35	29	22	33
—	San Antonio (Tex.)	2	1	.667	2.67	8	8	0	0	0	54	39	16	16	20	52
1993—	Albuquerque (PCL)	1	0	1.000	7.47	|16	0	0	0	2	31 1/3	38	28	26	19	32
—	Vero Beach (FSL)	2	3	.400	4.92	|30	1	0	0	5	60 1/3	54	37	33	33	60
1994—	Vancouver (PCL)■	5	3	.625	5.22	37	10	0	0	8	91 1/3	101	56	53	34	66
1995—	California (A.L.)	3	0	1.000	3.88	46	0	0	0	1	55 2/3	49	27	24	26	36
—	Lake Elsinore (Calif.)	0	0	...	9.53	5	1	0	0	0	5 2/3	9	6	6	3	8
1996—	California (A.L.)	5	5	.500	2.67	69	0	0	0	1	81	62	27	24	42	65
1997—	Anaheim (A.L.)	5	5	.500	4.31	58	0	0	0	7	62 2/3	69	32	30	28	57
1998—	Anaheim (A.L.)	0	0	...	1.93	11	0	0	0	0	14	10	3	3	7	12
Major league totals (4 years)		13	10	.565	3.42	184	0	0	0	9	213 1/3	190	89	81	103	170

JAVIER, STAN   OF   GIANTS

PERSONAL: Born January 9, 1964, in San Francisco de Macoris, Dominican Republic. ... 6-0/202. ... Bats both, throws right. ... Full name: Stanley Julian Javier. ... Son of Julian Javier, infielder with St. Louis Cardinals (1960-71) and Cincinnati Reds (1972). ... Name pronounced HA-vee-AIR.
HIGH SCHOOL: La Altagracia (San Francisco de Macoris, Dominican Republic).
TRANSACTIONS/CAREER NOTES: Signed as non-drafted free agent by St. Louis Cardinals organization (March 26, 1981). ... Traded by Cardinals organization with SS Bobby Meacham to New York Yankees organization for OF Bob Helsom, P Marty Mason and P Steve Fincher (December 14, 1982). ... Traded by Yankees organization with P Jay Howell, P Jose Rijo, P Eric Plunk and P Tim Birtsas to Oakland Athletics for OF Rickey Henderson, P Bert Bradley and cash (December 5, 1984). ... On Oakland disabled list (August 3-September 1, 1987; included rehabilitation assignment to Tacoma (August 20-September 1). ... On disabled list (August 18-September 2, 1988 and July 7-24, 1989). ... Traded by A's to Los Angeles Dodgers for 2B Willie Randolph (May 13, 1990). ... Traded by Dodgers to Philadelphia Phillies for P Steve Searcy and a player to be named later (July 2, 1992); Dodgers acquired IF Julio Peguero to complete deal (July 28, 1992). ... Granted free agency (October 27, 1992). ... Signed by California Angels organization (January 15, 1993). ... Granted free agency (October 29, 1993). ... Signed by A's (December 7, 1993). ... Granted free agency (November 2, 1995). ... Signed by San Francisco Giants (December 8, 1995). ... On San Francisco disabled list (April 13-29 and July 17, 1996-remainder of season); included rehabilitation assignment to San Jose (April 26-29). ... Granted free agency (October 28, 1997). ... Re-signed by Giants (November 26, 1997).
STATISTICAL NOTES: Led A.L. outfielders with 1.000 fielding percentage in 1995.

Year	Team (League)	Pos.	G	AB	R	H	2B	3B	HR	RBI	Avg.	BB	SO	SB	PO	A	E	Avg.
1981—	Johnson City (App.) ...	OF	53	144	30	36	5	4	3	19	.250	40	33	2	53	2	3	.948
1982—	Johnson City (App.) ...	OF	57	185	45	51	3	•4	8	36	.276	42	55	11	94	8	4	.962
1983—	Greensboro (S. Atl.)■	OF	129	489	109	152	*34	6	12	77	.311	75	95	33	250	10	15	.945
1984—	New York (A.L.)	OF	7	7	1	1	0	0	0	0	.143	0	1	0	3	0	0	1.000
—	Nashville (Southern) ..	OF	76	262	40	76	17	4	7	38	.290	39	57	17	202	4	7	.967
—	Columbus (Int'l)	OF	32	99	12	22	3	1	0	7	.222	12	26	1	77	4	2	.976

Year Team (League)	Pos.	G	AB	R	H	2B	3B	HR	RBI	Avg.	BB	SO	SB	PO	A	E	Avg.
						BATTING									FIELDING		
1985—Huntsville (Sou.)■	OF	140	486	105	138	22	8	9	64	.284	*112	92	61	363	8	7	.981
1986—Tacoma (PCL)	OF-1B	69	248	50	81	16	2	4	51	.327	47	46	18	172	9	6	.968
—Oakland (A.L.)	OF-DH	59	114	13	23	8	0	0	8	.202	16	27	8	118	1	0	1.000
1987—Oakland (A.L.) ...	OF-1B-DH	81	151	22	28	3	1	2	9	.185	19	33	3	149	5	3	.981
—Tacoma (PCL)	OF-1B	15	51	6	11	2	0	0	2	.216	4	12	3	26	0	2	.929
1988—Oakland (A.L.) ...	OF-1B-DH	125	397	49	102	13	3	2	35	.257	32	63	20	274	7	5	.983
1989—Oakland (A.L.) ...	OF-2B-1B	112	310	42	77	12	3	1	28	.248	31	45	12	221	8	2	.991
1990—Oakland (A.L.) ...	OF-DH	19	33	4	8	0	2	0	3	.242	3	6	0	19	0	0	1.000
—Los Angeles (N.L.)■..	OF	104	276	56	84	9	4	3	24	.304	37	44	15	204	2	0	1.000
1991—Los Angeles (N.L.)	OF-1B	121	176	21	36	5	3	1	11	.205	16	36	7	90	4	3	.969
1992—Los Angeles (N.L.)	OF	56	58	6	11	3	0	1	5	.190	6	11	1	17	0	1	1.000
—Philadelphia (N.L.)■..	OF	74	276	36	72	14	1	0	24	.261	31	43	17	212	7	3	.986
1993—California (A.L.)	O-1-2-DH	92	237	33	69	10	4	3	28	.291	27	33	12	167	4	4	.977
1994—Oakland (A.L.)■	OF-1B-3B	109	419	75	114	23	0	10	44	.272	49	76	24	274	4	4	.986
1995—Oakland (A.L.)	OF-3B	130	442	81	123	20	2	8	56	.278	49	63	36	332	3	0	†1.000
1996—San Fran. (N.L.)■......	OF	71	274	44	74	25	0	2	22	.270	25	51	14	180	2	3	.984
—San Jose (Calif.)	OF	3	5	1	2	0	0	0	1	.400	1	1	0	1	0	0	1.000
1997—San Francisco (N.L.) ..	OF-1B	142	440	69	126	16	4	8	50	.286	56	70	25	279	2	7	.976
1998—San Francisco (N.L.) ..	OF	135	417	63	121	13	5	4	49	.290	65	63	21	217	0	3	.986
American League totals (9 years)		734	2110	320	545	89	15	26	211	.258	226	347	115	1557	32	18	.989
National League totals (6 years)		703	1917	295	524	85	17	19	185	.273	236	318	100	1199	17	19	.985
Major league totals (14 years)		1437	4027	615	1069	174	32	45	396	.265	462	665	215	2756	49	37	.987

DIVISION SERIES RECORD

Year Team (League)	Pos.	G	AB	R	H	2B	3B	HR	RBI	Avg.	BB	SO	SB	PO	A	E	Avg.
						BATTING									FIELDING		
1997—San Francisco (N.L.) ..	OF	3	12	2	5	1	0	0	1	.417	0	2	1	11	0	0	1.000

CHAMPIONSHIP SERIES RECORD

Year Team (League)	Pos.	G	AB	R	H	2B	3B	HR	RBI	Avg.	BB	SO	SB	PO	A	E	Avg.
						BATTING									FIELDING		
1988—Oakland (A.L.)	OF-PR	2	4	0	2	0	0	0	1	.500	1	0	0	5	0	0	1.000
1989—Oakland (A.L.)	OF	1	2	0	0	0	0	0	0	.000	0	1	0	1	0	0	1.000
Championship series totals (2 years)		3	6	0	2	0	0	0	1	.333	1	1	0	6	0	0	1.000

NOTES: Member of World Series championship team (1989).

WORLD SERIES RECORD

Year Team (League)	Pos.	G	AB	R	H	2B	3B	HR	RBI	Avg.	BB	SO	SB	PO	A	E	Avg.
						BATTING									FIELDING		
1988—Oakland (A.L.)	PR-OF	3	4	0	2	0	0	0	2	.500	0	1	0	1	0	0	1.000
1989—Oakland (A.L.)	OF	1	0	0	0	0	0	0	0	...	0	0	0	0	0	0	...
World Series totals (2 years)		4	4	0	2	0	0	0	2	.500	0	1	0	1	0	0	1.000

JEFFERIES, GREGG   OF   TIGERS

PERSONAL: Born August 1, 1967, in Burlingame, Calif. ... 5-10/185. ... Bats both, throws right. ... Full name: Gregory Scott Jefferies.
HIGH SCHOOL: Serra (San Mateo, Calif.).
TRANSACTIONS/CAREER NOTES: Selected by New York Mets organization in first round (20th pick overall) of free-agent draft (June 3, 1985). ... On disabled list (April 27-May 13, 1991). ... Traded by Mets with OF Kevin McReynolds and 2B Keith Miller to Kansas City Royals for P Bret Saberhagen and IF Bill Pecota (December 11, 1991). ... Traded by Royals with OF Ed Gerald to St. Louis Cardinals for OF Felix Jose and IF/OF Craig Wilson (February 12, 1993). ... Granted free agency (October 18, 1994). ... Signed by Philadelphia Phillies (December 14, 1994). ... On disabled list (June 17-July 2, 1995). ... On Philadelphia disabled list (April 5-June 4, 1996); included rehabilitation assignment to Scranton/Wilkes-Barre (May 30-June 4). ... On disabled list (August 18-September 2, 1997). ... Traded by Phillies to Anaheim Angels for a player to be named later (August 28, 1998); Phillies acquired P Doug Nickle to complete deal (September 9, 1998). ... Granted free agency (October 26, 1998). ... Signed by Detroit Tigers (December 28, 1998).
HONORS: Named Appalachian League Player of the Year (1985). ... Named Carolina League Most Valuable Player (1986). ... Named Texas League Most Valuable Player (1987).
STATISTICAL NOTES: Led Carolina League with .549 slugging percentage in 1986. ... Led Texas League with 18 intentional bases on balls received in 1987. ... Tied for International League lead with 10 intentional bases on balls received in 1988. ... Led International League third basemen with 240 assists in 1988. ... Led A.L. third basemen with 26 errors in 1992. ... Tied for N.L. lead with 94 double plays by first basemen in 1994 ... Hit for the cycle (August 25, 1995). ... Had 15-game hitting streak (August 20-September 5, 1998). ... Career major league grand slams: 2.

Year Team (League)	Pos.	G	AB	R	H	2B	3B	HR	RBI	Avg.	BB	SO	SB	PO	A	E	Avg.
						BATTING									FIELDING		
1985—Kingsport (Appal.)	SS-2B	47	166	27	57	18	2	3	29	.343	14	16	21	78	130	21	.908
—Columbia (S. Atl.)	2B-SS	20	64	7	18	2	2	1	12	.281	4	4	7	28	26	2	.964
1986—Columbia (S. Atl.)	SS	25	112	29	38	6	1	5	24	.339	9	10	13	36	83	7	.944
—Lynchburg (Caro.) ...	SS	95	390	66	138	25	9	11	80	*.354	33	29	43	138	273	20	.954
—Jackson (Texas)	SS-3B	5	19	1	8	1	1	0	7	.421	2	2	1	7	9	1	.941
1987—Jackson (Texas)	SS-3B	134	510	81	187	*48	5	20	101	.367	49	43	26	167	388	35	.941
—New York (N.L.)	PH	6	6	0	3	1	0	0	2	.500	0	0	0	...	...	...	...
1988—Tidewater (Int'l)	3-S-2-O	132	504	62	142	28	4	7	61	.282	32	35	32	110	†330	27	.942
—New York (N.L.)	3B-2B	29	109	19	35	8	2	6	17	.321	8	10	5	33	46	2	.975
1989—New York (N.L.)	2B-3B	141	508	72	131	28	2	12	56	.258	39	46	21	242	280	14	.974
1990—New York (N.L.)	2B-3B	153	604	96	171	*40	3	15	68	.283	46	40	11	242	341	16	.973
1991—New York (N.L.)	2B-3B	136	486	59	132	19	2	9	62	.272	47	38	26	170	271	17	.963
1992—Kansas City (A.L.)■	3B-DH-2B	152	604	66	172	36	3	10	75	.285	43	29	19	96	304	†26	.939
1993—St. Louis (N.L.)■	1B-2B	142	544	89	186	24	3	16	83	.342	62	32	46	1281	77	9	.993
1994—St. Louis (N.L.)	1B	103	397	52	129	27	1	12	55	.325	45	26	12	889	53	7	.993

				BATTING											FIELDING			
Year	Team (League)	Pos.	G	AB	R	H	2B	3B	HR	RBI	Avg.	BB	SO	SB	PO	A	E	Avg.
1995—Philadelphia (N.L.)■..		1B-OF	114	480	69	147	31	2	11	56	.306	35	26	9	579	36	3	.995
1996—Philadelphia (N.L.)......		1B-OF	104	404	59	118	17	3	7	51	.292	36	21	20	522	39	1	.998
—Scran./W.B. (Int'l)......		1B	4	17	1	2	0	1	0	0	.118	1	3	0	22	3	1	.962
1997—Philadelphia (N.L.)......		OF	130	476	68	122	25	3	11	48	.256	53	27	12	211	5	3	.986
1998—Philadelphia (N.L.)......		OF	125	483	65	142	22	3	8	48	.294	29	27	11	168	7	1	.994
—Anaheim (A.L.)■........		OF-1B	19	72	7	25	6	0	1	10	.347	0	5	1	48	2	0	1.000
American League totals (2 years)			171	676	73	197	42	3	11	85	.291	43	34	20	144	306	26	.945
National League totals (11 years)			1183	4497	648	1316	242	24	107	546	.293	400	293	173	4337	1155	73	.987
Major league totals (12 years)			1354	5173	721	1513	284	27	118	631	.292	443	327	193	4481	1461	99	.984

CHAMPIONSHIP SERIES RECORD

				BATTING											FIELDING			
Year	Team (League)	Pos.	G	AB	R	H	2B	3B	HR	RBI	Avg.	BB	SO	SB	PO	A	E	Avg.
1988—New York (N.L.).........		3B	7	27	2	9	2	0	0	1	.333	4	0	0	5	8	1	.929

ALL-STAR GAME RECORD

			BATTING										FIELDING			
Year	League	Pos.	AB	R	H	2B	3B	HR	RBI	Avg.	BB	SO	SB	PO	A	E	Avg.
1993—National.....................	PH-DH	1	0	0	0	0	0	0	0	.000	0	1	0	...	...	...	...
1994—National.....................	1B	1	2	1	1	0	0	0	0	1.000	0	0	0	6	0	0	1.000
All-Star Game totals (2 years)		2	2	1	1	0	0	0	0	.500	0	1	0	6	0	0	1.000

J

JEFFERSON, REGGIE   DH/1B   RED SOX

PERSONAL: Born September 25, 1968, in Tallahassee, Fla. ... 6-4/215. ... Bats left, throws left. ... Full name: Reginald Jirod Jefferson.
HIGH SCHOOL: Lincoln (Tallahassee, Fla.).
TRANSACTIONS/CAREER NOTES: Selected by Cincinnati Reds organization in third round of free-agent draft (June 2, 1986). ... On disabled list (May 25, 1990-remainder of season). ... Traded by Reds to Cleveland Indians for 1B Tim Costo (June 14, 1991). ... On Cleveland disabled list (June 24-July 1, 1991); included rehabilitation assignment to Canton/Akron (June 25-July 1). ... On Cleveland disabled list (March 28-July 4, 1992); included rehabilitation assignment to Colorado Springs (June 15-July 4). ... On Colorado Springs suspended list (September 6-9, 1992). ... Traded by Indians with SS Felix Fermin and cash to Seattle Mariners for SS Omar Vizquel (December 20, 1993). ... On disabled list (May 21-June 10, 1994). ... Granted free agency (March 11, 1995). ... Signed by Boston Red Sox (April 9, 1995). ... On disabled list (July 10-September 19, 1995). ... On Boston disabled list (July 15, 1998-remainder of season); included rehabilitation assignments to Gulf Coast Red Sox (August 10) and Sarasota (August 11-12 and August 29-September 1).
STATISTICAL NOTES: Led Gulf Coast League first basemen with 624 total chances in 1986. ... Had 22-game hitting streak (July 13-August 8, 1997). ... Career major league grand slams: 2.
MISCELLANEOUS: Batted as switch-hitter (1986 and 1989-May 1994).

				BATTING											FIELDING			
Year	Team (League)	Pos.	G	AB	R	H	2B	3B	HR	RBI	Avg.	BB	SO	SB	PO	A	E	Avg.
1986—GC Reds (GCL)..........		1B	59	208	28	54	4	•5	3	33	.260	24	40	10	*581	*36	4	.989
1987—Billings (Pioneer)........		1B	8	22	10	8	1	0	1	9	.364	4	2	1	21	1	0	1.000
—Cedar Rap. (Midw.).....		1B	15	54	9	12	5	0	3	11	.222	1	12	1	120	11	1	.992
1988—Cedar Rap. (Midw.).....		1B	135	517	76	149	26	2	18	*90	.288	40	89	2	1084	91	13	.989
1989—Chattanooga (Sou.).....		1B	135	487	66	140	19	3	17	80	.287	43	73	2	1004	79	16	.985
1990—Nashville (A.A.).........		1B	37	126	24	34	11	2	5	23	.270	14	30	1	314	20	4	.988
1991—Nashville (A.A.).........		1B	28	103	15	33	3	1	3	20	.320	10	22	3	196	13	2	.991
—Cincinnati (N.L.).........		1B	5	7	1	1	0	0	1	1	.143	1	2	0	14	1	0	1.000
—Cleveland (A.L.)■.......		1B	26	101	10	20	3	0	2	12	.198	3	22	0	252	24	2	.993
—Cant./Akr. (Eastern)....		1B	6	25	2	7	1	0	0	4	.280	1	5	0	46	3	0	1.000
—Colo. Springs (PCL) ...		1B	39	136	29	42	11	0	3	21	.309	16	28	0	289	25	3	.991
1992—Colo. Springs (PCL) ...		1B	57	218	49	68	11	4	11	44	.312	29	50	1	363	34	5	.988
—Cleveland (A.L.)..........		1B-DH	24	89	8	30	6	2	1	6	.337	1	17	0	129	12	1	.993
1993—Cleveland (A.L.)..........		DH-1B	113	366	35	91	11	2	10	34	.249	28	78	1	112	10	3	.976
1994—Seattle (A.L.)■........		DH-1B-OF	63	162	24	53	11	0	8	32	.327	17	32	0	95	10	2	.981
1995—Boston (A.L.)■.........		DH-1B-OF	46	121	21	35	8	0	5	26	.289	9	24	0	28	4	0	1.000
1996—Boston (A.L.)..............		DH-OF-1B	122	386	67	134	30	4	19	74	.347	25	89	0	178	17	3	.985
1997—Boston (A.L.)..............		DH-1B	136	489	74	156	33	1	13	67	.319	24	93	1	74	5	2	.975
1998—Boston (A.L.)..............		DH-1B	62	196	24	60	16	1	8	31	.306	21	40	0	37	4	2	.953
—GC Red Sox (GCL)		DH	1	4	0	0	0	0	0	0	.000	0	1	0	...	...	...	...
—Sarasota (Fla. St.)		DH	4	14	2	5	0	0	0	2	.357	1	3	0	...	...	...	...
American League totals (8 years)			592	1910	263	579	118	10	66	282	.303	128	395	2	905	86	15	.985
National League totals (1 year)			5	7	1	1	0	0	1	1	.143	1	2	0	14	1	0	1.000
Major league totals (8 years)			597	1917	264	580	118	10	67	283	.303	129	397	2	919	87	15	.985

DIVISION SERIES RECORD

				BATTING											FIELDING			
Year	Team (League)	Pos.	G	AB	R	H	2B	3B	HR	RBI	Avg.	BB	SO	SB	PO	A	E	Avg.
1995—Boston (A.L.).............		DH	1	4	1	1	0	0	0	0	.250	0	1	0	...	...	...	...

JENKINS, GEOFF   OF   BREWERS

PERSONAL: Born July 21, 1974, in Olympia, Wash. ... 6-1/204. ... Bats left, throws right. ... Full name: Geoffrey Scott Jenkins.
HIGH SCHOOL: Cordova Senior (Rancho Cordova, Calif.).
COLLEGE: Southern California.
TRANSACTIONS/CAREER NOTES: Selected by Milwaukee Brewers organization in first round (ninth pick overall) of free-agent draft (June 1, 1995). ... On El Paso disabled list (May 8-July 23, 1996). ... On disabled list (July 4-August 11, 1997).

Year Team (League)	Pos.	G	AB	R	H	2B	3B	HR	RBI	Avg.	BB	SO	SB	PO	A	E	Avg.
1995— Helena (Pioneer)	OF	7	26	2	9	0	1	0	9	.346	3	11	0	15	1	0	1.000
— Stockton (California) ..	OF	13	47	13	12	2	0	3	12	.255	10	12	2	14	3	2	.895
— El Paso (Texas)..........	OF	22	79	12	22	4	2	1	13	.278	8	23	3	41	1	7	.857
1996— El Paso (Texas)..........	DH	22	77	17	22	5	4	1	11	.286	12	21	1	...	...	...	...
— Stockton (California) ..	OF	37	138	27	48	8	4	3	25	.348	20	32	3	2	0	0	1.000
1997— Tucson (PCL)	OF-SS	93	347	44	82	24	3	10	56	.236	33	87	0	115	7	5	.961
1998— Louisville (Int'l)	OF	55	215	38	71	10	4	7	52	.330	14	39	1	90	3	2	.979
— Milwaukee (N.L.)........	OF	84	262	33	60	12	1	9	28	.229	20	61	1	115	6	4	.968
Major league totals (1 year)		84	262	33	60	12	1	9	28	.229	20	61	1	115	6	4	.968

JENNINGS, ROBIN — OF — CUBS

PERSONAL: Born April 11, 1972, in Republic of Singapore. ... 6-2/210. ... Bats left, throws left. ... Full name: Robin Christopher Jennings.
HIGH SCHOOL: Annandale (Va.).
JUNIOR COLLEGE: Manatee Community College (Fla.).
TRANSACTIONS/CAREER NOTES: Selected by Baltimore Orioles organization in 30th round of free-agent draft (June 4, 1990); did not sign. ... Selected by Chicago Cubs organization in 33rd round of free-agent draft (June 3, 1991). ... On Iowa disabled list (May 31-June 11 and August 10-20, 1996). ... On Chicago disabled list (March 22-June 8, 1998); included rehabilitation assignment to West Tenn (June 1-3) and Iowa (June 4-8).
STATISTICAL NOTES: Tied for New York-Pennsylvania League lead in double plays by outfielder with two in 1992. ... Led Midwest League outfielders with 20 assists in 1993.

Year Team (League)	Pos.	G	AB	R	H	2B	3B	HR	RBI	Avg.	BB	SO	SB	PO	A	E	Avg.
1992— Geneva (NY-Penn)......	OF	72	275	39	82	12	2	7	47	.298	20	43	10	96	*9	4	.963
1993— Peoria (Midwest)........	OF-1B	132	474	64	146	29	5	3	65	.308	46	73	11	219	†31	7	.973
1994— Daytona (Fla. St.)	OF	128	476	54	133	24	5	8	60	.279	45	54	2	165	8	8	.956
1995— Orlando (South.)	OF	132	490	71	145	27	7	17	79	.296	44	61	7	242	15	10	.963
1996— Iowa (Am. Assoc.)......	OF	86	331	53	94	15	6	18	56	.284	32	53	2	156	5	3	.982
— Chicago (N.L.)..........	OF	31	58	7	13	5	0	0	4	.224	3	9	1	19	2	0	1.000
1997— Iowa (Am. Assoc.)......	OF	126	464	67	128	25	5	20	71	.276	56	73	5	197	10	3	.986
— Chicago (N.L.)..........	OF	9	18	1	3	1	0	0	2	.167	0	2	0	5	0	0	1.000
1998— West Tenn (Sou.)	OF	2	6	0	0	0	0	0	0	.000	0	2	0	1	0	0	1.000
— Iowa (Pacific Coast) ...	OF-1B	81	298	57	74	23	2	16	62	.248	33	49	4	129	5	5	.964
Major league totals (2 years)		40	76	8	16	6	0	0	6	.211	3	11	1	24	2	0	1.000

JENSEN, MARCUS — C

PERSONAL: Born December 14, 1972, in Oakland. ... 6-4/204. ... Bats both, throws right. ... Full name: Marcus C. Jensen.
HIGH SCHOOL: Skyline (Oakland).
TRANSACTIONS/CAREER NOTES: Selected by San Francisco Giants organization in supplemental round ("sandwich pick" between first and second round, 33rd pick overall) of free-agent draft (June 4, 1990); pick received as part of compensation for San Diego Padres signing Type A free-agent P Craig Lefferts. ... On disabled list (June 1-14, 1993). ... Traded by Giants to Detroit Tigers for C Brian Johnson (July 16, 1997). ... Granted free agency (July 22, 1997). ... Re-signed by Tigers (July 26, 1997). ... Released by Tigers (March 25, 1998). ... Signed by Milwaukee Brewers organization (April 5, 1998). ... On Louisville disabled list (April 9-21, 1998). ... Released by Brewers (September 29, 1998).
STATISTICAL NOTES: Tied for Arizona League lead with three intentional bases on balls received in 1991. ... Led California League catchers with 722 total chances in 1994. ... Led Texas League catchers with 546 total chances in 1995.

Year Team (League)	Pos.	G	AB	R	H	2B	3B	HR	RBI	Avg.	BB	SO	SB	PO	A	E	Avg.
1990— Everett (N'west)..........	C	51	171	21	29	3	0	2	12	.170	24	60	0	191	27	3	.986
1991— Ariz. Giants (Ariz.).......	C-1B	48	155	28	44	8	3	2	30	.284	34	22	4	226	29	7	.973
1992— Clinton (Midwest)........	C-1B	86	264	35	62	14	0	4	33	.235	54	87	4	493	68	10	.982
1993— Clinton (Midwest).......	C	104	324	53	85	24	2	11	56	.262	66	98	1	641	73	7	.990
1994— San Jose (Calif.)........	C	118	418	56	101	18	0	7	47	.242	61	100	1	*627	86	9	.988
1995— Shreveport (Texas)......	C	95	321	55	91	22	8	4	45	.283	41	68	0	*471	70	5	.991
1996— Phoenix (PCL)............	C	120	405	41	107	22	4	5	53	.264	44	95	1	568	65	8	.988
— San Francisco (N.L.) ..	C	9	19	4	4	1	0	0	4	.211	8	7	0	37	5	2	.955
1997— San Francisco (N.L.) ..	C	30	74	5	11	2	0	1	3	.149	7	23	0	106	10	2	.983
— Toledo (Int'l)■............	C	24	80	5	14	5	0	0	9	.175	9	25	0	149	6	1	.994
— Detroit (A.L.)	C	8	11	1	2	0	0	0	1	.182	1	5	0	26	1	1	.964
1998— Louisville (Int'l)■........	C-1B	74	230	29	52	13	0	10	33	.226	33	64	0	444	34	3	.994
— Milwaukee (N.L.)........	C	2	2	0	0	0	0	0	0	.000	0	2	0	1	0	0	1.000
American League totals (1 year)		8	11	1	2	0	0	0	1	.182	1	5	0	26	1	1	.964
National League totals (3 years)		41	95	9	15	3	0	1	7	.158	15	32	0	144	15	4	.975
Major league totals (3 years)		49	106	10	17	3	0	1	8	.160	16	37	0	170	16	5	.974

JERZEMBECK, MIKE — P — YANKEES

PERSONAL: Born May 18, 1972, in Queens, N.Y. ... 6-1/185. ... Throws right, bats right. ... Full name: Michael Joseph Jerzembeck.
HIGH SCHOOL: Archbishop Molloy (Jamaica, N.Y.).
COLLEGE: North Carolina.
TRANSACTIONS/CAREER NOTES: Selected by New York Yankees organization in fifth round of free-agent draft (June 3, 1993). ... On disabled list (May 8-29 and June 13-July 16, 1994). ... On disabled list (April 18-September 8, 1995).

Year	Team (League)	W	L	Pct.	ERA	G	GS	CG	ShO	Sv.	IP	H	R	ER	BB	SO
1993—Oneonta (N.Y.-Penn)		8	4	.667	2.68	14	14	0	0	0	77⅓	70	25	23	26	76
1994—Tampa (Fla. St.)...............		4	3	.571	3.15	16	16	0	0	0	68⅔	59	27	24	22	45
1995—Tampa (Fla. St.)...............		0	1	.000	9.00	2	0	0	0	0	3	5	4	3	2	1
1996—Columbus (Int'l)		0	0	...	5.40	1	0	0	0	0	1⅔	1	1	1	1	0
—Norwich (Eastern)		3	6	.333	4.52	14	13	1	1	0	69⅔	74	38	35	26	65
—Tampa (Fla. St.)...............		4	2	.667	2.95	12	12	0	0	0	73⅓	67	26	24	13	60
1997—Norwich (Eastern)		2	1	.667	1.71	8	8	0	0	0	42	21	10	8	16	42
—Columbus (Int'l)		7	5	.583	3.59	20	20	2	0	0	130⅓	125	55	52	37	118
1998—Columbus (Int'l)		4	9	.308	4.87	24	24	0	0	0	140⅓	158	82	76	55	107
—New York (A.L.)................		0	1	.000	12.79	3	2	0	0	0	6⅓	9	9	9	4	1
Major league totals (1 year)........		0	1	.000	12.79	3	2	0	0	0	6⅓	9	9	9	4	1

JETER, DEREK   SS   YANKEES

PERSONAL: Born June 26, 1974, in Pequannock, N.J. ... 6-3/195. ... Bats right, throws right. ... Full name: Derek Sanderson Jeter.
HIGH SCHOOL: Central (Kalamazoo, Mich.).
COLLEGE: Michigan.
TRANSACTIONS/CAREER NOTES: Selected by New York Yankees organization in first round (sixth pick overall) of free-agent draft (June 1, 1992). ... On New York disabled list (June 3-19, 1998); included rehabilitation assignment to Columbus (June 18-19).
HONORS: Named Minor League Player of the Year by THE SPORTING NEWS (1994). ... Named A.L. Rookie Player of the Year by THE SPORTING NEWS (1996). ... Named A.L. Rookie of the Year by Baseball Writers' Association of America (1996).
STATISTICAL NOTES: Had 15-game hitting streak (May 2-20, 1998).

Year Team (League)	Pos.	G	AB	R	H	2B	3B	HR	RBI	Avg.	BB	SO	SB	PO	A	E	Avg.
1992—GC Yankees (GCL)......	SS	47	173	19	35	10	0	3	25	.202	19	36	2	67	132	12	.943
—Greensboro (S. Atl.) ...	SS	11	37	4	9	0	0	1	4	.243	7	16	0	14	25	9	.813
1993—Greensboro (S. Atl.) ...	SS	128	515	85	152	14	11	5	71	.295	56	95	18	158	292	56	.889
1994—Tampa (Fla. St.)........	SS	69	292	61	96	13	8	0	39	.329	23	30	28	93	204	12	.961
—Alb./Colon. (East.)	SS	34	122	17	46	7	2	2	13	.377	15	16	12	42	105	6	.961
—Columbus (Int'l)	SS	35	126	25	44	7	1	3	16	.349	20	15	10	54	93	7	.955
1995—Columbus (Int'l)	SS	123	486	*96	154	27	9	2	45	.317	61	56	20	189	394	*29	.953
—New York (A.L.)..........	SS	15	48	5	12	4	1	0	7	.250	3	11	0	17	34	2	.962
1996—New York (A.L.)..........	SS	157	582	104	183	25	6	10	78	.314	48	102	14	244	444	22	.969
1997—New York (A.L.)..........	SS	159	654	116	190	31	7	10	70	.291	74	125	23	243	*457	18	.975
1998—New York (A.L.)..........	SS	149	626	*127	203	25	8	19	84	.324	57	119	30	223	393	9	.986
—Columbus (Int'l)	SS	1	5	2	2	2	0	0	0	.400	0	2	0	4	3	1	.875
Major league totals (4 years)		480	1910	352	588	85	22	39	239	.308	182	357	67	727	1328	51	.976

DIVISION SERIES RECORD

Year Team (League)	Pos.	G	AB	R	H	2B	3B	HR	RBI	Avg.	BB	SO	SB	PO	A	E	Avg.
1996—New York (A.L.)..........	SS	4	17	2	7	1	0	0	1	.412	0	2	0	8	10	2	.900
1997—New York (A.L.)..........	SS	5	21	6	7	1	0	2	2	.333	3	5	1	12	15	0	1.000
1998—New York (A.L.)..........	SS	3	9	0	1	0	0	0	0	.111	2	2	0	4	5	0	1.000
Division series totals (3 years)		12	47	8	15	2	0	2	3	.319	5	9	1	24	30	2	.964

CHAMPIONSHIP SERIES RECORD

Year Team (League)	Pos.	G	AB	R	H	2B	3B	HR	RBI	Avg.	BB	SO	SB	PO	A	E	Avg.
1996—New York (A.L.)..........	SS	5	24	5	10	2	0	1	1	.417	0	5	2	6	13	0	1.000
1998—New York (A.L.)..........	SS	6	25	3	5	1	1	0	2	.200	2	5	3	9	13	0	1.000
Championship series totals (2 years)		11	49	8	15	3	1	1	3	.306	2	10	5	15	26	0	1.000

WORLD SERIES RECORD

NOTES: Member of World Series championship team (1996 and 1998).

Year Team (League)	Pos.	G	AB	R	H	2B	3B	HR	RBI	Avg.	BB	SO	SB	PO	A	E	Avg.
1996—New York (A.L.)..........	SS	6	20	5	5	0	0	0	1	.250	4	6	1	15	22	2	.949
1998—New York (A.L.)..........	SS	4	17	4	6	0	0	0	1	.353	3	3	0	7	8	0	1.000
World Series totals (2 years)		10	37	9	11	0	0	0	2	.297	7	9	1	22	30	2	.963

ALL-STAR GAME RECORD

Year League	Pos.	AB	R	H	2B	3B	HR	RBI	Avg.	BB	SO	SB	PO	A	E	Avg.
1998—American	SS	1	0	0	0	0	0	0	.000	0	1	0	0	2	0	1.000

JIMENEZ, D'ANGELO   SS   YANKEES

PERSONAL: Born December 21, 1977, in Masaya, Nicaragua. ... 6-0/160. ... Bats right, throws right.
TRANSACTIONS/CAREER NOTES: Signed as non-drafted free agent by New York Yankees organization (August 1, 1994).
STATISTICAL NOTES: Led Gulf Coast League shortstops with 289 total chances in 1995. ... Led South Atlantic League shortstops with 640 total chances in 1996.

Year Team (League)	Pos.	G	AB	R	H	2B	3B	HR	RBI	Avg.	BB	SO	SB	PO	A	E	Avg.
1995—GC Yankees (GCL)......	SS	57	214	41	60	14	*8	0	28	.280	23	31	6	*95	*173	21	.927
1996—Greensboro (S. Atl.) ...	SS	138	*537	68	131	25	5	6	48	.244	56	113	15	190	*400	*50	.922
1997—Tampa (A.A.)........	SS	2	7	1	1	0	0	0	1	.143	0	1	0	2	8	2	.833
—Tampa (Fla. St.)........	SS	94	352	52	99	14	6	6	48	.281	50	50	8	147	283	21	.953
1998—Norwich (Eastern)	SS	40	152	21	41	6	2	2	21	.270	25	26	5	62	119	12	.938
—Columbus (Int'l)	SS-2B	91	344	55	88	19	4	8	51	.256	46	67	6	150	302	26	.946

JIMENEZ, JOSE   P   CARDINALS

PERSONAL: Born July 7, 1973, in San Pedro de Macoris, Dominican Republic. ... 6-3/195. ... Throws right, bats right.
TRANSACTIONS/CAREER NOTES: Signed as non-drafted free agent by St. Louis Cardinals organization (October 21, 1991).
HONORS: Named Texas League Pitcher of the Year (1998).
STATISTICAL NOTES: Pitched 6-0 no-hit victory for Arkansas against Shreveport (August 27, 1998).

Year Team (League)	W	L	Pct.	ERA	G	GS	CG	ShO	Sv.	IP	H	R	ER	BB	SO
1992— Dom. Cardinals (DSL)	3	2	.600	6.10	18	2	0	0	0	48²/₃	68	43	33	23	21
1993— Dom. Cardinals (DSL)	3	5	.375	3.51	12	12	0	0	0	56¹/₃	61	47	22	35	30
1994— Dom. Cardinals (DSL)	3	9	.250	2.77	19	9	0	0	3	68¹/₃	54	43	21	30	54
1995— Johnson City (App.)	5	7	.417	3.49	14	•14	1	1	0	*90¹/₃	81	48	35	25	85
1996— Peoria (Midwest)	12	9	.571	2.92	28	27	3	1	0	172¹/₃	158	75	56	53	129
1997— Prince William (Caro.)	9	7	.563	3.09	24	24	2	0	0	145²/₃	128	73	50	42	81
1998— Arkansas (Texas)	15	6	.714	3.11	26	26	1	1	0	179²/₃	156	71	62	68	88
— St. Louis (N.L.)	3	0	1.000	2.95	4	3	0	0	0	21¹/₃	22	8	7	8	12
Major league totals (1 year)	3	0	1.000	2.95	4	3	0	0	0	21¹/₃	22	8	7	8	12

J

JOHNS, DOUG   P   ORIOLES

PERSONAL: Born December 19, 1967, in South Bend, Ind. ... 6-2/195. ... Throws left, bats right. ... Full name: Douglas Alan Johns.
HIGH SCHOOL: Nova (Fort Lauderdale, Fla.).
COLLEGE: Virginia.
TRANSACTIONS/CAREER NOTES: Selected by Oakland Athletics organization in 16th round of free-agent draft (June 4, 1990). ... Claimed on waivers by Kansas City Royals (March 14, 1997). ... Released by Royals (May 29, 1997). ... Signed by Baltimore Orioles (June 30, 1997). ... Granted free agency (October 15, 1997). ... Re-signed by Orioles (January 9, 1998). ... Played in Europe during 1998 season. ... On Baltimore disabled list (May 3-18, 1998).
STATISTICAL NOTES: Pitched 3-0 no-hit victory against Burlington (July 17, 1991).
MISCELLANEOUS: Appeared in two games as pinch runner (1996).

Year Team (League)	W	L	Pct.	ERA	G	GS	CG	ShO	Sv.	IP	H	R	ER	BB	SO
1990— Arizona A's (Arizona)	3	1	.750	1.84	8	7	1	0	0	44	36	17	9	9	38
— S. Oregon (N'west)	0	2	.000	5.73	6	2	0	0	1	11	13	9	7	11	9
1991— Madison (Midwest)	12	6	.667	3.23	38	14	1	1	2	128¹/₃	108	59	46	54	104
1992— Reno (California)	13	10	.565	3.26	27	26	4	1	0	*179¹/₃	194	98	65	64	101
— Huntsville (Southern)	0	0	. . .	3.94	3	1	0	0	0	16	21	11	7	5	4
1993— Huntsville (Southern)	7	5	.583	2.97	40	6	0	0	1	91	82	41	30	31	56
1994— Huntsville (Southern)	3	0	1.000	1.20	9	0	0	0	0	15	16	2	2	12	9
— Tacoma (PCL)	9	8	.529	2.89	22	19	2	1	0	134	114	55	43	48	65
1995— Edmonton (PCL)	9	5	.643	3.41	23	21	0	0	0	132	148	55	50	43	70
— Oakland (A.L.)	5	3	.625	4.61	11	9	1	1	0	54²/₃	44	32	28	26	25
1996— Oakland (A.L.)	6	12	.333	5.98	42	23	1	0	1	158	187	112	105	69	71
1997— Omaha (Am. Assoc.)■.........	1	5	.167	7.56	9	6	1	0	0	41²/₃	58	36	35	11	24
— Rochester (Int'l)■..............	3	1	.750	3.74	9	8	2	1	0	55¹/₃	57	25	23	13	42
1998— Rochester (Int'l)■..............	0	1	.000	1.69	2	2	0	0	0	10²/₃	7	3	2	6	4
— Baltimore (A.L.)	3	3	.500	4.57	31	10	0	0	1	86²/₃	108	46	44	32	34
Major league totals (3 years)	14	18	.438	5.32	84	42	2	1	2	299¹/₃	339	190	177	127	130

JOHNS, KEITH   SS

PERSONAL: Born July 19, 1971, in Jacksonville. ... 6-1/175. ... Bats right, throws right. ... Full name: Robert Keith Johns Jr.
HIGH SCHOOL: Sandalwood (Jacksonville).
COLLEGE: Mississippi.
TRANSACTIONS/CAREER NOTES: Selected by St. Louis Cardinals organization in sixth round of free-agent draft (June 1, 1992). ... On disabled list (April 13-27, 1994). ... Traded by Cardinals to Milwaukee Brewers for a player to be named later (March 27, 1997); Cardinals acquired P Scotty Pace to complete deal (January 6, 1998). ... Traded by Brewers to Baltimore Orioles for a player to be named later (August 31, 1997). ... Traded by Orioles organization to Boston Red Sox organization for 1B Bo Dodson (March 30, 1998). ... On Pawtucket disabled list (April 22-29, 1998). ... Granted free agency (October 15, 1998).
STATISTICAL NOTES: Led Florida State League shortstops with 588 total chances in 1994.

						BATTING								FIELDING		
Year Team (League)	Pos.	G	AB	R	H	2B	3B	HR	RBI	Avg.	BB	SO	SB	PO	A	E	Avg.
1992— Hamilton (NYP)	SS	70	275	36	78	11	1	1	28	.284	27	42	15	106	183	22	.929
1993— Springfield (Midw.)	SS	132	467	74	121	24	1	2	40	.259	70	68	40	151	*415	34	.943
1994— St. Peters. (FSL)	SS	122	464	52	106	20	0	3	47	.228	37	49	18	*186	372	30	.949
1995— Arkansas (Texas)	SS	111	396	69	111	13	2	2	28	.280	55	53	14	159	354	26	.952
— Louisville (A.A.)	2B-3B-SS	5	10	0	0	0	0	0	0	.000	0	2	0	7	9	0	1.000
1996— Arkansas (Texas)	SS	127	447	52	110	17	1	1	40	.246	47	61	8	199	348	28	.951
1997— Tucson (PCL)■............	SS-2B	112	333	45	88	21	3	5	36	.264	43	61	4	154	308	*29	.941
— Rochester (Int'l)■..........	SS	1	1	0	0	0	0	0	0	.000	0	0	0	0	1	0	1.000
1998— Pawtucket (Int'l)■.........	S-1-3-P	96	329	31	75	12	1	8	38	.228	28	82	2	170	271	15	.967
— Boston (A.L.)	DH-2B	2	0	0	0	0	0	0	0	. . .	1	0	0	1	1	0	1.000
Major league totals (1 year)		2	0	0	0	0	0	0	0	. . .	1	0	0	1	1	0	1.000

RECORD AS PITCHER

Year Team (League)	W	L	Pct.	ERA	G	GS	CG	ShO	Sv.	IP	H	R	ER	BB	SO
1998— Pawtucket (Int'l)■.........	0	0	. . .	0.00	1	0	0	0	0	1	0	0	0	2	0

PERSONAL: Born January 8, 1968, in Oakland. ... 6-2/210. ... Bats right, throws right. ... Full name: Brian David Johnson.
HIGH SCHOOL: Skyline (Oakland).
COLLEGE: Stanford.
TRANSACTIONS/CAREER NOTES: Selected by Montreal Expos organization in 36th round of free-agent draft (June 2, 1986); did not sign. ... Selected by New York Yankees organization in 16th round of free-agent draft (June 5, 1989). ... Selected by Las Vegas, San Diego Padres organization from Albany/Colonie, Yankees organization, in Rule 5 minor league draft (December 9, 1991). ... On disabled list (April 22-May 16, 1992). ... Traded by Padres with P Willie Blair to Detroit Tigers for P Joey Eischen and P Cam Smith (December 17, 1996). ... Traded by Tigers to San Francisco Giants for C Marcus Jensen (July 16, 1997). ... On San Francisco disabled list (May 4-21 and July 22-August 7, 1998); included rehabilitation assignment to Fresno (July 31-August 7). ... Granted free agency (December 21, 1998). ... Signed by Cincinnati Reds (January 11, 1999).
STATISTICAL NOTES: Led South Atlantic League catchers with 752 putouts and 844 total chances in 1990. ... Led Florida State League catchers with 654 putouts in 1991. ... Career major league grand slams: 3.

Year Team (League)	Pos.	G	AB	R	H	2B	3B	HR	RBI	Avg.	BB	SO	SB	PO	A	E	Avg.
1989— GC Yankees (GCL)......	C	17	61	7	22	1	1	0	8	.361	4	5	0	84	14	1	.990
1990— Greensboro (S. Atl.)...	C-3B-1B	137	496	58	118	15	0	7	51	.238	57	65	4	†773	91	13	.985
1991— Alb./Colon. (East.)	C-1B	2	8	0	0	0	0	0	0	.000	0	2	0	10	2	0	1.000
—Fort Laud. (FSL)	C-1B-3B	113	394	35	94	19	0	1	44	.239	34	67	4	†738	65	13	.984
1992— Wichita (Texas)■	C-3B	75	245	30	71	20	0	3	26	.290	22	32	3	472	40	3	.994
1993— Las Vegas (PCL)	C-3B-OF	115	416	58	141	35	6	10	71	.339	41	53	0	513	67	9	.985
1994— San Diego (N.L.)	C-1B	36	93	7	23	4	1	3	16	.247	5	21	0	185	15	0	1.000
—Las Vegas (PCL)	C	15	51	6	11	1	0	2	9	.216	8	6	0	61	5	0	1.000
1995— San Diego (N.L.)	C-1B	68	207	20	52	9	0	3	29	.251	11	39	0	403	32	4	.991
1996— San Diego (N.L.)	C-1B-3B	82	243	18	66	13	1	8	35	.272	4	36	0	456	21	5	.990
1997— Detroit (A.L.)■	C-DH	45	139	13	33	6	1	2	18	.237	5	19	1	217	9	3	.987
—Toledo (Int'l)..............	C	7	21	0	3	2	0	0	1	.143	0	2	0	38	4	0	1.000
—San Fran. (N.L.)	C-1B	56	179	19	50	7	2	11	27	.279	14	26	0	352	24	2	.995
1998— San Francisco (N.L.) ..	C-OF	99	308	34	73	8	1	13	34	.237	28	67	0	591	33	4	.994
—Fresno (PCL).............	OF	5	19	4	6	1	0	2	3	.316	1	5	0	10	0	0	1.000
American League totals (1 year)		45	139	13	33	6	1	2	18	.237	5	19	1	217	9	3	.987
National League totals (5 years)		341	1030	98	264	41	5	38	141	.256	62	189	0	1987	125	15	.993
Major league totals (5 years)		386	1169	111	297	47	6	40	159	.254	67	208	1	2204	134	18	.992

DIVISION SERIES RECORD

Year Team (League)	Pos.	G	AB	R	H	2B	3B	HR	RBI	Avg.	BB	SO	SB	PO	A	E	Avg.
1996— San Diego (N.L.)	C	2	8	2	3	1	0	0	0	.375	0	1	0	15	3	0	1.000
1997— San Francisco (N.L.) ..	C	3	10	2	1	0	0	1	1	.100	1	4	0	18	0	0	1.000
Division series totals (2 years)		5	18	4	4	1	0	1	1	.222	1	5	0	33	3	0	1.000

PERSONAL: Born July 20, 1971, in Fort Pierce, Fla. ... 6-2/220. ... Bats right, throws right. ... Full name: Charles Edward Johnson Jr.
HIGH SCHOOL: Westwood (Fort Pierce, Fla.).
COLLEGE: Miami (Fla.).
TRANSACTIONS/CAREER NOTES: Selected by Montreal Expos organization in first round (10th pick overall) of free-agent draft (June 5, 1989); did not sign. ... Selected by Florida Marlins organization in first round (28th pick overall) of free-agent draft (June 1, 1992). ... On Florida disabled list (August 9-September 1, 1995); included rehabilitation assignment to Portland (August 30-September 1). ... On disabled list (July 28-September 1, 1996). ... Traded by Marlins with OF Gary Sheffield, 3B Bobby Bonilla, OF Jim Eisenreich and P Manuel Barrios to Los Angeles Dodgers for C Mike Piazza and 3B Todd Zeile (May 15, 1998). ... Traded by Dodgers with OF Roger Cedeno to New York Mets for C Todd Hundley and P Arnold Gooch; then traded by Mets to Baltimore Orioles for P Armando Benitez (December 1, 1998).
RECORDS: Holds major league career records for most consecutive errorless games by catcher—159 (June 24, 1996-September 28, 1997); and most consecutive chances accepted by catcher without an error—1,294 (June 23, 1996-September 28, 1997). ... Holds major league single-season records for most consecutive errorless games by catcher—123 (April 1-September 28, 1997); and most chances accepted without an error by catcher—973 (April 1-September 28, 1997). ... Shares major league single-season records for highest fielding average by catcher (100 or more games)—1.000 (1997); and fewest errors (100 or more games)—0 (1997).
HONORS: Named catcher on The Sporting News college All-America team (1992). ... Won N.L. Gold Glove at catcher (1995-98).
STATISTICAL NOTES: Led Midwest League with 230 total bases in 1993. ... Led Midwest League catchers with 1,004 total chances in 1993. ... Led N.L. catchers with 12 double plays in 1996.
MISCELLANEOUS: Member of 1992 U.S. Olympic baseball team.

Year Team (League)	Pos.	G	AB	R	H	2B	3B	HR	RBI	Avg.	BB	SO	SB	PO	A	E	Avg.
1993— Kane County (Midw.)..	C	135	488	74	134	29	5	19	*94	.275	62	111	9	*852	*140	12	.988
1994— Portland (Eastern)......	C	132	443	64	117	29	1	*28	80	.264	*74	97	4	713	*84	7	.991
—Florida (N.L.)..............	C	4	11	5	5	1	0	1	4	.455	1	4	0	18	2	0	1.000
1995— Florida (N.L.)..............	C	97	315	40	79	15	1	11	39	.251	46	71	0	641	•63	6	.992
—Portland (Eastern)......	C	2	7	0	0	0	0	0	0	.000	1	3	0	21	2	1	.958
1996— Florida (N.L.)..............	C	120	386	34	84	13	1	13	37	.218	40	91	1	751	70	4	*.995
1997— Florida (N.L.)..............	C	124	416	43	104	26	1	19	63	.250	60	109	0	901	73	0	*1.000
1998— Florida (N.L.)..............	C	31	113	13	25	5	0	7	23	.221	16	30	0	193	10	2	.990
—Los Angeles (N.L.)■ ..	C	102	346	31	75	13	0	12	35	.217	29	99	0	715	50	6	.992
Major league totals (5 years)		478	1587	166	372	73	3	63	201	.234	192	404	1	3219	268	18	.995

DIVISION SERIES RECORD

Year Team (League)	Pos.	G	AB	R	H	2B	3B	HR	RBI	Avg.	BB	SO	SB	PO	A	E	Avg.
1997— Florida (N.L.)..............	C	3	8	5	2	1	0	1	2	.250	3	2	0	21	3	0	1.000

CHAMPIONSHIP SERIES RECORD

Year Team (League)	Pos.	G	AB	R	H	2B	3B	HR	RBI	Avg.	BB	SO	SB	PO	A	E	Avg.
						BATTING									FIELDING		
1997— Florida (N.L.)	C	6	17	1	2	2	0	0	5	.118	3	8	0	52	3	2	.965

WORLD SERIES RECORD

NOTES: Member of World Series championship team (1997).

Year Team (League)	Pos.	G	AB	R	H	2B	3B	HR	RBI	Avg.	BB	SO	SB	PO	A	E	Avg.
						BATTING									FIELDING		
1997— Florida (N.L.)	C	7	28	4	10	0	0	1	3	.357	1	6	0	49	2	0	1.000

ALL-STAR GAME RECORD

Year League	Pos.	AB	R	H	2B	3B	HR	RBI	Avg.	BB	SO	SB	PO	A	E	Avg.
					BATTING									FIELDING		
1997— National	C	1	0	0	0	0	0	0	.000	0	1	0	2	0	0	1.000

JOHNSON, JASON　　　　　P　　　　　DEVIL RAYS

PERSONAL: Born October 27, 1973, in Santa Barbara, Calif. ... 6-6/235. ... Throws right, bats right. ... Full name: Jason Michael Johnson.
HIGH SCHOOL: Conner (Hebron, Ky.)
TRANSACTIONS/CAREER NOTES: Signed as non-drafted free agent by Pittsburgh Pirates organization (July 21, 1992). ... Selected by Tampa Bay Devil Rays in first round (14th pick overall) of expansion draft (November 18, 1997). ... On Tampa Bay disabled list (July 4, 1998-remainder of season).

Year Team (League)	W	L	Pct.	ERA	G	GS	CG	ShO	Sv.	IP	H	R	ER	BB	SO
1992— GC Pirates (GCL)...............	2	0	1.000	3.68	5	0	0	0	0	7 1/3	6	3	3	6	3
1993— GC Pirates (GCL)...............	1	4	.200	2.33	9	9	0	0	0	54	48	23	14	14	39
— Welland (N.Y.-Penn)	1	5	.167	4.63	6	6	1	0	0	35	33	24	18	9	19
1994— Augusta (S. Atl.)..............	2	12	.143	4.03	20	19	1	0	0	102 2/3	119	67	46	32	69
1995— Augusta (S. Atl.)..............	3	5	.375	4.36	11	11	1	0	0	53 2/3	57	32	26	17	42
— Lynchburg (Carolina)	1	2	.333	2.05	5	4	0	0	0	22	23	6	5	5	9
1996— Lynchburg (Carolina)	1	4	.200	6.50	15	5	0	0	0	44 1/3	56	37	32	12	27
— Augusta (S. Atl.)..............	4	4	.500	3.11	14	14	1	1	0	84	82	40	29	25	83
1997— Lynchburg (Carolina)	8	4	.667	3.71	17	17	0	0	0	99 1/3	98	43	41	30	92
— Carolina (Southern)	3	3	.500	4.08	9	9	1	0	0	57 1/3	56	31	26	16	63
— Pittsburgh (N.L.)	0	0	. . .	6.00	3	0	0	0	0	6	10	4	4	1	3
1998— Durham (International)■....	1	0	1.000	2.92	2	2	0	0	0	12 1/3	6	4	4	2	14
— Tampa Bay (A.L.)	2	5	.286	5.70	13	13	0	0	0	60	74	38	38	27	36
A.L. totals (1 year)	2	5	.286	5.70	13	13	0	0	0	60	74	38	38	27	36
N.L. totals (1 year)	0	0	. . .	6.00	3	0	0	0	0	6	10	4	4	1	3
Major league totals (2 years)......	2	5	.286	5.73	16	13	0	0	0	66	84	42	42	28	39

JOHNSON, JONATHON　　　　　P　　　　　RANGERS

PERSONAL: Born July 16, 1974, in LaGrange, Ga. ... 6-0/180. ... Throws right, bats right. ... Full name: Jonathon Kent Johnson.
HIGH SCHOOL: Forest (Ocala, Fla.).
COLLEGE: Florida State.
TRANSACTIONS/CAREER NOTES: Selected by Texas Rangers organization in first round (seventh pick overall) of free-agent draft (June 1, 1995). ... On Oklahoma disabled list (May 1-17, 1998).

Year Team (League)	W	L	Pct.	ERA	G	GS	CG	ShO	Sv.	IP	H	R	ER	BB	SO
1995— Charlotte (Fla. St.).............	1	5	.167	2.70	8	7	1	0	0	43 1/3	34	14	13	16	25
1996— Tulsa (Texas)	*13	10	.565	3.56	26	25	*6	0	0	174 1/3	176	86	69	41	97
— Oklahoma City (A.A.).........	1	0	1.000	0.00	1	1	1	1	0	9	2	0	0	1	6
1997— Oklahoma City (A.A.).........	1	8	.111	7.29	13	12	1	0	1	58	83	54	47	29	33
— Tulsa (Texas)	5	4	.556	3.52	10	10	4	0	0	71 2/3	70	35	28	15	47
1998— Oklahoma (Pacific Coast)...	6	6	.500	4.90	19	18	1	0	1	112	109	66	61	32	94
— Charlotte (Fla. St.)	0	2	.000	4.63	3	3	0	0	0	11 2/3	10	6	6	4	11
— Texas (A.L.)	0	0	. . .	8.31	1	1	0	0	0	4 1/3	5	4	4	5	3
Major league totals (1 year)........	0	0	. . .	8.31	1	1	0	0	0	4 1/3	5	4	4	5	3

JOHNSON, LANCE　　　　　OF　　　　　CUBS

PERSONAL: Born July 6, 1963, in Lincoln Heights, Ohio. ... 5-11/165. ... Bats left, throws left. ... Full name: Kenneth Lance Johnson.
HIGH SCHOOL: Princeton (Cincinnati).
JUNIOR COLLEGE: Triton College (Ill.).
COLLEGE: South Alabama.
TRANSACTIONS/CAREER NOTES: Selected by Pittsburgh Pirates organization in 30th round of free-agent draft (June 8, 1981); did not sign. ... Selected by Seattle Mariners organization in 31st round of free-agent draft (June 7, 1982); did not sign. ... Selected by St. Louis Cardinals organization in sixth round of free-agent draft (June 4, 1984). ... Traded by Cardinals with P Rick Horton and cash to Chicago White Sox for P Jose DeLeon (February 9, 1988). ... Granted free agency (November 8, 1995). ... Signed by New York Mets (December 14, 1995). ... On New York disabled list (May 2-June 16, 1997). ... Traded by Mets with two players to be named later to Chicago Cubs for OF Brian McRae, P Mel Rojas and P Turk Wendell (August 8, 1997); Cubs acquired P Mark Clark (August 11) and IF Manny Alexander (August 14) to complete deal. ... On disabled list (April 28-July 13, 1998).
RECORDS: Holds major league record for most consecutive years leading league in triples—4 (1991-94). ... Shares A.L. single-game record for most triples—3 (September 23, 1995).
HONORS: Named American Association Most Valuable Player (1987).
STATISTICAL NOTES: Led New York-Pennsylvania League outfielders with 201 total chances in 1984. ... Led Texas League in caught stealing with 15 in 1986. ... Led American Association outfielders with 333 total chances in 1987. ... Led Pacific Coast League outfielders with five

double plays in 1988. ... Led Pacific Coast League outfielders with 273 total chances in 1989. ... Led Pacific Coast League in caught stealing with 18 in 1989. ... Led A.L. in caught stealing with 22 in 1990. ... Led N.L. outfielders with 412 total chances in 1996. ... Had 25-game hitting streak (July 16-August 11, 1992). ... Collected six hits in one game (September 23, 1995). ... Career major league grand slams: 1.

Year	Team (League)	Pos.	G	AB	R	H	2B	3B	HR	RBI	Avg.	BB	SO	SB	PO	A	E	Avg.
1984—	Erie (N.Y.-Penn).........	OF	71	283	*63	*96	7	5	1	28	.339	45	20	29	*188	5	8	.960
1985—	St. Peters. (FSL)........	OF	129	497	68	134	17	10	2	55	.270	58	39	33	338	16	5	.986
1986—	Arkansas (Texas)......	OF	127	445	82	128	24	6	2	33	.288	59	57	*49	262	11	7	.975
1987—	Louisville (A.A.)..........	OF	116	477	89	159	21	11	5	50	.333	49	45	42	*319	6	•8	.976
	— St. Louis (N.L.)..........	OF	33	59	4	13	2	1	0	7	.220	4	6	6	27	0	2	.931
1988—	Chicago (A.L.)■........	OF-DH	33	124	11	23	4	1	0	6	.185	6	11	6	63	1	2	.970
	— Vancouver (PCL)	OF	100	411	71	126	12	6	2	36	.307	42	52	49	262	9	5	.982
1989—	Vancouver (PCL)	OF	106	408	69	124	11	7	0	28	.304	46	36	33	*261	7	5	.982
	— Chicago (A.L.)...........	OF-DH	50	180	28	54	8	2	0	16	.300	17	24	16	113	0	2	.983
1990—	Chicago (A.L.)...........	OF-DH	151	541	76	154	18	9	1	51	.285	33	45	36	353	5	10	.973
1991—	Chicago (A.L.)...........	OF	159	588	72	161	14	•13	0	49	.274	26	58	26	425	11	2	.995
1992—	Chicago (A.L.)...........	OF	157	567	67	158	15	*12	3	47	.279	34	33	41	433	11	6	.987
1993—	Chicago (A.L.)...........	OF	147	540	75	168	18	*14	0	47	.311	36	33	35	*427	7	•9	.980
1994—	Chicago (A.L.)...........	OF-DH	106	412	56	114	11	*14	3	54	.277	26	23	26	317	1	0	*1.000
1995—	Chicago (A.L.)...........	OF-DH	142	*607	98	*186	18	12	10	57	.306	32	31	40	338	8	3	.991
1996—	New York (N.L.)■.......	OF	160	*682	117	*227	31	*21	9	69	.333	33	40	50	*391	9	•12	.971
1997—	New York (N.L.).........	OF	72	265	43	82	10	6	1	24	.309	33	21	15	152	4	4	.975
	— Chicago (N.L.)■........	OF-DH	39	145	17	44	6	2	4	15	.303	9	10	5	79	0	3	.963
1998—	Chicago (N.L.)...........	OF	85	304	51	85	8	4	2	21	.280	26	22	10	154	5	4	.975
American League totals (8 years)			945	3559	483	1018	106	77	17	327	.286	210	258	226	2469	44	34	.987
National League totals (4 years)			389	1455	232	451	57	34	16	136	.310	105	99	86	803	18	25	.970
Major league totals (12 years)			1334	5014	715	1469	163	111	33	463	.293	315	357	312	3272	62	59	.983

DIVISION SERIES RECORD

Year	Team (League)	Pos.	G	AB	R	H	2B	3B	HR	RBI	Avg.	BB	SO	SB	PO	A	E	Avg.
1998—	Chicago (N.L.)	OF	3	12	0	2	0	0	0	1	.167	0	1	0	10	0	0	1.000

CHAMPIONSHIP SERIES RECORD

Year	Team (League)	Pos.	G	AB	R	H	2B	3B	HR	RBI	Avg.	BB	SO	SB	PO	A	E	Avg.
1987—	St. Louis (N.L.)..........	PR	1	0	1	0	0	0	0	0	...	0	0	1	...	...	...	...
1993—	Chicago (A.L.)	OF	6	23	2	5	1	1	1	6	.217	2	1	1	15	0	0	1.000
Championship series totals (2 years)			7	23	3	5	1	1	1	6	.217	2	1	2	15	0	0	1.000

WORLD SERIES RECORD

Year	Team (League)	Pos.	G	AB	R	H	2B	3B	HR	RBI	Avg.	BB	SO	SB	PO	A	E	Avg.
1987—	St. Louis (N.L.)..........	PR	1	0	0	0	0	0	0	0	...	0	0	1	...	...	...	...

ALL-STAR GAME RECORD

Year	League	Pos.	AB	R	H	2B	3B	HR	RBI	Avg.	BB	SO	SB	PO	A	E	Avg.
1996—	National	OF	4	1	3	1	0	0	0	.750	0	0	1	5	0	0	1.000

JOHNSON, MARK — C — WHITE SOX

PERSONAL: Born September 12, 1975, in Wheatridge, Colo. ... 6-0/185. ... Bats left, throws right. ... Full name: Mark Landon Johnson.
HIGH SCHOOL: Warner Robins (Ga.).
TRANSACTIONS/CAREER NOTES: Selected by Chicago White Sox organization in first round (26th pick overall) of free-agent draft (June 2, 1994).
STATISTICAL NOTES: Led Carolina League with .420 on-base percentage in 1997. ... Led Carolina League catchers with 1000 total chances and tied for league lead with eight double plays in 1997. ... Led Southern League with .443 on-base percentage in 1998.

Year	Team (League)	Pos.	G	AB	R	H	2B	3B	HR	RBI	Avg.	BB	SO	SB	PO	A	E	Avg.
1994—	GC Whi. Sox (GCL)	C	32	87	10	21	5	0	0	14	.241	14	15	1	182	22	3	.986
1995—	Hickory (S. Atl.).........	C	107	319	31	58	9	0	2	17	.182	59	52	3	*681	67	11	.986
1996—	South Bend (Mid.)......	C	67	214	29	55	14	3	2	27	.257	39	25	3	408	37	9	.980
	— Prince Will. (Car.)......	C	18	58	9	14	3	0	0	3	.241	13	6	0	112	8	1	.992
1997—	Win.-Salem (Car.).......	C	120	375	59	95	27	4	4	46	.253	*106	85	4	*899	90	11	*.989
1998—	Birmingham (Sou.)......	C-1B	117	382	68	108	17	3	9	59	.283	*105	72	0	723	65	8	.990
	— Chicago (A.L.)	C	7	23	2	2	0	2	0	1	.087	1	8	0	36	2	0	1.000
Major league totals (1 year)			7	23	2	2	0	2	0	1	.087	1	8	0	36	2	0	1.000

JOHNSON, MARK — 1B

PERSONAL: Born October 17, 1967, in Worcester, Mass. ... 6-4/230. ... Bats left, throws left. ... Full name: Mark Patrick Johnson.
HIGH SCHOOL: Holy Name (Worcester, Mass.).
COLLEGE: Dartmouth (degree in psychology).
TRANSACTIONS/CAREER NOTES: Selected by Pittsburgh Pirates organization in 42nd round of free-agent draft (June 5, 1989); did not sign. ... Selected by Pirates organization in 20th round of free-agent draft (June 4, 1990). ... On Calgary disabled list (August 26-September 8, 1995). ... Claimed on waivers by Cincinnati Reds (August 29, 1997). ... Traded by Reds to Anaheim Angels for a player to be named later (September 11, 1998). ... Released by Angels (December 22, 1998). ... Signed by Hanshin Tigers of Japan Central League (December 22, 1998).

HONORS: Named Southern League Most Valuable Player (1994).
STATISTICAL NOTES: Led Southern League with 11 intentional bases on balls received in 1994. ... Career major league grand slams: 1.

Year	Team (League)	Pos.	G	AB	R	H	2B	3B	HR	RBI	Avg.	BB	SO	SB	PO	A	E	Avg.
							BATTING								FIELDING			
1990— Welland (NYP)............	1B	5	8	2	4	1	0	0	2	.500	2	0	0	2	1	0	1.000
— Augusta (S. Atl.)........	1B	43	144	12	36	7	0	0	19	.250	24	18	4	240	18	5	.981
1991— Augusta (S. Atl.)........	1B	49	139	23	36	7	4	2	25	.259	29	1	15	319	33	9	.975
— Salem (Carolina)	1B-OF-3B	37	103	12	26	2	0	2	13	.252	18	25	0	32	28	3	.952
1992— Carolina (Southern)....	1B	122	383	40	89	16	1	7	45	.232	55	94	16	610	41	8	.988
1993— Carolina (Southern)....	1B-OF	125	399	48	93	18	4	14	52	.233	66	93	6	500	40	4	.993
1994— Carolina (Southern)....	1B-OF	111	388	69	107	20	2	*23	85	.276	67	89	6	570	52	6	.990
1995— Pittsburgh (N.L.)........	1B	79	221	32	46	6	1	13	28	.208	37	66	5	527	36	8	.986
— Calgary (PCL)............	1B	9	23	7	7	4	0	2	8	.304	6	4	1	65	5	2	.972
1996— Pittsburgh (N.L.)........	1B-OF	127	343	55	94	24	0	13	47	.274	44	64	6	778	73	6	.993
1997— Pittsburgh (N.L.)........	1B-DH	78	219	30	47	10	0	4	29	.215	43	78	1	542	44	5	.992
— Calgary (PCL)............	1B-OF	34	115	28	39	11	1	6	16	.339	22	28	4	183	25	0	1.000
— Indianapolis (A.A.)■..	1B	3	4	0	0	0	0	0	0	.000	2	2	0	17	2	0	1.000
1998— Indianapolis (Int'l)	1B-OF	116	357	65	107	33	1	22	75	.300	68	82	2	443	37	5	.990
— Anaheim (A.L.)■........	1B-DH	10	14	1	1	0	0	0	0	.071	0	6	0	13	1	0	1.000
American League totals (1 year)		10	14	1	1	0	0	0	0	.071	0	6	0	13	1	0	1.000
National League totals (3 years)		284	783	117	187	40	1	30	104	.239	124	208	12	1847	153	19	.991
Major league totals (4 years)		294	797	118	188	40	1	30	104	.236	124	214	12	1860	154	19	.991

JOHNSON, MIKE   P   EXPOS

PERSONAL: Born October 3, 1975, in Edmonton. ... 6-2/170. ... Throws right, bats left. ... Full name: Michael Keith Johnson.
HIGH SCHOOL: Salisbury Composite (Edmonton).
TRANSACTIONS/CAREER NOTES: Selected by Toronto Blue Jays organization in 17th round of free-agent draft (June 3, 1993). ... Selected by San Francisco Giants organization from Toronto Blue Jays organization in Rule 5 major league draft (December 9, 1996). ... Traded by Giants to Baltimore Orioles for cash considerations (December 9, 1996). ... Traded by Orioles to Montreal Expos for a player to be named later (July 31, 1997); Orioles acquired P Everett Stull to complete deal (October 31, 1997).

Year	Team (League)	W	L	Pct.	ERA	G	GS	CG	ShO	Sv.	IP	H	R	ER	BB	SO
1993— GC Blue Jays (GCL)............	0	2	.000	4.87	16	1	0	0	1	44 1/3	51	40	24	22	31
1994— Medicine Hat (Pioneer)	1	3	.250	4.46	9	9	0	0	0	36 1/3	48	31	18	22	8
1995— GC Blue Jays (GCL)............	0	2	.000	7.20	3	3	0	0	0	15	20	15	12	8	13
— Medicine Hat (Pioneer)	4	1	.800	3.86	19	0	0	0	3	49	46	26	21	25	32
1996— Hagerstown (S. Atl.)	11	8	.579	3.15	29	23	5	3	0	162 2/3	157	74	57	39	155
1997— Baltimore (A.L.)■..............	0	1	.000	7.94	14	5	0	0	2	39 2/3	52	36	35	16	29
— Montreal (N.L.)■...............	2	5	.286	5.94	11	11	0	0	0	50	54	34	33	21	28
1998— Harrisburg (Eastern)	3	2	.600	6.95	7	7	0	0	0	33 2/3	35	27	26	10	38
— Ottawa (Int'l)...................	4	9	.308	4.29	18	18	1	0	0	109	105	63	52	38	88
— Montreal (N.L.)..................	0	2	.000	14.73	2	2	0	0	0	7 1/3	16	12	12	2	4
A.L. totals (1 year)	0	1	.000	7.94	14	5	0	0	2	39 2/3	52	36	35	16	29
N.L. totals (2 years)	2	7	.222	7.06	13	13	0	0	0	57 1/3	70	46	45	23	32
Major league totals (2 years)	2	8	.200	7.42	27	18	0	0	2	97	122	82	80	39	61

JOHNSON, RANDY   P   DIAMONDBACKS

PERSONAL: Born September 10, 1963, in Walnut Creek, Calif. ... 6-10/230. ... Throws left, bats right. ... Full name: Randall David Johnson.
HIGH SCHOOL: Livermore (Calif.).
COLLEGE: Southern California.
TRANSACTIONS/CAREER NOTES: Selected by Atlanta Braves organization in third round of free-agent draft (June 7, 1982); did not sign. ... Selected by Montreal Expos organization in second round of free-agent draft (June 3, 1985). ... Traded by Expos organization with P Brian Holman and P Gene Harris to Seattle Mariners for P Mark Langston and a player to be named later (May 25, 1989); Indianapolis, Expos organization, acquired P Mike Campbell to complete deal (July 31, 1989). ... On disabled list (June 11-27, 1992). ... On Seattle disabled list (May 15-August 6 and August 27, 1996-remainder of season); included rehabilitation assignment to Everett (August 3-6). ... On suspended list (April 24-27, 1998). ... Traded by Mariners to Houston Astros for SS Carlos Guillen, P Freddy Garcia and a player to be named later (July 31, 1998); Mariners acquired P John Halama to complete deal (October 1, 1998). ... Granted free agency (October 28, 1998). ... Signed by Arizona Diamondbacks (December 10, 1998).
RECORDS: Shares major league single-game record for most strikeouts by lefthander—19 (June 24 and August 8, 1997). ... Shares A.L. record for most strikeouts in two consecutive games—32 (August 8 [19] and 15 [13], 1997, 17 innings).
HONORS: Named A.L. Pitcher of the Year by The Sporting News (1995). ... Named lefthanded pitcher on The Sporting News A.L. All-Star team (1995 and 1997). ... Named A.L. Cy Young Award winner by Baseball Writers' Association of America (1995).
STATISTICAL NOTES: Led American Association with 20 balks in 1988. ... Pitched 2-0 no-hit victory against Detroit (June 2, 1990). ... Pitched 4-0 one-hit, complete-game victory against Oakland (August 14, 1991). ... Struck out 15 batters in one game (September 16, 1992; June 14 and September 16, 1993; June 4 and August 11, 1994; June 24 and September 23, 1995; May 28 and June 8, 1997; April 10, May 24 and July 11, 1998). ... Struck out 18 batters in one game (September 27, 1992). ... Led A.L. with 18 hit batsmen in 1992 and 16 in 1993. ... Pitched 7-0 one-hit, complete-game victory against Oakland (May 16, 1993). ... Struck out 16 batters in one game (July 15, 1995; July 18, 1997 and August 28, 1998). ... Struck out 19 batters in one game (June 24 and August 8, 1997). ... Pitched 3-0 one-hit, complete-game victory against Minnesota (July 16, 1998).
MISCELLANEOUS: Holds Seattle Mariners franchise all-time records for most wins (130), lowest earned-run average (3.37), most innings pitched (1,838 1/3), most strikeouts (2,162), most complete games (51), and most shutouts (19). ... Appeared in one game as outfielder with no chances (1993).

Year	Team (League)	W	L	Pct.	ERA	G	GS	CG	ShO	Sv.	IP	H	R	ER	BB	SO
1985— Jamestown (NYP)	0	3	.000	5.93	8	8	0	0	0	27 1/3	29	22	18	24	21
1986— W.P. Beach (FSL)...............	8	7	.533	3.16	26	•26	2	1	0	119 2/3	89	49	42	*94	133
1987— Jacksonville (Southern)......	11	8	.579	3.73	25	24	0	0	0	140	100	63	58	128	*163

Year	Team (League)	W	L	Pct.	ERA	G	GS	CG	ShO	Sv.	IP	H	R	ER	BB	SO
1988—	Indianapolis (A.A.)..............	8	7	.533	3.26	20	19	0	0	0	113 1/3	85	52	41	72	111
	— Montreal (N.L.)...................	3	0	1.000	2.42	4	4	1	0	0	26	23	8	7	7	25
1989—	Montreal (N.L.)...................	0	4	.000	6.67	7	6	0	0	0	29 2/3	29	25	22	26	26
	— Indianapolis (A.A.)............	1	1	.500	2.00	3	3	0	0	0	18	13	5	4	9	17
	— Seattle (A.L.)■...............	7	9	.438	4.40	22	22	2	0	0	131	118	75	64	70	104
1990—	Seattle (A.L.)...................	14	11	.560	3.65	33	33	5	2	0	219 2/3	174	103	89	*120	194
1991—	Seattle (A.L.)...................	13	10	.565	3.98	33	33	2	1	0	201 1/3	151	96	89	*152	228
1992—	Seattle (A.L.)...................	12	14	.462	3.77	31	31	6	2	0	210 1/3	154	104	88	*144	*241
1993—	Seattle (A.L.)...................	19	8	.704	3.24	35	34	10	3	1	255 1/3	185	97	92	99	*308
1994—	Seattle (A.L.)...................	13	6	.684	3.19	23	23	*9	*4	0	172	132	65	61	72	*204
1995—	Seattle (A.L.)...................	18	2	*.900	*2.48	30	30	6	3	0	214 1/3	159	65	59	65	*294
1996—	Seattle (A.L.)...................	5	0	1.000	3.67	14	8	0	0	1	61 1/3	48	27	25	25	85
	— Everett (Northwest)..........	0	0	...	0.00	1	1	0	0	0	2	0	0	0	0	5
1997—	Seattle (A.L.)...................	20	4	*.833	2.28	30	29	5	2	0	213	147	60	54	77	291
1998—	Seattle (A.L.)...................	9	10	.474	4.33	23	23	6	2	0	160	146	90	77	60	213
	— Houston (N.L.)■.............	10	1	.909	1.28	11	11	4	4	0	84 1/3	57	12	12	26	116
A.L. totals (10 years)		130	74	.637	3.42	274	266	51	19	2	1838 1/3	1414	782	698	884	2162
N.L. totals (3 years)		13	5	.722	2.64	22	21	5	4	0	140	109	45	41	59	167
Major league totals (11 years)....		143	79	.644	3.36	296	287	56	23	2	1978 1/3	1523	827	739	943	2329

DIVISION SERIES RECORD

RECORDS: Holds career records for most losses—4; and most strikeouts—49. ... Holds single-game record for most strikeouts—13 (October 5, 1997). ... Shares career records for most games started—5; and most innings pitched—37. ... Holds A.L. career record for most strike-outs—32.

Year	Team (League)	W	L	Pct.	ERA	G	GS	CG	ShO	Sv.	IP	H	R	ER	BB	SO
1995—	Seattle (A.L.).....................	2	0	1.000	2.70	2	1	0	0	0	10	5	3	3	6	16
1997—	Seattle (A.L.).....................	0	2	.000	5.54	2	2	1	0	0	13	14	8	8	6	16
1998—	Houston (N.L.)	0	2	.000	1.93	2	2	0	0	0	14	12	4	3	2	17
Div. series totals (3 years)		2	4	.333	3.41	6	5	1	0	0	37	31	15	14	14	49

CHAMPIONSHIP SERIES RECORD

Year	Team (League)	W	L	Pct.	ERA	G	GS	CG	ShO	Sv.	IP	H	R	ER	BB	SO
1995—	Seattle (A.L.).....................	0	1	.000	2.35	2	2	0	0	0	15 1/3	12	6	4	2	13

ALL-STAR GAME RECORD

Year	League	W	L	Pct.	ERA	GS	CG	ShO	Sv.	IP	H	R	ER	BB	SO
1990—	American...........................							Did not play.							
1993—	American...........................	0	0	...	0.00	0	0	0	0	2	0	0	0	0	1
1994—	American...........................	0	0	...	9.00	0	0	0	0	1	2	1	1	0	0
1995—	American...........................	0	0	...	0.00	0	0	0	0	2	0	0	0	1	3
1997—	American...........................	0	0	...	0.00	1	0	0	0	2	0	0	0	1	2
All-Star totals (4 years)		0	0	...	1.29	2	0	0	0	7	2	1	1	2	6

JOHNSON, RUSS   IF   ASTROS

PERSONAL: Born February 22, 1973, in Baton Rouge, La. ... 5-10/180. ... Bats right, throws right. ... Full name: William Russell Johnson.
HIGH SCHOOL: Denham Springs (La.).
COLLEGE: Louisiana State.
TRANSACTIONS/CAREER NOTES: Selected by Houston Astros organization in supplemental round ("sandwich pick" between first and second round, 30th pick overall) of free-agent draft (June 2, 1994); pick received as part of compensation for San Francisco Giants signing Type A free-agent P Mark Portugal.
STATISTICAL NOTES: Led Texas League shortstops with 664 total chances and 87 double plays in 1995. ... Led Pacific Coast League third basemen with .962 fielding percentage in 1998.

Year	Team (League)	Pos.	G	AB	R	H	2B	3B	HR	RBI	Avg.	BB	SO	SB	PO	A	E	Avg.
							BATTING									FIELDING		
1995—	Jackson (Texas)	SS	132	475	65	118	16	2	9	53	.248	50	60	10	182	383	13	.978
1996—	Jackson (Texas)	SS	132	496	86	154	24	5	15	74	.310	56	50	9	219	411	34	.949
1997—	New Orleans (A.A.)	3B-SS	122	445	72	123	16	6	4	49	.276	66	78	7	86	269	21	.944
	— Houston (N.L.)	3B-2B	21	60	7	18	1	0	2	9	.300	6	14	1	13	24	1	.974
1998—	New Orleans (PCL).....	3B-2B-SS	122	453	*95	140	28	2	7	52	.309	*90	64	11	76	235	11	†.966
	— Houston (N.L.)	3B-2B	8	13	2	3	1	0	0	0	.231	1	5	1	3	9	0	1.000
Major league totals (2 years)			29	73	9	21	2	0	2	9	.288	7	19	2	16	33	1	.980

DIVISION SERIES RECORD

Year	Team (League)	Pos.	G	AB	R	H	2B	3B	HR	RBI	Avg.	BB	SO	SB	PO	A	E	Avg.
							BATTING									FIELDING		
1997—	Houston (N.L.)	PH	1	1	0	0	0	0	0	0	.000	0	1	0	...	...	...	...

JOHNSTONE, JOHN   P   GIANTS

PERSONAL: Born November 25, 1968, in Liverpool, N.Y. ... 6-3/210. ... Throws right, bats right. ... Full name: John William Johnstone.
HIGH SCHOOL: Bishop Ludden (Syracuse, N.Y.).
JUNIOR COLLEGE: Onondaga Community College (N.Y.).
TRANSACTIONS/CAREER NOTES: Selected by New York Mets organization in 20th round of free-agent draft (June 2, 1987). ... On disabled list (June 24-July 7, 1992). ... Selected by Florida Marlins in second round (31st pick overall) of expansion draft (November 17, 1992). ... On disabled list (May 8, 1995-remainder of season). ... Granted free agency (December 21, 1995). ... Signed by Houston Astros organization (December 28, 1995). ... Granted free agency (September 30, 1996). ... Signed by San Francisco Giants organization (December 17, 1996). ... Claimed on waivers by Oakland Athletics (August 7, 1997). ... Granted free agency (August 31, 1997). ... Signed by Giants organization (September 1, 1997).

Year—Team (League)	W	L	Pct.	ERA	G	GS	CG	ShO	Sv.	IP	H	R	ER	BB	SO
1987— Kingsport (Appalachian).....	1	1	.500	7.45	17	1	0	0	0	29	42	28	24	20	21
1988— GC Mets (GCL).................	3	4	.429	2.68	12	12	3	0	0	74	65	29	22	25	57
1989— Pittsfield (NYP)	*11	2	.846	2.77	15	15	2	1	0	104	101	47	32	28	60
1990— St. Lucie (Fla. St.)	*15	6	.714	2.24	25	25	*9	3	0	172 2/3	145	53	43	60	120
1991— Williamsport (Eastern)	7	9	.438	3.97	27	•27	2	0	0	165 1/3	159	94	73	79	100
1992— Binghamton (Eastern)	7	7	.500	3.74	24	24	2	0	0	149 1/3	132	66	62	36	121
1993— Edmonton (PCL)■..............	4	*15	.211	5.18	30	21	1	0	4	144 1/3	167	95	83	59	126
— Florida (N.L.)	0	2	.000	5.91	7	0	0	0	0	10 2/3	16	8	7	7	5
1994— Edmonton (PCL)	5	3	.625	4.46	29	0	0	0	4	42 1/3	46	23	21	9	43
— Florida (N.L.)	1	2	.333	5.91	17	0	0	0	0	21 1/3	23	20	14	16	23
1995— Florida (N.L.)	0	0	. . .	3.86	4	0	0	0	0	4 2/3	7	2	2	2	3
1996— Tucson (PCL)■.................	3	3	.500	3.42	45	1	0	0	5	55 1/3	59	27	21	22	70
— Houston (N.L.)	1	0	1.000	5.54	9	0	0	0	0	13	17	8	8	5	5
1997— Phoenix (PCL)■.................	0	3	.000	4.03	38	0	0	0	*24	38	34	17	17	15	30
— San Francisco (N.L.)	0	0	. . .	3.38	13	0	0	0	0	18 2/3	15	7	7	7	15
— Oakland (A.L.)■.................	0	0	. . .	2.84	5	0	0	0	0	6 1/3	7	2	2	7	4
1998— San Francisco (N.L.)	6	5	.545	3.07	70	0	0	0	0	88	72	32	30	38	86
A.L. totals (1 year)	0	0	. . .	2.84	5	0	0	0	0	6 1/3	7	2	2	7	4
N.L. totals (6 years)	8	9	.471	3.91	120	0	0	0	0	156 1/3	150	77	68	75	137
Major league totals (6 years)	8	9	.471	3.87	125	0	0	0	0	162 2/3	157	79	70	82	141

JONES, ANDRUW   OF   BRAVES

PERSONAL: Born April 23, 1977, in Willemstad, Curacao. ... 6-1/185. ... Bats right, throws right. ... Full name: Andruw Rudolf Jones.
HIGH SCHOOL: St. Paulus (Willemstad, Curacao).
TRANSACTIONS/CAREER NOTES: Signed as non-drafted free agent by Atlanta Braves organization (July 1, 1993).
RECORDS: Holds N.L. single-season record for fewest singles (150 or more games)—55 (1997).
HONORS: Named South Atlantic League Most Valuable Player (1995). ... Won N.L. Gold Glove as outfielder (1998).
STATISTICAL NOTES: Led South Atlantic League with nine sacrifice flies in 1995. ... Led South Atlantic League outfielders with 246 total chances and tied for lead with four double plays in 1995. ... Led N.L. outfielders with 435 total chances and tied for lead with six double plays in 1998. ... Career major league grand slams: 1.

Year Team (League)	Pos.	G	AB	R	H	2B	3B	HR	RBI	Avg.	BB	SO	SB	PO	A	E	Avg.
1994— GC Braves (GCL)........	OF	27	95	22	21	5	1	2	10	.221	16	19	5	90	0	3	.968
— Danville (Appal.).........	OF	36	143	20	48	9	2	1	16	.336	9	25	16	81	3	2	.977
1995— Macon (S. Atl.)..........	OF	•139	537	*104	149	41	5	25	100	.277	70	122	*56	*332	10	4	.988
1996— Durham (Carolina)......	OF	66	243	65	76	14	3	17	43	.313	42	54	16	174	9	7	.963
— Greenville (Southern) .	OF	38	157	39	58	10	1	12	37	.369	17	34	12	129	7	1	.993
— Richmond (Int'l)........	OF	12	45	11	17	3	1	5	12	.378	1	9	2	34	1	1	.972
— Atlanta (N.L.)..............	OF	31	106	11	23	7	1	5	13	.217	7	29	3	73	4	2	.975
1997— Atlanta (N.L.)..............	OF	153	399	60	92	18	1	18	70	.231	56	107	20	287	14	7	.977
1998— Atlanta (N.L.)..............	OF	159	582	89	158	33	8	31	90	.271	40	129	27	*413	•20	2	.995
Major league totals (3 years)		343	1087	160	273	58	10	54	173	.251	103	265	50	773	38	11	.987

DIVISION SERIES RECORD

RECORDS: Holds record for most at-bats without a hit—14.

Year Team (League)	Pos.	G	AB	R	H	2B	3B	HR	RBI	Avg.	BB	SO	SB	PO	A	E	Avg.
1996— Atlanta (N.L.)..............	OF-PR	3	0	0	0	0	0	0	0	. . .	1	0	0	2	0	0	1.000
1997— Atlanta (N.L.)..............	OF	3	5	1	0	0	0	0	1	.000	1	1	0	10	0	0	1.000
1998— Atlanta (N.L.)..............	OF	3	9	2	0	0	0	0	1	.000	3	2	2	8	0	0	1.000
Division series totals (3 years)		9	14	3	0	0	0	0	2	.000	5	3	2	20	0	0	1.000

CHAMPIONSHIP SERIES RECORD

Year Team (League)	Pos.	G	AB	R	H	2B	3B	HR	RBI	Avg.	BB	SO	SB	PO	A	E	Avg.
1996— Atlanta (N.L.)..............	OF-PR-PH	5	9	3	2	0	0	1	3	.222	3	2	0	5	0	0	1.000
1997— Atlanta (N.L.)..............	OF-PH	5	9	0	4	0	0	0	1	.444	1	1	0	12	1	0	1.000
1998— Atlanta (N.L.)..............	OF	6	22	3	6	0	0	1	2	.273	1	4	1	15	0	0	1.000
Championship series totals (3 years)		16	40	6	12	0	0	2	6	.300	5	7	1	32	1	0	1.000

WORLD SERIES RECORD

RECORDS: Shares record for most home runs in two consecutive innings—2 (October 20, 1996, second and third innings).
NOTES: Hit home runs in first two at-bats (October 20, 1996, second and third innings).

Year Team (League)	Pos.	G	AB	R	H	2B	3B	HR	RBI	Avg.	BB	SO	SB	PO	A	E	Avg.
1996— Atlanta (N.L.)..............	OF	6	20	4	8	1	0	2	6	.400	3	6	1	7	1	0	1.000

JONES, BOBBY   P   METS

PERSONAL: Born February 10, 1970, in Fresno, Calif. ... 6-4/225. ... Throws right, bats right. ... Full name: Robert Joseph Jones.
HIGH SCHOOL: Fresno (Calif.).
COLLEGE: Fresno State.
TRANSACTIONS/CAREER NOTES: Selected by New York Mets organization in supplemental round ("sandwich pick" between first and second round, 36th pick overall) of free-agent draft (June 3, 1991); pick received as part of compensation for Los Angeles Dodgers signing Type A free-agent OF Darryl Strawberry.
HONORS: Named Eastern League Pitcher of the Year (1992).
STATISTICAL NOTES: Led International League with 11 hit batsmen in 1993. ... Led N.L. with 18 sacrifice hits in 1995.

Year Team (League)	W	L	Pct.	ERA	G	GS	CG	ShO	Sv.	IP	H	R	ER	BB	SO
1991— Columbia (S. Atl.)	3	1	.750	1.85	5	5	0	0	0	24 1/3	20	5	5	3	35
1992— Binghamton (Eastern)	12	4	.750	*1.88	24	24	4	*4	0	158	118	40	33	43	143
1993— Norfolk (Int'l)	12	10	.545	3.63	24	24	6	*3	0	166	149	72	67	32	126
— New York (N.L.)	2	4	.333	3.65	9	9	0	0	0	61 2/3	61	35	25	22	35
1994— New York (N.L.)	12	7	.632	3.15	24	24	1	1	0	160	157	75	56	56	80
1995— New York (N.L.)	10	10	.500	4.19	30	30	3	1	0	195 2/3	209	107	91	53	127
1996— New York (N.L.)	12	8	.600	4.42	31	31	3	1	0	195 2/3	219	102	96	46	116
1997— New York (N.L.)	15	9	.625	3.63	30	30	2	1	0	193 1/3	177	88	78	63	125
1998— New York (N.L.)	9	9	.500	4.05	30	30	0	0	0	195 1/3	192	94	88	53	115
Major league totals (6 years)	60	47	.561	3.90	154	154	9	4	0	1001 2/3	1015	501	434	293	598

ALL-STAR GAME RECORD

Year League	W	L	Pct.	ERA	GS	CG	ShO	Sv.	IP	H	R	ER	BB	SO
1997— National	0	0	...	0.00	0	0	0	0	1	1	0	0	0	2

JONES, BOBBY — P — ROCKIES

PERSONAL: Born April 11, 1972, in Orange, N.J. ... 6-0/178. ... Throws left, bats right. ... Full name: Robert Mitchell Jones.
HIGH SCHOOL: Rutherford (N.J.).
JUNIOR COLLEGE: Chipola Junior College (Fla.).
TRANSACTIONS/CAREER NOTES: Selected by Milwaukee Brewers organization in 44th round of free-agent draft (June 3, 1991). ... Selected by Colorado Rockies organization from Brewers organization in Rule 5 minor league draft (December 5, 1994).
STATISTICAL NOTES: Tied for Pacific Coast League lead with 12 hit batsmen in 1997.

Year Team (League)	W	L	Pct.	ERA	G	GS	CG	ShO	Sv.	IP	H	R	ER	BB	SO
1992— Helena (Pioneer)	5	4	.556	4.36	14	13	1	0	0	76 1/3	93	51	37	23	53
1993— Beloit (Midwest)	10	10	.500	4.11	25	25	4	0	0	144 2/3	159	82	66	65	115
1994— Stockton (California)	6	12	.333	4.21	26	26	2	0	0	147 2/3	131	90	69	64	147
1995— New Haven (East.)■	5	2	.714	2.58	27	8	0	0	3	73 1/3	61	27	21	36	70
— Colo. Springs (PCL)	1	2	.333	7.30	11	8	0	0	0	40 2/3	50	38	33	33	48
1996— Colo. Springs (PCL)	2	8	.200	4.97	57	0	0	0	3	88 2/3	88	54	49	63	78
1997— Colo. Springs (PCL)	7	11	.389	5.14	25	21	0	0	0	133	135	89	76	71	104
— Colorado (N.L.)	1	1	.500	8.38	4	4	0	0	0	19 1/3	30	18	18	12	5
1998— Colorado (N.L.)	7	8	.467	5.22	35	20	1	0	0	141 1/3	153	87	82	66	109
Major league totals (2 years)	8	9	.471	5.60	39	24	1	0	0	160 2/3	183	105	100	78	114

JONES, CHIPPER — 3B — BRAVES

PERSONAL: Born April 24, 1972, in De Land, Fla. ... 6-4/210. ... Bats both, throws right. ... Full name: Larry Wayne Jones.
HIGH SCHOOL: The Bolles School (Jacksonville).
TRANSACTIONS/CAREER NOTES: Selected by Atlanta Braves organization in first round (first pick overall) of free-agent draft (June 4, 1990). ... On Atlanta disabled list (March 20, 1994-entire season). ... On disabled list (March 22-April 6, 1996).
RECORDS: Holds major league single-season records for fewest putouts by third baseman (150 or more games)—77 (1997); and fewest chances accepted by third baseman (150 or more games)—318. ... Holds N.L. single-season record for fewest assists by third baseman (150 or more games)—241 (1997).
HONORS: Named N.L. Rookie Player of the Year by THE SPORTING NEWS (1995).
STATISTICAL NOTES: Led South Atlantic League with 10 sacrifice flies in 1991. ... Led South Atlantic League shortstops with 692 total chances and 71 double plays in 1991. ... Led International League with 268 total bases in 1993. ... Led International League shortstops with 619 total chances in 1993. ... Career major league grand slams: 4.

Year Team (League)	Pos.	G	AB	R	H	2B	3B	HR	RBI	Avg.	BB	SO	SB	PO	A	E	Avg.
1990— GC Braves (GCL)	SS	44	140	20	32	1	1	1	18	.229	14	25	5	64	140	18	.919
1991— Macon (S. Atl.)	SS	136	473	*104	154	24	11	15	98	.326	69	70	40	*217	*419	56	.919
1992— Durham (Carolina)	SS	70	264	43	73	22	1	4	31	.277	31	34	10	106	200	14	.956
— Greenville (Sou.)	SS	67	266	43	92	17	11	9	42	.346	11	32	14	92	218	18	.945
1993— Richmond (Int'l)	SS	139	536	*97	*174	31	*12	13	89	.325	57	70	23	195	381	*43	.931
— Atlanta (N.L.)	SS	8	3	2	2	1	0	0	0	.667	1	1	0	1	1	0	1.000
1994— Atlanta (N.L.)										Did not play.							
1995— Atlanta (N.L.)	3B-OF	140	524	87	139	22	3	23	86	.265	73	99	8	103	255	25	.935
1996— Atlanta (N.L.)	3B-SS-OF	157	598	114	185	32	5	30	110	.309	87	88	14	103	288	17	.958
1997— Atlanta (N.L.)	3B-OF	157	597	100	176	41	3	21	111	.295	76	88	20	83	241	15	.956
1998— Atlanta (N.L.)	3B	160	601	123	188	29	5	34	107	.313	96	93	16	105	290	12	.971
Major league totals (5 years)		622	2323	426	690	125	16	108	414	.297	333	369	58	395	1075	69	.955

DIVISION SERIES RECORD

RECORDS: Shares single-game record for most home runs—2 (October 3, 1995). ... Holds N.L. career records for most at-bats—45; most runs—11; most hits—15; most home runs—4; most total bases—29; and most bases on balls—12. ... Shares N.L. career record for most games—13.

Year Team (League)	Pos.	G	AB	R	H	2B	3B	HR	RBI	Avg.	BB	SO	SB	PO	A	E	Avg.
1995— Atlanta (N.L.)	3B	4	18	4	7	2	0	2	4	.389	2	2	0	3	4	0	1.000
1996— Atlanta (N.L.)	3B	3	9	2	2	0	0	1	2	.222	3	4	1	1	3	0	1.000
1997— Atlanta (N.L.)	3B	3	8	3	4	0	0	1	2	.500	3	2	1	2	3	1	.833
1998— Atlanta (N.L.)	3B	3	10	2	2	0	0	0	1	.200	4	3	0	2	2	0	1.000
Division series totals (4 years)		13	45	11	15	2	0	4	9	.333	12	11	2	8	12	1	.952

CHAMPIONSHIP SERIES RECORD

RECORDS: Shares single-series record for most singles—9 (1996). ... Shares single-game record for most singles—4 (October 9, 1996).

Year Team (League)	Pos.	G	AB	R	H	2B	3B	HR	RBI	Avg.	BB	SO	SB	PO	A	E	Avg.
1995— Atlanta (N.L.).............	3B	4	16	3	7	0	0	1	3	.438	3	1	1	4	13	0	1.000
1996— Atlanta (N.L.).............	3B	7	25	6	11	2	0	0	4	.440	3	1	1	5	7	1	.923
1997— Atlanta (N.L.).............	3B	6	24	5	7	1	0	2	4	.292	2	3	0	1	8	0	1.000
1998— Atlanta (N.L.).............	3B	6	24	2	5	1	0	0	1	.208	4	5	0	1	12	0	1.000
Championship series totals (4 years)		23	89	16	30	4	0	3	12	.337	12	10	2	11	40	1	.981

WORLD SERIES RECORD

NOTES: Member of World Series championship team (1995).

						BATTING								FIELDING			
Year Team (League)	Pos.	G	AB	R	H	2B	3B	HR	RBI	Avg.	BB	SO	SB	PO	A	E	Avg.
1995— Atlanta (N.L.).............	3B	6	21	3	6	3	0	0	1	.286	4	3	0	6	12	1	.947
1996— Atlanta (N.L.).............	3B-SS	6	21	3	6	3	0	0	3	.286	4	2	0	4	7	0	1.000
World Series totals (2 years)		12	42	6	12	6	0	0	4	.286	8	5	0	10	19	1	.967

ALL-STAR GAME RECORD

					BATTING								FIELDING		
Year League	Pos.	AB	R	H	2B	3B	HR	RBI	Avg.	BB	SO	SB	PO	A	E	Avg.
1996— National	3B	2	1	1	0	0	0	0	.500	0	0	0	1	1	0	1.000
1997— National	3B	1	0	0	0	0	0	0	.000	0	0	0	0	1	0	1.000
1998— National	3B	2	1	0	0	0	0	0	.000	1	0	0	0	0	0	...
All-Star Game totals (3 years)		5	2	1	0	0	0	0	.200	1	0	0	1	2	0	1.000

JONES, CHRIS   OF

PERSONAL: Born December 16, 1965, in Utica, N.Y. ... 6-2/210. ... Bats right, throws right. ... Full name: Christopher Carlos Jones.
HIGH SCHOOL: Liverpool (N.Y.).
TRANSACTIONS/CAREER NOTES: Selected by Cincinnati Reds organization in third round of free-agent draft (June 4, 1984). ... Released by Reds (December 13, 1991). ... Signed by Houston Astros organization (December 19, 1991). ... Granted free agency (October 16, 1992). ... Signed by Colorado Rockies (October 26, 1992). ... Granted free agency (December 20, 1993). ... Re-signed by Rockies organization (December 22, 1993). ... Granted free agency (October 15, 1994). ... Signed by New York Mets (December 7, 1994). ... Granted free agency (October 15, 1996). ... Signed by San Diego Padres (November 4, 1996). ... On disabled list (May 22-June 10, 1997). ... Granted free agency (October 6, 1997). ... Signed by Arizona Diamondbacks (November 19, 1997). ... Traded by Diamondbacks to San Francisco Giants for P Ricky Pickett (April 27, 1998). ... Released by Giants (October 2, 1998).

						BATTING								FIELDING		
Year Team (League)	Pos.	G	AB	R	H	2B	3B	HR	RBI	Avg.	BB	SO	SB	PO	A	E	Avg.
1984— Billings (Pioneer)........	3B	21	73	8	11	2	0	2	13	.151	2	24	4	6	27	5	.868
1985— Billings (Pioneer)........	OF	63	240	43	62	12	5	4	33	.258	19	72	13	112	4	*13	.899
1986— Cedar Rap. (Midw.)	OF	128	473	65	117	13	9	20	78	.247	20	126	23	218	15	11	.955
1987— Vermont (Eastern).......	OF	113	383	50	88	11	4	10	39	.230	23	99	13	207	12	8	.965
1988— Chattanooga (Sou.)	OF	116	410	50	111	20	7	4	61	.271	29	102	11	185	15	8	.962
1989— Chattanooga (Sou.)	OF	103	378	47	95	18	2	10	54	.251	23	68	10	197	8	7	.967
— Nashville (A.A.)	OF	21	49	8	8	1	0	2	5	.163	0	16	2	25	0	1	.962
1990— Nashville (A.A.)	OF	134	436	53	114	23	3	10	52	.261	23	86	12	209	17	8	.966
1991— Nashville (A.A.)	OF	73	267	29	65	5	4	9	33	.243	19	65	10	110	5	6	.950
— Cincinnati (N.L.)	OF	52	89	14	26	1	2	2	6	.292	2	31	2	27	1	0	1.000
1992— Houston (N.L.)■	OF	54	63	7	12	2	1	1	4	.190	7	21	3	27	0	2	.931
— Tucson (PCL)	OF	45	170	25	55	9	8	3	28	.324	18	34	7	86	7	2	.979
1993— Colo. Springs (PCL)■	OF	46	168	41	47	5	5	12	40	.280	19	47	8	107	5	3	.974
— Colorado (N.L.)	OF	86	209	29	57	11	4	6	31	.273	10	48	9	114	2	2	.983
1994— Colo. Springs (PCL) ...	OF	98	386	77	124	22	4	20	75	.321	35	72	12	191	11	*15	.931
— Colorado (N.L.)	OF	21	40	6	12	2	1	0	2	.300	2	14	0	16	0	1	.941
1995— Norfolk (Int'l)■	OF	33	114	20	38	12	1	3	19	.333	11	20	5	62	4	1	.985
— New York (N.L.)........	OF-1B	79	182	33	51	6	2	8	31	.280	13	45	2	122	6	2	.985
1996— New York (N.L.)........	OF-1B	89	149	22	36	7	0	4	18	.242	12	42	1	83	1	3	.966
1997— San Diego (N.L.)■	OF	92	152	24	37	9	0	7	25	.243	16	45	7	73	4	4	.951
1998— Arizona (N.L.)■	OF	20	31	3	6	1	0	0	3	.194	3	9	0	11	0	0	1.000
— San Fran. (N.L.)■	OF-DH	43	90	14	17	2	1	2	10	.189	8	28	2	31	1	2	.941
— Fresno (Pacific Coast)	OF	25	60	11	16	1	3	3	8	.267	6	12	2	17	0	1	.944
Major league totals (8 years)		536	1005	152	254	41	11	30	130	.253	73	283	26	504	15	16	.970

JONES, DOUG   P   ATHLETICS

PERSONAL: Born June 24, 1957, in Covina, Calif. ... 6-2/224. ... Throws right, bats right. ... Full name: Douglas Reid Jones.
HIGH SCHOOL: Lebanon (Ind.).
JUNIOR COLLEGE: Central Arizona College.
COLLEGE: Butler.
TRANSACTIONS/CAREER NOTES: Selected by Milwaukee Brewers organization in third round of free-agent draft (January 10, 1978). ... On disabled list (June 20-July 12, 1978). ... On Vancouver disabled list (April 11-September 1, 1983 and April 25-May 30, 1984). ... Granted free agency (October 15, 1984). ... Signed by Waterbury, Cleveland Indians organization (April 3, 1985). ... Granted free agency (December 20, 1991). ... Signed by Houston Astros organization (January 24, 1992). ... Traded by Astros with P Jeff Juden to Philadelphia Phillies for P Mitch Williams (December 2, 1993). ... Granted free agency (October 15, 1994). ... Signed by Baltimore Orioles (April 8, 1995). ... Granted free agency (November 3, 1995). ... Signed by Chicago Cubs (December 28, 1995). ... Released by Cubs (June 15, 1996). ... Signed by New Orleans, Brewers organization (June 28, 1996). ... Granted free agency (November 6, 1996). ... Re-signed by Brewers (December 7, 1996). ... On disabled list (July 16-August 3, 1997). ... Granted free agency (October 27, 1997). ... Re-signed by Brewers (November 18, 1997). ... Traded by Brewers to Indians for P Eric Plunk (July 23, 1998). ... Granted free agency (October 29, 1998). ... Signed by Oakland Athletics (January 11, 1999).
HONORS: Named N.L. co-Fireman of the Year by THE SPORTING NEWS (1992).
MISCELLANEOUS: Holds Cleveland Indians all-time record for most saves (129).

Year Team (League)	W	L	Pct.	ERA	G	GS	CG	ShO	Sv.	IP	H	R	ER	BB	SO
1978— Newark (N.Y.-Penn)............	2	4	.333	5.21	15	3	1	0	2	38	49	30	22	15	27
1979— Burlington (Midw.)............	10	10	.500	*1.75	28	20	*16	•3	0	*190	144	63	37	73	115
1980— Stockton (California)	6	2	.750	2.84	11	11	5	1	0	76	63	32	24	31	54
— Vancouver (PCL)	3	2	.600	3.23	8	8	1	1	0	53	52	19	19	15	28
— Holyoke (Eastern)............	5	3	.625	2.90	8	8	4	2	0	62	57	23	20	26	39
1981— El Paso (Texas)................	5	7	.417	5.80	15	15	3	1	0	90	121	67	58	28	62
— Vancouver (PCL)	5	3	.625	3.04	11	10	2	0	0	80	79	29	27	22	38
1982— Milwaukee (A.L.)	0	0	...	10.13	4	0	0	0	0	2 2/3	5	3	3	1	1
— Vancouver (PCL)	5	8	.385	2.97	23	9	4	0	2	106	109	48	35	31	60
1983— Vancouver (PCL)	0	1	.000	10.29	3	1	0	0	0	7	10	8	8	5	4
1984— Vancouver (PCL)	1	0	1.000	10.13	3	0	0	0	0	8	9	9	9	3	2
— El Paso (Texas)................	6	8	.429	4.28	16	16	7	0	0	109 1/3	120	61	52	35	62
1985— Waterbury (Eastern)■.......	9	4	.692	3.65	39	1	0	0	7	116	123	59	47	36	113
1986— Maine (International).........	5	6	.455	*2.09	43	3	0	0	9	116 1/3	105	35	27	27	98
— Cleveland (A.L.)...............	1	0	1.000	2.50	11	0	0	0	1	18	18	5	5	6	12
1987— Cleveland (A.L.)...............	6	5	.545	3.15	49	0	0	0	8	91 1/3	101	45	32	24	87
— Buffalo (A.A.).................	5	2	.714	2.04	23	0	0	0	7	61 2/3	49	18	14	12	61
1988— Cleveland (A.L.)...............	3	4	.429	2.27	51	0	0	0	37	83 1/3	69	26	21	16	72
1989— Cleveland (A.L.)...............	7	10	.412	2.34	59	0	0	0	32	80 2/3	76	25	21	13	65
1990— Cleveland (A.L.)...............	5	5	.500	2.56	66	0	0	0	43	84 1/3	66	26	24	22	55
1991— Cleveland (A.L.)...............	4	8	.333	5.54	36	4	0	0	7	63 1/3	87	42	39	17	48
— Colo. Springs (PCL)	2	2	.500	3.28	17	2	1	1	7	35 2/3	30	14	13	5	29
1992— Houston (N.L.)■..............	11	8	.579	1.85	80	0	0	0	36	111 2/3	96	29	23	17	93
1993— Houston (N.L.).................	4	10	.286	4.54	71	0	0	0	26	85 1/3	102	46	43	21	66
1994— Philadelphia (N.L.)■.........	2	4	.333	2.17	47	0	0	0	27	54	55	14	13	6	38
1995— Baltimore (A.L.)■.............	0	4	.000	5.01	52	0	0	0	22	46 2/3	55	30	26	16	42
1996— Chicago (A.L.)■...............	2	2	.500	5.01	28	0	0	0	2	32 1/3	41	20	18	7	26
— New Orleans (A.A.)■.........	0	3	.000	3.75	13	0	0	0	6	24	28	10	10	6	17
— Milwaukee (A.L.)	5	0	1.000	3.41	24	0	0	0	1	31 2/3	31	13	12	13	34
1997— Milwaukee (A.L.)■............	6	6	.500	2.02	75	0	0	0	36	80 1/3	62	20	18	9	82
1998— Milwaukee (N.L.)	3	4	.429	5.17	46	0	0	0	12	54	65	32	31	11	43
— Cleveland (A.L.)■.............	1	2	.333	3.45	23	0	0	0	1	31 1/3	34	12	12	6	28
A.L. totals (11 years)	38	44	.463	3.12	450	4	0	0	188	613 2/3	604	247	213	143	526
N.L. totals (5 years)	22	28	.440	3.42	272	0	0	0	103	337 1/3	359	141	128	62	266
Major league totals (14 years)....	60	72	.455	3.23	722	4	0	0	291	951	963	388	341	205	792

DIVISION SERIES RECORD

Year Team (League)	W	L	Pct.	ERA	G	GS	CG	ShO	Sv.	IP	H	R	ER	BB	SO
1998— Cleveland (A.L.)................	0	0	...	6.75	1	0	0	0	0	2 2/3	3	2	2	1	1

CHAMPIONSHIP SERIES RECORD

Year Team (League)	W	L	Pct.	ERA	G	GS	CG	ShO	Sv.	IP	H	R	ER	BB	SO
1998— Cleveland (A.L.)................							Did not play.								

ALL-STAR GAME RECORD

Year League	W	L	Pct.	ERA	GS	CG	ShO	Sv.	IP	H	R	ER	BB	SO
1988— American	0	0	...	0.00	0	0	0	0	2/3	0	0	0	0	1
1989— American	0	0	...	0.00	0	0	0	1	1 1/3	1	0	0	0	0
1990— American						Did not play.								
1992— National	0	0	...	27.00	0	0	0	0	1	4	3	3	0	2
1994— National	1	0	1.000	0.00	0	0	0	0	1	2	0	0	0	2
All-Star totals (4 years)	1	0	1.000	6.75	0	0	0	1	4	7	3	3	0	5

JONES, JACQUE   OF   TWINS

PERSONAL: Born April 25, 1975, in San Diego. ... 5-10/176. ... Bats left, throws left. ... Full name: Jacque Dewayne Jones.
HIGH SCHOOL: San Diego.
COLLEGE: Southern California.
TRANSACTIONS/CAREER NOTES: Selected by Minnesota Twins organization in second round of free-agent draft (June 2, 1996).
MISCELLANEOUS: Member of 1996 U.S. Olympic baseball team.

						BATTING							FIELDING			
Year Team (League)	Pos.	G	AB	R	H	2B	3B	HR	RBI	Avg.	BB	SO	SB	PO	A	E	Avg.
1996— Fort Myers (FSL)	OF	1	3	0	2	1	0	0	1	.667	0	0	0	0	0	0	...
1997— Fort Myers (FSL)	OF	131	539	84	*160	33	6	15	82	.297	33	110	24	313	8	7	.979
1998— New Britain (East.)	OF	134	518	78	155	39	3	21	85	.299	37	134	18	288	12	10	.968

JONES, JAIME   OF   MARLINS

PERSONAL: Born August 2, 1976, in San Diego. ... 6-3/190. ... Bats left, throws left. ... Full name: James Paul Jones.
HIGH SCHOOL: Rancho Bernardo (San Diego).
TRANSACTIONS/CAREER NOTES: Selected by Florida Marlins organization in first round (sixth pick overall) of free-agent draft (June 1, 1995).

						BATTING							FIELDING			
Year Team (League)	Pos.	G	AB	R	H	2B	3B	HR	RBI	Avg.	BB	SO	SB	PO	A	E	Avg.
1995— GC Marlins (GCL)	OF	5	18	2	4	0	0	0	3	.222	5	4	0	3	0	0	1.000
— Elmira (N.Y.-Penn)......	OF	31	116	21	33	6	2	4	11	.284	9	30	5	38	1	4	.907
1996— Kane County (Midw.)..	OF	62	237	29	59	17	1	8	45	.249	19	74	7	80	2	6	.932
1997— Brevard Co. (Fla. St.)..	OF	95	373	63	101	27	4	10	60	.271	44	86	6	100	1	7	.935
1998— Portland (Eastern)	OF	123	438	58	123	27	0	10	63	.281	55	118	4	141	7	8	.949

J

JONES, TERRY   OF   EXPOS

PERSONAL: Born February 15, 1971, in Birmingham, Ala. ... 5-10/165. ... Bats both, throws right. ... Full name: Terry Lee Jones.
HIGH SCHOOL: Pinson Valley (Pinson, Ala.).
JUNIOR COLLEGE: Wallace State Community College (Ala.).
COLLEGE: North Alabama.
TRANSACTIONS/CAREER NOTES: Selected by Colorado Rockies organization in 40th round of free-agent draft (June 3, 1993). ... Traded by Rockies with a player to be named later to Montreal Expos for P Dave Veres and a player to be named later (December 10, 1997).
STATISTICAL NOTES: Led California League outfielders with 342 total chances and tied for lead with four double plays in 1994. ... Led Pacific Coast League outfielders with 311 total chances in 1996.

								BATTING							FIELDING		
Year Team (League)	Pos.	G	AB	R	H	2B	3B	HR	RBI	Avg.	BB	SO	SB	PO	A	E	Avg.
1993— Bend (Northwest)	OF	33	138	21	40	5	4	0	18	.290	12	19	16	57	7	1	.985
— Central Valley (Cal.)	OF	21	73	16	21	1	0	0	7	.288	10	15	5	36	2	1	.974
1994— Central Valley (Cal.)	OF	129	*536	94	157	20	1	2	34	.293	42	85	44	*312	*16	14	.959
1995— New Haven (East.)	OF	124	472	78	127	12	1	1	26	.269	39	104	*51	264	18	*10	.966
1996— Colo. Springs (PCL)	OF	128	497	75	143	7	4	0	33	.288	37	80	26	281	14	*16	.949
— Colorado (N.L.)	OF	12	10	6	3	0	0	0	1	.300	0	3	0	5	0	0	1.000
1997— Colo. Springs (PCL)	OF	92	363	70	98	14	4	1	25	.270	25	49	*36	139	11	1	.993
1998— Ottawa (Int'l)■	OF	81	278	36	66	3	4	0	21	.237	32	48	35	193	5	4	.980
— Montreal (N.L.)	OF	60	212	30	46	7	2	1	15	.217	21	46	16	161	4	2	.988
Major league totals (2 years)		72	222	36	49	7	2	1	16	.221	21	49	16	166	4	2	.988

JONES, TODD   P   TIGERS

PERSONAL: Born April 24, 1968, in Marietta, Ga. ... 6-3/230. ... Throws right, bats right. ... Full name: Todd Barton Jones.
HIGH SCHOOL: Osborne (Ga.).
COLLEGE: Jacksonville (Ala.) State.
TRANSACTIONS/CAREER NOTES: Selected by New York Mets organization in 41st round of free-agent draft (June 2, 1986); did not sign. ... Selected by Houston Astros organization in supplemental round ("sandwich pick" between first and second round, 27th pick overall) of free-agent draft (June 5, 1989); pick received as part of compensation for Texas Rangers signing Type A free-agent P Nolan Ryan. ... On suspended list (September 14-16, 1993). ... On Houston disabled list (July 19-August 12 and August 18-September 12, 1996); included rehabilitation assignment to Tucson (August 9-12). ... Traded by Astros with OF Brian Hunter, IF Orlando Miller, P Doug Brocail and cash to Detroit Tigers for C Brad Ausmus, P Jose Lima, P C.J. Nitkowski, P Trever Miller and IF Daryle Ward (December 10, 1996).

Year Team (League)	W	L	Pct.	ERA	G	GS	CG	ShO	Sv.	IP	H	R	ER	BB	SO
1989— Auburn (N.Y.-Penn)	2	3	.400	5.44	11	9	1	0	0	49 2/3	47	39	30	42	71
1990— Osceola (Florida St.)	12	10	.545	3.51	27	•27	1	0	0	151 1/3	124	81	59	*109	106
1991— Osceola (Florida St.)	4	4	.500	4.35	14	14	0	0	0	72 1/3	69	38	35	35	51
— Jackson (Texas)	4	3	.571	4.88	10	10	0	0	0	55 1/3	51	37	30	39	37
1992— Jackson (Texas)	3	7	.300	3.14	*61	0	0	0	25	66	52	28	23	44	60
— Tucson (PCL)	0	1	.000	4.50	3	0	0	0	0	4	1	2	2	10	4
1993— Tucson (PCL)	4	2	.667	4.44	41	0	0	0	12	48 2/3	49	26	24	31	45
— Houston (N.L.)	1	2	.333	3.13	27	0	0	0	2	37 1/3	28	14	13	15	25
1994— Houston (N.L.)	5	2	.714	2.72	48	0	0	0	5	72 2/3	52	23	22	26	63
1995— Houston (N.L.)	6	5	.545	3.07	68	0	0	0	15	99 2/3	89	38	34	52	96
1996— Houston (N.L.)	6	3	.667	4.40	51	0	0	0	17	57 1/3	61	30	28	32	44
— Tucson (PCL)	0	0	...	0.00	1	0	0	0	0	2	1	1	0	2	0
1997— Detroit (A.L.)■	5	4	.556	3.09	68	0	0	0	31	70	60	29	24	35	70
1998— Detroit (A.L.)	1	4	.200	4.97	65	0	0	0	28	63 1/3	58	38	35	36	57
A.L. totals (2 years)	6	8	.429	3.98	133	0	0	0	59	133 1/3	118	67	59	71	127
N.L. totals (4 years)	18	12	.600	3.27	194	0	0	0	39	267	230	105	97	125	228
Major league totals (6 years)	24	20	.545	3.51	327	0	0	0	98	400 1/3	348	172	156	196	355

JORDAN, BRIAN   OF   BRAVES

PERSONAL: Born March 29, 1967, in Baltimore. ... 6-1/205. ... Bats right, throws right. ... Full name: Brian O'Neal Jordan.
HIGH SCHOOL: Milford (Baltimore).
COLLEGE: Richmond.
TRANSACTIONS/CAREER NOTES: Selected by Cleveland Indians organization in 20th round of free-agent draft (June 3, 1985); did not sign. ... Selected by St. Louis Cardinals organization in supplemental round ("sandwich pick" between first and second round, 30th pick overall) of free-agent draft (June 1, 1988); pick received as part of compensation for New York Yankees signing Type A free-agent 1B/OF Jack Clark. ... On disabled list (May 1-8 and June 3-10, 1991). ... On temporarily inactive list (July 3, 1991-remainder of season). ... On St. Louis disabled list (May 23-June 22, 1992); included rehabilitation assignment to Louisville (June 10-22). ... On Louisville disabled list (June 7-14, 1993). ... On disabled list (July 10, 1994-remainder of season; and March 31-April 15, 1996). ... On St. Louis disabled list (May 6-June 13, June 26-August 10 and August 25, 1997-remainder of season); included rehabilitation assignment to Louisville (June 5-13). ... Granted free agency (October 22, 1998). ... Signed by Atlanta Braves (November 23, 1998).
STATISTICAL NOTES: Tied for N.L. lead with six double plays by outfielder in 1998. ... Career major league grand slams: 2.

								BATTING							FIELDING		
Year Team (League)	Pos.	G	AB	R	H	2B	3B	HR	RBI	Avg.	BB	SO	SB	PO	A	E	Avg.
1988— Hamilton (NYP)	OF	19	71	12	22	3	1	4	12	.310	6	15	3	32	1	1	.971
1989— St. Peters. (FSL)	OF	11	43	7	15	4	1	2	11	.349	0	8	0	22	2	0	1.000
1990— Arkansas (Texas)	OF	16	50	4	8	1	0	0	0	.160	0	11	0	28	0	2	.933
— St. Peters. (FSL)	OF	9	30	3	5	0	1	0	1	.167	2	11	0	23	0	0	1.000
1991— Louisville (A.A.)	OF	61	212	35	56	11	4	4	24	.264	17	41	10	144	3	2	.987
1992— Louisville (A.A.)	OF	43	155	23	45	3	1	4	16	.290	8	21	13	89	3	1	.989
— St. Louis (N.L.)	OF	55	193	17	40	9	4	5	22	.207	10	48	7	101	4	1	.991

Year Team (League)	Pos.	G	AB	R	H	2B	3B	HR	RBI	Avg.	BB	SO	SB	PO	A	E	Avg.
						BATTING									FIELDING		
1993—St. Louis (N.L.)..........	OF	67	223	33	69	10	6	10	44	.309	12	35	6	140	4	4	.973
—Louisville (A.A.)..........	OF	38	144	24	54	13	2	5	35	.375	16	17	9	75	2	0	1.000
1994—St. Louis (N.L.)..........	OF-1B	53	178	14	46	8	2	5	15	.258	16	40	4	105	6	1	.991
1995—St. Louis (N.L.)..........	OF	131	490	83	145	20	4	22	81	.296	22	79	24	267	4	1	.996
1996—St. Louis (N.L.)..........	OF-1B	140	513	82	159	36	1	17	104	.310	29	84	22	310	9	2	.994
1997—St. Louis (N.L.)..........	OF	47	145	17	34	5	0	0	10	.234	10	21	6	82	2	0	1.000
—Louisville (A.A.)..........	OF	6	20	1	3	0	0	0	2	.150	1	2	0	6	0	0	1.000
1998—St. Louis (N.L.)..........	OF-DH-3B	150	564	100	178	34	7	25	91	.316	40	66	17	284	12	9	.970
Major league totals (7 years)		643	2306	346	671	122	24	84	367	.291	139	373	86	1289	41	18	.987

DIVISION SERIES RECORD

Year Team (League)	Pos.	G	AB	R	H	2B	3B	HR	RBI	Avg.	BB	SO	SB	PO	A	E	Avg.
						BATTING									FIELDING		
1996—St. Louis (N.L.)..........	OF	3	12	4	4	0	0	1	3	.333	1	3	1	5	0	0	1.000

CHAMPIONSHIP SERIES RECORD

Year Team (League)	Pos.	G	AB	R	H	2B	3B	HR	RBI	Avg.	BB	SO	SB	PO	A	E	Avg.
						BATTING									FIELDING		
1996—St. Louis (N.L.)..........	OF	7	25	3	6	1	1	1	2	.240	2	3	0	13	0	0	1.000

RECORD AS FOOTBALL PLAYER

TRANSACTIONS/CAREER NOTES: Selected by Buffalo Bills in seventh round (173rd pick overall) of 1989 NFL draft. ... Signed by Bills (July 17, 1989). ... Claimed on waivers by Atlanta Falcons (September 5, 1989). ... On injured reserve with ankle injury (September 9-October 22, 1989). ... On developmental squad (October 23-December 2, 1989). ... Granted free agency (February 1, 1992).

PRO STATISTICS: 1989—Recovered two fumbles. 1990—Recovered one fumble. 1991—Credited with two safeties and recovered one fumble.

MISCELLANEOUS: Played safety. ... Named alternate for 1992 Pro Bowl.

Year Team	G	No.	Yds.	Avg.	TD	No.	No.	Yds.	Avg.	TD	No.	Yds.	Avg.	TD	TD	Pts.	Fum.
		INTERCEPTIONS				SACKS	PUNT RETURNS				KICKOFF RETURNS				TOTAL		
1989—Atlanta NFL................	4	0	0	...	0	0.0	4	34	8.5	0	3	27	9.0	0	0	0	1
1990—Atlanta NFL................	16	3	14	4.7	0	0.0	2	19	9.5	0	0	0	...	0	0	0	0
1991—Atlanta NFL................	16	2	3	1.5	0	4.0	14	116	8.3	0	5	100	20.0	0	0	4	0
Pro totals (3 years)	36	5	17	3.4	0	4.0	20	169	8.5	0	8	127	15.9	0	0	4	1

JORDAN, KEVIN   IF   PHILLIES

PERSONAL: Born October 9, 1969, in San Francisco. ... 6-1/206. ... Bats right, throws right. ... Full name: Kevin Wayne Jordan.

HIGH SCHOOL: Lowell (San Francisco).

JUNIOR COLLEGE: Canada College (Calif.).

COLLEGE: Nebraska.

TRANSACTIONS/CAREER NOTES: Selected by Los Angeles Dodgers organization in 10th round of free-agent draft (June 5, 1989); did not sign. ... Selected by New York Yankees organization in 20th round of free-agent draft (June 4, 1990). ... Traded by Yankees with P Bobby Munoz and P Ryan Karp to Philadelphia Phillies for P Terry Mulholland and a player to be named later (February 9, 1994); Yankees acquired P Jeff Patterson to complete deal (November 8, 1994). ... On disabled list (May 1-June 20, 1994; and June 17, 1996-remainder of season).

STATISTICAL NOTES: Led Eastern League with 234 total bases in 1993. ... Led Eastern League second basemen with 93 double plays in 1993.

Year Team (League)	Pos.	G	AB	R	H	2B	3B	HR	RBI	Avg.	BB	SO	SB	PO	A	E	Avg.
						BATTING									FIELDING		
1990—Oneonta (NYP)	2B	73	276	47	92	13	•7	4	54	.333	23	31	19	131	158	8	.973
1991—Fort Laud. (FSL)	2B-1B	121	448	61	122	25	5	4	53	.272	37	66	14	182	306	16	.968
1992—Prince Will. (Car.)	2B-3B	112	438	67	136	29	8	8	63	.311	27	54	6	192	288	20	.960
1993—Alb./Colon. (East.)	2B	135	513	87	145	*33	4	16	87	.283	41	53	8	261	359	21	.967
1994—Scran./W.B. (Int'l)■..........	2B-3B	81	314	44	91	22	1	12	57	.290	29	28	0	160	237	16	.961
1995—Scran./W.B. (Int'l)	2B	106	410	61	127	29	4	5	60	.310	28	36	3	217	279	12	.976
—Philadelphia (N.L.)	2B-3B	24	54	6	10	1	0	2	6	.185	2	9	0	29	35	1	.985
1996—Philadelphia (N.L.)	1B-2B-3B	43	131	15	37	10	0	3	12	.282	5	20	2	243	27	0	1.000
1997—Scran./W.B. (Int'l)	3B-2B-1B	7	30	5	9	2	2	0	2	.300	2	6	2	23	18	1	.976
—Philadelphia (N.L.)	1-3-2-DH	84	177	19	47	8	0	6	30	.266	3	26	0	157	31	6	.969
1998—Philadelphia (N.L.)	1-2-DH-3	112	250	23	69	13	0	2	27	.276	8	30	0	195	77	4	.986
Major league totals (4 years)		263	612	63	163	32	0	13	75	.266	18	85	2	624	170	11	.986

JORDAN, RICARDO   P   DODGERS

PERSONAL: Born June 27, 1970, in Boynton Beach, Fla. ... 6-0/190. ... Throws left, bats left.

HIGH SCHOOL: Atlantic (Delray Beach, Fla.).

JUNIOR COLLEGE: Miami-Dade (South) Community College.

TRANSACTIONS/CAREER NOTES: Selected by Toronto Blue Jays organization in 37th round of free-agent draft (June 4, 1990). ... Traded by Blue Jays with 3B Howard Battle to Philadelphia Phillies for P Paul Quantrill (December 6, 1995). ... Traded by Phillies with P Toby Borland to New York Mets for 1B Rico Brogna (November 27, 1996). ... Granted free agency (October 15, 1997). ... Signed by Cincinnati Reds organization (November 27, 1997). ... Released by Reds (August 8, 1998). ... Signed by New York Yankees organization (August 11, 1998). ... Granted free agency (October 15, 1998). ... Signed by Los Angeles Dodgers organization (January 15, 1999).

Year Team (League)	W	L	Pct.	ERA	G	GS	CG	ShO	Sv.	IP	H	R	ER	BB	SO
1990—Dunedin (Fla. St.)	0	2	.000	2.38	13	2	0	0	0	22 2/3	15	9	6	19	16
1991—Myrtle Beach (SAL)	9	8	.529	2.74	29	23	3	1	1	144 2/3	101	58	44	79	152
1992—Dunedin (Fla. St.)	0	5	.000	3.83	45	0	0	0	15	47	44	26	20	28	49
1993—Knoxville (Southern)	1	4	.200	2.45	25	0	0	0	2	36 2/3	33	17	10	18	35
—Dunedin (Fla. St.)	2	0	1.000	4.38	15	0	0	0	1	24 2/3	20	13	12	15	24
1994—Knoxville (Southern)	4	3	.571	2.66	53	0	0	0	17	64 1/3	54	25	19	23	70

Year Team (League)	W	L	Pct.	ERA	G	GS	CG	ShO	Sv.	IP	H	R	ER	BB	SO
1995—Syracuse (Int'l)	0	0	...	6.57	13	0	0	0	0	12 1/3	15	9	9	7	17
—Toronto (A.L.)	1	0	1.000	6.60	15	0	0	0	1	15	18	11	11	13	10
1996—Scran./W.B. (Int'l)■	3	3	.500	5.26	32	0	0	0	1	39 1/3	40	30	23	22	40
—Philadelphia (N.L.)	2	2	.500	1.80	26	0	0	0	0	25	18	6	5	12	17
1997—New York (N.L.)■	1	2	.333	5.33	22	0	0	0	0	27	31	17	16	15	19
—Norfolk (Int'l)	0	1	.000	2.79	34	0	0	0	1	29	20	11	9	24	34
1998—Cincinnati (N.L.)■	1	0	1.000	24.30	6	0	0	0	0	3 1/3	9	9	9	7	1
—Indianapolis (Int'l)	2	4	.333	3.49	37	6	0	0	0	69 2/3	70	39	27	33	52
—Columbus (Int'l)■	2	0	1.000	4.85	5	5	0	0	0	26	28	15	14	17	22
A.L. totals (1 year)	1	0	1.000	6.60	15	0	0	0	1	15	18	11	11	13	10
N.L. totals (3 years)	4	4	.500	4.88	54	0	0	0	0	55 1/3	53	32	30	34	37
Major league totals (4 years)	5	4	.556	5.25	69	0	0	0	1	70 1/3	71	43	41	47	47

J

JOYNER, WALLY   1B   PADRES

PERSONAL: Born June 16, 1962, in Atlanta. ... 6-2/200. ... Bats left, throws left. ... Full name: Wallace Keith Joyner.
HIGH SCHOOL: Redan (Stone Mountain, Ga.).
COLLEGE: Brigham Young.
TRANSACTIONS/CAREER NOTES: Selected by California Angels organization in third round of free-agent draft (June 6, 1983); pick received as compensation for New York Yankees signing free-agent DH Don Baylor. ... On disabled list (July 12, 1990-remainder of season). ... Granted free agency (October 28, 1991). ... Signed by Kansas City Royals (December 9, 1991). ... On disabled list (June 26-July 14, 1994). ... Traded by Royals with P Aaron Dorlarque to San Diego Padres for 2B/OF Bip Roberts and P Bryan Wolff (December 21, 1995). ... On San Diego disabled list (June 3-July 11, 1996); included rehabilitation assignment to Rancho Cucamonga (July 7-11). ... On disabled list (April 28-May 13, 1997); included rehabilitation assignment to Las Vegas (May 8-12).
RECORDS: Shares major league record for most home runs in month of October—4 (1987).
STATISTICAL NOTES: Tied for Eastern League lead with eight intentional bases on balls received in 1984. ... Led Pacific Coast League first basemen with 1,229 total chances and 121 double plays in 1985. ... Led A.L. with 12 sacrifice flies in 1986. ... Hit three home runs in one game (October 3, 1987). ... Led A.L. first basemen with 1,520 total chances in 1988 and 1,441 in 1991. ... Led A.L. first basemen with 148 double plays in 1988 and 138 in 1992. ... Career major league grand slams: 6.

Year Team (League)	Pos.	G	AB	R	H	2B	3B	HR	RBI	Avg.	BB	SO	SB	PO	A	E	Avg.
1983— Peoria (Midwest)	1B	54	192	25	63	16	2	3	33	.328	19	25	1	480	45	6	.989
1984— Waterbury (Eastern)	1B-OF	134	467	81	148	24	7	12	72	.317	67	60	0	906	86	9	.991
1985— Edmonton (PCL)	1B	126	477	68	135	29	5	12	73	.283	60	64	2	*1107	*107	•15	.988
1986— California (A.L.)	1B	154	593	82	172	27	3	22	100	.290	57	58	5	1222	139	15	.989
1987— California (A.L.)	1B	149	564	100	161	33	1	34	117	.285	72	64	8	1276	92	10	.993
1988— California (A.L.)	1B	158	597	81	176	31	2	13	85	.295	55	51	8	*1369	*143	8	.995
1989— California (A.L.)	1B	159	593	78	167	30	2	16	79	.282	46	58	3	*1487	99	4	*.997
1990— California (A.L.)	1B	83	310	35	83	15	0	8	41	.268	41	34	2	727	62	4	.995
1991— California (A.L.)	1B	143	551	79	166	34	3	21	96	.301	52	66	2	*1335	98	8	.994
1992— Kansas City (A.L.)■	1B-DH	149	572	66	154	36	2	9	66	.269	55	50	11	1236	137	10	.993
1993— Kansas City (A.L.)	1B	141	497	83	145	36	3	15	65	.292	66	67	5	1116	145	7	.994
1994— Kansas City (A.L.)	1B-DH	97	363	52	113	20	3	8	57	.311	47	43	3	717	64	8	.991
1995— Kansas City (A.L.)	1B-DH	131	465	69	144	28	0	12	83	.310	69	65	3	1111	118	3	*.998
1996— San Diego (N.L.)■	1B	121	433	59	120	29	1	8	65	.277	69	71	5	1059	89	3	*.997
— Rancho Cuca. (Cal.)	1B	3	10	1	3	1	0	0	2	.300	1	1	0	14	2	0	1.000
1997— San Diego (N.L.)	1B	135	455	59	149	29	2	13	83	.327	51	51	3	1027	89	4	*.996
— Las Vegas (PCL)	1B	3	8	1	2	0	0	0	1	.250	0	1	0	16	1	0	1.000
1998— San Diego (N.L.)	1B	131	439	58	131	30	1	12	80	.298	51	44	1	985	81	7	.993
American League totals (10 years)		1364	5105	725	1481	290	19	158	789	.290	560	556	50	11656	1097	77	.994
National League totals (3 years)		387	1327	176	400	88	4	33	228	.301	171	166	9	3071	259	14	.996
Major league totals (13 years)		1751	6432	901	1881	378	23	191	1017	.292	731	722	59	14727	1356	91	.994

DIVISION SERIES RECORD

Year Team (League)	Pos.	G	AB	R	H	2B	3B	HR	RBI	Avg.	BB	SO	SB	PO	A	E	Avg.
1996— San Diego (N.L.)	1B	3	9	0	1	0	0	0	0	.111	0	2	0	12	2	0	1.000
1998— San Diego (N.L.)	1B	4	6	1	1	0	0	1	2	.167	1	2	0	19	1	1	.952
Division series totals (2 years)		7	15	1	2	0	0	1	2	.133	1	4	0	31	3	1	.971

CHAMPIONSHIP SERIES RECORD

Year Team (League)	Pos.	G	AB	R	H	2B	3B	HR	RBI	Avg.	BB	SO	SB	PO	A	E	Avg.
1986— California (A.L.)	1B	3	11	3	5	2	0	1	2	.455	2	0	0	24	1	0	1.000
1998— San Diego (N.L.)	1B	6	16	3	5	0	0	0	2	.313	4	3	0	45	6	0	1.000
Championship series totals (2 years)		9	27	6	10	2	0	1	4	.370	6	3	0	69	7	0	1.000

WORLD SERIES RECORD

Year Team (League)	Pos.	G	AB	R	H	2B	3B	HR	RBI	Avg.	BB	SO	SB	PO	A	E	Avg.
1998— San Diego (N.L.)	1B	3	8	0	0	0	0	0	0	.000	3	1	0	22	0	0	1.000

ALL-STAR GAME RECORD

Year League	Pos.	AB	R	H	2B	3B	HR	RBI	Avg.	BB	SO	SB	PO	A	E	Avg.
1986— American	1B	1	0	0	0	0	0	0	.000	0	0	0	3	1	0	1.000

JUDD, MIKE   P   DODGERS

PERSONAL: Born June 30, 1975, in San Diego. ... 6-1/217. ... Throws right, bats right. ... Full name: Michael Galen Judd.
HIGH SCHOOL: Helix (La Mesa, Calif.).
JUNIOR COLLEGE: Grossmont (San Diego).
TRANSACTIONS/CAREER NOTES: Selected by New York Yankees organization in ninth round of free-agent draft (June 1, 1995). ... Traded by Yankees to Los Angeles Dodgers for P Billy Brewer (June 22, 1996).

Year Team (League)	W	L	Pct.	ERA	G	GS	CG	ShO	Sv.	IP	H	R	ER	BB	SO
1995— GC Yankees (GCL)	1	1	.500	1.11	21	0	0	0	8	32 1/3	18	5	4	6	30
—Greensboro (S. Atl.)	0	0	...	0.00	1	0	0	0	0	2 2/3	2	0	0	0	1
1996—Greensboro (S. Atl.)	2	2	.500	3.81	29	0	0	0	10	28 1/3	22	14	12	8	36
—Savannah (S. Atl.)■	4	2	.667	2.44	15	8	1	0	3	55 1/3	40	21	15	15	62
1997—Vero Beach (FSL)	6	5	.545	3.53	14	14	1	0	0	86 2/3	67	37	34	39	104
—San Antonio (Tex.)	4	2	.667	2.73	12	12	0	0	0	79	69	27	24	33	65
—Los Angeles (N.L.)	0	0	...	0.00	1	0	0	0	0	2 2/3	4	0	0	0	4
1998—Albuquerque (PCL)	5	7	.417	4.56	17	17	3	1	0	94 2/3	98	62	48	44	77
—Los Angeles (N.L.)	0	0	...	15.09	7	0	0	0	0	11 1/3	19	19	19	9	14
Major league totals (2 years)	0	0	...	12.21	8	0	0	0	0	14	23	19	19	9	18

JUDEN, JEFF   P

PERSONAL: Born January 19, 1971, in Salem, Mass. ... 6-8/265. ... Throws right, bats both. ... Full name: Jeffrey Daniel Juden. ... Cousin of Daniel Juden, right winger in Tampa Bay Lightning organization. ... Name pronounced JOO-den.
HIGH SCHOOL: Salem (Mass.).
TRANSACTIONS/CAREER NOTES: Selected by Houston Astros organization in first round (12th pick overall) of free-agent draft (June 5, 1989). ... On disabled list (June 14-21, 1992). ... Traded by Astros with P Doug Jones to Philadelphia Phillies for P Mitch Williams (December 2, 1993). ... On Scranton/Wilkes-Barre disabled list (June 22-July 24 and July 25, 1994-remainder of season). ... Traded by Phillies with OF/1B Tommy Eason to San Francisco Giants for IF Mike Benjamin (October 6, 1995). ... Claimed on waivers by Montreal Expos (July 11, 1996). ... On Montreal suspended list (September 4-7, 1996). ... Traded by Expos to Cleveland Indians for P Steve Kline (July 31, 1997). ... Traded by Indians with OF Marquis Grissom to Milwaukee Brewers for P Ben McDonald, P Mike Fetters and P Ron Villone (December 8, 1997). ... Traded by Brewers to Anaheim Angels for a player to be named later and cash (August 7, 1998). ... Released by Angels (November 16, 1998).
STATISTICAL NOTES: Led Pacific Coast League with seven balks in 1992. ... Career major league grand slams: 1.

Year Team (League)	W	L	Pct.	ERA	G	GS	CG	ShO	Sv.	IP	H	R	ER	BB	SO
1989— Sarasota (Florida State)	1	4	.200	3.40	9	8	0	0	0	39 2/3	33	21	15	17	49
1990— Osceola (Florida St.)	10	1	*.909	2.27	15	15	2	1	0	91	72	37	23	42	85
—Columbus (Southern)	1	3	.250	5.37	11	11	0	0	0	52	55	36	31	42	40
1991— Jackson (Texas)	6	3	.667	3.10	16	16	0	0	0	95 2/3	84	43	33	44	75
—Tucson (PCL)	3	2	.600	3.18	10	10	0	0	0	56 2/3	56	28	20	25	51
—Houston (N.L.)	0	2	.000	6.00	4	3	0	0	0	18	19	14	12	7	11
1992— Tucson (PCL)	9	10	.474	4.04	26	26	0	0	0	147	149	84	66	71	120
1993— Tucson (PCL)	11	6	.647	4.63	27	27	0	0	0	169	174	102	87	*76	156
—Houston (N.L.)	0	1	.000	5.40	2	0	0	0	0	5	4	3	3	4	7
1994— Philadelphia (N.L.)■	1	4	.200	6.18	6	5	0	0	0	27 2/3	29	25	19	12	22
—Scran./W.B. (Int'l)	2	2	.500	8.53	6	6	0	0	0	25 1/3	30	28	24	19	28
1995— Scran./W.B. (Int'l)	6	4	.600	4.10	14	13	0	0	0	83 1/3	73	43	38	33	65
—Philadelphia (N.L.)	2	4	.333	4.02	13	10	1	0	0	62 2/3	53	31	28	31	47
1996— San Francisco (N.L.)■	4	0	1.000	4.10	36	0	0	0	0	41 2/3	39	23	19	20	35
—Montreal (N.L.)■	1	0	1.000	2.20	22	0	0	0	0	32 2/3	22	12	8	14	26
1997— Montreal (N.L.)	11	5	.688	4.22	22	22	3	0	0	130	125	64	61	57	107
—Cleveland (A.L.)■	0	1	.000	5.46	8	5	0	0	0	31 1/3	32	21	19	15	29
1998— Milwaukee (N.L.)■	7	11	.389	5.53	24	24	2	0	0	138 1/3	149	91	85	66	109
—Anaheim (A.L.)■	1	3	.250	6.75	8	6	0	0	0	40	33	32	30	18	39
A.L. totals (2 years)	1	4	.200	6.18	16	11	0	0	0	71 1/3	65	53	49	33	68
N.L. totals (7 years)	26	27	.491	4.64	129	64	6	0	0	456	440	263	235	211	364
Major league totals (7 years)	27	31	.466	4.85	145	75	6	0	0	527 1/3	505	316	284	244	432

CHAMPIONSHIP SERIES RECORD

Year Team (League)	W	L	Pct.	ERA	G	GS	CG	ShO	Sv.	IP	H	R	ER	BB	SO
1997— Cleveland (A.L.)	0	0	...	0.00	3	0	0	0	0	1	2	0	0	2	2

WORLD SERIES RECORD

Year Team (League)	W	L	Pct.	ERA	G	GS	CG	ShO	Sv.	IP	H	R	ER	BB	SO
1997— Cleveland (A.L.)	0	0	...	4.50	2	0	0	0	0	2	2	1	1	2	0

JUSTICE, DAVID   OF   INDIANS

PERSONAL: Born April 14, 1966, in Cincinnati. ... 6-3/200. ... Bats left, throws left. ... Full name: David Christopher Justice.
HIGH SCHOOL: Covington (Ky.) Latin.
COLLEGE: Thomas More College (Ky.).
TRANSACTIONS/CAREER NOTES: Selected by Atlanta Braves organization in fourth round of free-agent draft (June 3, 1985). ... On Atlanta disabled list (June 27-August 20, 1991); included rehabilitation assignment to Macon (August 16-20). ... On disabled list (April 12-27, 1992; June 2-17, 1995 and May 16, 1996-remainder of season). ... Traded by Braves with OF Marquis Grissom to Cleveland Indians for OF Kenny Lofton and P Alan Embree (March 25, 1997). ... On disabled list (June 24-July 10, 1997).
RECORDS: Holds major league single-season record for fewest errors by outfielder who led league in errors—8 (1992).
HONORS: Named N.L. Rookie Player of the Year by THE SPORTING NEWS (1990). ... Named N.L. Rookie of the Year by Baseball Writers' Association of America (1990). ... Named outfielder on THE SPORTING NEWS N.L. All-Star team (1993). ... Named outfielder on THE SPORTING NEWS N.L. Silver Slugger team (1993). ... Named outfielder on THE SPORTING NEWS A.L. Silver Slugger team (1997). ... Named A.L. Comeback Player of the Year by THE SPORTING NEWS (1997). ... Named outfielder on THE SPORTING NEWS A.L. All-Star team (1997).
STATISTICAL NOTES: Tied for Appalachian League lead with five sacrifice flies in 1985. ... Career major league grand slams: 2.

J
K

Year Team (League)	Pos.	G	AB	R	H	2B	3B	HR	RBI	Avg.	BB	SO	SB	PO	A	E	Avg.
						BATTING									FIELDING		
1985— Pulaski (Appalachian).	OF	66	204	39	50	8	0	•10	46	.245	40	30	0	86	2	4	.957
1986— Sumter (S. Atl.)	OF	61	220	48	66	16	0	10	61	.300	48	28	10	124	7	4	.970
— Durham (Carolina).	OF-1B	67	229	47	64	9	1	12	44	.279	46	24	2	163	5	1	.994
1987— Greenville (Southern).	OF	93	348	38	79	12	4	6	40	.227	53	48	3	199	4	8	.962
1988— Richmond (Int'l)	OF	70	227	27	46	9	1	8	28	.203	39	55	4	136	5	4	.972
— Greenville (Southern).	OF	58	198	34	55	13	1	9	37	.278	37	41	6	100	3	5	.954
1989— Richmond (Int'l)	OF-1B	115	391	47	102	24	3	12	58	.261	59	66	12	220	15	6	.975
— Atlanta (N.L.)	OF	16	51	7	12	3	0	1	3	.235	3	9	2	24	0	0	1.000
1990— Richmond (Int'l)	OF-1B	12	45	7	16	5	1	2	7	.356	7	6	0	23	4	2	.931
— Atlanta (N.L.)	1B-OF	127	439	76	124	23	2	28	78	.282	64	92	11	604	42	14	.979
1991— Atlanta (N.L.)	OF	109	396	67	109	25	1	21	87	.275	65	81	8	204	9	7	.968
— Macon (S. Atl.)	OF	3	10	2	2	0	0	2	5	.200	2	1	0	1	0	0	1.000
1992— Atlanta (N.L.)	OF	144	484	78	124	19	5	21	72	.256	79	85	2	313	8	*8	.976
1993— Atlanta (N.L.)	OF	157	585	90	158	15	4	40	120	.270	78	90	3	323	9	5	.985
1994— Atlanta (N.L.)	OF	104	352	61	110	16	2	19	59	.313	69	45	2	192	6	*11	.947
1995— Atlanta (N.L.)	OF	120	411	73	104	17	2	24	78	.253	73	68	4	233	8	4	.984
1996— Atlanta (N.L.)	OF	40	140	23	45	9	0	6	25	.321	21	22	1	88	3	0	1.000
1997— Cleveland (A.L.)■.	OF-DH	139	495	84	163	31	1	33	101	.329	80	79	3	120	3	2	.984
1998— Cleveland (A.L.)	DH-OF	146	540	94	151	39	2	21	88	.280	76	98	9	37	0	0	1.000
American League totals (2 years)		285	1035	178	314	70	3	54	189	.303	156	177	12	157	3	2	.988
National League totals (8 years)		817	2858	475	786	127	16	160	522	.275	452	492	33	1981	85	49	.977
Major league totals (10 years)		1102	3893	653	1100	197	19	214	711	.283	608	669	45	2138	88	51	.978

RECORDS: Shares career record for most doubles—6.

DIVISION SERIES RECORD

Year Team (League)	Pos.	G	AB	R	H	2B	3B	HR	RBI	Avg.	BB	SO	SB	PO	A	E	Avg.
						BATTING									FIELDING		
1995— Atlanta (N.L.)	OF	4	13	2	3	0	0	0	0	.231	5	2	0	6	0	1	.857
1997— Cleveland (A.L.)	DH	5	19	3	5	2	0	1	2	.263	2	3	0	0	0	0	...
1998— Cleveland (A.L.)	DH-OF	4	16	2	5	4	0	1	6	.313	0	1	0	5	1	0	1.000
Division series totals (3 years)		13	48	7	13	6	0	2	8	.271	7	6	0	11	1	1	.923

CHAMPIONSHIP SERIES RECORD

Year Team (League)	Pos.	G	AB	R	H	2B	3B	HR	RBI	Avg.	BB	SO	SB	PO	A	E	Avg.
						BATTING									FIELDING		
1991— Atlanta (N.L.)	OF	7	25	4	5	1	0	1	2	.200	3	7	0	17	0	1	.944
1992— Atlanta (N.L.)	OF	7	25	5	7	1	0	2	6	.280	6	2	0	19	3	0	1.000
1993— Atlanta (N.L.)	OF	6	21	2	3	1	0	0	4	.143	3	3	0	14	0	1	.933
1995— Atlanta (N.L.)	OF	3	11	1	3	0	0	0	1	.273	2	1	0	0	0	0	...
1997— Cleveland (A.L.)	DH	6	21	3	7	1	0	0	0	.333	2	4	0	...	...	...	
1998— Cleveland (A.L.)	OF-DH-PH	6	19	2	3	0	0	1	2	.158	3	3	0	3	0	0	1.000
Championship series totals (6 years)		35	122	17	28	4	0	4	15	.230	19	20	0	53	3	2	.966

NOTES: Member of World Series championship team (1995).

WORLD SERIES RECORD

Year Team (League)	Pos.	G	AB	R	H	2B	3B	HR	RBI	Avg.	BB	SO	SB	PO	A	E	Avg.
						BATTING									FIELDING		
1991— Atlanta (N.L.)	OF	7	27	5	7	0	0	2	6	.259	5	5	2	21	1	1	.957
1992— Atlanta (N.L.)	OF	6	19	4	3	0	0	1	3	.158	4	6	1	15	0	1	.938
1995— Atlanta (N.L.)	OF	6	20	3	5	1	0	1	5	.250	5	1	0	16	0	0	1.000
1997— Cleveland (A.L.)	OF-DH	7	27	4	5	0	0	0	4	.185	6	8	0	9	0	0	1.000
World Series totals (4 years)		26	93	16	20	1	0	4	18	.215	22	19	3	61	1	1	.969

ALL-STAR GAME RECORD

Year League	Pos.	AB	R	H	2B	3B	HR	RBI	Avg.	BB	SO	SB	PO	A	E	Avg.
					BATTING									FIELDING		
1993— National	OF	3	0	1	0	0	0	0	.333	0	0	0	1	0	1	.500
1994— National	OF	2	0	0	0	0	0	0	.000	0	0	0	1	0	0	1.000
1997— American								Selected, did not play.								
All-Star Game totals (2 years)		5	0	1	0	0	0	0	.200	0	0	0	2	0	1	.667

KAMIENIECKI, SCOTT   P   ORIOLES

PERSONAL: Born April 19, 1964, in Mt. Clemens, Mich. ... 6-0/200. ... Throws right, bats right. ... Full name: Scott Andrew Kamieniecki. ... Name pronounced KAM-ah-NIK-ee.

HIGH SCHOOL: Redford St. Mary's (Detroit).

COLLEGE: Michigan (degree in physical education).

TRANSACTIONS/CAREER NOTES: Selected by Detroit Tigers organization in second round of free-agent draft (June 7, 1982); did not sign. ... Selected by Milwaukee Brewers organization in 23rd round of free-agent draft (June 3, 1985); did not sign. ... Selected by New York Yankees organization in 14th round of free-agent draft (June 2, 1986). ... On New York disabled list (August 3, 1991-remainder of season). ... On New York disabled list (April 2-29, 1992); included rehabilitation assignments to Fort Lauderdale (April 9-17) and Columbus (April 17-29). ... On New York disabled list (May 6-July 15, 1995); included rehabilitation assignments to Tampa (July 5-10) and Columbus (July 10-12). ... On New York disabled list (March 27-April 24 and July 31, 1996-remainder of season); included rehabilitation assignment to Tampa (April 6-24). ... On Columbus disabled list (June 20-July 31, 1996). ... Granted free agency (December 20, 1996). ... Signed by Baltimore Orioles organization (January 22, 1997). ... Granted free agency (October 30, 1997). ... Re-signed by Orioles (December 5, 1997). ... On Baltimore disabled list (April 25-May 12, May 23-July 25, and August 23, 1998-remainder of season); included rehabilitation assignment to Bowie (July 9-25).

Year Team (League)	W	L	Pct.	ERA	G	GS	CG	ShO	Sv.	IP	H	R	ER	BB	SO
1987— Alb./Colon. (East.)	1	3	.250	5.35	10	7	0	0	0	37	41	25	22	33	19
— Prince William (Caro.)	9	5	.643	4.17	19	19	1	0	0	112 1/3	91	61	52	78	84
1988— Prince William (Caro.)	6	7	.462	4.40	15	15	•7	2	0	100 1/3	115	62	49	50	72
— Fort Lauderdale (FSL)	3	6	.333	3.62	12	11	1	1	0	77	71	36	31	40	51
1989— Alb./Colon. (East.)	10	9	.526	3.70	24	23	6	3	1	151	142	67	62	57	*140
1990— Alb./Colon. (East.)	10	9	.526	3.20	22	21	3	1	0	132	113	55	47	61	99

Year Team (League)	W	L	Pct.	ERA	G	GS	CG	ShO	Sv.	IP	H	R	ER	BB	SO
1991— Columbus (Int'l)	6	3	.667	2.36	11	11	3	1	0	76 1/3	61	25	20	20	58
— New York (A.L.).................	4	4	.500	3.90	9	9	0	0	0	55 1/3	54	24	24	22	34
1992— Fort Lauderdale (FSL)	1	0	1.000	1.29	1	1	1	0	0	7	8	1	1	0	3
— Columbus (Int'l)	1	0	1.000	0.69	2	2	0	0	0	13	6	1	1	4	12
— New York (A.L.).................	6	14	.300	4.36	28	28	4	0	0	188	193	100	91	74	88
1993— New York (A.L.).................	10	7	.588	4.08	30	20	2	0	1	154 1/3	163	73	70	59	72
— Columbus (Int'l)	1	0	1.000	1.50	1	1	0	0	0	6	5	1	1	0	4
1994— New York (A.L.).................	8	6	.571	3.76	22	16	1	0	0	117 1/3	115	53	49	59	71
1995— New York (A.L.).................	7	6	.538	4.01	17	16	1	0	0	89 2/3	83	43	40	41	43
— Tampa (Fla. St.).................	1	0	1.000	1.80	1	1	0	0	0	5	6	2	1	1	2
— Columbus (Int'l)	1	0	1.000	0.00	1	1	0	0	0	6 2/3	2	0	0	1	10
1996— Tampa (Fla. St.).................	2	1	.667	1.17	3	3	1	0	0	23	20	6	3	4	17
— New York (A.L.).................	1	2	.333	11.12	7	5	0	0	0	22 2/3	36	30	28	19	15
— Columbus (Int'l)	2	1	.667	5.64	5	5	2	0	0	30 1/3	33	21	19	8	27
1997— Baltimore (A.L.)■...............	10	6	.625	4.01	30	30	0	0	0	179 1/3	179	83	80	67	109
1998— Baltimore (A.L.).................	2	6	.250	6.75	12	11	0	0	0	54 2/3	67	41	41	26	25
— Bowie (Eastern).................	1	0	1.000	4.76	3	3	0	0	0	11 1/3	13	6	6	2	5
Major league totals (8 years)......	**48**	**51**	**.485**	**4.42**	**155**	**135**	**8**	**0**	**1**	**861 1/3**	**890**	**447**	**423**	**375**	**457**

DIVISION SERIES RECORD

Year Team (League)	W	L	Pct.	ERA	G	GS	CG	ShO	Sv.	IP	H	R	ER	BB	SO
1995— New York (A.L.).................	0	0	...	7.20	1	1	0	0	0	5	9	5	4	4	4
1997— Baltimore (A.L.).................							Did not play.								

CHAMPIONSHIP SERIES RECORD

Year Team (League)	W	L	Pct.	ERA	G	GS	CG	ShO	Sv.	IP	H	R	ER	BB	SO
1997— Baltimore (A.L.).................	1	0	1.000	0.00	2	1	0	0	0	8	4	0	0	2	5

K

KAPLER, GABE   OF   TIGERS

PERSONAL: Born August 31, 1975, in Hollywood, Calif. ... 6-2/190. ... Bats right, throws right. ... Full name: Gabriel Stefan Kapler.
JUNIOR COLLEGE: Moorpark (Calif.) College.
TRANSACTIONS/CAREER NOTES: Selected by Detroit Tigers organization in 57th round of free-agent draft (June 1, 1995).
HONORS: Named Minor League Player of the Year by THE SPORTING NEWS (1998). ... Named Southern League Most Valuable Player (1998).
STATISTICAL NOTES: Led South Atlantic League with 280 total bases in 1996. ... Led Florida State League with 262 total bases in 1997. ... Led Southern League with 319 total bases and 11 sacrifice flies in 1998.

							BATTING							FIELDING		
Year Team (League)	Pos.	G	AB	R	H	2B	3B	HR	RBI	Avg.	BB	SO	SB	PO	A	E	Avg.
1995— Jamestown (NYP)	OF	63	236	38	68	19	4	4	34	.288	23	37	1	103	9	9	.926
1996— Fayetteville (SAL)	OF-3B	138	524	81	*157	*45	0	26	99	.300	62	73	14	195	14	7	.968
1997— Lakeland (FSL)	OF	137	519	87	153	*40	6	19	87	.295	54	68	8	252	14	6	.978
1998— Jacksonville (Sou.)......	OF-1B	139	547	*113	*176	*47	6	*28	*146	.322	66	93	6	294	12	5	.984
— Detroit (A.L.).............	OF-DH	7	25	3	5	0	1	0	0	.200	1	4	2	9	0	0	1.000
Major league totals (1 year)		**7**	**25**	**3**	**5**	**0**	**1**	**0**	**0**	**.200**	**1**	**4**	**2**	**9**	**0**	**0**	**1.000**

KARCHNER, MATT   P   CUBS

PERSONAL: Born June 28, 1967, in Berwick, Pa. ... 6-4/215. ... Throws right, bats right. ... Full name: Matthew Dean Karchner.
HIGH SCHOOL: Berwick (Pa.).
COLLEGE: Bloomsburg (Pa.).
TRANSACTIONS/CAREER NOTES: Selected by Kansas City Royals organization in eighth round of free-agent draft (June 5, 1989). ... On disabled list (August 1-8, 1991). ... Selected by Montreal Expos from Royals organization in Rule 5 major league draft (December 9, 1991). ... Returned to Royals (April 4, 1992). ... On disabled list (September 2-18, 1992; and May 10, 1993-remainder of season). ... Selected by Chicago White Sox organization from Royals organization in Rule 5 minor league draft (December 13, 1993). ... On Chicago disabled list (August 11-September 1, 1996); included rehabilitation assignment to Nashville (August 30-September 1). ... On Chicago disabled list (May 7-23 and June 24-July 9, 1998). ... Traded by White Sox to Chicago Cubs for P Jon Garland (July 29, 1998).

Year Team (League)	W	L	Pct.	ERA	G	GS	CG	ShO	Sv.	IP	H	R	ER	BB	SO
1989— Eugene (Northwest)	1	1	.500	3.90	8	5	0	0	0	30	30	19	13	8	25
1990— Appleton (Midwest)...........	2	7	.222	4.82	27	11	1	0	0	71	70	42	38	31	58
1991— Baseball City (FSL)............	6	3	.667	1.97	38	0	0	0	5	73	49	28	16	25	65
1992— Memphis (Sou.)	8	8	.500	4.47	33	18	2	0	1	141	161	83	70	35	88
1993— Memphis (Sou.)	3	2	.600	4.20	6	5	0	0	0	30	34	16	14	4	14
1994— Birmingham (Southern)■.....	5	2	.714	1.26	39	0	0	0	6	43	36	10	6	14	29
— Nashville (A.A.)	4	2	.667	1.37	17	0	0	0	2	26 1/3	18	5	4	7	19
1995— Nashville (A.A.)	3	3	.500	1.45	28	0	0	0	9	37 1/3	39	7	6	10	29
— Chicago (A.L.).................	4	2	.667	1.69	31	0	0	0	0	32	33	8	6	12	24
1996— Chicago (A.L.).................	7	4	.636	5.76	50	0	0	0	1	59 1/3	61	42	38	41	46
— Nashville (A.A.)	0	0	...	0.00	1	0	0	0	0	2/3	0	0	0	0	0
1997— Nashville (A.A.)	2	1	.667	1.93	13	0	0	0	3	18 2/3	12	5	4	6	11
— Chicago (A.L.).................	3	1	.750	2.91	52	0	0	0	15	52 2/3	50	18	17	26	30
1998— Chicago (A.L.).................	2	4	.333	5.15	32	0	0	0	11	36 2/3	33	21	21	19	30
— Chicago (N.L.)■...............	3	1	.750	5.14	29	0	0	0	0	28	30	18	16	14	22
A.L. totals (4 years)	**16**	**11**	**.593**	**4.08**	**165**	**0**	**0**	**0**	**27**	**180 2/3**	**177**	**89**	**82**	**98**	**130**
N.L. totals (1 year)	**3**	**1**	**.750**	**5.14**	**29**	**0**	**0**	**0**	**0**	**28**	**30**	**18**	**16**	**14**	**22**
Major league totals (4 years)......	**19**	**12**	**.613**	**4.23**	**194**	**0**	**0**	**0**	**27**	**208 2/3**	**207**	**107**	**98**	**112**	**152**

DIVISION SERIES RECORD

Year Team (League)	W	L	Pct.	ERA	G	GS	CG	ShO	Sv.	IP	H	R	ER	BB	SO
1998— Chicago (N.L.)	0	0	...	13.50	1	0	0	0	0	2/3	1	1	1	0	1

KARL, SCOTT — P — BREWERS

PERSONAL: Born August 9, 1971, in Riverside, Calif. ... 6-2/209. ... Throws left, bats left. ... Full name: Randall Scott Karl.
HIGH SCHOOL: Carlsbad (Calif.).
COLLEGE: Hawaii.
TRANSACTIONS/CAREER NOTES: Selected by Milwaukee Brewers organization in sixth round of free-agent draft (June 1, 1992). ... On New Orleans disabled list (April 27-May 31, 1994).
STATISTICAL NOTES: Tied for Texas League lead with seven balks in 1993.
MISCELLANEOUS: Appeared in one game as pinch runner (1998).

Year Team (League)	W	L	Pct.	ERA	G	GS	CG	ShO	Sv.	IP	H	R	ER	BB	SO
1992— Helena (Pioneer)	7	0	•1.000	*1.46	9	9	1	1	0	61 2/3	54	13	10	16	57
1993— El Paso (Texas)	13	8	.619	2.45	27	•27	•4	•2	0	*180	172	67	49	35	95
1994— New Orleans (A.A.)	5	5	.500	3.84	15	13	2	0	0	89	92	38	38	33	54
— El Paso (Texas)	5	1	.833	2.96	8	8	3	0	0	54 2/3	44	21	18	15	51
1995— New Orleans (A.A.)	3	4	.429	3.30	8	6	1	1	0	46 1/3	47	18	17	12	29
— Milwaukee (A.L.)	6	7	.462	4.14	25	18	1	0	0	124	141	65	57	50	59
1996— Milwaukee (A.L.)	13	9	.591	4.86	32	32	3	1	0	207 1/3	220	124	112	72	121
1997— Milwaukee (A.L.)	10	13	.435	4.47	32	32	1	0	0	193 1/3	212	103	96	67	119
1998— Milwaukee (N.L.)	10	11	.476	4.40	33	33	0	0	0	192 1/3	219	104	94	66	102
A.L. totals (3 years)	29	29	.500	4.55	89	82	5	1	0	524 2/3	573	292	265	189	299
N.L. totals (1 year)	10	11	.476	4.40	33	33	0	0	0	192 1/3	219	104	94	66	102
Major league totals (4 years)	39	40	.494	4.51	122	115	5	1	0	717	792	396	359	255	401

KARROS, ERIC — 1B — DODGERS

PERSONAL: Born November 4, 1967, in Hackensack, N.J. ... 6-4/226. ... Bats right, throws right. ... Full name: Eric Peter Karros. ... Name pronounced CARE-ose.
HIGH SCHOOL: Patrick Henry (San Diego).
COLLEGE: UCLA.
TRANSACTIONS/CAREER NOTES: Selected by Los Angeles Dodgers organization in sixth round of free-agent draft (June 1, 1988). ... On Los Angeles disabled list (March 29-April 24, 1998); included rehabilitation assignment to San Bernardino (April 19-25).
HONORS: Named N.L. Rookie Player of the Year by THE SPORTING NEWS (1992). ... Named N.L. Rookie of the Year by Baseball Writers' Association of America (1992). ... Named first baseman on THE SPORTING NEWS N.L. All-Star team (1995). ... Named first baseman on THE SPORTING NEWS N.L. Silver Slugger team (1995).
STATISTICAL NOTES: Tied for Pioneer League lead in errors by first baseman with 14 in 1988. ... Led California League first basemen with 1,232 putouts, 110 assists and 1,358 total chances in 1989. ... Led Texas League with 282 total bases in 1990. ... Led Texas League first basemen with 1,337 total chances and 129 double plays in 1990. ... Led Pacific Coast League with 269 total bases in 1991. ... Tied for Pacific Coast League lead with eight intentional bases on balls received in 1991. ... Led Pacific Coast League first basemen with 1,095 putouts, 109 assists and 1,215 total chances in 1991. ... Led N.L. in grounding into double plays with 27 in 1996.

Year Team (League)	Pos.	G	AB	R	H	2B	3B	HR	RBI	Avg.	BB	SO	SB	PO	A	E	Avg.
1988— Great Falls (Pio.)	1B-3B	66	268	68	98	12	1	12	55	.366	32	35	8	516	31	‡19	.966
1989— Bakersfield (Calif.)	1B-3B	*142	545	86	*165	*40	1	15	86	.303	63	99	18	†1238	†113	19	.986
1990— San Antonio (Tex.)	1B	*131	509	91	*179	*45	2	18	78	*.352	57	79	6	*1223	*106	8	*.994
1991— Albuquerque (PCL)	1B-3B	132	488	88	154	33	8	22	101	.316	58	80	3	†1095	†109	11	.991
— Los Angeles (N.L.)	1B	14	14	0	1	1	0	0	1	.071	1	6	0	33	2	0	1.000
1992— Los Angeles (N.L.)	1B	149	545	63	140	30	1	20	88	.257	37	103	2	1211	126	9	.993
1993— Los Angeles (N.L.)	1B	158	619	74	153	27	2	23	80	.247	34	82	0	1335	*147	12	.992
1994— Los Angeles (N.L.)	1B	111	406	51	108	21	1	14	46	.266	29	53	2	896	118	•9	.991
1995— Los Angeles (N.L.)	1B	143	551	83	164	29	3	32	105	.298	61	115	4	1234	109	7	.995
1996— Los Angeles (N.L.)	1B	154	608	84	158	29	1	34	111	.260	53	121	8	1314	121	15	.990
1997— Los Angeles (N.L.)	1B	•162	628	86	167	28	0	31	104	.266	61	116	15	1317	121	11	.992
1998— San Bern. (Calif.)	1B	4	15	3	4	1	0	0	1	.267	0	2	0	32	2	0	1.000
— Los Angeles (N.L.)	1B-DH	139	507	59	150	20	1	23	87	.296	47	93	7	1150	110	12	.991
Major league totals (8 years)		1030	3878	500	1041	185	9	177	622	.268	323	689	38	8490	854	75	.992

DIVISION SERIES RECORD

RECORDS: Shares single-game record for most home runs—2 (October 4, 1995).

Year Team (League)	Pos.	G	AB	R	H	2B	3B	HR	RBI	Avg.	BB	SO	SB	PO	A	E	Avg.
1995— Los Angeles (N.L.)	1B	3	12	3	6	1	0	2	4	.500	1	0	0	14	0	0	1.000
1996— Los Angeles (N.L.)	1B	3	9	0	0	0	0	0	0	.000	2	3	0	28	2	0	1.000
Division series totals (2 years)		6	21	3	6	1	0	2	4	.286	3	3	0	42	2	0	1.000

KARSAY, STEVE — P — INDIANS

PERSONAL: Born March 24, 1972, in Flushing, N.Y. ... 6-3/209. ... Throws right, bats right. ... Full name: Stefan Andrew Karsay. ... Name pronounced CAR-say.
HIGH SCHOOL: Christ the King (Queens, N.Y.).
TRANSACTIONS/CAREER NOTES: Selected by Toronto Blue Jays organization in first round (22nd pick overall) of free-agent draft (June 4, 1990). ... On Knoxville disabled list (July 3-16, 1993). ... Traded by Blue Jays with a player to be named later to Oakland Athletics for OF Rickey Henderson (July 31, 1993); A's acquired OF Jose Herrera to complete deal (August 6, 1993). ... On disabled list (April 26, 1994-remainder of season; April 24, 1995-entire season; and August 6, 1997-remainder of season). ... Traded by A's to Cleveland Indians for P Mike Fetters (December 8, 1997). ... On Buffalo disabled list (May 14-25 and June 12-July 15, 1998).
MISCELLANEOUS: Appeared in one game as pinch runner (1997).

Year— Team (League)	W	L	Pct.	ERA	G	GS	CG	ShO	Sv.	IP	H	R	ER	BB	SO
1990— St. Catharines (NYP)	1	1	.500	0.79	5	5	0	0	0	22²/₃	11	4	2	12	25
1991— Myrtle Beach (SAL)	4	9	.308	3.58	20	20	1	0	0	110²/₃	96	58	44	48	100
1992— Dunedin (Fla. St.)	6	3	.667	2.73	16	16	3	2	0	85²/₃	56	32	26	29	87
1993— Knoxville (Southern)	8	4	.667	3.38	19	18	1	0	0	104	98	42	39	32	100
— Huntsville (Southern)■.......	0	0	...	5.14	2	2	0	0	0	14	13	8	8	3	22
— Oakland (A.L.)	3	3	.500	4.04	8	8	0	0	0	49	49	23	22	16	33
1994— Oakland (A.L.)	1	1	.500	2.57	4	4	1	0	0	28	26	8	8	8	15
1995—							Did not play.								
1996— Modesto (California)	0	1	.000	2.65	14	14	0	0	0	34	35	16	10	1	31
1997— Oakland (A.L.)	3	12	.200	5.77	24	24	0	0	0	132²/₃	166	92	85	47	92
1998— Buffalo (Int'l)■..................	6	4	.600	3.76	16	14	0	0	0	79	89	39	33	15	63
— Cleveland (A.L.).................	0	2	.000	5.92	11	1	0	0	0	24¹/₃	31	16	16	6	13
Major league totals (4 years)......	7	18	.280	5.04	47	37	1	0	0	234	272	139	131	77	153

KEAGLE, GREG   P   TIGERS

PERSONAL: Born June 20, 1971, in Corning, N.Y. ... 6-2/195. ... Throws right, bats right. ... Full name: Gregory Charles Keagle. ... Name pronounced KAY-gull.
HIGH SCHOOL: Horseheads (N.Y.) Central.
COLLEGE: Florida International.
TRANSACTIONS/CAREER NOTES: Selected by San Diego Padres organization in sixth round of free-agent draft (June 3, 1993). ... Traded by Padres organization to Seattle Mariners organization (September 16, 1995), completing deal in which Padres traded P Andy Benes and a player to be named later to Mariners for P Ron Villone and OF Marc Newfield (July 31, 1995). ... Selected by Detroit Tigers from Mariners organization in Rule 5 major league draft (December 4, 1995). ... On Detroit disabled list (July 7-August 21, 1996); included rehabilitation assignment to Toledo (July 22-August 20). ... On Toledo disabled list (July 9-23, 1998).

Year— Team (League)	W	L	Pct.	ERA	G	GS	CG	ShO	Sv.	IP	H	R	ER	BB	SO
1993— Spokane (N'west)	3	3	.500	3.25	15	15	1	0	0	83	80	37	30	40	77
1994— Rancho Cuca. (Cal.)	11	1	.917	2.05	14	14	1	1	0	92	62	23	21	41	91
— Wichita (Texas)	3	9	.250	6.27	13	13	0	0	0	70¹/₃	84	53	49	32	57
1995— Memphis (Sou.)	4	9	.308	5.11	15	15	1	0	0	81	82	52	46	41	82
— Rancho Cuca. (Cal.)	0	0	...	4.50	2	2	0	0	0	14	14	9	7	2	11
— Las Vegas (PCL)	7	6	.538	4.28	14	13	0	0	0	75²/₃	76	47	36	42	49
1996— Detroit (A.L.)■.................	3	6	.333	7.39	26	6	0	0	0	87²/₃	104	76	72	68	70
— Toledo (International)........	2	3	.400	10.00	6	6	0	0	0	27	42	32	30	11	24
1997— Toledo (International)........	11	7	.611	3.81	23	23	3	1	0	151¹/₃	136	68	64	61	140
— Detroit (A.L.)	3	5	.375	6.55	11	10	0	0	0	45¹/₃	58	33	33	18	33
1998— Detroit (A.L.)	0	5	.000	5.59	9	7	0	0	0	38²/₃	46	26	24	20	25
— Toledo (International)........	5	3	.625	4.63	15	14	0	0	0	81²/₃	94	48	42	32	61
Major league totals (3 years)......	6	16	.273	6.76	46	23	0	0	0	171²/₃	208	135	129	106	128

KELLY, MIKE   OF   DEVIL RAYS

PERSONAL: Born June 2, 1970, in Los Angeles. ... 6-4/195. ... Bats right, throws right. ... Full name: Michael Raymond Kelly.
HIGH SCHOOL: Los Alamitos (Calif.).
COLLEGE: Arizona State.
TRANSACTIONS/CAREER NOTES: Selected by New York Mets organization in 24th round of free-agent draft (June 1, 1988); did not sign. ... Selected by Atlanta Braves organization in first round (second pick overall) of free-agent draft (June 3, 1991). ... Traded by Braves to Cincinnati Reds organization for P Chad Fox and a player to be named later (January 9, 1996); Braves acquired P Ray King to complete deal (June 11, 1996). ... Traded by Reds to Tampa Bay Devil Rays for a player to be named later (November 11, 1997); Reds acquired 1B Dmitri Young to complete deal (November 18). ... On Tampa Bay disabled list (April 1-21, 1998); included rehabilitation assignment to Durham (April 16-21).
HONORS: Named College Player of the Year by THE SPORTING NEWS (1990). ... Named outfielder on THE SPORTING NEWS college All-America team (1990). ... Named Golden Spikes Award winner by USA Baseball (1991).

Year— Team (League)	Pos.	G	AB	R	H	2B	3B	HR	RBI	Avg.	BB	SO	SB	PO	A	E	Avg.
1991— Durham (Carolina)......	OF	35	124	29	31	6	1	6	17	.250	19	47	6	4	0	0	1.000
1992— Greenville (Southern) .	OF	133	471	83	108	18	4	25	71	.229	65	*162	22	244	7	3	.988
1993— Richmond (Int'l).........	OF	123	424	63	103	13	1	19	58	.243	36	109	11	270	6	2	*.993
1994— Atlanta (N.L.)	OF	30	77	14	21	10	1	2	9	.273	2	17	0	25	0	1	.962
— Richmond (Int'l).........	OF	81	313	46	82	14	4	15	45	.262	32	96	9	181	5	1	.995
1995— Richmond (Int'l).........	OF	15	45	5	13	1	0	2	8	.289	5	17	0	24	0	0	1.000
— Atlanta (N.L.)	OF	97	137	26	26	6	1	3	17	.190	11	49	7	63	0	4	.940
1996— Cincinnati (N.L.)■......	OF	19	49	5	9	4	0	1	7	.184	9	11	4	34	1	1	.972
— Indianapolis (A.A.)......	OF	88	292	43	61	10	1	8	30	.209	30	80	13	132	2	4	.971
1997— Chattanooga (Sou.)....	OF	15	60	14	21	7	0	3	12	.350	3	16	3	32	2	0	1.000
— Indianapolis (A.A.)......	OF	27	92	28	32	8	0	7	18	.348	23	23	7	51	1	2	.963
— Cincinnati (N.L.)	OF	73	140	27	41	13	2	6	19	.293	12	30	6	88	2	2	.978
1998— Tampa Bay (A.L.)■....	OF-DH	106	279	39	67	11	2	10	33	.240	22	80	13	137	4	0	1.000
— Durham (Int'l)	OF	4	12	2	1	0	0	0	0	.083	4	5	0	12	0	1	.923
American League totals (1 year)	OF-DH	106	279	39	67	11	2	10	33	.240	22	80	13	137	4	0	1.000
National League totals (4 years)		219	403	72	97	33	4	12	52	.241	32	107	17	210	3	8	.964
Major league totals (5 years)		325	682	111	164	44	6	22	85	.240	54	187	30	347	7	8	.978

KELLY, PAT   2B   CARDINALS

PERSONAL: Born October 14, 1967, in Philadelphia. ... 6-0/182. ... Bats right, throws right. ... Full name: Patrick Franklin Kelly.
HIGH SCHOOL: Catashuqua (Pa.).
COLLEGE: West Chester (Pa.).

TRANSACTIONS/CAREER NOTES: Selected by New York Yankees organization in ninth round of free-agent draft (June 1, 1988). ... On New York disabled list (April 21-May 7, 1992); included rehabilitation assignment to Albany/Colonie (May 5-7). ... On New York disabled list (June 22-July 7, 1994); included rehabilitation assignment to Albany/Colonie (July 6-7). ... On New York disabled list (May 27-July 7, 1995); included rehabilitation assignments to Gulf Coast Yankees (July 3-4) and Tampa (July 4-7). ... On New York disabled list (March 27-July 26, July 27-August 12, and August 23-September 7, 1996); included rehabilitation assignments to Gulf Coast Yankees (July 1-5), Tampa (July 5-8 and July 11-16), Columbus (July 16-26) and Norwich (August 8-12). ... On New York disabled list (May 10-June 3 and August 17-September 1, 1997); included rehabilitation assignment to Columbus (May 21-June 2, 1997). ... Granted free agency (November 7, 1997). ... Signed by Toronto Blue Jays organization (November 27, 1997). ... Contract sold by Blue Jays to St. Louis Cardinals (July 16, 1998). ... Granted free agency (October 26, 1998). ... Re-signed by Cardinals organization (December 7, 1998).

STATISTICAL NOTES: Led Carolina League second basemen with 76 double plays and tied for lead with 641 total chances in 1989. ... Led Eastern League second basemen with 667 total chances and 97 double plays in 1990. ... Led A.L. with 14 sacrifice hits in 1994.

							BATTING							FIELDING		
Year Team (League)	Pos.	G	AB	R	H	2B	3B	HR	RBI	Avg.	BB	SO	SB	PO	A	E	Avg.
1988— Oneonta (NYP)	2B-SS	71	280	49	92	11	6	2	34	.329	15	45	25	124	207	16	.954
1989— Prince Will. (Car.)	2B	124	436	61	116	21	*7	3	45	.266	32	79	31	244	*372	25	.961
1990— Alb./Colon. (East.)	2B	126	418	67	113	19	6	8	44	.270	37	79	31	*266	*381	*20	.970
1991— Columbus (Int'l)	2B	31	116	27	39	9	2	3	19	.336	9	16	8	53	97	4	.974
— New York (A.L.)	3B-2B	96	298	35	72	12	4	3	23	.242	15	52	12	78	204	18	.940
1992— New York (A.L.)	2B-DH	106	318	38	72	22	2	7	27	.226	25	72	8	203	296	11	.978
— Alb./Colon. (East.)	2B	2	6	1	0	0	0	0	0	.000	2	4	0	4	8	0	1.000
1993— New York (A.L.)	2B	127	406	49	111	24	1	7	51	.273	24	68	14	245	369	14	.978
1994— New York (A.L.)	2B	93	286	35	80	21	2	3	41	.280	19	51	6	180	258	10	.978
— Alb./Colon. (East.)	2B	1	4	1	1	0	0	0	0	.250	0	1	1	2	2	0	1.000
1995— New York (A.L.)	2B-DH	89	270	32	64	12	1	4	29	.237	23	65	8	161	255	7	.983
— GC Yankees (GCL)	2B	1	2	2	0	0	0	0	1	.000	1	0	3	3	3	0	1.000
— Tampa (Fla. St.)	2B	3	17	0	4	1	0	0	2	.235	0	1	0	8	14	0	1.000
1996— GC Yankees (GCL)	2B	5	17	7	6	2	0	1	1	.353	3	2	3	5	5	0	1.000
— Tampa (Fla. St.)	2B	6	22	6	6	0	0	1	2	.273	1	7	0	15	9	2	.923
— Columbus (Int'l)	2B	8	37	6	14	1	1	2	7	.378	2	11	3	19	19	0	1.000
— New York (A.L.)	2B-DH	13	21	4	3	0	0	0	2	.143	2	9	0	8	24	1	.970
— Norwich (Eastern)	2B	4	17	3	5	2	1	0	4	.294	0	2	1	7	13	1	.952
1997— New York (A.L.)	2B-DH	67	120	25	29	6	1	2	10	.242	14	37	8	63	92	3	.981
— Columbus (Int'l)	2B	11	44	8	15	4	0	2	6	.341	4	6	1	15	39	0	1.000
1998— Syracuse (Int'l)■........	2B	80	291	58	82	22	3	17	39	.282	39	60	18	133	211	8	.977
— St. Louis (N.L.)■	2B-OF-SS	53	153	18	33	5	0	4	14	.216	13	48	5	79	109	7	.964
American League totals (7 years)		591	1719	218	431	97	11	26	183	.251	122	354	56	938	1498	64	.974
National League totals (1 year)		53	153	18	33	5	0	4	14	.216	13	48	5	79	109	7	.964
Major league totals (8 years)		644	1872	236	464	102	11	30	197	.248	135	402	61	1017	1607	71	.974

DIVISION SERIES RECORD

							BATTING							FIELDING		
Year Team (League)	Pos.	G	AB	R	H	2B	3B	HR	RBI	Avg.	BB	SO	SB	PO	A	E	Avg.
1995— New York (A.L.)	2B-PR	5	3	3	0	0	0	0	1	.000	1	3	0	2	4	0	1.000

KELLY, ROBERTO — OF — RANGERS

PERSONAL: Born October 1, 1964, in Panama City, Panama. ... 6-2/198. ... Bats right, throws right. ... Full name: Roberto Conrado Kelly.
HIGH SCHOOL: Panama City (Panama).
COLLEGE: Jose Dolores Moscote College (Panama).
TRANSACTIONS/CAREER NOTES: Signed as non-drafted free agent by New York Yankees organization (February 21, 1982). ... On disabled list (July 10-August 23, 1986). ... On New York disabled list (June 29-September 1, 1988; May 26-June 12, 1989; and July 6-August 13, 1991). ... Traded by Yankees to Cincinnati Reds for OF Paul O'Neill and 1B Joe DeBerry (November 3, 1992). ... On disabled list (July 14, 1993-remainder of season). ... Traded by Reds with P Roger Etheridge to Atlanta Braves for OF Deion Sanders (May 29, 1994). ... Traded by Braves with OF Tony Tarasco and P Esteban Yan to Montreal Expos for OF Marquis Grissom (April 6, 1995). ... Traded by Expos with P Joey Eischen to Los Angeles Dodgers for OF Henry Rodriguez and IF Jeff Treadway (May 23, 1995). ... Granted free agency (November 6, 1995). ... Signed by Minnesota Twins (January 29, 1996). ... On disabled list (June 27-July 12, 1996). ... On Minnesota disabled list (March 24-April 16, 1997); included rehabilitation assignment to Fort Myers (April 11-16). ... Traded by Twins to Seattle Mariners for two players to be named later (August 20, 1997); Twins acquired P Joe Mays and P Jeromy Palki to complete deal (October 9, 1997). ... Granted free agency (October 31, 1997). ... Signed by Texas Rangers (December 9, 1997). ... On disabled list (April 27-June 6, 1998).
RECORDS: Holds major league single-season record for most times reaching base on catcher's interference—8 (1992). ... Shares major league single-season record for fewest double plays by outfielder (150 or more games)—0 (1990).
STATISTICAL NOTES: Led International League outfielders with 345 total chances in 1987. ... Led A.L. outfielders with 430 total chances in 1990. ... Career major league grand slams: 1.
MISCELLANEOUS: Batted as switch hitter (1985).

							BATTING							FIELDING		
Year Team (League)	Pos.	G	AB	R	H	2B	3B	HR	RBI	Avg.	BB	SO	SB	PO	A	E	Avg.
1982— GC Yankees (GCL)	SS-OF	31	86	13	17	1	1	1	18	.198	10	18	3	47	79	19	.869
1983— Oneonta (NYP)	OF-3B	48	167	17	36	1	2	2	17	.216	12	20	12	70	3	5	.936
— Greensboro (S. Atl.) ...	OF-SS	20	49	6	13	0	0	0	3	.265	3	5	3	30	2	0	1.000
1984— Greensboro (S. Atl.) ...	OF-1B	111	361	68	86	13	2	1	26	.238	57	49	42	228	5	4	.983
1985— Fort Laud. (FSL)	OF	114	417	86	103	4	*13	3	38	.247	58	70	49	187	1	1	.995
1986— Alb./Colon. (East.)	OF	86	299	42	87	11	4	2	43	.291	29	63	10	206	8	7	.968
1987— Columbus (Int'l)	OF	118	471	77	131	19	8	13	62	.278	33	116	*51	*331	4	10	.971
— New York (A.L.)	OF-DH	23	52	12	14	3	0	1	7	.269	5	15	9	42	0	2	.955
1988— New York (A.L.)	OF-DH	38	77	9	19	4	1	1	7	.247	3	15	5	70	1	1	.986
— Columbus (Int'l)	OF	30	120	25	40	8	1	3	16	.333	6	29	11	51	1	0	1.000
1989— New York (A.L.)	OF	137	441	65	133	18	3	9	48	.302	41	89	35	353	9	6	.984
1990— New York (A.L.)	OF	*162	641	85	183	32	4	15	61	.285	33	148	42	420	5	5	.988
1991— New York (A.L.)	OF	126	486	68	130	22	2	20	69	.267	45	77	32	268	8	4	.986
1992— New York (A.L.)	OF	152	580	81	158	31	2	10	66	.272	41	96	28	389	8	7	.983

K

Year Team (League)	Pos.	G	AB	R	H	2B	3B	HR	RBI	Avg.	BB	SO	SB	PO	A	E	Avg.
1993— Cincinnati (N.L.)■	OF	78	320	44	102	17	3	9	35	.319	17	43	21	198	3	1	.995
1994— Cincinnati (N.L.)	OF	47	179	29	54	8	0	3	21	.302	11	35	9	118	2	1	.992
—Atlanta (N.L.)■	OF	63	255	44	73	15	3	6	24	.286	24	36	10	128	3	2	.985
1995— Montreal (N.L.)■	OF	24	95	11	26	4	0	1	9	.274	7	14	4	42	1	0	1.000
—Los Angeles (N.L.)■ ..	OF	112	409	47	114	19	2	6	48	.279	15	65	15	183	2	6	.969
1996— Minnesota (A.L.)■	OF-DH	98	322	41	104	17	4	6	47	.323	23	53	10	203	4	2	.990
1997— Fort Myers (FSL)	OF	4	11	2	4	0	0	1	3	.364	4	1	0	6	0	0	1.000
—Minnesota (A.L.)	OF-DH	75	247	39	71	19	2	5	37	.287	17	50	7	101	1	0	1.000
—Seattle (A.L.)■	OF-DH	30	121	19	36	7	0	7	22	.298	5	17	2	53	1	0	1.000
1998— Texas (A.L.)■	OF-DH	75	257	48	83	7	3	16	46	.323	8	46	0	155	5	4	.976
American League totals (9 years)		916	3224	467	931	160	21	90	410	.289	221	606	170	2054	42	31	.985
National League totals (3 years)		324	1258	175	369	63	8	25	137	.293	74	193	59	669	11	10	.986
Major league totals (12 years)		1240	4482	642	1300	223	29	115	547	.290	295	799	229	2723	53	41	.985

DIVISION SERIES RECORD

Year Team (League)	Pos.	G	AB	R	H	2B	3B	HR	RBI	Avg.	BB	SO	SB	PO	A	E	Avg.
1995— Los Angeles (N.L.)	OF	3	11	0	4	0	0	0	0	.364	1	0	0	8	0	1	.889
1997— Seattle (A.L.)	OF-PH	4	13	1	4	3	0	0	1	.308	0	3	0	4	0	0	1.000
1998— Texas (A.L.)	OF	2	7	0	1	1	0	0	0	.143	0	2	0	3	0	0	1.000
Division series totals (3 years)		9	31	1	9	4	0	0	1	.290	1	5	0	15	0	1	.938

ALL-STAR GAME RECORD

Year League	Pos.	AB	R	H	2B	3B	HR	RBI	Avg.	BB	SO	SB	PO	A	E	Avg.
1992— American	OF	2	0	1	1	0	0	2	.500	0	1	0	1	0	0	1.000
1993— National	OF	1	0	0	0	0	0	0	.000	0	1	0	1	0	0	1.000
All-Star Game totals (2 years)		3	0	1	1	0	0	2	.333	0	2	0	1	1	0	1.000

KENDALL, JASON   C   PIRATES

PERSONAL: Born June 26, 1974, in San Diego. ... 6-0/193. ... Bats right, throws right. ... Full name: Jason Daniel Kendall. ... Son of Fred Kendall, coach, Detroit Tigers; and catcher/first baseman with San Diego Padres (1969-76, 1979 and 1980), Cleveland Indians (1977) and Boston Red Sox (1978).

HIGH SCHOOL: Torrance (Calif.).

TRANSACTIONS/CAREER NOTES: Selected by Pittsburgh Pirates organization in first round (23rd pick overall) of free-agent draft (June 1, 1992).

HONORS: Named Southern League Most Valuable Player (1995). ... Named N.L. Rookie Player of the Year by THE SPORTING NEWS (1996).

STATISTICAL NOTES: Led Gulf Coast League with 13 passed balls in 1992. ... Led Southern League with .414 on-base percentage in 1995. ... Led Southern League catchers with 754 total chances in 1995. ... Led N.L. catchers in double plays with 20 in 1997. ... Led N.L. in being hit by pitch with 31 in 1998. ... Led N.L. catchers with 1,082 total chances in 1998.

Year Team (League)	Pos.	G	AB	R	H	2B	3B	HR	RBI	Avg.	BB	SO	SB	PO	A	E	Avg.
1992— GC Pirates (GCL)........	C	33	111	7	29	2	0	0	10	.261	8	9	2	182	36	5	.978
1993— Augusta (S. Atl.)........	C	102	366	43	101	17	4	1	40	.276	22	30	8	472	65	20	.964
1994— Salem (Carolina)	C	101	371	68	118	19	2	7	66	.318	47	21	14	409	33	9	.980
—Carolina (Southern)....	C	13	47	6	11	2	0	0	6	.234	2	3	0	54	9	2	.969
1995— Carolina (Southern)......	C	117	429	87	140	26	1	8	71	.326	56	22	10	*692	54	8	.989
1996— Pittsburgh (N.L.)........	C	130	414	54	124	23	5	3	42	.300	35	30	5	797	71	*18	.980
1997— Pittsburgh (N.L.)........	C	144	486	71	143	36	4	8	49	.294	49	53	18	952	*103	11	.990
1998— Pittsburgh (N.L.)........	C	149	535	95	175	36	3	12	75	.327	51	51	26	*1015	58	9	.992
Major league totals (3 years)		423	1435	220	442	95	12	23	166	.308	135	134	49	2764	232	38	.987

ALL-STAR GAME RECORD

Year League	Pos.	AB	R	H	2B	3B	HR	RBI	Avg.	BB	SO	SB	PO	A	E	Avg.
1996— National	C	0	0	0	0	0	0	0	...	0	0	0	0	0	0	...
1998— National	PH	1	0	1	0	0	0	0	1.000	0	0	0	...	...	...	...
All-Star Game totals (2 years)		1	0	1	0	0	0	0	1.000	0	0	0	0	0	0	...

KENT, JEFF   2B   GIANTS

PERSONAL: Born March 7, 1968, in Bellflower, Calif. ... 6-1/205. ... Bats right, throws right. ... Full name: Jeffrey Franklin Kent.

HIGH SCHOOL: Edison (Huntington Beach, Calif.).

COLLEGE: California.

TRANSACTIONS/CAREER NOTES: Selected by Toronto Blue Jays organization in 20th round of free-agent draft (June 5, 1989). ... Traded by Blue Jays with a player to be named later to New York Mets for P David Cone (August 27, 1992); Mets acquired OF Ryan Thompson to complete deal (September 1, 1992). ... On disabled list (July 6-21, 1995). ... Traded by New York Mets with IF Jose Vizcaino to Cleveland Indians for 2B Carlos Baerga and IF Alvaro Espinoza (July 29, 1996). ... Traded by Indians with IF Jose Vizcaino, P Julian Tavarez and a player to be named later to San Francisco Giants for 3B Matt Williams and a player to be named later (November 13, 1996); Indians traded P Joe Roa to Giants for OF Trenidad Hubbard to complete deal (December 16, 1996). ... On suspended list (August 22-25, 1997). ... On disabled list (June 10-July 10, 1998).

STATISTICAL NOTES: Led Florida State League second basemen with 680 total chances and 83 double plays in 1990. ... Led Southern League second basemen with 673 total chances and 96 double plays in 1991. ... Led N.L. second basemen in errors with 18 1993 and 20 in 1998. ... Tied for N.L. lead with 10 sacrifice flies in 1998. ... Career major league grand slams: 7.

Year Team (League)	Pos.	G	AB	R	H	2B	3B	HR	RBI	Avg.	BB	SO	SB	PO	A	E	Avg.
1989—St. Catharines (NYP)..	SS-3B	73	268	34	60	14	1	*13	37	.224	33	81	5	103	178	29	.906
1990—Dunedin (Fla. St.).......	2B	132	447	72	124	32	2	16	60	.277	53	98	17	*261	*404	15	.978
1991—Knoxville (Southern)..	2B	•139	445	68	114	*34	1	2	61	.256	80	104	25	249	*395	*29	.957
1992—Toronto (A.L.)........	3B-2B-1B	65	192	36	46	13	1	8	35	.240	20	47	2	62	112	11	.941
—New York (N.L.)■..	2B-SS-3B	37	113	16	27	8	1	3	15	.239	7	29	0	62	93	3	.981
1993—New York (N.L.)..........	2B-3B-SS	140	496	65	134	24	0	21	80	.270	30	88	4	261	341	†22	.965
1994—New York (N.L.).........	2B	107	415	53	121	24	5	14	68	.292	23	84	1	222	337	•14	.976
1995—New York (N.L.).........	2B	125	472	65	131	22	3	20	65	.278	29	89	3	245	354	10	.984
1996—New York (N.L.).........	3B	89	335	45	97	20	1	9	39	.290	21	56	4	75	184	21	.925
—Cleveland (A.L.)■....	1-2-3-DH	39	102	16	27	7	0	3	16	.265	10	22	2	125	46	1	.994
1997—San Fran. (N.L.)■....	2B-1B	155	580	90	145	38	2	29	121	.250	48	133	11	405	429	16	.981
1998—San Francisco (N.L.)..	2B-1B	137	526	94	156	37	3	31	128	.297	48	110	9	279	404	†20	.972
American League totals (2 years)		104	294	52	73	20	1	11	51	.248	30	69	4	187	158	12	.966
National League totals (7 years)		790	2937	428	811	173	15	127	516	.276	206	589	32	1549	2142	106	.972
Major league totals (7 years)		894	3231	480	884	193	16	138	567	.274	236	658	36	1736	2300	118	.972

DIVISION SERIES RECORD

RECORDS: Shares single-game record for most home runs—2 (October 3, 1997).

Year Team (League)	Pos.	G	AB	R	H	2B	3B	HR	RBI	Avg.	BB	SO	SB	PO	A	E	Avg.
1996—Cleveland (A.L.).........	2-1-PR-3	4	8	2	1	1	0	0	0	.125	0	0	0	3	3	0	1.000
1997—San Francisco (N.L.)..	2B-1B	3	10	2	3	0	0	2	2	.300	2	1	0	19	7	0	1.000
Division series totals (2 years)		7	18	4	4	1	0	2	2	.222	2	1	0	22	10	0	1.000

K

KEY, JIMMY   P

PERSONAL: Born April 22, 1961, in Huntsville, Ala. ... 6-1/190. ... Throws left, bats right. ... Full name: James Edward Key.
HIGH SCHOOL: Butler (Huntsville, Ala.).
COLLEGE: Clemson.
TRANSACTIONS/CAREER NOTES: Selected by Chicago White Sox organization in 10th round of free-agent draft (June 5, 1979); did not sign. ... Selected by Toronto Blue Jays organization in third round of free-agent draft (June 7, 1982). ... On Toronto disabled list (April 15-June 29, 1988); included rehabilitation assignment to Dunedin (June 10-27). ... On disabled list (August 4-19, 1989). ... On Toronto disabled list (May 23-June 22, 1990); included rehabilitation assignment to Dunedin (June 7-18). ... Granted free agency (October 27, 1992). ... Signed by New York Yankees (December 10, 1992). ... On disabled list (May 17, 1995-remainder of season). ... On New York disabled list (May 16-31 and June 11-26, 1996); included rehabilitation assignment to Tampa (May 21-31) and Gulf Coast Yankees (June 22-23). ... Granted free agency (December 7, 1996). ... Signed by Baltimore Orioles (December 10, 1996). ... On Baltimore disabled list (May 21-July 28, 1998); included rehabilitation assignment to Frederick (July 24-28). ... Granted free agency (October 27, 1998).
HONORS: Named A.L. Pitcher of the Year by THE SPORTING NEWS (1987 and 1994). ... Named lefthanded pitcher on THE SPORTING NEWS A.L. All-Star team (1987 and 1993-94).
STATISTICAL NOTES: Pitched 5-0 one-hit, complete-game victory against Chicago (May 22, 1986). ... Pitched 5-0 one-hit, complete-game victory against California (April 27, 1993).
MISCELLANEOUS: Appeared in one game as pinch runner (1985).

Year Team (League)	W	L	Pct.	ERA	G	GS	CG	ShO	Sv.	IP	H	R	ER	BB	SO
1982—Medicine Hat (Pioneer)......	2	1	.667	2.30	5	5	1	0	0	31 1/3	27	12	8	10	25
—Florence (S. Atl.)...............	5	2	.714	3.72	9	9	0	0	0	58	59	33	24	18	49
1983—Knoxville (Southern)......	6	5	.545	2.85	14	14	2	0	0	101	86	35	32	40	57
—Syracuse (Int'l)...............	4	8	.333	4.13	16	15	2	0	0	89 1/3	87	58	41	33	71
1984—Toronto (A.L.)....................	4	5	.444	4.65	63	0	0	0	10	62	70	37	32	32	44
1985—Toronto (A.L.)....................	14	6	.700	3.00	35	32	3	0	0	212 2/3	188	77	71	50	85
1986—Toronto (A.L.)....................	14	11	.560	3.57	36	35	4	2	0	232	222	98	92	74	141
1987—Toronto (A.L.)....................	17	8	.680	*2.76	36	36	8	1	0	261	210	93	80	66	161
1988—Toronto (A.L.)....................	12	5	.706	3.29	21	21	2	2	0	131 1/3	127	55	48	30	65
—Dunedin (Fla. St.).........	2	0	1.000	0.00	4	4	0	0	0	21 1/3	15	2	0	1	11
1989—Toronto (A.L.)....................	13	14	.481	3.88	33	33	5	1	0	216	226	99	93	27	118
1990—Toronto (A.L.)....................	13	7	.650	4.25	27	27	0	0	0	154 2/3	169	79	73	22	88
—Dunedin (Fla. St.).........	2	0	1.000	2.50	3	3	0	0	0	18	21	7	5	3	14
1991—Toronto (A.L.)....................	16	12	.571	3.05	33	33	2	2	0	209 1/3	207	84	71	44	125
1992—Toronto (A.L.)....................	13	13	.500	3.53	33	33	4	2	0	216 2/3	205	88	85	59	117
1993—New York (A.L.)■..........	18	6	.750	3.00	34	34	4	2	0	236 2/3	219	84	79	43	173
1994—New York (A.L.).............	*17	4	.810	3.27	25	•25	1	0	0	168	177	68	61	52	97
1995—New York (A.L.).............	1	2	.333	5.64	5	5	0	0	0	30 1/3	40	20	19	6	14
1996—New York (A.L.).............	12	11	.522	4.68	30	30	0	0	0	169 1/3	171	93	88	58	116
—Tampa (Fla. St.)..........	0	0	....	2.77	2	2	0	0	0	13	10	4	4	1	11
—GC Yankees (GCL)............	1	0	1.000	0.00	1	1	0	0	0	5	3	2	0	0	10
1997—Baltimore (A.L.)■..........	16	10	.615	3.43	34	34	1	1	0	212 1/3	210	90	81	82	141
1998—Baltimore (A.L.)............	6	3	.667	4.20	25	11	0	0	0	79 1/3	77	39	37	23	53
—Frederick (Carolina)...........	1	0	1.000	3.00	1	1	0	0	0	6	4	2	2	2	6
Major league totals (15 years)....	186	117	.614	3.51	470	389	34	13	10	2591 2/3	2518	1104	1010	668	1538

DIVISION SERIES RECORD

Year Team (League)	W	L	Pct.	ERA	G	GS	CG	ShO	Sv.	IP	H	R	ER	BB	SO
1996—New York (A.L.).................	0	0	...	3.60	1	1	0	0	0	5	5	2	2	1	3
1997—Baltimore (A.L.).................	0	1	.000	3.86	1	1	0	0	0	4 2/3	8	2	2	0	4
Div. series totals (2 years)	0	1	.000	3.72	2	2	0	0	0	9 2/3	13	4	4	1	7

CHAMPIONSHIP SERIES RECORD

RECORDS: Shares single-series record for most hit batsmen—3 (1997).

Year Team (League)	W	L	Pct.	ERA	G	GS	CG	ShO	Sv.	IP	H	R	ER	BB	SO
1985— Toronto (A.L.)..................	0	1	.000	5.19	2	2	0	0	0	8 2/3	15	5	5	2	5
1989— Toronto (A.L.)..................	1	0	1.000	4.50	1	1	0	0	0	6	7	3	3	2	2
1991— Toronto (A.L.)..................	0	0	...	3.00	1	1	0	0	0	6	5	2	2	1	1
1992— Toronto (A.L.)..................	0	0	...	0.00	1	0	0	0	0	3	2	0	0	2	1
1996— New York (A.L.)	1	0	1.000	2.25	1	1	0	0	0	8	3	2	2	1	5
1997— Baltimore (A.L.)	0	0	...	2.57	2	1	0	0	0	7	5	2	2	3	7
Champ. series totals (6 years)	2	1	.667	3.26	8	6	0	0	0	38 2/3	37	14	14	11	21

WORLD SERIES RECORD

NOTES: Member of World Series championship team (1992 and 1996).

Year Team (League)	W	L	Pct.	ERA	G	GS	CG	ShO	Sv.	IP	H	R	ER	BB	SO
1992— Toronto (A.L.)..................	2	0	1.000	1.00	2	1	0	0	0	9	6	2	1	0	6
1996— New York (A.L.)	1	1	.500	3.97	2	2	0	0	0	11 1/3	15	5	5	5	1
World Series totals (2 years)	3	1	.750	2.66	4	3	0	0	0	20 1/3	21	7	6	5	7

ALL-STAR GAME RECORD

Year League	W	L	Pct.	ERA	GS	CG	ShO	Sv.	IP	H	R	ER	BB	SO
1985— American	0	0	...	0.00	0	0	0	0	1/3	0	0	0	0	0
1991— American	1	0	1.000	0.00	0	0	0	0	1	1	0	0	0	1
1993— American	0	0	...	9.00	0	0	0	0	1	2	1	1	0	1
1994— American	0	0	...	4.50	1	0	0	0	2	1	1	1	0	1
All-Star totals (4 years)	1	0	1.000	4.15	1	0	0	0	4 1/3	4	2	2	0	3

KIDA, MASAO   P   TIGERS   K

PERSONAL: Born September 12, 1968, in Tokyo, Japan. ... 6-2/210. ... Throws right, bats right.
TRANSACTIONS/CAREER NOTES: Played with Yomiuri Giants (1989-97) and Orix Blue Wave (1998) of Japanese League. ... Signed by Detroit Tigers (November 23, 1998).

Year Team (League)	W	L	Pct.	ERA	G	GS	CG	ShO	Sv.	IP	H	R	ER	BB	SO
1989— Yomiuri (Jp. Cen.)	2	1	.667	4.62	8	...	...	...	0	37	...	...	19	...	26
1990— Yomiuri (Jp. Cen.)	12	8	.600	2.71	32	...	...	...	7	182 2/3	...	...	55	...	182
1991— Yomiuri (Jp. Cen.)	4	7	.364	6.44	19	...	...	...	1	50 1/3	...	...	36	...	44
1992— Yomiuri (Jp. Cen.)	3	6	.333	4.53	29	...	...	...	0	93 1/3	...	...	47	...	87
1993— Yomiuri (Jp. Cen.)	7	7	.500	3.35	35	...	...	...	2	131 2/3	...	...	49	...	97
1994— Yomiuri (Jp. Cen.)	6	8	.429	4.93	28	...	...	...	1	87 2/3	...	...	48	...	61
1995— Yomiuri (Jp. Cen.)	7	9	.438	3.40	40	...	...	...	0	121 2/3	...	...	46	...	97
1996— Yomiuri (Jp. Cen.)	7	9	.438	3.78	33	...	...	...	2	123 2/3	...	...	52	...	99
1997— Yomiuri (Jp. Cen.)	2	2	.500	1.99	39	...	...	...	7	49 2/3	...	...	11	...	53
1998— Orix (Jap. Pacific)■...........	4	7	.364	4.62	36	13	1	0	16	97 1/3	97	54	50	36	74

KILE, DARRYL   P   ROCKIES

PERSONAL: Born December 2, 1968, in Garden Grove, Calif. ... 6-5/212. ... Throws right, bats right. ... Full name: Darryl Andrew Kile.
HIGH SCHOOL: Norco (Calif.).
JUNIOR COLLEGE: Chaffey College (Calif.).
TRANSACTIONS/CAREER NOTES: Selected by Houston Astros organization in 30th round of free-agent draft (June 2, 1987). ... On Tucson disabled list (June 25-July 5, 1992). ... Granted free agency (October 28, 1997). ... Signed by Colorado Rockies (December 4, 1997).
RECORDS: Shares modern N.L. record for most hit batsmen (nine-inning game)—4 (June 2, 1996).
STATISTICAL NOTES: Led N.L. with 15 hit batsmen in 1993. ... Pitched 7-1 no-hit victory against New York (September 8, 1993). ... Tied for N.L. lead with 10 wild pitches in 1994. ... Tied for N.L. lead with 16 hit batsmen in 1996.
MISCELLANEOUS: Appeared in two games as pinch runner (1996). ... Had sacrifice hit in two appearances as pinch hitter and appeared in one game as pinch runner (1998).

Year Team (League)	W	L	Pct.	ERA	G	GS	CG	ShO	Sv.	IP	H	R	ER	BB	SO
1988— GC Astros (GCL)	5	3	.625	3.17	12	12	0	0	0	59 2/3	48	34	21	33	54
1989— Columbus (Southern)........	11	6	.647	2.58	20	20	6	•2	0	125 2/3	74	47	36	68	108
—Tucson (PCL)	2	1	.667	5.96	6	6	1	1	0	25 2/3	33	20	17	13	18
1990— Tucson (PCL)	5	10	.333	6.64	26	23	1	0	0	123 1/3	147	97	91	68	77
1991— Houston (N.L.)	7	11	.389	3.69	37	22	0	0	0	153 2/3	144	81	63	84	100
1992— Houston (N.L.)	5	10	.333	3.95	22	22	2	0	0	125 1/3	124	61	55	63	90
—Tucson (PCL)	4	1	.800	3.99	9	9	0	0	0	56 1/3	50	31	25	32	43
1993— Houston (N.L.)	15	8	.652	3.51	32	26	4	2	0	171 2/3	152	73	67	69	141
1994— Houston (N.L.)	9	6	.600	4.57	24	24	0	0	0	147 2/3	153	84	75	*82	105
1995— Houston (N.L.)	4	12	.250	4.96	25	21	0	0	0	127	114	81	70	73	113
—Tucson (PCL)	2	1	.667	8.51	4	4	0	0	0	24 1/3	29	23	23	12	15
1996— Houston (N.L.)	12	11	.522	4.19	35	33	4	0	0	219	233	113	102	97	219
1997— Houston (N.L.)	19	7	.731	2.57	34	34	6	4	0	255 2/3	208	87	73	94	205
1998— Colorado (N.L.)■	13	*17	.433	5.20	36	•35	4	1	0	230 1/3	257	141	133	96	158
Major league totals (8 years)......	84	82	.506	4.01	245	217	20	7	0	1430 1/3	1385	721	638	658	1131

DIVISION SERIES RECORD

Year Team (League)	W	L	Pct.	ERA	G	GS	CG	ShO	Sv.	IP	H	R	ER	BB	SO
1997— Houston (N.L.)	0	1	.000	2.57	1	1	0	0	0	7	2	2	2	2	4

ALL-STAR GAME RECORD

Year League	W	L	Pct.	ERA	GS	CG	ShO	Sv.	IP	H	R	ER	BB	SO
1993— National					Did not play.									
1997— National					Did not play.									

KING, CESAR   C   RANGERS

PERSONAL: Born February 28, 1978, in LaRomana, Dominican Republic. ... 6-0/175. ... Bats right, throws right.
TRANSACTIONS/CAREER NOTES: Signed as non-drafted free agent by Texas Rangers organization (September 4, 1994). ... On disabled list (August 1-30, 1998).
STATISTICAL NOTES: Led Florida State League catchers with 10 double plays in 1997. ... Led Texas League catchers with 12 double plays and 18 passed balls in 1998.

| | | | | | | | BATTING | | | | | | | | FIELDING | | |
Year Team (League)	Pos.	G	AB	R	H	2B	3B	HR	RBI	Avg.	BB	SO	SB	PO	A	E	Avg.
1995— Dom. Rangers (DSL)..	C	54	182	33	55	9	0	3	22	.302	22	34	3	277	43	11	.967
1996— Char., S.C. (S. Atl.).....	C	84	276	35	69	10	1	7	28	.250	21	58	8	399	71	14	.971
1997— Charlotte (Fla. St.)......	C-3B	91	307	51	91	14	4	6	37	.296	35	58	8	553	84	10	.985
— Tulsa (Texas)	C	14	45	6	16	1	0	1	8	.356	5	3	0	85	8	3	.969
1998— Tulsa (Texas)	C	90	316	40	70	16	2	3	39	.222	30	68	1	585	73	8	.988

KING, CURTIS   P   CARDINALS

PERSONAL: Born October 25, 1970, in Norristown, Pa. ... 6-5/205. ... Throws right, bats right. ... Full name: Curtis Albert King.
HIGH SCHOOL: Plymouth-Whitemarsh (Plymouth Meeting, Pa.).
COLLEGE: Philadelphia Textile.
TRANSACTIONS/CAREER NOTES: Selected by St. Louis Cardinals organization in fifth round of free-agent draft (June 2, 1994).

Year Team (League)	W	L	Pct.	ERA	G	GS	CG	ShO	Sv.	IP	H	R	ER	BB	SO
1994— New Jersey (NYP)	1	0	1.000	2.61	5	4	0	0	0	20 2/3	19	7	6	11	14
— Savannah (S. Atl.)	4	1	.800	1.87	8	8	2	2	0	53	37	14	11	9	40
1995— St. Petersburg (FSL)	7	8	.467	2.58	28	21	3	0	0	136	117	49	39	49	65
1996— Arkansas (Texas)	0	1	.000	19.80	5	0	0	0	1	5	15	12	11	6	5
— St. Petersburg (FSL)	3	3	.500	2.75	48	0	0	0	30	55 2/3	41	20	17	24	27
1997— Arkansas (Texas)	2	3	.400	4.46	32	0	0	0	16	36 1/3	38	19	18	10	29
— Louisville (A.A.)	2	1	.667	2.05	16	0	0	0	3	22	19	5	5	6	9
— St. Louis (N.L.)	4	2	.667	2.76	30	0	0	0	0	29 1/3	38	14	9	11	13
1998— Memphis (Pacific Coast)	0	1	.000	2.10	27	0	0	0	12	25 2/3	31	6	6	6	23
— St. Louis (N.L.)	2	0	1.000	3.53	36	0	0	0	2	51	50	20	20	20	28
Major league totals (2 years)......	**6**	**2**	**.750**	**3.25**	**66**	**0**	**0**	**0**	**2**	**80 1/3**	**88**	**34**	**29**	**31**	**41**

KING, JEFF   1B   ROYALS

PERSONAL: Born December 26, 1964, in Marion, Ind. ... 6-1/188. ... Bats right, throws right. ... Full name: Jeffrey Wayne King. ... Son of Jack King, minor league catcher (1954-55).
HIGH SCHOOL: Rampart (Colorado Springs, Colo.).
COLLEGE: Arkansas.
TRANSACTIONS/CAREER NOTES: Selected by Chicago Cubs organization in 23rd round of free-agent draft (June 6, 1983); did not sign. ... Selected by Pittsburgh Pirates organization in first round (first pick overall) of free-agent draft (June 2, 1986). ... On Pittsburgh disabled list (May 5-31, 1991); included rehabilitation assignment to Buffalo (May 25-31). ... On Pittsburgh disabled list (June 13-October 7, 1991); included rehabilitation assignment to Buffalo (August 28-September 6). ... On disabled list (May 25-June 9, 1994 and June 16-July 1, 1995). ... Traded by Pirates with SS Jay Bell to Kansas City Royals for 3B Joe Randa, P Jeff Granger, P Jeff Martin and P Jeff Wallace (December 13, 1996). ... On disabled list (August 16-September 1, 1998).
RECORDS: Shares major league single-inning record for most home runs—2 (August 8, 1995, second inning and April 30, 1996, fourth inning).
HONORS: Named College Player of the Year by THE SPORTING NEWS (1986). ... Named third baseman on THE SPORTING NEWS college All-America team (1986).
STATISTICAL NOTES: Led Carolina League with .565 slugging percentage in 1987. ... Led N.L. third basemen with 353 assists and 475 total chances in 1993. ... Led N.L. third basemen with 27 double plays in 1994. ... Led A.L. first basemen in double plays with 135 in 1997. ... Career major league grand slams: 8.

| | | | | | | | BATTING | | | | | | | | FIELDING | | |
Year Team (League)	Pos.	G	AB	R	H	2B	3B	HR	RBI	Avg.	BB	SO	SB	PO	A	E	Avg.
1986— Prince Will. (Car.)	3B	37	132	18	31	4	1	6	20	.235	19	34	1	25	50	8	.904
1987— Salem (Carolina)	1B-3B	90	310	68	86	9	1	26	71	.277	61	88	6	572	106	13	.981
— Harrisburg (East.)........	1B	26	100	12	24	7	0	2	25	.240	4	27	0	107	10	1	.992
1988— Harrisburg (East.)........	3B	117	411	49	105	21	1	14	66	.255	46	87	5	97	208	24	.927
1989— Buffalo (A.A.)............	1B-3B	51	169	26	43	5	2	6	29	.254	57	60	11	213	61	8	.972
— Pittsburgh (N.L.)	1-3-2-S	75	215	31	42	13	3	5	19	.195	20	34	4	403	59	4	.991
1990— Pittsburgh (N.L.)	3B-1B	127	371	46	91	17	1	14	53	.245	21	50	3	61	215	18	.939
1991— Pittsburgh (N.L.)	3B	33	109	16	26	1	1	4	18	.239	14	15	3	15	62	2	.975
— Buffalo (A.A.)............	3B	9	18	3	4	1	1	0	2	.222	6	3	1	2	8	1	.909
1992— Pittsburgh (N.L.)	3-2-1-S-O	130	480	56	111	21	2	14	65	.231	27	56	4	368	234	12	.980
— Buffalo (A.A.)............	3B-1B-2B	7	29	6	10	2	0	2	5	.345	2	2	1	21	12	0	1.000
1993— Pittsburgh (N.L.)	3B-SS-2B	158	611	82	180	35	3	9	98	.295	59	54	8	108	†362	18	.963
1994— Pittsburgh (N.L.)	3B-2B	94	339	36	89	23	0	5	42	.263	30	38	3	61	198	13	.952
1995— Pittsburgh (N.L.)	3-1-2-S	122	445	61	118	27	2	18	87	.265	55	63	7	352	206	17	.970
1996— Pittsburgh (N.L.)	1B-2B-3B	155	591	91	160	36	4	30	111	.271	70	95	15	896	252	11	.991
1997— Kansas City (A.L.)■	1B-DH	155	543	84	129	30	1	28	112	.238	89	96	16	1217	*147	5	*.996
1998— Kansas City (A.L.)	1B-DH-3B	131	486	83	128	17	1	24	93	.263	42	73	10	935	91	5	.995
American League totals (2 years)		286	1029	167	257	47	2	52	205	.250	131	169	26	2152	238	10	.996
National League totals (8 years)		894	3161	419	817	173	16	99	493	.258	296	405	47	2264	1588	95	.976
Major league totals (10 years)		1180	4190	586	1074	220	18	151	698	.256	427	574	73	4416	1826	105	.983

Year	Team (League)	Pos.	G	AB	R	H	2B	3B	HR	RBI	Avg.	BB	SO	SB	PO	A	E	Avg.
							BATTING									FIELDING		
1990— Pittsburgh (N.L.)		3B-PH	5	10	0	1	0	0	0	0	.100	1	5	0	1	4	0	1.000
1992— Pittsburgh (N.L.)		3B	7	29	4	7	4	0	0	2	.241	0	1	0	11	19	1	.968
Championship series totals (2 years)			12	39	4	8	4	0	0	2	.205	1	6	0	12	23	1	.972

KING, RAY   P   CUBS

PERSONAL: Born January 15, 1974, in Chicago. ... 6-1/225. ... Throws left, bats left. ... Full name: Raymond Keith King.
HIGH SCHOOL: Ripley (Tenn.).
COLLEGE: Lambuth (Tenn.).
TRANSACTIONS/CAREER NOTES: Selected by Cincinnati Red organization in eighth round of free-agent draft (June 1, 1995). ... Loaned by Reds organization to Atlanta Braves organization (March 22-June 11, 1996). ... Traded by Reds organization to Braves organization (June 11, 1996); completing deal in which Braves traded OF Mike Kelly to Reds for P Chad Fox and a player to be named later (January 9, 1996). ... Traded by Braves organization to Chicago Cubs organization for P Jon Ratliff (January 20, 1998).

Year	Team (League)	W	L	Pct.	ERA	G	GS	CG	ShO	Sv.	IP	H	R	ER	BB	SO
1995— Billings (Pioneer)................		3	0	1.000	1.67	28	0	0	0	5	43	31	11	8	15	43
1996— Macon (S. Atl.)■................		3	5	.375	2.80	18	10	1	0	0	70²/₃	63	34	22	20	63
— Durham (Carolina)............		3	6	.333	4.46	14	14	2	0	0	82²/₃	104	54	41	15	52
1997— Greenville (Southern)		5	5	.500	6.85	12	9	0	0	0	65²/₃	85	53	50	24	42
— Durham (Carolina)............		6	9	.400	5.40	24	6	0	0	3	71²/₃	89	54	43	26	60
1998— West Tenn (Southern)■.....		1	2	.333	2.43	25	0	0	0	3	29²/₃	23	9	8	10	26
— Iowa (Pacific Coast)		1	3	.250	5.01	37	0	0	0	2	32¹/₃	36	20	18	15	26

KINGSALE, GENE   OF   ORIOLES

PERSONAL: Born August 20, 1976, in Oranjestad, Aruba. ... 6-3/190. ... Bats both, throws right. ... Full name: Eugene Humphrey Kingsale.
HIGH SCHOOL: John F. Kennedy Technical School (Oranjestad, Aruba).
TRANSACTIONS/CAREER NOTES: Signed as non-drafted free agent by Baltimore Orioles organization (June 19, 1993). ... On Frederick disabled list (May 29-August 31, 1996). ... On Bowie disabled list (April 8-August 8, 1997).
STATISTICAL NOTES: Tied for Gulf Coast League lead in double plays by outfielder with two in 1994.

Year	Team (League)	Pos.	G	AB	R	H	2B	3B	HR	RBI	Avg.	BB	SO	SB	PO	A	E	Avg.
							BATTING									FIELDING		
1994— GC Orioles (GCL)........		OF-2B	50	168	26	52	2	3	0	9	.310	18	24	15	100	2	3	.971
1995— Bluefield (Appal.)........		OF	47	171	45	54	11	2	0	16	.316	27	31	20	95	3	*11	.899
1996— Frederick (Carolina)........		OF	49	166	26	45	6	4	0	9	.271	19	32	23	100	1	4	.962
— Baltimore (A.L.)..........		OF	3	0	0	0	0	0	0	0	...	0	0	0	2	0	0	1.000
1997— Bowie (Eastern)........		OF	13	46	8	19	6	0	0	4	.413	5	4	5	23	0	1	.958
— GC Orioles (GCL)........		OF	6	17	2	5	0	0	0	0	.294	2	2	1	16	0	1	.941
1998— Bowie (Eastern)........		OF	111	427	69	112	11	5	1	34	.262	48	79	29	279	9	6	.980
— Rochester (Int'l)........		OF	18	55	3	12	1	1	0	2	.218	4	8	3	38	2	0	1.000
— Baltimore (A.L.)........		OF-DH	11	2	1	0	0	0	0	0	.000	0	1	0	2	0	0	1.000
Major league totals (2 years)			14	2	1	0	0	0	0	0	.000	0	1	0	4	0	0	1.000

KINKADE, MIKE   3B   METS

PERSONAL: Born May 6, 1973, in Livonia, Mich. ... 6-1/210. ... Bats right, throws right. ... Full name: Michael A. Kinkade.
HIGH SCHOOL: Tigard (Ore.)
COLLEGE: Washington State.
TRANSACTIONS/CAREER NOTES: Selected by Milwaukee Brewers organization in ninth round of free-agent draft (June 1, 1995). ... On Louisville disabled list (April 20-May 14, 1998). ... Traded by Brewers to New York Mets for P Bill Pulsipher (July 31, 1998).
HONORS: Named Texas League Player of the Year (1997).
STATISTICAL NOTES: Led Texas League with .455 on-base percentage and tied for league lead with 275 total bases in 1997.

Year	Team (League)	Pos.	G	AB	R	H	2B	3B	HR	RBI	Avg.	BB	SO	SB	PO	A	E	Avg.
							BATTING									FIELDING		
1995— Helena (Pioneer)		3B-1B-C	69	266	76	94	19	1	4	39	.353	43	38	26	291	79	10	.974
1996— Beloit (Midwest).........		3B-C-1B	135	499	105	151	33	4	15	100	.303	47	69	23	148	310	39	.922
1997— El Paso (Texas)........		3B	125	468	•112	*180	35	12	12	*109	*.385	52	66	17	*79	249	*60	.845
1998— Louisville (Int'l).........		3B-1B	80	291	57	90	24	6	7	46	.309	36	52	10	183	120	15	.953
— Norfolk (Int'l)■.........		3B-1B	30	125	12	35	5	0	1	18	.280	3	24	6	32	61	5	.949
— New York (N.L.).........		3B	3	2	2	0	0	0	0	0	.000	0	0	0	0	0	0	...
Major league totals (1 year)			3	2	2	0	0	0	0	0	.000	0	0	0	0	0	0	...

KINNEY, MATT   P   TWINS

PERSONAL: Born December 16, 1976, in Bangor, Maine. ... 6-4/200. ... Throws right, bats right. ... Full name: Matthew John Kinney.
HIGH SCHOOL: Bangor (Maine).
TRANSACTIONS/CAREER NOTES: Selected by Boston Red Sox organization in sixth round of free-agent draft (June 1, 1995). ... Traded by Red Sox with P Joe Thomas and P John Barnes to Minnesota Twins for P Greg Swindell and 1B Orlando Merced (July 31, 1998).
STATISTICAL NOTES: Led Florida State League with 93 bases on balls and 25 wild pitches in 1998.

Year	Team (League)	W	L	Pct.	ERA	G	GS	CG	ShO	Sv.	IP	H	R	ER	BB	SO
1995— GC Red Sox (GCL)		1	3	.250	2.93	8	2	0	0	2	27²/₃	29	13	9	10	11
1996— Lowell (NY-Penn)		3	9	.250	2.68	15	•15	0	0	0	87¹/₃	68	51	26	44	72
1997— Michigan (Midwest)		8	5	.615	3.53	22	22	2	1	0	117¹/₃	93	59	46	78	123
1998— Sarasota (Florida State)......		9	6	.600	4.01	22	20	2	1	1	121¹/₃	109	70	54	75	96
— Fort Myers (Fla. St.)■		3	2	.600	3.13	7	7	0	0	0	37¹/₃	31	18	13	§18	39

K

PERSONAL: Born January 22, 1964, in Williamsburg, Va. ... 5-10/190. ... Bats left, throws right. ... Full name: Wayne Edward Kirby. ... Brother of Terry Kirby, running back, San Francisco 49ers; and cousin of Chris Slade, linebacker, New England Patriots.

HIGH SCHOOL: Tabb (Va.).

COLLEGE: Newport News (Va.) Apprentice School.

TRANSACTIONS/CAREER NOTES: Selected by Los Angeles Dodgers organization in 13th round of free-agent draft (January 11, 1983). ... Granted free agency (October 15, 1990). ... Signed by Cleveland Indians organization (December 3, 1990). ... Granted free agency (October 15, 1991). ... Re-signed by Colorado Springs, Indians organization (December 12, 1991). ... Released by Indians (June 19, 1996). ... Claimed on waivers by Dodgers (June 24, 1996). ... Granted free agency (October 3, 1997). ... Signed by St. Louis Cardinals organization (December 22, 1997). ... Traded by Cardinals organization to New York Mets organization for IF Shawn Gilbert and a player to be named later (June 10, 1998). ... Signed by Toronto Blue Jays organization (January 6, 1999).

STATISTICAL NOTES: Led Pacific Coast League in caught stealing with 20 in 1992.

							BATTING									FIELDING		
Year	Team (League)	Pos.	G	AB	R	H	2B	3B	HR	RBI	Avg.	BB	SO	SB	PO	A	E	Avg.
1983—	GC Dodgers (GCL)	OF	60	216	43	63	7	1	0	13	.292	34	19	23	89	9	1	.990
1984—	Vero Beach (FSL)	OF	76	224	39	61	6	3	0	21	.272	21	30	11	101	3	5	.954
	— Great Falls (Pio.)	OF	20	84	19	26	2	2	1	11	.310	12	9	19	35	3	2	.950
	— Bakersfield (Calif.)	OF	23	84	14	23	3	0	0	10	.274	4	5	8	10	1	3	.786
1985—	Vero Beach (FSL)	OF	122	437	70	123	9	3	0	28	.281	41	41	31	231	10	4	.984
1986—	Vero Beach (FSL)	OF-2B	114	387	60	101	9	4	2	31	.261	37	30	28	264	18	4	.986
1987—	Bakersfield (Calif.)	OF	105	416	77	112	14	3	0	34	.269	49	42	56	213	13	12	.950
	— San Antonio (Tex.)	OF	24	80	7	19	1	2	1	9	.238	4	7	6	47	1	3	.941
1988—	Bakersfield (Calif.)	OF	12	47	12	13	0	1	0	4	.277	11	4	9	20	2	2	.917
	— San Antonio (Tex.)	OF	100	334	50	80	9	2	0	21	.240	21	43	26	181	4	4	.979
1989—	San Antonio (Tex.)	OF	44	140	14	30	3	1	0	7	.214	18	17	11	77	3	4	.952
	— Albuquerque (PCL)	OF	78	310	62	106	18	8	0	30	.342	26	27	29	149	8	2	.987
1990—	Albuquerque (PCL)	OF	119	342	56	95	14	5	0	30	.278	28	36	29	185	11	9	.956
1991—	Colo. Springs (PCL)■	OF-2B	118	385	66	113	14	4	1	39	.294	34	36	29	227	14	6	.976
	— Cleveland (A.L.)	OF	21	43	4	9	2	0	0	5	.209	2	6	1	40	1	0	1.000
1992—	Colo. Springs (PCL) ...	OF	123	470	•101	*162	18	*16	11	74	.345	36	28	51	274	14	7	.976
	— Cleveland (A.L.)	DH-OF	21	18	9	3	1	0	1	1	.167	3	2	0	3	0	0	1.000
1993—	Charlotte (Int'l)	OF	17	76	10	22	6	2	3	7	.289	3	10	4	38	1	0	1.000
	— Cleveland (A.L.)	OF-DH	131	458	71	123	19	5	6	60	.269	37	58	17	273	*19	5	.983
1994—	Cleveland (A.L.)	OF-DH	78	191	33	56	6	0	5	23	.293	13	30	11	92	2	4	.959
1995—	Cleveland (A.L.)	OF-DH	101	188	29	39	10	2	1	14	.207	13	32	10	94	2	1	.990
1996—	Cleveland (A.L.)	OF-DH	27	16	3	4	1	0	0	1	.250	2	2	0	8	0	0	1.000
	— Los Angeles (N.L.)■..	OF	65	188	23	51	10	1	1	11	.271	17	17	4	93	2	3	.969
1997—	Los Angeles (N.L.)	OF	46	65	6	11	2	0	0	4	.169	10	12	0	36	1	0	1.000
	— Albuquerque (PCL)	OF	68	269	57	90	16	5	10	43	.335	26	33	18	138	9	5	.967
1998—	Memphis (PCL)■	OF	58	227	36	64	15	3	5	32	.282	15	33	10	113	4	3	.975
	— New York (N.L.)■	OF	26	31	5	6	0	1	0	0	.194	1	9	1	15	1	0	1.000
	— Norfolk (Int'l)	OF	42	162	32	50	8	3	5	23	.309	21	18	11	71	5	1	.987
American League totals (6 years)			379	914	149	234	39	7	13	104	.256	70	130	39	510	24	10	.982
National League totals (3 years)			137	284	34	68	12	2	1	15	.239	28	38	5	144	4	3	.980
Major league totals (8 years)			516	1198	183	302	51	9	14	119	.252	98	168	44	654	28	13	.981

DIVISION SERIES RECORD

							BATTING									FIELDING		
Year	Team (League)	Pos.	G	AB	R	H	2B	3B	HR	RBI	Avg.	BB	SO	SB	PO	A	E	Avg.
1995—	Cleveland (A.L.)..........	PR-OF	3	1	0	1	0	0	0	0	1.000	0	0	0	0	0	0	...
1996—	Los Angeles (N.L.)	OF-PH	3	8	1	1	0	0	0	0	.125	2	1	0	4	0	0	1.000
Division series totals (2 years)			6	9	1	2	0	0	0	0	.222	2	1	0	4	0	0	1.000

CHAMPIONSHIP SERIES RECORD

							BATTING									FIELDING		
Year	Team (League)	Pos.	G	AB	R	H	2B	3B	HR	RBI	Avg.	BB	SO	SB	PO	A	E	Avg.
1995—	Cleveland (A.L.)..........	OF-PR	5	5	2	1	0	0	0	0	.200	0	0	1	3	0	0	1.000

WORLD SERIES RECORD

							BATTING									FIELDING		
Year	Team (League)	Pos.	G	AB	R	H	2B	3B	HR	RBI	Avg.	BB	SO	SB	PO	A	E	Avg.
1995—	Cleveland (A.L.)..........	PH-PR-OF	3	1	0	0	0	0	0	0	.000	0	1	0	1	0	0	1.000

PERSONAL: Born September 22, 1975, in Learington, Ont. ... 6-0/175. ... Bats right, throws right. ... Full name: Daniel Victor Klassen.

HIGH SCHOOL: John Carroll (Fort Pierce, Fla.).

TRANSACTIONS/CAREER NOTES: Selected by Milwaukee Brewers organization in second round of free-agent draft (June 3, 1993). ... On disabled list (April 7-June 23, 1995 and April 11-22, 1996). ... Selected by Arizona Diamondbacks in second round (37th pick overall) of expansion draft (November 18, 1997). ... On Tucson disabled list (August 13-September 8, 1998).

STATISTICAL NOTES: Tied for Arizona League lead in intentional bases on balls received with three in 1994.

							BATTING									FIELDING		
Year	Team (League)	Pos.	G	AB	R	H	2B	3B	HR	RBI	Avg.	BB	SO	SB	PO	A	E	Avg.
1993—	Ariz. Brewers (Ariz.) ...	SS	38	117	26	26	5	0	2	20	.222	24	28	14	45	97	12	.922
	— Helena (Pioneer)	SS	18	45	8	9	1	0	0	3	.200	7	11	2	25	42	7	.905
1994—	Beloit (Midwest)	SS	133	458	61	119	20	3	6	54	.260	58	123	28	177	328	40	.927
1995—	Beloit (Midwest)	SS-3B	59	218	27	60	15	2	2	25	.275	16	43	12	73	133	18	.920
1996—	Stockton (California) ..	SS	118	432	58	116	22	4	2	46	.269	34	77	14	186	373	*33	.944
1997—	El Paso (Texas)	SS	135	519	112	172	30	6	14	81	.331	48	104	16	177	399	*50	.920
1998—	Tucson (PCL)■	SS-2B	73	281	47	82	25	2	10	47	.292	19	54	6	128	202	8	.976
	— Arizona (N.L.).............	2B	29	108	12	21	2	1	3	8	.194	9	33	1	60	74	5	.964
Major league totals (1 year)			29	108	12	21	2	1	3	8	.194	9	33	1	60	74	5	.964

PERSONAL: Born June 12, 1971, in Westminster, Calif. ... 6-3/220. ... Bats left, throws left. ... Full name: Ryan Anthony Klesko.
HIGH SCHOOL: Westminster (Calif.).
TRANSACTIONS/CAREER NOTES: Selected by Atlanta Braves organization in fifth round of free-agent draft (June 5, 1989). ... On Atlanta disabled list (May 3-18, 1995); included rehabilitation assignment to Greenville (May 13-17).
HONORS: Named Southern League Most Valuable Player (1991).
STATISTICAL NOTES: Career major league grand slams: 6.

Year	Team (League)	Pos.	G	AB	R	H	2B	3B	HR	RBI	Avg.	BB	SO	SB	PO	A	E	Avg.
1989—	GC Braves (GCL)	DH	17	57	14	23	5	4	1	16	.404	6	6	4	...	...	...	...
	—Sumter (S. Atl.)	1B	25	90	17	26	6	0	1	12	.289	11	14	1	173	11	4	.979
1990—	Sumter (S. Atl.)	1B	63	231	41	85	15	1	10	38	.368	31	30	13	575	43	14	.978
	—Durham (Carolina)	1B	77	292	40	80	16	1	7	47	.274	32	53	10	490	34	13	.976
1991—	Greenville (Southern)	1B	126	419	64	122	22	3	14	67	.291	75	60	14	1043	57	*17	.985
1992—	Richmond (Int'l)	1B	123	418	63	105	22	2	17	59	.251	41	72	3	947	51	*11	.989
	—Atlanta (N.L.)	1B	13	14	0	0	0	0	0	1	.000	0	5	0	25	0	0	1.000
1993—	Richmond (Int'l)	1B-OF	98	343	59	94	14	2	22	74	.274	47	69	4	587	45	12	.981
	—Atlanta (N.L.)	1B-OF	22	17	3	6	1	0	2	5	.353	3	4	0	8	0	0	1.000
1994—	Atlanta (N.L.)	OF-1B	92	245	42	68	13	3	17	47	.278	26	48	1	89	3	7	.929
1995—	Atlanta (N.L.)	OF-1B	107	329	48	102	25	2	23	70	.310	47	72	5	131	4	8	.944
	—Greenville (Southern)	OF	4	13	1	3	0	0	1	4	.231	2	1	0	2	0	0	1.000
1996—	Atlanta (N.L.)	OF-1B	153	528	90	149	21	4	34	93	.282	68	129	6	204	8	5	.977
1997—	Atlanta (N.L.)	OF-1B	143	467	67	122	23	6	24	84	.261	48	130	4	245	6	6	.977
1998—	Atlanta (N.L.)	OF-1B	129	427	69	117	29	1	18	70	.274	56	66	5	195	13	2	.990
Major league totals (7 years)			659	2027	319	564	112	16	118	370	.278	248	454	21	897	34	28	.971

DIVISION SERIES RECORD

RECORDS: Shares career record for most grand slams—1 (September 30, 1998). ... Shares single-inning record for most runs batted in—4 (September 30, 1998). ... Holds N.L. career record for most strikeouts—12. ... Shares N.L. career record for most games—13.

Year	Team (League)	Pos.	G	AB	R	H	2B	3B	HR	RBI	Avg.	BB	SO	SB	PO	A	E	Avg.
1995—	Atlanta (N.L.)	OF	4	15	5	7	1	0	1	1	.467	0	3	0	3	0	0	1.000
1996—	Atlanta (N.L.)	OF	3	8	1	1	0	0	1	1	.125	3	4	1	2	0	1	.667
1997—	Atlanta (N.L.)	OF	3	8	2	2	1	0	1	1	.250	0	2	0	3	0	1	.750
1998—	Atlanta (N.L.)	OF	3	11	1	3	0	0	1	4	.273	0	3	0	5	0	0	1.000
Division series totals (4 years)			13	42	9	13	2	0	3	7	.310	3	12	1	13	0	2	.867

CHAMPIONSHIP SERIES RECORD

Year	Team (League)	Pos.	G	AB	R	H	2B	3B	HR	RBI	Avg.	BB	SO	SB	PO	A	E	Avg.
1995—	Atlanta (N.L.)	OF-PH	4	7	0	0	0	0	0	0	.000	3	4	0	1	0	0	1.000
1996—	Atlanta (N.L.)	OF	6	16	1	4	0	0	1	3	.250	2	6	0	13	0	0	1.000
1997—	Atlanta (N.L.)	OF	5	17	2	4	0	0	2	4	.235	2	3	0	5	0	0	1.000
1998—	Atlanta (N.L.)	OF-PH	5	12	2	1	0	0	0	1	.083	6	3	0	3	0	1	.750
Championship series totals (4 years)			20	52	5	9	0	0	3	8	.173	13	16	0	22	0	1	.957

WORLD SERIES RECORD

NOTES: Member of World Series championship team (1995).

Year	Team (League)	Pos.	G	AB	R	H	2B	3B	HR	RBI	Avg.	BB	SO	SB	PO	A	E	Avg.
1995—	Atlanta (N.L.)	OF-DH	6	16	4	5	0	0	3	4	.313	3	4	0	1	0	1	1.000
1996—	Atlanta (N.L.)	DH-O-1-PH	5	10	2	1	0	0	0	1	.100	3	4	0	1	0	1	.500
World Series totals (2 years)			11	26	6	6	0	0	3	5	.231	6	8	0	2	0	1	.667

PERSONAL: Born August 22, 1972, in Sunbury, Pa. ... 6-2/210. ... Throws left, bats both. ... Full name: Steven James Kline.
HIGH SCHOOL: Lewisburg (Pa.).
COLLEGE: West Virginia.
TRANSACTIONS/CAREER NOTES: Selected by Cleveland Indians organization in eighth round of free-agent draft (June 3, 1993). ... On disabled list (May 23-August 5, 1995). ... On temporarily inactive list (April 5-20, 1996). ... Traded by Indians to Montreal Expos for P Jeff Juden (July 31, 1997).

Year	Team (League)	W	L	Pct.	ERA	G	GS	CG	ShO	Sv.	IP	H	R	ER	BB	SO
1993—	Burlington (Appalachian)	1	1	.500	4.91	2	1	0	0	0	7 1/3	11	4	4	2	4
	—Watertown (NYP)	5	4	.556	3.19	13	13	2	1	0	79	77	36	28	12	45
1994—	Columbus (S. Atl.)	*18	5	.783	3.01	28	•28	2	1	0	*185 2/3	175	67	62	36	*174
1995—	Cant./Akr. (Eastern)	2	3	.400	2.42	14	14	0	0	0	89 1/3	86	34	24	30	45
1996—	Cant./Akr. (Eastern)	8	12	.400	5.46	25	24	0	0	0	146 2/3	168	98	89	55	107
1997—	Cleveland (A.L.)	3	1	.750	5.81	20	1	0	0	0	26 1/3	42	19	17	13	17
	—Buffalo (A.A.)	3	3	.500	4.03	20	4	0	0	1	51 1/3	53	26	23	13	41
	—Montreal (N.L.)■	1	3	.250	6.15	26	0	0	0	0	26 1/3	31	18	18	10	20
1998—	Ottawa (Int'l)	0	0	. . .	0.00	2	0	0	0	0	2 2/3	1	0	0	0	1
	—Montreal (N.L.)	3	6	.333	2.76	78	0	0	0	1	71 2/3	62	25	22	41	76
A.L. totals (1 year)		3	1	.750	5.81	20	1	0	0	0	26 1/3	42	19	17	13	17
N.L. totals (2 years)		4	9	.308	3.67	104	0	0	0	1	98	93	43	40	51	96
Major league totals (2 years)		7	10	.412	4.13	124	1	0	0	1	124 1/3	135	62	57	64	113

K

KLINGENBECK, SCOTT   P

PERSONAL: Born February 3, 1971, in Cincinnati. ... 6-2/205. ... Throws right, bats right. ... Full name: Scott Edward Klingenbeck.
HIGH SCHOOL: Oak Hills (Cincinnati).
COLLEGE: Ohio State.
TRANSACTIONS/CAREER NOTES: Selected by Detroit Tigers organization in 57th round of free-agent draft (June 5, 1989); did not sign. ... Selected by Baltimore Orioles organization in fifth round of free-agent draft (June 1, 1992). ... On Bowie disabled list (July 11-30, 1994). ... Traded by Orioles with a player to be named later to Minnesota Twins for P Scott Erickson (July 7, 1995); Twins acquired OF Kimera Bartee to complete deal (September 18, 1995). ... Traded by Twins to Cincinnati Reds organization for future considerations (April 8, 1997). ... Released by Reds (September 9, 1997). ... Signed by Texas Rangers organization (November 22, 1997). ... Released by Rangers organization (March 12, 1998). ... Signed by Reds organization (March 13, 1998). ... Released by Reds (July 2, 1998). ... Signed by Pittsburgh Pirates organization (July 14, 1998). ... Granted free agency (October 15, 1998).
STATISTICAL NOTES: Led American Association with 23 home runs allowed in 1997.

Year — Team (League)	W	L	Pct.	ERA	G	GS	CG	ShO	Sv.	IP	H	R	ER	BB	SO
1992— Kane County (Midwest)......	3	4	.429	2.63	11	11	0	0	0	68 1/3	50	31	20	28	64
1993— Frederick (Carolina)...........	13	4	*.765	2.98	23	23	0	0	0	139	151	62	46	35	146
1994— Bowie (Eastern).................	7	5	.583	3.63	25	25	3	0	0	143 2/3	151	76	58	37	120
— Baltimore (A.L.).................	1	0	1.000	3.86	1	1	0	0	0	7	6	4	3	4	5
1995— Rochester (Int'l)...............	3	1	.750	2.72	8	7	0	0	0	43	46	14	13	10	29
— Baltimore (A.L.).................	2	2	.500	4.88	6	5	0	0	0	31 1/3	32	17	17	18	15
— Minnesota (A.L.)■..............	0	2	.000	8.57	18	4	0	0	0	48 1/3	69	48	46	24	27
1996— Salt Lake (PCL).................	9	3	.750	3.11	22	22	5	•2	0	150 2/3	159	64	52	41	100
— Minnesota (A.L.)	1	1	.500	7.85	10	3	0	0	0	28 2/3	42	28	25	10	15
1997— Salt Lake (PCL)	0	0	...	1.29	1	1	0	0	0	7	6	1	1	0	6
— Indianapolis (A.A.)■...........	12	8	.600	3.96	27	27	2	0	0	170 2/3	180	85	75	41	119
1998— Indianapolis (Int'l).............	6	2	.750	2.86	10	10	0	0	0	63	57	26	20	10	50
— Cincinnati (N.L.)...............	1	3	.250	5.96	4	4	0	0	0	22 2/3	26	17	15	7	13
— Nashville (PCL)■...............	2	2	.500	6.14	6	6	0	0	0	29 1/3	45	24	20	7	15
A.L. totals (3 years)	4	5	.444	7.10	35	13	0	0	0	115 1/3	149	97	91	56	62
N.L. totals (1 year).....................	1	3	.250	5.96	4	4	0	0	0	22 2/3	26	17	15	7	13
Major league totals (4 years)......	5	8	.385	6.91	39	17	0	0	0	138	175	114	106	63	75

KNIGHT, BRANDON   P   RANGERS

PERSONAL: Born October 1, 1975, in Oxnard, Calif. ... 6-0/170. ... Throws right, bats left. ... Full name: Brandon Michael Knight.
HIGH SCHOOL: Buena (Ventura, Calif.).
JUNIOR COLLEGE: Ventura (Calif.) College.
TRANSACTIONS/CAREER NOTES: Selected by Texas Rangers organization in 14th round of free-agent draft (June 1, 1995).

Year — Team (League)	W	L	Pct.	ERA	G	GS	CG	ShO	Sv.	IP	H	R	ER	BB	SO
1995— GC Rangers (GCL)............	2	1	.667	5.25	3	2	0	0	0	12	12	7	7	6	11
— Charleston, S.C. (SAL).......	4	2	.667	3.13	9	9	0	0	0	54 2/3	37	22	19	21	52
1996— Charlotte (Fla. St.)............	4	10	.286	5.12	19	17	2	0	0	102	118	65	58	45	74
— Hudson Valley (NYP).........	2	2	.500	4.42	9	9	0	0	0	53	59	29	26	21	52
1997— Charlotte (Fla. St.)............	7	4	.636	2.23	14	12	3	1	0	92 2/3	82	33	23	22	91
1998— Tulsa (Texas)...................	6	4	.600	4.50	14	14	2	•1	0	90	83	52	45	35	84
— Tulsa (Texas)...................	6	6	.500	5.11	14	14	0	0	0	86 1/3	94	54	49	37	87
— Okla. City (PCL).................	0	7	.000	9.74	16	12	0	0	0	64 2/3	100	75	70	29	52

KNOBLAUCH, CHUCK   2B   YANKEES

PERSONAL: Born July 7, 1968, in Houston. ... 5-9/170. ... Bats right, throws right. ... Full name: Edward Charles Knoblauch. ... Son of Ray Knoblauch, minor league pitcher (1947-56); and nephew of Ed Knoblauch, minor league outfielder (1938-42 and 1947-55). ... Name pronounced NOB-lock.
HIGH SCHOOL: Bellaire (Houston).
COLLEGE: Texas A&M.
TRANSACTIONS/CAREER NOTES: Selected by Philadelphia Phillies organization in 18th round of free-agent draft (June 2, 1986); did not sign. ... Selected by Minnesota Twins organization in first round (25th pick overall) of free-agent draft (June 5, 1989). ... Traded by Twins to New York Yankees for P Eric Milton, P Danny Mota, OF Brian Buchanan, SS Cristian Guzman and cash (February 6, 1998).
HONORS: Named A.L. Rookie Player of the Year by THE SPORTING NEWS (1991). ... Named A.L. Rookie of the Year by Baseball Writers' Association of America (1991). ... Named second baseman on THE SPORTING NEWS A.L. All-Star team (1994 and 1997). ... Named second baseman on THE SPORTING NEWS A.L. Silver Slugger team (1995 and 1997). ... Won A.L. Gold Glove at second base (1997).
STATISTICAL NOTES: Had 20-game hitting streak (September 2-25, 1991). ... Led A.L. second basemen with 424 assists, 101 double plays and 718 total chances in 1997. ... Led A.L. in being hit by pitch with 18 in 1998. ... Career major league grand slams: 2.
MISCELLANEOUS: Holds Minnesota Twins all-time record for most stolen bases (276).

Year — Team (League)	Pos.	G	AB	R	H	2B	3B	HR	RBI	Avg.	BB	SO	SB	PO	A	E	Avg.
1989— Kenosha (Midwest)	SS	51	196	29	56	13	1	2	19	.286	32	23	9	60	124	21	.898
— Visalia (California)......	SS	18	77	20	28	10	0	0	21	.364	6	11	4	23	52	10	.882
1990— Orlando (South.)	2B	118	432	74	125	23	6	2	53	.289	63	31	23	275	300	20	.966
1991— Minnesota (A.L.)	2B	151	565	78	159	24	6	1	50	.281	59	40	25	249	460	18	.975
1992— Minnesota (A.L.)	2B-DH-SS	155	600	104	178	19	6	2	56	.297	88	60	34	306	415	6	.992
1993— Minnesota (A.L.)	2B-SS-OF	153	602	82	167	27	4	2	41	.277	65	44	29	302	431	9	.988
1994— Minnesota (A.L.)	2B-SS	109	445	85	139	*45	3	5	51	.312	41	56	35	191	285	3	.994
1995— Minnesota (A.L.)	2B-SS	136	538	107	179	34	8	11	63	.333	78	95	46	254	400	10	.985
1996— Minnesota (A.L.)	2B-DH	153	578	140	197	35	*14	13	72	.341	98	74	45	271	390	8	*.988
1997— Minnesota (A.L.)	2B-DH-SS	156	611	117	178	26	10	9	58	.291	84	84	62	285	†428	12	.983
1998— New York (A.L.)■.......	2B-DH	150	603	117	160	25	4	17	64	.265	76	70	31	275	408	13	.981
Major league totals (8 years)		1163	4542	830	1357	235	55	60	455	.299	589	523	307	2133	3217	79	.985

DIVISION SERIES RECORD

Year	Team (League)	Pos.	G	AB	R	H	2B	3B	HR	RBI	Avg.	BB	SO	SB	PO	A	E	Avg.
									BATTING								FIELDING	
1998— New York (A.L.)..........		2B	3	11	0	1	0	0	0	0	.091	0	4	0	4	10	1	.933

CHAMPIONSHIP SERIES RECORD

Year	Team (League)	Pos.	G	AB	R	H	2B	3B	HR	RBI	Avg.	BB	SO	SB	PO	A	E	Avg.
									BATTING								FIELDING	
1991— Minnesota (A.L.)		2B	5	20	5	7	2	0	0	3	.350	3	3	2	8	14	0	1.000
1998— New York (A.L.)..........		2B	6	25	4	5	1	0	0	0	.200	4	2	0	9	17	0	1.000
Championship series totals (2 years)			11	45	9	12	3	0	0	3	.267	7	5	2	17	31	0	1.000

WORLD SERIES RECORD

NOTES: Member of World Series championship team (1991 and 1998).

Year	Team (League)	Pos.	G	AB	R	H	2B	3B	HR	RBI	Avg.	BB	SO	SB	PO	A	E	Avg.
									BATTING								FIELDING	
1991— Minnesota (A.L.)		2B	7	26	3	8	1	0	0	2	.308	4	2	4	15	14	1	.967
1998— New York (A.L.)..........		2B	4	16	3	6	0	0	1	3	.375	3	2	1	7	10	1	.944
World Series totals (2 years)			11	42	6	14	1	0	1	5	.333	7	4	5	22	24	2	.958

ALL-STAR GAME RECORD

Year	League	Pos.	AB	R	H	2B	3B	HR	RBI	Avg.	BB	SO	SB	PO	A	E	Avg.
									BATTING							FIELDING	
1992— American		PH-2B	1	0	0	0	0	0	0	.000	1	0	0	0	0	0	. . .
1994— American		2B	3	1	0	0	0	0	0	.000	0	2	0	1	2	0	1.000
1996— American		2B	1	0	1	0	0	0	0	1.000	0	0	0	3	1	0	1.000
1997— American		2B	0	0	0	0	0	0	0	. . .	0	0	0	1	1	0	1.000
All-Star Game totals (4 years)			5	1	1	0	0	0	0	.200	1	2	0	5	4	0	1.000

KNORR, RANDY   C   ASTROS

PERSONAL: Born November 12, 1968, in San Gabriel, Calif. ... 6-2/215. ... Bats right, throws right. ... Full name: Randy Duane Knorr. ... Name pronounced NOR.

HIGH SCHOOL: Baldwin Park (Calif.).

TRANSACTIONS/CAREER NOTES: Selected by Toronto Blue Jays organization in 10th round of free-agent draft (June 2, 1986). ... On disabled list (June 24-July 4, 1986 and May 10, 1989-remainder of season). ... On Syracuse disabled list (May 11-23, 1992). ... On Toronto disabled list (August 20-September 30, 1992). ... On Toronto disabled list (July 1-August 11, 1995); included rehabilitation assignment to Syracuse (July 21-August 9). ... Traded by Blue Jays to Houston Astros for cash (May 17, 1996). ... Granted free agency (December 20, 1996). ... Re-signed by Astros organization (December 23, 1996). ... On Houston disabled list (August 29-September 6, 1997); included rehabilitation assignment to New Orleans (August 29-September 6). ... Granted free agency (October 14, 1997). ... Signed by Florida Marlins organization (December 22, 1997). ... On Charlotte disabled list (April 24-May 22, 1998). ... Granted free agency (September 29, 1998). ... Signed by Astros organization (January 21, 1999).

STATISTICAL NOTES: Led South Atlantic League catchers with 960 total chances and 25 passed balls in 1988.

Year	Team (League)	Pos.	G	AB	R	H	2B	3B	HR	RBI	Avg.	BB	SO	SB	PO	A	E	Avg.
									BATTING								FIELDING	
1986— Medicine Hat (Pio.)		1B	55	215	21	58	13	0	4	52	.270	17	53	0	451	29	10	.980
1987— Myrtle Beach (SAL)		C-1B-2B	46	129	17	34	4	0	6	21	.264	6	46	0	95	7	1	.990
— Medicine Hat (Pio.)		C	26	106	21	31	7	0	10	24	.292	5	26	0	70	5	4	.949
1988— Myrtle Beach (SAL)		C	117	364	43	85	13	0	9	42	.234	41	91	0	*870	75	15	.984
1989— Dunedin (Fla. St.)		C	33	122	13	32	6	0	6	23	.262	6	21	0	186	20	2	.990
1990— Knoxville (Southern) ..		C	116	392	51	108	12	1	13	64	.276	31	83	0	599	72	15	.978
1991— Knoxville (Southern) ..		C-1B	24	74	7	13	4	0	0	4	.176	10	18	2	136	16	2	.987
— Syracuse (Int'l)..........		C	91	342	29	89	20	0	5	44	.260	23	58	1	477	49	7	.987
— Toronto (A.L.)............		C	3	1	0	0	0	0	0	0	.000	1	1	0	6	1	0	1.000
1992— Syracuse (Int'l)..........		C	61	228	27	62	13	1	11	27	.272	17	38	1	220	22	3	.988
— Toronto (A.L.)............		C	8	19	1	5	0	0	1	2	.263	1	5	0	33	3	0	1.000
1993— Toronto (A.L.)............		C	39	101	11	25	3	2	4	20	.248	9	29	0	168	20	0	1.000
1994— Toronto (A.L.)............		C	40	124	20	30	2	0	7	19	.242	10	35	0	247	21	2	.993
1995— Toronto (A.L.)............		C	45	132	18	28	8	0	3	16	.212	11	28	0	243	22	8	.971
— Syracuse (Int'l)..........		C	18	67	6	18	5	1	1	6	.269	5	14	0	129	14	3	.979
1996— Syracuse (Int'l)..........		C	12	36	1	10	5	0	0	5	.278	5	8	0	53	2	0	1.000
— Houston (N.L.)■		C	37	87	7	17	5	0	1	7	.195	5	18	0	204	14	0	1.000
1997— New Orleans (A.A.).....		C	72	244	22	58	10	0	5	27	.238	22	38	0	502	54	9	.984
— Houston (N.L.)		C-1B	4	8	1	3	0	0	1	1	.375	0	2	0	19	3	0	1.000
1998— Charlotte (Int'l)■........		C	68	201	30	66	15	0	7	39	.328	34	41	1	349	25	9	.977
— Florida (N.L.)		C	15	49	4	10	4	1	2	11	.204	1	10	0	82	7	1	.989
American League totals (5 years)			135	377	50	88	13	2	15	57	.233	32	98	0	697	67	10	.987
National League totals (3 years)			56	144	12	30	9	1	4	19	.208	6	30	0	305	24	1	.997
Major league totals (8 years)			191	521	62	118	22	3	19	76	.226	38	128	0	1002	91	11	.990

CHAMPIONSHIP SERIES RECORD

Year	Team (League)	Pos.	G	AB	R	H	2B	3B	HR	RBI	Avg.	BB	SO	SB	PO	A	E	Avg.
									BATTING								FIELDING	
1992— Toronto (A.L.)									Did not play.									
1993— Toronto (A.L.)									Did not play.									

WORLD SERIES RECORD

NOTES: Member of World Series championship team (1992 and 1993).

Year	Team (League)	Pos.	G	AB	R	H	2B	3B	HR	RBI	Avg.	BB	SO	SB	PO	A	E	Avg.
									BATTING								FIELDING	
1992— Toronto (A.L.)									Did not play.									
1993— Toronto (A.L.).............		C	1	0	0	0	0	0	0	0	. . .	0	0	0	3	0	0	1.000

KOLB, DANNY   P   RANGERS

PERSONAL: Born March 29, 1975, in Sterling, Ill. ... 6-4/185. ... Throws right, bats right. ... Full name: Daniel Lee Kolb. ... Cousin of Gary Kolb, outfielder with four major league teams (1960-69).
HIGH SCHOOL: Walnut (Ill.).
JUNIOR COLLEGE: Sauk Valley Community College (Ill.).
TRANSACTIONS/CAREER NOTES: Selected by Minnesota Twins organization in 17th round of free-agent draft (June 3, 1993); did not sign. ... Selected by Texas Rangers organization in sixth round of free-agent draft (June 3, 1995).
STATISTICAL NOTES: Pitched six-inning, 3-0 no-hit victory against Columbus (June 12, 1996). ... Tied for Appalachian League lead with 22 hit batsmen in 1996.

Year	Team (League)	W	L	Pct.	ERA	G	GS	CG	ShO	Sv.	IP	H	R	ER	BB	SO
1995—	GC Twins (GCL)	1	7	.125	2.21	12	11	0	0	0	53	38	22	13	28	46
1996—	Charleston, S.C. (S. Atl.)	8	6	.571	2.57	20	20	4	2	0	126	80	50	36	60	127
—	Charlotte (Fla. St.)	2	2	.500	4.26	6	6	0	0	0	38	38	18	18	14	28
—	Tulsa (Texas)	1	0	1.000	0.77	2	2	0	0	0	11 2/3	5	1	1	8	7
1997—	Charlotte (Fla. St.)	4	10	.286	4.87	24	23	3	0	0	133	146	91	72	62	83
—	Tulsa (Texas)	0	2	.000	4.76	2	2	0	0	0	11 1/3	7	7	6	11	6
1998—	Tulsa (Texas)	12	11	.522	4.82	28	28	2	0	0	162 1/3	187	104	87	76	83
—	Oklahoma (Pacific Coast)	0	0	. . .	0.00	1	0	0	0	0	1	1	0	0	1	0

K

KONERKO, PAUL   1B/3B   WHITE SOX

PERSONAL: Born March 5, 1976, in Providence, R.I. ... 6-3/211. ... Bats right, throws right. ... Full name: Paul Henry Konerko.
HIGH SCHOOL: Chaparral (Scottsdale, Ariz.).
TRANSACTIONS/CAREER NOTES: Selected by Los Angeles Dodgers organization in first round (13th pick overall) of free-agent draft (June 2, 1994). ... Traded by Dodgers with P Dennis Reyes to Cincinnati Reds for P Jeff Shaw (July 4, 1998). ... Traded by Reds to Chicago White Sox for OF Mike Cameron (November 11, 1998).
HONORS: Named Pacific Coast League Most Valuable Player (1997).
STATISTICAL NOTES: Led Northwest League with seven sacrifice flies in 1994. ... Led Pacific Coast League with 300 total bases and .621 slugging percentage in 1997.

Year	Team (League)	Pos.	G	AB	R	H	2B	3B	HR	RBI	Avg.	BB	SO	SB	PO	A	E	Avg.
1994—	Yakima (N'west)	C	67	257	25	74	15	2	6	*58	.288	36	52	1	271	33	5	.984
1995—	San Bern. (Calif.)	C	118	448	7	124	21	1	19	77	.277	59	88	3	676	68	11	.985
1996—	San Antonio (Tex.)	1B	133	470	78	141	23	2	29	86	.300	72	85	1	1114	92	14	.989
—	Albuquerque (PCL)	1B	4	14	2	6	0	0	1	2	.429	1	2	0	30	0	0	1.000
1997—	Albuquerque (PCL)	3B-1B-2B	130	483	97	156	31	1	*37	*127	.323	64	61	2	257	216	24	.952
—	Los Angeles (N.L.)	1B-3B	6	7	0	1	0	0	0	0	.143	1	2	0	3	0	0	1.000
1998—	Los Angeles (N.L.)	1-3-0-DH	49	144	14	31	1	0	4	16	.215	10	30	0	187	30	2	.991
—	Albuquerque (PCL)	OF-1B-3B	24	87	16	33	10	0	6	36	.379	11	12	0	61	3	3	.955
—	Cincinnati (N.L.)■	3B-1B-OF	26	73	7	16	3	0	3	13	.219	6	10	0	48	24	0	1.000
—	Indianapolis (Int'l)	3B	39	150	25	49	8	0	8	39	.327	19	18	1	21	68	4	.957
Major league totals (2 years)			81	224	21	48	4	0	7	29	.214	17	42	0	238	54	2	.993

KOSKIE, COREY   3B   TWINS

PERSONAL: Born June 28, 1973, in Anola, Man. ... 6-3/217. ... Bats left, throws right. ... Full name: Cordel Leonard Koskie.
HIGH SCHOOL: Springfield Collegiate (Oakbank, Man.).
JUNIOR COLLEGE: Des Moines (Iowa) Area Community College.
COLLEGE: Manitoba, then Kwantlen (B.C.).
TRANSACTIONS/CAREER NOTES: Selected by Minnesota Twins organization in 26th round of free-agent draft (June 2, 1994). ... On Fort Myers disabled list (May 10-28 and June 25-July 4, 1996).
STATISTICAL NOTES: Tied for Eastern League lead with 10 intentional bases on balls in 1997.

Year	Team (League)	Pos.	G	AB	R	H	2B	3B	HR	RBI	Avg.	BB	SO	SB	PO	A	E	Avg.
1994—	Elizabethton (App.)	3B	34	107	13	25	2	1	3	10	.234	18	27	0	23	84	8	.930
1995—	Fort Wayne (Midw.)	3B	123	462	64	143	37	5	16	78	.310	38	79	2	80	244	36	.900
1996—	Fort Myers (FSL)	3B	95	338	43	88	19	4	9	55	.260	40	76	1	62	176	19	.926
1997—	New Britain (East.)	3B	131	437	88	125	26	6	23	79	.286	90	106	9	72	234	22	.933
1998—	Salt Lake (PCL)	3B	135	505	91	152	32	5	26	105	.301	51	104	15	83	250	23	.935
—	Minnesota (A.L.)	3B	11	29	2	4	0	0	1	2	.138	2	10	0	6	10	1	.941
Major league totals (1 year)			11	29	2	4	0	0	1	2	.138	2	10	0	6	10	1	.941

KOTSAY, MARK   OF   MARLINS

PERSONAL: Born December 2, 1975, in Whittier, Calif. ... 6-0/190. ... Bats left, throws left. ... Full name: Mark Steven Kotsay.
HIGH SCHOOL: Santa Fe Springs (Calif.).
COLLEGE: Cal State Fullerton.
TRANSACTIONS/CAREER NOTES: Selected by Florida Marlins organization in first round (ninth pick overall) of free-agent draft (June 4, 1996).
HONORS: Named Golden Spikes Award winner by USA Baseball (1995). ... Named Most Outstanding Player of College World Series (1995).
STATISTICAL NOTES: Tied for Eastern League lead in double plays by outfielder with four in 1997. ... Tied for N.L. lead with 20 assists by outfielder in 1998.
MISCELLANEOUS: Member of 1996 U.S. Olympic baseball team.

Year	Team (League)	Pos.	G	AB	R	H	2B	3B	HR	RBI	Avg.	BB	SO	SB	PO	A	E	Avg.
1996—Kane County (Midw.)..		OF	17	60	16	17	5	0	2	8	.283	16	8	3	37	2	0	1.000
1997—Portland (Eastern)......		OF	114	438	*103	134	27	2	20	77	.306	75	65	17	230	12	2	*.992
—Florida (N.L.).............		OF	14	52	5	10	1	1	0	4	.192	4	7	3	31	2	0	1.000
1998—Florida (N.L.)		OF-1B	154	578	72	161	25	7	11	68	.279	34	61	10	350	‡21	6	.984
Major league totals (2 years)			168	630	77	171	26	8	11	72	.271	38	68	13	381	23	6	.985

KRAUSE, SCOTT   OF   BREWERS

PERSONAL: Born August 16, 1973, in Euclid, Ohio. ... 6-1/187. ... Bats right, throws right. ... Full name: Scott Raymond Krause.
HIGH SCHOOL: North (Eastlake, Ohio).
COLLEGE: New Orleans.
TRANSACTIONS/CAREER NOTES: Selected by Milwaukee Brewers organization in 10th round of free-agent draft (June 2, 1994).
STATISTICAL NOTES: Led Midwest League outfielders with .985 fielding percentage and tied for for lead in double plays with three in 1995. ... Tied for International League lead in being hit by pitch with 15 in 1998.

Year	Team (League)	Pos.	G	AB	R	H	2B	3B	HR	RBI	Avg.	BB	SO	SB	PO	A	E	Avg.
1994—Helena (Pioneer)		OF	63	252	51	90	18	3	4	52	.357	18	49	13	77	6	4	.954
1995—Beloit (Midwest).........		OF-2B-1B	134	481	83	119	30	4	13	76	.247	50	126	24	179	14	3	†.985
1996—Stockton (California) ..		OF-1B	108	427	82	128	22	4	19	83	.300	32	101	25	209	12	5	.978
—El Paso (Texas)...........		OF	24	85	16	27	5	2	3	11	.318	2	19	2	36	4	0	1.000
1997—El Paso (Texas)...........		OF-1B	125	474	97	171	33	11	16	88	.361	20	108	13	196	13	7	.968
1998—Louisville (Int'l)		OF	117	390	71	114	25	2	26	82	.292	46	104	11	151	4	6	.963

KREUTER, CHAD   C   ROYALS

PERSONAL: Born August 26, 1964, in Greenbrae, Calif. ... 6-2/200. ... Bats both, throws right. ... Full name: Chad Michael Kreuter. ... Name pronounced CREW-ter.
HIGH SCHOOL: Redwood (Calif.).
COLLEGE: Pepperdine.
TRANSACTIONS/CAREER NOTES: Selected by Texas Rangers organization in fifth round of free-agent draft (June 3, 1985). ... Granted free agency (October 15, 1991). ... Signed by Toledo, Detroit Tigers organization (January 2, 1992). ... Granted free agency (December 23, 1994). ... Signed by Seattle Mariners (April 8, 1995). ... On Seattle disabled list (June 19-July 6, 1995). ... On Tacoma disabled list (August 4-25, 1995). ... Granted free agency (October 16, 1995). ... Signed by Chicago White Sox organization (December 11, 1995). ... On disabled list (July 20, 1996-remainder of season). ... Granted free agency (October 14, 1996). ... Re-signed by White Sox organization (January 29, 1997). ... Traded by White Sox with OF Tony Phillips to Anaheim Angels for P Chuck McElroy and C Jorge Fabregas (May 18, 1997). ... Granted free agency (November 7, 1997). ... Signed by White Sox (December 10, 1997). ... Traded by White Sox to Angels for cash considerations (September 18, 1998). ... Granted free agency (October 26, 1998). ... Signed by Kansas City Royals (December 15, 1998).
RECORDS: Shares major league single-game record for most sacrifice flies—3 (July 30, 1994). ... Shares major league record for most hits in one inning in first major league game—2 (September 14, 1988, fifth inning).
STATISTICAL NOTES: Led Carolina League catchers with 21 errors and 17 double plays and tied for lead with 113 assists in 1986. ... Tied for Texas League lead in double plays by catcher with nine in 1988. ... Led A.L. with 21 passed balls in 1989. ... Switch-hit home runs in one game (September 7, 1993). ... Career major league grand slams: 1.
MISCELLANEOUS: Batted righthanded only (1985 and 1990).

Year	Team (League)	Pos.	G	AB	R	H	2B	3B	HR	RBI	Avg.	BB	SO	SB	PO	A	E	Avg.
1985—Burlington (Midw.)		C	69	199	25	53	9	0	4	26	.266	38	48	3	349	34	8	.980
1986—Salem (Carolina)		C-OF-3B	125	387	55	85	21	2	6	49	.220	67	82	5	613	†115	‡21	.972
1987—Charlotte (Fla. St.)......		C-OF-3B	85	281	36	61	18	1	9	40	.217	31	32	1	380	54	8	.982
1988—Tulsa (Texas)		C	108	358	46	95	24	6	3	51	.265	55	66	2	603	71	•13	.981
—Texas (A.L.)		C	16	51	3	14	2	1	1	5	.275	7	13	0	93	8	1	.990
1989—Texas (A.L.)		C	87	158	16	24	3	0	5	9	.152	27	40	0	453	26	4	.992
—Okla. City (A.A.).........		C	26	87	10	22	3	0	0	6	.253	13	11	1	146	14	2	.988
1990—Texas (A.L.)		C	22	22	2	1	1	0	0	2	.045	8	9	0	39	4	1	.977
—Okla. City (A.A.).........		C	92	291	41	65	17	1	7	35	.223	52	80	1	559	64	10	.984
1991—Texas (A.L.)		C	3	4	0	0	0	0	0	0	.000	0	1	0	5	0	0	1.000
—Okla. City (A.A.).........		C	24	70	14	19	6	0	1	12	.271	18	16	2	146	23	7	.960
—Tulsa (Texas)		C	42	128	23	30	5	1	2	10	.234	29	23	1	269	27	4	.987
1992—Detroit (A.L.)■		C-DH	67	190	22	48	9	0	2	16	.253	20	38	0	271	22	5	.983
1993—Detroit (A.L.)		C-DH-1B	119	374	59	107	23	3	15	51	.286	49	92	2	522	70	7	.988
1994—Detroit (A.L.)		C-1B-OF	65	170	17	38	8	0	1	19	.224	28	36	0	280	22	4	.987
1995—Seattle (A.L.)■		C	26	75	12	17	5	0	1	8	.227	5	22	0	151	12	4	.976
—Tacoma (PCL)		C	15	48	6	14	5	0	1	11	.292	8	11	0	70	10	1	.988
1996—Chicago (A.L.)■........		C-1B-DH	46	114	14	25	8	0	3	18	.219	13	29	0	182	12	2	.990
1997—Chicago (A.L.)■		C-1B	19	37	6	8	2	1	1	3	.216	8	9	0	59	4	2	.969
—Anaheim (A.L.)■		C-DH	70	218	19	51	7	1	4	18	.234	21	57	0	431	29	3	.994
1998—Chicago (A.L.)■........		C	93	245	26	62	9	1	2	33	.253	32	45	1	424	35	7	.985
—Anaheim (A.L.)■		C	3	7	1	1	1	0	0	0	.143	1	4	0	14	1	2	.882
Major league totals (11 years)			636	1665	197	396	78	7	35	182	.238	219	395	3	2924	245	42	.987

KRIVDA, RICK   P   ROYALS

PERSONAL: Born January 19, 1970, in McKeesport, Pa. ... 6-1/185. ... Throws left, bats right. ... Full name: Rick Michael Krivda.
HIGH SCHOOL: McKeesport (Pa.) Area.
COLLEGE: California (Pa.).

TRANSACTIONS/CAREER NOTES: Selected by Baltimore Orioles organization in 23rd round of free-agent draft (June 3, 1991). ... Claimed on waivers by Cleveland Indians (March 24, 1998). ... Traded by Indians to Cincinnati Reds for P Eddie Priest and OF Christian Rojas (June 16, 1998). ... Released by Reds (November 10, 1998). ... Signed by Kansas City Royals organization (December 17, 1998).

Year	Team (League)	W	L	Pct.	ERA	G	GS	CG	ShO	Sv.	IP	H	R	ER	BB	SO
1991—	Bluefield (Appalachian)	7	1	.875	1.88	15	8	0	0	1	67	48	20	14	24	79
1992—	Kane County (Midwest)	12	5	.706	3.03	18	18	2	0	0	121 2/3	108	53	41	41	124
—	Frederick (Carolina)	5	1	.833	2.98	9	9	1	1	0	57 1/3	51	23	19	15	64
1993—	Bowie (Eastern)	7	5	.583	3.08	22	22	0	0	0	125 2/3	114	46	43	50	108
—	Rochester (Int'l)	3	0	1.000	1.89	5	5	0	0	0	33 1/3	20	7	7	16	23
1994—	Rochester (Int'l)	9	10	.474	3.53	28	26	3	2	0	163	149	75	64	73	122
1995—	Rochester (Int'l)	6	5	.545	3.19	16	16	1	0	0	101 2/3	96	44	36	32	74
—	Baltimore (A.L.)	2	7	.222	4.54	13	13	1	0	0	75 1/3	76	40	38	25	53
1996—	Rochester (Int'l)	3	1	.750	4.30	8	8	0	0	0	44	51	24	21	15	34
—	Baltimore (A.L.)	3	5	.375	4.96	22	11	0	0	0	81 2/3	89	48	45	39	54
1997—	Rochester (Int'l)	14	2	.875	3.39	22	21	*6	*3	0	146	122	61	55	34	128
—	Baltimore (A.L.)	4	2	.667	6.30	10	10	0	0	0	50	67	36	35	18	29
1998—	Cleveland (A.L.)■	2	0	1.000	3.24	11	1	0	0	0	25	24	10	9	16	10
—	Cincinnati (N.L.)■	0	2	.000	11.28	16	1	0	0	0	26 1/3	41	34	33	19	19
A.L. totals (4 years)		11	14	.440	4.93	56	35	1	0	0	232	256	134	127	98	146
N.L. totals (1 year)		0	2	.000	11.28	16	1	0	0	0	26 1/3	41	34	33	19	19
Major league totals (4 years)		11	16	.407	5.57	72	36	1	0	0	258 1/3	297	168	160	117	165

KROON, MARC   P

K

PERSONAL: Born April 2, 1973, in Bronx, N.Y. ... 6-2/195. ... Throws right, bats right. ... Full name: Marc Jason Kroon.
HIGH SCHOOL: Shadow Mountain (Phoenix).
TRANSACTIONS/CAREER NOTES: Selected by New York Mets organization in supplemental round ("sandwich pick" between second and third round) of free-agent draft (June 3, 1991); pick received as part of compensation for Toronto Blue Jays signing Type C free-agent 1B/DH Pat Tabler. ... Traded by Mets organization to San Diego Padres organization (December 13, 1993), completing deal in which Mets traded OF Randy Curtis and a player to be named later to Padres for P Frank Seminara, OF Tracy Jones and SS Pablo Martinez (December 10, 1993). ... Traded by Padres to Cincinnati Reds for P Buddy Carlyle (April 8, 1998). ... On Cincinnati disabled list (May 7-June 12, 1998); included rehabilitation assignment to Indianapolis (May 11-June 4). ... On Indianapolis disabled list (July 20-August 10, 1998). ... Granted free agency (October 15, 1998).

Year	Team (League)	W	L	Pct.	ERA	G	GS	CG	ShO	Sv.	IP	H	R	ER	BB	SO
1991—	GC Mets (GCL)	2	3	.400	4.53	12	10	1	0	0	47 2/3	39	33	24	22	39
1992—	Kingsport (Appalachian)	3	5	.375	4.10	12	12	0	0	0	68	52	41	31	57	60
1993—	Capital City (S. Atl.)	2	11	.154	3.47	29	19	0	0	2	124 1/3	123	65	48	70	122
1994—	Rancho Cuca. (Cal.)■	11	6	.647	4.83	26	26	0	0	0	143 1/3	143	86	77	81	153
1995—	Memphis (Sou.)	7	5	.583	3.51	22	19	0	0	2	115 1/3	90	49	45	61	123
—	San Diego (N.L.)	0	1	.000	10.80	2	0	0	0	0	1 2/3	1	2	2	2	2
1996—	Memphis (Sou.)	2	4	.333	2.89	44	0	0	0	22	46 2/3	33	19	15	28	56
1997—	Las Vegas (PCL)■	1	3	.250	4.54	46	0	0	0	15	41 2/3	34	22	21	22	53
—	San Diego (N.L.)	0	1	.000	7.15	12	0	0	0	0	11 1/3	14	9	9	5	12
1998—	San Diego (N.L.)■	0	0	. . .	0.00	2	0	0	0	0	2 1/3	0	0	0	1	2
—	Cincinnati (N.L.)■	0	0	. . .	13.50	4	0	0	0	0	5 1/3	7	8	8	4	4
—	Indianapolis (Int'l)	3	2	.600	5.63	39	0	0	0	1	46 1/3	39	29	29	47	36
Major league totals (3 years)		0	2	.000	8.27	20	0	0	0	0	20 2/3	22	19	19	16	20

KUBENKA, JEFF   P   DODGERS

PERSONAL: Born August 24, 1974, in Weimer, Texas. ... 6-1/191. ... Throws left, bats right. ... Full name: Jeffrey S. Kubenka.
HIGH SCHOOL: Schulenburg (Texas).
COLLEGE: St. Mary's (Texas).
TRANSACTIONS/CAREER NOTES: Selected by Los Angeles Dodgers organization in 38th round of free-agent draft (June 4, 1996). ... On Albuquerque disabled list (May 6-July 9, 1998).

Year	Team (League)	W	L	Pct.	ERA	G	GS	CG	ShO	Sv.	IP	H	R	ER	BB	SO
1996—	Yakima (N'west)	5	1	.833	2.51	28	0	0	0	*14	32 1/3	20	11	9	10	61
1997—	San Bernardino (Calif.)	5	1	.833	0.92	34	0	0	0	19	39	24	4	4	11	62
—	San Antonio (Tex.)	3	0	1.000	0.70	19	0	0	0	4	25 2/3	10	2	2	6	38
—	Albuquerque (PCL)	0	2	.000	8.59	8	0	0	0	2	7 1/3	11	9	7	2	10
1998—	Albuquerque (PCL)	2	5	.286	2.45	28	0	0	0	9	40 1/3	32	11	11	12	40
—	San Antonio (Tex.)	0	0	. . .	7.00	9	0	0	0	0	9	10	11	7	7	10
—	Los Angeles (N.L.)	1	0	1.000	0.96	6	0	0	0	0	9 1/3	4	1	1	8	10
Major league totals (1 year)		1	0	1.000	0.96	6	0	0	0	0	9 1/3	4	1	1	8	10

KUSIEWICZ, MIKE   P   ROCKIES

PERSONAL: Born November 1, 1976, in Montreal. ... 6-2/190. ... Throws left, bats right. ... Full name: Michael Edward Kusiewicz.
HIGH SCHOOL: St. Pius X (Nepean, Ont.).
TRANSACTIONS/CAREER NOTES: Selected by Colorado Rockies organization in eighth round of free-agent draft (June 2, 1994).
STATISTICAL NOTES: Led Eastern League with 16 hit batsmen in 1998.

Year	Team (League)	W	L	Pct.	ERA	G	GS	CG	ShO	Sv.	IP	H	R	ER	BB	SO
1995—	Asheville (S. Atl.)	8	4	.667	*2.06	21	21	0	0	0	122 1/3	92	40	28	34	103
—	Salem (Carolina)	0	0	. . .	1.50	1	1	0	0	0	6	7	1	1	0	7
1996—	New Haven (East.)	2	4	.333	3.30	14	14	0	0	0	76 1/3	83	38	28	27	64
—	Salem (Carolina)	0	1	.000	5.09	5	3	0	0	1	23	19	15	13	12	18
1997—	New Haven (East.)	2	4	.333	6.35	10	4	0	0	0	28 1/3	41	28	20	10	11
—	Salem (Carolina)	8	6	.571	2.52	19	18	1	1	0	117 2/3	99	44	33	32	107
1998—	New Haven (East.)	14	7	.667	2.32	27	26	2	0	0	178 2/3	161	59	46	35	151

LAKER, TIM   C   DODGERS

PERSONAL: Born November 27, 1969, in Encino, Calif. ... 6-3/200. ... Bats right, throws right. ... Full name: Timothy John Laker.
HIGH SCHOOL: Simi Valley (Calif.).
JUNIOR COLLEGE: Oxnard (Calif.) College.
TRANSACTIONS/CAREER NOTES: Selected by Kansas City Royals organization in 49th round of free-agent draft (June 2, 1987); did not sign. ... Selected by Montreal Expos organization in sixth round of free-agent draft (June 1, 1988). ... On Ottawa disabled list (April 30-May 14, 1993). ... On disabled list (March 29, 1996-entire season). ... Claimed on waivers by Baltimore Orioles (March 25, 1997). ... On Rochester disabled list (June 5-16, 1997). ... Granted free agency (October 15, 1997). ... Signed by Tampa Bay Devil Rays (December 19, 1997). ... Released by Devil Rays (June 26, 1998). ... Signed by Pittsburgh Pirates organization (July 9, 1998). ... Released by Pirates (December 18, 1998). ... Signed by Los Angeles Dodgers (January 6, 1999).
STATISTICAL NOTES: Led New York-Pennsylvania League with 16 passed balls in 1989. ... Led Midwest League catchers with 125 assists, 18 errors and 944 total chances in 1990. ... Tied for International League lead in errors by catcher with 11 in 1993. ... Led International League with 20 passed balls in 1994.

							BATTING							FIELDING		
Year	Team (League)	Pos.	G	AB	R	H	2B	3B	HR	RBI	Avg.	BB	SO	SB	PO	A	E	Avg.
1988— Jamestown (NYP)		C-OF	47	152	14	34	9	0	0	17	.224	8	30	2	236	22	2	.992
1989— Rockford (Midwest) ...		C	14	48	4	11	1	1	0	4	.229	3	6	1	91	6	4	.960
— Jamestown (NYP)		C	58	216	25	48	9	1	2	24	.222	16	40	8	437	61	8	.984
1990— Rockford (Midwest) ...		C-OF	120	425	46	94	18	3	7	57	.221	32	83	7	802	†125	†18	.981
— W.P. Beach (FSL)		C	2	3	0	0	0	0	0	0	.000	0	1	0	2	0	0	1.000
1991— Harrisburg (East.)		C	11	35	4	10	1	0	1	5	.286	2	5	0	67	4	3	.959
— W.P. Beach (FSL)		C	100	333	35	77	15	2	5	33	.231	22	51	10	560	87	*14	.979
1992— Harrisburg (East.)		C	117	409	55	99	19	3	15	68	.242	39	89	3	630	62	*14	.980
— Montreal (N.L.)		C	28	46	8	10	3	0	0	4	.217	2	14	1	102	8	1	.991
1993— Montreal (N.L.)		C	43	86	3	17	2	1	0	7	.198	2	16	2	136	18	2	.987
— Ottawa (Int'l)		C-1B	56	204	26	47	10	0	4	23	.230	21	41	3	341	37	‡11	.972
1994— Ottawa (Int'l)		C	118	424	68	131	32	2	12	71	.309	47	96	11	643	*89	•11	.985
1995— Montreal (N.L.)		C	64	141	17	33	8	1	3	20	.234	14	38	0	265	27	7	.977
1996— Montreal (N.L.)						Did not play.												
1997— Rochester (Int'l)■		C	79	290	45	75	11	1	11	37	.259	34	49	1	283	17	6	.980
— Baltimore (A.L.)		C	7	14	0	0	0	0	0	1	.000	2	9	0	28	0	1	.966
1998— Durham (Int'l)■		C	40	134	36	32	7	0	11	26	.239	28	32	1	197	19	2	.991
— Tampa Bay (A.L.)		C-DH	3	5	1	1	0	0	0	0	.200	1	1	0	5	0	0	1.000
— Nashville (PCL)■		C-1B	44	152	30	54	16	1	11	34	.355	21	26	1	277	26	4	.987
— Pittsburgh (N.L.)		1B-C	14	24	2	9	1	0	1	2	.375	1	3	0	35	1	0	1.000
American League totals (2 years)			10	19	1	1	0	0	0	1	.053	3	10	0	33	0	1	.971
National League totals (4 years)			149	297	30	69	14	2	4	33	.232	19	71	3	538	54	10	.983
Major league totals (5 years)			159	316	31	70	14	2	4	34	.222	22	81	3	571	54	11	.983

LAMB, DAVID   IF   DEVIL RAYS

PERSONAL: Born June 6, 1975, in West Hills, Calif. ... 6-2/165. ... Bats both, throws right. ... Full name: David Christian Lamb.
HIGH SCHOOL: Newbury Park (Calif.).
TRANSACTIONS/CAREER NOTES: Selected by Baltimore Orioles organization in second round of free-agent draft (June 3, 1993). ... Selected by Tampa Bay Devil Rays from Orioles organization in Rule 5 major league draft (December 14, 1998).

							BATTING							FIELDING		
Year	Team (League)	Pos.	G	AB	R	H	2B	3B	HR	RBI	Avg.	BB	SO	SB	PO	A	E	Avg.
1993— GC Orioles (GCL)		SS	16	56	4	10	1	0	0	6	.179	10	8	2	16	22	3	.927
1994— Albany (S. Atl.)		SS	92	308	37	74	9	2	0	29	.240	32	40	4	118	230	22	.941
1995— Bowie (Eastern)		SS	1	4	0	1	0	0	0	1	.250	0	1	0	1	3	1	.800
— Frederick (Carolina) ...		SS-2B	124	436	39	97	14	2	2	34	.222	38	81	6	151	348	24	.954
1996— High Desert (Calif.)		SS	116	460	63	118	24	3	3	55	.257	50	68	5	202	356	18	.969
1997— Frederick (Carolina) ...		2B-SS-3B	70	249	30	65	21	1	2	39	.261	25	32	3	119	183	9	.971
— Bowie (Eastern)		SS-3B-2B	73	269	46	89	20	2	4	38	.331	34	35	0	81	159	11	.956
1998— Bowie (Eastern)		SS	66	241	29	73	10	1	2	25	.303	27	33	1	73	171	14	.946
— Rochester (Int'l)		SS-3B-2B	48	178	24	53	7	1	1	16	.298	17	25	1	69	116	7	.964

LAMPKIN, TOM   C   MARINERS

PERSONAL: Born March 4, 1964, in Cincinnati. ... 5-11/195. ... Bats left, throws right. ... Full name: Thomas Michael Lampkin.
HIGH SCHOOL: Blanchet (Seattle).
JUNIOR COLLEGE: Edmonds College (Wash.).
COLLEGE: Portland.
TRANSACTIONS/CAREER NOTES: Selected by Cleveland Indians organization in 11th round of free-agent draft (June 2, 1986). ... On disabled list (July 6, 1989-remainder of season). ... Traded by Indians organization to San Diego Padres for OF Alex Cole (July 11, 1990). ... Traded by Padres to Milwaukee Brewers for cash (March 25, 1993). ... Granted free agency (December 20, 1993). ... Signed by San Francisco Giants organization (January 5, 1994). ... On San Francisco disabled list (March 31-April 24 and August 26, 1996-remainder of season); included rehabilitation assignment to San Jose (April 22-24). ... Traded by Giants to St. Louis Cardinals for a player to be named later or cash (December 19, 1996); Giants acquired P Rene Arocha to complete deal (February 12, 1997). ... Granted free agency (October 23, 1998). ... Signed by Seattle Mariners (December 14, 1998).
STATISTICAL NOTES: Led Pacific Coast League catchers with 11 double plays in 1992. ... Led Pacific Coast League catchers with 595 putouts in 1994.

							BATTING							FIELDING		
Year	Team (League)	Pos.	G	AB	R	H	2B	3B	HR	RBI	Avg.	BB	SO	SB	PO	A	E	Avg.
1986— Batavia (NY-Penn)		C	63	190	24	49	5	1	1	20	.258	31	14	4	323	36	8	.978
1987— Waterloo (Midw.)		C	118	398	49	106	19	2	7	55	.266	34	41	5	689	*100	15	.981
1988— Williamsport (East.) ...		C	80	263	38	71	10	0	3	23	.270	25	20	1	431	60	9	.982

L

Year	Team (League)	Pos.	G	AB	R	H	2B	3B	HR	RBI	Avg.	BB	SO	SB	PO	A	E	Avg.
	—Colo. Springs (PCL) ...	C	34	107	14	30	5	0	0	7	.280	9	2	0	171	28	5	.975
	—Cleveland (A.L.)..........	C	4	4	0	0	0	0	0	0	.000	1	0	0	3	0	0	1.000
1989	—Colo. Springs (PCL) ...	C	63	209	26	67	10	3	4	32	.321	10	18	4	305	21	8	.976
1990	—Colo. Springs (PCL) ...	C-2B	69	199	32	44	7	5	1	18	.221	19	19	7	312	36	12	.967
	—San Diego (N.L.)■...	C	26	63	4	14	0	1	1	4	.222	4	9	0	91	10	3	.971
	—Las Vegas (PCL)	C	1	2	0	1	0	0	0	0	.500	0	1	0	3	0	0	1.000
1991	—San Diego (N.L.)	C	38	58	4	11	3	1	0	3	.190	3	9	0	49	5	0	1.000
	—Las Vegas (PCL)	C-1B-OF	45	164	25	52	11	1	2	29	.317	10	19	2	211	26	6	.975
1992	—Las Vegas (PCL)	C	108	340	45	104	17	4	3	48	.306	53	27	15	506	*64	12	.979
	—San Diego (N.L.)	C-OF	9	17	3	4	0	0	0	0	.235	6	1	2	30	3	0	1.000
1993	—New Orleans (A.A.)■..	C-OF	25	80	18	26	5	0	2	10	.325	18	4	5	152	12	3	.982
	—Milwaukee (A.L.)	C-OF-DH	73	162	22	32	8	0	4	25	.198	20	26	7	242	24	6	.978
1994	—Phoenix (PCL)■..........	C-OF	118	453	76	136	32	8	8	70	.300	42	49	8	†595	59	10	.985
1995	—San Francisco (N.L.) ..	C-OF	65	76	8	21	2	0	1	9	.276	9	8	2	62	5	0	1.000
1996	—San Jose (Calif.).........	C	2	7	2	2	0	1	0	2	.286	1	2	0	10	1	0	1.000
	—San Francisco (N.L.) ..	C	66	177	26	41	8	0	6	29	.232	20	22	1	342	27	3	.992
1997	—St. Louis (N.L.)■	C	108	229	28	56	8	1	7	22	.245	28	30	2	413	37	5	.989
1998	—St. Louis (N.L.).........	C-OF-1B	93	216	25	50	12	1	6	28	.231	24	32	3	337	19	5	.986
American League totals (2 years)			77	166	22	32	8	0	4	25	.193	21	26	7	245	24	6	.978
National League totals (7 years)			405	836	98	197	33	4	21	95	.236	94	111	10	1324	106	16	.989
Major league totals (9 years)			482	1002	120	229	41	4	25	120	.229	115	137	17	1569	130	22	.987

LANGSTON, MARK   P   PADRES

PERSONAL: Born August 20, 1960, in San Diego. ... 6-2/185. ... Throws left, bats right. ... Full name: Mark Edward Langston.
HIGH SCHOOL: Buchser (Santa Clara, Calif.).
COLLEGE: San Jose State.
TRANSACTIONS/CAREER NOTES: Selected by Chicago Cubs organization in 15th round of free-agent draft (June 6, 1978); did not sign. ... Selected by Seattle Mariners organization in third round of free-agent draft (June 8, 1981); pick received as compensation for Texas Rangers signing free-agent IF Bill Stein. ... On disabled list (June 7-July 22, 1985). ... Traded by Mariners with a player to be named later to Montreal Expos for P Randy Johnson, P Brian Holman and P Gene Harris (May 25, 1989); Expos acquired P Mike Campbell to complete deal (July 31, 1989). ... Granted free agency (November 13, 1989). ... Signed by California Angels (December 1, 1989). ... On disabled list (April 10-May 11, 1994). ... On California disabled list (May 6-31, July 12-28 and August 10, 1996-remainder of season); included rehabilitation assignment to Lake Elsinore (May 26-31). ... Angels franchise renamed Anaheim Angels for 1997 season. ... On disabled list (May 20-August 20 and August 21, 1997-remainder of season). ... Granted free agency (October 28, 1997). ... Signed by San Diego Padres organization (January 7, 1998). ... On disabled list (April 15-May 23 and August 23-September 8, 1998). ... Granted free agency (November 2, 1998). ... Re-signed by Padres organization (December 7, 1998).
RECORDS: Holds major league single-season record for fewest assists by pitcher who led league in assists—42 (1990).
HONORS: Named A.L. Rookie Pitcher of the Year by THE SPORTING NEWS (1984). ... Won A.L. Gold Glove at pitcher (1987-88 and 1991-95).
STATISTICAL NOTES: Pitched seven innings, combining with Mike Witt (two innings) in 1-0 no-hit victory against Seattle (April 11, 1990). ... Struck out 15 batters in one game (June 25, 1986). ... Struck out 16 batters in one game (May 10, 1988). ... Pitched 3-0 one-hit, complete-game victory against Texas (September 24, 1988).
MISCELLANEOUS: Scored in only appearance as pinch runner and struck out twice in two appearances as designated hitter (1992). ... Had a sacrifice hit in only appearance as pinch hitter (1998).

Year	Team (League)	W	L	Pct.	ERA	G	GS	CG	ShO	Sv.	IP	H	R	ER	BB	SO
1981	—Bellingham (N'west)..........	7	3	.700	3.39	13	13	5	1	0	85	81	37	32	46	97
1982	—Bakersfield (California).......	12	7	.632	2.54	26	26	7	3	0	177 1/3	143	71	50	102	161
1983	—Chattanooga (Southern).....	14	9	.609	3.59	28	28	10	0	0	198	187	104	79	102	142
1984	—Seattle (A.L.)	17	10	.630	3.40	35	33	5	2	0	225	188	99	85	*118	*204
1985	—Seattle (A.L.)	7	14	.333	5.47	24	24	2	0	0	126 2/3	122	85	77	91	72
1986	—Seattle (A.L.)	12	14	.462	4.85	37	36	9	0	0	239 1/3	234	*142	*129	123	*245
1987	—Seattle (A.L.)	19	13	.594	3.84	35	35	14	3	0	272	242	132	116	114	*262
1988	—Seattle (A.L.)	15	11	.577	3.34	35	35	9	3	0	261 1/3	222	108	97	110	235
1989	—Seattle (A.L.)	4	5	.444	3.56	10	10	2	1	0	73 1/3	60	30	29	19	60
	—Montreal (N.L.)■...............	12	9	.571	2.39	24	24	6	4	0	176 2/3	138	57	47	93	175
1990	—California (A.L.)■...............	10	17	.370	4.40	33	33	5	1	0	223	215	120	109	104	195
1991	—California (A.L.)	19	8	.704	3.00	34	34	7	0	0	246 1/3	190	89	82	96	183
1992	—California (A.L.)	13	14	.481	3.66	32	32	9	2	0	229	206	103	93	74	174
1993	—California (A.L.)	16	11	.593	3.20	35	35	7	0	0	256 1/3	220	100	91	85	196
1994	—California (A.L.)	7	8	.467	4.68	18	18	2	1	0	119 1/3	121	67	62	54	109
1995	—California (A.L.)	15	7	.682	4.63	31	31	2	1	0	200 1/3	212	109	103	64	142
1996	—California (A.L.)	6	5	.545	4.82	18	18	2	0	0	123 1/3	116	68	66	45	83
	—Lake Elsinore (Calif.)	0	0	. . .	0.00	1	1	0	0	0	4	3	0	0	0	5
1997	—Anaheim (A.L.)■...............	2	4	.333	5.85	9	9	0	0	0	47 2/3	61	34	31	29	30
	—Lake Elsinore (Calif.)	0	2	.000	3.21	3	3	0	0	0	14	11	7	5	2	10
1998	—San Diego (N.L.)■	4	6	.400	5.86	22	16	0	0	0	81 1/3	107	55	53	41	56
A.L. totals (14 years)		162	141	.535	3.98	386	383	75	14	0	2643	2409	1286	1170	1126	2190
N.L. totals (2 years)		16	15	.516	3.49	46	40	6	4	0	258	245	112	100	134	231
Major league totals (15 years)....		178	156	.533	3.94	432	423	81	18	0	2901	2654	1398	1270	1260	2421

DIVISION SERIES RECORD

Year	Team (League)	W	L	Pct.	ERA	G	GS	CG	ShO	Sv.	IP	H	R	ER	BB	SO
1998	—San Diego (N.L.)						Did not play.									

CHAMPIONSHIP SERIES RECORD

Year	Team (League)	W	L	Pct.	ERA	G	GS	CG	ShO	Sv.	IP	H	R	ER	BB	SO
1998	—San Diego (N.L.)	0	0	. . .	0.00	3	0	0	0	0	1 1/3	1	0	0	0	1

WORLD SERIES RECORD

Year	Team (League)	W	L	Pct.	ERA	G	GS	CG	ShO	Sv.	IP	H	R	ER	BB	SO
1998— San Diego (N.L.)		0	0	...	40.50	1	0	0	0	0	$2/3$	1	3	3	3	0

ALL-STAR GAME RECORD

Year	League	W	L	Pct.	ERA	GS	CG	ShO	Sv.	IP	H	R	ER	BB	SO
1987— American		0	0	...	0.00	0	0	0	0	2	0	0	0	0	3
1991— American					Did not play.										
1992— American		0	0	...	9.00	0	0	0	0	1	2	1	1	0	1
1993— American		0	0	...	9.00	1	0	0	0	2	3	2	2	1	2
All-Star totals (3 years)		0	0	...	5.40	1	0	0	0	5	5	3	3	1	6

LANKFORD, FRANK   P   YANKEES

PERSONAL: Born March 26, 1971, in Atlanta. ... 6-2/190. ... Throws right, bats right. ... Full name: Frank Greenfield Lankford.
HIGH SCHOOL: Westminster (Atlanta).
COLLEGE: Virginia.
TRANSACTIONS/CAREER NOTES: Selected by New York Yankees organization in 17th round of free-agent draft (June 3, 1993). ... Selected by Los Angeles Dodgers from Yankees organization in Rule 5 major league draft (December 15, 1997). ... Returned to Yankees organization for cash (May 15, 1998). ... On Columbus disabled list (May 28-June 27, 1998).

Year	Team (League)	W	L	Pct.	ERA	G	GS	CG	ShO	Sv.	IP	H	R	ER	BB	SO
1993— Oneonta (N.Y.-Penn)		4	5	.444	3.34	16	7	0	0	0	$64^{2}/3$	60	41	24	22	61
1994— Greensboro (S. Atl.)		7	6	.538	2.95	54	0	0	0	7	$82^{1}/3$	79	37	27	18	74
1995— Tampa (Fla. St.)		4	6	.400	2.59	55	0	0	0	15	73	64	29	21	22	58
1996— Norwich (Eastern)		7	8	.467	2.66	61	0	0	0	4	88	82	42	26	40	61
1997— Norwich (Eastern)		4	2	.667	2.90	11	11	2	0	0	$68^{1}/3$	58	28	22	15	39
— Columbus (Int'l)		7	4	.636	2.69	15	13	1	1	0	$93^{2}/3$	84	33	28	22	40
1998— Los Angeles (N.L.)■		0	2	.000	5.95	12	0	0	0	1	$19^{2}/3$	23	13	13	7	7
— Columbus (Int'l)■		5	9	.357	5.07	15	15	3	0	0	94	110	60	53	32	58
Major league totals (1 year)........		0	2	.000	5.95	12	0	0	0	1	$19^{2}/3$	23	13	13	7	7

LANKFORD, RAY   OF   CARDINALS

L

PERSONAL: Born June 5, 1967, in Modesto, Calif. ... 5-11/198. ... Bats left, throws left. ... Full name: Raymond Lewis Lankford. ... Nephew of Carl Nichols, catcher with Baltimore Orioles (1986-88) and Houston Astros (1989-91).
HIGH SCHOOL: Grace Davis (Modesto, Calif.).
JUNIOR COLLEGE: Modesto (Calif.) Junior College.
TRANSACTIONS/CAREER NOTES: Selected by Chicago Cubs organization in third round of free-agent draft (January 14, 1986); did not sign. ... Selected by St. Louis Cardinals organization in third round of free-agent draft (June 2, 1987). ... On disabled list (June 24-July 9, 1993). ... On St. Louis disabled list (March 27-April 22, 1997); included rehabilitation assignment to Prince William (April 14-22).
RECORDS: Shares major league single-season record for fewest double plays by outfielder (150 or more games)—0 (1992).
HONORS: Named Texas League Most Valuable Player (1989).
STATISTICAL NOTES: Led Appalachian League outfielders with 155 total chances in 1987. ... Led Appalachian League in caught stealing with 11 in 1987. ... Led Midwest League with 242 total bases in 1988. ... Led Texas League outfielders with 387 total chances in 1989. ... Led American Association outfielders with 352 total chances in 1990. ... Tied for American Association lead with nine intentional bases on balls received in 1990. ... Hit for the cycle (September 15, 1991). ... Led N.L. in caught stealing with 24 in 1992. ... Career major league grand slams: 5.

							BATTING							FIELDING		
Year	Team (League)	Pos.	G	AB	R	H	2B	3B	HR	RBI	Avg.	BB	SO	SB	PO	A	E	Avg.
1987— Johnson City (App.) ...	OF	66	253	45	78	17	4	3	32	.308	19	43	14	*143	7	5	.968
1988— Springfield (Midw.)	OF	135	532	90	151	26	*16	11	66	.284	60	92	33	284	5	7	.976
1989— Arkansas (Texas)......	OF	*134	498	98	*158	28	*12	11	98	.317	65	57	38	*367	9	11	.972
1990— Louisville (A.A.)..........	OF	132	473	61	123	25	8	10	72	.260	72	81	30	*333	8	•11	.969
— St. Louis (N.L.)...........	OF	39	126	12	36	10	1	3	12	.286	13	27	8	92	1	1	.989
1991— St. Louis (N.L.)..........	OF	151	566	83	142	23	*15	9	69	.251	41	114	44	367	7	6	.984
1992— St. Louis (N.L.)..........	OF	153	598	87	175	40	6	20	86	.293	72	*147	42	*438	5	2	.996
1993— St. Louis (N.L.)..........	OF	127	407	64	97	17	3	7	45	.238	81	111	14	312	6	7	.978
1994— St. Louis (N.L.)..........	OF	109	416	89	111	25	5	19	57	.267	58	113	11	260	5	6	.978
1995— St. Louis (N.L.)..........	OF	132	483	81	134	35	2	25	82	.277	63	110	24	300	7	3	.990
1996— St. Louis (N.L.)..........	OF	149	545	100	150	36	8	21	86	.275	79	133	35	356	9	1	*.997
1997— Prince Will. (Car.)	OF	4	13	3	4	1	0	0	4	.308	4	5	1	6	0	0	1.000
— St. Louis (N.L.)..........	OF	133	465	94	137	36	3	31	98	.295	95	125	21	293	4	9	.971
1998— St. Louis (N.L.)..........	OF-DH	154	533	94	156	37	1	31	105	.293	86	151	26	338	7	5	.986
Major league totals (9 years)		1147	4139	704	1138	259	44	166	640	.275	588	1031	225	2756	51	40	.986

DIVISION SERIES RECORD

							BATTING							FIELDING		
Year	Team (League)	Pos.	G	AB	R	H	2B	3B	HR	RBI	Avg.	BB	SO	SB	PO	A	E	Avg.
1996— St. Louis (N.L.)..........	OF-PH	1	2	1	1	0	0	0	0	.500	1	0	0	4	0	0	1.000

CHAMPIONSHIP SERIES RECORD

							BATTING							FIELDING		
Year	Team (League)	Pos.	G	AB	R	H	2B	3B	HR	RBI	Avg.	BB	SO	SB	PO	A	E	Avg.
1996— St. Louis (N.L.)..........	OF-PH	5	13	1	0	0	0	0	1	.000	1	4	0	7	0	0	1.000

ALL-STAR GAME RECORD

						BATTING							FIELDING		
Year	League	Pos.	AB	R	H	2B	3B	HR	RBI	Avg.	BB	SO	SB	PO	A	E	Avg.
1997— National	OF	2	0	0	0	0	0	0	.000	1	1	0	0	0	0	...

LANSING, MIKE — 2B — ROCKIES

PERSONAL: Born April 3, 1968, in Rawlins, Wyo. ... 6-0/195. ... Bats right, throws right. ... Full name: Michael Thomas Lansing.
HIGH SCHOOL: Natrona County (Casper, Wyo.).
COLLEGE: Wichita State.
TRANSACTIONS/CAREER NOTES: Selected by Baltimore Orioles organization in ninth round of free-agent draft (June 5, 1989); did not sign. ... Selected by Miami Miracle, independent, in sixth round of free-agent draft (June 4, 1990). ... On disabled list (April 29-May 9, 1991). ... Contract sold by Miami to Montreal Expos organization (September 18, 1991). ... On disabled list (May 31-June 15, 1995). ... Traded by Expos to Colorado Rockies for P Jake Westbrook, P John Nicholson and OF Mark Hamlin (November 18, 1997).
STATISTICAL NOTES: Led Eastern League shortstops with 76 double plays in 1992. ... Hit three home runs in one game (September 22, 1998). ... Career major league grand slams: 2.

										BATTING					FIELDING		
Year Team (League)	Pos.	G	AB	R	H	2B	3B	HR	RBI	Avg.	BB	SO	SB	PO	A	E	Avg.
1990— Miami (Fla. St.)	SS	61	207	20	50	5	2	2	11	.242	29	35	15	104	166	10	.964
1991— Miami (Fla. St.)	SS-2B	104	384	54	110	20	7	6	55	.286	40	75	29	148	273	27	.940
1992— Harrisburg (East.)■ ...	SS	128	483	66	135	20	6	6	54	.280	52	64	46	189	*373	20	*.966
1993— Montreal (N.L.)	3B-SS-2B	141	491	64	141	29	1	3	45	.287	46	56	23	136	336	24	.952
1994— Montreal (N.L.)	2B-3B-SS	106	394	44	105	21	2	5	35	.266	30	37	12	164	283	10	.978
1995— Montreal (N.L.)	2B-SS	127	467	47	119	30	2	10	62	.255	28	65	27	306	373	6	.991
1996— Montreal (N.L.)	2B-SS	159	641	99	183	40	2	11	53	.285	44	85	23	349	395	11	.985
1997— Montreal (N.L.)	2B	144	572	86	161	45	2	20	70	.281	45	92	11	279	395	9	.987
1998— Colorado (N.L.)■	2B-3B	153	584	73	161	39	2	12	66	.276	39	88	10	345	425	10	.987
Major league totals (6 years)		830	3149	413	870	204	11	61	331	.276	232	423	106	1579	2207	70	.982

LARA, NELSON — P — MARLINS

PERSONAL: Born July 15, 1978, in Santo Domingo, Dominican Republic. ... 6-4/185. ... Throws right, bats right. ... Full name: Nelson Rafael Lara.
HIGH SCHOOL: Colegio San Jose (Santo Domingo, Dominican Republic).
TRANSACTIONS/CAREER NOTES: Signed as non-drafted free agent by Florida Marlins organization (September 15, 1994).

Year Team (League)	W	L	Pct.	ERA	G	GS	CG	ShO	Sv.	IP	H	R	ER	BB	SO
1995— GC Marlins (GCL)	1	1	.500	3.74	11	0	0	0	1	21 2/3	21	13	9	11	9
1996— GC Marlins (GCL)	1	2	.333	5.59	7	0	0	0	0	9 2/3	6	11	6	12	3
1997— Kane County (Midwest)......	1	2	.333	3.99	29	0	0	0	3	38 1/3	37	20	17	14	43
1998— Brevard County (FSL)........	2	5	.286	9.42	19	4	0	0	0	28 2/3	27	36	30	33	32
—Kane County (Midwest)......	2	2	.500	6.14	10	4	0	0	0	29 1/3	29	23	20	23	21

LARKIN, ANDY — P — MARLINS

PERSONAL: Born June 27, 1974, in Chelan, Wash. ... 6-4/190. ... Throws right, bats right. ... Full name: Andrew Dane Larkin.
HIGH SCHOOL: South Medford (Medford, Ore).
TRANSACTIONS/CAREER NOTES: Selected by Florida Marlins organization in 25th round of free-agent draft (June 1, 1992). ... On disabled list (June 14-August 23, 1995). ... On Portland disabled list (April 4-May 11, 1996). ... On Florida disabled list (May 11-July 17, 1996); included rehabilitation assignment to Brevard County (June 18-July 17).
STATISTICAL NOTES: Pitched 6-0 no-hit victory against Welland (July 25, 1993). ... Led New York-Pennsylvania League with 12 hit batsmen in 1993. ... Led Midwest League with 19 hit batsmen in 1994. ... Led International League with 15 hit batsmen in 1997.

Year Team (League)	W	L	Pct.	ERA	G	GS	CG	ShO	Sv.	IP	H	R	ER	BB	SO
1992— GC Marlins (GCL)	1	2	.333	5.23	14	4	0	0	2	41 1/3	41	26	24	19	20
1993— Elmira (N.Y.-Penn)	5	7	.417	2.97	14	14	•4	•1	0	88	74	43	29	23	89
1994— Kane County (Midwest)......	9	7	.563	2.83	21	21	3	1	0	140	125	53	44	27	125
1995— Portland (Eastern)	1	2	.333	3.38	9	9	0	0	0	40	29	16	15	11	23
1996— Brevard County (FSL)........	0	4	.000	4.23	6	6	0	0	0	27 2/3	34	20	13	7	18
—Portland (Eastern)	4	1	.800	3.10	8	8	0	0	0	49 1/3	45	18	17	10	40
—Florida (N.L.)	0	0	. . .	1.80	1	1	0	0	0	5	3	1	1	4	2
1997— Charlotte (Int'l)	6	11	.353	6.05	28	27	3	0	0	144 1/3	166	109	97	76	103
1998— Charlotte (Int'l)	4	1	.800	6.37	11	10	0	0	0	53 2/3	55	39	38	32	41
—Florida (N.L.)	3	8	.273	9.64	17	14	0	0	0	74 2/3	101	87	80	55	43
Major league totals (2 years)......	3	8	.273	9.15	18	15	0	0	0	79 2/3	104	88	81	59	45

LARKIN, BARRY — SS — REDS

PERSONAL: Born April 28, 1964, in Cincinnati. ... 6-0/185. ... Bats right, throws right. ... Full name: Barry Louis Larkin. ... Brother of Steve Larkin, outfielder/first baseman, Cincinnati Reds organization; and cousin of Nathan Davis, defensive tackle with Atlanta Falcons (1997).
HIGH SCHOOL: Moeller (Cincinnati).
COLLEGE: Michigan.
TRANSACTIONS/CAREER NOTES: Selected by Cincinnati Reds organization in second round of free-agent draft (June 7, 1982); did not sign. ... Selected by Reds organization in first round (fourth pick overall) of free-agent draft (June 3, 1985). ... On disabled list (April 13-May 2, 1987). ... On Cincinnati disabled list (July 11-September 1, 1989); included rehabilitation assignment to Nashville (August 27-September 1). ... On disabled list (May 18-June 4, 1991; April 19-May 8, 1992; and August 5, 1993-remainder of season). ... On disabled list (June 17-August 2 and September 1, 1997-remainder of season; and March 12-April 7, 1998).
RECORDS: Holds major league single-season record for fewest putouts by shortstop for leader—230 (1996). ... Shares major league record for most home runs in two consecutive games—5 (June 27 [2] and 28 [3], 1991).
HONORS: Named shortstop on THE SPORTING NEWS college All-America team (1985). ... Named American Association Most Valuable Player (1986). ... Named shortstop on THE SPORTING NEWS N.L. All-Star team (1988-92, 1994-96 and 1998). ... Named shortstop on THE SPORTING NEWS N.L. Silver Slugger team (1988-92, 1995-96 and 1998). ... Won N.L. Gold Glove at shortstop (1994-96). ... Named N.L. Most Valuable Player by Baseball Writers' Association of America (1995).

STATISTICAL NOTES: Led American Association with .525 slugging percentage in 1986. ... Had 21-game hitting streak (September 10-October 2, 1988). ... Tied for N.L. lead in double plays by shortstop with 86 in 1990. ... Hit three home runs in one game (June 28, 1991).
MISCELLANEOUS: Member of 1984 U.S. Olympic baseball team.

Year Team (League)	Pos.	G	AB	R	H	2B	3B	HR	RBI	Avg.	BB	SO	SB	PO	A	E	Avg.
1985— Vermont (Eastern)	SS	72	255	42	68	13	2	1	31	.267	23	21	12	110	166	17	.942
1986— Denver (A.A.)	SS-2B	103	413	67	136	31	10	10	51	.329	31	43	19	172	287	18	.962
— Cincinnati (N.L.)	SS-2B	41	159	27	45	4	3	3	19	.283	9	21	8	51	125	4	.978
1987— Cincinnati (N.L.)	SS	125	439	64	107	16	2	12	43	.244	36	52	21	168	358	19	.965
1988— Cincinnati (N.L.)	SS	151	588	91	174	32	5	12	56	.296	41	24	40	231	470	•29	.960
1989— Cincinnati (N.L.)	SS	97	325	47	111	14	4	4	36	.342	20	23	10	142	267	10	.976
— Nashville (A.A.)	SS	2	5	2	5	1	0	0	0	1.000	0	0	0	1	3	0	1.000
1990— Cincinnati (N.L.)	SS	158	614	85	185	25	6	7	67	.301	49	49	30	254	*469	17	.977
1991— Cincinnati (N.L.)	SS	123	464	88	140	27	4	20	69	.302	55	64	24	226	372	15	.976
1992— Cincinnati (N.L.)	SS	140	533	76	162	32	6	12	78	.304	63	58	15	233	408	11	.983
1993— Cincinnati (N.L.)	SS	100	384	57	121	20	3	8	51	.315	51	33	14	159	281	16	.965
1994— Cincinnati (N.L.)	SS	110	427	78	119	23	5	9	52	.279	64	58	26	*178	312	10	.980
1995— Cincinnati (N.L.)	SS	131	496	98	158	29	6	15	66	.319	61	49	51	192	341	11	.980
1996— Cincinnati (N.L.)	SS	152	517	117	154	32	4	33	89	.298	96	52	36	*230	426	17	.975
1997— Cincinnati (N.L.)	SS-DH	73	224	34	71	17	3	4	20	.317	47	24	14	77	171	5	.980
1998— Cincinnati (N.L.)	SS	145	538	93	166	34	10	17	72	.309	79	69	26	207	361	12	.979
Major league totals (13 years)		1546	5708	955	1713	305	61	156	718	.300	671	576	315	2348	4361	176	.974

DIVISION SERIES RECORD

Year Team (League)	Pos.	G	AB	R	H	2B	3B	HR	RBI	Avg.	BB	SO	SB	PO	A	E	Avg.
1995— Cincinnati (N.L.)	SS	3	13	2	5	0	0	0	1	.385	1	2	4	3	8	0	1.000

CHAMPIONSHIP SERIES RECORD

Year Team (League)	Pos.	G	AB	R	H	2B	3B	HR	RBI	Avg.	BB	SO	SB	PO	A	E	Avg.
1990— Cincinnati (N.L.)	SS	6	23	5	6	2	0	0	1	.261	3	1	3	21	15	1	.973
1995— Cincinnati (N.L.)	SS	4	18	1	7	2	1	0	0	.389	1	1	1	10	15	1	.962
Championship series totals (2 years)		10	41	6	13	4	1	0	1	.317	4	2	4	31	30	2	.968

WORLD SERIES RECORD

RECORDS: Shares single-inning record for most at-bats—2 (October 19, 1990, third inning).
NOTES: Member of World Series championship team (1990).

Year Team (League)	Pos.	G	AB	R	H	2B	3B	HR	RBI	Avg.	BB	SO	SB	PO	A	E	Avg.
1990— Cincinnati (N.L.)	SS	4	17	3	6	1	1	0	1	.353	2	0	0	1	14	0	1.000

ALL-STAR GAME RECORD

Year League	Pos.	AB	R	H	2B	3B	HR	RBI	Avg.	BB	SO	SB	PO	A	E	Avg.
1988— National	SS	2	0	0	0	0	0	0	.000	0	1	0	0	1	0	1.000
1989— National							Did not play.									
1990— National	PR-SS	0	0	0	0	0	0	0	. . .	0	0	1	1	2	0	1.000
1991— National	SS	1	0	0	0	0	0	0	.000	0	0	0	0	2	0	1.000
1993— National	SS	2	0	0	0	0	0	1	.000	0	1	0	2	1	0	1.000
1994— National							Selected, did not play—injured.									
1995— National	SS	3	0	0	0	0	0	0	.000	0	0	0	2	3	0	1.000
1996— National	SS	3	1	1	0	0	0	0	.333	0	0	0	0	2	0	1.000
1997— National							Selected, did not play—injured.									
All-Star Game totals (6 years)		11	1	1	0	0	0	1	.091	0	2	1	5	11	0	1.000

LARKIN, STEVE   OF/1B   REDS

PERSONAL: Born July 24, 1973, in Cincinnati. ... 6-0/190. ... Bats left, throws left. ... Full name: Stephen Karari Larkin. ... Brother of Barry Larkin, shortstop, Cincinnati Reds; and cousin of Nathan Davis, defensive tackle with Atlanta Falcons (1997).
HIGH SCHOOL: Moeller (Cincinnati).
COLLEGE: Texas.
TRANSACTIONS/CAREER NOTES: Selected by Texas Rangers organization in 10th round of free-agent draft (June 10, 1994). ... Traded by Rangers organization with cash to Cincinnati Reds organization for 3B Craig Worthington (August 16, 1995). ... On Chattanooga disabled list (August 6-September 27, 1998).

Year Team (League)	Pos.	G	AB	R	H	2B	3B	HR	RBI	Avg.	BB	SO	SB	PO	A	E	Avg.
1994— Hudson Valley (NYP)	OF-1B	66	237	26	47	10	1	2	22	.198	30	47	10	201	18	12	.948
1995— Charl., S.C. (SAL)	1B-OF	113	369	50	94	19	1	5	45	.255	54	80	18	424	32	14	.970
— Win.-Salem (Car.)■	OF-1B	13	50	2	11	1	0	0	4	.220	3	12	2	40	1	2	.953
1996— Win.-Salem (Car.)	1B-OF	39	117	13	21	2	0	3	6	.179	14	25	6	190	9	8	.961
— Char., W.Va. (SAL)	1B-OF	58	203	30	55	7	2	5	33	.271	35	40	5	358	31	11	.973
1997— Char., W.Va. (SAL)	OF-1B	129	464	88	129	23	10	13	79	.278	52	83	28	404	25	11	.975
1998— Chattanooga (Sou.)	OF	80	267	33	61	22	1	3	31	.228	23	52	3	123	3	7	.947
— Cincinnati (N.L.)	1B	1	3	0	1	0	0	0	0	.333	0	1	0	6	0	0	1.000
Major league totals (1 year)		1	3	0	1	0	0	0	0	.333	0	1	0	6	0	0	1.000

LaRUE, JASON   C   REDS

PERSONAL: Born March 19, 1974, in Houston. ... 5-11/200. ... Bats right, throws right. ... Full name: Michael Jason LaRue.
HIGH SCHOOL: Spring Valley (Spring Branch, Tex.).
COLLEGE: Dallas Baptist.
TRANSACTIONS/CAREER NOTES: Selected by Cincinnati Reds organization in fifth round of free-agent draft (June 1, 1995). ... On disabled list (June 30-September 13, 1996).
STATISTICAL NOTES: Tied for Pioneer League lead in being hit by pitch with 12 in 1995. ... Led Pioneer League catchers with seven double plays in 1995. ... Led Southern League with .617 slugging percentage in 1998. ... Tied for Southern League lead with 21 passed balls in 1998.

								BATTING						FIELDING			
Year	Team (League)	Pos.	G	AB	R	H	2B	3B	HR	RBI	Avg.	BB	SO	SB	PO	A	E	Avg.
1995— Billings (Pioneer)		C	58	183	35	50	8	1	5	31	.273	16	28	3	346	46	8	.980
1996— Char., W.Va. (SAL)		C-1B	37	123	17	26	8	0	2	14	.211	11	28	3	234	48	6	.979
1997— Char., W.Va. (SAL)		C-1-3-O	132	473	78	149	*50	3	8	81	.315	47	90	14	711	84	19	.977
1998— Chattanooga (Sou.)		C-3B-1B	105	386	71	141	39	8	14	82	*.365	40	60	4	546	90	10	.985
— Indianapolis (Int'l)		C	15	51	5	12	4	0	0	5	.235	4	8	0	83	11	0	1.000

LATHAM, CHRIS   OF   TWINS

PERSONAL: Born May 26, 1973, in Coeur d'Alene, Idaho. ... 6-0/195. ... Bats both, throws right. ... Full name: Christopher Joseph Latham.
HIGH SCHOOL: Basic Technical (Las Vegas).
TRANSACTIONS/CAREER NOTES: Selected by Los Angeles Dodgers organization in 11th round of free-agent draft (June 3, 1991). ... Traded by Dodgers organization to Minnesota Twins (October 30, 1995), completing deal in which Twins traded P Mark Guthrie and P Kevin Tapani to Dodgers for 1B/3B Ron Coomer, P Greg Hansell, P Jose Parra and a player to be named later (July 31, 1995). ... On disabled list (August 30-September 9, 1996).
STATISTICAL NOTES: Led Northwest League with 148 total bases and 20 caught stealing in 1994. ... Tied for Northwest League lead with seven intentional bases on balls received in 1994. ... Led Northwest League outfielders with 154 total chances in 1994. ... Led Pacific Coast League lead in caught stealing with 19 in 1997.

								BATTING						FIELDING			
Year	Team (League)	Pos.	G	AB	R	H	2B	3B	HR	RBI	Avg.	BB	SO	SB	PO	A	E	Avg.
1991— GC Dodgers (GCL)		2B	43	109	17	26	2	1	0	11	.239	16	45	14	47	63	10	.917
1992— Great Falls (Pio.)		2B	17	37	8	12	2	0	0	3	.324	8	8	1	17	24	6	.872
— GC Dodgers (GCL)		2B-SS-3B	14	48	4	11	2	0	0	2	.229	5	17	2	26	14	1	.976
1993— Yakima (N'west)		OF	54	192	46	50	2	*6	4	17	.260	39	53	25	83	5	6	.936
— Bakersfield (Calif.)		OF	6	27	1	5	1	0	0	3	.185	4	5	2	12	0	1	.923
1994— Bakersfield (Calif.)		OF	52	191	29	41	5	2	2	15	.215	28	49	28	88	4	7	.929
— Yakima (N'west)		OF	71	288	*69	*98	19	*8	5	32	*.340	55	66	33	*144	6	4	.974
1995— Vero Beach (FSL)		OF	71	259	53	74	13	4	6	39	.286	56	54	42	125	5	7	.949
— San Antonio (Tex.)		OF	58	214	38	64	14	5	9	37	.299	33	59	11	135	2	4	.972
— Albuquerque (PCL)		OF	5	18	2	3	0	1	0	3	.167	1	4	1	7	0	0	1.000
1996— Salt Lake (PCL)■		OF	115	376	59	103	16	6	9	50	.274	36	91	26	235	9	9	.964
1997— Salt Lake (PCL)		OF	118	492	78	152	22	5	8	58	.309	58	110	21	262	6	11	.961
— Minnesota (A.L.)		OF	15	22	4	4	1	0	0	1	.182	0	8	0	11	0	1	.917
1998— Salt Lake (PCL)		OF	97	377	81	122	21	4	11	51	.324	56	99	29	201	8	9	.959
— Minnesota (A.L.)		OF	34	94	14	15	1	0	1	5	.160	13	36	4	69	1	2	.972
Major league totals (2 years)			49	116	18	19	2	0	1	6	.164	13	44	4	80	1	3	.964

LAWRENCE, JOE   SS   BLUE JAYS

PERSONAL: Born February 13, 1977, in Lake Charles, La. ... 6-2/190. ... Bats right, throws right. ... Full name: Joseph D. Lawrence.
HIGH SCHOOL: Barbe (Lake Charles, La.).
TRANSACTIONS/CAREER NOTES: Selected by Toronto Blue Jays organization in first round (16th pick overall) of free-agent draft (June 4, 1996); pick received as compensation for Baltimore Orioles signing Type A free-agent 2B Roberto Alomar.

								BATTING						FIELDING			
Year	Team (League)	Pos.	G	AB	R	H	2B	3B	HR	RBI	Avg.	BB	SO	SB	PO	A	E	Avg.
1996— St. Catharines (NYP)		SS-3B	29	98	23	22	7	2	0	11	.224	14	17	1	31	67	11	.899
1997— Hagerstown (SAL)		SS	116	446	63	102	24	1	8	38	.229	49	107	10	134	278	33	.926
1998— Dunedin (Fla. St.)		SS-3B	125	454	102	140	31	6	11	44	.308	*105	88	15	163	345	48	.914

LAWRENCE, SEAN   P

PERSONAL: Born September 2, 1970, in Oak Park, Ill. ... 6-4/215. ... Throws left, bats left. ... Full name: Sean Christopher Lawrence.
HIGH SCHOOL: Oak Park-River Forest (Ill.).
COLLEGE: St. Francis (Ill.).
TRANSACTIONS/CAREER NOTES: Selected by Pittsburgh Pirates organization in sixth round of free-agent draft (June 1, 1992). ... On disabled list (June 14-September 8, 1994). ... Granted free agency (October 15, 1998).

Year Team (League)	W	L	Pct.	ERA	G	GS	CG	ShO	Sv.	IP	H	R	ER	BB	SO
1992— Welland (N.Y.-Penn)	3	6	.333	5.23	15	•15	0	0	0	74	75	55	43	34	71
1993— Salem (Northwest)	1	3	.250	10.20	4	4	0	0	0	15	25	19	17	9	14
— Augusta (S. Atl.)	6	8	.429	3.12	22	22	0	0	0	121	108	59	42	50	96
1994— Salem (Carolina)	4	2	.667	2.63	12	12	0	0	0	72	76	38	21	18	66
1995— Carolina (Southern)	0	2	.000	5.48	12	3	0	0	0	21 1/3	27	13	13	8	19
— Lynchburg (Carolina)	5	8	.385	4.22	20	19	0	00	0	111	115	56	52	25	82
1996— Carolina (Southern)	3	5	.375	3.95	37	9	0	0	2	82	80	40	36	36	81
1997— Calgary (PCL)	8	9	.471	4.21	26	26	2	0	0	143 1/3	154	83	67	57	116
1998— Nashville (Pacific Coast)	12	9	.571	5.02	26	26	0	0	0	147	153	86	82	57	126
— Pittsburgh (N.L.)	2	1	.667	7.32	7	3	0	0	0	19 2/3	25	16	16	10	12
Major league totals (1 year)	2	1	.667	7.32	7	3	0	0	0	19 2/3	25	16	16	10	12

LAWTON, MATT   OF   TWINS

PERSONAL: Born November 3, 1971, in Gulfport, Miss. ... 5-10/192. ... Bats left, throws right. ... Full name: Matthew Lawton III.
HIGH SCHOOL: Harrison Central (Gulfport, Miss.).
JUNIOR COLLEGE: Gulf Coast Community College (Fla.).
TRANSACTIONS/CAREER NOTES: Selected by Minnesota Twins organization in 12th round of free-agent draft (June 3, 1991).
STATISTICAL NOTES: Led Florida State League with .407 on-base percentage in 1994. ... Career major league grand slams: 2.

Year Team (League)	Pos.	G	AB	R	H	2B	3B	HR	RBI	Avg.	BB	SO	SB	PO	A	E	Avg.
1992— GC Twins (GCL).........	2B	53	173	39	45	8	3	2	26	.260	27	27	20	129	142	12	.958
1993— Fort Wayne (Midw.)....	OF	111	340	50	97	21	3	9	38	.285	65	42	23	65	6	3	.959
1994— Fort Myers (FSL).......	OF	122	446	79	134	30	1	7	51	.300	80	64	42	188	13	6	.971
1995— New Britain (East.)	OF	114	412	75	111	19	5	13	54	.269	56	70	26	221	12	2	*.991
— Minnesota (A.L.)	OF-DH	21	60	11	19	4	1	1	12	.317	7	11	1	34	1	1	.972
1996— Minnesota (A.L.)	OF-DH	79	252	34	65	7	1	6	42	.258	28	28	4	196	4	3	.985
— Salt Lake (PCL)	OF	53	212	40	63	16	1	7	33	.297	26	34	2	88	0	6	.936
1997— Minnesota (A.L.)	OF	142	460	74	114	29	3	14	60	.248	76	81	7	278	9	7	.976
1998— Minnesota (A.L.)	OF	152	557	91	155	36	6	21	77	.278	86	64	16	398	12	4	.990
Major league totals (4 years)		394	1329	210	353	11	42	191		.266	197	184	28	906	26	15	.984

LAXTON, BRETT   P   ATHLETICS

PERSONAL: Born October 5, 1973, in Stafford, N.J. ... 6-2/205. ... Throws right, bats left. ... Full name: Brett William Laxton. ... Son of Bill Laxton, pitcher with five major league teams (1970-71, 1974, and 1976-77).
HIGH SCHOOL: Audobon (N.J.).
COLLEGE: Louisiana State.
TRANSACTIONS/CAREER NOTES: Selected by San Diego Padres organization in fourth round of free-agent draft (June 1, 1992); did not sign. ... Selected by Oakland Athletics organization in 24th round of free-agent draft (June 4, 1996).

Year Team (League)	W	L	Pct.	ERA	G	GS	CG	ShO	Sv.	IP	H	R	ER	BB	SO
1996— S. Oregon (N'west).............	0	5	.000	7.71	13	8	0	0	0	32 2/3	39	34	28	26	38
1997— Visalia (California)	11	5	.688	2.99	29	22	0	0	0	138 2/3	141	62	46	50	121
1998— Huntsville (Southern)	11	4	.733	3.40	21	21	0	0	0	129 2/3	109	64	49	79	82
— Edmonton (PCL)	2	4	.333	6.60	8	8	0	0	0	46 1/3	45	35	34	24	21

LeBRON, JUAN   OF   METS

PERSONAL: Born June 7, 1977, in Arroyo, Puerto Rico. ... 6-4/195. ... Bats right, throws right. ... Full name: Juan Arturo LeBron. ... Son of Juan LeBron, infielder/outfielder/catcher in Pittsburgh Pirates organization (1970-75).
HIGH SCHOOL: Carmen Huyke (Puerto Rico).
TRANSACTIONS/CAREER NOTES: Selected by Kansas City Royals organization in first round (19th pick overall) of free-agent draft (June 1, 1995). ... Traded by Royals to New York Mets for 3B/2B Joe Randa (December 10, 1998).
STATISTICAL NOTES: Led Gulf Coast League in grounding into double plays with nine in 1996.

Year Team (League)	Pos.	G	AB	R	H	2B	3B	HR	RBI	Avg.	BB	SO	SB	PO	A	E	Avg.
1995— GC Royals (GCL)........	OF	47	147	17	26	5	2	2	13	.177	10	38	0	54	0	5	.915
1996— GC Royals (GCL)........	OF	58	215	19	62	9	2	3	30	.288	6	34	1	52	2	2	.964
1997— Lansing (Midwest)	OF	35	113	12	24	7	0	3	20	.212	0	32	0	45	2	2	.959
— Spokane (N'west)........	OF	69	288	49	88	*27	1	7	45	.306	17	74	8	104	9	8	.934
1998— Lansing (Midwest)	OF	121	442	70	111	26	9	17	84	.251	57	129	18	184	10	8	.960

LEDEE, RICKY   OF   YANKEES

PERSONAL: Born November 22, 1973, in Ponce, Puerto Rico. ... 6-1/160. ... Bats left, throws left. ... Full name: Ricardo Alberto Ledee. ... Name pronounced le-DAY.
HIGH SCHOOL: Colonel Nuestra Sonora de Valvanera (Coano, Puerto Rico).
TRANSACTIONS/CAREER NOTES: Selected by New York Yankees organization in 16th round of free-agent draft (June 3, 1990). ... On Tampa disabled list (April 6-May 27, 1996). ... On Columbus disabled list (May 5-16 and May 22-August 4, 1997).

Year Team (League)	Pos.	G	AB	R	H	2B	3B	HR	RBI	Avg.	BB	SO	SB	PO	A	E	Avg.
1990— GC Yankees (GCL)......	OF	19	37	5	4	2	0	0	1	.108	6	18	2	18	1	0	1.000
1991— GC Yankees (GCL)......	OF	47	165	22	44	6	2	0	18	.267	22	40	3	79	6	6	.934
1992— GC Yankees (GCL)......	OF	52	179	25	41	9	2	2	23	.229	24	47	1	62	4	2	.971
1993— Oneonta (NYP).........	OF	52	192	32	49	7	6	8	20	.255	25	46	7	91	6	3	.970
1994— Greensboro (S. Atl.) ...	OF	134	484	87	121	23	9	22	71	.250	91	126	10	170	10	5	.973
1995— Greensboro (S. Atl.) ...	OF	89	335	65	90	16	6	14	49	.269	51	66	10	160	7	3	.982
1996— Norwich (Eastern)	OF	39	137	27	50	11	1	8	37	.365	16	25	2	48	2	1	.980
— Columbus (Int'l)	OF	96	358	79	101	22	6	21	64	.282	44	95	6	97	3	5	.952
1997— Columbus (Int'l)	OF	43	170	38	52	12	1	10	39	.306	21	49	4	56	0	2	.966
— GC Yankees (GCL)	OF	7	21	3	7	1	0	0	2	.333	2	4	0	1	0	0	1.000
1998— Columbus (Int'l)	OF	96	360	70	102	21	1	19	41	.283	54	108	7	132	1	4	.971
— New York (A.L.)..........	OF	42	79	13	19	5	2	1	12	.241	7	29	3	47	4	1	.981
Major league totals (1 year)		42	79	13	19	5	2	1	12	.241	7	29	3	47	4	1	.981

DIVISION SERIES RECORD

Year Team (League)	Pos.	G	AB	R	H	2B	3B	HR	RBI	Avg.	BB	SO	SB	PO	A	E	Avg.
1998— New York (A.L.)							Did not play.										

							BATTING									FIELDING		
Year	Team (League)	Pos.	G	AB	R	H	2B	3B	HR	RBI	Avg.	BB	SO	SB	PO	A	E	Avg.
1998— New York (A.L.)	PH-O-PR-DH	3	5	0	0	0	0	0	0	0	.000	0	0	0	3	0	0	1.000

WORLD SERIES RECORD

NOTES: Member of World Series championship team (1998).

							BATTING									FIELDING		
Year	Team (League)	Pos.	G	AB	R	H	2B	3B	HR	RBI	Avg.	BB	SO	SB	PO	A	E	Avg.
1998— New York (A.L.)	OF-PH	4	10	1	6	3	0	0	4	.600	2	1	0	8	0	0	1.000

LEDESMA, AARON — IF — DEVIL RAYS

PERSONAL: Born June 3, 1971, in Union City, Calif. ... 6-2/200. ... Bats right, throws right. ... Full name: Aaron David Ledesma.
HIGH SCHOOL: James Logan (Union City, Calif.).
JUNIOR COLLEGE: Chabot College (Calif.).
TRANSACTIONS/CAREER NOTES: Selected by New York Mets organization in second round of free-agent draft (June 4, 1990). ... On disabled list (April 13-May 24, 1991 and July 19, 1993-remainder of season). ... On suspended list (July 29-31, 1994). ... Traded by Mets to California Angels for OF Kevin Flora (January 18, 1996). ... Granted free agency (October 15, 1996). ... Signed by Rochester, Baltimore Orioles organization (January 17, 1997). ... Selected by Tampa Bay Devil Rays in third round (62nd pick overall) of expansion draft (November 18, 1997).
STATISTICAL NOTES: Led Florida State League shortstops with 641 total chances and 79 double plays in 1992. ... Led International League shortstops with 68 double plays in 1994. ... Led Pacific Coast League in grounding into double plays with 18 in 1996.

							BATTING									FIELDING		
Year	Team (League)	Pos.	G	AB	R	H	2B	3B	HR	RBI	Avg.	BB	SO	SB	PO	A	E	Avg.
1990— Kingsport (Appal.)	SS	66	243	50	81	11	1	5	38	.333	30	28	27	78	*170	24	.912
1991— Columbia (S. Atl.)	SS	33	115	19	39	8	0	1	14	.339	8	16	3	44	64	10	.915
1992— St. Lucie (Fla. St.)	SS	134	456	51	120	17	2	2	50	.263	46	66	20	185	*411	45	.930
1993— Binghamton (East.)	SS	66	206	23	55	12	0	5	22	.267	14	43	2	36	65	10	.910
1994— Norfolk (Int'l)	SS	119	431	49	118	20	1	3	57	.274	28	41	18	157	347	26	*.951
1995— Norfolk (Int'l)	3B-1B-SS	56	201	26	60	12	1	0	28	.299	10	22	6	73	94	10	.944
— New York (N.L.)	3B-1B-SS	21	33	4	8	0	0	0	3	.242	6	7	0	5	12	2	.895
1996— Vancouver (PCL)■	SS-3B	109	440	60	134	27	4	1	51	.305	32	59	2	150	261	20	.954
1997— Rochester (Int'l)■	SS-1B	85	326	40	106	26	1	3	43	.325	35	48	12	121	185	13	.959
— Baltimore (A.L.)	2-3-1-S	43	88	24	31	5	1	2	11	.352	13	9	1	68	52	3	.976
1998— Tampa Bay (A.L.)■	S-2-3-DH-1	95	299	30	97	16	3	0	29	.324	9	51	9	151	227	12	.969
American League totals (2 years)		138	387	54	128	21	4	2	40	.331	22	60	10	219	279	15	.971
National League totals (1 year)		21	33	4	8	0	0	0	3	.242	6	7	0	5	12	2	.895
Major league totals (3 years)		159	420	58	136	21	4	2	43	.324	28	67	10	224	291	17	.968

LEE, CARLOS — 3B — WHITE SOX

PERSONAL: Born June 20, 1976, in Aguadulce, Panama. ... 6-2/202. ... Bats right, throws right. ... Full name: Carlos Noriel Lee.
TRANSACTIONS/CAREER NOTES: Signed as non-drafted free agent by Chicago White Sox organization (February 8, 1994).
STATISTICAL NOTES: Led Southern League in grounding into double plays with 32 in 1998.

							BATTING									FIELDING		
Year	Team (League)	Pos.	G	AB	R	H	2B	3B	HR	RBI	Avg.	BB	SO	SB	PO	A	E	Avg.
1994— Sarasota (Gulf Coast)	3B	29	56	6	7	1	0	0	1	.125	4	8	0	18	29	2	.959
1995— Hickory (S. Atl.)	3B	63	218	18	54	9	1	4	30	.248	8	34	1	30	76	19	.848
— Bristol (Appal.)	3B-1B	*67	*269	43	*93	17	1	7	45	.346	8	34	17	84	107	18	.914
1996— Hickory (S. Atl.)	3B-1B	119	480	65	150	23	6	8	70	.313	23	50	18	149	235	32	.923
1997— Win.-Salem (Car.)	3B	*139	*546	81	*173	*50	4	17	82	.317	36	65	11	*93	233	34	.906
1998— Birmingham (Sou.)	3B	138	*549	77	166	33	2	21	106	.302	39	55	11	*99	223	*35	.902

LEE, COREY — P — RANGERS

PERSONAL: Born December 26, 1974, in Raleigh, N.C. ... 6-2/180. ... Throws left, bats both. ... Full name: Corey W. Lee.
HIGH SCHOOL: Clayton (N.C.).
COLLEGE: North Carolina State.
TRANSACTIONS/CAREER NOTES: Selected by Texas Rangers organization in supplemental round ("sandwich pick" between first and second round, 32nd pick overall) of free-agent draft (June 2, 1996); pick received as compensation for New York Yankees signing Type A free-agent P Kenny Rogers.

Year	Team (League)	W	L	Pct.	ERA	G	GS	CG	ShO	Sv.	IP	H	R	ER	BB	SO
1996— Hudson Valley (NYP)	1	4	.200	3.29	9	9	0	0	0	54 2/3	42	24	20	21	59
1997— Charlotte (Fla. St.)	*15	5	.750	3.47	23	23	6	2	0	160 2/3	132	66	62	60	147
1998— Tulsa (Texas)	10	9	.526	4.51	26	25	1	0	0	143 2/3	105	81	72	102	132

LEE, DAVID — P — ROCKIES

PERSONAL: Born March 12, 1973, in Pittsburgh. ... 6-1/200. ... Throws right, bats right. ... Full name: David Emmer Lee.
HIGH SCHOOL: Langley (Pittsburgh).
JUNIOR COLLEGE: Community College of Allegheny County-North (Pa.).
COLLEGE: Mercyhurst.
TRANSACTIONS/CAREER NOTES: Selected by Colorado Rockies organization in 23rd round of free-agent draft (June 1, 1995).
STATISTICAL NOTES: Led South Atlantic League pitchers in games finished with 49 in 1997.

Year	Team (League)	W	L	Pct.	ERA	G	GS	CG	ShO	Sv.	IP	H	R	ER	BB	SO
1996—	Portland (Northwest)..........	5	1	.833	0.78	17	0	0	0	7	23	13	3	2	16	24
—Salem (Carolina)		0	2	.000	2.25	8	0	0	0	1	12	14	6	3	6	10
1997—	Asheville (S. Atl.)..............	4	8	.333	4.08	51	0	0	0	22	53	61	30	24	23	59
1998—	Salem (Carolina)	3	5	.375	3.77	54	0	0	0	25	57 1/3	57	26	24	15	54

LEE, DEREK   1B   MARLINS

PERSONAL: Born September 6, 1975, in Sacramento. ... 6-5/225. ... Throws right, bats right. ... Full name: Derrek Leon Lee. ... Son of Leon Lee, infielder, St. Louis Cardinals organization (1969-71) and Lotte Orions (1978-82), Taiyo Whales (1983-85) and Yakult Swallows (1986-87) of Japanese League; and nephew of Leron Lee, outfielder with four major league teams (1969-1976) and Lotte Orions (1977-87) of Japanese League.
HIGH SCHOOL: El Camino (Sacramento).
TRANSACTIONS/CAREER NOTES: Selected by San Diego Padres in first round (14th pick overall) of free-agent draft (June 2, 1994). ... Traded by Padres with P Rafael Medina and P Steve Hoff to Florida Marlins for P Kevin Brown (December 15, 1997).
HONORS: Named Southern League Most Valuable Player (1996).
STATISTICAL NOTES: Led Southern League with 285 total bases in 1996. ... Led Southern League first basemen 1,121 putouts in 1996. ... Led Pacific Coast League first basemen with 1,189 total chances and 108 double plays in 1997. ... Career major league grand slams: 2.

RECORD AS POSITION PLAYER

Year	Team (League)	Pos.	G	AB	R	H	2B	3B	HR	RBI	Avg.	BB	SO	SB	PO	A	E	Avg.
1993—	Ariz. Padres (Ariz.).....	1B	15	52	11	17	1	1	2	5	.327	6	7	4	115	14	2	.985
—Rancho Cuca. (Cal.) ...		1B	20	73	13	20	5	1	1	10	.274	10	20	0	115	6	5	.960
1994—	Rancho Cuca. (Cal.) ...	1B	126	442	66	118	19	2	8	53	.267	42	95	18	289	27	4	.988
1995—	Rancho Cuca. (Cal.) ...	1B	128	502	82	151	25	2	23	95	.301	49	130	14	970	86	*18	.983
—Memphis (Sou.)		1B	2	9	0	1	0	0	0	1	.111	0	2	0	16	3	0	1.000
1996—	Memphis (Sou.)	1B-3B	134	500	98	140	39	2	34	*104	.280	65	*170	13	†1121	77	11	.991
1997—	Las Vegas (PCL)	1B	125	472	86	153	29	2	13	64	.324	60	116	17	*1069	*111	9	*.992
—San Diego (N.L.)		1B	22	54	9	14	3	0	1	4	.259	9	24	0	131	13	0	1.000
1998—	Florida (N.L.)■..........	1B	141	454	62	106	29	1	17	74	.233	47	120	5	950	114	8	.993
Major league totals (2 years)			163	508	71	120	32	1	18	78	.236	56	144	5	1081	127	8	.993

LEE, TRAVIS   1B   DIAMONDBACKS

PERSONAL: Born May 26, 1975, in San Diego. ... 6-3/210. ... Bats left, throws left. ... Full name: Travis Reynolds Lee.
HIGH SCHOOL: Olympia (Wash.).
COLLEGE: San Diego State.
TRANSACTIONS/CAREER NOTES: Selected by Minnesota Twins organization in first round (second pick overall) of free-agent draft (June 4, 1996). ... Granted free agency (June 19, 1996). ... Signed by Arizona Diamondbacks organization (October 15, 1996). ... Loaned by Diamondbacks organization to Tucson, Milwaukee Brewers organization (June 5, 1997). ... Returned to Diamondbacks (March 30, 1998). ... On disabled list (July 25-August 9, 1998).
HONORS: Named Golden Spikes Award winner by USA Baseball (1996).
MISCELLANEOUS: Tied for Arizona Diamondbacks all-time record for most home runs (22). ... Member of 1996 U.S. Olympic baseball team.

Year	Team (League)	Pos.	G	AB	R	H	2B	3B	HR	RBI	Avg.	BB	SO	SB	PO	A	E	Avg.
1997—	High Desert (Calif.)■.	1B	61	226	63	82	18	1	18	63	.363	47	36	5	553	67	1	.998
—Tucson (PCL)■.........		1B-OF	59	227	42	68	16	2	14	46	.300	31	46	2	382	32	3	.993
1998—	Arizona (N.L.)............	1B	146	562	71	151	20	2	22	72	.269	67	123	8	1269	100	3	.998
Major league totals (1 year)			146	562	71	151	20	2	22	72	.269	67	123	8	1269	100	3	.998

LEITER, AL   P   METS

PERSONAL: Born October 23, 1965, in Toms River, N.J. ... 6-3/220. ... Throws left, bats left. ... Full name: Alois Terry Leiter. ... Brother of Mark Leiter, pitcher, Seattle Mariners; and brother of Kurt Leiter, minor league pitcher (1982-84 and 1986). ... Name pronounced LIE-ter.
HIGH SCHOOL: Central Regional (Bayville, N.J.).
TRANSACTIONS/CAREER NOTES: Selected by New York Yankees organization in second round of free-agent draft (June 4, 1984). ... On New York disabled list (June 22-July 26, 1988); included rehabilitation assignment to Columbus (July 17-25). ... Traded by Yankees to Toronto Blue Jays for OF Jesse Barfield (April 30, 1989). ... On Toronto disabled list (May 11, 1989-remainder of season); included rehabilitation assignment to Dunedin (August 12-29). ... On Syracuse disabled list (May 20-June 13, 1990). ... On Toronto disabled list (April 27, 1991-remainder of season); included rehabilitation assignments to Dunedin (May 20-28 and July 19-August 7). ... On disabled list (April 24-May 9, 1993 and June 9-24, 1994). ... Granted free agency (November 6, 1995). ... Signed by Florida Marlins (December 14, 1995). ... On disabled list (May 1-20 and August 13-29, 1997). ... Traded by Marlins with 2B Ralph Milliard to New York Mets for P Jesus Sanchez, P A.J. Burnett and OF Robert Stratton (February 6, 1998). ... On disabled list (June 27-July 18, 1998).
HONORS: Named lefthanded pitcher on THE SPORTING NEWS N.L. All-Star team (1996).
STATISTICAL NOTES: Tied for A.L. lead with five balks in 1994. ... Led A.L. with 14 wild pitches in 1995. ... Pitched 11-0 no-hit victory against Colorado (May 11, 1996).

Year	Team (League)	W	L	Pct.	ERA	G	GS	CG	ShO	Sv.	IP	H	R	ER	BB	SO
1984—	Oneonta (N.Y.-Penn)	3	2	.600	3.63	10	10	0	0	0	57	52	32	23	26	48
1985—	Oneonta (N.Y.-Penn)	3	2	.600	2.37	6	6	2	0	0	38	27	14	10	25	34
—Fort Lauderdale (FSL)		1	6	.143	6.48	17	17	1	0	0	82	87	70	59	57	44
1986—	Fort Lauderdale (FSL)	4	8	.333	4.05	22	21	1	1	0	117 2/3	96	64	53	90	101
1987—	Columbus (Int'l)	1	4	.200	6.17	5	5	0	0	0	23 1/3	21	18	16	15	23
—Alb./Colon. (East.)		3	3	.500	3.35	15	14	2	0	0	78	64	34	29	37	71
—New York (A.L.).................		2	2	.500	6.35	4	4	0	0	0	22 2/3	24	16	16	15	28
1988—	New York (A.L.).................	4	4	.500	3.92	14	14	0	0	0	57 1/3	49	27	25	33	60
—Columbus (Int'l)		0	2	.000	3.46	4	4	0	0	0	13	5	7	5	14	12

Year Team (League)	W	L	Pct.	ERA	G	GS	CG	ShO	Sv.	IP	H	R	ER	BB	SO
1989— New York (A.L.)	1	2	.333	6.08	4	4	0	0	0	26²/₃	23	20	18	21	22
— Toronto (A.L.)■	0	0	...	4.05	1	1	0	0	0	6²/₃	9	3	3	2	4
— Dunedin (Fla. St.)	0	2	.000	5.63	3	3	0	0	0	8	11	5	5	5	4
1990— Dunedin (Fla. St.)	0	0	...	2.63	6	6	0	0	0	24	18	8	7	12	14
— Syracuse (Int'l)	3	8	.273	4.62	15	14	1	1	0	78	59	43	40	68	69
— Toronto (A.L.)	0	0	...	0.00	4	0	0	0	0	6¹/₃	1	0	0	2	5
1991— Toronto (A.L.)	0	0	...	27.00	3	0	0	0	0	1²/₃	3	5	5	5	1
— Dunedin (Fla. St.)	0	0	...	1.86	4	3	0	0	0	9²/₃	5	2	2	7	5
1992— Syracuse (Int'l)	8	9	.471	3.86	27	27	2	0	0	163¹/₃	159	82	70	64	108
— Toronto (A.L.)	0	0	...	9.00	1	0	0	0	0	1	1	1	1	2	0
1993— Toronto (A.L.)	9	6	.600	4.11	34	12	1	1	2	105	93	52	48	56	66
1994— Toronto (A.L.)	6	7	.462	5.08	20	20	1	0	0	111²/₃	125	68	63	65	100
1995— Toronto (A.L.)	11	11	.500	3.64	28	28	2	1	0	183	162	80	74	*108	153
1996— Florida (N.L.)■	16	12	.571	2.93	33	33	2	1	0	215¹/₃	153	74	70	*119	200
1997— Florida (N.L.)	11	9	.550	4.34	27	27	0	0	0	151¹/₃	133	78	73	91	132
1998— New York (N.L.)■	17	6	.739	2.47	28	28	4	2	0	193	151	55	53	71	174
A.L. totals (9 years)	33	32	.508	4.36	113	83	4	2	2	522	490	272	253	309	439
N.L. totals (3 years)	44	27	.620	3.15	88	88	6	3	0	559²/₃	437	207	196	281	506
Major league totals (12 years)	77	59	.566	3.74	201	171	10	5	2	1081²/₃	927	479	449	590	945

DIVISION SERIES RECORD

Year Team (League)	W	L	Pct.	ERA	G	GS	CG	ShO	Sv.	IP	H	R	ER	BB	SO
1997— Florida (N.L.)	0	0	...	9.00	1	1	0	0	0	4	7	4	4	3	3

CHAMPIONSHIP SERIES RECORD

Year Team (League)	W	L	Pct.	ERA	G	GS	CG	ShO	Sv.	IP	H	R	ER	BB	SO
1993— Toronto (A.L.)	0	0	...	3.38	2	0	0	0	0	2²/₃	4	1	1	2	2
1997— Florida (N.L.)	0	1	.000	4.32	2	1	0	0	0	8¹/₃	13	4	4	2	6
Champ. series totals (2 years)	0	1	.000	4.09	4	1	0	0	0	11	17	5	5	4	8

WORLD SERIES RECORD

RECORDS: Shares single-inning record for most bases on balls allowed—4 (October 21, 1997, fourth inning).
NOTES: Member of World Series championship team (1993 and 1997).

Year Team (League)	W	L	Pct.	ERA	G	GS	CG	ShO	Sv.	IP	H	R	ER	BB	SO
1993— Toronto (A.L.)	1	0	1.000	7.71	3	0	0	0	0	7	12	6	6	2	5
1997— Florida (N.L.)	0	0	...	5.06	2	2	0	0	0	10²/₃	10	9	6	10	10
World Series totals (2 years)	1	0	1.000	6.11	5	2	0	0	0	17²/₃	22	15	12	12	15

ALL-STAR GAME RECORD

Year League	W	L	Pct.	ERA	GS	CG	ShO	Sv.	IP	H	R	ER	BB	SO
1996— National	0	0	...	0.00	0	0	0	0	¹/₃	0	0	0	0	0

LEITER, MARK   P   MARINERS

PERSONAL: Born April 13, 1963, in Joliet, Ill. ... 6-3/220. ... Throws right, bats right. ... Full name: Mark Edward Leiter. ... Brother of Al Leiter, pitcher, New York Mets; and brother of Kurt Leiter, minor league pitcher (1982-84 and 1986). ... Name pronounced LIE-ter.
HIGH SCHOOL: Central Regional (Bayville, N.J.).
JUNIOR COLLEGE: Connors State College (Okla.).
COLLEGE: Ramapo College of New Jersey.
TRANSACTIONS/CAREER NOTES: Selected by Baltimore Orioles organization in fourth round of free-agent draft (January 11, 1983). ... On disabled list (April 10, 1986-entire season; April 10, 1987-entire season; and April 10-June 13, 1988). ... Released by Orioles organization (June 13, 1988). ... Signed by Fort Lauderdale, New York Yankees organization (September 29, 1988). ... Traded by Yankees to Detroit Tigers for IF Torey Lovullo (March 19, 1991). ... On Detroit disabled list (June 6-23, 1991; July 24-August 24, 1992; and August 4-September 1, 1993). ... Released by Tigers (March 15, 1994). ... Signed by California Angels (March 21, 1994). ... Granted free agency (December 23, 1994). ... Signed by Phoenix, San Francisco Giants organization (April 10, 1995). ... Traded by Giants to Montreal Expos for P Tim Scott and P Kirk Rueter (July 30, 1996). ... Granted free agency (November 5, 1996). ... Signed by Philadelphia Phillies (December 12, 1996). ... On disabled list (June 21-July 5, 1997). ... Traded by Phillies to Seattle Mariners for P Paul Spoljaric (November 9, 1998).
STATISTICAL NOTES: Tied for A.L. lead with nine hit batsmen in 1994. ... Led N.L. with 17 hit batsmen in 1995 and tied for lead with 16 in 1996. ... Led N.L. with 37 home runs allowed in 1996.

Year Team (League)	W	L	Pct.	ERA	G	GS	CG	ShO	Sv.	IP	H	R	ER	BB	SO
1983— Bluefield (Appalachian)	2	1	.667	2.70	6	6	2	0	0	36²/₃	33	17	11	13	35
— Hagerstown (Caro.)	1	5	.167	7.25	8	8	0	0	0	36	42	31	29	28	18
1984— Hagerstown (Caro.)	8	•13	.381	5.62	27	24	5	1	0	139¹/₃	132	96	87	*108	105
1985— Hagerstown (Caro.)	2	8	.200	3.46	34	6	1	0	8	83¹/₃	77	44	32	29	82
— Charlotte (Southern)	0	1	.000	1.42	5	0	0	0	1	6¹/₃	3	1	1	2	8
1986—							Did not play.								
1987—							Did not play.								
1988—							Did not play.								
1989— Fort Lauderdale (FSL)■	2	2	.500	1.53	6	4	1	0	1	35¹/₃	27	9	6	5	22
— Columbus (Int'l)	9	6	.600	5.00	22	12	0	0	0	90	102	50	50	34	70
1990— Columbus (Int'l)	9	4	.692	3.60	30	14	2	1	1	122²/₃	114	56	49	27	115
— New York (A.L.)	1	1	.500	6.84	8	3	0	0	0	26¹/₃	33	20	20	9	21
1991— Toledo (International)■■	1	0	1.000	0.00	5	0	0	0	1	6²/₃	6	0	0	3	7
— Detroit (A.L.)	9	7	.563	4.21	38	15	1	0	1	134²/₃	125	66	63	50	103
1992— Detroit (A.L.)	8	5	.615	4.18	35	14	1	0	0	112	116	57	52	43	75
1993— Detroit (A.L.)	6	6	.500	4.73	27	13	1	0	0	106²/₃	111	61	56	44	70
1994— California (A.L.)■	4	7	.364	4.72	40	7	0	0	2	95¹/₃	99	56	50	35	71
1995— San Francisco (N.L.)■	10	12	.455	3.82	30	29	7	1	0	195²/₃	185	91	83	55	129
1996— San Francisco (N.L.)	4	10	.286	5.19	23	22	1	0	0	135¹/₃	151	93	78	50	118
— Montreal (N.L.)■	4	2	.667	4.39	12	12	1	0	0	69²/₃	68	35	34	19	46

Year	Team (League)	W	L	Pct.	ERA	G	GS	CG	ShO	Sv.	IP	H	R	ER	BB	SO
1997—	Philadelphia (N.L.)■	10	*17	.370	5.67	31	31	3	0	0	182 2/3	216	*132	*115	64	148
1998—	Philadelphia (N.L.)	7	5	.583	3.55	69	0	0	0	23	88 2/3	67	36	35	47	84
	A.L. totals (5 years)	28	26	.519	4.57	148	52	3	0	3	475	484	260	241	181	340
	N.L. totals (4 years)	35	46	.432	4.62	165	94	12	1	23	672	687	387	345	235	525
	Major league totals (9 years)	63	72	.467	4.60	313	146	15	1	26	1147	1171	647	586	416	865

LEIUS, SCOTT 3B/SS ROYALS

PERSONAL: Born September 24, 1965, in Yonkers, N.Y. ... 6-3/208. ... Bats right, throws right. ... Full name: Scott Thomas Leius. ... Name pronounced LAY-us.

HIGH SCHOOL: Mamaroneck (N.Y.).

COLLEGE: Concordia College (N.Y.).

TRANSACTIONS/CAREER NOTES: Selected by Minnesota Twins organization in 13th round of free-agent draft (June 2, 1986). ... On disabled list (August 3, 1989-remainder of season and April 22, 1993-remainder of season). ... Granted free agency (October 10, 1995). ... Signed by Cleveland Indians (March 31, 1996). ... On Cleveland disabled list (June 7-27, 1996); included rehabilitation assignment to Buffalo (June 13-27). ... Granted free agency (September 30, 1996). ... Signed by Boston Red Sox organization (February 8, 1997). ... Released by Red Sox (March 29, 1997). ... Signed by Chicago White Sox organization (May 20, 1997). ... Granted free agency (October 15, 1997). ... Signed by Kansas City Royals organization (March 9, 1998). ... On Kansas City disabled list (August 14-September 4, 1998); included rehabilitation assignment to Omaha (August 31-September 4). ... Granted free agency (October 28, 1998). ... Re-signed by Royals organization (December 17, 1998).

STATISTICAL NOTES: Led Appalachian League shortstops with 174 assists and 33 double plays in 1986. ... Led Midwest League shortstops with 74 double plays in 1987.

							BATTING								FIELDING		
Year	Team (League)	Pos.	G	AB	R	H	2B	3B	HR	RBI	Avg.	BB	SO	SB	PO	A	E	Avg.
1986—	Elizabethton (App.)	SS-3B	61	237	37	66	14	1	4	23	.278	26	45	5	67	†176	18	.931
1987—	Kenosha (Midwest)	SS	126	414	65	99	16	4	8	51	.239	50	88	6	183	331	31	.943
1988—	Visalia (California)	SS	93	308	44	73	14	4	3	46	.237	42	50	3	154	234	15	.963
1989—	Orlando (South.)	SS	99	346	49	105	22	2	4	45	*.303	38	74	3	148	257	22	.948
1990—	Portland (PCL)	SS-2B	103	352	34	81	13	5	2	23	.230	35	66	5	155	323	18	.964
	— Minnesota (A.L.)	SS-3B	14	25	4	6	1	0	1	4	.240	2	2	0	20	25	0	1.000
1991—	Minnesota (A.L.)	3B-SS-OF	109	199	35	57	7	2	5	20	.286	30	35	5	56	129	7	.964
1992—	Minnesota (A.L.)	3B-SS	129	409	50	102	18	2	2	35	.249	34	61	6	63	261	15	.956
1993—	Minnesota (A.L.)	SS	10	18	4	3	0	0	0	2	.167	2	4	0	10	26	2	.947
1994—	Minnesota (A.L.)	3B-SS	97	350	57	86	16	1	14	49	.246	37	58	2	63	185	8	.969
1995—	Minnesota (A.L.)	3B-SS-DH	117	372	51	92	16	5	4	45	.247	49	54	2	60	187	14	.946
1996—	Cleveland (A.L.)■■...	3-1-2-DH	27	43	3	6	4	0	1	3	.140	2	8	0	45	16	1	.984
	— Buffalo (A.A.)	1-2-3-O	35	123	22	33	3	1	4	17	.268	12	16	0	110	36	7	.954
1997—	Nashville (A.A.)■ ..	3B-1B	30	104	15	25	2	0	7	17	.240	11	6	0	57	27	5	.944
1998—	Omaha (PCL)■	3B-2B-SS	71	258	40	77	10	0	15	46	.298	17	30	7	37	110	11	.930
	— Kansas City (A.L.)	3B-SS-DH	17	46	2	8	0	0	0	4	.174	1	6	0	8	19	4	.871
	Major league totals (8 years)		520	1462	206	360	62	10	27	162	.246	157	228	15	325	848	51	.958

CHAMPIONSHIP SERIES RECORD

							BATTING								FIELDING		
Year	Team (League)	Pos.	G	AB	R	H	2B	3B	HR	RBI	Avg.	BB	SO	SB	PO	A	E	Avg.
1991—	Minnesota (A.L.)	3B-PH	3	4	0	0	0	0	0	0	.000	1	1	0	1	4	0	1.000

WORLD SERIES RECORD

NOTES: Member of World Series championship team (1991).

							BATTING								FIELDING		
Year	Team (League)	Pos.	G	AB	R	H	2B	3B	HR	RBI	Avg.	BB	SO	SB	PO	A	E	Avg.
1991—	Minnesota (A.L.)	3B-PH-SS	7	14	2	5	0	0	1	2	.357	1	2	0	5	8	1	.929

LEMKE, MARK 2B

PERSONAL: Born August 13, 1965, in Utica, N.Y. ... 5-9/167. ... Bats both, throws right. ... Full name: Mark Alan Lemke. ... Name pronounced LEM-kee.

HIGH SCHOOL: Notre Dame (Utica, N.Y.).

TRANSACTIONS/CAREER NOTES: Selected by Atlanta Braves organization in 27th round of free-agent draft (June 6, 1983). ... On Atlanta disabled list (May 29-July 17, 1990); included rehabilitation assignment to Gulf Coast Braves (July 9-17). ... On disabled list (June 25-July 18, 1995 and May 27-June 13, 1996). ... Granted free agency (October 30, 1996). ... Re-signed by Braves (December 18, 1996). ... On disabled list (August 22, 1997-remainder of season). ... Granted free agency (November 5, 1997). ... Signed by Boston Red Sox organization (March 26, 1998). ... On Boston disabled list (May 26, 1998-remainder of season). ... Granted free agency (October 26, 1998).

STATISTICAL NOTES: Led Gulf Coast League second basemen with .977 fielding percentage, 175 putouts, 207 assists, 391 total chances and 39 double plays in 1984. ... Led Carolina League second basemen with .982 fielding percentage, 355 assists and 83 double plays in 1987. ... Led Southern League with 239 total bases in 1988. ... Led Southern League second basemen with 739 total chances and 105 double plays in 1988. ... Led International League second basemen with 731 total chances and 105 double plays in 1989. ... Led N.L. second basemen with 785 total chances and 100 double plays in 1993.

							BATTING								FIELDING		
Year	Team (League)	Pos.	G	AB	R	H	2B	3B	HR	RBI	Avg.	BB	SO	SB	PO	A	E	Avg.
1983—	GC Braves (GCL)	2B	53	209	37	55	6	0	0	19	.263	30	19	10	81	101	11	.943
1984—	Anderson (S. Atl.)	2B-3B	42	121	18	18	2	0	0	5	.149	14	14	3	67	83	4	.974
	— GC Braves (GCL)	2B-SS	•63	*243	41	67	11	0	3	32	.276	29	14	2	†175	†209	9	†.977
1985—	Sumter (S. Atl.)	2B	90	231	25	50	6	0	0	20	.216	34	22	2	119	174	11	.964
1986—	Sumter (S. Atl.)	3B-2B	126	448	99	122	24	2	18	66	.272	87	31	11	134	274	16	.962
1987—	Durham (Carolina)	2B-3B	127	489	75	143	28	3	20	68	.292	54	45	10	248	†355	11	†.982
	— Greenville (Southern) .	3B	6	26	0	6	0	0	0	4	.231	0	4	0	4	12	1	.941

Year Team (League)	Pos.	G	AB	R	H	2B	3B	HR	RBI	Avg.	BB	SO	SB	PO	A	E	Avg.
1988—Greenville (Southern).	2B	•143	*567	81	*153	30	4	16	80	.270	52	92	18	*281	*440	18	.976
—Atlanta (N.L.)	2B	16	58	8	13	4	0	0	2	.224	4	5	0	47	51	3	.970
1989—Richmond (Int'l)	2B	*146	*518	69	143	22	7	5	61	.276	66	45	4	*299	*417	*15	.979
—Atlanta (N.L.)	2B	14	55	4	10	2	1	2	10	.182	5	7	0	25	40	0	1.000
1990—Atlanta (N.L.)	3B-2B-SS	102	239	22	54	13	0	0	21	.226	21	22	0	90	193	4	.986
—GC Braves (GCL)	2B-3B	4	11	2	4	0	0	1	5	.364	1	3	0	5	11	1	.941
1991—Atlanta (N.L.)	2B-3B	136	269	36	63	11	2	2	23	.234	29	27	1	162	215	10	.974
1992—Atlanta (N.L.)	2B-3B	155	427	38	97	7	4	6	26	.227	50	39	0	236	335	9	.984
1993—Atlanta (N.L.)	2B	151	493	52	124	19	2	7	49	.252	65	50	1	*329	442	14	.982
1994—Atlanta (N.L.)	2B	104	350	40	103	15	0	3	31	.294	38	37	0	209	300	3	*.994
1995—Atlanta (N.L.)	2B	116	399	42	101	16	5	5	38	.253	44	40	2	205	305	5	.990
1996—Atlanta (N.L.)	2B	135	498	64	127	17	0	5	37	.255	53	48	5	228	410	15	.977
1997—Atlanta (N.L.)	2B	109	351	33	86	17	1	2	26	.245	33	51	2	191	309	10	.980
1998—Boston (A.L.)■	2B	31	91	10	17	4	0	0	7	.187	6	15	0	38	71	0	1.000
American League totals (1 year)		31	91	10	17	4	0	0	7	.187	6	15	0	38	71	0	1.000
National League totals (10 years)		1038	3139	339	778	121	15	32	263	.248	342	326	11	1722	2600	73	.983
Major league totals (11 years)		1069	3230	349	795	125	15	32	270	.246	348	341	11	1760	2671	73	.984

DIVISION SERIES RECORD

Year Team (League)	Pos.	G	AB	R	H	2B	3B	HR	RBI	Avg.	BB	SO	SB	PO	A	E	Avg.
1995—Atlanta (N.L.)	2B	4	19	3	4	1	0	0	1	.211	1	3	0	8	16	0	1.000
1996—Atlanta (N.L.)	2B	3	12	1	2	1	0	0	2	.167	0	1	0	4	8	0	1.000
Division series totals (2 years)		7	31	4	6	2	0	0	3	.194	1	4	0	12	24	0	1.000

CHAMPIONSHIP SERIES RECORD

RECORDS: Holds N.L. career record for most games with one club—31. ... Shares single-series record for most singles—9 (1996).

Year Team (League)	Pos.	G	AB	R	H	2B	3B	HR	RBI	Avg.	BB	SO	SB	PO	A	E	Avg.
1991—Atlanta (N.L.)	2B	7	20	1	4	1	0	0	1	.200	4	0	0	12	10	1	.957
1992—Atlanta (N.L.)	2B-3B	7	21	2	7	1	0	0	2	.333	5	3	0	11	17	0	1.000
1993—Atlanta (N.L.)	2B	6	24	2	5	2	0	0	4	.208	1	6	0	6	19	2	.926
1995—Atlanta (N.L.)	2B	4	18	2	3	0	0	0	1	.167	1	0	0	13	16	0	1.000
1996—Atlanta (N.L.)	2B	7	27	4	12	2	0	1	5	.444	4	2	0	9	18	0	1.000
Championship series totals (5 years)		31	110	11	31	6	0	1	13	.282	15	11	0	51	80	3	.978

WORLD SERIES RECORD

RECORDS: Shares single-game record for most triples—2 (October 24, 1991).
NOTES: Member of World Series championship team (1995).

Year Team (League)	Pos.	G	AB	R	H	2B	3B	HR	RBI	Avg.	BB	SO	SB	PO	A	E	Avg.
1991—Atlanta (N.L.)	2B	6	24	4	10	1	3	0	4	.417	2	4	0	14	19	1	.971
1992—Atlanta (N.L.)	2B	6	19	0	4	0	0	0	2	.211	1	3	0	18	12	0	1.000
1995—Atlanta (N.L.)	2B	6	22	1	6	0	0	0	0	.273	3	2	0	10	24	1	.971
1996—Atlanta (N.L.)	2B	6	26	2	6	1	0	0	2	.231	0	3	0	11	24	0	1.000
World Series totals (4 years)		24	91	7	26	2	3	0	8	.286	6	12	0	53	79	2	.985

LENNON, PATRICK   OF   BLUE JAYS

PERSONAL: Born April 27, 1968, in Whiteville, N.C. ... 6-2/230. ... Bats right, throws right. ... Full name: Patrick Orlando Lennon.

HIGH SCHOOL: Whiteville (N.C.).

TRANSACTIONS/CAREER NOTES: Selected by Seattle Mariners organization in first round (eighth pick overall) of free-agent draft (June 2, 1986). ... On Calgary disabled list (May 18, 1992-remainder of season). ... Granted free agency (October 15, 1992). ... Signed by Colorado Rockies (October 29, 1992). ... Released by Colorado Springs, Rockies organization (April 2, 1993). ... Signed by Torreon of Mexican League (1993). ... Signed by Canton/Akron, Cleveland Indians organization (July 19, 1993). ... Granted free agency (October 15, 1993). ... Signed by New Britain, Boston Red Sox organization (March 7, 1994). ... On disabled list (August 4-12, 1994). ... Released by Red Sox organization (July 20, 1995). ... Signed by Salt Lake, Minnesota Twins organization (July 22, 1995). ... Granted free agency (October 16, 1995). ... Signed by Kansas City Royals (March 31, 1996). ... Released by Royals (April 29, 1996). ... Signed by Edmonton, Oakland Athletics organization (June 1, 1996). ... On Edmonton disabled list (September 10-18, 1996). ... On Oakland disabled list (August 20-September 12, 1997); included rehabilitation assignments to Modesto (August 28-September 3) and Edmonton (Septmeber 3-12). ... Released by A's (December 15, 1997). ... Signed by Anaheim Angels organization (January 30, 1998). ... Released by Angels (March 11, 1998). ... Signed by Toronto Blue Jays organization (March 25, 1998).

STATISTICAL NOTES: Led Midwest League third basemen with 39 errors in 1987.

Year Team (League)	Pos.	G	AB	R	H	2B	3B	HR	RBI	Avg.	BB	SO	SB	PO	A	E	Avg.
1986—Bellingham (N'west)	SS-3B	51	169	35	41	5	2	3	27	.243	36	50	8	57	90	27	.845
1987—Wausau (Midwest)	3B-SS	98	319	54	80	21	3	7	34	.251	45	82	25	73	190	†40	.868
1988—Vermont (Eastern)	3B	95	321	44	83	9	3	9	40	.259	21	87	15	81	143	*28	.889
1989—Williamsport (East.)	OF-3B	66	248	32	65	14	2	3	31	.262	23	53	7	67	20	14	.861
1990—San Bern. (Calif.)	3B-OF	44	163	29	47	6	2	8	30	.288	15	51	6	29	40	7	.908
—Williamsport (East.)	OF-3B	49	167	24	49	6	4	5	22	.293	10	37	10	62	40	10	.911
1991—Calgary (PCL)	OF-3B	112	416	75	137	29	5	15	74	.329	46	68	12	114	3	6	.951
—Seattle (A.L.)	DH-OF	9	8	2	1	1	0	0	1	.125	3	1	0	2	0	0	1.000
1992—Seattle (A.L.)	1B	1	2	0	0	0	0	0	0	.000	0	0	0	5	0	0	1.000
—Calgary (PCL)	OF-3B	13	48	8	17	3	0	1	9	.354	6	10	4	12	0	1	.923
1993—Torreon (Mexican)■	OF	27	97	18	34	5	0	5	15	.351	11	31	0	27	1	0	1.000
—Cant./Akr. (Eastern)■	OF-1B	45	152	24	39	7	1	4	23	.257	30	45	4	45	3	4	.923

Year Team (League)	Pos.	G	AB	R	H	2B	3B	HR	RBI	Avg.	BB	SO	SB	PO	A	E	Avg.
1994— New Britain (East.)■ ..	OF-1B	114	429	80	140	30	5	17	67	.326	48	96	13	189	12	3	.985
1995— Pawtucket (Int'l)........	OF	40	128	20	35	6	2	3	20	.273	16	42	6	54	4	3	.951
— Trenton (Eastern)	OF	27	98	19	39	7	0	1	8	.398	14	22	7	32	2	3	.919
— Salt Lake (PCL)■	OF	34	115	26	46	15	0	6	29	.400	12	29	2	10	0	0	1.000
1996— Kansas City (A.L.)■ ...	OF-DH	14	30	5	7	3	0	0	1	.233	7	10	0	18	0	1	.947
— Edmonton (PCL)■	OF	68	251	37	82	16	2	12	42	.327	28	82	3	57	5	4	.939
1997— Edmonton (PCL)	OF	39	134	28	46	7	0	9	35	.343	22	34	0	13	1	0	1.000
— Oakland (A.L.)	OF-DH	56	116	14	34	6	1	1	14	.293	15	35	0	55	0	3	.948
— Modesto (California) ..	OF	5	16	3	3	1	0	1	4	.188	3	5	0	2	0	0	1.000
1998— Syracuse (Int'l)■........	OF	126	438	87	127	22	4	27	95	.290	*87	121	12	132	11	8	.947
— Toronto (A.L.).............	OF	2	4	1	2	2	0	0	0	.500	0	1	0	3	0	0	1.000
Major league totals (5 years)		82	160	22	44	12	1	1	16	.275	25	47	0	83	0	4	.954

LeROY, JOHN   P

PERSONAL: Born April 19, 1975, in Bellevue, Wash. ... 6-3/175. ... Throws right, bats right. ... Full name: John Michael LeRoy.
HIGH SCHOOL: Sammamish (Bellevue, Wash.).
TRANSACTIONS/CAREER NOTES: Selected by Atlanta Braves organization in 15th round of free-agent draft (June 3, 1993). ... Selected by Tampa Bay Devil Rays in second round (34th pick overall) of expansion draft (November 18, 1997). ... On Orlando disabled list (April 27, 1998-remainder of season). ... Released by Devil Rays (December 14, 1998).

Year Team (League)	W	L	Pct.	ERA	G	GS	CG	ShO	Sv.	IP	H	R	ER	BB	SO
1993— GC Braves (GCL)	2	2	.500	2.05	10	2	0	0	1	26 1/3	21	9	6	8	32
1994— Macon (S. Atl.)..................	3	3	.500	4.46	10	9	0	0	0	40 1/3	36	21	20	20	44
1995— Durham (Carolina).............	6	9	.400	5.44	24	22	1	0	0	125 2/3	128	82	76	57	77
1996— Durham (Carolina).............	7	4	.636	3.50	19	19	0	0	0	110 2/3	91	47	43	52	94
— Greenville (Southern)	1	1	.500	2.98	8	8	0	0	0	45 1/3	43	18	15	18	38
1997— Greenville (Southern)	5	5	.500	5.03	29	14	0	0	1	98 1/3	105	59	55	43	84
— Atlanta (N.L.)......................	1	0	1.000	0.00	1	0	0	0	0	2	1	0	0	3	3
1998— Durham (International)■...	0	1	.000	27.00	4	0	0	0	0	4	11	12	12	5	1
— Orlando (South.)	1	0	1.000	6.45	12	0	0	0	0	22 1/3	22	17	16	10	12
— St. Petersburg (FSL)	1	1	.500	4.58	11	0	0	0	0	17 2/3	18	9	9	6	17
Major league totals (1 year)........	1	0	1.000	0.00	1	0	0	0	0	2	1	0	0	3	3

LESHER, BRIAN   OF   ATHLETICS

PERSONAL: Born March 5, 1971, in Antwerp, Belgium. ... 6-5/216. ... Bats right, throws left. ... Full name: Brian Herbert Lesher.
HIGH SCHOOL: Newark (Del.).
COLLEGE: Delaware.
TRANSACTIONS/CAREER NOTES: Selected by Oakland Athletics organization in 25th round of free-agent draft (June 1, 1992). ... On Oakland disabled list (March 22-May 11, 1998); included rehabilitation assignment to Edmonton (May 2-11).

Year Team (League)	Pos.	G	AB	R	H	2B	3B	HR	RBI	Avg.	BB	SO	SB	PO	A	E	Avg.
1992— S. Oregon (N'west).....	OF-1B	46	136	21	26	7	1	3	18	.191	12	35	3	63	3	4	.943
1993— Madison (Midwest)	OF	119	394	63	108	13	5	5	47	.274	46	102	20	193	9	5	.976
1994— Modesto (California) ..	OF-1B	117	393	76	114	21	0	14	68	.290	81	84	11	332	20	11	.970
1995— Huntsville (Sou.) ..	OF-1B	127	471	78	123	23	2	19	71	.261	64	110	7	198	7	6	.972
1996— Edmonton (PCL)	1B-OF	109	414	57	119	29	2	18	75	.287	36	108	6	699	44	9	.988
— Oakland (A.L.)	OF-1B	26	82	11	19	3	0	5	16	.232	5	17	0	46	2	1	.980
1997— Edmonton (PCL)	OF-1B	110	415	85	134	27	5	21	78	.323	64	86	14	220	6	6	.974
— Oakland (A.L.)	OF-DH-1B	46	131	17	30	4	1	4	16	.229	9	30	4	87	5	3	.968
1998— Edmonton (PCL)	OF-1B	99	360	62	108	31	1	11	60	.300	46	96	3	224	6	5	.979
— Oakland (A.L.)	OF-1B	7	7	0	1	1	0	0	1	.143	0	3	0	4	2	1	.857
Major league totals (3 years)		79	220	28	50	8	1	9	33	.227	14	50	4	137	9	5	.967

LESKANIC, CURTIS   P   ROCKIES

PERSONAL: Born April 2, 1968, in Homestead, Pa. ... 6-0/186. ... Throws right, bats right. ... Full name: Curtis John Leskanic. ... Name pronounced lees-CAN-ik.
HIGH SCHOOL: Steel Valley (Munhall, Pa.).
COLLEGE: Louisiana State.
TRANSACTIONS/CAREER NOTES: Selected by Cleveland Indians organization in eighth round of free-agent draft (June 5, 1989). ... On disabled list (April 23-June 25, 1990). ... Traded by Indians organization with P Oscar Munoz to Minnesota Twins organization for 1B Paul Sorrento (March 28, 1992). ... Selected by Colorado Rockies in third round (66th pick overall) of expansion draft (November 17, 1992). ... Loaned by Rockies organization to Wichita, Padres organization (April 7-May 20, 1993). ... On Colorado disabled list (May 30-June 28, 1996); included rehabilitation assignment to Colorado Springs (June 22-27). ... On Colorado disabled list (March 23-April 12, 1997); included rehabilitation assignment to Salem (April 6-8).
MISCELLANEOUS: Had a sacrifice hit in only appearance as pinch hitter (1998).

Year Team (League)	W	L	Pct.	ERA	G	GS	CG	ShO	Sv.	IP	H	R	ER	BB	SO
1990— Kinston (Carolina)	6	5	.545	3.68	14	14	2	0	0	73 1/3	61	34	30	30	71
1991— Kinston (Carolina)	8	8	.652	2.79	28	28	0	0	0	174 1/3	143	63	54	91	*163
1992— Orlando (South.)■	9	11	.450	4.30	26	23	3	0	0	152 2/3	158	84	73	64	126
— Portland (PCL)	1	2	.333	9.98	5	3	0	0	0	15 1/3	16	17	17	8	14
1993— Wichita (Texas)■	3	2	.600	3.45	7	7	0	0	0	44 1/3	37	20	17	17	42
— Colo. Springs (PCL)■........	4	3	.571	4.47	9	7	1	1	0	44 1/3	39	24	22	26	38
— Colorado (N.L.)	1	5	.167	5.37	18	8	0	0	0	57	59	40	34	27	30

Year Team (League)	W	L	Pct.	ERA	G	GS	CG	ShO	Sv.	IP	H	R	ER	BB	SO
1994— Colo. Springs (PCL)	5	7	.417	3.31	21	21	2	0	0	130 1/3	129	60	48	54	98
— Colorado (N.L.)	1	1	.500	5.64	8	3	0	0	0	22 1/3	27	14	14	10	17
1995— Colorado (N.L.)	6	3	.667	3.40	*76	0	0	0	10	98	83	38	37	33	107
1996— Colorado (N.L.)	7	5	.583	6.23	70	0	0	0	6	73 2/3	82	51	51	38	76
— Colo. Springs (PCL)	0	0	...	3.00	3	0	0	0	0	3	5	1	1	1	2
1997— Salem (Carolina)	0	0	...	3.86	2	1	0	0	0	2 1/3	5	2	1	1	3
— Colorado (N.L.)	4	0	1.000	5.55	55	0	0	0	2	58 1/3	59	36	36	24	53
— Colo. Springs (PCL)	0	0	...	3.79	10	3	0	0	2	19	11	9	8	18	20
1998— Colorado (N.L.)	6	4	.600	4.40	66	0	0	0	2	75 2/3	75	37	37	40	55
Major league totals (6 years)	25	18	.581	4.89	293	11	0	0	20	385	385	216	209	172	338

DIVISION SERIES RECORD

Year Team (League)	W	L	Pct.	ERA	G	GS	CG	ShO	Sv.	IP	H	R	ER	BB	SO
1995— Colorado (N.L.)	0	1	.000	6.00	3	0	0	0	0	3	3	2	2	0	4

LEVINE, AL   P   RANGERS

PERSONAL: Born May 22, 1968, in Park Ridge, Ill. ... 6-3/180. ... Throws right, bats left. ... Full name: Alan Brian Levine.
HIGH SCHOOL: Hoffman Estates (Ill.).
JUNIOR COLLEGE: Harper Junior College (Ill.).
COLLEGE: Southern Illinois-Carbondale.
TRANSACTIONS/CAREER NOTES: Selected by Chicago White Sox in 11th round of free-agent draft (June 3, 1991). ... Traded by White Sox with P Larry Thomas to Texas Rangers for SS Benji Gil (December 19, 1997).

Year Team (League)	W	L	Pct.	ERA	G	GS	CG	ShO	Sv.	IP	H	R	ER	BB	SO
1991— Utica (N.Y.-Penn)	6	4	.600	3.18	16	12	2	1	1	85	75	45	30	26	83
1992— South Bend (Mid.)...............	9	5	.643	2.81	23	23	2	0	0	156 2/3	151	67	49	36	131
— Sarasota (Florida State)......	0	2	.000	4.02	3	2	0	0	0	15 2/3	17	11	7	5	11
1993— Sarasota (Florida State)......	11	8	.579	3.68	27	26	5	1	0	161 1/3	169	87	66	50	*129
1994— Birmingham (Southern)	5	9	.357	3.31	18	18	1	0	0	114 1/3	117	50	42	44	94
— Nashville (A.A.)	0	2	.000	7.88	8	4	0	0	0	24	34	23	21	11	24
1995— Nashville (A.A.)	0	2	.000	5.14	3	3	0	0	0	14	20	10	8	7	14
— Birmingham (Southern)	4	3	.571	2.34	43	1	0	0	7	73	61	22	19	25	68
1996— Nashville (A.A.)	4	5	.444	3.65	43	0	0	0	12	61 2/3	58	27	25	24	45
— Chicago (A.L.)	0	1	.000	5.40	16	0	0	0	0	18 1/3	22	14	11	7	12
1997— Chicago (A.L.)	2	2	.500	6.91	25	0	0	0	0	27 1/3	35	22	21	16	22
— Nashville (A.A.)	1	1	.500	7.13	26	0	0	0	2	35 1/3	58	32	28	11	29
1998— Oklahoma (PCL)■.............	1	3	.250	4.73	12	7	0	0	1	53 1/3	51	33	28	17	30
— Texas (A.L.)	0	1	.000	4.50	30	0	0	0	0	58	68	30	29	16	19
Major league totals (3 years)	2	4	.333	5.30	71	0	0	0	0	103 2/3	125	66	61	39	53

LEVIS, JESSE   C   DEVIL RAYS

PERSONAL: Born April 14, 1968, in Philadelphia. ... 5-9/200. ... Bats left, throws right.
HIGH SCHOOL: Northeast (Philadelphia).
COLLEGE: North Carolina.
TRANSACTIONS/CAREER NOTES: Selected by Philadelphia Phillies organization in 36th round of free-agent draft (June 2, 1986); did not sign. ... Selected by Cleveland Indians organization in fourth round of free-agent draft (June 5, 1989). ... Traded by Indians to Milwaukee Brewers for P Scott Nate and a player to be named later (April 4, 1996); Indians acquired P Jared Camp to complete deal (June 9, 1996). ... On disabled list (May 8, 1998-remainder of season). ... Released by Brewers (September 29, 1998). ... Signed by Tampa Bay Devil Rays organization (December 18, 1998).
STATISTICAL NOTES: Led Eastern League catchers with 733 total chances in 1991.

Year Team (League)	Pos.	G	AB	R	H	2B	3B	HR	RBI	Avg.	BB	SO	SB	PO	A	E	Avg.
1989— Burlington (Appal.)......	C	27	93	11	32	4	0	4	16	.344	10	7	1	189	27	2	.991
— Kinston (Carolina)	C	27	87	11	26	6	0	2	11	.299	12	15	1	95	17	2	.982
— Colo. Springs (PCL) ..	PH	1	1	0	0	0	0	0	0	.000	0	0	0	...	...	...	...
1990— Kinston (Carolina)	C	107	382	63	113	18	3	7	64	.296	64	42	4	517	63	5	.991
1991— Cant./Akr. (Eastern)	C	115	382	31	101	17	3	6	45	.264	40	36	2	*644	*77	12	.984
1992— Colo. Springs (PCL) ...	C	87	253	39	92	20	1	6	44	.364	37	25	1	375	47	4	.991
— Cleveland (A.L.)	C-DH	28	43	2	12	4	0	1	3	.279	0	5	0	59	5	1	.985
1993— Charlotte (Int'l)..........	C	47	129	10	32	6	1	2	20	.248	15	12	0	266	22	4	.986
— Cleveland (A.L.)	C	31	63	7	11	2	0	0	4	.175	2	10	0	109	7	1	.991
1994— Charlotte (Int'l)..........	C	111	375	55	107	20	0	10	59	.285	55	39	2	452	34	4	.992
— Cleveland (A.L.)	PH	1	1	0	1	0	0	0	0	1.000	0	0	0	...	...	...	...
1995— Buffalo (A.A.)	C	66	196	26	61	16	0	4	20	.311	32	11	0	338	20	2	.994
— Cleveland (A.L.)	C	12	18	1	6	2	0	0	3	.333	1	0	0	33	5	0	1.000
1996— Milwaukee (A.L.)■......	C-DH	104	233	27	55	6	1	1	21	.236	38	15	0	373	26	1	*.998
1997— Milwaukee (A.L.)	C-DH	99	200	19	57	7	0	1	19	.285	24	17	1	296	19	2	.994
1998— Milwaukee (N.L.)	C	22	37	4	13	0	0	0	4	.351	7	6	1	83	2	0	1.000
American League totals (6 years)		275	558	56	142	21	1	3	50	.254	65	47	1	870	62	5	.995
National League totals (1 year)		22	37	4	13	0	0	0	4	.351	7	6	1	83	2	0	1.000
Major league totals (7 years)		297	595	60	155	21	1	3	54	.261	72	53	2	953	64	5	.995

LEWIS, DARREN   OF   RED SOX

PERSONAL: Born August 28, 1967, in Berkeley, Calif. ... 6-0/189. ... Bats right, throws right. ... Full name: Darren Joel Lewis.
HIGH SCHOOL: Moreau (Hayward, Calif.).

JUNIOR COLLEGE: Chabot College (Calif.).
COLLEGE: California.
TRANSACTIONS/CAREER NOTES: Selected by Los Angeles Dodgers organization in sixth round of free-agent draft (January 14, 1986); did not sign. ... Selected by Toronto Blue Jays organization in 45th round of free-agent draft (June 2, 1987); did not sign. ... Selected by Oakland Athletics organization in 18th round of free-agent draft (June 1, 1988). ... Traded by A's with a player to be named later to San Francisco Giants for IF Ernest Riles (December 4, 1990); Giants acquired P Pedro Pena to complete deal (December 17, 1990). ... On disabled list (August 20-September 4, 1993). ... Traded by Giants with P Mark Portugal and P Dave Burba to Cincinnati Reds for OF Deion Sanders, P John Roper, P Ricky Pickett, P Scott Service and IF Dave McCarty (July 21, 1995). ... Released by Reds (December 1, 1995). ... Signed by Chicago White Sox (December 14, 1995). ... Traded by White Sox to Los Angeles Dodgers for a player to be named later (August 27, 1997); White Sox acquired IF Chad Fonville to complete deal (September 2, 1997). ... Granted free agency (October 27, 1997). ... Signed by Boston Red Sox (December 23, 1997). ... Granted free agency (November 3, 1998). ... Re-signed by Red Sox (November 5, 1998).
RECORDS: Holds major league records for most consecutive errorless games by outfielder—392 (August 21, 1990-June 29, 1994); and most consecutive chances accepted without an error by outfielder—938 (August 21, 1990-June 29, 1994). ... Shares major league record for fewest double plays by outfielder (150 or more games)—0 (1998). ... Holds N.L. records for most consecutive errorless games by outfielder—369 (July 13, 1991-June 29, 1994); and most consecutive chances accepted without an error by outfielder—905 (July 13, 1991-June 29, 1994).
HONORS: Won N.L. Gold Glove as outfielder (1994).
STATISTICAL NOTES: Led California League outfielders with 324 total chances in 1989. ... Career major league grand slams: 1.

Year Team (League)	Pos.	G	AB	R	H	2B	3B	HR	RBI	Avg.	BB	SO	SB	PO	A	E	Avg.
1988—Arizona A's (Ariz.).......	OF	5	15	8	5	3	0	0	4	.333	6	5	4	15	1	0	1.000
—Madison (Midwest)	OF-2B	60	199	38	49	4	1	0	11	.246	46	37	31	195	3	4	.980
1989—Modesto (California) ..	OF	129	503	74	150	23	5	4	39	.298	59	84	27	*311	8	5	.985
—Huntsville (Sou.)	OF	9	31	7	10	1	1	1	7	.323	2	6	0	16	0	0	1.000
1990—Huntsville (Sou.)	OF	71	284	52	84	11	3	3	23	.296	36	28	21	186	6	0	1.000
—Tacoma (PCL)	OF	60	247	32	72	5	2	2	26	.291	16	35	16	132	9	2	.986
—Oakland (A.L.)	OF-DH	25	35	4	8	0	0	0	1	.229	7	4	2	33	0	0	1.000
1991—Phoenix (PCL)■........	OF	81	315	63	107	12	10	2	52	.340	41	36	32	243	5	2	.992
—San Francisco (N.L.) ..	OF	72	222	41	55	5	3	1	15	.248	36	30	13	159	2	0	1.000
1992—San Francisco (N.L.) ..	OF	100	320	38	74	8	1	1	18	.231	29	46	28	225	3	0	1.000
—Phoenix (PCL)	OF	42	158	22	36	5	2	0	6	.228	11	15	9	93	2	0	1.000
1993—San Francisco (N.L.) ..	OF	136	522	84	132	17	7	2	48	.253	30	40	46	344	4	0	•1.000
1994—San Francisco (N.L.) ..	OF	114	451	70	116	15	•9	4	29	.257	53	50	30	279	5	2	.993
1995—San Francisco (N.L.) ..	OF	74	309	47	78	10	3	1	16	.252	17	37	21	200	2	1	.995
—Cincinnati (N.L.)■......	OF	58	163	19	40	3	0	0	8	.245	17	20	11	121	3	1	.992
1996—Chicago (A.L.)■........	OF	141	337	55	77	12	2	4	53	.228	45	40	21	287	0	3	.990
1997—Chicago (A.L.)	OF-DH	81	77	15	18	1	0	0	5	.234	11	14	11	90	1	0	1.000
—Los Angeles (N.L.)■ ..	OF	26	77	7	23	3	1	1	10	.299	6	17	3	49	1	1	.980
1998—Boston (A.L.)■..........	OF-DH	155	585	95	157	25	3	8	63	.268	70	94	29	382	6	3	.992
American League totals (4 years)		402	1034	169	260	38	5	12	122	.251	133	152	63	792	7	6	.993
National League totals (6 years)		580	2064	306	518	61	24	10	144	.251	188	240	152	1377	20	5	.996
Major league totals (9 years)		982	3098	475	778	99	29	22	266	.251	321	392	215	2169	27	11	.995

DIVISION SERIES RECORD

Year Team (League)	Pos.	G	AB	R	H	2B	3B	HR	RBI	Avg.	BB	SO	SB	PO	A	E	Avg.
1995—Cincinnati (N.L.)	OF-PH	3	3	0	0	0	0	0	0	.000	0	1	0	3	0	0	1.000
1998—Boston (A.L.).............	OF	4	14	4	5	2	0	0	0	.357	1	3	1	10	0	0	1.000
Division series totals (2 years)		7	17	4	5	2	0	0	0	.294	1	4	1	13	0	0	1.000

CHAMPIONSHIP SERIES RECORD

Year Team (League)	Pos.	G	AB	R	H	2B	3B	HR	RBI	Avg.	BB	SO	SB	PO	A	E	Avg.
1995—Cincinnati (N.L.)	OF-PR	2	1	0	0	0	0	0	0	.000	0	0	0	2	0	0	1.000

LEWIS, MARK — 2B — REDS

PERSONAL: Born November 30, 1969, in Hamilton, Ohio. ... 6-1/185. ... Bats right, throws right. ... Full name: Mark David Lewis.
HIGH SCHOOL: Hamilton (Ohio).
TRANSACTIONS/CAREER NOTES: Selected by Cleveland Indians organization in first round (second pick overall) of free-agent draft (June 1, 1988). ... On Kinston disabled list (May 29-June 20, 1989). ... Traded by Indians to Cincinnati Reds for IF Tim Costo (December 14, 1994). ... Traded by Reds to Detroit Tigers (November 16, 1995), completing deal in which Reds acquired P David Wells for P C.J. Nitkowski, P David Tuttle and a player to be named later (July 31, 1995). ... Traded by Tigers to San Francisco Giants for 1B Jesus Ibarra (December 16, 1996). ... On disabled list (March 31-April 12, 1997). ... Granted free agency (December 21, 1997). ... Signed by Philadelphia Phillies (December 23, 1997). ... Granted free agency (October 26, 1998). ... Signed by Reds (December 12, 1998).
STATISTICAL NOTES: Tied for A.L. lead in errors by shortstop with 25 in 1992. ... Tied for International League lead in grounding into double plays with 19 in 1993. ... Led International League shortstops with 81 double plays in 1993. ... Career major league grand slams: 1.

Year Team (League)	Pos.	G	AB	R	H	2B	3B	HR	RBI	Avg.	BB	SO	SB	PO	A	E	Avg.
1988—Burlington (Appal.).....	SS	61	227	39	60	13	1	7	43	.264	25	44	14	70	*177	23	.915
1989—Kinston (Carolina)	SS	93	349	50	94	16	3	1	32	.269	34	50	17	130	244	32	.921
—Cant./Akr. (Eastern)	SS	7	25	4	5	1	0	0	1	.200	1	3	0	15	28	2	.956
1990—Cant./Akr. (Eastern)	SS	102	390	55	106	19	3	10	60	.272	23	49	8	152	286	31	.934
—Colo. Springs (PCL)	SS	34	124	16	38	8	1	1	21	.306	9	13	2	52	84	11	.925
1991—Colo. Springs (PCL)	SS-2B-3B	46	179	29	50	10	3	2	31	.279	18	23	3	65	135	10	.952
—Cleveland (A.L.)	2B-SS	84	314	29	83	15	1	0	30	.264	15	45	2	129	231	9	.976
1992—Cleveland (A.L.).........	SS-3B	122	413	44	109	21	0	5	30	.264	25	69	4	184	336	‡26	.952
1993—Charlotte (Int'l)..........	SS	126	507	93	144	30	4	17	67	.284	34	76	9	168	*403	23	.961
—Cleveland (A.L.)..........	SS	14	52	6	13	2	0	1	5	.250	0	7	3	22	31	2	.964
1994—Cleveland (A.L.).........	SS-3B-2B	20	73	6	15	5	0	1	8	.205	2	13	1	17	40	6	.905
—Charlotte (Int'l)..........	SS-2B-3B	86	328	56	85	16	1	8	34	.259	35	48	2	117	199	12	.963

L

			BATTING												FIELDING		
Year	Team (League)	Pos.	G	AB	R	H	2B	3B	HR	RBI	Avg.	BB	SO	SB	PO	A	E	Avg.
1995—Cincinnati (N.L.)■......	3B-2B-SS	81	171	25	58	13	1	3	30	.339	21	33	0	19	107	4	.969
1996—Detroit (A.L.)■.........	2B-DH	145	545	69	147	30	3	11	55	.270	42	109	6	264	413	9	.987
1997—San Fran. (N.L.)■......	3B-2B-DH	118	341	50	91	14	6	10	42	.267	23	62	3	74	157	14	.943
1998—Philadelphia (N.L.)■..	2B	142	518	52	129	21	2	9	54	.249	48	111	3	276	437	16	.978
American League totals (5 years)		385	1397	154	367	73	4	18	128	.263	84	243	16	616	1051	52	.970
National League totals (3 years)		341	1030	127	278	48	9	22	126	.270	92	206	6	369	701	34	.969
Major league totals (8 years)		726	2427	281	645	121	13	40	254	.266	176	449	22	985	1752	86	.970

DIVISION SERIES RECORD

			BATTING												FIELDING		
Year	Team (League)	Pos.	G	AB	R	H	2B	3B	HR	RBI	Avg.	BB	SO	SB	PO	A	E	Avg.
1995—Cincinnati (N.L.)	3B-PH	2	2	2	1	0	0	1	5	.500	1	0	0	0	0	1	.000
1997—San Francisco (N.L.) ..	2B	1	5	0	3	0	0	0	1	.600	0	0	0	1	3	0	1.000
Division series totals (2 years)		3	7	2	4	0	0	1	6	.571	1	0	0	1	3	1	.800

CHAMPIONSHIP SERIES RECORD

			BATTING												FIELDING		
Year	Team (League)	Pos.	G	AB	R	H	2B	3B	HR	RBI	Avg.	BB	SO	SB	PO	A	E	Avg.
1995—Cincinnati (N.L.)	3B	2	4	0	1	0	0	0	0	.250	1	1	0	2	3	0	1.000

LEWIS, RICHIE   P

PERSONAL: Born January 25, 1966, in Muncie, Ind. ... 5-10/175. ... Throws right, bats right. ... Full name: Richie Todd Lewis.
HIGH SCHOOL: South Side (Muncie, Ind.).
COLLEGE: Florida State (received degree, 1987).
TRANSACTIONS/CAREER NOTES: Selected by Montreal Expos organization in second round of free-agent draft (June 2, 1987). ... On disabled list (June 2-August 12 and August 22, 1988-remainder of season; and July 28, 1989-remainder of season). ... On Jacksonville disabled list (June 1-8 and June 11, 1990-remainder of season). ... Traded by Expos to Baltimore Orioles for P Chris Myers (August 24, 1991). ... Selected by Florida Marlins in second round (51st pick overall) of expansion draft (November 17, 1992). ... On Charlotte disabled list (April 6-25, 1995). ... Granted free agency (October 16, 1995). ... Signed by Las Vegas, San Diego Padres organization (January 18, 1996). ... Traded by Padres with OF Melvin Nieves and C Raul Casanova to Detroit Tigers for P Sean Bergman, P Cade Gaspar and OF Todd Steverson (March 22, 1996). ... On Detroit disabled list (June 21-July 11, 1996); included rehabilitation assignment to Toledo (July 6-11). ... Released by Tigers (November 20, 1996). ... Signed by Oakland Athletics organization (January 6, 1997). ... Released by A's (June 19, 1997). ... Signed by Indianapolis, Reds organization (June 20, 1997). ... Granted free agency (September 11, 1997). ... Signed by Philadelphia Phillies organization (January 12, 1998). ... Released by Phillies (March 22, 1998). ... Signed by Baltimore Orioles organization (April 23, 1998). ... Granted free agency (October 15, 1998).
HONORS: Named righthanded pitcher on THE SPORTING NEWS college All-America team (1987).
STATISTICAL NOTES: Tied for N.L. lead with 10 wild pitches in 1994.
MISCELLANEOUS: Made an out in only appearance as pinch hitter with Detroit (1996).

Year	Team (League)	W	L	Pct.	ERA	G	GS	CG	ShO	Sv.	IP	H	R	ER	BB	SO
1987—Indianapolis (A.A.)............	0	0	...	9.82	2	0	0	0	0	3 2/3	6	4	4	2	3
1988—Jacksonville (Southern)......	5	3	.625	3.38	12	12	1	0	0	61 1/3	37	32	23	56	60
1989—Jacksonville (Southern)......	5	4	.556	2.58	17	17	0	0	0	94 1/3	80	37	27	55	105
1990—W.P. Beach (FSL)..............	0	1	.000	4.80	10	0	0	0	2	15	12	12	8	11	14
—Jacksonville (Southern).......	0	0	...	1.26	11	0	0	0	5	14 1/3	7	2	2	5	14
1991—Harrisburg (Eastern).........	6	5	.545	3.74	34	6	0	0	5	74 2/3	67	33	31	40	82
—Indianapolis (A.A.).............	1	0	1.000	3.58	5	4	0	0	0	27 2/3	35	12	11	20	22
—Rochester (Int'l)■.............	1	0	1.000	2.81	2	2	0	0	0	16	13	5	5	7	18
1992—Rochester (Int'l).............	10	9	.526	3.28	24	23	6	1	0	159 1/3	136	63	58	61	154
—Baltimore (A.L.)................	1	1	.500	10.80	2	2	0	0	0	6 2/3	13	8	8	7	4
1993—Florida (N.L.)■...............	6	3	.667	3.26	57	0	0	0	0	77 1/3	68	37	28	43	65
1994—Florida (N.L.)..................	1	4	.200	5.67	45	0	0	0	0	54	62	44	34	38	45
1995—Charlotte (Int'l)..............	5	2	.714	3.20	17	8	1	0	0	59	50	22	21	20	45
—Florida (N.L.)....................	0	1	.000	3.75	21	1	0	0	0	36	30	15	15	15	32
1996—Detroit (A.L.)■..............	4	6	.400	4.18	72	0	0	0	2	90 1/3	78	45	42	65	78
—Toledo (International).........	0	0	...	2.25	2	0	0	0	0	4	1	1	1	1	4
1997—Oakland (A.L.)■.............	2	0	1.000	9.64	14	0	0	0	0	18 2/3	24	21	20	15	12
—Edmonton (PCL)................	1	1	.500	5.85	11	1	0	0	1	20	24	13	13	14	25
—Indianapolis (A.A.)■..........	0	1	.000	1.52	27	0	0	0	9	29 2/3	22	7	5	7	33
—Cincinnati (N.L.)...............	0	0	...	6.35	4	0	0	0	0	5 2/3	4	5	4	3	4
1998—Rochester (Int'l)■..........	5	7	.417	5.01	21	21	2	0	0	124	107	77	69	42	131
—Baltimore (A.L.)................	0	0	...	15.43	2	1	0	0	0	4 2/3	8	8	8	5	4
A.L. totals (4 years)...............	7	7	.500	5.83	90	3	0	0	2	120 1/3	123	82	78	92	98
N.L. totals (4 years)...................	7	8	.467	4.21	127	1	0	0	0	173	164	101	81	99	146
Major league totals (7 years)......	14	15	.483	4.88	217	4	0	0	2	293 1/3	287	183	159	191	244

LEYRITZ, JIM   C/1B   PADRES

PERSONAL: Born December 27, 1963, in Lakewood, Ohio. ... 6-0/195. ... Bats right, throws right. ... Full name: James Joseph Leyritz. ... Name pronounced LAY-rits.
HIGH SCHOOL: Turpin (Cincinnati).
JUNIOR COLLEGE: Middle Georgia College.
COLLEGE: Kentucky.
TRANSACTIONS/CAREER NOTES: Signed as non-drafted free agent by New York Yankees organization (August 24, 1985). ... Traded by Yankees to Anaheim Angels for two players to be named later (December 5, 1996); Yankees acquired 3B Ryan Kane and P Jeremy Blevins to

complete deal (December 9, 1996). ... Traded by Angels with a player to be named later to Texas Rangers for P Ken Hill (July 29, 1997); Rangers acquired IF Rob Sasser to complete deal (October 31, 1997). ... Traded by Rangers with OF Damon Buford to Boston Red Sox for P Aaron Sele, P Mark Brandenburg and C Bill Haselman (November 6, 1997). ... Traded by Red Sox with OF Ethan Faggett to San Diego Padres for P Carlos Reyes, P Dario Veras and C Mandy Romero (June 21, 1998).

STATISTICAL NOTES: Led Florida State League with 25 passed balls in 1987. ... Tied for Eastern League lead in being hit by pitch with nine in 1989. ... Career major league grand slams: 2.

Year Team (League)	Pos.	G	AB	R	H	2B	3B	HR	RBI	Avg.	BB	SO	SB	PO	A	E	Avg.
1986— Oneonta (NYP)	C	23	91	12	33	3	1	4	15	.363	5	10	1	170	21	2	.990
— Fort Laud. (FSL)	C	12	34	3	10	1	1	0	1	.294	4	5	0	32	8	1	.976
1987— Fort Laud. (FSL)	C	102	374	48	115	22	0	6	51	.307	38	54	2	458	*76	13	.976
1988— Alb./Colon. (East.)	C-3B-1B	112	382	40	92	18	3	5	50	.241	43	62	3	418	73	6	.988
1989— Alb./Colon. (East.)	C-OF-3B	114	375	53	118	18	2	10	66	*.315	65	51	2	421	41	3	.994
1990— Columbus (Int'l)	3-2-1-O-C	59	204	36	59	11	1	8	32	.289	37	33	4	75	96	13	.929
— New York (A.L.)	3B-OF-C	92	303	28	78	13	1	5	25	.257	27	51	2	117	107	13	.945
1991— New York (A.L.)	3-C-1-DH	32	77	8	14	3	0	0	4	.182	13	15	0	38	21	3	.952
— Columbus (Int'l)	C-3-S-2	79	270	50	72	24	1	11	48	.267	38	50	1	209	48	5	.981
1992— New York (A.L.) DH-C-O-3-1-2		63	144	17	37	6	0	7	26	.257	14	22	0	96	15	1	.991
1993— New York (A.L.)	1-O-DH-C	95	259	43	80	14	0	14	53	.309	37	59	0	333	15	2	.994
1994— New York (A.L.)	C-DH-1B	75	249	47	66	12	0	17	58	.265	35	61	0	282	15	0	1.000
1995— New York (A.L.)	C-1B-DH	77	264	37	71	12	0	7	37	.269	37	73	1	417	24	3	.993
1996— New York (A.L.) C-DH-3-1-O-2		88	265	23	70	10	0	7	40	.264	30	68	2	387	31	6	.986
1997— Anaheim (A.L.)■	C-1B-DH	84	294	47	81	7	0	11	50	.276	37	56	1	440	45	2	.996
— Texas (A.L.)■	C-DH-1B	37	85	11	24	4	0	0	14	.282	23	22	1	116	7	1	.992
1998— Boston (A.L.)■	DH-C-1B	52	129	17	37	6	0	8	24	.287	21	34	0	13	0	0	1.000
— San Diego (N.L.)■	C-1-3-O	62	143	17	38	10	0	4	18	.266	21	40	0	276	19	3	.990
American League totals (9 years)		695	2069	278	558	87	1	76	331	.270	274	461	7	2239	280	31	.988
National League totals (1 year)		62	143	17	38	10	0	4	18	.266	21	40	0	276	19	3	.990
Major league totals (9 years)		757	2212	295	596	97	1	80	349	.269	295	501	7	2515	299	34	.988

DIVISION SERIES RECORD

Year Team (League)	Pos.	G	AB	R	H	2B	3B	HR	RBI	Avg.	BB	SO	SB	PO	A	E	Avg.
1995— New York (A.L.)	C-PH	2	7	1	1	0	0	1	2	.143	0	1	0	13	0	0	1.000
1996— New York (A.L.)	C-DH	2	3	0	0	0	0	0	1	.000	0	1	0	4	0	0	1.000
1998— San Diego (N.L.)	1B-C-PH	4	10	3	4	0	0	3	5	.400	0	2	0	34	0	0	1.000
Division series totals (3 years)		8	20	4	5	0	0	4	8	.250	0	4	0	51	0	0	1.000

CHAMPIONSHIP SERIES RECORD

Year Team (League)	Pos.	G	AB	R	H	2B	3B	HR	RBI	Avg.	BB	SO	SB	PO	A	E	Avg.
1996— New York (A.L.)	C-OF-PH	3	8	1	2	0	0	1	2	.250	1	4	0	11	2	0	1.000
1998— San Diego (N.L.)	PH-1B-C	5	12	1	2	0	0	1	4	.167	0	2	0	24	1	0	1.000
Championship series totals (2 years)		8	20	2	4	0	0	2	6	.200	1	6	0	35	3	0	1.000

WORLD SERIES RECORD

NOTES: Member of World Series championship team (1996).

Year Team (League)	Pos.	G	AB	R	H	2B	3B	HR	RBI	Avg.	BB	SO	SB	PO	A	E	Avg.
1996— New York (A.L.)	C-PH	4	8	1	3	0	0	1	3	.375	4	2	1	15	0	0	1.000
1998— San Diego (N.L.) DH-PH-1-C		4	10	0	0	0	0	0	0	.000	1	4	0	19	0	0	1.000
World Series totals (2 years)		8	18	1	3	0	0	1	3	.167	5	6	1	34	0	0	1.000

LIDLE, CORY　　　　　　　P　　　　　　　DEVIL RAYS

PERSONAL: Born March 22, 1972, in Hollywood, Calif. ... 5-11/180. ... Throws right, bats right. ... Full name: Cory Fulton Lidle. ... Twin brother of Kevin Lidle, catcher, Colorado Rockies organization.

HIGH SCHOOL: South Hills (Covina, Calif.).

TRANSACTIONS/CAREER NOTES: Signed as non-drafted free agent by Minnesota Twins organization (August 25, 1990). ... Released by Elizabethton, Twins organization (April 1, 1993). ... Signed by Pocatello, Pioneer League (May 28, 1993). ... Purchased by Milwaukee Brewers organization from Pocatello (September 17, 1993). ... Traded by Brewers to New York Mets organization for C Kelly Stinnett (January 17, 1996). ... Selected by Arizona Diamondbacks in first round (13th pick overall) of expansion draft (November 18, 1997). ... On Arizona disabled list (March 31, 1998-entire season); included rehabilitation assignments to High Desert (April 20-28) and Tucson (September 3-7). ... Claimed on waivers by Tampa Bay Devil Rays (October 7, 1998).

Year Team (League)	W	L	Pct.	ERA	G	GS	CG	ShO	Sv.	IP	H	R	ER	BB	SO
1991— GC Twins (GCL).................	1	1	.500	5.79	4	0	0	0	0	4 2/3	5	3	3	0	5
1992— Elizabethton (Appal.)	2	1	.667	3.71	19	2	0	0	6	43 2/3	40	29	18	21	32
1993— Pocatello (Pioneer)■..........	•8	4	.667	4.13	17	16	3	0	1	106 2/3	104	59	49	54	91
1994— Stockton (California)■	1	2	.333	4.43	25	1	0	0	4	42 2/3	60	32	21	13	38
— Beloit (Midwest)................	3	4	.429	2.61	13	9	1	1	0	69	65	24	20	11	62
1995— El Paso (Texas).................	5	4	.556	3.36	45	9	0	0	2	109 2/3	126	52	41	36	78
1996— Binghamton (Eastern)■	14	10	.583	3.31	27	27	•6	1	0	*190 1/3	186	78	70	49	141
1997— Norfolk (Int'l)	4	2	.667	3.64	7	7	1	0	0	42	46	20	17	10	34
— New York (N.L.).................	7	2	.778	3.53	54	2	0	0	2	81 2/3	86	38	32	20	54
1998— High Desert (Calif.)■	0	0	. . .	0.00	1	1	0	0	0	2 2/3	2	1	0	2	6
— Tucson (PCL)	0	0	. . .	0.00	1	1	0	0	0	4 2/3	2	0	0	2	2
Major league totals (1 year)........	7	2	.778	3.53	54	2	0	0	2	81 2/3	86	38	32	20	54

LIEBER, JON   P   CUBS

PERSONAL: Born April 2, 1970, in Council Bluffs, Iowa. ... 6-3/225. ... Throws right, bats left. ... Full name: Jonathan Ray Lieber. ... Name pronounced LEE-ber.
HIGH SCHOOL: Abraham Lincoln (Council Bluffs, Iowa.).
JUNIOR COLLEGE: Iowa Western Community College-Council Bluffs (Iowa).
COLLEGE: South Alabama.
TRANSACTIONS/CAREER NOTES: Selected by Chicago Cubs organization in ninth round of free-agent draft (June 3, 1991); did not sign. ... Selected by Kansas City Royals organization in second round of free-agent draft (June 1, 1992); pick received as part of compensation for New York Yankees signing Type A free-agent OF Danny Tartabull. ... Traded by Royals organization with P Dan Miceli to Pittsburgh Pirates organization for P Stan Belinda (July 31, 1993). ... On disabled list (August 21-September 15, 1998). ... Traded by Pirates to Chicago Cubs for OF Brant Brown (December 14, 1998).

Year Team (League)	W	L	Pct.	ERA	G	GS	CG	ShO	Sv.	IP	H	R	ER	BB	SO
1992— Eugene (Northwest)	3	0	1.000	1.16	5	5	0	0	0	31	26	6	4	2	23
— Baseball City (FSL)	3	3	.500	4.65	7	6	0	0	0	31	45	20	16	8	19
1993— Wilmington (Caro.)	9	3	.750	2.67	17	16	2	0	0	114 2/3	125	47	34	9	89
— Memphis (Sou.)	2	1	.667	6.86	4	4	0	0	0	21	32	16	16	6	17
— Carolina (Southern)■	4	2	.667	3.97	6	6	0	0	0	34	39	15	15	10	28
1994— Carolina (Southern)	2	0	1.000	1.29	3	3	1	1	0	21	13	4	3	2	21
— Buffalo (A.A.)	1	1	.500	1.69	3	3	0	0	0	21 1/3	16	4	4	1	21
— Pittsburgh (N.L.)	6	7	.462	3.73	17	17	1	0	0	108 2/3	116	62	45	25	71
1995— Pittsburgh (N.L.)	4	7	.364	6.32	21	12	0	0	0	72 2/3	103	56	51	14	45
— Calgary (PCL)	1	5	.167	7.01	14	14	0	0	0	77	122	69	60	19	34
1996— Pittsburgh (N.L.)	9	5	.643	3.99	51	15	0	0	1	142	156	70	63	28	94
1997— Pittsburgh (N.L.)	11	14	.440	4.49	33	32	1	0	0	188 1/3	193	102	94	51	160
1998— Pittsburgh (N.L.)	8	14	.364	4.11	29	28	2	0	1	171	182	93	78	40	138
Major league totals (5 years)	38	47	.447	4.36	151	104	4	0	2	682 2/3	750	383	331	158	508

LIEBERTHAL, MIKE   C   PHILLIES

PERSONAL: Born January 18, 1972, in Glendale, Calif. ... 6-0/186. ... Bats right, throws right. ... Full name: Michael Scott Lieberthal. ... Name pronounced LEE-ber-thal.
HIGH SCHOOL: Westlake (Westlake Village, Calif.).
TRANSACTIONS/CAREER NOTES: Selected by Philadelphia Phillies organization in first round (third pick overall) of free-agent draft (June 4, 1990). ... On Scranton/Wilkes-Barre disabled list (August 31, 1992-remainder of season). ... On disabled list (August 22, 1996-remainder of season). ... On disabled list (July 24-September 2, 1998).
STATISTICAL NOTES: Tied for N.L. lead in passed balls with 12 in 1997. ... Career major league grand slams: 1.

Year Team (League)	Pos.	G	AB	R	H	2B	3B	HR	RBI	Avg.	BB	SO	SB	PO	A	E	Avg.
1990— Martinsville (App.)	C	49	184	26	42	9	0	4	22	.228	11	40	2	421	*52	5	*.990
1991— Spartanburg (SAL)	C	72	243	34	74	17	0	0	31	.305	23	25	1	565	68	10	.984
— Clearwater (FSL)	C	16	52	7	15	2	0	0	7	.288	3	12	0	128	9	1	.993
1992— Reading (Eastern)	C	86	309	30	88	16	1	2	37	.285	19	26	4	524	48	7	.988
— Scran./W.B. (Int'l)	C	16	45	4	9	1	0	0	4	.200	2	5	0	86	6	1	.989
1993— Scran./W.B. (Int'l)	C	112	382	35	100	17	0	7	40	.262	24	32	2	659	75	•11	.985
1994— Scran./W.B. (Int'l)	C	84	296	23	69	16	0	1	32	.233	21	29	1	472	50	9	.983
— Philadelphia (N.L.)	C	24	79	6	21	3	1	1	5	.266	3	5	0	122	4	4	.969
1995— Philadelphia (N.L.)	C	16	47	1	12	2	0	0	4	.255	5	5	0	95	10	1	.991
— Scran./W.B. (Int'l)	C-3B	85	278	44	78	20	2	6	42	.281	44	26	1	503	46	5	.991
1996— Philadelphia (N.L.)	C	50	166	21	42	8	0	7	23	.253	10	30	0	284	20	3	.990
1997— Philadelphia (N.L.)	C-DH	134	455	59	112	27	1	20	77	.246	44	76	3	934	73	12	.988
1998— Philadelphia (N.L.)	C	86	313	39	80	15	3	8	45	.256	17	44	2	607	41	8	.988
Major league totals (5 years)		310	1060	126	267	55	5	36	154	.252	79	160	5	2042	148	28	.987

LIEFER, JEFF   OF/1B   WHITE SOX

PERSONAL: Born August 17, 1974, in Fontana, Calif. ... 6-3/195. ... Bats left, throws right. ... Full name: Jeffery David Liefer.
HIGH SCHOOL: Upland (Calif.).
COLLEGE: Long Beach State.
TRANSACTIONS/CAREER NOTES: Selected by Cleveland Indians organization in sixth round of free-agent draft (June 1, 1992); did not sign. ... Selected by Chicago White Sox organization in first round (25th pick overall) of free-agent draft (June 1, 1995).

Year Team (League)	Pos.	G	AB	R	H	2B	3B	HR	RBI	Avg.	BB	SO	SB	PO	A	E	Avg.
1996— South Bend (Mid.)	3B	74	277	60	90	14	0	15	58	.325	30	62	6	31	62	23	.802
— Prince Will. (Car.)	DH	37	147	17	33	6	0	1	13	.224	11	27	0	0	0	0	...
1997— Birmingham (Sou.)	OF	119	474	67	113	24	9	15	71	.238	38	115	2	166	2	•8	.955
1998— Birmingham (Sou.)	1B-OF	127	471	84	137	33	6	21	89	.291	60	125	1	763	66	11	.987
— Calgary (PCL)	OF-1B	8	31	3	8	3	0	1	10	.258	2	12	0	26	3	0	1.000

LIGTENBERG, KERRY   P   BRAVES

PERSONAL: Born May 11, 1971, in Rapid City, S.D. ... 6-2/205. ... Throws right, bats right. ... Full name: Kerry Dale Ligtenberg. ... Name pronounced Light-en-berg.
HIGH SCHOOL: Park (Cottage Grove, Minn.).
COLLEGE: Minnesota-Morris, then Minnesota.
TRANSACTIONS/CAREER NOTES: Signed by Minneapolis, Prairie League prior to 1994 season. ... Contract purchased by Atlanta Braves organization from Minneapolis of the Prairie League (March 28, 1995).

Year Team (League)	W	L	Pct.	ERA	G	GS	CG	ShO	Sv.	IP	H	R	ER	BB	SO
1994— Minneapolis (Prairie).........	5	5	.500	3.31	19	19	2		0	114 1/3	103	47	42	44	94
1995— Minneapolis (Prairie).........	11	2	.846	2.73	17	15	4		0	108 2/3	101	41	33	26	100
1996— Durham (Carolina)■............	7	4	.636	2.41	49	0	0	0	20	59 2/3	58	20	16	16	76
1997— Greenville (Southern)	3	1	.750	2.04	31	0	0	0	16	35 1/3	20	8	8	14	43
— Richmond (Int'l)................	0	3	.000	4.32	14	0	0	0	1	25	21	13	12	2	35
— Atlanta (N.L.)...................	1	0	1.000	3.00	15	0	0	0	1	15	12	5	5	4	19
1998— Atlanta (N.L.)....................	3	2	.600	2.71	75	0	0	0	30	73	51	24	22	24	79
Major league totals (2 years)......	4	2	.667	2.76	90	0	0	0	31	88	63	29	27	28	98

DIVISION SERIES RECORD

Year Team (League)	W	L	Pct.	ERA	G	GS	CG	ShO	Sv.	IP	H	R	ER	BB	SO
1998— Atlanta (N.L.)....................	0	0	. . .	0.00	3	0	0	0	0	3 1/3	1	0	0	5	3

CHAMPIONSHIP SERIES RECORD

Year Team (League)	W	L	Pct.	ERA	G	GS	CG	ShO	Sv.	IP	H	R	ER	BB	SO
1997— Atlanta (N.L.)....................	0	0	. . .	0.00	2	0	0	0	0	3	1	0	0	0	4
1998— Atlanta (N.L.)....................	0	1	.000	7.36	4	0	0	0	0	3 2/3	3	3	3	2	5
Champ. series totals (2 years)	0	1	.000	4.05	6	0	0	0	0	6 2/3	4	3	3	2	9

LILLY, TED   P   EXPOS

PERSONAL: Born January 4, 1976, in Lameta, Calif. ... 6-1/180. ... Throws left, bats left. ... Full name: Theodore R. Lilly.
HIGH SCHOOL: Yosemite (Oakhurst, Calif.).
JUNIOR COLLEGE: Fresno (Calif.) City College.
TRANSACTIONS/CAREER NOTES: Selected by Los Angeles Dodgers in 23rd round of free-agent draft (June 4, 1996). ... Traded by Dodgers with 2B Wilton Guerrero, OF Peter Bergeron and 1B Jonathan Tucker to Montreal Expos for P Carlos Perez, SS Mark Grudzielanek and IF Hiram Bocachica (July 31, 1998).
HONORS: Named California League Pitcher of the Year (1997).
STATISTICAL NOTES: Pitched 8-0 no-hit victory against Lake Elsinore (May 10, 1997).

Year Team (League)	W	L	Pct.	ERA	G	GS	CG	ShO	Sv.	IP	H	R	ER	BB	SO
1996— Yakima (N'west)............	4	0	1.000	0.84	13	8	0	0	0	53 2/3	25	9	5	14	75
1997— San Bernardino (Calif.)......	7	8	.467	*2.81	23	21	2	1	0	134 2/3	116	52	42	32	158
1998— San Antonio (Tex.)	8	4	.667	3.30	17	17	0	0	0	111 2/3	114	50	41	37	96
— Albuquerque (PCL)............	1	3	.250	4.94	5	5	0	0	0	31	39	20	17	9	25
— Ottawa (Int'l)■............	2	2	.500	4.85	7	7	0	0	0	39	45	28	21	19	49

LIMA, JOSE   P   ASTROS

PERSONAL: Born September 30, 1972, in Santiago, Dominican Republic. ... 6-2/205. ... Throws right, bats right. ... Full name: Jose D. Lima. ... Name pronounced LEE-mah.
HIGH SCHOOL: Escuela Primaria Las Charcas (Santiago, Dominican Replublic).
TRANSACTIONS/CAREER NOTES: Signed as non-drafted free agent by Detroit Tigers organization (July 5, 1989). ... Traded by Tigers with C Brad Ausmus, P C.J. Nitkowski, P Trever Miller and IF Daryle Ward to Houston Astros for OF Brian Hunter, IF Orlando Miller, P Doug Brocail, P Todd Jones and cash (December 10, 1996).
STATISTICAL NOTES: Led Florida State League with 14 home runs allowed in 1992. ... Led Eastern League with 13 balks in 1993. ... Pitched 3-0 no-hit victory for Toledo against Pawtucket (August 17, 1994).

Year Team (League)	W	L	Pct.	ERA	G	GS	CG	ShO	Sv.	IP	H	R	ER	BB	SO
1990— Bristol (Appalachian).........	3	8	.273	5.02	14	12	1	0	1	75 1/3	89	49	42	22	64
1991— Lakeland (Fla. St.)	0	1	.000	10.38	4	1	0	0	0	8 2/3	16	10	10	2	5
— Fayetteville (S. Atl.)	1	3	.250	4.97	18	7	0	0	0	58	53	38	32	25	60
1992— Lakeland (Fla. St.)	5	11	.313	3.16	25	25	5	2	0	151	132	57	53	21	137
1993— London (Eastern)	8	•13	.381	4.07	27	27	2	0	0	177	160	96	80	59	138
1994— Toledo (International)	7	9	.438	3.60	23	22	3	2	0	142 1/3	124	70	57	48	117
— Detroit (A.L.)....................	0	1	.000	13.50	3	1	0	0	0	6 2/3	11	10	10	3	7
1995— Lakeland (Fla. St.)	3	1	.750	2.57	4	4	0	0	0	21	23	11	6	0	20
— Toledo (International)	5	3	.625	3.01	11	11	1	0	0	74 2/3	69	26	25	14	40
— Detroit (A.L.)....................	3	9	.250	6.11	15	15	0	0	0	73 2/3	85	52	50	18	37
1996— Toledo (International)	5	4	.556	6.78	12	12	0	0	0	69	93	53	52	12	57
— Detroit (A.L.)....................	5	6	.455	5.70	39	4	0	0	3	72 2/3	87	48	46	22	59
1997— Houston (N.L.)■................	1	6	.143	5.28	52	1	0	0	2	75	79	45	44	16	63
1998— Houston (N.L.)	16	8	.667	3.70	33	33	3	1	0	233 1/3	229	100	96	32	169
A.L. totals (3 years)	8	16	.333	6.24	57	20	0	0	3	153	183	110	106	43	103
N.L. totals (2 years)	17	14	.548	4.09	85	34	3	1	2	308 1/3	308	145	140	48	232
Major league totals (5 years)......	25	30	.455	4.80	142	54	3	1	5	461 1/3	491	255	246	91	335

DIVISION SERIES RECORD

Year Team (League)	W	L	Pct.	ERA	G	GS	CG	ShO	Sv.	IP	H	R	ER	BB	SO
1997— Houston (N.L.)	0	0	. . .	0.00	1	0	0	0	0	1	0	0	0	1	1

LINCOLN, MIKE   P   TWINS

PERSONAL: Born April 10, 1975, in Carmichael, Calif. ... 6-2/211. ... Throws right, bats right. ... Full name: Michael George Lincoln.
HIGH SCHOOL: Casa Roble (Orangevale, Calif.).
JUNIOR COLLEGE: American River College (Calif.).
COLLEGE: Tennessee.
TRANSACTIONS/CAREER NOTES: Selected by Minnesota Twins organization in 13th round of free-agent draft (June 2, 1996).

Year Team (League)	W	L	Pct.	ERA	G	GS	CG	ShO	Sv.	IP	H	R	ER	BB	SO
1996— Fort Myers (Fla. St.)	5	2	.714	4.07	12	11	0	0	0	59 2/3	64	31	27	25	24
1997— Fort Myers (Fla. St.)	13	4	.765	2.28	20	20	1	1	0	134	130	41	34	25	75
1998— New Britain (East.)	*15	7	.682	3.22	26	26	1	0	0	173 1/3	180	80	62	35	109

L

LINIAK, COLE   3B   RED SOX

PERSONAL: Born August 23, 1976, in Encinitas, Calif. ... 6-1/182. ... Bats right, throws right. ... Full name: Cole Edward Liniak.
HIGH SCHOOL: San Dieguito (Encinitas, Calif.).
TRANSACTIONS/CAREER NOTES: Selected by Boston Red Sox organization in seventh round of free-agent draft (June 1, 1995).
STATISTICAL NOTES: Led Midwest League third basemen with .967 fielding percentage in 1996.

							BATTING									FIELDING		
Year Team (League)	Pos.	G	AB	R	H	2B	3B	HR	RBI	Avg.	BB	SO	SB	PO	A	E	Avg.
1995— GC Red Sox (GCL)	3B	23	79	9	21	7	0	1	8	.266	4	8	2	21	53	2	.974
1996— Michigan (Midwest) ...	3B-2B	121	437	65	115	26	2	3	46	.263	59	59	7	79	248	11	†.967
1997— Sarasota (Fla. St.)	3B	64	217	32	73	16	0	6	42	.336	22	31	1	38	116	18	.895
— Trenton (Eastern)	3B	53	200	20	56	11	0	2	18	.280	17	29	0	35	82	9	.929
1998— Pawtucket (Int'l).........	3B	112	429	65	112	31	1	17	59	.261	39	71	4	86	192	18	.939
— GC Red Sox (GCL)	DH	2	8	1	0	0	0	0	0	.000	0	1	0	...	...	...	...

LIRA, FELIPE   P   TIGERS

PERSONAL: Born April 26, 1972, in Miranda, Venezuela. ... 6-0/170. ... Throws right, bats right. ... Full name: Antonio Felipe Lira.
HIGH SCHOOL: Rafael O. Figueroa (Venezuela).
TRANSACTIONS/CAREER NOTES: Signed as non-drafted free agent by Detroit Tigers organization (February 20, 1990). ... On Lakeland disabled list (April 10-June 10, 1991). ... Traded by Tigers with P Omar Olivares to Seattle Mariners for P Scott Sanders, P Dean Crow and 3B Carlos Villalobos (July 18, 1997). ... Granted free agency (October 15, 1998). ... Signed by Tigers organization (November 24, 1998).
STATISTICAL NOTES: Pitched seven-inning, 4-0 no-hit victory against Columbus (May 4, 1994). ... Led International League with 16 wild pitches in 1994.

Year Team (League)	W	L	Pct.	ERA	G	GS	CG	ShO	Sv.	IP	H	R	ER	BB	SO
1990— Bristol (Appalachian).........	5	5	.500	2.41	13	10	2	1	1	78 1/3	70	26	21	16	71
— Lakeland (Fla. St.)	0	0	...	5.40	1	0	0	0	0	1 2/3	3	1	1	3	4
1991— Fayetteville (S. Atl.)	5	5	.500	4.66	15	13	0	0	1	73 1/3	79	43	38	19	56
1992— Lakeland (Fla. St.)	11	5	.688	2.39	32	8	2	1	1	109	95	36	29	16	84
1993— London (Eastern)	10	4	.714	3.38	22	22	2	0	0	152	157	63	57	39	122
— Toledo (International)	1	2	.333	4.60	5	5	0	0	0	31 1/3	32	18	16	11	23
1994— Toledo (International)........	7	12	.368	4.70	26	26	1	1	0	151 1/3	171	91	79	45	110
1995— Detroit (A.L.)	9	13	.409	4.31	37	22	0	0	1	146 1/3	151	74	70	56	89
1996— Detroit (A.L.)	6	14	.300	5.22	32	32	3	2	0	194 2/3	204	123	113	66	113
1997— Detroit (A.L.)	5	7	.417	5.77	20	15	1	1	0	92	101	61	59	45	64
— Seattle (A.L.)■...................	0	4	.000	9.16	8	3	0	0	0	18 2/3	31	21	19	10	9
— Everett (Northwest)	1	0	1.000	3.60	1	1	0	0	0	5	6	3	2	2	9
— Tacoma (PCL)	2	0	1.000	3.43	3	3	0	0	0	21	21	8	8	5	17
1998— Tacoma (PCL)	6	8	.429	4.26	20	20	2	1	0	129	142	69	61	42	88
— Seattle (A.L.)	1	0	1.000	4.60	7	0	0	0	0	15 2/3	22	10	8	5	16
Major league totals (4 years)	21	38	.356	5.18	104	72	4	3	1	467 1/3	509	289	269	182	291

LIRIANO, NELSON   2B

PERSONAL: Born June 3, 1964, in Puerto Plata, Dominican Republic. ... 5-10/185. ... Bats both, throws right. ... Full name: Nelson Arturo Liriano. ... Name pronounced LEER-ee-ON-oh.
HIGH SCHOOL: Jose Debeaw (Puerto Plata, Dominican Republic).
TRANSACTIONS/CAREER NOTES: Signed as non-drafted free agent by Toronto Blue Jays organization (November 1, 1982). ... Traded by Blue Jays with OF Pedro Munoz to Minnesota Twins for P John Candelaria (July 27, 1990). ... Released by Twins (April 2, 1991). ... Signed by Kansas City Royals organization (May 1, 1991). ... Granted free agency (October 15, 1991). ... Signed by Cleveland Indians organization (January 31, 1992). ... Granted free agency (October 15, 1992). ... Signed by Rockies organization (October 26, 1992). ... On Colorado Springs disabled list (April 7-30, 1993). ... Claimed on waivers by Pittsburgh Pirates (October 14, 1994). ... Claimed on waivers by Los Angeles Dodgers (November 20, 1996). ... On disabled list (March 24-April 13, 1997). ... Granted free agency (October 3, 1997). ... Signed by Rockies organization (December 19, 1997). ... Granted free agency (October 15, 1998).
STATISTICAL NOTES: Led Carolina League second basemen with 79 double plays in 1985. ... Led International League second basemen with 611 total chances and 96 double plays in 1987. ... Career major league grand slams: 1.

							BATTING									FIELDING		
Year Team (League)	Pos.	G	AB	R	H	2B	3B	HR	RBI	Avg.	BB	SO	SB	PO	A	E	Avg.
1983— Florence (S. Atl.)	2B	129	478	87	124	24	5	6	57	.259	70	81	27	214	323	34	.940
1984— Kinston (Carolina)	2B	132	*512	68	126	22	4	5	50	.246	46	86	10	260	*357	*21	.967
1985— Kinston (Carolina)	2B	134	451	68	130	23	1	6	36	.288	39	55	25	*261	328	•25	.959
1986— Knoxville (Southern) ..	2B-3B-SS	135	557	88	159	25	*15	7	59	.285	48	63	35	239	324	22	.962
1987— Syracuse (Int'l)...........	2B	130	531	72	133	19	•10	10	55	.250	44	76	36	*246	*346	*19	.969
— Toronto (A.L.)	2B	37	158	29	38	6	2	2	10	.241	16	22	13	83	107	1	.995
1988— Toronto (A.L.)	2B-DH-3B	99	276	36	73	6	2	3	23	.264	11	40	12	121	177	12	.961
— Syracuse (Int'l)...........	2B	8	31	2	6	1	1	0	1	.194	2	4	2	14	23	0	1.000
1989— Toronto (A.L.)	2B-DH	132	418	51	110	26	3	5	53	.263	43	51	16	267	330	12	.980
1990— Toronto (A.L.)..............	2B	50	170	16	36	7	2	1	15	.212	16	20	3	93	132	4	.983
— Minnesota (A.L.)..........	2B-DH-SS	53	185	30	47	5	7	0	13	.254	22	24	5	83	128	7	.968
1991— Omaha (A.A.)■............	2B-SS	86	292	50	80	16	9	2	36	.274	31	39	6	149	218	9	.976
— Kansas City (A.L.)	2B	10	22	5	9	0	0	1	1	.409	0	2	0	11	23	0	1.000
1992— Colo. Springs (PCL)■	2B-3B-SS	106	361	73	110	19	9	5	52	.305	48	50	20	144	230	9	.977
1993— Central Valley (Cal.) ...	3B-SS-2B	6	22	3	8	0	2	0	4	.364	6	0	0	4	10	0	1.000
— Colo. Springs (PCL) ...	2B-SS-3B	79	293	48	105	23	6	6	46	.358	32	34	9	143	232	15	.962
— Colorado (N.L.)	SS-2B-3B	48	151	28	46	6	3	2	15	.305	18	22	6	65	103	6	.966
1994— Colorado (N.L.)	2B-SS-3B	87	255	39	65	17	5	3	31	.255	42	44	0	145	225	10	.974
1995— Pittsburgh (N.L.)■■....	2B-3B-SS	107	259	29	74	12	1	5	38	.286	24	34	2	130	137	5	.982
1996— Pittsburgh (N.L.)	2B-3B-SS	112	217	23	58	14	2	3	30	.267	14	22	3	58	98	3	.981

– 328 –

Year	Team (League)	Pos.	G	AB	R	H	2B	3B	HR	RBI	Avg.	BB	SO	SB	PO	A	E	Avg.
1997—	Los Angeles (N.L.)■..	2-1-3-S	76	88	10	20	6	0	1	11	.227	6	12	0	19	24	2	.956
1998—	Colo. Springs (PCL)■	2B-3B-SS	87	286	44	90	16	3	7	44	.315	39	42	8	71	150	10	.957
	— Colorado (N.L.)	2B-SS	12	17	0	0	0	0	0	0	.000	0	7	0	4	4	0	1.000
	American League totals (5 years)		381	1229	167	313	50	16	11	115	.255	108	159	49	658	897	36	.977
	National League totals (6 years)		442	987	129	263	55	11	14	125	.266	104	141	10	421	591	26	.975
	Major league totals (11 years)		823	2216	296	576	105	27	25	240	.260	212	300	59	1079	1488	62	.976

CHAMPIONSHIP SERIES RECORD

Year	Team (League)	Pos.	G	AB	R	H	2B	3B	HR	RBI	Avg.	BB	SO	SB	PO	A	E	Avg.
1989—	Toronto (A.L.)............	2B	3	7	1	3	0	0	0	1	.429	2	0	3	4	3	1	.875

LITTLE, MARK   OF   CARDINALS

PERSONAL: Born July 11, 1972, in Edwardsville, Ill. ... 6-0/195. ... Bats right, throws right. ... Full name: Mark Travis Little.
HIGH SCHOOL: Edwardsville (Ill.).
COLLEGE: Memphis.
TRANSACTIONS/CAREER NOTES: Selected by Texas Rangers organization in eighth round of free-agent draft (June 2, 1994). ... On disabled list (August 5-September 5, 1996). ... On Oklahoma disabled list (June 23-July 25, 1998). ... Traded by Rangers organization to St. Louis Cardinals organization (August 9, 1998); completing deal in which Cardinals traded P Todd Stottlemyre and SS Royce Clayton to Rangers for P Darren Oliver, 3B Fernando Tatis and a player to be named later (July 31, 1998).
STATISTICAL NOTES: Led American Association outfielders with 280 putouts and 297 total chances in 1997.

Year	Team (League)	Pos.	G	AB	R	H	2B	3B	HR	RBI	Avg.	BB	SO	SB	PO	A	E	Avg.
1994—	Hudson Valley (NYP)..	OF	54	208	33	61	15	5	3	27	.293	22	38	14	136	3	6	.959
1995—	Charlotte (Fla. St.)	OF	115	438	75	112	31	8	9	50	.256	51	108	20	274	8	10	.966
1996—	Tulsa (Texas)	OF	101	409	69	119	24	2	13	50	.291	48	88	22	263	9	9	.968
1997—	Okla. City (A.A.)	OF-1B	121	415	72	109	23	4	15	45	.263	39	100	21	†282	9	8	.973
1998—	Oklahoma (PCL)	OF	69	274	58	81	20	4	8	46	.296	16	60	9	161	6	1	.994
	— Memphis (PCL)■.......	OF	19	63	9	17	3	3	0	6	.270	6	10	0	33	0	1	.971
	— St. Louis (N.L.)..........	OF	7	12	0	1	0	0	0	0	.083	2	5	1	11	0	0	1.000
	Major league totals (1 year)		7	12	0	1	0	0	0	0	.083	2	5	1	11	0	0	1.000

LIVINGSTONE, SCOTT   3B   DODGERS

PERSONAL: Born July 15, 1965, in Dallas. ... 6-0/190. ... Bats left, throws right. ... Full name: Scott Louis Livingstone.
HIGH SCHOOL: Lake Highlands (Dallas).
COLLEGE: Texas A&M.
TRANSACTIONS/CAREER NOTES: Selected by Toronto Blue Jays organization in sixth round of free-agent draft (June 4, 1984); did not sign. ... Selected by New York Yankees organization in 26th round of free-agent draft (June 2, 1986); did not sign. ... Selected by Oakland Athletics organization in third round of free-agent draft (June 2, 1987); did not sign. ... Selected by Detroit Tigers organization in second round of free-agent draft (June 1, 1988). ... On disabled list (July 14-23 and July 28-August 7, 1990). ... Traded by Tigers with SS Jorge Velandia to San Diego Padres for P Gene Harris (May 11, 1994). ... On disabled list (June 3-23, 1996). ... On San Diego disabled list (April 29-May 26, 1997); included rehabilitation assignment to Rancho Cucamonga (May 10-12). ... Traded by Padres with P Fernando Valenzuela and OF Phil Plantier to St. Louis Cardinals for P Danny Jackson, P Rich Batchelor and OF Mark Sweeney (June 13, 1997). ... Granted free agency (November 7, 1997). ... Signed by Montreal Expos organization (March 30, 1998). ... Granted free agency (October 2, 1998). ... Signed by Los Angeles Dodgers organization (January 15, 1999).
HONORS: Named designated hitter on THE SPORTING NEWS college All-America team (1987-88).
STATISTICAL NOTES: Tied for Eastern League lead in total chances by third baseman with 360 in 1989.

Year	Team (League)	Pos.	G	AB	R	H	2B	3B	HR	RBI	Avg.	BB	SO	SB	PO	A	E	Avg.
1988—	Lakeland (Fla. St.)	3B	53	180	28	51	8	1	2	25	.283	11	25	1	30	115	8	.948
1989—	London (Eastern)	3B-SS	124	452	46	98	18	1	14	71	.217	52	67	1	100	265	25	.936
1990—	Toledo (Int'l)	3B	103	345	44	94	19	0	6	36	.272	21	40	1	66	181	13	.950
1991—	Toledo (Int'l)	3B-1B	92	331	48	100	13	3	3	62	.302	40	52	2	65	137	16	.927
	— Detroit (A.L.)	3B	44	127	19	37	5	0	2	11	.291	10	25	2	32	67	2	.980
1992—	Detroit (A.L.)	3B	117	354	43	100	21	0	4	46	.282	21	36	1	67	189	10	.962
1993—	Detroit (A.L.)	3B-DH	98	304	39	89	10	2	2	39	.293	19	32	1	33	94	6	.955
1994—	Detroit (A.L.)	DH-1B-3B	15	23	0	5	1	0	0	1	.217	1	4	0	6	3	0	1.000
	— San Diego (N.L.)■ ...	3B	57	180	11	49	12	1	2	10	.272	6	22	2	20	78	6	.942
1995—	San Diego (N.L.)	1B-3B-2B	99	196	26	66	15	0	5	32	.337	15	22	2	300	33	3	.991
1996—	San Diego (N.L.)	1B-3B	102	172	20	51	4	1	2	20	.297	9	22	0	143	34	2	.989
1997—	San Diego (N.L.)	3B-1B-2B	23	26	1	4	1	0	0	3	.154	2	1	0	17	9	2	.929
	— Rancho Cuca. (Cal.) ...	DH	3	8	2	2	0	0	0	0	.250	3	0	0	. . .	. . .	. . .	. . .
	— St. Louis (N.L.)■	3B-DH-OF	42	41	3	7	1	0	0	3	.171	1	10	1	0	1	0	1.000
	— Louisville (A.A.)	1B	9	25	4	9	1	0	0	2	.360	2	3	0	31	3	1	.971
1998—	Montreal (N.L.)■.......	3B-DH-1B	76	110	1	23	6	0	0	12	.209	5	15	1	16	25	3	.932
	American League totals (4 years)		274	808	101	231	37	2	8	97	.286	51	97	4	138	353	18	.965
	National League totals (5 years)		399	725	62	200	39	2	9	80	.276	38	92	6	496	180	16	.977
	Major league totals (8 years)		673	1533	163	431	76	4	17	177	.281	89	189	10	634	533	34	.972

DIVISION SERIES RECORD

Year	Team (League)	Pos.	G	AB	R	H	2B	3B	HR	RBI	Avg.	BB	SO	SB	PO	A	E	Avg.
1996—	San Diego (N.L.)	PH	2	2	1	1	0	0	0	0	.500	0	0	0	. . .	. . .	. . .	. . .

PERSONAL: Born April 9, 1967, in Geelong, Victoria, Australia. ... 6-7/234. ... Throws left, bats left. ... Full name: Graeme John Lloyd. ... Name pronounced GRAM.

HIGH SCHOOL: Geelong Technical School (Victoria, Australia).

COLLEGE: Geelong Tech.

TRANSACTIONS/CAREER NOTES: Signed as non-drafted free agent by Toronto Blue Jays organization (January 26, 1988). ... On Myrtle Beach disabled list (June 29-September 1, 1989). ... Selected by Philadelphia Phillies from Blue Jays organization in Rule 5 major league draft (December 7, 1992). ... Traded by Phillies to Milwaukee Brewers for P John Trisler (December 8, 1992). ... On disabled list (August 20-September 4, 1993 and July 25-September 10, 1995). ... On suspended list (September 5-9, 1993). ... Traded by Brewers with OF Pat Listach to New York Yankees for OF Gerald Williams and P Bob Wickman (August 23, 1996). ... On disabled list (April 22-May 8, 1998).

Year Team (League)	W	L	Pct.	ERA	G	GS	CG	ShO	Sv.	IP	H	R	ER	BB	SO
1988— Myrtle Beach (SAL)	3	2	.600	3.62	41	0	0	0	2	59 2/3	71	33	24	30	43
1989— Dunedin (Fla. St.)	0	0	...	10.13	2	0	0	0	0	2 2/3	6	3	3	1	0
— Myrtle Beach (SAL)	0	0	...	5.40	1	1	0	0	0	5	5	4	3	0	3
1990— Myrtle Beach (SAL)	5	2	.714	2.72	19	6	0	0	6	49 2/3	51	20	15	16	42
1991— Dunedin (Fla. St.)	2	5	.286	2.24	50	0	0	0	24	60 1/3	54	17	15	25	39
— Knoxville (Southern)	0	0	...	0.00	2	0	0	0	0	1 2/3	1	0	0	1	2
1992— Knoxville (Southern)	4	8	.333	1.96	49	7	1	0	14	92	79	30	20	25	65
1993— Milwaukee (A.L.)■	3	4	.429	2.83	55	0	0	0	0	63 2/3	64	24	20	13	31
1994— Milwaukee (A.L.)	2	3	.400	5.17	43	0	0	0	3	47	49	28	27	15	31
1995— Milwaukee (A.L.)	0	5	.000	4.50	33	0	0	0	4	32	28	16	16	8	13
1996— Milwaukee (A.L.)	2	4	.333	2.82	52	0	0	0	0	51	49	19	16	17	24
— New York (A.L.)■	0	2	.000	17.47	13	0	0	0	0	5 2/3	12	11	11	5	6
1997— New York (A.L.)	1	1	.500	3.31	46	0	0	0	1	49	55	24	18	20	26
1998— New York (A.L.)	3	0	1.000	1.67	50	0	0	0	0	37 2/3	26	10	7	6	20
Major league totals (6 years)	11	19	.367	3.62	292	0	0	0	8	286	283	132	115	84	151

DIVISION SERIES RECORD

Year Team (League)	W	L	Pct.	ERA	G	GS	CG	ShO	Sv.	IP	H	R	ER	BB	SO
1996— New York (A.L.)	0	0	...	0.00	2	0	0	0	0	1	1	0	0	0	0
1997— New York (A.L.)	0	0	...	0.00	2	0	0	0	0	1 1/3	0	0	0	0	1
1998— New York (A.L.)	0	0	...	0.00	1	0	0	0	0	1/3	0	0	0	0	0
Div. series totals (3 years)	0	0	...	0.00	5	0	0	0	0	2 2/3	1	0	0	0	1

CHAMPIONSHIP SERIES RECORD

Year Team (League)	W	L	Pct.	ERA	G	GS	CG	ShO	Sv.	IP	H	R	ER	BB	SO
1996— New York (A.L.)	0	0	...	0.00	2	0	0	0	0	1 2/3	0	0	0	0	1
1998— New York (A.L.)	0	0	...	0.00	1	0	0	0	0	2/3	1	0	0	0	0
Champ. series totals (2 years)	0	0	...	0.00	3	0	0	0	0	2 1/3	1	0	0	0	1

WORLD SERIES RECORD

NOTES: Member of World Series championship team (1996 and 1998).

Year Team (League)	W	L	Pct.	ERA	G	GS	CG	ShO	Sv.	IP	H	R	ER	BB	SO
1996— New York (A.L.)	1	0	1.000	0.00	4	0	0	0	0	2 2/3	0	0	0	0	4
1998— New York (A.L.)	0	0	...	0.00	1	0	0	0	0	1/3	0	0	0	0	0
World Series totals (2 years)	1	0	1.000	0.00	5	0	0	0	0	3	0	0	0	0	4

PERSONAL: Born December 31, 1971, in Tijuana, Mexico. ... 6-3/205. ... Throws right, bats right. ... Full name: Esteban Antonio Veyna Loaiza. ... Name pronounced low-EYE-zah.

HIGH SCHOOL: Mar Vista (Imperial Beach, Calif.).

TRANSACTIONS/CAREER NOTES: Signed as non-drafted free agent by Pittsburgh Pirates organization (March 21, 1991). ... Loaned by Pirates organization to Mexico City Red Devils of the Mexican League (May 7, 1993). ... Returned to Pirates organization (May 28, 1993). ... On disabled list (April 7-28 and July 7-14, 1994). ... Loaned to Red Devils of the Mexican League (June 19, 1996). ... Returned to Pirates organization (August 14, 1996). ... Traded by Pirates to Texas Rangers for P Todd Van Poppel and 2B Warren Morris (July 17, 1998).

MISCELLANEOUS: Made an out in only appearance as pinch hitter (1995). ... Had sacrifice hit in only appearance as pinch hitter (1996).

Year Team (League)	W	L	Pct.	ERA	G	GS	CG	ShO	Sv.	IP	H	R	ER	BB	SO
1991— GC Pirates (GCL)	5	1	.833	2.26	11	11	1	•1	0	51 2/3	48	17	13	14	41
1992— Augusta (S. Atl.)	10	8	.556	3.89	26	25	3	0	0	143 1/3	134	72	62	60	123
1993— Salem (Carolina)	6	7	.462	3.39	17	17	3	0	0	109	113	53	41	30	61
— Carolina (Southern)	2	1	.667	3.77	7	7	1	0	0	43	39	18	18	12	40
— M.C. Red Devils (Mex.)■	1	1	.500	5.18	4	3	0	0	0	24 1/3	32	18	14	4	15
1994— Carolina (Southern)■	10	5	.667	3.79	24	24	3	0	0	154 1/3	169	69	65	30	115
1995— Pittsburgh (N.L.)	8	9	.471	5.16	32	•31	1	0	0	172 2/3	205	*115	*99	55	85
1996— Calgary (PCL)	3	4	.429	4.02	12	11	1	1	0	69 1/3	61	34	31	25	38
— M.C. Red Devils (Mex.)■	2	0	1.000	2.43	5	5	0	0	0	33 1/3	28	12	9	14	16
— Pittsburgh (N.L.)■	2	3	.400	4.96	10	10	1	1	0	52 2/3	65	32	29	19	32
1997— Pittsburgh (N.L.)	11	11	.500	4.13	33	32	0	0	0	196 1/3	214	99	90	56	122
1998— Pittsburgh (N.L.)	6	5	.545	4.52	21	14	0	0	0	91 2/3	96	50	46	30	53
— Texas (A.L.)■	3	6	.333	5.90	14	14	1	0	0	79 1/3	103	57	52	22	55
A.L. totals (1 year)	3	6	.333	5.90	14	14	1	0	0	79 1/3	103	57	52	22	55
N.L. totals (4 years)	27	28	.491	4.63	96	87	3	1	0	513 1/3	580	296	264	160	292
Major league totals (4 years)	30	34	.469	4.80	110	101	4	1	0	592 2/3	683	353	316	182	347

PERSONAL: Born November 10, 1964, in Whittier, Calif. ... 5-10/170. ... Bats left, throws right. ... Full name: Keith Virgil Lockhart.

HIGH SCHOOL: Northview (Covina, Calif.).

JUNIOR COLLEGE: Mount San Antonio (Texas) Junior College.
COLLEGE: Oral Roberts.
TRANSACTIONS/CAREER NOTES: Selected by Cincinnati Reds organization in 11th round of free-agent draft (June 2, 1986). ... Contract sold by Reds organization to Tacoma, Oakland Athletics organization (February 4, 1992). ... Granted free agency (October 15, 1992). ... Signed by St. Louis Cardinals organization (December 12, 1992). ... Granted free agency (October 15, 1993). ... Signed by San Diego Padres organization (January 7, 1994). ... Granted free agency (October 15, 1994). ... Signed by Omaha, Kansas City Royals organization (November 14, 1994). ... Traded by Royals with OF Michael Tucker to Atlanta Braves for OF Jermaine Dye and P Jamie Walker (March 27, 1997). ... On disabled list (August 6-22, 1997).
STATISTICAL NOTES: Led Midwest League third basemen with 33 double plays in 1987. ... Led Southern League with 11 sacrifice flies in 1988. ... Led American Association second basemen with 631 total chances in 1989. ... Order of frequency of positions played in 1994 for Las Vegas: OF-SS-2B-3B-P-C. ... Career major league grand slams: 1.

Year Team (League)	Pos.	G	AB	R	H	2B	3B	HR	RBI	Avg.	BB	SO	SB	PO	A	E	Avg.
1986— Billings (Pioneer)........	2B-3B	53	202	51	70	11	3	7	31	.347	35	22	4	81	150	17	.931
— Cedar Rap. (Midw.)	2B-3B	13	42	4	8	2	0	0	1	.190	6	6	1	17	15	0	1.000
1987— Cedar Rap. (Midw.)	3B-2B	*140	511	101	160	37	5	23	84	.313	86	70	20	85	292	28	.931
1988— Chattanooga (Sou.)	3B-2B	139	515	74	137	27	3	12	67	.266	61	59	7	102	323	36	.922
1989— Nashville (A.A.)	2B	131	479	77	128	21	6	14	58	.267	61	41	4	*279	*335	17	.973
1990— Nashville (A.A.)	2B-3B-OF	126	431	48	112	25	4	9	63	.260	51	74	8	173	248	9	.979
1991— Nashville (A.A.)	3B-2B-OF	116	411	53	107	25	3	8	36	.260	24	64	3	153	241	13	.968
1992— Tacoma (PCL)■	2B-3B-SS	107	363	44	101	25	3	5	37	.278	29	21	5	199	239	11	.976
1993— Louisville (A.A.)■........	3-2-O-1	132	467	66	140	24	3	13	68	.300	60	43	3	157	239	12	.971
1994— San Diego (N.L.)■	3-2-S-O	27	43	4	9	0	0	2	6	.209	4	10	1	10	21	1	.969
— Las Vegas (PCL)	O-I-P-C	89	331	61	106	15	5	7	43	.320	26	37	3	143	113	10	.962
1995— Omaha (A.A.)■	3B	44	148	24	56	7	1	5	19	.378	16	10	1	31	72	8	.928
— Kansas City (A.L.)	2B-3B-DH	94	274	41	88	19	3	6	33	.321	14	21	8	111	178	8	.973
1996— Kansas City (A.L.)	3B-2B-DH	138	433	49	118	33	3	7	55	.273	30	40	11	137	281	13	.970
1997— Atlanta (N.L.)■..........	2B-3B-DH	96	147	25	41	5	3	6	32	.279	14	17	0	24	48	3	.960
1998— Atlanta (N.L.)...........	2B-DH-3B	109	366	50	94	21	0	9	37	.257	29	37	2	130	250	6	.984
American League totals (2 years)		232	707	90	206	52	6	13	88	.291	44	61	19	248	459	21	.971
National League totals (3 years)		232	556	79	144	26	3	17	75	.259	47	64	3	164	319	10	.980
Major league totals (5 years)		464	1263	169	350	78	9	30	163	.277	91	125	22	412	778	31	.975

DIVISION SERIES RECORD

Year Team (League)	Pos.	G	AB	R	H	2B	3B	HR	RBI	Avg.	BB	SO	SB	PO	A	E	Avg.
1997— Atlanta (N.L.).............	2B	2	6	0	0	0	0	0	0	.000	0	1	0	1	8	1	.900
1998— Atlanta (N.L.).............	2B	3	12	2	4	0	0	0	0	.333	1	0	0	9	9	0	1.000
Division series totals (2 years)		5	18	2	4	0	0	0	0	.222	1	1	0	10	17	1	.964

CHAMPIONSHIP SERIES RECORD

Year Team (League)	Pos.	G	AB	R	H	2B	3B	HR	RBI	Avg.	BB	SO	SB	PO	A	E	Avg.
1997— Atlanta (N.L.).............	2B-PH	5	16	4	8	1	1	0	3	.500	1	1	0	14	5	0	1.000
1998— Atlanta (N.L.).............	2B-PH	6	17	2	4	1	1	0	0	.235	0	4	0	5	12	0	1.000
Championship series totals (2 years)		11	33	6	12	2	2	0	3	.364	1	5	0	19	17	0	1.000

RECORD AS PITCHER

Year Team (League)	W	L	Pct.	ERA	G	GS	CG	ShO	Sv.	IP	H	R	ER	BB	SO
1994— Las Vegas (PCL)	0	0	...	0.00	1	1	0	0	0	1	0	0	0	0	0

LoDUCA, PAUL — C — DODGERS

PERSONAL: Born April 12, 1972, in Brooklyn, N.Y. ... 5-10/185. ... Bats right, throws right. ... Full name: Paul Anthony LoDuca.
HIGH SCHOOL: Apollo (Phoenix).
JUNIOR COLLEGE: Glendale (Ariz.) Community College.
COLLEGE: Arizona State.
TRANSACTIONS/CAREER NOTES: Selected by Los Angeles Dodgers organization in 25th round of free-agent draft (June 3, 1993).
STATISTICAL NOTES: Led Florida State League with .400 on-base percentage in 1996. ... Led Florida State League catchers with 17 errors in 1996. ... Led Texas League catchers with .990 fielding percentage, 84 assists and 667 total chances in 1997. ... Led Pacific Coast League in grounding into double plays with 20 in 1998.

Year Team (League)	Pos.	G	AB	R	H	2B	3B	HR	RBI	Avg.	BB	SO	SB	PO	A	E	Avg.
1993— Vero Beach (FSL)	C	39	134	17	42	6	0	0	13	.313	13	22	0	209	26	2	.992
1994— Bakersfield (Calif.)	1-B-C	123	455	65	144	32	1	6	68	.316	52	49	16	657	59	5	.993
1995— San Antonio (Tex.)	C-1B-3B	61	199	27	49	8	0	1	8	.246	26	25	5	353	43	11	.973
1996— Vero Beach (FSL)	C-1B-3B	124	439	54	134	22	0	3	66	.305	70	38	8	747	116	†18	.980
1997— San Antonio (Tex.)	C-1B	105	385	63	126	28	2	7	69	.327	46	27	16	636	†91	7	†.990
1998— Albuquerque (PCL)......	C-1B-3B	126	451	69	144	30	3	8	58	.319	59	40	19	742	92	17	.980
— Los Angeles (N.L.)	C	6	14	2	4	1	0	0	1	.286	0	1	0	18	2	0	1.000
Major league totals (1 year)		6	14	2	4	1	0	0	1	.286	0	1	0	18	2	0	1.000

LOEWER, CARLTON — P — PHILLIES

PERSONAL: Born September 24, 1973, in Lafayette, La. ... 6-6/220. ... Throws right, bats both. ... Full name: Carlton Edward Loewer.
HIGH SCHOOL: St. Edmund (Eunice, La.).
COLLEGE: Mississippi State.
TRANSACTIONS/CAREER NOTES: Selected by Toronto Blue Jays organization in seventh round of free-agent draft (June 3, 1991); did not sign. ... Selected by Philadelphia Phillies organization in first round (23rd pick overall) of free-agent draft (June 2, 1994).
STATISTICAL NOTES: Led Eastern League with 24 home runs allowed in 1996.

Year Team (League)	W	L	Pct.	ERA	G	GS	CG	ShO	Sv.	IP	H	R	ER	BB	SO
1995—Clearwater (Fla. St.)	7	5	.583	3.30	20	20	1	0	0	114 2/3	124	59	42	36	83
—Reading (Eastern)	4	1	.800	2.16	8	8	0	0	0	50	42	17	12	31	35
1996—Reading (Eastern)	7	10	.412	5.26	27	27	3	1	0	171	*191	115	100	57	119
1997—Scran./W.B. (Int'l)................	5	13	.278	4.60	29	*29	4	0	0	184	*198	*120	94	50	152
1998—Scran./W.B. (Int'l)...............	7	3	.700	2.87	12	12	*5	•2	0	94	89	34	30	22	69
—Philadelphia (N.L.)..............	7	8	.467	6.09	21	21	1	0	0	122 2/3	154	86	83	39	58
Major league totals (1 year)........	7	8	.467	6.09	21	21	1	0	0	122 2/3	154	86	83	39	58

LOFTON, KENNY   OF   INDIANS

PERSONAL: Born May 31, 1967, in East Chicago, Ind. ... 6-0/180. ... Bats left, throws left. ... Full name: Kenneth Lofton.

HIGH SCHOOL: Washington (East Chicago, Ind.).

COLLEGE: Arizona.

TRANSACTIONS/CAREER NOTES: Selected by Houston Astros organization in 17th round of free-agent draft (June 1, 1988). ... Traded by Astros with IF Dave Rohde to Cleveland Indians for P Willie Blair and C Eddie Taubensee (December 10, 1991). ... On disabled list (July 17-August 1, 1995). ... Traded by Indians with P Alan Embree to Atlanta Braves for OF Marquis Grissom and OF Dave Justice (March 25, 1997). ... On disabled list (June 18-July 5 and July 6-28, 1997). ... Granted free agency (October 28, 1997). ... Signed by Indians (December 8, 1997).

RECORDS: Holds A.L. rookie-season record for most stolen bases—66 (1992). ... Shares A.L. single-season record for fewest errors by outfielder who led league in errors—8 (1998).

HONORS: Won A.L. Gold Glove as outfielder (1993-96).

STATISTICAL NOTES: Tied for Pacific Coast League lead in caught stealing with 23 in 1991. ... Led Pacific Coast League outfielders with 344 total chances in 1991. ... Led N.L. in caught stealing with 20 in 1997. ... Career major league grand slams: 1.

MISCELLANEOUS: Holds Cleveland Indians all-time record for most stolen bases (379).

								BATTING							FIELDING			
Year Team (League)	Pos.	G	AB	R	H	2B	3B	HR	RBI	Avg.	BB	SO	SB	PO	A	E	Avg.
1988—Auburn (NY-Penn)......	OF	48	187	23	40	6	1	1	14	.214	19	51	26	94	5	4	.961
1989—Auburn (NY-Penn)......	OF	34	110	21	29	3	1	0	8	.264	14	30	26	37	4	8	.837
—Asheville (S. Atl.)........	OF	22	82	14	27	2	0	1	9	.329	12	10	14	38	1	2	.951
1990—Osceola (Fla. St.)......	OF	124	481	98	*159	15	5	2	35	.331	61	77	62	246	13	7	.974
1991—Tucson (PCL)........	OF	130	*545	93	*168	19	*17	2	50	.308	52	95	40	*308	*27	9	.974
—Houston (N.L.)	OF	20	74	9	15	1	0	0	0	.203	5	19	2	41	1	1	.977
1992—Cleveland (A.L.)■.....	OF	148	576	96	164	15	8	5	42	.285	68	54	*66	420	14	8	.982
1993—Cleveland (A.L.)......	OF	148	569	116	185	28	8	1	42	.325	81	83	*70	402	11	•9	.979
1994—Cleveland (A.L.)......	OF	112	459	105	*160	32	9	12	57	.349	52	56	*60	276	•13	2	.993
1995—Cleveland (A.L.)......	OF-DH	118	481	93	149	22	*13	7	53	.310	40	49	*54	248	*11	8	.970
1996—Cleveland (A.L.)......	OF	154	*662	132	210	35	4	14	67	.317	61	82	*75	376	13	10	.975
1997—Atlanta (N.L.)■......	OF	122	493	90	164	20	6	5	48	.333	64	83	27	290	5	5	.983
1998—Cleveland (A.L.)■......	OF	154	600	101	169	31	6	12	64	.282	87	80	54	339	*19	8	.978
American League totals (6 years)		834	3347	643	1037	163	48	51	325	.310	389	404	379	2061	81	45	.979
National League totals (2 years)		142	567	99	179	21	6	5	48	.316	69	102	29	331	6	6	.983
Major league totals (8 years)		976	3914	742	1216	184	54	56	373	.311	458	506	408	2392	87	51	.980

DIVISION SERIES RECORD

								BATTING							FIELDING			
Year Team (League)	Pos.	G	AB	R	H	2B	3B	HR	RBI	Avg.	BB	SO	SB	PO	A	E	Avg.
1995—Cleveland (A.L.)..........	OF	3	13	1	2	0	0	0	0	.154	1	3	0	9	0	2	.818
1996—Cleveland (A.L.)..........	OF	4	18	3	3	0	0	0	1	.167	2	3	5	10	0	0	1.000
1997—Atlanta (N.L.)..........	OF	3	13	2	2	1	0	0	0	.154	1	2	0	6	1	0	1.000
1998—Cleveland (A.L.)..........	OF	4	16	5	6	1	0	2	4	.375	1	1	2	10	0	0	1.000
Division series totals (4 years)		14	60	11	13	2	0	2	5	.217	5	9	7	35	1	2	.947

CHAMPIONSHIP SERIES RECORD

								BATTING							FIELDING			
Year Team (League)	Pos.	G	AB	R	H	2B	3B	HR	RBI	Avg.	BB	SO	SB	PO	A	E	Avg.
1995—Cleveland (A.L.)..........	OF	6	24	4	11	0	2	0	3	.458	4	6	5	15	0	0	1.000
1997—Atlanta (N.L.)..........	OF	6	27	3	5	0	1	0	1	.185	1	7	1	9	1	2	.833
1998—Cleveland (A.L.)..........	OF	6	27	2	5	1	0	1	3	.185	1	7	1	8	0	1	.889
Championship series totals (3 years)		18	78	9	21	1	3	1	7	.269	6	20	7	32	1	3	.917

WORLD SERIES RECORD

RECORDS: Shares single-inning record for most stolen bases—2 (October 21, 1995).

								BATTING							FIELDING			
Year Team (League)	Pos.	G	AB	R	H	2B	3B	HR	RBI	Avg.	BB	SO	SB	PO	A	E	Avg.
1995—Cleveland (A.L.)..........	OF	6	25	6	5	1	0	0	0	.200	3	1	6	12	0	0	1.000

ALL-STAR GAME RECORD

RECORDS: Shares single-game record for most stolen bases—2 (July 9, 1996).

							BATTING							FIELDING			
Year League	Pos.	AB	R	H	2B	3B	HR	RBI	Avg.	BB	SO	SB	PO	A	E	Avg.
1994—American..................	OF	2	0	1	0	0	0	2	.500	0	1	1	1	0	0	1.000
1995—American..................	OF	3	0	0	0	0	0	0	.000	0	1	0	0	0	0	...
1996—American..................	OF	3	0	2	0	0	0	0	.667	0	0	2	0	0	0	...
1997—National..................						Selected, did not play—injured.											
1998—American..................	OF	3	0	1	0	0	0	0	.333	1	0	1	2	0	0	1.000
All-Star Game totals (4 years)		11	0	4	0	0	0	2	.364	1	2	4	3	0	0	1.000

LOISELLE, RICH — P — PIRATES

PERSONAL: Born January 12, 1972, in Neenah, Wis. ... 6-5/250. ... Throws right, bats right. ... Full name: Richard Frank Loiselle.
HIGH SCHOOL: Lawton (Okla.).
JUNIOR COLLEGE: Odessa (Texas) College.
TRANSACTIONS/CAREER NOTES: Selected by San Diego Padres organization in 38th round of free-agent draft (June 3, 1991). ... Traded by Padres organization with P Jeff Tabaka to Houston Astros organization for OF Phil Plantier (July 19, 1995). ... On Tucson disabled list (August 2, 1995-remainder of season). ... Traded by Astros to Pittsburgh Pirates for P Danny Darwin (July 23, 1996). ... On Pittsburgh disabled list (July 20-August 17, 1998); included rehabilitation assignment to Nashville (August 7-16).

Year Team (League)	W	L	Pct.	ERA	G	GS	CG	ShO	Sv.	IP	H	R	ER	BB	SO
1991— Ariz. Padres (Ariz.)	2	3	.400	3.52	12	12	0	0	0	61 1/3	72	40	24	26	47
1992— Charleston (A.A.)	4	8	.333	3.71	19	19	2	2	0	97	93	51	40	42	64
1993— Waterloo (Midw.)	1	5	.167	3.94	14	10	1	1	0	59 1/3	55	28	26	29	47
— Rancho Cuca. (Cal.)	5	8	.385	5.77	14	14	1	0	0	82 2/3	109	64	53	34	53
1994— Rancho Cuca. (Cal.)	9	10	.474	3.96	27	27	0	0	0	156 2/3	160	83	69	76	120
1995— Memphis (Sou.)	6	3	.667	3.55	13	13	1	0	0	78 2/3	82	46	31	33	48
— Las Vegas (PCL)	2	2	.500	7.24	8	7	1	1	0	27 1/3	36	27	22	9	16
— Tucson (PCL)■	0	0	...	2.61	2	1	0	0	0	10 1/3	8	4	3	4	4
1996— Jackson (Texas)	7	4	.636	3.47	16	16	2	0	0	98 2/3	107	46	38	27	65
— Tucson (PCL)	2	2	.500	2.43	5	5	1	1	0	33 1/3	28	20	9	11	31
— Calgary (PCL)■	2	2	.500	4.09	8	8	0	0	0	50 2/3	64	28	23	16	41
— Pittsburgh (N.L.)	1	0	1.000	3.05	5	3	0	0	0	20 2/3	22	8	7	8	9
1997— Pittsburgh (N.L.)	1	5	.167	3.10	72	0	0	0	29	72 2/3	76	29	25	24	66
1998— Pittsburgh (N.L.)	2	7	.222	3.44	54	0	0	0	19	55	56	26	21	36	48
— Nashville (Pacific Coast)	0	0	...	0.00	4	0	0	0	2	5	3	0	0	0	6
Major league totals (3 years)	4	12	.250	3.22	131	3	0	0	48	148 1/3	154	63	53	68	123

LOMASNEY, STEVE — C — RED SOX

PERSONAL: Born August 29, 1977, in Melrose, Mass. ... 6-0/185. ... Bats right, throws right. ... Full name: Steven James Lomasney.
HIGH SCHOOL: Peabody (Mass.).
TRANSACTIONS/CAREER NOTES: Selected by Boston Red Sox organization in fifth round of free-agent draft (June 1, 1995).
STATISTICAL NOTES: Led New York-Pennsylvania League with 21 passed balls in 1996.

Year Team (League)	Pos.	G	AB	R	H	2B	3B	HR	RBI	Avg.	BB	SO	SB	PO	A	E	Avg.
1995— GC Red Sox (GCL)	C	29	92	10	15	6	0	0	7	.163	8	16	2	146	29	5	.972
1996— Lowell (NY-Penn)	C	59	173	26	24	10	0	4	21	.139	42	63	2	402	47	9	.980
1997— Michigan (Midwest)	C	102	324	50	89	27	3	12	51	.275	32	98	3	623	83	12	.983
1998— Sarasota (Fla. St.)	C-1B	122	443	74	106	22	1	22	63	.239	59	145	13	590	79	13	.981

LOMBARD, GEORGE — OF — BRAVES

PERSONAL: Born September 14, 1975, in Atlanta. ... 6-0/208. ... Bats left, throws right. ... Full name: George Paul Lombard.
HIGH SCHOOL: Lovett (Atlanta).
TRANSACTIONS/CAREER NOTES: Selected by Atlanta Braves organization in second round of free-agent draft (June 2, 1994). ... On disabled list (August 16, 1996-remainder of season).
STATISTICAL NOTES: Tied for South Atlantic League lead in caught stealing with 13 in 1995. ... Led Carolina League outfielders with 284 total chances in 1997. ... Led Southern League with 10 intentional bases on balls in 1998.

Year Team (League)	Pos.	G	AB	R	H	2B	3B	HR	RBI	Avg.	BB	SO	SB	PO	A	E	Avg.
1994— GC Braves (GCL)	OF	40	129	10	18	2	0	0	5	.140	18	47	10	33	1	2	.944
1995— Eugene (Northwest)	OF	68	262	38	66	5	3	5	19	.252	23	91	35	71	5	3	.962
— Macon (S. Atl.)	OF	49	180	32	37	6	1	3	16	.206	27	44	16	44	2	2	.958
1996— Macon (S. Atl.)	OF	116	444	76	109	16	8	15	51	.245	36	122	24	229	2	7	.971
1997— Durham (Carolina)	OF	131	462	65	122	25	7	14	72	.264	66	145	35	*270	5	9	.968
1998— Greenville (Southern)	OF	122	422	84	130	25	4	22	65	.308	71	140	35	170	8	10	.947
— Atlanta (N.L.)	OF	6	6	2	2	0	0	1	1	.333	0	1	1	2	0	0	1.000
Major league totals (1 year)		6	6	2	2	0	0	1	1	.333	0	1	1	2	0	0	1.000

LONG, TERRENCE — OF — METS

PERSONAL: Born February 29, 1976, in Montgomery, Ala. ... 6-1/190. ... Bats left, throws left. ... Full name: Terrence Deon Long.
HIGH SCHOOL: Stanhope Elmore (Millbrook, Ala.).
TRANSACTIONS/CAREER NOTES: Selected by New York Mets organization in first round (20th pick overall) of free-agent draft (June 2, 1994); pick received as compensation for Baltimore Orioles signing Type A free-agent P Sid Fernandez. ... On disabled list (May 15-27, 1996).

Year Team (League)	Pos.	G	AB	R	H	2B	3B	HR	RBI	Avg.	BB	SO	SB	PO	A	E	Avg.
1994— Kingsport (Appal.)	OF-1B	60	215	39	50	9	2	12	39	.233	32	52	9	237	5	5	.980
1995— Capital City (SAL)	OF	55	178	27	35	1	2	2	13	.197	28	43	8	69	5	5	.937
— Pittsfield (NYP)	OF	51	187	24	48	9	4	4	31	.257	18	36	11	113	3	1	*.991
1996— Columbia (S. Atl.)	OF	123	473	66	136	26	9	12	78	.288	36	120	32	246	8	5	.981
1997— St. Lucie (Fla. St.)	OF	126	470	52	118	29	7	8	61	.251	40	102	24	235	7	7	.972
1998— Binghamton (East.)	OF	130	455	69	135	20	*10	16	58	.297	62	105	23	218	9	10	.958

LOOPER, BRADEN — P — MARLINS

PERSONAL: Born October 28, 1974, in Weatherford, Okla. ... 6-5/225. ... Throws right, bats right. ... Full name: Braden LaVern Looper. ... Name pronounced BRAY-dun.
HIGH SCHOOL: Mangum (Okla.).
COLLEGE: Wichita State.
TRANSACTIONS/CAREER NOTES: Selected by St. Louis Cardinals organization in first round (third pick overall) of free-agent draft (June 2, 1996). ... On Memphis disabled list (May 6-June 21, 1998). ... Traded by Cardinals with P Armando Almanza and SS Pablo Ozuna to Florida Marlins for SS Edgar Renteria (December 14, 1998).
MISCELLANEOUS: Member of 1996 U.S. Olympic baseball team.

Year	Team (League)	W	L	Pct.	ERA	G	GS	CG	ShO	Sv.	IP	H	R	ER	BB	SO
1997—	Prince William (Caro.)	3	6	.333	4.48	12	12	0	0	0	64 1/3	71	38	32	25	58
—	Arkansas (Texas)	1	4	.200	5.91	19	0	0	0	5	21 1/3	24	14	14	7	20
1998—	St. Louis (N.L.)	0	1	.000	5.40	4	0	0	0	0	3 1/3	5	4	2	1	4
—	Memphis (Pacific Coast)	2	3	.400	3.10	40	0	0	0	20	40 2/3	43	16	14	13	43
Major league totals (1 year)		0	1	.000	5.40	4	0	0	0	0	3 1/3	5	4	2	1	4

LOPEZ, ALBIE — P — DEVIL RAYS

PERSONAL: Born August 18, 1971, in Mesa, Ariz. ... 6-2/185. ... Throws right, bats right. ... Full name: Albert Anthony Lopez.
HIGH SCHOOL: Westwood (Mesa, Ariz.).
JUNIOR COLLEGE: Mesa (Ariz.) Community College.
TRANSACTIONS/CAREER NOTES: Selected by San Francisco Giants organization in 46th round of free-agent draft (June 5, 1989); did not sign. ... Selected by Seattle Mariners organization in 19th round of free-agent draft (June 4, 1990); did not sign. ... Selected by Cleveland Indians organization in 20th round of free-agent draft (June 3, 1991). ... On Cleveland disabled list (July 2-28 and August 13-September 1, 1997). ... Selected by Tampa Bay Devil Rays in second round (48th pick overall) of expansion draft (November 18, 1997). ... On Tampa Bay disabled list (August 1-26, 1998); included rehabilitation assignments to Durham (August 15-18) and St. Petersburg (August 25-26).
STATISTICAL NOTES: Led American Association with 10 hit batsmen and tied for lead with three balks in 1996.

Year	Team (League)	W	L	Pct.	ERA	G	GS	CG	ShO	Sv.	IP	H	R	ER	BB	SO
1991—	Burlington (Appalachian)	4	5	.444	3.44	13	13	0	0	0	73 1/3	61	33	28	23	81
1992—	Columbus (S. Atl.)	7	2	.778	2.88	16	16	1	0	0	97	80	41	31	33	117
—	Kinston (Carolina)	5	2	.714	3.52	10	10	1	1	0	64	56	28	25	26	44
1993—	Cant./Akr. (Eastern)	9	4	.692	3.11	16	16	2	0	0	110	79	44	38	47	80
—	Cleveland (A.L.)	3	1	.750	5.98	9	9	0	0	0	49 2/3	49	34	33	32	25
—	Charlotte (Int'l)	1	0	1.000	2.25	3	2	0	0	0	12	8	3	3	2	7
1994—	Charlotte (Int'l)	13	3	.813	3.94	22	22	3	0	0	144	136	68	63	42	105
—	Cleveland (A.L.)	1	2	.333	4.24	4	4	1	1	0	17	20	11	8	6	18
1995—	Buffalo (A.A.)	5	10	.333	4.44	18	18	1	1	0	101 1/3	101	57	50	51	82
—	Cleveland (A.L.)	0	0	...	3.13	6	2	0	0	0	23	17	8	8	7	22
1996—	Buffalo (A.A.)	10	2	.833	3.87	17	17	2	0	0	104 2/3	90	54	45	40	89
—	Cleveland (A.L.)	5	4	.556	6.39	13	10	0	0	0	62	80	47	44	22	45
1997—	Cleveland (A.L.)	3	7	.300	6.93	37	6	0	0	0	76 2/3	101	61	59	40	63
—	Buffalo (A.A.)	1	0	1.000	0.00	7	0	0	0	1	11 1/3	6	0	0	2	13
—	Akron (Eastern)	0	0	...	0.00	1	0	0	0	0	1	2	0	0	0	2
1998—	Tampa Bay (A.L.)■	7	4	.636	2.60	54	0	0	0	0	79 2/3	73	31	23	32	62
—	Durham (International)	0	0	...	0.00	2	0	0	0	0	3	4	0	0	1	2
—	St. Petersburg (FSL)	0	1	.000	18.00	1	1	0	0	0	1	2	2	2	0	1
Major league totals (6 years)		19	18	.514	5.11	123	31	1	1	1	308	340	192	175	139	235

LOPEZ, JAVY — C — BRAVES

PERSONAL: Born November 5, 1970, in Ponce, Puerto Rico. ... 6-3/200. ... Bats right, throws right. ... Full name: Javier Torres Lopez.
HIGH SCHOOL: Academia Cristo Rey (Urb la Ramble Ponce, Puerto Rico).
TRANSACTIONS/CAREER NOTES: Signed as non-drafted free agent by Atlanta Braves organization (November 6, 1987). ... On Greenville disabled list (July 18-August 2, 1992). ... On disabled list (July 6-22, 1997).
HONORS: Named Southern League Most Valuable Player (1992).
STATISTICAL NOTES: Led Midwest League catchers with 11 double plays and 31 passed balls in 1990. ... Led Carolina League catchers with 701 total chances and 14 double plays in 1991. ... Led Southern League catchers with 763 total chances and 19 passed balls in 1992. ... Led International League catchers with 15 passed balls in 1993. ... Tied for N.L. lead with 10 passed balls in 1994. ... Career major league grand slams: 2.

Year	Team (League)	Pos.	G	AB	R	H	2B	3B	HR	RBI	Avg.	BB	SO	SB	PO	A	E	Avg.
1988—	GC Braves (GCL)	C	31	94	8	18	4	0	1	9	.191	3	19	1	131	30	7	.958
1989—	Pulaski (Appalachian)	C	51	153	27	40	8	1	3	27	.261	5	35	3	264	26	5	.983
1990—	Burlington (Midw.)	C	116	422	48	112	17	3	11	55	.265	14	84	0	724	79	11	.986
1991—	Durham (Carolina)	C	113	384	43	94	14	2	11	51	.245	25	88	10	*610	85	6	.991
1992—	Greenville (Southern)	C	115	442	63	142	28	3	16	60	.321	24	47	7	*680	75	8	.990
—	Atlanta (N.L.)	C	9	16	3	6	2	0	0	2	.375	0	1	0	28	2	0	1.000
1993—	Richmond (Int'l)	C	100	380	56	116	23	2	17	74	.305	12	53	1	718	70	10	.987
—	Atlanta (N.L.)	C	8	16	1	6	1	1	1	2	.375	0	2	0	37	2	1	.975
1994—	Atlanta (N.L.)	C	80	277	27	68	9	0	13	35	.245	17	61	0	559	35	3	.995
1995—	Atlanta (N.L.)	C	100	333	37	105	11	4	14	51	.315	14	57	0	625	50	8	.988
1996—	Atlanta (N.L.)	C	138	489	56	138	19	1	23	69	.282	28	84	1	993	*81	6	.994
1997—	Atlanta (N.L.)	C	123	414	52	122	28	1	23	68	.295	40	82	1	792	56	6	.993
1998—	Atlanta (N.L.)	C-DH	133	489	73	139	21	1	34	106	.284	30	85	5	978	68	5	*.995
Major league totals (7 years)			591	2034	249	584	91	8	108	333	.287	129	372	7	4012	294	29	.993

DIVISION SERIES RECORD

						BATTING								FIELDING			
Year Team (League)	Pos.	G	AB	R	H	2B	3B	HR	RBI	Avg.	BB	SO	SB	PO	A	E	Avg.
1995—Atlanta (N.L.).............	C	3	9	0	4	0	0	0	3	.444	0	3	0	22	3	0	1.000
1996—Atlanta (N.L.).............	C	2	7	1	2	0	0	1	1	.286	1	1		21	1	1	.957
1997—Atlanta (N.L.).............	C	2	7	3	2	2	0	0	1	.286	2	1	0	18	0	0	1.000
1998—Atlanta (N.L.).............	C	2	7	1	2	0	0	1	1	.286	1	1	0	20	3	0	1.000
Division series totals (4 years)		9	30	5	10	2	0	2	6	.333	4	5	1	81	7	1	.989

CHAMPIONSHIP SERIES RECORD

RECORDS: Shares career record for most doubles—7. ... Shares single-game record for most runs—4 (October 14, 1996). ... Holds N.L. single-series record for most runs—8 (1996). ... Shares N.L. single-series record for most consecutive hits—5 (1996). ... Holds single-series record for most doubles—5 (1996). ... Shares single-series record for most total bases—24 (1996). ... Holds single-series record for most long hits—7 (1996).

NOTES: Named N.L. Championship Series Most Valuable Player (1996).

						BATTING								FIELDING			
Year Team (League)	Pos.	G	AB	R	H	2B	3B	HR	RBI	Avg.	BB	SO	SB	PO	A	E	Avg.
1992—Atlanta (N.L.).............	C	1	1	0	0	0	0	0	0	.000	0	0	0	2	0	0	1.000
1995—Atlanta (N.L.).............	C	3	14	2	5	1	0	1	3	.357	0	1	0	28	2	0	1.000
1996—Atlanta (N.L.).............	C	7	24	8	13	5	0	2	6	.542	4	1	1	48	3	0	1.000
1997—Atlanta (N.L.).............	C-PH	5	17	0	1	1	0	0	2	.059	1	7	0	40	3	0	1.000
1998—Atlanta (N.L.).............	C-PH	6	20	2	6	0	0	1	1	.300	0	7	0	43	2	1	.978
Championship series totals (5 years)		22	76	12	25	7	0	4	12	.329	5	16	1	161	10	1	.994

WORLD SERIES RECORD

NOTES: Member of World Series championship team (1995).

						BATTING								FIELDING			
Year Team (League)	Pos.	G	AB	R	H	2B	3B	HR	RBI	Avg.	BB	SO	SB	PO	A	E	Avg.
1992—Atlanta (N.L.)								Did not play.									
1995—Atlanta (N.L.).............	C-PH	6	17	1	3	2	0	1	3	.176	1	1	0	32	4	0	1.000
1996—Atlanta (N.L.).............	C	6	21	3	4	0	0	0	1	.190	3	4	0	41	4	0	1.000
World Series totals (2 years)		12	38	4	7	2	0	1	4	.184	4	5	0	73	8	0	1.000

ALL-STAR GAME RECORD

RECORDS: Hit home run in first at-bat (July 8, 1997).

					BATTING								FIELDING			
Year League	Pos.	AB	R	H	2B	3B	HR	RBI	Avg.	BB	SO	SB	PO	A	E	Avg.
1997—National	C	1	1	1	0	0	1	1	1.000	0	0	0	4	1	0	1.000
1998—National	C	1	0	0	0	0	0	0	.000	0	1	0	3	0	0	1.000
All-Star Game totals (2 years)		2	1	1	0	0	1	1	.500	0	1	0	7	1	0	1.000

LOPEZ, LUIS   IF   METS

PERSONAL: Born September 4, 1970, in Cidra, Puerto Rico. ... 5-11/166. ... Bats both, throws right. ... Full name: Luis Manuel Lopez.
HIGH SCHOOL: San Jose (Caguas, Puerto Rico).
TRANSACTIONS/CAREER NOTES: Signed as non-drafted free agent by San Diego Padres organization (September 9, 1987). ... On Las Vegas disabled list (July 3-14, 1994). ... Granted free agency (October 15, 1994). ... Re-signed by Padres (April 20, 1995). ... On disabled list (April 24, 1995-entire season). ... On San Diego disabled list (March 29-April 18 and July 31-September 1, 1996); included rehabilitation assignments to Las Vegas (March 30-April 18 and August 17-September 1). ... Traded by Padres to Houston Astros for P Sean Runyan (March 15, 1997). ... Traded by Astros to New York Mets for IF Tim Bogar (March 31, 1997).
STATISTICAL NOTES: Led South Atlantic League shortstops with 703 total chances and 78 double plays in 1989. ... Led Pacific Coast League shortstops with 30 errors in 1992. ... Tied for Pacific Coast League lead with 13 sacrifice hits in 1993. ... Career major league grand slams: 1.

						BATTING								FIELDING			
Year Team (League)	Pos.	G	AB	R	H	2B	3B	HR	RBI	Avg.	BB	SO	SB	PO	A	E	Avg.
1988—Spokane (N'west).......	SS	70	312	50	95	13	1	0	35	.304	18	59	14	*118	217	*47	.877
1989—Char., S.C. (S. Atl.).....	SS	127	460	50	102	15	1	1	29	.222	17	85	12	*256	*373	*74	.895
1990—Riverside (Calif.).........	SS	14	46	5	17	3	1	1	4	.370	3	3	4	18	38	6	.903
1991—Wichita (Texas).........	2B-SS	125	452	43	121	17	1	1	41	.268	18	70	6	274	339	26	.959
1992—Las Vegas (PCL)........	SS-OF	120	395	44	92	8	8	1	31	.233	19	65	6	200	358	†30	.949
1993—Las Vegas (PCL)........	SS-2B	131	491	52	150	36	6	6	58	.305	27	62	8	230	380	29	.955
—San Diego (N.L.)........	2B	17	43	1	5	1	0	0	1	.116	0	8	0	23	34	1	.983
1994—Las Vegas (PCL)........	2B	12	49	2	10	2	2	0	6	.204	1	5	0	28	43	2	.973
—San Diego (N.L.)........	SS-2B-3B	77	235	29	65	16	1	2	20	.277	15	39	3	101	174	14	.952
1995—								Did not play.									
1996—Las Vegas (PCL)........	2B-SS	18	68	4	14	3	0	1	12	.206	2	15	0	39	43	2	.976
—San Diego (N.L.)........	SS-2B-3B	63	139	10	25	3	0	2	11	.180	9	35	0	57	100	4	.975
1997—Norfolk (Int'l)■........	SS-2B	48	203	32	67	12	1	4	19	.330	9	29	2	79	123	14	.935
—New York (N.L.)........	SS-2B-3B	78	178	19	48	12	1	1	19	.270	12	42	2	79	156	9	.963
1998—New York (N.L.).........	2-S-3-O	117	266	37	67	13	2	2	22	.252	20	60	2	123	144	11	.960
Major league totals (5 years)		352	861	96	210	45	4	7	73	.244	56	184	7	383	608	39	.962

DIVISION SERIES RECORD

						BATTING								FIELDING			
Year Team (League)	Pos.	G	AB	R	H	2B	3B	HR	RBI	Avg.	BB	SO	SB	PO	A	E	Avg.
1996—San Diego (N.L.)	PR	1	0	0	0	0	0	0	0	...	0	0	0	...	...	...	...

LOPEZ, MENDY — SS — ROYALS

PERSONAL: Born October 15, 1974, in Santo Domingo, Dominican Republic. ... 6-2/190. ... Bats right, throws right. ... Full name: Mendy Aude Lopez.
HIGH SCHOOL: Liceo Los Trinitanos (Santo Domingo, Dominican Republic).
TRANSACTIONS/CAREER NOTES: Signed as non-drafted free agent by Kansas City Royals organization (February 26, 1992).
STATISTICAL NOTES: Led Gulf Coast League shortstops with .971 fielding percentage, 80 putouts, 154 assists, 241 total chances and 39 double plays in 1994. ... Tied for Texas League lead with 28 double plays by third baseman in 1996.

								BATTING							FIELDING		
Year	Team (League)	Pos.	G	AB	R	H	2B	3B	HR	RBI	Avg.	BB	SO	SB	PO	A	E	Avg.
1992—	Dom. Royals (DSL)	SS	49	145	22	40	1	0	1	23	.276	22	15	7	81	155	26	.901
1993—	Dom. Royals (DSL)	IF	28	98	15	27	5	2	0	20	.276	11	5	2	52	75	15	.894
1994—	GC Royals (GCL)	SS-3B-2B	59	*235	56	85	*19	3	5	*50	.362	22	27	10	†84	†195	12	†.959
1995—	Wilmington (Caro.)......	3B-SS	130	428	42	116	29	3	2	36	.271	28	73	18	84	335	25	.944
1996—	Wichita (Texas)	3B-SS	93	327	47	92	20	5	6	32	.281	26	67	14	80	265	24	.935
1997—	Omaha (A.A.).............	3B	17	52	6	12	2	0	1	6	.231	8	21	0	15	38	6	.898
—	Wichita (Texas)	SS	101	357	56	83	16	3	5	42	.232	36	70	7	193	296	20	.961
1998—	Omaha (PCL).............	SS-3B	60	195	18	35	6	1	3	14	.179	18	44	2	71	167	10	.960
—	Kansas City (A.L.)	SS-3B	74	206	18	50	10	2	1	15	.243	12	40	5	102	225	15	.956
Major league totals (1 year)			74	206	18	50	10	2	1	15	.243	12	40	5	102	225	15	.956

LOPEZ, RODRIGO — P — PADRES

PERSONAL: Born December 14, 1975, in Mexico City, Mexico. ... 6-0/180. ... Throws right, bats right. ... Full name: Rodrigo Munoz Lopez.
TRANSACTIONS/CAREER NOTES: Signed by Aguila of Mexican League (1994). ... Purchased by San Diego Padres organization from Aguila (March 17, 1995). ... Loaned by Padres to Mexico City Red Devils of Mexican League (March 13, 1998). ... Returned to Padres organization (August 19, 1998).

Year	Team (League)	W	L	Pct.	ERA	G	GS	CG	ShO	Sv.	IP	H	R	ER	BB	SO
1994—	Aguila (Mexican)	0	0	...	4.97	10	0	0	0	0	12²/₃	15	7	7	3	5
1995—	Ariz. Padres (Ariz.)■	1	1	.500	5.45	11	7	0	0	1	34²/₃	41	29	21	14	33
1996—	Idaho Falls (Pioneer)..........	4	4	.500	5.70	15	14	0	0	1	71	76	52	45	34	72
1997—	Clinton (Midwest)...............	6	8	.429	3.18	37	14	2	0	9	121²/₃	103	49	43	42	123
1998—	Mex. City Reds (Mx.)■	10	6	.625	3.35	26	26	1	0	0	163²/₃	165	73	61	79	95
—	Mobile (Southern)■..........	3	0	1.000	1.40	4	4	2	1	0	25²/₃	21	11	4	4	20

LORETTA, MARK — IF — BREWERS

PERSONAL: Born August 14, 1971, in Santa Monica, Calif. ... 6-0/186. ... Bats right, throws right. ... Full name: Mark David Loretta.
HIGH SCHOOL: St. Francis (La Canada, Calif.).
COLLEGE: Northwestern.
TRANSACTIONS/CAREER NOTES: Selected by Milwaukee Brewers organization in seventh round of free-agent draft (June 3, 1993). ... On New Orleans suspended list (May 17-20, 1996).
STATISTICAL NOTES: Led American Association shortstops with 200 putouts and 591 total chances in 1995.

								BATTING							FIELDING		
Year	Team (League)	Pos.	G	AB	R	H	2B	3B	HR	RBI	Avg.	BB	SO	SB	PO	A	E	Avg.
1993—	Helena (Pioneer)	SS	6	28	5	9	1	0	1	8	.321	1	4	0	11	18	0	1.000
—	Stockton (California) ..	SS-3B	53	201	36	73	4	1	4	31	.363	22	17	8	75	173	15	.943
1994—	El Paso (Texas)..........	SS-P	77	302	50	95	13	6	0	38	.315	27	33	8	125	271	11	.973
—	New Orleans (A.A.)	SS-2B	43	138	16	29	7	0	1	14	.210	12	13	2	68	121	11	.945
1995—	New Orleans (A.A.)	SS-3B-2B	127	479	48	137	22	5	7	79	.286	34	47	8	†204	376	25	.959
—	Milwaukee (A.L.)	SS-2B-DH	19	50	13	13	3	0	1	3	.260	4	7	1	18	42	1	.984
1996—	New Orleans (A.A.)	SS	19	71	10	18	5	1	0	11	.254	9	8	1	31	60	5	.948
—	Milwaukee (A.L.)	2B-3B-SS	73	154	20	43	3	0	1	13	.279	14	15	2	63	116	2	.989
1997—	Milwaukee (A.L.)	2-S-1-3-DH	132	418	56	120	17	5	5	47	.287	47	60	5	334	277	15	.976
1998—	Milwaukee (N.L.)	1-S-3-2-O	140	434	55	137	29	0	6	54	.316	42	47	9	450	215	6	.991
American League totals (3 years)			224	622	89	176	23	5	7	63	.283	65	82	8	415	435	18	.979
National League totals (1 year)			140	434	55	137	29	0	6	54	.316	42	47	9	450	215	6	.991
Major league totals (4 years)			364	1056	144	313	52	5	13	117	.296	107	129	17	865	650	24	.984

RECORD AS PITCHER

Year	Team (League)	W	L	Pct.	ERA	G	GS	CG	ShO	Sv.	IP	H	R	ER	BB	SO
1994—	El Paso (Texas)..................	0	0	...	...	1	0	0	0	0	0	0	1	1	1	0

LORRAINE, ANDREW — P — CUBS

PERSONAL: Born August 11, 1972, in Los Angeles. ... 6-3/195. ... Throws left, bats left. ... Full name: Andrew Jason Lorraine.
HIGH SCHOOL: William S. Hart (Newhall, Calif.).
COLLEGE: Stanford.
TRANSACTIONS/CAREER NOTES: Selected by New York Mets organization in 38th round of free-agent draft (June 4, 1990); did not sign. ... Selected by California Angels organization in fourth round of free-agent draft (June 3, 1993). ... Traded by Angels with OF McKay Christensen, P Bill Simas and P John Snyder to Chicago White Sox for P Jim Abbott and P Tim Fortugno (July 27, 1995). ... Traded by White Sox with OF Charles Poe to Oakland Athletics for OF/DH Danny Tartabull (January 22, 1996). ... Released by A's (October 16, 1997). ... Signed by Seattle Mariners organization (October 17, 1997). ... Granted free agency (October 3, 1998). ... Signed by Chicago Cubs organization (November 13, 1998).

Year	Team (League)	W	L	Pct.	ERA	G	GS	CG	ShO	Sv.	IP	H	R	ER	BB	SO
1993—	Boise (Northwest)	4	1	.800	1.29	6	6	3	1	0	42	33	6	6	6	39
1994—	Vancouver (PCL)	12	4	.750	3.42	22	22	•4	•2	0	142	156	63	54	34	90
—	California (A.L.)..................	0	2	.000	10.61	4	3	0	0	0	18²/₃	30	23	22	11	10
1995—	Vancouver (PCL)	6	6	.500	3.96	18	18	4	1	0	97²/₃	105	49	43	30	51
—	Nashville (A.A.)■	4	1	.800	6.00	7	7	0	0	0	39	51	29	26	12	26
—	Chicago (A.L.)	0	0	...	3.38	5	0	0	0	0	8	3	3	3	2	5

Year	Team (League)	W	L	Pct.	ERA	G	GS	CG	ShO	Sv.	IP	H	R	ER	BB	SO
1996—	Edmonton (PCL)■	8	10	.444	5.68	30	25	0	0	0	141	181	95	89	46	73
1997—	Edmonton (PCL)	8	6	.571	4.74	23	20	2	2	0	117²/₃	143	72	62	34	75
	— Oakland (A.L.)	3	1	.750	6.37	12	6	0	0	0	29²/₃	45	22	21	15	18
1998—	Tacoma (PCL)■	7	4	.636	4.82	52	4	0	0	2	80¹/₃	93	44	43	36	70
	— Seattle (A.L.)	0	0	...	2.45	4	0	0	0	0	3²/₃	3	1	1	4	0
Major league totals (4 years)		3	3	.500	7.05	25	9	0	0	0	60	81	49	47	32	33

LOVULLO, TOREY IF PHILLIES

PERSONAL: Born July 25, 1965, in Santa Monica, Calif. ... 6-0/185. ... Bats both, throws right. ... Full name: Salvatore Anthony Lovullo. ... Name pronounced leh-VOO-lo.
HIGH SCHOOL: Montclair Prep (Van Nuys, Calif.).
COLLEGE: UCLA (degree in psychology).
TRANSACTIONS/CAREER NOTES: Selected by Kansas City Royals organization in 27th round of free-agent draft (June 2, 1986); did not sign. ... Selected by Detroit Tigers organization in fifth round of free-agent draft (June 2, 1987). ... Traded by Tigers to New York Yankees for P Mark Leiter (March 19, 1991). ... Granted free agency (October 16, 1992). ... Signed by California Angels (November 19, 1992). ... Claimed on waivers by Seattle Mariners (April 1, 1994). ... Granted free agency (October 15, 1994). ... Signed by Cleveland Indians (November 21, 1994). ... Granted free agency (October 16, 1995). ... Signed by Oakland Athletics organization (December 5, 1995). ... Granted free agency (October 15, 1996). ... Signed by Ottawa, Expos organization (December 17, 1996). ... Released by Expos (May 20, 1997). ... Signed by Buffalo, Indians organization (May 20, 1997). ... Granted free agency (October 15, 1997). ... Re-signed by Indians organization (December 19, 1997). ... On Buffalo disabled list (June 25-July 30, 1998). ... Granted free agency (October 15, 1998). ... Signed by Philadelphia Phillies organization (November 5, 1998).
HONORS: Named second baseman on THE SPORTING NEWS college All-America team (1987).
STATISTICAL NOTES: Tied for International League lead with 10 intentional bases on balls received in 1989. ... Led International League with .509 slugging percentage in 1992. ... Tied for International League lead with 20 errors by third baseman in 1998.

Year	Team (League)	Pos.	G	AB	R	H	2B	3B	HR	RBI	Avg.	BB	SO	SB	PO	A	E	Avg.
							BATTING									FIELDING		
1987—	Fayetteville (SAL)	3B-2B	55	191	34	49	13	0	8	32	.257	37	30	6	41	133	22	.888
	— Lakeland (Fla. St.)	3B	18	60	11	16	3	0	1	16	.267	10	8	0	11	30	2	.953
1988—	Glens Falls (East.)	3B-2B	78	270	37	74	17	1	9	50	.274	36	44	2	63	173	21	.918
	— Toledo (Int'l)	2B-3B-SS	57	177	18	41	8	1	5	20	.232	9	24	2	120	149	5	.982
	— Detroit (A.L.)	2B-3B	12	21	2	8	1	1	1	2	.381	1	2	0	12	19	0	1.000
1989—	Toledo (Int'l)	1-3-2-S	112	409	48	94	23	2	10	52	.230	44	57	2	217	257	20	.960
	— Detroit (A.L.)	1B-3B	29	87	8	10	2	0	1	4	.115	14	20	1	134	24	1	.994
1990—	Toledo (Int'l)	2B-3B-1B	141	486	71	131	*38	1	14	58	.270	61	74	4	280	352	18	.972
1991—	New York (A.L.)■.....	3B	22	51	0	9	2	0	0	2	.176	5	7	0	14	33	3	.940
	— Columbus (Int'l)	3-1-2-0	106	395	74	107	24	5	10	75	.271	59	54	4	277	164	16	.965
1992—	Columbus (Int'l)	2-3-1-0	131	468	69	138	*33	5	19	89	.295	64	65	9	187	206	8	.980
1993—	California (A.L.) ...2-3-S-O-DH-1		116	367	42	92	20	0	6	30	.251	36	49	7	208	249	11	.976
1994—	Seattle (A.L.)■	2B-3B-DH	36	72	9	16	5	0	2	7	.222	9	13	1	19	49	1	.986
	— Calgary (PCL)	SS-2B-3B	54	211	43	62	18	1	11	47	.294	34	28	2	85	165	9	.965
1995—	Buffalo (A.A.)■	2-3-1-S	132	474	84	121	20	5	16	61	.255	70	62	3	235	303	18	.968
1996—	Oakland (A.L.)■ ...1-3-DH-2-S-O		65	82	15	18	4	0	3	9	.220	11	17	1	134	21	1	.994
	— Edmonton (PCL) ...1-2-3-P-O-S		26	93	18	26	4	0	4	19	.280	18	12	0	112	39	3	.981
1997—	Ottawa (Int'l)	2B-3B	28	64	6	9	3	0	0	6	.141	6	13	0	31	42	0	1.000
	— Buffalo (A.A.)■	3-2-1-S	97	321	40	73	18	0	12	40	.227	51	64	0	115	203	12	.964
1998—	Buffalo (Int'l)	3B-2B-1B	92	328	66	107	17	4	17	65	.326	54	32	3	114	168	‡23	.925
	— Cleveland (A.L.)	2B-3B	6	19	1	4	1	0	0	1	.211	1	2	0	4	15	1	.950
Major league totals (7 years)			286	699	77	157	35	1	13	55	.225	77	110	10	525	410	18	.981

RECORD AS PITCHER

Year	Team (League)	W	L	Pct.	ERA	G	GS	CG	ShO	Sv.	IP	H	R	ER	BB	SO
1996—	Edmonton (PCL)	0	0	...	4.50	26	0	0	0	0	4	3	2	2	3	0

LOWE, DEREK P RED SOX

PERSONAL: Born June 1, 1973, in Dearborn, Mich. ... 6-6/170. ... Throws right, bats right. ... Full name: Derek Christopher Lowe.
HIGH SCHOOL: Edsel Ford (Dearborn, Mich.).
TRANSACTIONS/CAREER NOTES: Selected by Seattle Mariners organization in eighth round of free-agent draft (June 3, 1991). ... Traded by Mariners with C Jason Varitek to Boston Red Sox for P Heathcliff Slocumb (July 31, 1997).
STATISTICAL NOTES: Led Southern League with seven balks in 1994.

Year	Team (League)	W	L	Pct.	ERA	G	GS	CG	ShO	Sv.	IP	H	R	ER	BB	SO
1991—	Ariz. Mariners (Ariz.)	5	3	.625	2.41	12	12	0	0	0	71	58	26	19	21	60
1992—	Bellingham (N'west)	7	3	.700	2.42	14	13	2	•1	0	85²/₃	69	34	23	22	66
1993—	Riverside (California)	12	9	.571	5.26	27	26	3	2	0	154	189	104	90	60	80
1994—	Jacksonville (Southern)....	7	10	.412	4.94	26	26	2	0	0	151¹/₃	177	92	83	50	75
1995—	Port City (Southern)......	1	6	.143	6.08	10	10	1	0	0	53¹/₃	70	41	36	22	30
	— Ariz. Mariners (Ariz.)	1	0	1.000	0.93	2	2	0	0	0	9²/₃	5	1	1	2	11
1996—	Port City (Southern)	5	3	.625	3.05	10	10	0	0	0	65	56	27	22	17	33
	— Tacoma (PCL)	6	9	.400	4.54	17	16	1	1	0	105	118	64	53	37	54
1997—	Tacoma (PCL)	3	4	.429	3.45	10	9	1	0	0	57¹/₃	53	26	22	20	49
	— Seattle (A.L.)	2	4	.333	6.96	12	9	0	0	0	53	59	43	41	20	39
	— Pawtucket (Int'l)■	4	0	1.000	2.37	6	5	0	0	0	30¹/₃	23	8	8	11	21
	— Boston (A.L.)	0	2	.000	3.38	8	0	0	0	0	16	15	6	6	3	13
1998—	Boston (A.L.)	3	9	.250	4.02	63	10	0	0	4	123	126	65	55	42	77
Major league totals (2 years)		5	15	.250	4.78	83	19	0	0	4	192	200	114	102	65	129

DIVISION SERIES RECORD

Year	Team (League)	W	L	Pct.	ERA	G	GS	CG	ShO	Sv.	IP	H	R	ER	BB	SO
1998—	Boston (A.L.)	0	0	...	2.08	2	0	0	0	0	4¹/₃	3	1	1	2	2

LOWE, SEAN   P   CARDINALS

PERSONAL: Born March 29, 1971, in Dallas. ... 6-2/205. ... Throws right, bats right. ... Full name: Jonathon Sean Lowe.
HIGH SCHOOL: Mesquite (Texas).
JUNIOR COLLEGE: McLennan Community College (Texas).
COLLEGE: Arizona State.
TRANSACTIONS/CAREER NOTES: Selected by Cincinnati Reds organization in 43rd round of free-agent draft (June 5, 1989); did not sign. ... Selected by Oakland Athletics organization in 43rd round of free-agent draft (June 4, 1990); did not sign. ... Selected by St. Louis Cardinals organization in first round (15th pick overall) of free-agent draft (June 1, 1992). ... On St. Petersburg disabled list (July 19-August 8, 1994). ... On Arkansas disabled list (May 28-June 4, 1996). ... On Louisville disabled list (April 9-18, 1997).
STATISTICAL NOTES: Tied for American Association lead with 10 hit batsmen in 1997.

Year	Team (League)	W	L	Pct.	ERA	G	GS	CG	ShO	Sv.	IP	H	R	ER	BB	SO
1992—	Hamilton (NYP)	2	0	1.000	1.61	5	5	0	0	0	28	14	8	5	14	22
1993—	St. Petersburg (FSL)	6	11	.353	4.27	25	25	0	0	0	132 2/3	152	80	63	62	87
1994—	St. Petersburg (FSL)	5	6	.455	3.47	21	21	0	0	0	114	119	51	44	37	92
	Arkansas (Texas)	2	1	.667	1.40	3	3	0	0	0	19 1/3	13	3	3	8	11
1995—	Arkansas (Texas)	9	8	.529	4.88	24	24	0	0	0	129	143	84	70	64	77
1996—	Louisville (A.A.)	8	9	.471	4.70	25	18	0	0	0	115	127	72	60	51	76
	Arkansas (Texas)	2	3	.400	6.00	6	6	0	0	0	33	32	24	22	15	25
1997—	Louisville (A.A.)	6	10	.375	4.37	26	23	1	0	1	131 2/3	142	74	64	53	117
	St. Louis (N.L.)	0	2	.000	9.35	6	4	0	0	0	17 1/3	27	21	18	10	8
1998—	Memphis (Pacific Coast)	12	8	.600	3.18	25	21	0	0	0	153	147	57	54	61	114
	St. Louis (N.L.)	0	3	.000	15.19	4	1	0	0	0	5 1/3	11	9	9	5	2
Major league totals (2 years)		0	5	.000	10.72	10	5	0	0	0	22 2/3	38	30	27	15	10

LOWELL, MIKE   3B   YANKEES

PERSONAL: Born February 24, 1974, in San Juan, Puerto Rico. ... 6-4/193. ... Bats right, throws right. ... Full name: Michael Averett Lowell.
HIGH SCHOOL: Coral Gables (Fla.).
COLLEGE: Florida International.
TRANSACTIONS/CAREER NOTES: Selected by New York Yankees organization in 20th round of free-agent draft (June 1, 1995).
STATISTICAL NOTES: Led New York-Pennsylvania League third basemen with 271 total chances in 1995. ... Led South Atlantic League third basemen with .926 fielding percentage, 301 putouts and 421 total chances in 1996. ... Tied for International League lead with 20 errors by third baseman in 1998.

Year	Team (League)	Pos.	G	AB	R	H	2B	3B	HR	RBI	Avg.	BB	SO	SB	PO	A	E	Avg.
							BATTING									FIELDING		
1995—	Oneonta (NYP)	3B	72	281	36	73	18	0	1	27	.260	23	34	3	59	188	24	.911
1996—	Greensboro (S. Atl.)	3B-SS	113	433	58	122	33	0	8	64	.282	46	43	10	91	†302	32	.925
	Tampa (Fla. St.)	3B	24	78	8	22	5	0	0	11	.282	3	13	1	22	40	3	.954
1997—	Norwich (Eastern)	3B-SS	78	285	60	98	17	0	15	47	.344	48	30	2	57	133	15	.927
	Columbus (Int'l)	3B-SS	57	210	36	58	13	1	15	45	.276	23	34	2	31	73	5	.954
1998—	Columbus (Int'l)	3B-1B-SS	126	510	79	155	34	3	26	99	.304	37	85	4	114	283	‡21	.950
	New York (A.L.)	3B-DH	8	15	1	4	0	0	0	0	.267	0	1	0	2	5	0	1.000
Major league totals (1 year)			8	15	1	4	0	0	0	0	.267	0	1	0	2	5	0	1.000

LOWERY, TERRELL   OF   DEVIL RAYS

PERSONAL: Born October 25, 1970, in Oakland. ... 6-3/195. ... Bats right, throws right. ... Full name: Quenton Terrell Lowery. ... Brother of Josh Lowery, minor league shortstop (1989-90).
HIGH SCHOOL: Oakland Technical.
COLLEGE: Loyola Marymount.
TRANSACTIONS/CAREER NOTES: Selected by Texas Rangers organization in second round of free-agent draft (June 3, 1991). ... On Butte disabled list (June 17-27, 1992). ... On restricted list (June 27, 1992-February 5, 1993). ... On Oklahoma City disabled list (April 6-August 24, 1995). ... Traded by Rangers to New York Mets for OF Damon Buford (January 25, 1996). ... Selected by Chicago Cubs organization from Mets organization in Rule 5 major league draft (December 9, 1996). ... On Iowa disabled list (September 4, 1998-remainder of season). ... Granted free agency (October 15, 1998). ... Signed by Tampa Bay Devil Rays organization (November 19, 1998).
STATISTICAL NOTES: Led Texas League outfielders with 303 total chances in 1994. ... Led American Association with .401 on-base percentage in 1997.

Year	Team (League)	Pos.	G	AB	R	H	2B	3B	HR	RBI	Avg.	BB	SO	SB	PO	A	E	Avg.
							BATTING									FIELDING		
1991—	Butte (Pioneer)	OF	54	214	38	64	10	7	3	33	.299	29	44	23	92	7	6	.943
1992—									Did not play.									
1993—	Charlotte (Fla. St.)	OF	65	257	46	77	7	9	3	36	.300	46	47	14	156	5	4	.976
	Tulsa (Texas)	OF	66	258	29	62	5	1	3	14	.240	28	50	10	152	6	2	.988
1994—	Tulsa (Texas)	OF	129	496	89	142	34	8	8	54	.286	59	113	33	*280	16	7	.977
1995—	GC Rangers (GCL)	OF	10	34	10	9	3	1	3	7	.265	6	7	1	7	0	0	1.000
	Charlotte (Fla. St.)	OF	11	35	4	9	2	2	0	4	.257	6	6	1	18	0	0	1.000
1996—	Norfolk (Int'l)■	OF	62	193	25	45	7	2	4	21	.233	22	44	6	106	4	1	.991
	Binghamton (East.)	OF	62	211	34	58	13	4	7	32	.275	44	44	5	97	3	3	.971
1997—	Iowa (Am. Assoc.)■	OF	110	386	69	116	28	3	17	71	.301	65	97	9	244	8	3	.988
	Chicago (N.L.)	OF	9	14	2	4	0	0	0	0	.286	3	3	1	7	2	0	1.000
1998—	Iowa (Pacific Coast)	OF	65	246	41	73	14	1	12	49	.297	27	63	5	155	5	1	.994
	Chicago (N.L.)	OF	24	15	2	3	1	0	0	1	.200	3	7	0	13	0	1	.929
Major league totals (2 years)			33	29	4	7	1	0	0	1	.241	6	10	1	20	2	1	.957

LUDWICK, ERIC   P   BLUE JAYS

PERSONAL: Born December 14, 1971, in Whiteman AFB, Mo. ... 6-5/210. ... Throws right, bats right. ... Full name: Eric David Ludwick.
HIGH SCHOOL: El Dorado (Las Vegas).
COLLEGE: California, then UNLV.
TRANSACTIONS/CAREER NOTES: Selected by New York Mets organization in second round of free-agent draft (June 3, 1993). ... Traded by Mets with P Erik Hiljus and OF Yudith Ozorio to St. Louis Cardinals for OF Bernard Gilkey (January 22, 1996). ... Traded by Cardinals with P T.J. Mathews and P Blake Stein to Oakland Athletics for 1B Mark McGwire (July 31, 1997). ... Traded by A's to Florida Marlins for IF Kurt Abbott (December 19, 1997). ... On Florida disabled list (April 9-26, May 3-July 9 and July 20-August 28, 1998); included rehabilitation assignments to Charlotte (June 26-July 9 and August 4-28). ... Selected by Detroit Tigers from Marlins organization in Rule 5 major league draft; then traded by Tigers to Toronto Blue Jays for P Beiker Graterol (December 14, 1998).

Year Team (League)	W	L	Pct.	ERA	G	GS	CG	ShO	Sv.	IP	H	R	ER	BB	SO
1993— Pittsfield (NYP)	4	4	.500	3.18	10	10	1	0	0	51	51	27	18	18	40
1994— St. Lucie (Fla. St.)	7	13	.350	4.55	27	27	3	0	0	150 1/3	162	*102	76	77	77
1995— Binghamton (Eastern)	12	5	.706	2.95	23	22	3	2	0	143 1/3	108	52	47	68	131
— Norfolk (Int'l)	1	1	.500	5.85	4	3	0	0	0	20	22	15	13	7	9
1996— Louisville (A.A.)■	3	4	.429	2.83	11	11	0	0	0	60 1/3	55	24	19	24	73
— St. Louis (N.L.)	0	1	.000	9.00	6	1	0	0	0	10	11	11	10	3	12
1997— St. Louis (N.L.)	0	1	.000	9.45	5	0	0	0	0	6 2/3	12	7	7	6	7
— Louisville (A.A.)	6	8	.429	2.93	24	11	1	0	4	80	67	31	26	26	85
— Edmonton (PCL)■	1	1	.500	3.32	6	3	0	0	0	19	22	7	7	4	20
— Oakland (A.L.)	1	4	.200	8.25	6	5	0	0	0	24	32	24	22	16	14
1998— Florida (N.L.)■	1	4	.200	7.44	13	6	0	0	0	32 2/3	46	31	27	17	27
— Charlotte (Int'l)	1	3	.250	3.71	8	8	0	0	0	26 2/3	25	17	11	13	26
A.L. totals (1 year)	1	4	.200	8.25	6	5	0	0	0	24	32	24	22	16	14
N.L. totals (3 years)	1	6	.143	8.03	24	7	0	0	0	49 1/3	69	49	44	26	46
Major league totals (3 years)	2	10	.167	8.10	30	12	0	0	0	73 1/3	101	73	66	42	60

LUGO, JULIO   IF   ASTROS

PERSONAL: Born November 16, 1975, in Barahona, Dominican Republic. ... 6-1/165. ... Bats right, throws right. ... Full name: Julio Cesar Lugo.
JUNIOR COLLEGE: Connors State (Okla.).
TRANSACTIONS/CAREER NOTES: Selected by Houston Astros organization in 43rd round of free-agent draft (June 2, 1994).
STATISTICAL NOTES: Led Florida State League shortstops with 40 errors in 1997.

Year Team (League)	Pos.	G	AB	R	H	2B	3B	HR	RBI	Avg.	BB	SO	SB	PO	A	E	Avg.
1995— Auburn (NY-Penn)	2B-SS-OF	59	230	36	67	6	3	1	16	.291	26	31	17	85	116	12	.944
1996— Quad City (Midwest)	SS-2B-3B	101	393	60	116	18	2	10	50	.295	32	75	24	122	289	29	.934
1997— Kissimmee (Fla. St.)	SS-2B-3B	125	505	89	135	22	*14	7	61	.267	46	99	35	186	433	†41	.938
1998— Kissimmee (Fla. St.)	SS	128	509	81	154	20	*14	7	62	.303	49	72	51	181	308	42	.921

LUKE, MATT   OF   ANGELS

PERSONAL: Born February 26, 1971, in Long Beach, Calif. ... 6-5/220. ... Bats left, throws left. ... Full name: Matthew Clifford Luke.
HIGH SCHOOL: El Dorado (Calif.).
COLLEGE: California.
TRANSACTIONS/CAREER NOTES: Selected by New York Yankees organization in eighth round of free-agent draft (June 1, 1992). ... On Tampa disabled list (April 22-May 9, 1994). ... On Columbus disabled list (April 5-May 1 and May 12-June 2, 1996). ... On temporarily inactive list (April 3-May 13, 1997). ... Claimed on waivers by Los Angeles Dodgers (September 25, 1997). ... Claimed on waivers by Cleveland Indians (June 8, 1998). ... Traded by Indians to Dodgers for cash (June 19, 1998). ... Granted free agency (December 21, 1998). ... Signed by Anaheim Angels (January 12, 1999).
STATISTICAL NOTES: Led South Atlantic League with 267 total bases in 1993.

Year Team (League)	Pos.	G	AB	R	H	2B	3B	HR	RBI	Avg.	BB	SO	SB	PO	A	E	Avg.
1992— Oneonta (NYP)	OF-1B	69	271	30	67	11	*7	2	34	.247	19	32	4	230	16	7	.972
1993— Greensboro (S. Atl.)	OF	135	*549	83	•157	37	5	21	91	.286	47	79	11	218	11	3	*.987
1994— Tampa (Fla. St.)	OF	57	222	52	68	11	2	16	42	.306	28	27	4	100	12	5	.957
— Alb./Colon. (East.)	OF-1B	63	236	34	67	11	2	8	40	.284	28	50	6	158	8	3	.982
1995— Norwich (Eastern)	OF	93	365	48	95	17	5	8	53	.260	20	68	5	178	12	4	.979
— Columbus (Int'l)	OF	23	77	11	23	4	1	3	12	.299	2	12	1	36	1	2	.949
1996— New York (A.L.)	PR	1	0	1	0	0	0	0	0	...	0	0	0	...	...	...	...
— Columbus (Int'l)	OF-1B	74	264	46	74	14	2	19	70	.280	17	52	1	159	8	2	.988
— Tampa (Fla. St.)	OF	2	7	1	2	0	0	0	1	.286	1	1	0	3	0	0	1.000
1997— Columbus (Int'l)	OF-1B	87	337	42	77	19	3	8	45	.228	29	64	0	263	23	4	.986
1998— Los Angeles (N.L.)■	OF-1B	102	237	34	56	12	1	12	34	.236	17	60	2	161	19	1	.994
— Cleveland (A.L.)■	PH	2	2	0	0	0	0	0	0	.000	0	0	0	...	...	...	...
American League totals (2 years)		3	2	1	0	0	0	0	0	.000	0	0	0	...	...	...	...
National League totals (1 year)		102	237	34	56	12	1	12	34	.236	17	60	2	161	19	1	.994
Major league totals (2 years)		105	239	35	56	12	1	12	34	.234	17	60	2	161	19	1	.994

LUNAR, FERNANDO   C   BRAVES

PERSONAL: Born May 25, 1977, in Cantanura, Venezuela. ... 6-1/190. ... Bats right, throws right. ... Full name: Fernando Jose Lunar.
HIGH SCHOOL: Liceo Anaco Venezuela.

L

TRANSACTIONS/CAREER NOTES: Signed as non-drafted free agent by Atlanta Braves organization (March 15, 1994). ... On disabled list (April 16-24, 1995).

STATISTICAL NOTES: Tied for Gulf Coast League lead in double plays by catcher with three in 1994. ... Led South Atlantic League catchers with 11 double plays in 1996. ... Led South Atlantic League with 1,026 total chances in 1997. ... Led Carolina League catchers with nine double plays in 1998.

Year Team (League)	Pos.	G	AB	R	H	2B	3B	HR	RBI	Avg.	BB	SO	SB	PO	A	E	Avg.
										BATTING					FIELDING		
1994— GC Braves (GCL)	C	33	100	9	24	5	0	2	12	.240	1	13	0	203	32	7	.971
1995— Macon (S. Atl.)	C	39	134	13	24	2	0	0	9	.179	10	38	1	261	35	10	.967
1996— Macon (S. Atl.)	C	104	343	33	63	9	0	7	33	.184	20	65	3	648	112	12	.984
1997— Macon (S. Atl.)	C	105	380	41	99	26	2	7	37	.261	18	42	0	*888	*135	13	.987
1998— Danville (Carolina)	C	91	286	19	63	9	0	3	28	.220	6	52	1	726	103	8	.990

LUNDQUIST, DAVID   P   WHITE SOX

PERSONAL: Born June 4, 1973, in Beverly, Mass. ... 6-2/200. ... Throws right, bats right. ... Full name: David Bruce Lundquist.
JUNIOR COLLEGE: Cochise County Community College (Ariz.).
TRANSACTIONS/CAREER NOTES: Selected by Chicago White Sox organization in fifth round of free-agent draft (June 3, 1993). ... On Prince William disabled list (April 5-June 5 and June 19, 1996-remainder of season).

Year Team (League)	W	L	Pct.	ERA	G	GS	CG	ShO	Sv.	IP	H	R	ER	BB	SO
1993— GC White Sox (GCL)	5	3	.625	3.14	11	10	0	0	0	63	70	26	22	15	40
1994— Hickory (S. Atl.)	13	10	.565	3.48	27	27	3	2	0	178 2/3	170	88	69	43	133
1995— South Bend (Mid.)..............	8	4	.667	3.58	18	18	5	1	0	118	107	54	47	38	60
1996— GC White Sox (GCL)	1	1	.500	2.63	3	3	0	0	0	13 2/3	8	4	4	2	16
— Prince William (Caro.)........	0	2	.000	5.67	5	5	0	0	0	27	31	17	17	14	23
1997— Win.-Salem (Car.)	3	1	.750	6.75	20	6	0	0	0	48	65	41	36	23	39
— Birmingham (Southern)	0	0		8.78	7	0	0	0	0	13 1/3	26	20	13	5	15
1998— Win.-Salem (Car.)	1	0	1.000	2.53	6	0	0	0	0	10 2/3	9	4	3	3	9
— Birmingham (Southern)	1	1	.500	3.29	33	0	0	0	10	41	28	15	15	15	41
— Calgary (PCL)	3	0	1.000	3.60	12	0	0	0	2	15	12	6	6	7	12

MABRY, JOHN   OF/3B   MARINERS

PERSONAL: Born October 17, 1970, in Wilmington, Del. ... 6-4/195. ... Bats left, throws right. ... Full name: John Steven Mabry. ... Name pronounced MAY-bree.
HIGH SCHOOL: Bohemia Manor (Chesapeake City, Md.).
COLLEGE: West Chester (Pa.).
TRANSACTIONS/CAREER NOTES: Selected by St. Louis Cardinals organization in sixth round of free-agent draft (June 3, 1991). ... On disabled list (April 22-30 and May 6-18, 1992). ... On disabled list (August 20-September 24, 1997). ... Granted free agency (December 21, 1998). ... Signed by Seattle Mariners (December 30, 1998).
STATISTICAL NOTES: Led Texas League in grounding into double plays with 17 in 1993. ... Led Texas League outfielders with six double plays in 1993. ... Hit for the cycle (May 18, 1996). ... Had 20-game hitting streak (May 19-June 9, 1997).

Year Team (League)	Pos.	G	AB	R	H	2B	3B	HR	RBI	Avg.	BB	SO	SB	PO	A	E	Avg.
										BATTING					FIELDING		
1991— Hamilton (NYP)	OF	49	187	25	58	11	0	1	31	.310	17	18	9	73	*10	5	.943
— Savannah (S. Atl.)	OF	22	86	10	20	6	1	0	8	.233	7	12	1	36	1	1	.974
1992— Springfield (Midw.)	OF	115	438	63	115	13	6	11	57	.263	24	39	2	171	14	6	.969
1993— Arkansas (Texas)	OF	*136	528	68	153	32	2	16	72	.290	27	68	7	262	15	3	*.989
— Louisville (A.A.)...........	OF	4	7	0	1	0	0	0	1	.143	0	1	0	3	0	0	1.000
1994— Louisville (A.A.)..........	OF	122	477	76	125	30	1	15	68	.262	32	67	2	237	4	2	.992
— St. Louis (N.L.)............	OF	6	23	2	7	3	0	0	3	.304	2	4	0	16	0	0	1.000
1995— St. Louis (N.L.)..........	1B-OF	129	388	35	119	21	1	5	41	.307	24	45	0	652	58	4	.994
— Louisville (A.A.)...........	OF	4	12	0	1	0	0	0	0	.083	0	0	0	8	0	1	.889
1996— St. Louis (N.L.)..........	1B-OF	151	543	63	161	30	2	13	74	.297	37	84	3	1182	76	8	.994
1997— St. Louis (N.L.)..........	OF-1B-3B	116	388	40	110	19	0	5	36	.284	39	77	0	455	30	1	.998
1998— St. Louis (N.L.)..........	OF-3B-1B	142	377	41	94	22	0	9	46	.249	30	76	0	206	64	9	.968
Major league totals (5 years)		544	1719	181	491	95	3	32	200	.286	132	286	3	2511	228	22	.992

DIVISION SERIES RECORD

RECORDS: Shares career record for most triples—1.

Year Team (League)	Pos.	G	AB	R	H	2B	3B	HR	RBI	Avg.	BB	SO	SB	PO	A	E	Avg.
										BATTING					FIELDING		
1996— St. Louis (N.L.)..........	1B	3	10	1	3	0	1	0	1	.300	2	1	0	20	1	0	1.000

CHAMPIONSHIP SERIES RECORD

Year Team (League)	Pos.	G	AB	R	H	2B	3B	HR	RBI	Avg.	BB	SO	SB	PO	A	E	Avg.
										BATTING					FIELDING		
1996— St. Louis (N.L.)..........	1B-OF	7	23	1	6	0	0	0	0	.261	0	6	0	45	1	0	1.000

MacFARLANE, MIKE   C   ATHLETICS

PERSONAL: Born April 12, 1964, in Stockton, Calif. ... 6-1/210. ... Bats right, throws right. ... Full name: Michael Andrew Macfarlane.
HIGH SCHOOL: Lincoln (Stockton, Calif.).
COLLEGE: Santa Clara.
TRANSACTIONS/CAREER NOTES: Selected by Kansas City Royals organization in fourth round of free-agent draft (June 3, 1985). ... On disabled list (April 9-July 9, 1986 and July 16-September 14, 1991). ... Granted free agency (October 17, 1994). ... Signed by Boston Red Sox

(April 8, 1995). ... Granted free agency (November 6, 1995). ... Signed by Royals (December 16, 1995). ... On disabled list (March 29-April 13 and May 3-23, 1997). ... Granted free agency (October 28, 1997). ... Re-signed by Royals (November 25, 1997). ... Traded by Royals to Oakland Athletics for OF Shane Mack and a player to be named later (April 8, 1998); Royals acquired P Greg Hansell to complete deal (May 10, 1998). ... Granted free agency (October 23, 1998). ... Re-signed by A's (December 16, 1998).

STATISTICAL NOTES: Tied for A.L. lead in being hit by pitch with 15 in 1992. ... Led A.L. in being hit by pitch with 18 in 1994. ... Led A.L. catchers with nine double plays in 1994. ... Led A.L. with 26 passed balls in 1995. ... Career major league grand slams: 4.

							BATTING								FIELDING			
Year Team (League)	Pos.	G	AB	R	H	2B	3B	HR	RBI	Avg.	BB	SO	SB	PO	A	E	Avg.
1985— Memphis (Sou.)	C	65	223	29	60	15	4	8	39	.269	11	30	0	295	24	9	.973
1986— Memphis (Sou.)	OF	40	141	26	34	7	2	12	29	.241	10	26	0	0	0	0	...
1987— Omaha (A.A.)	C	87	302	53	79	25	1	13	50	.262	22	50	0	408	37	6	.987
— Kansas City (A.L.)	C	8	19	0	4	1	0	0	3	.211	2	2	0	29	2	0	1.000
1988— Kansas City (A.L.)	C	70	211	25	56	15	0	4	26	.265	21	37	0	309	18	2	.994
— Omaha (A.A.)	C	21	76	8	18	7	2	2	8	.237	4	15	0	85	5	1	.989
1989— Kansas City (A.L.)	C-DH	69	157	13	35	6	0	2	19	.223	7	27	0	249	17	1	.996
1990— Kansas City (A.L.)	C-DH	124	400	37	102	24	4	6	58	.255	25	69	1	660	23	6	.991
1991— Kansas City (A.L.)	C-DH	84	267	34	74	18	2	13	41	.277	17	52	1	391	28	3	.993
1992— Kansas City (A.L.)	C-DH	129	402	51	94	28	3	17	48	.234	30	89	1	527	43	4	.993
1993— Kansas City (A.L.)	C	117	388	55	106	27	0	20	67	.273	40	83	2	647	68	11	.985
1994— Kansas City (A.L.)	C-DH	92	314	53	80	17	3	14	47	.255	35	71	1	498	39	4	.993
1995— Boston (A.L.)■............	C	115	364	45	82	18	1	15	51	.225	38	78	2	618	49	5	.993
1996— Kansas City (A.L.)■ ...	C-DH	112	379	58	104	24	2	19	54	.274	31	57	3	511	35	4	.993
1997— Kansas City (A.L.)	C	82	257	34	61	14	2	8	35	.237	24	47	0	439	20	4	.991
1998— Kansas City (A.L.)	C	3	11	1	1	0	0	0	0	.091	0	2	0	13	3	0	1.000
— Oakland (A.L.)■	C	78	207	28	52	12	0	7	34	.251	12	34	1	355	20	4	.989
Major league totals (12 years)		1083	3376	434	851	204	17	125	483	.252	282	648	12	5246	365	48	.992

DIVISION SERIES RECORD

							BATTING								FIELDING			
Year Team (League)	Pos.	G	AB	R	H	2B	3B	HR	RBI	Avg.	BB	SO	SB	PO	A	E	Avg.
1995— Boston (A.L.)	C	3	9	0	3	0	0	0	1	.333	0	3	0	18	0	2	.900

MACHADO, ROBERT   C   WHITE SOX

PERSONAL: Born June 3, 1973, in Caracas, Venezuela. ... 6-1/205. ... Bats right, throws right. ... Full name: Robert Alexis Machado.
TRANSACTIONS/CAREER NOTES: Signed as non-drafted free agent by Chicago White Sox organization (August 10, 1989).
STATISTICAL NOTES: Led Gulf Coast League catchers with 349 total chances in 1991. ... Tied for Southern League lead in double plays by catcher with 10 in 1996. ... Tied for American Association lead in passed balls with nine in 1997.

							BATTING								FIELDING			
Year Team (League)	Pos.	G	AB	R	H	2B	3B	HR	RBI	Avg.	BB	SO	SB	PO	A	E	Avg.
1991— GC Whi. Sox (GCL)	C	38	126	11	31	4	1	0	15	.246	6	21	2	*287	*54	8	.977
1992— Utica (N.Y.-Penn)........	C	45	161	16	44	13	1	2	20	.273	5	26	1	279	30	12	.963
1993— South Bend (Mid.)......	C	75	281	34	86	14	3	2	33	.306	19	59	1	490	66	12	.979
1994— Prince Will. (Car.)	C	93	312	45	81	17	1	11	47	.260	27	68	0	562	66	*16	.975
1995— Nashville (A.A.)	C	16	49	7	7	3	0	1	5	.143	7	12	0	87	17	3	.972
— Prince Will. (Car.)	C	83	272	37	69	14	0	6	31	.254	40	47	0	548	78	5	.992
1996— Birmingham (Sou.).....	C	87	309	35	74	16	0	6	28	.239	20	56	1	502	67	5	.991
— Chicago (A.L.)	C	4	6	1	4	1	0	0	2	.667	0	0	0	6	0	0	1.000
1997— Nashville (A.A.)	C	84	308	43	83	18	0	8	30	.269	12	61	5	461	49	6	.988
— Chicago (A.L.)	C	10	15	1	3	0	1	0	2	.200	1	6	0	34	3	0	1.000
1998— Calgary (PCL).............	C	66	239	31	63	19	0	4	27	.264	20	33	2	409	39	6	.987
— Chicago (A.L.)	C	34	111	14	23	6	0	3	15	.207	7	22	0	189	17	4	.981
Major league totals (3 years)		48	132	16	30	7	1	3	19	.227	8	28	0	229	20	4	.984

MACK, SHANE   OF   PADRES

PERSONAL: Born December 7, 1963, in Los Angeles. ... 6-0/190. ... Bats right, throws right. ... Full name: Shane Lee Mack. ... Brother of Quinn Mack, outfielder in four major league organizations (1987-96).
HIGH SCHOOL: Gahr (Cerritos, Calif.).
COLLEGE: UCLA.
TRANSACTIONS/CAREER NOTES: Selected by Kansas City Royals organization in fourth round of free-agent draft (June 8, 1981); did not sign. ... Selected by San Diego Padres organization in first round (11th pick overall) of free-agent draft (June 4, 1984). ... On San Diego disabled list (March 25-May 4, 1989). ... Selected by Minnesota Twins from Padres organization in Rule 5 major league draft (December 4, 1989). ... On disabled list (May 15-30, 1993 and March 29-May 3, 1994). ... Granted free agency (October 19, 1994). ... Signed by Yomiuri Giants of Japan Central League (January 4, 1995). ... Signed by Boston Red Sox (December 14, 1996). ... On disabled list (August 7-September 1, 1997). ... Granted free agency (October 28, 1997). ... Signed by Oakland Athletics (December 22, 1997). ... Traded with a player to be named later to Royals for C Mike Macfarlane (April 8, 1998); Royals acquired P Greg Hansell to complete deal (May 8, 1998). ... On Kansas City disabled list (July 31, 1998-remainder of season). ... Granted free agency (October 27, 1998). ... Signed by Padres organization (December 18, 1998).
HONORS: Named outfielder on THE SPORTING NEWS college All-America team (1984).
STATISTICAL NOTES: Tied for Texas League lead in being hit by pitch with seven in 1986. ... Led Texas League outfielders with four double plays in 1986. ... Had 22-game hitting streak (July 26-August 18, 1992). ... Tied for A.L. lead in being hit by pitch with 15 in 1992. ... Had 15-game hitting streak (April 10-26, 1998). ... Career major league grand slams: 5.
MISCELLANEOUS: Member of 1984 U.S. Olympic baseball team.

							BATTING								FIELDING			
Year Team (League)	Pos.	G	AB	R	H	2B	3B	HR	RBI	Avg.	BB	SO	SB	PO	A	E	Avg.
1985— Beaumont (Texas)	OF-3B	125	430	59	112	23	3	6	55	.260	38	89	12	252	12	7	.974
1986— Beaumont (Texas)	OF	115	452	61	127	26	3	15	68	.281	21	79	14	255	•14	8	.971
— Las Vegas (PCL)	OF	19	69	13	25	1	6	0	6	.362	2	13	3	43	0	2	.956

M

Year Team (League)	Pos.	G	AB	R	H	2B	3B	HR	RBI	Avg.	BB	SO	SB	PO	A	E	Avg.
					BATTING									FIELDING			
1987—Las Vegas (PCL)	OF	39	152	38	51	11	1	5	26	.336	19	32	13	97	3	1	.990
—San Diego (N.L.)	OF	105	238	28	57	11	3	4	25	.239	18	47	4	159	1	3	.982
1988—Las Vegas (PCL)	OF	55	196	43	68	7	1	10	40	.347	29	44	7	116	7	3	.976
—San Diego (N.L.)	OF	56	119	13	29	3	0	0	12	.244	14	21	5	110	4	2	.983
1989—Las Vegas (PCL)	OF	24	80	10	18	3	1	1	8	.225	14	19	4	59	3	1	.984
1990—Minnesota (A.L.)■	OF-DH	125	313	50	102	10	4	8	44	.326	29	69	13	230	8	3	.988
1991—Minnesota (A.L.)	OF-DH	143	442	79	137	27	8	18	74	.310	34	79	13	290	6	7	.977
1992—Minnesota (A.L.)	OF	156	600	101	189	31	6	16	75	.315	64	106	26	322	9	4	.988
1993—Minnesota (A.L.)	OF	128	503	66	139	30	4	10	61	.276	41	76	15	347	8	5	.986
1994—Minnesota (A.L.)	OF-DH	81	303	55	101	21	2	15	61	.333	32	51	4	201	2	2	.990
1995—Yomiuri (Jp. Cen.)■	...	120	477	...	131	...	...	20	52	.275	...	...	...	...	...	...	...
1996—Yomiuri (Jp. Cen.)	...	127	484	71	142	28	0	22	75	.293	...	...	12	...	...	...	...
1997—Boston (A.L.)■	OF-DH	60	130	13	41	7	0	3	17	.315	9	24	2	75	0	0	1.000
1998—Oakland (A.L.)	...	3	2	1	0	0	0	0	0	.000	0	0	0	0	0	0	...
—Kansas City (A.L.)■ ...	OF-DH	66	207	30	58	15	1	6	29	.280	15	36	8	54	1	1	.982
American League totals (7 years)		762	2500	395	767	141	25	76	361	.307	224	441	81	1519	34	22	.986
National League totals (2 years)		161	357	41	86	14	3	4	37	.241	32	68	9	269	5	5	.982
Major league totals (9 years)		923	2857	436	853	155	28	80	398	.299	256	509	90	1788	39	27	.985

CHAMPIONSHIP SERIES RECORD

Year Team (League)	Pos.	G	AB	R	H	2B	3B	HR	RBI	Avg.	BB	SO	SB	PO	A	E	Avg.
					BATTING									FIELDING			
1991—Minnesota (A.L.)	OF	5	18	4	6	1	1	0	3	.333	2	4	2	3	0	1	.750

WORLD SERIES RECORD

NOTES: Member of World Series championship team (1991).

Year Team (League)	Pos.	G	AB	R	H	2B	3B	HR	RBI	Avg.	BB	SO	SB	PO	A	E	Avg.
					BATTING									FIELDING			
1991—Minnesota (A.L.)	OF	6	23	0	3	1	0	1	1	.130	0	7	0	11	0	0	1.000

MADDUX, GREG   P   BRAVES

PERSONAL: Born April 14, 1966, in San Angelo, Texas. ... 6-0/175. ... Throws right, bats right. ... Full name: Gregory Alan Maddux. ... Brother of Mike Maddux, pitcher with eight major league teams (1986-98).

HIGH SCHOOL: Valley (Las Vegas).

TRANSACTIONS/CAREER NOTES: Selected by Chicago Cubs organization in second round of free-agent draft (June 4, 1984). ... Granted free agency (October 26, 1992). ... Signed by Atlanta Braves (December 9, 1992).

RECORDS: Holds major league career records for most years leading league in putouts by pitcher—7; and most years leading league in chances accepted by pitcher—9. ... Holds major league single-season record for fewest complete games by pitcher for leader—8 (1993). ... Holds N.L. career record for most putouts by pitcher—349. ... Shares major league career record for most years leading league in double plays by pitcher—5; and most years leading league in assists by pitcher—6. ... Shares major league single-game record for most putouts by pitcher—7 (April 29, 1990). ... Shares N.L. career record for most years leading league in assists by pitcher—5. ... Shares modern N.L. single-season record for most putouts by pitcher—39 (1990, 1991 and 1993).

HONORS: Won N.L. Gold Glove at pitcher (1990-98). ... Named righthanded pitcher on THE SPORTING NEWS N.L. All-Star team (1992-95). ... Named N.L. Cy Young Award winner by Baseball Writers' Association of America (1992-95). ... Named N.L. Pitcher of the Year by THE SPORTING NEWS (1993-95).

STATISTICAL NOTES: Led Appalachian League with eight hit batsmen in 1984. ... Led American Association with 12 hit batsmen in 1986. ... Led N.L. with 14 hit batsmen in 1992. ... Pitched 3-1 one-hit, complete-game victory against Houston (May 28, 1995). ... Pitched 2-0 one-hit, complete-game victory against San Diego (April 27, 1997).

MISCELLANEOUS: Appeared in three games as pinch runner (1988). ... Singled and scored and struck out in two appearances as pinch hitter (1991). ... Holds Atlanta Braves franchise all-time record for lowest earned-run average (2.15).

Year Team (League)	W	L	Pct.	ERA	G	GS	CG	ShO	Sv.	IP	H	R	ER	BB	SO
1984—Pikeville (Appal.)	6	2	.750	2.63	14	12	2	•2	0	85 2/3	63	35	25	41	62
1985—Peoria (Midwest)	13	9	.591	3.19	27	27	6	0	0	186	176	86	66	52	125
1986—Pittsfield (Eastern)	4	3	.571	2.73	8	8	4	2	0	62 2/3	49	22	19	15	35
—Iowa (Am. Assoc.)	10	1	*.909	3.02	18	18	5	•2	0	128 1/3	127	49	43	30	65
—Chicago (N.L.)	2	4	.333	5.52	6	5	1	0	0	31	44	20	19	11	20
1987—Chicago (N.L.)	6	14	.300	5.61	30	27	1	1	0	155 2/3	181	111	97	74	101
—Iowa (Am. Assoc.)	3	0	1.000	0.98	4	4	2	•2	0	27 2/3	17	3	3	12	22
1988—Chicago (N.L.)	18	8	.692	3.18	34	34	9	3	0	249	230	97	88	81	140
1989—Chicago (N.L.)	19	12	.613	2.95	35	35	7	1	0	238 1/3	222	90	78	82	135
1990—Chicago (N.L.)	15	15	.500	3.46	35	•35	8	2	0	237	*242	*116	91	71	144
1991—Chicago (N.L.)	15	11	.577	3.35	37	*37	7	2	0	*263	232	113	98	66	198
1992—Chicago (N.L.)	•20	11	.645	2.18	35	•35	9	4	0	*268	201	68	65	70	199
1993—Atlanta (N.L.)■	20	10	.667	*2.36	36	•36	*8	1	0	*267	228	85	70	52	197
1994—Atlanta (N.L.)	•16	6	.727	*1.56	25	25	*10	•3	0	*202	150	44	35	31	156
1995—Atlanta (N.L.)	*19	2	*.905	*1.63	28	28	*10	•3	0	•209 2/3	147	39	38	23	181
1996—Atlanta (N.L.)	15	11	.577	2.72	35	35	5	1	0	245	225	85	74	28	172
1997—Atlanta (N.L.)	19	4	*.826	2.20	33	33	5	2	0	232 2/3	200	58	57	20	177
1998—Atlanta (N.L.)	18	9	.667	*2.22	34	34	9	*5	0	251	201	75	62	45	204
Major league totals (13 years)	202	117	.633	2.75	403	399	89	28	0	2849 1/3	2503	1001	872	654	2024

DIVISION SERIES RECORD

RECORDS: Holds career record for most hits allowed—36. ... Shares career record for most games started—5; most innings pitched—37; most wins—4; and most complete games—1. ... Holds N.L. career records for most wins—4; most games started—5; most innings pitched—37; and most runs allowed—12. ... Shares N.L. career record for most earned runs allowed—10.

Year Team (League)	W	L	Pct.	ERA	G	GS	CG	ShO	Sv.	IP	H	R	ER	BB	SO
1995—Atlanta (N.L.)	1	0	1.000	4.50	2	2	0	0	0	14	19	7	7	2	7
1996—Atlanta (N.L.)	1	0	1.000	0.00	1	1	0	0	0	7	3	2	0	0	7
1997—Atlanta (N.L.)	1	0	1.000	1.00	1	1	0	0	0	9	7	1	1	1	6
1998—Atlanta (N.L.)	1	0	1.000	2.57	1	1	0	0	0	7	3	1	1	0	4
Div. series totals (4 years)	4	0	1.000	2.43	5	5	1	0	0	37	36	12	10	3	24

M

CHAMPIONSHIP SERIES RECORD

RECORDS: Holds career record for most runs allowed—39. ... Shares career record for most sacrifice hits—5. ... Shares single-series record for most earned runs allowed—11 (1989). ... Holds N.L. career record for most sacrifice hits—5. ... Holds N.L. single-series record for most runs allowed—12 (1989).

NOTES: Scored once in only appearance as pinch runner (1989).

Year Team (League)	W	L	Pct.	ERA	G	GS	CG	ShO	Sv.	IP	H	R	ER	BB	SO
1989— Chicago (N.L.)..................	0	1	.000	13.50	2	2	0	0	0	7 $\frac{1}{3}$	13	12	11	4	5
1993— Atlanta (N.L.)....................	1	1	.500	4.97	2	2	0	0	0	12 $\frac{2}{3}$	11	8	7	7	11
1995— Atlanta (N.L.)....................	1	0	1.000	1.13	1	1	0	0	0	8	7	1	1	2	4
1996— Atlanta (N.L.)....................	1	1	.500	2.51	2	2	0	0	0	14 $\frac{1}{3}$	15	9	4	3	10
1997— Atlanta (N.L.)....................	0	2	.000	1.38	2	2	0	0	0	13	9	7	2	4	16
1998— Atlanta (N.L.)....................	0	1	.000	3.00	2	1	0	0	1	6	5	2	2	3	4
Champ. series totals (6 years)	**3**	**6**	**.333**	**3.96**	**11**	**10**	**0**	**0**	**1**	**61 $\frac{1}{3}$**	**60**	**39**	**27**	**23**	**50**

WORLD SERIES RECORD

NOTES: Member of World Series championship team (1995).

Year Team (League)	W	L	Pct.	ERA	G	GS	CG	ShO	Sv.	IP	H	R	ER	BB	SO
1995— Atlanta (N.L.)....................	1	1	.500	2.25	2	2	1	0	0	16	9	6	4	3	8
1996— Atlanta (N.L.)....................	1	1	.500	1.72	2	2	0	0	0	15 $\frac{2}{3}$	14	3	3	1	5
World Series totals (2 years)	**2**	**2**	**.500**	**1.99**	**4**	**4**	**1**	**0**	**0**	**31 $\frac{2}{3}$**	**23**	**9**	**7**	**4**	**13**

ALL-STAR GAME RECORD

Year League	W	L	Pct.	ERA	GS	CG	ShO	Sv.	IP	H	R	ER	BB	SO
1988— National						Did not play.								
1992— National	0	0	...	6.75	0	0	0	0	1 $\frac{1}{3}$	1	1	1	0	0
1994— National	0	0	...	3.00	1	0	0	0	3	3	1	1	0	2
1995— National					Selected, did not play—injured.									
1996— National						Did not play.								
1997— National	0	0	...	4.50	1	0	0	0	2	2	1	1	0	0
1998— National	0	0	...	0.00	1	0	0	0	2	3	0	0	1	1
All-Star totals (4 years)	**0**	**0**	**...**	**3.24**	**3**	**0**	**0**	**0**	**8 $\frac{1}{3}$**	**9**	**3**	**3**	**1**	**3**

MADDUX, MIKE   P

PERSONAL: Born August 27, 1961, in Dayton, Ohio. ... 6-2/185. ... Throws right, bats left. ... Full name: Michael Ausley Maddux. ... Brother of Greg Maddux, pitcher, Atlanta Braves.

HIGH SCHOOL: Rancho (Las Vegas).

COLLEGE: Texas-El Paso.

TRANSACTIONS/CAREER NOTES: Selected by Cincinnati Reds organization in 36th round of free-agent draft (June 5, 1979); did not sign. ... Selected by Philadelphia Phillies organization in fifth round of free-agent draft (June 7, 1982). ... On Philadelphia disabled list (April 21-June 1, 1988); included rehabilitation assignment to Maine (May 13-22). ... Released by Phillies organization (November 20, 1989). ... Signed by Los Angeles Dodgers (December 21, 1989). ... Granted free agency (October 15, 1990). ... Signed by San Diego Padres (March 30, 1991). ... On disabled list (April 5-26, 1992). ... Traded by Padres to New York Mets for P Roger Mason and P Mike Freitas (December 17, 1992). ... On disabled list (April 27-May 13, 1994). ... Granted free agency (October 18, 1994). ... Signed by Pittsburgh Pirates organization (April 10, 1995). ... Released by Pirates (May 16, 1995). ... Signed by Boston Red Sox (May 30, 1995). ... Granted free agency (November 6, 1995). ... Re-signed by Red Sox (December 15, 1995). ... On Boston disabled list (May 6-August 2, 1996); included rehabilitation assignments to Pawtucket (May 24-25, July 12-16 and July 25-31). ... Granted free agency (November 1, 1996). ... Re-signed by Red Sox (December 7, 1996). ... Released by Red Sox (March 26, 1997). ... Signed by Seattle Mariners organization (April 11, 1997). ... On Seattle disabled list (June 22-July 13, 1997). ... Released by Mariners (July 23, 1997). ... Signed by Padres organization (August 19, 1997). ... Granted free agency (October 15, 1997). ... Signed by Montreal Expos (March 30, 1998). ... On disabled list (April 8-May 1 and June 7-July 9, 1998). ... Granted free agency (September 29, 1998).

MISCELLANEOUS: Appeared in one game as pinch runner with Philadelphia (1988).

Year Team (League)	W	L	Pct.	ERA	G	GS	CG	ShO	Sv.	IP	H	R	ER	BB	SO
1982— Bend (Northwest)..............	3	6	.333	3.99	11	10	3	0	0	65 $\frac{1}{3}$	68	35	29	26	59
1983— Spartanburg (SAL)	4	6	.400	5.44	13	13	3	0	0	84 $\frac{1}{3}$	98	62	51	47	85
— Peninsula (Caro.)	8	4	.667	3.62	14	14	6	0	0	99 $\frac{1}{3}$	92	46	40	35	78
— Reading (Eastern)	0	0	...	6.00	1	1	0	0	0	3	4	2	2	1	2
1984— Reading (Eastern)	3	•12	.200	5.04	20	19	4	0	0	116	143	82	65	49	77
— Portland (PCL)	2	4	.333	5.84	8	8	1	0	0	44 $\frac{2}{3}$	58	32	29	17	22
1985— Portland (PCL)	9	12	.429	5.31	27	26	6	1	0	166	195	106	98	51	96
1986— Portland (PCL)	5	2	.714	2.36	12	12	3	0	0	84	70	26	22	22	65
— Philadelphia (N.L.)	3	7	.300	5.42	16	16	0	0	0	78	88	56	47	34	44
1987— Maine (International)........	6	6	.500	4.35	18	16	3	1	0	103 $\frac{1}{3}$	116	58	50	26	71
— Philadelphia (N.L.)...........	2	0	1.000	2.65	7	2	0	0	0	17	17	5	5	5	15
1988— Philadelphia (N.L.)...........	4	3	.571	3.76	25	11	0	0	0	88 $\frac{2}{3}$	91	41	37	34	59
— Maine (International).........	0	2	.000	4.18	5	3	1	0	0	23 $\frac{2}{3}$	25	18	11	10	18
1989— Philadelphia (N.L.)...........	1	3	.250	5.15	16	4	2	1	1	43 $\frac{2}{3}$	52	29	25	14	26
— Scran./W.B. (Int'l).............	7	7	.500	3.66	19	17	3	1	0	123	119	55	50	26	100
1990— Albuquerque (PCL)■......	8	5	.615	4.25	20	19	2	0	0	108	122	59	51	32	85
— Los Angeles (N.L.)	0	1	.000	6.53	11	2	0	0	0	20 $\frac{2}{3}$	24	15	15	4	11
1991— San Diego (N.L.)■..........	7	2	.778	2.46	64	1	0	0	5	98 $\frac{2}{3}$	78	30	27	27	57
1992— San Diego (N.L.)	2	2	.500	2.37	50	1	0	0	5	79 $\frac{2}{3}$	71	25	21	24	60
1993— New York (N.L.)■...........	3	8	.273	3.60	58	0	0	0	5	75	67	34	30	27	57
1994— New York (N.L.).............	2	1	.667	5.11	27	0	0	0	2	44	45	25	25	13	32
1995— Pittsburgh (N.L.)■..........	1	0	1.000	9.00	8	0	0	0	0	9	14	9	9	3	4
— Boston (A.L.)■.................	4	1	.800	3.61	36	4	0	0	1	89 $\frac{2}{3}$	86	40	36	15	65
1996— Boston (A.L.)...................	3	2	.600	4.48	23	7	0	0	0	64 $\frac{1}{3}$	76	37	32	27	32
— Pawtucket (Int'l)	2	0	1.000	3.21	3	3	0	0	0	14	13	5	5	2	9
1997— Tacoma (PCL)■..............	0	0	...	0.00	1	1	0	0	0	5	1	0	0	2	5
— Seattle (A.L.)	1	0	1.000	10.13	6	0	0	0	0	10 $\frac{2}{3}$	20	12	12	8	7

M

Year	Team (League)	W	L	Pct.	ERA	G	GS	CG	ShO	Sv.	IP	H	R	ER	BB	SO
	—Las Vegas (PCL)■	0	2	.000	5.63	3	3	0	0	0	16	23	11	10	9	13
1998—	Montreal (N.L.)■................	3	4	.429	3.72	51	0	0	0	1	55 2/3	50	24	23	15	33
	A.L. totals (3 years)	8	3	.727	4.37	65	11	0	0	1	164 2/3	182	89	80	50	104
	N.L. totals (11 years)	28	31	.475	3.90	333	37	2	1	19	610	597	293	264	200	398
	Major league totals (13 years)....	36	34	.514	4.00	398	48	2	1	20	774 2/3	779	382	344	250	502

DIVISION SERIES RECORD

Year	Team (League)	W	L	Pct.	ERA	G	GS	CG	ShO	Sv.	IP	H	R	ER	BB	SO
1995—	Boston (A.L.)	0	0	...	0.00	2	0	0	0	0	3	2	0	0	1	1

MAGADAN, DAVE   3B/1B   PADRES

PERSONAL: Born September 30, 1962, in Tampa, Fla. ... 6-4/215. ... Bats left, throws right. ... Full name: David Joseph Magadan. ... Cousin of Lou Piniella, manager, Seattle Mariners, and major league outfielder/designated hitter with four teams (1964 and 1968-84). ... Name pronounced MAG-uh-dun.

HIGH SCHOOL: Jesuit (Tampa).

COLLEGE: Alabama.

TRANSACTIONS/CAREER NOTES: Selected by Boston Red Sox organization in 12th round of free-agent draft (June 3, 1980); did not sign. ... Selected by New York Mets organization in second round of free-agent draft (June 6, 1983). ... On disabled list (August 7-September 10, 1984; March 29-April 17, 1987; May 5-20, 1988; and August 9, 1992-remainder of season). ... Granted free agency (October 27, 1992). ... Signed by Florida Marlins organization (December 8, 1992). ... Traded by Marlins to Seattle Mariners for OF Henry Cotto and P Jeff Darwin (June 27, 1993). ... Traded by Mariners to Marlins for P Jeff Darwin and cash (November 9, 1993). ... On disabled list (March 29-April 13 and July 21, 1994-remainder of season). ... Granted free agency (October 19, 1994). ... Signed by Houston Astros (April 15, 1995). ... Granted free agency (October 30, 1995). ... Signed by Chicago Cubs (December 26, 1995). ... On Chicago disabled list (March 22-April 16 and April 17-May 31, 1996); included rehabilitation assignment to Daytona (May 17-29). ... Granted free agency (November 18, 1996). ... Signed by Oakland Athletics organization (January 23, 1997). ... Granted free agency (October 27, 1997). ... Re-signed by A's (November 12, 1997). ... On disabled list (May 16, 1998-remainder of season). ... Granted free agency (October 29, 1998). ... Signed by San Diego Padres (December 21, 1998).

HONORS: Named Golden Spikes Award winner by USA Baseball (1983). ... Named designated hitter on THE SPORTING NEWS college All-America team (1983).

STATISTICAL NOTES: Led Carolina League with 10 intentional bases on balls received in 1984. ... Led Texas League third basemen with 87 putouts, 275 assists, 393 total chances and 31 errors in 1985. ... Led International League third basemen with .934 fielding percentage, 283 assists and 31 double plays in 1986. ... Led N.L. first basemen with .998 fielding percentage in 1990.

								BATTING								FIELDING		
Year	Team (League)	Pos.	G	AB	R	H	2B	3B	HR	RBI	Avg.	BB	SO	SB	PO	A	E	Avg.
1983—	Columbia (S. Atl.).......	1B	64	220	41	74	13	1	3	32	.336	51	29	2	520	37	7	.988
1984—	Lynchburg (Caro.)......	1B	112	371	78	130	22	4	0	62	*.350	104	43	2	896	64	16	.984
1985—	Jackson (Texas)........	3B-1B	134	466	84	144	22	0	0	76	.309	*106	57	0	†106	†276	†31	.925
1986—	Tidewater (Int'l).........	3B-1B	133	473	68	147	33	6	1	64	.311	84	45	2	78	†284	25	†.935
	—New York (N.L.).........	1B	10	18	3	8	0	0	0	3	.444	3	1	0	48	5	0	1.000
1987—	New York (N.L.).........	3B-1B	85	192	21	61	13	1	3	24	.318	22	22	0	88	92	4	.978
1988—	New York (N.L.).........	1B-3B	112	314	39	87	15	0	1	35	.277	60	39	0	459	99	10	.982
1989—	New York (N.L.).........	1B-3B	127	374	47	107	22	3	4	41	.286	49	37	1	587	89	7	.990
1990—	New York (N.L.).........	1B-3B	144	451	74	148	28	6	6	72	.328	74	55	2	837	99	3	†.997
1991—	New York (N.L.).........	1B	124	418	58	108	23	0	4	51	.258	83	50	1	1035	90	5	.996
1992—	New York (N.L.).........	3B-1B	99	321	33	91	9	1	3	28	.283	56	44	1	54	136	11	.945
1993—	Florida (N.L.)■..........	3B-1B	66	227	22	65	12	0	4	29	.286	44	30	0	55	122	7	.962
	—Seattle (A.L.)■.........	1B-3B-DH	71	228	27	59	11	0	1	21	.259	36	33	2	325	72	5	.988
1994—	Florida (N.L.)■..........	3B-1B	74	211	30	58	7	0	1	17	.275	39	25	0	127	78	4	.981
1995—	Houston (N.L.)■........	3B-1B	127	348	44	109	24	0	2	51	.313	71	56	2	121	163	18	.940
1996—	Daytona (Fla. St.)■.....	3B	7	20	5	6	1	0	0	3	.300	7	2	0	0	6	1	.857
	—Iowa (Am. Assoc.)......	3B	3	9	0	2	1	0	0	1	.222	1	2	0	3	3	0	1.000
	—Chicago (N.L.)..........	3B-1B	78	169	23	43	10	0	3	17	.254	29	23	0	75	67	3	.979
1997—	Oakland (A.L.)■.........	3B-1B-DH	128	271	38	82	10	1	4	30	.303	50	40	1	148	65	5	.977
1998—	Oakland (A.L.)..........	3B-1B	35	109	12	35	8	0	1	13	.321	13	12	0	48	55	6	.945
	American League totals (3 years)		234	608	77	176	29	1	6	64	.289	99	85	3	521	192	16	.978
	National League totals (11 years)		1046	3043	394	885	163	11	31	368	.291	530	382	7	3486	1040	72	.984
	Major league totals (13 years)		1280	3651	471	1061	192	12	37	432	.291	629	467	10	4007	1232	88	.983

CHAMPIONSHIP SERIES RECORD

								BATTING								FIELDING		
Year	Team (League)	Pos.	G	AB	R	H	2B	3B	HR	RBI	Avg.	BB	SO	SB	PO	A	E	Avg.
1988—	New York (N.L.)..........	PH	3	3	0	0	0	0	0	0	.000	0	2	0	...	...	...	...

MAGEE, WENDELL   OF   PHILLIES

PERSONAL: Born August 3, 1972, in Hattiesburg, Miss. ... 6-0/220. ... Bats right, throws right. ... Full name: Wendell Errol Magee Jr.

HIGH SCHOOL: Hattiesburg (Miss.).

JUNIOR COLLEGE: Pearl River College.

COLLEGE: Samford.

TRANSACTIONS/CAREER NOTES: Selected by Philadelphia Phillies organization in 12th round of free-agent draft (June 2, 1994).

STATISTICAL NOTES: Led International League outfielders with 320 total chances in 1998.

								BATTING								FIELDING		
Year	Team (League)	Pos.	G	AB	R	H	2B	3B	HR	RBI	Avg.	BB	SO	SB	PO	A	E	Avg.
1994—	Batavia (NY-Penn)......	OF	63	229	42	64	12	4	2	35	.279	16	24	10	115	7	6	.953
1995—	Clearwater (FSL)........	OF	96	388	67	137	24	5	6	46	*.353	33	40	7	166	12	5	.973
	—Reading (Eastern)......	OF	39	136	17	40	9	1	3	21	.294	21	17	3	65	4	5	.932

Year	Team (League)	Pos.	G	AB	R	H	2B	3B	HR	RBI	Avg.	BB	SO	SB	PO	A	E	Avg.
1996—	Reading (Eastern)	OF	71	270	38	79	15	5	6	30	.293	24	40	10	101	8	3	.973
	— Scran./W.B. (Int'l)......	OF	44	155	31	44	9	2	10	32	.284	21	31	3	92	2	4	.959
	— Philadelphia (N.L.).....	OF	38	142	9	29	7	0	2	14	.204	9	33	0	88	2	2	.978
1997—	Philadelphia (N.L.).....	OF	38	115	7	23	4	0	1	9	.200	9	20	1	95	2	4	.960
	— Scran./W.B. (Int'l)......	OF	83	294	39	72	20	1	10	39	.245	30	56	4	167	3	3	.983
1998—	Scran./W.B. (Int'l)......	OF	126	507	86	147	30	7	24	72	.290	46	102	7	*302	7	•11	.966
	— Philadelphia (N.L.).....	OF	20	75	9	22	6	1	1	11	.293	7	11	0	31	1	2	.941
Major league totals (3 years)			96	332	25	74	17	1	4	34	.223	25	64	1	214	5	8	.965

MAGNANTE, MIKE   P

PERSONAL: Born June 17, 1965, in Glendale, Calif. ... 6-1/185. ... Throws left, bats left. ... Full name: Michael Anthony Magnante. ... Name pronounced mag-NAN-tee.
HIGH SCHOOL: John Burroughs (Burbank, Calif.).
COLLEGE: UCLA (bachelor of science degree in applied mathematics).
TRANSACTIONS/CAREER NOTES: Selected by Kansas City Royals organization in 11th round of free-agent draft (June 1, 1988). ... On disabled list (June 17, 1990-remainder of season; July 2-20, 1992; and July 16-31, 1994). ... On Kansas City disabled list (May 19-June 13, 1996); included rehabilitation assignment to Omaha (June 8-13). ... Released by Royals (October 2, 1996). ... Signed by Houston Astros organization (December 19, 1996). ... On disabled list (May 10-25, 1998). ... Granted free agency (October 23, 1998).
RECORDS: Shares major league record for striking out side on nine pitches (August 22, 1997, ninth inning).

Year	Team (League)	W	L	Pct.	ERA	G	GS	CG	ShO	Sv.	IP	H	R	ER	BB	SO
1988—	Eugene (Northwest)	1	1	.500	0.56	3	3	0	0	0	16	10	6	1	2	26
	— Appleton (Midwest)...........	3	2	.600	3.21	9	8	0	0	0	47 2/3	48	20	17	15	40
	— Baseball City (FSL)............	1	1	.500	4.13	4	4	1	0	0	24	19	12	11	8	19
1989—	Memphis (Sou.).............	8	9	.471	3.66	26	26	4	1	0	157 1/3	137	70	64	53	118
1990—	Omaha (Am. Assoc.)..........	2	5	.286	4.11	13	13	2	0	0	76 2/3	72	39	35	25	56
1991—	Omaha (Am. Assoc.).........	6	1	.857	3.02	10	10	2	0	0	65 2/3	53	23	22	23	50
	— Kansas City (A.L.)	0	1	.000	2.45	38	0	0	0	0	55	55	19	15	23	42
1992—	Kansas City (A.L.)	4	9	.308	4.94	44	12	0	0	0	89 1/3	115	53	49	35	31
1993—	Omaha (Am. Assoc.).........	2	6	.250	3.67	33	13	0	0	2	105 1/3	97	46	43	29	74
	— Kansas City (A.L.)	1	2	.333	4.08	7	6	0	0	0	35 1/3	37	16	16	11	16
1994—	Kansas City (A.L.)	2	3	.400	4.60	36	1	0	0	0	47	55	27	24	16	21
1995—	Omaha (Am. Assoc.).........	5	1	.833	2.84	15	8	0	0	0	57	55	23	18	13	38
	— Kansas City (A.L.)	1	1	.500	4.23	28	0	0	0	0	44 2/3	45	23	21	16	28
1996—	Kansas City (A.L.)	2	2	.500	5.67	38	0	0	0	0	54	58	38	34	24	32
	— Omaha (Am. Assoc.).........	1	0	1.000	0.00	1	0	0	0	0	3	3	1	0	0	6
1997—	New Orleans (A.A.)■........	2	3	.400	4.50	17	0	0	0	1	24	31	14	12	5	23
	— Houston (N.L.)	3	1	.750	2.27	40	0	0	0	1	47 2/3	39	16	12	11	43
1998—	Houston (N.L.)	4	7	.364	4.88	48	0	0	0	2	51 2/3	56	28	28	26	39
A.L. totals (6 years)		10	18	.357	4.40	191	19	0	0	0	325 1/3	365	176	159	125	170
N.L. totals (2 years)		7	8	.467	3.62	88	0	0	0	3	99 1/3	95	44	40	37	82
Major league totals (8 years)......		17	26	.395	4.22	279	19	0	0	3	424 2/3	460	220	199	162	252

DIVISION SERIES RECORD

Year	Team (League)	W	L	Pct.	ERA	G	GS	CG	ShO	Sv.	IP	H	R	ER	BB	SO
1997—	Houston (N.L.)	0	0	...	4.50	2	0	0	0	0	2	4	3	1	0	2

MAHAY, RON   P   RED SOX

PERSONAL: Born June 28, 1971, in Crestwood, Ill. ... 6-2/190. ... Throws left, bats left. ... Full name: Ronald Matthew Mahay.
HIGH SCHOOL: Alan B. Shepard (Palos Heights, Ill.).
JUNIOR COLLEGE: South Suburban (Ill.).
TRANSACTIONS/CAREER NOTES: Selected by Boston Red Sox organization in 18th round of free-agent draft (June 3, 1991). ... On disabled list (May 5, 1992-remainder of season). ... On Lynchburg disabled list (August 6-September 9, 1993). ... On disabled list (August 23-September 1, 1994). ... On Pawtucket temporarily inactive list (April 19-25, 1995). ... On Sarasota disabled list (April 4-25, 1996).
MISCELLANEOUS: Played outfield only (1991-95).

Year	Team (League)	W	L	Pct.	ERA	G	GS	CG	ShO	Sv.	IP	H	R	ER	BB	SO
1996—	Sarasota (Florida State)......	2	2	.500	3.82	31	4	0	0	2	70 2/3	61	33	30	35	68
	— Trenton (Eastern)	0	1	.000	29.45	1	1	0	0	0	3 2/3	12	13	12	6	0
1997—	Trenton (Eastern)	3	3	.500	3.10	17	4	0	0	5	40 2/3	29	16	14	13	47
	— Pawtucket (Int'l)...............	1	0	1.000	0.00	2	0	0	0	0	4 2/3	3	0	0	1	6
	— Boston (A.L.).................	3	1	1.000	2.52	28	0	0	0	0	25	19	7	7	11	22
1998—	Pawtucket (Int'l).................	3	1	.750	4.17	23	1	0	0	3	41	37	20	19	19	41
	— Boston (A.L.).............	1	1	.500	3.46	29	0	0	0	1	26	26	16	10	15	14
Major league totals (2 years)......		4	1	.800	3.00	57	0	0	0	1	51	45	23	17	26	36

RECORD AS POSITION PLAYER

Year	Team (League)	Pos.	G	AB	R	H	2B	3B	HR	RBI	Avg.	BB	SO	SB	PO	A	E	Avg.
1991—	GC Red Sox (GCL)	OF	54	187	30	51	6	5	1	29	.273	33	40	2	97	2	3	.971
1992—	Winter Haven (FSL)....	OF	19	63	6	16	2	1	0	4	.254	2	19	0	33	2	1	.972
1993—	Lynchburg (Caro.).......	OF-C	73	254	28	54	8	1	5	23	.213	11	63	2	174	7	5	.973
	— New Britain (East.).......	OF	8	25	2	3	0	0	1	2	.120	1	6	1	15	1	2	.889
1994—	Sarasota (Fla. St.)	OF	105	367	43	102	18	0	4	46	.278	39	67	3	189	16	4	.981
1995—	Pawtucket (Int'l)........	OF	11	44	5	14	4	0	0	3	.318	4	9	1	30	2	0	1.000
	— Trenton (Eastern)	OF	93	310	37	73	12	3	5	28	.235	44	90	5	187	9	6	.970
	— Boston (A.L.)...........	OF	5	20	3	4	2	0	1	3	.200	1	6	0	9	0	0	1.000
Major league totals (1 year)			5	20	3	4	2	0	1	3	.200	1	6	0	9	0	0	1.000

M

MALLOY, MARTY 2B BRAVES

PERSONAL: Born July 6, 1972, in Gainesville, Fla. ... 5-10/160. ... Bats left, throws right. ... Full name: Marty Thomas Malloy.
HIGH SCHOOL: Trenton (Fla.).
JUNIOR COLLEGE: Santa Fe Community College (Fla.).
TRANSACTIONS/CAREER NOTES: Signed as non-drafted free agent by Atlanta Braves organization (June 25, 1992).

							BATTING							FIELDING			
Year Team (League)	Pos.	G	AB	R	H	2B	3B	HR	RBI	Avg.	BB	SO	SB	PO	A	E	Avg.
1992— Idaho Falls (Pio.)........	2B-SS	62	251	45	79	18	1	2	28	.315	11	43	8	127	143	17	.941
1993— Macon (S. Atl.).........	2B-SS-OF	109	376	55	110	19	3	2	36	.293	39	70	24	187	264	19	.960
1994— Durham (Carolina)......	2B-SS	118	428	53	113	22	1	6	35	.264	52	69	18	193	317	19	.964
1995— Greenville (Southern) .	2B	124	461	73	128	20	3	10	59	.278	39	58	11	246	321	16	.973
1996— Greenville (Southern) .	2B	111	429	82	134	27	2	4	36	.312	54	50	11	209	278	14	.972
— Richmond (Int'l).........	2B-SS	18	64	7	13	2	1	0	8	.203	5	7	3	34	40	2	.974
1997— Richmond (Int'l).........	2B	108	414	66	118	19	5	2	25	.285	41	61	17	*195	278	•12	.975
1998— Richmond (Int'l).........	2B	124	483	75	140	25	3	7	54	.290	51	65	20	206	351	13	.977
— Atlanta (N.L.).............	2B	11	28	3	5	1	0	1	1	.179	2	2	0	16	22	0	1.000
Major league totals (1 year)		11	28	3	5	1	0	1	1	.179	2	2	0	16	22	0	1.000

CHAMPIONSHIP SERIES RECORD

							BATTING							FIELDING			
Year Team (League)	Pos.	G	AB	R	H	2B	3B	HR	RBI	Avg.	BB	SO	SB	PO	A	E	Avg.
1998— Atlanta (N.L.).............	PR-2B	1	1	1	0	0	0	0	0	.000	0	1	0	0	1	0	1.000

MALONEY, SEAN P

PERSONAL: Born May 25, 1971, in South Kingstown, R.I. ... 6-7/230. ... Throws right, bats right. ... Full name: Sean Patrick Maloney.
HIGH SCHOOL: North Kingstown (Kingstown, R.I.).
COLLEGE: Georgetown (D.C.); degree in business administration.
TRANSACTIONS/CAREER NOTES: Selected by Milwaukee Brewers organization in 19th round of free-agent draft (June 3, 1993). ... On Tucson disabled list (May 8-24 and June 12-September 2, 1997). ... Released by Brewers (March 10, 1998). ... Signed by Los Angeles Dodgers organization (March 20, 1998). ... On Albuquerque disabled list (April 7-May 28, 1998). ... Granted free agency (December 21, 1998).

Year Team (League)	W	L	Pct.	ERA	G	GS	CG	ShO	Sv.	IP	H	R	ER	BB	SO
1993— Helena (Pioneer)	2	2	.500	4.34	17	3	1	0	0	47²/₃	55	31	23	11	35
1994— Beloit (Midwest)................	2	6	.250	5.49	51	0	0	0	22	59	73	42	36	10	53
1995— El Paso (Texas)................	7	5	.583	4.18	43	0	0	0	15	64²/₃	69	41	30	28	54
1996— El Paso (Texas)................	3	2	.600	1.43	51	0	0	0	*38	56²/₃	49	11	9	12	57
1997— Tucson (PCL)	0	2	.000	4.82	15	0	0	0	5	18²/₃	24	10	10	3	21
— Milwaukee (A.L.)	0	0	. . .	5.14	3	0	0	0	0	7	7	4	4	2	5
1998— Albuquerque (PCL)■	3	2	.600	4.63	26	0	0	0	9	35	38	21	18	8	38
— Los Angeles (N.L.)	0	1	.000	4.97	11	0	0	0	0	12²/₃	13	7	7	5	11
A.L. totals (1 year)	0	0	. . .	5.14	3	0	0	0	0	7	7	4	4	2	5
N.L. totals (1 year)	0	1	.000	4.97	11	0	0	0	0	12²/₃	13	7	7	5	11
Major league totals (2 years)	0	1	.000	5.03	14	0	0	0	0	19²/₃	20	11	11	7	16

MANTEI, MATT P MARLINS

PERSONAL: Born July 7, 1973, in Tampa. ... 6-1/190. ... Throws right, bats right. ... Full name: Matthew Bruce Mantei. ... Name pronounced MAN-tay.
HIGH SCHOOL: River Valley (Three Oaks, Mich.).
TRANSACTIONS/CAREER NOTES: Selected by Seattle Mariners organization in 25th round of free-agent draft (June 3, 1991). ... Selected by Florida Marlins from Mariners organization in Rule 5 major league draft (December 5, 1994). ... On Florida disabled list (April 20-June 18 and July 29-September 1, 1995); included rehabilitation assignments to Portland and Charlotte (May 13-June 18). ... On Florida disabled list (June 19, 1996-remainder of season). ... On Florida disabled list (March 31, 1997-entire season). ... Granted free agency (December 21, 1997). ... Re-signed by Marlins organization (December 21, 1997). ... On Florida disabled list (August 19-September 4, 1998).

Year Team (League)	W	L	Pct.	ERA	G	GS	CG	ShO	Sv.	IP	H	R	ER	BB	SO
1991— Ariz. Mariners (Ariz.)..........	1	4	.200	6.69	17	5	0	0	0	40¹/₃	54	40	30	28	29
1992— Ariz. Mariners (Ariz.)..........	1	1	.500	5.63	3	3	0	0	0	16	18	10	10	5	19
1993— Bellingham (N'west)	1	1	.500	5.96	26	0	0	0	*12	25²/₃	26	19	17	15	34
1994— Appleton (Midwest)...........	5	1	.833	2.06	48	0	0	0	26	48	42	14	11	21	70
1995— Portland (Eastern)■	1	0	1.000	2.38	8	0	0	0	1	11¹/₃	10	3	3	5	15
— Charlotte (Int'l)	0	1	.000	2.57	6	0	0	0	0	7	1	3	2	5	10
— Florida (N.L.)	0	1	.000	4.73	12	0	0	0	0	13¹/₃	12	8	7	13	15
1996— Florida (N.L.)	1	0	1.000	6.38	14	0	0	0	0	18¹/₃	13	13	13	21	25
— Charlotte (Int'l)	0	2	.000	4.70	7	0	0	0	2	7²/₃	6	4	4	7	8
1997— Brevard County (FSL)........	0	0	. . .	6.00	4	0	0	0	0	6	4	4	4	6	11
— Portland (Eastern)	1	0	1.000	6.75	5	0	0	0	0	4	1	3	3	8	7
1998— Charlotte (Int'l)	1	2	.333	5.51	16	0	0	0	3	16¹/₃	11	10	10	18	25
— Florida (N.L.)	3	4	.429	2.96	42	0	0	0	9	54²/₃	38	19	18	23	63
Major league totals (3 years)	4	5	.444	3.96	68	0	0	0	9	86¹/₃	63	40	38	57	103

MANTO, JEFF 3B INDIANS

PERSONAL: Born August 23, 1964, in Bristol, Pa. ... 6-3/210. ... Bats right, throws right. ... Full name: Jeffrey Paul Manto.
HIGH SCHOOL: Bristol (Pa.).
COLLEGE: Temple.

M

TRANSACTIONS/CAREER NOTES: Selected by New York Yankees organization in 35th round of free-agent draft (June 7, 1982); did not sign. ... Selected by California Angels organization in 14th round of free-agent draft (June 3, 1985). ... On disabled list (July 16, 1986-remainder of season). ... Traded by Angels organization with P Colin Charland to Cleveland Indians for P Scott Bailes (January 9, 1990). ... Released by Indians (November 27, 1991). ... Signed by Richmond, Atlanta Braves organization (January 23, 1992). ... On disabled list (May 4-14, 1992). ... Granted free agency (October 15, 1992). ... Signed by Philadelphia Phillies organization (December 16, 1992). ... Granted free agency (October 15, 1993). ... Signed by New York Mets organization (December 16, 1993). ... Traded by Mets organization to Baltimore Orioles organization for future considerations (May 19, 1994). ... On Baltimore disabled list (June 26-July 13, 1995); included rehabilitation assignments to Bowie (July 9-10) and Frederick (July 10-13). ... Signed by Yomiuri Giants of Japan Central League (January 25, 1996). ... Released by Giants (April 23, 1996). ... Signed by Boston Red Sox organization (May 7, 1996). ... On Boston disabled list (May 26-June 27, 1996); included rehabilitation assignment to Trenton (June 21-27). ... Traded by Red Sox to Seattle Mariners for IF Arquimedez Pozo (July 23, 1996). ... Released by Mariners (August 29, 1996). ... Claimed on waivers by Red Sox (August 29, 1996). ... Granted free agency (October 8, 1996). ... Signed by Syracuse, Blue Jays organization (February 17, 1997). ... On Syracuse disabled list (May 26-June 2, 1997). ... Traded by Blue Jays organization to Cleveland Indians organization for OF Ryan Thompson (June 6, 1997). ... Claimed on waivers by Detroit Tigers (April 24, 1998). ... Released by Tigers (June 12, 1998). ... Signed by Indians organization (June 16, 1998). ... Released by Indians (October 15, 1998). ... Re-signed by Indians (January 5, 1999).

RECORDS: Shares major league record for most consecutive home runs in three games—4 (June 8 [1], 9 [2] and 10 [1], 1995).

HONORS: Named Texas League Most Valuable Player (1988). ... Named International League Most Valuable Player (1994).

STATISTICAL NOTES: Led California League third basemen with 245 assists and 365 total chances in 1987. ... Tied for Texas League lead in errors by third baseman with 32 in 1988. ... Led Texas League in grounding into double plays with 17 in 1988. ... Led Pacific Coast League with .446 on-base percentage in 1990. ... Led Pacific Coast League third basemen with .943 fielding percentage, 265 assists and 22 double plays in 1989. ... Led International League with 12 sacrifice flies in 1992. ... Led International League with .404 on-base percentage, 260 total bases, 31 home runs, 100 RBIs and tied for league lead in being hit by pitch with 11 in 1994.

							BATTING									FIELDING		
Year— Team (League)	Pos.	G	AB	R	H	2B	3B	HR	RBI	Avg.	BB	SO	SB	PO	A	E	Avg.
1985— Quad Cities (Mid.)	OF-3B	74	233	34	46	5	2	11	34	.197	40	74	3	87	8	3	.969
1986— Quad Cities (Mid.)	3B	73	239	31	59	13	0	8	49	.247	37	70	2	48	114	28	.853
1987— Palm Springs (Calif.)	3B-1B	112	375	61	96	21	4	7	63	.256	102	85	8	93	†246	37	.902
1988— Midland (Texas)	3B-2B-1B	120	408	88	123	23	3	24	101	.301	62	76	7	82	208	‡32	.901
1989— Edmonton (PCL)	3B-1B	127	408	89	113	25	3	23	67	.277	91	81	4	140	†266	21	†.951
1990— Colo. Springs (PCL)■	3B-1B	96	316	73	94	27	1	18	82	.297	78	65	10	340	131	10	.979
— Cleveland (A.L.)	1B-3B	30	76	12	17	5	1	2	14	.224	21	18	0	185	24	2	.991
1991— Cleveland (A.L.)	3-1-C-O	47	128	15	27	7	0	2	13	.211	14	22	2	109	63	8	.956
— Colo. Springs (PCL)	3-1-C-S-O	43	153	36	49	16	0	6	36	.320	33	24	1	169	53	11	.953
1992— Richmond (Int'l)■	3B-2B-1B	127	450	65	131	24	1	13	68	.291	57	63	1	89	245	23	.936
1993— Scran./W.B. (Int'l)■	3B-1B-C	106	388	62	112	30	1	17	88	.289	55	58	4	401	134	8	.985
— Philadelphia (N.L.)	3B-SS	8	18	0	1	0	0	0	0	.056	0	3	0	2	8	0	1.000
1994— Norfolk (Int'l)■	3B-1B-2B	37	115	20	30	6	0	4	17	.261	27	28	1	73	46	4	.967
— Rochester (Int'l)■	3B	94	329	61	102	25	2	§27	§83	.310	43	47	2	277	102	15	.962
1995— Baltimore (A.L.)	3B-DH-1B	89	254	31	65	9	0	17	38	.256	24	69	0	68	103	6	.966
— Bowie (Eastern)	DH	1	4	1	1	0	0	0	0	.250	1	2	0	0	0	0	...
— Frederick (Carolina)	3B	2	8	1	3	0	0	1	3	.375	0	1	0	0	2	0	1.000
1996— Yomiuri (Jp. Cen.)■	...		27	1	3			0	1	.111							...
— Pawtucket (Int'l)■	3B-2B	12	45	6	11	5	0	2	6	.244	5	8	1	13	29	2	.955
— Boston (A.L.)	3-2-S-1	22	48	8	10	3	1	2	6	.208	8	12	0	25	47	4	.947
— Trenton (Eastern)	3B-2B-SS	6	21	3	6	0	0	0	5	.286	1	5	0	5	5	3	.769
— Seattle (A.L.)■	3B-DH-OF	21	54	7	10	3	0	1	4	.185	9	12	0	8	26	1	.971
1997— Syracuse (Int'l)■	3B-OF-1B	40	132	18	27	5	1	3	11	.205	22	30	1	23	19	1	.977
— Buffalo (A.A.)■	3B-1B-OF	54	187	37	60	11	0	20	54	.321	31	43	0	59	54	6	.950
— Cleveland (A.L.)	3B-1B-OF	16	30	3	8	3	0	2	7	.267	1	10	0	35	5	0	1.000
1998— Cleveland (A.L.)	3B-1B-2B	15	37	8	8	1	0	2	6	.216	2	10	0	49	8	1	.983
— Detroit (A.L.)■	1B-DH-OF	16	30	6	8	2	0	1	3	.267	3	11	1	43	0	1	.977
— Buffalo (Int'l)■	1B-3B	62	209	46	65	11	0	23	63	.311	58	48	4	282	35	2	.994
American League totals (6 years)		256	657	90	153	33	2	29	91	.233	82	164	3	522	276	23	.972
National League totals (1 year)		8	18	0	1	0	0	0	0	.056	0	3	0	2	8	0	1.000
Major league totals (7 years)		264	675	90	154	33	2	29	91	.228	82	167	3	524	284	23	.972

MANUEL, BARRY   P

PERSONAL: Born August 12, 1965, in Mamou, La. ... 5-11/185. ... Throws right, bats right. ... Full name: Barry Paul Manuel. ... Brother of Ferral Manuel, minor league catcher (1989).

HIGH SCHOOL: Mamou (La.).

COLLEGE: Louisiana State.

TRANSACTIONS/CAREER NOTES: Selected by Texas Rangers organization in second round of free-agent draft (June 2, 1987). ... On Texas disabled list (March 27-June 20, 1993); included rehabilitation assignment to Charlotte (June 11-20). ... Claimed on waivers by Baltimore Orioles (August 9, 1993). ... Granted free agency (October 15, 1994). ... Signed by Ottawa, Montreal Expos organization (February 19, 1995). ... Granted free agency (October 16, 1995). ... Re-signed by Expos (March 31, 1996). ... Traded by Expos to New York Mets for cash (March 28, 1997). ... Granted free agency (October 15, 1997). ... Signed by Arizona Diamondbacks organization (December 18, 1997). ... Granted free agency (October 15, 1998). ... Signed by Seibu Lions of Japan Pacific League (January 19, 1999).

STATISTICAL NOTES: Pitched one inning, combining with Cedric Shaw (seven innings) and Everett Cunningham (one inning) in 2-0 no-hit victory for Tulsa against Arkansas (April 18, 1991).

Year— Team (League)	W	L	Pct.	ERA	G	GS	CG	ShO	Sv.	IP	H	R	ER	BB	SO
1987— GC Rangers (GCL)	0	0	...	18.00	1	0	0	0	0	1	3	2	2	1	1
— Charlotte (Fla. St.)	1	2	.333	6.60	13	5	0	0	0	30	33	24	22	18	19
1988— Charlotte (Fla. St.)	4	3	.571	2.54	37	0	0	0	4	60 1/3	47	24	17	32	55
1989— Tulsa (Texas)	3	4	.429	7.48	11	11	0	0	0	49 1/3	49	44	41	39	40
— Charlotte (Fla. St.)	4	7	.364	4.72	15	14	0	0	0	76 1/3	77	43	40	30	51
1990— Charlotte (Fla. St.)	1	5	.167	2.88	57	0	0	0	*36	56 1/3	39	23	18	30	60
1991— Tulsa (Texas)	2	7	.222	3.29	56	0	0	0	*25	68 1/3	63	29	25	34	45
— Texas (A.L.)	1	0	1.000	1.13	8	0	0	0	0	16	7	2	2	6	5
1992— Oklahoma City (A.A.)	1	8	.111	5.27	27	0	0	0	5	27 1/3	32	24	16	26	11
— Texas (A.L.)	1	0	1.000	4.76	3	0	0	0	0	5 2/3	6	3	3	1	9
— Tulsa (Texas)	2	0	1.000	4.00	16	1	0	0	2	27	28	12	12	16	28

Year Team (League)	W	L	Pct.	ERA	G	GS	CG	ShO	Sv.	IP	H	R	ER	BB	SO
1993— Charlotte (Fla. St.).............	0	0	...	0.00	3	0	0	0	0	4 2/3	6	0	0	2	4
— Oklahoma City (A.A.)..........	2	2	.500	7.99	21	0	0	0	2	23 2/3	29	21	21	16	19
— Rochester (Int'l)■...............	1	1	.500	3.66	9	0	0	0	0	19 2/3	14	8	8	7	11
1994— Rochester (Int'l)................	11	8	.579	5.48	35	20	1	0	4	139 2/3	161	87	85	58	107
1995— Ottawa (Int'l)■.................	5	12	.294	4.59	35	22	1	0	1	127 1/3	125	71	65	50	85
1996— Montreal (N.L.)...............	4	1	.800	3.24	53	0	0	0	0	86	70	34	31	26	62
1997— New York (N.L.)■............	0	1	.000	5.26	19	0	0	0	0	25 2/3	35	18	15	13	21
— Norfolk (Int'l).....................	2	5	.286	4.87	19	8	0	0	0	61	60	36	33	21	52
1998— Arizona (N.L.)■................	1	0	1.000	7.47	13	0	0	0	0	15 2/3	17	14	13	14	12
— Arizona D-backs (Ariz.)	0	0	...	0.00	1	0	0	0	0	2	1	0	0	0	2
— Tucson (PCL)	3	2	.600	2.61	23	0	0	0	0	41 1/3	28	12	12	16	40
A.L. totals (2 years)	2	0	1.000	2.08	11	0	0	0	0	21 2/3	13	5	5	7	14
N.L. totals (3 years)	5	2	.714	4.17	85	0	0	0	0	127 1/3	122	66	59	53	95
Major league totals (5 years)	7	2	.778	3.87	96	0	0	0	0	149	135	71	64	60	109

MANWARING, KIRT — C — ROCKIES

PERSONAL: Born July 15, 1965, in Elmira, N.Y. ... 5-11/198. ... Bats right, throws right. ... Full name: Kirt Dean Manwaring.
HIGH SCHOOL: Horseheads (N.Y.).
COLLEGE: Coastal Carolina (S.C.).
TRANSACTIONS/CAREER NOTES: Selected by Boston Red Sox organization in 12th round of free-agent draft (June 6, 1983); did not sign. ... Selected by San Francisco Giants organization in second round of free-agent draft (June 2, 1986). ... On disabled list (August 31-September 15, 1989 and June 24-July 18, 1990). ... On San Francisco disabled list (May 30-July 11, 1991); included rehabilitation assignments to Phoenix (July 1-8) and San Jose (July 8-11). ... On San Francisco disabled list (July 22-August 6, 1992). ... On San Francisco disabled list (April 10-May 23, 1996); included rehabilitation assignment to Phoenix (May 18-23). ... Traded by Giants to Houston Astros for C Rick Wilkins and cash (July 27, 1996). ... Granted free agency (October 28, 1996). ... Signed by Colorado Rockies (December 9, 1996). ... Granted free agency (October 28, 1998). ... Re-signed by Rockies (December 16, 1998).
HONORS: Won N.L. Gold Glove at catcher (1993).
STATISTICAL NOTES: Led Texas League catchers with 688 total chances and eight double plays in 1987. ... Led N.L. catchers with 12 double plays in 1992 and 10 in 1994.

							BATTING							FIELDING		
Year Team (League)	Pos.	G	AB	R	H	2B	3B	HR	RBI	Avg.	BB	SO	SB	PO	A	E	Avg.
1986— Clinton (Midwest).......	C	49	147	18	36	7	1	2	16	.245	14	26	1	243	31	5	.982
1987— Shreveport (Texas).....	C	98	307	27	82	13	2	2	22	.267	19	33	1	603	*81	4	.994
— San Francisco (N.L.) ..	C	6	7	0	1	0	0	0	0	.143	0	1	0	9	1	1	.909
1988— Phoenix (PCL)	C	81	273	29	77	12	2	2	35	.282	14	32	3	411	51	6	.987
— San Francisco (N.L.) ..	C	40	116	12	29	7	0	1	15	.250	2	21	0	162	24	4	.979
1989— San Francisco (N.L.) ..	C	85	200	14	42	4	2	0	18	.210	11	28	2	289	32	6	.982
1990— Phoenix (PCL)	C	74	247	20	58	10	2	3	14	.235	24	34	0	352	45	4	*.990
— San Francisco (N.L.) ..	C	8	13	0	2	0	1	0	1	.154	0	3	0	22	3	0	1.000
1991— San Francisco (N.L.) ..	C	67	178	16	40	9	0	0	19	.225	9	22	1	315	28	4	.988
— Phoenix (PCL)	C	24	81	8	18	0	0	4	14	.222	8	15	0	100	15	3	.975
— San Jose (Calif.).........	C	1	3	1	0	0	0	0	0	.000	1	1	0	16	0	0	1.000
1992— San Francisco (N.L.) ..	C	109	349	24	85	10	5	4	26	.244	29	42	2	564	68	4	.994
1993— San Francisco (N.L.) ..	C	130	432	48	119	15	1	5	49	.275	41	76	1	739	70	2	*.998
1994— San Francisco (N.L.) ..	C	97	316	30	79	17	1	1	29	.250	25	50	1	541	52	4	.993
1995— San Francisco (N.L.) ..	C	118	379	21	95	15	2	4	36	.251	27	72	1	607	55	7	.990
1996— San Francisco (N.L.) ..	C	49	145	9	34	6	0	1	14	.234	16	24	0	268	26	2	.993
— Phoenix (PCL)	C	4	11	1	2	0	0	0	1	.182	2	0	0	15	3	0	1.000
— Houston (N.L.)■........	C	37	82	5	18	3	0	0	4	.220	3	16	0	171	21	1	.995
1997— Colorado (N.L.)■.......	C	104	337	22	76	6	4	1	27	.226	30	78	1	488	40	3	.994
1998— Colorado (N.L.)	C	110	291	30	72	12	3	2	26	.247	38	49	1	528	48	7	.988
Major league totals (12 years)		960	2845	231	692	104	19	19	264	.243	231	482	10	4703	468	45	.991

CHAMPIONSHIP SERIES RECORD

							BATTING							FIELDING		
Year Team (League)	Pos.	G	AB	R	H	2B	3B	HR	RBI	Avg.	BB	SO	SB	PO	A	E	Avg.
1989— San Francisco (N.L.) ..	C-PH	3	2	0	0	0	0	0	0	.000	0	0	0	5	0	0	1.000

WORLD SERIES RECORD

							BATTING							FIELDING		
Year Team (League)	Pos.	G	AB	R	H	2B	3B	HR	RBI	Avg.	BB	SO	SB	PO	A	E	Avg.
1989— San Francisco (N.L.) ..	C	1	1	1	1	1	0	0	0	1.000	0	0	0	0	0	0	...

MARRERO, ELI — C — CARDINALS

PERSONAL: Born November 17, 1973, in Havana, Cuba. ... 6-1/180. ... Bats right, throws right. ... Full name: Elieser Marrero.
HIGH SCHOOL: Coral Gables (Fla.).
TRANSACTIONS/CAREER NOTES: Selected by St. Louis Cardinals organization in third round of free-agent draft (June 3, 1993). ... On St. Louis disabled list (March 22-April 13, 1998).
STATISTICAL NOTES: Led Texas League catchers with 746 total chances in 1996. ... Led American Association catchers with 750 total chances in 1997.

							BATTING							FIELDING		
Year Team (League)	Pos.	G	AB	R	H	2B	3B	HR	RBI	Avg.	BB	SO	SB	PO	A	E	Avg.
1993— Johnson City (App.) ...	C	18	61	10	22	8	0	2	14	.361	12	9	2	154	18	1	.994
1994— Savannah (S. Atl.)	C	116	421	71	110	16	3	21	79	.261	39	92	5	821	92	•15	.984
1995— St. Peters. (FSL).........	C	107	383	43	81	16	1	10	55	.211	23	55	9	574	52	10	.984

Year Team (League)	Pos.	G	AB	R	H	2B	3B	HR	RBI	Avg.	BB	SO	SB	PO	A	E	Avg.
1996—Arkansas (Texas)	C	116	374	65	101	17	3	19	65	.270	32	55	9	*676	67	3	*.996
1997—Louisville (A.A.)	C	112	395	60	108	21	7	20	68	.273	25	53	4	*675	*68	7	.991
—St. Louis (N.L.)	C	17	45	4	11	2	0	2	7	.244	2	13	4	82	12	3	.969
1998—St. Louis (N.L.)	C-1B	83	254	28	62	18	1	4	20	.244	28	42	6	427	31	4	.991
—Memphis (PCL)	C	32	130	22	31	5	0	7	21	.238	13	23	5	195	17	2	.991
Major league totals (2 years)		100	299	32	73	20	1	6	27	.244	30	55	10	509	43	7	.987

MARTE, DAMASO   P   MARINERS

PERSONAL: Born February 14, 1975, in Santo Domingo, Dominican Republic. ... 6-0/170. ... Throws left, bats left. ... Full name: Damaso Sabinon Marte.
TRANSACTIONS/CAREER NOTES: Signed as non-drafted free agent by Seattle Mariners organization (October 28, 1992). ... On disabled list (April 3-17, 1997). ... On Orlando disabled list (April 2-May 3 and September 2, 1998-remainder of season).

Year Team (League)	W	L	Pct.	ERA	G	GS	CG	ShO	Sv.	IP	H	R	ER	BB	SO
1993—Dom. Mariners (DSL)	2	5	.286	6.55	17	15	2	0	0	56 1/3	62	48	41	50	29
1994—Dom. Mariners (DSL)	7	0	1.000	3.86	17	13	0	0	0	65 1/3	53	41	28	48	80
1995—Everett (Northwest)	2	2	.500	2.21	11	11	5	0	0	36 2/3	25	11	9	10	39
1996—Wis. Rap. (Midw.)	8	6	.571	4.49	26	26	2	1	0	142 1/3	134	82	71	75	115
1997—Lancaster (Calif.)	8	8	.500	4.13	25	25	2	1	0	139 1/3	144	75	64	62	127
1998—Orlando (South.)	7	6	.538	5.27	22	20	0	0	0	121 1/3	136	82	71	47	99

MARTIN, AL   OF   •   PIRATES

PERSONAL: Born November 24, 1967, in West Covina, Calif. ... 6-2/214. ... Bats left, throws left. ... Full name: Albert Lee Martin. ... Formerly known as Albert Scales-Martin. ... Nephew of Rod Martin, linebacker with Oakland/Los Angeles Raiders (1977-88).
HIGH SCHOOL: Rowland (West Covina, Calif.).
COLLEGE: Southern California.
TRANSACTIONS/CAREER NOTES: Selected by Atlanta Braves organization in eighth round of free-agent draft (June 3, 1985). ... Granted free agency (October 15, 1991). ... Signed by Pittsburgh Pirates organization (November 11, 1991). ... On suspended list (September 17-20, 1993). ... On disabled list (July 11, 1994-remainder of season). ... On disabled list (May 22-June 24, 1997); included rehabilitation assignment to Carolina (June 21-23).
RECORDS: Shares major league record for fewest double plays by outfielder (150 or more games)—0 (1996). ... Holds modern N.L. single-season record for fewest putouts by outfielder (150 or more games)—217 (1996). ... Holds N.L. single-season record for fewest chances accepted by outfielder (150 or more games)—222 (1997).
STATISTICAL NOTES: Led Gulf Coast League first basemen with 15 errors in 1985. ... Led American Association with .557 slugging percentage in 1992. ... Led American Association outfielders with six double plays in 1992. ... Career major league grand slams: 1.

Year Team (League)	Pos.	G	AB	R	H	2B	3B	HR	RBI	Avg.	BB	SO	SB	PO	A	E	Avg.
1985—GC Braves (GCL)	1B-OF	40	138	16	32	3	0	0	9	.232	19	36	1	246	13	†15	.945
1986—Sumter (S. Atl.)	1B	44	156	23	38	5	0	1	24	.244	23	36	6	299	12	8	.975
—Idaho Falls (Pio.)	OF-1B	63	242	39	80	17	•6	4	44	.331	20	53	11	272	15	8	.973
1987—Sumter (S. Atl.)	OF-1B	117	375	59	95	18	5	12	64	.253	44	69	27	137	7	9	.941
1988—Burlington (Midw.)	OF	123	480	69	134	21	3	7	42	.279	30	88	40	224	4	8	.966
1989—Durham (Carolina)	OF	128	457	*84	124	26	3	9	48	.271	34	107	27	169	7	7	.962
1990—Greenville (Southern)	OF	133	455	64	110	17	4	11	50	.242	43	102	20	200	8	7	.967
1991—Greenville (Southern)	OF-1B	86	301	38	73	13	3	7	38	.243	32	84	19	134	7	6	.959
—Richmond (Int'l)	OF	44	151	20	42	11	1	5	18	.278	7	33	11	73	4	2	.975
1992—Buffalo (A.A.) ■	OF	125	420	85	128	16	*15	20	59	.305	35	93	20	222	10	8	.967
—Pittsburgh (N.L.)	OF	12	12	1	2	0	1	0	2	.167	0	5	0	6	0	0	1.000
1993—Pittsburgh (N.L.)	OF	143	480	85	135	26	8	18	64	.281	42	122	16	268	6	7	.975
1994—Pittsburgh (N.L.)	OF	82	276	48	79	12	4	9	33	.286	34	56	15	129	8	3	.979
1995—Pittsburgh (N.L.)	OF	124	439	70	124	25	3	13	41	.282	44	92	20	206	8	5	.977
1996—Pittsburgh (N.L.)	OF	155	630	101	189	40	1	18	72	.300	54	116	38	217	5	5	.965
1997—Pittsburgh (N.L.)	OF	113	423	64	123	24	7	13	59	.291	45	83	23	125	8	6	.957
—Carolina (Southern)	OF	3	9	0	1	0	0	0	0	.111	0	0	0	2	0	0	1.000
1998—Pittsburgh (N.L.)	OF-DH	125	440	57	105	15	2	12	47	.239	32	91	20	192	6	3	.985
Major league totals (7 years)		754	2700	426	757	142	26	83	318	.280	251	565	132	1143	41	32	.974

MARTIN, CHANDLER   P   ROCKIES

PERSONAL: Born October 23, 1973, in Salem, Ore. ... 6-1/192. ... Throws right, bats right. ... Full name: Chandler Jay Martin.
COLLEGE: Portland.
TRANSACTIONS/CAREER NOTES: Selected by Colorado Rockies organization in sixth round of free-agent draft (June 1, 1995).

Year Team (League)	W	L	Pct.	ERA	G	GS	CG	ShO	Sv.	IP	H	R	ER	BB	SO
1995—Portland (Northwest)	4	1	.800	1.66	7	7	0	0	0	38	20	10	7	21	34
—Asheville (S. Atl.)	4	3	.571	3.83	8	8	0	0	0	49 1/3	48	23	21	27	32
1996—Asheville (S. Atl.)	9	0	1.000	2.20	14	14	00	0	0	86	65	26	21	31	73
—New Haven (East.)	1	0	1.000	7.20	1	1	0	0	0	5	6	4	4	3	4
—Salem (Carolina)	2	8	.200	5.87	13	13	1	1	0	69	80	56	45	53	59
1997—Salem (Carolina)	1	5	.167	3.97	16	5	0	0	1	45 1/3	46	25	20	25	30
1998—Salem (Carolina)	12	7	.632	*2.48	24	24	*7	0	0	160	136	54	44	43	104

M

MARTIN, NORBERTO   IF

PERSONAL: Born December 10, 1966, in Santo Domingo, Dominican Republic. ... 5-10/182. ... Bats right, throws right. ... Full name: Norberto Edonal Martin. ... Name pronounced mar-TEEN.

TRANSACTIONS/CAREER NOTES: Signed as non-drafted free agent by Chicago White Sox organization (March 27, 1984). ... On Peninsula disabled list (April 10-May 5, 1986). ... On Appleton disabled list (May 14, 1986-remainder of season). ... On disabled list (April 7, 1989-entire season and May 5-June 9, 1991). ... On Chicago disabled list (April 6-June 5, 1996); included rehabilitation assignment to Nashville (May 14-June 1). ... On disabled list (June 20-July 3 and July 21-August 8, 1997). ... Granted free agency (December 21, 1997). ... Signed by Anaheim Angels (January 9, 1998). ... On disabled list (August 6-21, 1998). ... Granted free agency (December 21, 1998).

STATISTICAL NOTES: Led Gulf Coast League shortstops with 37 errors in 1984. ... Led Pacific Coast League second basemen with 681 total chances in 1992. ... Led American Association second basemen with 291 putouts, 438 assists, 18 errors and 747 total chances in 1993. ... Career major league grand slams: 1.

							BATTING								FIELDING		
Year — Team (League)	Pos.	G	AB	R	H	2B	3B	HR	RBI	Avg.	BB	SO	SB	PO	A	E	Avg.
1984— GC Whi. Sox (GCL)	SS-OF	56	205	36	56	8	2	1	30	.273	21	31	18	66	149	†37	.853
1985— Appleton (Midwest)....	SS	30	196	15	19	2	0	0	5	.097	9	23	2	39	86	12	.912
—Niagara Falls (NYP)	SS	60	217	22	55	9	0	1	13	.253	7	41	6	85	173	35	.881
1986— Appleton (Midwest)....	SS	9	33	4	10	2	0	0	2	.303	2	5	1	13	16	6	.829
—GC Whi. Sox (GCL)	PR	1	0	0	0	0	0	0	0	...	0	0	0	...	...	...	...
1987— Char., W.Va. (SAL).....	SS-OF-2B	68	250	44	78	14	1	5	35	.312	17	40	14	84	152	25	.904
—Peninsula (Caro.)	2B	41	162	21	42	6	1	1	18	.259	18	19	11	94	108	15	.931
1988— Tampa (Fla. St.)........	2B	101	360	44	93	10	4	2	33	.258	17	49	24	196	268	20	.959
1989—								Did not play.									
1990— Vancouver (PCL)	2B	130	508	77	135	20	4	3	45	.266	27	63	10	283	324	17	.973
1991— Vancouver (PCL)	2B-SS	93	338	39	94	9	0	0	20	.278	21	38	11	196	265	16	.966
1992— Vancouver (PCL)	2B	135	497	72	143	12	7	0	29	.288	29	44	29	266	*395	•20	.971
1993— Nashville (A.A.)	2B-SS	•137	*580	87	*179	21	6	9	74	.309	26	59	31	†292	†442	†18	.976
—Chicago (A.L.)	2B-DH	8	14	3	5	0	0	0	2	.357	1	1	0	13	9	1	.957
1994— Nashville (A.A.)	S-3-2-O	43	172	26	44	8	0	2	12	.256	10	14	4	47	72	10	.922
—Chicago (A.L.)	2-S-3-0-DH	45	131	19	36	7	1	1	16	.275	9	16	4	58	77	2	.985
1995— Chicago (A.L.)	2-0-DH-3-S	72	160	17	43	7	4	2	17	.269	3	25	5	52	67	7	.944
1996— Chicago (A.L.)	S-DH-2-3	70	140	30	49	7	0	1	14	.350	6	17	10	61	79	6	.959
—Nashville (A.A.)	2B-SS-3B	17	68	9	14	3	0	2	8	.206	4	10	1	27	43	2	.972
1997— Chicago (A.L.)	S-3-2-DH	71	213	24	64	7	1	2	27	.300	6	31	1	50	97	5	.967
1998— Anaheim (A.L.)■........	2-DH-3-O-S	79	195	20	42	2	0	1	13	.215	6	29	3	91	144	4	.983
Major league totals (6 years)		**345**	**853**	**113**	**239**	**30**	**6**	**7**	**89**	**.280**	**31**	**119**	**23**	**325**	**473**	**25**	**.970**

MARTIN, TOM   P   INDIANS

PERSONAL: Born May 21, 1970, in Charleston, S.C. ... 6-1/200. ... Throws left, bats left. ... Full name: Thomas Edgar Martin.

HIGH SCHOOL: Bay (Panama City, Fla.).

TRANSACTIONS/CAREER NOTES: Selected by Baltimore Orioles organization in sixth round of free-agent draft (June 1, 1988). ... Traded by Orioles with 3B Craig Worthington to San Diego Padres organization for P Jim Lewis and OF Steve Martin (February 17, 1992). ... Selected by Atlanta Braves organization from Padres organization in Rule 5 minor league draft (December 13, 1993). ... Released by Braves (January 25, 1994). ... Signed by Houston Astros organization (February 21, 1996). ... On disabled list (May 30-June 15, 1997). ... Selected by Arizona Diamondbacks in second round (29th pick overall) of expansion draft (November 18, 1997). ... Traded by Diamondbacks with 3B Travis Fryman and cash to Cleveland Indians for 3B Matt Williams (December 1, 1997). ... On Cleveland disabled list (April 30-May 18 and August 31-September 19, 1998); included rehabilitation assignments to Buffalo (May 13-18 and September 3-19).

Year — Team (League)	W	L	Pct.	ERA	G	GS	CG	ShO	Sv.	IP	H	R	ER	BB	SO
1989— Bluefield (Appalachian)	3	3	.500	4.62	8	8	0	0	0	39	36	28	20	25	31
—Erie (N.Y.-Penn).................	0	5	.000	6.64	7	7	0	0	0	40²/₃	42	39	30	25	44
1990— Wausau (Midwest)............	2	3	.400	2.48	9	9	0	0	0	40	31	25	11	27	45
1991— Kane County (Midwest)......	4	10	.286	3.64	38	10	0	0	6	99	92	50	40	56	106
1992— High Desert (Calif.)■	0	2	.000	9.37	11	0	0	0	0	16¹/₃	23	19	17	16	10
—Waterloo (Midw.)	2	6	.250	4.25	39	2	0	0	3	55	62	38	26	22	57
1993— Rancho Cuca. (Cal.)	1	4	.200	5.61	47	1	0	0	0	59¹/₃	72	41	37	39	53
1994— Greenville (Southern)■......	5	6	.455	4.62	36	6	0	0	0	74	82	40	38	27	51
1995— Richmond (Int'l)	0	0	...	9.00	7	0	0	0	0	9	10	9	9	10	3
1996— Tucson (PCL)■	0	0	...	0.00	5	0	0	0	0	6	6	0	0	2	1
—Jackson (Texas)	6	2	.750	3.24	57	0	0	0	3	75	71	35	27	42	58
1997— Houston (N.L.)	5	3	.625	2.09	55	0	0	0	2	56	52	13	13	23	36
1998— Cleveland (A.L.)■..............	1	1	.500	12.89	14	0	0	0	0	14²/₃	29	21	21	12	9
—Buffalo (Int'l)	3	1	.750	6.00	41	0	0	0	0	36	46	25	24	13	35
A.L. totals (1 year).................	1	1	.500	12.89	14	0	0	0	0	14²/₃	29	21	21	12	9
N.L. totals (1 year).................	5	3	.625	2.09	55	0	0	0	2	56	52	13	13	23	36
Major league totals (2 years)......	6	4	.600	4.33	69	0	0	0	2	70²/₃	81	34	34	35	45

DIVISION SERIES RECORD

Year — Team (League)	W	L	Pct.	ERA	G	GS	CG	ShO	Sv.	IP	H	R	ER	BB	SO
1997— Houston (N.L.)	0	0	...	0.00	2	0	0	0	0	²/₃	1	1	0	1	0

MARTINEZ, DAVE   OF   DEVIL RAYS

PERSONAL: Born September 26, 1964, in Brooklyn, N.Y. ... 5-10/175. ... Bats left, throws left. ... Full name: David Martinez.

HIGH SCHOOL: Lake Howell (Casselberry, Fla.).

JUNIOR COLLEGE: Valencia Community College (Fla.).

TRANSACTIONS/CAREER NOTES: Selected by Texas Rangers organization in 40th round of free-agent draft (June 7, 1982); did not sign. ... Selected by Chicago Cubs organization in secondary phase of free-agent draft (January 11, 1983). ... On disabled list (April 27, 1984-remainder of season). ... Traded by Cubs to Montreal Expos for OF Mitch Webster (July 14, 1988). ... On disqualified list (October 4-5, 1991). ...

Traded by Expos with P Scott Ruskin and SS Willie Greene to Cincinnati Reds for P John Wetteland and P Bill Risley (December 11, 1991). ... Granted free agency (October 27, 1992). ... Signed by San Francisco Giants (December 9, 1992). ... On San Francisco disabled list (April 30-June 4, 1993); included rehabilitation assignment to Phoenix (June 1-4). ... Granted free agency (October 14, 1994). ... Signed by Chicago White Sox (April 5, 1995). ... Granted free agency (November 3, 1995). ... Re-signed by White Sox (November 14, 1995). ... Granted free agency (October 27, 1997). ... Signed by Tampa Bay Devil Rays (December 4, 1997). ... On disabled list (July 22, 1998-remainder of season).

RECORDS: Shares single-game major league record for most unassisted double plays by first baseman—2 (June 21, 1997).

STATISTICAL NOTES: Career major league grand slams: 2.

							BATTING								FIELDING		
Year Team (League)	Pos.	G	AB	R	H	2B	3B	HR	RBI	Avg.	BB	SO	SB	PO	A	E	Avg.
1983— Quad Cities (Mid.)	OF	44	119	17	29	6	2	0	10	.244	26	30	10	47	8	1	.982
—Geneva (NY-Penn)......	OF	64	241	35	63	15	2	5	33	.261	40	52	16	132	6	8	.945
1984— Quad Cities (Mid.)	OF	12	41	6	9	2	2	0	5	.220	9	13	3	13	2	1	.938
1985— Win.-Salem (Car.)	OF	115	386	52	132	14	4	5	54	*.342	62	35	38	206	11	7	.969
1986— Iowa (Am. Assoc.).......	OF	83	318	52	92	11	5	5	32	.289	36	34	42	214	7	2	.991
—Chicago (N.L.)	OF	53	108	13	15	1	1	1	7	.139	6	22	4	77	2	1	.988
1987— Chicago (N.L.)	OF	142	459	70	134	18	8	8	36	.292	57	96	16	283	10	6	.980
1988— Chicago (N.L.)	OF	75	256	27	65	10	1	4	34	.254	21	46	7	162	2	5	.970
—Montreal (N.L.)■......	OF	63	191	24	49	3	5	2	12	.257	17	48	16	119	2	1	.992
1989— Montreal (N.L.)...........	OF	126	361	41	99	16	7	3	27	.274	27	57	23	199	7	7	.967
1990— Montreal (N.L.)...........	OF-P	118	391	60	109	13	5	11	39	.279	24	48	13	257	6	3	.989
1991— Montreal (N.L.)...........	OF	124	396	47	117	18	5	7	42	.295	20	54	16	213	10	4	.982
1992— Cincinnati (N.L.)■......	OF-1B	135	393	47	100	20	5	3	31	.254	42	54	12	382	18	6	.985
1993— San Fran. (N.L.)■......	OF	91	241	28	58	12	1	5	27	.241	27	39	6	131	6	1	.993
—Phoenix (PCL)	OF	3	15	4	7	0	0	0	2	.467	1	1	1	5	1	0	1.000
1994— San Francisco (N.L.) ..	OF-1B	97	235	23	58	9	3	4	27	.247	21	22	3	256	18	3	.989
1995— Chicago (A.L.)■.........	O-1-DH-P	119	303	49	93	16	4	5	37	.307	32	41	8	392	25	3	.993
1996— Chicago (A.L.)	OF-1B	146	440	85	140	20	8	10	53	.318	52	52	15	368	16	6	.985
1997— Chicago (A.L.)	OF-1B-DH	145	504	78	144	16	6	12	55	.286	55	69	12	485	30	7	.987
1998— Tampa Bay (A.L.)■......	OF-DH-1B	90	309	31	79	11	0	3	20	.256	35	52	8	163	9	1	.994
American League totals (4 years)		500	1556	243	456	63	18	30	165	.293	174	214	43	1408	80	17	.989
National League totals (9 years)		1024	3031	380	804	120	41	48	282	.265	262	486	116	2079	81	37	.983
Major league totals (13 years)		1524	4587	623	1260	183	59	78	447	.275	436	700	159	3487	161	54	.985

RECORD AS PITCHER

Year Team (League)	W	L	Pct.	ERA	G	GS	CG	ShO	Sv.	IP	H	R	ER	BB	SO
1990— Montreal (N.L.).................	0	0	...	54.00	1	0	0	0	0	$\frac{1}{3}$	2	2	2	2	0
1995— Chicago (A.L.)■	0	0	...	0.00	1	0	0	0	0	1	0	0	0	2	0
A.L. totals (1 year)	0	0	...	0.00	1	0	0	0	0	1	0	0	0	2	0
N.L. totals (1 year)	0	0	...	54.00	1	0	0	0	0	$\frac{1}{3}$	2	2	2	2	0
Major league totals (2 years)......	0	0	...	13.50	2	0	0	0	0	$1\frac{1}{3}$	2	2	2	4	0

MARTINEZ, DENNIS   P

PERSONAL: Born May 14, 1955, in Granada, Nicaragua. ... 6-1/180. ... Throws right, bats right. ... Full name: Jose Dennis Martinez.

TRANSACTIONS/CAREER NOTES: Signed as non-drafted free agent by Baltimore Orioles organization (December 10, 1973). ... On Baltimore disabled list (March 28-April 20, 1980). ... On Baltimore disabled list (June 3-July 10, 1980); included rehabilitation assignment to Miami (July 1-10). ... On Baltimore disabled list (April 28-June 16, 1986); included rehabilitation assignment to Rochester (May 21-June 10). ... Traded by Orioles to Montreal Expos for a player to be named later (June 16, 1986); Orioles acquired IF Rene Gonzales to complete deal (December 16, 1986). ... Granted free agency (November 12, 1986). ... Signed by Miami, independent (April 14, 1987). ... Released by Miami (May 6, 1987). ... Signed by Expos organization (May 6, 1987). ... Granted free agency (November 9, 1987). ... Re-signed by Expos (December 18, 1987). ... Granted free agency (October 25, 1993). ... Signed by Cleveland Indians (December 2, 1993). ... On disabled list (June 29-July 24, July 31-August 27 and August 30, 1996-remainder of season). ... Granted free agency (November 18, 1996). ... Signed by Seattle Mariners organization (February 20, 1997). ... Released by Mariners (May 24, 1997). ... Signed by Atlanta Braves organization (January 30, 1998). ... Granted free agency (November 2, 1998).

HONORS: Named International League Pitcher of the Year (1976).

STATISTICAL NOTES: Pitched 4-0 one-hit, complete-game victory against California (June 5, 1985). ... Tied for N.L. lead with 10 balks in 1988. ... Pitched 2-0 perfect game against Los Angeles (July 28, 1991).

MISCELLANEOUS: Had sacrifice hit in one game as pinch hitter (1991). ... Had sacrifice fly in one game as pinch hitter (1993).

Year Team (League)	W	L	Pct.	ERA	G	GS	CG	ShO	Sv.	IP	H	R	ER	BB	SO
1974— Miami (Florida St.)	15	6	.714	2.06	25	25	10	4	0	179	124	48	41	53	162
1975— Miami (Florida St.)	12	4	.750	2.61	20	20	9	3	0	145	125	54	42	35	114
—Asheville (South.)...............	4	1	.800	2.60	6	6	4	1	0	45	45	16	13	12	18
—Rochester (Int'l)...............	0	0	...	5.40	2	0	0	0	0	5	7	4	3	2	4
1976— Rochester (Int'l)...............	*14	8	.636	*2.50	25	23	*16	1	0	180	148	64	50	50	*140
—Baltimore (A.L.)................	1	2	.333	2.57	4	2	1	0	0	28	23	8	8	8	18
1977— Baltimore (A.L.)................	14	7	.667	4.10	42	13	5	0	4	167	157	86	76	64	107
1978— Baltimore (A.L.)................	16	11	.593	3.52	40	38	15	2	0	276	257	121	108	93	142
1979— Baltimore (A.L.)................	15	16	.484	3.67	40	*39	*18	3	0	*292	279	129	119	78	132
1980— Baltimore (A.L.)................	6	4	.600	3.96	25	12	2	0	1	100	103	44	44	44	42
—Miami (Florida St.).............	0	0	...	0.00	2	2	0	0	0	12	3	1	0	5	7
1981— Baltimore (A.L.)................	•14	5	.737	3.32	25	24	9	2	0	179	173	84	66	62	88
1982— Baltimore (A.L.)................	16	12	.571	4.21	40	39	10	2	0	252	262	123	118	87	111
1983— Baltimore (A.L.)................	7	16	.304	5.53	32	25	4	0	0	153	209	108	94	45	71
1984— Baltimore (A.L.)................	6	9	.400	5.02	34	20	2	0	0	$141\frac{2}{3}$	145	81	79	37	77
1985— Baltimore (A.L.)................	13	11	.542	5.15	33	31	3	1	0	180	203	110	103	63	68
1986— Baltimore (A.L.)................	0	0	...	6.75	4	0	0	0	0	$6\frac{2}{3}$	11	5	5	2	2
—Rochester (Int'l)...............	2	1	.667	6.05	4	4	0	0	0	$19\frac{1}{3}$	18	14	13	9	14
—Montreal (N.L.)................	3	6	.333	4.59	19	15	1	1	0	98	103	52	50	28	63
1987— Miami (Florida St.)■........	1	1	.500	6.16	3	3	0	0	0	19	21	14	13	3	11
—Indianapolis (A.A.)■........	3	2	.600	4.46	7	7	1	1	0	$38\frac{1}{3}$	32	20	19	13	30
—Montreal (N.L.)................	11	4	*.733	3.30	22	22	2	1	0	$144\frac{2}{3}$	133	59	53	40	84

Year	Team (League)	W	L	Pct.	ERA	G	GS	CG	ShO	Sv.	IP	H	R	ER	BB	SO
1988—	Montreal (N.L.)...............	15	13	.536	2.72	34	34	9	2	0	235 1/3	215	94	71	55	120
1989—	Montreal (N.L.)...............	16	7	.696	3.18	34	33	5	2	0	232	227	88	82	49	142
1990—	Montreal (N.L.)...............	10	11	.476	2.95	32	32	7	2	0	226	191	80	74	49	156
1991—	Montreal (N.L.)...............	14	11	.560	*2.39	31	31	•9	*5	0	222	187	70	59	62	123
1992—	Montreal (N.L.)...............	16	11	.593	2.47	32	32	6	0	0	226 1/3	172	75	62	60	147
1993—	Montreal (N.L.)...............	15	9	.625	3.85	35	34	2	0	1	224 2/3	211	110	96	64	138
1994—	Cleveland (A.L.)■.............	11	6	.647	3.52	24	24	7	3	0	176 2/3	166	75	69	44	92
1995—	Cleveland (A.L.)...............	12	5	.706	3.08	28	28	3	2	0	187	174	71	64	46	99
1996—	Cleveland (A.L.)...............	9	6	.600	4.50	20	20	1	1	0	112	122	63	56	37	48
1997—	Seattle (A.L.)■.................	1	5	.167	7.71	9	9	0	0	0	49	65	46	42	29	17
1998—	Atlanta (N.L.)■.................	4	6	.400	4.45	53	5	1	1	2	91	109	53	45	19	62
A.L. totals (15 years)		141	115	.551	4.11	400	324	80	16	5	2300	2349	1154	1051	739	1114
N.L. totals (9 years)		104	78	.571	3.13	292	238	42	14	3	1700	1548	681	592	426	1035
Major league totals (23 years)		245	193	.559	3.70	692	562	122	30	8	4000	3897	1835	1643	1165	2149

DIVISION SERIES RECORD

Year	Team (League)	W	L	Pct.	ERA	G	GS	CG	ShO	Sv.	IP	H	R	ER	BB	SO
1995—	Cleveland (A.L.)................	0	0	. . .	3.00	1	1	0	0	0	6	5	2	2	0	2
1998—	Atlanta (N.L.).....................							Did not play.								
Div. series totals (1 years)		0	0	. . .	3.00	1	1	0	0	0	6	5	2	2	0	2

CHAMPIONSHIP SERIES RECORD

Year	Team (League)	W	L	Pct.	ERA	G	GS	CG	ShO	Sv.	IP	H	R	ER	BB	SO
1979—	Baltimore (A.L.).................	0	0	. . .	3.24	1	1	0	0	0	8 1/3	8	3	3	0	4
1983—	Baltimore (A.L.).................							Did not play.								
1995—	Cleveland (A.L.)................	1	1	.500	2.03	2	2	0	0	0	13 1/3	10	3	3	3	7
1998—	Atlanta (N.L.).....................	1	0	1.000	0.00	4	0	0	0	0	3 1/3	1	0	0	2	0
Champ. series totals (3 years)		2	1	.667	2.16	7	3	0	0	0	25	19	6	6	5	11

NOTES: Member of World Series championship team (1983).

WORLD SERIES RECORD

Year	Team (League)	W	L	Pct.	ERA	G	GS	CG	ShO	Sv.	IP	H	R	ER	BB	SO
1979—	Baltimore (A.L.).................	0	0	. . .	18.00	2	1	0	0	0	2	6	4	4	0	0
1983—	Baltimore (A.L.).................							Did not play.								
1995—	Cleveland (A.L.)................	0	1	.000	3.48	2	2	0	0	0	10 1/3	12	4	4	8	5
World Series totals (2 years)		0	1	.000	5.84	4	3	0	0	0	12 1/3	18	8	8	8	5

ALL-STAR GAME RECORD

Year	League	W	L	Pct.	ERA	GS	CG	ShO	Sv.	IP	H	R	ER	BB	SO
1990—	National	0	0	. . .	0.00	0	0	0	0	1	0	0	0	0	1
1991—	National	0	1	.000	13.50	0	0	0	0	2	4	3	3	0	0
1992—	National	0	0	. . .	0.00	0	0	0	0	1	0	0	0	1	1
1995—	American	0	0	. . .	4.50	0	0	0	0	2	1	1	1	0	0
All-Star totals (4 years)		0	1	.000	6.00	0	0	0	0	6	5	4	4	1	2

M

MARTINEZ, EDGAR   DH   MARINERS

PERSONAL: Born January 2, 1963, in New York. ... 5-11/200. ... Bats right, throws right. ... Cousin of Carmelo Martinez, first baseman/outfielder with six major league teams (1983-91).

HIGH SCHOOL: Dorado (Puerto Rico).

COLLEGE: American College (Puerto Rico).

TRANSACTIONS/CAREER NOTES: Signed as non-drafted free agent by Seattle Mariners organization (December 19, 1982). ... On Seattle disabled list (April 4-May 17, 1993). ... On Seattle disabled list (June 15-July 21, 1993); included rehabilitation assignment to Jacksonville (July 17-21). ... On Seattle disabled list (August 17, 1993-remainder of season). ... On disabled list (April 16-May 6, 1994 and July 21-August 12, 1996).

RECORDS: Shares A.L. single-game record for most errors by third baseman—4 (May 6, 1990).

HONORS: Named third baseman on THE SPORTING NEWS A.L. All-Star team (1992). ... Named third baseman on THE SPORTING NEWS A.L. Silver Slugger team (1992). ... Named designated hitter on THE SPORTING NEWS A.L. All-Star team (1995 and 1997). ... Named designated hitter on THE SPORTING NEWS A.L. Silver Slugger team (1995 and 1997).

STATISTICAL NOTES: Led Southern League third basemen with 360 total chances and 34 double plays in 1985. ... Led Southern League with 12 sacrifice flies in 1985. ... Led Southern League third basemen with .960 fielding percentage in 1986. ... Led Pacific Coast League third basemen with 389 total chances and 31 double plays in 1987. ... Led A.L. in on-base percentage with .479 in 1995 and .429 in 1998. ... Hit three home runs in one game (July 6, 1996). ... Career major league grand slams: 2.

MISCELLANEOUS: Holds Seattle Mariners franchise all-time records for most doubles (337) and highest batting average (.318).

Year	Team (League)	Pos.	G	AB	R	H	2B	3B	HR	RBI	Avg.	BB	SO	SB	PO	A	E	Avg.
1983—	Bellingham (N'west)...	3B	32	104	14	18	1	1	0	5	.173	18	24	1	22	58	6	.930
1984—	Wausau (Midwest).....	3B	126	433	72	131	32	2	15	66	.303	84	57	11	85	246	25	.930
1985—	Chattanooga (Sou.).....	3B	111	357	43	92	15	5	3	47	.258	71	30	1	*94	*247	19	*.947
	—Calgary (PCL).........	3B-2B	20	68	8	24	7	1	0	14	.353	12	7	1	15	44	4	.937
1986—	Chattanooga (Sou.).....	3B-2B	132	451	71	119	29	5	6	74	.264	89	35	2	94	263	15	†.960
1987—	Calgary (PCL)............	3B	129	438	75	144	31	1	10	66	.329	82	47	3	*91	*278	20	.949
	—Seattle (A.L.)	3B-DH	13	43	6	16	5	2	0	5	.372	2	5	0	13	19	0	1.000
1988—	Calgary (PCL)............	3B-2B	95	331	63	120	19	4	8	64	*.363	66	40	9	48	185	20	.921
	—Seattle (A.L.)	3B	14	32	0	9	4	0	0	5	.281	4	7	0	5	8	1	.929
1989—	Seattle (A.L.)	3B	65	171	20	41	5	0	2	20	.240	17	26	2	40	72	6	.949
	—Calgary (PCL).........	3B-2B	32	113	30	39	11	0	3	23	.345	22	13	2	22	56	12	.867
1990—	Seattle (A.L.)	3B-DH	144	487	71	147	27	2	11	49	.302	74	62	1	89	259	*27	.928
1991—	Seattle (A.L.)	3B-DH	150	544	98	167	35	1	14	52	.307	84	72	0	84	299	15	.962

Year	Team (League)	Pos.	G	AB	R	H	2B	3B	HR	RBI	Avg.	BB	SO	SB	PO	A	E	Avg.
1992—Seattle (A.L.)	3B-DH-1B	135	528	100	181	•46	3	18	73	*.343	54	61	14	88	211	17	.946
1993—Seattle (A.L.)	DH-3B	42	135	20	32	7	0	4	13	.237	28	19	0	5	11	2	.889
—Jacksonville (Sou.)	DH	4	14	2	5	0	0	1	3	.357	2	0	0	...	...	...	...
1994—Seattle (A.L.)	3B-DH	89	326	47	93	23	1	13	51	.285	53	42	6	44	128	9	.950
1995—Seattle (A.L.)	DH-3B-1B	•145	511	•121	182	•52	0	29	113	*.356	116	87	4	30	4	2	.944
1996—Seattle (A.L.)	DH-1-3-O	139	499	121	163	52	2	26	103	.327	123	84	3	29	1	1	.968
1997—Seattle (A.L.)	DH-1B-3B	155	542	104	179	35	1	28	108	.330	119	86	2	68	4	1	.986
1998—Seattle (A.L.)	DH-1B	154	556	86	179	46	1	29	102	.322	106	96	1	22	6	0	1.000
Major league totals (12 years)		1245	4374	794	1389	337	13	174	694	.318	780	647	33	517	1022	81	.950

DIVISION SERIES RECORD

RECORDS: Shares single-game records for most runs batted in—7; and most home runs—2 (October 7, 1995). ... Holds career record for highest slugging percentage (20 or more at-bats)—.811.
NOTES: Shares postseason single-game record for most RBIs—7 (October 7, 1995).

Year	Team (League)	Pos.	G	AB	R	H	2B	3B	HR	RBI	Avg.	BB	SO	SB	PO	A	E	Avg.
1995—Seattle (A.L.)	DH	5	21	6	12	3	0	2	10	.571	6	2	0	...	...	...	...
1997—Seattle (A.L.)	DH	4	16	2	3	0	0	2	3	.188	0	3	0	...	...	...	...
Division series totals (2 years)		9	37	8	15	3	0	4	13	.405	6	5	0	0	0	0	...

CHAMPIONSHIP SERIES RECORD

Year	Team (League)	Pos.	G	AB	R	H	2B	3B	HR	RBI	Avg.	BB	SO	SB	PO	A	E	Avg.
1995—Seattle (A.L.)	DH	6	23	0	2	0	0	0	0	.087	2	5	1	...	...	...	...

ALL-STAR GAME RECORD

Year	League	Pos.	AB	R	H	2B	3B	HR	RBI	Avg.	BB	SO	SB	PO	A	E	Avg.
1992—American	PH	1	0	0	0	0	0	0	.000	0	0	0	...	...	...	...
1995—American	DH	3	0	0	0	0	0	0	.000	0	1	0	...	...	...	...
1996—American	PH	1	0	0	0	0	0	0	.000	0	0	0	...	...	...	...
1997—American	DH	2	1	2	0	0	1	1	1.000	0	0	0	...	...	...	...
All-Star Game totals (4 years)		7	1	2	0	0	1	1	.286	0	1	0	...	...	...	...

MARTINEZ, FELIX   SS   ROYALS

PERSONAL: Born May 18, 1974, in Nagua, Dominican Republic. ... 6-0/180. ... Bats both, throws right.
HIGH SCHOOL: Solome Urena (Nagua, Dominican Republic).
TRANSACTIONS/CAREER NOTES: Contract purchased by Kansas City Royals organization from Hiroshima Toyo Carp of Japan Central League (March 5, 1993). ... Suspended four games by American League (June 5, 1998) to be served in 1999 season.
STATISTICAL NOTES: Led Texas League shortstops with 643 total chances in 1993.

M

Year	Team (League)	Pos.	G	AB	R	H	2B	3B	HR	RBI	Avg.	BB	SO	SB	PO	A	E	Avg.
1993—GC Royals (GCL)	SS-2B-3B	57	165	23	42	5	1	0	12	.255	17	26	22	79	136	30	.878
1994—Wilmington (Caro.)	SS	117	400	65	107	16	4	2	43	.268	30	91	19	177	329	30	.944
1995—Wichita (Texas)	SS	127	426	53	112	15	3	3	30	.263	31	71	*44	*222	371	*50	.922
1996—Omaha (A.A.)	SS	118	395	54	93	13	3	5	35	.235	44	79	18	177	374	*42	.929
1997—Omaha (A.A.)	SS	112	410	55	104	19	4	2	36	.254	29	86	21	175	312	*36	.931
—Kansas City (A.L.)	SS-DH	16	31	3	7	1	1	0	3	.226	6	8	0	17	22	1	.975
1998—Kansas City (A.L.)	SS-2B	34	85	7	11	1	1	0	5	.129	5	21	3	49	80	6	.956
—Omaha (Pacific Coast)	SS-2B	51	164	27	41	8	3	2	16	.250	15	40	6	74	135	14	.937
Major league totals (2 years)		50	116	10	18	2	2	0	8	.155	11	29	3	66	102	7	.960

MARTINEZ, GREG   OF   BREWERS

PERSONAL: Born January 27, 1972, in Las Vegas. ... 5-10/173. ... Bats both, throws right. ... Full name: Gregory Alfred Martinez.
HIGH SCHOOL: Chaparral (Las Vegas).
JUNIOR COLLEGE: Barstow (Calif.) Community College.
TRANSACTIONS/CAREER NOTES: Selected by Milwaukee Brewers organization in 24th round of free-agent draft (June 3, 1993).
STATISTICAL NOTES: Led International League with 10 sacrifice hits in 1998.

Year	Team (League)	Pos.	G	AB	R	H	2B	3B	HR	RBI	Avg.	BB	SO	SB	PO	A	E	Avg.
1993—Ariz. Brewers (Ariz.)	OF	5	19	6	12	0	00	0	3	.632	4	0	7	9	1	1	.909
—Helena (Pioneer)	OF	52	183	45	53	4	2	0	19	.290	30	26	29	85	7	1	.989
1994—Beloit (Midwest)	OF	81	224	39	62	8	1	0	20	.277	25	32	27	133	8	0	1.000
1995—Stockton (California)	OF	114	410	80	113	8	2	0	43	.276	69	64	55	253	7	4	.985
1996—Stockton (California)	OF	73	286	51	82	5	1	0	26	.287	29	34	30	141	5	0	1.000
—El Paso (Texas)	OF	41	166	27	52	2	2	1	21	.313	13	19	14	99	0	2	.980
1997—El Paso (Texas)	OF	95	381	75	111	10	10	1	29	.291	32	55	39	193	13	1	*.995
—Tucson (PCL)	OF	3	12	2	5	2	0	0	3	.417	0	1	0	4	0	0	1.000
1998—Milwaukee (N.L.)	OF	13	3	2	0	0	0	0	0	.000	1	2	2	0	0	0	...
—Louisville (Int'l)	OF	115	376	65	98	4	11	4	25	.261	51	80	43	219	5	2	.991
Major league totals (1 year)		13	3	2	0	0	0	0	0	.000	1	2	2	0	0	0	...

MARTINEZ, JAVIER　　　　　P　　　　　PIRATES

PERSONAL: Born February 5, 1977, in Bayamon, Puerto Rico. ... 6-2/235. ... Throws right, bats right. ... Full name: Javier Antonio Martinez.
HIGH SCHOOL: Liceo (Bayamon, Puerto Rico).
TRANSACTIONS/CAREER NOTES: Selected by Chicago Cubs organization in third round of free-agent draft (June 2, 1994). ... On Rockford disabled list (April 5-July 10, 1996). ... Selected by Oakland Athletics from Cubs organization in Rule 5 major league draft (December 15, 1997). ... Traded by A's to Pittsburgh Pirates for cash (December 15, 1997).

Year　Team (League)	W	L	Pct.	ERA	G	GS	CG	ShO	Sv.	IP	H	R	ER	BB	SO
1994— Huntington (Appal.)............	2	1	.667	3.55	8	8	0	0	0	33	21	18	13	19	28
1995— Rockford (Midwest)	6	6	.500	3.97	18	18	1	0	0	104 1/3	100	56	46	39	53
1996— GC Cubs (GCL).................	2	1	.667	0.60	3	3	0	0	0	15	11	4	1	6	15
— Rockford (Midwest)	4	3	.571	3.36	10	10	3	0	0	59	49	26	22	30	53
1997— Daytona (Fla. St.)	2	6	.250	5.79	9	9	2	0	0	51 1/3	65	40	33	26	34
— Rockford (Midwest)	1	7	.125	5.70	17	17	1	0	0	79	85	61	50	50	70
1998— Pittsburgh (N.L.)■	0	1	.000	4.83	37	0	0	0	0	41	39	32	22	34	42
Major league totals (1 year)........	**0**	**1**	**.000**	**4.83**	**37**	**0**	**0**	**0**	**0**	**41**	**39**	**32**	**22**	**34**	**42**

MARTINEZ, MANNY　　　　　OF　　　　　EXPOS

PERSONAL: Born October 3, 1970, in San Pedro de Macoris, Dominican Republic. ... 6-2/169. ... Bats right, throws right. ... Full name: Manuel DeJesus Martinez.
TRANSACTIONS/CAREER NOTES: Signed as non-drafted free agent by Oakland Athletics organization (March 9, 1988). ... Played in Dominican Summer League (1988-89). ... Granted free agency (October 15, 1994). ... Signed by Chicago Cubs organization (February 13, 1995). ... Granted free agency (October 15, 1995). ... Signed by Seattle Mariners organization (January 29, 1996). ... Claimed on waivers by Philadelphia Phillies organization (July 11, 1996). ... Granted free agency (October 15, 1996). ... Signed by Pittsburgh Pirates organization (December 19, 1996). ... On Calgary disabled list (April 30-May 8 and June 20-27, 1997). ... Claimed on waivers by Montreal Expos (December 17, 1998).
STATISTICAL NOTES: Tied for Northwest League lead in double plays by outfielder with three in 1990. ... Led American Association outfielders with 302 total chances in 1995.

Year　Team (League)	Pos.	G	AB	R	H	2B	3B	HR	RBI	Avg.	BB	SO	SB	PO	A	E	Avg.
1990— S. Oregon (N'west).....	OF-P	66	244	36	60	5	0	2	17	.246	16	59	6	124	9	6	.957
1991— Modesto (California) ..	OF	125	502	73	136	32	3	3	55	.271	34	80	26	267	13	8	.972
1992— Modesto (California) ..	OF	121	495	70	125	23	1	9	45	.253	39	75	17	232	12	10	.961
1993— San Bern. (Calif.)........	OF	109	459	88	148	26	3	11	52	.322	41	60	28	222	15	4	.983
— Tacoma (PCL)	OF	20	59	9	18	2	0	1	6	.305	4	12	2	33	6	0	1.000
1994— Tacoma (PCL)	OF	*137	*536	76	137	25	5	9	60	.256	28	72	18	*322	11	9	.974
1995— Iowa (Am. Assoc.)■ ..	OF	122	397	63	115	17	•8	8	49	.290	20	64	11	*281	16	5	.983
1996— Tacoma (PCL)■	OF	66	277	54	87	15	1	4	24	.314	23	41	14	181	11	5	.975
— Seattle (A.L.)	OF	9	17	3	4	2	1	0	3	.235	3	5	2	12	2	0	1.000
— Scran./W.B. (Int'l)■■...	OF	17	67	8	14	1	1	0	5	.209	4	17	3	40	0	1	.976
— Philadelphia (N.L.).......	OF	13	36	2	8	0	2	0	0	.222	1	11	2	20	1	1	.955
1997— Calgary (PCL)■.........	OF	109	420	78	139	34	1	16	66	.331	33	80	17	196	7	5	.976
1998— Nashville (PCL)	OF-2B	22	75	12	18	5	0	1	6	.240	7	20	5	31	2	2	.943
— Pittsburgh (N.L.)	OF-DH	73	180	21	45	11	2	6	24	.250	9	44	0	92	0	1	.989
American League totals (1 year)		9	17	3	4	2	1	0	3	.235	3	5	2	12	2	0	1.000
National League totals (2 years)		86	216	23	53	11	4	6	24	.245	10	55	2	112	1	2	.983
Major league totals (2 years)		95	233	26	57	13	5	6	27	.245	13	60	4	124	3	2	.984

RECORD AS PITCHER

Year　Team (League)	W	L	Pct.	ERA	G	GS	CG	ShO	Sv.	IP	H	R	ER	BB	SO
1990— S. Oregon (N'west)............	0	0	. . .	45.00	66	0	0	0	0	1	5	5	5	2	0

MARTINEZ, PEDRO J.　　　　　P　　　　　RED SOX

PERSONAL: Born July 25, 1971, in Manoguayabo, Dominican Republic. ... 5-11/170. ... Throws right, bats right. ... Full name: Pedro Jaime Martinez. ... Brother of Ramon J. Martinez, pitcher with Los Angeles Dodgers (1988-98); and brother of Jesus Martinez, pitcher in Los Angeles Dodgers (1991-97) and Cincinnati Reds (1998) organizations.
COLLEGE: Ohio Dominican College (Dominican Republic).
TRANSACTIONS/CAREER NOTES: Signed as non-drafted free agent by Los Angeles Dodgers organization (June 18, 1988). ... On Albuquerque disabled list (June 20-July 2 and August 3-August 25, 1992). ... Traded by Dodgers to Montreal Expos for 2B Delino DeShields (November 19, 1993). ... On suspended list (April 1-9, 1997). ... Traded by Expos to Boston Red Sox for P Carl Pavano and a player to be named later (November 18, 1997); Expos acquired P Tony Armas Jr. to complete deal (December 18, 1997).
HONORS: Named Minor League Player of the Year by THE SPORTING NEWS (1991). ... Named N.L. Pitcher of the Year by THE SPORTING NEWS (1997). ... Named righthanded pitcher on THE SPORTING NEWS N.L. All-Star team (1997). ... Named N.L. Cy Young Award winner by Baseball Writers' Association of America (1997). ... Named righthanded pitcher on THE SPORTING NEWS A.L. All-Star team (1998).
STATISTICAL NOTES: Led N.L. with 11 hit batsmen in 1994. ... Pitched nine perfect innings against San Diego, before being relieved after yielding leadoff double in 10th inning (June 3, 1995). ... Tied for N.L. lead with 16 sacrifice hits in 1996. ... Pitched 2-0 one-hit, complete-game victory against Cincinnati (July 13, 1997).

Year　Team (League)	W	L	Pct.	ERA	G	GS	CG	ShO	Sv.	IP	H	R	ER	BB	SO
1988— Dom. Dodgers (DSL)	5	1	.833	3.10	8	7	1	0	0	49 1/3	45	25	17	16	28
1989— Dom. Dodgers (DSL)	7	2	.778	2.73	13	7	2	3	1	85 2/3	59	30	26	25	63
1990— Great Falls (Pio.)	8	3	.727	3.62	14	•14	0	0	0	77	74	39	31	40	82
1991— Bakersfield (California) ..	8	0	1.000	2.05	10	10	0	0	0	61 1/3	41	17	14	19	83
— San Antonio (Tex.)	7	5	.583	1.76	12	12	4	•3	0	76 2/3	57	21	15	31	74
— Albuquerque (PCL)............	3	3	.500	3.66	6	6	0	0	0	39 1/3	28	17	16	16	35
1992— Albuquerque (PCL)	7	6	.538	3.81	20	20	3	1	0	125 1/3	104	57	53	57	124
— Los Angeles (N.L.)	0	1	.000	2.25	2	1	0	0	0	8	6	2	2	1	8

Year Team (League)	W	L	Pct.	ERA	G	GS	CG	ShO	Sv.	IP	H	R	ER	BB	SO
1993—Albuquerque (PCL)	0	0	...	3.00	1	1	0	0	0	3	1	1	1	1	4
—Los Angeles (N.L.)	10	5	.667	2.61	65	2	0	0	2	107	76	34	31	57	119
1994—Montreal (N.L.)■	11	5	.688	3.42	24	23	1	1	1	144 2/3	115	58	55	45	142
1995—Montreal (N.L.)	14	10	.583	3.51	30	30	2	2	0	194 2/3	158	79	76	66	174
1996—Montreal (N.L.)	13	10	.565	3.70	33	33	4	1	0	216 2/3	189	100	89	70	222
1997—Montreal (N.L.)	17	8	.680	*1.90	31	31	*13	4	0	241 1/3	158	65	51	67	305
1998—Boston (A.L.)■	19	7	.731	2.89	33	33	3	2	0	233 2/3	188	82	75	67	251
A.L. totals (1 year)	19	7	.731	2.89	33	33	3	2	0	233 2/3	188	82	75	67	251
N.L. totals (6 years)	65	39	.625	3.00	185	120	20	8	3	912 1/3	702	338	304	306	970
Major league totals (7 years)	84	46	.646	2.98	218	153	23	10	3	1146	890	420	379	373	1221

DIVISION SERIES RECORD

Year Team (League)	W	L	Pct.	ERA	G	GS	CG	ShO	Sv.	IP	H	R	ER	BB	SO
1998—Boston (A.L.)	1	0	1.000	3.86	1	1	0	0	0	7	6	3	3	0	8

ALL-STAR GAME RECORD

Year League	W	L	Pct.	ERA	GS	CG	ShO	Sv.	IP	H	R	ER	BB	SO
1996—National	0	0	...	0.00	0	0	0	0	1	2	0	0	0	1
1997—National	0	0	...	0.00	0	0	0	0	1	0	0	0	0	2
1998—American							Did not play.							
All-Star totals (2 years)	0	0	...	0.00	0	0	0	0	2	2	0	0	0	3

MARTINEZ, RAMON E.　　　　2B　　　　GIANTS

PERSONAL: Born October 10, 1972, in Philadelphia. ... 6-1/187. ... Bats right, throws right. ... Full name: Ramon E. Martinez.
HIGH SCHOOL: Escuela Superior Catholica (Bayamon, Puerto Rico).
JUNIOR COLLEGE: Vernon (Texas) Regional Junior College.
TRANSACTIONS/CAREER NOTES: Signed as non-drafted free agent by Kansas City Royals organization (January 15, 1994). ... Traded by Royals to San Francisco Giants (December 9, 1996); completing deal in which Giants traded P Jamie Brewington to Royals for a player to be named later (November 26, 1996).
STATISTICAL NOTES: Led Texas League with 18 sacrifice hits and nine sacrifice flies in 1995. ... Led Texas League second basemen with .984 fielding percentage in 1995. ... Led American Association with 13 sacrifice hits in 1996.

Year Team (League)	Pos.	G	AB	R	H	2B	3B	HR	RBI	Avg.	BB	SO	SB	PO	A	E	Avg.
1993—GC Royals (GCL)	2B-OF	57	165	23	42	5	1	0	12	.255	17	26	22	72	108	6	.968
—Wilmington (Caro.)	2B-SS	24	75	8	19	4	0	0	6	.253	11	9	1	52	72	6	.954
1994—Wilmington (Caro.)	2B	90	325	40	87	13	2	2	35	.268	35	25	6	176	249	16	.964
—Rockford (Midwest)	2B	6	18	3	5	0	0	0	3	.278	4	2	1	9	12	1	.955
1995—Wichita (Texas)	2B-SS	103	393	58	108	20	2	3	51	.275	42	50	11	186	311	9	†.982
1996—Omaha (A.A.)	2B	85	320	35	81	12	3	6	41	.253	21	34	3	163	207	12	.969
—Wichita (Texas)	2B	26	93	16	32	4	1	1	8	.344	7	8	4	47	84	6	.956
1997—Shreveport (Texas)■	SS	105	404	72	129	32	4	5	54	.319	40	48	4	167	370	18	.968
—Phoenix (PCL)	2B-SS	18	57	6	16	2	0	1	7	.281	5	9	1	26	44	3	.959
1998—Fresno (Pacific Coast)	2B-SS	98	364	58	114	21	2	14	59	.313	38	42	0	209	280	10	.980
—San Francisco (N.L.)	2B	19	19	4	6	1	0	0	0	.316	4	2	0	15	20	0	1.000
Major league totals (1 year)		19	19	4	6	1	0	0	0	.316	4	2	0	15	20	0	1.000

M

MARTINEZ, RAMON J.　　　　P

PERSONAL: Born March 22, 1968, in Santo Domingo, Dominican Republic. ... 6-4/184. ... Throws right, bats both. ... Full name: Ramon Jaime Martinez. ... Brother of Pedro J. Martinez, pitcher, Boston Red Sox; and brother of Jesus Martinez, pitcher in Los Angeles Dodgers (1991-97) and Cincinnati Reds (1998) organizations.
HIGH SCHOOL: Liceo Secunderia Las Americas (Dominican Republic).
TRANSACTIONS/CAREER NOTES: Signed as non-drafted free agent by Los Angeles Dodgers organization (September 1, 1984). ... On suspended list (July 8-12, 1993). ... Granted free agency (November 1, 1995). ... Re-signed by Dodgers (November 16, 1995). ... On Los Angeles disabled list (April 7-May 14, 1996); included rehabilitation assignments to San Antonio (May 4-9) and Vero Beach (May 9-14). ... On Los Angeles disabled list (June 15-August 20, 1997); included rehabilitation assignment to San Bernardino (July 26-August 20). ... On disabled list (June 19, 1998-remainder of season). ... Granted free agency (November 17, 1998).
STATISTICAL NOTES: Struck out 18 batters in one game (June 4, 1990). ... Pitched 7-0 no-hit victory against Florida (July 14, 1995).
MISCELLANEOUS: Member of 1984 Dominican Republic Olympic baseball team. ... Appeared in one game as pinch runner (1989). ... Appeared in one game as pinch runner (1992). ... Appeared in one game as pinch hitter and appeared in one game as pinch runner with Los Angeles (1996).

Year Team (League)	W	L	Pct.	ERA	G	GS	CG	ShO	Sv.	IP	H	R	ER	BB	SO
1985—GC Dodgers (GCL)	4	1	.800	2.59	23	6	0	0	1	59	57	30	17	23	42
1986—Bakersfield (California)	4	8	.333	4.75	20	20	2	1	0	106	119	73	56	63	78
1987—Vero Beach (FSL)	16	5	.762	2.17	25	25	6	1	0	170 1/3	128	45	41	78	148
1988—San Antonio (Tex.)	8	4	.667	2.46	14	14	2	1	0	95	79	29	26	34	89
—Albuquerque (PCL)	5	2	.714	2.76	10	10	1	1	0	58 2/3	43	24	18	32	49
—Los Angeles (N.L.)	1	3	.250	3.79	9	6	0	0	0	35 2/3	27	17	15	22	23
1989—Albuquerque (PCL)	10	2	.833	2.79	18	18	2	1	0	113	92	40	35	50	127
—Los Angeles (N.L.)	6	4	.600	3.19	15	15	2	2	0	98 2/3	79	39	35	41	89
1990—Los Angeles (N.L.)	20	6	.769	2.92	33	33	*12	3	0	234 1/3	191	89	76	67	223
1991—Los Angeles (N.L.)	17	13	.567	3.27	33	33	6	4	0	220 1/3	190	89	80	69	150
1992—Los Angeles (N.L.)	8	11	.421	4.00	25	25	1	1	0	150 2/3	141	82	67	69	101
1993—Los Angeles (N.L.)	10	12	.455	3.44	32	32	4	3	0	211 2/3	202	88	81	*104	127
1994—Los Angeles (N.L.)	12	7	.632	3.97	24	24	4	•3	0	170	160	83	75	56	119
1995—Los Angeles (N.L.)	17	7	.708	3.66	30	30	4	2	0	206 1/3	176	95	84	*81	138

Year Team (League)	W	L	Pct.	ERA	G	GS	CG	ShO	Sv.	IP	H	R	ER	BB	SO
1996— San Antonio (Tex.)	0	0	...	0.00	1	1	0	0	0	$2^2/_3$	0	0	0	3	1
— Vero Beach (FSL)	1	0	1.000	0.00	1	1	0	0	0	7	5	1	0	0	10
— Los Angeles (N.L.)	15	6	.714	3.42	29	27	2	2	0	$168^2/_3$	153	76	64	86	133
1997— Los Angeles (N.L.)	10	5	.667	3.64	22	22	1	0	0	$133^2/_3$	123	64	54	68	120
— San Bernardino (Calif.)	0	1	.000	1.15	4	4	0	0	0	$15^2/_3$	10	2	2	4	16
1998— Los Angeles (N.L.)	7	3	.700	2.83	15	15	1	0	0	$101^2/_3$	76	41	32	41	91
Major league totals (11 years)	123	77	.615	3.45	267	262	37	20	0	$1731^2/_3$	1518	763	663	704	1314

DIVISION SERIES RECORD

Year Team (League)	W	L	Pct.	ERA	G	GS	CG	ShO	Sv.	IP	H	R	ER	BB	SO
1995— Los Angeles (N.L.)	0	1	.000	14.54	1	1	0	0	0	$4^1/_3$	10	7	7	2	3
1996— Los Angeles (N.L.)	0	0	...	1.13	1	1	0	0	0	8	3	1	1	3	6
Div. series totals (2 years)	0	1	.000	5.84	2	2	0	0	0	$12^1/_3$	13	8	8	5	9

MARTINEZ, SANDY   C   CUBS

PERSONAL: Born October 3, 1972, in Villa Mella, Dominican Republic. ... 6-2/215. ... Bats left, throws right. ... Full name: Angel Sandy Martinez.

HIGH SCHOOL: Villa Mella (Dominican Republic).

TRANSACTIONS/CAREER NOTES: Signed as non-drafted free agent by Toronto Blue Jays organization (January 10, 1990). ... On disabled list (May 15-June 8, 1993). ... On Toronto disabled list (August 17-September 1, 1996); included rehabilitation assignment to Knoxville (August 26-September 1). ... On Syracuse disabled list (June 14-24, 1997). ... Traded by Blue Jays to Chicago Cubs for a player to be named later (December 11, 1997); Blue Jays acquired P Trevor Schaffer to complete deal (December 18, 1997). ... On suspended list (July 1-3, 1998).

RECORDS: Shares major league single-game records for most putouts by catcher (nine-inning game)—20 (May 6, 1998); and most chances accepted by catcher (nine-inning game) since 1900—20 (May 6, 1998).

STATISTICAL NOTES: Led Pioneer League with 24 passed balls in 1992. ... Led Florida State League catchers with 14 errors in 1994.

						BATTING								FIELDING		
Year Team (League)	Pos.	G	AB	R	H	2B	3B	HR	RBI	Avg.	BB	SO	SB	PO	A	E	Avg.
1990— Dom. Dodgers (DSL) .	C	44	145	21	35	2	0	0	10	.241	18	15	1	...	...	...	...
1991— Dunedin (Fla. St.)	C	12	38	3	7	1	0	0	3	.184	7	7	0	82	9	2	.978
— Medicine Hat (Pio.)	C	34	98	8	17	1	0	2	16	.173	12	29	0	141	19	3	.982
1992— Dunedin (Fla. St.)	C	4	15	4	3	1	0	2	4	.200	0	3	0	11	2	1	.929
— Medicine Hat (Pio.)	C-1B-SS	57	206	27	52	15	0	4	39	.252	14	62	0	275	58	5	.985
1993— Hagerstown (SAL)......	C	94	338	41	89	16	1	9	46	.263	19	71	1	493	68	14	.976
1994— Dunedin (Fla. St.)	C-1B	122	450	50	117	14	6	7	52	.260	22	79	1	615	79	†14	.980
1995— Knoxville (Southern) ..	C	41	144	14	33	8	1	2	22	.229	6	34	0	219	30	5	.980
— Toronto (A.L.)............	C	62	191	12	46	12	0	2	25	.241	7	45	0	329	28	5	.986
1996— Toronto (A.L.)............	C	76	229	17	52	9	3	3	18	.227	16	58	0	413	33	3	.993
— Knoxville (Southern) ..	C	4	16	2	3	0	0	0	0	.188	0	5	0	17	2	1	.950
1997— Syracuse (Int'l)...........	C	96	322	28	72	12	1	4	29	.224	27	76	7	588	50	9	.986
— Toronto (A.L.)............	C	3	2	1	0	0	0	0	0	.000	1	1	0	12	2	1	.933
1998— Chicago (N.L.)............	C	45	87	7	23	9	1	0	7	.264	13	21	1	185	7	3	.985
American League totals (3 years)		141	422	30	98	21	3	5	43	.232	24	104	0	754	63	9	.989
National League totals (1 year)		45	87	7	23	9	1	0	7	.264	13	21	1	185	7	3	.985
Major league totals (4 years)		186	509	37	121	30	4	5	50	.238	37	125	1	939	70	12	.988

DIVISION SERIES RECORD

						BATTING								FIELDING		
Year Team (League)	Pos.	G	AB	R	H	2B	3B	HR	RBI	Avg.	BB	SO	SB	PO	A	E	Avg.
1998— Chicago (N.L.)............	C	1	1	1	1	0	0	0	0	1.000	0	0	0	1	0	0	1.000

MARTINEZ, TINO   1B   YANKEES

PERSONAL: Born December 7, 1967, in Tampa. ... 6-2/210. ... Bats left, throws right. ... Full name: Constantino Martinez.

HIGH SCHOOL: Tampa Catholic (Tampa).

COLLEGE: Tampa (Fla.).

TRANSACTIONS/CAREER NOTES: Selected by Boston Red Sox organization in third round of free-agent draft (June 3, 1985); did not sign. ... Selected by Seattle Mariners organization in first round (14th pick overall) of free-agent draft (June 1, 1988). ... On disabled list (August 10, 1993-remainder of season). ... Traded by Mariners with P Jeff Nelson and P Jim Mecir to New York Yankees for P Sterling Hitchcock and 3B Russ Davis (December 7, 1995).

HONORS: Named first baseman on The Sporting News college All-America team (1988). ... Named Pacific Coast League Most Valuable Player (1991). ... Named first baseman on The Sporting News A.L. All-Star team (1997). ... Named first baseman on The Sporting News A.L. Silver Slugger team (1997).

STATISTICAL NOTES: Led Eastern League with 13 intentional bases on balls received in 1989. ... Led Eastern League first basemen with 1,348 total chances and 106 double plays in 1989. ... Tied for Pacific Coast League lead with 11 intentional bases on balls received in 1990. ... Led Pacific Coast League first basemen with .991 fielding percentage, 1,051 putouts, 98 assists, 1,159 total chances and 117 double plays in 1990. ... Led Pacific Coast League first basemen with .992 fielding percentage and 122 double plays in 1991. ... Hit three home runs in one game (April 2, 1997). ... Led A.L. with 13 sacrifice flies in 1997. ... Career major league grand slams: 6.

MISCELLANEOUS: Member of 1988 U.S. Olympic baseball team.

						BATTING								FIELDING		
Year Team (League)	Pos.	G	AB	R	H	2B	3B	HR	RBI	Avg.	BB	SO	SB	PO	A	E	Avg.
1989— Williamsport (East.) ...	1B	*137	*509	51	131	29	2	13	64	.257	59	54	7	*1260	*81	7	*.995
1990— Calgary (PCL)	1B-3B	128	453	83	145	28	1	17	93	.320	74	37	8	†1051	†98	10	†.991
— Seattle (A.L.)	1B	24	68	4	15	4	0	0	5	.221	9	9	0	155	12	0	1.000
1991— Calgary (PCL)	1B-3B	122	442	94	144	34	5	18	86	.326	82	44	3	1078	106	9	†.992
— Seattle (A.L.)	1B-DH	36	112	11	23	2	0	4	9	.205	11	24	0	249	22	2	.993
1992— Seattle (A.L.)	1B-DH	136	460	53	118	19	2	16	66	.257	42	77	2	678	58	4	.995
1993— Seattle (A.L.)	1B-DH	109	408	48	108	25	1	17	60	.265	45	56	0	932	60	3	.997

Year	Team (League)	Pos.	G	AB	R	H	2B	3B	HR	RBI	Avg.	BB	SO	SB	PO	A	E	Avg.
									BATTING							FIELDING		
1994— Seattle (A.L.)	1B-DH	97	329	42	86	21	0	20	61	.261	29	52	1	705	45	2	.997
1995— Seattle (A.L.)	1B-DH	141	519	92	152	35	3	31	111	.293	62	91	0	1048	101	8	.993
1996— New York (A.L.)■....	1B-DH	155	595	82	174	28	0	25	117	.292	68	85	2	1238	83	5	*.996
1997— New York (A.L.).........	1B-DH	158	594	96	176	31	2	44	141	.296	75	75	3	1302	105	8	.994
1998— New York (A.L.).........	1B	142	531	92	149	33	1	28	123	.281	61	83	2	1180	93	10	.992
Major league totals (9 years)		998	3616	520	1001	198	9	185	693	.277	402	552	10	7487	579	42	.995

DIVISION SERIES RECORD

RECORDS: Holds career record for most at-bats—66. ... Shares career records for most games—17; most hits—20; and most doubles—6.

Year	Team (League)	Pos.	G	AB	R	H	2B	3B	HR	RBI	Avg.	BB	SO	SB	PO	A	E	Avg.
									BATTING							FIELDING		
1995— Seattle (A.L.)	1B	5	22	4	9	1	0	1	5	.409	3	4	0	39	5	0	1.000
1996— New York (A.L.).........	1B	4	15	3	4	2	0	0	0	.267	4	1	0	33	3	0	1.000
1997— New York (A.L.).........	1B	5	18	1	4	1	0	1	4	.222	2	4	0	48	6	0	1.000
1998— New York (A.L.).........	1B	3	11	1	3	2	0	0	0	.273	0	2	0	27	1	0	1.000
Division series totals (4 years)		17	66	9	20	6	0	2	9	.303	9	11	0	147	15	0	1.000

CHAMPIONSHIP SERIES RECORD

Year	Team (League)	Pos.	G	AB	R	H	2B	3B	HR	RBI	Avg.	BB	SO	SB	PO	A	E	Avg.
									BATTING							FIELDING		
1995— Seattle (A.L.)	1B	6	22	1	3	0	0	0	0	.136	3	7	0	45	5	1	.980
1996— New York (A.L.).........	1B	5	22	3	4	1	0	0	0	.182	0	2	0	49	2	0	1.000
1998— New York (A.L.).........	1B	6	19	1	2	1	0	0	1	.105	6	8	2	47	4	1	.981
Championship series totals (3 years)		17	63	5	9	2	0	0	1	.143	9	17	2	141	11	2	.987

WORLD SERIES RECORD

RECORDS: Shares single-game record for most grand slams—1 (October 17, 1998). ... Shares single-inning record for most runs batted in—4 (October 17, 1998, seventh inning).

NOTES: Member of World Series championship team (1996 and 1998).

Year	Team (League)	Pos.	G	AB	R	H	2B	3B	HR	RBI	Avg.	BB	SO	SB	PO	A	E	Avg.
									BATTING							FIELDING		
1996— New York (A.L.).........	1B-PH	6	11	0	1	0	0	0	0	.091	2	5	0	27	0	0	1.000
1998— New York (A.L.).........	1B	4	13	4	5	0	0	1	4	.385	6	2	0	36	3	0	1.000
World Series totals (2 years)		10	24	4	6	0	0	1	4	.250	8	7	0	63	3	0	1.000

ALL-STAR GAME RECORD

Year	League	Pos.	AB	R	H	2B	3B	HR	RBI	Avg.	BB	SO	SB	PO	A	E	Avg.
								BATTING							FIELDING		
1995— American	PH	1	0	1	0	0	0	0	0	1.000	0	0	0	...	...	...	...
1997— American	1B	2	0	0	0	0	0	0	0	.000	0	0	0	10	0	0	1.000
All-Star Game totals (2 years)		3	0	1	0	0	0	0	0	.333	0	0	0	10	0	0	1.000

MARTINEZ, WILLIE — P — INDIANS

M

PERSONAL: Born January 4, 1978, in Barquisimeto, Venezuela. ... 6-2/185. ... Throws right, bats right. ... Full name: William Jose Martinez.
HIGH SCHOOL: Barquisimeto (Venezuela).
TRANSACTIONS/CAREER NOTES: Signed as non-drafted free agent by Cleveland Indians organization (January 16, 1995). ... On Akron disabled list (May 3-17 and July 11-18, 1998).

Year	Team (League)	W	L	Pct.	ERA	G	GS	CG	ShO	Sv.	IP	H	R	ER	BB	SO
1995— Burlington (Appalachian)....	0	7	.000	9.45	11	11	0	0	0	40	64	50	42	25	36
1996— Watertown (NYP)	6	5	.545	2.40	14	14	1	1	0	90	79	25	24	21	92
1997— Kinston (Carolina)	8	2	.800	3.09	23	23	1	0	0	137	125	61	47	42	120
1998— Akron (Eastern)	9	7	.563	4.38	26	26	2	1	0	154	169	92	75	44	117

MARZANO, JOHN — C — RANGERS

PERSONAL: Born February 14, 1963, in Philadelphia. ... 5-11/195. ... Bats right, throws right. ... Full name: John Robert Marzano.
HIGH SCHOOL: Central (Philadelphia).
COLLEGE: Temple.
TRANSACTIONS/CAREER NOTES: Selected by Minnesota Twins organization in third round of free-agent draft (June 8, 1981, did not sign); pick received as compensation for California Angels signing free-agent P Geoff Zahn. ... Selected by Boston Red Sox organization in first round (14th pick overall) of free-agent draft (June 4, 1984). ... On disabled list (June 13-28, 1986). ... On Boston disabled list (April 6-July 26, 1992); included rehabilitation assignment to Pawtucket (July 7-26). ... Released by Red Sox (March 24, 1993). ... Signed by Cleveland Indians organization (May 5, 1993). ... On disabled list (May 12-23, 1993). ... Released by Indians organization (May 23, 1993). ... Signed by Philadelphia Phillies organization (December 14, 1993). ... Granted free agency (October 15, 1994). ... Signed by Texas Rangers organization (April 2, 1995). ... On Oklahoma City suspended list (June 8-10, 1995). ... Granted free agency (October 16, 1995). ... Signed by Seattle Mariners organization (December 14, 1995). ... On suspended list (September 3-5, 1996). ... Granted free agency (October 29, 1997). ... Re-signed by Mariners organization (December 8, 1997). ... Granted free agency (October 23, 1998). ... Signed by Rangers (January 13, 1999).
HONORS: Named catcher on THE SPORTING NEWS college All-America team (1984).
STATISTICAL NOTES: Led Eastern League in being hit by pitch with 12 in 1986. ... Led American Association catchers with 620 total chances and 12 double plays in 1995.
MISCELLANEOUS: Member of 1984 U.S. Olympic baseball team.

Year	Team (League)	Pos.	G	AB	R	H	2B	3B	HR	RBI	Avg.	BB	SO	SB	PO	A	E	Avg.
									BATTING							FIELDING		
1985— New Britain (East.)	C	103	350	36	86	14	6	4	51	.246	19	43	4	530	70	12	.980
1986— New Britain (East.)	C-3B	118	445	55	126	28	2	10	62	.283	24	66	2	509	76	14	.977

Year Team (League)	Pos.	G	AB	R	H	2B	3B	HR	RBI	Avg.	BB	SO	SB	PO	A	E	Avg.
1987— Pawtucket (Int'l)■	C	70	255	46	72	22	0	10	35	.282	21	50	2	326	36	8	.978
— Boston (A.L.)	C	52	168	20	41	11	0	5	24	.244	7	41	0	337	24	5	.986
1988— Boston (A.L.)	C	10	29	3	4	1	0	0	1	.138	1	3	0	77	4	0	1.000
— Pawtucket (Int'l)	C	33	111	7	22	2	1	0	5	.198	8	17	1	151	24	8	.956
— New Britain (East.)	C	35	112	11	23	6	1	0	5	.205	10	13	1	117	11	3	.977
1989— Pawtucket (Int'l)	C	106	322	27	68	11	0	8	36	.211	15	53	1	574	62	10	.985
— Boston (A.L.)	C	7	18	5	8	3	0	1	3	.444	0	2	0	29	4	0	1.000
1990— Boston (A.L.)	C	32	83	8	20	4	0	0	6	.241	5	10	0	153	14	0	1.000
— Pawtucket (Int'l)	C-3B	26	75	16	24	4	1	2	8	.320	11	9	6	100	12	0	1.000
1991— Boston (A.L.)	C	49	114	10	30	8	0	0	9	.263	1	16	0	174	20	3	.985
1992— Pawtucket (Int'l)	C	18	62	5	18	1	0	2	12	.290	3	11	0	53	4	2	.966
— Boston (A.L.)	C-DH	19	50	4	4	2	1	0	1	.080	2	12	0	81	9	3	.968
1993— Charlotte (Int'l)■	C	3	9	0	1	0	0	0	0	.111	1	1	0	12	1	1	.929
1994— Scran./W.B. (Int'l)■	C-OF	88	280	25	59	19	2	1	19	.211	24	32	2	311	31	7	.980
1995— Okla. City (A.A.)■	C	120	427	55	132	*41	3	9	56	.309	33	54	3	*551	*64	5	.992
— Texas (A.L.)	C	2	6	1	2	0	0	0	0	.333	0	0	0	7	1	0	1.000
1996— Seattle (A.L.)■	C	41	106	8	26	6	0	0	6	.245	7	15	0	194	10	3	.986
1997— Seattle (A.L.)	C-DH	39	87	7	25	3	0	1	10	.287	7	15	0	191	13	5	.976
1998— Seattle (A.L.)	C-DH	50	133	13	31	7	1	4	12	.233	9	24	0	317	24	1	.997
Major league totals (10 years)		301	794	79	191	45	2	11	72	.241	39	138	0	1560	123	20	.988

MASAOKA, ONAN   P   DODGERS

PERSONAL: Born October 27, 1977, in Hilo, Hawaii. ... 6-0/188. ... Throws left, bats right. ... Full name: Onan Kainoa Satoshi Masaoka.
HIGH SCHOOL: Waiakea (Hilo, Hawaii).
TRANSACTIONS/CAREER NOTES: Selected by Los Angeles Dodgers organization in third round of free-agent draft (June 1, 1995).

Year Team (League)	W	L	Pct.	ERA	G	GS	CG	ShO	Sv.	IP	H	R	ER	BB	SO
1995— Yakima (N'west)	2	4	.333	3.65	15	7	0	0	3	49 1/3	28	25	20	47	75
1996— Savannah (S. Atl.)	2	5	.286	4.29	13	13	0	0	0	65	55	35	31	35	80
1997— Vero Beach (FSL)	6	8	.429	3.87	28	24	2	1	1	148 2/3	113	72	64	55	132
1998— San Antonio (Tex.)	6	6	.500	5.32	27	20	1	1	1	110	114	79	65	63	94

MASHORE, DAMON   OF

PERSONAL: Born October 31, 1969, in Ponce, Puerto Rico. ... 5-11/209. ... Throws right, bats right. ... Full name: Damon Wayne Mashore. ... Son of Clyde Mashore, outfielder with Cincinnati Reds (1969) and Montreal Expos (1970-73). ... Name pronounced MAY-shore.
HIGH SCHOOL: Clayton Valley (Concord, Calif.).
COLLEGE: Arizona.
TRANSACTIONS/CAREER NOTES: Selected by Oakland Athletics organization in ninth round of free-agent draft (June 3, 1991). ... On disabled list (July 13-September 8, 1993). ... On Huntsville disabled list (May 23-August 2, 1994). ... On Oakland disabled list (August 13, 1996-remainder of season). ... On disabled list (July 27, 1997-remainder of season). ... Granted free agency (October 15, 1997). ... Signed by Anaheim Angels (January 26, 1998). ... On suspended list (June 18-19, 1998). ... Granted free agency (October 15, 1998).
STATISTICAL NOTES: Tied for Northwest League lead in double plays by outfielder with two in 1991.

RECORD AS POSITION PLAYER

Year Team (League)	Pos.	G	AB	R	H	2B	3B	HR	RBI	Avg.	BB	SO	SB	PO	A	E	Avg.
1991— S. Oregon (N'west)	OF	73	264	48	72	17	6	6	31	.273	34	94	15	93	6	3	.971
1992— Modesto (California)	OF	124	471	91	133	22	3	18	64	.282	73	*136	29	212	12	8	.966
1993— Huntsville (Sou.)	OF	70	253	35	59	7	2	3	20	.233	25	64	18	167	9	3	.983
1994— Scottsdale (Ariz.)	OF	11	34	6	14	2	0	0	6	.412	4	3	1	15	0	0	1.000
— Huntsville (Sou.)	OF	59	210	24	47	11	2	4	21	.224	13	53	6	97	2	5	.952
1995— Edmonton (PCL)	OF	117	337	50	101	19	5	1	37	.300	42	77	17	197	12	4	.981
1996— Edmonton (PCL)	OF	50	183	32	49	9	1	8	29	.268	19	48	6	74	7	1	.988
— Oakland (A.L.)	OF	50	105	20	28	7	1	3	12	.267	16	31	4	65	1	1	.985
1997— Oakland (A.L.)	OF	92	279	55	69	10	2	3	18	.247	50	82	5	203	10	2	.991
1998— Anaheim (A.L.)■	OF-DH	43	98	13	23	6	0	2	11	.235	9	22	1	53	1	0	1.000
— Vancouver (PCL)	OF	42	143	19	39	7	0	2	15	.273	18	28	1	62	4	1	.985
Major league totals (3 years)		185	482	88	120	23	3	8	41	.249	75	135	10	321	12	3	.991

MATEO, RUBEN   OF   RANGERS

PERSONAL: Born February 10, 1978, in San Cristobal, Dominican Republic. ... 6-0/170. ... Bats right, throws right. ... Full name: Ruben Amaurys Mateo.
TRANSACTIONS/CAREER NOTES: Signed as non-drafted free agent by Texas Rangers organization (October 24, 1994). ... On Tulsa disabled list (April 13-May 13, 1998).

Year Team (League)	Pos.	G	AB	R	H	2B	3B	HR	RBI	Avg.	BB	SO	SB	PO	A	E	Avg.
1995— Dom. Rangers (DSL)	OF	48	176	30	53	9	3	4	42	.301	20	23	1	55	1	1	.982
1996— Char., S.C. (S. Atl.)	OF	134	496	65	129	30	8	8	58	.260	26	78	30	215	15	7	.970
1997— Charlotte (Fla. St.)	OF	99	385	63	121	23	8	12	67	.314	22	55	20	174	10	8	.958
1998— Tulsa (Texas)	OF	107	433	79	134	32	3	18	75	.309	30	56	18	215	11	7	.970
— Charlotte (Fla. St.)	OF	1	4	0	0	0	0	0	1	.000	0	1	0	2	0	0	1.000

M

PERSONAL: Born September 22, 1970, in Reynoldsburg, Ohio. ... 6-3/221. ... Bats right, throws right. ... Full name: Michael Scott Matheny.
HIGH SCHOOL: Reynoldsburg (Ohio).
COLLEGE: Michigan.
TRANSACTIONS/CAREER NOTES: Selected by Toronto Blue Jays organization in 31st round of free-agent draft (June 1, 1988); did not sign. ... Selected by Milwaukee Brewers organization in eighth round of free-agent draft (June 3, 1991). ... On Milwaukee suspended list (June 20-23, 1996). ... On Milwaukee disabled list (June 15-July 12, 1998); included rehabilitation assignment to Beloit (July 11-13). ... Granted free agency (December 21, 1998). ... Signed by Blue Jays (December 23, 1998).
STATISTICAL NOTES: Led California League catchers with 20 double plays in 1992. ... Led Texas League catchers with 18 double plays in 1993. ... Career major league grand slams: 2.

								BATTING							FIELDING		
Year	Team (League)	Pos.	G	AB	R	H	2B	3B	HR	RBI	Avg.	BB	SO	SB	PO	A	E	Avg.
1991— Helena (Pioneer)	C	64	253	35	72	14	0	2	34	.285	19	52	2	456	68	5	*.991
1992— Stockton (California) ..	C	106	333	42	73	13	2	6	46	.219	35	81	2	582	114	8	*.989
1993— El Paso (Texas).........	C	107	339	39	86	21	2	2	28	.254	17	73	1	524	*100	9	.986
1994— Milwaukee (A.L.)........	C	28	53	3	12	3	0	1	2	.226	3	13	0	81	8	1	.989
— New Orleans (A.A.).....	C-1B	57	177	20	39	10	1	4	21	.220	16	39	1	345	43	5	.987
1995— New Orleans (A.A.).....	C	6	17	3	6	2	0	3	4	.353	1	0	5	0	30	4	0	1.000
— Milwaukee (A.L.)........	C	80	166	13	41	9	1	0	21	.247	12	28	2	261	18	4	.986
1996— Milwaukee (A.L.).......	C-DH	106	313	31	64	15	2	8	46	.204	14	80	3	475	40	8	.985
— New Orleans (A.A.).....	C	20	66	3	15	4	0	1	6	.227	2	17	1	87	6	0	1.000
1997— Milwaukee (A.L.).......	C-1B	123	320	29	78	16	1	4	32	.244	17	68	0	697	58	5	.993
1998— Milwaukee (N.L.)........	C	108	320	24	76	13	0	6	27	.238	11	63	1	570	45	8	.987
— Beloit (Midwest).........	C	2	8	1	2	1	0	0	2	.250	1	3	0	13	1	0	1.000
American League totals (4 years)		337	852	76	195	43	4	13	101	.229	46	189	5	1514	124	18	.989
National League totals (1 year)		108	320	24	76	13	0	6	27	.238	11	63	1	570	45	8	.987
Major league totals (5 years)		445	1172	100	271	56	4	19	128	.231	57	252	6	2084	169	26	.989

PERSONAL: Born January 19, 1970, in Belleville, Ill. ... 6-2/200. ... Throws right, bats right. ... Full name: Timothy Jay Mathews. ... Son of Nelson Mathews, outfielder with Chicago Cubs (1960-63) and Kansas City Athletics (1964-65).
HIGH SCHOOL: Columbia (Ill.).
COLLEGE: UNLV.
TRANSACTIONS/CAREER NOTES: Selected by St. Louis Cardinals organization in 36th round of free-agent draft (June 1, 1992). ... On Louisville disabled list (May 30-June 6, 1995). ... On suspended list (April 1-7, 1997). ... Traded by Cardinals with P Eric Ludwick and P Blake Stein to Oakland Athletics for 1B Mark McGwire (July 31, 1997).
STATISTICAL NOTES: Pitched 4-0 no-hit victory against Burlington (August 13, 1993).

Year	Team (League)	W	L	Pct.	ERA	G	GS	CG	ShO	Sv.	IP	H	R	ER	BB	SO
1992— Hamilton (NYP).............	10	1	*.909	2.18	14	14	1	0	0	86²/₃	70	25	21	30	89
1993— Springfield (Mid.)..............	12	9	.571	2.71	25	25	5	2	0	159¹/₃	121	59	48	29	144
1994— St. Petersburg (FSL)	5	5	.500	2.44	11	11	1	0	0	66¹/₃	52	22	18	23	62
— Arkansas (Texas)..............	5	5	.500	3.15	16	16	1	0	0	97	83	37	34	24	93
1995— Louisville (A.A.)..............	9	4	.692	2.70	32	7	0	0	1	66²/₃	60	35	20	27	50
— St. Louis (N.L.)..............	1	1	.500	1.52	23	0	0	0	2	29²/₃	21	7	5	11	28
1996— St. Louis (N.L.)..............	2	6	.250	3.01	67	0	0	0	6	83²/₃	62	32	28	32	80
1997— St. Louis (N.L.)..............	4	4	.500	2.15	40	0	0	0	0	46	41	14	11	18	46
— Oakland (A.L.)■.............	6	2	.750	4.40	24	0	0	0	3	28²/₃	34	18	14	12	24
1998— Oakland (A.L.)...............	7	4	.636	4.58	66	0	0	0	1	72²/₃	71	44	37	29	53
A.L. totals (2 years)	13	6	.684	4.53	90	0	0	0	4	101¹/₃	105	62	51	41	77
N.L. totals (3 years)	7	11	.389	2.49	130	0	0	0	8	159¹/₃	124	53	44	61	154
Major league totals (4 years)	20	17	.541	3.28	220	0	0	0	12	260²/₃	229	115	95	102	231

DIVISION SERIES RECORD

Year	Team (League)	W	L	Pct.	ERA	G	GS	CG	ShO	Sv.	IP	H	R	ER	BB	SO
1996— St. Louis (N.L.)..................	1	0	1.000	0.00	1	0	0	0	0	1	1	0	0	0	2

CHAMPIONSHIP SERIES RECORD

Year	Team (League)	W	L	Pct.	ERA	G	GS	CG	ShO	Sv.	IP	H	R	ER	BB	SO
1996— St. Louis (N.L.)..................	0	0	...	0.00	2	0	0	0	0	²/₃	2	0	0	2	2

PERSONAL: Born October 5, 1964, in Alexandria, La. ... 6-2/225. ... Throws right, bats left. ... Full name: Terry Alan Mathews.
HIGH SCHOOL: Menard (Alexandria, La.).
COLLEGE: Northeast Louisiana.
TRANSACTIONS/CAREER NOTES: Selected by Texas Rangers organization in fifth round of free-agent draft (June 2, 1987). ... On Texas disabled list (July 29-September 12, 1992). ... Released by Rangers organization (April 4, 1993). ... Signed by Houston Astros organization (April 4, 1993). ... Granted free agency (October 15, 1993). ... Signed by Edmonton, Florida Marlins organization (November 9, 1993). ... On Florida disabled list (August 19-September 3, 1995); included rehabilitation assignment to Charlotte (August 29-September 1). ... On Florida disabled list (April 2-17, 1996). ... Traded by Marlins to Baltimore Orioles for a player to be named later (August 21, 1996); Marlins acquired C Greg Zaun to complete deal (August 23, 1996). ... On Baltimore disabled list (April 30-May 26 and June 2-17, 1998); included rehabilitation assignment to Bowie (June 7-11) and Rochester (June 12-17). ... Released by Orioles (July 7, 1998). ... Signed by Oakland Athletics organization (July 17, 1998). ... Granted free agency (October 15, 1998). ... Signed by Kansas City Royals organization (January 14, 1999).
MISCELLANEOUS: Grounded into double play in only appearance as pinch hitter with Florida (1995).

M

Year	Team (League)	W	L	Pct.	ERA	G	GS	CG	ShO	Sv.	IP	H	R	ER	BB	SO
1987—	Gastonia (S. Atl.)................	3	3	.500	5.59	34	1	0	0	0	48 1/3	53	35	30	32	46
1988—	Charlotte (Fla. St.)..............	13	6	.684	2.80	27	26	2	1	0	163 2/3	141	68	51	49	94
1989—	Tulsa (Texas)..................	2	5	.286	6.15	10	10	1	0	0	45 1/3	53	40	31	24	32
	— Charlotte (Fla. St.)...........	4	2	.667	3.64	10	10	0	0	0	59 1/3	55	28	24	17	30
1990—	Tulsa (Texas)..................	5	7	.417	4.27	14	14	4	2	0	86 1/3	88	50	41	36	48
	— Oklahoma City (A.A.).........	2	7	.222	3.69	12	11	1	1	0	70 2/3	81	39	29	15	36
1991—	Oklahoma City (A.A.).........	5	6	.455	3.49	18	13	1	0	1	95 1/3	98	39	37	34	63
	— Texas (A.L.)................	4	0	1.000	3.61	34	2	0	0	1	57 1/3	54	24	23	18	51
1992—	Texas (A.L.).................	2	4	.333	5.95	40	0	0	0	0	42 1/3	48	29	28	31	26
	— Oklahoma City (A.A.).........	1	1	.500	4.32	9	2	0	0	1	16 2/3	17	8	8	7	13
1993—	Jackson (Texas)■..........	6	5	.545	3.67	17	17	0	0	0	103	116	55	42	29	74
	— Tucson (PCL).............	5	0	1.000	3.55	16	4	0	0	2	33	40	14	13	11	34
1994—	Edmonton (PCL)■...........	4	4	.500	4.29	13	12	3	0	0	84	88	43	40	22	46
	— Florida (N.L.)..............	2	1	.667	3.35	24	2	0	0	0	43	45	16	16	9	21
1995—	Florida (N.L.)...............	4	4	.500	3.38	57	0	0	0	3	82 2/3	70	32	31	27	72
	— Charlotte (Int'l)............	0	0	...	4.91	2	0	0	0	0	3 2/3	5	2	2	0	5
1996—	Florida (N.L.)...............	2	4	.333	4.91	57	0	0	0	4	55	59	33	30	27	49
	— Baltimore (A.L.)■...........	2	2	.500	3.38	14	0	0	0	0	18 2/3	20	7	7	7	13
1997—	Baltimore (A.L.).............	4	4	.500	4.41	57	0	0	0	1	63 1/3	63	35	31	36	39
1998—	Baltimore (A.L.).............	0	1	.000	6.20	17	0	0	0	0	20 1/3	26	15	14	8	10
	— Bowie (Eastern)................	0	0	...	6.00	1	1	0	0	0	3	3	2	2	1	2
	— Rochester (Int'l)............	0	1	.000	3.00	1	1	0	0	0	3	4	1	1	2	4
	— Edmonton (PCL)■...........	2	2	.500	4.57	13	8	0	0	1	43 1/3	47	22	22	11	33
A.L. totals (5 years)		12	11	.522	4.59	162	2	0	0	2	202	211	110	103	100	139
N.L. totals (3 years)		8	9	.471	3.84	138	2	0	0	7	180 2/3	174	81	77	63	142
Major league totals (7 years).....		20	20	.500	4.23	300	4	0	0	9	382 2/3	385	191	180	163	281

DIVISION SERIES RECORD

Year	Team (League)	W	L	Pct.	ERA	G	GS	CG	ShO	Sv.	IP	H	R	ER	BB	SO
1996—	Baltimore (A.L.)..................	0	0	...	0.00	3	0	0	0	0	2 2/3	3	0	0	1	2
1997—	Baltimore (A.L.)..................	0	0	...	18.00	1	0	0	0	0	1	2	2	2	0	1
Div. series totals (2 years)		0	0	...	4.91	4	0	0	0	0	3 2/3	5	2	2	1	3

CHAMPIONSHIP SERIES RECORD

Year	Team (League)	W	L	Pct.	ERA	G	GS	CG	ShO	Sv.	IP	H	R	ER	BB	SO
1996—	Baltimore (A.L.)	0	0	...	0.00	3	0	0	0	0	2 1/3	0	0	0	2	3

MATTHEWS, GARY   OF   PADRES

PERSONAL: Born August 25, 1974, in San Francisco ... 6-0/200. ... Bats both, throws right. ... Full name: Gary Nathaniel Matthews Jr. ... Son of Gary Matthews, batting coach, Toronto Blue Jays, and outfielder with five major league teams (1972-87).
HIGH SCHOOL: Granada Hills (Calif.).
JUNIOR COLLEGE: Mission College (Calif.).
TRANSACTIONS/CAREER NOTES: Selected by San Diego Padres organization in 13th round of free-agent draft (June 3, 1993).

							BATTING								FIELDING		
Year	Team (League)	Pos.	G	AB	R	H	2B	3B	HR	RBI	Avg.	BB	SO	SB	PO	A	E	Avg.
1994—	Spokane (N'west).......	OF-2B	52	191	23	40	6	1	0	18	.209	19	58	3	96	2	4	.961
1995—	Clinton (Midwest).......	OF	128	421	57	100	18	4	2	40	.238	68	109	28	245	9	9	.966
1996—	Rancho Cuca. (Cal.) ...	OF	123	435	65	118	21	11	7	54	.271	60	102	7	218	7	16	.934
1997—	Rancho Cuca. (Cal.) ...	OF	69	268	66	81	15	4	8	40	.302	49	57	10	110	6	5	.959
	— Mobile (Southern)......	OF	28	90	14	22	4	1	2	12	.244	15	29	3	45	3	2	.960
1998—	Mobile (Southern)......	OF	72	254	62	78	15	4	7	51	.307	55	50	11	184	8	1	.995

MATTHEWS, MIKE   P   INDIANS

PERSONAL: Born October 24, 1973, in Fredericksburg, Va. ... 6-2/175. ... Throws left, bats left. ... Full name: Michael Scott Matthews.
HIGH SCHOOL: Woodbridge Senior (Va.).
JUNIOR COLLEGE: Montgomery-Rockville College (Md.).
TRANSACTIONS/CAREER NOTES: Selected by Cleveland Indians organization in second round of free-agent draft (June 1, 1992). ... On Watertown disabled list (June 17-September 12, 1993). ... On disabled list (June 7-28, 1995). ... On Buffalo disabled list (June 8-July 1, 1998).
STATISTICAL NOTES: Tied for Eastern League lead with four balks in 1997.

Year	Team (League)	W	L	Pct.	ERA	G	GS	CG	ShO	Sv.	IP	H	R	ER	BB	SO
1992—	Burlington (Appalachian)....	7	0	•1.000	*1.01	10	10	0	0	0	62 1/3	33	13	7	27	55
	— Watertown (NYP)..............	1	0	1.000	3.27	2	2	2	0	0	11	10	4	4	8	5
1993—	....							Did not play.								
1994—	Columbus (S. Atl.).............	6	8	.429	3.08	23	23	0	0	0	119 2/3	120	53	41	44	99
1995—	Cant./Akr. (Eastern)..........	5	8	.385	5.93	15	15	1	0	0	74 1/3	82	62	49	43	37
1996—	Cant./Akr. (Eastern)..........	9	11	.450	4.66	27	27	3	0	0	162 1/3	178	96	84	74	112
1997—	Buffalo (A.A.).................	0	2	.000	7.71	5	5	0	0	0	21	32	19	18	10	17
	— Akron (Eastern).................	6	8	.429	3.82	19	19	3	1	0	113	116	62	48	57	69
1998—	Buffalo (Int'l).................	9	6	.600	4.63	24	23	0	0	0	130 1/3	137	79	67	68	86

MAXWELL, JASON   IF   CUBS

PERSONAL: Born March 26, 1972, in Lewisburg, Tenn. ... 6-1/180. ... Bats right, throws right. ... Full name: Jason Ramond Maxwell.
HIGH SCHOOL: Marshall County (Lewisburg, Tenn.).
COLLEGE: Middle Tennessee.
TRANSACTIONS/CAREER NOTES: Selected by Chicago Cubs organization in 74th round of free-agent draft (June 3, 1993).
STATISTICAL NOTES: Led Southern League with nine sacrifice flies in 1997.

Year Team (League)	Pos.	G	AB	R	H	2B	3B	HR	RBI	Avg.	BB	SO	SB	PO	A	E	Avg.
1993— Huntington (Appal.)....	SS	61	179	50	52	7	2	7	38	.291	35	39	6	60	140	9	.957
1994— Daytona (Fla. St.).......	SS	116	368	71	85	18	2	10	31	.231	55	96	7	167	333	*38	.929
1995— Daytona (Fla. St.).......	SS	117	388	66	102	13	3	10	58	.263	63	68	12	181	325	16	*.969
1996— Orlando (South.)........	SS-2B-3B	126	433	64	115	20	1	9	45	.266	56	77	19	188	336	29	.948
1997— Orlando (South.)........	SS-2B	122	409	87	114	22	6	14	58	.279	82	72	12	176	376	28	.952
1998— Iowa (Pacific Coast)...	2B-SS	124	483	86	144	40	3	15	60	.298	52	93	8	237	306	16	.971
— Chicago (N.L.)............	2B	7	3	2	1	0	0	1	2	.333	0	2	0	0	1	0	1.000
Major league totals (1 year)		7	3	2	1	0	0	1	2	.333	0	2	0	0	1	0	1.000

MAY, DERRICK — OF — EXPOS

PERSONAL: Born July 14, 1968, in Rochester, N.Y. ... 6-4/225. ... Bats left, throws right. ... Full name: Derrick Brant May. ... Son of Dave May, outfielder with five major league teams (1967-78).
HIGH SCHOOL: Newark (Del.).
TRANSACTIONS/CAREER NOTES: Selected by Chicago Cubs organization in first round (ninth pick overall) of free-agent draft (June 2, 1986). ... On Iowa disabled list (April 14-May 27 and June 6-24, 1991). ... Granted free agency (April 7, 1995). ... Signed by New Orleans, Milwaukee Brewers organization (April 12, 1995). ... Traded by Brewers to Houston Astros for a player to be named later (June 21, 1995); Brewers acquired IF Tommy Nevers to complete deal (July 21, 1996). ... On disabled list (June 20-July 5, 1996). ... Granted free agency (December 20, 1996). ... Signed by Philadelphia Phillies organization (January 29, 1997). ... Released by Phillies (August 6, 1997). ... Signed by Montreal Expos organization (March 30, 1998). ... Granted free agency (October 1, 1998). ... Re-signed by Expos organization (January 13, 1999).
STATISTICAL NOTES: Tied for Carolina League lead in double plays by outfielder with four in 1988. ... Career major league grand slams: 2.

Year Team (League)	Pos.	G	AB	R	H	2B	3B	HR	RBI	Avg.	BB	SO	SB	PO	A	E	Avg.
1986— Wytheville (App.)........	OF	54	178	25	57	6	1	0	23	.320	16	15	17	47	3	5	.909
1987— Peoria (Midwest)........	OF	128	439	60	131	19	8	9	52	.298	42	106	5	181	13	8	.960
1988— Win.-Salem (Car.).......	OF	130	485	76	•148	29	*9	8	65	.305	37	82	13	209	13	10	.957
1989— Charlotte (Southern) ..	OF	136	491	72	145	26	5	9	70	.295	34	77	19	239	8	•13	.950
1990— Iowa (Am. Assoc.)......	OF-1B	119	459	55	136	27	1	8	69	.296	23	50	5	159	10	8	.955
— Chicago (N.L.)	OF	17	61	8	15	3	0	1	11	.246	2	7	1	34	1	1	.972
1991— Iowa (Am. Assoc.)......	OF	82	310	47	92	18	4	3	49	.297	19	38	7	130	2	5	.964
— Chicago (N.L.)	OF	15	22	4	5	2	0	1	3	.227	2	1	0	11	1	0	1.000
1992— Iowa (Am. Assoc.)......	OF	8	30	6	11	4	1	2	8	.367	3	3	0	11	1	0	1.000
— Chicago (N.L.)	OF	124	351	33	96	11	0	8	45	.274	14	40	5	153	3	5	.969
1993— Chicago (N.L.)	OF	128	465	62	137	25	2	10	77	.295	31	41	10	220	8	7	.970
1994— Chicago (N.L.)	OF	100	345	43	98	19	2	8	51	.284	30	34	3	155	4	1	.994
1995— Milwaukee (A.L.)■.....	OF	32	113	15	28	3	1	1	9	.248	5	18	0	65	1	2	.971
— Houston (N.L.)■..........	OF-1B	78	206	29	62	15	1	8	41	.301	19	24	5	74	0	2	.974
1996— Houston (N.L.)	OF	109	259	24	65	12	3	5	33	.251	30	33	2	125	5	4	.970
1997— Philadelphia (N.L.)■ ..	OF	83	149	8	34	5	1	1	13	.228	8	26	4	69	4	3	.961
1998— Montreal (N.L.)■........	OF-DH	85	180	13	43	8	0	5	15	.239	11	24	0	57	3	1	.984
— Ottawa (Int'l)	OF	21	69	16	26	6	0	6	21	.377	13	7	0	23	1	1	.960
American League totals (1 year)		32	113	15	28	3	1	1	9	.248	5	18	0	65	1	2	.971
National League totals (9 years)		739	2038	224	555	100	9	47	289	.272	147	230	30	898	29	24	.975
Major league totals (9 years)		771	2151	239	583	103	10	48	298	.271	152	248	30	963	30	26	.974

M

MAYNE, BRENT — C — GIANTS

PERSONAL: Born April 19, 1968, in Loma Linda, Calif. ... 6-1/192. ... Bats left, throws right. ... Full name: Brent Danem Mayne.
HIGH SCHOOL: Costa Mesa (Calif.).
JUNIOR COLLEGE: Orange Coast College (Calif.).
COLLEGE: Cal State Fullerton.
TRANSACTIONS/CAREER NOTES: Selected by Kansas City Royals organization in first round (13th pick overall) of free-agent draft (June 5, 1989). ... On disabled list (July 24, 1989-remainder of season). ... Traded by Royals to New York Mets for OF Al Shirley (December 19, 1995). ... Granted free agency (December 7, 1996). ... Signed by Seattle Mariners organization (January 10, 1997). ... Released by Mariners (March 28, 1997). ... Signed by Oakland Athletics organization (April 8, 1997). ... Granted free agency (October 30, 1997). ... Signed by San Francisco Giants (November 21, 1997).
STATISTICAL NOTES: Led A.L. catchers with 11 double plays in 1995. ... Career major league grand slams: 2.

Year Team (League)	Pos.	G	AB	R	H	2B	3B	HR	RBI	Avg.	BB	SO	SB	PO	A	E	Avg.
1989— Baseball City (FSL).....	C	7	24	5	13	3	1	0	8	.542	0	3	0	31	2	0	1.000
1990— Memphis (Sou.).........	C	115	412	48	110	16	3	2	61	.267	52	51	5	591	61	11	.983
— Kansas City (A.L.)	C	5	13	2	3	0	0	0	1	.231	3	3	0	29	3	1	.970
1991— Kansas City (A.L.)	C-DH	85	231	22	58	8	0	3	31	.251	23	42	2	425	38	6	.987
1992— Kansas City (A.L.)	C-3B-DH	82	213	16	48	10	0	0	18	.225	11	26	0	281	33	3	.991
1993— Kansas City (A.L.)	C-DH	71	205	22	52	9	1	2	22	.254	18	31	3	356	27	2	.995
1994— Kansas City (A.L.)	C-DH	46	144	19	37	5	1	2	20	.257	14	27	1	246	14	1	.996
1995— Kansas City (A.L.)	C	110	307	23	77	18	1	1	27	.251	25	41	0	540	40	3	.995
1996— New York (N.L.)■	C	70	99	9	26	6	0	1	6	.263	12	22	0	85	3	0	1.000
1997— Edmonton (PCL)■	C	2	3	0	0	0	0	0	0	.000	0	1	0	5	0	0	1.000
— Oakland (A.L.)	C	85	256	29	74	12	0	6	22	.289	18	33	1	419	36	2	.996
1998— San Fran. (N.L.)■.......	C	94	275	26	75	15	0	3	32	.273	37	47	2	493	39	5	.991
American League totals (7 years)		484	1369	133	349	62	3	14	141	.255	112	203	7	2296	191	18	.993
National League totals (2 years)		164	374	35	101	21	0	4	38	.270	49	69	2	578	42	5	.992
Major league totals (9 years)		648	1743	168	450	83	3	18	179	.258	161	272	9	2874	233	23	.993

MAYS, JOE   P   TWINS

PERSONAL: Born December 10, 1975, in Flint, Mich. ... 6-1/160. ... Throws right, bats both. ... Full name: Joseph E. Mays.
HIGH SCHOOL: Southeast (Bradenton, Fla.).
TRANSACTIONS/CAREER NOTES: Selected by Seattle Mariners organization in sixth round of free-agent draft (June 2, 1994). ... Traded by Mariners to Minnesota Twins (October 8, 1997); completing deal in which Twins traded OF Roberto Kelly to Mariners for P Jeromy Palki and a player to be named later (August 20, 1997).

Year Team (League)	W	L	Pct.	ERA	G	GS	CG	ShO	Sv.	IP	H	R	ER	BB	SO
1995— Ariz. Mariners (Ariz.)	2	3	.400	3.25	10	10	0	0	0	44 1/3	41	24	16	18	44
1996— Everett (Northwest)	4	4	.500	3.08	13	10	0	0	0	64 1/3	55	33	22	22	56
1997— Wisconsin (Midwest)	9	3	.750	2.09	13	13	1	0	0	81 2/3	62	20	19	23	79
— Lancaster (Calif.)	7	4	.636	4.86	15	15	1	0	0	96 1/3	108	55	52	34	82
1998— Fort Myers (Fla. St.)■	7	2	.778	3.04	16	15	0	0	0	94 2/3	101	45	32	23	83
— New Britain (East.)	5	3	.625	4.99	11	10	0	0	0	57 2/3	63	40	32	21	45

McCARTHY, GREG   P   MARINERS

PERSONAL: Born October 30, 1968, in Norwalk, Conn. ... 6-2/215. ... Throws left, bats left. ... Full name: Gregory O'Neil McCarthy.
HIGH SCHOOL: Bridgeport (Conn.) Central.
TRANSACTIONS/CAREER NOTES: Selected by Philadelphia Phillies organization in 36th round of free-agent draft (June 2, 1987). ... Selected by Montreal Expos from Phillies organization in Rule 5 major league draft (December 3, 1990). ... On disabled list (March 29, 1991-entire season). ... Selected by Cleveland Indians organization from Expos organization in Rule 5 minor league draft (December 9, 1991). ... On disabled list (July 5-September 9, 1992). ... Granted free agency (December 20, 1993). ... Re-signed by Indians organization (January 6, 1994). ... Granted free agency (October 15, 1994). ... Signed by Chicago White Sox organization (November 24, 1994). ... On Birmingham disabled list (May 16-23 and May 28-July 4, 1995). ... Granted free agency (October 16, 1995). ... Signed by Seattle Mariners organization (November 3, 1995).

Year Team (League)	W	L	Pct.	ERA	G	GS	CG	ShO	Sv.	IP	H	R	ER	BB	SO
1987— Utica (N.Y.-Penn)	4	1	.800	0.91	20	0	0	0	3	29 2/3	14	9	3	23	40
1988— Spartanburg (SAL)	4	2	.667	4.04	34	1	0	0	2	64 2/3	52	36	29	52	65
1989— Spartanburg (SAL)	5	8	.385	4.18	24	15	2	1	0	112	90	58	52	80	115
1990— Clearwater (Fla. St.)	1	3	.250	3.47	42	1	0	0	5	59 2/3	47	33	23	38	67
1991—								Did not play.							
1992— Kinston (Carolina)■	3	0	1.000	0.00	23	0	0	0	12	27 1/3	14	0	0	9	37
1993— Kinston (Carolina)	0	0	. . .	1.69	9	0	0	0	2	10 2/3	8	4	2	13	14
— Cant./Akr. (Eastern)	2	3	.400	4.72	33	0	0	0	6	34 1/3	28	18	18	37	39
1994— Cant./Akr. (Eastern)	2	3	.400	2.25	22	0	0	0	9	32	19	12	8	23	39
— Charlotte (Int'l)	1	0	1.000	6.94	18	0	0	0	0	23 1/3	17	22	18	28	21
1995— Birmingham (Southern)■	3	3	.500	5.04	38	0	0	0	3	44 1/3	37	28	25	29	48
1996— Tacoma (PCL)■	4	2	.667	3.29	39	0	0	0	4	68 1/3	58	31	25	53	90
— Seattle (A.L.)	0	0	. . .	1.86	10	0	0	0	0	9 2/3	8	2	2	4	7
1997— Tacoma (PCL)	2	1	.667	3.27	22	0	0	0	3	22	21	8	8	16	34
— Seattle (A.L.)	1	1	.500	5.46	37	0	0	0	0	29 2/3	26	21	18	16	34
1998— Tacoma (PCL)	1	2	.333	4.19	19	0	0	0	1	19 1/3	15	14	9	22	24
— Seattle (A.L.)	1	2	.333	5.01	29	0	0	0	0	23 1/3	18	13	13	17	25
A.L. totals (3 years)	2	3	.400	4.74	76	0	0	0	0	62 2/3	52	36	33	37	66
N.L. totals (0 year)	0	0	. . .		0	0	0	0	0	0	0	0	0	0	0
Major league totals (3 years)	2	3	.400	4.74	76	0	0	0	0	62 2/3	52	36	33	37	66

M

McCARTY, DAVID   OF/1B   TIGERS

PERSONAL: Born November 23, 1969, in Houston. ... 6-5/215. ... Bats right, throws left. ... Full name: David Andrew McCarty.
HIGH SCHOOL: Sharpstown (Houston).
COLLEGE: Stanford.
TRANSACTIONS/CAREER NOTES: Selected by Minnesota Twins organization in first round (third pick overall) of free-agent draft (June 3, 1991). ... Traded by Twins to Cincinnati Reds for P John Courtright (June 8, 1995). ... Traded by Reds with OF Deion Sanders, P Ricky Pickett, P Scott Service and P John Roper to San Francisco Giants for OF Darren Lewis, P Mark Portugal and P Dave Burba (July 21, 1995). ... On San Francisco disabled list (June 6-27, 1996); included rehabilitation assignment to Phoenix (June 20-27). ... Traded by Giants to Seattle Mariners for OF Jay Leach and OF Scott Smith (January 30, 1998). ... Granted free agency (September 30, 1998). ... Signed by Detroit Tigers organization (December 18, 1998).

Year Team (League)	Pos.	G	AB	R	H	2B	3B	HR	RBI	Avg.	BB	SO	SB	PO	A	E	Avg.
1991— Visalia (California)	OF	15	50	16	19	3	0	3	8	.380	13	7	3	23	1	0	1.000
— Orlando (South.)	OF	20	88	18	23	4	0	3	11	.261	10	20	0	38	4	1	.977
1992— Orlando (South.)	OF-1B	129	456	75	124	16	2	18	79	.272	55	89	6	357	32	9	.977
— Portland (PCL)	OF-1B	7	26	7	13	2	0	1	8	.500	5	3	1	40	3	1	.977
1993— Portland (PCL)	OF	40	143	42	55	11	0	8	31	.385	27	25	5	185	21	2	.990
— Minnesota (A.L.)	OF-1B-DH	98	350	36	75	15	2	2	21	.214	19	80	2	412	38	8	.983
1994— Minnesota (A.L.)	1B-OF	44	131	21	34	8	2	1	12	.260	7	32	2	243	28	5	.982
— Salt Lake (PCL)	1B	55	186	32	47	9	3	3	19	.253	35	34	1	191	16	5	.976
1995— Minnesota (A.L.)	1B-OF	25	55	10	12	3	1	0	4	.218	4	18	0	130	10	1	.993
— Indianapolis (A.A.)■	1B	37	140	31	47	10	1	8	32	.336	15	30	0	335	14	2	.994
— Phoenix (PCL)■	1B-OF	37	151	31	53	19	2	4	19	.351	17	27	1	330	32	2	.995
— San Francisco (N.L.)	OF-1B	12	20	1	5	1	0	0	2	.250	2	4	1	19	0	1	.950
1996— San Francisco (N.L.)	1B-OF	91	175	16	38	3	0	6	24	.217	18	43	2	291	18	3	.990
— Phoenix (PCL)	OF-1B	6	25	4	10	1	1	1	7	.400	2	4	0	29	1	0	1.000
1997— Phoenix (PCL)	1B-OF	121	434	85	153	27	5	22	92	.353	49	75	9	563	53	3	.995
1998— Tacoma (PCL)■	1B-OF	108	398	73	126	30	2	11	52	.317	59	85	9	430	32	2	.996
— Seattle (A.L.)	OF-1B	8	18	1	5	0	0	1	2	.278	5	4	1	21	0	0	1.000
American League totals (4 years)		175	554	68	126	26	5	4	39	.227	35	134	5	806	76	14	.984
National League totals (2 years)		103	195	17	43	4	0	6	26	.221	20	47	3	310	18	4	.988
Major league totals (5 years)		278	749	85	169	30	5	10	65	.226	55	181	8	1116	94	18	.985

McCLAIN, SCOTT   3B   DEVIL RAYS

PERSONAL: Born May 19, 1972, in Simi Valley, Calif. ... 6-4/210. ... Bats right, throws right. ... Full name: Scott Michael McClain.
HIGH SCHOOL: Atascadero (Calif.).
TRANSACTIONS/CAREER NOTES: Selected by Baltimore Orioles organization in 22nd round of free-agent draft (June 4, 1990). ... Traded by Orioles with IF Manny Alexander to New York Mets for P Hector Ramirez (March 22, 1997). ... Granted free agency (October 15, 1997). ... Signed by Tampa Bay Devil Rays organization (December 19, 1997).
STATISTICAL NOTES: Led Carolina League third basemen with 113 putouts in 1993. ... Led Eastern League third basemen with 111 putouts in 1994.

Year Team (League)	Pos.	G	AB	R	H	2B	3B	HR	RBI	Avg.	BB	SO	SB	PO	A	E	Avg.
1990— Bluefield (Appal.)........	3B-OF-P	40	107	20	21	2	0	4	15	.196	22	35	2	27	46	8	.901
1991— Kane County (Midw.)..	3B	25	81	9	18	0	0	0	4	.222	17	25	1	12	53	4	.942
— Bluefield (Appal.)........	3B-2B-SS	41	148	16	39	5	0	0	24	.264	15	39	5	33	79	15	.882
1992— Kane County (Midw.)..	3B-SS	96	316	43	84	12	2	3	30	.266	48	62	7	97	192	26	.917
1993— Frederick (Carolina)..	3B-SS-1B	133	427	65	111	22	2	9	54	.260	70	88	10	†114	239	24	.936
1994— Bowie (Eastern).........	3B-SS	133	427	71	103	29	1	11	58	.241	72	89	6	†111	224	22	.938
1995— Bowie (Eastern).........	3B	70	259	41	72	14	1	13	61	.278	25	44	2	57	165	16	.933
— Rochester (Int'l)	3B	61	199	32	50	9	1	8	22	.251	23	34	0	41	130	11	.940
1996— Rochester (Int'l)	3B	131	463	76	130	23	4	17	69	.281	61	109	8	*96	255	17	.954
1997— Norfolk (Int'l)	3B-SS-1B	127	429	71	120	29	2	21	64	.280	64	93	1	161	270	19	.958
1998— Durham (Int'l)■.......	3B-SS	126	472	91	141	35	0	34	109	.299	66	113	6	75	242	12	.964
— Tampa Bay (A.L.).......	1B-3B	9	20	2	2	0	0	0	0	.100	2	6	0	26	6	1	.970
Major league totals (1 year)		9	20	2	2	0	0	0	0	.100	2	6	0	26	6	1	.970

RECORD AS PITCHER

Year Team (League)	W	L	Pct.	ERA	G	GS	CG	ShO	Sv.	IP	H	R	ER	BB	SO
1990— Bluefield (Appalachian)	0	0	...	9.00	1	0	0	0	0	1	1	1	1	0	0

McCRACKEN, QUINTON   OF   DEVIL RAYS

PERSONAL: Born March 16, 1970, in Wilmington, N.C. ... 5-7/173. ... Bats both, throws right. ... Full name: Quinton Antoine McCracken.
HIGH SCHOOL: South Brunswick (Southport, N.C.).
COLLEGE: Duke.
TRANSACTIONS/CAREER NOTES: Selected by Colorado Rockies organization in 25th round of free-agent draft (June 1, 1992). ... Selected by Tampa Bay Devil Rays in first round (fourth pick overall) of expansion draft (November 18, 1997).
STATISTICAL NOTES: Led California League with 12 sacrifice hits in 1993. ... Led Eastern League in caught stealing with 19 in 1994. ... Had 18-game hitting streak (August 18-September 9, 1998).
MISCELLANEOUS: Holds Tampa Bay Devil Rays all-time records for highest batting average (.292), most runs scored (76), most hits (179) and most doubles (38).

M

Year Team (League)	Pos.	G	AB	R	H	2B	3B	HR	RBI	Avg.	BB	SO	SB	PO	A	E	Avg.
1992— Bend (Northwest).......	2B-OF	67	232	37	65	13	2	0	27	.280	25	39	18	98	129	17	.930
1993— Central Valley (Cal.)....	OF-2B	127	483	94	141	17	7	2	58	.292	78	90	60	153	75	13	.946
1994— New Haven (East.)......	OF	136	544	94	151	27	4	5	39	.278	48	72	36	273	6	8	.972
1995— New Haven (East.)......	OF	55	221	33	79	11	4	1	26	.357	21	32	26	92	10	3	.971
— Colo. Springs (PCL) ...	OF	61	244	55	88	14	6	3	28	.361	23	30	17	104	5	1	.991
— Colorado (N.L.)	OF	3	1	0	0	0	0	0	0	.000	0	1	0	0	0	0	...
1996— Colorado (N.L.)	OF	124	283	50	82	13	6	3	40	.290	32	62	17	131	3	6	.957
1997— Colorado (N.L.)	OF	147	325	69	95	11	1	3	36	.292	42	62	28	195	5	4	.980
1998— Tampa Bay (A.L.)■.....	OF	155	614	77	179	38	7	7	59	.292	41	107	19	343	18	3	.992
American League totals (1 year)		155	614	77	179	38	7	7	59	.292	41	107	19	343	18	3	.992
National League totals (3 years)		274	609	119	177	24	7	6	76	.291	74	125	45	326	8	10	.971
Major league totals (4 years)		429	1223	196	356	62	14	13	135	.291	115	232	64	669	26	13	.982

McCURRY, JEFF   P   ASTROS

PERSONAL: Born January 21, 1970, in Tokyo, Japan. ... 6-6/220. ... Throws right, bats right. ... Full name: Jeffrey Dee McCurry.
HIGH SCHOOL: St. Thomas (Houston).
JUNIOR COLLEGE: San Jacinto College (Texas).
COLLEGE: Texas Christian.
TRANSACTIONS/CAREER NOTES: Selected by Pittsburgh Pirates organization in 20th round of free-agent draft (June 5, 1989); did not sign. ... Selected by Pirates organization in 14th round of free-agent draft (June 4, 1990). ... On Welland disabled list (June 19-July 12, 1991). ... Claimed on waivers by Detroit Tigers (November 20, 1995). ... Selected by Colorado Rockies organization from Tigers organization in Rule 5 minor league draft (December 9, 1996). ... Granted free agency (November 10, 1997). ... Signed by Pirates organization (December 18, 1997). ... Granted free agency (October 14, 1998). ... Signed by Houston Astros organization (January 21, 1999).

Year Team (League)	W	L	Pct.	ERA	G	GS	CG	ShO	Sv.	IP	H	R	ER	BB	SO
1991— GC Pirates (GCL)...............	1	0	1.000	2.57	6	1	0	0	0	14	19	10	4	4	8
— Welland (N.Y.-Penn).........	2	1	.667	0.57	9	0	0	0	0	15²/₃	11	4	1	10	18
1992— Augusta (S. Atl.)...............	2	1	.667	3.30	19	0	0	0	7	30	36	14	11	15	34
— Salem (Carolina)	6	2	.750	2.87	30	0	0	0	3	62²/₃	49	22	20	24	52
1993— Salem (Carolina)	1	4	.200	3.89	41	0	0	0	22	44	41	21	19	15	32
— Carolina (Southern)...........	2	1	.667	2.79	23	0	0	0	9	29	24	11	9	14	14
1994— Carolina (Southern)...........	6	5	.545	3.21	48	2	0	0	11	81¹/₃	74	35	29	30	60
1995— Calgary (PCL)...................	0	0	...	1.80	3	0	0	0	0	5	3	1	1	2	2
— Pittsburgh (N.L.)...............	1	4	.200	5.02	55	0	0	0	1	61	82	38	34	30	27
1996— Toledo (International)■......	1	4	.200	4.76	39	0	0	0	2	58²/₃	66	37	31	26	56
— Detroit (A.L.)	0	0	...	24.30	2	0	0	0	0	3¹/₃	9	9	9	2	0

Year Team (League)	W	L	Pct.	ERA	G	GS	CG	ShO	Sv.	IP	H	R	ER	BB	SO
1997—Colorado (N.L.)■	1	4	.200	4.43	33	0	0	0	0	40 2/3	43	22	20	20	19
—Colo. Springs (PCL)	1	1	.500	5.09	16	0	0	0	3	17 2/3	17	12	10	6	13
1998—Nashville (PCL)■	2	5	.286	4.96	40	0	0	0	23	45 1/3	45	26	25	15	34
—Pittsburgh (N.L.)	1	3	.250	6.52	16	0	0	0	0	19 1/3	24	14	14	9	11
A.L. totals (1 year)	0	0	...	24.30	2	0	0	0	0	3 1/3	9	9	9	2	0
N.L. totals (3 years)	3	11	.214	5.06	104	0	0	0	1	121	149	74	68	59	57
Major league totals (4 years)	3	11	.214	5.57	106	0	0	0	1	124 1/3	158	83	77	61	57

McDILL, ALLEN P

PERSONAL: Born August 23, 1971, in Greenville, Miss. ... 6-0/155. ... Throws left, bats left. ... Full name: Allen Gabriel McDill.
HIGH SCHOOL: Lake Hamilton (Ark.).
TRANSACTIONS/CAREER NOTES: Selected by New York Mets organization in 20th round of free-agent draft (June 1, 1992). ... Traded by Mets organization with P Jason Jacome to Kansas City Royals organization for P Derek Wallace and a player to be named later (July 21, 1995); Mets acquired P John Carter to complete deal (November 16, 1995). ... Granted free agency (December 21, 1998).

Year Team (League)	W	L	Pct.	ERA	G	GS	CG	ShO	Sv.	IP	H	R	ER	BB	SO
1992—GC Mets (GCL)	3	4	.429	2.70	10	9	0	0	0	53 1/3	36	23	16	15	60
—Kingsport (Appalachian)	0	0	...	0.00	1	0	0	0	0	1/3	0	0	0	2	0
1993—Kingsport (Appalachian)	5	2	.714	2.19	9	9	0	0	0	53 1/3	52	19	13	14	42
—Pittsfield (NYP)	2	3	.400	5.40	5	5	0	0	0	28 1/3	31	22	17	15	24
1994—Columbia (S. Atl.)	9	6	.600	3.55	19	19	1	0	0	111 2/3	101	52	44	38	102
1995—Binghamton (Eastern)	3	5	.375	4.56	12	12	1	0	0	73	69	42	37	38	44
—St. Lucie (Fla. St.)	4	2	.667	1.64	7	7	1	1	0	49 1/3	36	11	9	13	28
—Wichita (Texas)■	1	0	1.000	2.11	12	1	0	0	1	21 1/3	16	7	5	5	20
1996—Wichita (Texas)	1	5	.167	5.54	54	0	0	0	11	65	79	43	40	21	62
—Omaha (Am. Assoc.)	0	1	.000	54.00	2	0	0	0	0	1/3	3	2	2	1	1
1997—Omaha (Am. Assoc.)	5	2	.714	5.88	23	6	0	0	2	64 1/3	80	42	42	26	51
—Kansas City (A.L.)	0	0	...	13.50	3	0	0	0	0	4	3	6	6	8	2
—Wichita (Texas)	0	1	.000	3.12	16	0	0	0	3	17 1/3	18	7	6	7	14
1998—Omaha (Pacific Coast)	6	4	.600	2.39	61	0	0	0	4	60 1/3	54	22	16	24	62
—Kansas City (A.L.)	0	0	...	10.50	7	0	0	0	0	6	9	7	7	2	3
Major league totals (2 years)	0	0	...	11.70	10	0	0	0	0	10	12	13	13	10	5

McDONALD, DONZELL OF YANKEES

PERSONAL: Born February 20, 1975, in Long Beach, Calif. ... 5-11/165. ... Bats both, throws right. ... Brother of Darnell McDonald, outfielder in Baltimore Orioles organization.
HIGH SCHOOL: Cherry Creek (Colo.).
JUNIOR COLLEGE: Yavapai College (Ariz.).
TRANSACTIONS/CAREER NOTES: Selected by New York Yankees organization in 22nd round of free-agent draft (June 1, 1995). ... On disabled list (July 3-August 6, 1997).
STATISTICAL NOTES: Led New York-Pennsylvania League outfielders with 179 total chances in 1996. ... Led Eastern League in caught stealing with 22 in 1998. ... Led Eastern League outfielders with 328 total chances in 1998.

M

Year Team (League)	Pos.	G	AB	R	H	2B	3B	HR	RBI	Avg.	BB	SO	SB	PO	A	E	Avg.
								BATTING						FIELDING			
1995—GC Yankees (GCL)	OF	28	110	23	26	5	1	0	9	.236	16	24	11	44	0	3	.936
1996—Oneonta (NYP)	OF	74	282	57	78	8	*10	2	30	.277	43	62	*54	*169	4	6	.966
1997—Tampa (Fla. St.)	OF	77	297	69	88	23	8	3	23	.296	48	75	39	173	3	4	.978
1998—Norwich (Eastern)	OF	134	495	80	125	20	7	6	36	.253	55	127	35	*312	8	8	.976
—Tampa (Fla. St.)	OF	5	18	6	6	1	2	0	2	.333	2	7	2	14	0	0	1.000

McDONALD, JASON OF ATHLETICS

PERSONAL: Born March 20, 1972, in Modesto, Calif. ... 5-7/182. ... Bats both, throws right. ... Full name: Jason Adam McDonald.
HIGH SCHOOL: Elk Grove (Calif.) Unified School.
COLLEGE: Houston.
TRANSACTIONS/CAREER NOTES: Selected by Oakland Athletics organization in fourth round of free-agent draft (June 3, 1993). ... On Oakland disabled list (April 19-May 4 and May 24-August 4, 1998); included rehabilitation assignments to Edmonton (April 30-May 4) and Huntsville (July 27-August 4).
STATISTICAL NOTES: Led California League shortstops with 43 errors in 1995. ... Tied for Pacific Coast League lead in being hit by pitch with 15 in 1996. ... Led Pacific Coast League second basemen with 254 putouts, 352 assists, 24 errors, 630 total chances and 75 double plays in 1996.

Year Team (League)	Pos.	G	AB	R	H	2B	3B	HR	RBI	Avg.	BB	SO	SB	PO	A	E	Avg.
								BATTING						FIELDING			
1993—S. Oregon (N'west)	2B	35	112	26	33	5	2	0	8	.295	31	17	22	70	77	7	.955
1994—W. Mich. (Mid.)	2B-OF-SS	116	404	67	96	11	*9	2	31	.238	81	87	52	253	167	21	.952
1995—Modesto (California)	SS-OF-2B	133	493	109	129	25	7	6	50	.262	*110	84	*70	247	246	†50	.908
1996—Edmonton (PCL)	2B-OF	137	479	71	114	7	5	8	46	.238	63	82	33	†302	†352	†25	.963
1997—Edmonton (PCL)	OF	79	276	74	73	14	6	4	30	.264	74	58	31	187	10	5	.975
—Oakland (A.L.)	OF	78	236	47	62	11	4	4	14	.263	36	49	13	151	3	5	.969
1998—Oakland (A.L.)	OF-DH	70	175	25	44	9	0	1	16	.251	27	33	10	122	7	6	.956
—Edmonton (PCL)	OF	12	43	12	10	1	1	2	5	.233	15	11	7	37	3	0	1.000
—Huntsville (Sou.)	OF	7	20	9	6	2	0	2	4	.300	8	6	4	10	1	0	1.000
Major league totals (2 years)		148	411	72	106	20	4	5	30	.258	63	82	23	273	10	11	.963

McDONALD, JOHN   SS   INDIANS

PERSONAL: Born September 24, 1974, in New London, Conn. ... 5-11/175. ... Bats right, throws right. ... Full name: John J. McDonald.
HIGH SCHOOL: East Lyme (Conn.).
JUNIOR COLLEGE: Connecticut (Avery Point).
COLLEGE: Providence.
TRANSACTIONS/CAREER NOTES: Selected by Cleveland Indians organization in 12th round of free-agent draft (June 4, 1996).
STATISTICAL NOTES: Led Carolina League shortstops with 647 total chances and 105 double plays in 1997. ... Led Eastern League shortstops with 672 total chances in 1998.

								BATTING						FIELDING		
Year	Team (League)	Pos.	G	AB	R	H	2B	3B	HR	RBI	Avg.	BB	SO	SB	PO	A	E	Avg.
1996—	Watertown (NYP)	SS	75	278	48	75	11	0	2	26	.270	32	49	11	85	228	18	.946
1997—	Kinston (Carolina)	SS	130	541	77	140	27	3	5	53	.259	51	75	6	*209	*413	25	*.961
1998—	Akron (Eastern)	SS	132	514	68	118	18	2	2	43	.230	43	61	17	*242	407	23	.966

McDOWELL, JACK   P   ANGELS

PERSONAL: Born January 16, 1966, in Van Nuys, Calif. ... 6-5/190. ... Throws right, bats right. ... Full name: Jack Burns McDowell.
HIGH SCHOOL: Notre Dame (Van Nuys, Calif.).
COLLEGE: Stanford.
TRANSACTIONS/CAREER NOTES: Selected by Boston Red Sox organization in 20th round of free-agent draft (June 4, 1984); did not sign. ... Selected by Chicago White Sox organization in first round (fifth pick overall) of free-agent draft (June 2, 1987). ... On suspended list (August 20-24, 1991). ... Traded by White Sox to New York Yankees for P Keith Heberling and a player to be named later (December 14, 1994); White Sox acquired OF Lyle Mouton to complete deal (April 22, 1995). ... Granted free agency (October 31, 1995). ... Signed by Cleveland Indians (December 14, 1995). ... On disabled list (July 22-August 9, 1996 and May 13, 1997-remainder of season). ... Granted free agency (November 5, 1997). ... Signed by Anaheim Angels (February 27, 1998). ... On Anaheim disabled list (April 27-May 21 and June 1-August 15, 1998); included rehabilitation assignments to Vancouver (July 25-29), Lake Elsinore (July 30-August 9) and Midland (August 10-15). ... On suspended list (August 15-18, 1998). ... Granted free agency (October 23, 1998). ... Re-signed by Angels (December 7, 1998).
HONORS: Named righthanded pitcher on The Sporting News A.L. All-Star team (1992-93). ... Named A.L. Pitcher of the Year by The Sporting News (1993). ... Named A.L. Cy Young Award winner by Baseball Writers' Association of America (1993).
STATISTICAL NOTES: Pitched 15-1 one-hit, complete-game victory against Milwaukee (July 14, 1991).

Year	Team (League)	W	L	Pct.	ERA	G	GS	CG	ShO	Sv.	IP	H	R	ER	BB	SO
1987—	GC White Sox (GCL)	0	1	.000	2.57	2	1	0	0	0	7	4	3	2	1	12
—	Birmingham (Southern)	1	2	.333	7.84	4	4	1	1	0	$20^2/_3$	19	20	18	8	17
—	Chicago (A.L.)	3	0	1.000	1.93	4	4	0	0	0	28	16	6	6	6	15
1988—	Chicago (A.L.)	5	10	.333	3.97	26	26	1	0	0	$158^2/_3$	147	85	70	68	84
1989—	Vancouver (PCL)	5	6	.455	6.13	16	16	1	0	0	$86^2/_3$	97	60	59	50	65
—	GC White Sox (GCL)	2	0	1.000	0.75	4	4	0	0	0	24	19	2	2	4	25
1990—	Chicago (A.L.)	14	9	.609	3.82	33	33	4	0	0	205	189	93	87	77	165
1991—	Chicago (A.L.)	17	10	.630	3.41	35	•35	*15	3	0	$253^2/_3$	212	97	96	82	191
1992—	Chicago (A.L.)	20	10	.667	3.18	34	34	*13	1	0	$260^2/_3$	247	95	92	75	178
1993—	Chicago (A.L.)	*22	10	.688	3.37	34	34	10	*4	0	$256^2/_3$	261	104	96	69	158
1994—	Chicago (A.L.)	10	9	.526	3.73	25	•25	6	2	0	181	186	82	75	42	127
1995—	New York (A.L.)■	15	10	.600	3.93	30	30	*8	2	0	$217^2/_3$	211	106	95	78	157
1996—	Cleveland (A.L.)■..............	13	9	.591	5.11	30	30	5	1	0	192	214	119	109	67	141
1997—	Cleveland (A.L.)	3	3	.500	5.09	8	6	0	0	0	$40^2/_3$	44	25	23	18	38
1998—	Anaheim (A.L.)■	5	3	.625	5.09	14	14	0	0	0	76	96	45	43	19	45
—	Vancouver (PCL)	0	0	. . .	6.00	1	1	0	0	0	3	4	2	2	2	0
—	Lake Elsinore (Calif.)	0	1	.000	9.00	1	1	0	0	0	5	7	5	5	0	4
—	Midland (Texas)	0	1	.000	3.86	1	1	0	0	0	7	5	3	3	2	5
Major league totals (11 years)		**127**	**83**	**.605**	**3.81**	**273**	**271**	**62**	**13**	**0**	**1870**	**1823**	**857**	**792**	**601**	**1299**

DIVISION SERIES RECORD

RECORDS: Holds A.L. career record for most hit batsmen—2.

Year	Team (League)	W	L	Pct.	ERA	G	GS	CG	ShO	Sv.	IP	H	R	ER	BB	SO
1995—	New York (A.L.)	0	2	.000	9.00	2	1	0	0	0	7	8	7	7	4	6
1996—	Cleveland (A.L.)	0	0	. . .	6.35	1	1	0	0	0	$5^2/_3$	6	4	4	1	5
Div. series totals (2 years)		**0**	**2**	**.000**	**7.82**	**3**	**2**	**0**	**0**	**0**	**$12^2/_3$**	**14**	**11**	**11**	**5**	**11**

CHAMPIONSHIP SERIES RECORD

RECORDS: Holds single-game record for most hits allowed—13 (October 5, 1993). ... Shares single-game record for most earned runs allowed—7 (October 5, 1993).

Year	Team (League)	W	L	Pct.	ERA	G	GS	CG	ShO	Sv.	IP	H	R	ER	BB	SO
1993—	Chicago (A.L.)	0	2	.000	10.00	2	2	0	0	0	9	18	10	10	5	5

ALL-STAR GAME RECORD

Year	League	W	L	Pct.	ERA	GS	CG	ShO	Sv.	IP	H	R	ER	BB	SO
1991—	American	0	0	. . .	0.00	0	0	0	0	2	1	0	0	2	0
1992—	American	0	0	. . .	0.00	0	0	0	0	1	0	0	0	0	0
1993—	American	1	0	1.000	0.00	0	0	0	0	1	0	0	0	0	0
All-Star totals (3 years)		**1**	**0**	**1.000**	**0.00**	**0**	**0**	**0**	**0**	**4**	**1**	**0**	**0**	**2**	**0**

McELROY, CHUCK   P   ROCKIES

PERSONAL: Born October 1, 1967, in Port Arthur, Texas. ... 6-0/205. ... Throws left, bats left. ... Full name: Charles Dwayne McElroy. ... Name pronounced MACK-il-roy.
HIGH SCHOOL: Lincoln (Port Arthur, Texas).
TRANSACTIONS/CAREER NOTES: Selected by Philadelphia Phillies organization in eighth round of free-agent draft (June 2, 1986). ... Traded by Phillies with P Bob Scanlan to Chicago Cubs for P Mitch Williams (April 7, 1991). ... Traded by Cubs to Cincinnati Reds for P Larry

M

Luebbers, P Mike Anderson and C Darron Cox (December 10, 1993). ... On disabled list (June 7-23, 1995). ... On Cincinnati disabled list (March 28-April 28, 1996); included rehabilitation assignment to Indianapolis (April 12-28). ... Traded by Reds to California Angels for P Lee Smith (May 27, 1996). ... On California disabled list (August 11-28, 1996). ... Angels franchise renamed Anaheim Angels for 1997 season. ... Traded by Angels with C Jorge Fabregas to Chicago White Sox for OF Tony Phillips and C Chad Kreuter (May 18, 1997). ... Selected by Arizona Diamondbacks in third round (67th pick overall) of expansion draft (November 18, 1997). ... Traded by Diamondbacks to Colorado Rockies for OF Harvey Pulliam (November 18, 1997).

MISCELLANEOUS: Appeared in one game as pinch runner with Chicago (1997).

Year	Team (League)	W	L	Pct.	ERA	G	GS	CG	ShO	Sv.	IP	H	R	ER	BB	SO
1986—	Utica (N.Y.-Penn)	4	6	.400	2.95	14	14	5	1	0	94 2/3	85	40	31	28	91
1987—	Spartanburg (SAL)	14	4	.778	3.11	24	21	5	2	0	130 1/3	117	51	45	48	115
—	Clearwater (Fla. St.)	1	0	1.000	0.00	2	2	0	0	0	7 1/3	1	1	0	4	7
1988—	Reading (Eastern)	9	12	.429	4.50	28	26	4	2	0	160	•173	89	*80	70	92
1989—	Reading (Eastern)	3	1	.750	2.68	32	0	0	0	12	47	39	14	14	14	39
—	Scran./W.B. (Int'l)	1	2	.333	2.93	14	0	0	0	3	15 1/3	13	6	5	11	12
—	Philadelphia (N.L.)	0	0	. . .	1.74	11	0	0	0	0	10 1/3	12	2	2	4	8
1990—	Scran./W.B. (Int'l)	6	8	.429	2.72	57	1	0	0	7	76	62	24	23	34	78
—	Philadelphia (N.L.)	0	1	.000	7.71	16	0	0	0	0	14	24	13	12	10	16
1991—	Chicago (N.L.)■	6	2	.750	1.95	71	0	0	0	3	101 1/3	73	33	22	57	92
1992—	Chicago (N.L.)	4	7	.364	3.55	72	0	0	0	6	83 2/3	73	40	33	51	83
1993—	Chicago (N.L.)	2	2	.500	4.56	49	0	0	0	0	47 1/3	51	30	24	25	31
—	Iowa (Am. Assoc.)	0	1	.000	4.60	9	0	0	0	2	15 2/3	19	10	8	9	13
1994—	Cincinnati (N.L.)■	1	2	.333	2.34	52	0	0	0	5	57 2/3	52	15	15	15	38
1995—	Cincinnati (N.L.)	3	4	.429	6.02	44	0	0	0	0	40 1/3	46	29	27	15	27
1996—	Indianapolis (A.A.)	1	1	.500	2.70	5	3	0	0	0	13 1/3	11	4	4	4	10
—	Cincinnati (N.L.)	2	0	1.000	6.57	12	0	0	0	0	12 1/3	13	10	9	10	13
—	California (A.L.)■	5	1	.833	2.95	40	0	0	0	0	36 2/3	32	12	12	13	32
1997—	Anaheim (A.L.)	0	0	. . .	3.45	13	0	0	0	0	15 2/3	17	7	6	3	18
—	Chicago (A.L.)■	1	3	.250	3.94	48	0	0	0	1	59 1/3	56	29	26	19	44
1998—	Colorado (N.L.)■	6	4	.600	2.90	78	0	0	0	2	68 1/3	68	23	22	24	61
A.L. totals (2 years)		6	4	.600	3.55	101	0	0	0	1	111 2/3	105	48	44	35	94
N.L. totals (9 years)		24	22	.522	3.43	405	0	0	0	16	435 1/3	412	195	166	211	369
Major league totals (10 years)		30	26	.536	3.46	506	0	0	0	17	547	517	243	210	246	463

McEWING, JOE   2B/OF   CARDINALS

PERSONAL: Born October 19, 1972, in Bristol, Pa. ... 5-11/170. ... Bats right, throws right. ... Full name: Joseph Earl McEwing.
HIGH SCHOOL: Bishop Egan (Fairless Hills, Pa.).
JUNIOR COLLEGE: County College of Morris (N.J.).
TRANSACTIONS/CAREER NOTES: Selected by St. Louis Cardinals organization in 28th round of free-agent draft (June 1, 1992).
STATISTICAL NOTES: Led Arizona League outfielders with 94 putouts, 11 assists, four double plays, 106 total chances and .991 fielding percentage in 1992. ... Led South Atlantic League with 15 sacrifice hits in 1993. ... Led Texas League outfielders with .993 fielding percentage in 1996. ... Tied for Pacific Coast League lead with three double plays by outfielder in 1998.

							BATTING						FIELDING		
Year	Team (League)	Pos.	G	AB	R	H	2B	3B	HR	RBI	Avg.	BB	SO	SB	PO	A	E	Avg.
1992—	Ariz. Cardinals (Ariz.)	OF-SS	55	211	*55	71	4	2	0	13	.336	24	18	23	†94	†12	1	.991
1993—	Savannah (S. Atl.)	OF	138	511	*94	127	35	1	0	43	.249	89	73	22	262	13	5	.982
1994—	Madison (Midwest)	OF	90	347	58	112	24	2	4	47	.323	32	53	18	184	6	5	.974
—	St. Peters. (FSL)	OF-2B	50	197	22	49	7	0	1	20	.249	19	32	8	105	23	2	.985
1995—	St. Peters. (FSL)	2B-OF	75	281	33	64	13	0	1	23	.228	25	49	2	139	176	15	.955
—	Arkansas (Texas)	OF-2B	42	121	16	30	4	0	2	12	.248	9	13	3	61	12	0	1.000
1996—	Arkansas (Texas)	OF-2B	106	216	27	45	7	3	2	14	.208	13	32	2	134	15	2	†.987
1997—	Arkansas (Texas)	0-2-1-3	103	263	33	68	6	3	4	35	.259	19	39	2	134	24	2	.988
1998—	Arkansas (Texas)	OF-SS-P	60	223	45	79	21	4	9	46	.354	21	18	4	130	25	1	.994
—	Memphis (PCL)	0-3-S-2	78	329	52	110	30	7	6	46	.334	21	39	11	143	24	3	.982
—	St. Louis (N.L.)	2B-OF	10	20	5	4	1	0	0	1	.200	1	3	0	10	10	0	1.000
Major league totals (1 year)			10	20	5	4	1	0	0	1	.200	1	3	0	10	10	0	1.000

RECORD AS PITCHER

Year	Team (League)	W	L	Pct.	ERA	G	GS	CG	ShO	Sv.	IP	H	R	ER	BB	SO
1997—	Arkansas (Texas)	0	0	. . .	27.00	1	0	0	0	0	1/3	1	1	1	0	0
1998—	Arkansas (Texas)	0	0	. . .	27.00	1	0	0	0	0	1	3	3	3	1	1

McGEE, WILLIE   OF   CARDINALS

PERSONAL: Born November 2, 1958, in San Francisco. ... 6-1/185. ... Bats both, throws right. ... Full name: Willie Dean McGee.
HIGH SCHOOL: Harry Ellis (Richmond, Calif.).
JUNIOR COLLEGE: Diablo Valley College (Calif.).
TRANSACTIONS/CAREER NOTES: Selected by Chicago White Sox organization in seventh round of free-agent draft (June 8, 1976); did not sign. ... Selected by New York Yankees organization in secondary phase of free-agent draft (January 11, 1977). ... On disabled list (May 22-June 7 and July 14-August 7, 1980; and April 24-June 4, 1981). ... Traded by Yankees organization to St. Louis Cardinals organization for P Bob Sykes (October 21, 1981). ... On Louisville disabled list (April 13-23, 1982). ... On St. Louis disabled list (March 30-April 29, 1983); included rehabilitation assignment to Arkansas (April 18-29). ... On disabled list (July 12-27, 1984 and August 3-27, 1986). ... On disabled list (June 7-July 18, 1989); included rehabilitation assignment to Louisville (July 8-18). ... On St. Louis disabled list (July 26-August 14, 1989). ... Traded by Cardinals to Oakland Athletics for OF Felix Jose, 3B Stan Royer and P Daryl Green (August 29, 1990). ... Granted free agency (November 5, 1990). ... Signed by San Francisco Giants (December 3, 1990). ... On San Francisco disabled list (July 12-August 1, 1991); included rehabilitation assignment to Phoenix (July 28-August 1). ... On disabled list (July 10-30, 1993 and June 8, 1994-remainder of season). ... Granted free agency (October 14, 1994). ... Signed by Pawtucket, Boston Red Sox organization (June 6, 1995). ... Granted free agency (November 3, 1995). ... Signed by Cardinals (December 15, 1995). ... Granted free agency (November 13, 1996). ... Re-signed by

Cardinals (December 4, 1996). ... On disabled list (July 12-29, 1997). ... Granted free agency (October 29, 1997). ... Re-signed by Cardinals (December 5, 1997). ... Granted free agency (October 23, 1998). ... Re-signed by Cardinals (December 7, 1998).

RECORDS: Holds modern N.L. single-season record for highest batting average by switch hitter (100 or more games)—.353 (1985). ... Shares major league single-season record for fewest double plays by outfielder who led league in double plays—3 (1991).

HONORS: Won N.L. Gold Glove as outfielder (1983, 1985-86). ... Named N.L. Player of the Year by THE SPORTING NEWS (1985). ... Named outfielder on THE SPORTING NEWS N.L. All-Star team (1985). ... Named outfielder on THE SPORTING NEWS N.L. Silver Slugger team (1985). ... Named N.L. Most Valuable Player by Baseball Writers' Association of America (1985).

STATISTICAL NOTES: Hit for the cycle (June 23, 1984). ... Led N.L. in grounding into double plays with 24 in 1987. ... Had 22-game hitting streak (July 5-August 1, 1990). ... Tied for N.L. lead in double plays by outfielder with three in 1991. ... Career major league grand slams: 2.

Year Team (League)	Pos.	G	AB	R	H	2B	3B	HR	RBI	Avg.	BB	SO	SB	PO	A	E	Avg.
1977— Oneonta (NYP)	OF	65	225	31	53	4	3	2	22	.236	13	65	13	103	5	10	.915
1978— Fort Laud. (FSL)	OF	124	423	62	106	6	6	0	37	.251	50	78	25	243	12	9	.966
1979— West Haven (East.).....	OF	49	115	21	28	3	1	1	8	.243	13	17	7	88	3	3	.968
— Fort Laud. (FSL)	OF	46	176	25	56	8	3	1	18	.318	17	34	16	103	3	2	.981
1980— Nashville (Southern) ..	OF	78	223	35	63	4	5	1	22	.283	19	39	7	127	6	6	.957
1981— Nashville (Southern) ..	OF	100	388	77	125	20	5	7	63	.322	24	46	24	203	10	6	.973
1982— Louisville (A.A.)■.......	OF	13	55	11	16	2	2	1	3	.291	2	7	5	40	0	1	.976
— St. Louis (N.L.)...........	OF	123	422	43	125	12	8	4	56	.296	12	58	24	245	3	11	.958
1983— St. Louis (N.L.)..........	OF	147	601	75	172	22	8	5	75	.286	26	98	39	385	7	5	.987
— Arkansas (Texas)	OF	7	29	5	8	1	1	0	2	.276	4	6	1	7	0	0	1.000
1984— St. Louis (N.L.)..........	OF	145	571	82	166	19	11	6	50	.291	29	80	43	374	10	6	.985
1985— St. Louis (N.L.)..........	OF	152	612	114	*216	26	*18	10	82	*.353	34	86	56	382	11	9	.978
1986— St. Louis (N.L.)..........	OF	124	497	65	127	22	7	7	48	.256	37	82	19	325	9	3	*.991
1987— St. Louis (N.L.)..........	OF-SS	153	620	76	177	37	11	11	105	.285	24	90	16	354	10	7	.981
1988— St. Louis (N.L.)..........	OF	137	562	73	164	24	6	3	50	.292	32	84	41	348	9	9	.975
1989— St. Louis (N.L.)..........	OF	58	199	23	47	10	2	3	17	.236	10	34	8	118	2	3	.976
— Louisville (A.A.)	OF	8	27	5	11	4	0	0	4	.407	3	4	3	20	1	1	.955
1990— St. Louis (N.L.)..........	OF	125	501	76	168	32	5	3	62	*.335	38	86	28	341	13	*16	.957
— Oakland (A.L.)..........	OF-DH	29	113	23	31	3	2	0	15	.274	10	18	3	72	1	1	.986
1991— San Fran. (N.L.)■.......	OF	131	497	67	155	30	3	4	43	.312	34	74	17	259	6	6	.978
— Phoenix (PCL)	OF	4	10	4	5	1	0	0	1	.500	3	1	2	10	0	1	.909
1992— San Francisco (N.L.) ..	OF	138	474	56	141	20	2	1	36	.297	29	88	13	231	11	6	.976
1993— San Francisco (N.L.) ..	OF	130	475	53	143	28	1	4	46	.301	38	67	10	224	9	5	.979
1994— San Francisco (N.L.) ..	OF	45	156	19	44	3	0	5	23	.282	15	24	3	80	2	1	.988
1995— Pawtucket (Int'l)■......	OF	5	21	9	10	0	0	0	2	.476	0	4	2	7	0	1	.875
— Boston (A.L.)	OF	67	200	32	57	11	3	2	15	.285	9	41	5	101	7	3	.973
1996— St. Louis (N.L.)■.......	OF-1B	123	309	52	95	15	2	5	41	.307	18	60	5	142	10	5	.968
1997— St. Louis (N.L.)..........	OF-DH	122	300	29	90	19	4	3	38	.300	22	59	8	99	6	2	.981
1998— St. Louis (N.L.)..........	OF-DH-1B	120	269	27	68	10	1	3	34	.253	14	49	7	102	8	7	.940
American League totals (2 years)		96	313	55	88	14	5	2	30	.281	19	59	8	173	8	4	.978
National League totals (16 years)		1973	7065	930	2098	329	89	77	806	.297	412	1119	337	4009	126	101	.976
Major league totals (17 years)		2069	7378	985	2186	343	94	79	836	.296	431	1178	345	4182	134	105	.976

DIVISION SERIES RECORD

Year Team (League)	Pos.	G	AB	R	H	2B	3B	HR	RBI	Avg.	BB	SO	SB	PO	A	E	Avg.
1995— Boston (A.L.)..............	OF-PH	2	4	0	1	0	0	0	1	.250	0	2	0	0	0	0	...
1996— St. Louis (N.L.)...........	OF	3	10	1	1	0	0	0	1	.100	1	3	0	9	0	1	.900
Division series totals (2 years)		5	14	1	2	0	0	0	2	.143	1	5	0	9	0	1	.900

CHAMPIONSHIP SERIES RECORD

RECORDS: Shares single-series record for most triples—2 (1982). ... Shares N.L. career records for most triples—3; and most times caught stealing—4. ... Shares N.L. single-series record for most times caught stealing—3 (1985).

Year Team (League)	Pos.	G	AB	R	H	2B	3B	HR	RBI	Avg.	BB	SO	SB	PO	A	E	Avg.
1982— St. Louis (N.L.)..........	OF	3	13	4	4	0	2	1	5	.308	0	5	0	12	0	1	.923
1985— St. Louis (N.L.)..........	OF	6	26	6	7	1	0	0	3	.269	3	6	2	18	0	0	1.000
1987— St. Louis (N.L.)..........	OF	7	26	2	8	1	1	0	2	.308	0	5	0	16	0	0	1.000
1990— Oakland (A.L.)	OF-PR-DH	3	9	3	2	1	0	0	0	.222	1	2	2	2	0	0	1.000
1996— St. Louis (N.L.)..........	OF-PH	6	15	0	5	0	0	0	0	.333	0	3	0	5	0	1	.833
Championship series totals (5 years)		25	89	15	26	3	3	1	10	.292	4	21	4	53	0	2	.964

WORLD SERIES RECORD

NOTES: Member of World Series championship team (1982).

Year Team (League)	Pos.	G	AB	R	H	2B	3B	HR	RBI	Avg.	BB	SO	SB	PO	A	E	Avg.
1982— St. Louis (N.L.)..........	OF	6	25	6	6	0	0	2	5	.240	1	3	2	24	0	0	1.000
1985— St. Louis (N.L.)..........	OF	7	27	2	7	2	0	1	2	.259	1	3	1	15	0	0	1.000
1987— St. Louis (N.L.)..........	OF	7	27	2	10	2	0	0	4	.370	0	9	0	21	1	1	.957
1990— Oakland (A.L.)	OF-PH	4	10	1	2	1	0	0	0	.200	0	2	1	5	0	0	1.000
World Series totals (4 years)		24	89	11	25	5	0	3	11	.281	2	17	4	65	1	1	.985

ALL-STAR GAME RECORD

Year League	Pos.	AB	R	H	2B	3B	HR	RBI	Avg.	BB	SO	SB	PO	A	E	Avg.
1983— National	OF	2	0	1	0	0	0	0	.500	0	0	0	2	0	0	1.000
1985— National	OF	2	0	1	1	0	0	2	.500	0	0	0	1	0	0	1.000
1987— National	OF	4	0	0	0	0	0	0	.000	0	0	0	2	0	0	1.000
1988— National	PR-OF	2	0	0	0	0	0	0	.000	0	0	0	1	0	0	1.000
All-Star Game totals (4 years)		10	0	2	1	0	0	2	.200	0	0	0	6	0	0	1.000

M

PERSONAL: Born October 31, 1963, in Tampa. ... 6-3/215. ... Bats left, throws left. ... Full name: Frederick Stanley McGriff. ... Cousin of Terry McGriff, minor league catcher with four major league teams (1987-90, 1993 and 1994); and uncle of Charles Johnson, catcher, Baltimore Orioles.

HIGH SCHOOL: Jefferson (Tampa).

TRANSACTIONS/CAREER NOTES: Selected by New York Yankees organization in ninth round of free-agent draft (June 8, 1981). ... Traded by Yankees organization with OF Dave Collins, P Mike Morgan and cash to Toronto Blue Jays for OF/C Tom Dodd and P Dale Murray (December 9, 1982). ... On disabled list (June 5-August 14, 1985). ... Traded by Blue Jays with SS Tony Fernandez to San Diego Padres for OF Joe Carter and 2B Roberto Alomar (December 5, 1990). ... On suspended list (June 23-26, 1992). ... Traded by Padres to Atlanta Braves for OF Melvin Nieves, P Donnie Elliott and OF Vince Moore (July 18, 1993). ... Granted free agency (November 6, 1995). ... Re-signed by Braves (December 2, 1995). ... Traded by Braves to Tampa Bay Devil Rays for a player to be named later or cash (November 18, 1997); Devil Rays sent Braves an undisclosed amount of cash to complete deal (April 1, 1998).

RECORDS: Shares major league record for most grand slams in two consecutive games—2 (August 13 and 14, 1991). ... Shares N.L. single-season record for fewest errors by first baseman who led league in errors—12 (1992).

HONORS: Named first baseman on THE SPORTING NEWS A.L. All-Star team (1989). ... Named first baseman on THE SPORTING NEWS A.L. Silver Slugger team (1989). ... Named first baseman on THE SPORTING NEWS N.L. All-Star team (1992-93). ... Named first baseman on THE SPORTING NEWS N.L. Silver Slugger team (1992-93).

STATISTICAL NOTES: Led International League first basemen with .992 fielding percentage, 1,219 putouts, 85 assists, 1,314 total chances and 108 double plays in 1986. ... Tied for International League lead in intentional bases on balls received with eight and in grounding into double plays with 16 in 1986. ... Led A.L. first basemen with 1,592 total chances and 148 double plays in 1989. ... Led N.L. with 26 intentional base on balls received in 1991. ... Led N.L. first basemen with 1,077 total chances in 1994. ... Led N.L. in grounding into double plays with 22 in 1997. ... Led A.L. first basemen with 140 double plays in 1998. ... Career major league grand slams: 5.

MISCELLANEOUS: Holds Tampa Bay Devil Rays all-time records for most home runs (19) and most runs batted in (81).

						BATTING									FIELDING		
Year	Team (League)	Pos.	G	AB	R	H	2B	3B	HR	RBI	Avg.	BB	SO	SB	PO	A	E	Avg.
1981— GC Yankees (GCL)	1B	29	81	6	12	2	0	0	9	.148	11	20	0	176	8	7	.963
1982— GC Yankees (GCL)	1B	62	217	38	59	11	1	*9	•41	.272	*48	63	6	514	*56	8	.986
1983— Florence (S. Atl.)■	1B	33	119	26	37	3	1	7	26	.311	20	35	3	250	14	6	.978
— Kinston (Carolina)	1B	94	350	53	85	14	1	21	57	.243	55	112	3	784	57	10	.988
1984— Knoxville (Southern)	1B	56	189	29	47	13	2	9	25	.249	29	55	0	481	45	10	.981
— Syracuse (Int'l)	1B	70	238	28	56	10	1	13	28	.235	26	89	0	644	45	3	.996
1985— Syracuse (Int'l)	1B	51	176	19	40	8	2	5	20	.227	23	53	0	433	37	5	.989
1986— Syracuse (Int'l)	1B-OF	133	468	69	121	23	4	19	74	.259	83	119	0	†1219	†85	10	†.992
— Toronto (A.L.)	DH-1B	3	5	1	1	0	0	0	0	.200	0	2	0	3	0	0	1.000
1987— Toronto (A.L.)	DH-1B	107	295	58	73	16	0	20	43	.247	60	104	3	108	7	2	.983
1988— Toronto (A.L.)	1B	154	536	100	151	35	4	34	82	.282	79	149	6	1344	93	5	.997
1989— Toronto (A.L.)	1B-DH	161	551	98	148	27	3	*36	92	.269	119	131	7	1460	115	*17	.989
1990— Toronto (A.L.)	1B-DH	153	557	91	167	21	1	35	88	.300	94	108	5	1246	126	6	.996
1991— San Diego (N.L.)■	1B	153	528	84	147	19	1	31	106	.278	105	135	4	1370	87	14	.990
1992— San Diego (N.L.)	1B	152	531	79	152	30	4	*35	104	.286	96	108	8	1219	108	•12	.991
1993— San Diego (N.L.)	1B	83	302	52	83	11	1	18	46	.275	42	55	4	640	47	12	.983
— Atlanta (N.L.)■	1B	68	255	59	79	18	1	19	55	.310	34	51	1	563	45	5	.992
1994— Atlanta (N.L.)	1B	113	424	81	135	25	1	34	94	.318	50	76	7	*1004	66	7	.994
1995— Atlanta (N.L.)	1B	•144	528	85	148	27	1	27	93	.280	65	99	3	1285	96	5	.996
1996— Atlanta (N.L.)	1B	159	617	81	182	37	1	28	107	.295	68	116	7	1416	124	12	.992
1997— Atlanta (N.L.)■	1B	152	564	77	156	25	1	22	97	.277	68	112	5	1191	96	13	.990
1998— Tampa Bay (A.L.)	1B-DH	151	564	73	160	33	0	19	81	.284	79	118	7	1150	81	6	.995
American League totals (6 years)		729	2508	421	700	132	8	144	386	.279	431	612	28	5311	422	36	.994
National League totals (7 years)		1024	3749	598	1082	192	11	214	702	.289	528	752	39	8688	669	80	.992
Major league totals (13 years)		1753	6257	1019	1782	324	19	358	1088	.285	959	1364	67	13999	1091	116	.992

DIVISION SERIES RECORD

RECORDS: Holds N.L. single-game record for most runs batted in—5 (October 7, 1995). ... Shares single-game record for most home runs—2 (October 7, 1995). ... Shares N.L. career record for most runs batted in—10.

						BATTING									FIELDING		
Year	Team (League)	Pos.	G	AB	R	H	2B	3B	HR	RBI	Avg.	BB	SO	SB	PO	A	E	Avg.
1995— Atlanta (N.L.)	1B	4	18	4	6	0	0	2	6	.333	2	3	0	39	2	0	1.000
1996— Atlanta (N.L.)	1B	3	9	1	3	1	0	1	3	.333	2	1	0	25	3	0	1.000
1997— Atlanta (N.L.)	1B	3	9	4	2	0	0	0	1	.222	3	2	0	27	3	0	1.000
Division series totals (3 years)		10	36	9	11	1	0	3	10	.306	7	6	0	91	8	0	1.000

CHAMPIONSHIP SERIES RECORD

RECORDS: Shares N.L. single-game record for most at-bats—6 (October 14, 1996). ... Shares N.L. single-game record for most runs—4 (October 17, 1996). ... Shares career record for most doubles—7.

						BATTING									FIELDING		
Year	Team (League)	Pos.	G	AB	R	H	2B	3B	HR	RBI	Avg.	BB	SO	SB	PO	A	E	Avg.
1989— Toronto (A.L.)■	1B	5	21	1	3	0	0	0	3	.143	0	4	0	35	2	1	.974
1993— Atlanta (N.L.)	1B	6	23	6	10	2	0	1	4	.435	4	7	0	49	4	0	1.000
1995— Atlanta (N.L.)	1B	4	16	5	7	4	0	0	0	.438	3	0	0	42	4	0	1.000
1996— Atlanta (N.L.)	1B	7	28	6	7	0	1	2	7	.250	3	5	0	55	2	1	.983
1997— Atlanta (N.L.)	1B	6	21	0	7	1	0	0	4	.333	2	7	0	41	2	1	.977
Championship series totals (5 years)		28	109	18	34	7	1	3	18	.312	12	23	0	222	14	3	.987

WORLD SERIES RECORD

NOTES: Hit home run in first at-bat (October 21, 1995). ... Member of World Series championship team (1995).

						BATTING									FIELDING		
Year	Team (League)	Pos.	G	AB	R	H	2B	3B	HR	RBI	Avg.	BB	SO	SB	PO	A	E	Avg.
1995— Atlanta (N.L.)	1B	6	23	5	6	2	0	2	3	.261	3	7	1	68	2	1	.986
1996— Atlanta (N.L.)	1B	6	20	4	6	0	0	2	6	.300	6	4	0	62	5	0	1.000
World Series totals (2 years)		12	43	9	12	2	0	4	9	.279	9	11	1	130	7	1	.993

M

NOTES: Named Most Valuable Player (1994).

Year	League	Pos.	AB	R	H	2B	3B	HR	RBI	Avg.	BB	SO	SB	PO	A	E	Avg.
								BATTING						FIELDING			
1992—National		1B	3	0	2	0	0	0	1	.667	0	0	0	7	1	0	1.000
1994—National		PH-1B	1	1	1	0	0	1	2	1.000	0	0	0	0	0	0	...
1995—National		1B	3	0	0	0	0	0	0	.000	0	2	0	5	0	0	1.000
1996—National		1B	2	0	0	0	0	0	0	.000	0	2	0	2	1	0	1.000
All-Star Game totals (4 years)			9	1	3	0	0	1	3	.333	0	4	0	14	2	0	1.000

McGUIRE, RYAN — 1B — EXPOS

PERSONAL: Born November 23, 1971, in Bellflower, Calif. ... 6-0/215. ... Bats left, throws left. ... Full name: Ryan Byron McGuire.
HIGH SCHOOL: El Camino Real (Woodland Hills, Calif.).
COLLEGE: UCLA.
TRANSACTIONS/CAREER NOTES: Selected by Boston Red Sox organization in third round of free-agent draft (June 3, 1993). ... Traded by Red Sox with P Rheal Cormier and P Shayne Bennett to Montreal Expos for SS Wil Cordero and P Bryan Eversgerd (January 10, 1996).
STATISTICAL NOTES: Led Carolina League first basemen with 1,312 total chances in 1994.

Year	Team (League)	Pos.	G	AB	R	H	2B	3B	HR	RBI	Avg.	BB	SO	SB	PO	A	E	Avg.
									BATTING							FIELDING		
1993—Fort Laud. (FSL)		1B	56	213	23	69	12	2	4	38	.324	27	34	2	513	61	5	.991
1994—Lynchburg (Caro.)		1B	*137	489	70	133	29	0	10	73	.272	79	77	10	*1165	*129	18	.986
1995—Trenton (Eastern)		1B	109	414	59	138	29	1	7	59	.333	58	51	11	708	55	10	.987
1996—Ottawa (Int'l)■		1B-OF	134	451	62	116	21	2	12	60	.257	59	80	11	987	73	8	.993
1997—Ottawa (Int'l)		1B	50	184	37	55	11	1	3	15	.299	36	29	5	421	52	2	.996
—Montreal (N.L.)		OF-1B-DH	84	199	22	51	15	2	3	17	.256	19	34	1	226	19	3	.988
1998—Montreal (N.L.)		1B-OF	130	210	17	39	9	0	1	10	.186	32	55	0	326	26	7	.981
Major league totals (2 years)			214	409	39	90	24	2	4	27	.220	51	89	1	552	45	10	.984

McGWIRE, MARK — 1B — CARDINALS

PERSONAL: Born October 1, 1963, in Pomona, Calif. ... 6-5/250. ... Bats right, throws right. ... Full name: Mark David McGwire. ... Brother of Dan McGwire, quarterback with Seattle Seahawks (1991-94) and Miami Dolphins (1995).
HIGH SCHOOL: Damien (Claremont, Calif.).
COLLEGE: Southern California.
TRANSACTIONS/CAREER NOTES: Selected by Montreal Expos organization in eighth round of free-agent draft (June 8, 1981); did not sign. ... Selected by Oakland Athletics organization in first round (10th pick overall) of free-agent draft (June 4, 1984). ... On disabled list (April 11-26, 1989 and August 22-September 11, 1992). ... Granted free agency (October 26, 1992). ... Re-signed by A's (December 24, 1992). ... On disabled list (May 14-September 3, 1993; April 30-June 18 and July 27, 1994-remainder of season). ... On suspended list (September 4-8, 1993). ... On disabled list (July 18-August 2 and August 5-26, 1995). ... On disabled list (March 22-April 23, 1996). ... Traded by A's to St. Louis Cardinals for P T.J. Mathews, P Eric Ludwick and P Blake Stein (July 31, 1997).
RECORDS: Holds major league single-season records for most home runs—70 (1998); and most home runs by first baseman—69 (1998). ... Holds major league records for most home runs in consecutive years—128 (1997-98); most consecutive seasons with 50 or more home runs—3 (1996-98); and fewest singles in season (150 or more games)—53 (1991). ... Holds major league rookie-season records for most home runs—49; and extra bases on long hits—183 (1987). ... Shares major league single-season record for most games with three home runs—2 (1998). ... Shares major league records for most home runs in two consecutive games—5 (June 27 [3] and 28 [2], 1987 and June 10 [2] and 11 [3], 1995); and most home runs in one inning—2 (September 22, 1996, fifth inning). ... Shares modern major league record for most runs in two consecutive games—9 (June 27 and 28, 1987). ... Holds N.L. single-season record for most bases on balls—162 (1998). ... Holds A.L. rookie-season record for highest slugging percentage—.618 (1987).
HONORS: Named College Player of the Year by THE SPORTING NEWS (1984). ... Named first baseman on THE SPORTING NEWS college All-America team (1984). ... Named A.L. Rookie Player of the Year by THE SPORTING NEWS (1987). ... Named A.L. Rookie of the Year by Baseball Writers' Association of America (1987). ... Won A.L. Gold Glove at first base (1990). ... Named first baseman on THE SPORTING NEWS A.L. All-Star team (1992 and 1996). ... Named first baseman on THE SPORTING NEWS A.L. Silver Slugger team (1992 and 1996). ... Named Sportsman of the Year by THE SPORTING NEWS (1997). ... Named first baseman on THE SPORTING NEWS N.L. All-Star team (1998). ... Named first baseman on THE SPORTING NEWS N.L. Silver Slugger team (1998). ... Named co-Sportsman of the Year by THE SPORTING NEWS (1998).
STATISTICAL NOTES: Led California League third basemen with 239 assists and 354 total chances in 1985. ... Hit three home runs in one game (June 27, 1987; June 11, 1995; April 14 and May 19, 1998). ... Led A.L. in slugging percentage with .618 in 1987, .585 in 1992 and .730 in 1996. ... Led A.L. first basemen with 1,429 total chances in 1990. ... Led A.L. with .467 on-base percentage in 1996. ... Led major leagues with 58 home runs in 1997. ... Led N.L. with .752 slugging percentage and .470 on-base percentage in 1998. ... Led N.L. first basemen with 1,435 total chances in 1998. ... Career major league grand slams: 11.
MISCELLANEOUS: Holds Oakland Athletics all-time franchise records for most home runs (363) and most runs batted in (941). ... Member of 1984 U.S. Olympic baseball team.

Year	Team (League)	Pos.	G	AB	R	H	2B	3B	HR	RBI	Avg.	BB	SO	SB	PO	A	E	Avg.
									BATTING							FIELDING		
1984—Modesto (California)		1B	16	55	7	11	3	0	1	1	.200	8	21	0	107	6	1	.991
1985—Modesto (California)		3B-1B	138	489	95	134	23	3	•24	•106	.274	96	108	1	105	†240	33	.913
1986—Huntsville (Sou.)		3B	55	195	40	59	15	0	10	53	.303	46	45	3	34	124	16	.908
—Tacoma (PCL)		3B	78	280	42	89	21	5	13	59	.318	42	67	1	53	126	25	.877
—Oakland (A.L.)		3B	18	53	10	10	1	0	3	9	.189	4	18	0	10	20	6	.833
1987—Oakland (A.L.)		1B-3B-OF	151	557	97	161	28	4	*49	118	.289	71	131	1	1176	101	13	.990
1988—Oakland (A.L.)		1B-OF	155	550	87	143	22	1	32	99	.260	76	117	0	1228	88	9	.993
1989—Oakland (A.L.)		1B-DH	143	490	74	113	17	0	33	95	.231	83	94	1	1170	114	6	.995
1990—Oakland (A.L.)		1B-DH	156	523	87	123	16	0	39	108	.235	*110	116	2	*1329	95	5	.997
1991—Oakland (A.L.)		1B	154	483	62	97	22	0	22	75	.201	93	116	2	1191	•101	4	.997
1992—Oakland (A.L.)		1B	139	467	87	125	22	0	42	104	.268	90	105	0	1118	71	6	.995
1993—Oakland (A.L.)		1B	27	84	16	28	6	0	9	24	.333	21	19	0	197	14	0	1.000
1994—Oakland (A.L.)		1B-DH	47	135	26	34	3	0	9	25	.252	37	40	0	307	18	4	.988
1995—Oakland (A.L.)		1B-DH	104	317	75	87	13	0	39	90	.274	88	77	1	775	64	*12	.986

M

Year Team (League)	Pos.	G	AB	R	H	2B	3B	HR	RBI	Avg.	BB	SO	SB	PO	A	E	Avg.
1996— Oakland (A.L.)	1B-DH	130	423	104	132	21	0	*52	113	.312	116	112	0	913	60	10	.990
1997— Oakland (A.L.)	1B	105	366	48	104	24	0	34	81	.284	58	98	1	884	60	6	.994
—St. Louis (N.L.)■	1B	51	174	38	44	3	0	§24	42	.253	43	61	2	438	34	1	.998
1998— St. Louis (N.L.)	1B	155	509	130	152	21	0	*70	147	.299	*162	155	1	1326	97	12	.992
American League totals (12 years)		1329	4448	773	1157	195	5	363	941	.260	847	1043	8	10298	806	81	.993
National League totals (2 years)		206	683	168	196	24	0	94	189	.287	205	216	3	1764	131	13	.993
Major league totals (13 years)		1535	5131	941	1353	219	5	457	1130	.264	1052	1259	11	12062	937	94	.993

CHAMPIONSHIP SERIES RECORD

Year Team (League)	Pos.	G	AB	R	H	2B	3B	HR	RBI	Avg.	BB	SO	SB	PO	A	E	Avg.
1988— Oakland (A.L.)	1B	4	15	4	5	0	0	1	3	.333	1	5	0	24	2	0	1.000
1989— Oakland (A.L.)	1B	5	18	3	7	1	0	1	3	.389	1	4	0	46	1	1	.979
1990— Oakland (A.L.)	1B	4	13	2	2	0	0	0	2	.154	3	3	0	40	0	0	1.000
1992— Oakland (A.L.)	1B	6	20	1	3	0	0	1	3	.150	5	4	0	46	2	1	.980
Championship series totals (4 years)		19	66	10	17	1	0	3	11	.258	10	16	0	156	5	2	.988

WORLD SERIES RECORD

NOTES: Member of World Series championship team (1989).

Year Team (League)	Pos.	G	AB	R	H	2B	3B	HR	RBI	Avg.	BB	SO	SB	PO	A	E	Avg.
1988— Oakland (A.L.)	1B	5	17	1	1	0	0	1	1	.059	3	4	0	40	3	0	1.000
1989— Oakland (A.L.)	1B	4	17	0	5	1	0	1	1	.294	1	3	0	28	2	0	1.000
1990— Oakland (A.L.)	1B	4	14	1	3	0	0	0	0	.214	2	4	0	42	1	2	.956
World Series totals (3 years)		13	48	2	9	1	0	1	2	.188	6	11	0	110	6	2	.983

ALL-STAR GAME RECORD

NOTES: Named to A.L. All-Star team for 1991 game; replaced by Rafael Palmeiro due to injury.

Year League	Pos.	AB	R	H	2B	3B	HR	RBI	Avg.	BB	SO	SB	PO	A	E	Avg.
1987— American	1B	3	0	0	0	0	0	0	.000	0	0	0	7	0	1	.875
1988— American	1B	2	0	1	0	0	0	0	.500	0	1	0	8	0	0	1.000
1989— American	1B	3	0	1	0	0	0	0	.333	0	0	0	5	0	0	1.000
1990— American	1B	2	0	0	0	0	0	0	.000	0	2	0	7	0	0	1.000
1991— American				Selected, did not play—injured.												
1992— American	1B	3	1	1	0	0	0	0	.333	0	0	0	4	0	0	1.000
1995— American				Selected, did not play—injured.												
1996— American	1B	1	0	1	0	0	0	0	1.000	0	0	0	2	1	0	1.000
1997— American	1B	2	0	0	0	0	0	0	.000	0	2	0	4	0	0	1.000
1998— National	1B	2	1	0	0	0	0	0	.000	1	1	0	6	0	0	1.000
All-Star Game totals (8 years)		18	2	4	0	0	0	2	.222	1	6	0	43	1	1	.978

M

McKNIGHT, TONY   P   ASTROS

PERSONAL: Born June 29, 1977, in Texarkana, Ark. ... 6-5/205. ... Throws right, bats right. ... Full name: Tony Mark McKnight.
HIGH SCHOOL: Arkansas (Texarkana, Ark.).
TRANSACTIONS/CAREER NOTES: Selected by Houston Astros organization in first round (22nd pick overall) of free-agent draft (June 1, 1995). ... On disabled list (June 19-July 15, 1996).

Year Team (League)	W	L	Pct.	ERA	G	GS	CG	ShO	Sv.	IP	H	R	ER	BB	SO
1995— GC Astros (GCL)	1	1	.500	3.86	3	3	0	0	0	11 2/3	14	5	5	2	8
1996— GC Astros (GCL)	2	1	.667	6.23	8	5	0	0	0	21 2/3	28	21	15	7	15
1997— Quad City (Midwest)	4	9	.308	4.68	20	20	0	0	0	115 1/3	116	71	60	55	92
1998— Kissimmee (Florida State)..	11	13	.458	4.67	28	•28	0	0	0	154 1/3	191	101	80	50	104

McLEMORE, MARK   2B   RANGERS

PERSONAL: Born October 4, 1964, in San Diego. ... 5-11/207. ... Bats both, throws right. ... Full name: Mark Tremell McLemore.
HIGH SCHOOL: Morse (San Diego).
TRANSACTIONS/CAREER NOTES: Selected by California Angels organization in ninth round of free-agent draft (June 7, 1982). ... On disabled list (May 15-27, 1985). ... On California disabled list (May 24-August 2, 1988); included rehabilitation assignments to Palm Springs (July 7-21) and Edmonton (July 22-27). ... On California disabled list (May 17-August 17, 1990); included rehabilitation assignments to Edmonton (May 24-June 6) and Palm Springs (August 9-13). ... Traded by Angels to Colorado Springs, Cleveland Indians organization (August 17, 1990), completing deal in which Indians traded C Ron Tingley to Angels for a player to be named later (September 6, 1989). ... Released by Indians organization (December 13, 1990). ... Signed by Tucson, Houston Astros organization (March 6, 1991). ... On Houston disabled list (May 9-June 25, 1991); included rehabilitation assignments to Tucson (May 24-29) and Jackson (June 14-22). ... Released by Astros (June 25, 1991). ... Signed by Baltimore Orioles organization (July 5, 1991). ... Granted free agency (October 15, 1991). ... Re-signed by Orioles organization (February 5, 1992). ... Granted free agency (December 19, 1992). ... Re-signed by Rochester, Orioles organization (January 6, 1993). ... Granted free agency (October 18, 1994). ... Signed by Texas Rangers (December 13, 1994). ... Granted free agency (December 7, 1996). ... Re-signed by Rangers (December 13, 1996). ... On Texas disabled list (May 15-June 12 and August 19-September 28, 1997); included rehabilitation assignments to Charlotte (June 7-8) and Oklahoma City (June 9-12). ... On disabled list (June 7-22, 1998).
STATISTICAL NOTES: Led California League second basemen with 400 assists and 84 double plays in 1984. ... Led Pacific Coast League second basemen with 597 total chances and 95 double plays in 1989. ... Led A.L. second basemen with 473 assists and 798 total chances in 1996.

Year Team (League)	Pos.	G	AB	R	H	2B	3B	HR	RBI	Avg.	BB	SO	SB	PO	A	E	Avg.
1982— Salem (Northwest)	2B-SS	55	165	42	49	6	2	0	25	.297	39	38	14	81	125	11	.949
1983— Peoria (Midwest)	2B-SS	95	329	42	79	7	3	0	18	.240	53	64	15	170	250	24	.946
1984— Redwood (Calif.)	2B-SS	134	482	102	142	8	3	0	45	.295	106	75	59	274	†429	25	.966

Year	Team (League)	Pos.	G	AB	R	H	2B	3B	HR	RBI	Avg.	BB	SO	SB	PO	A	E	Avg.
1985—	Midland (Texas).........	2B-SS	117	458	80	124	17	6	2	46	.271	66	59	31	301	339	19	.971
1986—	Midland (Texas)..........	2B	63	237	54	75	9	1	1	29	.316	48	18	38	155	194	13	.964
	—Edmonton (PCL)	2B	73	286	41	79	13	1	0	23	.276	39	30	29	173	215	7	.982
	—California (A.L.)	2B	5	4	0	0	0	0	0	0	.000	1	2	0	3	10	0	1.000
1987—	California (A.L.)	2B-SS-DH	138	433	61	102	13	3	3	41	.236	48	72	25	293	363	17	.975
1988—	California (A.L.)	2B-3B-DH	77	233	38	56	11	2	2	16	.240	25	25	13	108	178	6	.979
	—Palm Springs (Calif.)..	2B	11	44	9	15	3	1	0	6	.341	11	7	7	18	24	1	.977
	—Edmonton (PCL)	2B	12	45	7	12	3	0	0	6	.267	4	4	7	35	33	1	.986
1989—	Edmonton (PCL)	2B	114	430	60	105	13	2	2	34	.244	49	67	26	*264	323	10	*.983
	—California (A.L.)	2B-DH	32	103	12	25	3	1	0	14	.243	7	19	6	55	88	5	.966
1990—	California (A.L.)	2B	20	48	4	7	2	0	0	2	.146	4	9	1	14	15	0	1.000
	—Edmonton (PCL)	2B-SS	9	39	4	10	2	0	0	3	.256	6	10	0	24	32	4	.933
	—Palm Springs (Calif.)..	2B	6	22	3	6	0	0	0	2	.273	3	7	0	20	22	0	1.000
	—Colo. Springs (PCL)■	2B-3B-SS	14	54	11	15	2	0	1	7	.278	11	8	5	23	40	2	.969
	—Cleveland (A.L.)	SS-3B-2B	8	12	2	2	0	0	0	0	.167	0	6	0	23	24	4	.922
1991—	Houston (N.L.)■......	2B	21	61	6	9	1	0	0	2	.148	6	13	0	25	54	2	.975
	—Tucson (PCL)	2B	4	14	2	5	1	0	0	0	.357	2	1	0	8	6	0	1.000
	—Jackson (Texas)	2B	7	22	6	5	3	0	1	4	.227	6	3	1	27	24	0	1.000
	—Rochester (Int'l)■......	2B	57	228	32	64	11	4	1	28	.281	27	29	12	134	166	5	.984
1992—	Baltimore (A.L.)■	2B-DH	101	228	40	56	7	2	0	27	.246	21	26	11	126	186	7	.978
1993—	Baltimore (A.L.).........	O-2-3-DH	148	581	81	165	27	5	4	72	.284	64	92	21	335	80	6	.986
1994—	Baltimore (A.L.).........	2B-OF-DH	104	343	44	88	11	1	3	29	.257	51	50	20	219	269	9	.982
1995—	Texas (A.L.)■..........	OF-2B-DH	129	467	73	122	20	5	5	41	.261	59	71	21	248	184	4	.991
1996—	Texas (A.L.)	2B-OF	147	517	84	150	23	4	5	46	.290	87	69	27	313	†473	12	.985
1997—	Texas (A.L.)	2B-OF	89	349	47	91	17	2	1	25	.261	40	54	7	148	254	8	.980
	—Charlotte (Fla. St.)......	2B	2	7	1	4	1	0	0	3	.571	2	1	1	3	3	0	1.000
	—Okla. City (A.A.)	2B	3	10	0	1	0	0	0	1	.100	1	1	1	2	3	0	1.000
1998—	Texas (A.L.)	2B-DH	126	461	79	114	15	1	5	53	.247	89	64	12	249	332	15	.975
American League totals (12 years)			1124	3779	565	978	149	26	28	366	.259	496	559	164	2134	2456	93	.980
National League totals (1 year)			21	61	6	9	1	0	0	2	.148	6	13	0	25	54	2	.975
Major league totals (13 years)			1145	3840	571	987	150	26	28	368	.257	502	572	164	2159	2510	95	.980

DIVISION SERIES RECORD

Year	Team (League)	Pos.	G	AB	R	H	2B	3B	HR	RBI	Avg.	BB	SO	SB	PO	A	E	Avg.
1996—	Texas (A.L.)	2B	4	15	1	2	0	0	0	2	.133	0	4	0	10	16	0	1.000
1998—	Texas (A.L.)	2B	3	10	0	1	1	0	0	0	.100	2	3	0	4	12	0	1.000
Division series totals (2 years)			7	25	1	3	1	0	0	2	.120	2	7	0	14	28	0	1.000

McMICHAEL, GREG   P   METS

M

PERSONAL: Born December 1, 1966, in Knoxville, Tenn. ... 6-3/215. ... Throws right, bats right. ... Full name: Gregory Winston McMichael.
HIGH SCHOOL: Webb School of Knoxville (Knoxville, Tenn.).
COLLEGE: Tennessee.
TRANSACTIONS/CAREER NOTES: Selected by Cleveland Indians organization in seventh round of free-agent draft (June 1, 1988). ... Released by Indians organization (April 4, 1991). ... Signed by Atlanta Braves organization (April 16, 1991). ... Traded by Braves to New York Mets for P Paul Byrd and a player to be named later (November 25, 1996); Braves acquired P Andy Zwirchitz to complete deal (May 25, 1997). ... Traded by Mets with P Dave Mlicki to Los Angeles Dodgers for P Hideo Nomo and P Brad Clontz (June 5, 1998). ... Traded by Dodgers with cash to Mets for P Brian Bohanon (July 10, 1998).

Year	Team (League)	W	L	Pct.	ERA	G	GS	CG	ShO	Sv.	IP	H	R	ER	BB	SO
1988—	Burlington (Appalachian)....	2	0	1.000	2.57	3	3	1	1	0	21	17	9	6	4	20
	—Kinston (Carolina)	4	2	.667	2.68	11	11	2	0	0	77 1/3	57	31	23	18	35
1989—	Cant./Akr. (Eastern)	11	11	.500	3.49	26	•26	8	•5	0	170	164	81	66	64	101
1990—	Cant./Akr. (Eastern)	2	3	.400	3.35	13	4	0	0	0	40 1/3	39	17	15	17	19
	—Colo. Springs (PCL)	2	3	.400	5.80	12	12	1	1	0	59	72	45	38	30	34
1991—	Durham (Carolina)■	5	6	.455	3.62	36	6	0	0	2	79 2/3	83	34	32	29	82
1992—	Greenville (Southern)	4	2	.667	1.36	15	4	0	0	1	46 1/3	37	14	7	13	53
	—Richmond (Int'l)	6	5	.545	4.38	19	13	0	0	2	90 1/3	89	52	44	34	86
1993—	Atlanta (N.L.)......................	2	3	.400	2.06	74	0	0	0	19	91 2/3	68	22	21	29	89
1994—	Atlanta (N.L.)......................	4	6	.400	3.84	51	0	0	0	21	58 2/3	66	29	25	19	47
1995—	Atlanta (N.L.)......................	7	2	.778	2.79	67	0	0	0	2	80 2/3	64	27	25	32	74
1996—	Atlanta (N.L.)......................	5	3	.625	3.22	73	0	0	0	2	86 2/3	84	37	31	27	78
1997—	New York (N.L.)■...............	7	10	.412	2.98	73	0	0	0	7	87 2/3	73	34	29	27	81
1998—	New York (N.L.)■...............	5	3	.625	4.02	52	0	0	0	1	53 2/3	64	31	24	29	44
	—Los Angeles (N.L.)■...............	0	1	.000	4.40	12	0	0	0	1	14 1/3	17	8	7	6	11
Major league totals (6 years)......		30	28	.517	3.08	402	0	0	0	53	473 1/3	436	188	162	169	424

DIVISION SERIES RECORD

Year	Team (League)	W	L	Pct.	ERA	G	GS	CG	ShO	Sv.	IP	H	R	ER	BB	SO
1995—	Atlanta (N.L.)......................	0	0	...	6.75	2	0	0	0	0	1 1/3	1	1	1	2	1
1996—	Atlanta (N.L.)......................	0	0	...	6.75	2	0	0	0	0	1 1/3	1	1	1	1	3
Div. series totals (2 years)		0	0	...	6.75	4	0	0	0	0	2 2/3	2	2	2	3	4

CHAMPIONSHIP SERIES RECORD

Year	Team (League)	W	L	Pct.	ERA	G	GS	CG	ShO	Sv.	IP	H	R	ER	BB	SO
1993—	Atlanta (N.L.)......................	0	1	.000	6.75	4	0	0	0	0	4	7	3	3	2	1
1995—	Atlanta (N.L.)......................	1	0	1.000	0.00	3	0	0	0	1	2 2/3	0	0	0	1	2
1996—	Atlanta (N.L.)......................	0	1	.000	9.00	3	0	0	0	0	2	4	2	2	1	3
Champ. series totals (3 years)		1	2	.333	5.19	10	0	0	0	1	8 2/3	11	5	5	4	6

NOTES: Member of World Series championship team (1995).

Year Team (League)	W	L	Pct.	ERA	G	GS	CG	ShO	Sv.	IP	H	R	ER	BB	SO
1995— Atlanta (N.L.)......................	0	0	...	2.70	3	0	0	0	0	3 1/3	3	2	1	2	2
1996— Atlanta (N.L.)......................	0	0	...	27.00	2	0	0	0	0	1	5	3	3	0	1
World Series totals (2 years)	0	0	...	8.31	5	0	0	0	0	4 1/3	8	5	4	2	3

McMILLON, BILLY   OF

PERSONAL: Born November 17, 1971, in Otero, N.M. ... 5-11/179. ... Bats left, throws left. ... Full name: William Edward McMillon.
HIGH SCHOOL: Bishopville (S.C.)
COLLEGE: Clemson.
TRANSACTIONS/CAREER NOTES: Selected by Florida Marlins organization in eighth round of free-agent draft (June 3, 1993). ... On Charlotte disabled list (April 20-29, 1997). ... Traded by Marlins to Philadelphia Phillies for OF/1B Darren Daulton (July 21, 1997). ... On Scranton/Wilkes-Barre disabled list (May 20-July 13, 1998). ... Granted free agency (December 21, 1998).
STATISTICAL NOTES: Tied for New York-Pennsylvania League lead with four intentional bases on balls received in 1993. ... Tied for Midwest League lead with nine sacrifice flies in 1994. ... Led Eastern League with .423 on-base percentage in 1995. ... Led International League with .418 on-base percentage in 1996. ... Career major league grand slams: 1.

									BATTING						FIELDING		
Year Team (League)	Pos.	G	AB	R	H	2B	3B	HR	RBI	Avg.	BB	SO	SB	PO	A	E	Avg.
1993— Elmira (N.Y.-Penn)......	OF	57	226	38	69	14	2	6	35	.305	31	43	5	66	1	5	.931
1994— Kane County (Midw.)..	OF	•137	496	88	125	25	3	17	*101	.252	*84	99	7	187	9	7	.966
1995— Portland (Eastern)......	OF	*141	518	92	*162	29	3	14	93	.313	*96	90	15	207	14	4	.982
1996— Charlotte (Int'l)..........	OF	97	347	72	122	32	2	17	70	*.352	36	76	5	135	10	4	.973
— Florida (N.L.)..............	OF	28	51	4	11	0	0	4	4	.216	5	14	0	17	0	0	1.000
1997— Charlotte (Int'l)..........	OF	57	204	34	57	18	0	8	26	.279	32	51	8	84	5	2	.978
— Florida (N.L.)..............	OF	13	18	0	2	1	0	0	1	.111	0	7	0	4	0	0	1.000
— Scran./W.B. (Int'l)■....	OF	26	92	18	27	8	1	4	21	.293	12	24	2	49	3	0	1.000
— Philadelphia (N.L.)......	OF	24	72	10	21	4	1	2	13	.292	6	17	2	42	2	2	.957
1998— Scran./W.B. (Int'l).......	OF	77	267	42	69	16	1	13	38	.258	34	59	6	133	9	2	.986
Major league totals (2 years)		65	141	14	34	5	1	2	18	.241	11	38	2	63	2	2	.970

McNICHOL, BRIAN   P   CUBS

PERSONAL: Born May 20, 1974, in Fairfax, Va. ... 6-5/225. ... Throws left, bats left. ... Full name: Brian David McNichol.
HIGH SCHOOL: Garfield (Woodbridge, Va.).
COLLEGE: James Madison.
TRANSACTIONS/CAREER NOTES: Selected by Chicago Cubs organization in second round of free-agent draft (June 1, 1995).

Year Team (League)	W	L	Pct.	ERA	G	GS	CG	ShO	Sv.	IP	H	R	ER	BB	SO
1995— Williamsport (NYP)	3	1	.750	3.08	9	9	0	0	0	49 2/3	57	28	17	8	35
1996— Daytona (Fla. St.)	1	2	.333	4.67	8	7	0	0	0	34 2/3	39	24	18	14	22
— GC Cubs (GCL).................	0	0	...	0.00	1	1	0	0	0	3 1/3	4	2	0	0	2
1997— Daytona (Fla. St.)	2	2	.500	2.31	6	6	0	0	0	39	32	14	10	10	40
— Orlando (South.)	7	10	.412	5.81	22	22	0	0	0	119 1/3	153	89	77	42	97
1998— West Tenn (Southern)	12	9	.571	3.72	28	26	•4	1	0	179	170	88	74	62	168
— Iowa (Pacific Coast)	0	0	...	7.71	1	1	0	0	0	7	12	6	6	1	5

McRAE, BRIAN   OF   METS

PERSONAL: Born August 27, 1967, in Bradenton, Fla. ... 6-0/195. ... Bats both, throws right. ... Full name: Brian Wesley McRae. ... Son of Hal McRae, hitting coach, Philadelphia Phillies; outfielder/designated hitter with Cincinnati Reds and Kansas City Royals (1968 and 1970-87); and manager with Royals (1991-94).
HIGH SCHOOL: Blue Springs (Mo.), then Manatee (Bradenton, Fla.).
COLLEGE: Kansas.
TRANSACTIONS/CAREER NOTES: Selected by Kansas City Royals organization in first round (17th pick overall) of free-agent draft (June 3, 1985). ... Traded by Royals to Chicago Cubs for P Derek Wallace and P Geno Morones (April 5, 1995). ... Traded by Cubs with P Mel Rojas and P Turk Wendell to New York Mets for OF Lance Johnson and two players to be named later (August 8, 1997); Mets traded P Mark Clark (August 11) and IF Manny Alexander (August 14) to Cubs to complete deal.
RECORDS: Shares major league single-season record for fewest double plays by outfielder (150 or more games)—0 (1991). ... Shares major league single-game record for most unassisted double plays by outfielder—1 (August 23, 1992). ... Shares N.L. single-season record for fewest assists by outfielder (150 or more games)—2 (1996).
STATISTICAL NOTES: Led Northwest League second basemen with 373 total chances in 1986. ... Tied for Southern League lead in double plays by outfielder with five in 1989. ... Had 22-game hitting streak (July 20-August 13, 1991). ... Led N.L. outfielders with 352 total chances in 1995. ... Career major league grand slams: 4.

									BATTING						FIELDING		
Year Team (League)	Pos.	G	AB	R	H	2B	3B	HR	RBI	Avg.	BB	SO	SB	PO	A	E	Avg.
1985— GC Royals (GCL)	2B-SS	60	217	40	58	6	5	0	23	.267	28	34	27	116	142	18	.935
1986— Eugene (Northwest) ...	2B	72	306	*66	82	10	3	1	29	.268	41	49	28	146	*214	13	*.965
1987— Fort Myers (FSL)	2B	131	481	62	121	14	1	1	31	.252	22	70	33	*284	346	18	.972
1988— Baseball City (FSL)......	2B	30	107	18	33	2	0	1	11	.308	9	11	8	70	103	4	.977
— Memphis (Sou.)	2B	91	288	33	58	13	1	4	15	.201	16	60	13	147	231	18	.955
1989— Memphis (Sou.)	OF	138	*533	72	121	18	8	5	42	.227	43	65	23	249	11	5	.981
1990— Memphis (Sou.)	OF	116	470	78	126	24	6	10	64	.268	44	66	21	265	8	7	.975
— Kansas City (A.L.)	OF	46	168	21	48	8	3	2	23	.286	9	29	4	120	1	0	1.000
1991— Kansas City (A.L.)	OF	152	629	86	164	28	9	8	64	.261	24	99	20	405	2	3	.993
1992— Kansas City (A.L.)	OF	149	533	63	119	23	5	4	52	.223	42	88	18	419	8	3	.993
1993— Kansas City (A.L.)	OF	153	627	78	177	28	9	12	69	.282	37	105	23	394	4	7	.983

M

Year	Team (League)	Pos.	G	AB	R	H	2B	3B	HR	RBI	Avg.	BB	SO	SB	PO	A	E	Avg.
									BATTING							FIELDING		
1994— Kansas City (A.L.)		OF-DH	114	436	71	119	22	6	4	40	.273	54	67	28	252	2	3	.988
1995— Chicago (N.L.)■........		OF	137	*580	92	167	38	7	12	48	.288	47	92	27	*345	4	3	.991
1996— Chicago (N.L.)..........		OF	157	624	111	172	32	5	17	66	.276	73	84	37	345	2	5	.986
1997— Chicago (N.L.)..........		OF	108	417	63	100	27	5	6	28	.240	52	62	14	242	3	1	.996
— New York (N.L.)■		OF	45	145	23	36	5	2	5	15	.248	13	22	3	65	1	3	.957
1998— New York (N.L.)..........		OF	159	552	79	146	36	5	21	79	.264	80	90	20	302	8	4	.987
American League totals (5 years)			614	2393	319	627	109	32	30	248	.262	166	388	93	1590	17	16	.990
National League totals (4 years)			606	2318	368	621	138	24	61	236	.268	265	350	101	1299	18	16	.988
Major league totals (9 years)			1220	4711	687	1248	247	56	91	484	.265	431	738	194	2889	35	32	.989

MEADOWS, BRIAN — P — MARLINS

PERSONAL: Born November 21, 1975, in Montgomery, Ala. ... 6-4/210. ... Throws right, bats right. ... Full name: Matthew Brian Meadows.
HIGH SCHOOL: Charles Henderson (Troy, Ala.).
TRANSACTIONS/CAREER NOTES: Selected by Florida Marlins organization in third round of free-agent draft (June 2, 1994); pick received as compensation for Colorado Rockies signing Type B free-agent SS Walt Weiss. ... On disabled list (July 28-August 13, 1998).

Year	Team (League)	W	L	Pct.	ERA	G	GS	CG	ShO	Sv.	IP	H	R	ER	BB	SO
1994— GC Marlins (GCL)...............		3	0	1.000	1.95	8	7	0	0	0	37	34	9	8	6	33
1995— Kane County (Midwest).......		9	9	.500	4.22	26	26	1	1	0	147	163	90	69	41	103
1996— Portland (Eastern).............		0	1	.000	4.33	4	4	1	0	0	27	26	15	13	4	13
— Brevard County (FSL)........		8	7	.533	3.58	24	23	3	1	0	146	129	73	58	25	69
1997— Portland (Eastern).............		9	7	.563	4.61	29	*29	4	0	0	175²/₃	204	99	90	48	115
1998— Florida (N.L.)...................		11	13	.458	5.21	31	31	1	0	0	174¹/₃	222	106	101	46	88
Major league totals (1 year)........		11	13	.458	5.21	31	31	1	0	0	174¹/₃	222	106	101	46	88

MEARES, PAT — SS

PERSONAL: Born September 6, 1968, in Salina, Kan. ... 6-0/187. ... Bats right, throws right. ... Full name: Patrick James Meares.
HIGH SCHOOL: Sacred Heart (Salina, Kan.).
COLLEGE: Wichita State.
TRANSACTIONS/CAREER NOTES: Selected by Minnesota Twins organization in 15th round of free-agent draft (June 4, 1990). ... On disabled list (June 22-July 7, 1994 and August 11-26, 1997). ... Granted free agency (December 21, 1998).
RECORDS: Holds major league single-season record for fewest assists by shortstop (150 or more games)—344 (1996).

Year	Team (League)	Pos.	G	AB	R	H	2B	3B	HR	RBI	Avg.	BB	SO	SB	PO	A	E	Avg.
									BATTING							FIELDING		
1990— Kenosha (Midwest)		3B-2B	52	197	26	47	10	2	4	22	.239	25	45	2	35	94	16	.890
1991— Visalia (California)......		2B-3B-OF	89	360	53	109	21	4	6	44	.303	24	63	15	155	224	26	.936
1992— Orlando (South.)		SS	81	300	42	76	19	0	3	23	.253	11	57	5	91	190	35	.889
1993— Portland (PCL)		SS	18	54	6	16	5	0	0	3	.296	3	11	0	28	48	5	.938
— Minnesota (A.L.)		SS	111	346	33	87	14	3	0	33	.251	7	52	4	165	304	19	.961
1994— Minnesota (A.L.)		SS	80	229	29	61	12	1	2	24	.266	14	50	5	133	209	13	.963
1995— Minnesota (A.L.)		SS-OF	116	390	57	105	19	4	12	49	.269	15	68	10	187	317	•18	.966
1996— Minnesota (A.L.)		SS-OF	152	517	66	138	26	7	8	67	.267	17	90	9	257	344	22	.965
1997— Minnesota (A.L.)		SS	134	439	63	121	23	3	10	60	.276	18	86	7	211	415	20	.969
1998— Minnesota (A.L.)		SS	149	543	56	141	26	3	9	70	.260	24	86	7	263	412	24	.966
Major league totals (6 years)			742	2464	304	653	120	21	41	303	.265	95	432	42	1216	2001	116	.965

MECIR, JIM — P — DEVIL RAYS

PERSONAL: Born May 16, 1970, in Queens, N.Y. ... 6-1/195. ... Throws right, bats both. ... Full name: James Jason Mecir. ... Name pronounced ma-SEER.
HIGH SCHOOL: Smithtown East (St. James, N.Y.).
COLLEGE: Eckerd (Fla.).
TRANSACTIONS/CAREER NOTES: Selected by Seattle Mariners organization in third round of free-agent draft (June 3, 1991). ... On disabled list (June 25-August 25, 1992). ... Traded by Mariners with 1B Tino Martinez and P Jeff Nelson to New York Yankees for P Sterling Hitchcock and 3B Russ Davis (December 7, 1995). ... Traded by Yankees to Boston Red Sox (September 29, 1997), completing deal in which Yankees traded P Tony Armas and a player to be named later to Red Sox for C Mike Stanley and IF Randy Brown (August 13, 1997). ... Selected by Tampa Bay Devil Rays in second round (36th pick overall) of expansion draft (November 18, 1997).
STATISTICAL NOTES: Led California League with 15 hit batsmen in 1993.
MISCELLANEOUS: Holds Tampa Bay Devil Rays all-time record for most games pitched (68).

Year	Team (League)	W	L	Pct.	ERA	G	GS	CG	ShO	Sv.	IP	H	R	ER	BB	SO
1991— San Bernardino (Calif.).......		3	5	.375	4.22	14	12	0	0	1	70¹/₃	72	40	33	37	48
1992— San Bernardino (Calif.).......		4	5	.444	4.67	14	11	0	0	0	61²/₃	72	40	32	26	53
1993— Riverside (California).........		9	11	.450	4.33	26	26	1	0	0	145¹/₃	160	89	70	58	85
1994— Jacksonville (Southern).......		6	5	.545	2.69	46	0	0	0	13	80¹/₃	73	28	24	35	53
1995— Tacoma (PCL)		1	4	.200	3.10	40	0	0	0	8	69²/₃	63	29	24	28	46
— Seattle (A.L.)		0	0	. . .	0.00	2	0	0	0	0	4²/₃	5	1	0	2	3
1996— Columbus (Int'l)■.............		3	3	.500	2.27	33	0	0	0	7	47²/₃	37	14	12	15	52
— New York (A.L.)..............		1	1	.500	5.13	26	0	0	0	0	40¹/₃	42	24	23	23	38
1997— Columbus (Int'l)...............		1	1	.500	1.00	24	0	0	0	11	27	14	4	3	6	34
— New York (A.L.)..............		0	4	.000	5.88	25	0	0	0	0	33²/₃	36	23	22	10	25
1998— Tampa Bay (A.L.)■...........		7	2	.778	3.11	68	0	0	0	0	84	68	30	29	33	77
Major league totals (4 years)......		8	7	.533	4.09	121	0	0	0	0	162²/₃	151	78	74	68	143

M

MEDINA, CARLOS   P   ORIOLES

PERSONAL: Born May 16, 1977, in La Vega, Dominican Republic. ... 6-2/160. ... Throws left, bats left.
HIGH SCHOOL: Federico Garcia Godoy (La Vega, Dominican Republic).
TRANSACTIONS/CAREER NOTES: Signed as non-drafted free agent by Florida Marlins organization (December 26, 1993). ... Granted free agency (December 21, 1998). ... Re-signed by Orioles organization (December 21, 1998).

Year	Team (League)	W	L	Pct.	ERA	G	GS	CG	ShO	Sv.	IP	H	R	ER	BB	SO
1994	Dom. Marlins (DSL)	5	5	.500	3.22	14	9	0	0	0	64 1/3	68	33	23	28	22
1995	Dom. Marlins (DSL)	2	3	.400	2.18	12	11	1	0	0	62	59	29	15	30	41
1996	GC Marlins (GCL)	0	1	.000	3.72	4	1	0	0	0	9 2/3	16	7	4	1	9
1997	—								Statistics unavailable.							
1998	Delmarva (S. Atl.)■	4	6	.400	3.79	22	11	0	0	0	80 2/3	70	41	34	39	85
	Bowie (Eastern)	1	0	1.000	0.00	1	1	0	0	0	5	1	0	0	0	6

MEDINA, RAFAEL   P   MARLINS

PERSONAL: Born February 15, 1975, in Panama City, Panama. ... 6-3/195. ... Throws right, bats right. ... Brother of Ricardo Medina, third baseman in Chicago Cubs organization (1989-94).
TRANSACTIONS/CAREER NOTES: Signed as non-drafted free agent by New York Yankees organization (September 6, 1992). ... On disabled list (July 11-22 and August 5-September 30, 1996). ... Traded by Yankees with OF Ruben Rivera and cash to San Diego Padres for rights to P Hideki Irabu, 2B Homer Bush, OF Gordon Amerson and a player to be named later (April 22, 1997); Padres traded OF Vernon Maxwell to Yankees to complete deal (June 9). ... Traded by Padres with P Steve Hoff and 1B Derrek Lee to Florida Marlins for P Kevin Brown (December 15, 1997). ... On Florida disabled list (April 18-July 17, 1998); included rehabilitation assignment to Charlotte (June 26-July 17).

Year	Team (League)	W	L	Pct.	ERA	G	GS	CG	ShO	Sv.	IP	H	R	ER	BB	SO
1993	GC Yankees (GCL)	2	0	1.000	0.66	5	5	0	0	0	27 1/3	16	6	2	12	21
1994	Oneonta (N.Y.-Penn)	3	7	.300	4.66	14	14	1	0	0	73 1/3	67	54	38	35	59
1995	Greensboro (S. Atl.)	4	4	.500	4.01	19	19	1	0	0	98 2/3	86	48	44	38	108
	Tampa (Fla. St.)	2	2	.500	2.37	6	6	0	0	0	30 1/3	29	12	8	12	25
1996	Norwich (Eastern)	5	8	.385	3.06	19	19	1	0	0	103	78	48	35	55	112
1997	Rancho Cuca. (Cal.)■	2	0	1.000	2.00	3	3	0	0	0	18	13	4	4	5	14
	Las Vegas (PCL)	4	5	.444	7.56	13	13	0	0	0	66 2/3	90	60	56	39	50
1998	Florida (N.L.)■	2	6	.250	6.01	12	12	0	0	0	67 1/3	76	50	45	52	49
	Charlotte (Int'l)	4	2	.667	3.90	11	9	3	1	0	57 2/3	53	27	25	26	41
Major league totals (1 year)		**2**	**6**	**.250**	**6.01**	**12**	**12**	**0**	**0**	**0**	**67 1/3**	**76**	**50**	**45**	**52**	**49**

MELO, JUAN   SS   PADRES

PERSONAL: Born May 11, 1976, in Bani, Dominican Republic. ... 6-1/160. ... Bats both, throws right. ... Full name: Juan Esteban Melo.
HIGH SCHOOL: Colegio Redentol (Bani, Dominican Republic).
TRANSACTIONS/CAREER NOTES: Signed as non-drafted free agent San Diego Padres organization (June 15, 1993). ... On suspended list (July 9-13, 1996).
STATISTICAL NOTES: Tied for Midwest League lead in double plays by shortstop with 70 in 1995. ... Led California League shortstops with 613 total chances and 92 double plays in 1996.

Year	Team (League)	Pos.	G	AB	R	H	2B	3B	HR	RBI	Avg.	BB	SO	SB	PO	A	E	Avg.
1994	Ariz. Padres (Ariz.)	SS	37	145	20	41	3	3	0	15	.283	10	36	3	46	117	13	.926
	Spokane (N'west)	SS	3	11	4	4	1	0	1	2	.364	1	3	0	2	11	2	.867
1995	Clinton (Midwest)	SS	134	479	65	135	32	1	5	46	.282	33	88	12	183	372	47	.922
1996	Rancho Cuca. (Cal.)	SS	128	503	75	153	27	6	8	75	.304	22	102	6	*209	*378	26	.958
1997	Mobile (Southern)	SS	113	456	52	131	22	2	7	67	.287	29	90	7	182	307	28	.946
	Las Vegas (PCL)	SS	12	48	6	13	4	0	1	6	.271	1	10	0	11	33	3	.936
1998	Las Vegas (PCL)	SS	130	467	61	127	26	1	6	47	.272	24	91	9	214	360	21	.965

MELUSKEY, MITCH   C   ASTROS

PERSONAL: Born September 18, 1973, in Yakima, Wash. ... 6-0/185. ... Bats both, throws right. ... Full name: Mitchell Wade Meluskey.
HIGH SCHOOL: Eisenhower (Yakima, Wash.).
TRANSACTIONS/CAREER NOTES: Selected by Cleveland Indians organization in 12th round of free-agent draft (June 1, 1992). ... Traded by Indians to Houston Astros organization for OF Buck McNabb (April 27, 1995).
STATISTICAL NOTES: Led South Atlantic catchers with nine double plays in 1993. ... Tied for Texas League lead with four intentional bases on balls in 1997. ... Led Pacific Coast League with 10 intentional bases on balls received in 1998.

Year	Team (League)	Pos.	G	AB	R	H	2B	3B	HR	RBI	Avg.	BB	SO	SB	PO	A	E	Avg.
1992	Burlington (Appal.)	C	43	126	23	29	7	0	3	16	.230	29	36	3	227	29	4	.985
1993	Columbus (S. Atl.)	C	101	342	36	84	18	3	3	47	.246	35	69	1	639	87	7	.990
1994	Kinston (Carolina)	C	100	319	36	77	16	1	3	41	.241	49	62	3	458	40	6	.988
1995	Kinston (Carolina)	C	8	29	5	7	5	0	0	2	.241	2	9	0	58	6	1	.985
	Kissimmee (Fla. St.)■	C	78	261	23	56	18	1	3	31	.215	27	33	3	443	40	10	.980
1996	Kissimmee (Fla. St.)	C	74	231	29	77	19	0	1	31	.333	29	26	1	315	27	9	.974
	Jackson (Texas)	C	38	134	18	42	11	0	0	21	.313	18	24	0	207	18	5	.978
1997	Jackson (Texas)	C	73	241	49	82	18	0	14	46	.340	31	39	1	356	43	6	.985
	New Orleans (A.A.)	C	51	172	22	43	7	0	3	21	.250	25	38	0	323	26	4	.989
1998	New Orleans (PCL)	C-OF	121	397	76	140	41	0	17	71	.353	85	59	2	702	49	10	.987
	Houston (N.L.)	C	8	8	1	2	1	0	0	0	.250	1	4	0	9	0	0	1.000
Major league totals (1 year)			**8**	**8**	**1**	**2**	**1**	**0**	**0**	**0**	**.250**	**1**	**4**	**0**	**9**	**0**	**0**	**1.000**

MENDOZA, CARLOS OF DEVIL RAYS

PERSONAL: Born November 14, 1974, in Ciudad Bolivar, Venezuela. ... 5-11/165. ... Bats left, throws left. ... Full name: Carlos Ramon Mendoza.
HIGH SCHOOL: Agosto Mendez (Bolivar, Venezuela).
TRANSACTIONS/CAREER NOTES: Signed as non-drafted free agent by New York Mets organization (November 10, 1992). ... On disabled list (May 27-June 9, 1996). ... On Binghamton disabled list (April 17-June 22, 1997). ... Selected by Tampa Bay Devil Rays in second round (52nd pick overall) of expansion draft (November 18, 1997). ... On Durham disabled list (April 9-22 and June 24-July 26, 1998).

							BATTING							FIELDING		
Year Team (League)	Pos.	G	AB	R	H	2B	3B	HR	RBI	Avg.	BB	SO	SB	PO	A	E	Avg.
1993— Dom. Mets (DSL)	OF	36	96	25	23	1	0	1	14	.240	23	10	7	17	3	1	.952
1994— Dom. Mets (DSL)	OF	57	197	66	69	11	1	1	25	.350	68	13	15	74	6	3	.964
1995— Kingsport (Appal.)	OF	51	192	*56	63	9	0	1	24	.328	27	24	28	54	4	3	.951
1996— Columbia (S. Atl.)	OF	85	304	61	102	10	2	0	37	*.336	57	47	31	54	6	2	.968
1997— Binghamton (East.)	OF	59	228	36	87	12	2	1	13	.382	14	25	14	79	5	1	.988
— Norfolk (Int'l)	OF	10	35	3	5	0	1	0	0	.143	3	4	1	17	0	0	1.000
— New York (N.L.)	OF	15	12	6	3	0	0	0	1	.250	4	2	0	5	0	0	1.000
1998— St. Peters. (FSL)■......	OF	8	32	6	10	2	0	0	8	.313	4	3	4	20	1	0	1.000
— Durham (Int'l)	OF	51	201	32	54	8	0	0	11	.269	16	29	9	99	5	5	.954
— GC Devil Rays	OF	6	18	6	8	1	0	0	4	.444	5	3	3	13	0	0	1.000
— Orlando (South.)	OF	35	139	27	47	3	3	1	19	.338	19	18	16	53	1	2	.964
Major league totals (1 year)		15	12	6	3	0	0	0	1	.250	4	2	0	5	0	0	1.000

MENDOZA, RAMIRO P YANKEES

PERSONAL: Born June 15, 1972, in Los Santos, Panama. ... 6-2/154. ... Throws right, bats right.
TRANSACTIONS/CAREER NOTES: Signed as non-drafted free agent by New York Yankees organization (November 13, 1991).

Year Team (League)	W	L	Pct.	ERA	G	GS	CG	ShO	Sv.	IP	H	R	ER	BB	SO
1992— Dominican Yankees (DSL)..	10	2	.833	2.13	15	15	5	0	0	109 2/3	93	37	26	28	79
1993— GC Yankees (GCL)	4	5	.444	2.79	15	9	0	0	1	67 2/3	59	26	21	7	61
— Greensboro (S. Atl.)	0	1	.000	2.45	2	0	0	0	0	3 2/3	3	1	1	5	3
1994— Tampa (Fla. St.)	12	6	.667	3.01	22	21	1	0	0	134 1/3	133	54	45	35	110
1995— Norwich (Eastern)	5	6	.455	3.21	19	19	2	1	0	89 2/3	87	39	32	33	68
— Columbus (Int'l)	1	0	1.000	2.57	2	2	0	0	0	14	10	4	4	2	13
1996— Columbus (Int'l)	6	2	.750	2.51	15	15	0	0	0	97	96	30	27	19	61
— New York (A.L.)	4	5	.444	6.79	12	11	0	0	0	53	80	43	40	10	34
1997— Columbus (Int'l)	0	0	. . .	5.68	1	1	0	0	0	6 1/3	7	6	4	1	4
— New York (A.L.)	8	6	.571	4.24	39	15	0	0	2	133 2/3	157	67	63	28	82
1998— New York (A.L.)	10	2	.833	3.25	41	14	1	1	1	130 1/3	131	50	47	30	56
Major league totals (3 years)	22	13	.629	4.26	92	40	1	1	3	317	368	160	150	68	172

DIVISION SERIES RECORD

Year Team (League)	W	L	Pct.	ERA	G	GS	CG	ShO	Sv.	IP	H	R	ER	BB	SO
1997— New York (A.L.)	1	1	.500	2.45	2	0	0	0	0	3 2/3	3	1	1	0	2
1998— New York (A.L.)					Did not play.										

CHAMPIONSHIP SERIES RECORD

Year Team (League)	W	L	Pct.	ERA	G	GS	CG	ShO	Sv.	IP	H	R	ER	BB	SO
1998— New York (A.L.)	0	0	. . .	0.00	2	0	0	0	0	4 1/3	4	0	0	0	1

WORLD SERIES RECORD

NOTES: Member of World Series championship team (1998).

Year Team (League)	W	L	Pct.	ERA	G	GS	CG	ShO	Sv.	IP	H	R	ER	BB	SO
1998— New York (A.L.)	1	0	1.000	9.00	1	0	0	0	0	1	2	1	1	0	1

M

MERCED, ORLANDO OF/1B

PERSONAL: Born November 2, 1966, in San Juan, Puerto Rico. ... 6-1/195. ... Bats left, throws right. ... Full name: Orlando Luis Merced. ... Name pronounced mer-SED.
HIGH SCHOOL: University Garden (San Juan, Puerto Rico).
TRANSACTIONS/CAREER NOTES: Signed as non-drafted free agent by Pittsburgh Pirates organization (February 22, 1985). ... On Macon disabled list (April 18-28, 1987). ... On Watertown disabled list (June 23, 1987-remainder of season). ... On disabled list (May 1-18, August 1-16 and August 22-September 6, 1996). ... Traded by Pirates with IF Carlos Garcia and P Dan Plesac to Toronto Blue Jays for P Jose Silva, P Jose Pett, IF Brandon Cromer and three players to be named later (November 14, 1996); Pirates acquired P Mike Halperin, IF Abraham Nunez and C/OF Craig Wilson to complete deal (December 11, 1996). ... On disabled list (July 29-September 28, 1997). ... Granted free agency (October 27, 1997). ... Signed by Minnesota Twins organization (January 12, 1998). ... Traded by Twins with P Greg Swindell to Boston Red Sox for P Matt Kinney, P Joe Thomas and P John Barnes (July 31, 1998). ... Released by Red Sox (August 31, 1998). ... Signed by Chicago Cubs (September 5, 1998). ... Granted free agency (October 28, 1998).
STATISTICAL NOTES: Led N.L. outfielders in double plays with five in 1993 and five in 1996. ... Career major league grand slams: 2.
MISCELLANEOUS: Batted as switch hitter (1985-92).

							BATTING							FIELDING		
Year Team (League)	Pos.	G	AB	R	H	2B	3B	HR	RBI	Avg.	BB	SO	SB	PO	A	E	Avg.
1985— GC Pirates (GCL)	SS-3B-1B	40	136	16	31	6	0	1	13	.228	9	9	3	46	78	28	.816
1986— Macon (S. Atl.)	OF-3B	65	173	20	34	4	1	2	24	.197	12	38	5	53	15	13	.840
— Watertown (NYP)	3B-1B-OF	27	89	12	16	0	1	3	9	.180	14	21	6	49	28	10	.885
1987— Macon (S. Atl.)	OF	4	4	1	0	0	0	0	0	.000	1	3	0	1	1	0	1.000
— Watertown (NYP)	2B	4	12	4	5	0	1	0	3	.417	1	1	1	11	7	2	.900
1988— Augusta (S. Atl.)	2B-3B-SS	37	136	19	36	6	3	1	17	.265	7	20	2	35	39	7	.914
— Salem (Carolina)	3-2-O-S	80	298	47	87	12	7	7	42	.292	27	64	13	77	183	31	.893

Year	Team (League)	Pos.	G	AB	R	H	2B	3B	HR	RBI	Avg.	BB	SO	SB	PO	A	E	Avg.
1989—	Harrisburg (East.)	1B-OF-3B	95	341	43	82	16	4	6	48	.240	32	66	13	435	32	10	.979
	— Buffalo (A.A.)	1B-OF-3B	35	129	18	44	5	3	1	16	.341	7	26	0	173	15	3	.984
1990—	Buffalo (A.A.)	1B-3B-OF	101	378	52	99	12	6	9	55	.262	46	63	14	689	83	20	.975
	— Pittsburgh (N.L.)	OF-C	25	24	3	5	1	0	0	0	.208	1	9	0	0	0	0	...
1991—	Buffalo (A.A.)	1B	3	12	1	2	0	0	0	0	.167	1	4	1	29	2	0	1.000
	— Pittsburgh (N.L.)	1B-OF	120	411	83	113	17	2	10	50	.275	64	81	8	916	60	12	.988
1992—	Pittsburgh (N.L.)	1B-OF	134	405	50	100	28	5	6	60	.247	52	63	5	906	75	5	.995
1993—	Pittsburgh (N.L.)	OF-1B	137	447	68	140	26	4	8	70	.313	77	64	3	485	31	10	.981
1994—	Pittsburgh (N.L.)	OF-1B	108	386	48	105	21	3	9	51	.272	42	58	4	508	29	5	.991
1995—	Pittsburgh (N.L.)	OF-1B	132	487	75	146	29	4	15	83	.300	52	74	7	374	23	6	.985
1996—	Pittsburgh (N.L.)	OF-1B	120	453	69	130	24	1	17	80	.287	51	74	8	242	15	3	.988
1997—	Toronto (A.L.)■	OF-DH-1B	98	368	45	98	23	2	9	40	.266	47	62	7	193	10	3	.985
1998—	Minnesota (A.L.)■	1B-OF-DH	63	204	22	59	12	0	5	33	.289	17	29	1	324	23	6	.983
	— Boston (A.L.)■	DH-OF	9	9	0	0	0	0	0	2	.000	2	3	0	2	0	0	1.000
	— Chicago (N.L.)■	OF	12	10	2	3	0	0	1	5	.300	1	2	0	3	0	0	1.000
American League totals (2 years)			170	581	67	157	35	2	14	75	.270	66	94	8	519	33	9	.984
National League totals (8 years)			788	2623	398	742	146	19	66	399	.283	340	425	35	3434	233	41	.989
Major league totals (9 years)			958	3204	465	899	181	21	80	474	.281	406	519	43	3953	266	50	.988

CHAMPIONSHIP SERIES RECORD

NOTES: Hit home run in first at-bat (October 12, 1991).

Year	Team (League)	Pos.	G	AB	R	H	2B	3B	HR	RBI	Avg.	BB	SO	SB	PO	A	E	Avg.
1991—	Pittsburgh (N.L.)	1B-PH	3	9	1	2	0	0	1	1	.222	0	1	0	13	0	1	.929
1992—	Pittsburgh (N.L.)	1B-PH	4	10	0	1	1	0	0	2	.100	2	4	0	27	2	1	.967
Championship series totals (2 years)			7	19	1	3	1	0	1	3	.158	2	5	0	40	2	2	.955

MERCEDES, JOSE   P   BREWERS

PERSONAL: Born March 5, 1971, in El Seibo, Dominican Republic. ... 6-1/208. ... Throws right, bats right. ... Full name: Jose Miguel Mercedes.

TRANSACTIONS/CAREER NOTES: Signed as non-drafted free agent by Baltimore Orioles organization (August 10, 1989). ... Selected by Milwaukee Brewers from Orioles organization in Rule 5 major league draft (December 13, 1993). ... On Milwaukee disabled list (April 2-May 30, 1994); included rehabilitation assignments to El Paso (April 30-May 14) and New Orleans (May 14-28). ... On disabled list (May 14, 1995-remainder of season). ... On Milwaukee disabled list (May 5, 1998-remainder of season); included rehabilitation assignment to El Paso (June 15-16).

Year	Team (League)	W	L	Pct.	ERA	G	GS	CG	ShO	Sv.	IP	H	R	ER	BB	SO
1990—								Dominican Summer League statistics unavailable.								
1991—								Dominican Summer League statistics unavailable.								
1992—	GC Orioles (GCL)	2	3	.400	1.78	8	5	2	0	0	35 1/3	31	12	7	13	21
	— Kane County (Midwest)	3	2	.600	2.66	8	8	2	•2	0	47 1/3	40	26	14	15	45
1993—	Bowie (Eastern)	6	8	.429	4.78	26	23	3	0	0	147	170	86	78	65	75
1994—	El Paso (Texas)■	2	0	1.000	4.66	3	0	0	0	0	9 2/3	13	6	5	4	8
	— New Orleans (A.A.)	0	0	...	4.91	3	3	0	0	0	18 1/3	19	10	10	8	7
	— Milwaukee (A.L.)	2	0	1.000	2.32	19	0	0	0	0	31	22	9	8	16	11
1995—	Milwaukee (A.L.)	0	1	.000	9.82	5	0	0	0	0	7 1/3	12	9	8	8	6
1996—	New Orleans (A.A.)	3	7	.300	3.56	25	15	0	0	1	101	109	58	40	28	47
	— Milwaukee (A.L.)	0	2	.000	9.18	11	0	0	0	0	16 2/3	20	18	17	5	6
1997—	Milwaukee (A.L.)	7	10	.412	3.79	29	23	2	1	0	159	146	76	67	53	80
1998—	Milwaukee (A.L.)	2	2	.500	6.75	7	5	0	0	0	32	42	25	24	9	11
	— El Paso (Texas)	0	0	...	10.80	1	1	0	0	0	3 1/3	9	4	4	0	0
A.L. totals (4 years)		9	13	.409	4.21	64	23	2	1	0	214	200	112	100	82	103
N.L. totals (1 year)		2	2	.500	6.75	7	5	0	0	0	32	42	25	24	9	11
Major league totals (5 years)		11	15	.423	4.54	71	28	2	1	0	246	242	137	124	91	114

MERCKER, KENT   P   CARDINALS

PERSONAL: Born February 1, 1968, in Dublin, Ohio. ... 6-2/195. ... Throws left, bats left. ... Full name: Kent Franklin Mercker.

HIGH SCHOOL: Dublin (Ohio).

TRANSACTIONS/CAREER NOTES: Selected by Atlanta Braves organization in first round (fifth pick overall) of free-agent draft (June 2, 1986). ... On Richmond disabled list (March 30-May 6, 1990). ... On disabled list (August 9-24, 1991). ... Traded by Braves to Baltimore Orioles for P Joe Borowski and P Rachaad Stewart (December 17, 1995). ... Traded by Orioles to Cleveland Indians for 1B Eddie Murray (July 21, 1996). ... Granted free agency (November 4, 1996). ... Signed by Cincinnati Reds (December 10, 1996). ... On disabled list (August 17-September 2, 1997). ... Granted free agency (October 27, 1997). ... Signed by St. Louis Cardinals (December 16, 1997). ... On disabled list (June 14-July 1, 1998).

HONORS: Named Carolina League co-Pitcher of the Year (1988).

STATISTICAL NOTES: Pitched six innings, combining with Mark Wohlers (two innings) and Alejandro Pena (one inning) in 1-0 no-hit victory against San Diego (September 11, 1991). ... Pitched 6-0 no-hit victory against Los Angeles (April 8, 1994). ... Career major league grand slams: 1.

MISCELLANEOUS: Had a sacrifice hit and received a base on balls in two games as pinch hitter (1991). ... Appeared in one game as pinch runner (1997). ... Appeared in one game as pinch runner (1998).

Year	Team (League)	W	L	Pct.	ERA	G	GS	CG	ShO	Sv.	IP	H	R	ER	BB	SO
1986—	GC Braves (GCL)	4	3	.571	2.47	9	8	0	0	0	47 1/3	37	21	13	16	42
1987—	Durham (Carolina)	0	1	.000	5.40	3	3	0	0	0	11 2/3	11	8	7	6	14
1988—	Durham (Carolina)	11	4	.733	*2.75	19	19	5	0	0	127 2/3	102	44	39	47	159
	— Greenville (Southern)	3	1	.750	3.35	9	9	0	0	0	48 1/3	36	20	18	26	60
1989—	Richmond (Int'l)	9	12	.429	3.20	27	•27	4	0	0	168 2/3	107	66	60	*95	*144
	— Atlanta (N.L.)	0	0	...	12.46	2	1	0	0	0	4 1/3	8	6	6	6	4

M

Year Team (League)	W	L	Pct.	ERA	G	GS	CG	ShO	Sv.	IP	H	R	ER	BB	SO
1990— Richmond (Int'l)	5	4	.556	3.55	12	10	0	0	1	58 1/3	60	30	23	27	69
—Atlanta (N.L.)	4	7	.364	3.17	36	0	0	0	7	48 1/3	43	22	17	24	39
1991—Atlanta (N.L.)	5	3	.625	2.58	50	4	0	0	6	73 1/3	56	23	21	35	62
1992—Atlanta (N.L.)	3	2	.600	3.42	53	0	0	0	6	68 1/3	51	27	26	35	49
1993—Atlanta (N.L.)	3	1	.750	2.86	43	6	0	0	0	66	52	24	21	36	59
1994—Atlanta (N.L.)	9	4	.692	3.45	20	17	2	1	0	112 1/3	90	46	43	45	111
1995—Atlanta (N.L.)	7	8	.467	4.15	29	26	0	0	0	143	140	73	66	61	102
1996—Baltimore (A.L.)■	3	6	.333	7.76	14	12	0	0	0	58	73	56	50	35	22
—Buffalo (A.A.)■	0	2	.000	3.94	3	3	0	0	0	16	11	7	7	9	11
—Cleveland (A.L.)	1	0	1.000	3.09	10	0	0	0	0	11 2/3	10	4	4	3	7
1997—Cincinnati (N.L.)■	8	11	.421	3.92	28	25	0	0	0	144 2/3	135	65	63	62	75
1998—St. Louis (N.L.)■	11	11	.500	5.07	30	29	0	0	0	161 2/3	199	99	91	53	72
A.L. totals (1 year)	4	6	.400	6.98	24	12	0	0	0	69 2/3	83	60	54	38	29
N.L. totals (9 years)	50	47	.515	3.88	291	108	2	1	19	822	774	385	354	357	573
Major league totals (10 years)....	54	53	.505	4.12	315	120	2	1	19	891 2/3	857	445	408	395	602

DIVISION SERIES RECORD

Year Team (League)	W	L	Pct.	ERA	G	GS	CG	ShO	Sv.	IP	H	R	ER	BB	SO
1995—Atlanta (N.L.)	0	0	...	0.00	1	0	0	0	0	1/3	0	0	0	0	0

CHAMPIONSHIP SERIES RECORD

Year Team (League)	W	L	Pct.	ERA	G	GS	CG	ShO	Sv.	IP	H	R	ER	BB	SO
1991—Atlanta (N.L.)	0	1	.000	13.50	1	0	0	0	0	2/3	0	1	1	2	0
1992—Atlanta (N.L.)	0	0	...	0.00	2	0	0	0	0	3	1	0	0	1	1
1993—Atlanta (N.L.)	0	0	...	1.80	5	0	0	0	0	5	3	1	1	2	4
Champ. series totals (3 years)....	0	1	.000	2.08	8	0	0	0	0	8 2/3	4	2	2	5	5

WORLD SERIES RECORD

NOTES: Member of World Series championship team (1995).

Year Team (League)	W	L	Pct.	ERA	G	GS	CG	ShO	Sv.	IP	H	R	ER	BB	SO
1991—Atlanta (N.L.)	0	0	...	0.00	2	0	0	0	0	1	0	0	0	0	1
1995—Atlanta (N.L.)	0	0	...	4.50	1	0	0	0	0	2	1	1	1	2	2
World Series totals (2 years)	0	0	...	3.00	3	0	0	0	0	3	1	1	1	2	3

MERLONI, LOU   IF   RED SOX

PERSONAL: Born April 6, 1971, in Framingham, Mass. ... 5-10/195. ... Bats right, throws right. ... Full name: Louis William Merloni.
HIGH SCHOOL: Framingham (Mass.) South.
COLLEGE: Providence.
TRANSACTIONS/CAREER NOTES: Selected by Boston Red Sox organization in 10th round of free-agent draft (June 3, 1993). ... On Boston disabled list (June 29-September 12, 1998); included rehabilitation assignment to Gulf Coast Red Sox (August 8-20).

Year Team (League)	Pos.	G	AB	R	H	2B	3B	HR	RBI	Avg.	BB	SO	SB	PO	A	E	Avg.
1993—GC Red Sox (GCL)	SS	4	14	4	5	1	0	0	1	.357	1	1	1	7	13	1	.952
—Fort Laud. (FSL)	3B-SS	44	156	14	38	1	1	2	21	.244	13	26	1	40	114	8	.951
1994—Sar. R. Sox (GCL)	2B-3B-SS	113	419	59	120	16	2	1	63	.286	36	57	5	196	304	18	.965
1995—Trenton (Eastern)	2B-3B-SS	93	318	42	88	16	1	1	30	.277	39	50	7	166	222	20	.951
1996—GC Red Sox (GCL)	2B	1	4	1	1	0	0	0	0	.250	0	0	0	3	3	0	1.000
—Trenton (Eastern)	3-2-S-1	28	95	11	22	6	1	3	16	.232	9	18	0	39	67	8	.930
—Pawtucket (Int'l)	3B-2B-SS	38	115	19	29	6	0	1	12	.252	10	20	0	39	99	8	.945
1997—Trenton (Eastern)	3B-2B-SS	69	255	49	79	17	4	5	37	.310	30	43	3	68	130	9	.957
—Pawtucket (Int'l)	2B-3B-SS	49	165	24	49	10	0	5	24	.297	15	20	0	61	122	4	.979
1998—Pawtucket (Int'l)	SS-2B-3B	27	88	17	34	3	1	8	22	.386	16	13	2	27	56	2	.976
—Boston (A.L.)	2B-3B-SS	39	96	10	27	6	0	1	15	.281	7	20	1	52	73	5	.962
—GC Red Sox (GCL)	2B	1	1	0	0	0	0	0	0	.000	0	0	0	0	0	0	...
Major league totals (1 year)		39	96	10	27	6	0	1	15	.281	7	20	1	52	73	5	.962

MESA, JOSE   P   MARINERS

PERSONAL: Born May 22, 1966, in Azua, Dominican Republic. ... 6-3/225. ... Throws right, bats right. ... Full name: Jose Ramon Mesa.
HIGH SCHOOL: Santa School (Azua, Dominican Republic).
TRANSACTIONS/CAREER NOTES: Signed as non-drafted free agent by Toronto Blue Jays organization (October 31, 1981). ... On Kinston disabled list (August 27, 1984-remainder of season). ... Traded by Blue Jays organization to Baltimore Orioles (September 4, 1987), completing deal in which Orioles traded P Mike Flanagan to Blue Jays for P Oswald Peraza and a player to be named later (August 31, 1987). ... On Rochester disabled list (April 18-May 16 and June 30, 1988-remainder of season; May 27, 1989-remainder of season; and August 21-September 5, 1991). ... Traded by Orioles to Cleveland Indians for OF Kyle Washington (July 14, 1992). ... On suspended list (April 5-8, 1993). ... Traded by Indians with IF Shawon Dunston and P Alvin Morman to San Francisco Giants for P Steve Reed and OF Jacob Cruz (July 23, 1998). ... Granted free agency (October 23, 1998). ... Signed by Seattle Mariners (November 13, 1998).
HONORS: Named A.L. Fireman of the Year by THE SPORTING NEWS (1995).
STATISTICAL NOTES: Tied for Carolina League lead with nine hit batsmen in 1985.
MISCELLANEOUS: Appeared in one game as pinch runner for Baltimore (1991).

Year Team (League)	W	L	Pct.	ERA	G	GS	CG	ShO	Sv.	IP	H	R	ER	BB	SO
1982—GC Blue Jays (GCL)	6	4	.600	2.70	13	12	6	*3	1	83 1/3	58	34	25	20	40
1983—Florence (S. Atl.)	6	12	.333	5.48	28	27	1	0	0	141 1/3	153	*116	86	93	91
1984—Florence (S. Atl.)	4	3	.571	3.76	7	7	0	0	0	38 1/3	38	24	16	25	35
—Kinston (Carolina)	5	2	.714	3.91	10	9	0	0	0	50 2/3	51	23	22	28	24
1985—Kinston (Carolina)	5	10	.333	6.16	30	20	0	0	1	106 2/3	110	89	73	79	71
1986—Vent. County (Cal.)	10	6	.625	3.86	24	24	2	1	0	142 1/3	141	71	61	58	113
—Knoxville (Southern)	2	2	.500	4.35	9	8	2	1	0	41 1/3	40	32	24	23	30

M

Year Team (League)	W	L	Pct.	ERA	G	GS	CG	ShO	Sv.	IP	H	R	ER	BB	SO
1987— Knoxville (Southern)	10	•13	.435	5.21	35	*35	4	2	0	*193 1/3	*206	*131	*112	104	115
— Baltimore (A.L.)■..............	1	3	.250	6.03	6	5	0	0	0	31 1/3	38	23	21	15	17
1988— Rochester (Int'l)	0	3	.000	8.62	11	2	0	0	0	15 2/3	21	20	15	14	15
1989— Rochester (Int'l)	0	2	.000	5.40	7	1	0	0	0	10	10	6	6	6	3
— Hagerstown (Eastern)	0	0	. . .	1.38	3	3	0	0	0	13	9	2	2	4	12
1990— Hagerstown (Eastern)	5	5	.500	3.42	15	15	3	1	0	79	77	35	30	30	72
— Rochester (Int'l)	1	2	.333	2.42	4	4	0	0	0	26	21	11	7	12	23
— Baltimore (A.L.)..................	3	2	.600	3.86	7	7	0	0	0	46 2/3	37	20	20	27	24
1991— Baltimore (A.L.)..................	6	11	.353	5.97	23	23	2	1	0	123 2/3	151	86	82	62	64
— Rochester (Int'l)	3	3	.500	3.86	8	8	1	1	0	51 1/3	37	25	22	30	48
1992— Baltimore (A.L.)..................	3	8	.273	5.19	13	12	0	0	0	67 2/3	77	41	39	27	22
— Cleveland (A.L.)■..............	4	4	.500	4.16	15	15	1	1	0	93	92	45	43	43	40
1993— Cleveland (A.L.)..................	10	12	.455	4.92	34	33	3	0	0	208 2/3	232	122	114	62	118
1994— Cleveland (A.L.)..................	7	5	.583	3.82	51	0	0	0	2	73	71	33	31	26	63
1995— Cleveland (A.L.)..................	3	0	1.000	1.13	62	0	0	0	*46	64	49	9	8	17	58
1996— Cleveland (A.L.)..................	2	7	.222	3.73	69	0	0	0	39	72 1/3	69	32	30	28	64
1997— Cleveland (A.L.)..................	4	4	.500	2.40	66	0	0	0	16	82 1/3	83	28	22	28	69
1998— Cleveland (A.L.)..................	3	4	.429	5.17	44	0	0	0	1	54	61	36	31	20	35
— San Francisco (N.L.)■....	5	3	.625	3.52	32	0	0	0	0	30 2/3	30	14	12	18	28
A.L. totals (10 years)	46	60	.434	4.33	390	95	6	2	104	916 2/3	960	475	441	355	574
N.L. totals (1 year)	5	3	.625	3.52	32	0	0	0	0	30 2/3	30	14	12	18	28
Major league totals (10 years)....	51	63	.447	4.30	422	95	6	2	104	947 1/3	990	489	453	373	602

DIVISION SERIES RECORD

Year Team (League)	W	L	Pct.	ERA	G	GS	CG	ShO	Sv.	IP	H	R	ER	BB	SO
1995— Cleveland (A.L.)..................	0	0	. . .	0.00	2	0	0	0	0	2	0	0	0	2	0
1996— Cleveland (A.L.)..................	0	1	.000	3.86	2	0	0	0	0	4 2/3	8	2	2	0	7
1997— Cleveland (A.L.)..................	0	0	. . .	2.70	2	0	0	0	1	3 1/3	5	1	1	1	2
Div. series totals (3 years)	0	1	.000	2.70	6	0	0	0	1	10	13	3	3	3	9

CHAMPIONSHIP SERIES RECORD

Year Team (League)	W	L	Pct.	ERA	G	GS	CG	ShO	Sv.	IP	H	R	ER	BB	SO
1995— Cleveland (A.L.)..................	0	0	. . .	2.25	4	0	0	0	1	4	3	1	1	1	1
1997— Cleveland (A.L.)..................	1	0	1.000	3.38	4	0	0	0	2	5 1/3	5	2	2	3	5
Champ. series totals (2 years)	1	0	1.000	2.89	8	0	0	0	3	9 1/3	8	3	3	4	6

WORLD SERIES RECORD

Year Team (League)	W	L	Pct.	ERA	G	GS	CG	ShO	Sv.	IP	H	R	ER	BB	SO
1995— Cleveland (A.L.)..................	1	0	1.000	4.50	2	0	0	0	1	4	5	2	2	1	4
1997— Cleveland (A.L.)..................	0	0	. . .	5.40	5	0	0	0	1	5	10	3	3	1	5
World Series totals (2 years)	1	0	1.000	5.00	7	0	0	0	2	9	15	5	5	2	9

ALL-STAR GAME RECORD

Year League	W	L	Pct.	ERA	GS	CG	ShO	Sv.	IP	H	R	ER	BB	SO
1995— American	0	0	. . .	0.00	0	0	0	0	1	0	0	0	0	1
1996— American							Did not play.							

METCALFE, MIKE   2B   DODGERS

PERSONAL: Born January 2, 1973, in Qunatico, Va. ... 5-10/175. ... Bats right, throws right. ... Full name: Michael Henry Metcalfe Jr.
HIGH SCHOOL: Colonial (Orlando).
COLLEGE: Miami (Fla.).
TRANSACTIONS/CAREER NOTES: Selected by Los Angeles Dodgers organization in third round of free-agent draft (June 2, 1994). ... On disabled list (June 17-August 23 and August 27, 1996-remainder of season). ... On San Antonio disabled list (April 23-July 9, 1998).
STATISTICAL NOTES: Led Florida State League in caught stealing with 27 in 1995. ... Led California League in caught stealing with 32 in 1997.

					BATTING								FIELDING		
Year Team (League)	Pos.	G	AB	R	H	2B	3B	HR	RBI	Avg.	BB	SO	SB	PO	A	E	Avg.
1994— Bakersfield (Calif.).....	SS	69	275	44	78	10	0	0	18	.284	28	34	41	98	208	17	.947
1995— San Antonio (Tex.)	SS	10	41	10	10	1	0	0	2	.244	7	2	1	14	31	2	.957
— Vero Beach (FSL)	SS	120	435	86	131	13	3	3	35	.301	60	37	*60	153	301	*40	.919
1996— Vero Beach (FSL)	DH	2	5	0	0	0	0	0	0	.000	0	0	0	. . .	. . .	. . .	. . .
1997— San Bern. (Calif.)........	2B	132	519	83	147	28	7	3	47	.283	55	79	67	*228	324	12	*.979
1998— San Antonio (Tex.)	2B	57	213	35	60	5	5	3	19	.282	30	24	19	117	151	14	.950
— Los Angeles (N.L.)	2B	4	1	0	0	0	0	0	0	.000	0	1	2	0	0	0	. . .
Major league totals (1 year)		4	1	0	0	0	0	0	0	.000	0	1	2	0	0	0	. . .

MEULENS, HENSLEY   OF

PERSONAL: Born June 23, 1967, in Curacao, Netherlands Antilles. ... 6-3/210. ... Bats right, throws right. ... Full name: Hensley Filemon Meulens.
HIGH SCHOOL: Triniteit (Willamstad).
TRANSACTIONS/CAREER NOTES: Signed as non-drafted free agent by New York Yankees organization (October 31, 1985). ... Released by Yankees (November 26, 1993). ... Signed by Chiba Lotte Marines of Japan Pacific League (November 26, 1993). ... Signed by Yakult Swallows of Japan Central League for 1995 and 1996 seasons. ... Signed by Atlanta Braves organization (December 20, 1996). ... Released by Braves (March 20, 1997). ... Signed by Montreal Expos organization (April 17, 1997). ... Granted free agency (October 6, 1997). ... Signed by Arizona Diamondbacks organization (December 17, 1997). ... Traded by Diamondbacks to Chicago White Sox for a player to be named later (August 1, 1998). ... On Calgary disabled list (August 4, 1998-remainder of season). ... Granted free agency (October 15, 1998).
HONORS: Named International League Most Valuable Player (1990).

STATISTICAL NOTES: Led Gulf Coast League third basemen with 178 total chances in 1986. ... Tied for Eastern League lead in double plays by third baseman with 18 in 1988. ... Tied for Eastern League lead in being hit by pitch with nine in 1989. ... Led International League with 245 total bases in 1990 and 257 in 1992. ... Led International League third basemen with 88 putouts, 30 errors and 373 total chances in 1992.

Year Team (League)	Pos.	G	AB	R	H	2B	3B	HR	RBI	Avg.	BB	SO	SB	PO	A	E	Avg.
1986— GC Yankees (GCL)......	3B	59	219	36	51	10	4	4	31	.233	28	*66	4	*40	*118	20	.888
1987— Prince Will. (Car.).......	3B-OF	116	430	76	129	23	2	28	103	.300	53	124	14	96	224	*37	.896
— Fort Laud. (FSL)	3B	17	58	2	10	3	0	0	2	.172	7	25	0	18	37	7	.887
1988— Alb./Colon. (East.)	3B	79	278	50	68	9	1	13	40	.245	37	96	3	57	162	23	.905
— Columbus (Int'l)	3B	55	209	27	48	9	1	6	22	.230	14	61	0	39	111	14	.915
1989— Alb./Colon. (East.)	3B	104	335	55	86	8	2	11	45	.257	61	108	3	67	172	*29	.892
— Columbus (Int'l)	3B	14	45	8	13	4	0	1	3	.289	8	13	0	11	27	3	.927
— New York (A.L.)	3B	8	28	2	5	0	0	0	1	.179	2	8	0	5	23	4	.875
1990— Columbus (Int'l)	OF-1B-3B	136	480	81	137	20	5	26	96	.285	66	132	6	359	51	13	.969
— New York (A.L.)	OF	23	83	12	20	7	0	3	10	.241	9	25	1	49	3	2	.963
1991— New York (A.L.)..........	OF-DH-1B	96	288	37	64	8	1	6	29	.222	18	97	3	179	5	6	.968
1992— Columbus (Int'l)	3B-2B	141	534	*96	147	28	2	*26	*100	.275	60	*168	15	†88	255	†30	.920
— New York (A.L.)	3B	2	5	1	3	0	0	1	1	.600	1	0	0	3	3	0	1.000
1993— Columbus (Int'l)	OF-1B-3B	75	279	39	57	14	0	14	45	.204	32	92	6	264	20	19	.937
— New York (A.L.)	OF-1B-3B	30	53	8	9	1	1	2	5	.170	8	19	0	32	0	0	1.000
1994— Chiba Lot. (Jp. Pc.)■.	...	122	431	49	107	21	0	23	69	.248	35	135	8	...	...	...	...
1995— Yakult (Jp. Cen.)■....	...	130	438	74	107	16	0	29	80	.244	64	134	6	...	...	...	...
1996— Yakult (Jp. Cen.)	...	128	439	47	108	14	3	25	67	.246	44	140	1	...	...	...	...
1997— W.P. Beach (FSL)■....	3B	1	4	0	1	1	0	0	0	.250	0	2	0	0	2	0	1.000
— Ottawa (Int'l)	3B-1B-OF	121	423	81	116	20	2	24	75	.274	62	119	19	384	114	20	.961
— Montreal (N.L.)	OF-1B	16	24	6	7	1	0	2	6	.292	4	10	0	15	0	0	1.000
1998— Tucson (PCL)■.........	OF-1B-3B	76	268	45	67	16	2	13	37	.250	30	67	2	91	14	8	.929
— Arizona (N.L.)............	OF	7	15	1	1	0	0	1	1	.067	0	6	0	6	1	0	1.000
— Calgary (PCL)■..........	OF	2	8	3	3	1	0	2	3	.375	0	2	0	1	0	0	1.000
American League totals (5 years)		159	457	60	101	16	2	12	46	.221	38	149	4	265	34	12	.961
National League totals (2 years)		23	39	7	8	1	0	3	7	.205	4	16	0	21	1	0	1.000
Major league totals (7 years)		182	496	67	109	17	2	15	53	.220	42	165	4	286	35	12	.964

MEYERS, CHAD — IF — CUBS

PERSONAL: Born August 8, 1975, in Omaha, Neb. ... 6-0/190. ... Bats right, throws right. ... Full name: Chad William Meyers.
HIGH SCHOOL: Daniel J. Gross (Omaha, Neb.).
COLLEGE: Creighton.
TRANSACTIONS/CAREER NOTES: Selected by Chicago Cubs organization in fifth round of free-agent draft (June 4, 1996).
STATISTICAL NOTES: Led New York-Pennsylvania League second basemen with 33 double plays in 1996.

Year Team (League)	Pos.	G	AB	R	H	2B	3B	HR	RBI	Avg.	BB	SO	SB	PO	A	E	Avg.
1996— Will. (NYP)	2B-OF	67	230	46	56	9	2	2	26	.243	33	39	27	123	136	12	.956
1997— Rockford (Midwest) ...	2-0-3-S	125	439	89	132	28	4	4	58	.301	74	72	54	205	266	26	.948
1998— Daytona (Fla. St.)	2B-OF	48	186	39	60	8	3	3	25	.323	33	29	23	97	109	13	.941
— West Tenn (Sou.)	2B	77	293	63	79	14	0	0	26	.270	58	43	37	154	173	23	.934

MICELI, DAN — P — PADRES

PERSONAL: Born September 9, 1970, in Newark, N.J. ... 6-0/216. ... Throws right, bats right. ... Full name: Daniel Miceli.
HIGH SCHOOL: Dr. Phillips (Orlando).
TRANSACTIONS/CAREER NOTES: Signed as non-drafted free agent by Kansas City Royals organization (March 7, 1990). ... Traded by Royals with P Jon Lieber to Pittsburgh Pirates for P Stan Belinda (July 31, 1993). ... Traded by Pirates to Detroit Tigers for P Clint Sodowsky (November 1, 1996). ... Traded by Tigers with P Donne Wall and 3B Ryan Balfe to San Diego Padres for P Tim Worrell and OF Trey Beamon (November 19, 1997).

Year Team (League)	W	L	Pct.	ERA	G	GS	CG	ShO	Sv.	IP	H	R	ER	BB	SO
1990— GC Royals (GCL)	3	4	.429	3.91	*27	0	0	0	4	53	45	27	23	29	48
1991— Eugene (Northwest)	0	1	.000	2.14	25	0	0	0	10	33 2/3	18	8	8	18	43
1992— Appleton (Midwest)............	1	1	.500	1.93	23	0	0	0	9	23 1/3	12	6	5	4	44
— Memphis (Sou.)	3	0	1.000	1.91	32	0	0	0	4	37 2/3	20	10	8	13	46
1993— Memphis (Sou.)	6	4	.600	4.60	40	0	0	0	7	58 2/3	54	30	30	39	68
— Carolina (Southern)■........	0	2	.000	5.11	13	0	0	0	10	12 1/3	11	8	7	4	19
— Pittsburgh (N.L.)	0	0	...	5.06	9	0	0	0	0	5 1/3	6	3	3	3	4
1994— Buffalo (A.A.)..................	1	1	.500	1.88	19	0	0	0	2	24	15	5	5	6	31
— Pittsburgh (N.L.)	2	1	.667	5.93	28	0	0	0	2	27 1/3	28	19	18	11	27
1995— Pittsburgh (N.L.)	4	4	.500	4.66	58	0	0	0	21	58	61	30	30	28	56
1996— Pittsburgh (N.L.)	2	10	.167	5.78	44	9	0	0	1	85 2/3	99	65	55	45	66
— Carolina (Southern)............	1	0	1.000	1.00	3	0	0	0	1	9	4	1	1	1	17
1997— Detroit (A.L.)■................	3	2	.600	5.01	71	0	0	0	3	82 2/3	77	49	46	38	79
1998— San Diego (N.L.)■	10	5	.667	3.22	67	0	0	0	2	72 2/3	64	28	26	27	70
A.L. totals (1 year)	3	2	.600	5.01	71	0	0	0	3	82 2/3	77	49	46	38	79
N.L. totals (5 years)	18	20	.474	4.77	206	9	0	0	26	249	258	145	132	114	223
Major league totals (6 years)	21	22	.488	4.83	277	9	0	0	29	331 2/3	335	194	178	152	302

DIVISION SERIES RECORD

Year Team (League)	W	L	Pct.	ERA	G	GS	CG	ShO	Sv.	IP	H	R	ER	BB	SO
1998— San Diego (N.L.)	1	1	.500	2.70	3	0	0	0	0	3 1/3	2	1	1	0	4

M

CHAMPIONSHIP SERIES RECORD

Year Team (League)	W	L	Pct.	ERA	G	GS	CG	ShO	Sv.	IP	H	R	ER	BB	SO
1998— San Diego (N.L.)	0	0	...	13.50	3	0	0	0	0	$2/3$	4	1	1	0	1

WORLD SERIES RECORD

Year Team (League)	W	L	Pct.	ERA	G	GS	CG	ShO	Sv.	IP	H	R	ER	BB	SO
1998— San Diego (N.L.)	0	0	...	0.00	2	0	0	0	0	$1 2/3$	2	0	0	2	1

MICHALAK, CHRIS   P

PERSONAL: Born January 4, 1971, in Joliet, Ill. ... 6-2/195. ... Throws left, bats left. ... Full name: Christian Matthew Michalak.
HIGH SCHOOL: Joliet (Ill.) Catholic.
COLLEGE: Notre Dame.
TRANSACTIONS/CAREER NOTES: Selected by Oakland Athletics organization in 12th round of free-agent draft (June 3, 1993). ... Released by A's organization (April 1, 1997). ... Signed by Arizona Diamondbacks organization (April 8, 1997). ... Loaned to Tulsa, Texas Rangers organization by Diamondbacks (April 1, 1998). ... Returned to Diamondbacks organization (May 4, 1998). ... Granted free agency (October 17, 1998).

Year Team (League)	W	L	Pct.	ERA	G	GS	CG	ShO	Sv.	IP	H	R	ER	BB	SO
1993— S. Oregon (N'west)............	7	3	.700	2.85	16	15	0	0	0	79	77	41	25	36	57
1994— West. Mich. (Mid.).............	5	3	.625	3.90	15	10	0	0	0	67	66	32	29	28	38
— Modesto (California)	5	3	.625	2.91	17	10	1	0	2	$77 1/3$	67	28	25	20	46
1995— Huntsville (Southern)	1	1	.500	11.12	7	0	0	0	1	$5 2/3$	10	7	7	5	4
— Modesto (California)	3	2	.600	2.62	44	0	0	0	2	$65 1/3$	56	26	19	27	49
1996— Modesto (California)	2	2	.500	3.03	21	0	0	0	4	$38 2/3$	37	21	13	17	39
— Huntsville (Southern)	4	0	1.000	7.71	21	0	0	0	0	$23 1/3$	32	29	20	26	15
1997— High Desert (Calif.)■	3	7	.300	2.65	49	0	0	0	4	85	76	36	25	31	74
1998— Tulsa (Texas)■	1	2	.333	1.83	10	0	0	0	0	$19 2/3$	10	4	4	2	15
— Tucson (PCL)■	3	8	.273	5.03	29	9	0	0	0	$73 1/3$	91	47	41	29	50
— Arizona (N.L.)	0	0	...	11.81	5	0	0	0	0	$5 1/3$	9	7	7	4	5
Major league totals (1 year)........	0	0	...	11.81	5	0	0	0	0	$5 1/3$	9	7	7	4	5

MIENTKIEWICZ, DOUG   1B   TWINS

PERSONAL: Born June 19, 1974, in Toledo, Ohio. ... 6-2/193. ... Bats left, throws right. ... Full name: Douglas Andrew Mientkiewicz. ... Name pronounced mint-KAY-vich.
HIGH SCHOOL: Westminster Christian (Miami).
COLLEGE: Florida State.
TRANSACTIONS/CAREER NOTES: Selected by Minnesota Twin organization in fifth round of free-agent draft (June 1, 1995).
STATISTICAL NOTES: Led Florida State League first basemen with 1,271 total chances and 113 double plays in 1996. ... Led Eastern League first basemen with .995 fielding percentage in 1997.

Year Team (League)	Pos.				BATTING								FIELDING		
		G	AB	R	H	2B	3B	HR	RBI	Avg.	BB	SO	SB	PO	A	E	Avg.
1995— Fort Myers (FSL)	1B	38	110	9	27	6	1	1	15	.245	18	19	2	160	12	1	.994
1996— Fort Myers (FSL)	1B	133	492	69	143	•36	4	5	79	.291	66	47	12	*1183	85	3	*.998
1997— New Britain (East.)	1B-OF	132	467	87	119	28	2	15	61	.255	*98	67	21	989	63	5	†.995
1998— New Britain (East.)	1B-OF	139	502	*96	162	*45	0	16	88	*.323	96	58	11	1171	92	12	.991
— Minnesota (A.L.)	1B	8	25	1	5	1	0	0	2	.200	4	3	1	61	3	0	1.000
Major league totals (1 year)		8	25	1	5	1	0	0	2	.200	4	3	1	61	3	0	1.000

MIESKE, MATT   OF   MARINERS

PERSONAL: Born February 13, 1968, in Midland, Mich. ... 6-0/195. ... Bats right, throws right. ... Full name: Matthew Todd Mieske. ... Name pronounced MEE-skee.
HIGH SCHOOL: Bay City Western (Auburn, Mich.).
COLLEGE: Western Michigan.
TRANSACTIONS/CAREER NOTES: Selected by Oakland Athletics organization in 20th round of free-agent draft (June 5, 1989); did not sign. ... Selected by San Diego Padres organization in 17th round of free-agent draft (June 4, 1990). ... Traded by Padres organization with P Ricky Bones and SS Jose Valentin to Milwaukee Brewers organization for 3B Gary Sheffield and P Geoff Kellogg (March 27, 1992). ... On New Orleans disabled list (May 25-June 10 and June 13-July 29, 1993). ... On disabled list (August 9-September 2, 1997). ... Granted free agency (December 21, 1997). ... Signed by Chicago Cubs (December 29, 1997). ... Released by Cubs (December 7, 1998). ... Signed by Seattle Mariners (December 16, 1998).
HONORS: Named Northwest League Most Valuable Player (1990). ... Named California League Most Valuable Player (1991).
STATISTICAL NOTES: Led Northwest League with 155 total bases in 1990. ... Led Northwest League outfielders with 148 total chances in 1990. ... Led California League with 261 total bases and .456 on-base percentage in 1991. ... Career major league grand slams: 2.

Year Team (League)	Pos.				BATTING								FIELDING		
		G	AB	R	H	2B	3B	HR	RBI	Avg.	BB	SO	SB	PO	A	E	Avg.
1990— Spokane (N'west)	OF	*76	*291	*59	99	20	6	*12	*63	.340	45	43	26	*134	7	7	.953
1991— High Desert (Calif.)	OF	•133	492	108	*168	*36	6	15	119	*.341	*94	82	39	258	14	*15	.948
1992— Denver (A.A.)■	OF	134	*524	80	140	29	11	19	77	.267	39	90	13	252	*23	*13	.955
1993— New Orleans (A.A.)	OF	60	219	36	57	14	2	8	22	.260	27	46	6	114	4	2	.983
— Milwaukee (A.L.)	OF	23	58	9	14	0	0	3	7	.241	4	14	0	43	1	3	.936
1994— Milwaukee (A.L.)	OF-DH	84	259	39	67	13	1	10	38	.259	21	62	3	154	7	4	.976
— New Orleans (A.A.)	OF	2	8	2	2	0	0	1	3	.250	1	1	1	2	0	0	1.000
1995— Milwaukee (A.L.)	OF-DH	117	267	42	67	13	1	12	48	.251	27	45	2	177	7	4	.979
1996— Milwaukee (A.L.)	OF	127	374	46	104	24	3	14	64	.278	26	76	1	250	7	1	.996
1997— Milwaukee (A.L.)	OF-DH	84	253	39	63	15	3	5	21	.249	19	50	1	121	6	5	.962
1998— Chicago (N.L.)■	OF	97	97	16	29	7	0	1	12	.299	11	17	0	36	1	1	.974
— Iowa (Pacific Coast) ...	OF	35	106	17	27	5	0	7	19	.255	10	27	0	35	3	2	.950
American League totals (5 years)		435	1211	175	315	65	8	44	178	.260	97	247	7	745	28	17	.978
National League totals (1 year)		77	97	16	29	7	0	1	12	.299	11	17	0	36	1	1	.974
Major league totals (6 years)		512	1308	191	344	72	8	45	190	.263	108	264	7	781	29	18	.978

MILLAR, KEVIN   1B/3B   MARLINS

PERSONAL: Born September 24, 1971, in Los Angeles. ... 6-0/185. ... Bats right, throws right. ... Full name: Kevin Charles Millar. ... Nephew of Wayne Nordhagen, outfielder with four major league teams (1976-1983).
HIGH SCHOOL: University (Los Angeles).
JUNIOR COLLEGE: Los Angeles Community College.
TRANSACTIONS/CAREER NOTES: Purchased by Florida Marlins organization from St. Paul, Northern League (September 20, 1993). ... Granted free agency (December 21, 1997). ... Re-signed by Marlins (December 21, 1997). ... On Florida disabled list (April 19, 1998-remainder of season); included rehabilitation assignment to Charlotte (June 14-29).
HONORS: Named Eastern League Player of the Year (1997).
STATISTICAL NOTES: Led Midwest League with 240 total bases in 1994. ... Led Florida State League with 10 sacrifice flies in 1995. ... Led Florida State League first basemen with 1,320 total chances in 1995. ... Led Eastern League with 309 total bases and .423 on-base percentage and tied for league lead with seven sacrifice flies in 1997. ... Led Eastern League first basemen with 93 assists and 116 double plays in 1997.

								BATTING								FIELDING		
Year— Team (League)	Pos.	G	AB	R	H	2B	3B	HR	RBI	Avg.	BB	SO	SB	PO	A	E	Avg.
1993— St. Paul (Northern)....	3B-2B	63	227	33	59	11	1	5	30	.260	24	27	2	51	133	18	.911
1994— Kane Co. (Midw.)■....	1B	135	477	75	144	35	2	19	93	.302	74	88	3	1010	64	11	.990
1995— Brevard Co. (Fla. St.)..	1B	129	459	53	132	32	2	13	68	.288	70	66	4	*1213	95	12	.991
1996— Portland (Eastern)......	1B-3B	130	472	69	150	32	0	18	86	.318	37	53	6	753	134	15	.983
1997— Portland (Eastern)......	1B-3B	135	511	94	*175	•34	2	32	*131	*.342	66	53	2	1146	†121	17	.987
1998— Florida (N.L.).............	3B	2	2	1	1	0	0	0	0	.500	1	0	0	2	3	1	.833
— Charlotte (Int'l)...........	3B-1B	14	46	14	15	3	0	4	15	.326	9	7	1	34	19	4	.930
Major league totals (1 year)		**2**	**2**	**1**	**1**	**0**	**0**	**0**	**0**	**.500**	**1**	**0**	**0**	**2**	**3**	**1**	**.833**

MILLER, DAMIAN   C   DIAMONDBACKS

PERSONAL: Born October 13, 1969, in La Crosse, Wis. ... 6-2/190. ... Bats right, throws right. ... Full name: Damian Donald Miller.
HIGH SCHOOL: West Salem (Wis.).
COLLEGE: Viterbo (Wis.).
TRANSACTIONS/CAREER NOTES: Selected by Minnesota Twins organization in 20th round of free-agent draft (June 4, 1990). ... Selected by Arizona Diamondbacks in second round (47th pick overall) of expansion draft (November 18, 1997).
STATISTICAL NOTES: Led Pacific Coast League catchers with .998 fielding percentage in 1995. ... Led Pacific Coast League catchers with 70 assists and 695 total chances in 1996. ... Career major league grand slams: 1.

								BATTING								FIELDING		
Year— Team (League)	Pos.	G	AB	R	H	2B	3B	HR	RBI	Avg.	BB	SO	SB	PO	A	E	Avg.
1990— Elizabethton (App.).....	C	14	45	7	10	1	0	1	6	.222	9	3	1	102	6	2	.982
1991— Kenosha (Midwest)	C-1B-OF	80	267	28	62	11	1	3	34	.232	24	53	3	357	52	4	.990
1992— Kenosha (Midwest)	C	115	377	53	110	27	2	5	56	.292	53	66	6	696	89	9	.989
1993— Fort Myers (FSL)........	C	87	325	31	69	12	1	1	26	.212	31	44	6	465	62	8	.985
— Nashville (Southern) ..	C	4	13	0	3	0	0	0	0	.231	2	4	0	26	3	0	1.000
1994— Nashville (Southern) ..	C	103	328	36	88	10	0	8	35	.268	35	51	4	628	81	8	.989
1995— Salt Lake (PCL)	C-OF	83	295	39	84	23	1	3	41	.285	15	39	2	395	52	1	†.998
1996— Salt Lake (PCL)	C	104	385	54	110	27	1	7	55	.286	25	58	1	619	†70	6	.991
1997— Salt Lake (PCL)	C	85	314	48	106	19	3	11	82	.338	29	62	6	445	35	6	.988
— Minnesota (A.L.)	C-DH	25	66	5	18	1	0	2	13	.273	2	12	0	85	3	0	1.000
1998— Tucson (PCL)■...........	C	18	63	14	22	7	1	0	11	.349	9	9	0	95	15	3	.973
— Arizona (N.L.)	C-DH-O-1	57	168	17	48	14	2	3	14	.286	11	43	1	255	27	4	.986
American League totals (1 year)		**25**	**66**	**5**	**18**	**1**	**0**	**2**	**13**	**.273**	**2**	**12**	**0**	**85**	**3**	**0**	**1.000**
National League totals (1 year)		**57**	**168**	**17**	**48**	**14**	**2**	**3**	**14**	**.286**	**11**	**43**	**1**	**255**	**27**	**4**	**.986**
Major league totals (2 years)		**82**	**234**	**22**	**66**	**15**	**2**	**5**	**27**	**.282**	**13**	**55**	**1**	**340**	**30**	**4**	**.989**

M

MILLER, DAVID   OF   PHILLIES

PERSONAL: Born December 9, 1973, in Philadelphia. ... 6-4/200. ... Bats left, throws left.
HIGH SCHOOL: Chestnut Hill Academy (Philadelphia).
COLLEGE: Clemson.
TRANSACTIONS/CAREER NOTES: Selected by Cleveland Indians organization in first round (23rd pick overall) of free-agent draft (June 1, 1995). ... Selected by Philadelphia Phillies from Indians organization in Rule 5 major league draft (December 14, 1998).

								BATTING								FIELDING		
Year— Team (League)	Pos.	G	AB	R	H	2B	3B	HR	RBI	Avg.	BB	SO	SB	PO	A	E	Avg.
1996— Kinston (Car.).............	OF-1B	129	488	71	124	23	1	7	54	.254	38	94	14	406	27	13	.910
1997— Akron (East).............	OF-1B	134	509	84	153	27	9	4	61	.301	48	77	22	245	10	5	.942
1998— Buffalo (Int'l).............	OF	115	415	56	111	19	2	9	54	.267	61	72	6	257	5	4	.985

MILLER, KURT   P   CUBS

PERSONAL: Born August 24, 1972, in Tucson, Ariz. ... 6-5/225. ... Throws right, bats right. ... Full name: Kurt Everett Miller.
HIGH SCHOOL: Bowie (Texas), then Tulsa (Okla.) Union, then West (Bakersfield, Calif.).
TRANSACTIONS/CAREER NOTES: Selected by Pittsburgh Pirates organization in first round (fifth pick overall) of free-agent draft (June 4, 1990). ... On Augusta disabled list (July 10-August 3, 1991). ... Traded by Pirates with a player to be named later to Texas Rangers for 3B Steve Buechele (August 30, 1991); Rangers acquired P Hector Fajardo to complete deal (September 6, 1991). ... Traded by Rangers with P Robb Nen to Florida Marlins for P Cris Carpenter (July 17, 1993). ... On disabled list (March 31-September 1, 1997); included rehabilitation assignments to Brevard County (April 13-18) and Charlotte (May 27-September 1). ... Traded by Marlins to Chicago Cubs for cash considerations (November 18, 1997).
STATISTICAL NOTES: Tied for Texas League lead with four balks in 1992.

Year	Team (League)	W	L	Pct.	ERA	G	GS	CG	ShO	Sv.	IP	H	R	ER	BB	SO
1990—	Welland (N.Y.-Penn)	3	2	.600	3.29	14	12	0	0	0	65 2/3	59	39	24	37	62
1991—	Augusta (S. Atl.)	6	7	.462	2.50	21	21	2	2	0	115 1/3	89	49	32	57	103
1992—	Charlotte (Fla. St.)■	5	4	.556	2.39	12	12	0	0	0	75 1/3	51	23	20	29	58
	—Tulsa (Texas)	7	5	.583	3.68	16	15	0	0	0	88	82	42	36	35	73
1993—	Tulsa (Texas)	6	8	.429	5.06	18	18	0	0	0	96	102	69	54	45	68
	—Edmonton (PCL)■	3	3	.500	4.50	9	9	0	0	0	48	42	24	24	34	19
1994—	Edmonton (PCL)	7	*13	.350	6.88	23	23	0	0	0	125 2/3	164	105	96	64	58
	—Florida (N.L.)	1	3	.250	8.10	4	4	0	0	0	20	26	18	18	7	11
1995—	Charlotte (Int'l)	8	11	.421	4.62	22	22	0	0	0	126 2/3	143	76	65	55	83
1996—	Charlotte (Int'l)	3	5	.375	4.66	12	12	2	0	0	65 2/3	77	39	34	26	38
	—Florida (N.L.)	1	3	.250	6.80	26	5	0	0	0	46 1/3	57	41	35	33	30
1997—	Brevard County (FSL)	0	0	...	1.80	2	2	0	0	0	5	6	1	1	2	7
	—Charlotte (Int'l)	2	1	.667	3.58	21	0	0	0	0	27 2/3	25	12	11	22	31
	—Florida (N.L.)	0	1	.000	9.82	7	0	0	0	0	7 1/3	12	8	8	7	7
1998—	Iowa (Pacific Coast)■	14	3	.824	3.81	28	27	2	0	0	167 2/3	153	77	71	77	145
	—Chicago (N.L.)	0	0	...	0.00	3	0	0	0	0	4	3	0	0	0	6
Major league totals (4 years)		2	7	.222	7.07	40	9	0	0	0	77 2/3	98	67	61	47	54

MILLER, TRAVIS   P   TWINS

PERSONAL: Born November 2, 1972, in Dayton, Ohio. ... 6-3/211. ... Throws left, bats right. ... Full name: Travis Eugene Miller.
HIGH SCHOOL: National Trail (New Paris, Ohio).
COLLEGE: Kent.
TRANSACTIONS/CAREER NOTES: Selected by Minnesota Twins organization in supplemental round ("sandwich pick" between first and second round, 34th pick overall) of free-agent draft (June 2, 1994); pick received as compensation for Twins failing to sign 1993 first-round pick C Jason Varitek. ... On Salt Lake disabled list (April 20-May 3, 1998).

Year	Team (League)	W	L	Pct.	ERA	G	GS	CG	ShO	Sv.	IP	H	R	ER	BB	SO
1994—	Fort Wayne (Midw.)	4	1	.800	2.60	11	9	1	0	0	55 1/3	52	17	16	12	50
	—Nashville (Southern)	0	0	...	2.84	1	1	0	0	0	6 1/3	3	3	2	2	4
1995—	New Britain (East.)	7	9	.438	4.37	28	27	1	1	0	162 2/3	*172	93	79	65	151
1996—	Minnesota (A.L.)	1	2	.333	9.23	7	7	0	0	0	26 1/3	45	29	27	9	15
	—Salt Lake (PCL)	8	10	.444	4.83	27	27	1	0	0	160 1/3	187	97	86	57	*143
1997—	Salt Lake (PCL)	10	6	.625	4.73	21	21	0	0	0	125 2/3	140	73	66	57	86
	—Minnesota (A.L.)	1	5	.167	7.63	13	7	0	0	0	48 1/3	64	49	41	23	26
1998—	Salt Lake (PCL)	3	4	.429	4.84	34	2	0	0	9	57 2/3	60	33	31	31	65
	—Minnesota (A.L.)	0	2	.000	3.86	14	0	0	0	0	23 1/3	25	10	10	11	23
Major league totals (3 years)		2	9	.182	7.16	34	14	0	0	0	98	134	88	78	43	64

MILLER, TREVER   P   ASTROS

PERSONAL: Born May 29, 1973, in Louisville, Ky. ... 6-4/195. ... Throws left, bats right. ... Full name: Trever Douglas Miller.
HIGH SCHOOL: Trinity (Louisville, Ky.).
TRANSACTIONS/CAREER NOTES: Selected by Detroit Tigers organization in supplemental round ("sandwich pick" between first and second round, 41st pick overall) of free-agent draft (June 3, 1991); pick received as part of compensation for Atlanta Braves signing Type A free-agent C Mike Heath. ... Traded by Tigers with C Brad Ausmus, P Jose Lima, P C.J. Nitkowski and IF Daryle Ward to Houston Astros for OF Brian Hunter, IF Orlando Miller, P Doug Brocail, P Todd Jones and cash (December 10, 1996). ... On Houston disabled list (August 23-September 7, 1998).
STATISTICAL NOTES: Tied for Appalachian League lead with seven home runs allowed in 1991.

Year	Team (League)	W	L	Pct.	ERA	G	GS	CG	ShO	Sv.	IP	H	R	ER	BB	SO
1991—	Bristol (Appalachian)	2	7	.222	5.67	13	13	0	0	0	54	60	44	34	29	46
1992—	Bristol (Appalachian)	3	•8	.273	4.93	12	12	1	0	0	69 1/3	75	45	38	27	64
1993—	Fayetteville (S. Atl.)	8	13	.381	4.19	28	28	2	0	0	161	151	99	75	67	116
1994—	Trenton (Eastern)	7	•16	.304	4.39	26	26	*6	0	0	174 1/3	*198	95	85	51	73
1995—	Jacksonville (Southern)	8	2	.800	2.72	31	16	3	2	0	122 1/3	122	46	37	34	77
1996—	Toledo (International)	13	6	.684	4.90	27	27	0	0	0	165 1/3	167	98	90	65	115
	—Detroit (A.L.)	0	4	.000	9.18	5	4	0	0	0	16 2/3	28	17	17	9	8
1997—	New Orleans (A.A.)■	6	7	.462	3.30	29	27	2	0	0	163 2/3	177	71	60	54	99
1998—	Houston (N.L.)	2	0	1.000	3.04	37	1	0	0	1	53 1/3	57	21	18	20	30
A.L. totals (1 year)		0	4	.000	9.18	5	4	0	0	0	16 2/3	28	17	17	9	8
N.L. totals (1 year)		2	0	1.000	3.04	37	1	0	0	1	53 1/3	57	21	18	20	30
Major league totals (2 years)		2	4	.333	4.50	42	5	0	0	1	70	85	38	35	29	38

DIVISION SERIES RECORD

Year	Team (League)	W	L	Pct.	ERA	G	GS	CG	ShO	Sv.	IP	H	R	ER	BB	SO
1998—	Houston (N.L.)	0	0	...	...	1	0	0	0	0	0	0	0	0	1	0

MILLER, WADE   P   ASTROS

PERSONAL: Born September 13, 1976, in Reading, Pa. ... 6-2/185. ... Throws right, bats right. ... Full name: Wade T. Miller.
HIGH SCHOOL: Brandywine Heights (Pa.).
COLLEGE: Alvernia (Pa.).
TRANSACTIONS/CAREER NOTES: Selected by Houston Astros organization in 20th round of free-agent draft (June 4, 1996). ... On disabled list (June 1, 1998-remainder of season).

Year	Team (League)	W	L	Pct.	ERA	G	GS	CG	ShO	Sv.	IP	H	R	ER	BB	SO
1996—	Auburn (N.Y.-Penn)	1	1	.500	5.00	2	2	0	0	0	9	8	9	5	4	11
	—GC Astros (GCL)	3	4	.429	3.79	11	10	0	0	0	57	49	26	24	12	53
1997—	Quad City (Midwest)	5	3	.625	3.36	10	8	2	0	0	59	45	27	22	10	50
	—Kissimmee (Florida State)	10	2	.833	1.80	14	14	4	1	0	100	79	28	20	14	76
1998—	Jackson (Texas)	5	0	1.000	2.32	10	10	0	0	0	62	49	23	16	27	48

M

MILLIARD, RALPH — IF — METS

PERSONAL: Born December 30, 1973, in Willemstad, Curacao. ... 5-11/175. ... Bats right, throws right. ... Full name: Ralph Gregory Milliard.
HIGH SCHOOL: Aamsvdorda Technical School (Soest, The Netherlands).
TRANSACTIONS/CAREER NOTES: Signed as non-drafted free agent by Florida Marlins organization (July 26, 1992). ... On Charlotte disabled list (April 22-May 7, 1997). ... Traded by Marlins with P Al Leiter to New York Mets for P Jesus Sanchez, P A.J. Burnett, and OF Robert Stratton (February 6, 1998).
STATISTICAL NOTES: Led Gulf Coast League second basemen with 111 putouts, 142 assists, 257 total chances and .984 fielding percentage in 1993. ... Led Midwest League second basemen with 659 total chances and 72 double plays in 1994. ... Led International League second basemen with 276 putouts in 1998.

Year Team (League)	Pos.	G	AB	R	H	2B	3B	HR	RBI	Avg.	BB	SO	SB	PO	A	E	Avg.
1993— GC Marlins (GCL)	2B-3B	53	192	35	45	15	0	0	25	.234	30	17	11	†114	†145	5	.981
1994— Kane County (Midw.)	2B	133	515	*97	153	34	2	8	67	.297	68	63	10	*248	*390	21	.968
1995— Portland (Eastern)	2B	128	464	*104	124	22	3	11	40	.267	85	83	22	*299	357	17	.975
1996— Portland (Eastern)	2B	6	20	2	4	0	1	0	2	.200	1	5	1	12	18	0	1.000
— Charlotte (Int'l)	2B	69	250	47	69	15	2	6	26	.276	38	43	8	154	188	5	.986
— Florida (N.L.)	2B	24	62	7	10	2	0	0	1	.161	14	16	2	42	65	5	.955
1997— Charlotte (Int'l)	2B	33	132	19	35	5	1	4	18	.265	9	21	5	71	91	1	.994
— Florida (N.L.)	2B	8	30	2	6	0	0	0	2	.200	3	3	1	14	32	0	1.000
— Portland (Eastern)	2B	19	69	13	19	1	2	0	5	.275	7	8	3	37	53	1	.989
1998— Norfolk (Int'l)■	2B-SS	127	417	73	108	24	4	15	52	.259	79	59	17	†277	373	13	.980
— New York (N.L.)	2B-SS	10	1	3	0	0	0	0	0	.000	0	1	0	3	2	1	.833
Major league totals (3 years)		42	93	12	16	2	0	0	3	.172	17	20	3	59	99	6	.963

MILLS, ALAN — P — DODGERS

PERSONAL: Born October 18, 1966, in Lakeland, Fla. ... 6-1/195. ... Throws right, bats both. ... Full name: Alan Bernard Mills.
HIGH SCHOOL: Kathleen (Fla.).
JUNIOR COLLEGE: Polk Community College (Fla.).
TRANSACTIONS/CAREER NOTES: Selected by Boston Red Sox organization in first round (13th pick overall) of free-agent draft (January 14, 1986); did not sign. ... Selected by California Angels organization in secondary phase of free-agent draft (June 2, 1986). ... Traded by Angels organization to New York Yankees organization (June 22, 1987), completing deal in which Angels traded P Ron Romanick and a player to be named later to Yankees for C Butch Wynegar (December 19, 1986). ... Traded by Yankees to Baltimore Orioles for two players to be named later (February 29, 1992); Yankees acquired P Francisco de la Rosa (February 29, 1992) and P Mark Carper (June 8, 1992) to complete deal. ... On suspended list (June 26-30, 1993). ... On Rochester disabled list (July 4-September 16, 1995). ... On disabled list (March 22-May 12, 1996 and April 10-June 15, 1997). ... On suspended list (May 29-30, 1998). ... Granted free agency (October 23, 1998). ... Signed by Los Angeles Dodgers (December 10, 1998).

Year Team (League)	W	L	Pct.	ERA	G	GS	CG	ShO	Sv.	IP	H	R	ER	BB	SO
1986— Salem (Northwest)	6	6	.500	4.63	14	14	1	0	0	83 2/3	77	58	43	60	50
1987— Prince William (Caro.)■	2	11	.154	6.09	35	8	0	0	1	85 2/3	102	75	58	64	53
1988— Prince William (Caro.)	3	8	.273	4.13	42	5	0	0	4	93 2/3	93	56	43	43	59
1989— Prince William (Caro.)	6	1	.857	0.91	26	0	0	0	7	39 2/3	22	5	4	13	44
— Fort Lauderdale (FSL)	1	4	.200	3.77	22	0	0	0	6	31	40	15	13	9	25
1990— New York (A.L.)	1	5	.167	4.10	36	0	0	0	0	41 2/3	48	21	19	33	24
— Columbus (Int'l)	3	3	.500	3.38	17	0	0	0	6	29 1/3	22	11	11	14	30
1991— Columbus (Int'l)	7	5	.583	4.43	38	15	0	0	8	113 2/3	109	65	56	75	77
— New York (A.L.)	1	1	.500	4.41	6	2	0	0	0	16 1/3	16	9	8	8	11
1992— Rochester (Int'l)■	0	1	.000	5.40	3	0	0	0	1	5	6	3	3	2	8
— Baltimore (A.L.)	10	4	.714	2.61	35	3	0	0	2	103 1/3	78	33	30	54	60
1993— Baltimore (A.L.)	5	4	.556	3.23	45	0	0	0	4	100 1/3	80	39	36	51	68
1994— Baltimore (A.L.)	3	3	.500	5.16	47	0	0	0	2	45 1/3	43	26	26	24	44
1995— Baltimore (A.L.)	3	0	1.000	7.43	21	0	0	0	0	23	30	20	19	18	16
— Rochester (Int'l)	0	1	.000	0.00	1	1	0	0	0	2 2/3	2	6	0	5	2
— GC Orioles (GCL)	0	0	. . .	0.00	1	1	0	0	0	2	3	0	0	2	1
1996— Baltimore (A.L.)	3	2	.600	4.28	49	0	0	0	3	54 2/3	40	26	26	35	50
1997— Baltimore (A.L.)	2	3	.400	4.89	39	0	0	0	0	38 2/3	41	23	21	33	32
1998— Baltimore (A.L.)	3	4	.429	3.74	72	0	0	0	2	77	55	32	32	50	57
Major league totals (9 years)	31	26	.544	3.90	350	5	0	0	13	500 1/3	431	229	217	306	362

DIVISION SERIES RECORD

Year Team (League)	W	L	Pct.	ERA	G	GS	CG	ShO	Sv.	IP	H	R	ER	BB	SO
1997— Baltimore (A.L.)	0	0	. . .	0.00	1	0	0	0	0	1	1	0	0	0	1

CHAMPIONSHIP SERIES RECORD

Year Team (League)	W	L	Pct.	ERA	G	GS	CG	ShO	Sv.	IP	H	R	ER	BB	SO
1996— Baltimore (A.L.)	0	0	. . .	3.86	3	0	0	0	0	2 1/3	3	1	1	1	3
1997— Baltimore (A.L.)	0	1	.000	2.70	3	0	0	0	0	3 1/3	1	1	1	2	3
Champ. series totals (2 years)	0	1	.000	3.18	6	0	0	0	0	5 2/3	4	2	2	3	6

MILLWOOD, KEVIN — P — BRAVES

PERSONAL: Born December 24, 1974, in Gastonia, N.C. ... 6-4/220. ... Throws right, bats right. ... Full name: Kevin Austin Millwood.
HIGH SCHOOL: Bessemer City (N.C.).
TRANSACTIONS/CAREER NOTES: Selected by Atlanta Braves organization in 11th round of free-agent draft (June 3, 1993).
STATISTICAL NOTES: Pitched 6-0 one-hit, complete-game victory against Pittsburgh (April 14, 1998).

M

Year — Team (League)	W	L	Pct.	ERA	G	GS	CG	ShO	Sv.	IP	H	R	ER	BB	SO
1993— GC Braves (GCL)	3	3	.500	3.06	12	9	0	0	0	50	36	27	17	28	49
1994— Danville (Appalachian)	3	3	.500	3.72	13	5	0	0	1	46	42	25	19	34	56
— Macon (S. Atl.)	0	5	.000	5.79	12	4	0	0	1	32 2/3	31	31	21	32	24
1995— Macon (S. Atl.)	5	6	.455	4.63	29	12	0	0	0	103	86	65	53	57	89
1996— Durham (Carolina)	6	9	.400	4.28	33	20	1	0	1	149 1/3	138	77	71	58	139
1997— Greenville (Southern)	3	5	.375	4.11	11	11	0	0	0	61 1/3	59	37	28	24	61
— Richmond (Int'l)	7	0	1.000	1.93	9	9	1	0	0	60 2/3	38	13	13	16	46
— Atlanta (N.L.)	5	3	.625	4.03	12	8	0	0	0	51 1/3	55	26	23	21	42
1998— Atlanta (N.L.)	17	8	.680	4.08	31	29	3	1	0	174 1/3	175	86	79	56	163
Major league totals (2 years)	22	11	.667	4.07	43	37	3	1	0	225 2/3	230	112	102	77	205

MILTON, ERIC — P — TWINS

PERSONAL: Born August 4, 1975, in State College, Pa. ... 6-3/200. ... Throws left, bats left. ... Full name: Eric Robert Milton.
HIGH SCHOOL: Bellefonte (Pa.).
COLLEGE: Maryland.
TRANSACTIONS/CAREER NOTES: Selected by New York Yankees organization in first round (20th pick overall) of free-agent draft (June 2, 1996). ... Traded by Yankees with P Danny Mota, OF Brian Buchanan, SS Cristian Guzman and cash to Minnesota Twins for 2B Chuck Knoblauch (February 6, 1998).
STATISTICAL NOTES: Tied for Eastern League lead with four balks in 1997.

Year — Team (League)	W	L	Pct.	ERA	G	GS	CG	ShO	Sv.	IP	H	R	ER	BB	SO
1997— Tampa (Fla. St.)	8	3	.727	3.09	14	14	1	0	0	93 1/3	78	35	32	14	95
— Norwich (Eastern)	6	3	.667	3.13	14	14	1	0	0	77 2/3	59	29	27	36	67
1998— Minnesota (A.L.)■	8	14	.364	5.64	32	32	1	0	0	172 1/3	195	113	108	70	107
Major league totals (1 year)	8	14	.364	5.64	32	32	1	0	0	172 1/3	195	113	108	70	107

MINOR, DAMON — 1B — GIANTS

PERSONAL: Born January 5, 1974, in Canton, Ohio. ... 6-7/230. ... Bats left, throws left. ... Full name: Damon Reed Minor. ... Brother of Ryan Minor, third baseman, Baltimore Orioles.
HIGH SCHOOL: Hammon (Okla.).
COLLEGE: Oklahoma.
TRANSACTIONS/CAREER NOTES: Selected by San Francisco Giants organization in 12th round of free-agent draft (June 4, 1996).
STATISTICAL NOTES: Tied for Northwest League lead in intentional bases on balls received with four in 1996. ... Led Northwest League first basemen with 693 total chances in 1996. ... Led California League with eight intentional bases in balls received in 1997. ... Led California League first basemen with 127 double plays and 1,371 total chances in 1997.

Year — Team (League)	Pos.	G	AB	R	H	2B	3B	HR	RBI	Avg.	BB	SO	SB	PO	A	E	Avg.
1996— Bellingham (N'west)	1B	75	269	44	65	11	1	12	55	.242	47	86	0	*650	38	5	.993
1997— Bakersfield (Calif.)	1B	*140	532	98	154	34	1	31	99	.289	87	143	2	*1261	*88	*22	.984
1998— Shreveport (Texas)	1B	81	289	39	69	11	1	14	52	.239	30	51	1	641	39	8	.988
— San Jose (Calif.)	1B	48	176	26	50	10	1	7	36	.284	28	40	0	413	36	6	.987

M

MINOR, RYAN — 3B — ORIOLES

PERSONAL: Born January 5, 1974, in Canton, Ohio. ... 6-7/225. ... Bats right, throws right. ... Full name: Ryan Dale Minor. ... Brother of Damon Minor, first baseman, San Francisco Giants organization.
HIGH SCHOOL: Hammon (Okla.).
COLLEGE: Oklahoma.
TRANSACTIONS/CAREER NOTES: Selected by Baltimore Orioles organization in 15th round of free-agent draft (June 1, 1992); did not sign. ... Selected by Orioles organization in 33rd round of free-agent draft (June 4, 1996).
STATISTICAL NOTES: Led Eastern League third basemen with 27 double plays in 1998.

Year — Team (League)	Pos.	G	AB	R	H	2B	3B	HR	RBI	Avg.	BB	SO	SB	PO	A	E	Avg.
1996— Bluefield (Appal.)	3B-SS	25	87	14	22	6	0	4	9	.253	7	32	1	13	45	5	.921
1997— Delmarva (S. Atl.)	3B-1B	134	488	83	150	42	1	24	97	.307	51	102	7	193	209	34	.922
1998— Bowie (Eastern)	3B	138	521	73	130	20	3	17	71	.250	34	*152	2	89	245	*26	.928
— Baltimore (A.L.)	3B-1B-DH	9	14	3	6	1	0	0	1	.429	0	3	0	6	5	1	.917
Major league totals (1 year)		9	14	3	6	1	0	0	1	.429	0	3	0	6	5	1	.917

CBA REGULAR-SEASON RECORD

TRANSACTIONS/CAREER NOTES: Selected by Philadelphia 76ers in second round (32nd pick overall) of 1996 NBA draft. ... Played in Continental Basketball Association with Oklahoma City Calvary (1996-97).

Season Team	G	Min.	FGM	FGA	Pct.	FTM	FTA	Pct.	Reb.	Ast.	Pts.	RPG	APG	PPG
96-97—Oklahoma City	32	892	124	270	.459	38	50	.760	141	62	304	4.4	1.9	9.5

MIRABELLI, DOUG — C — GIANTS

PERSONAL: Born October 18, 1970, in Kingman, Ariz. ... 6-1/218. ... Bats right, throws right. ... Full name: Douglas Anthony Mirabelli.
HIGH SCHOOL: Valley (Las Vegas).
COLLEGE: Wichita State.
TRANSACTIONS/CAREER NOTES: Selected by Detroit Tigers organization in sixth round of free-agent draft (June 5, 1989); did not sign. ... Selected by San Francisco Giants organization in fifth round of free-agent draft (June 1, 1992). ... On Phoenix disabled list (May 16-23, 1995).
STATISTICAL NOTES: Led Texas League with .419 on-base percentage in 1996. ... Led Pacific Coast League catchers with 680 total chances in 1997.

Year Team (League)	Pos.	G	AB	R	H	2B	3B	HR	RBI	Avg.	BB	SO	SB	PO	A	E	Avg.
1992— San Jose (Calif.)........	C	53	177	30	41	11	1	0	21	.232	24	18	1	321	38	10	.973
1993— San Jose (Calif.)........	C	113	371	58	100	19	2	1	48	.270	72	55	0	737	99	9	.989
1994— Shreveport (Texas).....	C-1B	85	255	23	56	8	0	4	24	.220	36	48	3	391	51	3	.993
1995— Shreveport (Texas).....	C-1B	40	126	14	38	13	0	0	16	.302	20	14	1	193	21	3	.986
—Phoenix (PCL)...........	C	23	66	3	11	0	1	0	7	.167	12	10	1	115	17	2	.985
1996— Shreveport (Texas).....	C-1B	115	380	60	112	23	0	21	70	.295	76	49	0	548	56	7	.989
—Phoenix (PCL)...........	C	14	47	10	14	7	0	0	7	.298	4	7	0	97	10	2	.982
—San Francisco (N.L.)..	C	9	18	2	4	1	0	0	1	.222	3	4	0	29	2	0	1.000
1997— Phoenix (PCL)...........	C	100	332	49	88	23	2	8	48	.265	58	69	1	*629	47	4	.994
—San Francisco (N.L.)..	C	6	7	0	1	0	0	0	0	.143	1	3	0	16	0	0	1.000
1998— Fresno (Pacific Coast)	C	85	265	45	69	12	2	13	53	.260	52	55	2	605	50	3	*.995
—San Francisco (N.L.)..	C	10	17	2	4	2	0	1	4	.235	2	6	0	34	4	1	.974
Major league totals (3 years)		25	42	4	9	3	0	1	5	.214	6	13	0	79	6	1	.988

MITCHELL, KEITH   OF

PERSONAL: Born August 6, 1969, in San Diego. ... 5-10/195. ... Bats right, throws right. ... Full name: Keith Alexander Mitchell. ... Cousin of Kevin Mitchell, outfielder with eight major league teams (1985-94 and 1996-98) and Fukuoka Dalei Hawks in Japan Central League (1995).
HIGH SCHOOL: Lincoln (San Diego).
TRANSACTIONS/CAREER NOTES: Selected by Atlanta Braves organization in fourth round of free-agent draft (June 2, 1987). ... On suspended list (September 5, 1993-remainder of season). ... Granted free agency (October 15, 1993). ... Signed by Seattle Mariners organization (November 18, 1993). ... On Seattle disabled list (April 9-May 20, 1994); included rehabilitation assignment to Calgary (May 12-20). ... Granted free agency (October 6, 1994). ... Signed by Cincinnati Reds organization (May 31, 1995). ... Granted free agency (October 16, 1995). ... Re-signed by Reds organization (January 24, 1996). ... Released by Reds (November 19, 1996). ... Signed by Pittsburgh Pirates organization (December 19, 1996). ... Granted free agency (October 15, 1997). ... Signed by Boston Red Sox organization (January 28, 1998). ... Granted free agency (December 21, 1998).
STATISTICAL NOTES: Led Gulf Coast League outfielders with 109 putouts and tied for lead with 117 total chances in 1987. ... Tied for Carolina League lead in double plays by outfielder with four in 1990.

Year Team (League)	Pos.	G	AB	R	H	2B	3B	HR	RBI	Avg.	BB	SO	SB	PO	A	E	Avg.
1987— GC Braves (GCL)........	OF-2B	57	208	24	50	12	1	2	21	.240	29	50	7	†111	6	4	.967
1988— Sumter (S. Atl.).........	OF	98	341	35	85	16	1	5	33	.249	41	50	9	193	7	6	.971
1989— Burlington (Midw.)......	OF-3B	127	448	64	117	23	0	10	49	.261	70	66	12	250	18	8	.971
1990— Durham (Carolina)......	OF	129	456	81	134	24	3	6	48	.294	92	48	18	256	9	5	.981
1991— Greenville (Southern) .	OF	60	214	46	70	15	3	10	47	.327	29	29	12	99	4	4	.963
—Richmond (Int'l).............	OF	25	95	16	31	6	1	2	17	.326	9	13	0	56	0	1	.982
—Atlanta (N.L.).............	OF	48	66	11	21	0	0	2	5	.318	8	12	3	31	1	1	.970
1992— Richmond (Int'l)........	OF-3B-2B	121	403	45	91	19	1	4	50	.226	66	55	14	195	10	9	.958
1993— Richmond (Int'l)........	OF	110	353	59	82	23	1	4	44	.232	44	48	9	138	7	6	.960
1994— Seattle (A.L.)■..........	OF-DH	46	128	21	29	2	0	5	15	.227	18	22	0	49	0	1	.980
—Calgary (PCL).............	OF	9	39	6	10	0	0	4	12	.256	2	4	0	8	1	0	1.000
1995— Indianapolis (A.A.)■ ..	OF	70	213	40	52	11	2	11	36	.244	40	40	4	136	4	3	.979
1996— Indianapolis (A.A.)......	OF-1B	112	357	60	107	21	3	16	66	.300	64	68	9	247	17	5	.981
—Cincinnati (N.L.)........	OF	11	15	2	4	1	0	1	3	.267	1	3	0	7	0	1	.875
1997— Indianapolis (A.A.)......	OF-1B	124	407	72	108	24	1	15	60	.265	*72	65	10	177	6	4	.979
1998— Trenton (Eastern)■	OF	12	41	4	8	2	0	2	7	.195	8	5	0	22	1	0	1.000
—Pawtucket (Int'l).............	OF-1B	63	211	55	66	15	0	12	45	.313	44	37	3	85	8	1	.989
—Boston (A.L.).............	DH-OF	23	33	4	9	2	0	0	6	.273	7	5	1	6	0	0	1.000
American League totals (2 years)		69	161	25	38	4	0	5	21	.236	25	27	1	55	0	1	.982
National League totals (2 years)		59	81	13	25	1	0	3	8	.309	9	15	3	38	1	2	.951
Major league totals (4 years)		128	242	38	63	5	0	8	29	.260	34	42	4	93	1	3	.969

CHAMPIONSHIP SERIES RECORD

Year Team (League)	Pos.	G	AB	R	H	2B	3B	HR	RBI	Avg.	BB	SO	SB	PO	A	E	Avg.
1991— Atlanta (N.L.).............	OF-PR-PH	5	4	0	0	0	0	0	0	.000	0	1	0	2	0	0	1.000

WORLD SERIES RECORD

Year Team (League)	Pos.	G	AB	R	H	2B	3B	HR	RBI	Avg.	BB	SO	SB	PO	A	E	Avg.
1991— Atlanta (N.L.).............	OF-PR	3	2	0	0	0	0	0	0	.000	0	1	0	0	0	0	...

MITCHELL, KEVIN   OF

PERSONAL: Born January 13, 1962, in San Diego. ... 5-11/244. ... Bats right, throws right. ... Full name: Kevin Darrell Mitchell. ... Cousin of Keith Mitchell, outfielder with four major league teams (1991, 1994, 1996 and 1998).
HIGH SCHOOL: Clairmont (San Diego).
TRANSACTIONS/CAREER NOTES: Signed as non-drafted free agent by New York Mets organization (November 16, 1980). ... On disabled list (July 21, 1982-remainder of season and July 12-30, 1985). ... Traded by Mets with OF Shawn Abner, OF Stanley Jefferson, P Kevin Armstrong and P Kevin Brown to San Diego Padres for OF Kevin McReynolds, P Gene Walter and IF Adam Ging (December 11, 1986). ... Traded by Padres with P Dave Dravecky and P Craig Lefferts to San Francisco Giants for 3B Chris Brown, P Keith Comstock, P Mark Davis and P Mark Grant (July 4, 1987). ... On suspended list for one game (May 3, 1991). ... On disabled list (June 3-25, 1991). ... Traded by Giants with P Mike Remlinger to Seattle Mariners for P Bill Swift, P Mike Jackson and P Dave Burba (December 11, 1991). ... On disabled list (August 8-23 and September 2, 1992-remainder of season). ... Traded by Mariners to Cincinnati Reds for P Norm Charlton (November 17, 1992). ... On disabled list (July 9-24 and September 10, 1993-remainder of season). ... Suspended by Reds for two games (July 24-25, 1993). ... Granted free agency (October 25, 1994). ... Played in Japan (1995). ... Signed by Boston Red Sox (March 8, 1996). ... On Boston disabled list (April 23-May 9 and May 30-July 16, 1996); included rehabilitation assignments to Pawtucket (May 7-9 and June 14-17). ... Traded by Red Sox to Reds for IF Robert Mejia and P Brad Tweedlie (July 30, 1996). ... Granted free agency (November 18, 1996). ... Signed by Cleveland Indians orga-

nization (December 13, 1996). ... Released by Indians (June 3, 1997). ... Signed by Oakland Athletics organization (March 9, 1998). ... On Oakland disabled list (May 3-June 3, 1998); included rehabilitation assignment to Edmonton (May 27-June 3). ... Released by Athletics (August 7, 1998).

RECORDS: Holds major league single-season record for most intentional bases on balls received by righthanded batter—32 (1989).

HONORS: Named Major League Player of the Year by THE SPORTING NEWS (1989). ... Named N.L. Player of the Year by THE SPORTING NEWS (1989). ... Named outfielder on THE SPORTING NEWS N.L. All-Star team (1989). ... Named outfielder on THE SPORTING NEWS N.L. Silver Slugger team (1989). ... Named N.L. Most Valuable Player by Baseball Writers' Association of America (1989).

STATISTICAL NOTES: Led Texas League third basemen with 224 assists in 1983. ... Led International League third basemen with 215 assists in 1984. ... Led International League third basemen with 22 errors in 1985. ... Led N.L. with 345 total bases, 32 intentional bases on balls received and .635 slugging percentage in 1989. ... Hit three home runs in one game (May 25, 1990). ... Had 20-game hitting streak (June 1-30, 1993). ... Career major league grand slams: 1.

Year	Team (League)	Pos.	G	AB	R	H	2B	3B	HR	RBI	Avg.	BB	SO	SB	PO	A	E	Avg.
1981—Kingsport (Appal.)......	3B-OF	62	221	39	74	9	2	7	45	.335	22	31	5	44	102	18	.890
1982—Lynchburg (Caro.)......	3B	29	85	19	27	5	1	1	16	.318	13	25	0	11	33	10	.815
1983—Jackson (Texas)......	3B	120	441	75	132	25	2	15	85	.299	48	84	11	81	†224	21	.936
1984—Tidewater (Int'l)	3B-1B-OF	120	432	51	105	21	3	10	54	.243	25	89	1	114	†220	22	.938
—New York (N.L.).........	3B	7	14	0	3	0	0	0	1	.214	0	3	0	1	4	1	.833
1985—Tidewater (Int'l)	3B-1B	95	348	44	101	24	2	9	43	.290	32	60	3	56	209	†22	.923
1986—New York (N.L.)	O-S-3-1	108	328	51	91	22	2	12	43	.277	33	61	3	158	69	10	.958
1987—San Diego (N.L.)■.....	3B-OF	62	196	19	48	7	1	7	26	.245	20	38	0	32	108	8	.946
—San Fran. (N.L.)■......	3B-SS-OF	69	268	49	82	13	1	15	44	.306	28	50	9	44	132	7	.962
1988—San Francisco (N.L.)..	3B-OF	148	505	60	127	25	7	19	80	.251	48	85	5	118	205	22	.936
1989—San Francisco (N.L.)..	OF-3B	154	543	100	158	34	6	*47	*125	.291	87	115	3	305	10	7	.978
1990—San Francisco (N.L.)..	OF	140	524	90	152	24	2	35	93	.290	58	87	4	295	9	9	.971
1991—San Francisco (N.L.)..	OF-1B	113	371	52	95	13	1	27	69	.256	43	57	2	188	6	6	.970
1992—Seattle (A.L.)■.........	OF-DH	99	360	48	103	24	0	9	67	.286	35	46	0	130	4	0	1.000
1993—Cincinnati (N.L.)■......	OF	93	323	56	110	21	3	19	64	.341	25	48	1	149	7	7	.957
1994—Cincinnati (N.L.).......	OF-1B	95	310	57	101	18	1	30	77	.326	59	62	2	139	10	4	.974
1995—Fukuoka (Jp. Pac.)■..	OF	37	130	17	39	6	0	8	28	.300	...	...	0	...	...	...	...
1996—Boston (A.L.).........	OF-DH	27	92	9	28	4	0	2	13	.304	11	14	0	29	0	2	.935
—Pawtucket (Int'l)........	OF	5	16	1	2	0	0	0	0	.125	1	5	0	2	0	1	.667
—Cincinnati (N.L.)■......	OF-1B	37	114	18	37	11	0	6	26	.325	26	16	0	73	2	2	.974
1997—Cleveland (A.L.)■......	DH-OF	20	59	7	9	1	0	4	11	.153	9	11	1	0	0	1	.000
1998—Oakland (A.L.)■.......	DH-OF-1B	51	127	14	29	7	1	2	21	.228	9	26	0	15	0	0	1.000
—Edmonton (PCL)........	DH	6	23	4	8	2	0	0	1	.348	1	2	0	...	...	...	...
American League totals (4 years)		197	638	78	169	36	1	17	112	.265	64	97	1	174	4	3	.983
National League totals (10 years)		1026	3496	552	1004	188	24	217	648	.287	427	622	29	1502	562	83	.961
Major league totals (13 years)		1223	4134	630	1173	224	25	234	760	.284	491	719	30	1676	566	86	.963

CHAMPIONSHIP SERIES RECORD

Year	Team (League)	Pos.	G	AB	R	H	2B	3B	HR	RBI	Avg.	BB	SO	SB	PO	A	E	Avg.
1986—New York (N.L.).........	OF	2	8	1	2	0	0	0	0	.250	0	1	0	3	0	0	1.000
1987—San Francisco (N.L.)..	3B	7	30	2	8	1	0	1	2	.267	0	3	1	4	11	1	.938
1989—San Francisco (N.L.)..	OF	5	17	5	6	0	0	2	7	.353	3	0	0	15	1	1	.941
Championship series totals (3 years)		14	55	8	16	1	0	3	9	.291	3	4	1	22	12	2	.944

WORLD SERIES RECORD

NOTES: Member of World Series championship team (1986).

Year	Team (League)	Pos.	G	AB	R	H	2B	3B	HR	RBI	Avg.	BB	SO	SB	PO	A	E	Avg.
1986—New York (N.L.)..........	PH-OF-DH	5	8	1	2	0	0	0	0	.250	0	3	0	0	2	0	1.000
1989—San Francisco (N.L.)..	OF	4	17	2	5	0	0	1	2	.294	0	3	0	10	0	1	.909
World Series totals (2 years)		9	25	3	7	0	0	1	2	.280	0	6	0	10	2	1	.923

ALL-STAR GAME RECORD

Year	League	Pos.	AB	R	H	2B	3B	HR	RBI	Avg.	BB	SO	SB	PO	A	E	Avg.
1989—National....................	OF	4	1	2	0	0	0	1	.500	0	2	0	0	0	0	...
1990—National....................	OF	2	0	0	0	0	0	0	.000	0	1	0	1	0	0	1.000
All-Star Game totals (2 years)		6	1	2	0	0	0	1	.333	0	3	0	1	0	0	1.000

M

MLICKI, DAVE   P   DODGERS

PERSONAL: Born June 8, 1968, in Cleveland. ... 6-4/205. ... Throws right, bats right. ... Full name: David John Mlicki. ... Brother of Doug Mlicki, pitcher, St. Louis Cardinals organization. ... Name pronounced muh-LICK-ee.

HIGH SCHOOL: Cheyenne Mountain (Colorado Springs, Colo.).

COLLEGE: Oklahoma State.

TRANSACTIONS/CAREER NOTES: Selected by Seattle Mariners organization in 23rd round of free-agent draft (June 5, 1989); did not sign. ... Selected by Cleveland Indians organization in 17th round of free-agent draft (June 4, 1990). ... On Cleveland disabled list (April 4-August 4, 1993); included rehabilitation assignment to Canton/Akron (July 19-August 4). ... Traded by Indians organization with P Jerry DiPoto, P Paul Byrd and a player to be named later to New York Mets organization for OF Jeromy Burnitz and P Joe Roa (November 18, 1994); Mets acquired 2B Jesus Azuaje to complete deal (December 6, 1994). ... Traded by Mets with P Greg McMichael to Los Angeles Dodgers for P Hideo Nomo and P Brad Clontz (June 5, 1998).

STATISTICAL NOTES: Led International League with 26 home runs allowed in 1994.

MISCELLANEOUS: Struck out in only appearance as pinch hitter (1996). ... Appeared in one game as pinch runner (1997).

Year Team (League)	W	L	Pct.	ERA	G	GS	CG	ShO	Sv.	IP	H	R	ER	BB	SO
1990— Burlington (Appalachian)....	3	1	.750	3.50	8	1	0	0	0	18	16	11	7	6	17
— Watertown (NYP).............	3	0	1.000	3.38	7	4	0	0	0	32	33	15	12	11	28
1991— Columbus (S. Atl.).............	8	6	.571	4.20	22	19	2	0	0	115⅔	101	70	54	70	136
1992— Cant./Akr. (Eastern)...........	11	9	.550	3.60	27	*27	2	0	0	172⅔	143	77	69	•80	146
— Cleveland (A.L.).................	0	2	.000	4.98	4	4	0	0	0	21⅔	23	14	12	16	16
1993— Cant./Akr. (Eastern)...........	2	1	.667	0.39	6	6	0	0	0	23	15	2	1	8	21
— Cleveland (A.L.).................	0	0	...	3.38	3	3	0	0	0	13⅓	11	6	5	6	7
1994— Charlotte (Int'l).................	6	10	.375	4.25	28	28	0	0	0	165⅓	179	85	78	64	152
1995— New York (N.L.)■.............	9	7	.563	4.26	29	25	0	0	0	160⅔	160	82	76	54	123
1996— New York (N.L.).............	6	7	.462	3.30	51	2	0	0	1	90	95	46	33	33	83
1997— New York (N.L.).............	8	12	.400	4.00	32	32	1	1	0	193⅔	194	89	86	76	157
1998— New York (N.L.).............	1	4	.200	5.68	10	10	1	0	0	57	68	38	36	25	39
— Los Angeles (N.L.)■.......	7	3	.700	4.05	20	20	2	1	0	124⅓	120	64	56	38	78
A.L. totals (2 years)..................	0	2	.000	4.37	7	7	0	0	0	35	34	20	17	22	23
N.L. totals (4 years)..................	31	33	.484	4.13	142	89	4	2	1	625⅔	637	319	287	226	480
Major league totals (6 years)......	31	35	.470	4.14	149	96	4	2	1	660⅔	671	339	304	248	503

MOEHLER, BRIAN — P — TIGERS

PERSONAL: Born December 31, 1971, in Rockingham, N.C. ... 6-3/235. ... Throws right, bats right. ... Full name: Brian Merritt Moehler.
HIGH SCHOOL: Richmond (N.C.) South.
COLLEGE: UNC Greensboro.
TRANSACTIONS/CAREER NOTES: Selected by Detroit Tigers organization in sixth round of free-agent draft (June 3, 1993). ... On disabled list (August 9-22, 1997).

Year Team (League)	W	L	Pct.	ERA	G	GS	CG	ShO	Sv.	IP	H	R	ER	BB	SO
1993— Niagara Falls (NYP)...........	6	5	.545	3.22	12	11	0	0	0	58⅔	51	33	21	27	38
1994— Lakeland (Fla. St.).............	12	12	.500	3.01	26	25	5	2	0	164⅔	153	66	55	65	92
1995— Jacksonville (Southern)......	8	10	.444	4.82	28	27	0	0	0	162⅓	176	94	87	52	89
1996— Detroit (A.L.)....................	0	1	.000	4.35	2	2	0	0	0	10⅓	11	10	5	8	2
— Jacksonville (Southern).....	15	6	.714	3.48	28	28	1	0	0	173⅓	186	80	67	50	120
1997— Detroit (A.L.)....................	11	12	.478	4.67	31	31	2	1	0	175⅓	198	97	91	61	97
1998— Detroit (A.L.)....................	14	13	.519	3.90	33	33	4	3	0	221⅓	220	103	96	56	123
Major league totals (3 years)......	25	26	.490	4.25	66	66	6	4	0	407	429	210	192	125	222

MOELLER, CHAD — C — TWINS

PERSONAL: Born February 18, 1975, in Upland, Calif. ... 6-3/207. ... Bats right, throws right. ... Full name: Chad Edward Moeller.
HIGH SCHOOL: Upland (Calif.).
COLLEGE: Southern California.
TRANSACTIONS/CAREER NOTES: Selected by Minnesota Twins organization in seventh round of free-agent draft (June 2, 1996). ... On disabled list (July 12, 1996-remainder of season).

Year Team (League)	Pos.	G	AB	R	H	2B	3B	HR	RBI	Avg.	BB	SO	SB	PO	A	E	Avg.
1996— Elizabethton (App.).....	C	17	59	17	21	4	0	4	13	.356	18	9	1	99	16	1	.991
1997— Fort Wayne (Midw.)....	C	108	384	58	111	18	3	9	39	.289	48	76	11	824	90	*15	.984
1998— Fort Myers (FSL)........	C	66	254	37	83	24	1	6	39	.327	31	37	2	395	36	9	.980
— New Britain (East.)	C	58	187	21	44	10	0	6	23	.235	24	41	2	414	25	6	.987

The BATTING columns span G through SB; the FIELDING columns span PO through Avg.

MOHLER, MIKE — P — CARDINALS

PERSONAL: Born July 26, 1968, in Dayton, Ohio. ... 6-2/208. ... Throws left, bats right. ... Full name: Michael Ross Mohler.
HIGH SCHOOL: East Ascension (Gonzales, La.).
COLLEGE: Nicholls State (La.).
TRANSACTIONS/CAREER NOTES: Selected by Oakland Athletics organization in 42nd round of free-agent draft (June 5, 1989). ... On Tacoma disabled list (April 7-May 24, 1994). ... Granted free agency (December 21, 1998). ... Signed by St. Louis Cardinals (January 15, 1999).
MISCELLANEOUS: Appeared in two games as pinch runner (1997).

Year Team (League)	W	L	Pct.	ERA	G	GS	CG	ShO	Sv.	IP	H	R	ER	BB	SO
1990— Madison (Midwest)	1	1	.500	3.41	42	2	0	0	1	63⅓	56	34	24	32	72
1991— Modesto (California)	9	4	.692	2.86	21	20	1	0	0	122⅔	106	48	39	45	98
— Huntsville (Southern)	4	2	.667	3.57	8	8	0	0	0	53	55	22	21	20	27
1992— Huntsville (Southern)	3	8	.273	3.59	44	6	0	0	3	80⅓	72	41	32	39	56
1993— Oakland (A.L.)	1	6	.143	5.60	42	9	0	0	0	64⅓	57	45	40	44	42
1994— Modesto (California)	1	1	.500	2.76	7	5	0	0	1	29⅓	21	9	9	6	29
— Tacoma (PCL)	1	3	.250	3.53	17	11	0	0	0	63⅔	66	31	25	21	50
— Oakland (A.L.)	0	1	.000	7.71	1	1	0	0	0	2⅓	2	3	2	2	4
1995— Edmonton (PCL)	2	1	.667	2.60	29	0	0	0	5	45	40	16	13	20	28
— Oakland (A.L.)	1	1	.500	3.04	28	0	0	0	1	23⅔	16	8	8	18	15
1996— Oakland (A.L.)	6	3	.667	3.67	72	0	0	0	7	81	79	36	33	41	64
1997— Oakland (A.L.)	1	10	.091	5.13	62	10	0	0	1	101⅔	116	65	58	54	66
1998— Oakland (A.L.)	3	3	.500	5.16	57	0	0	0	0	61	70	38	35	26	42
Major league totals (6 years)......	12	24	.333	4.74	262	20	0	0	9	334	340	195	176	185	233

M

MOLINA, BEN   C   ANGELS

PERSONAL: Born July 20, 1974, in Rio Pedras, Puerto Rico. ... 5-11/190. ... Bats right, throws right. ... Full name: Benjamin Jose Molina.
TRANSACTIONS/CAREER NOTES: Signed as non-drafted free agent by California Angels organization (May 23, 1993). ... Angels franchise renamed Anaheim Angels for 1997 season. ... On Vancouver disabled list (May 13-22, 1998).
STATISTICAL NOTES: Led Texas League catchers with 703 total chances and nine double plays in 1996.

							BATTING							FIELDING		
Year Team (League)	Pos.	G	AB	R	H	2B	3B	HR	RBI	Avg.	BB	SO	SB	PO	A	E	Avg.
1993— Ariz. Angels (Ariz.)	C	27	80	9	21	6	2	0	10	.263	10	4	0	47	2	0	1.000
1994— Cedar Rap. (Midw.)	C	48	171	14	48	8	0	3	16	.281	8	12	1	349	40	10	.975
1995— Vancouver (PCL)	C	2	6	0	1	0	0	0	0	.167	0	2	0	4	0	0	1.000
—Cedar Rap. (Midw.)	C	39	133	15	39	9	0	4	17	.293	15	11	1	283	32	7	.978
—Lake Elsinore (Calif.) ..	C	27	96	21	37	7	2	2	12	.385	8	7	0	195	16	1	.995
1996— Midland (Texas)........	C	108	365	45	100	21	2	8	54	.274	25	25	0	*615	*81	7	.990
1997— Lake Elsinore (Calif.) ..	C	36	149	18	42	10	2	4	33	.282	7	9	0	239	36	1	.996
—Midland (Texas)..........	C	29	106	18	35	8	0	6	30	.330	10	7	0	74	15	02	.978
1998— Vancouver (PCL)	C	49	184	13	54	9	1	1	22	.293	5	14	1	316	24	5	.986
—Midland (Texas)..........	C	41	154	28	55	8	0	9	39	.357	14	7	0	233	21	3	.988
—Anaheim (A.L.)	C	2	1	0	0	0	0	0	0	.000	0	0	0	1	0	0	1.000
Major league totals (1 year)		2	1	0	0	0	0	0	0	.000	0	0	0	1	0	0	1.000

MOLINA, GABE   P   ORIOLES

PERSONAL: Born May 3, 1975, in Denver. ... 5-11/180. ... Throws right, bats right. ... Full name: Cruz Gabriel Molina.
HIGH SCHOOL: John F. Kennedy (Denver).
COLLEGE: Arizona State.
TRANSACTIONS/CAREER NOTES: Selected by Baltimore Orioles organization in 21st round of free-agent draft (June 4, 1996).

Year Team (League)	W	L	Pct.	ERA	G	GS	CG	ShO	Sv.	IP	H	R	ER	BB	SO
1996— Bluefield (Appalachian)	4	0	1.000	3.60	23	0	0	0	7	30	29	12	12	13	33
1997— Delmarva (S. Atl.)...............	8	6	.571	2.18	46	0	0	0	7	91	59	24	22	32	119
1998— Bowie (Eastern).................	3	2	.600	3.36	47	0	0	0	24	61 2/3	48	24	23	27	75

MOLINA, IZZY   C   DIAMONDBACKS

PERSONAL: Born June 3, 1971, in New York. ... 5-11/224. ... Bats right, throws right. ... Full name: Islay Molina.
HIGH SCHOOL: Christopher Columbus (Miami).
TRANSACTIONS/CAREER NOTES: Selected by Oakland Athletics organization in 22nd round of free-agent draft (June 4, 1990). ... Granted free agency (December 21, 1997). ... Re-signed by A's organization (December 22, 1997). ... Granted free agency (October 15, 1998). ... Signed by Arizona Diamondbacks organization (December 17, 1998).
STATISTICAL NOTES: Tied for Arizona League lead in errors by catcher with six in 1990. ... Tied for Midwest League lead in double plays by catcher with eight in 1991. ... Tied for California League lead in grounding into double plays with 20 in 1992. ... Led California League catchers with 871 total chances and 28 passed balls in 1992. ... Led California League catchers with 740 putouts, 119 assists, 15 errors, 874 total chances, 11 double plays and 20 passed balls in 1993. ... Led Southern League catchers with 831 total chances and 14 passed balls in 1994. ... Led Southern League catchers with 74 assists and 11 double plays in 1995.

							BATTING							FIELDING		
Year Team (League)	Pos.	G	AB	R	H	2B	3B	HR	RBI	Avg.	BB	SO	SB	PO	A	E	Avg.
1990— Arizona A's (Ariz.).......	C-1B	39	127	20	43	12	2	0	18	.339	9	22	5	261	17	‡6	.979
1991— Madison (Midwest)......	C	95	316	35	89	16	1	3	45	.282	15	38	6	560	63	8	.987
1992— Reno (California)	C	116	436	71	113	17	2	10	75	.259	39	57	8	*716	*139	16	.982
—Tacoma (PCL)	C	10	36	3	7	0	1	0	5	.194	2	6	1	52	4	0	1.000
1993— Modesto (California) ..	C-OF	125	444	61	116	26	5	6	69	.261	44	85	2	†740	†119	†15	.983
1994— Huntsville (Sou.)	C	116	388	31	84	17	2	8	50	.216	16	47	5	*703	*116	12	.986
1995— Edmonton (PCL)	C	2	6	0	1	0	0	0	0	.167	0	2	0	9	1	0	1.000
—Huntsville (Sou.)	C-1B	83	301	38	78	16	1	8	26	.259	26	62	3	462	†75	12	.978
1996— Edmonton (PCL)	C-1B	98	342	45	90	12	3	12	56	.263	25	55	2	582	65	7	.989
—Oakland (A.L.)	C-DH	14	25	0	5	2	0	0	1	.200	1	3	0	31	1	0	1.000
1997— Oakland (A.L.)	C	48	111	6	22	3	1	3	7	.198	3	17	0	218	17	2	.992
—Edmonton (PCL)	C-P	1	218	33	57	11	3	6	34	.261	12	27	2	330	32	2	.995
1998— Oakland (A.L.)	C-DH	6	2	1	1	0	0	0	0	.500	0	0	0	8	1	0	1.000
—Edmonton (PCL)	C-1-P-O	86	303	29	73	15	2	8	38	.241	17	60	3	549	45	12	.980
Major league totals (3 years)		68	138	7	28	5	1	3	8	.203	4	20	0	257	19	2	.993

RECORD AS PITCHER

Year Team (League)	W	L	Pct.	ERA	G	GS	CG	ShO	Sv.	IP	H	R	ER	BB	SO
1997— Edmonton (PCL)	0	0	. . .	0.00	1	0	0	0	0	1/3	0	0	0	0	0
1998— Edmonton (PCL)	0	0	. . .	27.00	1	0	0	0	0	1	2	3	3	2	0

MOLITOR, PAUL   DH/1B

PERSONAL: Born August 22, 1956, in St. Paul, Minn. ... 6-0/195. ... Bats right, throws right. ... Full name: Paul Leo Molitor.
HIGH SCHOOL: Cretin (St. Paul).
COLLEGE: Minnesota.
TRANSACTIONS/CAREER NOTES: Selected by St. Louis Cardinals organization in 28th round of free-agent draft (June 5, 1974); did not sign. ... Selected by Milwaukee Brewers organization in first round (third pick overall) of free-agent draft (June 7, 1977). ... On disabled list (June 24-July 18, 1980; May 3-August 12, 1981; May 2, 1984-remainder of season; August 13-28, 1985; May 10-30, June 2-17 and June 19-July

8, 1986; and April 30-May 26 and June 27-July 16, 1987). ... Granted free agency (November 9, 1987). ... Re-signed by Brewers (January 5, 1988). ... On disabled list (March 30-April 14, 1989). ... On Milwaukee disabled list (April 2-27 and June 17-July 30, 1990); included rehabilitation assignment to Beloit (July 28). ... Granted free agency (October 30, 1992). ... Signed by Toronto Blue Jays (December 7, 1992). ... Granted free agency (November 3, 1995). ... Signed by Minnesota Twins (December 5, 1995). ... On disabled list (April 17-May 2, 1997). ... Granted free agency (October 28, 1997). ... Re-signed by Twins (December 6, 1997). ... On Minnesota disabled list (June 21-July 15, 1998); included rehabilitation assignment to Salt Lake (July 13-15). ... Granted free agency (October 26, 1998). ... Announced retirement (December 3, 1998).

RECORDS: Shares major league record for most stolen bases in one inning—3 (July 26, 1987, first inning). ... Holds A.L. single-season record for most stolen bases without being caught stealing—20 (1994).

HONORS: Named shortstop on THE SPORTING NEWS college All-America team (1977). ... Named Midwest League Most Valuable Player (1977). ... Named A.L. Rookie Player of the Year by THE SPORTING NEWS (1978). ... Named designated hitter on THE SPORTING NEWS A.L. All-Star team (1987 and 1993-96). ... Named designated hitter on THE SPORTING NEWS A.L. Silver Slugger team (1987-88, 1993 and 1996).

STATISTICAL NOTES: Hit three home runs in one game (May 12, 1982). ... Led A.L. third basemen with 29 errors and 48 double plays in 1982. ... Had 39-game hitting streak (July 16-August 25, 1987). ... Hit for the cycle (May 15, 1991). ... Had 17-game hitting streak (August 31-September 19, 1998). ... Career major league grand slams: 3.

MISCELLANEOUS: Holds Milwaukee Brewers all-time record for highest batting average (.303) and most stolen bases (412). ... Holds Toronto Blue Jays all-time record for highest batting average (.315).

							BATTING								FIELDING		
Year Team (League)	Pos.	G	AB	R	H	2B	3B	HR	RBI	Avg.	BB	SO	SB	PO	A	E	Avg.
1977— Burlington (Midw.)	SS	64	228	52	79	12	0	8	50	.346	47	25	14	83	207	28	.912
1978— Milwaukee (A.L.)	2-S-DH-3	125	521	73	142	26	4	6	45	.273	19	54	30	253	401	22	.967
1979— Milwaukee (A.L.)	2B-SS-DH	140	584	88	188	27	16	9	62	.322	48	48	33	309	440	16	.979
1980— Milwaukee (A.L.)	2-S-DH-3	111	450	81	137	29	2	9	37	.304	48	48	34	260	336	20	.968
1981— Milwaukee (A.L.)	OF-DH	64	251	45	67	11	0	2	19	.267	25	29	10	119	4	3	.976
1982— Milwaukee (A.L.)	3B-DH-SS	160	*666	*136	201	26	8	19	71	.302	69	93	41	134	350	†32	.938
1983— Milwaukee (A.L.)	3B-DH	152	608	95	164	28	6	15	47	.270	59	74	41	105	343	16	.966
1984— Milwaukee (A.L.)	3B-DH	13	46	3	10	1	0	0	6	.217	2	8	1	7	21	2	.933
1985— Milwaukee (A.L.)	3B-DH	140	576	93	171	28	3	10	48	.297	54	80	21	126	263	19	.953
1986— Milwaukee (A.L.)	3B-DH-OF	105	437	62	123	24	6	9	55	.281	40	81	20	86	171	15	.945
1987— Milwaukee (A.L.)	DH-3B-2B	118	465	*114	164	*41	5	16	75	.353	69	67	45	60	113	5	.972
1988— Milwaukee (A.L.)	3B-DH-2B	154	609	115	190	34	6	13	60	.312	71	54	41	87	188	17	.942
1989— Milwaukee (A.L.)	3B-DH-2B	155	615	84	194	35	4	11	56	.315	64	67	27	106	287	18	.956
1990— Milwaukee (A.L.)	2-1-DH-3	103	418	64	119	27	6	12	45	.285	37	51	18	463	222	10	.986
— Beloit (Midwest)	DH	1	4	1	2	0	0	1	1	.500	0	0	0	...	...	...	...
1991— Milwaukee (A.L.)	DH-1B	158	*665	*133	*216	32	•13	17	75	.325	77	62	19	389	32	6	.986
1992— Milwaukee (A.L.)	DH-1B	158	609	89	195	36	7	12	89	.320	73	66	31	461	26	2	.996
1993— Toronto (A.L.)■........	DH-1B	160	636	121	*211	37	5	22	111	.332	77	71	22	178	14	3	.985
1994— Toronto (A.L.)	DH-1B	*115	454	86	155	30	4	14	75	.341	55	48	20	47	3	0	1.000
1995— Toronto (A.L.)	DH	130	525	63	142	31	2	15	60	.270	61	57	12	...	...		...
1996— Minnesota (A.L.)■	DH-1B	161	660	99	*225	41	8	9	113	.341	56	72	18	138	13	1	.993
1997— Minnesota (A.L.)	DH-1B	135	538	63	164	32	4	10	89	.305	45	73	11	99	7	1	.991
1998— Minnesota (A.L.)	DH-1B	126	502	75	141	29	5	4	69	.281	45	41	9	79	7	0	1.000
— Salt Lake (PCL)	DH	2	10	0	5	1	0	0	0	.500	0	0	0	...	...		...
Major league totals (21 years)		2683	10835	1782	3319	605	114	234	1307	.306	1094	1244	504	3506	3241	208	.970

DIVISION SERIES RECORD

							BATTING								FIELDING		
Year Team (League)	Pos.	G	AB	R	H	2B	3B	HR	RBI	Avg.	BB	SO	SB	PO	A	E	Avg.
1981— Milwaukee (A.L.)	OF	5	20	2	5	0	0	1	1	.250	2	5	0	12	0	0	1.000

CHAMPIONSHIP SERIES RECORD

RECORDS: Holds single-series record for most consecutive hits—6 (1993). ... Shares career record for most consecutive hits—6 (1993).

							BATTING								FIELDING		
Year Team (League)	Pos.	G	AB	R	H	2B	3B	HR	RBI	Avg.	BB	SO	SB	PO	A	E	Avg.
1982— Milwaukee (A.L.)	3B	5	19	4	6	1	0	2	5	.316	2	3	1	4	11	2	.882
1993— Toronto (A.L.)	DH	6	23	7	9	2	1	1	5	.391	3	3	0	...	...	...	...
Championship series totals (2 years)		11	42	11	15	3	1	3	10	.357	5	6	1	4	11	2	.882

WORLD SERIES RECORD

RECORDS: Holds single-game records for most hits—5 (October 12, 1982). ... Shares single-series record for most runs—10 (1993). ... Shares single-game record for most at-bats (nine-inning game)—6 (October 12, 1982).

NOTES: Named Most Valuable Player (1993). ... Member of World Series championship team (1993).

							BATTING								FIELDING		
Year Team (League)	Pos.	G	AB	R	H	2B	3B	HR	RBI	Avg.	BB	SO	SB	PO	A	E	Avg.
1982— Milwaukee (A.L.)	3B	7	31	5	11	0	0	0	3	.355	2	4	1	4	9	0	1.000
1993— Toronto (A.L.)	DH-3B-1B	6	24	10	12	2	2	2	8	.500	3	0	1	7	3	0	1.000
World Series totals (2 years)		13	55	15	23	2	2	2	11	.418	5	4	2	11	12	0	1.000

ALL-STAR GAME RECORD

						BATTING							FIELDING		
Year League	Pos.	AB	R	H	2B	3B	HR	RBI	Avg.	BB	SO	SB	PO	A	E	Avg.
1980— American....................						Selected, did not play—injured.										
1985— American....................	3B-OF	1	0	0	0	0	0	0	.000	0	0	0	0	0	0	...
1988— American....................	2B	3	0	0	0	0	0	0	.000	0	1	0	1	2	0	1.000
1991— American....................	3B	0	0	0	0	0	0	0	...	0	0	0	0	0	0	...
1992— American....................	PH-1B	2	0	1	0	0	0	0	.500	0	1	0	5	0	1	.833
1993— American....................	DH	1	0	0	0	0	0	0	.000	1	0	0	...	...	...	...
1994— American....................	PH	1	0	0	0	0	0	0	.000	0	0	0	...	...	...	...
All-Star Game totals (6 years)		8	0	1	0	0	0	0	.125	1	2	0	6	2	1	.889

M

MONAHAN, SHANE   OF   MARINERS

PERSONAL: Born August 12, 1974, in Syosset, N.Y. ... 6-0/195. ... Bats left, throws right. ... Full name: Shane Hartland Monahan. ... Son of Hartland Monahan, right winger with six NHL teams (1973-74 through 1980-81); great-grandson of Howie Morenz, Hockey Hall of Fame center with three NHL teams (1923-24 through 1936-37); grandson of Bernie "Boom Boom" Geoffrion, Hockey Hall of Fame right winger with Montreal Canadiens and New York Rangers (1950-51 through 1967-68).
HIGH SCHOOL: Wheeler (Marietta, Ga.).
COLLEGE: Clemson.
TRANSACTIONS/CAREER NOTES: Selected by Seattle Mariners organization in second round of free-agent draft (June 1, 1995).
STATISTICAL NOTES: Led California League outfielders with 265 total chances in 1996.

								BATTING						FIELDING		
Year Team (League)	Pos.	G	AB	R	H	2B	3B	HR	RBI	Avg.	BB	SO	SB	PO	A	E	Avg.
1995—Wisconsin (Midwest) .	OF	59	233	34	66	9	6	1	32	.283	11	40	9	100	0	3	.971
1996—Lancaster (Calif.)	OF	132	*584	107	164	31	*12	14	97	.281	30	124	19	*248	10	7	.974
1997—Tacoma (PCL)	OF	21	85	15	25	4	0	2	12	.294	5	21	5	46	3	2	.961
— Memphis (Sou.)	OF	107	401	52	121	24	6	12	76	.302	30	100	14	139	10	3	.980
1998—Tacoma (PCL)	OF	69	277	32	69	8	5	4	33	.249	19	47	6	141	1	1	.993
— Seattle (A.L.)	OF	62	211	17	51	8	1	4	28	.242	8	53	1	117	3	1	.992
Major league totals (1 year)		62	211	17	51	8	1	4	28	.242	8	53	1	117	3	1	.992

MONDESI, RAUL   OF   DODGERS

PERSONAL: Born March 12, 1971, in San Cristobal, Dominican Republic. ... 5-11/215. ... Bats right, throws right. ... Name pronounced MON-de-see.
HIGH SCHOOL: Liceo Manuel Maria Valencia (Dominican Republic).
TRANSACTIONS/CAREER NOTES: Signed as non-drafted free agent by Los Angeles Dodgers organization (June 6, 1988). ... On Bakersfield disabled list (May 8-July 5, 1991). ... On Albuquerque disabled list (May 8-16, 1992). ... On San Antonio disabled list (June 2-16, June 24-August 10 and August 24, 1992-remainder of season).
HONORS: Named N.L. Rookie Player of the Year by THE SPORTING NEWS (1994). ... Named N.L. Rookie of the Year by Baseball Writers' Association of America (1994). ... Won N.L. Gold Glove as outfielder (1995 and 1997).
STATISTICAL NOTES: Career major league grand slams: 2.

								BATTING						FIELDING		
Year Team (League)	Pos.	G	AB	R	H	2B	3B	HR	RBI	Avg.	BB	SO	SB	PO	A	E	Avg.
1990— Great Falls (Pio.)	OF	44	175	35	53	10	4	8	31	.303	11	30	30	65	4	1	.986
1991— Bakersfield (Calif.)	OF	28	106	23	30	7	2	3	13	.283	5	21	9	42	5	3	.940
— San Antonio (Tex.)	OF	53	213	32	58	11	5	5	26	.272	8	47	8	101	6	4	.964
— Albuquerque (PCL)	OF	2	9	3	3	0	1	0	0	.333	0	1	1	0	0	1	1.000
1992— Albuquerque (PCL)	OF	35	138	23	43	4	7	4	15	.312	9	35	2	89	8	7	.933
— San Antonio (Tex.)	OF	18	68	8	18	2	2	2	14	.265	1	24	3	31	6	1	.974
1993— Albuquerque (PCL)	OF	110	425	65	119	22	7	12	65	.280	18	85	13	211	10	10	.957
— Los Angeles (N.L.)	OF	42	86	13	25	3	1	4	10	.291	4	16	4	55	3	3	.951
1994— Los Angeles (N.L.)	OF	112	434	63	133	27	8	16	56	.306	16	78	11	206	*16	8	.965
1995— Los Angeles (N.L.)	OF	139	536	91	153	23	6	26	88	.285	33	96	27	282	*16	6	.980
1996— Los Angeles (N.L.)	OF	157	634	98	188	40	7	24	88	.297	32	122	14	337	11	•12	.967
1997— Los Angeles (N.L.)	OF	159	616	95	191	42	5	30	87	.310	44	105	32	338	10	4	.989
1998— Los Angeles (N.L.)	OF	148	580	85	162	26	5	30	90	.279	30	112	16	284	6	6	.980
Major league totals (6 years)		757	2886	445	852	161	32	130	419	.295	159	529	104	1502	62	39	.976

DIVISION SERIES RECORD

								BATTING						FIELDING		
Year Team (League)	Pos.	G	AB	R	H	2B	3B	HR	RBI	Avg.	BB	SO	SB	PO	A	E	Avg.
1995— Los Angeles (N.L.)	OF	3	9	0	2	0	0	0	1	.222	0	2	0	8	0	0	1.000
1996— Los Angeles (N.L.)	OF	3	11	0	2	2	0	0	1	.182	0	4	0	2	0	0	1.000
Division series totals (2 years)		6	20	0	4	2	0	0	2	.200	0	6	0	10	0	0	1.000

ALL-STAR GAME RECORD

						BATTING						FIELDING		
Year League	Pos.	AB	R	H	2B	3B	HR	RBI	Avg.	BB	SO	SB	PO	A	E	Avg.
1995— National	OF	1	0	0	0	0	0	0	.000	0	0	0	2	0	0	1.000

MONTGOMERY, JEFF   P   ROYALS

PERSONAL: Born January 7, 1962, in Wellston, Ohio. ... 5-11/175. ... Throws right, bats right. ... Full name: Jeffrey Thomas Montgomery.
HIGH SCHOOL: Wellston (Ohio).
COLLEGE: Marshall (bachelor of science degree in computer science, 1984).
TRANSACTIONS/CAREER NOTES: Selected by Cincinnati Reds organization in ninth round of free-agent draft (June 6, 1983). ... Traded by Reds to Kansas City Royals for OF Van Snider (February 15, 1988). ... Granted free agency (November 8, 1995). ... Re-signed by Royals (December 15, 1995). ... On Kansas City disabled list (April 18-May 3, 1997); included rehabilitation assignment to Omaha (April 29-May 3). ... Granted free agency (October 28, 1998). ... Re-signed by Royals (December 7, 1998).
RECORDS: Shares major league record for striking out side on nine pitches (April 29, 1990, eighth inning).
HONORS: Named A.L. Fireman of the Year by THE SPORTING NEWS (1993).
MISCELLANEOUS: Holds Kansas City Royals all-time record for most saves (292).

Year Team (League)	W	L	Pct.	ERA	G	GS	CG	ShO	Sv.	IP	H	R	ER	BB	SO
1983—Billings (Pioneer)	6	2	.750	2.42	20	0	0	0	5	44 2/3	31	13	12	13	90
1984—Tampa (Fla. St.)	5	3	.625	2.44	31	0	0	0	•14	44 1/3	29	15	12	30	56
— Vermont (Eastern)	2	0	1.000	2.13	22	0	0	0	4	25 1/3	14	7	6	24	20
1985—Vermont (Eastern)	5	3	.625	2.05	*53	1	0	0	9	101	63	25	23	48	89

Year Team (League)	W	L	Pct.	ERA	G	GS	CG	ShO	Sv.	IP	H	R	ER	BB	SO
1986— Denver (Am. Assoc.)	11	7	.611	4.39	30	22	2	2	1	151 2/3	162	88	74	57	78
1987— Nashville (A.A.)	8	5	.615	4.14	24	21	1	0	0	139	132	76	64	51	121
— Cincinnati (N.L.)	2	2	.500	6.52	14	1	0	0	0	19 1/3	25	15	14	9	13
1988— Omaha (Am. Assoc.)■......	1	2	.333	1.91	20	0	0	0	13	28 1/3	15	6	6	11	36
— Kansas City (A.L.)	7	2	.778	3.45	45	0	0	0	1	62 2/3	54	25	24	30	47
1989— Kansas City (A.L.)	7	3	.700	1.37	63	0	0	0	18	92	66	16	14	25	94
1990— Kansas City (A.L.)	6	5	.545	2.39	73	0	0	0	24	94 1/3	81	36	25	34	94
1991— Kansas City (A.L.)	4	4	.500	2.90	67	0	0	0	33	90	83	32	29	28	77
1992— Kansas City (A.L.)	1	6	.143	2.18	65	0	0	0	39	82 2/3	61	23	20	27	69
1993— Kansas City (A.L.)	7	5	.583	2.27	69	0	0	0	•45	87 1/3	65	22	22	23	66
1994— Kansas City (A.L.)	2	3	.400	4.03	42	0	0	0	27	44 2/3	48	21	20	15	50
1995— Kansas City (A.L.)	2	3	.400	3.43	54	0	0	0	31	65 2/3	60	27	25	25	49
1996— Kansas City (A.L.)	4	6	.400	4.26	48	0	0	0	24	63 1/3	59	31	30	19	45
1997— Kansas City (A.L.)	1	4	.200	3.49	55	0	0	0	14	59 1/3	53	24	23	18	48
— Omaha (Am. Assoc.)	0	0	. . .	0.00	2	0	0	0	0	2	1	0	0	1	2
1998— Kansas City (A.L.)	2	5	.286	4.98	56	0	0	0	36	56	58	35	31	22	54
A.L. totals (11 years)	43	46	.483	2.97	637	0	0	0	292	798	688	292	263	266	693
N.L. totals (1 year)	2	2	.500	6.52	14	1	0	0	0	19 1/3	25	15	14	9	13
Major league totals (12 years)....	45	48	.484	3.05	651	1	0	0	292	817 1/3	713	307	277	275	706

ALL-STAR GAME RECORD

Year League	W	L	Pct.	ERA	GS	CG	ShO	Sv.	IP	H	R	ER	BB	SO
1992— American	0	0	. . .	27.00	0	0	0	0	2/3	2	2	2	0	0
1993— American	0	0	. . .	0.00	0	0	0	0	1	0	0	0	0	1
1996— American							Did not play.							
All-Star totals (2 years)	0	0	. . .	10.80	0	0	0	0	1 2/3	2	2	2	0	1

MONTGOMERY, RAY · OF · PIRATES

PERSONAL: Born August 8, 1969, in Bronxville, N.Y. ... 6-3/195. ... Bats right, throws right. ... Full name: Raymond James Montgomery.
HIGH SCHOOL: Archbishop Stepinac (White Plains, N.Y.).
COLLEGE: Fordham.
TRANSACTIONS/CAREER NOTES: Selected by Houston Astros organization in 13th round of free-agent draft (June 4, 1990). ... On disabled list (April 10-17 and June 3-July 24, 1992). ... On Houston disabled list (June 18, 1997-remainder of season). ... On Houston disabled list (March 22-April 6, 1998). ... On New Orleans disabled list (July 18-31, 1998). ... Granted free agency (October 15, 1998). ... Signed by Pittsburgh Pirates organization (December 22, 1998).

							BATTING								FIELDING			
Year Team (League)	Pos.	G	AB	R	H	2B	3B	HR	RBI	Avg.	BB	SO	SB	PO	A	E	Avg.
1990— Auburn (NY-Penn)....	OF-1B	61	193	19	45	8	1	0	13	.233	23	32	12	245	14	8	.970
1991— Burlington (Midw.).....	OF	120	433	60	109	24	3	3	57	.252	37	65	16	249	12	4	.985
1992— Jackson (Texas)	OF	51	148	13	31	4	1	1	10	.209	7	27	4	76	3	2	.975
1993— Jackson (Texas)	OF	100	338	50	95	16	3	10	59	.281	36	54	12	151	9	6	.964
— Tucson (PCL)	OF	15	50	9	17	3	1	2	6	.340	5	7	1	33	1	0	1.000
1994— Tucson (PCL)	OF	103	332	51	85	19	6	7	51	.256	35	54	5	179	11	8	.960
1995— Jackson (Texas)	OF-1B	35	127	24	38	8	1	10	24	.299	13	13	6	102	10	1	.991
— Tucson (PCL)	OF	88	291	48	88	19	0	11	68	.302	24	58	5	182	10	7	.965
1996— Tucson (PCL)	OF-1B	100	360	70	110	20	0	22	75	.306	59	54	7	182	8	4	.979
— Houston (N.L.)	OF	12	14	4	3	1	0	1	4	.214	1	5	0	6	0	0	1.000
1997— Houston (N.L.)	OF	29	68	8	16	4	1	0	4	.235	5	18	0	25	2	0	1.000
— New Orleans (A.A.).....	OF	20	73	17	21	5	0	6	13	.288	11	15	1	33	0	1	.971
1998— New Orleans (PCL).....	OF	75	272	42	79	18	1	9	45	.290	26	48	4	156	4	4	.976
— Houston (N.L.)	OF	6	5	2	2	0	0	0	0	.400	0	0	0	1	0	0	1.000
Major league totals (3 years)		47	87	14	21	5	1	1	8	.241	6	23	0	32	2	0	1.000

M

MONTGOMERY, STEVE · P · DODGERS

PERSONAL: Born February 21, 1974, in Mecca, Ohio. ... 6-6/230. ... Throws right, bats right. ... Full name: Steven Robert Montgomery III.
HIGH SCHOOL: Maplewood, (Cortland, Ohio).
COLLEGE: Kent.
TRANSACTIONS/CAREER NOTES: Signed as non-drafted free agent by Kansas City Royals organization (September 12, 1993). ... Released by Royals (April 3, 1995). ... Signed by Johnstown, Frontier League (June, 1995). ... Sold by Johnstown to Baltimore Orioles organization (October 31, 1995). ... Claimed on waivers by Los Angeles Dodgers organization (March 12, 1998). ... On Albuquerque disabled list (April 7-July 31, 1998). ... On Los Angeles disabled list (July 31, 1998-remainder of season).

Year Team (League)	W	L	Pct.	ERA	G	GS	CG	ShO	Sv.	IP	H	R	ER	BB	SO
1994— GC Royals (GCL)	1	1	.500	1.56	12	0	0	0	3	17 1/3	12	6	3	5	12
1995— Johnstown (Frontier)...........	2	0	1.000	0.00	33	0	0	0	9	38 2/3	18	1	0	16	52
1996— High Desert (Calif.)■	5	6	.455	5.27	44	3	0	0	2	71 2/3	85	54	42	34	79
1997— Bowie (Eastern).................	10	5	.667	3.10	24	2	0	0	0	136 1/3	116	56	47	52	127
— Rochester (Int'l)	0	2	.000	12.15	2	1	0	0	0	6 2/3	15	12	9	3	2
1998—							Did not play.								

MOODY, ERIC · P · RANGERS

PERSONAL: Born January 6, 1971, in Greenville, S.C. ... 6-6/185. ... Throws right, bats right. ... Full name: Eric Lane Moody.
HIGH SCHOOL: Palmetto (Williamston, S.C.).
COLLEGE: Erskine (S.C.); degree in physical education.

TRANSACTIONS/CAREER NOTES: Selected by Texas Rangers organization in 24th round of free-agent draft (June 3, 1993). ... On Texas disabled list (September 18, 1998-remainder of season).

Year Team (League)	W	L	Pct.	ERA	G	GS	CG	ShO	Sv.	IP	H	R	ER	BB	SO
1993—Erie (N.Y.-Penn)	3	3	.500	3.83	17	7	0	0	0	54	54	30	23	13	33
1994—Hudson Valley (NYP)	7	3	.700	2.83	15	12	1	0	0	89	82	32	28	18	68
1995—Charlotte (Fla. St.)	5	5	.500	2.75	13	13	2	2	0	88 1/3	84	30	27	13	57
1996—Tulsa (Texas)	8	4	.667	3.57	44	5	0	0	16	95 2/3	92	40	38	23	80
1997—Oklahoma City (A.A.)	5	6	.455	3.46	35	10	1	1	1	112	114	49	43	21	72
—Texas (A.L.)	0	1	.000	4.26	10	1	0	0	0	19	26	10	9	2	12
1998—Oklahoma (Pacific Coast)	6	6	.500	3.38	45	6	0	0	12	101 1/3	112	51	38	23	73
Major league totals (1 year)	0	1	.000	4.26	10	1	0	0	0	19	26	10	9	2	12

MOORE, TREY   P   EXPOS

PERSONAL: Born October 2, 1972, in Houston. ... 6-0/190. ... Throws left, bats left. ... Full name: Warren Neal Moore III.
HIGH SCHOOL: Keller (Texas).
COLLEGE: Texas A&M.
TRANSACTIONS/CAREER NOTES: Selected by Seattle Mariners organization in second round of free-agent draft (June 2, 1994). ... Traded by Mariners with C Chris Widger and P Matt Wagner to Montreal Expos for P Alex Pacheco and P Jeff Fassero (October 29, 1996). ... On Montreal disabled list (June 7, 1998-remainder of season); included rehabilitation assignment to Ottawa (July 9-20).
MISCELLANEOUS: Struck out in only appearance as pinch hitter with Montreal (1998).

Year Team (League)	W	L	Pct.	ERA	G	GS	CG	ShO	Sv.	IP	H	R	ER	BB	SO
1994—Bellingham (N'west)	5	2	.714	2.63	11	10	1	0	0	61 2/3	48	18	18	24	73
1995—Riverside (California)	14	6	.700	3.09	24	24	0	0	0	148 1/3	122	65	51	58	134
1996—Port City (Southern)	1	6	.143	7.71	11	11	0	0	0	53 2/3	73	54	46	33	42
—Lancaster (Calif.)	7	5	.583	4.10	15	15	2	0	0	94 1/3	106	57	43	31	77
1997—Harrisburg (Eastern)■	11	6	.647	4.15	27	27	2	•2	0	162 2/3	152	91	75	66	137
1998—Montreal (N.L.)	2	5	.286	5.02	13	11	0	0	0	61	78	37	34	17	35
—Ottawa (Int'l)	1	1	.500	5.54	3	3	0	0	0	13	18	8	8	4	8
Major league totals (1 year)	2	5	.286	5.02	13	11	0	0	0	61	78	37	34	17	35

MORANDINI, MICKEY   2B   CUBS

PERSONAL: Born April 22, 1966, in Leechburg, Pa. ... 5-11/180. ... Bats left, throws right. ... Full name: Michael Robert Morandini. ... Name pronounced MOR-an-DEEN-ee.
HIGH SCHOOL: Leechburg (Pa.) Area.
COLLEGE: Indiana.
TRANSACTIONS/CAREER NOTES: Selected by Pittsburgh Pirates organization in seventh round of free-agent draft (June 2, 1987); did not sign. ... Selected by Philadelphia Phillies organization in fifth round of free-agent draft (June 1, 1988). ... On disabled list (June 15-30, 1996). ... Traded by Phillies to Chicago Cubs for OF Doug Glanville (December 23, 1997).
RECORDS: Holds N.L. single-season record for fewest chances accepted by second baseman (150 games or more)—671 (1998).
STATISTICAL NOTES: Led International League second basemen with 271 putouts, 419 assists and 701 total chances in 1990.
MISCELLANEOUS: Member of 1988 U.S. Olympic baseball team. ... Turned unassisted triple play while playing second base (September 20, 1992, sixth inning); ninth player ever to accomplish feat and first ever by second baseman during regular season.

M

Year Team (League)	Pos.	G	AB	R	H	2B	3B	HR	RBI	Avg.	BB	SO	SB	PO	A	E	Avg.
1989—Spartanburg (SAL)	SS	63	231	43	78	19	1	1	30	.338	35	45	18	87	198	10	.966
—Clearwater (FSL)	SS	17	63	14	19	4	1	0	4	.302	7	8	3	20	59	2	.975
—Reading (Eastern)	SS	48	188	39	66	12	1	5	29	.351	23	32	5	73	137	10	.955
1990—Scran./W.B. (Int'l)	2B-SS	139	503	76	131	24	*10	1	31	.260	60	90	16	†271	†419	11	.984
—Philadelphia (N.L.)	2B	25	79	9	19	4	0	1	3	.241	6	19	3	37	61	1	.990
1991—Scran./W.B. (Int'l)	2B	12	46	7	12	4	0	1	9	.261	5	6	2	19	38	1	.983
—Philadelphia (N.L.)	2B	98	325	38	81	11	4	1	20	.249	29	45	13	183	254	6	.986
1992—Philadelphia (N.L.)	2B-SS	127	422	47	112	8	8	3	30	.265	25	64	8	239	336	6	.990
1993—Philadelphia (N.L.)	2B	120	425	57	105	19	9	3	33	.247	34	73	13	208	288	5	.990
1994—Philadelphia (N.L.)	2B	87	274	40	80	16	5	2	26	.292	34	33	10	167	216	6	.985
1995—Philadelphia (N.L.)	2B	127	494	65	140	34	7	6	49	.283	42	80	9	269	336	7	.989
1996—Philadelphia (N.L.)	2B	140	539	64	135	24	6	3	32	.250	49	87	26	286	352	12	.982
1997—Philadelphia (N.L.)	2B-SS	150	553	83	163	40	2	1	39	.295	62	91	16	254	350	6	.990
1998—Chicago (N.L.)■	2B	154	582	93	172	20	4	8	53	.296	72	84	13	267	404	5	*.993
Major league totals (9 years)		1028	3693	496	1007	176	45	28	285	.273	353	576	111	1910	2597	54	.988

DIVISION SERIES RECORD

Year Team (League)	Pos.	G	AB	R	H	2B	3B	HR	RBI	Avg.	BB	SO	SB	PO	A	E	Avg.
1998—Chicago (N.L.)	2B	3	9	1	2	0	0	0	1	.222	3	2	0	5	3	0	1.000

CHAMPIONSHIP SERIES RECORD

Year Team (League)	Pos.	G	AB	R	H	2B	3B	HR	RBI	Avg.	BB	SO	SB	PO	A	E	Avg.
1993—Philadelphia (N.L.)	2B-PH	4	16	1	4	0	1	0	2	.250	0	3	1	8	9	1	.944

WORLD SERIES RECORD

Year Team (League)	Pos.	G	AB	R	H	2B	3B	HR	RBI	Avg.	BB	SO	SB	PO	A	E	Avg.
1993—Philadelphia (N.L.)	PH-2B	3	5	1	1	0	0	0	0	.200	1	2	0	2	0	0	1.000

ALL-STAR GAME RECORD

Year League	Pos.	AB	R	H	2B	3B	HR	RBI	Avg.	BB	SO	SB	PO	A	E	Avg.
1995—National	2B	1	0	0	0	0	0	0	.000	0	1	0	0	1	0	1.000

MORDECAI, MIKE — IF — EXPOS

PERSONAL: Born December 13, 1967, in Birmingham, Ala. ... 5-11/180. ... Bats right, throws right. ... Full name: Michael Howard Mordecai.
HIGH SCHOOL: Hewitt Trussville (Ala.).
COLLEGE: Southern Alabama.
TRANSACTIONS/CAREER NOTES: Selected by Pittsburgh Pirates organization in 33rd round of free-agent draft (June 2, 1986); did not sign. ... Selected by Atlanta Braves organization in sixth round of free-agent draft (June 5, 1989). ... On disabled list (April 8-29, 1993). ... On Atlanta disabled list (April 19-May 11, 1996); included rehabilitation assignment to Richmond (May 8-11). ... Granted free agency (December 21, 1997). ... Signed by Montreal Expos organization (March 27, 1998). ... On Montreal disabled list (June 24-July 24, 1998); included rehabilitation assignments to Jupiter (July 16-19) and Ottawa (July 19-24).

										BATTING						FIELDING		
Year	Team (League)	Pos.	G	AB	R	H	2B	3B	HR	RBI	Avg.	BB	SO	SB	PO	A	E	Avg.
1989— Burlington (Midw.)		SS-3B	65	241	39	61	11	1	1	22	.253	33	43	12	80	163	21	.920
— Greenville (Southern) .		3B-2B	4	8	0	3	0	0	0	1	.375	1	1	0	4	6	0	1.000
1990— Durham (Carolina)......		SS	72	271	42	76	11	7	3	36	.280	42	45	10	111	221	29	.920
1991— Durham (Carolina)......		SS	109	397	52	104	15	2	4	42	.262	40	58	30	164	302	27	.945
1992— Greenville (Southern) .		SS	65	222	31	58	13	1	4	31	.261	29	31	9	93	204	11	.964
— Richmond (Int'l)........		SS-2B-3B	36	118	12	29	3	0	1	6	.246	5	19	0	48	101	10	.937
1993— Richmond (Int'l).........2-S-3-O-C-1			72	205	29	55	8	1	2	14	.268	14	33	10	98	145	9	.964
1994— Richmond (Int'l).......		SS-1B-3B	99	382	67	107	25	1	14	57	.280	35	50	14	117	279	22	.947
— Atlanta (N.L.).............		SS	4	4	1	1	0	0	1	3	.250	1	0	0	1	4	0	1.000
1995— Atlanta (N.L.).............		2-1-3-S-O	69	75	10	21	6	0	3	11	.280	9	16	0	39	31	0	1.000
1996— Atlanta (N.L.).............		2-3-S-1	66	108	12	26	5	0	2	8	.241	9	24	1	33	52	2	.977
— Richmond (Int'l)........		SS	3	11	2	2	0	0	1	2	.182	0	3	0	3	13	0	1.000
1997— Atlanta (N.L.).........3-2-S-1-DH-O			61	81	8	14	2	1	0	3	.173	6	16	0	26	17	0	1.000
— Richmond (Int'l)........		2B-3B-SS	31	122	23	38	10	0	3	15	.311	9	17	0	29	61	1	.989
1998— Montreal (N.L.)■........		S-2-3-1	73	119	12	24	4	2	3	10	.202	9	20	1	38	82	5	.960
— Jupiter (Florida State)		2B-SS	2	8	0	0	0	0	0	0	.000	1	3	0	4	4	0	1.000
— Ottawa (Int'l)		SS-2B	6	22	2	5	2	0	0	1	.227	3	3	0	9	22	1	.969
Major league totals (5 years)			273	387	43	86	17	3	9	35	.222	34	76	2	137	186	7	.979

DIVISION SERIES RECORD

										BATTING						FIELDING		
Year	Team (League)	Pos.	G	AB	R	H	2B	3B	HR	RBI	Avg.	BB	SO	SB	PO	A	E	Avg.
1995— Atlanta (N.L.)..............		PH-SS	2	3	1	2	1	0	0	2	.667	0	0	0	1	0	0	1.000
1996— Atlanta (N.L.)							Did not play.											

CHAMPIONSHIP SERIES RECORD

										BATTING						FIELDING		
Year	Team (League)	Pos.	G	AB	R	H	2B	3B	HR	RBI	Avg.	BB	SO	SB	PO	A	E	Avg.
1995— Atlanta (N.L.).............		PH-SS	2	2	0	0	0	0	0	0	.000	0	1	0	0	0	0	. . .
1996— Atlanta (N.L.).............		3B-PH-2B	4	4	1	1	0	0	0	0	.250	0	1	0	1	1	0	1.000
Championship series totals (2 years)			6	6	1	1	0	0	0	0	.167	0	2	0	1	1	0	1.000

WORLD SERIES RECORD

NOTES: Member of World Series championship team (1995).

										BATTING						FIELDING		
Year	Team (League)	Pos.	G	AB	R	H	2B	3B	HR	RBI	Avg.	BB	SO	SB	PO	A	E	Avg.
1995— Atlanta (N.L.)..............		SS-DH	3	3	0	1	0	0	0	0	.333	0	1	0	0	6	0	1.000
1996— Atlanta (N.L.)..............		PH	1	1	0	0	0	0	0	0	.000	0	0	0	. . .	. . .	. . .	. . .
World Series totals (2 years)			4	4	0	1	0	0	0	0	.250	0	1	0	0	6	0	1.000

MORENO, JULIO — P — ORIOLES

PERSONAL: Born October 23, 1975, in San Pedro de Macoris, Dominican Republic. ... 6-1/165. ... Throws right, bats right. ... Full name: Julio Cesar Moreno.
TRANSACTIONS/CAREER NOTES: Signed as non-drafted free agent by Baltimore Orioles organization (January 15, 1993). ... On disabled list (April 24-May 4, 1997). ... On Rochester disabled list (April 9, 1998-entire season).

Year	Team (League)	W	L	Pct.	ERA	G	GS	CG	ShO	Sv.	IP	H	R	ER	BB	SO
1993— Dom. Orioles (DSL)...........		1	2	.333	12.54	16	2	0	0	0	28	45	42	39	28	11
1994— Dom. Orioles (DSL)...........		2	1	.667	3.61	8	8	2	1	0	47 1/3	35	31	19	33	25
— GC Orioles (GCL)...............		0	22	.000	11.88	4	2	0	0	0	8 1/3	14	14	11	1	6
1995— GC Orioles (GCL)...............		3	2	.600	1.59	5	5	1	1	0	34	17	9	6	7	29
— Bluefield (Appalachian) ...		4	3	.571	4.20	9	8	0	0	0	49 1/3	61	31	23	12	36
1996— Frederick (Carolina)...........		9	10	.474	3.50	28	26	0	0	0	162	167	80	63	38	147
1997— Bowie (Eastern)................		9	6	.600	3.83	27	25	1	0	0	138 2/3	141	76	59	64	106
1998—								Did not play.								

MORENO, ORBER — P — ROYALS

PERSONAL: Born April 27, 1977, in Caracas, Venezuela. ... 6-2/190. ... Throws right, bats right. ... Full name: Orber Aquiles Moreno.
HIGH SCHOOL: Luisa Caceres (Venezuela).
TRANSACTIONS/CAREER NOTES: Signed as non-drafted free agent by Kansas City Royals organization (November 10, 1993).

Year	Team (League)	W	L	Pct.	ERA	G	GS	CG	ShO	Sv.	IP	H	R	ER	BB	SO
1994— Dom. Royals (DSL)		3	3	.500	3.19	16	11	0	0	1	67 2/3	51	33	24	27	44
1995— GC Royals (GCL)		1	1	.500	2.45	8	3	0	0	1	22	15	9	6	7	21
1996— GC Royals (GCL)		5	1	.833	1.36	12	7	0	0	1	46 1/3	37	15	7	10	50
1997— Lansing (Midwest)..............		4	8	.333	4.81	27	25	0	0	0	138 1/3	150	83	74	45	128
1998— Wilmington (Caro.).............		3	2	.600	0.82	23	0	0	0	7	33	8	3	3	10	50
— Wichita (Texas)		0	1	.000	2.88	24	0	0	0	7	34 1/3	28	13	11	12	40

MORGAN, MIKE   P

PERSONAL: Born October 8, 1959, in Tulare, Calif. ... 6-2/220. ... Throws right, bats right. ... Full name: Michael Thomas Morgan.
HIGH SCHOOL: Valley (Las Vegas).
TRANSACTIONS/CAREER NOTES: Selected by Oakland Athletics organization in first round (fourth pick overall) of free-agent draft (June 6, 1978). ... On disabled list (May 14-June 27, 1980). ... Traded by A's organization to New York Yankees for SS Fred Stanley and a player to be named later (November 3, 1980); A's acquired 2B Brian Doyle to complete deal (November 17, 1980). ... On disabled list (April 9-22, 1981). ... Traded by Yankees with OF/1B Dave Collins, 1B Fred McGriff and cash to Toronto Blue Jays for P Dale Murray and OF/C Tom Dodd (December 9, 1982). ... On Toronto disabled list (July 2-August 23, 1983); included rehabilitation assignment to Syracuse (August 1-18). ... Selected by Seattle Mariners from Blue Jays organization in Rule 5 major league draft (December 3, 1984). ... On Seattle disabled list (April 17, 1985-remainder of season); included rehabilitation assignment to Calgary (July 19-22). ... Traded by Mariners to Baltimore Orioles for P Ken Dixon (December 9, 1987). ... On Baltimore disabled list (June 9-July 19, 1988); included rehabilitation assignment to Rochester (June 30-July 17). ... On Baltimore disabled list (August 12, 1988-remainder of season). ... Traded by Orioles to Los Angeles Dodgers for OF Mike Devereaux (March 12, 1989). ... Granted free agency (October 28, 1991). ... Signed by Chicago Cubs (December 3, 1991). ... On disabled list (June 14-29, 1993; May 9-27, June 2-22 and July 28, 1994-remainder of season). ... On Chicago disabled list (April 24-May 25, 1995); included rehabilitation assignment to Orlando (May 15-25). ... Traded by Cubs with 3B/OF Paul Torres and C Francisco Morales to St. Louis Cardinals for 3B Todd Zeile and cash (June 16, 1995). ... On St. Louis disabled list (July 4-24, 1995). ... Granted free agency (November 6, 1995). ... Re-signed by Cardinals (December 7, 1995). ... On St. Louis disabled list (March 22-May 18, 1996); included rehabilitation assignment to St. Petersburg (April 20-May 15). ... Released by Cardinals (August 28, 1996). ... Signed by Cincinnati Reds (September 4, 1996). ... On disabled list (June 8-24, 1997). ... Granted free agency (October 28, 1997). ... Signed by Minnesota Twins (December 16, 1997). ... On Minnesota disabled list (June 27-July 13 and July 15-August 16, 1998). ... Traded by Twins to Cubs for cash and a player to be named later (August 25, 1998); Twins acquired P Scott Downs to complete deal (November 3, 1998). ... Granted free agency (October 30, 1998).
RECORDS: Shares Major League record for most clubs played and pitched for in career (since 1900)—10.

Year	Team (League)	W	L	Pct.	ERA	G	GS	CG	ShO	Sv.	IP	H	R	ER	BB	SO
1978—	Oakland (A.L.)	0	3	.000	7.50	3	3	1	0	0	12	19	12	10	8	0
—	Vancouver (PCL)	5	6	.455	5.58	14	14	5	1	0	92	109	67	57	54	31
1979—	Ogden (Pac. Coast)	5	5	.500	3.48	13	13	6	0	0	101	93	48	39	49	42
—	Oakland (A.L.)	2	10	.167	5.96	13	13	2	0	0	77	102	57	51	50	17
1980—	Ogden (Pac. Coast)	6	9	.400	5.40	20	20	3	0	0	115	135	79	69	77	46
1981—	Nashville (Southern)■	8	7	.533	4.42	26	26	7	0	0	169	164	97	83	83	100
1982—	New York (A.L.)	7	11	.389	4.37	30	23	2	0	0	150 1/3	167	77	73	67	71
1983—	Toronto (A.L.)■	0	3	.000	5.16	16	4	0	0	0	45 1/3	48	26	26	21	22
—	Syracuse (Int'l)	0	3	.000	5.59	5	4	0	0	1	19 1/3	20	12	12	13	17
1984—	Syracuse (Int'l)	13	11	.542	4.07	34	28	10	•4	0	*185 2/3	167	•101	84	•100	105
1985—	Seattle (A.L.)■	1	1	.500	12.00	2	2	0	0	0	6	11	8	8	5	2
—	Calgary (PCL)	0	0	. . .	4.50	1	1	0	0	0	2	3	1	1	0	0
1986—	Seattle (A.L.)	11	•17	.393	4.53	37	33	9	1	1	216 1/3	243	122	109	86	116
1987—	Seattle (A.L.)	12	17	.414	4.65	34	31	8	2	0	207	245	117	107	53	85
1988—	Baltimore (A.L.)■	1	6	.143	5.43	22	10	2	0	1	71 1/3	70	45	43	23	29
—	Rochester (Int'l)	0	2	.000	4.76	3	3	0	0	0	17	19	10	9	6	7
1989—	Los Angeles (N.L.)■	8	11	.421	2.53	40	19	0	0	0	152 2/3	130	51	43	33	72
1990—	Los Angeles (N.L.)	11	15	.423	3.75	33	33	6	•4	0	211	216	100	88	60	106
1991—	Los Angeles (N.L.)	14	10	.583	2.78	34	33	5	1	1	236 1/3	197	85	73	61	140
1992—	Chicago (N.L.)■	16	8	.667	2.55	34	34	6	1	0	240	203	80	68	79	123
1993—	Chicago (N.L.)	10	15	.400	4.03	32	32	1	1	0	207 2/3	206	100	93	74	111
1994—	Chicago (N.L.)	2	10	.167	6.69	15	15	1	0	0	80 2/3	111	65	60	35	57
1995—	Orlando (South.)	0	2	.000	7.59	2	2	0	0	0	10 2/3	13	9	9	7	5
—	Chicago (N.L.)	2	1	.667	2.19	4	4	0	0	0	24 2/3	19	8	6	9	15
—	St. Louis (N.L.)■	5	6	.455	3.88	17	17	1	0	0	106 2/3	114	48	46	25	46
1996—	St. Petersburg (FSL)	1	0	1.000	0.00	1	1	0	0	0	5 2/3	4	0	0	1	4
—	Louisville (A.A.)	1	3	.250	7.04	4	4	1	0	0	23	29	18	18	11	10
—	St. Louis (N.L.)	4	8	.333	5.24	18	18	0	0	0	103	118	63	60	40	55
—	Cincinnati (N.L.)■	2	3	.400	2.30	5	5	0	0	0	27 1/3	28	9	7	7	19
1997—	Cincinnati (N.L.)	9	12	.429	4.78	31	30	1	0	0	162	165	91	86	49	103
1998—	Minnesota (A.L.)■	4	2	.667	3.49	18	17	0	0	0	98	108	41	38	24	50
—	Chicago (N.L.)	0	1	.000	7.15	5	5	0	0	0	22 2/3	30	21	18	15	10
A.L. totals (9 years)		38	70	.352	4.74	175	136	24	3	2	883 1/3	1013	505	465	337	392
N.L. totals (10 years)		83	100	.454	3.70	268	245	21	7	1	1574 2/3	1537	721	648	487	857
Major league totals (18 years)		121	170	.416	4.08	443	381	45	10	3	2458	2550	1226	1113	824	1249

DIVISION SERIES RECORD

Year	Team (League)	W	L	Pct.	ERA	G	GS	CG	ShO	Sv.	IP	H	R	ER	BB	SO
1998—	Chicago (N.L.)	0	0	. . .	0.00	2	0	0	0	0	1 1/3	0	0	0	0	1

ALL-STAR GAME RECORD

Year	League	W	L	Pct.	ERA	GS	CG	ShO	Sv.	IP	H	R	ER	BB	SO
1991—	National	0	0	. . .	0.00	0	0	0	0	1	0	0	0	0	1

MORGAN, SCOTT   OF   INDIANS

PERSONAL: Born July 19, 1973, in Westlake, Calif. ... 6-7/230. ... Bats right, throws right. ... Full name: Scott Alexander Morgan.
HIGH SCHOOL: Lompoc (Calif.).
JUNIOR COLLEGE: Allan Hancock College (Calif.).
COLLEGE: Gonzaga.
TRANSACTIONS/CAREER NOTES: Selected by Milwaukee Brewers organization in 45th round of free-agent draft (June 1, 1992); did not sign. ... Selected by Cleveland Indians organization in seventh round of free-agent draft (June 1, 1995). ... On disabled list (July 11, 1996-remainder of season). ... On disabled list (April 21-30 and June 22-29, 1998).
STATISTICAL NOTES: Led Carolina League with .606 slugging percentage in 1997.

Year Team (League)	Pos.	G	AB	R	H	2B	3B	HR	RBI	Avg.	BB	SO	SB	PO	A	E	Avg.
1995— Watertown (NYP)	OF	66	244	42	64	18	0	2	33	.262	26	63	6	50	3	3	.946
1996— Columbus (S. Atl.)......	OF	87	305	62	95	25	1	22	80	.311	46	70	9	106	6	4	.966
1997— Kinston (Carolina)	OF	95	368	*86	116	32	3	23	67	.315	47	87	4	143	7	2	.987
— Akron (Eastern)	OF	21	69	11	12	3	0	2	6	.174	8	20	1	37	4	1	.976
1998— Akron (Eastern)	OF	119	456	95	134	31	4	25	89	.294	56	124	4	201	4	5	.976

MORMAN, ALVIN   P   ROYALS

PERSONAL: Born January 6, 1969, in Rockingham, N.C. ... 6-3/210. ... Throws left, bats left.
HIGH SCHOOL: Richmond Senior (Rockingham, N.C.).
COLLEGE: Wingate (N.C.).
TRANSACTIONS/CAREER NOTES: Selected by Houston Astros organization in 39th round of free-agent draft (June 3, 1991). ... On disabled list (August 26, 1993-remainder of season and May 23-June 14, 1995). ... On temporarily inactive list (July 25-August 2, 1994). ... Traded by Astros to Cleveland Indians for P Jose Cabrera (May 9, 1997). ... On Cleveland disabled list (July 28-September 1, 1997). ... On Cleveland disabled list (May 4-19, 1998); included rehabilitation assignment to Buffalo (May 14-19). ... Traded by Indians with P Jose Mesa and IF Shawon Dunston to San Francisco Giants for P Steve Reed and OF Jacob Cruz (July 23, 1998). ... On San Francisco disabled list (August 7-September 1, 1998); included rehabilitation assignment to Fresno (August 18-26). ... Granted free agency (December 21, 1998). ... Signed by Kansas City Royals (December 21, 1998).

Year Team (League)	W	L	Pct.	ERA	G	GS	CG	ShO	Sv.	IP	H	R	ER	BB	SO
1991— GC Astros (GCL)	1	0	1.000	2.16	11	0	0	0	1	16^2/$_3$	15	7	4	5	24
— Osceola (Florida St.)..........	0	0	...	1.50	3	0	0	0	0	6	5	3	1	2	3
1992— Asheville (S. Atl.).............	8	0	1.000	1.55	57	0	0	0	15	75^1/$_3$	60	17	13	26	70
1993— Jackson (Texas)	8	2	*.800	2.96	19	19	0	0	0	97^1/$_3$	77	35	32	28	101
1994— Tucson (PCL)	3	7	.300	5.11	58	0	0	0	5	74	84	51	42	26	49
1995— Tucson (PCL)	5	1	.833	3.91	45	0	0	0	3	48^1/$_3$	50	26	21	20	36
1996— Houston (N.L.).................	4	1	.800	4.93	53	0	0	0	0	42	43	24	23	24	31
1997— New Orleans (A.A.)..........	0	1	.000	4.50	8	0	0	0	0	10	11	5	5	2	14
— Cleveland (A.L.)■.............	0	0	...	5.89	34	0	0	0	2	18^1/$_3$	19	13	12	14	13
— Buffalo (A.A.)....................	0	0	...	0.00	3	0	0	0	0	3^1/$_3$	2	0	0	0	3
1998— Cleveland (A.L.)...............	0	1	.000	5.32	31	0	0	0	0	22	25	13	13	11	16
— Buffalo (Int'l)...................	0	0	...	0.00	2	0	0	0	0	2	3	0	0	0	4
— San Francisco (N.L.)■........	0	1	.000	5.14	9	0	0	0	0	7	8	4	4	3	7
— Fresno (Pacific Coast)	2	0	1.000	4.15	4	1	0	0	0	4^1/$_3$	7	2	2	0	3
A.L. totals (2 years)	0	1	.000	5.58	65	0	0	0	2	40^1/$_3$	44	26	25	25	29
N.L. totals (2 years)	4	2	.667	4.96	62	0	0	0	0	49	51	28	27	27	38
Major league totals (3 years)......	4	3	.571	5.24	127	0	0	0	2	89^1/$_3$	95	54	52	52	67

DIVISION SERIES RECORD

Year Team (League)	W	L	Pct.	ERA	G	GS	CG	ShO	Sv.	IP	H	R	ER	BB	SO
1997— Cleveland (A.L.).................	0	0	...	...	1	0	0	0	0	0	0	0	0	1	0

CHAMPIONSHIP SERIES RECORD

Year Team (League)	W	L	Pct.	ERA	G	GS	CG	ShO	Sv.	IP	H	R	ER	BB	SO
1997— Cleveland (A.L.).................	0	0	...	0.00	2	0	0	0	0	1^1/$_3$	0	0	0	0	1

WORLD SERIES RECORD

Year Team (League)	W	L	Pct.	ERA	G	GS	CG	ShO	Sv.	IP	H	R	ER	BB	SO
1997— Cleveland (A.L.).................	0	0	...	0.00	2	0	0	0	0	^{1}/$_3$	0	2	0	2	1

M

MORRIS, HAL   1B   REDS

PERSONAL: Born April 9, 1965, in Fort Rucker, Ala. ... 6-2/195. ... Bats left, throws left. ... Full name: William Harold Morris. ... Brother of Bobby Morris, second baseman, Cleveland Indians organization.
HIGH SCHOOL: Munster (Ind.).
COLLEGE: Michigan.
TRANSACTIONS/CAREER NOTES: Selected by New York Yankees organization in eighth round of free-agent draft (June 2, 1986). ... On Albany/Colonie disabled list (August 14, 1986-remainder of season). ... Traded by Yankees with P Rodney Imes to Cincinnati Reds for P Tim Leary and OF Van Snider (December 12, 1989). ... On Cincinnati disabled list (April 16-May 17, 1992); included rehabilitation assignment to Nashville (May 14-17). ... On Cincinnati disabled list (August 5-21, 1992). ... On Cincinnati disabled list (March 27-June 7, 1993); included rehabilitation assignment to Indianapolis (June 4-7). ... On suspended list (August 10, 1993). ... On Cincinnati disabled list (June 18-July 13, 1995); included rehabilitation assignment to Indianapolis (July 7-10). ... Granted free agency (November 2, 1995). ... Re-signed by Reds (December 6, 1995). ... On Cincinnati disabled list (July 2-17, 1996); included rehabilitation assignment to Indianapolis (July 16-17). ... On Cincinnati disabled list (July 31-September 10, 1997). ... Granted free agency (October 29, 1997). ... Signed by Kansas City Royals (December 22, 1997). ... On disabled list (May 8-23, 1998). ... Granted free agency (October 23, 1998). ... Signed by Reds (January 14, 1999).
RECORDS: Shares major league single-inning record for most doubles—2 (August 17, 1996, eighth inning).
STATISTICAL NOTES: Had 29-game hitting streak (August 27-September 29, 1996). ... Career major league grand slams: 1.

Year Team (League)	Pos.	G	AB	R	H	2B	3B	HR	RBI	Avg.	BB	SO	SB	PO	A	E	Avg.
1986— Oneonta (NYP)	1B	36	127	26	48	9	2	3	30	.378	18	15	1	317	26	3	.991
— Alb./Colon. (East.)	1B	25	79	7	17	5	0	0	4	.215	4	10	0	203	19	2	.991
1987— Alb./Colon. (East.)	1B-OF	135	*530	65	*173	31	4	5	73	.326	36	43	7	1086	79	17	.986
1988— Columbus (Int'l)	OF-1B	121	452	41	134	19	4	3	38	.296	36	62	8	543	26	8	.986
— New York (A.L.)..........	OF-DH	15	20	1	2	0	0	0	0	.100	0	9	0	7	0	0	1.000
1989— Columbus (Int'l)	1B-OF	111	417	70	136	24	1	17	66	*.326	28	47	5	636	67	9	.987
— New York (A.L.)..........	OF-1B-DH	15	18	2	5	0	0	0	4	.278	1	4	0	12	0	0	1.000
1990— Cincinnati (N.L.)■......	1B-OF	107	309	50	105	22	3	7	36	.340	21	32	9	595	53	4	.994
— Nashville (A.A.)	OF	16	64	8	22	5	0	1	10	.344	5	10	4	23	1	1	.960
1991— Cincinnati (N.L.)	1B-OF	136	478	72	152	33	1	14	59	.318	46	61	10	979	100	9	.992

Year Team (League)	Pos.	G	AB	R	H	2B	3B	HR	RBI	Avg.	BB	SO	SB	PO	A	E	Avg.
1992— Cincinnati (N.L.)	1B	115	395	41	107	21	3	6	53	.271	45	53	6	841	86	1	*.999
— Nashville (A.A.)	1B	2	6	1	1	1	0	0	0	.167	2	1	0	13	3	0	1.000
1993— Indianapolis (A.A.)	1B	3	13	4	6	0	1	1	5	.462	1	2	0	26	3	0	1.000
— Cincinnati (N.L.)	1B	101	379	48	120	18	0	7	49	.317	34	51	2	746	75	5	.994
1994— Cincinnati (N.L.)	1B	112	436	60	146	30	4	10	78	.335	34	62	6	901	80	6	.994
1995— Cincinnati (N.L.)	1B	101	359	53	100	25	2	11	51	.279	29	58	1	757	72	5	.994
— Indianapolis (A.A.)	1B	2	5	2	2	0	0	0	1	.400	1	0	0	13	2	0	1.000
1996— Cincinnati (N.L.)	1B	142	528	82	165	32	4	16	80	.313	50	76	7	1129	91	8	.993
— Indianapolis (A.A.)	1B	1	4	1	2	1	0	1	1	.500	0	1	0	2	0	0	1.000
1997— Cincinnati (N.L.)	1B	96	333	42	92	20	1	1	33	.276	23	43	3	672	52	7	.990
1998— Kansas City (A.L.)■ ...	1B-DH-OF	127	472	50	146	27	2	1	40	.309	32	52	1	396	35	4	.991
American League totals (3 years)		157	510	53	153	27	2	1	44	.300	33	65	1	415	35	4	.991
National League totals (8 years)		910	3217	448	987	201	18	72	439	.307	282	436	44	6620	609	45	.994
Major league totals (11 years)		1067	3727	501	1140	228	20	73	483	.306	315	501	45	7035	644	49	.994

DIVISION SERIES RECORD

Year Team (League)	Pos.	G	AB	R	H	2B	3B	HR	RBI	Avg.	BB	SO	SB	PO	A	E	Avg.
1995— Cincinnati (N.L.)	1B	3	10	5	5	1	0	0	2	.500	3	1	1	22	2	0	1.000

CHAMPIONSHIP SERIES RECORD

Year Team (League)	Pos.	G	AB	R	H	2B	3B	HR	RBI	Avg.	BB	SO	SB	PO	A	E	Avg.
1990— Cincinnati (N.L.)	1B-PH	5	12	3	5	1	0	0	1	.417	1	0	0	20	2	0	1.000
1995— Cincinnati (N.L.)	1B-PH	4	12	0	2	1	0	0	1	.167	1	1	1	27	3	0	1.000
Championship series totals (2 years)		9	24	3	7	2	0	0	2	.292	2	1	1	47	5	0	1.000

NOTES: Member of World Series championship team (1990).

WORLD SERIES RECORD

Year Team (League)	Pos.	G	AB	R	H	2B	3B	HR	RBI	Avg.	BB	SO	SB	PO	A	E	Avg.
1990— Cincinnati (N.L.)	1B-DH	4	14	0	1	0	0	0	2	.071	1	1	0	18	1	0	1.000

MORRIS, MATT   P   CARDINALS

PERSONAL: Born August 9, 1974, in Middletown, N.Y. ... 6-5/210. ... Throws right, bats right. ... Full name: Matthew Christian Morris.

HIGH SCHOOL: Valley Central (Montgomery, N.Y.).

COLLEGE: Seton Hall.

TRANSACTIONS/CAREER NOTES: Selected by Milwaukee Brewers organization in 25th round of free-agent draft (June 1, 1992); did not sign. ... Selected by St. Louis Cardinals organization in first round (12th pick overall) of free-agent draft (June 1, 1995). ... On St. Louis disabled list (March 24-April 11 and April 12-July 10, 1998); included rehabilitation assignments to Arkansas (April 6-11) and Memphis (June 21-July 10).

HONORS: Named N.L. Rookie Pitcher of the Year by THE SPORTING NEWS (1997).

MISCELLANEOUS: Struck out in only appearance as pinch hitter (1997).

Year Team (League)	W	L	Pct.	ERA	G	GS	CG	ShO	Sv.	IP	H	R	ER	BB	SO
1995— New Jersey (NYP)	2	0	1.000	1.64	2	2	0	0	0	11	12	3	2	3	13
— St. Petersburg (FSL)	3	2	.600	2.38	6	6	1	1	0	34	22	16	9	11	31
1996— Arkansas (Texas)	12	12	.500	3.88	27	27	4	*4	0	167	178	79	72	48	120
— Louisville (A.A.)	0	1	.000	3.38	1	1	0	0	0	8	8	3	3	1	9
1997— St. Louis (N.L.)	12	9	.571	3.19	33	33	3	0	0	217	208	88	77	69	149
1998— Arkansas (Texas)	0	0	...	0.00	1	0	0	0	1	4	4	0	0	0	2
— St. Louis (N.L.)	7	5	.583	2.53	17	17	2	1	0	113 2/3	101	37	32	42	79
— Memphis (Pacific Coast)	1	0	1.000	4.50	4	4	0	0	0	14	16	8	7	4	21
Major league totals (2 years)	19	14	.576	2.97	50	50	5	1	0	330 2/3	309	125	109	111	228

MORRIS, WARREN   2B   PIRATES

PERSONAL: Born January 11, 1974, in Alexandria, La. ... 5-10/175. ... Bats left, throws right. ... Full name: Warren Randall Morris.

HIGH SCHOOL: Bolton (Alexandria, La.).

TRANSACTIONS/CAREER NOTES: Selected by Texas Rangers organization in fifth round of free-agent draft (June 2, 1996). ... Traded by Rangers with P Todd Van Poppel to Pittsburgh Pirates for P Esteban Loaiza (July 17, 1998).

MISCELLANEOUS: Member of 1996 U.S. Olympic baseball team.

Year Team (League)	Pos.	G	AB	R	H	2B	3B	HR	RBI	Avg.	BB	SO	SB	PO	A	E	Avg.
1997— Charlotte (Fla. St.)	2B-3B	128	494	78	151	27	9	12	75	.306	62	100	16	193	247	18	.961
— Okla. City (A.A.)	2B	8	32	3	7	1	0	1	3	.219	3	5	0	17	31	0	1.000
1998— Tulsa (Texas)	2B	95	390	59	129	22	5	14	73	.331	43	63	12	179	274	17	.964
— Carolina (Southern)■	2B	44	151	28	50	8	3	5	30	.331	24	34	5	87	100	7	.964

MOSQUERA, JULIO   C   DEVIL RAYS

PERSONAL: Born January 29, 1972, in Panama City, Panama. ... 6-0/190. ... Bats right, throws right. ... Full name: Julio Alberto Mosquera.

TRANSACTIONS/CAREER NOTES: Signed as non-drafted free agent by Toronto Blue Jays organization (May 16, 1991). ... On Syracuse disabled list (June 18-August 21, 1998). ... Claimed on waivers by Tampa Bay Devil Rays (September 23, 1998).

STATISTICAL NOTES: Led Pioneer League with 13 passed balls in 1994. ... Led South Atlantic League catchers with .991 fielding percentage in 1995. ... Led Southern League with 19 passed balls in 1996.

Year Team (League)	Pos.	G	AB	R	H	2B	3B	HR	RBI	Avg.	BB	SO	SB	PO	A	E	Avg.
1991— Dom. B. Jays (DSL) ...	C	42	136	20	29	3	0	0	10	.213	8	12	3	...	...	...	...
1992— Dom. B. Jays (DSL) ...	C	67	235	47	85	12	1	3	39	.362	17	20	17	207	94	14	.956
1993— GC Jays (GCL)..........	C-SS	35	108	9	28	3	2	0	15	.259	8	16	3	180	39	8	.965
1994— Medicine Hat (Pio.) ...	C	59	229	33	78	17	1	2	44	.341	18	35	3	299	*70	11	.971
1995— Hagerstown (SAL)......	C-1B	108	406	64	118	22	5	3	46	.291	29	53	5	641	103	7	†.991
1996— Knoxville (Southern) ..	C	92	318	36	73	17	0	2	31	.230	29	55	6	679	63	7	.991
— Syracuse (Int'l)...........	C	23	72	6	18	1	0	0	5	.250	6	14	0	164	9	3	.983
— Toronto (A.L.)............	C	8	22	2	5	2	0	0	2	.227	0	3	0	48	1	0	1.000
1997— Knoxville (Southern) ..	C	87	309	47	90	23	1	5	50	.291	22	56	3	587	56	7	.989
— Syracuse (Int'l)..........	C	10	35	5	8	1	0	0	1	.229	2	5	0	55	5	1	.984
— Toronto (A.L.)............	C	3	8	0	2	1	0	0	0	.250	0	2	0	11	1	0	1.000
1998— Syracuse (Int'l).........	C	28	94	10	20	6	0	2	4	.213	5	12	1	145	20	0	1.000
— Knoxville (Southern) ..	C-OF	12	43	4	12	1	0	0	8	.279	4	7	0	51	7	1	.983
Major league totals (2 years)		11	30	2	7	3	0	0	2	.233	0	5	0	59	2	0	1.000

MOSS, DAMIAN   P   BRAVES

PERSONAL: Born November 24, 1976, in Darlinghurst, Australia. ... 6-0/187. ... Throws right, bats left. ... Full name: Damian Joseph Moss.
HIGH SCHOOL: Liverpool Boys (Australia).
TRANSACTIONS/CAREER NOTES: Signed as non-drafted free agent by Atlanta Braves organization (July 1, 1993). ... On Atlanta disabled list (March 27, 1998-entire season).
STATISTICAL NOTES: Led Appalachian League with 14 hit batsmen in 1994.

Year Team (League)	W	L	Pct.	ERA	G	GS	CG	ShO	Sv.	IP	H	R	ER	BB	SO
1994— Danville (Appalachian)........	2	5	.286	3.58	12	12	1	1	0	60 1/3	30	28	24	55	77
1995— Macon (S. Atl.)..................	9	10	.474	3.56	27	27	0	0	0	149 1/3	134	73	59	70	•177
1996— Durham (Carolina)..............	9	1	*.900	2.25	14	14	0	0	0	84	52	25	21	40	89
— Greenville (Southern)	2	5	.286	4.97	11	10	0	0	0	58	57	41	32	35	48
1997— Greenville (Southern)	6	8	.429	5.35	21	19	1	0	0	112 2/3	111	73	67	58	116
1998—								Did not play.							

MOTA, DANNY   P   TWINS

PERSONAL: Born October 9, 1975, in Santo Domingo, Dominican Republic. ... 6-0/180. ... Throws right, bats right. ... Full name: Daniel Avila Mota.
TRANSACTIONS/CAREER NOTES: Signed as non-drafted free agent by New York Yankees organization (April 15, 1994). ... Traded by Yankees with P Eric Milton, SS Cristian Guzman, OF Brian Buchanan and cash to Minnesota Twins for 2B Chuck Knoblauch (February 5, 1998).

Year Team (League)	W	L	Pct.	ERA	G	GS	CG	ShO	Sv.	IP	H	R	ER	BB	SO
1994— Dominican Yankees (DSL)..	2	3	.400	4.53	13	12	0	0	0	57 2/3	50	39	29	24	51
1995— GC Yankees (GCL)............	2	3	.400	2.20	14	0	0	0	0	32 2/3	27	9	8	4	35
1996— Oneonta (N.Y.-Penn)	0	1	.000	4.50	10	0	0	0	7	10	10	5	5	2	11
1997— Oneonta (N.Y.-Penn)	1	0	1.000	2.22	27	0	0	0	*17	28 1/3	21	8	7	16	40
— Greensboro (S. Atl.)	2	0	1.000	1.82	20	0	0	0	1	29 2/3	17	6	6	11	30
1998— Fort Wayne (Midw.)............	4	3	.571	2.25	25	0	0	0	7	32	24	14	8	8	39
— Fort Myers (Fla. St.)..........	3	5	.375	2.85	19	4	0	0	0	47 1/3	45	21	15	22	49

MOTA, GUILLERMO   P   EXPOS

PERSONAL: Born July 25, 1973, in San Pedro de Macoris, Dominican Republic. ... 6-5/185. ... Throws right, bats right.
HIGH SCHOOL: Jose Joaquin Perez (San Pedro de Macoris, Dominican Republic).
TRANSACTIONS/CAREER NOTES: Signed as non-drafted free agent by New York Mets organization (September 7, 1990). ... Selected by Montreal Expos organization from Mets organization in Rule 5 minor league draft (December 9, 1996).
STATISTICAL NOTES: Led Gulf Coast League third basemen with .945 fielding percentage and tied for lead with 40 putouts and 11 double plays in 1993. ... Led Appalachian League third basemen with 44 putouts, 157 assists, 214 total chances and .939 fielding percentage in 1994. ... Led South Atlantic League shortstops with 615 total chances and 66 double plays in 1995.
MISCELLANEOUS: Played infield only (1991-96).

Year Team (League)	W	L	Pct.	ERA	G	GS	CG	ShO	Sv.	IP	H	R	ER	BB	SO
1997— Cape Fear (S. Atl.)■..........	5	10	.333	4.36	25	23			0	126	135	65	61	33	112
1998— Jupiter (Florida State)	3	2	.600	0.66	20	0	0	0	2	41	18	6	3	6	27
— Harrisburg (Eastern)	2	0	1.000	1.06	12	0	0	0	4	17	10	2	2	2	19

RECORD AS POSITION PLAYER

Year Team (League)	Pos.	G	AB	R	H	2B	3B	HR	RBI	Avg.	BB	SO	SB	PO	A	E	Avg.
1991— Dom. Mets (DSL)......	...	32	90	4	22	2	0	0	12	.244	9	19	0	...	...	...	...
1992— Dom. Mets (DSL)......	...	70	228	49	68	10	3	6	40	.298	28	40	10	...	...	...	...
1993— GC Mets (GCL)..........	3B-SS	43	169	23	42	7	2	1	22	.249	7	37	1	‡42	95	8	*.945
1994— St. Lucie (Fla. St.)	3B	1	4	1	0	0	0	0	0	.000	0	0	0	1	5	1	.857
— Kingsport (Appal.)......	3B-SS	65	245	40	60	10	2	9	37	.245	20	78	5	†55	†175	16	†.935
1995— Columbia (S. Atl.)......	SS-1B	123	400	45	97	24	3	4	45	.243	32	127	8	205	373	40	.935
1996— St. Lucie (Fla. St.)	SS-3B	102	304	34	71	10	3	1	21	.234	34	90	8	127	293	21	.952

MOUTON, JAMES   OF

PERSONAL: Born December 29, 1968, in Denver. ... 5-9/175. ... Bats right, throws right. ... Full name: James Raleigh Mouton. ... Name pronounced MOO-tawn.
HIGH SCHOOL: Burbank (Calif.).
COLLEGE: St. Mary's (Calif.).

M

TRANSACTIONS/CAREER NOTES: Selected by New York Yankees organization in 42nd round of free-agent draft (June 2, 1987); did not sign. ... Selected by Minnesota Twins organization in eighth round of free-agent draft (June 4, 1990); did not sign. ... Selected by Houston Astros organization in seventh round of free-agent draft (June 3, 1991). ... On Houston disabled list (June 12-30, 1995); included rehabilitation assignment to Tucson (June 27-30). ... Traded by Astros to San Diego Padres for P Sean Bergman (January 14, 1998). ... On San Diego disabled list (May 16-June 1, 1998); included rehabilitation assignment to Las Vegas (May 27-June 1). ... Granted free agency (December 21, 1998).

HONORS: Named Pacific Coast League Most Valuable Player (1993).

STATISTICAL NOTES: Led New York-Pennsylvania League in caught stealing with 18 in 1991. ... Led New York-Pennsylvania League second basemen with 382 total chances in 1991. ... Led Florida State League second basemen with 623 total chances in 1992. ... Led Pacific Coast League with 286 total bases and tied for lead in caught stealing with 18 in 1993. ... Led Pacific Coast League second basemen with 674 total chances and 75 double plays in 1993. ... Career major league grand slams: 1.

Year	Team (League)	Pos.	G	AB	R	H	2B	3B	HR	RBI	Avg.	BB	SO	SB	PO	A	E	Avg.
1991—	Auburn (NY-Penn)......	2B	76	288	71	76	15	*10	2	40	.264	55	32	*60	*170	184	*28	.927
1992—	Osceola (Fla. St.)........	2B	133	507	*110	143	•30	6	11	62	.282	71	78	*51	*288	294	*41	.934
1993—	Tucson (PCL)	2B	134	*546	*126	*172	*42	12	16	92	.315	72	82	40	*277	*354	*43	.936
1994—	Houston (N.L.)	OF	99	310	43	76	11	0	2	16	.245	27	69	24	163	5	3	.982
—	Tucson (PCL)	OF	4	17	2	7	1	0	1	1	.412	2	3	1	7	1	0	1.000
1995—	Tucson (PCL)	OF	3	11	1	5	0	0	1	1	.455	0	2	0	1	0	1	.500
—	Houston (N.L.)	OF	104	298	42	78	18	2	4	27	.262	25	59	25	136	4	0	1.000
1996—	Houston (N.L.)	OF	122	300	40	79	15	1	3	34	.263	38	55	21	158	7	5	.971
—	Tucson (PCL)	OF	1	4	1	1	0	0	0	0	.250	1	0	0	2	0	0	1.000
1997—	Houston (N.L.)	OF	86	180	24	38	9	1	3	23	.211	18	30	9	86	1	0	1.000
1998—	San Diego (N.L.)■...	OF-DH	55	63	8	12	2	1	0	7	.190	7	11	4	30	1	1	.969
—	Las Vegas (PCL)	OF-2B	50	192	38	68	17	3	4	31	.354	17	31	15	57	2	1	.983
Major league totals (5 years)			466	1151	157	283	55	5	12	107	.246	115	224	83	573	18	9	.985

MOUTON, LYLE — OF — ORIOLES

PERSONAL: Born May 13, 1969, in Lafayette, La. ... 6-4/240. ... Bats right, throws right. ... Full name: Lyle Joseph Mouton. ... Name pronounced MOO-tawn.

HIGH SCHOOL: St. Thomas More (Lafayette, La.).

COLLEGE: Louisiana State.

TRANSACTIONS/CAREER NOTES: Selected by New York Yankees organization in fifth round of free-agent draft (June 3, 1991). ... Traded by Yankees to Chicago White Sox (April 22, 1995), completing deal in which White Sox traded P Jack McDowell to Yankees for P Keith Heberling and a player to be named later (December 14, 1994). ... On Chicago disabled list (May 11-27, 1997); included rehabilitation assignment to Birmingham (May 25-27). ... Contract sold to Yakult Swallows of Japan Central League (November 21, 1997). ... Contract purchased by Baltimore Orioles organization (July 2, 1998).

Year	Team (League)	Pos.	G	AB	R	H	2B	3B	HR	RBI	Avg.	BB	SO	SB	PO	A	E	Avg.
1991—	Oneonta (NYP)	OF	70	272	53	84	11	2	7	41	.309	31	38	15	106	5	5	.957
1992—	Prince Will. (Car.).......	OF	50	189	28	50	14	1	6	34	.265	17	42	4	49	5	4	.931
—	Albany (Eastern)......	OF	64	214	25	46	12	2	2	27	.215	24	55	1	102	1	0	1.000
1993—	Albany (Eastern)......	OF	135	491	74	125	22	3	16	76	.255	50	125	18	189	9	5	.975
1994—	Alb./Colon. (East.)......	OF-3B	74	274	42	84	23	1	12	42	.307	27	62	7	118	4	2	.984
—	Columbus (Int'l)......	OF	59	204	26	64	14	5	4	32	.314	14	45	5	99	5	1	.990
1995—	Nashville (A.A.)■......	OF	71	267	40	79	17	0	8	41	.296	23	58	10	123	8	3	.978
—	Chicago (A.L.)	OF-DH	58	179	23	54	16	0	5	27	.302	19	46	1	93	5	1	.990
1996—	Chicago (A.L.)	OF-DH	87	214	25	63	8	1	7	39	.294	22	50	3	64	1	2	.970
1997—	Chicago (A.L.)	OF-DH	88	242	26	65	9	0	5	23	.269	14	66	4	126	1	4	.969
—	Birmingham (Sou.).....	OF	3	11	1	2	0	0	1	1	.182	1	4	0	5	0	0	1.000
1998—	Yokult (Jp.Cen.)■	OF	30	97	7	21	8	0	3	12	.241	9	27	0	...	...	...	...
—	Rochester (Int'l)■......	OF	37	137	23	44	9	2	7	32	.321	13	31	1	56	1	1	.983
—	Baltimore (A.L.).......	OF-DH	18	39	5	12	2	0	2	7	.308	4	8	0	19	1	0	1.000
Major league totals (4 years)			251	674	79	194	35	1	19	96	.288	59	170	8	302	8	7	.978

MOYER, JAMIE — P — MARINERS

PERSONAL: Born November 18, 1962, in Sellersville, Pa. ... 6-0/170. ... Throws left, bats left. ... Son-in-law of Digger Phelps, ESPN college basketball analyst, and Notre Dame basketball coach (1971-72 through 1990-91).

HIGH SCHOOL: Souderton (Pa.) Area.

COLLEGE: St. Joseph's (Pa.).

TRANSACTIONS/CAREER NOTES: Selected by Chicago Cubs organization in sixth round of free-agent draft (June 4, 1984). ... Traded by Cubs with OF Rafael Palmeiro and P Drew Hall to Texas Rangers for P Mitch Williams, P Paul Kilgus, P Steve Wilson, IF Curtis Wilkerson, IF Luis Benitez and OF Pablo Delgado (December 5, 1988). ... On Texas disabled list (May 31-September 1, 1989); included rehabilitation assignments to Gulf Coast Rangers (August 5-14) and Tulsa (August 15-24). ... Released by Rangers (November 13, 1990). ... Signed by Louisville, St. Louis Cardinals organization (January 9, 1991). ... Released by Cardinals (October 14, 1991). ... Signed by Cubs organization (January 8, 1992). ... Released by Iowa, Cubs organization (March 30, 1992). ... Signed by Toledo, Detroit Tigers organization (May 24, 1992). ... Granted free agency (December 8, 1992). ... Signed by Baltimore Orioles organization (December 14, 1992). ... Granted free agency (November 1, 1995). ... Signed by Boston Red Sox (January 2, 1996). ... Traded by Red Sox to Seattle Mariners for OF Darren Bragg (July 30, 1996). ... Granted free agency (October 29, 1996). ... Re-signed by Mariners (November 20, 1996). ... On Seattle disabled list (March 23-April 29, 1997); included rehabilitation assignment to Tacoma (April 24-29).

STATISTICAL NOTES: Led American Association with 16 home runs allowed in 1991. ... Led A.L. with .813 winning percentage in 1996.

Year	Team (League)	W	L	Pct.	ERA	G	GS	CG	ShO	Sv.	IP	H	R	ER	BB	SO
1984—	Geneva (N.Y.-Penn)............	•9	3	.750	1.89	14	14	5	2	0	*104 2/3	59	27	22	31	*120
1985—	Win.-Salem (Car.).......	8	2	.800	2.30	12	12	6	2	0	94	82	36	24	22	94
—	Pittsfield (Eastern).............	7	6	.538	3.72	15	15	3	0	0	96 2/3	99	49	40	32	51
1986—	Pittsfield (Eastern).............	3	1	.750	0.88	6	6	0	0	0	41	27	10	4	16	42
—	Iowa (Am. Assoc.).............	3	2	.600	2.55	6	6	2	0	0	42 1/3	25	14	12	11	25
—	Chicago (N.L.).................	7	4	.636	5.05	16	16	1	1	0	87 1/3	107	52	49	42	45
1987—	Chicago (N.L.).................	12	15	.444	5.10	35	33	1	0	0	201	210	127	*114	97	147

Year Team (League)	W	L	Pct.	ERA	G	GS	CG	ShO	Sv.	IP	H	R	ER	BB	SO
1988— Chicago (N.L.)	9	15	.375	3.48	34	30	3	1	0	202	212	84	78	55	121
1989— Texas (A.L.)■	4	9	.308	4.86	15	15	1	0	0	76	84	51	41	33	44
— GC Rangers (GCL).............	1	0	1.000	1.64	3	3	0	0	0	11	8	4	2	1	18
— Tulsa (Texas)	1	1	.500	5.11	2	2	1	1	0	12 1/3	16	8	7	3	9
1990— Texas (A.L.)	2	6	.250	4.66	33	10	1	0	0	102 1/3	115	59	53	39	58
1991— St. Louis (N.L.)■	0	5	.000	5.74	8	7	0	0	0	31 1/3	38	21	20	16	20
— Louisville (A.A.)	5	10	.333	3.80	20	20	1	0	0	125 2/3	125	64	53	43	69
1992— Toledo (International)■......	10	8	.556	2.86	21	20	5	0	0	138 2/3	128	48	44	37	80
1993— Rochester (Int'l)■	6	0	1.000	1.67	8	8	1	1	0	54	42	13	10	13	41
— Baltimore (A.L.)	12	9	.571	3.43	25	25	3	1	0	152	154	63	58	38	90
1994— Baltimore (A.L.)	5	7	.417	4.77	23	23	0	0	0	149	158	81	79	38	87
1995— Baltimore (A.L.)	8	6	.571	5.21	27	18	0	0	0	115 2/3	117	70	67	30	65
1996— Boston (A.L.)■...............	7	1	.875	4.50	23	10	0	0	0	90	111	50	45	27	50
— Seattle (A.L.)■...............	6	2	§.750	3.31	11	11	0	0	0	70 2/3	66	36	26	19	29
1997— Tacoma (PCL)	1	0	1.000	0.00	1	1	0	0	0	5	1	0	0	0	6
— Seattle (A.L.)	17	5	.773	3.86	30	30	2	0	0	188 2/3	187	82	81	43	113
1998— Seattle (A.L.)	15	9	.625	3.53	34	34	4	3	0	234 1/3	234	99	92	42	158
A.L. totals (8 years)	76	54	.585	4.14	221	176	11	4	0	1178 2/3	1226	591	542	309	694
N.L. totals (4 years)	28	39	.418	4.50	93	86	5	2	0	521 2/3	567	284	261	210	333
Major league totals (12 years)....	104	93	.528	4.25	314	262	16	6	0	1700 1/3	1793	875	803	519	1027

DIVISION SERIES RECORD

Year Team (League)	W	L	Pct.	ERA	G	GS	CG	ShO	Sv.	IP	H	R	ER	BB	SO
1997— Seattle (A.L.)	0	1	.000	5.79	1	1	0	0	0	4 2/3	5	3	3	1	2

MUELLER, BILL — 3B — GIANTS

PERSONAL: Born March 17, 1971, in Maryland Heights, Mo. ... 5-10/180. ... Bats both, throws right. ... Full name: William Richard Mueller. ... Name pronounced MILLER.

HIGH SCHOOL: DeSmet (Creve Coeur, Mo.).

COLLEGE: Southwest Missouri State.

TRANSACTIONS/CAREER NOTES: Selected by San Francisco Giants organization in 15th round of free-agent draft (June 3, 1993). ... On disabled list (July 1-16, 1997).

STATISTICAL NOTES: Led California League with .435 on-base percentage in 1994. ... Led Pacific Coast League third basemen with 25 double plays in 1996. ... Had 17-game hitting streak (April 24-May 14, 1998). ... Career major league grand slams: 1.

								BATTING						FIELDING		
Year Team (League)	Pos.	G	AB	R	H	2B	3B	HR	RBI	Avg.	BB	SO	SB	PO	A	E	Avg.
1993— Everett (N'west).........	2B	58	200	31	60	8	2	1	24	.300	42	17	13	86	143	8	.966
1994— San Jose (Calif.).........	3B-2B-SS	120	431	79	130	20	•9	5	72	.302	*103	47	4	83	276	29	.925
1995— Shreveport (Texas).....	3B-2B	88	330	56	102	16	2	1	39	.309	53	36	6	52	169	5	.978
— Phoenix (PCL)..........	3B-2B	41	172	23	51	13	6	2	19	.297	19	31	0	26	85	7	.941
1996— Phoenix (PCL)	3B-SS-2B	106	440	73	133	14	6	4	36	.302	44	40	2	92	250	11	.969
— San Francisco (N.L.) ..	3B-2B	55	200	31	66	15	1	0	19	.330	24	26	0	51	99	6	.962
1997— San Francisco (N.L.) ..	3B	128	390	51	114	26	3	7	44	.292	48	71	4	85	218	14	.956
1998— San Francisco (N.L.) ..	3B-2B	145	534	93	157	27	0	9	59	.294	79	83	3	99	287	19	.953
Major league totals (3 years)		328	1124	175	337	68	4	16	122	.300	151	180	7	235	604	39	.956

DIVISION SERIES RECORD

								BATTING						FIELDING		
Year Team (League)	Pos.	G	AB	R	H	2B	3B	HR	RBI	Avg.	BB	SO	SB	PO	A	E	Avg.
1997— San Francisco (N.L.) ..	3B	3	12	1	3	0	0	1	1	.250	0	0	0	2	9	0	1.000

MULHOLLAND, TERRY — P — CUBS

PERSONAL: Born March 9, 1963, in Uniontown, Pa. ... 6-3/220. ... Throws left, bats right. ... Full name: Terence John Mulholland.

HIGH SCHOOL: Laurel Highlands (Uniontown, Pa.).

COLLEGE: Marietta College (Ohio).

TRANSACTIONS/CAREER NOTES: Selected by San Francisco Giants organization in first round (24th pick overall) of free-agent draft (June 4, 1984); pick received as compensation for Detroit Tigers signing free-agent IF Darrell Evans. ... On San Francisco disabled list (August 1, 1988-remainder of season). ... Traded by Giants with P Dennis Cook and 3B Charlie Hayes to Philadelphia Phillies for P Steve Bedrosian and a player to be named later (June 18, 1989); Giants organization acquired IF Rick Parker to complete deal (August 7, 1989). ... On Philadelphia disabled list (June 12-28, 1990); included rehabilitation assignment to Scranton/Wilkes-Barre (June 23-24). ... Traded by Phillies with a player to be named later to New York Yankees for P Bobby Munoz, 2B Kevin Jordan and P Ryan Karp (February 9, 1994); Yankees acquired P Jeff Patterson to complete deal (November 8, 1994). ... Granted free agency (October 17, 1994). ... Signed by Giants (April 8, 1995). ... On San Francisco disabled list (June 6-July 4, 1995); included rehabilitation assignment to Phoenix (June 23-July 4). ... Granted free agency (November 3, 1995). ... Signed by Reading, Phillies organization (February 17, 1996). ... Traded by Phillies to Seattle Mariners for IF Desi Relaford (July 31, 1996). ... Granted free agency (October 28, 1996). ... Signed by Chicago Cubs (December 10, 1996). ... Claimed on waivers by Giants (August 8, 1997). ... Granted free agency (October 27, 1997). ... Signed by Cubs organization (February 2, 1998). ... Granted free agency (October 28, 1998). ... Re-signed by Cubs (November 6, 1998).

STATISTICAL NOTES: Pitched 6-0 no-hit victory for Philadelphia against San Francisco (August 15, 1990).

MISCELLANEOUS: Appeared in one game as pinch runner (1991). ... Appeared in one game as pinch runner with San Francisco (1995).

Year Team (League)	W	L	Pct.	ERA	G	GS	CG	ShO	Sv.	IP	H	R	ER	BB	SO
1984— Everett (Northwest)	1	0	1.000	0.00	3	3	0	0	0	19	10	2	0	4	15
— Fresno (California).............	5	2	.714	2.95	9	9	0	0	0	42 2/3	32	17	14	36	39
1985— Shreveport (Texas)	9	8	.529	2.90	26	26	8	*3	0	176 2/3	166	79	57	87	122
1986— Phoenix (PCL)	8	5	.615	4.46	17	17	3	0	0	111	112	60	55	56	77
— San Francisco (N.L.)	1	7	.125	4.94	15	10	0	0	0	54 2/3	51	33	30	35	27

Year Team (League)	W	L	Pct.	ERA	G	GS	CG	ShO	Sv.	IP	H	R	ER	BB	SO
1987— Phoenix (PCL)	7	12	.368	5.07	37	*29	3	1	1	172 1/3	200	*124	•97	90	94
1988— Phoenix (PCL)	7	3	.700	3.58	19	14	3	2	0	100 2/3	116	45	40	44	57
— San Francisco (N.L.)	2	1	.667	3.72	9	6	2	1	0	46	50	20	19	7	18
1989— San Francisco (N.L.)	0	0	. . .	4.09	5	1	0	0	0	11	15	5	5	4	6
— Phoenix (PCL)	4	5	.444	2.99	13	10	3	0	0	78 1/3	67	30	26	26	61
— Philadelphia (N.L.)■	4	7	.364	5.00	20	17	2	1	0	104 1/3	122	61	58	32	60
1990— Philadelphia (N.L.)	9	10	.474	3.34	33	26	6	1	0	180 2/3	172	78	67	42	75
— Scran./W.B. (Int'l)	0	1	.000	3.00	1	1	0	0	0	6	9	4	2	2	2
1991— Philadelphia (N.L.)	16	13	.552	3.61	34	34	8	3	0	232	231	100	93	49	142
1992— Philadelphia (N.L.)	13	11	.542	3.81	32	32	*12	2	0	229	227	101	97	46	125
1993— Philadelphia (N.L.)	12	9	.571	3.25	29	28	7	2	0	191	177	80	69	40	116
1994— New York (A.L.)■	6	7	.462	6.49	24	19	2	0	0	120 2/3	150	94	87	37	72
1995— San Francisco (N.L.)■	5	13	.278	5.80	29	24	2	0	0	149	190	112	96	38	65
— Phoenix (PCL)	0	0	. . .	2.25	1	1	0	0	0	4	4	3	1	1	4
1996— Philadelphia (N.L.)	8	7	.533	4.66	21	21	3	0	0	133 1/3	157	74	69	21	52
— Seattle (A.L.)■	5	4	.556	4.67	12	12	0	0	0	69 1/3	75	38	36	28	34
1997— Chicago (N.L.)■	6	12	.333	4.07	25	25	1	0	0	157	162	79	71	45	74
— San Francisco (N.L.)■	0	1	.000	5.16	15	2	0	0	0	29 2/3	28	21	17	6	25
1998— Chicago (N.L.)	6	5	.545	2.89	70	6	0	0	3	112	100	49	36	39	72
A.L. totals (2 years)	11	11	.500	5.83	36	31	2	0	0	190	225	132	123	65	106
N.L. totals (11 years)	82	96	.461	4.01	337	232	43	10	3	1629 2/3	1682	813	727	404	857
Major league totals (12 years)....	93	107	.465	4.20	373	263	45	10	3	1819 2/3	1907	945	850	469	963

DIVISION SERIES RECORD

Year Team (League)	W	L	Pct.	ERA	G	GS	CG	ShO	Sv.	IP	H	R	ER	BB	SO
1998— Chicago (N.L.)	0	1	.000	11.57	2	0	0	0	0	2 1/3	2	3	3	2	2

CHAMPIONSHIP SERIES RECORD

Year Team (League)	W	L	Pct.	ERA	G	GS	CG	ShO	Sv.	IP	H	R	ER	BB	SO
1993— Philadelphia (N.L.)..............	0	1	.000	7.20	1	1	0	0	0	5	9	5	4	1	2

WORLD SERIES RECORD

Year Team (League)	W	L	Pct.	ERA	G	GS	CG	ShO	Sv.	IP	H	R	ER	BB	SO
1993— Philadelphia (N.L.)..............	1	0	1.000	6.75	2	2	0	0	0	10 2/3	14	8	8	3	5

ALL-STAR GAME RECORD

Year League	W	L	Pct.	ERA	GS	CG	ShO	Sv.	IP	H	R	ER	BB	SO
1993— National	0	0	. . .	4.50	1	0	0	0	2	1	1	1	2	0

MULLEN, SCOTT   P   ROYALS

PERSONAL: Born January 17, 1975, in San Benito, Texas. ... 6-2/190. ... Throws left, bats right. ... Full name: Kenneth Scott Mullen.
HIGH SCHOOL: Beaufort (S.C.).
TRANSACTIONS/CAREER NOTES: Selected by Kansas City Royals organization in seventh round of free-agent draft (June 4, 1996).

Year Team (League)	W	L	Pct.	ERA	G	GS	CG	ShO	Sv.	IP	H	R	ER	BB	SO
1996— Spokane (N'west)	5	6	.455	3.92	15	15	0	0	0	80 1/3	78	45	35	29	78
1997— Lansing (Midwest)	5	2	.714	3.70	16	16	0	0	0	92 1/3	90	46	38	31	78
— Wilmington (Caro.).............	4	4	.500	4.55	11	11	0	0	0	59 1/3	64	35	30	26	43
1998— Wilmington (Caro.).............	8	4	.667	2.21	14	14	1	1	0	85 2/3	68	28	21	25	56
— Wichita (Texas)	8	2	.800	4.11	12	12	0	0	0	70	66	34	32	26	42

MULLINS, GREG   P   BREWERS

PERSONAL: Born December 13, 1971, in Palatka, Fla. ... 5-10/167. ... Throws left, bats left. ... Full name: Gregory E. Mullins.
HIGH SCHOOL: Palatka (Fla.).
COLLEGE: North Florida.
TRANSACTIONS/CAREER NOTES: Signed as non-drafted free agent by Milwaukee Brewers organization (May 25, 1995).

Year Team (League)	W	L	Pct.	ERA	G	GS	CG	ShO	Sv.	IP	H	R	ER	BB	SO
1995— Helena (Pioneer)	4	0	1.000	2.74	4	4	0	0	0	23	22	7	7	2	14
— Beloit (Midwest)	3	1	.750	3.96	15	4	0	0	2	36 1/3	26	16	16	14	48
1996— El Paso (Texas)	1	5	.167	7.07	23	1	0	0	2	28	30	25	22	17	28
— Stockton (California)	0	0	. . .	3.97	10	0	0	0	1	11 1/3	13	5	5	4	12
1997— Stockton (California)	0	2	.000	2.18	30	0	0	0	19	33	22	9	8	12	52
— El Paso (Texas)	1	1	.500	2.70	25	0	0	0	13	23 1/3	19	8	7	11	21
1998— Louisville (Int'l)	1	3	.250	3.55	61	0	0	0	18	66	57	26	26	23	86
— Milwaukee (N.L.)	0	0	. . .	0.00	2	0	0	0	0	1	1	0	0	0	1
Major league totals (1 year)........	0	0	. . .	0.00	2	0	0	0	0	1	1	0	0	0	1

MUNOZ, BOBBY   P   DEVIL RAYS

PERSONAL: Born March 3, 1968, in Rio Piedras, Puerto Rico. ... 6-7/210. ... Throws right, bats right. ... Full name: Roberto Munoz.
HIGH SCHOOL: Hialeah (Fla.) Miami Lakes.
JUNIOR COLLEGE: Palm Beach Junior College (Fla.) and Polk Community College (Fla.).
TRANSACTIONS/CAREER NOTES: Selected by New York Yankees organization in 15th round of free-agent draft (June 1, 1988). ... Traded by Yankees with 2B Kevin Jordan and P Ryan Karp to Philadelphia Phillies for P Terry Mulholland and a player to be named later (February 9, 1994); Yankees acquired P Jeff Patterson to complete deal (November 8, 1994). ... On Philadelphia disabled list (April 18-July 22 and August 3, 1995-remainder of season); included rehabilitation assignments to Reading (June 19-July 10) and Scranton/Wilkes-Barre (July 10-17). ... On Philadelphia disabled list (March 23-June 11, June 17-July 22 and August 8, 1996-remainder of season); included rehabilitation assignments to Clearwater (May 21-June 11), Scranton/Wilkes-Barre (June 22-July 19) and Reading (August 13-September 2). ... Granted free

agency (May 19, 1997). ... Signed by San Diego Padres organization (May 29, 1997). ... Released by Padres organization (July 15, 1997). ... Signed by Los Angeles Dodgers organization (July 21, 1997). ... Granted free agency (October 15, 1997). ... Signed by Baltimore Orioles organization (February 6, 1998). ... Granted free agency (October 15, 1998). ... Signed by Tampa Bay Devil Rays organization (November 19, 1998).

Year	Team (League)	W	L	Pct.	ERA	G	GS	CG	ShO	Sv.	IP	H	R	ER	BB	SO
1989—	GC Yankees (GCL).............	1	1	.500	3.48	2	2	0	0	0	10 1/3	5	4	4	4	13
	— Fort Lauderdale (FSL)	1	2	.333	4.73	3	3	0	0	0	13 1/3	16	8	7	7	2
1990—	Greensboro (S. Atl.)	5	12	.294	3.73	25	24	0	0	0	132 2/3	133	70	55	58	100
1991—	Fort Lauderdale (FSL)	5	8	.385	2.33	19	19	4	2	0	108	91	45	28	40	53
	— Columbus (Int'l)	0	0	.000	24.00	1	1	0	0	0	3	8	8	8	3	2
1992—	Alb./Colon. (East.)	7	5	.583	3.28	22	22	0	0	0	112 1/3	96	55	41	70	66
1993—	Columbus (Int'l)	3	1	.750	1.44	22	1	0	0	10	31 1/3	24	6	5	8	16
	— New York (A.L.)................	3	3	.500	5.32	38	0	0	0	0	45 2/3	48	27	27	26	33
1994—	Philadelphia (N.L.)■............	7	5	.583	2.67	21	14	1	0	1	104 1/3	101	40	31	35	59
	— Scran./W.B. (Int'l)	2	3	.400	2.12	6	5	0	0	0	34	27	9	8	14	24
1995—	Reading (Eastern)	0	4	.000	10.80	4	4	0	0	0	15	28	19	18	3	8
	— Scran./W.B. (Int'l)	1	0	1.000	0.56	2	2	1	1	0	16	8	2	1	3	10
	— Philadelphia (N.L.)	0	2	.000	5.74	3	3	0	0	0	15 2/3	15	13	10	9	6
1996—	Clearwater (Fla. St.)	1	1	.500	1.93	2	2	0	0	0	14	15	4	3	2	7
	— Philadelphia (N.L.)	0	3	.000	7.82	6	6	0	0	0	25 1/3	42	28	22	7	8
	— Scran./W.B. (Int'l)	4	2	.667	3.91	8	8	0	0	0	50 2/3	50	24	22	7	34
	— Reading (Eastern)	0	1	.000	2.93	4	4	0	0	0	27 2/3	24	13	9	8	29
1997—	Philadelphia (N.L.)	1	5	.167	8.91	8	7	0	0	0	33 1/3	47	35	33	15	20
	— Las Vegas (PCL)■............	0	2	.000	9.93	17	1	0	0	0	22 2/3	30	26	25	11	13
	— Albuquerque (PCL)■..........	0	3	.000	4.35	18	0	0	0	0	31	43	17	15	15	20
1998—	Rochester (Int'l)■...............	3	1	.750	1.06	44	0	0	0	19	59 1/3	40	9	7	13	46
	— Baltimore (A.L.)................	0	0	...	9.75	9	1	0	0	0	12	18	13	13	6	6
A.L. totals (2 years)		3	3	.500	6.24	47	1	0	0	0	57 2/3	66	40	40	32	39
N.L. totals (4 years)		8	15	.348	4.84	38	30	1	0	1	178 2/3	205	116	96	66	93
Major league totals (6 years)......		11	18	.379	5.18	85	31	1	0	1	236 1/3	271	156	136	98	132

MUNOZ, MIKE   P

PERSONAL: Born July 12, 1965, in Baldwin Park, Calif. ... 6-2/198. ... Throws left, bats left. ... Full name: Michael Anthony Munoz.
HIGH SCHOOL: Bishop Amat (La Puente, Calif.).
COLLEGE: Cal Poly Pomona.
TRANSACTIONS/CAREER NOTES: Selected by Los Angeles Dodgers organization in third round of free-agent draft (June 2, 1986). ... Traded by Dodgers organization to Detroit Tigers for P Mike Wilkins (September 30, 1990). ... Granted free agency (May 12, 1993). ... Signed by Colorado Springs, Colorado Rockies organization (May 14, 1993). ... On Colorado disabled list (July 27-August 15, 1996); included rehabilitation assignment to Colorado Springs (August 10-15). ... Granted free agency (October 27, 1997). ... Re-signed by Rockies (January 27, 1998). ... Granted free agency (October 26, 1998).

Year	Team (League)	W	L	Pct.	ERA	G	GS	CG	ShO	Sv.	IP	H	R	ER	BB	SO
1986—	Great Falls (Pio.)	4	4	.500	3.21	14	14	2	2	0	81 1/3	85	44	29	38	49
1987—	Bakersfield (California)	8	7	.533	3.74	52	12	2	0	9	118	125	68	49	43	80
1988—	San Antonio (Tex.)	7	2	.778	1.00	56	0	0	0	14	71 2/3	63	18	8	24	71
1989—	Albuquerque (PCL)............	6	4	.600	3.08	60	0	0	0	6	79	72	32	27	40	81
	— Los Angeles (N.L.)	0	0	...	16.88	3	0	0	0	0	2 2/3	5	5	5	2	3
1990—	Los Angeles (N.L.)	0	1	.000	3.18	8	0	0	0	0	5 2/3	6	2	2	3	2
	— Albuquerque (PCL)............	4	1	.800	4.25	49	0	0	0	6	59 1/3	65	33	28	19	40
1991—	Toledo (International)■........	2	3	.400	3.83	38	1	0	0	8	54	44	30	23	35	38
	— Detroit (A.L.)	0	0	...	9.64	6	0	0	0	0	9 1/3	14	10	10	5	3
1992—	Detroit (A.L.)	1	2	.333	3.00	65	0	0	0	2	48	44	16	16	25	23
1993—	Detroit (A.L.)	0	1	.000	6.00	8	0	0	0	0	3	4	2	2	6	1
	— Colo. Springs (PCL)■........	1	2	.333	1.67	40	0	0	0	3	37 2/3	46	10	7	9	30
	— Colorado (N.L.)	2	1	.667	4.50	21	0	0	0	0	18	21	12	9	9	16
1994—	Colorado (N.L.)	4	2	.667	3.74	57	0	0	0	1	45 2/3	37	22	19	31	32
1995—	Colorado (N.L.)	2	4	.333	7.42	64	0	0	0	2	43 2/3	54	38	36	27	37
1996—	Colorado (N.L.)	2	2	.500	6.65	54	0	0	0	0	44 2/3	55	33	33	16	45
	— Colo. Springs (PCL)	1	1	.500	2.03	10	0	0	0	3	13 1/3	8	3	3	6	13
1997—	Colorado (N.L.)	3	3	.500	4.53	64	0	0	0	2	45 2/3	52	25	23	13	26
1998—	Colorado (N.L.)	2	2	.500	5.66	40	0	0	0	0	41 1/3	53	32	26	16	24
A.L. totals (3 years)		1	3	.250	4.18	79	0	0	0	2	60 1/3	62	28	28	36	27
N.L. totals (8 years)		15	15	.500	5.57	311	0	0	0	8	247 1/3	283	169	153	117	185
Major league totals (10 years)....		16	18	.471	5.29	390	0	0	0	10	307 2/3	345	197	181	153	212

DIVISION SERIES RECORD

Year	Team (League)	W	L	Pct.	ERA	G	GS	CG	ShO	Sv.	IP	H	R	ER	BB	SO
1995—	Colorado (N.L.)	0	1	.000	13.50	4	0	0	0	0	1 1/3	4	2	2	1	1

MUNRO, PETER   P   BLUE JAYS

PERSONAL: Born June 14, 1975, in Flushing, N.Y. ... 6-2/204. ... Throws right, bats right. ... Full name: Peter Daniel Munro.
HIGH SCHOOL: Benjamin Cardozo (Bayside, N.Y.).
JUNIOR COLLEGE: Okaloosa-Walton Community College (Fla.).
TRANSACTIONS/CAREER NOTES: Signed as non-drafted free agent by Boston Red Sox organization (May 25, 1994). ... On Pawtucket disabled list (May 24-June 8, 1998). ... Traded by Red Sox with P Jay Yennaco to Toronto Blue Jays for 1B/DH Mike Stanley (July 30, 1998).

Year	Team (League)	W	L	Pct.	ERA	G	GS	CG	ShO	Sv.	IP	H	R	ER	BB	SO
1995—	Utica (N.Y.-Penn)...............	5	4	.556	2.60	14	14	0	0	0	90	79	38	26	33	74
1996—	Sarasota (Florida State)......	11	6	.647	3.60	27	25	2	•2	1	155	153	76	62	62	115
1997—	Trenton (Eastern)	7	10	.412	4.95	22	22	1	0	0	116 1/3	113	76	64	47	109
1998—	Pawtucket (Int'l)................	5	4	.556	4.05	18	17	0	0	0	106 2/3	111	49	48	35	75
	— Syracuse (Int'l)■..............	2	5	.286	7.46	8	8	0	0	0	44 2/3	58	42	37	23	42

M

MURRAY, CALVIN   OF   GIANTS

PERSONAL: Born July 30, 1971, in Dallas. ... 5-11/190. ... Bats right, throws right. ... Full name: Calvin Duane Murray.
HIGH SCHOOL: Warren Travis White (Dallas).
COLLEGE: Texas.
TRANSACTIONS/CAREER NOTES: Selected by San Francisco Giants organization in first round (seventh pick overall) of free-agent draft (June 1, 1992).
STATISTICAL NOTES: Tied for Texas League lead in double plays by outfielder with four in 1997.
MISCELLANEOUS: Member of 1992 U.S. Olympic Baseball team.

Year Team (League)	Pos.	G	AB	R	H	2B	3B	HR	RBI	Avg.	BB	SO	SB	PO	A	E	Avg.
1993—San Jose (Calif.)	OF	85	345	61	97	24	1	9	42	.281	40	63	42	203	9	2	.991
—Shreveport (Texas)	OF	37	138	15	26	6	0	0	6	.188	14	29	12	79	2	2	.976
—Phoenix (PCL)	OF	5	19	4	6	1	1	0	0	.316	2	5	1	13	0	2	.867
1994—Shreveport (Texas)	OF	480	480	67	111	19	5	2	35	.231	47	81	33	268	5	3	.989
1995—Phoenix (PCL)	OF	13	50	8	9	1	0	4	10	.180	4	6	2	19	2	0	1.000
—Shreveport (Texas)	OF	110	441	77	104	17	3	2	29	.236	59	70	26	286	9	2	.993
1996—Shreveport (Texas)	OF	50	169	32	44	7	0	7	24	.260	25	33	6	89	4	3	.969
—Phoenix (PCL)	OF	83	311	50	76	16	6	3	28	.244	43	60	12	207	3	2	.991
1997—Shreveport (Texas)	OF	122	419	83	114	25	3	10	56	.272	66	73	*52	214	9	5	.978
1998—Fresno (Pacific Coast)	OF	33	90	16	21	3	1	3	5	.233	12	18	3	27	1	0	1.000
—Shreveport (Texas)	OF	88	337	63	104	22	5	8	39	.309	58	45	34	198	3	7	.966

MURRAY, DAN   P   METS

PERSONAL: Born November 21, 1973, in Los Alamitos, Calif. ... 6-1/195. ... Throws right, bats right. ... Full name: Daniel Saffle Murray.
HIGH SCHOOL: Pacifica (Garden Grove, Calif.).
COLLEGE: San Diego State.
TRANSACTIONS/CAREER NOTES: Selected by New York Mets organization in 10th round of free-agent draft (June 1, 1995).

Year Team (League)	W	L	Pct.	ERA	G	GS	CG	ShO	Sv.	IP	H	R	ER	BB	SO
1995—Pittsfield (NYP)	0	6	.000	1.97	22	0	0	0	6	32	24	17	7	16	34
1996—St. Lucie (Fla. St.)	7	5	.583	4.25	33	13	0	0	0	101 2/3	114	60	48	53	56
1997—St. Lucie (Fla. St.)	12	10	.545	3.45	30	24	4	•2	0	156 1/3	150	75	60	55	91
1998—Binghamton (Eastern)	11	6	.647	3.18	27	27	1	1	0	164 1/3	153	64	58	54	159

MURRAY, HEATH   P   PADRES

PERSONAL: Born April 19, 1973, in Troy, Ohio. ... 6-4/205. ... Throws left, bats left. ... Full name: Heath Robertson Murray.
HIGH SCHOOL: Troy (Ohio).
COLLEGE: Michigan.
TRANSACTIONS/CAREER NOTES: Selected by San Diego Padres organization in third round of free-agent draft (June 2, 1994). ... On San Diego disabled list (June 23-July 10, 1997). ... On San Diego disabled list (September 19, 1998-remainder of season).

Year Team (League)	W	L	Pct.	ERA	G	GS	CG	ShO	Sv.	IP	H	R	ER	BB	SO
1994—Spokane (N'west)	5	6	.455	2.90	15	15	•2	•1	0	*99 1/3	101	46	32	18	78
1995—Rancho Cuca. (Cal.)	9	4	.692	3.12	14	14	4	•2	0	92 1/3	80	37	32	38	81
—Memphis (Sou.)	5	4	.556	3.38	14	14	0	0	0	77 1/3	83	36	29	42	71
1996—Memphis (Sou.)	13	9	.591	3.21	27	27	1	1	0	174	154	83	62	60	156
1997—Las Vegas (PCL)	6	8	.429	5.45	19	19	2	1	0	109	142	72	66	41	99
—San Diego (N.L.)	1	2	.333	6.75	17	3	0	0	0	33 1/3	50	25	25	21	16
1998—Las Vegas (PCL)	9	11	.450	4.99	27	27	3	0	0	162 1/3	191	103	90	62	121
Major league totals (1 year)	1	2	.333	6.75	17	3	0	0	0	33 1/3	50	25	25	21	16

MUSSINA, MIKE   P   ORIOLES

PERSONAL: Born December 8, 1968, in Williamsport, Pa. ... 6-2/185. ... Throws right, bats right. ... Full name: Michael Cole Mussina. ... Name pronounced myoo-SEEN-uh.
HIGH SCHOOL: Montoursville (Pa.).
COLLEGE: Stanford (degree in economics, 1990).
TRANSACTIONS/CAREER NOTES: Selected by Baltimore Orioles organization in 11th round of free-agent draft (June 2, 1987); did not sign. ... Selected by Orioles organization in first round (20th pick overall) of free-agent draft (June 4, 1990). ... On Rochester disabled list (May 5-12, 1991). ... On Baltimore disabled list (July 22-August 20, 1993); included rehabilitation assignment to Bowie (August 9-20). ... On disabled list (April 17-May 3 and May 15-June 6, 1998).
HONORS: Named International League Most Valuable Pitcher (1991). ... Named righthanded pitcher on THE SPORTING NEWS A.L. All-Star team (1995). ... Won A.L. Gold Glove at pitcher (1996-98).
STATISTICAL NOTES: Pitched 8-0 one-hit, complete-game victory against Texas (July 17, 1992). ... Pitched 3-0 one-hit, complete-game victory against Cleveland (May 30, 1997).

Year Team (League)	W	L	Pct.	ERA	G	GS	CG	ShO	Sv.	IP	H	R	ER	BB	SO
1990—Hagerstown (Eastern)	3	0	1.000	1.49	7	7	2	1	0	42 1/3	34	10	7	7	40
—Rochester (Int'l)	0	0	...	1.35	2	2	0	0	0	13 1/3	8	2	2	4	15
1991—Rochester (Int'l)	10	4	.714	2.87	19	19	3	1	0	122 1/3	108	42	39	31	107
—Baltimore (A.L.)	4	5	.444	2.87	12	12	2	0	0	87 2/3	77	31	28	21	52
1992—Baltimore (A.L.)	18	5	*.783	2.54	32	32	8	4	0	241	212	70	68	48	130
1993—Baltimore (A.L.)	14	6	.700	4.46	25	25	3	2	0	167 2/3	163	84	83	44	117
—Bowie (Eastern)	1	0	1.000	2.25	2	2	0	0	0	8	5	2	2	1	10

Year	Team (League)	W	L	Pct.	ERA	G	GS	CG	ShO	Sv.	IP	H	R	ER	BB	SO
1994—	Baltimore (A.L.)................	16	5	.762	3.06	24	24	3	0	0	176 1/3	163	63	60	42	99
1995—	Baltimore (A.L.)................	*19	9	.679	3.29	32	32	7	*4	0	221 2/3	187	86	81	50	158
1996—	Baltimore (A.L.)................	19	11	.633	4.81	36	*36	4	1	0	243 1/3	264	137	130	69	204
1997—	Baltimore (A.L.)................	15	8	.652	3.20	33	33	4	1	0	224 2/3	197	87	80	54	218
1998—	Baltimore (A.L.)................	13	10	.565	3.49	29	29	4	2	0	206 1/3	189	85	80	41	175
Major league totals (8 years)......		118	59	.667	3.50	223	223	35	14	0	1568 2/3	1452	643	610	369	1153

DIVISION SERIES RECORD

Year	Team (League)	W	L	Pct.	ERA	G	GS	CG	ShO	Sv.	IP	H	R	ER	BB	SO
1996—	Baltimore (A.L.)................	0	0	...	4.50	1	1	0	0	0	6	7	4	3	2	6
1997—	Baltimore (A.L.)................	2	0	1.000	1.93	2	2	0	0	0	14	7	3	3	3	16
Div. series totals (2 years)		2	0	1.000	2.70	3	3	0	0	0	20	14	7	6	5	22

CHAMPIONSHIP SERIES RECORD

Year	Team (League)	W	L	Pct.	ERA	G	GS	CG	ShO	Sv.	IP	H	R	ER	BB	SO
1996—	Baltimore (A.L.)................	0	1	.000	5.87	1	1	0	0	0	7 2/3	8	5	5	2	6
1997—	Baltimore (A.L.)................	0	0	...	0.60	2	2	0	0	0	15	4	1	1	4	25
Champ. series totals (2 years)		0	1	.000	2.38	3	3	0	0	0	22 2/3	12	6	6	6	31

ALL-STAR GAME RECORD

Year	League	W	L	Pct.	ERA	GS	CG	ShO	Sv.	IP	H	R	ER	BB	SO
1992—	American..........................	0	0	...	0.00	0	0	0	0	1	0	0	0	0	0
1993—	American..........................						Did not play.								
1994—	American..........................	0	0	...	0.00	0	0	0	0	1	1	0	0	0	1
1997—	National............................						Did not play.								
All-Star totals (2 years)		0	0	...	0.00	0	0	0	0	2	1	0	0	0	1

MYERS, GREG   C   PADRES

PERSONAL: Born April 14, 1966, in Riverside, Calif. ... 6-2/208. ... Bats left, throws right. ... Full name: Gregory Richard Myers.

HIGH SCHOOL: Riverside (Calif.) Polytechnical.

TRANSACTIONS/CAREER NOTES: Selected by Toronto Blue Jays organization in third round of free-agent draft (June 4, 1984). ... On disabled list (June 17, 1988-remainder of season). ... On Toronto disabled list (March 26-June 5, 1989); included rehabilitation assignment to Knoxville (May 17-June 5). ... On Toronto disabled list (May 5-25, 1990); included rehabilitation assignment to Syracuse (May 21-24). ... Traded by Blue Jays with OF Rob Ducey to California Angels for P Mark Eichhorn (July 30, 1992). ... On California disabled list (August 27, 1992-remainder of season). ... On California disabled list (April 24-June 21, 1994); included rehabilitation assignments to Lake Elsinore (May 20-June 6 and June 13-21). ... On disabled list (April 21-May 6, June 1-21 and September 30, 1995-remainder of season). ... Granted free agency (November 3, 1995). ... Signed by Minnesota Twins (December 8, 1995). ... On disabled list (July 14-August 2, 1996). ... On Minnesota disabled list (August 9-24, 1997). ... Traded by Twins to Atlanta Braves for a player to be named later (September 5, 1997); Twins acquired 1B Steve Hacker to complete deal (December 18, 1997). ... Granted free agency (October 28, 1997). ... Signed by San Diego Padres (November 25, 1997). ... On San Diego disabled list (June 4-July 24, 1998); included rehabilitation assignments to Rancho Cucamonga (July 17-19) and Las Vegas (July 21-23).

STATISTICAL NOTES: Led California League catchers with 967 total chances in 1986. ... Led International League catchers with 698 total chances in 1987.

M

Year	Team (League)	Pos.	G	AB	R	H	2B	3B	HR	RBI	Avg.	BB	SO	SB	PO	A	E	Avg.
1984—	Medicine Hat (Pio.)	C	38	133	20	42	9	0	2	20	.316	16	6	0	216	24	4	.984
1985—	Florence (S. Atl.)	C	134	489	52	109	19	2	5	62	.223	39	54	0	551	61	7	*.989
1986—	Ventura (Calif.)	C	124	451	65	133	23	4	20	79	.295	43	46	9	*849	99	19	.980
1987—	Syracuse (Int'l)...........	C	107	342	35	84	19	1	10	47	.246	22	46	3	*637	50	11	.984
	— Toronto (A.L.)...........	C	7	9	1	1	0	0	0	0	.111	0	3	0	24	1	0	1.000
1988—	Syracuse (Int'l)...........	C	34	120	18	34	7	1	7	21	.283	8	24	1	63	9	1	.986
1989—	Knoxville (Southern) ..	C	29	90	11	30	10	0	5	19	.333	3	16	1	130	12	1	.993
	— Toronto (A.L.)...........	C-DH	17	44	0	5	2	0	0	1	.114	2	9	0	46	6	0	1.000
	— Syracuse (Int'l).........	C	24	89	8	24	6	0	1	11	.270	4	9	0	60	7	1	.985
1990—	Toronto (A.L.).............	C	87	250	33	59	7	1	5	22	.236	22	33	0	411	30	3	.993
	— Syracuse (Int'l).........	C	3	11	0	2	1	0	0	2	.182	1	1	0	14	0	0	1.000
1991—	Toronto (A.L.).............	C	107	309	25	81	22	0	8	36	.262	21	45	0	484	37	11	.979
1992—	Toronto (A.L.).............	C	22	61	4	14	6	0	1	13	.230	5	5	0	92	13	1	.991
	— California (A.L.)■......	C-DH	8	17	0	4	1	0	0	0	.235	0	6	0	33	3	0	1.000
1993—	California (A.L.)	C-DH	108	290	27	74	10	0	7	40	.255	17	47	3	369	44	6	.986
1994—	California (A.L.)	C-DH	45	126	10	31	6	0	2	8	.246	10	27	0	194	28	2	.991
	— Lake Elsinore (Calif.) ..	C	10	32	4	8	2	0	0	5	.250	2	6	0	31	3	0	1.000
1995—	California (A.L.)	C-DH	85	273	35	71	12	2	9	38	.260	17	49	0	341	21	4	.989
1996—	Minnesota (A.L.)■	C	97	329	37	94	22	3	6	47	.286	19	52	0	488	27	8	.985
1997—	Minnesota (A.L.)	C-DH	62	165	24	44	11	1	5	28	.267	16	29	0	196	11	3	.986
	— Atlanta (N.L.)■.........	C	9	9	0	1	0	0	0	1	.111	1	3	0	11	2	0	1.000
1998—	San Diego (N.L.)■	C	69	171	19	42	10	0	4	20	.246	17	36	0	276	29	4	.987
	— Rancho Cuca. (Cal.)	C	3	9	1	0	0	0	0	0	.000	2	1	0	8	0	0	1.000
	— Las Vegas (PCL)	C	3	9	0	5	0	0	0	1	.556	0	0	0	16	1	0	1.000
American League totals (10 years)			645	1873	196	478	99	7	43	233	.255	129	305	3	2678	221	38	.987
National League totals (2 years)			78	180	19	43	10	0	4	21	.239	18	39	0	287	31	4	.988
Major league totals (11 years)			723	2053	215	521	109	7	47	254	.254	147	344	3	2965	252	42	.987

DIVISION SERIES RECORD

Year	Team (League)	Pos.	G	AB	R	H	2B	3B	HR	RBI	Avg.	BB	SO	SB	PO	A	E	Avg.
1998—	San Diego (N.L.)	C	1	0	0	0	0	0	0	0	.000	0	0	0	0	0	0	...

Year Team (League)	Pos.	G	AB	R	H	2B	3B	HR	RBI	Avg.	BB	SO	SB	PO	A	E	Avg.
								BATTING							FIELDING		
1991— Toronto (A.L.)								Did not play.									
1998— San Diego (N.L.)	PH	2	1	1	1	0	0	1	2	1.000	1	0	0	...	...	...	...

WORLD SERIES RECORD

Year Team (League)	Pos.	G	AB	R	H	2B	3B	HR	RBI	Avg.	BB	SO	SB	PO	A	E	Avg.
								BATTING							FIELDING		
1998— San Diego (N.L.)	PH-C	2	4	0	0	0	0	0	0	.000	0	2	0	4	1	0	1.000

MYERS, MIKE   P   BREWERS

PERSONAL: Born June 26, 1969, in Arlington Heights, Ill. ... 6-4/214. ... Throws left, bats left. ... Full name: Michael Stanley Myers.
HIGH SCHOOL: Crystal Lake (Ill.) Central.
COLLEGE: Iowa State.
TRANSACTIONS/CAREER NOTES: Selected by San Francisco Giants organization in fourth round of free-agent draft (June 4, 1990). ... On Clinton disabled list (June 3-September 16, 1991; April 9-June 2 and June 21-July 6, 1992). ... Selected by Florida Marlins from Giants organization in Rule 5 major league draft (December 7, 1992). ... On Edmonton disabled list (April 13-June 7, 1994). ... On Florida disabled list (June 7-August 5, 1994); included rehabilitation assignment to Brevard County (June 23-July 11). ... Traded by Marlins to Detroit Tigers (August 9, 1995), completing deal in which Marlins acquired P Buddy Groom for a player to be named later (August 7, 1995). ... Traded by Tigers with P Rick Greene and SS Santiago Perez to Milwaukee Brewers for P Bryce Florie and a player to be named later (November 20, 1997).
STATISTICAL NOTES: Led Pacific Coast League with 10 hit batsmen in 1993.

Year Team (League)	W	L	Pct.	ERA	G	GS	CG	ShO	Sv.	IP	H	R	ER	BB	SO
1990—Everett (Northwest)	4	5	.444	3.90	15	14	1	0	0	85 1/3	91	43	37	30	73
1991—Clinton (Midwest)	5	3	.625	2.62	11	11	1	0	0	65 1/3	61	23	19	18	59
1992—San Jose (California)	5	1	.833	2.30	8	8	0	0	0	54 2/3	43	20	14	17	40
—Clinton (Midwest)	1	2	.333	1.19	7	7	0	0	0	37 2/3	28	11	5	8	32
1993—Edmonton (PCL)■	7	14	.333	5.18	27	27	3	0	0	161 2/3	195	109	93	52	112
1994—Edmonton (PCL)	1	5	.167	5.55	12	11	0	0	0	60	78	42	37	21	55
—Brevard County (FSL)	0	0	...	0.79	3	2	0	0	0	11 1/3	7	1	1	4	15
1995—Charlotte (Int'l)	0	5	.000	5.65	37	0	0	0	0	36 2/3	41	25	23	15	24
—Florida (N.L.)	0	0	...	0.00	2	0	0	0	0	2	1	0	0	3	0
—Toledo (International)■	0	0	...	4.32	6	0	0	0	0	8 1/3	6	4	4	3	8
—Detroit (A.L.)	1	0	1.000	9.95	11	0	0	0	0	6 1/3	10	7	7	4	4
1996—Detroit (A.L.)	1	5	.167	5.01	•83	0	0	0	6	64 2/3	70	41	36	34	69
1997—Detroit (A.L.)	0	4	.000	5.70	*88	0	0	0	2	53 2/3	58	36	34	25	50
1998—Milwaukee (N.L.)■	2	2	.500	2.70	70	0	0	0	1	50	44	19	15	22	40
A.L. totals (3 years)	2	9	.182	5.56	182	0	0	0	8	124 2/3	138	84	77	63	123
N.L. totals (2 years)	2	2	.500	2.60	72	0	0	0	1	52	45	19	15	25	40
Major league totals (4 years)	4	11	.267	4.69	254	0	0	0	9	176 2/3	183	103	92	88	163

M

MYERS, RANDY   P   PADRES

PERSONAL: Born September 19, 1962, in Vancouver, Wash. ... 6-1/210. ... Throws left, bats left. ... Full name: Randall Kirk Myers.
HIGH SCHOOL: Evergreen (Vancouver, Wash.).
JUNIOR COLLEGE: Clark Community College (Wash.).
TRANSACTIONS/CAREER NOTES: Selected by Cincinnati Reds organization in third round of free-agent draft (January 12, 1982); did not sign. ... Selected by New York Mets organization in secondary phase of free-agent draft (June 7, 1982). ... Traded by Mets with P Kip Gross to Cincinnati Reds for P John Franco and OF Don Brown (December 6, 1989). ... Traded by Reds to San Diego Padres for OF/2B Bip Roberts and a player to be named later (December 8, 1991); Reds acquired OF Craig Pueschner to complete deal (December 9, 1991). ... Granted free agency (October 26, 1992). ... Signed by Chicago Cubs (December 9, 1992). ... Granted free agency (November 3, 1995). ... Signed by Baltimore Orioles (December 14, 1995). ... Granted free agency (October 27, 1997). ... Signed by Toronto Blue Jays (November 26, 1997). ... Traded by Blue Jays to Padres for C Brian Loyd and a player to be named later (August 6, 1998).
RECORDS: Shares N.L. single-season record for most saves—53 (1993). ... Shares N.L. single-game record for most consecutive strikeouts by relief pitcher—6 (September 8, 1990).
HONORS: Named Carolina League Pitcher of the Year (1984). ... Named N.L. Fireman of the Year by THE SPORTING NEWS (1993 and 1995).
STATISTICAL NOTES: Tied for Appalachian League lead with three balks in 1982.
MISCELLANEOUS: Had sacrifice hit in one game as pinch hitter (1992). ... Grounded into a double play in one game as pinch hitter (1993).

Year Team (League)	W	L	Pct.	ERA	G	GS	CG	ShO	Sv.	IP	H	R	ER	BB	SO
1982—Kingsport (Appalachian)	6	3	.667	4.12	13	•13	1	0	0	74 1/3	68	49	34	69	•86
1983—Columbia (S. Atl.)	14	10	.583	3.63	28	•28	3	0	0	173 1/3	146	94	70	108	164
1984—Lynchburg (Carolina)	13	5	.722	*2.06	23	22	•7	1	0	157	123	46	36	61	171
—Jackson (Texas)	2	1	.667	2.06	5	5	1	0	0	35	29	14	8	16	35
1985—Jackson (Texas)	4	8	.333	3.96	19	19	2	1	0	120 1/3	99	61	53	69	116
—Tidewater (Int'l)	1	1	.500	1.84	8	7	0	0	0	44	40	13	9	20	25
—New York (N.L.)	0	0	...	0.00	1	0	0	0	0	2	0	0	0	1	2
1986—Tidewater (Int'l)	6	7	.462	2.35	45	0	0	0	12	65	44	19	17	44	79
—New York (N.L.)	0	0	...	4.22	10	0	0	0	0	10 2/3	11	5	5	9	13
1987—New York (N.L.)	3	6	.333	3.96	54	0	0	0	6	75	61	36	33	30	92
—Tidewater (Int'l)	0	0	...	4.91	5	0	0	0	3	7 1/3	6	4	4	4	13
1988—New York (N.L.)	7	3	.700	1.72	55	0	0	0	26	68	45	15	13	17	69
1989—New York (N.L.)	7	4	.636	2.35	65	0	0	0	24	84 1/3	62	23	22	40	88
1990—Cincinnati (N.L.)■	4	6	.400	2.08	66	0	0	0	31	86 2/3	59	24	20	38	98
1991—Cincinnati (N.L.)	6	13	.316	3.55	58	12	1	0	6	132	116	61	52	80	108
1992—San Diego (N.L.)■	3	6	.333	4.29	66	0	0	0	38	79 2/3	84	38	38	34	66
1993—Chicago (N.L.)■	2	4	.333	3.11	73	0	0	0	*53	75 1/3	65	26	26	26	86
1994—Chicago (N.L.)	1	5	.167	3.79	38	0	0	0	21	40 1/3	40	18	17	16	32

Year Team (League)	W	L	Pct.	ERA	G	GS	CG	ShO	Sv.	IP	H	R	ER	BB	SO
1995— Chicago (N.L.)....................	1	2	.333	3.88	57	0	0	0	*38	55 2/3	49	25	24	28	59
1996— Baltimore (A.L.).■............	4	4	.500	3.53	62	0	0	0	31	58 2/3	60	24	23	29	74
1997— Baltimore (A.L.).................	2	3	.400	1.51	61	0	0	0	*45	59 2/3	47	12	10	22	56
1998— Toronto (A.L.).■................	3	4	.429	4.46	41	0	0	0	28	42 1/3	44	21	21	19	32
— San Diego (N.L.).■	1	3	.250	6.28	21	0	0	0	0	14 1/3	15	10	10	7	9
A.L. totals (3 years)	9	11	.450	3.02	164	0	0	0	104	160 2/3	151	57	54	70	162
N.L. totals (12 years)	35	52	.402	3.23	564	12	1	0	243	724	607	281	260	326	722
Major league totals (14 years)....	44	63	.411	3.19	728	12	1	0	347	884 2/3	758	338	314	396	884

DIVISION SERIES RECORD

RECORDS: Shares A.L. career record for most saves—3.

Year Team (League)	W	L	Pct.	ERA	G	GS	CG	ShO	Sv.	IP	H	R	ER	BB	SO
1996— Baltimore (A.L.).................	0	0	. . .	0.00	3	0	0	0	2	3	0	0	0	0	3
1997— Baltimore (A.L.).................	0	0	. . .	0.00	2	0	0	0	1	2	0	0	0	0	5
1998— San Diego (N.L.)								Did not play.							
Div. series totals (2 years)	0	0	. . .	0.00	5	0	0	0	3	5	0	0	0	0	8

CHAMPIONSHIP SERIES RECORD

RECORDS: Shares N.L. single-series record for most saves—3 (1990).

NOTES: Named N.L. Championship Series co-Most Valuable Player (1990).

Year Team (League)	W	L	Pct.	ERA	G	GS	CG	ShO	Sv.	IP	H	R	ER	BB	SO
1988— New York (N.L.).................	2	0	1.000	0.00	3	0	0	0	0	4 2/3	1	0	0	2	0
1990— Cincinnati (N.L.)...............	0	0	. . .	0.00	4	0	0	0	3	5 2/3	2	0	0	3	7
1996— Baltimore (A.L.)...............	0	1	.000	2.25	3	0	0	0	0	4	4	1	1	3	2
1997— Baltimore (A.L.)...............	0	1	.000	5.06	4	0	0	0	1	5 1/3	6	3	3	3	7
1998— San Diego (N.L.)	0	0	. . .	13.50	4	0	0	0	0	2	3	3	3	2	3
Champ. series totals (5 years)	2	2	.500	2.91	18	0	0	0	4	21 2/3	16	7	7	13	19

WORLD SERIES RECORD

NOTES: Member of World Series championship team (1990).

Year Team (League)	W	L	Pct.	ERA	G	GS	CG	ShO	Sv.	IP	H	R	ER	BB	SO
1990— Cincinnati (N.L.)	0	0	. . .	0.00	3	0	0	0	1	3	2	0	0	0	3
1998— San Diego (N.L.)	0	0	. . .	9.00	3	0	0	0	0	1	0	1	1	1	2
World Series totals (2 years)	0	0	. . .	2.25	6	0	0	0	1	4	2	1	1	1	5

ALL-STAR GAME RECORD

Year League	W	L	Pct.	ERA	GS	CG	ShO	Sv.	IP	H	R	ER	BB	SO
1990— National	0	0	. . .	0.00	0	0	0	0	1	1	0	0	2	0
1994— National	0	0	. . .	0.00	0	0	0	0	1	1	0	0	0	1
1995— National	0	0	. . .	0.00	0	0	0	1	1	0	0	0	1	0
1997— National	0	0	. . .	0.00	0	0	0	0	1	0	0	0	0	2
All-Star totals (4 years)	0	0	. . .	0.00	0	0	0	1	4	2	0	0	3	3

MYERS, ROD D.　　　　　OF　　　　　REDS　　M

PERSONAL: Born January 14, 1973, in Conroe, Texas. ... 6-1/190. ... Bats left, throws left. ... Full name: Roderick Demond Myers.

HIGH SCHOOL: Conroe (Texas).

TRANSACTIONS/CAREER NOTES: Selected by Kansas City Royals organization in 13th round of free-agent draft (June 3, 1991). ... On disabled list (March 22-July 10, 1997); included rehabilitation assignment to Wichita (July 3-10). ... On Kansas City disabled list (March 22-June 22, 1998); included rehabilitation assignment to Wichita (June 1-21). ... Released by Royals (December 14, 1998). ... Signed by Cincinnati Reds organization (December 18, 1998).

Year Team (League)	Pos.	G	AB	R	H	2B	3B	HR	RBI	Avg.	BB	SO	SB	PO	A	E	Avg.
1991— GC Royals (GCL)	OF	44	133	14	37	2	3	1	18	.278	6	27	12	45	2	1	.979
— Baseball City (FSL).....	OF	4	11	1	2	0	0	0	0	.182	0	5	1	4	0	0	1.000
1992— Appleton (Midwest)....	OF	71	218	31	48	10	2	4	30	.220	39	67	25	132	5	10	.932
1993— Rockford (Midwest) ...	OF	129	474	69	123	24	5	9	68	.259	58	117	49	208	10	7	.969
1994— Wilmington (Caro.).....	OF	126	457	76	120	20	4	12	65	.263	67	93	31	168	5	7	.961
1995— Wichita (Texas)	OF-1B	131	499	71	*153	22	6	7	62	.307	34	77	29	262	8	10	.964
1996— Omaha (A.A.).............	OF	112	411	68	120	27	1	16	54	.292	49	106	37	263	5	2	*.993
— Kansas City (A.L.)	OF	22	63	9	18	7	0	1	11	.286	7	16	3	33	0	0	1.000
1997— Wichita (Texas)	OF	4	16	3	5	2	0	0	3	.313	3	3	0	8	0	0	1.000
— Kansas City (A.L.)	OF	31	101	14	26	7	0	2	9	.257	17	22	4	55	1	1	.982
— Omaha (A.A.)	OF	38	142	21	36	10	0	2	10	.254	15	37	6	89	3	1	.989
1998— Wichita (Texas)	OF	41	143	19	32	11	0	4	21	.224	30	31	8	70	5	0	1.000
— Omaha (Pacific Coast)	OF	30	101	15	22	4	1	0	10	.218	12	25	4	67	4	1	.986
Major league totals (2 years)		53	164	23	44	14	0	3	20	.268	24	38	7	88	1	1	.989

MYERS, ROD L.　　　　　P　　　　　CUBS

PERSONAL: Born June 26, 1969, in Rockford, Ill. ... 6-1/205. ... Throws right, bats right. ... Full name: Rodney Luther Myers.

HIGH SCHOOL: Rockford (Ill.) East.

COLLEGE: Wisconsin.

TRANSACTIONS/CAREER NOTES: Selected by Kansas City Royals organization in 12th round of free-agent draft (June 4, 1990). ... On disabled list (May 17-June 3 and June 21-September 15, 1994; and June 30-July 21, 1995). ... Selected by Chicago Cubs from Royals organization in Rule 5 major league draft (December 4, 1995). ... On Iowa disabled list (June 7-15, 1998).

Year	Team (League)	W	L	Pct.	ERA	G	GS	CG	ShO	Sv.	IP	H	R	ER	BB	SO
1990—	Eugene (Northwest)	0	2	.000	1.19	6	4	0	0	0	22²/₃	19	9	3	13	17
1991—	Appleton (Midwest)	1	1	.500	2.60	9	4	0	0	0	27²/₃	22	9	8	26	29
1992—	Lethbridge (Pioneer)	5	•8	.385	4.01	15	15	*5	0	0	*103¹/₃	93	57	46	61	76
1993—	Rockford (Midwest)	7	3	.700	1.79	12	12	5	2	0	85¹/₃	65	22	17	18	65
	—Memphis (Sou.)	3	6	.333	5.62	12	12	1	1	0	65²/₃	73	46	41	32	42
1994—	Wilmington (Caro.)	1	1	.500	4.82	4	0	0	0	1	9¹/₃	9	6	5	1	9
	—Memphis (Sou.)	5	1	.833	1.03	42	0	0	0	9	69²/₃	45	20	8	29	53
1995—	Omaha (Am. Assoc.)	4	5	.444	4.10	38	0	0	0	2	48¹/₃	52	26	22	19	38
1996—	Chicago (N.L.)■	2	1	.667	4.68	45	0	0	0	0	67¹/₃	61	38	35	38	50
1997—	Iowa (Am. Assoc.)	7	8	.467	4.09	24	23	1	0	0	140²/₃	140	76	64	38	79
	—Chicago (N.L.)	0	0	...	6.00	5	1	0	0	0	9	12	6	6	7	6
1998—	Iowa (Pacific Coast)	7	5	.583	3.91	33	13	2	1	11	101¹/₃	84	47	44	45	86
	—Chicago (N.L.)	0	0	...	7.00	12	0	0	0	0	18	26	14	14	6	15
	Major league totals (3 years)	2	1	.667	5.25	62	1	0	0	0	94¹/₃	99	58	55	51	71

NAGY, CHARLES — P — INDIANS

PERSONAL: Born May 5, 1967, in Fairfield, Conn. ... 6-3/200. ... Throws right, bats left. ... Full name: Charles Harrison Nagy. ... Name pronounced NAG-ee.

HIGH SCHOOL: Roger Ludlowe (Fairfield, Conn.).

COLLEGE: Connecticut.

TRANSACTIONS/CAREER NOTES: Selected by Cleveland Indians organization in first round (17th pick overall) of free-agent draft (June 1, 1988); pick received as part of compensation for San Francisco Giants signing Type A free-agent OF Brett Butler. ... On Cleveland disabled list (May 16-October 1, 1993); included rehabilitation assignment to Canton/Akron (June 10-24).

HONORS: Named Carolina League Pitcher of the Year (1989).

STATISTICAL NOTES: Pitched 6-0 one-hit, complete-game victory against Baltimore (August 8, 1992).

MISCELLANEOUS: Member of 1988 U.S. Olympic baseball team.

Year	Team (League)	W	L	Pct.	ERA	G	GS	CG	ShO	Sv.	IP	H	R	ER	BB	SO
1989—	Kinston (Carolina)	8	4	.667	1.51	13	13	6	*4	0	95¹/₃	69	22	16	24	99
	—Cant./Akr. (Eastern)	4	5	.444	3.35	15	14	2	0	0	94	102	44	35	32	65
1990—	Cant./Akr. (Eastern)	13	8	.619	2.52	23	23	•9	0	0	175	132	62	49	39	99
	—Cleveland (A.L.)	2	4	.333	5.91	9	8	0	0	0	45²/₃	58	31	30	21	26
1991—	Cleveland (A.L.)	10	15	.400	4.13	33	33	6	1	0	211¹/₃	228	103	97	66	109
1992—	Cleveland (A.L.)	17	10	.630	2.96	33	33	10	3	0	252	245	91	83	57	169
1993—	Cleveland (A.L.)	2	6	.250	6.29	9	9	1	0	0	48²/₃	66	38	34	13	30
	—Cant./Akr. (Eastern)	0	0	...	1.13	2	2	0	0	0	8	8	1	1	2	4
1994—	Cleveland (A.L.)	10	8	.556	3.45	23	23	3	0	0	169¹/₃	175	76	65	48	108
1995—	Cleveland (A.L.)	16	6	.727	4.55	29	29	2	1	0	178	194	95	90	61	139
1996—	Cleveland (A.L.)	17	5	.773	3.41	32	32	5	0	0	222	217	89	84	61	167
1997—	Cleveland (A.L.)	15	11	.577	4.28	34	34	1	1	0	227	253	115	108	77	149
1998—	Cleveland (A.L.)	15	10	.600	5.22	33	33	2	0	0	210¹/₃	250	*139	122	66	120
	Major league totals (9 years)	104	75	.581	4.10	235	234	30	6	0	1564¹/₃	1686	777	713	470	1017

DIVISION SERIES RECORD

RECORDS: Holds career record for most bases on balls allowed—16. ... Shares major league and A.L. records for most games started—5.

Year	Team (League)	W	L	Pct.	ERA	G	GS	CG	ShO	Sv.	IP	H	R	ER	BB	SO
1995—	Cleveland (A.L.)	1	0	1.000	1.29	1	1	0	0	0	7	4	1	1	5	6
1996—	Cleveland (A.L.)	0	1	.000	7.15	2	2	0	0	0	11¹/₃	15	9	9	5	13
1997—	Cleveland (A.L.)	0	1	.000	9.82	1	1	0	0	0	3²/₃	2	5	4	6	1
1998—	Cleveland (A.L.)	1	0	1.000	1.13	1	1	0	0	0	8	4	1	1	0	3
	Div. series totals (4 years)	2	2	.500	4.50	5	5	0	0	0	30	25	16	15	16	23

CHAMPIONSHIP SERIES RECORD

RECORDS: Shares A.L. single-game record for most consecutive strikeouts—4 (October 13, 1995).

Year	Team (League)	W	L	Pct.	ERA	G	GS	CG	ShO	Sv.	IP	H	R	ER	BB	SO
1995—	Cleveland (A.L.)	0	0	...	1.13	1	1	0	0	0	8	5	2	1	0	6
1997—	Cleveland (A.L.)	0	0	...	2.77	2	2	0	0	0	13	17	4	4	5	5
1998—	Cleveland (A.L.)	0	1	.000	3.72	2	2	0	0	0	9²/₃	13	7	4	1	6
	Champ. series totals (3 years)	0	1	.000	2.64	5	5	0	0	0	30²/₃	35	13	9	6	17

WORLD SERIES RECORD

RECORDS: Shares record for most consecutive bases on balls allowed in one inning—3 (October 21, 1997, third inning).

Year	Team (League)	W	L	Pct.	ERA	G	GS	CG	ShO	Sv.	IP	H	R	ER	BB	SO
1995—	Cleveland (A.L.)	0	0	...	6.43	1	1	0	0	0	7	8	5	5	1	4
1997—	Cleveland (A.L.)	0	1	.000	6.43	2	1	0	0	0	7	8	6	5	5	5
	World Series totals (2 years)	0	1	.000	6.43	3	2	0	0	0	14	16	11	10	6	9

ALL-STAR GAME RECORD

Year	League	W	L	Pct.	ERA	GS	CG	ShO	Sv.	IP	H	R	ER	BB	SO
1992—	American	0	0	...	0.00	0	0	0	0	1	0	0	0	0	1
1996—	American	0	1	.000	13.50	1	0	0	0	2	4	3	3	0	1
	All-Star totals (2 years)	0	1	.000	9.00	1	0	0	0	3	4	3	3	0	2

NATHAN, JOE — P — GIANTS

PERSONAL: Born November 22, 1974, in Houston. ... 6-4/195. ... Throws right, bats right. ... Full name: Joseph Michael Nathan.

HIGH SCHOOL: Pine Bush (N.Y.).

COLLEGE: New York State-Stony Brook.

TRANSACTIONS/CAREER NOTES: Selected by San Francisco Giants organization in sixth round of free-agent draft (June 1, 1995).

MISCELLANEOUS: Played shortstop only (1995).

N

Year	Team (League)	W	L	Pct.	ERA	G	GS	CG	ShO	Sv.	IP	H	R	ER	BB	SO
1996—						Did not play—attended New York State-Stony Brook.										
1997—	Salem-Kaizer (Northwest) ..	2	1	.667	2.47	18	5	0	0	2	62	53	22	17	26	44
1998—	San Jose (California).........	8	6	.571	3.32	22	22	0	0	0	122	100	51	45	48	118
	— Shreveport (Texas).............	1	3	.250	8.80	4	4	0	0	0	15 $\frac{1}{3}$	20	15	15	9	10

RECORD AS POSITION PLAYER

Year	Team (League)	Pos.	G		BATTING										FIELDING		
				AB	R	H	2B	3B	HR	RBI	Avg.	BB	SO	SB	PO	A	E	Avg.
1995—	Bellingham (N'west)...	SS	56	177	23	41	7	2	3	20	.232	22	48	3	76	150	26	.897

NAULTY, DAN   P   YANKEES

PERSONAL: Born January 6, 1970, in Los Angeles. ... 6-6/224. ... Throws right, bats right. ... Full name: Daniel Donovan Naulty.
HIGH SCHOOL: Ocean View (Huntington Beach, Calif.).
JUNIOR COLLEGE: Cerritos (Calif.)
COLLEGE: Cal State Fullerton.
TRANSACTIONS/CAREER NOTES: Selected by Minnesota Twins organization in 14th round of free-agent draft (June 1, 1992). ... On disabled list (August 5-September 30, 1996). ... On Minnesota disabled list (May 26-September 1, 1997); included rehabilitation assignments to Gulf Coast Twins (July 24-26) and Salt Lake (July 28-August 31). ... On Minnesota disabled list (July 12, 1998-remainder of season). ... Traded by Twins to New York Yankees for 3B Allen Butler (November 16, 1998).

Year	Team (League)	W	L	Pct.	ERA	G	GS	CG	ShO	Sv.	IP	H	R	ER	BB	SO
1992—	Kenosha (Midwest)	0	1	.000	5.50	6	2	0	0	0	18	22	12	11	7	14
1993—	Fort Myers (Fla. St.)	0	3	.000	5.70	7	6	0	0	0	30	41	22	19	14	20
	— Fort Wayne (Midw.)...........	6	8	.429	3.26	18	18	3	2	0	116	101	45	42	48	96
1994—	Fort Myers (Fla. St.)	8	4	.667	2.95	16	15	1	0	0	88 $\frac{1}{3}$	78	35	29	32	83
	— Nashville (Southern)	0	7	.000	5.89	9	9	0	0	0	47 $\frac{1}{3}$	48	32	31	22	29
1995—	Salt Lake (PCL)	2	6	.250	5.18	42	8	0	0	4	90 $\frac{1}{3}$	92	55	52	2	76
1996—	Minnesota (A.L.)	3	2	.600	3.79	49	0	0	0	4	57	43	26	24	35	56
1997—	Minnesota (A.L.)	1	1	.500	5.87	29	0	0	0	1	30 $\frac{2}{3}$	29	20	20	10	23
	— GC Twins (GCL)................	0	0	...	2.25	2	2	0	0	0	4	2	1	1	3	3
	— Salt Lake (PCL)	0	1	.000	11.37	6	0	0	0	0	6 $\frac{1}{3}$	11	10	8	2	5
1998—	Salt Lake (PCL)	1	0	1.000	6.75	5	0	0	0	0	5 $\frac{1}{3}$	8	4	4	2	5
	— Minnesota (A.L.)	0	2	.000	4.94	19	0	0	0	0	23 $\frac{2}{3}$	25	16	13	10	15
Major league totals (3 years)......		4	5	.444	4.61	97	0	0	0	5	111 $\frac{1}{3}$	97	62	57	55	94

NAVARRO, JAIME   P   WHITE SOX

PERSONAL: Born March 27, 1968, in Bayamon, Puerto Rico. ... 6-4/230. ... Throws right, bats right. ... Son of Julio Navarro, pitcher with Los Angeles Angels (1962-64), Detroit Tigers (1964-66) and Atlanta Braves (1970).
HIGH SCHOOL: Luis Pales Matos (Bayamon, Puerto Rico).
JUNIOR COLLEGE: Miami-Dade Community College-New World Center.
TRANSACTIONS/CAREER NOTES: Selected by Baltimore Orioles organization in second round of free-agent draft (January 14, 1986); did not sign. ... Selected by Orioles organization in secondary phase of free-agent draft (June 2, 1986); did not sign. ... Selected by Milwaukee Brewers organization in third round of free-agent draft (June 2, 1987). ... Granted free agency (April 7, 1995). ... Signed by Chicago Cubs (April 9, 1995). ... Granted free agency (November 1, 1995). ... Re-signed by Cubs (December 8, 1995). ... Granted free agency (November 1, 1996). ... Signed by Chicago White Sox (December 11, 1996).
RECORDS: Shares major league record for most errors by pitcher in one inning—3 (August 18, 1996, third inning). ... Shares A.L. single-season record for most sacrifice flies allowed—17 (1993).
STATISTICAL NOTES: Led A.L. with five balks in 1990. ... Tied for A.L. lead with 14 wild pitches in 1997. ... Led A.L. with 18 wild pitches in 1998.

Year	Team (League)	W	L	Pct.	ERA	G	GS	CG	ShO	Sv.	IP	H	R	ER	BB	SO
1987—	Helena (Pioneer)	4	3	.571	3.57	13	13	3	0	0	85 $\frac{2}{3}$	87	37	34	18	95
1988—	Stockton (California)	15	5	.750	3.09	26	23	8	2	0	174 $\frac{2}{3}$	148	70	60	74	151
1989—	El Paso (Texas).................	5	2	.714	2.47	11	11	1	0	0	76 $\frac{2}{3}$	61	29	21	35	78
	— Denver (Am. Assoc.)	1	1	.500	3.60	3	3	1	0	0	20	24	8	8	7	17
	— Milwaukee (A.L.)	7	8	.467	3.12	19	17	1	0	0	109 $\frac{2}{3}$	119	47	38	32	56
1990—	Milwaukee (A.L.)	8	7	.533	4.46	32	22	3	0	1	149 $\frac{1}{3}$	176	83	74	41	75
	— Denver (Am. Assoc.)	2	3	.400	4.20	6	6	1	0	0	40 $\frac{2}{3}$	41	27	19	14	28
1991—	Milwaukee (A.L.)	15	12	.556	3.92	34	34	10	2	0	234	237	117	102	73	114
1992—	Milwaukee (A.L.)	17	11	.607	3.33	34	34	5	3	0	246	224	98	91	64	100
1993—	Milwaukee (A.L.)	11	12	.478	5.33	35	34	5	1	0	214 $\frac{1}{3}$	254	135	*127	73	114
1994—	Milwaukee (A.L.)	4	9	.308	6.62	29	10	0	0	0	89 $\frac{2}{3}$	115	71	66	35	65
1995—	Chicago (N.L.)■..............	14	6	.700	3.28	29	29	1	1	0	200 $\frac{1}{3}$	194	79	73	56	128
1996—	Chicago (N.L.)	15	12	.556	3.92	35	35	4	1	0	*236 $\frac{2}{3}$	244	116	103	72	158
1997—	Chicago (A.L.)■..............	9	14	.391	5.79	33	33	2	0	0	209 $\frac{2}{3}$	*267	*155	*135	73	142
1998—	Chicago (A.L.)	8	•16	.333	6.36	37	27	1	0	1	172 $\frac{2}{3}$	223	135	122	77	71
A.L. totals (8 years)		79	89	.470	4.77	253	211	27	6	2	1425 $\frac{1}{3}$	1615	841	755	468	737
N.L. totals (2 years)		29	18	.617	3.62	64	64	5	2	0	437	438	195	176	128	286
Major league totals (10 years)		108	107	.502	4.50	317	275	32	8	2	1862 $\frac{1}{3}$	2053	1036	931	596	1023

N

NEAGLE, DENNY   P   REDS

PERSONAL: Born September 13, 1968, in Gambrills, Md. ... 6-2/225. ... Throws left, bats left. ... Full name: Dennis Edward Neagle Jr. ... Name pronounced NAY-ghul.
HIGH SCHOOL: Arundel (Gambrills, Md.).
COLLEGE: Minnesota.

TRANSACTIONS/CAREER NOTES: Selected by Minnesota Twins organization in third round of free-agent draft (June 5, 1989). ... On Portland disabled list (April 5-23, 1991). ... On Minnesota disabled list (July 28-August 12, 1991). ... Traded by Twins with OF Midre Cummings to Pittsburgh Pirates for P John Smiley (March 17, 1992). ... Traded by Pirates to Atlanta Braves for 1B Ron Wright and a player to be named later (August 28, 1996); Pirates acquired P Jason Schmidt to complete deal (August 30, 1996). ... Traded by Braves with OF Michael Tucker and P Rob Bell to Cincinnati Reds for 2B Bret Boone and P Mike Remlinger (November 10, 1998).
HONORS: Named lefthanded pitcher on THE SPORTING NEWS N.L. All-Star team (1997).
STATISTICAL NOTES: Tied for N.L. lead with 16 sacrifice hits in 1996. ... Career major league grand slams: 1.
MISCELLANEOUS: Appeared in one game as pinch runner (1992). ... Appeared in one game as pinch runner (1995). ... Doubled and had a sacrifice hit in three appearances as pinch hitter with Pittsburgh (1996).

Year	Team (League)	W	L	Pct.	ERA	G	GS	CG	ShO	Sv.	IP	H	R	ER	BB	SO
1989—	Elizabethton (Appal.)	1	2	.333	4.50	6	3	0	0	1	22	20	11	11	8	32
—	Kenosha (Midwest)	2	1	.667	1.65	6	6	1	1	0	43 2/3	25	9	8	16	40
1990—	Visalia (California)	8	0	1.000	1.43	10	10	0	0	0	63	39	13	10	16	92
—	Orlando (South.)	12	3	.800	2.45	17	17	4	1	0	121 1/3	94	40	33	31	94
1991—	Portland (PCL)	9	4	.692	3.27	19	17	1	1	0	104 2/3	101	41	38	32	94
—	Minnesota (A.L.)	0	1	.000	4.05	7	3	0	0	0	20	28	9	9	7	14
1992—	Pittsburgh (N.L.)■	4	6	.400	4.48	55	6	0	0	2	86 1/3	81	46	43	43	77
1993—	Pittsburgh (N.L.)	3	5	.375	5.31	50	7	0	0	1	81 1/3	82	49	48	37	73
—	Buffalo (A.A.)	0	0	...	0.00	3	0	0	0	0	3 1/3	3	0	0	2	6
1994—	Pittsburgh (N.L.)	9	10	.474	5.12	24	24	2	0	0	137	135	80	78	49	122
1995—	Pittsburgh (N.L.)	13	8	.619	3.43	31	•31	5	1	0	•209 2/3	*221	91	80	45	150
1996—	Pittsburgh (N.L.)	14	6	.700	3.05	27	27	1	0	0	182 1/3	186	67	62	34	131
—	Atlanta (N.L.)■	2	3	.400	5.59	6	6	1	0	0	38 2/3	40	26	24	14	18
1997—	Atlanta (N.L.)	*20	5	.800	2.97	34	34	4	4	0	233 1/3	204	87	77	49	172
1998—	Atlanta (N.L.)	16	11	.593	3.55	32	31	5	2	0	210 1/3	196	91	83	60	165
A.L. totals (1 year)		0	1	.000	4.05	7	3	0	0	0	20	28	9	9	7	14
N.L. totals (7 years)		81	54	.600	3.78	259	166	18	7	3	1179 1/3	1145	537	495	331	908
Major league totals (8 years)		81	55	.596	3.78	266	169	18	7	3	1199 1/3	1173	546	504	338	922

DIVISION SERIES RECORD

Year	Team (League)	W	L	Pct.	ERA	G	GS	CG	ShO	Sv.	IP	H	R	ER	BB	SO
1998—	Atlanta (N.L.)							Did not play.								

CHAMPIONSHIP SERIES RECORD

Year	Team (League)	W	L	Pct.	ERA	G	GS	CG	ShO	Sv.	IP	H	R	ER	BB	SO
1992—	Pittsburgh (N.L.)	0	0	...	27.00	2	0	0	0	0	1 2/3	4	5	5	3	0
1996—	Atlanta (N.L.)	0	0	...	2.35	2	1	0	0	0	7 2/3	2	2	2	3	8
1997—	Atlanta (N.L.)	1	0	1.000	0.00	2	1	1	1	0	12	5	0	0	1	9
1998—	Atlanta (N.L.)	0	0	.000	3.52	2	1	0	0	0	7 2/3	8	3	3	2	9
Champ. series totals (4 years)		1	0	1.000	3.10	8	3	1	1	0	29	19	10	10	9	26

WORLD SERIES RECORD

Year	Team (League)	W	L	Pct.	ERA	G	GS	CG	ShO	Sv.	IP	H	R	ER	BB	SO
1996—	Atlanta (N.L.)	0	0	...	3.00	2	1	0	0	0	6	5	3	2	4	3

ALL-STAR GAME RECORD

Year	League	W	L	Pct.	ERA	GS	CG	ShO	Sv.	IP	H	R	ER	BB	SO
1995—	National	0	0	...	0.00	0	0	0	0	1	1	0	0	0	1
1997—	National						Did not play.								

NEGRETTE, RICHARD   P   INDIANS

PERSONAL: Born March 6, 1976, in Maracaibo, Venezuela. ... 6-2/175. ... Throws right, bats right. ... Full name: Richard Alexander Negrette.
TRANSACTIONS/CAREER NOTES: Signed as non-drafted free agent by Cleveland Indians organization (July 2, 1993).

Year	Team (League)	W	L	Pct.	ERA	G	GS	CG	ShO	Sv.	IP	H	R	ER	BB	SO
1994—	DSL Indians (DSL)	3	5	.375	2.87	13	12	0	0	0	75 1/3	56	40	24	32	52
1995—	Watertown (NYP)	3	3	.500	5.52	18	5	0	0	3	45 2/3	42	30	28	23	35
1996—	Kinston (Carolina)	0	1	.000	23.14	1	1	0	0	0	2 1/3	9	7	6	4	0
—	Burlington (Appalachian)	2	6	.250	5.16	14	13	0	0	0	59 1/3	57	50	34	36	52
1997—	Columbus (S. Atl.)	2	1	.667	4.46	16	0	0	0	1	36 1/3	24	23	18	16	21
—	Watertown (NYP)	2	3	.400	3.66	17	0	0	0	1	39 1/3	25	17	16	29	30
1998—	Columbus (S. Atl.)	1	3	.250	5.09	21	0	0	0	2	40 2/3	39	24	23	22	35
—	Kinston (Carolina)	3	5	.375	2.88	28	0	0	0	0	50	32	22	16	27	41

NEILL, MIKE   OF   ATHLETICS

PERSONAL: Born April 27, 1970, in Martinsville, Pa. ... 6-2/190. ... Bats left, throws left. ... Full name: Michael Robert Neill.
HIGH SCHOOL: Seaford (Del.).
COLLEGE: Villanova.
TRANSACTIONS/CAREER NOTES: Selected by Oakland Athletics organization in second round of free-agent draft (June 3, 1991); pick received as compensation for San Francisco Giants signing Type A free-agent OF Willie McGee. ... On Huntsville disabled list (April 2-29, 1993). ... On Modesto disabled list (May 20, 1993-remainder of season). ... On Tacoma disabled list (April 7-June 24, 1994). ... On Oakland disabled list (August 2-26, 1998); included rehabilitation assignment to Huntsville (August 22-26).

Year	Team (League)	Pos.	G	AB	R	H	2B	3B	HR	RBI	Avg.	BB	SO	SB	PO	A	E	Avg.
							BATTING								FIELDING			
1991—	S. Oregon (N'west)	OF	63	240	42	84	14	0	5	42	*.350	35	54	9	81	5	5	.945
1992—	Reno (California)	OF	130	473	101	159	26	7	5	76	.336	81	96	23	184	13	4	.980
—	Huntsville (Sou.)	OF	5	16	4	5	0	0	0	2	.313	2	7	1	8	0	0	1.000
1993—	Huntsville (Sou.)	OF	54	179	30	44	8	0	1	15	.246	34	45	3	70	2	2	.973
—	Modesto (California)	OF	17	62	4	12	3	0	0	4	.194	12	12	0	28	0	0	1.000

Year Team (League)	Pos.	G	AB	R	H	2B	3B	HR	RBI	Avg.	BB	SO	SB	PO	A	E	Avg.
1994— Modesto (California) ..	DH	47	165	22	48	4	1	2	18	.291	26	50	1	...	...	...	...
— Tacoma (PCL)	DH	7	22	1	5	1	0	0	2	.227	3	7	0	...	...	...	...
1995— Huntsville (Sou.)	OF	33	107	11	32	6	1	2	16	.299	12	29	1	24	0	0	1.000
— Modesto (California) ..	OF	71	257	39	71	17	1	6	36	.276	34	65	4	113	7	4	.968
1996— Modesto (California) ..	OF	114	442	101	150	20	6	19	78	.339	68	123	28	136	6	4	.973
— Edmonton (PCL)	OF	6	20	4	3	1	0	1	4	.150	2	3	0	10	0	0	1.000
1997— Huntsville (Sou.)	OF	122	486	*129	165	30	2	14	80	*.340	72	113	16	212	12	4	.982
— Edmonton (PCL)	OF	7	21	3	4	0	0	0	3	.190	7	7	1	6	0	1	.857
1998— Edmonton (PCL)	OF	99	371	72	112	18	4	10	48	.302	65	91	6	165	5	5	.971
— Oakland (A.L.)	OF	6	15	2	4	1	0	0	0	.267	2	4	0	14	0	0	1.000
— Huntsville (Sou.)	OF	12	35	1	9	5	0	0	2	.257	4	13	0	21	1	0	1.000
Major league totals (1 year)		6	15	2	4	1	0	0	0	.267	2	4	0	14	0	0	1.000

NELSON, JEFF — P — YANKEES

PERSONAL: Born November 17, 1966, in Baltimore. ... 6-8/235. ... Throws right, bats right. ... Full name: Jeffrey Allan Nelson.
HIGH SCHOOL: Catonsville (Md.).
JUNIOR COLLEGE: Catonsville (Md.) Community College.
TRANSACTIONS/CAREER NOTES: Selected by Los Angeles Dodgers organization in 22nd round of free-agent draft (June 4, 1984). ... On Great Falls disabled list (April 10-June 4, 1986). ... Selected by Calgary, Seattle Mariners organization from Dodgers organization in Rule 5 minor league draft (December 9, 1986). ... On disabled list (July 16, 1989-remainder of season). ... Traded by Mariners with 1B Tino Martinez and P Jim Mecir to New York Yankees for P Sterling Hitchcock and 3B Russ Davis (December 7, 1995). ... On suspended list (September 3-5, 1996). ... On suspended list (May 28-29, 1998). ... On New York disabled list (June 26-September 4, 1998); included rehabilitation assignment to Tampa (August 31-September 4).
MISCELLANEOUS: Appeared in one game as outfielder with no chances for Seattle (1993).

Year Team (League)	W	L	Pct.	ERA	G	GS	CG	ShO	Sv.	IP	H	R	ER	BB	SO
1984— Great Falls (Pio.)	0	0	...	54.00	1	0	0	0	0	2/3	3	4	4	3	1
— GC Dodgers (GCL)	0	0	...	1.35	9	0	0	0	0	13 1/3	6	3	2	6	7
1985— GC Dodgers (GCL)	0	5	.000	5.51	14	7	0	0	0	47 1/3	72	50	29	32	31
1986— Great Falls (Pio.)	0	0	...	13.50	3	0	0	0	0	2	5	3	3	3	1
— Bakersfield (California)	0	7	.000	6.69	24	11	0	0	0	71 1/3	79	83	53	84	37
1987— Salinas (Calif.)■	3	7	.300	5.74	17	16	1	0	0	80	80	61	51	71	43
1988— San Bernardino (Calif.)	8	9	.471	5.54	27	27	1	1	0	149 1/3	163	115	92	91	94
1989— Williamsport (Eastern)	7	5	.583	3.31	15	15	2	0	0	92 1/3	72	41	34	53	61
1990— Williamsport (Eastern)	1	4	.200	6.44	10	10	0	0	0	43 1/3	65	35	31	18	14
— Peninsula (Caro.)	2	2	.500	3.15	18	7	1	1	6	60	47	21	21	25	49
1991— Jacksonville (Southern)	4	0	1.000	1.27	21	0	0	0	12	28 1/3	23	5	4	9	34
— Calgary (PCL)	3	4	.429	3.90	28	0	0	0	21	32 1/3	39	19	14	15	26
1992— Calgary (PCL)	1	0	1.000	0.00	2	0	0	0	0	3 2/3	0	0	0	1	0
— Seattle (A.L.)	1	7	.125	3.44	66	0	0	0	6	81	71	34	31	44	46
1993— Calgary (PCL)	1	0	1.000	1.17	5	0	0	0	1	7 2/3	6	1	1	2	6
— Seattle (A.L.)	5	3	.625	4.35	71	0	0	0	1	60	57	30	29	34	61
1994— Seattle (A.L.)	0	0	...	2.76	28	0	0	0	0	42 1/3	35	18	13	20	44
— Calgary (PCL)	1	4	.200	2.84	18	0	0	0	8	25 1/3	29	9	8	7	30
1995— Seattle (A.L.)	7	3	.700	2.17	62	0	0	0	2	78 2/3	58	21	19	27	96
1996— New York (A.L.)■	4	4	.500	4.36	73	0	0	0	2	74 1/3	75	38	36	36	91
1997— New York (A.L.)	3	7	.300	2.86	77	0	0	0	2	78 2/3	53	32	25	37	81
1998— New York (A.L.)	5	3	.625	3.79	45	0	0	0	3	40 1/3	44	18	17	22	35
— Tampa (Fla. St.)	0	0	...	0.00	2	1	0	0	0	2	1	1	0	1	4
Major league totals (7 years)	25	27	.481	3.36	422	0	0	0	16	455 1/3	393	191	170	220	454

DIVISION SERIES RECORD

Year Team (League)	W	L	Pct.	ERA	G	GS	CG	ShO	Sv.	IP	H	R	ER	BB	SO
1995— Seattle (A.L.)	0	1	.000	3.18	3	0	0	0	0	5 2/3	7	2	2	3	7
1996— New York (A.L.)	1	0	1.000	0.00	2	0	0	0	0	3 2/3	2	0	0	3	5
1997— New York (A.L.)	0	0	...	0.00	4	0	0	0	0	4	4	0	0	2	0
1998— New York (A.L.)	0	0	...	0.00	2	0	0	0	0	2 2/3	2	0	0	1	2
Div. series totals (4 years)	1	1	.500	1.13	11	0	0	0	0	16	15	2	2	9	14

CHAMPIONSHIP SERIES RECORD

Year Team (League)	W	L	Pct.	ERA	G	GS	CG	ShO	Sv.	IP	H	R	ER	BB	SO
1995— Seattle (A.L.)	0	0	...	0.00	3	0	0	0	0	3	3	0	0	5	3
1996— New York (A.L.)	0	1	.000	11.57	2	0	0	0	0	2 1/3	5	3	3	0	2
1998— New York (A.L.)	0	1	.000	20.25	3	0	0	0	0	1 1/3	3	3	3	1	3
Champ. series totals (3 years)	0	2	.000	8.10	8	0	0	0	0	6 2/3	11	6	6	6	8

WORLD SERIES RECORD

NOTES: Member of World Series championship team (1996 and 1998).

Year Team (League)	W	L	Pct.	ERA	G	GS	CG	ShO	Sv.	IP	H	R	ER	BB	SO
1996— New York (A.L.)	0	0	...	0.00	3	0	0	0	0	4 1/3	1	0	0	1	5
1998— New York (A.L.)	0	0	...	0.00	3	0	0	0	0	2 1/3	2	1	0	1	4
World Series totals (2 years)	0	0	...	0.00	6	0	0	0	0	6 2/3	3	1	0	2	9

N

NEN, ROBB — P — GIANTS

PERSONAL: Born November 28, 1969, in San Pedro, Calif. ... 6-5/215. ... Throws right, bats right. ... Full name: Robert Allen Nen. ... Son of Dick Nen, first baseman with Los Angeles Dodgers (1963), Washington Senators (1965-68) and Chicago Cubs (1970).
HIGH SCHOOL: Los Alamitos (Calif.).

TRANSACTIONS/CAREER NOTES: Selected by Texas Rangers organization in 32nd round of free-agent draft (June 2, 1987). ... On Charlotte disabled list (April 6-26 and May 6-24, 1990). ... On disabled list (April 23-June 10, June 28-July 8 and July 11-September 3, 1991; and May 7-September 9, 1992). ... On Texas disabled list (June 12-July 17, 1993); included rehabilitation assignment to Oklahoma City (June 21-July 17). ... Traded by Rangers with P Kurt Miller to Florida Marlins for P Cris Carpenter (July 17, 1993). ... Traded by Marlins to San Francisco Giants for P Mike Villano, P Joe Fontenot and P Mick Pageler (November 18, 1997).

MISCELLANEOUS: Holds Florida Marlins all-time record for most games pitched (269) and most saves (108).

Year	Team (League)	W	L	Pct.	ERA	G	GS	CG	ShO	Sv.	IP	H	R	ER	BB	SO
1987—GC Rangers (GCL)		0	0	...	7.71	2	0	0	0	0	2 1/3	4	2	2	3	4
1988—Gastonia (S. Atl.)		0	5	.000	7.45	14	10	0	0	0	48 1/3	69	57	40	45	36
—Butte (Pioneer)		4	5	.444	8.75	14	13	0	0	0	48 1/3	65	55	47	45	30
1989—Gastonia (S. Atl.)		7	4	.636	2.41	24	24	1	1	0	138 1/3	96	47	37	76	146
1990—Charlotte (Fla. St.)		1	4	.200	3.69	11	11	1	0	0	53 2/3	44	28	22	36	38
—Tulsa (Texas)		0	5	.000	5.06	7	7	0	0	0	26 2/3	23	20	15	21	21
1991—Tulsa (Texas)		0	2	.000	5.79	6	6	0	0	0	28	24	21	18	20	23
1992—Tulsa (Texas)		1	1	.500	2.16	4	4	1	0	0	25	21	7	6	2	20
1993—Texas (A.L.)		1	1	.500	6.35	9	3	0	0	0	22 2/3	28	17	16	26	12
—Oklahoma City (A.A.)		0	2	.000	6.67	6	5	0	0	0	28 1/3	45	22	21	18	12
—Florida (N.L.)■		1	0	1.000	7.02	15	1	0	0	0	33 1/3	35	28	26	20	27
1994—Florida (N.L.)		5	5	.500	2.95	44	0	0	0	15	58	46	20	19	17	60
1995—Florida (N.L.)		0	7	.000	3.29	62	0	0	0	23	65 2/3	62	26	24	23	68
1996—Florida (N.L.)		5	1	.833	1.95	75	0	0	0	35	83	67	21	18	21	92
1997—Florida (N.L.)		9	3	.750	3.89	73	0	0	0	35	74	72	35	32	40	81
1998—San Francisco (N.L.)■		7	7	.500	1.52	78	0	0	0	40	88 2/3	59	21	15	25	110
A.L. totals (1 year)		1	1	.500	6.35	9	3	0	0	0	22 2/3	28	17	16	26	12
N.L. totals (6 years)		27	23	.540	3.00	347	1	0	0	148	402 2/3	341	151	134	146	438
Major league totals (6 years)		28	24	.538	3.17	356	4	0	0	148	425 1/3	369	168	150	172	450

DIVISION SERIES RECORD

Year	Team (League)	W	L	Pct.	ERA	G	GS	CG	ShO	Sv.	IP	H	R	ER	BB	SO
1997—Florida (N.L.)		1	0	1.000	0.00	2	0	0	0	0	2	1	1	0	2	2

CHAMPIONSHIP SERIES RECORD

Year	Team (League)	W	L	Pct.	ERA	G	GS	CG	ShO	Sv.	IP	H	R	ER	BB	SO
1997—Florida (N.L.)		0	0	...	0.00	2	0	0	0	2	2	0	0	0	0	0

WORLD SERIES RECORD

NOTES: Member of World Series championship team (1997).

Year	Team (League)	W	L	Pct.	ERA	G	GS	CG	ShO	Sv.	IP	H	R	ER	BB	SO
1997—Florida (N.L.)		0	0	...	7.71	4	0	0	0	2	4 2/3	8	5	4	2	7

ALL-STAR GAME RECORD

Year	League	W	L	Pct.	ERA	GS	CG	ShO	Sv.	IP	H	R	ER	BB	SO
1998—National		0	0	...	9.00	0	0	0	0	1	3	3	1	0	0

NEVIN, PHIL   C/1B   ANGELS

PERSONAL: Born January 19, 1971, in Fullerton, Calif. ... 6-2/231. ... Bats right, throws right. ... Full name: Phillip Joseph Nevin.

HIGH SCHOOL: El Dorado (Placentia, Calif.).

COLLEGE: Cal State Fullerton.

TRANSACTIONS/CAREER NOTES: Selected by Los Angeles Dodgers organization in third round of free-agent draft (June 5, 1989); did not sign. ... Selected by Houston Astros organization in first round (first pick overall) of free-agent draft (June 1, 1992). ... On Tucson disabled list (July 12-30, 1995). ... Traded by Astros to Detroit Tigers (August 15, 1995), completing deal in which Astros acquired P Mike Henneman for a player to be named later (August 10, 1995). ... On Detroit disabled list (March 21-April 16, 1997); included rehabilitation assignment to Lakeland (April 8-16). ... Traded by Tigers with C Matt Walbeck to Anaheim Angels for P Nick Skuse (November 20, 1997). ... On suspended list (June 12-15, 1998).

HONORS: Named Golden Spikes Award winner by USA Baseball (1992). ... Named third baseman on THE SPORTING NEWS college All-America team (1992). ... Named Most Outstanding Player of College World Series (1992).

STATISTICAL NOTES: Led Pacific Coast League third basemen with .891 fielding percentage in 1993. ... Led Pacific Coast League in grounding into double plays with 21 in 1994. ... Led Pacific Coast League third basemen with 31 errors and 32 double plays in 1994. ... Led A.L. catchers with 20 passed balls in 1998.

MISCELLANEOUS: Member of 1992 U.S. Olympic baseball team.

Year	Team (League)	Pos.	G	AB	R	H	2B	3B	HR	RBI	Avg.	BB	SO	SB	PO	A	E	Avg.
1993—Tucson (PCL)	3B-OF	123	448	67	128	21	3	10	93	.286	52	99	8	68	187	29	†.898
1994—Tucson (PCL)	3B-OF	118	445	67	117	20	1	12	79	.263	55	101	3	73	240	†32	.907
1995—Tucson (PCL)	3B	62	223	31	65	16	0	7	41	.291	27	39	2	39	128	14	.923
—Houston (N.L.)	3B	18	60	4	7	1	0	0	1	.117	7	13	1	10	32	3	.933
—Toledo (Int'l)■	OF	7	23	3	7	2	0	1	3	.304	1	5	0	2	0	0	1.000
—Detroit (A.L.)	OF-DH	29	96	9	21	3	1	2	12	.219	11	27	0	50	2	2	.963
1996—Jacksonville (Sou.)	C-3-O-1	98	344	77	101	18	1	24	69	.294	60	83	6	384	76	11	.977
—Detroit (A.L.)	3-O-C-DH	38	120	15	35	5	0	8	19	.292	8	39	1	45	51	5	.950
1997—Lakeland (Fla. St.)	1B-3B	3	9	3	5	1	0	1	4	.556	3	2	0	9	4	1	.929
—Toledo (Int'l)	1B-3B	5	19	1	3	0	0	1	3	.158	2	9	0	19	4	0	1.000
—Detroit (A.L.)	O-DH-3-1-C	93	251	32	59	16	1	9	35	.235	25	68	0	94	18	2	.982
1998—Anaheim (A.L.)■	C-DH-1B	75	237	27	54	8	1	8	27	.228	17	67	0	402	32	5	.989
American League totals (4 years)		235	704	83	169	32	3	27	93	.240	61	201	1	591	103	14	.980
National League totals (1 year)		18	60	4	7	1	0	0	1	.117	7	13	1	10	32	3	.933
Major league totals (4 years)		253	764	87	176	33	3	27	94	.230	68	214	2	601	135	17	.977

NEWFIELD, MARC — OF — ATHLETICS

PERSONAL: Born October 19, 1972, in Sacramento, Calif. ... 6-4/224. ... Bats right, throws right. ... Full name: Marc Alexander Newfield.
HIGH SCHOOL: Marina (Huntington Beach, Calif.).
TRANSACTIONS/CAREER NOTES: Selected by Seattle Mariners organization in first round (sixth pick overall) of free-agent draft (June 4, 1990). ... On disabled list (June 3, 1992-remainder of season). ... Traded by Mariners with P Ron Villone to San Diego Padres for P Andy Benes and a player to be named later (July 31, 1995); Mariners acquired P Greg Keagle to complete deal (September 16, 1995). ... Traded by Padres with P Bryce Florie and P Ron Villone to Milwaukee Brewers for OF Greg Vaughn and a player to be named later (July 31, 1996); Padres acquired OF Gerald Parent to complete deal (September 16, 1996). ... On Milwaukee disabled list (May 29-July 5 and July 23, 1997-remainder of season); included rehabilitation assignment to Tucson (June 25-July 3). ... Released by Brewers (December 18, 1998). ... Signed by Oakland Athletics organization (January 7, 1999).
HONORS: Named Arizona League Most Valuable Player (1990).

Year	Team (League)	Pos.	G	AB	R	H	2B	3B	HR	RBI	Avg.	BB	SO	SB	PO	A	E	Avg.
										BATTING						FIELDING		
1990— Ariz. Mariners (Ariz.)..	1B-OF	51	192	34	60	•13	2	6	38	.313	25	20	4	358	13	5	.987
1991— San Bern. (Calif.)........	OF-1B	125	440	64	132	22	3	11	68	.300	59	90	12	245	10	8	.970
— Jacksonville (Sou.).....	OF-1B	6	26	4	6	3	0	0	2	.231	0	8	0	16	0	1	.941
1992— Jacksonville (Sou.).....	OF	45	162	15	40	12	0	4	19	.247	12	34	1	17	1	0	1.000
1993— Jacksonville (Sou.).....	1B-OF	91	336	48	103	18	0	19	51	.307	33	35	1	435	21	3	.993
— Seattle (A.L.)	DH-OF	22	66	5	15	3	0	1	7	.227	2	8	0	0	0	0	...
1994— Calgary (PCL)............	OF	107	430	89	150	*44	2	19	83	.349	42	58	0	136	1	9	.938
— Seattle (A.L.)	DH-OF	12	38	3	7	1	0	1	4	.184	2	4	0	2	0	0	1.000
1995— Tacoma (PCL)	OF	53	198	30	55	11	0	5	30	.278	19	30	1	55	1	2	.966
— Seattle (A.L.)	OF	24	85	7	16	3	0	3	14	.188	3	16	0	44	0	0	1.000
— Las Vegas (PCL)■	OF-1B	20	70	10	24	5	1	3	12	.343	3	11	2	54	2	1	.982
— San Diego (N.L.)	OF	21	55	6	17	5	1	1	7	.309	2	8	0	24	1	0	1.000
1996— San Diego (N.L.)	OF-1B	84	191	27	48	11	0	5	26	.251	16	44	1	73	1	3	.961
— Milwaukee (A.L.)■....	OF	49	179	21	55	15	0	7	31	.307	11	26	0	96	3	1	.990
1997— Milwaukee (A.L.)	OF-DH	50	157	14	36	8	0	1	18	.229	14	27	0	43	0	1	.977
— Tucson (PCL)	DH	8	31	4	10	1	0	1	3	.323	4	6	0				...
1998— Milwaukee (N.L.)	OF-DH	93	186	15	44	7	0	3	25	.237	19	29	0	73	3	3	.962
American League totals (5 years)		157	525	50	129	30	0	13	74	.246	32	81	0	185	3	2	.989
National League totals (3 years)		198	432	48	109	23	1	9	58	.252	37	81	0	170	5	6	.967
Major league totals (6 years)		355	957	98	238	53	1	22	132	.249	69	162	1	355	8	8	.978

NEWMAN, AL — P — DEVIL RAYS

PERSONAL: Born October 2, 1969, in La Habra, Calif. ... 6-6/240. ... Throws left, bats left. ... Full name: Alan Spencer Newman.
HIGH SCHOOL: La Habra (Calif.).
COLLEGE: Cal State Fullerton.
TRANSACTIONS/CAREER NOTES: Selected by San Diego Padres organization in 26th round of free-agent draft (June 2, 1987); did not sign. ... Selected by Minnesota Twins organization in second round of free-agent draft (June 1, 1988). ... On disabled list (April 16-26 and August 5-September 6, 1992). ... Traded by Twins with IF Tom Houk to Cincinnati Reds for 3B Gary Scott (June 30, 1993). ... Selected by Chicago Cubs organization from Reds organization in Rule 5 minor league draft (December 13, 1993). ... Released by Cubs organization (April 1, 1994). ... Signed by Alexandria Aces of the Texas-Louisiana League (May 10, 1995). ... Sold by Alexandria to San Diego Padres organization (September 27, 1994). ... Released by Padres organization (April 1, 1995). ... Signed by Alexandria (May 1995). ... Contract sold to Chicago White Sox organization (January 14, 1997). ... Granted free agency (October 17, 1997). ... Signed by San Diego Padres organization (November 12, 1997). ... Granted free agency (October 15, 1998). ... Signed by Tampa Bay Devil Rays organization (November 19, 1998).
STATISTICAL NOTES: Led Appalachian League with 17 wild pitches in 1988.

Year	Team (League)	W	L	Pct.	ERA	G	GS	CG	ShO	Sv.	IP	H	R	ER	BB	SO
1988— Elizabethton (Appal.).........	2	•8	.200	8.13	13	12	2	0	0	55 1/3	57	62	50	56	51
1989— Kenosha (Midwest)	3	9	.250	2.84	18	18	1	0	0	88 2/3	65	41	28	74	82
1990— Kenosha (Midwest)	10	4	.714	*1.64	22	22	5	1	0	154	95	41	28	78	158
— Visalia (California)	3	1	.750	2.23	5	5	0	0	0	36 1/3	29	15	9	22	42
1991— Visalia (California)	6	5	.545	3.51	15	15	0	0	0	92 1/3	86	49	36	49	79
— Orlando (South.)	5	4	.556	2.69	11	11	2	0	0	67	53	28	20	30	53
1992— Orlando (South.)	4	8	.333	4.15	18	18	2	1	0	102	94	54	47	67	86
1993— Nashville (Southern)	1	6	.143	6.03	14	11	1	0	0	65 2/3	75	52	44	40	35
— Indianapolis (A.A.)■	1	3	.250	8.55	8	3	0	0	0	20	24	23	19	27	15
1994— Alexandria (Tex.-La.)■	9	2	.818	2.83	20	21	6	•3	0	143	127	58	45	76	128
1995— Alexandria (Tex.-La.)	10	8	.556	5.19	23	21	5	2	0	137	141	87	79	74	*129
1996— Alexandria (Tex.-La.)	6	6	.500	4.56	35	11	0	0	2	118 1/3	136	70	60	43	82
1997— Birmingham (Southern)■..	7	3	.700	2.49	44	0	0	0	10	72 1/3	55	34	20	40	64
1998— Las Vegas (PCL)■	3	5	.500	3.30	63	0	0	0	7	76 1/3	58	29	28	50	76

NEWSON, WARREN — OF

PERSONAL: Born July 3, 1964, in Newnan, Ga. ... 5-7/200. ... Bats left, throws left. ... Full name: Warren Dale Newson.
HIGH SCHOOL: Newnan (Ga.).
JUNIOR COLLEGE: Middle Georgia Junior College
COLLEGE: Georgia.
TRANSACTIONS/CAREER NOTES: Selected by San Diego Padres organization in fourth round of free-agent draft (January 14, 1986). ... Traded by Padres with IF Joey Cora and IF Kevin Garner to Chicago White Sox organization for P Adam Peterson and P Steve Rosenberg (March 31, 1991). ... On Nashville disabled list (April 29-May 22, 1993). ... Traded by White Sox to Seattle Mariners for a player to be named later (July 18, 1995); White Sox acquired P Jeff Darwin to complete deal (October 9, 1995). ... Released by Mariners (November 16, 1995). ... Signed by Texas Rangers (December 6, 1995). ... On Texas disabled list (April 2-20 and August 25, 1997-remainder of season); included rehabilitation assignment to Tulsa (April 17-20). ... Granted free agency (October 2, 1997). ... Re-signed by Rangers (December 16, 1997). ... Granted free agency (October 13, 1998).
STATISTICAL NOTES: Led Texas League with 10 intentional bases on balls received in 1989.

Year	Team (League)	Pos.	G	AB	R	H	2B	3B	HR	RBI	Avg.	BB	SO	SB	PO	A	E	Avg.
1986—	Spokane (N'west)	OF	54	159	29	37	8	1	2	31	.233	47	37	3	54	3	3	.950
1987—	Char., S.C. (S. Atl.) ...	OF	58	191	50	66	12	2	7	32	.346	52	35	13	81	4	2	.977
—Reno (California)		OF	51	165	44	51	7	2	6	28	.309	39	34	2	60	5	8	.890
1988—	Riverside (Calif.)	OF	130	438	99	130	23	•7	*22	91	.297	107	102	36	182	7	11	.945
1989—	Wichita (Texas)	OF	128	427	94	130	20	6	18	70	.304	*103	99	20	191	15	5	.976
1990—	Las Vegas (PCL)	OF	123	404	80	123	20	3	13	58	.304	83	110	13	146	4	10	.938
1991—	Vancouver (PCL)■....	OF	33	111	19	41	12	1	2	19	.369	30	26	5	53	1	0	1.000
—Chicago (A.L.)		OF-DH	71	132	20	39	5	0	4	25	.295	28	34	2	48	3	2	.962
1992—	Chicago (A.L.)	OF-DH	63	136	19	30	3	0	1	11	.221	37	38	3	67	5	0	1.000
—Vancouver (PCL)		OF	19	59	7	15	0	0	0	9	.254	16	21	3	42	1	1	.977
1993—	Nashville (A.A.)	OF	61	176	40	60	8	2	4	21	.341	38	38	5	74	7	1	.988
—Chicago (A.L.)		DH-OF	26	40	9	12	0	0	2	6	.300	9	12	0	5	0	0	1.000
1994—	Chicago (A.L.)	OF-DH	63	102	16	26	5	0	2	7	.255	14	23	1	46	1	1	.979
1995—	Chicago (A.L.)	OF-DH	51	85	19	20	0	2	3	9	.235	23	27	1	44	1	1	.978
—Seattle (A.L.)■		OF	33	72	15	21	2	0	2	6	.292	16	18	1	33	1	1	.971
1996—	Texas (A.L.)■	OF-DH	91	235	34	60	14	1	10	31	.255	37	82	3	122	5	1	.992
1997—	Texas (A.L.)	OF-DH	81	169	23	36	10	1	10	23	.213	31	53	3	93	1	5	.949
—Tulsa (Texas)		DH	2	7	1	1	0	0	1	2	.143	2	1	0	...	...	...	...
1998—	Oklahoma (PCL)	OF	111	398	75	122	21	1	21	75	.307	66	106	7	104	4	2	.982
—Texas (A.L.)		OF-DH	10	21	1	4	1	0	0	2	.190	1	5	0	6	0	0	1.000
Major league totals (8 years)			489	992	156	248	40	4	34	120	.250	196	292	14	464	17	11	.978

DIVISION SERIES RECORD

Year	Team (League)	Pos.	G	AB	R	H	2B	3B	HR	RBI	Avg.	BB	SO	SB	PO	A	E	Avg.
1995—	Seattle (A.L.)	PH	1	1	0	0	0	0	0	0	.000	0	1	0	...	...	...	...
1996—	Texas (A.L.)	PH	2	1	0	0	0	0	0	0	.000	1	0	0	...	...	...	...
Division series totals (2 years)			3	2	0	0	0	0	0	0	.000	1	1	0	...	...	...	...

CHAMPIONSHIP SERIES RECORD

Year	Team (League)	Pos.	G	AB	R	H	2B	3B	HR	RBI	Avg.	BB	SO	SB	PO	A	E	Avg.
1993—	Chicago (A.L.)	DH-PH	2	5	1	1	0	0	1	1	.200	0	1	0	...	...	...	...

NIEVES, JOSE   SS/2B   CUBS

PERSONAL: Born June 16, 1975, in Guacara, Venezuela. ... 6-1/185. ... Bats right, throws right. ... Full name: Jose Miguel Nieves (Pinto). ... Name pronounced nee-EV-es. ... Brother of Juan Nieves, outfielder, Toronto Blue Jays organization.
HIGH SCHOOL: Enrique Delgado Palacios (Carabobo, Venezuela).
TRANSACTIONS/CAREER NOTES: Signed as non-drafted free agent by Milwaukee Brewers organization (June 10, 1992). ... Released by Brewers organization (October 19, 1993). ... Signed by Chicago Cubs organization (June 30, 1994). ... On disabled list (May 29-June 12, 1997).

Year	Team (League)	Pos.	G	AB	R	H	2B	3B	HR	RBI	Avg.	BB	SO	SB	PO	A	E	Avg.
1992—	Dom. Brewers (DSL)..	IF	8	15	2	5	0	0	1	3	.333	4	4	0	9	13	5	.815
1993—	Dom. Brewers (DSL)..	IF	54	144	21	29	4	3	2	14	.201	22	25	6	43	78	19	.864
1994—	Dom. Cubs (DSL)■..	2B	37	137	21	39	6	1	4	24	.285	13	23	5	50	76	9	.933
1995—	Will. (NYP)	SS-2B	69	276	46	59	13	1	4	44	.214	21	39	11	85	193	33	.894
1996—	Rockford (Midwest) ...	SS-2B-3B	113	396	55	96	20	4	5	57	.242	33	59	17	156	318	37	.928
1997—	Daytona (Fla. St.)	SS-2B	85	331	51	91	20	1	4	42	.275	17	55	16	151	218	27	.932
1998—	West Tenn (Sou.)	SS-2B	82	314	42	91	27	5	8	39	.290	18	55	17	130	211	24	.984
—Iowa (PCL)		SS	19	75	7	19	4	0	0	4	.253	2	11	1	35	61	4	.960
—Chicago (N.L.)		SS	2	1	0	0	0	0	0	0	.000	0	0	0	0	0	0	...
Major league totals (1 year)			2	1	0	0	0	0	0	0	.000	0	0	0	0	0	0	...

NIEVES, MELVIN   OF   TWINS

PERSONAL: Born December 28, 1971, in San Juan, Puerto Rico. ... 6-2/220. ... Bats both, throws right. ... Full name: Melvin Ramos Nieves. ... Name pronounced nee-EV-es.
HIGH SCHOOL: Ivis Pales Matos (Santa Rosa, Puerto Rico).
TRANSACTIONS/CAREER NOTES: Signed as non-drafted free agent by Atlanta Braves organization (May 20, 1988). ... On disabled list (April 11-June 13, 1991). ... On Richmond disabled list (May 18-26, 1993). ... Traded by Braves with P Donnie Elliott and OF Vince Moore to San Diego Padres for 1B Fred McGriff (July 18, 1993). ... Traded by Padres with P Richie Lewis and C Raul Casanova to Detroit Tigers for P Sean Bergman, P Cade Gaspar and OF Todd Steverson (March 22, 1996). ... On disabled list (June 5-20 and August 2-19, 1996 and August 4-19, 1997). ... Traded by Tigers to Cincinnati Reds for C Paul Bako and P Donne Wall (November 11, 1997). ... On Cincinnati disabled list (March 23-May 7, and September 18, 1998-remainder of season); included rehabilitation assignment to Indianapolis (April 20-May 7). ... Released by Reds (November 5, 1998). ... Signed by Minnesota Twins organization (December 15, 1998).
RECORDS: Holds A.L. single-season record for most games with switch-hit home runs—2 (1996).
STATISTICAL NOTES: Switch-hit home runs in one game two times (July 15 and August 20, 1996). ... Career major league grand slams: 2.

Year	Team (League)	Pos.	G	AB	R	H	2B	3B	HR	RBI	Avg.	BB	SO	SB	PO	A	E	Avg.
1988—	GC Braves (GCL)	OF	56	170	16	30	6	0	1	12	.176	20	53	5	100	1	2	.981
1989—	Pulaski (Appalachian).	OF	64	231	43	64	16	3	9	46	.277	30	59	6	45	1	6	.885
1990—	Sumter (S. Atl.)	OF	126	459	60	130	24	7	9	59	.283	53	125	10	227	7	11	.955
1991—	Durham (Carolina)	OF	64	201	31	53	11	0	9	25	.264	40	53	3	75	8	5	.943
1992—	Durham (Carolina)	OF	31	106	18	32	9	1	8	32	.302	17	33	4	61	4	2	.970
—Greenville (Southern).		OF	100	350	61	99	23	5	18	76	.283	52	98	6	127	9	5	.965
—Atlanta (N.L.)		OF	12	19	0	4	1	0	0	1	.211	2	7	0	8	0	3	.727

N

Year Team (League)	Pos.	G	AB	R	H	2B	3B	HR	RBI	Avg.	BB	SO	SB	PO	A	E	Avg.
1993— Richmond (Int'l)	OF	78	273	38	76	10	3	10	36	.278	25	84	4	124	5	7	.949
— Las Vegas (PCL)■	OF	43	159	31	49	10	1	7	24	.308	18	42	2	79	4	1	.988
— San Diego (N.L.)	OF	19	47	4	9	0	0	2	3	.191	3	21	0	27	0	2	.931
1994— Las Vegas (PCL)	OF-1B	111	406	81	125	17	6	25	92	.308	58	*138	1	170	4	10	.946
— San Diego (N.L.)	OF	10	19	2	5	1	0	1	4	.263	3	10	0	11	1	0	1.000
1995— San Diego (N.L.)	OF-1B	98	234	32	48	6	1	14	38	.205	19	88	2	106	5	2	.982
1996— Detroit (A.L.)■	OF-DH	120	431	71	106	23	4	24	60	.246	44	158	1	207	9	*13	.943
1997— Detroit (A.L.)	OF-DH	116	359	46	82	18	1	20	64	.228	39	157	1	187	4	4	.979
1998— Indianapolis (Int'l)■	OF	15	53	10	15	4	0	2	13	.283	9	11	0	19	0	1	.950
— Cincinnati (N.L.)	OF-DH	83	119	8	30	4	0	2	17	.252	26	42	0	31	1	0	1.000
American League totals (2 years)		236	790	117	188	41	5	44	124	.238	83	315	2	394	13	17	.960
National League totals (5 years)		222	438	46	96	12	1	19	63	.219	53	168	2	183	7	7	.964
Major league totals (7 years)		458	1228	163	284	53	6	63	187	.231	136	483	4	577	20	24	.961

NILSSON, DAVID — 1B/OF — BREWERS

PERSONAL: Born December 14, 1969, in Brisbane, Queensland, Australia. ... 6-3/240. ... Bats left, throws right. ... Full name: David Wayne Nilsson.

HIGH SCHOOL: Kedron (Brisbane, Australia).

TRANSACTIONS/CAREER NOTES: Signed as non-drafted free agent by Milwaukee Brewers organization (February 9, 1987). ... On disabled list (April 30-May 26, 1990). ... On Denver disabled list (August 13, 1991-remainder of season). ... On Milwaukee disabled list (July 6-24, 1992); included rehabilitation assignment to Denver (July 16-24). ... On Milwaukee disabled list (March 27-April 14, 1993); included rehabilitation assignment to El Paso (April 5-14). ... On Milwaukee disabled list (May 18-June 22, 1993); included rehabilitation assignment to New Orleans (May 26-June 13). ... On Milwaukee disabled list (April 16-June 24, 1995); included rehabilitation assignments to Beloit (June 10-14), El Paso (June 14-21) and New Orleans (June 21-24). ... On Milwaukee disabled list (April 4-May 8, 1996); included rehabilitation assignment to New Orleans (May 2-8). ... On Milwaukee disabled list (March 17-May 13, 1998); included rehabilitation assignment to Beloit (May 3-6) and El Paso (May 8-13).

RECORDS: Shares major league record for most home runs in one inning—2 (May 17, 1996, sixth inning).

STATISTICAL NOTES: Career major league grand slams: 2.

Year Team (League)	Pos.	G	AB	R	H	2B	3B	HR	RBI	Avg.	BB	SO	SB	PO	A	E	Avg.
1987— Helena (Pioneer)	C	55	188	36	74	13	0	1	21	.394	5	7	0	329	28	7	.981
1988— Beloit (Midwest)	C-1B	95	332	28	74	15	2	4	41	.223	25	49	2	526	64	6	.990
1989— Stockton (California)	C-2B	125	472	59	115	16	6	5	56	.244	50	76	2	703	66	13	.983
1990— Stockton (California)	C-1B-3B	107	359	70	104	22	3	7	47	.290	43	36	6	600	86	12	.983
1991— El Paso (Texas)	C-3B	65	249	52	104	24	3	5	57	.418	27	14	4	348	46	8	.980
— Denver (A.A.)	C-1B-3B	28	95	10	22	8	0	1	14	.232	17	16	1	146	16	2	.988
1992— Denver (A.A.)	C-1B-3B	66	240	38	76	16	7	3	39	.317	23	19	10	350	51	6	.985
— Milwaukee (A.L.)	C-1B-DH	51	164	15	38	8	0	4	25	.232	17	18	2	231	16	2	.992
1993— El Paso (Texas)	C	5	17	5	8	1	0	1	7	.471	2	4	1	31	9	0	1.000
— Milwaukee (A.L.)	C-DH-1B	100	296	35	76	10	2	7	40	.257	37	36	3	457	33	9	.982
— New Orleans (A.A.)	C	17	61	9	21	6	0	1	9	.344	5	6	0	55	7	1	.984
1994— Milwaukee (A.L.)	C-DH-1B	109	397	51	109	28	3	12	69	.275	34	61	1	315	15	2	.994
1995— Beloit (Midwest)	DH	3	11	2	6	3	0	1	7	.545	2	0	0	...	...	...	...
— El Paso (Texas)	OF	5	15	1	7	1	0	1	4	.467	0	1	1	4	0	0	1.000
— New Orleans (A.A.)	OF	3	9	1	4	0	0	1	4	.444	2	0	0	2	0	0	1.000
— Milwaukee (A.L.)	O-DH-1-C	81	263	41	73	12	1	12	53	.278	24	41	2	117	7	2	.984
1996— New Orleans (A.A.)	1B	7	26	3	7	1	0	1	2	.269	4	3	0	25	3	0	1.000
— Milwaukee (A.L.)	O-DH-1-C	123	453	81	150	33	2	17	84	.331	57	68	2	252	19	7	.975
1997— Milwaukee (A.L.)	1B-DH-OF	156	554	71	154	33	0	20	81	.278	65	88	2	641	39	6	.991
1998— Beloit (Midwest)	1B	4	12	3	5	3	0	1	7	.417	2	0	0	23	1	0	1.000
— El Paso (Texas)	1B	5	17	4	5	3	0	0	5	.294	2	0	1	32	7	1	.975
— Milwaukee (N.L.)	1B-OF-C	102	309	39	83	14	1	12	56	.269	33	48	2	436	24	9	.981
American League totals (6 years)		620	2127	294	600	124	8	72	352	.282	234	312	12	2013	129	28	.987
National League totals (1 year)		102	309	39	83	14	1	12	56	.269	33	48	2	436	24	9	.981
Major league totals (7 years)		722	2436	333	683	138	9	84	408	.280	267	360	14	2449	153	37	.986

NITKOWSKI, C.J. — P — TIGERS

PERSONAL: Born March 9, 1973, in Suffern, N.Y. ... 6-3/205. ... Throws left, bats left. ... Full name: Christopher John Nitkowski.

HIGH SCHOOL: Don Bosco (N.J.).

COLLEGE: St. John's.

TRANSACTIONS/CAREER NOTES: Selected by Cincinnati Reds organization in first round (ninth pick overall) of free-agent draft (June 2, 1994). ... Traded by Reds with P David Tuttle and a player to be named later to Detroit Tigers for P David Wells (July 31, 1995); Tigers acquired IF Mark Lewis to complete deal (November 16, 1995). ... On Detroit disabled list (August 11-29, 1996). ... Traded by Tigers with C Brad Ausmus, P Jose Lima, P Trever Miller and IF Daryle Ward to Houston Astros for OF Brian Hunter, IF Orlando Miller, P Doug Brocail, P Todd Jones and cash (December 10, 1996). ... Traded by Astros with C Brad Ausmus to Tigers for C Paul Bako, P Brian Powell, 3B Carlos Villalobos, P Dean Crow and P Mark Persails (January 14, 1999).

RECORDS: Shares major league record for most hit batsmen in one inning—3 (August 3, 1998, eighth inning).

Year Team (League)	W	L	Pct.	ERA	G	GS	CG	ShO	Sv.	IP	H	R	ER	BB	SO
1994— Chattanooga (Southern)	6	3	.667	3.50	14	14	0	0	0	74 2/3	61	30	29	40	60
1995— Chattanooga (Southern)	4	2	.667	2.50	8	8	0	0	0	50 1/3	39	20	14	20	52
— Indianapolis (A.A.)	0	2	.000	5.20	6	6	0	0	0	27 2/3	28	16	16	10	21
— Cincinnati (N.L.)	1	3	.250	6.12	9	7	0	0	0	32 1/3	41	25	22	15	18
— Detroit (A.L.)■	1	4	.200	7.09	11	11	0	0	0	39 1/3	53	32	31	20	13
1996— Toledo (International)	4	6	.400	4.46	19	19	1	0	0	111	104	60	55	53	103
— Detroit (A.L.)	2	3	.400	8.08	11	8	0	0	0	45 2/3	62	44	41	38	36
1997— New Orleans (A.A.)■	8	10	.444	3.98	28	28	1	0	0	174 1/3	183	82	77	56	*141

Year Team (League)	W	L	Pct.	ERA	G	GS	CG	ShO	Sv.	IP	H	R	ER	BB	SO
1998— Houston (N.L.)	3	3	.500	3.77	43	0	0	0	3	59²/₃	49	27	25	23	44
— New Orleans (PCL)	0	1	.000	6.00	5	3	0	0	1	15	22	12	10	7	18
A.L. totals (2 years)	3	7	.300	7.62	22	19	0	0	0	85	115	76	72	58	49
N.L. totals (2 years)	4	6	.400	4.60	52	7	0	0	3	92	90	52	47	38	62
Major league totals (3 years)	7	13	.350	6.05	74	26	0	0	3	177	205	128	119	96	111

NIXON, OTIS   OF   BRAVES

PERSONAL: Born January 9, 1959, in Evergreen, N.C. ... 6-2/180. ... Bats both, throws right. ... Full name: Otis Junior Nixon. ... Brother of Donell Nixon, outfielder with Seattle Mariners (1987), San Francisco Giants (1988-89) and Baltimore Orioles (1990).

HIGH SCHOOL: Columbus (N.C.).

JUNIOR COLLEGE: Louisburg (N.C.) College.

TRANSACTIONS/CAREER NOTES: Selected by Cincinnati Reds organization in 21st round of free-agent draft (June 6, 1978); did not sign. ... Selected by California Angels organization in secondary phase of free-agent draft (January 9, 1979); did not sign. ... Selected by New York Yankees organization in secondary phase of free-agent draft (June 5, 1979). ... Traded by Yankees with P George Frazier and a player to be named later to Cleveland Indians for 3B Toby Harrah and a player to be named later (February 5, 1984); Yankees organization acquired P Rick Browne and Indians organization acquired P Guy Elston to complete deal (February 8, 1984). ... Granted free agency (October 15, 1987). ... Signed by Indianapolis, Montreal Expos organization (March 5, 1988). ... Traded by Expos with 3B Boi Rodriguez to Atlanta Braves for C Jimmy Kremers and a player to be named later (April 1, 1991); Sumter, Expos organization, acquired P Keith Morrison to complete deal (June 3, 1991). ... On suspended list (August 13-16, 1991). ... On disqualified list (September 16, 1991-April 24, 1992). ... Granted free agency (November 11, 1991). ... Re-signed by Braves (December 12, 1991). ... Granted free agency (October 25, 1993). ... Signed by Boston Red Sox (December 7, 1993). ... Traded by Red Sox with 3B Luis Ortiz to Texas Rangers for DH/OF Jose Canseco (December 9, 1994). ... Granted free agency (November 3, 1995). ... Signed by Toronto Blue Jays (December 7, 1995). ... On disabled list (June 11-26, 1996). ... Traded by Blue Jays to Los Angeles Dodgers for C Bobby Cripps (August 12, 1997). ... Granted free agency (October 27, 1997). ... Signed by Minnesota Twins (December 11, 1997). ... On disabled list (April 29-May 30, 1998). ... Granted free agency (October 27, 1998). ... Signed by Braves (December 1, 1998).

RECORDS: Shares modern major league single-game record for most stolen bases—6 (June 16, 1991).

STATISTICAL NOTES: Led Appalachian League third basemen with .945 fielding percentage, 52 putouts, 120 assists, 182 total chances and 12 double plays in 1979. ... Led International League in caught stealing with 29 in 1983. ... Led International League outfielders with .992 fielding percentage, 363 putouts and 371 total chances in 1983. ... Had 20-game hitting streak (July 11-31, 1991). ... Led A.L. in caught stealing with 21 in 1995.

Year Team (League)	Pos.	G	AB	R	H	2B	3B	HR	RBI	Avg.	BB	SO	SB	PO	A	E	Avg.
1979— Paintsville (Appal.)	3B-SS	63	203	58	58	10	3	1	25	.286	*57	40	5	†54	†122	11	†.941
1980— Greensboro (S. Atl.)	3B-SS	136	493	*124	137	12	5	3	48	.278	*113	88	*67	164	308	36	.929
1981— Nashville (Southern)	SS	127	407	89	102	9	2	0	20	.251	*110	101	71	198	348	*56	.907
1982— Nashville (Southern)	SS-2B	72	283	47	80	3	2	0	20	.283	59	56	61	126	211	23	.936
— Columbus (Int'l)	2B-SS	59	207	43	58	4	0	0	14	.280	49	41	46	104	169	14	.951
1983— Columbus (Int'l)	OF-2B	138	*557	*129	*162	11	6	0	41	.291	96	83	*94	†385	24	4	†.990
— New York (A.L.)	OF	13	14	2	2	0	0	0	0	.143	1	5	2	14	1	1	.938
1984— Cleveland (A.L.)■	OF	49	91	16	14	0	0	0	1	.154	8	11	12	81	3	0	1.000
— Maine (Int'l)	OF	72	253	42	70	5	1	0	22	.277	44	45	39	206	7	1	.995
1985— Cleveland (A.L.)	OF-DH	104	162	34	38	4	0	3	9	.235	8	27	20	129	5	4	.971
1986— Cleveland (A.L.)	OF-DH	105	95	33	25	4	1	0	8	.263	13	12	23	90	3	3	.969
1987— Cleveland (A.L.)	OF-DH	19	17	2	1	0	0	0	1	.059	3	4	2	21	0	0	1.000
— Buffalo (A.A.)	OF	59	249	51	71	13	4	2	23	.285	34	30	36	170	3	3	.983
1988— Indianapolis (A.A.)■	OF	67	235	52	67	6	3	0	19	.285	43	28	40	130	1	1	.992
— Montreal (N.L.)	OF	90	271	47	66	8	2	0	15	.244	28	42	46	176	2	1	.994
1989— Montreal (N.L.)	OF	126	258	41	56	7	2	0	21	.217	33	36	37	160	2	2	.988
1990— Montreal (N.L.)	OF-SS	119	231	46	58	6	2	1	20	.251	28	33	50	149	6	1	.994
1991— Atlanta (N.L.)■	OF	124	401	81	119	10	1	0	26	.297	47	40	72	218	6	3	.987
1992— Atlanta (N.L.)	OF	120	456	79	134	14	2	2	22	.294	39	54	41	333	6	3	.991
1993— Atlanta (N.L.)	OF	134	461	77	124	12	3	1	24	.269	61	63	47	308	4	3	.990
1994— Boston (A.L.)■	OF	103	398	60	109	15	1	0	25	.274	55	65	42	254	4	3	.989
1995— Texas (A.L.)■	OF	139	589	87	174	21	2	0	45	.295	58	85	50	357	4	4	.989
1996— Toronto (A.L.)■	OF	125	496	87	142	15	1	1	29	.286	71	68	54	342	5	2	.994
1997— Toronto (A.L.)	OF-DH	103	401	54	105	12	1	1	26	.262	52	54	47	254	1	1	.996
— Los Angeles (N.L.)■	OF	42	175	30	48	6	2	1	18	.274	13	24	12	97	1	1	.990
1998— Minnesota (A.L.)■	OF	110	448	71	133	6	6	1	20	.297	44	56	37	278	4	3	.989
American League totals (10 years)		870	2711	446	743	77	12	6	164	.274	313	387	289	1820	30	21	.989
National League totals (7 years)		755	2253	401	605	63	14	5	146	.269	249	292	305	1441	27	14	.991
Major league totals (16 years)		1625	4964	847	1348	140	26	11	310	.272	562	679	594	3261	57	35	.990

CHAMPIONSHIP SERIES RECORD

RECORDS: Shares N.L. single-game record for most hits—4 (October 10, 1992).

Year Team (League)	Pos.	G	AB	R	H	2B	3B	HR	RBI	Avg.	BB	SO	SB	PO	A	E	Avg.
1992— Atlanta (N.L.)	OF	7	28	5	8	2	0	0	2	.286	4	4	3	16	0	0	1.000
1993— Atlanta (N.L.)	OF	6	23	3	8	2	0	0	4	.348	5	6	0	13	0	0	1.000
Championship series totals (2 years)		13	51	8	16	4	0	0	6	.314	9	10	3	29	0	0	1.000

WORLD SERIES RECORD

Year Team (League)	Pos.	G	AB	R	H	2B	3B	HR	RBI	Avg.	BB	SO	SB	PO	A	E	Avg.
1992— Atlanta (N.L.)	OF	6	27	3	8	1	0	0	1	.296	1	3	5	18	0	0	1.000

NIXON, TROT — OF — RED SOX

PERSONAL: Born April 11, 1974, in Durham, N.C. ... 6-2/196. ... Bats left, throws left. ... Full name: Christopher Trotman Nixon.
HIGH SCHOOL: New Hanover (Wilmington, N.C.).
TRANSACTIONS/CAREER NOTES: Selected by Boston Red Sox organization in first round (seventh pick overall) of free-agent draft (June 3, 1993). ... On disabled list (July 12, 1994-remainder of season).
STATISTICAL NOTES: Tied for Eastern League lead with four double plays by outfielders in 1996. ... Tied for International League lead with 11 errors and three double plays by outfielder in 1998.

							BATTING								FIELDING		
Year Team (League)	Pos.	G	AB	R	H	2B	3B	HR	RBI	Avg.	BB	SO	SB	PO	A	E	Avg.
1994— Lynchburg (Caro.)	OF	71	264	33	65	12	0	12	43	.246	44	53	10	143	8	4	.974
1995— Sarasota (Fla. St.)	OF	73	264	43	80	11	4	5	39	.303	45	46	7	140	4	2	.986
— Trenton (Eastern)	OF	25	94	9	15	3	1	2	8	.160	7	20	2	66	2	0	1.000
1996— Trenton (Eastern)	OF	123	438	55	110	11	4	11	63	.251	50	65	7	224	*14	5	.979
— Boston (A.L.)	OF	2	4	2	2	1	0	0	0	.500	0	1	1	3	0	0	1.000
1997— Pawtucket (Int'l)	OF	130	475	80	116	18	3	20	61	.244	63	86	11	268	10	4	.986
1998— Pawtucket (Int'l)	OF-1B	135	509	97	158	26	4	23	74	.310	76	81	26	231	11	‡11	.957
— Boston (A.L.)	OF-DH	13	27	3	7	1	0	0	0	.259	1	3	0	16	0	0	1.000
Major league totals (2 years)		15	31	5	9	2	0	0	0	.290	1	4	1	19	0	0	1.000

DIVISION SERIES RECORD

							BATTING								FIELDING		
Year Team (League)	Pos.	G	AB	R	H	2B	3B	HR	RBI	Avg.	BB	SO	SB	PO	A	E	Avg.
1998— Boston (A.L.)	OF	2	3	0	1	0	0	0	0	.333	1	0	0	3	0	0	1.000

NOMO, HIDEO — P — METS

PERSONAL: Born August 31, 1968, in Osaka, Japan. ... 6-2/230. ... Throws right, bats right.
HIGH SCHOOL: Seijyo Kogyo (Japan).
TRANSACTIONS/CAREER NOTES: Selected by Kintetsu Buffaloes in first round of 1989 Japanese free-agent draft. ... Signed as free agent by Los Angeles Dodgers organization (February 8, 1995). ... On Albuquerque temporarily inactive list (April 3-27, 1995). ... Traded by Dodgers with P Brad Clontz to New York Mets for P Dave Mlicki and P Greg McMichael (June 4, 1998).
HONORS: Named N.L. Rookie Pitcher of the Year by THE SPORTING NEWS (1995). ... Named N.L. Rookie of the Year by Baseball Writers' Association of America (1995).
STATISTICAL NOTES: Struck out 16 batters in one game (June 14, 1995). ... Pitched 3-0 one-hit, complete-game victory against San Francisco (August 5, 1995). ... Led N.L. with 19 wild pitches and five balks in 1995. ... Led N.L. with five balks in 1995 and four in 1997. ... Struck out 17 batters in one game (April 13, 1996). ... Pitched 9-0 no-hit victory against Colorado (September 17, 1996).
MISCELLANEOUS: Member of 1988 Japanese Olympic baseball team.

Year Team (League)	W	L	Pct.	ERA	G	GS	CG	ShO	Sv.	IP	H	R	ER	BB	SO
1990— Kintetsu (Jap. Pac.)	*18	8	.692	*2.91	29	27	21	2	0	235	167	...	76	*109	*287
1991— Kintetsu (Jap. Pac.)	*17	11	.607	3.05	31	29	22	*4	1	242 1/3	183	...	82	*128	*287
1992— Kintetsu (Jap. Pac.)	*18	8	.692	2.66	30	29	17	*5	0	216 2/3	150	...	64	*117	*228
1993— Kintetsu (Jap. Pac.)	*17	12	.586	3.70	32	32	14	2	0	243 1/3	*201	...	100	*148	*276
1994— Kintetsu (Jap. Pac.)	8	7	.533	3.63	17	17	6	2	0	114	...	...	46	86	126
1995— Bakersfield (California)■......	0	1	.000	3.38	1	1	0	0	0	5 1/3	6	2	2	1	6
— Los Angeles (N.L.)	13	6	.684	2.54	28	28	4	•3	0	191 1/3	124	63	54	78	*236
1996— Los Angeles (N.L.)	16	11	.593	3.19	33	33	3	2	0	228 1/3	180	93	81	85	234
1997— Los Angeles (N.L.)	14	12	.538	4.25	33	33	1	0	0	207 1/3	193	104	98	92	233
1998— Los Angeles (N.L.)	2	7	.222	5.05	12	12	2	0	0	67 2/3	57	39	38	38	73
— New York (N.L.)■	4	5	.444	4.82	17	16	1	0	0	89 2/3	73	49	48	56	94
Major league totals (4 years)	49	41	.544	3.66	123	122	11	5	0	784 1/3	627	348	319	349	870

DIVISION SERIES RECORD

RECORDS: Shares N.L. career record for most earned runs allowed—10.

Year Team (League)	W	L	Pct.	ERA	G	GS	CG	ShO	Sv.	IP	H	R	ER	BB	SO
1995— Los Angeles (N.L.)	0	1	.000	9.00	1	1	0	0	0	5	7	5	5	2	6
1996— Los Angeles (N.L.)	0	1	.000	12.27	1	1	0	0	0	3 2/3	5	5	5	5	3
Div. series totals (2 years)	0	2	.000	10.38	2	2	0	0	0	8 2/3	12	10	10	7	9

ALL-STAR GAME RECORD

Year League	W	L	Pct.	ERA	GS	CG	ShO	Sv.	IP	H	R	ER	BB	SO
1995— National	0	0	. . .	0.00	1	0	0	0	2	1	0	0	0	3

NORTON, GREG — IF — WHITE SOX

PERSONAL: Born July 6, 1972, in San Leandro, Calif. ... 6-1/190. ... Bats both, throws right. ... Full name: Gregory Blakemoor Norton.
HIGH SCHOOL: Bishop O'Dowd (Oakland).
COLLEGE: Oklahoma.
TRANSACTIONS/CAREER NOTES: Selected by San Francisco Giants organization in seventh round of free-agent draft (June 4, 1990); did not sign. ... Selected by Chicago White Sox organization in second round of free-agent draft (June 3, 1993).
STATISTICAL NOTES: Led Midwest League third basemen with 387 total chances in 1994. ... Led American Association with .534 slugging percentage in 1997. ... Led American Association third basemen with 29 errors in 1997.

							BATTING								FIELDING		
Year Team (League)	Pos.	G	AB	R	H	2B	3B	HR	RBI	Avg.	BB	SO	SB	PO	A	E	Avg.
1993— GC Whi. Sox (GCL)	3B	3	9	1	2	0	0	0	2	.222	1	1	0	1	7	0	1.000
— Hickory (S. Atl.)	3B-SS	71	254	36	62	12	2	4	36	.244	41	44	0	57	161	17	.928
1994— South Bend (Mid.)	3B	127	477	73	137	22	2	6	64	.287	62	71	5	92	*265	30	.922
1995— Birmingham (Sou.)	3B	133	469	65	162	23	2	6	60	.345	64	90	19	102	277	25	*.938

Year	Team (League)	Pos.	G	AB	R	H	2B	3B	HR	RBI	Avg.	BB	SO	SB	PO	A	E	Avg.
								BATTING								FIELDING		
1996—	Birmingham (Sou.).....	SS	76	287	40	81	14	3	8	44	.282	33	55	5	104	214	17	.949
	—Nashville (A.A.)	SS-3B	43	164	28	47	14	2	7	26	.287	17	42	2	43	95	13	.914
	—Chicago (A.L.)	SS-3B-DH	11	23	4	5	0	0	2	3	.217	4	6	0	8	5	2	.867
1997—	Nashville (A.A.)	3B-SS-2B	114	414	82	114	27	1	26	76	.275	57	101	3	83	247	†38	.897
	—Chicago (A.L.)	3B-DH	18	34	5	9	2	2	0	1	.265	2	8	0	4	15	3	.864
1998—	Chicago (A.L.)	1-3-DH-2	105	299	38	71	17	2	9	36	.237	26	77	3	654	42	6	.991
Major league totals (3 years)			134	356	47	85	19	4	11	40	.239	32	91	3	666	62	11	.985

NORTON, PHILLIP   P   CUBS

PERSONAL: Born February 1, 1976, in Texarkana, Texas. ... 6-1/185. ... Throws left, bats both. ... Full name: Phillip Douglas Norton.
HIGH SCHOOL: Pleasant Grove (Texarkana, Texas).
JUNIOR COLLEGE: Texarkana (Texas) College.
TRANSACTIONS/CAREER NOTES: Selected by Chicago Cubs organization in 10th round of free-agent draft (June 4, 1996).

Year	Team (League)	W	L	Pct.	ERA	G	GS	CG	ShO	Sv.	IP	H	R	ER	BB	SO
1996—	GC Cubs (GCL).................	0	0	...	0.00	1	0	0	0	0	3	1	0	0	0	6
	—Williamsport (NYP)	7	4	.636	2.54	15	13	2	1	0	85	68	33	24	33	77
1997—	Rockford (Midwest)	9	3	.750	3.22	18	18	3	0	0	109	92	51	39	44	114
	—Daytona (Fla. St.)	3	2	.600	2.34	7	6	3	0	0	42 1/3	40	11	11	12	44
	—Orlando (South.)	1	0	1.000	2.57	2	1	0	0	0	7	8	2	2	2	7
1998—	Daytona (Fla. St.)	4	3	.571	3.27	10	10	0	0	0	66	57	30	24	26	54
	—West Tenn (Southern)	6	6	.500	3.52	19	19	1	1	0	120 1/3	118	60	47	50	119

NUNEZ, ABRAHAM   SS   PIRATES

PERSONAL: Born March 16, 1976, in Santo Domingo, Dominican Republic. ... 5-11/175. ... Bats both, throws right. ... Full name: Abraham Orlando Nunez Adames.
HIGH SCHOOL: Emmanuel (Santo Domingo, Dominican Republic)
TRANSACTIONS/CAREER NOTES: Signed as non-drafted free agent by Toronto Blue Jays organization (May 5, 1994). ... Traded by Blue Jays with P Mike Halperin and C/OF Craig Wilson to Pittsburgh Pirates (December 11, 1996), completing deal in which Blue Jays traded P Jose Silva, P Jose Pett, IF Brandon Cromer and three players to be named later to Pirates for OF/1B Orlando Merced, IF Carlos Garcia, and P Dan Plesac (November 14, 1996).
STATISTICAL NOTES: Tied for New York-Pennsylvania League lead in caught stealing with 14 in 1996. ... Led New York-Pennsylvania League shortstops in fielding with .953 in 1996.

Year	Team (League)	Pos.	G	AB	R	H	2B	3B	HR	RBI	Avg.	BB	SO	SB	PO	A	E	Avg.
								BATTING								FIELDING		
1994—	Dom. B. Jays (DSL) ...	2B	59	188	31	47	5	0	0	15	.250	42	37	22	155	27	12	.938
1995—	Dom. B. Jays (DSL) ...	2B	54	186	49	56	10	3	4	25	.301	30	27	24	80	97	7	.962
1996—	St. Catharines (NYP) ..	SS-2B	75	*297	43	83	6	4	3	26	.279	31	43	37	136	239	15	•.962
1997—	Lynchburg (Caro.)■...	SS	78	304	45	79	9	4	3	32	.260	23	67	29	100	219	15	.955
	—Carolina (Southern)....	SS	47	198	31	65	6	1	1	14	.328	20	28	10	76	129	11	.949
	—Pittsburgh (N.L.)	SS-2B	19	40	3	9	2	2	0	6	.225	3	10	1	14	37	0	1.000
1998—	Nashville (PCL)	SS	94	366	50	91	12	3	3	32	.249	39	73	16	155	274	21	.953
	—Lynchburg (Caro.)	SS-2B	5	18	2	4	1	0	0	2	.222	3	1	1	6	18	1	.960
	—Pittsburgh (N.L.)	SS	24	52	6	10	2	0	1	2	.192	12	14	4	33	60	7	.930
Major league totals (2 years)			43	92	9	19	4	2	1	8	.207	15	24	5	47	97	7	.954

NUNEZ, VLADIMIR   P   DIAMONDBACKS

PERSONAL: Born March 15, 1975, in Havana, Cuba. ... 6-4/235. ... Throws right, bats right.
TRANSACTIONS/CAREER NOTES: Signed as non-drafted free agent by Arizona Diamondbacks organization (February 1, 1996). ... On Tucson disabled list (April 7-24, 1998).
STATISTICAL NOTES: Led California League with 36 home runs allowed in 1997.

Year	Team (League)	W	L	Pct.	ERA	G	GS	CG	ShO	Sv.	IP	H	R	ER	BB	SO
1996—	Visalia (California)	1	6	.143	5.43	12	10	0	0	0	53	64	45	32	17	37
	—Lethbridge (Pioneer).............	*10	0	*1.000	*2.22	14	13	0	0	0	85	78	25	21	10	*93
1997—	High Desert (Calif.).............	8	5	.615	5.17	28	28	1	1	0	158 1/3	169	102	91	40	142
1998—	Tucson (PCL)	4	4	.500	4.91	31	13	1	0	2	95 1/3	103	58	52	37	78
	—Arizona (N.L.)	0	0	...	10.13	4	0	0	0	0	5 1/3	7	6	6	2	2
Major league totals (1 year)........		0	0	...	10.13	4	0	0	0	0	5 1/3	7	6	6	2	2

NUNNALLY, JON   OF   REDS

PERSONAL: Born November 9, 1971, in Danville, Va. ... 5-10/190. ... Bats left, throws right. ... Full name: Jonathan Keith Nunnally.
HIGH SCHOOL: Hargrave Military Institute (Chatham, Va.).
JUNIOR COLLEGE: Miami-Dade (South) Community College.
TRANSACTIONS/CAREER NOTES: Selected by Baltimore Orioles organization in 39th round of free-agent draft (June 4, 1990); did not sign. ... Selected by Cleveland Indians organization in third round of free-agent draft (June 1, 1992). ... Selected by Kansas City Royals from Indians organization in Rule 5 major league draft (December 5, 1994). ... Traded by Royals with IF/OF Chris Stynes to Cincinnati Reds for P Hector Carrasco and P Scott Service (July 15, 1997).
STATISTICAL NOTES: Tied for American Association lead with eight bases on balls received in 1996. ... Tied for American Association lead with five double plays by outfielder in 1996. ... Career major league grand slams: 1.
MISCELLANEOUS: Hit home run in first major league at-bat (April 29, 1995).

Year	Team (League)	Pos.	G	AB	R	H	2B	3B	HR	RBI	Avg.	BB	SO	SB	PO	A	E	Avg.
1992— Watertown (NYP)		OF	69	246	39	59	10	4	5	43	.240	32	55	12	146	2	8	.949
1993— Columbus (S. Atl.)......		2B-OF	125	438	81	110	15	2	15	56	.251	63	108	17	226	202	25	.945
1994— Kinston (Carolina)		OF	132	483	70	129	29	2	22	74	.267	64	125	23	263	*14	9	.969
1995— Kansas City (A.L.)■ ...		OF-DH	119	303	51	74	15	6	14	42	.244	51	86	6	197	5	6	.971
1996— Kansas City (A.L.)		OF-DH	35	90	16	19	5	1	5	17	.211	13	25	0	61	0	2	.968
— Omaha (A.A.)..............		OF	103	345	76	97	21	4	25	77	.281	47	100	10	182	12	4	.980
1997— Omaha (A.A.)		OF	68	230	35	64	11	1	15	33	.278	39	67	8	173	8	7	.963
— Kansas City (A.L.)		OF	13	29	8	7	0	1	1	4	.241	5	7	0	12	0	0	1.000
— Cincinnati (N.L.)■		OF	65	201	38	64	12	3	13	35	.318	26	51	7	120	3	2	.984
1998— Cincinnati (N.L.)		OF	74	174	29	36	9	0	7	20	.207	34	38	3	126	5	6	.956
— Indianapolis (Int'l)		OF	79	290	53	73	18	2	11	53	.252	47	71	7	146	8	8	.951
American League totals (3 years)			167	422	75	100	20	8	20	63	.237	69	118	6	270	5	8	.972
National League totals (2 years)			139	375	67	100	21	3	20	55	.267	60	89	10	246	8	8	.969
Major league totals (4 years)			306	797	142	200	41	11	40	118	.251	129	207	16	516	13	16	.971

NYE, RYAN   P   PHILLIES

PERSONAL: Born June 24, 1973, in Biloxi, Miss. ... 6-2/214. ... Throws right, bats right. ... Full name: Ryan Craig Nye.
HIGH SCHOOL: Cameron (Okla.).
JUNIOR COLLEGE: Westark Community College (Ark.).
COLLEGE: Texas Tech.
TRANSACTIONS/CAREER NOTES: Selected by Seattle Mariners organization in 43rd round of free-agent draft (June 3, 1991); did not sign. ... Selected by Seattle Mariners organization in 22nd round of free-agent draft (June 1, 1992); did not sign. ... Selected by Philadelphia Phillies organization in second round of free-agent draft (June 2, 1994). ... On Philadelphia disabled list (June 23-July 18, 1997). ... On Scranton/Wilkes-Barre disabled list (July 8-28, 1998).

Year	Team (League)	W	L	Pct.	ERA	G	GS	CG	ShO	Sv.	IP	H	R	ER	BB	SO
1994— Batavia (N.Y.-Penn)		7	2	.778	2.64	13	12	1	0	0	$71\frac{2}{3}$	64	27	21	15	71
1995— Clearwater (Fla. St.)		12	7	.632	3.40	27	27	5	1	0	167	164	71	63	33	116
1996— Reading (Eastern)		8	2	.800	3.84	14	14	0	0	0	$86\frac{2}{3}$	76	41	37	30	90
— Scran./W.B. (Int'l)..............		5	2	.714	5.02	14	14	0	0	0	$80\frac{2}{3}$	97	52	45	30	51
1997— Scran./W.B. (Int'l)..............		4	10	.286	5.52	17	17	0	0	0	$109\frac{1}{3}$	117	70	67	32	85
— Philadelphia (N.L.)..............		0	2	.000	8.25	4	2	0	0	0	12	20	11	11	9	7
1998— Scran./W.B. (Int'l)..............		9	6	.600	4.05	23	22	3	•2	0	140	139	73	63	49	118
— Philadelphia (N.L.)..............		0	0	. . .	27.00	1	0	0	0	0	1	3	3	3	0	3
Major league totals (2 years)......		0	2	.000	9.69	5	2	0	0	0	13	23	14	14	9	10

O'BRIEN, CHARLIE   C   ANGELS

PERSONAL: Born May 1, 1961, in Tulsa, Okla. ... 6-2/205. ... Bats right, throws right. ... Full name: Charles Hugh O'Brien. ... Brother of John O'Brien, first baseman in St. Louis Cardinals organization (1991-93).
HIGH SCHOOL: Bishop Kelley (Tulsa, Okla.).
JUNIOR COLLEGE: McLennan Community College (Texas).
COLLEGE: Wichita State.
TRANSACTIONS/CAREER NOTES: Selected by Texas Rangers organization in 14th round of free-agent draft (June 6, 1978); did not sign. ... Selected by Seattle Mariners organization in 21st round of free-agent draft (June 8, 1981); did not sign. ... Selected by Oakland Athletics organization in fifth round of free-agent draft (June 7, 1982). ... On disabled list (July 31, 1983-remainder of season). ... On Albany/Colonie disabled list (April 13-May 15, 1984). ... Traded by A's organization with IF Steve Kiefer, P Mike Fulmer and P Pete Kendrick to Milwaukee Brewers for P Moose Haas (March 30, 1986). ... Traded by Brewers with a player to be named later to New York Mets for two players to be named later (August 30, 1990); Brewers acquired P Julio Machado and P Kevin Brown (September 7, 1990) and Mets acquired P Kevin Carmody (September 11, 1990) to complete deal. ... Granted free agency (October 29, 1993). ... Signed by Atlanta Braves (November 26, 1993). ... Granted free agency (October 30, 1995). ... Signed by Toronto Blue Jays (December 14, 1995). ... Granted free agency (October 27, 1997). ... Signed by Chicago White Sox (December 10, 1997). ... On Chicago disabled list (July 19-30, 1998). ... Traded by White Sox to Anaheim Angels for P Jason Stockstill and P Brian Tokarse (July 30, 1998). ... On Anaheim disabled list (July 30-September 1 and September 18, 1998-remainder of season); included rehabilitation assignment to Midland (August 25-31).
STATISTICAL NOTES: Career major league grand slams: 1.

Year	Team (League)	Pos.	G	AB	R	H	2B	3B	HR	RBI	Avg.	BB	SO	SB	PO	A	E	Avg.
1982— Medford (N'west)		C	17	60	11	17	3	0	3	14	.283	10	10	0	116	18	4	.971
— Modesto (California) ..		C	41	140	23	42	6	0	3	32	.300	20	19	7	239	44	5	.983
1983— Alb./Colon. (East.)		C-1B	92	285	50	83	12	1	14	56	.291	52	39	3	478	82	11	.981
1984— Modesto (California) ..		C	9	32	8	9	2	0	1	5	.281	2	4	1	41	8	0	1.000
— Tacoma (PCL)		C-OF	69	195	33	44	11	0	9	22	.226	28	31	0	260	39	0	1.000
1985— Huntsville (Sou.)		C	33	115	20	24	5	0	7	16	.209	16	20	0	182	29	5	.977
— Oakland (A.L.)		C	16	11	3	3	1	0	0	1	.273	3	3	0	23	0	1	.958
— Modesto (California) ..		C	9	27	5	8	4	1	1	2	.296	2	5	0	33	8	1	.976
— Tacoma (PCL)		C	18	57	5	9	4	0	0	7	.158	6	17	0	110	9	3	.975
1986— Vancouver (PCL)■		C	6	17	1	2	0	0	0	1	.118	4	4	0	22	3	2	.926
— El Paso (Texas)..........		C-OF-1B	92	336	72	109	20	3	15	75	.324	50	30	0	437	43	4	.992
1987— Denver (A.A.)		C	80	266	37	75	12	1	8	35	.282	41	33	5	415	53	6	.987
— Milwaukee (A.L.)		C	10	35	2	7	3	1	0	0	.200	4	4	0	78	11	0	1.000
1988— Denver (A.A.)		C	48	153	16	43	5	0	4	25	.281	19	19	1	243	44	3	.990
— Milwaukee (A.L.)		C	40	118	12	26	6	0	2	9	.220	5	16	0	210	20	2	.991
1989— Milwaukee (A.L.)		C	62	188	22	44	10	0	6	35	.234	21	11	0	314	36	5	.986
1990— Milwaukee (A.L.)		C	46	145	11	27	7	2	0	11	.186	11	26	0	217	24	2	.992
— New York (N.L.)■		C	28	68	6	11	3	0	0	9	.162	10	8	0	191	21	3	.986
1991— New York (N.L.)........		C	69	168	16	31	6	0	2	14	.185	17	25	0	396	37	4	.991
1992— New York (N.L.)........		C	68	156	15	33	12	0	2	13	.212	16	18	0	287	44	7	.979

N

O

– 417 –

Year Team (League)	Pos.	G	AB	R	H	2B	3B	HR	RBI	Avg.	BB	SO	SB	PO	A	E	Avg.
1993— New York (N.L.)..........	C	67	188	15	48	11	0	4	23	.255	14	14	1	325	39	5	.986
1994— Atlanta (N.L.)■..........	C	51	152	24	37	11	0	8	28	.243	15	24	0	308	26	3	.991
1995— Atlanta (N.L.)..........	C	67	198	18	45	7	0	9	23	.227	29	40	0	446	23	4	.992
1996— Toronto (A.L.)■........	C	109	324	33	77	17	0	13	44	.238	29	68	0	613	37	3	.995
1997— Toronto (A.L.)..........	C	69	225	22	49	15	1	4	27	.218	22	45	0	543	41	3	.995
1998— Chicago (A.L.)■........	C	57	164	12	43	9	0	4	18	.262	9	31	0	305	22	4	.988
— Midland (Texas)■......	C	5	17	1	2	0	0	0	2	.118	2	4	1	33	0	0	1.000
— Anaheim (A.L.)	C	5	11	1	2	0	0	0	0	.182	1	2	0	20	2	0	1.000
American League totals (8 years)		414	1221	118	278	68	4	29	145	.228	105	206	0	2323	193	20	.992
National League totals (6 years)		350	930	94	205	50	0	25	110	.220	101	129	1	1953	190	26	.988
Major league totals (13 years)		764	2151	212	483	118	4	54	255	.225	206	335	1	4276	383	46	.990

DIVISION SERIES RECORD

Year Team (League)	Pos.	G	AB	R	H	2B	3B	HR	RBI	Avg.	BB	SO	SB	PO	A	E	Avg.
1995— Atlanta (N.L.)..............	C	2	5	0	1	0	0	0	0	.200	1	1	0	8	1	0	1.000

CHAMPIONSHIP SERIES RECORD

Year Team (League)	Pos.	G	AB	R	H	2B	3B	HR	RBI	Avg.	BB	SO	SB	PO	A	E	Avg.
1995— Atlanta (N.L.)..............	C-PH	2	5	1	2	0	0	1	3	.400	0	1	0	3	1	0	1.000

WORLD SERIES RECORD

NOTES: Member of World Series championship team (1995).

Year Team (League)	Pos.	G	AB	R	H	2B	3B	HR	RBI	Avg.	BB	SO	SB	PO	A	E	Avg.
1995— Atlanta (N.L.)..............	C	2	3	0	0	0	0	0	0	.000	0	0	0	7	2	0	1.000

OCHOA, ALEX   OF   BREWERS

PERSONAL: Born March 29, 1972, in Miami Lakes, Fla. ... 6-0/195. ... Bats right, throws right.
HIGH SCHOOL: Hialeah (Fla.) Miami Lakes.
TRANSACTIONS/CAREER NOTES: Selected by Baltimore Orioles organization in third round of free-agent draft (June 3, 1991). ... Traded by Orioles with OF Damon Buford to New York Mets for 3B/OF Bobby Bonilla and a player to be named later (July 28, 1995); Orioles acquired P Jimmy Williams to complete deal (August 17, 1995). ... Traded by Mets to Minnesota Twins for OF Rich Becker (December 12, 1997). ... Traded by Twins to Milwaukee Brewers for a player to be named later (December 14, 1998); Twins acquired OF Darrell Nicholas to complete deal (December 15, 1998).
STATISTICAL NOTES: Led Carolina League in grounding into double plays with 15 in 1993. ... Led Eastern League with 12 sacrifice flies in 1994. ... Tied for Eastern League lead in double plays by outfielder with five in 1994. ... Led International League outfielders with 249 putouts and 266 total chances in 1995. ... Hit for the cycle (July 3, 1996). ... Tied for International League lead in double plays by outfielder with three in 1996.

Year Team (League)	Pos.	G	AB	R	H	2B	3B	HR	RBI	Avg.	BB	SO	SB	PO	A	E	Avg.
1991— GC Orioles (GCL)........	OF	53	179	26	55	8	3	1	30	.307	16	14	11	45	3	2	.960
1992— Kane County (Midw.)..	OF	133	499	65	147	22	7	1	59	.295	58	55	31	225	•17	•12	.953
1993— Frederick (Carolina)..	OF	137	532	84	147	29	5	13	90	.276	46	67	34	169	13	11	.943
1994— Bowie (Eastern).........	OF	134	519	77	156	25	2	14	82	.301	49	67	28	237	•22	6	.977
1995— Rochester (Int'l)........	OF	91	336	41	92	18	2	8	46	.274	26	50	17	183	9	5	.975
— Norfolk (Int'l)■............	OF	34	123	17	38	6	2	2	15	.309	14	12	7	‡66	1	2	.971
— New York (N.L.).........	OF	11	37	7	11	1	0	0	0	.297	2	10	1	20	1	0	1.000
1996— Norfolk (Int'l)	OF	67	233	45	79	12	4	8	39	.339	32	22	5	110	9	5	.960
— New York (N.L.).........	OF	82	282	37	83	19	3	4	33	.294	17	30	4	135	8	5	.966
1997— New York (N.L.)........	OF-DH	113	238	31	58	14	1	3	22	.244	18	32	3	104	7	2	.982
1998— Minnesota (A.L.)■	OF-DH	94	249	35	64	14	2	2	25	.257	10	35	6	117	8	4	.969
American League totals (1 year)		94	249	35	64	14	2	2	25	.257	10	35	6	117	8	4	.969
National League totals (3 years)		206	557	75	152	34	4	7	55	.273	37	72	8	259	16	7	.975
Major league totals (4 years)		300	806	110	216	48	6	9	80	.268	47	107	14	376	24	11	.973

O'CONNOR, BRIAN   P   PIRATES

PERSONAL: Born January 4, 1977, in Cincinnati. ... 6-2/190. ... Throws left, bats left. ... Full name: Brian Michael O'Connor.
HIGH SCHOOL: Reading (Ohio).
TRANSACTIONS/CAREER NOTES: Selected by Pittsburgh Pirates organization in 11th round of free-agent draft (June 1, 1995).

Year Team (League)	W	L	Pct.	ERA	G	GS	CG	ShO	Sv.	IP	H	R	ER	BB	SO
1995— GC Pirates (GCL).............	2	2	.500	1.88	14	5	0	0	1	43	33	22	9	13	43
1996— Augusta (S. Atl.).............	0	1	.000	3.06	19	0	0	0	1	35 1/3	33	13	12	8	37
— Erie (N.Y.-Penn)................	4	*10	.286	5.85	15	•15	0	0	0	67 2/3	75	*60	44	47	60
1997— Augusta (S. Atl.).............	2	7	.222	4.41	25	14	0	0	0	85 2/3	90	54	42	39	91
— Lynchburg (Carolina)	2	1	.667	3.46	11	0	0	0	02	13	11	5	5	6	14
1998— Lynchburg (Carolina)	6	2	.750	2.60	14	14	1	0	0	86 2/3	86	34	25	22	84
— Carolina (Southern)...........	2	4	.333	8.25	14	13	0	0	0	64 1/3	86	65	59	53	41

OFFERMAN, JOSE   2B/1B   RED SOX

PERSONAL: Born November 8, 1968, in San Pedro de Macoris, Dominican Republic. ... 6-0/190. ... Bats both, throws right. ... Full name: Jose Antonio Dono Offerman.
HIGH SCHOOL: Colegio Biblico Cristiano (Dominican Republic).

TRANSACTIONS/CAREER NOTES: Signed as non-drafted free agent by Los Angeles Dodgers organization (July 24, 1986). ... Traded by Dodgers to Kansas City Royals for P Billy Brewer (December 17, 1995). ... On Kansas City disabled list (April 6-29, July 10-22 and August 14-September 6, 1997). ... Granted free agency (October 23, 1998). ... Signed by Boston Red Sox (November 16, 1998).
RECORDS: Holds A.L. single-season record for most consecutive games batted safely by switch hitter—27 (1998).
HONORS: Named Minor League Player of the Year by THE SPORTING NEWS (1990). ... Named Pacific Coast League Player of the Year (1990).
STATISTICAL NOTES: Tied for Pioneer League lead in caught stealing with 10 in 1988. ... Tied for Pacific Coast League lead in caught stealing with 18 in 1990. ... Led Pacific Coast League shortstops with 36 errors in 1990. ... Hit home run in first major league at-bat (August 19, 1990). ... Led N.L. with 25 sacrifice hits in 1993. ... Had 27-game hitting streak (July 11-August 7, 1998).

Year Team (League)	Pos.	G	AB	R	H	2B	3B	HR	RBI	Avg.	BB	SO	SB	PO	A	E	Avg.
1987—					Dominican Summer League statistics unavailable.												
1988— Great Falls (Pio.)	SS	60	251	75	83	11	5	2	28	.331	38	42	*57	82	143	18	*.926
1989— Bakersfield (Calif.)......	SS	62	245	53	75	9	4	2	22	.306	35	48	37	94	179	30	.901
— San Diego (Tex.)	SS	68	278	47	80	6	3	2	22	.288	40	39	32	106	168	20	.932
1990— Albuquerque (PCL)......	SS-2B	117	454	104	148	16	11	0	56	.326	71	81	*60	174	361	†36	.937
— Los Angeles (N.L.)......	SS	29	58	7	9	0	0	1	7	.155	4	14	1	30	40	4	.946
1991— Albuquerque (PCL)......	SS	79	289	58	86	8	4	0	29	.298	47	58	32	126	241	17	.956
— Los Angeles (N.L.)......	SS	52	113	10	22	2	0	0	3	.195	25	32	3	50	121	10	.945
1992— Los Angeles (N.L.)......	SS	149	534	67	139	20	8	1	30	.260	57	98	23	208	398	*42	.935
1993— Los Angeles (N.L.)......	SS	158	590	77	159	21	6	1	62	.269	71	75	30	250	454	*37	.950
1994— Los Angeles (N.L.)......	SS	72	243	27	51	8	4	1	25	.210	38	38	2	123	195	11	.967
— Albuquerque (PCL)......	SS	56	224	43	74	7	5	1	31	.330	37	48	9	91	196	13	.957
1995— Los Angeles (N.L.)......	SS	119	429	69	123	14	6	4	33	.287	69	67	2	165	312	*35	.932
1996— Kansas City (A.L.)■...	1-2-S-O	151	561	85	170	33	8	5	47	.303	74	98	24	920	234	16	.986
1997— Kansas City (A.L.)	2B-DH	106	424	59	126	23	6	2	39	.297	41	64	9	201	254	9	.981
1998— Kansas City (A.L.)	2B-DH	158	607	102	191	28	*13	7	66	.315	89	96	45	277	440	19	.974
American League totals (3 years)		415	1592	246	487	84	27	14	152	.306	204	258	78	1398	928	44	.981
National League totals (6 years)		579	1967	257	503	65	24	8	160	.256	264	324	61	826	1520	139	.944
Major league totals (9 years)		994	3559	503	990	149	51	22	312	.278	468	582	139	2224	2448	183	.962

DIVISION SERIES RECORD

Year Team (League)	Pos.	G	AB	R	H	2B	3B	HR	RBI	Avg.	BB	SO	SB	PO	A	E	Avg.
1995— Los Angeles (N.L.)	PR	1	0	0	0	0	0	0	0	...	0	0	0	...	...	...	...

ALL-STAR GAME RECORD

Year League	Pos.	AB	R	H	2B	3B	HR	RBI	Avg.	BB	SO	SB	PO	A	E	Avg.
1995— National	SS	0	0	0	0	0	0	0	...	0	0	0	0	0	0	...

OGEA, CHAD   P   PHILLIES

PERSONAL: Born November 9, 1970, in Lake Charles, La. ... 6-2/220. ... Throws right, bats left. ... Full name: Chad Wayne Ogea. ... Name pronounced OH-jay.
HIGH SCHOOL: St. Louis (Lake Charles, La.).
COLLEGE: Louisiana State.
TRANSACTIONS/CAREER NOTES: Selected by Cleveland Indians organization in third round of free-agent draft (June 3, 1991). ... On Cleveland disabled list (April 28-May 28, 1996); included rehabilitation assignment to Buffalo (May 15-June 8). ... On Cleveland disabled list (June 24-September 1, 1997). ... On Cleveland disabled list (March 22-April 21, May 20-July 13 and July 30-September 1, 1998); included rehabilitation assignments to Buffalo (June 20-July 11, April 11-20 and August 22-27). ... Traded by Indians to Philadelphia Phillies for P Jerry Spradlin (November 13, 1998).
STATISTICAL NOTES: Led International League with 26 home runs allowed in 1993.

Year Team (League)	W	L	Pct.	ERA	G	GS	CG	ShO	Sv.	IP	H	R	ER	BB	SO
1992— Kinston (Carolina)	13	3	.813	3.49	21	21	•5	•2	0	139 1/3	135	61	54	29	123
— Cant./Akr. (Eastern)	6	1	.857	2.20	7	7	1	1	0	49	38	12	12	12	40
1993— Charlotte (Int'l)	•13	8	.619	3.82	29	•29	0	0	0	181 1/3	169	91	77	54	135
1994— Charlotte (Int'l)	9	10	.474	3.85	24	23	6	0	1	163 2/3	146	80	70	34	113
— Cleveland (A.L.).................	0	1	.000	6.06	4	1	0	0	0	16 1/3	21	11	11	10	11
1995— Buffalo (A.A.).................	0	1	.000	4.58	4	4	0	0	0	17 2/3	16	12	9	8	11
— Cleveland (A.L.).................	8	3	.727	3.05	20	14	1	0	0	106 1/3	95	38	36	29	57
1996— Cleveland (A.L.).................	10	6	.625	4.79	29	21	1	1	0	146 2/3	151	82	78	42	101
— Buffalo (A.A.).................	0	1	.000	5.26	5	5	0	0	0	25 2/3	27	15	15	6	20
1997— Cleveland (A.L.).................	8	9	.471	4.99	21	21	1	0	0	126 1/3	139	79	70	47	80
— Buffalo (A.A.).................	1	1	.500	4.29	4	4	0	0	0	21	24	10	10	6	11
1998— Buffalo (Int'l).................	2	1	.667	3.61	9	9	1	0	0	42 1/3	42	19	17	5	34
— Cleveland (A.L.).................	5	4	.556	5.61	19	9	0	0	0	69	74	44	43	25	43
Major league totals (5 years)	31	23	.574	4.61	93	66	3	1	0	464 2/3	480	254	238	153	292

DIVISION SERIES RECORD

Year Team (League)	W	L	Pct.	ERA	G	GS	CG	ShO	Sv.	IP	H	R	ER	BB	SO
1996— Cleveland (A.L.).................	0	0	...	0.00	1	0	0	0	0	1/3	0	0	0	2	0
1997— Cleveland (A.L.).................	0	0	...	1.69	1	0	0	0	0	5 1/3	2	1	1	0	1
1998— Cleveland (A.L.).................							Did not play.								
Div. series totals (2 years)	0	0	...	1.59	2	0	0	0	0	5 2/3	2	1	1	2	1

CHAMPIONSHIP SERIES RECORD

Year Team (League)	W	L	Pct.	ERA	G	GS	CG	ShO	Sv.	IP	H	R	ER	BB	SO
1995— Cleveland (A.L.).................	0	0	...	0.00	1	0	0	0	0	2/3	1	0	0	0	2
1997— Cleveland (A.L.).................	0	2	.000	3.21	2	2	0	0	0	14	12	5	5	5	7
1998— Cleveland (A.L.).................	0	1	.000	8.10	2	1	0	0	0	6 2/3	9	6	6	5	4
Champ. series totals (3 years)	0	3	.000	4.64	5	3	0	0	0	21 1/3	22	11	11	10	13

WORLD SERIES RECORD

Year Team (League)	W	L	Pct.	ERA	G	GS	CG	ShO	Sv.	IP	H	R	ER	BB	SO
1997— Cleveland (A.L.).................	2	0	1.000	1.54	2	2	0	0	0	11 2/3	11	2	2	3	5

OJALA, KIRT   P   MARLINS

PERSONAL: Born December 24, 1968, in Kalamazoo, Mich. ... 6-2/215. ... Throws left, bats left. ... Full name: Kirt Stanley Ojala. ... Name pronounced O-juh-luh.
HIGH SCHOOL: Portage (Mich.) Central.
COLLEGE: Michigan.
TRANSACTIONS/CAREER NOTES: Selected by New York Yankees organization in fourth round of free-agent draft (June 4, 1990). ... On disabled list (April 9-23, 1992). ... Selected by Oakland Athletics from Yankees organization in Rule 5 major league draft (December 7, 1992). ... Returned to Yankees organization (March 27, 1993). ... Granted free agency (April 5, 1996). ... Signed by Indianapolis, Cincinnati Reds organization (April 11, 1996). ... Claimed on waivers by Florida Marlins organization (March 27, 1997). ... Granted free agency (October 15, 1997). ... Signed by Arizona Diamondbacks (November 26, 1997). ... Claimed on waivers by Marlins (February 20, 1998).
RECORDS: Shares major league record for most strikeouts in one inning—4 (September 16, 1998, fourth inning).

Year Team (League)	W	L	Pct.	ERA	G	GS	CG	ShO	Sv.	IP	H	R	ER	BB	SO
1990— Oneonta (N.Y.-Penn)	7	2	.778	2.16	14	14	1	0	0	79	75	28	19	43	87
1991— Prince William (Caro.)	8	7	.533	2.53	25	23	1	0	0	156 2/3	120	52	44	61	112
1992— Alb./Colon. (East.)	12	8	.600	3.62	24	23	2	1	0	151 2/3	130	71	61	•80	116
1993— Columbus (Int'l)	8	9	.471	5.50	31	20	0	0	0	126	145	85	77	71	83
— Alb./Colon. (East.)	1	0	1.000	0.00	1	1	0	0	0	6 1/3	5	0	0	2	6
1994— Columbus (Int'l)	11	7	.611	3.83	25	23	1	1	0	148	157	78	63	46	81
1995— Columbus (Int'l)	8	7	.533	3.95	32	20	0	0	1	145 2/3	138	74	64	54	107
1996— Indianapolis (A.A.)■	7	7	.500	3.77	22	21	3	0	0	133 2/3	143	67	56	31	92
1997— Charlotte (Int'l)■	8	7	.533	3.50	25	24	0	0	0	149	148	74	58	55	119
— Florida (N.L.)	1	2	.333	3.14	7	5	0	0	0	28 2/3	28	10	10	18	19
1998— Florida (N.L.)	2	7	.222	4.25	41	13	1	0	0	125	128	71	59	59	75
Major league totals (2 years)	3	9	.250	4.04	48	18	1	0	0	153 2/3	156	81	69	77	94

O'LEARY, TROY   OF   RED SOX

PERSONAL: Born August 4, 1969, in Compton, Calif. ... 6-0/198. ... Bats left, throws left. ... Full name: Troy Franklin O'Leary.
HIGH SCHOOL: Cypress (Calif.).
JUNIOR COLLEGE: Chaffey College (San Diego).
TRANSACTIONS/CAREER NOTES: Selected by Milwaukee Brewers organization in 13th round of free-agent draft (June 2, 1987). ... Claimed on waivers by Boston Red Sox (April 14, 1995).
HONORS: Named Texas League Most Valuable Player (1992).
STATISTICAL NOTES: Led Pioneer League with 144 total bases in 1989. ... Led Texas League with 227 total bases and .399 on-base percentage in 1992. ... Led Texas League outfielders with 242 total chances in 1992. ... Career major league grand slams: 2.

Year Team (League)	Pos.	G	AB	R	H	2B	3B	HR	RBI	Avg.	BB	SO	SB	PO	A	E	Avg.
1987— Helena (Pioneer)	OF	3	5	0	2	0	0	0	1	.400	0	0	0	0	0	0	...
1988— Helena (Pioneer)	OF	67	203	40	70	11	1	0	27	.345	30	32	10	64	4	3	.958
1989— Beloit (Midwest)	OF	42	115	7	21	4	0	0	8	.183	15	20	1	55	1	1	.982
— Helena (Pioneer)	OF	•68	263	54	*89	16	3	11	*56	.338	28	43	9	92	6	3	.970
1990— Beloit (Midwest)	OF	118	436	73	130	29	1	6	62	.298	41	90	12	184	14	8	.961
— Stockton (California)	OF	2	6	1	3	1	0	0	0	.500	2	1	0	3	0	1	.750
1991— Stockton (California)	OF	126	418	63	110	20	4	5	46	.263	73	96	4	163	4	3	.982
1992— El Paso (Texas)	OF	*135	*506	*92	*169	27	8	5	79	*.334	59	87	28	*220	11	*11	.955
1993— New Orleans (A.A.)	OF-1B	111	388	65	106	32	1	7	59	.273	43	61	6	189	8	6	.970
— Milwaukee (A.L.)	OF	19	41	3	12	3	0	0	3	.293	5	9	0	32	1	0	1.000
1994— New Orleans (A.A.)	OF-1B	63	225	44	74	18	5	8	43	.329	32	37	10	99	10	2	.982
— Milwaukee (A.L.)	OF-DH	27	66	9	18	1	1	2	7	.273	5	12	1	37	2	0	1.000
1995— Boston (A.L.)■	OF-DH	112	399	60	123	31	6	10	49	.308	29	64	5	196	6	5	.976
1996— Boston (A.L.)	OF	149	497	68	129	28	5	15	81	.260	47	80	3	227	8	7	.971
1997— Boston (A.L.)	OF-DH	146	499	65	154	32	4	15	80	.309	39	70	0	267	8	6	.979
1998— Boston (A.L.)	OF	156	611	95	165	36	8	23	83	.270	36	108	2	303	9	3	.990
Major league totals (6 years)		609	2113	300	601	131	24	65	303	.284	161	343	11	1062	34	21	.981

DIVISION SERIES RECORD

Year Team (League)	Pos.	G	AB	R	H	2B	3B	HR	RBI	Avg.	BB	SO	SB	PO	A	E	Avg.
1998— Boston (A.L.)	OF	4	16	0	1	0	0	0	0	.063	1	4	0	8	0	0	1.000

OLERUD, JOHN   1B   METS

PERSONAL: Born August 5, 1968, in Seattle. ... 6-5/220. ... Bats left, throws left. ... Full name: John Garrett Olerud. ... Son of John E. Olerud, minor league catcher (1965-70). ... Name pronounced OH-luh-rude.
HIGH SCHOOL: Interlake (Bellevue, Wash.).
COLLEGE: Washington State.
TRANSACTIONS/CAREER NOTES: Selected by New York Mets organization in 27th round of free-agent draft (June 2, 1986); did not sign. ... Selected by Toronto Blue Jays organization in third round of free-agent draft (June 5, 1989). ... Traded by Blue Jays with cash to Mets for P Robert Person (December 20, 1996). ... Granted free agency (October 27, 1997). ... Re-signed by Mets (November 24, 1997).
RECORDS: Shares A.L. single-season records for most intentional bases on balls received—33 (1993); and most intentional bases on balls received by lefthanded hitter—33 (1993). ... Shares N.L. single-season record for most consecutive times reached base safely—15 (September 16 [1], 18 [5], 20 [4], 22 [1], 1998; 6 singles, 1 double, 2 home runs, 6 bases on balls).
STATISTICAL NOTES: Tied for A.L. lead with 10 sacrifice flies in 1991. ... Had 26-game hitting streak (May 26-June 22, 1993). ... Led A.L. with 33 intentional bases on balls received and .473 on-base percentage in 1993. ... Hit for the cycle (September 11, 1997). ... Had 23-game hitting streak (July 19-August 9, 1998). ... Career major league grand slams: 3.

Year	Team (League)	Pos.	G	AB	R	H	2B	3B	HR	RBI	Avg.	BB	SO	SB	PO	A	E	Avg.
1989— Toronto (A.L.)............	1B-DH	6	8	2	3	0	0	0	0	.375	0	1	0	19	2	0	1.000
1990— Toronto (A.L.)............	DH-1B	111	358	43	95	15	1	14	48	.265	57	75	0	133	10	2	.986
1991— Toronto (A.L.)............	1B-DH	139	454	64	116	30	1	17	68	.256	68	84	0	1120	78	5	.996
1992— Toronto (A.L.)............	1B-DH	138	458	68	130	28	0	16	66	.284	70	61	1	1057	81	7	.994
1993— Toronto (A.L.)............	1B-DH	158	551	109	200	*54	2	24	107	*.363	114	65	0	1160	97	10	.992
1994— Toronto (A.L.)............	1B-DH	108	384	47	114	29	2	12	67	.297	61	53	1	824	68	6	.993
1995— Toronto (A.L.)............	1B	135	492	72	143	32	0	8	54	.291	84	54	0	1099	89	4	.997
1996— Toronto (A.L.)............	1B-DH	125	398	59	109	25	0	18	61	.274	60	37	1	781	56	2	.998
1997— New York (N.L.)■	1B	154	524	90	154	34	1	22	102	.294	85	67	0	1292	120	7	.995
1998— New York (N.L.).........	1B	160	557	91	197	36	4	22	93	.354	96	73	2	1258	116	5	.996
American League totals (8 years)		920	3103	464	910	213	6	109	471	.293	514	430	3	6193	481	36	.995
National League totals (2 years)		314	1081	181	351	70	5	44	195	.325	181	140	2	2550	236	12	.996
Major league totals (10 years)		1234	4184	645	1261	283	11	153	666	.301	695	570	5	8743	717	48	.995

CHAMPIONSHIP SERIES RECORD

Year	Team (League)	Pos.	G	AB	R	H	2B	3B	HR	RBI	Avg.	BB	SO	SB	PO	A	E	Avg.
1991— Toronto (A.L.)............	1B	5	19	1	3	0	0	0	3	.158	3	1	0	40	3	0	1.000
1992— Toronto (A.L.)............	1B	6	23	4	8	2	0	1	4	.348	2	5	0	51	1	0	1.000
1993— Toronto (A.L.)............	1B	6	23	5	8	1	0	0	3	.348	4	1	0	48	9	1	.983
Championship series totals (3 years)		17	65	10	19	3	0	1	10	.292	9	7	0	139	13	1	.993

WORLD SERIES RECORD

NOTES: Member of World Series championship team (1992 and 1993).

Year	Team (League)	Pos.	G	AB	R	H	2B	3B	HR	RBI	Avg.	BB	SO	SB	PO	A	E	Avg.
1992— Toronto (A.L.)............	1B	4	13	2	4	0	0	0	0	.308	0	4	0	25	3	0	1.000
1993— Toronto (A.L.)............	1B	5	17	5	4	1	0	1	2	.235	4	1	0	36	0	0	1.000
World Series totals (2 years)		9	30	7	8	1	0	1	2	.267	4	5	0	61	3	0	1.000

ALL-STAR GAME RECORD

Year	League	Pos.	AB	R	H	2B	3B	HR	RBI	Avg.	BB	SO	SB	PO	A	E	Avg.
1993— American	1B	2	0	0	0	0	0	0	.000	0	0	0	4	0	0	1.000

OLIVARES, OMAR P ANGELS

PERSONAL: Born July 6, 1967, in Mayaguez, Puerto Rico. ... 6-0/205. ... Throws right, bats right. ... Full name: Omar Palqu Olivares. ... Son of Ed Olivares, outfielder with St. Louis Cardinals (1960-61).

HIGH SCHOOL: Hostos (Mayaguez, Puerto Rico).

TRANSACTIONS/CAREER NOTES: Signed as non-drafted free agent by San Diego Padres organization (September 15, 1986). ... Traded by Padres organization to St. Louis Cardinals for OF Alex Cole and P Steve Peters (February 27, 1990). ... On St. Louis disabled list (May 27-June 13, 1992 and June 4-20, 1993). ... Granted free agency (April 7, 1995). ... Signed by Colorado Rockies (April 9, 1995). ... Claimed on waivers by Philadelphia Phillies (July 11, 1995). ... Granted free agency (October 16, 1995). ... Signed by Detroit Tigers (December 20, 1995). ... On Detroit disabled list (April 16-May 30, 1996); included rehabilitation assignment to Toledo (May 24-30). ... Traded by Tigers with P Felipe Lira to Seattle Mariners for P Scott Sanders, P Dean Crow and 3B Carlos Villalobos (July 18, 1997). ... Granted free agency (October 30, 1997). ... Signed by Anaheim Angels (December 11, 1997).

RECORDS: Shares major league single-season record for fewest double plays by pitcher who led league in double plays—4 (1992).

STATISTICAL NOTES: Tied for Texas League lead with 10 hit batsmen in 1989.

MISCELLANEOUS: Appeared in one game as pinch runner and singled and scored in three games as pinch hitter (1992). ... Appeared in one game as pinch runner and made an out in one game as pinch hitter (1993). ... Made an out in one game as pinch hitter with St. Louis (1994). ... Appeared in one game as pinch runner with Colorado (1995). ... Hit two-run home run in only game as pinch hitter with Philadelphia (1995). ... Appeared in three games as pinch runner with Detroit (1997). ... Struck out in only appearance as pinch hitter and scored one run in two games as pinch runner (1998).

Year	Team (League)	W	L	Pct.	ERA	G	GS	CG	ShO	Sv.	IP	H	R	ER	BB	SO
1987— Charleston, S.C. (S. Atl.)....	4	14	.222	4.60	31	24	5	0	0	170 1/3	182	107	87	57	86
1988— Charleston, S.C. (S. Atl.)....	13	6	.684	2.23	24	24	*10	3	0	185 1/3	166	63	46	43	94
— Riverside (California).........	3	0	1.000	1.16	4	3	1	0	0	23	18	9	3	9	16
1989— Wichita (Texas)	12	11	.522	3.39	26	26	6	1	0	*185 2/3	175	87	70	61	79
1990— Louisville (A.A.)■..............	10	11	.476	2.82	23	23	5	2	0	159 1/3	127	58	50	59	88
— St. Louis (N.L.).................	1	1	.500	2.92	9	6	0	0	0	49 1/3	45	17	16	17	20
1991— St. Louis (N.L.).................	11	7	.611	3.71	28	24	0	0	1	167 1/3	148	72	69	61	91
— Louisville (A.A.)................	1	2	.333	3.47	6	6	0	0	0	36 1/3	39	15	14	16	27
1992— St. Louis (N.L.).................	9	9	.500	3.84	32	30	1	0	0	197	189	84	84	63	124
1993— St. Louis (N.L.).................	5	3	.625	4.17	58	9	0	0	1	118 2/3	134	60	55	54	63
1994— Louisville (A.A.)................	2	1	.667	4.37	9	9	0	0	0	47 1/3	47	24	23	16	38
— St. Louis (N.L.).................	3	4	.429	5.74	14	12	1	0	1	73 2/3	84	53	47	37	26
1995— Colo. Springs (PCL)■..............	0	1	.000	5.40	3	2	0	0	0	11 2/3	14	7	7	2	6
— Colorado (N.L.)..................	1	3	.250	7.39	11	6	0	0	0	31 2/3	44	28	26	21	15
— Philadelphia (N.L.)■............	0	1	.000	5.40	5	0	0	0	0	10	11	6	6	2	7
— Scran./W.B. (Int'l).............	0	3	.000	4.87	7	7	0	0	0	44 1/3	49	25	24	20	28
1996— Detroit (A.L.)■...............	7	11	.389	4.89	25	25	4	0	0	160	169	90	87	75	81
— Toledo (International).........	1	0	1.000	8.44	1	1	0	0	0	5 1/3	4	5	5	3	5
1997— Detroit (A.L.)■...............	5	6	.455	4.70	19	19	3	2	0	115	110	68	60	53	74
— Seattle (A.L.)..................	1	4	.200	5.49	13	12	0	0	0	62 1/3	81	41	38	28	29
1998— Anaheim (A.L.)■..............	9	9	.500	4.03	37	26	1	0	0	183	189	92	82	91	112
A.L. totals (3 years)	22	30	.423	4.62	94	82	8	2	0	520 1/3	549	291	267	247	296
N.L. totals (6 years)	30	28	.517	4.21	157	87	2	0	3	647 2/3	655	320	303	255	346
Major league totals (9 years)......	52	58	.473	4.39	251	169	10	2	3	1168	1204	611	570	502	642

O

PERSONAL: Born October 6, 1970, in Kansas City, Mo. ... 6-2/210. ... Throws left, bats right. ... Full name: Darren Christopher Oliver. ... Son of Bob Oliver, first baseman/outfielder with five major league teams (1965 and 1969-75).

HIGH SCHOOL: Rio Linda (Calif.) Senior.

TRANSACTIONS/CAREER NOTES: Selected by Texas Rangers organization in third round of free-agent draft (June 1, 1988). ... On Gulf Coast Rangers disabled list (April 6-August 9, 1990). ... On disabled list (May 1, 1991-remainder of season). ... On Tulsa disabled list (July 1, 1992-remainder of season). ... On disabled list (June 27, 1995-remainder of season). ... On Texas disabled list (June 11-26, 1998); included rehabilitation assignment to Oklahoma City (June 21-26). ... Traded by Rangers with 3B Fernando Tatis and a player to be named later to St. Louis Cardinals for P Todd Stottlemyre and SS Royce Clayton (July 31, 1998); Cardinals acquired OF Mark Little to complete deal (August 9, 1998).

MISCELLANEOUS: Made an out in only appearance as pinch hitter with St. Louis (1998).

Year — Team (League)	W	L	Pct.	ERA	G	GS	CG	ShO	Sv.	IP	H	R	ER	BB	SO
1988— GC Rangers (GCL)	5	1	.833	2.15	12	9	0	0	0	54 1/3	39	16	13	18	59
1989— Gastonia (S. Atl.)	8	7	.533	3.16	24	23	2	1	0	122 1/3	86	54	43	82	108
1990— GC Rangers (GCL)	0	0	...	0.00	3	3	0	0	0	6	1	1	0	1	7
— Gastonia (S. Atl.)	0	0	...	13.50	1	1	0	0	0	2	1	3	3	4	2
1991— Charlotte (Fla. St.)	0	1	.000	4.50	2	2	0	0	0	8	6	4	4	3	12
1992— Charlotte (Fla. St.)	1	0	1.000	0.72	8	2	1	1	2	25	11	2	2	10	33
— Tulsa (Texas)	0	1	.000	3.14	3	3	0	0	0	14 1/3	15	9	5	4	14
1993— Tulsa (Texas)	7	5	.583	1.96	46	0	0	0	6	73 1/3	51	18	16	41	77
— Texas (A.L.)	0	0	...	2.70	2	0	0	0	0	3 1/3	2	1	1	1	4
1994— Texas (A.L.)	4	0	1.000	3.42	43	0	0	0	2	50	40	24	19	35	50
— Oklahoma City (A.A.)	0	0	...	0.00	6	0	0	0	1	7 1/3	1	0	0	3	6
1995— Texas (A.L.)	4	2	.667	4.22	17	7	0	0	0	49	47	25	23	32	39
1996— Charlotte (Fla. St.)	0	1	.000	3.00	2	1	0	0	0	12	8	4	4	3	9
— Texas (A.L.)	14	6	.700	4.66	30	30	1	1	0	173 2/3	190	97	90	76	112
1997— Texas (A.L.)	13	12	.520	4.20	32	32	3	1	0	201 1/3	213	111	94	82	104
1998— Texas (A.L.)	6	7	.462	6.53	19	19	2	0	0	103 1/3	140	84	75	43	58
— Oklahoma (Pacific Coast)	0	0	...	0.00	1	1	0	0	0	5	2	0	0	1	1
— St. Louis (N.L.)■	4	4	.500	4.26	10	10	0	0	0	57	64	31	27	23	29
A.L. totals (6 years)	41	27	.603	4.68	143	88	6	2	2	580 2/3	632	342	302	269	367
N.L. totals (1 year)	4	4	.500	4.26	10	10	0	0	0	57	64	31	27	23	29
Major league totals (6 years)	45	31	.592	4.64	153	98	6	2	2	637 2/3	696	373	329	292	396

DIVISION SERIES RECORD

Year — Team (League)	W	L	Pct.	ERA	G	GS	CG	ShO	Sv.	IP	H	R	ER	BB	SO
1996— Texas (A.L.)	0	1	.000	3.38	1	1	0	0	0	8	6	3	3	2	3

OLIVER, JOE   C

PERSONAL: Born July 24, 1965, in Memphis. ... 6-3/220. ... Bats right, throws right. ... Full name: Joseph Melton Oliver.

HIGH SCHOOL: Boone (Orlando).

TRANSACTIONS/CAREER NOTES: Selected by Cincinnati Reds organization in second round of free-agent draft (June 6, 1983); pick received as compensation for New York Yankees signing Type A free-agent P Bob Shirley. ... On disabled list (April 23-May 6, 1986 and April 12, 1994-remainder of season). ... Released by Reds (November 3, 1994). ... Signed by New Orleans, Milwaukee Brewers organization (March 24, 1995). ... On Milwaukee disabled list (July 14-August 15, 1995); included rehabilitation assignment to New Orleans (August 10-15). ... Granted free agency (October 31, 1995). ... Signed by Reds (February 26, 1996). ... Granted free agency (November 18, 1996). ... Re-signed by Reds organization (February 8, 1997). ... Granted free agency (October 30, 1997). ... Signed by Detroit Tigers organization (December 22, 1997). ... Released by Tigers (July 16, 1998). ... Signed by Seattle Mariners (July 24, 1998). ... Granted free agency (October 27, 1998).

STATISTICAL NOTES: Led Pioneer League catchers with .989 fielding percentage, 425 putouts, 38 assists and 468 total chances in 1983. ... Led Midwest League catchers with 855 total chances and 30 passed balls in 1984. ... Led Florida State League catchers with 84 assists and 33 passed balls in 1985. ... Led American Association catchers with 13 errors in 1989. ... Tied for N.L. lead with 16 passed balls in 1990. ... Led N.L. catchers with 925 putouts and 997 total chances in 1992. ... Career major league grand slams: 4.

							BATTING								FIELDING		
Year — Team (League)	Pos.	G	AB	R	H	2B	3B	HR	RBI	Avg.	BB	SO	SB	PO	A	E	Avg.
1983— Billings (Pioneer)	C-1B	56	186	21	40	4	0	4	28	.215	15	47	1	†426	†39	5	†.989
1984— Cedar Rap. (Midw.)	C	102	335	34	73	11	0	3	29	.218	17	83	2	*757	85	13	.985
1985— Tampa (Fla. St.)	C-1B	112	386	38	104	23	2	7	62	.269	32	75	1	615	†94	16	.978
1986— Vermont (Eastern)	C	84	282	32	78	18	1	6	41	.277	21	47	2	383	62	14	.969
1987— Vermont (Eastern)	C-1B	66	236	31	72	13	2	10	60	.305	17	30	0	247	35	10	.966
1988— Nashville (A.A.)	C	73	220	19	45	7	2	4	24	.205	18	39	0	413	37	7	.985
— Chattanooga (Sou.)	C	28	105	9	26	6	0	3	12	.248	5	19	0	176	15	1	1.000
1989— Nashville (A.A.)	C-1B	71	233	22	68	13	0	6	31	.292	13	35	0	388	37	†13	.970
— Cincinnati (N.L.)	C	49	151	13	41	8	0	3	23	.272	6	28	0	260	21	4	.986
1990— Cincinnati (N.L.)	C	121	364	34	84	23	0	8	52	.231	37	75	1	686	59	6	*.992
1991— Cincinnati (N.L.)	C	94	269	21	58	11	0	11	41	.216	18	53	0	496	40	11	.980
1992— Cincinnati (N.L.)	C-1B	143	485	42	131	25	1	10	57	.270	35	75	2	†926	64	8	.992
1993— Cincinnati (N.L.)	C-1B-OF	139	482	40	115	28	0	14	75	.239	27	91	0	825	70	7	.992
1994— Cincinnati (N.L.)	C	6	19	1	4	0	0	1	5	.211	2	3	0	48	2	1	.980
1995— Milwaukee (A.L.)■	C-DH-1B	97	337	43	92	20	0	12	51	.273	27	66	2	414	40	8	.983
— New Orleans (A.A.)	C	4	13	0	1	1	0	0	0	.077	0	3	0	14	7	0	1.000
1996— Cincinnati (N.L.)■	C-1B-OF	106	289	31	70	12	1	11	46	.242	28	54	2	583	45	5	.992
1997— Indianapolis (A.A.)	C	2	9	1	3	0	0	1	1	.333	0	1	0	21	4	0	1.000
— Cincinnati (N.L.)	C-1B	111	349	28	90	13	0	14	43	.258	25	58	1	681	55	7	.991
1998— Detroit (A.L.)■	C-1B-DH	50	155	8	35	8	0	4	22	.226	7	33	0	261	17	5	.982
— Seattle (A.L.)■	C	29	85	12	19	3	0	2	10	.224	10	15	1	174	9	3	.984
American League totals (2 years)		176	577	63	146	31	0	18	83	.253	44	114	3	849	66	16	.983
National League totals (8 years)		769	2408	210	593	120	2	72	342	.246	178	437	6	4505	356	49	.990
Major league totals (10 years)		945	2985	273	739	151	2	90	425	.248	222	551	9	5354	422	65	.989

							BATTING							FIELDING		
Year	Team (League)	Pos.	G	AB	R	H	2B	3B	HR	RBI	Avg.	BB	SO	SB	PO	A	E	Avg.
1990— Cincinnati (N.L.)		C	5	14	1	2	0	0	0	0	.143	0	2	0	27	1	0	1.000

WORLD SERIES RECORD

NOTES: Member of World Series championship team (1990).

							BATTING							FIELDING		
Year	Team (League)	Pos.	G	AB	R	H	2B	3B	HR	RBI	Avg.	BB	SO	SB	PO	A	E	Avg.
1990— Cincinnati (N.L.)		C	4	18	2	6	3	0	0	2	.333	0	1	0	27	1	3	.903

OLSEN, JASON   P   WHITE SOX

PERSONAL: Born March 16, 1975, in Fairfield, Calif. ... 6-4/210. ... Throws right, bats right. ... Full name: Jason Joseph Olsen.
HIGH SCHOOL: Fairfield (Calif.).
JUNIOR COLLEGE: Napa (Calif.) Valley College.
TRANSACTIONS/CAREER NOTES: Selected by Chicago White Sox organization in 44th round of free-agent draft (June 2, 1994).

Year	Team (League)	W	L	Pct.	ERA	G	GS	CG	ShO	Sv.	IP	H	R	ER	BB	SO
1996— Hickory (S. Atl.)		2	1	.667	1.37	4	4	1	0	0	26 1/3	19	5	4	6	32
— South Bend (Mid.)		4	1	.800	1.75	9	9	0	0	0	56 2/3	39	16	11	13	55
— Prince William (Caro.)		6	4	.600	3.87	12	12	0	0	0	79	74	39	34	31	55
1997— Birmingham (Southern)		9	14	.391	4.88	28	27	1	1	0	160 1/3	183	101	87	58	121
1998— Birmingham (Southern)		8	10	.444	4.69	28	28	•4	0	0	159 1/3	188	95	83	53	134

OLSON, GREGG   P   DIAMONDBACKS

PERSONAL: Born October 11, 1966, in Omaha, Neb. ... 6-4/210. ... Throws right, bats right. ... Full name: Gregg William Olson.
HIGH SCHOOL: Northwest (Omaha, Neb.).
COLLEGE: Auburn.
TRANSACTIONS/CAREER NOTES: Selected by Baltimore Orioles organization in first round (fourth pick overall) of free-agent draft (June 1, 1988). ... On disabled list (August 9-September 20, 1993). ... Granted free agency (December 20, 1993). ... Signed by Atlanta Braves (February 8, 1994). ... On Atlanta disabled list (March 26-May 30, 1994); included rehabilitation assignment to Richmond (May 14-30). ... Granted free agency (December 23, 1994). ... Signed by Cleveland Indians organization (March 24, 1995). ... On Buffalo disabled list (April 6-14, 1995). ... Contract sold by Buffalo to Kansas City Royals (July 24, 1995). ... Granted free agency (November 1, 1995). ... Signed by St. Louis Cardinals organization (January 23, 1996). ... Released by Cardinals organization (March 26, 1996). ... Signed by Cincinnati Reds organization (March 26, 1996). ... Traded by Reds to Detroit Tigers for IF Yuri Sanchez (April 26, 1996). ... Traded by Tigers to Houston Astros for two players to be named later (August 26, 1996); Tigers acquired P Kevin Gallaher and IF Pedro Santana to complete deal (August 27, 1996). ... Granted free agency (October 28, 1996). ... Signed by Minnesota Twins organization (December 20, 1996). ... Released by Twins (May 16, 1997). ... Signed by Royals organization (May 25, 1997). ... Granted free agency (October 28, 1997). ... Signed by Arizona Diamondbacks organization (January 31, 1998).
RECORDS: Holds A.L. rookie-season record for most saves—27 (1989).
HONORS: Named righthanded pitcher on THE SPORTING NEWS college All-America team (1988). ... Named A.L. Rookie of the Year by Baseball Writers' Association of America (1989).
STATISTICAL NOTES: Pitched one inning, combining with starter Bob Milacki (six innings), Mike Flanagan (one inning) and Mark Williamson (one inning) in 2-0 no-hit victory against Oakland (July 13, 1991).
MISCELLANEOUS: Holds Baltimore Orioles all-time record for most saves (160). ... Holds Arizona Diamondbacks all-time record for most games (64) and most saves (30). ... Struck out in only plate appearance (1993).

Year	Team (League)	W	L	Pct.	ERA	G	GS	CG	ShO	Sv.	IP	H	R	ER	BB	SO
1988— Hagerstown (Caro.)		1	0	1.000	2.00	8	0	0	0	4	9	5	2	2	2	9
— Charlotte (Southern)		0	1	.000	5.87	8	0	0	0	1	15 1/3	24	13	10	6	22
— Baltimore (A.L.)		1	1	.500	3.27	10	0	0	0	0	11	10	4	4	10	9
1989— Baltimore (A.L.)		5	2	.714	1.69	64	0	0	0	27	85	57	17	16	46	90
1990— Baltimore (A.L.)		6	5	.545	2.42	64	0	0	0	37	74 1/3	57	20	20	31	74
1991— Baltimore (A.L.)		4	6	.400	3.18	72	0	0	0	31	73 2/3	74	28	26	29	72
1992— Baltimore (A.L.)		1	5	.167	2.05	60	0	0	0	36	61 1/3	46	14	14	24	58
1993— Baltimore (A.L.)		0	2	.000	1.60	50	0	0	0	29	45	37	9	8	18	44
1994— Richmond (Int'l)■..............		0	0	. . .	1.59	8	2	0	0	2	11 1/3	8	3	2	8	13
— Atlanta (N.L.)		0	2	.000	9.20	16	0	0	0	1	14 2/3	19	15	15	13	10
1995— Buffalo (A.A.)■...............		1	0	1.000	2.49	18	0	0	0	13	21 2/3	16	6	6	9	25
— Cleveland (A.L.)		0	0	. . .	13.50	3	0	0	0	0	2 2/3	5	4	4	2	0
— Omaha (Am. Assoc.)■........		0	0	. . .	0.00	1	0	0	0	0	1	0	0	0	1	1
— Kansas City (A.L.)		3	3	.500	3.26	20	0	0	0	3	30 1/3	23	11	11	17	21
1996— Indianapolis (A.A.)■		0	0	. . .	4.26	7	0	0	0	4	6 1/3	6	4	3	6	4
— Detroit (A.L.)■..................		3	0	1.000	5.02	43	0	0	0	8	43	43	25	24	28	29
— Houston (N.L.)■...............		1	0	1.000	4.82	9	0	0	0	0	9 1/3	12	5	5	7	8
1997— Minnesota (A.L.)■		0	0	. . .	18.36	11	0	0	0	0	8 1/3	19	17	17	11	6
— Omaha (Am. Assoc.)■.......		3	1	.750	3.31	9	5	0	0	0	35 1/3	30	13	13	10	20
— Kansas City (A.L.)		4	3	.571	3.02	34	0	0	0	1	41 2/3	39	18	14	17	28
1998— Arizona (N.L.)■...............		3	4	.429	3.01	64	0	0	0	30	68 2/3	56	25	23	25	55
A.L. totals (9 years)		27	27	.500	2.99	431	0	0	0	172	476 1/3	410	167	158	233	431
N.L. totals (3 years)		4	6	.400	4.18	89	0	0	0	31	92 2/3	87	45	43	45	73
Major league totals (11 years)		31	33	.484	3.18	520	0	0	0	203	569	497	212	201	278	504

ALL-STAR GAME RECORD

Year	League	W	L	Pct.	ERA	GS	CG	ShO	Sv.	IP	H	R	ER	BB	SO
1990— American							Did not play.								

PERSONAL: Born February 25, 1963, in Columbus, Ohio. ... 6-4/215. ... Bats left, throws left. ... Full name: Paul Andrew O'Neill. ... Son of Charles O'Neill, minor league pitcher (1945-48).

HIGH SCHOOL: Brookhaven (Columbus, Ohio).

COLLEGE: Otterbein College (Ohio).

TRANSACTIONS/CAREER NOTES: Selected by Cincinnati Reds organization in fourth round of free-agent draft (June 8, 1981). ... On Denver disabled list (May 10-July 16, 1986). ... On Cincinnati disabled list (July 21-September 1, 1989); included rehabilitation assignment to Nashville (August 27-September 1). ... Traded by Reds with 1B Joe DeBerry to New York Yankees for OF Roberto Kelly (November 3, 1992). ... On disabled list (May 7-23, 1995). ... On suspended list (September 6-8, 1996).

STATISTICAL NOTES: Led American Association outfielders with 19 assists and eight double plays in 1985. ... Hit three home runs in one game (August 31, 1995). ... Had 17-game hitting streak (May 24-June 10, 1998). ... Tied for A.L. lead in grounding into double plays with 22 in 1998. ... Led A.L. outfielders with six double plays in 1998. ... Career major league grand slams: 3.

Year Team (League)	Pos.	G	AB	R	H	2B	3B	HR	RBI	Avg.	BB	SO	SB	PO	A	E	Avg.
1981— Billings (Pioneer)	OF	66	241	37	76	7	2	3	29	.315	21	35	6	87	4	5	.948
1982— Cedar Rap. (Midw.)	OF	116	386	50	105	19	2	8	71	.272	21	79	12	137	7	8	.947
1983— Tampa (Fla. St.)	OF-1B	121	413	62	115	23	7	8	51	.278	56	70	20	218	14	10	.959
—Waterbury (Eastern)	OF	14	43	6	12	0	0	0	6	.279	6	8	2	26	0	0	1.000
1984— Vermont (Eastern)	OF	134	475	70	126	31	5	16	76	.265	52	72	29	246	5	7	.973
1985— Denver (A.A.)	OF-1B	*137	*509	63	*155	*32	3	7	74	.305	28	73	5	248	†20	7	.975
—Cincinnati (N.L.)	OF	5	12	1	4	1	0	0	1	.333	0	2	0	3	1	0	1.000
1986— Cincinnati (N.L.)	PH	3	2	0	0	0	0	0	0	.000	1	1	0	. . .	. . .	. . .	. . .
—Denver (A.A.)	OF	55	193	20	49	9	2	5	27	.254	9	28	1	98	7	4	.963
1987— Cincinnati (N.L.)	OF-1B-P	84	160	24	41	14	1	7	28	.256	18	29	2	90	2	4	.958
—Nashville (A.A.)	OF	11	37	12	11	0	0	3	6	.297	5	5	1	19	1	0	1.000
1988— Cincinnati (N.L.)	OF-1B	145	485	58	122	25	3	16	73	.252	38	65	8	410	13	6	.986
1989— Cincinnati (N.L.)	OF	117	428	49	118	24	2	15	74	.276	46	64	20	223	7	4	.983
—Nashville (A.A.)	OF	4	12	1	4	0	0	0	0	.333	3	1	1	7	1	0	1.000
1990— Cincinnati (N.L.)	OF	145	503	59	136	28	0	16	78	.270	53	103	13	271	12	2	.993
1991— Cincinnati (N.L.)	OF	152	532	71	136	36	0	28	91	.256	73	107	12	301	13	2	.994
1992— Cincinnati (N.L.)	OF	148	496	59	122	19	1	14	66	.246	77	85	6	291	12	1	*.997
1993— New York (A.L.)■	OF-DH	141	498	71	155	34	1	20	75	.311	44	69	2	230	7	2	.992
1994— New York (A.L.)	OF-DH	103	368	68	132	25	1	21	83	*.359	72	56	5	203	7	1	.995
1995— New York (A.L.)	OF-DH	127	460	82	138	30	4	22	96	.300	71	76	1	220	3	3	.987
1996— New York (A.L.)	OF-DH-1B	150	546	89	165	35	1	19	91	.302	102	76	0	293	7	0	*1.000
1997— New York (A.L.)	OF-DH-1B	149	553	89	179	42	0	21	117	.324	75	92	10	293	7	5	.984
1998— New York (A.L.)	OF-DH	152	602	95	191	40	2	24	116	.317	57	103	15	293	11	4	.987
American League totals (6 years)		822	3027	494	960	206	9	127	578	.317	421	472	33	1532	42	15	.991
National League totals (8 years)		799	2618	321	679	147	7	96	411	.259	306	456	61	1589	60	19	.989
Major league totals (14 years)		1621	5645	815	1639	353	16	223	989	.290	727	928	94	3121	102	34	.990

DIVISION SERIES RECORD

RECORDS: Holds career record for most home runs—6; most runs batted in—14; and total bases—42. ... Shares career records for most games—17; and most hits—20.

Year Team (League)	Pos.	G	AB	R	H	2B	3B	HR	RBI	Avg.	BB	SO	SB	PO	A	E	Avg.
1995— New York (A.L.)	OF-PH	5	18	5	6	0	0	3	6	.333	5	5	0	13	0	0	1.000
1996— New York (A.L.)	OF	4	15	0	2	0	0	0	0	.133	0	2	0	13	0	0	1.000
1997— New York (A.L.)	OF	5	19	5	8	2	0	2	7	.421	3	0	0	9	0	0	1.000
1998— New York (A.L.)	OF	3	11	1	4	2	0	1	1	.364	1	1	0	2	0	0	1.000
Division series totals (4 years)		17	63	11	20	4	0	6	14	.317	9	8	0	37	0	0	1.000

CHAMPIONSHIP SERIES RECORD

Year Team (League)	Pos.	G	AB	R	H	2B	3B	HR	RBI	Avg.	BB	SO	SB	PO	A	E	Avg.
1990— Cincinnati (N.L.)	OF	5	17	1	8	3	0	1	4	.471	1	1	1	9	2	0	1.000
1996— New York (A.L.)	OF	4	11	1	3	0	0	1	2	.273	3	2	0	9	1	0	1.000
1998— New York (A.L.)	OF	6	25	6	7	2	0	1	3	.280	3	4	2	10	0	0	1.000
Championship series totals (3 years)		15	53	8	18	5	0	3	9	.340	7	7	3	28	3	0	1.000

WORLD SERIES RECORD

NOTES: Member of World Series championship team (1990, 1996 and 1998).

Year Team (League)	Pos.	G	AB	R	H	2B	3B	HR	RBI	Avg.	BB	SO	SB	PO	A	E	Avg.
1990— Cincinnati (N.L.)	OF	4	12	2	1	0	0	0	1	.083	5	2	1	11	0	0	1.000
1996— New York (A.L.)	OF-PH	5	12	1	2	2	0	0	0	.167	3	2	0	12	0	0	1.000
1998— New York (A.L.)	OF	4	19	3	4	1	0	0	0	.211	1	2	0	8	0	1	.889
World Series totals (3 years)		13	43	6	7	3	0	0	1	.163	9	6	1	31	0	1	.969

ALL-STAR GAME RECORD

Year League	Pos.	AB	R	H	2B	3B	HR	RBI	Avg.	BB	SO	SB	PO	A	E	Avg.
1991— National	OF	2	0	0	0	0	0	0	.000	0	1	0	0	0	0	. . .
1994— American	PH	1	0	0	0	0	0	0	.000	0	0	0	. . .	. . .	. . .	. . .
1995— American	OF	1	0	0	0	0	0	0	.000	0	0	0	0	0	0	. . .
1997— American	OF	2	0	0	0	0	0	0	.000	0	1	0	1	0	0	1.000
1998— American	OF	2	0	0	0	0	0	0	.000	0	0	0	1	0	0	1.000
All-Star Game totals (5 years)		8	0	0	0	0	0	0	.000	0	2	0	1	1	0	1.000

RECORD AS PITCHER

Year Team (League)	W	L	Pct.	ERA	G	GS	CG	ShO	Sv.	IP	H	R	ER	BB	SO
1987— Cincinnati (N.L.)	0	0	. . .	13.50	1	0	0	0	0	2	2	3	3	4	2

OQUIST, MIKE   P   ATHLETICS

PERSONAL: Born May 30, 1968, in La Junta, Colo. ... 6-2/189. ... Throws right, bats right. ... Full name: Michael Lee Oquist. ... Name pronounced OH-kwist.
HIGH SCHOOL: La Junta (Colo.).
COLLEGE: Arkansas.
TRANSACTIONS/CAREER NOTES: Selected by Baltimore Orioles organization in 13th round of free-agent draft (June 5, 1989). ... Granted free agency (October 16, 1995). ... Signed by Las Vegas, San Diego Padres organization (December 21, 1995). ... On Las Vegas disabled list (April 4-11, 1996). ... Granted free agency (October 15, 1996). ... Signed by Oakland Athletics organization (November 19, 1996). ... On Oakland disabled list (July 14-August 20, 1997); included rehabilitation assignment to Modesto (August 12-20). ... Granted free agency (December 21, 1998). ... Re-signed by Athletics organization (January 8, 1999).
MISCELLANEOUS: Appeared in two games as pinch runner with Oakland (1997).

Year Team (League)	W	L	Pct.	ERA	G	GS	CG	ShO	Sv.	IP	H	R	ER	BB	SO
1989— Erie (N.Y.-Penn)	7	4	.636	3.59	15	15	1	1	0	97 2/3	86	43	39	25	109
1990— Frederick (Carolina)	9	8	.529	2.81	25	25	3	1	0	166 1/3	134	64	52	48	*170
1991— Hagerstown (Eastern)	10	9	.526	4.06	27	26	1	0	0	166 1/3	168	82	75	62	136
1992— Rochester (Int'l)	10	12	.455	4.11	26	24	5	0	0	153 1/3	164	80	70	45	111
1993— Rochester (Int'l)	9	8	.529	3.50	28	21	2	1	0	149 1/3	144	62	58	41	128
— Baltimore (A.L.)	0	0	...	3.86	5	0	0	0	0	11 2/3	12	5	5	4	8
1994— Rochester (Int'l)	3	2	.600	3.73	13	8	0	0	3	50 2/3	54	23	21	15	36
— Baltimore (A.L.)	3	3	.500	6.17	15	9	0	0	0	58 1/3	75	41	40	30	39
1995— Rochester (Int'l)	2	1	.667	4.17	27	0	0	0	0	54	51	27	25	41	27
— Rochester (Int'l)	0	0	...	5.25	7	0	0	0	2	12	17	8	7	5	11
1996— Las Vegas (PCL)■	9	4	.692	2.89	27	20	2	0	1	140 1/3	136	55	45	44	110
— San Diego (N.L.)	0	0	...	2.35	8	0	0	0	0	7 2/3	6	2	2	4	4
1997— Edmonton (PCL)■	6	1	.857	3.25	9	9	1	0	0	52 2/3	57	23	19	16	37
— Oakland (A.L.)	4	6	.400	5.02	19	17	1	0	0	107 2/3	111	62	60	43	72
— Modesto (California)	0	0	...	4.91	2	2	0	0	0	3 2/3	5	2	2	1	5
1998— Oakland (A.L.)	7	11	.389	6.22	31	29	0	0	0	175	210	125	121	57	112
A.L. totals (5 years)	16	21	.432	5.55	97	55	1	0	0	406 2/3	459	260	251	175	258
N.L. totals (1 year)	0	0	...	2.35	8	0	0	0	0	7 2/3	6	2	2	4	4
Major league totals (6 years)	16	21	.432	5.50	105	55	1	0	0	414 1/3	465	262	253	179	262

ORDAZ, LUIS   SS   CARDINALS

PERSONAL: Born August 12, 1975, in Maracaibo, Venezuela. ... 5-11/170. ... Bats right, throws right. ... Full name: Luis Javier Ordaz.
HIGH SCHOOL: Santa Maria Gorette (Maracaibo, Venezuela).
TRANSACTIONS/CAREER NOTES: Signed as non-drafted free agent by Cincinnati Reds organization (January 27, 1993). ... Traded by Reds to St. Louis Cardinals as part of three-team deal in which Reds sent P Mike Remlinger to Kansas City Royals, Cardinals sent OF Andre King to Reds and Royals sent OF Miguel Mejia to Cardinals (December 4, 1995). ... On Memphis disabled list (April 7-16, 1998).
STATISTICAL NOTES: Led Appalachian League shortstops with 277 total chances and 24 errors and tied for lead with 173 assists in 1994. ... Led Texas League in grounding into double plays with 19 in 1997.

Year Team (League)	Pos.	G	AB	R	H	2B	3B	HR	RBI	Avg.	BB	SO	SB	PO	A	E	Avg.
1993— Princeton (Appal.)	3B-SS-2B	57	217	28	65	9	7	2	39	.300	7	32	3	58	117	13	.931
1994— Char., W.Va. (SAL)	SS	9	31	3	7	0	0	0	0	.226	1	4	1	16	18	7	.829
— Princeton (Appal.)	SS-2B	60	211	33	52	12	3	0	12	.246	10	27	7	81	‡173	†24	.914
1995— Char., W.Va. (SAL)	SS	112	359	43	83	14	7	2	42	.231	13	47	12	164	290	22	.954
1996— St. Peters. (FSL)■	SS	126	423	46	115	13	3	3	49	.272	30	53	10	228	317	21	.963
1997— Arkansas (Texas)	SS	115	390	44	112	20	6	4	58	.287	22	39	11	149	327	33	.935
— St. Louis (N.L.)	SS	12	22	3	6	1	0	0	1	.273	1	2	3	9	17	1	.963
1998— Memphis (PCL)	SS-2B	59	214	29	62	9	2	6	35	.290	16	20	3	104	174	14	.952
— St. Louis (N.L.)	SS-3B-2B	57	153	9	31	5	0	0	8	.203	12	18	2	70	157	13	.946
Major league totals (2 years)		69	175	12	37	6	0	0	9	.211	13	20	5	79	174	14	.948

ORDONEZ, MAGGLIO   OF   WHITE SOX

PERSONAL: Born January 28, 1974, in Caracas, Venezuela. ... 5-11/170. ... Bats right, throws right.
TRANSACTIONS/CAREER NOTES: Signed as non-drafted free agent by Chicago White Sox organization (May 18, 1991).
HONORS: Named American Association Most Valuable Player (1997).
STATISTICAL NOTES: Led American Association with nine sacrifice flies and tied for league lead with 249 total bases in 1997.

Year Team (League)	Pos.	G	AB	R	H	2B	3B	HR	RBI	Avg.	BB	SO	SB	PO	A	E	Avg.
1992— GC Whi. Sox (GCL)	OF	38	111	17	20	10	2	1	14	.180	13	26	6	26	2	0	1.000
1993— Hickory (S. Atl.)	OF	84	273	32	59	14	4	3	20	.216	26	66	5	131	10	6	.959
1994— Hickory (S. Atl.)	OF	132	490	86	144	24	5	11	69	.294	45	57	16	275	16	6	.980
1995— Prince Will. (Car.)	OF	131	487	61	116	24	2	12	65	.238	41	71	11	256	5	6	.978
1996— Birmingham (Sou.)	OF	130	479	66	126	41	0	18	67	.263	39	74	9	231	12	6	.976
1997— Nashville (A.A.)	OF	135	523	65	*172	29	3	14	90	*.329	32	61	14	278	8	5	.983
— Chicago (A.L.)	OF	21	69	12	22	6	0	4	11	.319	2	8	1	43	1	0	1.000
1998— Chicago (A.L.)	OF	145	535	70	151	25	2	14	65	.282	28	53	9	323	10	5	.985
Major league totals (2 years)		166	604	82	173	31	2	18	76	.286	30	61	10	366	11	5	.987

ORDONEZ, REY   SS   METS

PERSONAL: Born November 11, 1972, in Havana, Cuba. ... 5-9/159. ... Bats right, throws right. ... Full name: Reynaldo Ordonez.
HIGH SCHOOL: Espa (Havana, Cuba).

COLLEGE: Fajardo College (Havana, Cuba).
TRANSACTIONS/CAREER NOTES: Played with St. Paul Saints of Northern League (1993). ... Acquired by New York Mets organization in lottery of Cuban defectors (October 29, 1993). ... Signed by Mets organization (February 8, 1994). ... On disabled list (June 2-July 11, 1997).
HONORS: Won N.L. Gold Glove at shortstop (1997-98).
STATISTICAL NOTES: Led International League shortstops in total chances with 645 in 1995. ... Led N.L. shortstops with 705 total chances and 102 double plays in 1996.

Year	Team (League)	Pos.	G	AB	R	H	2B	3B	HR	RBI	Avg.	BB	SO	SB	PO	A	E	Avg.
1993—	St. Paul (Northern).....	SS-2B	15	60	10	17	4	0	0	7	.283	3	9	3	18	48	2	.971
1994—	St. Lucie (Fla. St.)■ ...	SS	79	314	47	97	21	2	2	40	.309	14	28	11	141	291	15	.966
	— Binghamton (East.) ...	SS	48	191	22	50	10	2	1	20	.262	4	18	4	57	139	8	.961
1995—	Norfolk (Int'l)	SS	125	439	49	94	21	4	2	50	.214	27	50	11	188	*436	21	.967
1996—	New York (N.L.)..........	SS	151	502	51	129	12	4	1	30	.257	22	53	1	228	450	27	.962
1997—	New York (N.L.)..........	SS	120	356	35	77	5	3	1	33	.216	18	36	11	171	355	9	*.983
1998—	New York (N.L.)..........	SS	153	505	46	124	20	2	1	42	.246	23	60	3	265	401	17	.975
Major league totals (3 years)			424	1363	132	330	37	9	3	105	.242	63	149	15	664	1206	53	.972

ORIE, KEVIN — 3B — MARLINS

PERSONAL: Born September 1, 1972, in West Chester, Pa. ... 6-4/215. ... Bats right, throws right. ... Full name: Kevin Leonard Orie.
HIGH SCHOOL: Upper St. Clair (Pa.).
COLLEGE: Indiana.
TRANSACTIONS/CAREER NOTES: Selected by Chicago Cubs organization in supplemental round ("sandwich pick" between first and second round, 29th pick overall) of free-agent draft (June 3, 1993); pick received as part of compensation for Atlanta Braves signing Type A free-agent P Greg Maddux. ... On disabled list (May 3, 1994-remainder of season). ... On Iowa disabled list (July 27-August 19, 1996). ... On Chicago disabled list (April 30-May 30, 1997); included rehabilitation assignments to Orlando (May 16-20) and Iowa (May 20-30). ... Traded by Cubs with P Todd Noel and P Justin Speier to Florida Marlins for P Felix Heredia and P Steve Hoff (July 31, 1998).

Year	Team (League)	Pos.	G	AB	R	H	2B	3B	HR	RBI	Avg.	BB	SO	SB	PO	A	E	Avg.
1993—	Peoria (Midwest)........	SS-OF	65	238	28	64	17	1	7	45	.269	21	51	3	77	149	12	.950
1994—	Daytona (Fla. St.)	DH	6	17	4	7	3	1	1	5	.412	8	4	0	...	...	...	...
1995—	Daytona (Fla. St.)	3B	119	409	54	100	17	4	9	51	.244	42	71	5	80	204	26	.916
1996—	Orlando (South.)	3B	82	296	42	93	25	0	8	58	.314	48	52	2	60	144	14	.936
	— Iowa (Am. Assoc.)......	3B	14	48	5	10	1	0	2	6	.208	6	10	0	11	26	1	.974
1997—	Chicago (N.L.)............	3B-SS	114	364	40	100	23	5	8	44	.275	39	57	2	91	213	9	.971
	— Orlando (South.)	DH	3	13	3	5	2	0	2	6	.385	2	1	0	...	...	...	...
	— Iowa (Am. Assoc.)......	3B	9	32	7	12	4	0	1	8	.375	5	5	0	2	13	1	.938
1998—	Chicago (N.L.)............	3B	64	204	24	37	14	0	2	21	.181	18	35	1	39	101	5	.966
	— Iowa (Pacific Coast) ...	3B	24	92	27	34	8	0	9	24	.370	12	15	1	7	41	2	.960
	— Florida (N.L.)■..........	3B	48	175	23	46	8	1	6	17	.263	14	24	1	49	106	10	.939
Major league totals (2 years)			226	743	87	183	45	6	16	82	.246	71	116	4	179	420	24	.961

OROSCO, JESSE — P — ORIOLES

PERSONAL: Born April 21, 1957, in Santa Barbara, Calif. ... 6-2/205. ... Throws left, bats right. ... Name pronounced oh-ROSS-koh.
HIGH SCHOOL: Santa Barbara (Calif.).
COLLEGE: Santa Barbara (Calif.) City College.
TRANSACTIONS/CAREER NOTES: Selected by St. Louis Cardinals organization in seventh round of free-agent draft (January 11, 1977); did not sign. ... Selected by Minnesota Twins organization in second round of free-agent draft (January 10, 1978). ... Traded by Twins organization to New York Mets (February 7, 1979), completing deal in which Twins traded P Greg Field and a player to be named later to Mets for P Jerry Koosman (December 8, 1978). ... Traded by Mets as part of an eight-player, three-team deal in which Mets sent Orosco to Oakland Athletics (December 11, 1987); A's then traded Orosco, SS Alfredo Griffin and P Jay Howell to Los Angeles Dodgers for P Bob Welch, P Matt Young and P Jack Savage; A's then traded Savage, P Wally Whitehurst and P Kevin Tapani to Mets. ... Granted free agency (November 4, 1988). ... Signed by Cleveland Indians (December 3, 1988). ... Traded by Indians to Milwaukee Brewers for a player to be named later (December 6, 1991); deal settled in cash. ... Granted free agency (November 5, 1992). ... Re-signed by Brewers (December 4, 1992). ... Granted free agency (October 15, 1994). ... Signed by Baltimore Orioles (April 9, 1995). ... Granted free agency (October 27, 1996). ... Re-signed by Orioles (November 15, 1996).
MISCELLANEOUS: Appeared in one game as outfielder with one putout (1986). ... Struck out in only plate appearance (1993).

Year	Team (League)	W	L	Pct.	ERA	G	GS	CG	ShO	Sv.	IP	H	R	ER	BB	SO
1978—	Elizabethton (Appal.)	4	4	.500	1.13	20	0	0	0	6	40	29	7	5	20	48
1979—	Tidewater (Int'l)■..............	4	4	.500	3.89	16	15	1	0	0	81	82	45	35	43	55
	— New York (N.L.)	1	2	.333	4.89	18	2	0	0	0	35	33	20	19	22	22
1980—	Jackson (Texas)	4	4	.500	3.68	37	1	0	0	3	71	52	36	29	62	85
1981—	Tidewater (Int'l)	9	5	.643	3.31	46	10	0	0	8	87	80	39	32	32	81
	— New York (N.L.)	0	1	.000	1.59	8	0	0	0	1	17	13	4	3	6	18
1982—	New York (N.L.)	4	10	.286	2.72	54	2	0	0	4	109 1/3	92	37	33	40	89
1983—	New York (N.L.)	13	7	.650	1.47	62	0	0	0	17	110	76	27	18	38	84
1984—	New York (N.L.)	10	6	.625	2.59	60	0	0	0	31	87	58	29	25	34	85
1985—	New York (N.L.)	8	6	.571	2.73	54	0	0	0	17	79	66	26	24	34	68
1986—	New York (N.L.)	8	6	.571	2.33	58	0	0	0	21	81	64	23	21	35	62
1987—	New York (N.L.)	3	9	.250	4.44	58	0	0	0	16	77	78	41	38	31	78
1988—	Los Angeles (N.L.)■	3	2	.600	2.72	55	0	0	0	9	53	41	18	16	30	43
1989—	Cleveland (A.L.)	3	4	.429	2.08	69	0	0	0	3	78	54	20	18	26	79
1990—	Cleveland (A.L.)	5	4	.556	3.90	55	0	0	0	2	64 2/3	58	35	28	38	55
1991—	Cleveland (A.L.)	2	0	1.000	3.74	47	0	0	0	0	45 2/3	52	20	19	15	36
1992—	Milwaukee (A.L.)■	3	1	.750	3.23	59	0	0	0	1	39	33	15	14	13	40
1993—	Milwaukee (A.L.)	3	5	.375	3.18	57	0	0	0	8	56 2/3	47	25	20	17	67
1994—	Milwaukee (A.L.)	3	1	.750	5.08	40	0	0	0	0	39	32	26	22	26	36

O

Year Team (League)	W	L	Pct.	ERA	G	GS	CG	ShO	Sv.	IP	H	R	ER	BB	SO
1995— Baltimore (A.L.)■..............	2	4	.333	3.26	*65	0	0	0	3	49²/₃	28	19	18	27	58
1996— Baltimore (A.L.)................	3	1	.750	3.40	66	0	0	0	0	55²/₃	42	22	21	28	52
1997— Baltimore (A.L.)................	6	3	.667	2.32	71	0	0	0	0	50¹/₃	29	13	13	30	46
1998— Baltimore (A.L.)................	4	1	.800	3.18	69	0	0	0	7	56²/₃	46	20	20	28	50
A.L. totals (10 years)	34	24	.586	3.24	598	0	0	0	24	535¹/₃	421	215	193	248	519
N.L. totals (9 years)	50	49	.505	2.73	427	4	0	0	116	648¹/₃	521	225	197	270	549
Major league totals (19 years)....	84	73	.535	2.97	1025	4	0	0	140	1183²/₃	942	440	390	518	1068

DIVISION SERIES RECORD

Year Team (League)	W	L	Pct.	ERA	G	GS	CG	ShO	Sv.	IP	H	R	ER	BB	SO
1996— Baltimore (A.L.)................	0	1	.000	36.00	4	0	0	0	0	1	2	4	4	3	2
1997— Baltimore (A.L.)................	0	0	...	0.00	2	0	0	0	0	1¹/₃	1	0	0	0	1
Div. series totals (2 years)	0	1	.000	15.43	6	0	0	0	0	2¹/₃	3	4	4	3	3

CHAMPIONSHIP SERIES RECORD

RECORDS: Holds single-series record for most games won—3 (1986).

Year Team (League)	W	L	Pct.	ERA	G	GS	CG	ShO	Sv.	IP	H	R	ER	BB	SO
1986— New York (N.L.)...............	3	0	1.000	3.38	4	0	0	0	0	8	5	3	3	2	10
1988— Los Angeles (N.L.)	0	0	...	7.71	4	0	0	0	0	2¹/₃	4	2	2	3	0
1996— Baltimore (A.L.)................	0	0	...	4.50	4	0	0	0	0	2	2	1	1	2	2
1997— Baltimore (A.L.)................	0	0	...	0.00	2	0	0	0	0	1¹/₃	0	0	0	1	1
Champ. series totals (4 years)....	3	0	1.000	3.95	14	0	0	0	0	13²/₃	11	6	6	8	13

WORLD SERIES RECORD

NOTES: Member of World Series championship team (1986 and 1988).

Year Team (League)	W	L	Pct.	ERA	G	GS	CG	ShO	Sv.	IP	H	R	ER	BB	SO
1986— New York (N.L.)................	0	0	...	0.00	4	0	0	0	2	5²/₃	2	0	0	0	6
1988— Los Angeles (N.L.)							Did not play.								

ALL-STAR GAME RECORD

Year League	W	L	Pct.	ERA	GS	CG	ShO	Sv.	IP	H	R	ER	BB	SO
1983— National	0	0	...	0.00	0	0	0	0	¹/₃	0	0	0	0	1
1984— National							Did not play.							

ORTIZ, DAVID — 1B — TWINS

PERSONAL: Born November 18, 1975, in Santo Domingo, Dominican Republic. ... 6-4/237. ... Bats left, throws left. ... Full name: David Americo Ortiz.
HIGH SCHOOL: Estudia Espallat (Dominican Republic).
TRANSACTIONS/CAREER NOTES: Signed as non-drafted free agent by Seattle Mariners organization (November 28, 1992). ... Traded by Mariners to Minnesota Twins (September 13, 1996); completing deal in which Twins traded 3B Dave Hollins to Mariners for a player to be named later (August 29, 1996). ... On Minnesota disabled list (May 10-July 9, 1998); included rehabilitation assignment to Salt Lake (June 25-July 9).
STATISTICAL NOTES: Led Arizona League first basemen with 393 total chances in 1994.

Year Team (League)	Pos.	G	AB	R	H	2B	3B	HR	RBI	Avg.	BB	SO	SB	PO	A	E	Avg.
1994— Ariz. Mariners (Ariz.)..	1B	53	167	14	41	10	1	2	20	.246	14	46	1	*372	15	6	.985
1995— Ariz. Mariners (Ariz.)..	1B	48	184	30	61	18	4	4	37	.332	23	52	2	436	*27	5	*.989
1996— Wis. Rap. (Mid.)........	1B-3B	129	485	89	156	34	2	18	93	.322	52	108	3	1126	80	13	.989
1997— Fort Myers (FSL)........	1B	61	239	45	79	15	0	13	58	.331	22	53	2	524	44	9	.984
— New Britain (East.)	1B	69	258	40	83	22	2	14	56	.322	21	78	2	268	16	3	.990
— Salt Lake (PCL)	1B	10	42	5	9	1	0	4	10	.214	2	11	0	71	2	0	1.000
— Minnesota (A.L.)	1B-DH	15	49	10	16	3	0	1	6	.327	2	19	0	84	10	1	.989
1998— Minnesota (A.L.)	1B-DH	86	278	47	77	20	0	9	46	.277	39	72	1	503	46	6	.989
— Salt Lake (PCL)	1B	11	37	5	9	3	0	2	6	.243	3	9	0	76	10	3	.966
Major league totals (2 years)		101	327	57	93	23	0	10	52	.284	41	91	1	587	56	7	.989

ORTIZ, HECTOR — C — DODGERS

PERSONAL: Born October 14, 1969, in Rio Piedras, Puerto Rico. ... 6-0/205. ... Bats right, throws right.
HIGH SCHOOL: Luis Hernaiz Verone (Canovanas, Puerto Rico).
JUNIOR COLLEGE: Ranger (Texas) College.
TRANSACTIONS/CAREER NOTES: Selected by Los Angeles Dodgers organization in 35th round of free-agent draft (June 1, 1988). ... Granted free agency (October 17, 1994). ... Signed by Chicago Cubs organization (January 22, 1995). ... Granted free agency (October 15, 1996). ... Signed by Kansas City Royals organization (January 29, 1997). ... On Omaha disabled list (May 19-June 6, 1998). ... Granted free agency (October 15, 1998). ... Signed by Dodgers organization (January 6, 1999).

Year Team (League)	Pos.	G	AB	R	H	2B	3B	HR	RBI	Avg.	BB	SO	SB	PO	A	E	Avg.
1988— Salem (Northwest)	C-3B	32	77	5	11	1	0	0	4	.143	5	16	0	157	19	7	.962
1989— Vero Beach (FSL)	C	42	85	5	12	0	1	0	4	.141	6	15	0	174	23	6	.970
— Salem (Northwest)	C	44	140	13	32	3	1	0	12	.229	4	24	2	268	24	*12	.961
1990— Yakima (N'west)	C	52	173	16	47	3	1	0	12	.272	5	15	1	*392	*62	7	.985
1991— Vero Beach (FSL)	C	42	123	3	28	2	0	0	8	.228	5	8	0	238	28	7	.974
1992— Bakersfield (Calif.)......	C	63	206	19	58	8	1	1	31	.282	21	16	2	428	44	3	.994
— San Antonio (Tex.)	C	26	59	1	12	1	0	0	5	.203	11	13	0	140	23	3	.982
1993— San Antonio (Tex.)	C-3B	49	131	6	28	5	0	1	6	.214	9	17	0	311	43	8	.978
— Albuquerque (PCL).....	C	18	44	0	8	1	1	0	3	.182	0	6	0	78	11	2	.978
1994— Albuquerque (PCL).....	C	34	93	7	28	1	1	0	10	.301	3	12	0	144	20	4	.976
— San Antonio (Tex.)	C-P	24	75	4	9	0	0	0	4	.120	2	7	0	166	23	2	.990

Year	Team (League)	Pos.	G	AB	R	H	2B	3B	HR	RBI	Avg.	BB	SO	SB	PO	A	E	Avg.
1995—	Orlando (South.)■	C	96	299	13	70	12	0	0	18	.234	20	39	0	567	72	6	.991
1996—	Orlando (South.)	C	78	216	16	47	8	0	0	15	.218	26	23	1	475	32	6	.988
—	Iowa (Am. Assoc.)......	C	27	79	6	19	2	0	0	3	.241	3	16	0	139	9	2	.987
1997—	Omaha (A.A.)■	C	21	63	7	12	3	0	0	3	.190	13	15	0	130	6	3	.978
—	Wichita (Texas)	C	59	180	20	45	3	0	1	25	.250	21	15	1	340	40	*15	.962
1998—	Wichita (Texas)	C	4	13	1	2	0	0	0	0	.154	2	1	0	24	6	1	.968
—	Omaha (PCL).............	C	63	191	17	43	7	0	0	12	.225	9	26	0	318	30	8	.978
—	Kansas City (A.L.)	C-1B	4	4	1	0	0	0	0	0	.000	0	0	0	4	0	0	1.000
Major league totals (1 year)			4	4	1	0	0	0	0	0	.000	0	0	0	4	0	0	1.000

RECORD AS PITCHER

Year	Team (League)	W	L	Pct.	ERA	G	GS	CG	ShO	Sv.	IP	H	R	ER	BB	SO
1994—	San Antonio (Tex.)	0	0	...	0.00	1	0	0	0	0	1	0	0	0	1	1

ORTIZ, JOSE — IF — ATHLETICS

PERSONAL: Born June 13, 1977, in Santo Domingo, Dominican Republic. ... 5-9/160. ... Bats right, throws right. ... Full name: Jose Daniel Ortiz (Santos).
TRANSACTIONS/CAREER NOTES: Signed as non-drafted free agent by Oakland Athletics organization (November 8, 1994). ... On disabled list (May 10-June 30, 1998).
STATISTICAL NOTES: Led Arizona League with .530 slugging percentage in 1996. ... Led Arizona League shortstops with 279 total chances and 42 double plays in 1996. ... Led California League shortstops with 53 errors and 80 double plays in 1997.

Year	Team (League)	Pos.	G	AB	R	H	2B	3B	HR	RBI	Avg.	BB	SO	SB	PO	A	E	Avg.
1995—	Dom. Athletics (DSL) .	SS	61	217	45	65	12	2	9	41	.300	32	22	14	182	38	17	.928
1996—	Arizona A's (Ariz.)	SS	52	200	*43	66	12	8	4	25	.330	20	34	16	*93	*165	21	.925
—	Modesto (California) ..	2B	1	4	0	1	0	0	0	0	.250	0	1	0	2	5	0	1.000
1997—	Modesto (California) ..	SS-2B	128	497	92	122	25	7	16	58	.245	60	107	22	186	373	†53	.913
1998—	Huntsville (Sou.)	2B-SS-OF	94	354	70	98	24	2	6	55	.277	48	63	22	159	274	27	.941

ORTIZ, RAMON — P — ANGELS

PERSONAL: Born March 23, 1976, in Cotui, Dominican Republic. ... 6-0/165. ... Throws right, bats right. ... Full name: Ramon Diogenes Ortiz.
HIGH SCHOOL: 8th Intermedian (Dominican Republic).
TRANSACTIONS/CAREER NOTES: Signed as non-drafted free agent (June 20, 1995). ... Angels franchise renamed Anaheim Angels for 1997 season. ... On disabled list (May 9, 1998-remainder of season).
STATISTICAL NOTES: Pitched 12-0 no-hit victory against Quad City (August 7, 1997).

Year	Team (League)	W	L	Pct.	ERA	G	GS	CG	ShO	Sv.	IP	H	R	ER	BB	SO
1996—	Boise (Northwest)	1	1	.500	3.66	3	3	0	0	0	19²/₃	21	10	8	6	18
1997—	Cedar Rapids (Midw.)	11	10	.524	3.58	27	•27	*8	*4	0	181	156	78	72	53	*225
1998—	Midland (Texas)	2	1	.667	5.55	7	7	0	0	0	47	50	31	29	16	53

ORTIZ, RUSS — P — GIANTS

PERSONAL: Born June 5, 1974, in Encino, Calif. ... 6-1/210. ... Throws right, bats right. ... Full name: Russell Reid Ortiz.
HIGH SCHOOL: Montclair Prep (Van Nuys, Calif.).
COLLEGE: Oklahoma.
TRANSACTIONS/CAREER NOTES: Selected by San Francisco Giants organization in fourth round of free-agent draft (June 1, 1995).
RECORDS: Shares N.L. record for most consecutive home runs allowed in one inning—3 (August 10, 1998, fifth inning).

Year	Team (League)	W	L	Pct.	ERA	G	GS	CG	ShO	Sv.	IP	H	R	ER	BB	SO
1995—	Bellingham (N'west)...........	2	0	1.000	0.52	25	0	0	0	11	34¹/₃	19	4	2	13	55
—	San Jose (California).........	0	1	.000	1.50	5	0	0	0	0	6	4	1	1	2	7
1996—	San Jose (California).........	0	0	...	0.25	34	0	0	0	23	36²/₃	16	2	1	20	63
—	Shreveport (Texas)............	1	2	.333	4.05	26	0	0	0	13	26²/₃	22	14	12	21	29
1997—	Shreveport (Texas)............	2	3	.400	4.13	12	12	0	0	0	56²/₃	52	28	26	37	50
—	Phoenix (PCL)...............	4	3	.571	5.51	14	14	0	0	0	85	96	57	52	34	70
1998—	San Francisco (N.L.)	4	4	.500	4.99	22	13	0	0	0	88¹/₃	90	51	49	46	75
—	Fresno (Pacific Coast)........	3	1	.750	1.60	10	10	0	0	0	50²/₃	35	10	9	22	59
Major league totals (1 year)........		4	4	.500	4.99	22	13	0	0	0	88¹/₃	90	51	49	46	75

O OSBORNE, DONOVAN — P — CARDINALS

PERSONAL: Born June 21, 1969, in Roseville, Calif. ... 6-2/195. ... Throws left, bats left. ... Full name: Donovan Alan Osborne.
HIGH SCHOOL: Carson City (Nev.).
COLLEGE: UNLV.
TRANSACTIONS/CAREER NOTES: Selected by Montreal Expos organization in ninth round of free-agent draft (June 2, 1987); did not sign. ... Selected by St. Louis Cardinals organization in first round (13th pick overall) of free-agent draft (June 4, 1990). ... On St. Louis disabled list (April 2, 1994-entire season). ... On St. Louis disabled list (May 15-July 14, 1995); included rehabilitation assignments to Arkansas and Louisville (June 28-July 14). ... On St. Louis disabled list (March 25-April 17, 1996); included rehabilitation assignments to St. Petersburg (April 7-12) and Louisville (April 12-17). ... On St. Louis disabled list (May 3-July 29, 1997). ... On St. Louis disabled list (March 22-April 16 and May 8-August 8, 1998); included rehabilitation assignments to Arkansas (April 6-10, April 12-16 and July 17-August 1) and Memphis (April 11).
HONORS: Named lefthanded pitcher on THE SPORTING NEWS college All-America team (1989).
STATISTICAL NOTES: Career major league grand slams: 1.
MISCELLANEOUS: Appeared in three games as pinch runner (1993).

Year	Team (League)	W	L	Pct.	ERA	G	GS	CG	ShO	Sv.	IP	H	R	ER	BB	SO
1990—	Hamilton (NYP)	0	2	.000	3.60	4	4	0	0	0	20	21	8	8	5	14
—	Savannah (S. Atl.)	2	2	.500	2.61	6	6	1	0	0	41 1/3	40	20	12	7	28
1991—	Arkansas (Texas)	8	12	.400	3.63	26	26	3	0	0	166	178	82	67	43	130
1992—	St. Louis (N.L.)	11	9	.550	3.77	34	29	0	0	0	179	193	91	75	38	104
1993—	St. Louis (N.L.)	10	7	.588	3.76	26	26	1	0	0	155 2/3	153	73	65	47	83
1994—								Did not play.								
1995—	St. Louis (N.L.)	4	6	.400	3.81	19	19	0	0	0	113 1/3	112	58	48	34	82
—	Arkansas (Texas)	0	1	.000	2.45	2	2	0	0	0	11	12	4	3	2	6
—	Louisville (A.A.)	0	1	.000	3.86	1	1	0	0	0	7	8	3	3	0	3
1996—	St. Petersburg (FSL)	1	0	1.000	0.00	1	1	0	0	0	6	2	0	0	0	2
—	Louisville (A.A.)	1	0	1.000	2.57	1	1	0	0	0	7	6	2	2	2	3
—	St. Louis (N.L.)	13	9	.591	3.53	30	30	2	1	0	198 2/3	191	87	78	57	134
1997—	St. Louis (N.L.)	3	7	.300	4.93	14	14	0	0	0	80 1/3	84	46	44	23	51
—	Louisville (A.A.)	0	1	.000	4.73	3	3	0	0	0	13 1/3	13	7	7	5	13
1998—	Arkansas (Texas)	2	0	1.000	4.26	5	5	0	0	0	19	16	9	9	3	21
—	Memphis (Pacific Coast)	0	0		6.23	1	1	0	0	0	4 1/3	5	4	3	0	6
—	St. Louis (N.L.)	5	4	.556	4.09	14	14	1	1	0	83 2/3	84	42	38	22	60
Major league totals (6 years)		46	42	.523	3.86	137	132	4	2	0	810 2/3	817	397	348	221	514

DIVISION SERIES RECORD

Year	Team (League)	W	L	Pct.	ERA	G	GS	CG	ShO	Sv.	IP	H	R	ER	BB	SO
1996—	St. Louis (N.L.)	0	0	...	9.00	1	1	0	0	0	4	7	4	4	0	5

CHAMPIONSHIP SERIES RECORD

Year	Team (League)	W	L	Pct.	ERA	G	GS	CG	ShO	Sv.	IP	H	R	ER	BB	SO
1996—	St. Louis (N.L.)	1	1	.500	9.39	2	2	0	0	0	7 2/3	12	8	8	4	6

OSIK, KEITH   C   PIRATES

PERSONAL: Born October 22, 1968, in Port Jefferson, N.Y. ... 6-0/198. ... Bats right, throws right. ... Full name: Keith Richard Osik. ... Name pronounced OH-sik.
HIGH SCHOOL: Shoreham (N.Y.)-Wading River.
COLLEGE: Louisiana State.
TRANSACTIONS/CAREER NOTES: Selected by Texas Rangers organization in 47th round of free-agent draft (June 2, 1987); did not sign. ... Selected by Pittsburgh Pirates organization in 24th round of free-agent draft (June 4, 1990). ... On Pittsburgh disabled list (July 16-August 13, 1996); included rehabilitation assignment to Erie (August 10-13).

Year	Team (League)	Pos.	G	AB	R	H	2B	3B	HR	RBI	Avg.	BB	SO	SB	PO	A	E	Avg.
1990—	Welland (NYP)	3-C-1-2-S	29	97	13	27	4	0	1	20	.278	11	12	2	59	29	2	.978
1991—	Salem (Carolina)	C-3B-2B	87	300	31	81	12	1	6	35	.270	38	48	2	307	85	12	.970
—	Carolina (Southern)	C-3B	17	43	9	13	3	1	0	5	.302	5	5	0	84	13	2	.980
1992—	Carolina (Southern)	3-C-2-P	129	425	41	110	17	1	5	45	.259	52	69	2	222	195	19	.956
1993—	Carolina (Southern)	C-3B	103	371	47	104	21	2	10	47	.280	30	46	0	662	69	6	.992
1994—	Buffalo (A.A.)	C-O-1-P-2	83	260	27	55	16	0	5	33	.212	28	41	0	403	50	8	.983
1995—	Calgary (PCL)	C-1-O-P-3	90	301	40	101	25	1	10	59	.336	21	42	2	458	35	4	.992
1996—	Pittsburgh (N.L.)	C-3B-OF	48	140	18	41	14	1	1	14	.293	14	22	1	237	25	6	.978
—	Erie (N.Y.-Penn)	C	3	10	1	3	1	0	0	2	.300	1	2	0	19	2	0	1.000
1997—	Pittsburgh (N.L.)	C-2-1-3	49	105	10	27	9	1	0	7	.257	9	21	0	163	14	2	.989
1998—	Pittsburgh (N.L.)	C-3B	39	98	8	21	4	0	0	7	.214	13	16	1	152	30	1	.995
Major league totals (3 years)			136	343	36	89	27	2	1	28	.259	36	59	2	552	69	9	.986

RECORD AS PITCHER

Year	Team (League)	W	L	Pct.	ERA	G	GS	CG	ShO	Sv.	IP	H	R	ER	BB	SO
1992—	Carolina (Southern)	0	0	...	0.00	2	0	0	0	0	2 2/3	2	0	0	0	3
1994—	Buffalo (A.A.)	0	1	.000	13.50	1	0	0	0	0	2/3	2	1	1	0	1
1995—	Calgary (PCL)	0	0	...	4.50	2	0	0	0	0	2	1	1	1	1	3

OSUNA, ANTONIO   P   DODGERS

PERSONAL: Born April 12, 1973, in Sinaloa, Mexico. ... 5-11/206. ... Throws right, bats right. ... Full name: Antonio Pedro Osuna.
HIGH SCHOOL: Secondaria Federal (Mexico).
TRANSACTIONS/CAREER NOTES: Signed as non-drafted free agent by Los Angeles Dodgers organization (June 12, 1991). ... On suspended list (April 8-July 17, 1993). ... On San Antonio disabled list (April 8-June 6, 1994). ... On Los Angeles disabled list (May 19-June 16, 1995); included rehabilitation assignment to San Bernardino (June 6-16). ... On disabled list (September 9, 1998-remainder of season).

Year	Team (League)	W	L	Pct.	ERA	G	GS	CG	ShO	Sv.	IP	H	R	ER	BB	SO
1991—	GC Dodgers (GCL)	0	0	...	0.82	8	0	0	0	4	11	8	5	1	0	13
—	Yakima (N'west)	0	0	...	3.20	13	0	0	0	5	25 1/3	18	10	9	8	39
1992—	M.C. Tigers (Mex.)	13	7	.650	4.05	28	26	3	1	0	166 2/3	181	80	75	74	129
1993—	Bakersfield (California)	0	2	.000	4.91	14	2	0	0	2	18 1/3	19	10	10	5	20
1994—	San Antonio (Tex.)	1	2	.333	0.98	35	0	0	0	19	46	19	6	5	18	53
—	Albuquerque (PCL)	0	0	...	0.00	6	0	0	0	4	6	5	1	0	1	8
1995—	Los Angeles (N.L.)	2	4	.333	4.43	39	0	0	0	0	44 2/3	39	22	22	20	46
—	San Bernardino (Calif.)	0	0	...	1.29	5	0	0	0	0	7	3	1	1	5	11
—	Albuquerque (PCL)	0	1	.000	4.42	19	0	0	0	11	18 1/3	15	9	9	9	19
1996—	Albuquerque (PCL)	0	0	...	0.00	1	0	0	0	0	1	2	0	0	0	1
—	Los Angeles (N.L.)	9	6	.600	3.00	73	0	0	0	4	84	65	33	28	32	85
1997—	Albuquerque (PCL)	1	1	.500	1.93	13	0	0	0	6	14	9	3	3	4	26
—	Los Angeles (N.L.)	3	4	.429	2.19	48	0	0	0	0	61 2/3	46	15	15	19	68
1998—	Los Angeles (N.L.)	7	1	.875	3.06	54	0	0	0	6	64 2/3	50	26	22	32	72
Major league totals (4 years)		21	15	.583	3.07	214	0	0	0	10	255	200	96	87	103	271

Year Team (League)	W	L	Pct.	ERA	G	GS	CG	ShO	Sv.	IP	H	R	ER	BB	SO
1995— Los Angeles (N.L.)	0	1	.000	2.70	3	0	0	0	0	3 1/3	3	1	1	1	3
1996— Los Angeles (N.L.)	0	1	.000	4.50	2	0	0	0	0	2	3	1	1	1	4
Div. series totals (2 years)	0	2	.000	3.38	5	0	0	0	0	5 1/3	6	2	2	2	7

OTANEZ, WILLIS 3B ORIOLES

PERSONAL: Born April 19, 1973, in Vega Baja, Puerto Rico. ... 6-1/200. ... Bats right, throws right. ... Full name: Willis A. Otanez.
HIGH SCHOOL: Liceo Miguel Angel Garcia (Cotui, Dominican Republic).
TRANSACTIONS/CAREER NOTES: Signed as non-drafted free agent by Los Angeles Dodgers organization (February 10, 1990). ... On disabled list (August 3-September 10, 1993). ... Traded by Dodgers with 2B Miguel Cairo to Seattle Mariners for 3B Mike Blowers (November 29, 1995). ... Claimed on waivers by Baltimore Orioles (February 12, 1996). ... On Rochester disabled list (May 15-July 24, 1997). ... Granted free agency (December 21, 1997). ... Re-signed by Orioles (January 8, 1998). ... On Baltimore disabled list (August 28, 1998-remainder of season).
STATISTICAL NOTES: Led Eastern League second basemen with 106 putouts in 1996. ... Led International League third basemen with .968 fielding percentage and 91 putouts in 1998.

							BATTING							FIELDING		
Year Team (League)	Pos.	G	AB	R	H	2B	3B	HR	RBI	Avg.	BB	SO	SB	PO	A	E	Avg.
1990— Dom. Dodgers (DSL) .	...	70	267	44	84	18	0	1	46	.315	51	24	4	...	...	...	...
1991— Great Falls (Pio.)	SS-3B	58	222	38	64	9	2	6	39	.288	19	34	3	64	124	22	.895
1992— Vero Beach (FSL)	SS-3B	117	390	27	86	18	0	3	27	.221	24	60	2	160	305	33	.934
1993— Bakersfield (Calif.)	3B-SS-2B	95	325	34	85	11	2	10	39	.262	29	63	1	76	211	25	.920
1994— Vero Beach (FSL)	3B	131	476	77	132	27	1	19	72	.277	53	98	4	*109	302	23	.947
1995— Vero Beach (FSL)	3B	92	354	39	92	24	0	10	53	.260	28	59	1	59	186	20	.925
— San Antonio (Tex.)	3B	27	100	8	24	4	1	1	7	.240	6	25	0	18	48	3	.957
1996— Bowie (Eastern)■	3B-SS	138	506	60	134	27	2	24	75	.265	45	97	3	†106	279	24	.941
1997— Rochester (Int'l)	3B-1B	49	168	20	35	9	0	5	25	.208	15	35	0	67	68	12	.918
— Bowie (Eastern)	3B	19	78	13	26	9	0	3	13	.333	9	19	0	1	20	1	.955
— GC Orioles (GCL)	DH	8	25	5	8	2	0	2	3	.320	2	4	0	...	...	...	...
1998— Rochester (Int'l)	3B-1B-OF	124	481	87	137	24	2	27	100	.285	41	104	1	†122	240	12	†.968
— Baltimore (A.L.)	OF	3	5	0	1	0	0	0	0	.200	0	2	0	1	0	0	1.000
Major league totals (1 year)		3	5	0	1	0	0	0	0	.200	0	2	0	1	0	0	1.000

OWENS, ERIC IF/OF

PERSONAL: Born February 3, 1971, in Danville, Va. ... 6-1/185. ... Bats right, throws right. ... Full name: Eric Blake Owens.
HIGH SCHOOL: Tunstall (Dry Fork, Va.).
COLLEGE: Ferrum (Va.).
TRANSACTIONS/CAREER NOTES: Selected by Cincinnati Reds organization in fourth round of free-agent draft (June 1, 1992). ... On Indianapolis disabled list (August 20-September 11, 1995). ... Traded by Reds to Florida Marlins for a player to be named later (March 21, 1998). ... Reds acquired P Jesus Martinez to complete deal (March 26, 1998). ... Contract sold by Marlins to Milwaukee Brewers (March 25, 1998). ... Granted free agency (October 15, 1998).
HONORS: Named American Association Most Valuable Player (1995).
STATISTICAL NOTES: Led Pioneer League shortstops with 28 errors in 1992. ... Tied for American Association lead in errors by second baseman with 17 in 1997.

							BATTING							FIELDING		
Year Team (League)	Pos.	G	AB	R	H	2B	3B	HR	RBI	Avg.	BB	SO	SB	PO	A	E	Avg.
1992— Billings (Pioneer)	SS-3B	67	239	41	72	10	3	3	26	.301	23	22	15	82	164	†29	.895
1993— Win.-Salem (Car.)	SS	122	487	74	132	25	4	10	63	.271	53	69	21	*215	347	34	.943
1994— Chattanooga (Sou.)	3B-2B	134	523	73	133	17	3	3	36	.254	54	86	38	151	266	40	.912
1995— Indianapolis (A.A.)	2B	108	427	*86	134	24	•8	12	63	.314	52	61	*33	219	274	*17	.967
— Cincinnati (N.L.)	3B	2	2	0	2	0	0	0	1	1.000	0	0	0	0	0	0	...
1996— Indianapolis (A.A.)	S-3-2-O	33	128	24	41	8	2	4	14	.320	11	16	6	44	64	6	.947
— Cincinnati (N.L.)	OF-2B-3B	88	205	26	41	6	0	0	9	.200	23	38	16	76	14	2	.978
1997— Cincinnati (N.L.)	OF-2B	27	57	8	15	0	0	0	3	.263	4	11	3	15	0	1	.938
— Indianapolis (A.A.)	2-S-O-3	104	391	56	112	15	4	11	44	.286	42	55	23	184	241	‡27	.940
1998— Milwaukee (N.L.)■	OF-2B	34	40	5	5	2	0	1	4	.125	2	6	0	14	2	1	.941
— Louisville (Int'l)	OF-3B	77	254	48	85	11	4	5	40	.335	34	30	21	85	57	8	.947
Major league totals (4 years)		151	304	39	63	8	0	1	17	.207	29	55	19	105	16	4	.968

PAGNOZZI, TOM C

PERSONAL: Born July 30, 1962, in Tucson, Ariz. ... 6-1/190. ... Bats right, throws right. ... Full name: Thomas Alan Pagnozzi. ... Brother of Tim Pagnozzi, minor league shortstop (1976); and brother of Mike Pagnozzi, minor league pitcher (1975-78). ... Name pronounced pag-NAHZ-ee.
HIGH SCHOOL: Rincon (Tucson, Ariz.).
JUNIOR COLLEGE: Central Arizona College.
COLLEGE: Arkansas.
TRANSACTIONS/CAREER NOTES: Selected by Milwaukee Brewers organization in 24th round of free-agent draft (January 12, 1982); did not sign. ... Selected by St. Louis Cardinals organization in eighth round of free-agent draft (June 6, 1983). ... On St. Louis disabled list (May 8-June 17, 1993); included rehabilitation assignment to Louisville (June 2-17). ... On St. Louis disabled list (March 29-May 5, 1994); included rehabilitation assignment to Louisville (April 23-May 5). ... On St. Louis disabled list (July 18-August 26, 1995); included rehabilitation assignment to Louisville (August 17-26). ... On St. Louis disabled list (March 24-April 15, 1996); included rehabilitation assignment to Louisville (April 4-15). ... Granted free agency (October 31, 1996). ... Re-signed by Cardinals (December 6, 1996). ... On St. Louis disabled list (March 29-April 25 and April 30-August 11, 1997); included rehabilitation assignment to Arkansas (April 19-25). ... On St. Louis disabled list (April 4-28, 1998); included rehabilitation assignment to Peoria (April 24-28). ... Released by Cardinals (August 16, 1998).
HONORS: Won N.L. Gold Glove at catcher (1991-92 and 1994).
STATISTICAL NOTES: Led N.L. catchers with .998 fielding percentage in 1994. ... Career major league grand slams: 2.

O

P

Year	Team (League)	Pos.	G	AB	R	H	2B	3B	HR	RBI	Avg.	BB	SO	SB	PO	A	E	Avg.
1983—	Erie (N.Y.-Penn)	C	45	168	28	52	9	1	6	22	.310	14	34	3	183	20	3	.985
—	Macon (S. Atl.)	C	18	57	7	14	2	1	0	6	.246	6	13	0	125	18	8	.947
1984—	Springfield (Midw.)	C	114	396	57	112	20	4	10	68	.283	31	75	3	667	*90	12	.984
1985—	Arkansas (Texas)	C-1B	41	139	15	43	7	1	5	29	.309	13	21	0	243	27	1	.996
—	Louisville (A.A.)	C	76	268	29	72	13	2	5	40	.269	21	47	0	266	25	4	.986
1986—	Louisville (A.A.)	C	30	106	12	31	4	0	1	18	.292	6	21	0	160	19	3	.984
1987—	Louisville (A.A.)	C-3B	84	320	53	100	20	2	14	71	.313	30	50	0	427	43	6	.987
—	St. Louis (N.L.)	C-1B	27	48	8	9	1	0	2	9	.188	4	13	1	61	5	0	1.000
1988—	St. Louis (N.L.)	1B-C	81	195	17	55	9	0	0	15	.282	11	32	0	340	30	4	.989
1989—	St. Louis (N.L.)	C-1B-3B	52	80	3	12	2	0	0	3	.150	6	19	0	100	9	2	.982
1990—	St. Louis (N.L.)	C-1B	69	220	20	61	15	0	2	23	.277	14	37	1	345	39	4	.990
1991—	St. Louis (N.L.)	C-1B	140	459	38	121	24	5	2	57	.264	36	63	9	682	81	7	.991
1992—	St. Louis (N.L.)	C	139	485	33	121	26	3	7	44	.249	28	64	2	688	53	1	*.999
1993—	St. Louis (N.L.)	C	92	330	31	85	15	1	7	41	.258	19	30	1	421	44	4	.991
—	Louisville (A.A.)	C	12	43	5	12	3	0	1	1	.279	2	3	0	51	6	2	.966
1994—	Louisville (A.A.)	C	10	25	4	6	3	0	0	3	.240	6	6	0	32	3	0	1.000
—	St. Louis (N.L.)	C-1B	70	243	21	66	12	1	7	40	.272	21	39	0	370	41	1	†.998
1995—	St. Louis (N.L.)	C	62	219	17	47	14	1	2	15	.215	11	31	0	336	38	2	.995
—	Louisville (A.A.)	C	5	16	4	8	2	0	1	3	.500	1	0	0	19	0	0	1.000
1996—	Louisville (A.A.)	C	8	26	5	4	0	0	2	3	.154	3	2	0	36	5	0	1.000
—	St. Louis (N.L.)	C-1B	119	407	48	110	23	0	13	55	.270	24	78	4	717	48	8	.990
1997—	Arkansas (Texas)	C	21	63	8	20	0	0	5	17	.317	4	8	0	68	4	1	.986
—	St. Louis (N.L.)	C-1B-3B	25	50	4	11	3	0	1	8	.220	1	7	0	63	2	0	1.000
—	Louisville (A.A.)	C	3	5	0	0	0	0	0	0	.000	0	1	0	8	3	0	1.000
1998—	St. Louis (N.L.)	C	51	160	7	35	9	0	1	10	.219	14	37	0	259	17	5	.982
—	Peoria (Midwest)	C	4	8	2	1	0	0	0	1	.125	6	1	0	28	0	0	1.000
Major league totals (12 years)			927	2896	247	733	153	11	44	320	.253	189	450	18	4382	407	38	.992

DIVISION SERIES RECORD

Year	Team (League)	Pos.	G	AB	R	H	2B	3B	HR	RBI	Avg.	BB	SO	SB	PO	A	E	Avg.
1996—	St. Louis (N.L.)	C	3	11	0	3	0	0	0	2	.273	2	3	0	28	0	0	1.000

CHAMPIONSHIP SERIES RECORD

Year	Team (League)	Pos.	G	AB	R	H	2B	3B	HR	RBI	Avg.	BB	SO	SB	PO	A	E	Avg.
1987—	St. Louis (N.L.)	PH	1	1	0	0	0	0	0	0	.000	0	0	0	...	...		...
1996—	St. Louis (N.L.)	C	7	19	1	3	1	0	0	1	.158	1	4	0	49	1	0	1.000
Championship series totals (2 years)			8	20	1	3	1	0	0	1	.150	1	4	0	49	1	0	1.000

WORLD SERIES RECORD

Year	Team (League)	Pos.	G	AB	R	H	2B	3B	HR	RBI	Avg.	BB	SO	SB	PO	A	E	Avg.
1987—	St. Louis (N.L.)	DH-PH	2	4	0	1	0	0	0	0	.250	0	0	0	...			

ALL-STAR GAME RECORD

Year	League	Pos.	AB	R	H	2B	3B	HR	RBI	Avg.	BB	SO	SB	PO	A	E	Avg.
1992—	National	PH	1	0	0	0	0	0	0	.000	0	0	0	...	...		...

PAINTER, LANCE — P — CARDINALS

PERSONAL: Born July 21, 1967, in Bedford, England. ... 6-1/197. ... Throws left, bats left. ... Full name: Lance Telford Painter.
HIGH SCHOOL: Nicolet (Glendale, Wis.).
COLLEGE: Wisconsin.
TRANSACTIONS/CAREER NOTES: Selected by San Diego Padres organization in 25th round of free-agent draft (June 4, 1990). ... Selected by Colorado Rockies in second round (34th pick overall) of expansion draft (November 17, 1992). ... On disabled list (April 17-May 6, 1995). ... On disabled list (August 6, 1996-remainder of season). ... Claimed on waivers by St. Louis Cardinals (December 2, 1996). ... On disabled list (April 5-May 12 and May 20-June 20, 1997); included rehabilitation assignment to Louisville (May 1-12).
STATISTICAL NOTES: Led Texas League with 10 hit batsmen in 1992.
MISCELLANEOUS: Received base on balls in only appearance as pinch hitter with Colorado (1995). ... Struck out twice in two appearances as pinch hitter (1996).

Year	Team (League)	W	L	Pct.	ERA	G	GS	CG	ShO	Sv.	IP	H	R	ER	BB	SO
1990—	Spokane (N'west)	7	3	.700	1.51	23	1	0	0	3	71 2/3	45	18	12	15	104
1991—	Waterloo (Midw.)	14	8	.636	2.30	28	28	7	*4	0	200	162	64	51	57	201
1992—	Wichita (Texas)	10	5	*.667	3.53	27	•27	1	1	0	163 1/3	138	74	64	55	137
1993—	Colo. Springs (PCL)■	9	7	.563	4.30	23	22	•4	1	0	138	165	90	66	44	91
—	Colorado (N.L.)	2	2	.500	6.00	10	6	1	0	0	39	52	26	26	9	16
1994—	Colo. Springs (PCL)	4	3	.571	4.79	13	13	1	0	0	71 1/3	83	42	38	28	59
—	Colorado (N.L.)	4	6	.400	6.11	15	14	0	0	0	73 2/3	91	51	50	26	41
1995—	Colorado (N.L.)	3	0	1.000	4.37	33	1	0	0	0	45 1/3	55	23	22	10	36
—	Colo. Springs (PCL)	0	3	.000	5.96	11	4	0	0	0	25 2/3	32	20	17	11	12
1996—	Colorado (N.L.)	4	2	.667	5.86	34	1	0	0	0	50 2/3	56	37	33	25	48
1997—	Colorado (N.L.)■	1	1	.500	4.76	14	0	0	0	0	17	13	9	9	8	11
—	Louisville (A.A.)	1	0	1.000	5.23	18	2	0	0	0	20 2/3	18	14	12	4	22
1998—	St. Louis (N.L.)	4	0	1.000	3.99	65	0	0	0	1	47 1/3	42	24	21	28	39
Major league totals (6 years)		18	11	.621	5.31	171	22	1	0	2	273	309	170	161	106	191

DIVISION SERIES RECORD

NOTES: Struck out in only appearance as pinch hitter (1995).

Year	Team (League)	W	L	Pct.	ERA	G	GS	CG	ShO	Sv.	IP	H	R	ER	BB	SO
1995—	Colorado (N.L.)	0	0	...	5.40	1	1	0	0	0	5	5	3	3	2	4

P

PALL, DONN   P

PERSONAL: Born January 11, 1962, in Chicago. ... 6-1/179. ... Throws right, bats right. ... Full name: Donn Steven Pall.
HIGH SCHOOL: Evergreen Park (Ill.).
COLLEGE: Illinois (received degree, 1985).
TRANSACTIONS/CAREER NOTES: Selected by Chicago White Sox organization in 23rd round of free-agent draft (June 3, 1985). ... On Chicago disabled list (May 19-June 2, 1989); included rehabilitation assignment to South Bend (May 30-June 2). ... Traded by White Sox to Philadelphia Phillies for a player to be named later (September 1, 1993); White Sox acquired C Doug Lindsey to complete deal (September 8, 1993). ... Granted free agency (December 20, 1993). ... Signed by New York Yankees (January 16, 1994). ... Released by Yankees (July 29, 1994). ... Signed by Chicago Cubs (August 6, 1994). ... Granted free agency (October 21, 1994). ... Signed by White Sox organization (March 27, 1995). ... Granted free agency (October 16, 1995). ... Signed by Florida Marlins organization (April 25, 1996). ... Granted free agency (October 15, 1996). ... Re-signed by Marlins (January 2, 1997). ... Granted free agency (October 15, 1997). ... Re-signed by Marlins organization (February 19, 1998). ... Granted free agency (September 29, 1998).

Year	Team (League)	W	L	Pct.	ERA	G	GS	CG	ShO	Sv.	IP	H	R	ER	BB	SO
1985—	GC White Sox (GCL)	•7	5	.583	1.67	13	13	•4	•2	0	*86	68	34	16	10	63
1986—	Appleton (Midwest)	5	5	.500	2.31	11	11	3	1	0	78	71	29	20	14	51
—	Birmingham (Southern)	3	4	.429	4.44	21	9	0	0	1	73	77	38	36	27	41
1987—	Birmingham (Southern)	8	11	.421	4.27	30	23	3	0	0	158	173	100	75	63	139
1988—	Vancouver (PCL)	5	2	.714	2.23	44	0	0	0	10	72 2/3	61	21	18	20	41
—	Chicago (A.L.)	0	2	.000	3.45	17	0	0	0	0	28 2/3	39	11	11	8	16
1989—	Chicago (A.L.)	4	5	.444	3.31	53	0	0	0	6	87	90	35	32	19	58
—	South Bend (Mid.)	0	0	. . .	0.00	2	0	0	0	0	3 1/3	1	0	0	0	4
1990—	Chicago (A.L.)	3	5	.375	3.32	56	0	0	0	2	76	63	33	28	24	39
1991—	Chicago (A.L.)	7	2	.778	2.41	51	0	0	0	0	71	59	22	19	20	40
1992—	Chicago (A.L.)	5	2	.714	4.93	39	0	0	0	1	73	79	43	40	27	27
1993—	Chicago (A.L.)	2	3	.400	3.22	39	0	0	0	1	58 2/3	62	25	21	11	29
—	Philadelphia (N.L.)■	1	0	1.000	2.55	8	0	0	0	0	17 2/3	15	7	5	3	11
1994—	New York (A.L.)■	1	2	.333	3.60	26	0	0	0	0	35	43	18	14	9	21
—	Chicago (N.L.)■	0	0	. . .	4.50	2	0	0	0	0	4	8	2	2	1	2
1995—	Nashville (A.A.)■	4	3	.571	3.98	44	0	0	0	3	86	89	40	38	20	79
1996—	Charlotte (Int'l)■	3	3	.500	2.96	38	0	0	0	17	51 2/3	42	21	17	12	53
—	Florida (N.L.)	1	1	.500	5.79	12	0	0	0	0	18 2/3	16	15	12	9	9
1997—	Charlotte (Int'l)	4	7	.364	3.39	59	0	0	0	8	79 2/3	82	40	30	11	70
—	Florida (N.L.)	0	0	. . .	3.86	2	0	0	0	0	2 1/3	3	1	1	1	0
1998—	Charlotte (Int'l)	1	2	.333	4.15	29	0	0	0	14	34 2/3	33	17	16	10	33
—	Florida (N.L.)	0	1	.000	5.13	23	0	0	0	0	33 1/3	42	19	19	7	26
A.L. totals (7 years)		22	21	.512	3.46	281	0	0	0	10	429 1/3	435	187	165	118	230
N.L. totals (5 years)		2	2	.500	4.62	47	0	0	0	0	76	84	44	39	21	48
Major league totals (10 years)		24	23	.511	3.63	328	0	0	0	10	505 1/3	519	231	204	139	278

PALMEIRO, ORLANDO   OF   ANGELS

PERSONAL: Born January 19, 1969, in Hoboken, N.J. ... 5-11/175. ... Bats left, throws left. ... Cousin of Rafael Palmeiro, first baseman, Texas Rangers. ... Name pronounced pal-MAIR-oh.
HIGH SCHOOL: Southridge (Miami).
JUNIOR COLLEGE: Miami-Dade (South) Community College.
COLLEGE: Miami (Fla.).
TRANSACTIONS/CAREER NOTES: Selected by California Angels organization in 33rd round of free-agent draft (June 3, 1991). ... On disabled list (September 1-26, 1994). ... Angels franchise renamed Anaheim Angels for 1997 season. ... On disabled list (August 23-September 7, 1997).
STATISTICAL NOTES: Tied for Northwest League lead in double plays by outfielder with two in 1991. ... Led Texas League with 18 sacrifice hits in 1993. ... Led Texas League outfielders with 328 total chances in 1993. ... Led Pacific Coast League in caught stealing with 16 in 1994. ... Led Pacific Coast League with 11 sacrifice hits in 1995.

Year	Team (League)	Pos.	G	AB	R	H	2B	3B	HR	RBI	Avg.	BB	SO	SB	PO	A	E	Avg.
							BATTING								FIELDING			
1991—	Boise (Northwest)	OF	70	277	56	77	11	2	1	24	.278	33	22	8	130	8	2	*.986
1992—	Quad City (Midwest)	OF	127	451	83	143	22	4	0	41	*.317	56	41	31	211	9	6	.973
1993—	Midland (Texas)	OF	131	*535	85	163	19	5	0	64	.305	42	35	18	*307	12	9	.973
1994—	Vancouver (PCL)	OF	117	458	79	150	28	4	1	47	.328	58	46	21	254	6	1	.996
1995—	Vancouver (PCL)	OF	107	398	66	122	21	4	0	47	.307	41	34	16	192	4	1	*.995
—	California (A.L.)	OF-DH	15	20	3	7	0	0	0	1	.350	1	1	0	7	0	0	1.000
1996—	Vancouver (PCL)	OF	62	245	40	75	13	4	0	33	.306	30	19	7	113	4	5	.959
—	California (A.L.)	OF-DH	50	87	6	25	6	1	0	6	.287	8	13	0	33	0	0	1.000
1997—	Anaheim (A.L.)	OF-DH	74	134	19	29	2	2	0	8	.216	17	11	2	78	1	2	.975
1998—	Vancouver (PCL)	OF	43	140	21	42	13	3	1	29	.300	16	10	3	70	4	0	1.000
—	Anaheim (A.L.)	OF-DH	75	165	28	53	7	2	0	21	.321	20	11	5	92	0	0	1.000
Major league totals (4 years)			214	406	56	114	15	5	0	36	.281	46	36	7	210	1	2	.991

PALMEIRO, RAFAEL   1B   RANGERS

P

PERSONAL: Born September 24, 1964, in Havana, Cuba. ... 6-0/190. ... Bats left, throws left. ... Full name: Rafael Corrales Palmeiro. ... Cousin of Orlando Palmeiro, outfielder, Anaheim Angels. ... Name pronounced pal-MAIR-oh.
HIGH SCHOOL: Jackson (Miami).
COLLEGE: Mississippi State (degree in commercial art).
TRANSACTIONS/CAREER NOTES: Selected by New York Mets organization in eighth round of free-agent draft (June 7, 1982); did not sign. ... Selected by Chicago Cubs organization in first round (22nd pick overall) of free-agent draft (June 3, 1985); pick received as compensation for San Diego Padres signing Type A free-agent P Tim Stoddard. ... Traded by Cubs with P Jamie Moyer and P Drew Hall to Texas Rangers for P Mitch Williams, P Paul Kilgus, P Steve Wilson, IF Curtis Wilkerson, IF Luis Benitez and OF Pablo Delgado (December 5, 1988). ... Granted free

agency (October 25, 1993). ... Signed by Baltimore Orioles (December 12, 1993). ... Granted free agency (October 23, 1998). ... Signed by Rangers (December 4, 1998).

HONORS: Named outfielder on THE SPORTING NEWS college All-America team (1985). ... Named Eastern League Most Valuable Player (1986). ... Won A.L. Gold Glove at first base (1997-98). ... Named first baseman on THE SPORTING NEWS A.L. All-Star team (1998). ... Named first baseman on THE SPORTING NEWS A.L. Silver Slugger team (1998).

STATISTICAL NOTES: Led Eastern League with 225 total bases, 13 sacrifice flies and 13 intentional bases on balls received in 1986. ... Had 20-game hitting streak (July 18-August 11, 1988). ... Led A.L. first basemen in total chances with 1,540 in 1993 and 1,510 in 1996. ... Led A.L. first basemen in double plays with 133 in 1993 and 157 in 1996. ... Led A.L. first basemen with 1,568 total chances in 1998. ... Had 24-game hitting streak (April 23-May 22, 1994). ... Career major league grand slams: 5.

Year	Team (League)	Pos.	G	AB	R	H	2B	3B	HR	RBI	Avg.	BB	SO	SB	PO	A	E	Avg.
1985—	Peoria (Midwest)	OF	73	279	34	83	22	4	5	51	.297	31	34	9	113	7	1	.992
1986—	Pittsfield (Eastern)	OF	•140	509	66	*156	29	2	12	*95	.306	54	32	15	248	9	3	*.988
	—Chicago (N.L.)	OF	22	73	9	18	4	0	3	12	.247	4	6	1	34	2	4	.900
1987—	Iowa (Am. Assoc.)	OF-1B	57	214	36	64	14	3	11	41	.299	22	22	4	150	13	2	.988
	—Chicago (N.L.)	OF-1B	84	221	32	61	15	1	14	30	.276	20	26	2	176	9	1	.995
1988—	Chicago (N.L.)	OF-1B	152	580	75	178	41	5	8	53	.307	38	34	12	322	11	5	.985
1989—	Texas (A.L.)■	1B-DH	156	559	76	154	23	4	8	64	.275	63	48	4	1167	*119	12	.991
1990—	Texas (A.L.)	1B-DH	154	598	72	*191	35	6	14	89	.319	40	59	3	1215	91	7	.995
1991—	Texas (A.L.)	1B-DH	159	631	115	203	*49	3	26	88	.322	68	72	4	1305	96	*12	.992
1992—	Texas (A.L.)	1B-DH	159	608	84	163	27	4	22	85	.268	72	83	2	1251	*143	7	.995
1993—	Texas (A.L.)	1B	160	597	*124	176	40	2	37	105	.295	73	85	22	*1388	*147	5	.997
1994—	Baltimore (A.L.)■	1B	111	436	82	139	32	0	23	76	.319	54	63	7	959	66	4	.996
1995—	Baltimore (A.L.)	1B	143	554	89	172	30	2	39	104	.310	62	65	3	1181	*119	4	.997
1996—	Baltimore (A.L.)	1B-DH	162	626	110	181	40	2	39	142	.289	95	96	8	*1383	*119	8	.995
1997—	Baltimore (A.L.)	1B-DH	158	614	95	156	24	2	38	110	.254	67	109	5	1305	112	10	.993
1998—	Baltimore (A.L.)	1B-DH	162	619	98	183	36	1	43	121	.296	79	91	11	*1435	*124	9	.994
American League totals (10 years)			1524	5842	945	1718	336	26	289	984	.294	673	771	69	12589	1136	78	.994
National League totals (3 years)			258	874	116	257	60	6	25	95	.294	62	66	15	532	22	10	.982
Major league totals (13 years)			1782	6716	1061	1975	396	32	314	1079	.294	735	837	84	13121	1158	88	.994

DIVISION SERIES RECORD

Year	Team (League)	Pos.	G	AB	R	H	2B	3B	HR	RBI	Avg.	BB	SO	SB	PO	A	E	Avg.
1996—	Baltimore (A.L.)	1B	4	17	4	3	1	0	1	2	.176	1	6	0	35	1	1	.973
1997—	Baltimore (A.L.)	1B	4	12	2	3	2	0	0	0	.250	0	2	0	27	2	0	1.000
Division series totals (2 years)			8	29	6	6	3	0	1	2	.207	1	8	0	62	3	1	.985

CHAMPIONSHIP SERIES RECORD

NOTES: Hit home run in first at-bat (October 9, 1996).

Year	Team (League)	Pos.	G	AB	R	H	2B	3B	HR	RBI	Avg.	BB	SO	SB	PO	A	E	Avg.
1996—	Baltimore (A.L.)	1B	5	17	4	4	0	0	2	4	.235	4	4	0	44	3	0	1.000
1997—	Baltimore (A.L.)	1B	6	25	3	7	2	0	1	2	.280	0	10	0	55	2	0	1.000
Championship series totals (2 years)			11	42	7	11	2	0	3	6	.262	4	14	0	99	5	0	1.000

ALL-STAR GAME RECORD

Year	League	Pos.	AB	R	H	2B	3B	HR	RBI	Avg.	BB	SO	SB	PO	A	E	Avg.
1988—	National	PH-OF	0	0	0	0	0	0	0	...	1	0	0	1	0	0	1.000
1991—	American	1B	0	0	0	0	0	0	0	...	1	0	0	2	0	0	1.000
1998—	American	1B	2	1	2	0	0	0	1	1.000	0	0	0	2	0	0	1.000
All-Star Game totals (3 years)			2	1	2	0	0	0	1	1.000	2	0	0	5	0	0	1.000

PALMER, DEAN   3B   TIGERS

PERSONAL: Born December 27, 1968, in Tallahassee, Fla. ... 6-1/210. ... Bats right, throws right. ... Full name: Dean William Palmer.
HIGH SCHOOL: Florida (Tallahassee, Fla.).
TRANSACTIONS/CAREER NOTES: Selected by Texas Rangers organization in third round of free-agent draft (June 2, 1986). ... On disabled list (July 19, 1988-remainder of season; April 28-May 13, 1994; and June 4-September 22, 1995). ... Traded by Rangers to Kansas City Royals for OF Tom Goodwin (July 25, 1997). ... Granted free agency (October 27, 1997). ... Re-signed by Royals (December 15, 1997). ... Granted free agency (October 23, 1998). ... Signed by Detroit Tigers (November 13, 1998).
RECORDS: Shares major league single-season record for fewest assists by third baseman (150 or more games)—221 (1996). ... Holds A.L. single-season record for fewest chances accepted by third baseman (150 or more games)—326 (1996). ... Shares A.L. single-season record for fewest double plays by third baseman (150 or more games)—17 (1996).
HONORS: Named third baseman on THE SPORTING NEWS A.L. Silver Slugger team (1998).
STATISTICAL NOTES: Led Texas League third basemen with 30 errors in 1989. ... Led A.L. third basemen with 29 errors in 1993. ... Career major league grand slams: 6.

Year	Team (League)	Pos.	G	AB	R	H	2B	3B	HR	RBI	Avg.	BB	SO	SB	PO	A	E	Avg.
1986—	GC Rangers (GCL)	3B	50	163	19	34	7	1	0	12	.209	22	34	6	25	75	13	.885
1987—	Gastonia (S. Atl.)	3B	128	484	51	104	16	0	9	54	.215	36	126	5	58	209	*59	.819
1988—	Charlotte (Fla. St.)	3B	74	305	38	81	12	1	4	35	.266	15	69	0	49	144	28	.873
1989—	Tulsa (Texas)	3B-SS	133	498	82	125	32	5	*25	90	.251	41	*152	15	85	213	†31	.906
	—Texas (A.L.)	3-DH-S-O	16	19	0	2	2	0	0	1	.105	0	12	0	3	4	2	.778
1990—	Tulsa (Texas)	3B	7	24	4	7	0	1	3	9	.292	4	10	0	9	6	3	.833
	—Okla. City (A.A.)	3B-1B	88	316	33	69	17	4	12	39	.218	20	106	1	206	110	21	.938
1991—	Okla. City (A.A.)	3B-OF	60	234	45	70	11	2	*22	59	.299	20	61	4	49	105	11	.933
	—Texas (A.L.)	3B-OF-DH	81	268	38	50	9	2	15	37	.187	32	98	0	69	75	9	.941
1992—	Texas (A.L.)	3B	152	541	74	124	25	0	26	72	.229	62	*154	10	124	254	22	.945

P

Year	Team (League)	Pos.	G	AB	R	H	2B	3B	HR	RBI	Avg.	BB	SO	SB	PO	A	E	Avg.
								BATTING								FIELDING		
1993—Texas (A.L.)	3B-SS	148	519	88	127	31	2	33	96	.245	53	154	11	86	258	†29	.922
1994—Texas (A.L.)	3B	93	342	50	84	14	2	19	59	.246	26	89	3	50	179	*22	.912
1995—Texas (A.L.)	3B	36	119	30	40	6	0	9	24	.336	21	21	1	19	72	5	.948
1996—Texas (A.L.)	3B-DH	154	582	98	163	26	2	38	107	.280	59	145	2	105	221	16	.953
1997—Texas (A.L.)	3B	94	355	47	87	21	0	14	55	.245	26	84	1	72	162	10	.959
—Kansas City (A.L.)■ ...	3B-DH	49	187	23	52	10	1	9	31	.278	15	50	1	27	82	9	.924
1998—Kansas City (A.L.)	3B-DH	152	572	84	159	27	2	34	119	.278	48	134	8	69	187	22	.921
Major league totals (9 years)		975	3504	532	888	171	11	197	601	.253	342	941	37	624	1494	146	.936

DIVISION SERIES RECORD

Year	Team (League)	Pos.	G	AB	R	H	2B	3B	HR	RBI	Avg.	BB	SO	SB	PO	A	E	Avg.
								BATTING								FIELDING		
1996—Texas (A.L.)	3B	4	19	3	4	1	0	1	2	.211	0	5	0	3	10	1	.929

ALL-STAR GAME RECORD

Year	League	Pos.	AB	R	H	2B	3B	HR	RBI	Avg.	BB	SO	SB	PO	A	E	Avg.
						BATTING									FIELDING		
1998—American	PH	1	0	0	0	0	0	0	.000	0	0	0	...	...	...	...

PANIAGUA, JOSE   P   MARINERS

PERSONAL: Born August 20, 1973, in San Jose De Ocoa, Dominican Republic. ... 6-2/185. ... Throws right, bats right. ... Full name: Jose Luis Sanchez Paniagua.

HIGH SCHOOL: Liceo Nuestra Senora del Altagracia (Santo Domingo, Dominican Republic).

TRANSACTIONS/CAREER NOTES: Signed as non-drafted free agent by Montreal Expos organization (September 17, 1990). ... On Montreal disabled list (May 25-June 11, 1996). ... On Ottawa disabled list (July 16-August 2, 1996). ... Selected by Tampa Bay Devil Rays in second round (50th pick overall) of expansion draft (November 18, 1997). ... Claimed on waivers by Seattle Mariners (March 26, 1998).

Year	Team (League)	W	L	Pct.	ERA	G	GS	CG	ShO	Sv.	IP	H	R	ER	BB	SO
1992—Dom. Expos (DSL)	3	7	.300	4.15	13	13	3	1	0	73 2/3	69	50	34	46	60
1993—GC Expos (GCL)	3	0	1.000	0.67	4	4	1	0	0	27	13	2	2	5	25
1994—W.P. Beach (FSL)	9	9	.500	3.64	26	26	1	0	0	141	131	82	57	54	110
1995—Harrisburg (Eastern)	7	•12	.368	5.34	25	25	2	1	0	126 1/3	140	84	75	62	89
1996—Ottawa (Int'l)	9	5	.643	3.18	15	14	2	1	0	85	72	39	30	23	61
—Montreal (N.L.)	2	4	.333	3.53	13	11	0	0	0	51	55	24	20	23	27
—Harrisburg (Eastern)	3	0	1.000	0.00	3	3	0	0	0	18	12	1	0	2	16
1997—W.P. Beach (FSL)	1	0	1.000	0.00	2	2	0	0	0	10	5	0	0	2	11
—Ottawa (Int'l)	8	10	.444	4.64	22	22	1	0	0	137 2/3	164	79	71	44	87
—Montreal (N.L.)	1	2	.333	12.00	9	3	0	0	0	18	29	24	24	16	8
1998—Tacoma (PCL)■	3	1	.750	2.77	44	0	0	0	5	68 1/3	66	25	21	22	61
—Seattle (A.L.)	2	0	1.000	2.05	18	0	0	0	1	22	15	5	5	5	16
A.L. totals (1 year)	2	0	1.000	2.05	18	0	0	0	1	22	15	5	5	5	16
N.L. totals (2 years)	3	6	.333	5.74	22	14	0	0	0	69	84	48	44	39	35
Major league totals (3 years)	5	6	.455	4.85	40	14	0	0	1	91	99	53	49	44	51

PAQUETTE, CRAIG   3B   METS

PERSONAL: Born March 28, 1969, in Long Beach, Calif. ... 6-0/190. ... Bats right, throws right. ... Full name: Craig Howard Paquette.

HIGH SCHOOL: Ranchos Alamitos (Garden Grove, Calif.).

JUNIOR COLLEGE: Golden West College (Calif.).

TRANSACTIONS/CAREER NOTES: Selected by Minnesota Twins organization in 36th round of free-agent draft (June 2, 1987); did not sign. ... Selected by Oakland Athletics organization in eighth round of free-agent draft (June 5, 1989). ... On Modesto disabled list (April 10-May 5, 1991). ... On Huntsville disabled list (June 1-11, 1991). ... On Tacoma disabled list (July 18, 1994-remainder of season). ... Released by A's (March 26, 1996). ... Signed by Kansas City Royals organization (April 3, 1996). ... Granted free agency (October 15, 1997). ... Signed by New York Mets organization (December 23, 1997). ... On New York disabled list (May 7, 1998-remainder of season). ... Granted free agency (October 15, 1998). ... Re-signed by Mets organization (December 18, 1998).

STATISTICAL NOTES: Tied for Northwest League lead with 163 total bases in 1989. ... Led Northwest League third basemen with .936 fielding percentage and 12 double plays in 1989. ... Led Southern League third basemen with 349 total chances in 1992. ... Career major league grand slams: 2.

Year	Team (League)	Pos.	G	AB	R	H	2B	3B	HR	RBI	Avg.	BB	SO	SB	PO	A	E	Avg.
								BATTING								FIELDING		
1989—S. Oregon (N'west)	3B-SS-2B	71	277	53	93	*22	3	14	56	.336	30	46	9	61	155	15	†.935
1990—Modesto (California) ..	3B	130	495	65	118	23	4	15	59	.238	47	123	8	*88	218	26	*.922
1991—Huntsville (Sou.)	3B-1B	102	378	50	99	18	1	8	60	.262	28	87	0	51	132	16	.920
1992—Huntsville (Sou.)	3B	115	450	59	116	25	4	17	71	.258	29	118	13	69	*248	*32	.908
—Tacoma (PCL)	3B	17	66	10	18	7	0	2	11	.273	2	16	3	14	33	3	.940
1993—Tacoma (PCL)	3B-SS-2B	50	183	29	49	8	0	8	29	.268	14	54	3	32	116	15	.908
—Oakland (A.L.)	3B-DH-OF	105	393	35	86	20	4	12	46	.219	14	108	4	82	165	13	.950
1994—Tacoma (PCL)	3B	65	245	39	70	12	3	17	48	.286	14	48	3	40	166	14	.936
—Oakland (A.L.)	3B	14	49	0	7	2	0	0	0	.143	0	14	1	14	22	0	1.000
1995—Oakland (A.L.)	3-0-S-1	105	283	42	64	13	1	13	49	.226	12	88	5	72	92	8	.953
1996—Omaha (A.A.)■	3B-1B-OF	18	63	9	21	3	0	4	13	.333	8	14	1	24	9	3	.917
—Kansas City (A.L.)	3-0-1-S-DH	118	429	61	111	15	1	22	67	.259	23	101	5	261	102	14	.963
1997—Kansas City (A.L.)	3B-OF	77	252	26	58	15	1	8	33	.230	10	57	2	51	130	12	.938
—Omaha (A.A.)	3B	23	91	9	28	6	0	3	20	.308	6	26	0	12	29	2	.953
1998—Norfolk (Int'l)■	3B-SS-OF	15	61	11	17	1	1	3	14	.279	1	13	2	9	39	4	.923
—New York (N.L.)	3B-1B-OF	7	19	3	5	2	0	0	0	.263	0	6	1	5	2	0	1.000
American League totals (5 years)		419	1406	164	326	65	7	55	195	.232	59	368	17	480	511	47	.955
National League totals (1 year)		7	19	3	5	2	0	0	0	.263	0	6	1	5	2	0	1.000
Major league totals (6 years)		426	1425	167	331	67	7	55	195	.232	59	374	18	485	513	47	.955

P

PERSONAL: Born September 16, 1961, in Ashland, Ore. ... 6-5/245. ... Bats right, throws right. ... Full name: Mark Alan Parent.
HIGH SCHOOL: Anderson (Calif.).
TRANSACTIONS/CAREER NOTES: Selected by San Diego Padres organization in fourth round of free-agent draft (June 5, 1979). ... On suspended list (August 27, 1983-remainder of season). ... On disabled list (September 4, 1984-remainder of season). ... Traded by Padres to Texas Rangers for 3B Scott Coolbaugh (December 12, 1990). ... On Texas disabled list (March 9-September 6, 1991); included rehabilitation assignment to Oklahoma City (August 31-September 5). ... Granted free agency (October 8, 1991). ... Signed by Baltimore Orioles organization (February 5, 1992). ... On Rochester disabled list (April 10-17, 1992). ... Released by Orioles (December 2, 1993). ... Signed by Chicago Cubs organization (December 14, 1993). ... Claimed on waivers by Pittsburgh Pirates (October 11, 1994). ... Traded by Pirates to Cubs for a player to be named later (August 31, 1995). ... Granted free agency (October 31, 1995). ... Signed by Detroit Tigers (December 13, 1995). ... Released by Tigers (August 21, 1996). ... Signed by Orioles (August 27, 1996). ... Granted free agency (November 18, 1996). ... Signed by Philadelphia Phillies (December 11, 1996). ... Granted free agency (October 23, 1998).
STATISTICAL NOTES: Led Northwest League catchers with .979 fielding percentage in 1980. ... Led Carolina League catchers with 16 double plays in 1981. ... Led Pacific Coast League catchers with .988 fielding percentage in 1987. ... Led International League catchers with eight double plays in 1992. ... Tied for International League lead in double plays by catcher with 11 in 1993.

							BATTING								FIELDING		
Year Team (League)	Pos.	G	AB	R	H	2B	3B	HR	RBI	Avg.	BB	SO	SB	PO	A	E	Avg.
1979— Walla Walla (NWL)	C-OF	40	126	8	24	4	0	1	11	.190	8	31	8	229	34	6	.978
1980— Reno (California)	C	30	99	8	20	3	0	0	12	.202	16	12	0	128	23	2	.987
— Grays Har. (NWL)	C-1B	66	230	29	55	11	2	7	32	.239	17	30	1	381	38	9	†.979
1981— Salem (Carolina)	C	123	438	44	103	16	3	6	47	.235	37	90	10	*694	87	*28	.965
1982— Amarillo (Texas)	C	26	89	12	17	3	1	1	13	.191	11	13	2	100	6	2	.981
— Salem (Carolina)	C-1B	99	360	39	81	15	2	6	41	.225	32	58	2	475	64	12	.978
1983— Beaumont (Texas)	C	81	282	38	71	22	1	7	33	.252	33	35	1	464	71	10	*.982
1984— Beaumont (Texas)	C-1B	111	380	52	109	24	3	7	60	.287	38	39	1	674	68	7	.991
1985— Las Vegas (PCL)	C-1B	105	361	36	87	23	3	7	45	.241	29	58	1	586	54	6	.991
1986— Las Vegas (PCL)	C-1B	86	267	29	77	10	4	5	40	.288	23	25	0	344	40	5	.987
— San Diego (N.L.)	C	8	14	1	2	0	0	0	0	.143	1	3	0	16	0	2	.889
1987— Las Vegas (PCL)	C-1-3-O	105	387	50	113	23	2	4	43	.292	38	53	2	556	58	8	†.987
— San Diego (N.L.)	C	12	25	0	2	0	0	0	2	.080	0	9	0	36	3	0	1.000
1988— San Diego (N.L.)	C	41	118	9	23	3	0	6	15	.195	6	23	0	203	15	3	.986
1989— San Diego (N.L.)	C-1B	52	141	12	27	4	0	7	21	.191	8	34	1	246	17	0	1.000
1990— San Diego (N.L.)	C	65	189	13	42	11	0	3	16	.222	16	29	1	324	31	3	.992
1991— Okla. City (A.A.)■.......	C	5	8	0	2	0	0	0	1	.250	0	1	0	4	0	0	1.000
— Texas (A.L.)	C	3	1	0	0	0	0	0	0	.000	0	1	0	5	0	0	1.000
1992— Rochester (Int'l)■.......	C	101	356	52	102	24	0	17	69	.287	35	64	4	588	49	4	.994
— Baltimore (A.L.).........	C	17	34	4	8	1	0	2	4	.235	3	7	0	73	7	1	.988
1993— Rochester (Int'l)	C	92	332	47	82	15	0	14	56	.247	40	71	0	549	63	3	*.995
— Baltimore (A.L.).........	C-DH	22	54	7	14	2	0	4	12	.259	3	14	0	83	5	1	.989
1994— Chicago (N.L.)■.........	C	44	99	8	26	4	0	3	16	.263	13	24	0	184	21	5	.976
1995— Pittsburgh (N.L.)■.......	C	69	233	25	54	9	0	15	33	.232	23	62	0	365	39	4	.990
— Chicago (N.L.)■.......	C	12	32	5	8	2	0	3	5	.250	3	7	0	66	5	0	1.000
1996— Detroit (A.L.)■..........	C-1B	38	104	13	25	6	0	7	17	.240	3	27	0	159	14	1	.994
— Baltimore (A.L.).........	C	18	33	4	6	1	0	2	6	.182	2	10	0	73	3	1	.987
1997— Philadelphia (N.L.)■ ..	C	39	113	4	17	3	0	0	8	.150	7	39	0	225	21	1	.996
1998— Philadelphia (N.L.)......	C	34	113	7	25	4	0	1	13	.221	10	30	1	211	15	3	.987
American League totals (4 years)		98	226	28	53	10	0	15	39	.235	11	59	0	393	29	4	.991
National League totals (9 years)		376	1077	84	226	40	0	38	129	.210	87	260	3	1876	167	21	.990
Major league totals (13 years)		474	1303	112	279	50	0	53	168	.214	98	319	3	2269	196	25	.990

DIVISION SERIES RECORD

							BATTING								FIELDING		
Year Team (League)	Pos.	G	AB	R	H	2B	3B	HR	RBI	Avg.	BB	SO	SB	PO	A	E	Avg.
1996— Baltimore (A.L.)	C	4	5	0	1	0	0	0	0	.200	0	2	0	19	0	0	1.000

CHAMPIONSHIP SERIES RECORD

							BATTING								FIELDING		
Year Team (League)	Pos.	G	AB	R	H	2B	3B	HR	RBI	Avg.	BB	SO	SB	PO	A	E	Avg.
1996— Baltimore (A.L.)	C	2	6	0	1	0	0	0	0	.167	0	2	0	14	0	0	1.000

PERSONAL: Born June 30, 1973, in Kong Ju City, Korea. ... 6-2/204. ... Throws right, bats right.
HIGH SCHOOL: Kong Ju (Kong Ju City, Korea).
COLLEGE: Hanyang University (Seoul, Korea).
TRANSACTIONS/CAREER NOTES: Signed as non-drafted free agent by Los Angeles Dodgers organization (January 14, 1994). ... On Albuquerque disabled list (July 16-29, 1995).

Year Team (League)	W	L	Pct.	ERA	G	GS	CG	ShO	Sv.	IP	H	R	ER	BB	SO
1994— Los Angeles (N.L.)	0	0	...	11.25	2	0	0	0	0	4	5	5	5	6	6
— San Antonio (Tex.)	5	7	.417	3.55	20	20	0	0	0	101 1/3	91	52	40	57	100
1995— Albuquerque (PCL)............	6	7	.462	4.91	23	22	0	0	0	110	93	64	60	76	101
— Los Angeles (N.L.)	0	0	...	4.50	2	1	0	0	0	4	2	2	2	2	7
1996— Los Angeles (N.L.)	5	5	.500	3.64	48	10	0	0	0	108 2/3	82	48	44	71	119
1997— Los Angeles (N.L.)	14	8	.636	3.38	32	29	2	0	0	192	149	80	72	70	166
1998— Los Angeles (N.L.)	15	9	.625	3.71	34	34	2	0	0	220 2/3	199	101	91	97	191
Major league totals (5 years)......	34	22	.607	3.64	118	74	4	0	0	529 1/3	437	236	214	245	489

P

PERSONAL: Born February 8, 1975, in Norwalk, Calif. ... 5-11/165. ... Throws left, bats left. ... Full name: Jim Vo Parque.
HIGH SCHOOL: Crescenta Valley (Calif.).
COLLEGE: UCLA.
TRANSACTIONS/CAREER NOTES: Selected by Chicago White Sox organization in second round of free-agent draft (June 3, 1997).
STATISTICAL NOTES: Tied for A.L. lead with three balks in 1998.
MISCELLANEOUS: Member of 1996 U.S. Olympic baseball team.

Year Team (League)	W	L	Pct.	ERA	G	GS	CG	ShO	Sv.	IP	H	R	ER	BB	SO
1997— Winston-Salem (Car.)	7	2	.778	2.77	11	11	0	0	0	61 2/3	29	19	19	23	76
— Nashville (A.A.)	1	0	1.000	4.22	2	2	0	0	0	10 2/3	9	5	5	9	5
1998— Calgary (PCL)	2	3	.400	3.94	8	8	0	0	0	48	49	26	21	25	31
— Chicago (A.L.)	7	5	.583	5.10	21	21	0	0	0	113	135	72	64	49	77
Major league totals (1 year)	**7**	**5**	**.583**	**5.10**	**21**	**21**	**0**	**0**	**0**	**113**	**135**	**72**	**64**	**49**	**77**

PARRIS, STEVE · P · REDS

PERSONAL: Born December 17, 1967, in Joliet, Ill. ... 6-0/195. ... Throws right, bats right. ... Full name: Steven Michael Parris.
HIGH SCHOOL: Joliet (Ill.) West.
COLLEGE: College of St. Francis (Ill.).
TRANSACTIONS/CAREER NOTES: Selected by Philadelphia Phillies organization in fifth round of free-agent draft (June 5, 1989). ... Claimed on waivers by Los Angeles Dodgers (April 19, 1993). ... Claimed on waivers by Seattle Mariners (April 26, 1993). ... On Jacksonville disabled list (May 12-June 23 and July 17-31, 1993). ... Released by Mariners (July 31, 1993). ... Signed by Salem, Pittsburgh Pirates organization (June 24, 1994). ... On Pittsburgh disabled list (March 6-July 11 and August 18-September 10, 1996); included rehabilitation assignments to Augusta (June 12-13) and Carolina (June 13-July 11). ... Released by Pirates (March 13, 1997). ... Signed by Cincinnati Reds organization (May 6, 1997). ... Granted free agency (October 15, 1997). ... Re-signed by Reds organization (October 27, 1997).

Year Team (League)	W	L	Pct.	ERA	G	GS	CG	ShO	Sv.	IP	H	R	ER	BB	SO
1989— Batavia (N.Y.-Penn)	3	5	.375	3.92	13	10	1	0	0	66 2/3	69	38	29	20	46
1990— Batavia (N.Y.-Penn)	7	1	*.875	2.64	14	14	0	0	0	81 2/3	70	34	24	22	50
1991— Clearwater (Fla. St.)	7	5	.583	3.39	43	6	0	0	1	93	101	43	35	25	59
1992— Reading (Eastern)	5	7	.417	4.64	18	14	0	0	0	85 1/3	94	55	44	21	60
— Scran./W.B. (Int'l)	3	3	.500	4.03	11	6	0	0	1	51 1/3	57	25	23	17	29
1993— Scran./W.B. (Int'l)	0	0	...	12.71	3	0	0	0	0	5 2/3	9	9	8	3	4
— Jacksonville (Southern)■	0	1	.000	5.93	7	1	0	0	0	13 2/3	15	9	9	6	5
1994— Salem (Carolina)■	3	3	.500	3.63	17	7	0	0	0	57	58	24	23	21	48
1995— Carolina (Southern)	9	1	.900	2.51	14	14	2	2	0	89 2/3	61	25	25	16	86
— Pittsburgh (N.L.)	6	6	.500	5.38	15	15	1	1	0	82	89	49	49	33	61
1996— Augusta (S. Atl.)	0	0	...	0.00	1	1	0	0	0	5	1	0	0	1	6
— Carolina (Southern)	2	0	1.000	3.04	5	5	0	0	0	26 2/3	24	11	9	6	22
— Pittsburgh (N.L.)	0	3	.000	7.18	8	4	0	0	0	26 1/3	35	22	21	11	27
1997— Chattanooga (Southern)■	6	2	.750	4.13	14	14	0	0	0	80 2/3	78	44	37	29	68
— Indianapolis (A.A.)	2	3	.400	3.57	5	5	1	1	0	35 1/3	26	15	14	11	27
1998— Indianapolis (Int'l)	6	1	.857	3.84	13	13	1	1	0	84 1/3	74	38	36	26	102
— Cincinnati (N.L.)	6	5	.545	3.73	18	16	1	1	0	99	89	44	41	32	77
Major league totals (3 years)	**12**	**14**	**.462**	**4.82**	**41**	**35**	**2**	**2**	**0**	**207 1/3**	**213**	**115**	**111**	**76**	**165**

PASSINI, BRIAN · P · BREWERS

PERSONAL: Born January 24, 1975, in Spring Valley, Ill. ... 6-3/195. ... Throws left, bats left. ... Full name: Brian Michael Passini.
HIGH SCHOOL: Parkland (Ill.).
COLLEGE: Miami (Ohio).
TRANSACTIONS/CAREER NOTES: Selected by Colorado Rockies organization in 25th round of free-agent draft (June 2, 1994); did not sign. ... Selected by Milwaukee Brewers organization in eighth round of free-agent draft (June 4, 1996).

Year Team (League)	W	L	Pct.	ERA	G	GS	CG	ShO	Sv.	IP	H	R	ER	BB	SO
1996— Helena (Pioneer)	7	2	.778	3.48	15	14	1	0	0	77 2/3	91	37	30	27	71
1997— Beloit (Midwest)	1	1	.500	6.65	17	0	0	0	0	21 2/3	32	16	16	9	16
— Stockton (California)	1	5	.167	4.76	8	8	1	0	0	45 1/3	40	28	24	21	34
1998— Stockton (California)	5	6	.455	3.60	15	15	1	0	0	90	83	39	36	31	91
— El Paso (Texas)	5	4	.556	2.91	12	12	1	1	0	80 1/3	69	35	26	28	51

PATRICK, BRONSWELL · P · GIANTS

PERSONAL: Born September 16, 1970, in Pitt County, N.C. ... 6-1/220. ... Throws right, bats right. ... Full name: Bronswell Dante Patrick.
HIGH SCHOOL: D.H. Conley (Winterville, N.C.).
TRANSACTIONS/CAREER NOTES: Selected by Oakland Athletics in 23rd round of free-agent draft (June 1, 1988). ... Granted free agency (October 17, 1994). ... Signed by Houston Astros organization (January 18, 1995). ... Granted free agency (October 15, 1996). ... Re-signed by Astros organization (November 22, 1996). ... Granted free agency (October 17, 1997). ... Signed by Milwaukee Brewers organization (November 5, 1997). ... Granted free agency (October 15, 1998). ... Signed by San Francisco Giants organization (December 4, 1998).
STATISTICAL NOTES: Tied for Arizona League lead in home runs allowed with seven in 1988. ... Led Southern League with 20 home runs allowed in 1992.

P

Year Team (League)	W	L	Pct.	ERA	G	GS	CG	ShO	Sv.	IP	H	R	ER	BB	SO
1988— Arizona A's (Arizona)	8	3	.727	2.99	14	*13	2	0	0	*96 1/3	*99	37	32	16	64
1989— Madison (Midwest)	2	5	.286	3.64	12	10	0	0	0	54 1/3	62	29	22	14	32
1990— Modesto (California)	3	7	.300	5.18	14	14	0	0	0	74 2/3	92	58	43	32	37
— Madison (Midwest)	3	7	.300	3.60	13	12	3	0	0	80	88	44	32	19	40

Year Team (League)	W	L	Pct.	ERA	G	GS	CG	ShO	Sv.	IP	H	R	ER	BB	SO
1991—Modesto (California)	12	12	.500	3.24	28	26	3	1	0	169 2/3	158	77	61	60	95
1992—Huntsville (Southern)	•13	7	.650	3.76	29	29	3	0	0	179 1/3	*187	84	75	46	98
1993—Tacoma (PCL)	3	8	.273	7.05	35	13	1	0	1	104 2/3	156	87	82	42	56
1994—Huntsville (Southern)	2	0	1.000	2.93	7	3	0	0	1	27 2/3	31	11	9	10	16
— Tacoma (PCL)	1	1	.500	4.75	30	0	0	0	2	47 1/3	50	31	25	20	38
1995—Tucson (PCL)■	5	1	.833	4.19	43	4	0	0	1	81 2/3	91	42	38	21	62
1996—Tucson (PCL)	7	3	.700	3.51	33	15	0	0	1	118	137	59	46	33	82
1997—New Orleans (A.A.)	6	5	.545	3.22	30	12	1	1	0	100 2/3	108	45	36	30	88
1998—Louisville (Int'l)■	3	1	.750	4.30	6	6	0	0	0	37 2/3	43	21	18	9	28
— Milwaukee (N.L.)	4	1	.800	4.69	32	3	0	0	0	78 2/3	83	43	41	29	49
Major league totals (1 year)	4	1	.800	4.69	32	3	0	0	0	78 2/3	83	43	41	29	49

PATTERSON, BOB　　　　P

PERSONAL: Born May 16, 1959, in Jacksonville. ... 6-1/195. ... Throws left, bats right. ... Full name: Robert Chandler Patterson.
HIGH SCHOOL: Wade Hampton (Greenville, S.C.).
COLLEGE: East Carolina (degree in industrial technology).
TRANSACTIONS/CAREER NOTES: Selected by San Diego Padres organization in 21st round of free-agent draft (June 7, 1982). ... Traded by Padres to Pittsburgh Pirates for OF Marvell Wynne (April 3, 1986). ... On disabled list (April 28, 1988-remainder of season). ... Released by Pirates (November 20, 1992). ... Signed by Texas Rangers organization (December 8, 1992). ... Granted free agency (October 4, 1993). ... Signed by California Angels organization (January 18, 1994). ... Granted free agency (December 23, 1994). ... Re-signed by Angels organization (April 16, 1995). ... Granted free agency (November 2, 1995). ... Signed by Chicago Cubs (January 16, 1996). ... On disabled list (April 10-27, 1998). ... Released by Cubs (July 13, 1998).

Year Team (League)	W	L	Pct.	ERA	G	GS	CG	ShO	Sv.	IP	H	R	ER	BB	SO
1982—GC Padres (GCL)	4	3	.571	2.94	8	6	3	0	0	52	60	18	17	7	65
— Reno (California)	1	0	1.000	3.55	4	4	1	1	0	25 1/3	28	11	10	5	10
1983—Beaumont (Texas)	8	4	.667	4.01	43	9	2	0	11	116 2/3	107	61	52	36	97
1984—Las Vegas (PCL)	8	9	.471	3.27	*60	7	1	0	13	143 1/3	129	63	52	37	97
1985—Las Vegas (PCL)	10	11	.476	3.14	42	20	7	1	6	186 1/3	187	80	65	52	146
— San Diego (N.L.)	0	0	...	24.75	3	0	0	0	0	4	13	11	11	3	1
1986—Hawaii (Pac. Coast)■	9	6	.600	3.40	25	21	6	1	1	156	146	68	59	44	*137
— Pittsburgh (N.L.)	2	3	.400	4.95	11	5	0	0	0	36 1/3	49	20	20	5	20
1987—Pittsburgh (N.L.)	1	4	.200	6.70	15	7	0	0	0	43	49	34	32	22	27
— Vancouver (PCL)	5	2	.714	2.12	14	12	5	1	0	89	62	21	21	30	92
1988—Buffalo (A.A.)	2	0	1.000	2.32	4	4	1	0	0	31	26	12	8	4	20
1989—Buffalo (A.A.)	12	6	.667	3.35	31	25	4	1	1	177 1/3	177	69	66	35	103
— Pittsburgh (N.L.)	4	3	.571	4.05	12	3	0	0	1	26 2/3	23	13	12	8	20
1990—Pittsburgh (N.L.)	8	5	.615	2.95	55	5	0	0	5	94 2/3	88	33	31	21	70
1991—Pittsburgh (N.L.)	4	3	.571	4.11	54	1	0	0	2	65 2/3	67	32	30	15	57
1992—Pittsburgh (N.L.)	6	3	.667	2.92	60	0	0	0	9	64 2/3	59	22	21	23	43
1993—Texas (A.L.)■	2	4	.333	4.78	52	0	0	0	1	52 2/3	59	28	28	11	46
1994—California (A.L.)■	2	3	.400	4.07	47	0	0	0	1	42	35	21	19	15	30
1995—California (A.L.)	5	2	.714	3.04	62	0	0	0	0	53 1/3	48	18	18	13	41
1996—Chicago (N.L.)■	3	3	.500	3.13	79	0	0	0	8	54 2/3	46	19	19	22	53
1997—Chicago (N.L.)	1	6	.143	3.34	76	0	0	0	0	59 1/3	47	23	22	10	58
1998—Chicago (N.L.)	1	1	.500	7.52	33	0	0	0	1	20 1/3	36	20	17	12	17
A.L. totals (3 years)	9	9	.500	3.95	161	0	0	0	2	148	142	67	65	39	117
N.L. totals (10 years)	30	31	.492	4.12	398	21	0	0	26	469 1/3	477	227	215	141	366
Major league totals (13 years)	39	40	.494	4.08	559	21	0	0	28	617 1/3	619	294	280	180	483

CHAMPIONSHIP SERIES RECORD

Year Team (League)	W	L	Pct.	ERA	G	GS	CG	ShO	Sv.	IP	H	R	ER	BB	SO
1990—Pittsburgh (N.L.)	0	0	...	0.00	2	0	0	0	1	1	1	0	0	2	0
1991—Pittsburgh (N.L.)	0	0	...	0.00	1	0	0	0	0	2	1	0	0	0	3
1992—Pittsburgh (N.L.)	0	0	...	5.40	2	0	0	0	0	1 2/3	3	1	1	1	1
Champ. series totals (3 years)	0	0	...	1.93	5	0	0	0	1	4 2/3	5	1	1	3	4

PATTERSON, DANNY　　　　P　　　　RANGERS

PERSONAL: Born February 17, 1971, in San Gabriel, Calif. ... 6-0/225. ... Throws right, bats right. ... Full name: Danny Shane Patterson.
HIGH SCHOOL: San Gabriel (Calif.).
JUNIOR COLLEGE: Cerritos College (Calif.).
TRANSACTIONS/CAREER NOTES: Selected by Texas Rangers organization in 47th round of free-agent draft (June 5, 1989). ... On Texas disabled list (May 22-June 14, 1997); included rehabilitation assignment to Tulsa (June 9-14). ... On Texas disabled list (March 22-April 17, 1998); included rehabilitation assignments to Tulsa (April 7-12) and Oklahoma (April 13-17).

Year Team (League)	W	L	Pct.	ERA	G	GS	CG	ShO	Sv.	IP	H	R	ER	BB	SO
1990—Butte (Pioneer)	0	3	.000	6.35	13	3	0	0	1	28 1/3	36	23	20	14	18
1991—GC Rangers (GCL)	5	3	.625	3.24	11	9	0	0	0	50	43	21	18	12	46
1992—Gastonia (S. Atl.)	4	6	.400	3.59	23	21	3	1	0	105 1/3	106	47	42	33	84
1993—Charlotte (Fla. St.)	5	6	.455	2.51	47	0	0	0	7	68	55	22	19	28	41
1994—Tulsa (Texas)	1	4	.200	1.64	30	1	0	0	6	44	35	13	8	17	33
— Charlotte (Fla. St.)	1	0	1.000	4.61	7	0	0	0	0	13 2/3	13	7	7	5	9
1995—Tulsa (Texas)	2	2	.500	6.19	26	0	0	0	5	36 1/3	45	27	25	13	24
— Oklahoma City (A.A.)	1	0	1.000	1.65	14	0	0	0	2	27 1/3	23	8	5	9	9
1996—Oklahoma City (A.A.)	6	2	.750	1.68	44	0	0	0	10	80 1/3	79	22	15	15	53
— Texas (A.L.)	0	0	...	0.00	7	0	0	0	0	8 2/3	10	4	0	3	5
1997—Texas (A.L.)	10	6	.625	3.42	54	0	0	0	1	71	70	29	27	23	69
— Tulsa (Texas)	0	0	...	4.50	2	2	0	0	0	2	5	4	1	0	0

P

Year Team (League)	W	L	Pct.	ERA	G	GS	CG	ShO	Sv.	IP	H	R	ER	BB	SO
1998— Tulsa (Texas)	0	0	...	4.50	2	1	0	0	0	4	3	2	2	0	4
— Oklahoma (Pacific Coast)...	0	0	...	4.50	1	0	0	0	0	2	4	1	1	1	2
— Texas (A.L.)	2	5	.286	4.45	56	0	0	0	2	60 2/3	64	31	30	19	33
Major league totals (3 years)......	12	11	.522	3.66	117	0	0	0	3	140 1/3	144	64	57	45	107

DIVISION SERIES RECORD

Year Team (League)	W	L	Pct.	ERA	G	GS	CG	ShO	Sv.	IP	H	R	ER	BB	SO
1996— Texas (A.L.)	0	0	...	0.00	1	0	0	0	0	1/3	1	0	0	0	0

PAUL, JOSH — C — WHITE SOX

PERSONAL: Born May 19, 1975, in Evanston, Ill. ... 6-1/185. ... Bats right, throws right. ... Full name: Joshua William Paul.
HIGH SCHOOL: Buffalo Grove (Ill.).
COLLEGE: Vanderbilt.
TRANSACTIONS/CAREER NOTES: Selected by Chicago White Sox organization in second round of free-agent draft (June 4, 1996). ... On Birmingham disabled list (April 13-July 13, 1997).
STATISTICAL NOTES: Led Carolina League catchers with 939 total chances in 1998.

Year Team (League)	Pos.	G	AB	R	H	2B	3B	HR	RBI	Avg.	BB	SO	SB	PO	A	E	Avg.
1996— Hickory (S. Atl.)	C	59	226	41	74	16	0	8	37	.327	21	53	13	197	29	2	.991
1997— Birmingham (Sou.)......	C	34	115	18	34	5	0	1	16	.296	12	25	6	221	17	3	.988
— GC Whi. Sox (GCL) ...	C	5	14	3	6	0	1	0	0	.429	1	3	1	21	6	3	.900
1998— Win.-Salem (Car.).......	C	123	444	66	113	20	7	11	63	.255	38	91	20	*818	*118	3	*.997

The BATTING columns span: AB R H 2B 3B HR RBI Avg. BB SO SB. The FIELDING columns span: PO A E Avg.

PAVANO, CARL — P — EXPOS

PERSONAL: Born January 8, 1976, in New Britain, Conn. ... 6-5/225. ... Throws right, bats right. ... Full name: Carl Anthony Pavano.
HIGH SCHOOL: Southington (Conn.).
TRANSACTIONS/CAREER NOTES: Selected by Boston Red Sox organization in 13th round of free-agent draft (June 2, 1994). ... Traded by Red Sox with a player to be named later to Montreal Expos for P Pedro J. Martinez (November 18, 1997); Expos acquired P Tony Armas Jr. to complete deal (December 18, 1997).
HONORS: Named Eastern League Pitcher of the Year (1996).

Year Team (League)	W	L	Pct.	ERA	G	GS	CG	ShO	Sv.	IP	H	R	ER	BB	SO
1994— GC Red Sox (GCL)	4	3	.571	1.84	9	7	0	0	0	44	31	14	9	7	47
1995— Michigan (Midwest)	6	6	.500	3.45	22	22	1	0	0	141	118	63	54	52	138
1996— Trenton (Eastern)	*16	5	.762	2.63	27	26	•6	2	0	185	154	66	54	47	146
1997— Pawtucket (Int'l)	11	6	.647	3.12	23	23	3	0	0	161 2/3	148	62	56	34	147
1998— Jupiter (Florida State)■	0	0	...	6.60	4	4	0	0	0	15	20	11	11	3	14
— Ottawa (Int'l)	1	0	1.000	2.41	3	3	0	0	0	18 2/3	12	5	5	7	14
— Montreal (N.L.)	6	9	.400	4.21	24	23	0	0	0	134 2/3	130	70	63	43	83
Major league totals (1 year)........	6	9	.400	4.21	24	23	0	0	0	134 2/3	130	70	63	43	83

PAVLIK, ROGER — P

PERSONAL: Born October 4, 1967, in Houston. ... 6-2/220. ... Throws right, bats right. ... Full name: Roger Allen Pavlik.
HIGH SCHOOL: Aldine (Houston).
TRANSACTIONS/CAREER NOTES: Selected by Texas Rangers organization in second round of free-agent draft (June 2, 1986). ... On disabled list (June 21, 1986-remainder of season; June 4-August 6, 1987; and April 29-May 6 and May 23-July 29, 1991). ... On Texas disabled list (March 25-May 15, 1994); included rehabilitation assignments to Charlotte (April 23-May 10) and Oklahoma City (May 10-15). ... On Texas disabled list (June 12-July 2, 1994); included rehabilitation assignment to Oklahoma City (June 27-July 2). ... On Texas disabled list (July 3-24, 1994); included rehabilitation assignment to Oklahoma City (July 7-27). ... On Texas disabled list (May 7-September 2, 1997); included rehabilitation assignments to Gulf Coast Rangers (August 15-23), Tulsa (August 23-28) and Oklahoma City (August 28-September 2). ... Granted free agency (December 21, 1997). ... Re-signed by Rangers (December 23, 1997). ... On Texas disabled list (April 24, 1998-remainder of season). ... Granted free agency (October 27, 1998).
STATISTICAL NOTES: Pitched 5 1/3 innings, combining with reliever Steve Peters (2 2/3 innings) for eight no-hit innings in a 1-0 loss to Indianapolis (April 17, 1991). ... Pitched 3-1 one-hit, complete-game victory against Detroit (May 4, 1996).

Year Team (League)	W	L	Pct.	ERA	G	GS	CG	ShO	Sv.	IP	H	R	ER	BB	SO
1986—						Did not play.									
1987— Gastonia (S. Atl.)............	2	7	.222	4.95	15	14	0	0	0	67 1/3	66	46	37	42	55
1988— Gastonia (S. Atl.)............	2	12	.143	4.59	18	16	0	0	0	84 1/3	94	65	43	58	89
— Butte (Pioneer)	4	0	1.000	4.59	8	8	1	1	0	49	45	29	25	34	56
1989— Charlotte (Fla. St.)...........	3	8	.273	3.41	26	22	1	1	1	118 2/3	92	60	45	72	98
1990— Charlotte (Fla. St.)...........	5	3	.625	2.44	11	11	1	0	0	66 1/3	50	21	18	40	76
— Tulsa (Texas)	6	5	.545	2.33	16	16	2	1	0	100 1/3	66	29	26	71	91
1991— Oklahoma City (A.A.)........	0	5	.000	5.19	8	7	0	0	0	26	19	21	15	26	43
1992— Oklahoma City (A.A.)........	7	5	.583	2.98	18	18	0	0	0	117 2/3	90	44	39	51	104
— Texas (A.L.)	4	4	.500	4.21	13	12	1	0	0	62	66	32	29	34	45
1993— Oklahoma City (A.A.)........	3	2	.600	1.70	6	6	0	0	0	37	26	12	7	14	32
— Texas (A.L.)	12	6	.667	3.41	26	26	2	0	0	166 1/3	151	67	63	80	131
1994— Charlotte (Fla. St.)...........	2	1	.667	1.08	3	3	0	0	0	16 2/3	13	2	2	2	15
— Oklahoma City (A.A.)........	2	2	.500	3.10	5	5	0	0	0	29	26	11	10	7	38
— Texas (A.L.)	2	5	.286	7.69	11	11	0	0	0	50 1/3	61	45	43	30	31
1995— Texas (A.L.)	10	10	.500	4.37	31	31	2	1	0	191 2/3	174	96	93	90	149
1996— Texas (A.L.)	15	8	.652	5.19	34	34	7	0	0	201	216	120	116	81	127

P

Year Team (League)	W	L	Pct.	ERA	G	GS	CG	ShO	Sv.	IP	H	R	ER	BB	SO
1997— Texas (A.L.)	3	5	.375	4.37	11	11	0	0	0	57²/₃	59	29	28	31	35
— GC Rangers (GCL)	0	0	. . .	1.29	2	2	0	0	0	7	8	1	1	0	5
— Tulsa (Texas)	0	0	. . .	3.60	1	1	0	0	0	5	3	2	2	2	4
— Oklahoma City (A.A.)	0	0	. . .	0.00	1	1	0	0	0	6	2	0	0	0	4
1998— Texas (A.L.)	1	1	.500	3.86	5	0	0	0	1	14	16	8	6	5	8
Major league totals (7 years)	47	39	.547	4.58	131	125	12	1	1	743	743	397	378	351	526

DIVISION SERIES RECORD

Year Team (League)	W	L	Pct.	ERA	G	GS	CG	ShO	Sv.	IP	H	R	ER	BB	SO
1996— Texas (A.L.)	0	1	.000	6.75	1	1	0	0	0	2²/₃	4	2	2	0	1

ALL-STAR GAME RECORD

Year League	W	L	Pct.	ERA	GS	CG	ShO	Sv.	IP	H	R	ER	BB	SO
1996— American	0	0	. . .	9.00	0	0	0	0	2	3	2	2	0	2

PAYTON, JAY   OF   METS

PERSONAL: Born November 22, 1972, in Zanesville, Ohio. ... 5-10/185. ... Bats right, throws right. ... Full name: Jayson Lee Payton.
HIGH SCHOOL: Zanesville (Ohio).
COLLEGE: Georgia Tech.
TRANSACTIONS/CAREER NOTES: Selected by New York Mets organization in supplemental round ("sandwich pick" between first and second round, 29th pick overall) of free-agent draft (June 2, 1994); pick received as part of compensation for Baltimore Orioles signing Type A free-agent P Sid Fernandez. ... On Norfolk disabled list (April 29-July 3, 1996). ... On St. Lucie temporarily inactive list (July 11-16, 1996). ... On disabled list (April 3, 1997-entire season). ... On Norfolk disabled list (May 27-June 15 and June 24-July 20, 1998).

Year Team (League)	Pos.	G	AB	R	H	2B	3B	HR	RBI	Avg.	BB	SO	SB	PO	A	E	Avg.
1994— Pittsfield (NYP)	OF	58	219	47	80	16	2	3	37	.365	23	18	10	124	8	5	.964
— Binghamton (East.)	OF	8	25	3	7	1	0	0	1	.280	2	3	1	11	0	1	.917
1995— Binghamton (East.)	OF	85	357	59	123	20	3	14	54	.345	29	32	16	230	7	3	.988
— Norfolk (Int'l)	OF	50	196	33	47	11	4	4	30	.240	11	22	11	106	3	2	.982
1996— GC Mets (GCL)	DH	3	13	3	5	1	0	1	2	.385	0	1	1	. . .	. . .	. . .	. . .
— Norfolk (Int'l)	OF	55	153	30	47	6	3	6	26	.307	11	26	10	7	1	0	1.000
— St. Lucie (Fla. St.)	DH	9	26	4	8	2	0	0	1	.308	4	5	2	. . .	. . .	. . .	. . .
1997—								Did not play.									
1998— Norfolk (Int'l)	OF-1B	82	322	45	84	14	4	8	30	.261	26	50	12	315	20	7	.980
— St. Lucie (Fla. St.)	OF	3	7	0	1	0	0	0	0	.143	3	1	0	8	0	0	1.000
— New York (N.L.)	OF	15	22	2	7	1	0	0	0	.318	1	4	0	6	1	0	1.000
Major league totals (1 year)		15	22	2	7	1	0	0	0	.318	1	4	0	6	1	0	1.000

PEEPLES, MIKE   2B   BLUE JAYS

PERSONAL: Born September 3, 1976, in Orange Park, Fla. ... 5-11/170. ... Bats right, throws right. ... Full name: Michael Eddie Peeples.
HIGH SCHOOL: Clay (Green Cove Springs, Fla.).
TRANSACTIONS/CAREER NOTES: Selected by Toronto Blue Jays organization in sixth round of free-agent draft (June 2, 1994).
STATISTICAL NOTES: Led Florida State League second basemen with 23 errors in 1997. ... Led Southern League with 17 sacrifice hits in 1998.

Year Team (League)	Pos.	G	AB	R	H	2B	3B	HR	RBI	Avg.	BB	SO	SB	PO	A	E	Avg.
1994— GC Jays (GCL)	SS-2B	47	172	22	40	5	3	0	11	.233	13	25	17	49	81	5	.963
1995— Medicine Hat (Pio.)	2B-OF-SS	•72	285	55	89	14	4	3	50	.312	35	46	27	112	90	27	.882
1996— Hagerstown (SAL)	DH	74	268	30	63	15	1	3	31	.235	37	55	15	. . .	. . .	. . .	. . .
1997— Dunedin (Fla. St.)	2B-OF	129	477	73	122	29	2	2	42	.256	54	83	26	219	341	†23	.961
1998— Knoxville (Southern)	2B	113	395	58	99	16	3	7	42	.251	36	62	20	195	323	18	.966

PENA, ALEX   P   PIRATES

PERSONAL: Born September 9, 1977, in Santo Domingo, Dominican Republic. ... 6-2/205. ... Throws right, bats right. ... Full name: Alex J. Pena.
TRANSACTIONS/CAREER NOTES: Signed as non-drafted free agent by Pittsburgh Pirates organization (January 7, 1994).
MISCELLANEOUS: Played outfield (1995-98).

Year Team (League)	W	L	Pct.	ERA	G	GS	CG	ShO	Sv.	IP	H	R	ER	BB	SO
1998— Augusta (S. Atl.)	0	0	. . .	18.00	1	0	0	0	0	1	2	2	2	3	1

RECORD AS POSITION PLAYER

Year Team (League)	Pos.	G	AB	R	H	2B	3B	HR	RBI	Avg.	BB	SO	SB	PO	A	E	Avg.
1995— GC Pirates (GCL)	OF-3B	48	172	15	41	7	3	1	20	.238	6	26	3	88	8	3	.970
1996— Augusta (S. Atl.)	OF	52	167	9	27	4	2	0	12	.162	7	51	2	75	10	5	.944
— Erie (N.Y.-Penn)	OF	74	281	31	75	10	3	4	33	.267	14	52	10	131	15	6	.961
1997— Augusta (S. Atl.)	OF	111	356	34	87	12	2	5	40	.244	18	81	11	176	11	10	.949
1998— Lynchburg (Caro.)	OF	5	16	1	1	0	0	0	0	.063	0	8	0	8	1	0	1.000
— Augusta (S. Atl.)	OF	90	292	47	74	15	1	5	26	.253	24	69	7	153	5	5	.969

PENA, ANGEL   C   DODGERS

PERSONAL: Born February 16, 1975, in San Pedro de Macoris, Dominican Republic. ... 5-10/228. ... Bats right, throws right. ... Full name: Angel Maria Pena.
HIGH SCHOOL: Escuela Puerto Rico (San Pedro de Macoris, Dominican Republic).

TRANSACTIONS/CAREER NOTES: Signed as non-drafted free agent by Los Angeles Dodgers organization (July 24, 1992). ... Missed entire 1994 season due to injury. ... On San Bernardino disabled list (July 26-September 17, 1997).
STATISTICAL NOTES: Led California League catchers with 31 passed balls in 1997. ... Led Texas League catchers with 781 putouts, 81 assists, 14 errors and 876 total chances in 1998.

Year Team (League)	Pos.	G	AB	R	H	2B	3B	HR	RBI	Avg.	BB	SO	SB	PO	A	E	Avg.
								BATTING							FIELDING		
1993—Dom. Dodgers (DSL) .	C	50	168	27	47	3	2	1	24	.280	10	41	6	197	57	15	.944
1994—								Did not play.									
1995— Great Falls (Pio.)	C	49	138	24	40	11	1	4	15	.290	21	32	2	297	42	7	.980
1996— Savannah (S. Atl.)	C	36	127	13	26	4	0	6	16	.205	7	37	1	238	39	6	.979
—Dom. Dodgers (DSL) .	C	23	78	30	37	9	1	8	40	.474	24	12	1	86	11	1	.990
1997—San Bern. (Calif.).........	C	86	322	53	89	22	4	16	64	.276	32	84	3	661	83	10	.987
1998—San Antonio (Tex.)	C-OF	126	483	81	162	32	2	22	105	.335	48	80	9	†781	†81	†14	.984
—Los Angeles (N.L.)	C	6	13	1	3	0	0	0	0	.231	0	6	0	26	2	0	1.000
Major league totals (1 year)		6	13	1	3	0	0	0	0	.231	0	6	0	26	2	0	1.000

PENA, JUAN — P — RED SOX

PERSONAL: Born June 27, 1977, in Santo Domingo, Dominican Republic. ... 6-5/211. ... Throws right, bats right. ... Full name: Juan Francisco Pena.
HIGH SCHOOL: Miami (Fla.).
JUNIOR COLLEGE: Miami-Dade (Wolfson) Community College.
TRANSACTIONS/CAREER NOTES: Selected by Boston Red Sox organization in 27th round of free-agent draft (June 1, 1995). ... On disabled list (April 9-24 and June 17-27, 1998).
STATISTICAL NOTES: Pitched 5-0 no-hit victory for Pawtucket against Durham (July 22, 1998).

Year Team (League)	W	L	Pct.	ERA	G	GS	CG	ShO	Sv.	IP	H	R	ER	BB	SO
1995—GC Red Sox (GCL)	3	2	.600	1.95	13	4	2	1	1	55 1/3	41	17	12	6	47
—Sarasota (Florida State)......	1	1	.500	4.91	2	2	0	0	0	7 1/3	8	4	4	3	5
1996—Michigan (Midwest)	12	10	.545	2.97	26	26	4	0	0	*187 2/3	149	70	62	34	156
1997—Sarasota (Florida State)......	4	6	.400	2.96	13	13	3	0	0	91 1/3	67	39	30	23	88
—Trenton (Eastern)	5	6	.455	4.73	16	14	0	0	0	97	98	56	51	31	79
1998—Pawtucket (Int'l).................	8	10	.444	4.38	24	23	1	1	0	139 2/3	141	73	68	51	*146

PENDERGRASS, TYRONE — OF — WHITE SOX

PERSONAL: Born July 31, 1976, in Darlington, S.C. ... 6-1/175. ... Bats both, throws right. ... Full name: Tyrone Darice Pendergrass.
COLLEGE: Benedict College (S.C.).
TRANSACTIONS/CAREER NOTES: Signed as non-drafted free agent by Atlanta Braves organization (June 15, 1995). ... Selected by Chicago White Sox from Braves organization in Rule 5 major league draft (December 14, 1998).
STATISTICAL NOTES: Led Appalachian League outfielders with 123 total chances in 1996. ... Led Carolina League outfielders with 312 total chances in 1998.

Year Team (League)	Pos.	G	AB	R	H	2B	3B	HR	RBI	Avg.	BB	SO	SB	PO	A	E	Avg.
								BATTING							FIELDING		
1995—GC Braves (GCL)........	OF	52	188	19	34	4	0	1	7	.181	15	51	8	101	2	0	•1.000
1996—Danville (Appal.)	OF	54	220	50	68	8	•7	3	23	.309	24	39	*40	*118	3	2	*.984
—Macon (S. Atl.)..........	OF	12	45	8	12	1	1	1	3	.267	4	12	5	38	1	1	.975
1997—Macon (S. Atl.)..........	OF	127	489	81	127	16	5	6	37	.260	60	101	70	251	16	11	.960
1998—Danville (Carolina)......	OF	132	518	74	143	23	10	4	35	.276	43	91	39	*300	7	5	.984
—Greenville (Southern) .	OF	5	16	3	2	0	0	0	0	.125	2	4	1	8	0	1	.889

PENDLETON, TERRY — 3B

PERSONAL: Born July 16, 1960, in Los Angeles. ... 5-9/195. ... Bats both, throws right. ... Full name: Terry Lee Pendleton.
HIGH SCHOOL: Channel Island (Oxnard, Calif.).
JUNIOR COLLEGE: Oxnard (Calif.) College.
COLLEGE: Fresno State.
TRANSACTIONS/CAREER NOTES: Selected by St. Louis Cardinals organization in seventh round of free-agent draft (June 7, 1982). ... On disabled list (April 8-May 23 and July 16-September 5, 1983; June 15-30, 1985; May 28-June 24, 1988; and April 24-May 9, 1990). ... Granted free agency (November 5, 1990). ... Signed by Atlanta Braves (December 3, 1990). ... On Atlanta disabled list (June 21-July 25, 1994; included rehabilitation assignment to Greenville (July 23-25). ... Granted free agency (October 24, 1994). ... Signed by Florida Marlins (April 7, 1995). ... On suspended list (June 17-21, 1995). ... Traded by Marlins to Braves for OF Roosevelt Brown (August 13, 1996). ... Granted free agency (October 29, 1996). ... Signed by Cincinnati Reds organization (January 27, 1997). ... On Cincinnati disabled list (March 18-April 29 and July 7-23, 1997; included rehabilitation assignment to Indianapolis (April 25-29). ... Released by Reds (July 24, 1997). ... Signed by Kansas City Royals organization (January 20, 1998). ... On Kansas City disabled list (June 14-July 21, 1998; included rehabilitation assignment to Omaha (July 13-20). ... Granted free agency (October 23, 1998). ... Announced retirement (December 13, 1998).
RECORDS: Holds major league single-season record for fewest putouts by third baseman for leader—110 (1996).
HONORS: Won N.L. Gold Glove at third base (1987, 1989 and 1992). ... Named N.L. Comeback Player of the Year by The Sporting News (1991). ... Named third baseman on The Sporting News N.L. All-Star team (1991). ... Named N.L. Most Valuable Player by Baseball Writers' Association of America (1991).
STATISTICAL NOTES: Led American Association third basemen with .964 fielding percentage and 88 putouts in 1984. ... Led N.L. third basemen with 133 putouts and 371 assists in 1986. ... Led N.L. third basemen with 524 total chances in 1986, 512 in 1987, 520 in 1989, 481 in 1991 and 477 in 1992. ... Led N.L. third basemen with 36 double plays in 1986 and 31 in 1991. ... Tied for N.L. lead with 303 total bases in 1991. ... Led N.L. third basemen with 110 putouts in 1996. ... Career major league grand slams: 5.

P

Year — Team (League)	Pos.	G	AB	R	H	2B	3B	HR	RBI	Avg.	BB	SO	SB	PO	A	E	Avg.
1982— Johnson City (App.) ...	2B	43	181	38	58	14	•4	4	27	.320	12	28	13	79	105	17	.915
— St. Peters. (FSL).........	2B	20	69	4	18	2	1	1	7	.261	2	18	1	41	51	2	.979
1983— Arkansas (Texas)........	2B	48	185	29	51	10	3	4	20	.276	9	26	7	94	135	7	.970
1984— Louisville (A.A.).........	3B-2B	91	330	52	98	23	5	4	44	.297	24	51	6	†91	157	10	†.961
— St. Louis (N.L.)..........	3B	67	262	37	85	16	3	1	33	.324	16	32	20	59	155	9	.943
1985— St. Louis (N.L.)..........	3B	149	559	56	134	16	3	5	69	.240	37	75	17	129	361	18	.965
1986— St. Louis (N.L.)..........	3B-OF	159	578	56	138	26	5	1	59	.239	34	59	24	†133	†371	20	.962
1987— St. Louis (N.L.)..........	3B	159	583	82	167	29	4	12	96	.286	70	74	19	117	*369	26	.949
1988— St. Louis (N.L.)..........	3B	110	391	44	99	20	2	6	53	.253	21	51	3	75	239	12	.963
1989— St. Louis (N.L.)..........	3B	162	613	83	162	28	5	13	74	.264	44	81	9	113	*392	15	*.971
1990— St. Louis (N.L.)..........	3B	121	447	46	103	20	2	6	58	.230	30	58	7	91	248	19	.947
1991— Atlanta (N.L.)■........	3B	153	586	94	*187	34	8	22	86	*.319	43	70	10	108	*349	24	.950
1992— Atlanta (N.L.)..........	3B	160	640	98	•199	39	1	21	105	.311	37	67	5	*133	*325	19	.960
1993— Atlanta (N.L.)..........	3B	161	633	81	172	33	1	17	84	.272	36	97	5	*128	319	19	.959
1994— Atlanta (N.L.)..........	3B	77	309	25	78	18	3	7	30	.252	12	57	2	60	149	11	.950
— Greenville (Southern) .	3B	2	6	0	3	1	0	0	2	.500	0	1	0	1	1	1	.667
1995— Florida (N.L.)■..........	3B	133	513	70	149	32	1	14	78	.290	38	84	1	•104	250	18	.952
1996— Florida (N.L.)■	3B	111	406	30	102	20	1	7	58	.251	26	75	0	*83	214	12	.961
— Atlanta (N.L.)■..........	3B	42	162	21	33	6	0	4	17	.204	15	36	2	*27	80	7	.939
1997— Indianapolis (A.A.)■ ..	3B	4	12	2	2	0	0	0	2	.167	4	1	0	3	10	0	1.000
— Cincinnati (N.L.)..........	3B	50	113	11	28	9	0	1	17	.248	12	14	2	14	35	3	.942
1998— Kansas City (A.L.)■	DH-3B	79	237	17	61	10	0	3	29	.257	15	49	1	12	33	2	.957
— Omaha (PCL).............	3B	7	25	2	9	4	0	1	6	.360	4	3	0	1	2	0	1.000
American League totals (1 year)		79	237	17	61	10	0	3	29	.257	15	49	1	12	33	2	.957
National League totals (14 years)		1814	6795	834	1836	346	39	137	917	.270	471	930	126	1374	3856	236	.957
Major league totals (15 years)		1893	7032	851	1897	356	39	140	946	.270	486	979	127	1386	3889	238	.957

DIVISION SERIES RECORD

Year — Team (League)	Pos.	G	AB	R	H	2B	3B	HR	RBI	Avg.	BB	SO	SB	PO	A	E	Avg.
1996— Atlanta (N.L.)............	PH	1	1	0	0	0	0	0	0	.000	0	1	0	0	0	0	. . .

RECORDS: Shares record for most at-bats in one inning—2 (October 13, 1985, second inning). ... Holds N.L. career record for most games—38; and most at-bats—135.

CHAMPIONSHIP SERIES RECORD

Year — Team (League)	Pos.	G	AB	R	H	2B	3B	HR	RBI	Avg.	BB	SO	SB	PO	A	E	Avg.
1985— St. Louis (N.L.)..........	3B	6	24	2	5	1	0	0	4	.208	1	3	0	6	18	1	.960
1987— St. Louis (N.L.)..........	3B	6	19	3	4	0	1	0	1	.211	0	6	0	3	11	0	1.000
1991— Atlanta (N.L.)............	3B	7	30	1	5	1	1	0	1	.167	1	3	0	5	11	0	1.000
1992— Atlanta (N.L.)............	3B	7	30	2	7	2	0	0	3	.233	0	2	0	4	18	0	1.000
1993— Atlanta (N.L.)............	3B	6	26	4	9	1	0	1	5	.346	0	2	0	7	5	0	1.000
1996— Atlanta (N.L.)............	PH-3B	6	6	0	0	0	0	0	0	.000	2	3	0	0	1	0	1.000
Championship series totals (6 years)		38	135	12	30	5	2	1	14	.222	4	19	0	25	64	1	.989

WORLD SERIES RECORD

Year — Team (League)	Pos.	G	AB	R	H	2B	3B	HR	RBI	Avg.	BB	SO	SB	PO	A	E	Avg.
1985— St. Louis (N.L.).........	3B	7	23	3	6	1	1	0	3	.261	3	2	0	6	14	1	.952
1987— St. Louis (N.L.)..........	DH-PH	3	7	2	3	0	0	0	1	.429	1	1	2	. . .	. . .	. . .	. . .
1991— Atlanta (N.L.).........	3B	7	30	6	11	3	0	2	3	.367	3	1	0	3	20	2	.920
1992— Atlanta (N.L.).........	3B	6	25	2	6	2	0	0	2	.240	1	5	0	4	19	0	1.000
1996— Atlanta (N.L.).........	DH-PH-3B	4	9	1	2	1	0	0	0	.222	1	1	0	0	2	0	1.000
World Series totals (5 years)		27	94	14	28	7	1	2	9	.298	9	10	2	13	55	3	.958

ALL-STAR GAME RECORD

Year League	Pos.	AB	R	H	2B	3B	HR	RBI	Avg.	BB	SO	SB	PO	A	E	Avg.
1992— National	3B	2	0	1	0	0	0	0	.500	0	0	0	0	2	0	1.000

PENNINGTON, BRAD   P

PERSONAL: Born April 14, 1969, in Salem, Ind. ... 6-5/215. ... Throws left, bats left. ... Full name: Brad Lee Pennington.
HIGH SCHOOL: Eastern (Pekin, Ind.).
JUNIOR COLLEGE: Vincennes (Ind.) University.
COLLEGE: Bellarmine College (Ky.).
TRANSACTIONS/CAREER NOTES: Selected by Baltimore Orioles organization in 12th round of free-agent draft (June 5, 1989). ... Traded by Orioles organization to Cincinnati Reds for OF Danny Clyburn and P Tony Nieto (June 16, 1995). ... Granted free agency (October 16, 1995). ... Signed by Boston Red Sox (November 8, 1995). ... Claimed on waivers by California Angels (May 17, 1996). ... On California disabled list (May 31-June 22, 1996); included rehabilitation assignments to Lake Elsinore (June 15-19) and Vancouver (June 19-22). ... Granted free agency (October 15, 1996). ... Signed by Kansas City Royals organization (April 30, 1997). ... Granted free agency (October 15, 1997). ... Signed by Tampa Bay Devil Rays (January 8, 1998). ... Granted free agency (October 7, 1998).
STATISTICAL NOTES: Tied for Appalachian League lead with 14 wild pitches in 1989.

Year — Team (League)	W	L	Pct.	ERA	G	GS	CG	ShO	Sv.	IP	H	R	ER	BB	SO
1989— Bluefield (Appalachian)	2	•7	.222	6.58	15	14	0	0	0	64 1/3	50	58	47	*74	81
1990— Wausau (Midwest)............	4	9	.308	5.18	32	18	1	0	0	106	81	89	61	*121	142
1991— Frederick (Carolina)............	1	4	.200	3.92	36	0	0	0	13	43 2/3	32	23	19	44	58
— Kane County (Midwest)......	0	2	.000	5.87	23	0	0	0	4	23	16	17	15	25	43

P

Year	Team (League)	W	L	Pct.	ERA	G	GS	CG	ShO	Sv.	IP	H	R	ER	BB	SO
1992—	Frederick (Carolina)	1	0	1.000	2.00	8	0	0	0	2	9	5	3	2	4	16
	— Hagerstown (Eastern)	1	2	.333	2.54	19	0	0	0	7	28 $1/3$	20	9	8	17	33
	— Rochester (Int'l)	1	3	.250	2.08	29	0	0	0	5	39	12	10	9	33	56
1993—	Rochester (Int'l)	1	2	.333	3.45	17	0	0	0	8	15 $2/3$	12	11	6	13	19
	— Baltimore (A.L.)	3	2	.600	6.55	34	0	0	0	4	33	34	25	24	25	39
1994—	Baltimore (A.L.)	0	1	.000	12.00	8	0	0	0	0	6	9	8	8	8	7
	— Rochester (Int'l)	6	8	.429	5.32	35	9	0	0	3	86 $1/3$	68	59	51	74	89
1995—	Baltimore (A.L.)	0	1	.000	8.10	8	0	0	0	0	6 $2/3$	3	7	6	11	10
	— Cincinnati (N.L.)■	0	0	...	5.59	6	0	0	0	0	9 $2/3$	9	8	6	11	7
	— Indianapolis (A.A.)	0	0	...	10.29	11	2	0	0	0	14	17	19	16	21	11
1996—	Boston (A.L.)■	0	2	.000	2.77	14	0	0	0	0	13	6	5	4	15	13
	— Lake Elsinore (Calif.)■	0	0	...	0.00	2	2	0	0	0	3	0	0	0	2	5
	— Vancouver (PCL)	3	0	1.000	4.23	11	2	0	0	1	27 $2/3$	20	20	13	22	43
	— California (A.L.)	0	0	...	12.27	8	0	0	0	0	7 $1/3$	5	10	10	16	7
1997—	Wichita (Texas)■	0	0	...	0.75	12	0	0	0	3	12	7	1	1	8	14
	— Omaha (Am. Assoc.)	2	1	.667	4.32	35	1	0	0	0	50	41	28	24	41	48
1998—	Durham (International)■	4	4	.500	4.86	45	6	0	0	1	100	77	55	54	65	125
A.L. totals (4 years)		3	6	.333	7.09	72	0	0	0	4	66	57	55	52	75	76
N.L. totals (1 year)		0	0	...	5.59	6	0	0	0	0	9 $2/3$	9	8	6	11	7
Major league totals (4 years)		3	6	.333	6.90	78	0	0	0	4	75 $2/3$	66	63	58	86	83

PEOPLES, DANNY　　　　OF　　　　INDIANS

PERSONAL: Born January 20, 1975, in Round Rock, Texas. ... 6-1/207. ... Bats right, throws right. ... Full name: Daniel Laurence Peoples.
HIGH SCHOOL: Round Rock (Texas).
COLLEGE: Texas.
TRANSACTIONS/CAREER NOTES: Selected by Cleveland Indians organization in first round (28th pick overall) of free-agent draft (June 4, 1996). ... On disabled list (July 31, 1996-remainder of season). ... On disabled list (April 10-24, June 3-10, June 15-July 31 and August 21, 1998-remainder of season).

							BATTING							FIELDING		
Year	Team (League)	Pos.	G	AB	R	H	2B	3B	HR	RBI	Avg.	BB	SO	SB	PO	A	E	Avg.
1996—	Watertown (NYP)	DH	35	117	20	28	7	0	3	26	.239	28	36	3	...	...	...	...
1997—	Kinston (Carolina)	OF	121	409	82	102	21	1	*34	84	.249	84	145	8	86	2	4	.957
1998—	Akron (Eastern)	OF	60	222	30	62	19	0	8	32	.279	29	61	1	71	2	2	.973

PERCIVAL, TROY　　　　P　　　　ANGELS

PERSONAL: Born August 9, 1969, in Fontana, Calif. ... 6-3/230. ... Throws right, bats right. ... Full name: Troy Eugene Percival. ... Name pronounced PER-sih-vol.
HIGH SCHOOL: Moreno Valley (Calif.).
COLLEGE: UC Riverside.
TRANSACTIONS/CAREER NOTES: Selected by California Angels organization in sixth round of free-agent draft (June 5, 1990). ... On Palm Springs disabled list (June 3-July 2, 1992). ... On disabled list (May 28, 1993-remainder of season). ... Angels franchise renamed Anaheim Angels for 1997 season. ... On disabled list (April 7-May 16, 1997); included rehabilitation assignment to Lake Elsinore (May 13-16).
MISCELLANEOUS: Played catcher (1990). ... Struck out in only appearance as pinch hitter (1996).

Year	Team (League)	W	L	Pct.	ERA	G	GS	CG	ShO	Sv.	IP	H	R	ER	BB	SO
1991—	Boise (Northwest)	2	0	1.000	1.41	28	0	0	0	*12	38 $1/3$	23	7	6	18	63
1992—	Palm Springs (Calif.)	1	1	.500	5.06	11	0	0	0	2	10 $2/3$	6	7	6	8	16
	— Midland (Texas)	3	1	1.000	2.37	20	0	0	0	5	19	18	5	5	11	21
1993—	Vancouver (PCL)	0	1	.000	6.27	18	0	0	0	4	18 $2/3$	24	14	13	13	19
1994—	Vancouver (PCL)	2	6	.250	4.13	49	0	0	0	15	61	63	31	28	29	73
1995—	California (A.L.)	3	2	.600	1.95	62	0	0	0	3	74	37	19	16	26	94
1996—	California (A.L.)	0	2	.000	2.31	62	0	0	0	36	74	38	20	19	31	100
1997—	Anaheim (A.L.)	5	5	.500	3.46	55	0	0	0	27	52	40	20	20	22	72
	— Lake Elsinore (Calif.)	0	0	...	0.00	2	1	0	0	0	2	1	0	0	0	3
1998—	Anaheim (A.L.)	2	7	.222	3.65	67	0	0	0	42	66 $2/3$	45	31	27	37	87
Major league totals (4 years)		10	16	.385	2.77	246	0	0	0	108	266 $2/3$	160	90	82	116	353

ALL-STAR GAME RECORD

Year	League	W	L	Pct.	ERA	GS	CG	ShO	Sv.	IP	H	R	ER	BB	SO
1996—	American	0	0	...	0.00	0	0	0	0	1	1	0	0	0	1
1998—	American	0	0	...	0.00	0	0	0	0	1	1	0	0	0	2
All-Star totals (2 years)		0	0	...	0.00	0	0	0	0	2	2	0	0	0	3

RECORD AS POSITION PLAYER

							BATTING							FIELDING		
Year	Team (League)	Pos.	G	AB	R	H	2B	3B	HR	RBI	Avg.	BB	SO	SB	PO	A	E	Avg.
1990—	Boise (Northwest)	C	29	79	12	16	0	0	0	5	.203	19	25	0	215	25	5	.980

P　　PEREZ, CARLOS　　　　P　　　　DODGERS

PERSONAL: Born January 14, 1971, in Nigua, Dominican Republic. ... 6-3/210. ... Throws left, bats left. ... Full name: Carlos Gross Perez. ... Brother of Melido Perez, pitcher with Chicago White Sox (1988-91) and New York Yankees (1992-96); brother of Pascual Perez, pitcher with four major league teams (1980-85 and 1987-92); brother of Vladimir Perez, minor league pitcher (1986-94); brother of Reuben Dario Perez, minor league pitcher (1988-94); and brother of Valerio Perez, minor league pitcher (1983-84).

TRANSACTIONS/CAREER NOTES: Signed as non-drafted free agent by Montreal Expos organization (January 7, 1988). ... On disabled list (April 9-24 and May 18-July 7, 1992). ... On suspended list (July 7-October 22, 1992). ... On Montreal disabled list (March 31, 1996-entire season). ... Traded by Expos with SS Mark Grudzielanek and OF Hiram Bocachica to Los Angeles Dodgers for 2B Wilton Guerrero, P Ted Lilly, OF Peter Bergeron and 1B Jonathan Tucker (July 31, 1998).

Year Team (League)	W	L	Pct.	ERA	G	GS	CG	ShO	Sv.	IP	H	R	ER	BB	SO
1989— DSL Expos (DSL)	3	3	.500	3.07	16	4	0	0	2	44	25	21	15	32	45
1990— GC Expos (GCL)	3	1	.750	2.52	13	2	0	0	2	35²/₃	24	14	10	15	38
1991— Sumter (S. Atl.)	2	2	.500	2.44	16	12	0	0	0	73²/₃	57	29	20	32	69
1992— Rockford (Midwest)	0	1	.000	5.79	7	1	0	0	1	9¹/₃	12	7	6	5	8
1993— Burlington (Midw.)	1	0	1.000	3.24	12	1	0	0	1	16²/₃	13	6	6	9	21
—San Bernardino (Calif.).......	8	7	.533	3.44	20	18	0	0	0	131	120	57	50	44	98
1994— Harrisburg (Eastern)	7	2	.778	1.94	12	11	2	2	1	79	55	27	17	18	69
—Ottawa (Int'l)	7	5	.583	3.33	17	17	3	0	0	119	130	50	44	41	82
1995— Montreal (N.L.).................	10	8	.556	3.69	28	23	2	1	0	141¹/₃	142	61	58	28	106
1996— Montreal (N.L.).................							Did not play.								
1997— Montreal (N.L.).................	12	13	.480	3.88	33	32	8	*5	0	206²/₃	206	109	89	48	110
1998— Montreal (N.L.).................	7	10	.412	3.75	23	23	3	0	0	163¹/₃	177	79	68	33	82
—GC Expos (GCL)	1	0	1.000	0.00	1	0	0	0	0	5	5	2	0	1	2
—Los Angeles (N.L.)■........	4	4	.500	3.24	11	11	4	2	0	77²/₃	67	30	28	30	46
Major league totals (3 years)......	33	35	.485	3.71	95	89	17	8	0	589	592	279	243	139	344

ALL-STAR GAME RECORD

Year League	W	L	Pct.	ERA	GS	CG	ShO	Sv.	IP	H	R	ER	BB	SO
1995— National.............................	0	0	...	0.00	0	0	0	0	¹/₃	1	0	0	1	0

PEREZ, EDDIE   C   BRAVES

PERSONAL: Born May 4, 1968, in Cuidad Ojeda, Venezuela. ... 6-1/185. ... Bats right, throws right. ... Full name: Eduardo Rafael Perez.
HIGH SCHOOL: Doctor Raul Cuenca (Cuidad Ojeda, Venezuela).
TRANSACTIONS/CAREER NOTES: Signed as non-drafted free agent by Atlanta Braves organization (September 27, 1986). ... On disabled list (August 30-September 14, 1996).
STATISTICAL NOTES: Led South Atlantic League catchers with 13 double plays in 1989. ... Tied for International League lead in errors by catcher with 11 in 1994. ... Led International League catchers with 539 putouts, 69 assists and 615 total chances in 1995. ... Tied for International League lead with seven double plays in 1995.

Year Team (League)	Pos.	G	AB	R	H	2B	3B	HR	RBI	Avg.	BB	SO	SB	PO	A	E	Avg.
1987— GC Braves (GCL)........	C	31	89	8	18	1	0	1	5	.202	8	14	0	161	31	4	.980
1988— Burlington (Midw.).....	C-1B	64	186	14	43	8	0	4	19	.231	10	33	1	245	42	11	.963
1989— Sumter (S. Atl.).........	C-1B	114	401	39	93	21	0	5	44	.232	44	68	2	760	96	16	.982
1990— Sumter (S. Atl.).........	C-1B	41	123	11	22	7	1	3	17	.179	14	18	0	315	32	3	.991
—Durham (Carolina)......	C-1B	31	93	9	22	1	0	3	10	.237	1	12	0	197	17	3	.986
1991— Durham (Carolina)......	C-1B	92	277	38	75	10	1	9	41	.271	17	33	0	497	55	8	.986
—Greenville (Southern).	1B	1	4	0	1	0	0	0	0	.250	0	1	0	9	0	0	1.000
1992— Greenville (Southern).	C-1B	91	275	28	63	16	0	6	41	.229	24	41	3	631	64	14	.980
1993— Greenville (Southern).	1B-C	28	84	15	28	6	0	6	17	.333	2	8	1	146	19	3	.982
1994— Richmond (Int'l)........	C-1B	113	388	37	101	16	2	9	49	.260	18	47	1	718	80	‡12	.985
1995— Richmond (Int'l)........	C-1B	92	324	31	86	19	0	5	40	.265	12	58	1	†540	†69	7	.989
—Atlanta (N.L.)..........	C-1B	7	13	1	4	1	0	1	4	.308	0	2	0	34	2	0	1.000
1996— Atlanta (N.L.)...........	C-1B	68	156	19	40	9	1	4	17	.256	8	19	0	281	22	3	.990
1997— Atlanta (N.L.)...........	C-1B	73	191	20	41	5	0	6	18	.215	10	35	0	417	24	5	.989
1998— Atlanta (N.L.).............	C-1B-DH	61	149	18	50	12	0	6	32	.336	15	28	1	290	29	2	.994
Major league totals (4 years)		209	509	58	135	27	1	17	71	.265	33	84	1	1022	77	10	.991

DIVISION SERIES RECORD

RECORDS: Shares career record for most grand slams—1 (October 3, 1998).

Year Team (League)	Pos.	G	AB	R	H	2B	3B	HR	RBI	Avg.	BB	SO	SB	PO	A	E	Avg.
1995— Atlanta (N.L.)								Did not play.									
1996— Atlanta (N.L.)	C	1	3	0	1	0	0	0	0	.333	0	0	0	10	0	0	1.000
1997— Atlanta (N.L.)	C	1	3	0	0	0	0	0	0	.000	0	1	0	6	0	0	1.000
1998— Atlanta (N.L.)	C	1	5	1	1	0	0	1	4	.200	0	2	0	6	0	0	1.000
Division series totals (3 years)		3	11	1	2	0	0	1	4	.182	0	3	0	22	0	0	1.000

CHAMPIONSHIP SERIES RECORD

Year Team (League)	Pos.	G	AB	R	H	2B	3B	HR	RBI	Avg.	BB	SO	SB	PO	A	E	Avg.
1995— Atlanta (N.L.)								Did not play.									
1996— Atlanta (N.L.)	C-1B	4	1	0	0	0	0	0	0	.000	1	0	0	7	0	0	1.000
1997— Atlanta (N.L.)	C	2	3	0	0	0	0	0	0	.000	0	0	0	14	0	0	1.000
1998— Atlanta (N.L.)	C	3	4	0	3	0	0	0	0	.750	0	0	0	6	0	0	1.000
Championship series totals (3 years)		9	8	0	3	0	0	0	0	.375	1	0	0	27	0	0	1.000

WORLD SERIES RECORD

NOTES: Member of World Series championship team (1995).

Year Team (League)	Pos.	G	AB	R	H	2B	3B	HR	RBI	Avg.	BB	SO	SB	PO	A	E	Avg.
1995— Atlanta (N.L.)								Did not play.									
1996— Atlanta (N.L.)	C	2	1	0	0	0	0	0	0	.000	0	0	0	2	0	0	1.000

P

PERSONAL: Born September 11, 1969, in Cincinnati. ... 6-4/215. ... Bats right, throws right. ... Full name: Eduardo Antanacio Perez. ... Son of Tony Perez, special assistant to general manager, Florida Marlins; major league infielder with four teams (1964-86) and manager, Cincinnati Reds (1993); and brother of Victor Perez, minor league outfielder/first baseman (1990).
HIGH SCHOOL: Robinson (Santurce, Puerto Rico).
COLLEGE: Florida State.
TRANSACTIONS/CAREER NOTES: Selected by California Angels organization in first round (17th pick overall) of free-agent draft (June 3, 1991). ... On Palm Springs disabled list (May 9-19, 1992). ... On Vancouver disabled list (June 26-July 7, 1994). ... Traded by Angels to Cincinnati Reds for P Will Pennyfeather (April 5, 1996). ... Released by Reds (December 14, 1998).
STATISTICAL NOTES: Career major league grand slams: 1.

Year	Team (League)	Pos.	G	AB	R	H	2B	3B	HR	RBI	Avg.	BB	SO	SB	PO	A	E	Avg.
1991—	Boise (Northwest)	OF-1B	46	160	35	46	13	0	1	22	.288	19	39	12	87	6	3	.969
1992—	Palm Springs (Calif.)..	3B-SS-OF	54	204	37	64	8	4	3	35	.314	23	33	14	30	90	16	.882
	— Midland (Texas)	3B-OF-1B	62	235	27	54	8	1	3	23	.230	22	49	15	53	97	13	.920
1993—	Vancouver (PCL)	3B-1B-OF	96	363	66	111	23	6	12	70	.306	28	83	21	98	174	23	.922
	— California (A.L.)	3B-DH	52	180	16	45	6	2	4	30	.250	9	39	5	24	101	5	.962
1994—	California (A.L.)	1B	38	129	10	27	7	0	5	16	.209	12	29	3	305	15	1	.997
	— Vancouver (PCL)	3B	61	219	37	65	14	3	7	38	.297	34	53	9	35	116	12	.926
	— Ariz. Angels (Ariz.)	3B	1	3	0	0	0	0	0	0	.000	1	1	0	0	3	0	1.000
1995—	Vancouver (PCL)■......	3B-1B	69	246	39	80	12	7	6	37	.325	25	34	6	94	90	6	.968
	— California (A.L.)	3B-DH	29	71	9	12	4	1	1	7	.169	12	9	0	16	37	7	.883
1996—	Indianapolis (A.A.)■......	3B-1B	122	451	84	132	29	5	21	84	.293	51	69	11	110	215	21	.939
	— Cincinnati (N.L.)	1B-3B	18	36	8	8	0	0	3	5	.222	5	9	0	59	11	0	1.000
1997—	Cincinnati (N.L.)	1-O-3-DH	106	297	44	75	18	0	16	52	.253	29	76	5	506	49	2	.996
1998—	Cincinnati (N.L.)	1B-3B-OF	84	172	20	41	4	0	4	30	.238	21	45	0	291	47	5	.985
American League totals (3 years)			119	380	35	84	17	3	10	53	.221	33	77	8	345	153	13	.975
National League totals (3 years)			208	505	72	124	22	0	23	87	.246	55	130	5	856	107	7	.993
Major league totals (6 years)			327	885	107	208	39	3	33	140	.235	88	207	13	1201	260	20	.986

PERSONAL: Born March 28, 1973, in La Romana, Dominican Republic. ... 6-0/155. ... Throws left, bats left. ... Full name: Juan Luis Perez.
TRANSACTIONS/CAREER NOTES: Signed as non-drafted free agent by Oakland Athletics organization (January 17, 1992).

Year	Team (League)	W	L	Pct.	ERA	G	GS	CG	ShO	Sv.	IP	H	R	ER	BB	SO
1993—	Arizona A's (Arizona)..........	4	1	.800	2.31	12	0	0	0	0	35	34	12	9	9	31
1994—	Arizona A's (Arizona)	3	2	.600	4.37	14	4	0	0	1	47 1/3	66	30	23	14	41
1995—	West. Mich. (Mid.)	11	8	.579	3.64	30	19	1	0	1	141	129	73	57	55	117
1996—	Modesto (California)	2	4	.333	5.02	38	8	0	0	4	98 2/3	120	68	55	34	89
1997—	Visalia (California)	3	6	.333	2.78	53	0	0	0	1	64 2/3	47	30	20	24	66
1998—	Huntsville (Southern)	3	2	.600	2.45	27	0	0	0	8	36 2/3	29	13	10	16	37
	— Edmonton (PCL)	3	4	.429	3.12	24	0	0	0	1	40 1/3	35	17	14	18	37

PERSONAL: Born February 2, 1975, in Villa Mella, Dominican Republic. ... 6-0/175. ... Bats both, throws right. ... Full name: Neifi Neftali Diaz Perez.
TRANSACTIONS/CAREER NOTES: Signed as non-drafted free agent by Colorado Rockies organization (November 9, 1992).
STATISTICAL NOTES: Led California League shortstops with 650 total chances and 86 double plays in 1994. ... Tied for Eastern League lead in double plays by shortstop with 80 in 1995. ... Led Pacific Coast League shortstops with 678 total chances and 91 double plays in 1996. ... Hit for the cycle (July 25, 1998). ... Had 15-game hitting streak (July 27-August 11, 1998). ... Led N.L. with 22 sacrifice hits in 1998. ... Led N.L. shortstops with 272 putouts, 516 assists, 808 total chances and 127 double plays in 1998.

Year	Team (League)	Pos.	G	AB	R	H	2B	3B	HR	RBI	Avg.	BB	SO	SB	PO	A	E	Avg.
1993—	Bend (Northwest).......	SS-2B	75	296	35	77	11	4	3	32	.260	19	43	19	127	244	25	.937
1994—	Central Valley (Cal.)....	SS	•134	506	64	121	16	7	1	35	.239	32	79	9	*223	388	*39	.940
1995—	Colo. Springs (PCL) ...	SS	11	36	4	10	4	0	0	2	.278	0	5	1	16	28	3	.936
	— New Haven (East.)......	SS	116	427	59	108	23	3	5	43	.253	24	52	5	175	358	18	*.967
1996—	Colo. Springs (PCL) ...	SS	133	*570	77	180	28	12	7	72	.316	21	48	16	*244	*409	*25	.963
	— Colorado (N.L.)	SS-2B	17	45	4	7	2	0	0	3	.156	0	8	2	21	28	2	.961
1997—	Colo. Springs (PCL) ...	SS	68	303	68	110	24	3	8	46	.363	17	27	8	119	198	8	.975
	— Colorado (N.L.)	SS-2B-3B	83	313	46	91	13	10	5	31	.291	21	43	4	185	287	9	.981
1998—	Colorado (N.L.)	SS-C	•162	647	80	177	25	9	9	59	.274	38	70	5	†272	†516	20	.975
Major league totals (3 years)			262	1005	130	275	40	19	14	93	.274	59	121	11	478	831	31	.977

PERSONAL: Born June 7, 1978, in Las Matas de Farfan, Dominican Republic. ... 6-0/150. ... Throws left, bats left. ... Full name: Odalis Amadol Perez.
HIGH SCHOOL: Damian Davis Ortiz (Las Matas de Farfan, Dominican Republic).
TRANSACTIONS/CAREER NOTES: Signed as non-drafted free agent by Atlanta Braves organization (July 2, 1994).

Year	Team (League)	W	L	Pct.	ERA	G	GS	CG	ShO	Sv.	IP	H	R	ER	BB	SO
1995—	GC Braves (GCL)...............	3	5	.375	2.22	12	12	1	1	0	65	48	22	16	18	62
1996—	Eugene (Northwest)	2	1	.667	3.80	10	6	0	0	0	23 2/3	26	16	10	11	38
1997—	Macon (S. Atl.)..................	4	5	.444	1.65	36	0	0	0	5	87 1/3	67	31	16	27	100

P

Year Team (League)	W	L	Pct.	ERA	G	GS	CG	ShO	Sv.	IP	H	R	ER	BB	SO
1998— Greenville (Southern)	6	5	.545	4.02	23	21	0	0	0	132	127	67	59	53	143
— Richmond (Int'l)	1	2	.333	2.96	13	0	0	0	3	24 1/3	26	10	8	7	22
— Atlanta (N.L.)	0	1	.000	4.22	10	0	0	0	0	10 2/3	10	5	5	4	5
Major league totals (1 year)	0	1	.000	4.22	10	0	0	0	0	10 2/3	10	5	5	4	5

DIVISION SERIES RECORD

Year Team (League)	W	L	Pct.	ERA	G	GS	CG	ShO	Sv.	IP	H	R	ER	BB	SO
1998— Atlanta (N.L.)	1	0	1.000	0.00	1	0	0	0	0	2/3	0	0	0	0	1

CHAMPIONSHIP SERIES RECORD

Year Team (League)	W	L	Pct.	ERA	G	GS	CG	ShO	Sv.	IP	H	R	ER	BB	SO
1998— Atlanta (N.L.)	0	0	...	54.00	2	0	0	0	0	1/3	5	2	2	3	0

PEREZ, ROBERT   OF

PERSONAL: Born June 4, 1969, in Bolivar, Venezuela. ... 6-3/230. ... Bats right, throws right. ... Full name: Robert Alexander Jimenez Perez.
HIGH SCHOOL: Raul Leoni Otero (Bolivar, Venezuela).
TRANSACTIONS/CAREER NOTES: Signed as non-drafted free agent by Toronto Blue Jays organization (May 1, 1989). ... Claimed on waivers by Seattle Mariners (March 30, 1998). ... Traded by Mariners to Montreal Expos for C Raul Chavez (May 8, 1998). ... On Montreal disabled list (June 22-July 14, 1998). ... Granted free agency (September 29, 1998).
STATISTICAL NOTES: Led International League outfielders with 303 total chances in 1993. ... Tied for International League lead in grounding into double plays with 19 in 1993. ... Led International League in grounding into double plays with 21 in 1994. ... Tied for International League lead with eight sacrifice flies in 1994. ... Led International League with 249 total bases in 1995.

Year Team (League)	Pos.	G	AB	R	H	2B	3B	HR	RBI	Avg.	BB	SO	SB	PO	A	E	Avg.
1989— Dom. Dodgers (DSL) .	OF	52	219	34	*79	*20	3	5	40	.361	21	23	5	...	...	...	...
1990— St. Catharines (NYP) ..	OF	52	207	21	54	10	2	5	25	.261	8	34	7	80	5	1	.988
— Myrtle Beach (SAL)	OF	21	72	8	21	2	0	1	10	.292	3	9	2	40	1	1	.976
1991— Dunedin (Fla. St.)	OF	127	480	50	*145	28	6	4	50	*.302	22	72	8	160	10	5	.971
— Syracuse (Int'l)	OF	4	20	2	4	1	0	0	1	.200	0	2	0	5	0	1	.833
1992— Knoxville (Southern) ..	OF	*139	•526	59	137	25	5	9	59	.260	13	87	11	241	13	7	.973
1993— Syracuse (Int'l)	OF	138	524	72	154	26	10	12	64	.294	24	65	13	278	•13	*12	.960
1994— Syracuse (Int'l)	OF	128	510	63	155	28	3	10	65	.304	27	76	4	231	8	9	.964
— Toronto (A.L.)	OF	4	8	0	1	0	0	0	0	.125	0	1	0	3	1	0	1.000
1995— Syracuse (Int'l)	OF	122	502	70	*172	*38	6	9	67	*.343	13	60	7	208	7	8	.964
— Toronto (A.L.)	OF	17	48	2	9	2	0	1	3	.188	0	5	0	30	0	0	1.000
1996— Toronto (A.L.)	OF-DH	86	202	30	66	10	4	2	21	.327	8	17	3	114	3	2	.983
1997— Toronto (A.L.)	OF-DH	37	78	4	15	4	1	2	6	.192	0	16	0	35	0	0	1.000
1998— Seattle (A.L.)■.........	OF	17	35	3	6	1	0	2	6	.171	0	5	0	20	1	0	1.000
— Montreal (N.L.)■.........	OF	52	106	9	25	1	0	1	8	.236	2	23	0	20	3	4	.852
American League totals (5 years)		161	371	39	97	17	1	7	36	.261	8	44	3	202	5	2	.990
National League totals (1 year)		52	106	9	25	1	0	1	8	.236	2	23	0	20	3	4	.852
Major league totals (5 years)		213	477	48	122	18	1	8	44	.256	10	67	3	222	8	6	.975

PEREZ, SANTIAGO   SS   BREWERS

PERSONAL: Born December 30, 1975, in Santo Domingo, Dominican Republic. ... 6-2/150. ... Bats both, throws right. ... Full name: Santiago Alberto Perez.
HIGH SCHOOL: Liceo Victor Estrella Luz (Santo Domingo, Dominican Republic).
TRANSACTIONS/CAREER NOTES: Signed as non-drafted free agent by Detroit Tigers organization (March 10, 1993). ... Traded by Tigers with P Mike Myers and P Rick Greene to Milwaukee Brewers for P Bryce Florie and a player to be named later (November 20, 1997).

Year Team (League)	Pos.	G	AB	R	H	2B	3B	HR	RBI	Avg.	BB	SO	SB	PO	A	E	Avg.
1993— Dom. Tigers (DSL)	IF-OF	58	171	28	45	6	2	0	17	.263	20	22	17	59	47	16	.869
1994— Dom. Tigers (DSL)	SS	60	227	54	78	7	9	2	47	.344	32	43	20	106	183	39	.881
1995— Fayetteville (SAL)	SS	130	425	54	101	15	1	4	44	.238	30	98	10	176	327	46	.916
1996— Lakeland (Fla. St.)	SS	122	418	33	105	18	2	1	27	.251	16	88	6	192	310	41	.924
1997— Lakeland (Fla. St.)	SS	111	445	66	122	20	12	4	46	.274	20	98	21	148	322	34	.933
1998— El Paso (Texas)■.......	SS	107	454	73	139	20	*13	11	64	.306	28	70	21	186	310	*36	.932
— Louisville (Int'l)	SS-2B	36	133	18	36	4	3	3	14	.271	6	31	6	67	91	6	.963

PEREZ, TOMAS   IF   BLUE JAYS

PERSONAL: Born December 29, 1973, in Barquisimeto, Venezuela. ... 5-11/177. ... Bats both, throws right. ... Full name: Tomas Orlando Perez.
TRANSACTIONS/CAREER NOTES: Signed as non-drafted free agent by Montreal Expos organization (July 11, 1991). ... Selected by California Angels from Expos organization in Rule 5 major league draft (December 5, 1994). ... Contract sold by Angels to Toronto Blue Jays (December 5, 1994). ... On Toronto disabled list (June 25-July 25, 1997); included rehabilitation assignment to Syracuse (July 12-24).
STATISTICAL NOTES: Led Midwest League shortstops with 217 putouts and 65 double plays in 1994. ... Led International League with 14 sacrifice hits in 1997. ... Led International League shortstops with .977 fielding percentage in 1998.

Year Team (League)	Pos.	G	AB	R	H	2B	3B	HR	RBI	Avg.	BB	SO	SB	PO	A	E	Avg.
1992— Dom. Expos (DSL)	IF	44	151	35	46	7	0	1	19	.305	27	20	12	112	138	12	.954
1993— GC Expos (GCL)	SS	52	189	27	46	3	1	2	21	.243	23	25	8	*121	*205	12	*.964
1994— Burlington (Midw.)	SS-2B	119	465	76	122	22	1	8	47	.262	48	78	8	†221	347	34	.944
1995— Toronto (A.L.)■..........	SS-2B-3B	41	98	12	24	3	1	1	8	.245	7	18	0	48	77	5	.962
1996— Syracuse (Int'l)..........	SS-2B	40	123	15	34	10	1	1	13	.276	7	19	8	80	97	7	.962
— Toronto (A.L.).............	2B-3B-SS	91	295	24	74	13	4	1	19	.251	25	29	1	151	250	15	.964

P

Year Team (League)	Pos.	G	AB	R	H	2B	3B	HR	RBI	Avg.	BB	SO	SB	PO	A	E	Avg.
						BATTING								FIELDING			
1997—Syracuse (Int'l)..........	SS	89	303	32	68	13	0	1	20	.224	37	67	3	158	274	12	.973
—Toronto (A.L.)............	SS-2B	40	123	9	24	3	2	0	9	.195	11	28	1	58	124	3	.984
1998—Syracuse (Int'l)..........	SS-2B	116	404	40	102	15	4	3	37	.252	18	67	4	205	437	15	†.977
—Toronto (A.L.)............	SS-2B	6	9	1	1	0	0	0	0	.111	1	3	0	6	6	0	1.000
Major league totals (4 years)		178	525	46	123	19	7	2	36	.234	44	78	2	263	457	23	.969

PEREZ, YORKIS — P — PHILLIES

PERSONAL: Born September 30, 1967, in Bajos de Haina, Dominican Republic. ... 6-0/180. ... Throws left, bats both. ... Full name: Yorkis Miguel Perez.

TRANSACTIONS/CAREER NOTES: Signed as non-drafted free agent by Minnesota Twins organization (February 23, 1983). ... Traded by Twins organization with P Neal Heaton, P Al Cardwood and C Jeff Reed to Montreal Expos for P Jeff Reardon and C Tom Nieto (February 3, 1987). ... Granted free agency (October 15, 1990). ... Signed by Atlanta Braves organization (February 1, 1991). ... Traded by Braves with P Turk Wendell to Chicago Cubs for P Mike Bielecki and C Damon Berryhill (September 29, 1991). ... Released by Cubs (December 11, 1991). ... Signed by Yomiuri Giants of Japan Central League (1992). ... Released by Yomiuri (August 17, 1992). ... Signed as free agent by Jacksonville, Seattle Mariners organization (August 19, 1992). ... Released by Mariners organization (January 11, 1993). ... Signed by Montreal Expos organization (February 15, 1993). ... Granted free agency (October 15, 1993). ... Signed by Florida Marlins organization (December 15, 1993). ... On Florida disabled list (June 10-30, 1994); included rehabilitation assignment to Portland (June 25-30). ... Traded by Marlins to Braves for P Martin Sanchez (December 13, 1996). ... Claimed on waivers by New York Mets (March 31, 1997). ... On New York disabled list (April 5-June 5, 1997); included rehabilitation assignment to Norfolk (May 15-June 5). ... Granted free agency (October 15, 1997). ... Signed by Philadelphia Phillies organization (January 23, 1998). ... On Scranton/Wilkes-Barre disabled list (April 9-16, 1998). ... On Philadelphia disabled list (May 25-June 17, 1998); included rehabilitation assignment to Reading (June 14) and Scranton/Wilkes-Barre (June 16).

Year Team (League)	W	L	Pct.	ERA	G	GS	CG	ShO	Sv.	IP	H	R	ER	BB	SO
1983—Elizabethton (Appal.)	0	1	.000	20.25	3	1	0	0	0	4	5	9	9	9	6
1984—Elizabethton (Appal.)	0	0	...	0.00	1	0	0	0	0	1⅓	1	0	0	1	1
1985—Santiago (DSL)	6	8	.429	3.17	21	16	7	2	1	122	104	58	43	63	69
1986—Kenosha (Midwest)	4	11	.267	5.15	31	18	3	0	0	131	120	81	75	88	144
1987—W.P. Beach (FSL)■	6	2	.750	2.34	15	15	3	0	0	100	78	36	26	46	111
—Jacksonville (Southern)......	2	7	.222	4.05	12	10	1	1	1	60	61	34	27	30	60
1988—Jacksonville (Southern)......	8	12	.400	5.82	27	25	2	1	0	130	142	96	84	94	105
1989—W.P. Beach (FSL)	7	6	.538	2.76	18	12	0	0	1	94⅔	62	34	29	54	85
—Jacksonville (Southern)......	4	3	.571	3.60	20	0	0	0	0	35	25	16	14	34	50
1990—Jacksonville (Southern)......	2	2	.500	6.00	28	2	0	0	1	42	36	34	28	34	39
—Indianapolis (A.A.)	1	0	1.000	2.31	9	0	0	0	0	11⅔	8	5	3	6	8
1991—Richmond (Int'l)■	•12	3	•.800	3.79	36	10	0	0	1	107	99	47	45	53	102
—Chicago (N.L.)■	1	0	1.000	2.08	3	0	0	0	0	4⅓	2	1	1	2	3
1992—Yomiuri (Jp. Cen.)■	0	1	.000	7.11	3	0	0	0	0	6⅓	8	6	5	3	6
1993—Harrisburg (Eastern)■	4	2	.667	3.45	34	0	0	0	3	44⅓	49	26	17	20	58
—Ottawa (Int'l)	0	1	.000	3.60	20	0	0	0	5	20	14	12	8	7	17
1994—Florida (N.L.)■	3	0	1.000	3.54	44	0	0	0	0	40⅔	33	18	16	14	41
—Portland (Eastern)	0	0	...	0.00	2	0	0	0	0	2	1	0	0	0	2
1995—Florida (N.L.)	2	6	.250	5.21	69	0	0	0	1	46⅔	35	29	27	28	47
1996—Florida (N.L.)	3	4	.429	5.29	64	0	0	0	0	47⅔	51	28	28	31	47
—Charlotte (Int'l)	3	0	1.000	4.22	9	0	0	0	0	10⅔	6	5	5	3	13
1997—New York (N.L.)■	0	1	.000	8.31	9	0	0	0	0	8⅔	15	8	8	4	7
—Norfolk (Int'l)	1	0	1.000	3.48	17	0	0	0	3	20⅔	22	9	8	7	24
—Binghamton (Eastern)	2	1	.667	0.66	12	3	0	0	0	27⅓	15	4	2	12	39
1998—Scran./W.B. (Int'l)■	0	0	...	0.00	4	1	0	0	0	4⅓	2	1	0	1	3
—Philadelphia (N.L.)	0	2	.000	3.81	57	0	0	0	0	52	40	23	22	25	42
—Reading (Eastern)	0	0	...	0.00	1	1	0	0	0	1	0	0	0	0	1
Major league totals (6 years)......	9	13	.409	4.59	246	0	0	0	1	200	176	107	102	104	187

PERISHO, MATT — P — RANGERS

PERSONAL: Born June 8, 1975, in Burlington, Iowa. ... 6-0/190. ... Throws left, bats left. ... Full name: Matthew Alan Perisho.
HIGH SCHOOL: McClintock (Tempe, Ariz.).
TRANSACTIONS/CAREER NOTES: Selected by California Angels organization in third round of free-agent draft (June 3, 1993). ... Angels franchise renamed Anaheim Angels for 1997 season. ... Traded by Angels to Texas Rangers for IF Mike Bell (October 31, 1997). ... On Oklahoma disabled list (June 29-July 25, 1998).

Year Team (League)	W	L	Pct.	ERA	G	GS	CG	ShO	Sv.	IP	H	R	ER	BB	SO
1993—Ariz. Angels (Ariz.)	7	3	.700	3.66	11	11	1	1	0	64	58	32	26	23	65
1994—Cedar Rapids (Midw.)	12	9	.571	4.33	27	27	0	0	0	147⅔	165	90	71	88	107
1995—Lake Elsinore (Calif.)	8	9	.471	6.32	24	22	0	0	0	115⅓	137	91	81	60	68
1996—Lake Elsinore (Calif.)	7	5	.583	4.20	21	18	1	1	0	128⅔	131	72	60	58	97
—Midland (Texas)	3	2	.600	3.21	8	8	0	0	0	53⅓	48	22	19	20	50
1997—Midland (Texas).................	5	2	.714	2.96	10	10	3	•1	0	73	60	26	24	26	62
—Anaheim (A.L.)	0	2	.000	6.00	11	8	0	0	0	45	59	34	30	28	35
—Vancouver (PCL)	4	4	.500	5.33	9	9	1	0	0	52⅓	68	42	31	29	47
1998—Tulsa (Texas)■	0	0	...	6.00	1	1	0	0	0	3	3	2	2	3	1
—Oklahoma (Pacific Coast) ...	8	5	.615	3.89	15	15	1	0	0	90⅓	91	41	39	42	60
—Texas (A.L.)	0	2	.000	27.00	2	2	0	0	0	5	15	17	15	8	2
Major league totals (2 years)......	0	4	.000	8.10	13	10	0	0	0	50	74	51	45	36	37

PERKINS, DAN — P — TWINS

PERSONAL: Born March 15, 1975, in Miami. ... 6-2/193. ... Throws right, bats right. ... Full name: Daniel Lee Perkins.
HIGH SCHOOL: Westminster Christian (Miami).
TRANSACTIONS/CAREER NOTES: Selected by Minnesota Twins organization in second round of free-agent draft (June 3, 1993).

Year Team (League)	W	L	Pct.	ERA	G	GS	CG	ShO	Sv.	IP	H	R	ER	BB	SO
1993— Elizabethton (Appal.)	3	3	.500	5.00	10	10	0	0	0	45	46	33	25	25	30
1994— Fort Wayne (Midw.)	1	8	.111	6.22	12	12	0	0	0	50 2/3	61	38	35	22	34
— Elizabethton (Appal.)	0	2	.000	3.67	10	9	1	0	0	54	51	31	22	14	34
1995— Fort Wayne (Midw.)	7	12	.368	5.49	29	22	0	0	0	121 1/3	133	86	74	69	82
1996— Fort Myers (Fla. St.)	13	7	.650	2.96	39	13	3	1	2	136 2/3	125	52	45	37	111
1997— New Britain (East.)	7	10	.412	4.91	24	24	2	0	0	144 2/3	158	94	79	53	114
1998— New Britain (East.)	13	5	.722	3.98	20	19	1	1	0	117 2/3	140	64	52	31	79
— Salt Lake (PCL)	5	0	1.000	4.82	7	7	1	0	0	46 2/3	48	30	25	20	33

PERSON, ROBERT — P — BLUE JAYS

PERSONAL: Born October 6, 1969, in St. Louis. ... 6-0/195. ... Throws right, bats right. ... Full name: Robert Alan Person.
HIGH SCHOOL: University City (Mo.).
JUNIOR COLLEGE: Seminole (Okla.) Junior College.
TRANSACTIONS/CAREER NOTES: Selected by Cleveland Indians organization in 25th round of free-agent draft (June 5, 1989). ... Loaned by Indians organization to Bend, independent (June 12-25, 1991). ... Traded by Indians organization to Chicago White Sox organization for P Grady Hall (June 27, 1991). ... On disabled list (April 10-May 13, 1992). ... Selected by Florida Marlins in second round (47th pick overall) of expansion draft (November 17, 1992). ... Granted free agency (December 19, 1992). ... Re-signed by Marlins organization (January 8, 1993). ... Traded by Marlins organization to New York Mets organization for P Steve Long (March 30, 1994). ... Traded by Mets to Toronto Blue Jays for 1B John Olerud and cash (December 20, 1996). ... On Toronto disabled list (May 8-26 and September 9-28, 1997). ... On Syracuse disabled list (April 19-27, 1998).
MISCELLANEOUS: Appeared in two games as pinch runner with New York (1996).

Year Team (League)	W	L	Pct.	ERA	G	GS	CG	ShO	Sv.	IP	H	R	ER	BB	SO
1989— Burlington (Appalachian)....	0	1	.000	3.18	10	5	0	0	1	34	23	13	12	17	19
1990— Watertown (NYP)	1	0	1.000	1.10	5	2	0	0	0	16 1/3	8	2	2	7	19
— Kinston (Carolina)	1	0	1.000	2.70	4	3	0	0	0	16 2/3	17	6	5	9	7
— GC Indians (GCL)	0	2	.000	7.36	8	0	0	0	2	7 1/3	10	7	6	4	8
1991— Kinston (Carolina)	3	5	.375	4.67	11	11	0	0	0	52	56	37	27	42	45
— Bend (Northwest)■	1	1	.500	3.60	2	2	0	0	0	10	6	6	4	5	6
— South Bend (Mid.)■..........	4	3	.571	3.30	13	13	0	0	0	76 1/3	50	35	28	56	66
1992— Sarasota (Florida State)......	5	7	.417	3.59	19	18	1	0	0	105 1/3	90	48	42	62	85
1993— High Desert (Calif.)■	12	10	.545	4.69	28	26	4	0	0	169	184	*115	88	48	107
1994— Binghamton (Eastern)■	9	6	.600	3.45	31	23	3	2	0	159	124	68	61	68	130
1995— Binghamton (Eastern)	5	4	.556	3.11	26	7	1	0	7	66 2/3	46	27	23	25	65
— Norfolk (Int'l)	2	1	.667	4.50	5	4	0	0	0	32	30	17	16	13	33
— New York (N.L.)..............	1	0	1.000	0.75	3	1	0	0	0	12	5	1	1	2	10
1996— New York (N.L.)..............	4	5	.444	4.52	27	13	0	0	0	89 2/3	86	50	45	35	76
— Norfolk (Int'l)	5	0	1.000	3.35	8	8	0	0	0	43	33	16	16	21	32
1997— Toronto (A.L.)■..............	5	10	.333	5.61	23	22	0	0	0	128 1/3	125	86	80	60	99
— Syracuse (Int'l)..............	1	0	1.000	0.00	1	1	0	0	0	7	4	1	0	2	5
1998— Toronto (A.L.)..............	3	1	.750	7.04	27	0	0	0	6	38 1/3	45	31	30	22	31
— Syracuse (Int'l)..............	3	3	.500	2.29	20	6	1	0	0	59	38	17	15	29	55
A.L. totals (2 years)	8	11	.421	5.94	50	22	0	0	6	166 2/3	170	117	110	82	130
N.L. totals (2 years)	5	5	.500	4.07	30	14	0	0	0	101 2/3	91	51	46	37	86
Major league totals (4 years)......	13	16	.448	5.23	80	36	0	0	6	268 1/3	261	168	156	119	216

RECORD AS POSITION PLAYER

Year Team (League)	Pos.	G		BATTING										FIELDING		
			AB	R	H	2B	3B	HR	RBI	Avg.	BB	SO	SB	PO	A	E	Avg.
1990— GC Indians (GCL)	OF	24	46	6	4	0	0	0	3	.087	10	12	1	10	2	0	1.000

PETAGINE, ROBERTO — 1B/OF

PERSONAL: Born June 2, 1971, in Nueva Esparita, Venezuela. ... 6-1/215. ... Bats left, throws left. ... Full name: Roberto Antonio Petagine. ... Name pronounced PET-uh-GHEEN.
TRANSACTIONS/CAREER NOTES: Signed as non-drafted free agent by Houston Astros organization (February 13, 1990). ... On Tucson disabled list (April 30-June 11, 1994). ... Traded by Astros with 3B Ken Caminiti, OF Steve Finley, SS Andujar Cedeno, P Brian Williams and a player to be named later to San Diego Padres for OF Phil Plantier, OF Derek Bell, P Pedro Martinez, P Doug Brocail, IF Craig Shipley and SS Ricky Gutierrez (December 28, 1994); Padres acquired P Sean Fesh to complete deal (May 1, 1995). ... Traded by Padres with P Scott Adair to New York Mets for P Luis Arroyo and P Pete Walker (March 17, 1996). ... Traded by Mets to Cincinnati Reds for SS Yuri Sanchez (February 5, 1998). ... Contract sold by Reds to Yakult Swallows of Japan Central League (December 2, 1998).
HONORS: Named Texas League Player of the Year (1993). ... Named International League Most Valuable Player (1997 and 1998).
STATISTICAL NOTES: Led Gulf Coast League first basemen with .990 fielding percentage and 46 double plays in 1990. ... Led Texas League with .442 on-base percentage and 14 intentional bases on balls received in 1993. ... Led International League with seven intentional bases on balls received in 1996. ... Led International League with .430 on-base percentage in 1997. ... Led International League first basemen with 117 double plays in 1997. ... Led International League with .436 on-base percentage.

Year Team (League)	Pos.	G	AB	R	H	2B	3B	HR	RBI	Avg.	BB	SO	SB	PO	A	E	Avg.
1990— GC Astros (GCL)	1B-OF	55	187	35	54	5	4	2	24	.289	26	23	9	474	36	5	†.990
1991— Burlington (Midw.)	1B	124	432	72	112	24	1	12	58	.259	71	74	7	940	60	22	.978
1992— Osceola (Fla. St.)	1B	86	307	52	90	22	4	7	49	.293	47	47	3	701	74	10	.987
— Jackson (Texas)	1B	21	70	8	21	4	0	4	12	.300	6	15	1	151	15	0	1.000
1993— Jackson (Texas)	1B	128	437	73	146	*36	2	15	90	.334	*84	89	6	1033	*110	14	.988
1994— Houston (N.L.)	1B	8	7	0	0	0	0	0	0	.000	1	3	0	3	0	0	1.000
— Tucson (PCL)	1B	65	247	53	78	19	0	10	44	.316	35	54	3	597	35	10	.984
1995— San Diego (N.L.)■	1B-OF	89	124	15	29	8	0	3	17	.234	26	41	0	263	22	1	.997
— Las Vegas (PCL)	1B	19	56	8	12	2	1	1	5	.214	13	17	1	110	7	3	.975
1996— Norfolk (Int'l)■	1B	95	314	49	100	24	3	12	65	.318	51	75	4	743	67	*15	.982
— New York (N.L.)..........	1B	50	99	10	23	3	0	4	17	.232	9	27	0	209	23	1	.996

P

Year	Team (League)	Pos.	G	AB	R	H	2B	3B	HR	RBI	Avg.	BB	SO	SB	PO	A	E	Avg.
								BATTING								FIELDING		
1997— Norfolk (Int'l)		1B-OF	129	441	90	140	32	1	31	100	.317	*85	92	0	1023	68	11	.990
— New York (N.L.).........		1B-OF	12	15	2	1	0	0	0	2	.067	3	6	0	10	3	0	1.000
1998— Indianapolis (Int'l)■...		1B-OF	102	363	79	120	30	1	24	109	.331	70	71	3	665	55	6	.992
— Cincinnati (N.L.)		1B-OF	34	62	14	16	2	1	3	7	.258	16	11	1	74	4	0	1.000
Major league totals (5 years)			193	307	41	69	13	1	10	43	.225	55	88	1	559	52	2	.997

PETERS, CHRIS   P   PIRATES

PERSONAL: Born January 28, 1972, in Fort Thomas, Ky. ... 6-1/165. ... Throws left, bats left. ... Full name: Christopher Michael Peters.
HIGH SCHOOL: Peters Township (McMurray, Pa.).
COLLEGE: Indiana.
TRANSACTIONS/CAREER NOTES: Selected by Pittsburgh Pirates organization in 37th round of free-agent draft (June 3, 1993).

Year	Team (League)	W	L	Pct.	ERA	G	GS	CG	ShO	Sv.	IP	H	R	ER	BB	SO
1993— Welland (N.Y.-Penn)		1	0	1.000	4.55	16	0	0	0	0	27 2/3	33	16	14	20	25
1994— Augusta (S. Atl.)		4	5	.444	4.30	54	0	0	0	4	60 2/3	51	34	29	33	83
— Salem (Carolina)		1	0	1.000	13.50	3	0	0	0	0	3 1/3	5	5	5	1	2
1995— Lynchburg (Carolina)		11	5	.688	2.43	24	24	3	*3	0	144 2/3	126	57	39	35	132
— Carolina (Southern)		2	0	1.000	1.29	2	2	0	0	0	14	9	2	2	2	7
1996— Carolina (Southern)		7	3	.700	2.64	14	14	0	0	0	92	73	37	27	34	69
— Calgary (PCL)		1	1	.500	0.98	4	4	0	0	0	27 2/3	18	3	3	8	16
— Pittsburgh (N.L.)		2	4	.333	5.63	16	10	0	0	0	64	72	43	40	25	28
1997— Calgary (PCL)		2	4	.333	4.38	14	9	0	0	1	51 1/3	52	32	25	30	55
— Pittsburgh (N.L.)		2	2	.500	4.58	31	1	0	0	0	37 1/3	38	23	19	21	17
1998— Pittsburgh (N.L.)■..........		8	10	.444	3.47	39	21	1	0	1	148	142	63	57	55	103
Major league totals (3 years)		12	16	.429	4.19	86	32	1	0	1	249 1/3	252	129	116	101	148

PETKOVSEK, MARK   P   ANGELS

PERSONAL: Born November 18, 1965, in Beaumont, Texas. ... 6-0/185. ... Throws right, bats right. ... Full name: Mark Joseph Petkovsek. ... Name pronounced PET-kie-zeck.
HIGH SCHOOL: Kelly (Beaumont, Texas).
COLLEGE: Texas.
TRANSACTIONS/CAREER NOTES: Selected by Texas Rangers organization in supplemental round ("sandwich pick" between first and second round, 29th pick overall) of free-agent draft (June 2, 1987); pick received as compensation for New York Yankees signing Type A free-agent OF Gary Ward. ... Granted free agency (October 16, 1991). ... Signed by Pittsburgh Pirates organization (January 22, 1992). ... Granted free agency (October 15, 1992). ... Re-signed by Pirates organization (November 9, 1992). ... On Buffalo disabled list (July 4-23, 1993). ... Granted free agency (October 12, 1993). ... Signed by Tucson, Houston Astros organization (March 4, 1994). ... On disabled list (July 20-August 12, 1994). ... Granted free agency (October 15, 1994). ... Signed by St. Louis Cardinals organization (November 18, 1994). ... On Louisville suspended list (May 12-17, 1995). ... On St. Louis disabled list (March 22-April 19, 1996); included rehabilitation assignments to St. Petersburg (April 5-12) and Louisville (April 12-19). ... On suspended list (September 9-12, 1997). ... Traded by Cardinals to Anaheim Angels for a player to be named later or cash (December 14, 1998); Cardinals acquired C Matt Garrick to complete deal (December 14, 1998).
STATISTICAL NOTES: Pitched 5-0 no-hit victory against Colorado Springs (May 16, 1994).

Year	Team (League)	W	L	Pct.	ERA	G	GS	CG	ShO	Sv.	IP	H	R	ER	BB	SO
1987— GC Rangers (GCL)..............		0	0	...	3.18	3	1	0	0	0	5 2/3	4	2	2	2	7
— Charlotte (Fla. St.)		3	4	.429	4.02	11	10	0	0	0	56	67	36	25	17	23
1988— Charlotte (Fla. St.)		10	11	.476	2.97	28	28	7	•5	0	175 2/3	156	71	58	42	95
1989— Tulsa (Texas)		8	5	.615	3.47	21	21	1	0	0	140	144	63	54	35	66
— Oklahoma City (A.A.)..........		0	4	.000	7.34	6	6	0	0	0	30 2/3	39	27	25	18	8
1990— Oklahoma City (A.A.)..........		7	*14	.333	5.25	28	28	2	1	0	151	*187	*103	88	42	81
1991— Oklahoma City (A.A.)		9	8	.529	4.93	25	24	3	1	0	149 2/3	162	89	82	38	67
— Texas (A.L.)		0	1	.000	14.46	4	1	0	0	0	9 1/3	21	16	15	4	6
1992— Buffalo (A.A.)■		8	8	.500	3.53	32	22	1	0	1	150 1/3	150	76	59	44	49
1993— Buffalo (A.A.)		3	4	.429	4.33	14	11	1	0	0	70 2/3	74	38	34	16	27
— Pittsburgh (N.L.)		3	0	1.000	6.96	26	0	0	0	0	32 1/3	43	25	25	9	14
1994— Tucson (PCL)■................		10	7	.588	4.62	25	23	1	1	0	138 1/3	176	87	71	40	69
1995— Louisville (A.A.)■..............		4	1	.800	2.32	8	8	2	1	0	54 1/3	38	16	14	8	30
— St. Louis (N.L.)		6	6	.500	4.00	26	21	1	1	0	137 1/3	136	71	61	35	71
1996— St. Petersburg (FSL)		0	0	...	4.50	3	0	0	0	0	6	6	3	3	0	5
— Louisville (A.A.)		0	1	.000	9.00	2	1	0	0	0	3	5	4	3	1	4
— St. Louis (N.L.)		11	2	.846	3.55	48	6	0	0	0	88 2/3	83	37	35	35	45
1997— St. Louis (N.L.)		4	7	.364	5.06	55	2	0	0	2	96	109	61	54	31	51
1998— St. Louis (N.L.)		7	4	.636	4.77	48	10	0	0	2	105 2/3	131	63	56	36	55
A.L. totals (1 year)		0	1	.000	14.46	4	1	0	0	0	9 1/3	21	16	15	4	6
N.L. totals (5 years)		31	19	.620	4.52	203	39	1	1	2	460	502	257	231	146	236
Major league totals (6 years)		31	20	.608	4.72	207	40	1	1	2	469 1/3	523	273	246	150	242

DIVISION SERIES RECORD

Year	Team (League)	W	L	Pct.	ERA	G	GS	CG	ShO	Sv.	IP	H	R	ER	BB	SO
1996— St. Louis (N.L.)..................		0	0	...	0.00	1	0	0	0	0	2	0	0	0	0	1

CHAMPIONSHIP SERIES RECORD

RECORDS: Shares single-series record for most games pitched—6 (1996).

Year	Team (League)	W	L	Pct.	ERA	G	GS	CG	ShO	Sv.	IP	H	R	ER	BB	SO
1996— St. Louis (N.L.)..................		0	1	.000	7.36	6	0	0	0	0	7 1/3	11	6	6	4	7

P

PERSONAL: Born June 15, 1972, in Baton Rouge, La. ... 6-5/235. ... Throws left, bats left. ... Full name: Andrew Eugene Pettitte.
HIGH SCHOOL: Deer Park (Texas).
JUNIOR COLLEGE: San Jacinto (North) College (Texas).
TRANSACTIONS/CAREER NOTES: Selected by New York Yankees organization in 22nd round of free-agent draft (June 4, 1990). ... Signed by Yankees prior to 1991 free-agent draft (May 25, 1991). ... On Albany temporarily inactive list (June 5-10, 1994).
HONORS: Named lefthanded pitcher on THE SPORTING NEWS A.L. All-Star team (1996).

Year — Team (League)	W	L	Pct.	ERA	G	GS	CG	ShO	Sv.	IP	H	R	ER	BB	SO
1991— GC Yankees (GCL)	4	1	.800	0.98	6	6	0	0	0	36 2/3	16	6	4	8	51
— Oneonta (N.Y.-Penn)	2	2	.500	2.18	6	6	1	0	0	33	33	18	8	16	32
1992— Greensboro (S. Atl.)	10	4	.714	2.20	27	27	2	1	0	168	141	53	41	55	130
1993— Prince William (Caro.)	11	9	.550	3.04	26	26	2	1	0	159 2/3	146	68	54	47	129
— Albany (S. Atl.)	1	0	1.000	3.60	1	1	0	0	0	5	5	4	2	2	6
1994— Alb./Colon. (East.)	7	2	.778	2.71	11	11	0	0	0	73	60	32	22	18	50
— Columbus (Int'l)	7	2	.778	2.98	16	16	3	0	0	96 2/3	101	40	32	21	61
1995— Columbus (Int'l)	0	0	.000	0.00	2	2	0	0	0	11 2/3	7	0	0	0	8
— New York (A.L.)	12	9	.571	4.17	31	26	3	0	0	175	183	86	81	63	114
1996— New York (A.L.)	*21	8	.724	3.87	35	34	2	0	0	221	229	105	95	72	162
1997— New York (A.L.)	18	7	.720	2.88	35	•35	4	1	0	240 1/3	233	86	77	65	166
1998— New York (A.L.)	16	11	.593	4.24	33	32	5	0	0	216 1/3	226	110	102	87	146
Major league totals (4 years)	67	35	.657	3.75	134	127	14	1	0	852 2/3	871	387	355	287	588

DIVISION SERIES RECORD

RECORDS: Shares career records for most runs allowed—20; and most earned runs allowed—20. ... Holds A.L. record for most innings pitched—32. ... Shares major league and A.L. career records for most games started—5.

Year — Team (League)	W	L	Pct.	ERA	G	GS	CG	ShO	Sv.	IP	H	R	ER	BB	SO
1995— New York (A.L.)	0	0	...	5.14	1	1	0	0	0	7	9	4	4	3	0
1996— New York (A.L.)	0	0	...	5.68	1	1	0	0	0	6 1/3	4	4	4	6	3
1997— New York (A.L.)	0	2	.000	8.49	2	2	0	0	0	11 2/3	15	11	11	1	5
1998— New York (A.L.)	1	0	1.000	1.29	1	1	0	0	0	7	3	1	1	0	8
Div. series totals (4 years)	1	2	.333	5.63	5	5	0	0	0	32	31	20	20	10	16

CHAMPIONSHIP SERIES RECORD

Year — Team (League)	W	L	Pct.	ERA	G	GS	CG	ShO	Sv.	IP	H	R	ER	BB	SO
1996— New York (A.L.)	1	0	1.000	3.60	2	2	0	0	0	15	10	6	6	5	7
1998— New York (A.L.)	0	1	.000	11.57	1	1	0	0	0	4 2/3	8	6	6	3	1
Champ. series totals (2 years)	1	1	.500	5.49	3	3	0	0	0	19 2/3	18	12	12	8	8

WORLD SERIES RECORD

RECORDS: Shares single-game record for most earned runs allowed—7 (October 20, 1996).
NOTES: Member of World Series championship team (1996 and 1998).

Year — Team (League)	W	L	Pct.	ERA	G	GS	CG	ShO	Sv.	IP	H	R	ER	BB	SO
1996— New York (A.L.)	1	1	.500	5.91	2	2	0	0	0	10 2/3	11	7	7	4	5
1998— New York (A.L.)	1	0	1.000	0.00	1	1	0	0	0	7 1/3	5	0	0	3	4
World Series totals (2 years)	2	1	.667	3.50	3	3	0	0	0	18	16	7	7	7	9

ALL-STAR GAME RECORD

Year — League	W	L	Pct.	ERA	GS	CG	ShO	Sv.	IP	H	R	ER	BB	SO
1996— American				Did not play.										

PERSONAL: Born April 29, 1970, in West Covina, Calif. ... 6-1/185. ... Bats left, throws left. ... Full name: Charles Gene Phillips.
HIGH SCHOOL: Bishop Amat (La Puente, Calif.).
TRANSACTIONS/CAREER NOTES: Selected by California Angels organization in fourth round of free-agent draft (June 1, 1988). ... Claimed on waivers by San Francisco Giants (December 17, 1992). ... On Phoenix disabled list (August 14, 1994-remainder of season). ... Traded by Giants to Philadelphia Phillies for a player to be named later or cash (May 2, 1996); Phillies sent Giants an undisclosed amount of cash to complete deal (June 14, 1996). ... Granted free agency (October 10, 1996). ... Signed by Houston Astros organization (March 14, 1997). ... Granted free agency (October 15, 1997). ... Re-signed by Astros (November 26, 1997). ... Granted free agency (October 15, 1998). ... Signed by Colorado Rockies organization (December 18, 1998).
STATISTICAL NOTES: Led Northwest League first basemen with 641 putouts, 42 assists and 691 total chances in 1990. ... Led California League first basemen with 1,166 putouts, 1,272 total chances and 117 double plays in 1991. ... Led Texas League first basemen with 1,222 putouts, 100 assists, 17 errors, 1,339 total chances and 106 double plays in 1992. ... Led Pacific Coast League first basemen with 1,135 putouts, 93 assists, 28 errors and 1,256 total chances in 1993.

Year — Team (League)	Pos.	G	AB	R	H	2B	3B	HR	RBI	Avg.	BB	SO	SB	PO	A	E	Avg.
1988— Bend (Northwest)	OF-1B	56	210	24	40	8	0	4	23	.190	21	70	3	197	9	3	.986
1989— Quad City (Midwest)	1B-OF	125	442	41	85	29	4	8	50	.192	49	146	3	954	46	20	.980
1990— Palm Springs (Calif.)	1B	46	162	14	32	4	1	1	15	.198	10	58	3	436	26	16	.967
— Boise (Northwest)	1B-OF	70	237	30	46	6	0	10	34	.194	19	78	1	†642	†42	8	.988
1991— Palm Springs (Calif.)	1B-P	130	471	64	117	22	2	20	70	.248	57	*144	15	†1166	94	12	.991
1992— Midland (Texas)	1B-OF	127	497	58	118	32	4	14	77	.237	32	*165	5	†1223	*100	†17	.987
1993— Phoenix (PCL)■	1B-OF	134	506	80	133	35	2	*27	94	.263	53	127	7	†1138	†93	†29	.977
— San Francisco (N.L.)	1B	11	16	1	5	1	1	1	4	.313	0	5	0	32	2	1	.971
1994— Phoenix (PCL)	1B	95	360	69	108	28	5	27	79	.300	45	96	4	782	78	6	.993
— San Francisco (N.L.)	1B	15	38	1	5	0	0	1	3	.132	1	13	1	79	10	1	.989
1995— San Francisco (N.L.)	1B-OF	92	231	27	45	9	0	9	28	.195	19	69	1	536	37	4	.993
1996— San Francisco (N.L.)	1B	15	25	3	5	0	0	2	5	.200	1	13	0	49	2	1	.981
— Philadelphia (N.L.)■	OF-1B	35	79	9	12	5	0	5	10	.152	10	38	0	113	4	2	.983
— Scran./W.B. (Int'l)	OF-1B	53	200	33	57	14	2	13	42	.285	19	53	2	112	6	5	.959

P

Year	Team (League)	Pos.	G	AB	R	H	2B	3B	HR	RBI	Avg.	BB	SO	SB	PO	A	E	Avg.
								BATTING								FIELDING		
1997—New Orleans (A.A.)■..		OF-1B	104	411	59	119	28	0	21	71	.290	39	112	0	411	36	7	.985
—Houston (N.L.)		1B-OF	13	15	2	2	0	0	1	4	.133	0	7	0	9	0	0	1.000
1998—New Orleans (PCL).....		1B-OF	56	225	51	68	18	0	21	60	.302	21	65	1	381	24	4	.990
—Houston (N.L.)		1B-OF	36	58	4	11	0	0	2	9	.190	7	22	0	72	6	3	.963
Major league totals (6 years)			217	462	47	85	15	1	21	63	.184	38	167	2	890	61	12	.988

RECORD AS PITCHER

Year	Team (League)	W	L	Pct.	ERA	G	GS	CG	ShO	Sv.	IP	H	R	ER	BB	SO
1991—Palm Springs (Calif.)..........		0	0	...	4.50	2	0	0	0	0	2	3	1	1	2	3

PHILLIPS, JASON   P   PIRATES

PERSONAL: Born March 22, 1974, in Williamsport, Pa. ... 6-6/225. ... Throws right, bats right. ... Full name: Jason Charles Phillips.
HIGH SCHOOL: Hughesville (Pa.).
TRANSACTIONS/CAREER NOTES: Selected by Pittsburgh Pirates organization in 14th round of free-agent draft (June 1, 1992).

Year	Team (League)	W	L	Pct.	ERA	G	GS	CG	ShO	Sv.	IP	H	R	ER	BB	SO
1992—GC Pirates (GCL)................		1	2	.333	8.47	4	4	0	0	0	17	21	21	16	13	10
1993—Welland (N.Y.-Penn)		4	6	.400	3.53	14	14	0	0	0	71 1/3	60	44	28	36	66
1994—Augusta (S. Atl.)		6	12	.333	6.73	23	1	0	0	0	108 1/3	118	97	81	88	108
1995—Augusta (S. Atl.)		4	3	.571	3.60	30	6	0	0	0	80	76	46	32	53	65
1996—Augusta (S. Atl.)		5	4	.556	2.41	14	14	1	1	0	89 2/3	79	35	24	29	75
—Lynchburg (Carolina)		5	6	.455	4.52	13	13	1	1	0	73 2/3	82	47	37	35	63
1997—Lynchburg (Carolina)		11	6	.647	3.76	23	23	2	1	0	138 2/3	129	66	58	35	140
—Carolina (Southern)		1	2	.333	2.32	4	4	2	1	0	31	21	8	8	9	22
1998—Carolina (Southern)............		7	•13	.350	4.71	25	25	1	1	0	151	161	89	79	52	114
—Nashville (Pacific Coast)		2	0	1.000	2.59	5	5	0	0	0	31 1/3	38	10	9	12	21

PHILLIPS, TONY   OF   ATHLETICS

PERSONAL: Born April 25, 1959, in Atlanta. ... 5-10/175. ... Bats both, throws right. ... Full name: Keith Anthony Phillips.
HIGH SCHOOL: Roswell (Ga.).
JUNIOR COLLEGE: New Mexico Military Institute.
TRANSACTIONS/CAREER NOTES: Selected by Seattle Mariners organization in 16th round of free-agent draft (June 7, 1977); did not sign. ... Selected by Montreal Expos organization in secondary phase of free-agent draft (January 10, 1978). ... On West Palm Beach temporarily inactive list (April 11-May 4, 1978). ... Traded by Expos organization with cash to San Diego Padres for 1B Willie Montanez (August 31, 1980). ... Traded by Padres organization with P Eric Mustad and IF Kevin Bell to Oakland Athletics organization for P Bob Lacey and P Roy Moretti (March 27, 1981). ... On Oakland disabled list (March 26-August 22, 1985); included rehabilitation assignments to Tacoma (July 30-August 5 and August 7-20). ... On disabled list (August 14-October 3, 1986). ... On Oakland disabled list (July 12-August 28, 1987); included rehabilitation assignment to Tacoma (August 20-28). ... Released by A's (December 21, 1987). ... Re-signed by A's (March 9, 1988). ... On Oakland disabled list (May 18-July 8, 1988); included rehabilitation assignment to Tacoma (June 16-July 4). ... Granted free agency (November 13, 1989). ... Signed by Detroit Tigers (December 5, 1989). ... Traded by Tigers to California Angels for OF Chad Curtis (April 12, 1995). ... On suspended list (August 8-10, 1995). ... Granted free agency (October 31, 1995). ... Signed by Chicago White Sox (January 20, 1996). ... On suspended list (April 30-May 3, 1997). ... Traded by White Sox with C Chad Kreuter to Angels for P Chuck McElroy and C Jorge Fabregas (May 18, 1997). ... On Anaheim suspended list (August 17-20, 1997). ... Released by Angels (April 1, 1998). ... Signed by Toronto Blue Jays (July 1, 1998). ... Traded by Blue Jays to New York Mets for P Leoncio Ramirez Estrella (July 31, 1998). ... Granted free agency (October 28, 1998). ... Signed by A's (December 14, 1998).
RECORDS: Shares major league single-game record for most assists by second baseman (nine-inning game)—12 (July 6, 1986).
STATISTICAL NOTES: Led Southern League shortstops with 42 errors in 1980. ... Led Eastern League in being hit by pitch with 10 in 1981. ... Hit for the cycle (May 16, 1986). ... Led A.L. third basemen with 19 errors in 1995. ... Career major league grand slams: 1.

Year	Team (League)	Pos.	G	AB	R	H	2B	3B	HR	RBI	Avg.	BB	SO	SB	PO	A	E	Avg.
								BATTING								FIELDING		
1978—W.P. Beach (FSL)........		3B-SS-2B	32	54	8	9	0	0	0	3	.167	9	7	2	13	33	5	.902
—Jamestown (NYP)		SS-2B-3B	52	152	24	29	5	2	1	17	.191	27	24	3	73	146	16	.932
1979—W.P. Beach (FSL)........		2B-SS	60	203	30	47	5	1	0	18	.232	36	26	7	120	156	21	.929
—Memphis (Sou.)		SS-2B	52	156	31	44	4	2	3	11	.282	19	13	3	68	134	18	.918
1980—Memphis (Sou.)		SS-2B	136	502	100	125	18	4	5	41	.249	*98	89	50	226	408	†42	.938
1981—West Haven (East.)■..		SS	131	461	79	114	25	3	9	64	.247	67	69	40	200	391	*33	.947
—Tacoma (PCL)		2B-SS	4	11	1	4	1	0	0	2	.364	0	0	0	8	10	0	1.000
1982—Tacoma (PCL)		SS	86	300	76	89	18	5	4	47	.297	73	63	29	138	236	30	.926
—Oakland (A.L.)		SS	40	81	11	17	2	2	0	8	.210	12	26	2	46	95	7	.953
1983—Oakland (A.L.)		S-2-3-DH	148	412	54	102	12	3	4	35	.248	48	70	16	218	383	30	.952
1984—Oakland (A.L.)		SS-2B-OF	154	451	62	120	24	3	4	37	.266	42	86	10	255	391	28	.958
1985—Tacoma (PCL)		3B-2B	20	69	9	9	1	0	0	5	.130	8	28	3	15	36	4	.927
—Oakland (A.L.)		3B-2B	42	161	23	45	12	2	4	17	.280	13	34	3	54	103	3	.981
1986—Oakland (A.L.) 2-3-O-DH-S			118	441	76	113	14	5	5	52	.256	76	82	15	191	326	13	.975
1987—Oakland (A.L.) 2-3-S-O-DH			111	379	48	91	20	0	10	46	.240	57	76	7	179	299	14	.972
—Tacoma (PCL)		2B-3B	7	26	9	9	2	1	1	6	.346	4	3	1	8	10	0	1.000
1988—Oakland (A.L.) S-O-2-3			16	59	10	16	0	0	2	8	.271	12	13	0	25	27	2	.963
—Oakland (A.L.) 3-O-2-S-1-DH			79	212	32	43	8	4	2	17	.203	36	50	0	84	80	10	.943
1989—Oakland (A.L.)■.........		2-3-S-O-1	143	451	48	118	15	6	4	47	.262	58	66	3	184	321	15	.971
1990—Detroit (A.L.)■...........3-2-S-O-DH			152	573	97	144	23	5	8	55	.251	99	85	19	180	368	23	.960
1991—Detroit (A.L.) O-3-2-DH-S			146	564	87	160	28	4	17	72	.284	79	95	10	269	237	8	.984
1992—Detroit (A.L.) O-2-DH-3-S			159	606	*114	167	32	3	10	64	.276	114	93	12	301	195	11	.978
1993—Detroit (A.L.)		O-2-DH-3	151	566	113	177	27	0	7	57	.313	*132	102	16	321	165	13	.974
1994—Detroit (A.L.)		OF-2B-DH	114	438	91	123	19	3	19	61	.281	95	105	13	254	42	6	.980
1995—California (A.L.)■........		3B-OF-DH	139	525	119	137	21	1	27	61	.261	113	135	13	166	179	†20	.945
1996—Chicago (A.L.)■..........		OF-2B-3B	153	581	119	161	29	3	12	63	.277	*125	132	13	351	18	7	.981
1997—Chicago (A.L.)		OF-3B	36	129	23	40	6	0	2	9	.310	29	29	4	74	15	3	.967
—Anaheim (A.L.)■........		2-O-DH-3	105	405	73	107	28	2	6	48	.264	73	89	9	137	103	8	.968

P

Year Team (League)	Pos.	G	AB	R	H	2B	3B	HR	RBI	Avg.	BB	SO	SB	PO	A	E	Avg.
1998—Syracuse (Int'l)■	OF-2B	10	32	7	8	1	0	1	4	.250	15	10	2	17	3	1	.952
—Toronto (A.L.)	OF	13	48	9	17	5	0	1	7	.354	9	6	0	24	0	1	.960
—New York (N.L.)■	OF	52	188	25	42	11	0	3	14	.223	38	44	1	86	2	3	.967
American League totals (17 years)		2003	7023	1199	1882	325	46	142	756	.268	1210	1361	165	3288	3320	220	.968
National League totals (1 year)		52	188	25	42	11	0	3	14	.223	38	44	1	86	2	3	.967
Major league totals (17 years)		2055	7211	1224	1924	336	46	145	770	.267	1248	1405	166	3374	3322	223	.968

CHAMPIONSHIP SERIES RECORD

Year Team (League)	Pos.	G	AB	R	H	2B	3B	HR	RBI	Avg.	BB	SO	SB	PO	A	E	Avg.
1988—Oakland (A.L.)	OF-2B	2	7	0	2	1	0	0	0	.286	1	3	0	10	0	0	1.000
1989—Oakland (A.L.)	2B-3B	5	18	1	3	1	0	0	1	.167	2	4	2	4	14	0	1.000
Championship series totals (2 years)		7	25	1	5	2	0	0	1	.200	3	7	2	14	14	0	1.000

WORLD SERIES RECORD

NOTES: Member of World Series championship team (1989).

Year Team (League)	Pos.	G	AB	R	H	2B	3B	HR	RBI	Avg.	BB	SO	SB	PO	A	E	Avg.
1988—Oakland (A.L.)	OF-2B	2	4	1	1	0	0	0	0	.250	1	2	2	3	5	0	1.000
1989—Oakland (A.L.)	2B-3B-OF	4	17	2	4	1	0	1	3	.235	0	3	0	8	15	0	1.000
World Series totals (2 years)		6	21	3	5	1	0	1	3	.238	1	5	2	11	20	0	1.000

PIAZZA, MIKE   C   METS

PERSONAL: Born September 4, 1968, in Norristown, Pa. ... 6-3/215. ... Bats right, throws right. ... Full name: Michael Joseph Piazza. ... Name pronounced pee-AH-za.

HIGH SCHOOL: Phoenixville (Pa.) Area.

JUNIOR COLLEGE: Miami-Dade (North) Community College.

TRANSACTIONS/CAREER NOTES: Selected by Los Angeles Dodgers organization in 62nd round of free-agent draft (June 1, 1988). ... On disabled list (May 11-June 4, 1995). ... Traded by Dodgers with 3B Todd Zeile to Florida Marlins for OF Gary Sheffield, 3B Bobby Bonilla, C Charles Johnson, OF Jim Eisenreich and P Manuel Barrios (May 15, 1998). ... Traded by Marlins to New York Mets for OF Preston Wilson, P Ed Yarnall and P Geoff Goetz (May 22, 1998).

RECORDS: Shares major league record for most grand slams in two consecutive games—2 (August 9 and 10, 1998). ... Shares major league single-month record for most grand slams—3 (April 1998). ... Holds single-season record for highest batting average by a catcher (100 or more games)—.362 (1997).

HONORS: Named N.L. Rookie Player of the Year by THE SPORTING NEWS (1993). ... Named catcher on THE SPORTING NEWS N.L. All-Star team (1993-98). ... Named catcher on THE SPORTING NEWS N.L. Silver Slugger team (1993-98). ... Named N.L. Rookie of the Year by Baseball Writers' Association of America (1993).

STATISTICAL NOTES: Led California League with .540 slugging percentage and in grounding into double plays with 19 in 1991. ... Led N.L. catchers with 98 assists and tied for lead with 11 errors in 1993. ... Led N.L. catchers in total chances with 866 in 1995 and 1,055 in 1996. ... Led N.L. catchers in passed balls with 12 in 1995 and 12 in 1996. ... Hit three home runs in one game (June 29, 1996). ... Led N.L. catchers in total chances with 1,135 in 1997. ... Led N.L. catchers with 83 assists in 1998. ... Career major league grand slams: 9.

Year Team (League)	Pos.	G	AB	R	H	2B	3B	HR	RBI	Avg.	BB	SO	SB	PO	A	E	Avg.
1989—Salem (Northwest)	C	57	198	22	53	11	0	8	25	.268	13	51	0	230	21	6	.977
1990—Vero Beach (FSL)	C-1B	88	272	27	68	20	0	6	45	.250	11	68	0	428	38	16	.967
1991—Bakersfield (Calif.)	C-1B	117	448	71	124	27	2	29	80	.277	47	83	0	723	69	15	.981
1992—San Antonio (Tex.)	C	31	114	18	43	11	0	7	21	.377	13	18	0	189	22	4	.981
—Albuquerque (PCL)	C-1B	94	358	54	122	22	5	16	69	.341	37	57	1	550	50	9	.985
—Los Angeles (N.L.)	C	21	69	5	16	3	0	1	7	.232	4	12	0	94	7	1	.990
1993—Los Angeles (N.L.)	C-1B	149	547	81	174	24	2	35	112	.318	46	86	3	901	†98	‡11	.989
1994—Los Angeles (N.L.)	C	107	405	64	129	18	0	24	92	.319	33	65	1	640	38	*10	.985
1995—Los Angeles (N.L.)	C	112	434	82	150	17	0	32	93	.346	39	80	1	*805	52	9	.990
1996—Los Angeles (N.L.)	C	148	547	87	184	16	0	36	105	.336	81	93	0	*1055	70	9	.992
1997—Los Angeles (N.L.)	C-DH	152	556	104	201	32	1	40	124	.362	69	77	5	*1045	74	*16	.986
1998—Los Angeles (N.L.)	C	37	149	20	42	5	0	9	30	.282	11	27	0	277	25	2	.993
—Florida (N.L.)■	C	5	18	1	5	0	1	0	5	.278	0	0	0	27	3	1	.968
—New York (N.L.)■	C-DH	109	394	67	137	33	0	23	76	.348	47	53	1	680	§57	8	.989
Major league totals (7 years)		840	3119	511	1038	148	4	200	644	.333	330	493	11	5524	424	67	.989

DIVISION SERIES RECORD

Year Team (League)	Pos.	G	AB	R	H	2B	3B	HR	RBI	Avg.	BB	SO	SB	PO	A	E	Avg.
1995—Los Angeles (N.L.)	C	3	14	1	3	1	0	1	1	.214	0	2	0	31	0	0	1.000
1996—Los Angeles (N.L.)	C	3	10	1	3	0	0	0	2	.300	1	2	0	25	4	0	1.000
Division series totals (2 years)		6	24	2	6	1	0	1	3	.250	1	4	0	56	4	0	1.000

ALL-STAR GAME RECORD

NOTES: Named Most Valuable Player (1996).

Year League	Pos.	AB	R	H	2B	3B	HR	RBI	Avg.	BB	SO	SB	PO	A	E	Avg.
1993—National	C	1	0	0	0	0	0	0	.000	0	1	0	3	0	0	1.000
1994—National	C	4	0	1	0	0	0	1	.250	0	0	0	6	0	0	1.000
1995—National	C	3	1	1	0	0	1	1	.333	0	1	0	6	1	0	1.000
1996—National	C	3	1	2	1	0	1	2	.667	0	1	0	6	1	0	1.000
1997—National	C	1	0	0	0	0	0	0	.000	1	0	0	2	0	0	1.000
1998—National	C	3	0	1	0	0	0	0	.333	0	0	0	2	0	0	1.000
All-Star Game totals (6 years)		15	2	5	1	0	2	4	.333	1	2	0	25	2	0	1.000

P

PICHARDO, HIPOLITO · P · ROYALS

PERSONAL: Born August 22, 1969, in Esperanza, Dominican Republic. ... 6-1/195. ... Throws right, bats right. ... Full name: Hipolito Antonio Pichardo. ... Name pronounced ee-POL-uh-toe puh-CHAR-doh.
HIGH SCHOOL: Liceo Enriguillo (Jicome Esperanza, Dominican Republic).
TRANSACTIONS/CAREER NOTES: Signed as non-drafted free agent by Kansas City Royals organization (December 16, 1987). ... On disabled list (August 14-September 1, 1993 and August 15-September 1, 1995). ... On Kansas City disabled list (July 5-August 25, 1997); included rehabilitation assignment to Omaha (July 25-August 25). ... Granted free agency (October 31, 1997). ... Re-signed by Royals (December 4, 1997). ... On Kansas City disabled list (May 6-23 and August 21, 1998-remainder of season); included rehabilitation assignment to Lansing (August 21).
STATISTICAL NOTES: Pitched 8-0 one-hit, complete-game victory for Kansas City against Boston (July 21, 1992).

Year Team (League)	W	L	Pct.	ERA	G	GS	CG	ShO	Sv.	IP	H	R	ER	BB	SO
1988—GC Royals (GCL)	0	0	...	13.50	1	0	0	0	0	1 1/3	3	2	2	1	3
1989—Appleton (Midwest)	5	4	.556	2.97	12	12	2	0	0	75 2/3	58	29	25	18	50
1990—Baseball City (FSL)	1	6	.143	3.80	11	10	0	0	0	45	47	28	19	25	40
1991—Memphis (Sou.)	3	11	.214	4.27	34	11	0	0	0	99	116	56	47	38	75
1992—Memphis (Sou.)	0	0	...	0.64	2	2	0	0	0	14	13	2	1	1	10
—Kansas City (A.L.)	9	6	.600	3.95	31	24	1	1	0	143 2/3	148	71	63	49	59
1993—Kansas City (A.L.)	7	8	.467	4.04	30	25	2	0	0	165	183	85	74	53	70
1994—Kansas City (A.L.)	5	3	.625	4.92	45	0	0	0	3	67 2/3	82	42	37	24	36
1995—Kansas City (A.L.)	8	4	.667	4.36	44	0	0	0	1	64	66	34	31	30	43
1996—Kansas City (A.L.)	3	5	.375	5.43	57	0	0	0	3	68	74	41	41	26	43
1997—Kansas City (A.L.)	3	5	.375	4.22	47	0	0	0	11	49	51	24	23	24	34
—Omaha (Am. Assoc.)	0	0	...	5.79	5	1	0	0	1	4 2/3	5	3	3	3	3
1998—Kansas City (A.L.)	7	8	.467	5.13	27	18	0	0	1	112 1/3	126	73	64	43	55
—Lansing (Midwest)	0	0	...	0.00	1	0	0	0	0	1	0	0	0	0	0
Major league totals (7 years)	42	39	.519	4.48	281	67	3	1	19	669 2/3	730	370	333	249	340

PICKERING, CALVIN · 1B · ORIOLES

PERSONAL: Born September 29, 1976, in St. Thomas, Virgin Islands. ... 6-3/286. ... Bats left, throws left. ... Full name: Calvin E. Pickering.
HIGH SCHOOL: King (Tampa).
TRANSACTIONS/CAREER NOTES: Selected by Baltimore Orioles organization in 35th round of free-agent draft (June 3, 1995).
HONORS: Named Eastern League Most Valuable Player (1998).
STATISTICAL NOTES: Led Appalachian League with 135 totals bases, .675 slugging pecentage and four intentional bases on balls received in 1996. ... Led Eastern League with 276 total bases, .434 on-base percentage, .566 slugging percentage, 16 intentional bases on balls received and grounding into double plays with 20 in 1998. ... Led Eastern League first basemen with 20 errors in 1998.

Year Team (League)	Pos.	G	AB	R	H	2B	3B	HR	RBI	Avg.	BB	SO	SB	PO	A	E	Avg.
1995—GC Orioles (GCL)	1B	15	60	8	30	10	0	1	22	.500	2	6	0	86	6	3	.968
1996—Bluefield (Appal.)	1B	60	200	45	65	14	1	*18	*66	.325	28	64	8	396	26	9	.979
1997—Delmarva (S. Atl.)	1B	122	444	88	138	31	1	25	79	.311	53	139	6	940	70	*27	.974
1998—Bowie (Eastern)	1B-OF	139	488	93	151	28	2	*31	*114	.309	*98	119	4	1068	60	†22	.981
—Baltimore (A.L.)	1B-DH	9	21	4	5	0	0	2	3	.238	3	4	1	31	0	1	.969
Major league totals (1 year)		9	21	4	5	0	0	2	3	.238	3	4	1	31	0	1	.969

PICKETT, RICKY · P · ROYALS

PERSONAL: Born January 19, 1970, in Fort Worth, Texas ... 6-1/200. ... Throws left, bats left. ... Full name: Cecil Lee Pickett.
HIGH SCHOOL: Eastern Hills (Fort Worth, Texas).
JUNIOR COLLEGE: Northeastern Oklahoma A&M.
TRANSACTIONS/CAREER NOTES: Selected by Cincinnati Reds organization in 28th round of free-agent draft (June 1, 1992). ... Traded by Reds organization with OF Deion Sanders, P John Roper, P Scott Service and 1B Dave McCarty to San Francisco Giants organization for P Mark Portugal, P Dave Burba and OF Darren Lewis (July 21, 1995). ... Traded by Giants organization to Arizona Diamondbacks for OF Chris Jones (April 27, 1998). ... Released by Diamondbacks (May 25, 1998). ... Signed by Texas Rangers organization (May 25, 1998). ... Granted free agency (October 15, 1998). ... Signed by Kansas City Royals organization (December 17, 1998).

Year Team (League)	W	L	Pct.	ERA	G	GS	CG	ShO	Sv.	IP	H	R	ER	BB	SO
1992—Billings (Pioneer)	1	2	.333	2.35	20	4	0	0	0	53 2/3	35	21	14	28	41
1993—Char., W.Va. (S. Atl.)	1	2	.333	6.75	44	1	0	0	0	44	42	40	33	48	65
1994—Char., W.Va. (S. Atl.)	1	1	.500	1.98	28	0	0	0	13	27 1/3	14	8	6	20	48
—Win.-Salem (Car.)	2	1	.667	3.75	21	0	0	0	4	24	16	11	10	23	33
1995—Chattanooga (Southern)	4	5	.444	3.28	40	0	0	0	9	46 2/3	22	20	17	44	69
—Shreveport (Texas)■	2	0	1.000	1.71	14	0	0	0	3	21	9	5	4	9	23
1996—Phoenix (PCL)	0	3	.000	8.64	8	0	0	0	0	8 1/3	12	8	8	5	7
—Shreveport (Texas)	4	1	.800	2.77	29	0	0	0	2	48 2/3	35	21	15	35	51
1997—Phoenix (PCL)	3	3	.500	3.19	61	0	0	0	12	67 2/3	52	27	24	49	85
1998—Fresno (Pacific Coast)	1	1	.500	3.86	5	0	0	0	0	7	6	4	3	14	11
—Tucson (PCL)■	0	0	...	15.43	5	0	0	0	0	4 2/3	7	8	8	9	5
—Arizona (N.L.)	0	0	...	81.00	2	0	0	0	0	2/3	3	6	6	4	2
—Oklahoma (Pacific Coast)■	6	6	.500	3.71	24	10	2	2	1	80	69	39	33	52	78
Major league totals (1 year)	0	0	...	81.00	2	0	0	0	0	2/3	3	6	6	4	2

PICKFORD, KEVIN · P · PIRATES

PERSONAL: Born March 12, 1975, in Fresno, Calif. ... 6-3/190. ... Throws left, bats left. ... Full name: Kevin Patrick Pickford.
HIGH SCHOOL: Clovis West (Fresno, Calif.).
TRANSACTIONS/CAREER NOTES: Selected by Pittsburgh Pirates organization in second round of free-agent draft (June 3, 1993); pick received as part of compensation for Houston Astros signing Type A free-agent P Doug Drabek.

Year Team (League)	W	L	Pct.	ERA	G	GS	CG	ShO	Sv.	IP	H	R	ER	BB	SO
1993—GC Pirates (GCL)	0	4	.000	3.41	9	7	0	0	0	34 1/3	24	19	13	20	28
1994—Augusta (S. Atl.)	0	1	.000	4.15	2	2	0	0	0	8 2/3	9	6	4	5	7
—Welland (N.Y.-Penn)	5	8	.385	4.89	•15	15	1	1	0	84 2/3	86	52	46	36	52
1995—Augusta (S. Atl.)	7	3	.700	2.00	16	16	0	0	0	85 2/3	85	28	19	16	59
—Lynchburg (Carolina)	0	3	.000	4.94	4	4	0	0	0	27 1/3	31	15	15	0	15
1996—Lynchburg (Carolina)	11	11	.500	4.07	28	•28	•4	1	0	*172 1/3	*195	99	78	25	100
1997—Carolina (Southern)	1	2	.333	7.36	21	1	0	0	1	29 1/3	48	29	24	15	24
—Lynchburg (Carolina)	3	4	.429	3.56	14	10	0	0	1	73 1/3	72	31	29	11	50
1998—Carolina (Southern)	5	1	.833	3.90	13	8	1	0	0	57 2/3	48	26	25	15	43
—Nashville (Pacific Coast)	6	1	.857	3.49	13	12	0	0	0	80	84	33	31	20	59

PIERZYNSKI, A.J.   C   TWINS

PERSONAL: Born December 30, 1976, in Bridgehampton, N.Y. ... 6-3/220. ... Bats left, throws right. ... Full name: Anthony John Pierzynski.
HIGH SCHOOL: Dr. Phillips (Orlando).
TRANSACTIONS/CAREER NOTES: Selected by Minnesota Twins organization in third round of free-agent draft (June 2, 1994).
STATISTICAL NOTES: Tied for Appalachian League lead in errors by catcher with 12 in 1995. ... Led Appalachian League catchers with 71 assists in 1995. ... Tied for Midwest League lead with 20 errors by catcher in 1996.

Year Team (League)	Pos.	G	AB	R	H	2B	3B	HR	RBI	Avg.	BB	SO	SB	PO	A	E	Avg.
1994—GC Twins (GCL)	C	43	152	21	44	8	1	1	19	.289	12	19	0	198	28	8	.966
1995—Fort Wayne (Midw.)	C	22	84	10	26	5	1	2	14	.310	2	10	0	119	34	10	.939
—Elizabethton (App.)	C-1B	56	205	29	68	13	1	7	45	.332	14	23	0	376	†72	‡12	.974
1996—Fort Wayne (Midw.)	C-OF	114	431	48	118	30	3	7	70	.274	22	53	0	658	80	†21	.972
1997—Fort Myers (FSL)	C-1B	118	412	49	115	23	1	9	64	.279	16	59	2	677	78	10	.987
1998—New Britain (East.)	C	59	212	30	63	11	0	3	17	.297	10	25	0	409	37	2	.996
—Salt Lake (PCL)	C	59	208	29	53	7	0	2	30	.255	9	24	3	366	30	7	.983
—Minnesota (A.L.)	C	7	10	1	3	0	0	0	1	.300	1	2	0	33	2	0	1.000
Major league totals (1 year)		7	10	1	3	0	0	0	1	.300	1	2	0	33	2	0	1.000

PISCIOTTA, MARC   P   CUBS

PERSONAL: Born August 7, 1970, in Edison, N.J. ... 6-5/225. ... Throws right, bats right. ... Full name: Marc George Pisciotta. ... Name pronounced pih-SHO-tuh.
HIGH SCHOOL: George Walton Comprehensive (Marietta, Ga.).
COLLEGE: Georgia Tech.
TRANSACTIONS/CAREER NOTES: Selected by Pittsburgh Pirates organization in 19th round of free-agent draft (June 3, 1991). ... On disabled list (May 22-June 19, 1992). ... Selected by Colorado Rockies from Pirates organization in Rule 5 major league draft (December 13, 1993). ... Returned to Pirates organization (March 28, 1994). ... Claimed on waivers by Chicago Cubs (November 20, 1996).

Year Team (League)	W	L	Pct.	ERA	G	GS	CG	ShO	Sv.	IP	H	R	ER	BB	SO
1991—Welland (N.Y.-Penn)	1	1	.500	0.26	24	0	0	0	8	34	16	4	1	20	47
1992—Augusta (S. Atl.)	4	5	.444	4.54	20	12	1	0	1	79 1/3	91	51	40	43	54
1993—Augusta (S. Atl.)	5	2	.714	2.68	34	0	0	0	12	43 2/3	31	18	13	17	49
—Salem (Carolina)	0	0	...	2.95	20	0	0	0	12	18 1/3	23	13	6	13	13
1994—Salem (Carolina)	1	4	.200	1.53	31	0	0	0	19	29 1/3	24	14	5	13	23
—Carolina (Southern)	3	4	.429	5.61	26	0	0	0	5	25 2/3	32	21	16	15	21
1995—Carolina (Southern)	6	4	.600	4.15	56	0	0	0	9	69 1/3	60	37	32	45	57
1996—Calgary (PCL)	2	7	.222	4.11	57	0	0	0	1	65 2/3	71	38	30	46	46
1997—Iowa (Am. Assoc.)■	6	2	.750	2.36	42	0	0	0	22	45 2/3	29	12	12	23	48
—Chicago (N.L.)	3	1	.750	3.18	24	0	0	0	0	28 1/3	20	10	10	16	21
1998—Chicago (N.L.)	1	2	.333	4.09	43	0	0	0	0	44	44	21	20	32	31
—Iowa (Pacific Coast)	3	5	.375	6.46	28	0	0	0	8	30 2/3	34	24	22	16	29
Major league totals (2 years)	4	3	.571	3.73	67	0	0	0	0	72 1/3	64	31	30	48	52

PITTSLEY, JIM   P   ROYALS

PERSONAL: Born April 3, 1974, in DuBois, Pa. ... 6-7/220. ... Throws right, bats right. ... Full name: James Michael Pittsley.
HIGH SCHOOL: DuBois (Pa.).
TRANSACTIONS/CAREER NOTES: Selected by Kansas City Royals organization in first round (17th pick overall) of free-agent draft (June 1, 1992); pick received as part of compensation for San Diego Padres signing Type A free-agent IF Kurt Stillwell. ... On disabled list (May 29-June 6 and July 29-September 13, 1993). ... On Kansas City disabled list (August 17, 1995-remainder of season). ... On Kansas City disabled list (March 30-July 6, 1996); included rehabilitation assignments to Wilmington (June 6-14), Wichita (June 14-28) and Omaha (June 28-July 5). ... On suspended list (June 12-14, 1998).

Year Team (League)	W	L	Pct.	ERA	G	GS	CG	ShO	Sv.	IP	H	R	ER	BB	SO
1992—GC Royals (GCL)	4	1	.800	3.32	9	9	0	0	0	43 1/3	27	16	16	15	47
—Baseball City (FSL)	0	0	...	0.00	1	1	0	0	0	3	2	0	0	1	4
1993—Rockford (Midwest)	5	5	.500	4.26	15	15	2	1	0	80 1/3	76	43	38	32	87
1994—Wilmington (Caro.)	11	5	.688	3.17	27	27	1	1	0	161 2/3	154	73	57	42	*171
1995—Omaha (Am. Assoc.)	4	1	.800	3.21	8	8	0	0	0	47 2/3	38	20	17	16	39
—Kansas City (A.L.)	0	0	...	13.50	1	1	0	0	0	3 1/3	7	5	5	1	0
1996—Omaha (Am. Assoc.)	0	1	.000	11.00	2	2	0	0	0	9	13	12	11	5	10
—Wichita (Texas)	3	0	1.000	0.41	3	3	0	0	0	22	9	1	1	5	7
—Omaha (Am. Assoc.)	7	1	.875	3.97	13	13	0	0	0	70 1/3	74	34	31	39	53
1997—Omaha (Am. Assoc.)	1	2	.333	4.42	7	7	0	0	0	38 2/3	36	21	19	20	30
—Kansas City (A.L.)	5	8	.385	5.46	21	21	0	0	0	112	120	72	68	54	52
1998—Kansas City (A.L.)	1	1	.500	6.59	39	2	0	0	0	68 1/3	88	56	50	37	44
Major league totals (3 years)	6	9	.400	6.03	61	24	0	0	0	183 2/3	215	133	123	92	96

P

PLESAC, DAN — P — BLUE JAYS

PERSONAL: Born February 4, 1962, in Gary, Ind. ... 6-5/217. ... Throws left, bats left. ... Full name: Daniel Thomas Plesac. ... Name pronounced PLEE-sack.
HIGH SCHOOL: Crown Point (Ind.).
COLLEGE: North Carolina State.
TRANSACTIONS/CAREER NOTES: Selected by St. Louis Cardinals organization in second round of free-agent draft (June 3, 1980); did not sign. ... Selected by Milwaukee Brewers organization in first round (26th pick overall) of free-agent draft (June 6, 1983). ... Granted free agency (October 27, 1992). ... Signed by Chicago Cubs (December 8, 1992). ... Granted free agency (October 25, 1994). ... Signed by Pittsburgh Pirates (November 9, 1994). ... Traded by Pirates with OF Orlando Merced and IF Carlos Garcia to Toronto Blue Jays for P Jose Silva, P Jose Pett, IF Brandon Cromer and three players to be named later (November 14, 1996); Pirates acquired P Mike Halperin, IF Abraham Nunez and C/OF Craig Wilson to complete deal (December 11, 1996).
STATISTICAL NOTES: Led Appalachian League pitchers with three balks in 1983.
MISCELLANEOUS: Holds Milwaukee Brewers all-time records for lowest earned run average (3.21), most games pitched (365) and most saves (133).

Year Team (League)	W	L	Pct.	ERA	G	GS	CG	ShO	Sv.	IP	H	R	ER	BB	SO
1983— Paintsville (Appal.)	*9	1	.900	3.50	14	•14	2	0	0	82 1/3	76	44	32	57	*85
1984— Stockton (California)	6	6	.500	3.32	16	16	2	0	0	108 1/3	106	51	40	50	101
— El Paso (Texas)	2	2	.500	3.46	7	7	0	0	0	39	43	19	15	16	24
1985— El Paso (Texas)	12	5	.706	4.97	25	24	2	0	0	150 1/3	171	91	83	68	128
1986— Milwaukee (A.L.)	10	7	.588	2.97	51	0	0	0	14	91	81	34	30	29	75
1987— Milwaukee (A.L.)	5	6	.455	2.61	57	0	0	0	23	79 1/3	63	30	23	23	89
1988— Milwaukee (A.L.)	1	2	.333	2.41	50	0	0	0	30	52 1/3	46	14	14	12	52
1989— Milwaukee (A.L.)	3	4	.429	2.35	52	0	0	0	33	61 1/3	47	16	16	17	52
1990— Milwaukee (A.L.)	3	7	.300	4.43	66	0	0	0	24	69	67	36	34	31	65
1991— Milwaukee (A.L.)	2	7	.222	4.29	45	10	0	0	8	92 1/3	92	49	44	39	61
1992— Milwaukee (A.L.)	5	4	.556	2.96	44	4	0	0	1	79	64	28	26	35	54
1993— Chicago (N.L.)■	2	1	.667	4.74	57	0	0	0	0	62 2/3	74	37	33	21	47
1994— Chicago (N.L.)	2	3	.400	4.61	54	0	0	0	1	54 2/3	61	30	28	13	53
1995— Pittsburgh (N.L.)■	4	4	.500	3.58	58	0	0	0	3	60 1/3	53	26	24	27	57
1996— Pittsburgh (N.L.)	6	5	.545	4.09	73	0	0	0	11	70 1/3	67	35	32	24	76
1997— Toronto (A.L.)■	2	4	.333	3.58	73	0	0	0	1	50 1/3	47	22	20	19	61
1998— Toronto (A.L.)	4	3	.571	3.78	78	0	0	0	4	50	41	23	21	16	55
A.L. totals (9 years)	35	44	.443	3.28	516	14	0	0	138	624 2/3	548	252	228	221	564
N.L. totals (4 years)	14	13	.519	4.25	242	0	0	0	15	248	255	128	117	85	233
Major league totals (13 years)	49	57	.462	3.56	758	14	0	0	153	872 2/3	803	380	345	306	797

ALL-STAR GAME RECORD

Year League	W	L	Pct.	ERA	GS	CG	ShO	Sv.	IP	H	R	ER	BB	SO
1987— American	0	0	...	0.00	0	0	0	0	1	0	0	0	0	1
1988— American	0	0	...	0.00	0	0	0	0	1/3	0	0	0	0	1
1989— American	0	0	...	...	0	0	0	0	0	1	0	0	0	0
All-Star totals (3 years)	0	0	...	0.00	0	0	0	0	1 1/3	1	0	0	0	2

PLUNK, ERIC — P — BREWERS

PERSONAL: Born September 3, 1963, in Wilmington, Calif. ... 6-6/224. ... Throws right, bats right. ... Full name: Eric Vaughn Plunk.
HIGH SCHOOL: Bellflower (Calif.).
COLLEGE: Cal State Dominguez Hills.
TRANSACTIONS/CAREER NOTES: Selected by New York Yankees organization in fourth round of free-agent draft (June 8, 1981). ... On disabled list (August 11-26, 1983). ... Traded by Yankees with OF Stan Javier, P Jay Howell, P Jose Rijo and P Tim Birtsas to Oakland Athletics for OF Rickey Henderson, P Bert Bradley and cash (December 5, 1984). ... On disabled list (July 2-17, 1988). ... Traded by A's with P Greg Cadaret and OF Luis Polonia to New York Yankees for OF Rickey Henderson (June 21, 1989). ... Released by Yankees (November 20, 1991). ... Signed by Syracuse, Toronto Blue Jays organization (December 12, 1991). ... Released by Syracuse, Blue Jays organization (March 27, 1992). ... Signed by Canton/Akron, Cleveland Indians organization (April 9, 1992). ... Granted free agency (October 27, 1992). ... Re-signed by Indians (November 12, 1992). ... Granted free agency (October 29, 1996). ... Re-signed by Indians (December 10, 1996). ... Traded by Indians to Milwaukee Brewers for P Doug Jones (July 23, 1998).
STATISTICAL NOTES: Tied for Florida State League lead with seven balks in 1984. ... Led A.L. with six balks in 1986.

Year Team (League)	W	L	Pct.	ERA	G	GS	CG	ShO	Sv.	IP	H	R	ER	BB	SO
1981— GC Yankees (GCL)	3	4	.429	3.83	11	11	1	0	0	54	56	29	23	20	47
1982— Paintsville (Appal.)	6	3	.667	4.64	12	8	4	0	0	64	63	35	33	30	59
1983— Fort Lauderdale (FSL)	8	10	.444	2.74	20	20	5	•4	0	125	115	55	38	63	109
1984— Fort Lauderdale (FSL)	12	12	.500	2.86	28	28	7	1	0	176 1/3	153	85	56	*123	*152
1985— Huntsville (Southern)■	8	2	.800	3.40	13	13	2	1	0	79 1/3	61	36	30	56	68
— Tacoma (PCL)	0	5	.000	5.77	11	10	0	0	0	53	51	41	34	50	43
1986— Tacoma (PCL)	2	3	.400	4.68	6	6	0	0	0	32 2/3	25	18	17	33	31
— Oakland (A.L.)	4	7	.364	5.31	26	15	0	0	0	120 1/3	91	75	71	102	98
1987— Oakland (A.L.)	4	6	.400	4.74	32	11	0	0	2	95	91	53	50	62	90
— Tacoma (PCL)	1	1	.500	1.56	24	0	0	0	9	34 2/3	21	8	6	17	56
1988— Oakland (A.L.)	7	2	.778	3.00	49	0	0	0	5	78	62	27	26	39	79
1989— Oakland (A.L.)	1	1	.500	2.20	23	0	0	0	1	28 2/3	17	7	7	12	24
— New York (A.L.)■	7	5	.583	3.69	27	7	0	0	0	75 2/3	65	36	31	52	61
1990— New York (A.L.)	6	3	.667	2.72	47	0	0	0	0	72 2/3	58	27	22	43	67
1991— New York (A.L.)	2	5	.286	4.76	43	8	0	0	0	111 2/3	128	69	59	62	103
1992— Cant./Akr. (Eastern)■	1	2	.333	1.72	9	0	0	0	0	15 2/3	11	4	3	5	19
— Cleveland (A.L.)	9	6	.600	3.64	58	0	0	0	4	71 2/3	61	31	29	38	50
1993— Cleveland (A.L.)	4	5	.444	2.79	70	0	0	0	15	71	61	29	22	30	77
1994— Cleveland (A.L.)	7	2	.778	2.54	41	0	0	0	3	71	61	25	20	37	73
1995— Cleveland (A.L.)	6	2	.750	2.67	56	0	0	0	2	64	48	19	19	27	71
1996— Cleveland (A.L.)	3	2	.600	2.43	56	0	0	0	2	77 2/3	56	21	21	34	85

P

Year— Team (League)	W	L	Pct.	ERA	G	GS	CG	ShO	Sv.	IP	H	R	ER	BB	SO
1997— Cleveland (A.L.)	4	5	.444	4.66	55	0	0	0	0	65 2/3	62	37	34	36	66
1998— Cleveland (A.L.)	3	1	.750	4.83	37	0	0	0	0	41	44	23	22	15	38
— Milwaukee (N.L.)■	1	2	.333	3.69	26	0	0	0	1	31 2/3	33	14	13	15	36
A.L. totals (13 years)	67	52	.563	3.73	620	41	0	0	34	1044	905	479	433	589	982
N.L. totals (1 year)	1	2	.333	3.69	26	0	0	0	1	31 2/3	33	14	13	15	36
Major league totals (13 years)	68	54	.557	3.73	646	41	0	0	35	1075 2/3	938	493	446	604	1018

DIVISION SERIES RECORD

Year— Team (League)	W	L	Pct.	ERA	G	GS	CG	ShO	Sv.	IP	H	R	ER	BB	SO
1995— Cleveland (A.L.)	0	0	...	0.00	1	0	0	0	0	1 1/3	1	0	0	1	1
1996— Cleveland (A.L.)	0	1	.000	6.75	3	0	0	0	0	4	1	3	3	3	6
1997— Cleveland (A.L.)	0	1	.000	13.50	1	0	0	0	0	1 1/3	4	4	2	0	1
Div. series totals (3 years)	0	2	.000	6.75	5	0	0	0	0	6 2/3	6	7	5	4	8

CHAMPIONSHIP SERIES RECORD

Year— Team (League)	W	L	Pct.	ERA	G	GS	CG	ShO	Sv.	IP	H	R	ER	BB	SO
1988— Oakland (A.L.)	0	0	...	0.00	1	0	0	0	0	1/3	1	0	0	0	1
1995— Cleveland (A.L.)	0	0	...	9.00	3	0	0	0	0	2	1	2	2	3	2
1997— Cleveland (A.L.)	1	0	1.000	0.00	1	0	0	0	0	2/3	1	0	0	0	0
Champ. series totals (3 years)	1	0	1.000	6.00	5	0	0	0	0	3	3	2	2	3	3

WORLD SERIES RECORD

Year— Team (League)	W	L	Pct.	ERA	G	GS	CG	ShO	Sv.	IP	H	R	ER	BB	SO
1988— Oakland (A.L.)	0	0	...	0.00	2	0	0	0	0	1 2/3	0	0	0	0	3
1995— Cleveland (A.L.)							Did not play.								
1997— Cleveland (A.L.)	0	1	.000	9.00	3	0	0	0	0	3	3	4	3	4	3
World Series totals (2 years)	0	1	.000	5.79	5	0	0	0	0	4 2/3	3	4	3	4	6

POLANCO, PLACIDO — IF — CARDINALS

PERSONAL: Born October 10, 1975, in Santo Domingo, Dominican Republic. ... 5-10/168. ... Bats right, throws right. ... Full name: Placido Enrique Polanco.
HIGH SCHOOL: Santo Claro (Santo Domingo, Dominican Republic).
JUNIOR COLLEGE: Miami-Dade (Wolfson) Community College.
TRANSACTIONS/CAREER NOTES: Selected by St. Louis Cardinals in 19th round of free-agent draft (June 3, 1994).
STATISTICAL NOTES: Led Florida State League in grounding into double plays with 31 in 1996. ... Tied for Texas League lead in double plays by second baseman with 110 in 1997.

							BATTING								FIELDING			
Year— Team (League)	Pos.	G	AB	R	H	2B	3B	HR	RBI	Avg.	BB	SO	SB	PO	A	E	Avg.
1994— Ariz. Cardinals (Ariz.)	SS-2B	32	127	17	27	4	0	1	10	.213	7	15	4	47	89	10	.932
1995— Peoria (Midwest)	SS-2B	103	361	43	96	7	4	2	41	.266	18	30	7	114	285	21	.950
1996— St. Peters. (FSL)	2B	*137	540	65	*157	29	5	0	51	.291	24	34	4	198	*383	4	*.993
1997— Arkansas (Texas)	2B	129	508	71	148	16	3	2	51	.291	29	51	19	240	*425	14	*.979
1998— Memphis (PCL)	2B-SS	70	246	36	69	19	1	1	21	.280	16	15	6	113	193	5	.984
— St. Louis (N.L.)	SS-2B	45	114	10	29	3	2	1	11	.254	5	9	2	72	102	7	.961
Major league totals (1 year)		45	114	10	29	3	2	1	11	.254	5	9	2	72	102	7	.961

POLCOVICH, KEVIN — IF — PIRATES

PERSONAL: Born June 28, 1970, in Auburn, N.Y. ... 5-9/182. ... Bats right, throws right. ... Full name: Kevin Michael Polcovich.
HIGH SCHOOL: Auburn (N.Y.).
COLLEGE: Florida.
TRANSACTIONS/CAREER NOTES: Selected by Pittsburgh Pirates organization in 30th round of free-agent draft (June 1, 1992).

							BATTING								FIELDING			
Year— Team (League)	Pos.	G	AB	R	H	2B	3B	HR	RBI	Avg.	BB	SO	SB	PO	A	E	Avg.
1992— Augusta (S. Atl.)	SS-2B-3B	46	153	24	40	6	2	0	10	.261	18	30	7	78	119	9	.956
— Carolina (Southern)	SS	13	35	1	6	0	0	1	1	.171	4	4	0	16	45	2	.968
1993— Augusta (S. Atl.)	SS-2B	14	48	9	13	2	0	0	4	.271	7	8	2	11	33	6	.880
— Salem (Carolina)	SS-2B-3B	94	282	44	72	10	3	1	25	.255	49	42	13	111	281	22	.947
— Carolina (Southern)	2B-SS	4	11	1	3	0	0	1	1	.273	1	1	0	4	15	0	1.000
1994— Carolina (Southern)	SS	125	406	46	95	14	2	2	33	.234	38	70	9	185	351	28	.950
1995— Carolina (Southern)	SS	64	221	27	70	8	0	3	18	.317	14	29	10	88	208	18	.943
— Calgary (PCL)	SS	62	213	31	60	8	1	3	27	.282	11	32	5	90	215	13	.959
1996— Calgary (PCL)	SS-2B	104	336	53	92	21	3	1	46	.274	18	49	7	165	292	18	.962
1997— Carolina (Southern)	3B-2B-SS	17	50	13	16	5	0	3	7	.320	10	4	4	12	33	5	.900
— Calgary (PCL)	SS	17	62	7	19	4	0	1	9	.306	1	7	0	27	53	6	.930
— Pittsburgh (N.L.)	SS-2B-3B	84	245	37	67	16	1	4	21	.273	21	45	2	121	246	12	.968
1998— Pittsburgh (N.L.)	SS-2B-3B	81	212	18	40	12	0	0	14	.189	15	33	4	76	213	20	.935
Major league totals (2 years)		165	457	55	107	28	1	4	35	.234	36	78	6	197	459	32	.953

POLITTE, CLIFF — P — PHILLIES

PERSONAL: Born February 27, 1974, in St. Louis. ... 5-11/185. ... Throws right, bats right. ... Full name: Cliff Anthony Politte. ... Son of Clifford Edward Politte, pitcher in St. Louis Cardinals organization (1959-65). ... Name pronounced po-LEET.
HIGH SCHOOL: Vianney (Kirkwood, Mo.).
JUNIOR COLLEGE: Jefferson College (Mo.).

P

TRANSACTIONS/CAREER NOTES: Selected by St. Louis Cardinals organization in 54th round of free agent draft (June 1, 1995). ... Traded by Cardinals with OF Ron Gant and P Jeff Brantley to Philadelphia Phillies for P Ricky Bottalico and P Garrett Stephenson (November 19, 1998). **HONORS:** Named Carolina League Pitcher of the Year (1997).

Year Team (League)	W	L	Pct.	ERA	G	GS	CG	ShO	Sv.	IP	H	R	ER	BB	SO
1996— Peoria (Midwest)	14	6	.700	2.59	25	25	0	0	0	149 2/3	108	50	43	47	151
1997— Prince William (Caro.)	11	1	*.917	*2.24	19	19	0	0	0	120 1/3	89	37	30	31	118
— Arkansas (Texas)	4	1	.800	2.15	6	6	0	0	0	37 2/3	35	15	9	9	26
1998— St. Louis (N.L.)	2	3	.400	6.32	8	8	0	0	0	37	45	32	26	18	22
— Memphis (Pacific Coast)	1	4	.200	7.64	10	10	0	0	0	50 2/3	71	46	43	24	42
— Arkansas (Texas)	5	3	.625	2.96	10	10	1	1	0	67	56	25	22	16	61
Major league totals (1 year)	2	3	.400	6.32	8	8	0	0	0	37	45	32	26	18	22

PONSON, SIDNEY   P   ORIOLES

PERSONAL: Born November 2, 1976, in Noord, Aruba. ... 6-1/220. ... Throws right, bats right. ... Full name: Sidney Alton Ponson. **COLLEGE:** Maria (Aruba). **TRANSACTIONS/CAREER NOTES:** Signed as non-drafted free agent by Baltimore Orioles organization (August 17, 1993). ... On Bowie disabled list (June 13-July 15, 1997).

Year Team (League)	W	L	Pct.	ERA	G	GS	CG	ShO	Sv.	IP	H	R	ER	BB	SO
1994— GC Orioles (GCL)	4	3	.571	2.96	12	10	1	0	0	73	68	30	24	17	53
1995— Bluefield (Appalachian)	6	3	.667	4.17	13	13	0	0	0	77 2/3	79	44	36	16	56
1996— Frederick (Carolina)	7	6	.538	3.45	18	16	3	0	0	107	98	56	41	28	110
1997— Bowie (Eastern)	2	7	.222	5.42	13	13	1	1	0	74 2/3	7	51	45	32	56
— GC Orioles (GCL)	1	0	1.000	0.00	1	0	0	0	0	2	0	0	0	0	1
1998— Rochester (Int'l)	1	0	1.000	0.00	1	1	0	0	0	5	4	0	0	1	3
— Baltimore (A.L.)	8	9	.471	5.27	31	20	0	0	1	135	157	82	79	42	85
Major league totals (1 year)	8	9	.471	5.27	31	20	0	0	1	135	157	82	79	42	85

POOLE, JIM   P   PHILLIES

PERSONAL: Born April 28, 1966, in Rochester, N.Y. ... 6-2/195. ... Throws left, bats left. ... Full name: James Richard Poole. **HIGH SCHOOL:** LaSalle (Philadelphia). **COLLEGE:** Georgia Tech. **TRANSACTIONS/CAREER NOTES:** Selected by Los Angeles Dodgers organization in 34th round of free-agent draft (June 2, 1987); did not sign. ... Selected by Dodgers organization in ninth round of free-agent draft (June 1, 1988). ... Traded by Dodgers with cash to Texas Rangers for P Steve Allen and P David Lynch (December 30, 1990). ... Claimed on waivers by Baltimore Orioles (May 31, 1991). ... On Baltimore disabled list (April 3-June 23, 1992); included rehabilitation assignments to Hagerstown (May 25-June 12) and Rochester (June 12-23). ... Granted free agency (December 23, 1994). ... Signed by Buffalo, Cleveland Indians organization (March 18, 1995). ... Traded by Indians with a player to be named later or cash to San Francisco Giants for 1B/OF Mark Carreon (July 9, 1996). ... Released by Giants (July 15, 1998). ... Signed by Indians organization (July 22, 1998). ... Granted free agency (October 30, 1998). ... Signed by Philadelphia Phillies (December 15, 1998).

Year Team (League)	W	L	Pct.	ERA	G	GS	CG	ShO	Sv.	IP	H	R	ER	BB	SO
1988— Vero Beach (FSL)	1	1	.500	3.77	10	0	0	0	0	14 1/3	13	7	6	9	12
1989— Vero Beach (FSL)	11	4	.733	1.61	*60	0	0	0	19	78 1/3	57	16	14	24	93
— Bakersfield (California)	0	0	. . .	0.00	1	0	0	0	0	1 2/3	2	1	0	0	1
1990— San Antonio (Tex.)	6	7	.462	2.40	54	0	0	0	16	63 2/3	55	31	17	27	77
— Los Angeles (N.L.)	0	0	. . .	4.22	16	0	0	0	0	10 2/3	7	5	5	8	6
1991— Oklahoma City (A.A.)■	0	0	. . .	0.00	10	0	0	0	3	12 1/3	4	0	0	1	14
— Texas (A.L.)	0	0	. . .	4.50	5	0	0	0	1	6	10	4	3	3	4
— Rochester (Int'l)■	3	2	.600	2.79	27	0	0	0	9	29	29	11	9	9	25
— Baltimore (A.L.)	3	2	.600	2.00	24	0	0	0	0	36	19	10	8	9	34
1992— Hagerstown (Eastern)	0	1	.000	2.77	7	3	0	0	0	13	14	4	4	1	4
— Rochester (Int'l)	1	6	.143	5.31	32	0	0	0	10	42 1/3	40	26	25	18	30
— Baltimore (A.L.)	0	0	. . .	0.00	6	0	0	0	0	3 1/3	3	3	0	1	3
1993— Baltimore (A.L.)	2	1	.667	2.15	55	0	0	0	2	50 1/3	30	18	12	21	29
1994— Baltimore (A.L.)	1	0	1.000	6.64	38	0	0	0	0	20 1/3	32	15	15	11	18
1995— Buffalo (A.A.)■	0	0	. . .	27.00	1	1	0	0	0	2 2/3	7	8	8	2	0
— Cleveland (A.L.)	3	3	.500	3.75	42	0	0	0	0	50 1/3	40	22	21	17	41
1996— Cleveland (A.L.)	4	0	1.000	3.04	32	0	0	0	0	26 2/3	29	15	9	14	19
— San Francisco (N.L.)■	2	1	.667	2.66	35	0	0	0	0	23 2/3	15	7	7	13	19
1997— San Francisco (N.L.)	3	1	.750	7.11	63	0	0	0	0	49 1/3	73	44	39	25	26
1998— San Francisco (N.L.)	1	3	.250	5.29	26	0	0	0	0	32 1/3	38	20	19	9	16
— Buffalo (Int'l)■	1	0	1.000	0.87	13	0	0	0	0	10 1/3	6	3	1	2	16
— Cleveland (A.L.)	0	0	. . .	5.14	12	0	0	0	0	7	9	4	4	3	11
A.L. totals (7 years)	13	6	.684	3.24	214	0	0	0	3	200	172	91	72	79	159
N.L. totals (4 years)	6	5	.545	5.43	140	0	0	0	0	116	133	76	70	55	67
Major league totals (9 years)	19	11	.633	4.04	354	0	0	0	3	316	305	167	142	134	226

DIVISION SERIES RECORD

Year Team (League)	W	L	Pct.	ERA	G	GS	CG	ShO	Sv.	IP	H	R	ER	BB	SO
1995— Cleveland (A.L.)	0	0	. . .	5.40	1	0	0	0	0	1 2/3	2	1	1	1	2
1998— Cleveland (A.L.)	0	0	. . .	0.00	2	0	0	0	0	2	1	0	0	1	2
Div. series totals (2 years)	0	0	. . .	2.45	3	0	0	0	0	3 2/3	3	1	1	2	4

CHAMPIONSHIP SERIES RECORD

Year Team (League)	W	L	Pct.	ERA	G	GS	CG	ShO	Sv.	IP	H	R	ER	BB	SO
1995— Cleveland (A.L.)	0	0	. . .	0.00	1	0	0	0	0	1	0	0	0	0	2
1998— Cleveland (A.L.)	0	0	. . .	0.00	4	0	0	0	0	1 1/3	0	0	0	1	2
Champ. series totals (2 years)	0	0	. . .	0.00	5	0	0	0	0	2 1/3	0	0	0	1	4

WORLD SERIES RECORD

Year Team (League)	W	L	Pct.	ERA	G	GS	CG	ShO	Sv.	IP	H	R	ER	BB	SO
1995— Cleveland (A.L.)	0	1	.000	3.86	2	0	0	0	0	2 1/3	1	1	1	0	1

P

PERSONAL: Born October 30, 1962, in Los Angeles. ... 6-0/208. ... Throws right, bats right. ... Full name: Mark Steven Portugal.

HIGH SCHOOL: Norwalk (Calif.).

TRANSACTIONS/CAREER NOTES: Signed as non-drafted free agent by Minnesota Twins organization (October 23, 1980). ... On Toledo disabled list (July 22-August 2, 1985). ... On Minnesota disabled list (August 7-28, 1988). ... Traded by Twins to Houston Astros for a player to be named later (December 4, 1988); Twins organization acquired P Todd McClure to complete deal (December 7, 1988). ... On disabled list (July 18-August 13, 1991). ... On Houston disabled list (June 13-July 4 and July 10-September 23, 1992). ... Granted free agency (October 25, 1993). ... Signed by San Francisco Giants (November 21, 1993). ... On disabled list (June 17-July 3 and August 6, 1994-remainder of season). ... Traded by Giants with OF Darren Lewis and P Dave Burba to Cincinnati Reds for OF Deion Sanders, P John Roper, P Ricky Pickett, P Scott Service and IF Dave McCarty (July 21, 1995). ... On disabled list (August 28-September 15, 1996). ... Granted free agency (November 18, 1996). ... Signed by Philadelphia Phillies (December 12, 1996). ... On disabled list (March 24-April 20 and May 4, 1997-remainder of season; and April 3-May 14, 1998). ... Granted free agency (October 28, 1998). ... Signed by Boston Red Sox (December 11, 1998).

HONORS: Named pitcher on THE SPORTING NEWS N.L. Silver Slugger team (1994).

STATISTICAL NOTES: Led Appalachian League with 12 wild pitches, 11 home runs allowed and tied for lead with five hit batsmen in 1981. ... Tied for N.L. lead in games started by pitcher with 31 in 1995.

MISCELLANEOUS: Appeared in one game as pinch runner (1991). ... Had one sacrifice hit in only appearance as pinch hitter (1996).

Year	Team (League)	W	L	Pct.	ERA	G	GS	CG	ShO	Sv.	IP	H	R	ER	BB	SO
1981—	Elizabethton (Appal.)	7	1	.875	3.71	14	13	2	0	1	85	65	41	35	39	65
1982—	Wis. Rap. (Midw.)	9	8	.529	4.01	36	15	4	1	2	119	110	62	53	62	95
1983—	Visalia (California)	10	5	.667	4.18	24	23	2	0	0	131 1/3	142	77	61	84	132
1984—	Orlando (South.)	14	7	.667	2.98	27	27	10	3	0	196	171	80	65	113	110
1985—	Toledo (International)	8	5	.615	3.78	19	19	5	1	0	128 2/3	129	60	54	60	89
—	Minnesota (A.L.)	1	3	.250	5.55	6	4	0	0	0	24 1/3	24	16	15	14	12
1986—	Toledo (International)	5	1	.833	2.60	6	6	3	1	0	45	34	15	13	23	30
—	Minnesota (A.L.)	6	10	.375	4.31	27	15	3	0	1	112 2/3	112	56	54	50	67
1987—	Minnesota (A.L.)	1	3	.250	7.77	13	7	0	0	0	44	58	40	38	24	28
—	Portland (PCL)	1	10	.091	6.00	17	16	2	0	0	102	108	75	68	50	69
1988—	Portland (PCL)	2	0	1.000	1.37	3	3	1	1	0	19 2/3	15	3	3	8	9
—	Minnesota (A.L.)	3	3	.500	4.53	26	0	0	0	3	57 2/3	60	30	29	17	31
1989—	Tucson (PCL)■	7	5	.583	3.78	17	17	5	0	0	116 2/3	107	55	49	32	90
—	Houston (N.L.)	7	1	.875	2.75	20	15	2	1	0	108	91	34	33	37	86
1990—	Houston (N.L.)	11	10	.524	3.62	32	32	1	0	0	196 2/3	187	90	79	67	136
1991—	Houston (N.L.)	10	12	.455	4.49	32	27	1	0	1	168 1/3	163	91	84	59	120
1992—	Houston (N.L.)	6	3	.667	2.66	18	16	1	1	0	101 1/3	76	32	30	41	62
1993—	Houston (N.L.)	18	4	*.818	2.77	33	33	1	1	0	208	194	75	64	77	131
1994—	San Francisco (N.L.)■	10	8	.556	3.93	21	21	1	0	0	137 1/3	135	68	60	45	87
1995—	San Francisco (N.L.)	5	5	.500	4.15	17	17	1	0	0	104	106	56	48	34	63
—	Cincinnati (N.L.)■	6	5	.545	3.82	14	§14	0	0	0	77 2/3	79	35	33	22	33
1996—	Cincinnati (N.L.)	8	9	.471	3.98	27	26	1	1	0	156	146	77	69	42	93
1997—	Philadelphia (N.L.)■	0	2	.000	4.61	3	3	0	0	0	13 2/3	17	8	7	5	2
1998—	Philadelphia (N.L.)	10	5	.667	4.44	26	26	3	0	0	166 1/3	186	88	82	32	104
A.L. totals (4 years)		11	19	.367	5.13	72	26	3	0	4	238 2/3	254	142	136	105	138
N.L. totals (10 years)		91	64	.587	3.69	243	230	12	4	1	1437 1/3	1380	654	589	461	917
Major league totals (14 years)		102	83	.551	3.89	315	256	15	4	5	1676	1634	796	725	566	1055

CHAMPIONSHIP SERIES RECORD

Year	Team (League)	W	L	Pct.	ERA	G	GS	CG	ShO	Sv.	IP	H	R	ER	BB	SO
1995—	Cincinnati (N.L.)	0	1	.000	36.00	1	0	0	0	0	1	3	4	4	1	0

PERSONAL: Born August 17, 1971, in Santurce, Puerto Rico. ... 6-2/205. ... Bats both, throws right. ... Full name: Jorge Rafael Posada Jr. ... Name pronounced HOR-hay po-SAHD-a.

HIGH SCHOOL: Colegio Alejandrino (Puerto Rico).

TRANSACTIONS/CAREER NOTES: Selected by New York Yankees organization in 24th round of free-agent draft (June 4, 1990). ... On disabled list (July 26-September 4, 1994). ... On Columbus disabled list (May 3-12, 1995).

STATISTICAL NOTES: Led New York-Pennsylvania League second basemen with 42 double plays in 1991. ... Led Carolina League with 38 passed balls in 1993. ... Tied for Carolina League lead in intentional bases on balls received with four in 1993. ... Tied for International League lead in errors by catcher with 11 in 1994. ... Tied for International League lead in double plays by catcher with seven in 1995. ... Led International League with 14 passed balls in 1995. ... Switch-hit home runs in one game (August 23, 1998).

							BATTING							FIELDING		
Year	Team (League)	Pos.	G	AB	R	H	2B	3B	HR	RBI	Avg.	BB	SO	SB	PO	A	E	Avg.
1991—	Oneonta (NYP)	2B-C	71	217	34	51	5	5	4	33	.235	51	51	6	172	205	21	.947
1992—	Greensboro (S. Atl.) ...	C-3B	101	339	60	94	22	4	12	58	.277	58	87	11	263	39	11	.965
1993—	Prince Will. (Car.)	C-3B	118	410	71	106	27	2	17	61	.259	67	90	17	677	98	15	.981
—	Albany (Eastern)	C	7	25	3	7	0	0	0	0	.280	2	7	0	39	7	2	.958
1994—	Columbus (Int'l)	C-OF	92	313	46	75	13	3	11	48	.240	32	81	5	425	39	‡11	.977
1995—	Columbus (Int'l)	C	108	368	60	94	32	5	8	51	.255	54	101	4	500	58	4	*.993
—	New York (A.L.)	C	1	0	0	0	0	0	0	0	...	0	0	0	1	0	0	1.000
1996—	Columbus (Int'l)	C-OF	106	354	76	96	22	6	11	62	.271	*79	86	3	598	51	10	.985
—	New York (A.L.)	C-DH	8	14	1	1	0	0	0	0	.071	1	6	0	17	2	0	1.000
1997—	New York (A.L.)	C	60	188	29	47	12	0	6	25	.250	30	33	1	367	23	3	.992
1998—	New York (A.L.)	C-DH-1B	111	358	56	96	23	0	17	63	.268	47	92	0	594	47	4	.994
Major league totals (4 years)			180	560	86	144	35	0	23	88	.257	78	131	1	979	72	7	.993

P

DIVISION SERIES RECORD

Year Team (League)	Pos.	G	AB	R	H	2B	3B	HR	RBI	Avg.	BB	SO	SB	PO	A	E	Avg.
1995— New York (A.L.)..........	PR	1	0	1	0	0	0	0	0	...	0	0	0	...	...	...	...
1997— New York (A.L.)..........	C-PH	2	2	0	0	0	0	0	0	.000	0	1	0	1	1	0	1.000
1998— New York (A.L.)..........	C	1	2	1	0	0	0	0	0	.000	1	2	0	11	1	0	1.000
Division series totals (3 years)		4	4	2	0	0	0	0	0	.000	1	3	0	12	2	0	1.000

CHAMPIONSHIP SERIES RECORD

Year Team (League)	Pos.	G	AB	R	H	2B	3B	HR	RBI	Avg.	BB	SO	SB	PO	A	E	Avg.
1998— New York (A.L.)..........	C-PH	5	11	1	2	0	0	1	2	.182	4	2	0	35	1	0	1.000

NOTES: Member of World Series championship team (1998).

WORLD SERIES RECORD

Year Team (League)	Pos.	G	AB	R	H	2B	3B	HR	RBI	Avg.	BB	SO	SB	PO	A	E	Avg.
1998— New York (A.L.)..........	C-PH	4	9	2	3	0	0	1	2	.333	2	2	0	20	0	0	1.000

POWELL, BRIAN   P   ASTROS

PERSONAL: Born October 10, 1973, in Bainbridge, Ga. ... 6-2/205. ... Throws right, bats right. ... Full name: William Brian Powell.
HIGH SCHOOL: Bainbridge (Ga.).
COLLEGE: Georgia.
TRANSACTIONS/CAREER NOTES: Selected by Detroit Tigers organization in second round of free-agent draft (June 1, 1995). ... Traded by Tigers with C Paul Bako, P Dean Crow, P Mark Persails and 3B Carlos Villalobos to Houston Astros for C Brad Ausmus and P C.J. Nitkowski (January 14, 1999).

Year Team (League)	W	L	Pct.	ERA	G	GS	CG	ShO	Sv.	IP	H	R	ER	BB	SO
1995— Jamestown (NYP)	2	1	.667	3.08	5	5	0	0	0	26 1/3	19	12	9	8	15
— Fayetteville (S. Atl.)	4	0	1.000	1.61	5	5	0	0	0	28	15	5	5	11	37
1996— Lakeland (Fla. St.)	8	13	.381	4.90	29	27	*5	0	0	*174 1/3	*195	106	*95	47	84
1997— Lakeland (Fla. St.)	13	9	.591	2.50	27	27	*8	2	0	*183 1/3	153	70	51	35	122
1998— Jacksonville (Southern)......	10	2	*.833	3.07	14	14	2	1	0	93 2/3	84	37	32	24	51
— Toledo (International)........	0	0	...	0.00	1	1	0	0	0	7	5	0	0	0	7
— Detroit (A.L.)	3	8	.273	6.35	18	16	0	0	0	83 2/3	101	67	59	36	46
Major league totals (1 year)........	3	8	.273	6.35	18	16	0	0	0	83 2/3	101	67	59	36	46

POWELL, DANTE   OF   DIAMONDBACKS

PERSONAL: Born August 25, 1973, in Long Beach, Calif. ... 6-2/185. ... Bats right, throws right. ... Full name: LeJon Dante Powell.
HIGH SCHOOL: Millikan (Long Beach, Calif.).
COLLEGE: Cal State Fullerton.
TRANSACTIONS/CAREER NOTES: Selected by Toronto Blue Jays in supplemental round ("sandwich pick" between first and second round, 42nd pick overall) of free-agent draft (June 3, 1991); did not sign. ... Selected by San Francisco Giants organization in first round (22nd pick overall) of free-agent draft (June 2, 1994). ... Traded by Giants to Arizona Diamondbacks for P Alan Embree (November 10, 1998).
STATISTICAL NOTES: Led Texas League with 23 caught stealing in 1996. ... Led Texas League outfielders with 347 total chances in 1996. ... Led Pacific Coast League outfielders with 293 total chances in 1998.

Year Team (League)	Pos.	G	AB	R	H	2B	3B	HR	RBI	Avg.	BB	SO	SB	PO	A	E	Avg.
1994— Everett (N'west).........	OF	41	165	31	51	15	1	5	25	.309	19	47	27	88	3	2	.978
— San Jose (Calif.).........	OF	1	4	0	2	0	0	0	0	.500	0	1	0	1	0	0	1.000
1995— San Jose (Calif.).........	OF	135	505	74	125	23	8	10	70	.248	46	131	43	*308	*18	11	.967
1996— Shreveport (Texas)	OF	135	508	*92	142	27	2	21	78	.280	72	92	*43	*331	8	8	.977
— Phoenix (PCL)	OF	2	8	0	2	0	1	0	0	.250	2	3	0	4	0	0	1.000
1997— Phoenix (PCL)	OF	108	452	91	109	24	4	11	42	.241	52	105	34	*266	7	4	.986
— San Francisco (N.L.) ..	OF	27	39	8	12	1	0	1	3	.308	4	11	1	27	0	0	1.000
1998— Fresno (Pacific Coast) ...	OF	134	448	83	103	17	3	14	52	.230	71	138	41	*284	2	7	.976
— San Francisco (N.L.) ..	OF	8	4	2	2	0	0	1	1	.500	3	0	2	0	0	0	1.000
Major league totals (2 years)		35	43	10	14	1	0	2	4	.326	7	11	1	29	0	0	1.000

DIVISION SERIES RECORD

Year Team (League)	Pos.	G	AB	R	H	2B	3B	HR	RBI	Avg.	BB	SO	SB	PO	A	E	Avg.
1997— San Francisco (N.L.) ..	OF	1	0	0	0	0	0	0	0	...	0	0	0	0	0	0	...

POWELL, JAY   P   ASTROS

PERSONAL: Born January 19, 1972, in Meridian, Miss. ... 6-4/225. ... Throws right, bats right. ... Full name: James Willard Powell Jr. ... Brother-in-law of Bud Brown, defensive back with Miami Dolphins (1984-88).
HIGH SCHOOL: West Lauderdale (Collinsville, Miss.).
COLLEGE: Mississippi State.
TRANSACTIONS/CAREER NOTES: Selected by San Diego Padres organization in 11th round of free-agent draft (June 4, 1990); did not sign. ... Selected by Baltimore Orioles organization in first round (19th pick overall) of free-agent draft (June 3, 1993). ... On disabled list (April 7-26, 1994). ... Traded by Orioles organization to Florida Marlins organization for IF Bret Barberie (December 6, 1994). ... On Florida disabled list (April 20-May 10, 1996); included rehabilitation assignment to Brevard County (May 8-10). ... Traded by Marlins with C Scott Makarewicz to Houston Astros for C Ramon Castro (July 6, 1998).
MISCELLANEOUS: Struck out in only appearance as pinch hitter with Florida (1996).

Year Team (League)	W	L	Pct.	ERA	G	GS	CG	ShO	Sv.	IP	H	R	ER	BB	SO
1993— Albany (S. Atl.)..................	0	2	.000	4.55	6	6	0	0	0	27²/₃	29	19	14	13	29
1994— Frederick (Carolina)...........	7	7	.500	4.96	26	20	0	0	1	123¹/₃	132	79	68	54	87
1995— Portland (Eastern)■..........	5	4	.556	1.87	50	0	0	0	*24	53	42	12	11	15	53
— Florida (N.L.).....................	0	0	...	1.08	9	0	0	0	0	8¹/₃	7	2	1	6	4
1996— Florida (N.L.)..................	4	3	.571	4.54	67	0	0	0	2	71¹/₃	71	41	36	36	52
— Brevard County (FSL)........	0	0	...	0.00	1	1	0	0	0	2	0	0	0	0	4
1997— Florida (N.L.)..................	7	2	.778	3.28	74	0	0	0	2	79²/₃	71	35	29	30	65
1998— Florida (N.L.)..................	4	4	.500	4.21	33	0	0	0	3	36¹/₃	36	19	17	22	24
— Houston (N.L.)■................	3	3	.500	2.38	29	0	0	0	4	34	22	9	9	15	38
Major league totals (4 years)......	18	12	.600	3.61	212	0	0	0	11	229²/₃	207	106	92	109	183

DIVISION SERIES RECORD

Year Team (League)	W	L	Pct.	ERA	G	GS	CG	ShO	Sv.	IP	H	R	ER	BB	SO
1998— Houston (N.L.)	0	0	...	11.57	3	0	0	0	0	2¹/₃	2	3	3	3	3

CHAMPIONSHIP SERIES RECORD

Year Team (League)	W	L	Pct.	ERA	G	GS	CG	ShO	Sv.	IP	H	R	ER	BB	SO
1997— Florida (N.L.)	0	0	...	0.00	1	0	0	0	0	²/₃	0	0	0	0	1

WORLD SERIES RECORD

NOTES: Member of World Series championship team (1997).

Year Team (League)	W	L	Pct.	ERA	G	GS	CG	ShO	Sv.	IP	H	R	ER	BB	SO
1997— Florida (N.L.)	1	0	1.000	7.36	4	0	0	0	0	3²/₃	5	3	3	4	2

POWELL, JEREMY   P   EXPOS

PERSONAL: Born June 18, 1976, in La Miranda, Calif. ... 6-6/225. ... Throws right, bats right. ... Full name: Jeremy Robert Powell.
HIGH SCHOOL: Highlands (North Highlands, Calif.).
TRANSACTIONS/CAREER NOTES: Selected by Montreal Expos organization in fourth round of free-agent draft (June 2, 1994).

Year Team (League)	W	L	Pct.	ERA	G	GS	CG	ShO	Sv.	IP	H	R	ER	BB	SO
1994— GC Expos (GCL).................	2	2	.500	2.93	9	9	1	0	0	43	37	16	14	14	36
1995— Albany (S. Atl.)..................	1	0	1.000	1.59	1	1	0	0	0	5²/₃	4	1	1	1	6
— Vermont (NYP).................	5	5	.500	4.34	15	•15	0	0	0	87	88	48	42	34	47
1996— Delmarva (S. Atl.)	12	9	.571	3.03	27	27	1	0	0	157²/₃	127	68	53	66	109
1997— W.P. Beach (FSL)...............	9	10	.474	3.02	26	26	1	0	0	155	162	75	52	62	121
1998— Harrisburg (Eastern)	9	7	.563	3.01	22	22	1	0	0	131²/₃	115	54	44	37	77
— Montreal (N.L.).................	1	5	.167	7.92	7	6	0	0	0	25	27	25	22	11	14
Major league totals (1 year)........	1	5	.167	7.92	7	6	0	0	0	25	27	25	22	11	14

PRATT, TODD   C   METS

PERSONAL: Born February 9, 1967, in Bellevue, Neb. ... 6-3/230. ... Bats right, throws right. ... Full name: Todd Alan Pratt.
HIGH SCHOOL: Hilltop (Chula Vista, Calif.).
TRANSACTIONS/CAREER NOTES: Selected by Boston Red Sox organization in sixth round of free-agent draft (June 3, 1985). ... Selected by Cleveland Indians organization from Red Sox organization in Rule 5 minor league draft (December 7, 1987). ... Returned to Red Sox organization (March 28, 1988). ... Granted free agency (October 15, 1991). ... Signed by Baltimore Orioles organization (November 13, 1991). ... Selected by Philadelphia Phillies from Orioles organization in Rule 5 major league draft (December 9, 1991). ... On Philadelphia disabled list (April 28-May 27, 1993); included rehabilitation assignment to Scranton/Wilkes-Barre (May 23-27). ... Granted free agency (December 23, 1994). ... Signed by Iowa, Chicago Cubs organization (April 8, 1995). ... Granted free agency (October 16, 1995). ... Signed by Seattle Mariners organization (January 25, 1996). ... Released by Mariners organization (March 27, 1996). ... Signed by New York Mets organization (December 23, 1996). ... On New York disabled list (May 7-June 23, 1998); included rehabilitation assignments to St. Lucie (June 14-18), Gulf Coast Mets (June 19-21) and Norfolk (June 22-23).
STATISTICAL NOTES: Led South Atlantic League catchers with 660 putouts and nine double plays and tied for lead with 13 errors in 1986. ... Led Eastern League catchers with 11 errors in 1989.

Year Team (League)	Pos.	G	AB	R	H	2B	3B	HR	RBI	Avg.	BB	SO	SB	PO	A	E	Avg.
1985— Elmira (N.Y.-Penn)......	C	39	119	7	16	1	1	0	5	.134	10	27	0	254	29	6	.979
1986— Greensboro (S. Atl.) ...	C-1B	107	348	63	84	16	0	12	56	.241	75	114	0	†826	55	‡15	.983
1987— Winter Haven (FSL).....	C-1B-OF	118	407	57	105	22	0	12	65	.258	70	94	0	672	64	15	.980
1988— New Britain (East.)	C-1B	124	395	41	89	15	2	8	49	.225	41	110	1	540	46	15	.975
1989— New Britain (East.)	C-1B	109	388	30	77	17	1	2	35	.228	44	66	1	435	42	†11	.977
1990— New Britain (East.)	C-1B	70	195	15	45	14	1	2	22	.231	18	56	0	166	15	4	.978
1991— Pawtucket (Int'l)........	C-1B	68	219	68	64	16	0	11	41	.292	23	42	0	236	21	4	.985
1992— Reading (Eastern)■.....	C	41	132	20	44	6	1	6	26	.333	24	28	2	90	6	3	.970
— Scran./W.B. (Int'l).......	C-1B	41	125	20	40	9	1	7	28	.320	30	14	1	152	16	4	.977
— Philadelphia (N.L.)......	C	16	46	6	13	1	0	2	10	.283	4	12	0	65	4	2	.972
1993— Philadelphia (N.L.)......	C	33	87	8	25	6	0	5	13	.287	5	19	0	169	7	2	.989
— Scran./W.B. (Int'l).......	C	3	9	1	2	1	0	0	1	.222	3	1	0	11	0	0	1.000
1994— Philadelphia (N.L.)......	C	28	102	10	20	6	1	2	9	.196	12	29	0	172	8	0	1.000
1995— Iowa (Am. Assoc.)■ ..	C-1B	23	58	3	19	1	0	0	5	.328	4	17	0	82	8	2	.978
— Chicago (N.L.).............	C	25	60	3	8	2	0	0	4	.133	6	21	0	149	9	3	.981
1996—								Out of organized baseball.									
1997— Norfolk (Int'l)■..........	C	59	206	42	62	8	3	9	34	.301	26	48	1	317	24	4	.988
— New York (N.L.)...........	C	39	106	12	30	6	0	2	19	.283	13	32	0	186	22	2	.990
1998— Norfolk (Int'l)	C-OF-1B	35	118	16	42	6	0	7	30	.356	15	19	2	115	8	2	.984
— New York (N.L.)	C-1B	41	69	9	19	9	1	2	18	.275	2	20	0	78	4	2	.976
— St. Lucie (Fla. St.)	C-1B-OF	5	20	2	9	1	0	1	3	.450	1	5	1	40	6	0	1.000
— GC Mets (GCL)..........	C-OF	2	4	1	1	0	0	0	0	.250	4	1	0	7	2	0	1.000
Major league totals (6 years)		182	470	48	115	30	2	13	73	.245	42	133	0	819	54	11	.988

P

CHAMPIONSHIP SERIES RECORD

Year Team (League)	Pos.	G	AB	R	H	2B	3B	HR	RBI	Avg.	BB	SO	SB	PO	A	E	Avg.
1993— Philadelphia (N.L.)......	C	1	1	0	0	0	0	0	0	.000	0	1	0	1	0	0	1.000

WORLD SERIES RECORD

Year Team (League)	Pos.	G	AB	R	H	2B	3B	HR	RBI	Avg.	BB	SO	SB	PO	A	E	Avg.
1993— Philadelphia (N.L.).....								Did not play.									

PRIDE, CURTIS   OF

PERSONAL: Born December 17, 1968, in Washington, D.C. ... 6-0/200. ... Bats left, throws right. ... Full name: Curtis John Pride.
HIGH SCHOOL: John F. Kennedy (Silver Spring, Md.).
COLLEGE: William & Mary (degree in finance).
TRANSACTIONS/CAREER NOTES: Selected by New York Mets organization in 10th round of free-agent draft (June 2, 1986). ... Granted free agency (October 15, 1992). ... Signed by Ottawa, Montreal Expos organization (December 8, 1992). ... On Ottawa disabled list (April 7-May 13, July 6-15 and August 7-14, 1994). ... Granted free agency (October 16, 1995). ... Signed by Detroit Tigers (March 31, 1996). ... On Detroit disabled list (April 13-May 10, 1996); included rehabilitation assignment to Toledo (April 30-May 10). ... Granted free agency (August 21, 1997). ... Signed by Boston Red Sox organization (August 30, 1997). ... Granted free agency (October 15, 1997). ... Signed by Atlanta Braves organization (February 6, 1998). ... On suspended list (May 27-28, 1998). ... On Atlanta disabled list (June 28-July 14, 1998); included rehabilitation assignment to Richmond (July 13-14). ... Released by Braves (December 1, 1998).

Year Team (League)	Pos.	G	AB	R	H	2B	3B	HR	RBI	Avg.	BB	SO	SB	PO	A	E	Avg.
1986— Kingsport (Appal.)......	OF	27	46	5	5	0	0	1	4	.109	6	24	5	17	1	0	1.000
1987— Kingsport (Appal.)......	OF	31	104	22	25	4	0	1	9	.240	16	34	14	39	3	5	.894
1988— Kingsport (Appal.)......	OF	70	268	*59	76	13	1	8	27	.284	50	48	23	118	6	5	.961
1989— Pittsfield (NYP)	OF	55	212	35	55	7	3	6	23	.259	25	47	9	105	3	4	.964
1990— Columbia (S. Atl.).......	OF	53	191	38	51	4	4	6	25	.267	21	45	11	72	4	11	.874
1991— St. Lucie (Fla. St.)......	OF	116	392	57	102	21	7	9	37	.260	43	94	24	199	5	4	.981
1992— Binghamton (East.)	OF	118	388	54	88	15	3	10	42	.227	47	110	14	214	3	8	.964
1993— Harrisburg (East.)■....	OF	50	180	51	64	6	3	15	39	.356	12	36	21	69	0	2	.972
— Ottawa (Int'l)............	OF	69	262	55	79	11	4	6	22	.302	34	61	29	136	3	2	.986
— Montreal (N.L.)..........	OF	10	9	3	4	1	1	1	5	.444	0	3	1	2	0	0	1.000
1994— W.P. Beach (FSL).......	OF	3	8	5	6	1	0	1	3	.750	4	2	2	11	0	0	1.000
— Ottawa (Int'l)	OF	82	300	56	77	16	4	9	32	.257	39	81	22	164	1	3	.982
1995— Ottawa (Int'l)	OF	42	154	25	43	8	3	4	24	.279	12	35	8	69	5	2	.974
— Ottawa (Int'l)	OF	48	63	10	11	1	0	0	2	.175	5	16	3	23	0	2	.920
1996— Detroit (A.L.)■...........	OF-DH	95	267	52	80	17	5	10	31	.300	31	63	11	89	0	3	.967
— Toledo (Int'l)..............	OF	9	26	4	6	1	0	1	2	.231	9	7	4	3	0	0	1.000
1997— Detroit (A.L.).............	OF-DH	79	162	21	34	4	4	2	19	.210	24	45	6	49	0	1	.980
— Pawtucket (Int'l)■.......	OF	1	3	0	0	0	0	0	0	.000	0	2	0	2	0	0	1.000
— Boston (A.L.)............	PH	2	2	1	1	0	0	1	1	.500	0	1	0	...	...	...	...
1998— Atlanta (N.L.)■..........	OF-DH	70	107	19	27	6	1	3	9	.252	9	29	4	41	0	0	1.000
— Richmond (Int'l)........	OF	21	78	11	19	2	1	2	6	.244	15	17	8	28	1	0	1.000
American League totals (2 years)		176	431	74	115	21	9	13	51	.267	55	109	17	138	0	4	.972
National League totals (3 years)		128	179	32	42	8	2	4	16	.235	14	48	8	66	0	2	.971
Major league totals (5 years)		304	610	106	157	29	11	17	67	.257	69	157	25	204	0	6	.971

PRIEST, EDDIE   P   REDS

PERSONAL: Born April 8, 1974, in Boaz, Ala. ... 6-1/195. ... Throws left, bats right. ... Full name: Eddie Lee Priest.
HIGH SCHOOL: Susan Moore (Blountsville, Ala.).
JUNIOR COLLEGE: Southern Union State (Ala.).
TRANSACTIONS/CAREER NOTES: Selected by Cincinnati Reds organization in ninth round of free-agent draft (June 2, 1994). ... On disabled list (April 8-July 15 and August 27-September 13, 1996). ... Traded by Reds with OF Christian Rojas to Cleveland Indians for P Rick Krivda (June 16, 1998). ... Claimed on waivers by Reds (October 1, 1998).

Year Team (League)	W	L	Pct.	ERA	G	GS	CG	ShO	Sv.	IP	H	R	ER	BB	SO
1994— Billings (Pioneer)...............	7	4	.636	2.54	13	13	2	0	0	85	74	31	24	14	82
1995— Win.-Salem (Car.).............	5	5	.500	3.63	12	12	1	1	0	67	60	32	27	22	60
1996— Win.-Salem (Car.).............	1	0	1.000	0.73	4	4	0	0	0	12 1/3	5	2	1	6	9
1997— Char., W.Va. (S. Atl.)........	5	3	.625	3.62	14	14	0	0	0	77	79	38	31	10	70
— Chattanooga (Southern).....	4	6	.400	3.44	14	14	1	0	0	91 2/3	101	39	35	17	63
1998— Chattanooga (Southern).....	1	2	.333	1.73	4	4	0	0	0	26	15	6	5	10	29
— Indianapolis (International)	4	1	.800	4.76	6	6	0	0	0	34	36	19	18	7	21
— Cincinnati (N.L.)	0	1	.000	10.50	2	2	0	0	0	6	12	8	7	1	1
— Buffalo (Int'l)■.................	3	5	.375	4.91	16	16	0	0	0	88	103	56	48	28	44
Major league totals (1 year)........	0	1	.000	10.50	2	2	0	0	0	6	12	8	7	1	1

PRIETO, ARIEL   P   ATHLETICS

P

PERSONAL: Born October 22, 1969, in Havana, Cuba. ... 6-3/245. ... Throws right, bats right.
COLLEGE: Fajardo University (Isle of Pines, Cuba).
TRANSACTIONS/CAREER NOTES: Selected by Oakland Athletics organization in first round (fifth pick overall) of free-agent draft (June 1, 1995). ... On disabled list (August 19-September 3, 1995). ... On Oakland disabled list (May 19-July 28, 1996); included rehabilitation assignments to Modesto (July 1-11) and Edmonton (July 11-28). ... On Oakland disabled list (July 13-August 8 and August 23, 1997-remainder of season); included rehabilitation assignment to Edmonton (August 8-17). ... On Edmonton disabled list (July 29-September 10, 1998).

Year Team (League)	W	L	Pct.	ERA	G	GS	CG	ShO	Sv.	IP	H	R	ER	BB	SO
1995—Oakland (A.L.)	2	6	.250	4.97	14	9	1	0	0	58	57	35	32	32	37
1996—Oakland (A.L.)	6	7	.462	4.15	21	21	2	0	0	$125\frac{2}{3}$	130	66	58	54	75
—Modesto (California)	0	0	...	3.00	2	1	0	0	1	9	9	4	3	2	8
—Edmonton (PCL)	3	0	1.000	0.57	3	3	0	0	0	$15\frac{2}{3}$	11	1	1	6	18
1997—Oakland (A.L.)	6	8	.429	5.04	22	22	0	0	0	125	155	84	70	70	90
—Edmonton (PCL)	0	0	...	1.50	2	2	0	0	0	6	4	1	1	1	7
1998—Edmonton (PCL)	5	1	.833	2.56	10	10	1	0	0	$52\frac{2}{3}$	47	20	15	12	50
—Oakland (A.L.)	0	1	.000	11.88	2	2	0	0	0	$8\frac{1}{3}$	17	11	11	5	8
Major league totals (4 years)	14	22	.389	4.85	59	54	3	0	0	317	359	196	171	161	210

PRINCE, TOM   C   PHILLIES

PERSONAL: Born August 13, 1964, in Kankakee, Ill. ... 5-11/206. ... Bats right, throws right. ... Full name: Thomas Albert Prince.
HIGH SCHOOL: Bradley-Bourbonnais (Bradley, Ill.).
JUNIOR COLLEGE: Kankakee (Ill.) Community College.
TRANSACTIONS/CAREER NOTES: Selected by Atlanta Braves organization in eighth round of free-agent draft (January 11, 1983); did not sign. ... Selected by Braves organization in secondary phase of free-agent draft (June 6, 1983); did not sign. ... Selected by Pittsburgh Pirates organization in secondary phase of free-agent draft (January 17, 1984). ... On Pittsburgh disabled list (August 13-September 1, 1991); included rehabilitation assignment to Buffalo (August 28-September 1). ... Granted free agency (October 15, 1993). ... Signed by Albuquerque, Los Angeles Dodgers organization (November 12, 1993). ... On Albuquerque disabled list (April 30-May 7, 1994). ... Released by Dodgers (December 5, 1994). ... Re-signed by Dodgers organization (January 5, 1995). ... On Los Angeles disabled list (June 4-July 10, 1995); included rehabilitation assignment to Albuquerque (June 26-July 10). ... Granted free agency (October 15, 1995). ... Re-signed by Dodgers organization (November 1, 1995). ... Granted free agency (October 22, 1998). ... Signed by Philadelphia Phillies (December 15, 1998).
STATISTICAL NOTES: Led South Atlantic League catchers with 930 total chances, 10 double plays and 27 passed balls in 1985. ... Led Carolina League catchers with 954 total chances and 15 passed balls in 1986. ... Led Eastern League catchers with 721 total chances and nine double plays in 1987. ... Led American Association catchers with 12 double plays in 1992. ... Led Pacific Coast League catchers with 677 total chances and nine double plays in 1994.

Year Team (League)	Pos.	G	AB	R	H	2B	3B	HR	RBI	Avg.	BB	SO	SB	PO	A	E	Avg.
1984—Watertown (NYP)	C-3B	23	69	6	14	3	0	2	13	.203	9	13	0	155	26	2	.989
—GC Pirates (GCL)	C-1B	18	48	4	11	0	0	1	6	.229	8	10	1	75	16	4	.958
1985—Macon (S. Atl.)	C	124	360	60	75	20	1	10	42	.208	96	92	13	*810	*101	*19	.980
1986—Prince Will. (Car.)	C	121	395	59	100	34	1	10	47	.253	50	74	4	*821	•113	20	.979
1987—Harrisburg (East.)	C	113	365	41	112	23	2	6	54	.307	51	46	6	*622	*88	•11	.985
—Pittsburgh (N.L.)	C	4	9	1	2	1	0	1	2	.222	0	2	0	14	3	0	1.000
1988—Buffalo (A.A.)	C	86	304	35	79	16	0	14	42	.260	23	53	3	456	51	*12	.977
—Pittsburgh (N.L.)	C	29	74	3	13	2	0	0	6	.176	4	15	0	108	8	2	.983
1989—Buffalo (A.A.)	C	65	183	21	37	8	1	6	33	.202	22	30	2	312	22	5	.985
—Pittsburgh (N.L.)	C	21	52	1	7	4	0	0	5	.135	6	12	1	85	11	4	.960
1990—Pittsburgh (N.L.)	C	4	10	1	1	0	0	0	0	.100	1	2	0	16	1	0	1.000
—Buffalo (A.A.)	C-1B	94	284	38	64	13	0	7	37	.225	39	46	4	461	62	8	.985
1991—Pittsburgh (N.L.)	C-1B	26	34	4	9	3	0	1	2	.265	7	3	0	53	9	1	.984
—Buffalo (A.A.)	C	80	221	29	46	8	3	6	32	.208	37	31	3	379	61	5	.989
1992—Pittsburgh (N.L.)	C-3B	27	44	1	4	2	0	0	5	.091	6	9	1	76	8	2	.977
—Buffalo (A.A.)	C-OF	75	244	34	64	17	0	9	35	.262	20	35	3	307	50	8	.978
1993—Pittsburgh (N.L.)	C	66	179	14	35	14	0	2	24	.196	13	38	1	271	31	5	.984
1994—Albuquerque (PCL)■	C	103	330	61	94	31	2	20	54	.285	51	67	2	593	*75	9	.987
—Los Angeles (N.L.)	C	3	6	2	2	0	0	0	1	.333	1	3	0	11	1	0	1.000
1995—Los Angeles (N.L.)	C	18	40	3	8	2	1	1	4	.200	4	10	0	71	8	1	.988
—Albuquerque (PCL)	C	61	192	30	61	15	0	7	36	.318	27	41	0	310	34	4	.989
1996—Albuquerque (PCL)	C-3B-OF	32	95	24	39	5	1	7	22	.411	15	14	0	88	20	1	.991
—Los Angeles (N.L.)	C	40	64	6	19	6	0	1	11	.297	6	15	0	161	11	1	.994
1997—Los Angeles (N.L.)	C	47	100	17	22	5	0	3	14	.220	5	15	0	221	25	1	.996
1998—Los Angeles (N.L.)	C	37	81	7	15	5	1	0	5	.185	7	24	0	175	16	0	1.000
Major league totals (12 years)		322	693	60	137	44	2	9	79	.198	60	148	3	1262	132	17	.988

PRITCHETT, CHRIS   1B   ANGELS

PERSONAL: Born January 31, 1970, in Merced, Calif. ... 6-4/212. ... Bats left, throws right. ... Full name: Christopher Davis Pritchett.
HIGH SCHOOL: Central Catholic (Modesto, Calif.).
COLLEGE: UCLA.
TRANSACTIONS/CAREER NOTES: Selected by California Angels organization in second round of free-agent draft (June 3, 1991). ... Angels franchise renamed Anaheim Angels for 1997 season. ... On Anaheim disabled list (March 30-April 16, 1998).
STATISTICAL NOTES: Tied for Midwest League lead with six intentional bases on balls received in 1992. ... Led Texas League first basemen with 1,075 putouts, 19 errors and 1,182 total chances in 1993. ... Led Texas League with .421 on-base percentage in 1994. ... Led Texas League first basemen with 100 double plays in 1994. ... Tied for Pacific Coast League lead with 11 intentional bases on balls received in 1996. ... Led Pacific Coast League first baseman with 1,107 putouts, 98 assists, 1,211 total chances, .995 fielding percentage and 107 double plays in 1996.

Year Team (League)	Pos.	G	AB	R	H	2B	3B	HR	RBI	Avg.	BB	SO	SB	PO	A	E	Avg.
1991—Boise (Northwest)	1B	70	255	41	68	10	3	9	50	.267	47	41	1	636	26	5	*.993
1992—Quad City (Midwest)	1B	128	448	79	130	19	1	13	72	.290	71	88	9	*1059	84	13	*.989
1993—Midland (Texas)	1B-2B	127	464	61	143	30	6	2	66	.308	61	72	3	†1076	92	†19	.984
1994—Midland (Texas)	1B-OF-3B	127	460	86	142	25	4	6	91	.309	*92	81	5	1028	94	13	.989
1995—Vancouver (PCL)	1B-OF	123	434	66	120	27	4	8	53	.276	56	79	2	999	92	12	.989
1996—Vancouver (PCL)	1B-OF	130	485	78	143	39	1	16	73	.295	71	96	5	†1116	†98	6	†.995
—California (A.L.)	1B	5	13	1	2	0	0	0	1	.154	0	3	0	29	1	0	1.000

							BATTING								FIELDING		
Year	Team (League)	Pos.	G	AB	R	H	2B	3B	HR	RBI	Avg.	BB	SO	SB	PO	A	E	Avg.
1997—Vancouver (PCL)		1B-OF	109	383	60	107	30	3	7	47	.279	42	72	5	621	51	7	.990
1998—Vancouver (PCL)		1B	104	374	42	97	21	1	7	41	.259	37	72	2	739	55	10	.988
—Anaheim (A.L.)		1B	31	80	12	23	2	1	2	8	.288	4	16	2	190	20	1	.995
Major league totals (2 years)			36	93	13	25	2	1	2	9	.269	4	19	2	219	21	1	.996

PROKOPEC, LUKE   P   DODGERS

PERSONAL: Born February 23, 1978, in Blackwood, South Australia. ... 5-11/166. ... Throws right, bats left. ... Full name: Kenneth Luke Prokopec.
HIGH SCHOOL: Renmark (South Australia).
TRANSACTIONS/CAREER NOTES: Signed as non-drafted free agent by Los Angeles Dodgers organization (August 28, 1994).

Year	Team (League)	W	L	Pct.	ERA	G	GS	CG	ShO	Sv.	IP	H	R	ER	BB	SO
1997—Savannah (S. Atl.)		3	1	.750	4.07	61	6	0	0	0	42	37	21	19	12	45
1998—San Bernardino (Calif.)		8	5	.615	2.69	20	20	0	0	0	110 1/3	99	43	33	33	148
—San Antonio (Tex.)		3	0	1.000	1.38	5	5	0	0	0	26	16	5	4	13	25

RECORD AS POSITION PLAYER

							BATTING								FIELDING		
Year	Team (League)	Pos.	G	AB	R	H	2B	3B	HR	RBI	Avg.	BB	SO	SB	PO	A	E	Avg.
1995—Great Falls (Pio.)		OF	43	119	16	29	6	2	2	24	.244	8	37	5	30	4	0	1.000
1996—Savannah (S. Atl.)		OF	82	245	34	53	12	1	4	29	.216	27	78	0	59	5	8	.889
1997—Savannah (S. Atl.)		OF-P	61	164	11	38	7	3	2	20	.232	12	49	3	79	11	2	.978

PULSIPHER, BILL   P   BREWERS

PERSONAL: Born October 9, 1973, in Fort Benning, Ga. ... 6-3/225. ... Throws left, bats left. ... Full name: William Thomas Pulsipher.
HIGH SCHOOL: Fairfax (Va.).
TRANSACTIONS/CAREER NOTES: Selected by New York Mets organization in second round of free-agent draft (June 3, 1991). ... On disabled list (March 22, 1996-entire season). ... On New York disabled list (March 24-May 3, 1997); included rehabilitation assignment to Norfolk (April 4-May 3). ... On Norfolk disabled list (June 30-July 30, 1997). ... Traded by Mets to Milwaukee Brewers for 3B Mike Kinkade (July 31, 1998).
STATISTICAL NOTES: Tied for Eastern League lead with four balks in 1994.
MISCELLANEOUS: Appeared in one game as pinch runner with Mets (1998).

Year	Team (League)	W	L	Pct.	ERA	G	GS	CG	ShO	Sv.	IP	H	R	ER	BB	SO
1992—Pittsfield (NYP)		6	3	.667	2.84	14	14	0	0	0	95	88	40	30	56	83
1993—Capital City (S. Atl.)		2	3	.400	2.08	6	6	1	0	0	43 1/3	34	17	10	12	29
—St. Lucie (Fla. St.)		7	3	.700	2.24	13	13	3	1	0	96 1/3	63	27	24	39	102
1994—Binghamton (Eastern)		14	9	.609	3.22	28	28	5	1	0	*201	179	90	72	89	171
1995—Norfolk (Int'l)		6	4	.600	3.14	13	13	•4	2	0	91 2/3	84	36	32	33	63
—New York (N.L.).................		5	7	.417	3.98	17	17	2	0	0	126 2/3	122	58	56	45	81
1996—								Did not play.								
1997—Norfolk (Int'l)		0	5	.000	7.81	8	5	0	0	0	27 2/3	23	29	24	38	18
—St. Lucie (Fla. St.)		1	4	.200	5.89	12	7	0	0	0	36 2/3	29	27	24	35	35
—Binghamton (Eastern)		0	0	...	1.42	10	0	0	0	0	12 2/3	11	3	2	7	12
—GC Mets (GCL)		0	0	...	1.80	2	2	0	0	0	5	3	1	1	1	4
1998—Norfolk (Int'l)		7	5	.583	3.96	14	14	1	0	0	86 1/3	91	50	38	41	58
—New York (N.L.).................		0	0	...	6.91	15	1	0	0	0	14 1/3	23	11	11	5	13
—Milwaukee (N.L.)■		3	4	.429	4.66	11	10	0	0	0	58	63	30	30	26	38
Major league totals (2 years)......		8	11	.421	4.39	43	28	2	0	0	199	208	99	97	76	132

QUANTRILL, PAUL   P   BLUE JAYS

PERSONAL: Born November 3, 1968, in London, Ont. ... 6-1/185. ... Throws right, bats left. ... Full name: Paul John Quantrill.
HIGH SCHOOL: Okemos (Mich.).
COLLEGE: Wisconsin.
TRANSACTIONS/CAREER NOTES: Selected by Los Angeles Dodgers organization in 26th round of free-agent draft (June 2, 1986); did not sign. ... Selected by Boston Red Sox organization in sixth round of free-agent draft (June 5, 1989). ... Traded by Red Sox with OF Billy Hatcher to Philadelphia Phillies for OF Wes Chamberlain and P Mike Sullivan (May 31, 1994). ... Traded by Phillies to Toronto Blue Jays for 3B Howard Battle and P Ricardo Jordan (December 6, 1995).

Year	Team (League)	W	L	Pct.	ERA	G	GS	CG	ShO	Sv.	IP	H	R	ER	BB	SO
1989—GC Red Sox (GCL)		0	0	...	0.00	2	0	0	0	2	5	2	0	0	0	5
—Elmira (N.Y.-Penn)		5	4	.556	3.43	20	7	•5	0	2	76	90	37	29	12	57
1990—Winter Haven (FSL)		2	5	.286	4.14	7	7	1	0	0	45 2/3	46	24	21	6	14
—New Britain (East.)		7	11	.389	3.53	22	22	1	1	0	132 2/3	148	65	52	23	53
1991—New Britain (East.)		2	1	.667	2.06	5	5	1	0	0	35	32	14	8	8	18
—Pawtucket (Int'l)		10	7	.588	4.45	25	23	•6	2	0	155 2/3	169	81	77	30	75
1992—Pawtucket (Int'l)		6	8	.429	4.46	19	18	4	1	0	119	143	63	59	20	56
—Boston (A.L.)...................		2	3	.400	2.19	27	0	0	0	1	49 1/3	55	18	12	15	24
1993—Boston (A.L.)...................		6	12	.333	3.91	49	14	1	1	1	138	151	73	60	44	66
1994—Boston (A.L.)...................		1	1	.500	3.52	17	0	0	0	1	23	25	10	9	5	15
—Philadelphia (N.L.)■		2	2	.500	6.00	18	1	0	0	0	30	39	21	20	10	13
—Scran./W.B. (Int'l)		3	3	.500	3.47	8	8	1	1	0	57	55	25	22	6	36
1995—Philadelphia (N.L.)		11	12	.478	4.67	33	29	0	0	0	179 1/3	212	102	93	44	103
1996—Toronto (A.L.)■.................		5	14	.263	5.43	38	20	0	0	0	134 1/3	172	90	81	51	86
1997—Toronto (A.L.)		6	7	.462	1.94	77	0	0	0	5	88	103	25	19	17	56
1998—Toronto (A.L.)		3	4	.429	2.59	82	0	0	0	7	80	88	26	23	22	59
A.L. totals (6 years)		23	41	.359	3.58	290	34	1	1	14	512 2/3	594	242	204	154	306
N.L. totals (2 years)		13	14	.481	4.86	51	30	0	0	1	209 1/3	251	123	113	54	116
Major league totals (7 years)......		36	55	.396	3.95	341	64	1	1	15	722	845	365	317	208	422

PERSONAL: Born May 21, 1974, in La Miranda, Calif. ... 6-1/175. ... Bats right, throws right. ... Full name: Mark David Quinn.
HIGH SCHOOL: Clements (Sugar Land, Texas).
COLLEGE: Rice.
TRANSACTIONS/CAREER NOTES: Selected by Kansas City Royals organization in 11th round of free-agent draft (June 1, 1995).

							BATTING								FIELDING		
Year	Team (League)	Pos.	G	AB	R	H	2B	3B	HR	RBI	Avg.	BB	SO	SB	PO	A	E	Avg.
1995—Spokane (N'west)		3B	44	162	28	46	12	2	6	36	.284	15	28	0	8	33	8	.837
1996—Lansing (Midwest)		OF	113	437	63	132	23	3	9	71	.302	43	54	14	143	15	7	.958
1997—Wilmington (Caro.)		OF	87	299	51	92	22	3	16	71	.308	42	47	3	75	7	6	.932
— Wichita (Texas)		OF	26	96	26	36	13	0	2	19	.375	15	19	1	35	0	1	.972
1998—Wichita (Texas)		OF	100	372	82	130	26	6	16	84	*.349	43	54	4	157	11	8	.955

Q
R

PERSONAL: Born March 3, 1968, in Glendale, Calif. ... 6-3/204. ... Throws left, bats left. ... Full name: Scott David Radinsky.
HIGH SCHOOL: Simi Valley (Calif.).
TRANSACTIONS/CAREER NOTES: Selected by Chicago White Sox organization in third round of free-agent draft (June 2, 1986). ... On Chicago disabled list (March 2, 1994-entire season). ... On Chicago disabled list (July 17-August 15, 1995); included rehabilitation assignment to South Bend (August 1-15). ... Granted free agency (December 21, 1995). ... Signed by Los Angeles Dodgers organization (January 16, 1996). ... On Los Angeles disabled list (March 28-April 12, 1996); included rehabilitation assignment to San Bernardino (April 4-12). ... Granted free agency (October 23, 1998). ... Signed by St. Louis Cardinals (November 23, 1998).

Year	Team (League)	W	L	Pct.	ERA	G	GS	CG	ShO	Sv.	IP	H	R	ER	BB	SO
1986—GC White Sox (GCL)		1	0	1.000	3.38	7	7	0	0	0	26²/₃	24	20	10	17	18
1987—Peninsula (Caro.)		1	7	.125	5.77	12	8	0	0	0	39	43	30	25	32	37
— GC White Sox (GCL)		3	3	.500	2.31	11	10	0	0	0	58¹/₃	43	23	15	39	41
1988—GC White Sox (GCL)		0	0	. . .	5.40	5	0	0	0	0	3¹/₃	2	2	2	4	7
1989—South Bend (Mid.)		7	5	.583	1.75	53	0	0	0	31	61²/₃	39	21	12	19	83
1990—Chicago (A.L.)		6	1	.857	4.82	62	0	0	0	4	52¹/₃	47	29	28	36	46
1991—Chicago (A.L.)		5	5	.500	2.02	67	0	0	0	8	71¹/₃	53	18	16	23	49
1992—Chicago (A.L.)		3	7	.300	2.73	68	0	0	0	15	59¹/₃	54	21	18	34	48
1993—Chicago (A.L.)		8	2	.800	4.28	73	0	0	0	4	54²/₃	61	33	26	19	44
1994—Chicago (A.L.)								Did not play.								
1995—Chicago (A.L.)		2	1	.667	5.45	46	0	0	0	1	38	46	23	23	17	14
— South Bend (Mid.)		0	0	. . .	0.00	6	0	0	0	2	9²/₃	5	0	0	0	11
1996—San Bernardino (Calif.)■		0	0	. . .	2.08	3	0	0	0	0	4¹/₃	2	1	1	2	4
— Los Angeles (N.L.)		5	1	.833	2.41	56	0	0	0	1	52¹/₃	52	19	14	17	48
1997—Los Angeles (N.L.)		5	1	.833	2.89	75	0	0	0	3	62¹/₃	54	22	20	21	44
1998—Los Angeles (N.L.)		6	6	.500	2.63	62	0	0	0	13	61²/₃	63	21	18	20	45
A.L. totals (5 years)		24	16	.600	3.62	316	0	0	0	32	275²/₃	261	124	111	129	201
N.L. totals (3 years)		16	8	.667	2.65	193	0	0	0	17	176¹/₃	169	62	52	58	137
Major league totals (8 years)		40	24	.625	3.25	509	0	0	0	49	452	430	186	163	187	338

DIVISION SERIES RECORD

Year	Team (League)	W	L	Pct.	ERA	G	GS	CG	ShO	Sv.	IP	H	R	ER	BB	SO
1996—Los Angeles (N.L.)		0	0	. . .	0.00	2	0	0	0	0	1¹/₃	0	0	0	1	2

CHAMPIONSHIP SERIES RECORD

Year	Team (League)	W	L	Pct.	ERA	G	GS	CG	ShO	Sv.	IP	H	R	ER	BB	SO
1993—Chicago (A.L.)		0	0	. . .	10.80	4	0	0	0	0	1²/₃	3	4	2	1	1

PERSONAL: Born October 27, 1972, in Eau Claire, Wis. ... 6-2/184. ... Throws right, bats right. ... Full name: Brad William Radke.
HIGH SCHOOL: Jesuit (Tampa).
TRANSACTIONS/CAREER NOTES: Selected by Minnesota Twins organization in eighth round of free-agent draft (June 3, 1991).
STATISTICAL NOTES: Led A.L. in home runs allowed with 32 in 1995 and 40 in 1996.

Year	Team (League)	W	L	Pct.	ERA	G	GS	CG	ShO	Sv.	IP	H	R	ER	BB	SO
1991—GC Twins (GCL)		3	4	.429	3.08	10	9	1	0	1	49²/₃	41	21	17	14	46
1992—Kenosha (Midwest)		10	10	.500	2.93	26	25	4	1	0	165²/₃	149	70	54	47	127
1993—Fort Myers (Fla. St.)		3	5	.375	3.82	14	14	0	0	0	92	85	42	39	21	69
— Nashville (Southern)		2	6	.250	4.62	13	13	1	0	0	76	81	42	39	16	76
1994—Nashville (Southern)		12	9	.571	2.66	29	*28	5	1	0	186¹/₃	167	66	55	34	123
1995—Minnesota (A.L.)		11	14	.440	5.32	29	28	2	1	0	181	195	112	107	47	75
1996—Minnesota (A.L.)		11	16	.407	4.46	35	35	3	0	0	232	231	125	115	57	148
1997—Minnesota (A.L.)		20	10	.667	3.87	35	*35	4	1	0	239²/₃	238	114	103	48	174
1998—Minnesota (A.L.)		12	14	.462	4.30	32	32	5	1	0	213²/₃	238	109	102	43	146
Major league totals (4 years)		54	54	.500	4.44	131	130	14	3	0	866¹/₃	902	460	427	195	543

ALL-STAR GAME RECORD

Year	League	W	L	Pct.	ERA	GS	CG	ShO	Sv.	IP	H	R	ER	BB	SO
1998—American		0	0	. . .	9.00	0	0	0	0	1	2	1	1	1	1

PERSONAL: Born August 9, 1971, in Calgary, Alta. ... 6-2/200. ... Bats left, throws right. ... Full name: Ryan Ashley Radmanovich.
HIGH SCHOOL: John Diefenbaker (Calgary, Alta.).

JUNIOR COLLEGE: Allan Hancock College (Calif.).
COLLEGE: Pepperdine.
TRANSACTIONS/CAREER NOTES: Selected by Minnesota Twins organization in 14th round of free-agent draft (June 3, 1993). ... On disabled list (April 21-May 12 and May 23-September 15, 1995). ... Claimed on waivers by Seattle Mariners (March 27, 1998).
STATISTICAL NOTES: Led Midwest League third basemen with 21 double plays in 1994.
MISCELLANEOUS: Member of 1992 Canadian Olympic baseball team.

Year Team (League)	Pos.	G	AB	R	H	2B	3B	HR	RBI	Avg.	BB	SO	SB	PO	A	E	Avg.
1993— Fort Wayne (Midw.)....	OF	62	204	36	59	7	5	8	38	.289	30	60	8	84	6	3	.968
1994— Fort Myers (FSL)........	3B-OF	26	85	11	16	4	0	2	9	.188	7	19	3	12	47	12	.831
— Fort Wayne (Midw.).......	3B	101	383	64	105	20	6	19	69	.274	45	98	19	75	169	28	.897
1995— Fort Myers (FSL).......	3B	12	41	3	13	2	0	0	5	.317	2	8	0	7	22	7	.806
1996— New Britain (East.)	OF	125	453	77	127	31	2	25	86	.280	49	122	4	246	3	4	.984
1997— Salt Lake (PCL)......	OF-3B	133	485	92	128	25	4	28	78	.264	67	*138	11	226	7	9	.963
1998— Tacoma (PCL)■	OF	110	397	73	119	33	2	15	65	.300	46	83	2	164	4	3	.982
— Seattle (A.L.).............	OF-1B	25	69	5	15	4	0	2	10	.217	4	25	1	34	2	0	1.000
Major league totals (1 year)		25	69	5	15	4	0	2	10	.217	4	25	1	34	2	0	1.000

RAGGIO, BRADY　　　　　　　　P

PERSONAL: Born September 17, 1972, in Los Angeles. ... 6-4/210. ... Throws right, bats right. ... Full name: Brady John Raggio. ... Name pronounced RAZH-ee-oh.
HIGH SCHOOL: San Ramon Valley (Los Angeles).
JUNIOR COLLEGE: Chabot College (Calif.).
TRANSACTIONS/CAREER NOTES: Selected by St. Louis Cardinals organization in 20th round of free-agent draft (June 1, 1992). ... Suffered non-baseball injury; missed entire 1993 season. ... Released by Cardinals (December 14, 1998).

Year Team (League)	W	L	Pct.	ERA	G	GS	CG	ShO	Sv.	IP	H	R	ER	BB	SO
1992— Ariz. Cardinals (Ariz.)	4	3	.571	3.54	14	6	3	0	1	48 1/3	51	26	19	7	48
1993—						Did not play.									
1994— New Jersey (NYP)	3	0	1.000	1.67	4	4	0	0	0	27	28	7	5	4	20
— Madison (Midwest)	4	3	.571	3.21	11	11	1	0	0	67 1/3	63	31	24	14	66
1995— Peoria (Midwest)...............	3	0	1.000	1.85	8	8	3	0	0	48 2/3	42	13	10	2	34
— St. Petersburg (FSL)	2	3	.400	3.80	20	3	0	0	0	47 1/3	43	24	20	13	25
1996— Arkansas (Texas)..............	9	10	.474	3.22	26	24	4	1	0	162 1/3	160	68	58	40	123
1997— Louisville (A.A.).................	8	11	.421	4.17	22	22	2	0	0	138	145	68	64	32	91
— St. Louis (N.L.).................	1	2	.333	6.89	15	4	0	0	0	31 1/3	44	24	24	16	21
1998— Memphis (Pacific Coast)....	8	9	.471	3.07	24	23	2	1	0	152 1/3	156	57	52	31	100
— St. Louis (N.L.).................	1	1	.500	15.43	4	1	0	0	0	7	22	12	12	3	3
Major league totals (2 years)......	2	3	.400	8.45	19	5	0	0	0	38 1/3	66	36	36	19	24

RAINES, TIM　　　　　　　　OF

PERSONAL: Born September 16, 1959, in Sanford, Fla. ... 5-8/186. ... Bats both, throws right. ... Full name: Timothy Raines. ... Father of TIm Raines Jr., outfielder in Baltimore Orioles organization; and brother of Ned Raines, minor league outfielder (1978-80).
HIGH SCHOOL: Seminole (Sanford, Fla.).
TRANSACTIONS/CAREER NOTES: Selected by Montreal Expos organization in fifth round of free-agent draft (June 7, 1977). ... On disabled list (May 23-June 5, 1978). ... Granted free agency (November 12, 1986). ... Re-signed by Expos (May 2, 1987). ... On disabled list (June 24-July 9, 1988 and June 25-July 10, 1990). ... Traded by Expos with P Jeff Carter and a player to be named later to Chicago White Sox for OF Ivan Calderon and P Barry Jones (December 23, 1990); White Sox acquired P Mario Brito to complete deal (February 15, 1991). ... On Chicago disabled list (April 10-May 22, 1993); included rehabilitation assignment to Nashville (May 19-22). ... Granted free agency (November 1, 1993). ... Re-signed by White Sox (December 22, 1993). ... Traded by White Sox to New York Yankees for a player to be named later (December 28, 1995); White Sox acquired 3B Blaise Kozeniewski to complete deal (February 6, 1996). ... On New York disabled list (March 21-April 16 and May 22-August 11, 1996); included rehabilitation assignments to Tampa (April 12-13 and July 25-August 2), Columbus (April 13-16 and June 23-24), Gulf Coast Yankees (June 22-23) and Norwich (August 2-10). ... On New York disabled list (March 27-April 11 and July 2-August 12, 1997); included rehabilitation assignment to Tampa (April 7-10, July 24-27, and August 5-7), Gulf Coast Yankees (July 24), Norwich (July 26-27) and Columbus (August 8-11). ... Granted free agency (October 29, 1997). ... Re-signed by Yankees (December 19, 1997). ... Granted free agency (October 26, 1998).
RECORDS: Holds major league single-season record for most intentional bases on balls received by switch hitter—26 (1987). ... Holds A.L. career record for most consecutive stolen bases without being caught stealing—40 (July 23, 1993 through August 4, 1995). ... Shares A.L. single-game record for most consecutive times reached base safely—7 (April 20, 1994, 12 innings).
HONORS: Named Minor League Player of the Year by THE SPORTING NEWS (1980). ... Named N.L. Rookie Player of the Year by THE SPORTING NEWS (1981). ... Named outfielder on THE SPORTING NEWS N.L. All-Star team (1983 and 1986). ... Won THE SPORTING NEWS Gold Shoe Award (1984). ... Named outfielder on THE SPORTING NEWS N.L. Silver Slugger team (1986).
STATISTICAL NOTES: Led N.L. outfielders with 21 assists in 1983. ... Led N.L. with .413 on-base percentage in 1986. ... Hit for the cycle (August 16, 1987). ... Switch-hit home runs in one game (July 16, 1988 and August 31, 1993). ... Hit three home runs in one game (April 18, 1994). ... Career major league grand slams: 6.
MISCELLANEOUS: Holds Montreal Expos all-time records for most runs (934), most triples (81), highest career batting average (.301) and most stolen bases (634).

Year Team (League)	Pos.	G	AB	R	H	2B	3B	HR	RBI	Avg.	BB	SO	SB	PO	A	E	Avg.
1977— GC Expos (GCL).....	2B-3B-OF	49	161	28	45	6	2	0	21	.280	27	16	29	79	72	13	.921
1978— W.P. Beach (FSL)........	2B-SS	100	359	67	103	10	0	0	23	.287	64	44	57	219	273	24	.953
1979— Memphis (Sou.).........	2B	•145	552	*104	160	25	10	5	50	.290	90	51	59	*341	*413	*23	.970
— Montreal (N.L.)..........	PR	6	0	3	0	0	0	0	0	. . .	0	0	2	. . .	. . .	. . .	. . .
1980— Denver (A.A.)..............	2B	108	429	105	152	23	•11	6	64	*.354	61	42	*77	226	338	16	.972
— Montreal (N.L.)...........	2B-OF	15	20	5	1	0	0	0	0	.050	6	3	5	15	16	0	1.000
1981— Montreal (N.L.)..........	OF-2B	88	313	61	95	13	7	5	37	.304	45	31	*71	162	8	4	.977
1982— Montreal (N.L.)..........	OF-2B	156	647	90	179	32	8	4	43	.277	75	83	*78	293	126	8	.981

Year	Team (League)	Pos.	G	AB	R	H	2B	3B	HR	RBI	Avg.	BB	SO	SB	PO	A	E	Avg.
1983— Montreal (N.L.)..........		OF-2B	156	615	*133	183	32	8	11	71	.298	97	70	*90	314	†23	4	.988
1984— Montreal (N.L.)..........		OF-2B	160	622	106	192	•38	9	8	60	.309	87	69	*75	420	8	6	.986
1985— Montreal (N.L.)..........		OF	150	575	115	184	30	13	11	41	.320	81	60	70	284	8	2	.993
1986— Montreal (N.L.)..........		OF	151	580	91	194	35	10	9	62	*.334	78	60	70	270	13	6	.979
1987— Montreal (N.L.)..........		OF	139	530	*123	175	34	8	18	68	.330	90	52	50	297	9	4	.987
1988— Montreal (N.L.)..........		OF	109	429	66	116	19	7	12	48	.270	53	44	33	235	5	3	.988
1989— Montreal (N.L.)..........		OF	145	517	76	148	29	6	9	60	.286	93	48	41	253	7	1	.996
1990— Montreal (N.L.)..........		OF	130	457	65	131	11	5	9	62	.287	70	43	49	239	3	6	.976
1991— Chicago (A.L.)■		OF-DH	155	609	102	163	20	6	5	50	.268	83	68	51	273	12	3	.990
1992— Chicago (A.L.)..........		OF-DH	144	551	102	162	22	9	7	54	.294	81	48	45	312	12	2	.994
1993— Chicago (A.L.)..........		OF	115	415	75	127	16	4	16	54	.306	64	35	21	200	5	0	*1.000
— Nashville (A.A.).........		OF	3	11	3	5	1	0	0	2	.455	2	0	2	3	0	0	1.000
1994— Chicago (A.L.)..........		OF	101	384	80	102	15	5	10	52	.266	61	43	13	204	3	4	.981
1995— Chicago (A.L.)..........		OF-DH	133	502	81	143	25	4	12	67	.285	70	52	13	193	7	4	.980
1996— Tampa (Fla. St.)■......		OF	9	36	9	13	2	0	2	11	.361	8	3	0	10	2	0	1.000
— Columbus (Int'l)		OF	4	12	3	3	1	0	0	0	.250	1	3	1	2	0	0	1.000
— New York (A.L.)..........		OF-DH	59	201	45	57	10	0	9	33	.284	34	29	10	79	3	1	.988
— GC Yankees (GCL)......		DH	1	5	2	3	2	0	0	3	.600	1	0	0	0	0	0	...
— Norwich (Eastern)......		OF	8	27	8	5	1	0	1	1	.185	9	2	2	4	0	0	1.000
1997— Tampa (Fla. St.)......		OF	11	35	8	12	0	0	2	5	.343	11	1	1	13	1	0	1.000
— New York (A.L.)..........		OF-DH	74	271	56	87	20	2	4	38	.321	41	34	8	79	1	1	.988
— GC Yankees (GCL)......		OF	1	4	0	1	0	0	0	2	.250	1	1	0	2	0	0	1.000
— Norwich (Eastern)......		OF	2	7	0	2	1	0	0	2	.286	0	2	0	2	0	0	1.000
— Columbus (Int'l)......		OF	4	13	1	2	0	0	0	0	.154	3	2	0	4	0	0	1.000
1998— New York (A.L.)..........		DH-OF	109	321	53	93	13	1	5	47	.290	55	49	8	61	3	1	.985
American League totals (8 years)			890	3254	594	934	141	31	68	395	.287	489	358	169	1401	46	16	.989
National League totals (12 years)			1405	5305	934	1598	273	81	96	552	.301	775	563	634	2782	226	44	.986
Major league totals (20 years)			2295	8559	1528	2532	414	112	164	947	.296	1264	921	803	4183	272	60	.987

DIVISION SERIES RECORD

Year	Team (League)	Pos.	G	AB	R	H	2B	3B	HR	RBI	Avg.	BB	SO	SB	PO	A	E	Avg.
1996— New York (A.L.)..........		OF	4	16	3	4	0	0	0	0	.250	3	1	0	5	0	0	1.000
1997— New York (A.L.)..........		DH-OF	5	19	4	4	0	0	1	3	.211	3	1	2	7	00	0	1.000
1998— New York (A.L.)..........		PH-DH	2	4	1	1	1	0	0	0	.250	1	1	0				...
Division series totals (3 years)			11	39	8	9	1	0	1	3	.231	7	3	2	12	0	0	1.000

CHAMPIONSHIP SERIES RECORD

RECORDS: Holds single-series record for most singles—10 (1993). ... Shares A.L. single-series record for most hits—12 (1993).

Year	Team (League)	Pos.	G	AB	R	H	2B	3B	HR	RBI	Avg.	BB	SO	SB	PO	A	E	Avg.
1981— Montreal (N.L.)..........		OF	5	21	1	5	2	0	0	1	.238	0	3	0	9	0	0	1.000
1993— Chicago (A.L.)..........		OF	6	27	5	12	2	0	0	1	.444	2	2	1	12	2	0	1.000
1996— New York (A.L.)..........		OF	5	15	2	4	1	0	0	0	.267	1	1	0	5	0	0	1.000
1998— New York (A.L.)..........		DH-OF	3	10	0	1	0	0	0	1	.100	2	5	0	1	0	0	1.000
Championship series totals (4 years)			19	73	8	22	5	0	0	3	.301	5	11	1	27	2	0	1.000

WORLD SERIES RECORD

NOTES: Member of World Series championship team (1996 and 1998).

Year	Team (League)	Pos.	G	AB	R	H	2B	3B	HR	RBI	Avg.	BB	SO	SB	PO	A	E	Avg.
1996— New York (A.L.)..........		OF	4	14	2	3	0	0	0	0	.214	2	1	0	5	0	1	.833
1998— New York (A.L.)								Did not play.										

ALL-STAR GAME RECORD

NOTES: Named Most Valuable Player (1987).

Year	League	Pos.	AB	R	H	2B	3B	HR	RBI	Avg.	BB	SO	SB	PO	A	E	Avg.
1981— National		PR-OF	0	0	0	0	0	0	0	...	0	0	0	1	0	0	1.000
1982— National		OF	1	0	0	0	0	0	0	.000	1	1	1	0	0	0	...
1983— National		OF	3	0	0	0	0	0	0	.000	0	1	1	2	0	0	1.000
1984— National		OF	1	0	0	0	0	0	0	.000	0	1	0	4	0	0	1.000
1985— National		PH-OF	0	1	0	0	0	0	0	...	1	0	0	0	0	0	...
1986— National		PH-OF	2	0	0	0	0	0	0	.000	0	1	0	1	0	0	1.000
1987— National		OF	3	0	3	0	1	0	2	1.000	0	0	1	1	0	0	1.000
All-Star Game totals (7 years)			10	1	3	0	1	0	2	.300	2	4	3	9	0	0	1.000

RAKERS, JASON   P   INDIANS

PERSONAL: Born June 29, 1973, in Pittsburgh. ... 6-2/200. ... Throws right, bats right. ... Full name: Jason Paul Rakers.
HIGH SCHOOL: Shaler Area (Pittsburgh).
COLLEGE: Pittsburgh, then New Mexico State.
TRANSACTIONS/CAREER NOTES: Selected by Cleveland Indians organization in 25th round of free-agent draft (June 1, 1995). ... On disabled list (April 4-June 23, 1996).
STATISTICAL NOTES: Pitched 8-0 no-hit victory for Kinston against Durham (June 4, 1997, first game).

Year	Team (League)	W	L	Pct.	ERA	G	GS	CG	ShO	Sv.	IP	H	R	ER	BB	SO
1995— Watertown (NYP)		4	3	.571	3.00	14	14	1	•1	0	75	72	27	25	24	73
1996— Columbus (S. Atl.)..............		5	4	.556	3.61	14	14	1	1	0	77 1/3	84	37	31	17	64

Year	Team (League)	W	L	Pct.	ERA	G	GS	CG	ShO	Sv.	IP	H	R	ER	BB	SO
1997—	Kinston (Carolina)	8	5	.615	3.07	17	17	2	2	0	102 2/3	93	41	35	18	105
	— Buffalo (A.A.)....................	1	0	1.000	0.00	1	1	0	0	0	7	5	0	0	1	3
	— Akron (Eastern)	1	4	.200	4.39	7	7	1	1	0	41	36	21	20	11	31
1998—	Akron (Eastern)	3	1	.750	2.59	5	5	0	0	0	31 1/3	35	10	9	7	27
	— Cleveland (A.L.)................	0	0	...	9.00	1	0	0	0	0	1	0	1	1	3	0
	— Buffalo (Int'l)...................	8	6	.571	4.57	21	21	1	0	0	126	134	70	64	38	89
Major league totals (1 year)........		0	0	...	9.00	1	0	0	0	0	1	0	1	1	3	0

RAMIREZ, ALEX — OF — INDIANS

PERSONAL: Born October 3, 1974, in Caracas, Venezuela. ... 5-11/176. ... Bats right, throws right. ... Full name: Alexander Ramon Ramirez.
TRANSACTIONS/CAREER NOTES: Signed as non-drafted free agent by Cleveland Indians organization (July 1, 1991). ... On Buffalo disabled list (May 21-June 4, 1998).
STATISTICAL NOTES: Led Appalachian League outfielders with three double plays in 1993.

R

							BATTING							FIELDING		
Year	Team (League)	Pos.	G	AB	R	H	2B	3B	HR	RBI	Avg.	BB	SO	SB	PO	A	E	Avg.
1992—	Dom. Inds. (DSL)	OF	69	272	28	79	13	3	8	48	.290	13	34	17	136	9	8	.948
1993—	Kinston (Carolina)	OF	3	12	0	2	0	0	0	1	.167	0	5	0	3	0	1	.750
	— Burlington (Appal.)......	OF	64	252	44	68	14	4	13	58	.270	13	52	13	85	8	7	.930
1994—	Columbus (S. Atl.)......	OF	125	458	64	115	23	3	18	57	.251	26	100	7	168	6	9	.951
1995—	Bakersfield (Calif.)......	OF	98	406	56	131	25	2	10	52	.323	18	76	13	150	9	10	.941
	— Cant./Akr. (Eastern)....	OF	33	133	15	33	3	4	1	11	.248	5	24	3	72	5	2	.975
1996—	Cant./Akr. (Eastern)......	OF	131	513	79	*169	28	*12	14	85	.329	16	74	18	209	4	5	.977
1997—	Buffalo (A.A.)............	OF	119	416	59	119	19	*8	11	44	.286	24	95	10	167	8	*10	.946
1998—	Buffalo (Int'l)............	OF	121	521	94	156	21	8	34	103	.299	16	101	6	224	7	9	.963
	— Cleveland (A.L.)..........	OF	3	8	1	1	0	0	0	0	.125	0	3	0	5	0	1	.833
Major league totals (1 year)			3	8	1	1	0	0	0	0	.125	0	3	0	5	0	1	.833

RAMIREZ, ARAMIS — 3B — PIRATES

PERSONAL: Born June 25, 1978, in Santo Domingo, Dominican Republic. ... 6-1/215. ... Bats right, throws right. ... Full name: Aramis Nin Ramirez.
TRANSACTIONS/CAREER NOTES: Signed as non-drafted free agent by Pittsburgh Pirates organization (November 7, 1994). ... On suspended list (July 24-29, 1998). ... On Pittsburgh disabled list (August 10-September 4, 1998); included rehabilitation assignment to Nashville (August 27-September 4).
HONORS: Named Carolina League Most Valuable Player (1997).
STATISTICAL NOTES: Led Carolina League third basemen with 379 total chances in 1997.

							BATTING							FIELDING		
Year	Team (League)	Pos.	G	AB	R	H	2B	3B	HR	RBI	Avg.	BB	SO	SB	PO	A	E	Avg.
1995—	Dom. Pirates (DSL)....	3B	64	214	41	63	13	0	11	54	.294	42	26	2	65	82	19	.886
1996—	Erie (N.Y.-Penn).........	3B	61	223	37	68	14	4	9	42	.305	31	41	0	39	107	17	.896
	— Augusta (S. Atl.).........	3B	6	20	3	4	1	0	1	2	.200	1	7	0	3	7	2	.833
1997—	Lynchburg (Caro.)......	3B	137	482	85	134	24	2	29	*114	.278	80	103	5	75	*265	*39	.897
1998—	Nashville (PCL)	3B-SS	47	168	19	46	10	0	5	18	.274	24	28	0	33	77	8	.932
	— Pittsburgh (N.L.)	3B	72	251	23	59	9	1	6	24	.235	18	72	0	29	114	9	.941
Major league totals (1 year)			72	251	23	59	9	1	6	24	.235	18	72	0	29	114	9	.941

RAMIREZ, JULIO — OF — MARLINS

PERSONAL: Born August 10, 1977, in San Juan de la Maguana, Dominican Republic. ... 5-11/170. ... Bats right, throws right. ... Full name: Julio Caesar Ramirez.
HIGH SCHOOL: Escuela Otilia Pelaez (Santo Domingo, Dominican Republic).
TRANSACTIONS/CAREER NOTES: Signed as non-drafted free agent by Florida Marlins organization (December 6, 1993).
STATISTICAL NOTES: Led Florida State League outfielders with 390 total chances in 1998.

							BATTING							FIELDING		
Year	Team (League)	Pos.	G	AB	R	H	2B	3B	HR	RBI	Avg.	BB	SO	SB	PO	A	E	Avg.
1994—	Dom. Marlins (DSL) ...	OF	67	274	54	75	18	0	7	32	.274	28	41	29	136	11	10	.936
1995—	GC Marlins (GCL).......	OF	48	204	35	58	9	4	2	13	.284	13	42	17	109	7	2	.983
1996—	Brevard Co. (Fla. St.)..	OF	17	61	11	15	0	1	0	2	.246	4	18	2	12	2	1	.933
	— GC Marlins (GCL).......	OF	43	174	35	50	5	4	0	16	.287	15	34	26	95	2	2	.980
1997—	Kane County (Midw.)..	OF	99	376	70	96	18	7	14	53	.255	37	122	41	179	8	4	.979
1998—	Brevard Co. (Fla. St.)..	OF	135	*559	90	156	20	12	13	58	.279	45	147	71	*365	•17	8	.979

RAMIREZ, MANNY — OF — INDIANS

PERSONAL: Born May 30, 1972, in Santo Domingo, Dominican Republic. ... 6-0/190. ... Bats right, throws right. ... Full name: Manuel Aristides Ramirez.
HIGH SCHOOL: George Washington (New York).
TRANSACTIONS/CAREER NOTES: Selected by Cleveland Indians organization in first round (13th pick overall) of free-agent draft (June 3, 1991). ... On disabled list (July 10, 1992-remainder of season).
RECORDS: Shares major league record for most consecutive home runs—4 (September 15 [3], 16 [1], 1998); most home runs in two consecutive games—5 (September 15 [3], 16 [2], 1998); and most home runs in three consecutive games—6 (September 15 [3], 16 [2], 17 [1], 1998).

HONORS: Named Appalachian League Most Valuable Player (1991). ... Named outfielder on THE SPORTING NEWS A.L. All-Star team (1995). ... Named outfielder on THE SPORTING NEWS A.L. Silver Slugger team (1995).
STATISTICAL NOTES: Led Appalachian League with 146 total bases and .679 slugging percentage in 1991. ... Hit three home runs in one game (September 15, 1998). ... Career major league grand slams: 8.

Year — Team (League)	Pos.	G	AB	R	H	2B	3B	HR	RBI	Avg.	BB	SO	SB	PO	A	E	Avg.
1991— Burlington (Appal.).....	OF	59	215	44	70	11	4	*19	*63	.326	34	41	7	83	2	3	.966
1992— Kinston (Carolina)	OF	81	291	52	81	18	4	13	63	.278	45	74	1	128	3	6	.956
1993— Cant./Akr. (Eastern)	OF	89	344	67	117	32	0	17	79	*.340	45	68	2	142	4	5	.967
— Charlotte (Int'l)..........	OF	40	145	38	46	12	0	14	36	.317	27	35	1	70	3	3	.961
— Cleveland (A.L.)..........	DH-OF	22	53	5	9	1	0	2	5	.170	2	8	0	3	0	0	1.000
1994— Cleveland (A.L.)..........	OF-DH	91	290	51	78	22	0	17	60	.269	42	72	4	150	7	1	.994
1995— Cleveland (A.L.)..........	OF-DH	137	484	85	149	26	1	31	107	.308	75	112	6	220	3	5	.978
1996— Cleveland (A.L.)..........	OF-DH	152	550	94	170	45	3	33	112	.309	85	104	8	272	*19	9	.970
1997— Cleveland (A.L.)..........	OF-DH	150	561	99	184	40	0	26	88	.328	79	115	2	259	10	7	.975
1998— Cleveland (A.L.)..........	OF-DH	150	571	108	168	35	2	45	145	.294	76	121	5	291	10	7	.977
Major league totals (6 years)		702	2509	442	758	169	6	154	517	.302	359	532	25	1195	49	29	.977

DIVISION SERIES RECORD

RECORDS: Shares single-game record for most home runs—2 (October 2, 1998).

Year — Team (League)	Pos.	G	AB	R	H	2B	3B	HR	RBI	Avg.	BB	SO	SB	PO	A	E	Avg.
1995— Cleveland (A.L.)..........	OF	3	12	1	0	0	0	0	0	.000	1	2	0	3	0	0	1.000
1996— Cleveland (A.L.)..........	OF	4	16	4	6	2	0	2	2	.375	1	4	0	8	2	0	1.000
1997— Cleveland (A.L.)..........	OF	5	21	2	3	1	0	0	3	.143	0	3	0	3	0	1	.750
1998— Cleveland (A.L.)..........	OF	4	14	2	5	2	0	2	3	.357	1	4	0	4	0	0	1.000
Division series totals (4 years)		16	63	9	14	5	0	4	8	.222	3	13	0	18	2	1	.952

CHAMPIONSHIP SERIES RECORD

Year — Team (League)	Pos.	G	AB	R	H	2B	3B	HR	RBI	Avg.	BB	SO	SB	PO	A	E	Avg.
1995— Cleveland (A.L.)..........	OF	6	21	2	6	0	0	2	2	.286	2	5	0	9	0	0	1.000
1997— Cleveland (A.L.)..........	OF	6	21	3	6	1	0	2	3	.286	5	5	0	14	0	1	.933
1998— Cleveland (A.L.)..........	OF	6	21	2	7	1	0	2	4	.333	4	9	0	12	0	0	1.000
Championship series totals (3 years)		18	63	7	19	2	0	6	9	.302	11	19	0	35	0	1	.972

WORLD SERIES RECORD

Year — Team (League)	Pos.	G	AB	R	H	2B	3B	HR	RBI	Avg.	BB	SO	SB	PO	A	E	Avg.
1995— Cleveland (A.L.)..........	OF	6	18	2	4	0	0	1	2	.222	4	5	1	8	0	0	1.000
1997— Cleveland (A.L.)..........	OF	7	26	3	4	0	0	2	6	.154	6	5	0	16	1	1	.944
World Series totals (2 years)		13	44	5	8	0	0	3	8	.182	10	10	1	24	1	1	.962

ALL-STAR GAME RECORD

Year — League	Pos.	AB	R	H	2B	3B	HR	RBI	Avg.	BB	SO	SB	PO	A	E	Avg.
1995— American	PH-OF	0	0	0	0	0	0	0	...	2	0	0	2	0	0	1.000
1998— American	OF	1	0	0	0	0	0	1	.000	0	0	0	0	0	0	...
All-Star Game totals (2 years)		1	0	0	0	0	0	1	.000	2	0	0	2	0	0	1.000

RAMIREZ, ROBERTO   P   ROCKIES

PERSONAL: Born August 17, 1972, in El Laurel, Veracruz, Mexico ... 5-11/170. ... Throws left, bats left. ... Full name: Roberto Sanchez Ramirez.
HIGH SCHOOL: Cetis 145 Technical (Veracruz, Mexico).
TRANSACTIONS/CAREER NOTES: Signed as non-drafted free agent by Mexico City Reds of Mexican League (1989). ... Contract sold by Mexico City to Pittsburgh Pirates organization (January 8, 1990). ... On Augusta disabled list (April 9-May 8, 1992). ... Loaned by Pirates organization to Mexico City Red Devils of Mexican League (May 8, 1992-remainder of season; February 18, 1993-entire season; May 6-August 29, 1994; and April 15, 1995-entire season). ... Granted free agency (October 16, 1995). ... Signed by New York Mets organization (March 5, 1997). ... Released by Mets organization prior to 1997 season. ... Signed by San Diego Padres organization (April 23, 1998). ... Granted free agency (October 15, 1998). ... Signed by Colorado Rockies (October 29, 1998).

Year — Team (League)	W	L	Pct.	ERA	G	GS	CG	ShO	Sv.	IP	H	R	ER	BB	SO
1989— Mex. City Reds (Mex.) ...	0	0	...	4.91	2	1	0	0	0	$3^2/3$	4	2	2	2	2
1990— GC Pirates (GCL)■.........	2	1	.667	0.53	11	3	0	0	0	$33^2/3$	20	4	2	18	27
1991— Welland (N.Y.-Penn)..........	2	6	.250	4.12	16	12	0	0	1	$74^1/3$	66	43	34	35	71
1992— M.C. Red Devils (Mex.)■.....	3	9	.250	5.98	19	13	6	0	0	$81^1/3$	102	61	54	47	57
1993— M.C. Red Devils (Mex.)	14	5	.737	3.40	25	24	8	4	0	$156^1/3$	136	65	59	65	100
1994— Carolina (Southern)■..........	0	1	.000	5.27	6	6	0	0	0	$27^1/3$	38	19	16	8	21
— M.C. Red Devils (Mex.)■.....	12	2	.857	2.68	16	16	7	4	0	111	103	39	33	32	82
1995— M.C. Red Devils (Mex.)	13	3	.813	2.56	20	20	8	3	0	$137^1/3$	125	50	39	35	70
1996— M.C. Red Devils (Mex.)	14	9	.609	2.84	28	*28	8	1	0	*$190^1/3$	179	70	60	76	132
1997— M.C. Red Devils (Mex.)	12	4	.750	3.76	24	24	1	0	0	$150^2/3$	157	71	63	64	82
1998— M.C. Red Devils (Mex.)	5	0	1.000	3.06	6	6	0	0	0	$35^1/3$	33	12	12	6	23
— Las Vegas (PCL)■	1	1	.500	2.43	26	1	0	0	2	$29^2/3$	23	14	8	10	33
— San Diego (N.L.)	1	0	1.000	6.14	21	0	0	0	0	$14^2/3$	12	13	10	12	17
Major league totals (1 year).......	1	0	1.000	6.14	21	0	0	0	0	$14^2/3$	12	13	10	12	17

RAMSAY, ROBERT   P   RED SOX

PERSONAL: Born December 3, 1973, in Vancouver, Wash. ... 6-5/230. ... Throws left, bats left. ... Full name: Robert Arthur Ramsay.
HIGH SCHOOL: Mountain View (Vancouver, Wash.).
COLLEGE: Washington State.
TRANSACTIONS/CAREER NOTES: Selected by Boston Red Sox organization in seventh round of free-agent draft (June 2, 1996).

Year Team (League)	W	L	Pct.	ERA	G	GS	CG	ShO	Sv.	IP	H	R	ER	BB	SO
1996— GC Red Sox (GCL)	0	1	.000	4.91	2	0	0	0	0	3²/₃	5	2	2	3	5
— Sarasota (Florida State)......	2	2	.500	6.09	12	7	0	0	0	34	42	23	23	27	32
1997— Sarasota (Florida State)......	9	9	.500	4.78	23	22	1	0	0	135²/₃	134	90	72	63	115
1998— Trenton (Eastern)	12	6	.667	3.49	27	27	1	1	0	162²/₃	137	67	63	50	166

R

RANDA, JOE   3B/2B   ROYALS

PERSONAL: Born December 18, 1969, in Milwaukee. ... 5-11/190. ... Bats right, throws right. ... Full name: Joseph Gregory Randa.
HIGH SCHOOL: Kettle-Moraine (Wales, Wis.).
JUNIOR COLLEGE: Indian River Community College (Fla.).
COLLEGE: Tennessee.
TRANSACTIONS/CAREER NOTES: Selected by California Angels organization in 30th round of free-agent draft (June 5, 1989); did not sign. ... Selected by Kansas City Royals organization in 11th round of free-agent draft (June 3, 1991). ... On Kansas City disabled list (May 5-27, 1996); included rehabilitation assignment to Omaha (May 23-27). ... Traded by Royals with P Jeff Granger, P Jeff Martin and P Jeff Wallace to Pittsburgh Pirates for SS Jay Bell and 1B Jeff King (December 13, 1996). ... On Pittsburgh disabled list (June 28-July 27, 1997); included rehabilitation assignment to Calgary (July 25-27). ... Selected by Arizona Diamondbacks in third round (57th pick overall) of expansion draft (November 18, 1997). ... Traded by Diamondbacks with P Matt Drews and 3B Gabe Alvarez to Detroit Tigers for 3B Travis Fryman (November 18, 1997). ... Traded by Tigers to New York Mets for P Willie Blair (December 4, 1998). ... Traded by Mets to Royals for OF Juan LeBron (December 10, 1998).
HONORS: Named Northwest League Most Valuable Player (1991).
STATISTICAL NOTES: Led Northwest League with 150 total bases and .438 on-base percentage in 1991. ... Led Northwest League third basemen with 182 total chances and 12 double plays in 1991. ... Led Southern League with 10 sacrifice flies in 1993. ... Led American Association third basemen with 433 total chances and 28 double plays in 1994.

							BATTING								FIELDING		
Year Team (League)	Pos.	G	AB	R	H	2B	3B	HR	RBI	Avg.	BB	SO	SB	PO	A	E	Avg.
1991— Eugene (Northwest) ...	3B	72	275	53	*93	20	2	11	59	.338	46	29	6	*57	*111	14	*.923
1992— Appleton (Midwest)....	3B	72	266	55	80	13	0	5	43	.301	34	37	6	53	137	12	.941
— Baseball City (FSL).....	3B-SS	51	189	22	52	7	0	1	12	.275	12	21	4	43	105	6	.961
1993— Memphis (Sou.)	3B	131	505	74	149	31	5	11	72	.295	39	64	8	*97	309	25	.942
1994— Omaha (A.A.).............	3B	127	455	65	125	27	2	10	51	.275	30	49	5	*85	*324	*24	.945
1995— Omaha (A.A.).............	3B	64	233	33	64	10	2	8	33	.275	22	33	2	42	96	6	.958
— Kansas City (A.L.)	3B-2B-DH	34	70	6	12	2	0	1	5	.171	6	17	0	15	44	3	.952
1996— Kansas City (A.L.)	3-2-1-DH	110	337	36	102	24	1	6	47	.303	26	47	13	80	160	10	.960
— Omaha (A.A.)	3B	3	9	1	1	0	1	0	0	.111	1	1	0	1	10	0	1.000
1997— Pittsburgh (N.L.)■	3B-2B	126	443	58	134	27	9	7	60	.302	41	64	4	91	288	21	.948
— Calgary (PCL)	3B	3	11	4	4	1	0	1	4	.364	3	4	0	2	7	1	.900
1998— Detroit (A.L.)■	3-2-DH-1	138	460	56	117	21	2	9	50	.254	41	70	8	102	252	7	.981
American League totals (3 years)		282	867	98	231	47	3	16	102	.266	73	134	21	197	456	20	.970
National League totals (1 year)		126	443	58	134	27	9	7	60	.302	41	64	4	91	288	21	.948
Major league totals (4 years)		408	1310	156	365	74	12	23	162	.279	114	198	25	288	744	41	.962

RANDALL, SCOTT   P   ROCKIES

PERSONAL: Born October 29, 1975, in Fullerton, Calif. ... 6-3/190. ... Throws right, bats right. ... Full name: Scott Phillip Randall.
HIGH SCHOOL: Dos Pueblos (Goleta, Calif.).
JUNIOR COLLEGE: Santa Barbara (Calif.) City.
COLLEGE: UC Santa Barbara.
TRANSACTIONS/CAREER NOTES: Selected by Colorado Rockies organization in 11th round of free-agent draft (June 1, 1995).

Year Team (League)	W	L	Pct.	ERA	G	GS	CG	ShO	Sv.	IP	H	R	ER	BB	SO
1995— Portland (Northwest)..........	7	3	.700	*1.99	15	•15	1	0	0	95	76	35	21	28	78
1996— Asheville (S. Atl.)..............	14	4	.778	2.74	24	24	1	1	0	154¹/₃	121	53	47	50	136
1997— Salem (Carolina)	9	10	.474	3.84	27	26	2	1	0	176	167	93	75	66	128
1998— New Haven (East.).............	10	•14	.417	3.83	29	•29	*7	2	0	*202	*210	•102	86	62	135

RANDOLPH, STEVE   P   DIAMONDBACKS

PERSONAL: Born May 1, 1974, in Okinawa, Japan. ... 6-3/185. ... Throws left, bats left. ... Full name: Stephen LaCharles Randolph.
HIGH SCHOOL: James Bowie (Simms, Texas).
JUNIOR COLLEGE: Galveston (Texas) College.
COLLEGE: Texas.
TRANSACTIONS/CAREER NOTES: Selected by New York Yankees organization in 18th round of free-agent draft (June 1, 1995). ... Selected by Arizona Diamondbacks from Yankees organization in Rule 5 major league draft (December 15, 1997).

Year Team (League)	W	L	Pct.	ERA	G	GS	CG	ShO	Sv.	IP	H	R	ER	BB	SO
1995— Tampa (Fla. St.).................	4	0	1.000	2.22	8	3	0	0	0	24¹/₃	11	7	6	16	34
— Oneonta (N.Y.-Penn)	0	3	.000	7.48	6	6	0	0	0	21²/₃	19	22	18	23	31
1996— Greensboro (S. Atl.)	4	7	.364	3.77	32	17	0	0	0	100¹/₃	64	46	42	96	111
1997— Tampa (Fla. St.).................	4	7	.364	3.87	34	13	1	0	1	95¹/₃	74	55	41	63	108
1998— High Desert (Calif.)■	4	4	.500	3.59	17	17	0	0	0	85¹/₃	71	44	34	42	104
— Tucson (PCL)	1	3	.250	3.18	17	1	0	0	0	22²/₃	16	11	8	19	23

RAPP, PAT P RED SOX

R

PERSONAL: Born July 13, 1967, in Jennings, La. ... 6-3/215. ... Throws right, bats right. ... Full name: Patrick Leland Rapp.
HIGH SCHOOL: Sulphur (La.).
JUNIOR COLLEGE: Hinds Community College (Miss.).
COLLEGE: Southern Mississippi.
TRANSACTIONS/CAREER NOTES: Selected by San Francisco Giants organization in 15th round of free-agent draft (June 5, 1989). ... Selected by Florida Marlins in first round (10th pick overall) of expansion draft (November 17, 1992). ... Traded by Marlins to Giants for P Brandon Leese and P Bobby Rector (July 18, 1997). ... On San Francisco disabled list (July 20-August 5, 1997). ... Granted free agency (December 21, 1997). ... Signed by Kansas City Royals organization (January 22, 1998). ... Granted free agency (December 21, 1998). ... Signed by Boston Red Sox (January 11, 1999).
STATISTICAL NOTES: Pitched 17-0 one-hit, complete-game victory against Colorado (September 17, 1995).
MISCELLANEOUS: Appeared in one game as pinch runner (1994). ... Holds Florida Marlins all-time records for most wins (37), most strikeouts (384) and most innings pitched (665.2).

Year Team (League)	W	L	Pct.	ERA	G	GS	CG	ShO	Sv.	IP	H	R	ER	BB	SO
1989— Pocatello (Pioneer)............	4	6	.400	5.30	16	12	1	0	0	73	90	54	43	29	40
1990— Clinton (Midwest)..............	14	10	.583	2.64	27	26	4	0	0	167 1/3	132	60	49	79	132
1991— San Jose (California)......	7	5	.583	2.50	16	15	1	0	0	90	88	41	25	37	73
— Shreveport (Texas)............	6	2	.750	2.69	10	10	1	1	0	60 1/3	52	23	18	22	46
1992— Phoenix (PCL).............	7	8	.467	3.05	39	12	2	1	3	121	115	54	41	40	79
— San Francisco (N.L.)......	0	2	.000	7.20	3	2	0	0	0	10	8	8	8	6	3
1993— Edmonton (PCL)■	8	3	.727	3.43	17	17	•4	1	0	107 2/3	89	45	41	34	93
— Florida (N.L.)......................	4	6	.400	4.02	16	16	1	0	0	94	101	49	42	39	57
1994— Florida (N.L.)......................	7	8	.467	3.85	24	23	2	1	0	133 1/3	132	67	57	69	75
1995— Charlotte (Int'l)......................	0	1	.000	6.00	1	1	0	0	0	6	6	4	4	1	5
— Florida (N.L.)......................	14	7	.667	3.44	28	28	3	2	0	167 1/3	158	72	64	76	102
1996— Florida (N.L.)..................	8	•16	.333	5.10	30	29	0	0	0	162 1/3	184	95	92	91	86
— Charlotte (Int'l)..................	1	1	.500	8.18	2	2	0	0	0	11	18	12	10	4	9
1997— Florida (N.L.)..................	4	6	.400	4.47	19	19	1	1	0	108 2/3	121	59	54	51	64
— San Francisco (N.L.)■..	1	2	.333	6.00	8	6	0	0	0	33	37	24	22	21	28
— Phoenix (PCL)........	2	0	1.000	3.60	3	3	0	0	0	15	16	6	6	9	6
1998— Kansas City (A.L.)■..	12	13	.480	5.30	32	32	1	1	0	188 1/3	208	117	111	107	132
A.L. totals (1 year)	12	13	.480	5.30	32	32	1	1	0	188 1/3	208	117	111	107	132
N.L. totals (6 years)	38	47	.447	4.31	128	123	7	4	0	708 2/3	741	374	339	353	415
Major league totals (7 years)	50	60	.455	4.52	160	155	8	5	0	897	949	491	450	460	547

RATH, FRED P TWINS

PERSONAL: Born January 5, 1973, in Dallas. ... 6-3/220. ... Throws right, bats right. ... Full name: Frederick Helsher Rath.
HIGH SCHOOL: Thomas Jefferson (Tampa).
COLLEGE: South Florida.
TRANSACTIONS/CAREER NOTES: Signed as non-drafted free agent by Minnesota Twins organization (June 6, 1995). ... Claimed on waivers by Colorado Rockies (June 25, 1998). ... Claimed on waivers by Twins (September 28, 1998).

Year Team (League)	W	L	Pct.	ERA	G	GS	CG	ShO	Sv.	IP	H	R	ER	BB	SO
1995— Elizabethton (Appal.)..........	1	1	.500	1.35	27	0	0	0	12	33 1/3	20	8	5	11	50
1996— Fort Wayne (Midw.)............	1	2	.333	1.51	32	0	0	0	14	41 2/3	26	12	7	10	63
— Fort Myers (Fla. St.)........	2	5	.286	2.79	22	0	0	0	4	29	25	10	9	10	29
1997— Fort Myers (Fla. St.)........	4	0	1.000	1.64	17	0	0	0	2	22	18	4	4	3	22
— New Britain (East.)...........	3	3	.500	2.68	33	0	0	0	12	50 1/3	43	17	15	13	33
— Salt Lake (PCL).................	0	1	.000	1.64	10	0	0	0	3	11	11	2	2	2	11
1998— Salt Lake (PCL).................	1	2	.333	4.55	27	0	0	0	8	31 2/3	35	16	16	8	15
— Colo. Springs (PCL)■..	5	1	.833	5.08	23	0	0	0	4	28 1/3	37	17	16	15	20
— Colorado (N.L.)	0	0	...	1.69	2	0	0	0	0	5 1/3	6	1	1	2	2
Major league totals (1 year)	0	0	...	1.69	2	0	0	0	0	5 1/3	6	1	1	2	2

RATH, GARY P TWINS

PERSONAL: Born January 10, 1973, in Gulfport, Miss. ... 6-2/186. ... Throws left, bats left. ... Full name: Gary Alfred Rath Jr.
HIGH SCHOOL: Long Beach (Miss.).
COLLEGE: Mississippi State.
TRANSACTIONS/CAREER NOTES: Selected by Los Angeles Dodgers organization in second round of free-agent draft (June 2, 1994). ... Granted free agency (November 30, 1998). ... Signed by Minnesota Twins organization (December 18, 1998).

Year Team (League)	W	L	Pct.	ERA	G	GS	CG	ShO	Sv.	IP	H	R	ER	BB	SO
1994— Vero Beach (FSL)	5	6	.455	2.73	13	11	0	0	0	62 2/3	55	26	19	23	50
1995— Albuquerque (PCL).............	3	5	.375	5.08	8	8	0	0	0	39	46	31	22	20	23
— San Antonio (Tex.)	•13	3	*.813	*2.77	18	16	3	1	0	117	96	42	36	48	81
1996— Albuquerque (PCL).............	10	11	.476	4.19	30	•30	1	1	0	180 1/3	177	97	84	*89	125
1997— Albuquerque (PCL).............	7	11	.389	6.05	24	24	0	0	0	132 1/3	177	107	89	49	100
1998— Albuquerque (PCL).............	9	7	.563	4.52	28	24	1	0	1	157 1/3	184	91	79	52	119
— Los Angeles (N.L.)	0	0	...	10.80	3	0	0	0	0	3 1/3	3	4	4	2	4
Major league totals (1 year)	0	0	...	10.80	3	0	0	0	0	3 1/3	3	4	4	2	4

RAY, KEN P ROYALS

PERSONAL: Born January 27, 1974, in Atlanta. ... 6-2/200. ... Throws right, bats right. ... Full name: Kenneth Alan Ray.
HIGH SCHOOL: Roswell (Ga.).
TRANSACTIONS/CAREER NOTES: Selected by Kansas City Royals organization in 18th round of free-agent draft (June 3, 1993). ... On disabled list (April 7-23, 1996).

Year — Team (League)	W	L	Pct.	ERA	G	GS	CG	ShO	Sv.	IP	H	R	ER	BB	SO
1993— GC Royals (GCL)..............	2	3	.400	2.28	13	7	0	0	0	47⅓	44	21	12	17	45
1994— Rockford (Midwest)	10	4	.714	1.82	27	18	0	0	3	128⅔	94	34	26	56	128
1995— Wichita (Texas)	4	5	.444	5.97	14	14	0	0	0	75⅓	83	55	50	46	53
— Wilmington (Caro.)............	6	4	.600	2.69	13	13	1	0	0	77	74	32	23	22	63
1996— Wichita (Texas)	4	12	.250	6.12	22	22	1	0	0	120⅔	151	94	82	57	79
1997— Omaha (Am. Assoc.)	5	12	.294	6.37	25	21	2	0	0	113	131	86	80	63	96
1998— Wichita (Texas)	10	5	.667	5.20	24	21	0	0	0	117⅔	149	79	68	47	71

REBOULET, JEFF   2B   ORIOLES

R

PERSONAL: Born April 30, 1964, in Dayton, Ohio. ... 6-0/175. ... Bats right, throws right. ... Full name: Jeffrey Allen Reboulet. ... Brother of Jim Reboulet, former second baseman in St. Louis Cardinals and Pittsburgh Pirates organizations. ... Name pronounced REB-uh-lay.

HIGH SCHOOL: Alter (Kettering, Ohio).

COLLEGE: Louisiana State.

TRANSACTIONS/CAREER NOTES: Selected by Houston Astros organization in 26th round of free-agent draft (June 3, 1985); did not sign. ... Selected by Minnesota Twins organization in 10th round of free-agent draft (June 2, 1986). ... Granted free agency (October 4, 1996). ... Signed by Baltimore Orioles organization (January 30, 1997).

STATISTICAL NOTES: Led Southern League shortstops with 602 total chances in 1988. ... Led Pacific Coast League with 17 sacrifice hits in 1991. ... Led Pacific Coast League shortstops with 649 total chances and 99 double plays in 1991.

Year — Team (League)	Pos.	G	AB	R	H	2B	3B	HR	RBI	Avg.	BB	SO	SB	PO	A	E	Avg.
1986— Visalia (California)......	SS	72	254	54	73	13	1	0	29	.287	54	33	14	118	188	20	.939
1987— Orlando (South.)	SS-2B-3B	129	422	52	108	15	1	1	35	.256	58	56	9	220	370	26	.958
1988— Orlando (South.)	SS	125	439	57	112	24	2	4	41	.255	53	55	18	*225	347	30	.950
— Portland (PCL)	2B-SS	4	12	0	1	0	0	0	1	.083	3	2	0	8	13	1	.955
1989— Portland (PCL)	S-2-3-0	26	65	9	16	1	0	0	3	.246	12	11	2	38	62	7	.935
— Orlando (South.)	SS-2B-OF	81	291	43	63	5	1	0	26	.216	49	33	11	129	228	22	.942
1990— Orlando (South.)	2-3-S-0-1	97	287	43	66	12	2	2	28	.230	57	37	10	131	230	12	.968
1991— Portland (PCL)	SS	134	391	50	97	27	3	3	46	.248	57	52	5	*202	415	*32	.951
1992— Portland (PCL)	SS	48	161	21	46	11	1	2	21	.286	35	18	3	72	141	7	.968
— Minnesota (A.L.) S-3-2-0-DH		73	137	15	26	7	1	1	16	.190	23	26	3	71	163	5	.979
1993— Minnesota (A.L.) S-3-2-0-DH		109	240	33	62	8	0	1	15	.258	35	37	5	122	215	6	.983
1994— Minnesota (A.L.) S-2-1-3-0-DH		74	189	28	49	11	1	3	23	.259	18	23	0	150	131	7	.976
1995— Minnesota (A.L.) S-3-1-2-C		87	216	39	63	11	0	4	23	.292	27	34	1	164	160	4	.988
1996— Minnesota (A.L.) S-3-2-1-0-DH		107	234	20	52	9	0	0	23	.222	25	34	4	138	114	2	.992
1997— Baltimore (A.L.)■......	2-S-3-0	99	228	26	54	9	0	4	27	.237	23	44	3	106	163	7	.975
1998— Baltimore (A.L.).........	2B-SS-3B	79	126	20	31	6	0	1	8	.246	19	34	0	51	120	6	.966
Major league totals (7 years)		628	1370	181	337	61	2	14	135	.246	170	232	16	802	1066	37	.981

DIVISION SERIES RECORD

Year — Team (League)	Pos.	G	AB	R	H	2B	3B	HR	RBI	Avg.	BB	SO	SB	PO	A	E	Avg.
1997— Baltimore (A.L.).........	2B	2	5	1	1	0	0	1	1	.200	0	2	0	2	3	0	1.000

CHAMPIONSHIP SERIES RECORD

Year — Team (League)	Pos.	G	AB	R	H	2B	3B	HR	RBI	Avg.	BB	SO	SB	PO	A	E	Avg.
1997— Baltimore (A.L.)..........	SS-PR	1	2	1	0	0	0	0	0	.000	0	1	0	0	0	0	...

REDMAN, MARK   P   TWINS

PERSONAL: Born January 5, 1974, in San Diego. ... 6-5/220. ... Throws left, bats left. ... Full name: Mark Allen Redman.

HIGH SCHOOL: Escondido (Calif.).

COLLEGE: The Master's (Calif.), then Oklahoma.

TRANSACTIONS/CAREER NOTES: Selected by Detroit Tigers organization in 41st round of free-agent draft (June 1, 1992); did not sign. ... Selected by Minnesota Twins organization in first round (13th pick overall) of free-agent draft (June 1, 1995). ... On Salt Lake disabled list (August 1-8, 1998).

Year — Team (League)	W	L	Pct.	ERA	G	GS	CG	ShO	Sv.	IP	H	R	ER	BB	SO
1995— Fort Myers (Fla. St.)...........	2	1	.667	2.76	8	5	0	0	0	32⅔	28	13	10	13	26
1996— Fort Myers (Fla. St.)...........	3	4	.429	1.85	13	13	0	0	0	82⅔	63	24	17	34	75
— New Britain (East.)............	7	7	.500	3.81	16	16	3	0	0	106⅓	101	51	45	50	96
— Salt Lake (PCL).................	0	0	...	9.00	1	1	0	0	0	4	7	4	4	2	4
1997— Salt Lake (PCL)..............	8	*15	.348	6.31	29	28	0	0	1	158⅓	204	*123	111	80	125
1998— New Britain (East.)	4	2	.667	1.52	8	8	0	0	0	47⅓	40	11	8	17	51
— Salt Lake (PCL)	6	7	.462	5.53	19	18	0	0	0	99⅓	111	75	61	41	88

REDMOND, MIKE   C   MARLINS

PERSONAL: Born May 5, 1971, in Seattle. ... 6-1/185. ... Bats right, throws right. ... Full name: Michael Patrick Redmond.

HIGH SCHOOL: Gonzaga Prep (Spokane, Wash.).

COLLEGE: Gonzaga.

TRANSACTIONS/CAREER NOTES: Signed as a non-drafted free agent by Florida Marlins organization (August 18, 1992). ... On Florida disabled list (August 24-September 8, 1998).

STATISTICAL NOTES: Led Eastern League catchers with 95 assists in 1995. ... Led Eastern League catchers with 906 total chances in 1996.

Year Team (League)	Pos.	G	AB	R	H	2B	3B	HR	RBI	Avg.	BB	SO	SB	PO	A	E	Avg.
1993—Kane County (Midw.)..	C	43	100	10	20	2	0	0	10	.200	6	17	2	213	26	1	.996
1994—Kane County (Midw.)..	C	92	306	39	83	10	0	1	24	.271	26	31	3	638	78	6	.992
—Brevard Co. (Fla. St.)..	C	12	42	4	11	4	0	0	2	.262	3	4	0	60	10	0	1.000
1995—Portland (Eastern)......	C-3B	105	333	37	85	11	1	3	39	.255	22	27	2	657	•95	6	.992
1996—Portland (Eastern)......	C	120	394	43	113	22	0	4	44	.287	26	45	3	*814	88	4	*.996
1997—Charlotte (Int'l)..........	C	22	61	8	13	5	1	1	2	.213	1	10	0	119	13	2	.985
—GC Marlins (GCL)........	DH	16	55	7	19	3	0	0	5	.345	9	5	2	...	...	...	...
—Brevard Co. (Fla. St.)..	1B	5	17	2	0	0	0	0	0	.000	2	2	0	8	0	0	1.000
1998—Portland (Eastern)......	C	8	28	7	9	4	0	1	7	.321	2	2	0	53	6	1	.983
—Charlotte (Int'l)..........	C	18	58	4	14	2	0	2	7	.241	0	3	00	101	20	0	1.000
—Florida (N.L.)	C	37	118	10	39	9	0	2	12	.331	5	16	0	216	25	2	.992
Major league totals (1 year)		37	118	10	39	9	0	2	12	.331	5	16	0	216	25	2	.992

REED, JEFF — C — ROCKIES

R

PERSONAL: Born November 12, 1962, in Joliet, Ill. ... 6-2/202. ... Bats left, throws right. ... Full name: Jeffrey Scott Reed. ... Brother of Curtis Reed, minor league outfielder (1977-84).

HIGH SCHOOL: West (Joliet, Ill.).

TRANSACTIONS/CAREER NOTES: Selected by Minnesota Twins organization in first round (12th pick overall) of free-agent draft (June 3, 1980). ... Traded by Twins organization with P Neal Heaton, P Al Cardwood and P Yorkis Perez to Montreal Expos for P Jeff Reardon and C Tom Nieto (February 3, 1987). ... On Montreal disabled list (April 20-May 25, 1987); included rehabilitation assignment to Indianapolis (May 19-25). ... Traded by Expos with OF Herm Winningham and P Randy St. Claire to Cincinnati Reds for OF Tracy Jones and P Pat Pacillo (July 13, 1988). ... On disabled list (July 1-19, 1991). ... On Cincinnati disabled list (April 26-September 1, 1992); included rehabilitation assignment to Nashville (August 17-September 1). ... Granted free agency (October 27, 1992). ... Signed by San Francisco Giants organization (January 15, 1993). ... On San Francisco disabled list (June 30-August 3, 1993); included rehabilitation assignment to San Jose (July 21-22 and July 30-August 3). ... Granted free agency (November 3, 1995). ... Signed by Colorado Rockies (December 18, 1995). ... Granted free agency (October 27, 1997). ... Re-signed by Rockies (November 18, 1997).

RECORDS: Holds modern N.L. single-inning record for most errors by catcher—3 (July 28, 1987, seventh inning).

STATISTICAL NOTES: Led California League catchers with 758 total chances and tied for lead with nine double plays in 1982. ... Led Southern League catchers with 714 total chances and 12 double plays in 1983. ... Led International League catchers with 720 total chances in 1985. ... Career major league grand slams: 2.

Year Team (League)	Pos.	G	AB	R	H	2B	3B	HR	RBI	Avg.	BB	SO	SB	PO	A	E	Avg.
1980—Elizabethton (App.).....	C	65	225	39	64	15	1	1	20	.284	51	23	2	269	*41	9	.972
1981—Wis. Rap. (Mid.)........	C	106	312	63	73	12	1	4	34	.234	86	36	4	547	*93	7	.989
—Orlando (South.)	C	3	4	0	1	0	0	0	0	.250	1	0	0	4	1	0	1.000
1982—Visalia (California)	C	125	395	69	130	19	2	5	54	.329	78	32	1	*642	•106	10	.987
1983—Orlando (South.)	C	118	379	52	100	16	5	6	45	.264	76	40	2	*618	•88	8	*.989
—Toledo (Int'l).............	C	14	41	5	7	1	1	0	3	.171	5	9	0	77	6	1	.988
1984—Minnesota (A.L.)	C	18	21	3	3	3	0	0	1	.143	2	6	0	41	2	1	.977
—Toledo (Int'l).............	C	94	301	30	80	16	3	3	35	.266	37	35	1	546	43	5	*.992
1985—Toledo (Int'l).............	C	122	404	53	100	15	3	5	36	.248	59	49	1	*627	*81	12	.983
—Minnesota (A.L.)	C	7	10	2	2	0	0	0	0	.200	0	3	0	9	3	0	1.000
1986—Minnesota (A.L.)	C	68	165	13	39	6	1	2	9	.236	16	19	1	332	19	2	.994
—Toledo (Int'l).............	C	25	71	10	22	5	3	1	14	.310	17	9	0	108	22	2	.985
1987—Montreal (N.L.)■.......	C	75	207	15	44	11	0	1	21	.213	12	20	0	357	36	12	.970
—Indianapolis (A.A.)......	C	5	17	0	3	0	0	0	0	.176	1	2	0	27	2	0	1.000
1988—Montreal (N.L.)........	C	43	123	10	27	3	2	0	9	.220	13	22	1	197	20	1	.995
—Indianapolis (A.A.)......	C	8	22	1	7	3	0	0	1	.318	2	2	0	30	11	0	1.000
—Cincinnati (N.L.)■.......	C	49	142	10	33	6	0	1	7	.232	15	19	0	271	18	2	.993
1989—Cincinnati (N.L.)	C	102	287	16	64	11	0	3	23	.223	34	46	0	504	50	7	.988
1990—Cincinnati (N.L.)	C	72	175	12	44	8	1	3	16	.251	24	26	0	358	26	5	.987
1991—Cincinnati (N.L.)	C	91	270	20	72	15	2	3	31	.267	23	38	0	527	29	5	.991
1992—Nashville (A.A.)	C	14	25	1	6	1	0	1	2	.240	2	7	0	47	4	0	1.000
—Cincinnati (N.L.)	C	15	25	2	4	0	0	0	2	.160	1	4	0	29	2	0	1.000
1993—San Fran. (N.L.)■.......	C	66	119	10	31	3	0	6	12	.261	16	22	0	180	14	0	1.000
—San Jose (Calif.)........	C	4	10	2	5	1	0	0	2	.500	1	0	0	19	2	0	1.000
1994—San Francisco (N.L.) ..	C	50	103	11	18	3	0	1	7	.175	11	21	0	138	9	1	.993
1995—San Francisco (N.L.) ..	C	66	113	12	30	2	0	0	9	.265	20	17	0	175	21	1	.995
1996—Colorado (N.L.)■	C	116	341	34	97	20	1	8	37	.284	43	65	2	546	51	11	.982
1997—Colorado (N.L.)	C	90	256	43	76	10	0	17	40	.297	35	55	2	428	37	6	.987
1998—Colorado (N.L.)	C	113	259	43	75	17	1	9	39	.290	37	57	0	452	27	7	.986
American League totals (3 years)		93	196	18	44	9	1	2	10	.224	18	28	1	382	24	3	.993
National League totals (12 years)		948	2420	238	615	109	7	52	260	.254	284	412	5	4162	340	58	.987
Major league totals (15 years)		1041	2616	256	659	118	8	54	270	.252	302	440	6	4544	364	61	.988

CHAMPIONSHIP SERIES RECORD

Year Team (League)	Pos.	G	AB	R	H	2B	3B	HR	RBI	Avg.	BB	SO	SB	PO	A	E	Avg.
1990—Cincinnati (N.L.)	C	4	7	0	0	0	0	0	0	.000	2	0	0	24	1	0	1.000

WORLD SERIES RECORD

NOTES: Member of World Series championship team (1990).

Year Team (League)	Pos.	G	AB	R	H	2B	3B	HR	RBI	Avg.	BB	SO	SB	PO	A	E	Avg.
1990—Cincinnati (N.L.).........							Did not play.										

PERSONAL: Born August 16, 1965, in Huntington, W.Va. ... 6-1/195. ... Throws right, bats right. ... Full name: Richard Allen Reed.
HIGH SCHOOL: Huntington (W.Va.).
COLLEGE: Marshall.
TRANSACTIONS/CAREER NOTES: Selected by Pittsburgh Pirates organization in 26th round of free-agent draft (June 2, 1986). ... On Buffalo disabled list (May 2-13, 1991). ... Granted free agency (April 3, 1992). ... Signed by Kansas City Royals organization (April 4, 1992). ... Granted free agency (August 5, 1993). ... Signed by Texas Rangers organization (August 11, 1993). ... Claimed on waivers by Cincinnati Reds (May 13, 1994). ... On Indianapolis disabled list (May 29-June 9, 1995). ... Granted free agency (October 16, 1995). ... Signed by New York Mets organization (November 7, 1995).
HONORS: Named American Association Most Valuable Pitcher (1991).

Year	Team (League)	W	L	Pct.	ERA	G	GS	CG	ShO	Sv.	IP	H	R	ER	BB	SO
1986—	GC Pirates (GCL)	0	2	.000	3.75	8	3	0	0	0	24	20	12	10	6	15
	—Macon (S. Atl.)	0	0	. . .	2.84	1	1	0	0	0	6 1/3	5	3	2	2	1
1987—	Macon (S. Atl.)	8	4	.667	2.50	46	0	0	0	7	93 2/3	80	38	26	29	92
1988—	Salem (Carolina)	6	2	.750	2.74	15	8	4	1	0	72 1/3	56	28	22	17	73
	—Harrisburg (Eastern)	1	0	1.000	1.13	2	2	0	0	0	16	11	2	2	2	17
	—Buffalo (A.A.)	5	2	.714	1.64	10	9	3	2	0	77	62	15	14	12	50
	—Pittsburgh (N.L.)	1	0	1.000	3.00	2	2	0	0	0	12	10	4	4	2	6
1989—	Buffalo (A.A.)	9	8	.529	3.72	20	20	3	0	0	125 2/3	130	58	52	28	75
	—Pittsburgh (N.L.)	1	4	.200	5.60	15	7	0	0	0	54 2/3	62	35	34	11	34
1990—	Buffalo (A.A.)	7	4	.636	3.46	15	15	2	2	0	91	82	37	35	21	63
	—Pittsburgh (N.L.)	2	3	.400	4.36	13	8	1	1	1	53 2/3	62	32	26	12	27
1991—	Buffalo (A.A.)	*14	4	*.778	*2.15	25	25	•5	2	0	167 2/3	151	45	40	26	102
	—Pittsburgh (N.L.)	0	0	. . .	10.38	1	1	0	0	0	4 1/3	8	6	5	1	2
1992—	Omaha (Am. Assoc.)■	5	4	.556	4.35	11	10	3	0	1	62	67	33	30	12	35
	—Kansas City (A.L.)	3	7	.300	3.68	19	18	1	1	0	100 1/3	105	47	41	20	49
1993—	Omaha (Am. Assoc.)	11	4	.733	3.09	19	19	3	*2	0	128 1/3	116	48	44	14	58
	—Kansas City (A.L.)	0	0	. . .	9.82	1	0	0	0	0	3 2/3	6	4	4	1	3
	—Oklahoma City (A.A.)■	1	3	.250	4.19	5	5	1	0	0	34 1/3	43	20	16	2	21
	—Texas (A.L.)	1	0	1.000	2.25	2	0	0	0	0	4	6	1	1	1	2
1994—	Oklahoma City (A.A.)	1	1	.500	3.86	2	2	0	0	0	11 2/3	10	5	5	0	8
	—Texas (A.L.)	1	1	.500	5.94	4	3	0	0	0	16 2/3	17	13	11	7	12
	—Indianapolis (A.A.)■	9	5	.643	4.68	21	21	3	1	0	140 1/3	162	80	73	19	79
1995—	Indianapolis (A.A.)	11	4	.733	3.33	22	21	3	1	0	135	127	60	50	26	92
	—Cincinnati (N.L.)	0	0	. . .	5.82	4	3	0	0	0	17	18	12	11	3	10
1996—	Norfolk (Int'l)■	8	10	.444	3.16	28	28	1	0	0	182	164	72	64	33	128
1997—	New York (N.L.)	13	9	.591	2.89	33	31	2	0	0	208 1/3	186	76	67	31	113
1998—	New York (N.L.)	16	11	.593	3.48	31	31	2	1	0	212 1/3	208	84	82	29	153
A.L. totals (3 years)		5	8	.385	4.11	26	21	1	1	0	124 2/3	134	65	57	29	66
N.L. totals (7 years)		33	27	.550	3.67	99	83	5	2	1	562 1/3	554	249	229	89	345
Major league totals (10 years)		38	35	.521	3.75	125	104	6	3	1	687	688	314	286	118	411

ALL-STAR GAME RECORD

Year	League	W	L	Pct.	ERA	GS	CG	ShO	Sv.	IP	H	R	ER	BB	SO
1998—	National							Did not play.							

PERSONAL: Born March 11, 1966, in Los Angeles. ... 6-2/212. ... Throws right, bats right. ... Full name: Steven Vincent Reed.
HIGH SCHOOL: Chatsworth (Calif.).
COLLEGE: Lewis-Clark State College (Idaho).
TRANSACTIONS/CAREER NOTES: Signed as non-drafted free agent by San Francisco Giants organization (June 24, 1988). ... On disabled list (July 17-August 13, 1990). ... Selected by Colorado Rockies in third round (60th pick overall) of expansion draft (November 17, 1992). ... Granted free agency (December 21, 1997). ... Signed by San Francisco Giants (December 24, 1997). ... Traded by Giants with OF Jacob Cruz to Cleveland Indians for P Jose Mesa, IF Shawon Dunston and P Alvin Morman (July 23, 1998).
RECORDS: Holds Colorado Rockies all-time record for most games pitched (329).

Year	Team (League)	W	L	Pct.	ERA	G	GS	CG	ShO	Sv.	IP	H	R	ER	BB	SO
1988—	Pocatello (Pioneer)	4	1	.800	2.54	31	0	0	0	*13	46	42	20	13	8	49
1989—	Clinton (Midwest)	5	3	.625	1.05	60	0	0	0	26	94 2/3	54	16	11	38	104
	—San Jose (California)	0	0	. . .	0.00	2	0	0	0	0	2	0	0	0	1	3
1990—	Shreveport (Texas)	3	1	.750	1.64	45	1	0	0	8	60 1/3	53	20	11	20	59
1991—	Shreveport (Texas)	2	0	1.000	0.83	15	0	0	0	7	21 2/3	17	2	2	3	26
	—Phoenix (PCL)	2	3	.400	4.31	41	0	0	0	6	56 1/3	62	33	27	12	46
1992—	Shreveport (Texas)	1	0	1.000	0.62	27	0	0	0	23	29	18	3	2	0	33
	—Phoenix (PCL)	0	1	.000	3.48	29	0	0	0	20	31	27	13	12	10	30
	—San Francisco (N.L.)	1	0	1.000	2.30	18	0	0	0	0	15 2/3	13	5	4	3	11
1993—	Colorado (N.L.)■	9	5	.643	4.48	64	0	0	0	3	84 1/3	80	47	42	30	51
	—Colo. Springs (PCL)	0	0	. . .	0.00	11	0	0	0	7	12 1/3	8	1	0	3	10
1994—	Colorado (N.L.)	3	2	.600	3.94	*61	0	0	0	3	64	79	33	28	26	51
1995—	Colorado (N.L.)	5	2	.714	2.14	71	0	0	0	3	84	61	24	20	21	79
1996—	Colorado (N.L.)	4	3	.571	3.96	70	0	0	0	0	75	66	38	33	19	51
1997—	Colorado (N.L.)	4	6	.400	4.04	63	0	0	0	0	62 1/3	49	28	28	27	43
1998—	San Francisco (N.L.)■	2	1	.667	1.48	50	0	0	0	1	54 2/3	30	10	9	19	50
	—Cleveland (A.L.)■	2	2	.500	6.66	20	0	0	0	0	25 2/3	26	19	19	8	23
A.L. totals (1 year)		2	2	.500	6.66	20	0	0	0	0	25 2/3	26	19	19	8	23
N.L. totals (7 years)		28	19	.596	3.35	397	0	0	0	16	440	378	185	164	145	336
Major league totals (7 years)		30	21	.588	3.54	417	0	0	0	16	465 2/3	404	204	183	153	359

DIVISION SERIES RECORD

Year	Team (League)	W	L	Pct.	ERA	G	GS	CG	ShO	Sv.	IP	H	R	ER	BB	SO
1995—	Colorado (N.L.)	0	0	...	0.00	3	0	0	0	0	2 2/3	2	0	0	1	3
1998—	Cleveland (A.L.)	1	0	1.000	40.50	2	0	0	0	0	2/3	1	3	3	1	1
Div. series totals (2 years)		**1**	**0**	**1.000**	**8.10**	**5**	**0**	**0**	**0**	**0**	**3 1/3**	**3**	**3**	**3**	**2**	**4**

CHAMPIONSHIP SERIES RECORD

Year	Team (League)	W	L	Pct.	ERA	G	GS	CG	ShO	Sv.	IP	H	R	ER	BB	SO
1998—	Cleveland (A.L.)	0	0	...	0.00	3	0	0	0	0	1 2/3	0	0	0	1	0

REESE, POKEY   IF   REDS

PERSONAL: Born June 10, 1973, in Columbia, S.C. ... 5-11/180. ... Bats right, throws right. ... Full name: Calvin Reese Jr.
HIGH SCHOOL: Lower Richland (Hopkins, S.C.).
TRANSACTIONS/CAREER NOTES: Selected by Cincinnati Reds organization in first round (20th pick overall) of free-agent draft (June 3, 1991). ... On disabled list (June 23-July 22, 1995; September 17, 1996-remainder of season; and July 31, 1998-remainder of season).
RECORDS: Shares N.L. record for most errors by shortstop in opening game of season (nine-inning game) since 1900—4 (March 31, 1998).

							BATTING								FIELDING		
Year	Team (League)	Pos.	G	AB	R	H	2B	3B	HR	RBI	Avg.	BB	SO	SB	PO	A	E	Avg.
1991—	Princeton (Appal.)	SS	62	231	30	55	8	3	3	27	.238	23	44	10	93	146	*31	.885
1992—	Char., W.Va. (SAL.)	SS	106	380	50	102	19	3	6	53	.268	24	75	19	181	287	34	.932
1993—	Chattanooga (Sou.)	SS	102	345	35	73	17	4	3	37	.212	23	77	8	181	300	25	.951
1994—	Chattanooga (Sou.)	SS	134	484	77	130	23	4	12	49	.269	43	75	21	*221	362	38	.939
1995—	Indianapolis (A.A.)......	SS	89	343	51	82	21	1	10	46	.239	36	81	8	131	258	27	.935
1996—	Indianapolis (A.A.)......	SS-3B	79	280	26	65	16	0	1	23	.232	21	46	5	131	239	22	.944
1997—	Cincinnati (N.L.)	SS-2B-3B	128	397	48	87	15	0	4	26	.219	31	82	25	182	284	15	.969
	Indianapolis (A.A.)......	SS	17	72	12	17	2	0	4	11	.236	9	12	4	43	42	3	.966
1998—	Cincinnati (N.L.)	3B-SS-2B	59	133	20	34	2	2	1	16	.256	14	28	3	50	78	8	.941
Major league totals (2 years)			187	530	68	121	17	2	5	42	.228	45	110	28	232	362	23	.963

REKAR, BRYAN   P   DEVIL RAYS

PERSONAL: Born June 3, 1972, in Oak Lawn, Ill. ... 6-3/210. ... Throws right, bats right. ... Full name: Bryan Robert Rekar. ... Cousin of Pete Bercich, linebacker, Minnesota Vikings; and nephew of Bob Bercich, defensive back with Dallas Cowboys (1960 and 1961).
HIGH SCHOOL: Providence Catholic (New Lenox, Ill.).
COLLEGE: Bradley.
TRANSACTIONS/CAREER NOTES: Selected by Colorado Rockies organization in second round of free-agent draft (June 3, 1993). ... Selected by Tampa Bay Devil Rays in second round (38th pick overall) of expansion draft (November 18, 1997). ... On Tampa Bay disabled list (March 19-July 6, 1998); included rehabilitation assignments to St. Petersburg (May 16-25 and June 25-July 4) and Durham (May 26-June 1 and July 4-6).

Year	Team (League)	W	L	Pct.	ERA	G	GS	CG	ShO	Sv.	IP	H	R	ER	BB	SO
1993—	Bend (Northwest)	3	5	.375	4.08	13	13	1	0	0	75	81	36	34	18	59
1994—	Central Valley (Cal.)	6	6	.500	3.48	22	19	0	0	0	111 1/3	120	52	43	31	91
1995—	New Haven (East.)	6	3	.667	2.13	12	12	1	1	0	80 1/3	65	28	19	16	80
	Colo. Springs (PCL)	4	2	.667	1.49	7	7	2	1	0	48 1/3	29	10	8	13	39
	Colorado (N.L.)	4	6	.400	4.98	15	14	1	0	0	85	95	51	47	24	60
1996—	Colo. Springs (PCL)	8	8	.500	4.46	19	19	0	0	0	123	138	68	61	36	75
	Colorado (N.L.)	2	4	.333	8.95	14	11	0	0	0	58 1/3	87	61	58	26	25
1997—	Colo. Springs (PCL)	10	9	.526	5.46	28	25	0	0	0	145	169	96	88	39	116
	Colorado (N.L.)	1	0	1.000	5.79	2	2	0	0	0	9 1/3	11	7	6	6	4
1998—	St. Petersburg (FSL)■	0	0	...	0.69	4	4	0	0	0	13	6	2	1	2	15
	Durham (International)......	0	1	.000	3.27	3	3	0	0	0	11	10	4	4	2	9
	Tampa Bay (A.L.).............	2	8	.200	4.98	16	15	1	0	0	86 2/3	95	56	48	21	55
A.L. totals (1 year)		2	8	.200	4.98	16	15	1	0	0	86 2/3	95	56	48	21	55
N.L. totals (3 years)		7	10	.412	6.54	31	27	1	0	0	152 2/3	193	119	111	56	89
Major league totals (4 years)		9	18	.333	5.98	47	42	2	0	0	239 1/3	288	175	159	77	144

RELAFORD, DESI   SS   PHILLIES

PERSONAL: Born September 16, 1973, in Valdosta, Ga. ... 5-9/175. ... Bats both, throws right. ... Full name: Desmond Lamont Relaford.
HIGH SCHOOL: Sandalwood (Jacksonville).
TRANSACTIONS/CAREER NOTES: Selected by Seattle Mariners organization in fourth round of free-agent draft (June 3, 1991). ... Traded by Mariners to Philadelphia Phillies for P Terry Mulholland (July 31, 1996).
STATISTICAL NOTES: Led California League shortstops with 601 total chances in 1992. ... Led Southern League shortstops with 35 errors in 1993. ... Led International League shortstops with 587 total chances and 81 double plays in 1997.

							BATTING								FIELDING		
Year	Team (League)	Pos.	G	AB	R	H	2B	3B	HR	RBI	Avg.	BB	SO	SB	PO	A	E	Avg.
1991—	Ariz. Mariners (Ariz.) ..	SS-2B	46	163	36	44	7	3	0	18	.270	22	24	17	58	126	24	.885
1992—	Peninsula (Caro.)	SS	130	445	53	96	18	1	3	34	.216	39	88	27	167	*382	*52	.913
1993—	Jacksonville (Sou.).....	SS-2B-3B	133	472	49	115	16	4	8	47	.244	50	103	16	157	386	†38	.935
1994—	Jacksonville (Sou.)	SS	37	143	24	29	7	3	3	11	.203	22	28	10	71	119	4	.979
	Riverside (Calif.).........	SS	99	374	95	116	27	5	5	59	.310	78	78	27	125	296	36	.921
1995—	Port City (Southern) ...	SS-2B	90	352	51	101	11	2	7	27	.287	41	58	25	134	276	31	.930
	Tacoma (PCL)	2B-SS	30	113	20	27	5	1	2	7	.239	13	24	6	52	93	6	.960
1996—	Tacoma (PCL)	2B-SS	93	317	27	65	12	0	4	32	.205	23	58	10	174	306	20	.960
	Scran./W.B. (Int'l)■.......	SS	21	85	12	20	4	1	1	11	.235	8	19	7	25	65	6	.938
	Philadelphia (N.L.)......	SS-2B	15	40	2	7	2	0	0	1	.175	3	9	1	21	26	2	.959

Year Team (League)	Pos.	G	AB	R	H	2B	3B	HR	RBI	Avg.	BB	SO	SB	PO	A	E	Avg.
1997— Scran./W.B. (Int'l).......	SS	131	517	82	138	34	4	9	53	.267	43	77	29	180	*373	34	.942
— Philadelphia (N.L.)......	SS	15	38	3	7	1	2	0	6	.184	5	6	3	12	31	1	.977
1998— Philadelphia (N.L.)......	SS	142	494	45	121	25	3	5	41	.245	33	87	9	189	380	24	.960
Major league totals (3 years)		172	572	50	135	28	5	5	48	.236	41	102	13	222	437	27	.961

REMLINGER, MIKE   P   BRAVES

PERSONAL: Born March 26, 1966, in Middletown, N.Y. ... 6-1/210. ... Throws left, bats left. ... Full name: Michael John Remlinger. ... Name pronounced REM-lynn-jer.

HIGH SCHOOL: Carver (Plymouth, Mass.).

COLLEGE: Dartmouth.

TRANSACTIONS/CAREER NOTES: Selected by San Francisco Giants organization in first round (16th pick overall) of free-agent draft (June 2, 1987). ... On disabled list (April 30, 1988-remainder of season). ... Traded by Giants with OF Kevin Mitchell to Seattle Mariners for P Bill Swift, P Mike Jackson and P Dave Burba (December 11, 1991). ... On Jacksonville disabled list (July 30, 1992-remainder of season). ... Granted free agency (October 15, 1993). ... Signed by New York Mets organization (November 22, 1993). ... Traded by Mets to Cincinnati Reds for OF Cobi Cradle (May 11, 1995). ... Granted free agency (October 6, 1995). ... Re-signed by Reds (October 22, 1995). ... Traded by Reds to Kansas City Royals as part of a three-team deal in which Reds sent SS Luis Ordaz to St. Louis Cardinals for OF Andre King. Royals then sent OF Miguel Mejia to Cardinals to complete deal (December 4, 1995). ... Claimed on waivers by Reds (April 4, 1996). ... Traded by Reds with 2B Bret Boone to Atlanta Braves for P Denny Neagle, OF Michael Tucker and P Rob Bell (November 10, 1998).

RECORDS: Shares major league record for pitching shutout in first major league game (June 15, 1991).

STATISTICAL NOTES: Led American Association with 18 wild pitches in 1996. ... Led N.L. with 12 wild pitches in 1997.

MISCELLANEOUS: Appeared in two games as pinch runner (1997).

Year Team (League)	W	L	Pct.	ERA	G	GS	CG	ShO	Sv.	IP	H	R	ER	BB	SO
1987— Everett (Northwest)............	0	0	. . .	3.60	2	1	0	0	0	5	1	2	2	5	11
— Clinton (Midwest)............	2	1	.667	3.30	6	5	0	0	0	30	21	12	11	14	43
— Shreveport (Texas)............	4	2	.667	2.36	6	6	0	0	0	34 1/3	14	11	9	22	51
1988— Shreveport (Texas)............	1	0	1.000	0.69	3	3	0	0	0	13	7	4	1	4	18
1989— Shreveport (Texas)............	4	6	.400	2.98	16	16	0	0	0	90 2/3	68	43	30	73	92
— Phoenix (PCL)............	1	6	.143	9.21	11	10	0	0	0	43	51	47	44	52	28
1990— Shreveport (Texas)............	9	11	.450	3.90	25	25	2	1	0	147 2/3	149	82	64	72	75
1991— Phoenix (PCL)............	5	5	.500	6.38	19	19	1	1	0	108 2/3	134	86	77	59	68
— San Francisco (N.L.)	2	1	.667	4.37	8	6	1	1	0	35	36	17	17	20	19
1992— Calgary (PCL)■............	1	7	.125	6.65	21	11	0	0	0	70 1/3	97	65	52	48	24
— Jacksonville (Southern)......	1	1	.500	3.46	5	5	0	0	0	26	25	15	10	11	21
1993— Calgary (PCL)............	4	3	.571	5.53	19	18	0	0	0	84 2/3	100	57	52	52	51
— Jacksonville (Southern)......	1	3	.250	6.58	7	7	0	0	0	39 2/3	40	30	29	19	23
1994— Norfolk (Int'l)■............	2	4	.333	3.14	12	9	0	0	0	63	57	29	22	25	45
— New York (N.L.)............	1	5	.167	4.61	10	9	0	0	0	54 2/3	55	30	28	35	33
1995— New York (N.L.)............	0	1	.000	6.35	5	0	0	0	0	5 2/3	7	5	4	2	6
— Cincinnati (N.L.)■............	0	0	. . .	9.00	2	0	0	0	0	1	2	1	1	3	1
— Indianapolis (A.A.)............	5	3	.625	4.05	41	1	0	0	0	46 2/3	40	24	21	32	58
1996— Indianapolis (A.A.)............	4	3	.571	2.52	28	13	0	0	0	89 1/3	64	29	25	44	97
— Cincinnati (N.L.)............	0	1	.000	5.60	19	4	0	0	0	27 1/3	24	17	17	19	19
1997— Cincinnati (N.L.)............	8	8	.500	4.14	69	12	2	0	2	124	100	61	57	60	145
1998— Cincinnati (N.L.)............	8	15	.348	4.82	35	28	1	1	0	164 1/3	164	96	88	87	144
Major league totals (6 years)	19	31	.380	4.63	148	59	4	2	2	412	388	227	212	226	367

RENTERIA, EDGAR   SS   CARDINALS

PERSONAL: Born August 7, 1975, in Barranquilla, Colombia. ... 6-1/160. ... Bats right, throws right. ... Full name: Edgar Enrique Renteria. ... Brother of Edinson Renteria, infielder in Houston Astros and Florida Marlins organizations (1985-1994).

HIGH SCHOOL: Instituto Los Alpes (Barranquilla, Colombia).

TRANSACTIONS/CAREER NOTES: Signed as non-drafted free agent by Florida Marlins organization (February 14, 1992). ... On Florida disabled list (June 24-July 11, 1996); included rehabilitation assignment to Charlotte (July 3-11). ... On disabled list (August 25-September 9, 1998). ... Traded by Marlins to St. Louis Cardinals for P Braden Looper, P Armando Almanza and SS Pablo Ozuna (December 14, 1998).

STATISTICAL NOTES: Had 22-game hitting streak (July 25-August 16, 1996). ... Led N.L. in sacrifice hits with 19 in 1997. ... Led N.L. in caught stealing with 22 in 1998.

Year Team (League)	Pos.	G	AB	R	H	2B	3B	HR	RBI	Avg.	BB	SO	SB	PO	A	E	Avg.
1992— GC Marlins (GCL).......	SS	43	163	25	47	8	1	0	9	.288	8	29	10	56	152	*24	.897
1993— Kane County (Midw.)..	SS	116	384	40	78	8	0	1	35	.203	35	94	7	•173	306	34	.934
1994— Brevard Co. (Fla. St.)..	SS	128	439	46	111	15	1	0	36	.253	35	56	6	167	372	23	.959
1995— Portland (Eastern)......	SS	135	508	70	147	15	7	7	68	.289	32	85	30	179	379	33	.944
1996— Charlotte (Int'l)...........	SS	35	132	17	37	8	0	2	16	.280	9	17	10	48	114	7	.959
— Florida (N.L.)............	SS	106	431	68	133	18	3	5	31	.309	33	68	16	163	344	11	.979
1997— Florida (N.L.).............	SS	154	617	90	171	21	3	4	52	.277	45	108	32	*242	415	17	.975
1998— Florida (N.L.).............	SS	133	517	79	146	18	2	3	31	.282	48	78	41	194	372	20	.966
Major league totals (3 years)		393	1565	237	450	57	8	12	114	.288	126	254	89	599	1131	48	.973

DIVISION SERIES RECORD

Year Team (League)	Pos.	G	AB	R	H	2B	3B	HR	RBI	Avg.	BB	SO	SB	PO	A	E	Avg.
1997— Florida (N.L.).............	SS	3	13	1	2	0	0	0	1	.154	2	4	0	9	11	2	.909

CHAMPIONSHIP SERIES RECORD

Year Team (League)	Pos.	G	AB	R	H	2B	3B	HR	RBI	Avg.	BB	SO	SB	PO	A	E	Avg.
						BATTING									FIELDING		
1997—Florida (N.L.).............	SS	6	22	4	5	1	0	0	0	.227	3	6	1	14	15	0	1.000

RECORDS: Holds record for most strikeouts in one inning—2 (October 23, 1997, sixth inning).
NOTES: Member of World Series championship team (1997).

WORLD SERIES RECORD

Year Team (League)	Pos.	G	AB	R	H	2B	3B	HR	RBI	Avg.	BB	SO	SB	PO	A	E	Avg.
						BATTING									FIELDING		
1997—Florida (N.L.).............	SS	7	31	3	9	2	0	0	3	.290	3	5	0	12	26	1	.974

ALL-STAR GAME RECORD

Year League	Pos.	AB	R	H	2B	3B	HR	RBI	Avg.	BB	SO	SB	PO	A	E	Avg.
						BATTING								FIELDING		
1998—National.....................	SS	1	1	0	0	0	0	0	.000	0	0	0	0	3	0	1.000

R

REYES, AL   P   BREWERS

PERSONAL: Born April 10, 1971, in San Cristobal, Dominican Republic. ... 6-1/209. ... Throws right, bats right. ... Full name: Rafael Alberto Reyes.
HIGH SCHOOL: Francisco del Rosario Sanche (Santo Domingo, Dominican Republic).
TRANSACTIONS/CAREER NOTES: Signed as non-drafted free agent by Montreal Expos organization (February 17, 1988). ... On disabled list (May 23, 1991-remainder of season). ... Selected by Milwaukee Brewers from Expos organization in Rule 5 major league draft (December 5, 1994). ... On disabled list (July 19, 1995-remainder of season). ... On New Orleans disabled list (April 4-August 2, 1996). ... On Milwaukee disabled list (July 25-September 8, 1998); included rehabilitation assignment to Louisville (September 1-8).

Year Team (League)	W	L	Pct.	ERA	G	GS	CG	ShO	Sv.	IP	H	R	ER	BB	SO
1989— DSL Expos (DSL)	3	4	.429	2.79	12	10	1	0	0	71	68	36	22	33	49
1990— W.P. Beach (FSL)..............	5	4	.556	4.74	16	10	0	0	1	57	58	32	30	32	47
1991— Rockford (Midwest)	0	1	.000	5.56	3	3	0	0	0	11 1/3	14	8	7	2	10
1992— Albany (S. Atl.)...............	0	2	.000	3.95	27	0	0	0	4	27 1/3	24	14	12	13	29
1993— Burlington (Midw.)	7	6	.538	2.68	53	0	0	0	11	74	52	33	22	26	80
1994— Harrisburg (Eastern)	2	2	.500	3.25	60	0	0	0	*35	69 1/3	68	26	25	13	60
1995— Milwaukee (A.L.)■..........	1	1	.500	2.43	27	0	0	0	1	33 1/3	19	9	9	18	29
1996— Beloit (Midwest)	1	0	1.000	1.83	13	0	0	0	0	19 2/3	17	7	4	6	22
— Milwaukee (A.L.)	1	0	1.000	7.94	5	0	0	0	0	5 2/3	8	5	5	2	2
1997— Tucson (PCL)	2	4	.333	5.02	38	0	0	0	7	57 1/3	52	39	32	34	70
— Milwaukee (A.L.)	1	2	.333	5.46	19	0	0	0	1	29 2/3	32	19	18	9	28
1998— Milwaukee (N.L.)	5	1	.833	3.95	50	0	0	0	0	57	55	26	25	31	58
— Louisville (Int'l)	0	1	.000	8.31	3	2	0	0	0	4 1/3	5	5	4	2	5
A.L. totals (3 years)	3	3	.500	4.19	51	0	0	0	2	68 2/3	59	33	32	29	59
N.L. totals (1 year)......................	5	1	.833	3.95	50	0	0	0	0	57	55	26	25	31	58
Major league totals (4 years)......	8	4	.667	4.08	101	0	0	0	2	125 2/3	114	59	57	60	117

REYES, CARLOS   P

PERSONAL: Born April 4, 1969, in Miami. ... 6-1/190. ... Throws right, bats both. ... Full name: Carlos Alberto Reyes.
HIGH SCHOOL: Tampa Catholic.
JUNIOR COLLEGE: Brevard Community College (Fla.).
COLLEGE: Florida Southern.
TRANSACTIONS/CAREER NOTES: Signed as non-drafted free agent by Atlanta Braves organization (June 21, 1991). ... Selected by Oakland Athletics from Braves organization in Rule 5 major league draft (December 13, 1993). ... On Oakland disabled list (July 18-August 4, 1994); included rehabilitation assignment to Modesto (July 25-30). ... Granted free agency (December 20, 1996). ... Signed by New York Yankees organization (February 6, 1997). ... Released by Yankees (April 8, 1997). ... Signed by Athletics (April 10, 1997). ... On Oakland disabled list (August 21-September 12, 1997); included rehabilitation assignment to Edmonton (September 3-12). ... Granted free agency (October 15, 1997). ... Signed by San Diego Padres (November 7, 1997). ... Traded by Padres with P Dario Veras and C Mandy Romero to Boston Red Sox for C Jim Leyritz and OF Ethan Faggett (June 21, 1998). ... Released by Red Sox (December 14, 1998).

Year Team (League)	W	L	Pct.	ERA	G	GS	CG	ShO	Sv.	IP	H	R	ER	BB	SO
1991— GC Braves (GCL)	3	2	.600	1.77	20	0	0	0	5	45 2/3	44	15	9	9	37
1992— Macon (S. Atl.).................	2	3	.400	2.10	23	0	0	0	2	60	57	16	14	11	57
— Durham (Carolina)............	2	1	.667	2.43	21	0	0	0	5	40 2/3	31	11	11	10	33
1993— Greenville (Southern)	8	1	.889	2.06	33	2	0	0	2	70	64	22	16	24	57
— Richmond (Int'l)	1	0	1.000	3.77	18	1	0	0	1	28 2/3	30	12	12	11	30
1994— Oakland (A.L.)■.............	0	3	.000	4.15	27	9	0	0	1	78	71	38	36	44	57
— Modesto (California)	0	0	. . .	0.00	3	3	0	0	0	5	2	0	0	0	3
1995— Oakland (A.L.)	4	6	.400	5.09	40	1	0	0	0	69	71	43	39	28	48
1996— Oakland (A.L.)	7	10	.412	4.78	46	10	0	0	0	122 1/3	134	71	65	61	78
1997— Columbus (Int'l)■...........	0	0	. . .	18.00	1	1	0	0	0	2	5	4	4	0	2
— Edmonton (PCL)■	2	0	1.000	3.48	5	4	1	0	0	31	30	14	12	3	23
— Oakland (A.L.)	3	4	.429	5.82	37	6	0	0	0	77 1/3	101	52	50	25	43
1998— Las Vegas (PCL)■	0	0	. . .	0.00	1	0	0	0	0	1	0	0	0	0	2
— San Diego (N.L.)	2	2	.500	3.58	22	0	0	0	1	27 2/3	23	11	11	6	24
— Boston (A.L.)■...............	1	1	.500	3.52	24	0	0	0	0	38 1/3	35	15	15	14	23
A.L. totals (5 years)	15	24	.385	4.79	174	26	0	0	1	385	412	219	205	172	249
N.L. totals (1 year)......................	2	2	.500	3.58	22	0	0	0	1	27 2/3	23	11	11	6	24
Major league totals (5 years)......	17	26	.395	4.71	196	26	0	0	2	412 2/3	435	230	216	178	273

REYES, DENNIS — P — REDS

PERSONAL: Born April 19, 1977, in Higuera de Zaragoza, Mexico. ... 6-3/246. ... Throws left, bats left.
HIGH SCHOOL: Ignacio Zaragoza (Higuera de Zaragoza, Mexico).
TRANSACTIONS/CAREER NOTES: Signed as non-drafted free agent by Los Angeles Dodgers organization (July 5, 1993). ... Traded by Dodgers with 1B/3B Paul Konerko to Cincinnati Reds for P Jeff Shaw (July 4, 1998).

Year Team (League)	W	L	Pct.	ERA	G	GS	CG	ShO	Sv.	IP	H	R	ER	BB	SO
1994— Vero Beach (FSL)	2	4	.333	6.70	9	9	0	0	0	41 2/3	58	37	31	18	25
— Great Falls (Pio.)	7	1	.875	3.78	14	9	0	0	0	66 2/3	71	37	28	25	70
1995— Vero Beach (FSL)	1	0	1.000	1.80	3	2	0	0	0	10	8	2	2	6	9
— M.C. Red Devils (Mex.)	5	5	.500	6.60	17	15	1	0	0	58 2/3	76	49	43	41	44
1996— San Bernardino (Calif.)	11	12	.478	4.17	29	•28	0	0	0	166	166	106	77	77	176
1997— San Antonio (Tex.)	8	1	.889	3.02	12	12	1	0	0	80 1/3	79	33	27	28	66
— Albuquerque (PCL)	6	3	.667	5.65	10	10	1	0	0	57 1/3	70	40	36	33	45
— Los Angeles (N.L.)	2	3	.400	3.83	14	5	0	0	0	47	51	21	20	18	36
1998— Albuquerque (PCL)	1	4	.200	1.44	7	7	1	1	0	43 2/3	31	13	7	18	58
— Los Angeles (N.L.)	0	4	.000	4.71	11	3	0	0	0	28 2/3	27	17	15	20	33
— Indianapolis (Int'l)■	2	0	1.000	3.00	4	4	0	0	0	24	20	10	8	14	27
— Cincinnati (N.L.)	3	1	.750	4.42	8	7	0	0	0	38 2/3	35	19	19	27	44
Major league totals (2 years)	5	8	.385	4.25	33	15	0	0	0	114 1/3	113	57	54	65	113

REYNOLDS, SHANE — P — ASTROS

PERSONAL: Born March 26, 1968, in Bastrop, La. ... 6-3/210. ... Throws right, bats right. ... Full name: Richard Shane Reynolds.
HIGH SCHOOL: Ouachita Christian (Monroe, La.).
JUNIOR COLLEGE: Faulkner State Junior College (Ala.).
COLLEGE: Texas.
TRANSACTIONS/CAREER NOTES: Selected by Houston Astros organization in third round of free-agent draft (June 5, 1989). ... On Houston disabled list (June 10-July 14, 1997); included rehabilitation assignment to New Orleans (July 10-14).
MISCELLANEOUS: Appeared in one game as pinch runner (1995).

Year Team (League)	W	L	Pct.	ERA	G	GS	CG	ShO	Sv.	IP	H	R	ER	BB	SO
1989— Auburn (N.Y.-Penn)	3	2	.600	2.31	6	6	1	0	0	35	36	16	9	14	23
— Asheville (S. Atl.)	5	3	.625	3.68	8	8	2	1	0	51 1/3	53	25	21	21	33
1990— Columbus (Southern)	9	10	.474	4.81	29	27	2	1	0	155 1/3	•181	104	83	70	92
1991— Jackson (Texas)	8	9	.471	4.47	27	•27	2	0	0	151	165	93	75	62	116
1992— Tucson (PCL)	9	8	.529	3.68	25	22	2	0	1	142	156	73	58	34	106
— Houston (N.L.)	1	3	.250	7.11	8	5	0	0	0	25 1/3	42	22	20	6	10
1993— Tucson (PCL)	10	6	.625	3.62	25	20	2	0	1	139 1/3	147	74	56	21	106
— Houston (N.L.)	0	0	...	0.82	5	1	0	0	0	11	11	4	1	6	10
1994— Houston (N.L.)	8	5	.615	3.05	33	14	1	1	0	124	128	46	42	21	110
1995— Houston (N.L.)	10	11	.476	3.47	30	30	3	2	0	189 1/3	196	87	73	37	175
1996— Houston (N.L.)	16	10	.615	3.65	35	35	4	1	0	239	227	103	97	44	204
1997— Houston (N.L.)	9	10	.474	4.23	30	30	2	0	0	181	189	92	85	47	152
— New Orleans (A.A.)	1	0	1.000	0.00	1	1	0	0	0	5	3	0	0	1	6
1998— Houston (N.L.)	19	8	.704	3.51	35	•35	3	1	0	233 1/3	257	99	91	53	209
Major league totals (7 years)	63	47	.573	3.67	176	150	13	5	0	1003	1050	453	409	214	870

DIVISION SERIES RECORD

Year Team (League)	W	L	Pct.	ERA	G	GS	CG	ShO	Sv.	IP	H	R	ER	BB	SO
1997— Houston (N.L.)	0	1	.000	3.00	1	1	0	0	0	6	5	2	2	1	5
1998— Houston (N.L.)	0	0	...	2.57	1	1	0	0	0	7	4	2	2	1	5
Div. series totals (2 years)	0	1	.000	2.77	2	2	0	0	0	13	9	4	4	2	10

REYNOSO, ARMANDO — P — DIAMONDBACKS

PERSONAL: Born May 1, 1966, in San Luis Potosi, Mexico. ... 6-0/204. ... Throws right, bats right. ... Full name: Martin Armando Gutierrez Reynoso. ... Name pronounced ray-NO-so.
HIGH SCHOOL: Escuela Secandaria Mita del Estado (Jalisco, Mexico).
TRANSACTIONS/CAREER NOTES: Signed as free agent by Saltillo of Mexican League. ... Contract sold by Saltillo to Atlanta Braves organization (August 15, 1990). ... Selected by Colorado Rockies in third round (58th pick overall) of expansion draft (November 17, 1992). ... On disabled list (May 21, 1994-remainder of season). ... On Colorado disabled list (April 17-June 18, 1995); included rehabilitation assignments to Colorado Springs (May 9-20 and June 8-14). ... Traded by Rockies to New York Mets for P Jerry Dipoto (November 27, 1996). ... On New York disabled list (March 24-April 15, and July 17, 1997-remainder of season); included rehabilitation assignment to St. Lucie (April 5-15). ... On New York disabled list (March 24-July 24, 1998); included rehabilitation assignments to St. Lucie (June 18-July 3) and Norfolk (July 12-17). ... Granted free agency (October 26, 1998). ... Signed by Arizona Diamondbacks (December 2, 1998).
STATISTICAL NOTES: Led International League with six balks in 1991 and five in 1992. ... Tied for International League lead with 10 hit batsmen in 1991.
MISCELLANEOUS: Appeared in one game as pinch runner with Colorado (1993).

Year Team (League)	W	L	Pct.	ERA	G	GS	CG	ShO	Sv.	IP	H	R	ER	BB	SO
1988— Saltillo (Mexican)	11	11	.500	4.30	32	29	10	2	2	180	176	98	86	85	92
1989— Saltillo (Mexican)	13	9	.591	3.48	27	25	7	2	0	160 1/3	155	78	62	64	107
1990— Saltillo (Mexican)	*20	3	.870	2.60	27	•27	12	5	0	200 2/3	174	61	58	73	*170
— Richmond (Int'l)■	3	1	.750	2.25	4	3	0	0	0	24	26	7	6	7	15
1991— Richmond (Int'l)	10	6	.625	*2.61	22	19	3	•3	0	131	117	44	38	39	97
— Atlanta (N.L.)	2	1	.667	6.17	6	5	0	0	0	23 1/3	26	18	16	10	10
1992— Richmond (Int'l)	12	9	.571	2.66	28	27	4	1	0	169 1/3	156	65	50	52	108
— Atlanta (N.L.)	1	0	1.000	4.70	3	1	0	0	1	7 2/3	11	4	4	2	2

Year — Team (League)	W	L	Pct.	ERA	G	GS	CG	ShO	Sv.	IP	H	R	ER	BB	SO
1993— Colo. Springs (PCL)■	2	1	.667	3.22	4	4	0	0	0	22 1/3	19	10	8	8	22
— Colorado (N.L.)	12	11	.522	4.00	30	30	4	0	0	189	206	101	84	63	117
1994— Colorado (N.L.)	3	4	.429	4.82	9	9	1	0	0	52 1/3	54	30	28	22	25
1995— Colo. Springs (PCL)	2	1	.667	1.57	5	5	0	0	0	23	14	4	4	6	17
— Colorado (N.L.)	7	7	.500	5.32	20	18	0	0	0	93	116	61	55	36	40
1996— Colorado (N.L.)	8	9	.471	4.96	30	30	0	0	0	168 2/3	195	97	93	49	88
1997— St. Lucie (Fla. St.)■	1	1	.500	2.70	2	2	0	0	0	10	9	3	3	1	6
— New York (N.L.)	6	3	.667	4.53	16	16	1	1	0	91 1/3	95	47	46	29	47
1998— St. Lucie (Fla. St.)	0	1	.000	3.75	4	4	0	0	0	12	14	6	5	1	6
— Norfolk (Int'l)	0	2	.000	10.61	2	2	0	0	0	9 1/3	14	11	11	4	8
— New York (N.L.)	7	3	.700	3.82	11	11	0	0	0	68 1/3	64	31	29	32	40
Major league totals (8 years)	46	38	.548	4.61	125	120	6	1	1	693 2/3	767	389	355	243	369

DIVISION SERIES RECORD

Year — Team (League)	W	L	Pct.	ERA	G	GS	CG	ShO	Sv.	IP	H	R	ER	BB	SO
1995— Colorado (N.L.)	0	0	. . .	0.00	1	0	0	0	0	1	2	0	0	0	0

RHODES, ARTHUR   P   ORIOLES

PERSONAL: Born October 24, 1969, in Waco, Texas. ... 6-2/205. ... Throws left, bats left. ... Full name: Arthur Lee Rhodes Jr. ... Brother of Ricky Rhodes, minor league pitcher in New York Yankees organization (1988-92).

HIGH SCHOOL: LaVega (Waco, Texas).

TRANSACTIONS/CAREER NOTES: Selected by Baltimore Orioles organization in second round of free-agent draft (June 1, 1988). ... On Hagerstown disabled list (May 13-June 5, 1991). ... On Baltimore disabled list (May 16-August 2, 1993); included rehabilitation assignment to Rochester (July 4-August 2). ... On Baltimore disabled list (May 2-20, 1994); included rehabilitation assignment to Frederick (May 16-20). ... On Baltimore disabled list (August 25, 1995-remainder of season). ... On disabled list (July 14-August 2 and August 6-September 27, 1996). ... On Baltimore disabled list (July 5-August 17, 1998); included rehabilitation assignment to Rochester (August 15-17).

HONORS: Named Eastern League Pitcher of the Year (1991).

MISCELLANEOUS: Appeared in one game as pinch runner (1997).

Year — Team (League)	W	L	Pct.	ERA	G	GS	CG	ShO	Sv.	IP	H	R	ER	BB	SO
1988— Bluefield (Appalachian)	3	4	.429	3.31	11	7	0	0	0	35 1/3	29	17	13	15	44
1989— Erie (N.Y.-Penn)	2	0	1.000	1.16	5	5	1	0	0	31	13	7	4	10	45
— Frederick (Carolina)	2	2	.500	5.18	7	6	0	0	0	24 1/3	19	16	14	19	28
1990— Frederick (Carolina)	4	6	.400	2.12	13	13	3	0	0	80 2/3	62	25	19	21	103
— Hagerstown (Eastern)	3	4	.429	3.73	12	12	0	0	0	72 1/3	62	32	30	39	60
1991— Hagerstown (Eastern)	7	4	.636	2.70	19	19	2	2	0	106 2/3	73	37	32	47	115
— Baltimore (A.L.)	0	3	.000	8.00	8	8	0	0	0	36	47	35	32	23	23
1992— Rochester (Int'l)	6	6	.500	3.72	17	17	1	0	0	101 2/3	84	48	42	46	115
— Baltimore (A.L.)	7	5	.583	3.63	15	15	2	1	0	94 1/3	87	39	38	38	77
1993— Baltimore (A.L.)	5	6	.455	6.51	17	17	0	0	0	85 2/3	91	62	62	49	49
— Rochester (Int'l)	1	1	.500	4.05	6	6	0	0	0	26 2/3	26	12	12	15	33
1994— Baltimore (A.L.)	3	5	.375	5.81	10	10	3	2	0	52 2/3	51	34	34	30	47
— Frederick (Carolina)	0	0	. . .	0.00	1	1	0	0	0	5	3	0	0	0	7
— Rochester (Int'l)	7	5	.583	2.79	15	15	3	0	0	90 1/3	70	41	28	34	86
1995— Rochester (Int'l)	2	1	.667	2.70	4	4	1	0	0	30	27	12	9	8	33
— Baltimore (A.L.)	2	5	.286	6.21	19	9	0	0	0	75 1/3	68	53	52	48	77
1996— Baltimore (A.L.)	9	1	.900	4.08	28	2	0	0	1	53	48	28	24	23	62
1997— Baltimore (A.L.)	10	3	.769	3.02	53	0	0	0	1	95 1/3	75	32	32	26	102
1998— Baltimore (A.L.)	4	4	.500	3.51	45	0	0	0	4	77	65	30	30	34	83
— Rochester (Int'l)	0	0	. . .	4.50	1	1	0	0	0	2	3	1	1	1	1
Major league totals (8 years)	40	32	.556	4.81	195	61	5	3	6	569 1/3	532	313	304	271	520

DIVISION SERIES RECORD

Year — Team (League)	W	L	Pct.	ERA	G	GS	CG	ShO	Sv.	IP	H	R	ER	BB	SO
1996— Baltimore (A.L.)	0	0	. . .	9.00	2	0	0	0	0	1	1	1	1	1	1
1997— Baltimore (A.L.)	0	0	. . .	0.00	1	0	0	0	0	2 1/3	0	0	0	0	4
Div. series totals (2 years)	0	0	. . .	2.70	3	0	0	0	0	3 1/3	1	1	1	1	5

CHAMPIONSHIP SERIES RECORD

Year — Team (League)	W	L	Pct.	ERA	G	GS	CG	ShO	Sv.	IP	H	R	ER	BB	SO
1996— Baltimore (A.L.)	0	0	. . .	0.00	3	0	0	0	0	2	2	0	0	0	2
1997— Baltimore (A.L.)	0	0	. . .	0.00	2	0	0	0	0	2 1/3	2	0	0	3	2
Champ. series totals (2 years)	0	0	. . .	0.00	5	0	0	0	0	4 1/3	4	0	0	3	4

RIGBY, BRAD   P   ATHLETICS

PERSONAL: Born May 14, 1973, in Milwaukee. ... 6-6/213. ... Throws right, bats right. ... Full name: Bradley Kenneth Rigby.

HIGH SCHOOL: Lake Brantley (Altamonte Springs, Fla.).

COLLEGE: Georgia Tech.

TRANSACTIONS/CAREER NOTES: Selected by Oakland Athletics organization in second round of free-agent draft (June 2, 1994). ... On Oakland disabled list (August 8-23, 1997; and March 26-April 10, 1998). ... On Edmonton disabled list (July 4-September 10, 1998).

Year — Team (League)	W	L	Pct.	ERA	G	GS	CG	ShO	Sv.	IP	H	R	ER	BB	SO
1994— Modesto (California)	2	1	.667	3.80	11	1	0	0	2	23 2/3	20	10	10	10	28
1995— Modesto (California)	11	4	.733	3.84	31	23	0	0	2	154 2/3	135	79	66	48	145
1996— Huntsville (Southern)	9	12	.429	3.95	26	26	3	0	0	159 1/3	161	89	70	59	127
1997— Edmonton (PCL)	8	4	.667	4.37	15	15	0	0	0	82 1/3	95	49	40	26	49
— Oakland (A.L.)	1	7	.125	4.87	14	14	0	0	0	77 2/3	92	44	42	22	34
1998— Edmonton (PCL)	5	6	.455	5.94	13	13	0	0	0	69 2/3	86	52	46	17	34
Major league totals (1 year)	1	7	.125	4.87	14	14	0	0	0	77 2/3	92	44	42	22	34

RIGGS, ADAM   2B   DODGERS

PERSONAL: Born October 4, 1972, in Steubenville, Ohio. ... 6-0/190. ... Bats right, throws right. ... Full name: Adam David Riggs.
HIGH SCHOOL: Lenape Valley (Stanhope, N.J.).
COLLEGE: South Carolina-Aiken.
TRANSACTIONS/CAREER NOTES: Selected by Los Angeles Dodgers organization in 22nd round of free-agent draft (June 2, 1994). ... On Albuquerque disabled list (April 4-June 9, 1997; and May 28-June 5, 1998). ... On Los Angeles disabled list (June 5, 1998-remainder of season).
HONORS: Named California League Most Valuable Player (1995).
STATISTICAL NOTES: Led California League with 317 total bases and .431 on-base percentage in 1995. ... Led Texas League second basemen with 717 total chances and 91 double plays in 1996.

							BATTING									FIELDING		
Year	Team (League)	Pos.	G	AB	R	H	2B	3B	HR	RBI	Avg.	BB	SO	SB	PO	A	E	Avg.
1994— Yakima (N'west)		2B	4	7	1	2	1	0	0	0	.286	0	1	0				...
— Great Falls (Pio.)		2B	62	234	55	73	20	3	5	44	.312	31	38	19	93	133	23	.908
1995— San Bern. (Calif.)		2B	134	*542	*111	*196	*39	5	24	106	*.362	59	93	31	223	303	*41	.928
1996— San Antonio (Tex.)		2B	134	506	68	143	31	6	14	66	.283	37	82	16	*295	*395	27	.962
1997— Albuquerque (PCL).....		2B-3B-OF	57	227	59	69	8	3	13	28	.304	29	39	12	131	162	8	.973
— Los Angeles (N.L.)		2B	9	20	3	4	1	0	0	1	.200	4	3	1	6	19	0	1.000
1998— Albuquerque (PCL).....		2B	44	170	30	63	13	3	4	25	.371	21	29	12	82	125	10	.954
Major league totals (1 year)			9	20	3	4	1	0	0	1	.200	4	3	1	6	19	0	1.000

RINCON, RICARDO   P   INDIANS

PERSONAL: Born April 13, 1970, in Veracruz, Mexico ... 5-10/187. ... Throws left, bats left. ... Full name: Ricardo Rincon Espinoza.
TRANSACTIONS/CAREER NOTES: Signed as non-drafted free agent by Pittsburgh Pirates organization (March 30, 1997). ... On Pittsburgh disabled list (March 22-April 14, 1998); included rehabilitation assignments to Carolina (April 6) and Nashville (April 11-April 14). ... Traded by Pirates to Cleveland Indians for OF Brian Giles (November 18, 1998).

Year	Team (League)	W	L	Pct.	ERA	G	GS	CG	ShO	Sv.	IP	H	R	ER	BB	SO
1990— Union Laguna (Mex.)		3	0	1.000	3.78	19	4	0	0	0	47²/₃	53	22	20	32	29
1991— Union Laguna (Mex.)		2	8	.200	6.54	32	9	0	0	1	74¹/₃	99	60	54	48	66
1992— Union Laguna (Mex.)		6	5	.545	3.91	49	9	0	0	4	89²/₃	87	45	39	46	91
1993— Torreon (Mexican)■..........		7	3	.700	3.17	57	4	0	0	8	82¹/₃	80	33	29	36	81
1994— M.C. Red Devils (Mex.)■....		2	4	.333	3.21	20	9	00	0	1	53¹/₃	57	23	19	20	38
1995— M.C. Red Devils (Mex.)		6	6	.500	5.16	27	11	0	0	3	75	86	45	43	41	41
1996— M.C. Red Devils (Mex.)		5	3	.625	2.97	50	0	0	0	10	78²/₃	58	28	26	27	60
1997— Pittsburgh (N.L.)■..........		4	8	.333	3.45	62	0	0	0	4	60	51	26	23	24	71
1998— Carolina (Southern)...........		0	0	...	6.00	2	0	0	0	0	3	5	2	2	2	1
— Nashville (Pacific Coast)		0	0	...	0.00	1	0	0	0	0	1	0	0	0	0	1
— Pittsburgh (N.L.)		0	2	.000	2.91	60	0	0	0	14	65	50	31	21	29	64
Major league totals (2 years)......		4	10	.286	3.17	122	0	0	0	18	125	101	57	44	53	135

RIOS, ARMANDO   OF   GIANTS

PERSONAL: Born September 13, 1971, in Santurce, Puerto Rico. ... 5-9/185. ... Bats left, throws left.
HIGH SCHOOL: Villa Fontana (Carolina, Puerto Rico).
COLLEGE: UNC Charlotte, then Louisiana State.
TRANSACTIONS/CAREER NOTES: Signed as non-drafted free agent by San Francisco Giants organization (January 6, 1994). ... On disabled list (May 15-29, 1996).

							BATTING									FIELDING		
Year	Team (League)	Pos.	G	AB	R	H	2B	3B	HR	RBI	Avg.	BB	SO	SB	PO	A	E	Avg.
1994— Clinton (Midwest).......		OF	119	407	67	120	23	4	8	60	.295	59	69	16	216	17	12	.951
1995— San Jose (Calif.).........		OF	128	488	76	143	34	3	8	75	.293	74	75	51	220	16	9	.963
1996— Shreveport (Texas)......		OF	92	329	62	93	22	2	12	49	.283	44	42	9	165	*15	7	.963
1997— Shreveport (Texas).....		OF	127	461	86	133	30	6	14	79	.289	63	85	17	191	*17	6	.972
1998— Fresno (Pacific Coast) ..		OF-1B	125	445	85	134	23	1	26	103	.301	55	73	17	226	14	7	.972
— San Francisco (N.L.) ..		OF	12	7	3	4	0	0	2	3	.571	3	2	0	5	0	0	1.000
Major league totals (1 year)			12	7	3	4	0	0	2	3	.571	3	2	0	5	0	0	1.000

RIOS, DAN   P   ROYALS

PERSONAL: Born November 11, 1972, in Madrid, Spain. ... 6-2/192. ... Throws right, bats right. ... Full name: Daniel Rios.
HIGH SCHOOL: Pace (Fla.).
JUNIOR COLLEGE: Seminole Community College (Fla.).
COLLEGE: Miami (Fla.).
TRANSACTIONS/CAREER NOTES: Signed as non-drafted free agent by New York Yankees organization (June 7, 1993). ... Claimed on waivers by Kansas City Royals (March 26, 1998).

Year	Team (League)	W	L	Pct.	ERA	G	GS	CG	ShO	Sv.	IP	H	R	ER	BB	SO
1993— GC Yankees (GCL)..............		2	0	1.000	3.52	24	0	0	0	6	38¹/₃	34	18	15	16	29
1994— Greensboro (S. Atl.)...........		3	2	.600	0.87	37	0	0	0	17	41¹/₃	32	4	4	13	36
— Tampa (Fla. St.).................		0	0	...	0.00	9	0	0	0	2	10¹/₃	6	2	0	4	11
1995— Tampa (Fla. St.)...............		0	4	.000	2.00	57	0	0	0	24	67¹/₃	67	24	15	20	72
1996— Norwich (Eastern)		3	1	.750	2.09	38	0	0	0	17	43	34	14	10	21	38
— Columbus (Int'l)		4	1	.800	1.95	24	0	0	0	0	27²/₃	22	7	6	6	22
1997— Columbus (Int'l)		7	4	.636	3.08	58	0	0	0	3	84²/₃	73	37	29	31	53
— New York (A.L.)		0	0	...	19.29	2	0	0	0	0	2¹/₃	9	5	5	2	1
1998— Omaha (Pacific Coast)■		6	7	.462	5.63	25	18	2	0	1	123	159	90	77	41	51
— Kansas City (A.L.)		0	1	.000	6.14	5	0	0	0	0	7¹/₃	9	9	5	6	6
Major league totals (2 years)......		0	1	.000	9.31	7	0	0	0	0	9²/₃	18	14	10	8	7

RIPKEN, BILL   IF

R

PERSONAL: Born December 16, 1964, in Havre de Grace, Md. ... 6-1/190. ... Bats right, throws right. ... Full name: William Oliver Ripken. ... Son of Cal Ripken Sr., minor league catcher (1957-62 and 1964); manager with Baltimore Orioles (1987-88) and coach with Orioles (1976-86 and 1989-92); and brother of Cal Ripken Jr., third baseman, Orioles.

HIGH SCHOOL: Aberdeen (Md.).

TRANSACTIONS/CAREER NOTES: Selected by Baltimore Orioles organization in 11th round of free-agent draft (June 7, 1982). ... On disabled list (April 20-May 3, 1984; June 23-July 6, 1985; March 27-April 14 and August 23-September 7, 1989; and August 5-20, 1990). ... On Baltimore disabled list (July 15-August 15, 1991); included rehabilitation assignments to Frederick (August 12-13) and Hagerstown (August 13-15). ... Released by Orioles (December 11, 1992). ... Signed by Texas Rangers organization (February 1, 1993). ... On Texas disabled list (May 13-28 and June 21-September 1, 1993). ... Granted free agency (October 4, 1993). ... Re-signed by Rangers organization (December 18, 1993). ... On disabled list (May 10-25 and July 16, 1994-remainder of season). ... Granted free agency (October 14, 1994). ... Signed by Buffalo, Cleveland Indians organization (March 25, 1995). ... Granted free agency (November 2, 1995). ... Signed by Orioles organization (December 23, 1995). ... Granted free agency (October 29, 1996). ... Signed by Texas Rangers (December 10, 1996). ... On disabled list (June 18-July 6 and July 25-August 8, 1997). ... Granted free agency (October 30, 1997). ... Signed by Detroit Tigers organization (December 16, 1997). ... On Detroit disabled list (April 26-May 28 and June 21-July 13, 1998); included rehabilitation assignments to Toledo (May 25-28 and July 10-13). ... Released by Tigers (July 20, 1998).

STATISTICAL NOTES: Led Southern League second basemen with 723 total chances and 79 double plays in 1986. ... Tied for Southern League lead in grounding into double plays with 21 in 1986. ... Tied for A.L. lead with 17 sacrifice hits in 1990. ... Tied for American Association lead with eight sacrifice flies in 1995. ... Led American Association shortstops with .978 fielding percentage, 389 assists and 80 double plays in 1995.

Year Team (League)	Pos.	G	AB	R	H	2B	3B	HR	RBI	Avg.	BB	SO	SB	PO	A	E	Avg.
1982—Bluefield (Appal.)	SS-3B-2B	27	45	8	11	1	0	0	4	.244	8	6	0	15	17	3	.914
1983—Bluefield (Appal.)	SS-3B	48	152	24	33	6	0	0	13	.217	12	13	7	82	145	23	.908
1984—Hagerstown (Car.)	SS-2B	115	409	48	94	15	3	2	40	.230	36	64	3	187	358	28	.951
1985—Charlotte (Southern)	SS	18	51	2	7	1	0	0	3	.137	6	4	0	18	52	4	.946
—Daytona Beach (FSL)	SS-3B-2B	67	222	23	51	11	0	0	18	.230	22	24	7	90	198	6	.973
1986—Charlotte (Southern)	2B	141	530	58	142	20	3	5	62	.268	24	47	9	*305	*395	*23	.968
1987—Rochester (Int'l)	2B-SS	74	238	32	68	15	0	0	11	.286	21	24	7	154	200	9	.975
—Baltimore (A.L.)	2B	58	234	27	72	9	0	2	20	.308	21	23	4	133	162	3	.990
1988—Baltimore (A.L.)	2B-3B-DH	150	512	52	106	18	1	2	34	.207	33	63	8	310	440	12	.984
1989—Baltimore (A.L.)	2B	115	318	31	76	11	2	2	26	.239	22	53	1	255	335	9	.985
1990—Baltimore (A.L.)	2B	129	406	48	118	28	1	3	38	.291	28	43	5	250	366	8	.987
1991—Baltimore (A.L.)	2B	104	287	24	62	11	1	0	14	.216	15	31	0	201	284	7	.986
—Frederick (Carolina)	DH	1	4	2	1	0	0	0	1	.250	0	1	0	...	...	...	...
—Hagerstown (East.)	2B	1	5	1	3	0	0	0	0	.600	0	0	1	2	1	0	1.000
1992—Baltimore (A.L.)	2B-DH	111	330	35	76	15	0	4	36	.230	18	26	2	217	317	4	*.993
1993—Texas (A.L.)■	2B-SS-3B	50	132	12	25	4	0	0	11	.189	11	19	0	80	123	2	.990
1994—Texas (A.L.)	3-2-S-1	32	81	9	25	5	0	0	6	.309	3	11	2	29	50	2	.975
1995—Buffalo (A.A.)■	SS-2B	130	448	51	131	34	1	4	56	.292	28	38	6	163	†401	12	†.979
—Cleveland (A.L.)	2B-3B	8	17	4	7	0	0	2	3	.412	0	3	0	7	6	0	1.000
1996—Baltimore (A.L.)	2B-3B-1B	57	135	19	31	8	0	2	12	.230	9	18	0	40	95	3	.978
1997—Texas (A.L.)■	S-2-3-1	71	203	18	56	9	1	3	24	.276	9	32	0	116	158	5	.982
1998—Detroit (A.L.)■	S-1-2-3-DH	27	74	8	20	3	0	0	5	.270	5	10	3	32	59	6	.938
—Toledo (Int'l)	3B	5	19	3	6	1	0	0	1	.316	2	0	0	3	12	0	1.000
Major league totals (12 years)		912	2729	287	674	121	6	20	229	.247	174	332	25	1670	2395	61	.985

RIPKEN, CAL   3B   ORIOLES

PERSONAL: Born August 24, 1960, in Havre de Grace, Md. ... 6-4/220. ... Bats right, throws right. ... Full name: Calvin Edwin Ripken Jr. ... Son of Cal Ripken Sr., minor league catcher (1957-62 and 1964), manager with Baltimore Orioles (1987-88) and coach, Orioles (1976-86 and 1989-92); and brother of Bill Ripken, infielder with four major league teams (1987-98).

HIGH SCHOOL: Aberdeen (Md.).

TRANSACTIONS/CAREER NOTES: Selected by Baltimore Orioles organization in second round of free-agent draft (June 6, 1978).

RECORDS: Holds major league career records for most consecutive games played—2,632 (May 30, 1982-September 19, 1998); most years leading league in games played—9; most consecutive years played all club's games—15 (1983-97); most years played all club's games—15 (1983-97); most home runs by shortstop—345; most years leading league in games by shortstop—12; most consecutive games by shortstop—2,216; and most years leading league in double plays by shortstop—8. ... Holds major league single-season records for most at-bats without a triple—646 (1989); highest fielding percentage by shortstop (150 or more games)—.996 (1990); fewest errors by shortstop (150 or more games)—3 (1990); most consecutive errorless games by shortstop—95 (April 14 through July 27, 1990); and most consecutive chances accepted by shortstop without an error—431 (April 14-July 28, 1990, first game). ... Holds A.L. career records for most double plays by shortstop—1,565; most years leading league in putouts by shortstop—6; most consecutive years played 150 or more games—12 (1982-93); and most years with 600 or more at-bats—13. ... Holds A.L. single-season record for most assists by shortstop—583 (1984). ... Shares A.L. career records for most years leading league in assists by shortstop—7; and most years with 150 or more games played—14.

HONORS: Named A.L. Rookie of the Year by THE SPORTING NEWS (1982). ... Named A.L. Rookie of the Year by Baseball Writers' Association of America (1982). ... Named Major League Player of the Year by THE SPORTING NEWS (1983 and 1991). ... Named A.L. Player of the Year by THE SPORTING NEWS (1983 and 1991). ... Named shortstop on THE SPORTING NEWS A.L. All-Star team (1983-85, 1989, 1991 and 1993-95). ... Named shortstop on THE SPORTING NEWS A.L. Silver Slugger team (1983-86, 1989, 1991 and 1993-94). ... Named A.L. Most Valuable Player by Baseball Writers' Association of America (1983 and 1991). ... Won A.L. Gold Glove at shortstop (1991-92). ... Named Sportsman of the Year by THE SPORTING NEWS (1995).

STATISTICAL NOTES: Tied for Appalachian League lead in double plays by shortstop with 31 in 1978. ... Led Southern League third basemen with .933 fielding percentage, 119 putouts, 268 assists, 415 total chances and 34 double plays in 1980. ... Tied for Southern League lead with nine sacrifice flies in 1980. ... Led A.L. shortstops with 831 total chances in 1983, 906 in 1984, 815 in 1989, 806 in 1991 and 738 in 1993. ... Led A.L. shortstops with 113 double plays in 1983, 122 in 1984, 123 in 1985, 119 in 1989, 114 in 1991, 119 in 1992, 72 in 1994 and 100 in 1995. ... Hit for the cycle (May 6, 1984). ... Tied for A.L. lead with 15 game-winning RBIs in 1986. ... Tied for A.L. lead with 10 sacrifice flies in 1988. ... Led A.L. with 368 total bases in 1991. ... Hit three home runs in one game (May 28, 1996). ... Led A.L. in grounding into double plays with 28 in 1996. ... Career major league grand slams: 8.

MISCELLANEOUS: Holds Baltimore Orioles all-time records for most runs (1,510), most doubles (544), most home runs (384) and most runs batted in (1,514).

Year— Team (League)	Pos.	G	AB	R	H	2B	3B	HR	RBI	Avg.	BB	SO	SB	PO	A	E	Avg.
1978— Bluefield (Appal.)........	SS	63	239	27	63	7	1	0	24	.264	24	46	1	*92	204	*33	.900
1979— Miami (Fla. St.)	3B-SS-2B	105	393	51	119	*28	1	5	54	.303	31	64	4	149	260	30	.932
—Charlotte (Southern) ..	3B	17	61	6	11	0	1	3	8	.180	3	13	1	13	26	3	.929
1980— Charlotte (Southern) ..	3B-SS	•144	522	91	144	28	5	25	78	.276	77	81	4	†151	†341	35	†.934
1981— Rochester (Int'l)	3B-SS	114	437	74	126	31	4	23	75	.288	66	85	0	128	320	21	.955
—Baltimore (A.L.).........	SS-3B	23	39	1	5	0	0	0	0	.128	1	8	0	13	30	3	.935
1982— Baltimore (A.L.).........	SS-3B	160	598	90	158	32	5	28	93	.264	46	95	3	221	440	19	.972
1983— Baltimore (A.L.).........	SS	•162	*663	*121	*211	*47	2	27	102	.318	58	97	0	272	*534	25	.970
1984— Baltimore (A.L.).........	SS	•162	641	103	195	37	7	27	86	.304	71	89	2	*297	*583	26	.971
1985— Baltimore (A.L.).........	SS	161	642	116	181	32	5	26	110	.282	67	68	2	*286	474	26	.967
1986— Baltimore (A.L.).........	SS	162	627	98	177	35	1	25	81	.282	70	60	4	240	*482	13	.982
1987— Baltimore (A.L.).........	SS	*162	624	97	157	28	3	27	98	.252	81	77	3	240	*480	20	.973
1988— Baltimore (A.L.).........	SS	161	575	87	152	25	1	23	81	.264	102	69	2	*284	480	21	.973
1989— Baltimore (A.L.).........	SS	•162	646	80	166	30	0	21	93	.257	57	72	3	*276	*531	8	.990
1990— Baltimore (A.L.).........	SS	161	600	78	150	28	4	21	84	.250	82	66	3	242	435	3	*.996
1991— Baltimore (A.L.).........	SS	•162	650	99	210	46	5	34	114	.323	53	46	6	*267	*528	11	*.986
1992— Baltimore (A.L.).........	SS	*162	637	73	160	29	1	14	72	.251	64	50	4	*287	445	12	.984
1993— Baltimore (A.L.).........	SS	*162	*641	87	165	26	3	24	90	.257	65	58	1	226	*495	17	.977
1994— Baltimore (A.L.).........	SS	112	444	71	140	19	3	13	75	.315	32	41	1	132	321	7	*.985
1995— Baltimore (A.L.).........	SS	144	550	71	144	33	2	17	88	.262	52	59	0	206	409	7	*.989
1996— Baltimore (A.L.).........	SS-3B	*163	640	94	178	40	1	26	102	.278	59	78	1	233	483	14	.981
1997— Baltimore (A.L.).........	3B-SS	•162	615	79	166	30	0	17	84	.270	56	73	1	100	313	22	.949
1998— Baltimore (A.L.).........	3B	161	601	65	163	27	1	14	61	.271	51	68	0	101	265	8	*.979
Major league totals (18 years)		**2704**	**10433**	**1510**	**2878**	**544**	**44**	**384**	**1514**	**.276**	**1067**	**1174**	**36**	**3923**	**7728**	**262**	**.978**

DIVISION SERIES RECORD

RECORDS: Holds career record for highest batting average (20 or more at-bats)—.441.

Year— Team (League)	Pos.	G	AB	R	H	2B	3B	HR	RBI	Avg.	BB	SO	SB	PO	A	E	Avg.
1996— Baltimore (A.L.).........	SS	4	18	2	8	3	0	0	2	.444	0	3	0	7	15	0	1.000
1997— Baltimore (A.L.).........	3B	4	16	1	7	2	0	0	1	.438	2	2	0	4	4	0	1.000
Division series totals (2 years)		**8**	**34**	**3**	**15**	**5**	**0**	**0**	**3**	**.441**	**2**	**5**	**0**	**11**	**19**	**0**	**1.000**

CHAMPIONSHIP SERIES RECORD

Year— Team (League)	Pos.	G	AB	R	H	2B	3B	HR	RBI	Avg.	BB	SO	SB	PO	A	E	Avg.
1983— Baltimore (A.L.).........	SS	4	15	5	6	2	0	0	1	.400	2	3	0	7	11	0	1.000
1996— Baltimore (A.L.).........	SS	5	20	1	5	1	0	0	0	.250	1	4	0	4	14	1	.947
1997— Baltimore (A.L.).........	3B	6	23	3	8	2	0	1	3	.348	4	6	0	1	14	0	1.000
Championship series totals (3 years)		**15**	**58**	**9**	**19**	**5**	**0**	**1**	**4**	**.328**	**7**	**13**	**0**	**12**	**39**	**1**	**.981**

WORLD SERIES RECORD

NOTES: Member of World Series championship team (1983).

Year— Team (League)	Pos.	G	AB	R	H	2B	3B	HR	RBI	Avg.	BB	SO	SB	PO	A	E	Avg.
1983— Baltimore (A.L.).........	SS	5	18	2	3	0	0	0	1	.167	3	4	0	6	14	0	1.000

ALL-STAR GAME RECORD

RECORDS: Shares single-game record for most at-bats (nine-inning game)—5 (July 12, 1994).
NOTES: Named Most Valuable Player (1991).

Year— League	Pos.	AB	R	H	2B	3B	HR	RBI	Avg.	BB	SO	SB	PO	A	E	Avg.
1983— American	SS	0	0	0	0	0	0	0	. . .	1	0	0	1	0	0	1.000
1984— American	SS	3	0	0	0	0	0	0	.000	0	0	0	0	0	0	. . .
1985— American	SS	3	0	1	0	0	0	0	.333	0	0	0	2	1	0	1.000
1986— American	SS	4	0	0	0	0	0	0	.000	0	0	0	0	1	0	1.000
1987— American	SS	2	0	1	0	0	0	0	.500	0	0	0	0	5	0	1.000
1988— American	SS	3	0	0	0	0	0	0	.000	1	0	0	1	4	0	1.000
1989— American	SS	3	0	1	1	0	0	0	.333	0	0	0	0	0	0	. . .
1990— American	SS	2	0	0	0	0	0	0	.000	0	0	0	1	1	0	1.000
1991— American	SS	3	1	2	0	0	1	3	.667	0	0	0	2	1	0	1.000
1992— American	SS	3	0	1	0	0	0	1	.333	0	0	0	1	1	0	1.000
1993— American	SS	3	0	0	0	0	0	0	.000	0	1	0	1	2	0	1.000
1994— American	SS	5	0	1	1	0	0	0	.200	0	2	0	1	2	0	1.000
1995— American	SS	3	0	2	0	0	0	0	.667	0	0	0	2	1	0	1.000
1996— American	SS	3	0	0	0	0	0	0	.000	0	0	0	1	1	0	1.000
1997— American	3B	2	0	1	0	0	0	0	.500	0	0	0	0	4	0	1.000
1998— American	3B	4	1	1	1	0	0	2	.250	0	0	0	1	1	0	1.000
All-Star Game totals (16 years)		**46**	**2**	**11**	**3**	**0**	**1**	**6**	**.239**	**2**	**3**	**0**	**14**	**25**	**0**	**1.000**

RISLEY, BILL   P   BLUE JAYS

PERSONAL: Born May 29, 1967, in Chicago. ... 6-2/210. ... Throws right, bats right. ... Full name: William Charles Risley. ... Name pronounced RIZZ-lee.
HIGH SCHOOL: Marist (Chicago).
COLLEGE: Truman College (III.).
TRANSACTIONS/CAREER NOTES: Selected by Cincinnati Reds organization in 14th round of free-agent draft (June 2, 1987). ... Traded by Reds with P John Wetteland to Montreal Expos for OF Dave Martinez, P Scott Ruskin and SS Willie Greene (December 11, 1991). ... On Indianapolis disabled list (April 9-20 and May 16-June 3, 1992). ... On Ottawa disabled list (April 8-23 and June 30-July 10, 1993). ... Claimed on waivers

by Seattle Mariners (March 17, 1994). ... On Seattle disabled list (May 29-June 13, 1995); included rehabilitation assignment to Tacoma (June 12-13). ... Traded by Mariners with 2B Miguel Cairo to Toronto Blue Jays for P Edwin Hurtado and P Paul Menhart (December 18, 1995). ... On Toronto disabled list (May 10-June 11 and June 26-July 31, 1996); included rehabilitation assignments to Syracuse (June 6-9) and St. Catharines (July 19-31). ... On Toronto disabled list (March 12-September 12, 1997); included rehabiliation assignment to Dunedin (May 22-September 1). ... On suspended list (September 16-18, 1998).

STATISTICAL NOTES: Tied for Southern League lead with five balks in 1991.

Year	Team (League)	W	L	Pct.	ERA	G	GS	CG	ShO	Sv.	IP	H	R	ER	BB	SO
1987—	GC Reds (GCL)	1	4	.200	1.89	11	11	0	0	0	52 1/3	38	24	11	26	50
1988—	Greensboro (S. Atl.)	8	4	.667	4.11	23	23	3	3	0	120 1/3	82	60	55	84	135
1989—	Cedar Rapids (Midw.)	9	10	.474	3.90	27	27	2	0	0	140 2/3	87	72	61	81	128
1990—	Cedar Rapids (Midw.)	8	9	.471	2.81	22	22	•7	1	0	137 2/3	99	51	43	68	123
1991—	Chattanooga (Southern)	5	7	.417	3.16	19	19	3	0	0	108 1/3	81	48	38	60	77
—	Nashville (A.A.)	3	5	.375	4.91	8	8	1	0	0	44	45	27	24	26	32
1992—	Indianapolis (A.A.)■	5	8	.385	6.40	25	15	0	0	0	95 2/3	105	69	68	47	64
—	Montreal (N.L.)	1	0	1.000	1.80	1	1	0	0	0	5	4	1	1	1	2
1993—	Ottawa (Int'l)	2	4	.333	2.69	41	0	0	0	1	63 2/3	51	26	19	34	74
—	Montreal (N.L.)	0	0	...	6.00	2	0	0	0	0	3	2	3	2	2	2
1994—	Calgary (PCL)■	0	0	...	3.00	6	1	0	0	1	12	13	5	4	4	15
—	Seattle (A.L.)	9	6	.600	3.44	37	0	0	0	0	52 1/3	31	20	20	19	61
1995—	Tacoma (PCL)	0	0	...	0.00	1	0	0	0	0	1	0	0	0	1	2
—	Seattle (A.L.)	2	1	.667	3.13	45	0	0	0	1	60 1/3	55	21	21	18	65
1996—	Toronto (A.L.)■	0	1	.000	3.89	25	0	0	0	0	41 2/3	33	20	18	25	29
—	Syracuse (Int'l)	0	0	...	0.00	2	0	0	0	0	1	0	1	0	1	0
—	St. Catharines (NYP)	0	0	...	1.29	3	1	0	0	0	7	3	1	1	2	10
1997—	Dunedin (Fla. St.)	0	2	.000	4.50	8	6	0	0	0	12	9	9	6	3	11
—	Syracuse (Int'l)	1	2	.333	8.22	11	1	0	0	0	15 1/3	19	15	14	10	20
—	Toronto (A.L.)	0	1	.000	8.31	3	0	0	0	0	4 1/3	3	4	4	2	2
1998—	Toronto (A.L.)	3	4	.429	5.27	44	0	0	0	0	54 2/3	52	37	32	34	42
A.L. totals (5 years)		14	13	.519	4.01	154	0	0	0	1	213 1/3	174	102	95	98	199
N.L. totals (2 years)		1	0	1.000	3.38	3	1	0	0	0	8	6	4	3	3	4
Major league totals (7 years)		15	13	.536	3.98	157	1	0	0	1	221 1/3	180	106	98	101	203

DIVISION SERIES RECORD

Year	Team (League)	W	L	Pct.	ERA	G	GS	CG	ShO	Sv.	IP	H	R	ER	BB	SO
1995—	Seattle (A.L.)	0	0	...	6.00	4	0	0	0	1	3	2	2	2	0	1

CHAMPIONSHIP SERIES RECORD

Year	Team (League)	W	L	Pct.	ERA	G	GS	CG	ShO	Sv.	IP	H	R	ER	BB	SO
1995—	Seattle (A.L.)	0	0	...	0.00	3	0	0	0	0	2 2/3	2	0	0	1	2

RITCHIE, TODD   P   PIRATES

PERSONAL: Born November 7, 1971, in Portsmouth, Va. ... 6-3/219. ... Throws right, bats right. ... Full name: Todd Everett Ritchie.
HIGH SCHOOL: Duncanville (Texas).
TRANSACTIONS/CAREER NOTES: Selected by Minnesota Twins organization in first round (12th pick overall) of free-agent draft (June 4, 1990). ... On disabled list (August 19, 1991-remainder of season; June 24-July 9, 1993; and April 28, 1994-remainder of season). ... Released by Twins (October 3, 1998). ... Signed by Pittsburgh Pirates organization (December 22, 1998).

Year	Team (League)	W	L	Pct.	ERA	G	GS	CG	ShO	Sv.	IP	H	R	ER	BB	SO
1990—	Elizabethton (Appal.)	5	2	.714	1.94	11	11	1	0	0	65	45	22	14	24	49
1991—	Kenosha (Midwest)	7	6	.538	3.55	21	21	0	0	0	116 2/3	113	53	46	50	101
1992—	Visalia (California)	11	9	.550	5.06	28	•28	3	1	0	172 2/3	193	113	97	65	129
1993—	Nashville (Southern)	3	2	.600	3.66	12	10	0	0	0	46 2/3	46	21	19	15	41
1994—	Nashville (Southern)	0	2	.000	4.24	4	4	0	0	0	17	24	10	8	7	9
1995—	New Britain (East.)	4	9	.308	5.73	24	21	0	0	0	113	135	78	72	54	60
1996—	New Britain (East.)	3	7	.300	5.44	29	10	0	0	4	82 2/3	101	55	50	30	53
—	Salt Lake (PCL)	0	4	.000	5.47	16	0	0	0	0	24 2/3	27	15	15	11	19
1997—	Minnesota (A.L.)	2	3	.400	4.58	42	0	0	0	0	74 2/3	87	41	38	28	44
1998—	Minnesota (A.L.)	0	0	...	5.63	15	0	0	0	0	24	30	17	15	9	21
—	Salt Lake (PCL)	1	3	.250	4.15	36	0	0	0	4	60 2/3	55	38	28	31	62
Major league totals (2 years)		2	3	.400	4.83	57	0	0	0	0	98 2/3	117	58	53	37	65

RITZ, KEVIN   P   ROCKIES

PERSONAL: Born June 8, 1965, in Eatontown, N.J. ... 6-4/229. ... Throws right, bats right. ... Full name: Kevin D. Ritz.
HIGH SCHOOL: Davis County (Iowa).
JUNIOR COLLEGE: Indian Hills Community College (Iowa).
COLLEGE: William Penn (Iowa).
TRANSACTIONS/CAREER NOTES: Selected by San Francisco Giants organization in fourth round of free-agent draft (January 9, 1985); did not sign. ... Selected by Detroit Tigers organization in secondary phase of free-agent draft (June 3, 1985). ... On Detroit disabled list (August 4, 1992-remainder of season). ... Selected by Colorado Rockies in second round (46th pick overall) of expansion draft (November 17, 1992). ... On disabled list (April 4, 1993-entire season). ... Released by Rockies (October 12, 1993). ... Re-signed by Rockies organization (December 1, 1993). ... On disabled list (July 11, 1997-remainder of season). ... On Colorado disabled list (March 20-May 7 and May 18, 1998-remainder of season); included rehabilitation assignments to Colorado Springs (April 21-May 3 and June 13-14) and New Haven (May 29-June 13).
MISCELLANEOUS: Holds Colorado Rockies all-time records for most wins (39) and most innings pitched (576 1/3).

Year	Team (League)	W	L	Pct.	ERA	G	GS	CG	ShO	Sv.	IP	H	R	ER	BB	SO
1986—	Gastonia (S. Atl.)	1	2	.333	4.21	7	7	0	0	0	36 1/3	29	19	17	21	34
—	Lakeland (Fla. St.)	3	9	.250	5.57	18	15	0	0	1	85 2/3	114	60	53	45	39
1987—	Glens Falls (East.)	8	8	.500	4.89	25	25	1	0	0	152 2/3	171	95	83	71	78
1988—	Glens Falls (East.)	8	10	.444	3.82	26	26	4	2	0	136 2/3	115	68	58	70	75

Year Team (League)	W	L	Pct.	ERA	G	GS	CG	ShO	Sv.	IP	H	R	ER	BB	SO
1989— Toledo (International).........	7	8	.467	3.16	16	16	1	0	0	102²/₃	95	48	36	60	74
— Detroit (A.L.).....................	4	6	.400	4.38	12	12	1	0	0	74	75	41	36	44	56
1990— Toledo (International).........	3	6	.333	5.22	20	18	0	0	0	89²/₃	93	68	52	59	57
— Detroit (A.L.).....................	0	4	.000	11.05	4	4	0	0	0	7¹/₃	14	12	9	14	3
1991— Toledo (International).........	8	7	.533	3.28	20	19	3	0	0	126¹/₃	116	50	46	60	105
— Detroit (A.L.).....................	0	3	.000	11.74	11	5	0	0	0	15¹/₃	17	22	20	22	9
1992— Detroit (A.L.).................	2	5	.286	5.60	23	11	0	0	0	80¹/₃	88	52	50	44	57
1993—									Did not play.						
1994— Colo. Springs (PCL)■........	5	0	1.000	1.29	9	3	1	1	0	35	26	6	5	6	27
— Colorado (N.L.)..................	5	6	.455	5.62	15	15	0	0	0	73²/₃	88	49	46	35	53
1995— Colorado (N.L.)...............	11	11	.500	4.21	31	28	0	0	2	173¹/₃	171	91	81	65	120
1996— Colorado (N.L.)...............	17	11	.607	5.28	35	35	2	0	0	213	236	*135	*125	105	105
1997— Colorado (N.L.)...............	6	8	.429	5.87	18	18	1	0	0	107¹/₃	142	72	70	46	56
1998— Colo. Springs (PCL)	0	2	.000	8.31	4	4	0	0	0	17¹/₃	25	23	16	9	7
— Colorado (N.L.)..................	0	2	.000	11.00	2	2	0	0	0	9	17	11	11	2	3
— New Haven (East.).............	1	2	.333	3.71	3	3	1	0	0	17	17	7	7	3	14
A.L. totals (4 years)	6	18	.250	5.85	50	32	1	0	0	177	194	127	115	124	125
N.L. totals (5 years)	39	38	.506	5.20	101	98	3	0	2	576¹/₃	654	358	333	253	337
Major league totals (9 years)......	45	56	.446	5.35	151	130	4	0	2	753¹/₃	848	485	448	377	462

DIVISION SERIES RECORD

Year Team (League)	W	L	Pct.	ERA	G	GS	CG	ShO	Sv.	IP	H	R	ER	BB	SO
1995— Colorado (N.L.)	0	0	...	7.71	2	1	0	0	0	7	12	7	6	3	5

RIVERA, LUIS   SS/2B   ANGELS

PERSONAL: Born January 3, 1964, in Cidra, Puerto Rico. ... 5-9/175. ... Bats right, throws right. ... Full name: Luis Antonio Rivera.
HIGH SCHOOL: Luis Munoz Iglesias (Cidra, Puerto Rico).
TRANSACTIONS/CAREER NOTES: Signed as non-drafted free agent by Montreal Expos organization (September 22, 1981). ... Traded by Expos with P John Dopson to Boston Red Sox for SS Spike Owen and P Dan Gakeler (December 8, 1988). ... On disabled list (June 21-July 18 and August 21-September 5, 1993). ... Granted free agency (October 25, 1993). ... Signed by New York Mets (January 19, 1994). ... Granted free agency (October 24, 1994). ... Signed by St. Louis Cardinals organization (April 18, 1995). ... Released by St. Louis Cardinals (April 24, 1995). ... Signed by Texas Rangers organization (May 3, 1995). ... On disabled list (May 27-June 4, 1995). ... Released by Rangers organization (June 10, 1995). ... Signed by New York Mets organization (November 15, 1995). ... Granted free agency (October 15, 1996). ... Signed by Houston Astros organization (January 25, 1997). ... Granted free agency (October 27, 1997). ... Re-signed by Astros organization (February 5, 1998). ... Traded by Astros to Kansas City Royals for cash (June 3, 1998). ... Released by Royals (September 4, 1998). ... Signed by Anaheim Angels organization (January 15, 1999).
STATISTICAL NOTES: Led Florida State League shortstops with 704 total chances and 95 double plays in 1983. ... Tied for Florida State League lead in total chances by shortstop with 626 in 1984. ... Led Southern League shortstops with 643 total chances and 107 double plays in 1985. ... Led American Association shortstops with 84 double plays in 1987. ... Career major league grand slams: 1.

Year Team (League)	Pos.	G	AB	R	H	2B	3B	HR	RBI	Avg.	BB	SO	SB	PO	A	E	Avg.
1982— San Jose (Calif.).........	SS	130	476	53	123	20	3	3	49	.258	27	94	12	226	389	55	.918
1983— W.P. Beach (FSL)........	SS	129	419	63	95	18	5	5	53	.227	58	88	6	217	*436	*51	.928
1984— W.P. Beach (FSL)........	SS	124	439	54	100	23	0	6	43	.228	50	79	14	*198	*389	39	.938
1985— Jacksonville (Sou.)......	SS	138	*538	74	129	20	2	16	72	.240	44	69	18	*198	*412	33	.949
1986— Indianapolis (A.A.)......	SS	108	407	60	100	17	5	7	43	.246	29	68	18	178	330	24	.955
— Montreal (N.L.)...............	SS	55	166	20	34	11	1	0	13	.205	17	33	1	64	119	9	.953
1987— Indianapolis (A.A.)......	SS	108	433	73	135	26	3	8	53	.312	32	73	24	190	291	18	.964
— Montreal (N.L.)...............	SS	18	32	0	5	2	0	0	1	.156	1	8	0	9	27	3	.923
1988— Montreal (N.L.)...........	SS	123	371	35	83	17	3	4	30	.224	24	69	3	160	301	18	.962
1989— Pawtucket (Int'l)■........	SS-3B	43	175	22	44	9	0	1	13	.251	11	23	5	53	106	9	.946
— Boston (A.L.).................	SS-2B-DH	93	323	35	83	17	1	5	29	.257	20	60	2	127	240	16	.958
1990— Boston (A.L.).............	SS-2B-3B	118	346	38	78	20	0	7	45	.225	25	58	4	187	310	18	.965
1991— Boston (A.L.).............	SS	129	414	64	107	22	3	8	40	.258	35	86	4	180	386	*24	.959
1992— Boston (A.L.).............	S-DH-O-3-2	102	288	17	62	11	1	0	29	.215	26	56	4	120	287	14	.967
1993— Boston (A.L.).............	S-2-DH-3	62	130	13	27	8	1	1	7	.208	11	36	1	65	111	6	.967
1994— New York (N.L.)■........	SS-2B	32	43	11	12	2	1	3	5	.279	4	14	0	19	29	2	.960
1995— Okla. City (A.A.)■........	SS	19	58	3	8	4	0	1	3	.138	1	6	0	24	51	3	.962
1996— Norfolk (Int'l)■............	SS-3B	114	356	34	80	23	3	6	39	.225	31	58	1	126	330	21	.956
1997— New Orleans (A.A.)■....	SS-3B-2B	124	382	46	91	23	4	3	45	.238	34	51	5	148	366	17	.968
— Houston (N.L.)...............	SS	7	13	2	3	0	1	0	3	.231	1	6	0	9	9	2	.900
1998— New Orleans (PCL).....	S-2-3-O	33	82	17	19	2	1	1	7	.232	9	8	2	22	39	6	.910
— Kansas City (A.L.)■.........	SS-2B-3B	42	89	14	22	4	0	0	7	.247	7	17	1	48	90	5	.965
American League totals (6 years)		546	1590	181	379	82	6	21	157	.238	124	313	16	727	1424	83	.963
National League totals (5 years)		235	625	68	137	32	6	7	52	.219	47	130	4	261	485	34	.956
Major league totals (11 years)		781	2215	249	516	114	12	28	209	.233	171	443	20	988	1909	117	.961

CHAMPIONSHIP SERIES RECORD

Year Team (League)	Pos.	G	AB	R	H	2B	3B	HR	RBI	Avg.	BB	SO	SB	PO	A	E	Avg.
1990— Boston (A.L.).............	SS	4	9	1	2	1	0	0	0	.222	0	2	0	6	16	1	.957

RIVERA, LUIS   P   BRAVES

PERSONAL: Born June 21, 1978, in Chihuahua, Mexico. ... 6-3/163. ... Throws right, bats right. ... Full name: Luis Gutierrez Rivera.
TRANSACTIONS/CAREER NOTES: Signed as non-drafted free agent by Atlanta Braves organization (February 18, 1995).

Year Team (League)	W	L	Pct.	ERA	G	GS	CG	ShO	Sv.	IP	H	R	ER	BB	SO
1996— GC Braves (GCL)...............	1	1	.500	2.59	8	6	0	0	0	24¹/₃	18	9	7	7	26
1997— Danville (Appalachian)........	3	1	.750	2.41	9	9	0	0	0	41	28	15	11	17	57
— Macon (S. Atl.)..................	2	0	1.000	1.29	4	4	0	0	0	21	13	4	3	7	22
1998— Macon (S. Atl.).................	5	5	.500	3.98	20	20	0	0	0	92²/₃	78	53	41	41	118

PERSONAL: Born November 29, 1969, in Panama City, Panama. ... 6-2/170. ... Throws right, bats right. ... Cousin of Ruben Rivera, outfielder, San Diego Padres.

TRANSACTIONS/CAREER NOTES: Signed as non-drafted free agent by New York Yankees organization (February 17, 1990). ... On disabled list (April 10-May 19, July 11-28 and August 12-September 8, 1992). ... On Albany/Colonie disabled list (April 9-June 28, 1993). ... On Greensboro disabled list (September 6, 1993-remainder of season). ... On Tampa disabled list (April 23-May 9, 1994). ... On Columbus disabled list (August 4-14, 1994). ... On disabled list (April 6-24, 1998).

HONORS: Named A.L. Fireman of the Year by THE SPORTING NEWS (1997).

STATISTICAL NOTES: Pitched seven-inning, 3-0 no-hit victory against Gulf Coast Pirates (August 31, 1990). ... Pitched five-inning, 3-0 no-hit victory for Columbus against Rochester (June 26, 1995).

Year Team (League)	W	L	Pct.	ERA	G	GS	CG	ShO	Sv.	IP	H	R	ER	BB	SO
1990— GC Yankees (GCL)	5	1	.833	*0.17	22	1	1	1	1	52	17	3	1	7	58
1991— Greensboro (S. Atl.)	4	9	.308	2.75	29	15	1	0	0	114 2/3	103	48	35	36	123
1992— Fort Lauderdale (FSL)	5	3	.625	2.28	10	10	3	1	0	59 1/3	40	17	15	5	42
1993— Greensboro (S. Atl.)	1	0	1.000	2.06	10	10	0	0	0	39 1/3	31	12	9	15	32
— GC Yankees (GCL)	0	1	.000	2.25	2	2	0	0	0	4	2	1	1	1	6
1994— Tampa (Fla. St.)	3	0	1.000	2.21	7	7	0	0	0	36 2/3	34	12	9	12	27
— Alb./Colon. (East.)	3	0	1.000	2.27	9	9	0	0	0	63 1/3	58	20	16	8	39
— Columbus (Int'l)	4	2	.667	5.81	6	6	1	0	0	31	34	22	20	10	23
1995— Columbus (Int'l)	2	2	.500	2.10	7	7	1	1	0	30	25	10	7	3	30
— New York (A.L.)	5	3	.625	5.51	19	10	0	0	0	67	71	43	41	30	51
1996— New York (A.L.)	8	3	.727	2.09	61	0	0	0	5	107 2/3	73	25	25	34	130
1997— New York (A.L.)	6	4	.600	1.88	66	0	0	0	43	71 2/3	65	17	15	20	68
1998— New York (A.L.)	3	0	1.000	1.91	54	0	0	0	36	61 1/3	48	13	13	17	36
Major league totals (4 years)	22	10	.688	2.75	200	10	0	0	84	307 2/3	257	98	94	101	285

DIVISION SERIES RECORD

Year Team (League)	W	L	Pct.	ERA	G	GS	CG	ShO	Sv.	IP	H	R	ER	BB	SO
1995— New York (A.L.)	1	0	1.000	0.00	3	0	0	0	0	5 1/3	3	0	0	1	8
1996— New York (A.L.)	0	0	...	0.00	2	0	0	0	0	4 2/3	0	0	0	1	1
1997— New York (A.L.)	0	0	...	4.50	2	0	0	0	1	2	2	1	1	0	1
1998— New York (A.L.)	0	0	...	0.00	3	0	0	0	2	3 1/3	1	0	0	1	2
Div. series totals (4 years)	1	0	1.000	0.59	10	0	0	0	3	15 1/3	6	1	1	3	12

CHAMPIONSHIP SERIES RECORD

Year Team (League)	W	L	Pct.	ERA	G	GS	CG	ShO	Sv.	IP	H	R	ER	BB	SO
1996— New York (A.L.)	1	0	1.000	*0.00	2	0	0	0	0	4	6	0	0	1	5
1998— New York (A.L.)	0	0	...	0.00	4	0	0	0	1	5 2/3	0	0	0	1	5
Champ. series totals (2 years)	1	0	1.000	0.00	6	0	0	0	1	9 2/3	6	0	0	2	10

WORLD SERIES RECORD

NOTES: Member of World Series championship team (1996 and 1998).

Year Team (League)	W	L	Pct.	ERA	G	GS	CG	ShO	Sv.	IP	H	R	ER	BB	SO
1996— New York (A.L.)	0	0	...	1.59	4	0	0	0	0	5 2/3	4	1	1	3	4
1998— New York (A.L.)	0	0	...	0.00	3	0	0	0	3	4 1/3	5	0	0	0	4
World Series totals (2 years)	0	0	...	0.90	7	0	0	0	3	10	9	1	1	3	8

ALL-STAR GAME RECORD

Year League	W	L	Pct.	ERA	GS	CG	ShO	Sv.	IP	H	R	ER	BB	SO
1997— American	0	0	...	0.00	0	0	0	1	1	0	0	0	0	1

R

PERSONAL: Born November 14, 1973, in La Chorrera, Panama ... 6-3/200. ... Bats right, throws right. ... Full name: Ruben Moreno Rivera. ... Cousin of Mariano Rivera, pitcher, New York Yankees.

TRANSACTIONS/CAREER NOTES: Signed as non-drafted free agent by New York Yankees organization (November 21, 1990). ... On New York disabled list (March 27-May 30, 1997). ... Traded by Yankees with P Rafael Medina and $3 million to San Diego Padres for the rights to P Hideki Irabu, 2B Homer Bush, OF Gordon Amerson and a player to be named later (April 22, 1997); Padres traded OF Vernon Maxwell to Yankees to complete deal (June 9). ... On San Diego disabled list (May 30-August 13, 1997); included rehabilitation assignments to Rancho Cucamonga (May 30-July 22) and Las Vegas (July 23-August 4).

HONORS: Named New York-Pennsylvania League Most Valuable Player (1993). ... Named South Atlantic League Most Valuable Player (1994).

STATISTICAL NOTES: Led New York-Pennsylvania League outfielders with three double plays in 1993. ... Led South Atlantic League with .573 slugging percentage in 1994. ... Career major league grand slams: 1.

Year Team (League)	Pos.	G	AB	R	H	2B	3B	HR	RBI	Avg.	BB	SO	SB	PO	A	E	Avg.
1991— Dom. Dodgers (DSL)	...	51	170	27	34	3	2	2	16	.200	23	37	14	...	...	...	...
1992— GC Yankees (GCL)	OF	53	194	37	53	10	3	1	20	.273	42	49	21	67	10	4	.951
1993— Oneonta (NYP)	OF	55	199	45	55	7	6	13	47	.276	32	66	12	111	9	3	.976
1994— Greensboro (S. Atl.)	OF	105	400	83	115	24	3	•28	81	.288	47	125	36	217	14	5	.979
— Tampa (Fla. St.)	OF	34	134	18	35	4	3	5	20	.261	8	38	12	76	6	2	.976
1995— Norwich (Eastern)	OF	71	256	49	75	16	8	9	39	.293	37	77	16	176	7	3	.984
— Columbus (Int'l)	OF	48	174	37	47	8	2	15	35	.270	26	62	8	113	6	3	.975
— New York (A.L.)	OF	5	1	0	0	0	0	0	0	.000	0	1	0	2	0	0	1.000
1996— Columbus (Int'l)	OF	101	362	59	85	20	4	10	46	.235	40	96	15	239	6	7	.972
— New York (A.L.)	OF	46	88	17	25	6	1	2	16	.284	13	26	6	77	2	0	1.000
1997— Rancho Cuca. (Cal.)■	DH	6	23	6	4	1	0	1	3	.174	3	9	1	...	...	...	...
— Las Vegas (PCL)	1B	12	48	6	12	5	1	1	6	.250	1	20	1	1	0	0	1.000
— San Diego (N.L.)	OF	17	20	2	5	1	0	0	1	.250	2	9	2	13	0	0	1.000
1998— Las Vegas (PCL)	OF	30	104	9	15	3	0	3	11	.144	11	42	4	53	2	0	1.000
— San Diego (N.L.)	OF	95	172	31	36	7	2	6	29	.209	28	52	5	104	3	3	.973
American League totals (2 years)		51	89	17	25	6	1	2	16	.281	13	27	6	79	2	0	1.000
National League totals (2 years)		112	192	33	41	8	2	6	30	.214	30	61	7	117	3	3	.976
Major league totals (4 years)		163	281	50	66	14	3	8	46	.235	43	88	13	196	5	3	.985

DIVISION SERIES RECORD

								BATTING									FIELDING		
Year	Team (League)	Pos.	G	AB	R	H	2B	3B	HR	RBI	Avg.	BB	SO	SB	PO	A	E	Avg.
1996— New York (A.L.).........		OF-PH	2	1	0	0	0	0	00	0	.000	0	1	0	0	0	0	...
1998— San Diego (N.L.)		OF	3	6	0	0	0	0	0	0	.000	0	3	0	3	0	0	1.000
Division series totals (2 years)			5	7	0	0	0	0	0	0	.000	0	4	0	3	0	0	1.000

CHAMPIONSHIP SERIES RECORD

								BATTING									FIELDING		
Year	Team (League)	Pos.	G	AB	R	H	2B	3B	HR	RBI	Avg.	BB	SO	SB	PO	A	E	Avg.
1998— San Diego (N.L.)		OF-PH	6	13	1	3	2	0	0	0	.231	0	7	1	8	1	0	1.000

WORLD SERIES RECORD

NOTES: Member of World Series championship team (1996); inactive due to injury.

								BATTING									FIELDING		
Year	Team (League)	Pos.	G	AB	R	H	2B	3B	HR	RBI	Avg.	BB	SO	SB	PO	A	E	Avg.
1996— New York (A.L.)							Did not play.											
1998— San Diego (N.L.)		PH-OF-PR	3	5	1	4	2	0	0	1	.800	0	0	0	3	0	0	1.000

RIZZO, TODD — P — WHITE SOX

PERSONAL: Born May 24, 1971, in Clifton Heights, Pa. ... 6-2/220. ... Throws left, bats right. ... Full name: Todd Michael Rizzo.
HIGH SCHOOL: Garnet Valley (Concordville, Pa.).
JUNIOR COLLEGE: Delaware County Community College (Pa.).
TRANSACTIONS/CAREER NOTES: Signed as non-drafted free agent by Los Angeles Dodgers organization (May 6, 1992). ... Released by Dodgers organization (June 13, 1993). ... Signed by San Antonio, independent (1994). ... Released by San Antonio (1994). ... Signed by Tyler, independent (1994). ... Signed by Chicago White Sox organization (March 4, 1995).

Year	Team (League)	W	L	Pct.	ERA	G	GS	CG	ShO	Sv.	IP	H	R	ER	BB	SO
1992— GC Dodgers (GCL)		0	1	.000	3.86	3	1	0	0	0	7	4	4	3	8	7
— Yakima (N'west)		2	0	1.000	4.50	15	0	0	0	0	26	21	13	13	24	26
1993—								Out of organized baseball.								
1994— San Antonio (Texas-La.).....		0	2	.000	7.53	17	0	0	0	1	28²/₃	30	32	24	41	20
— Tyler (Texas-Louisiana)		0	0	...	8.35	14	1	0	0	0	18¹/₃	24	23	17	21	13
1995— Prince William (Caro.)■....		3	5	.375	2.78	36	0	0	0	1	68	68	30	21	39	59
1996— Birmingham (Southern)		4	4	.500	2.75	46	0	0	0	0	68²/₃	61	28	21	40	48
1997— Nashville (A.A.)		4	5	.444	3.57	54	0	0	0	6	70²/₃	63	39	28	33	60
1998— Calgary (PCL)		7	3	.700	6.75	50	0	0	0	4	72	102	62	54	39	58
— Chicago (A.L.)		0	0	...	13.50	9	0	0	0	0	6²/₃	12	12	10	6	3
Major league totals (1 year)		0	0	...	13.50	9	0	0	0	0	6²/₃	12	12	10	6	3

ROBERTS, BIP — 2B/OF

PERSONAL: Born October 27, 1963, in Berkeley, Calif. ... 5-7/165. ... Bats both, throws right. ... Full name: Leon Joseph Roberts III. ... Nephew of Roy Shivers, running back with St. Louis Cardinals (1966-1972).
HIGH SCHOOL: Skyline (Oakland).
JUNIOR COLLEGE: Chabot College (Calif.).
COLLEGE: UNLV.
TRANSACTIONS/CAREER NOTES: Selected by Pittsburgh Pirates organization in fifth round of free-agent draft (June 8, 1981); did not sign. ... Selected by Pirates organization in secondary phase of free-agent draft (June 7, 1982). ... On suspended list (June 30-July 3, 1985). ... Selected by San Diego Padres from Pirates organization in Rule 5 major league draft (December 10, 1985). ... On disabled list (May 21-June 5, 1986 and August 17-September 9, 1991). ... Traded by Padres with a player to be named later to Cincinnati Reds for P Randy Myers (December 8, 1991); Reds acquired OF Craig Pueschner to complete deal (December 9, 1991). ... On disabled list (July 2-17 and August 4, 1993-remainder of season). ... Granted free agency (October 26, 1993). ... Signed by Padres (January 10, 1994). ... Granted free agency (October 20, 1994). ... Re-signed by Padres (December 23, 1994). ... On San Diego disabled list (June 28-July 13 and July 14-August 22, 1995); included rehabilitation assignments to Rancho Cucamonga (August 18-19) and Las Vegas (August 19-22). ... Traded by Padres with P Bryan Wolff to Kansas City Royals for 1B Wally Joyner and P Aaron Dorlarque (December 21, 1995). ... On disabled list (June 10-July 19 and August 7-September 1, 1996). ... On Kansas City disabled list (June 17-July 10, 1997). ... Traded by Royals to Cleveland Indians for P Roland de la Maza (August 31, 1997). ... Granted free agency (November 7, 1997). ... Signed by Detroit Tigers (December 12, 1997). ... On Detroit disabled list (April 26-May 12 and May 26-June 5, 1998); included rehabilitation assignments to Toledo (May 8-12 and June 10-15). ... Traded by Tigers to Oakland Athletics for a player to be named later (June 23, 1998); Tigers acquired IF Jason Wood to complete deal (July 18, 1998). ... Granted free agency (October 26, 1998).
RECORDS: Shares N.L. single-season record for most consecutive hits—10 (September 19, 20, 22 [second game] and 23, 1992; one base on balls).
STATISTICAL NOTES: Led South Atlantic League second basemen with .962 fielding percentage and tied for lead with 76 double plays in 1983. ... Led Carolina League second basemen with 654 total chances and 91 double plays in 1984. ... Had 23-game hitting streak (May 26-June 20, 1994). ... Career major league grand slams: 1.

								BATTING									FIELDING		
Year	Team (League)	Pos.	G	AB	R	H	2B	3B	HR	RBI	Avg.	BB	SO	SB	PO	A	E	Avg.
1982— GC Pirates (GCL)........		2B	6	23	4	7	1	0	0	1	.304	2	4	4	14	15	0	1.000
— Greenwood (SAL).......		2B	33	107	15	23	3	1	0	6	.215	15	18	10	52	82	7	.950
1983— Greenwood (SAL).......		2B-SS	122	438	78	140	20	5	6	63	.320	69	43	27	273	311	24	†.961
1984— Prince Will. (Car.).......		2B	134	498	81	*150	25	5	8	77	.301	44	63	50	*282	352	20	*.969
1985— Nashua (Eastern)........		2B	105	401	64	109	19	5	1	23	.272	29	43	•40	217	249	•29	.941
1986— San Diego (N.L.)■.......		2B	101	241	34	61	5	2	1	12	.253	14	29	14	166	172	10	.971
1987— Las Vegas (PCL)........		2B-OF-3B	98	359	66	110	18	10	1	38	.306	37	39	27	147	150	8	.974
1988— Las Vegas (PCL)........		3B-OF-2B	100	343	73	121	21	8	7	51	.353	32	45	29	103	130	17	.932
— San Diego (N.L.)........		2B-3B	5	9	1	3	0	0	0	0	.333	1	2	0	2	3	1	.833
1989— San Diego (N.L.)........		O-3-S-2	117	329	81	99	15	8	3	25	.301	49	45	21	134	113	9	.965
1990— San Diego (N.L.)........		O-3-S-2	149	556	104	172	36	3	9	44	.309	55	65	46	227	160	13	.968
1991— San Diego (N.L.)		2B-OF	117	424	66	119	13	3	3	32	.281	37	71	26	239	185	10	.977

Year— Team (League)	Pos.	G	AB	R	H	2B	3B	HR	RBI	Avg.	BB	SO	SB	PO	A	E	Avg.
						BATTING									FIELDING		
1992— Cincinnati (N.L.)■	OF-2B-3B	147	532	92	172	34	6	4	45	.323	62	54	44	209	152	7	.981
1993— Cincinnati (N.L.)	2-0-3-S	83	292	46	70	13	0	1	18	.240	38	46	26	152	176	6	.982
1994— San Diego (N.L.)■	2B-OF	105	403	52	129	15	5	2	31	.320	39	57	21	178	221	9	.978
1995— San Diego (N.L.)	OF-2B-SS	73	296	40	90	14	0	2	25	.304	17	36	20	135	88	4	.982
— Rancho Cuca. (Cal.)	DH	1	3	1	0	0	0	0	0	.000	1	1	1	0	0	0	...
— Las Vegas (PCL)	SS-2B	3	12	1	4	0	0	0	2	.333	0	3	1	2	15	1	.944
1996— Kansas City (A.L.)■	2B-DH-OF	90	339	39	96	21	2	0	52	.283	25	38	12	115	190	4	.987
1997— Kansas City (A.L.)	OF-3B	97	346	44	107	17	2	1	36	.309	21	53	15	149	17	3	.982
— Cleveland (A.L.)■	2B-OF	23	85	19	23	3	0	3	8	.271	7	14	3	37	33	4	.946
1998— Detroit (A.L.)■	DH-OF-2B	34	113	17	28	6	0	0	9	.248	16	14	6	3	3	0	1.000
— Toledo (Int'l)	DH	6	19	2	5	0	0	0	0	.263	2	4	2	0	0	0	...
— Oakland (A.L.)■	2B-OF-3B	61	182	28	51	11	0	1	15	.280	15	24	10	81	61	5	.966
American League totals (3 years)		305	1065	147	305	58	4	5	120	.286	84	143	46	385	304	16	.977
National League totals (9 years)		897	3082	516	915	145	27	25	232	.297	312	405	218	1442	1270	69	.975
Major league totals (12 years)		1202	4147	663	1220	203	31	30	352	.294	396	548	264	1827	1574	85	.976

DIVISION SERIES RECORD

Year— Team (League)	Pos.	G	AB	R	H	2B	3B	HR	RBI	Avg.	BB	SO	SB	PO	A	E	Avg.
						BATTING									FIELDING		
1997— Cleveland (A.L.)	2B-OF	5	19	1	6	0	0	0	1	.316	2	2	2	5	8	0	1.000

CHAMPIONSHIP SERIES RECORD

Year— Team (League)	Pos.	G	AB	R	H	2B	3B	HR	RBI	Avg.	BB	SO	SB	PO	A	E	Avg.
						BATTING									FIELDING		
1997— Cleveland (A.L.)	2B-OF	5	20	0	3	1	0	0	0	.150	0	8	1	11	7	1	.947

WORLD SERIES RECORD

Year— Team (League)	Pos.	G	AB	R	H	2B	3B	HR	RBI	Avg.	BB	SO	SB	PO	A	E	Avg.
						BATTING									FIELDING		
1997— Cleveland (A.L.)	2B-OF	6	22	3	6	4	0	0	4	.273	3	5	0	8	8	0	1.000

ALL-STAR GAME RECORD

Year— League	Pos.	AB	R	H	2B	3B	HR	RBI	Avg.	BB	SO	SB	PO	A	E	Avg.
					BATTING									FIELDING		
1992— National	OF	2	1	2	0	0	0	2	1.000	0	0	0	0	0	0	...

ROBERTS, GRANT — P — METS

PERSONAL: Born September 13, 1977, in El Cajon, Calif. ... 6-3/205. ... Throws right, bats right. ... Full name: Grant William Roberts.
HIGH SCHOOL: Grossmont (La Mesa, Calif.).
TRANSACTIONS/CAREER NOTES: Selected by New York Mets organization in 11th round of free-agent draft (June 1, 1995).

Year— Team (League)	W	L	Pct.	ERA	G	GS	CG	ShO	Sv.	IP	H	R	ER	BB	SO
1995— GC Mets (GCL)	2	1	.667	2.15	11	3	0	0	0	29 1/3	19	13	7	14	24
1996— Kingsport (Appalachian)	*9	1	*.900	2.10	13	13	2	*2	0	68 2/3	43	18	16	37	*92
1997— Columbia (S. Atl.)	11	3	*.786	2.36	22	22	2	1	0	129 2/3	98	37	34	44	122
1998— St. Lucie (Fla. St.)	4	5	.444	4.23	17	17	0	0	0	72 1/3	72	37	34	37	70

ROBERTS, WILLIS — P — TIGERS

PERSONAL: Born June 19, 1975, in San Cristobal, Dominican Republic. ... 6-3/175. ... Throws right, bats right. ... Full name: Willis Augusto Roberts.
TRANSACTIONS/CAREER NOTES: Signed as non-drafted free agent by Detroit Tigers organization (February 18, 1992). ... On disabled list (July 14-August 1 and August 1-September 13, 1994).

Year— Team (League)	W	L	Pct.	ERA	G	GS	CG	ShO	Sv.	IP	H	R	ER	BB	SO
1992— Dom. Tigers (DSL)	0	6	.000	8.23	12	7	1	0	0	35	43	49	32	46	17
1993— Bristol (Appalachian)	2	3	.400	1.38	10	2	0	0	1	26	24	16	4	11	23
1994— Bristol (Appalachian)	1	2	.333	3.92	4	4	0	0	0	20 2/3	9	9	9	8	17
1995— Fayetteville (S. Atl.)	6	3	.667	2.70	17	15	0	0	0	80	72	33	24	40	52
1996— Lakeland (Fla. St.)	9	7	.563	2.89	23	22	2	0	0	149 1/3	133	60	48	69	105
1997— Jacksonville (Southern)	6	*15	.286	6.28	26	26	2	0	0	149	181	*120	*104	64	86
1998— Jacksonville (Southern)	3	1	.750	2.19	12	2	0	0	0	24 2/3	21	10	6	10	15
— Toledo (International)	3	3	.500	4.61	39	0	0	0	2	54 2/3	63	33	28	28	40

ROBERTSON, MIKE — 1B

PERSONAL: Born October 9, 1970, in Norwich, Conn. ... 6-0/189. ... Bats left, throws left. ... Full name: Michael Francis Robertson. ... Son of Michael Robertson, infielder in Washington Senators and Texas Rangers organizations (1968-74).
HIGH SCHOOL: Servite (Anaheim, Calif.).
COLLEGE: Southern California.
TRANSACTIONS/CAREER NOTES: Selected by California Angels organization in 13th round of free-agent draft (June 1, 1988); did not sign. ... Selected by Chicago White Sox organization in third round of free-agent draft (June 3, 1991). ... Traded by White Sox to Philadelphia Phillies for 1B Gene Schall (January 31, 1997). ... Granted free agency (October 10, 1997). ... Signed by Arizona Diamondbacks organization (January 12, 1998). ... Granted free agency (September 29, 1998).
STATISTICAL NOTES: Led American Association first basemen with 1,172 putouts, 75 assists, .992 fielding percentage, 1,257 total chances and 111 double plays in 1995. ... Led International League first basemen with 97 assists and tied for league lead with 14 errors in 1997.

Year Team (League)	Pos.	G	AB	R	H	2B	3B	HR	RBI	Avg.	BB	SO	SB	PO	A	E	Avg.
1991— Utica (N.Y.-Penn)........	1B	13	54	6	9	2	1	0	8	.167	5	11	1	116	13	3	.977
— South Bend (Mid.)......	1B	54	210	30	69	16	2	1	26	.329	18	24	7	403	40	3	.993
1992—Sarasota (Fla. St.)	1B	106	395	50	99	21	3	10	59	.251	50	55	5	870	112	9	.991
—Birmingham (Sou.)........	1B	27	90	6	17	8	1	1	9	.189	10	19	0	213	21	3	.987
1993—Birmingham (Sou.).....	1B-OF	138	511	73	138	31	3	11	73	.270	59	97	10	1065	108	13	.989
1994—Birmingham (Sou.).....	OF-1B	53	196	32	62	20	2	3	30	.316	31	34	6	206	13	3	.986
—Nashville (A.A.)	OF-1B	67	213	21	48	8	1	8	21	.225	15	27	0	193	12	1	.995
1995—Nashville (A.A.)	1B-OF	139	499	55	124	17	4	19	52	.248	50	72	2	†1180	†75	11	†.991
1996—Nashville (A.A.)	1B	•138	450	64	116	16	4	21	74	.258	38	83	1	1074	54	4	*.996
—Chicago (A.L.)	1B-DH	6	7	0	1	1	0	0	0	.143	0	1	0	11	1	0	1.000
1997—Scran./W.B. (Int'l)■....	1B-OF	121	416	61	124	17	3	12	72	.298	58	67	0	951	†97	‡14	.987
—Philadelphia (N.L.)......	1B-OF-DH	22	38	3	8	2	1	0	4	.211	0	6	1	28	1	0	1.000
1998—Tucson (PCL)■..........	1B-OF	111	411	49	112	14	3	13	70	.273	33	56	1	862	55	6	.993
—Arizona (N.L.).............	DH	11	13	0	2	0	0	0	0	.154	0	2	0	...	...	...	...
American League totals (1 year)		6	7	0	1	1	0	0	0	.143	0	1	0	11	1	0	1.000
National League totals (2 years)		33	51	3	10	2	1	0	4	.196	0	8	1	28	1	0	1.000
Major league totals (3 years)		39	58	3	11	3	1	0	4	.190	0	9	1	39	2	0	1.000

ROBERTSON, RICH — P — RANGERS

PERSONAL: Born September 15, 1968, in Waller, Texas. ... 6-4/182. ... Throws left, bats left. ... Full name: Richard Wayne Robertson.
HIGH SCHOOL: Waller (Texas).
JUNIOR COLLEGE: San Jacinto College (Texas).
COLLEGE: Texas A&M.
TRANSACTIONS/CAREER NOTES: Selected by San Diego Padres organization in 32nd round of free-agent draft (June 5, 1989); did not sign. ... Selected by Pittsburgh Pirates organization in ninth round of free-agent draft (June 4, 1990). ... On Buffalo disabled list (June 10-19, 1993). ... Claimed on waivers by Minnesota Twins (November 4, 1994). ... Granted free agency (October 15, 1997). ... Signed by Anaheim Angels organization (January 19, 1998). ... Released by Angels (November 16, 1998). ... Signed by Texas Rangers organization (December 9, 1998).

Year Team (League)	W	L	Pct.	ERA	G	GS	CG	ShO	Sv.	IP	H	R	ER	BB	SO
1990—Welland (N.Y.-Penn)	3	4	.429	3.08	16	13	0	0	0	64 1/3	51	34	22	55	80
1991—Augusta (S. Atl.)...............	4	7	.364	4.99	13	12	1	0	0	74	73	52	41	51	62
—Salem (Carolina)	2	4	.333	4.93	12	11	0	0	0	45 2/3	34	32	25	42	32
1992—Salem (Carolina)	3	0	1.000	3.41	6	6	0	0	0	37	29	18	14	10	27
—Carolina (Southern)...........	6	7	.462	3.03	20	20	1	1	0	124 2/3	127	51	42	41	107
1993—Buffalo (A.A.)................	9	8	.529	4.28	23	23	2	0	0	132 1/3	141	67	63	52	71
—Pittsburgh (N.L.)................	0	1	.000	6.00	9	0	0	0	0	9	15	6	6	4	5
1994—Buffalo (A.A.)................	5	10	.333	3.11	18	17	0	0	0	118 2/3	112	47	41	36	71
—Pittsburgh (N.L.)................	0	0	...	6.89	8	0	0	0	0	15 2/3	20	12	12	10	8
1995—Salt Lake (PCL)■............	5	0	1.000	2.44	7	7	1	0	0	44 1/3	31	13	12	12	40
—Minnesota (A.L.)...............	2	0	1.000	3.83	25	4	1	0	0	51 2/3	48	28	22	31	38
1996—Minnesota (A.L.)...............	7	17	.292	5.12	36	31	5	•3	0	186 1/3	197	113	106	*116	114
1997—Minnesota (A.L.)...............	8	12	.400	5.69	31	26	0	0	0	147	169	105	93	70	69
1998—Vancouver (PCL)■............	11	12	.478	3.81	27	27	2	0	0	175	171	85	74	68	123
—Anaheim (A.L.)...................	0	0	...	15.88	5	0	0	0	0	5 2/3	11	11	10	2	3
A.L. totals (4 years)	17	29	.370	5.32	97	61	6	3	0	390 2/3	425	257	231	219	224
N.L. totals (2 years)	0	1	.000	6.57	17	0	0	0	0	24 2/3	35	18	18	14	13
Major league totals (6 years)......	17	30	.362	5.40	114	61	6	3	0	415 1/3	460	275	249	233	237

ROBINSON, KERRY — OF — MARINERS

PERSONAL: Born October 3, 1973, in St. Louis. ... 6-0/175. ... Bats left, throws left. ... Full name: Kerry Keith Robinson. ... Son of Rogers Robinson, outfielder in St. Louis Cardinals organization (1957-69).
HIGH SCHOOL: Hazelwood East (St. Louis).
COLLEGE: Southeast Missouri State.
TRANSACTIONS/CAREER NOTES: Selected by St. Louis Cardinals organization in 34th round of free-agent draft (June 1, 1995). ... Selected by Tampa Bay Devil Rays in second round (44th pick overall) of expansion draft (November 18, 1997). ... Claimed on waivers by Seattle Mariners (November 19, 1998).
STATISTICAL NOTES: Led Midwest League in caught stealing with 27 in 1996. ... Led Texas League in caught stealing with 23 in 1997.

Year Team (League)	Pos.	G	AB	R	H	2B	3B	HR	RBI	Avg.	BB	SO	SB	PO	A	E	Avg.
1995— Johnson City (App.) ...	OF	60	250	44	74	12	8	1	26	.296	16	30	14	86	5	6	.938
1996— Peoria (Midwest)........	OF	123	440	98	158	17	4	2	47	.359	51	51	•50	168	7	7	.962
1997— Arkansas (Texas).........	OF	135	*523	80	168	16	3	2	62	.321	54	64	40	193	6	7	.966
—Louisville (A.A.).........	OF	2	9	0	1	0	0	0	0	.111	0	1	0	3	0	0	1.000
1998— Orlando (South.)■.....	OF	72	309	45	83	7	5	2	26	.269	27	28	28	135	5	0	1.000
—Durham (Int'l).........	OF	58	242	28	73	7	4	1	28	.302	23	30	18	146	3	2	.987
—Tampa Bay (A.L.)........	OF	2	3	0	0	0	0	0	0	.000	0	1	0	4	0	0	1.000
Major league totals (1 year)		2	3	0	0	0	0	0	0	.000	0	1	0	4	0	0	1.000

ROCKER, JOHN — P — BRAVES

PERSONAL: Born October 17, 1974, in Statesboro, Ga. ... 6-4/210. ... Throws left, bats right. ... Full name: John Loy Rocker.
HIGH SCHOOL: First Presbyterian Day School (Macon, Ga.).
COLLEGE: Mercer (Ga.).
TRANSACTIONS/CAREER NOTES: Selected by Atlanta Braves organization in 18th round of free-agent draft (June 3, 1993).
STATISTICAL NOTES: Pitched 2-0 no-hit victory against Charleston, S.C. (June 9, 1996). ... Led Southern League in wild pitches with 17 in 1997.

Year	Team (League)	W	L	Pct.	ERA	G	GS	CG	ShO	Sv.	IP	H	R	ER	BB	SO
1994—	Danville (Appalachian)........	1	5	.167	3.53	12	12	1	0	0	63 2/3	50	36	25	38	72
1995—	Eugene (Northwest)	1	5	.167	5.16	12	12	0	0	0	59 1/3	45	40	34	36	74
—	Macon (S. Atl.)..................	4	4	.500	4.50	16	16	0	0	0	86	86	50	43	52	61
1996—	Macon (S. Atl.)	5	3	.625	3.89	20	19	2	2	0	106 1/3	85	60	46	63	107
—	Durham (Carolina).............	4	3	.571	3.39	9	9	0	0	0	58 1/3	63	24	22	25	43
1997—	Durham (Carolina).............	1	1	.500	4.33	11	1	0	0	0	35 1/3	33	21	17	22	39
—	Greenville (Southern)	5	6	.455	4.86	22	18	0	0	0	113	119	69	61	61	96
1998—	Richmond (Int'l)	1	1	.500	1.42	9	0	0	0	1	19	13	4	3	10	22
—	Atlanta (N.L.)	1	3	.250	2.13	47	0	0	0	2	38	22	10	9	22	42
Major league totals (1 year)		1	3	.250	2.13	47	0	0	0	2	38	22	10	9	22	42

DIVISION SERIES RECORD

Year	Team (League)	W	L	Pct.	ERA	G	GS	CG	ShO	Sv.	IP	H	R	ER	BB	SO
1998—	Atlanta (N.L.)	0	0	...	0.00	2	0	0	0	0	1 1/3	1	0	0	0	2

CHAMPIONSHIP SERIES RECORD

RECORDS: Shares single-series record for most games pitched—6 (1998).

Year	Team (League)	W	L	Pct.	ERA	G	GS	CG	ShO	Sv.	IP	H	R	ER	BB	SO
1998—	Atlanta (N.L.)	1	0	1.000	0.00	6	0	0	0	0	4 2/3	3	0	0	1	5

RODRIGUEZ, ALEX   SS   MARINERS

PERSONAL: Born July 27, 1975, in New York. ... 6-3/195. ... Bats right, throws right. ... Full name: Alexander Emmanuel Rodriguez.
HIGH SCHOOL: Westminster Christian (Miami).
TRANSACTIONS/CAREER NOTES: Selected by Seattle Mariners organization in first round (first pick overall) of free-agent draft (June 3, 1993). ... On Seattle disabled list (April 22-May 7, 1996); included rehabilitation assignment to Tacoma (May 5-7). ... On disabled list (June 12-27, 1997).
RECORDS: Holds A.L. single-season record for most home runs by shortstop—42 (1998).
HONORS: Named Major League Player of the Year by THE SPORTING NEWS (1996). ... Named shortstop on THE SPORTING NEWS A.L. All-Star team (1996 and 1998). ... Named shortstop on THE SPORTING NEWS A.L. Silver Slugger team (1996 and 1998).
STATISTICAL NOTES: Had 20-game hitting streak (August 16-September 4, 1996). ... Led A.L. with 379 total bases in 1996. ... Hit for the cycle (June 5, 1997). ... Led A.L. shortstops with 731 total chances in 1998. ... Career major league grand slams: 3.

							BATTING						FIELDING		
Year	Team (League)	Pos.	G	AB	R	H	2B	3B	HR	RBI	Avg.	BB	SO	SB	PO	A	E	Avg.
1994—	Appleton (Midwest)....	SS	65	248	49	79	17	6	14	55	.319	24	44	16	86	185	19	.934
—	Jacksonville (Sou.).....	SS	17	59	7	17	4	1	1	8	.288	10	13	2	17	63	3	.964
—	Seattle (A.L.)	SS	17	54	4	11	0	0	0	2	.204	3	20	3	20	45	6	.915
—	Calgary (PCL)	SS	32	119	22	37	7	4	6	21	.311	8	25	2	45	104	3	.980
1995—	Tacoma (PCL)	SS	54	214	37	77	12	3	15	45	.360	18	44	2	90	157	10	.961
—	Seattle (A.L.)	SS-DH	48	142	15	33	6	2	5	19	.232	6	42	4	56	106	8	.953
1996—	Seattle (A.L.)	SS	146	601	*141	215	*54	1	36	123	*.358	59	104	15	238	404	15	.977
—	Tacoma (PCL)	SS	2	5	0	1	0	0	0	0	.200	2	1	0	1	4	1	.833
1997—	Seattle (A.L.)	SS-DH	141	587	100	176	40	3	23	84	.300	41	99	29	209	394	*24	.962
1998—	Seattle (A.L.)	SS-DH	161	*686	123	*213	35	5	42	124	.310	45	121	46	268	445	18	.975
Major league totals (5 years)			513	2070	383	648	135	11	106	352	.313	154	386	97	791	1394	71	.969

DIVISION SERIES RECORD

							BATTING						FIELDING		
Year	Team (League)	Pos.	G	AB	R	H	2B	3B	HR	RBI	Avg.	BB	SO	SB	PO	A	E	Avg.
1995—	Seattle (A.L.)	SS-PR	1	1	1	0	0	0	0	0	.000	0	0	0	0	0	0	...
1997—	Seattle (A.L.)	SS	4	16	1	5	1	0	1	1	.313	0	5	0	5	10	0	1.000
Division series totals (2 years)			5	17	2	5	1	0	1	1	.294	0	5	0	5	10	0	1.000

CHAMPIONSHIP SERIES RECORD

							BATTING						FIELDING		
Year	Team (League)	Pos.	G	AB	R	H	2B	3B	HR	RBI	Avg.	BB	SO	SB	PO	A	E	Avg.
1995—	Seattle (A.L.)	PH	1	1	0	0	0	0	0	0	.000	0	1	0	...	...	...	...

ALL-STAR GAME RECORD

						BATTING						FIELDING		
Year	League	Pos.	AB	R	H	2B	3B	HR	RBI	Avg.	BB	SO	SB	PO	A	E	Avg.
1996—	American	SS	1	0	0	0	0	0	0	.000	0	0	0	0	0	0	...
1997—	American	SS	3	0	1	0	0	0	0	.333	0	2	0	1	0	1	0	1.000
1998—	American	SS	3	2	2	0	0	1	1	.667	0	1	0	1	2	0	1.000
All-Star Game totals (3 years)			7	2	3	0	0	1	1	.429	0	3	0	1	3	0	1.000

RODRIGUEZ, FELIX   P   GIANTS

PERSONAL: Born December 5, 1972, in Monte Cristi, Dominican Republic. ... 6-1/190. ... Throws right, bats right. ... Full name: Felix Antonio Rodriguez.
HIGH SCHOOL: Liceo Bijiador (Monte Cristi, Dominican Republic).
TRANSACTIONS/CAREER NOTES: Signed as non-drafted free agent by Los Angeles Dodgers organization (October 17, 1989). ... On disabled list (August 11, 1992-remainder of season). ... On Albuquerque disabled list (July 5-18, 1995). ... On disabled list (April 20-May 2 and May 12-27, 1996). ... Claimed on waivers by Cincinnati Reds (December 18, 1996). ... Traded by Reds to Arizona Diamondbacks for a player to be named later (November 11, 1997); Reds acquired P Scott Winchester to complete deal (November 18, 1997). ... On Arizona disabled list (June 21-July 30, 1998); included rehabilitation assignments to Arizona League Diamondbacks (July 20-27) and Tucson (July 28-30). ... Traded by Diamondbacks to San Francisco Giants for future considerations (December 8, 1998); Diamondbacks acquired P Troy Brohawn and OF Chris Van Rossum to complete deal (December 21, 1998).
STATISTICAL NOTES: Pitched 11-0 no-hit victory against Sarasota (August 28, 1993).
MISCELLANEOUS: Played catcher (1990-92).

Year	Team (League)	W	L	Pct.	ERA	G	GS	CG	ShO	Sv.	IP	H	R	ER	BB	SO
1993—Vero Beach (FSL)		8	8	.500	3.75	32	20	2	1	0	132	109	71	55	71	80
1994—San Antonio (Tex.)		6	8	.429	4.03	26	26	0	0	0	136 1/3	106	70	61	*88	126
1995—Albuquerque (PCL)		3	2	.600	4.24	14	11	0	0	0	51	52	29	24	26	46
—Los Angeles (N.L.)		1	1	.500	2.53	11	0	0	0	0	10 2/3	11	3	3	5	5
1996—Albuquerque (PCL)		3	9	.250	5.53	27	19	0	0	0	107 1/3	111	70	66	60	65
1997—Indianapolis (A.A.)■		3	3	.500	1.01	23	0	0	0	1	26 2/3	22	10	3	16	26
—Cincinnati (N.L.)		0	0	...	4.30	26	1	0	0	0	46	48	23	22	28	34
1998—Arizona (N.L.)■		0	2	.000	6.14	43	0	0	0	5	44	44	31	30	29	36
—Arizona D-backs (Ariz.)		0	0	...	4.15	3	2	0	0	0	4 1/3	3	4	2	2	5
—Tucson (PCL)		0	0	...	9.00	1	0	0	0	0	1	1	1	1	2	0
Major league totals (3 years)		1	3	.250	4.92	80	1	0	0	5	100 2/3	103	57	55	62	75

RECORD AS POSITION PLAYER

						BATTING									FIELDING		
Year	Team (League)	Pos.	G	AB	R	H	2B	3B	HR	RBI	Avg.	BB	SO	SB	PO	A	E	Avg.
1990—Dom. Dodgers (DSL) .	...	63	241	23	55	10	0	2	33	.228	15	52	4	...	...	...	...
1991—GC Dodgers (GCL)	C	45	139	15	37	8	1	2	21	.266	6	32	1	161	18	5	.973
1992—Great Falls (Pio.)	C-OF	32	110	20	32	8	0	2	20	.291	1	16	2	221	33	2	.992

RODRIGUEZ, FRANK — P — TWINS

PERSONAL: Born December 11, 1972, in Brooklyn, N.Y. ... 6-0/202. ... Throws right, bats right. ... Full name: Francisco Rodriguez.
HIGH SCHOOL: Eastern District (Brooklyn, N.Y.).
JUNIOR COLLEGE: Howard College (Texas).
TRANSACTIONS/CAREER NOTES: Selected by Boston Red Sox in second round of free-agent draft (June 4, 1990); pick received as compensation for Atlanta Braves signing of Type B free-agent 1B Nick Esasky. ... Traded by Red Sox with a player to be named later to Minnesota Twins for P Rick Aguilera (July 6, 1995); Twins acquired OF J.J. Johnson to complete deal (October 11, 1995).

Year	Team (League)	W	L	Pct.	ERA	G	GS	CG	ShO	Sv.	IP	H	R	ER	BB	SO
1992—Lynchburg (Carolina)	12	7	.632	3.09	25	25	1	0	0	148 2/3	125	56	51	65	129
1993—New Britain (East.)	7	11	.389	3.74	28	26	•4	1	0	170 2/3	147	79	71	78	151
1994—Pawtucket (Int'l)	8	13	.381	3.92	28	28	*8	1	0	*186	182	95	81	60	*160
1995—Boston (A.L.)	0	2	.000	10.57	9	2	0	0	0	15 1/3	21	19	18	10	14
—Pawtucket (Int'l)	1	1	.500	4.00	13	2	0	0	2	27	19	12	12	8	18
—Minnesota (A.L.)■	5	6	.455	5.38	16	16	0	0	0	90 1/3	93	64	54	47	45
1996—Minnesota (A.L.)	13	14	.481	5.05	38	33	3	0	2	206 2/3	218	129	116	78	110
1997—Minnesota (A.L.)	3	6	.333	4.62	43	15	0	0	0	142 1/3	147	82	73	60	65
1998—Minnesota (A.L.)	4	6	.400	6.56	20	11	0	0	0	70	88	58	51	30	62
—Salt Lake (PCL)	5	7	.417	4.67	16	16	2	1	0	96 1/3	97	53	50	35	79
Major league totals (4 years)	25	34	.424	5.35	126	77	3	0	2	524 2/3	567	352	312	225	296

RECORD AS POSITION PLAYER

						BATTING									FIELDING		
Year	Team (League)	Pos.	G	AB	R	H	2B	3B	HR	RBI	Avg.	BB	SO	SB	PO	A	E	Avg.
1991—GC Red Sox (GCL)	SS	3	14	3	7	0	1	0	3	.500	0	1	0	9	10	1	.950
—Elmira (N.Y.-Penn)......	SS	67	255	36	69	5	3	6	31	.271	13	38	3	95	209	24	.927

RODRIGUEZ, HENRY — OF — CUBS

PERSONAL: Born November 8, 1967, in Santo Domingo, Dominican Republic. ... 6-2/220. ... Bats left, throws left. ... Full name: Henry Anderson Lorenzo Rodriguez.
HIGH SCHOOL: Liceo Republica de Paraguay.
TRANSACTIONS/CAREER NOTES: Signed as non-drafted free agent by Los Angeles Dodgers organization (July 14, 1985). ... Traded by Dodgers with IF Jeff Treadway to Montreal Expos for OF Roberto Kelly and P Joey Eischen (May 23, 1995). ... On Montreal disabled list (June 2-September 1, 1995); included rehabilitation assignment to Ottawa (August 7-16). ... On suspended list (August 16-19, 1996). ... Traded by Expos to Chicago Cubs for P Miguel Batista (December 12, 1997). ... On disabled list (August 24-September 8, 1998). ... Granted free agency (October 23, 1998). ... Re-signed by Cubs (December 2, 1998).
RECORDS: Holds N.L. single-season record for most strikeouts by lefthander—160 (1996).
HONORS: Named Texas League Most Valuable Player (1990).
STATISTICAL NOTES: Tied for Gulf Coast League lead with seven intentional bases on balls received in 1987. ... Led Texas League with 14 sacrifice flies in 1990. ... Tied for Pacific Coast League lead with 10 sacrifice flies in 1992. ... Career major league grand slams: 4.

						BATTING									FIELDING		
Year	Team (League)	Pos.	G	AB	R	H	2B	3B	HR	RBI	Avg.	BB	SO	SB	PO	A	E	Avg.
1987—GC Dodgers (GCL)	1B-SS	49	148	23	49	7	3	0	15	*.331	16	15	3	309	23	6	.982
1988—Dom. Dodgers (DSL) .	...	19	21	9	8	2	0	0	10	.381	10	6	4	...	...	...	...
—Salem (Northwest)	1B	72	291	47	84	14	4	2	39	.289	21	42	14	585	*38	7	.989
1989—Vero Beach (FSL)	1B-OF	126	433	53	123	*33	1	10	73	.284	48	58	7	1072	66	12	.990
—Bakersfield (Calif.)	1B	3	9	2	2	0	0	1	2	.222	0	3	0	8	0	0	1.000
1990—San Antonio (Tex.)	OF	129	495	82	144	22	9	*28	*109	.291	61	66	5	223	5	10	.958
1991—Albuquerque (PCL).....	OF-1B	121	446	61	121	22	5	10	67	.271	25	62	4	234	12	5	.980
1992—Albuquerque (PCL).....	1B-OF	94	365	59	111	21	5	14	72	.304	31	57	1	484	41	10	.981
—Los Angeles (N.L.)	OF-1B	53	146	11	32	7	0	3	14	.219	8	30	0	68	8	3	.962
1993—Albuquerque (PCL).....	1B-OF	46	179	26	53	13	5	4	30	.296	14	37	1	277	18	5	.983
—Los Angeles (N.L.)	OF-1B	76	176	20	39	10	0	8	23	.222	11	39	1	127	9	1	.993
1994—Los Angeles (N.L.)	OF-1B	104	306	33	82	14	2	8	49	.268	17	58	0	198	9	2	.990
1995—Los Angeles (N.L.)	OF-1B	21	80	6	21	4	1	1	10	.263	5	17	0	37	0	0	1.000
—Montreal (N.L.)■........	1B-OF	24	58	7	12	0	0	1	5	.207	6	11	0	88	7	1	.990
—Ottawa (Int'l)............	DH	4	15	0	3	1	0	0	2	.200	1	4	0	...	...	...	...
1996—Montreal (N.L.)...........	OF-1B	145	532	81	147	42	1	36	103	.276	37	*160	2	528	33	11	.981
1997—Montreal (N.L.)...........	OF-1B	132	476	55	116	28	3	26	83	.244	42	149	3	220	6	3	.987
1998—Chicago (N.L.)■...........	OF-DH	128	415	56	104	21	1	31	85	.251	54	113	1	215	7	1	.996
Major league totals (7 years)		683	2189	269	553	126	8	114	372	.253	180	577	7	1481	79	22	.986

							BATTING							FIELDING			
Year	Team (League)	Pos.	G	AB	R	H	2B	3B	HR	RBI	Avg.	BB	SO	SB	PO	A	E	Avg.
1998— Chicago (N.L.)............		OF-PH	3	7	0	1	1	0	0	0	.143	1	2	0	5	1	0	1.000

ALL-STAR GAME RECORD

						BATTING							FIELDING			
Year	League	Pos.	AB	R	H	2B	3B	HR	RBI	Avg.	BB	SO	SB	PO	A	E	Avg.
1996— National......................		PH	1	0	1	0	0	0	1	1.000	0	0	0	...	...	...	...

RODRIGUEZ, IVAN   C   RANGERS

PERSONAL: Born November 30, 1971, in Vega Baja, Puerto Rico. ... 5-9/205. ... Bats right, throws right.
HIGH SCHOOL: Lina Padron Rivera (Vega Baja, Puerto Rico).
TRANSACTIONS/CAREER NOTES: Signed as non-drafted free agent by Texas Rangers organization (July 27, 1988). ... On disabled list (June 6-27, 1992).
HONORS: Won A.L. Gold Glove at catcher (1992-98). ... Named catcher on THE SPORTING NEWS A.L. All-Star team (1994-98). ... Named catcher on THE SPORTING NEWS A.L. Silver Slugger team (1994-98).
STATISTICAL NOTES: Led South Atlantic League catchers with 34 double plays in 1989. ... Led Florida State League catchers with 842 total chances in 1990. ... Led A.L. catchers with 941 total chances and 11 double plays in 1996. ... Led A.L. catchers with 942 total chances in 1998. ... Hit three home runs in one game (September 11, 1997).

							BATTING							FIELDING			
Year	Team (League)	Pos.	G	AB	R	H	2B	3B	HR	RBI	Avg.	BB	SO	SB	PO	A	E	Avg.
1989— Gastonia (S. Atl.)........		C	112	386	38	92	22	1	7	42	.238	21	58	2	691	*96	11	.986
1990— Charlotte (Fla. St.)......		C	109	408	48	117	17	7	2	55	.287	12	50	1	*727	101	14	.983
1991— Tulsa (Texas)		C	50	175	16	48	7	2	3	28	.274	6	27	1	210	33	3	.988
— Texas (A.L.)		C	88	280	24	74	16	0	3	27	.264	5	42	0	517	62	10	.983
1992— Texas (A.L.)		C-DH	123	420	39	109	16	1	8	37	.260	24	73	0	763	85	*15	.983
1993— Texas (A.L.)		C-DH	137	473	56	129	28	4	10	66	.273	29	70	8	801	76	8	.991
1994— Texas (A.L.)		C	99	363	56	108	19	1	16	57	.298	31	42	6	600	44	5	.992
1995— Texas (A.L.)		C-DH	130	492	56	149	32	2	12	67	.303	16	48	0	707	*67	8	.990
1996— Texas (A.L.)		C-DH	153	639	116	192	47	3	19	86	.300	38	55	5	*850	*81	•10	.989
1997— Texas (A.L.)		C-DH	150	597	98	187	34	4	20	77	.313	38	89	7	821	*75	7	.992
1998— Texas (A.L.)		C-DH	145	579	88	186	40	4	21	91	.321	32	88	9	*864	*72	6	.994
Major league totals (8 years)			1025	3843	533	1134	232	19	109	508	.295	213	507	35	5923	562	69	.989

DIVISION SERIES RECORD

							BATTING							FIELDING			
Year	Team (League)	Pos.	G	AB	R	H	2B	3B	HR	RBI	Avg.	BB	SO	SB	PO	A	E	Avg.
1996— Texas (A.L.)		C	4	16	1	6	1	0	0	2	.375	2	3	0	21	3	0	1.000
1998— Texas (A.L.)		C	3	10	0	1	0	0	0	1	.100	0	5	0	27	3	0	1.000
Division series totals (2 years)			7	26	1	7	1	0	0	3	.269	2	8	0	48	6	0	1.000

RECORDS: Shares single-game record for most at-bats (nine-inning game)—5 (July 12, 1994).

ALL-STAR GAME RECORD

						BATTING							FIELDING			
Year	League	Pos.	AB	R	H	2B	3B	HR	RBI	Avg.	BB	SO	SB	PO	A	E	Avg.
1992— American....................		C	2	0	0	0	0	0	0	.000	0	1	0	4	0	0	1.000
1993— American....................		C	2	1	1	1	0	0	0	.500	0	0	0	3	0	0	1.000
1994— American....................		C	5	1	2	0	0	0	0	.400	0	1	0	5	0	0	1.000
1995— American....................		C	3	0	0	0	0	0	0	.000	0	1	0	6	1	0	1.000
1996— American....................		C	2	0	0	0	0	0	0	.000	0	1	0	6	2	0	1.000
1997— American....................		C	2	0	0	0	0	0	0	.000	0	0	0	3	1	0	1.000
1998— American....................		C	4	1	3	0	0	0	1	.750	0	0	1	5	0	0	1.000
All-Star Game totals (7 years)			20	3	6	1	0	0	1	.300	0	4	1	32	4	0	1.000

RODRIGUEZ, NERIO   P   BLUE JAYS

PERSONAL: Born March 22, 1973, in Bani, Dominican Republic. ... 6-1/195. ... Throws right, bats right.
TRANSACTIONS/CAREER NOTES: Signed as non-drafted free agent by Chicago White Sox organization (February 2, 1990). ... Selected by Baltimore Orioles organization from White Sox organization in Rule 5 minor league draft (December 5, 1994). ... On Frederick disabled list (April 5-August 11, 1996). ... On Baltimore disabled list (May 26-June 30, 1998); included rehabilitation assignment to Bowie (June 24-30). ... Traded by Orioles with OF Shannon Carter to Toronto Blue Jays for P Juan Guzman (July 31, 1998).
STATISTICAL NOTES: Led Gulf Coast League catchers with 312 total chances in 1992.
MISCELLANEOUS: Played catcher (1990-94).

Year	Team (League)	W	L	Pct.	ERA	G	GS	CG	ShO	Sv.	IP	H	R	ER	BB	SO
1995— High Desert (Calif.)	0	0	...	1.80	7	0	0	0	0	10	8	2	2	7	10
1996— Frederick (Carolina)...........	8	7	.533	2.26	24	17	1	0	2	111 1/3	83	42	28	40	114
— Baltimore (A.L.).................	0	1	.000	4.32	8	1	0	0	0	16 2/3	18	11	8	7	12
— Rochester (Int'l)	1	0	1.000	1.80	2	2	0	0	0	15	10	3	3	2	6
1997— Rochester (Int'l)	11	10	.524	3.90	27	27	1	1	0	168 1/3	124	82	73	62	*160
— Baltimore (A.L.).................	2	1	.667	4.91	6	2	0	0	0	22	21	15	12	8	11
1998— Rochester (Int'l)	1	4	.200	5.47	5	5	0	0	0	24 2/3	24	16	15	10	19
— Baltimore (A.L.).................	1	3	.250	8.05	6	4	0	0	0	19	25	17	17	9	8
— Bowie (Eastern).................	0	1	.000	4.50	2	2	0	0	0	4	6	2	2	0	7
— Toronto (A.L.)■...............	1	0	1.000	9.72	7	0	0	0	0	8 1/3	10	9	9	8	3
Major league totals (3 years)......	4	5	.444	6.27	27	7	0	0	0	66	74	52	46	32	34

Year	Team (League)	Pos.	G	AB	R	H	2B	3B	HR	RBI	Avg.	BB	SO	SB	PO	A	E	Avg.
							BATTING									FIELDING		
1991—GC Whi. Sox (GCL)		C	26	89	4	20	1	0	0	8	.225	2	24	3	153	23	5	.972
1992—GC Whi. Sox (GCL)		C	41	122	18	33	8	1	2	13	.270	10	31	1	*257	43	*12	.962
1993—Hickory (S. Atl.)		C	82	262	31	54	9	2	4	32	.206	27	70	4	476	45	13	.976
1994—South Bend (Mid.)......		C	18	59	4	13	4	0	0	8	.220	2	14	0	95	19	0	1.000
—Prince Will. (Car.)		C	6	19	2	4	1	1	0	1	.211	1	9	0	34	6	0	1.000
1995—Bowie (Eastern)■......		C	3	4	0	0	0	0	0	0	.000	2	2	0	13	1	0	1.000
—High Desert (Calif.).....		C-P	58	144	20	34	7	0	4	12	.236	18	50	5	325	34	8	.978

RODRIGUEZ, RICH   P   GIANTS

R

PERSONAL: Born March 1, 1963, in Downey, Calif. ... 6-0/205. ... Throws left, bats left. ... Full name: Richard Anthony Rodriguez.

HIGH SCHOOL: Mountain View (El Monte, Calif.).

COLLEGE: Tennessee.

TRANSACTIONS/CAREER NOTES: Selected by Kansas City Royals organization in 17th round of free-agent draft (June 8, 1981); did not sign. ... Selected by New York Mets organization in ninth round of free-agent draft (June 4, 1984). ... Traded by Mets organization to Wichita, San Diego Padres organization, for 1B Brad Pounders and 1B Bill Stevenson (January 13, 1989). ... Traded by Padres with 3B Gary Sheffield to Florida Marlins for P Trevor Hoffman, P Jose Martinez and P Andres Berumen (June 24, 1993). ... Released by Marlins (March 29, 1994). ... Signed by St. Louis Cardinals (April 1, 1994). ... On disabled list (April 27, 1995-remainder of season). ... Released by Cardinals (November 20, 1995). ... Signed by Cincinnati Reds organization (January 2, 1996). ... Released by Reds (March 24, 1996). ... Signed by Kansas City Royals organization (April 9, 1996). ... On disabled list (May 18-29, 1996). ... Granted free agency (October 15, 1996). ... Signed by San Francisco Giants organization (November 25, 1996). ... Granted free agency (October 30, 1997). ... Re-signed by Giants (December 7, 1997).

MISCELLANEOUS: Appeared in one game as pinch runner (1991). ... Had sacrifice hit in only appearance as pinch hitter (1992).

Year	Team (League)	W	L	Pct.	ERA	G	GS	CG	ShO	Sv.	IP	H	R	ER	BB	SO
1984—Little Falls (NYP)		2	1	.667	2.80	25	1	0	0	0	35 1/3	28	21	11	36	27
1985—Columbia (S. Atl.).............		6	3	.667	4.03	49	3	0	0	6	80 1/3	89	41	36	36	71
1986—Lynchburg (Carolina)		2	1	.667	3.57	36	0	0	0	3	45 1/3	37	20	18	19	38
—Jackson (Texas)		3	4	.429	9.00	13	5	1	0	0	33	51	35	33	15	15
1987—Lynchburg (Carolina)		3	1	.750	2.78	*69	0	0	0	5	68	69	23	21	26	59
1988—Jackson (Texas)		2	7	.222	2.87	47	1	0	0	6	78 1/3	66	35	25	42	68
1989—Wichita (Texas)■		8	3	.727	3.63	54	0	0	0	8	74 1/3	74	30	30	37	40
1990—Las Vegas (PCL)		3	4	.429	3.51	27	2	0	0	8	59	50	24	23	22	46
—San Diego (N.L.)		1	1	.500	2.83	32	0	0	0	1	47 2/3	52	17	15	16	22
1991—San Diego (N.L.)		3	1	.750	3.26	64	1	0	0	0	80	66	31	29	44	40
1992—San Diego (N.L.)		6	3	.667	2.37	61	1	0	0	0	91	77	28	24	29	64
1993—San Diego (N.L.)		2	3	.400	3.30	34	0	0	0	2	30	34	15	11	9	22
—Florida (N.L.)■.................		0	1	.000	4.11	36	0	0	0	1	46	39	23	21	24	21
1994—St. Louis (N.L.)■..............		3	5	.375	4.03	56	0	0	0	0	60 1/3	62	30	27	26	43
1995—St. Louis (N.L.)..............		0	0	. . .	0.00	1	0	0	0	0	1 2/3	0	0	0	0	0
1996—Omaha (Am. Assoc.)■........		2	3	.400	3.99	47	0	0	0	3	70	75	40	31	20	68
1997—San Francisco (N.L.) ■		4	3	.571	3.17	71	0	0	0	1	65 1/3	65	24	23	21	32
1998—San Francisco (N.L.)		4	0	1.000	3.70	68	0	0	0	2	65 2/3	69	28	27	20	44
Major league totals (8 years).....		23	17	.575	3.27	423	2	0	0	7	487 2/3	464	196	177	189	288

DIVISION SERIES RECORD

Year	Team (League)	W	L	Pct.	ERA	G	GS	CG	ShO	Sv.	IP	H	R	ER	BB	SO
1997—San Francisco (N.L.)		0	0	. . .	0.00	2	0	0	0	0	1	1	0	0	0	0

ROGERS, KENNY   P   ATHLETICS

PERSONAL: Born November 10, 1964, in Savannah, Ga. ... 6-1/205. ... Throws left, bats left. ... Full name: Kenneth Scott Rogers.

HIGH SCHOOL: Plant City (Fla.).

TRANSACTIONS/CAREER NOTES: Selected by Texas Rangers organization in 39th round of free-agent draft (June 7, 1982). ... On Tulsa disabled list (April 12-30, 1986). ... Granted free agency (October 31, 1995). ... Signed by New York Yankees (December 30, 1995). ... Traded by Yankees with IF Mariano Duncan and P Kevin Henthorne to San Diego Padres for OF Greg Vaughn, P Kerry Taylor and P Chris Clark (July 4, 1997); trade later voided because Vaughn failed physical (July 6). ... Traded by Yankees with cash to Oakland Athletics for a player to be named later (November 7, 1997); Yankees acquired 3B Scott Brosius to complete deal (November 18, 1997).

STATISTICAL NOTES: Tied for A.L. lead with five balks in 1993. ... Pitched 4-0 perfect game against California (July 28, 1994).

Year	Team (League)	W	L	Pct.	ERA	G	GS	CG	ShO	Sv.	IP	H	R	ER	BB	SO
1982—GC Rangers (GCL)..............		0	0	. . .	0.00	2	0	0	0	0	3	0	0	0	0	4
1983—GC Rangers (GCL)..............		4	1	.800	2.36	15	6	0	0	1	53 1/3	40	21	14	20	36
1984—Burlington (Midw.)..............		4	7	.364	3.98	39	4	1	0	3	92 2/3	87	52	41	33	93
1985—Daytona Beach (FSL)..........		0	1	.000	7.20	6	0	0	0	0	10	12	9	8	11	9
—Burlington (Midw.)..............		2	5	.286	2.84	33	4	2	1	4	95	67	34	30	62	96
1986—Tulsa (Texas)		0	3	.000	9.91	10	4	0	0	1	26 1/3	39	30	29	18	23
—Salem (Carolina)		2	7	.222	6.27	12	12	0	0	0	66	75	54	46	26	46
1987—Charlotte (Fla. St.)		0	3	.000	4.76	5	3	0	0	0	17	17	13	9	8	14
—Tulsa (Texas)		1	5	.167	5.35	28	6	0	0	2	69	80	51	41	35	59
1988—Tulsa (Texas)		4	6	.400	4.00	13	13	2	0	0	83 1/3	73	43	37	34	76
—Charlotte (Fla. St.)		2	0	1.000	1.27	8	6	0	0	1	35 1/3	22	8	5	11	26
1989—Texas (A.L.)		3	4	.429	2.93	73	0	0	0	2	73 2/3	60	28	24	42	63
1990—Texas (A.L.)		10	6	.625	3.13	69	3	0	0	15	97 2/3	93	40	34	42	74
1991—Texas (A.L.)		10	10	.500	5.42	63	9	0	0	5	109 2/3	121	80	66	61	73
1992—Texas (A.L.)		3	6	.333	3.09	*81	0	0	0	6	78 2/3	80	32	27	26	70
1993—Texas (A.L.)		16	10	.615	4.10	35	33	5	0	0	208 1/3	210	108	95	71	140
1994—Texas (A.L.)		11	8	.579	4.46	24	24	6	2	0	167 1/3	169	93	83	52	120
1995—Texas (A.L.)		17	7	.708	3.38	31	31	3	1	0	208	192	87	78	76	140

Year	Team (League)	W	L	Pct.	ERA	G	GS	CG	ShO	Sv.	IP	H	R	ER	BB	SO
1996—New York (A.L.)■		12	8	.600	4.68	30	30	2	1	0	179	179	97	93	83	92
1997—New York (A.L.)		6	7	.462	5.65	31	22	1	0	0	145	161	100	91	62	78
1998—Oakland (A.L.)■		16	8	.667	3.17	34	34	7	1	0	238 $\frac{2}{3}$	215	96	84	67	138
Major league totals (10 years)		104	74	.584	4.03	471	186	24	5	28	1506	1480	761	675	582	988

DIVISION SERIES RECORD

Year	Team (League)	W	L	Pct.	ERA	G	GS	CG	ShO	Sv.	IP	H	R	ER	BB	SO
1996—New York (A.L.)		0	0	...	9.00	2	1	0	0	0	2	5	2	2	2	1

CHAMPIONSHIP SERIES RECORD

Year	Team (League)	W	L	Pct.	ERA	G	GS	CG	ShO	Sv.	IP	H	R	ER	BB	SO
1996—New York (A.L.)		0	0	...	12.00	1	1	0	0	0	3	5	4	4	2	3

WORLD SERIES RECORD

NOTES: Member of World Series championship team (1996).

Year	Team (League)	W	L	Pct.	ERA	G	GS	CG	ShO	Sv.	IP	H	R	ER	BB	SO
1996—New York (A.L.)		0	0	...	22.50	1	1	0	0	0	2	5	5	5	2	0

ALL-STAR GAME RECORD

Year	League	W	L	Pct.	ERA	GS	CG	ShO	Sv.	IP	H	R	ER	BB	SO
1995—American		0	0	...	9.00	0	0	0	0	1	1	1	1	0	2

R

ROJAS, MEL — P — DODGERS

PERSONAL: Born December 10, 1966, in Haina, Dominican Republic. ... 5-11/212. ... Throws right, bats right. ... Full name: Melaquides Rojas. ... Nephew of Felipe Alou, manager, Montreal Expos, and major league outfielder/first baseman with six teams (1958-74); nephew of Matty Alou, major league outfielder with six teams (1960-74); nephew of Jesus Alou, major league outfielder with four teams (1963-75 and 1978-79); brother of Francisco Rojas, minor league outfielder (1978 and 1979); and cousin of Moises Alou, outfielder, Houston Astros. ... Name pronounced RO-hoss.

HIGH SCHOOL: Liceo Manresa (Santo Domingo, Dominican Republic).

TRANSACTIONS/CAREER NOTES: Signed as non-drafted free agent by Montreal Expos organization (November 7, 1985). ... On Rockford disabled list (May 7-June 14, 1988). ... On West Palm Beach disabled list (August 8, 1988-remainder of season). ... On Indianapolis disabled list (June 26-July 5, 1991). ... On disabled list (July 4-19, 1993). ... Granted free agency (December 7, 1996). ... Signed by Chicago Cubs (December 11, 1996). ... Traded by Cubs with OF Brian McRae and P Turk Wendell to New York Mets for OF Lance Johnson and two players to be named later (August 8, 1997); Mets traded P Mark Clark (August 11) and IF Manny Alexander (August 14) to Cubs to complete deal. ... Traded by Mets to Los Angeles Dodgers for 3B/OF Bobby Bonilla (November 11, 1998).

RECORDS: Shares major league record for striking out side on nine pitches (May 11, 1994, ninth inning).

Year	Team (League)	W	L	Pct.	ERA	G	GS	CG	ShO	Sv.	IP	H	R	ER	BB	SO
1986—GC Expos (GCL)		4	5	.444	4.88	13	12	1	0	0	55 $\frac{1}{3}$	63	39	30	37	34
1987—Burlington (Midw.)		8	9	.471	3.80	25	25	4	1	0	158 $\frac{2}{3}$	146	84	67	67	100
1988—Rockford (Midwest)		6	4	.600	2.45	12	12	0	0	0	73 $\frac{1}{3}$	52	30	20	29	72
—W.P. Beach (FSL)		1	0	1.000	3.60	2	2	0	0	0	5	4	2	2	1	4
1989—Jacksonville (Southern)		10	7	.588	2.49	34	12	1	1	5	112	62	39	31	57	104
1990—Indianapolis (A.A.)		2	4	.333	3.13	17	17	0	0	0	97 $\frac{2}{3}$	84	42	34	47	64
—Montreal (N.L.)		3	1	.750	3.60	23	0	0	0	1	40	34	17	16	24	26
1991—Montreal (N.L.)		3	3	.500	3.75	37	0	0	0	6	48	42	21	20	13	37
—Indianapolis (A.A.)		4	2	.667	4.10	14	10	0	0	1	52 $\frac{2}{3}$	50	29	24	14	55
1992—Indianapolis (A.A.)		2	1	.667	5.40	4	0	0	0	0	8 $\frac{1}{3}$	10	5	5	3	7
—Montreal (N.L.)		7	1	.875	1.43	68	0	0	0	10	100 $\frac{2}{3}$	71	17	16	34	70
1993—Montreal (N.L.)		5	8	.385	2.95	66	0	0	0	10	88 $\frac{1}{3}$	80	39	29	30	48
1994—Montreal (N.L.)		3	2	.600	3.32	58	0	0	0	16	84	71	35	31	21	84
1995—Montreal (N.L.)		1	4	.200	4.12	59	0	0	0	30	67 $\frac{2}{3}$	69	32	31	29	61
1996—Montreal (N.L.)		7	4	.636	3.22	74	0	0	0	36	81	56	30	29	28	92
1997—Chicago (N.L.)■		0	4	.000	4.42	54	0	0	0	13	59	54	30	29	30	61
—New York (N.L.)■		0	2	.000	5.13	23	0	0	0	2	26 $\frac{1}{3}$	24	17	15	6	32
1998—New York (N.L.)		5	2	.714	6.05	50	0	0	0	2	58	68	39	39	30	41
Major league totals (9 years)		34	31	.523	3.51	512	0	0	0	126	653	569	277	255	245	552

ROLEN, SCOTT — 3B — PHILLIES

PERSONAL: Born April 4, 1975, in Jasper, Ind. ... 6-4/225. ... Bats right, throws right. ... Full name: Scott Bruce Rolen.

HIGH SCHOOL: Jasper (Ind.).

TRANSACTIONS/CAREER NOTES: Selected by Philadelphia Phillies organization in second round of free-agent draft (June 3, 1993).

HONORS: Named N.L. Rookie Player of the Year by THE SPORTING NEWS (1997). ... Named N.L. Rookie of the Year by Baseball Writers' Association of America (1997). ... Won N.L. Gold Glove at third base (1998).

STATISTICAL NOTES: Led South Atlantic League third basemen with 457 total chances and 36 double plays in 1994. ... Led N.L. third basemen in total chances with 459 in 1997 and 468 in 1998.

Year	Team (League)	Pos.	G	AB	R	H	2B	3B	HR	RBI	Avg.	BB	SO	SB	PO	A	E	Avg.
1993—Martinsville (App.)		3B	25	80	8	25	5	0	0	12	.313	10	15	3	23	57	10	.889
1994—Spartanburg (SAL)		3B	138	513	83	151	34	5	14	72	.294	55	90	6	96	323	38	.917
1995—Clearwater (FSL)		3B	66	238	45	69	13	2	10	39	.290	37	46	4	43	135	20	.899
—Reading (Eastern)		3B	20	76	16	22	3	0	3	15	.289	7	14	1	10	47	4	.934
1996—Reading (Eastern)		3B	61	230	44	83	22	2	9	42	.361	34	32	8	41	125	9	.949
—Scran./W.B. (Int'l)		3B	45	168	23	46	17	0	2	19	.274	28	28	4	32	88	6	.952
—Philadelphia (N.L.)		3B	37	130	10	33	7	0	4	18	.254	13	27	0	29	54	4	.954
1997—Philadelphia (N.L.)		3B	156	561	93	159	35	3	21	92	.283	76	138	16	*144	291	24	.948
1998—Philadelphia (N.L.)		3B	160	601	120	174	45	4	31	110	.290	93	141	14	*135	319	14	.970
Major league totals (3 years)			353	1292	223	366	87	7	56	220	.283	182	306	30	308	664	42	.959

ROLISON, NATE 1B MARLINS

PERSONAL: Born March 27, 1977, in Hattiesburg, Miss. ... 6-5/225. ... Bats left, throws right. ... Full name: Nathan M. Rolison.
HIGH SCHOOL: Petal (Miss.).
TRANSACTIONS/CAREER NOTES: Selected by Florida Marlins organization in second round of free-agent draft (June 1, 1995).
STATISTICAL NOTES: Led Midwest League first basemen with 1,254 total chances and 114 double plays in 1996. ... Led Florida State League first basemen with 89 double plays in 1997.

Year	Team (League)	Pos.	G	AB	R	H	2B	3B	HR	RBI	Avg.	BB	SO	SB	PO	A	E	Avg.
1995—	GC Marlins (GCL)	1B	37	134	22	37	10	2	1	19	.276	15	34	0	283	20	5	.984
1996—	Kane County (Midw.)	1B	131	474	63	115	28	1	14	75	.243	66	170	3	*1161	*80	13	.990
1997—	Brevard Co. (Fla. St.)	1B	122	473	59	121	22	0	16	65	.256	38	*143	3	1036	69	17	.985
1998—	Portland (Eastern)	1B	131	484	80	134	35	2	16	83	.277	64	150	5	1081	85	13	.989

ROMERO, MANDY C RED SOX

PERSONAL: Born October 29, 1967, in Miami. ... 6-0/180. ... Bats both, throws right. ... Full name: Armando Romero. ... Brother of Andy Romero, minor league first baseman/outfielder (1977-80).
HIGH SCHOOL: Miami Senior.
JUNIOR COLLEGE: Brevard Community College (Fla.).
TRANSACTIONS/CAREER NOTES: Selected by Pittsburgh Pirates in 19th round of free-agent draft (June 1, 1988). ... On disabled list (April 11-29 and June 20-28, 1991; July 13-August 7, 1992; and June 28-July 8 and August 23, 1993-remainder of season). ... Released by Pirates organization (May 6, 1994). ... Signed by Kansas City Royals organization (January 30, 1995). ... Granted free agency (October 16, 1995). ... Signed by San Diego Padres organization (November 25, 1995). ... Granted free agency (October 15, 1996). ... Re-signed by Padres (October 27, 1996). ... Traded by Padres with P Carlos Reyes and P Dario Veras to Boston Red Sox for C Jim Leyritz and OF Ethan Faggett (June 21, 1998). ... On Pawtucket disabled list (July 29-August 5, 1998).
STATISTICAL NOTES: Led South Atlantic League catchers with .989 fielding percentage in 1989. ... Led Carolina League with 222 total bases and .483 slugging percentage in 1990. ... Tied for Southern League lead with 14 passed balls in 1991. ... Tied for Southern League lead in errors by catcher with 14 in 1992.

Year	Team (League)	Pos.	G	AB	R	H	2B	3B	HR	RBI	Avg.	BB	SO	SB	PO	A	E	Avg.
1988—	Princeton (Appal.)	C	30	71	7	22	6	0	2	11	.310	13	15	1	143	14	2	.987
1989—	Augusta (S. Atl.)	C-3B	121	388	58	87	26	3	4	55	.224	67	74	8	629	74	9	†.987
1990—	Salem (Carolina)	C	124	460	62	134	31	3	17	*90	.291	55	68	0	565	60	7	.989
1991—	Carolina (Southern)	C	98	323	29	70	12	0	3	31	.217	45	53	1	552	63	4	*.994
1992—	Carolina (Southern)	C-3B	80	269	28	58	16	0	3	27	.216	29	39	0	523	43	‡14	.976
1993—	Buffalo (A.A.)	C	42	136	11	31	6	1	2	14	.228	6	12	1	168	13	5	.973
1994—	Buffalo (A.A.)	C	7	23	3	3	0	0	0	1	.130	2	1	0	34	5	0	1.000
1995—	Wichita (Texas)■	C-1B	121	440	73	133	32	1	21	82	.302	69	60	1	159	18	4	.978
1996—	Memphis (Sou.)■	C	88	297	40	80	15	0	10	46	.269	41	52	3	657	52	12	.983
1997—	Mobile (Southern)	C	61	222	50	71	22	0	13	52	.320	38	31	0	436	33	6	.987
	—Las Vegas (PCL)	C-3B-1B	33	91	19	28	4	1	3	13	.308	11	19	0	145	8	3	.981
	—San Diego (N.L.)	C	21	48	7	10	0	0	2	4	.208	2	18	1	96	8	0	1.000
1998—	Las Vegas (PCL)	C-1B	40	131	25	38	8	0	8	22	.290	20	25	0	307	29	7	.980
	—San Diego (N.L.)	C	6	9	1	0	0	0	0	0	.000	1	3	0	24	2	1	.963
	—Pawtucket (Int'l)■	C	45	139	20	46	5	0	8	27	.331	24	15	0	311	27	3	.991
	—Boston (A.L.)	C-DH	12	13	2	3	1	0	0	1	.231	3	3	0	11	0	0	1.000
American League totals (1 year)			12	13	2	3	1	0	0	1	.231	3	3	0	11	0	0	1.000
National League totals (2 years)			27	57	8	10	0	0	2	4	.175	3	21	1	120	10	1	.992
Major league totals (2 years)			39	70	10	13	1	0	2	5	.186	6	24	1	131	10	1	.993

ROOT, DEREK P ASTROS

PERSONAL: Born May 26, 1975, in Cleveland. ... 6-5/215. ... Throws left, bats left. ... Full name: Derek Anthony Root.
HIGH SCHOOL: St. Edward (Lakewood, Ohio).
TRANSACTIONS/CAREER NOTES: Selected by Houston Astros organization in fifth round of free-agent draft (June 3, 1993).
MISCELLANEOUS: Played first base (1993-94).

Year	Team (League)	W	L	Pct.	ERA	G	GS	CG	ShO	Sv.	IP	H	R	ER	BB	SO
1995—	Auburn (N.Y.-Penn)	2	0	1.000	3.29	17	3	0	0	1	38 1/3	28	14	14	24	37
	—Kissimmee (Florida State)	0	0	...	4.50	5	0	0	0	0	6	10	3	3	2	3
1996—	Quad City (Midwest)	5	3	.625	3.00	40	2	0	0	7	63	55	25	21	26	47
1997—	Kissimmee (Florida State)	4	*14	.222	4.19	26	22	2	0	0	129	131	76	60	42	68
1998—	Kissimmee (Florida State)	5	4	.556	2.35	29	9	2	•2	4	80 1/3	69	28	21	20	79
	—Jackson (Texas)	4	1	.800	3.89	7	6	0	0	0	44	46	24	19	17	31
	—New Orleans (PCL)	1	0	1.000	2.84	1	1	0	0	0	6 1/3	3	2	2	3	4

RECORD AS POSITION PLAYER

Year	Team (League)	Pos.	G	AB	R	H	2B	3B	HR	RBI	Avg.	BB	SO	SB	PO	A	E	Avg.
1993—	GC Astros (GCL)	1B	41	131	12	37	8	0	0	16	.282	12	21	1	284	17	11	.965
1994—	GC Astros (GCL)	1B	47	169	21	46	8	1	0	35	.272	8	18	2	338	24	9	.976

ROQUE, RAFAEL P BREWERS

PERSONAL: Born October 27, 1973, in Cotui, Dominican Republic. ... 6-4/189. ... Throws left, bats left. ... Full name: Rafael Antonio Roque.
TRANSACTIONS/CAREER NOTES: Signed as non-drafted free agent by New York Mets organization (March 15, 1991). ... Granted free agency (October 17, 1997). ... Signed by Milwaukee Brewers organization (October 31, 1997).

Year Team (League)	W	L	Pct.	ERA	G	GS	CG	ShO	Sv.	IP	H	R	ER	BB	SO
1991— Dominican Mets (DSL)......	1	0	1.000	5.40	4	0	0	0	1	5	4	6	3	9	1
1992— GC Mets (GCL)..................	3	1	.750	2.14	20	0	0	0	8	33²/₃	28	13	8	16	33
1993— Kingsport (Appalachian).....	1	3	.250	6.15	14	7	0	0	0	45¹/₃	58	44	31	26	36
1994— St. Lucie (Fla. St.).............	0	0	...	0.00	2	0	0	0	0	3	1	0	0	3	2
— Columbia (S. Atl.)...........	6	3	.667	2.40	15	15	1	0	0	86¹/₃	73	26	23	30	74
1995— St. Lucie (Fla. St.).............	6	9	.400	3.56	24	24	2	1	0	136²/₃	114	65	54	72	81
1996— Binghamton (Eastern)........	0	4	.000	7.27	13	13	0	0	0	60²/₃	71	57	49	39	46
— St. Lucie (Fla. St.).........	6	4	.600	2.12	14	12	1	0	0	76¹/₃	57	22	18	39	59
1997— Binghamton (Eastern)........	1	1	.500	6.84	16	0	0	0	0	26¹/₃	35	26	20	17	23
— St. Lucie (Fla. St.).........	2	10	.167	4.29	17	13	1	0	0	77²/₃	81	42	37	25	54
1998— El Paso (Texas)■	5	6	.455	4.40	16	16	1	0	0	94	113	56	46	35	70
— Louisville (Int'l)................	5	2	.714	3.62	9	8	0	0	0	49²/₃	42	21	20	19	43
— Milwaukee (N.L.)............	4	2	.667	4.88	9	9	0	0	0	48	42	28	26	24	34
Major league totals (1 year)........	4	2	.667	4.88	9	9	0	0	0	48	42	28	26	24	34

ROSADO, JOSE — P — ROYALS

PERSONAL: Born November 9, 1974, in Jersey City, N.J. ... 6-0/185. ... Throws left, bats left. ... Full name: Jose Antonio Rosado.
HIGH SCHOOL: Jose S. Alegria (Dorado, Puerto Rico).
JUNIOR COLLEGE: Galveston College (Texas).
TRANSACTIONS/CAREER NOTES: Selected by Kansas City Royals organization in 12th round of free-agent draft (June 2, 1994).
MISCELLANEOUS: Appeared in one game as pinch runner (1997).

Year Team (League)	W	L	Pct.	ERA	G	GS	CG	ShO	Sv.	IP	H	R	ER	BB	SO
1994— GC Royals (GCL)...............	6	2	.750	*1.25	14	12	0	0	0	64²/₃	45	14	9	7	56
1995— Wilmington (Caro.).............	10	7	.588	3.13	25	25	0	0	0	138	128	53	48	30	117
1996— Wichita (Texas).................	2	0	1.000	0.00	2	2	0	0	0	13	10	0	0	1	12
— Omaha (Am. Assoc.)..........	8	3	.727	3.17	15	15	1	0	0	96²/₃	80	38	34	38	82
— Kansas City (A.L.)............	8	6	.571	3.21	16	16	2	1	0	106²/₃	101	39	38	26	64
1997— Kansas City (A.L.)	9	12	.429	4.69	33	33	2	0	0	203¹/₃	208	117	106	73	129
1998— Kansas City (A.L.)	8	11	.421	4.69	38	25	2	1	1	174²/₃	180	106	91	57	135
Major league totals (3 years)......	25	29	.463	4.36	87	74	6	2	1	484²/₃	489	262	235	156	328

ALL-STAR GAME RECORD

Year League	W	L	Pct.	ERA	GS	CG	ShO	Sv.	IP	H	R	ER	BB	SO
1997— American..........................	1	0	1.000	9.00	0	0	0	0	1	2	1	1	1	1

ROSE, BRIAN — P — RED SOX

PERSONAL: Born February 13, 1976, in New Bedford, Mass. ... 6-3/212. ... Throws right, bats right. ... Full name: Brian Leonard Rose.
HIGH SCHOOL: Dartmouth (North Dartmouth, Mass.).
TRANSACTIONS/CAREER NOTES: Selected by Boston Red Sox organization in third round of free-agent draft (June 2, 1994). ... On Boston disabled list (May 13, 1998-remainder of season); included rehabilitation assignment to Pawtucket (June 13-July 10).
HONORS: Named International League Most Valuable Pitcher (1997).

Year Team (League)	W	L	Pct.	ERA	G	GS	CG	ShO	Sv.	IP	H	R	ER	BB	SO
1995— Michigan (Midwest)	8	5	.615	3.44	21	20	2	0	0	136	127	63	52	31	105
1996— Trenton (Eastern)	12	7	.632	4.01	27	27	4	2	0	163²/₃	157	82	73	45	115
1997— Pawtucket (Int'l)	*17	5	.773	*3.02	27	26	3	0	0	*190²/₃	188	74	64	46	116
— Boston (A.L.)...................	0	0	...	12.00	1	1	0	0	0	3	5	4	4	2	3
1998— Boston (A.L.)...................	1	4	.200	6.93	8	8	0	0	0	37²/₃	43	32	29	14	18
— Pawtucket (Int'l)	0	3	.000	7.64	6	6	0	0	0	17²/₃	24	19	15	4	17
Major league totals (2 years)	1	4	.200	7.30	9	9	0	0	0	40²/₃	48	36	33	16	21

ROSE, TEDDY — P — REDS

PERSONAL: Born August 23, 1973, in Lima, Ohio. ... 6-2/185. ... Throws right, bats left. ... Full name: Ted Michael Rose.
HIGH SCHOOL: St. Clairsville (Ohio).
COLLEGE: Kent.
TRANSACTIONS/CAREER NOTES: Selected by Cincinnati Reds organization in 14th round of free-agent draft (June 4, 1996).

Year Team (League)	W	L	Pct.	ERA	G	GS	CG	ShO	Sv.	IP	H	R	ER	BB	SO
1996— Princeton (Appalachian).....	3	5	.375	6.22	11	11	1	0	0	59¹/₃	70	44	41	21	53
1997— Charleston, W.Va. (SAL).....	11	6	.647	2.51	38	13	2	2	4	129¹/₃	108	44	36	27	132
1998— Chattanooga (Southern).....	11	10	.524	4.60	29	•29	1	0	0	168¹/₃	191	97	86	66	108

ROSKOS, JOHN — 1B — MARLINS

PERSONAL: Born November 19, 1974, in Victorville, Calif. ... 5-11/195. ... Bats right, throws right. ... Full name: John Edward Roskos.
HIGH SCHOOL: Cibola (Albuquerque, N.M.).
TRANSACTIONS/CAREER NOTES: Selected by Florida Marlins organization in second round of free-agent draft (June 3, 1993). ... On Elmira disabled list (August 9-September 19, 1994). ... On Kane County disabled list (August 28-September 7, 1995). ... Granted free agency (December 21, 1997). ... Re-signed by Marlins organization (December 21, 1997).

Year Team (League)	Pos.	G	AB	R	H	2B	3B	HR	RBI	Avg.	BB	SO	SB	PO	A	E	Avg.
1993— GC Marlins (GCL).......	C	11	40	6	7	1	0	1	3	.175	5	11	1	18	2	2	.909
1994— Elmira (N.Y.-Penn)......	C	39	136	11	38	7	0	4	23	.279	27	37	0	143	13	4	.975
1995— Kane County (Midw.)..	C	114	418	74	124	36	3	12	88	.297	42	86	2	431	47	7	.986
1996— Portland (Eastern)......	1B-C	121	396	53	109	26	3	9	58	.275	67	102	3	719	50	10	.987
1997— Portland (Eastern)......	C-1B	123	451	66	139	31	1	24	84	.308	50	81	4	630	37	8	.988
1998— Charlotte (Int'l).........	1B-OF	115	416	54	118	23	1	10	62	.284	43	84	0	647	38	4	.994
— Florida (N.L.).............	1B	10	10	1	1	0	0	0	0	.100	0	5	0	1	0	0	1.000
Major league totals (1 year)		10	10	1	1	0	0	0	0	.100	0	5	0	1	0	0	1.000

ROSSY, RICO   IF   ROYALS

PERSONAL: Born February 16, 1964, in San Juan, Puerto Rico. ... 5-10/175. ... Bats right, throws right. ... Full name: Elam Jose Rossy.
HIGH SCHOOL: Frontier (Chalmers, Ind.).
COLLEGE: Purdue.
TRANSACTIONS/CAREER NOTES: Selected by Baltimore Orioles organization in 33rd round of free-agent draft (June 3, 1985). ... Traded by Orioles organization with SS Terry Crowley Jr. to Pittsburgh Pirates organization for OF Joe Orsulak (November 6, 1987). ... Traded by Pirates organization to Atlanta Braves organization for OF Greg Tubbs (May 2, 1990). ... Traded by Braves to Kansas City Royals for OF Bobby Moore (December 10, 1991). ... On Kansas City disabled list (April 12-27, 1993); included rehabilitation assignment to Omaha (April 22-27). ... Granted free agency (October 15, 1994). ... Signed by Las Vegas, San Diego Padres organization (November 3, 1994). ... On disabled list (June 21-July 24, 1995). ... Granted free agency (October 16, 1995). ... Re-signed by Padres organization (October 28, 1995). ... Granted free agency (October 15, 1996). ... Signed by New York Mets organization (December 2, 1996). ... Released by Mets (March 28, 1997). ... Signed by Montreal Expos organization (March 31, 1997). ... Granted free agency (October 15, 1997). ... Signed by Seattle Mariners organization (December 27, 1997). ... Granted free agency (October 3, 1998). ... Signed by Royals organization (October 30, 1998).
STATISTICAL NOTES: Led New York-Pennsylvania League third basemen with 64 putouts, 159 assists, 252 total chances and 15 double plays in 1985.

Year Team (League)	Pos.	G	AB	R	H	2B	3B	HR	RBI	Avg.	BB	SO	SB	PO	A	E	Avg.
1985— Newark (NY-Penn)......	3B-SS-2B	73	246	38	53	14	2	3	25	.215	32	22	17	†67	†159	26	.897
1986— Miami (Fla. St.).........	3B-SS	38	134	26	34	7	1	1	9	.254	24	8	10	30	95	8	.940
— Charlotte (Southern) ..	S-3-2-O	77	232	40	68	16	2	3	25	.293	26	19	13	121	149	10	.964
1987— Charlotte (Southern) ..	3B-2B-OF	127	471	69	135	22	3	4	50	.287	43	38	20	129	255	19	.953
1988— Buffalo (A.A.)■.........	SS-3B-2B	68	187	12	46	4	0	1	20	.246	13	17	1	101	152	10	.962
1989— Harrisburg (East.)......	SS-3B	78	238	20	60	16	1	2	25	.252	27	19	2	107	175	12	.959
— Buffalo (A.A.)............	SS-C-2B	38	109	11	21	5	0	0	10	.193	18	11	4	85	98	6	.968
1990— Buffalo (A.A.)............	SS	8	17	3	3	0	1	0	2	.176	4	2	1	9	20	2	.935
— Greenville (Sou.)■.....	SS	5	21	4	4	1	0	0	0	.190	1	2	0	9	23	2	.941
— Richmond (Int'l).........	SS	107	380	58	88	13	0	4	32	.232	69	43	11	144	290	18	*.960
1991— Richmond (Int'l).........	2B-SS-3B	*139	482	58	124	25	1	2	48	.257	67	44	4	286	408	17	.976
— Atlanta (N.L.)............	SS	5	1	0	0	0	0	0	0	.000	0	1	0	0	0	0	...
1992— Omaha (A.A.)■.........	SS	48	174	29	55	10	1	4	17	.316	34	14	3	86	141	8	.966
— Kansas City (A.L.)	SS-3B-2B	59	149	21	32	8	1	1	12	.215	20	20	0	73	156	10	.958
1993— Kansas City (A.L.)	2B-3B-SS	46	86	10	19	4	0	2	12	.221	9	11	0	42	76	1	.992
— Omaha (A.A.)............	SS-3B	37	131	25	39	10	1	5	21	.298	20	19	3	54	124	7	.962
1994— Omaha (A.A.)............	SS-3B-P	120	412	49	97	23	0	11	63	.235	61	60	9	185	384	26	.956
1995— Las Vegas (PCL)■......	SS-3B-2B	98	316	44	95	11	2	1	45	.301	55	36	3	138	304	26	.944
1996— Las Vegas (PCL)	SS-3B	130	413	56	104	21	2	4	35	.252	70	63	6	164	406	18	.969
1997— Ottawa (Int'l).............	SS-2B-P	1	375	56	94	23	0	10	52	.251	37	64	5	154	288	20	.957
1998— Tacoma (PCL)■.........	SS-2B	56	210	33	60	18	0	8	36	.286	26	36	1	94	148	12	.953
— Seattle (A.L.)............	3-2-S-DH	37	81	12	16	6	0	1	4	.198	6	13	0	15	60	0	1.000
American League totals (3 years)		142	316	43	67	18	1	4	28	.212	35	44	0	130	292	11	.975
National League totals (1 year)		5	1	0	0	0	0	0	0	.000	0	1	0	0	0	0	...
Major league totals (4 years)		147	317	43	67	18	1	4	28	.211	35	45	0	130	292	11	.975

RECORD AS PITCHER

Year Team (League)	W	L	Pct.	ERA	G	GS	CG	ShO	Sv.	IP	H	R	ER	BB	SO
1994— Omaha (Am. Assoc.)..........	0	0	...	4.50	2	0	0	0	0	4	3	2	2	1	0
1997— Ottawa (Int'l)	0	0	...	0.00	1	0	0	0	0	1	0	0	0	1	0

RUEBEL, MATT   P   DIAMONDBACKS

PERSONAL: Born October 16, 1969, in Cincinnati. ... 6-2/180. ... Throws left, bats left. ... Full name: Matthew Alexander Ruebel.
HIGH SCHOOL: Ames (Iowa).
COLLEGE: Oklahoma.
TRANSACTIONS/CAREER NOTES: Selected by Pittsburgh Pirates organization in third round of free-agent draft (June 3, 1991). ... On Calgary disabled list (July 1-15, 1996). ... On disabled list (May 5-21, 1997). ... Granted free agency (October 15, 1997). ... Signed by Tampa Bay Devil Rays organization (January 27, 1998). ... Granted free agency (September 30, 1998). ... Signed by Arizona Diamondbacks organization (December 17, 1998).

Year Team (League)	W	L	Pct.	ERA	G	GS	CG	ShO	Sv.	IP	H	R	ER	BB	SO
1991— Welland (N.Y.-Penn)..........	1	1	.500	1.95	6	6	0	0	0	27 2/3	16	9	6	11	27
— Augusta (S. Atl.)...............	3	4	.429	3.83	8	8	2	1	0	47	43	26	20	25	35
1992— Augusta (S. Atl.)...............	5	2	.714	2.78	12	10	1	0	0	64 2/3	53	26	20	19	65
— Salem (Carolina)	1	6	.143	4.71	13	13	1	0	0	78 1/3	77	49	41	43	46
1993— Salem (Carolina)	1	4	.200	5.94	19	1	0	0	0	33 1/3	34	31	22	32	29
— Augusta (S. Atl.)...............	5	5	.500	2.42	23	7	1	1	0	63 1/3	51	28	17	34	50
1994— Salem (Carolina)	6	6	.500	3.44	21	13	0	0	0	86 1/3	87	49	33	27	72
— Carolina (Southern)...........	1	1	.500	6.61	6	3	0	0	0	16 1/3	28	15	12	3	14
1995— Carolina (Southern)...........	13	5	.722	2.76	27	27	4	*3	0	169 1/3	150	68	52	45	136
1996— Calgary (PCL)...................	5	3	.625	4.60	13	13	1	0	0	76 1/3	89	43	39	28	48
— Pittsburgh (N.L.)...............	1	1	.500	4.60	26	7	0	0	1	58 2/3	64	38	30	25	22
1997— Pittsburgh (N.L.)...............	3	2	.600	6.32	44	0	0	0	0	62 2/3	77	50	44	27	50
1998— Durham (International)■....	9	6	.600	4.74	24	23	1	1	0	129	141	73	68	45	87
— Tampa Bay (A.L.)...............	0	2	.000	6.23	7	1	0	0	0	8 2/3	11	7	6	4	6
A.L. totals (1 year)	0	2	.000	6.23	7	1	0	0	0	8 2/3	11	7	6	4	6
N.L. totals (2 years)	4	3	.571	5.49	70	7	0	0	1	121 1/3	141	88	74	52	72
Major league totals (3 years)......	4	5	.444	5.54	77	8	0	0	1	130	152	95	80	56	78

RUETER, KIRK　　　　　P　　　　　GIANTS

PERSONAL: Born December 1, 1970, in Centralia, Ill. ... 6-3/205. ... Throws left, bats left. ... Full name: Kirk Wesley Rueter. ... Name pronounced REE-ter.
HIGH SCHOOL: Nashville (Ill.) Community.
COLLEGE: Murray State.
TRANSACTIONS/CAREER NOTES: Selected by Montreal Expos organization in 19th round of free-agent draft (June 3, 1991). ... On Montreal disabled list (May 10-26, 1996); included rehabilitation assignment to Ottawa (May 20-24). ... Traded by Expos with P Tim Scott to San Francisco Giants for P Mark Leiter (July 30, 1996).
HONORS: Named N.L. Rookie Pitcher of the Year by THE SPORTING NEWS (1993).
STATISTICAL NOTES: Pitched 1-0 one-hit, complete-game victory for Montreal against San Francisco (August 27, 1995).
MISCELLANEOUS: Caught stealing in only appearance as pinch runner (1998).

Year　Team (League)	W	L	Pct.	ERA	G	GS	CG	ShO	Sv.	IP	H	R	ER	BB	SO
1991— GC Expos (GCL)	1	1	.500	0.95	5	4	0	0	0	19	16	5	2	4	19
— Sumter (S. Atl.)	3	1	.750	1.33	8	5	0	0	0	40 2/3	32	8	6	10	27
1992— Rockford (Midwest)	11	9	.550	2.58	26	26	6	•2	0	174 1/3	150	68	50	36	153
1993— Harrisburg (Eastern)	5	0	1.000	1.36	9	8	1	1	0	59 2/3	47	10	9	7	36
— Ottawa (Int'l)	4	2	.667	2.70	7	7	1	0	0	43 1/3	46	20	13	3	27
— Montreal (N.L.)	8	0	1.000	2.73	14	14	1	0	0	85 2/3	85	33	26	18	31
1994— Montreal (N.L.)	7	3	.700	5.17	20	20	0	0	0	92 1/3	106	60	53	23	50
— Ottawa (Int'l)	0	0	...	4.50	1	1	0	0	0	2	1	1	1	0	1
1995— Montreal (N.L.)	5	3	.625	3.23	9	9	1	1	0	47 1/3	38	17	17	9	28
— Ottawa (Int'l)	9	7	.563	3.06	20	20	3	1	0	120 2/3	120	50	41	25	67
1996— Ottawa (Int'l)	1	2	.333	4.20	3	3	1	0	0	15	21	7	7	3	3
— Montreal (N.L.)	5	6	.455	4.58	16	16	0	0	0	78 2/3	91	44	40	22	30
— San Francisco (N.L.)■	1	2	.333	1.93	4	3	0	0	0	23 1/3	18	6	5	5	16
— Phoenix (PCL)	1	2	.333	3.51	5	5	0	0	0	25 2/3	25	12	10	12	15
1997— San Francisco (N.L.)	13	6	.684	3.45	32	32	0	0	0	190 2/3	194	83	73	51	115
1998— San Francisco (N.L.)	16	9	.640	4.36	33	33	1	0	0	187 2/3	193	100	91	57	102
Major league totals (6 years)	55	29	.655	3.89	128	127	3	1	0	705 2/3	725	343	305	185	372

DIVISION SERIES RECORD

Year　Team (League)	W	L	Pct.	ERA	G	GS	CG	ShO	Sv.	IP	H	R	ER	BB	SO
1997— San Francisco (N.L.)	0	0	...	1.29	1	1	0	0	0	7	4	1	1	3	5

RUNYAN, SEAN　　　　　P　　　　　TIGERS

PERSONAL: Born June 21, 1974, in Fort Smith, Ark. ... 6-3/200. ... Throws left, bats left. ... Full name: Sean David Runyan.
HIGH SCHOOL: Urbandale (Iowa).
TRANSACTIONS/CAREER NOTES: Selected by Houston Astros organization in fifth round of free-agent draft (June 1, 1992). ... Traded by Astros to San Diego Padres for IF Luis Lopez (March 15, 1997). ... Selected by Detroit Tigers from Padres organization in Rule 5 major league draft (December 15, 1997).
RECORDS: Holds major league rookie-season record for most games pitched—88 (1998).

Year　Team (League)	W	L	Pct.	ERA	G	GS	CG	ShO	Sv.	IP	H	R	ER	BB	SO
1992— GC Astros (GCL)	3	3	.500	3.20	10	10	0	0	0	45	54	19	16	16	30
1993— GC Astros (GCL)	4	3	.571	2.98	12	12	0	0	0	66 1/3	66	35	22	24	52
1994— Auburn (N.Y.-Penn)	7	5	.583	3.49	14	14	2	1	0	95 1/3	90	49	37	19	66
1995— Quad City (Midwest)	4	6	.400	3.66	22	11	0	0	0	76 1/3	67	37	31	29	65
1996— Quad City (Midwest)	9	4	.692	3.88	29	17	0	0	0	132 1/3	128	61	57	30	104
1997— Mobile (Southern)	5	2	.714	2.34	40	1	0	0	1	61 2/3	54	25	16	28	52
1998— Detroit (A.L.)■	1	4	.200	3.58	*88	0	0	0	1	50 1/3	47	23	20	28	39
Major league totals (1 year)	1	4	.200	3.58	88	0	0	0	1	50 1/3	47	23	20	28	39

RUSCH, GLENDON　　　　　P　　　　　ROYALS

PERSONAL: Born November 7, 1974, in Seattle. ... 6-1/195. ... Throws left, bats left. ... Full name: Glendon James Rusch.
HIGH SCHOOL: Shorecrest (Seattle).
TRANSACTIONS/CAREER NOTES: Selected by Kansas City Royals organization in 17th round of free-agent draft (June 3, 1993). ... On Kansas City disabled list (June 16-July 1, 1997); included rehabilitation assignment to Omaha (June 26-July 1). ... On Kansas City disabled list (August 9-September 4, 1998); included rehabilitation assignment to Omaha (August 24-September 4).
STATISTICAL NOTES: Pitched 9-0 no-hit victory against Kane County (August 7, 1994).

Year　Team (League)	W	L	Pct.	ERA	G	GS	CG	ShO	Sv.	IP	H	R	ER	BB	SO
1993— GC Royals (GCL)	4	2	.667	1.60	11	10	0	0	0	62	43	14	11	11	48
— Rockford (Midwest)	0	1	.000	3.38	2	2	0	0	0	8	10	6	3	7	8
1994— Rockford (Midwest)	8	5	.615	4.66	28	17	1	1	1	114	111	61	59	34	122
1995— Wilmington (Caro.)	*14	6	.700	*1.74	26	26	1	1	0	165 2/3	110	41	32	34	147
1996— Omaha (Am. Assoc.)	11	9	.550	3.98	28	28	1	0	0	169 2/3	177	88	75	40	117
1997— Kansas City (A.L.)	6	9	.400	5.50	30	27	1	0	0	170 1/3	206	111	104	52	116
— Omaha (Am. Assoc.)	0	1	.000	4.50	1	1	0	0	0	6	7	3	3	1	2
1998— Kansas City (A.L.)	6	15	.286	5.88	29	24	1	1	1	154 2/3	191	104	101	50	94
— Omaha (Pacific Coast)	1	1	.500	7.98	3	3	0	0	0	14 2/3	20	18	13	6	14
Major league totals (2 years)	12	24	.333	5.68	59	51	2	1	1	325	397	215	205	102	210

RYAN, JASON　　　　　P　　　　　CUBS

PERSONAL: Born January 23, 1976, in Long Branch, N.J. ... 6-3/185. ... Throws right, bats both. ... Full name: Jason Paul Ryan. ... Son of Tim Ryan, pitcher in Los Angeles Dodgers and Atlanta Braves organizations; brother of Sean Ryan, minor league infielder with Philadelphia Phillies organization (1990-93); and nephew of Ed Madjeski, catcher, Philadelphia Athletics, Chicago White Sox and New York Giants (1932-34 and 1937).

HIGH SCHOOL: Immaculata (Somerville, N.J.).

TRANSACTIONS/CAREER NOTES: Selected by Chicago Cubs organization in ninth round of free-agent draft (June 2, 1994).

Year Team (League)	W	L	Pct.	ERA	G	GS	CG	ShO	Sv.	IP	H	R	ER	BB	SO
1994— GC Cubs (GCL)	1	2	.333	4.09	7	7	0	0	0	33	32	19	15	4	30
— Huntington (Appal.)	2	0	1.000	0.35	4	4	1	1	0	26	7	1	1	8	32
— Orlando (South.)	2	0	1.000	2.45	2	2	0	0	0	11	6	3	3	6	12
1995— Daytona (Fla. St.)	11	5	.688	3.48	26	26	0	0	0	134 2/3	128	61	52	54	98
1996— Orlando (South.)	2	5	.286	5.71	7	7	0	0	0	34 2/3	39	30	22	24	25
— Daytona (Fla. St.)	1	8	.111	5.24	17	10	0	0	1	67	72	42	39	33	49
1997— Daytona (Fla. St.)	9	8	.529	4.44	27	27	5	0	0	170 1/3	168	105	84	55	140
1998— West Tenn (Southern)	3	•13	.188	4.88	30	25	2	0	0	147 2/3	172	97	80	57	121

RYAN, KEN   P   PHILLIES

PERSONAL: Born October 24, 1968, in Pawtucket, R.I. ... 6-3/230. ... Throws right, bats right. ... Full name: Kenneth Frederick Ryan Jr.

HIGH SCHOOL: Seekonk (Mass.).

TRANSACTIONS/CAREER NOTES: Signed as non-drafted free agent by Boston Red Sox organization (June 16, 1986). ... Traded by Red Sox with OF Lee Tinsley and OF Glenn Murray to Philadelphia Phillies for P Heathcliff Slocumb, P Larry Wimberly and OF Rick Holifield (January 29, 1996). ... On Philadelphia disabled list (March 25-May 9 and June 13-September 1, 1997); included rehabilitation assignment to Reading (May 6-9). ... On Philadelphia disabled list (March 17-July 31, 1998); included rehabilitation assignments to Clearwater (July 5-14) and Scranton/Wilkes-Barre (July 17-30). ... Granted free agency (December 21, 1998). ... Re-signed by Phillies (December 22, 1998).

Year Team (League)	W	L	Pct.	ERA	G	GS	CG	ShO	Sv.	IP	H	R	ER	BB	SO
1986— Elmira (N.Y.-Penn)	2	2	.500	5.82	13	1	0	0	0	21 2/3	20	14	14	21	22
1987— Greensboro (S. Atl.)	3	12	.200	5.49	28	19	2	0	0	121 1/3	139	88	74	63	75
1988— Lynchburg (Carolina)	2	7	.222	6.18	19	14	0	0	0	71 1/3	79	51	49	45	49
1989— Winter Haven (FSL)	8	8	.500	3.15	24	22	3	0	0	137	114	58	48	81	78
1990— Lynchburg (Carolina)	6	•14	.300	5.13	28	•28	3	1	0	161 1/3	182	104	92	82	109
1991— Winter Haven (FSL)	1	3	.250	2.05	21	1	0	0	1	52 2/3	40	15	12	19	53
— New Britain (East.)	1	2	.333	1.73	14	0	0	0	1	26	23	7	5	12	26
— Pawtucket (Int'l)	1	0	1.000	4.91	9	0	0	0	1	18 1/3	15	11	10	11	14
1992— New Britain (East.)	1	4	.200	1.95	44	0	0	0	22	50 2/3	44	17	11	24	51
— Pawtucket (Int'l)	2	0	1.000	2.08	9	0	0	0	7	8 2/3	6	2	2	4	6
— Boston (A.L.)	0	0	...	6.43	7	0	0	0	1	7	4	5	5	5	5
1993— Boston (A.L.)	7	2	.778	3.60	47	0	0	0	1	50	43	23	20	29	49
— Pawtucket (Int'l)	0	2	.000	2.49	18	0	0	0	8	25 1/3	18	9	7	17	22
1994— Sarasota (Florida State)	0	0	...	3.68	8	0	0	0	1	7 1/3	6	3	3	2	11
— Boston (A.L.)	2	3	.400	2.44	42	0	0	0	13	48	46	14	13	17	32
1995— Boston (A.L.)	0	4	.000	4.96	28	0	0	0	7	32 2/3	34	20	18	24	34
— Trenton (Eastern)	0	2	.000	5.82	11	0	0	0	2	17	23	13	11	5	16
— Pawtucket (Int'l)	0	1	.000	6.30	9	0	0	0	0	10	12	7	7	4	6
1996— Philadelphia (N.L.)■	3	5	.375	2.43	62	0	0	0	8	89	71	32	24	45	70
1997— Reading (Eastern)	0	0	...	0.00	2	2	0	0	0	2	1	0	0	1	0
— Philadelphia (N.L.)	1	0	1.000	9.58	22	0	0	0	0	20 2/3	31	23	22	13	10
— Scran./W.B. (Int'l)	1	0	1.000	4.50	3	0	0	0	1	4	5	2	2	3	3
1998— Clearwater (Fla. St.)	0	0	...	3.00	4	4	0	0	0	9	5	3	3	3	10
— Scran./W.B. (Int'l)	1	0	1.000	0.00	6	0	0	0	1	8	7	0	0	3	9
— Philadelphia (N.L.)	0	0	...	4.37	17	1	0	0	0	22 2/3	21	12	11	20	16
A.L. totals (4 years)	9	9	.500	3.66	124	0	0	0	22	137 2/3	127	62	56	75	120
N.L. totals (3 years)	4	5	.444	3.88	101	1	0	0	8	132 1/3	123	67	57	78	96
Major league totals (7 years)	13	14	.481	3.77	225	1	0	0	30	270	250	129	113	153	216

RYAN, ROB   OF   DIAMONDBACKS

PERSONAL: Born June 24, 1973, in Havre, Mont. ... 5-11/190. ... Bats left, throws left. ... Full name: Robert James Ryan.

HIGH SCHOOL: Shadle Park (Spokane, Wash.).

COLLEGE: Washington State.

TRANSACTIONS/CAREER NOTES: Selected by Arizona Diamondbacks organization in 36th round of free-agent draft (June 4, 1996).

						BATTING							FIELDING		
Year Team (League)	Pos.	G	AB	R	H	2B	3B	HR	RBI	Avg.	BB	SO	SB	PO	A	E	Avg.
1996— Lethbridge (Pioneer)	OF	59	211	55	64	8	1	4	37	.303	43	33	23	107	3	4	.965
1997— South Bend (Mid.)	OF	121	421	71	132	35	5	8	73	.314	89	58	12	188	11	7	.966
1998— Tucson (PCL)	OF	116	394	71	125	18	2	17	66	.317	63	61	9	224	3	4	.983

SABERHAGEN, BRET   P   RED SOX

PERSONAL: Born April 11, 1964, in Chicago Heights, Ill. ... 6-1/200. ... Throws right, bats right. ... Full name: Bret William Saberhagen. ... Name pronounced SAY-ber-HAY-gun.

HIGH SCHOOL: Cleveland (Reseda, Calif.).

TRANSACTIONS/CAREER NOTES: Selected by Kansas City Royals organization in 19th round of free-agent draft (June 7, 1982). ... On disabled list (August 10-September 1, 1986; July 16-September 10, 1990; and June 15-July 13, 1991). ... Traded by Royals with OF Bill Pecota to New York Mets for OF Kevin McReynolds, IF Gregg Jefferies and 2B Keith Miller (December 11, 1991). ... On disabled list (May 16-July 18 and August 2-September 7, 1992 and August 3, 1993-remainder of season). ... On suspended list (April 3-8, 1994). ... Traded by Mets with a player to be named later to Colorado Rockies for P Juan Acevedo and P Arnold Gooch (July 31, 1995); Rockies acquired P David Swanson to complete deal (August 4, 1995). ... On disabled list (March 22, 1996-entire season). ... Granted free agency (October 29, 1996). ... Signed by Boston Red Sox organization (December 9, 1996). ... On Boston disabled list (March 31-August 22, 1997); included rehabilitation assignments to Lowell (July 27-August 1), Trenton (August 1-12) and Pawtucket (August 12-22). ... Granted free agency (October 31, 1997). ... Re-signed by Red Sox (November 17, 1997).

HONORS: Named A.L. Pitcher of the Year by THE SPORTING NEWS (1985 and 1989). ... Named righthanded pitcher on THE SPORTING NEWS A.L. All-Star team (1985 and 1989). ... Named A.L. Cy Young Award winner by Baseball Writers' Association of America (1985 and 1989). ... Named A.L. Comeback Player of the Year by THE SPORTING NEWS (1987 and 1998). ... Won A.L. Gold Glove at pitcher (1989).
STATISTICAL NOTES: Pitched 7-0 no-hit victory against Chicago (August 26, 1991).
MISCELLANEOUS: Appeared in one game as pinch runner (1984). ... Appeared in three games as pinch runner (1989).

Year — Team (League)	W	L	Pct.	ERA	G	GS	CG	ShO	Sv.	IP	H	R	ER	BB	SO
1983— Fort Myers (Fla. St.)	10	5	.667	2.30	16	16	3	1	0	109 2/3	98	34	28	19	82
—Jacksonville (Southern)......	6	2	.750	2.91	11	11	2	1	0	77 1/3	66	31	25	29	48
1984— Kansas City (A.L.)	10	11	.476	3.48	38	18	2	1	1	157 2/3	138	71	61	36	73
1985— Kansas City (A.L.)	20	6	.769	2.87	32	32	10	1	0	235 1/3	211	79	75	38	158
1986— Kansas City (A.L.)	7	12	.368	4.15	30	25	4	2	0	156	165	77	72	29	112
1987— Kansas City (A.L.)	18	10	.643	3.36	33	33	15	4	0	257	246	99	96	53	163
1988— Kansas City (A.L.)	14	16	.467	3.80	35	35	9	0	0	260 2/3	*271	122	110	59	171
1989— Kansas City (A.L.)	*23	6	.793	*2.16	36	35	*12	4	0	*262 1/3	209	74	63	43	193
1990— Kansas City (A.L.)	5	9	.357	3.27	20	20	5	0	0	135	146	52	49	28	87
1991— Kansas City (A.L.)	13	8	.619	3.07	28	28	7	2	0	196 1/3	165	76	67	45	136
1992— New York (N.L.)■	3	5	.375	3.50	17	15	1	1	0	97 2/3	84	39	38	27	81
1993— New York (N.L.)................	7	7	.500	3.29	19	19	4	1	0	139 1/3	131	55	51	17	93
1994— New York (N.L.)................	14	4	.778	2.74	24	24	4	0	0	177 1/3	169	58	54	13	143
1995— New York (N.L.)................	5	5	.500	3.35	16	16	3	0	0	110	105	45	41	20	71
—Colorado (N.L.)■	2	1	.667	6.28	9	9	0	0	0	43	60	33	30	13	29
1996— Colorado (N.L.)							Did not play.								
1997— Lowell (NY-Penn)■............	0	0	. . .	0.00	1	1	0	0	0	3	1	0	0	0	2
— Trenton (Eastern)	0	0	. . .	0.00	2	2	0	0	0	8	2	0	0	1	9
—Pawtucket (Int'l)	0	1	.000	3.27	2	2	0	0	0	11	11	4	4	1	9
—Boston (A.L.)	0	1	.000	6.58	6	6	0	0	0	26	30	20	19	10	14
1998— Boston (A.L.)..................	15	8	.652	3.96	31	31	0	0	0	175	181	82	77	29	100
A.L. totals (10 years)	125	87	.590	3.33	289	263	64	14	1	1861 1/3	1762	752	689	370	1207
N.L. totals (4 years)	31	22	.585	3.39	85	83	12	2	0	567 1/3	549	230	214	90	417
Major league totals (14 years)....	156	109	.589	3.35	374	346	76	16	1	2428 2/3	2311	982	903	460	1624

DIVISION SERIES RECORD

Year — Team (League)	W	L	Pct.	ERA	G	GS	CG	ShO	Sv.	IP	H	R	ER	BB	SO
1995— Colorado (N.L.)	0	1	.000	11.25	1	1	0	0	0	4	7	6	5	1	3
1998— Boston (A.L.)..................	0	1	.000	3.86	1	1	0	0	0	7	4	3	3	1	7
Div. series totals (2 years)	0	2	.000	6.55	2	2	0	0	0	11	11	9	8	2	10

CHAMPIONSHIP SERIES RECORD

Year — Team (League)	W	L	Pct.	ERA	G	GS	CG	ShO	Sv.	IP	H	R	ER	BB	SO
1984— Kansas City (A.L.)	0	0	. . .	2.25	1	1	0	0	0	8	6	3	2	1	5
1985— Kansas City (A.L.)	0	0	. . .	6.14	2	2	0	0	0	7 1/3	12	5	5	2	6
Champ. series totals (2 years)	0	0	. . .	4.11	3	3	0	0	0	15 1/3	18	8	7	3	11

WORLD SERIES RECORD

NOTES: Named Most Valuable Player (1985). ... Member of World Series championship team (1985).

Year — Team (League)	W	L	Pct.	ERA	G	GS	CG	ShO	Sv.	IP	H	R	ER	BB	SO
1985— Kansas City (A.L.)	2	0	1.000	0.50	2	2	2	1	0	18	11	1	1	1	10

ALL-STAR GAME RECORD

Year — League	W	L	Pct.	ERA	GS	CG	ShO	Sv.	IP	H	R	ER	BB	SO
1987— American	0	0	. . .	0.00	1	0	0	0	3	1	0	0	0	0
1990— American	1	0	1.000	0.00	0	0	0	0	2	0	0	0	0	1
1994— National							Did not play.							
All-Star totals (2 years)	1	0	1.000	0.00	1	0	0	0	5	1	0	0	0	1

SADLER, DONNIE   2B/SS   RED SOX

PERSONAL: Born June 17, 1975, in Gohlson, Texas. ... 5-6/165. ... Bats right, throws right. ... Full name: Donnie Lamont Sadler.
HIGH SCHOOL: Valley Mills (Texas).
TRANSACTIONS/CAREER NOTES: Selected by Boston Red Sox organization in 10th round of free-agent draft (June 2, 1994). ... On Pawtucket disabled list (May 4-June 4 and June 23-30, 1998).
STATISTICAL NOTES: Tied for International League lead in errors by second baseman with 12 in 1997. ... Tied for International League lead in caught stealing with 14 in 1997.

						BATTING								FIELDING			
Year — Team (League)	Pos.	G	AB	R	H	2B	3B	HR	RBI	Avg.	BB	SO	SB	PO	A	E	Avg.
1994— Fort Myers (GCL)	SS	53	206	52	56	8	6	1	16	.272	23	27	32				. . .
1995— Michigan (Midwest) ...	SS	118	438	*103	124	25	8	9	55	.283	79	85	41	168	307	28	.944
1996— Trenton (Eastern)	SS-OF	115	454	68	121	20	8	6	46	.267	38	75	34	185	237	27	.940
1997— Pawtucket (Int'l)........	2B-SS-OF	125	481	74	102	18	2	11	36	.212	57	121	20	252	354	‡15	.976
1998— Boston (A.L.).............	2B-DH-SS	58	124	21	28	4	4	3	15	.226	6	28	4	81	101	5	.973
—Pawtucket (Int'l)	2B-SS	36	131	25	29	5	1	2	10	.221	26	23	11	73	104	4	.978
Major league totals (1 year)		58	124	21	28	4	4	3	15	.226	6	28	4	81	101	5	.973

DIVISION SERIES RECORD

						BATTING								FIELDING			
Year — Team (League)	Pos.	G	AB	R	H	2B	3B	HR	RBI	Avg.	BB	SO	SB	PO	A	E	Avg.
1998— Boston (A.L.).............	2B-PR	3	0	0	0	0	0	0	0	. . .	0	0	0	1	1	0	1.000

PERSONAL: Born October 8, 1970, in Chitre Herrera, Panama. ... 6-0/185. ... Bats right, throws right. ... Full name: Olmedo Sanchez Saenz. ... Name pronounced SIGNS.
TRANSACTIONS/CAREER NOTES: Signed as non-drafted free agent by Chicago White Sox organization (May 11, 1990). ... Granted free agency (October 15, 1997). ... Re-signed by White Sox organization for 1998 season. ... Granted free agency (October 15, 1998). ... Signed by Oakland Athletics (November 13, 1998).
STATISTICAL NOTES: Led American Association third basemen with 395 total chances in 1995. ... Tied for American Association lead in being hit by pitch with 13 in 1996. ... Led American Association third basemen with 363 total chances and 24 double plays in 1996. ... Led Pacific Coast League in being hit by pitch with 22 in 1998.

| | | | | | | | | BATTING | | | | | | | FIELDING | | |
Year	Team (League)	Pos.	G	AB	R	H	2B	3B	HR	RBI	Avg.	BB	SO	SB	PO	A	E	Avg.
1991—	South Bend (Mid.)......	3B	56	192	23	47	10	1	2	22	.245	21	48	5	29	68	12	.890
	—Sarasota (Fla. St.)	3B	5	19	1	2	0	1	0	2	.105	2	0	0	5	11	3	.842
1992—	South Bend (Mid.)......	3B-1B	132	493	66	121	26	4	7	59	.245	36	52	16	113	294	48	.895
1993—	South Bend (Mid.)......	3B	13	50	3	18	4	1	0	7	.360	7	7	1	11	31	4	.913
	—Sarasota (Fla. St.)	3B	33	121	13	31	9	4	0	27	.256	9	18	3	15	55	5	.933
	—Birmingham (Sou.)......	3B	49	173	30	60	17	2	6	29	.347	20	21	2	38	87	14	.899
1994—	Nashville (A.A.)	3B	107	383	48	100	27	2	12	59	.261	30	57	3	76	167	22	.917
	—Chicago (A.L.)	3B	5	14	2	2	0	1	0	0	.143	0	5	0	3	5	0	1.000
1995—	Nashville (A.A.)	3B	111	415	60	126	26	1	13	74	.304	45	60	0	*82	*289	*24	*.939
1996—	Nashville (A.A.)	3B	134	476	86	124	29	1	18	63	.261	53	80	4	*97	244	22	.939
1997—	GC Whi. Sox (GCL)	DH	2	1	0	1	1	0	0	0	1.000	0	0	0	...	...	...	...
1998—	Calgary (PCL).............	3B	124	466	89	146	29	0	29	102	.313	45	49	3	75	235	21	.937
Major league totals (1 year)			5	14	2	2	0	1	0	0	.143	0	5	0	3	5	0	1.000

PERSONAL: Born March 3, 1965, in Columbus, Ohio. ... 6-4/220. ... Throws right, bats right. ... Full name: Anthony Joseph Sager.
HIGH SCHOOL: Watkins Memorial (Kirkersville, Ohio).
COLLEGE: Toledo.
TRANSACTIONS/CAREER NOTES: Selected by San Diego Padres organization in 10th round of free-agent draft (June 1, 1988). ... Granted free agency (October 15, 1994). ... Signed by Colorado Rockies organization (December 7, 1994). ... Granted free agency (October 16, 1995). ... Signed by Detroit Tigers organization (December 8, 1995). ... Granted free agency (October 15, 1998).

Year	Team (League)	W	L	Pct.	ERA	G	GS	CG	ShO	Sv.	IP	H	R	ER	BB	SO
1988—	Spokane (N'west)...............	8	3	.727	5.11	15	15	2	2	0	98²/₃	*123	*67	*56	27	74
1989—	Charleston, S.C. (S. Atl.)	•14	9	.609	3.38	26	25	6	2	0	167²/₃	166	77	63	40	105
1990—	Wichita (Texas)	11	•12	.478	5.48	26	26	2	1	0	154¹/₃	*200	*105	*94	29	79
1991—	Las Vegas (PCL)	7	5	.583	4.71	18	18	3	2	0	109	127	63	57	20	61
	—Wichita (Texas)	4	3	.571	4.13	10	10	1	0	0	65¹/₃	69	35	30	16	31
1992—	Las Vegas (PCL)	1	7	.125	7.95	30	3	0	0	1	60	89	57	53	17	40
1993—	Wichita (Texas)	5	3	.625	3.19	11	11	2	1	0	73¹/₃	69	30	26	16	49
	—Las Vegas (PCL)	6	5	.545	3.70	21	11	2	1	1	90	91	49	37	18	58
1994—	San Diego (N.L.)	1	4	.200	5.98	22	3	0	0	0	46²/₃	62	34	31	16	26
	—Las Vegas (PCL)	1	4	.200	4.43	23	2	0	0	5	40²/₃	57	24	20	8	23
1995—	Colo. Springs (PCL)■........	8	5	.615	3.50	23	22	1	1	0	133²/₃	153	61	52	23	80
	—Colorado (N.L.)	0	0	...	7.36	10	0	0	0	0	14²/₃	19	16	12	7	10
1996—	Toledo (International)■.......	1	0	1.000	2.63	18	2	0	0	0	37²/₃	38	14	11	3	24
	—Detroit (A.L.)	4	5	.444	5.01	22	9	0	0	0	79	91	46	44	29	52
1997—	Detroit (A.L.)	3	4	.429	4.18	38	1	0	0	3	84	81	43	39	24	53
1998—	Detroit (A.L.)	4	2	.667	6.52	31	3	0	0	2	59¹/₃	79	47	43	23	23
	—Toledo (International)........	1	2	.333	3.00	14	0	0	0	1	24	27	8	8	13	16
A.L. totals (3 years)		11	11	.500	5.10	91	13	0	0	5	222¹/₃	251	136	126	76	128
N.L. totals (2 years)		1	4	.200	6.31	32	3	0	0	0	61¹/₃	81	50	43	23	36
Major league totals (5 years)		12	15	.444	5.36	123	16	0	0	5	283²/₃	332	186	169	99	164

PERSONAL: Born September 10, 1973, in San Diego. ... 6-1/188. ... Throws right, bats right. ... Full name: Michael Eric Saipe. ... Name pronounced SAPE.
HIGH SCHOOL: University City (San Diego).
COLLEGE: San Diego.
TRANSACTIONS/CAREER NOTES: Selected by Colorado Rockies organization in 12th round of free-agent draft (June 2, 1994). ... On Colorado Springs disabled list (July 29-August 7, 1998).
STATISTICAL NOTES: Tied for Eastern League lead in balks with four in 1996.

Year	Team (League)	W	L	Pct.	ERA	G	GS	CG	ShO	Sv.	IP	H	R	ER	BB	SO
1994—	Bend (Northwest)...............	3	•7	.300	4.16	16	•16	0	0	0	84¹/₃	73	52	39	34	74
1995—	Salem (Carolina)	4	5	.444	3.48	21	9	0	0	3	85¹/₃	68	35	33	32	90
1996—	New Haven (East.)...............	10	7	.588	3.07	32	19	1	1	3	138	114	53	47	42	126
1997—	Nashville (Eastern)	8	5	.615	3.10	19	19	4	•2	0	136²/₃	127	57	47	29	123
	—Colo. Springs (PCL)	4	3	.571	5.52	10	10	1	0	0	60¹/₃	74	42	37	24	40
1998—	Colo. Springs (PCL)	5	11	.313	5.16	24	24	2	0	0	139²/₃	167	96	80	51	124
	—Colorado (N.L.)	0	1	.000	10.80	2	2	0	0	0	10	22	12	12	0	2
Major league totals (1 year)........		0	1	.000	10.80	2	2	0	0	0	10	22	12	12	0	2

S

PERSONAL: Born August 18, 1973, in Chicago. ... 6-1/195. ... Throws right, bats right. ... Full name: James Kenneth Sak Jr.
HIGH SCHOOL: St. Patrick (Chicago).
COLLEGE: Illinois Benedictine.
TRANSACTIONS/CAREER NOTES: Selected by San Diego Padres organization in 10th round of free-agent draft (June 1, 1995). ... On disabled list (July 23-August 10, 1998).

Year Team (League)	W	L	Pct.	ERA	G	GS	CG	ShO	Sv.	IP	H	R	ER	BB	SO
1995—Idaho Falls (Pioneer)	3	1	.750	1.65	13	0	0	0	1	32 2/3	15	9	6	12	55
—Clinton (Midwest)	6	1	.857	1.98	7	7	3	0	0	50	42	12	11	14	37
1996—Clinton (Midwest)	3	4	.429	3.56	21	7	0	0	0	65 2/3	46	31	26	45	72
—Rancho Cuca. (Cal.)	0	3	.000	6.32	4	4	0	0	0	15 2/3	21	13	11	12	14
1997—Rancho Cuca. (Cal.)	6	3	.667	2.93	57	3	0	0	27	70 2/3	42	28	23	30	113
1998—Mobile (Southern)	2	5	.286	5.14	45	0	0	0	16	49	33	29	28	36	56

PERSONAL: Born August 24, 1968, in Long Beach, Calif. ... 6-3/241. ... Bats right, throws right. ... Full name: Timothy James Salmon. ... Brother of Mike Salmon, safety with San Francisco 49ers (1997). ... Name pronounced SA-mon.
HIGH SCHOOL: Greenway (Phoenix).
COLLEGE: Grand Canyon (Ariz.).
TRANSACTIONS/CAREER NOTES: Selected by Atlanta Braves organization in 18th round of free-agent draft (June 2, 1986); did not sign. ... Selected by California Angels organization in third round of free-agent draft (June 5, 1989). ... On disabled list (May 12-23 and May 27-August 7, 1990; and July 18-August 3, 1994). ... Angels franchise renamed Anaheim Angels for 1997 season. ... On disabled list (April 23-May 9, 1998).
RECORDS: Shares major league record for fewest double plays by outfielder (150 or more games)—0 (1996). ... Shares A.L. record for most hits in three consecutive games—13 (May 10 [4], 11 [4] and 13 [5], 1994).
HONORS: Named Minor League Player of the Year by THE SPORTING NEWS (1992). ... Named Pacific Coast League Most Valuable Player (1992). ... Named A.L. Rookie Player of the Year by THE SPORTING NEWS (1993). ... Named A.L. Rookie of the Year by Baseball Writers' Association of America (1993). ... Named outfielder on THE SPORTING NEWS A.L. All-Star team (1995 and 1997). ... Named outfielder on THE SPORTING NEWS Silver Slugger team (1995).
STATISTICAL NOTES: Led Pacific Coast League with 275 total bases, .672 slugging percentage and .469 on-base percentage in 1992. ... Led A.L. outfielders with four double plays in 1994. ... Tied for A.L. lead in double plays by outfielder with five in 1997. ... Career major league grand slams: 3.

Year Team (League)	Pos.	G	AB	R	H	2B	3B	HR	RBI	Avg.	BB	SO	SB	PO	A	E	Avg.
1989—Bend (Northwest)	OF	55	196	37	48	6	5	6	31	.245	33	60	2	84	7	4	.958
1990—Palm Springs (Calif.)	OF	36	118	19	34	6	0	2	21	.288	21	44	11	63	3	1	.985
—Midland (Texas)	OF	27	97	17	26	3	1	3	16	.268	18	38	1	51	6	3	.950
1991—Midland (Texas)	OF	131	465	100	114	26	4	23	94	.245	*89	*166	12	265	16	10	.966
1992—Edmonton (PCL)	OF	118	409	•101	142	38	4	*29	*105	.347	91	103	9	231	14	3	.988
—California (A.L.)	OF	23	79	8	14	1	0	2	6	.177	11	23	1	40	1	2	.953
1993—California (A.L.)	OF-DH	142	515	93	146	35	1	31	95	.283	82	135	5	335	12	7	.980
1994—California (A.L.)	OF	100	373	67	107	18	2	23	70	.287	54	102	1	219	9	8	.966
1995—California (A.L.)	OF-DH	143	537	111	177	34	3	34	105	.330	91	111	5	320	7	4	.988
1996—California (A.L.)	OF-DH	156	581	90	166	27	4	30	98	.286	93	125	4	299	13	8	.975
1997—Anaheim (A.L.)	OF-DH	157	582	95	172	28	1	33	129	.296	95	142	9	352	15	11	.971
1998—Anaheim (A.L.)	DH-OF	136	463	84	139	28	1	26	88	.300	90	100	0	46	1	2	.959
Major league totals (7 years)		857	3130	548	921	171	12	179	591	.294	516	738	25	1611	58	42	.975

PERSONAL: Born April 27, 1975, in Des Moines, Iowa. ... 6-2/210. ... Throws left, bats left. ... Full name: Benjamin Damon Sampson.
HIGH SCHOOL: Ankeny (Iowa).
TRANSACTIONS/CAREER NOTES: Selected by Minnesota Twins organization in sixth round of free-agent draft (June 3, 1993). ... On disabled list (May 14-23, 1997).

Year Team (League)	W	L	Pct.	ERA	G	GS	CG	ShO	Sv.	IP	H	R	ER	BB	SO
1993—Elizabethton (Appal.)	4	1	.800	1.91	11	6	0	0	1	42 1/3	33	12	9	15	34
1994—Fort Wayne (Midw.)	6	9	.400	3.80	25	25	0	0	0	139 2/3	149	72	59	60	111
1995—Fort Myers (Fla. St.)	11	9	.550	3.49	28	27	3	2	0	160	148	71	62	52	95
1996—Fort Myers (Fla. St.)	7	1	.875	3.47	11	11	2	0	0	70	55	28	27	26	65
—New Britain (East.)	5	7	.417	5.73	16	16	1	0	0	75 1/3	108	54	48	25	51
1997—New Britain (East.)	10	6	.625	4.19	25	20	0	0	0	118	112	56	55	49	92
1998—Salt Lake (PCL)	10	7	.588	5.14	28	28	0	0	0	161	198	99	92	52	132
—Minnesota (A.L.)	1	0	1.000	1.56	5	2	0	0	0	17 1/3	10	3	3	6	16
Major league totals (1 year)	1	0	1.000	1.56	5	2	0	0	0	17 1/3	10	3	3	6	16

PERSONAL: Born December 9, 1960, in San Pedro de Macoris, Dominican Republic. ... 5-11/190. ... Bats right, throws right. ... Full name: Juan Milton Samuel. ... Name pronounced sam-WELL.
HIGH SCHOOL: Licey Puerto Rico (San Pedro de Macoris, Dominican Republic).
TRANSACTIONS/CAREER NOTES: Signed as non-drafted free agent by Philadelphia Phillies organization (April 29, 1980). ... On Philadelphia disabled list (April 13-May 2, 1986 and April 1-19, 1989). ... Traded by Phillies to New York Mets for OF Lenny Dykstra, P Roger McDowell and a player to be named later (June 18, 1989); Phillies organization acquired P Tom Edens to complete deal (July 27, 1989). ... Traded by Mets to Los Angeles Dodgers for P Alejandro Pena and OF Mike Marshall (December 20, 1989). ... Granted free agency (November 5, 1990). ... Re-signed by Dodgers (December 16, 1990). ... Granted free agency (October 28, 1991). ... Re-signed by Dodgers (February 27, 1992). ...

S

On Los Angeles disabled list (April 28-June 11, 1992). ... Released by Dodgers (July 30, 1992). ... Signed by Kansas City Royals (August 6, 1992). ... Granted free agency (October 21, 1992). ... Signed by Cincinnati Reds organization (December 11, 1992). ... Granted free agency (October 25, 1993). ... Signed by Detroit Tigers organization (February 14, 1994). ... Granted free agency (October 25, 1994). ... Re-signed by Tigers organization (April 17, 1995). ... Traded by Tigers to Royals for a player to be named later (September 8, 1995); Tigers acquired OF Phil Hiatt to complete deal (September 14, 1995). ... Granted free agency (November 2, 1995). ... Signed by Toronto Blue Jays organization (January 16, 1996). ... On disabled list (June 26-July 11, 1996). ... Granted free agency (November 18, 1996). ... Re-signed by Blue Jays organization (December 18, 1996). ... Granted free agency (October 28, 1997). ... Re-signed by Blue Jays organization (December 6, 1997). ... Granted free agency (November 5, 1998). ... Announced retirement to become assistant coach with Tigers (January 5, 1999).

RECORDS: Holds major league single-season records for most at-bats by righthander—701 (1984); and fewest sacrifice hits with most at-bats—0 (1984). ... Holds N.L. single-season record for most at-bats—701 (1984). ... Shares major league record for most consecutive seasons leading league in strikeouts—4 (1984-1987). ... Shares major league single-game record for most assists by second baseman (nine inning game)—12 (April 20, 1985).

HONORS: Named Carolina League Most Valuable Player (1982). ... Named N.L. Rookie Player of the Year by THE SPORTING NEWS (1984). ... Named second baseman on THE SPORTING NEWS N.L. All-Star team (1987). ... Named second baseman on THE SPORTING NEWS N.L. Silver Slugger team (1987).

STATISTICAL NOTES: Led Northwest League in caught stealing with 10 in 1980. ... Led South Atlantic League second basemen with 739 total chances and 82 double plays in 1981. ... Led Carolina League second basemen with 721 total chances and 82 double plays in 1982. ... Led Carolina League with 283 total bases and tied for lead in being hit by pitch with 15 in 1982. ... Led N.L. second basemen with 826 total chances in 1987. ... Led N.L. second basemen with 343 putouts and 92 double plays in 1988. ... Career major league grand slams: 2.

Year Team (League)	Pos.	G	AB	R	H	2B	3B	HR	RBI	Avg.	BB	SO	SB	PO	A	E	Avg.
1980— Cen. Oregon (NWL)....	2B	69	*298	66	84	11	2	17	44	.282	17	*87	25	162	188	*30	.921
1981— Spartanburg (SAL).....	2B	135	512	88	127	22	8	11	74	.248	36	132	53	*280	*409	*50	.932
1982— Peninsula (Caro.).......	2B	135	494	*111	158	29	6	28	94	.320	31	124	64	*244	*442	*35	.951
1983— Reading (Eastern)........	2B	47	184	36	43	10	0	11	39	.234	8	50	19	121	127	14	.947
— Portland (PCL)	2B	65	261	59	86	14	8	15	52	.330	22	46	33	110	168	15	.949
— Philadelphia (N.L.)......	2B	18	65	14	18	1	2	2	5	.277	4	16	3	44	54	9	.916
1984— Philadelphia (N.L.)......	2B	160	*701	105	191	36	•19	15	69	.272	28	*168	72	388	438	*33	.962
1985— Philadelphia (N.L.)......	2B	161	*663	101	175	31	13	19	74	.264	33	•141	53	*389	463	15	.983
1986— Philadelphia (N.L.)......	2B	145	591	90	157	36	12	16	78	.266	26	*142	42	290	440	*25	.967
1987— Philadelphia (N.L.)......	2B	160	*655	113	178	37	*15	28	100	.272	60	*162	35	*374	434	*18	.978
1988— Philadelphia (N.L.)......	2B-OF-3B	157	629	68	153	32	9	12	67	.243	39	151	33	†351	387	16	.979
1989— Philadelphia (N.L.)	OF	51	199	32	49	3	1	8	20	.246	18	45	11	133	2	1	.993
— New York (N.L.)■	OF	86	333	37	76	13	1	3	28	.228	24	75	31	206	4	3	.986
1990— Los Angeles (N.L.)■•....	2B-OF	143	492	62	119	24	3	13	52	.242	51	126	38	273	262	16	.971
1991— Los Angeles (N.L.)	2B	153	594	74	161	22	6	12	58	.271	49	133	23	300	442	17	.978
1992— Los Angeles (N.L.)	2B-OF	47	122	7	32	3	1	0	15	.262	7	22	2	76	77	5	.968
— Kansas City (A.L.)■ ...	OF-2B	29	102	15	29	5	3	0	8	.284	7	27	6	45	29	6	.925
1993— Cincinnati (N.L.)..........	2-1-3-O	103	261	31	60	10	4	4	26	.230	23	53	9	151	172	10	.970
1994— Detroit (A.L.)■..........	O-DH-2-1	59	136	32	42	9	5	5	21	.309	10	26	5	82	28	1	.991
1995— Detroit (A.L.).............	1-DH-O-2	76	171	28	48	10	1	10	34	.281	24	38	5	289	35	9	.973
— Kansas City (A.L.)■....	DH-OF-1B	15	34	3	6	0	0	2	5	.176	5	11	1	11	0	0	1.000
1996— Toronto (A.L.)■..........	DH-OF-1B	69	188	34	48	8	3	8	26	.255	15	65	9	117	3	2	.984
1997— Toronto (A.L.)............	DH-3-1-2-O	45	95	13	27	5	4	3	15	.284	10	28	5	34	13	0	1.000
1998— Toronto (A.L.)............	DH-O-1-2	43	50	14	9	2	0	1	2	.180	7	13	13	19	4	2	.920
American League totals (6 years)		336	776	139	209	39	16	29	111	.269	78	208	44	597	112	20	.973
National League totals (11 years)		1384	5305	734	1369	248	86	132	592	.258	362	1234	352	2975	3175	168	.973
Major league totals (16 years)		1720	6081	873	1578	287	102	161	703	.259	440	1442	396	3572	3287	188	.973

CHAMPIONSHIP SERIES RECORD

Year Team (League)	Pos.	G	AB	R	H	2B	3B	HR	RBI	Avg.	BB	SO	SB	PO	A	E	Avg.
1983— Philadelphia (N.L.)......	PR	1	0	0	0	0	0	0	0	...	0	0	0	...	...	...	...

WORLD SERIES RECORD

Year Team (League)	Pos.	G	AB	R	H	2B	3B	HR	RBI	Avg.	BB	SO	SB	PO	A	E	Avg.
1983— Philadelphia (N.L.)......	PR-PH	3	1	0	0	0	0	0	0	.000	0	0	0	...	...	...	...

ALL-STAR GAME RECORD

RECORDS: Holds single-game record for most putouts by second baseman—7 (July 14, 1987). ... Shares single-game record for most chances accepted by second baseman—9 (July 14, 1987).

Year League	Pos.	AB	R	H	2B	3B	HR	RBI	Avg.	BB	SO	SB	PO	A	E	Avg.
1984— National.....................								Did not play.								
1987— National.....................	2B	4	0	0	0	0	0	0	.000	0	1	0	7	2	0	1.000
1991— National.....................	2B	1	0	1	0	0	0	0	1.000	0	0	0	2	1	0	1.000
All-Star Game totals (2 years)		5	0	1	0	0	0	0	.200	0	1	0	9	3	0	1.000

SANCHEZ, ALEX   OF   DEVIL RAYS

PERSONAL: Born August 26, 1976, in Havana, Cuba. ... 5-10/180. ... Bats left, throws left. ... Full name: Alexis Sanchez.

JUNIOR COLLEGE: Miami-Dade (Wolfson) Community College.

TRANSACTIONS/CAREER NOTES: Selected by Tampa Bay Devil Rays organization in fifth round of free-agent draft (June 2, 1996).

STATISTICAL NOTES: Led South Atlantic League in caught stealing with 40 in 1997. ... Led South Atlantic League outfielders with 296 total chances in 1997. ... Led Florida State League in caught stealing with 33 and sacrifice flies with 12 in 1998.

Year Team (League)	Pos.	G	AB	R	H	2B	3B	HR	RBI	Avg.	BB	SO	SB	PO	A	E	Avg.
1996— GC Devil Rays	OF	56	227	36	64	7	6	1	22	.282	10	35	20	91	1	3	.968
1997— Char., S.C. (SAL)	OF	131	537	73	155	15	6	0	34	.289	37	72	*92	279	6	•11	.963
1998— St. Peters. (FSL).........	OF	128	545	77	*180	17	9	1	50	.330	31	70	66	330	5	•12	.965

SANCHEZ, JESUS   P   MARLINS

PERSONAL: Born October 11, 1974, in Nizao Bani, Dominican Republic. ... 5-10/155. ... Throws left, bats left. ... Full name: Jesus Paulino Sanchez.

TRANSACTIONS/CAREER NOTES: Signed as non-drafted free agent by New York Mets organization (June 7, 1992). ... On disabled list (April 4-May 28, 1996). ... Traded by Mets with P A.J. Burnett and OF Robert Stratton to Florida Marlins for P Al Leiter and 2B Ralph Milliard (February 6, 1998).

STATISTICAL NOTES: Led Dominican Summer League in home runs allowed with 14 in 1992.

MISCELLANEOUS: Appeared in two games as pinch runner (1998).

Year Team (League)	W	L	Pct.	ERA	G	GS	CG	ShO	Sv.	IP	H	R	ER	BB	SO
1992—Dominican Mets (DSL)	5	5	.500	4.19	15	15	1	0	0	$81^2/_3$	86	52	38	38	72
1993—Dominican Mets (DSL)	7	3	.700	2.40	16	13	2	•2	0	$82^1/_3$	63	30	22	36	94
1994—Kingsport (Appalachian)	7	4	.636	1.96	13	12	•3	0	0	$87^1/_3$	61	27	19	27	71
1995—Capital City (S. Atl.)	9	7	.563	3.13	27	4	0	0	0	$169^2/_3$	154	76	59	58	•177
1996—St. Lucie (Fla. St.)	9	3	.750	1.96	16	16	2	1	0	92	53	22	20	24	81
1997—Binghamton (Eastern)	*13	10	.565	4.30	26	26	3	0	0	$165^1/_3$	146	87	79	61	*176
1998—Florida (N.L.)■	7	9	.438	4.47	35	29	0	0	0	173	178	98	86	91	137
Major league totals (1 year)	7	9	.438	4.47	35	29	0	0	0	173	178	98	86	91	137

SANCHEZ, REY   SS/2B   ROYALS

PERSONAL: Born October 5, 1967, in Rio Piedras, Puerto Rico. ... 5-9/170. ... Bats right, throws right. ... Full name: Rey Francisco Guadalupe Sanchez.

HIGH SCHOOL: Live Oak (Morgan Hill, Calif.).

TRANSACTIONS/CAREER NOTES: Selected by Texas Rangers organization in 13th round of free-agent draft (June 2, 1986). ... Traded by Rangers organization to Chicago Cubs organization for IF Bryan House (January 3, 1990). ... On disabled list (April 6, 1990-entire season). ... On Chicago disabled list (May 6-21, 1992); included rehabilitation assignment to Iowa (May 13-21). ... On disabled list (July 24-August 9, 1995). ... On Chicago disabled list (June 5-July 20 and August 11-September 1, 1996); included rehabilitation assignment to Iowa (July 16-20). ... Traded by Cubs to New York Yankees for P Frisco Parotte (August 16, 1997). ... Granted free agency (November 3, 1997). ... Signed by San Francisco Giants (January 22, 1998). ... Granted free agency (November 5, 1998). ... Signed by Kansas City Royals (December 11, 1998).

STATISTICAL NOTES: Led Gulf Coast League shortstops with .932 fielding percentage in 1986. ... Led American Association shortstops with 104 double plays in 1989. ... Led American Association shortstops with 596 total chances and 81 double plays in 1992.

Year Team (League)	Pos.	G	AB	R	H	2B	3B	HR	RBI	Avg.	BB	SO	SB	PO	A	E	Avg.
1986—GC Rangers (GCL)■	SS-2B	52	169	27	49	3	1	0	23	.290	41	18	10	69	158	15	†.938
1987—Gastonia (S. Atl.)	SS	50	160	19	35	1	2	1	10	.219	22	17	6	88	162	18	.933
—Butte (Pioneer)	SS	49	189	36	69	10	6	0	25	.365	21	12	22	84	162	12	.953
1988—Charlotte (Fla. St.)	SS	128	418	60	128	6	5	0	38	.306	35	24	29	226	*415	35	.948
1989—Okla. City (A.A.)	SS	134	464	38	104	10	4	1	39	.224	21	50	4	*237	*418	29	.958
1990—										Did not play.							
1991—Iowa (Am. Assoc.)■	SS	126	417	60	121	16	5	2	46	.290	37	27	13	204	*375	17	*.971
—Chicago (N.L.)	SS-2B	13	23	1	6	0	0	0	2	.261	4	3	0	11	25	0	1.000
1992—Chicago (N.L.)	SS-2B	74	255	24	64	14	3	1	19	.251	10	17	2	148	202	9	.975
—Iowa (Am. Assoc.)	SS-2B	20	76	12	26	3	0	0	3	.342	4	1	6	31	77	5	.956
1993—Chicago (N.L.)	SS	105	344	35	97	11	2	0	28	.282	15	22	1	158	316	15	.969
1994—Chicago (N.L.)	2B-SS	96	291	26	83	13	1	0	24	.285	20	29	2	152	278	9	.979
1995—Chicago (N.L.)	2B-SS	114	428	57	119	22	2	3	27	.278	14	48	6	195	351	7	.987
1996—Chicago (N.L.)	SS	95	289	28	61	9	0	1	12	.211	22	42	7	151	307	11	.977
—Iowa (Am. Assoc.)	SS	3	12	2	2	0	0	0	1	.167	1	2	2	4	10	1	.933
1997—Chicago (N.L.)	SS-2B-3B	97	205	14	51	9	0	1	12	.249	11	26	4	100	157	6	.977
—New York (A.L.)■	2B-SS	38	138	21	43	12	0	1	15	.312	5	21	0	66	110	4	.978
1998—San Fran. (N.L.)	SS-2B	109	316	44	90	14	2	2	30	.285	16	47	0	142	261	8	.981
American League totals (1 year)		38	138	21	43	12	0	1	15	.312	5	21	0	66	110	4	.978
National League totals (8 years)		703	2151	229	571	92	10	8	154	.265	112	234	22	1057	1897	65	.978
Major league totals (8 years)		741	2289	250	614	104	10	9	169	.268	117	255	22	1123	2007	69	.978

DIVISION SERIES RECORD

Year Team (League)	Pos.	G	AB	R	H	2B	3B	HR	RBI	Avg.	BB	SO	SB	PO	A	E	Avg.
1997—New York (A.L.)	2B	5	15	1	3	1	0	0	1	.200	0	2	0	15	14	0	1.000

SANDERS, ANTHONY   OF   BLUE JAYS

PERSONAL: Born March 2, 1974, in Tucson, Ariz. ... 6-2/200. ... Bats right, throws right. ... Full name: Anthony Marcus Sanders.

HIGH SCHOOL: Santa Rita (Tucson, Ariz.).

TRANSACTIONS/CAREER NOTES: Selected by Toronto Blue Jays organization in seventh round of free-agent draft (June 1, 1992). ... On Syracuse disabled list (July 22, 1998-remainder of season).

Year Team (League)	Pos.	G	AB	R	H	2B	3B	HR	RBI	Avg.	BB	SO	SB	PO	A	E	Avg.
1993—Medicine Hat (Pio.)	OF	63	225	44	59	9	3	4	33	.262	20	49	6	88	8	2	.980
1994—St. Catharines (NYP)	OF	74	258	36	66	17	3	6	45	.256	27	53	8	120	9	3	.977
1995—Hagerstown (SAL)	OF	133	512	72	119	28	1	8	48	.232	52	103	26	274	15	3	.990
1996—Dunedin (Fla. St.)	OF	102	417	75	108	25	0	17	50	.259	34	93	16	209	8	4	.982
—Knoxville (Southern)	OF	38	133	16	36	8	0	1	18	.271	7	33	1	66	1	3	.957
1997—Dunedin (Fla. St.)	OF	1	5	0	1	1	0	0	1	.200	1	1	0	1	0	0	1.000
—Knoxville (Southern)	OF	111	429	68	114	20	4	26	69	.266	44	121	20	224	7	4	.983
1998—Syracuse (Int'l)	OF	60	209	23	40	9	2	4	19	.191	20	65	5	145	6	1	.993
—Knoxville (Southern)	OF	6	25	9	10	2	0	4	9	.400	2	6	0	15	3	0	1.000

PERSONAL: Born December 1, 1967, in Florence, S.C. ... 6-1/185. ... Bats right, throws right. ... Full name: Reginald Laverne Sanders.
HIGH SCHOOL: Wilson (Florence, S.C.).
COLLEGE: Spartanburg (S.C.) Methodist.
TRANSACTIONS/CAREER NOTES: Selected by Cincinnati Reds organization in seventh round of free-agent draft (June 2, 1987). ... On disabled list (July 11-September 15, 1988 and July 15-September 5, 1989). ... On Chattanooga disabled list (June 30-July 26, 1991). ... On Cincinnati disabled list (August 24-September 20, 1991; and May 13-29 and July 17-August 2, 1992). ... On suspended list (June 3-9, 1994). ... On Cincinnati disabled list (April 20-May 22, May 31-June 15 and September 17, 1996-remainder of season); included rehabilitation assignment to Indianapolis (May 17-22). ... On Cincinnati disabled list (April 19-May 6 and May 24-July 23, 1997); included rehabilitation assignments to Chattanooga (May 3-5) and Indianapolis (July 15-22).
HONORS: Named Midwest League Most Valuable Player (1990). ... Named outfielder on The Sporting News N.L. All-Star team (1995).
STATISTICAL NOTES: Hit three home runs in one game (August 15, 1995).

							BATTING								FIELDING		
Year Team (League)	Pos.	G	AB	R	H	2B	3B	HR	RBI	Avg.	BB	SO	SB	PO	A	E	Avg.
1988— Billings (Pioneer)........	SS	17	64	11	15	1	1	0	3	.234	6	4	10	18	33	3	.944
1989— Greensboro (S. Atl.)...	SS	81	315	53	91	18	5	9	53	.289	29	63	21	125	169	42	.875
1990— Cedar Rap. (Midw.)	OF	127	466	89	133	21	4	17	63	.285	59	97	40	241	10	10	.962
1991— Chattanooga (Sou.) ...	OF	86	302	50	95	15	•8	8	49	.315	41	67	15	158	2	3	.982
— Cincinnati (N.L.)	OF	9	40	6	8	0	0	1	3	.200	0	9	1	22	0	0	1.000
1992— Cincinnati (N.L.)	OF	116	385	62	104	26	6	12	36	.270	48	98	16	262	11	6	.978
1993— Cincinnati (N.L.)	OF	138	496	90	136	16	4	20	83	.274	51	118	27	312	3	8	.975
1994— Cincinnati (N.L.)	OF	107	400	66	105	20	8	17	62	.263	41	*114	21	218	12	6	.975
1995— Cincinnati (N.L.)	OF	133	484	91	148	36	6	28	99	.306	69	122	36	268	12	5	.982
1996— Cincinnati (N.L.)	OF	81	287	49	72	17	1	14	33	.251	44	86	24	160	7	2	.988
— Indianapolis (A.A.) ...	OF	4	12	3	5	2	0	0	1	.417	1	4	0	4	1	0	1.000
1997— Cincinnati (N.L.)	OF	86	312	52	79	19	2	19	56	.253	42	93	13	183	4	5	.974
— Chattanooga (Sou.)	OF	3	11	3	6	1	1	1	3	.545	1	2	0	11	0	0	1.000
— Indianapolis (A.A.) ...	OF	5	19	1	4	0	0	0	1	.211	1	6	0	6	0	2	.750
1998— Cincinnati (N.L.)	OF	135	481	83	129	18	6	14	59	.268	51	137	20	263	4	6	.978
Major league totals (8 years)		805	2885	499	781	152	33	125	431	.271	346	777	158	1688	53	38	.979

DIVISION SERIES RECORD

							BATTING								FIELDING		
Year Team (League)	Pos.	G	AB	R	H	2B	3B	HR	RBI	Avg.	BB	SO	SB	PO	A	E	Avg.
1995— Cincinnati (N.L.)	OF	3	13	3	2	1	0	1	2	.154	1	9	2	7	0	1	.875

CHAMPIONSHIP SERIES RECORD

							BATTING								FIELDING		
Year Team (League)	Pos.	G	AB	R	H	2B	3B	HR	RBI	Avg.	BB	SO	SB	PO	A	E	Avg.
1995— Cincinnati (N.L.)	OF	4	16	0	2	0	0	0	0	.125	2	10	0	7	0	1	.875

ALL-STAR GAME RECORD

						BATTING								FIELDING		
Year League	Pos.	AB	R	H	2B	3B	HR	RBI	Avg.	BB	SO	SB	PO	A	E	Avg.
1995— National	OF	1	0	0	0	0	0	0	.000	0	1	0	0	0	0	...

PERSONAL: Born March 25, 1969, in Hannibal, Mo. ... 6-4/220. ... Throws right, bats right. ... Full name: Scott Gerald Sanders.
HIGH SCHOOL: Thibodaux (La.).
COLLEGE: Nicholls State (La.).
TRANSACTIONS/CAREER NOTES: Selected by San Diego Padres organization in supplemental round ("sandwich pick" between first and second round, 32nd pick overall) of free-agent draft (June 4, 1990); pick received as part of compensation for Kansas City Royals signing Type A free-agent P Mark Davis. ... On disabled list (May 1-17, 1994). ... On San Diego disabled list (July 18, 1995-remainder of season); included rehabilitation assignment to Las Vegas (August 28-September 1). ... Traded by Padres to Seattle Mariners for P Sterling Hitchcock (December 6, 1996). ... Traded by Mariners with P Dean Crow and 3B Carlos Villalobos to Detroit Tigers for P Omar Olivares and P Felipe Lira (July 18, 1997). ... Traded by Tigers to Padres for a player to be named later (May 6, 1998). ... On Las Vegas disabled list (June 21- July 1, 1998). ... Released by Padres (November 17, 1998). ... Signed by Chicago Cubs (December 2, 1998).
STATISTICAL NOTES: Tied for N.L. lead with 10 wild pitches in 1994. ... Pitched 4-0 one-hit, complete-game victory for Detroit against Texas (September 9, 1997).
MISCELLANEOUS: Appeared in one game as pinch runner for Detroit (1997).

Year Team (League)	W	L	Pct.	ERA	G	GS	CG	ShO	Sv.	IP	H	R	ER	BB	SO
1990— Waterloo (Midw.)	2	2	.500	4.86	7	7	0	0	0	37	43	21	20	21	29
— Spokane (N'west)	2	1	.667	0.95	3	3	0	0	0	19	12	3	2	5	21
1991— Waterloo (Midw.)	3	0	1.000	0.68	4	4	0	0	0	26 1/3	17	2	2	6	18
— High Desert (Calif.)	9	6	.600	3.66	21	21	4	2	0	132 2/3	114	72	54	72	93
1992— Wichita (Texas)	7	5	.583	3.49	14	14	0	0	0	87 2/3	85	35	34	37	95
— Las Vegas (PCL)	3	6	.333	5.50	14	12	1	1	0	72	92	49	44	31	51
1993— Las Vegas (PCL)	5	10	.333	4.96	24	24	•4	0	0	152 1/3	170	101	84	62	*161
— San Diego (N.L.)	3	3	.500	4.13	9	9	0	0	0	52 1/3	54	32	24	23	37
1994— San Diego (N.L.)	4	8	.333	4.78	23	20	0	0	1	111	103	63	59	48	109
1995— San Diego (N.L.)	5	5	.500	4.30	17	15	1	0	0	90	79	46	43	31	88
— Las Vegas (PCL)	0	0	...	0.00	1	1	0	0	0	3	3	0	0	1	2
1996— San Diego (N.L.)	9	5	.643	3.38	46	16	0	0	0	144	107	58	54	48	157
1997— Seattle (A.L.)■	3	6	.333	6.47	33	6	0	0	2	65 1/3	73	48	47	38	62
— Detroit (A.L.)■	3	8	.273	5.33	14	14	1	1	0	74 1/3	79	44	44	24	58
1998— Detroit (A.L.)	0	2	.000	17.69	3	2	0	0	0	9 2/3	24	19	19	6	6

Year	Team (League)	W	L	Pct.	ERA	G	GS	CG	ShO	Sv.	IP	H	R	ER	BB	SO
	—Las Vegas (PCL)■	1	2	.333	3.44	15	3	0	0	3	36 2/3	34	14	14	12	43
	—San Diego (N.L.)	3	1	.750	4.11	23	0	0	0	0	30 2/3	33	20	14	5	26
	A.L. totals (2 years)	6	16	.273	6.63	50	22	1	1	2	149 1/3	176	111	110	68	126
	N.L. totals (5 years)	24	22	.522	4.08	118	60	1	0	1	428	386	219	194	155	417
	Major league totals (6 years)	30	38	.441	4.74	168	82	2	1	3	577 1/3	562	330	304	223	543

DIVISION SERIES RECORD

Year	Team (League)	W	L	Pct.	ERA	G	GS	CG	ShO	Sv.	IP	H	R	ER	BB	SO
1996—	San Diego (N.L.)	0	0	...	8.31	1	1	0	0	0	4 1/3	3	4	4	4	4

SANFORD, CHANCE — 2B

PERSONAL: Born June 2, 1972, in Houston. ... 5-10/175. ... Bats left, throws right. ... Full name: Chance Steven Sanford.
HIGH SCHOOL: Stratford (Houston).
JUNIOR COLLEGE: San Jacinto (North) College (Texas).
TRANSACTIONS/CAREER NOTES: Selected by Pittsburgh Pirates organization in 27th round of free-agent draft (June 1, 1992). ... On Nashville disabled list (June 22-September 8, 1998). ... Released by Pirates (October 15, 1998).
STATISTICAL NOTES: Led Carolina League second baseman with 34 errors in 1994.

Year	Team (League)	Pos.	G	AB	R	H	2B	3B	HR	RBI	Avg.	BB	SO	SB	PO	A	E	Avg.
1992—	Welland (NYP)	2B-SS	59	214	36	61	11	3	5	21	.285	35	39	13	70	165	15	.940
	—Augusta (S. Atl.)	2B	14	46	3	5	1	0	0	2	.109	3	10	0	24	34	2	.967
1993—	Salem (Carolina)	2B	115	428	54	109	21	5	10	37	.255	33	80	11	172	284	34	.931
1994—	Salem (Carolina)	2B-OF	127	474	81	130	32	6	19	78	.274	56	95	12	209	318	•34	.939
1995—	Carolina (Southern)	PH-PR	16	36	6	10	3	1	3	10	.278	5	7	3	...	...	...	...
	—GCL Pirates (GCL)	2B	6	19	2	4	0	0	1	1	.211	2	2	0	8	9	1	.944
	—Lynchburg (Caro.)	2B	16	66	8	22	4	0	3	14	.333	7	13	1	34	39	3	.961
1996—	Carolina (Southern)	2B	131	470	62	115	16	13	4	56	.245	72	106	11	213	336	•22	.961
1997—	Carolina (Southern)	2B-3B	44	149	30	39	10	2	9	36	.262	20	39	3	58	123	8	.958
	—Calgary (PCL)	3B-2B-SS	89	325	58	95	27	9	6	60	.292	39	82	9	74	189	16	.943
1998—	Nashville (PCL)	2-3-S-O	27	81	17	21	7	1	4	21	.259	16	12	0	29	41	3	.959
	—Pittsburgh (N.L.)	3B-2B-SS	14	28	3	4	1	1	0	3	.143	1	6	0	5	6	2	.846
	Major league totals (1 year)		14	28	3	4	1	1	0	3	.143	1	6	0	5	6	2	.846

SANTANA, JULIO — P — DEVIL RAYS

PERSONAL: Born January 20, 1974, in San Pedro de Macoris, Dominican Republic. ... 6-0/185. ... Throws right, bats right. ... Full name: Julio Franklin Santana. ... Nephew of Rico Carty, outfielder with seven major league teams (1963-79).
HIGH SCHOOL: Divina Providence (Dominican Republic).
TRANSACTIONS/CAREER NOTES: Signed as non-drafted free agent by Texas Rangers organization (February 18, 1990). ... On Texas disabled list (July 15-August 10, 1997). ... Claimed on waivers by Tampa Bay Devil Rays (April 27, 1998).

Year	Team (League)	W	L	Pct.	ERA	G	GS	CG	ShO	Sv.	IP	H	R	ER	BB	SO
1992—	San Pedro (DSL)	0	1	.000	3.24	4	1	0	0	0	8 1/3	8	5	3	7	5
1993—	GC Rangers (GCL)	4	1	.800	1.38	*26	0	0	0	7	39	31	9	6	7	50
1994—	Char., W.Va. (S. Atl.)	6	7	.462	2.46	16	16	0	0	0	91 1/3	65	38	25	44	103
	—Tulsa (Texas)	7	2	.778	2.90	11	11	2	0	0	71 1/3	50	26	23	41	45
1995—	Oklahoma City (A.A.)	0	2	.000	39.00	2	2	0	0	0	3	9	14	13	7	6
	—Charlotte (Fla. St.)	0	3	.000	3.73	5	5	1	0	0	31 1/3	32	16	13	16	27
	—Tulsa (Texas)	6	4	.600	3.23	15	15	3	0	0	103	91	40	37	52	71
1996—	Oklahoma City (A.A.)	11	12	.478	4.02	29	29	4	1	0	185 2/3	171	102	83	66	113
1997—	Texas (A.L.)	4	6	.400	6.75	30	14	0	0	0	104	141	86	78	49	64
	—Oklahoma City (A.A.)	0	0	...	15.00	1	1	0	0	0	3	9	6	5	2	1
1998—	Texas (A.L.)	0	0	...	8.44	3	0	0	0	0	5 1/3	7	5	5	4	1
	—Tampa Bay (A.L.)■	5	6	.455	4.23	32	19	1	0	0	140 1/3	144	72	66	58	60
	Major league totals (2 years)	9	12	.429	5.37	65	33	1	0	0	249 2/3	292	163	149	111	125

RECORD AS POSITION PLAYER

Year	Team (League)	Pos.	G	AB	R	H	2B	3B	HR	RBI	Avg.	BB	SO	SB	PO	A	E	Avg.
1990—	San Pedro (DSL)	...	11	34	4	7	0	0	1	3	.206	5	7	0	...	...	...	...
1991—	San Pedro (DSL)	...	55	161	27	42	7	0	2	12	.261	27	37	5	...	...	...	...
1992—	San Pedro (DSL)	OF-IF	17	48	7	11	2	0	2	2	.229	11	8	0	50	2	4	.929

SANTANA, MARINO — P — RED SOX

PERSONAL: Born May 10, 1972, in San Jose de los Llanos, Dominican Republic. ... 6-1/190. ... Throws right, bats right.
TRANSACTIONS/CAREER NOTES: Signed as non-drafted free agent by Seattle Mariners organization (April 28, 1990). ... Granted free agency (October 15, 1996). ... Signed by Detroit Tigers organization (November 26, 1996). ... Traded by Tigers to Boston Red Sox for cash (December 10, 1998).

Year	Team (League)	W	L	Pct.	ERA	G	GS	CG	ShO	Sv.	IP	H	R	ER	BB	SO
1990—	Dom. Mariners (DSL)	3	2	.600	2.94	12	5	0	0	5	49	47	20	16	14	25
1991—	Dom. Mariners (DSL)	4	4	.500	3.87	14	14	2		0	86	92	47	37	40	39
1992—	Dom. Mariners (DSL)	6	9	.400	2.38	18	16	4	0	0	106	109	59	28	37	91
1993—	Bellingham (N'west)	0	1	.000	5.82	15	0	0	0	0	21 2/3	27	19	14	22	24
1994—	Bellingham (N'west)	6	3	.667	3.15	15	15	1	0	0	80	68	35	28	26	88
1995—	Wisconsin (Midwest)	8	3	.727	1.77	15	15	2	1	0	96 2/3	57	26	19	25	110
	—Riverside (California)	3	5	.375	6.19	9	9	0	0	0	48	44	47	33	25	57
1996—	Lancaster (Calif.)	8	15	.348	5.03	28	•28	1	0	0	157 1/3	164	105	88	57	167
1997—	Jacksonville (Southern)■	4	1	.800	3.28	39	0	0	0	1	74	55	28	27	43	98
1998—	Toledo (International)	6	3	.667	2.90	44	0	0	0	7	68 1/3	44	30	22	34	94
	—Detroit (A.L.)	0	0	...	3.68	7	0	0	0	0	7 1/3	9	3	3	8	10
	Major league totals (1 year)	0	0	...	3.68	7	0	0	0	0	7 1/3	9	3	3	8	10

S

SANTANGELO, F.P.   OF/IF   GIANTS

PERSONAL: Born October 24, 1967, in Livonia, Mich. ... 5-10/190. ... Bats both, throws right. ... Full name: Frank Paul Santangelo.
HIGH SCHOOL: Valley (Sacramento).
JUNIOR COLLEGE: Sacramento City College.
COLLEGE: Miami (Fla.).
TRANSACTIONS/CAREER NOTES: Selected by Montreal Expos organization in 20th round of free-agent draft (June 5, 1989). ... On disabled list (April 21-May 2, 1994). ... On Montreal disabled list (July 16-31, 1998); included rehabilitation assignment to Ottawa (July 28-31). ... Granted free agency (December 21, 1998). ... Signed by San Francisco Giants (December 23, 1998).
STATISTICAL NOTES: Led Eastern League with 13 sacrifice hits in 1991. ... Switch-hit home runs in one game (June 7, 1997).

								BATTING							FIELDING		
Year	Team (League)	Pos.	G	AB	R	H	2B	3B	HR	RBI	Avg.	BB	SO	SB	PO	A	E	Avg.
1989— Jamestown (NYP)		2B	2	6	0	3	1	0	0	0	.500	1	0	1	5	5	2	.833
— W.P. Beach (FSL)	SS-2B-OF		57	173	18	37	4	0	0	14	.214	23	12	3	32	67	8	.925
1990— W.P. Beach (FSL)	S-O-2-3		116	394	63	109	19	2	0	38	.277	51	49	22	151	202	22	.941
1991— Harrisburg (East.)	2-O-S-3		132	462	78	113	12	7	5	42	.245	74	45	21	234	253	16	.968
1992— Indianapolis (A.A.)	O-2-S-3		137	462	83	123	25	0	5	34	.266	62	58	12	291	119	4	.990
1993— Ottawa (Int'l)	O-S-3-2		131	453	86	124	21	2	4	45	.274	59	52	18	246	186	14	.969
1994— Ottawa (Int'l)	O-2-S-3		119	413	62	104	28	1	5	41	.252	59	64	7	235	140	12	.969
1995— Ottawa (Int'l)	3-2-O-S-C		95	267	37	68	15	3	2	25	.255	32	22	7	89	185	10	.965
— Montreal (N.L.)	OF-2B		35	98	11	29	5	1	1	9	.296	12	9	1	47	0	1	.979
1996— Montreal (N.L.)	O-3-2-S		152	393	54	109	20	5	7	56	.277	49	61	5	251	45	6	.980
1997— Montreal (N.L.)	O-3-2-S		130	350	56	87	19	5	5	31	.249	50	73	8	175	56	3	.987
1998— Montreal (N.L.)	OF-2B-3B		122	383	53	82	18	0	4	23	.214	44	72	7	211	77	5	.983
— Ottawa (Int'l)	OF		2	8	1	2	0	0	0	1	.250	0	3	0	2	0	0	1.000
Major league totals (4 years)			439	1224	174	307	62	11	17	119	.251	155	215	21	684	178	15	.983

SANTIAGO, BENITO   C   CUBS

PERSONAL: Born March 9, 1965, in Ponce, Puerto Rico. ... 6-1/195. ... Bats right, throws right. ... Full name: Benito Rivera Santiago. ... Name pronounced SAHN-tee-AH-go.
HIGH SCHOOL: John F. Kennedy (Ponce, Puerto Rico).
TRANSACTIONS/CAREER NOTES: Signed as non-drafted free agent by San Diego Padres organization (September 1, 1982). ... On disabled list (June 21-July 2, 1985). ... On San Diego disabled list (June 15-August 10, 1990); included rehabilitation assignment to Las Vegas (August 2-9). ... On San Diego disabled list (May 31-July 11, 1992); included rehabilitation assignment to Las Vegas (July 7-11). ... Granted free agency (October 26, 1992). ... Signed by Florida Marlins (December 16, 1992). ... On suspended list (May 5-9, 1994). ... Granted free agency (October 20, 1994). ... Signed by Cincinnati Reds (April 17, 1995). ... On disabled list (May 8-July 4, 1995). ... Granted free agency (October 31, 1995). ... Signed by Philadelphia Phillies (January 30, 1996). ... Granted free agency (November 18, 1996). ... Signed by Toronto Blue Jays (December 9, 1996). ... On disabled list (April 14-29, 1997). ... On Toronto disabled list (March 18-September 3, 1998); included rehabilitation assignments to Dunedin (August 15-26) and Syracuse (August 28-September 3). ... Granted free agency (October 23, 1998). ... Signed by Chicago Cubs (December 10, 1998).
RECORDS: Holds major league rookie-season record for most consecutive games batted safely—34 (August 25-October 2, 1987). ... Shares major league single-season record for fewest passed balls (100 or more games)—0 (1992). ... Shares major league record for most consecutive home runs—4 (September 14 [1] and 15 [3], 1996).
HONORS: Named N.L. Rookie Player of the Year by THE SPORTING NEWS (1987). ... Named catcher on THE SPORTING NEWS N.L. All-Star team (1987, 1989 and 1991). ... Named catcher on THE SPORTING NEWS N.L. Silver Slugger team (1987-88 and 1990-91). ... Named N.L. Rookie of the Year by Baseball Writers' Association of America (1987). ... Won N.L. Gold Glove at catcher (1988-90).
STATISTICAL NOTES: Led Florida State League catchers with 26 passed balls and 12 double plays in 1983. ... Led Texas League catchers with 78 assists and 16 passed balls in 1985. ... Led Pacific Coast League catchers with 655 total chances in 1986. ... Had 34-game hitting streak (August 25-October 2, 1987). ... Led N.L. with 22 passed balls in 1987, 14 in 1989 and 23 in 1993. ... Led N.L. in grounding into double plays with 21 in 1991. ... Tied for N.L. lead in double plays by catcher with 11 in 1988 and 14 in 1991. ... Led N.L. catchers with 100 assists and 14 errors in 1991. ... Led N.L. catchers with .996 fielding percentage in 1995. ... Hit three home runs in one game (September 15, 1996). ... Career major league grand slams: 6.

								BATTING							FIELDING		
Year	Team (League)	Pos.	G	AB	R	H	2B	3B	HR	RBI	Avg.	BB	SO	SB	PO	A	E	Avg.
1983— Miami (Fla. St.)	C		122	429	34	106	25	3	5	56	.247	11	79	3	471	*69	*21	.963
1984— Reno (California)	C		114	416	64	116	20	6	16	83	.279	36	75	5	692	96	25	.969
1985— Beaumont (Texas)	C-1B-3B		101	372	55	111	16	6	5	52	.298	16	59	12	525	†78	15	.976
1986— Las Vegas (PCL)	C		117	437	55	125	26	3	17	71	.286	17	81	19	*563	71	*21	.968
— San Diego (N.L.)	C		17	62	10	18	2	0	3	6	.290	2	12	0	80	7	5	.946
1987— San Diego (N.L.)	C		146	546	64	164	33	2	18	79	.300	16	112	21	817	80	*22	.976
1988— San Diego (N.L.)	C		139	492	49	122	22	2	10	46	.248	24	82	15	725	*75	*12	.985
1989— San Diego (N.L.)	C		129	462	50	109	16	3	16	62	.236	26	89	11	685	81	*20	.975
1990— San Diego (N.L.)	C		100	344	42	93	8	5	11	53	.270	27	55	5	538	51	12	.980
— Las Vegas (PCL)	C		6	20	5	6	2	0	1	8	.300	3	1	0	25	5	0	1.000
1991— San Diego (N.L.)	C-OF		152	580	60	155	22	3	17	87	.267	23	114	8	830	†100	†14	.985
1992— San Diego (N.L.)	C		106	386	37	97	21	0	10	42	.251	21	52	2	584	53	*12	.982
— Las Vegas (PCL)	C		4	13	3	4	0	0	1	2	.308	1	1	0	13	2	0	1.000
1993— Florida (N.L.)■	C-OF		139	469	49	108	19	6	13	50	.230	37	88	10	740	64	11	.987
1994— Florida (N.L.)	C		101	337	35	92	14	2	11	41	.273	25	57	1	511	*66	5	.991
1995— Cincinnati (N.L.)■	C-1B		81	266	40	76	20	0	11	44	.286	24	48	2	480	35	2	†.996
1996— Philadelphia (N.L.)■	C-1B		136	481	71	127	21	2	30	85	.264	49	104	2	834	67	11	.988
1997— Toronto (A.L.)■	C-DH		97	341	31	83	10	0	13	42	.243	17	80	1	621	40	2	.997
1998— Dunedin (Fla. St.)	C		11	37	4	6	1	0	1	5	.162	3	9	3	19	6	0	1.000
— Syracuse (Int'l)	C		5	22	0	5	2	0	0	2	.227	1	3	0	19	1	0	1.000
— Toronto (A.L.)	C		15	29	3	9	5	0	0	4	.310	1	6	0	45	2	0	1.000
American League totals (2 years)			112	370	34	92	15	0	13	46	.249	18	86	1	666	42	2	.997
National League totals (11 years)			1246	4425	507	1161	198	25	150	595	.262	274	813	77	6824	679	126	.983
Major league totals (13 years)			1358	4795	541	1253	213	25	163	641	.261	292	899	78	7490	721	128	.985

NOTES: Hit home run in first at-bat (October 3, 1995).

Year Team (League)	Pos.	G	AB	R	H	2B	3B	HR	RBI	Avg.	BB	SO	SB	PO	A	E	Avg.
										BATTING					FIELDING		
1995— Cincinnati (N.L.)	C	3	9	2	3	0	0	1	3	.333	3	3	0	20	0	0	1.000

CHAMPIONSHIP SERIES RECORD

Year Team (League)	Pos.	G	AB	R	H	2B	3B	HR	RBI	Avg.	BB	SO	SB	PO	A	E	Avg.
										BATTING					FIELDING		
1995— Cincinnati (N.L.)	C	4	13	0	3	0	0	0	0	.231	2	3	0	23	1	0	1.000

ALL-STAR GAME RECORD

Year League	Pos.	AB	R	H	2B	3B	HR	RBI	Avg.	BB	SO	SB	PO	A	E	Avg.
						BATTING								FIELDING		
1989— National	C	1	0	0	0	0	0	0	.000	0	1	0	0	0	1	.000
1990— National						Selected, did not play—injured.										
1991— National	C	3	0	0	0	0	0	0	.000	0	1	0	4	0	0	1.000
1992— National	C	1	0	0	0	0	0	0	.000	0	1	0	3	0	0	1.000
All-Star Game totals (3 years)		**5**	**0**	**0**	**0**	**0**	**0**	**0**	**.000**	**0**	**3**	**0**	**7**	**0**	**1**	**.875**

SANTIAGO, JOSE   P   ROYALS

PERSONAL: Born November 5, 1974, in Fajardo, Puerto Rico. ... 6-3/215. ... Throws right, bats right. ... Full name: Jose Rafael Santiago.
HIGH SCHOOL: Carlos Escobar Lopez (Loiza, Puerto Rico).
TRANSACTIONS/CAREER NOTES: Selected by Kansas City Royals organization in 70th round of free agent draft (June 3, 1994). ... On Kansas City disabled list (June 26-July 9, 1997).

Year Team (League)	W	L	Pct.	ERA	G	GS	CG	ShO	Sv.	IP	H	R	ER	BB	SO
1994— GC Royals (GCL)	1	0	1.000	2.37	10	1	0	0	2	19	17	7	5	7	10
1995— Spokane (N'west)	2	4	.333	3.14	22	0	0	0	1	48 $2/3$	60	26	17	20	32
1996— Lansing (Midwest)	7	6	.538	3.74	54	0	0	0	19	77	78	34	32	21	55
1997— Wilmington (Caro.)	1	1	.500	4.91	4	0	0	0	2	3 $2/3$	3	3	2	1	1
— Lansing (Midwest)	1	0	1.000	2.08	9	0	0	0	1	13	10	6	3	6	8
— Kansas City (A.L.)	0	0	...	1.93	4	0	0	0	0	4 $2/3$	7	2	1	2	1
— Wichita (Texas)	2	1	.667	4.00	22	0	0	0	3	27	32	13	12	8	12
1998— Wichita (Texas)	3	4	.429	3.61	52	0	0	0	22	72 $1/3$	79	36	29	27	31
— Kansas City (A.L.)	0	0	...	9.00	2	0	0	0	0	2	4	2	2	0	2
— Omaha (Pacific Coast)........	0	0	...	7.04	4	0	0	0	1	7 $2/3$	10	9	6	5	4
Major league totals (2 years)	**0**	**0**	**...**	**4.05**	**6**	**0**	**0**	**0**	**0**	**6 $2/3$**	**11**	**4**	**3**	**2**	**3**

SASSER, ROB   3B   RANGERS

PERSONAL: Born March 9, 1975, in Philadelphia. ... 6-3/205. ... Bats right, throws right. ... Full name: Robert Dofell Sasser.
HIGH SCHOOL: Oakland.
TRANSACTIONS/CAREER NOTES: Selected by Atlanta Braves organization in 10th round of free-agent draft (June 10, 1993). ... Selected by California Angels organization from Braves organization in Rule 5 minor league draft (December 9, 1996). ... Angels franchise renamed Anaheim Angels for 1997 season. ... Traded by Angels to Texas Rangers (October 31, 1997), completing deal in which Rangers traded P Ken Hill to Angels for C Jim Leyritz (July 29, 1997). ... On Tulsa disabled list (April 6-May 2, 1998).
STATISTICAL NOTES: Led South Atlantic League third basemen with 45 errors in 1996. ... Led Midwest League third basemen with 435 total chances in 1997. ... Led Texas League third basemen with 229 assists and 321 total chances in 1998.

Year Team (League)	Pos.	G	AB	R	H	2B	3B	HR	RBI	Avg.	BB	SO	SB	PO	A	E	Avg.
										BATTING					FIELDING		
1993— GC Braves (GCL)	3B	33	113	19	27	4	0	0	7	.239	6	25	2	15	61	10	.884
1994— Idaho Falls (Pio.).........	3B-SS	58	219	32	50	9	6	2	26	.228	19	58	13	35	122	20	.887
1995— Danville (Appal.).........	3B	12	47	8	15	2	1	0	7	.319	4	7	5	7	16	4	.852
1996— Macon (S. Atl.).........	3-1-S-2	135	465	64	122	35	3	8	64	.262	65	108	38	247	262	†51	.909
1997— Cedar Rap. (Midw.)	3B-SS	134	497	103	135	26	5	17	77	.272	69	92	37	104	303	28	.936
1998— Tulsa (Texas)■	3B-2B	111	417	57	117	25	2	8	62	.281	60	98	18	68	†233	‡26	.920
— Charlotte (Fla. St.)......	3B	4	13	1	4	2	0	0	3	.308	3	5	1	2	9	0	1.000
— Texas (A.L.).............	PH	1	1	0	0	0	0	0	0	.000	0	0	0	...	...	...	...
Major league totals (1 year)		**1**	**1**	**0**	**0**	**0**	**0**	**0**	**0**	**.000**	**0**	**0**	**0**	**...**	**...**	**...**	**...**

SATURRIA, LUIS   OF   CARDINALS

PERSONAL: Born July 21, 1976, in San Pedro de Macoris, Dominican Republic. ... 6-2/165. ... Bats right, throws right. ... Full name: Luis Arturo Saturria.
TRANSACTIONS/CAREER NOTES: Signed as non-drafted free agent by St. Louis Cardinals organization (March 5, 1994). ... Selected by Toronto Blue Jays from Cardinals organization in Rule 5 major league draft (December 15, 1997). ... Returned to Cardinals organization (March 20, 1998).
STATISTICAL NOTES: Tied for Carolina League lead with three double plays by outfielder in 1998.

Year Team (League)	Pos.	G	AB	R	H	2B	3B	HR	RBI	Avg.	BB	SO	SB	PO	A	E	Avg.
										BATTING					FIELDING		
1994— Dom. Cardinals (DSL)	OF	61	227	29	63	2	6	1	23	.278	25	49	16	118	13	8	.942
1995— Dom. Cardinals (DSL)	OF	66	245	48	78	16	7	2	33	.318	34	26	12	126	14	22	.864
1996— Johnson City (App.)	OF	57	227	43	58	7	1	5	40	.256	24	61	12	68	5	3	.961
1997— Peoria (Midwest)........	OF	122	445	81	122	19	5	11	51	.274	44	95	23	196	*24	9	.961
1998— Prince Will. (Car.)	OF	129	462	70	136	25	9	12	73	.294	28	104	26	235	11	*15	.943

SAUERBECK, SCOTT   P   PIRATES

PERSONAL: Born November 9, 1971, in Cincinnati. ... 6-3/190. ... Throws left, bats right. ... Full name: Scott William Sauerbeck.
HIGH SCHOOL: Northwest (Cincinnati.).
COLLEGE: Miami of Ohio.
TRANSACTIONS/CAREER NOTES: Selected by New York Mets organization in 23rd round of free-agent draft (June 2, 1994). ... Selected by Pittsburgh Pirates from Mets organization in Rule 5 major league draft (December 14, 1998).

Year Team (League)	W	L	Pct.	ERA	G	GS	CG	ShO	Sv.	IP	H	R	ER	BB	SO
1994— Pittsfield (NYP)	3	1	.750	2.05	21	0	0	0	1	48 1/3	39	16	11	19	39
1995— St. Lucie (Fla. St.)	0	1	1.000	2.03	20	1	0	0	0	26 2/3	26	10	6	14	25
— Capital City (S. Atl.)............	5	4	.556	3.27	19	0	0	0	2	33	28	14	12	14	33
1996— St. Lucie (Fla. St.)	6	6	.500	2.27	17	16	2	2	0	99 1/3	101	37	25	27	62
— Binghamton (Eastern)	3	3	.500	3.47	8	8	2	0	0	46 2/3	48	24	18	12	30
1997— Binghamton (Eastern)	8	9	.471	4.93	27	20	2	0	0	131 1/3	144	89	72	50	88
— Norfolk (Int'l)	1	0	1.000	3.60	1	1	0	0	0	5	3	2	2	4	4
1998— Norfolk (Int'l)	7	13	.350	3.93	27	27	2	0	0	160 1/3	178	82	70	69	119

SAUNDERS, TONY   P   DEVIL RAYS

S

PERSONAL: Born April 29, 1974, in Baltimore. ... 6-2/205. ... Throws left, bats left. ... Full name: Anthony Scott Saunders.
HIGH SCHOOL: Glen Burnie (Md.).
TRANSACTIONS/CAREER NOTES: Signed as non-drafted free agent by Florida Marlins organization (June 9, 1992). ... On Florida disabled list (May 19-July 10, 1997). ... Selected by Tampa Bay Devil Rays in first round (first pick overall) of expansion draft (November 18, 1997).
MISCELLANEOUS: Holds Tampa Bay Devil Rays all-time record for strikeouts (172). ... Tied for Tampa Bay Devil Rays all-time record for complete games (2).

Year Team (League)	W	L	Pct.	ERA	G	GS	CG	ShO	Sv.	IP	H	R	ER	BB	SO
1992— GC Marlins (GCL)	4	1	.800	1.18	24	0	0	0	7	45 2/3	29	10	6	13	37
1993— Kane County (Midwest)......	6	1	.857	2.27	23	10	2	0	1	83 1/3	72	23	21	32	87
1994— Brevard County (FSL)	5	5	.500	3.15	10	10	1	0	0	60	54	24	21	9	46
1995— Brevard County (FSL)	6	5	.545	3.04	13	13	0	0	0	71	60	29	24	15	54
1996— Portland (Eastern)	13	4	.765	2.63	26	26	2	0	0	167 2/3	121	51	49	62	*156
1997— Florida (N.L.)	4	6	.400	4.61	22	21	0	0	0	111 1/3	99	62	57	64	102
— Portland (Eastern)	0	0	. . .	9.00	1	1	0	0	0	2	3	2	2	1	3
— Charlotte (Int'l)	1	0	1.000	2.77	3	3	0	0	0	13	9	4	4	6	9
1998— Tampa Bay (A.L.)■............	6	15	.286	4.12	31	31	2	0	0	192 1/3	191	95	88	*111	172
A.L. totals (1 year)...................	6	15	.286	4.12	31	31	2	0	0	192 1/3	191	95	88	111	172
N.L. totals (1 year)...................	4	6	.400	4.61	22	21	0	0	0	111 1/3	99	62	57	64	102
Major league totals (2 years)......	10	21	.323	4.30	53	52	2	0	0	303 2/3	290	157	145	175	274

CHAMPIONSHIP SERIES RECORD

Year Team (League)	W	L	Pct.	ERA	G	GS	CG	ShO	Sv.	IP	H	R	ER	BB	SO
1997— Florida (N.L.)	0	0	. . .	3.38	1	1	0	0	0	5 1/3	4	2	2	3	3

WORLD SERIES RECORD

NOTES: Member of World Series championship team (1997).

Year Team (League)	W	L	Pct.	ERA	G	GS	CG	ShO	Sv.	IP	H	R	ER	BB	SO
1997— Florida (N.L.)	0	1	.000	27.00	1	1	0	0	0	2	7	6	6	3	2

SCANLAN, BOB   P   ASTROS

PERSONAL: Born August 9, 1966, in Los Angeles. ... 6-4/220. ... Throws right, bats right. ... Full name: Robert Guy Scanlan Jr.
HIGH SCHOOL: Harvard (North Hollywood, Calif.).
TRANSACTIONS/CAREER NOTES: Selected by Philadelphia Phillies organization in 25th round of free-agent draft (June 4, 1984). ... Traded by Phillies with P Chuck McElroy to Chicago Cubs organization for P Mitch Williams (April 7, 1991). ... On suspended list (September 30-October 4, 1992 and September 17-20, 1993). ... Traded by Cubs to Milwaukee Brewers for P Rafael Novoa and OF Mike Carter (December 19, 1993). ... On Milwaukee disabled list (June 12-August 21, 1995); included rehabilitation assignment to New Orleans (August 4-21). ... Released by Brewers (December 18, 1995). ... Signed by Toledo, Detroit Tigers organization (January 15, 1996). ... Claimed on waivers by Kansas City Royals organization (August 8, 1996). ... Released by Royals (March 26, 1997). ... Signed by San Diego Padres organization (May 29, 1997). ... Granted free agency (October 15, 1997). ... Signed by Houston Astros organization (December 22, 1997). ... Granted free agency (October 15, 1998). ... Re-signed by Astros organization (January 21, 1999).
STATISTICAL NOTES: Led International League with 17 wild pitches in 1988.

Year Team (League)	W	L	Pct.	ERA	G	GS	CG	ShO	Sv.	IP	H	R	ER	BB	SO
1984— GC Phillies (GCL)	0	2	.000	6.48	13	6	0	0	0	33 1/3	43	31	24	30	17
1985— Spartanburg (SAL)	8	12	.400	4.14	26	25	4	0	0	152 1/3	160	95	70	53	108
1986— Clearwater (Fla. St.)	8	12	.400	4.15	24	22	5	0	0	125 2/3	146	73	58	45	51
1987— Reading (Eastern)	*15	5	.750	5.10	27	26	3	1	0	164	187	98	93	55	91
1988— Maine (International).........	5	*18	.217	5.59	28	27	4	1	0	161	181	*110	*100	50	79
1989— Reading (Eastern)	6	10	.375	5.78	31	17	4	1	0	118 1/3	124	88	•76	58	63
1990— Scran./W.B. (Int'l).............	8	1	.889	4.85	23	23	0	0	0	130	128	79	70	59	74
1991— Iowa (Am. Assoc.)■	2	0	1.000	2.95	4	3	0	0	0	18 1/3	14	8	6	10	15
— Chicago (N.L.)................	7	8	.467	3.89	40	13	0	0	1	111	114	60	48	40	44
1992— Chicago (N.L.)	3	6	.333	2.89	69	0	0	0	14	87 1/3	76	32	28	30	42
1993— Chicago (N.L.)	4	5	.444	4.54	70	0	0	0	0	75 1/3	79	41	38	28	44
1994— Milwaukee (A.L.)■............	2	6	.250	4.11	30	12	0	0	2	103	117	53	47	28	65
1995— Milwaukee (A.L.)■	4	7	.364	6.59	17	14	0	0	0	83 1/3	101	66	61	44	29
— New Orleans (A.A.)	0	1	1.000	5.40	3	3	0	0	0	11 2/3	17	7	7	5	63
1996— Lakeland (Fla. St.)■	0	1	.000	5.00	2	2	0	0	0	9	9	6	5	3	4
— Toledo (International)........	1	3	.250	7.50	14	5	0	0	0	36	46	35	30	15	18
— Detroit (A.L.)	0	0	. . .	10.64	8	0	0	0	0	11	16	15	13	9	3
— Omaha (Am. Assoc.)■........	0	0	. . .	0.73	12	0	0	0	5	12 1/3	10	2	1	3	9
— Kansas City (A.L.)	0	1	.000	3.18	9	0	0	0	0	11 1/3	13	4	4	3	3

Year	Team (League)	W	L	Pct.	ERA	G	GS	CG	ShO	Sv.	IP	H	R	ER	BB	SO
1997—	Las Vegas (PCL)■	3	1	.750	3.53	36	1	0	0	1	51	51	24	20	17	20
1998—	Houston (N.L.)■	0	1	.000	3.08	27	0	0	0	0	26 1/3	24	12	9	13	9
	New Orleans (PCL)	5	4	.556	6.46	14	12	1	0	0	61 1/3	90	50	44	24	35
A.L. totals (3 years)		6	14	.300	5.39	64	26	0	0	2	208 2/3	247	138	125	84	100
N.L. totals (4 years)		14	20	.412	3.69	206	13	0	0	15	300	293	145	123	111	139
Major league totals (7 years)		20	34	.370	4.39	270	39	0	0	17	508 2/3	540	283	248	195	239

SCHEFFER, AARON · P · MARINERS

PERSONAL: Born October 15, 1975, in Ypsilanti, Mich. ... 6-2/185. ... Throws right, bats left. ... Full name: Aaron Alvin Marcus Scheffer.
HIGH SCHOOL: John Glenn (Westland, Mich.).
TRANSACTIONS/CAREER NOTES: Signed as non-drafted free agent by Seattle Mariners organization (August 2, 1993).

Year	Team (League)	W	L	Pct.	ERA	G	GS	CG	ShO	Sv.	IP	H	R	ER	BB	SO
1994—	Bellingham (N'west)	0	0	...	6.00	2	0	0	0	0	3	4	4	2	3	5
	Ariz. Mariners (Ariz.)	2	2	.500	1.95	24	0	0	0	6	32 1/3	18	11	7	10	26
1995—	Wisconsin (Midwest)	0	1	.000	6.59	9	0	0	0	0	13 2/3	17	14	10	5	8
	Everett (Northwest)	2	5	.286	3.74	24	0	0	0	1	43 1/3	44	23	18	16	38
1996—	Wisconsin (Midwest)	8	1	.889	3.72	45	1	0	0	14	67 2/3	55	35	28	34	89
1997—	Lancaster (Calif.)	11	3	.786	5.44	37	3	0	0	4	92 1/3	93	58	56	42	103
1998—	Lancaster (Calif.)	2	2	.500	3.14	25	0	0	0	10	43	46	19	15	12	65
	Orlando (South.)	1	0	1.000	2.20	19	0	0	0	5	32 2/3	23	8	8	13	33

SCHILLING, CURT · P · PHILLIES

PERSONAL: Born November 14, 1966, in Anchorage, Alaska. ... 6-4/228. ... Throws right, bats right. ... Full name: Curtis Montague Schilling.
HIGH SCHOOL: Shadow Mountain (Phoenix).
JUNIOR COLLEGE: Yavapai College (Ariz.).
TRANSACTIONS/CAREER NOTES: Selected by Boston Red Sox organization in second round of free-agent draft (January 14, 1986). ... Traded by Red Sox organization with OF Brady Anderson to Baltimore Orioles for P Mike Boddicker (July 29, 1988). ... Traded by Orioles with P Pete Harnisch and OF Steve Finley to Houston Astros for 1B Glenn Davis (January 10, 1991). ... Traded by Astros to Philadelphia Phillies for P Jason Grimsley (April 2, 1992). ... On Philadelphia disabled list (May 17-July 25, 1994); included rehabilitation assignments to Scranton/Wilkes-Barre (July 10-15) and Reading (July 15-20). ... On disabled list (July 19, 1995-remainder of season). ... On Philadelphia disabled list (March 23-May 14, 1996); included rehabilitation assignments to Clearwater (April 23-May 3) and Scranton/Wilkes-Barre (May 3-14).
RECORDS: Holds N.L. single-season record for most strikeouts by righthander—319 (1997).
STATISTICAL NOTES: Tied for International League lead with six balks in 1989. ... Pitched 2-1 one-hit, complete-game victory against New York (September 9, 1992). ... Struck out 15 batters in one game (July 21, 1997 and April 5, 1998). ... Struck out 16 batters in one game (September 1, 1997).
MISCELLANEOUS: Struck out once in two appearances as pinch hitter with Philadelphia (1996).

Year	Team (League)	W	L	Pct.	ERA	G	GS	CG	ShO	Sv.	IP	H	R	ER	BB	SO
1986—	Elmira (N.Y.-Penn)	7	3	.700	2.59	16	15	2	1	0	93 2/3	92	34	27	30	75
1987—	Greensboro (S. Atl.)	8	*15	.348	3.82	29	28	7	3	0	184	179	96	78	65	*189
1988—	New Britain (East.)	8	5	.615	2.97	21	17	4	1	0	106	91	44	35	40	62
	Charlotte (Southern)■	5	2	.714	3.18	7	7	2	1	0	45 1/3	36	19	16	23	32
	Baltimore (A.L.)	0	3	.000	9.82	4	4	0	0	0	14 2/3	22	19	16	10	4
1989—	Rochester (Int'l)	•13	11	.542	3.21	27	•27	•9	•3	0	*185 1/3	176	76	66	59	109
	Baltimore (A.L.)	0	1	.000	6.23	5	1	0	0	0	8 2/3	10	6	6	3	6
1990—	Rochester (Int'l)	4	4	.500	3.92	15	14	1	0	0	87 1/3	95	46	38	25	83
	Baltimore (A.L.)	1	2	.333	2.54	35	0	0	0	3	46	38	13	13	19	32
1991—	Houston (N.L.)■	3	5	.375	3.81	56	0	0	0	8	75 2/3	79	35	32	39	71
	Tucson (PCL)	0	1	.000	3.42	13	0	0	0	3	23 2/3	16	9	9	12	21
1992—	Philadelphia (N.L.)■	14	11	.560	2.35	42	26	10	4	2	226 1/3	165	67	59	59	147
1993—	Philadelphia (N.L.)	16	7	.696	4.02	34	34	7	2	0	235 1/3	234	114	105	57	186
1994—	Philadelphia (N.L.)	2	8	.200	4.48	13	13	1	0	0	82 1/3	87	42	41	28	58
	Scran./W.B. (Int'l)	0	0	...	1.80	2	2	0	0	0	10	6	2	2	5	6
	Reading (Eastern)	0	0	...	0.00	1	1	0	0	0	4	6	0	0	1	4
1995—	Philadelphia (N.L.)	7	5	.583	3.57	17	17	1	0	0	116	96	52	46	26	114
1996—	Clearwater (Fla. St.)	2	0	1.000	1.29	2	2	0	0	0	14	9	2	2	1	17
	Scran./W.B. (Int'l)	1	0	1.000	1.38	2	2	0	0	0	13	9	2	2	5	10
	Philadelphia (N.L.)	9	10	.474	3.19	26	26	*8	2	0	183 1/3	149	69	65	50	182
1997—	Philadelphia (N.L.)	17	11	.607	2.97	35	•35	7	2	0	254 1/3	208	96	84	58	*319
1998—	Philadelphia (N.L.)	15	14	.517	3.25	35	•35	*15	2	0	*268 2/3	236	101	97	61	*300
A.L. totals (3 years)		1	6	.143	4.54	44	5	0	0	3	69 1/3	70	38	35	32	42
N.L. totals (8 years)		83	71	.539	3.30	258	186	49	12	10	1442	1254	576	529	378	1377
Major league totals (11 years)		84	77	.522	3.36	302	191	49	12	13	1511 1/3	1324	614	564	410	1419

CHAMPIONSHIP SERIES RECORD

RECORDS: Holds single-game records for most consecutive strikeouts—5; and most consecutive strikeouts from start of the game—5 (October 6, 1993).
NOTES: Named N.L. Championship Series Most Valuable Player (1993).

Year	Team (League)	W	L	Pct.	ERA	G	GS	CG	ShO	Sv.	IP	H	R	ER	BB	SO
1993—	Philadelphia (N.L.)	0	0	...	1.69	2	2	0	0	0	16	11	4	3	5	19

WORLD SERIES RECORD

Year	Team (League)	W	L	Pct.	ERA	G	GS	CG	ShO	Sv.	IP	H	R	ER	BB	SO
1993—	Philadelphia (N.L.)	1	1	.500	3.52	2	2	1	1	0	15 1/3	13	7	6	5	9

ALL-STAR GAME RECORD

Year	League	W	L	Pct.	ERA	GS	CG	ShO	Sv.	IP	H	R	ER	BB	SO
1997—	National	0	0	...	0.00	0	0	0	0	2	2	0	0	0	3
1998—	National							Did not play.							

SCHMIDT, JASON   P   PIRATES

PERSONAL: Born January 29, 1973, in Lewiston, Idaho. ... 6-5/211. ... Throws right, bats right. ... Full name: Jason David Schmidt.
HIGH SCHOOL: Kelso (Wash.).
TRANSACTIONS/CAREER NOTES: Selected by Atlanta Braves organization in eighth round of free-agent draft (June 3, 1991). ... On Atlanta disabled list (July 15-August 30, 1996); included rehabilitation assignment to Greenville (August 11-30). ... Claimed on waivers by Pittsburgh Pirates (August 30, 1996), completing deal in which Pirates traded P Denny Neagle to Braves for a player to be named later (August 28, 1996).
STATISTICAL NOTES: Led N.L. with 15 wild pitches in 1998.
MISCELLANEOUS: Received base on balls in only appearance as pinch hitter with Atlanta (1995).

Year Team (League)	W	L	Pct.	ERA	G	GS	CG	ShO	Sv.	IP	H	R	ER	BB	SO
1991—GC Braves (GCL)	3	4	.429	2.38	11	11	0	0	0	45 1/3	32	21	12	23	44
1992—Pulaski (Appalachian)	3	4	.429	4.01	11	11	0	0	0	58 1/3	38	36	26	31	56
—Macon (S. Atl.)	0	3	.000	4.01	7	7	0	0	0	24 2/3	31	18	11	19	33
1993—Durham (Carolina)	7	11	.389	4.94	22	22	0	0	0	116 2/3	128	69	64	47	110
1994—Greenville (Southern)	8	7	.533	3.65	24	24	1	0	0	140 2/3	135	64	57	54	131
1995—Atlanta (N.L.)	2	2	.500	5.76	9	2	0	0	0	25	27	17	16	18	19
—Richmond (Int'l)	8	6	.571	*2.25	19	19	0	0	0	116	97	40	29	48	95
1996—Atlanta (N.L.)	3	4	.429	6.75	13	11	0	0	0	58 2/3	69	48	44	32	48
—Richmond (Int'l)	3	0	1.000	2.56	7	7	0	0	0	45 2/3	36	17	13	19	41
—Greenville (Southern)	0	0	...	9.00	1	1	0	0	0	2	4	2	2	0	2
—Pittsburgh (N.L.)■	2	2	.500	4.06	6	6	1	0	0	37 2/3	39	19	17	21	26
1997—Pittsburgh (N.L.)	10	9	.526	4.60	32	32	2	0	0	187 2/3	193	106	96	76	136
1998—Pittsburgh (N.L.)	11	14	.440	4.07	33	33	0	0	0	214 1/3	228	106	97	71	158
Major league totals (4 years)	28	31	.475	4.64	93	84	3	0	0	523 1/3	556	296	270	218	387

SCHOENEWEIS, SCOTT   P   ANGELS

PERSONAL: Born October 2, 1973, in Long Branch, N.J. ... 6-0/186. ... Throws left, bats left. ... Full name: Scott David Schoeneweis.
HIGH SCHOOL: Lenape (Medford, N.J.).
COLLEGE: Duke.
TRANSACTIONS/CAREER NOTES: Selected by California Angels organization in third round of free-agent draft (June 4, 1996). ... Angels franchise renamed Anaheim Angels for 1997 season.

Year Team (League)	W	L	Pct.	ERA	G	GS	CG	ShO	Sv.	IP	H	R	ER	BB	SO
1996—Lake Elsinore (Calif.)	8	3	.727	3.94	14	12	0	0	0	93 2/3	86	47	41	27	83
1997—Midland (Texas)	7	5	.583	5.96	20	20	3	0	0	113 1/3	145	84	75	39	84
1998—Vancouver (PCL)	11	8	.579	4.50	27	27	2	0	0	180	188	102	90	59	133

SCHOUREK, PETE   P   PIRATES

PERSONAL: Born May 10, 1969, in Austin, Texas. ... 6-5/205. ... Throws left, bats left. ... Full name: Peter Alan Schourek. ... Name pronounced SHUR-ek.
HIGH SCHOOL: George C. Marshall (Falls Church, Va.).
TRANSACTIONS/CAREER NOTES: Selected by New York Mets organization in second round of free-agent draft (June 2, 1987). ... On disabled list (June 17, 1988-remainder of season). ... Claimed on waivers by Cincinnati Reds (April 7, 1994). ... On disabled list (June 1-22 and July 2, 1996-remainder of season). ... On disabled list (June 14-July 18 and July 31-September 2, 1997). ... Released by Reds (October 10, 1997). ... Signed by Houston Astros organization (January 9, 1998). ... On New Orleans disabled list (April 7-24, 1998). ... Traded by Astros to Boston Red Sox for cash (August 6, 1998). ... Granted free agency (October 23, 1998). ... Signed by Pittsburgh Pirates (December 17, 1998).
HONORS: Named lefthanded pitcher on THE SPORTING NEWS N.L. All-Star team (1995).
STATISTICAL NOTES: Pitched 9-0 one-hit, complete-game victory for New York against Montreal (September 10, 1991).
MISCELLANEOUS: Appeared in one game as pinch runner with New York (1992). ... Struck out in only appearance as pinch hitter (1996). ... Appeared in one game as pinch runner (1997).

Year Team (League)	W	L	Pct.	ERA	G	GS	CG	ShO	Sv.	IP	H	R	ER	BB	SO
1987—Kingsport (Appalachian)	4	5	.444	3.68	12	12	2	0	0	78 1/3	70	37	32	34	57
1988—						Did not play.									
1989—Columbia (S. Atl.)	5	9	.357	2.85	27	19	5	1	1	136	120	66	43	66	131
—St. Lucie (Fla. St.)	0	0	...	2.25	2	1	0	0	0	4	3	1	1	2	4
1990—St. Lucie (Fla. St.)	4	1	.800	0.97	5	5	2	2	0	37	29	4	4	8	28
—Tidewater (Int'l)	1	0	1.000	2.57	2	2	1	1	0	14	9	4	4	5	14
—Jackson (Texas)	11	4	.733	3.04	19	19	1	0	0	124 1/3	109	53	42	39	94
1991—Tidewater (Int'l)	1	1	.500	2.52	4	4	0	0	0	25	18	7	7	10	17
—New York (N.L.)	5	4	.556	4.27	35	8	1	1	2	86 1/3	82	49	41	43	67
1992—Tidewater (Int'l)	2	5	.286	2.73	8	8	2	1	0	52 2/3	46	20	16	23	42
—New York (N.L.)	6	8	.429	3.64	22	21	0	0	0	136	137	60	55	44	60
1993—New York (N.L.)	5	12	.294	5.96	41	18	0	0	0	128 1/3	168	90	85	45	72
1994—Cincinnati (N.L.)■	7	2	.778	4.09	22	10	0	0	0	81 1/3	90	39	37	29	69
1995—Cincinnati (N.L.)	18	7	.720	3.22	29	29	2	0	0	190 1/3	158	72	68	45	160
1996—Cincinnati (N.L.)	4	5	.444	6.01	12	12	0	0	0	67 1/3	79	48	45	24	54
1997—Cincinnati (N.L.)	5	8	.385	5.42	18	17	0	0	0	84 2/3	78	59	51	38	59
1998—Kissimmee (Fla. St.)■	0	0	...	1.08	2	1	0	0	0	8 1/3	8	1	1	4	9
—Houston (N.L.)	7	6	.538	4.50	15	15	0	0	0	80	82	43	40	36	59
—Boston (A.L.)■	1	3	.250	4.30	10	8	0	0	0	44	45	21	21	14	36
A.L. totals (1 year)	1	3	.250	4.30	10	8	0	0	0	44	45	21	21	14	36
N.L. totals (8 years)	57	52	.523	4.45	194	130	3	1	2	854 1/3	874	460	422	304	600
Major league totals (8 years)	58	55	.513	4.44	204	138	3	1	2	898 1/3	919	481	443	318	636

DIVISION SERIES RECORD

Year Team (League)	W	L	Pct.	ERA	G	GS	CG	ShO	Sv.	IP	H	R	ER	BB	SO
1995—Cincinnati (N.L.)	1	0	1.000	2.57	1	1	0	0	0	7	5	2	2	3	5
1998—Boston (A.L.)	0	0	...	0.00	1	1	0	0	0	5 1/3	2	0	0	4	1
Div. series totals (2 years)	1	0	1.000	1.46	2	2	0	0	0	12 1/3	7	2	2	7	6

Year	Team (League)	W	L	Pct.	ERA	G	GS	CG	ShO	Sv.	IP	H	R	ER	BB	SO
1995—	Cincinnati (N.L.)	0	1	.000	1.26	2	2	0	0	0	14 1/3	14	2	2	3	13

SEANEZ, RUDY — P — BRAVES

PERSONAL: Born October 20, 1968, in Brawley, Calif. ... 5-10/190. ... Throws right, bats right. ... Full name: Rudy Caballero Seanez. ... Name pronounced see-AHN-yez.

HIGH SCHOOL: Brawley (Calif.) Union.

TRANSACTIONS/CAREER NOTES: Selected by Cleveland Indians organization in fourth round of free-agent draft (June 10, 1986). ... On disabled list (May 4-July 11 and August 9-29, 1987). ... On Cleveland disabled list (April 1-16, 1991). ... On Cleveland disabled list (July 30-September 2, 1991); included rehabilitation assignment to Colorado Springs (August 14-September 2). ... Traded by Indians to Los Angeles Dodgers for P Dennis Cook and P Mike Christopher (December 10, 1991). ... On disabled list (March 29, 1992-entire season). ... Traded by Dodgers to Colorado Rockies for 2B Jody Reed (November 17, 1992). ... On Colorado disabled list (April 4-July 16, 1993); included rehabilitation assignments to Central Valley (June 16-July 4) and Colorado Springs (July 4-15). ... Granted free agency (July 16, 1993). ... Signed by San Diego Padres organization (July 22, 1993). ... Released by Padres (November 18, 1993). ... Signed by Dodgers organization (January 12, 1994). ... On Los Angeles disabled list (May 28-June 16, 1994); included rehabilitation assignment to San Bernardino (June 9-16). ... Granted free agency (October 15, 1996). ... Signed by New York Mets organization (January 15, 1997). ... Granted free agency (October 15, 1997). ... Signed by Atlanta Braves organization (December 9, 1997).

STATISTICAL NOTES: Pitched 4-0 no-hit victory against Pulaski (August 2, 1986).

Year	Team (League)	W	L	Pct.	ERA	G	GS	CG	ShO	Sv.	IP	H	R	ER	BB	SO
1986—	Burlington (Appalachian)....	5	2	.714	3.20	13	12	1	1	0	76	59	37	27	32	56
1987—	Waterloo (Midw.)	0	4	.000	6.75	10	10	0	0	0	34 2/3	35	29	26	23	23
1988—	Waterloo (Midw.)	6	6	.500	4.69	22	22	1	1	0	113 1/3	98	69	59	68	93
1989—	Kinston (Carolina)	8	10	.444	4.14	25	25	1	0	0	113	94	66	52	*111	149
	—Colo. Springs (PCL)	0	0	. . .	0.00	1	0	0	0	0	1	1	0	0	0	0
	—Cleveland (A.L.)	0	0	. . .	3.60	5	0	0	0	0	5	1	2	2	4	7
1990—	Cant./Akr. (Eastern)	1	0	1.000	2.16	15	0	0	0	5	16 2/3	9	4	4	12	27
	—Cleveland (A.L.)	2	1	.667	5.60	24	0	0	0	0	27 1/3	22	17	17	25	24
	—Colo. Springs (PCL)	1	4	.200	6.75	12	0	0	0	1	12	15	10	9	10	7
1991—	Colo. Springs (PCL)	0	0	. . .	7.27	16	0	0	0	0	17 1/3	17	14	14	22	19
	—Cant./Akr. (Eastern)	4	2	.667	2.58	25	0	0	0	7	38 1/3	17	12	11	30	73
	—Cleveland (A.L.)	0	0	. . .	16.20	5	0	0	0	0	5	10	12	9	7	7
1992—								Did not play.									
1993—	Central Valley (Cal.)■........	0	2	.000	9.72	5	1	0	0	0	8 1/3	9	9	9	11	7
	—Colo. Springs (PCL)	0	0	. . .	9.00	3	0	0	0	0	3	3	3	3	1	5
	—Las Vegas (PCL)■	0	1	.000	6.41	14	0	0	0	0	19 2/3	24	15	14	11	14
	—San Diego (N.L.)	0	0	. . .	13.50	3	0	0	0	0	3 1/3	8	6	5	2	1
1994—	Albuquerque (PCL)■.........	2	1	.667	5.32	20	0	0	0	9	22	28	14	13	13	26
	—Los Angeles (N.L.)	1	1	.500	2.66	17	0	0	0	0	23 2/3	24	7	7	9	18
1995—	Los Angeles (N.L.)	1	3	.250	6.75	37	0	0	0	3	34 2/3	39	27	26	18	29
	—San Bernardino (Calif.)......	2	0	1.000	0.00	4	0	0	0	1	6	2	0	0	3	5
1996—	Albuquerque (PCL)............	0	2	.000	6.52	21	0	0	0	6	19 1/3	27	18	14	11	20
1997—	Norfolk (Int'l)■	1	0	1.000	4.05	9	0	0	0	0	13 1/3	12	8	6	11	17
	—Omaha (Am. Assoc.)■........	2	5	.286	6.51	28	3	0	0	0	47	53	42	34	25	46
1998—	Richmond (Int'l)■...............	2	0	1.000	1.29	16	0	0	0	7	21	13	9	3	7	33
	—Atlanta (N.L.)...................	4	1	.800	2.75	34	0	0	0	2	36	25	13	11	16	50
A.L. totals (3 years)		2	1	.667	6.75	34	0	0	0	0	37 1/3	33	31	28	36	38
N.L. totals (4 years)		6	5	.545	4.52	91	0	0	0	5	97 2/3	96	53	49	45	98
Major league totals (7 years)......		8	6	.571	5.13	125	0	0	0	5	135	129	84	77	81	136

DIVISION SERIES RECORD

Year	Team (League)	W	L	Pct.	ERA	G	GS	CG	ShO	Sv.	IP	H	R	ER	BB	SO
1998—	Atlanta (N.L.).....................	0	0	. . .	0.00	1	0	0	0	0	1	0	0	0	0	0

CHAMPIONSHIP SERIES RECORD

Year	Team (League)	W	L	Pct.	ERA	G	GS	CG	ShO	Sv.	IP	H	R	ER	BB	SO
1998—	Atlanta (N.L.).....................	0	0	. . .	6.00	4	0	0	0	0	3	2	2	2	1	4

SEFCIK, KEVIN — OF/IF — PHILLIES

PERSONAL: Born February 10, 1971, in Oak Lawn, Ill. ... 5-10/180. ... Bats right, throws right. ... Full name: Kevin John Sefcik.

HIGH SCHOOL: Victor Andrews (Tinley Park, Ill.).

COLLEGE: St. Xavier (Ill.).

TRANSACTIONS/CAREER NOTES: Selected by Philadelphia Phillies organization in 33rd round of free-agent draft (June 3, 1993).

STATISTICAL NOTES: Led New York-Pennsylvania League second basemen with 212 assists and 359 total chances in 1993.

							BATTING								FIELDING			
Year	Team (League)	Pos.	G	AB	R	H	2B	3B	HR	RBI	Avg.	BB	SO	SB	PO	A	E	Avg.
1993—	Batavia (NY-Penn)	2B-3B	74	281	49	84	24	4	2	28	.299	27	22	20	136	†216	16	.957
1994—	Clearwater (FSL)	3B-2B	130	516	83	147	29	8	2	46	.285	49	43	30	91	293	21	.948
1995—	Scran./W.B. (Int'l)......	2B	7	26	5	9	6	1	0	6	.346	3	1	0	13	16	0	1.000
	—Reading (Eastern)	SS-3B	128	508	68	138	18	4	4	46	.272	38	48	14	166	349	18	.966
	—Philadelphia (N.L.)......	3B	5	4	1	0	0	0	0	0	.000	0	2	0	0	1	0	1.000
1996—	Philadelphia (N.L.)......	SS-3B-2B	44	116	10	33	5	3	0	9	.284	9	16	3	30	83	7	.942
	—Scran./W.B. (Int'l)......	3B	45	180	34	60	7	5	0	19	.333	15	20	11	63	143	10	.954
1997—	Philadelphia (N.L.)......	2B-SS-3B	61	119	11	32	3	0	2	6	.269	4	9	1	39	62	4	.962
	—Scran./W.B. (Int'l)......	2B-3B-OF	29	123	19	41	11	2	1	7	.333	9	11	5	51	56	6	.947
1998—	Philadelphia (N.L.)......	O-3-DH-2	104	169	27	53	7	2	3	20	.314	25	32	4	89	1	2	.978
Major league totals (4 years)			214	408	49	118	15	5	5	35	.289	38	59	8	158	147	13	.959

S

PERSONAL: Born July 19, 1966, in Kansas City, Kan. ... 6-1/202. ... Bats both, throws left. ... Full name: David Vincent Segui. ... Son of Diego Segui, pitcher with five major league teams (1962-75 and 1977); and brother of Dan Segui, minor league infielder (1987-90). ... Name pronounced seh-GHEE.

HIGH SCHOOL: Bishop Ward (Kansas City, Kan.).

JUNIOR COLLEGE: Kansas City Kansas Community College.

COLLEGE: Louisiana Tech.

TRANSACTIONS/CAREER NOTES: Selected by Baltimore Orioles organization in 18th round of free-agent draft (June 2, 1987). ... On Rochester disabled list (April 19-26, 1991). ... On suspended list (August 16-19, 1993). ... Traded by Orioles to New York Mets for SS Kevin Baez and P Tom Wegmann (March 27, 1994). ... On disabled list (June 20-July 5, 1994). ... Traded by Mets to Montreal Expos for P Reid Cornelius (June 8, 1995). ... On disabled list (July 4-August 16, 1996). ... On disabled list (June 4-21, 1997). ... On suspended list (July 26, 1997). ... Granted free agency (October 28, 1997). ... Signed by Seattle Mariners (December 12, 1997).

STATISTICAL NOTES: Led N.L. first basemen with .996 fielding percentage in 1994. ... Switch-hit home runs in one game (April 1, 1998). ... Led A.L. first basemen with .999 fielding percentage in 1998. ... Career major league grand slams: 4.

Year — Team (League)	Pos.	G	AB	R	H	2B	3B	HR	RBI	Avg.	BB	SO	SB	PO	A	E	Avg.
														BATTING		FIELDING	
1988—Hagerstown (Car.)	1B-OF	60	190	35	51	12	4	3	31	.268	22	23	0	342	25	9	.976
1989—Frederick (Carolina)	1B	83	284	43	90	19	0	10	50	.317	41	32	2	707	47	4	.995
—Hagerstown (East.)	1B	44	173	22	56	14	1	1	27	.324	16	16	0	381	30	1	.998
1990—Rochester (Int'l)	1B-OF	86	307	55	103	28	0	2	51	.336	45	28	5	704	62	3	.996
—Baltimore (A.L.)	1B-DH	40	123	14	30	7	0	2	15	.244	11	15	0	283	26	3	.990
1991—Rochester (Int'l)	1B-OF	28	96	9	26	2	0	1	10	.271	15	6	1	165	15	0	1.000
—Baltimore (A.L.)	OF-1B-DH	86	212	15	59	7	0	2	22	.278	12	19	1	264	23	3	.990
1992—Baltimore (A.L.)	1B-DH	115	189	21	44	9	0	1	17	.233	20	23	1	406	35	1	.998
1993—Baltimore (A.L.)	1B-DH	146	450	54	123	27	0	10	60	.273	58	53	2	1152	98	5	.996
1994—New York (N.L.)■	1B-OF	92	336	46	81	17	1	10	43	.241	33	43	0	695	52	5	†.993
1995—New York (N.L.)	OF-1B	33	73	9	24	3	1	2	11	.329	12	9	1	56	5	0	1.000
—Montreal (N.L.)■	1B-OF	97	383	59	117	22	3	10	57	.305	28	38	1	840	70	3	.997
1996—Montreal (N.L.)	1B	115	416	69	119	30	1	11	58	.286	60	54	4	944	90	7	.993
1997—Montreal (N.L.)	1B	125	459	75	141	22	3	21	68	.307	57	66	1	1035	88	6	.995
1998—Seattle (A.L.)■	1B-OF	143	522	79	159	36	1	19	84	.305	49	80	3	1045	116	1	†.999
American League totals (5 years)		530	1496	183	415	86	4	34	198	.277	150	190	7	3150	298	13	.996
National League totals (4 years)		462	1667	258	482	94	9	54	237	.289	190	210	7	3570	305	21	.995
Major league totals (9 years)		992	3163	441	897	180	10	88	435	.284	340	400	14	6720	603	34	.995

PERSONAL: Born January 19, 1975, in Bocas del Toro, Panama. ... 6-5/215. ... Bats both, throws right. ... Full name: Fernando Alfredo Seguignol.

HIGH SCHOOL: Almirante de Bocas del Toro (Bocas del Toro, Panama).

TRANSACTIONS/CAREER NOTES: Signed as non-drafted free agent by New York Yankees organization (January 29, 1993). ... Traded by Yankees with cash to Montreal Expos for P John Wetteland (April 5, 1995). ... On Harrisburg disabled list (June 24-July 17, 1998).

STATISTICAL NOTES: Led Florida State League with 14 sacrifice flies in 1997. ... Tied for Florida State League lead in assists by first basemen with 91 in 1997.

Year — Team (League)	Pos.	G	AB	R	H	2B	3B	HR	RBI	Avg.	BB	SO	SB	PO	A	E	Avg.
														BATTING		FIELDING	
1993—GC Yankees (GCL)	OF-1B	45	161	16	35	3	3	2	20	.217	9	37	2	86	8	2	.979
1994—Oneonta (NYP)	OF	73	266	36	77	14	*9	2	32	.289	16	61	4	77	3	4	.952
1995—Albany (S. Atl.)■	OF	121	457	59	95	22	2	12	66	.208	28	141	12	205	7	8	.964
1996—Delmarva (S. Atl.)	OF	118	410	59	98	14	5	8	55	.239	48	126	12	173	4	4	.978
1997—W.P. Beach (FSL)	1B-OF	124	456	70	116	27	5	18	83	.254	30	129	5	967	‡91	15	.986
1998—Harrisburg (East.)	1B-OF	80	281	54	81	13	0	25	69	.288	29	77	6	503	50	9	.984
—Ottawa (Int'l)	OF-1B	32	109	16	28	8	0	6	16	.257	12	43	0	44	2	1	.979
—Montreal (N.L.)	OF-1B	16	42	6	11	4	0	2	3	.262	3	15	0	65	5	0	1.000
Major league totals (1 year)		16	42	6	11	4	0	2	3	.262	3	15	0	65	5	0	1.000

PERSONAL: Born June 25, 1970, in Golden Valley, Minn. ... 6-5/215. ... Throws right, bats right. ... Full name: Aaron Helmer Sele. ... Name pronounced SEE-lee.

HIGH SCHOOL: North Kitsap (Poulsbo, Wash.).

COLLEGE: Washington State.

TRANSACTIONS/CAREER NOTES: Selected by Minnesota Twins organization in 37th round of free-agent draft (June 1, 1988); did not sign. ... Selected by Boston Red Sox organization in first round (23rd pick overall) of free-agent draft (June 3, 1991). ... On Boston disabled list (May 24, 1995-remainder of season); included rehabilitation assignments to Trenton (June 19-22), Sarasota (July 10-21 and August 7-16) and Pawtucket (August 16-23). ... On Boston disabled list (August 14-September 1, 1996); included rehabilitation assignment to Pawtucket (August 26-27). ... Traded by Red Sox with P Mark Brandenburg and C Bill Haselman to Texas Rangers for C Jim Leyritz and OF Damon Buford (November 6, 1997).

HONORS: Named A.L. Rookie Pitcher of the Year by THE SPORTING NEWS (1993). ... Named International League Most Valuable Pitcher (1993).

STATISTICAL NOTES: Led Carolina League with 14 hit batsmen in 1992. ... Tied for A.L. lead with nine hit batsmen in 1994.

Year — Team (League)	W	L	Pct.	ERA	G	GS	CG	ShO	Sv.	IP	H	R	ER	BB	SO
1991—Winter Haven (FSL)	3	6	.333	4.96	13	11	4	0	1	69	65	42	38	32	51
1992—Lynchburg (Carolina)	13	5	.722	2.91	20	19	2	1	0	127	104	51	41	46	112
—New Britain (East.)	2	1	.667	6.27	7	6	1	0	0	33	43	29	23	15	29
1993—Pawtucket (Int'l)	8	2	.800	2.19	14	14	2	1	0	94 1/3	74	30	23	23	87
—Boston (A.L.)	7	2	.778	2.74	18	18	0	0	0	111 2/3	100	42	34	48	93

S

Year— Team (League)	W	L	Pct.	ERA	G	GS	CG	ShO	Sv.	IP	H	R	ER	BB	SO
1994— Boston (A.L.)	8	7	.533	3.83	22	22	2	0	0	143 1/3	140	68	61	60	105
1995— Boston (A.L.)	3	1	.750	3.06	6	6	0	0	0	32 1/3	32	14	11	14	21
— Trenton (Eastern)	0	1	.000	3.38	2	2	0	0	0	8	8	3	3	2	9
— Sarasota (Florida State)	0	0	. . .	0.00	2	2	0	0	0	7	6	0	0	1	8
— Pawtucket (Int'l)	0	0	. . .	9.00	2	2	0	0	0	5	9	5	5	2	1
1996— Boston (A.L.)	7	11	.389	5.32	29	29	1	0	0	157 1/3	192	110	93	67	137
— Pawtucket (Int'l)	0	0	. . .	6.00	1	1	0	0	0	3	3	2	2	1	4
1997— Boston (A.L.)	13	12	.520	5.38	33	33	1	0	0	177 1/3	196	115	106	80	122
1998— Texas (A.L.)■	19	11	.633	4.23	33	33	3	2	0	212 2/3	239	116	100	84	167
Major league totals (6 years)	57	44	.564	4.37	141	141	7	2	0	834 2/3	899	465	405	353	645

DIVISION SERIES RECORD

Year Team (League)	W	L	Pct.	ERA	G	GS	CG	ShO	Sv.	IP	H	R	ER	BB	SO
1998— Texas (A.L.)	0	1	.000	6.00	1	1	0	0	0	6	8	4	4	1	4

ALL-STAR GAME RECORD

Year League	W	L	Pct.	ERA	GS	CG	ShO	Sv.	IP	H	R	ER	BB	SO
1998— American				Did not play.										

SERAFINI, DANIEL   P   TWINS

PERSONAL: Born January 25, 1974, in San Francisco. ... 6-1/195. ... Throws left, bats both. ... Full name: Daniel Joseph Serafini.
HIGH SCHOOL: Serra (San Mateo, Calif.).
TRANSACTIONS/CAREER NOTES: Selected by Minnesota Twins organization in first round (26th pick overall) of free-agent draft (June 1, 1992). ... On Salt Lake disabled list (May 11-31, 1996).

Year— Team (League)	W	L	Pct.	ERA	G	GS	CG	ShO	Sv.	IP	H	R	ER	BB	SO
1992— GC Twins (GCL)	1	0	1.000	3.64	8	6	0	0	0	29 2/3	27	16	12	15	33
1993— Fort Wayne (Midw.)	10	8	.556	3.65	27	27	1	1	0	140 2/3	117	72	57	83	147
1994— Fort Myers (Fla. St.)	9	9	.500	4.61	23	23	2	1	0	136 2/3	149	84	70	57	130
1995— New Britain (East.)	12	9	.571	3.38	27	27	1	1	0	162 2/3	155	74	61	72	123
— Salt Lake (PCL)	0	0	. . .	6.75	1	0	0	0	0	4	4	3	3	1	4
1996— Salt Lake (PCL)	7	7	.500	5.28	25	23	1	0	0	130 2/3	164	84	81	58	109
— Minnesota (A.L.)	0	1	.000	10.38	1	1	0	0	0	4 1/3	7	5	5	2	1
1997— Salt Lake (PCL)	9	7	.563	4.97	28	24	2	0	0	152	166	87	84	55	118
— Minnesota (A.L.)	2	1	.667	3.42	6	4	1	0	0	26 1/3	27	11	10	11	15
1998— Salt Lake (PCL)	2	4	.333	3.71	9	8	0	0	0	53 1/3	56	29	22	21	39
— Minnesota (A.L.)	7	4	.636	6.48	28	9	0	0	0	75	95	58	54	29	46
Major league totals (3 years)	9	6	.600	5.88	35	14	1	0	0	105 2/3	129	74	69	42	62

SERRANO, WASCAR   P   PADRES

PERSONAL: Born June 2, 1978, in Santo Domingo, Dominican Republic. ... 6-2/178. ... Throws right, bats right.
HIGH SCHOOL: Las Carreres (Dominican Republic).
TRANSACTIONS/CAREER NOTES: Signed as non-drafted free agent by San Diego Padres organization (May 31, 1995).

Year Team (League)	W	L	Pct.	ERA	G	GS	CG	ShO	Sv.	IP	H	R	ER	BB	SO
1995— Dominican Padres (DSL)	3	3	.500	3.11	12	7	0	0	0	46 1/3	63	24	16	15	23
1996— Dominican Padres (DSL)	3	7	.300	7.88	22	2	0	0	1	53 2/3	77	58	47	24	44
1997— Idaho Falls (Pioneer)	0	1	.000	11.88	2	2	0	0	0	8 1/3	13	12	11	4	13
— Ariz. Padres (Ariz.)	•6	3	.667	3.18	12	11	0	0	1	70 2/3	60	43	25	22	75
— Clinton (Midwest)	0	1	.000	6.00	1	1	1	0	0	6	6	5	4	2	2
1998— Clinton (Midwest)	9	7	.563	3.22	26	26	0	0	0	156 2/3	150	74	56	54	143

SERVAIS, SCOTT   C   GIANTS

PERSONAL: Born June 4, 1967, in La Crosse, Wis. ... 6-2/210. ... Bats right, throws right. ... Full name: Scott Daniel Servais. ... Name pronounced SER-viss.
HIGH SCHOOL: Westby (Wis.).
COLLEGE: Creighton.
TRANSACTIONS/CAREER NOTES: Selected by New York Mets organization in second round of free-agent draft (June 3, 1985); did not sign. ... Selected by Houston Astros organization in third round of free-agent draft (June 1, 1988). ... On Tucson disabled list (June 29-July 1, 1991). ... On Houston disabled list (August 4-September 7, 1991). ... Traded by Astros with OF Luis Gonzalez to Chicago Cubs for C Rick Wilkins (June 28, 1995). ... On Chicago disabled list (July 10-August 3, 1995). ... Granted free agency (October 23, 1998). ... Signed by San Francisco Giants (January 17, 1999).
STATISTICAL NOTES: Tied for Pacific Coast League lead in double plays by catcher with nine in 1990. ... Led N.L. catchers with 12 errors in 1995.
MISCELLANEOUS: Member of 1988 U.S. Olympic baseball team.

Year Team (League)	Pos.	G	AB	R	H	2B	3B	HR	RBI	Avg.	BB	SO	SB	PO	A	E	Avg.
							BATTING								FIELDING		
1989— Osceola (Fla. St.)	C-1B	46	153	16	41	9	0	2	23	.268	16	35	0	168	24	4	.980
— Columbus (Southern)	C	63	199	20	47	5	0	1	22	.236	19	42	0	330	45	3	.992
1990— Tucson (PCL)	C	89	303	37	66	11	3	5	37	.218	18	61	0	453	63	9	.983
1991— Tucson (PCL)	C	60	219	34	71	12	0	2	27	.324	13	19	0	350	33	6	.985
— Houston (N.L.)	C	16	37	0	6	3	0	0	6	.162	4	8	0	77	4	1	.988
1992— Houston (N.L.)	C	77	205	12	49	9	0	0	15	.239	11	25	0	386	27	2	.995
1993— Houston (N.L.)	C	85	258	24	63	11	0	11	32	.244	22	45	0	493	40	2	.996
1994— Houston (N.L.)	C	78	251	27	49	15	1	9	41	.195	10	44	0	481	29	2	.996
1995— Houston (N.L.)	C	28	89	7	20	10	0	1	12	.225	9	15	0	198	17	5	.977
— Chicago (N.L.)■	C	52	175	31	50	12	0	12	35	.286	23	37	2	328	33	§7	.981
1996— Chicago (N.L.)	C-1B	129	445	42	118	20	0	11	63	.265	30	75	0	798	73	11	.988

Year	Team (League)	Pos.	G	AB	R	H	2B	3B	HR	RBI	Avg.	BB	SO	SB	PO	A	E	Avg.
									BATTING							FIELDING		
1997—Chicago (N.L.)		C-DH-1B	122	385	36	100	21	0	6	45	.260	24	56	0	736	73	8	.990
1998—Chicago (N.L.)		C-1B	113	325	35	72	15	1	7	36	.222	26	51	1	654	48	4	.994
Major league totals (8 years)			700	2170	214	527	116	2	57	285	.243	159	356	3	4151	344	42	.991

DIVISION SERIES RECORD

Year	Team (League)	Pos.	G	AB	R	H	2B	3B	HR	RBI	Avg.	BB	SO	SB	PO	A	E	Avg.
									BATTING							FIELDING		
1998—Chicago (N.L.)		C	1	3	0	2	0	0	0	0	.667	0	0	0	6	1	0	1.000

SERVICE, SCOTT   P   ROYALS

PERSONAL: Born February 26, 1967, in Cincinnati. ... 6-6/230. ... Throws right, bats right. ... Full name: David Scott Service.

HIGH SCHOOL: Aiken (Cincinnati).

TRANSACTIONS/CAREER NOTES: Signed as non-drafted free agent by Philadelphia Phillies organization (August 24, 1985). ... Granted free agency (October 11, 1990). ... Signed by Montreal Expos organization (November 15, 1990). ... Released by Expos organization (July 19, 1991). ... Played with Chunichi Dragons of Japan Central League (August 1991). ... Signed by Expos organization (January 10, 1992). ... Granted free agency (June 8, 1992). ... Signed by Nashville, Cincinnati Reds organization (June 9, 1992). ... On Indianapolis disabled list (May 15-22, 1993). ... Claimed on waivers by Colorado Rockies (June 28, 1993). ... Claimed on waivers by Reds (July 7, 1993). ... On Indianapolis disabled list (April 17-24, 1994). ... Released by Reds (November 17, 1994). ... Re-signed by Indianapolis, Reds organization (February 24, 1995). ... Traded by Reds organization with OF Deion Sanders, P John Roper, P Ricky Pickett and IF Dave McCarty to San Francisco Giants for OF Darren Lewis, P Mark Portugal and P Dave Burba (July 21, 1995). ... Released by Giants (March 26, 1996). ... Signed by Reds organization (April 2, 1996). ... Claimed on waivers by Oakland Athletics (March 27, 1997). ... Claimed on waivers by Reds (April 4, 1997). ... Traded by Reds with P Hector Carrasco to Kansas City Royals for OF Jon Nunnally and IF/OF Chris Stynes (July 15, 1997). ... On suspended list (June 15-16, 1998).

STATISTICAL NOTES: Led American Association with .800 winning percentage in 1992. ... Led American Association with 24 saves in 1997.

MISCELLANEOUS: Made an out in only appearance as pinch hitter with Cincinnati (1993).

Year	Team (League)	W	L	Pct.	ERA	G	GS	CG	ShO	Sv.	IP	H	R	ER	BB	SO
1986—Spartanburg (SAL)		1	6	.143	5.83	14	9	1	0	0	58 2/3	68	44	38	34	49
—Utica (N.Y.-Penn)		5	4	.556	2.67	10	10	2	0	0	70 2/3	65	30	21	18	43
—Clearwater (Fla. St.)		1	2	.333	3.20	4	4	1	1	0	25 1/3	20	10	9	15	19
1987—Reading (Eastern)		0	3	.000	7.78	5	4	0	0	0	19 2/3	22	19	17	16	12
—Clearwater (Fla. St.)		13	4	.765	2.48	21	21	5	2	0	137 2/3	127	46	38	32	73
1988—Reading (Eastern)		3	4	.429	2.86	10	9	1	1	0	56 2/3	52	25	18	22	39
—Maine (International)		8	8	.500	3.67	19	18	1	0	0	110 1/3	109	51	45	31	87
—Philadelphia (N.L.)		0	0	...	1.69	5	0	0	0	0	5 1/3	7	1	1	1	6
1989—Scran./W.B. (Int'l)		3	1	.750	2.16	23	0	0	0	6	33 1/3	27	8	8	23	23
—Reading (Eastern)		6	6	.500	3.26	23	10	1	1	1	85 2/3	71	36	31	23	82
1990—Scran./W.B. (Int'l)		5	4	.556	4.76	45	9	0	0	2	96 1/3	96	56	51	44	94
1991—Indianapolis (A.A.)■		6	7	.462	2.97	18	17	3	1	0	121 1/3	83	42	40	39	91
—Chunichi (Jp. Cn.)■		0	0	...	9.00	1	...	...	...	0	1	...	...	1	0	0
1992—Indianapolis (A.A.)■		2	0	1.000	0.74	13	0	0	0	2	24 1/3	12	3	2	9	25
—Montreal (N.L.)		0	0	...	14.14	5	0	0	0	0	7	15	11	11	5	11
—Nashville (A.A.)■		6	2	§.750	2.29	39	2	0	0	4	70 2/3	54	22	18	35	87
1993—Indianapolis (A.A.)		4	2	.667	4.45	21	1	0	0	2	30 1/3	25	16	15	17	28
—Colorado (N.L.)■		0	0	...	9.64	3	0	0	0	0	4 2/3	8	5	5	1	3
—Cincinnati (N.L.)		2	2	.500	3.70	26	0	0	0	2	41 1/3	36	19	17	15	40
1994—Indianapolis (A.A.)		5	5	.500	2.31	40	0	0	0	13	58 1/3	35	16	15	27	67
—Cincinnati (N.L.)		1	2	.333	7.36	6	0	0	0	0	7 1/3	8	9	6	3	5
1995—Indianapolis (A.A.)		4	1	.800	2.18	36	0	0	0	18	41 1/3	33	13	10	15	48
—San Francisco (N.L.)■		3	1	.750	3.19	28	0	0	0	0	31	18	11	11	20	30
1996—Indianapolis (A.A.)■		1	4	.200	3.00	35	1	0	0	15	48	34	18	16	10	58
—Cincinnati (N.L.)		1	0	1.000	3.94	34	1	0	0	0	48	51	21	21	18	46
1997—Cincinnati (N.L.)		0	0	...	11.81	4	0	0	0	0	5 1/3	11	7	7	1	3
—Indianapolis (A.A.)		3	2	.600	3.71	33	0	0	0	15	34	30	15	14	12	53
—Omaha (Am. Assoc.)■		0	0	...	0.00	16	0	0	0	§9	14 2/3	9	0	0	4	16
—Kansas City (A.L.)		0	3	.000	4.76	12	0	0	0	0	17	17	9	9	5	19
1998—Kansas City (A.L.)		6	4	.600	3.48	73	0	0	0	4	82 2/3	70	35	32	34	95
A.L. totals (2 years)		6	7	.462	3.70	85	0	0	0	4	99 2/3	87	44	41	39	114
N.L. totals (7 years)		7	5	.583	4.74	111	1	0	0	2	150	154	84	79	64	144
Major league totals (8 years)		13	12	.520	4.33	196	1	0	0	6	249 2/3	241	128	120	103	258

SEXSON, RICHIE   1B   INDIANS

PERSONAL: Born December 29, 1974, in Portland. ... 6-6/206. ... Bats right, throws right. ... Full name: Richmond Lockwood Sexson. ... Name pronounced SECKS-an.

HIGH SCHOOL: Prairie (Brush Prairie, Wash.).

TRANSACTIONS/CAREER NOTES: Selected by Cleveland Indians organization in 24th round of free-agent draft (June 2, 1993).

STATISTICAL NOTES: Led Carolina League with 251 total bases in 1995. ... Led Carolina League first basemen with 1,226 total chances and 109 double plays in 1995. ... Led American Association first basemen with .996 fielding percentage, 1,003 total chances and 105 double plays in 1997. ... Career major league grand slams: 1.

Year	Team (League)	Pos.	G	AB	R	H	2B	3B	HR	RBI	Avg.	BB	SO	SB	PO	A	E	Avg.
									BATTING							FIELDING		
1993—Burlington (Appal.)		1B	40	97	11	18	3	0	1	5	.186	18	21	1	309	15	4	.988
1994—Columbus (S. Atl.)		1B	130	488	88	133	25	2	14	77	.273	37	87	7	933	*63	10	*.990
1995—Kinston (Carolina)		1B	131	494	80	*151	*34	0	22	*85	.306	43	115	4	*1135	*79	12	.990
1996—Cant./Akr. (Eastern)		1B	133	518	85	143	35	3	16	76	.276	39	118	2	892	76	11	.989

Year	Team (League)	Pos.	G	AB	R	H	2B	3B	HR	RBI	Avg.	BB	SO	SB	PO	A	E	Avg.
1997—Buffalo (A.A.)	1B	115	434	57	113	20	2	*31	88	.260	27	87	5	*922	*77	4	*.996
—Cleveland (A.L.)	1B-DH	5	11	1	3	0	0	0	0	.273	0	2	0	11	1	0	1.000
1998—Buffalo (Int'l)	OF-1B	89	344	58	102	20	1	21	74	.297	50	68	1	270	29	3	.990
—Cleveland (A.L.)	1B-OF-DH	49	174	28	54	14	1	11	35	.310	6	42	1	325	38	6	.984
Major league totals (2 years)		54	185	29	57	14	1	11	35	.308	6	44	1	336	39	6	.984

DIVISION SERIES RECORD

Year	Team (League)	Pos.	G	AB	R	H	2B	3B	HR	RBI	Avg.	BB	SO	SB	PO	A	E	Avg.
1998—Cleveland (A.L.)	1B	3	2	0	0	0	0	0	0	.000	2	1	0	12	1	0	1.000

CHAMPIONSHIP SERIES RECORD

Year	Team (League)	Pos.	G	AB	R	H	2B	3B	HR	RBI	Avg.	BB	SO	SB	PO	A	E	Avg.
1998—Cleveland (A.L.)	1B	3	6	0	0	0	0	0	0	.000	0	3	0	20	3	0	1.000

SEXTON, CHRIS   IF   ROCKIES

PERSONAL: Born August 3, 1971, in Cincinnati. ... 5-11/178. ... Bats right, throws right. ... Full name: Christopher Philip Sexton.
HIGH SCHOOL: St. Xavier (Cincinnati).
COLLEGE: Miami of Ohio (degree in business).
TRANSACTIONS/CAREER NOTES: Selected by Cinciannti Reds organization in 10th round of free-agent draft (June 3, 1993). ... Traded by Reds to Colorado Rockies organization for P Marcus Moore (April 10, 1995).
STATISTICAL NOTES: Led South Atlantic League with .412 on-base percentage in 1994. ... Led South Atlantic League shortstops with 71 double plays in 1994. ... Led Carolina League with 84 runs and 97 bases on balls received in 1995. ... Led Carolina League shortstops with .966 fielding percentage, 201 putouts, 423 assists, 646 total chances and 73 double plays in 1995.

Year	Team (League)	Pos.	G	AB	R	H	2B	3B	HR	RBI	Avg.	BB	SO	SB	PO	A	E	Avg.
1993—Billings (Pioneer)	S-3-2-O	72	273	*63	91	14	4	4	46	.333	35	27	13	94	174	23	.921
1994—Char., S.C. (SAL)	SS-OF	133	467	82	140	21	4	5	59	.300	91	67	18	189	326	36	.935
1995—Win.-Salem (Car.)	SS	4	15	3	6	0	0	1	5	.400	4	0	0	6	17	0	1.000
—Salem (Carolina)■	SS	123	461	§81	123	16	6	4	32	.267	§93	55	14	§195	§406	22	§.965
—New Haven (East.)	SS	1	3	0	0	0	0	0	0	.000	0	0	0		3	0	1.000
1996—New Haven (East.)	SS-OF	127	444	50	96	12	2	0	28	.216	71	68	8	190	294	23	.955
1997—Nashville (Eastern)	SS-OF	98	360	65	107	22	4	1	38	.297	62	37	8	178	200	14	.964
—Colo. Springs (PCL)	SS	33	112	18	30	3	1	1	8	.268	16	21	1	57	87	5	.966
1998—Colo. Springs (PCL)	S-2-3-O	132	462	88	131	22	6	2	43	.284	72	67	7	219	352	25	.958

SHAVE, JON   IF   RANGERS

PERSONAL: Born November 4, 1967, in Waycross, Ga. ... 6-0/185. ... Bats right, throws right. ... Full name: Jonathan Taylor Shave.
HIGH SCHOOL: Fernandina Beach (Fla.).
COLLEGE: Mississippi State.
TRANSACTIONS/CAREER NOTES: Selected by California Angels organization in ninth round of free-agent draft (June 2, 1986); did not sign. ... Selected by Toronto Blue Jays organization in 56th round of free-agent draft (June 5, 1989); did not sign. ... Selected by Texas Rangers organization in fifth round of free-agent draft (June 4, 1990). ... On Texas disabled list (March 25-April 19, 1994). ... On disabled list (April 6-June 1 and June 3-July 22, 1995). ... Granted free agency (October 15, 1996). ... Signed by Minnesota Twins organization (November 6, 1996). ... Granted free agency (October 15, 1997). ... Re-signed by Twins (November 9, 1997). ... Claimed on waivers by Rangers (November 19, 1998).
STATISTICAL NOTES: Led Texas League second basemen with 233 putouts, 19 errors, 530 total chances and 63 double plays in 1992. ... Tied for American Association lead with 12 sacrifice hits in 1994.

Year	Team (League)	Pos.	G	AB	R	H	2B	3B	HR	RBI	Avg.	BB	SO	SB	PO	A	E	Avg.
1990—Butte (Pioneer)	SS	64	250	41	88	9	3	2	42	.352	25	27	21	112	159	22	.925
1991—Gastonia (S. Atl.)	SS-2B	55	213	29	62	11	0	2	24	.291	20	26	11	103	152	23	.917
—Charlotte (Fla. St.)	SS-2B	56	189	17	43	4	1	1	20	.228	18	31	7	93	120	15	.934
1992—Tulsa (Texas)	2B-SS	118	453	57	130	23	5	2	36	.287	37	59	6	†251	314	†21	.964
1993—Okla. City (A.A.)	2B-SS	100	399	58	105	17	3	4	41	.263	20	60	4	190	277	13	.973
—Texas (A.L.)	SS-2B	17	47	3	15	2	0	0	7	.319	0	8	1	22	37	3	.952
1994—Okla. City (A.A.)	2-S-3-O	95	332	29	73	15	2	1	31	.220	14	61	6	177	258	20	.956
1995—Okla. City (A.A.)	2B	32	83	10	17	1	0	0	5	.205	7	28	1	43	64	4	.964
1996—Okla. City (A.A.)	2B-3B-SS	116	414	54	110	20	2	7	41	.266	41	97	8	158	283	22	.952
1997—Salt Lake (PCL)	S-3-2-O-1	103	395	75	130	27	3	7	60	.329	39	62	6	191	192	15	.962
1998—Salt Lake (PCL)	2-3-O-S-1	90	317	63	107	20	1	4	41	.338	34	46	8	149	183	15	.957
—Minnesota (A.L.)	3-DH-1-S	19	40	7	10	3	0	1	5	.250	3	10	1	7	20	0	1.000
Major league totals (2 years)		36	87	10	25	5	0	1	12	.287	3	18	2	29	57	3	.966

SHAW, JEFF   P   DODGERS

PERSONAL: Born July 7, 1966, in Washington Court House, Ohio. ... 6-2/200. ... Throws right, bats right. ... Full name: Jeffrey Lee Shaw.
HIGH SCHOOL: Washington (Washington Court House, Ohio).
JUNIOR COLLEGE: Cuyahoga Community College-Western Campus (Ohio).
COLLEGE: Rio Grande (Ohio) College.
TRANSACTIONS/CAREER NOTES: Selected by Cleveland Indians organization in first round (first pick overall) of free-agent draft (January 14, 1986). ... Granted free agency (October 16, 1992). ... Signed by Omaha, Kansas City Royals organization (November 9, 1992). ... Traded by

S

Royals organization with C Tim Spehr to Montreal Expos organization for P Mark Gardner and P Doug Piatt (December 9, 1992). ... Granted free agency (February 17, 1995). ... Re-signed by Expos organization (April 9, 1995). ... Traded by Expos to Chicago White Sox for P Jose DeLeon (August 28, 1995). ... Granted free agency (December 21, 1995). ... Signed by Cincinnati Reds organization (January 2, 1996). ... Traded by Reds to Los Angeles Dodgers for IF Paul Konerko and P Dennis Reyes (July 4, 1998).

HONORS: Named N.L. Fireman of the Year by THE SPORTING NEWS (1997).

STATISTICAL NOTES: Led Eastern League with 14 hit batsmen in 1989. ... Tied for Pacific Coast League lead with 10 hit batsmen in 1992.

Year	Team (League)	W	L	Pct.	ERA	G	GS	CG	ShO	Sv.	IP	H	R	ER	BB	SO
1986—	Batavia (N.Y.-Penn)	8	4	.667	2.44	14	12	3	1	0	88²/₃	79	32	24	35	71
1987—	Waterloo (Midw.)	11	11	.500	3.52	28	*28	6	*4	0	184¹/₃	192	89	72	56	117
1988—	Williamsport (Eastern)	5	*19	.208	3.63	27	•27	6	1	0	163²/₃	•173	*94	66	75	61
1989—	Cant./Akr. (Eastern)	7	10	.412	3.62	30	22	6	3	0	154¹/₃	134	84	62	67	95
1990—	Colo. Springs (PCL)	10	3	.769	4.29	17	16	4	0	0	98²/₃	98	54	47	52	55
—Cleveland (A.L.)		3	4	.429	6.66	12	9	0	0	0	48²/₃	73	38	36	20	25
1991—	Colo. Springs (PCL)	6	3	.667	4.64	12	12	1	0	0	75²/₃	77	47	39	25	55
—Cleveland (A.L.)		0	5	.000	3.36	29	1	0	0	1	72¹/₃	72	34	27	27	31
1992—	Colo. Springs (PCL)	10	5	.667	4.76	25	24	1	0	0	155	174	88	82	45	84
—Cleveland (A.L.)		0	1	.000	8.22	2	1	0	0	0	7²/₃	7	7	7	4	3
1993—	Ottawa (Int'l)■	0	0	. . .	0.00	2	1	0	0	0	4	5	0	0	2	1
—Montreal (N.L.)		2	7	.222	4.14	55	8	0	0	0	95²/₃	91	47	44	32	50
1994—	Montreal (N.L.)	5	2	.714	3.88	46	0	0	0	1	67¹/₃	67	32	29	15	47
1995—	Montreal (N.L.)	1	6	.143	4.62	50	0	0	0	3	62¹/₃	58	35	32	26	45
—Chicago (A.L.)■		0	0	. . .	6.52	9	0	0	0	0	9²/₃	12	7	7	1	6
1996—	Cincinnati (N.L.)■	8	6	.571	2.49	78	0	0	0	4	104²/₃	99	34	29	29	69
1997—	Cincinnati (N.L.)	4	2	.667	2.38	78	0	0	0	*42	94²/₃	79	26	25	12	74
1998—	Cincinnati (N.L.)	2	4	.333	1.81	39	0	0	0	23	49²/₃	40	11	10	12	29
—Los Angeles (N.L.)■		1	4	.200	2.55	34	0	0	0	25	35¹/₃	35	11	10	7	26
A.L. totals (4 years)		3	10	.231	5.01	52	11	0	0	1	138¹/₃	164	86	77	52	65
N.L. totals (6 years)		23	31	.426	3.16	380	8	0	0	98	509²/₃	469	196	179	133	340
Major league totals (9 years)		26	41	.388	3.56	432	19	0	0	99	648	633	282	256	185	405

ALL-STAR GAME RECORD

Year	League	W	L	Pct.	ERA	GS	CG	ShO	Sv.	IP	H	R	ER	BB	SO
1998—	National	0	0	. . .	9.00	0	0	0	0	1	3	1	1	0	0

SHEETS, ANDY   IF   PADRES

PERSONAL: Born November 19, 1971, in Baton Rouge, La. ... 6-2/180. ... Bats right, throws right. ... Full name: Andrew Mark Sheets.

HIGH SCHOOL: St. Amant (La.).

COLLEGE: Tulane, then Louisiana State.

TRANSACTIONS/CAREER NOTES: Selected by Seattle Mariners organization in fourth round of free-agent draft (June 1, 1992). ... Selected by Tampa Bay Devil Rays in first round (24th pick overall) of expansion draft (November 18, 1997). ... Traded by Devil Rays with P Brian Boehringer to San Diego Padres for C John Flaherty (November 18, 1997).

STATISTICAL NOTES: Led Pacific Coast League shortstops with .973 fielding percentage in 1997.

Year	Team (League)	Pos.	G	AB	R	H	2B	3B	HR	RBI	Avg.	BB	SO	SB	PO	A	E	Avg.
1993—	Riverside (Calif.)	SS	52	176	23	34	9	1	1	12	.193	17	51	2	80	159	17	.934
—Appleton (Midwest)	SS-2B-OF	69	259	32	68	10	4	1	25	.263	20	59	7	98	194	11	.964
1994—	Riverside (Calif.)	SS	31	100	17	27	5	1	2	10	.270	16	22	6	39	95	14	.905
—Jacksonville (Sou.)	SS	70	232	26	51	12	0	0	17	.220	20	54	3	105	205	17	.948
—Calgary (PCL)	SS	26	93	22	32	8	1	2	16	.344	11	20	1	32	80	2	.982
1995—	Tacoma (PCL)	SS	132	437	57	128	29	9	2	47	.293	32	83	8	157	382	27	.952
1996—	Tacoma (PCL)	SS-2B-3B	62	232	44	83	16	5	5	33	.358	25	56	6	95	176	14	.951
—Seattle (A.L.)	3B-2B-SS	47	110	18	21	8	0	0	9	.191	10	41	2	40	77	5	.959
1997—	Tacoma (PCL)	SS-2B-3B	113	401	57	104	23	0	14	53	.259	46	97	7	174	314	13	.974
—Seattle (A.L.)	3B-SS-2B	32	89	18	22	3	0	4	9	.247	7	34	2	14	62	8	.905
1998—	San Diego (N.L.)■	S-3-2-1	88	194	31	47	5	3	7	29	.242	21	62	7	96	145	9	.964
American League totals (2 years)		79	199	36	43	11	0	4	18	.216	17	75	4	54	139	13	.937
National League totals (1 year)		88	194	31	47	5	3	7	29	.242	21	62	7	96	145	9	.964
Major league totals (3 years)		167	393	67	90	16	3	11	47	.229	38	137	11	150	284	22	.952

DIVISION SERIES RECORD

Year	Team (League)	Pos.	G	AB	R	H	2B	3B	HR	RBI	Avg.	BB	SO	SB	PO	A	E	Avg.
1997—	Seattle (A.L.)	3B	2	3	0	1	0	0	0	0	.333	0	2	0	0	0	0	. . .
1998—	San Diego (N.L.)	PR-2B	2	0	0	0	0	0	0	0	. . .	0	0	0	0	0	0	. . .
Division series totals (2 years)		4	3	0	1	0	0	0	0	.333	0	2	0	0	0	0	. . .

CHAMPIONSHIP SERIES RECORD

Year	Team (League)	Pos.	G	AB	R	H	2B	3B	HR	RBI	Avg.	BB	SO	SB	PO	A	E	Avg.
1998—	San Diego (N.L.)	SS-PH	3	3	0	0	0	0	0	0	.000	0	1	0	0	2	0	1.000

WORLD SERIES RECORD

Year	Team (League)	Pos.	G	AB	R	H	2B	3B	HR	RBI	Avg.	BB	SO	SB	PO	A	E	Avg.
1998—	San Diego (N.L.)	SS	2	2	0	0	0	0	0	0	.000	0	1	0	0	2	0	1.000

PERSONAL: Born November 18, 1968, in Tampa. ... 5-11/205. ... Bats right, throws right. ... Full name: Gary Antonian Sheffield. ... Nephew of Dwight Gooden, pitcher, Cleveland Indians.

HIGH SCHOOL: Hillsborough (Tampa).

TRANSACTIONS/CAREER NOTES: Selected by Milwaukee Brewers organization in first round (sixth pick overall) of free-agent draft (June 2, 1986). ... On Milwaukee disabled list (July 14-September 9, 1989). ... On suspended list (August 31-September 3, 1990). ... On disabled list (June 15-July 3 and July 25, 1991-remainder of season). ... Traded by Brewers with P Geoff Kellogg to San Diego Padres for P Ricky Bones, SS Jose Valentin and OF Matt Mieske (March 27, 1992). ... Traded by Padres with P Rich Rodriguez to Florida Marlins for P Trevor Hoffman, P Jose Martinez and P Andres Berumen (June 24, 1993). ... On Florida suspended list (July 9-12, 1993). ... On Florida disabled list (May 10-25 and May 28-June 12, 1994); included rehabilitation assignment to Portland (June 10-12). ... On disabled list (June 11-September 1, 1995; and May 14-29, 1997). ... Traded by Marlins with 3B Bobby Bonilla, C Charles Johnson, OF Jim Eisenreich and P Manuel Barrios to Los Angeles Dodgers for C Mike Piazza and 3B Todd Zeile (May 15, 1998). ... On suspended list (August 4-6, 1998).

RECORDS: Shares major league record for fewest double plays by outfielder (150 or more games)—0 (1996).

HONORS: Named Minor League co-Player of the Year by THE SPORTING NEWS (1988). ... Named Major League Player of the Year by THE SPORTING NEWS (1992). ... Named N.L. Comeback Player of the Year by THE SPORTING NEWS (1992). ... Named third baseman on THE SPORTING NEWS N.L. All-Star team (1992). ... Named third baseman on THE SPORTING NEWS N.L. Silver Slugger team (1992). ... Named outfielder on THE SPORTING NEWS N.L. All-Star team (1996). ... Named outfielder on THE SPORTING NEWS N.L. Silver Slugger team (1996).

STATISTICAL NOTES: Led Pioneer League shortstops with 34 double plays in 1986. ... Led California League shortstops with 77 double plays in 1987. ... Led N.L. with 323 total bases in 1992. ... Led N.L. with .465 on-base percentage in 1996. ... Career major league grand slams: 5.

MISCELLANEOUS: Holds Florida Marlins all-time records for most home runs (122) and most runs (365).

							BATTING							FIELDING		
Year	Team (League)	Pos.	G	AB	R	H	2B	3B	HR	RBI	Avg.	BB	SO	SB	PO	A	E	Avg.
1986—	Helena (Pioneer)	SS	57	222	53	81	12	2	15	*71	.365	20	14	14	97	149	24	.911
1987—	Stockton (California) ..	SS	129	469	84	130	23	3	17	*103	.277	81	49	25	235	345	39	.937
1988—	El Paso (Texas)..........	SS-3B-OF	77	296	70	93	19	3	19	65	.314	35	41	5	130	206	23	.936
	— Denver (A.A.)............	3B-SS	57	212	42	73	9	5	9	54	.344	21	22	8	54	97	8	.950
	— Milwaukee (A.L.).......	SS	24	80	12	19	1	0	4	12	.238	7	7	3	39	48	3	.967
1989—	Milwaukee (A.L.).......	SS-3B-DH	95	368	34	91	18	0	5	32	.247	27	33	10	100	238	16	.955
	— Denver (A.A.)............	SS	7	29	3	4	1	1	0	0	.138	2	0	0	2	6	0	1.000
1990—	Milwaukee (A.L.).......	3B	125	487	67	143	30	1	10	67	.294	44	41	25	98	254	25	.934
1991—	Milwaukee (A.L.).......	3B-DH	50	175	25	34	12	2	2	22	.194	19	15	5	29	65	8	.922
1992—	San Diego (N.L.)■..	3B	146	557	87	184	34	3	33	100	*.330	48	40	5	99	299	16	.961
1993—	San Diego (N.L.)	3B	68	258	34	76	12	2	10	36	.295	18	30	5	41	102	15	.905
	— Florida (N.L.)■..........	3B	72	236	33	69	8	3	10	37	.292	29	34	12	38	123	19	.894
1994—	Florida (N.L.)	OF	87	322	61	89	16	1	27	78	.276	51	50	12	154	7	5	.970
	— Portland (Eastern)	OF	2	7	1	2	1	0	0	0	.286	1	3	0	3	0	0	1.000
1995—	Florida (N.L.)	OF	63	213	46	69	8	0	16	46	.324	55	45	19	109	5	7	.942
1996—	Florida (N.L.)	OF	161	519	118	163	33	1	42	120	.314	142	66	16	238	8	6	.976
1997—	Florida (N.L.)	OF-DH	135	444	86	111	22	1	21	71	.250	121	79	11	226	14	5	.980
1998—	Florida (N.L.)	OF	40	136	21	37	11	1	6	28	.272	26	16	4	68	3	1	.986
	— Los Angeles (N.L.)■..	OF	90	301	52	95	16	1	16	57	.316	69	30	18	149	6	1	.994
American League totals (4 years)			294	1110	138	287	61	3	21	133	.259	97	96	43	266	605	52	.944
National League totals (7 years)			862	2986	538	893	160	13	181	573	.299	559	390	102	1122	567	75	.957
Major league totals (11 years)			1156	4096	676	1180	221	16	202	706	.288	656	486	145	1388	1172	127	.953

DIVISION SERIES RECORD

							BATTING							FIELDING		
Year	Team (League)	Pos.	G	AB	R	H	2B	3B	HR	RBI	Avg.	BB	SO	SB	PO	A	E	Avg.
1997—	Florida (N.L.)	OF	3	9	3	5	1	0	1	1	.556	5	0	1	6	0	0	1.000

CHAMPIONSHIP SERIES RECORD

							BATTING							FIELDING		
Year	Team (League)	Pos.	G	AB	R	H	2B	3B	HR	RBI	Avg.	BB	SO	SB	PO	A	E	Avg.
1997—	Florida (N.L.)	OF	6	17	6	4	0	0	1	1	.235	7	3	0	5	2	0	1.000

WORLD SERIES RECORD

NOTES: Member of World Series championship team (1997).

							BATTING							FIELDING		
Year	Team (League)	Pos.	G	AB	R	H	2B	3B	HR	RBI	Avg.	BB	SO	SB	PO	A	E	Avg.
1997—	Florida (N.L.)	OF	7	24	4	7	1	0	1	5	.292	8	5	0	16	0	1	.941

ALL-STAR GAME RECORD

						BATTING							FIELDING		
Year	League	Pos.	AB	R	H	2B	3B	HR	RBI	Avg.	BB	SO	SB	PO	A	E	Avg.
1992—	National	3B	2	0	0	0	0	0	0	.000	0	0	0	0	0	0	...
1993—	National	3B	3	1	2	0	0	1	2	.667	0	0	0	0	2	0	1.000
1996—	National	OF	1	0	0	0	0	0	0	.000	0	0	0	2	0	0	1.000
1998—	National	PH	1	0	0	0	0	0	0	.000	0	0	0	0	0	0	...
All-Star Game totals (4 years)			7	1	2	0	0	1	2	.286	0	0	0	2	2	0	1.000

SHELDON, SCOTT   IF   RANGERS

PERSONAL: Born November 20, 1968, in Hammond, Ind. ... 6-3/185. ... Bats right, throws right. ... Full name: Scott Patrick Sheldon.

HIGH SCHOOL: Clear Lake (Houston).

COLLEGE: Houston.

TRANSACTIONS/CAREER NOTES: Selected by Oakland Athletics organization in eighth round of free-agent draft (June 3, 1991). ... Granted free agency (October 17, 1997). ... Signed by Texas Rangers organization (November 20, 1997).

Year	Team (League)	Pos.	G	AB	R	H	2B	3B	HR	RBI	Avg.	BB	SO	SB	PO	A	E	Avg.
								BATTING								FIELDING		
1991—	S. Oregon (N'west)....	2-3-S-1	65	229	34	58	10	3	0	24	.253	23	44	9	122	124	14	.946
1992—	Madison (Midwest)....	SS-1B	74	275	41	76	16	0	6	24	.276	32	78	5	107	217	25	.928
1993—	Madison (Midwest)....	3B-SS	131	428	67	91	22	1	8	67	.213	49	121	8	90	275	26	.934
1994—	Huntsville (Sou.)	3-O-S-2-1	91	268	31	62	10	1	0	28	.231	28	69	7	69	185	11	.958
1995—	Huntsville (Sou.)	2-S-1-3	66	235	25	51	10	2	4	15	.217	23	60	5	203	188	12	.970
—	Edmonton (PCL)	3-S-1-2	45	128	21	33	7	1	4	12	.258	15	15	4	44	89	5	.964
1996—	Edmonton (PCL)	S-1-2-3-O	98	350	61	105	27	3	10	60	.300	43	83	5	259	230	14	.972
1997—	Edmonton (PCL)	SS-2B	118	422	89	133	39	6	19	77	.315	59	104	5	139	313	11	.976
—	Oakland (A.L.)	SS-2B-3B	13	24	2	6	0	0	1	2	.250	1	6	0	16	18	2	.944
1998—	Oklahoma (PCL)■........	SS-OF	131	493	74	126	31	4	29	96	.256	62	143	2	163	397	24	.959
—	Texas (A.L.)	3-S-DH-1	7	16	0	2	0	0	0	1	.125	1	6	0	8	11	1	.950
Major league totals (2 years)			20	40	2	8	0	0	1	3	.200	2	12	0	24	29	3	.946

SHIPLEY, CRAIG — IF — ANGELS

PERSONAL: Born January 7, 1963, in Sydney, Australia. ... 6-1/190. ... Bats right, throws right. ... Full name: Craig Barry Shipley.
HIGH SCHOOL: Epping (Sydney, Australia).
COLLEGE: Alabama.
TRANSACTIONS/CAREER NOTES: Signed as non-drafted free agent by Los Angeles Dodgers organization (May 28, 1984). ... On Albuquerque disabled list (May 5-June 6, 1986). ... Traded by Dodgers to New York Mets organization for C John Gibbons (April 1, 1988). ... On disabled list (beginning of season-August 20, 1990). ... Selected by San Diego Padres organization from Mets organization in Rule 5 minor league draft (December 2, 1990). ... On Las Vegas disabled list (April 11-May 2, 1991). ... On disabled list (May 6-23, 1993 and April 25-May 20, 1994). ... Traded by Padres with OF Phil Plantier, OF Derek Bell, P Pedro Martinez, P Doug Brocail and SS Ricky Gutierrez to Houston Astros for 3B Ken Caminiti, OF Steve Finley, SS Andujar Cedeno, 1B Robert Petagine, P Brian Williams and a player to be named later (December 28, 1994); Padres acquired P Sean Fesh to complete deal (May 1, 1995). ... Granted free agency (December 21, 1995). ... Signed by Padres (January 5, 1996). ... On San Diego disabled list (April 23-May 8 and May 17-July 31, 1996); included rehabilitation assignments to Las Vegas (July 1-4) and Arizona Padres (July 29-31). ... Granted free agency (December 7, 1996). ... Re-signed by Padres (December 23, 1996). ... On San Diego disabled list (March 18-May 13 and June 8-July 2, 1997); included rehabilitation assignment to Las Vegas (May 4-12). ... Granted free agency (November 6, 1997). ... Signed by St. Louis Cardinals organization (January 22, 1998). ... Traded by Cardinals to Anaheim Angels for IF Chip Hale (March 30, 1998). ... On disabled list (April 12-30 and August 20-September 4, 1998). ... Granted free agency (October 26, 1998). ... Re-signed by Angels organization (December 7, 1998).
STATISTICAL NOTES: Career major league grand slams: 1.

Year	Team (League)	Pos.	G	AB	R	H	2B	3B	HR	RBI	Avg.	BB	SO	SB	PO	A	E	Avg.
								BATTING								FIELDING		
1984—	Vero Beach (FSL)	SS	85	293	56	82	11	2	0	28	.280	52	44	18	137	216	17	.954
1985—	Albuquerque (PCL).....	SS	124	414	50	100	9	2	0	30	.242	22	43	24	202	367	21	.964
1986—	Albuquerque (PCL).....	SS	61	203	33	59	8	2	0	16	.291	11	23	6	99	173	18	.938
—	Los Angeles (N.L.) ...	SS-2B-3B	12	27	3	3	1	0	0	4	.111	2	5	0	16	18	3	.919
1987—	Albuquerque (PCL).....	SS	49	139	17	31	6	1	1	15	.223	13	19	6	70	101	9	.950
—	San Antonio (Tex.)	3B	33	127	14	30	5	3	2	9	.236	5	17	2	19	56	3	.962
—	Los Angeles (N.L.)	SS-3B	26	35	3	9	1	0	0	2	.257	0	6	0	15	28	3	.935
1988—	Jackson (Texas)■.......	SS	89	335	41	88	14	3	6	41	.263	24	40	6	141	266	16	.962
—	Tidewater (Int'l)	2B-SS-3B	40	151	12	41	5	0	1	13	.272	4	15	0	54	110	2	.988
1989—	Tidewater (Int'l)	SS-3B-2B	44	131	6	27	1	0	2	9	.206	7	22	0	48	110	6	.963
—	New York (N.L.)	SS-3B	4	7	3	1	0	0	0	0	.143	0	1	0	0	4	0	1.000
1990—	Tidewater (Int'l)	PH-PR	4	3	1	0	0	0	0	0	.000	0	1	0	...	...	...	...
1991—	Las Vegas (PCL)■.......	SS-2B	65	230	27	69	9	5	5	34	.300	10	32	2	83	177	6	.977
—	San Diego (N.L.)	SS-2B	37	91	6	25	3	0	1	6	.275	2	14	0	39	70	7	.940
1992—	San Diego (N.L.)	SS-2B-3B	52	105	7	26	6	0	0	7	.248	2	21	1	52	74	1	.992
1993—	San Diego (N.L.)	S-3-2-0	105	230	25	54	9	0	4	22	.235	10	31	12	84	121	7	.967
1994—	San Diego (N.L.)	3-S-2-0-1	81	240	32	80	14	4	4	30	.333	9	28	6	65	108	9	.951
1995—	Houston (N.L.)■..........	3-S-2-1	92	232	23	61	8	1	3	24	.263	8	28	6	43	116	3	.981
1996—	San Diego (N.L.)■.......	2-S-3-0	33	92	13	29	5	0	1	7	.315	2	15	7	35	64	1	.990
—	Ariz. Padres (Ariz.).....	SS	1	2	1	0	0	0	0	0	.000	0	1	0	0	3	0	1.000
1997—	San Diego (N.L.)	SS-3B	3	7	4	5	1	0	0	1	.714	0	0	0	2	0	0	1.000
—	Las Vegas (PCL)	S-2-3-0	6	19	0	6	3	0	0	1	.316	0	5	0	4	5	0	1.000
—	San Diego (N.L.)	S-2-1-3	63	139	22	38	9	0	5	19	.273	7	20	1	69	73	6	.959
1998—	Anaheim (A.L.)■........	3-2-1-S-O-DH	77	147	18	38	7	1	2	17	.259	5	22	0	72	76	3	.980
American League totals (1 year)			77	147	18	38	7	1	2	17	.259	5	22	0	72	76	3	.980
National League totals (10 years)			505	1198	137	326	56	5	18	121	.272	42	169	33	418	676	40	.965
Major league totals (11 years)			582	1345	155	364	63	6	20	138	.271	47	191	33	490	752	43	.967

SHOEMAKER, STEVE — P — ROCKIES

PERSONAL: Born February 3, 1973, in Phoenixville, Pa. ... 6-1/214. ... Throws right, bats left. ... Full name: Stephen Patrick Shoemaker.
HIGH SCHOOL: Phoenixville (Pa.).
COLLEGE: Alabama.
TRANSACTIONS/CAREER NOTES: Selected by New York Yankees organization in fourth round of free-agent draft (June 3, 1994). ... Traded by Yankees organization to Colorado Rockies organization (December 6, 1995), completing deal in which Rockies traded C Joe Girardi to Yankees for P Mike DeJean and a player to be named later (November 30, 1995).

Year	Team (League)	W	L	Pct.	ERA	G	GS	CG	ShO	Sv.	IP	H	R	ER	BB	SO
1994—	Oneonta (N.Y.-Penn)	3	5	.375	4.30	12	12	0	0	0	58 2/3	62	32	28	28	46
1995—	Greensboro (S. Atl.)	4	4	.500	3.11	17	17	0	0	0	81	62	33	28	52	82
—	Tampa (Fla. St.)	0	1	.000	1.08	3	2	0	0	0	16 2/3	9	5	2	13	12
1996—	Salem (Carolina)■	2	7	.222	4.69	25	13	0	0	1	86 1/3	63	49	45	63	105
1997—	Salem (Carolina)	3	3	.500	2.77	9	9	1	0	0	52	39	21	16	25	76
—	Nashville (Eastern)	6	4	.600	3.02	14	14	1	0	0	95 1/3	64	36	32	53	111
—	Colo. Springs (PCL)	1	1	.500	8.41	5	4	0	0	0	20 1/3	23	19	19	17	27
1998—	Colo. Springs (PCL)	2	7	.222	9.05	15	12	0	0	0	62 2/3	80	68	63	63	56
—	New Haven (East.)............	3	5	.375	4.89	15	15	0	0	0	84 2/3	69	60	46	63	85

SHOUSE, BRIAN   P   DIAMONDBACKS

PERSONAL: Born September 26, 1968, in Effingham, Ill. ... 5-11/180. ... Throws left, bats left. ... Full name: Brian Douglas Shouse.
HIGH SCHOOL: Effingham (Ill.).
COLLEGE: Bradley.
TRANSACTIONS/CAREER NOTES: Selected by Pittsburgh Pirates organization in 13th round of free-agent draft (June 4, 1990). ... Released by Pirates (May 16, 1996). ... Signed by Baltimore Orioles organization (May 22, 1996). ... Granted free agency (October 15, 1997). ... Signed by Boston Red Sox (October 28, 1997). ... Released by Red Sox (June 25, 1998). ... Signed by Arizona Diamondbacks (November 19, 1998).

Year — Team (League)	W	L	Pct.	ERA	G	GS	CG	ShO	Sv.	IP	H	R	ER	BB	SO
1990— Welland (N.Y.-Penn)	4	3	.571	5.22	17	1	0	0	2	39 2/3	50	27	23	7	39
1991— Augusta (S. Atl.)	2	3	.400	3.19	26	0	0	0	8	31	22	13	11	9	32
— Salem (Carolina)	2	1	.667	2.94	17	0	0	0	3	33 2/3	35	12	11	15	25
1992— Carolina (Southern)	5	6	.455	2.44	59	0	0	0	4	77 1/3	71	31	21	28	79
1993— Buffalo (A.A.)	1	0	1.000	3.83	48	0	0	0	2	51 2/3	54	24	22	17	25
— Pittsburgh (N.L.)	0	0	...	9.00	6	0	0	0	0	4	7	4	4	2	3
1994— Buffalo (A.A.)	3	4	.429	3.63	43	0	0	0	0	52	44	22	21	15	31
1995— Carolina (Southern)	7	6	.538	4.47	21	20	0	0	0	114 2/3	126	64	57	19	76
— Calgary (PCL)	4	4	.500	6.18	8	8	1	0	0	39 1/3	62	35	27	7	17
1996— Calgary (PCL)	1	0	1.000	10.66	12	1	0	0	0	12 2/3	22	15	15	4	12
— Rochester (Int'l)■	1	2	.333	4.50	32	0	0	0	2	50	53	27	25	16	45
1997— Rochester (Int'l)	6	2	.750	2.27	54	0	0	0	9	71 1/3	48	21	18	21	81
1998— Pawtucket (Int'l)■	2	0	1.000	2.90	22	1	0	0	6	31	21	11	10	7	25
— Boston (A.L.)	0	1	.000	5.63	7	0	0	0	0	8	9	5	5	4	5
A.L. totals (1 year)	0	1	.000	5.63	7	0	0	0	0	8	9	5	5	4	5
N.L. totals (1 year)	0	0	...	9.00	6	0	0	0	0	4	7	4	4	2	3
Major league totals (2 years)	0	1	.000	6.75	13	0	0	0	0	12	16	9	9	6	8

SHUEY, PAUL   P   INDIANS

PERSONAL: Born September 16, 1970, in Lima, Ohio. ... 6-3/215. ... Throws right, bats right. ... Full name: Paul Kenneth Shuey. ... Name pronounced SHOO-ee.
HIGH SCHOOL: Millbrook (Raleigh, N.C.).
COLLEGE: North Carolina.
TRANSACTIONS/CAREER NOTES: Selected by Cleveland Indians organization in first round (second pick overall) of free-agent draft (June 1, 1992). ... On Cleveland disabled list (June 27-July 21, 1994); included rehabilitation assignment to Charlotte (July 5-21). ... On Cleveland disabled list (May 4-22, 1995). ... On Buffalo disabled list (June 2-July 10, 1995). ... On Cleveland disabled list (April 25-May 18, June 19-July 4 and July 11-August 1, 1997); included rehabilitation assignments to Buffalo (May 5-10) and Akron (July 11-18). ... On Cleveland disabled list (April 11-June 15, 1998); included rehabilitation assignments to Akron (April 24) and Buffalo (May 23-June 14).
RECORDS: Shares major league single-inning record for most strikeouts—4 (May 14, 1994, ninth inning).

Year — Team (League)	W	L	Pct.	ERA	G	GS	CG	ShO	Sv.	IP	H	R	ER	BB	SO
1992— Columbus (S. Atl.)	5	5	.500	3.35	14	14	0	0	0	78	62	35	29	47	73
1993— Cant./Akr. (Eastern)	4	8	.333	7.30	27	7	0	0	0	61 2/3	76	50	50	36	41
— Kinston (Carolina)	1	0	1.000	4.84	15	0	0	0	0	22 1/3	29	12	12	8	27
1994— Kinston (Carolina)	1	0	1.000	3.75	13	0	0	0	8	12	10	5	5	3	16
— Cleveland (A.L.)	0	1	.000	8.49	14	0	0	0	5	11 2/3	14	11	11	12	16
— Charlotte (Int'l)	2	1	.667	1.93	20	0	0	0	10	23 1/3	15	9	5	10	25
1995— Cleveland (A.L.)	0	2	.000	4.26	7	0	0	0	0	6 1/3	5	4	3	5	5
— Buffalo (A.A.)	1	2	.333	2.63	25	0	0	0	11	27 1/3	21	9	8	7	27
1996— Buffalo (A.A.)	3	2	.600	0.81	19	0	0	0	4	33 1/3	14	4	3	9	57
— Cleveland (A.L.)	5	2	.714	2.85	42	0	0	0	4	53 2/3	45	19	17	26	44
1997— Cleveland (A.L.)	4	2	.667	6.20	40	0	0	0	2	45	52	31	31	28	46
— Buffalo (A.A.)	0	0	...	3.60	3	0	0	0	0	5	4	2	2	4	6
— Akron (Eastern)	0	0	...	3.38	3	0	0	0	0	8	10	3	3	0	9
1998— Cleveland (A.L.)	5	4	.556	2.98	43	0	0	0	2	51	44	19	17	25	58
— Akron (Eastern)	0	0	...	54.00	1	0	0	0	0	1/3	3	2	2	1	0
— Buffalo (Int'l)	0	0	...	2.51	11	0	0	0	2	14 1/3	11	4	4	6	22
Major league totals (5 years)	14	11	.560	4.24	146	0	0	0	13	167 2/3	160	84	79	96	169

DIVISION SERIES RECORD

Year — Team (League)	W	L	Pct.	ERA	G	GS	CG	ShO	Sv.	IP	H	R	ER	BB	SO
1996— Cleveland (A.L.)	0	0	...	9.00	3	0	0	0	0	2	5	2	2	2	2
1998— Cleveland (A.L.)	0	0	...	0.00	3	0	0	0	0	3	3	0	0	1	4
Div. series totals (2 years)	0	0	...	3.60	6	0	0	0	0	5	8	2	2	3	6

CHAMPIONSHIP SERIES RECORD

Year — Team (League)	W	L	Pct.	ERA	G	GS	CG	ShO	Sv.	IP	H	R	ER	BB	SO
1998— Cleveland (A.L.)	0	0	...	0.00	5	0	0	0	0	6 1/3	4	0	0	9	7

SHUMAKER, ANTHONY   P   PHILLIES

PERSONAL: Born May 14, 1973, in Tucson, Ariz. ... 6-5/223. ... Throws left, bats left. ... Full name: Anthony Warren Shumaker.
HIGH SCHOOL: Kokomo (Ind.).
COLLEGE: Cardinal Stritch (Wis.).
TRANSACTIONS/CAREER NOTES: Selected by Philadelphia Phillies organization in 23rd round of free-agent draft (June 1, 1995).

Year — Team (League)	W	L	Pct.	ERA	G	GS	CG	ShO	Sv.	IP	H	R	ER	BB	SO
1995— Martinsville (App.)	1	3	.250	4.50	6	4	0	0	0	28	31	16	14	8	26
— Batavia (N.Y.-Penn)	2	2	.500	1.62	9	4	1	1	0	39	38	10	7	4	31
1996— Piedmont (S. Atl.)	3	0	1.000	1.38	20	0	0	0	4	32 2/3	16	7	5	10	51
— Clearwater (Fla. St.)	5	3	.625	5.10	31	0	0	0	3	30	39	17	17	12	24
1997— Clearwater (Fla. St.)	5	4	.556	2.13	61	0	0	0	9	72	64	22	17	17	77
1998— Reading (Eastern)	7	10	.412	3.35	38	21	1	1	2	166 2/3	152	75	62	44	129

S

PERSONAL: Born August 16, 1966, in Paducah, Ky. ... 6-0/195. ... Bats both, throws right. ... Full name: Terrance Darnell Shumpert.
HIGH SCHOOL: Paducah (Ky.) Tilghman.
COLLEGE: Kentucky.
TRANSACTIONS/CAREER NOTES: Selected by Kansas City Royals organization in second round of free-agent draft (June 2, 1987). ... On disabled list (July 19-August 13, 1989). ... On Kansas City disabled list (June 3-September 10, 1990); included rehabilitation assignment to Omaha (August 7-25). ... On Kansas City disabled list (August 7-September 7, 1992). ... Traded by Royals to Boston Red Sox for a player to be named later (December 13, 1994). ... Granted free agency (October 6, 1995). ... Signed by Iowa, Chicago Cubs organization (March 12, 1996). ... On Chicago disabled list (August 19-September 3, 1996). ... Granted free agency (October 15, 1996). ... Signed by San Diego Padres (November 4, 1996). ... On San Diego disabled list (May 27-August 5, 1997). ... Released by Padres (August 5, 1997). ... Signed by Colorado Rockies organization (August 13, 1997). ... Granted free agency (October 15, 1998). ... Re-signed by Rockies organization (December 18, 1998).
STATISTICAL NOTES: Led American Association with 21 sacrifice hits in 1993. ... Career major league grand slams: 1.

Year Team (League)	Pos.	G	AB	R	H	2B	3B	HR	RBI	Avg.	BB	SO	SB	PO	A	E	Avg.
1987— Eugene (Northwest) ...	2B	48	186	38	54	16	1	4	22	.290	27	41	16	81	107	11	.945
1988— Appleton (Midwest) ...	2B-OF	114	422	64	102	*37	2	7	38	.242	56	90	36	235	266	20	.962
1989— Omaha (A.A.).............	2B	113	355	54	88	29	2	4	22	.248	25	63	23	218	295	*22	.959
1990— Omaha (A.A.).............	2B	39	153	24	39	6	4	2	12	.255	14	28	18	72	95	7	.960
— Kansas City (A.L.).........	2B-DH	32	91	7	25	6	1	0	8	.275	2	17	3	56	74	3	.977
1991— Kansas City (A.L.)	2B	144	369	45	80	16	4	5	34	.217	30	75	17	249	368	16	.975
1992— Kansas City (A.L.)	2B-DH-SS	36	94	6	14	5	1	1	11	.149	3	17	2	50	77	4	.969
— Omaha (A.A.).............	2B-SS	56	210	23	42	12	0	1	14	.200	13	33	3	113	154	9	.972
1993— Omaha (A.A.).............	2B	111	413	70	124	29	1	14	59	.300	41	62	*36	190	303	14	.972
— Kansas City (A.L.)	2B	8	10	0	1	0	0	0	0	.100	2	2	1	11	11	0	1.000
1994— Kansas City (A.L.)	2-3-DH-S	64	183	28	44	6	2	8	24	.240	13	39	18	70	129	6	.961
1995— Boston (A.L.)■.........	2-3-S-DH	21	47	6	11	3	0	0	3	.234	4	13	3	21	35	2	.966
— Pawtucket (Int'l)	3B-2B-OF	37	133	17	36	7	0	2	11	.271	14	27	10	29	69	11	.899
1996— Iowa (Am. Assoc.)■ ...	2-3-1-S	72	246	45	68	13	4	5	32	.276	24	44	13	119	165	7	.976
— Chicago (N.L.)	3B-2B-SS	27	31	5	7	1	0	2	6	.226	2	11	0	11	9	1	.952
1997— Las Vegas (PCL)■......	3B-2B-SS	32	109	18	31	8	1	1	16	.284	9	20	3	37	58	4	.960
— San Diego (N.L.)	2B-OF-3B	13	33	4	9	3	0	1	6	.273	3	4	0	23	17	2	.952
— New Haven (East.)■....	2B	5	17	2	4	0	0	1	1	.235	0	2	0	8	17	0	1.000
— Colo. Springs (PCL) ...	S-2-3-O	10	37	8	11	3	0	1	2	.297	2	7	0	8	20	5	.848
1998— Colo. Springs (PCL) ...	2-0-3-S	97	376	66	115	29	8	12	50	.306	35	59	11	141	133	4	.986
— Colorado (N.L.)	2B	23	26	3	6	1	0	1	2	.231	2	8	0	2	14	0	1.000
American League totals (6 years)		305	794	92	175	36	8	14	80	.220	54	163	44	457	694	33	.972
National League totals (3 years)		63	90	12	22	5	0	4	14	.244	7	23	0	36	40	3	.962
Major league totals (9 years)		368	884	104	197	41	8	18	94	.223	61	186	44	493	734	36	.971

SIDDALL, JOE   C   TIGERS

PERSONAL: Born October 25, 1967, in Windsor, Ont. ... 6-1/200. ... Bats left, throws right. ... Full name: Joseph Todd Siddall.
HIGH SCHOOL: Assumption (Windsor, Ont.).
COLLEGE: Central Michigan.
TRANSACTIONS/CAREER NOTES: Signed as non-drafted free agent by Montreal Expos organization (August 5, 1987). ... Granted free agency (October 16, 1995). ... Signed by Florida Marlins organization (November 30, 1995). ... On Charlotte disabled list (April 4-May 15, 1996). ... Granted free agency (September 30, 1996). ... Signed by Montreal Expos organization (October 29, 1996). ... Granted free agency (October 15, 1997). ... Signed by Detroit Tigers organization (December 2, 1997). ... Granted free agency (October 9, 1998). ... Re-signed by Tigers organization (November 24, 1998).
STATISTICAL NOTES: Led New York-Pennsylvania League catchers with seven double plays in 1988. ... Led Midwest League with 19 passed balls in 1989.

Year Team (League)	Pos.	G	AB	R	H	2B	3B	HR	RBI	Avg.	BB	SO	SB	PO	A	E	Avg.
1988— Jamestown (NYP)	C	53	178	18	38	5	3	1	16	.213	14	29	5	298	50	4	.989
1989— Rockford (Midwest) ...	C	98	313	36	74	15	2	4	38	.236	26	56	8	656	91	12	.984
1990— W.P. Beach (FSL).......	C	106	349	29	78	12	1	0	32	.223	20	55	6	644	*105	7	*.991
1991— Harrisburg (East.).......	C	76	235	28	54	6	1	1	23	.230	23	53	8	401	36	7	.984
1992— Harrisburg (East.).......	C	95	288	26	68	12	0	2	27	.236	29	55	4	199	28	1	.996
1993— Ottawa (Int'l)	C-0-1-3	48	136	14	29	6	0	1	16	.213	19	33	2	221	33	5	.981
— Montreal (N.L.)...........	C-OF-1B	19	20	0	2	1	0	0	1	.100	1	5	0	33	5	0	1.000
1994— Ottawa (Int'l)	C	38	110	9	19	2	1	3	13	.173	10	21	1	194	26	0	1.000
1995— Ottawa (Int'l)	C-3B	83	248	26	53	14	2	1	23	.214	23	42	3	348	57	5	.988
— Montreal (N.L.)...........	C	7	10	4	3	0	0	0	1	.300	3	3	0	14	1	2	.882
1996— Charlotte (Int'l)■.........	C-3B	65	189	22	53	13	1	3	20	.280	11	36	1	316	45	7	.981
— Florida (N.L.)	C	18	47	0	7	1	0	0	3	.149	2	8	0	78	8	2	.977
1997— Ottawa (Int'l)■.............	C	57	164	18	45	12	1	1	16	.274	21	42	1	278	34	1	.987
1998— Toledo (Int'l)■.............	C-1-0-3	43	129	16	31	5	0	4	16	.240	11	42	2	175	19	2	.990
— Detroit (A.L.)	C-OF	29	65	3	12	3	0	1	6	.185	7	25	0	142	16	1	.994
American League totals (1 year)		29	65	3	12	3	0	1	6	.185	7	25	0	142	16	1	.994
National League totals (3 years)		44	77	4	12	2	0	0	5	.156	6	16	0	125	14	4	.972
Major league totals (4 years)		73	142	7	24	5	0	1	11	.169	13	41	0	267	30	5	.983

SIERRA, RUBEN   OF   METS

PERSONAL: Born October 6, 1965, in Rio Piedras, Puerto Rico. ... 6-1/200. ... Bats both, throws right. ... Full name: Ruben Angel Garcia Sierra.
HIGH SCHOOL: Dr. Secario Rosario (Rio Piedras, Puerto Rico).

TRANSACTIONS/CAREER NOTES: Signed as non-drafted free agent by Texas Rangers organization (November 21, 1982). ... Traded by Rangers with P Jeff Russell, P Bobby Witt and cash to Oakland Athletics for OF Jose Canseco (August 31, 1992). ... Granted free agency (October 26, 1992). ... Re-signed by A's (December 21, 1992). ... On Oakland disabled list (July 7-22, 1995). ... Traded by A's with P Jason Beverlin to New York Yankees for OF/DH Danny Tartabull (July 28, 1995). ... Traded by Yankees with P Matt Drews to Detroit Tigers for 1B/DH Cecil Fielder (July 31, 1996). ... Traded by Tigers to Cincinnati Reds for OF Decomba Conner and P Ben Bailey (October 28, 1996). ... Released by Reds (May 9, 1997). ... Signed by Toronto Blue Jays organization (May 11, 1997). ... Released by Blue Jays (June 16, 1997). ... Signed by Chicago White Sox organization (January 9, 1998). ... Released by White Sox (May 29, 1998). ... Signed by New York Mets organization (June 20, 1998).

HONORS: Named A.L. Player of the Year by The Sporting News (1989). ... Named outfielder on The Sporting News A.L. All-Star team (1989). ... Named outfielder on The Sporting News A.L. Silver Slugger team (1989).

STATISTICAL NOTES: Switch-hit home runs in one game five times (September 13, 1986; August 27, 1988; June 8, 1989; June 7, 1994; and June 22, 1996). ... Led A.L. with 12 sacrifice flies in 1987. ... Led A.L. outfielders with six double plays in 1987. ... Led A.L. with 344 total bases and .543 slugging percentage in 1989. ... Career major league grand slams: 3.

MISCELLANEOUS: Holds Texas Rangers all-time record for most triples (43). ... Batted righthanded only (1983).

Year — Team (League)	Pos.	G	AB	R	H	2B	3B	HR	RBI	Avg.	BB	SO	SB	PO	A	E	Avg.
1983— GC Rangers (GCL)	OF	48	182	26	44	7	3	1	26	.242	16	38	3	67	6	4	.948
1984— Burlington (Midw.)	OF	•138	482	55	127	33	5	6	75	.263	49	97	13	239	18	*20	.928
1985— Tulsa (Texas)	OF	*137	*545	63	138	34	*8	13	74	.253	35	111	22	234	12	*15	.943
1986— Okla. City (A.A.)	OF	46	189	31	56	11	2	9	41	.296	15	27	8	114	4	2	.983
— Texas (A.L.)	OF-DH	113	382	50	101	13	10	16	55	.264	22	65	7	200	7	6	.972
1987— Texas (A.L.)	OF	158	*643	97	169	35	4	30	109	.263	39	114	16	272	•17	11	.963
1988— Texas (A.L.)	OF-DH	156	615	77	156	32	2	23	91	.254	44	91	18	310	11	7	.979
1989— Texas (A.L.)	OF	•162	634	101	194	35	*14	29	*119	.306	43	82	8	313	13	9	.973
1990— Texas (A.L.)	OF-DH	159	608	70	170	37	2	16	96	.280	49	86	9	283	7	10	.967
1991— Texas (A.L.)	OF	161	661	110	203	44	5	25	116	.307	56	91	16	305	15	7	.979
1992— Texas (A.L.)	OF-DH	124	500	66	139	30	6	14	70	.278	31	59	12	224	6	7	.970
— Oakland (A.L.)■	OF-DH	27	101	17	28	4	1	3	17	.277	14	9	2	59	0	0	1.000
1993— Oakland (A.L.)	OF-DH	158	630	77	147	23	5	22	101	.233	52	97	25	291	9	7	.977
1994— Oakland (A.L.)	OF-DH	110	426	71	114	21	1	23	92	.268	23	64	8	155	8	*9	.948
1995— Oakland (A.L.)	OF-DH	70	264	40	70	17	0	12	42	.265	24	42	4	89	1	4	.957
— New York (A.L.)■	DH-OF	56	215	33	56	15	0	7	44	.260	22	34	1	18	1	1	.950
1996— Campeche (Mex.)■...	...	1	1	1	0	0	0	0	0	.000	0	0	0	0	0	0	...
— New York (A.L.)■	DH-OF	96	360	39	93	17	1	11	52	.258	40	58	1	56	5	1	.984
— Detroit (A.L.)■	OF-DH	46	158	22	35	9	1	1	20	.222	20	25	3	52	1	5	.914
1997— Cincinnati (N.L.)■	OF	25	90	6	22	5	1	2	7	.244	6	21	0	34	3	0	1.000
— Syracuse (Int'l)■	OF	8	32	5	7	2	0	1	5	.219	2	6	0	10	2	1	.923
— Toronto (A.L.)	OF-DH	14	48	4	10	0	2	1	5	.208	3	13	0	13	0	1	.929
1998— Chicago (A.L.)■	OF-DH	27	74	7	16	4	1	4	11	.216	3	11	2	19	1	0	1.000
— Norfolk (Int'l)■	OF	28	108	16	28	5	0	3	19	.259	13	18	3	50	1	0	1.000
American League totals (13 years)		1637	6319	881	1701	336	55	237	1040	.269	485	941	132	2659	102	85	.970
National League totals (1 year)		25	90	6	22	5	1	2	7	.244	6	21	0	34	3	0	1.000
Major league totals (13 years)		1662	6409	887	1723	341	56	239	1047	.269	491	962	132	2693	105	85	.971

DIVISION SERIES RECORD

Year — Team (League)	Pos.	G	AB	R	H	2B	3B	HR	RBI	Avg.	BB	SO	SB	PO	A	E	Avg.
1995— New York (A.L.)	DH	5	23	2	4	2	0	2	5	.174	2	7	0	...	...	...	...

CHAMPIONSHIP SERIES RECORD

Year — Team (League)	Pos.	G	AB	R	H	2B	3B	HR	RBI	Avg.	BB	SO	SB	PO	A	E	Avg.
1992— Oakland (A.L.)	OF	6	24	4	8	2	1	1	7	.333	2	1	1	12	0	0	1.000

ALL-STAR GAME RECORD

Year — League	Pos.	AB	R	H	2B	3B	HR	RBI	Avg.	BB	SO	SB	PO	A	E	Avg.
1989— American	OF	3	1	2	0	0	0	1	.667	0	0	0	1	0	0	1.000
1991— American	OF	2	0	0	0	0	0	0	.000	0	2	0	0	0	0	...
1992— American	OF	2	2	1	0	0	1	2	.500	0	0	0	1	0	0	1.000
1994— American	OF	2	0	0	0	0	0	0	.500	0	0	0	1	0	0	1.000
All-Star Game totals (4 years)		9	3	4	0	0	1	3	.444	0	2	0	3	0	0	1.000

SIKORSKI, BRIAN   P   ASTROS

PERSONAL: Born July 27, 1973, in Detroit. ... 6-1/190. ... Throws right, bats right. ... Full name: Brian Patrick Sikorski.

HIGH SCHOOL: Roseville (Mich.).

COLLEGE: Western Michigan.

TRANSACTIONS/CAREER NOTES: Selected by Houston Astros organization in fourth round of free-agent draft (June 1, 1995).

STATISTICAL NOTES: Led Midwest League with 12 balks in 1996.

Year — Team (League)	W	L	Pct.	ERA	G	GS	CG	ShO	Sv.	IP	H	R	ER	BB	SO
1995— Auburn (N.Y.-Penn)	1	2	.333	2.10	23	0	0	0	12	34 1/3	22	8	8	14	35
— Quad City (Midwest)	1	0	1.000	0.00	2	0	0	0	0	3	1	1	0	0	4
1996— Quad City (Midwest)	11	8	.579	3.13	26	25	1	0	0	166 2/3	140	79	58	70	150
1997— Kissimmee (Florida State)	8	2	.800	3.06	11	11	0	0	0	67 2/3	64	29	23	16	46
— Jackson (Texas)	5	5	.500	4.63	17	17	0	0	0	93 1/3	91	55	48	31	74
1998— Jackson (Texas)	6	4	.600	4.07	15	15	0	0	0	97 1/3	83	50	44	44	80
— New Orleans (PCL)	5	8	.385	5.79	15	14	1	0	0	84	86	57	54	32	64

SILVA, JOSE — P — PIRATES

PERSONAL: Born December 19, 1973, in Tijuana, Mexico. ... 6-5/227. ... Throws right, bats right. ... Full name: Jose Leonel Silva.
HIGH SCHOOL: Hilltop (Chula Vista, Calif.).
TRANSACTIONS/CAREER NOTES: Selected by Toronto Blue Jays organization in sixth round of free-agent draft (June 3, 1991). ... On disabled list (April 6-August 17, 1995). ... On Knoxville disabled list (April 4-June 5, 1996). ... Traded by Blue Jays with IF Jose Pett, IF Brandon Cromer and three players to be named later to Pittsburgh Pirates for OF Orlando Merced, IF Carlos Garcia and P Dan Plesac (November 14, 1996); Pirates acquired P Mike Halperin, IF Abraham Nunez and C/OF Craig Wilson to complete deal (December 11, 1996). ... On Calgary disabled list (April 29-June 2, 1997). ... On Pittsburgh disabled list (June 17-September 10, 1998); included rehabilitation assignment to Nashville (August 25-September 6).

Year — Team (League)	W	L	Pct.	ERA	G	GS	CG	ShO	Sv.	IP	H	R	ER	BB	SO
1992— GC Blue Jays (GCL)............	6	4	.600	2.28	12	•12	0	0	0	59 1/3	42	23	15	18	78
1993— Hagerstown (S. Atl.)...........	12	5	.706	2.52	24	24	0	0	0	142 2/3	103	50	40	62	161
1994— Dunedin (Fla. St.)..............	0	2	.000	3.77	8	7	0	0	0	43	41	32	18	24	41
— Knoxville (Southern)	4	8	.333	4.14	16	16	1	1	0	91 1/3	89	47	42	31	71
1995— Knoxville (Southern)	0	0	. . .	9.00	3	0	0	0	0	2	3	2	2	6	2
1996— Knoxville (Southern)	2	3	.400	4.91	22	6	0	0	0	44	45	27	24	22	26
— Toronto (A.L.).................	0	0	. . .	13.50	2	0	0	0	0	2	5	3	3	0	0
1997— Calgary (PCL)■.................	5	1	.833	3.41	17	11	0	0	0	66	74	27	25	22	54
— Pittsburgh (N.L.).............	2	1	.667	5.94	11	4	0	0	0	36 1/3	52	26	24	16	30
1998— Pittsburgh (N.L.).............	6	7	.462	4.40	18	18	1	0	0	100 1/3	104	55	49	30	64
— Nashville (Pacific Coast)	0	0	. . .	4.82	3	3	0	0	0	9 1/3	10	5	5	4	6
A.L. totals (1 year)	0	0	. . .	13.50	2	0	0	0	0	2	5	3	3	0	0
N.L. totals (2 years)	8	8	.500	4.81	29	22	1	0	0	136 2/3	156	81	73	46	94
Major league totals (3 years)......	8	8	.500	4.93	31	22	1	0	0	138 2/3	161	84	76	46	94

SILVESTRI, DAVE — SS

PERSONAL: Born September 29, 1967, in St. Louis. ... 6-0/196. ... Bats right, throws right. ... Full name: David Joseph Silvestri.
HIGH SCHOOL: Parkway Central (Chesterfield, Mo.).
COLLEGE: Missouri.
TRANSACTIONS/CAREER NOTES: Selected by Houston Astros in second round of free-agent draft (June 1, 1988); pick received as compensation for New York Yankees signing Type B free-agent OF Jose Cruz. ... Traded by Astros organization with a player to be named later to Yankees organization for IF Orlando Miller (March 13, 1990); Yankees acquired P Daven Bond to complete deal (June 11, 1990). ... On New York disabled list (May 13-30, 1995). ... Traded by Yankees to Montreal Expos for OF Tyrone Horne (July 16, 1995). ... Claimed on waivers by Seattle Mariners (November 15, 1996). ... Claimed on waivers by Texas Rangers (March 27, 1997). ... Granted free agency (October 8, 1997). ... Signed by Tampa Bay Devil Rays organization (January 27, 1998). ... Granted free agency (October 15, 1998).
STATISTICAL NOTES: Led Florida State League shortstops with 221 putouts, 473 assists, 726 total chances and 93 double plays in 1989. ... Led Carolina League shortstops with 622 total chances and 96 double plays in 1990. ... Led Eastern League shortstops with 84 double plays in 1991.
MISCELLANEOUS: Member of 1988 U.S. Olympic baseball team.

							BATTING							FIELDING		
Year — Team (League)	Pos.	G	AB	R	H	2B	3B	HR	RBI	Avg.	BB	SO	SB	PO	A	E	Avg.
1989— Osceola (Fla. St.)........	SS-1B	129	437	67	111	20	1	2	50	.254	68	72	28	†238	†475	32	.957
1990— Prince Will. (Car.)■......	SS	131	465	74	120	30	7	5	56	.258	77	90	37	218	*382	22	*.965
— Alb./Colon. (East.)......	SS	2	7	0	2	0	0	0	2	.286	0	1	0	3	5	1	.889
1991— Alb./Colon. (East.)......	SS	*140	512	*97	134	31	8	19	83	.262	83	126	20	218	*362	•32	.948
1992— Columbus (Int'l).........	SS	118	420	83	117	25	5	13	73	.279	58	110	19	*195	265	11	*.977
— New York (A.L.).........	SS	7	13	3	4	0	2	0	1	.308	0	3	0	4	12	2	.889
1993— Columbus (Int'l).........	SS-3B-OF	120	428	76	115	26	4	20	65	.269	68	127	6	183	299	16	.968
— New York (A.L.).........	SS-3B	7	21	4	6	1	0	1	4	.286	5	3	0	9	20	3	.906
1994— Columbus (Int'l).........	2-S-3-0-1	114	394	72	99	19	2	25	83	.251	*83	129	18	174	235	19	.956
— New York (A.L.).........	2B-3B-SS	12	18	3	2	0	1	1	2	.111	4	9	0	4	16	1	.968
1995— New York (A.L.).........	2-DH-1-S	17	21	4	2	0	0	1	4	.095	4	9	0	28	13	0	1.000
— Montreal (N.L.)■........	S-3-1-2-0	39	72	12	19	6	0	2	7	.264	9	27	2	34	36	1	.986
1996— Montreal (N.L.).........	3-S-0-1-2	86	162	16	33	4	0	1	17	.204	34	41	2	23	92	10	.920
1997— Okla. City (A.A.)■......	3-1-2-S-0	124	467	54	112	25	3	17	68	.240	55	104	4	215	263	22	.956
— Texas (A.L.)	3B-SS	2	4	0	0	0	0	0	0	.000	0	1	0	0	2	0	1.000
1998— Durham (Int'l)■.........	2-3-S-1-0	129	480	74	133	31	2	8	56	.277	61	73	12	223	325	13	.977
— Tampa Bay (A.L.).........	3-DH-2-S	8	14	0	1	0	0	0	0	.071	0	2	0	5	9	1	.933
American League totals (6 years)		53	91	14	15	1	3	3	11	.165	13	27	0	60	72	7	.950
National League totals (2 years)		125	234	28	52	10	0	3	24	.222	43	68	4	57	128	11	.944
Major league totals (7 years)		178	325	42	67	11	3	6	35	.206	56	95	4	117	200	18	.946

SIMAS, BILL — P — WHITE SOX

PERSONAL: Born November 28, 1971, in Hanford, Calif. ... 6-3/220. ... Throws right, bats left. ... Full name: William Anthony Simas Jr.
HIGH SCHOOL: St. Joseph (Calif.).
COLLEGE: Fresno (Calif.) City College.
TRANSACTIONS/CAREER NOTES: Selected by California Angels organization in sixth round of free-agent draft (June 1, 1992). ... Traded by Angels with P Andrew Lorraine, P John Snyder and OF McKay Christensen to Chicago White Sox for P Jim Abbott and P Tim Fortugno (July 27, 1995). ... On disabled list (July 23-August 5 and August 17, 1997-remainder of season).

Year — Team (League)	W	L	Pct.	ERA	G	GS	CG	ShO	Sv.	IP	H	R	ER	BB	SO
1992— Boise (Northwest)	6	5	.545	3.95	14	12	0	0	1	70 2/3	82	44	31	29	39
1993— Cedar Rapids (Midw.)	5	8	.385	4.95	35	6	0	0	6	80	93	60	44	36	62
1994— Lake Elsinore (Calif.)	5	2	.714	2.11	37	0	0	0	13	47	44	17	11	10	34
— Midland (Texas)................	2	0	1.000	0.59	13	0	0	0	6	15 1/3	5	1	1	2	12

Year	Team (League)	W	L	Pct.	ERA	G	GS	CG	ShO	Sv.	IP	H	R	ER	BB	SO
1995—	Vancouver (PCL)	6	3	.667	3.55	30	0	0	0	6	38	44	19	15	14	44
—Nashville (A.A.)■		1	1	.500	3.86	7	0	0	0	0	11²/₃	12	5	5	3	12
—Chicago (A.L.)		1	1	.500	2.57	14	0	0	0	0	14	15	5	4	10	16
1996—Chicago (A.L.)		2	8	.200	4.58	64	0	0	0	2	72²/₃	75	39	37	39	65
1997—Chicago (A.L.)		3	1	.750	4.14	40	0	0	0	1	41¹/₃	46	23	19	24	38
1998—Calgary (PCL)		1	0	1.000	0.00	5	0	0	0	1	9	3	1	0	2	11
—Chicago (A.L.)		4	3	.571	3.57	60	0	0	0	18	70²/₃	54	29	28	22	56
Major league totals (4 years)		10	13	.435	3.99	178	0	0	0	21	198²/₃	190	96	88	95	175

SIMMONS, BRIAN — OF — WHITE SOX

PERSONAL: Born September 4, 1973, in Lebanon, Pa. ... 6-2/190. ... Bats both, throws right. ... Full name: Brian Lee Simmons.
HIGH SCHOOL: Peters Township (McMurray, Pa.).
COLLEGE: Michigan.
TRANSACTIONS/CAREER NOTES: Selected by Baltimore Orioles organization in 35th round of free-agent draft (June 1, 1992); did not sign. ... Selected by Chicago White Sox organization in second round of free-agent draft (June 1, 1995). ... On South Bend disabled list (April 5-17, 1996). ... On Calgary disabled list (June 22-August 10, 1998); included rehabilitation assignment to Arizona White Sox (August 1-8).
STATISTICAL NOTES: Led Southern League outfielders with 334 total chances in 1997. ... Switch-hit home runs in one game (September 26, 1998).

Year	Team (League)	Pos.	G	AB	R	H	2B	3B	HR	RBI	Avg.	BB	SO	SB	PO	A	E	Avg.
1995—Sarasota (Gulf Coast)		OF	5	17	5	3	1	0	1	5	.176	6	1	0	13	1	0	1.000
—Hickory (S. Atl.)		OF	41	163	13	31	6	1	2	11	.190	19	44	4	77	2	1	.988
1996—South Bend (Mid.)		OF	92	356	73	106	29	6	17	58	.298	48	69	14	204	10	7	.968
—Prince Will. (Car.)		OF	33	131	17	26	4	3	4	14	.198	9	39	2	70	2	2	.973
1997—Birmingham (Sou.)		OF	138	546	108	143	28	*12	15	72	.262	*88	124	15	*322	7	5	.985
1998—Calgary (PCL)		OF	94	355	72	103	21	4	13	51	.290	41	82	10	197	6	7	.967
—Ariz. White Sox (Ariz.)		OF	5	12	1	2	0	0	0	0	.167	1	1	0	3	0	0	1.000
—Chicago (A.L.)		OF	5	19	4	7	0	0	2	6	.368	0	2	0	13	0	0	1.000
Major league totals (1 year)			5	19	4	7	0	0	2	6	.368	0	2	0	13	0	0	1.000

SIMMS, MIKE — OF — RANGERS

PERSONAL: Born January 12, 1967, in Whittier, Calif. ... 6-4/230. ... Bats right, throws right. ... Full name: Michael Howard Simms.
HIGH SCHOOL: Esperanza (Calif.).
TRANSACTIONS/CAREER NOTES: Selected by Houston Astros organization in sixth round of free-agent draft (June 3, 1985). ... On disabled list (May 11-28, 1989). ... On Tucson disabled list (July 31-August 16, 1992). ... Granted free agency (March 30, 1993). ... Signed by San Diego Padres organization (April 7, 1993). ... Granted free agency (October 15, 1993). ... Signed by Pittsburgh Pirates (December 15, 1993). ... Released by Buffalo, Pirates organization (April 28, 1994). ... Signed by Astros organization (May 2, 1994). ... Granted free agency (October 15, 1994). ... Re-signed by Tucson (November 18, 1994). ... Granted free agency (October 15, 1996). ... Signed by Texas Rangers organization (December 19, 1996). ... Granted free agency (October 27, 1997). ... Re-signed by Rangers organization (December 17, 1997).
STATISTICAL NOTES: Led South Atlantic League with 264 total bases in 1987. ... Led South Atlantic League first basemen with 1,089 putouts, 19 errors and 1,158 total chances in 1987. ... Led Pacific Coast League first basemen with 19 errors in 1990. ... Career major league grand slams: 1.

Year	Team (League)	Pos.	G	AB	R	H	2B	3B	HR	RBI	Avg.	BB	SO	SB	PO	A	E	Avg.
1985—GC Astros (GCL)		1B	21	70	10	19	2	1	3	18	.271	6	26	0	186	7	5	.975
1986—GC Astros (GCL)		1B	54	181	33	47	14	1	4	37	.260	22	48	2	433	28	7	.985
1987—Asheville (S. Atl.)		1B-3B	133	469	93	128	19	0	*39	100	.273	73	*167	7	†1089	52	†19	.984
1988—Osceola (Fla. St.)		1B	123	428	63	104	19	1	16	73	.243	76	130	9	1143	41	22	.982
1989—Columbus (Southern)		1B	109	378	64	97	21	3	20	81	.257	66	110	12	938	44	10	.990
1990—Tucson (PCL)		1B-3B-OF	124	421	75	115	34	5	13	72	.273	74	*135	3	1013	75	†19	.983
—Houston (N.L.)		1B	12	13	3	4	1	0	1	2	.308	0	4	0	20	1	0	1.000
1991—Tucson (PCL)		OF-1B	85	297	53	73	20	2	15	59	.246	36	94	2	325	25	8	.978
—Houston (N.L.)		OF	49	123	18	25	5	0	3	16	.203	18	38	1	44	4	6	.889
1992—Tucson (PCL)		OF-1B	116	404	73	114	22	6	11	75	.282	61	107	7	476	29	11	.979
—Houston (N.L.)		OF-1B	15	24	1	6	1	0	1	3	.250	2	9	0	10	2	0	1.000
1993—Las Vegas (PCL)■		1-O-3-P	129	414	74	111	25	2	24	80	.268	67	114	1	774	46	13	.984
1994—Buffalo (A.A.)■		OF	18	55	10	13	5	0	4	8	.236	4	13	0	26	0	0	1.000
—Tucson (PCL)■		1B-OF-3B	100	373	76	107	34	6	20	85	.287	51	79	9	555	32	9	.985
—Houston (N.L.)		OF	6	12	1	1	1	0	0	0	.083	0	5	1	6	0	1	.857
1995—Houston (N.L.)		1B-OF	50	121	14	31	4	0	9	24	.256	13	28	1	221	17	1	.996
—Tucson (PCL)		1B-OF	85	319	56	94	26	8	13	66	.295	35	65	10	424	30	8	.983
1996—Tucson (PCL)		1B	17	64	11	19	3	0	7	19	.297	9	17	0	138	9	5	.967
—Houston (N.L.)		OF-1B	49	68	6	12	2	1	1	8	.176	4	16	1	24	1	0	1.000
1997—Okla. City (A.A.)■		OF	10	39	7	15	4	0	3	8	.385	6	8	0	17	1	0	1.000
—Texas (A.L.)		DH-OF-1B	59	111	13	28	8	0	5	22	.252	8	27	0	36	1	2	.949
1998—Texas (A.L.)		OF-DH-1B	86	186	36	55	11	0	16	46	.296	24	47	0	118	8	2	.984
American League totals (2 years)			145	297	49	83	19	0	21	68	.279	32	74	0	154	9	4	.976
National League totals (6 years)			181	361	43	79	14	1	15	53	.219	37	100	4	325	25	8	.978
Major league totals (8 years)			326	658	92	162	33	1	36	121	.246	69	174	4	479	34	12	.977

DIVISION SERIES RECORD

Year	Team (League)	Pos.	G	AB	R	H	2B	3B	HR	RBI	Avg.	BB	SO	SB	PO	A	E	Avg.
1998—Texas (A.L.)		DH	2	5	0	1	0	0	0	0	.200	0	2	0	...	...	...	...

RECORD AS PITCHER

Year	Team (League)	W	L	Pct.	ERA	G	GS	CG	ShO	Sv.	IP	H	R	ER	BB	SO
1993—Las Vegas (PCL)		0	0	...	0.00	1	0	0	0	0	²/₃	1	0	0	0	0

PERSONAL: Born May 26, 1975, in Willemstad, Curacao. ... 6-0/180. ... Bats left, throws left. ... Full name: Randall Carlito Simon.
HIGH SCHOOL: Juan Pablo Duarte Tech (Willemstad, Curacao).
TRANSACTIONS/CAREER NOTES: Signed as non-drafted free agent by Atlanta Braves organization (July 17, 1992).
STATISTICAL NOTES: Led International League in grounding into double plays with 18 in 1997 and 22 in 1998.

										BATTING					FIELDING		
Year	Team (League)	Pos.	G	AB	R	H	2B	3B	HR	RBI	Avg.	BB	SO	SB	PO	A	E	Avg.
1993—	Danville (Appal.).........	1B	61	232	28	59	17	1	3	31	.254	10	34	1	463	37	10	.980
1994—	Macon (S. Atl.)...........	1B	106	358	48	105	23	1	10	54	.293	6	56	7	582	49	9	.986
1995—	Durham (Carolina)......	1B	122	420	56	111	18	1	18	79	.264	36	63	6	864	51	10	.989
1996—	Greenville (Southern).	1B-OF	134	498	74	139	26	2	18	77	.279	37	61	4	723	55	16	.980
1997—	Richmond (Int'l).........	1B	133	519	62	160	*45	1	14	*102	.308	17	76	1	*1063	72	•14	.988
—	Atlanta (N.L.).............	1B	13	14	2	6	1	0	0	1	.429	1	2	0	16	2	0	1.000
1998—	Richmond (Int'l).........	1B	126	484	52	124	20	1	13	70	.256	24	62	4	981	51	*11	.989
—	Atlanta (N.L.).............	1B	7	16	2	3	0	0	0	4	.188	0	1	0	36	1	0	1.000
Major league totals (2 years)			20	30	4	9	1	0	0	5	.300	1	3	0	52	3	0	1.000

S

PERSONAL: Born August 2, 1971, in Victoria, B.C. ... 6-2/190. ... Throws left, bats left. ... Full name: Steven Scott Sinclair.
HIGH SCHOOL: Oak Bay (Victoria, B.C.).
COLLEGE: Kwantlen (Vancouver, B.C.).
TRANSACTIONS/CAREER NOTES: Selected by Toronto Blue Jays organization in 28th round of free-agent draft (June 3, 1991).

Year	Team (League)	W	L	Pct.	ERA	G	GS	CG	ShO	Sv.	IP	H	R	ER	BB	SO
1991—	Medicine Hat (Pioneer)	0	1	.000	6.75	12	0	0	0	0	14 2/3	17	15	11	11	14
1992—	GC Blue Jays (GCL)...........	1	2	.333	2.74	5	4	0	0	0	23	23	10	7	5	18
—	Medicine Hat (Pioneer)	2	3	.400	4.60	9	7	0	0	0	43	54	25	22	12	28
1993—	Medicine Hat (Pioneer)	5	2	.714	3.33	15	12	0	0	0	78 1/3	87	41	29	16	45
1994—	Hagerstown (S. Atl.)..........	9	2	.818	3.77	38	1	0	0	3	105	127	53	44	25	75
1995—	Dunedin (Fla. St.).............	5	3	.625	2.59	46	0	0	0	2	73	69	26	21	17	52
1996—	Dunedin (Fla. St.).............	0	1	.000	3.38	3	0	0	0	0	2 2/3	4	2	1	0	1
1997—	Dunedin (Fla. St.).............	2	5	.286	2.90	43	0	0	0	3	68 1/3	63	36	22	26	66
—	Syracuse (Int'l).................	0	0	. . .	6.00	6	0	0	0	0	9	11	6	6	3	9
1998—	Syracuse (Int'l).................	3	1	.750	2.17	43	1	0	0	3	49 2/3	37	15	12	23	45
—	Toronto (A.L.)...................	0	2	.000	3.60	24	0	0	0	0	15	13	7	6	5	8
Major league totals (1 year)........		0	2	.000	3.60	24	0	0	0	0	15	13	7	6	5	8

PERSONAL: Born August 15, 1972, in Mesa, Ariz. ... 6-2/195. ... Bats left, throws left. ... Full name: Christopher Verdell Singleton.
HIGH SCHOOL: Pinole (Calif.) Valley.
COLLEGE: Nevada.
TRANSACTIONS/CAREER NOTES: Selected by San Francisco Giants organization in second round of free-agent draft (June 3, 1993). ... Traded by Giants with P Alberto Castillo to New York Yankees for 3B Charlie Hayes and cash (November 11, 1997). ... Traded by Yankees to Chicago White Sox for a player to be named later (December 8, 1998).
STATISTICAL NOTES: Led Texas League with nine sacrifice flies in 1997. ... Led Texas League outfielders with 271 total chances and tied for league lead with four double plays in 1997. ... Tied for Texas League lead with four intentional bases on balls in 1997.

										BATTING					FIELDING		
Year	Team (League)	Pos.	G	AB	R	H	2B	3B	HR	RBI	Avg.	BB	SO	SB	PO	A	E	Avg.
1993—	Everett (N'west).........	OF	58	219	39	58	14	4	3	18	.265	18	46	14	106	6	3	.974
1994—	San Jose (Calif.)........	OF	113	425	51	106	17	5	2	49	.249	27	62	19	248	10	13	.952
1995—	San Jose (Calif.)........	OF	94	405	55	112	13	5	2	31	.277	17	49	33	142	6	7	.955
1996—	Shreveport (Texas).....	OF	129	500	68	149	31	9	5	72	.298	24	58	27	262	10	4	.986
—	Phoenix (PCL)...........	OF	9	32	3	4	0	0	0	0	.125	1	2	0	18	1	0	1.000
1997—	Shreveport (Texas).....	OF	126	464	85	147	26	10	9	61	.317	22	50	27	*253	11	7	.974
1998—	Columbus (Int'l)■......	OF	121	413	55	105	17	10	6	45	.254	27	78	9	251	10	7	.974

PERSONAL: Born May 13, 1971, in Chicago. ... 6-1/200. ... Throws left, bats left. ... Full name: Michael Robert Sirotka.
HIGH SCHOOL: Westfield (Houston).
COLLEGE: Louisiana State.
TRANSACTIONS/CAREER NOTES: Selected by Chicago White Sox organization in 15th round of free-agent draft (June 3, 1993). ... On Hickory disabled list (July 1-28, 1993). ... On South Bend temporarily inactive list (August 27-October 4, 1993).

Year	Team (League)	W	L	Pct.	ERA	G	GS	CG	ShO	Sv.	IP	H	R	ER	BB	SO
1993—	GC White Sox (GCL)	0	0	. . .	0.00	3	0	0	0	0	5	4	1	0	2	8
—	South Bend (Mid.)............	0	1	.000	6.10	7	1	0	0	0	10 1/3	12	8	7	6	12
1994—	South Bend (Mid.)............	12	9	.571	3.07	27	27	8	2	0	196 2/3	183	99	67	56	173
1995—	Birmingham (Southern)	7	6	.538	3.20	16	16	1	0	0	101 1/3	95	42	36	22	79
—	Chicago (A.L.)	1	2	.333	4.19	6	6	0	0	0	34 1/3	39	16	16	17	19
—	Nashville (A.A.)	1	5	.167	2.83	8	8	0	0	0	54	51	21	17	13	34
1996—	Nashville (A.A.)	7	5	.583	3.60	15	15	1	1	0	90	90	44	36	24	58
—	Chicago (A.L.)	1	2	.333	7.18	15	4	0	0	0	26 1/3	34	27	21	12	11
1997—	Nashville (A.A.)	7	5	.583	3.28	19	19	1	0	0	112 1/3	115	49	41	22	92
—	Chicago (A.L.)	3	0	1.000	2.25	7	4	0	0	0	32	36	9	8	5	24
1998—	Chicago (A.L.)	14	15	.483	5.06	33	33	5	0	0	211 2/3	255	137	119	47	128
Major league totals (4 years)......		19	19	.500	4.85	61	47	5	0	0	304 1/3	364	189	164	81	182

PERSONAL: Born June 7, 1966, in Jamaica, N.Y. ... 6-3/220. ... Throws right, bats right.
HIGH SCHOOL: John Bowne (Flushing, N.Y.).
TRANSACTIONS/CAREER NOTES: Signed as non-drafted free agent by New York Mets organization (July 10, 1984). ... Selected by Chicago Cubs organization from Mets organization in Rule 5 minor league draft (December 9, 1986). ... Traded by Cubs to Cleveland Indians for SS Jose Hernandez (June 1, 1993). ... Traded by Indians to Philadelphia Phillies for OF Ruben Amaro (November 2, 1993). ... Traded by Phillies with P Larry Wimberly and OF Rick Holifield to Boston Red Sox for P Ken Ryan, OF Lee Tinsley and OF Glenn Murray (January 29, 1996). ... Traded by Red Sox to Seattle Mariners for C Jason Varitek and P Derek Lowe (July 31, 1997). ... Granted free agency (October 23, 1998). ... Signed by Baltimore Orioles (January 15, 1999).
STATISTICAL NOTES: Led Carolina League with 19 wild pitches in 1988.

Year Team (League)	W	L	Pct.	ERA	G	GS	CG	ShO	Sv.	IP	H	R	ER	BB	SO
1984— Kingsport (Appalachian).....	0	0	...	0.00	1	0	0	0	0	$1/3$	0	1	0	1	0
— Little Falls (NYP)	0	0	...	11.00	4	1	0	0	0	9	8	11	11	16	10
1985— Kingsport (Appalachian).....	3	2	.600	3.78	11	9	1	0	0	$52 1/3$	47	32	22	31	29
1986— Little Falls (NYP)	3	1	.750	1.65	25	0	0	0	1	$43 2/3$	24	17	8	36	41
1987— Win.-Salem (Car.)■........	1	2	.333	6.26	9	4	0	0	0	$27 1/3$	26	25	19	26	27
— Peoria (Midwest)	10	4	.714	2.60	16	16	3	1	0	$103 2/3$	97	44	30	42	81
1988— Win.-Salem (Car.)..............	6	6	.500	4.96	25	19	2	1	1	$119 2/3$	122	75	66	90	78
1989— Peoria (Midwest)	5	3	.625	1.78	49	0	0	0	22	$55 2/3$	31	16	11	33	52
1990— Charlotte (Southern)	3	1	.750	2.15	43	0	0	0	12	$50 1/3$	50	20	12	32	37
— Iowa (Am. Assoc.)..............	3	2	.600	2.00	20	0	0	0	1	27	16	10	6	18	21
1991— Chicago (N.L.)..............	2	1	.667	3.45	52	0	0	0	1	$62 2/3$	53	29	24	30	34
— Iowa (Am. Assoc.)..............	1	0	1.000	4.05	12	0	0	0	1	$13 1/3$	10	8	6	6	9
1992— Chicago (N.L.)..............	0	3	.000	6.50	30	0	0	0	1	36	52	27	26	21	27
— Iowa (Am. Assoc.)..............	1	3	.250	2.59	36	1	0	0	7	$41 2/3$	36	13	12	16	47
1993— Iowa (Am. Assoc.)..............	1	0	1.000	1.50	10	0	0	0	7	12	7	2	2	8	10
— Chicago (N.L.)..............	1	0	1.000	3.38	10	0	0	0	0	$10 2/3$	7	5	4	4	4
— Cleveland (A.L.)■..............	3	1	.750	4.28	20	0	0	0	0	$27 1/3$	28	14	13	16	18
— Charlotte (Int'l)..............	3	2	.600	3.56	23	0	0	0	1	$30 1/3$	25	14	12	11	25
1994— Philadelphia (N.L.)■	5	1	.833	2.86	52	0	0	0	0	$72 1/3$	75	32	23	28	58
1995— Philadelphia (N.L.)..............	5	6	.455	2.89	61	0	0	0	32	$65 1/3$	64	26	21	35	63
1996— Boston (A.L.)■..............	5	5	.500	3.02	75	0	0	0	31	$83 1/3$	68	31	28	55	88
1997— Boston (A.L.)..............	0	5	.000	5.79	49	0	0	0	17	$46 2/3$	58	32	30	34	36
— Seattle (A.L.)■..............	0	4	.000	4.13	27	0	0	0	10	$28 1/3$	26	13	13	15	28
1998— Seattle (A.L.)..............	2	5	.286	5.32	57	0	0	0	3	$67 2/3$	72	40	40	44	51
A.L. totals (4 years)	10	20	.333	4.41	228	0	0	0	61	$253 1/3$	252	130	124	164	221
N.L. totals (5 years)	13	11	.542	3.57	205	0	0	0	34	247	251	119	98	118	186
Major league totals (8 years)......	23	31	.426	3.99	433	0	0	0	95	$500 1/3$	503	249	222	282	407

DIVISION SERIES RECORD

Year Team (League)	W	L	Pct.	ERA	G	GS	CG	ShO	Sv.	IP	H	R	ER	BB	SO
1997— Seattle (A.L.)	0	0	...	4.50	2	0	0	0	0	2	3	1	1	1	0

ALL-STAR GAME RECORD

Year League	W	L	Pct.	ERA	GS	CG	ShO	Sv.	IP	H	R	ER	BB	SO
1995— National	1	0	1.000	0.00	0	0	0	0	1	1	0	0	0	2

PERSONAL: Born November 23, 1971, in Oxnard, Calif. ... 6-5/214. ... Throws right, bats right. ... Full name: Aaron James Small.
HIGH SCHOOL: South Hills (Covina, Calif.).
TRANSACTIONS/CAREER NOTES: Selected by Toronto Blue Jays organization in 22nd round of free-agent draft (June 5, 1989). ... Traded by Blue Jays to Florida Marlins for a player to be named later (April 26, 1995); Blue Jays acquired P Ernie Delgado to complete deal (September 19, 1995). ... On Charlotte disabled list (May 3-June 14, 1995). ... Claimed on waivers by Seattle Mariners (January 23, 1996). ... Claimed on waivers by Oakland Athletics (January 29, 1996). ... Claimed on waivers by Arizona Diamondbacks (June 26, 1998).
STATISTICAL NOTES: Pitched 6-0 no-hit victory for Edmonton against Vancouver (August 8, 1996).

Year Team (League)	W	L	Pct.	ERA	G	GS	CG	ShO	Sv.	IP	H	R	ER	BB	SO
1989— Medicine Hat (Pioneer)	1	7	.125	5.86	15	14	0	0	0	$70 2/3$	80	55	46	31	40
1990— Myrtle Beach (SAL)	9	9	.500	2.80	27	27	1	0	0	$147 2/3$	150	72	46	56	96
1991— Dunedin (Fla. St.)	8	7	.533	2.73	24	23	1	0	0	$148 1/3$	129	51	45	42	92
1992— Knoxville (Southern)	5	12	.294	5.27	27	24	2	1	0	135	152	94	79	61	79
1993— Knoxville (Southern)	4	4	.500	3.39	48	9	0	0	16	93	99	44	35	40	44
1994— Knoxville (Southern)	5	5	.500	2.99	29	11	1	1	5	$96 1/3$	92	37	32	38	75
— Syracuse (Int'l)..............	3	2	.600	2.22	13	0	0	0	0	$24 1/3$	19	8	6	9	15
— Toronto (A.L.).................	0	0	...	9.00	1	0	0	0	0	2	5	2	2	2	0
1995— Syracuse (Int'l)..............	0	0	...	5.40	1	0	0	0	0	$1 2/3$	3	1	1	1	2
— Charlotte (Int'l)■..............	2	1	.667	2.88	33	0	0	0	10	$40 2/3$	36	15	13	10	31
— Florida (N.L.)..............	1	0	1.000	1.42	7	0	0	0	0	$6 1/3$	7	2	1	6	5
1996— Oakland (A.L.)..............	1	3	.250	8.16	12	3	0	0	0	$28 2/3$	37	28	26	22	17
— Edmonton (PCL)..............	8	6	.571	4.29	25	19	1	0	1	$119 2/3$	111	65	57	28	83
1997— Edmonton (PCL)..............	1	0	1.000	0.00	1	1	0	0	0	5	1	0	0	4	4
— Oakland (A.L.)..............	9	5	.643	4.28	71	0	0	0	4	$96 2/3$	109	50	46	40	57
1998— Oakland (A.L.)..............	1	1	.500	7.25	24	0	0	0	0	36	51	34	29	14	19
— Arizona (N.L.)■..............	3	1	.750	3.69	23	0	0	0	0	$31 2/3$	32	14	13	8	14
A.L. totals (4 years)	11	9	.550	5.68	108	3	0	0	4	$163 1/3$	202	114	103	78	93
N.L. totals (2 years)	4	1	.800	3.32	30	0	0	0	0	38	39	16	14	14	19
Major league totals (5 years)	15	10	.600	5.23	138	3	0	0	4	$201 1/3$	241	130	117	92	112

PERSONAL: Born November 12, 1973, in San Saba, Texas. ... 6-2/180. ... Throws right, bats right. ... Full name: Jon David Smart.
HIGH SCHOOL: Westlake (Austin, Texas).
COLLEGE: Texas.
TRANSACTIONS/CAREER NOTES: Selected by Montreal Expos organization in fourth round of free-agent draft (June 1, 1995).

Year Team (League)	W	L	Pct.	ERA	G	GS	CG	ShO	Sv.	IP	H	R	ER	BB	SO
1995— G.C. Expos (GCL)	2	0	1.000	1.69	2	2	0	0	0	10 2/3	10	2	2	1	6
—Vermont (NYP)	0	1	.000	2.28	5	5	0	0	0	27 2/3	29	9	7	7	21
1996— Delmarva (S. Atl.)	9	8	.529	3.39	25	25	3	2	0	156 2/3	155	75	59	31	109
1997— W.P. Beach (FSL)	5	4	.556	3.26	17	13	1	0	1	102	105	45	37	21	65
—Harrisburg (Eastern)	6	3	.667	3.69	12	12	0	0	0	70 2/3	75	34	29	24	43
1998— Cape Fear (South Atlantic)	3	0	1.000	2.45	3	1	0	0	0	11	7	3	3	0	12
—Harrisburg (Eastern)	3	5	.375	2.45	14	11	2	0	1	77	67	23	21	18	47
—Ottawa (Int'l)	2	3	.400	4.89	6	6	0	0	0	35	34	22	19	11	16

PERSONAL: Born March 17, 1965, in Phoenixville, Pa. ... 6-4/210. ... Throws left, bats left. ... Full name: John Patrick Smiley.
HIGH SCHOOL: Perkiomen Valley (Graterford, Pa.).
TRANSACTIONS/CAREER NOTES: Selected by Pittsburgh Pirates organization in 12th round of free-agent draft (June 6, 1983). ... On disabled list (April 27-May 27, 1984 and May 19-July 1, 1990). ... Traded by Pirates to Minnesota Twins for P Denny Neagle and OF Midre Cummings (March 17, 1992). ... Granted free agency (October 26, 1992). ... Signed by Cincinnati Reds (December 1, 1992). ... On disabled list (July 3, 1993-remainder of season and August 22-September 6, 1995). ... On Cincinnati disabled list (June 2-17, 1997). ... Traded by Reds with IF Jeff Branson to Cleveland Indians for P Danny Graves, P Jim Crowell, P Scott Winchester and IF Damian Jackson (July 31, 1997). ... On disabled list (March 22, 1998-entire season).
STATISTICAL NOTES: Tied for Gulf Coast League lead with five home runs allowed in 1983. ... Pitched 2-1 one-hit, complete-game victory against Montreal (June 3, 1988). ... Pitched 4-0 one-hit, complete-game victory against New York (April 17, 1991). ... Pitched 6-0 one-hit, complete-game victory against St. Louis (September 22, 1996).

Year Team (League)	W	L	Pct.	ERA	G	GS	CG	ShO	Sv.	IP	H	R	ER	BB	SO
1983— GC Pirates (GCL)	3	4	.429	5.92	12	12	0	0	0	65 1/3	69	45	*43	27	42
1984— Macon (S. Atl.)	5	11	.313	3.95	21	19	2	0	1	130	119	73	57	41	73
1985— Prince William (Caro.)	2	2	.500	5.14	10	10	0	0	0	56	64	36	32	27	45
—Macon (S. Atl.)	3	8	.273	4.67	16	16	1	1	0	88 2/3	84	55	46	37	70
1986— Prince William (Caro.)	2	4	.333	3.10	48	2	0	0	14	90	64	35	31	40	93
—Pittsburgh (N.L.)	1	0	1.000	3.86	12	0	0	0	0	11 2/3	4	6	5	4	9
1987— Pittsburgh (N.L.)	5	5	.500	5.76	63	0	0	0	4	75	69	49	48	50	58
1988— Pittsburgh (N.L.)	13	11	.542	3.25	34	32	5	1	0	205	185	81	74	46	129
1989— Pittsburgh (N.L.)	12	8	.600	2.81	28	28	8	1	0	205 1/3	174	78	64	49	123
1990— Pittsburgh (N.L.)	9	10	.474	4.64	26	25	2	0	0	149 1/3	161	83	77	36	86
1991— Pittsburgh (N.L.)	•20	8	•.714	3.08	33	32	2	1	0	207 2/3	194	78	71	44	129
1992— Minnesota (A.L.)■	16	9	.640	3.21	34	34	5	2	0	241	205	93	86	65	163
1993— Cincinnati (N.L.)	3	9	.250	5.62	18	18	2	0	0	105 2/3	117	69	66	31	60
1994— Cincinnati (N.L.)	11	10	.524	3.86	24	24	1	1	0	158 2/3	169	80	68	37	112
1995— Cincinnati (N.L.)	12	5	.706	3.46	28	27	1	0	0	176 2/3	173	72	68	39	124
1996— Cincinnati (N.L.)	13	14	.481	3.64	35	34	2	2	0	217 1/3	207	100	88	54	171
1997— Cincinnati (N.L.)	9	10	.474	5.23	20	20	0	0	0	117	139	76	68	31	94
—Cleveland (A.L.)■	2	4	.333	5.54	6	6	0	0	0	37 1/3	45	23	23	10	26
1998— Cleveland (A.L.)						Did not play.									
A.L. totals (2 years)	18	13	.581	3.52	40	40	5	2	0	278 1/3	250	116	109	75	189
N.L. totals (11 years)	108	90	.545	3.85	321	240	23	6	4	1629 1/3	1592	772	697	421	1095
Major league totals (12 years)	126	103	.550	3.80	361	280	28	8	4	1907 2/3	1842	888	806	496	1284

DIVISION SERIES RECORD

Year Team (League)	W	L	Pct.	ERA	G	GS	CG	ShO	Sv.	IP	H	R	ER	BB	SO
1995— Cincinnati (N.L.)	0	0	...	3.00	1	1	0	0	0	6	9	2	2	0	1

CHAMPIONSHIP SERIES RECORD

Year Team (League)	W	L	Pct.	ERA	G	GS	CG	ShO	Sv.	IP	H	R	ER	BB	SO
1990— Pittsburgh (N.L.)	0	0	...	0.00	1	0	0	0	0	2	2	0	0	0	2
1991— Pittsburgh (N.L.)	0	2	.000	23.63	2	2	0	0	0	2 2/3	8	8	7	1	3
1995— Cincinnati (N.L.)	0	0	...	3.60	1	1	0	0	0	5	5	2	2	0	1
Champ. series totals (3 years)	0	2	.000	8.38	4	3	0	0	0	9 2/3	15	10	9	1	4

ALL-STAR GAME RECORD

Year League	W	L	Pct.	ERA	GS	CG	ShO	Sv.	IP	H	R	ER	BB	SO
1991— National	0	0	...	...	0	0	0	0	0	1	1	1	0	0
1995— National	0	0	...	9.00	0	0	0	0	2	2	2	2	0	0
All-Star totals (2 years)	0	0	...	13.50	0	0	0	0	2	3	3	3	0	0

PERSONAL: Born May 10, 1974, in Oakland. ... 6-3/190. ... Bats right, throws right. ... Full name: Robert Eugene Smith.
HIGH SCHOOL: Fremont (Oakland).
TRANSACTIONS/CAREER NOTES: Selected by Atlanta Braves organization in 11th round of free-agent draft (June 1, 1992). ... Selected by Tampa Bay Devil Rays in first round (12th pick overall) of expansion draft (November 18, 1997). ... On Tampa Bay disabled list (May 13-28, 1998).
STATISTICAL NOTES: Tied for Carolina League lead in grounding into double plays with 19 in 1994. ... Led Carolina League third basemen with 388 total chances and 27 double plays in 1994.

Year	Team (League)	Pos.	G	AB	R	H	2B	3B	HR	RBI	Avg.	BB	SO	SB	PO	A	E	Avg.
1992— GC Braves (GCL)	3B	57	217	31	51	9	1	3	28	.235	17	55	5	37	115	15	.910
1993— Macon (S. Atl.)	3B	108	384	53	94	16	7	4	38	.245	23	81	12	65	167	30	.885
1994— Durham (Carolina)	3B	127	478	49	127	27	2	12	71	.266	41	112	18	104	253	31	*.920
1995— Greenville (Southern)	3B	127	444	75	116	27	3	14	58	.261	40	109	12	*120	265	26	.937
1996— Richmond (Int'l)	3B-SS	124	445	49	114	27	0	8	58	.256	32	114	15	116	228	24	.935
1997— Richmond (Int'l)	SS	100	357	47	88	10	2	12	47	.246	44	109	6	161	297	*23	.952
1998— Tampa Bay (A.L.)■	3-DH-S-2	117	370	44	102	15	3	11	55	.276	34	110	5	89	203	13	.957
Major league totals (1 year)		117	370	44	102	15	3	11	55	.276	34	110	5	89	203	13	.957

SMITH, CAM — P — MARINERS

PERSONAL: Born September 20, 1973, in Brooklyn, N.Y. ... 6-3/190. ... Throws right, bats right. ... Full name: Cameron Smith.
HIGH SCHOOL: Ravena-Coyemans-Selkirk (Ravena, N.Y.).
COLLEGE: Ithaca (N.Y.) College.
TRANSACTIONS/CAREER NOTES: Selected by Detroit Tigers organization in third round of free-agent draft (June 3, 1993). ... On disabled list (May 31-June 14, 1996). ... Traded by Tigers with P Joey Eischen to San Diego Padres for C Brian Johnson and P Willie Blair (December 17, 1996). ... On disabled list (June 2-12, 1997). ... Claimed on waivers by Seattle Mariners (November 26, 1997).
STATISTICAL NOTES: Led South Atlantic League with 21 wild pitches and 18 hit batsmen in 1995.

Year	Team (League)	W	L	Pct.	ERA	G	GS	CG	ShO	Sv.	IP	H	R	ER	BB	SO
1993— Bristol (Appalachian)	3	1	.750	3.58	9	7	1	0	0	37 2/3	25	22	15	22	33
— Niagara Falls (NYP)	0	0	...	18.00	2	2	0	0	0	5	12	11	10	6	0
1994— Fayetteville (S. Atl.)	5	13	.278	6.06	26	26	1	0	0	133 2/3	133	100	90	86	128
1995— Fayetteville (S. Atl.)	13	8	.619	3.81	29	*29	2	2	0	149	110	75	63	87	166
1996— Lakeland (Fla. St.)	5	8	.385	4.59	22	21	0	0	0	113 2/3	93	64	58	71	114
1997— Mobile (Southern)■	3	5	.375	7.03	26	15	0	0	1	79 1/3	85	70	62	73	88
1998— Orlando (South.)■	1	3	.250	4.62	23	1	0	0	0	39	32	27	20	32	49
— Lancaster (Calif.)	1	1	.500	2.50	8	0	0	0	2	18	11	7	5	13	32

SMITH, DAN — P — EXPOS

PERSONAL: Born September 15, 1975, in Flemington, N.J. ... 6-3/210. ... Throws right, bats right. ... Full name: Daniel Charles Smith Jr.
HIGH SCHOOL: Girard (Kan.).
TRANSACTIONS/CAREER NOTES: Selected by Texas Rangers organization in seventh round of free-agent draft (June 3, 1993). ... On Charlotte disabled list (June 12-July 7, 1995). ... Claimed on waivers by Montreal Expos (December 14, 1998).

Year	Team (League)	W	L	Pct.	ERA	G	GS	CG	ShO	Sv.	IP	H	R	ER	BB	SO
1993— GC Rangers (GCL)	3	2	.600	2.87	12	10	1	0	0	53 1/3	50	19	17	8	27
1994— Charlotte (Fla. St.)	0	0	...	0.00	2	0	0	0	0	3 2/3	2	0	0	2	3
— Charleston, S.C. (S. Atl.)	7	10	.412	4.92	27	27	4	0	0	157 1/3	171	*111	86	55	86
1995— GC Rangers (GCL)	0	3	.000	4.26	4	3	0	0	0	19	19	9	9	5	12
— Charlotte (Fla. St.)	5	1	.833	2.95	9	9	1	1	0	58	53	23	19	16	34
1996— Charlotte (Fla. St.)	3	7	.300	5.07	18	18	1	0	0	87	100	61	49	38	55
1997— Charlotte (Fla. St.)	8	10	.444	4.43	26	25	2	0	0	160 2/3	169	93	79	66	113
1998— Tulsa (Texas)	13	9	.591	5.81	26	25	1	0	0	153 1/3	162	101	99	58	105
— Okla. City (PCL)	0	0	...	6.00	1	1	0	0	0	6	6	4	4	1	3

SMITH, MARK — OF

PERSONAL: Born May 7, 1970, in Pasadena, Calif. ... 6-3/235. ... Bats right, throws right. ... Full name: Mark Edward Smith.
HIGH SCHOOL: Arcadia (Calif.).
COLLEGE: Southern California.
TRANSACTIONS/CAREER NOTES: Selected by Baltimore Orioles organization in first round (ninth pick overall) of free-agent draft (June 3, 1991). ... On Baltimore disabled list (July 23, 1996-remainder of season); included rehabilitation assignments to Frederick (August 12-13), Bowie (August 21-23) and Rochester (September 3-13). ... Traded by Orioles to San Diego Padres for C Leroy McKinnis (January 9, 1997). ... Traded by Padres with P Hal Garrett to Pittsburgh Pirates for OF Trey Beamon and OF Angelo Encarnacion (March 29, 1997). ... On Pittsburgh disabled list (May 23-June 14, 1997); included rehabilitation assignment to Carolina (June 12-14). ... On Pittsburgh disabled list (May 4-19, 1998); included rehabilitation assignment to Nashville (May 9-19). ... Granted free agency (September 29, 1998).

Year	Team (League)	Pos.	G	AB	R	H	2B	3B	HR	RBI	Avg.	BB	SO	SB	PO	A	E	Avg.
1991— Frederick (Carolina)	OF	38	148	20	37	5	1	4	29	.250	9	24	1	49	1	1	.980
1992— Hagerstown (East.)	OF	128	472	51	136	*32	6	4	62	.288	45	55	15	226	9	4	.983
1993— Rochester (Int'l)	OF	129	485	69	136	27	1	12	68	.280	37	90	4	261	9	7	.975
1994— Rochester (Int'l)	OF	114	437	69	108	27	1	19	66	.247	35	88	4	207	9	5	.977
— Baltimore (A.L.)	OF	3	7	0	1	0	0	0	2	.143	0	2	0	8	0	0	1.000
1995— Rochester (Int'l)	OF	96	364	55	101	25	3	12	66	.277	24	69	7	167	4	7	.961
— Baltimore (A.L.)	OF-DH	37	104	11	24	5	0	3	15	.231	12	22	3	60	2	0	1.000
1996— Rochester (Int'l)	OF	39	132	24	46	14	1	8	32	.348	14	22	10	55	1	2	.966
— Baltimore (A.L.)	OF-DH	27	78	9	19	2	0	4	10	.244	3	20	0	50	0	1	.980
— Frederick (Carolina)	DH	1	1	0	0	0	0	0	0	.000	0	0	0	0	0	0	...
— Bowie (Eastern)	DH	6	22	1	2	0	0	1	2	.091	1	6	0	0	0	0	...
1997— Calgary (PCL)■	OF	39	137	37	51	14	1	14	42	.372	21	15	2	55	1	1	.982
— Pittsburgh (N.L.)	OF-1B-DH	71	193	29	55	13	1	9	35	.285	28	36	3	111	9	0	1.000
— Carolina (Southern)	OF	3	12	5	5	1	0	3	4	.417	0	1	0	4	0	1	.800
1998— Pittsburgh (N.L.)	OF-1B-DH	59	128	18	25	6	0	2	13	.195	10	26	7	72	4	1	.987
— Nashville (PCL)	OF-1B-3B	24	93	18	33	10	1	8	30	.355	11	20	3	83	17	2	.980
American League totals (3 years)		67	189	20	44	7	0	7	27	.233	15	44	3	118	2	1	.992
National League totals (2 years)		130	321	47	80	19	1	11	48	.249	38	62	10	183	13	1	.995
Major league totals (5 years)		197	510	67	124	26	1	18	75	.243	53	106	13	301	15	2	.994

S

PERSONAL: Born February 27, 1966, in Weymouth, Mass. ... 6-2/200. ... Throws right, bats right. ... Full name: Peter John Smith.
HIGH SCHOOL: Burlington (Mass.).
TRANSACTIONS/CAREER NOTES: Selected by Philadelphia Phillies organization in first round (21st pick overall) of free-agent draft (June 4, 1984). ... Traded by Phillies organization with C Ozzie Virgil to Atlanta Braves for P Steve Bedrosian and OF Milt Thompson (December 10, 1985). ... On Atlanta disabled list (June 25-September 3, 1990); included rehabilitation assignment to Greenville (August 26-September 2). ... On Atlanta disabled list (April 4-May 23, 1991); included rehabilitation assignments to Macon (April 12-24) and Richmond (April 24-May 9 and May 13-14). ... On disabled list (July 25-September 1, 1993). ... Traded by Braves to New York Mets for OF Dave Gallagher (November 24, 1993). ... On disabled list (July 18-August 7, 1994). ... Granted free agency (October 25, 1994). ... Signed by Cincinnati Reds (December 1, 1994). ... Released by Reds (June 27, 1995). ... Signed by Florida Marlins organization (July 1, 1995). ... Granted free agency (October 16, 1995). ... Signed by San Diego Padres organization (December 23, 1995). ... Granted free agency (October 15, 1996). ... Re-signed by Padres organization (January 12, 1997). ... Granted free agency (October 30, 1997). ... Re-signed by Padres (December 16, 1997). ... Traded by Padres to Baltimore Orioles for P Eric Estes (June 9, 1998). ... Granted free agency (October 27, 1998).
STATISTICAL NOTES: Led N.L. with seven balks in 1989. ... Pitched seven-inning, 1-0 no-hit victory for Richmond against Rochester (May 3, 1992). ... Led N.L. with 25 home runs allowed in 1994.
MISCELLANEOUS: Appeared in one game as pinch runner (1989). ... Appeared in one game as pinch runner with San Diego (1997). ... Appeared in one game as pinch runner with San Diego (1998).

Year	Team (League)	W	L	Pct.	ERA	G	GS	CG	ShO	Sv.	IP	H	R	ER	BB	SO
1984—	GC Phillies (GCL)	1	2	.333	1.46	8	8	0	0	0	37	28	11	6	16	35
1985—	Clearwater (Fla. St.)	12	10	.545	3.29	26	25	4	1	0	153	135	68	56	80	86
1986—	Greenville (Southern)■	1	8	.111	5.85	24	19	0	0	0	104 2/3	117	88	68	78	64
1987—	Greenville (Southern)	9	9	.500	3.35	29	25	5	1	1	177 1/3	162	76	66	67	119
—	Atlanta (N.L.)	1	2	.333	4.83	6	6	0	0	0	31 2/3	39	21	17	14	11
1988—	Atlanta (N.L.)	7	15	.318	3.69	32	32	5	3	0	195 1/3	183	89	80	88	124
1989—	Atlanta (N.L.)	5	14	.263	4.75	28	27	1	0	0	142	144	83	75	57	115
1990—	Atlanta (N.L.)	5	6	.455	4.79	13	13	3	0	0	77	77	45	41	24	56
—	Atlanta (N.L.)	0	0	. . .	0.00	2	2	0	0	0	3 1/3	1	0	0	0	2
1991—	Macon (S. Atl.)	0	0	. . .	8.38	3	3	0	0	0	9 2/3	15	11	9	2	14
—	Richmond (Int'l)	3	3	.500	7.24	10	10	1	0	0	51	66	44	41	24	41
—	Atlanta (N.L.)	1	3	.250	5.06	14	10	0	0	0	48	48	33	27	22	29
1992—	Richmond (Int'l)	7	4	.636	2.14	15	15	4	1	0	109 1/3	75	27	26	24	93
—	Atlanta (N.L.)	7	0	1.000	2.05	12	11	2	1	0	79	63	19	18	28	43
1993—	Atlanta (N.L.)	4	8	.333	4.37	20	14	0	0	0	90 2/3	92	45	44	36	53
1994—	New York (N.L.)■	4	10	.286	5.55	21	21	1	0	0	131 1/3	145	83	81	42	62
1995—	Cincinnati (N.L.)■	1	2	.333	6.66	11	2	0	0	0	24 1/3	30	19	18	7	14
—	Charlotte (Int'l)	2	1	.667	3.86	10	8	0	0	0	49	51	21	21	17	20
1996—	Las Vegas (PCL)■	11	9	.550	4.95	26	26	2	1	0	169	192	106	93	42	95
1997—	Las Vegas (PCL)	3	2	.600	4.28	6	6	0	0	0	33 2/3	38	16	16	6	24
—	San Diego (N.L.)	7	6	.538	4.81	37	15	0	0	1	118	120	66	63	52	68
1998—	San Diego (N.L.)	3	2	.600	4.78	10	8	0	0	0	43 1/3	45	23	23	18	36
—	Baltimore (A.L.)■	2	3	.400	6.20	27	4	0	0	0	45	57	31	31	16	29
A.L. totals (1 year)		2	3	.400	6.20	27	4	0	0	0	45	57	31	31	16	29
N.L. totals (11 years)		45	68	.398	4.47	204	159	12	4	1	980 2/3	986	526	487	388	611
Major league totals (11 years)		47	71	.398	4.55	231	163	12	4	1	1025 2/3	1043	557	518	404	640

CHAMPIONSHIP SERIES RECORD

Year	Team (League)	W	L	Pct.	ERA	G	GS	CG	ShO	Sv.	IP	H	R	ER	BB	SO
1992—	Atlanta (N.L.)	0	0	. . .	2.45	2	0	0	0	0	3 2/3	2	1	1	3	3

WORLD SERIES RECORD

Year	Team (League)	W	L	Pct.	ERA	G	GS	CG	ShO	Sv.	IP	H	R	ER	BB	SO
1992—	Atlanta (N.L.)	0	0	. . .	0.00	1	0	0	0	0	3	3	0	0	0	0

PERSONAL: Born November 7, 1972, in Springfield, Ore. ... 5-10/165. ... Throws right, bats right. ... Full name: Travis William Smith.
HIGH SCHOOL: Bend (Ore.).
COLLEGE: Texas Tech.
TRANSACTIONS/CAREER NOTES: Selected by Milwaukee Brewers organization in 19th round of free-agent draft (June 1, 1995). ... On Louisville disabled list (April 9-18, 1998). ... On Milwaukee disabled list (June 23, 1998-remainder of season). ... Released by Brewers (October 5, 1998).

Year	Team (League)	W	L	Pct.	ERA	G	GS	CG	ShO	Sv.	IP	H	R	ER	BB	SO
1995—	Helena (Pioneer)	4	2	.667	2.41	20	7	0	0	5	56	41	16	15	19	63
1996—	Stockton (California)	6	1	.857	1.84	14	6	0	0	1	58 2/3	56	17	12	21	48
—	El Paso (Texas)	7	4	.636	4.18	17	17	3	1	0	107 2/3	119	56	50	39	68
1997—	El Paso (Texas)	*16	3	*.842	4.15	28	28	5	•1	0	184 1/3	210	106	85	58	107
1998—	Louisville (Int'l)	4	6	.400	5.32	12	11	0	0	0	67 2/3	77	44	40	25	36
—	Milwaukee (N.L.)	0	0	. . .	0.00	1	0	0	0	0	2	1	0	0	0	1
Major league totals (1 year)		0	0	. . .	0.00	1	0	0	0	0	2	1	0	0	0	1

PERSONAL: Born May 15, 1967, in Warren, Mich. ... 6-3/205. ... Throws right, bats right. ... Full name: John Andrew Smoltz.
HIGH SCHOOL: Waverly (Lansing, Mich.).
TRANSACTIONS/CAREER NOTES: Selected by Detroit Tigers organization in 22nd round of free-agent draft (June 3, 1985). ... Traded by Tigers organization to Atlanta Braves for P Doyle Alexander (August 12, 1987). ... On suspended list (June 20-29, 1994). ... Granted free agency (October 31, 1996). ... Re-signed by Braves (November 20, 1996). ... On Atlanta disabled list (March 29-April 15 and May 24-June 20, 1998); included rehabilitation assignments to Greenville (April 2-10 and June 10-14) and Macon (April 10-14 and June 14-16).

RECORDS: Shares major league record for most home runs allowed in one inning—4 (June 19, 1994, first inning).

HONORS: Named N.L. Pitcher of the Year by THE SPORTING NEWS (1996). ... Named righthanded pitcher on THE SPORTING NEWS N.L. All-Star team (1996). ... Named N.L. Cy Young Award winner by Baseball Writers' Association of America (1996). ... Named pitcher on THE SPORTING NEWS N.L. Silver Slugger team (1997).

STATISTICAL NOTES: Tied for Florida State League lead with six balks in 1986. ... Led N.L. with 14 wild pitches in 1990, 20 in 1991 and 17 in 1992. ... Struck out 15 batters in one game (May 24, 1992).

MISCELLANEOUS: Appeared in three games as pinch runner and struck out in only appearance in pinch hitter (1989). ... Appeared in four games as pinch runner (1990). ... Appeared in two games as pinch runner (1991). ... Struck out in only appearance as pinch hitter (1992). ... Appeared in one game as pinch runner (1997).

Year Team (League)	W	L	Pct.	ERA	G	GS	CG	ShO	Sv.	IP	H	R	ER	BB	SO
1986—Lakeland (Fla. St.)	7	8	.467	3.56	17	14	2	1	0	96	86	44	38	31	47
1987—Glens Falls (East.)	4	10	.286	5.68	21	21	0	0	0	130	131	89	82	81	86
—Richmond (Int'l)■...............	0	1	.000	6.19	3	3	0	0	0	16	17	11	11	11	5
1988—Richmond (Int'l)	10	5	.667	2.79	20	20	3	0	0	135 1/3	118	49	42	37	115
—Atlanta (N.L.)	2	7	.222	5.48	12	12	0	0	0	64	74	40	39	33	37
1989—Atlanta (N.L.)	12	11	.522	2.94	29	29	5	0	0	208	160	79	68	72	168
1990—Atlanta (N.L.)	14	11	.560	3.85	34	34	6	2	0	231 1/3	206	109	99	*90	170
1991—Atlanta (N.L.)	14	13	.519	3.80	36	36	5	0	0	229 2/3	206	101	97	77	148
1992—Atlanta (N.L.)	15	12	.556	2.85	35	•35	9	3	0	246 2/3	206	90	78	80	*215
1993—Atlanta (N.L.)	15	11	.577	3.62	35	35	3	1	0	243 2/3	208	104	98	100	208
1994—Atlanta (N.L.)	6	10	.375	4.14	21	21	1	0	0	134 2/3	120	69	62	48	113
1995—Atlanta (N.L.)	12	7	.632	3.18	29	29	2	1	0	192 2/3	166	76	68	72	193
1996—Atlanta (N.L.)	*24	8	*.750	2.94	35	35	6	2	0	*253 2/3	199	93	83	55	*276
1997—Atlanta (N.L.)	15	12	.556	3.02	35	•35	7	2	0	*256	*234	97	86	63	241
1998—Greenville (Southern)	0	1	.000	2.57	3	3	0	0	0	14	11	4	4	3	16
—Macon (S. Atl.)	0	0	. . .	3.60	2	2	0	0	0	10	7	4	4	1	14
—Atlanta (N.L.)	17	3	*.850	2.90	26	26	2	2	0	167 2/3	145	58	54	44	173
Major league totals (11 years)....	**146**	**105**	**.582**	**3.36**	**327**	**327**	**46**	**13**	**0**	**2228**	**1924**	**916**	**832**	**734**	**1942**

DIVISION SERIES RECORD

RECORDS: Holds N.L. single-game record for most strikeouts—11 (October 3, 1997). ... Holds N.L. career record for most strikeouts—30.

Year Team (League)	W	L	Pct.	ERA	G	GS	CG	ShO	Sv.	IP	H	R	ER	BB	SO
1995—Atlanta (N.L.).................	0	0	. . .	7.94	1	1	0	0	0	5 2/3	5	5	5	1	6
1996—Atlanta (N.L.).................	1	0	1.000	1.00	1	1	0	0	0	9	4	1	1	2	7
1997—Atlanta (N.L.).................	1	0	1.000	1.00	1	1	1	0	0	9	3	1	1	1	11
1998—Atlanta (N.L.).................	1	0	1.000	1.17	1	1	0	0	0	7 2/3	5	1	1	0	6
Div. series totals (4 years)	**3**	**0**	**1.000**	**2.30**	**4**	**4**	**1**	**0**	**0**	**31 1/3**	**17**	**8**	**8**	**4**	**30**

CHAMPIONSHIP SERIES RECORD

RECORDS: Shares N.L. single-series record for most bases on balls allowed—10 (1992). ... Holds career record for most innings pitched—83 2/3; most strikeouts—80; and most bases on balls allowed—34. ... Shares career record for most games started—12. ... Holds N.L. career record for most wins—6.

NOTES: Named Most Valuable Player (1992).

Year Team (League)	W	L	Pct.	ERA	G	GS	CG	ShO	Sv.	IP	H	R	ER	BB	SO
1991—Atlanta (N.L.).................	2	0	1.000	1.76	2	2	1	1	0	15 1/3	14	3	3	3	15
1992—Atlanta (N.L.).................	2	0	1.000	2.66	3	3	0	0	0	20 1/3	14	7	6	10	19
1993—Atlanta (N.L.).................	0	1	.000	0.00	1	1	0	0	0	6 1/3	8	2	0	5	10
1995—Atlanta (N.L.).................	0	0	. . .	2.57	1	1	0	0	0	7	7	2	2	2	2
1996—Atlanta (N.L.).................	2	0	1.000	1.20	2	2	0	0	0	15	12	2	2	3	12
1997—Atlanta (N.L.).................	0	1	.000	7.50	1	1	0	0	0	6	5	5	5	5	9
1998—Atlanta (N.L.).................	0	0	. . .	3.95	2	2	0	0	0	13 2/3	13	6	6	6	13
Champ. series totals (7 years)	**6**	**2**	**.750**	**2.58**	**12**	**12**	**1**	**1**	**0**	**83 2/3**	**73**	**27**	**24**	**34**	**80**

WORLD SERIES RECORD

NOTES: Appeared in one game as pinch runner (1992). ... Member of World Series championship team (1995).

Year Team (League)	W	L	Pct.	ERA	G	GS	CG	ShO	Sv.	IP	H	R	ER	BB	SO
1991—Atlanta (N.L.).................	0	0	. . .	1.26	2	2	0	0	0	14 1/3	13	2	2	1	11
1992—Atlanta (N.L.).................	1	0	1.000	2.70	2	2	0	0	0	13 1/3	13	5	4	7	12
1995—Atlanta (N.L.).................	0	0	. . .	15.43	1	1	0	0	0	2 1/3	6	4	4	2	4
1996—Atlanta (N.L.).................	1	1	.500	0.64	2	2	0	0	0	14	6	2	1	8	14
World Series totals (4 years)	**2**	**1**	**.667**	**2.25**	**7**	**7**	**0**	**0**	**0**	**44**	**38**	**13**	**11**	**18**	**41**

ALL-STAR GAME RECORD

RECORDS: Shares single-game record for most wild pitches—2 (July 13, 1993). ... Shares single-inning record for most wild pitches—2 (July 13, 1993, sixth inning).

Year League	W	L	Pct.	ERA	GS	CG	ShO	Sv.	IP	H	R	ER	BB	SO
1989—National	0	1	.000	9.00	0	0	0	0	1	2	1	1	0	0
1992—National	0	0	. . .	0.00	0	0	0	0	1/3	1	0	0	0	0
1993—National	0	0	. . .	0.00	0	0	0	0	1/3	0	0	0	0	0
1996—National	1	0	1.000	0.00	1	0	0	0	2	2	0	0	0	1
All-Star totals (4 years)	**1**	**1**	**.500**	**2.45**	**1**	**0**	**0**	**0**	**3 2/3**	**5**	**1**	**1**	**1**	**1**

SNOPEK, CHRIS   3B/SS   RED SOX

PERSONAL: Born September 20, 1970, in Cynthiana, Ky. ... 6-1/185. ... Bats right, throws right. ... Full name: Christopher Charles Snopek.

HIGH SCHOOL: Harrison County (Cynthiana, Ky.).

COLLEGE: Mississippi.

TRANSACTIONS/CAREER NOTES: Selected by Texas Rangers organization in 11th round of free-agent draft (June 5, 1989); did not sign. ... Selected by Chicago White Sox organization in sixth round of free-agent draft (June 1, 1992). ... Traded by White Sox to Boston Red Sox for OF Corey Jenkins (August 31, 1998).

STATISTICAL NOTES: Led New York-Pennsylvania League third baseman with 18 double plays in 1992. ... Led Southern League third basemen with 29 double plays in 1994.

Year	Team (League)	Pos.	G	AB	R	H	2B	3B	HR	RBI	Avg.	BB	SO	SB	PO	A	E	Avg.
1992—	Utica (N.Y.-Penn).......	3B-SS	73	245	49	69	15	1	2	29	.282	*52	44	14	48	151	11	.948
1993—	South Bend (Mid.)......	3B	22	72	20	28	8	1	5	18	.389	15	13	1	19	51	3	.959
	— Sarasota (Fla. St.)......	3B-SS	107	371	61	91	21	4	10	50	.245	65	67	3	94	240	24	.933
1994—	Birmingham (Sou.).....	3B-SS	106	365	58	96	25	3	6	54	.263	58	49	9	89	312	25	.941
1995—	Nashville (A.A.).........	SS-3B	113	393	56	127	23	4	12	55	.323	50	72	2	133	358	32	.939
	— Chicago (A.L.)...........	3B-SS	22	68	12	22	4	0	1	7	.324	9	12	1	25	31	2	.966
1996—	Chicago (A.L.)...........	3B-SS-DH	46	104	18	27	6	1	6	18	.260	6	16	0	25	65	5	.947
	— Nashville (A.A.).........	SS-3B	40	153	18	38	8	0	2	12	.248	21	24	2	38	107	6	.960
1997—	Chicago (A.L.)..........	3B-SS	86	298	27	65	15	0	5	35	.218	18	51	3	61	125	16	.921
	— Nashville (A.A.).........	SS-3B	20	73	8	17	4	0	3	8	.233	7	13	0	29	52	3	.964
1998—	Chicago (A.L.)..........	S-2-3-DH-1-O	53	125	17	26	2	0	1	4	.208	14	24	3	62	112	5	.972
	— Boston (A.L.)■..........	2B-3B-DH	8	12	2	2	0	0	0	2	.167	2	5	0	1	4	1	.833
Major league totals (4 years)			215	607	76	142	27	1	13	66	.234	49	108	7	174	337	29	.946

SNOW, J.T.   1B   GIANTS

PERSONAL: Born February 26, 1968, in Long Beach, Calif. ... 6-2/205. ... Bats both, throws left. ... Full name: Jack Thomas Snow Jr. ... Son of Jack Snow, wide receiver with Los Angeles Rams (1965-75).

HIGH SCHOOL: Los Alamitos (Calif.).

COLLEGE: Arizona.

TRANSACTIONS/CAREER NOTES: Selected by New York Yankees organization in fifth round of free-agent draft (June 5, 1989). ... Traded by Yankees with P Jerry Nielsen and P Russ Springer to California Angels for P Jim Abbott (December 6, 1992). ... Traded by Angels to San Francisco Giants for P Allen Watson and P Fausto Macey (November 27, 1996).

HONORS: Named International League Most Valuable Player (1992). ... Won A.L. Gold Glove at first base (1995-96). ... Won N.L. Gold Glove at first base (1997-98).

STATISTICAL NOTES: Led New York-Pennsylvania League first basemen with 649 total chances in 1989. ... Led Carolina League in grounding into double plays with 20 in 1990. ... Led Carolina League first basemen with 1,298 total chances and 120 double plays in 1990. ... Tied for Eastern League lead with 10 sacrifice flies in 1991. ... Led Eastern League first basemen with 1,200 total chances in 1991. ... Led International League with 11 intentional bases on balls received in 1992. ... Led International League first basemen with .995 fielding percentage, 1,097 putouts, 93 assists, 1,196 total chances and 107 double plays in 1992. ... Switch-hit home runs in one game (June 9, 1996). ... Career major league grand slams: 5.

Year	Team (League)	Pos.	G	AB	R	H	2B	3B	HR	RBI	Avg.	BB	SO	SB	PO	A	E	Avg.
1989—	Oneonta (NYP)..........	1B	73	274	41	80	18	2	8	51	.292	29	35	4	*590	53	6	*.991
1990—	Prince Will. (Car.).......	1B	*138	520	57	133	25	1	8	72	.256	46	65	2	*1208	*78	12	.991
1991—	Alb./Colon. (East.).......	1B	132	477	78	133	33	3	13	76	.279	67	78	5	*1102	90	8	*.993
1992—	Columbus (Int'l)........	1B-OF	135	492	81	154	26	4	15	78	•.313	70	65	3	†1103	†93	8	†.993
	— New York (A.L.).........	1B-DH	7	14	1	2	1	0	0	2	.143	5	5	0	43	2	0	1.000
1993—	California (A.L.)■........	1B	129	419	60	101	18	2	16	57	.241	55	88	3	1010	81	6	.995
	— Vancouver (PCL)........	1B	23	94	19	32	9	1	5	24	.340	10	13	0	200	13	2	.991
1994—	Vancouver (PCL)........	1B	53	189	35	56	13	2	8	43	.296	22	32	1	413	42	1	.998
	— California (A.L.).........	1B	61	223	22	49	4	0	8	30	.220	19	48	0	489	37	2	.996
1995—	California (A.L.).........	1B	143	544	80	157	22	1	24	102	.289	52	91	2	1161	57	4	.997
1996—	California (A.L.).........	1B	155	575	69	148	20	1	17	67	.257	56	96	1	1274	103	10	.993
1997—	San Fran. (N.L.)■.......	1B	157	531	81	149	36	1	28	104	.281	96	124	6	1308	108	7	.995
1998—	San Francisco (N.L.) ..	1B	138	435	65	108	29	1	15	79	.248	58	84	1	1040	94	1	*.999
American League totals (5 years)			495	1775	232	457	65	4	65	258	.257	187	328	6	3977	280	22	.995
National League totals (2 years)			295	966	146	257	65	2	43	183	.266	154	208	7	2348	202	8	.997
Major league totals (7 years)			790	2741	378	714	130	6	108	441	.260	341	536	13	6325	482	30	.996

DIVISION SERIES RECORD

Year	Team (League)	Pos.	G	AB	R	H	2B	3B	HR	RBI	Avg.	BB	SO	SB	PO	A	E	Avg.
1997—	San Francisco (N.L.) ..	1B	3	6	0	1	0	0	0	0	.167	1	1	0	12	0	0	1.000

SNYDER, JOHN   P   WHITE SOX

PERSONAL: Born August 16, 1974, in Southfield, Mich. ... 6-3/185. ... Throws right, bats right. ... Full name: John Michael Snyder.

HIGH SCHOOL: Westlake (Westlake Village, Calif.).

TRANSACTIONS/CAREER NOTES: Selected by California Angels organization in 13th round of free-agent draft (June 1, 1992). ... Traded by Angels with P Andrew Lorraine, P Bill Simas and OF McKay Christensen to Chicago White Sox for P Jim Abbott and P Tim Fortugno (July 27, 1995). ... On Gulf Coast disabled list (July 21, 1996-remainder of season). ... On disabled list (April 3-May 4, 1997).

Year	Team (League)	W	L	Pct.	ERA	G	GS	CG	ShO	Sv.	IP	H	R	ER	BB	SO
1992—	Ariz. Angels (Ariz.)	2	4	.333	3.27	15	0	0	0	3	44	40	27	16	16	38
1993—	Cedar Rapids (Midw.)	5	6	.455	5.91	21	16	1	1	0	99	125	88	65	39	79
1994—	Lake Elsinore (Calif.)	10	11	.476	4.47	26	26	2	0	0	159	181	101	79	56	108
1995—	Midland (Texas)	8	9	.471	5.74	21	21	0	0	0	133 1/3	158	93	85	48	81
	— Birmingham (Southern)■ ..	1	0	1.000	6.64	5	4	0	0	0	20 1/3	24	16	15	6	13
1996—	Birmingham (Southern)	3	5	.375	4.83	9	9	0	0	0	54	59	35	29	16	58
	— GC White Sox (GCL)	1	0	1.000	1.65	4	4	0	0	0	16 1/3	5	3	3	4	23
1997—	Birmingham (Southern)	7	8	.467	4.64	20	20	2	1	0	114 1/3	130	76	59	43	90
1998—	Calgary (PCL)	7	3	.700	4.36	15	15	1	0	0	97	112	49	47	34	63
	— Chicago (A.L.)	7	2	.778	4.80	15	14	1	0	0	86 1/3	96	49	46	23	52
Major league totals (1 year).......		7	2	.778	4.80	15	14	1	0	0	86 1/3	96	49	46	23	52

SODERSTROM, STEVE — P — GIANTS

PERSONAL: Born April 3, 1972, in Turlock, Calif. ... 6-3/210. ... Throws right, bats right. ... Full name: Stephen Andrew Soderstrom.
HIGH SCHOOL: Turlock (Calif.).
COLLEGE: Fresno State.
TRANSACTIONS/CAREER NOTES: Selected by New York Mets organization in 15th round of free-agent draft (June 4, 1990); did not sign. ... Selected by San Francisco Giants organization in first round (sixth pick overall) of free-agent draft (June 3, 1993). ... On disabled list (June 25-July 1, 1997). ... On disabled list (June 30-July 19, 1998).
STATISTICAL NOTES: Tied for Texas League lead with 10 hit batsmen in 1995.

Year — Team (League)	W	L	Pct.	ERA	G	GS	CG	ShO	Sv.	IP	H	R	ER	BB	SO
1994— San Jose (California)	2	3	.400	4.20	8	8	0	0	0	40 $^2/_3$	34	20	19	26	40
1995— Shreveport (Texas)	9	5	.643	3.41	22	22	0	0	0	116	106	53	44	51	91
1996— Phoenix (PCL)	7	8	.467	4.41	29	29	0	0	0	171 $^1/_3$	178	94	84	58	80
— San Francisco (N.L.)	2	0	1.000	5.27	3	3	0	0	0	13 $^2/_3$	16	11	8	6	9
1997— Phoenix (PCL)	4	8	.333	6.47	31	15	0	0	1	105 $^2/_3$	141	81	76	52	78
1998— Fresno (Pacific Coast)	11	4	.733	4.05	25	23	2	0	1	137 $^2/_3$	133	71	62	39	96
Major league totals (1 year)	2	0	1.000	5.27	3	3	0	0	0	13 $^2/_3$	16	11	8	6	9

SODOWSKY, CLINT — P — DIAMONDBACKS

PERSONAL: Born July 13, 1972, in Ponca City, Okla. ... 6-4/200. ... Throws right, bats left. ... Full name: Clint Rea Sodowsky.
JUNIOR COLLEGE: Connors State (Okla.).
TRANSACTIONS/CAREER NOTES: Selected by Detroit Tigers organization in ninth round of free-agent draft (June 3, 1991). ... On disabled list (August 29-September 13, 1994). ... On Jacksonville suspended list (May 15-16, 1995). ... Traded by Tigers to Pittsburgh Pirates for P Dan Miceli (November 1, 1996). ... On Pittsburgh disabled list (August 26-September 10, 1997). ... Selected by Arizona Diamondbacks in second round (35th pick overall) of expansion draft (November 18, 1997).
MISCELLANEOUS: Appeared in one game as pinch runner with Arizona (1998).

Year — Team (League)	W	L	Pct.	ERA	G	GS	CG	ShO	Sv.	IP	H	R	ER	BB	SO
1991— Bristol (Appalachian)	0	5	.000	3.76	14	8	0	0	0	55	49	34	23	34	44
1992— Bristol (Appalachian)	2	2	.500	3.54	15	6	0	0	0	56	46	35	22	29	48
1993— Fayetteville (S. Atl.)	14	10	.583	5.09	27	27	1	0	0	155 $^2/_3$	177	101	88	51	80
1994— Lakeland (Fla. St.)	6	3	.667	3.83	19	18	1	1	0	110 $^1/_3$	111	58	47	34	73
1995— Jacksonville (Southern)	5	5	.500	2.55	19	19	5	•3	0	123 $^2/_3$	102	46	35	50	77
— Toledo (International)	5	1	.833	2.85	9	9	1	0	0	60	47	21	19	30	32
— Detroit (A.L.)	2	2	.500	5.01	6	6	0	0	0	23 $^1/_3$	24	15	13	18	14
1996— Detroit (A.L.)	1	3	.250	11.84	7	7	0	0	0	24 $^1/_3$	40	34	32	20	9
— Toledo (International)	6	8	.429	3.94	19	19	1	0	0	118 $^2/_3$	128	67	52	51	59
1997— Calgary (PCL)■	0	1	.000	6.59	8	0	0	0	1	13 $^2/_3$	19	10	10	6	9
— Pittsburgh (N.L.)	2	2	.500	3.63	45	0	0	0	0	52	49	22	21	34	51
1998— Arizona (N.L.)■	3	6	.333	5.68	45	6	0	0	0	77 $^2/_3$	86	56	49	39	42
— Tucson (PCL)	0	1	.000	3.86	2	2	0	0	0	9 $^1/_3$	11	4	4	3	7
A.L. totals (2 years)	3	5	.375	8.50	13	13	0	0	0	47 $^2/_3$	64	49	45	38	23
N.L. totals (2 years)	5	8	.385	4.86	90	6	0	0	0	129 $^2/_3$	135	78	70	73	93
Major league totals (4 years)	8	13	.381	5.84	103	19	0	0	0	177 $^1/_3$	199	127	115	111	116

SOJO, LUIS — IF — YANKEES

PERSONAL: Born January 3, 1966, in Barquisimeto, Venezuela. ... 5-11/175. ... Bats right, throws right. ... Name pronounced SO-ho.
TRANSACTIONS/CAREER NOTES: Signed as non-drafted free agent by Toronto Blue Jays organization (January 3, 1986). ... Traded by Blue Jays with OF Junior Felix and a player to be named later to California Angels for OF Devon White, P Willie Fraser and a player to be named later (December 2, 1990); Blue Jays acquired P Marcus Moore and Angels acquired C Ken Rivers to complete deal (December 4, 1990). ... Traded by Angels to Blue Jays for 3B Kelly Gruber and cash (December 8, 1992). ... On Toronto disabled list (May 10-30, 1993). ... Granted free agency (October 15, 1993). ... Signed by Seattle Mariners organization (January 10, 1994). ... On Seattle disabled list (June 7-23, 1995); included rehabilitation assignment to Tacoma (June 19-23). ... Claimed on waivers by New York Yankees (August 22, 1996). ... Granted free agency (December 20, 1996). ... Re-signed by Yankees (January 9, 1997). ... On disabled list (August 15, 1997-remainder of season). ... Granted free agency (October 31, 1997). ... Re-signed by Yankees (November 12, 1997). ... On New York disabled list (March 22-April 27, 1998); included rehabilitation assignments to Tampa (April 17-20) and Columbus (April 20-27).
STATISTICAL NOTES: Led International League shortstops in .957 fielding percentage in 1989. ... Led International League with nine sacrifice flies in 1990. ... Led A.L. with 19 sacrifice hits in 1991. ... Career major league grand slams: 1.

Year — Team (League)	Pos.	G	AB	R	H	2B	3B	HR	RBI	Avg.	BB	SO	SB	PO	A	E	Avg.
1986—					Dominican Summer League statistics unavailable.												
1987— Myrtle Beach (SAL)	S-2-3-0	72	223	23	47	5	4	2	15	.211	17	18	5	104	123	14	.942
1988— Myrtle Beach (SAL)	SS	135	*536	83	*155	22	5	5	56	.289	35	35	14	191	407	28	.955
1989— Syracuse (Int'l)	SS-2B	121	482	54	133	20	5	3	54	.276	21	42	9	170	348	23	†.957
1990— Syracuse (Int'l)	2B-SS	75	297	39	88	12	3	6	25	.296	14	23	10	138	212	10	.972
— Toronto (A.L.)	2-S-0-3-DH	33	80	14	18	3	0	1	9	.225	5	5	1	34	31	5	.929
1991— California (A.L.)■	2-S-3-0-DH	113	364	38	94	14	1	3	20	.258	14	26	4	233	335	11	.981
1992— Edmonton (PCL)	3B-2B-SS	37	145	22	43	9	1	1	24	.297	9	17	4	32	106	4	.972
— California (A.L.)	2B-3B-SS	106	368	37	100	12	3	7	43	.272	14	24	7	196	293	9	.982
1993— Toronto (A.L.)■	SS-2B-3B	19	47	5	8	2	0	0	6	.170	4	2	0	24	35	2	.967
— Syracuse (Int'l)	2-0-3-S-1	43	142	17	31	7	2	1	12	.218	8	12	2	46	60	4	.964
1994— Calgary (PCL)■	SS-2B	24	102	19	33	9	3	1	18	.324	10	7	5	36	81	2	.983
— Seattle (A.L.)	2-S-DH-3	63	213	32	59	9	2	6	22	.277	8	25	2	97	186	7	.976
1995— Seattle (A.L.)	SS-2B-OF	102	339	50	98	18	2	7	39	.289	23	19	4	141	221	9	.976
— Tacoma (PCL)	2B-SS	4	17	1	3	0	0	1	1	.176	0	2	0	4	9	0	1.000
1996— Seattle (A.L.)	3B-2B-SS	77	247	20	52	8	1	1	16	.211	10	13	2	97	158	8	.970
— New York (A.L.)■	2B-SS-3B	18	40	3	11	2	0	0	5	.275	1	4	0	16	37	0	1.000

Year Team (League)	Pos.	G	AB	R	H	2B	3B	HR	RBI	Avg.	BB	SO	SB	PO	A	E	Avg.
							BATTING								**FIELDING**		
1997— New York (A.L.)..........	2-S-3-1	77	215	27	66	6	1	2	25	.307	16	14	3	131	153	5	.983
1998— Tampa (Fla. St.)..........	SS	3	9	1	2	0	0	0	0	.222	2	0	0	4	8	1	.923
—Columbus (Int'l)	SS-2B	6	23	1	5	2	0	0	2	.217	1	1	1	9	16	1	.962
— New York (A.L.)........S-1-2-3-DH		54	147	16	34	3	1	0	14	.231	4	15	1	146	74	3	.987
Major league totals (9 years)		662	2060	242	540	77	11	27	199	.262	99	147	24	1115	1523	59	.978

DIVISION SERIES RECORD

Year Team (League)	Pos.	G	AB	R	H	2B	3B	HR	RBI	Avg.	BB	SO	SB	PO	A	E	Avg.
							BATTING								**FIELDING**		
1995— Seattle (A.L.)	SS	5	20	0	5	0	0	0	3	.250	0	3	0	9	15	1	.960
1996— New York (A.L.).........	2B	2	0	0	0	0	0	0	0	. . .	0	0	0	1	1	0	1.000
1998— New York (A.L.)								Did not play.									
Division series totals (2 years)		7	20	0	5	0	0	0	3	.250	0	3	0	10	16	1	.963

CHAMPIONSHIP SERIES RECORD

Year Team (League)	Pos.	G	AB	R	H	2B	3B	HR	RBI	Avg.	BB	SO	SB	PO	A	E	Avg.
							BATTING								**FIELDING**		
1995— Seattle (A.L.)	SS	6	20	0	5	2	0	0	1	.250	0	2	0	9	18	1	.964
1996— New York (A.L.).........	2B	3	5	0	1	0	0	0	0	.200	0	1	0	4	4	0	1.000
1998— New York (A.L.)	1B	1	0	0	0	0	0	0	0	. . .	0	0	0	1	1	0	1.000
Championship series totals (3 years)		10	25	0	6	2	0	0	1	.240	0	3	0	14	23	1	.974

WORLD SERIES RECORD

NOTES: Member of World Series championship team (1996 and 1998).

Year Team (League)	Pos.	G	AB	R	H	2B	3B	HR	RBI	Avg.	BB	SO	SB	PO	A	E	Avg.
							BATTING								**FIELDING**		
1996— New York (A.L.)..........	PH-2B	5	5	0	3	1	0	0	1	.600	0	0	0	5	2	0	1.000
1998— New York (A.L.)								Did not play.									

S

SORIANO, ALFONSO   SS   YANKEES

PERSONAL: Born January 7, 1978, in Dominican Republic. ... 6-1/175. ... Bats right, throws right.
TRANSACTIONS/CAREER NOTES: Signed by Hiroshima Toyo Carp of Japan Central League (November 1994). ... Played in Toyo Carp organization (1995-97). ... Retired from Japan Central League and declared free agent by Major League Baseball (1998). ... Signed by New York Yankees (1998).

Year Team (League)	Pos.	G	AB	R	H	2B	3B	HR	RBI	Avg.	BB	SO	SB	PO	A	E	Avg.
							BATTING								**FIELDING**		
1995—						Japan minor league statistics unavailable.											
1996—						Japan minor league statistics unavailable.											
1997— Hiroshima (Jp. Cn.)....	OF	9	17	2	2	0	0	0	0	.118	2	4	0	. . .	. . .	. . .	. . .
1998—						Out of organized baseball.											

SORRENTO, PAUL   1B   DEVIL RAYS

PERSONAL: Born November 17, 1965, in Somerville, Mass. ... 6-2/220. ... Bats left, throws right. ... Full name: Paul Anthony Sorrento.
HIGH SCHOOL: St. John's Preparatory (Danvers, Mass.).
COLLEGE: Florida State.
TRANSACTIONS/CAREER NOTES: Selected by California Angels organization in fourth round of free-agent draft (June 2, 1986). ... Traded by Angels organization with P Mike Cook and P Rob Wassenaar to Minnesota Twins for P Bert Blyleven and P Kevin Trudeau (November 3, 1988). ... Traded by Twins to Cleveland Indians for P Oscar Munoz and P Curt Leskanic (March 28, 1992). ... Granted free agency (December 21, 1995). ... Signed by Seattle Mariners (January 3, 1996). ... Granted free agency (October 27, 1997). ... Signed by Tampa Bay Devil Rays (December 8, 1997).
STATISTICAL NOTES: Led Southern League first basemen with 103 double plays in 1989. ... Led Pacific Coast League first basemen with 14 errors in 1991. ... Career major league grand slams: 9.

Year Team (League)	Pos.	G	AB	R	H	2B	3B	HR	RBI	Avg.	BB	SO	SB	PO	A	E	Avg.
							BATTING								**FIELDING**		
1986— Quad Cities (Mid.)	OF	53	177	33	63	11	2	6	34	.356	24	40	0	83	7	1	.989
— Palm Springs (Calif.)..	OF	16	62	5	15	3	0	1	7	.242	4	15	0	16	1	1	.944
1987— Palm Springs (Calif.)..	OF	114	370	66	83	14	2	8	45	.224	78	95	1	123	10	4	.971
1988— Palm Springs (Calif.)..	1B-OF	133	465	91	133	30	6	14	99	.286	110	101	3	719	55	18	.977
1989— Orlando (South.)■.....	1B	140	509	81	130	*35	2	27	*112	.255	84	119	1	1070	41	*24	.979
— Minnesota (A.L.)	1B-DH	14	21	2	5	0	0	0	1	.238	5	4	0	13	0	0	1.000
1990— Portland (PCL)	1B-OF	102	354	59	107	27	1	19	72	.302	64	95	3	695	52	13	.983
— Minnesota (A.L.)	DH-1B	41	121	11	25	4	1	5	13	.207	12	31	1	118	7	1	.992
1991— Portland (PCL)	1B-DH	113	409	59	126	30	2	13	79	.308	62	65	1	933	58	†14	.986
— Minnesota (A.L.)	1B-DH	26	47	6	12	2	0	4	13	.255	4	11	0	70	7	0	1.000
1992— Cleveland (A.L.)■........	1B-DH	140	458	52	123	24	1	18	60	.269	51	89	0	996	78	8	.993
1993— Cleveland (A.L.)	1B-OF-DH	148	463	75	119	26	1	18	65	.257	58	121	3	1015	86	6	.995
1994— Cleveland (A.L.)..........	1B-DH	95	322	43	90	14	0	14	62	.280	34	68	0	798	59	4	.995
1995— Cleveland (A.L.)..........	1B-DH	104	323	50	76	14	0	25	79	.235	51	71	1	816	58	7	.992
1996— Seattle (A.L.)■............	1B	143	471	67	136	32	1	23	93	.289	57	103	0	957	81	11	.990
1997— Seattle (A.L.)..............	1B-DH	146	457	68	123	19	0	31	80	.269	51	112	0	929	86	4	.996
1998— Tampa Bay (A.L.)■.....	DH-1B-OF	137	435	40	98	27	0	17	57	.225	54	133	2	249	24	0	1.000
Major league totals (10 years)		994	3118	414	807	162	4	155	523	.259	377	743	7	5961	486	41	.994

DIVISION SERIES RECORD

Year Team (League)	Pos.	G	AB	R	H	2B	3B	HR	RBI	Avg.	BB	SO	SB	PO	A	E	Avg.
							BATTING								**FIELDING**		
1995— Cleveland (A.L.)..........	1B	3	10	2	3	0	0	0	1	.300	2	3	0	27	5	2	.941
1997— Seattle (A.L.)	1B-PH	4	10	2	3	1	0	1	1	.300	2	3	0	27	4	1	.969
Division series totals (2 years)		7	20	4	6	1	0	1	2	.300	4	6	0	54	9	3	.955

CHAMPIONSHIP SERIES RECORD

Year — Team (League)	Pos.	G	AB	R	H	2B	3B	HR	RBI	Avg.	BB	SO	SB	PO	A	E	Avg.
						— BATTING —								— FIELDING —			
1991— Minnesota (A.L.)	PH	1	1	0	0	0	0	0	0	.000	0	1	0	...	...	...	...
1995— Cleveland (A.L.).........	1B	4	13	2	2	1	0	0	0	.154	2	3	0	34	1	2	.946
Championship series totals (2 years)		5	14	2	2	1	0	0	0	.143	2	4	0	34	1	2	.946

WORLD SERIES RECORD

NOTES: Member of World Series championship team (1991).

Year — Team (League)	Pos.	G	AB	R	H	2B	3B	HR	RBI	Avg.	BB	SO	SB	PO	A	E	Avg.
						— BATTING —								— FIELDING —			
1991— Minnesota (A.L.)	PH-1B	3	2	0	0	0	0	0	0	.000	1	2	0	1	1	0	1.000
1995— Cleveland (A.L.).........	1B-PH	6	11	0	2	1	0	0	0	.182	0	4	0	19	2	1	.955
World Series totals (2 years)		9	13	0	2	1	0	0	0	.154	1	6	0	20	3	1	.958

SOSA, JUAN   IF   ROCKIES

PERSONAL: Born August 10, 1975, in San Francisco de Macoris, Dominican Republic. ... 6-1/175. ... Bats right, throws right. ... Full name: Juan Luis Sosa.

HIGH SCHOOL: Renacimiento (Dominican Republic).

TRANSACTIONS/CAREER NOTES: Signed as non-drafted free agent by Los Angeles Dodgers organization (July 24, 1993). ... Selected by Colorado Rockies organization from Dodgers in Rule 5 minor league draft (December 15, 1997).

STATISTICAL NOTES: Led Carolina League shortstops with 555 total chances in 1998.

Year — Team (League)	Pos.	G	AB	R	H	2B	3B	HR	RBI	Avg.	BB	SO	SB	PO	A	E	Avg.
						— BATTING —								— FIELDING —			
1993— Dom. Dodgers (DSL) .	IF	63	237	51	66	7	4	0	39	.278	45	52	8	209	28	16	.937
1994— Dom. Dodgers (DSL) .	2B	59	224	55	65	11	3	6	60	.290	44	27	13	141	168	17	.948
1995— Vero Beach (FSL)	2B-SS	8	27	2	6	1	1	1	6	.222	0	4	0	10	21	1	.969
— Yakima (N'west)	2B-3B-SS	61	217	26	51	10	4	3	16	.235	15	39	8	93	174	16	.943
1996— Savannah (S. Atl.)	2-S-3-0	112	370	58	94	21	2	7	38	.254	30	64	14	139	261	22	.948
1997— Vero Beach (FSL)	SS-2B-3B	92	250	32	55	5	2	5	29	.220	14	39	20	130	193	19	.944
1998— Salem (Carolina)■....	SS	133	529	88	147	20	*12	8	47	.278	43	83	*64	*196	328	31	.944

SOSA, SAMMY   OF   CUBS

PERSONAL: Born November 12, 1968, in San Pedro de Macoris, Dominican Republic. ... 6-0/210. ... Bats right, throws right. ... Full name: Samuel Sosa.

TRANSACTIONS/CAREER NOTES: Signed as non-drafted free agent by Texas Rangers organization (July 30, 1985). ... Traded by Rangers with SS Scott Fletcher and P Wilson Alvarez to Chicago White Sox for OF Harold Baines and IF Fred Manrique (July 29, 1989). ... Traded by White Sox with P Ken Patterson to Chicago Cubs for OF George Bell (March 30, 1992). ... On Chicago disabled list (June 13-July 27 and August 7-September 16, 1992); included rehabilitation assignment to Iowa (July 21-27). ... On disabled list (August 21, 1996-remainder of season).

RECORDS: Holds major league single-month record for most home runs—20 (June 1998). ... Holds major league single-season record for most home runs by outfielder—66 (1998). ... Shares major league records for most home runs in one inning—2 (May 16, 1996, seventh inning); and most grand slams in two consecutive games—2 (July 27 and 28, 1998). ... Shares major league single-season record for most times hitting two or more home runs in a game—11 (1998). ... Holds N.L. record for most home runs in consecutive seasons—102 (1997-98).

HONORS: Named outfielder on THE SPORTING NEWS N.L. All-Star team (1995 and 1998). ... Named outfielder on THE SPORTING NEWS N.L. Silver Slugger team (1995 and 1998). ... Named co-Sportsman of the Year by THE SPORTING NEWS (1998). ... Named Major League Player of the Year by THE SPORTING NEWS (1998). ... Named N.L. Most Valuable Player by Baseball Writers' Association of America (1998).

STATISTICAL NOTES: Led Gulf Coast League with 96 total bases in 1986. ... Tied for South Atlantic League lead in double plays by outfielder with four in 1987. ... Collected six hits in one game (July 2, 1993). ... Tied for N.L. lead in double plays by outfielder with four in 1995. ... Hit three home runs in one game (June 5, 1996 and June 15, 1998). ... Led N.L. with 416 total bases in 1998. ... Career major league grand slams: 3.

Year — Team (League)	Pos.	G	AB	R	H	2B	3B	HR	RBI	Avg.	BB	SO	SB	PO	A	E	Avg.
						— BATTING —								— FIELDING —			
1986— GC Rangers (GCL)......	OF	61	229	38	63	*19	1	4	28	.275	22	51	11	92	9	•6	.944
1987— Gastonia (S. Atl.)........	OF	129	519	73	145	27	4	11	59	.279	21	123	22	183	12	17	.920
1988— Charlotte (Fla. St.)......	OF	131	507	70	116	13	*12	9	51	.229	35	106	42	227	11	7	.971
1989— Tulsa (Texas)	OF	66	273	45	81	15	4	7	31	.297	15	52	16	110	7	4	.967
— Texas (A.L.)............	OF-DH	25	84	8	20	3	0	1	3	.238	0	20	0	33	1	2	.944
— Okla. City (A.A.)........	OF	10	39	2	4	2	0	0	3	.103	2	8	4	22	0	2	.917
— Vancouver (PCL)	OF	13	49	7	18	3	0	1	5	.367	0	20	0	43	1	0	1.000
— Chicago (A.L.)■........	OF	33	99	19	27	5	0	3	10	.273	11	27	7	61	1	2	.969
1990— Chicago (A.L.)	OF	153	532	72	124	26	10	15	70	.233	33	150	32	315	14	*13	.962
1991— Chicago (A.L.)	OF-DH	116	316	39	64	10	1	10	33	.203	14	98	13	214	6	6	.973
— Vancouver (PCL)	OF	32	116	19	31	7	2	3	19	.267	17	32	9	95	2	3	.970
1992— Chicago (N.L.)■..........	OF	67	262	41	68	7	2	8	25	.260	19	63	15	145	4	6	.961
— Iowa (Am. Assoc.)......	OF	5	19	3	6	2	0	0	1	.316	1	2	5	14	0	0	1.000
1993— Chicago (N.L.)	OF	159	598	92	156	25	5	33	93	.261	38	135	36	344	17	9	.976
1994— Chicago (N.L.)	OF	105	426	59	128	17	6	25	70	.300	25	92	22	248	5	7	.973
1995— Chicago (N.L.)	OF	•144	564	89	151	17	3	36	119	.268	58	134	34	320	13	*13	.962
1996— Chicago (N.L.)	OF	124	498	84	136	21	2	40	100	.273	34	134	18	253	15	10	.964
1997— Chicago (N.L.)	OF	•162	642	90	161	31	4	36	119	.251	45	*174	22	325	16	8	.977
1998— Chicago (N.L.)	OF	159	643	*134	198	20	0	66	*158	.308	73	*171	18	334	14	9	.975
American League totals (3 years)		327	1031	138	235	44	11	29	116	.228	58	295	52	623	22	23	.966
National League totals (7 years)		920	3633	589	998	138	22	244	684	.275	292	903	165	1969	84	62	.971
Major league totals (10 years)		1247	4664	727	1233	182	33	273	800	.264	350	1198	217	2592	106	85	.969

DIVISION SERIES RECORD

					BATTING										FIELDING		
Year	Team (League)	Pos.	G	AB	R	H	2B	3B	HR	RBI	Avg.	BB	SO	SB	PO	A	E	Avg.
1998— Chicago (N.L.)	OF	3	11	0	2	1	0	0	0	.182	1	4	0	5	0	0	1.000

ALL-STAR GAME RECORD

NOTES: Named to All-Star team for 1998 game; replaced by Bret Boone due to injury.

					BATTING									FIELDING		
Year	League	Pos.	AB	R	H	2B	3B	HR	RBI	Avg.	BB	SO	SB	PO	A	E	Avg.
1995— National	OF	1	0	0	0	0	0	0	.000	0	0	0	2	0	0	1.000
1998— National.....................						Selected, did not play—injured.										

SPARKS, STEVE   P   ANGELS

PERSONAL: Born July 2, 1965, in Tulsa, Okla. ... 6-0/180. ... Throws right, bats right. ... Full name: Steven William Sparks.
HIGH SCHOOL: Holland Hall (Tulsa, Okla.).
COLLEGE: Sam Houston State.
TRANSACTIONS/CAREER NOTES: Selected by Milwaukee Brewers organization in fifth round of free-agent draft (June 2, 1987). ... On disabled list (March 24, 1997-entire season). ... Granted free agency (October 15, 1997). ... Signed by Anaheim Angels (February 23, 1998). ... On Cedar Rapids disabled list (April 9-19, 1998).

Year	Team (League)	W	L	Pct.	ERA	G	GS	CG	ShO	Sv.	IP	H	R	ER	BB	SO
1987— Helena (Pioneer)	6	3	.667	4.68	10	9	2	0	0	57 2/3	68	44	30	20	47
1988— Beloit (Midwest)	9	13	.409	3.79	25	24	5	1	0	164	162	80	69	51	96
1989— Stockton (California)	•13	5	.722	2.41	23	22	3	2	0	164	125	55	44	53	126
1990— Stockton (California)	10	7	.588	3.69	19	19	5	1	0	129 1/3	136	63	53	31	77
— El Paso (Texas).................	1	2	.333	6.53	7	6	1	0	0	30 1/3	43	24	22	15	14
1991— Stockton (California)	9	10	.474	3.06	24	24	•8	2	0	179 2/3	160	70	61	98	139
— El Paso (Texas).................	1	2	.333	9.53	4	4	0	0	0	17	30	22	18	9	10
1992— El Paso (Texas).................	9	8	.529	5.37	28	22	3	0	1	140 2/3	159	99	84	50	79
1993— New Orleans (A.A.)..........	9	13	.409	3.84	29	•28	*7	1	0	*180 1/3	174	89	77	*80	104
1994— New Orleans (A.A.)..........	10	12	.455	4.46	28	27	5	1	0	*183 2/3	183	101	91	68	105
1995— Milwaukee (A.L.)	9	11	.450	4.63	33	27	3	0	0	202	210	111	104	86	96
1996— Milwaukee (A.L.)	4	7	.364	6.60	20	13	1	0	0	88 2/3	103	66	65	52	21
— New Orleans (A.A.)..........	2	6	.250	4.99	11	10	3	2	0	57 2/3	64	43	32	35	27
1997— Milwaukee (A.L.)							Did not play.								
1998— Vancouver (PCL)■..........	0	4	.000	2.89	4	4	2	0	0	28	23	11	9	6	19
— Anaheim (A.L.)	9	4	.692	4.34	22	20	0	0	0	128 2/3	130	66	62	58	90
— Midland (Texas)	0	4	.000	7.08	7	7	0	0	0	40 2/3	49	38	32	15	34
Major league totals (3 years)......	**22**	**22**	**.500**	**4.96**	**75**	**60**	**4**	**0**	**0**	**419 1/3**	**443**	**243**	**231**	**196**	**207**

SPEHR, TIM   C   ROYALS

PERSONAL: Born July 2, 1966, in Excelsior Springs, Mo. ... 6-2/200. ... Bats right, throws right. ... Full name: Timothy Joseph Spehr. ... Name pronounced SPEAR.
HIGH SCHOOL: Richfield (Waco, Texas).
JUNIOR COLLEGE: McLennan College (Texas).
COLLEGE: Arizona State.
TRANSACTIONS/CAREER NOTES: Selected by Kansas City Royals organization in fifth round of free-agent draft (June 1, 1988). ... On disabled list (June 25-July 27, 1988). ... On Baseball City disabled list (April 7-May 21, 1989). ... Traded by Royals with P Jeff Shaw to Montreal Expos organization for P Mark Gardner and P Doug Piatt (December 9, 1992). ... On disabled list (July 31, 1995-remainder of season and August 18-September 6, 1996). ... Granted free agency (October 21, 1996). ... Signed by Pawtucket, Boston Red Sox organization (March 6, 1997). ... Traded by Red Sox to Royals for cash (March 26, 1997). ... Released by Royals (May 27, 1997). ... Signed by Atlanta Braves (June 10, 1997). ... Granted free agency (December 21, 1997). ... Signed by New York Mets organization (January 8, 1998). ... On New York disabled list (May 5-August 28, 1998); included rehabilitation assignment to St. Lucie (August 12-27). ... Traded by Mets to Royals for cash (August 31, 1998).
STATISTICAL NOTES: Led American Association catchers with 730 total chances and 14 double plays in 1990. ... Tied for American Association lead in being hit by pitch with 11 in 1992. ... Career major league grand slams: 2.

						BATTING								FIELDING		
Year	Team (League)	Pos.	G	AB	R	H	2B	3B	HR	RBI	Avg.	BB	SO	SB	PO	A	E	Avg.
1988— Appleton (Midwest)....	C	31	110	15	29	3	0	5	22	.264	10	28	3	146	14	7	.958
1989— Baseball City (FSL).....	C	18	64	8	16	5	0	1	7	.250	5	17	1	63	7	1	.986
— Memphis (Sou.)..........	C	61	216	22	42	9	0	6	23	.194	16	59	1	274	36	5	.984
1990— Omaha (A.A.)...........	C	102	307	42	69	10	2	6	34	.225	41	88	5	*658	67	5	*.993
1991— Omaha (A.A.)	C	72	215	27	59	14	2	6	26	.274	25	48	3	402	53	8	.983
— Kansas City (A.L.)	C	37	74	7	14	5	0	3	14	.189	9	18	1	190	19	3	.986
1992— Omaha (A.A.)	C	109	336	48	85	22	0	15	42	.253	61	89	4	577	65	7	.989
1993— Montreal (N.L.)■.......	C	53	87	14	20	6	0	2	10	.230	6	20	2	166	22	9	.954
— Ottawa (Int'l)	C	46	141	15	28	6	1	4	13	.199	14	35	2	248	24	6	.978
1994— Montreal (N.L.)..........	C-OF	52	36	8	9	3	1	0	5	.250	4	11	2	104	6	0	1.000
1995— Montreal (N.L.)...........	C	41	35	4	9	5	0	1	3	.257	6	7	0	92	12	1	.990
1996— Montreal (N.L.)...........	C-OF	63	44	4	4	1	0	1	3	.091	3	15	1	121	7	2	.985
1997— Kansas City (A.L.)■ ...	C	17	35	3	6	0	0	1	1	.171	2	12	0	78	7	0	1.000
— Richmond (Int'l)■.......	C	36	120	13	23	5	0	3	14	.192	12	37	0	262	36	5	.983
— Atlanta (N.L.).............	C	8	14	2	3	1	0	1	4	.214	0	4	1	32	4	2	.947
1998— New York (N.L.)■	C-1B	21	51	3	7	1	0	0	3	.137	7	16	1	120	10	0	1.000
— St. Lucie (Fla. St.)	C	14	38	7	7	2	0	1	6	.184	9	16	0	42	3	1	.978
— Norfolk (Int'l)	PH	1	1	0	1	0	0	0	0	1.000	0	0	0	...	...	...	...
— Kansas City (A.L.)	C	11	25	5	6	2	0	1	2	.240	8	3	0	62	2	0	1.000
American League totals (3 years)		65	134	15	26	7	0	5	18	.194	19	33	1	330	28	3	.984
National League totals (6 years)		238	267	35	52	17	1	5	28	.195	26	73	7	635	61	14	.980
Major league totals (7 years)		303	401	50	78	24	1	10	46	.195	45	106	8	965	89	17	.984

SPEIER, JUSTIN   P   MARLINS

PERSONAL: Born November 6, 1973, in Walnut Creek, Calif. ... 6-4/205. ... Throws right, bats right. ... Full name: Justin James Speier. ... Son of Chris Speier, infielder with five major league teams (1971-89).
HIGH SCHOOL: Brophy College Prep (Phoenix).
COLLEGE: San Francisco, then Nicholls State.
TRANSACTIONS/CAREER NOTES: Selected by Chicago Cubs organization in 55th round of free-agent draft (June 1, 1995). ... Traded by Cubs with 3B Kevin Orie and P Todd Noel to Florida Marlins for P Felix Heredia and P Steve Hoff (July 31, 1998).

Year Team (League)	W	L	Pct.	ERA	G	GS	CG	ShO	Sv.	IP	H	R	ER	BB	SO
1995—Williamsport (NYP)	2	1	.667	1.49	30	0	0	0	12	36 1/3	27	6	6	4	39
1996—Daytona (Fla. St.)	2	4	.333	3.76	33	0	0	0	13	38 1/3	32	19	16	19	34
—Orlando (South.)	4	1	.800	2.05	24	0	0	0	6	26 1/3	23	7	6	5	14
1997—Orlando (South.)	6	5	.545	4.48	50	0	0	0	6	78 1/3	77	46	39	23	63
—Iowa (Am. Assoc.).............	2	0	1.000	0.00	8	0	0	0	1	12 1/3	5	0	0	1	9
1998—Iowa (Pacific Coast)	3	3	.500	5.05	45	0	0	0	12	51 2/3	52	31	29	19	49
—Chicago (N.L.)....................	0	0	. . .	13.50	1	0	0	0	0	1 1/3	2	2	2	1	2
—Florida (N.L.)■................	0	3	.000	8.38	18	0	0	0	0	19 1/3	25	18	18	12	15
Major league totals (1 year)........	0	3	.000	8.71	19	0	0	0	0	20 2/3	27	20	20	13	17

SPENCER, SHANE   OF   YANKEES

PERSONAL: Born February 20, 1972, in Key West, Fla. ... 5-11/210. ... Bats right, throws right. ... Full name: Michael Shane Spencer.
HIGH SCHOOL: Granite Hills (El Cajon, Calif.).
TRANSACTIONS/CAREER NOTES: Selected by New York Yankees organization in 28th round of free-agent draft (June 4, 1990). ... On disabled list (April 10-May 9, 1994).
RECORDS: Shares major league single-month record for most grand slams—3 (September 1998).
HONORS: Named Florida State League Most Valuable Player (1995).
STATISTICAL NOTES: Led Florida State League with 235 total bases in 1995. ... Career major league grand slams: 3.

							BATTING								FIELDING		
Year Team (League)	Pos.	G	AB	R	H	2B	3B	HR	RBI	Avg.	BB	SO	SB	PO	A	E	Avg.
1990—GC Yankees (GCL)......	OF	42	147	20	27	4	0	0	7	.184	20	23	11	79	3	3	.965
1991—GC Yankees (GCL)......	OF	44	160	25	49	7	0	0	30	.306	14	19	9	64	6	3	.959
—Oneonta (NYP)	OF	18	53	10	13	2	1	0	3	.245	10	9	2	11	0	1	.917
1992—Greensboro (S. Atl.)...	OF-P	83	258	43	74	10	2	3	27	.287	33	37	8	135	6	0	1.000
1993—Greensboro (S. Atl.)...	OF-P	122	431	89	116	35	2	12	80	.269	52	62	14	138	10	5	.967
1994—Tampa (Fla. St.) ...	OF	90	334	44	97	22	3	8	53	.290	30	53	5	90	10	4	.962
1995—Tampa (Fla. St.) ...	OF	•134	500	87	*150	31	3	16	*88	.300	61	60	14	166	6	6	.966
1996—Norwich (Eastern)	OF-1B-3B	126	450	70	114	19	0	29	89	.253	68	99	4	218	24	3	.988
—Columbus (Int'l)	OF	9	31	7	11	4	0	3	6	.355	5	5	0	25	1	1	.963
1997—Columbus (Int'l)	OF-3B	125	452	78	109	34	4	30	86	.241	71	105	0	189	7	4	.980
1998—Columbus (Int'l)	OF-1B	87	342	66	110	29	1	18	67	.322	41	59	1	225	11	5	.979
—New York (A.L.)..........	OF-DH-1B	27	67	18	25	6	0	10	27	.373	5	12	0	29	2	0	1.000
Major league totals (1 year)		27	67	18	25	6	0	10	27	.373	5	12	0	29	2	0	1.000

DIVISION SERIES RECORD

							BATTING								FIELDING		
Year Team (League)	Pos.	G	AB	R	H	2B	3B	HR	RBI	Avg.	BB	SO	SB	PO	A	E	Avg.
1998—New York (A.L.)..........	OF	2	6	3	3	0	0	2	4	.500	0	1	0	1	0	0	1.000

CHAMPIONSHIP SERIES RECORD

							BATTING								FIELDING		
Year Team (League)	Pos.	G	AB	R	H	2B	3B	HR	RBI	Avg.	BB	SO	SB	PO	A	E	Avg.
1998—New York (A.L.)..........	OF	3	10	1	1	0	0	0	0	.100	1	3	0	7	1	0	1.000

NOTES: Member of World Series championship team (1998).

							BATTING								FIELDING		
Year Team (League)	Pos.	G	AB	R	H	2B	3B	HR	RBI	Avg.	BB	SO	SB	PO	A	E	Avg.
1998—New York (A.L.)..........	OF	1	3	1	1	1	0	0	0	.333	0	2	0	2	1	0	1.000

RECORD AS PITCHER

Year Team (League)	W	L	Pct.	ERA	G	GS	CG	ShO	Sv.	IP	H	R	ER	BB	SO
1992—Greensboro (S. Atl.)	0	0	. . .	0.00	1	0	0	0	0	1	2	0	0	1	1
1993—Greensboro (S. Atl.)	0	0	. . .	4.50	2	0	0	0	0	4	5	2	2	2	5

SPENCER, STAN   P   PADRES

PERSONAL: Born August 7, 1969, in Vancouver, B.C. ... 6-4/205. ... Throws right, bats right. ... Full name: Stanley Roger Spencer.
HIGH SCHOOL: Columbia River (Vancouver, B.C.).
COLLEGE: Stanford.
TRANSACTIONS/CAREER NOTES: Selected by Boston Red Sox organization in 26th round of free-agent draft (June 2, 1987); did not sign. ... Selected by Montreal Expos organization in supplemental round ("sandwich pick" between first and second round, 35th pick overall) of free-agent draft (June 4, 1990); pick received as part of compensation for Los Angeles Dodgers signing Type A free-agent OF Hubie Brooks. ... On disabled list (July 2, 1990-remainder of season and July 18, 1991-remainder of season). ... On Harrisburg disabled list (April 9, 1992-entire season). ... Selected by Florida Marlins from Expos organization in Rule 5 major league draft (December 7, 1992). ... On disabled list (April 8-June 24, 1993). ... On Portland disabled list (July 9-16, 1994). ... Granted free agency (October 11, 1995). ... Signed by San Diego Padres organization (February 7, 1997). ... On Rancho Cucamonga disabled list (May 9-22, 1997). ... Granted free agency (October 15, 1997). ... Re-signed by Padres organization (December 29, 1997). ... On Las Vegas disabled list (May 16-June 1, 1998).
HONORS: Named righthanded pitcher on THE SPORTING NEWS college All-America team (1990).
STATISTICAL NOTES: Tied for Eastern League lead with three balks in 1991.

Year	Team (League)	W	L	Pct.	ERA	G	GS	CG	ShO	Sv.	IP	H	R	ER	BB	SO
1990—								Did not play.								
1991—	Harrisburg (Eastern)	6	1	.857	4.40	17	17	1	0	0	92	90	52	45	30	66
1992—								Did not play.								
1993—	High Desert (Calif.)■	4	4	.500	4.09	13	13	0	0	0	61 2/3	67	33	28	18	38
1994—	Brevard County (FSL)	1	0	1.000	3.15	6	5	0	0	0	20	20	9	7	6	22
	—Portland (Eastern)	9	4	.692	3.48	20	20	1	0	0	124	113	52	48	30	96
1995—	Charlotte (Int'l)	1	4	.200	7.84	9	9	0	0	0	41 1/3	61	37	36	24	19
	—Portland (Eastern)	1	4	.200	7.38	8	8	0	0	0	39	57	39	32	19	32
1996—								Out of organized baseball.								
1997—	Rancho Cuca. (Cal.)■	3	1	.750	3.35	7	7	0	0	0	40 1/3	37	18	15	5	46
	—Las Vegas (PCL)	3	2	.600	3.75	8	8	0	0	0	48	48	23	20	18	47
1998—	Las Vegas (PCL)	12	6	.667	3.93	22	22	0	0	0	137 1/3	120	67	60	42	136
	—San Diego (N.L.)	1	0	1.000	4.70	6	5	0	0	0	30 2/3	29	16	16	4	31
Major league totals (1 year)		1	0	1.000	4.70	6	5	0	0	0	30 2/3	29	16	16	4	31

SPIERS, BILL   IF   ASTROS

PERSONAL: Born June 5, 1966, in Orangeburg, S.C. ... 6-2/190. ... Bats left, throws right. ... Full name: William James Spiers III. ... Name pronounced SPY-ers.

HIGH SCHOOL: Wade Hampton Academy (Orangeburg, S.C.).

COLLEGE: Clemson.

TRANSACTIONS/CAREER NOTES: Selected by Milwaukee Brewers organization in first round (13th pick overall) of free-agent draft (June 2, 1987). ... On Milwaukee disabled list (April 6-May 15, 1990); included rehabilitation assignment to Denver (April 27-May 14). ... On Milwaukee disabled list (April 5-September 2, 1992); included rehabilitation assignments to Beloit (May 6-15 and August 20-September 2). ... Granted free agency (December 20, 1993). ... Re-signed by Brewers (December 21, 1993). ... Claimed on waivers by New York Mets (October 25, 1994). ... On New York disabled list (May 15-June 5 and June 26-July 16, 1995); included rehabilitation assignment to Norfolk (May 22-June 5). ... Granted free agency (November 3, 1995). ... Signed by Houston Astros organization (January 10, 1996). ... Granted free agency (November 14, 1996). ... Re-signed by Astros (December 2, 1996). ... Granted free agency (November 3, 1997). ... Re-signed by Astros (November 25, 1997).

HONORS: Named shortstop on THE SPORTING NEWS college All-America team (1987).

STATISTICAL NOTES: Career major league grand slams: 2.

							BATTING								FIELDING		
Year	Team (League)	Pos.	G	AB	R	H	2B	3B	HR	RBI	Avg.	BB	SO	SB	PO	A	E	Avg.
1987—	Helena (Pioneer)	SS	6	22	4	9	1	0	0	3	.409	3	3	2	8	6	6	.700
	—Beloit (Midwest)	SS	64	258	43	77	10	1	3	26	.298	15	38	11	111	160	20	.931
1988—	Stockton (California)	SS	84	353	68	95	17	3	5	52	.269	42	41	27	140	240	19	.952
	—El Paso (Texas)	SS	47	168	22	47	5	2	3	21	.280	15	20	4	73	141	13	.943
1989—	Milwaukee (A.L.)	S-3-2-DH-1	114	345	44	88	9	3	4	33	.255	21	63	10	164	295	21	.956
	—Denver (A.A.)	SS	14	47	9	17	2	1	2	8	.362	5	6	1	32	33	2	.970
1990—	Denver (A.A.)	SS	11	38	6	12	0	0	1	7	.316	10	8	1	22	23	2	.957
	—Milwaukee (A.L.)	SS	112	363	44	88	15	3	2	36	.242	16	46	11	159	326	12	.976
1991—	Milwaukee (A.L.)	SS-DH-OF	133	414	71	117	13	6	8	54	.283	34	55	14	201	345	17	.970
1992—	Beloit (Midwest)	SS	16	55	9	13	3	0	0	7	.236	7	7	4	12	28	3	.930
	—Milwaukee (A.L.)	S-2-DH-3	12	16	2	5	2	0	0	2	.313	1	4	1	6	6	0	1.000
1993—	Milwaukee (A.L.)	2-O-S-DH	113	340	43	81	8	4	2	36	.238	29	51	9	213	231	13	.972
1994—	Milwaukee (A.L.)	3-S-DH-O-1	73	214	27	54	10	1	0	17	.252	19	42	7	70	129	8	.961
1995—	New York (N.L.)■	3B-2B	63	72	5	15	2	1	0	11	.208	12	15	0	13	30	7	.860
	—Norfolk (Int'l)	2B-3B	12	41	4	9	2	0	0	4	.220	8	6	0	23	29	4	.929
1996—	Houston (N.L.)■	3-2-S-1-O	122	218	27	55	10	1	6	26	.252	20	34	7	44	108	5	.968
1997—	Houston (N.L.)	3-S-1-2	132	291	51	93	27	4	4	48	.320	61	42	10	104	200	18	.944
1998—	Houston (N.L.)	3-2-1-S	123	384	66	105	27	4	4	43	.273	45	62	11	101	184	9	.969
American League totals (6 years)			557	1692	231	433	57	17	16	178	.256	120	261	52	813	1332	71	.968
National League totals (4 years)			440	965	149	268	66	10	14	128	.278	138	153	28	262	522	39	.953
Major league totals (10 years)			997	2657	380	701	123	27	30	306	.264	258	414	80	1075	1854	110	.964

DIVISION SERIES RECORD

RECORDS: Shares N.L. career record for most doubles—3.

							BATTING								FIELDING		
Year	Team (League)	Pos.	G	AB	R	H	2B	3B	HR	RBI	Avg.	BB	SO	SB	PO	A	E	Avg.
1997—	Houston (N.L.)	3B	3	11	1	0	0	0	0	0	.000	1	2	0	1	3	0	1.000
1998—	Houston (N.L.)	3B-PH	4	14	2	4	3	0	0	1	.286	1	3	0	1	5	0	1.000
Division series totals (2 years)			7	25	3	4	3	0	0	1	.160	2	5	0	2	8	0	1.000

SPIEZIO, SCOTT   2B   ATHLETICS

PERSONAL: Born September 21, 1972, in Joliet, Ill. ... 6-2/222. ... Bats both, throws right. ... Full name: Scott Edward Spiezio. ... Son of Ed Spiezio, third baseman with St. Louis Cardinals (1964-68), San Diego Padres (1969-72) and Chicago White Sox (1972).

HIGH SCHOOL: Morris (Ill.).

COLLEGE: Illinois.

TRANSACTIONS/CAREER NOTES: Selected by Oakland Athletics organization in sixth round of free-agent draft (June 3, 1993). ... On Oakland disabled list (June 8-25, 1997); included rehabilitation assignment to Southern Oregon (June 23-25). ... On Oakland disabled list (June 15-July 31, 1998); included rehabilitation assignment to Edmonton (July 26-31).

STATISTICAL NOTES: Led California League third basemen with .948 fielding percentage in 1994. ... Led Southern League with 14 sacrifice flies in 1995. ... Led Southern League third basemen with 291 assists, 29 errors, 424 total chances and 34 double plays in 1995. ... Led Pacific Coast League third basemen with 91 putouts, 302 assists, 405 total chances and .970 fielding percentage in 1996. ... Led A.L. second basemen with .990 fielding percentage in 1997. ... Had 18-game hitting streak (May 21-June 9, 1998). ... Career major league grand slams: 3.

Year	Team (League)	Pos.	G	AB	R	H	2B	3B	HR	RBI	Avg.	BB	SO	SB	PO	A	E	Avg.
1993—	S. Oregon (N'west).....	3B-1B	31	125	32	41	10	2	3	19	.328	16	18	0	76	40	9	.928
	— Modesto (California) ..	3B-1B	32	110	12	28	9	1	1	13	.255	23	19	1	42	51	5	.949
1994—	Modesto (California) ..	3B-1B-SS	127	453	84	127	32	5	14	68	.280	88	72	5	66	281	18	†.951
1995—	Huntsville (Sou.)	3B-1B-2B	141	528	78	149	33	8	13	86	.282	67	78	10	122	†295	†29	.935
1996—	Edmonton (PCL)	3B-1B	*140	523	87	137	30	4	20	91	.262	56	66	6	†174	†304	15	†.970
	— Oakland (A.L.)	3B-DH	9	29	6	9	2	0	2	8	.310	4	4	0	6	5	2	.846
1997—	Oakland (A.L.)	2B-3B	147	538	58	131	28	4	14	65	.243	44	75	9	280	415	7	†.990
	— S. Oregon (N'west)......	2B	2	9	1	5	0	0	0	2	.556	2	1	0	3	4	1	.875
1998—	Oakland (A.L.)	2B-DH	114	406	54	105	19	1	9	50	.259	44	56	1	198	316	13	.975
	— Edmonton (PCL)	2B	5	13	3	3	1	0	1	4	.231	3	2	0	5	3	1	.889
Major league totals (3 years)			270	973	118	245	49	5	25	123	.252	92	135	10	484	736	22	.982

SPIVEY, JUNIOR — IF — DIAMONDBACKS

PERSONAL: Born January 28, 1975, in Oklahoma City. ... 6-0/185. ... Bats right, throws right. ... Full name: Ernest Lee Spivey.
HIGH SCHOOL: Douglass (Oklahoma City).
JUNIOR COLLEGE: Cowley County Community College (Kan.).
TRANSACTIONS/CAREER NOTES: Selected by Arizona Diamondbacks organization in 26th round of free-agent draft (June 4, 1996). ... Loaned by Diamondbacks to Tulsa, Texas Rangers organization (July 18, 1998). ... Returned to Diamondbacks organization (August 29, 1998).
STATISTICAL NOTES: Led California League second basemen with 653 total chances in 1997. ... Tied for California League lead with 20 errors by second baseman in 1998.

Year	Team (League)	Pos.	G	AB	R	H	2B	3B	HR	RBI	Avg.	BB	SO	SB	PO	A	E	Avg.
1996—	Ariz. D-backs (Ariz.) ...	2B-SS-3B	20	69	13	23	0	0	0	3	.333	12	16	11	35	61	3	.970
	— Lethbridge (Pioneer) ..	2B-SS	31	107	30	36	3	4	2	25	.336	23	24	8	63	70	10	.930
1997—	High Desert (Calif.)......	2B	136	491	88	134	24	6	6	53	.273	69	115	14	226	*394	*33	.949
1998—	High Desert (Calif.).....	2B-3B-SS	79	285	64	80	14	5	5	35	.281	64	61	34	147	224	‡20	.949
	— Tulsa (Texas)■	2B	34	119	26	37	10	1	3	16	.311	28	25	8	62	84	3	.980

SPOLJARIC, PAUL — P — PHILLIES

PERSONAL: Born September 24, 1970, in Kelowna, B.C. ... 6-3/210. ... Throws left, bats right. ... Full name: Paul Nikola Spoljaric. ... Name pronounced spole-JAIR-ick.
HIGH SCHOOL: Springvalley Secondary (Kelowna, B.C.).
COLLEGE: Douglas College (B.C.).
TRANSACTIONS/CAREER NOTES: Signed as non-drafted free agent by Toronto Blue Jays organization (August 26, 1989). ... On Toronto disabled list (July 25-August 18, 1996); included rehabilitation assignment to St. Catharines (August 10-18). ... On Toronto disabled list (March 23-April 18, 1997); included rehabilitation assignment to Dunedin (April 4-17). ... Traded by Blue Jays with P Mike Timlin to Seattle Mariners for OF Jose Cruz Jr. (July 31, 1997). ... Traded by Mariners to Philadelphia Phillies for P Mark Leiter (November 9, 1998).
HONORS: Named South Atlantic League Most Outstanding Pitcher (1992).
STATISTICAL NOTES: Tied for A.L. lead with three balks in 1997.

Year	Team (League)	W	L	Pct.	ERA	G	GS	CG	ShO	Sv.	IP	H	R	ER	BB	SO
1990—	Medicine Hat (Pioneer)	3	7	.300	4.34	15	13	0	0	1	66 1/3	57	43	32	35	62
1991—	St. Catharines (NYP)	0	2	.000	4.82	4	4	0	0	0	18 2/3	21	14	10	9	21
1992—	Myrtle Beach (SAL)	10	8	.556	2.82	26	26	1	0	0	162 2/3	111	68	51	58	161
1993—	Dunedin (Fla. St.)	3	0	1.000	1.38	4	4	0	0	0	26	16	5	4	12	29
	— Knoxville (Southern)	4	1	.800	2.28	7	7	0	0	0	43 1/3	30	12	11	22	51
	— Syracuse (Int'l)	8	7	.533	5.29	18	18	1	1	0	95 1/3	97	63	56	52	88
1994—	Toronto (A.L.)	0	1	.000	38.57	2	1	0	0	0	2 1/3	5	10	10	9	2
	— Syracuse (Int'l)	1	5	.167	5.70	8	8	0	0	0	47 1/3	47	37	30	28	38
	— Knoxville (Southern)	6	5	.545	3.62	17	16	0	0	0	102	88	50	41	48	79
1995—	Syracuse (Int'l)	2	10	.167	4.93	43	9	0	0	10	87 2/3	69	51	48	54	108
1996—	Syracuse (Int'l)	3	0	1.000	3.27	17	0	0	0	4	22	20	9	8	6	24
	— Toronto (A.L.)	2	2	.500	3.08	28	0	0	0	1	38	30	17	13	19	38
	— St. Catharines (NYP)	0	0	. . .	0.00	2	2	0	0	0	5	3	0	0	0	7
1997—	Dunedin (Fla. St.)	0	0	. . .	1.69	4	3	0	0	0	10 2/3	10	3	2	2	10
	— Toronto (A.L.)	0	3	.000	3.19	37	0	0	0	3	48	37	17	17	21	43
	— Seattle (A.L.)■	0	0	. . .	4.76	20	0	0	0	0	22 2/3	24	13	12	15	27
1998—	Seattle (A.L.)	4	6	.400	6.48	53	6	0	0	0	83 1/3	85	67	60	55	89
Major league totals (4 years)		6	12	.333	5.19	140	7	0	0	4	194 1/3	181	124	112	119	199

DIVISION SERIES RECORD

Year	Team (League)	W	L	Pct.	ERA	G	GS	CG	ShO	Sv.	IP	H	R	ER	BB	SO
1997—	Seattle (A.L.)	0	0	. . .	0.00	2	0	0	0	0	1 2/3	4	0	0	0	1

SPRADLIN, JERRY — P — INDIANS

PERSONAL: Born June 14, 1967, in Fullerton, Calif. ... 6-7/246. ... Throws right, bats both. ... Full name: Jerry Carl Spradlin.
HIGH SCHOOL: Katella (Anaheim, Calif.).
COLLEGE: Fullerton (Calif.) College.
TRANSACTIONS/CAREER NOTES: Selected by Cincinnati Reds organization in 19th round of free-agent draft (June 1, 1988). ... Claimed on waivers by Florida Marlins (August 4, 1994). ... Granted free agency (October 16, 1995). ... Signed by Indianapolis, Reds orgnization (February 11, 1996). ... On Indianapolis disabled list (May 24-June 1, 1996). ... Released by Reds (October 30, 1996). ... Signed by Philadelphia Phillies (December 9, 1996). ... Traded by Phillies to Cleveland Indians for P Chad Ogea (November 13, 1998).
HONORS: Named Southern League co-Most Valuable Pitcher (1992).

S

Year Team (League)	W	L	Pct.	ERA	G	GS	CG	ShO	Sv.	IP	H	R	ER	BB	SO
1988— Billings (Pioneer)	4	1	.800	3.21	17	5	0	0	0	47 2/3	45	25	17	14	23
1989— Greensboro (S. Atl.)	7	2	.778	2.76	42	1	0	0	2	94 2/3	88	35	29	23	56
1990— Cedar Rapids (Midw.)	0	1	.000	3.00	5	0	0	0	0	12	13	8	4	5	6
— Char., W.Va. (S. Atl.)	3	4	.429	2.54	43	1	1	0	17	74 1/3	74	23	21	17	39
1991— Chattanooga (Southern)	7	3	.700	3.09	48	1	0	0	4	96	95	38	33	32	73
1992— Chattanooga (Southern)	3	3	.500	1.38	59	0	0	0	*34	65 1/3	52	11	10	13	35
— Cedar Rapids (Midw.)	1	0	1.000	7.71	1	0	0	0	0	2 1/3	5	2	2	0	4
1993— Indianapolis (A.A.)	3	2	.600	3.49	34	0	0	0	1	56 2/3	58	24	22	12	46
— Cincinnati (N.L.)	2	1	.667	3.49	37	0	0	0	2	49	44	20	19	9	24
1994— Indianapolis (A.A.)	3	3	.500	3.68	28	5	0	0	3	73 1/3	87	36	30	16	49
— Cincinnati (N.L.)	0	0	. . .	10.13	6	0	0	0	0	8	12	11	9	2	4
— Edmonton (PCL)■	1	0	1.000	2.53	6	0	0	0	1	10 2/3	12	3	3	4	3
1995— Charlotte (Int'l)	3	3	.500	3.03	41	0	0	0	1	59 1/3	59	26	20	15	38
1996— Indianapolis (A.A.)■	6	8	.429	3.33	49	8	0	0	15	100	94	49	37	23	79
— Cincinnati (N.L.)	0	0	. . .	0.00	1	0	0	0	0	1/3	0	0	0	0	0
1997— Philadelphia (N.L.)■	4	8	.333	4.74	76	0	0	0	1	81 2/3	86	45	43	27	67
1998— Philadelphia (N.L.)	4	4	.500	3.53	69	0	0	0	1	81 2/3	63	34	32	20	76
Major league totals (5 years)	10	13	.435	4.20	189	0	0	0	4	220 2/3	205	110	103	58	171

SPRAGUE, ED   3B   PIRATES

PERSONAL: Born July 25, 1967, in Castro Valley, Calif. ... 6-2/205. ... Bats right, throws right. ... Full name: Edward Nelson Sprague Jr. ... Son of Ed Sprague, major league pitcher with four teams (1968-69 and 1971-76); and husband of Kristen Babb, Olympic gold-medal synchronized swimmer (1992). ... Name pronounced SPRAYGH.

HIGH SCHOOL: St. Mary's (Stockton, Calif.).

COLLEGE: Stanford.

TRANSACTIONS/CAREER NOTES: Selected by Boston Red Sox organization in 26th round of free-agent draft (June 3, 1985); did not sign. ... Selected by Toronto Blue Jays organization in first round (25th pick overall) of free-agent draft (June 1, 1988). ... On suspended list (August 8-10, 1993). ... On disabled list (September 4-28, 1997). ... Traded by Blue Jays to Oakland Athletics for P Scott Rivette (July 31, 1998). ... Granted free agency (October 27, 1998). ... Signed by Pittsburgh Pirates (December 15, 1998).

STATISTICAL NOTES: Led International League third basemen with 31 errors and 364 total chances and tied for lead with 240 assists in 1990. ... Led A.L. in grounding into double plays with 23 in 1993. ... Led A.L. third basemen with 98 putouts in 1994 and 133 in 1995. ... Led A.L. in being hit by pitch with 15 in 1995. ... Career major league grand slams: 3.

MISCELLANEOUS: Member of 1988 U.S. Olympic baseball team.

Year Team (League)	Pos.	G	AB	R	H	2B	3B	HR	RBI	Avg.	BB	SO	SB	PO	A	E	Avg.
1989— Dunedin (Fla. St.)	3B	52	192	21	42	9	2	7	23	.219	16	40	1	33	86	14	.895
— Syracuse (Int'l)	3B	86	288	23	60	14	1	5	33	.208	18	73	0	51	149	*25	.889
1990— Syracuse (Int'l)	3B-1B-C	142	*519	60	124	23	5	20	75	.239	31	100	4	171	‡246	†35	.923
1991— Syracuse (Int'l)	C-3B	23	88	24	32	8	0	5	25	.364	10	21	2	111	17	6	.955
— Toronto (A.L.)	3-1-C-DH	61	160	17	44	7	0	4	20	.275	19	43	0	167	72	14	.945
1992— Syracuse (Int'l)	C-1B-3B	100	369	49	102	18	2	16	50	.276	44	73	0	438	44	12	.976
— Toronto (A.L.)	C-1-DH-3	22	47	6	11	2	0	1	7	.234	3	7	0	82	5	1	.989
1993— Toronto (A.L.)	3B	150	546	50	142	31	1	12	73	.260	32	85	1	*127	232	17	.955
1994— Toronto (A.L.)	3B-1B	109	405	38	97	19	1	11	44	.240	23	95	1	†117	147	14	.950
1995— Toronto (A.L.)	3B-1B-DH	144	521	77	127	27	2	18	74	.244	58	96	0	†167	234	17	.959
1996— Toronto (A.L.)	3B-DH	159	591	88	146	35	2	36	101	.247	60	146	0	108	218	15	.956
1997— Toronto (A.L.)	3B-DH	138	504	63	115	29	4	14	48	.228	51	102	0	106	202	18	.945
1998— Toronto (A.L.)	3B	105	382	49	91	20	0	17	51	.238	24	73	0	87	157	20	.924
— Oakland (A.L.)■	3B-1B	27	87	8	13	5	0	3	7	.149	2	17	1	24	37	6	.910
Major league totals (8 years)		915	3243	396	786	175	10	116	425	.242	272	664	3	985	1304	122	.949

CHAMPIONSHIP SERIES RECORD

Year Team (League)	Pos.	G	AB	R	H	2B	3B	HR	RBI	Avg.	BB	SO	SB	PO	A	E	Avg.
1991— Toronto (A.L.)								Did not play.									
1992— Toronto (A.L.)	PH	2	2	0	1	0	0	0	0	.500	0	1	0	. . .	. . .	. . .	
1993— Toronto (A.L.)	3B	6	21	0	6	0	1	0	4	.286	2	4	0	5	9	0	1.000
Championship series totals (2 years)		8	23	0	7	0	1	0	4	.304	2	5	0	5	9	0	1.000

WORLD SERIES RECORD

NOTES: Hit home run in first at-bat (October 18, 1992). ... Member of World Series championship team (1992 and 1993).

Year Team (League)	Pos.	G	AB	R	H	2B	3B	HR	RBI	Avg.	BB	SO	SB	PO	A	E	Avg.
1992— Toronto (A.L.)	PH-1B	3	2	1	1	0	0	1	2	.500	1	0	0	0	0	0	. . .
1993— Toronto (A.L.)	3B-PH-1B	5	15	0	1	0	0	0	2	.067	1	6	0	4	9	2	.867
World Series totals (2 years)		8	17	1	2	0	0	1	4	.118	2	6	0	4	9	2	.867

SPRINGER, DENNIS   P

PERSONAL: Born February 12, 1965, in Fresno, Calif. ... 5-10/185. ... Throws right, bats right. ... Full name: Dennis LeRoy Springer.

HIGH SCHOOL: Washington (Fresno, Calif.).

JUNIOR COLLEGE: Kings River Community College (Calif.).

COLLEGE: Fresno State.

TRANSACTIONS/CAREER NOTES: Selected by Los Angeles Dodgers organization in 21st round of free-agent draft (June 2, 1987). ... On San Antonio disabled list (April 19-27, 1992). ... On disabled list (August 24-September 6, 1993). ... Granted free agency (October 15, 1993). ... Signed by Philadelphia Phillies organization (May 19, 1994). ... Granted free agency (December 21, 1995). ... Signed by California Angels organization (January 5, 1996). ... Angels franchise renamed Anaheim Angels for 1997 season. ... Selected by Tampa Bay Devil Rays in first round (26th pick overall) of expansion draft (November 18, 1997). ... Released by Devil Rays (November 3, 1998).

Year Team (League)	W	L	Pct.	ERA	G	GS	CG	ShO	Sv.	IP	H	R	ER	BB	SO
1987— Great Falls (Pio.)	4	3	.571	2.88	23	5	1	0	6	65²/₃	70	38	21	16	54
1988— Bakersfield (California)	13	7	.650	3.27	32	20	6	•4	2	154	135	75	56	62	108
1989— San Antonio (Tex.)	6	8	.429	3.15	19	19	4	1	0	140	128	58	49	46	89
— Albuquerque (PCL)	4	1	.800	4.83	8	7	0	0	0	41	58	28	22	14	18
1990— San Antonio (Tex.)	8	6	.571	3.31	24	24	3	0	0	*163¹/₃	147	76	60	73	77
1991— San Antonio (Tex.)	10	10	.500	4.43	30	24	2	0	0	164²/₃	153	96	81	91	*138
1992— San Antonio (Tex.)	6	7	.462	4.35	18	18	4	0	0	122	114	61	59	49	73
— Albuquerque (PCL)	2	7	.222	5.66	11	11	1	0	0	62	70	45	39	22	36
1993— Albuquerque (PCL)	3	8	.273	5.99	35	18	0	0	0	130²/₃	173	104	87	39	69
1994— Reading (Eastern)■	5	8	.385	3.40	24	19	2	0	2	135	125	74	51	44	118
1995— Scran./W.B. (Int'l)	10	11	.476	4.68	30	23	4	0	0	171	163	*101	89	47	115
— Philadelphia (N.L.)	0	3	.000	4.84	4	4	0	0	0	22¹/₃	21	15	12	9	15
1996— California (A.L.)■	5	6	.455	5.51	20	15	2	1	0	94²/₃	91	65	58	43	64
— Vancouver (PCL)	10	3	.769	2.72	16	12	6	0	0	109¹/₃	89	35	33	36	78
1997— Anaheim (A.L.)	9	9	.500	5.18	32	28	3	1	0	194²/₃	199	118	112	73	75
— Vancouver (PCL)	1	1	.500	3.00	2	2	2	0	0	15	12	6	5	6	7
1998— Tampa Bay (A.L.)■	3	11	.214	5.45	29	17	1	0	0	115²/₃	120	77	70	60	46
— Durham (International)	2	3	.400	2.87	5	5	0	0	0	37²/₃	34	13	12	15	23
A.L. totals (3 years)	17	26	.395	5.33	81	60	6	2	0	405	410	260	240	176	185
N.L. totals (1 year)	0	3	.000	4.84	4	4	0	0	0	22¹/₃	21	15	12	9	15
Major league totals (4 years)	17	29	.370	5.31	85	64	6	2	0	427¹/₃	431	275	252	185	200

SPRINGER, RUSS — P — BRAVES

S

PERSONAL: Born November 7, 1968, in Alexandria, La. ... 6-4/205. ... Throws right, bats right. ... Full name: Russell Paul Springer.
HIGH SCHOOL: Grant (Dry Prong, La.).
COLLEGE: Louisiana State.
TRANSACTIONS/CAREER NOTES: Selected by New York Yankees organization in seventh round of free-agent draft (June 5, 1989). ... Traded by Yankees with 1B J.T. Snow and P Jerry Nielsen to California Angels for P Jim Abbott (December 6, 1992). ... On California disabled list (August 2, 1993-remainder of season). ... Traded by Angels to Philadelphia Phillies (August 15, 1995), completing deal in which Angels acquired OF Dave Gallagher from Phillies for 2B Kevin Flora and a player to be named later (August 9, 1995). ... Released by Phillies (December 20, 1996). ... Signed by Houston Astros organization (December 30, 1996). ... On Houston disabled list (June 17-July 10, 1997); included rehabilitation assignment to Jackson (July 8-10). ... Selected by Arizona Diamondbacks in third round (61st pick overall) of expansion draft (November 18, 1997). ... Traded by Diamondbacks to Atlanta Braves for P Alan Embree (June 23, 1998). ... On Atlanta disabled list (August 6-21, 1998).

Year Team (League)	W	L	Pct.	ERA	G	GS	CG	ShO	Sv.	IP	H	R	ER	BB	SO
1989— GC Yankees (GCL)	3	0	1.000	1.50	6	6	0	0	0	24	14	8	4	10	34
1990— GC Yankees (GCL)	0	2	.000	1.20	4	4	0	0	0	15	10	6	2	4	17
— Greensboro (S. Atl.)	2	3	.400	3.67	10	10	0	0	0	56¹/₃	51	33	23	31	51
1991— Fort Lauderdale (FSL)	5	9	.357	3.49	25	25	2	0	0	152¹/₃	118	68	59	62	139
— Alb./Colon. (East.)	1	0	1.000	1.80	2	2	0	0	0	15	9	4	3	6	16
1992— Columbus (Int'l)	8	5	.615	2.69	20	20	1	0	0	123²/₃	89	46	37	54	95
— New York (A.L.)	0	0	. . .	6.19	14	0	0	0	0	16	18	11	11	10	12
1993— Vancouver (PCL)■	5	4	.556	4.27	11	9	1	0	0	59	58	37	28	33	40
— California (A.L.)	1	6	.143	7.20	14	9	1	0	0	60	73	48	48	32	31
1994— Vancouver (PCL)	7	4	.636	3.04	12	12	•4	0	0	83	77	35	28	19	58
— California (A.L.)	2	2	.500	5.52	18	5	0	0	2	45²/₃	53	28	28	14	28
1995— Vancouver (PCL)	2	0	1.000	3.44	6	6	0	0	0	34	24	16	13	23	23
— California (A.L.)	1	2	.333	6.10	19	6	0	0	1	51²/₃	60	37	35	25	38
— Philadelphia (N.L.)■	0	0	. . .	3.71	14	0	0	0	0	26²/₃	22	11	11	10	32
1996— Philadelphia (N.L.)	3	10	.231	4.66	51	7	0	0	0	96²/₃	106	60	50	38	94
1997— Houston (N.L.)■	3	3	.500	4.23	54	0	0	0	3	55¹/₃	48	28	26	27	74
— Jackson (Texas)	0	0	. . .	9.00	1	0	0	0	0	1	2	1	1	0	2
1998— Arizona (N.L.)■	4	3	.571	4.13	26	0	0	0	0	32²/₃	29	16	15	14	37
— Atlanta (N.L.)■	1	1	.500	4.05	22	0	0	0	0	20	22	10	9	16	19
A.L. totals (4 years)	4	10	.286	6.33	65	20	1	0	3	173¹/₃	204	124	122	81	109
N.L. totals (4 years)	11	17	.393	4.32	167	7	0	0	3	231¹/₃	227	125	111	105	256
Major league totals (7 years)	15	27	.357	5.18	232	27	1	0	6	404²/₃	431	249	233	186	365

DIVISION SERIES RECORD

Year Team (League)	W	L	Pct.	ERA	G	GS	CG	ShO	Sv.	IP	H	R	ER	BB	SO
1997— Houston (N.L.)	0	0	. . .	5.40	2	0	0	0	0	1²/₃	2	1	1	1	3

STAHOVIAK, SCOTT — 1B — CUBS

PERSONAL: Born March 6, 1970, in Waukegan, Ill. ... 6-5/230. ... Bats left, throws right. ... Full name: Scott Edmund Stahoviak. ... Name pronounced stuh-HO-vee-ak.
HIGH SCHOOL: Carmel (Mundelein, Ill.).
COLLEGE: Creighton.
TRANSACTIONS/CAREER NOTES: Selected by Minnesota Twins organization in 27th round of free-agent draft (June 1, 1988); did not sign. ... Selected by Twins organization in supplemental round ("sandwich pick" between first and second round, 27th pick overall) of free-agent draft (June 3, 1991); pick received as compensation for California Angels signing Type A free-agent 3B Gary Gaetti. ... On Nashville disabled list (May 12-June 24, 1993). ... On Minnesota disabled list (April 2-May 16, 1997); included rehabilitation assignment to Salt Lake (May 8-16). ... Granted free agency (September 29, 1998). ... Signed by Chicago Cubs organization (November 13, 1998).

Year Team (League)	Pos.	G	AB	R	H	2B	3B	HR	RBI	Avg.	BB	SO	SB	PO	A	E	Avg.
						BATTING									FIELDING		
1991— Visalia (California)	3B	43	158	29	44	9	1	1	25	.278	22	28	9	31	89	12	.909
1992— Visalia (California)	3B	110	409	62	126	26	3	5	68	.308	82	66	17	92	181	*40	.872

Year	Team (League)	Pos.	G	AB	R	H	2B	3B	HR	RBI	Avg.	BB	SO	SB	PO	A	E	Avg.
						BATTING										FIELDING		
1993—Nashville (Southern)..	3-1-S-O	93	331	40	90	25	1	12	56	.272	56	95	10	89	150	24	.909
—Minnesota (A.L.)	3B	20	57	1	11	4	0	0	1	.193	3	22	0	9	38	4	.922
1994—Salt Lake (PCL)	3B-1B	123	437	96	139	41	6	13	94	.318	70	90	6	303	204	31	.942
1995—Salt Lake (PCL)	3B-1B	9	33	6	10	1	0	0	5	.303	6	3	2	36	16	0	1.000
—Minnesota (A.L.)	1B-3B-DH	94	263	28	70	19	0	3	23	.266	30	61	5	503	91	5	.992
1996—Minnesota (A.L.)	1B-DH	130	405	72	115	30	3	13	61	.284	59	114	3	801	92	5	.994
1997—Minnesota (A.L.)	1B-DH	91	275	33	63	17	0	10	33	.229	24	73	5	607	58	7	.990
—Salt Lake (PCL)	1B	8	28	5	6	0	0	2	10	.214	5	8	0	72	7	0	1.000
1998—Salt Lake (PCL)	1B-OF	111	399	71	126	33	6	18	82	.316	45	94	5	565	56	3	.995
—Minnesota (A.L.)	1B-OF	19	11	1	2	0	0	1	1	.105	0	7	0	35	4	1	.975
Major league totals (5 years)		344	1019	135	261	70	3	27	119	.256	116	277	13	1955	283	22	.990

STAIRS, MATT   OF   ATHLETICS

PERSONAL: Born February 27, 1968, in Saint John, N.B. ... 5-9/206. ... Bats left, throws right. ... Full name: Matthew Wade Stairs.

HIGH SCHOOL: Fredericton (N.B.).

TRANSACTIONS/CAREER NOTES: Signed as non-drafted free agent by Montreal Expos organization (January 17, 1989). ... On disabled list (May 16-23, 1991). ... On Ottawa disabled list (May 7-18, 1993). ... Released by Expos (June 8, 1993). ... Contract purchased by Chunichi Dragons of Japan Central League (June 8, 1993). ... Signed by Expos organization (December 15, 1993). ... Traded by Expos with P Pete Young to Boston Red Sox for cash (February 18, 1994). ... Granted free agency (October 14, 1995). ... Signed by Oakland Athletics organization (December 1, 1995).

HONORS: Named Eastern League Most Valuable Player (1991).

STATISTICAL NOTES: Led Eastern League with .509 slugging percentage, 257 total bases and tied for lead with eight intentional bases on balls received in 1991. ... Career major league grand slams: 4.

MISCELLANEOUS: Member of 1988 Canadian Olympic baseball team.

Year	Team (League)	Pos.	G	AB	R	H	2B	3B	HR	RBI	Avg.	BB	SO	SB	PO	A	E	Avg.
						BATTING										FIELDING		
1989—W.P. Beach (FSL)	3B-SS-2B	36	111	12	21	3	1	1	9	.189	9	18	0	21	66	4	.956
—Jamestown (NYP)	2B-3B	14	43	8	11	1	0	1	5	.256	3	5	1	15	35	6	.893
—Rockford (Midwest)	3B	44	141	20	40	9	2	2	14	.284	15	29	5	30	62	7	.929
1990—W.P. Beach (FSL)	3B-2B	55	183	30	62	9	3	3	30	.339	41	19	15	40	112	17	.899
—Jacksonville (Sou.)	3-0-2-S	79	280	26	71	17	0	3	34	.254	22	43	5	76	107	22	.893
1991—Harrisburg (East.)	2B-3B-OF	129	505	87	*168	30	•10	13	78	*.333	66	47	23	193	314	22	.958
1992—Indianapolis (A.A.)	OF	110	401	57	107	23	4	11	56	.267	49	61	11	188	11	3	.985
—Montreal (N.L.)	OF	13	30	2	5	2	0	0	5	.167	7	7	0	14	0	1	.933
1993—Ottawa (Int'l)	OF	34	125	18	35	4	2	3	20	.280	11	15	4	49	4	0	1.000
—Montreal (N.L.)	OF	6	8	1	3	1	0	0	2	.375	0	1	0	1	0	0	1.000
—Chunichi (Jp. Cn.)■..	...	60	132	10	33	6	0	6	23	.250	7	34	1	...	...	...	...
1994—New Britain (East.)■..	OF-1B	93	317	44	98	25	2	9	61	.309	53	38	10	106	12	3	.975
1995—Pawtucket (Int'l)	OF	75	271	40	77	17	0	13	56	.284	29	41	3	79	13	0	1.000
—Boston (A.L.)	DH	39	88	8	23	7	1	1	17	.261	4	14	0	19	2	2	.913
1996—Oakland (A.L.)■	OF-DH-1B	61	137	21	38	5	1	10	23	.277	19	23	1	65	11	1	.987
—Edmonton (PCL)	OF-1B	51	180	35	62	16	1	8	41	.344	21	34	0	49	2	3	.944
1997—Oakland (A.L.)	OF-DH-1B	133	352	62	105	19	0	27	73	.298	50	60	3	142	9	4	.974
1998—Oakland (A.L.)	DH-OF-1B	149	523	88	154	33	1	26	106	.294	59	93	8	67	11	0	1.000
American League totals (4 years)		382	1100	179	320	64	3	64	219	.291	132	190	12	293	33	7	.979
National League totals (2 years)		19	38	3	8	3	0	0	7	.211	7	8	0	15	0	1	.938
Major league totals (6 years)		401	1138	182	328	67	3	64	226	.288	139	198	12	308	33	8	.977

DIVISION SERIES RECORD

Year	Team (League)	Pos.	G	AB	R	H	2B	3B	HR	RBI	Avg.	BB	SO	SB	PO	A	E	Avg.
						BATTING										FIELDING		
1995—Boston (A.L.)	PH	1	1	0	0	0	0	0	0	.000	0	1	0	...	...	...	...

STANIFER, ROB   P   MARLINS

PERSONAL: Born March 10, 1972, in Easley, S.C. ... 6-3/205. ... Throws right, bats right. ... Full name: Robert Wayne Stanifer.

HIGH SCHOOL: Easley (S.C.).

COLLEGE: Anderson (S.C.); degree in sports administration, 1994.

TRANSACTIONS/CAREER NOTES: Selected by Florida Marlins organization in 12th round of free-agent draft (June 2, 1994).

Year	Team (League)	W	L	Pct.	ERA	G	GS	CG	ShO	Sv.	IP	H	R	ER	BB	SO
1994—Elmira (N.Y.-Penn)	2	1	.667	2.57	9	8	1	0	0	49	54	17	14	12	38
—Brevard County (FSL)	1	2	.333	6.29	5	5	0	0	0	24 1/3	32	20	17	10	12
1995—Brevard County (FSL)	3	6	.333	4.14	18	13	0	0	0	82 2/3	97	47	38	15	45
1996—Brevard County (FSL)	4	2	.667	2.39	22	0	0	0	0	49	54	17	13	9	32
—Portland (Eastern)	3	1	.750	1.57	18	0	0	0	2	34 1/3	27	15	6	9	33
1997—Charlotte (Int'l)	4	0	1.000	4.88	22	0	0	0	5	27 2/3	34	16	15	7	25
—Florida (N.L.)	1	2	.333	4.60	36	0	0	0	1	45	43	23	23	16	22
1998—Charlotte (Int'l)	4	2	.667	4.31	21	1	0	0	4	39 2/3	39	20	19	13	29
—Florida (N.L.)	2	4	.333	5.63	38	0	0	0	1	48	54	33	30	22	30
Major league totals (2 years)	3	6	.333	5.13	74	0	0	0	2	93	97	56	53	38	58

STANKIEWICZ, ANDY   IF

PERSONAL: Born August 10, 1964, in Inglewood, Calif. ... 5-9/165. ... Bats right, throws right. ... Full name: Andrew Neal Stankiewicz. ... Name pronounced STANK-a-wits.

HIGH SCHOOL: St. Paul (Sante Fe Springs, Calif.).

COLLEGE: Pepperdine.

TRANSACTIONS/CAREER NOTES: Selected by Kansas City Royals organization in 26th round of free-agent draft (June 7, 1982); did not sign. ... Selected by Detroit Tigers organization in 18th round of free-agent draft (June 3, 1985); did not sign. ... Selected by New York Yankees organization in 12th round of free-agent draft (June 2, 1986). ... On disabled list (May 16-31, 1992). ... On Columbus disabled list (August 18-26, 1993). ... Traded by Yankees with P Domingo Jean to Houston Astros for P Xavier Hernandez (November 27, 1993). ... On Houston disabled list (July 6-August 7, 1994); included rehabilitation assignment to Jackson (August 1-7). ... On Houston disabled list (May 29-June 26, 1995); included rehabilitation assignment to Tucson (June 18-26). ... Granted free agency (October 16, 1995). ... Signed by Montreal Expos organization (December 20, 1995). ... On disabled list (August 12-September 1, 1996). ... Granted free agency (December 21, 1997). ... Signed by Arizona Diamondbacks (January 8, 1998). ... On Arizona disabled list (March 20-April 6 and June 24-July 19, 1998); included rehabilitation assignments to Arizona League Diamondbacks (July 9-11) and Tucson (July 12-17). ... Granted free agency (November 2, 1998).

STATISTICAL NOTES: Led Eastern League with 11 sacrifice flies in 1989. ... Led Eastern League second basemen with 615 total chances and 85 double plays in 1989.

							BATTING								FIELDING		
Year Team (League)	Pos.	G	AB	R	H	2B	3B	HR	RBI	Avg.	BB	SO	SB	PO	A	E	Avg.
1986— Oneonta (NYP)..........	2B-SS	59	216	51	64	8	3	0	17	.296	38	41	14	107	152	12	.956
1987— Fort Laud. (FSL).......	2B	119	456	80	140	18	7	2	47	.307	62	84	26	233	347	16	.973
1988— Alb./Colon. (East.)......	2B	109	414	63	111	20	2	1	33	.268	39	53	15	230	325	*16	.972
— Columbus (Int'l)........	2B	29	114	4	25	0	0	0	4	.219	6	25	2	56	97	3	.981
1989— Alb./Colon. (East.)......	2B	133	498	*74	133	26	2	4	49	.267	57	59	*41	*242	*369	4	*.993
1990— Columbus (Int'l).........	2B-SS-3B	135	446	68	102	14	4	1	48	.229	71	63	25	237	399	10	.985
1991— Columbus (Int'l).........	2B	125	372	47	101	12	4	1	41	.272	29	45	29	220	324	15	.973
1992— New York (A.L.).........	SS-2B-DH	116	400	52	107	22	2	2	25	.268	38	42	9	185	346	12	.978
1993— Columbus (Int'l).........	2B-3B-SS	90	331	45	80	12	5	0	32	.242	29	46	12	138	265	6	.985
— New York (A.L.).........	2-3-DH-S	16	9	5	0	0	0	0	0	.000	1	1	0	7	15	0	1.000
1994— Houston (N.L.)■.......	SS-2B-3B	37	54	10	14	3	0	1	5	.259	12	12	1	12	45	0	1.000
— Jackson (Texas)	2B-SS	5	12	1	5	0	0	0	3	.417	0	0	0	8	7	1	.938
1995— Houston (N.L.).........	SS-2B-3B	43	52	6	6	1	0	0	7	.115	12	19	4	20	59	1	.988
— Tucson (PCL)	2B	25	87	16	24	4	0	1	15	.276	14	8	3	36	81	3	.975
1996— Montreal (N.L.)■.......	2B-SS-3B	64	77	12	22	5	1	0	9	.286	6	12	1	16	43	3	.952
1997— Montreal (N.L.).........	2-S-3-DH	76	107	11	24	9	0	1	5	.224	4	22	1	33	68	3	.971
1998— Arizona (N.L.)■.......	2B	77	145	9	30	5	0	0	8	.207	7	33	1	62	94	1	.994
— Ariz. D-backs (Ariz.) ...	2B	3	10	2	3	0	0	0	3	.300	0	0	0	5	8	0	1.000
— Tucson (PCL)	2B	5	20	1	6	0	0	0	2	.300	0	0	0	11	9	0	1.000
American League totals (2 years)		132	409	57	107	22	2	2	25	.262	39	43	9	192	361	12	.979
National League totals (5 years)		297	435	48	96	23	1	2	34	.221	41	98	8	143	309	8	.983
Major league totals (7 years)		429	844	105	203	45	3	4	59	.241	80	141	17	335	670	20	.980

RECORD AS PITCHER

Year Team (League)	W	L	Pct.	ERA	G	GS	CG	ShO	Sv.	IP	H	R	ER	BB	SO
1991— Columbus (Int'l)...............	0	0	...	0.00	1	0	0	0	0	$1/3$	1	0	0	1	0

STANLEY, MIKE — DH/1B — RED SOX

PERSONAL: Born June 25, 1963, in Fort Lauderdale. ... 6-0/190. ... Bats right, throws right. ... Full name: Michael Robert Stanley.

HIGH SCHOOL: St. Thomas Aquinas (Fort Lauderdale).

COLLEGE: Florida.

TRANSACTIONS/CAREER NOTES: Selected by Texas Rangers organization in 16th round of free-agent draft (June 3, 1985). ... On disabled list (July 24-August 14, 1988 and August 18-September 2, 1989). ... Granted free agency (November 15, 1990). ... Re-signed by Rangers organization (February 4, 1991). ... Granted free agency (October 14, 1991). ... Signed by Columbus, New York Yankees organization (January 21, 1992). ... On disabled list (May 14-29, 1994). ... Granted free agency (November 1, 1995). ... Signed by Boston Red Sox (December 14, 1995). ... Traded by Red Sox with IF Randy Brown to Yankees for P Tony Armas Jr. and a player to be named later (August 13, 1997); Red Sox acquired P Jim Mecir to complete deal (September 29, 1997). ... Granted free agency (October 27, 1997). ... Signed by Toronto Blue Jays (December 8, 1997). ... Traded by Blue Jays to Red Sox for P Peter Munro and P Jay Yennaco (July 30, 1998).

HONORS: Named catcher on THE SPORTING NEWS A.L. All-Star team (1993). ... Named catcher on THE SPORTING NEWS A.L. Silver Slugger team (1993).

STATISTICAL NOTES: Hit three home runs in one game (August 10, 1995, first game). ... Led A.L. catchers with 18 passed balls in 1996. ... Career major league grand slams: 8.

							BATTING								FIELDING		
Year Team (League)	Pos.	G	AB	R	H	2B	3B	HR	RBI	Avg.	BB	SO	SB	PO	A	E	Avg.
1985— Salem (Carolina)	1B-C	4	9	2	5	0	0	0	3	.556	1	1	0	19	1	1	.952
— Burlington (Midw.)	C-1B-OF	13	42	8	13	2	0	1	6	.310	6	5	0	45	2	0	1.000
— Tulsa (Texas)	C-1-O-2	46	165	24	51	10	0	3	17	.309	24	18	6	289	18	6	.981
1986— Tulsa (Texas)	C-1B-3B	67	235	41	69	16	2	6	35	.294	34	26	5	379	45	2	.995
— Texas (A.L.).............	3-C-DH-O	15	30	4	10	3	0	1	1	.333	3	7	1	14	8	1	.957
— Okla. City (A.A.).........	C-3B-1B	56	202	37	74	13	3	5	49	.366	44	42	1	206	55	9	.967
1987— Okla. City (A.A.).........	C-1B	46	182	43	61	8	3	13	54	.335	29	36	2	277	32	2	.994
— Texas (A.L.).............	C-1B-DH-O	78	216	34	59	8	1	6	37	.273	31	48	3	389	26	7	.983
1988— Texas (A.L.).............	C-DH-1-3	94	249	21	57	8	0	3	27	.229	37	62	0	342	17	4	.989
1989— Texas (A.L.).............	C-DH-1-3	67	122	9	30	3	1	1	11	.246	12	29	1	117	8	3	.977
1990— Texas (A.L.).............	C-DH-3-1	103	189	21	47	8	1	2	19	.249	30	25	1	261	25	4	.986
1991— Texas (A.L.)...........C-1-3-DH-O		95	181	25	45	13	1	3	25	.249	34	44	0	288	20	6	.981
1992— New York (A.L.)■........	C-DH-1B	68	173	24	43	7	0	8	27	.249	33	45	0	287	30	6	.981
1993— New York (A.L.).........	C-DH	130	423	70	129	17	1	26	84	.305	57	85	1	652	46	3	*.996
1994— New York (A.L.).........	C-1B-DH	82	290	54	87	20	0	17	57	.300	39	56	0	442	35	5	.990
1995— New York (A.L.).........	C-DH	118	399	63	107	29	1	18	83	.268	57	106	1	651	35	5	.993
1996— Boston (A.L.)■.........	C-DH	121	397	73	107	20	1	24	69	.270	69	62	2	654	19	•10	.985
1997— Boston (A.L.)............	DH-1B-C	97	260	45	78	17	0	13	53	.300	39	50	0	284	21	2	.993
— New York (A.L.).........	DH-1B	28	87	16	25	8	0	3	12	.287	15	22	0	71	3	0	1.000
1998— Toronto (A.L.)■........	DH-1B-OF	98	341	49	82	13	0	22	47	.240	56	86	2	172	12	1	.995
— Boston (A.L.)■.........	DH-1B	47	156	25	45	12	0	7	32	.288	26	43	1	108	6	0	1.000
Major league totals (13 years)		1241	3513	533	951	186	7	154	584	.271	538	770	13	4732	311	57	.989

S

Year	Team (League)	Pos.	G	AB	R	H	2B	3B	HR	RBI	Avg.	BB	SO	SB	PO	A	E	Avg.
							BATTING									FIELDING		
1995—New York (A.L.).........		C	4	16	2	5	0	0	1	3	.313	2	1	0	30	0	1	.968
1997—New York (A.L.).........		PH-DH	2	4	1	3	1	0	0	1	.750	0	1	0	...	...	...	...
1998—Boston (A.L.).............		DH	4	15	1	4	0	0	0	0	.267	2	5	0	...	...	...	...
Division series totals (3 years)			10	35	4	12	1	0	1	4	.343	4	7	0	30	0	1	.968

ALL-STAR GAME RECORD

Year	League	Pos.	AB	R	H	2B	3B	HR	RBI	Avg.	BB	SO	SB	PO	A	E	Avg.
						BATTING									FIELDING		
1995—American...................		C	1	0	0	0	0	0	0	.000	0	0	0	3	0	0	1.000

STANTON, MIKE　　　　　　　　P　　　　　　　　YANKEES

PERSONAL: Born June 2, 1967, in Houston. ... 6-1/215. ... Throws left, bats left. ... Full name: William Michael Stanton.
HIGH SCHOOL: Midland (Texas).
JUNIOR COLLEGE: Alvin (Texas) Community College.
TRANSACTIONS/CAREER NOTES: Selected by Atlanta Braves organization in 13th round of free-agent draft (June 2, 1987). ... On Atlanta disabled list (April 27, 1990-remainder of season); included rehabilitation assignments to Greenville (May 31-June 5 and August 21-29). ... Granted free agency (December 23, 1994). ... Re-signed by Braves (April 12, 1995). ... Traded by Braves with a player to be named later to Boston Red Sox for two players to be named later (July 31, 1995); Red Sox acquired P Matt Murray and Braves acquired OF Marc Lewis and P Mike Jacobs to complete deal (August 31, 1995). ... Traded by Red Sox to Texas Rangers for P Mark Brandenburg and P Kerry Lacy (July 31, 1996). ... Granted free agency (October 27, 1996). ... Signed by New York Yankees (December 11, 1996).

Year Team (League)	W	L	Pct.	ERA	G	GS	CG	ShO	Sv.	IP	H	R	ER	BB	SO
1987—Pulaski (Appalachian)........	4	8	.333	3.24	15	13	3	2	0	83⅓	64	37	30	42	82
1988—Burlington (Midw.).............	11	5	.688	3.62	30	23	1	1	0	154	154	86	62	69	160
—Durham (Carolina)..............	1	0	1.000	1.46	2	2	1	1	0	12⅓	14	3	2	5	14
1989—Greenville (Southern)	4	1	.800	1.58	47	0	0	0	19	51⅓	32	10	9	31	58
—Richmond (Int'l)...............	2	0	1.000	0.00	13	0	0	0	8	20	6	0	0	13	20
—Atlanta (N.L.)......................	0	1	.000	1.50	20	0	0	0	7	24	17	4	4	8	27
1990—Atlanta (N.L.)....................	0	3	.000	18.00	7	0	0	0	2	7	16	16	14	4	7
—Greenville (Southern)	1	0	1.000	1.59	4	4	0	0	0	5⅔	7	1	1	3	4
1991—Atlanta (N.L.)....................	5	5	.500	2.88	74	0	0	0	7	78	62	27	25	21	54
1992—Atlanta (N.L.)....................	5	4	.556	4.10	65	0	0	0	8	63⅔	59	32	29	20	44
1993—Atlanta (N.L.)....................	4	6	.400	4.67	63	0	0	0	27	52	51	35	27	29	43
1994—Atlanta (N.L.)....................	3	1	.750	3.55	49	0	0	0	3	45⅔	41	18	18	26	35
1995—Atlanta (N.L.)....................	1	1	.500	5.59	26	0	0	0	1	19⅓	31	14	12	6	13
—Boston (A.L.)■....................	1	0	1.000	3.00	22	0	0	0	0	21	17	9	7	8	10
1996—Boston (A.L.)....................	4	3	.571	3.83	59	0	0	0	1	56⅓	58	24	24	23	46
—Texas (A.L.)■.....................	0	1	.000	3.22	22	0	0	0	0	22⅓	20	8	8	4	14
1997—New York (A.L.)■..............	6	1	.857	2.57	64	0	0	0	3	66⅔	50	19	19	34	70
1998—New York (A.L.)................	4	1	.800	5.47	67	0	0	0	6	79	71	51	48	26	69
A.L. totals (4 years)	15	6	.714	3.89	234	0	0	0	10	245⅓	216	111	106	95	209
N.L. totals (7 years)	18	21	.462	4.01	304	0	0	0	55	289⅔	277	146	129	114	223
Major league totals (10 years)....	33	27	.550	3.95	538	0	0	0	65	535	493	257	235	209	432

DIVISION SERIES RECORD

Year Team (League)	W	L	Pct.	ERA	G	GS	CG	ShO	Sv.	IP	H	R	ER	BB	SO
1995—Boston (A.L.).....................	0	0	...	0.00	1	0	0	0	0	2⅓	1	0	0	0	4
1996—Texas (A.L.)......................	0	1	.000	2.70	3	0	0	0	0	3⅓	2	2	1	3	3
1997—New York (A.L.).................	0	0	...	0.00	3	0	0	0	0	1	1	0	0	1	3
1998—New York (A.L.).................							Did not play.								
Div. series totals (3 years)	0	1	.000	1.35	7	0	0	0	0	6⅔	4	2	1	4	10

CHAMPIONSHIP SERIES RECORD

Year Team (League)	W	L	Pct.	ERA	G	GS	CG	ShO	Sv.	IP	H	R	ER	BB	SO
1991—Atlanta (N.L.)....................	0	0	...	2.45	3	0	0	0	0	3⅔	4	1	1	3	3
1992—Atlanta (N.L.)....................	0	0	...	0.00	5	0	0	0	0	4⅓	2	1	0	2	5
1993—Atlanta (N.L.)....................	0	0	...	0.00	1	0	0	0	0	1	1	0	0	1	0
1998—New York (N.L.)................	0	0	...	0.00	3	0	0	0	0	3⅔	2	0	0	2	4
Champ. series totals (4 years)	0	0	...	0.71	12	0	0	0	0	12⅔	9	2	1	8	12

WORLD SERIES RECORD

NOTES: Member of World Series championship team (1998).

Year Team (League)	W	L	Pct.	ERA	G	GS	CG	ShO	Sv.	IP	H	R	ER	BB	SO
1991—Atlanta (N.L.).....................	1	0	1.000	0.00	5	0	0	0	0	7⅓	5	0	0	2	7
1992—Atlanta (N.L.).....................	0	0	...	0.00	4	0	0	0	1	5	3	0	0	2	1
1998—New York (A.L.).................	0	0	...	27.00	1	0	0	0	0	⅔	3	2	2	0	1
World Series totals (3 years)	1	0	1.000	1.38	10	0	0	0	1	13	11	2	2	4	9

STARK, DENNIS　　　　　　　　P　　　　　　　　MARINERS

PERSONAL: Born October 27, 1974, in Hicksville, Ohio. ... 6-2/210. ... Throws right, bats right.
HIGH SCHOOL: Edgerton (Ohio).
COLLEGE: Toledo.
TRANSACTIONS/CAREER NOTES: Selected by Seattle Mariners organization in fourth round of free-agent draft (June 4, 1996). ... On Lancaster disabled list (April 26, 1998-remainder of season); included rehabilitation assignment to Arizona Mariners (July 30-August 11).

Year	Team (League)	W	L	Pct.	ERA	G	GS	CG	ShO	Sv.	IP	H	R	ER	BB	SO
1996—	Everett (Northwest)	1	3	.250	4.45	12	4	0	0	0	30 1/3	25	19	15	17	49
1997—	Wisconsin (Midwest)	6	3	.667	1.97	16	15	1	0	0	91 1/3	52	27	20	33	105
	—Lancaster (Eastern)	1	1	.500	3.24	3	3	0	0	0	16 2/3	13	7	6	10	17
1998—	Lancaster (Calif.)	1	2	.333	4.29	5	5	00	0	0	21	18	12	10	17	21
	—Ariz. Mariners (Ariz.)	0	0	...	2.16	3	1	0	0	0	8 1/3	9	2	2	2	13

STATON, T.J.   OF   EXPOS

PERSONAL: Born February 17, 1975, in Norfolk, Va. ... 6-3/210. ... Bats left, throws left. ... Full name: Tarrence Jervon Staton.
HIGH SCHOOL: Elyria West (Elyria, Ohio).
TRANSACTIONS/CAREER NOTES: Selected by Pittsburgh Pirates organization in 10th round of free-agent draft (June 3, 1993). ... Claimed on waivers by Montreal Expos (November 25, 1998).

Year	Team (League)	Pos.	G	AB	R	H	2B	3B	HR	RBI	Avg.	BB	SO	SB	PO	A	E	Avg.
1993—	GC Pirates (GCL)	OF	32	115	23	41	9	2	1	18	.357	8	14	10	44	4	5	.906
1994—	GC Pirates (GCL)	OF	11	39	3	10	3	0	1	5	.256	1	8	0	23	1	1	.960
	—Welland (NYP)	OF	12	45	4	8	3	0	0	4	.178	0	7	5	18	1	0	1.000
	—Augusta (S. Atl.)	OF	37	125	9	27	6	1	0	5	.216	10	38	6	66	2	7	.907
1995—	Augusta (S. Atl.)	OF	112	391	43	114	21	5	5	53	.292	27	97	27	153	10	9	.948
1996—	Carolina (Southern)	OF	112	386	72	119	24	3	15	57	.308	58	99	17	178	7	4	.979
1997—	Calgary (PCL)	OF	65	199	30	47	14	0	2	22	.236	22	51	3	78	3	1	.988
	—Carolina (Southern)	OF	58	207	33	60	11	2	6	33	.290	12	60	8	79	4	3	.965
1998—	Carolina (Southern)	OF	63	223	37	67	17	1	7	48	.300	25	52	6	78	4	1	.988
	—Nashville (PCL)	OF	62	186	28	45	8	0	6	21	.242	15	55	5	102	2	6	.945

STEENSTRA, KENNIE   P   ROYALS

PERSONAL: Born October 13, 1970, in Springfield, Mo. ... 6-5/220. ... Throws right, bats right. ... Full name: Kenneth Gregory Steenstra.
COLLEGE: Wichita State.
TRANSACTIONS/CAREER NOTES: Selected by Chicago Cubs organization in 12th round of free-agent draft (June 2, 1992). ... Granted free agency (October 15, 1998). ... Signed by Kansas City Royals organization (December 17, 1998).
STATISTICAL NOTES: Tied for American Association League lead in sacrifice flies allowed with 9 in 1996.

Year	Team (League)	W	L	Pct.	ERA	G	GS	CG	ShO	Sv.	IP	H	R	ER	BB	SO
1992—	Geneva (N.Y.-Penn)	3	0	1.000	0.90	3	3	1	0	0	20	11	4	2	3	12
	—Peoria (Midwest)	6	3	.667	2.11	12	12	4	2	0	89 2/3	79	29	21	22	68
1993—	Daytona Beach (FSL)	5	3	.625	2.55	13	13	1	1	0	81 1/3	64	26	23	13	57
	—Iowa (Am. Assoc.)	1	0	1.000	6.75	1	1	0	0	0	6 2/3	9	5	5	4	6
	—Orlando (South.)	8	3	.727	3.59	14	14	2	2	0	100 1/3	103	47	40	25	60
1994—	Orlando (South.)	9	7	.563	2.61	23	23	2	1	0	158 1/3	146	55	46	43	83
	—Iowa (Am. Assoc.)	1	2	.333	13.15	3	3	0	0	0	13	24	21	19	4	10
1995—	Iowa (Am. Assoc.)	9	•12	.429	3.89	29	26	*6	•2	0	171 1/3	174	85	74	51	96
1996—	Iowa (Am. Assoc.)	8	12	.400	5.01	26	26	1	0	0	158	170	96	88	51	101
1997—	Iowa (Am. Assoc.)	5	10	.333	3.92	25	25	•4	0	0	160 2/3	161	85	70	45	111
1998—	Iowa (Pacific Coast)	11	5	.688	4.38	25	24	1	1	0	148	171	84	72	37	104
	—Chicago (N.L.)	0	0	...	10.80	4	0	0	0	0	3 1/3	7	4	4	1	4
Major league totals (1 year)		0	0	...	10.80	4	0	0	0	0	3 1/3	7	4	4	1	4

STEIN, BLAKE   P   ATHLETICS

PERSONAL: Born August 3, 1973, in McComb, Miss. ... 6-7/210. ... Throws right, bats right. ... Full name: William Blake Stein.
HIGH SCHOOL: Covington (La.).
COLLEGE: Spring Hill College (Ala.).
TRANSACTIONS/CAREER NOTES: Selected by St. Louis Cardinals organization in sixth round of free-agent draft (June 2, 1994). ... Traded by Cardinals with P T.J. Mathews and P Eric Ludwick to Oakland Athletics for 1B Mark McGwire (July 31, 1997).
RECORDS: Shares major league single-inning record for most strikeouts—4 (July 27, 1998, fourth inning).

Year	Team (League)	W	L	Pct.	ERA	G	GS	CG	ShO	Sv.	IP	H	R	ER	BB	SO
1994—	Johnson City (App.)	4	1	.800	2.87	13	13	1	0	0	59 2/3	44	21	19	24	69
1995—	Peoria (Midwest)	10	6	.625	3.80	27	•27	1	0	0	139 2/3	122	69	59	61	133
1996—	St. Petersburg (FSL)	•16	5	.762	*2.15	28	27	2	1	1	172	122	48	41	54	*159
1997—	Arkansas (Texas)	8	7	.533	4.24	22	22	1	0	0	133 2/3	128	67	63	49	114
	—Huntsville (Southern)■	3	2	.600	5.71	7	7	0	0	0	34 2/3	36	24	22	20	25
1998—	Edmonton (PCL)	3	1	.750	3.47	5	4	0	0	0	23 1/3	22	13	9	11	31
	—Oakland (A.L.)	5	9	.357	6.37	24	20	1	1	0	117 1/3	117	92	83	71	89
Major league totals (1 year)		5	9	.357	6.37	24	20	1	1	0	117 1/3	117	92	83	71	89

STEINBACH, TERRY   C   TWINS

PERSONAL: Born March 2, 1962, in New Ulm, Minn. ... 6-1/212. ... Bats right, throws right. ... Full name: Terry Lee Steinbach. ... Brother of Tom Steinbach, minor league outfielder (1983).
HIGH SCHOOL: New Ulm (Minn.).
COLLEGE: Minnesota.
TRANSACTIONS/CAREER NOTES: Selected by Cleveland Indians organization in 16th round of free-agent draft (June 3, 1980); did not sign. ... Selected by Oakland Athletics organization in ninth round of free-agent draft (June 6, 1983). ... On disabled list (May 6-June 1, 1988; July 3-28, 1990; and April 10-25, 1992). ... Granted free agency (October 26, 1992). ... Re-signed by A's (December 14, 1992). ... On disabled list

(August 16, 1993-remainder of season and August 13-29, 1995). ... Granted free agency (November 17, 1996). ... Signed by Minnesota Twins (December 5, 1996). ... Granted free agency (October 29, 1998). ... Re-signed by Twins organization (January 4, 1999).
RECORDS: Holds A.L. single-season record for most home runs by catcher—34 (1996; also hit one home run as pinch hitter).
HONORS: Named Southern League Most Valuable Player (1986).
STATISTICAL NOTES: Led Northwest League third basemen with 122 assists and tied for lead with 17 errors in 1983. ... Led Midwest League third basemen with 31 double plays in 1984. ... Led Southern League with 22 passed balls in 1986. ... Hit home run in first major league at-bat (September 12, 1986). ... Led A.L. catchers with 15 errors in 1991. ... Led A.L. catchers with .998 fielding percentage in 1994. ... Career major league grand slams: 8.

							BATTING							FIELDING		
Year	Team (League)	Pos.	G	AB	R	H	2B	3B	HR	RBI	Avg.	BB	SO	SB	PO	A	E	Avg.
1983— Medford (N'west)	3B-OF-1B	62	219	42	69	16	0	6	38	.315	28	22	8	105	†124	‡21	.916
1984— Madison (Midwest)	3B-1B-P	135	474	57	140	24	6	11	79	.295	49	59	5	107	257	27	.931
1985— Huntsville (Sou.)	C-3-1-O-P	128	456	64	124	31	3	9	72	.272	45	36	4	187	43	6	.975
1986— Huntsville (Sou.)	C-1B-3B	138	505	113	164	33	2	24	*132	.325	94	74	10	620	73	14	.980
— Oakland (A.L.)	C	6	15	3	5	0	0	2	4	.333	1	0	0	21	4	1	.962
1987— Oakland (A.L.)	C-3-DH-1	122	391	66	111	16	3	16	56	.284	32	66	1	642	44	10	.986
1988— Oakland (A.L.)	C-3-1-DH-O	104	351	42	93	19	1	9	51	.265	33	47	3	536	58	9	.985
1989— Oakland (A.L.)	C-O-1-DH-3	130	454	37	124	13	1	7	42	.273	30	66	1	612	47	11	.984
1990— Oakland (A.L.)	C-DH-1B	114	379	32	95	15	2	9	57	.251	19	66	0	401	31	5	.989
1991— Oakland (A.L.)	C-1B-DH	129	456	50	125	31	1	6	67	.274	22	70	2	639	53	†15	.979
1992— Oakland (A.L.)	C-1B-DH	128	438	48	122	20	1	12	53	.279	45	58	2	598	72	10	.985
1993— Oakland (A.L.)	C-1B-DH	104	389	47	111	19	1	10	43	.285	25	65	3	524	47	7	.988
1994— Oakland (A.L.)	C-DH-1B	103	369	51	105	21	2	11	57	.285	26	62	2	597	59	1	†.998
1995— Oakland (A.L.)	C-1B	114	406	43	113	26	1	15	65	.278	25	74	1	686	57	6	.992
1996— Oakland (A.L.)	C-DH-1B	145	514	79	140	25	1	35	100	.272	49	115	0	732	46	7	.991
1997— Minnesota (A.L.)■	C-1B-DH	122	447	60	111	27	1	12	54	.248	35	106	6	657	51	6	.992
1998— Minnesota (A.L.)	C-DH	124	422	45	102	25	2	14	54	.242	38	89	0	665	52	7	.990
Major league totals (13 years)		1445	5031	603	1357	257	17	158	703	.270	380	884	21	7310	621	95	.988

CHAMPIONSHIP SERIES RECORD

							BATTING							FIELDING		
Year	Team (League)	Pos.	G	AB	R	H	2B	3B	HR	RBI	Avg.	BB	SO	SB	PO	A	E	Avg.
1988— Oakland (A.L.)	C	2	4	0	1	0	0	0	0	.250	2	0	0	12	0	0	1.000
1989— Oakland (A.L.)	C-DH	4	15	0	3	0	0	0	1	.200	1	5	0	17	0	0	1.000
1990— Oakland (A.L.)	C	3	11	2	5	0	0	0	1	.455	1	2	0	11	0	0	1.000
1992— Oakland (A.L.)	C	6	24	1	7	0	0	1	5	.292	2	7	0	30	7	0	1.000
Championship series totals (4 years)		15	54	3	16	0	0	1	7	.296	6	14	0	70	7	0	1.000

WORLD SERIES RECORD

NOTES: Member of World Series championship team (1989).

							BATTING							FIELDING		
Year	Team (League)	Pos.	G	AB	R	H	2B	3B	HR	RBI	Avg.	BB	SO	SB	PO	A	E	Avg.
1988— Oakland (A.L.)	C-DH	3	11	0	4	1	0	0	0	.364	0	2	0	11	3	0	1.000
1989— Oakland (A.L.)	C	4	16	3	4	0	1	1	7	.250	2	1	0	27	2	0	1.000
1990— Oakland (A.L.)	C	3	8	0	1	0	0	0	0	.125	0	1	0	8	1	0	1.000
World Series totals (3 years)		10	35	3	9	1	1	1	7	.257	2	4	0	46	6	0	1.000

ALL-STAR GAME RECORD

NOTES: Named Most Valuable Player (1988). ... Hit home run in first at-bat (July 12, 1988).

					BATTING							FIELDING		
Year	League	Pos.	AB	R	H	2B	3B	HR	RBI	Avg.	BB	SO	SB	PO	A	E	Avg.
1988— American	C	1	1	1	0	0	1	2	1.000	0	0	0	3	1	1	.800
1989— American	C	3	0	1	0	0	0	0	.333	0	0	0	6	1	0	1.000
1993— American	C	2	0	1	1	0	0	1	.500	0	1	0	6	0	0	1.000
All-Star Game totals (3 years)		6	1	3	1	0	1	3	.500	0	1	0	15	2	1	.944

RECORD AS PITCHER

Year	Team (League)	W	L	Pct.	ERA	G	GS	CG	ShO	Sv.	IP	H	R	ER	BB	SO
1984— Madison (Midwest)	0	0	...	9.00	2	0	0	0	0	3	2	4	3	4	0
1985— Huntsville (Southern)	0	0	...	0.00	1	0	0	0	0	1	0	0	0	0	0

STENSON, DERNELL   OF   RED SOX

PERSONAL: Born June 17, 1978, in La Grange, Ga. ... 6-1/215. ... Bats left, throws left. ... Full name: Dernell Renauld Stenson.
HIGH SCHOOL: La Grange (Ga.).
TRANSACTIONS/CAREER NOTES: Selected by Boston Red Sox organization in third round of free-agent draft (June 2, 1996).

							BATTING							FIELDING		
Year	Team (League)	Pos.	G	AB	R	H	2B	3B	HR	RBI	Avg.	BB	SO	SB	PO	A	E	Avg.
1996— GC Red Sox (GCL)	OF	32	97	16	21	3	1	2	15	.216	16	26	4	30	2	0	1.000
1997— Michigan (Midwest)	OF	131	471	79	137	35	2	15	80	.291	72	105	6	145	11	14	.918
1998— Trenton (Eastern)	OF	138	505	90	130	21	1	24	71	.257	84	135	5	218	*15	6	.975

STENTZ, BRENT   P   TWINS

PERSONAL: Born July 24, 1975, in New Port Richey, Fla. ... 6-5/224. ... Throws right, bats right. ... Full name: Brent Daniel Stentz.
HIGH SCHOOL: Brooksville (Hernando, Fla.).
JUNIOR COLLEGE: Pasco-Hernandez Community College (Fla.).
TRANSACTIONS/CAREER NOTES: Selected by Detroit Tigers organization in 33rd round of free-agent draft (June 2, 1994). ... Traded by Tigers to Minnesota Twins organization for C Matt Walbeck (December 11, 1996).
HONORS: Named Eastern League Pitcher of the Year (1998).

Year Team (League)	W	L	Pct.	ERA	G	GS	CG	ShO	Sv.	IP	H	R	ER	BB	SO
1995— Gulf Coast Tigers (GCL)	2	1	.667	2.36	•24	0	0	0	*16	26²/₃	21	7	7	12	28
— Lakeland (Fla. St.).............	0	0	...	0.00	2	0	0	0	0	2	0	0	0	0	4
1996— Fayetteville (S. Atl.)...........	7	8	.467	3.49	45	8	0	0	2	98	91	51	38	27	92
1997— Fort Myers (Fla. St.)■	7	2	.778	2.47	49	1	0	0	17	69¹/₃	53	20	19	24	70
1998— New Britain (East.).............	1	2	.333	1.98	57	0	0	0	*43	59	44	13	13	28	65

STEPHENSON, GARRETT   P   CARDINALS

PERSONAL: Born January 2, 1972, in Takoma Park, Md. ... 6-5/208. ... Throws right, bats right. ... Full name: Garrett Charles Stephenson.
HIGH SCHOOL: Boonsboro (Md.).
JUNIOR COLLEGE: Ricks (Idaho).
COLLEGE: Idaho State.
TRANSACTIONS/CAREER NOTES: Selected by Baltimore Orioles organization in 18th round of free-agent draft (June 1, 1992). ... Traded by Orioles with P Calvin Maduro to Philadelphia Phillies (September 4, 1996), completing deal in which Phillies traded 3B Todd Zeile and OF Pete Incaviglia to Orioles for two players to be named later (August 29, 1996). ... On Philadelphia disabled list (June 5-22 and August 18-September 2, 1997). ... On Scranton/Wilkes-Barre disabled list (July 8-August 3, 1998). ... Traded by Phillies with P Ricky Bottalico to St. Louis Cardinals for OF Ron Gant, P Jeff Brantley and P Cliff Politte (November 19, 1998).
STATISTICAL NOTES: Led Eastern League with 23 home runs allowed and 18 hit batsmen in 1995.

Year Team (League)	W	L	Pct.	ERA	G	GS	CG	ShO	Sv.	IP	H	R	ER	BB	SO
1992— Bluefield (Appalachian)	3	1	.750	4.73	12	3	0	0	0	32¹/₃	35	22	17	7	30
1993— Albany (S. Atl.)..................	16	7	.696	2.84	30	24	3	•2	1	171¹/₃	142	65	54	44	147
1994— Frederick (Carolina)...........	7	5	.583	4.02	18	17	1	0	0	107¹/₃	91	62	48	36	133
— Bowie (Eastern)...............	3	2	.600	5.15	7	7	1	1	0	36²/₃	47	22	21	11	32
1995— Bowie (Eastern)...............	7	10	.412	3.64	29	*29	1	0	0	175¹/₄	154	87	71	47	139
1996— Rochester (Int'l)..............	7	6	.538	4.81	23	21	3	1	0	121²/₃	123	66	65	44	86
— Baltimore (A.L.)................	0	1	.000	12.79	3	0	0	0	0	6¹/₃	13	9	9	3	3
1997— Scran./W.B. (Int'l)■...........	3	1	.750	5.90	7	3	0	0	0	29	27	19	19	12	27
— Philadelphia (N.L.)...........	8	6	.571	3.15	20	18	2	0	0	117	104	45	41	38	81
1998— Philadelphia (N.L.)...........	0	2	.000	9.00	6	6	0	0	0	23	31	24	23	19	17
— Scran./W.B. (Int'l)...........	1	8	.111	5.25	13	11	2	0	0	73²/₃	81	49	43	16	48
A.L. totals (1 year)	0	1	.000	12.79	3	0	0	0	0	6¹/₃	13	9	9	3	3
N.L. totals (2 years)	8	8	.500	4.11	26	24	2	0	0	140	135	69	64	57	98
Major league totals (3 years)	8	9	.471	4.49	29	24	2	0	0	146¹/₃	148	78	73	60	101

STEVENS, DAVE   P

PERSONAL: Born March 4, 1970, in Fullerton, Calif. ... 6-3/195. ... Throws right, bats right. ... Full name: David James Stevens.
HIGH SCHOOL: La Habra (Calif.).
COLLEGE: Fullerton (Calif.) College.
TRANSACTIONS/CAREER NOTES: Selected by Chicago Cubs organization in 20th round of free-agent draft (June 5, 1989). ... On disabled list (June 17-July 4, 1991). ... On Iowa disabled list (April 8-May 20, 1993). ... Traded by Cubs with C Matt Walbeck to Minnesota Twins for P Willie Banks (November 24, 1993). ... On disabled list (May 30-June 21 and July 21-August 9, 1996). ... Claimed on waivers by Chicago Cubs organization (July 31, 1997). ... Released by Cubs (December 3, 1998).
MISCELLANEOUS: Appeared in one game as pinch runner with Chicago (1998).

Year Team (League)	W	L	Pct.	ERA	G	GS	CG	ShO	Sv.	IP	H	R	ER	BB	SO
1990— Huntington (Appal.)...........	2	4	.333	4.61	13	11	0	0	0	56²/₃	48	44	29	47	55
1991— Geneva (N.Y.-Penn)...........	2	3	.400	2.85	9	9	1	0	0	47¹/₃	49	20	15	14	44
1992— Charlotte (Southern).........	9	13	.409	3.91	26	26	2	0	0	149²/₃	147	79	65	53	89
1993— Iowa (Am. Assoc.)...........	4	0	1.000	4.19	24	0	0	0	4	34¹/₃	24	16	16	14	29
— Orlando (South.)	6	1	.857	4.22	11	11	1	1	0	70¹/₃	69	36	33	35	49
1994— Salt Lake (PCL)■.............	6	2	.750	1.67	23	0	0	0	3	43	41	13	8	16	30
— Minnesota (A.L.)...........	5	2	.714	6.80	24	0	0	0	0	45	55	35	34	23	24
1995— Minnesota (A.L.)...........	5	4	.556	5.07	56	0	0	0	10	65²/₃	74	40	37	32	47
1996— Minnesota (A.L.)...........	3	3	.500	4.66	49	0	0	0	11	58	58	31	30	25	29
1997— Salt Lake (PCL)...........	9	3	.750	4.30	16	14	1	0	0	90	93	52	43	31	71
— Minnesota (A.L.)...........	1	3	.250	9.00	6	6	0	0	0	23	41	23	23	17	16
— Iowa (Am. Assoc.)■...........	1	1	.500	4.70	6	0	0	0	1	7²/₃	8	4	4	5	8
— Chicago (N.L.)...........	0	2	.000	9.64	10	0	0	0	0	9¹/₃	13	11	10	9	13
1998— Iowa (Pacific Coast)...........	4	1	.800	3.08	26	0	0	0	2	49²/₃	41	19	17	16	39
— Chicago (N.L.)...........	1	2	.333	4.74	31	0	0	0	0	38	42	20	20	17	31
A.L. totals (4 years)	14	12	.538	5.82	135	6	0	0	21	191²/₃	228	129	124	97	116
N.L. totals (2 years)	1	4	.200	5.70	41	0	0	0	0	47¹/₃	55	31	30	26	44
Major league totals (5 years)	15	16	.484	5.80	176	6	0	0	21	239	283	160	154	123	160

STEVENS, LEE   DH/1B   RANGERS

PERSONAL: Born July 10, 1967, in Kansas City, Mo. ... 6-4/235. ... Bats left, throws left. ... Full name: DeWain Lee Stevens.
HIGH SCHOOL: Lawrence (Kan.).
TRANSACTIONS/CAREER NOTES: Selected by California Angels organization in first round (22nd pick overall) of free-agent draft (June 2, 1986). ... Traded by Angels to Montreal Expos for P Jeff Tuss (January 15, 1993); Tuss announced his retirement and Expos sent P Keith Morrison to Angels to complete deal (January 21, 1993). ... Released by Expos (March 30, 1993). ... Signed by Toronto Blue Jays organization (April 8, 1993). ... Granted free agency (October 15, 1993). ... Signed by Vancouver, Angels organization (October 25, 1993). ... Released by Vancouver (November 16, 1993). ... Played in Japan (1994-95). ... Signed by Texas Rangers organization (April 3, 1996). ... On Texas disabled list (August 4-September 1, 1996); included rehabilitation assignment to Oklahoma City (August 13-September 1, 1996). ... On Texas disabled list (August 8-September 1, 1998); included rehabilitation assignment to Oklahoma (August 25-September 1).
HONORS: Named American Association Most Valuable Player (1996).

STATISTICAL NOTES: Led California League first basemen with .986 fielding percentage, 1,028 putouts and 66 assists in 1987. ... Led Texas League outfielders with 12 errors in 1988. ... Tied for Pacific Coast League lead with 11 intentional bases on balls received in 1990. ... Led American Association with 277 total bases, .643 slugging percentage and .404 on-base percentage in 1996. ... Tied for American Association lead with eight intentional bases on balls received in 1996. ... Hit three home runs in one game (April 13, 1998). ... Career major league grand slams: 2.

							BATTING								FIELDING		
Year Team (League)	Pos.	G	AB	R	H	2B	3B	HR	RBI	Avg.	BB	SO	SB	PO	A	E	Avg.
1986— Salem (Northwest)	OF-1B	72	267	45	75	18	2	6	47	.281	45	49	13	231	18	5	.980
1987— Palm Springs (Calif.)..	1B-OF	140	532	82	130	29	2	19	97	.244	61	117	1	†1031	†68	18	†.984
1988— Midland (Texas).........	OF-1B	116	414	79	123	26	2	23	76	.297	58	108	0	217	16	†14	.943
1989— Edmonton (PCL)	1B-OF	127	446	72	110	29	9	14	74	.247	61	115	5	635	40	7	.990
1990— Edmonton (PCL)	OF-1B	90	338	57	99	31	2	16	66	.293	55	83	1	284	10	6	.980
— California (A.L.).........	1B	67	248	28	53	10	0	7	32	.214	22	75	1	597	36	4	.994
1991— Edmonton (PCL)	OF-1B	123	481	75	151	29	3	19	96	.314	37	79	3	519	33	7	.987
— California (A.L.).........	OF-1B	18	58	8	17	7	0	0	9	.293	6	12	1	100	6	1	.991
1992— California (A.L.).........	1B-DH	106	312	25	69	19	0	7	37	.221	29	64	1	764	49	4	.995
1993— Syracuse (Int'l)■..	OF-1B	116	401	61	106	30	1	14	66	.264	39	85	2	201	12	3	.986
1994— Kintetsu (Jp. Pac.)■ ..	OF	93	302	44	87	21	0	20	66	.288	28	100	0	...	...	...	...
1995— Kintetsu (Jp. Pac.).....	OF	129	476	54	117	29	1	23	70	.246	46	129	0	...	...	...	...
1996— Okla. City (A.A.)■......	1B-OF	117	431	84	140	*37	2	*32	94	.325	58	90	3	348	24	3	.992
— Texas (A.L.)...........	1B-OF	27	78	6	18	2	3	3	12	.231	6	22	0	157	14	1	.994
1997— Texas (A.L.)............	1B-DH-OF	137	426	58	128	24	2	21	74	.300	23	83	1	486	33	3	.994
1998— Texas (A.L.)............	DH-1B-OF	120	344	52	91	17	4	20	59	.265	31	93	0	220	15	1	.996
— Oklahoma (PCL)........	1B	3	12	2	4	0	0	1	1	.333	0	2	0	12	1	0	1.000
Major league totals (6 years)		475	1466	177	376	79	9	58	223	.256	117	349	4	2324	153	14	.994

DIVISION SERIES RECORD

							BATTING								FIELDING		
Year Team (League)	Pos.	G	AB	R	H	2B	3B	HR	RBI	Avg.	BB	SO	SB	PO	A	E	Avg.
1998— Texas (A.L.)	DH	1	3	0	0	0	0	0	0	.000	0	1	0	...	...	...	...

STEWART, SHANNON — OF — BLUE JAYS

PERSONAL: Born February 25, 1974, in Cincinnati. ... 6-1/205. ... Bats right, throws right. ... Full name: Shannon Harold Stewart.
HIGH SCHOOL: Southridge Senior (Miami).
TRANSACTIONS/CAREER NOTES: Selected by Toronto Blue Jays organization in first round (19th pick overall) of free-agent draft (June 1, 1992); pick received as part of compensation for Los Angeles Dodgers signing Type A free-agent P Tom Candiotti. ... On disabled list (June 13, 1994-remainder of season). ... On Syracuse disabled list (May 13-31, 1996).
STATISTICAL NOTES: Led International League outfielders with 286 total chances in 1996.

							BATTING								FIELDING		
Year Team (League)	Pos.	G	AB	R	H	2B	3B	HR	RBI	Avg.	BB	SO	SB	PO	A	E	Avg.
1992— GC Jays (GCL)...........	OF	50	172	44	40	1	0	1	11	.233	24	27	*32	81	1	1	.988
1993— St. Catharines (NYP)..	OF	75	*301	•53	84	15	2	3	29	.279	33	43	25	81	0	0	1.000
1994— Hagerstown (SAL)......	OF	56	225	39	73	10	5	4	25	.324	23	39	15	92	4	1	.990
1995— Knoxville (Southern) ..	OF	138	498	89	143	24	6	5	55	.287	*89	61	42	283	6	6	.980
— Toronto (A.L.)...........	OF	12	38	2	8	0	0	0	1	.211	5	5	2	20	1	1	.955
1996— Syracuse (Int'l).........	OF	112	420	77	125	26	8	6	42	.298	54	61	*35	*274	7	5	.983
— Toronto (A.L.)..........	OF	7	17	2	3	1	0	0	2	.176	1	4	1	4	0	1	.800
1997— Toronto (A.L.)............	OF-DH	44	168	25	48	13	7	0	22	.286	19	24	10	97	1	2	.980
— Syracuse (Int'l).........	OF	58	208	41	72	13	1	5	24	.346	36	26	9	115	1	2	.983
1998— Toronto (A.L.)............	OF	144	516	90	144	29	3	12	55	.279	67	77	51	295	4	6	.980
Major league totals (4 years)		207	739	119	203	43	10	12	80	.275	92	110	64	416	6	10	.977

STIEB, DAVE — P — BLUE JAYS

PERSONAL: Born July 22, 1957, in Santa Ana, Calif. ... 6-1/195. ... Throws right, bats right. ... Full name: David Andrew Stieb. ... Brother of Steve Stieb, minor league catcher (1979-81). ... Name pronounced STEEB.
HIGH SCHOOL: Oak Grove (San Jose, Calif.).
COLLEGE: Santa Ana (Calif.) College, then Southern Illinois.
TRANSACTIONS/CAREER NOTES: Selected by Toronto Blue Jays organization in fifth round of free-agent draft (June 6, 1978). ... On disabled list (May 23, 1991-remainder of season). ... On Toronto disabled list (March 27-April 22, 1992); included rehabilitation assignment to Dunedin (April 11-20). ... On Toronto disabled list (August 9, 1992-remainder of season). ... Granted free agency (October 28, 1992). ... Signed by Chicago White Sox (December 8, 1992). ... On Chicago disabled list (April 5-28, 1993); included rehabilitation assignments to Sarasota (April 11-22) and Nashville (April 22-28). ... On Chicago disabled list (May 23, 1993). ... Signed by Kansas City Royals organization (June 14, 1993). ... Released by Royals organization (July 31, 1993). ... Signed by Blue Jays organization (April 1, 1998). ... Granted free agency (October 26, 1998). ... Re-signed by Blue Jays organization (December 7, 1998).
RECORDS: Shares major league record for most consecutive one-hit games—2 (September 24 and 30, 1988). ... Shares A.L. single-season record for most low-hit (no-hit and one-hit) games—3 (1988).
HONORS: Named outfielder on THE SPORTING NEWS college All-America team (1978). ... Named A.L. Pitcher of the Year by THE SPORTING NEWS (1982). ... Named righthanded pitcher on THE SPORTING NEWS A.L. All-Star team (1982).
STATISTICAL NOTES: Led A.L. with 14 hit batsmen in 1983, 11 in 1984, 15 in 1986, 13 in 1989 and tied for lead with 11 in 1981. ... Pitched 9-0 one-hit, complete-game victory against Milwaukee (May 31, 1988). ... Pitched 1-0 one-hit, complete-game victory against Cleveland (September 24, 1988). ... Pitched 4-0 one-hit, complete-game victory against Baltimore (September 30, 1988). ... Pitched 8-0 one-hit, complete-game victory against New York (April 10, 1989). ... Pitched 7-0 one-hit, complete-game victory against Milwaukee (August 26, 1989). ... Pitched 3-0 no-hit victory against Cleveland (September 2, 1990).
MISCELLANEOUS: Holds Toronto Blue Jays all-time records for most wins (175), innings pitched (2,873 1/3), strikeouts (1,658), complete games (103) and shutouts (30). ... Appeared in one game as outfielder with no chances and made an out in only at-bat (1980). ... Appeared in one game as pinch runner (1986 and 1988).

Year Team (League)	W	L	Pct.	ERA	G	GS	CG	ShO	Sv.	IP	H	R	ER	BB	SO
1979— Dunedin (Fla. St.)	5	0	1.000	4.24	8	8	2	1	0	51	54	30	24	28	38
— Syracuse (Int'l)	5	2	.714	2.12	7	7	4	0	0	51	39	15	12	14	20
— Toronto (A.L.)	8	8	.500	4.33	18	18	7	1	0	129	139	70	62	48	52
1980— Toronto (A.L.)	12	15	.444	3.70	34	32	14	4	0	243	232	108	100	83	108
1981— Toronto (A.L.)	11	10	.524	3.18	25	25	11	2	0	184	148	70	65	61	89
1982— Toronto (A.L.)	17	14	.548	3.25	38	38	*19	*5	0	*288 1/3	*271	116	104	75	141
1983— Toronto (A.L.)	17	12	.586	3.04	36	36	14	4	0	278	223	105	94	93	187
1984— Toronto (A.L.)	16	8	.667	2.83	35	35	11	2	0	*267	215	87	84	88	198
1985— Toronto (A.L.)	14	13	.519	*2.48	36	36	8	2	0	265	206	89	73	96	167
1986— Toronto (A.L.)	7	12	.368	4.74	37	34	1	1	1	205	239	128	108	87	127
1987— Toronto (A.L.)	13	9	.591	4.09	33	31	3	1	0	185	164	92	84	87	115
1988— Toronto (A.L.)	16	8	.667	3.04	32	31	8	4	0	207 1/3	157	76	70	79	147
1989— Toronto (A.L.)	17	8	.680	3.35	33	33	3	2	0	206 2/3	164	83	77	76	101
1990— Toronto (A.L.)	18	6	.750	2.93	33	33	2	2	0	208 2/3	179	73	68	64	125
1991— Toronto (A.L.)	4	3	.571	3.17	9	9	1	0	0	59 2/3	52	22	21	23	29
1992— Dunedin (Fla. St.)	1	1	.500	2.13	2	2	0	0	0	12 2/3	7	6	3	4	11
— Toronto (A.L.)	4	6	.400	5.04	21	14	1	0	0	96 1/3	98	58	54	43	45
1993— Sarasota (Florida State)■...	1	1	.500	5.84	2	2	0	0	0	12 1/3	18	10	8	2	14
— Nashville (A.A.)	0	1	.000	3.86	1	1	0	0	0	7	9	3	3	2	3
— Chicago (A.L.)	1	3	.250	6.04	4	4	0	0	0	22 1/3	27	17	15	14	11
— Omaha (Am. Assoc.)■..........	3	3	.500	6.42	9	8	1	1	0	47 2/3	63	37	34	12	18
1998— Dunedin (Fla. St.)■.........	2	0	1.000	3.00	3	3	0	0	0	15	17	8	5	5	19
— Syracuse (Int'l)	5	4	.556	2.73	9	9	2	0	0	66	44	23	20	17	47
— Toronto (A.L.)	1	2	.333	4.83	19	3	0	0	2	50 1/3	58	31	27	17	27
Major league totals (16 years)....	176	137	.562	3.44	443	412	103	30	3	2895 2/3	2572	1225	1106	1034	1669

CHAMPIONSHIP SERIES RECORD

Year Team (League)	W	L	Pct.	ERA	G	GS	CG	ShO	Sv.	IP	H	R	ER	BB	SO
1985— Toronto (A.L.)	1	1	.500	3.10	3	3	0	0	0	20 1/3	11	7	7	10	18
1989— Toronto (A.L.)	0	2	.000	6.35	2	2	0	0	0	11 1/3	12	8	8	6	10
Champ. series totals (2 years)	1	3	.250	4.26	5	5	0	0	0	31 2/3	23	15	15	16	28

ALL-STAR GAME RECORD

RECORDS: Shares single-game record for most wild pitches—2 (July 8, 1980). ... Shares record for most wild pitches in one inning—2 (July 8, 1980, seventh inning).

Year League	W	L	Pct.	ERA	GS	CG	ShO	Sv.	IP	H	R	ER	BB	SO
1980— American	0	0	. . .	0.00	0	0	0	0	1	1	1	0	2	0
1981— American	0	0	. . .	0.00	0	0	0	0	1 2/3	1	0	0	1	1
1983— American	1	0	1.000	0.00	1	0	0	0	3	0	1	0	1	4
1984— American	0	1	.000	4.50	1	0	0	0	2	3	2	1	0	2
1985— American	0	0	. . .	0.00	0	0	0	0	1	0	0	0	1	2
1988— American	0	0	. . .	0.00	0	0	0	0	1	1	0	0	0	0
1990— American	0	0	. . .	0.00	0	0	0	0	2	0	0	0	1	1
All-Star totals (7 years)	1	1	.500	0.77	2	0	0	0	11 2/3	6	4	1	6	10

STINNETT, KELLY   C   DIAMONDBACKS

PERSONAL: Born February 14, 1970, in Lawton, Okla. ... 5-11/195. ... Bats right, throws right. ... Full name: Kelly Lee Stinnett. ... Name pronounced stih-NET.

HIGH SCHOOL: Lawton (Okla.).

JUNIOR COLLEGE: Seminole (Okla.) Junior College.

TRANSACTIONS/CAREER NOTES: Selected by Cleveland Indians organization in 11th round of free-agent draft (June 5, 1989). ... Selected by New York Mets from Indians organization in Rule 5 major league draft (December 13, 1993). ... Traded by Mets to Milwaukee Brewers for P Cory Lidle (January 17, 1996). ... On Milwaukee disabled list (July 27-September 2, 1997). ... Selected by Arizona Diamondbacks in third round (65th pick overall) of expansion draft (November 18, 1997).

STATISTICAL NOTES: Led New York-Pennsylvania League catchers with 18 errors in 1990. ... Led South Atlantic League catchers with 27 errors in 1991. ... Tied for American Association lead in being hit by pitch with 13 in 1996. ... Led American Association catchers with 10 errors and tied for lead with nine double plays in 1996.

Year Team (League)	Pos.	G	AB	R	H	2B	3B	HR	RBI	Avg.	BB	SO	SB	PO	A	E	Avg.
							BATTING								FIELDING		
1990— Watertown (NYP)	C-1B	60	192	29	46	10	2	2	21	.240	40	43	3	348	48	†18	.957
1991— Columbus (S. Atl.)	C-1B	102	384	49	101	15	1	14	74	.263	26	70	4	685	100	†28	.966
1992— Cant./Akr. (Eastern)	C	91	296	37	84	10	0	6	32	.284	16	43	7	560	57	*13	.979
1993— Charlotte (Int'l)	C	98	288	42	79	10	3	6	33	.274	17	52	0	495	48	8	.985
1994— New York (N.L.)■........	C	47	150	20	38	6	2	2	14	.253	11	28	2	211	20	5	.979
1995— New York (N.L.)	C	77	196	23	43	8	1	4	18	.219	29	65	2	380	22	7	.983
1996— Milwaukee (A.L.)■........	C-DH	14	26	1	2	0	0	0	0	.077	2	11	0	46	2	2	.960
— New Orleans (A.A.).....	C-3B	95	334	63	96	21	1	27	70	.287	31	83	3	485	52	†11	.980
1997— Tucson (PCL)	C-1B	64	209	50	67	15	3	10	43	.321	42	46	1	256	34	2	.993
— Milwaukee (A.L.)	C-DH	30	36	2	9	4	0	0	3	.250	3	9	0	81	5	1	.989
1998— Arizona (N.L.)■.........	C-DH	92	274	35	71	14	1	11	34	.259	35	74	0	458	37	8	.984
American League totals (2 years)		44	62	3	11	4	0	0	3	.177	5	20	0	127	7	3	.978
National League totals (3 years)		216	620	78	152	28	4	17	66	.245	75	167	4	1049	79	20	.983
Major league totals (5 years)		260	682	81	163	32	4	17	69	.239	80	187	4	1176	86	23	.982

STOCKER, KEVIN   SS   DEVIL RAYS

PERSONAL: Born February 13, 1970, in Spokane, Wash. ... 6-1/175. ... Bats both, throws right. ... Full name: Kevin Douglas Stocker.

HIGH SCHOOL: Central Valley (Veradale, Wash.).

COLLEGE: Washington.
TRANSACTIONS/CAREER NOTES: Selected by Philadelphia Phillies organization in second round of free-agent draft (June 3, 1991). ... On Philadelphia disabled list (April 28-June 1, 1994); included rehabilitation assignment to Scranton/Wilkes-Barre (May 28-June 1). ... Traded by Phillies to Tampa Bay Devil Rays for OF Bob Abreu (November 18, 1997). ... On disabled list (August 30, 1998-remainder of season).

							BATTING								FIELDING		
Year Team (League)	Pos.	G	AB	R	H	2B	3B	HR	RBI	Avg.	BB	SO	SB	PO	A	E	Avg.
1991— Spartanburg (SAL)	SS	70	250	26	55	11	1	0	20	.220	31	37	15	83	176	18	.935
1992— Clearwater (FSL)	SS	63	244	43	69	13	4	1	33	.283	27	31	15	102	220	16	.953
— Reading (Eastern)	SS	62	240	31	60	9	2	1	13	.250	22	30	17	100	172	14	.951
1993— Scran./W.B. (Int'l)	SS	83	313	54	73	14	1	3	17	.233	29	56	17	122	248	15	.961
— Philadelphia (N.L.)	SS	70	259	46	84	12	3	2	31	.324	30	43	5	118	202	14	.958
1994— Philadelphia (N.L.)	SS	82	271	38	74	11	2	2	28	.273	44	41	2	118	253	16	.959
— Scran./W.B. (Int'l)	SS	4	13	1	4	1	0	0	2	.308	1	0	0	5	11	0	1.000
1995— Philadelphia (N.L.)	SS	125	412	42	90	14	3	1	32	.218	43	75	6	147	383	17	.969
1996— Philadelphia (N.L.)	SS	119	394	46	100	22	6	5	41	.254	43	89	6	165	352	13	.975
— Scran./W.B. (Int'l)	SS	12	44	5	10	3	0	2	6	.227	0	4	1	17	39	1	.982
1997— Philadelphia (N.L.)	SS	149	504	51	134	23	5	4	40	.266	51	91	11	190	376	11	.981
1998— Tampa Bay (A.L.)■	SS	112	336	37	70	11	3	6	25	.208	27	80	5	186	335	11	.979
American League totals (1 year)		112	336	37	70	11	3	6	25	.208	27	80	5	186	335	11	.979
National League totals (5 years)		545	1840	223	482	82	19	14	172	.262	211	339	30	738	1566	71	.970
Major league totals (6 years)		657	2176	260	552	93	22	20	197	.254	238	419	35	924	1901	82	.972

CHAMPIONSHIP SERIES RECORD

							BATTING								FIELDING		
Year Team (League)	Pos.	G	AB	R	H	2B	3B	HR	RBI	Avg.	BB	SO	SB	PO	A	E	Avg.
1993— Philadelphia (N.L.)	SS	6	22	0	4	1	0	0	1	.182	2	5	0	10	13	1	.958

WORLD SERIES RECORD

							BATTING								FIELDING		
Year Team (League)	Pos.	G	AB	R	H	2B	3B	HR	RBI	Avg.	BB	SO	SB	PO	A	E	Avg.
1993— Philadelphia (N.L.)	SS	6	19	1	4	1	0	0	1	.211	5	5	0	8	13	0	1.000

STONE, RICKY   P   DODGERS

PERSONAL: Born February 28, 1975, in Hamilton, Ohio. ... 6-1/168. ... Throws right, bats right. ... Full name: Ricky L. Stone.
HIGH SCHOOL: Hamilton (Ohio).
TRANSACTIONS/CAREER NOTES: Selected by Los Angeles Dodgers organization in fourth round of free-agent draft (June 2, 1994).

Year Team (League)	W	L	Pct.	ERA	G	GS	CG	ShO	Sv.	IP	H	R	ER	BB	SO
1994— Great Falls (Pio.)	2	2	.500	4.44	13	7	0	0	2	50 2/3	55	40	25	24	48
1995— San Bernardino (Calif.)	3	5	.375	6.52	12	12	0	0	0	58	79	50	42	25	31
— Yakima (N'west)	4	4	.500	5.25	16	6	0	0	2	48	54	31	28	20	28
1996— Savannah (S. Atl.)	2	1	.667	3.98	5	5	0	0	0	31 2/3	34	15	14	9	31
— Vero Beach (FSL)	8	6	.571	3.83	21	21	1	0	0	112 2/3	115	58	48	46	74
1997— San Bernardino (Calif.)	3	3	.500	3.35	8	8	0	0	0	53 2/3	40	22	20	10	40
— San Antonio (Tex.)	0	3	.000	5.47	25	5	0	0	3	52 2/3	63	33	32	30	46
1998— San Antonio (Tex.)	7	2	.778	3.84	13	13	1	1	0	82	76	40	35	26	69
— Albuquerque (PCL)	5	5	.500	5.38	18	16	0	0	0	105 1/3	120	69	63	41	85

STOOPS, JIM   P   ROCKIES

PERSONAL: Born June 30, 1972, in Edison, N.J. ... 6-2/180. ... Throws right, bats right. ... Full name: James Wellington Stoops.
HIGH SCHOOL: Franklin (Somerset, N.J.).
COLLEGE: South Carolina (degree in retail management).
TRANSACTIONS/CAREER NOTES: Signed as non-drafted free agent by San Francisco Giants (May 31, 1995). ... Traded by Giants with OF Darryl Hamilton and a player to be named later to Colorado Rockies for OF Ellis Burks (July 31, 1998); Rockies acquired P Jason Brester to complete deal (August 17, 1998).

Year Team (League)	W	L	Pct.	ERA	G	GS	CG	ShO	Sv.	IP	H	R	ER	BB	SO
1995— Bellingham (N'west)	6	5	.545	3.43	24	0	0	0	4	42	32	23	16	17	58
1996— Burlington (Midw.)	3	3	.500	2.52	46	0	0	0	5	60 2/3	43	24	17	40	69
1997— San Jose (California)	2	5	.286	5.20	50	0	0	0	4	91 2/3	92	56	53	45	114
1998— San Jose (California)	2	1	.667	0.98	45	0	0	0	*31	55 1/3	28	7	6	25	96
— Salem (Carolina)■	0	0	. . .	0.00	3	0	0	0	0	4 1/3	2	0	0	1	8
— Colo. Springs (PCL)	1	0	1.000	1.23	11	0	0	0	1	14 2/3	6	6	2	8	17
— Colorado (N.L.)	1	0	1.000	2.25	3	0	0	0	0	4	5	1	1	3	0
Major league totals (1 year)	1	0	1.000	2.25	3	0	0	0	0	4	5	1	1	3	0

STOTTLEMYRE, TODD   P   DIAMONDBACKS

PERSONAL: Born May 20, 1965, in Yakima, Wash. ... 6-3/200. ... Throws right, bats left. ... Full name: Todd Vernon Stottlemyre. ... Son of Mel Stottlemyre Sr., pitching coach, New York Yankees; pitcher with New York Yankees (1964-74) and pitching coach for New York Mets (1984-93); and brother of Mel Stottlemyre Jr., pitcher with Kansas City Royals (1990).
HIGH SCHOOL: A.C. Davis (Yakima, Wash.).
JUNIOR COLLEGE: Yakima (Wash.) Valley College.
COLLEGE: UNLV.
TRANSACTIONS/CAREER NOTES: Selected by New York Yankees organization in fifth round of free-agent draft (June 6, 1983); did not sign. ... Selected by St. Louis Cardinals organization in secondary phase of free-agent draft (January 9, 1985); did not sign. ... Selected by Toronto Blue Jays organization in secondary phase of free-agent draft (June 3, 1985). ... On disabled list (June 20-July 13, 1992). ... On suspended list (September 23-28, 1992). ... On disabled list (May 23-June 13, 1993). ... Granted free agency (October 18, 1994). ... Signed by Oakland

Athletics (April 11, 1995). ... Traded by A's to St. Louis Cardinals for P Bret Wagner, P Jay Witasick and P Carl Dale (January 9, 1996). ... Traded by Cardinals with SS Royce Clayton to Texas Rangers for P Darren Oliver, 3B Fernando Tatis and a player to be named later (July 31, 1998); Cardinals acquired OF Mark Little to complete deal (August 9, 1998). ... Granted free agency (October 22, 1998). ... Signed by Arizona Diamondbacks (December 2, 1998).

STATISTICAL NOTES: Pitched 9-0 one-hit, complete-game victory against Chicago (August 26, 1992). ... Struck out 15 batters in one game (June 16, 1995).

MISCELLANEOUS: Struck out in only appearance as pinch hitter (1997).

Year Team (League)	W	L	Pct.	ERA	G	GS	CG	ShO	Sv.	IP	H	R	ER	BB	SO
1986— Vent. County (Cal.)	9	4	.692	2.43	17	17	2	0	0	103²/₃	76	39	28	36	104
— Knoxville (Southern)	8	7	.533	4.18	18	18	1	0	0	99	93	56	46	49	81
1987— Syracuse (Int'l)	11	•13	.458	4.44	34	*34	1	0	0	186²/₃	189	•103	*92	*87	143
1988— Toronto (A.L.)	4	8	.333	5.69	28	16	0	0	0	98	109	70	62	46	67
— Syracuse (Int'l)	5	0	1.000	2.05	7	7	1	0	0	48¹/₃	36	12	11	8	51
1989— Toronto (A.L.)	7	7	.500	3.88	27	18	0	0	0	127²/₃	137	56	55	44	63
— Syracuse (Int'l)	3	2	.600	3.23	10	9	2	0	0	55²/₃	46	23	20	15	45
1990— Toronto (A.L.)	13	17	.433	4.34	33	33	4	0	0	203	214	101	98	69	115
1991— Toronto (A.L.)	15	8	.652	3.78	34	34	1	0	0	219	194	97	92	75	116
1992— Toronto (A.L.)	12	11	.522	4.50	28	27	6	2	0	174	175	99	87	63	98
1993— Toronto (A.L.)	11	12	.478	4.84	30	28	1	1	0	176²/₃	204	107	95	69	98
1994— Toronto (A.L.)	7	7	.500	4.22	26	19	3	1	1	140²/₃	149	67	66	48	105
1995— Oakland (A.L.)■	14	7	.667	4.55	31	31	2	0	0	209²/₃	228	117	106	80	205
1996— St. Louis (N.L.)■	14	11	.560	3.87	34	33	5	2	0	223¹/₃	191	100	96	93	194
1997— St. Louis (N.L.)	12	9	.571	3.88	28	28	0	0	0	181	155	86	78	65	160
1998— St. Louis (N.L.)	9	9	.500	3.51	23	23	3	0	0	161¹/₃	146	74	63	51	147
— Texas (A.L.)	5	4	.556	4.33	10	10	0	0	0	68	68	33	29	30	57
A.L. totals (9 years)	88	81	.521	4.41	247	216	17	4	1	1409	1478	747	690	524	924
N.L. totals (3 years)	35	29	.547	3.77	85	84	8	2	0	565²/₃	492	260	237	209	501
Major league totals (11 years)	123	110	.528	4.23	332	300	25	6	1	1974²/₃	1970	1007	927	733	1425

DIVISION SERIES RECORD

Year Team (League)	W	L	Pct.	ERA	G	GS	CG	ShO	Sv.	IP	H	R	ER	BB	SO
1996— St. Louis (N.L.)	1	0	1.000	1.35	1	1	0	0	0	6²/₃	5	1	1	2	7
1998— Texas (A.L.)	0	1	.000	2.25	1	1	0	0	0	8	6	2	2	4	8
Div. series totals (2 years)	1	1	.500	1.84	2	2	1	0	0	14²/₃	11	3	3	6	15

CHAMPIONSHIP SERIES RECORD

RECORDS: Shares single-series record for most earned runs allowed—11 (1996). ... Shares single-game record for most earned runs allowed—7 (October 14, 1996). ... Shares record for most hits allowed in one inning—6 (October 14, 1996, first inning).

Year Team (League)	W	L	Pct.	ERA	G	GS	CG	ShO	Sv.	IP	H	R	ER	BB	SO
1989— Toronto (A.L.)	0	1	.000	7.20	1	1	0	0	0	5	7	4	4	2	3
1991— Toronto (A.L.)	0	1	.000	9.82	1	1	0	0	0	3²/₃	7	4	4	1	3
1992— Toronto (A.L.)	0	0	. . .	2.45	1	0	0	0	0	3²/₃	3	1	1	0	1
1993— Toronto (A.L.)	0	1	.000	7.50	1	1	0	0	0	6	6	5	5	4	4
1996— St. Louis (N.L.)	1	1	.500	12.38	3	2	0	0	0	8	15	11	11	3	11
Champ. series totals (5 years)	1	4	.200	8.54	7	5	0	0	0	26¹/₃	38	25	25	10	22

WORLD SERIES RECORD

RECORDS: Shares records for most bases on balls allowed in one inning—4 (October 20, 1993, first inning); and most consecutive bases on balls allowed in one inning—3 (October 20, 1993, first inning).

NOTES: Member of World Series championship team (1992 and 1993).

Year Team (League)	W	L	Pct.	ERA	G	GS	CG	ShO	Sv.	IP	H	R	ER	BB	SO
1992— Toronto (A.L.)	0	0	. . .	0.00	4	0	0	0	0	3²/₃	4	0	0	0	4
1993— Toronto (A.L.)	0	0	. . .	27.00	1	1	0	0	0	2	3	6	6	4	1
World Series totals (2 years)	0	0	. . .	9.53	5	1	0	0	0	5²/₃	7	6	6	4	5

STOVALL, DaROND   OF   MARLINS

PERSONAL: Born January 3, 1973, in St. Louis. ... 6-1/185. ... Bats both, throws left. ... Full name: DaRond Tyrone Stovall.

HIGH SCHOOL: Althoff Catholic (Belleville, Ill.).

TRANSACTIONS/CAREER NOTES: Selected by St. Louis Cardinals organization in fifth round of free-agent draft (June 3, 1991). ... Traded by Cardinals organization with P Bryan Eversgerd and P Kirk Bullinger to Montreal Expos organization for P Ken Hill (April 5, 1995). ... On Harrisburg disabled list (May 16-July 9, 1996) ... Granted free agency (October 15, 1998). ... Signed by Florida Marlins organization (November 12, 1998).

STATISTICAL NOTES: Led Florida State League outfielders with 339 total chances in 1994. ... Career major league grand slams: 1.

Year Team (League)	Pos.	G	AB	R	H	2B	3B	HR	RBI	Avg.	BB	SO	SB	PO	A	E	Avg.
1991— Johnson City (App.)	OF	48	134	16	19	2	2	0	5	.142	23	63	9	69	2	5	.934
1992— Savannah (S. Atl.)	OF	135	450	51	92	13	7	7	40	.204	63	138	20	250	8	12	.956
1993— Springfield (Midw.)	OF	*135	460	73	118	19	4	20	81	.257	53	143	18	247	6	11	.958
1994— St. Peters. (FSL)	OF	134	507	68	113	20	6	15	69	.223	62	*154	24	*328	7	4	.988
1995— W.P. Beach (FSL)■	OF	121	461	52	107	22	2	4	51	.232	44	117	18	283	13	3	.990
1996— Harrisburg (East.)	OF	74	272	38	60	7	1	10	36	.221	32	86	10	171	4	3	.983
— G.C. Expos (GCL)	OF	9	34	5	15	3	2	0	7	.441	3	6	3	10	0	0	1.000
— W.P. Beach (FSL)	OF	8	31	8	14	4	0	1	8	.452	6	7	2	19	0	1	.950
1997— Harrisburg (East.)	OF	45	169	29	48	4	1	9	39	.284	23	30	4	93	3	1	.990
— Ottawa (Int'l)	OF	99	342	40	83	23	2	4	48	.243	31	114	10	181	10	7	.965
1998— Montreal (N.L.)	OF	62	78	11	16	2	1	2	6	.205	6	29	1	35	2	3	.925
— Ottawa (Int'l)	OF	44	150	15	34	7	1	8	22	.227	21	51	6	74	2	3	.962
Major league totals (1 year)		62	78	11	16	2	1	2	6	.205	6	29	1	35	2	3	.925

STOWERS, CHRISTOPHER   OF   EXPOS

PERSONAL: Born August 18, 1974, in Marietta, Ga. ... 6-3/195. ... Bats left, throws left. ... Full name: Christopher James Stowers.
HIGH SCHOOL: Walton (Marietta, Ga.).
COLLEGE: Georgia.
TRANSACTIONS/CAREER NOTES: Selected by Montreal Expos organization in 17th round of free-agent draft (June 4, 1996).
STATISTICAL NOTES: Led New York-Pennsylvania League with six intentional bases on balls received in 1996.

							BATTING							FIELDING		
Year	Team (League)	Pos.	G	AB	R	H	2B	3B	HR	RBI	Avg.	BB	SO	SB	PO	A	E	Avg.
1996—Vermont (NYP)		OF	72	282	*58	*90	21	9	7	44	.319	21	37	16	112	9	3	.976
1997—Harrisburg (East.)		OF	19	59	9	17	4	2	0	5	.288	5	11	3	37	2	3	.929
—W.P. Beach (FSL)		OF	111	414	56	113	15	5	4	30	.273	30	77	19	223	7	6	.975
1998—Harrisburg (East.)		OF	134	510	86	137	31	5	17	66	.269	42	109	24	243	10	4	.984

STRANGE, DOUG   IF   PIRATES

PERSONAL: Born April 13, 1964, in Greenville, S.C. ... 6-1/188. ... Bats both, throws right. ... Full name: Joseph Douglas Strange.
HIGH SCHOOL: Wade Hampton (Greenville, S.C.).
COLLEGE: North Carolina State.
TRANSACTIONS/CAREER NOTES: Selected by Detroit Tigers organization in seventh round of free-agent draft (June 3, 1985). ... Traded by Tigers to Houston Astros organization for IF/OF Lou Frazier (March 30, 1990). ... Released by Astros organization (May 25, 1990). ... Signed by Chicago Cubs organization (June 11, 1990). ... Granted free agency (December 19, 1992). ... Signed by Texas Rangers organization (January 11, 1993). ... On disabled list (July 2-17, 1994). ... Granted free agency (December 23, 1994). ... Signed by Seattle Mariners organization (April 5, 1995). ... Granted free agency (October 8, 1996). ... Signed by Montreal Expos organization (February 4, 1997). ... On Montreal disabled list (June 17-July 2, 1997). ... Granted free agency (November 5, 1997). ... Signed by Pittsburgh Pirates (December 2, 1997). ... On Pittsburgh disabled list (July 2-31, 1998); included rehabilitation assignment to Carolina (July 26-31).
STATISTICAL NOTES: Led Florida State League third basemen with 116 putouts and tied for lead with 20 double plays in 1986. ... Led American Association third basemen with 16 double plays in 1990. ... Led American Association with 10 intentional bases on balls received in 1991. ... Career major league grand slams: 1.
MISCELLANEOUS: Batted righthanded only (Glens Falls, 1987).

							BATTING							FIELDING		
Year	Team (League)	Pos.	G	AB	R	H	2B	3B	HR	RBI	Avg.	BB	SO	SB	PO	A	E	Avg.
1985—Bristol (Appal.)		OF-2B-3B	65	226	43	69	16	1	6	45	.305	22	30	6	84	59	11	.929
1986—Lakeland (Fla. St.)		3B-1B	126	466	59	119	29	4	2	63	.255	65	59	18	†202	215	37	.919
1987—Glens Falls (East.)		3-2-0-S	115	431	63	130	31	1	13	70	.302	31	53	5	110	214	20	.942
—Toledo (Int'l)		3B	16	45	7	11	2	0	1	5	.244	4	7	3	14	28	3	.933
1988—Toledo (Int'l)		3B-SS-1B	82	278	23	56	8	2	6	19	.201	8	38	9	52	126	13	.932
—Glens Falls (East.)		3B	57	218	32	61	11	1	1	36	.280	16	28	11	45	112	12	.929
1989—Toledo (Int'l)		3B-SS	83	304	38	75	15	2	8	42	.247	34	49	8	108	197	17	.947
—Detroit (A.L.)		3B-2B-SS	64	196	16	42	4	1	1	14	.214	17	36	3	53	118	19	.900
1990—Tucson (PCL)■		3B	37	98	7	22	3	0	0	7	.224	8	23	0	9	47	9	.862
—Iowa (Am. Assoc.)■		3B-SS	82	269	31	82	17	1	5	35	.305	28	42	6	58	149	16	.928
1991—Iowa (Am. Assoc.)		3-2-1-S-O	131	509	76	149	35	5	8	56	.293	49	75	10	263	273	21	.962
—Chicago (N.L.)		3B	3	9	0	4	1	0	0	1	.444	0	1	1	1	3	1	.800
1992—Iowa (Am. Assoc.)		3B-2B	55	212	32	65	16	1	4	26	.307	9	32	3	84	126	16	.929
—Chicago (N.L.)		3B-2B	52	94	7	15	1	0	1	5	.160	10	15	1	24	51	6	.926
1993—Texas (A.L.)■		2B-3B-SS	145	484	58	124	29	0	7	60	.256	43	69	6	276	374	13	.980
1994—Texas (A.L.)		2B-3B-OF	73	226	26	48	12	1	5	26	.212	15	38	1	88	175	11	.960
1995—Seattle (A.L.)■		3-2-0-DH	74	155	19	42	9	2	2	21	.271	10	25	0	39	69	5	.956
1996—Seattle (A.L.)		3-0-DH-1-2	88	183	19	43	7	1	3	23	.235	14	31	1	26	39	2	.970
1997—Montreal (N.L.)■		3-2-0-1	118	327	40	84	16	2	12	47	.257	36	76	0	70	176	13	.950
—Ottawa (Int'l)		3B	2	7	3	3	1	0	0	0	.429	1	1	0	2	3	0	1.000
1998—Pittsburgh (N.L.)		3B-2B-1B	90	185	9	32	8	0	0	14	.173	10	39	1	44	73	5	.959
—Carolina (Southern)		3B	4	14	4	5	0	0	0	0	.357	2	1	0	1	5	0	1.000
American League totals (5 years)			444	1244	138	299	61	5	18	144	.240	99	199	11	482	775	50	.962
National League totals (4 years)			263	615	56	135	26	2	13	67	.220	56	131	3	139	303	25	.946
Major league totals (9 years)			707	1859	194	434	87	7	31	211	.233	155	330	14	621	1078	75	.958

DIVISION SERIES RECORD

							BATTING							FIELDING		
Year	Team (League)	Pos.	G	AB	R	H	2B	3B	HR	RBI	Avg.	BB	SO	SB	PO	A	E	Avg.
1995—Seattle (A.L.)		3B-PH	2	4	0	0	0	0	0	1	.000	1	1	0	0	0	0	...

CHAMPIONSHIP SERIES RECORD

							BATTING							FIELDING		
Year	Team (League)	Pos.	G	AB	R	H	2B	3B	HR	RBI	Avg.	BB	SO	SB	PO	A	E	Avg.
1995—Seattle (A.L.)		PH-3B	4	4	0	0	0	0	0	0	.000	0	2	0	2	3	0	1.000

STRAWBERRY, DARRYL   OF

PERSONAL: Born March 12, 1962, in Los Angeles. ... 6-6/215. ... Bats left, throws left. ... Full name: Darryl Eugene Strawberry. ... Brother of Michael Strawberry, minor league outfielder (1980-81).
HIGH SCHOOL: Crenshaw (Los Angeles).
TRANSACTIONS/CAREER NOTES: Selected by New York Mets organization in first round (first pick overall) of free-agent draft (June 3, 1980). ... On disabled list (May 12-June 28, 1985). ... Granted free agency (November 5, 1990). ... Signed by Los Angeles Dodgers (November 8, 1990). ... On disabled list (June 18-July 3, 1991; May 14-July 6 and July 21-September 1, 1992). ... On Los Angeles disabled list (May 13-June 5, 1993); included rehabilitation assignment to Albuquerque (May 28-June 5). ... On Los Angeles disabled list (June 17, 1993-remainder of season and April 4-May 26, 1994). ... Released by Dodgers (May 26, 1994). ... Signed by San Francisco Giants organization (June 19, 1994). ... Released by Giants (February 8, 1995). ... Signed by New York Yankees organization (June 19, 1995). ... On Columbus disabled list

(June 22-July 4, 1995). ... Granted free agency (November 30, 1995). ... Signed by St. Paul of Northern League (May 3, 1996). ... Contract purchased by Yankees organization (July 4, 1996). ... On New York disabled list (April 7-August 15, 1997); included rehabilitation assignments to Norwich (May 19), Columbus (June 9-13 and August 8-15) and Tampa (August 4-7). ... Granted free agency (October 30, 1997). ... Re-signed by Yankees (January 8, 1998). ... Granted free agency (December 21, 1998).

RECORDS: Shares major league single-season record for most grand slams as a pinch hitter—2 (1998). ... Shares major league single-game record for most strikeouts (nine-inning game)—5 (May 1, 1991).

HONORS: Named Texas League Most Valuable Player (1982). ... Named N.L. Rookie Player of the Year by THE SPORTING NEWS (1983). ... Named N.L. Rookie of the Year by Baseball Writers' Association of America (1983). ... Named outfielder on THE SPORTING NEWS N.L. All-Star team (1988 and 1990). ... Named outfielder on THE SPORTING NEWS N.L. Silver Slugger team (1988 and 1990).

STATISTICAL NOTES: Led Texas League in slugging percentage with .602 and in caught stealing with 22 in 1982. ... Hit three home runs in one game (August 5, 1985 and August 6, 1996). ... Led N.L. with .545 slugging percentage in 1988. ... Led Gulf Coast League with five intentional bases on balls received in 1995. ... Career major league grand slams: 8.

MISCELLANEOUS: Holds New York Mets all-time records for most runs (662), most home runs (252) and most runs batted in (733).

							BATTING								FIELDING		
Year Team (League)	Pos.	G	AB	R	H	2B	3B	HR	RBI	Avg.	BB	SO	SB	PO	A	E	Avg.
1980— Kingsport (Appal.)......	OF	44	157	27	42	5	2	5	20	.268	20	39	5	55	4	3	.952
1981— Lynchburg (Caro.)......	OF	123	420	84	107	22	6	13	78	.255	82	105	31	173	8	13	.933
1982— Jackson (Texas)........	OF	129	435	93	123	19	9	*34	97	.283	*100	145	45	211	8	9	.961
1983— Tidewater (Int'l)......	OF	16	57	12	19	4	1	3	13	.333	14	18	7	22	0	4	.846
— New York (N.L.).........	OF	122	420	63	108	15	7	26	74	.257	47	128	19	232	8	4	.984
1984— New York (N.L.).........	OF	147	522	75	131	27	4	26	97	.251	75	131	27	276	11	6	.980
1985— New York (N.L.).........	OF	111	393	78	109	15	4	29	79	.277	73	96	26	211	5	2	.991
1986— New York (N.L.).........	OF	136	475	76	123	27	5	27	93	.259	72	141	28	226	10	6	.975
1987— New York (N.L.).........	OF	154	532	108	151	32	5	39	104	.284	97	122	36	272	6	8	.972
1988— New York (N.L.).........	OF	153	543	101	146	27	3	*39	101	.269	85	127	29	297	4	9	.971
1989— New York (N.L.).........	OF	134	476	69	107	26	1	29	77	.225	61	105	11	272	4	8	.972
1990— New York (N.L.).........	OF	152	542	92	150	18	1	37	108	.277	70	110	15	268	10	3	.989
1991— Los Angeles (N.L.)■..	OF	139	505	86	134	22	4	28	99	.265	75	125	10	209	11	5	.978
1992— Los Angeles (N.L.)	OF	43	156	20	37	8	0	5	25	.237	19	34	3	67	2	1	.986
1993— Los Angeles (N.L.)	OF	32	100	12	14	2	0	5	12	.140	16	19	1	37	1	4	.905
— Albuquerque (PCL)......	OF	5	19	3	6	2	0	1	2	.316	2	5	1	7	0	0	1.000
1994— Phoenix (PCL)■.........	OF	3	10	3	3	0	0	2	3	.300	0	4	0	4	0	0	1.000
— San Francisco (N.L.) ..	OF	29	92	13	22	3	1	4	17	.239	19	22	0	61	1	2	.969
1995— GC Yankees (GCL)■...	OF	7	20	3	5	2	0	0	4	.250	9	5	2	3	1	0	1.000
— Tampa (Fla. St.).......	DH	2	9	1	2	1	0	1	2	.222	1	2	0	...	...	...	...
— Columbus (Int'l)........	OF	22	83	20	25	3	1	7	29	.301	15	17	1	9	0	0	1.000
— New York (A.L.)........	DH-OF	32	87	15	24	4	1	3	13	.276	10	22	0	18	2	2	.909
1996— St. Paul (Northern)■..	OF	29	108	31	47	7	0	18	39	.435	22	16	4	...	...	...	...
— Columbus (Int'l)■......	DH	2	8	3	3	0	0	3	5	.375	0	3	0	...	...	...	...
— New York (A.L.)........	OF-DH	63	202	35	53	13	0	11	36	.262	31	55	6	45	1	0	1.000
1997— New York (A.L.)........	DH-OF	11	29	1	3	1	0	0	2	.103	3	9	0	5	0	0	1.000
— Norwich (Eastern)......	OF	1	2	0	0	0	0	0	0	.000	0	1	0	0	0	0	...
— Columbus (Int'l)........	DH	11	38	8	11	3	0	6	19	.289	8	10	0	...	...	...	...
— Tampa (Fla. St.).........	DH	4	16	2	7	1	0	0	4	.438	1	3	0	...	...	...	...
1998— New York (A.L.)........	DH-OF	101	295	44	73	11	2	24	57	.247	46	90	8	19	0	2	.905
American League totals (4 years)		207	613	95	153	29	3	38	108	.250	90	176	14	87	3	4	.957
National League totals (12 years)		1352	4756	793	1232	222	35	294	886	.259	709	1160	205	2428	73	58	.977
Major league totals (16 years)		1559	5369	888	1385	251	38	332	994	.258	799	1336	219	2515	76	62	.977

DIVISION SERIES RECORD

							BATTING								FIELDING		
Year Team (League)	Pos.	G	AB	R	H	2B	3B	HR	RBI	Avg.	BB	SO	SB	PO	A	E	Avg.
1995— New York (A.L.).........	PH	2	2	0	0	0	0	0	0	.000	0	1	0	...	...	...	...
1996— New York (A.L.).........	DH	2	5	0	0	0	0	0	0	.000	0	2	0	...	...	...	...
Division series totals (2 years)		4	7	0	0	0	0	0	0	.000	0	3	0	...	...	...	...

CHAMPIONSHIP SERIES RECORD

RECORDS: Shares single-series record for most strikeouts—12 (1986).

							BATTING								FIELDING		
Year Team (League)	Pos.	G	AB	R	H	2B	3B	HR	RBI	Avg.	BB	SO	SB	PO	A	E	Avg.
1986— New York (N.L.).........	OF	6	22	4	5	1	0	2	5	.227	3	12	1	9	0	0	1.000
1988— New York (N.L.).........	OF	7	30	5	9	2	0	1	6	.300	2	5	0	11	0	0	1.000
1996— New York (A.L.).........	OF-PH	4	12	4	5	0	0	3	5	.417	2	2	0	5	0	0	1.000
Championship series totals (3 years)		17	64	13	19	3	0	6	16	.297	7	19	1	25	0	0	1.000

WORLD SERIES RECORD

NOTES: Member of World Series championship team (1986 and 1996). ... Member of World Series championship team (1998); inactive.

							BATTING								FIELDING		
Year Team (League)	Pos.	G	AB	R	H	2B	3B	HR	RBI	Avg.	BB	SO	SB	PO	A	E	Avg.
1986— New York (N.L.).........	OF	7	24	4	5	1	0	1	1	.208	4	6	3	19	0	0	1.000
1996— New York (A.L.).........	OF	5	16	0	3	0	0	0	1	.188	5	6	0	11	0	0	1.000
World Series totals (2 years)		12	40	4	8	1	0	1	2	.200	9	12	3	30	0	0	1.000

ALL-STAR GAME RECORD

					BATTING								FIELDING		
Year League	Pos.	AB	R	H	2B	3B	HR	RBI	Avg.	BB	SO	SB	PO	A	E	Avg.
1984— National	OF	2	0	1	0	0	0	0	.500	0	1	0	0	0	0	...
1985— National	OF	1	2	1	0	0	0	0	1.000	1	0	1	3	0	0	1.000
1986— National	OF	2	0	1	0	0	0	0	.500	0	1	0	1	0	0	1.000
1987— National	OF	2	0	0	0	0	0	0	.000	0	0	0	0	0	0	...
1988— National	OF	4	0	1	0	0	0	0	.250	0	1	0	4	0	0	1.000
1989— National		Selected, did not play—injured.														
1990— National	OF	1	0	0	0	0	0	0	.000	0	1	0	3	1	1	.800
1991— National		Selected, did not play—injured.														
All-Star Game totals (6 years)		12	2	4	0	0	0	0	.333	1	4	1	11	1	1	.923

S

STRITTMATTER, MARK   C   ROCKIES

PERSONAL: Born April 4, 1969, in Huntington, N.Y. ... 6-1/220. ... Bats right, throws right. ... Full name: Mark Arthur Strittmatter.
HIGH SCHOOL: Ridgewood (N.J.).
JUNIOR COLLEGE: County College of Morris (N.J.).
COLLEGE: Virginia Commonwealth.
TRANSACTIONS/CAREER NOTES: Selected by Colorado Rockies organization in 28th round of free-agent draft (June 1, 1992). ... On disabled list (July 18, 1997-remainder of season).

Year Team (League)	Pos.	G	AB	R	H	2B	3B	HR	RBI	Avg.	BB	SO	SB	PO	A	E	Avg.
1992— Bend (Northwest).......	C	35	101	17	26	6	0	2	13	.257	12	28	0	269	36	2	.993
1993— Central Valley (Cal.)....	C	59	179	21	47	8	0	2	15	.263	31	29	3	405	61	2	.996
— Colo. Springs (PCL) ...	C	5	10	1	2	1	0	0	2	.200	0	2	0	15	1	0	1.000
1994— New Haven (East.)......	C	73	215	20	49	8	0	2	26	.228	33	39	1	464	45	4	*.992
1995— Colo. Springs (PCL) ...	C	5	17	1	5	2	0	0	3	.294	0	3	0	32	4	1	.973
— New Haven (East.)......	C	90	288	44	70	12	1	7	42	.243	47	51	1	664	48	7	.990
1996— Colo. Springs (PCL) ...	C	58	159	21	37	8	1	2	18	.233	17	30	2	302	34	6	.982
1997— Colo. Springs (PCL) ...	C	45	114	16	28	8	0	2	12	.246	11	21	0	241	15	1	.996
1998— Colo. Springs (PCL) ...	C	87	255	32	71	15	3	6	38	.278	30	48	0	504	53	5	.991
— Colorado (N.L.)	C	4	4	0	0	0	0	0	0	.000	0	3	0	10	1	0	1.000
Major league totals (1 year)		4	4	0	0	0	0	0	0	.000	0	3	0	10	1	0	1.000

RECORD AS PITCHER

Year Team (League)	W	L	Pct.	ERA	G	GS	CG	ShO	Sv.	IP	H	R	ER	BB	SO
1998— Colo. Springs (PCL)	0	0	...	36.00	1	0	0	0	0	1	6	4	4	0	0

STUCKENSCHNEIDER, ERIC   OF   ATHLETICS

PERSONAL: Born August 24, 1971, in Jefferson City, Mo. ... 6-0/190. ... Bats right, throws right. ... Full name: Eric Bruce Stuckenschneider.
HIGH SCHOOL: Fatima (Westphalia, Mo.).
COLLEGE: Central Missouri State.
TRANSACTIONS/CAREER NOTES: Selected by Los Angeles Dodgers organization in 30th round of free-agent draft (June 2, 1994). ... On disabled list (April 25-July 10, 1995). ... Selected by Oakland Athletics from Dodgers organization in Rule 5 major league draft (December 14, 1998).
STATISTICAL NOTES: Led South Atlantic League with .424 on base percentage in 1996. ... Led Florida State League with .419 on base percentage in 1997.

Year Team (League)	Pos.	G	AB	R	H	2B	3B	HR	RBI	Avg.	BB	SO	SB	PO	A	E	Avg.
1994— Yakima (N'west)	OF	58	190	40	57	13	4	3	39	.300	45	43	22	65	5	1	.986
1995— San Bern. (Calif.)........	OF	8	20	2	5	1	0	0	2	.250	7	6	1	3	0	0	1.000
— Great Falls (Pio.)........	OF	40	118	32	37	8	2	4	16	.314	32	26	10	2	0	0	1.000
1996— Savannah (S. Atl.)	OF	140	470	*111	130	28	6	16	63	.277	*111	96	50	141	5	4	.973
1997— Vero Beach (FSL)........	OF	131	452	*100	126	25	3	6	45	.279	*101	79	40	208	4	2	.991
1998— San Antonio (Tex.)	OF	72	282	60	78	16	7	3	22	.277	44	47	16	114	6	4	.968
— Albuquerque (PCL).....	OF	40	269	50	83	13	10	7	28	.309	44	50	18	131	2	1	.993

STYNES, CHRIS   OF/IF   REDS

PERSONAL: Born January 19, 1973, in Queens, N.Y. ... 5-10/185. ... Bats right, throws right. ... Full name: Christopher Desmond Stynes.
HIGH SCHOOL: Boca Raton (Fla.).
TRANSACTIONS/CAREER NOTES: Selected by Toronto Blue Jays in third round of free-agent draft (June 3, 1991). ... Traded by Blue Jays with P David Sinnes and IF Tony Medrano to Kansas City Royals for P David Cone (April 6, 1995). ... Traded by Royals with OF Jon Nunnally to Cincinnati Reds for P Hector Carrasco and P Scott Service (July 15, 1997).
STATISTICAL NOTES: Tied for Florida State League lead in double plays by third basemen with 22 in 1993. ... Led Southern League with 237 total bases in 1994.

Year Team (League)	Pos.	G	AB	R	H	2B	3B	HR	RBI	Avg.	BB	SO	SB	PO	A	E	Avg.
1991— GC Jays (GCL)...........	3B	57	219	29	67	15	1	4	39	.306	9	39	10	42	*138	8	*.957
1992— Myrtle Beach (SAL)....	3B	127	489	67	139	36	0	7	46	.284	16	43	28	86	208	26	.919
1993— Dunedin (Fla. St.).......	3B	123	496	72	151	28	5	7	48	.304	25	40	19	83	234	21	*.938
1994— Knoxville (Southern) ..	2B	136	*545	79	*173	32	4	8	79	.317	23	36	28	247	*366	20	.968
1995— Omaha (A.A.)■	2B-3B	83	306	51	84	12	5	9	42	.275	27	24	4	144	204	13	.964
— Kansas City (A.L.) ...	2B-DH	22	35	7	6	1	0	0	2	.171	4	3	0	21	35	1	.982
1996— Omaha (A.A.).............	OF-3B-2B	72	284	50	101	22	2	10	40	.356	18	17	7	98	77	9	.951
— Kansas City (A.L.) ...	O-2-DH-3	36	92	8	27	6	0	0	6	.293	2	5	5	38	8	3	.939
1997— Omaha (A.A.).............	2B-OF-3B	82	332	53	88	18	1	8	44	.265	19	25	3	101	80	10	.948
— Indianapolis (A.A.)■ ..	2B	21	86	14	31	8	0	1	17	.360	2	5	4	47	61	2	.982
— Cincinnati (N.L.)	OF-2B-3B	49	198	31	69	7	1	6	28	.348	11	13	11	87	33	2	.984
1998— Cincinnati (N.L.)	O-3-2-S	123	347	52	88	10	1	6	27	.254	32	36	15	148	54	2	.990
American League totals (2 years)		58	127	15	33	7	0	0	8	.260	6	8	5	59	43	4	.962
National League totals (2 years)		172	545	83	157	17	2	12	55	.288	43	49	26	235	87	4	.988
Major league totals (4 years)		230	672	98	190	24	2	12	63	.283	49	57	31	294	130	8	.981

S

SULLIVAN, SCOTT   P   REDS

PERSONAL: Born March 13, 1971, in Carrollton, Ala. ... 6-3/210. ... Throws right, bats right. ... Full name: William Scott Sullivan.
HIGH SCHOOL: Pickens Academy (Carrollton, Ala.).
COLLEGE: Auburn.
TRANSACTIONS/CAREER NOTES: Selected by Cincinnati Reds organization in second round of free-agent draft (June 3, 1993). ... On Indianapolis disabled list (August 21, 1995-remainder of season).

Year Team (League)	W	L	Pct.	ERA	G	GS	CG	ShO	Sv.	IP	H	R	ER	BB	SO
1993—Billings (Pioneer)	5	0	1.000	1.67	18	7	2	2	3	54	33	13	10	25	79
1994—Chattanooga (Southern)	11	7	.611	3.41	34	13	2	0	7	121⅓	101	60	46	40	111
1995—Indianapolis (A.A.)	4	3	.571	3.53	44	0	0	0	1	58⅔	51	31	23	24	54
—Cincinnati (N.L.)	0	0	. . .	4.91	3	0	0	0	0	3⅔	4	2	2	2	2
1996—Indianapolis (A.A.)	5	2	.714	2.73	53	3	0	0	1	108⅔	95	38	33	37	77
—Cincinnati (N.L.)	0	0	. . .	2.25	7	0	0	0	0	8	7	2	2	5	3
1997—Cincinnati (N.L.)	5	3	.625	3.24	59	0	0	0	1	97⅓	79	36	35	30	96
—Indianapolis (A.A.)	3	1	.750	1.30	19	0	0	0	2	27⅔	16	4	4	4	23
1998—Cincinnati (N.L.)	5	5	.500	5.21	67	0	0	0	1	102	98	62	59	36	86
Major league totals (4 years)	10	8	.556	4.18	136	0	0	0	2	211	188	102	98	73	187

SUPPAN, JEFF   P   ROYALS

PERSONAL: Born January 2, 1975, in Oklahoma City. ... 6-2/210. ... Throws right, bats right. ... Full name: Jeffrey Scot Suppan.
HIGH SCHOOL: Crespi (Encino, Calif.).
TRANSACTIONS/CAREER NOTES: Selected by Boston Red Sox organization in second round of free-agent draft (June 3, 1993). ...On Trenton disabled list (April 9-29, 1995). ... On Boston disabled list (August 25, 1996-remainder of season). ... Selected by Arizona Diamondbacks in first round (third pick overall) of expansion draft (November 18, 1997). ... Contract purchased by Royals from Arizona Diamondbacks (September 3, 1998).

Year Team (League)	W	L	Pct.	ERA	G	GS	CG	ShO	Sv.	IP	H	R	ER	BB	SO
1993—GC Red Sox (GCL)	4	3	.571	2.18	10	9	2	1	0	57⅔	52	20	14	16	64
1994—Sarasota (Florida State)	•13	7	.650	3.26	27	27	4	2	0	174	153	74	63	50	*173
1995—Trenton (Eastern)	6	2	.750	2.36	15	15	1	1	0	99	86	35	26	26	88
—Boston (A.L.)	1	2	.333	5.96	8	3	0	0	0	22⅔	29	15	15	5	19
—Pawtucket (Int'l)	2	3	.400	5.32	7	7	0	0	0	45⅔	50	29	27	9	32
1996—Boston (A.L.)	1	1	.500	7.54	8	4	0	0	0	22⅔	29	19	19	13	13
—Pawtucket (Int'l)	10	6	.625	3.22	22	22	7	1	0	145⅓	130	66	52	25	142
1997—Pawtucket (Int'l)	5	1	.833	3.71	9	9	2	1	0	60⅔	51	26	25	15	40
—Boston (A.L.)	7	3	.700	5.69	23	22	0	0	0	112⅓	140	75	71	36	67
1998—Arizona (N.L.)■	1	7	.125	6.68	13	13	1	0	0	66	82	55	49	21	39
—Tucson (PCL)	4	3	.571	3.63	13	12	0	0	0	67	75	29	27	17	62
—Kansas City (A.L.)■	0	0	. . .	0.71	4	1	0	0	0	12⅔	9	1	1	1	12
A.L. totals (4 years)	9	6	.600	5.60	43	30	0	0	0	170⅓	207	110	106	55	111
N.L. totals (1 year)	1	7	.125	6.68	13	13	1	0	0	66	82	55	49	21	39
Major league totals (4 years)	10	13	.435	5.90	56	43	1	0	0	236⅓	289	165	155	76	150

SURHOFF, B.J.   OF   ORIOLES

PERSONAL: Born August 4, 1964, in Bronx, N.Y. ... 6-1/200. ... Bats left, throws right. ... Full name: William James Surhoff. ... Son of Dick Surhoff, forward with New York Knicks and Milwaukee Hawks of National Basketball Association (1952-53 and 1953-54); and brother of Rich Surhoff, pitcher with Philadelphia Phillies and Texas Rangers (1985).
HIGH SCHOOL: Rye (N.Y.).
COLLEGE: North Carolina.
TRANSACTIONS/CAREER NOTES: Selected by New York Yankees organization in fifth round of free-agent draft (June 7, 1982); did not sign. ... Selected by Milwaukee Brewers organization in first round (first pick overall) of free-agent draft (June 3, 1985). ... On suspended list (August 23-25, 1990). ... On Milwaukee disabled list (March 25-April 16, April 20-May 23 and July 7, 1994-remainder of season); included rehabilitation assignments to El Paso (April 12-16) and New Orleans (May 17-23). ... Granted free agency (October 20, 1994). ... Re-signed by New Orleans, Brewers organization (April 7, 1995). ... Granted free agency (November 6, 1995). ... Signed by Baltimore Orioles (December 20, 1995). ... On disabled list (May 18-June 2, 1996). ... Granted free agency (October 26, 1998). ... Re-signed by Orioles (December 7, 1998).
HONORS: Named College Player of the Year by THE SPORTING NEWS (1985). ... Named catcher on THE SPORTING NEWS college All-America team (1985).
STATISTICAL NOTES: Tied for Pacific Coast League lead in double plays by catcher with 10 in 1986. ... Led A.L. catchers with 68 assists in 1991. ... Career major league grand slams: 4.
MISCELLANEOUS: Member of 1984 U.S. Olympic baseball team.

Year Team (League)	Pos.	G	AB	R	H	2B	3B	HR	RBI	Avg.	BB	SO	SB	PO	A	E	Avg.
1985—Beloit (Midwest)	C	76	289	39	96	13	4	7	58	.332	22	35	10	475	44	3	.994
1986—Vancouver (PCL)	C	116	458	71	141	19	3	5	59	.308	29	30	21	539	70	7	*.989
1987—Milwaukee (A.L.)	C-3-DH-1	115	395	50	118	22	3	7	68	.299	36	30	11	648	56	11	.985
1988—Milwaukee (A.L.)	C-3-1-S-O	139	493	47	121	21	0	5	38	.245	31	49	21	550	94	8	.988
1989—Milwaukee (A.L.)	C-DH-3B	126	436	42	108	17	4	5	55	.248	25	29	14	530	58	10	.983
1990—Milwaukee (A.L.)	C-3B	135	474	55	131	21	4	6	59	.276	41	37	18	619	62	12	.983
1991—Milwaukee (A.L.)	C-DH-3-O-2	143	505	57	146	19	4	5	68	.289	26	33	5	665	†71	4	.995
1992—Milwaukee (A.L.)	C-1-DH-O-3	139	480	63	121	19	1	4	62	.252	46	41	14	699	74	6	.992
1993—Milwaukee (A.L.)	3-0-1-C-DH	148	552	66	151	38	3	7	79	.274	36	47	12	175	220	18	.956
1994—El Paso (Texas)	OF	3	12	2	3	1	0	0	0	.250	0	2	0	3	0	0	1.000
—Milwaukee (A.L.)	3-C-1-O-DH	40	134	20	35	11	2	5	22	.261	16	14	0	121	29	4	.974
—New Orleans (A.A.)	3-O-C-1	5	19	3	6	2	0	0	1	.316	1	2	0	21	3	0	1.000
1995—Milwaukee (A.L.)	O-1-C-DH	117	415	72	133	26	3	13	73	.320	37	43	7	530	44	5	.991

Year	Team (League)	Pos.	G	AB	R	H	2B	3B	HR	RBI	Avg.	BB	SO	SB	PO	A	E	Avg.
						BATTING									FIELDING			
1996—Baltimore (A.L.)■	3-O-DH-1	143	537	74	157	27	6	21	82	.292	47	79	0	137	178	15	.955
1997—Baltimore (A.L.)	O-DH-1-3	147	528	80	150	30	4	18	88	.284	49	60	1	268	16	2	.993
1998—Baltimore (A.L.)	OF-1B	162	573	79	160	34	1	22	92	.279	49	81	9	256	12	3	.989
Major league totals (12 years)		1554	5522	705	1531	285	35	118	786	.277	439	543	112	5198	914	98	.984

NOTES: Shares single-game record for most home runs—2 (October 1, 1996).

DIVISION SERIES RECORD

Year	Team (League)	Pos.	G	AB	R	H	2B	3B	HR	RBI	Avg.	BB	SO	SB	PO	A	E	Avg.
						BATTING									FIELDING			
1996—Baltimore (A.L.)	OF-PH	4	13	3	5	0	0	3	5	.385	0	1	0	6	0	0	1.000
1997—Baltimore (A.L.)	OF-PH	3	11	0	3	1	0	0	2	.273	0	2	0	1	1	0	1.000
Division series totals (2 years)		7	24	3	8	1	0	3	7	.333	0	3	0	7	1	0	1.000

CHAMPIONSHIP SERIES RECORD

Year	Team (League)	Pos.	G	AB	R	H	2B	3B	HR	RBI	Avg.	BB	SO	SB	PO	A	E	Avg.
						BATTING									FIELDING			
1996—Baltimore (A.L.)	OF-PH	5	15	0	4	0	0	0	2	.267	1	2	0	11	1	0	1.000
1997—Baltimore (A.L.)	OF-1B	6	25	1	5	2	0	0	1	.200	2	2	0	13	0	0	1.000
Championship series totals (2 years)		11	40	1	9	2	0	0	3	.225	3	4	0	24	1	0	1.000

S SUTTON, LARRY 1B ROYALS

PERSONAL: Born May 14, 1970, in West Covina, Calif. ... 6-0/185. ... Bats left, throws left. ... Full name: Larry James Sutton.
HIGH SCHOOL: Mater Dei (Santa Ana, Calif.).
COLLEGE: Illinois.
TRANSACTIONS/CAREER NOTES: Selected by Kansas City organization in 21st round of free-agent draft (June 1, 1992).
HONORS: Named Northwest League Most Valuable Player (1992). ... Named Carolina League Most Valuable Player (1994).
STATISTICAL NOTES: Led Northwest League with 142 total bases in 1992. ... Led Midwest League first basemen with 92 double plays in 1993. ... Led Carolina League with .542 slugging percentage, 10 intentional bases on balls received and nine sacrifice flies in 1994. ... Led Texas League first basemen with .989 fielding percentage in 1996.

Year	Team (League)	Pos.	G	AB	R	H	2B	3B	HR	RBI	Avg.	BB	SO	SB	PO	A	E	Avg.
						BATTING									FIELDING			
1992—Eugene (Northwest) ...	1B	70	238	45	74	17	3	*15	*58	.311	48	33	3	517	29	14	.975
—Appleton (Midwest)....	DH	1	2	1	0	0	0	0	0	.000	2	1	0	...	...	...	...
1993—Rockford (Midwest) ...	1B	113	361	67	97	24	1	7	50	.269	*95	65	3	911	76	11	.989
1994—Wilmington (Caro.)....	1B	129	480	91	147	33	1	26	94	.306	*81	71	2	1086	71	12	*.990
1995—Wichita (Texas)	1B	53	197	31	53	11	1	5	32	.269	26	33	1	452	25	7	.986
1996—Wichita (Texas)	1B-OF	125	463	84	137	22	2	22	84	.296	77	66	4	1105	76	13	*.989
1997—Omaha (A.A.)	1B	106	380	61	114	27	1	19	72	.300	61	57	0	839	54	5	.994
—Kansas City (A.L.)	1B-DH-OF	27	69	9	20	2	0	2	8	.290	5	12	0	92	8	0	1.000
1998—Kansas City (A.L.)	OF-1B-DH	111	310	29	76	14	2	5	42	.245	29	46	3	179	7	2	.989
Major league totals (2 years)		138	379	38	96	16	2	7	50	.253	34	58	3	271	15	2	.993

SUZUKI, MAC P MARINERS

PERSONAL: Born May 31, 1975, in Kobe, Japan. ... 6-3/195. ... Throws right, bats right. ... Full name: Makoto Suzuki.
HIGH SCHOOL: Takigawa Daini (Kobe, Japan).
TRANSACTIONS/CAREER NOTES: Played with Salinas, independent (August 30, 1992). ... Signed by San Bernardino, independent (April 9, 1993). ... Contract purchased by Seattle Mariners organization from San Bernardino (September 5, 1993). ... On disabled list (April 19-June 15 and July 10, 1994-remainder of season). ... On Riverside temporarily inactive list (April 22-August 3, 1995). ... On Riverside disabled list (August 3-18, 1995). ... On Port City disabled list (May 8-17, 1996).

Year	Team (League)	W	L	Pct.	ERA	G	GS	CG	ShO	Sv.	IP	H	R	ER	BB	SO
1992—Salinas (Calif.)	0	0	...	0.00	1	0	0	0	0	1	0	0	0	0	1
1993—San Bernardino (Calif.)■....	4	4	.500	3.68	48	1	0	0	12	80²/₃	59	37	33	56	87
1994—Jacksonville (Southern) ...	1	0	1.000	2.84	8	0	0	0	0	12²/₃	15	4	4	6	10
1995—Riverside (California).........	0	1	.000	4.70	6	0	0	0	0	7²/₃	10	4	4	6	6
—Ariz. Mariners (Ariz.)	1	0	1.000	6.75	4	3	0	0	0	4	5	4	3	0	3
1996—Tacoma (PCL)	0	3	.000	7.25	13	2	0	0	0	22¹/₃	31	19	18	12	14
—Port City (Southern)..........	3	6	.333	4.72	16	16	0	0	0	74¹/₃	69	41	39	32	66
—Seattle (A.L.)..................	0	0	...	20.25	1	0	0	0	0	1¹/₃	3	3	3	2	1
1997—Tacoma (PCL)	4	9	.308	5.94	32	10	0	0	0	83¹/₃	79	60	55	64	63
1998—Tacoma (PCL)	9	10	.474	4.37	28	21	2	1	0	131²/₃	130	70	64	70	117
—Seattle (A.L.)..................	1	2	.333	7.18	6	5	0	0	0	26¹/₃	34	23	21	15	19
Major league totals (2 years)......	1	2	.333	7.81	7	5	0	0	0	27²/₃	36	26	24	17	20

SVEUM, DALE IF

PERSONAL: Born November 23, 1963, in Richmond, Calif. ... 6-2/212. ... Bats both, throws right. ... Full name: Dale Curtis Sveum. ... Cousin of John Olerud, first baseman, New York Mets. ... Name pronounced SWAIM.
HIGH SCHOOL: Pinole Valley (Calif.).
TRANSACTIONS/CAREER NOTES: Selected by Milwaukee Brewers organization in first round (25th pick overall) of free-agent draft (June 7, 1982). ... On Milwaukee disabled list (July 23-August 9, 1986). ... On Milwaukee disabled list (March 19, 1989-entire season); included rehabilitation assignments to Beloit (June 30-July 5) and Stockton (July 6-18). ... Traded by Brewers to Philadelphia Phillies for P Bruce Ruffin (December 11, 1991). ... On disabled list (April 9-24, 1992). ... Traded by Phillies to Chicago White Sox for P Keith Shepherd (August 10,

1992). ... Granted free agency (October 26, 1992). ... Signed by Oakland Athletics organization (January 21, 1993). ... Released by A's (June 17, 1993). ... Signed by Calgary, Seattle Mariners organization (June 27, 1993). ... On Calgary disabled list (August 3-13 and August 18, 1993-remainder of season; and June 14-21, 1994). ... Granted free agency (October 7, 1994). ... Signed by Buffalo, Pittsburgh Pirates organization (November 10, 1994). ... Granted free agency (October 16, 1995). ... Re-signed by Carolina, Pirates organization (February 2, 1996). ... On Calgary disabled list (May 17-June 18, 1996). ... Granted free agency (October 28, 1997). ... Signed by New York Yankees (November 25, 1997). ... Released by Yankees (August 3, 1998).

STATISTICAL NOTES: Led California League third basemen with 261 assists in 1983. ... Led Texas League with 256 total bases in 1984. ... Led Texas League third basemen with 111 putouts and 30 errors in 1984. ... Led American League third basemen with 26 errors in 1986. ... Hit three home runs in one game (July 17, 1987). ... Switch-hit home runs in one game (July 17, 1987 and June 12, 1988). ... Led American League shortstops with 27 errors in 1988. ... Led Pacific Coast League third basemen with 20 double plays in 1995.

								BATTING							FIELDING		
Year	Team (League)	Pos.	G	AB	R	H	2B	3B	HR	RBI	Avg.	BB	SO	SB	PO	A	E	Avg.
1982—	Pikeville (Appal.)	SS-3B	58	223	29	52	13	1	2	21	.233	20	50	6	84	158	36	.871
1983—	Stockton (California)	3B-SS	135	533	70	139	26	5	5	70	.261	29	73	15	105	†281	40	.906
1984—	El Paso (Texas)	3B-SS	131	523	92	*172	*41	8	9	84	.329	43	72	6	†113	259	†30	.925
1985—	Vancouver (PCL)	3B-SS	122	415	42	98	17	3	6	48	.236	48	79	4	81	200	26	.915
1986—	Vancouver (PCL)	3B	28	105	16	31	3	2	1	23	.295	13	22	0	22	54	4	.950
—Milwaukee (A.L.)	3B-SS-2B	91	317	35	78	13	2	7	35	.246	32	63	4	92	179	†30	.900
1987—	Milwaukee (A.L.)	SS-2B	153	535	86	135	27	3	25	95	.252	40	133	2	242	396	23	.965
1988—	Milwaukee (A.L.)	SS-2B-DH	129	467	41	113	14	4	9	51	.242	21	122	1	209	375	†27	.956
1989—	Beloit (Midwest)	DH	6	15	0	2	1	0	0	2	.133	5	6	0	...	...	...	...
—Stockton (California)	DH	11	43	5	8	0	0	1	5	.186	6	14	0	...	...	...	...
1990—	Milwaukee (A.L.)	3-2-1-S	48	117	15	23	7	0	1	12	.197	12	30	0	59	63	6	.953
—Denver (A.A.)	3-S-1-2	57	218	25	63	17	2	2	26	.289	20	49	1	134	102	12	.952
1991—	Milwaukee (A.L.)	S-3-DH-2	90	266	33	64	19	1	4	43	.241	32	78	2	85	189	10	.965
1992—	Philadelphia (N.L.)■	SS-3B-1B	54	135	13	24	4	0	2	16	.178	16	39	0	78	100	8	.957
—Chicago (A.L.)■	SS-3B-1B	40	114	15	25	9	0	2	12	.219	12	29	1	43	98	8	.946
1993—	Tacoma (PCL)■	SS-2B-SS	12	43	10	15	1	0	2	6	.349	6	7	2	29	21	0	1.000
—Oakland (A.L.)	1-3-2-DH-O-S	30	79	12	14	2	1	2	6	.177	16	21	0	128	17	3	.980
—Calgary (PCL)■	3B-1B	33	120	31	36	11	1	6	26	.300	24	32	0	62	29	3	.968
1994—	Calgary (PCL)■	3B-1B-OF	102	393	71	111	21	3	22	78	.282	49	98	1	100	185	30	.905
—Seattle (A.L.)	DH-3B	10	27	3	5	0	0	1	2	.185	2	10	0	2	8	1	.909
1995—	Calgary (PCL)■	3-1-P-S	118	408	71	116	34	1	12	70	.284	48	78	2	356	240	16	.974
1996—	Calgary (PCL)■	3B-1B-2B	101	343	62	103	28	2	23	84	.300	33	71	2	226	161	8	.980
—Pittsburgh (N.L.)	3B	12	34	9	12	5	0	1	5	.353	6	6	0	4	17	2	.913
1997—	Pittsburgh (N.L.)	3-S-1-2	126	306	30	80	20	1	12	47	.261	27	81	0	154	142	8	.974
1998—	New York (A.L.)	1B-3B-DH	30	58	6	9	0	0	0	3	.155	4	16	0	112	15	4	.969
American League totals (9 years)			621	1980	246	466	91	11	51	259	.235	171	502	10	972	1340	112	.954
National League totals (3 years)			192	475	52	116	29	1	15	68	.244	49	126	0	236	259	18	.965
Major league totals (11 years)			813	2455	298	582	120	12	66	327	.237	220	628	10	1208	1599	130	.956

RECORD AS PITCHER

Year	Team (League)	W	L	Pct.	ERA	G	GS	CG	ShO	Sv.	IP	H	R	ER	BB	SO
1995—	Calgary (PCL)	0	0	...	0.00	2	0	0	0	0	2	1	0	0	0	2

SWEENEY, MARK — OF/1B — PADRES

PERSONAL: Born October 26, 1969, in Framingham, Mass. ... 6-1/195. ... Bats left, throws left. ... Full name: Mark Patrick Sweeney.
HIGH SCHOOL: Holliston (Mass.).
COLLEGE: Maine.
TRANSACTIONS/CAREER NOTES: Selected by Los Angeles Dodgers organization in 39th round of free-agent draft (June 4, 1990); did not sign. ... Selected by California Angels organization in ninth round of free-agent draft (June 3, 1991). ... Traded by Angels organization with a player to be named later to St. Louis Cardinals for P John Habyan (July 8, 1995); Cardinals acquired IF Rod Correia to complete deal (January 31, 1996). ... Traded by Cardinals with P Danny Jackson and P Rich Batchelor to San Diego Padres for P Fernando Valenzuela, 3B Scott Livingstone and OF Phil Plantier (June 13, 1997).

								BATTING							FIELDING		
Year	Team (League)	Pos.	G	AB	R	H	2B	3B	HR	RBI	Avg.	BB	SO	SB	PO	A	E	Avg.
1991—	Boise (Northwest)	OF	70	234	45	66	10	3	4	34	.282	*51	42	9	81	2	4	.954
1992—	Quad City (Midwest)	OF	120	424	65	115	20	5	14	76	.271	47	85	15	205	5	4	.981
1993—	Palm Springs (Calif.)	OF-1B	66	245	41	87	18	3	3	47	.355	42	29	9	145	2	7	.955
—Midland (Texas)	OF	51	188	41	67	13	2	9	32	.356	27	22	1	85	3	1	.989
1994—	Vancouver (PCL)	1B-OF	103	344	59	98	12	3	8	49	.285	59	50	3	330	12	2	.994
—Midland (Texas)	OF-1B	14	50	13	15	3	0	3	18	.300	10	10	1	66	5	2	.973
1995—	Vancouver (PCL)	OF-1B	69	226	48	78	14	2	7	59	.345	43	33	3	102	2	2	.981
—Louisville (A.A.)■	1B	22	76	15	28	8	0	2	22	.368	14	8	2	176	19	2	.990
—St. Louis (N.L.)	1B-OF	37	77	5	21	2	0	2	13	.273	10	15	1	153	11	2	.988
1996—	St. Louis (N.L.)	OF-1B	98	170	32	45	9	0	3	22	.265	33	29	3	126	3	3	.977
1997—	St. Louis (N.L.)	OF-1B	44	61	5	13	3	0	0	4	.213	9	14	0	31	1	0	1.000
—San Diego (N.L.)■	OF-1B	71	103	11	33	4	0	2	19	.320	11	18	2	41	3	2	.957
1998—	San Diego (N.L.)	OF-1B-DH	122	192	17	45	8	3	2	15	.234	26	37	1	165	5	1	.994
Major league totals (4 years)			372	603	70	157	26	3	9	73	.260	89	113	7	516	23	8	.985

DIVISION SERIES RECORD

								BATTING							FIELDING		
Year	Team (League)	Pos.	G	AB	R	H	2B	3B	HR	RBI	Avg.	BB	SO	SB	PO	A	E	Avg.
1996—	St. Louis (N.L.)	PH	1	1	0	1	0	0	0	0	1.000	0	0	0	...	...	...	...
1998—	San Diego (N.L.)	PH	2	1	0	0	0	0	0	0	.000	1	0	0	...	...	...	...
Division series totals (2 years)			3	2	0	1	0	0	0	0	.500	1	0	0	...	...	...	...

CHAMPIONSHIP SERIES RECORD

Year Team (League)	Pos.	G	AB	R	H	2B	3B	HR	RBI	Avg.	BB	SO	SB	PO	A	E	Avg.
1996— St. Louis (N.L.)..........	PH-OF	5	4	1	0	0	0	0	0	.000	0	2	0	2	0	0	1.000
1998— San Diego (N.L.)	PH	3	2	1	0	0	0	0	0	.000	1	1	0	...	...	...	...
Championship series totals (2 years)		8	6	2	0	0	0	0	0	.000	1	3	0	2	0	0	1.000

WORLD SERIES RECORD

Year Team (League)	Pos.	G	AB	R	H	2B	3B	HR	RBI	Avg.	BB	SO	SB	PO	A	E	Avg.
1998— San Diego (N.L.)	PH	3	3	0	2	0	0	0	1	.667	0	0	0	0	0	0	...

SWEENEY, MIKE   C   ROYALS

PERSONAL: Born July 22, 1973, in Orange, Calif. ... 6-2/215. ... Bats right, throws right. ... Full name: Michael John Sweeney.
HIGH SCHOOL: Ontario (Calif.).
TRANSACTIONS/CAREER NOTES: Selected by Kansas City Royals organization in 10th round of free-agent draft (June 3, 1991). ... On disabled list (May 24-July 5, 1994).
STATISTICAL NOTES: Led Carolina League with .548 slugging percentage in 1995. ... Tied for A.L. lead in double plays by catcher with 13 in 1997.

Year Team (League)	Pos.	G	AB	R	H	2B	3B	HR	RBI	Avg.	BB	SO	SB	PO	A	E	Avg.
1991— GC Royals (GCL)	C-1B	38	102	8	22	3	0	1	11	.216	11	9	1	124	16	4	.972
1992— Eugene (Northwest) ...	C	59	199	17	44	12	1	4	28	.221	13	54	3	367	42	14	.967
1993— Eugene (Northwest) ...	C	53	175	32	42	10	2	6	29	.240	30	41	1	364	46	7	.983
1994— Rockford (Midwest)....	C	86	276	47	83	20	3	10	52	.301	55	43	0	453	54	6	.988
1995— Wilmington (Caro.).....	C-3B	99	332	61	103	23	1	18	53	*.310	60	39	6	575	45	7	.989
— Kansas City (A.L.)	C	4	4	1	1	0	0	0	0	.250	0	0	0	7	0	1	.875
1996— Wichita (Texas)	C	66	235	45	75	18	1	14	51	.319	32	29	3	201	13	1	.995
— Omaha (A.A.)...............	C	25	101	14	26	9	0	3	16	.257	6	13	0	167	8	0	1.000
— Kansas City (A.L.)	C-DH	50	165	23	46	10	0	4	24	.279	18	21	1	158	7	1	.994
1997— Kansas City (A.L.)	C-DH	84	240	30	58	8	0	7	31	.242	17	33	3	425	31	3	.993
— Omaha (A.A.)...............	C	40	144	22	34	8	1	10	29	.236	18	20	0	229	15	1	.996
1998— Kansas City (A.L.)	C	92	282	32	73	18	0	8	35	.259	24	38	2	517	33	•9	.984
Major league totals (4 years)		230	691	86	178	36	0	19	90	.258	59	92	6	1107	71	14	.988

SWIFT, BILL   P   MARINERS

PERSONAL: Born October 27, 1961, in South Portland, Maine. ... 6-0/197. ... Throws right, bats right. ... Full name: William Charles Swift.
HIGH SCHOOL: South Portland (Portland, Maine).
COLLEGE: Maine.
TRANSACTIONS/CAREER NOTES: Selected by Minnesota Twins organization in second round of free-agent draft (June 6, 1983); did not sign. ... Selected by Seattle Mariners organization in first round (second pick overall) of free-agent draft (June 4, 1984). ... On disabled list (May 6-21, 1985 and April 22, 1987-remainder of season). ... On Seattle disabled list (March 28-April 27, 1989); included rehabilitation assignment to San Bernardino (April 18-27). ... On disabled list (April 11-26, 1991). ... Traded by Mariners with P Mike Jackson and P Dave Burba to San Francisco Giants for OF Kevin Mitchell and P Mike Remlinger (December 11, 1991). ... On disabled list (May 23-June 21 and August 25-September 9, 1992; May 18-June 6 and June 24-July 21, 1994). ... Granted free agency (October 15, 1994). ... Signed by Colorado Rockies (April 8, 1995). ... On disabled list (May 28-June 16 and July 26-September 1, 1995). ... On Colorado disabled list (March 22-June 3 and June 4-August 26, 1996); included rehabilitation assignment to Salem (August 16-26). ... On Colorado disabled list (May 13-July 11, 1997); included rehabilitation assignment to Salem (June 29-July 4) and Colorado Springs (July 4-July 11). ... Released by Rockies (August 20, 1997). ... Signed by Baltimore Orioles (August 26, 1997). ... Released by Baltimore Orioles (August 30, 1997). ... Signed by Mariners organization (February 14, 1998). ... Granted free agency (October 23, 1998). ... Re-signed by Mariners (January 8, 1999).
MISCELLANEOUS: Member of 1984 U.S. Olympic baseball team. ... Appeared in five games as pinch runner (1992). ... Appeared in one game as pinch runner (1994). ... Appeared in one game as pinch runner (1997). ... Had sacrifice hit in only appearance as pinch hitter with Colorado (1997).

Year Team (League)	W	L	Pct.	ERA	G	GS	CG	ShO	Sv.	IP	H	R	ER	BB	SO
1985— Chattanooga (Southern).....	2	1	.667	3.69	7	7	0	0	0	39	34	16	16	21	21
— Seattle (A.L.)...............	6	10	.375	4.77	23	21	0	0	0	120²/₃	131	71	64	48	55
1986— Seattle (A.L.)...............	2	9	.182	5.46	29	17	1	0	0	115¹/₃	148	85	70	55	55
— Calgary (PCL)...............	4	4	.500	3.95	10	8	3	1	1	57	57	33	25	22	29
1987— Calgary (PCL)...............	0	0	...	8.84	5	5	0	0	0	18¹/₃	32	22	18	13	5
1988— Seattle (A.L.)...............	8	12	.400	4.59	38	24	6	1	0	174²/₃	199	99	89	65	47
1989— San Bernardino (Calif.).......	1	0	1.000	0.00	2	2	0	0	0	10	8	0	0	2	4
— Seattle (A.L.)...............	7	3	.700	4.43	37	16	0	0	0	130	140	72	64	38	45
1990— Seattle (A.L.)...............	6	4	.600	2.39	55	8	0	0	6	128	135	46	34	21	42
1991— Seattle (A.L.)...............	1	2	.333	1.99	71	0	0	0	17	90¹/₃	74	22	20	26	48
1992— San Francisco (N.L.)■.......	10	4	.714	*2.08	30	22	3	2	1	164²/₃	144	41	38	43	77
1993— San Francisco (N.L.)	21	8	.724	2.82	34	34	1	1	0	232²/₃	195	82	73	55	157
1994— San Francisco (N.L.)	8	7	.533	3.38	17	17	0	0	0	109¹/₃	109	49	41	31	62
1995— Colorado (N.L.)■.............	9	3	.750	4.94	19	19	0	0	0	105²/₃	122	62	58	43	68
1996— Colorado (N.L.)	1	1	.500	5.40	7	3	0	0	2	18¹/₃	23	12	11	5	5
— Salem (Carolina)	0	0	...	4.50	2	2	0	0	0	6	9	4	3	1	4
1997— Colorado (N.L.)	4	6	.400	6.34	14	13	0	0	0	65¹/₃	85	57	46	26	29
— Salem (Carolina)	0	1	.000	6.75	1	1	0	0	0	4	4	3	3	0	1
— Colo. Springs (PCL)	0	1	.000	12.00	1	1	0	0	0	3	4	4	4	3	4
— Rochester (Int'l)■...........	0	1	.000	4.91	2	0	0	0	0	3²/₃	2	2	2	3	2
1998— Seattle (A.L.)■..............	11	9	.550	5.85	29	26	0	0	0	144²/₃	183	103	94	51	77
A.L. totals (7 years)	41	49	.456	4.33	282	112	7	1	24	903²/₃	1010	498	435	304	369
N.L. totals (6 years)	53	29	.646	3.45	121	108	4	3	3	696	678	303	267	203	398
Major league totals (13 years)	94	78	.547	3.95	403	220	11	4	27	1599²/₃	1688	801	702	507	767

DIVISION SERIES RECORD

Year Team (League)	W	L	Pct.	ERA	G	GS	CG	ShO	Sv.	IP	H	R	ER	BB	SO
1995— Colorado (N.L.)	0	0	...	6.00	1	1	0	0	0	6	7	4	4	2	3

S

SWINDELL, GREG   P   DIAMONDBACKS

PERSONAL: Born January 2, 1965, in Fort Worth, Texas. ... 6-3/230. ... Throws left, bats right. ... Full name: Forest Gregory Swindell. ... Name pronounced swin-DELL.

HIGH SCHOOL: Sharpstown (Houston).

COLLEGE: Texas.

TRANSACTIONS/CAREER NOTES: Selected by Cleveland Indians organization in first round (second pick overall) of free-agent draft (June 2, 1986). ... On disabled list (June 30, 1987-remainder of season and July 26-August 30, 1989). ... Traded by Indians to Cincinnati Reds for P Jack Armstrong, P Scott Scudder and P Joe Turek (November 15, 1991). ... On disabled list (August 23-September 7, 1992). ... Granted free agency (October 26, 1992). ... Signed by Houston Astros (December 4, 1992). ... On disabled list (July 6-26, 1993). ... On Houston disabled list (April 20-May 22, 1996). ... Released by Astros (June 3, 1996). ... Signed by Indians (June 15, 1996). ... On Cleveland disabled list (July 4-21, 1996). ... Granted free agency (October 3, 1996). ... Signed by Minnesota Twins organization (December 18, 1996). ... Traded by Twins with 1B Orlando Merced to Boston Red Sox for P Matt Kinney, P Joe Thomas and P John Barnes (July 31, 1998). ... Granted free agency (October 27, 1998). ... Signed by Arizona Diamondbacks (November 13, 1998).

HONORS: Named lefthanded pitcher on THE SPORTING NEWS college All-America team (1985-86).

STATISTICAL NOTES: Struck out 15 batters in one game (May 10, 1987).

MISCELLANEOUS: Struck out in only appearance as pinch hitter (1995).

Year	Team (League)	W	L	Pct.	ERA	G	GS	CG	ShO	Sv.	IP	H	R	ER	BB	SO
1986—	Waterloo (Midw.)	2	1	.667	1.00	3	3	0	0	0	18	12	2	2	3	25
	—Cleveland (A.L.)	5	2	.714	4.23	9	9	1	0	0	61 2/3	57	35	29	15	46
1987—	Cleveland (A.L.)	3	8	.273	5.10	16	15	4	1	0	102 1/3	112	62	58	37	97
1988—	Cleveland (A.L.)	18	14	.563	3.20	33	33	12	4	0	242	234	97	86	45	180
1989—	Cleveland (A.L.)	13	6	.684	3.37	28	28	5	2	0	184 1/3	170	71	69	51	129
1990—	Cleveland (A.L.)	12	9	.571	4.40	34	34	3	0	0	214 2/3	245	110	105	47	135
1991—	Cleveland (A.L.)	9	16	.360	3.48	33	33	7	0	0	238	241	112	92	31	169
1992—	Cincinnati (N.L.)■	12	8	.600	2.70	31	30	5	3	0	213 2/3	210	72	64	41	138
1993—	Houston (N.L.)■	12	13	.480	4.16	31	30	1	1	0	190 1/3	215	98	88	40	124
1994—	Houston (N.L.)	8	9	.471	4.37	24	24	1	0	0	148 1/3	175	80	72	26	74
1995—	Houston (N.L.)	10	9	.526	4.47	33	26	1	1	0	153	180	86	76	39	96
1996—	Houston (N.L.)■	0	3	.000	7.83	8	4	0	0	0	23	35	25	20	11	15
	—Cleveland (A.L.)■	1	1	.500	6.59	13	2	0	0	0	28 2/3	31	21	21	8	21
1997—	Minnesota (A.L.)■	7	4	.636	3.58	65	1	0	0	1	115 2/3	102	46	46	25	75
1998—	Minnesota (A.L.)	3	3	.500	3.66	52	0	0	0	2	66 1/3	67	27	27	18	45
	—Boston (A.L.)■	2	3	.400	3.38	29	0	0	0	0	24	25	13	9	13	18
A.L. totals (9 years)		73	66	.525	3.82	312	155	32	7	3	1277 2/3	1284	594	542	290	915
N.L. totals (5 years)		42	42	.500	3.95	127	114	8	5	0	728 1/3	815	361	320	157	447
Major league totals (13 years)		115	108	.516	3.87	439	269	40	12	3	2006	2099	955	862	447	1362

DIVISION SERIES RECORD

Year	Team (League)	W	L	Pct.	ERA	G	GS	CG	ShO	Sv.	IP	H	R	ER	BB	SO
1998—	Boston (A.L.)	0	0	...	0.00	1	0	0	0	0	1 1/3	0	0	0	1	1

ALL-STAR GAME RECORD

Year	League	W	L	Pct.	ERA	GS	CG	ShO	Sv.	IP	H	R	ER	BB	SO
1989—	American	0	0	...	0.00	0	0	0	0	1 2/3	2	0	0	0	3

TABAKA, JEFF   P   PIRATES

PERSONAL: Born January 17, 1964, in Barberton, Ohio. ... 6-2/201. ... Throws left, bats right. ... Full name: Jeffrey Jon Tabaka. ... Name pronounced tuh-BAW-kuh.

HIGH SCHOOL: Copley (Ohio).

COLLEGE: Kent.

TRANSACTIONS/CAREER NOTES: Selected by Montreal Expos organization in free-agent draft (June 2, 1986). ... On West Palm Beach disabled list (May 2-June 23, 1988). ... Selected by Philadelphia Phillies from Expos organization in Rule 5 major league draft (December 5, 1988); Expos waived right to reclaim him as part of deal in which Expos traded P Floyd Youmans and P Jeff Parrett to Phillies for P Kevin Gross (December 6, 1988). ... Released by Phillies organization (July 26, 1991). ... Signed by Milwaukee Brewers organization (August 8, 1991). ... On disabled list (June 18-July 4, 1992). ... Granted free agency (October 15, 1992). ... Re-signed by Brewers (October 30, 1992). ... Selected by Florida Marlins in third round (71st pick overall) of expansion draft (November 17, 1992). ... Granted free agency (March 21, 1993). ... Signed by Brewers organization (March 26, 1993). ... Granted free agency (October 15, 1993). ... Re-signed by Brewers organization (January 6, 1994). ... Released by Brewers organization (April 2, 1994). ... Signed by Pittsburgh Pirates organization (April 3, 1994). ... Claimed on waivers by San Diego Padres (May 12, 1994). ... Traded by Padres with P Rich Loiselle to Houston Astros for OF Phil Plantier (July 19, 1995). ... Granted free agency (December 20, 1996). ... Signed by Cincinnati Reds organization (January 10, 1997). ... Granted free agency (October 15, 1997). ... Signed by Pirates (December 10, 1997). ... On Pittsburgh disabled list (May 25-July 3, 1998); included rehabilitation assignment to Nashville (June 24-30).

MISCELLANEOUS: Made two outs in one game as designated hitter with New Orleans (1993).

Year	Team (League)	W	L	Pct.	ERA	G	GS	CG	ShO	Sv.	IP	H	R	ER	BB	SO
1986—	Jamestown (NYP)	2	4	.333	4.30	13	9	0	0	0	52 1/3	51	31	25	34	57
1987—	W.P. Beach (FSL)	8	6	.571	4.17	28	15	0	0	5	95	90	46	44	58	71
1988—	W.P. Beach (FSL)	7	5	.583	1.71	16	16	2	2	0	95	71	38	18	34	52
	—Jacksonville (Southern)	1	0	1.000	6.55	2	2	0	0	0	11	14	8	8	5	7
1989—	Reading (Eastern)■	8	7	.533	4.65	21	17	6	1	0	100 2/3	109	59	52	54	80
	—Scran./W.B. (Int'l)	0	4	.000	6.32	6	6	0	0	0	31 1/3	32	26	22	23	15
1990—	Clearwater (Fla. St.)	5	2	.714	3.03	8	5	0	0	0	35 2/3	39	17	12	18	23
1991—	Reading (Eastern)	4	8	.333	5.07	21	20	1	1	0	108 1/3	117	65	61	78	68
	—Stockton (California)■	0	2	.000	5.19	4	4	0	0	0	17 1/3	19	11	10	16	19
1992—	El Paso (Texas)■	9	5	.643	2.52	50	0	0	0	10	82	67	23	23	38	75
1993—	New Orleans (A.A.)	6	6	.500	3.24	53	0	0	0	1	58 1/3	50	26	21	30	63
1994—	Buffalo (A.A.)■	1	0	1.000	3.38	9	0	0	0	1	5 1/3	3	2	2	4	4
	—Pittsburgh (N.L.)	0	0	...	18.00	5	0	0	0	0	4	4	8	8	8	2
	—San Diego (N.L.)■	3	1	.750	3.89	34	0	0	0	1	37	28	21	16	19	30

Year Team (League)	W	L	Pct.	ERA	G	GS	CG	ShO	Sv.	IP	H	R	ER	BB	SO
1995— Las Vegas (PCL)	0	1	.000	1.99	19	0	0	0	6	22 2/3	16	6	5	14	27
— San Diego (N.L.)	0	0	...	7.11	10	0	0	0	0	6 1/3	10	5	5	5	6
— Houston (N.L.)■	1	0	1.000	2.22	24	0	0	0	0	24 1/3	17	6	6	12	19
1996— Houston (N.L.)	0	2	.000	6.64	18	0	0	0	1	20 1/3	28	18	15	14	18
— Tucson (PCL)	6	2	.750	2.93	41	0	0	0	4	43	40	16	14	21	51
1997— Indianapolis (A.A.)■	3	2	.600	2.65	58	0	0	0	3	57 2/3	44	19	17	19	68
— Cincinnati (N.L.)	0	0	...	4.50	3	0	0	0	0	2	1	1	1	1	1
1998— Pittsburgh (N.L.)■	2	2	.500	3.02	37	0	0	0	0	50 2/3	37	19	17	22	40
— Nashville (Pacific Coast)	0	1	.000	7.71	4	0	0	0	0	4 2/3	9	4	4	0	4
Major league totals (5 years)	6	5	.545	4.23	131	0	0	0	2	144 2/3	125	78	68	81	116

TAM, JEFF   P   METS

PERSONAL: Born August 19, 1970, in Fullerton, Calif. ... 6-1/202. ... Throws right, bats right. ... Full name: Jeffery Eugene Tam.
HIGH SCHOOL: Eau Gaille (Melbourne, Fla.)
COLLEGE: Florida State.
TRANSACTIONS/CAREER NOTES: Signed as a non-drafted free agent by New York Mets organization (June 27, 1993).

Year Team (League)	W	L	Pct.	ERA	G	GS	CG	ShO	Sv.	IP	H	R	ER	BB	SO
1993— Pittsfield (NYP)	3	3	.500	3.35	21	1	0	0	0	40 1/3	50	21	15	7	31
1994— Columbia (S. Atl.)	1	1	.500	1.29	26	0	0	0	18	28	23	14	4	6	22
— St. Lucie (Fla. St.)	0	0	...	0.00	24	0	0	0	16	26 2/3	13	0	0	6	15
— Binghamton (Eastern)	0	0	...	8.10	4	0	0	0	0	6 2/3	9	6	6	5	7
1995— Binghamton (Eastern)	0	2	.000	4.50	14	0	0	0	3	18	20	11	9	4	9
— GC Mets (GCL)	0	0	...	3.00	2	1	0	0	0	3	2	1	1	1	2
1996— Binghamton (Eastern)	6	2	.750	2.44	49	0	0	0	2	62 2/3	51	19	17	16	48
1997— Norfolk (Int'l)	7	5	.583	4.67	40	11	0	0	6	111 2/3	137	72	58	14	67
1998— Norfolk (Int'l)	3	3	.500	1.83	45	0	0	0	11	64	42	14	13	6	54
— New York (N.L.)	1	1	.500	6.28	15	0	0	0	0	14 1/3	13	10	10	4	8
Major league totals (1 year)	1	1	.500	6.28	15	0	0	0	0	14 1/3	13	10	10	4	8

TAPANI, KEVIN   P   CUBS

PERSONAL: Born February 18, 1964, in Des Moines, Iowa. ... 6-1/195. ... Throws right, bats right. ... Full name: Kevin Ray Tapani. ... Name pronounced TAP-uh-nee.
HIGH SCHOOL: Escanaba (Mich.).
COLLEGE: Central Michigan (degree in finance, 1987).
TRANSACTIONS/CAREER NOTES: Selected by Chicago Cubs organization in ninth round of free-agent draft (June 3, 1985); did not sign. ... Selected by Oakland Athletics organization in second round of free-agent draft (June 2, 1986). ... Traded by A's as part of an eight-player, two-team deal in which New York Mets traded P Jesse Orosco to A's (December 11, 1987). A's traded Orosco, SS Alfredo Griffin and P Jay Howell to Los Angeles Dodgers for P Bob Welch, P Matt Young and P Jack Savage. A's then traded Savage, P Wally Whitehurst and Tapani to Mets. ... Traded by Mets with P Tim Drummond to Portland, Minnesota Twins organization (August 1, 1989), as partial completion of deal in which Twins traded P Frank Viola to Mets for P Rick Aguilera, P David West and three players to be named later (July 31, 1989); Twins acquired P Jack Savage to complete deal (October 16, 1989). ... On disabled list (August 17-September 10, 1990). ... Traded by Twins with P Mark Guthrie to Los Angeles Dodgers for 1B/3B Ron Coomer, P Greg Hansell, P Jose Parra and a player to be named later (July 31, 1995); Twins acquired OF Chris Latham to complete deal (October 30, 1995). ... Granted free agency (December 21, 1995). ... Signed by Chicago White Sox (February 3, 1996). ... Granted free agency (October 29, 1996). ... Signed by Cubs (December 16, 1996). ... On disabled list (March 27-July 23, 1997); included rehabilitation assignments to Rockford (June 25-26 and July 12-13), Orlando (July 1-7), Daytona (July 7-8) and Iowa (July 18-19).
STATISTICAL NOTES: Pitched 5-0 one-hit, complete-game victory for Chicago against Cincinnati (September 16, 1997). ... Career major league grand slams: 1.

Year Team (League)	W	L	Pct.	ERA	G	GS	CG	ShO	Sv.	IP	H	R	ER	BB	SO
1986— Medford (N'west)	1	0	1.000	0.00	2	2	0	0	0	8 1/3	6	3	0	3	9
— Modesto (California)	6	1	.857	2.48	11	11	1	0	0	69	74	26	19	22	44
— Huntsville (Southern)	1	0	1.000	6.00	1	1	0	0	0	6	8	4	4	1	2
— Tacoma (PCL)	0	1	.000	15.43	1	1	0	0	0	2 1/3	5	6	4	1	1
1987— Modesto (California)	10	7	.588	3.76	24	24	6	1	0	148 1/3	122	74	62	60	121
1988— St. Lucie (Fla. St.)■	1	0	1.000	1.42	3	3	0	0	0	19	17	5	3	4	11
— Jackson (Texas)	5	1	.833	2.74	24	5	0	0	3	62 1/3	46	23	19	19	35
1989— Tidewater (Int'l)	7	5	.583	3.47	17	17	2	1	0	109	113	49	42	25	63
— New York (N.L.)	0	0	...	3.68	3	0	0	0	0	7 1/3	5	3	3	4	2
— Portland (PCL)■	4	2	.667	2.20	6	6	1	0	0	41	38	15	10	12	30
— Minnesota (A.L.)	2	2	.500	3.86	5	5	0	0	0	32 2/3	34	15	14	8	21
1990— Minnesota (A.L.)	12	8	.600	4.07	28	28	1	1	0	159 1/3	164	75	72	29	101
1991— Minnesota (A.L.)	16	9	.640	2.99	34	34	4	1	0	244	225	84	81	40	135
1992— Minnesota (A.L.)	16	11	.593	3.97	34	34	4	1	0	220	226	103	97	48	138
1993— Minnesota (A.L.)	12	15	.444	4.43	36	35	3	1	0	225 2/3	243	123	111	57	150
1994— Minnesota (A.L.)	11	7	.611	4.62	24	24	4	1	0	156	181	86	80	39	91
1995— Minnesota (A.L.)	6	11	.353	4.92	20	20	3	1	0	133 2/3	155	79	73	34	88
— Los Angeles (N.L.)■	4	2	.667	5.05	13	11	0	0	0	57	72	37	32	14	43
1996— Chicago (A.L.)■	13	10	.565	4.59	34	34	1	0	0	225 1/3	236	123	115	76	150
1997— Rockford (Midwest)■	1	0	1.000	0.82	2	2	0	0	0	11	5	1	1	0	7
— Orlando (South.)	0	0	...	4.50	1	1	0	0	0	4	3	2	2	2	2
— Daytona (Fla. St.)	0	0	...	3.86	1	1	0	0	0	4 2/3	5	2	2	2	4
— Iowa (Am. Assoc.)	0	1	.000	4.00	1	1	1	0	0	9	5	4	4	1	4
— Chicago (N.L.)	9	3	.750	3.39	13	13	1	1	0	85	77	33	32	23	55
1998— Chicago (N.L.)	19	9	.679	4.85	35	34	2	2	0	219	244	120	118	62	136
A.L. totals (8 years)	88	73	.547	4.14	215	214	20	6	0	1396 2/3	1464	688	643	331	874
N.L. totals (4 years)	32	14	.696	4.52	64	58	3	3	0	368 1/3	398	193	185	103	236
Major league totals (10 years)	120	87	.580	4.22	279	272	23	9	0	1765	1862	881	828	434	1110

T

DIVISION SERIES RECORD

Year	Team (League)	W	L	Pct.	ERA	G	GS	CG	ShO	Sv.	IP	H	R	ER	BB	SO
1995— Los Angeles (N.L.)		0	0	...	81.00	2	0	0	0	0	$^1/_3$	0	3	3	4	1
1998— Chicago (N.L.)		0	0	...	1.00	1	1	0	0	0	9	5	1	1	3	6
Div. series totals (2 years)		0	0	...	3.86	3	1	0	0	0	$9^1/_3$	5	4	4	7	7

CHAMPIONSHIP SERIES RECORD

Year	Team (League)	W	L	Pct.	ERA	G	GS	CG	ShO	Sv.	IP	H	R	ER	BB	SO
1991— Minnesota (A.L.)		0	1	.000	7.84	2	2	0	0	0	$10^1/_3$	16	9	9	3	9

WORLD SERIES RECORD

NOTES: Member of World Series championship team (1991).

Year	Team (League)	W	L	Pct.	ERA	G	GS	CG	ShO	Sv.	IP	H	R	ER	BB	SO
1991— Minnesota (A.L.)		1	1	.500	4.50	2	2	0	0	0	12	13	6	6	2	7

TARASCO, TONY   OF

PERSONAL: Born December 9, 1970, in New York. ... 6-1/205. ... Bats left, throws right. ... Full name: Anthony Giacinto Tarasco.

HIGH SCHOOL: Santa Monica (Calif.).

TRANSACTIONS/CAREER NOTES: Selected by Atlanta Braves organization in 15th round of free-agent draft (June 1, 1988). ... On disabled list (August 4-September 12, 1991). ... Traded by Braves with OF Roberto Kelly and P Esteban Yan to Montreal Expos for OF Marquis Grissom (April 6, 1995). ... Traded by Expos to Baltimore Orioles for OF Sherman Obando (March 13, 1996). ... On Rochester disabled list (June 16-August 25, 1996). ... On Baltimore disabled list (August 25-September 13, 1996); included rehabilitation assignments to Frederick (August 25-September 8) and Rochester (September 9-13). ... Claimed on waivers by Cincinnati Reds (March 24, 1998). ... On Indianapolis disabled list (April 26-May 29, 1998). ... Released by Reds (November 10, 1998).

STATISTICAL NOTES: Career major league grand slams: 1.

Year	Team (League)	Pos.	G	AB	R	H	2B	3B	HR	RBI	Avg.	BB	SO	SB	PO	A	E	Avg.
1988— Idaho Falls (Pio.)........		OF	7	10	1	0	0	0	0	1	.000	5	2	1	2	0	1	.667
— GC Braves (GCL)		OF	21	64	10	15	6	1	0	4	.234	7	7	3	25	1	1	.963
1989— Pulaski (Appalachian).		OF	49	156	22	53	8	2	2	22	.340	21	20	7	45	4	3	.942
1990— Sumter (S. Atl.)		OF	107	355	42	94	13	3	3	37	.265	37	57	9	173	14	9	.954
1991— Durham (Carolina)......		OF	78	248	31	62	8	2	12	38	.250	21	64	11	119	6	3	.977
1992— Greenville (Southern) .		OF-2B	133	489	73	140	22	2	15	54	.286	27	84	33	209	17	5	.978
1993— Richmond (Int'l)		OF	93	370	73	122	15	7	15	53	.330	36	54	19	143	8	2	.987
— Atlanta (N.L.)............		OF	24	35	6	8	2	0	0	2	.229	0	5	0	11	0	0	1.000
1994— Atlanta (N.L.)............		OF	87	132	16	36	6	0	5	19	.273	9	17	5	42	1	0	1.000
1995— Montreal (N.L.)■.......		OF	126	438	64	109	18	4	14	40	.249	51	78	24	230	7	5	.979
1996— Baltimore (A.L.)■......		OF-DH	31	84	14	20	3	0	1	9	.238	7	15	5	50	1	0	1.000
— Rochester (Int'l)		OF	29	103	18	27	6	0	2	9	.262	17	20	4	4	0	0	1.000
— Frederick (Carolina)....		DH	9	35	6	8	3	0	1	5	.229	4	4	0	0	0	0	...
— GC Orioles (GCL)		DH	3	8	2	3	1	0	0	3	.375	2	1	0	0	0	0	...
1997— Baltimore (A.L.)........		OF-DH	100	166	26	34	8	1	7	26	.205	25	33	2	104	4	1	.991
— Rochester (Int'l)		OF	10	35	4	7	0	0	2	6	.200	7	7	0	19	1	0	1.000
1998— Indianapolis (Int'l)■...		OF	90	319	53	100	19	1	16	45	.313	43	46	3	101	3	0	1.000
— Cincinnati (N.L.)		OF	15	24	5	5	2	0	1	4	.208	3	5	0	10	0	0	1.000
American League totals (2 years)			131	250	40	54	11	1	8	35	.216	32	48	7	154	5	1	.994
National League totals (4 years)			252	629	91	158	28	4	20	65	.251	63	105	29	293	8	5	.984
Major league totals (6 years)			383	879	131	212	39	5	28	100	.241	95	153	36	447	13	6	.987

DIVISION SERIES RECORD

Year	Team (League)	Pos.	G	AB	R	H	2B	3B	HR	RBI	Avg.	BB	SO	SB	PO	A	E	Avg.
1996— Baltimore (A.L.)									Did not play.									

CHAMPIONSHIP SERIES RECORD

Year	Team (League)	Pos.	G	AB	R	H	2B	3B	HR	RBI	Avg.	BB	SO	SB	PO	A	E	Avg.
1993— Atlanta (N.L.).............		OF-PR	2	1	0	0	0	0	0	0	.000	0	1	0	0	0	0	...
1996— Baltimore (A.L.).........		OF	2	1	0	0	0	0	0	0	.000	0	1	0	2	0	0	1.000
Championship series totals (2 years)			4	2	0	0	0	0	0	0	.000	0	2	0	2	0	0	1.000

TATIS, FERNANDO   3B   CARDINALS

PERSONAL: Born January 1, 1975, in San Pedro De Macoris, Dominican Republic. ... 6-1/175. ... Bats right, throws right.

TRANSACTIONS/CAREER NOTES: Signed as non-drafted free agent by Texas Rangers organization (August 25, 1992). ... Traded by Rangers with P Darren Oliver and a player to be named later to St. Louis Cardinals for P Todd Stottlemyre and SS Royce Clayton (July 31, 1998); Cardinals acquired OF Mark Little to complete deal (August 9, 1998).

STATISTICAL NOTES: Tied for Gulf Coast League lead in intentional bases on balls received with four in 1994. ... Led Gulf Coast League third basemen with 165 assists and 227 total chances in 1994. ... Tied for Texas League lead with four intentional bases on balls in 1997.

Year	Team (League)	Pos.	G	AB	R	H	2B	3B	HR	RBI	Avg.	BB	SO	SB	PO	A	E	Avg.
1993— Dom. Rangers (DSL)..		IF	59	198	22	54	5	1	4	34	.273	27	12	7	135	37	11	.940
1994— GC Rangers (GCL)....		3B-2B	•60	212	34	70	10	2	6	32	.330	25	33	21	47	†168	17	.927
1995— Char., S.C. (S. Atl.) ...		3B	131	494	74	•151	*43	4	15	84	.303	45	94	22	*98	235	37	.900
1996— Charlotte (Fla. St.)		3B	85	325	46	93	25	0	12	53	.286	30	48	9	53	148	24	.893
— Okla. City (A.A.).........		3B	2	4	0	2	1	0	0	0	.500	0	1	0	0	1	0	1.000
1997— Tulsa (Texas)		3B	102	382	73	120	26	1	24	61	.314	46	72	17	53	193	21	.921
— Texas (A.L.)		3B	60	223	29	57	9	0	8	29	.256	14	42	3	45	90	7	.951

Year	Team (League)	Pos.	G	AB	R	H	2B	3B	HR	RBI	Avg.	BB	SO	SB	PO	A	E	Avg.
							BATTING									FIELDING		
1998— Texas (A.L.)................		3B	95	330	41	89	17	2	3	32	.270	12	66	6	74	184	15	.945
— St. Louis (N.L.)■		3B-SS	55	202	28	58	16	2	8	26	.287	24	57	7	36	123	12	.930
American League totals (2 years)			155	553	70	146	26	2	11	61	.264	26	108	9	119	274	22	.947
National League totals (1 year)			55	202	28	58	16	2	8	26	.287	24	57	7	36	123	12	.930
Major league totals (2 years)			210	755	98	204	42	4	19	87	.270	50	165	16	155	397	34	.942

TATIS, RAMON P DEVIL RAYS

PERSONAL: Born January 5, 1973, in Guayubin, Dominican Republic. ... 6-3/185. ... Throws left, bats left. ... Full name: Ramon Francisco Tatis.
HIGH SCHOOL: Los Limones (Guayabin).
TRANSACTIONS/CAREER NOTES: Signed as non-drafted free agent by New York Mets organization (September 6, 1990). ... Selected by Chicago Cubs from Mets organization in Rule 5 major league draft (December 9, 1996). ... Selected by Tampa Bay Devil Rays in second round (42nd pick overall) of expansion draft (November 18, 1997). ... On Durham disabled list (June 29-July 10, 1998). ... On Tampa Bay disabled list (August 26-September 8, 1998).

Year	Team (League)	W	L	Pct.	ERA	G	GS	CG	ShO	Sv.	IP	H	R	ER	BB	SO
1991— Dominican Mets (DSL)........		2	6	.250	4.26	12	12	0	0	0	57	59	41	27	34	43
1992— GC Mets (GCL)..................		1	3	.250	8.50	11	5	0	0	0	36	56	40	34	15	25
1993— Kingsport (Appalachian).....		0	2	.000	6.12	13	3	0	0	1	42 2/3	51	42	29	23	25
1994— Kingsport (Appalachian).....		1	3	.250	3.32	13	4	0	0	0	40 2/3	35	25	15	31	36
1995— Columbia (S. Atl.)............		2	3	.400	5.63	16	2	0	0	0	32	34	27	20	14	27
— Pittsfield (NYP)		4	5	.444	3.63	13	13	1	•1	0	79 1/3	88	40	32	27	69
1996— St. Lucie (Fla. St.)........		4	2	.667	3.39	46	1	0	0	6	74 1/3	71	35	28	38	46
1997— Chicago (N.L.)■................		1	1	.500	5.34	56	0	0	0	0	55 2/3	66	36	33	29	33
1998— Durham (International)■.....		1	3	.250	3.67	19	9	0	0	2	61 1/3	66	29	25	24	44
— Tampa Bay (A.L.)........		0	0	. . .	13.89	22	0	0	0	0	11 2/3	23	19	18	16	5
A.L. totals (1 year)		0	0	. . .	13.89	22	0	0	0	0	11 2/3	23	19	18	16	5
N.L. totals (1 year)		1	1	.500	5.34	56	0	0	0	0	55 2/3	66	36	33	29	33
Major league totals (2 years)		1	1	.500	6.82	78	0	0	0	0	67 1/3	89	55	51	45	38

TATUM, JIM IF/OF ROCKIES

T

PERSONAL: Born October 9, 1967, in San Diego. ... 6-2/200. ... Bats right, throws right. ... Full name: Jimmy Ray Tatum Jr.
HIGH SCHOOL: Santana (Santee, Calif.).
TRANSACTIONS/CAREER NOTES: Selected by San Diego Padres organization in third round of free-agent draft (June 3, 1985). ... Released by Padres organization (June 8, 1988). ... Signed by Cleveland Indians organization (September 14, 1989). ... Released by Indians organization (May 24, 1990). ... Signed by Milwaukee Brewers organization (June 21, 1990). ... Selected by Colorado Rockies in second round (44th pick overall) of expansion draft (November 17, 1992). ... Granted free agency (December 20, 1993). ... Re-signed by Rockies organization (December 23, 1993). ... Granted free agency (October 15, 1994). ... Re-signed by Rockies (November 2, 1994). ... Granted free agency (October 16, 1995). ... Signed by Boston Red Sox (November 1, 1995). ... Traded by Red Sox to San Diego Padres organization for cash (June 8, 1996). ... Granted free agency (October 15, 1996). ... Signed by New York Mets organization (December 26, 1997). ... On Norfolk disabled list (July 8, 1998-remainder of season). ... Granted free agency (October 15, 1998). ... Signed by Rockies organization (December 18, 1998).
HONORS: Named American Association Most Valuable Player (1992).
STATISTICAL NOTES: Led Northwest League third basemen with 149 assists, 27 errors, 214 total chances and 11 double plays in 1985. ... Led South Atlantic League third basemen with 35 errors and 29 double plays in 1986. ... Led South Atlantic League third basemen with 257 assists and tied for lead with 368 total chances in 1987. ... Led Texas League in sacrifice flies with 20, in being hit by pitch with 15 and in grounding into double plays with 21 in 1991. ... Led American Association with 261 total bases and 11 sacrifice flies in 1992. ... Led Pacific Coast League with 10 sacrifice flies in 1994. ... Career major league grand slams: 1.

Year	Team (League)	Pos.	G	AB	R	H	2B	3B	HR	RBI	Avg.	BB	SO	SB	PO	A	E	Avg.
							BATTING									FIELDING		
1985— Spokane (N'west).......		3B-SS	74	281	21	64	9	1	1	32	.228	20	60	0	51	†168	†30	.880
1986— Char., S.C. (S. Atl.).....		3B-2B-SS	120	431	55	112	19	2	10	62	.260	41	83	2	81	232	†41	.884
1987— Char., S.C. (S. Atl.).....		3B-SS-2B	128	468	52	131	22	2	9	72	.280	46	65	8	87	†259	24	.935
1988— Wichita (Texas)		3B	118	402	38	105	26	1	8	54	.261	30	73	2	*97	195	27	.915
1989—							Out of organized baseball.											
1990— Cant./Akr. (Eastern)■.		3B-1B	30	106	6	19	6	0	2	11	.179	6	19	1	57	51	12	.900
— Stockton (Calif.)■.......		3B-1B	70	260	41	68	16	0	12	59	.262	13	49	4	160	108	7	.975
1991— El Paso (Texas).......		S-3-C-1-P	130	493	99	158	27	8	18	128	.320	63	79	5	190	263	31	.936
1992— Denver (A.A.)..............		3B-OF	130	492	74	*162	*36	3	19	101	*.329	40	87	8	90	272	25	.935
— Milwaukee (A.L.)		3B	5	8	0	1	0	0	0	0	.125	1	2	0	6	2	0	1.000
1993— Colorado (N.L.)■		1B-3B-OF	92	98	7	20	5	0	1	12	.204	5	27	0	45	5	2	.962
— Colo. Springs (PCL) ...		3B-1B	13	45	5	10	2	0	2	7	.222	2	9	0	8	21	3	.906
1994— Colo. Springs (PCL) ...		C-3-0-1	121	439	76	154	43	1	21	97	.351	44	84	2	372	106	16	.968
1995— Colo. Springs (PCL) ...		3B-C	27	93	17	30	7	0	6	18	.323	6	21	0	15	39	4	.931
— Colorado (N.L.)..........		OF-C	34	34	4	8	1	1	0	4	.235	1	7	0	4	0	0	1.000
1996— Pawtucket (Int'l)■.......		3-2-0-1	19	66	11	18	2	0	5	16	.273	7	12	2	26	34	4	.938
— Boston (A.L.)............		3B	2	8	1	1	0	0	0	0	.125	0	2	0	3	2	0	1.000
— Las Vegas (PCL)■		OF-1B-3B	64	233	40	80	20	1	12	56	.343	23	53	4	185	27	3	.986
— San Diego (N.L.)		3B	5	3	0	0	0	0	0	0	.000	0	1	0	0	0	0	. . .
1997— Las Vegas (PCL)		OF-3B-1B	44	161	21	51	12	1	9	25	.317	8	39	1	56	13	1	.986
1998— New York (N.L.)■ 1-C-0-3-DH			35	50	4	9	1	2	2	13	.180	3	19	0	51	6	0	1.000
American League totals (2 years)			7	16	1	2	0	0	0	0	.125	1	4	0	9	4	0	1.000
National League totals (4 years)			166	185	15	37	7	3	3	29	.200	9	54	0	100	11	2	.982
Major league totals (5 years)			173	201	16	39	7	3	3	29	.194	10	58	0	109	15	2	.984

RECORD AS PITCHER

Year	Team (League)	W	L	Pct.	ERA	G	GS	CG	ShO	Sv.	IP	H	R	ER	BB	SO
1991— El Paso (Texas)..................		0	0	. . .	0.00	1	0	0	0	0	1	1	0	0	0	0

PERSONAL: Born October 31, 1968, in Beeville, Texas. ... 6-3/200. ... Bats left, throws right. ... Full name: Edward Kenneth Taubensee. ... Name pronounced TAW-ben-see.
HIGH SCHOOL: Lake Howell (Casselberry, Fla.).
TRANSACTIONS/CAREER NOTES: Selected by Cincinnati Reds organization in sixth round of free-agent draft (June 2, 1986). ... Selected by Oakland Athletics from Reds organization in Rule 5 major league draft (December 3, 1990). ... Claimed on waivers by Cleveland Indians (April 4, 1991). ... Traded by Indians with P Willie Blair to Houston Astros for OF Kenny Lofton and IF Dave Rohde (December 10, 1991). ... Traded by Astros to Reds for P Ross Powell and P Marty Lister (April 19, 1994).
STATISTICAL NOTES: Led Pioneer League with 19 passed balls in 1987. ... Tied for South Atlantic League lead in double plays by catcher with seven in 1988.

Year	Team (League)	Pos.	G	AB	R	H	2B	3B	HR	RBI	Avg.	BB	SO	SB	PO	A	E	Avg.
1986—	GC Reds (GCL)..........	C-1B	35	107	8	21	3	0	1	11	.196	11	33	0	208	27	8	.967
1987—	Billings (Pioneer).......	C	55	162	24	43	7	0	5	28	.265	25	47	2	344	29	6	.984
1988—	Greensboro (S. Atl.)....	C	103	330	36	85	16	1	10	41	.258	44	93	8	640	70	15	.979
	—Chattanooga (Sou.)....	C	5	12	2	2	0	0	1	1	.167	3	4	0	17	5	1	.957
1989—	Cedar Rap. (Midw.)....	C	59	196	25	39	5	0	8	22	.199	25	55	4	400	9	1	.998
	—Chattanooga (Sou.)....	C	45	127	11	24	2	0	3	13	.189	11	28	0	213	31	6	.976
1990—	Cedar Rap. (Midw.)....	C	122	417	57	108	21	1	16	62	.259	51	98	11	795	94	16	.982
1991—	Cleveland (A.L.).......	C	26	66	5	16	2	1	0	8	.242	5	16	0	89	6	2	.979
	—Colo. Springs (PCL)....	C	91	287	53	89	23	3	13	39	.310	31	61	0	412	47	12	.975
1992—	Houston (N.L.)■......	C	104	297	23	66	15	0	5	28	.222	31	78	2	557	66	5	.992
	—Tucson (PCL)...........	C	20	74	13	25	8	1	1	10	.338	8	17	0	127	10	4	.972
1993—	Houston (N.L.)..........	C	94	288	26	72	11	1	9	42	.250	21	44	1	551	41	5	.992
1994—	Houston (N.L.)........	C	5	10	0	1	0	0	0	0	.100	0	3	0	19	2	0	1.000
	—Cincinnati (N.L.)■.....	C	61	177	29	52	8	2	8	21	.294	15	28	2	362	17	4	.990
1995—	Cincinnati (N.L.)........	C-1B	80	218	32	62	14	2	9	44	.284	22	52	2	338	22	6	.984
1996—	Cincinnati (N.L.)........	C	108	327	46	95	20	0	12	48	.291	26	64	3	538	42	11	.981
1997—	Cincinnati (N.L.)......	C-O-1-DH	108	254	26	68	18	0	10	34	.268	22	66	0	408	26	5	.989
1998—	Cincinnati (N.L.)........	C	130	431	61	120	27	0	11	72	.278	52	93	1	776	44	10	.988
American League totals (1 year)			26	66	5	16	2	1	0	8	.242	5	16	0	89	6	2	.979
National League totals (7 years)			690	2002	243	536	113	5	64	289	.268	189	428	11	3549	260	46	.988
Major league totals (8 years)			716	2068	248	552	115	6	64	297	.267	194	444	11	3638	266	48	.988

CHAMPIONSHIP SERIES RECORD

Year	Team (League)	Pos.	G	AB	R	H	2B	3B	HR	RBI	Avg.	BB	SO	SB	PO	A	E	Avg.
1995—	Cincinnati (N.L.).........	PH-C	2	2	0	1	0	0	0	0	.500	0	0	0	0	0	0	...

TAVAREZ, JESUS   OF

PERSONAL: Born March 26, 1971, in Santo Domingo, Dominican Republic. ... 6-0/170. ... Bats both, throws right. ... Full name: Jesus Rafael Tavarez. ... Name pronounced tuh-VARE-ez.
TRANSACTIONS/CAREER NOTES: Signed as non-drafted free agent by Seattle Mariners organization (June 8, 1989). ... On disabled list (April 20-May 20, 1992). ... Selected by Florida Marlins in first round (26th pick overall) of expansion draft (November 17, 1992). ... On disabled list (May 18-June 4, 1993). ... On Florida disabled list (June 11-27, 1995). ... Traded by Marlins to Boston Red Sox for a player to be named later (November 25, 1996); Marlins acquired P Robert Rodgers to complete deal (December 10, 1996). ... Granted free agency (October 7, 1997). ... Signed by Baltimore Orioles organization (January 20, 1998). ... Granted free agency (September 29, 1998).
STATISTICAL NOTES: Tied for Carolina League lead in double plays by outfielder with four in 1990.
MISCELLANEOUS: Batted righthanded only (1990-92).

Year	Team (League)	Pos.	G	AB	R	H	2B	3B	HR	RBI	Avg.	BB	SO	SB	PO	A	E	Avg.
1989—						Dominican Summer League statistics unavailable.												
1990—	Peninsula (Caro.).......	OF	108	379	39	90	10	1	0	32	.237	20	79	40	228	•12	9	.964
1991—	San Bern. (Calif.).......	OF	124	466	80	132	11	3	5	41	.283	39	78	69	231	9	9	.964
1992—	Jacksonville (Sou.)......	OF	105	392	38	101	9	2	3	25	.258	23	54	29	208	7	5	.977
1993—	High Desert (Calif.)■.	OF	109	444	104	130	21	8	7	71	.293	57	66	47	194	10	9	.958
1994—	Portland (Eastern)......	OF	89	353	60	101	11	8	2	32	.286	35	63	20	171	3	6	.967
	—Florida (N.L.).............	OF	17	39	4	7	0	0	0	4	.179	1	5	1	28	1	0	1.000
1995—	Charlotte (Int'l)..........	OF	39	140	15	42	6	2	1	8	.300	9	19	7	92	2	2	.979
	—Florida (N.L.).............	OF	63	190	31	55	6	2	2	13	.289	16	27	7	118	1	0	1.000
1996—	Florida (N.L.).............	OF	98	114	14	25	3	0	0	6	.219	7	18	5	58	0	0	1.000
1997—	Pawtucket (Int'l)■......	OF	59	229	43	61	6	3	3	20	.266	27	31	22	127	7	3	.978
	—Boston (A.L.).............	OF-DH	42	69	12	12	3	1	0	9	.174	4	9	0	49	1	1	.980
1998—	Rochester (Int'l)■......	OF-2B	102	364	62	102	17	6	1	30	.280	27	59	22	183	4	5	.974
	—Baltimore (A.L.).........	OF	8	11	2	2	0	0	1	1	.182	2	3	0	7	0	0	1.000
American League totals (2 years)			50	80	14	14	3	1	1	10	.175	6	12	0	56	1	1	.983
National League totals (3 years)			178	343	49	87	9	2	2	23	.254	24	50	13	204	2	0	1.000
Major league totals (5 years)			228	423	63	101	12	3	3	33	.239	30	62	13	260	3	1	.996

TAVAREZ, JULIAN   P   GIANTS

PERSONAL: Born May 22, 1973, in Santiago, Dominican Republic. ... 6-2/190. ... Throws right, bats right.
HIGH SCHOOL: Santiago (Dominican Republic) Public School.
TRANSACTIONS/CAREER NOTES: Signed as non-drafted free agent by Cleveland Indians organization (March 16, 1990). ... On Cleveland suspended list (June 18-21, 1996). ... Traded by Indians with IF Jeff Kent, IF Jose Vizcaino and a player to be named later to San Francisco Giants for 3B Matt Williams and a player to be named later (November 13, 1996); Indians traded P Joe Roa to Giants for OF Trenidad Hubbard to

complete deal (December 16, 1996). ... On San Francisco disabled list (July 13-August 7, 1998); included rehabilitation assignment to Fresno (August 5-7). ... On suspended list (September 14-16, 1998).

HONORS: Named A.L. Rookie Pitcher of the Year by THE SPORTING NEWS (1995).

STATISTICAL NOTES: Led Appalachian League with 10 hit batsmen in 1993.

Year Team (League)	W	L	Pct.	ERA	G	GS	CG	ShO	Sv.	IP	H	R	ER	BB	SO
1990— DSL Indians (DSL)	5	5	.500	3.29	14	12	3	0	0	82	85	53	30	48	33
1991— DSL Indians (DSL)	8	2	.800	2.67	19	18	1	0	0	121 1/3	95	41	36	28	75
1992— Burlington (Appalachian)....	6	3	.667	2.68	14	•14	2	•2	0	87 1/3	86	41	26	12	69
1993— Kinston (Carolina)	11	5	.688	2.42	18	18	2	0	0	119	102	48	32	28	107
— Cant./Akr. (Eastern)	2	1	.667	0.95	3	2	1	1	0	19	14	2	2	1	11
— Cleveland (A.L.)................	2	2	.500	6.57	8	7	0	0	0	37	53	29	27	13	19
1994— Charlotte (Int'l)	•15	6	.714	3.48	26	26	2	2	0	176	167	79	68	43	102
— Cleveland (A.L.)................	0	1	.000	21.60	1	1	0	0	0	1 2/3	6	8	4	1	0
1995— Cleveland (A.L.)	10	2	.833	2.44	57	0	0	0	0	85	76	36	23	21	68
1996— Cleveland (A.L.)	4	7	.364	5.36	51	4	0	0	0	80 2/3	101	49	48	22	46
— Buffalo (A.A.)................	1	0	1.000	1.29	2	2	0	0	0	14	10	2	2	3	10
1997— San Francisco (N.L.)■	6	4	.600	3.87	•89	0	0	0	0	88 1/3	91	43	38	34	38
1998— San Francisco (N.L.)	5	3	.625	3.80	60	0	0	0	1	85 1/3	96	41	36	36	52
— Fresno (Pacific Coast)	0	0	. . .	19.29	1	0	0	0	0	2 1/3	6	5	5	0	1
A.L. totals (4 years)	16	12	.571	4.49	117	12	0	0	0	204 1/3	236	122	102	57	133
N.L. totals (2 years)	11	7	.611	3.83	149	0	0	0	1	173 2/3	187	84	74	70	90
Major league totals (6 years)......	27	19	.587	4.19	266	12	0	0	1	378	423	206	176	127	223

DIVISION SERIES RECORD

Year Team (League)	W	L	Pct.	ERA	G	GS	CG	ShO	Sv.	IP	H	R	ER	BB	SO
1995— Cleveland (A.L.)	0	0	. . .	6.75	3	0	0	0	0	2 2/3	5	2	2	0	3
1996— Cleveland (A.L.)	0	0	. . .	0.00	2	0	0	0	0	1 1/3	1	0	0	2	1
1997— San Francisco (N.L.)	0	1	.000	4.50	3	0	0	0	0	4	4	2	2	2	0
Div. series totals (3 years)	0	1	.000	4.50	8	0	0	0	0	8	10	4	4	4	4

CHAMPIONSHIP SERIES RECORD

Year Team (League)	W	L	Pct.	ERA	G	GS	CG	ShO	Sv.	IP	H	R	ER	BB	SO
1995— Cleveland (A.L.)..................	0	1	.000	2.70	4	0	0	0	0	3 1/3	3	1	1	1	2

WORLD SERIES RECORD

Year Team (League)	W	L	Pct.	ERA	G	GS	CG	ShO	Sv.	IP	H	R	ER	BB	SO
1995— Cleveland (A.L.)..................	0	0	. . .	0.00	5	0	0	0	0	4 1/3	3	0	0	2	1

TAYLOR, BILL   P   ATHLETICS

PERSONAL: Born October 16, 1961, in Monticello, Fla. ... 6-8/230. ... Throws right, bats right. ... Full name: William Howell Taylor.

HIGH SCHOOL: Central (Thomasville, Ga.).

COLLEGE: Abraham Baldwin Agricultural College (Ga.).

TRANSACTIONS/CAREER NOTES: Selected by Texas Rangers organization in second round of free-agent draft (January 8, 1980). ... Loaned by Rangers organization to Wausau, Seattle Mariners organization (April 5-June 23, 1982). ... Granted free agency (October 22, 1988). ... Signed by Las Vegas, San Diego Padres organization (March 30, 1989). ... Granted free agency (October 22, 1989). ... Signed by Atlanta Braves organization (August 16, 1990). ... Selected by Toronto Blue Jays from Braves organization in Rule 5 major league draft (December 7, 1992). ... Returned to Braves organization (April 3, 1993). ... Granted free agency (October 15, 1993). ... Signed by Oakland Athletics organization (December 13, 1993). ... On disabled list (July 27, 1994-remainder of season and April 12, 1995-entire season). ... On Oakland disabled list (August 15-September 13, 1996).

Year Team (League)	W	L	Pct.	ERA	G	GS	CG	ShO	Sv.	IP	H	R	ER	BB	SO
1980— Asheville (S. Atl.)................	0	2	.000	10.93	6	2	0	0	0	14	24	24	17	9	12
— GC Rangers (GCL).............	0	0	. . .	2.31	14	2	0	0	0	35	36	14	9	16	22
1981— Asheville (S. Atl.)..............	1	7	.125	4.64	14	12	1	0	0	64	76	43	33	35	44
— GC Rangers (GCL).............	4	2	.667	2.72	12	11	0	0	0	53	42	23	16	29	35
1982— Wausau (Midwest)■	2	5	.286	5.03	19	1	0	0	2	39 1/3	36	27	22	27	34
— Burlington (Midw.)■	5	4	.556	3.72	18	8	2	0	1	72 2/3	64	37	30	36	61
1983— Salem (Carolina)	1	1	.500	6.26	7	7	1	0	0	41 2/3	30	34	29	42	42
— Tulsa (Texas)	5	8	.385	6.87	21	12	0	0	0	76	86	65	58	51	75
1984— Tulsa (Texas)	5	3	.625	3.83	42	2	0	0	7	80	65	38	34	51	80
1985— Tulsa (Texas)	3	9	.250	3.47	20	17	2	0	0	103 2/3	84	55	40	48	87
1986— Tulsa (Texas)	3	7	.300	3.95	11	11	2	1	0	68 1/3	65	40	30	37	64
— Oklahoma City (A.A.)	5	5	.500	4.60	16	16	1	0	0	101 2/3	94	56	52	57	68
1987— Oklahoma City (A.A.)	•12	9	.571	5.61	28	•28	0	0	0	168 1/3	198	122	105	91	100
1988— Oklahoma City (A.A.)	4	8	.333	5.49	20	12	1	1	1	82	98	55	50	35	42
1989— Las Vegas (PCL)■	7	4	.636	5.13	47	0	0	0	1	79	93	48	45	27	71
1990— Durham (Carolina)■	0	0	. . .	3.24	5	0	0	0	0	8 1/3	8	3	3	1	10
— Richmond (Int'l)	0	0	. . .	0.00	2	0	0	0	0	2 1/3	4	0	0	0	0
1991— Greenville (Southern)	6	2	.750	1.51	•59	0	0	0	22	77 1/3	49	16	13	15	65
1992— Richmond (Int'l)	2	3	.400	2.28	47	0	0	0	12	79	72	27	20	27	82
1993— Richmond (Int'l)	2	4	.333	1.98	59	0	0	0	*26	68 1/3	56	19	15	26	81
1994— Oakland (A.L.)■	1	3	.250	3.50	41	0	0	0	1	46 1/3	38	24	18	18	48
1996— Edmonton (PCL)	0	0	. . .	0.79	7	0	0	0	4	11 1/3	10	1	1	3	13
— Oakland (A.L.)	6	3	.667	4.33	55	0	0	0	17	60 1/3	52	30	29	25	67
1997— Oakland (A.L.)	3	4	.429	3.82	72	0	0	0	23	73	70	32	31	36	66
1998— Oakland (A.L.)	4	9	.308	3.58	70	0	0	0	33	73	71	37	29	22	58
Major league totals (4 years)......	14	19	.424	3.81	238	0	0	0	74	252 2/3	231	123	107	101	239

TAYLOR, REGGIE — OF — PHILLIES

PERSONAL: Born January 12, 1977, in Newberry, S.C. ... 6-1/178. ... Bats left, throws right. ... Full name: Reginald Tremain Taylor.
HIGH SCHOOL: Newberry (S.C.).
TRANSACTIONS/CAREER NOTES: Selected by Philadelphia Phillies organization in first round (14th pick overall) of free-agent draft (June 1, 1995). ... On disabled list (July 23, 1998-remainder of season).
STATISTICAL NOTES: Led South Atlantic League outfielders with 308 total chances in 1996. ... Led Florida State League outfielders with 354 total chances in 1997.

															BATTING		FIELDING		
Year	Team (League)	Pos.	G	AB	R	H	2B	3B	HR	RBI	Avg.	BB	SO	SB	PO	A	E	Avg.
1995—	Martinsville (App.)	OF	64	239	36	53	4	6	2	32	.222	23	58	18	116	9	8	.940
1996—	Piedmont (S. Atl.)	OF	128	499	68	131	20	6	0	31	.263	29	136	36	287	9	*12	.961
1997—	Clearwater (FSL)	OF	134	545	73	133	18	6	12	47	.244	30	130	40	324	*19	11	.969
1998—	Reading (Eastern)	OF	79	337	49	92	14	6	5	22	.273	12	73	22	164	6	10	.944

TEJADA, MIGUEL — SS — ATHLETICS

PERSONAL: Born May 25, 1976, in Bani, Dominican Republic. ... 5-9/192. ... Bats right, throws right. ... Full name: Miguel Odalis Martinez Tejada.
TRANSACTIONS/CAREER NOTES: Signed as non-drafted free agent by Oakland Athletics organization (July 17, 1993). ... On suspended list (July 4-7, 1996). ... On disabled list (July 20-August 10, 1996). ... On Oakland disabled list (March 22-May 20, 1998); included rehabilitation assignments to Edmonton (May 11-12) and Huntsville (May 12-20).
STATISTICAL NOTES: Led California League shortstops with 44 errors in 1996. ... Led Southern League shortstops with 688 total chances and 97 double plays in 1997.

															BATTING		FIELDING		
Year	Team (League)	Pos.	G	AB	R	H	2B	3B	HR	RBI	Avg.	BB	SO	SB	PO	A	E	Avg.
1993—							Dominican League statistics unavailable.											
1994—	Dom. Athletics (DSL)	2B	74	218	51	64	9	1	18	62	.294	37	36	13	76	126	16	.927
1995—	S. Oregon (N'west)	SS	74	269	45	66	15	5	8	44	.245	41	54	19	*129	*214	26	.930
1996—	Modesto (California)	SS-3B	114	458	97	128	12	5	20	72	.279	51	93	27	194	358	†45	.925
1997—	Huntsville (Sou.)	SS	128	502	85	138	20	3	22	97	.275	50	99	15	*229	*423	*36	.948
	Oakland (A.L.)	SS	26	99	10	20	3	2	2	10	.202	2	22	2	54	69	4	.969
1998—	Edmonton (PCL)	SS	1	3	0	0	0	0	0	0	.000	1	1	0	0	5	0	1.000
	Huntsville (Sou.)	SS	15	52	9	17	6	0	2	7	.327	4	8	1	18	41	5	.922
	Oakland (A.L.)	SS	105	365	53	85	20	1	11	45	.233	28	86	5	173	327	26	.951
Major league totals (2 years)			131	464	63	105	23	3	13	55	.226	30	108	7	227	396	30	.954

TEJERA, MICHAEL — P — MARLINS

PERSONAL: Born October 18, 1976, in Havana, Cuba. ... 5-9/175. ... Throws left, bats left.
HIGH SCHOOL: Southwest (Miami).
TRANSACTIONS/CAREER NOTES: Selected by Florida Marlins organization in sixth round of free-agent draft (June 1, 1995).

Year	Team (League)	W	L	Pct.	ERA	G	GS	CG	ShO	Sv.	IP	H	R	ER	BB	SO
1995—	GC Marlins (GCL)	3	1	.750	2.65	11	3	0	0	2	34	28	13	10	16	28
1996—	GC Marlins (GCL)	1	0	1.000	3.60	2	0	0	0	0	5	6	2	2	0	2
1997—	Utica (N.Y.-Penn)	3	3	.500	3.76	12	12	0	0	0	69 1/3	65	36	29	11	67
1998—	Kane County (Midwest)	6	1	.857	2.77	10	10	0	0	0	55 1/3	44	20	17	13	47
	Portland (Eastern)	9	5	.643	4.11	18	18	2	2	0	107 1/3	113	55	49	36	97

TELEMACO, AMAURY — P — DIAMONDBACKS

PERSONAL: Born January 19, 1974, in Higuey, Dominican Republic. ... 6-3/214. ... Throws right, bats right. ... Full name: Amaury Regalado Telemaco. ... Name pronounced AH-mer-ee tel-ah-MAH-ko.
HIGH SCHOOL: Cristo Rey (La Romana, Dominican Republic).
TRANSACTIONS/CAREER NOTES: Signed as non-drafted free agent by Chicago Cubs organization (May 23, 1991). ... On temporarily inactive list (August 17, 1993-remainder of season). ... On Orlando disabled list (August 23-September 8, 1994). ... On Chicago disabled list (August 20-September 4, 1996); included rehabilitation assignment to Iowa (September 2-4). ... Claimed on waivers by Arizona Diamondbacks (May 15, 1998).

Year	Team (League)	W	L	Pct.	ERA	G	GS	CG	ShO	Sv.	IP	H	R	ER	BB	SO
1991—	Puerta Plata (DSL)	3	3	.500	3.55	15	13	0	0	0	66	81	43	26	32	43
1992—	Huntington (Appal.)	3	5	.375	4.01	12	12	2	0	0	76 1/3	71	45	34	17	*93
	Peoria (Midwest)	0	1	.000	7.94	2	1	0	0	0	5 2/3	9	5	5	5	5
1993—	Peoria (Midwest)	8	11	.421	3.45	23	23	3	0	0	143 2/3	129	69	55	54	133
1994—	Daytona (Fla. St.)	7	3	.700	3.40	11	11	2	0	0	76 2/3	62	35	29	23	59
	Orlando (South.)	3	5	.375	3.45	12	12	2	0	0	62 2/3	56	29	24	20	49
1995—	Orlando (South.)	8	8	.500	3.29	22	22	3	1	0	147 2/3	112	60	54	42	151
1996—	Iowa (Am. Assoc.)	3	1	.750	3.06	8	8	1	0	0	50	38	19	17	18	42
	Chicago (N.L.)	5	7	.417	5.46	25	17	0	0	0	97 1/3	108	67	59	31	64
1997—	Iowa (Am. Assoc.)	5	9	.357	4.51	18	18	3	•2	0	113 2/3	121	70	57	38	75
	Chicago (N.L.)	0	3	.000	6.16	10	5	0	0	0	38	47	26	26	11	29
	Orlando (South.)	1	0	1.000	2.25	1	1	0	0	0	8	9	2	2	2	6
1998—	Chicago (N.L.)	1	1	.500	3.90	14	0	0	0	0	27 2/3	23	12	12	13	18
	Arizona (N.L.)■	6	9	.400	3.94	27	18	0	0	0	121	127	63	53	33	60
Major league totals (3 years)		12	20	.375	4.75	76	40	0	0	0	284	305	168	150	88	171

TELFORD, ANTHONY   P   EXPOS

PERSONAL: Born March 6, 1966, in San Jose, Calif. ... 6-0/195. ... Throws right, bats right. ... Full name: Anthony Charles Telford.
HIGH SCHOOL: Silver Creek (Calif.).
COLLEGE: San Jose State.
TRANSACTIONS/CAREER NOTES: Selected by Baltimore Orioles organization in third round of free-agent draft (June 2, 1987). ... On disabled list (April 20, 1988-remainder of season). ... On Frederick disabled list (April 7-18, 1989). ... On Erie disabled list (June 16-30, 1989). ... Granted free agency (October 15, 1993). ... Signed by Atlanta Braves organization (November 23, 1993). ... Granted free agency (October 15, 1994). ... Signed by Edmonton, Oakland Athletics organization (January 20, 1995). ... Released by Edmonton (May 16, 1995). ... Signed by Cleveland Indians organization (June 15, 1995). ... Granted free agency (October 16, 1995). ... Signed by Montreal Expos organization (February 22, 1996). ... Granted free agency (October 15, 1996). ... Re-signed by Expos organization (December 18, 1996).

Year	Team (League)	W	L	Pct.	ERA	G	GS	CG	ShO	Sv.	IP	H	R	ER	BB	SO
1987—	Newark (N.Y.-Penn)	1	0	1.000	1.02	6	2	0	0	0	17 2/3	16	2	2	3	27
	—Hagerstown (Caro.)	1	0	1.000	1.59	2	2	0	0	0	11 1/3	9	2	2	5	10
	—Rochester (Int'l)	0	0	...	0.00	1	0	0	0	0	2	0	0	0	3	3
1988—	Hagerstown (Caro.)	1	0	1.000	0.00	1	1	0	0	0	7	3	0	0	0	10
1989—	Frederick (Carolina)	2	1	.667	4.21	9	5	0	0	1	25 2/3	25	15	12	12	19
1990—	Frederick (Carolina)	4	2	.667	1.68	8	8	1	0	0	53 2/3	35	15	10	11	49
	—Hagerstown (Eastern)	10	2	.833	1.97	14	13	3	1	0	96	80	26	21	25	73
	—Baltimore (A.L.)	3	3	.500	4.95	8	8	0	0	0	36 1/3	43	22	20	19	20
1991—	Rochester (Int'l)	•12	9	.571	3.95	27	25	3	0	0	157 1/3	166	82	69	48	115
	—Baltimore (A.L.)	0	0	...	4.05	9	1	0	0	0	26 2/3	27	12	12	6	24
1992—	Rochester (Int'l)	12	7	.632	4.18	27	26	3	0	0	*181	*183	89	84	64	129
1993—	Rochester (Int'l)	7	7	.500	4.27	38	6	0	0	2	90 2/3	98	51	43	33	66
	—Baltimore (A.L.)	0	0	...	9.82	3	0	0	0	0	7 1/3	11	8	8	1	6
1994—	Richmond (Int'l)■	10	6	.625	4.23	38	20	3	1	0	142 2/3	148	82	67	41	111
1995—	Edmonton (PCL)■	3	2	.600	7.18	8	6	0	0	0	36 1/3	47	32	29	16	17
	—Cant./Akr. (Eastern)■	2	0	1.000	0.82	2	2	0	0	0	11	6	2	1	4	4
	—Buffalo (A.A.)	4	1	.800	3.46	16	2	0	0	0	39	35	15	15	10	24
1996—	Ottawa (Int'l)■	7	2	.778	4.11	30	15	1	1	0	118 1/3	128	62	54	34	69
1997—	Montreal (N.L.)	4	6	.400	3.24	65	0	0	0	1	89	77	34	32	33	61
1998—	Montreal (N.L.)	3	6	.333	3.86	77	0	0	0	1	91	85	45	39	36	59
A.L. totals (3 years)		3	3	.500	5.12	20	9	0	0	0	70 1/3	81	42	40	26	50
N.L. totals (2 years)		7	12	.368	3.55	142	0	0	0	2	180	162	79	71	69	120
Major league totals (5 years)		10	15	.400	3.99	162	9	0	0	2	250 1/3	243	121	111	95	170

TELGHEDER, DAVID   P   INDIANS

PERSONAL: Born November 11, 1966, in Middletown, N.Y. ... 6-2/223. ... Throws right, bats right. ... Full name: David William Telgheder. ... Name pronounced tell-GATOR.
HIGH SCHOOL: Minisink Valley (Slate Hill, N.Y.).
COLLEGE: Massachusetts (received degree, 1989).
TRANSACTIONS/CAREER NOTES: Selected by New York Mets organization in 31st round of free-agent draft (June 5, 1989). ... On Norfolk disabled list (September 1-8, 1994). ... Granted free agency (October 16, 1995). ... Signed by Oakland Athletics organization (November 21, 1995). ... On Oakland disabled list (June 24-September 8, 1997); included rehabilitation assignment to Modesto (August 28-September 3). ... On Oakland disabled list (June 3, 1998-remainder of season). ... Granted free agency (October 15, 1998). ... Signed by Cleveland Indians organization (January 5, 1999).
RECORDS: Shares major league record for most home runs allowed in one inning—4 (September 21, 1996, third inning).
STATISTICAL NOTES: Pitched 1-0 no-hit victory against Pawtucket (May 15, 1992).

Year	Team (League)	W	L	Pct.	ERA	G	GS	CG	ShO	Sv.	IP	H	R	ER	BB	SO
1989—	Pittsfield (NYP)	5	3	.625	2.45	13	7	4	1	2	58 2/3	43	18	16	9	65
1990—	Columbia (S. Atl.)	9	3	.750	1.54	14	13	5	1	0	99 1/3	79	22	17	10	81
	—St. Lucie (Fla. St.)	9	4	.692	3.00	14	14	3	0	0	96	84	38	32	14	77
1991—	Williamsport (Eastern)	•13	11	.542	3.60	28	26	1	0	0	167 2/3	185	81	67	33	90
1992—	Tidewater (Int'l)	6	*14	.300	4.21	28	27	3	2	0	169	173	87	79	36	118
1993—	Norfolk (Int'l)	7	3	.700	2.95	13	12	0	0	1	76 1/3	81	29	25	19	52
	—New York (N.L.)	6	2	.750	4.76	24	7	0	0	0	75 2/3	82	40	40	21	35
1994—	New York (N.L.)	0	1	.000	7.20	6	0	0	0	0	10	11	8	8	8	4
	—Norfolk (Int'l)	8	10	.444	3.40	23	23	3	2	0	158 2/3	156	65	60	26	83
1995—	Norfolk (Int'l)	5	4	.556	2.24	29	11	0	0	3	92 1/3	77	34	23	8	75
	—New York (N.L.)	1	2	.333	5.61	7	4	0	0	0	25 2/3	34	18	16	7	16
1996—	Edmonton (PCL)■	8	6	.571	4.17	17	17	1	0	0	101 1/3	102	53	47	23	59
	—Modesto (California)	1	0	1.000	1.50	1	1	0	0	0	6	4	3	1	1	3
	—Oakland (A.L.)	4	7	.364	4.65	16	14	1	1	0	79 1/3	92	42	41	26	43
1997—	Modesto (California)	0	0	...	3.38	2	2	0	0	0	5 1/3	3	2	2	2	4
	—Oakland (A.L.)	4	6	.400	6.06	20	19	0	0	0	101	134	71	68	35	55
1998—	Edmonton (PCL)	1	2	.333	7.31	3	3	0	0	0	16	26	14	13	3	9
	—Oakland (A.L.)	0	1	.000	3.60	8	2	0	0	0	20	19	12	8	6	5
A.L. totals (3 years)		8	14	.364	5.26	44	35	1	1	0	200 1/3	245	125	117	67	103
N.L. totals (3 years)		7	5	.583	5.17	37	11	0	0	0	111 1/3	127	66	64	36	55
Major league totals (6 years)		15	19	.441	5.23	81	46	1	1	0	311 2/3	372	191	181	103	158

TESSMER, JAY   P   YANKEES

PERSONAL: Born December 26, 1971, in Meadville, Pa. ... 6-3/190. ... Throws right, bats right. ... Full name: Jay Weldon Tessmer.
HIGH SCHOOL: Cochranton (Pa.).
COLLEGE: Miami (Fla.).
TRANSACTIONS/CAREER NOTES: Selected by New York Yankees organization in 19th round of free-agent draft (June 1, 1995).
HONORS: Name Florida State League Most Valuable Player (1996).

Year	Team (League)	W	L	Pct.	ERA	G	GS	CG	ShO	Sv.	IP	H	R	ER	BB	SO
1995—Oneonta (N.Y.-Penn)		2	0	1.000	0.95	34	0	0	0	20	38	27	8	4	12	52
1996—Tampa (Fla. St.)		12	4	.750	1.48	*68	0	0	0	*35	97 1/3	68	18	16	19	104
1997—Norwich (Eastern)		3	6	.333	5.31	55	0	0	0	17	62 2/3	78	41	37	24	51
1998—Norwich (Eastern)		3	4	.429	1.09	45	0	0	0	29	49 2/3	50	8	6	13	57
—Columbus (Int'l)		1	1	.500	0.49	12	0	0	0	5	18 1/3	8	2	1	1	14
—New York (A.L.)		1	0	1.000	3.12	7	0	0	0	0	8 2/3	4	3	3	4	6
Major league totals (1 year)		1	0	1.000	3.12	7	0	0	0	0	8 2/3	4	3	3	4	6

TEWKSBURY, BOB — P

PERSONAL: Born November 30, 1960, in Concord, N.H. ... 6-4/206. ... Throws right, bats right. ... Full name: Robert Alan Tewksbury.
HIGH SCHOOL: Merrimack (Penacook, N.H.).
COLLEGE: Rutgers, then St. Leo College (Fla.).
TRANSACTIONS/CAREER NOTES: Selected by New York Yankees organization in 19th round of free-agent draft (June 8, 1981). ... On Fort Lauderdale disabled list (April 8-June 7, 1983). ... On disabled list (April 9-27, 1984). ... On Albany/Colonie disabled list (June 10-25, 1985). ... Traded by Yankees with P Rich Scheid and P Dean Wilkins to Chicago Cubs for P Steve Trout (July 13, 1987). ... On Chicago disabled list (August 13, 1987-remainder of season and May 22-June 12, 1988). ... Granted free agency (October 15, 1988). ... Signed by St. Louis Cardinals (December 16, 1988). ... Granted free agency (October 17, 1994). ... Signed by Texas Rangers (April 10, 1995). ... On Texas disabled list (July 23-August 26, 1995); included rehabilitation assignment to Charlotte (August 22-26). ... Granted free agency (November 3, 1995). ... Signed by San Diego Padres (December 18, 1995). ... Granted free agency (October 31, 1996). ... Signed by Minnesota Twins (December 12, 1996). ... On disabled list (May 5-25 and July 18-August 18, 1997; and May 23-June 7 and July 15-August 22, 1998). ... Granted free agency (October 22, 1998). ... Announced retirement (January 20, 1999).
STATISTICAL NOTES: Pitched 5-0 one-hit, complete-game victory for St. Louis against Houston (August 17, 1990).
MISCELLANEOUS: Struck out in only appearance as pinch hitter with Texas (1995).

Year	Team (League)	W	L	Pct.	ERA	G	GS	CG	ShO	Sv.	IP	H	R	ER	BB	SO
1981—Oneonta (N.Y.-Penn)		7	3	.700	3.60	14	14	6	1	0	85	85	43	34	37	62
1982—Fort Lauderdale (FSL)		*15	4	.789	*1.88	24	23	•13	*5	1	182 1/3	146	46	38	47	92
1983—Fort Lauderdale (FSL)		2	0	1.000	0.00	2	2	1	0	0	16	6	1	0	1	5
—Nashville (Southern)		5	1	.833	2.82	7	7	3	0	0	51	49	20	16	10	15
1984—Nashville (Southern)		11	9	.550	2.83	26	26	6	0	0	172	185	69	54	42	78
1985—Alb./Colon. (East.)		6	5	.545	3.54	17	17	4	2	0	106 2/3	101	48	42	19	63
—Columbus (Int'l)		3	0	1.000	1.02	6	6	1	1	0	44	27	5	5	5	21
1986—New York (A.L.)		9	5	.643	3.31	23	20	2	0	0	130 1/3	144	58	48	31	49
—Columbus (Int'l)		1	0	1.000	2.70	2	2	0	0	0	10	6	3	3	2	4
1987—New York (A.L.)		1	4	.200	6.75	8	6	0	0	0	33 1/3	47	26	25	7	12
—Columbus (Int'l)		6	1	.857	2.53	11	11	3	0	0	74 2/3	68	23	21	11	32
—Chicago (N.L.)■		0	4	.000	6.50	7	3	0	0	0	18	32	15	13	13	10
1988—Iowa (Am. Assoc.)		4	2	.667	3.76	10	10	2	0	0	67	73	28	28	10	43
—Chicago (N.L.)		0	0	. . .	8.10	1	1	0	0	0	3 1/3	6	5	3	2	1
1989—Louisville (A.A.)■		•13	5	.722	2.43	28	28	2	1	0	*189	170	63	51	34	72
—St. Louis (N.L.)		1	0	1.000	3.30	7	4	1	1	0	30	25	12	11	10	17
1990—St. Louis (N.L.)		10	9	.526	3.47	28	20	3	2	1	145 1/3	151	67	56	15	50
—Louisville (A.A.)		3	2	.600	2.43	6	6	0	0	0	40 2/3	41	15	11	3	22
1991—St. Louis (N.L.)		11	12	.478	3.25	30	30	3	0	0	191	206	86	69	38	75
1992—St. Louis (N.L.)		16	5	*.762	2.16	33	32	5	0	0	233	217	63	56	20	91
1993—St. Louis (N.L.)		17	10	.630	3.83	32	32	2	0	0	213 2/3	*258	99	91	20	97
1994—St. Louis (N.L.)		12	10	.545	5.32	24	24	4	1	0	155 2/3	*190	97	92	22	79
1995—Texas (A.L.)■		8	7	.533	4.58	21	21	4	1	0	129 2/3	169	75	66	20	53
—Charlotte (Fla. St.)		1	0	1.000	0.00	1	1	0	0	0	6	3	0	0	0	4
1996—San Diego (N.L.)■		10	10	.500	4.32	36	33	1	0	0	206 1/3	224	116	99	43	126
1997—Minnesota (A.L.)■		8	13	.381	4.22	26	26	5	2	0	168 2/3	200	83	79	31	92
1998—Minnesota (A.L.)		7	13	.350	4.79	26	25	1	0	0	148 1/3	174	82	79	20	60
A.L. totals (5 years)		33	42	.440	4.38	104	98	12	3	0	610 1/3	734	324	297	109	266
N.L. totals (9 years)		77	60	.562	3.69	198	179	19	4	1	1196 1/3	1309	560	490	183	546
Major league totals (13 years)		110	102	.519	3.92	302	277	31	7	1	1806 2/3	2043	884	787	292	812

DIVISION SERIES RECORD

Year	Team (League)	W	L	Pct.	ERA	G	GS	CG	ShO	Sv.	IP	H	R	ER	BB	SO
1996—San Diego (N.L.)							Did not play.									

ALL-STAR GAME RECORD

Year	League	W	L	Pct.	ERA	GS	CG	ShO	Sv.	IP	H	R	ER	BB	SO
1992—National		0	0	. . .	21.60	0	0	0	0	1 2/3	4	4	4	1	0

THOMAS, FRANK — DH/1B — WHITE SOX

PERSONAL: Born May 27, 1968, in Columbus, Ga. ... 6-5/257. ... Bats right, throws right. ... Full name: Frank Edward Thomas.
HIGH SCHOOL: Columbus (Ga.).
COLLEGE: Auburn.
TRANSACTIONS/CAREER NOTES: Selected by Chicago White Sox organization in first round (seventh pick overall) of free-agent draft (June 5, 1989). ... On disabled list (July 11-30, 1996; and June 7-22, 1997).
RECORDS: Shares A.L. single-season record for most intentional bases on balls received by righthanded batter—29 (1995).
HONORS: Named first baseman on THE SPORTING NEWS college All-America team (1989). ... Named designated hitter on THE SPORTING NEWS A.L. All-Star team (1991). ... Named designated hitter on THE SPORTING NEWS A.L. Silver Slugger team (1991). ... Named Major League Player of the Year by THE SPORTING NEWS (1993). ... Named first baseman on THE SPORTING NEWS A.L. All-Star team (1993-94). ... Named first baseman on THE SPORTING NEWS A.L. Silver Slugger team (1993-94). ... Named A.L. Most Valuable Player by Baseball Writers' Association of America (1993-94).
STATISTICAL NOTES: Led Southern League with .581 slugging percentage and .487 on-base percentage in 1990. ... Led A.L. with .453 on-base percentage in 1991, .439 in 1992, .487 in 1994 and .456 in 1997. ... Led A.L. first basemen with 1,533 total chances in 1992. ... Led A.L.

with .729 slugging percentage in 1994. ... Led A.L. with 12 sacrifice flies in 1995. ... Led A.L. with 29 intentional bases on balls received in 1995 and 26 in 1996. ... Hit three home runs in one game (September 15, 1996) ... Career major league grand slams: 5.

MISCELLANEOUS: Holds Chicago White Sox all-time record for most home runs (286).

Year	Team (League)	Pos.	G	AB	R	H	2B	3B	HR	RBI	Avg.	BB	SO	SB	PO	A	E	Avg.
1989—	GC Whi. Sox (GCL)	1B	17	52	8	19	5	0	1	11	.365	10	24	4	130	8	2	.986
—	Sarasota (Fla. St.)	1B	55	188	27	52	9	1	4	30	.277	31	33	0	420	31	7	.985
1990—	Birmingham (Sou.).....	1B	109	353	85	114	27	5	18	71	.323	*112	74	7	954	77	14	.987
—	Chicago (A.L.)	1B-DH	60	191	39	63	11	3	7	31	.330	44	54	0	428	26	5	.989
1991—	Chicago (A.L.)	DH-1B	158	559	104	178	31	2	32	109	.318	*138	112	1	459	27	2	.996
1992—	Chicago (A.L.)	1B-DH	160	573	108	185	•46	2	24	115	.323	•122	88	6	*1428	92	13	.992
1993—	Chicago (A.L.)	1B-DH	153	549	106	174	36	0	41	128	.317	112	54	4	1222	83	15	.989
1994—	Chicago (A.L.)	1B-DH	113	399	*106	141	34	1	38	101	.353	*109	61	2	735	45	7	.991
1995—	Chicago (A.L.)	1B-DH	•145	493	102	152	27	0	40	111	.308	*136	74	3	738	34	7	.991
1996—	Chicago (A.L.)	1B	141	527	110	184	26	0	40	134	.349	109	70	1	1098	85	9	.992
1997—	Chicago (A.L.)	1B-DH	146	530	110	184	35	0	35	125	*.347	109	69	1	739	49	11	.986
1998—	Chicago (A.L.)	DH-1B	160	585	109	155	35	2	29	109	.265	110	93	7	116	6	2	.984
Major league totals (9 years)			1236	4406	894	1416	281	10	286	963	.321	989	675	25	6963	447	71	.991

CHAMPIONSHIP SERIES RECORD

RECORDS: Holds single-series record for most bases on balls received—10 (1993). ... Shares single-game record for most bases on balls received—4 (October 5, 1993).

Year	Team (League)	Pos.	G	AB	R	H	2B	3B	HR	RBI	Avg.	BB	SO	SB	PO	A	E	Avg.
1993—	Chicago (A.L.)	1B-DH	6	17	2	6	0	0	1	3	.353	10	5	0	24	3	0	1.000

ALL-STAR GAME RECORD

Year	League	Pos.	AB	R	H	2B	3B	HR	RBI	Avg.	BB	SO	SB	PO	A	E	Avg.
1993—	American	PH-DH	1	0	1	0	0	0	0	1.000	0	0	0	...	...	...	...
1994—	American	1B	2	1	2	0	0	0	0	1.000	1	0	0	6	0	0	1.000
1995—	American	1B	2	1	1	0	0	1	2	.500	0	0	0	5	1	0	1.000
1996—	American..................					Selected, did not play—injured.											
1997—	American..................					Selected, did not play—injured.											
All-Star Game totals (3 years)			5	2	4	0	0	1	3	.800	1	0	0	11	1	0	1.000

THOME, JIM   1B   INDIANS

PERSONAL: Born August 27, 1970, in Peoria, Ill. ... 6-4/230. ... Bats left, throws right. ... Full name: James Howard Thome. ... Name pronounced TOE-me.

HIGH SCHOOL: Limestone (Bartonville, Ill.).

JUNIOR COLLEGE: Illinois Central College.

TRANSACTIONS/CAREER NOTES: Selected by Cleveland Indians organization in 13th round of free-agent draft (June 5, 1989). ... On Cleveland disabled list (March 28-May 18, 1992); included rehabilitation assignment to Canton/Akron (May 9-18). ... On Cleveland disabled list (May 20-June 15, 1992); included rehabilitation assignment to Canton/Akron (June 1-15). ... On disabled list (August 8-September 16, 1998).

HONORS: Named International League Most Valuable Player (1993). ... Named third baseman on THE SPORTING NEWS A.L. All-Star team (1995 and 1996). ... Named third baseman on THE SPORTING NEWS A.L. Silver Slugger team (1996).

STATISTICAL NOTES: Led International League with .441 on-base percentage in 1993. ... Hit three home runs in one game (July 22, 1994). ... Had 16-game hitting streak (May 25-June 10, 1998). ... Career major league grand slams: 2.

Year	Team (League)	Pos.	G	AB	R	H	2B	3B	HR	RBI	Avg.	BB	SO	SB	PO	A	E	Avg.
1989—	GC Indians (GCL)	SS-3B	55	186	22	44	5	3	0	22	.237	21	33	6	65	144	21	.909
1990—	Burlington (Appal.).......	3B	34	118	31	44	7	1	12	34	.373	27	18	6	28	79	11	.907
—	Kinston (Carolina)	3B	33	117	19	36	4	1	4	16	.308	24	26	4	10	66	8	.905
1991—	Cant./Akr. (Eastern)	3B	84	294	47	99	20	2	5	45	.337	44	58	8	41	167	17	.924
—	Colo. Springs (PCL) ...	3B	41	151	20	43	7	3	2	28	.285	12	29	0	28	84	6	.949
—	Cleveland (A.L.)..........	3B	27	98	7	25	4	2	1	9	.255	5	16	1	12	60	8	.900
1992—	Colo. Springs (PCL) ...	3B	12	48	11	15	4	1	2	14	.313	6	16	0	9	20	8	.784
—	Cleveland (A.L.)..........	3B	40	117	8	24	3	1	2	12	.205	10	34	2	21	61	11	.882
—	Cant./Akr. (Eastern)	3B	30	107	16	36	9	2	1	14	.336	24	30	0	11	35	4	.920
1993—	Charlotte (Int'l)..........	3B	115	410	85	136	21	4	25	*102	*.332	76	94	1	67	226	15	.951
—	Cleveland (A.L.)..........	3B	47	154	28	41	11	0	7	22	.266	29	36	2	29	86	6	.950
1994—	Cleveland (A.L.)..........	3B	98	321	58	86	20	1	20	52	.268	46	84	3	62	173	15	.940
1995—	Cleveland (A.L.)..........	3B-DH	137	452	92	142	29	3	25	73	.314	97	113	4	75	214	16	.948
1996—	Cleveland (A.L.)..........	3B-DH	151	505	122	157	28	5	38	116	.311	123	141	2	86	262	17	.953
1997—	Cleveland (A.L.)..........	1B	147	496	104	142	25	0	40	102	.286	*120	146	1	1233	95	10	.993
1998—	Cleveland (A.L.)..........	1B-DH	123	440	89	129	34	2	30	85	.293	89	141	1	998	85	10	.991
Major league totals (8 years)			770	2583	508	746	154	14	163	471	.289	519	711	16	2516	1036	93	.974

DIVISION SERIES RECORD

RECORDS: Holds career record for most strikeouts—21.

Year	Team (League)	Pos.	G	AB	R	H	2B	3B	HR	RBI	Avg.	BB	SO	SB	PO	A	E	Avg.
1995—	Cleveland (A.L.)..........	3B	3	13	1	2	0	0	1	3	.154	1	6	0	6	6	0	1.000
1996—	Cleveland (A.L.)..........	3B	4	10	1	3	0	0	0	0	.300	1	5	0	1	1	0	1.000
1997—	Cleveland (A.L.)..........	1B	4	15	1	3	0	0	0	1	.200	0	5	0	44	3	0	1.000
1998—	Cleveland (A.L.)..........	1B-DH	4	15	2	2	0	0	2	2	.133	3	5	0	26	1	0	1.000
Division series totals (4 years)			15	53	5	10	0	0	3	6	.189	5	21	0	77	11	0	1.000

CHAMPIONSHIP SERIES RECORD

RECORDS: Shares single-game record for most grand slams—1 (October 13, 1998). ... Shares single-inning record for most runs batted in—4 (October 13, 1998, fifth inning).

Year Team (League)	Pos.	G	AB	R	H	2B	3B	HR	RBI	Avg.	BB	SO	SB	PO	A	E	Avg.
1995— Cleveland (A.L.)	3B	5	15	2	4	0	0	2	5	.267	2	3	0	1	5	1	.857
1997— Cleveland (A.L.)	1B-PH	6	14	3	1	0	0	0	0	.071	5	4	0	35	2	0	1.000
1998— Cleveland (A.L.)	DH-1B	6	23	4	7	0	0	4	8	.304	1	8	0	45	4	0	1.000
Championship series totals (3 years)		17	52	9	12	0	0	6	13	.231	8	15	0	81	11	1	.989

WORLD SERIES RECORD

Year Team (League)	Pos.	G	AB	R	H	2B	3B	HR	RBI	Avg.	BB	SO	SB	PO	A	E	Avg.
1995— Cleveland (A.L.)	3B-PH	6	19	1	4	1	0	1	2	.211	2	5	0	3	5	1	.889
1997— Cleveland (A.L.)	1B	7	28	8	8	0	1	2	4	.286	5	7	0	57	5	1	.984
World Series totals (2 years)		13	47	9	12	1	1	3	6	.255	7	12	0	60	10	2	.972

ALL-STAR GAME RECORD

Year League	Pos.	AB	R	H	2B	3B	HR	RBI	Avg.	BB	SO	SB	PO	A	E	Avg.
1997— American	PH-DH	1	0	0	0	0	0	0	.000	0	0	0	...	...	...	...
1998— American	1B	2	1	0	0	0	0	0	.000	2	1	0	4	0	0	1.000
All-Star Game totals (2 years)		3	1	0	0	0	0	0	.000	2	1	0	4	0	0	1.000

THOMPSON, JUSTIN   P   TIGERS

PERSONAL: Born March 8, 1973, in San Antonio. ... 6-4/215. ... Throws left, bats left. ... Full name: Justin Willard Thompson.
HIGH SCHOOL: Klein Oak (Spring, Texas).
TRANSACTIONS/CAREER NOTES: Selected by Detroit Tigers organization in supplemental round ("sandwich pick" between first and second round, 32nd pick overall) of free-agent draft (June 3, 1991); pick received as part of compensation for Minnesota Twins signing Type A free-agent P Jack Morris. ... On Trenton disabled list (April 8, 1994-entire season). ... On Detroit disabled list (June 3-August 17, 1996); included rehabilitation assignments to Fayetteville (July 19-23), Visalia (July 23-26) and Toledo (July 26-August 11). ... On disabled list (July 6-21, 1997).

Year Team (League)	W	L	Pct.	ERA	G	GS	CG	ShO	Sv.	IP	H	R	ER	BB	SO
1991— Bristol (Appalachian)	2	5	.286	3.60	10	10	0	0	0	50	45	29	20	24	60
1992— Fayetteville (S. Atl.)	4	4	.500	2.18	20	19	0	0	0	95	79	32	23	40	88
1993— Lakeland (Fla. St.)	4	4	.500	3.56	11	11	0	0	0	$55^2/_3$	65	25	22	16	46
— London (Eastern)	3	6	.333	4.09	14	14	1	0	0	$83^2/_3$	96	51	38	37	72
1994—							Did not play.								
1995— Lakeland (Fla. St.)	2	1	.667	4.88	6	6	0	0	0	24	30	13	13	8	20
— Jacksonville (Southern)	6	7	.462	3.73	18	18	3	0	0	123	110	55	51	38	98
1996— Toledo (International)	6	3	.667	3.42	13	13	3	1	0	$84^1/_3$	74	36	32	26	69
— Detroit (A.L.)	1	6	.143	4.58	11	11	0	0	0	59	62	35	30	31	44
— Fayetteville (S. Atl.)	0	0	...	3.00	1	1	0	0	0	3	1	1	1	0	5
— Visalia (California)	0	0	...	0.00	1	1	0	0	0	3	2	0	0	2	7
1997— Detroit (A.L.)	15	11	.577	3.02	32	32	4	0	0	$223^1/_3$	188	82	75	66	151
1998— Detroit (A.L.)	11	15	.423	4.05	34	34	5	0	0	222	227	114	100	79	149
Major league totals (3 years)	27	32	.458	3.66	77	77	9	0	0	$504^1/_3$	477	231	205	176	344

ALL-STAR GAME RECORD

Year League	W	L	Pct.	ERA	GS	CG	ShO	Sv.	IP	H	R	ER	BB	SO
1997— American	0	0	...	0.00	0	0	0	0	1	0	0	0	0	1

THOMPSON, MARK   P   REDS

PERSONAL: Born April 7, 1971, in Russellville, Ky. ... 6-2/213. ... Throws right, bats right. ... Full name: Mark Radford Thompson.
HIGH SCHOOL: Logan County (Russellville, Ky.).
COLLEGE: Kentucky.
TRANSACTIONS/CAREER NOTES: Selected by Colorado Rockies organization in second round of free-agent draft (June 1, 1992). ... On Colorado Springs disabled list (June 30-September 7, 1993; August 9-18 and August 27-September 5, 1994). ... On Colorado disabled list (May 8, 1997-remainder of season); included rehabilitation assignments to Asheville (June 29-July 15) and Colorado Springs (July 15-July 20). ... On Colorado disabled list (May 7, 1998-remainder of season); included rehabilitation assignments to Arizona League Rockies (August 14), Salem (August 19-29) and Colorado Springs (September 3). ... Granted free agency (October 20, 1998). ... Signed by Cincinnati Reds organization (December 15, 1998).
RECORDS: Shares N.L. single-inning record for most consecutive home runs allowed—3 (June 30, 1996, third inning).

Year Team (League)	W	L	Pct.	ERA	G	GS	CG	ShO	Sv.	IP	H	R	ER	BB	SO
1992— Bend (Northwest)	8	4	.667	1.95	16	•16	*4	0	0	*$106^1/_3$	81	32	23	31	*102
1993— Central Valley (Cal.)	3	2	.600	2.20	11	11	0	0	0	$69^2/_3$	46	19	17	18	72
— Colo. Springs (PCL)	3	0	1.000	2.70	4	4	2	0	0	$33^1/_3$	31	13	10	11	22
1994— Colo. Springs (PCL)	8	9	.471	4.49	23	23	•4	1	0	$140^1/_3$	169	83	70	57	82
— Colorado (N.L.)	1	1	.500	9.00	2	2	0	0	0	9	16	9	9	8	5
1995— Colorado (N.L.)	2	3	.400	6.53	21	5	0	0	0	51	73	42	37	22	30
— Colo. Springs (PCL)	5	3	.625	6.10	11	10	0	0	0	62	73	43	42	25	38
1996— Colorado (N.L.)	9	11	.450	5.30	34	28	3	1	0	$169^2/_3$	189	109	100	74	99
1997— Colorado (N.L.)	3	3	.500	7.89	6	6	0	0	0	$29^1/_3$	40	27	26	13	9
— Asheville (S. Atl.)	0	2	.000	2.70	4	4	0	0	0	$13^1/_3$	11	5	4	5	9
— Colo. Springs (PCL)	0	0	...	12.00	1	1	0	0	0	3	6	4	4	1	1
1998— Colorado (N.L.)	1	2	.333	7.71	6	6	0	0	0	$23^1/_3$	36	22	20	12	14
— Ariz. Rockies (Ariz.)	0	0	...	0.00	1	1	0	0	0	3	1	0	0	0	2
— Salem (Carolina)	0	0	...	3.95	3	3	0	0	0	$13^2/_3$	17	7	6	3	10
— Colo. Springs (PCL)	0	1	.000	18.90	1	1	0	0	0	$3^1/_3$	10	7	7	1	1
Major league totals (5 years)	16	20	.444	6.11	69	47	3	1	0	$282^2/_3$	354	209	192	129	157

DIVISION SERIES RECORD

Year Team (League)	W	L	Pct.	ERA	G	GS	CG	ShO	Sv.	IP	H	R	ER	BB	SO
1995— Colorado (N.L.)	0	0	...	0.00	1	0	0	0	1	1	0	0	0	0	0

THOMSON, JOHN　　　　　　　　P　　　　　　　　ROCKIES

PERSONAL: Born October 1, 1973, in Vicksburg, Miss. ... 6-3/187. ... Throws right, bats right. ... Full name: John Carl Thomson.
HIGH SCHOOL: Sulphur (La.).
JUNIOR COLLEGE: Blinn College (Texas).
COLLEGE: McNeese State.
TRANSACTIONS/CAREER NOTES: Selected by Colorado Rockies organization in seventh round of free-agent draft (June 3, 1993). ... On Colorado disabled list (June 16-July 26, 1998); included rehabilitation assignment to Asheville (July 16-22).
STATISTICAL NOTES: Tied for Arizona League lead with 14 wild pitches in 1993.

Year	Team (League)	W	L	Pct.	ERA	G	GS	CG	ShO	Sv.	IP	H	R	ER	BB	SO
1993—	Ariz. Rockies (Ariz.)	3	5	.375	4.62	11	11	0	0	0	$50^{2}/_{3}$	43	40	26	31	36
1994—	Asheville (S. Atl.)	6	6	.500	2.85	19	15	1	1	0	$88^{1}/_{3}$	70	34	28	33	79
—	Central Valley (Cal.)	3	1	.750	3.28	9	8	0	0	0	$49^{1}/_{3}$	43	20	18	18	41
1995—	New Haven (East.)	7	8	.467	4.18	26	24	0	0	0	$131^{1}/_{3}$	132	69	61	56	82
1996—	New Haven (East.)	9	4	.692	2.86	16	16	1	0	0	$97^{2}/_{3}$	82	35	31	27	86
—	Colo. Springs (PCL)	4	7	.364	5.04	11	11	0	0	0	$69^{2}/_{3}$	76	45	39	26	62
1997—	Colo. Springs (PCL)	4	2	.667	3.43	7	7	0	0	0	42	36	18	16	14	49
—	Colorado (N.L.)	7	9	.438	4.71	27	27	2	1	0	$166^{1}/_{3}$	193	94	87	51	106
1998—	Colorado (N.L.)	8	11	.421	4.81	26	26	2	0	0	161	174	86	86	49	106
—	Asheville (S. Atl.)	1	0	1.000	0.00	2	2	0	0	0	9	5	1	0	1	12
Major league totals (2 years)		**15**	**20**	**.429**	**4.76**	**53**	**53**	**4**	**1**	**0**	**$327^{1}/_{3}$**	**367**	**180**	**173**	**100**	**212**

THURMAN, MIKE　　　　　　　　P　　　　　　　　EXPOS

PERSONAL: Born July 22, 1973, in Corvallis, Ore. ... 6-0/210. ... Throws right, bats right. ... Full name: Michael Richard Thurman.
HIGH SCHOOL: Philomath (Ore.).
COLLEGE: Oregon State.
TRANSACTIONS/CAREER NOTES: Selected by Montreal Expos organization in supplemental round ("sandwich pick" between first and second round, 31st pick overall) of free-agent draft (June 2, 1994); pick received as compensation for Cleveland Indians signing Type A free-agent P Dennis Martinez. ... On Harrisburg disabled list (June 17-July 5, 1997).

Year	Team (League)	W	L	Pct.	ERA	G	GS	CG	ShO	Sv.	IP	H	R	ER	BB	SO
1994—	Vermont (NYP)	0	1	.000	5.40	2	2	0	0	0	$6^{2}/_{3}$	6	4	4	2	3
1995—	Albany (S. Atl.)	3	8	.273	5.47	22	22	2	0	0	$110^{1}/_{3}$	133	79	67	32	77
1996—	W.P. Beach (FSL)	6	8	.429	3.33	19	19	0	0	0	$113^{2}/_{3}$	122	53	42	23	68
—	Harrisburg (Eastern)	3	1	.750	5.11	4	4	1	0	0	$24^{2}/_{3}$	25	14	14	5	14
1997—	Harrisburg (Eastern)	9	6	.600	3.81	20	20	1	0	0	$115^{2}/_{3}$	102	54	49	30	85
—	Ottawa (Int'l)	1	3	.250	5.49	4	4	0	0	0	$19^{2}/_{3}$	17	13	12	9	15
—	Montreal (N.L.)	1	0	1.000	5.40	5	2	0	0	0	$11^{2}/_{3}$	8	9	7	4	8
1998—	Ottawa (Int'l)	7	7	.500	3.41	19	19	0	0	0	$105^{2}/_{3}$	107	50	40	49	76
—	Montreal (N.L.)	4	5	.444	4.70	14	13	0	0	0	67	60	38	35	26	32
Major league totals (2 years)		**5**	**5**	**.500**	**4.81**	**19**	**15**	**0**	**0**	**0**	**$78^{2}/_{3}$**	**68**	**47**	**42**	**30**	**40**

TIMLIN, MIKE　　　　　　　　P　　　　　　　　ORIOLES

PERSONAL: Born March 10, 1966, in Midland, Texas. ... 6-4/210. ... Throws right, bats right. ... Full name: Michael August Timlin.
HIGH SCHOOL: Midland (Texas).
COLLEGE: Southwestern University (Texas).
TRANSACTIONS/CAREER NOTES: Selected by Toronto Blue Jays organization in fifth round of free-agent draft (June 2, 1987). ... On disabled list (April 4-May 2, 1989 and August 2-17, 1991). ... On Toronto disabled list (March 27-June 12, 1992); included rehabilitation assignments to Dunedin (April 11-15 and May 24-June 5) and Syracuse (June 5-12). ... On disabled list (May 25-June 9, 1994). ... On Toronto disabled list (June 22-August 18, 1995); included rehabilitation assignment to Syracuse (July 31-August 18). ... Traded by Blue Jays with P Paul Spoljaric to Seattle Mariners for OF Jose Cruz Jr. (July 31, 1997). ... Granted free agency (October 22, 1998). ... Signed by Baltimore Orioles (November 16, 1998).
STATISTICAL NOTES: Led South Atlantic League with 19 hit batsmen in 1988.

Year	Team (League)	W	L	Pct.	ERA	G	GS	CG	ShO	Sv.	IP	H	R	ER	BB	SO
1987—	Medicine Hat (Pioneer)	4	8	.333	5.14	13	12	2	0	0	$75^{1}/_{3}$	79	50	43	26	66
1988—	Myrtle Beach (SAL)	10	6	.625	2.86	35	22	0	0	0	151	119	68	48	77	106
1989—	Dunedin (Fla. St.)	5	8	.385	3.25	33	7	1	0	7	$88^{2}/_{3}$	90	44	32	36	64
1990—	Dunedin (Fla. St.)	7	2	.778	1.43	42	0	0	0	22	$50^{1}/_{3}$	36	11	8	16	46
—	Knoxville (Southern)	1	2	.333	1.73	17	0	0	0	8	26	20	6	5	7	21
1991—	Toronto (A.L.)	11	6	.647	3.16	63	3	0	0	3	$108^{1}/_{3}$	94	43	38	50	85
1992—	Dunedin (Fla. St.)	0	0	...	0.90	6	1	0	0	1	10	9	2	1	2	7
—	Syracuse (Int'l)	0	1	.000	8.74	7	1	0	0	3	$11^{1}/_{3}$	15	11	11	5	7
—	Toronto (A.L.)	0	2	.000	4.12	26	0	0	0	1	$43^{2}/_{3}$	45	23	20	20	35
1993—	Toronto (A.L.)	4	2	.667	4.69	54	0	0	0	1	$55^{2}/_{3}$	63	32	29	27	49
—	Dunedin (Fla. St.)	0	0	...	1.00	4	0	0	0	1	9	4	1	1	0	8
1994—	Toronto (A.L.)	0	1	.000	5.18	34	0	0	0	2	40	41	25	23	20	38
1995—	Toronto (A.L.)	4	3	.571	2.14	31	0	0	0	5	42	38	13	10	17	36
—	Syracuse (Int'l)	1	1	.500	1.04	8	0	0	0	2	$17^{1}/_{3}$	13	6	2	4	13
1996—	Toronto (A.L.)	1	6	.143	3.65	59	0	0	0	31	$56^{2}/_{3}$	47	25	23	18	52
1997—	Toronto (A.L.)	3	2	.600	2.87	38	0	0	0	9	47	41	17	15	15	36
—	Seattle (A.L.)■	3	2	.600	3.86	26	0	0	0	1	$25^{2}/_{3}$	28	13	11	5	9
1998—	Seattle (A.L.)	3	3	.500	2.95	70	0	0	0	19	$79^{1}/_{3}$	78	26	26	16	60
Major league totals (8 years)		**29**	**27**	**.518**	**3.52**	**401**	**3**	**0**	**0**	**72**	**$498^{1}/_{3}$**	**475**	**217**	**195**	**188**	**400**

DIVISION SERIES RECORD

Year	Team (League)	W	L	Pct.	ERA	G	GS	CG	ShO	Sv.	IP	H	R	ER	BB	SO
1997—	Seattle (A.L.)	0	0	...	54.00	1	0	0	0	0	$^{2}/_{3}$	3	4	4	1	1

Year	Team (League)	W	L	Pct.	ERA	G	GS	CG	ShO	Sv.	IP	H	R	ER	BB	SO
1991—	Toronto (A.L.)....................	0	1	.000	3.18	4	0	0	0	0	5²/₃	5	4	2	2	5
1992—	Toronto (A.L.)....................	0	0	...	6.75	2	0	0	0	0	1¹/₃	4	1	1	0	1
1993—	Toronto (A.L.)....................	0	0	...	3.86	1	0	0	0	0	2¹/₃	3	1	1	0	2
Champ. series totals (3 years)		0	1	.000	3.86	7	0	0	0	0	9¹/₃	12	6	4	2	8

WORLD SERIES RECORD

NOTES: Member of World Series championship team (1992 and 1993).

Year	Team (League)	W	L	Pct.	ERA	G	GS	CG	ShO	Sv.	IP	H	R	ER	BB	SO
1992—	Toronto (A.L.)....................	0	0	...	0.00	2	0	0	0	1	1¹/₃	0	0	0	0	0
1993—	Toronto (A.L.)....................	0	0	...	0.00	2	0	0	0	0	2¹/₃	2	0	0	0	4
World Series totals (2 years)		0	0	...	0.00	4	0	0	0	1	3²/₃	2	0	0	0	4

TOMBERLIN, ANDY   OF   METS

PERSONAL: Born November 7, 1966, in Monroe, N.C. ... 5-11/185. ... Bats left, throws left. ... Full name: Andy Lee Tomberlin.

HIGH SCHOOL: Piedmont (Monroe, N.C.).

TRANSACTIONS/CAREER NOTES: Signed as non-drafted free agent by Atlanta Braves organization (August 16, 1985). ... On disabled list (April 10-May 28, 1991). ... Granted free agency (October 15, 1992). ... Signed by Buffalo, Pittsburgh Pirates organization (November 24, 1992). ... On Buffalo disabled list (May 22-June 5 and June 30-July 27, 1993). ... Granted free agency (October 13, 1993). ... Signed by Pawtucket, Boston Red Sox organization (February 4, 1994). ... On Boston disabled list (June 9-July 26, 1994). ... Granted free agency (October 6, 1994). ... Signed by Oakland Athletics organization (December 11, 1994). ... On Edmonton disabled list (August 2-September 12, 1995). ... Granted free agency (October 16, 1995). ... Re-signed by A's organization (January 12, 1996). ... On Edmonton temporarily inactive list (April 26-May 1, 1996). ... Traded by A's organization to New York Mets organization for a player to be named later (May 1, 1996). ... Granted free agency (October 15, 1996). ... Re-signed by Mets organization (November 21, 1996). ... On New York disabled list (April 9, 1997-remainder of season; included rehabilitation assignments to Gulf Coast Mets (August 13-20) and St. Lucie (August 21-28). ... Granted free agency (October 15, 1997). ... Signed by Detroit Tigers (December 22, 1997). ... Released by Tigers (June 29, 1998). ... Signed by Atlanta Braves organization (June 30, 1998). ... On Richmond disabled list (July 25-August 7, 1998). ... Granted free agency (October 15, 1998). ... Signed by Mets organization (November 18, 1998).

STATISTICAL NOTES: Tied for Carolina League lead with seven intentional bases on balls received in 1989.

Year	Team (League)	Pos.	G	AB	R	H	2B	3B	HR	RBI	Avg.	BB	SO	SB	PO	A	E	Avg.
1986—	Sumter (S. Atl.)	P	13	1	0	0	0	0	0	0	.000	1	1	0	2	2	2	.667
—	Pulaski (Appalachian).	P	3	4	2	1	0	0	0	0	.250	2	1	0	0	5	0	1.000
1987—	Pulaski (Appalachian).	P	14	7	1	2	0	0	0	1	.286	0	0	0	1	9	1	.909
1988—	Burlington (Midw.)	OF	43	134	24	46	7	3	3	18	.343	22	33	7	62	6	3	.958
—	Durham (Carolina)......	OF-P	83	256	43	77	16	3	6	35	.301	49	42	16	152	2	3	.981
1989—	Durham (Carolina)......	OF-1B-P	119	363	63	102	13	2	16	61	.281	54	82	35	442	16	1	.998
1990—	Greenville (Southern).	OF-P	60	196	31	61	9	1	4	25	.311	20	35	9	95	4	3	.971
—	Richmond (Int'l)	OF-1B	80	283	36	86	19	3	4	31	.304	39	43	11	180	9	4	.979
1991—	Richmond (Int'l)	OF	93	329	47	77	13	2	2	24	.234	41	85	10	192	1	1	.995
1992—	Richmond (Int'l)	OF	118	406	69	110	16	5	9	47	.271	41	102	12	184	9	3	.985
1993—	Buffalo (A.A.).............	OF-P	68	221	41	63	11	6	12	45	.285	18	48	3	104	7	5	.957
—	Pittsburgh (N.L.)	OF	27	42	4	12	0	1	1	5	.286	2	14	0	9	1	0	1.000
1994—	Pawtucket (Int'l)■	OF	54	189	38	63	12	2	13	39	.333	22	60	11	90	4	2	.979
—	Boston (A.L.).............	OF-DH-P	18	36	1	7	0	1	1	1	.194	6	12	1	12	2	0	1.000
1995—	Edmonton (PCL)■	OF	14	52	9	13	3	0	2	7	.250	5	15	0	25	1	2	.929
—	Oakland (A.L.)...........	OF-DH	46	85	15	18	0	0	4	10	.212	5	22	4	45	1	1	.979
1996—	Edmonton (PCL)■	OF	17	60	12	17	2	1	0	5	.283	8	15	1	25	1	1	.963
—	Norfolk (Int'l)■	OF	38	129	17	42	6	1	8	18	.326	8	29	1	66	1	1	.985
—	New York (N.L.)..........	OF-1B	63	66	12	17	4	0	3	10	.258	9	27	0	8	1	0	1.000
1997—	New York (N.L.)..........	OF	6	7	0	2	0	0	0	0	.286	1	3	0	2	0	0	1.000
—	GC Mets (GCL)	OF	7	22	6	7	0	0	2	7	.318	3	7	1	5	1	0	1.000
—	St. Lucie (Fla. St.)	DH	1	3	0	0	0	0	0	1	.000	1	2	0	0	0	0	...
1998—	Toledo (Int'l)■............	OF	14	47	13	16	2	1	2	4	.340	8	15	1	12	1	2	.867
—	Detroit (A.L.)..............	DH-OF	32	69	8	15	2	0	2	12	.217	3	25	1	5	0	0	1.000
—	Richmond (Int'l)■........	OF	39	104	12	27	3	0	4	15	.260	15	29	1	50	1	1	.981
American League totals (3 years)			96	190	24	40	2	1	7	23	.211	14	59	6	62	3	1	.985
National League totals (3 years)			96	115	16	31	4	1	4	15	.270	12	44	0	19	2	0	1.000
Major league totals (6 years)			192	305	40	71	6	2	11	38	.233	26	103	6	81	5	1	.989

RECORD AS PITCHER

Year	Team (League)	W	L	Pct.	ERA	G	GS	CG	ShO	Sv.	IP	H	R	ER	BB	SO
1986—	Sumter (S. Atl.)	1	0	1.000	4.62	13	0	0	0	0	25¹/₃	18	17	13	27	22
—	Pulaski (Appalachian).........	2	0	1.000	2.12	3	3	0	0	0	17	13	4	4	9	15
1987—	Pulaski (Appalachian).........	4	2	.667	4.43	12	6	0	0	0	44²/₃	35	23	22	29	51
1988—	Durham (Carolina).............	0	0	...	0.00	1	0	0	0	0	1	0	0	0	0	0
1989—	Durham (Carolina).............	0	0	...	18.00	1	0	0	0	0	1	2	2	2	2	2
1990—	Greenville (Southern)	0	0	...	0.00	1	0	0	0	0	1	1	0	0	1	1
1993—	Buffalo (A.A.)....................	0	0	...	0.00	2	0	0	0	0	2	0	0	0	3	1
1994—	Boston (A.L.)....................	0	0	...	0.00	1	0	0	0	0	2	1	0	0	1	1
Major league totals (1 year)........		0	0	...	0.00	1	0	0	0	0	2	1	0	0	1	1

TOMKO, BRETT   P   REDS

PERSONAL: Born April 7, 1973, in San Diego. ... 6-4/215. ... Throws right, bats right. ... Full name: Brett Daniel Tomko.

HIGH SCHOOL: El Dorado (Placentia, Calif.).

JUNIOR COLLEGE: Mt. San Antonio College (Calif.).

COLLEGE: Florida Southern.

TRANSACTIONS/CAREER NOTES: Selected by Cincinnati Reds organization in second round of free-agent draft (June 1, 1995).
MISCELLANEOUS: Appeared in two games as pinch runner (1997). ... Appeared in one game as pinch runner and struck out in only appearance as pinch hitter (1998).

Year Team (League)	W	L	Pct.	ERA	G	GS	CG	ShO	Sv.	IP	H	R	ER	BB	SO
1995— Char., W.Va. (S. Atl.)	4	2	.667	1.84	9	7	0	0	0	49	41	12	10	9	46
1996— Chattanooga (Southern).....	11	7	.611	3.88	27	27	0	0	0	157 2/3	131	73	68	54	164
1997— Indianapolis (A.A.).............	6	3	.667	2.95	10	10	0	0	0	61	53	21	20	9	60
— Cincinnati (N.L.)	11	7	.611	3.43	22	19	0	0	0	126	106	50	48	47	95
1998— Cincinnati (N.L.)	13	12	.520	4.44	34	34	1	0	0	210 2/3	198	111	104	64	162
Major league totals (2 years)......	24	19	.558	4.06	56	53	1	0	0	336 2/3	304	161	152	111	257

TORREALBA, YORVIT   C   GIANTS

PERSONAL: Born July 19, 1978, in Caracas, Venezuela. ... 5-11/180. ... Bats right, throws right. ... Full name: Yorvit Adolfo Torrealba.
TRANSACTIONS/CAREER NOTES: Signed as non-drafted free agent by San Francisco Giants organization (September 14, 1994).
STATISTICAL NOTES: Led California League catchers with 10 double plays in 1997.

											BATTING						FIELDING	
Year Team (League)	Pos.	G	AB	R	H	2B	3B	HR	RBI	Avg.	BB	SO	SB	PO	A	E	Avg.
1995— Bellingham (N'west)...	C	26	71	2	11	3	0	0	8	.155	2	14	0	152	26	5	.973
1996— San Jose (Calif.).........	C	2	5	0	0	0	0	0	0	.000	1	1	0	16	1	0	1.000
— Burlington (Midw.).....	C	1	4	0	0	0	0	0	0	.000	0	1	0	7	1	0	1.000
— Bellingham (N'west)....	C	48	150	23	40	4	0	1	10	.267	9	27	4	290	33	2	.994
1997— Bakersfield (Calif.).....	C	119	446	52	122	15	3	4	40	.274	31	58	4	779	*119	6	.993
1998— Shreveport (Texas).....	C	59	196	18	46	7	0	0	13	.235	18	30	0	397	70	2	.996
— San Jose (Calif.).........	C	21	70	10	20	2	0	0	10	.286	1	6	2	171	16	2	.989
— Fresno (Pacific Coast)	C	4	11	1	2	1	0	0	1	.182	1	4	0	22	0	0	1.000

TRACHSEL, STEVE   P   CUBS

PERSONAL: Born October 31, 1970, in Oxnard, Calif. ... 6-4/205. ... Throws right, bats right. ... Full name: Stephen Christopher Trachsel. ... Name pronounced TRACK-sul.
HIGH SCHOOL: Troy (Fullerton, Calif.).
JUNIOR COLLEGE: Fullerton (Calif.) College.
COLLEGE: Long Beach State.
TRANSACTIONS/CAREER NOTES: Selected by Chicago Cubs organization in eighth round of free-agent draft (June 3, 1991). ... On Chicago disabled list (July 20-August 4, 1994).
HONORS: Named N.L. Rookie Pitcher of the Year by THE SPORTING NEWS (1994).
STATISTICAL NOTES: Pitched 4-2 no-hit victory for Winston-Salem against Peninsula (July 12, 1991, second game). ... Pitched 6-0 one-hit, complete-game victory against Houston (May 13, 1996). ... Led N.L. with 32 home runs allowed in 1997.

Year Team (League)	W	L	Pct.	ERA	G	GS	CG	ShO	Sv.	IP	H	R	ER	BB	SO
1991— Geneva (N.Y.-Penn)............	1	0	1.000	1.26	2	2	0	0	0	14 1/3	10	2	2	6	7
— Win.-Salem (Car.)..............	4	4	.500	3.67	12	12	1	0	0	73 2/3	70	38	30	19	69
1992— Charlotte (Southern)	•13	8	.619	3.06	29	•29	5	2	0	*191	180	76	65	35	135
1993— Iowa (Am. Assoc.)............	13	6	.684	3.96	27	26	1	1	0	170 2/3	170	78	75	45	135
— Chicago (N.L.)...................	0	2	.000	4.58	3	3	0	0	0	19 2/3	16	10	10	3	14
1994— Chicago (N.L.)...................	9	7	.563	3.21	22	22	1	0	0	146	133	57	52	54	108
— Iowa (Am. Assoc.)............	0	2	.000	10.00	2	2	0	0	0	9	11	10	10	7	8
1995— Chicago (N.L.)...................	7	13	.350	5.15	30	29	2	0	0	160 2/3	174	104	92	76	117
1996— Orlando (South.)..............	0	1	.000	2.77	2	2	0	0	0	13	11	6	4	0	12
— Chicago (N.L.)...................	13	9	.591	3.03	31	31	3	2	0	205	181	82	69	62	132
1997— Chicago (N.L.)...................	8	12	.400	4.51	34	34	0	0	0	201 1/3	225	110	101	69	160
1998— Chicago (N.L.)...................	15	8	.652	4.46	33	33	1	0	0	208	204	107	103	84	149
Major league totals (6 years)......	52	51	.505	4.09	153	152	7	2	0	940 2/3	933	470	427	348	680

ALL-STAR GAME RECORD

Year League	W	L	Pct.	ERA	GS	CG	ShO	Sv.	IP	H	R	ER	BB	SO
1996— National	0	0	. . .	0.00	0	0	0	0	1	0	0	0	0	3

TRAMMELL, BUBBA   OF   DEVIL RAYS

PERSONAL: Born November 6, 1971, in Knoxville, Tenn. ... 6-2/220. ... Bats right, throws right. ... Full name: Thomas Bubba Trammell.
HIGH SCHOOL: Knoxville (Tenn.) Central.
JUNIOR COLLEGE: Cleveland (Tenn.) State Community College.
COLLEGE: Tennessee.
TRANSACTIONS/CAREER NOTES: Selected by Detroit Tigers organization in 11th round of free-agent draft (June 2, 1994). ... Selected by Tampa Bay Devil Rays in first round (22nd pick overall) of expansion draft (November 18, 1997).

											BATTING						FIELDING	
Year Team (League)	Pos.	G	AB	R	H	2B	3B	HR	RBI	Avg.	BB	SO	SB	PO	A	E	Avg.
1994— Jamestown (NYP)	OF	65	235	37	70	18	6	5	41	.298	23	32	9	77	3	5	.941
1995— Lakeland (Fla. St.)	OF	122	454	61	129	32	6	16	72	.284	48	80	13	176	7	5	.973
1996— Jacksonville (Sou.)......	OF	83	311	63	102	23	2	27	75	.328	32	61	3	100	6	5	.955
— Toledo (Int'l).............	OF	51	180	32	53	14	1	6	24	.294	22	44	5	72	5	1	.987
1997— Detroit (A.L.)	OF-DH	44	123	14	28	5	0	4	13	.228	15	35	3	52	1	0	1.000
— Toledo (Int'l).............	OF	90	319	56	80	15	1	28	75	.251	38	91	2	103	3	3	.972
1998— Tampa Bay (A.L.)■......	OF-DH	59	199	28	57	18	1	12	35	.286	16	45	0	50	3	0	1.000
— Durham (Int'l)	OF	57	217	46	63	12	0	16	48	.290	38	42	6	110	5	2	.983
Major league totals (2 years)		103	322	42	85	23	1	16	48	.264	31	80	3	102	4	0	1.000

TREMIE, CHRIS   C   PIRATES

PERSONAL: Born October 17, 1969, in Houston. ... 6-0/200. ... Bats right, throws right. ... Full name: Christopher James Tremie.
HIGH SCHOOL: South Houston.
COLLEGE: Houston.
TRANSACTIONS/CAREER NOTES: Selected by Houston Astros organization in 41st round of free-agent draft (June 1, 1988); did not sign. ... Selected by Chicago White Sox organization in 39th round of free-agent draft (June 1, 1992). ... On disabled list (July 22, 1992-remainder of season). ... Selected by Philadelphia Phillies organization from White Sox organization in Rule 5 minor league draft (December 9, 1996). ... Traded by Phillies to Texas Rangers for future considerations (March 29, 1998). ... Granted free agency (October 15, 1998). ... Signed by Pittsburgh Pirates organization (December 22, 1998).
STATISTICAL NOTES: Led Southern League catchers with 13 double plays in 1994.

							BATTING								FIELDING		
Year Team (League)	Pos.	G	AB	R	H	2B	3B	HR	RBI	Avg.	BB	SO	SB	PO	A	E	Avg.
1992— Utica (N.Y.-Penn).......	C	6	16	1	1	0	0	0	0	.063	0	5	0	37	5	1	.977
1993— Hickory (S. Atl.)	C	49	155	7	29	6	1	1	17	.187	9	26	0	343	44	4	.990
— GC Whi. Sox (GCL)	C	2	4	0	0	0	0	0	0	.000	0	0	0	11	0	0	1.000
— Sarasota (Fla. St.)	C	14	37	2	6	1	0	0	5	.162	2	4	0	71	13	0	1.000
1994— Birmingham (Sou.)......	C	92	302	32	68	13	0	2	29	.225	17	44	4	561	70	6	.991
1995— Nashville (A.A.)	C	67	190	13	38	4	0	2	16	.200	13	37	0	394	30	1	.998
— Chicago (A.L.)	C-DH	10	24	0	4	0	0	0	0	.167	1	2	0	39	2	1	.976
1996— Nashville (A.A.)	C	70	215	17	47	10	1	0	26	.219	18	48	2	433	*52	2	.996
1997— Reading (Eastern)	C	97	295	20	60	11	1	2	31	.203	36	61	0	650	84	4	.995
1998— Oklahoma (PCL)■.....	C	78	247	35	55	10	0	0	12	.223	24	47	1	498	45	3	.995
— Texas (A.L.)...............	DH	2	3	2	1	1	0	0	0	.333	1	1	0	...	...	...	...
Major league totals (2 years)		12	27	2	5	1	0	0	0	.185	2	3	0	39	2	1	.976

TROMBLEY, MIKE   P   TWINS

PERSONAL: Born April 14, 1967, in Springfield, Mass. ... 6-2/204. ... Throws right, bats right. ... Full name: Michael Scott Trombley.
HIGH SCHOOL: Minnechaug Regional (Wilbraham, Mass.).
COLLEGE: Duke.
TRANSACTIONS/CAREER NOTES: Selected by Minnesota Twins organization in 14th round of free-agent draft (June 5, 1989).
STATISTICAL NOTES: Pitched 3-0 no-hit victory against Knoxville (August 8, 1991). ... Led Pacific Coast League with 18 home runs allowed in 1992.

Year Team (League)	W	L	Pct.	ERA	G	GS	CG	ShO	Sv.	IP	H	R	ER	BB	SO
1989— Kenosha (Midwest)	5	1	.833	3.12	12	3	0	0	2	49	45	23	17	13	41
— Visalia (California)..............	2	2	.500	2.14	6	6	2	1	0	42	31	12	10	11	36
1990— Visalia (California)...........	14	6	.700	3.43	27	25	3	1	0	176	163	79	67	50	164
1991— Orlando (South.)	12	7	.632	2.54	27	27	7	2	0	*191	153	65	54	57	*175
1992— Portland (PCL)	10	8	.556	3.65	25	25	2	0	0	165	149	70	67	58	*138
— Minnesota (A.L.)	3	2	.600	3.30	10	7	0	0	0	46 1/3	43	20	17	17	38
1993— Minnesota (A.L.)	6	6	.500	4.88	44	10	0	0	0	114 1/3	131	72	62	41	85
1994— Minnesota (A.L.)	2	0	1.000	6.33	24	0	0	0	0	48 1/3	56	36	34	18	32
— Salt Lake (PCL)	4	4	.500	5.04	11	10	0	0	0	60 2/3	75	37	34	20	63
1995— Salt Lake (PCL)	5	3	.625	3.62	12	12	0	0	0	69 2/3	71	32	28	26	59
— Minnesota (A.L.)	4	8	.333	5.62	20	18	0	0	0	97 2/3	107	68	61	42	68
1996— Salt Lake (PCL)	2	2	.500	2.45	24	0	0	0	10	36 2/3	24	12	10	10	38
— Minnesota (A.L.)	5	1	.833	3.01	43	0	0	0	6	68 2/3	61	24	23	25	57
1997— Minnesota (A.L.)	2	3	.400	4.37	67	0	0	0	1	82 1/3	77	43	40	31	74
1998— Minnesota (A.L.)	6	5	.545	3.63	77	1	0	0	1	96 2/3	90	41	39	41	89
Major league totals (7 years)......	28	25	.528	4.48	285	36	0	0	10	554 1/3	565	304	276	215	443

TRUBY, CHRIS   3B   ASTROS

PERSONAL: Born December 9, 1973, in Palm Springs, Calif. ... 6-2/190. ... Bats right, throws right. ... Full name: Christopher John Truby.
TRANSACTIONS/CAREER NOTES: Signed as non-drafted free agent by Houston Astros organization (August 25, 1992).
STATISTICAL NOTES: Led Gulf Coast League third basemen with 21 errors in 1993. ... Led New York-Pennsylvania League with 114 total bases and eight sacrifice flies in 1994. ... Led Midwest League third basemen with 279 assists and 26 double plays in 1995.

							BATTING								FIELDING		
Year Team (League)	Pos.	G	AB	R	H	2B	3B	HR	RBI	Avg.	BB	SO	SB	PO	A	E	Avg.
1993— GC Astros (GCL)	3B-SS	57	215	30	49	10	2	1	24	.228	22	30	16	42	158	†26	.885
— Osceola (Fla. St.)........	3B	3	13	0	0	0	0	0	0	.000	0	2	0	3	9	2	.857
1994— Quad City (Midwest) ..	3B-1B	36	111	12	24	4	1	2	19	.216	3	29	1	54	29	6	.933
— Auburn (NY-Penn)......	3B	73	282	*56	*91	17	6	7	*61	.323	23	48	20	48	153	*27	.882
1995— Quad City (Midwest) ..	3B-OF	118	400	68	93	23	4	9	64	.233	41	66	27	73	†279	38	.903
1996— Quad City (Midwest) ..	1B-3B	109	362	45	91	15	3	8	37	.251	28	74	6	545	128	17	.975
1997— Quad City (Midwest) ..	3B	68	268	34	75	14	1	7	46	.280	22	32	13	39	149	15	.926
— Kissimmee (Fla. St.)...	3-1-S-2	57	199	23	49	11	0	2	29	.246	8	40	8	52	122	16	.916
1998— Kissimmee (Fla. St.)..	3B	52	212	36	66	16	1	14	478	.311	19	30	6	45	130	9	.951
— Jackson (Texas)	3B-1B	80	308	46	89	20	5	16	63	.289	20	50	8	94	161	15	.944
— New Orleans (PCL).....	3B	5	17	6	7	1	1	1	1	.412	1	3	1	4	7	1	.917

TUCCI, PETER   OF   PADRES

PERSONAL: Born October 8, 1975, in Norwalk, Conn. ... 6-2/205. ... Bats right, throws right. ... Full name: Peter Joseph Tucci.
HIGH SCHOOL: Norwalk (Conn.).
COLLEGE: Providence.

T

TRANSACTIONS/CAREER NOTES: Selected by Toronto Blue Jays organization in supplemental round ("sandwich pick" between first and second round, 31st pick overall) of free-agent draft (June 4, 1996). ... Traded by Blue Jays organization with P Woody Williams and P Carlos Almanzar to San Diego Padres organization for P Joey Hamilton (December 13, 1998).
STATISTICAL NOTES: Led Florida State League with .624 slugging percentage in 1998.

Year Team (League)	Pos.	G	AB	R	H	2B	3B	HR	RBI	Avg.	BB	SO	SB	PO	A	E	Avg.
1996— St. Catharines (NYP)..	OF	54	205	28	52	8	7	7	33	.254	23	58	5	90	3	0	*1.000
1997— Hagerstown (SAL)......	OF	127	466	60	123	28	5	10	75	.264	35	95	9	147	11	1	.994
1998— Dunedin (Fla. St.).......	OF	92	356	72	117	30	3	23	76	.329	29	97	8	139	9	7	.955
— Knoxville (Southern) ..	OF	38	141	25	41	7	4	7	36	.291	13	29	3	64	2	3	.957

TUCKER, MICHAEL   OF   REDS

PERSONAL: Born June 25, 1971, in South Boston, Va. ... 6-2/185. ... Bats left, throws right. ... Full name: Michael Anthony Tucker.
HIGH SCHOOL: Bluestone (Skipwith, Va.).
COLLEGE: Longwood (Va.).
TRANSACTIONS/CAREER NOTES: Selected by Kansas City Royals organization in first round (10th pick overall) of free-agent draft (June 1, 1992). ... On Kansas City disabled list (June 4-21 and August 28, 1996-remainder of season); included rehabilitation assignment to Wichita (June 15-21). ... Traded by Royals with IF Keith Lockhart to Atlanta Braves for OF Jermaine Dye and P Jamie Walker (March 27, 1997). ... Traded by Braves with P Denny Neagle and P Rob Bell to Cincinnati Reds for 2B Bret Boone and P Mike Remlinger (November 10, 1998).

Year Team (League)	Pos.	G	AB	R	H	2B	3B	HR	RBI	Avg.	BB	SO	SB	PO	A	E	Avg.
1993— Wilmington (Caro.)......	2B	61	239	42	73	14	2	6	44	.305	34	49	12	120	157	10	.965
— Memphis (Sou.).........	2B	72	244	38	68	7	4	9	35	.279	42	51	12	153	176	13	.962
1994— Omaha (A.A.)............	OF	132	485	75	134	16	7	21	77	.276	69	111	11	196	11	•7	.967
1995— Kansas City (A.L.)	OF-DH	62	177	23	46	10	0	4	17	.260	18	51	2	67	3	1	.986
— Omaha (A.A.)............	OF	71	275	37	84	18	4	4	28	.305	24	39	11	133	11	2	.986
1996— Kansas City (A.L.)	OF-1B-DH	108	339	55	88	18	4	12	53	.260	40	69	10	235	8	2	.992
— Wichita (Texas)	OF-1B	6	20	4	9	1	3	0	7	.450	5	4	0	17	1	0	1.000
1997— Atlanta (N.L.)■..........	OF	138	499	80	141	25	7	14	56	.283	44	116	12	237	6	5	.980
1998— Atlanta (N.L.)..........	OF	130	414	54	101	27	3	13	46	.244	49	112	8	194	5	1	.995
American League totals (2 years)		170	516	78	134	28	4	16	70	.260	58	120	12	302	11	3	.991
National League totals (2 years)		268	913	134	242	52	10	27	102	.265	93	228	20	431	11	6	.987
Major league totals (4 years)		438	1429	212	376	80	14	43	172	.263	151	348	32	733	22	9	.988

DIVISION SERIES RECORD

Year Team (League)	Pos.	G	AB	R	H	2B	3B	HR	RBI	Avg.	BB	SO	SB	PO	A	E	Avg.
1997— Atlanta (N.L.)..............	OF	2	6	0	1	0	0	0	1	.167	0	1	0	3	0	0	1.000
1998— Atlanta (N.L.)..............	OF	3	8	1	2	0	0	1	2	.250	3	0	1	6	0	0	1.000
Division series totals (2 years)		5	14	1	3	0	0	1	3	.214	3	1	1	9	0	0	1.000

CHAMPIONSHIP SERIES RECORD

Year Team (League)	Pos.	G	AB	R	H	2B	3B	HR	RBI	Avg.	BB	SO	SB	PO	A	E	Avg.
1997— Atlanta (N.L.)..............	OF-PH	5	10	1	1	0	0	1	1	.100	3	4	0	5	1	0	1.000
1998— Atlanta (N.L.)..............	OF-PH	6	13	1	5	1	0	1	5	.385	2	5	0	7	0	0	1.000
Championship series totals (2 years)		11	23	2	6	1	0	2	6	.261	5	9	0	12	1	0	1.000

TURNER, CHRIS   C   INDIANS

PERSONAL: Born March 23, 1969, in Bowling Green, Ky. ... 6-3/200. ... Bats right, throws right. ... Full name: Christopher Wan Turner.
HIGH SCHOOL: Warren Central (Bowling Green, Ky.).
COLLEGE: Western Kentucky (degree in psychology, 1991).
TRANSACTIONS/CAREER NOTES: Selected by California Angels organization in seventh round of free-agent draft (June 3, 1991). ... Angels franchise renamed Anaheim Angels for 1997 season. ... On Anaheim disabled list (March 31-July 4, 1997); included rehabilitation assignment to Lake Elsinore (July 2-4). ... Granted free agency (October 10, 1997). ... Signed by Minnesota Twins organization (December 5, 1997). ... On Salt Lake suspended list (April 7-17, 1998). ... Released by Twins (April 20, 1998). ... Signed by Kansas City Royals organization (April 20, 1998). ... Granted free agency (October 15, 1998). ... Signed by Cleveland Indians organization (January 5, 1999).
STATISTICAL NOTES: Led Northwest League catchers with .997 fielding percentage in 1991. ... Led Pacific Coast League with 17 passed balls in 1993.

Year Team (League)	Pos.	G	AB	R	H	2B	3B	HR	RBI	Avg.	BB	SO	SB	PO	A	E	Avg.
1991— Boise (Northwest)	C-OF	52	163	26	37	5	0	2	29	.227	32	32	10	360	39	2	†.995
1992— Quad City (Midwest) ..	C-1B	109	330	66	83	18	1	9	53	.252	85	65	8	727	98	9	.989
1993— Vancouver (PCL)	C-1B	90	283	50	78	12	1	4	57	.276	49	44	6	524	56	6	.990
— California (A.L.).........	C	25	75	9	21	5	0	1	13	.280	9	16	1	116	14	1	.992
1994— California (A.L.).........	C	58	149	23	36	7	1	1	12	.242	10	29	3	268	29	1	.997
— Vancouver (PCL)	C	3	10	1	2	1	0	0	1	.200	0	2	0	10	1	1	.917
1995— Vancouver (PCL)	C-3-1-O	80	282	44	75	20	2	3	48	.266	34	54	3	345	49	6	.985
— California (A.L.).........	C	5	10	0	1	0	0	0	1	.100	0	3	0	17	2	0	1.000
1996— Vancouver (PCL)	C-O-3-1	113	390	51	100	19	1	2	47	.256	61	85	1	396	57	8	.983
— California (A.L.).........	C-OF	4	3	1	1	0	0	0	1	.333	1	0	0	3	2	0	1.000
1997— Lake Elsinore (Calif.)..	C	3	12	0	1	0	1	0	1	.083	0	3	0	25	1	1	.963
— Vancouver (PCL)	1B-C-OF	37	135	26	50	10	0	4	22	.370	14	22	0	291	15	5	.984
— Anaheim (A.L.)	C-1-DH-O	13	23	4	6	1	1	1	2	.261	5	8	0	34	2	0	1.000
1998— Kansas City (A.L.)■.....	C	4	9	0	0	0	0	0	0	.000	0	4	0	16	0	0	1.000
— Omaha (PCL).............	C-OF-3B	66	196	31	60	14	1	1	16	.306	38	36	6	328	19	3	.991
Major league totals (6 years)		109	269	37	65	13	2	3	29	.242	25	60	4	454	49	2	.996

PERSONAL: Born February 15, 1974, in Caracas, Venezuela. ... 6-2/205. ... Throws right, bats right. ... Full name: Ugueth Urtain Urbina. ... Name pronounced OOO-get.
HIGH SCHOOL: Liceo Peres Bonalde de Miranda (Miranda, Venezuela).
TRANSACTIONS/CAREER NOTES: Signed as non-drafted free agent by Montreal Expos organization (July 2, 1990). ... On disabled list (April 8-17, 1994). ... On temporarily inactive list (May 9-June 6, 1994). ... On Ottawa disabled list (August 10-September 14, 1995).

Year Team (League)	W	L	Pct.	ERA	G	GS	CG	ShO	Sv.	IP	H	R	ER	BB	SO
1991— GC Expos (GCL)	3	3	.500	2.29	10	10	3	•1	0	63	58	24	16	10	51
1992— Albany (S. Atl.)	7	•13	.350	3.22	24	24	5	2	0	142 1/3	111	68	51	54	100
1993— Burlington (Midw.)	2	3	.400	4.50	10	8	0	0	0	46	41	31	23	22	30
— Harrisburg (Eastern)	4	5	.444	3.99	11	11	3	1	0	70	66	32	31	32	45
1994— Harrisburg (Eastern)	9	3	.750	3.28	21	21	0	0	0	120 2/3	95	49	44	43	86
1995— W.P. Beach (FSL)	1	0	1.000	0.00	2	2	0	0	0	9	4	0	0	1	11
— Ottawa (Int'l)	6	2	.750	3.04	13	11	2	1	0	68	46	26	23	26	55
— Montreal (N.L.)	2	2	.500	6.17	7	4	0	0	0	23 1/3	26	17	16	14	15
1996— W.P. Beach (FSL)	1	1	.500	1.29	3	3	0	0	0	14	13	3	2	3	21
— Ottawa (Int'l)	2	0	1.000	2.66	5	5	0	0	0	23 2/3	17	9	7	6	28
— Montreal (N.L.)	10	5	.667	3.71	33	17	0	0	0	114	102	54	47	44	108
1997— Montreal (N.L.)	5	8	.385	3.78	63	0	0	0	27	64 1/3	52	29	27	29	84
1998— Montreal (N.L.)	6	3	.667	1.30	64	0	0	0	34	69 1/3	37	11	10	33	94
Major league totals (4 years)	23	18	.561	3.32	167	21	0	0	61	271	217	111	100	120	301

ALL-STAR GAME RECORD

Year League	W	L	Pct.	ERA	GS	CG	ShO	Sv.	IP	H	R	ER	BB	SO
1998— National	0	1	.000	27.00	0	0	0	0	1	3	3	3	1	2

PERSONAL: Born August 21, 1973, in Victoria, Mexico. ... 6-3/215. ... Throws right, bats right.
HIGH SCHOOL: CBTIS #119 (Victoria, Mexico).
TRANSACTIONS/CAREER NOTES: Signed as non-drafted free agent by Los Angeles Dodgers (June 14, 1991). ... Loaned by Dodgers organization to Mexico City Tigers of Mexican League (April 21-June 26, 1992; and March 17-August 19, 1993). ... On disabled list (July 6-28, 1997). ... On Los Angeles disabled list (July 26-September 1, 1998); included rehabilitation assignments to Vero Beach (August 22) and San Bernardino (August 27).
STATISTICAL NOTES: Led N.L. with five balks in 1996. ... Pitched 2-0 one-hit, complete-game victory against Pittsburgh (June 27, 1998).

Year Team (League)	W	L	Pct.	ERA	G	GS	CG	ShO	Sv.	IP	H	R	ER	BB	SO
1991— GC Dodgers (GCL)	2	2	.500	2.32	10	10	0	0	0	50 1/3	44	15	13	13	44
1992— M.C. Tigers (Mex.)■	0	0	...	19.64	5	0	0	0	0	3 2/3	15	9	8	1	2
— La Vega (DSL)	3	0	1.000	1.42	6	0	0	0	0	38	27	9	6	17	34
1993— M.C. Tigers (Mex.)■	16	7	.696	3.94	26	25	11	1	0	173 2/3	192	87	76	55	113
— San Antonio (Tex.)■	1	0	1.000	1.38	3	2	0	0	0	13	12	2	2	0	11
1994— San Antonio (Tex.)■	2	3	.400	3.38	8	8	0	0	0	53 1/3	54	22	20	9	55
— Albuquerque (PCL)	4	1	.800	3.40	8	8	0	0	0	45	44	21	17	13	39
— Los Angeles (N.L.)	3	1	.750	3.18	21	1	0	0	0	28 1/3	21	10	10	10	28
1995— Los Angeles (N.L.)	13	11	.542	3.05	33	27	6	2	1	197 2/3	168	76	67	51	150
1996— Los Angeles (N.L.)	15	7	.682	3.32	33	33	0	0	0	225	219	94	83	54	173
1997— Los Angeles (N.L.)	10	11	.476	2.65	30	30	0	0	0	196 2/3	171	68	58	47	140
1998— Los Angeles (N.L.)	11	10	.524	3.98	27	27	2	2	0	174	171	82	77	66	122
— Vero Beach (FSL)	0	0	...	0.00	1	1	0	0	0	3	2	0	0	1	3
— San Bernardino (Calif.)	1	0	1.000	2.84	1	1	0	0	0	6 1/3	7	2	2	1	4
Major league totals (5 years)	52	40	.565	3.23	144	118	8	4	1	821 2/3	750	330	295	228	613

DIVISION SERIES RECORD

Year Team (League)	W	L	Pct.	ERA	G	GS	CG	ShO	Sv.	IP	H	R	ER	BB	SO
1995— Los Angeles (N.L.)	0	0	...	0.00	1	1	0	0	0	7	3	2	0	1	6
1996— Los Angeles (N.L.)	0	1	.000	4.26	1	1	0	0	0	6 1/3	5	3	3	0	5
Div. series totals (2 years)	0	1	.000	2.03	2	2	0	0	0	13 1/3	8	5	3	1	11

U
V

PERSONAL: Born December 20, 1971, in Dayton, Ohio. ... 6-0/185. ... Throws right, bats right. ... Full name: Marc Christopher Valdes.
HIGH SCHOOL: Jesuit (Tampa).
COLLEGE: Florida.
TRANSACTIONS/CAREER NOTES: Selected by Cincinnati Reds organization in 20th round of free-agent draft (June 4, 1990); did not sign. ... Selected by Florida Marlins organization in first round (27th pick overall) of free-agent draft (June 3, 1993). ... Claimed on waivers by Montreal Expos (December 12, 1996). ... On disabled list (May 27-June 11 and June 23, 1998-remainder of season). ... Granted free agency (December 21, 1998). ... Signed by Tampa Bay Devil Rays organization (January 20, 1999).

Year Team (League)	W	L	Pct.	ERA	G	GS	CG	ShO	Sv.	IP	H	R	ER	BB	SO
1993— Elmira (N.Y.-Penn)	0	2	.000	5.59	3	3	0	0	0	9 2/3	8	9	6	7	15
1994— Kane County (Midwest)	7	4	.636	2.95	11	11	2	0	0	76 1/3	62	30	25	21	68
— Portland (Eastern)	8	4	.667	2.55	15	15	0	0	0	99	77	31	28	39	70
1995— Charlotte (Int'l)	9	•13	.409	4.86	27	27	3	2	0	170 1/3	189	98	•92	59	104
— Florida (N.L.)	0	0	...	14.14	3	3	0	0	0	7	17	13	11	9	2
1996— Charlotte (Int'l)	2	4	.333	5.12	8	8	1	0	0	51	66	32	29	15	24
— Portland (Eastern)	6	2	.750	2.66	10	10	1	0	0	64 1/3	60	25	19	12	49
— Florida (N.L.)	1	3	.250	4.81	11	8	0	0	0	48 2/3	63	32	26	23	13
1997— Montreal (N.L.)■	4	4	.500	3.13	48	7	0	0	2	95	84	36	33	39	54
1998— Montreal (N.L.)	1	3	.250	7.43	20	4	0	0	0	36 1/3	41	34	30	21	28
Major league totals (4 years)	6	10	.375	4.81	82	22	0	0	2	187	205	115	100	92	97

VALDES, PEDRO   OF/1B   RED SOX

PERSONAL: Born June 29, 1973, in Fajardo, Puerto Rico. ... 6-1/190. ... Bats left, throws left. ... Full name: Pedro Jose Manzo Valdes.
HIGH SCHOOL: Carlos Escobar Lopez (Loiza, Puerto Rico).
TRANSACTIONS/CAREER NOTES: Selected by Chicago Cubs organization in 12th round of free-agent draft (June 4, 1990). ... On Iowa disabled list (August 4-11, 1996). ... On Iowa disabled list (April 19-May 4, 1998). ... On Chicago disabled list (July 6-September 1, 1998); included rehabilitation assignment to Iowa (August 14-September 1). ... Released by Cubs (December 8, 1998). ... Signed by Boston Red Sox organization (January 12, 1999).
STATISTICAL NOTES: Led Southern League outfielders with six double plays in 1995.

							BATTING								FIELDING		
Year	Team (League)	Pos.	G	AB	R	H	2B	3B	HR	RBI	Avg.	BB	SO	SB	PO	A	E	Avg.
1991—	Huntington (Appal.)....	OF	49	152	17	44	11	1	0	16	.289	17	30	5	66	4	6	.921
1992—	Peoria (Midwest)........	OF	33	112	8	26	7	0	0	20	.232	7	32	0	32	1	1	.971
—	Geneva (NY-Penn)......	OF-1B	66	254	27	69	10	0	5	24	.272	3	33	4	210	18	9	.962
1993—	Peoria (Midwest)........	OF-1B	65	234	33	74	11	1	7	36	.316	10	40	2	51	2	1	.981
—	Daytona (Fla. St.)	OF-1B	60	230	27	66	16	1	8	49	.287	9	30	3	176	7	3	.984
1994—	Orlando (South.)	OF	116	365	39	103	14	4	1	37	.282	20	45	2	177	12	7	.964
1995—	Orlando (South.)	OF	114	426	57	128	28	3	7	68	.300	37	77	3	172	11	4	.979
1996—	Iowa (Am. Assoc.)......	OF	103	397	61	117	23	0	15	60	.295	31	57	2	183	7	5	.974
—	Chicago (N.L.)............	OF	9	8	2	1	1	0	0	1	.125	1	5	0	1	0	0	1.000
1997—	Iowa (Am. Assoc.)......	OF	125	464	65	132	30	1	14	60	.284	48	67	9	256	13	3	.989
1998—	Iowa (Pacific Coast)....	OF	65	229	49	72	12	0	17	40	.314	27	38	2	106	3	4	.965
—	Chicago (N.L.)............	OF	14	23	1	5	1	1	0	2	.217	1	3	0	10	0	0	1.000
Major league totals (2 years)			23	31	3	6	2	1	0	3	.194	2	8	0	11	0	0	1.000

VALDEZ, CARLOS   P

PERSONAL: Born December 26, 1971, in Nizao Bani, Dominican Republic. ... 5-11/191. ... Throws right, bats right. ... Full name: Carlos Luis Valdez. ... Brother of Efrain Valdez, pitcher with Cleveland Indians (1990-91) and Arizona Diamondbacks (1998).
TRANSACTIONS/CAREER NOTES: Signed as non-drafted free agent by San Francisco Giants organization (April 6, 1990). ... On Arizona Giants suspended list (July 29-30, 1991). ... On Dominican Giants suspended list (August 18-September 8, 1992). ... On disabled list (May 13-26, 1996). ... Contract purchased by Boston Red Sox (March 25, 1997). ... Granted free agency (October 15, 1997). ... Re-signed by Red Sox (January 29, 1998). ... On Pawtucket disabled list (June 19-July 2, 1998). ... Released by Red Sox (November 20, 1998).

Year	Team (League)	W	L	Pct.	ERA	G	GS	CG	ShO	Sv.	IP	H	R	ER	BB	SO
1990—	Dominican Giants (DSL)	5	4	.556	3.48	13	12	2	0	1	75	77	46	29	31	47
1991—	Arizona Giants (Ariz.)	2	3	.400	5.68	13	10	0	0	0	63 1/3	73	48	40	32	48
1992—	Dominican Giants (DSL)	1	1	.500	2.45	5	4	1	0	1	29 1/3	30	14	8	8	35
—	Arizona Giants (Ariz.)	3	1	.750	0.00	6	0	0	0	0	14 2/3	7	2	0	5	14
—	Everett (Northwest)........	0	1	.000	1.42	3	0	0	0	0	6 1/3	4	2	1	7	6
1993—	Clinton (Midwest)..........	4	7	.364	3.99	35	2	0	0	3	90 1/3	74	47	40	44	85
1994—	San Jose (California)..........	8	6	.571	4.51	36	17	0	0	0	123 2/3	109	70	62	61	116
1995—	Shreveport (Texas).............	3	2	.600	1.27	22	3	0	0	5	64	40	11	9	14	51
—	Phoenix (PCL)	1	0	1.000	2.76	18	0	0	0	2	29 1/3	29	10	9	13	30
—	San Francisco (N.L.)	0	1	.000	6.14	11	0	0	0	0	14 2/3	19	10	10	8	7
1996—	Phoenix (PCL)	4	3	.571	4.98	44	0	0	0	5	59 2/3	63	38	33	34	38
1997—	Pawtucket (Int'l)■...........	0	4	.000	4.69	35	8	0	0	1	78 2/3	73	49	41	46	64
1998—	Pawtucket (Int'l)...........	4	3	.571	4.10	37	5	0	0	0	74 2/3	74	38	34	22	75
—	Boston (A.L.).................	1	0	1.000	0.00	4	0	0	0	0	3 1/3	1	0	0	5	4
A.L. totals (1 year)		1	0	1.000	0.00	4	0	0	0	0	3 1/3	1	0	0	5	4
N.L. totals (1 year)		0	1	.000	6.14	11	0	0	0	0	14 2/3	19	10	10	8	7
Major league totals (2 years)......		1	1	.500	5.00	15	0	0	0	0	18	20	10	10	13	11

VALDEZ, EFRAIN   P

PERSONAL: Born July 11, 1966, in Nizao de Bani, Dominican Republic. ... 5-11/170. ... Throws left, bats left. ... Full name: Efrain Antonio Valdez. ... Brother of Carlos Valdez, pitcher with San Francisco Giants (1995) and Boston Red Sox (1998).
HIGH SCHOOL: Aliro Paulin (Nizao de Bani, Dominican Republic).
TRANSACTIONS/CAREER NOTES: Signed as non-drafted free agent by San Diego Padres organization (May 4, 1983). ... Contract sold by Padres organization to Texas Rangers organization (December 10, 1984). ... Loaned by Rangers organization to San Luis Potosi of Mexican League (1986). ... Selected by Cleveland Indians organization from Rangers organization in Rule 5 minor league draft (December 6, 1988). ... Granted free agency (October 15, 1989). ... Re-signed by Indians organization (January 9, 1990). ... Claimed on waivers by Toronto Blue Jays (July 3, 1991). ... Granted free agency (October 15, 1991). ... Signed by Denver, Milwaukee Brewers organization (November 28, 1991). ... Released by Denver (August 29, 1992). ... Signed by New York Mets organization (January 24, 1998). ... Traded by Mets to Arizona Diamondbacks for cash (May 26, 1998). ... Granted free agency (October 15, 1998).

Year	Team (League)	W	L	Pct.	ERA	G	GS	CG	ShO	Sv.	IP	H	R	ER	BB	SO
1983—	Spokane (N'west)..............	0	0	. . .	6.98	13	1	0	0	0	29 2/3	40	32	23	17	27
1984—	Spokane (N'west)..............	1	2	.333	7.56	13	1	0	0	0	16 2/3	26	18	14	8	15
1985—	Piratas (DSL)■	13	3	.813	1.85	17	15	6	2	1	121 1/3	76	38	25	48	113
1986—	San Luis Potosi (Mex.)■....	11	8	.579	4.60	26	26	5	0	0	164 1/3	176	105	84	76	82
—	Tulsa (Texas)■.............	0	1	.000	5.84	4	2	0	0	0	12 1/3	12	8	8	6	4
1987—	Tulsa (Texas)..............	1	4	.200	7.11	11	8	1	1	0	49 1/3	62	44	39	24	38
—	Charlotte (Fla. St.)..............	3	6	.333	3.71	17	8	0	0	0	70 1/3	67	32	29	27	45
1988—	Tulsa (Texas)...............	6	5	.545	4.55	43	3	0	0	6	63 1/3	63	37	32	24	52
1989—	Cant./Akr. (Eastern)■■.......	2	4	.333	2.15	44	2	0	0	1	75 1/3	60	26	18	13	55
1990—	Colo. Springs (PCL)	4	2	.667	3.81	46	1	0	0	6	75 2/3	72	38	32	30	52
—	Cleveland (A.L.)................	1	1	.500	3.04	13	0	0	0	0	23 2/3	20	10	8	14	13
1991—	Colo. Springs (PCL)	3	1	.750	3.82	14	1	0	0	0	30 2/3	26	15	13	13	25
—	Cleveland (A.L.)................	0	0	. . .	1.50	7	0	0	0	0	6	5	1	1	3	1
—	Syracuse (Int'l)■..............	3	2	.600	5.36	21	1	0	0	0	43 2/3	50	27	26	25	30

Year Team (League)	W	L	Pct.	ERA	G	GS	CG	ShO	Sv.	IP	H	R	ER	BB	SO
1992— Denver (Am. Assoc.)■.......	1	1	.500	5.43	36	1	0	0	0	68	76	45	41	22	43
1993—								Statistics unavailable.							
1994— Saltillo (Mexican)■............	3	5	.375	3.84	12	11	2	1	0	68	63	30	29	21	35
1995—								Statistics unavailable.							
1996— Quintana Roo (Mexican)■.	11	5	.688	2.23	20	20	6	3	0	149 1/3	123	49	37	44	69
1997— Quintana Roo (Mexican)	14	7	.667	2.07	24	24	13	5	0	187	149	55	43	54	75
1998— Norfolk (Int'l)■	1	0	1.000	3.92	18	0	0	0	1	20 2/3	23	9	9	10	15
— Tucson (PCL)■	1	4	.200	4.37	28	2	0	0	0	57 2/3	59	31	28	18	41
— Arizona (N.L.)	0	0	. . .	4.15	6	0	0	0	0	4 1/3	7	2	2	1	2
A.L. totals (2 years)	1	1	.500	2.73	20	0	0	0	0	29 2/3	25	11	9	17	14
N.L. totals (1 year)	0	0	. . .	4.15	6	0	0	0	0	4 1/3	7	2	2	1	2
Major league totals (3 years)	1	1	.500	2.91	26	0	0	0	0	34	32	13	11	18	16

VALDEZ, MARIO   1B   WHITE SOX

PERSONAL: Born November 19, 1974, in Obregon, Mexico ... 6-2/190. ... Bats left, throws right. ... Full name: Mario A. Valdez.
HIGH SCHOOL: Miami Senior.
JUNIOR COLLEGE: Miami-Dade (North) Community College.
TRANSACTIONS/CAREER NOTES: Selected by Chicago White Sox organization in 48th round of free-agent draft (June 3, 1993).
STATISTICAL NOTES: Led Pacific Coast League first basemen with 14 errors in 1998.

Year Team (League)	Pos.	G	AB	R	H	2B	3B	HR	RBI	Avg.	BB	SO	SB	PO	A	E	Avg.
1994— GC Whi. Sox (GCL)	1B-OF	53	157	20	37	11	2	2	25	.236	30	28	0	351	28	8	.979
1995— Hickory (S. Atl.)	1B	130	441	65	120	30	5	11	56	.272	67	107	9	1040	67	12	.989
1996— South Bend (Mid.)......	1B	61	202	46	76	19	0	10	43	.376	36	42	2	438	41	8	.984
— Birmingham (Sou.)......	1B-OF	50	168	22	46	10	2	3	28	.274	32	34	0	284	26	2	.994
1997— Nashville (A.A.)	1B	81	282	44	79	20	1	15	61	.280	43	77	1	616	44	6	.991
— Chicago (A.L.)	1B-DH-3B	54	115	11	28	7	0	1	13	.243	17	39	1	256	12	0	1.000
1998— Calgary (PCL).............	1B-OF	123	448	86	148	32	0	20	81	.330	60	102	1	1003	75	†15	.986
Major league totals (1 year)		54	115	11	28	7	0	1	13	.243	17	39	1	256	12	0	1.000

VALENTIN, JAVIER   C   TWINS

PERSONAL: Born September 19, 1975, in Manati, Puerto Rico. ... 5-10/192. ... Bats both, throws right. ... Full name: Jose Javier Valentin. ... Brother of Jose Valentin, shortstop, Milwaukee Brewers. ... Name pronounced VAL-un-TEEN.
HIGH SCHOOL: Fernando Callejo (Manati, Puerto Rico).
TRANSACTIONS/CAREER NOTES: Selected by Minnesota Twins organization in third round of free-agent draft (June 3, 1993).
STATISTICAL NOTES: Led Appalachian League catchers with 48 assists and 348 total chances in 1993. ... Led Midwest League with 730 putouts, 108 assists, 861 total chances, 23 errors and 11 double plays by catcher in 1995.

Year Team (League)	Pos.	G	AB	R	H	2B	3B	HR	RBI	Avg.	BB	SO	SB	PO	A	E	Avg.
1993— GC Twins (GCL)..........	C-3B	32	103	18	27	6	1	1	19	.262	14	19	0	120	23	5	.966
— Elizabethton (App.).....	C	9	24	3	5	1	0	0	3	.208	4	2	0	81	3	2	.977
1994— Elizabethton (App.).....	C-3B	54	210	23	44	5	0	9	27	.210	15	44	0	288	†50	12	.966
1995— Fort Wayne (Midw.).....	C-3B	112	383	59	124	26	5	19	65	.324	47	75	0	†736	†122	†23	.974
1996— Fort Myers (FSL).........	C-3B	87	338	34	89	26	1	7	54	.263	32	65	1	360	71	4	.991
— New Britain (East.)	C-3B	48	165	22	39	8	0	3	14	.236	16	35	0	188	36	5	.978
1997— New Britain (East.)	C-3B	102	370	41	90	17	0	8	50	.243	30	61	2	516	65	6	.990
— Minnesota (A.L.)	C	4	7	1	2	0	0	0	0	.286	0	3	0	11	2	0	1.000
1998— Minnesota (A.L.)	C-DH	55	162	11	32	7	1	3	18	.198	11	30	0	281	17	5	.983
Major league totals (2 years)		59	169	12	34	7	1	3	18	.201	11	33	0	292	19	5	.984

VALENTIN, JOHN   IF   RED SOX

PERSONAL: Born February 18, 1967, in Mineola, N.Y. ... 6-0/180. ... Bats right, throws right. ... Full name: John William Valentin. ... Name pronounced VAL-en-tin.
HIGH SCHOOL: St. Anthony (Jersey City, N.J.).
COLLEGE: Seton Hall.
TRANSACTIONS/CAREER NOTES: Selected by Boston Red Sox organization in fifth round of free-agent draft (June 1, 1988). ... On Boston disabled list (April 1-20, 1993); included rehabilitation assignment to Pawtucket (April 16-20). ... On Boston disabled list (May 4-June 6, 1994); included rehabilitation assignment to Pawtucket (May 31-June 6). ... On disabled list (August 3-18, 1996).
RECORDS: Shares A.L. single-season record for fewest putouts by third baseman for leader—121 (1998).
HONORS: Named shortstop on THE SPORTING NEWS A.L. Silver Slugger team (1995).
STATISTICAL NOTES: Led New York-Pennsylvania League shortstops with .949 fielding percentage in 1988. ... Hit three home runs in one game (June 2, 1995). ... Led A.L. shortstops with 659 total chances in 1995. ... Hit for the cycle (June 6, 1996). ... Led A.L. third basemen with 121 putouts in 1998. ... Career major league grand slams: 2.
MISCELLANEOUS: Turned unassisted triple play while playing shortstop (July 8, 1994, sixth inning); 10th player ever to accomplish feat.

Year Team (League)	Pos.	G	AB	R	H	2B	3B	HR	RBI	Avg.	BB	SO	SB	PO	A	E	Avg.
1988— Elmira (N.Y.-Penn)......	SS-3B	60	207	18	45	5	1	2	16	.217	36	35	5	96	175	14	†.951
1989— Winter Haven (FSL)......	SS-3B	55	215	27	58	13	1	3	18	.270	13	29	4	99	177	12	.958
— Lynchburg (Caro.)......	SS	75	264	47	65	7	2	8	34	.246	41	40	5	105	220	16	.953
1990— New Britain (East.)	SS	94	312	20	68	18	1	2	31	.218	25	46	1	139	246	21	.951
1991— New Britain (East.)	SS	23	81	8	16	3	0	0	5	.198	9	14	1	50	65	3	.975
— Pawtucket (Int'l)........	SS	100	329	52	87	22	4	9	49	.264	60	42	0	184	300	25	.951

Year Team (League)	Pos.	G	AB	R	H	2B	3B	HR	RBI	Avg.	BB	SO	SB	PO	A	E	Avg.
							BATTING								FIELDING		
1992—Pawtucket (Int'l)........	SS	97	331	47	86	18	1	9	29	.260	48	50	1	148	*358	20	.962
— Boston (A.L.).............	SS	58	185	21	51	13	0	5	25	.276	20	17	1	79	182	10	.963
1993—Pawtucket (Int'l)........	SS	2	9	3	3	0	0	1	1	.333	0	1	0	8	9	0	1.000
— Boston (A.L.).............	SS	144	468	50	130	40	3	11	66	.278	49	77	3	238	432	20	.971
1994—Boston (A.L.).............	SS-DH	84	301	53	95	26	2	9	49	.316	42	38	3	134	242	8	.979
— Pawtucket (Int'l)........	SS	5	18	2	6	0	0	1	2	.333	3	4	0	7	16	3	.885
1995—Boston (A.L.).............	SS	135	520	108	155	37	2	27	102	.298	81	67	20	227	*414	•18	.973
1996—Boston (A.L.).............	SS-3B-DH	131	527	84	156	29	3	13	59	.296	63	59	9	202	357	17	.970
1997—Boston (A.L.).............	2B-3B	143	575	95	176	*47	5	18	77	.306	58	66	7	239	380	22	.966
1998—Boston (A.L.).............	3B-2B	153	588	113	145	44	1	23	73	.247	77	82	4	†121	292	15	.965
Major league totals (7 years)		848	3164	524	908	236	16	106	451	.287	390	406	47	1240	2299	110	.970

DIVISION SERIES RECORD

Year Team (League)	Pos.	G	AB	R	H	2B	3B	HR	RBI	Avg.	BB	SO	SB	PO	A	E	Avg.
							BATTING								FIELDING		
1995—Boston (A.L.).............	SS	3	12	1	3	1	0	1	2	.250	3	1	0	5	5	1	.909
1998—Boston (A.L.).............	3B	4	15	5	7	1	0	0	0	.467	3	1	0	5	10	0	1.000
Division series totals (2 years)		7	27	6	10	2	0	1	2	.370	6	2	0	10	15	1	.962

VALENTIN, JOSE   SS   BREWERS

PERSONAL: Born October 12, 1969, in Manati, Puerto Rico. ... 5-10/176. ... Bats left, throws right. ... Full name: Jose Antonio Valentin. ... Brother of Javier Valentin, catcher, Minnesota Twins. ... Name pronounced VAL-un-TEEN.

HIGH SCHOOL: Fernando Callejo (Manati, Puerto Rico).

TRANSACTIONS/CAREER NOTES: Signed as non-drafted free agent by San Diego Padres organization (October 12, 1986). ... On disabled list (April 16-May 1 and May 18-July 11, 1990). ... Traded by Padres with P Ricky Bones and OF Matt Mieske to Milwaukee Brewers for 3B Gary Sheffield and P Geoff Kellogg (March 27, 1992). ... On Milwaukee disabled list (April 14-May 5, 1997); included rehabilitation assignment to Beloit (May 3-5).

STATISTICAL NOTES: Led Texas League shortstops with 658 total chances in 1991. ... Led American Association shortstops with 639 total chances and 70 double plays in 1992. ... Led American Association shortstops with 211 putouts and 80 double plays in 1993. ... Led A.L. shortstops with 20 errors in 1994. ... Hit three home runs in one game (April 3, 1998). ... Career major league grand slams: 3.

Year Team (League)	Pos.	G	AB	R	H	2B	3B	HR	RBI	Avg.	BB	SO	SB	PO	A	E	Avg.
							BATTING								FIELDING		
1987—Spokane (N'west).......	SS	70	244	52	61	8	2	2	24	.250	35	38	8	101	175	26	.914
1988—Char., S.C. (S. Atl.).....	SS	133	444	56	103	20	1	6	44	.232	45	83	11	204	412	60	.911
1989—Riverside (Calif.).........	SS	114	381	40	74	10	5	10	41	.194	37	93	8	*227	437	*46	.924
— Wichita (Texas)	SS-3B	18	49	8	12	1	0	2	5	.245	5	12	1	26	45	8	.899
1990—Wichita (Texas)	SS	11	36	4	10	2	0	0	2	.278	5	7	2	14	33	2	.959
1991—Wichita (Texas)	SS	129	447	73	112	22	5	17	68	.251	55	115	8	176	*442	40	.939
1992—Denver (A.A.)■	SS	*139	492	78	118	19	11	3	45	.240	53	99	9	*187	*414	*38	.941
— Milwaukee (A.L.)	SS-2B	4	3	1	0	0	0	0	1	1.000	0	0	0	1	1	1	.667
1993—New Orleans (A.A.).....	SS-1B	122	389	56	96	22	5	9	53	.247	47	87	9	†212	351	29	.951
— Milwaukee (A.L.)	SS	19	53	10	13	1	2	1	7	.245	7	16	1	20	51	6	.922
1994—Milwaukee (A.L.)	S-2-DH-3	97	285	47	68	19	0	11	46	.239	38	75	12	151	336	†20	.961
1995—Milwaukee (A.L.)	SS-DH-3B	112	338	62	74	23	3	11	49	.219	37	83	16	164	335	15	.971
1996—Milwaukee (A.L.)	SS	154	552	90	143	33	7	24	95	.259	66	145	17	243	460	*37	.950
1997—Milwaukee (A.L.)	SS-DH	136	494	58	125	23	1	17	58	.253	39	109	19	208	383	20	.967
— Beloit (Midwest)	SS	2	6	3	3	1	0	0	1	.500	2	1	0	1	8	0	1.000
1998—Milwaukee (N.L.)	SS-DH	151	428	65	96	24	0	16	49	.224	63	105	10	173	370	21	.963
American League totals (6 years)		522	1725	268	423	99	13	64	256	.245	187	428	65	787	1566	99	.960
National League totals (1 year)		151	428	65	96	24	0	16	49	.224	63	105	10	173	370	21	.963
Major league totals (7 years)		673	2153	333	519	123	13	80	305	.241	250	533	75	960	1936	120	.960

V

VAN POPPEL, TODD   P

PERSONAL: Born December 9, 1971, in Hinsdale, Ill. ... 6-5/210. ... Throws right, bats right. ... Full name: Todd Matthew Van Poppel.

HIGH SCHOOL: St. Martin (Arlington, Texas).

TRANSACTIONS/CAREER NOTES: Selected by Oakland Athletics organization in first round (14th pick overall) of free-agent draft (June 4, 1990); pick received as part of compensation for Milwaukee Brewers signing Type A free-agent DH Dave Parker. ... On disabled list (May 28-September 11, 1992). ... Claimed on waivers by Detroit Tigers (August 6, 1996). ... Claimed on waivers by California Angels (November 12, 1996). ... Released by Angels (March 26, 1997). ... Signed by Kansas City Royals organization (April 17, 1997). ... Released by Royals organization (June 6, 1997). ... Signed by Texas Rangers organization (June 20, 1997). ... Traded by Rangers with 2B Warren Morris to Pittsburgh Pirates for P Esteban Loaiza (July 17, 1998). ... Granted free agency (October 15, 1998).

Year Team (League)	W	L	Pct.	ERA	G	GS	CG	ShO	Sv.	IP	H	R	ER	BB	SO
1990—S. Oregon (N'west)	1	1	.500	1.13	5	5	0	0	0	24	10	5	3	9	32
— Madison (Midwest)	2	1	.667	3.95	3	3	0	0	0	13 2/3	8	11	6	10	17
1991—Huntsville (Southern)	6	*13	.316	3.47	24	24	1	1	0	132 1/3	118	69	51	90	115
— Oakland (A.L.)	0	0	...	9.64	1	1	0	0	0	4 2/3	7	5	5	2	6
1992—Tacoma (PCL)	4	2	.667	3.97	9	9	0	0	0	45 1/3	44	22	20	35	29
1993—Tacoma (PCL)	4	8	.333	5.83	16	16	0	0	0	78 2/3	67	53	51	54	71
— Oakland (A.L.)	6	6	.500	5.04	16	16	0	0	0	84	76	50	47	62	47
1994—Oakland (A.L.)	7	10	.412	6.09	23	23	0	0	0	116 2/3	108	80	79	•89	83
1995—Oakland (A.L.)	4	8	.333	4.88	36	14	1	0	0	138 1/3	125	77	75	56	122
1996—Oakland (A.L.)	1	5	.167	7.71	28	6	0	0	1	63	86	56	54	33	37
— Detroit (A.L.)■	2	4	.333	11.39	9	9	1	1	0	36 1/3	53	51	46	29	16
1997—Omaha (Am. Assoc.)■	1	5	.167	8.03	11	6	0	0	0	50	36	33		24	27
— Charlotte (Fla. St.)■	0	4	.000	4.04	6	6	2	0	0	35 2/3	36	19	16	10	33
— Tulsa (Texas)	3	3	.500	5.06	7	7	0	0	0	42 2/3	53	27	24	15	26

Year— Team (League)	W	L	Pct.	ERA	G	GS	CG	ShO	Sv.	IP	H	R	ER	BB	SO
1998— Tulsa (Texas)■	0	0	. . .	4.50	1	1	0	0	0	4	2	2	2	4	2
— Oklahoma (Pacific Coast)	5	5	.500	3.72	15	13	2	0	0	87	88	44	36	25	69
— Texas (A.L.)	1	2	.333	8.84	4	4	0	0	0	19 1/3	26	20	19	10	10
— Pittsburgh (N.L.)■	1	2	.333	5.36	18	7	0	0	0	47	53	32	28	18	32
A.L. totals (6 years)	21	35	.375	6.33	117	73	2	1	1	462 1/3	481	339	325	281	321
N.L. totals (1 year)	1	2	.333	5.36	18	7	0	0	0	47	53	32	28	18	32
Major league totals (6 years)	22	37	.373	6.24	135	80	2	1	1	509 1/3	534	371	353	299	353

VanRYN, BEN   P

PERSONAL: Born August 9, 1971, in Fort Wayne, Ind. ... 6-5/185. ... Throws left, bats left. ... Full name: Benjamin Ashley VanRyn. ... Name pronounced van-RIN.
HIGH SCHOOL: East Noble (Kendallville, Ind.).
TRANSACTIONS/CAREER NOTES: Selected by Montreal Expos organization in supplemental round ("sandwich pick" between first and second round, 37th pick overall) of free-agent draft (June 4, 1990); pick received as part of compensation for New York Yankees signing Type A free-agent P Pascual Perez. ... On Sumter disabled list (July 25-August 1, 1991). ... Traded by Expos organization to Los Angeles Dodgers organization for OF Marc Griffin (December 10, 1991). ... Traded by Dodgers to Cincinnati Reds for P William Brunson (December 16, 1994). ... Claimed on waivers by California Angels (May 9, 1995). ... Traded by Angels to St. Louis Cardinals for C Pat Borders (June 15, 1996). ... Claimed on waivers by Atlanta Braves (October 10, 1996). ... Released by Braves (December 19, 1996). ... Signed by Chicago Cubs organization (January 8, 1997). ... Granted free agency (October 15, 1997). ... Signed by Chicago Cubs organization (January 8, 1998). ... Traded by Cubs to San Diego Padres for P Don Wengert (May 5, 1998). ... Claimed on waivers by Toronto Blue Jays (May 29, 1998). ... Granted free agency (October 15, 1998).
HONORS: Named Texas League Pitcher of the Year (1993).

Year— Team (League)	W	L	Pct.	ERA	G	GS	CG	ShO	Sv.	IP	H	R	ER	BB	SO
1990— GC Expos (GCL)	5	3	.625	1.74	10	9	0	0	0	51 2/3	44	13	10	15	56
1991— Sumter (S. Atl.)	2	13	.133	6.50	20	20	0	0	0	109 1/3	122	96	79	61	77
— Jamestown (NYP)	3	3	.500	5.01	6	6	1	0	0	32 1/3	37	19	18	12	23
1992— Vero Beach (FSL)■	10	7	.588	3.20	26	25	1	1	0	137 2/3	125	58	49	54	108
1993— San Antonio (Tex.)	*14	4	.778	*2.21	21	21	1	0	0	134 1/3	118	43	33	37	144
— Albuquerque (PCL)	1	4	.200	10.73	6	6	0	0	0	24 1/3	35	30	29	17	9
1994— Albuquerque (PCL)	4	1	.800	6.39	12	9	0	0	0	50 2/3	75	42	36	24	44
— San Antonio (Tex.)	8	3	.727	2.99	17	17	0	0	0	102 1/3	93	42	34	35	72
1995— Chattanooga (Southern)■	0	1	.000	9.24	5	3	0	0	0	12 2/3	22	18	13	6	6
— Vancouver (PCL)■	2	0	1.000	3.07	11	5	0	0	0	29 1/3	29	10	10	9	20
— Midland (Texas)	1	1	.500	2.78	19	0	0	0	1	32 1/3	33	10	10	12	24
1996— Vancouver (PCL)	3	3	.500	3.89	18	1	0	0	0	34 2/3	35	17	15	13	28
— California (A.L.)	0	0	. . .	0.00	1	0	0	0	0	1	1	0	0	1	0
— Louisville (A.A.)	4	6	.400	4.88	19	10	0	0	1	66 1/3	69	43	36	27	42
1997— Iowa (Am. Assoc.)	2	2	.500	4.59	51	5	0	0	3	80 1/3	88	43	41	25	64
1998— Chicago (N.L.)	0	0	. . .	3.38	9	0	0	0	0	8	9	3	3	6	6
— San Diego (N.L.)■	0	1	.000	10.13	6	0	0	0	0	2 2/3	3	3	3	4	1
— Toronto (A.L.)■	0	1	.000	9.00	10	0	0	0	0	4	6	4	4	2	3
— Syracuse (Int'l)	2	1	.667	3.51	30	0	0	0	2	41	34	16	16	13	30
A.L. totals (2 years)	0	1	.000	7.20	11	0	0	0	0	5	7	4	4	3	3
N.L. totals (1 year)	0	1	.000	5.06	15	0	0	0	0	10 2/3	12	6	6	10	7
Major league totals (2 years)	0	2	.000	5.74	26	0	0	0	0	15 2/3	19	10	10	13	10

VANDER WAL, JOHN   OF   PADRES

PERSONAL: Born April 29, 1966, in Grand Rapids, Mich. ... 6-2/197. ... Bats left, throws left. ... Full name: John Henry Vander Wal.
HIGH SCHOOL: Hudsonville (Mich.).
COLLEGE: Western Michigan.
TRANSACTIONS/CAREER NOTES: Selected by Houston Astros organization in eighth round of free-agent draft (June 4, 1984); did not sign. ... Selected by Montreal Expos organization in third round of free-agent draft (June 2, 1987). ... Contract sold by Expos with OF Ronnie Hall to Colorado Rockies (March 31, 1994). ... Traded by Rockies to San Diego Padres for a player to be named later (August 31, 1998). ... Granted free agency (October 26, 1998). ... Re-signed by Padres (November 13, 1998).
RECORDS: Holds major league single-season record for most hits by pinch hitter—28 (1995).

Year— Team (League)	Pos.	G	AB	R	H	2B	3B	HR	RBI	Avg.	BB	SO	SB	PO	A	E	Avg.
1987— Jamestown (NYP)	OF	18	69	24	33	12	3	3	15	.478	3	14	3	20	0	0	1.000
— W.P. Beach (FSL)	OF	50	189	29	54	11	2	2	22	.286	30	25	8	103	1	3	.972
1988— W.P. Beach (FSL)	OF	62	231	50	64	15	2	10	33	.277	32	40	11	109	3	1	.991
— Jacksonville (Sou.)	OF	58	208	22	54	14	0	3	14	.260	17	49	3	99	0	0	1.000
1989— Jacksonville (Sou.)	OF	71	217	30	55	9	2	6	24	.253	22	51	2	72	3	1	.987
1990— Indianapolis (A.A.)	OF	51	135	16	40	6	0	2	14	.296	13	28	0	48	4	2	.963
— Jacksonville (Sou.)	OF	77	277	45	84	25	3	8	40	.303	39	46	6	106	4	1	.991
1991— Indianapolis (A.A.)	OF	133	478	84	140	36	8	15	71	.293	79	118	8	197	7	1	*.995
— Montreal (N.L.)	OF	21	61	4	13	4	1	1	8	.213	1	18	0	29	0	0	1.000
1992— Montreal (N.L.)	OF-1B	105	213	21	51	8	2	4	20	.239	24	36	3	122	6	2	.985
1993— Montreal (N.L.)	1B-OF	106	215	34	50	7	4	5	30	.233	27	30	6	271	14	4	.986
1994— Colorado (N.L.)■	1B-OF	91	110	12	27	3	1	5	15	.245	16	31	2	106	3	0	1.000
1995— Colorado (N.L.)	1B-OF	105	101	15	35	8	1	5	21	.347	16	23	1	51	4	2	.965
1996— Colorado (N.L.)	1B-OF	104	151	20	38	6	2	5	31	.252	19	38	2	72	2	1	.987
1997— Colorado (N.L.)	OF-1B-DH	76	92	7	16	2	0	1	14	.174	10	33	1	38	0	1	.974
— Colo. Springs (PCL)	1B-OF	25	103	29	42	12	1	3	19	.408	11	28	1	158	10	4	.977
1998— Colorado (N.L.)	OF-DH-1B	89	104	18	30	10	1	5	20	.288	16	29	0	29	3	0	1.000
— San Diego (N.L.)■	OF-1B	20	25	3	6	3	0	0	0	.240	6	5	0	21	2	0	1.000
Major league totals (8 years)		717	1072	134	266	51	12	31	156	.248	135	243	15	739	34	10	.987

V

DIVISION SERIES RECORD

RECORDS: Shares career record for most triples—1.

Year Team (League)	Pos.	G	AB	R	H	2B	3B	HR	RBI	Avg.	BB	SO	SB	PO	A	E	Avg.
						BATTING									FIELDING		
1995— Colorado (N.L.)	PH	4	4	0	0	0	0	0	0	.000	0	2	0	...	...	...	...
1998— San Diego (N.L.)	PH	3	3	1	1	0	1	0	2	.333	0	1	0	...	...	...	...
Division series totals (2 years)		7	7	1	1	0	1	0	2	.143	0	3	0	0	0	0	...

CHAMPIONSHIP SERIES RECORD

Year Team (League)	Pos.	G	AB	R	H	2B	3B	HR	RBI	Avg.	BB	SO	SB	PO	A	E	Avg.
						BATTING									FIELDING		
1998— San Diego (N.L.)	OF-PH	3	7	1	3	0	0	1	2	.429	0	2	0	5	1	0	1.000

WORLD SERIES RECORD

Year Team (League)	Pos.	G	AB	R	H	2B	3B	HR	RBI	Avg.	BB	SO	SB	PO	A	E	Avg.
						BATTING									FIELDING		
1998— San Diego (N.L.)	OF-PH	4	5	0	2	1	0	0	0	.400	0	2	0	1	0	0	1.000

VARITEK, JASON   C   RED SOX

PERSONAL: Born April 11, 1972, in Rochester, Minn. ... 6-2/210. ... Bats both, throws right. ... Full name: Jason A. Varitek.

HIGH SCHOOL: Lake Brantley (Longwood, Fla.).

COLLEGE: Georgia Tech.

TRANSACTIONS/CAREER NOTES: Selected by Minnesota Twins organization first round (21st pick overall) of free-agent draft (June 3, 1993); did not sign. ... Selected by Seattle Mariners organization in first round (14th pick overall) of free-agent draft (June 2, 1994). ... Traded by Mariners with P Derek Lowe to Boston Red Sox for P Heathcliff Slocumb (July 31, 1997).

STATISTICAL NOTES: Tied for Southern League lead in double plays by catcher with 10 in 1996. ... Led Southern League catchers with .993 fielding percentage and tied for lead with 10 double plays in 1996.

Year Team (League)	Pos.	G	AB	R	H	2B	3B	HR	RBI	Avg.	BB	SO	SB	PO	A	E	Avg.
						BATTING									FIELDING		
1995— Port City (Southern)...	C	104	352	42	79	14	3	10	44	.224	61	126	0	589	59	8	.988
1996— Port City (Southern)...	C-3B-OF	134	503	63	132	34	1	12	67	.262	66	93	7	663	79	5	*.993
1997— Tacoma (PCL)	C	87	307	54	78	13	0	15	48	.254	34	71	0	613	49	3	*.995
—Pawtucket (Int'l)■......	C	20	66	6	13	5	0	1	5	.197	8	12	0	123	10	1	.993
—Boston (A.L.).............	C	1	1	0	1	0	0	0	0	1.000	0	0	0	1	0	0	1.000
1998— Boston (A.L.)	C-DH	86	221	31	56	13	0	7	33	.253	17	45	2	367	32	5	.988
Major league totals (2 years)		87	222	31	57	13	0	7	33	.257	17	45	2	368	32	5	.988

DIVISION SERIES RECORD

Year Team (League)	Pos.	G	AB	R	H	2B	3B	HR	RBI	Avg.	BB	SO	SB	PO	A	E	Avg.
						BATTING									FIELDING		
1998— Boston (A.L.)	C	1	4	0	1	0	0	0	1	.250	0	1	0	5	0	0	1.000

VAUGHN, GREG   OF   PADRES

PERSONAL: Born July 3, 1965, in Sacramento. ... 6-0/202. ... Bats right, throws right. ... Full name: Gregory Lamont Vaughn. ... Cousin of Mo Vaughn, first baseman, Anaheim Angels; and cousin of Jerry Royster, infielder with five major league teams (1973-1988); and current manager of Las Vegas Stars of Pacific Coast League.

HIGH SCHOOL: John F. Kennedy (Sacramento).

JUNIOR COLLEGE: Sacramento City College.

COLLEGE: Miami (Fla.).

TRANSACTIONS/CAREER NOTES: Selected by St. Louis Cardinals organization in fifth round of free-agent draft (January 17, 1984); did not sign. ... Selected by Milwaukee Brewers organization in secondary phase of free-agent draft (June 4, 1984); did not sign. ... Selected by Pittsburgh Pirates organization in secondary phase of free-agent draft (January 9, 1985); did not sign. ... Selected by California Angels organization in secondary phase of free-agent draft (June 3, 1985); did not sign. ... Selected by Brewers organization in secondary phase of free-agent draft (June 2, 1986). ... On disabled list (May 26-June 10, 1990). ... On Milwaukee disabled list (April 8-27, 1994); included rehabilitation assignment to Beloit (April 25-27). ... Traded by Brewers with a player to be named later to San Diego Padres for P Bryce Florie, P Ron Villone and OF Marc Newfield (July 31, 1996); Padres acquired OF Gerald Parent to complete deal (September 16, 1996). ... Granted free agency (October 28, 1996). ... Re-signed by Padres (December 19, 1996). ... Traded by Padres with P Kerry Taylor and P Chris Clark to New York Yankees for P Kenny Rogers, IF Mariano Duncan and P Kevin Henthorne (July 4, 1997); trade later voided because Vaughn failed physical (July 6, 1997).

HONORS: Named Midwest League co-Most Valuable Player (1987). ... Named American Association Most Valuable Player (1989). ... Named N.L. Comeback Player of the Year by THE SPORTING NEWS (1998). ... Named outfielder on THE SPORTING NEWS N.L. All-Star team (1998). ... Named outfielder on THE SPORTING NEWS N.L. Silver Slugger team (1998).

STATISTICAL NOTES: Led Midwest League with 292 total bases in 1987. ... Led Texas League with 279 total bases in 1988. ... Led American Association with .548 slugging percentage in 1989. ... Career major league grand slams: 4.

Year Team (League)	Pos.	G	AB	R	H	2B	3B	HR	RBI	Avg.	BB	SO	SB	PO	A	E	Avg.
						BATTING									FIELDING		
1986— Helena (Pioneer)	OF	66	258	64	75	13	2	16	54	.291	30	69	23	99	5	3	.972
1987— Beloit (Midwest)........	OF	139	492	*120	150	31	6	*33	105	.305	102	115	36	247	11	10	.963
1988— El Paso (Texas)............	OF	131	505	*104	152	*39	2	*28	*105	.301	63	120	22	216	12	7	.970
1989— Denver (A.A.).............	OF	110	387	74	107	17	5	*26	*92	.276	62	94	20	140	4	3	.980
—Milwaukee (A.L.)	OF-DH	38	113	18	30	3	0	5	23	.265	13	23	4	32	1	2	.943
1990— Milwaukee (A.L.)	OF-DH	120	382	51	84	26	2	17	61	.220	33	91	7	195	8	7	.967
1991— Milwaukee (A.L.)	OF-DH	145	542	81	132	24	5	27	98	.244	62	125	2	315	5	2	.994
1992— Milwaukee (A.L.)	OF-DH	141	501	77	114	18	2	23	78	.228	60	123	15	288	6	3	.990
1993— Milwaukee (A.L.)	OF-DH	154	569	97	152	28	2	30	97	.267	89	118	10	214	1	3	.986
1994— Milwaukee (A.L.)	OF-DH	95	370	59	94	24	1	19	55	.254	51	93	9	162	5	3	.982
—Beloit (Midwest)........	DH	2	6	1	1	0	0	0	0	.167	4	1	0	...	...	...	...

Year Team (League)	Pos.	G	AB	R	H	2B	3B	HR	RBI	Avg.	BB	SO	SB	PO	A	E	Avg.
1995— Milwaukee (A.L.)........	DH	108	392	67	88	19	1	17	59	.224	55	89	10	...	...	...	...
1996— Milwaukee (A.L.)........	OF-DH	102	375	78	105	16	0	31	95	.280	58	99	5	192	5	4	.980
— San Diego (N.L.)■....	OF	43	141	20	29	3	1	10	22	.206	24	31	4	74	2	2	.974
1997— San Diego (N.L.)	OF-DH	120	361	60	78	10	0	18	57	.216	56	110	7	153	7	1	.994
1998— San Diego (N.L.)	OF-DH	158	573	112	156	28	4	50	119	.272	79	121	11	270	5	2	.993
American League totals (8 years)		903	3244	528	799	158	13	169	566	.246	421	761	62	1398	31	24	.983
National League totals (3 years)		321	1075	192	263	41	5	78	198	.245	159	262	22	497	14	5	.990
Major league totals (10 years)		1224	4319	720	1062	199	18	247	764	.246	580	1023	84	1895	45	29	.985

DIVISION SERIES RECORD

Year Team (League)	Pos.	G	AB	R	H	2B	3B	HR	RBI	Avg.	BB	SO	SB	PO	A	E	Avg.
1996— San Diego (N.L.)	PH	3	3	0	0	0	0	0	0	.000	0	1	0	...	...	...	...
1998— San Diego (N.L.)	OF	4	15	2	5	1	0	1	1	.333	0	4	0	2	0	0	1.000
Division series totals (2 years)		7	18	2	5	1	0	1	1	.278	0	5	0	2	0	0	1.000

CHAMPIONSHIP SERIES RECORD

Year Team (League)	Pos.	G	AB	R	H	2B	3B	HR	RBI	Avg.	BB	SO	SB	PO	A	E	Avg.
1998— San Diego (N.L.)	OF-PH	3	8	1	2	0	0	0	0	.250	1	1	0	2	0	0	1.000

WORLD SERIES RECORD

Year Team (League)	Pos.	G	AB	R	H	2B	3B	HR	RBI	Avg.	BB	SO	SB	PO	A	E	Avg.
1998— San Diego (N.L.)	OF-DH	4	15	3	2	0	0	2	4	.133	1	2	0	4	0	1	.800

ALL-STAR GAME RECORD

Year League	Pos.	AB	R	H	2B	3B	HR	RBI	Avg.	BB	SO	SB	PO	A	E	Avg.
1993— American..................	OF	1	1	1	0	0	0	0	1.000	0	0	0	0	0	0	...
1996— American..................							Did not play.									
1998— National.....................	OF	1	0	1	0	0	0	2	1.000	0	0	0	0	0	0	...
All-Star Game totals (2 years)		2	1	2	0	0	0	2	1.000	0	0	0	0	0	0	...

VAUGHN, MO   1B   ANGELS

PERSONAL: Born December 15, 1967, in Norwalk, Conn. ... 6-1/240. ... Bats left, throws right. ... Full name: Maurice Samuel Vaughn.

HIGH SCHOOL: Trinity Pawling Prep (Pawling, N.Y.).

COLLEGE: Seton Hall.

TRANSACTIONS/CAREER NOTES: Selected by Boston Red Sox organization in first round (23rd pick overall) of free-agent draft (June 9, 1989). ... On disabled list (June 17-July 10, 1997). ... Granted free agency (October 23, 1998). ... Signed by Anaheim Angels (December 11, 1998).

HONORS: Named first baseman on THE SPORTING NEWS A.L. All-Star team (1995). ... Named first baseman on THE SPORTING NEWS A.L. Silver Slugger team (1995). ... Named A.L. Most Valuable Player by Baseball Writers' Association of America (1995).

STATISTICAL NOTES: Led A.L. with 20 intentional bases on balls received in 1994. ... Led A.L. first basemen with 103 double plays in 1994. ... Led A.L. first basemen with 1,368 total chances and 128 double plays in 1995. ... Hit three home runs in one game (September 24, 1996 and May 30, 1997). ... Had 16-game hitting streak (September 13-27, 1998). ... Career major league grand slams: 7.

Year Team (League)	Pos.	G	AB	R	H	2B	3B	HR	RBI	Avg.	BB	SO	SB	PO	A	E	Avg.
1989— New Britain (East.)	1B	73	245	28	68	15	0	8	38	.278	25	47	1	541	45	•10	.983
1990— Pawtucket (Int'l).........	1B	108	386	62	114	26	1	22	72	.295	44	87	3	828	60	11	.988
1991— Pawtucket (Int'l).........	1B	69	234	35	64	10	0	14	50	.274	60	44	2	432	24	3	.993
— Boston (A.L.)...........	1B-DH	74	219	21	57	12	0	4	32	.260	26	43	2	378	26	6	.985
1992— Boston (A.L.)...........	1B-DH	113	355	42	83	16	2	13	57	.234	47	67	3	741	57	*15	.982
— Pawtucket (Int'l)........	1B	39	149	15	42	6	0	6	28	.282	18	35	1	368	15	8	.980
1993— Boston (A.L.)...........	1B-DH	152	539	86	160	34	1	29	101	.297	79	130	4	1110	70	*16	.987
1994— Boston (A.L.)...........	1B-DH	111	394	65	122	25	1	26	82	.310	57	112	4	880	57	10	.989
1995— Boston (A.L.)...........	1B-DH	140	550	98	165	28	3	39	•126	.300	68	*150	11	*1262	95	11	.992
1996— Boston (A.L.)...........	1B-DH	161	635	118	207	29	1	44	143	.326	95	154	2	1207	74	*15	.988
1997— Boston (A.L.)...........	1B-DH	141	527	91	166	24	0	35	96	.315	86	154	2	1088	75	*14	.988
1998— Boston (A.L.)...........	1B-DH	154	609	107	205	31	2	40	115	.337	61	144	0	1176	90	12	.991
Major league totals (8 years)		1046	3828	628	1165	199	10	230	752	.304	519	954	28	7842	544	99	.988

DIVISION SERIES RECORD

RECORDS: Shares single-game records for most home runs—2 (September 29, 1998); and most runs batted in—7 (September 29, 1998).

NOTES: Shares postseason single-game record for most runs batted in—7 (September 29, 1998).

Year Team (League)	Pos.	G	AB	R	H	2B	3B	HR	RBI	Avg.	BB	SO	SB	PO	A	E	Avg.
1995— Boston (A.L.)..............	1B	3	14	0	0	0	0	0	0	.000	1	7	0	27	2	0	1.000
1998— Boston (A.L.)..............	1B	4	17	3	7	2	0	2	7	.412	1	5	0	30	4	0	1.000
Division series totals (2 years)		7	31	3	7	2	0	2	7	.226	2	12	0	57	6	0	1.000

ALL-STAR GAME RECORD

NOTES: Named to A.L. All-Star team for 1998 game; replaced by Rafael Palmeiro due to injury.

Year League	Pos.	AB	R	H	2B	3B	HR	RBI	Avg.	BB	SO	SB	PO	A	E	Avg.
1995— American..................	1B	2	0	0	0	0	0	0	.000	0	2	0	4	0	0	1.000
1998— American..................							Selected, did not play—injured.									

VAZQUEZ, JAVIER P EXPOS

PERSONAL: Born July 25, 1976, in Ponce, Puerto Rico. ... 6-2/190. ... Throws right, bats right. ... Full name: Javier Carlos Vazquez.
HIGH SCHOOL: Colegio de Ponce (Ponce, Puerto Rico).
TRANSACTIONS/CAREER NOTES: Selected by Montreal Expos organization in fifth round of free-agent draft (June 2, 1994).

Year Team (League)	W	L	Pct.	ERA	G	GS	CG	ShO	Sv.	IP	H	R	ER	BB	SO
1994—G.C. Expos (GCL)	5	2	.714	2.53	15	11	1	1	0	67 2/3	37	25	19	15	56
1995—Albany (S. Atl.)	6	6	.500	5.08	21	21	1	0	0	102 2/3	109	67	58	47	87
1996—Delmarva (S. Atl.)	14	3	*.824	2.68	27	27	1	0	0	164 1/3	138	64	49	57	173
1997—Harrisburg (Eastern)	4	0	1.000	1.07	6	6	1	0	0	42	15	5	5	12	47
—W.P. Beach (FSL)	6	3	.667	2.16	19	19	1	0	0	112 2/3	98	40	27	28	100
1998—Montreal (N.L.)	5	15	.250	6.06	33	32	0	0	0	172 1/3	196	121	116	68	139
Major league totals (1 year)	5	15	.250	6.06	33	32	0	0	0	172 1/3	196	121	116	68	139

VELANDIA, JORGE SS ATHLETICS

PERSONAL: Born January 12, 1975, in Caracas, Venezuela. ... 5-9/160. ... Bats right, throws right. ... Full name: Jorge Macias Velandia.
TRANSACTIONS/CAREER NOTES: Signed as non-drafted free agent by Detroit Tigers organization (January 15, 1992). ... Traded by Tigers organization with 3B Scott Livingstone to San Diego Padres organization for P Gene Harris (May 11, 1994). ... Traded by Padres with P Doug Bochtler to Oakland Athletics for P Don Wengert and IF David Newhan (November 26, 1997).
STATISTICAL NOTES: Led Pacific Coast League shortstop with 648 total chances and 93 double plays in 1998.

Year Team (League)	Pos.	G	AB	R	H	2B	3B	HR	RBI	Avg.	BB	SO	SB	PO	A	E	Avg.
1992—Bristol (Appal.)	SS-2B	45	119	20	24	6	1	0	9	.202	15	16	3	54	88	12	.922
1993—Niagara Falls (NYP)	SS	72	212	30	41	11	0	1	22	.193	19	48	22	82	186	24	.918
—Fayetteville (SAL)	SS-2B-3B	37	106	15	17	4	0	0	11	.160	13	21	5	47	94	9	.940
1994—Lakeland (Fla. St.)	SS-2B	22	60	8	14	4	0	0	3	.233	6	14	0	40	56	4	.960
—Springfield (Midw.)■	SS-2B	98	290	42	71	14	0	4	36	.245	21	46	5	118	303	26	.942
1995—Memphis (Sou.)	SS	63	186	23	38	10	2	4	17	.204	14	37	0	88	152	12	.952
—Las Vegas (PCL)	SS	66	206	25	54	12	3	0	25	.262	13	37	0	97	190	*31	.903
1996—Memphis (Sou.)	SS	122	392	42	94	19	0	9	48	.240	31	65	3	173	368	33	.943
1997—Las Vegas (PCL)	SS	114	405	46	110	15	2	3	35	.272	29	62	13	170	*347	21	.961
—San Diego (N.L.)	SS-2B-3B	14	29	0	3	2	0	0	0	.103	1	7	0	11	23	3	.919
1998—Oakland (A.L.)■	SS-2B	8	4	0	1	0	0	0	0	.250	0	1	0	4	10	1	.933
—Edmonton (PCL)	SS	128	488	64	140	35	1	6	57	.287	37	52	8	203	*428	17	.974
American League totals (1 year)		8	4	0	1	0	0	0	0	.250	0	1	0	4	10	1	.933
National League totals (1 year)		14	29	0	3	2	0	0	0	.103	1	7	0	11	23	3	.919
Major league totals (2 years)		22	33	0	4	2	0	0	0	.121	1	8	0	15	33	4	.923

V

VELARDE, RANDY 2B ANGELS

PERSONAL: Born November 24, 1962, in Midland, Texas. ... 6-0/200. ... Bats right, throws right. ... Full name: Randy Lee Velarde. ... Name pronounced vel-ARE-dee.
HIGH SCHOOL: Robert E. Lee (Midland, Texas).
COLLEGE: Lubbock (Texas) Christian College.
TRANSACTIONS/CAREER NOTES: Selected by Chicago White Sox organization in 19th round of free-agent draft (June 3, 1985). ... Traded by White Sox organization with P Pete Filson to New York Yankees for P Scott Nielsen and IF Mike Soper (January 5, 1987). ... On New York disabled list (August 9-29, 1989). ... On New York disabled list (June 6-July 30, 1993); included rehabilitation assignment to Albany/Colonie (July 24-30). ... Granted free agency (December 23, 1994). ... Re-signed by Oneonta, Yankees organization (April 12, 1995). ... Granted free agency (November 2, 1995). ... Signed by California Angels (November 21, 1995). ... Angels franchise renamed Anaheim Angels for 1997 season. ... On disabled list (March 23-September 1 and September 2, 1997-remainder of season). ... On Anaheim disabled list (March 19-May 13 and May 16-August 3, 1998); included rehabilitation assignments to Lake Elsinore (May 7-13) and Vancouver (July 29-August 3). ... Granted free agency (October 23, 1998). ... Re-signed by Angels (December 7, 1998).
STATISTICAL NOTES: Led Midwest League shortstops with 52 errors in 1986. ... Had 21-game hitting streak (June 9-July 4, 1996). ... Career major league grand slams: 1.

Year Team (League)	Pos.	G	AB	R	H	2B	3B	HR	RBI	Avg.	BB	SO	SB	PO	A	E	Avg.
1985—Niagara Falls (NYP)	O-S-2-3	67	218	28	48	7	3	1	16	.220	35	72	8	124	117	15	.941
1986—Appleton (Midwest)	SS-3B-OF	124	417	55	105	31	4	11	50	.252	58	96	13	205	300	†54	.903
—Buffalo (A.A.)	SS	9	20	2	4	1	0	0	2	.200	2	4	1	9	28	3	.925
1987—Alb./Colon. (East.)■	SS-OF	71	263	40	83	20	2	7	32	.316	25	47	8	128	254	17	.957
—Columbus (Int'l)	SS	49	185	21	59	10	6	5	33	.319	15	36	8	100	164	16	.943
—New York (A.L.)	SS	8	22	1	4	0	0	0	1	.182	0	6	0	8	20	2	.933
1988—Columbus (Int'l)	SS-2B-3B	78	293	39	79	23	4	5	37	.270	25	71	7	123	271	25	.940
—New York (A.L.)	2B-SS-3B	48	115	18	20	6	0	5	12	.174	8	24	1	72	98	8	.955
1989—Columbus (Int'l)	SS-3B	103	387	59	103	26	3	11	53	.266	38	105	3	150	295	22	.953
—New York (A.L.)	3B-SS	33	100	12	34	4	2	2	11	.340	7	14	0	26	61	4	.956
1990—New York (A.L.)	3-S-O-2-DH	95	229	21	48	6	2	5	19	.210	20	53	0	70	159	12	.950
1991—New York (A.L.)	3B-SS-OF	80	184	19	45	11	1	1	15	.245	18	43	3	64	148	15	.934
1992—New York (A.L.)	S-3-O-2	121	412	57	112	24	1	7	46	.272	38	78	7	179	257	15	.967
1993—New York (A.L.)	O-S-3-DH	85	226	28	68	13	2	7	24	.301	18	39	2	102	92	9	.956
—Alb./Colon. (East.)	SS-OF	5	17	2	4	0	0	1	2	.235	2	2	0	6	12	2	.900
1994—New York (A.L.)	S-3-O-2	77	280	47	78	16	1	9	34	.279	22	61	4	92	188	19	.936
1995—New York (A.L.)	2-S-O-3	111	367	60	102	19	1	7	46	.278	55	64	5	168	258	10	.977
1996—California (A.L.)■	2B-3B-SS	136	530	82	151	27	3	14	54	.285	70	118	7	255	306	16	.972
1997—Anaheim (A.L.)	PR	1	0	0	0	0	0	0	0	...	0	0	0	...	...	...	...
1998—Lake Elsinore (Calif.)	2B	5	20	6	11	2	1	1	7	.550	2	1	0	10	18	1	.966
—Anaheim (A.L.)	2B	51	188	29	49	13	1	4	26	.261	34	42	7	88	132	4	.982
—Vancouver (PCL)	2B	4	16	0	4	2	0	0	2	.250	1	4	1	3	7	0	1.000
Major league totals (12 years)		846	2653	374	711	139	14	61	288	.268	290	542	36	1124	1719	114	.961

Year	Team (League)	Pos.	G	AB	R	H	2B	3B	HR	RBI	Avg.	BB	SO	SB	PO	A	E	Avg.
1995—	New York (A.L.)..........	2B-3B-OF	5	17	3	3	0	0	0	1	.176	6	4	0	15	11	1	.963

VENAFRO, MIKE   P   RANGERS

PERSONAL: Born August 2, 1973, in Takoma Park, Md. ... 5-10/170. ... Throws left, bats left. ... Full name: Michael R. Venafro.
HIGH SCHOOL: Paul VI (Fairfax, Va.).
TRANSACTIONS/CAREER NOTES: Selected by Texas Rangers organization in 29th round of free-agent draft (June 1, 1995).

Year	Team (League)	W	L	Pct.	ERA	G	GS	CG	ShO	Sv.	IP	H	R	ER	BB	SO
1995—	Hudson Valley (NYP).........	9	1	.900	2.13	32	0	0	0	2	50²/₃	37	13	12	21	32
1996—	Charleston, S.C. (SAL)	1	3	.250	3.51	50	0	0	0	19	59	57	27	23	21	62
1997—	Charlotte (Fla. St.)..............	4	2	.667	3.43	35	0	0	0	10	44²/₃	51	17	17	21	35
—	Tulsa (Texas)....................	0	1	.000	3.45	11	0	0	0	1	15²/₃	13	12	6	12	13
1998—	Tulsa (Texas)	3	4	.429	3.10	46	0	0	0	14	52¹/₃	42	21	18	26	45
—	Okla. City (PCL).................	0	0	. . .	6.35	13	0	0	0	0	17	19	12	12	10	15

VENTURA, ROBIN   3B   METS

PERSONAL: Born July 14, 1967, in Santa Maria, Calif. ... 6-1/198. ... Bats left, throws right. ... Full name: Robin Mark Ventura.
HIGH SCHOOL: Righetti (Santa Maria, Calif.).
COLLEGE: Oklahoma State.
TRANSACTIONS/CAREER NOTES: Selected by Chicago White Sox organization in first round (10th pick overall) of free-agent draft (June 1, 1988). ... On suspended list (August 23-25, 1993). ... On disabled list (March 31-July 24, 1997); included rehabilitation assignments to Nashville (July 13-17) and Birmingham (July 18-22). ... Granted free agency (October 23, 1998). ... Signed by New York Mets (December 1, 1998).
RECORDS: Holds A.L. single-season record for fewest chances accepted by third baseman for leader—372 (1996). ... Shares major league single-game record for most grand slams—2 (September 4, 1995).
HONORS: Named College Player of the Year by THE SPORTING NEWS (1987-88). ... Named third baseman on THE SPORTING NEWS college All-America team (1987-88). ... Named Golden Spikes Award winner by USA Baseball (1988). ... Won A.L. Gold Glove at third base (1991-93, 1996 and 1998).
STATISTICAL NOTES: Led Southern League with 12 intentional bases on balls received in 1989. ... Led Southern League third basemen with .930 fielding percentage and tied for lead with 21 double plays in 1989. ... Led A.L. third basemen with 18 errors in 1991. ... Led A.L. third basemen in putouts with 134 in 1991, 141 in 1992 and 133 in 1996. ... Led A.L. third basemen in total chances with 536 in 1992, 404 in 1993 and 382 in 1996. ... Led A.L. third basemen with 372 assists and tied for lead in double plays with 29 in 1992. ... Led A.L. third basemen in double plays with 22 in 1994 and 34 in 1996 and tied for lead with 29 in 1992. ... Led A.L. with 15 intentional bases on balls in 1998. ... Led A.L. third basemen with 447 total chances and 38 double plays in 1998. ... Career major league grand slams: 10.
MISCELLANEOUS: Member of 1988 U.S. Olympic baseball team.

Year	Team (League)	Pos.	G	AB	R	H	2B	3B	HR	RBI	Avg.	BB	SO	SB	PO	A	E	Avg.
1989—	Birmingham (Sou.).....	3B-1B-2B	129	454	75	126	25	2	3	67	.278	93	51	9	108	249	27	†.930
—	Chicago (A.L.)	3B	16	45	5	8	3	0	0	7	.178	8	6	0	17	33	2	.962
1990—	Chicago (A.L.)	3B-1B	150	493	48	123	17	1	5	54	.249	55	53	1	116	268	25	.939
1991—	Chicago (A.L.)	3B-1B	157	606	92	172	25	1	23	100	.284	80	67	2	†225	291	†18	.966
1992—	Chicago (A.L.)	3B-1B	157	592	85	167	38	1	16	93	.282	93	71	2	†141	†375	23	.957
1993—	Chicago (A.L.)	3B-1B	157	554	85	145	27	1	22	94	.262	105	82	1	119	278	14	.966
1994—	Chicago (A.L.)	3B-1B-SS	109	401	57	113	15	1	18	78	.282	61	69	3	89	180	20	.931
1995—	Chicago (A.L.)	3B-1B-DH	135	492	79	145	22	0	26	93	.295	75	98	4	201	216	19	.956
1996—	Chicago (A.L.)	3B-1B	158	586	96	168	31	2	34	105	.287	78	81	1	†189	247	11	.975
1997—	Nashville (A.A.)	3B	5	15	3	6	1	0	2	5	.400	2	1	0	1	12	0	1.000
—	Birmingham (Sou.).....	3B	4	17	3	5	1	0	1	2	.294	1	1	0	2	3	2	.714
—	Chicago (A.L.)	3B	54	183	27	48	10	1	6	26	.262	34	21	0	53	99	7	.956
1998—	Chicago (A.L.)	3B	161	590	84	155	31	4	21	91	.263	79	111	1	102	*330	15	.966
Major league totals (10 years)			1254	4542	658	1244	219	12	171	741	.274	668	659	15	1252	2317	154	.959

CHAMPIONSHIP SERIES RECORD

Year	Team (League)	Pos.	G	AB	R	H	2B	3B	HR	RBI	Avg.	BB	SO	SB	PO	A	E	Avg.
1993—	Chicago (A.L.)	3B-1B	6	20	2	4	0	0	1	5	.200	6	6	0	9	6	1	.938

ALL-STAR GAME RECORD

Year	League	Pos.	AB	R	H	2B	3B	HR	RBI	Avg.	BB	SO	SB	PO	A	E	Avg.
1992—	American	3B	2	1	2	1	0	0	1	1.000	0	0	0	1	1	0	1.000

VERAS, DARIO   P   ROYALS

PERSONAL: Born March 13, 1973, in Santiago, Dominican Republic. ... 6-1/155. ... Throws right, bats right. ... Full name: Dario Antonio Veras.
HIGH SCHOOL: Juan De Jesus Pimentel (Dominican Republic).
TRANSACTIONS/CAREER NOTES: Signed as non-drafted free agent by Los Angeles Dodgers organization (May 19, 1990). ... Selected by San Diego Padres organization in Rule 5 Minor League draft (December 12, 1993). ... On San Diego disabled list (April 23-May 9, 1997). ... On San Diego disabled list (May 17-July 28, 1997); included rehabilitation assignments to Mobile (June 8-16), Rancho Cucamonga (July 7-9) and Las Vegas (July 11-28). ... Traded by Padres with P Carlos Reyes and C Mandy Romero to Boston Red Sox for C Jim Leyritz and OF Ethan Faggett (June 21, 1998). ... Claimed on waivers by Kansas City Royals (December 7, 1998).

Year	Team (League)	W	L	Pct.	ERA	G	GS	CG	ShO	Sv.	IP	H	R	ER	BB	SO
1991—	Dom. Dodgers (DSL)	4	1	.800	2.53	20	0	0	0	6	32	28	11	9	4	22
1992—	La Vega (DSL)	7	1	.875	*0.89	26	0	0	0	7	61	34	11	6	15	54
1993—	Bakersfield (California).......	1	0	1.000	7.43	7	0	0	0	0	13 1/3	13	11	11	8	11
	—Vero Beach (FSL)	2	2	.500	2.80	24	0	0	0	02	54 2/3	59	23	17	14	31
1994—	Rancho Cuca. (Cal.)■	9	2	.818	2.05	*59	0	0	0	3	79	66	28	18	25	56
1995—	Memphis (Sou.)	7	3	.700	3.81	58	0	0	0	1	82 2/3	81	38	35	27	70
1996—	Memphis (Sou.)	3	1	.750	2.32	29	0	0	0	1	42 2/3	38	14	11	9	47
	—Las Vegas (PCL)	6	2	.750	2.90	19	1	0	0	1	40 1/3	41	17	13	6	30
	—San Diego (N.L.)	3	1	.750	2.79	23	0	0	0	0	29	24	10	9	10	23
1997—	San Diego (N.L.)	2	1	.667	5.11	23	0	0	0	0	24 2/3	28	18	14	12	21
	—Las Vegas (PCL)	0	2	.000	5.02	12	0	0	0	2	14 1/3	14	8	8	6	13
	—Mobile (Southern)	0	0	...	9.00	5	2	0	0	0	5	8	5	5	3	5
	—Rancho Cuca. (Cal.)	0	0	...	6.00	2	0	0	0	1	3	3	3	2	1	3
1998—	Las Vegas (PCL)	2	1	.667	3.79	31	0	0	0	9	35 2/3	36	15	15	11	29
	—Pawtucket (Int'l)■...........	2	0	1.000	3.72	23	0	0	0	7	29	30	12	12	11	27
	—Boston (A.L.)	0	1	.000	10.13	7	0	0	0	0	8	12	9	9	7	2
A.L. totals (1 year)		0	1	.000	10.13	7	0	0	0	0	8	12	9	9	7	2
N.L. totals (2 years)		5	2	.714	3.86	46	0	0	0	0	53 2/3	52	28	23	22	44
Major league totals (3 years)		5	3	.625	4.67	53	0	0	0	0	61 2/3	64	37	32	29	46

DIVISION SERIES RECORD

Year	Team (League)	W	L	Pct.	ERA	G	GS	CG	ShO	Sv.	IP	H	R	ER	BB	SO
1996—	San Diego (N.L.)	0	0	...	0.00	2	0	0	0	0	1	1	0	0	0	1

VERAS, QUILVIO — 2B — PADRES

PERSONAL: Born April 3, 1971, in Santo Domingo, Dominican Republic. ... 5-9/166. ... Bats both, throws right. ... Full name: Quilvio Alberto Perez Veras.

HIGH SCHOOL: Victor E. Liz (Santo Domingo, Dominican Republic).

TRANSACTIONS/CAREER NOTES: Signed as non-drafted free agent by New York Mets organization (November 22, 1989). ... On suspended list (July 31-August 2, 1994). ... On disabled list (August 7-15, 1994). ... Traded by Mets to Florida Marlins for OF Carl Everett (November 29, 1994). ... On Florida disabled list (May 10-June 21, 1996); included rehabilitation assignment to Charlotte (June 13-21). ... Traded by Marlins to San Diego Padres for P Dustin Hermanson (November 21, 1996).

STATISTICAL NOTES: Tied for Appalachian League lead in double plays by second baseman with 30 in 1991. ... Led Appalachian League second basemen with 282 total chances in 1991. ... Led South Atlantic League in on-base percentage with .441 and in caught stealing with 35 in 1992. ... Led Eastern League in on-base percentage with .430 and in caught stealing with 19 in 1993. ... Led Eastern League second basemen with 669 total chances in 1993. ... Led International League in caught stealing with 18 in 1994. ... Led International League second basemen with 589 total chances and 84 double plays in 1994. ... Led N.L. in caught stealing with 21 in 1995. ... Career major league grand slams: 1.

								— BATTING —							— FIELDING —		
Year	Team (League)	Pos.	G	AB	R	H	2B	3B	HR	RBI	Avg.	BB	SO	SB	PO	A	E	Avg.
1990—	GC Mets (GCL)	2B	30	98	26	29	3	3	1	5	.296	19	16	16	45	76	3	.976
	—Kingsport (Appal.)	2B	24	94	21	36	6	0	1	14	.383	13	14	9	55	79	8	.944
1991—	Kingsport (Appal.)	2B	64	226	*54	76	11	4	1	16	.336	36	28	38	*113	*161	8	.972
	—Pittsfield (NYP)	2B-SS	5	15	3	4	0	1	0	2	.267	5	1	2	16	16	1	.970
1992—	Columbia (S. Atl.)........	2B	117	414	97	132	24	10	2	40	*.319	84	52	*66	208	313	20	.963
1993—	Binghamton (East.)	2B	128	444	87	136	19	7	2	51	.306	*91	62	52	*274	*372	23	.966
1994—	Norfolk (Int'l)	2B	123	457	71	114	22	4	0	43	.249	59	56	40	*267	*308	*14	.976
1995—	Florida (N.L.)■	2B-OF	124	440	86	115	20	7	5	32	.261	80	68	*56	299	315	9	.986
1996—	Florida (N.L.)	2B	73	253	40	64	8	1	4	14	.253	51	42	8	174	191	5	.986
	—Charlotte (Int'l)	2B	28	104	22	34	5	2	2	8	.327	13	14	8	44	66	3	.973
1997—	San Diego (N.L.)■	2B	145	539	74	143	23	1	3	45	.265	72	84	33	276	407	11	.984
1998—	San Diego (N.L.)	2B	138	517	79	138	24	2	6	45	.267	84	78	24	258	405	9	.987
Major league totals (4 years)			480	1749	279	460	75	11	18	136	.263	287	272	121	1007	1318	34	.986

DIVISION SERIES RECORD

								— BATTING —							— FIELDING —		
Year	Team (League)	Pos.	G	AB	R	H	2B	3B	HR	RBI	Avg.	BB	SO	SB	PO	A	E	Avg.
1998—	San Diego (N.L.)	2B	4	15	1	2	0	0	0	0	.133	1	6	0	8	12	0	1.000

CHAMPIONSHIP SERIES RECORD

								— BATTING —							— FIELDING —		
Year	Team (League)	Pos.	G	AB	R	H	2B	3B	HR	RBI	Avg.	BB	SO	SB	PO	A	E	Avg.
1998—	San Diego (N.L.)	2B	6	24	2	6	1	0	0	2	.250	5	7	0	7	13	0	1.000

WORLD SERIES RECORD

								— BATTING —							— FIELDING —		
Year	Team (League)	Pos.	G	AB	R	H	2B	3B	HR	RBI	Avg.	BB	SO	SB	PO	A	E	Avg.
1998—	San Diego (N.L.)	2B	4	15	3	3	2	0	0	1	.200	3	4	0	9	16	0	1.000

VERAS, WILTON — 3B — RED SOX

PERSONAL: Born January 19, 1978, in Monte Cristi, Dominican Republic. ... 6-2/185. ... Bats right, throws right. ... Full name: Wilton Andres Veras.

HIGH SCHOOL: Monte Cristi (Dominican Republic).

TRANSACTIONS/CAREER NOTES: Signed as non-drafted free agent by Boston Red Sox organization (February 9, 1995).

STATISTICAL NOTES: Led New York-Pennsylvania League in grounding into double plays with nine in 1996. ... Led Midwest League in grounding into double plays with 19 in 1997. ... Led Eastern League third basemen with 377 total chances in 1998.

Year Team (League)	Pos.	G	AB	R	H	2B	3B	HR	RBI	Avg.	BB	SO	SB	PO	A	E	Avg.
1995— GC Red Sox (GCL)	1B-3B	31	91	7	24	1	0	0	5	.264	7	9	1	80	2	1	.988
1996— Lowell (NY-Penn)	3B	67	250	22	60	15	0	0	019	.240	13	29	2	*57	106	12	.931
1997— Michigan (Midwest) ...	3B	131	489	51	141	21	3	8	68	.288	31	51	3	99	220	19	*.944
1998— Trenton (Eastern)	3B	126	470	70	137	27	4	16	67	.291	15	66	5	*100	*259	18	*.952

VERES, DAVE P ROCKIES

PERSONAL: Born October 19, 1966, in Montgomery, Ala. ... 6-2/220. ... Throws right, bats right. ... Full name: David Scott Veres. ... Name pronounced VEERZ.

HIGH SCHOOL: Gresham (Ore.).

JUNIOR COLLEGE: Mount Hood Community College (Ore.).

TRANSACTIONS/CAREER NOTES: Selected by Oakland Athletics organization in fourth round of free-agent draft (January 14, 1986). ... Traded by A's organization to Los Angeles Dodgers organization for P Kevin Campbell (January 15, 1991). ... Loaned by Dodgers organization to Mexico City Tigers of Mexican League (April 3-May 15, 1992). ... Released by Albuquerque, Dodgers organization (May 15, 1992). ... Signed by Houston Astros organization (May 28, 1992). ... Traded by Astros with C Raul Chavez to Montreal Expos for 3B Sean Berry (December 20, 1995). ... On disabled list (August 21-September 17, 1997). ... Traded by Expos with a player to be named later to Colorado Rockies for OF Terry Jones and a player to be named later (December 10, 1997).

STATISTICAL NOTES: Tied for California League lead with 29 wild pitches in 1987. ... Led Southern League with 16 wild pitches in 1989.

MISCELLANEOUS: Made an out in only appearance as pinch hitter (1998).

Year Team (League)	W	L	Pct.	ERA	G	GS	CG	ShO	Sv.	IP	H	R	ER	BB	SO
1986— Medford (N'west)	5	2	.714	3.26	15	•15	0	0		77 1/3	58	38	28	57	60
1987— Modesto (California)	8	9	.471	4.79	26	26	2	0	0	148 1/3	124	90	79	108	124
1988— Modesto (California)	4	11	.267	3.31	19	19	3	0	0	125	100	61	46	78	91
— Huntsville (Southern)	3	4	.429	4.15	8	8	0	0	0	39	50	20	18	15	17
1989— Huntsville (Southern)	8	11	.421	4.86	29	28	2	1	0	159 1/3	160	93	86	83	105
1990— Tacoma (PCL)	11	8	.579	4.69	32	23	2	0	1	151 2/3	136	90	79	88	88
1991— Albuquerque (PCL)■.........	7	6	.538	4.47	57	3	0	0	5	100 2/3	89	52	50	52	81
1992— M.C. Tigers (Mex.)■	1	5	.167	8.10	14	1	0	0	1	23 1/3	29	21	21	12	12
— Tucson (PCL)■	2	3	.400	5.30	29	1	0	0	0	52 2/3	60	36	31	17	46
1993— Tucson (PCL)	6	10	.375	4.90	43	15	1	0	5	130 1/3	156	88	71	32	122
1994— Tucson (PCL)	1	1	.500	1.88	16	0	0	0	1	24	17	8	5	10	19
— Houston (N.L.)	3	3	.500	2.41	32	0	0	0	1	41	39	13	11	7	28
1995— Houston (N.L.)	5	1	.833	2.26	72	0	0	0	1	103 1/3	89	29	26	30	94
1996— Montreal (N.L.)■............	6	3	.667	4.17	68	0	0	0	4	77 2/3	85	39	36	32	81
1997— Montreal (N.L.)	2	3	.400	3.48	53	0	0	0	1	62	68	28	24	27	47
1998— Colorado (N.L.)■	3	1	.750	2.83	63	0	0	0	8	76 1/3	67	26	24	27	74
Major league totals (5 years)......	19	11	.633	3.02	288	0	0	0	15	360 1/3	348	135	121	123	324

VIDRO, JOSE 3B EXPOS

PERSONAL: Born August 27, 1974, in Mayaguez, Puerto Rico. ... 5-11/190. ... Bats both, throws right. ... Full name: Jose Angel Cetty Vidro.

HIGH SCHOOL: Blanco Morales (Sabana Grande, Puerto Rico).

TRANSACTIONS/CAREER NOTES: Selected by Montreal Expos organization in sixth round of free agent draft (June 1, 1992). ... On disabled list (June 1-15 and July 26, 1993-remainder of season).

Year Team (League)	Pos.	G	AB	R	H	2B	3B	HR	RBI	Avg.	BB	SO	SB	PO	A	E	Avg.
1992— G.C. Expos (GCL)	2B	54	200	29	66	6	2	4	31	.330	16	31	10	114	107	4	*.982
1993— Burlington (Midw.)	2B	76	287	39	69	19	0	2	34	.240	28	54	3	107	153	7	.974
1994— W.P. Beach (FSL)........	2B	125	465	57	124	30	2	4	49	.267	51	56	8	204	328	20	.964
1995— W.P. Beach (FSL)........	IF	44	163	20	53	15	2	3	24	.325	8	21	0	101	110	4	.981
— Harrisburg (East.).......	IF	64	246	33	64	16	2	4	38	.260	20	37	7	97	162	9	.966
1996— Harrisburg (East.).......	IF	126	452	57	117	25	3	18	82	.259	29	71	3	135	271	15	.964
1997— Ottawa (Int'l)	3B-2B	73	279	40	90	17	0	13	47	.323	22	40	2	70	161	8	.967
— Montreal (N.L.)..........	3B-DH-2B	67	169	19	42	12	1	2	17	.249	11	20	1	25	59	4	.955
1998— Montreal (N.L.)..........	2B-3B	83	205	24	45	12	0	0	18	.220	27	33	2	81	126	6	.972
— Ottawa (Int'l)	2B-3B	63	235	35	68	14	2	2	32	.289	24	25	5	91	124	6	.973
Major league totals (2 years)		150	374	43	87	24	1	2	35	.233	38	53	3	106	185	10	.967

VILLALOBOS, CARLOS 3B ASTROS

PERSONAL: Born April 5, 1974, in Cartagena, Colombia. ... 6-0/170. ... Bats right, throws right. ... Full name: Carlos Enrique Villalobos.

TRANSACTIONS/CAREER NOTES: Signed as non-drafted free agent by Seattle Mariners organization (January 6, 1993). ... Traded by Mariners with P Scott Sanders and P Dean Crow to Detroit Tigers organization for P Omar Olivares and P Felipe Lira (July 18, 1997). ... Traded by Tigers with C Paul Baku, P Mark Persails, P Dean Crow and P Brian Powell to Houston Astros for C Brad Ausmus and P C.J. Nitkowski (January 14, 1999).

STATISTICAL NOTES: Led Arizona League third basemen with .889 fielding percentage in 1994. ... Led California League third basemen with 43 errors in 1996. ... Led Southern League third basemen with 389 total chances in 1998.

Year Team (League)	Pos.	G	AB	R	H	2B	3B	HR	RBI	Avg.	BB	SO	SB	PO	A	E	Avg.
1994— Ariz. Mariners (Ariz.) ..	3-S-2-O	51	175	17	51	6	2	4	29	.291	11	34	6	30	109	19	†.880
1995— Wisconsin (Midwest) .	3B	110	389	64	101	16	4	9	53	.260	35	76	16	76	234	*43	.878
1996— Lancaster (Calif.)	3B-OF	111	415	69	121	21	5	5	63	.292	50	89	9	65	177	†43	.849
1997— Lancaster (Calif.)	3B-OF	86	296	71	101	22	2	11	53	.341	60	42	4	43	130	14	.925
— Lakeland (Fla. St.)■...	3B-1B	19	147	19	37	5	0	1	15	.252	11	25	0	34	59	11	.894
1998— Jacksonville (Sou.).....	3B	128	497	96	159	34	2	18	80	.320	55	85	8	94	*267	28	.928

V

VILLEGAS, ISMAEL   P   BRAVES

PERSONAL: Born August 12, 1976, in Rio Piedras, Puerto Rico. ... 6-0/188. ... Throws right, bats right.
HIGH SCHOOL: Magarita Janer Palacios (Guaynabo, Puerto Rico.).
TRANSACTIONS/CAREER NOTES: Selected by Chicago Cubs in fifth round of free-agent draft (June 1, 1995). ... Traded by Cubs to Atlanta Braves organization for C Tyler Houston (July 27, 1996).

Year Team (League)	W	L	Pct.	ERA	G	GS	CG	ShO	Sv.	IP	H	R	ER	BB	SO
1995— GC Cubs (GCL)	3	2	.600	2.40	11	10	0	0	0	41 1/3	33	17	11	11	26
1996— Rockford (Midwest)	2	5	.286	5.13	10	10	1	0	0	47 1/3	63	40	27	25	30
— Williamsport (NYP)	0	0	...	2.57	2	2	0	0	0	7	7	3	2	4	5
— Danville (Appalachian)■	0	0	...	3.00	1	0	0	0	0	3	2	1	1	1	4
— Macon (S. Atl.)	3	7	.300	5.00	12	12	2	1	0	72	80	46	40	19	60
1997— Durham (Carolina)	2	5	.286	5.07	30	1	0	0	1	55	60	33	31	32	44
1998— Greenville (Southern)	7	6	.538	5.28	40	17	1	0	3	124 1/3	134	78	73	71	120

VILLONE, RON   P   INDIANS

PERSONAL: Born January 16, 1970, in Englewood, N.J. ... 6-3/235. ... Throws left, bats left. ... Full name: Ronald Thomas Villone Jr.
HIGH SCHOOL: South Bergenfield (Bergenfield, N.J.).
COLLEGE: Massachusetts.
TRANSACTIONS/CAREER NOTES: Selected by Seattle Mariners in first round (14th pick overall) of free-agent draft (June 1, 1992). ... On disabled list (April 19-26, 1994). ... Traded by Mariners with OF Marc Newfield to San Diego Padres for P Andy Benes and a player to be named later (July 31, 1995); Mariners acquired P Greg Keagle to complete deal (September 16, 1995). ... Traded by Padres with P Bryce Florie and OF Marc Newfield to Milwaukee Brewers for OF Greg Vaughn and a player to be named later (July 31, 1996); Padres acquired OF Gerald Parent to complete deal (September 16, 1996). ... Traded by Brewers with P Ben McDonald and P Mike Fetters to Cleveland Indians for OF Marquis Grissom and P Jeff Juden (December 8, 1997). ... On Cleveland disabled list (August 15-September 1, 1998); included rehabilitation assignment to Buffalo (August 22-September 1).
MISCELLANEOUS: Member of 1992 U.S. Olympic baseball team.

Year Team (League)	W	L	Pct.	ERA	G	GS	CG	ShO	Sv.	IP	H	R	ER	BB	SO
1993— Riverside (California)	7	4	.636	4.21	16	16	0	0	0	83 1/3	74	47	39	62	82
— Jacksonville (Southern)	3	4	.429	4.38	11	11	0	0	0	63 2/3	49	34	31	41	66
1994— Jacksonville (Southern)	6	7	.462	3.86	41	5	0	0	8	79 1/3	56	37	34	68	94
1995— Seattle (A.L.)	0	2	.000	7.91	19	0	0	0	0	19 1/3	20	19	17	23	26
— Tacoma (PCL)	1	0	1.000	0.61	22	0	0	0	13	29 2/3	9	6	2	19	43
— San Diego (N.L.)■	2	1	.667	4.21	19	0	0	0	1	25 2/3	24	12	12	11	37
1996— Las Vegas (PCL)	2	1	.667	1.64	23	0	0	0	3	22	13	5	4	9	29
— San Diego (N.L.)	1	1	.500	2.95	21	0	0	0	0	18 1/3	17	6	6	7	19
— Milwaukee (A.L.)	0	0	...	3.28	23	0	0	0	2	24 2/3	14	9	9	18	19
1997— Milwaukee (A.L.)	1	0	1.000	3.42	50	0	0	0	0	52 2/3	54	23	20	36	40
1998— Buffalo (Int'l)■	2	2	.500	2.01	23	0	0	0	7	22 1/3	20	11	5	11	28
— Cleveland (A.L.)	0	0	...	6.00	20	0	0	0	0	27	30	18	18	22	15
A.L. totals (4 years)	1	2	.333	4.66	117	0	0	0	2	123 2/3	118	69	64	99	100
N.L. totals (2 years)	3	2	.600	3.68	40	0	0	0	1	44	41	18	18	18	56
Major league totals (4 years)	4	4	.500	4.40	157	0	0	0	3	167 2/3	159	87	82	117	156

VINA, FERNANDO   2B   BREWERS

PERSONAL: Born April 16, 1969, in Sacramento. ... 5-9/174. ... Bats left, throws right. ... Name pronounced VEEN-ya.
HIGH SCHOOL: Valley (Sacramento).
JUNIOR COLLEGE: Cosumnes River College (Calif.), then Sacramento City College.
COLLEGE: Arizona State.
TRANSACTIONS/CAREER NOTES: Selected by New York Yankees organization in 51st round of free-agent draft (June 1, 1988); did not sign. ... Selected by New York Mets organization in ninth round of free-agent draft (June 4, 1990). ... Selected by Seattle Mariners from Mets organization in Rule 5 major league draft (December 7, 1992). ... Returned to Mets organization (June 15, 1993). ... On New York disabled list (May 22-June 6, 1994). ... On Norfolk disabled list (August 30-September 6, 1994). ... Traded by Mets to Milwaukee Brewers (December 22, 1994), completing deal in which Brewers traded P Doug Henry for two players to be named later (November 30, 1994); Brewers acquired C Javier Gonzalez as partial completion of deal (December 6, 1994). ... On Milwaukee disabled list (April 20-July 17, 1997); included rehabilitation assignments to Stockton (July 9-11) and Tucson (July 12-17).
STATISTICAL NOTES: Tied for South Atlantic League lead in caught stealing with 22 in 1991. ... Led South Atlantic League second basemen with 600 total chances and 61 double plays in 1991. ... Led Florida State League second basemen with 85 double plays in 1992. ... Led N.L. in being hit by pitch with 12 in 1998. ... Led A.L. second basemen with 116 double plays in 1996. ... Led N.L. second basemen with 884 total chances and 135 double plays in 1998. ... Career major league grand slams: 1.

Year Team (League)	Pos.	G	AB	R	H	2B	3B	HR	RBI	Avg.	BB	SO	SB	PO	A	E	Avg.
1991— Columbia (S. Atl.)	2B	129	498	77	135	23	6	6	50	.271	46	27	42	194	*385	21	*.965
1992— St. Lucie (Fla. St.)	2B	111	421	61	124	15	5	1	42	.295	32	26	36	219	*360	17	.971
— Tidewater (Int'l)	2B	11	30	3	6	0	0	0	2	.200	0	2	0	16	28	1	.978
1993— Seattle (A.L.)■	2B-SS-DH	24	45	5	10	2	0	0	2	.222	4	3	6	28	40	0	1.000
— Norfolk (Int'l)■	SS-2B-OF	73	287	24	66	6	4	4	27	.230	7	17	16	146	232	14	.964
1994— New York (N.L.)	2-3-S-O	79	124	20	31	6	0	0	6	.250	12	11	3	46	59	4	.963
— Norfolk (Int'l)	SS-2B	6	17	2	3	0	0	0	1	.176	1	1	1	9	11	1	.952
1995— Milwaukee (A.L.)■	2B-SS-3B	113	288	46	74	7	7	3	29	.257	22	28	6	194	245	8	.982
1996— Milwaukee (A.L.)	2B	140	554	94	157	19	10	7	46	.283	38	35	16	*333	412	*16	.979
1997— Milwaukee (A.L.)	2B-DH	79	324	37	89	12	2	4	28	.275	12	23	8	149	227	7	.982
— Stockton (California)	2B	3	9	2	4	0	1	0	3	.444	0	0	0	2	7	0	1.000
— Tucson (PCL)	2B	6	19	3	9	3	0	1	5	.474	3	1	0	8	16	2	.923
1998— Milwaukee (N.L.)	2B	159	637	101	198	39	7	7	45	.311	54	46	22	404	468	12	.986
American League totals (4 years)		356	1211	182	330	40	19	14	105	.273	76	89	36	704	924	31	.981
National League totals (2 years)		238	761	121	229	45	7	7	51	.301	66	57	25	450	527	16	.984
Major league totals (6 years)		594	1972	303	559	85	26	21	156	.283	142	146	61	1154	1451	47	.982

V

						BATTING									FIELDING		
Year	League	Pos.	AB	R	H	2B	3B	HR	RBI	Avg.	BB	SO	SB	PO	A	E	Avg.
1998—	National	2B	1	0	1	0	0	0	0	1.000	1	0	0	1	1	1	.667

VITIELLO, JOE — 1B/3B — ROYALS

PERSONAL: Born April 11, 1970, in Cambridge, Mass. ... 6-3/230. ... Bats right, throws right. ... Full name: Joseph David Vitiello. ... Name pronounced VIT-ee-ELL-oh.

HIGH SCHOOL: Stoneham (Mass.).

COLLEGE: Alabama.

TRANSACTIONS/CAREER NOTES: Selected by New York Yankees organization in 31st round of free-agent draft (June 1, 1988); did not sign. ... Selected by Kansas City Royals organization in first round (seventh pick overall) of free-agent draft (June 3, 1991). ... On disabled list (April 12-23, 1992; June 2-11, 1993; and May 23-June 16, 1994). ... On disabled list (June 17-July 28 and August 13, 1997-remainder of season); included rehabilitation assignment to Omaha (July 15-28). ... On Kansas City disabled list (April 8-May 18, 1998); included rehabilitation assignment to Omaha (April 21-May 9). ... On Omaha disabled list (August 4-12, 1998). ... Granted free agency (October 15, 1998). ... Re-signed by Royals organization (December 17, 1998).

STATISTICAL NOTES: Led American Association with .440 on-base percentage in 1994.

							BATTING							FIELDING		
Year	Team (League)	Pos.	G	AB	R	H	2B	3B	HR	RBI	Avg.	BB	SO	SB	PO	A	E	Avg.
1991—	Eugene (Northwest) ...	OF-1B	19	64	16	21	2	0	6	21	.328	11	18	1	49	4	1	.981
	— Memphis (Sou.)	OF-1B	36	128	15	28	4	1	0	18	.219	23	36	0	77	4	1	.988
1992—	Baseball City (FSL).....	1B	115	400	52	113	16	1	8	65	.283	46	101	0	879	44	13	.986
1993—	Memphis (Sou.)	1B	117	413	62	119	25	2	15	66	.288	57	95	2	830	53	•17	.981
1994—	Omaha (A.A.).............	1B	98	352	46	121	28	3	10	61	*.344	56	63	3	605	46	8	.988
1995—	Kansas City (A.L.)	DH-1B	53	130	13	33	4	0	7	21	.254	8	25	0	51	3	1	.982
	— Omaha (A.A.).............	1B-OF	59	229	33	64	14	2	12	42	.279	12	50	0	225	21	4	.984
1996—	Kansas City (A.L.)	DH-1B-OF	85	257	29	62	15	1	8	40	.241	38	69	2	40	5	0	1.000
	— Omaha (A.A.).............	1B	36	132	26	37	7	0	9	31	.280	16	32	1	281	20	3	.990
1997—	Kansas City (A.L.)	OF-DH-1B	51	130	11	31	6	0	5	18	.238	14	37	0	56	0	1	.982
	— Omaha (A.A.).............	OF	13	42	5	9	1	0	3	9	.214	5	16	0	1	0	0	1.000
1998—	Kansas City (A.L.)	DH	3	7	0	1	0	0	0	0	.143	1	2	0	...	...	...	...
	— Omaha (PCL).............	1B-3B	103	376	44	107	20	2	18	71	.285	39	68	0	738	56	8	.990
Major league totals (4 years)			192	524	53	127	25	1	20	79	.242	61	133	2	147	8	2	.987

VIZCAINO, JOSE — SS — DODGERS

PERSONAL: Born March 26, 1968, in San Cristobal, Dominican Republic. ... 6-1/180. ... Bats both, throws right. ... Full name: Jose Luis Pimental Vizcaino. ... Name pronounced VIS-ky-EE-no.

HIGH SCHOOL: Americo Tolentino (Palenque de San Cristobal, Dominican Republic).

TRANSACTIONS/CAREER NOTES: Signed as non-drafted free agent by Los Angeles Dodgers organization (February 18, 1986). ... Traded by Dodgers to Chicago Cubs for IF Greg Smith (December 14, 1990). ... On disabled list (April 20-May 6 and August 26-September 16, 1992). ... Traded by Cubs to New York Mets for P Anthony Young and P Ottis Smith (March 30, 1994). ... Traded by Mets with IF Jeff Kent to Cleveland Indians for 2B Carlos Baerga and IF Alvaro Espinoza (July 29, 1996). ... Traded by Indians with IF Jeff Kent, P Julian Tavarez and a player to be named later to San Francisco Giants for 3B Matt Williams and a player to be named later (November 13, 1996); Indians traded P Joe Roa to Giants for OF Trenidad Hubbard to complete deal (December 16, 1996). ... Granted free agency (October 29, 1997). ... Signed by Dodgers (December 8, 1997). ... On disabled list (June 22-September 9, 1998).

STATISTICAL NOTES: Led Gulf Coast League shortstops with 23 double plays in 1987. ... Led Pacific Coast League shortstops with 611 total chances and 82 double plays in 1989. ... Tied for N.L. lead in fielding percentage by shortstop with .984 and assists by shortstop with 411 in 1995.

							BATTING							FIELDING		
Year	Team (League)	Pos.	G	AB	R	H	2B	3B	HR	RBI	Avg.	BB	SO	SB	PO	A	E	Avg.
1987—	GC Dodgers (GCL)	SS-1B	49	150	26	38	5	1	0	12	.253	22	24	8	73	107	13	.933
1988—	Bakersfield (Calif.)......	SS	122	433	77	126	11	4	0	38	.291	50	54	13	185	340	30	.946
1989—	Albuquerque (PCL).....	SS	129	434	60	123	10	4	1	44	.283	33	41	16	*191	*390	*30	.951
	— Los Angeles (N.L.).....	SS	7	10	2	2	0	0	0	0	.200	0	1	0	6	9	2	.882
1990—	Albuquerque (PCL).....	2B-SS	81	276	46	77	10	2	2	38	.279	30	33	13	141	229	14	.964
	— Los Angeles (N.L.).....	SS-2B	37	51	3	14	1	1	0	2	.275	4	8	1	23	27	2	.962
1991—	Chicago (N.L.)■......	3B-SS-2B	93	145	7	38	5	0	0	10	.262	5	18	2	49	118	7	.960
1992—	Chicago (N.L.)	SS-3B-2B	86	285	25	64	10	4	1	17	.225	14	35	3	93	195	9	.970
1993—	Chicago (N.L.)	SS-3B-2B	151	551	74	158	19	4	4	54	.287	46	71	12	217	410	17	.974
1994—	New York (N.L.)■	SS	103	410	47	105	13	3	3	33	.256	33	62	1	136	291	13	.970
1995—	New York (N.L.)	SS-2B	135	509	66	146	21	5	3	56	.287	35	76	8	189	‡411	10	‡.984
1996—	New York (N.L.)	2B	96	363	47	110	12	6	1	32	.303	28	58	9	179	259	6	.986
	— Cleveland (A.L.)■......	2B-SS-DH	48	179	23	51	5	2	0	13	.285	7	24	6	82	135	4	.982
1997—	San Fran. (N.L.)■.......	SS-2B	151	568	77	151	19	7	5	50	.266	48	87	8	206	450	16	.976
1998—	Los Angeles (N.L.)■..	SS	67	237	30	62	9	0	3	29	.262	17	35	7	89	172	4	.985
American League totals (1 year)			48	179	23	51	5	2	0	13	.285	7	24	6	82	135	4	.982
National League totals (10 years)			926	3129	378	850	109	30	20	283	.272	230	451	51	1187	2342	86	.976
Major league totals (10 years)			974	3308	401	901	114	32	20	296	.272	237	475	57	1269	2477	90	.977

DIVISION SERIES RECORD

							BATTING							FIELDING		
Year	Team (League)	Pos.	G	AB	R	H	2B	3B	HR	RBI	Avg.	BB	SO	SB	PO	A	E	Avg.
1996—	Cleveland (A.L.)..........	2B	3	12	1	4	2	0	0	1	.333	1	1	0	4	3	1	.875
1997—	San Francisco (N.L.) ..	SS	3	11	1	2	1	0	0	0	.182	0	5	0	3	10	0	1.000
Division series totals (2 years)			6	23	2	6	3	0	0	1	.261	1	6	0	7	13	1	.952

V

VIZCAINO, LUIS   P   ATHLETICS

PERSONAL: Born June 1, 1977, in Bani, Dominican Republic. ... 6-1/170. ... Throws right, bats right. ... Full name: Luis Vizcaino (Arias).
TRANSACTIONS/CAREER NOTES: Signed as non-drafted free agent by Oakland Athletics organization (December 9, 1994).

Year— Team (League)	W	L	Pct.	ERA	G	GS	CG	ShO	Sv.	IP	H	R	ER	BB	SO
1995— Dom. Athletics (DSL)	10	2	.833	2.27	16	15	5	1	0	*115	93	41	29	29	89
1996— Arizona A's (Arizona)	6	3	.667	4.07	15	10	0	0	1	59 2/3	58	36	27	24	52
1997— S. Oregon (N'west)	1	6	.143	7.93	22	5	0	0	0	47 2/3	62	51	42	27	42
— Modesto (California)	0	3	.000	13.19	7	0	0	0	0	14 1/3	24	24	21	13	15
1998— Modesto (California)	6	3	.667	2.74	23	16	0	0	0	102	72	39	31	43	108
— Huntsville (Southern)	3	2	.600	4.66	7	7	0	0	0	38 2/3	43	27	20	22	26

VIZQUEL, OMAR   SS   INDIANS

PERSONAL: Born April 24, 1967, in Caracas, Venezuela. ... 5-9/170. ... Bats both, throws right. ... Full name: Omar Enrique Vizquel. ... Name pronounced vis-KEL.
HIGH SCHOOL: Francisco Espejo (Caracas, Venezuela).
TRANSACTIONS/CAREER NOTES: Signed as non-drafted free agent by Seattle Mariners organization (April 1, 1984). ... On Seattle disabled list (April 7-May 13, 1990); included rehabilitation assignments to Calgary (May 3-7) and San Bernardino (May 8-12). ... On Seattle disabled list (April 13-May 11, 1992); included rehabilitation assignment to Calgary (May 5-11). ... Traded by Mariners to Cleveland Indians for SS Felix Fermin, 1B Reggie Jefferson and cash (December 20, 1993). ... On Cleveland disabled list (April 23-June 13, 1994); included rehabilitation assignment to Charlotte (June 6-13).
RECORDS: Holds major league career record for highest fielding percentage by shortstop (1,000 or more games)—.982.
HONORS: Won A.L. Gold Glove at shortstop (1993-98).
STATISTICAL NOTES: Led Midwest League shortstops with .969 fielding percentage in 1986. ... Tied for A.L. lead in double plays by shortstop with 108 in 1993. ... Led A.L. in sacrifice hits with 16 in 1997. ... Career major league grand slams: 2.
MISCELLANEOUS: Batted righthanded only (1984-88).

							BATTING							FIELDING		
Year— Team (League)	Pos.	G	AB	R	H	2B	3B	HR	RBI	Avg.	BB	SO	SB	PO	A	E	Avg.
1984— Butte (Pioneer)	SS-2B	15	45	7	14	2	0	0	4	.311	3	8	2	13	29	5	.894
1985— Bellingham (N'west)	SS-2B	50	187	24	42	9	0	5	17	.225	12	27	4	85	175	19	.932
1986— Wausau (Midwest)	SS-2B	105	352	60	75	13	2	4	28	.213	64	56	19	153	328	16	†.968
1987— Salinas (Calif.)	SS-2B	114	407	61	107	12	8	0	38	.263	57	55	25	81	295	25	.938
1988— Vermont (Eastern)	SS	103	374	54	95	18	2	2	35	.254	42	44	30	173	268	19	*.959
— Calgary (PCL)	SS	33	107	10	24	2	3	1	12	.224	5	14	2	43	92	6	.957
1989— Calgary (PCL)	SS	7	28	3	6	2	0	0	3	.214	3	4	0	15	14	0	1.000
— Seattle (A.L.)	SS	143	387	45	85	7	3	1	20	.220	28	40	1	208	388	18	.971
1990— Seattle (A.L.)	SS	48	150	18	35	6	2	0	8	.233	13	10	4	70	142	6	.972
— San Bern. (Calif.)	SS	6	28	5	7	0	0	0	3	.250	3	1	1	11	21	3	.914
— Seattle (A.L.)	SS	81	255	19	63	3	2	2	18	.247	18	22	4	103	239	7	.980
1991— Seattle (A.L.)	SS-2B	142	426	42	98	16	4	1	41	.230	45	37	7	224	422	13	.980
1992— Seattle (A.L.)	SS	136	483	49	142	20	4	0	21	.294	32	38	15	223	403	7	*.989
— Calgary (PCL)	SS	6	22	0	6	1	0	0	2	.273	1	3	0	14	21	1	.972
1993— Seattle (A.L.)	SS-DH	158	560	68	143	14	2	2	31	.255	50	71	12	245	475	15	.980
1994— Cleveland (A.L.)■	SS	69	286	39	78	10	1	1	33	.273	23	23	13	113	204	6	.981
— Charlotte (Int'l)	SS	7	26	3	7	1	0	0	1	.269	2	1	1	11	18	1	.967
1995— Cleveland (A.L.)	SS	136	542	87	144	28	0	6	56	.266	59	59	29	210	405	9	.986
1996— Cleveland (A.L.)	SS	151	542	98	161	36	1	9	64	.297	56	42	35	226	447	20	.971
1997— Cleveland (A.L.)	SS	153	565	89	158	23	6	5	49	.280	57	58	43	245	428	10	.985
1998— Cleveland (A.L.)	SS	151	576	86	166	30	6	2	50	.288	62	64	37	*273	442	5	*.993
Major league totals (10 years)		1320	4622	622	1238	187	29	29	383	.268	430	454	196	2070	3853	110	.982

DIVISION SERIES RECORD

							BATTING							FIELDING		
Year— Team (League)	Pos.	G	AB	R	H	2B	3B	HR	RBI	Avg.	BB	SO	SB	PO	A	E	Avg.
1995— Cleveland (A.L.)	SS	3	12	2	2	1	0	0	4	.167	2	2	1	4	11	0	1.000
1996— Cleveland (A.L.)	SS	4	14	4	6	1	0	0	2	.429	3	4	4	6	10	0	1.000
1997— Cleveland (A.L.)	SS	5	18	3	9	0	0	0	1	.500	2	1	4	12	14	0	1.000
1998— Cleveland (A.L.)	SS	4	15	1	1	0	0	0	0	.067	1	0	0	4	16	0	1.000
Division series totals (4 years)		16	59	10	18	2	0	0	7	.305	8	7	9	26	51	0	1.000

CHAMPIONSHIP SERIES RECORD

							BATTING							FIELDING		
Year— Team (League)	Pos.	G	AB	R	H	2B	3B	HR	RBI	Avg.	BB	SO	SB	PO	A	E	Avg.
1995— Cleveland (A.L.)	SS	6	23	2	2	1	0	0	2	.087	5	2	3	9	21	0	1.000
1997— Cleveland (A.L.)	SS	6	25	1	1	0	0	0	0	.040	2	10	0	16	15	0	1.000
1998— Cleveland (A.L.)	SS	6	25	2	11	0	1	0	0	.440	1	3	4	11	26	1	.974
Championship series totals (3 years)		18	73	5	14	1	1	0	2	.192	8	15	7	36	62	1	.990

WORLD SERIES RECORD

RECORDS: Shares single-inning record for most stolen bases—2 (October 26, 1997).

							BATTING							FIELDING		
Year— Team (League)	Pos.	G	AB	R	H	2B	3B	HR	RBI	Avg.	BB	SO	SB	PO	A	E	Avg.
1995— Cleveland (A.L.)	SS	6	23	3	4	0	1	0	1	.174	3	5	1	12	22	0	1.000
1997— Cleveland (A.L.)	SS	7	30	5	7	2	0	0	1	.233	3	5	5	12	17	0	1.000
World Series totals (2 years)		13	53	8	11	2	1	0	2	.208	6	10	6	24	39	0	1.000

V

ALL-STAR GAME RECORD

								BATTING							FIELDING		
Year	League	Pos.	AB	R	H	2B	3B	HR	RBI	Avg.	BB	SO	SB	PO	A	E	Avg.
1998— American		SS	2	0	1	0	0	0	0	.500	0	0	0	1	1	0	1.000

VOIGT, JACK   OF

PERSONAL: Born May 17, 1966, in Sarasota, Fla. ... 6-1/178. ... Bats right, throws right. ... Full name: John David Voigt.
HIGH SCHOOL: Venice (Fla.).
COLLEGE: Louisiana State.
TRANSACTIONS/CAREER NOTES: Selected by Baltimore Orioles organization in ninth round of free-agent draft (June 2, 1987). ... Traded by Orioles to Texas Rangers for P John Dettmer (May 16, 1995). ... Traded by Rangers organization to Boston Red Sox organization for P Chris Howard (August 31, 1995). ... Granted free agency (October 16, 1995). ... Signed by Rangers organization (April 13, 1996). ... Granted free agency (October 9, 1996). ... Signed by Milwaukee Brewers organization (January 30, 1997). ... Released by Brewers (December 1, 1997). ... Signed by Oakland Athletics organization (December 5, 1997). ... Traded by A's to Rangers for a player to be named later (August 9, 1998). ... Granted free agency (October 15, 1998).
STATISTICAL NOTES: Led New York-Pennsylvania League third basemen with .941 fielding percentage and 16 double plays in 1987. ... Led Carolina League third basemen with .990 fielding percentage in 1989. ... Led Eastern League with 11 sacrifice flies in 1990.

								BATTING							FIELDING		
Year	Team (League)	Pos.	G	AB	R	H	2B	3B	HR	RBI	Avg.	BB	SO	SB	PO	A	E	Avg.
1987— Newark (NY-Penn)	3B-1B	63	219	41	70	10	1	11	52	*.320	33	45	1	63	141	11	†.949
— Hagerstown (Car.)	1B	2	9	0	1	0	0	0	1	.111	1	4	0	9	0	2	.818
1988— Hagerstown (Car.)	OF-1B	115	367	62	83	18	2	12	42	.226	66	92	5	213	11	6	.974
1989— Frederick (Carolina)	OF-1B	127	406	61	107	26	5	10	77	.264	62	106	17	189	16	2	†.990
1990— Hagerstown (East.)	OF	126	418	55	107	26	2	12	70	.256	59	97	5	249	12	6	.978
1991— Hagerstown (East.)	OF	29	90	15	22	3	0	0	6	.244	15	19	6	8	0	0	1.000
— Rochester (Int'l)	OF-1B-3B	83	267	46	72	12	4	6	35	.270	40	53	9	198	32	3	.987
1992— Rochester (Int'l)	OF-1B-3B	129	443	74	126	23	4	16	64	.284	58	102	9	330	36	10	.973
— Baltimore (A.L.)	PR	1	0	0	0	0	0	0	0	...	0	0	0	...	...	...	...
1993— Rochester (Int'l)	OF-3B-1B	18	61	16	22	6	1	3	11	.361	9	14	0	38	5	1	.977
— Baltimore (A.L.)	O-DH-1-3	64	152	32	45	11	1	6	23	.296	25	33	1	101	6	1	.991
1994— Baltimore (A.L.)	OF-1B-DH	59	141	15	34	5	0	3	20	.241	18	25	0	114	5	2	.983
— Bowie (Eastern)	1B-3B-OF	41	154	26	48	9	1	6	35	.312	26	26	5	222	36	1	.996
1995— Baltimore (A.L.)	DH-1B	3	1	1	1	0	0	0	0	1.000	0	0	0	1	1	0	1.000
— Texas (A.L.)■	OF-1B-DH	33	62	8	10	3	0	2	8	.161	10	14	0	55	2	1	.983
— Tulsa (Texas)	OF-1B	4	16	1	3	0	0	1	3	.188	2	5	1	8	1	0	1.000
1996— Charlotte (Fla. St.)	1B-OF	7	27	7	11	3	0	1	8	.407	3	3	0	46	7	0	1.000
— Okla. City (A.A.)	OF-3B-1B	127	445	77	132	26	1	21	80	.297	*76	103	5	149	113	16	.942
— Texas (A.L.)■	OF	5	9	1	1	0	0	0	0	.111	0	2	0	5	1	0	1.000
1997— Tucson (PCL)■	O-1-3-2	66	235	36	64	20	0	5	40	.272	43	57	4	112	10	2	.984
— Milwaukee (A.L.)	O-1-3-DH	72	151	20	37	9	2	8	22	.245	19	36	1	144	10	1	.994
1998— Edmonton (PCL)■	1B-OF	18	68	10	22	6	0	4	11	.324	8	15	1	67	4	1	.986
— Oakland (A.L.)	1-O-DH-3	57	72	7	10	4	0	1	10	.139	6	19	5	102	5	1	.991
— Oklahoma (PCL)■	OF-1B	20	70	10	24	6	0	2	11	.343	14	19	0	42	2	1	.978
Major league totals (7 years)		294	588	84	138	32	3	20	83	.235	78	129	7	522	30	6	.989

VOSBERG, ED   P   PADRES

PERSONAL: Born September 28, 1961, in Tucson, Ariz. ... 6-1/210. ... Throws left, bats left. ... Full name: Edward John Vosberg. ... Nephew of Don Vosberg, defensive end with New York Giants (1941).
HIGH SCHOOL: Salpointe (Tucson, Ariz.).
COLLEGE: Arizona.
TRANSACTIONS/CAREER NOTES: Selected by St. Louis Cardinals organization in third round of free-agent draft (June 5, 1979); did not sign. ... Selected by Toronto Blue Jays organization in 11th round of free-agent draft (June 7, 1982); did not sign. ... Selected by San Diego Padres organization in third round of free-agent draft (June 6, 1983). ... Traded by Padres organization to Houston Astros organization for C Dan Walters (December 13, 1988). ... Traded by Astros organization to Los Angeles Dodgers organization (August 1, 1989), completing deal in which Dodgers organization traded OF Javier Ortiz to Astros organization for a player to be named later (July 22, 1989). ... Granted free agency (October 15, 1989). ... Signed by Phoenix, San Francisco Giants organization (March 13, 1990). ... Granted free agency (October 15, 1990). ... Signed by California Angels organization (December 4, 1990). ... Released by Angels organization (May 11, 1991). ... Signed by Calgary, Seattle Mariners organization (May 20, 1991). ... Released by Mariners organization (July 10, 1991). ... Pitched in Italy (1992). ... Signed by Iowa, Chicago Cubs organization (March 17, 1993). ... Granted free agency (October 15, 1993). ... Signed by Oakland Athletics organization (December 3, 1993). ... Granted free agency (October 15, 1994). ... Re-signed by A's organization (November 11, 1994). ... Selected by Los Angeles Dodgers from A's organization in Rule 5 major league draft (December 5, 1994). ... Granted free agency (April 24, 1995). ... Signed by Texas Rangers organization (April 26, 1995). ... Traded by Rangers to Florida Marlins for P Rick Helling (August 12, 1997). ... Traded by Marlins to Padres for P Chris Clark (November 20, 1997). ... On disabled list (March 25, 1998-entire season).
STATISTICAL NOTES: Led Pacific Coast League with 11 balks in 1987.

Year	Team (League)	W	L	Pct.	ERA	G	GS	CG	ShO	Sv.	IP	H	R	ER	BB	SO
1983— Reno (California)	6	6	.500	3.87	15	15	3	0	0	97 2/3	111	61	42	39	70
— Beaumont (Texas)	1	0	1.000	0.00	1	1	1	1	0	7	2	0	0	2	1
1984— Beaumont (Texas)	13	•11	.542	3.43	27	•27	5	2	0	183 2/3	196	87	70	74	100
1985— Beaumont (Texas)	9	11	.450	3.91	27	•27	2	1	0	175	178	92	76	69	124
1986— Las Vegas (PCL)	7	8	.467	4.72	25	24	2	1	0	129 2/3	136	80	68	64	93
— San Diego (N.L.)	0	1	.000	6.59	5	3	0	0	0	13 2/3	17	11	10	9	8
1987— Las Vegas (PCL)	9	8	.529	3.92	34	24	3	0	0	167 1/3	154	88	73	97	98
1988— Las Vegas (PCL)	11	7	.611	4.15	45	11	1	0	2	128	137	67	59	56	75
1989— Tucson (PCL)■	4	7	.364	6.78	23	14	0	0	1	87 2/3	122	70	66	49	68
— Albuquerque (PCL)■	2	1	.667	2.70	12	0	0	0	0	20	17	8	6	5	18
1990— Phoenix (PCL)■	1	3	.250	2.65	24	0	0	0	3	34	36	14	10	16	28
— San Francisco (N.L.)	1	1	.500	5.55	18	0	0	0	0	24 1/3	21	16	15	12	12

Year— Team (League)	W	L	Pct.	ERA	G	GS	CG	ShO	Sv.	IP	H	R	ER	BB	SO
1991— Edmonton (PCL)■	0	1	.000	6.28	12	0	0	0	0	14 1/3	19	10	10	5	14
—Calgary (PCL)■	0	2	.000	7.23	16	0	0	0	2	23 2/3	38	26	19	12	15
1992—							Italian statistics unavailable.								
1993— Iowa (Am. Assoc.)■	5	1	.833	3.57	52	0	0	0	3	63	67	32	25	22	64
1994— Tacoma (PCL)■	4	2	.667	3.35	26	1	0	0	3	53 2/3	39	21	20	19	54
—Oakland (A.L.)	0	2	.000	3.95	16	0	0	0	0	13 2/3	16	7	6	5	12
1995— Oklahoma City (A.A.)■	1	0	1.000	0.00	1	0	0	0	0	1 2/3	1	0	0	1	2
—Texas (A.L.)	5	5	.500	3.00	44	0	0	0	4	36	32	15	12	16	36
1996— Texas (A.L.)	1	1	.500	3.27	52	0	0	0	8	44	51	17	16	21	32
1997— Texas (A.L.)	1	2	.333	4.61	42	0	0	0	0	41	44	23	21	15	29
—Florida (N.L.)■	1	1	.500	3.75	17	0	0	0	1	12	15	7	5	6	8
1998— San Diego (N.L.)■							Did not play.								
A.L. totals (4 years)	7	10	.412	3.68	154	0	0	0	12	134 2/3	143	62	55	57	109
N.L. totals (3 years)	2	3	.400	5.40	40	3	0	0	1	50	53	34	30	27	28
Major league totals (6 years)	9	13	.409	4.14	194	3	0	0	13	184 2/3	196	96	85	84	137

DIVISION SERIES RECORD

Year— Team (League)	W	L	Pct.	ERA	G	GS	CG	ShO	Sv.	IP	H	R	ER	BB	SO
1996— Texas (A.L.)	0	0	...	...	1	0	0	0	0	0	1	0	0	0	0

CHAMPIONSHIP SERIES RECORD

Year— Team (League)	W	L	Pct.	ERA	G	GS	CG	ShO	Sv.	IP	H	R	ER	BB	SO
1997— Florida (N.L.)	0	0	...	0.00	2	0	0	0	0	2 2/3	2	0	0	1	3

WORLD SERIES RECORD

NOTES: Member of World Series championship team (1997).

Year— Team (League)	W	L	Pct.	ERA	G	GS	CG	ShO	Sv.	IP	H	R	ER	BB	SO
1997— Florida (N.L.)	0	0	...	6.00	2	0	0	0	0	3	3	2	2	3	2

WADE, TERRELL — P — DEVIL RAYS

PERSONAL: Born January 25, 1973, in Rembert, S.C. ... 6-3/205. ... Throws left, bats left. ... Full name: Hiawatha Terrell Wade.

HIGH SCHOOL: Hillcrest (S.C.).

TRANSACTIONS/CAREER NOTES: Signed as non-drafted free agent by Atlanta Braves organization (June 17, 1991). ... On Greenville disabled list (April 7-August 9, 1994). ... On Atlanta disabled list (June 7, 1997-remainder of season); included rehabilitation assignment to Greenville (July 22-August 15). ... Selected by Tampa Bay Devil Rays in third round (60th pick overall) of expansion draft (November 18, 1997). ... On Tampa Bay disabled list (March 19-September 18, 1998); included rehabilitation assignments to St. Petersburg (August 4-18) and Durham (August 19-September 18).

Year— Team (League)	W	L	Pct.	ERA	G	GS	CG	ShO	Sv.	IP	H	R	ER	BB	SO
1991— GC Braves (GCL)	2	0	1.000	6.26	10	2	0	0	0	23	29	17	16	15	22
1992— Idaho Falls (Pioneer)	1	4	.200	6.44	13	11	0	0	0	50 1/3	59	46	36	42	54
1993— Macon (S. Atl.)	8	2	.800	1.73	14	14	0	0	0	83 1/3	57	16	16	36	121
—Durham (Carolina)	2	1	.667	3.27	5	5	0	0	0	33	26	13	12	18	47
—Greenville (Southern)	2	1	.667	3.21	8	8	1	1	0	42	32	16	15	29	40
1994— Greenville (Southern)	9	3	.750	3.83	21	21	0	0	0	105 2/3	87	49	45	58	105
—Richmond (Int'l)	2	2	.500	2.63	4	4	0	0	0	24	23	9	7	15	26
1995— Richmond (Int'l)	10	9	.526	4.56	24	23	1	0	0	142	137	76	72	63	124
—Atlanta (N.L.)	0	1	.000	4.50	3	0	0	0	0	4	3	2	2	4	3
1996— Atlanta (N.L.)	5	0	1.000	2.97	44	8	0	0	1	69 2/3	57	28	23	47	79
1997— Atlanta (N.L.)	2	3	.400	5.36	12	9	0	0	0	42	60	31	25	16	35
—Greenville (Southern)	0	2	.000	4.97	8	6	0	0	0	12 2/3	15	10	7	8	14
1998— St. Petersburg (FSL)■	0	1	.000	3.60	3	3	0	0	0	15	12	8	6	7	16
—Durham (International)	1	1	.500	4.58	4	4	0	0	0	19 2/3	21	12	10	12	14
—Tampa Bay (A.L.)	1	1	.500	5.06	2	2	0	0	0	10 2/3	14	6	6	2	8
A.L. totals (1 year)	1	1	.500	5.06	2	2	0	0	0	10 2/3	14	6	6	2	8
N.L. totals (3 years)	7	4	.636	3.89	59	17	0	0	1	115 2/3	120	61	50	67	117
Major league totals (4 years)	8	5	.615	3.99	61	19	0	0	1	126 1/3	134	67	56	69	125

CHAMPIONSHIP SERIES RECORD

Year— Team (League)	W	L	Pct.	ERA	G	GS	CG	ShO	Sv.	IP	H	R	ER	BB	SO
1996— Atlanta (N.L.)	0	0	...	0.00	1	0	0	0	0	1/3	0	0	0	0	1

WORLD SERIES RECORD

Year— Team (League)	W	L	Pct.	ERA	G	GS	CG	ShO	Sv.	IP	H	R	ER	BB	SO
1996— Atlanta (N.L.)	0	0	...	0.00	2	0	0	0	0	2/3	0	0	0	1	0

W

WAGNER, BILLY — P — ASTROS

PERSONAL: Born July 25, 1971, in Tannersville, Va. ... 5-11/180. ... Throws left, bats left. ... Full name: William Edward Wagner.

HIGH SCHOOL: Tazewell (Va.).

COLLEGE: Ferrum (Va.).

TRANSACTIONS/CAREER NOTES: Selected by Houston Astros organization in first round (12th pick overall) of free-agent draft (June 3, 1993). ... On Houston disabled list (August 23-September 7, 1996). ... On Houston disabled list (July 16-August 7, 1998); included rehabilitation assignment to Jackson (August 1-7).

Year— Team (League)	W	L	Pct.	ERA	G	GS	CG	ShO	Sv.	IP	H	R	ER	BB	SO
1993— Auburn (N.Y.-Penn)	1	3	.250	4.08	7	7	0	0	0	28 2/3	25	19	13	25	31
1994— Quad City (Midwest)	8	9	.471	3.29	26	26	2	0	0	153	99	71	56	*91	*204
1995— Jackson (Texas)	2	2	.500	2.57	12	12	0	0	0	70	49	25	20	36	77
—Tucson (PCL)	5	3	.625	3.18	13	13	0	0	0	76 1/3	70	28	27	32	80
—Houston (N.L.)	0	0	...	0.00	1	0	0	0	0	1/3	0	0	0	0	0

Year Team (League)	W	L	Pct.	ERA	G	GS	CG	ShO	Sv.	IP	H	R	ER	BB	SO
1996—Tucson (PCL)	6	2	.750	3.28	12	12	1	1	0	74	62	32	27	33	86
— Houston (N.L.)	2	2	.500	2.44	37	0	0	0	9	51²/₃	28	16	14	30	67
1997—Houston (N.L.)	7	8	.467	2.85	62	0	0	0	23	66¹/₃	49	23	21	30	106
1998—Houston (N.L.)	4	3	.571	2.70	58	0	0	0	30	60	46	19	18	25	97
— Jackson (Texas)	0	0	...	0.00	3	1	0	0	0	3	1	0	0	0	7
Major league totals (4 years)	13	13	.500	2.67	158	0	0	0	62	178¹/₃	123	58	53	85	270

DIVISION SERIES RECORD

Year Team (League)	W	L	Pct.	ERA	G	GS	CG	ShO	Sv.	IP	H	R	ER	BB	SO
1997—Houston (N.L.)	0	0	...	18.00	1	0	0	0	0	1	3	2	2	0	2
1998—Houston (N.L.)	1	0	1.000	18.00	1	0	0	0	0	1	4	2	2	0	1
Div. series totals (2 years)	1	0	1.000	18.00	2	0	0	0	0	2	7	4	4	0	3

WAGNER, PAUL　　　　P　　　　BRAVES

PERSONAL: Born November 14, 1967, in Milwaukee. ... 6-1/210. ... Throws right, bats right. ... Full name: Paul Allen Wagner.
HIGH SCHOOL: Washington (Germantown, Wis.).
COLLEGE: Illinois State.
TRANSACTIONS/CAREER NOTES: Selected by Pittsburgh Pirates organization in 12th round of free-agent draft (June 5, 1989). ... On disabled list (August 3-19, 1993 and July 3-21, 1995). ... On Pittsburgh disabled list (June 7-July 2 and July 20, 1996-remainder of season); included rehabilitation assignment to Gulf Coast Pirates (June 24-28). ... On Pittsburgh disabled list (March 31-May 28, 1997); included rehabilitation assignment to Carolina (May 9-28). ... Released by Pirates (August 26, 1997). ... Signed by Milwaukee Brewers (September 2, 1997). ... On Milwaukee disabled list (May 18-June 2 and June 22-July 23, 1998); included rehabilitation assignments to Beloit (May 28-June 1) and Louisville (July 9-23). ... Released by Brewers (July 26, 1998). ... Signed by Atlanta Braves organization (August 5, 1998).
STATISTICAL NOTES: Pitched 4-0 one-hit, complete-game victory against Colorado (August 29, 1995).
MISCELLANEOUS: Made an out in only appearance as pinch hitter (1995). ... Walked in only appearance as pinch hitter with Pittsburgh (1996).

Year Team (League)	W	L	Pct.	ERA	G	GS	CG	ShO	Sv.	IP	H	R	ER	BB	SO
1989— Welland (N.Y.-Penn)	4	5	.444	4.47	13	10	0	0	0	50¹/₃	54	34	25	15	30
1990— Augusta (S. Atl.)	7	7	.500	2.75	35	1	0	0	4	72	71	30	22	30	71
— Salem (Carolina)	0	1	.000	5.00	11	4	0	0	2	36	39	22	20	17	28
1991— Salem (Carolina)	11	6	.647	3.12	25	25	5	•2	0	158²/₃	124	70	55	60	113
1992— Carolina (Southern)	6	6	.500	3.03	19	19	2	1	0	121²/₃	104	52	41	47	101
— Pittsburgh (N.L.)	2	0	1.000	0.69	6	1	0	0	0	13	9	1	1	5	5
— Buffalo (A.A.)	3	3	.500	5.49	8	8	0	0	0	39¹/₃	51	27	24	14	19
1993— Pittsburgh (N.L.)	8	8	.500	4.27	44	17	1	1	2	141¹/₃	143	72	67	42	114
1994— Pittsburgh (N.L.)	7	8	.467	4.59	29	17	1	0	0	119²/₃	136	69	61	50	86
1995— Pittsburgh (N.L.)	5	*16	.238	4.80	33	25	3	1	1	165	174	96	88	72	120
1996— Pittsburgh (N.L.)	4	8	.333	5.40	16	15	1	0	0	81²/₃	86	49	49	39	81
— GC Pirates (GCL)	0	0	...	0.00	1	1	0	0	0	3	2	0	0	0	4
1997— Carolina (Southern)	0	1	.000	10.13	12	3	0	0	0	16	25	20	18	16	20
— Pittsburgh (N.L.)	0	0	...	3.94	14	0	0	0	0	16	17	7	7	13	9
— Milwaukee (A.L.)■	1	0	1.000	9.00	2	0	0	0	0	2	3	2	2	0	0
1998— Milwaukee (A.L.)■	1	5	.167	7.11	13	9	0	0	0	55²/₃	67	49	44	31	37
— Beloit (Midwest)	0	1	.000	7.20	1	1	0	0	0	5	7	4	4	0	3
— Louisville (Int'l)	1	0	1.000	8.76	3	3	0	0	0	12¹/₃	17	12	12	5	6
— Richmond (Int'l)■	1	0	1.000	1.98	8	0	0	0	0	13²/₃	11	4	3	3	9
A.L. totals (1 year)	1	0	1.000	9.00	2	0	0	0	0	2	3	2	2	0	0
N.L. totals (7 years)	27	45	.375	4.82	155	84	6	2	3	592¹/₃	632	343	317	252	452
Major league totals (7 years)	28	45	.384	4.83	157	84	6	2	3	594¹/₃	635	345	319	252	452

WAINHOUSE, DAVE　　　　P　　　　ROCKIES

PERSONAL: Born November 7, 1967, in Toronto. ... 6-2/196. ... Throws right, bats left. ... Full name: David Paul Wainhouse.
HIGH SCHOOL: Mercer Island (Wash.).
COLLEGE: Washington State.
TRANSACTIONS/CAREER NOTES: Selected by Montreal Expos organization in first round (19th pick overall) of free-agent draft (June 1, 1988). ... On Harrisburg disabled list (April 25-May 3, 1991). ... On disabled list (August 13-September 8, 1992). ... Traded by Expos with P Kevin Foster to Seattle Mariners for IF Frank Bolick and a player to be named later (November 20, 1992); Expos organization acquired C Miah Bradbury to complete deal (December 8, 1992). ... On Calgary disabled list (April 23-August 3, 1993). ... Released by Mariners (March 29, 1994). ... Signed by Syracuse, Toronto Blue Jays organization (December 20, 1994). ... Released by Syracuse (June 5, 1995). ... Signed by Florida Marlins organization (June 8, 1995). ... Granted free agency (October 16, 1995). ... Signed by Pittsburgh Pirates organization (January 28, 1996). ... Granted free agency (October 15, 1997). ... Signed by Colorado Rockies organization (November 14, 1997).
MISCELLANEOUS: Member of 1988 Canadian Olympic baseball team.

Year Team (League)	W	L	Pct.	ERA	G	GS	CG	ShO	Sv.	IP	H	R	ER	BB	SO
1989— W.P. Beach (FSL)	1	1	.167	4.07	13	13	0	0	0	66¹/₃	75	35	30	19	26
1990— W.P. Beach (FSL)	6	3	.667	2.11	12	12	2	1	0	76²/₃	68	28	18	34	58
— Jacksonville (Southern)	7	7	.500	4.33	17	16	2	0	0	95²/₃	97	59	46	47	59
1991— Harrisburg (Eastern)	2	2	.500	2.60	33	0	0	0	11	52	49	17	15	17	46
— Indianapolis (A.A.)	2	0	1.000	4.08	14	0	0	0	1	28²/₃	28	14	13	15	13
— Montreal (N.L.)	0	1	.000	6.75	2	0	0	0	0	2²/₃	2	2	2	4	1
1992— Indianapolis (A.A.)	5	4	.556	4.11	44	0	0	0	21	46	48	22	21	24	37
1993— Seattle (A.L.)■	0	0	...	27.00	3	0	0	0	0	2¹/₃	7	7	7	5	2
— Calgary (PCL)	0	1	.000	4.02	13	0	0	0	5	15²/₃	10	7	7	7	7
1994—								Out of organized baseball.							
1995— Syracuse (Int'l)■	3	2	.600	3.70	26	0	0	0	5	24¹/₃	29	13	10	11	18
— Portland (Eastern)■	2	1	.667	7.20	17	0	0	0	0	25	39	22	20	8	16
— Charlotte (Int'l)	0	0	...	9.82	4	0	0	0	0	3²/₃	6	6	4	4	2
1996— Carolina (Southern)■	5	3	.625	3.16	45	0	0	0	25	51¹/₃	43	22	18	31	34
— Pittsburgh (N.L.)	1	0	1.000	5.70	17	0	0	0	0	23²/₃	22	16	15	10	16

W

Year Team (League)	W	L	Pct.	ERA	G	GS	CG	ShO	Sv.	IP	H	R	ER	BB	SO
1997—Pittsburgh (N.L.)	0	1	.000	8.04	25	0	0	0	0	28	34	28	25	17	21
—Calgary (PCL)	2	0	1.000	5.92	25	0	0	0	1	38	46	25	25	13	24
1998—Colo. Springs (PCL)■	2	3	.400	3.60	38	0	0	0	4	50	47	25	20	23	44
—Colorado (N.L.)	1	0	1.000	4.91	10	0	0	0	0	11	15	6	6	5	3
A.L. totals (1 year)	0	0	...	27.00	3	0	0	0	0	2 1/3	7	7	7	5	2
N.L. totals (4 years)	2	2	.500	6.61	54	0	0	0	0	65 1/3	73	52	48	36	41
Major league totals (5 years)	2	2	.500	7.32	57	0	0	0	0	67 2/3	80	59	55	41	43

WAKEFIELD, TIM   P   RED SOX

PERSONAL: Born August 2, 1966, in Melbourne, Fla. ... 6-2/206. ... Throws right, bats right. ... Full name: Timothy Stephen Wakefield.
HIGH SCHOOL: Eau Gallie (Melbourne, Fla.).
COLLEGE: Florida Tech.
TRANSACTIONS/CAREER NOTES: Selected by Pittsburgh Pirates organization in eighth round of free-agent draft (June 1, 1988). ... Released by Pirates (April 20, 1995). ... Signed by Boston Red Sox organization (April 26, 1995). ... On disabled list (April 15-May 6, 1997).
HONORS: Named N.L. Rookie Pitcher of the Year by THE SPORTING NEWS (1992). ... Named A.L. Comeback Player of the Year by THE SPORTING NEWS (1995).
STATISTICAL NOTES: Led Carolina League with 24 home runs allowed in 1990. ... Led American Association with 27 home runs allowed and 23 hit batsmen in 1994. ... Led A.L. with 16 hit batsmen in 1997.
MISCELLANEOUS: Appeared in one game as pinch runner with Pittsburgh (1992). ... Had a sacrifice hit in only appearance as pinch hitter (1998).

Year Team (League)	W	L	Pct.	ERA	G	GS	CG	ShO	Sv.	IP	H	R	ER	BB	SO
1989—Welland (N.Y.-Penn)	1	1	.500	3.40	18	1	0	0	2	39 2/3	30	17	15	21	42
1990—Salem (Carolina)	10	•14	.417	4.73	28	•28	2	0	0	*190 1/3	*187	109	*100	*85	127
1991—Carolina (Southern)	15	8	.652	2.90	26	25	•8	1	0	183	155	68	59	51	120
—Buffalo (A.A.)	0	1	.000	11.57	1	1	0	0	0	4 2/3	8	6	6	1	4
1992—Buffalo (A.A.)	10	3	.769	3.06	20	20	*6	1	0	135 1/3	122	52	46	51	71
—Pittsburgh (N.L.)	8	1	.889	2.15	13	13	4	1	0	92	76	26	22	35	51
1993—Pittsburgh (N.L.)	6	11	.353	5.61	24	20	3	2	0	128 1/3	145	83	80	75	59
—Carolina (Southern)	3	5	.375	6.99	9	9	1	0	0	56 2/3	68	48	44	22	36
1994—Buffalo (A.A.)	5	*15	.250	5.84	30	•29	4	1	0	175 2/3	*197	*127	*114	*98	83
1995—Pawtucket (Int'l)■	2	1	.667	2.52	4	4	0	0	0	25	23	10	7	9	14
—Boston (A.L.)	16	8	.667	2.95	27	27	6	1	0	195 1/3	163	76	64	68	119
1996—Boston (A.L.)	14	13	.519	5.14	32	32	6	0	0	211 2/3	238	*151	121	90	140
1997—Boston (A.L.)	12	•15	.444	4.25	35	29	4	2	0	201 1/3	193	109	95	87	151
1998—Boston (A.L.)	17	8	.680	4.58	36	33	2	0	0	216	211	123	110	79	146
A.L. totals (4 years)	59	44	.573	4.26	130	121	18	3	0	824 1/3	805	459	390	324	556
N.L. totals (2 years)	14	12	.538	4.17	37	33	7	3	0	220 1/3	221	109	102	110	110
Major league totals (6 years)	73	56	.566	4.24	167	154	25	6	0	1044 2/3	1026	568	492	434	666

DIVISION SERIES RECORD

Year Team (League)	W	L	Pct.	ERA	G	GS	CG	ShO	Sv.	IP	H	R	ER	BB	SO
1995—Boston (A.L.)	0	1	.000	11.81	1	1	0	0	0	5 1/3	5	7	7	5	4
1998—Boston (A.L.)	0	1	.000	33.75	1	1	0	0	0	1 1/3	3	5	5	2	1
Div. series totals (2 years)	0	2	.000	16.20	2	2	0	0	0	6 2/3	8	12	12	7	5

CHAMPIONSHIP SERIES RECORD

RECORDS: Shares single-series record for most complete games—2 (1992). ... Shares N.L. career record for most complete games—2.

Year Team (League)	W	L	Pct.	ERA	G	GS	CG	ShO	Sv.	IP	H	R	ER	BB	SO
1992—Pittsburgh (N.L.)	2	0	1.000	3.00	2	2	2	0	0	18	14	6	6	5	7

RECORD AS POSITION PLAYER

Year Team (League)	Pos.	G	AB	R	H	2B	3B	HR	RBI	Avg.	BB	SO	SB	PO	A	E	Avg.
1988—Watertown (NYP)	1B	54	159	24	30	6	2	3	20	.189	25	57	3	377	25	8	.980
1989—Augusta (S. Atl.)	3B-1B	11	34	5	8	2	1	0	5	.235	1	14	1	27	6	3	.917
—Welland (NYP)	3B-2B-1B	36	63	7	13	4	0	1	3	.206	3	21	1	26	31	8	.877

WALBECK, MATT   C   ANGELS

W

PERSONAL: Born October 2, 1969, in Sacramento. ... 5-11/206. ... Bats both, throws right. ... Full name: Matthew Lovick Walbeck.
HIGH SCHOOL: Sacramento.
TRANSACTIONS/CAREER NOTES: Selected by Chicago Cubs organization in eighth round of free-agent draft (June 2, 1987). ... On Winston-Salem disabled list (April 12-July 11, 1990). ... On Charleston, W.Va. disabled list (September 5, 1992-remainder of season). ... Traded by Cubs with P Dave Stevens to Minnesota Twins for P Willie Banks (November 24, 1993). ... On Minnesota disabled list (March 31-June 17, 1996); included rehabilitation assignments to Fort Myers (May 31-June 11) and New Britain (June 11-17). ... Traded by Twins to Detroit Tigers for P Brent Stentz (December 11, 1996). ... On Detroit disabled list (April 19-July 9, 1997); included rehabilitation assignments to Lakeland (June 12-15) and Toledo (June 16-July 9). ... Traded by Tigers with 3B Phil Nevin to Anaheim Angels for P Nick Skuse (November 20, 1997).
STATISTICAL NOTES: Tied for Carolina League lead with 10 sacrifice flies in 1991. ... Led American Association catchers with 561 total chances and tied for lead with nine double plays in 1993. ... Career major league grand slams: 1.
MISCELLANEOUS: Batted righthanded only (1987-89).

Year Team (League)	Pos.	G	AB	R	H	2B	3B	HR	RBI	Avg.	BB	SO	SB	PO	A	E	Avg.
1987—Wytheville (App.)	C	51	169	24	53	9	3	1	20	.314	22	39	0	293	22	1	*.997
1988—Char., W.Va. (SAL)	C	104	312	28	68	9	0	2	24	.218	30	44	7	549	68	14	.978
1989—Peoria (Midwest)	C	94	341	38	86	19	0	4	47	.252	20	47	5	605	72	11	.984
1990—Peoria (Midwest)	C	25	66	2	15	1	0	0	5	.227	5	7	1	137	16	2	.987
1991—Win.-Salem (Car.)	C	91	260	25	70	11	0	3	41	.269	20	23	3	473	64	12	.978

Year Team (League)	Pos.	G	AB	R	H	2B	3B	HR	RBI	Avg.	BB	SO	SB	PO	A	E	Avg.
1992—Charlotte (Southern) ..	C-1B	105	385	48	116	22	1	7	42	.301	33	56	0	552	80	10	.984
1993—Chicago (N.L.)...........	C	11	30	2	6	2	0	1	6	.200	1	6	0	49	2	0	1.000
—Iowa (Am. Assoc.).......	C	87	331	31	93	18	2	6	43	.281	18	47	1	496	*64	4	*.998
1994—Minnesota (A.L.)■	C-DH	97	338	31	69	12	0	5	35	.204	17	37	1	496	45	4	.993
1995—Minnesota (A.L.)........	C	115	393	40	101	18	1	1	44	.257	25	71	3	604	35	6	.991
1996—Fort Myers (FSL)........	C	9	33	4	9	1	1	0	9	.273	4	2	0	46	6	0	1.000
—New Britain (East.).....	C	7	24	1	5	0	0	0	0	.208	1	1	0	11	2	0	1.000
—Minnesota (A.L.)........	C	63	215	25	48	10	0	2	24	.223	9	34	3	326	19	2	.994
1997—Detroit (A.L.)■........	C	47	137	18	38	3	0	3	10	.277	12	19	3	240	15	3	.988
—Lakeland (Fla. St.)......	C	4	10	4	5	1	0	0	3	.500	4	1	0	14	0	1	.933
—Toledo (Int'l)............	C	17	59	6	18	2	1	1	8	.305	4	15	0	55	9	3	.955
1998—Anaheim (A.L.)■........	C-DH	108	338	41	87	15	2	6	46	.257	30	68	1	682	46	7	.990
American League totals (5 years)		430	1421	155	343	58	3	17	159	.241	93	229	11	2348	160	22	.991
National League totals (1 year)		11	30	2	6	2	0	1	6	.200	1	6	0	49	2	0	1.000
Major league totals (6 years)		441	1451	157	349	60	3	18	165	.241	94	235	11	2397	162	22	.991

WALKER, JAMIE   P   ROYALS

PERSONAL: Born July 1, 1971, in McMinnville, Tenn. ... 6-2/190. ... Throws left, bats left. ... Full name: Jamie Ross Walker.
HIGH SCHOOL: Warren County (McMinnville, Tenn.).
COLLEGE: Austin Peay.
TRANSACTIONS/CAREER NOTES: Selected by Houston Astros organization in 10th round of free-agent draft (June 1, 1992). ... Selected by Atlanta Braves organization from Astros organization in Rule 5 major league draft (December 9, 1996). ... Traded by Braves with OF Jermaine Dye to Kansas City Royals for OF Michael Tucker and IF Keith Lockhart (March 27, 1997). ... On Kansas City disabled list (June 5-24, 1997); included rehabilitation assignment to Wichita (June 11-24). ... On Kansas City disabled list (June 14, 1998-remainder of season). ... Granted free agency (December 21, 1998). ... Re-signed by Royals organization (December 21, 1998).

Year Team (League)	W	L	Pct.	ERA	G	GS	CG	ShO	Sv.	IP	H	R	ER	BB	SO
1992—Auburn (N.Y.-Penn)..........	4	6	.400	3.13	15	14	0	0	0	83 1/3	75	35	29	21	67
1993—Quad City (Midwest)	3	11	.214	5.13	25	24	1	1	0	131 2/3	140	92	75	48	121
1994—Quad City (Midwest)	8	10	.444	4.18	32	18	0	0	1	125	133	80	58	42	104
1995—Jackson (Texas)	4	2	.667	4.50	50	0	0	0	2	58	59	29	29	24	38
1996—Jackson (Texas)	5	1	.833	2.50	45	7	0	0	2	101	94	34	28	35	79
1997—Kansas City (A.L.)■...........	3	3	.500	5.44	50	0	0	0	0	43	46	28	26	20	24
—Wichita (Texas)	0	1	.000	9.45	5	0	0	0	0	6 2/3	6	8	7	5	6
1998—Omaha (Pacific Coast)........	5	1	.833	2.70	7	7	0	0	0	46 2/3	57	15	14	11	21
—Kansas City (A.L.)	0	1	.000	9.87	6	2	0	0	0	17 1/3	30	20	19	3	15
Major league totals (2 years)......	3	4	.429	6.71	56	2	0	0	0	60 1/3	76	48	45	23	39

WALKER, LARRY   OF   ROCKIES

PERSONAL: Born December 1, 1966, in Maple Ridge, B.C. ... 6-3/237. ... Bats left, throws right. ... Full name: Larry Kenneth Robert Walker.
HIGH SCHOOL: Maple Ridge (B.C.) Senior Secondary School.
TRANSACTIONS/CAREER NOTES: Signed as non-drafted free agent by Montreal Expos organization (November 14, 1984). ... On disabled list (April 4, 1988-entire season; June 28-July 13, 1991; and May 26-June 10, 1993). ... On suspended list (June 24-28, 1994). ... Granted free agency (October 24, 1994). ... Signed by Colorado Rockies (April 8, 1995). ... On Colorado disabled list (June 10-August 15, 1996); included rehabilitation assignments to Salem (August 6-9) and Colorado Springs (August 9-15). ... On Colorado disabled list (June 18-July 3, 1998).
RECORDS: Shares major league record for most long hits in two consecutive games (May 21-22, 1996; 2 doubles, 3 triples and 1 home run). ... Holds N.L. single-season records for most consecutive long hits—6 (May 21-22, 1996; 2 doubles, 3 triples and 1 home run); and highest slugging average by a lefthander (100 or more games)—.720 (1997).
HONORS: Named outfielder on THE SPORTING NEWS N.L. All-Star team (1992 and 1997). ... Won N.L. Gold Glove as outfielder (1992-93 and 1997-98). ... Named outfielder on THE SPORTING NEWS N.L. Silver Slugger team (1992 and 1997). ... Named N.L. Most Valuable Player by Baseball Writers' Association of America (1997).
STATISTICAL NOTES: Hit three home runs in one game (April 5, 1997). ... Led N.L. with 409 total bases in 1997. ... Led N.L. with .452 on-base percentage in 1997. ... Led N.L. in slugging percentage with .720 in 1997. ... Led N.L. outfielders in double plays with four in 1997. ... Had 20-game hitting streak (May 4-25, 1998). ... Career major league grand slams: 3.

Year Team (League)	Pos.	G	AB	R	H	2B	3B	HR	RBI	Avg.	BB	SO	SB	PO	A	E	Avg.
1985—Utica (N.Y.-Penn)........	1B-3B	62	215	24	48	8	2	2	26	.223	18	57	12	354	62	8	.981
1986—Burlington (Midw.)	OF-3B	95	332	67	96	12	6	29	74	.289	46	112	16	106	51	10	.940
—W.P. Beach (FSL).........	OF	38	113	20	32	7	5	4	16	.283	26	32	2	44	5	0	1.000
1987—Jacksonville (Sou.).....	OF	128	474	91	136	25	7	26	83	.287	67	120	24	263	9	9	.968
1988—							Did not play.										
1989—Indianapolis (A.A.)......	OF	114	385	68	104	18	2	12	59	.270	50	87	36	241	*18	*11	.959
—Montreal (N.L.)...........	OF	20	47	4	8	0	0	0	4	.170	5	13	1	19	2	0	1.000
1990—Montreal (N.L.)..........	OF	133	419	59	101	18	3	19	51	.241	49	112	21	249	12	4	.985
1991—Montreal (N.L.)..........	OF-1B	137	487	59	141	30	2	16	64	.290	42	102	14	536	36	6	.990
1992—Montreal (N.L.)..........	OF	143	528	85	159	31	4	23	93	.301	41	97	18	269	16	2	.993
1993—Montreal (N.L.)..........	OF-1B	138	490	85	130	24	5	22	86	.265	80	76	29	316	16	6	.982
1994—Montreal (N.L.)..........	OF-1B	103	395	76	127	44	2	19	86	.322	47	74	15	423	29	9	.980
1995—Colorado (N.L.)■........	OF	131	494	96	151	31	5	36	101	.306	49	72	16	225	13	3	.988
1996—Colorado (N.L.)..........	OF	83	272	58	75	18	4	18	58	.276	20	58	18	153	4	1	.994
—Salem (Carolina)	DH	2	8	3	4	3	0	1	1	.500	0	1	0	. . .	. . .	. . .	. . .
—Colo. Springs (PCL) ...	DH	3	11	2	4	0	0	2	8	.364	1	4	0	6	2	0	1.000
1997—Colorado (N.L.)..........	OF-1B-DH	153	568	143	208	46	4	*49	130	.366	78	90	33	254	14	2	.993
1998—Colorado (N.L.)..........	O-DH-2-3	130	454	113	165	46	3	23	67	*.363	64	61	14	236	8	4	.984
Major league totals (10 years)		1171	4154	778	1265	288	32	225	740	.305	475	755	179	2680	150	37	.987

W

DIVISION SERIES RECORD

Year—Team (League)	Pos.	G	AB	R	H	2B	3B	HR	RBI	Avg.	BB	SO	SB	PO	A	E	Avg.
1995—Colorado (N.L.)	OF	4	14	3	3	0	0	1	3	.214	3	4	1	3	0	0	1.000

ALL-STAR GAME RECORD

Year—League	Pos.	AB	R	H	2B	3B	HR	RBI	Avg.	BB	SO	SB	PO	A	E	Avg.
1992—National	PH	1	0	1	0	0	0	0	1.000	0	0	0	...	...	...	...
1997—National	OF	1	0	0	0	0	0	0	.000	1	0	0	0	0	0	...
1998—National	OF	1	1	0	0	0	0	0	.000	1	0	0	2	0	0	1.000
All-Star Game totals (3 years)		3	1	1	0	0	0	0	.333	2	0	0	2	0	0	1.000

WALKER, TODD   2B   TWINS

PERSONAL: Born May 25, 1973, in Bakersfield, Calif. ... 6-0/181. ... Bats left, throws right. ... Full name: Todd Arthur Walker.
HIGH SCHOOL: Airline (Bossier City, La.).
COLLEGE: Louisiana State.
TRANSACTIONS/CAREER NOTES: Selected by Texas Rangers organization in 51st round of free-agent draft (June 3, 1991); did not sign. ... Selected by Minnesota Twins organization in first round (eighth pick overall) of free-agent draft (June 2, 1994).
HONORS: Named Most Outstanding Player of College World Series (1993).
STATISTICAL NOTES: Led Pacific Coast League with 330 total bases and .599 slugging percentage and tied for lead in intentional bases on balls received with 11 in 1996.

Year—Team (League)	Pos.	G	AB	R	H	2B	3B	HR	RBI	Avg.	BB	SO	SB	PO	A	E	Avg.
1994—Fort Myers (FSL)	2B	46	171	29	52	5	2	10	34	.304	32	15	6	98	112	9	.959
1995—New Britain (East.)	2B-3B	137	513	83	149	27	3	21	85	.290	63	101	23	215	355	27	.955
1996—Salt Lake (PCL)	3B-2B	135	551	94	*187	*41	9	*28	*111	.339	57	91	13	129	276	19	.955
—Minnesota (A.L.)	3B-2B-DH	25	82	8	21	6	0	0	6	.256	4	13	2	16	39	2	.965
1997—Minnesota (A.L.)	3B-2B-DH	52	156	15	37	7	1	3	16	.237	11	30	7	35	86	4	.968
—Salt Lake (PCL)	3B	83	322	69	111	20	1	11	53	.345	46	49	5	44	174	*24	.901
1998—Minnesota (A.L.)	2B-DH	143	528	85	167	41	3	12	62	.316	47	65	19	219	363	13	.978
Major league totals (3 years)		220	766	108	225	54	4	15	84	.294	62	108	28	270	488	19	.976

WALL, DONNE   P   PADRES

PERSONAL: Born July 11, 1967, in Potosi, Mo. ... 6-1/180. ... Throws right, bats right. ... Full name: Donnell Lee Wall. ... Name pronounced DON-ee.
HIGH SCHOOL: Festus (Mo.).
JUNIOR COLLEGE: Jefferson College (Mo.), then St. Louis Community College at Meramec.
COLLEGE: Southwestern Louisiana.
TRANSACTIONS/CAREER NOTES: Selected by Houston Astros organization in 18th round of free-agent draft (June 5, 1989). ... On disabled list (May 27-June 16, 1994). ... Claimed on waivers by Cincinnati Reds (October 7, 1997). ... Traded by Reds with C Paul Bako to Detroit Tigers for OF Melvin Nieves (November 11, 1997). ... Traded by Tigers with P Dan Miceli and 3B Ryan Balfe to San Diego Padres for P Tim Worrell and OF Trey Beamon (November 19, 1997).
HONORS: Named Pacific Coast League Most Valuable Player (1995).
STATISTICAL NOTES: Led South Atlantic League with 18 home runs allowed in 1990.

Year—Team (League)	W	L	Pct.	ERA	G	GS	CG	ShO	Sv.	IP	H	R	ER	BB	SO
1989—Auburn (N.Y.-Penn)	7	0	*1.000	1.79	12	8	3	1	1	65 1/3	45	17	13	12	69
1990—Asheville (S. Atl.)	6	8	.429	5.18	28	22	1	0	1	132	149	87	76	47	111
1991—Burlington (Midw.)	7	5	.583	2.03	16	16	3	1	0	106 2/3	73	30	24	21	102
—Osceola (Florida St.)..........	6	3	.667	2.09	12	12	4	2	0	77 1/3	55	22	18	11	62
1992—Osceola (Florida St.).........	3	1	.750	2.63	7	7	0	0	0	41	37	13	12	8	30
—Jackson (Texas)	9	6	.600	3.54	18	18	2	0	0	114 1/3	114	51	45	26	99
1993—Tucson (PCL)	6	4	.600	3.83	25	22	0	0	0	131 2/3	147	73	56	25	89
1994—Tucson (PCL)	11	8	.579	4.43	26	24	2	2	0	148 1/3	171	87	73	35	84
1995—Tucson (PCL)	*17	6	.739	*3.30	28	•28	0	0	0	*177 1/3	190	72	65	32	*119
—Houston (N.L.)	3	1	.750	5.55	6	5	0	0	0	24 1/3	33	19	15	5	16
1996—Tucson (PCL)	3	3	.500	4.13	8	8	0	0	0	52 1/3	67	30	24	6	36
—Houston (N.L.)	9	8	.529	4.56	26	23	2	1	0	150	170	84	76	34	99
1997—New Orleans (A.A.)	8	7	.533	3.85	17	17	1	0	0	110	109	49	47	24	84
—Houston (N.L.)	2	5	.286	6.26	8	8	0	0	0	41 2/3	53	31	29	16	25
1998—Las Vegas (PCL)■	2	0	1.000	4.80	3	3	0	0	0	15	11	8	8	8	12
—San Diego (N.L.)	5	4	.556	2.43	46	1	0	0	1	70 1/3	50	20	19	32	56
Major league totals (4 years)	19	18	.514	4.37	86	37	2	1	1	286 1/3	306	154	139	87	196

DIVISION SERIES RECORD

Year—Team (League)	W	L	Pct.	ERA	G	GS	CG	ShO	Sv.	IP	H	R	ER	BB	SO
1998—San Diego (N.L.)	0	0	...	9.00	1	0	0	0	0	1	2	1	1	0	2

CHAMPIONSHIP SERIES RECORD

Year—Team (League)	W	L	Pct.	ERA	G	GS	CG	ShO	Sv.	IP	H	R	ER	BB	SO
1998—San Diego (N.L.)	0	0	...	3.00	3	0	0	0	1	3	3	2	1	4	4

WORLD SERIES RECORD

Year—Team (League)	W	L	Pct.	ERA	G	GS	CG	ShO	Sv.	IP	H	R	ER	BB	SO
1998—San Diego (N.L.)	0	1	.000	6.75	2	0	0	0	0	2 2/3	3	2	2	3	1

W

PERSONAL: Born September 1, 1971, in Van Nuys, Calif. ... 6-3/215. ... Throws right, bats right. ... Full name: Derek Robert Wallace.
HIGH SCHOOL: Chatsworth (Calif.).
COLLEGE: Pepperdine.
TRANSACTIONS/CAREER NOTES: Selected by Pittsburgh Pirates organization in 36th round of free-agent draft (June 5, 1989); did not sign. ... Selected by Chicago Cubs organization in first round (11th pick overall) of free-agent draft (June 1, 1992). ... Traded by Cubs with P Geno Morones to Kansas City Royals for OF Brian McRae (April 5, 1995). ... Traded by Royals organization with a player to be named later to New York Mets organization for P Jason Jacome and P Allen McDill (July 21, 1995); Mets acquired P John Carter to complete deal (November 16, 1995). ... On New York disabled list (March 27, 1997-entire season); included rehabilitation assignments to Gulf Coast Mets (July 22-August 17), St. Lucie (August 18-31) and Norfolk (September 1).
RECORDS: Shares major league record for most strikeouts in one inning—4 (September 13, 1996, ninth inning).
STATISTICAL NOTES: Led Florida State League with 11 balks in 1993.

Year	Team (League)	W	L	Pct.	ERA	G	GS	CG	ShO	Sv.	IP	H	R	ER	BB	SO
1992—	Peoria (Midwest)	0	1	.000	4.91	2	0	0	0	0	$3^2/_3$	3	2	2	1	2
1993—	Daytona (Fla. St.)	5	6	.455	4.20	14	12	0	0	1	$79^1/_3$	85	50	37	23	34
—	Iowa (Am. Assoc.)	0	0	...	11.25	1	1	0	0	0	4	8	5	5	1	2
—	Orlando (South.)	5	7	.417	5.03	15	15	2	0	0	$96^2/_3$	105	59	54	28	69
1994—	Orlando (South.)	2	9	.182	5.74	33	12	1	0	8	$89^1/_3$	95	61	57	31	49
—	Iowa (Am. Assoc.)	0	1	.000	4.15	5	0	0	0	1	$4^1/_3$	4	4	2	4	3
1995—	Wichita (Texas)■	4	3	.571	4.40	26	0	0	0	6	43	51	23	21	13	24
—	Binghamton (Eastern)■....	0	1	.000	5.28	15	0	0	0	2	$15^1/_3$	11	9	9	9	8
1996—	Norfolk (Int'l)	5	2	.714	1.72	49	0	0	0	26	$57^2/_3$	37	20	11	17	52
—	New York (N.L.)	2	3	.400	4.01	19	0	0	0	3	$24^2/_3$	29	12	11	14	15
1997—	GC Mets (GCL)	0	1	.000	3.38	8	5	0	0	0	8	6	3	3	1	9
—	St. Lucie (Fla. St.)	0	0	...	6.43	5	0	0	0	0	7	7	6	5	2	8
—	Norfolk (Int'l)	0	1	.000	9.00	1	0	0	0	0	1	2	2	1	1	0
1998—	Norfolk (Int'l)	5	2	.714	3.88	54	0	0	0	16	$60^1/_3$	58	31	26	27	50
Major league totals (1 year).......		2	3	.400	4.01	19	0	0	0	3	$24^2/_3$	29	12	11	14	15

PERSONAL: Born April 12, 1976, in Wheeling, W.Va. ... 6-2/228. ... Throws left, bats left. ... Full name: Jeffrey Allen Wallace.
HIGH SCHOOL: Minerva (Ohio).
TRANSACTIONS/CAREER NOTES: Selected by Kansas City Royals organization in 25th round of free-agent draft (June 1, 1995). ... Traded by Royals with P Jeff Granger, P Jeff Martin and 3B Joe Randa to Pittsburgh Pirates for SS Jay Bell and 1B Jeff King (December 13, 1996). ... On disabled list (March 22, 1998-entire season).

Year	Team (League)	W	L	Pct.	ERA	G	GS	CG	ShO	Sv.	IP	H	R	ER	BB	SO
1995—	Sara. Royals (GCL)	5	3	.625	1.22	12	7	0	0	1	$44^1/_3$	28	20	6	15	51
1996—	Lansing (Midwest)	4	9	.308	5.30	30	21	0	0	0	$122^1/_3$	140	79	72	66	84
1997—	Lynchburg (Carolina)■	5	0	1.000	1.65	9	0	0	0	0	$16^1/_3$	9	3	3	10	13
—	Carolina (Southern)	4	8	.333	5.40	38	0	0	0	3	$43^1/_3$	43	37	26	36	39
—	Pittsburgh (N.L.)	0	0	...	0.75	11	0	0	0	0	12	8	2	1	8	14
1998—	Pittsburgh (N.L.)							Did not play.								
Major league totals (1 year).......		0	0	...	0.75	11	0	0	0	0	12	8	2	1	8	14

PERSONAL: Born July 8, 1965, in Newnan, Ga. ... 6-1/200. ... Bats right, throws right. ... Full name: Jerome O'Terrell Walton.
HIGH SCHOOL: Enterprise (Ala.).
JUNIOR COLLEGE: Enterprise (Ala.) State Junior College.
TRANSACTIONS/CAREER NOTES: Selected by Chicago Cubs organization in second round of free-agent draft (January 14, 1986). ... On Chicago disabled list (May 11-June 11, 1989); included rehabilitation assignment to Iowa (June 6-11). ... On Chicago disabled list (June 18-August 2, 1990); included rehabilitation assignment to Iowa (July 29-August 1). ... On Chicago disabled list (March 28-April 24, 1992); included rehabilitation assignment to Iowa (April 17-24). ... On Iowa disabled list (July 1-September 14, 1992). ... Granted free agency (December 19, 1992). ... Signed by California Angels organization (January 29, 1993). ... On Vancouver disabled list (July 19-August 20, 1993). ... Released by Angels organization (August 20, 1993). ... Signed by Cincinnati Reds organization (November 4, 1993). ... On disabled list (July 1-23 and July 27, 1994-remainder of season). ... Granted free agency (December 21, 1995). ... Signed by Atlanta Braves (January 3, 1996). ... On Atlanta disabled list (May 30, 1996-remainder of season); included rehabilitation assignments to Greenville (June 20-23) and Richmond (July 15-21). ... Granted free agency (October 29, 1996). ... Signed by Baltimore Orioles organization (December 18, 1996). ... On Baltimore disabled list (April 25-September 1, 1997); included rehabilitation assignment to Frederick (August 22-September 1). ... Granted free agency (October 30, 1997). ... Signed by Tampa Bay Devil Rays (January 27, 1998). ... On disabled list (May 8-26, 1998). ... Released by Devil Rays (May 26, 1998).
HONORS: Named N.L. Rookie Player of the Year by THE SPORTING NEWS (1989). ... Named N.L. Rookie of the Year by Baseball Writers' Association of America (1989).
STATISTICAL NOTES: Led Appalachian League outfielders with 128 putouts and 131 total chances and tied for lead with two double plays in 1986. ... Led Midwest League in caught stealing with 25 in 1987. ... Had 30-game hitting streak (July 21-August 20, 1989).

							BATTING								FIELDING		
Year	Team (League)	Pos.	G	AB	R	H	2B	3B	HR	RBI	Avg.	BB	SO	SB	PO	A	E	Avg.
1986—	Wytheville (App.)........	OF-3B	62	229	48	66	7	4	5	34	.288	28	40	21	†130	7	3	.979
1987—	Peoria (Midwest)	OF	128	472	102	158	24	11	6	38	.335	91	91	49	255	9	7	.974
1988—	Pittsfield (Eastern)......	OF	120	414	64	137	26	2	3	49	*.331	41	69	42	270	11	2	*.993
1989—	Chicago (N.L.)	OF	116	475	64	139	23	3	5	46	.293	27	77	24	289	2	3	.990
—	Iowa (Am. Assoc.)	OF	4	18	4	6	1	0	1	3	.333	1	5	2	8	0	0	1.000
1990—	Chicago (N.L.)	OF	101	392	63	103	16	2	2	21	.263	50	70	14	247	3	6	.977
—	Iowa (Am. Assoc.)	OF	4	16	3	3	0	0	1	1	.188	2	4	0	6	1	0	1.000
1991—	Chicago (N.L.)	OF	123	270	42	59	13	1	5	17	.219	19	55	7	170	2	3	.983

W

Year Team (League)	Pos.	G	AB	R	H	2B	3B	HR	RBI	Avg.	BB	SO	SB	PO	A	E	Avg.
1992—Iowa (Am. Assoc.)......	OF	7	27	8	8	2	1	0	3	.296	4	6	1	10	0	0	1.000
—Chicago (N.L.).........	OF	30	55	7	7	0	1	0	1	.127	9	13	1	34	0	2	.944
1993—California (A.L.)■......	DH-OF	5	2	2	0	0	0	0	0	.000	1	2	1	2	0	0	1.000
—Vancouver (PCL).......	OF	54	176	34	55	11	1	2	20	.313	16	24	5	82	3	0	1.000
1994—Cincinnati (N.L.)■...	OF-1B	46	68	10	21	4	0	1	9	.309	4	12	1	57	1	1	.983
1995—Cincinnati (N.L.)........	OF-1B	102	162	32	47	12	1	8	22	.290	17	25	10	110	2	2	.982
1996—Atlanta (N.L.)■..........	OF	37	47	9	16	5	0	1	4	.340	5	10	0	34	0	0	1.000
—Greenville (Southern) .	OF	3	5	0	1	0	1	0	0	.200	3	1	0	2	0	0	1.000
—Richmond (Int'l).........	OF	6	18	3	8	2	1	1	5	.444	1	5	0	12	0	0	1.000
1997—Baltimore (A.L.)■...	OF-1B-DH	26	68	8	20	1	0	3	9	.294	4	10	0	52	1	0	1.000
—Frederick (Carolina)...	OF-1B	7	19	1	4	0	0	1	2	.211	5	0	1	15	0	0	1.000
1998—Tampa Bay (A.L.)■...	OF-DH	12	34	4	11	3	0	0	3	.324	2	6	0	13	2	0	1.000
American League totals (3 years)		43	104	14	31	4	0	3	12	.298	7	18	1	67	3	0	1.000
National League totals (7 years)		555	1469	227	392	73	8	22	120	.267	131	262	57	941	10	17	.982
Major league totals (10 years)		598	1573	241	423	77	8	25	132	.269	138	280	58	1008	13	17	.984

DIVISION SERIES RECORD

Year Team (League)	Pos.	G	AB	R	H	2B	3B	HR	RBI	Avg.	BB	SO	SB	PO	A	E	Avg.
1995—Cincinnati (N.L.)	OF-PH	3	3	0	0	0	0	0	0	.000	1	1	0	3	0	0	1.000
1997—Baltimore (A.L.)	1B	2	4	0	0	0	0	0	0	.000	0	2	0	5	1	0	1.000
Division series totals (2 years)		5	7	0	0	0	0	0	0	.000	1	3	0	8	1	0	1.000

CHAMPIONSHIP SERIES RECORD

RECORDS: Shares single-inning records for most at-bats—2; most hits—2; and most singles—2 (October 5, 1989, first inning).

Year Team (League)	Pos.	G	AB	R	H	2B	3B	HR	RBI	Avg.	BB	SO	SB	PO	A	E	Avg.
1989—Chicago (N.L.)	OF	5	22	4	8	0	0	0	2	.364	2	2	0	11	0	0	1.000
1995—Cincinnati (N.L.)	OF	2	7	0	0	0	0	0	0	.000	0	2	0	6	0	0	1.000
1997—Baltimore (A.L.)	OF	1	0	0	0	0	0	0	0	...	0	0	0	0	0	0	...
Championship series totals (3 years)		8	29	4	8	0	0	0	2	.276	2	4	0	17	0	0	1.000

WARD, BRYAN   P   WHITE SOX

PERSONAL: Born January 25, 1972, in Bristol, Pa. ... 6-2/210. ... Throws left, bats left. ... Full name: Bryan Matthew Ward.
HIGH SCHOOL: Rancoccas Valley Regional (Mount Holly, N.J.).
JUNIOR COLLEGE: County College of Morris (N.J.).
COLLEGE: South Carolina-Aiken.
TRANSACTIONS/CAREER NOTES: Selected by Florida Marlins organization in 20th round of free-agent draft (June 3, 1993). ... On Portland disabled list (April 23-May 1, 1997). ... Claimed on waivers by Chicago White Sox (October 14, 1997).

Year Team (League)	W	L	Pct.	ERA	G	GS	CG	ShO	Sv.	IP	H	R	ER	BB	SO
1993—Elmira (N.Y.-Penn)..............	2	5	.286	4.99	14	11	0	0	0	61 $\frac{1}{3}$	82	41	34	26	63
1994—Kane County (Midwest).....	3	4	.429	3.40	47	0	0	0	11	55 $\frac{2}{3}$	46	27	21	21	62
1995—Brevard County (FSL)......	5	1	.833	2.88	11	11	0	0	0	72	68	27	23	17	65
—Portland (Eastern).............	7	3	.700	4.50	20	11	1	1	2	72	70	42	36	31	71
1996—Portland (Eastern).........	9	9	.500	4.91	28	25	2	0	0	146 $\frac{2}{3}$	170	97	80	32	124
1997—Portland (Eastern).........	6	3	.667	3.91	12	12	0	0	0	76	71	39	33	19	69
—Charlotte (Int'l)..................	2	9	.182	6.93	15	14	2	0	0	75 $\frac{1}{3}$	102	62	58	30	48
1998—Birmingham (Southern)■..	2	3	.400	2.36	29	0	0	0	12	42	33	19	11	25	40
—Chicago (A.L.)..................	1	2	.333	3.33	28	0	0	0	1	27	30	13	10	7	17
Major league totals (1 year).......	1	2	.333	3.33	28	0	0	0	1	27	30	13	10	7	17

WARD, DARYLE   1B   ASTROS

PERSONAL: Born June 27, 1975, in Lynwood, Calif. ... 6-2/230. ... Bats left, throws left. ... Full name: Daryle Lamar Ward. ... Son of Gary Ward, outfielder with four major league teams (1979-90); and hitting coach, Charlotte Knights of International League.
HIGH SCHOOL: Brethren Christian (Riverside, Calif.).
JUNIOR COLLEGE: Rancho Santiago College (Calif.).
TRANSACTIONS/CAREER NOTES: Selected by Detroit Tigers organization in 15th round of free-agent draft (June 2, 1994). ... Traded by Tigers with C Brad Ausmus, P Jose Lima, P C.J. Nitkowski and P Trever Miller to Houston Astros for OF Brian Hunter, IF Orlando Miller, P Doug Brocail, P Todd Jones and cash (December 10, 1996).
STATISTICAL NOTES: Tied for Texas League lead with four intentional bases on balls in 1997.

Year Team (League)	Pos.	G	AB	R	H	2B	3B	HR	RBI	Avg.	BB	SO	SB	PO	A	E	Avg.
1994—Bristol (Appal.)	1B	48	161	17	43	6	0	5	30	.267	19	33	5	308	23	11	.968
1995—Fayetteville (SAL)........	1B	137	524	75	149	32	0	14	106	.284	46	111	1	1009	77	14	.987
1996—Lakeland (Fla. St.)	1B	128	464	65	135	29	4	10	68	.291	57	77	1	1058	103	8	.993
—Toledo (Int'l)..............	1B	6	23	1	4	0	0	0	1	.174	0	3	0	42	5	1	.979
1997—Jackson (Texas)■.......	1B	114	422	72	139	25	0	19	90	.329	46	68	4	951	76	12	.988
—New Orleans (A.A.).....	1B	14	48	4	18	1	0	2	8	.375	7	7	0	75	6	2	.976
1998—New Orleans (PCL).....	OF-1B	116	463	78	141	31	1	23	96	.305	41	78	2	482	48	13	.976
—Houston (N.L.)	PH	4	3	1	1	0	0	0	0	.333	1	2	0	...	...	...	...
Major league totals (1 year)		4	3	1	1	0	0	0	0	.333	1	2	0	...	...	...	

W

WARD, TURNER   OF   PIRATES

PERSONAL: Born April 11, 1965, in Orlando. ... 6-2/204. ... Bats both, throws right. ... Full name: Turner Max Ward.
HIGH SCHOOL: Satsuma (Ala.).
JUNIOR COLLEGE: Faulkner State Community College (Ala.).
COLLEGE: South Alabama.
TRANSACTIONS/CAREER NOTES: Selected by New York Yankees organization in 18th round of free-agent draft (June 2, 1986). ... Traded by Yankees organization with C Joel Skinner to Cleveland Indians organization for OF Mel Hall (March 19, 1989). ... On Gulf Coast Indians disabled list (April 7-July 24, 1989). ... Traded by Indians with P Tom Candiotti to Toronto Blue Jays for P Denis Boucher, OF Glenallen Hill, OF Mark Whiten and a player to be named later (June 27, 1991); Indians acquired cash to complete deal (October 15, 1991). ... On Toronto disabled list (August 2-September 1, 1993); included rehabilitation assignment to Knoxville (August 21-September 1). ... Claimed on waivers by Milwaukee Brewers (November 24, 1993). ... On Milwaukee disabled list (June 7-22, July 2-19 and July 24, 1995-remainder of season); included rehabilitation assignments to Beloit (July 17-19) and New Orleans (August 10-17 and August 31-September 5). ... On Milwaukee disabled list (May 25-September 1, 1996). ... Released by Brewers (November 1, 1996). ... Signed by Pittsburgh Pirates organization (April 22, 1997). ... On disabled list (August 5-20, 1998).
STATISTICAL NOTES: Led Pacific Coast League outfielders with 292 putouts and 308 total chances in 1990.

									BATTING						FIELDING			
Year	Team (League)	Pos.	G	AB	R	H	2B	3B	HR	RBI	Avg.	BB	SO	SB	PO	A	E	Avg.
1986— Oneonta (NYP)		OF-1B-3B	63	221	42	62	4	1	1	19	.281	31	39	6	97	6	5	.954
1987— Fort Laud. (FSL)		OF-3B	130	493	83	145	15	2	7	55	.294	64	83	25	332	11	8	.977
1988— Columbus (Int'l)		OF	134	490	55	123	24	1	7	50	.251	48	100	28	223	5	1	*.996
1989— GC Indians (GCL)■..		DH	4	15	2	3	0	0	0	1	.200	2	2	1	...	...	...	...
—Cant./Akr. (Eastern)		OF	30	93	19	28	5	1	0	3	.301	15	16	1	2	0	0	1.000
1990— Colo. Springs (PCL) ..		OF-2B	133	495	89	148	24	9	6	65	.299	72	70	22	†292	7	9	.971
—Cleveland (A.L.)........		OF-DH	14	46	10	16	2	1	1	10	.348	3	8	3	20	2	1	.957
1991— Cleveland (A.L.)........		OF	40	100	11	23	7	0	0	5	.230	10	16	0	65	1	0	1.000
—Colo. Springs (PCL) ..		OF	14	51	5	10	1	1	1	3	.196	6	9	2	30	0	1	.968
—Toronto (A.L.)■........		OF	8	13	1	4	0	0	0	2	.308	1	2	0	5	0	0	1.000
—Syracuse (Int'l)........		OF	59	218	40	72	11	3	7	32	.330	47	22	9	136	5	0	1.000
1992— Toronto (A.L.)........		OF	18	29	7	10	3	0	1	3	.345	4	4	0	18	1	0	1.000
—Syracuse (Int'l)........		OF	81	280	41	67	10	2	10	29	.239	44	43	7	143	3	5	.967
1993— Toronto (A.L.)........		OF-1B	72	167	20	32	4	2	4	28	.192	23	26	3	97	2	1	.990
—Knoxville (Southern) ..		OF	7	23	6	6	2	0	0	2	.261	7	3	3	20	0	0	1.000
1994— Milwaukee (A.L.)■.....		OF-3B	102	367	55	85	15	2	9	45	.232	52	68	6	260	9	4	.985
1995— Milwaukee (A.L.)........		OF-DH	44	129	19	34	3	1	4	16	.264	14	21	6	81	5	1	.989
—Beloit (Midwest)........		OF	2	5	0	0	0	0	0	0	.000	3	1	0	1	0	0	1.000
—New Orleans (A.A.).....		OF	11	33	3	8	1	1	1	3	.242	4	10	0	9	0	1	.900
1996— Milwaukee (A.L.)........		OF-DH	43	67	7	12	2	1	2	10	.179	13	17	3	54	1	0	1.000
—New Orleans (A.A.).....		DH	9	23	4	8	1	0	1	1	.348	7	4	0				...
1997— Calgary (PCL)■..........		OF-1B	59	209	44	71	18	3	9	44	.340	24	26	7	87	6	3	.969
—Pittsburgh (N.L.)		OF	71	167	33	59	16	1	7	33	.353	18	17	4	71	2	0	1.000
1998— Pittsburgh (N.L.)		OF-DH	123	282	33	74	13	3	9	46	.262	27	40	5	163	7	3	.983
American League totals (7 years)			341	918	130	216	36	7	21	119	.235	120	162	21	600	21	7	.989
National League totals (2 years)			194	449	66	133	29	4	16	79	.296	45	57	9	234	9	3	.988
Major league totals (9 years)			535	1367	196	349	65	11	37	198	.255	165	219	30	834	30	10	.989

WASDIN, JOHN   P   RED SOX

PERSONAL: Born August 5, 1972, in Fort Belvoir, Va. ... 6-2/193. ... Throws right, bats right. ... Full name: John Truman Wasdin.
HIGH SCHOOL: Amos P. Godby (Tallahassee, Fla.).
COLLEGE: Florida State.
TRANSACTIONS/CAREER NOTES: Selected by New York Yankees organization in 41st round of free-agent draft (June 4, 1990); did not sign. ... Selected by Oakland Athletics organization in first round (25th pick overall) of free-agent draft (June 3, 1993). ... Traded by A's with cash to Boston Red Sox for OF Jose Canseco (January 27, 1997).
STATISTICAL NOTES: Led Pacific Coast League with 26 home runs allowed in 1995.

Year	Team (League)	W	L	Pct.	ERA	G	GS	CG	ShO	Sv.	IP	H	R	ER	BB	SO
1993— Arizona A's (Arizona)		0	0	...	3.00	1	1	0	0	0	3	3	1	1	0	1
—Madison (Midwest)		2	3	.400	1.86	9	9	0	0	0	48 1/3	32	11	10	9	40
—Modesto (California)		0	3	.000	3.86	3	3	0	0	0	16 1/3	17	9	7	4	11
1994— Modesto (California)		3	1	.750	1.69	6	4	0	0	0	26 2/3	17	6	5	5	30
—Huntsville (Southern)		12	3	.800	3.43	21	21	0	0	0	141 2/3	126	61	54	29	108
1995— Edmonton (PCL)		12	8	.600	5.52	29	•28	2	1	0	174 1/3	193	117	107	38	111
—Oakland (A.L.)		1	1	.500	4.67	5	2	0	0	0	17 1/3	14	9	9	3	6
1996— Edmonton (PCL)		2	1	.667	4.14	9	9	0	0	0	50	52	23	23	17	30
—Oakland (A.L.)		8	7	.533	5.96	25	21	1	0	0	131 1/3	145	96	87	50	75
1997— Boston (A.L.)■...............		4	6	.400	4.40	53	7	0	0	0	124 2/3	121	68	61	38	84
1998— Boston (A.L.)		6	4	.600	5.25	47	8	0	0	0	96	111	57	56	27	59
—Pawtucket (Int'l)		1	0	1.000	3.00	4	2	0	0	0	12	11	6	4	5	10
Major league totals (4 years)		19	18	.514	5.19	130	38	1	0	0	369 1/3	391	230	213	118	224

DIVISION SERIES RECORD

Year	Team (League)	W	L	Pct.	ERA	G	GS	CG	ShO	Sv.	IP	H	R	ER	BB	SO
1998— Boston (A.L.)		0	0	...	10.80	1	0	0	0	0	1 2/3	2	2	2	1	2

WASHBURN, JARROD   P   ANGELS

PERSONAL: Born August 13, 1974, in La Crosse, Wis. ... 6-1/200. ... Throws left, bats left. ... Full name: Jarrod Michael Washburn.
HIGH SCHOOL: Webster (Wis.).

COLLEGE: Wisconsin-Oshkosh.
TRANSACTIONS/CAREER NOTES: Selected by California Angels organization in second round of free-agent draft (June 1, 1995).

Year	Team (League)	W	L	Pct.	ERA	G	GS	CG	ShO	Sv.	IP	H	R	ER	BB	SO
1995—	Cedar Rapids (Midw.)	0	1	.000	3.44	3	3	0	0	0	18 1/3	17	7	7	7	20
—	Boise (Northwest)	3	2	.600	3.33	8	8	0	0	0	46	35	17	17	14	54
1996—	Lake Elsinore (Calif.)	6	3	.667	3.30	14	14	3	0	0	92 2/3	79	38	34	33	93
—	Midland (Texas).................	5	6	.455	4.40	13	13	1	0	0	88	77	44	43	25	58
1997—	Midland (Texas).................	15	•12	.556	4.80	29	*29	29	•1	0	*189 1/3	*211	*115	*101	65	*146
—	Vancouver (PCL)	0	0	. . .	3.60	1	1	0	0	0	5	4	2	2	2	6
1998—	Vancouver (PCL)	4	5	.444	4.32	14	14	2	0	0	91 2/3	91	44	44	43	66
—	Anaheim (A.L.)..................	6	3	.667	4.62	15	11	0	0	0	74	70	40	38	27	48
—	Midland (Texas).................	0	1	.000	6.23	1	1	0	0	0	8 2/3	13	8	6	2	8
Major league totals (1 year)........		6	3	.667	4.62	15	11	0	0	0	74	70	40	38	27	48

WATKINS, PAT   OF   MARLINS

PERSONAL: Born September 2, 1972, in Raleigh, N.C. ... 6-2/195. ... Bats right, throws right. ... Full name: William Patrick Watkins.
HIGH SCHOOL: Garner (N.C.).
COLLEGE: East Carolina.
TRANSACTIONS/CAREER NOTES: Selected by Cincinnati Reds organization in supplemental round ("sandwich pick" between first and second round, 32nd pick overall) of free-agent draft (June 3, 1993); pick received as part of compensation for Houston Astros signing Type A free-agent P Greg Swindell. ... Traded by Reds to Florida Marlins for P Pedro Minaya (January 6, 1999).
STATISTICAL NOTES: Led Carolina League with 267 total bases in 1994. ... Tied for Carolina League lead in double plays by outfielder with four in 1994. ... Tied for International League lead in double plays by outfielder with three in 1998.

Year	Team (League)	Pos.	G	AB	R	H	2B	3B	HR	RBI	Avg.	BB	SO	SB	PO	A	E	Avg.
							BATTING								FIELDING			
1993—	Billings (Pioneer)........	OF	66	235	46	63	10	3	6	30	.268	22	44	15	123	5	2	.985
1994—	Win.-Salem (Car.).......	OF	132	*524	*107	*152	24	5	27	83	.290	62	84	31	262	13	7	.975
1995—	Win.-Salem (Car.).......	OF	27	107	14	22	3	1	4	13	.206	10	24	1	51	5	1	.982
—	Chattanooga (Sou.)......	OF	105	358	57	104	26	2	12	57	.291	33	53	5	185	8	8	.960
1996—	Chattanooga (Sou.)......	OF	127	492	63	136	31	2	8	59	.276	30	64	15	220	*21	4	.984
1997—	Chattanooga (Sou.)......	OF	46	177	35	62	15	1	7	30	.350	15	16	9	78	3	0	1.000
—	Indianapolis (A.A.)......	OF	84	325	46	91	14	7	9	35	.280	24	55	13	170	5	2	.989
—	Cincinnati (N.L.)	OF	17	29	2	6	2	0	0	0	.207	0	5	1	12	1	0	1.000
1998—	Cincinnati (N.L.).........	OF	83	147	11	39	8	1	2	15	.265	8	26	1	98	1	3	.971
—	Indianapolis (Int'l)......	OF	44	188	37	71	12	1	3	24	.378	15	26	8	98	5	2	.981
Major league totals (2 years)			100	176	13	45	10	1	2	15	.256	8	31	2	110	2	3	.974

WATSON, ALLEN   P   METS

PERSONAL: Born November 18, 1970, in New York, N.Y. ... 6-3/212. ... Throws left, bats left. ... Full name: Allen Kenneth Watson.
HIGH SCHOOL: Christ the King (Queens, N.Y.).
COLLEGE: New York State Institute of Technology.
TRANSACTIONS/CAREER NOTES: Selected by St. Louis Cardinals organization in first round (21st pick overall) of free-agent draft (June 3, 1991); pick received as part of compensation for Toronto Blue Jays signing Type A free-agent P Ken Dayley. ... On Savannah disabled list (August 19, 1991-remainder of season). ... On suspended list (June 25-July 3, 1994). ... On St. Louis disabled list (June 7-July 8, 1995); included rehabilitation assignments to Arkansas (June 21-26) and Louisville (June 26-July 8). ... Traded by Cardinals with P Rich DeLucia and P Doug Creek to San Francisco Giants for SS Royce Clayton and a player to be named later (December 14, 1995); Cardinals acquired 2B Chris Wimmer to complete deal (January 16, 1996). ... On San Francisco disabled list (July 2-25, 1996); included rehabilitation assignment to San Jose (July 15-25). ... Traded by Giants with P Fausto Macey to Anaheim Angels for 1B J.T. Snow (November 27, 1996). ... On Anaheim disabled list (May 24-July 13, 1998); included rehabilitation assignment to Midland (June 16), Lake Elsinore (April 21) and Vancouver (June 26). ... Granted free agency (December 21, 1998). ... Signed by New York Mets (January 19, 1999).
STATISTICAL NOTES: Led A.L. with 37 home runs allowed in 1997.
MISCELLANEOUS: Singled in three games as pinch hitter with San Francisco (1996).

Year	Team (League)	W	L	Pct.	ERA	G	GS	CG	ShO	Sv.	IP	H	R	ER	BB	SO
1991—	Hamilton (NYP).................	1	1	.500	2.52	8	8	0	0	0	39 1/3	22	15	11	17	46
—	Savannah (S. Atl.)	1	1	.500	3.95	3	3	0	0	0	13 2/3	16	7	6	8	12
1992—	St. Petersburg (FSL)	5	4	.556	1.91	14	14	2	0	0	89 2/3	81	31	19	18	80
—	Arkansas (Texas)............	8	5	.615	2.15	14	14	3	1	0	96 1/3	77	24	23	23	93
—	Louisville (A.A.).............	1	0	1.000	1.46	2	2	0	0	0	12 1/3	8	4	2	5	9
1993—	Louisville (A.A.).............	5	4	.556	2.91	17	17	2	0	0	120 2/3	101	46	39	31	66
—	St. Louis (N.L.)..............	6	7	.462	4.60	16	15	0	0	0	86	90	53	44	28	49
1994—	St. Louis (N.L.)..............	6	5	.545	5.52	22	22	0	0	0	115 2/3	130	73	71	53	74
1995—	St. Louis (N.L.)..............	7	9	.438	4.96	21	19	0	0	0	114 1/3	126	68	63	41	49
—	Louisville (A.A.).............	2	2	.500	2.63	4	4	1	1	0	24	20	10	7	6	19
—	Arkansas (Texas)............	1	0	1.000	0.00	1	1	0	0	0	5	4	1	0	0	7
1996—	San Francisco (N.L.)■.......	8	12	.400	4.61	29	29	2	0	0	185 2/3	189	105	95	69	128
—	San Jose (California)..........	0	0	. . .	1.42	2	2	0	0	0	6 1/3	7	1	1	0	12
1997—	Anaheim (A.L.)■.............	12	12	.500	4.93	35	34	0	0	0	199	220	121	109	73	141
1998—	Anaheim (A.L.)...............	6	7	.462	6.04	28	14	1	0	0	92 1/3	122	67	62	34	64
—	Midland (Texas)...............	0	0	. . .	2.25	1	1	0	0	0	4	6	2	1	1	3
—	Lake Elsinore (Calif.)	1	0	1.000	0.00	1	1	0	0	0	5	3	0	0	1	6
—	Vancouver (PCL)	0	1	.000	4.50	1	1	0	0	0	6	6	3	3	2	8
A.L. totals (2 years)		18	19	.486	5.28	63	48	1	0	0	291 1/3	342	188	171	107	205
N.L. totals (4 years)		27	33	.450	4.90	88	85	2	0	0	501 2/3	535	299	273	191	300
Major league totals (6 years)......		45	52	.464	5.04	151	133	3	0	0	793	877	487	444	298	505

W

PERSONAL: Born September 25, 1969, in Lawrenceburg, Tenn. ... 6-3/231. ... Throws right, bats right. ... Full name: John David Weathers.
HIGH SCHOOL: Loretto (Tenn.).
JUNIOR COLLEGE: Motlow State Community College (Tenn.).
TRANSACTIONS/CAREER NOTES: Selected by Toronto Blue Jays organization in third round of free-agent draft (June 1, 1988). ... On Syracuse disabled list (May 11-July 31, 1992). ... Selected by Florida Marlins in second round (29th pick overall) of expansion draft (November 17, 1992). ... On Florida disabled list (June 26-July 13, 1995); included rehabilitation assignments to Brevard County (July 4-10) and Charlotte (July 11-13). ... Traded by Marlins to New York Yankees for P Mark Hutton (July 31, 1996). ... Traded by Yankees to Cleveland Indians for OF Chad Curtis (June 9, 1997). ... Claimed on waivers by Cincinnati Reds (December 20, 1997). ... Claimed on waivers by Milwaukee Brewers (June 24, 1998).
MISCELLANEOUS: Appeared in two games as pinch runner (1994). ... Appeared in one game as pinch runner with Florida (1996).

Year Team (League)	W	L	Pct.	ERA	G	GS	CG	ShO	Sv.	IP	H	R	ER	BB	SO
1988— St. Catharines (NYP)	4	4	.500	3.02	15	12	0	0	0	62$^{2}/_{3}$	58	30	21	26	36
1989— Myrtle Beach (SAL)	11	•13	.458	3.86	31	*31	2	0	0	172$^{2}/_{3}$	163	99	74	86	111
1990— Dunedin (Fla. St.)	10	7	.588	3.70	27	•27	2	0	0	158	158	82	65	59	96
1991— Knoxville (Southern)	10	7	.588	2.45	24	22	5	2	0	139$^{1}/_{3}$	121	51	38	49	114
— Toronto (A.L.)	1	0	1.000	4.91	15	0	0	0	0	14$^{2}/_{3}$	15	9	8	17	13
1992— Syracuse (Int'l)	1	4	.200	4.66	12	10	0	0	0	48$^{1}/_{3}$	48	29	25	21	30
— Toronto (A.L.)	0	0	. . .	8.10	2	0	0	0	0	3$^{1}/_{3}$	5	3	3	2	3
1993— Edmonton (PCL)■	11	4	•.733	3.83	22	22	3	1	0	141	150	77	60	47	117
— Florida (N.L.)	2	3	.400	5.12	14	6	0	0	0	45$^{2}/_{3}$	57	26	26	13	34
1994— Florida (N.L.)	8	12	.400	5.27	24	24	0	0	0	135	166	87	79	59	72
1995— Florida (N.L.)	4	5	.444	5.98	28	15	0	0	0	90$^{1}/_{3}$	104	68	60	52	60
— Brevard County (FSL)	0	0	. . .	0.00	1	1	0	0	0	4	4	0	0	1	3
— Charlotte (Int'l)	0	1	.000	9.00	1	1	0	0	0	5	10	5	5	5	0
1996— Florida (N.L.)	2	2	.500	4.54	31	8	0	0	0	71$^{1}/_{3}$	85	41	36	28	40
— Charlotte (Int'l)	0	0	. . .	7.71	1	1	0	0	0	2$^{1}/_{3}$	5	2	2	3	0
— New York (A.L.)■■	0	2	.000	9.35	11	4	0	0	0	17$^{1}/_{3}$	23	19	18	14	13
— Columbus (Int'l)	0	2	.000	5.40	3	3	0	0	0	16$^{2}/_{3}$	20	13	10	5	7
1997— New York (A.L.)	0	1	.000	10.00	10	0	0	0	0	9	15	10	10	7	4
— Columbus (Int'l)	2	2	.500	3.19	5	5	1	0	0	36$^{2}/_{3}$	35	18	13	7	35
— Buffalo (A.A.)■	4	3	.571	3.15	11	11	2	1	0	68$^{2}/_{3}$	71	37	24	17	51
— Cleveland (A.L.)	1	2	.333	7.56	9	1	0	0	0	16$^{2}/_{3}$	23	14	14	8	14
1998— Cincinnati (N.L.)■	2	4	.333	6.21	16	9	0	0	0	62$^{1}/_{3}$	86	47	43	27	51
— Milwaukee (N.L.)■■	4	1	.800	3.21	28	0	0	0	0	47$^{2}/_{3}$	44	22	17	14	43
A.L. totals (4 years)	2	5	.286	7.82	47	5	0	0	0	61	81	55	53	48	47
N.L. totals (5 years)	22	27	.449	5.19	141	62	0	0	0	452$^{1}/_{3}$	542	291	261	193	300
Major league totals (8 years)	24	32	.429	5.51	188	67	0	0	0	513$^{1}/_{3}$	623	346	314	241	347

DIVISION SERIES RECORD

Year Team (League)	W	L	Pct.	ERA	G	GS	CG	ShO	Sv.	IP	H	R	ER	BB	SO
1996— New York (A.L.)	1	0	1.000	0.00	2	0	0	0	0	5	1	0	0	0	5

CHAMPIONSHIP SERIES RECORD

Year Team (League)	W	L	Pct.	ERA	G	GS	CG	ShO	Sv.	IP	H	R	ER	BB	SO
1996— New York (A.L.)	1	0	1.000	0.00	2	0	0	0	0	3	3	0	0	0	0

WORLD SERIES RECORD

NOTES: Member of World Series championship team (1996).

Year Team (League)	W	L	Pct.	ERA	G	GS	CG	ShO	Sv.	IP	H	R	ER	BB	SO
1996— New York (A.L.)	0	0	. . .	3.00	3	0	0	0	0	3	2	1	1	4	3

PERSONAL: Born August 4, 1973, in Springfield, Ill. ... 6-5/230. ... Throws right, bats right. ... Full name: James Eric Weaver.
HIGH SCHOOL: Illiopolis (Ill.).
TRANSACTIONS/CAREER NOTES: Signed as non-drafted free agent by Los Angeles Dodgers organization (July 22, 1991). ... On disabled list (May 1-August 31, 1994). ... Traded by Dodgers to Seattle Mariners for P Scott Proutty (October 12, 1998).
STATISTICAL NOTES: Pitched 2-1 no-hit victory against Fort Lauderdale (July 17, 1992, first game).

Year Team (League)	W	L	Pct.	ERA	G	GS	CG	ShO	Sv.	IP	H	R	ER	BB	SO
1992— Vero Beach (FSL)	4	11	.267	4.12	19	18	1	0	0	89$^{2}/_{3}$	73	52	41	57	73
1993— Bakersfield (California)	6	11	.353	4.28	28	•27	0	0	0	157$^{2}/_{3}$	135	89	75	*118	110
1994— Vero Beach (FSL)	1	3	.250	6.75	7	7	0	0	0	24	28	20	18	9	22
1995— San Antonio (Tex.)	8	11	.421	4.07	27	26	1	0	0	141$^{2}/_{3}$	147	83	64	72	105
1996— San Antonio (Tex.)	10	5	.667	3.30	18	18	1	1	0	122$^{2}/_{3}$	106	51	45	44	69
— Albuquerque (PCL)	1	4	.200	5.40	13	8	0	0	0	46$^{2}/_{3}$	63	39	28	22	38
1997— San Antonio (Tex.)	7	2	.778	3.61	13	13	2	•1	0	84$^{2}/_{3}$	80	43	34	38	60
— Albuquerque (PCL)	0	3	.000	6.42	21	8	0	0	0	68$^{2}/_{3}$	101	53	49	38	54
1998— Albuquerque (PCL)	2	5	.286	5.55	46	0	0	0	3	61$^{2}/_{3}$	65	41	38	32	63
— Los Angeles (N.L.)	2	0	1.000	0.93	7	0	0	0	0	9$^{2}/_{3}$	5	1	1	6	5
Major league totals (1 year)	2	0	1.000	0.93	7	0	0	0	0	9$^{2}/_{3}$	5	1	1	6	5

W

PERSONAL: Born December 6, 1972, in Newport Beach, Calif. ... 6-5/215. ... Throws left, bats left. ... Full name: Neil Aaron Weber.
HIGH SCHOOL: Corona Del Mar (Newport Beach, Calif.).
JUNIOR COLLEGE: Cuesta College (Calif.).

TRANSACTIONS/CAREER NOTES: Selected by Montreal Expos organization in eighth round of free-agent draft (June 3, 1993). ... On disabled list (July 12, 1996-remainder of season). ... Selected by Arizona Diamondbacks in first round (21st pick overall) of expansion draft (November 18, 1997). ... Released by Diamondbacks (November 19, 1998).

Year	Team (League)	W	L	Pct.	ERA	G	GS	CG	ShO	Sv.	IP	H	R	ER	BB	SO
1993— Jamestown (NYP)		6	5	.545	2.77	16	•16	2	•1	0	94 1/3	84	46	29	36	80
1994— W.P. Beach (FSL)		9	7	.563	3.20	25	24	1	0	0	135	113	58	48	62	134
1995— Harrisburg (Eastern)		6	11	.353	5.01	28	28	0	0	0	152 2/3	157	98	*85	*90	119
1996— Harrisburg (Eastern)		7	4	.636	3.03	18	18	1	0	0	107	90	37	36	44	74
1997— Ottawa (Int'l)		2	5	.286	7.94	9	9	0	0	0	39 2/3	46	46	35	40	27
— Harrisburg (Eastern)		7	6	.538	3.83	18	18	1	1	0	112 2/3	93	56	48	51	121
1998— Tucson (PCL)■		5	9	.357	5.11	46	11	1	0	1	112 2/3	116	82	64	55	79
— Arizona (N.L.)		0	0	. . .	11.57	4	0	0	0	0	2 1/3	5	3	3	3	4
Major league totals (1 year)		0	0	. . .	11.57	4	0	0	0	0	2 1/3	5	3	3	3	4

WEBSTER, LENNY   C   ORIOLES

PERSONAL: Born February 10, 1965, in New Orleans. ... 5-9/200. ... Bats right, throws right. ... Full name: Leonard Irell Webster.
HIGH SCHOOL: Lutcher (La.).
COLLEGE: Grambling State.
TRANSACTIONS/CAREER NOTES: Selected by Minnesota Twins organization in 16th round of free-agent draft (June 7, 1982); did not sign. ... Selected by Twins organization in 21st round of free-agent draft (June 3, 1985). ... Traded by Twins to Montreal Expos organization for a player to be named later (March 14, 1994). ... Granted free agency (December 23, 1994). ... Signed by Philadelphia Phillies organization (April 7, 1995). ... Claimed on waivers by Expos (March 29, 1996). ... Granted free agency (October 16, 1996). ... Signed by Baltimore Orioles organization (December 18, 1996). ... Granted free agency (October 30, 1997). ... Re-signed by Orioles (November 24, 1997).
HONORS: Named Midwest League Most Valuable Player (1988).

Year	Team (League)	Pos.	G	AB	R	H	2B	3B	HR	RBI	Avg.	BB	SO	SB	PO	A	E	Avg.
1986— Kenosha (Midwest)		C	22	65	2	10	2	0	0	8	.154	10	12	0	87	9	0	1.000
— Elizabethton (App.)		C	48	152	29	35	4	0	3	14	.230	22	21	1	88	11	3	.971
1987— Kenosha (Midwest)		C	52	140	17	35	7	0	3	17	.250	17	20	2	228	29	5	.981
1988— Kenosha (Midwest)		C	129	465	82	134	23	2	11	87	.288	71	47	3	606	96	14	.980
1989— Visalia (California)		C	63	231	36	62	7	0	5	39	.268	27	27	2	352	57	4	.990
— Orlando (South.)		C	59	191	29	45	7	0	2	17	.236	44	20	2	293	46	4	.988
— Minnesota (A.L.)		C	14	20	3	6	2	0	0	1	.300	3	2	0	32	0	0	1.000
1990— Orlando (South.)		C	126	455	69	119	31	0	8	71	.262	68	57	0	629	70	9	.987
— Minnesota (A.L.)		C	2	6	1	2	1	0	0	0	.333	1	1	0	9	0	0	1.000
1991— Portland (PCL)		C	87	325	43	82	18	0	7	34	.252	24	32	1	477	65	6	*.989
— Minnesota (A.L.)		C	18	34	7	10	1	0	3	8	.294	6	10	0	61	10	1	.986
1992— Minnesota (A.L.)		C-DH	53	118	10	33	10	1	1	13	.280	9	11	0	190	11	1	.995
1993— Minnesota (A.L.)		C-DH	49	106	14	21	2	0	1	8	.198	11	8	1	177	13	0	1.000
1994— Montreal (N.L.)■		C	57	143	13	39	10	0	5	23	.273	16	24	0	237	19	1	.996
1995— Philadelphia (N.L.)■		C	49	150	18	40	9	0	4	14	.267	16	27	0	274	18	3	.990
1996— Montreal (N.L.)		C	78	174	18	40	10	0	2	17	.230	25	21	0	390	25	1	.998
1997— Baltimore (A.L.)■		C-DH	98	259	29	66	8	1	7	37	.255	22	46	0	532	36	3	.995
1998— Baltimore (A.L.)		C-DH	108	309	37	88	16	0	10	46	.285	15	38	0	528	39	4	.993
American League totals (7 years)			342	852	101	226	40	2	22	113	.265	67	116	1	1529	109	9	.995
National League totals (3 years)			184	467	49	119	29	0	11	54	.255	57	72	0	901	62	5	.995
Major league totals (10 years)			526	1319	150	345	69	2	33	167	.262	124	188	1	2430	171	14	.995

DIVISION SERIES RECORD

Year	Team (League)	Pos.	G	AB	R	H	2B	3B	HR	RBI	Avg.	BB	SO	SB	PO	A	E	Avg.
1997— Baltimore (A.L.)		C	3	6	1	1	0	0	0	1	.167	1	0	0	20	0	0	1.000

CHAMPIONSHIP SERIES RECORD

Year	Team (League)	Pos.	G	AB	R	H	2B	3B	HR	RBI	Avg.	BB	SO	SB	PO	A	E	Avg.
1997— Baltimore (A.L.)		C-PH	4	9	0	2	0	0	0	0	.222	0	1	0	14	0	2	.875

WEHNER, JOHN   OF/3B

PERSONAL: Born June 29, 1967, in Pittsburgh. ... 6-3/206. ... Bats right, throws right. ... Full name: John Paul Wehner. ... Name pronounced WAY-ner.
HIGH SCHOOL: Carrick (Pittsburgh).
COLLEGE: Indiana.
TRANSACTIONS/CAREER NOTES: Selected by Pittsburgh Pirates organization in seventh round of free-agent draft (June 1, 1988). ... On Pittsburgh disabled list (August 29-October 7, 1991 and July 20, 1994-remainder of season). ... Claimed on waivers by Los Angeles Dodgers (October 15, 1996). ... Released by Dodgers (March 17, 1997). ... Signed by Florida Marlins organization (March 21, 1997). ... On Florida disabled list (June 26-September 1, 1997). ... Released by Marlins (November 20, 1997). ... Re-signed by Marlins organization (March 4, 1998). ... Granted free agency (September 29, 1998).
STATISTICAL NOTES: Led New York-Pennsylvania League third basemen with 219 total chances and 14 double plays in 1988. ... Led Carolina League third basemen with 403 total chances and tied for lead with 24 double plays in 1989. ... Led Eastern League third basemen with 476 total chances and 40 double plays in 1990.

Year	Team (League)	Pos.	G	AB	R	H	2B	3B	HR	RBI	Avg.	BB	SO	SB	PO	A	E	Avg.
1988— Watertown (NYP)		3B	70	265	41	73	6	0	3	31	.275	21	39	18	*65	137	17	.922
1989— Salem (Carolina)		3B	*137	*515	69	*155	32	6	14	73	.301	42	81	21	*89	*278	36	.911
1990— Harrisburg (Eastern)		3B	•138	*511	71	147	27	1	4	62	.288	40	51	24	*109	*317	50	.895
1991— Carolina (Southern)		3B-1B	61	234	30	62	5	1	3	21	.265	24	32	17	182	134	10	.969
— Buffalo (A.A.)		3B	31	112	18	34	9	2	1	15	.304	14	12	6	30	69	8	.925
— Pittsburgh (N.L.)		3B	37	106	15	36	7	0	0	7	.340	7	17	3	23	65	6	.936

Year	Team (League)	Pos.	G	AB	R	H	2B	3B	HR	RBI	Avg.	BB	SO	SB	PO	A	E	Avg.
1992—	Buffalo (A.A.)	2B-1B-3B	60	223	37	60	13	2	7	27	.269	29	30	10	226	122	7	.980
—	Pittsburgh (N.L.)	3B-1B-2B	55	123	11	22	6	0	0	4	.179	12	22	3	96	64	4	.976
1993—	Pittsburgh (N.L.)	3B-2B-OF	29	35	3	5	0	0	0	0	.143	6	10	0	17	8	0	1.000
—	Buffalo (A.A.)	3B-2B-OF	89	330	61	83	22	2	7	34	.252	40	53	17	133	256	17	.958
1994—	Buffalo (A.A.)	OF-3B-2B	88	330	52	100	19	3	7	44	.303	32	36	21	131	113	11	.957
—	Pittsburgh (N.L.)	3B	2	4	1	1	1	0	0	3	.250	0	1	0	0	2	0	1.000
1995—	Calgary (PCL)	3B-2B-OF	40	158	30	52	12	2	4	24	.329	12	16	8	36	98	12	.918
—	Pittsburgh (N.L.)	0-3-C-S	52	107	13	33	0	3	0	5	.308	10	17	3	35	29	0	1.000
1996—	Pittsburgh (N.L.)	0-3-2-C	86	139	19	36	9	1	2	13	.259	8	22	1	60	43	2	.981
1997—	Charlotte (Int'l)■	3-0-1-2	31	93	16	26	5	0	3	11	.280	6	18	3	32	33	2	.970
—	Florida (N.L.)	OF-3B	44	36	8	10	2	0	0	2	.278	2	5	1	14	3	0	1.000
1998—	Charlotte (Int'l)	OF-P	30	83	12	27	1	0	3	15	.325	4	16	5	29	3	2	.941
—	Florida (N.L.)	OF-3B	53	88	10	20	2	0	0	5	.227	7	12	1	27	12	0	1.000
Major league totals (8 years)			358	638	80	163	27	4	2	39	.255	52	106	12	272	226	12	.976

DIVISION SERIES RECORD

Year	Team (League)	Pos.	G	AB	R	H	2B	3B	HR	RBI	Avg.	BB	SO	SB	PO	A	E	Avg.
1997—	Florida (N.L.)	PR-OF	1	0	0	0	0	0	0	0	...	0	0	0	0	0	0	...

CHAMPIONSHIP SERIES RECORD

Year	Team (League)	Pos.	G	AB	R	H	2B	3B	HR	RBI	Avg.	BB	SO	SB	PO	A	E	Avg.
1992—	Pittsburgh (N.L.)	PH	2	2	0	0	0	0	0	0	.000	0	2	0	...	...	...	...

RECORD AS PITCHER

Year	Team (League)	W	L	Pct.	ERA	G	GS	CG	ShO	Sv.	IP	H	R	ER	BB	SO
1998—	Charlotte (Int'l)	0	0	...	0.00	1	0	0	0	0	1	0	0	0	1	0

WEISS, WALT   SS   BRAVES

PERSONAL: Born November 28, 1963, in Tuxedo, N.Y. ... 6-0/175. ... Bats both, throws right. ... Full name: Walter William Weiss Jr.
HIGH SCHOOL: Suffern (N.Y.).
COLLEGE: North Carolina.
TRANSACTIONS/CAREER NOTES: Selected by Baltimore Orioles organization in 10th round of free-agent draft (June 7, 1982); did not sign. ... Selected by Oakland Athletics organization in first round (11th pick overall) of free-agent draft (June 3, 1985). ... On Oakland disabled list (May 18-July 31, 1989); included rehabilitation assignments to Tacoma (July 18-25) and Modesto (July 26-31). ... On disabled list (August 23-September 7, 1990; April 15-30 and June 7, 1991-remainder of season). ... On Oakland disabled list (March 30-June 3, 1992); included rehabilitation assignment to Tacoma (May 26-June 3). ... Traded by A's to Florida Marlins for C Eric Helfand and a player to be named later (November 17, 1992); A's acquired P Scott Baker to complete deal (November 20, 1992). ... Granted free agency (October 25, 1993). ... Signed by Colorado Rockies (January 7, 1994). ... Granted free agency (November 3, 1995). ... Re-signed by Rockies (December 6, 1995). ... On disabled list (July 22-August 8, 1997). ... Granted free agency (October 27, 1997). ... Signed by Atlanta Braves (November 17, 1997).
HONORS: Named A.L. Rookie Player of the Year by The Sporting News (1988). ... Named A.L. Rookie of the Year by Baseball Writers' Association of America (1988).
STATISTICAL NOTES: Led N.L. shortstops with 99 double plays in 1995. ... Career major league grand slams: 1.

Year	Team (League)	Pos.	G	AB	R	H	2B	3B	HR	RBI	Avg.	BB	SO	SB	PO	A	E	Avg.
1985—	Pocatello (Pioneer)	SS	40	158	19	49	9	3	0	21	.310	12	18	6	51	126	11	.941
—	Modesto (California)	SS	30	122	17	24	4	1	0	7	.197	12	20	3	36	97	7	.950
1986—	Madison (Midwest)	SS	84	322	50	97	15	5	2	54	.301	33	66	12	143	251	20	.952
—	Huntsville (Sou.)	SS	46	160	19	40	2	1	0	13	.250	11	39	5	72	142	11	.951
1987—	Huntsville (Sou.)	SS	91	337	43	96	16	2	1	32	.285	47	67	23	152	259	17	.960
—	Oakland (A.L.)	SS-DH	16	26	3	12	4	0	0	1	.462	2	2	1	8	30	1	.974
—	Tacoma (PCL)	SS	46	179	35	47	4	3	0	17	.263	28	31	8	76	140	11	.952
1988—	Oakland (A.L.)	SS	147	452	44	113	17	3	3	39	.250	35	56	4	254	431	15	.979
1989—	Oakland (A.L.)	SS	84	236	30	55	11	0	3	21	.233	21	39	6	106	195	15	.953
—	Tacoma (PCL)	SS	2	9	1	1	1	0	0	1	.111	0	0	0	0	3	1	.750
—	Modesto (California)	SS	5	8	1	3	0	0	0	1	.375	4	1	0	6	9	0	1.000
1990—	Oakland (A.L.)	SS	138	445	50	118	17	1	2	35	.265	46	53	9	194	373	12	.979
1991—	Oakland (A.L.)	SS	40	133	15	30	6	1	0	13	.226	12	14	6	64	99	5	.970
1992—	Tacoma (PCL)	SS	4	13	2	3	1	0	0	3	.231	2	1	0	8	14	1	.957
—	Oakland (A.L.)	SS	103	316	36	67	5	2	0	21	.212	43	39	6	144	270	19	.956
1993—	Florida (N.L.)■	SS	158	500	50	133	14	2	1	39	.266	79	73	7	229	406	15	.977
1994—	Colorado (N.L.)■	SS	110	423	58	106	11	4	1	32	.251	56	58	12	157	318	13	.973
1995—	Colorado (N.L.)	SS	137	427	65	111	17	3	1	25	.260	98	57	15	201	406	16	.974
1996—	Colorado (N.L.)	SS	155	517	89	146	20	2	8	48	.282	80	78	10	220	450	*30	.957
1997—	Colorado (N.L.)	SS	121	393	52	106	23	5	4	38	.270	66	56	5	191	372	10	.983
1998—	Atlanta (N.L.)■	SS	96	347	64	97	18	2	0	27	.280	59	53	7	97	257	12	.967
American League totals (6 years)			528	1608	178	395	60	7	8	130	.246	159	203	32	770	1398	67	.970
National League totals (6 years)			777	2607	378	699	103	18	15	209	.268	438	375	56	1095	2209	96	.972
Major league totals (12 years)			1305	4215	556	1094	163	25	23	339	.260	597	578	88	1865	3607	163	.971

DIVISION SERIES RECORD

Year	Team (League)	Pos.	G	AB	R	H	2B	3B	HR	RBI	Avg.	BB	SO	SB	PO	A	E	Avg.
1995—	Colorado (N.L.)	SS	4	12	1	2	0	0	0	0	.167	3	3	1	6	12	0	1.000
1998—	Atlanta (N.L.)	SS	3	13	2	2	0	0	0	0	.154	1	3	0	6	3	0	1.000
Division series totals (2 years)			7	25	3	4	0	0	0	0	.160	4	6	1	12	15	0	1.000

Year Team (League)	Pos.	G	AB	R	H	2B	3B	HR	RBI	Avg.	BB	SO	SB	PO	A	E	Avg.
1988—Oakland (A.L.)	SS	4	15	2	5	2	0	0	2	.333	0	4	0	7	10	0	1.000
1989—Oakland (A.L.)	SS-PR	4	9	2	1	1	0	0	0	.111	1	1	1	5	9	0	1.000
1990—Oakland (A.L.)	SS	2	7	2	0	0	0	0	0	.000	2	2	0	2	7	1	.900
1992—Oakland (A.L.)	SS	3	6	1	1	0	0	0	0	.167	2	1	2	5	6	0	1.000
1998—Atlanta (N.L.)	SS	4	15	0	3	0	0	0	1	.200	2	5	1	4	11	0	1.000
Championship series totals (5 years)		17	52	7	10	3	0	0	3	.192	7	13	4	23	43	1	.985

NOTES: Member of World Series championship team (1989).

Year Team (League)	Pos.	G	AB	R	H	2B	3B	HR	RBI	Avg.	BB	SO	SB	PO	A	E	Avg.
1988—Oakland (A.L.)	SS	5	16	1	1	0	0	0	0	.063	0	1	0	5	11	1	.941
1989—Oakland (A.L.)	SS	4	15	3	2	0	0	1	1	.133	2	2	0	7	8	0	1.000
World Series totals (2 years)		9	31	4	3	0	0	1	1	.097	2	3	0	12	19	1	.969

Year League	Pos.	AB	R	H	2B	3B	HR	RBI	Avg.	BB	SO	SB	PO	A	E	Avg.
1998—National	SS	3	1	2	0	0	0	1	.667	0	0	0	2	2	0	1.000

WELCH, MIKE   P   PHILLIES

PERSONAL: Born August 25, 1972, in Haverhill, Mass. ... 6-2/210. ... Throws right, bats left. ... Full name: Michael Paul Welch.
HIGH SCHOOL: Nashua (N.H.).
COLLEGE: Southern Maine.
TRANSACTIONS/CAREER NOTES: Selected by New York Mets organization in third round of free-agent draft (June 3, 1993). ... Traded by Mets to Philadelphia Phillies for P Hector Mercado (December 15, 1997).
RECORDS: Shares N.L. single-inning record for most consecutive home runs allowed—3 (August 2, 1998, second inning).

Year Team (League)	W	L	Pct.	ERA	G	GS	CG	ShO	Sv.	IP	H	R	ER	BB	SO
1993—Pittsfield (NYP)	3	1	.750	1.45	17	0	0	0	9	31	23	9	5	6	31
1994—Capital City (S. Atl.)	7	11	.389	3.61	24	24	5	2	0	159 2/3	151	81	64	33	127
1995—St. Lucie (Fla. St.)	4	4	.500	5.40	44	6	0	0	15	70	96	50	42	18	51
—Binghamton (Eastern)	0	0	. . .	0.00	1	0	0	0	0	1	0	0	0	0	2
1996—Binghamton (Eastern)	4	2	.667	4.59	46	0	0	0	27	51	55	29	26	10	53
—Norfolk (Int'l)	0	1	.000	4.15	10	0	0	0	2	8 2/3	8	4	4	2	6
1997—Norfolk (Int'l)	2	2	.500	3.66	46	0	0	0	20	51 2/3	53	21	21	16	35
1998—Scran./W.B. (Int'l)■............	3	4	.429	5.97	31	6	0	0	2	75 1/3	98	56	50	17	32
—Philadelphia (N.L.).............	0	2	.000	8.27	10	2	0	0	0	20 2/3	26	19	19	7	15
Major league totals (1 year)........	0	2	.000	8.27	10	2	0	0	0	20 2/3	26	19	19	7	15

WELLS, BOB   P   TWINS

PERSONAL: Born November 1, 1966, in Yakima, Wash. ... 6-0/180. ... Throws right, bats right. ... Full name: Robert Lee Wells.
HIGH SCHOOL: Eisenhower (Yakima, Wash.).
JUNIOR COLLEGE: Spokane Falls Community College (Wash.).
TRANSACTIONS/CAREER NOTES: Signed as non-drafted free agent by Philadelphia Phillies organization (August 18, 1988). ... On Reading disabled list (July 21, 1991-remainder of season). ... On Scranton/Wilkes-Barre disabled list (April 9-28, 1992). ... On Reading disabled list (June 9, 1992-remainder of season and April 8-June 13, 1993). ... Claimed on waivers by Seattle Mariners (June 30, 1994). ... On Seattle disabled list (April 16-May 19, 1998); included rehabilitation assignment to Wisconsin (May 12-19, 1998). ... Released by Mariners (November 19, 1998). ... Signed by Minnesota Twins organization (January 19, 1999).

Year Team (League)	W	L	Pct.	ERA	G	GS	CG	ShO	Sv.	IP	H	R	ER	BB	SO
1989—Martinsville (App.)............	0	0	. . .	4.50	4	0	0	0	0	6	8	5	3	2	3
1990—Spartanburg (SAL)	5	8	.385	2.87	20	19	2	0	0	113	94	47	36	40	73
—Clearwater (Fla. St.)	0	2	.000	4.91	6	1	0	0	1	14 2/3	17	9	8	6	11
1991—Clearwater (Fla. St.)	7	2	.778	3.11	24	9	1	0	0	75 1/3	63	27	26	19	66
—Reading (Eastern)	1	0	1.000	3.60	1	1	0	0	0	5	4	2	2	1	3
1992—Clearwater (Fla. St.)	1	0	1.000	3.86	9	0	0	0	5	9 1/3	10	4	4	3	9
—Reading (Eastern)	0	1	.000	1.17	3	3	0	0	0	15 1/3	12	2	2	5	11
1993—Clearwater (Fla. St.)	1	0	1.000	0.98	12	1	0	0	2	27 2/3	23	5	3	6	24
—Scran./W.B. (Int'l)	1	1	.500	2.79	11	0	0	0	0	19 1/3	19	7	6	5	8
1994—Reading (Eastern)	1	3	.250	2.79	14	0	0	0	4	19 1/3	18	6	6	3	19
—Philadelphia (N.L.).............	1	0	1.000	1.80	6	0	0	0	0	5	4	1	1	3	3
—Scran./W.B. (Int'l)	0	2	.000	2.45	11	0	0	0	0	14 2/3	18	6	4	6	13
—Calgary (PCL)■.................	3	2	.600	6.54	6	6	0	0	0	31 2/3	43	27	23	9	17
—Seattle (A.L.)	1	0	1.000	2.25	1	0	0	0	0	4	4	1	1	1	3
1995—Seattle (A.L.)	4	3	.571	5.75	30	4	0	0	0	76 2/3	88	51	49	39	38
1996—Seattle (A.L.)	12	7	.632	5.30	36	16	1	1	0	130 2/3	141	78	77	46	94
1997—Seattle (A.L.)	2	0	1.000	5.75	46	1	0	0	2	67 1/3	88	49	43	18	51
1998—Seattle (A.L.)	2	2	.500	6.10	30	0	0	0	0	51 2/3	54	38	35	16	29
—Wisconsin (Midwest)	0	1	.000	3.00	1	1	0	0	0	3	4	2	1	0	2
A.L. totals (5 years)	21	12	.636	5.59	143	21	1	1	2	330 1/3	375	217	205	120	215
N.L. totals (1 year)....................	1	0	1.000	1.80	6	0	0	0	0	5	4	1	1	3	3
Major league totals (5 years)......	22	12	.647	5.53	149	21	1	1	2	335 1/3	379	218	206	123	218

W

DIVISION SERIES RECORD

Year Team (League)	W	L	Pct.	ERA	G	GS	CG	ShO	Sv.	IP	H	R	ER	BB	SO
1995— Seattle (A.L.)	0	0	...	9.00	1	0	0	0	0	1	2	1	1	1	0
1997— Seattle (A.L.)	0	0	...	0.00	1	0	0	0	0	1 1/3	1	0	0	0	1
Div. series totals (2 years)	0	0	...	3.86	2	0	0	0	0	2 1/3	3	1	1	1	1

CHAMPIONSHIP SERIES RECORD

Year Team (League)	W	L	Pct.	ERA	G	GS	CG	ShO	Sv.	IP	H	R	ER	BB	SO
1995— Seattle (A.L.)	0	0	...	3.00	1	0	0	0	0	3	2	1	1	2	2

WELLS, DAVID   P   YANKEES

PERSONAL: Born May 20, 1963, in Torrance, Calif. ... 6-4/225. ... Throws left, bats left. ... Full name: David Lee Wells.
HIGH SCHOOL: Point Loma (San Diego).
TRANSACTIONS/CAREER NOTES: Selected by Toronto Blue Jays organization in second round of free-agent draft (June 7, 1982). ... On Knoxville disabled list (June 28, 1984-remainder of season). ... On disabled list (April 10, 1985-entire season). ... On Knoxville disabled list (July 7-August 20, 1986). ... Released by Blue Jays (March 30, 1993). ... Signed by Detroit Tigers (April 3, 1993). ... On disabled list (August 1-20, 1993). ... Granted free agency (October 28, 1993). ... Re-signed by Tigers (December 13, 1993). ... On Detroit disabled list (April 19-June 6, 1994); included rehabilitation assignment to Lakeland (May 27-June 6). ... Traded by Tigers to Cincinnati Reds for P C.J. Nitkowski, P David Tuttle and a player to be named later (July 31, 1995); Tigers acquired IF Mark Lewis to complete deal (November 16, 1995). ... Traded by Reds to Baltimore Orioles for OF Curtis Goodwin and OF Trovin Valdez (December 26, 1995). ... Granted free agency (October 29, 1996). ... Signed by New York Yankees (December 24, 1996).
RECORDS: Holds A.L. single-season record for most consecutive batsmen retired—38 (May 12 [last 10], 17 [all 27] and 23 [first], 1998).
HONORS: Named lefthanded pitcher on THE SPORTING NEWS A.L. All-Star team (1998).
STATISTICAL NOTES: Struck out 16 batters in one game (July 30, 1997). ... Pitched 4-0 perfect game against Minnesota (May 17, 1998).

Year Team (League)	W	L	Pct.	ERA	G	GS	CG	ShO	Sv.	IP	H	R	ER	BB	SO
1982— Medicine Hat (Pioneer)	4	3	.571	5.18	12	12	1	0	0	64 1/3	71	42	37	32	53
1983— Kinston (Carolina)	6	5	.545	3.73	25	25	5	0	0	157	141	81	65	71	115
1984— Kinston (Carolina)	1	6	.143	4.71	7	7	0	0	0	42	51	29	22	19	44
— Knoxville (Southern)	3	2	.600	2.59	8	8	3	1	0	59	58	22	17	17	34
1985—							Did not play.								
1986— Florence (S. Atl.)	0	0	...	3.55	4	1	0	0	0	12 2/3	7	6	5	9	14
— Ventura (Calif.)	2	1	.667	1.89	5	2	0	0	0	19	13	5	4	4	26
— Knoxville (Southern)	1	3	.250	4.05	10	7	1	0	0	40	42	24	18	18	32
— Syracuse (Int'l)	0	1	.000	9.82	3	0	0	0	0	3 2/3	6	4	4	1	2
1987— Syracuse (Int'l)	4	6	.400	3.87	43	12	0	0	6	109 1/3	102	49	47	32	106
— Toronto (A.L.)	4	3	.571	3.99	18	2	0	0	1	29 1/3	37	14	13	12	32
1988— Toronto (A.L.)	3	5	.375	4.62	41	0	0	0	4	64 1/3	65	36	33	31	56
— Syracuse (Int'l)	0	0	...	0.00	6	0	0	0	3	5 2/3	7	1	0	2	8
1989— Toronto (A.L.)	7	4	.636	2.40	54	0	0	0	2	86 1/3	66	25	23	28	78
1990— Toronto (A.L.)	11	6	.647	3.14	43	25	0	0	3	189	165	72	66	45	115
1991— Toronto (A.L.)	15	10	.600	3.72	40	28	2	0	1	198 1/3	188	88	82	49	106
1992— Toronto (A.L.)	7	9	.438	5.40	41	14	0	0	2	120	138	84	72	36	62
1993— Detroit (A.L.)■	11	9	.550	4.19	32	30	0	0	0	187	183	93	87	42	139
1994— Lakeland (Fla. St.)	0	0	...	0.00	2	2	0	0	0	6	5	1	0	0	3
— Detroit (A.L.)	5	7	.417	3.96	16	16	5	1	0	111 1/3	113	54	49	24	71
1995— Detroit (A.L.)	10	3	.769	3.04	18	18	3	0	0	130 1/3	120	54	44	37	83
— Cincinnati (N.L.)■	6	5	.545	3.59	11	11	3	0	0	72 2/3	74	34	29	16	50
1996— Baltimore (A.L.)■	11	14	.440	5.14	34	34	3	0	0	224 1/3	247	132	128	51	130
1997— New York (A.L.)■	16	10	.615	4.21	32	32	5	2	0	218	239	109	102	45	156
1998— New York (A.L.)	18	4	*.818	3.49	30	30	8	*5	0	214 1/3	195	86	83	29	163
A.L. totals (12 years)	118	84	.584	3.97	399	229	26	8	13	1772 2/3	1756	847	782	429	1191
N.L. totals (1 year)	6	5	.545	3.59	11	11	3	0	0	72 2/3	74	34	29	16	50
Major league totals (12 years)	124	89	.582	3.96	410	240	29	8	13	1845 1/3	1830	881	811	445	1241

DIVISION SERIES RECORD

RECORDS: Shares career record for most games started—5; most innings pitched—37; and most wins—4. ... Holds A.L. career record for most wins—3.

Year Team (League)	W	L	Pct.	ERA	G	GS	CG	ShO	Sv.	IP	H	R	ER	BB	SO
1995— Cincinnati (N.L.)	1	0	1.000	0.00	1	1	0	0	0	6 1/3	6	1	0	1	8
1996— Baltimore (A.L.)	1	0	1.000	4.61	2	2	0	0	0	13 2/3	15	7	7	5	6
1997— New York (A.L.)	1	0	1.000	1.00	1	1	1	0	0	9	5	1	1	0	1
1998— New York (A.L.)	1	0	1.000	0.00	1	1	0	0	0	8	5	0	0	1	9
Div. series totals (4 years)	4	0	1.000	1.95	5	5	1	0	0	37	31	9	8	7	24

CHAMPIONSHIP SERIES RECORD

NOTES: Named A.L. Championship Series Most Valuable Player (1998).

Year Team (League)	W	L	Pct.	ERA	G	GS	CG	ShO	Sv.	IP	H	R	ER	BB	SO
1989— Toronto (A.L.)	0	0	...	0.00	1	0	0	0	0	1	0	1	0	2	1
1991— Toronto (A.L.)	0	0	...	2.35	4	0	0	0	0	7 2/3	6	2	2	2	9
1992— Toronto (A.L.)							Did not play.								
1995— Cincinnati (N.L.)	0	1	.000	4.50	1	1	0	0	0	6	8	3	3	2	3
1996— Baltimore (A.L.)	1	0	1.000	4.05	1	1	0	0	0	6 2/3	8	3	3	3	6
1998— New York (A.L.)	2	0	1.000	2.87	2	2	0	0	0	15 2/3	12	5	5	2	18
Champ. series totals (5 years)	3	1	.750	3.16	9	4	0	0	0	37	34	14	13	11	37

WORLD SERIES RECORD

NOTES: Member of World Series championship team (1992 and 1998).

Year Team (League)	W	L	Pct.	ERA	G	GS	CG	ShO	Sv.	IP	H	R	ER	BB	SO
1992— Toronto (A.L.)	0	0	...	0.00	4	0	0	0	0	4 1/3	1	0	0	2	3
1998— New York (A.L.)	1	0	1.000	6.43	1	1	0	0	0	7	7	5	5	2	4
World Series totals (2 years)	1	0	1.000	3.97	5	1	0	0	0	11 1/3	8	5	5	4	7

W

Year	League	W	L	Pct.	ERA	GS	CG	ShO	Sv.	IP	H	R	ER	BB	SO
1995—	American	0	0	...	0.00	0	0	0	0	$1/3$	0	0	0	0	1
1998—	American	0	0	...	0.00	1	0	0	0	2	0	0	0	1	1
All-Star totals (2 years)		0	0	...	0.00	1	0	0	0	$2\,1/3$	0	0	0	1	2

WENDELL, TURK · P · METS

PERSONAL: Born May 19, 1967, in Pittsfield, Mass. ... 6-2/205. ... Throws right, bats left. ... Full name: Steven John Wendell.
HIGH SCHOOL: Wahconah Regional (Dalton, Mass.).
COLLEGE: Quinnipiac College (Conn.).
TRANSACTIONS/CAREER NOTES: Selected by Atlanta Braves organization in fifth round of free-agent draft (June 1, 1988). ... Traded by Braves with P Yorkis Perez to Chicago Cubs for P Mike Bielecki and C Damon Berryhill (September 29, 1991). ... On disabled list (May 4, 1992-remainder of season). ... On Chicago disabled list (April 16-May 27, 1995); included rehabilitation assignments to Daytona (May 5-15) and Orlando (May 15-27). ... Traded by Cubs with OF Brian McRae and P Mel Rojas to New York Mets for OF Lance Johnson and two players to be named later (August 8, 1997); Cubs acquired P Mark Clark (August 11) and IF Manny Alexander (August 14) to complete deal.

Year	Team (League)	W	L	Pct.	ERA	G	GS	CG	ShO	Sv.	IP	H	R	ER	BB	SO
1988—	Pulaski (Appalachian)	3	•8	.273	3.83	14	14	*6	1	0	*101	85	50	43	30	87
1989—	Burlington (Midw.)	9	11	.450	2.21	22	22	•9	*5	0	159	127	63	39	41	153
	— Greenville (Southern)	0	0	...	9.82	1	1	0	0	0	$3\,2/3$	7	5	4	1	3
	— Durham (Carolina)	2	0	1.000	1.13	3	3	1	0	0	24	13	4	3	6	27
1990—	Durham (Carolina)	1	3	.250	1.86	6	5	1	0	0	$38\,2/3$	24	10	8	15	26
	— Greenville (Southern)	4	9	.308	5.74	36	13	1	1	2	91	105	70	58	48	85
1991—	Greenville (Southern)	11	3	*.786	2.56	25	20	1	1	0	$147\,2/3$	130	47	42	51	122
	— Richmond (Int'l)	0	2	.000	3.43	3	3	1	0	0	21	20	9	8	16	18
1992—	Iowa (Am. Assoc.)■	2	0	1.000	1.44	4	4	0	0	0	25	17	7	4	15	12
1993—	Iowa (Am. Assoc.)	10	8	.556	4.60	25	25	3	0	0	$148\,2/3$	148	88	76	47	110
	— Chicago (N.L.)	1	2	.333	4.37	7	4	0	0	0	$22\,2/3$	24	13	11	8	15
1994—	Iowa (Am. Assoc.)	11	6	.647	2.95	23	23	6	•3	0	168	141	58	55	28	118
	— Chicago (N.L.)	0	1	.000	11.93	6	2	0	0	0	$14\,1/3$	22	20	19	10	9
1995—	Daytona (Fla. St.)	0	0	...	1.17	4	2	0	0	0	$7\,2/3$	5	2	1	1	8
	— Orlando (South.)	1	0	1.000	3.86	5	0	0	0	1	7	6	3	3	4	7
	— Chicago (N.L.)	3	1	.750	4.92	43	0	0	0	0	$60\,1/3$	71	35	33	24	50
1996—	Chicago (N.L.)	4	5	.444	2.84	70	0	0	0	18	$79\,1/3$	58	26	25	44	75
1997—	Chicago (N.L.)	3	5	.375	4.20	52	0	0	0	4	60	53	32	28	39	54
	— New York (N.L.)■	0	0	...	4.96	13	0	0	0	1	$16\,1/3$	15	10	9	14	10
1998—	New York (N.L.)	5	1	.833	2.93	66	0	0	0	4	$76\,2/3$	62	25	25	33	58
Major league totals (6 years)		16	15	.516	4.10	257	6	0	0	27	$329\,2/3$	305	161	150	172	271

WENGERT, DON · P · ROYALS

PERSONAL: Born November 6, 1969, in Sioux City, Iowa. ... 6-2/212. ... Throws right, bats right. ... Full name: Donald Paul Wengert. ... Brother of Bill Wengert, pitcher with Los Angeles Dodgers, San Diego Padres and Boston Red Sox organizations (1988-95).
HIGH SCHOOL: Heelan Catholic (Sioux City, Iowa).
COLLEGE: Iowa State.
TRANSACTIONS/CAREER NOTES: Selected by Cincinnati Reds organization in 60th round of free-agent draft (June 1, 1988); did not sign. ... Selected by Oakland Athletics organization in fourth round of free-agent draft (June 1, 1992). ... On Oakland disabled list (July 30-August 18, 1995); included rehabilitation assignment to Edmonton (August 7-18). ... On disabled list (July 24-August 8, 1996). ... Traded by A's with IF David Newhan to San Diego Padres for P Doug Bochtler and IF Jorge Velandia (November 26, 1997). ... Traded by Padres to Chicago Cubs for P Ben VanRyn (May 5, 1998). ... Granted free agency (November 25, 1998). ... Signed by Kansas City Royals organization (December 21, 1998).
MISCELLANEOUS: Appeared in two games as pinch runner and had a sacrifice hit in only appearance as pinch hitter with Chicago (1998).

Year	Team (League)	W	L	Pct.	ERA	G	GS	CG	ShO	Sv.	IP	H	R	ER	BB	SO
1992—	S. Oregon (N'west)	2	0	1.000	1.46	6	5	1	0	0	37	32	6	6	7	29
	— Madison (Midwest)	3	4	.429	3.38	7	7	0	0	0	40	42	20	15	17	29
1993—	Madison (Midwest)	6	5	.545	3.32	13	13	2	0	0	$78\,2/3$	79	30	29	18	46
	— Modesto (California)	3	6	.333	4.73	12	12	0	0	0	$70\,1/3$	75	42	37	29	43
1994—	Modesto (California)	4	1	.800	2.95	10	7	0	0	2	$42\,2/3$	40	15	14	11	52
	— Huntsville (Southern)	6	4	.600	3.26	17	17	1	0	0	$99\,1/3$	86	43	36	33	92
1995—	Oakland (A.L.)	1	1	.500	3.34	19	0	0	0	0	$29\,2/3$	30	14	11	12	16
	— Edmonton (PCL)	1	1	.500	7.38	16	6	0	0	0	39	55	32	32	16	20
1996—	Oakland (A.L.)	7	11	.389	5.58	36	25	1	1	0	$161\,1/3$	200	102	100	60	75
1997—	Oakland (A.L.)	5	11	.313	6.04	49	12	1	0	2	134	177	96	90	41	68
1998—	San Diego (N.L.)■	0	0	...	5.93	10	0	0	0	1	$13\,2/3$	21	9	9	5	5
	— Chicago (N.L.)	1	5	.167	5.07	21	6	0	0	0	$49\,2/3$	55	29	28	23	41
	— Iowa (Pacific Coast)	3	1	.750	4.58	9	9	1	0	0	53	58	30	27	14	48
A.L. totals (3 years)		13	23	.361	5.57	104	37	2	1	2	325	407	212	201	113	159
N.L. totals (1 year)		1	5	.167	5.26	31	6	0	0	1	$63\,1/3$	76	39	37	28	46
Major league totals (4 years)		14	28	.333	5.52	135	43	2	1	3	$388\,1/3$	483	250	238	141	205

W

WEST, DAVID · P

PERSONAL: Born September 1, 1964, in Memphis. ... 6-6/247. ... Throws left, bats left. ... Full name: David Lee West.
HIGH SCHOOL: Craigmont (Memphis).
TRANSACTIONS/CAREER NOTES: Selected by New York Mets organization in fourth round of free-agent draft (June 6, 1983). ... Traded by Mets with P Rick Aguilera and three players to be named later to Minnesota Twins for P Frank Viola (July 31, 1989); Portland, Twins organization, acquired P Kevin Tapani and P Tim Drummond (August 1, 1989), and Twins acquired P Jack Savage to complete deal (October 16, 1989). ... On disabled list (September 7, 1990-remainder of season). ... On Minnesota disabled list (April 7-July 2, 1991); included rehabilita-

tion assignments to Orlando (May 12-15) and Portland (June 14-July 2). ... Traded by Twins to Philadelphia Phillies for P Mike Hartley (December 5, 1992). ... On Philadelphia disabled list (May 14-June 16 and July 7, 1995-remainder of season); included rehabilitation assignments to Scranton/Wilkes-Barre (June 5-9) and Reading (June 9-16). ... On Philadelphia disabled list (March 23-August 3 and August 26-September 12, 1996); included rehabilitation assignments to Clearwater (June 12-13 and June 29-July 21) and Scranton/Wilkes-Barre (July 21-28). ... Granted free agency (October 31, 1996). ... Played in Japan (1997). ... Signed by Cincinnati Reds organization (February 2, 1998). ... Released by Reds (March 9, 1998). ... Signed by Houston Astros organization (April 6, 1998). ... On New Orleans disabled list (May 10-17, 1998). ... Traded by Astros organization to Boston Red Sox organization for P Mike Blais (June 18, 1998). ... Released by Red Sox (September 8, 1998).

STATISTICAL NOTES: Led New York-Pennsylvania League with 16 wild pitches in 1984. ... Pitched 3-0 no-hit victory against Spartanburg (August 14, 1985). ... Pitched six innings, combining with Larry Casian (two innings) and Greg Johnson (one inning) in 5-0 no-hit victory for Portland against Vancouver (June 7, 1992).

Year — Team (League)	W	L	Pct.	ERA	G	GS	CG	ShO	Sv.	IP	H	R	ER	BB	SO
1983— GC Mets (GCL)	2	4	.333	2.85	12	10	0	0	0	53 2/3	41	28	17	52	56
1984— Columbia (S. Atl.)	3	5	.375	6.23	12	12	0	0	0	60 2/3	41	47	42	68	60
— Little Falls (NYP)	6	4	.600	3.34	13	11	0	0	0	62	43	35	23	62	79
1985— Columbia (S. Atl.)	10	9	.526	4.56	26	25	5	2	0	150	105	97	76	*111	194
1986— Lynchburg (Carolina)	1	6	.143	5.16	13	13	1	0	0	75	76	50	43	53	70
— Columbia (S. Atl.)	10	3	.769	2.91	13	13	3	1	0	92 2/3	74	41	30	56	101
1987— Jackson (Texas)	10	7	.588	2.81	25	25	4	•2	0	166 2/3	152	67	52	*81	*186
1988— Tidewater (Int'l)	12	4	*.750	*1.80	23	23	7	1	0	160 1/3	106	42	32	*97	143
— New York (N.L.)	1	0	1.000	3.00	2	1	0	0	0	6	6	2	2	3	3
1989— Tidewater (Int'l)	7	4	.636	2.37	12	12	5	1	0	87 1/3	60	31	23	29	69
— New York (N.L.)	0	2	.000	7.40	11	2	0	0	0	24 1/3	25	20	20	14	19
— Minnesota (A.L.)■	3	2	.600	6.41	10	5	0	0	0	39 1/3	48	29	28	19	31
1990— Minnesota (A.L.)	7	9	.438	5.10	29	27	2	0	0	146 1/3	142	88	83	78	92
1991— Minnesota (A.L.)	4	4	.500	4.54	15	12	0	0	0	71 1/3	66	37	36	28	52
— Orlando (South.)	0	0	...	0.00	1	1	0	0	0	1/3	0	0	0	0	0
— Portland (PCL)	1	1	.500	6.32	4	4	0	0	0	15 2/3	12	11	11	12	15
1992— Portland (PCL)	7	6	.538	4.43	19	18	1	0	0	101 2/3	88	51	50	65	87
— Minnesota (A.L.)	1	3	.250	6.99	9	3	0	0	0	28 1/3	32	24	22	20	19
1993—Philadelphia (N.L.)■	6	4	.600	2.92	76	0	0	0	3	86 1/3	60	37	28	51	87
1994— Philadelphia (N.L.)	4	10	.286	3.55	31	14	0	0	0	99	74	44	39	61	83
1995— Philadelphia (N.L.)	3	2	.600	3.79	8	8	0	0	0	38	34	17	16	19	25
— Scran./W.B. (Int'l)	1	0	1.000	0.00	1	1	1	1	0	7	2	0	0	0	6
— Reading (Eastern)	0	0	...	1.50	1	1	0	0	0	6	2	1	1	3	8
1996— Clearwater (Fla. St.)	1	0	1.000	3.13	5	5	0	0	0	23	21	8	8	11	17
— Scran./W.B. (Int'l)	1	0	1.000	5.25	2	2	0	0	0	12	14	8	7	2	12
— Philadelphia (N.L.)	2	2	.500	4.76	7	6	0	0	0	28 1/3	31	17	15	11	22
1997—Fukuoka (Jp. Pac.)■	8	5	.615	6.38	19	19	1	1	0	91 2/3	105	...	65	...	...
1998— New Orleans (PCL)■	1	1	.500	2.56	19	2	0	0	0	31 2/3	26	11	9	22	33
— Pawtucket (Int'l)■	5	0	1.000	1.13	17	0	0	0	3	24	19	4	3	12	23
— Boston (A.L.)	0	0	...	27.00	6	0	0	0	0	2	7	6	6	7	4
A.L. totals (5 years)	15	18	.455	5.48	69	47	2	0	0	287 1/3	295	184	175	152	198
N.L. totals (6 years)	16	20	.444	3.83	135	31	0	0	3	282	230	137	120	159	239
Major league totals (10 years)	31	38	.449	4.66	204	78	2	0	3	569 1/3	525	321	295	311	437

CHAMPIONSHIP SERIES RECORD

Year — Team (League)	W	L	Pct.	ERA	G	GS	CG	ShO	Sv.	IP	H	R	ER	BB	SO
1991— Minnesota (A.L.)	1	0	1.000	0.00	2	0	0	0	0	5 2/3	1	0	0	4	4
1993— Philadelphia (N.L.)	0	0	...	13.50	3	0	0	0	0	2 2/3	5	5	4	2	5
Champ. series totals (2 years)	1	0	1.000	4.32	5	0	0	0	0	8 1/3	6	5	4	6	9

WORLD SERIES RECORD

NOTES: Member of World Series championship team (1991).

Year — Team (League)	W	L	Pct.	ERA	G	GS	CG	ShO	Sv.	IP	H	R	ER	BB	SO
1991— Minnesota (A.L.)	0	0	...	...	2	0	0	0	0	0	2	4	4	4	0
1993— Philadelphia (N.L.)	0	0	...	27.00	3	0	0	0	0	1	5	3	3	1	0
World Series totals (2 years)	0	0	...	63.00	5	0	0	0	0	1	7	7	7	5	0

WETTELAND, JOHN   P   RANGERS

PERSONAL: Born August 21, 1966, in San Mateo, Calif. ... 6-2/215. ... Throws right, bats right. ... Full name: John Karl Wetteland.
HIGH SCHOOL: Cardinal Newman (Santa Rosa, Calif.).
COLLEGE: College of San Mateo (Calif.).
TRANSACTIONS/CAREER NOTES: Selected by New York Mets organization in 12th round of free-agent draft (June 4, 1984); did not sign. ... Selected by Los Angeles Dodgers organization in secondary phase of free-agent draft (January 9, 1985). ... Selected by Detroit Tigers from Dodgers organization in Rule 5 major league draft (December 7, 1987). ... Returned to Dodgers organization (March 29, 1988). ... On Albuquerque disabled list (May 1-8 and June 3-29, 1991). ... Traded by Dodgers with P Tim Belcher to Cincinnati Reds for OF Eric Davis and P Kip Gross (November 25, 1991). ... Traded by Reds with P Bill Risley to Montreal Expos for OF Dave Martinez, P Scott Ruskin and SS Willie Greene (December 11, 1991). ... On Montreal disabled list (March 23-April 23, 1993); included rehabilitation assignment to West Palm Beach (April 18-23). ... On disabled list (April 18-May 4, 1994). ... Traded by Expos to New York Yankees for OF Fernando Seguignol and cash (April 5, 1995). ... On disabled list (August 13-September 6, 1996). ... Granted free agency (November 5, 1996). ... Signed by Texas Rangers (December 17, 1996).

HONORS: Named A.L. Fireman of the Year by THE SPORTING NEWS (1996).
STATISTICAL NOTES: Tied for Florida State League lead with 11 home runs allowed and 17 wild pitches in 1987. ... Led Texas League with 22 wild pitches in 1988.

Year — Team (League)	W	L	Pct.	ERA	G	GS	CG	ShO	Sv.	IP	H	R	ER	BB	SO
1985— Great Falls (Pio.)	1	1	.500	3.92	11	2	0	0	0	20 2/3	17	10	9	15	23
1986— Bakersfield (California)	0	7	.000	5.78	15	12	4	0	0	67	71	50	43	46	38
— Great Falls (Pio.)	4	3	.571	5.45	12	12	1	0	0	69 1/3	70	51	42	40	59
1987— Vero Beach (FSL)	12	7	.632	3.13	27	27	7	2	0	175 2/3	150	81	61	92	144
1988— San Antonio (Tex.)	10	8	.556	3.88	25	25	3	1	0	162 1/3	141	74	70	•77	140

Year Team (League)	W	L	Pct.	ERA	G	GS	CG	ShO	Sv.	IP	H	R	ER	BB	SO
1989— Albuquerque (PCL)............	5	3	.625	3.65	10	10	1	0	0	69	61	28	28	20	73
— Los Angeles (N.L.)	5	8	.385	3.77	31	12	0	0	1	102²/₃	81	46	43	34	96
1990— Los Angeles (N.L.)............	2	4	.333	4.81	22	5	0	0	0	43	44	28	23	17	36
—Albuquerque (PCL)............	2	2	.500	5.59	8	5	1	0	0	29	27	19	18	13	26
1991— Albuquerque (PCL)............	4	3	.571	2.79	41	4	0	0	20	61¹/₃	48	22	19	26	55
— Los Angeles (N.L.)............	1	0	1.000	0.00	6	0	0	0	0	9	5	2	0	3	9
1992— Montreal (N.L.)■............	4	4	.500	2.92	67	0	0	0	37	83¹/₃	64	27	27	36	99
1993— W.P. Beach (FSL)............	0	0	...	0.00	2	2	0	0	0	3	0	0	0	0	6
— Montreal (N.L.)............	9	3	.750	1.37	70	0	0	0	43	85¹/₃	58	17	13	28	113
1994— Montreal (N.L.)............	4	6	.400	2.83	52	0	0	0	25	63²/₃	46	22	20	21	68
1995— New York (A.L.)■............	1	5	.167	2.93	60	0	0	0	31	61¹/₃	40	22	20	14	66
1996— New York (A.L.)............	2	3	.400	2.83	62	0	0	0	*43	63²/₃	54	23	20	21	69
1997— Texas (A.L.)■............	7	2	.778	1.94	61	0	0	0	31	65	43	18	14	21	63
1998— Texas (A.L.)............	3	1	.750	2.03	63	0	0	0	42	62	47	17	14	14	72
A.L. totals (4 years)	13	11	.542	2.43	246	0	0	0	147	252	184	80	68	70	270
N.L. totals (6 years)	25	25	.500	2.93	248	17	0	0	106	387	298	142	126	139	421
Major league totals (10 years)....	38	36	.514	2.73	494	17	0	0	253	639	482	222	194	209	691

DIVISION SERIES RECORD

Year Team (League)	W	L	Pct.	ERA	G	GS	CG	ShO	Sv.	IP	H	R	ER	BB	SO
1995— New York (A.L.)	0	1	.000	14.54	3	0	0	0	0	4¹/₃	8	7	7	2	5
1996— New York (A.L.)	0	0	...	0.00	3	0	0	0	2	4	2	0	0	5	4
1998— Texas (A.L.)	0	0	...	0.00	1	0	0	0	0	1	0	0	0	1	1
Div. series totals (3 years)	0	1	.000	6.75	7	0	0	0	2	9¹/₃	10	7	7	8	10

CHAMPIONSHIP SERIES RECORD

Year Team (League)	W	L	Pct.	ERA	G	GS	CG	ShO	Sv.	IP	H	R	ER	BB	SO
1996— New York (A.L.)	0	0	...	4.50	4	0	0	0	1	4	2	2	2	1	5

WORLD SERIES RECORD

RECORDS: Holds single-series record for most saves—4 (1996).

NOTES: Named Most Valuable Player (1996). ... Member of World Series championship team (1996).

Year Team (League)	W	L	Pct.	ERA	G	GS	CG	ShO	Sv.	IP	H	R	ER	BB	SO
1996— New York (A.L.)	0	0	...	2.08	4	0	0	0	4	4¹/₃	4	1	1	1	6

ALL-STAR GAME RECORD

Year League	W	L	Pct.	ERA	GS	CG	ShO	Sv.	IP	H	R	ER	BB	SO
1996— American					Did not play.									
1998— American	0	0	...	0.00	0	0	0	0	1	0	0	0	0	1

WHISENANT, MATT   P   ROYALS

PERSONAL: Born June 8, 1971, in Los Angeles. ... 6-3/215. ... Throws left, bats right. ... Full name: Matthew Michael Whisenant.

HIGH SCHOOL: La Canada (Calif.).

JUNIOR COLLEGE: Glendale (Ariz.) Community College.

TRANSACTIONS/CAREER NOTES: Selected by Philadelphia Phillies organization in 18th round of free-agent draft (June 5, 1989). ... Traded by Phillies organization with P Joel Adamson to Florida Marlins organization for P Danny Jackson (November 17, 1992). ... On disabled list (July 13, 1993-remainder of season). ... On Florida disabled list (March 28-July 4, 1997); included rehabilitation assignments to Brevard County (April 18-21) and Charlotte (May 5-July 4). ... Traded by Marlins to Kansas City Royals for C Matt Treanor (July 29, 1997).

STATISTICAL NOTES: Led International League with 30 wild pitches in 1996.

MISCELLANEOUS: Appeared in one game as pinch runner with Kansas City (1997).

Year Team (League)	W	L	Pct.	ERA	G	GS	CG	ShO	Sv.	IP	H	R	ER	BB	SO
1990— Princeton (Appalachian).....	0	0	...	11.40	9	2	0	0	0	15	16	27	19	20	25
1991— Batavia (N.Y.-Penn)	2	1	.667	2.45	11	10	0	0	0	47²/₃	31	19	13	42	55
1992— Spartanburg (SAL)	11	7	.611	3.23	27	27	2	0	0	150²/₃	117	69	54	85	151
1993— Kane County (Midwest)■....	2	6	.250	4.69	15	15	0	0	0	71	68	45	37	56	74
1994— Brevard County (FSL)........	6	9	.400	3.38	28	26	5	1	0	160	125	71	60	82	103
1995— Portland (Eastern)	10	6	.625	3.50	23	22	2	0	0	128²/₃	103	57	50	65	107
1996— Charlotte (Int'l)................	8	10	.444	6.92	28	22	1	0	0	121	149	107	93	101	97
1997— Brevard County (FSL)........	0	0	...	8.10	2	1	0	0	0	3¹/₃	3	3	3	3	4
— Charlotte (Int'l)................	2	1	.667	7.20	16	0	0	0	0	15	16	12	12	12	19
— Florida (N.L.).................	0	0	...	16.88	4	0	0	0	0	2²/₃	4	6	5	6	4
— Kansas City (A.L.)■	1	0	1.000	2.84	24	0	0	0	0	19	15	7	6	12	19
1998— Kansas City (A.L.)	2	1	.667	4.90	70	0	0	0	2	60²/₃	61	37	33	33	45
A.L. totals (2 years)	3	1	.750	4.41	94	0	0	0	2	79³/₃	76	44	39	45	61
N.L. totals (1 year)	0	0	...	16.88	4	0	0	0	0	2²/₃	4	6	5	6	4
Major league totals (2 years)......	3	1	.750	4.81	98	0	0	0	2	82¹/₃	80	50	44	51	65

WHITE, DERRICK   OF   ROCKIES

PERSONAL: Born October 12, 1969, in San Rafael, Calif. ... 6-1/220. ... Bats right, throws right. ... Full name: Derrick Ramon White. ... Brother of Marquis White, professional soccer player with New England Revolution.

HIGH SCHOOL: Terra Linda (San Rafael, Calif.).

JUNIOR COLLEGE: Santa Rosa (Calif.) Junior College.

COLLEGE: Oklahoma.

TRANSACTIONS/CAREER NOTES: Selected by Minnesota Twins organization in 23rd round of free-agent draft (June 5, 1989); did not sign. ... Selected by Philadelphia Phillies organization in ninth round of free-agent draft (June 4, 1990); did not sign. ... Selected by Montreal Expos organization in sixth round of free-agent draft (June 3, 1991). ... On Ottawa disabled list (April 8-May 4, 1993). ... Released by Ottawa (June 14, 1994). ... Signed by Florida Marlins organization (June 23, 1994). ... Granted free agency (October 15, 1994). ... Signed by Detroit Tigers

W

organization (November 16, 1994). ... Released by Tigers (October 12, 1995). ... Signed by Oakland Athletics organization (April 2, 1996). ... Released by Tigers (October 12, 1995). ... Signed by Anaheim Angels organization (March 13, 1997). ... On Midland suspended list (May 13-16, 1997). ... Granted free agency (October 15, 1997). ... Signed by Chicago Cubs organization (December 1, 1997). ... Claimed on waivers by Colorado Rockies (July 17, 1998). ... Released by Rockies (December 9, 1998). ... Re-signed by Rockies for 1999 season.

STATISTICAL NOTES: Led Eastern League first basemen with 1,294 total chances and 110 double plays in 1992.

Year Team (League)	Pos.	G	AB	R	H	2B	3B	HR	RBI	Avg.	BB	SO	SB	PO	A	E	Avg.
1991— Jamestown (NYP)	OF-1B	72	271	46	89	10	4	6	50	.328	40	46	8	402	18	8	.981
1992— Harrisburg (East.).......	1B	134	495	63	137	19	2	13	81	.277	40	73	17	*1178	*106	10	*.992
1993— W.P. Beach (FSL)..........	1B	6	25	1	5	0	0	0	1	.200	1	2	2	38	4	0	1.000
— Ottawa (Int'l)..........	1B	67	249	32	70	15	1	4	29	.281	20	52	10	632	49	8	.988
— Montreal (N.L.)...........	1B	17	49	6	11	3	0	2	4	.224	2	12	2	129	8	1	.993
— Harrisburg (East.).......	1B	21	79	14	18	1	0	2	12	.228	5	17	2	171	11	2	.989
1994— Ottawa (Int'l)	1B-OF	47	99	13	21	4	0	0	9	.212	8	25	4	179	11	2	.990
— Portland (Eastern)■.....	OF-1B	74	264	39	71	13	2	4	34	.269	28	52	14	137	12	3	.980
1995— Toledo (Int'l)■............	OF-1B	87	309	50	82	15	3	14	49	.265	29	65	6	327	20	9	.975
— Detroit (A.L.)	1B-OF-DH	39	48	3	9	2	0	0	2	.188	0	7	1	55	5	2	.968
1996— W. Mich. (Mid.)■.......	OF-1B-3B	73	263	49	69	17	0	10	43	.262	44	63	12	150	26	4	.978
— Modesto (California) ..	1B-3B-OF	54	197	45	58	15	1	7	39	.294	29	41	8	289	69	5	.986
1997— Vancouver (PCL)■.......	OF-1B	116	414	64	134	35	2	11	65	.324	44	73	11	253	14	4	.985
— Midland (Texas).........	OF	10	37	2	7	2	0	0	3	.189	5	6	1	3	0	0	1.000
1998— Iowa (Pacific Coast)■	OF-1B	66	251	57	91	17	2	18	76	.363	38	48	4	157	8	3	.982
— Chicago (N.L.)	DH-OF	11	10	1	1	0	0	1	2	.100	0	5	0	0	0	0	...
— Colorado (N.L.)	OF	9	0	0	0	0	0	0	0	.000	0	4	0	1	0	0	1.000
— Colo. Springs (PCL) ...	OF-1B	22	81	15	23	5	0	2	10	.284	10	14	2	40	3	0	1.000
American League totals (1 year)		39	48	3	9	2	0	0	2	.188	0	7	1	55	5	2	.968
National League totals (2 years)		37	68	7	12	3	0	3	6	.176	2	21	2	130	8	1	.993
Major league totals (3 years)		76	116	10	21	5	0	3	8	.181	2	28	3	185	13	3	.985

WHITE, DEVON   OF   DODGERS

PERSONAL: Born December 29, 1962, in Kingston, Jamaica. ... 6-2/190. ... Bats both, throws right. ... Full name: Devon Markes White. ... Name pronounced de-VON.

HIGH SCHOOL: Park West (New York).

TRANSACTIONS/CAREER NOTES: Selected by California Angels organization in sixth round of free-agent draft (June 8, 1981). ... On suspended list (June 11-12 and July 19, 1982-remainder of season). ... On Edmonton disabled list (May 12-22, 1986). ... On disabled list (May 7-June 10, 1988). ... Traded by Angels organization with P Willie Fraser and a player to be named later to Toronto Blue Jays for OF Junior Felix, IF Luis Sojo and a player to be named later (December 2, 1990); Blue Jays acquired P Marcus Moore and Angels acquired C Ken Rivers to complete deal (December 4, 1990). ... Granted free agency (November 1, 1995). ... Signed by Florida Marlins (November 21, 1995). ... On disabled list (April 25-May 30 and June 8-July 28, 1997). ... Traded by Marlins to Arizona Diamondbacks for P Jesus Martinez (November 18, 1997). ... Granted free agency (October 23, 1998). ... Signed by Los Angeles Dodgers (November 9, 1998).

RECORDS: Shares major league record for most stolen bases in one inning—3 (September 9, 1989, sixth inning).

HONORS: Won A.L. Gold Glove as outfielder (1988-89 and 1991-95).

STATISTICAL NOTES: Led Midwest League outfielders with 286 total chances in 1983. ... Led California League outfielders with 351 total chances in 1984. ... Led Pacific Coast League outfielders with 339 total chances in 1986. ... Switch-hit home runs in one game three times (June 23, 1987; June 29, 1990; and June 1, 1992). ... Led A.L. outfielders with 449 total chances in 1987, 448 in 1991 and 458 in 1992. ... Career major league grand slams: 7.

MISCELLANEOUS: Holds Arizona Diamondbacks all-time record for highest batting average (.279), most runs (84), most hits (157), most doubles (32), most runs batted in (85) and most stolen bases. ... Tied for Arizona Diamondbacks all-time record for most home runs (22).

Year Team (League)	Pos.	G	AB	R	H	2B	3B	HR	RBI	Avg.	BB	SO	SB	PO	A	E	Avg.
1981— Idaho Falls (Pio.)........	OF-3B-1B	30	106	10	19	2	0	0	10	.179	12	34	4	33	10	3	.935
1982— Danville (Midwest)	OF	57	186	21	40	6	1	1	11	.215	11	41	11	89	3	8	.920
1983— Peoria (Midwest)........	OF	117	430	69	109	17	6	13	66	.253	36	124	32	267	8	11	.962
— Nashua (Eastern).......	OF	17	70	11	18	7	2	0	2	.257	7	22	5	37	0	3	.925
1984— Redwood (Calif.)	OF	138	520	101	147	25	5	7	55	.283	56	118	36	*322	16	13	.963
1985— Midland (Texas).........	OF	70	260	52	77	10	4	4	35	.296	35	46	38	176	10	4	.979
— Edmonton (PCL)	OF	66	277	53	70	16	5	4	39	.253	24	77	21	205	6	2	.991
— California (A.L.)	OF	21	7	7	1	0	0	0	0	.143	1	3	3	10	1	0	1.000
1986— Edmonton (PCL)	OF	112	461	84	134	25	10	14	60	.291	31	90	*42	317	•16	6	.982
— California (A.L.)	OF	29	51	8	12	1	1	1	3	.235	6	8	6	49	0	2	.961
1987— California (A.L.)	OF	159	639	103	168	33	5	24	87	.263	39	135	32	*424	16	9	.980
1988— California (A.L.)	OF	122	455	76	118	22	2	11	51	.259	23	84	17	364	7	9	.976
1989— California (A.L.)	OF-DH	156	636	86	156	18	13	12	56	.245	31	129	44	430	10	5	.989
1990— California (A.L.)	OF	125	443	57	96	17	3	11	44	.217	44	116	21	302	11	9	.972
— Edmonton (PCL)	OF	14	55	9	20	4	4	0	6	.364	7	12	4	31	1	3	.914
1991— Toronto (A.L.)■..........	OF	156	642	110	181	40	10	17	60	.282	55	135	33	*439	8	1	*.998
1992— Toronto (A.L.)	OF-DH	153	641	98	159	26	7	17	60	.248	47	133	37	*443	8	7	.985
1993— Toronto (A.L.)	OF	146	598	116	163	42	6	15	52	.273	57	127	34	399	6	3	.993
1994— Toronto (A.L.)	OF	100	403	67	109	24	6	13	49	.270	21	80	11	268	3	6	.978
1995— Toronto (A.L.)	OF	101	427	61	121	23	5	10	53	.283	29	97	11	261	7	3	.989
1996— Florida (N.L.)■..........	OF	146	552	77	151	37	6	17	84	.274	38	99	22	296	5	4	.987
1997— Florida (N.L.)	OF	74	265	37	65	13	1	6	34	.245	32	65	13	152	4	2	.987
1998— Arizona (N.L.)	OF	146	563	84	157	32	1	22	85	.279	42	102	22	371	3	5	.987
American League totals (11 years)		1268	4942	789	1284	246	58	131	515	.260	353	1047	249	3389	77	54	.985
National League totals (3 years)		366	1380	198	373	82	8	45	203	.270	112	266	57	819	12	11	.987
Major league totals (14 years)		1634	6322	987	1657	328	66	176	718	.262	465	1313	306	4208	89	65	.985

W

DIVISION SERIES RECORD

Year	Team (League)	Pos.	G	AB	R	H	2B	3B	HR	RBI	Avg.	BB	SO	SB	PO	A	E	Avg.
						BATTING									FIELDING			
1997—Florida (N.L.)	OF	3	11	1	2	0	0	1	4	.182	2	3	0	3	0	0	1.000

CHAMPIONSHIP SERIES RECORD

RECORDS: Holds A.L. career record for highest batting average (50 or more at-bats)—.392. ... Holds single-series record for most times caught stealing—4 (1992). ... Shares A.L. single-series record for most hits—12 (1993). ... Shares A.L. single-game record for most at-bats— 6 (October 11, 1992, 11 innings).

Year	Team (League)	Pos.	G	AB	R	H	2B	3B	HR	RBI	Avg.	BB	SO	SB	PO	A	E	Avg.
						BATTING									FIELDING			
1986—California (A.L.)	OF-PR	4	2	2	1	0	0	0	0	.500	0	1	0	3	0	0	1.000
1991—Toronto (A.L.)............	OF	5	22	5	8	1	0	0	0	.364	2	3	3	16	0	0	1.000
1992—Toronto (A.L.)............	OF	6	23	2	8	2	0	0	2	.348	5	6	0	16	0	1	.941
1993—Toronto (A.L.)............	OF	6	27	3	12	1	1	1	2	.444	1	5	0	15	0	0	1.000
1997—Florida (N.L.)	OF	6	21	4	4	1	0	0	1	.190	2	7	1	16	0	0	1.000
Championship series totals (5 years)		27	95	16	33	5	1	1	5	.347	10	22	4	66	0	1	.985

WORLD SERIES RECORD

RECORDS: Shares record for most consecutive strikeouts in one series—5 (October 21 [1] and 22 [4], 1997).
NOTES: Member of World Series championship team (1992, 1993 and 1997).

Year	Team (League)	Pos.	G	AB	R	H	2B	3B	HR	RBI	Avg.	BB	SO	SB	PO	A	E	Avg.
						BATTING									FIELDING			
1992—Toronto (A.L.)............	OF	6	26	2	6	1	0	0	2	.231	0	6	1	22	0	0	1.000
1993—Toronto (A.L.)............	OF	6	24	8	7	3	2	1	7	.292	4	7	1	16	0	0	1.000
1997—Florida (N.L.)	OF	7	33	0	8	3	1	0	2	.242	3	10	1	16	0	0	1.000
World Series totals (3 years)		19	83	10	21	7	3	1	11	.253	7	23	3	54	0	0	1.000

ALL-STAR GAME RECORD

Year	League	Pos.	AB	R	H	2B	3B	HR	RBI	Avg.	BB	SO	SB	PO	A	E	Avg.
						BATTING									FIELDING			
1989—American	OF	1	0	0	0	0	0	0	.000	0	0	0	0	0	0	...
1993—American	OF	2	1	1	1	0	0	1	.500	0	0	1	1	0	0	1.000
1998—National	OF	3	1	3	0	1	0	0	1.000	0	0	0	0	0	0	...
All-Star Game totals (3 years)		6	2	4	1	1	0	1	.667	0	0	1	1	0	0	1.000

WHITE, GABE   P   REDS

PERSONAL: Born November 20, 1971, in Sebring, Fla. ... 6-2/200. ... Throws left, bats left. ... Full name: Gabriel Allen White.
HIGH SCHOOL: Sebring (Fla.).
TRANSACTIONS/CAREER NOTES: Selected by Montreal Expos organization in supplemental round ("sandwich pick" between first and second round, 28th pick overall) of free-agent draft (June 4, 1990); pick received as part of compensation for California Angels signing Type A free-agent P Mark Langston. ... On Harrisburg disabled list (July 2-27, 1993). ... On Ottawa disabled list (April 7-May 6, 1994). ... Traded by Expos to Cincinnati Reds for 2B Jhonny Carvajal (December 15, 1995). ... On disabled list (September 17, 1996-remainder of season).
RECORDS: Shares N.L. record for most consecutive home runs allowed in one inning—3 (July 7, 1996, second inning).

Year	Team (League)	W	L	Pct.	ERA	G	GS	CG	ShO	Sv.	IP	H	R	ER	BB	SO
1990—GC Expos (GCL)	4	2	.667	3.14	11	11	1	0	0	57 1/3	50	21	20	12	41
1991—Sumter (S. Atl.)	6	9	.400	3.26	24	24	5	0	0	149	127	73	54	53	140
1992—Rockford (Midwest)	14	8	.636	2.84	27	27	7	0	0	187	148	73	59	61	*176
1993—Harrisburg (Eastern)	7	2	.778	2.16	16	16	2	1	0	100	80	30	24	28	80
—Ottawa (Int'l)	2	1	.667	3.12	6	6	1	1	0	40 1/3	38	15	14	6	28
1994—W.P. Beach (FSL)	1	0	1.000	1.50	1	1	0	0	0	6	2	2	1	1	4
—Ottawa (Int'l)	8	3	.727	5.05	14	14	0	0	0	73	77	49	41	28	63
—Montreal (N.L.)...................	1	1	.500	6.08	7	5	0	0	1	23 2/3	24	16	16	11	17
1995—Ottawa (Int'l)	2	3	.400	3.90	12	12	0	0	0	62 1/3	58	31	27	17	37
—Montreal (N.L.)...................	1	2	.333	7.01	19	1	0	0	0	25 2/3	26	21	20	9	25
1996—Indianapolis (A.A.)■	6	3	.667	2.77	11	11	0	0	0	68 1/3	69	25	21	9	51
1997—Indianapolis (A.A.)	7	4	.636	2.82	20	19	0	0	0	118	119	46	37	18	62
—Cincinnati (N.L.)	2	2	.500	4.39	12	6	0	0	1	41	39	20	20	8	25
1998—Cincinnati (N.L.)	5	5	.500	4.01	69	3	0	0	9	98 2/3	86	46	44	27	83
Major league totals (4 years)	9	10	.474	4.76	107	15	0	0	11	189	175	103	100	55	150

WHITE, RICK   P   DEVIL RAYS

W

PERSONAL: Born December 23, 1968, in Springfield, Ohio. ... 6-4/215. ... Throws right, bats right. ... Full name: Richard Allen White.
HIGH SCHOOL: Kenton Ridge (Springfield, Ohio).
JUNIOR COLLEGE: Paducah (Ky.) Community College.
TRANSACTIONS/CAREER NOTES: Selected by Pittsburgh Pirates organization in 15th round of free-agent draft (June 4, 1990). ... On Carolina disabled list (May 15-July 6, 1993). ... On Buffalo disabled list (August 28-September 4, 1993). ... On Pittsburgh disabled list (April 14-May 17, 1995). ... Granted free agency (December 21, 1995). ... On Calgary disabled list (April 4-August 7, 1996). ... On Carolina disabled list (August 7-23, 1996). ... Granted free agency (October 15, 1996). ... Signed by Tampa Bay Devil Rays (February 4, 1997). ... Loaned by Devil Rays to Chicago Cubs organization (April 3-September 11, 1997).

Year	Team (League)	W	L	Pct.	ERA	G	GS	CG	ShO	Sv.	IP	H	R	ER	BB	SO
1990—GC Pirates (GCL)	3	1	.750	0.76	7	6	0	0	0	35 2/3	26	11	3	4	27
—Welland (N.Y.-Penn)	1	4	.200	3.26	9	5	1	0	0	38 2/3	39	19	14	14	43
1991—Augusta (S. Atl.)	4	4	.500	3.00	34	0	0	0	6	63	68	26	21	18	52
—Salem (Carolina)	2	3	.400	4.66	13	5	1	0	1	46 1/3	41	27	24	9	36
1992—Salem (Carolina)	7	9	.438	3.80	18	18	•5	1	0	120 2/3	116	58	51	24	70
—Carolina (Southern)	1	7	.125	4.21	10	10	1	0	0	57 2/3	59	32	27	18	45

Year Team (League)	W	L	Pct.	ERA	G	GS	CG	ShO	Sv.	IP	H	R	ER	BB	SO
1993— Carolina (Southern)...........	4	3	.571	3.50	12	12	1	0	0	69 1/3	59	29	27	12	52
— Buffalo (A.A.)....................	0	3	.000	3.54	7	3	0	0	0	28	25	13	11	8	16
1994— Pittsburgh (N.L.)................	4	5	.444	3.82	43	5	0	0	6	75 1/3	79	35	32	17	38
1995— Pittsburgh (N.L.)................	2	3	.400	4.75	15	9	0	0	0	55	66	33	29	18	29
— Calgary (PCL).....................	6	4	.600	4.20	14	11	1	0	0	79 1/3	97	40	37	10	56
1996— Carolina (Southern).............	0	1	.000	11.37	2	1	0	0	0	6 1/3	9	8	8	1	7
— GC Pirates (GCL)................	0	0	. . .	2.25	3	3	0	0	0	12	8	4	3	3	8
1997— Orlando (Southern)■.....	5	7	.417	4.71	39	8	0	0	12	86	93	55	45	22	65
1998— Durham (International)■.....	4	2	.667	4.22	9	9	1	0	0	53 1/3	63	29	25	11	31
— Tampa Bay (A.L.).............	2	6	.250	3.80	38	3	0	0	0	68 2/3	66	32	29	23	39
A.L. totals (1 year).....................	2	6	.250	3.80	38	3	0	0	0	68 2/3	66	32	29	23	39
N.L. totals (2 years)...................	6	8	.429	4.21	58	14	0	0	6	130 1/3	145	68	61	35	67
Major league totals (3 years)......	8	14	.364	4.07	96	17	0	0	6	199	211	100	90	58	106

WHITE, RONDELL OF EXPOS

PERSONAL: Born February 23, 1972, in Milledgeville, Ga. ... 6-0/210. ... Bats right, throws right. ... Full name: Rondell Bernard White.
HIGH SCHOOL: Jones County (Gray, Ga.).
TRANSACTIONS/CAREER NOTES: Selected by Montreal Expos organization in first round (24th pick overall) of free-agent draft (June 4, 1990); pick received as part of compensation for California Angels signing Type A free-agent P Mark Langston. ... On Montreal disabled list (April 28-July 16, 1996); included rehabilitation assignments to West Palm Beach (July 5-10), Gulf Coast Expos (July 5-10) and Harrisburg (July 10-16). ... On disabled list (July 21, 1998-remainder of season).
STATISTICAL NOTES: Led Gulf Coast League with 96 total bases in 1990. ... Hit for the cycle (June 11, 1995, 13 innings). ... Collected six hits in one game (June 11, 1995). ... Led N.L. outfielders in total chances with 385 in 1997. ... Career major league grand slams: 2.

Year Team (League)	Pos.	G	AB	R	H	2B	3B	HR	RBI	Avg.	BB	SO	SB	PO	A	E	Avg.
1990— GC Expos (GCL)	OF	57	221	33	66	7	4	5	34	.299	17	33	10	71	1	2	.973
1991— Sumter (S. Atl.)	OF	123	465	80	122	23	6	13	68	.262	57	109	50	215	1	3	*.987
1992— W.P. Beach (FSL)	OF	111	450	80	142	10	*12	4	41	.316	46	78	42	187	2	3	.984
— Harrisburg (East.)	OF	21	89	22	27	7	1	2	7	.303	6	14	6	29	1	2	.938
1993— Harrisburg (East.)	OF	90	372	72	122	16	10	12	52	.328	22	72	21	179	4	1	.995
— Ottawa (Int'l)	OF	37	150	28	57	8	2	7	32	.380	12	20	10	79	0	1	.988
— Montreal (N.L.)	OF	23	73	9	19	3	1	2	15	.260	7	16	1	33	0	0	1.000
1994— Montreal (N.L.)	OF	40	97	16	27	10	1	2	13	.278	9	18	1	34	1	2	.946
— Ottawa (Int'l)	OF	42	169	23	46	7	0	7	18	.272	15	17	9	91	4	2	.979
1995— Montreal (N.L.)	OF	130	474	87	140	33	4	13	57	.295	41	87	25	270	5	4	.986
1996— Montreal (N.L.)	OF	88	334	35	98	19	4	6	41	.293	22	53	14	185	5	2	.990
— W.P. Beach (FSL)	OF	3	10	0	2	1	0	0	2	.200	0	4	0	2	0	0	1.000
— G.C. Expos (GCL)	OF	3	12	3	3	0	0	2	4	.250	0	1	1	4	0	0	1.000
— Harrisburg (East.)	OF	5	20	5	7	1	0	3	6	.350	1	1	1	12	0	0	1.000
1997— Montreal (N.L.)	OF	151	592	84	160	29	5	28	82	.270	31	111	16	*376	6	3	*.992
1998— Montreal (N.L.)	OF-DH	97	357	54	107	21	2	17	58	.300	30	57	16	261	7	1	.996
Major league totals (6 years)		529	1927	285	551	115	17	68	266	.286	140	342	73	1159	24	12	.990

WHITEN, MARK OF INDIANS

PERSONAL: Born November 25, 1966, in Pensacola, Fla. ... 6-3/235. ... Bats both, throws right. ... Full name: Mark Anthony Whiten. ... Name pronounced WHITT-en.
HIGH SCHOOL: Pensacola (Fla.).
JUNIOR COLLEGE: Pensacola (Fla.) Junior College.
TRANSACTIONS/CAREER NOTES: Selected by Toronto Blue Jays organization in fifth round of free-agent draft (January 14, 1986). ... On Toronto suspended list (May 23-25, 1991). ... Traded by Blue Jays with P Denis Boucher, OF Glenallen Hill and a player to be named later to Cleveland Indians for P Tom Candiotti and OF Turner Ward (June 27, 1991); Indians acquired cash to complete deal (October 15, 1991). ... Traded by Indians to St. Louis Cardinals for P Mark Clark and SS Juan Andujar (March 31, 1993). ... On St. Louis disabled list (April 18-May 5, 1994); included rehabilitation assignment to Louisville (May 2-5). ... Traded by Cardinals with P Rheal Cormier to Boston Red Sox for 3B Scott Cooper, P Cory Bailey and a player to be named later (April 8, 1995). ... On Boston disabled list (May 22-June 9, 1995); included rehabilitation assignment to Pawtucket (June 2-9). ... Traded by Red Sox to Philadelphia Phillies for 1B Dave Hollins (July 24, 1995). ... Released by Phillies (June 17, 1996). ... Signed by Atlanta Braves (June 24, 1996). ... Traded by Braves to Seattle Mariners for P Roger Blanco (August 14, 1996). ... Granted free agency (December 7, 1996). ... Signed by New York Yankees (January 9, 1997). ... Released by Yankees (August 15, 1997). ... Signed by Cleveland Indians (May 6, 1998). ... Granted free agency (October 30, 1998). ... Re-signed by Indians (December 8, 1998).
RECORDS: Shares major league single-game records for most home runs—4 (September 7, 1993, second game); and most runs batted in—12 (September 7, 1993, second game). ... Shares major league record for most runs batted in during doubleheader—13 (September 7, 1993). ... Shares N.L. record for most runs batted in during two consecutive games—13 (September 7, 1993, first and second games).
STATISTICAL NOTES: Tied for Pioneer League lead in being hit by pitch with six in 1986. ... Led South Atlantic League outfielders with 322 total chances and tied for lead with four double plays in 1987. ... Led South Atlantic League in being hit by pitch with 16 and tied for lead in intentional bases on balls received with 10 in 1987. ... Led Southern League in being hit by pitch with 11 in 1989. ... Hit four home runs in one game (September 7, 1993, second game). ... Switch-hit home runs in one game (September 14, 1993). ... Career major league grand slams: 4.
MISCELLANEOUS: Batted righthanded only (1988-89).

Year Team (League)	Pos.	G	AB	R	H	2B	3B	HR	RBI	Avg.	BB	SO	SB	PO	A	E	Avg.
1986— Medicine Hat (Pio.)	OF	•70	270	53	81	16	3	10	44	.300	29	56	22	111	9	*10	.923
1987— Myrtle Beach (SAL)....	OF	*139	494	90	125	22	5	15	64	.253	76	149	49	*292	*18	12	.963
1988— Dunedin (Fla. St.).......	OF	99	385	61	97	8	5	7	37	.252	41	69	17	200	*21	9	.961
— Knoxville (Southern) ..	OF	28	108	20	28	3	1	2	9	.259	12	20	6	62	3	4	.942
1989— Knoxville (Southern) ..	OF	129	423	75	109	13	6	12	47	.258	60	114	11	223	17	8	.968
1990— Syracuse (Int'l).........	OF	104	390	65	113	19	4	14	48	.290	37	72	14	158	14	6	.966
— Toronto (A.L.)............	OF-DH	33	88	12	24	1	1	2	7	.273	7	14	2	60	3	0	1.000

W

Year Team (League)	Pos.	G	AB	R	H	2B	3B	HR	RBI	Avg.	BB	SO	SB	PO	A	E	Avg.
1991— Toronto (A.L.).............	OF	46	149	12	33	4	3	2	19	.221	11	35	0	90	2	0	1.000
— Cleveland (A.L.)■......	OF-DH	70	258	34	66	14	4	7	26	.256	19	50	4	166	11	7	.962
1992— Cleveland (A.L.).....	OF-DH	148	508	73	129	19	4	9	43	.254	72	102	16	321	14	7	.980
1993— St. Louis (N.L.)■.....	OF	152	562	81	142	13	4	25	99	.253	58	110	15	329	9	10	.971
1994— St. Louis (N.L.).....	OF	92	334	57	98	18	2	14	53	.293	37	75	10	234	9	9	.964
— Louisville (A.A.).....	OF	3	10	2	3	1	0	1	3	.300	1	1	0	3	0	0	1.000
1995— Boston (A.L.)■.........	OF-DH	32	108	13	20	3	0	1	10	.185	8	23	1	52	4	0	1.000
— Pawtucket (Int'l).....	OF	28	102	19	29	3	1	4	13	.284	19	30	4	43	4	3	.940
— Philadelphia (N.L.)■ ..	OF	60	212	38	57	10	1	11	37	.269	31	63	7	105	4	4	.965
1996— Philadelphia (N.L.).....	OF	60	182	33	43	8	0	7	21	.236	33	62	13	97	6	6	.945
— Atlanta (A.L.)■.....	OF	36	90	12	23	5	1	3	17	.256	16	25	2	41	1	3	.933
— Seattle (A.L.)■.......	OF	40	140	31	42	7	0	12	33	.300	21	40	2	90	4	3	.969
1997— New York (A.L.)■.....	OF	69	215	34	57	11	0	5	24	.265	30	47	4	102	2	5	.954
1998— Cleveland (A.L.)......	OF-DH-P	88	226	31	64	14	0	6	29	.283	29	60	2	124	7	4	.970
American League totals (7 years)		526	1692	240	435	73	12	44	191	.257	197	371	31	1005	47	26	.976
National League totals (4 years)		400	1380	221	363	54	8	60	227	.263	175	335	47	806	29	32	.963
Major league totals (9 years)		926	3072	461	798	127	20	104	418	.260	372	706	78	1811	76	58	.970

DIVISION SERIES RECORD

Year Team (League)	Pos.	G	AB	R	H	2B	3B	HR	RBI	Avg.	BB	SO	SB	PO	A	E	Avg.
1998— Cleveland (A.L.)..........								Did not play.									

CHAMPIONSHIP SERIES RECORD

Year Team (League)	Pos.	G	AB	R	H	2B	3B	HR	RBI	Avg.	BB	SO	SB	PO	A	E	Avg.
1998— Cleveland (A.L.)..........	OF	2	7	2	2	1	0	1	1	.286	1	3	0	3	0	0	1.000

RECORD AS PITCHER

Year Team (League)	W	L	Pct.	ERA	G	GS	CG	ShO	Sv.	IP	H	R	ER	BB	SO
1998— Cleveland (A.L.)■.............	0	0	...	9.00	1	0	0	0	0	1	1	1	1	2	3

WHITESIDE, MATT   P   PADRES

PERSONAL: Born August 8, 1967, in Charleston, Mo. ... 6-0/205. ... Throws right, bats right. ... Full name: Matthew Christopher Whiteside.
HIGH SCHOOL: Charleston (Mo.).
COLLEGE: Arkansas State (degree in physical education).
TRANSACTIONS/CAREER NOTES: Selected by Texas Rangers organization in 25th round of free-agent draft (June 4, 1990). ... On disabled list (May 9-25, 1995). ... Granted free agency (October 30, 1996). ... Re-signed by Rangers (November 22, 1996). ... Released by Rangers (March 23, 1998). ... Signed by Philadelphia Phillies (March 27, 1998). ... Granted free agency (October 15, 1998). ... Signed by San Diego Padres organization (November 23, 1998).
STATISTICAL NOTES: Tied for American Association lead with three balks in 1996.

Year Team (League)	W	L	Pct.	ERA	G	GS	CG	ShO	Sv.	IP	H	R	ER	BB	SO
1990— Butte (Pioneer).....	4	4	.500	3.45	18	5	0	0	2	57 1/3	57	33	22	25	45
1991— Gastonia (S. Atl.).....	3	1	.750	2.15	48	0	0	0	29	62 2/3	44	19	15	21	71
1992— Tulsa (Texas).....................	0	1	.000	2.41	33	0	0	0	21	33 2/3	31	9	9	3	30
— Oklahoma City (A.A.).........	1	0	1.000	0.79	12	0	0	0	8	11 1/3	7	1	1	3	13
— Texas (A.L.)......................	1	1	.500	1.93	20	0	0	0	4	28	26	8	6	11	13
1993— Texas (A.L.)......................	2	1	.667	4.32	60	0	0	0	1	73	78	37	35	23	39
— Oklahoma City (A.A.).........	2	1	.667	5.56	8	0	0	0	1	11 1/3	17	7	7	8	10
1994— Texas (A.L.)......................	2	2	.500	5.02	47	0	0	0	1	61	68	40	34	28	37
1995— Texas (A.L.)......................	5	4	.556	4.08	40	0	0	0	3	53	48	24	24	19	46
1996— Texas (A.L.)......................	0	1	.000	6.68	14	0	0	0	0	32 1/3	43	24	24	11	15
— Oklahoma City (A.A.).........	9	6	.600	3.45	36	7	0	0	0	94	95	41	36	24	52
1997— Oklahoma City (A.A.).........	1	1	.500	3.54	10	1	0	0	1	28	30	14	11	13	11
— Texas (A.L.)......................	4	1	.800	5.08	42	1	0	0	0	72 2/3	85	45	41	26	44
1998— Philadelphia (N.L.)■.........	1	1	.500	8.50	10	0	0	0	0	18	27	18	17	5	14
— Scran./W.B. (Int'l)..........	1	4	.200	6.48	30	1	0	0	5	33 1/3	47	24	24	7	21
A.L. totals (6 years).....................	14	10	.583	4.61	223	1	0	0	9	320	348	178	164	118	194
N.L. totals (1 year).....................	1	1	.500	8.50	10	0	0	0	0	18	27	18	17	5	14
Major league totals (7 years)......	15	11	.577	4.82	233	1	0	0	9	338	375	196	181	123	208

WICKMAN, BOB   P   BREWERS

W

PERSONAL: Born February 6, 1969, in Green Bay, Wis. ... 6-1/242. ... Throws right, bats right. ... Full name: Robert Joe Wickman.
HIGH SCHOOL: Oconto Falls (Wis.).
COLLEGE: Wisconsin-Whitewater.
TRANSACTIONS/CAREER NOTES: Selected by Chicago White Sox organization in second round of free-agent draft (June 4, 1990). ... Traded by White Sox organization with P Melido Perez and P Domingo Jean to New York Yankees organization for 2B Steve Sax and cash (January 10, 1992). ... Traded by Yankees with OF Gerald Williams to Milwaukee Brewers for P Graeme Lloyd and OF Pat Listach (August 23, 1996).

Year Team (League)	W	L	Pct.	ERA	G	GS	CG	ShO	Sv.	IP	H	R	ER	BB	SO
1990— GC White Sox (GCL).........	2	0	1.000	2.45	2	2	0	0	0	11	7	4	3	1	15
— Sarasota (Florida State)......	0	1	.000	1.98	2	2	0	0	0	13 2/3	17	7	3	4	8
— South Bend (Mid.).............	7	2	.778	1.38	9	9	3	0	0	65 1/3	50	16	10	16	50
1991— Sarasota (Florida State)......	5	1	.833	2.05	7	7	1	1	0	44	43	16	10	11	32
— Birmingham (Southern)	6	10	.375	3.56	20	20	4	1	0	131 1/3	127	68	52	50	81
1992— Columbus (Int'l)■.............	12	5	.706	2.92	23	23	2	1	0	157	131	61	51	55	108
— New York (A.L.)...................	6	1	.857	4.11	8	8	0	0	0	50 1/3	51	25	23	20	21

Year Team (League)	W	L	Pct.	ERA	G	GS	CG	ShO	Sv.	IP	H	R	ER	BB	SO
1993— New York (A.L.).................	14	4	.778	4.63	41	19	1	1	4	140	156	82	72	69	70
1994— New York (A.L.).................	5	4	.556	3.09	*53	0	0	0	6	70	54	26	24	27	56
1995— New York (A.L.).................	2	4	.333	4.05	63	1	0	0	1	80	77	38	36	33	51
1996— New York (A.L.).................	4	1	.800	4.67	58	0	0	0	0	79	94	41	41	34	61
— Milwaukee (A.L.)■..	3	0	1.000	3.24	12	0	0	0	0	16 $2/3$	12	9	6	10	14
1997— Milwaukee (A.L.).............	7	6	.538	2.73	74	0	0	0	1	95 $2/3$	89	32	29	41	78
1998— Milwaukee (N.L.).............	6	9	.400	3.72	72	0	0	0	25	82 $1/3$	79	38	34	39	71
A.L. totals (6 years)	41	20	.672	3.91	309	28	1	1	12	531 $2/3$	533	253	231	234	351
N.L. totals (1 year).....................	6	9	.400	3.72	72	0	0	0	25	82 $1/3$	79	38	34	39	71
Major league totals (7 years)......	47	29	.618	3.88	381	28	1	1	37	614	612	291	265	273	422

DIVISION SERIES RECORD

Year Team (League)	W	L	Pct.	ERA	G	GS	CG	ShO	Sv.	IP	H	R	ER	BB	SO
1995— New York (A.L.).................	0	0	...	0.00	3	0	0	0	0	3	5	0	0	0	3

WIDGER, CHRIS   C   EXPOS

PERSONAL: Born May 21, 1971, in Wilmington, Del. ... 6-3/215. ... Bats right, throws right. ... Full name: Christopher Jon Widger. ... Nephew of Mike Widger, linebacker with Montreal Alouettes and Ottawa Rough Riders of Canadian Football League (1970-78).
HIGH SCHOOL: Pennsville (N.J.).
COLLEGE: George Mason.
TRANSACTIONS/CAREER NOTES: Selected by Seattle Mariners organization in third round of free-agent draft (June 1, 1992). ... On disabled list (June 6-16, 1993). ... Traded by Mariners with P Trey Moore and P Matt Wagner to Montreal Expos for P Jeff Fassero and P Alex Pacheco (October 29, 1996).
STATISTICAL NOTES: Led N.L. catchers with 14 passed balls and tied for lead with 12 double plays in 1998. ... Career major league grand slams: 1.

Year Team (League)	Pos.	G	AB	R	H	2B	3B	HR	RBI	Avg.	BB	SO	SB	PO	A	E	Avg.
							BATTING								FIELDING		
1992— Bellingham (N'west)...	C	51	166	28	43	7	2	5	30	.259	22	36	8	266	39	4	*.987
1993— Riverside (Calif.).........	C	97	360	44	95	28	2	9	58	.264	19	64	5	472	63	14	.974
1994— Jacksonville (Sou.).....	C-OF-1B	116	388	58	101	15	3	16	59	.260	39	69	4	564	73	13	.980
1995— Tacoma (PCL)	C-OF	50	174	29	48	11	1	9	21	.276	9	29	0	189	22	4	.981
— Seattle (A.L.)	C-OF-DH	23	45	2	9	0	0	1	2	.200	3	11	0	64	1	0	1.000
1996— Tacoma (PCL)	C	97	352	42	107	20	2	13	48	.304	27	62	7	622	41	8	.988
— Seattle (A.L.)	C	8	11	1	2	0	0	0	0	.182	0	5	0	18	1	2	.905
1997— Montreal (N.L.)■........	C	91	278	30	65	20	3	7	37	.234	22	59	2	516	40	11	.981
1998— Montreal (N.L.)...........	C	125	417	36	97	18	1	15	53	.233	29	85	6	752	64	14	.983
American League totals (2 years)		31	56	3	11	0	0	1	2	.196	3	16	0	82	2	2	.977
National League totals (2 years)		216	695	66	162	38	4	22	90	.233	51	144	8	1268	104	25	.982
Major league totals (4 years)		247	751	69	173	38	4	23	92	.230	54	160	8	1350	106	27	.982

DIVISION SERIES RECORD

Year Team (League)	Pos.	G	AB	R	H	2B	3B	HR	RBI	Avg.	BB	SO	SB	PO	A	E	Avg.
							BATTING								FIELDING		
1995— Seattle (A.L.)	C	2	3	0	0	0	0	0	0	.000	0	3	0	14	0	0	1.000

CHAMPIONSHIP SERIES RECORD

Year Team (League)	Pos.	G	AB	R	H	2B	3B	HR	RBI	Avg.	BB	SO	SB	PO	A	E	Avg.
							BATTING								FIELDING		
1995— Seattle (A.L.)	C	3	1	0	0	0	0	0	0	.000	0	1	0	7	0	0	1.000

WILCOX, LUKE   OF   DEVIL RAYS

PERSONAL: Born November 15, 1973, in Lansing, Mich. ... 6-4/190. ... Bats left, throws right. ... Full name: Christopher Luke Wilcox.
HIGH SCHOOL: St. John's (Mich.).
COLLEGE: Western Michigan.
TRANSACTIONS/CAREER NOTES: Selected by New York Yankees organization in third round of free-agent draft (June 1, 1995). ... On Norwich disabled list (April 6-June 3, 1997). ... Selected by Tampa Bay Devil Rays in third round (66th pick overall) of expansion draft (November 18, 1997).

Year Team (League)	Pos.	G	AB	R	H	2B	3B	HR	RBI	Avg.	BB	SO	SB	PO	A	E	Avg.
							BATTING								FIELDING		
1995— Oneonta (NYP)..........	OF	59	223	25	73	16	7	1	28	.327	20	28	9	84	6	5	.947
1996— Tampa (Fla. St.).........	OF	119	470	72	133	32	5	11	76	.283	40	71	14	209	10	3	.986
1997— Norwich (Eastern)	OF	74	300	45	83	13	1	6	34	.277	18	36	13	141	6	3	.980
— Tampa (Fla. St.)	OF	12	40	7	12	4	0	0	4	.300	7	6	1	10	0	0	1.000
1998— Orlando (South.)■	OF	88	331	57	95	23	3	17	69	.287	39	54	2	141	10	2	.987
— Durham (Int'l)	OF	43	151	17	34	11	0	2	17	.225	16	27	0	98	4	0	1.000

WILKINS, MARC   P   PIRATES

PERSONAL: Born October 21, 1970, in Mansfield, Ohio ... 5-11/221. ... Throws right, bats right. ... Full name: Marc Allen Wilkins.
HIGH SCHOOL: Ontario (Ohio).
COLLEGE: Toledo.
TRANSACTIONS/CAREER NOTES: Selected by Pittsburgh Pirates organization in 47th round of free-agent draft (June 1, 1992). ... On Pittsburgh disabled list (April 26-May 11, and May 23, 1998-remainder of season); included rehabilitation assignments to Carolina (May 8-10) and Nashville (August 7-September 6).
STATISTICAL NOTES: Led Carolina League with 22 hit batsmen in 1994.

W

Year Team (League)	W	L	Pct.	ERA	G	GS	CG	ShO	Sv.	IP	H	R	ER	BB	SO
1992— Welland (N.Y.-Penn)	4	2	.667	7.29	28	1	0	0	1	42	49	36	34	24	42
1993— Augusta (S. Atl.)..............	5	6	.455	4.21	48	5	0	0	1	77	83	52	36	31	73
1994— Salem (Carolina)	8	5	.615	3.70	28	•28	0	0	0	151	155	84	62	45	90
1995— Carolina (Southern)...........	5	3	.625	3.99	37	12	0	0	0	99 1/3	91	47	44	44	80
1996— Carolina (Southern)...........	2	3	.400	4.01	11	3	0	0	0	24 2/3	19	12	11	11	19
— Pittsburgh (N.L.)	4	3	.571	3.84	47	2	0	0	1	75	75	36	32	36	62
1997— Pittsburgh (N.L.)	9	5	.643	3.69	70	0	0	0	2	75 2/3	65	33	31	33	47
1998— Pittsburgh (N.L.)	0	0	. . .	3.52	16	0	0	0	0	15 1/3	13	6	6	9	17
— Carolina (Southern)...........	0	0	. . .	4.50	2	0	0	0	0	2	1	1	1	0	4
— Nashville (Pacific Coast)	1	0	1.000	10.38	5	0	0	0	0	4 1/3	3	5	5	3	4
Major league totals (3 years)......	**13**	**8**	**.619**	**3.74**	**133**	**2**	**0**	**0**	**3**	**166**	**153**	**75**	**69**	**78**	**126**

WILKINS, RICK   C

PERSONAL: Born June 4, 1967, in Jacksonville. ... 6-2/215. ... Bats left, throws right. ... Full name: Richard David Wilkins.
HIGH SCHOOL: The Bolles School (Jacksonville).
JUNIOR COLLEGE: Florida Community College-Jacksonville.
COLLEGE: Furman.
TRANSACTIONS/CAREER NOTES: Selected by Chicago Cubs organization in 23rd round of free-agent draft (June 2, 1986). ... On Chicago disabled list (June 2-28, 1995). ... Traded by Cubs to Houston Astros for OF Luis Gonzalez and C Scott Servais (June 28, 1995). ... On Houston disabled list (July 2-September 5, 1995); included rehabilitation assignments to Jackson (August 28-September 1) and Tucson (September 1-5). ... Traded by Astros with cash to San Francisco Giants for C Kirt Manwaring (July 27, 1996). ... Released by Giants (August 1, 1997). ... Signed by Seattle Mariners organization (August 15, 1997). ... On Seattle disabled list (August 15-September 1, 1997); included rehabilitation assignment to Tacoma (August 15-September 1). ... Granted free agency (October 16, 1997). ... Re-signed by Mariners (December 15, 1997). ... Traded by Mariners to New York Mets for P Lindsay Gulin (May 12, 1998). ... On Norfolk disabled list (July 20-August 30, 1998). ... Granted free agency (October 15, 1998).
STATISTICAL NOTES: Led Appalachian League with eight intentional bases on balls received in 1987. ... Led Appalachian League catchers with .989 fielding percentage, 483 putouts and 540 total chances and tied for lead with six double plays in 1987. ... Led Midwest League catchers with 984 total chances in 1988. ... Led Carolina League catchers with 860 total chances and tied for lead with eight double plays in 1989. ... Led Southern League catchers with 857 total chances, 11 double plays and 15 passed balls in 1990. ... Tied for N.L. lead with 10 sacrifice flies in 1996. ... Career major league grand slams: 2.

						BATTING								FIELDING		
Year Team (League)	Pos.	G	AB	R	H	2B	3B	HR	RBI	Avg.	BB	SO	SB	PO	A	E	Avg.
1987— Geneva (NY-Penn)......	C-1B	75	243	35	61	8	2	8	43	.251	58	40	7	†503	51	7	†.988
1988— Peoria (Midwest).......	C	137	490	54	119	30	1	8	63	.243	67	110	4	*864	*101	*19	.981
1989— Win.-Salem (Car.)......	C	132	445	61	111	24	1	12	54	.249	50	87	6	*764	*78	*18	.979
1990— Charlotte (Southern) ..	C	127	449	48	102	18	1	17	71	.227	43	95	4	*740	*103	14	.984
1991— Iowa (Am. Assoc.)......	C-OF	38	107	12	29	3	1	5	14	.271	11	17	1	204	24	3	.987
— Chicago (N.L.)...........	C	86	203	21	45	9	0	6	22	.222	19	56	3	373	42	3	.993
1992— Chicago (N.L.)...........	C	83	244	20	66	9	1	8	22	.270	28	53	0	408	47	3	.993
— Iowa (Am. Assoc.)......	C	47	155	20	43	11	2	5	28	.277	19	42	0	177	18	2	.990
1993— Chicago (N.L.)...........	C	136	446	78	135	23	1	30	73	.303	50	99	2	717	89	3	.996
1994— Chicago (N.L.)...........	C-1B	100	313	44	71	25	2	7	39	.227	40	86	4	550	51	4	.993
1995— Chicago (N.L.)...........	C-1B	50	162	24	31	2	0	6	14	.191	36	51	0	294	31	4	.988
— Houston (N.L.).....■	C	15	40	6	10	1	0	1	5	.250	10	10	0	87	4	0	1.000
— Jackson (Texas)	C	4	11	0	0	0	0	0	0	.000	3	2	0	23	1	0	1.000
— Tucson (PCL)	C	4	12	0	4	0	0	0	4	.333	2	0	0	27	4	0	1.000
1996— Houston (N.L.)..........	C	84	254	34	54	8	2	6	23	.213	46	81	0	550	39	6	.990
— San Fran. (N.L.).....■	C-1B	52	157	19	46	10	0	8	36	.293	21	40	0	240	34	2	.993
1997— San Francisco (N.L.) ..	C	66	190	18	37	5	0	6	23	.195	17	65	0	326	37	5	.986
— Tacoma (PCL)	C-1B	17	68	16	23	8	0	1	14	.338	8	12	0	82	4	1	.989
— Seattle (A.L.)	C-DH	5	12	2	3	1	0	1	4	.250	1	2	0	9	1	0	1.000
1998— Seattle (A.L.)	C-1B-DH	19	41	5	8	1	1	1	4	.195	4	14	0	70	4	0	1.000
— New York (N.L.)■	C	5	15	3	2	0	0	0	1	.133	2	2	0	21	1	1	.957
— Norfolk (Int'l)	C-1B	45	158	17	41	13	1	1	20	.259	14	37	1	231	15	3	.988
American League totals (2 years)		24	53	7	11	2	1	2	8	.208	5	16	0	79	5	0	1.000
National League totals (8 years)		677	2024	267	497	92	6	78	258	.246	269	543	9	3566	375	31	.992
Major league totals (8 years)		701	2077	274	508	94	7	80	266	.245	274	559	9	3645	380	31	.992

DIVISION SERIES RECORD

						BATTING								FIELDING		
Year Team (League)	Pos.	G	AB	R	H	2B	3B	HR	RBI	Avg.	BB	SO	SB	PO	A	E	Avg.
1997— Seattle (A.L.)	C-PH	1	1	0	0	0	0	0	0	.000	1	0	0	2	0	0	1.000

W

WILLIAMS, BERNIE   OF   YANKEES

PERSONAL: Born September 13, 1968, in San Juan, Puerto Rico. ... 6-2/205. ... Bats both, throws right. ... Full name: Bernabe Figueroa Williams.
HIGH SCHOOL: Escuela Libre de Musica (San Juan, Puerto Rico).
COLLEGE: Puerto Rico.
TRANSACTIONS/CAREER NOTES: Signed as non-drafted free agent by New York Yankees organization (September 13, 1985). ... On disabled list (July 15, 1988-remainder of season and May 13-June 7, 1993). ... On disabled list (May 11-26, 1996; June 16-July 2 and July 15-August 1, 1997). ... On New York disabled list (June 11-July 18, 1998); included rehabilitation assignments to Tampa (July 6-7) and Norwich (July 14-16). ... Granted free agency (October 26, 1998). ... Re-signed by Yankees (December 1, 1998).
RECORDS: Shares major league single-game record for most strikeouts (nine-inning game)—5 (August 21, 1991). ... Shares major league single-inning record for most doubles—2 (June 22, 1994, seventh inning). ... Shares modern major league record for most long hits in one inning—2 (June 22, 1994, seventh inning).
HONORS: Won A.L. Gold Glove as outfielder (1997-98).

STATISTICAL NOTES: Led Gulf Coast League outfielders with 123 total chances in 1986. ... Tied for Gulf Coast League lead in caught stealing with 12 in 1986. ... Led Eastern League in caught stealing with 18 in 1990. ... Led Eastern League outfielders with 307 total chances and tied for lead with four double plays in 1990. ... Had 21-game hitting streak (August 1-23, 1993). ... Switch-hit home runs in one game three times (June 6, 1994; September 12, 1996; and September 4, 1998). ... Led A.L. outfielders with 441 total chances in 1995. ... Had 16-game hitting streak (July 31-August 14, 1998). ... Career major league grand slams: 5.
MISCELLANEOUS: Batted righthanded only (1986-88).

Year Team (League)	Pos.	G	AB	R	H	2B	3B	HR	RBI	Avg.	BB	SO	SB	PO	A	E	Avg.
1986— GC Yankees (GCL)......	OF	61	230	*45	62	5	3	2	25	.270	39	40	33	*117	3	3	.976
1987— Fort Laud. (FSL)........	OF	25	71	11	11	3	0	0	4	.155	18	22	9	49	1	0	1.000
— Oneonta (NYP)..........	OF	25	93	13	32	4	0	0	15	.344	10	14	9	40	0	2	.952
1988— Prince Will. (Car.).......	OF	92	337	72	113	16	7	7	45	*.335	65	65	29	186	8	5	.975
1989— Columbus (Int'l).........	OF	50	162	21	35	8	1	2	16	.216	25	38	11	112	2	1	.991
— Alb./Colon. (East.)......	OF	91	314	63	79	11	8	11	42	.252	60	72	26	180	5	5	.974
1990— Alb./Colon. (East.)......	OF	134	466	*91	131	28	5	8	54	.281	*98	97	*39	*288	15	4	.987
1991— Columbus (Int'l).........	OF	78	306	52	90	14	6	8	37	.294	38	43	9	164	2	1	.994
— New York (A.L.).........	OF	85	320	43	76	19	4	3	34	.238	48	57	10	230	3	5	.979
1992— New York (A.L.).........	OF	62	261	39	73	14	2	5	26	.280	29	36	7	187	5	1	.995
— Columbus (Int'l).........	OF	95	363	68	111	23	•9	8	50	.306	52	61	20	205	2	2	.990
1993— New York (A.L.).........	OF	139	567	67	152	31	4	12	68	.268	53	106	9	366	5	4	.989
1994— New York (A.L.).........	OF	108	408	80	118	29	1	12	57	.289	61	54	16	277	7	3	.990
1995— New York (A.L.).........	OF	144	563	93	173	29	9	18	82	.307	75	98	8	*432	1	•8	.982
1996— New York (A.L.).........	OF-DH	143	551	108	168	26	7	29	102	.305	82	72	17	334	10	5	.986
1997— New York (A.L.).........	OF	129	509	107	167	35	6	21	100	.328	73	80	15	270	2	2	.993
1998— New York (A.L.).........	OF-DH	128	499	101	169	30	5	26	97	*.339	74	81	15	298	4	3	.990
— Tampa (Fla. St.)......	OF	1	2	0	1	1	0	0	0	.500	1	0	0	2	0	0	1.000
— Norwich (Eastern)......	OF	3	11	6	6	2	0	2	5	.545	2	1	0	5	0	0	1.000
Major league totals (8 years)		938	3678	638	1096	213	38	126	566	.298	495	584	97	2394	37	31	.987

DIVISION SERIES RECORD

RECORDS: Shares single-game record for most home runs—2 (October 6, 1995 and October 5, 1996). ... Holds career records for most runs—16; and bases on balls—14. ... Shares career record for most games—17.

Year Team (League)	Pos.	G	AB	R	H	2B	3B	HR	RBI	Avg.	BB	SO	SB	PO	A	E	Avg.
1995— New York (A.L.).........	OF	5	21	8	9	2	0	2	5	.429	7	3	1	13	0	0	1.000
1996— New York (A.L.).........	OF	4	15	5	7	0	0	3	5	.467	2	1	1	10	0	0	1.000
1997— New York (A.L.).........	OF	5	17	3	2	1	0	0	1	.118	4	3	0	7	0	0	1.000
1998— New York (A.L.).........	OF	3	11	0	0	0	0	0	0	.000	1	4	0	8	0	0	1.000
Division series totals (4 years)		17	64	16	18	3	0	5	11	.281	14	11	2	38	0	0	1.000

CHAMPIONSHIP SERIES RECORD

NOTES: Named Most Valuable Player (1996).

Year Team (League)	Pos.	G	AB	R	H	2B	3B	HR	RBI	Avg.	BB	SO	SB	PO	A	E	Avg.
1996— New York (A.L.)..........	OF	5	19	6	9	3	0	2	6	.474	6	4	1	20	0	0	1.000
1998— New York (A.L.)..........	OF	6	21	4	8	1	0	0	5	.381	7	4	1	14	0	0	1.000
Championship series totals (2 years)		11	40	10	17	4	0	2	11	.425	13	8	2	34	0	0	1.000

WORLD SERIES RECORD

NOTES: Member of World Series championship team (1996 and 1998).

Year Team (League)	Pos.	G	AB	R	H	2B	3B	HR	RBI	Avg.	BB	SO	SB	PO	A	E	Avg.
1996— New York (A.L.)..........	OF	6	24	3	4	0	0	1	4	.167	4	6	1	15	0	0	1.000
1998— New York (A.L.)..........	OF	4	16	2	1	0	0	1	3	.063	3	5	0	6	0	0	1.000
World Series totals (2 years)		10	40	5	5	0	0	2	7	.125	7	11	1	21	0	0	1.000

ALL-STAR GAME RECORD

NOTES: Named to A.L. All-Star team for 1998 game; replaced by Manny Ramirez due to injury.

Year League	Pos.	AB	R	H	2B	3B	HR	RBI	Avg.	BB	SO	SB	PO	A	E	Avg.
1997— American..................	OF	0	1	0	0	0	0	0	...	1	0	1	1	0	0	1.000
1998— American..................						Selected, did not play—injured.										

WILLIAMS, EDDIE — 1B — TWINS

W

PERSONAL: Born November 1, 1964, in Shreveport, La. ... 6-0/210. ... Bats right, throws right. ... Full name: Edward Laquan Williams.
HIGH SCHOOL: Hoover (San Diego).
TRANSACTIONS/CAREER NOTES: Selected by New York Mets organization in first round (fourth pick overall) of free-agent draft (June 6, 1983). ... Traded by Mets organization with P Matt Bullinger and P Jay Tibbs to Cincinnati Reds for P Bruce Berenyi (June 15, 1984). ... Selected by Cleveland Indians from Reds organization in Rule 5 major league draft (December 10, 1985). ... Traded by Indians to Chicago White Sox for P Joel Davis and P Ed Wojna (January 23, 1989). ... Granted free agency (October 15, 1989). ... Signed by Las Vegas, San Diego Padres organization (December 21, 1989). ... Contract sold by Padres to Fukuoka Daiei Hawks of Japan Pacific League (December 2, 1990). ... Released by Fukuoka (September 1991). ... Signed by Greenville, Atlanta Braves organization (February 16, 1992). ... Released by Richmond, Braves organization (May 14, 1992). ... Signed by Denver, Milwaukee Brewers organization (November 30, 1992). ... Released by New Orleans, Brewers organization (April 19, 1993). ... Signed by Las Vegas, Padres organization (December 17, 1993). ... Granted free agency (December 21, 1995). ... Signed by Detroit Tigers (January 2, 1996). ... Granted free agency (October 15, 1996). ... Signed by Los Angeles Dodgers organization (November 18, 1996). ... Traded by Dodgers to Pittsburgh Pirates for P Hal Garrett (August 9, 1997). ... Released by Pirates (October 15, 1997). ... Signed by Padres organization (January 13, 1998). ... Released by Padres (September 11, 1998). ... Signed by Minnesota Twins organization (December 15, 1998).
HONORS: Named Midwest League Most Valuable Player (1985).

STATISTICAL NOTES: Led Midwest League in being hit by pitch with 15 in 1985. ... Led American Association third basemen with 352 total chances, 24 double plays, 237 assists, and 27 errors in 1987. ... Led American Association in being hit by pitch with 15 in 1987. ... Led Pacific Coast League in being hit by pitch with 12 in 1988. ... Career major league grand slams: 2.

							BATTING									FIELDING		
Year	Team (League)	Pos.	G	AB	R	H	2B	3B	HR	RBI	Avg.	BB	SO	SB	PO	A	E	Avg.
1983—	Little Falls (NYP)	3B	50	190	30	50	6	2	6	28	.263	19	41	3	50	53	13	.888
1984—	Columbia (S. Atl.)	3B	43	152	17	28	4	2	3	24	.184	15	31	1	24	76	16	.862
	—Tampa (Fla. St.)■....	3B	50	138	20	35	8	0	2	16	.254	25	23	0	25	43	11	.861
1985—	Cedar Rap. (Midw.) ...	3B	119	406	71	106	13	3	20	83	.261	62	101	5	83	204	33	.897
1986—	Cleveland (A.L.)■........	OF	5	7	2	1	0	0	0	1	.143	0	3	0	0	0	0	...
	—Waterbury (Eastern)...	3B	62	214	24	51	10	0	7	30	.238	28	41	3	39	100	15	.903
1987—	Buffalo (A.A.)..........	3B-SS	131	488	90	142	29	2	22	85	.291	55	117	6	88	†237	†27	.923
	—Cleveland (A.L.)..........	3B	22	64	9	11	4	0	1	4	.172	9	19	0	17	37	1	.982
1988—	Colo. Springs (PCL)...	3B-SS-1B	101	365	53	110	24	3	12	58	.301	18	51	0	93	177	29	.903
	—Cleveland (A.L.)..........	3B	10	21	3	4	0	0	0	1	.190	0	3	0	3	18	0	1.000
1989—	Chicago (A.L.)■........	3B	66	201	25	55	8	0	3	10	.274	18	31	1	37	123	16	.909
	—Vancouver (PCL)	3B-1B	35	114	12	28	8	0	1	13	.246	15	18	1	8	10	4	.818
1990—	Las Vegas (PCL)■...	3B-1B	93	348	59	110	29	2	17	75	.316	42	47	0	106	121	17	.930
	—San Diego (N.L.)	3B	14	42	5	12	3	0	3	4	.286	5	6	0	5	21	3	.897
1991—	Fukuoka (Jp. Pac.)■..	3B	49	163	20	41	...	...	5	16	.252	21	32	2	...	...	...	...
1992—	Richmond (Int'l)■..........	3B	24	74	8	15	3	0	1	5	.203	3	9	0	7	26	5	.868
1993—	Monter. Sul. (Mx.)■...	OF-3B-1B	59	210	40	74	17	0	12	34	.352	21	29	0	71	14	1	.988
	—New Orleans (A.A.)■.	3B-1B	8	27	2	7	0	1	1	4	.259	7	4	0	14	13	1	.964
1994—	Las Vegas (PCL)■■....	1B-3B	59	219	48	77	12	1	20	54	.352	24	34	0	276	49	4	.988
	—San Diego (N.L.)	1B-3B	49	175	32	58	11	1	11	42	.331	15	26	0	383	29	5	.988
1995—	San Diego (N.L.)	1B	97	296	35	77	11	1	12	47	.260	23	47	0	571	49	7	.989
1996—	Detroit (A.L.)■..........	DH-1-3-0	77	215	22	43	5	0	6	26	.200	18	50	0	25	2	0	1.000
1997—	Albuquerque (PCL)■..	1B-3B	76	279	73	102	17	0	29	76	.366	37	45	0	232	15	1	.996
	—Los Angeles (N.L.)........	PH	8	7	0	1	0	0	0	1	.143	1	1	0	...	...	...	...
	—Pittsburgh (N.L.)■........	1B	30	89	12	22	5	0	3	11	.247	10	24	1	202	8	2	.991
1998—	Las Vegas (PCL)■...	1B	90	307	69	103	24	0	20	77	.336	33	66	1	352	28	4	.990
	—San Diego (N.L.)	1B	17	28	1	4	0	0	0	3	.143	2	6	0	47	3	0	1.000
American League totals (5 years)			180	508	61	114	17	0	10	42	.224	45	106	1	82	180	17	.939
National League totals (5 years)			215	637	85	174	30	2	29	108	.273	56	110	1	1208	110	17	.987
Major league totals (10 years)			395	1145	146	288	47	2	39	150	.252	101	216	2	1290	290	34	.979

WILLIAMS, GERALD   OF   BRAVES

PERSONAL: Born August 10, 1966, in New Orleans. ... 6-2/187. ... Bats right, throws right. ... Full name: Gerald Floyd Williams.
HIGH SCHOOL: East St. John (Reserve, La.).
COLLEGE: Grambling State.
TRANSACTIONS/CAREER NOTES: Selected by New York Yankees organization in 14th round of free-agent draft (June 2, 1987). ... Traded by Yankees with P Bob Wickman to Milwaukee Brewers for P Graeme Lloyd and OF Pat Listach (August 23, 1996). ... Traded by Brewers to Atlanta Braves for P Chad Fox (December 11, 1997).
STATISTICAL NOTES: Led Carolina League outfielders with 307 total chances in 1989. ... Led International League outfielders with 354 total chances in 1992. ... Tied for International League lead in double plays by outfielder with five in 1992. ... Collected six hits in one game (May 1, 1996). ... Career major league grand slams: 2.

							BATTING									FIELDING		
Year	Team (League)	Pos.	G	AB	R	H	2B	3B	HR	RBI	Avg.	BB	SO	SB	PO	A	E	Avg.
1987—	Oneonta (NYP)	OF	29	115	26	42	6	2	2	29	.365	16	18	6	68	3	3	.959
1988—	Prince Will. (Car.)	OF	54	159	20	29	3	0	2	18	.182	15	47	6	71	2	3	.961
	—Fort Laud. (FSL)	OF	63	212	21	40	7	2	2	17	.189	16	56	4	163	2	6	.965
1989—	Prince Will. (Car.)	OF	134	454	63	104	19	6	13	69	.229	51	120	15	*292	7	8	.974
1990—	Fort Laud. (FSL)	OF	50	204	25	59	4	5	7	43	.289	16	52	19	115	1	3	.975
	—Alb./Colon. (East.)	OF	96	324	54	81	17	2	13	58	.250	35	74	18	210	6	7	.969
1991—	Alb./Colon. (East.)	OF	45	175	28	50	15	0	5	32	.286	18	26	18	109	4	3	.974
	—Columbus (Int'l)	OF	61	198	20	51	8	3	2	27	.258	16	39	9	124	1	3	.977
1992—	Columbus (Int'l)	OF	*142	547	92	*156	31	6	16	86	.285	38	98	36	*332	*14	8	.977
	—New York (A.L.)	OF	15	27	7	8	2	0	3	6	.296	0	3	2	20	1	2	.913
1993—	Columbus (Int'l)	OF	87	336	53	95	19	6	8	38	.283	20	66	29	191	6	3	.985
	—New York (A.L.)	OF-DH	42	67	11	10	2	3	0	6	.149	1	14	2	41	2	2	.956
1994—	New York (A.L.)	OF-DH	57	86	19	25	8	0	4	13	.291	4	17	1	43	2	2	.957
1995—	New York (A.L.)	OF-DH	100	182	33	45	18	2	6	28	.247	22	34	4	138	6	1	.993
1996—	New York (A.L.)	OF-DH	99	233	37	63	15	4	5	30	.270	15	39	7	132	1	3	.978
	—Milwaukee (A.L.)■...	OF	26	92	6	19	4	0	0	4	.207	4	18	3	75	3	1	.987
1997—	Milwaukee (A.L.)	OF-DH	155	566	73	143	32	2	10	41	.253	19	90	23	357	11	3	.992
1998—	Atlanta (N.L.)■..........	OF	129	266	46	81	19	2	10	44	.305	17	48	11	158	2	5	.970
American League totals (6 years)			494	1253	186	313	81	11	28	128	.250	65	215	42	806	26	14	.983
National League totals (1 year)			129	266	46	81	19	2	10	44	.305	17	48	11	158	2	5	.970
Major league totals (7 years)			623	1519	232	394	100	13	38	172	.259	82	263	53	964	28	19	.981

DIVISION SERIES RECORD

							BATTING									FIELDING		
Year	Team (League)	Pos.	G	AB	R	H	2B	3B	HR	RBI	Avg.	BB	SO	SB	PO	A	E	Avg.
1995—	New York (A.L.)	OF-PR	5	5	1	0	0	0	0	0	.000	2	3	0	7	1	0	1.000
1998—	Atlanta (N.L.)	OF	2	2	1	1	0	0	0	1	.500	0	1	0	2	0	0	1.000
Division series totals (2 years)			7	7	2	1	0	0	0	1	.143	2	4	0	9	1	0	1.000

CHAMPIONSHIP SERIES RECORD

RECORDS: Shares single-game record for most strikeouts—4 (October 10, 1998).

							BATTING									FIELDING		
Year	Team (League)	Pos.	G	AB	R	H	2B	3B	HR	RBI	Avg.	BB	SO	SB	PO	A	E	Avg.
1998—	Atlanta (N.L.)	PH-OF	5	13	0	2	0	0	0	1	.154	1	6	1	3	0	0	1.000

W

WILLIAMS, GLENN   2B   BRAVES

PERSONAL: Born July 18, 1977, in Gosford, Australia. ... 6-2/170. ... Bats right, throws right. ... Full name: Glenn David Williams.
HIGH SCHOOL: Ingleburn (Australia).
TRANSACTIONS/CAREER NOTES: Signed as non-drafted free agent by Atlanta Braves organization (August 17, 1993). ... On disabled list (May 2-20, June 2-19 and July 5, 1996-remainder of season; and April 22-June 5, 1997).

Year	Team (League)	Pos.	G	AB	R	H	2B	3B	HR	RBI	Avg.	BB	SO	SB	PO	A	E	Avg.
1994—	GC Braves (GCL)........	SS	24	89	8	18	2	0	2	7	.202	9	32	4	29	67	10	.906
—	Danville (Appal.)........	SS	24	79	11	20	2	0	1	9	.253	8	20	2	29	50	10	.888
1995—	Eugene (Northwest) ...	SS	71	268	39	60	11	4	7	36	.224	21	71	7	15	23	4	.905
—	Macon (S. Atl.)..........	SS	38	120	13	21	4	0	0	14	.175	16	42	2	37	87	19	.867
1996—	Macon (S. Atl.)..........	SS	51	181	14	35	7	3	3	18	.193	18	47	4	73	129	15	.931
1997—	Macon (S. Atl.)..........	SS	77	297	52	79	18	2	14	52	.266	24	105	9	113	171	17	.944
1998—	Danville (Carolina)......	2B	134	470	40	101	26	1	9	44	.215	37	132	1	219	297	*26	.952

WILLIAMS, MATT   3B   DIAMONDBACKS

PERSONAL: Born November 28, 1965, in Bishop, Calif. ... 6-2/210. ... Bats right, throws right. ... Full name: Matthew Derrick Williams. ... Grandson of Bartholomew (Bart) Griffith, outfielder/first baseman with Brooklyn Dodgers and Washington Senators (1922-24).
HIGH SCHOOL: Carson (Nev.).
COLLEGE: UNLV.
TRANSACTIONS/CAREER NOTES: Selected by New York Mets organization in 27th round of free-agent draft (June 6, 1983); did not sign. ... Selected by San Francisco Giants organization in first round (third pick overall) of free-agent draft (June 2, 1986). ... On disabled list (June 28-July 14, 1993). ... On San Francisco disabled list (June 4-August 19, 1995); included rehabilitation assignments to San Jose (July 24-25 and August 13-19). ... On disabled list (August 5, 1996-remainder of season). ... Traded by Giants with a player to be named later to Cleveland Indians for IF Jeff Kent, IF Jose Vizcaino, P Julian Tavarez and a player to be named later (November 13, 1996); Giants traded OF Trenidad Hubbard to Indians for P Joe Roa to complete deal (December 16, 1996). ... Traded by Indians to Arizona Diamondbacks for 3B Travis Fryman, P Tom Martin and cash (December 1, 1997). ... On Arizona disabled list (July 18-August 3, 1998); included rehabilitation assignment to Tucson (July 31-August 3).
RECORDS: Shares major league record for most home runs in two consecutive games—5 (April 25 [3] and 26 [2], 1997).
HONORS: Named shortstop on THE SPORTING NEWS college All-America team (1986). ... Named third baseman on THE SPORTING NEWS N.L. All-Star team (1990 and 1993-94). ... Named third baseman on THE SPORTING NEWS N.L. Silver Slugger team (1990 and 1993-94). ... Won N.L. Gold Glove at third base (1991 and 1993-94). ... Named third baseman on THE SPORTING NEWS A.L. All-Star team (1997). ... Won A.L. Gold Glove at third base (1997). ... Named third baseman on THE SPORTING NEWS A.L. Silver Slugger team (1997).
STATISTICAL NOTES: Led N.L. third basemen with 33 double plays in 1990 and 1992 and 34 in 1993. ... Tied for N.L. lead in total chances by third baseman with 465 in 1990. ... Led N.L. third basemen with 131 putouts in 1991. ... Led N.L. third basemen with 326 total chances in 1994. ... Hit three home runs in one game (April 25, 1997). ... Had 24-game hitting streak (August 13-September 8, 1997). ... Career major league grand slams: 7.

Year	Team (League)	Pos.	G	AB	R	H	2B	3B	HR	RBI	Avg.	BB	SO	SB	PO	A	E	Avg.
1986—	Everett (N'west).........	SS	4	17	3	4	0	1	1	10	.235	1	4	0	5	10	2	.882
—	Clinton (Midwest).......	SS	68	250	32	60	14	3	7	29	.240	23	62	3	89	150	10	.960
1987—	Phoenix (PCL)...........	3B-2B-SS	56	211	36	61	15	2	6	37	.289	19	53	6	53	136	14	.931
—	San Francisco (N.L.) ..	SS-3B	84	245	28	46	9	2	8	21	.188	16	68	4	110	234	9	.975
1988—	Phoenix (PCL)...........	3-S-2-O	82	306	45	83	19	1	12	51	.271	13	56	6	56	173	13	.946
—	San Francisco (N.L.) ..	3B-SS	52	156	17	32	6	1	8	19	.205	8	41	0	48	108	7	.957
1989—	San Francisco (N.L.) ..	3B-SS	84	292	31	59	18	1	18	50	.202	14	72	1	90	168	10	.963
—	Phoenix (PCL)	3B-SS-OF	76	284	61	91	20	2	26	61	.320	32	51	9	57	197	11	.958
1990—	San Francisco (N.L.) ..	3B	159	617	87	171	27	2	33	*122	.277	33	138	7	*140	306	19	.959
1991—	San Francisco (N.L.) ..	3B-SS	157	589	72	158	24	5	34	98	.268	33	128	5	†134	295	16	.964
1992—	San Francisco (N.L.) ..	3B	146	529	58	120	13	5	20	66	.227	39	109	7	105	289	*23	.945
1993—	San Francisco (N.L.) ..	3B	145	579	105	170	33	4	38	110	.294	27	80	1	117	266	12	.970
1994—	San Francisco (N.L.) ..	3B	112	445	74	119	16	3	*43	96	.267	33	87	1	79	*235	12	.963
1995—	San Francisco (N.L.) ..	3B	76	283	53	95	17	1	23	65	.336	30	58	2	49	178	10	.958
—	San Jose (Calif.)	3B	4	11	2	2	0	0	1	2	.182	0	3	0	0	4	0	1.000
1996—	San Francisco (N.L.) ..	3B-1B-SS	105	404	69	122	16	1	22	85	.302	39	91	1	164	191	14	.962
1997—	Cleveland (A.L.)■.......	3B	151	596	86	157	32	3	32	105	.263	34	108	12	89	301	12	.970
1998—	Arizona (N.L.)■.........	3B	135	510	72	136	26	1	20	71	.267	43	102	5	99	282	11	.972
—	Tucson (PCL)	3B	2	5	0	1	0	0	0	0	.200	0	0	0	0	1	0	1.000
American League totals (1 year)			151	596	86	157	32	3	32	105	.263	34	108	12	89	301	12	.970
National League totals (11 years)			1255	4649	666	1228	205	26	267	803	.264	315	974	34	1135	2552	143	.963
Major league totals (12 years)			1406	5245	752	1385	237	29	299	908	.264	349	1082	46	1224	2853	155	.963

DIVISION SERIES RECORD

Year	Team (League)	Pos.	G	AB	R	H	2B	3B	HR	RBI	Avg.	BB	SO	SB	PO	A	E	Avg.
1997—	Cleveland (A.L.).........	3B	5	17	4	4	1	0	1	3	.235	3	3	0	2	10	0	1.000

CHAMPIONSHIP SERIES RECORD

RECORDS: Holds N.L. single-series record for most runs batted in—9 (1989).

Year	Team (League)	Pos.	G	AB	R	H	2B	3B	HR	RBI	Avg.	BB	SO	SB	PO	A	E	Avg.
1987—	San Francisco (N.L.) ..						Did not play.											
1989—	San Francisco (N.L.) ..	3B-SS	5	20	2	6	1	0	2	9	.300	0	2	0	5	12	0	1.000
1997—	Cleveland (A.L.).........	3B	6	23	1	5	1	0	0	2	.217	3	7	1	6	18	2	.923
Championship series totals (2 years)			11	43	3	11	2	0	2	11	.256	3	9	1	11	30	2	.953

W

WORLD SERIES RECORD

Year Team (League)	Pos.	G	AB	R	H	2B	3B	HR	RBI	Avg.	BB	SO	SB	PO	A	E	Avg.
1989— San Francisco (N.L.) ..	SS-3B	4	16	1	2	0	0	1	1	.125	0	6	0	4	12	0	1.000
1997— Cleveland (A.L.).........	3B	7	26	8	10	1	0	1	3	.385	7	6	0	5	9	0	1.000
World Series totals (2 years)		11	42	9	12	1	0	2	4	.286	7	12	0	9	21	0	1.000

ALL-STAR GAME RECORD

NOTES: Named to N.L. All-Star team for 1996 game; replaced by Ken Caminiti due to injury.

					BATTING								FIELDING			
Year League	Pos.	AB	R	H	2B	3B	HR	RBI	Avg.	BB	SO	SB	PO	A	E	Avg.
1990— National......................	PH	1	0	0	0	0	0	0	.000	0	1	0	...	...	...	...
1994— National......................	3B	3	0	0	0	0	0	0	.000	0	2	0	0	1	1	.500
1995— National......................						Selected, did not play—injured.										
1996— National......................						Selected, did not play—injured.										
All-Star Game totals (2 years)		4	0	0	0	0	0	0	.000	0	3	0	0	1	1	.500

WILLIAMS, MIKE   P   PIRATES

PERSONAL: Born July 29, 1968, in Radford, Va. ... 6-3/209. ... Throws right, bats right. ... Full name: Michael Darren Williams.
HIGH SCHOOL: Giles (Pearisburg, Va.).
COLLEGE: Virginia Tech.
TRANSACTIONS/CAREER NOTES: Selected by Philadelphia Phillies organization in 14th round of free-agent draft (June 4, 1990). ... On suspended list (September 26, 1996-remainder of season). ... Granted free agency (December 20, 1996). ... Signed by Boston Red Sox organization (February 15, 1997). ... Released by Red Sox (March 14, 1997). ... Signed by Kansas City Royals organization (April 30, 1997). ... On suspended list (May 16-18, 1997). ... Granted free agency (October 15, 1997). ... Signed by Pittsburgh Pirates organization (December 18, 1997).
STATISTICAL NOTES: Led N.L. with 16 wild pitches in 1996.
MISCELLANEOUS: Appeared in one game as pinch runner (1996).

Year Team (League)	W	L	Pct.	ERA	G	GS	CG	ShO	Sv.	IP	H	R	ER	BB	SO
1990— Batavia (N.Y.-Penn)	2	3	.400	2.30	27	0	0	0	11	47	39	17	12	13	42
1991— Clearwater (Fla. St.)	7	3	.700	1.74	14	14	2	1	0	93 1/3	65	23	18	14	76
— Reading (Eastern)	7	5	.583	3.69	16	15	2	1	0	102 1/3	93	44	42	36	51
1992— Reading (Eastern)	1	2	.333	5.17	3	3	0	0	0	15 2/3	17	10	9	7	12
— Scran./W.B. (Int'l).............	9	1	*.900	2.43	16	16	3	1	0	92 2/3	84	26	25	30	59
— Philadelphia (N.L.).............	1	1	.500	5.34	5	5	1	0	0	28 2/3	29	20	17	7	5
1993— Scran./W.B. (Int'l).............	9	2	*.818	2.87	14	13	1	1	0	97 1/3	93	34	31	16	53
— Philadelphia (N.L.).............	1	3	.250	5.29	17	4	0	0	0	51	50	32	30	22	33
1994— Philadelphia (N.L.).............	2	4	.333	5.01	12	8	0	0	0	50 1/3	61	31	28	20	29
— Scran./W.B. (Int'l).............	2	7	.222	5.79	14	14	0	0	0	84	91	55	54	36	53
1995— Philadelphia (N.L.).............	3	3	.500	3.29	33	8	0	0	0	87 2/3	78	37	32	29	57
— Scran./W.B. (Int'l).............	0	1	.000	4.66	3	3	0	0	0	9 2/3	8	5	5	2	8
1996— Philadelphia (N.L.).............	6	14	.300	5.44	32	29	0	0	0	167	188	107	101	67	103
1997— Omaha (Am. Assoc.)■..	3	6	.333	4.22	20	11	1	0	5	79	71	41	37	38	68
— Kansas City (A.L.)	0	2	.000	6.43	10	0	0	0	1	14	20	11	10	8	10
1998— Pittsburgh (N.L.)■.............	4	2	.667	1.94	37	1	0	0	0	51	39	12	11	16	59
— Nashville (Pacific Coast)	0	2	.000	5.59	16	4	0	0	1	37	36	25	23	14	34
A.L. totals (1 year)	0	2	.000	6.43	10	0	0	0	1	14	20	11	10	8	10
N.L. totals (6 years)	17	27	.386	4.52	136	55	1	0	0	435 2/3	445	239	219	161	286
Major league totals (7 years)......	17	29	.370	4.58	146	55	1	0	1	449 2/3	465	250	229	169	296

WILLIAMS, REGGIE   OF   ANGELS

PERSONAL: Born May 5, 1966, in Laurens, S.C. ... 6-1/180. ... Bats both, throws right. ... Full name: Reginald Bernard Williams.
HIGH SCHOOL: Laurens (S.C.) District 55.
COLLEGE: South Carolina-Aiken.
TRANSACTIONS/CAREER NOTES: Selected by San Francisco Giants organization in 25th round of free-agent draft (June 1, 1988). ... Released by Giants organization (June 20, 1989). ... Signed by Boise, independent (July 20, 1989). ... Signed as free agent by California Angels organization (February 15, 1990). ... On Quad City disabled list (April 12-May 22, 1991). ... Traded by Angels to Los Angeles Dodgers for P Mike James (October 26, 1993). ... Released by Dodgers (October 13, 1994). ... Re-signed by Dodgers (April 11, 1995). ... Granted free agency (October 16, 1995). ... Re-signed by Dodgers (January 1, 1996). ... On disabled list (July 27-September 20, 1996). ... Granted free agency (October 15, 1996). ... Signed by Anaheim Angels organization (August 19, 1997).
STATISTICAL NOTES: Led Northwest League with 10 caught stealing in 1988. ... Led Pacific Coast League outfielders with 324 total chances in 1992 and 303 in 1993. ... Tied for Pacific Coast League lead in double plays by outfielder with four in 1993.

					BATTING								FIELDING			
Year Team (League)	Pos.	G	AB	R	H	2B	3B	HR	RBI	Avg.	BB	SO	SB	PO	A	E	Avg.
1988— Everett (N'west).........	OF	60	223	52	56	8	1	3	29	.251	47	43	36	131	1	4	.971
1989— Clinton (Midwest).....	OF	68	236	38	46	9	2	3	18	.195	29	66	14	146	7	3	.981
— Boise (Northwest)■ ...	OF	42	153	33	41	5	1	3	14	.268	24	29	18	64	3	2	.971
1990— Quad City (Midw.)■ ...	OF	58	189	50	46	11	2	3	12	.243	39	60	24	110	6	1	.991
1991— Midland (Texas).........	OF	83	319	77	99	12	3	1	30	.310	62	67	21	187	9	7	.966
— Palm Springs (Calif.)..	OF	14	44	10	13	1	0	1	2	.295	21	15	6	33	1	1	.971
1992— Edmonton (PCL)	OF	139	519	96	141	26	9	3	64	.272	88	110	44	*313	8	3	.991
— California (A.L.).........	OF-DH	14	26	5	6	1	1	0	2	.231	1	10	0	26	0	0	1.000
1993— Vancouver (PCL)	OF	130	481	92	132	17	6	2	53	.274	*88	99	*50	*293	6	4	.987
1994— Albuquerque (PCL)■..	OF	104	288	55	90	15	8	4	42	.313	33	62	21	137	6	4	.973
1995— Los Angeles (N.L.)	OF	15	11	2	1	0	0	0	1	.091	2	3	0	6	0	0	1.000
— Albuquerque (PCL).....	OF	66	234	44	73	15	5	6	29	.312	30	46	14	141	10	0	1.000

W

Year	Team (League)	Pos.	G	AB	R	H	2B	3B	HR	RBI	Avg.	BB	SO	SB	PO	A	E	Avg.
1996—	Albuquerque (PCL).....	OF	92	352	60	101	25	2	6	42	.287	37	72	17	197	10	4	.981
1997—	Vancouver (PCL)■.....	OF-2B	12	40	10	10	3	0	2	5	.250	6	13	3	27	5	0	1.000
1998—	Vancouver (PCL).......	OF-2B	100	373	58	105	25	5	5	39	.282	53	98	13	221	13	2	.992
	—Anaheim (A.L.)..........	OF-DH	29	36	7	13	1	0	1	5	.361	7	11	3	25	0	0	1.000
American League totals (2 years)			43	62	12	19	2	1	1	7	.306	8	21	3	51	0	0	1.000
National League totals (1 year)			15	11	2	1	0	0	0	1	.091	2	3	0	6	0	0	1.000
Major league totals (3 years)			58	73	14	20	2	1	1	8	.274	10	24	3	57	0	0	1.000

WILLIAMS, RICKY — OF — RANGERS

PERSONAL: Born May 21, 1977, in San Diego. ... 6-0/215. ... Bats right, throws right. ... Full name: Errick Lynne Williams. ... Cousin of Cecil Fielder, first baseman with five major league teams (1985-88 and 1990-98).

HIGH SCHOOL: Patrick Henry (San Diego).

COLLEGE: Texas.

TRANSACTIONS/CAREER NOTES: Selected by Philadelphia Phillies organization in eighth round of free-agent draft (June 1, 1995). ... Selected by Montreal Expos from Phillies organization in Rule 5 major league draft (December 14, 1998). ... Traded by Expos to Texas Rangers for cash considerations (December 15, 1998).

MISCELLANEOUS: Named running back on THE SPORTING NEWS College All-America first team (1997-1998). ... Doak Walker Award winner (1997-1998). ... Maxwell Award winner (1998). ... Walter Camp Award winner (1998). ... Heisman Trophy winner (1998). ... Named College Football Player of the Year by THE SPORTING NEWS (1998).

Year	Team (League)	Pos.	G	AB	R	H	2B	3B	HR	RBI	Avg.	BB	SO	SB	PO	A	E	Avg.
1996—	Piedmont (S. Atl.)	OF	84	266	30	50	4	3	3	20	.188	18	87	17	117	9	9	.933
1997—	Piedmont (S. Atl.)	OF	37	136	12	28	5	0	1	6	.206	9	44	10	58	5	3	.955
1998—	Batavia (NY-Penn)	OF	13	53	7	15	0	0	0	3	.283	2	16	6	17	1	0	1.000

WILLIAMS, TODD — P — REDS

PERSONAL: Born February 13, 1971, in Syracuse, N.Y. ... 6-3/210. ... Throws right, bats right. ... Full name: Todd Michael Williams.

HIGH SCHOOL: Minoa (East Syracuse N.Y.)

JUNIOR COLLEGE: Onondaga Community College (N.Y.).

TRANSACTIONS/CAREER NOTES: Selected by Los Angeles Dodgers organization in 54th round of free-agent draft (June 4, 1990). ... On disabled list (April 7-16, 1994). ... Traded by Dodgers to Oakland Athletics for P Matt McDonald (September 8, 1995). ... Released by A's (January 16, 1997). ... Signed by Cincinnati Reds organization (February 3, 1997).

Year	Team (League)	W	L	Pct.	ERA	G	GS	CG	ShO	Sv.	IP	H	R	ER	BB	SO
1991—	Great Falls (Pio.)	5	2	.714	2.72	28	0	0	0	8	53	50	26	16	24	59
1992—	Bakersfield (California) ...	0	0	. . .	2.30	13	0	0	0	9	15 2/3	11	4	4	7	11
	—San Antonio (Tex.)	7	4	.636	3.27	39	0	0	0	13	44	47	17	16	23	35
1993—	Albuquerque (PCL)	5	5	.500	4.99	*65	0	0	0	*21	70 1/3	87	44	39	31	56
1994—	Albuquerque (PCL)	4	2	.667	3.11	59	0	0	0	13	72 1/3	78	29	25	17	30
1995—	Los Angeles (N.L.)	2	2	.500	5.12	16	0	0	0	0	19 1/3	19	11	11	7	8
	—Albuquerque (PCL)	4	1	.800	3.38	25	0	0	0	0	45 1/3	59	21	17	15	23
1996—	Edmonton (PCL)■	5	3	.625	5.50	35	10	0	0	0	91 2/3	125	71	56	37	33
1997—	Chattanooga (Southern)■..	3	3	.500	2.10	48	0	0	0	*31	55 2/3	38	16	13	25	45
	—Indianapolis (A.A.)............	2	0	1.000	2.13	12	0	0	0	2	12 2/3	11	4	3	6	11
1998—	Indianapolis (Int'l)	0	3	.000	2.31	53	0	0	0	*26	58 1/3	54	19	15	24	35
	—Cincinnati (N.L.)................	0	1	.000	7.71	6	0	0	0	0	9 1/3	15	8	8	6	4
Major league totals (2 years)		2	3	.400	5.97	22	0	0	0	0	28 2/3	34	19	19	13	12

WILLIAMS, WOODY — P — PADRES

PERSONAL: Born August 19, 1966, in Houston. ... 6-0/195. ... Throws right, bats right. ... Full name: Gregory Scott Williams.

HIGH SCHOOL: Cypress-Fairbanks (Houston).

COLLEGE: Houston.

TRANSACTIONS/CAREER NOTES: Selected by Toronto Blue Jays organization in 28th round of free-agent draft (June 1, 1988). ... On disabled list (April 9-May 17, 1992). ... On Toronto disabled list (July 17, 1995-remainder of season); included rehabilitation assignment to Syracuse (August 15-25). ... On Toronto disabled list (March 22-May 31 and June 11-July 26, 1996); included rehabilitation assignments to Dunedin (May 2-10), Syracuse (May 10-28 and July 13-20) and St. Catharines (July 20-26). ... Traded by Blue Jays with P Carlos Almanzar and OF Peter Tucci to San Diego Padres for P Joey Hamilton (December 13, 1998).

Year	Team (League)	W	L	Pct.	ERA	G	GS	CG	ShO	Sv.	IP	H	R	ER	BB	SO
1988—	St. Catharines (NYP)	8	2	.800	1.54	12	12	2	0	0	76	48	22	13	21	58
	—Knoxville (Southern)	2	2	.500	3.81	6	4	0	0	0	28 1/3	27	13	12	12	25
1989—	Dunedin (Fla. St.)...........	3	5	.375	2.32	20	9	0	0	3	81 1/3	63	26	21	27	60
	—Knoxville (Southern)	3	5	.375	3.55	14	12	2	•2	1	71	61	32	28	33	51
1990—	Knoxville (Southern)	7	9	.438	3.14	42	12	0	0	5	126	111	55	44	39	74
	—Syracuse (Int'l).................	0	1	.000	10.00	3	0	0	0	0	9	15	10	10	4	8
1991—	Knoxville (Southern)	3	2	.600	3.59	18	1	0	0	3	42 2/3	42	18	17	14	37
	—Syracuse (Int'l).................	3	4	.429	4.12	31	0	0	0	6	54 2/3	52	27	25	27	37
1992—	Syracuse (Int'l).................	6	8	.429	3.13	25	16	1	0	1	120 2/3	115	46	42	41	81
1993—	Syracuse (Int'l).................	1	1	.500	2.20	12	0	0	0	3	16 1/3	15	5	4	5	16
	—Toronto (A.L.)....................	3	1	.750	4.38	30	0	0	0	0	37	40	18	18	22	24
	—Dunedin (Fla. St.)...........	0	0	. . .	0.00	2	0	0	0	0	4	0	0	0	2	2
1994—	Toronto (A.L.)....................	1	3	.250	3.64	38	0	0	0	0	59 1/3	44	24	24	33	56
	—Syracuse (Int'l).................	0	0	. . .	0.00	1	0	0	0	1	1 2/3	0	0	0	0	1

W

Year Team (League)	W	L	Pct.	ERA	G	GS	CG	ShO	Sv.	IP	H	R	ER	BB	SO
1995— Toronto (A.L.)	1	2	.333	3.69	23	3	0	0	0	53²/₃	44	23	22	28	41
— Syracuse (Int'l)	0	0	. . .	3.52	5	1	0	0	1	7²/₃	5	3	3	5	13
1996— Dunedin (Fla. St.)	0	2	.000	8.22	2	2	0	0	0	7²/₃	9	7	7	2	11
— Syracuse (Int'l)	3	1	.750	1.41	7	7	1	1	0	32	22	5	5	7	33
— Toronto (A.L.)	4	5	.444	4.73	12	10	1	0	0	59	64	33	31	21	43
— St. Catharines (NYP)	0	0	. . .	3.68	2	2	0	0	0	7¹/₃	7	3	3	4	12
1997— Toronto (A.L.)	9	14	.391	4.35	31	31	0	0	0	194²/₃	201	98	94	66	124
1998— Toronto (A.L.)	10	9	.526	4.46	32	32	1	1	0	209²/₃	196	112	104	81	151
Major league totals (6 years)	28	34	.452	4.30	166	76	2	1	0	613¹/₃	589	308	293	251	439

WILSON, CRAIG   IF   WHITE SOX

PERSONAL: Born September 3, 1970, in Chicago. ... 6-1/190. ... Bats right, throws right. ... Full name: Craig Franklin Wilson.
HIGH SCHOOL: Leyden (Franklin Park, Ill.).
COLLEGE: Kansas State.
TRANSACTIONS/CAREER NOTES: Selected by San Francisco Giants in 13th round of free-agent draft (June 3, 1991); did not sign. ... Selected by Chicago White Sox in 13th round of free agent draft (June 1, 1992).

							BATTING							FIELDING		
Year Team (League)	Pos.	G	AB	R	H	2B	3B	HR	RBI	Avg.	BB	SO	SB	PO	A	E	Avg.
1993— South Bend (Mid.)	SS	132	455	56	118	27	2	5	59	.259	49	50	4	166	388	21	.963
1994— Prince Will. (Car.)	SS	131	496	70	131	36	4	4	66	.264	58	44	1	187	388	11	.981
1995— Birmingham (Sou.)	SS	132	471	56	136	19	1	4	46	.289	43	44	2	193	389	34	.945
1996— Nashville (A.A.)	SS	44	123	13	22	4	1	1	6	.179	10	5	0	43	97	10	.933
— Birmingham (Sou.)	SS	58	202	36	57	9	0	3	26	.282	40	28	1	67	148	19	.919
1997— Nashville (A.A.)	SS	137	453	71	123	20	2	6	42	.272	48	31	4	189	398	20	.967
1998— Calgary (PCL)	2-S-3-1-0	120	432	67	132	21	1	14	69	.306	37	41	4	279	248	9	.983
— Chicago (A.L.)	SS-2B-3B	13	47	14	22	5	0	3	10	.468	3	6	1	20	27	0	1.000
Major league totals (1 year)		13	47	14	22	5	0	3	10	.468	3	6	1	20	27	0	1.000

WILSON, DAN   C   MARINERS

PERSONAL: Born March 25, 1969, in Arlington Heights, Ill. ... 6-3/202. ... Bats right, throws right. ... Full name: Daniel Allen Wilson.
HIGH SCHOOL: Barrington (Ill.).
COLLEGE: Minnesota.
TRANSACTIONS/CAREER NOTES: Selected by New York Mets organization in 26th round of free-agent draft (June 2, 1987); did not sign. ... Selected by Cincinnati Reds organization in first round (seventh pick overall) of free-agent draft (June 4, 1990). ... Traded by Reds with P Bobby Ayala to Seattle Mariners for P Erik Hanson and 2B Bret Boone (November 2, 1993). ... On disabled list (July 21-September 1, 1998).
RECORDS: Shares major league single-game record for most putouts by catcher (nine-inning game)—20 (August 8, 1997); most putouts by catcher (extra-inning game)—21 (March 31, 1996, 12 innings); and most chances accepted by catcher (nine-inning game) since 1900—20 (August 8, 1997). ... Shares A.L. single-game record for most putouts by catcher (extra-inning game)—21 (March 31, 1996, 12 innings).
STATISTICAL NOTES: Led American Association catchers with 810 total chances in 1992. ... Led A.L. catchers with 952 total chances in 1995 and 1,129 in 1997. ... Hit three home runs in one game (April 11, 1996). ... Tied for A.L. lead in double plays by catcher with 13 in 1997. ... Career major league grand slams: 2.

							BATTING							FIELDING		
Year Team (League)	Pos.	G	AB	R	H	2B	3B	HR	RBI	Avg.	BB	SO	SB	PO	A	E	Avg.
1990— Char., W.Va. (SAL)	C	32	113	16	28	9	1	2	17	.248	13	17	0	190	24	1	.995
1991— Char., W.Va. (SAL)	C	52	197	25	62	11	1	3	29	.315	25	21	1	355	41	3	.992
— Chattanooga (Sou.)	C	81	292	32	75	19	2	2	38	.257	21	39	2	486	49	4	.993
1992— Nashville (A.A.)	C	106	366	27	92	16	1	4	34	.251	31	58	1	*733	*69	*8	.990
— Cincinnati (N.L.)	C	12	25	2	9	1	0	0	3	.360	3	8	0	42	4	0	1.000
1993— Cincinnati (N.L.)	C	36	76	6	17	3	0	0	8	.224	9	16	0	146	9	1	.994
— Indianapolis (A.A.)	C	51	191	18	50	11	1	1	17	.262	19	31	1	314	24	2	.994
1994— Seattle (A.L.)■	C	91	282	24	61	14	2	3	27	.216	10	57	1	602	45	*9	.986
1995— Seattle (A.L.)	C	119	399	40	111	22	3	9	51	.278	33	63	2	*895	52	5	.995
1996— Seattle (A.L.)	C	138	491	51	140	24	0	18	83	.285	32	88	1	834	58	4	.996
1997— Seattle (A.L.)	C	146	508	66	137	31	1	15	74	.270	39	72	7	*1051	72	6	.995
1998— Seattle (A.L.)	C	96	325	39	82	17	1	9	44	.252	24	56	2	677	35	4	.994
American League totals (5 years)		590	2005	220	531	108	7	54	279	.265	138	336	13	4059	262	28	.994
National League totals (2 years)		48	101	8	26	4	0	0	11	.257	12	24	0	188	13	1	.995
Major league totals (7 years)		638	2106	228	557	112	7	54	290	.264	150	360	13	4247	275	29	.994

DIVISION SERIES RECORD

							BATTING							FIELDING		
Year Team (League)	Pos.	G	AB	R	H	2B	3B	HR	RBI	Avg.	BB	SO	SB	PO	A	E	Avg.
1995— Seattle (A.L.)	C	5	17	0	2	0	0	0	1	.118	2	6	0	34	1	0	1.000
1997— Seattle (A.L.)	C	4	13	0	0	0	0	0	0	.000	0	9	0	29	1	0	1.000
Division series totals (2 years)		9	30	0	2	0	0	0	1	.067	2	15	0	63	2	0	1.000

CHAMPIONSHIP SERIES RECORD

							BATTING							FIELDING		
Year Team (League)	Pos.	G	AB	R	H	2B	3B	HR	RBI	Avg.	BB	SO	SB	PO	A	E	Avg.
1995— Seattle (A.L.)	C	6	16	0	0	0	0	0	0	.000	0	4	0	35	3	1	.974

ALL-STAR GAME RECORD

						BATTING							FIELDING		
Year League	Pos.	AB	R	H	2B	3B	HR	RBI	Avg.	BB	SO	SB	PO	A	E	Avg.
1996— American	PH	1	0	0	0	0	0	0	.000	0	0	0	. . .	. . .	. . .	. . .

W

WILSON, ENRIQUE   2B/SS   INDIANS

PERSONAL: Born July 27, 1975, in Santo Domingo, Dominican Republic. ... 5-11/160. ... Bats both, throws right. ... Full name: Enrique Martes Wilson.

HIGH SCHOOL: Liceo Ramon Amelio Jiminez (Santo Domingo, Dominican Republic).

TRANSACTIONS/CAREER NOTES: Signed as non-drafted free agent by Minnesota Twins organization (April 15, 1992). ... Traded by Twins organization to Cleveland Indians organization (February 21, 1994), completing deal in which Twins acquired P Shawn Bryant for a player to be named later (February 21, 1994). ... On Cleveland disabled list (April 4-June 15, 1998); included rehabilitation assignment to Buffalo (June 2-15).

STATISTICAL NOTES: Led South Atlantic League shortstops with 625 total chances and 66 double plays in 1994. ... Led Carolina League with 10 sacrifice flies in 1995. ... Led Eastern League shortstops with 74 double plays in 1996. ... Career major league grand slams: 1.

							BATTING								FIELDING		
Year Team (League)	Pos.	G	AB	R	H	2B	3B	HR	RBI	Avg.	BB	SO	SB	PO	A	E	Avg.
1992— GC Twins (GCL).........	SS	13	44	12	15	1	0	0	8	.341	4	4	3	9	26	4	.897
1993— Elizabethton (App.).....	SS-3B	58	197	42	57	8	4	13	50	.289	14	18	5	50	139	19	.909
1994— Columbus (S. Atl.)■ ..	SS	133	512	82	143	28	12	10	72	.279	44	34	21	*185	*407	33	.947
1995— Kinston (Carolina).....	SS-2B	117	464	55	124	24	•7	6	52	.267	25	38	18	181	375	21	.964
1996— Cant./Akr. (Eastern)...	SS-2B	117	484	70	147	17	5	5	50	.304	31	46	23	179	344	28	.949
— Buffalo (A.A.)............	3B-SS	3	8	1	4	1	0	0	0	.500	1	1	0	1	2	1	.750
1997— Buffalo (A.A.)..........	SS-2B-3B	118	451	78	138	20	3	11	39	.306	42	41	9	218	332	20	.965
— Cleveland (A.L.)........	SS	5	15	2	5	0	0	0	1	.333	0	2	0	7	13	1	.952
1998— Cleveland (A.L.).........	2B-SS-3B	32	90	13	29	6	0	2	12	.322	4	8	2	43	76	2	.983
— Buffalo (Int'l)..........	2B-SS	56	221	40	62	13	0	4	23	.281	19	21	8	108	141	6	.976
Major league totals (2 years)		37	105	15	34	6	0	2	13	.324	4	10	2	50	89	3	.979

DIVISION SERIES RECORD

							BATTING								FIELDING		
Year Team (League)	Pos.	G	AB	R	H	2B	3B	HR	RBI	Avg.	BB	SO	SB	PO	A	E	Avg.
1998— Cleveland (A.L.).........	2B	1	2	0	0	0	0	0	0	.000	0	0	0	2	2	0	1.000

CHAMPIONSHIP SERIES RECORD

							BATTING								FIELDING		
Year Team (League)	Pos.	G	AB	R	H	2B	3B	HR	RBI	Avg.	BB	SO	SB	PO	A	E	Avg.
1998— Cleveland (A.L.).........	PR-2B	5	14	2	3	0	0	0	1	.214	1	3	0	5	19	1	.960

WILSON, PAUL   P   METS

PERSONAL: Born March 28, 1973, in Orlando. ... 6-5/235. ... Throws right, bats right. ... Full name: Paul Anthony Wilson.

HIGH SCHOOL: William R. Boone (Orlando).

COLLEGE: Florida State.

TRANSACTIONS/CAREER NOTES: Selected by New York Mets organization in first round (first pick overall) of free-agent draft (June 2, 1994). ... On New York disabled list (June 5-July 15, 1996); included rehabilitation assignments to St. Lucie (June 28-July 10) and Binghamton (July 10-15). ... On New York disabled list (March 27, 1997-entire season); included rehabilitation assignments to Gulf Coast Mets (August 2-23) and St. Lucie (August 28-September 8). ... On New York disabled list (March 13-August 4, 1998); included rehabilitation assignment to St. Lucie (July 9-August 1).

STATISTICAL NOTES: Named Eastern League Pitcher of the Year (1995).

Year Team (League)	W	L	Pct.	ERA	G	GS	CG	ShO	Sv.	IP	H	R	ER	BB	SO
1994— GC Mets (GCL)...............	0	2	.000	3.00	3	3	0	0	0	12	8	4	4	4	13
— St. Lucie (Fla. St.)........	0	5	.000	5.06	8	8	0	0	0	37 1/3	32	23	21	17	37
1995— Binghamton (Eastern)........	6	3	.667	*2.17	16	16	4	1	0	120 1/3	89	34	29	24	127
— Norfolk (Int'l)...................	5	3	.625	2.85	10	10	*4	2	0	66 1/3	59	25	21	20	67
1996— New York (N.L.)...............	5	12	.294	5.38	26	26	1	0	0	149	157	102	89	71	109
— St. Lucie (Fla. St.)	0	1	.000	3.38	2	2	0	0	0	8	6	5	3	4	5
— Binghamton (Eastern)........	0	1	.000	7.20	1	1	0	0	0	5	6	4	4	5	5
1997— GC Mets (GCL).................	1	0	1.000	1.45	4	3	0	0	1	18 2/3	14	7	3	4	18
— St. Lucie (Fla. St.)...........	0	0	. . .	2.57	1	1	0	0	0	7	6	2	2	0	6
1998— St. Lucie (Fla. St.)	0	1	.000	6.38	5	5	0	0	0	18 1/3	23	13	13	4	16
— Norfolk (Int'l)...................	4	1	.800	4.42	7	7	0	0	0	38 2/3	42	19	19	9	30
Major league totals (1 year).......	5	12	.294	5.38	26	26	1	0	0	149	157	102	89	71	109

WILSON, PRESTON   OF   MARLINS

W

PERSONAL: Born July 19, 1974, in Bamberg, S.C. ... 6-2/193. ... Bats right, throws right. ... Full name: Preston James David Wilson. ... Son of Mookie Wilson, first base/outfield coach, New York Mets; and outfielder with Mets (1980-89) and Toronto Blue Jays (1989-91).

HIGH SCHOOL: Bamberg Erhardt (Bamberg, S.C.).

TRANSACTIONS/CAREER NOTES: Selected by New York Mets organization in first round (ninth pick overall) of free-agent draft (June 1, 1992). ... On disabled list (April 4-29, May 21-July 13 and July 29-September 8, 1996). ... On Norfolk disabled list (April 20-May 2, 1998). ... Traded by Mets with P Ed Yarnall and P Geoff Goetz to Florida Marlins for C Mike Piazza (May 22, 1998).

STATISTICAL NOTES: Led Appalachian League third basemen with 197 total chances in 1993.

							BATTING								FIELDING		
Year Team (League)	Pos.	G	AB	R	H	2B	3B	HR	RBI	Avg.	BB	SO	SB	PO	A	E	Avg.
1993— Kingsport (Appal.)......	3B	66	259	44	60	10	0	*16	48	.232	24	75	6	*45	*127	*25	.873
— Pittsfield (NYP)	3B	8	29	6	16	5	1	1	12	.552	2	7	1	5	9	6	.700
1994— Capital City (SAL)......	3B	131	474	55	108	17	4	14	58	.228	20	135	10	78	281	47	.884
1995— Capital City (SAL)......	OF	111	442	70	119	26	5	20	61	.269	19	114	20	189	10	8	.961
1996— St. Lucie (Fla. St.)	OF	23	85	6	15	3	0	1	7	.176	8	21	1	39	4	2	.956
1997— St. Lucie (Fla. St.)	OF	63	245	32	60	12	1	11	48	.245	8	66	3	104	5	3	.973
— Binghamton (East.)	OF-3B	70	259	37	74	12	1	19	47	.286	21	71	7	116	3	6	.952

Year Team (League)	Pos.	G	AB	R	H	2B	3B	HR	RBI	Avg.	BB	SO	SB	PO	A	E	Avg.
1998—Norfolk (Int'l)	OF	18	73	9	18	5	1	1	9	.247	2	22	1	44	2	2	.958
—New York (N.L.)..........	OF	8	20	3	6	2	0	0	2	.300	2	8	1	10	0	1	.909
—Charlotte (Int'l)■.......	OF	94	356	71	99	25	3	25	77	.278	34	121	14	180	8	4	.979
—Florida (N.L.)	OF	14	31	4	2	0	0	1	1	.065	4	13	0	13	0	0	1.000
Major league totals (1 year)		22	51	7	8	2	0	1	3	.157	6	21	1	23	0	1	.958

WILSON, TREVOR   P

PERSONAL: Born June 7, 1966, in Torrance, Calif. ... 6-0/204. ... Throws left, bats left. ... Full name: Trevor Kirk Wilson.
HIGH SCHOOL: Oregon City (Ore.).
COLLEGE: Oregon State.
TRANSACTIONS/CAREER NOTES: Selected by San Francisco Giants organization in eighth round of free-agent draft (June 3, 1985). ... On San Francisco disabled list (August 22-September 6, 1990 and March 27-April 18, 1992). ... On suspended list (June 26-29, 1992). ... On San Francisco disabled list (May 21-June 5, 1993). ... On San Francisco disabled list (July 3-August 10, 1993); included rehabilitation assignment to San Jose (August 3-10). ... On San Francisco disabled list (August 24-September 15, 1993). ... On disabled list (March 23, 1994-entire season). ... Granted free agency (December 23, 1994). ... Re-signed by Giants (April 7, 1995). ... On San Francisco disabled list (June 20-July 17 and August 13, 1995-remainder of season); included rehabilitation assignments to San Jose (July 8-17 and August 31-September 8). ... Granted free agency (November 1, 1995). ... Signed by Cincinnati Reds (January 12, 1996). ... On Indianapolis disabled list (April 4-30, 1996). ... Released by Reds (April 30, 1996). ... Signed by Anaheim Angels organization (July 31, 1997). ... Granted free agency (October 23, 1998).
RECORDS: Shares major league record for striking out side on nine pitches (June 7, 1992, ninth inning).
STATISTICAL NOTES: Tied for Northwest League lead with two balks in 1985. ... Pitched 6-0 one-hit, complete-game victory for San Francisco against San Diego (June 13, 1990). ... Tied for N.L. lead with seven balks in 1992.
MISCELLANEOUS: Appeared in one game as pinch runner with San Francisco (1989). ... Appeared in one game as pinch runner (1992). ... Appeared in one game as pinch runner and struck out in only appearance as pinch hitter with San Francisco (1995).

Year Team (League)	W	L	Pct.	ERA	G	GS	CG	ShO	Sv.	IP	H	R	ER	BB	SO
1985—Everett (Northwest)	2	4	.333	4.23	17	7	0	0	3	55 1/3	67	36	26	26	50
1986—Clinton (Midwest)	6	11	.353	4.27	34	21	0	0	2	130 2/3	126	70	62	64	84
1987—Clinton (Midwest)	10	6	.625	2.01	26	26	3	2	0	161 1/3	130	60	36	77	146
1988—Shreveport (Texas)	5	4	.556	1.86	12	11	0	0	0	72 2/3	55	19	15	23	53
—Phoenix (PCL)	2	3	.400	5.05	11	9	0	0	0	51 2/3	49	35	29	33	49
—San Francisco (N.L.)	0	2	.000	4.09	4	4	0	0	0	22	25	14	10	8	15
1989—Phoenix (PCL)	7	7	.500	3.12	23	20	2	0	0	115 1/3	109	49	40	76	77
—San Francisco (N.L.)	2	3	.400	4.35	14	4	0	0	0	39 1/3	28	20	19	24	22
1990—Phoenix (PCL)	5	5	.500	3.82	11	10	2	1	0	66	63	31	28	44	45
—San Francisco (N.L.)	8	7	.533	4.00	27	17	3	2	0	110 1/3	87	52	49	49	66
1991—San Francisco (N.L.)	13	11	.542	3.56	44	29	2	1	0	202	173	87	80	77	139
1992—San Francisco (N.L.)	8	14	.364	4.21	26	26	1	1	0	154	152	82	72	64	88
1993—San Francisco (N.L.)	7	5	.583	3.60	22	18	1	0	0	110	110	45	44	40	57
—San Jose (California)	1	0	1.000	0.00	2	2	0	0	0	10	4	0	0	3	8
1994—							Did not play.								
1995—San Francisco (N.L.)	3	4	.429	3.92	17	17	0	0	0	82 2/3	82	42	36	38	38
—San Jose (California)	0	1	.000	1.35	2	2	0	0	0	6 2/3	5	4	1	3	5
1996—							Did not play.								
1997—							Did not play.								
1998—Vancouver (PCL)■.............	5	9	.357	3.62	21	21	4	1	0	141 2/3	130	67	57	59	94
—Anaheim (A.L.)..................	0	0	...	3.52	15	0	0	0	0	7 2/3	8	4	3	5	6
A.L. totals (1 year)	0	0	...	3.52	15	0	0	0	0	7 2/3	8	4	3	5	6
N.L. totals (7 years)	41	46	.471	3.87	154	115	7	4	0	720 1/3	657	342	310	300	425
Major league totals (8 years)	41	46	.471	3.87	169	115	7	4	0	728	665	346	313	305	431

WILSON, VANCE   C   METS

PERSONAL: Born March 17, 1973, in Mesa, Ariz. ... 5-11/190. ... Bats right, throws right. ... Full name: Vance Allen Wilson.
HIGH SCHOOL: Red Mountain (Mesa, Ariz.).
JUNIOR COLLEGE: Mesa (Ariz.) Community College.
TRANSACTIONS/CAREER NOTES: Selected by New York Mets organization in 44th round of free-agent draft (June 3, 1993). ... On Norfolk disabled list (May 2-July 18, 1998). ... On New York disabled list (September 8, 1998-remainder of season).

Year Team (League)	Pos.	G	AB	R	H	2B	3B	HR	RBI	Avg.	BB	SO	SB	PO	A	E	Avg.
1994—Pittsfield (NYP)	C	44	166	22	51	12	0	2	20	.307	5	27	4	190	25	5	.977
1995—Columbia (S. Atl.)........	C	91	324	34	81	11	0	6	32	.250	19	45	4	605	99	*14	.981
1996—St. Lucie (Fla. St.)	C	93	311	29	76	14	2	6	44	.244	31	41	2	502	87	8	.987
1997—Binghamton (East.)	C	92	322	46	89	17	0	15	40	.276	20	46	2	604	69	11	.984
1998—Norfolk (Int'l)	C	46	154	18	40	3	0	4	16	.260	9	29	0	348	29	4	.990
—GC Mets (GCL)	C	10	28	5	10	5	0	2	9	.357	0	0	0	35	9	2	.957
—St. Lucie (Fla. St.)	C	4	16	0	1	0	0	0	0	.063	0	5	0	19	3	0	1.000

WINCHESTER, SCOTT   P   REDS

PERSONAL: Born April 20, 1973, in Midland, Mich. ... 6-2/210. ... Throws right, bats right. ... Full name: Scott J. Winchester.
HIGH SCHOOL: H.H. Dow (Midland, Mich.).
COLLEGE: Clemson.
TRANSACTIONS/CAREER NOTES: Selected by Cleveland Indians organization in 14th round of free-agent draft (June 1, 1995). ... Traded by Indians with P Jim Crowell, P Danny Graves and IF Damian Jackson to Cincinnati Reds for P John Smiley and IF Jeff Branson (July 31, 1997). ... Selected by Arizona Diamondbacks in second round (33rd pick overall) of expansion draft (November 18, 1997). ... Traded by Diamondbacks to Reds (November 18, 1997), completing deal in which Reds traded P Felix Rodriguez to Diamondbacks for a player to be named later (November 11, 1997). ... On Indianapolis disabled list (August 18-September 8, 1998).

W

Year Team (League)	W	L	Pct.	ERA	G	GS	CG	ShO	Sv.	IP	H	R	ER	BB	SO
1995— Watertown (NYP)	3	1	.750	2.83	23	0	0	0	11	28²/₃	24	10	9	6	27
1996— Columbus (S. Atl.)..............	7	3	.700	3.23	52	0	0	0	26	61¹/₃	50	27	22	16	60
1997— Kinston (Carolina)	2	1	.667	1.47	34	0	0	0	29	36²/₃	21	6	6	11	45
— Akron (Eastern)	0	0	...	3.86	6	0	0	0	1	7	8	3	3	2	8
— Chattanooga (Southern)■..	2	1	.667	1.69	9	0	0	0	3	10²/₃	9	4	2	3	3
— Indianapolis (A.A.)..............	0	0	...	0.00	4	0	0	0	0	5²/₃	2	0	0	2	2
— Cincinnati (N.L.)	0	0	...	6.00	5	0	0	0	0	6	9	5	4	2	3
1998— Indianapolis (Int'l)	3	2	.600	6.67	6	5	0	0	0	29²/₃	39	23	22	8	12
— Cincinnati (N.L.)	3	6	.333	5.81	16	16	1	0	0	79	101	56	51	27	40
Major league totals (2 years)......	3	6	.333	5.82	21	16	1	0	0	85	110	61	55	29	43

WINN, RANDY   OF   DEVIL RAYS

PERSONAL: Born June 9, 1974, in Los Angeles. ... 6-2/175. ... Bats both, throws right. ... Full name: Dwight Randolph Winn.
HIGH SCHOOL: San Ramon Valley (Danville, Calif.).
COLLEGE: Santa Clara.
TRANSACTIONS/CAREER NOTES: Selected by Florida Marlins organization in third round of free-agent draft (June 1, 1995). ... On disabled list (August 22-September 11, 1995). ... Selected by Tampa Bay Devil Rays in third round (58th pick overall) of expansion draft (November 18, 1997).
STATISTICAL NOTES: Led Eastern League in caught stealing with 20 in 1997.
MISCELLANEOUS: Holds Tampa Bay Devil Rays all-time record for most triples (9) and most stolen bases (26).

Year Team (League)	Pos.	G	AB	R	H	2B	3B	HR	RBI	Avg.	BB	SO	SB	PO	A	E	Avg.
1995— Elmira (N.Y.-Penn)......	OF	51	213	38	67	7	4	0	22	.315	15	31	19	103	1	5	.954
1996— Kane County (Midw.)..	OF	130	514	90	139	16	3	0	35	.270	47	115	30	260	2	8	.970
1997— Brevard Co. (Fla. St.)..	OF	36	143	26	45	8	2	0	15	.315	16	28	16	95	0	0	1.000
— Portland (Eastern)	OF	96	384	66	112	15	6	8	36	.292	42	92	35	182	6	4	.979
1998— Durham (Int'l)■	OF	29	123	25	35	5	2	1	16	.285	15	24	10	55	1	2	.966
— Tampa Bay (A.L.)........	OF-DH	109	338	51	94	9	9	1	17	.278	29	69	26	192	7	4	.980
Major league totals (1 year)		109	338	51	94	9	9	1	17	.278	29	69	26	192	7	4	.980

WINSTON, DARRIN   P   ANGELS

PERSONAL: Born July 6, 1966, in Passaic, N.J. ... 6-0/195. ... Throws left, bats right. ... Full name: Darrin Alexander Winston.
HIGH SCHOOL: Bishop (Edison, N.J.).
COLLEGE: Rutgers.
TRANSACTIONS/CAREER NOTES: Selected by Montreal Expos in 18th round of free-agent draft (June 1, 1988). ... On disabled list (July 1, 1991 through 1992 season). ... Granted free agency (October 15, 1994). ... Signed by Pittsburgh Pirates organization (December 8, 1994). ... Granted free agency (October 15, 1995). ... Signed by New York Mets organization (December 20, 1996). ... Released by Mets organization (March 31, 1997). ... Signed by Scranton/Wilkes-Barre, Philadelphia Phillies organization (April 7, 1997). ... Granted free agency (October 15, 1998). ... Signed by Anaheim Angels organization (November 18, 1998).

Year Team (League)	W	L	Pct.	ERA	G	GS	CG	ShO	Sv.	IP	H	R	ER	BB	SO
1988— Jamestown (NYP)	2	4	.333	4.91	14	7	0	0	2	44	47	28	24	19	29
1989— Rockford (Midwest)	7	1	.875	1.52	47	0	0	0	16	65	52	16	11	11	70
1990— Jacksonville (Southern)..	6	2	.750	2.14	47	0	0	0	7	63	38	16	15	28	45
1991— Indianapolis (A.A.)..............	1	0	1.000	1.45	27	0	0	0	0	31	26	10	5	21	23
1992—								Did not play.							
1993— Harrisburg (Eastern)	1	0	1.000	4.63	24	0	0	0	1	44²/₃	53	30	23	19	36
— W.P. Beach (FSL).............	2	0	1.000	1.46	8	2	1	0	0	24²/₃	18	6	4	3	21
1994— Harrisburg (Eastern)	4	2	.667	1.53	25	0	0	0	0	35¹/₃	32	12	6	9	27
— Ottawa (Int'l)	2	0	1.000	3.81	23	0	0	0	0	28¹/₃	27	15	12	10	17
1995— Calgary (PCL)■	4	6	.400	4.80	53	0	0	0	2	50²/₃	59	33	27	17	40
1996—								Out of organized baseball.							
1997— Scran./W.B. (Int'l)■..........	7	4	.636	3.43	39	9	1	0	0	89¹/₃	74	38	34	36	66
— Philadelphia (N.L.).............	2	0	1.000	5.25	7	1	0	0	0	12	8	8	7	3	8
1998— Philadelphia (N.L.)..............	2	2	.500	6.12	27	0	0	0	1	25	31	18	17	6	11
— Scran./W.B. (Int'l).............	0	2	.000	9.51	16	2	0	0	0	23²/₃	40	27	25	10	18
Major league totals (2 years)......	4	2	.667	5.84	34	1	0	0	1	37	39	26	24	9	19

WITASICK, JAY   P   ATHLETICS

W

PERSONAL: Born August 28, 1972, in Baltimore. ... 6-4/210. ... Throws right, bats right. ... Full name: Gerald Alphonse Witasick.
HIGH SCHOOL: C. Milton Wright (Bel Air, Md.).
JUNIOR COLLEGE: Brevard Community College (Fla.).
COLLEGE: Maryland-Baltimore County.
TRANSACTIONS/CAREER NOTES: Selected by St. Louis Cardinals organization in second round of free-agent draft (June 3, 1993). ... On disabled list (July 17, 1995-remainder of season). ... Traded by Cardinals with OF Allen Battle, P Bret Wagner and P Carl Dale to Oakland Athletics for P Todd Stottlemyre (January 9, 1996). ... On Oakland disabled list (March 31-June 14, 1997); included rehabilitation assignment to Modesto (June 11-14).

Year Team (League)	W	L	Pct.	ERA	G	GS	CG	ShO	Sv.	IP	H	R	ER	BB	SO
1993— Johnson City (App.)	4	3	.571	4.12	12	12	0	0	0	67²/₃	65	42	31	19	74
— Savannah (S. Atl.)	1	0	1.000	4.50	1	1	0	0	0	6	7	3	3	2	8
1994— Madison (Midwest)	10	4	.714	2.32	18	18	2	0	0	112¹/₃	74	36	29	42	141
1995— St. Petersburg (FSL)	7	7	.500	2.74	18	18	1	1	0	105	80	39	32	36	109
— Arkansas (Texas)...............	2	4	.333	6.88	7	7	0	0	0	34	46	29	26	16	26

Year Team (League)	W	L	Pct.	ERA	G	GS	CG	ShO	Sv.	IP	H	R	ER	BB	SO
1996—Huntsville (Southern)■	0	3	.000	2.30	25	6	0	0	4	66 2/3	47	21	17	26	63
—Oakland (A.L.)	1	1	.500	6.23	12	0	0	0	0	13	12	9	9	5	12
—Edmonton (PCL)	0	0	...	4.15	6	0	0	0	2	8 2/3	9	4	4	6	9
1997—Modesto (California)	0	1	.000	4.15	9	2	0	0	1	17 1/3	16	9	8	5	29
—Edmonton (PCL)	3	2	.600	4.28	13	1	0	0	0	27 1/3	25	13	13	15	17
—Oakland (A.L.)	0	0	...	5.73	8	0	0	0	0	11	14	7	7	6	8
1998—Edmonton (PCL)	11	7	.611	3.87	27	26	2	1	0	149	126	74	64	49	155
—Oakland (A.L.)	1	3	.250	6.33	7	3	0	0	0	27	36	24	19	15	29
Major league totals (3 years)	2	4	.333	6.18	27	3	0	0	0	51	62	40	35	26	49

WITHEM, SHANNON — P

PERSONAL: Born September 21, 1972, in Ann Arbor, Mich. ... 6-3/185. ... Throws right, bats right. ... Full name: Shannon Bolt Withem. ... Name pronounced WITH-em.
HIGH SCHOOL: Willow Run (Ypsilanti, Mich.).
TRANSACTIONS/CAREER NOTES: Selected by Detroit Tigers organization in fifth round of free-agent draft (June 4, 1990). ... Granted free agency (October 15, 1997). ... Signed by Toronto Blue Jays organization (November 25, 1997). ... Released by Blue Jays (November 18, 1998).
HONORS: Named International League Most Valuable Pitcher (1998).
STATISTICAL NOTES: Tied for Appalachian League lead with 12 wild pitches in 1990.

Year Team (League)	W	L	Pct.	ERA	G	GS	CG	ShO	Sv.	IP	H	R	ER	BB	SO
1990—Bristol (Eastern)	3	*9	.250	5.23	14	13	0	0	0	62	70	43	36	35	48
1991—Fayetteville (S. Atl.)	2	6	.250	8.50	11	11	0	0	0	47 2/3	71	53	45	28	19
—Niagara Falls (NYP)	1	2	.333	3.33	8	3	0	0	0	27	26	12	10	11	17
1992—Fayetteville (S. Atl.)	1	3	.250	4.74	22	2	0	0	2	38	40	23	20	20	34
1993—Lakeland (Fla. St.)	10	2	.833	3.42	16	16	2	1	0	113	108	47	43	24	62
1994—Trenton (Eastern)	7	12	.368	3.44	25	25	5	1	0	178	190	80	68	37	135
1995—Jacksonville (Southern)	5	8	.385	5.75	19	18	0	0	0	108	142	77	69	24	80
1996—Binghamton (Eastern)	6	3	.667	3.24	12	12	1	1	0	86	86	32	31	17	59
—St. Lucie (Fla. St.)	1	0	1.000	1.29	2	2	0	0	0	14	8	2	2	1	13
—Norfolk (Int'l)	3	3	.500	4.64	8	8	0	0	0	42 2/3	56	25	22	6	30
1997—Norfolk (Int'l)	9	10	.474	4.34	29	27	1	0	0	155 2/3	167	85	75	48	109
1998—Syracuse (Int'l)■	*17	5	.773	3.27	28	27	4	•2	0	*189 2/3	176	72	69	58	113
—Toronto (A.L.)	0	0	...	3.00	1	0	0	0	0	3	3	1	1	2	2
Major league totals (1 year)	0	0	...	3.00	1	0	0	0	0	3	3	1	1	2	2

WITT, BOBBY — P — DEVIL RAYS

PERSONAL: Born May 11, 1964, in Arlington, Va. ... 6-2/205. ... Throws right, bats right. ... Full name: Robert Andrew Witt.
HIGH SCHOOL: Canton (Mass.).
COLLEGE: Oklahoma.
TRANSACTIONS/CAREER NOTES: Selected by Cincinnati Reds organization in seventh round of free-agent draft (June 7, 1982); did not sign. ... Selected by Texas Rangers organization in first round (third pick overall) of free-agent draft (June 3, 1985). ... On Texas disabled list (May 21-June 20, 1987); included rehabilitation assignments to Oklahoma City (June 7-12) and Tulsa (June 13). ... On Texas disabled list (May 27-July 31, 1991); included rehabilitation assignment to Oklahoma City (July 22-29). ... Traded by Rangers with OF Ruben Sierra, P Jeff Russell and cash to Oakland Athletics for OF Jose Canseco (August 31, 1992). ... Granted free agency (October 26, 1994). ... Signed by Florida Marlins (April 9, 1995). ... Traded by Marlins to Rangers for two players to be named later (August 8, 1995); Marlins acquired P Wilson Heredia (August 11, 1995) and OF Scott Podsednik (October 2, 1995) to complete deal. ... Granted free agency (November 3, 1995). ... Re-signed by Rangers (December 24, 1995). ... Granted free agency (October 27, 1997). ... Re-signed by Rangers (January 19, 1998). ... Traded by Rangers to St. Louis Cardinals for a player to be named later or cash (June 23, 1998). ... Granted free agency (October 29, 1998). ... Signed by Tampa Bay Devil Rays organization (January 20, 1999).
RECORDS: Shares major league record for most strikeouts in one inning—4 (August 2, 1987, second inning).
HONORS: Named righthanded pitcher on THE SPORTING NEWS college All-America team (1985).
STATISTICAL NOTES: Led A.L. with 22 wild pitches in 1986 and tied for lead with 16 in 1988. ... Pitched 4-0 one-hit, complete-game victory against Kansas City (June 23, 1994).
MISCELLANEOUS: Member of 1984 U.S. Olympic baseball team. ... Struck out in only appearance as pinch hitter with Texas (1987). ... Appeared in one game as pinch runner (1990). ... Appeared in one game as pinch runner (1994). ... Appeared in two games as pinch runner with Florida (1995). ... Made an out in only appearance as pinch hitter with Texas (1998).

Year Team (League)	W	L	Pct.	ERA	G	GS	CG	ShO	Sv.	IP	H	R	ER	BB	SO
1985—Tulsa (Texas)	0	6	.000	6.43	11	8	0	0	0	35	26	26	25	44	39
1986—Texas (A.L.)	11	9	.550	5.48	31	31	0	0	0	157 2/3	130	104	96	*143	174
1987—Texas (A.L.)	8	10	.444	4.91	26	25	1	0	0	143	114	82	78	*140	160
—Oklahoma City (A.A.)	1	0	1.000	9.00	1	1	0	0	0	5	5	5	5	3	2
—Tulsa (Texas)	0	1	.000	5.40	1	1	0	0	0	5	5	9	3	6	2
1988—Texas (A.L.)	8	10	.444	3.92	22	22	13	2	0	174 1/3	134	83	76	101	148
—Oklahoma City (A.A.)	4	6	.400	4.34	11	11	3	0	0	76 2/3	69	42	37	47	70
1989—Texas (A.L.)	12	13	.480	5.14	31	31	5	1	0	194 1/3	182	123	•111	*114	166
1990—Texas (A.L.)	17	10	.630	3.36	33	32	7	1	0	222	197	98	83	110	221
1991—Texas (A.L.)	3	7	.300	6.09	17	16	1	1	0	88 2/3	84	66	60	74	82
—Oklahoma City (A.A.)	1	1	.500	1.13	2	2	0	0	0	8	3	1	1	8	12
1992—Texas (A.L.)	9	13	.409	4.46	25	25	0	0	0	161 1/3	152	87	80	95	100
—Oakland (A.L.)■	1	1	.500	3.41	6	6	0	0	0	31 2/3	31	12	12	19	25
1993—Oakland (A.L.)	14	13	.519	4.21	35	33	5	1	0	220	226	112	103	91	131
1994—Oakland (A.L.)	8	10	.444	5.04	24	24	5	3	0	135 2/3	151	88	76	70	111
1995—Florida (N.L.)■	2	7	.222	3.90	19	19	1	0	0	110 2/3	104	52	48	47	95
—Texas (A.L.)■	3	4	.429	4.55	10	10	1	0	0	61 1/3	81	35	31	21	46
1996—Texas (A.L.)	16	12	.571	5.41	33	32	2	0	0	199 2/3	235	129	120	96	157
1997—Texas (A.L.)	12	12	.500	4.82	34	32	3	0	0	209	245	118	112	74	121
1998—Texas (A.L.)	5	4	.556	7.66	14	13	0	0	0	69 1/3	95	62	59	33	30
—St. Louis (N.L.)■	2	5	.286	4.94	17	5	0	0	0	47 1/3	55	32	26	20	28
A.L. totals (13 years)	127	128	.498	4.77	341	332	43	9	0	2068	2057	1199	1097	1181	1672
N.L. totals (2 years)	4	12	.250	4.22	36	24	1	0	0	158	159	84	74	67	123
Major league totals (13 years)	131	140	.483	4.73	377	356	44	9	0	2226	2216	1283	1171	1248	1795

W

Year	Team (League)	W	L	Pct.	ERA	G	GS	CG	ShO	Sv.	IP	H	R	ER	BB	SO
1996— Texas (A.L.)		0	0	...	8.10	1	1	0	0	0	3 1/3	4	3	3	2	3

CHAMPIONSHIP SERIES RECORD

Year	Team (League)	W	L	Pct.	ERA	G	GS	CG	ShO	Sv.	IP	H	R	ER	BB	SO
1992— Oakland (A.L.)		0	0	...	18.00	1	0	0	0	0	1	2	2	2	1	1

WITT, KEVIN — 1B — BLUE JAYS

PERSONAL: Born January 5, 1976, in High Point, N.C. ... 6-4/200. ... Bats left, throws right. ... Full name: Kevin Joseph Witt.
HIGH SCHOOL: Bishop Kenny (Jacksonville, Fla.).
TRANSACTIONS/CAREER NOTES: Selected by Toronto Blue Jays organization in first round (28th pick overall) of free-agent draft (June 2, 1994).
STATISTICAL NOTES: Tied for Southern League lead with seven intentional bases on balls in 1997. ... Led International League first basemen with .996 fielding percentage and 105 double plays in 1998.

									BATTING							FIELDING			
Year	Team (League)	Pos.	G	AB	R	H	2B	3B	HR	RBI	Avg.	BB	SO	SB	PO	A	E	Avg.
1994— Medicine Hat (Pio.)		SS	60	243	37	62	10	4	7	36	.255	15	52	4	*99	167	25	.914
1995— Hagerstown (SAL)		SS	119	479	58	111	35	1	14	50	.232	28	148	1	203	338	48	.919
1996— Dunedin (Fla. St.)		SS	124	446	63	121	18	6	13	70	.271	39	96	9	161	369	48	.917
1997— Knoxville (Southern)		1-3-O-S	127	501	76	145	27	4	•30	91	.289	44	109	1	553	118	15	.978
1998— Syracuse (Int'l)		1B-OF	126	455	71	124	20	3	23	67	.273	53	124	3	973	68	4	†.996
— Toronto (A.L.)		1B	5	7	0	1	0	0	0	0	.143	0	3	0	5	1	0	1.000
Major league totals (1 year)			5	7	0	1	0	0	0	0	.143	0	3	0	5	1	0	1.000

WOHLERS, MARK — P — BRAVES

PERSONAL: Born January 23, 1970, in Holyoke, Mass. ... 6-4/207. ... Throws right, bats right. ... Full name: Mark Edward Wohlers.
HIGH SCHOOL: Holyoke (Mass.).
TRANSACTIONS/CAREER NOTES: Selected by Atlanta Braves organization in eighth round of free-agent draft (June 1, 1988). ... On Atlanta disabled list (May 3-24 and August 21, 1998-remainder of season); included rehabilitation assignments to Greenville (May 23) and Richmond (August 25-September 8).
RECORDS: Shares major league single-inning record for most strikeouts—4 (June 7, 1995, ninth inning).
HONORS: Named Southern League Outstanding Pitcher (1991).
STATISTICAL NOTES: Pitched two innings, combining with starter Kent Mercker (six innings) and Alejandro Pena (one inning) in 1-0 no-hit victory for Atlanta against San Diego (September 11, 1991). ... Led International League with 17 wild pitches in 1998.

Year	Team (League)	W	L	Pct.	ERA	G	GS	CG	ShO	Sv.	IP	H	R	ER	BB	SO
1988— Pulaski (Appalachian)		5	3	.625	3.32	13	9	1	0	0	59 2/3	47	37	22	50	49
1989— Sumter (S. Atl.)		2	7	.222	6.49	14	14	0	0	0	68	74	55	49	59	51
— Pulaski (Appalachian)		1	1	.500	5.48	14	8	0	0	0	46	48	36	28	28	50
1990— Greenville (Southern)		0	1	.000	4.02	14	0	0	0	6	15 2/3	14	7	7	14	20
— Sumter (S. Atl.)		5	4	.556	1.88	37	2	0	0	5	52 2/3	27	13	11	20	85
1991— Greenville (Southern)		0	0	...	0.57	28	0	0	0	21	31 1/3	9	4	2	13	44
— Richmond (Int'l)		1	0	1.000	1.03	23	0	0	0	11	26 1/3	23	4	3	12	22
— Atlanta (N.L.)		3	1	.750	3.20	17	0	0	0	2	19 2/3	17	7	7	13	13
1992— Richmond (Int'l)		0	2	.000	3.93	27	2	0	0	9	34 1/3	32	16	15	17	33
— Atlanta (N.L.)		1	2	.333	2.55	32	0	0	0	4	35 1/3	28	11	10	14	17
1993— Richmond (Int'l)		1	3	.250	1.84	25	0	0	0	0	29 1/3	21	7	6	11	39
— Atlanta (N.L.)		6	2	.750	4.50	46	0	0	0	0	48	37	25	24	22	45
1994— Atlanta (N.L.)		7	2	.778	4.59	51	0	0	0	1	51	51	35	26	33	58
1995— Atlanta (N.L.)		7	3	.700	2.09	65	0	0	0	25	64 2/3	51	16	15	24	90
1996— Atlanta (N.L.)		2	4	.333	3.03	77	0	0	0	39	77 1/3	71	30	26	21	100
1997— Atlanta (N.L.)		5	7	.417	3.50	71	0	0	0	33	69 1/3	57	29	27	38	92
1998— Atlanta (N.L.)		0	1	.000	10.18	27	0	0	0	8	20 1/3	18	23	23	33	22
— Greenville (Southern)		0	0	...	0.00	1	1	0	0	0	1	1	1	0	1	1
— Richmond (Int'l)		0	3	.000	20.43	16	0	0	0	0	12 1/3	21	28	28	36	16
Major league totals (8 years)		31	22	.585	3.69	386	0	0	0	112	385 2/3	330	176	158	198	437

DIVISION SERIES RECORD

RECORDS: Holds career record for most saves—5. ... Holds N.L. career record for most games pitched—7.

Year	Team (League)	W	L	Pct.	ERA	G	GS	CG	ShO	Sv.	IP	H	R	ER	BB	SO
1995— Atlanta (N.L.)		0	1	.000	6.75	3	0	0	0	2	2 2/3	6	2	2	2	4
1996— Atlanta (N.L.)		0	0	...	0.00	3	0	0	0	3	3 1/3	1	0	0	0	4
1997— Atlanta (N.L.)		0	0	...	0.00	1	0	0	0	0	1	1	0	0	0	1
Div. series totals (3 years)		0	1	.000	2.57	7	0	0	0	5	7	8	2	2	2	9

CHAMPIONSHIP SERIES RECORD

RECORDS: Holds N.L. career records for most games pitched—18; and most games as relief pitcher—18.

Year	Team (League)	W	L	Pct.	ERA	G	GS	CG	ShO	Sv.	IP	H	R	ER	BB	SO
1991— Atlanta (N.L.)		0	0	...	0.00	3	0	0	0	0	1 2/3	3	0	0	1	1
1992— Atlanta (N.L.)		0	0	...	0.00	3	0	0	0	0	3	2	0	0	1	2
1993— Atlanta (N.L.)		0	1	.000	3.38	4	0	0	0	0	5 1/3	2	2	2	3	10
1995— Atlanta (N.L.)		1	0	1.000	1.80	4	0	0	0	0	5	2	1	1	0	8
1996— Atlanta (N.L.)		0	0	...	0.00	3	0	0	0	2	3	0	0	0	0	4
1997— Atlanta (N.L.)		0	0	...	0.00	1	0	0	0	0	1	0	0	0	1	1
Champ. series totals (6 years)		1	1	.500	1.42	18	0	0	0	2	19	9	3	3	6	26

W

NOTES: Member of World Series championship team (1995).

Year Team (League)	W	L	Pct.	ERA	G	GS	CG	ShO	Sv.	IP	H	R	ER	BB	SO
1991— Atlanta (N.L.)	0	0	...	0.00	3	0	0	0	0	1 2/3	2	0	0	2	1
1992— Atlanta (N.L.)	0	0	...	0.00	2	0	0	0	0	2/3	0	0	0	1	0
1995— Atlanta (N.L.)	0	0	...	1.80	4	0	0	0	0	5	4	1	1	3	3
1996— Atlanta (N.L.)	0	0	...	6.23	4	0	0	0	0	4 1/3	7	3	3	3	4
World Series totals (4 years)	0	0	...	3.09	13	0	0	0	0	11 2/3	13	4	4	9	8

ALL-STAR GAME RECORD

Year League	W	L	Pct.	ERA	GS	CG	ShO	Sv.	IP	H	R	ER	BB	SO
1996— National	0	0	...	0.00	0	0	0	0	2/3	1	0	0	0	0

WOLCOTT, BOB · P · RED SOX

PERSONAL: Born September 8, 1973, in Huntington Beach, Calif. ... 6-0/190. ... Throws right, bats right. ... Full name: Robert William Wolcott.
HIGH SCHOOL: North Medford (Ore.).
TRANSACTIONS/CAREER NOTES: Selected by Seattle Mariners organization in second round of free-agent draft (June 1, 1992). ... Selected by Arizona Diamondbacks in second round (53rd pick overall) of expansion draft (November 18, 1997). ... Traded by Diamondbacks to Boston Red Sox for a player to be named later (November 11, 1998); Diamondbacks acquired P Bart Miadich to complete deal (December 14, 1998).

Year Team (League)	W	L	Pct.	ERA	G	GS	CG	ShO	Sv.	IP	H	R	ER	BB	SO
1992— Bellingham (N'west)	0	1	.000	6.85	9	7	0	0	0	22 1/3	25	18	17	19	17
1993— Bellingham (N'west)	8	4	.667	2.64	15	15	1	0	0	95 1/3	70	31	28	26	79
1994— Riverside (California)	14	8	.636	2.84	26	26	•5	1	0	*180 2/3	173	75	57	50	142
— Calgary (PCL)	0	1	.000	3.00	1	1	0	0	0	6	6	2	2	3	5
1995— Port City (Southern)	7	3	.700	2.20	12	12	2	1	0	86	60	26	21	13	53
— Tacoma (PCL)	6	3	.667	4.08	13	13	2	1	0	79 1/3	94	49	36	16	43
— Seattle (A.L.)	3	2	.600	4.42	7	6	0	0	0	36 2/3	43	18	18	14	19
1996— Seattle (A.L.)	7	10	.412	5.73	30	28	1	0	0	149 1/3	179	101	95	54	78
— Lancaster (Calif.)	0	1	.000	10.50	1	1	0	0	0	6	9	7	7	0	6
— Tacoma (PCL)	0	2	.000	7.30	3	3	0	0	0	12 1/3	17	13	10	3	16
1997— Seattle (A.L.)	5	6	.455	6.03	19	18	0	0	0	100	129	71	67	29	58
— Tacoma (PCL)	1	3	.250	5.11	7	7	0	0	0	37	40	23	21	7	29
1998— Tucson (PCL)■	8	6	.571	5.18	23	21	2	1	0	128 2/3	156	79	74	26	100
— Arizona (N.L.)	1	3	.250	7.09	6	6	0	0	0	33	32	27	26	13	21
A.L. totals (3 years)	15	18	.455	5.66	56	52	1	0	0	286	351	190	180	97	155
N.L. totals (1 year)	1	3	.250	7.09	6	6	0	0	0	33	32	27	26	13	21
Major league totals (4 years)	16	21	.432	5.81	62	58	1	0	0	319	383	217	206	110	176

CHAMPIONSHIP SERIES RECORD

Year Team (League)	W	L	Pct.	ERA	G	GS	CG	ShO	Sv.	IP	H	R	ER	BB	SO
1995— Seattle (A.L.)	1	0	1.000	2.57	1	1	0	0	0	7	8	2	2	5	2

WOLFF, BRYAN · P · PADRES

PERSONAL: Born March 16, 1972, in Carbondale, Ill. ... 6-1/195. ... Throws right, bats right. ... Full name: Bryan Keith Wolff.
HIGH SCHOOL: Herrin (Ill.).
COLLEGE: Oral Roberts.
TRANSACTIONS/CAREER NOTES: Selected by San Diego Padres organization in 18th round of free-agent draft (June 3, 1993). ... Traded by Padres organization with 2B Bip Roberts to Kansas City Royals organization for P Aaron Donarque and 1B Wally Joyner (December 21, 1995). ... Released by Royals organization (May 21, 1997). ... Signed by Padres organization (May 27, 1997). ... Granted free agency (October 17, 1997). ... Re-signed by Padres organization (November 1, 1997).
STATISTICAL NOTES: Tied for Northwest league lead with 12 wild pitches in 1993.

Year Team (League)	W	L	Pct.	ERA	G	GS	CG	ShO	Sv.	IP	H	R	ER	BB	SO
1993— Spokane (N'west)	3	*9	.250	5.53	25	8	0	0	1	57	52	50	35	44	48
1994— Springfield (Mid.)	3	8	.273	5.37	60	0	0	0	24	63 2/3	46	43	38	58	99
1995— Rancho Cuca. (Cal.)	2	7	.222	3.32	54	0	0	0	18	57	39	23	21	54	77
1996— Wilmington (Caro.)■	1	2	.333	3.61	42	0	0	0	4	62 1/3	49	35	25	38	56
1997— Wichita (Texas)	1	1	.500	6.52	12	0	0	0	1	9 2/3	18	7	7	5	8
— Rancho Cuca. (Cal.)■	3	0	1.000	1.62	9	2	0	0	1	33 1/3	19	6	6	6	39
— Mobile (Southern)	1	2	.333	4.80	20	0	0	0	0	30	34	18	16	19	37
1998— Mobile (Southern)	9	3	.750	2.29	33	14	3	•2	0	133 2/3	90	40	34	43	134
— Las Vegas (PCL)	0	0	...	6.75	9	0	0	0	1	10 2/3	14	8	8	5	8

W

WOMACK, TONY · 2B · PIRATES

PERSONAL: Born September 25, 1969, in Danville, Va. ... 5-9/159. ... Bats left, throws right. ... Full name: Anthony Darrell Womack.
HIGH SCHOOL: Gretna (Va.).
COLLEGE: Guilford (N.C.), degree in sports management; then UNC Greensboro (did not play), master's degree in sports management.
TRANSACTIONS/CAREER NOTES: Selected by Pittsburgh Pirates organization in seventh round of free-agent draft (June 3, 1991). ... On disabled list (April 17-26 and August 28, 1992-remainder of season).
STATISTICAL NOTES: Tied for American Association lead with 12 sacrifice hits in 1994. ... Led Pacific Coast League with 14 sacrifice hits in 1996. ... Led N.L. second basemen with 20 errors in 1997. ... Had 16-game hitting streak (July 3-22, 1998).

Year Team (League)	Pos.	G	AB	R	H	2B	3B	HR	RBI	Avg.	BB	SO	SB	PO	A	E	Avg.
1991— Welland (NYP)	SS-2B	45	166	30	46	3	0	1	8	.277	17	39	26	78	109	16	.921
1992— Augusta (S. Atl.)	SS-2B	102	380	62	93	8	3	0	18	.245	41	59	50	186	291	40	.923
1993— Salem (Carolina)	SS	72	304	41	91	11	3	2	18	.299	13	34	28	130	223	28	.927
— Carolina (Southern)	SS	60	247	41	75	7	2	0	23	.304	17	34	21	102	169	11	.961
— Pittsburgh (N.L.)	SS	15	24	5	2	0	0	0	0	.083	3	3	2	11	22	1	.971

Year	Team (League)	Pos.	G	AB	R	H	2B	3B	HR	RBI	Avg.	BB	SO	SB	PO	A	E	Avg.
1994—	Buffalo (A.A.)..............	SS-2B	106	421	40	93	9	2	0	18	.221	19	76	41	211	283	22	.957
—	Pittsburgh (N.L.)	2B-SS	5	12	4	4	0	0	0	1	.333	2	3	0	3	6	2	.818
1995—	Calgary (PCL)	2B-SS	30	107	12	30	3	1	0	6	.280	12	11	7	37	94	5	.963
—	Carolina (Southern)....	SS-2B	82	332	52	85	9	4	1	19	.256	19	36	27	126	241	18	.953
1996—	Calgary (PCL)	SS-2B-OF	131	506	75	151	19	11	1	47	.298	31	79	37	258	335	24	.961
—	Pittsburgh (N.L.)	OF-2B	17	30	11	10	3	1	0	7	.333	6	1	2	11	8	2	.905
1997—	Pittsburgh (N.L.)	2B-SS	155	641	85	178	26	9	6	50	.278	43	109	*60	335	430	†20	.975
1998—	Pittsburgh (N.L.)	2B-OF-SS	159	655	85	185	26	7	3	45	.282	38	94	*58	309	451	17	.978
Major league totals (5 years)			351	1362	190	379	55	17	9	103	.278	92	210	122	669	917	42	.974

ALL-STAR GAME RECORD

Year	League	Pos.	AB	R	H	2B	3B	HR	RBI	Avg.	BB	SO	SB	PO	A	E	Avg.
1997—	National	2B	1	0	0	0	0	0	0	.000	0	0	0	1	0	0	1.000

WOOD, JASON   IF   TIGERS

PERSONAL: Born December 16, 1969, in San Bernadino, Calif. ... 6-1/170. ... Bats right, throws right. ... Full name: Jason William Wood.
HIGH SCHOOL: McLane (Fresno, Calif.).
TRANSACTIONS/CAREER NOTES: Selected by Oakland Athletics organzation in 11th round of free-agent draft (June 3, 1991). ... Traded by Athletics to Detroit Tigers (June 23, 1998), completing trade in which Tigers traded IF Bip Roberts to A's for a player to be named later (July 18, 1998).

Year	Team (League)	Pos.	G	AB	R	H	2B	3B	HR	RBI	Avg.	BB	SO	SB	PO	A	E	Avg.
1991—	S. Oregon (N'west).....	SS-2B	44	142	30	44	3	4	3	23	.310	28	30	5	64	117	14	.928
1992—	Modesto (California) ..	SS	128	454	66	105	28	3	6	49	.231	40	106	5	203	360	37	.938
1993—	Huntsville (Sou.)	SS	103	370	44	85	21	2	3	36	.230	33	97	2	161	227	32	.924
1994—	Huntsville (Sou.)	SS	134	468	54	128	29	2	6	84	.274	46	83	3	190	371	25	.957
1995—	Edmonton (PCL)	3B-2B-SS	127	421	49	99	20	5	2	50	.235	29	72	1	173	331	26	.951
1996—	Huntsville (Sou.)	3B-1B-SS	133	491	77	128	21	1	20	84	.261	72	87	2	337	292	20	.969
—	Edmonton (PCL)	1B	3	12	0	0	0	0	0	0	.000	5	6	0	39	1	1	.976
1997—	Edmonton (PCL)	3B-SS	130	505	83	162	35	7	19	87	.321	45	74	2	103	264	17	.956
1998—	Oakland (A.L.)	SS-3B	3	1	1	0	0	0	0	0	.000	0	1	0	1	3	0	1.000
—	Edmonton (PCL)	3-2-0-S	80	307	52	86	20	0	18	73	.280	37	71	1	91	175	10	.964
—	Detroit (A.L.)■...........	1B-DH-SS	10	23	5	8	2	0	1	1	.348	3	4	0	38	2	0	1.000
—	Toledo (Int'l)..............	3B-1B-SS	46	169	24	47	9	0	7	29	.278	16	30	0	99	66	5	.971
Major league totals (1 year)			13	24	6	8	2	0	1	1	.333	3	5	0	39	5	0	1.000

WOOD, KERRY   P   CUBS

PERSONAL: Born June 16, 1977, in Irving, Texas. ... 6-5/225. ... Throws right, bats right. ... Full name: Kerry Lee Wood.
HIGH SCHOOL: Grand Prairie (Texas).
TRANSACTIONS/CAREER NOTES: Selected by Chicago Cubs organization in first round (fourth pick overall) of free-agent draft (June 1, 1995). ... On disabled list (May 24-June 19, 1996).
RECORDS: Shares major league single-game record for most strikeouts (nine-inning game)—20 (May 6, 1998). ... Holds N.L. record for most strikeouts in consecutive games—33 (May 6 [20] and 11 [13], 1998).
HONORS: Named N.L. Rookie Pitcher of the Year by THE SPORTING NEWS (1998). ... Named N.L. Rookie of the Year by Baseball Writers' Association of America (1998).
STATISTICAL NOTES: Led Florida State League with 14 hit batsmen and seven balks in 1996. ... Pitched 2-0 one-hit, complete-game victory against Houston (May 6, 1998). ... Struck out 20 batters in one game (May 6, 1998). ... Struck out 16 batters in one game (August 26, 1998).

Year	Team (League)	W	L	Pct.	ERA	G	GS	CG	ShO	Sv.	IP	H	R	ER	BB	SO
1995—	Fort Myers (Fla. St.)	0	0	. . .	0.00	1	1	0	0	0	3	0	0	0	1	2
—	Williamsport (NYP)	0	0	. . .	10.38	2	2	0	0	0	4 1/3	5	8	5	5	5
1996—	Daytona (Fla. St.)	10	2	•.833	2.91	22	22	0	0	0	114 1/3	72	51	37	70	136
1997—	Orlando (South.)	6	7	.462	4.50	19	19	0	0	0	94	58	49	47	79	106
—	Iowa (Am. Assoc.).............	4	2	.667	4.68	10	10	0	0	0	57 2/3	35	35	30	52	80
1998—	Iowa (Pacific Coast)	1	0	1.000	0.00	1	1	0	0	0	5	1	0	0	2	11
—	Chicago (N.L.)	13	6	.684	3.40	26	26	1	1	0	166 2/3	117	69	63	85	233
Major league totals (1 year)........		13	6	.684	3.40	26	26	1	1	0	166 2/3	117	69	63	85	233

DIVISION SERIES RECORD

Year	Team (League)	W	L	Pct.	ERA	G	GS	CG	ShO	Sv.	IP	H	R	ER	BB	SO
1998—	Chicago (N.L.)	0	1	.000	1.80	1	1	0	0	0	5	3	1	1	4	5

W

WOODALL, BRAD   P   BREWERS

PERSONAL: Born June 25, 1969, in Atlanta. ... 6-0/181. ... Throws left, bats both. ... Full name: David Bradley Woodall.
HIGH SCHOOL: Spring Valley (Columbia, S.C.).
COLLEGE: North Carolina.
TRANSACTIONS/CAREER NOTES: Signed as non-drafted free agent by Atlanta Braves (June 10, 1991). ... On Greenville disabled list (April 8-May 3, 1993). ... On Richmond disabled list (July 8-August 18, 1995). ... Granted free agency (October 15, 1997). ... Signed by Milwaukee Brewers organization (December 19, 1997).
HONORS: Named International League Pitcher of the Year (1994).
MISCELLANEOUS: Scored one run in four appearances as pinch runner and had an RBI single, scored a run and struck out in two games as pinch hitter (1998).

Year Team (League)	W	L	Pct.	ERA	G	GS	CG	ShO	Sv.	IP	H	R	ER	BB	SO
1991— Idaho Falls (Pioneer)..........	4	1	.800	1.37	28	0	0	0	11	39⅓	29	9	6	19	57
— Durham (Carolina)...............	0	0	...	2.45	4	0	0	0	0	7⅓	4	3	2	4	14
1992— Durham (Carolina)...............	1	2	.333	2.13	24	0	0	0	4	42⅓	30	11	10	11	51
— Greenville (Southern)	3	4	.429	3.20	21	1	0	0	1	39⅓	26	15	14	17	45
1993— Durham (Carolina)...............	3	1	.750	3.00	6	5	1	1	0	30	21	10	10	6	27
— Idaho Falls (Pioneer)..........	2	4	.333	3.38	8	7	1	0	0	53⅓	43	24	20	24	38
— Richmond (Int'l).............	5	3	.625	4.21	10	9	0	0	0	57⅔	59	32	27	16	45
1994— Richmond (Int'l).................	•15	6	.714	*2.38	27	27	4	*3	0	185⅔	159	62	49	49	137
— Atlanta (N.L.)......................	0	1	.000	4.50	1	1	0	0	0	6	5	3	3	2	2
1995— Atlanta (N.L.)......................	1	1	.500	6.10	9	0	0	0	0	10⅓	13	10	7	8	5
— Richmond (Int'l).....................	4	4	.500	5.10	13	11	0	0	0	65⅓	70	39	37	17	44
1996— Richmond (Int'l).....................	9	7	.563	3.38	21	21	5	1	0	133⅓	124	59	50	36	74
— Atlanta (N.L.)......................	2	2	.500	7.32	8	3	0	0	0	19⅔	28	19	16	4	20
1997— Richmond (Int'l).....................	8	11	.421	5.51	26	26	1	0	0	148⅔	177	100	91	52	117
1998— Louisville (Int'l)■...............	1	1	.500	3.90	5	5	0	0	0	30	32	19	13	15	27
— Milwaukee (N.L.).............	7	9	.438	4.96	31	20	0	0	0	138	145	81	76	47	85
Major league totals (4 years)......	**10**	**13**	**.435**	**5.28**	**49**	**24**	**0**	**0**	**0**	**174**	**191**	**113**	**102**	**61**	**112**

WOODARD, STEVE — P — BREWERS

PERSONAL: Born May 15, 1975, in Hartselle, Ala. ... 6-4/235. ... Throws right, bats left. ... Full name: Steve Larry Woodard Jr.
HIGH SCHOOL: Hartselle (Ala.).
TRANSACTIONS/CAREER NOTES: Selected by Milwaukee Brewers organization in fifth round of free-agent draft (June 2, 1994).
RECORDS: Shares A.L. record for most strikeouts in first major league game—12 (July 28, 1997).
HONORS: Named Texas League Pitcher of the Year (1997).

Year Team (League)	W	L	Pct.	ERA	G	GS	CG	ShO	Sv.	IP	H	R	ER	BB	SO
1994— Stockton (California)	8	0	1.000	2.40	15	12	2	0	0	82⅔	68	29	22	13	85
1995— Beloit (Midwest)................	7	4	.636	4.54	21	21	0	0	0	115	113	68	58	31	94
1996— Stockton (California)	12	9	.571	4.02	28	•28	0	0	0	*181⅓	201	89	81	33	142
1997— El Paso (Texas)..................	14	3	.824	3.17	19	19	*6	•1	0	136⅓	136	56	48	25	97
— Tucson (PCL)......................	1	0	1.000	0.00	1	1	0	0	0	7	3	0	0	1	6
— Milwaukee (A.L.).............	3	3	.500	5.15	7	7	0	0	0	36⅔	39	25	21	6	32
1998— Milwaukee (N.L.).............	10	12	.455	4.18	34	26	0	0	0	165⅓	170	83	77	33	135
A.L. totals (1 year)................	**3**	**3**	**.500**	**5.15**	**7**	**7**	**0**	**0**	**0**	**36⅔**	**39**	**25**	**21**	**6**	**32**
N.L. totals (1 year).....................	**10**	**12**	**.455**	**4.18**	**34**	**26**	**0**	**0**	**0**	**165⅓**	**170**	**83**	**77**	**33**	**135**
Major league totals (2 years)......	**13**	**15**	**.464**	**4.36**	**41**	**33**	**0**	**0**	**0**	**202⅓**	**209**	**108**	**98**	**39**	**167**

WOOLF, JASON — SS — CARDINALS

PERSONAL: Born June 6, 1977, in Miami. ... 6-1/170. ... Bats both, throws right. ... Full name: Jason D. Woolf.
HIGH SCHOOL: American (Hialeah, Fla.).
TRANSACTIONS/CAREER NOTES: Selected by St. Louis Cardinals organization in second round of free-agent draft (June 1, 1995); choice received as part of compensation for Philadelphia Phillies signing Type A free-agent 1B-OF Gregg Jefferies. ... On disabled list (April 10-22 and April 29-June 21, 1998).

Year Team (League)	Pos.	G	AB	R	H	2B	3B	HR	RBI	Avg.	BB	SO	SB	PO	A	E	Avg.
															BATTING		FIELDING
1995— Johnson City (App.) ...	SS	31	111	16	31	7	1	0	14	.279	8	21	6	49	62	26	.810
1996— Peoria (Midwest)........	SS	108	362	68	93	12	8	1	27	.257	57	87	28	128	295	*39	.916
1997— Prince Will. (Car.).......	SS	70	251	59	62	11	3	6	18	.247	55	75	26	99	207	20	.939
1998— Arkansas (Texas)........	SS	76	294	63	78	22	5	4	16	.265	34	84	28	116	235	20	.946

WORRELL, TIM — P — ATHLETICS

PERSONAL: Born July 5, 1967, in Pasadena, Calif. ... 6-4/215. ... Throws right, bats right. ... Full name: Timothy Howard Worrell. ... Brother of Todd Worrell, pitcher with St. Louis Cardinals (1985-92) and Los Angeles Dodgers (1993-97). ... Name pronounced wor-RELL.
HIGH SCHOOL: Maranatha (Sierra Madre, Calif.).
COLLEGE: Biola (Calif.).
TRANSACTIONS/CAREER NOTES: Selected by San Diego Padres organization in 20th round of free-agent draft (June 5, 1989). ... On disabled list (April 19, 1994-remainder of season). ... On San Diego disabled list (April 24-September 1, 1995); included rehabilitation assignments to Rancho Cucamonga (May 3-17 and August 1-10) and Las Vegas (May 17-June 1 and August 10-30). ... Traded by Padres with OF Trey Beamon to Detroit Tigers for P Dan Miceli, P Donne Wall and 3B Ryan Balfe (November 19, 1997). ... Traded by Tigers with OF David Roberts to Cleveland Indians for OF Geronimo Berroa (June 24, 1998). ... Traded by Indians to Oakland Athletics for a player to be named later (July 12, 1998); Indians acquired SS Adam Robinson to complete deal (July 27, 1998).
STATISTICAL NOTES: Pitched 2-0 no-hit victory for Las Vegas against Phoenix (September 5, 1992).

Year Team (League)	W	L	Pct.	ERA	G	GS	CG	ShO	Sv.	IP	H	R	ER	BB	SO
1990— Charleston, S.C. (S. Atl.)	5	8	.385	4.64	20	19	3	0	0	110⅔	120	65	57	28	68
1991— Waterloo (Midw.)...........	8	4	.667	3.34	14	14	3	2	0	86⅓	70	36	32	33	83
— High Desert (Calif.)............	5	2	.714	4.24	11	11	2	0	0	63⅔	65	32	30	33	70
1992— Wichita (Texas)	8	6	.571	2.86	19	19	1	1	0	125⅔	115	46	40	32	109
— Las Vegas (PCL)	4	2	.667	4.26	10	10	1	1	0	63⅓	61	32	30	19	32
1993— Las Vegas (PCL)	5	6	.455	5.48	15	14	2	0	0	87	102	61	53	26	89
— San Diego (N.L.)	2	7	.222	4.92	21	16	0	0	0	100⅔	104	63	55	43	52
1994— San Diego (N.L.)	0	1	.000	3.68	3	3	0	0	0	14⅔	9	7	6	5	14
1995— Rancho Cuca. (Cal.)	0	2	.000	5.16	9	3	0	0	1	22⅔	25	17	13	6	17
— Las Vegas (PCL)	0	2	.000	6.00	10	3	0	0	0	24	27	21	16	17	18
— San Diego (N.L.)	1	0	1.000	4.73	9	0	0	0	0	13⅓	16	7	7	6	13

W

Year Team (League)	W	L	Pct.	ERA	G	GS	CG	ShO	Sv.	IP	H	R	ER	BB	SO
1996— San Diego (N.L.)	9	7	.563	3.05	50	11	0	0	1	121	109	45	41	39	99
1997— San Diego (N.L.)	4	8	.333	5.16	60	10	0	0	3	106 1/3	116	67	61	50	81
1998— Detroit (A.L.)■	2	6	.250	5.98	15	9	0	0	0	61 2/3	66	42	41	19	47
— Cleveland (A.L.)■	0	0	...	5.06	3	0	0	0	0	5 1/3	6	3	3	2	2
— Oakland (A.L.)■	0	1	.000	4.00	25	0	0	0	0	36	34	17	16	8	33
A.L. totals (1 year)	2	7	.222	5.24	43	9	0	0	0	103	106	62	60	29	82
N.L. totals (5 years)	16	23	.410	4.30	143	40	0	0	4	356	354	189	170	143	259
Major league totals (6 years)	18	30	.375	4.51	186	49	0	0	4	459	460	251	230	172	341

DIVISION SERIES RECORD

Year Team (League)	W	L	Pct.	ERA	G	GS	CG	ShO	Sv.	IP	H	R	ER	BB	SO
1996— San Diego (N.L.)	0	0	...	2.45	2	0	0	0	0	3 2/3	4	1	1	1	2

WRIGHT, JAMEY — P — ROCKIES

PERSONAL: Born December 24, 1974, in Oklahoma City. ... 6-5/221. ... Throws right, bats right. ... Full name: Jamey Alan Wright.
HIGH SCHOOL: Westmoore (Oklahoma City).
TRANSACTIONS/CAREER NOTES: Selected by Colorado Rockies organization in first round (28th pick overall) of free-agent draft (June 3, 1993). ... On Colorado disabled list (May 15-June 8, 1997); included rehabilitation assignment to Salem (June 1-8).

Year Team (League)	W	L	Pct.	ERA	G	GS	CG	ShO	Sv.	IP	H	R	ER	BB	SO
1993— Ariz. Rockies (Ariz.)	1	3	.250	4.00	8	8	8	0	0	36	35	19	16	9	26
1994— Asheville (S. Atl.)	7	•14	.333	5.97	28	27	2	0	0	143 1/3	*188	107	*95	59	103
1995— Salem (Carolina)	10	8	.556	2.47	26	26	2	1	0	*171	160	74	47	72	95
— New Haven (East.)	0	1	.000	9.00	1	1	1	0	0	3	6	6	3	3	0
1996— New Haven (East.)	5	1	.833	0.81	7	7	1	1	0	44 2/3	27	7	4	12	54
— Colo. Springs (PCL)	4	2	.667	2.72	9	9	0	0	0	59 2/3	53	20	18	22	40
— Colorado (N.L.)	4	4	.500	4.93	16	15	0	0	0	91 1/3	105	60	50	41	45
1997— Colorado (N.L.)	8	12	.400	6.25	26	26	1	0	0	149 2/3	198	113	104	71	59
— Salem (Carolina)	0	1	.000	9.00	1	1	0	0	0	1	1	1	1	1	1
— Colo. Springs (PCL)	1	0	1.000	1.64	2	2	0	0	0	11	9	3	2	5	11
1998— Colorado (N.L.)	9	14	.391	5.67	34	34	1	0	0	206 1/3	235	143	130	95	86
Major league totals (3 years)	21	30	.412	5.71	76	75	2	0	0	447 1/3	538	316	284	207	190

WRIGHT, JARET — P — INDIANS

PERSONAL: Born December 29, 1975, in Anaheim, Calif. ... 6-2/230. ... Throws right, bats right. ... Full name: Jaret Samuel Wright. ... Son of Clyde Wright, pitcher with California Angels (1966-73), Milwaukee Brewers (1974) and Texas Rangers (1975).
HIGH SCHOOL: Katella (Anaheim, Calif.).
TRANSACTIONS/CAREER NOTES: Selected by Cleveland Indians organization in first round (10th pick overall) of free-agent draft (June 2, 1994). ... On disabled list (June 19-September 23, 1996).

Year Team (League)	W	L	Pct.	ERA	G	GS	CG	ShO	Sv.	IP	H	R	ER	BB	SO
1994— Burlington (Appalachian)	0	1	.000	5.40	4	4	0	0	0	13 1/3	13	10	8	9	16
1995— Columbus (S. Atl.)	5	6	.455	3.00	24	24	0	0	0	129	93	55	43	79	113
1996— Kinston (Carolina)	7	4	.636	2.50	19	19	0	0	0	101	65	32	28	55	109
1997— Akron (Eastern)	3	3	.500	3.67	8	8	1	0	0	54	43	26	22	23	59
— Buffalo (A.A.)	4	1	.800	1.80	7	7	1	1	0	45	30	16	9	19	47
— Cleveland (A.L.)	8	3	.727	4.38	16	16	0	0	0	90 1/3	81	45	44	35	63
1998— Cleveland (A.L.)	12	10	.545	4.72	32	32	1	1	0	192 2/3	207	109	101	87	140
Major league totals (2 years)	20	13	.606	4.61	48	48	1	1	0	283	288	154	145	122	203

DIVISION SERIES RECORD

Year Team (League)	W	L	Pct.	ERA	G	GS	CG	ShO	Sv.	IP	H	R	ER	BB	SO
1997— Cleveland (A.L.)	2	0	1.000	3.97	2	2	0	0	0	11 1/3	11	6	5	7	10
1998— Cleveland (A.L.)	0	1	.000	12.46	1	1	0	0	0	4 1/3	7	6	6	2	6
Div. series totals (2 years)	2	1	.667	6.32	3	3	0	0	0	15 2/3	18	12	11	9	16

CHAMPIONSHIP SERIES RECORD

RECORDS: Shares single-game record for most home runs allowed—3 (October 12, 1997).

Year Team (League)	W	L	Pct.	ERA	G	GS	CG	ShO	Sv.	IP	H	R	ER	BB	SO
1997— Cleveland (A.L.)	0	0	...	15.00	1	1	0	0	0	3	6	5	5	2	3
1998— Cleveland (A.L.)	0	1	.000	8.10	2	1	0	0	0	6 2/3	7	6	6	8	4
Champ. series totals (2 years)	0	1	.000	10.24	3	2	0	0	0	9 2/3	13	11	11	10	7

WORLD SERIES RECORD

Year Team (League)	W	L	Pct.	ERA	G	GS	CG	ShO	Sv.	IP	H	R	ER	BB	SO
1997— Cleveland (A.L.)	1	0	1.000	2.92	2	2	0	0	0	12 1/3	7	4	4	10	12

W

WRIGHT, RON — 1B — PIRATES

PERSONAL: Born January 21, 1976, in Delta, Utah. ... 6-1/230. ... Bats right, throws right. ... Full name: Ronald Wade Wright.
HIGH SCHOOL: Kamiakin (Kennewick, Wash.).
TRANSACTIONS/CAREER NOTES: Selected by Atlanta Braves organization in seventh round of free-agent draft (June 2, 1994). ... Traded by Braves with OF Corey Pointer and a player to be named later to Pittsburgh Pirates for P Denny Neagle (August 28, 1996); Pirates acquired P Jason Schmidt to complete deal (August 30, 1996). ... On Calgary disabled list (July 24-September 2, 1997). ... On Nashville disabled list (April 29-September 8, 1998).
STATISTICAL NOTES: Led South Atlantic League first baseman with 1,152 total chances in 1995.

Year	Team (League)	Pos.	G	AB	R	H	2B	3B	HR	RBI	Avg.	BB	SO	SB	PO	A	E	Avg.
1994—	GC Braves (GCL)	1B	45	169	10	29	9	0	1	16	.172	10	21	1	382	31	6	.986
1995—	Macon (S. Atl.)	1B	135	537	93	143	23	1	•32	104	.266	62	118	2	1035	*99	18	.984
1996—	Durham (Carolina)	1B	66	240	47	66	15	2	20	62	.275	37	71	1	494	34	7	.987
—	Greenville (Southern) .	1B	63	232	39	59	11	1	16	52	.254	38	73	1	434	45	6	.988
—	Carolina (Southern)■.	1B	4	14	1	2	0	0	0	0	.143	2	7	0	32	0	2	.941
1997—	Calgary (PCL)	1B	91	336	50	102	31	0	16	63	.304	24	81	0	610	44	3	.995
1998—	Nashville (PCL)	1B	17	56	6	12	3	0	0	9	.214	9	18	0	125	11	2	.986
—	GC Pirates (GCL).......	1B	3	10	4	6	0	0	2	5	.600	2	0	0	11	0	0	1.000

YAN, ESTEBAN   P   DEVIL RAYS

PERSONAL: Born June 22, 1974, in Campina Del Seibo, Dominican Republic. ... 6-4/230. ... Throws right, bats right. ... Full name: Esteban Luis Yan.

HIGH SCHOOL: Escuela Hicayagua (Dominican Republic).

TRANSACTIONS/CAREER NOTES: Signed as non-drafted free agent by Atlanta Braves organization (November 21, 1990). ... Traded by Braves with OF Roberto Kelly and OF Tony Tarasco to Montreal Expos for OF Marquis Grissom (April 6, 1995). ... Contract sold by Expos organization to Baltimore Orioles organization (April 6, 1996). ... Selected by Tampa Bay Devil Rays in first round (18th pick overall) of expansion draft (November 18, 1997).

STATISTICAL NOTES: Led South Atlantic League with six balks in 1994.

Year	Team (League)	W	L	Pct.	ERA	G	GS	CG	ShO	Sv.	IP	H	R	ER	BB	SO
1991—	San Pedro (DSL)	4	1	.800	3.63	18	11	0	0	0	72	61	36	29	26	34
1992—	San Pedro (DSL)	12	3	.800	1.32	16	16	7	4	0	115²/₃	85	37	17	23	86
1993—	Danville (Appalachian)........	4	7	.364	3.03	14	14	0	0	0	71¹/₃	73	46	24	24	50
1994—	Macon (S. Atl.)	11	12	.478	3.27	28	•28	4	•3	0	170²/₃	155	85	62	34	121
1995—	W.P. Beach (FSL)■............	6	8	.429	3.07	24	21	1	0	1	137²/₃	139	63	47	33	89
1996—	Bowie (Eastern)■..............	0	2	.000	5.63	9	1	0	0	0	16	18	12	10	8	15
—	Rochester (Int'l)	5	4	.556	4.27	22	10	0	0	1	71²/₃	75	37	34	18	61
—	Baltimore (A.L.)	0	0	. . .	5.79	4	0	0	0	0	9¹/₃	13	7	6	3	7
1997—	Rochester (Int'l)	11	5	.688	3.10	34	12	0	0	2	119	107	54	41	37	131
—	Baltimore (A.L.)	0	1	.000	15.83	3	2	0	0	0	9²/₃	20	18	17	7	4
1998—	Tampa Bay (A.L.)■..........	5	4	.556	3.86	64	0	0	0	1	88²/₃	78	41	38	41	77
Major league totals (3 years)......		5	5	.500	5.10	71	2	0	0	1	107²/₃	111	66	61	51	88

YOSHII, MASATO   P   METS

PERSONAL: Born April 20, 1965, in Osaka, Japan. ... 6-2/210. ... Throws right, bats right.

HIGH SCHOOL: Minoshima (Japan).

TRANSACTIONS/CAREER NOTES: Played for Kintetsu Buffaloes of Japan Pacific League (1985-94). ... Played for Yakult Swallows of Japan Central League (1995-97). ... Signed by New York Mets (January 13, 1998).

Year	Team (League)	W	L	Pct.	ERA	G	GS	CG	ShO	Sv.	IP	H	R	ER	BB	SO
1985—	Kintetsu (Jap. Pac.)............	0	1	.000	21.00	2	. . .	. . .	. . .	0	3	. . .	. . .	7	3	1
1986—	Kintetsu (Jap. Pac.)............	0	0	. . .	23.14	2	. . .	. . .	. . .	0	2¹/₃	. . .	. . .	6	2	2
1987—	Kintetsu (Jap. Pac.)............	2	1	.667	4.75	13	. . .	. . .	. . .	0	36	. . .	. . .	19	12	23
1988—	Kintetsu (Jap. Pac.)............	10	2	.833	2.69	50	. . .	. . .	. . .	24	80¹/₃	. . .	. . .	24	44	44
1989—	Kintetsu (Jap. Pac.)............	5	5	.500	2.99	47	. . .	. . .	. . .	20	84¹/₃	. . .	. . .	28	37	44
1990—	Kintetsu (Jap. Pac.)............	8	9	.471	3.39	45	. . .	. . .	. . .	15	74¹/₃	. . .	. . .	28	30	55
1991—	Kintetsu (Jap. Pac.)............	2	1	.667	3.42	21	. . .	. . .	. . .	2	26¹/₃	. . .	. . .	10	6	13
1992—	Kintetsu (Jap. Pac.)............	1	0	1.000	2.31	9	. . .	. . .	. . .	0	11²/₃	. . .	. . .	3	2	4
1993—	Kintetsu (Jap. Pac.)............	5	5	.500	2.67	22	. . .	. . .	. . .	0	104²/₃	. . .	. . .	31	25	66
1994—	Kintetsu (Jap. Pac.)............	7	7	.500	5.47	21	. . .	. . .	. . .	0	97	. . .	. . .	59	37	42
1995—	Yakult (Jp. Cen.)■............	10	7	.588	3.12	25	. . .	. . .	. . .	0	147¹/₃	. . .	. . .	51	39	91
1996—	Yakult (Jp. Cen.)...............	10	7	.588	3.24	25	9	. . .	. . .	0	180¹/₃	. . .	. . .	65	47	145
1997—	Yakult (Jp. Cen.)...............	13	6	.684	2.99	28	26	6	2	0	174¹/₃	149	61	58	48	104
1998—	New York (N.L.)■	6	8	.429	3.93	29	29	1	0	0	171²/₃	166	79	75	53	117
Major league totals (1 year).......		6	8	.429	3.93	29	29	1	0	0	171²/₃	166	79	75	53	117

YOUNG, DMITRI   OF   REDS

PERSONAL: Born October 11, 1973, in Vicksburg, Miss. ... 6-2/235. ... Bats both, throws right. ... Full name: Dmitri Dell Young. ... Name pronounced duh-MEE-tree.

HIGH SCHOOL: Rio Mesa (Oxnard, Calif.).

TRANSACTIONS/CAREER NOTES: Selected by St. Louis Cardinals organization in first round (fourth pick overall) of free-agent draft (June 3, 1991). ... On disabled list (June 2-9, 1994). ... On Arkansas suspended list (August 1-11 and August 17-27, 1995). ... On Louisville disabled list (July 14-24, 1996). ... On St. Louis disabled list (May 11-29, 1997); included rehabilitation assignment to Louisville (May 25-29). ... Traded by Cardinals to Cincinnati Reds for P Jeff Brantley (November 10, 1997). ... Selected by Tampa Bay Devil Rays in first round (16th pick overall) of expansion draft (November 18, 1997). ... Traded by Devil Rays to Reds (November 18, 1997), completing deal in which Reds traded OF Mike Kelly to Devil Rays for a player to be named later (November 11, 1997).

STATISTICAL NOTES: Led Texas League with 14 intentional bases on balls received in 1994. ... Led Texas League first basemen with 15 errors in 1994. ... Tied for American Association lead with eight bases on balls received in 1996. ... Led American Association first basemen with 1,182 total chances and 102 double plays in 1996.

Year	Team (League)	Pos.	G	AB	R	H	2B	3B	HR	RBI	Avg.	BB	SO	SB	PO	A	E	Avg.
1991—	Johnson City (App.) ...	3B	37	129	22	33	10	0	2	22	.256	21	28	2	19	49	5	.932
1992—	Springfield (Midw.)	3B	135	493	74	153	*36	6	14	72	.310	51	94	14	66	239	42	.879
1993—	St. Peters. (FSL)........	3B-1B	69	270	31	85	13	3	5	43	.315	24	28	3	260	90	10	.972
—	Arkansas (Texas)........	1B-3B	45	166	13	41	11	2	3	21	.247	9	29	4	348	29	7	.982

Year Team (League)	Pos.	G	AB	R	H	2B	3B	HR	RBI	Avg.	BB	SO	SB	PO	A	E	Avg.
1994— Arkansas (Texas)........	OF-1B	125	453	53	123	33	2	8	54	.272	36	60	0	485	44	†16	.971
1995— Arkansas (Texas)........	OF	97	367	54	107	18	6	10	62	.292	30	46	2	116	5	9	.931
— Louisville (A.A.)..........	OF	2	7	3	2	0	0	0	0	.286	1	1	0	3	0	1	.750
1996— Louisville (A.A.)..........	1B	122	459	*90	153	31	8	15	64	*.333	34	67	16	*1091	83	8	.993
— St. Louis (N.L.)...........	1B	16	29	3	7	0	0	0	2	.241	4	5	0	39	1	1	.976
1997— St. Louis (N.L.)..........	1B-OF-DH	110	333	38	86	14	3	5	34	.258	38	63	6	641	47	13	.981
— Louisville (A.A.)..........	1B	24	84	10	23	7	0	4	14	.274	13	15	1	64	2	1	.985
1998— Cincinnati (N.L.)■......	OF-1B	144	536	81	166	48	1	14	83	.310	47	94	2	458	25	12	.976
Major league totals (3 years)		270	898	122	259	62	4	19	119	.288	89	162	8	1138	73	26	.979

CHAMPIONSHIP SERIES RECORD

Year Team (League)	Pos.	G	AB	R	H	2B	3B	HR	RBI	Avg.	BB	SO	SB	PO	A	E	Avg.
1996— St. Louis (N.L.)...........	PH-1B	4	7	1	2	0	1	0	2	.286	0	2	0	11	1	0	1.000

YOUNG, ERIC 2B DODGERS

PERSONAL: Born May 18, 1967, in New Brunswick, N.J. ... 5-9/170. ... Bats right, throws right. ... Full name: Eric Orlando Young.
HIGH SCHOOL: New Brunswick (N.J.).
COLLEGE: Rutgers.
TRANSACTIONS/CAREER NOTES: Selected by Los Angeles Dodgers organization in 43rd round of free-agent draft (June 5, 1989). ... Selected by Colorado Rockies in first round (11th pick overall) of expansion draft (November 17, 1992). ... On Colorado disabled list (March 22-April 22, 1996); included rehabilitation assignments to New Haven (April 5-10), Salem (April 10-13) and Colorado Springs (April 13-22). ... Traded by Rockies to Dodgers for P Pedro Astacio (August 19, 1997). ... On disabled list (July 13-31, 1998).
RECORDS: Shares major league record for most stolen bases in one inning—3 (June 30, 1996, third inning).
HONORS: Named second baseman on The Sporting News N.L. All-Star team (1996). ... Named second baseman on The Sporting News N.L. Silver Slugger team (1996).
STATISTICAL NOTES: Led Florida State League second basemen with 24 errors in 1990. ... Led Texas League in caught stealing with 26 in 1991. ... Led Texas League second basemen with .974 fielding percentage in 1991. ... Tied for N.L. lead in errors by second baseman with 11 in 1995. ... Hit three home runs in one game (May 10, 1996). ... Led N.L. in caught stealing with 19 in 1996. ... Led N.L. second basemen with 109 double plays in 1996 and 111 in 1997.
MISCELLANEOUS: Holds Colorado Rockies all-time record for most triples (28) and most stolen bases (180).

Year Team (League)	Pos.	G	AB	R	H	2B	3B	HR	RBI	Avg.	BB	SO	SB	PO	A	E	Avg.
1989— GC Dodgers (GCL)	2B	56	197	53	65	11	5	2	22	.330	33	16	*41	104	128	*15	.939
1990— Vero Beach (FSL)......	2B-OF	127	460	*101	132	23	7	2	50	.287	69	35	*76	156	218	†25	.937
1991— San Antonio (Tex.).....	2B-OF	127	461	82	129	17	4	3	35	.280	67	36	*70	206	282	13	†.974
— Albuquerque (PCL)......	2B	1	5	0	2	0	0	0	0	.400	0	0	0	1	2	0	1.000
1992— Albuquerque (PCL).....	2B	94	350	61	118	16	5	3	49	.337	33	18	28	210	287	*20	.961
— Los Angeles (N.L.)	2B	49	132	9	34	1	0	1	11	.258	8	9	6	85	114	9	.957
1993— Colorado (N.L.)■	2B-OF	144	490	82	132	16	8	3	42	.269	63	41	42	254	230	18	.964
1994— Colorado (N.L.)	OF-2B	90	228	37	62	13	1	7	30	.272	38	17	18	97	4	2	.981
1995— Colorado (N.L.)	2B-OF	120	366	68	116	21	•9	6	36	.317	49	29	35	180	230	11	.974
1996— New Haven (East.)......	2B	3	15	0	1	0	0	0	0	.067	0	3	0	9	5	0	1.000
— Salem (Carolina)	2B	3	10	2	3	3	0	0	0	.300	3	1	2	8	6	2	.875
— Colo. Springs (PCL)	2B	7	23	4	6	1	1	0	3	.261	5	1	0	15	18	3	.917
— Colorado (N.L.)	2B	141	568	113	184	23	4	8	74	.324	47	31	*53	340	431	12	.985
1997— Colorado (N.L.)	2B	118	468	78	132	29	6	6	45	.282	57	37	32	258	414	15	.978
— Los Angeles (N.L.)■■..	2B	37	154	28	42	4	2	2	16	.273	14	17	13	60	79	3	.979
1998— Los Angeles (N.L.)■■..	2B-DH	117	452	78	129	24	1	8	43	.285	45	32	42	225	304	13	.976
Major league totals (7 years)		816	2858	493	831	131	31	41	297	.291	321	213	241	1499	1806	83	.976

DIVISION SERIES RECORD

Year Team (League)	Pos.	G	AB	R	H	2B	3B	HR	RBI	Avg.	BB	SO	SB	PO	A	E	Avg.
1995— Colorado (N.L.)	2B	4	16	3	7	1	0	1	2	.438	2	2	1	8	13	3	.875

ALL-STAR GAME RECORD

Year League	Pos.	AB	R	H	2B	3B	HR	RBI	Avg.	BB	SO	SB	PO	A	E	Avg.
1996— National	PR-2B	1	0	0	0	0	0	0	.000	0	0	0	2	1	0	1.000

YOUNG, ERNIE OF DIAMONDBACKS

PERSONAL: Born July 8, 1969, in Chicago. ... 6-1/234. ... Bats right, throws right. ... Full name: Ernest Wesley Young.
HIGH SCHOOL: Mendel Catholic (Chicago).
COLLEGE: Lewis University (Ill.).
TRANSACTIONS/CAREER NOTES: Selected by Oakland Athletics organization in 10th round of free-agent draft (June 4, 1990). ... On disabled list (July 11, 1992-remainder of season). ... Traded by A's to Kansas City Royals for cash (March 17, 1998). ... On Kansas City disabled list (May 22-June 15, 1998); included rehabilitation assignment to Omaha (June 5-15). ... Granted free agency (October 15, 1998). ... Signed by Arizona Diamondbacks organization (December 17, 1998).
STATISTICAL NOTES: Led California League with .635 slugging percentage in 1993.

Year Team (League)	Pos.	G	AB	R	H	2B	3B	HR	RBI	Avg.	BB	SO	SB	PO	A	E	Avg.
1990— S. Oregon (N'west).....	OF	50	168	34	47	6	2	6	23	.280	29	53	4	62	5	2	.971
1991— Madison (Midwest)....	OF	114	362	75	92	19	2	15	71	.254	58	115	20	204	9	7	.968
1992— Modesto (California) ..	OF	74	253	55	63	12	4	11	33	.249	47	74	11	126	11	6	.958

Y

Year Team (League)	Pos.	G	AB	R	H	2B	3B	HR	RBI	Avg.	BB	SO	SB	PO	A	E	Avg.
1993— Modesto (California) ..	OF	85	301	83	92	18	6	23	71	.306	72	92	23	178	8	3	.984
—Huntsville (Sou.)	OF	45	120	26	25	5	0	5	15	.208	24	36	8	97	8	4	.963
1994— Huntsville (Sou.)	OF	72	257	45	89	19	4	14	55	.346	37	45	5	98	13	2	.982
—Oakland (A.L.)	OF-DH	11	30	2	2	1	0	0	3	.067	1	8	0	22	1	1	.958
—Tacoma (PCL)	OF	29	102	19	29	4	0	6	16	.284	13	27	0	53	2	2	.965
1995— Edmonton (PCL)	OF	95	347	70	96	21	4	15	72	.277	49	73	2	194	7	6	.971
—Oakland (A.L.)	OF	26	50	9	10	3	0	2	5	.200	8	12	0	35	0	2	.946
1996— Oakland (A.L.)	OF	141	462	72	112	19	4	19	64	.242	52	118	7	353	8	1	.997
1997— Oakland (A.L.)	OF	71	175	22	39	7	0	5	15	.223	19	57	1	135	4	4	.972
—Edmonton (PCL)	OF	54	195	39	63	10	0	9	45	.323	37	46	5	100	5	1	.991
1998— Omaha (PCL)■	OF	79	297	58	97	13	1	22	55	.327	29	68	6	174	10	2	.989
—Kansas City (A.L.)	OF	25	53	2	10	3	0	1	3	.189	2	9	2	43	2	0	1.000
Major league totals (5 years)		274	770	107	173	33	4	27	90	.225	82	204	10	588	15	8	.987

YOUNG, KEVIN 1B PIRATES

PERSONAL: Born June 16, 1969, in Alpena, Mich. ... 6-3/225. ... Bats right, throws right. ... Full name: Kevin Stacey Young.
HIGH SCHOOL: Washington (Kansas City, Kan.).
JUNIOR COLLEGE: Kansas City Kansas Community College.
COLLEGE: Southern Mississippi.
TRANSACTIONS/CAREER NOTES: Selected by Pittsburgh Pirates organization in seventh round of free-agent draft (June 4, 1990). ... On Pittsburgh disabled list (July 24-August 8, 1995). ... Released by Pirates (March 26, 1996). ... Signed by Kansas City Royals organization (April 1, 1996). ... Released by Royals (December 5, 1996). ... Signed by Pirates (March 31, 1997).
STATISTICAL NOTES: Tied for Southern League lead in errors by third baseman with 26 in 1991. ... Tied for American Association lead in being hit by pitch with 11 in 1992. ... Led American Association third basemen with 300 assists, 32 errors, 436 total chances and 41 double plays in 1992. ... Led N.L. first basemen with .998 fielding percentage in 1993. ... Career major league grand slams: 1.

Year Team (League)	Pos.	G	AB	R	H	2B	3B	HR	RBI	Avg.	BB	SO	SB	PO	A	E	Avg.
1990— Welland (NYP)...........	SS	72	238	46	58	16	2	5	30	.244	31	36	10	*79	118	26	.883
1991— Salem (Carolina)	3B	56	201	38	63	12	4	6	28	.313	20	34	3	54	93	12	.925
—Carolina (Southern)....	3B-1B	75	263	36	90	19	6	3	33	.342	15	38	9	157	116	‡28	.907
—Buffalo (A.A.).............	3B-1B	4	9	1	2	1	0	0	2	.222	0	0	1	6	6	2	.857
1992— Buffalo (A.A.).............	3B-1B	137	490	*91	154	29	6	8	65	.314	67	67	18	129	†313	†32	.932
—Pittsburgh (N.L.)	3B-1B	10	7	2	4	0	0	0	4	.571	2	0	1	3	1	1	.800
1993— Pittsburgh (N.L.)	1B-3B	141	449	38	106	24	3	6	47	.236	36	82	2	1122	112	3	†.998
1994— Pittsburgh (N.L.)	1B-3B-OF	59	122	15	25	7	2	1	11	.205	8	34	0	179	45	3	.987
—Buffalo (A.A.).............	3B-1B	60	228	26	63	14	5	5	27	.276	15	45	6	59	162	4	.982
1995— Calgary (PCL)	3B-1B	45	163	24	58	23	1	8	34	.356	15	21	6	144	85	12	.950
—Pittsburgh (N.L.)	3B-1B	56	181	13	42	9	0	6	22	.232	8	53	1	58	110	12	.933
1996— Omaha (A.A.)■	3B-1B	50	186	29	57	11	1	13	46	.306	12	41	3	280	45	5	.985
—Kansas City (A.L.)	1-O-3-DH	55	132	20	32	6	0	8	23	.242	11	32	3	199	19	1	.995
1997— Pittsburgh (N.L.)■......	1B-3B-OF	97	333	59	100	18	3	18	74	.300	16	89	11	644	66	5	.993
1998— Pittsburgh (N.L.)	1B	159	592	88	160	40	2	27	108	.270	44	127	15	*1334	80	8	.994
American League totals (1 year)		55	132	20	32	6	0	8	23	.242	11	32	3	199	19	1	.995
National League totals (6 years)		522	1684	215	437	98	10	58	266	.260	114	385	30	3340	414	32	.992
Major league totals (7 years)		577	1816	235	469	104	10	66	289	.258	125	417	33	3539	433	33	.992

YOUNG, TIM P

PERSONAL: Born October 15, 1973, in Gulfport, Miss. ... 5-10/170. ... Throws left, bats left. ... Full name: Timothy R. Young.
HIGH SCHOOL: Liberty County (Bristol, Fla.).
JUNIOR COLLEGE: Chipola Junior College (Fla.).
COLLEGE: Alabama.
TRANSACTIONS/CAREER NOTES: Selected by Montreal Expos organization in 19th round of free-agent draft (June 4, 1996). ... Granted free agency (December 21, 1998).

Year Team (League)	W	L	Pct.	ERA	G	GS	CG	ShO	Sv.	IP	H	R	ER	BB	SO
1996— Vermont (NYP)..................	1	0	1.000	0.31	27	0	0	0	18	29 1/3	14	1	1	4	46
1997— Cape Fear (South Atlantic) .	1	1	.500	1.50	45	0	0	0	18	54	33	12	9	15	66
—W.P. Beach (FSL)...........	0	0	. . .	0.57	11	0	0	0	5	15 2/3	8	1	1	4	13
—Harrisburg (Eastern)	0	0	. . .	0.00	1	0	0	0	0	2	1	0	0	0	3
1998— Harrisburg (Eastern)	3	3	.500	3.79	26	0	0	0	3	35 2/3	28	17	15	10	52
—Ottawa (Int'l)	1	1	.500	2.03	20	0	0	0	2	26 2/3	26	14	6	12	34
—Montreal (N.L.)..................	0	0	. . .	6.00	10	0	0	0	0	6	6	4	4	4	7
Major league totals (1 year)........	0	0	. . .	6.00	10	0	0	0	0	6	6	4	4	4	7

ZAUN, GREGG C RANGERS

PERSONAL: Born April 14, 1971, in Glendale, Calif. ... 5-10/180. ... Bats both, throws right. ... Full name: Gregory Owen Zaun. ... Nephew of Rick Dempsey, manager, Norfolk Tides and catcher with six major league teams (1969-92).
HIGH SCHOOL: St. Francis (La Canada, Calif.).
TRANSACTIONS/CAREER NOTES: Selected by Baltimore Orioles organization in 17th round of free-agent draft (June 5, 1989). ... On Bowie disabled list (June 17-July 15, 1993). ... Traded by Orioles to Florida Marlins (August 23, 1996), completing deal in which Marlins traded P Terry Mathews to Orioles for a player to be named later (August 21, 1996). ... Traded by Marlins to Texas Rangers for a player to be named later or cash (November 23, 1998).

STATISTICAL NOTES: Led Appalachian League catchers with 460 putouts and 501 total chances in 1990. ... Led Midwest League catchers with 796 total chances in 1991. ... Led Carolina League catchers with 746 putouts, 91 assists, 18 errors, 855 total chances and 10 double plays in 1992. ... Led International League catchers with 841 total chances and 11 double plays in 1994. ... Tied for N.L. lead with 12 double plays by catcher in 1998.

								BATTING							FIELDING			
Year	Team (League)	Pos.	G	AB	R	H	2B	3B	HR	RBI	Avg.	BB	SO	SB	PO	A	E	Avg.
1990—	Wausau (Midwest)	C	37	100	3	13	0	1	1	7	.130	7	17	0	270	26	3	.990
	— Bluefield (Appal.)......	C-3-S-P	61	184	29	55	5	2	2	21	.299	23	15	5	†462	34	10	.980
1991—	Kane County (Midw.)..	C	113	409	67	112	17	5	4	51	.274	50	41	4	*697	83	16	.980
1992—	Frederick (Carolina)....	C-2B	108	383	54	96	18	6	6	52	.251	42	45	3	†746	†91	†18	.979
1993—	Bowie (Eastern)	C-2-3-P	79	258	25	79	10	0	3	38	.306	27	26	4	423	51	10	.979
	— Rochester (Int'l)	C	21	78	10	20	4	2	1	11	.256	6	11	0	141	18	4	.975
1994—	Rochester (Int'l)	C	123	388	61	92	16	4	7	43	.237	56	72	4	*750	82	9	*.989
1995—	Rochester (Int'l)	C	42	140	26	41	13	1	6	18	.293	14	21	0	243	18	3	.989
	— Baltimore (A.L.).........	C	40	104	18	27	5	0	3	14	.260	16	14	1	216	13	3	.987
1996—	Baltimore (A.L.).........	C	50	108	16	25	8	1	1	13	.231	11	15	0	215	10	3	.987
	— Rochester (Int'l)	C	14	47	11	15	2	0	0	4	.319	11	6	0	52	3	2	.965
	— Florida (N.L.)■..........	C	10	31	4	9	1	0	1	2	.290	3	5	1	60	6	0	1.000
1997—	Florida (N.L.)	C-1B	58	143	21	43	10	2	2	20	.301	26	18	1	329	25	8	.978
1998—	Florida (N.L.)	C-2B	106	298	19	56	12	2	5	29	.188	35	52	5	531	49	8	.986
American League totals (2 years)			90	212	34	52	13	1	4	27	.245	27	29	1	431	23	6	.987
National League totals (3 years)			174	472	44	108	23	4	8	51	.229	64	75	7	920	80	16	.984
Major league totals (4 years)			264	684	78	160	36	5	12	78	.234	91	104	8	1351	103	22	.985

CHAMPIONSHIP SERIES RECORD

								BATTING							FIELDING			
Year	Team (League)	Pos.	G	AB	R	H	2B	3B	HR	RBI	Avg.	BB	SO	SB	PO	A	E	Avg.
1997—	Florida (N.L.)	C	1	0	0	0	0	0	0	0	. . .	0	0	0	2	0	0	1.000

WORLD SERIES RECORD

NOTES: Member of World Series championship team (1997).

								BATTING							FIELDING			
Year	Team (League)	Pos.	G	AB	R	H	2B	3B	HR	RBI	Avg.	BB	SO	SB	PO	A	E	Avg.
1997—	Florida (N.L.)	PH-C-PR	2	2	0	0	0	0	0	0	.000	0	0	0	3	0	0	1.000

RECORD AS PITCHER

Year	Team (League)	W	L	Pct.	ERA	G	GS	CG	ShO	Sv.	IP	H	R	ER	BB	SO
1990—	Bluefield (Appalachian)	0	0	. . .	0.00	1	0	0	0	0	1	1	0	0	1	1
1993—	Bowie (Eastern).................	0	0	. . .	0.00	1	0	0	0	0	2 1/3	1	0	0	0	0

ZEILE, TODD   3B   RANGERS

PERSONAL: Born September 9, 1965, in Van Nuys, Calif. ... 6-1/205. ... Bats right, throws right. ... Full name: Todd Edward Zeile. ... Husband of Julianne McNamara, Olympic gold-medal gymnast (1984). ... Name pronounced ZEEL.

HIGH SCHOOL: Hart (Newhall, Calif.).

COLLEGE: UCLA.

TRANSACTIONS/CAREER NOTES: Selected by Kansas City Royals organization in 30th round of free-agent draft (June 6, 1983); did not sign. ... Selected by St. Louis Cardinals organization in supplemental round ("sandwich pick" between second and third round 55th pick overall) of free-agent draft (June 2, 1986); pick received as compensation for New York Yankees signing Type C free-agent IF Ivan DeJesus. ... On St. Louis disabled list (April 23-May 9, 1995); included rehabilitation assignment to Louisville (May 6-9). ... Traded by Cardinals with cash to Chicago Cubs for P Mike Morgan, 3B/OF Paul Torres and C Francisco Morales (June 16, 1995). ... Granted free agency (December 21, 1995). ... Signed by Philadelphia Phillies (December 22, 1995). ... Traded by Phillies with OF Pete Incaviglia to Baltimore Orioles for two players to be named later (August 29, 1996); Phillies acquired P Calvin Maduro and P Garrett Stephenson to complete deal (September 4, 1996). ... Granted free agency (October 27, 1996). ... Signed by Los Angeles Dodgers (December 8, 1996). ... Traded by Dodgers with C Mike Piazza to Florida Marlins for OF Gary Sheffield, 3B Bobby Bonilla, C Charles Johnson, OF Jim Eisenreich and P Manuel Barrios (May 15, 1998). ... Traded by Marlins to Texas Rangers for 3B Jose Santo and P Dan DeYoung (July 31, 1998).

RECORDS: Holds N.L. single-season record for fewest putouts by third baseman (150 or more games)—83 (1993). ... Shares A.L. single-game record for most errors by first baseman—4 (August 7, 1996).

HONORS: Named Midwest League co-Most Valuable Player (1987).

STATISTICAL NOTES: Led New York-Pennsylvania League with six sacrifice flies in 1986. ... Tied for New York-Pennsylvania League lead in double plays by catcher with seven in 1986. ... Led Texas League catchers with 687 putouts and 761 total chances in 1988. ... Led American Association catchers with .992 fielding percentage and 17 passed balls in 1989. ... Career major league grand slams: 6.

								BATTING							FIELDING			
Year	Team (League)	Pos.	G	AB	R	H	2B	3B	HR	RBI	Avg.	BB	SO	SB	PO	A	E	Avg.
1986—	Erie (N.Y.-Penn).........	C	70	248	40	64	14	1	14	*63	.258	37	52	5	407	*66	8	.983
1987—	Springfield (Midw.)	C-3B	130	487	94	142	24	4	25	*106	.292	70	85	1	867	79	14	.985
1988—	Arkansas (Texas)........	C-OF-1B	129	430	95	117	33	2	19	75	.272	83	64	6	†697	66	10	.987
1989—	Louisville (A.A.).........	C-3B-1B	118	453	71	131	26	3	19	85	.289	45	78	0	583	71	6	†.991
	— St. Louis (N.L.).........	C	28	82	7	21	3	1	1	8	.256	9	14	0	125	10	4	.971
1990—	St. Louis (N.L.)..........	C-3-1-0	144	495	62	121	25	3	15	57	.244	67	77	2	648	106	15	.980
1991—	St. Louis (N.L.)..........	3B	155	565	76	158	36	3	11	81	.280	62	94	17	124	290	*25	.943
1992—	St. Louis (N.L.)..........	3B	126	439	51	113	18	4	7	48	.257	68	70	7	81	235	13	.960
	— Louisville (A.A.).........	3B	21	74	11	23	4	1	5	13	.311	9	13	0	15	41	5	.918
1993—	St. Louis (N.L.)..........	3B	157	571	82	158	36	1	17	103	.277	70	76	5	83	310	33	.923
1994—	St. Louis (N.L.)..........	3B	113	415	62	111	25	1	19	75	.267	52	56	1	66	224	12	.960
1995—	Louisville (A.A.).........	1B	2	8	0	1	0	0	0	0	.125	0	2	0	11	1	1	.923
	— St. Louis (N.L.).........	1B	34	127	16	37	6	0	5	22	.291	18	23	1	310	30	7	.980
	— Chicago (N.L.)■.........	3B-OF-1B	79	299	34	68	16	0	9	30	.227	16	53	0	52	134	12	.939
1996—	Philadelphia (N.L.)■ ..	3B-1B	134	500	61	134	24	0	20	80	.268	67	88	1	295	195	14	.972
	— Baltimore (A.L.)■......	3B	29	117	17	28	8	0	5	19	.239	15	16	0	24	56	3	.964
1997—	Los Angeles (N.L.)■ ..	3B	160	575	89	154	17	0	31	90	.268	85	112	8	105	248	*26	.931

Year Team (League)	Pos.	G	AB	R	H	2B	3B	HR	RBI	Avg.	BB	SO	SB	PO	A	E	Avg.
							BATTING								FIELDING		
1998— Los Angeles (N.L.)	3B-1B	40	158	22	40	6	1	7	27	.253	10	24	1	27	53	6	.930
—Florida (N.L.)■	3B	66	234	37	68	12	1	6	39	.291	31	34	2	43	122	5	.971
—Texas (A.L.)■	3B	52	180	26	47	14	1	6	28	.261	28	32	1	38	91	12	.915
American League totals (2 years)		81	297	43	75	22	1	11	47	.253	43	48	1	62	147	15	.933
National League totals (10 years)		1236	4460	599	1183	224	15	148	660	.265	555	721	45	1959	1957	172	.958
Major league totals (10 years)		1317	4757	642	1258	246	16	159	707	.264	598	769	46	2021	2104	187	.957

DIVISION SERIES RECORD

Year Team (League)	Pos.	G	AB	R	H	2B	3B	HR	RBI	Avg.	BB	SO	SB	PO	A	E	Avg.
							BATTING								FIELDING		
1996— Baltimore (A.L.)	3B	4	19	2	5	1	00	0	0	.263	2	5	0	4	9	2	.867
1998— Texas (A.L.)	3B	3	9	0	3	0	0	0	0	.333	0	2	0	0	4	0	1.000
Division series totals (2 years)		7	28	2	8	1	0	0	0	.286	2	7	0	4	13	2	.895

CHAMPIONSHIP SERIES RECORD

Year Team (League)	Pos.	G	AB	R	H	2B	3B	HR	RBI	Avg.	BB	SO	SB	PO	A	E	Avg.
							BATTING								FIELDING		
1996— Baltimore (A.L.)	3B	5	22	3	8	1 7	0	0	3	.364	5	2	1	3	7	1	.909

ZIMMERMAN, JORDAN   P   MARINERS

PERSONAL: Born April 28, 1975, in Kelowna, B.C. ... 6-0/200. ... Throws left, bats right. ... Full name: Jordan William Zimmerman.
HIGH SCHOOL: Brenham (Texas).
JUNIOR COLLEGE: Blinn College (Texas).
TRANSACTIONS/CAREER NOTES: Selected by Seattle Mariners organization in 32nd round of free-agent draft (June 2, 1994). ... On disabled list (July 7, 1995-remainder of season). ... On disabled list (June 18, 1996-remainder of season). ... On Lancaster disabled list (April 2-August 12, 1998).

Year Team (League)	W	L	Pct.	ERA	G	GS	CG	ShO	Sv.	IP	H	R	ER	BB	SO
1995—							Did not play.								
1996—							Did not play.								
1997— Everett (Northwest)	2	3	.400	4.15	11	9	0	0	0	39	37	27	18	23	54
—Wisconsin (Midwest)	0	1	.000	5.82	3	3	0	0	0	17	18	11	11	10	18
1998— Ariz. Mariners (Ariz.)	0	1	.000	3.00	5	3	0	0	0	12	14	6	4	7	11
—Lancaster (Calif.)	0	1	.000	4.86	3	3	0	0	0	$16^2/_3$	21	9	9	8	8

ZUBER, JON   1B

PERSONAL: Born December 10, 1969, in Encino, Calif. ... 6-0/190. ... Bats left, throws left. ... Full name: Jon Edward Zuber.
HIGH SCHOOL: Campolindo (Moraga, Calif.).
COLLEGE: California.
TRANSACTIONS/CAREER NOTES: Selected by Philadelphia Phillies organization in 12th round of free-agent draft (June 1, 1992). ... Granted free agency (December 21, 1998).
STATISTICAL NOTES: Tied for Florida State League lead with 214 total bases in 1993. ... Led Florida State League first basemen in fielding with .996 in 1993. ... Led Eastern League first basemen with 1,070 putouts and 1,180 total chances in 1994.

Year Team (League)	Pos.	G	AB	R	H	2B	3B	HR	RBI	Avg.	BB	SO	SB	PO	A	E	Avg.
							BATTING								FIELDING		
1992— Batavia (NY-Penn)	1B	22	88	14	30	6	3	1	21	.341	9	11	1	132	16	3	.980
—Spartanburg (SAL)	OF-1B	54	206	24	59	13	1	3	36	.286	33	31	3	54	1	1	.982
1993— Clearwater (FSL)	1B-OF-3B	129	494	70	152	*37	5	5	69	.308	49	47	6	1080	90	6	†.995
1994— Reading (Eastern)	1B-OF	138	498	81	146	29	5	9	70	.293	71	71	2	†1078	99	13	.989
1995— Scran./W.B. (Int'l)	1B	119	418	53	120	19	5	3	50	.287	49	68	1	825	63	4	.996
1996— Scran./W.B. (Int'l)	1B-OF	118	412	62	128	22	5	4	59	.311	58	50	4	522	46	6	.990
—Philadelphia (N.L.)......	1B	30	91	7	23	4	0	1	10	.253	6	11	1	145	11	2	.987
1997— Scran./W.B. (Int'l)	OF-1B	126	435	85	137	37	2	6	64	.315	79	53	3	300	18	1	.997
1998— Scran./W.B. (Int'l)	OF-1B	80	280	47	91	23	4	4	56	.325	45	34	0	328	23	0	1.000
—Philadelphia (N.L.)......	OF-1B	38	45	6	11	3	1	2	6	.244	6	9	0	22	1	0	1.000
Major league totals (2 years)		68	136	13	34	7	1	3	16	.250	12	20	1	167	12	2	.989

ZYWICA, MICHAEL   OF   RANGERS

PERSONAL: Born September 14, 1974, in Palos, Ill. ... 6-4/190. ... Bats right, throws right. ... Full name: Michael R. Zywica.
HIGH SCHOOL: Rich South (Richton Park, Ill.).
COLLEGE: Evansville.
TRANSACTIONS/CAREER NOTES: Selected by Texas Rangers organization in 24th round of free-agent draft (June 4, 1996).
STATISTICAL NOTES: Led Florida State League outfielders with five double plays in 1997.

Year Team (League)	Pos.	G	AB	R	H	2B	3B	HR	RBI	Avg.	BB	SO	SB	PO	A	E	Avg.
							BATTING								FIELDING		
1996— GC Rangers (GCL)......	OF-1B	33	110	18	30	7	1	3	22	.273	14	24	3	115	7	2	.984
—Char., S.C. (SAL)	OF	20	67	5	9	1	1	2	4	.134	7	13	3	33	5	1	.974
1997— Charlotte (Fla. St.)	OF-1B	126	462	75	119	25	5	12	64	.258	50	116	19	244	16	5	.981
1998— Charlotte (Fla. St.)	OF	68	252	67	96	21	3	11	49	.381	34	40	16	100	3	1	.990
—Tulsa (Texas)	OF	58	214	40	60	15	4	5	45	.280	19	56	7	92	5	2	.980

MAJOR LEAGUE MANAGERS

ALOU, FELIPE   EXPOS

PERSONAL: Born May 12, 1935, in Haina, Dominican Republic. ... 6-1/195. ... Batted right, threw right. ... Full name: Felipe Rojas Alou. ... Father of Moises Alou, outfielder, Houston Astros; brother of Jesus Alou, major league outfielder with four teams (1965-75 and 1978-79); brother of Matty Alou, major league outfielder with six teams (1960-74); and uncle of Mel Rojas, pitcher, Los Angeles Dodgers.

COLLEGE: Santo Domingo (Dominican Republic).

TRANSACTIONS/CAREER NOTES: Signed as free agent by New York Giants organization (November 14, 1955). ... Giants franchise moved from New York to San Francisco (1958). ... Traded by Giants with P Billy Hoeft, C Ed Bailey and a player to be named later to Milwaukee Braves for P Bob Hendley, P Bob Shaw and C Del Crandall (December 3, 1963); Braves acquired IF Ernie Bowman to complete deal (January 8, 1964). ... On disabled list (June 24-July 25, 1964). ... Braves franchise moved from Milwaukee to Atlanta (1966). ... Traded by Braves to Oakland Athletics for P Jim Nash (December 3, 1969). ... Traded by A's to New York Yankees for P Rob Gardner and P Ron Klimkowski (April 9, 1971). ... Contract sold by Yankees to Montreal Expos (September 5, 1973). ... Contract sold by Expos to Milwaukee Brewers (December 7, 1973). ... Released by Brewers (April 29, 1974).

HONORS: Named first baseman on THE SPORTING NEWS N.L. All-Star team (1966).

STATISTICAL NOTES: Led N.L. with 355 total bases in 1966. ... Career major league grand slams: 2.

Year	Team (League)	Pos.	G	AB	R	H	2B	3B	HR	RBI	Avg.	BB	SO	SB	PO	A	E	Avg.
1956	Lake Charles (Evan.) ..	OF	5	9	1	2	0	0	0	1	.222	...	...	0	6	1	0	1.000
	Cocoa (Fla. St.)	OF-3B	119	445	111	169	15	6	21	99	*.380	68	40	*48	199	60	23	.918
1957	Minneapolis (A.A.).......	OF	24	57	7	12	2	0	0	3	.211	5	8	1	32	1	1	.971
	Springfield (Eastern) ..	OF-3B	106	359	45	110	14	3	12	71	.306	27	29	18	215	26	9	.964
1958	Phoenix (PCL)...........	OF	55	216	61	69	16	2	13	42	.319	17	24	10	150	3	3	.981
	San Francisco (N.L.) ..	OF	75	182	21	46	9	2	4	16	.253	19	34	4	126	2	2	.985
1959	San Francisco (N.L.) ..	OF	95	247	38	68	13	2	10	33	.275	17	38	5	111	2	3	.974
1960	San Francisco (N.L.) ..	OF	106	322	48	85	17	3	8	44	.264	16	42	10	156	5	7	.958
1961	San Francisco (N.L.) ..	OF	132	415	59	120	19	0	18	52	.289	26	41	11	196	10	2	.990
1962	San Francisco (N.L.) ..	OF	154	561	96	177	30	3	25	98	.316	33	66	10	262	7	8	.971
1963	San Francisco (N.L.) ..	OF	157	565	75	159	31	9	20	82	.281	27	87	11	279	9	4	.986
1964	Milwaukee (N.L.)■.....	OF-1B	121	415	60	105	26	3	9	51	.253	30	41	5	329	12	5	.986
1965	Milwaukee (N.L.).......	0-1-3-S	143	555	80	165	29	2	23	78	.297	31	63	8	626	43	6	.991
1966	Atlanta (N.L.).............	1-0-3-S	154	*666	*122	*218	32	6	31	74	.327	24	51	5	935	64	13	.987
1967	Atlanta (N.L.).............	1B-OF	140	574	76	157	26	3	15	43	.274	32	50	6	864	34	9	.990
1968	Atlanta (N.L.).............	OF	160	*662	72	*210	37	5	11	57	.317	48	56	12	379	8	8	.980
1969	Atlanta (N.L.).............	OF	123	476	54	134	13	1	5	32	.282	23	23	4	260	4	3	.989
1970	Oakland (A.L.)■........	OF-1B	154	575	70	156	25	3	8	55	.271	32	31	10	290	11	7	.977
1971	Oakland (A.L.)............	OF	2	8	0	2	1	0	0	0	.250	0	1	0	7	0	0	1.000
	New York (A.L.)■........	OF-1B	131	461	52	133	20	6	8	69	.289	32	24	5	506	23	4	.992
1972	New York (A.L.)..........	1B-OF	120	324	33	90	18	1	6	37	.278	22	27	1	669	54	7	.990
1973	New York (A.L.)..........	1B-OF	93	280	25	66	12	0	4	27	.236	9	25	0	512	31	7	.987
	Montreal (N.L.)■.........	OF-1B	19	48	4	10	1	0	1	4	.208	2	4	0	30	3	0	1.000
1974	Milwaukee (A.L.)■	OF	3	3	0	0	0	0	0	0	.000	0	2	0	0	0	1	.000
American League totals (5 years)			503	1651	180	447	76	10	26	188	.271	95	110	16	1984	119	26	.988
National League totals (13 years)			1579	5688	805	1654	283	39	180	664	.291	328	596	91	4553	203	70	.985
Major league totals (17 years)			2082	7339	985	2101	359	49	206	852	.286	423	706	107	6537	322	96	.986

CHAMPIONSHIP SERIES RECORD

Year	Team (League)	Pos.	G	AB	R	H	2B	3B	HR	RBI	Avg.	BB	SO	SB	PO	A	E	Avg.
1969	Atlanta (N.L.)..............	PH	1	1	0	0	0	0	0	0	.000	0	0	0	...	...	...	...

WORLD SERIES RECORD

Year	Team (League)	Pos.	G	AB	R	H	2B	3B	HR	RBI	Avg.	BB	SO	SB	PO	A	E	Avg.
1962	San Francisco (N.L.) ..	OF	7	26	2	7	1	1	0	1	.269	1	4	0	8	0	1	.889

ALL-STAR GAME RECORD

Year	League	Pos.	AB	R	H	2B	3B	HR	RBI	Avg.	BB	SO	SB	PO	A	E	Avg.
1962	National	OF	0	0	0	0	0	0	1	...	0	0	0	0	0	0	...
1966	National							Did not play.									
1968	National	OF	0	0	0	0	0	0	0	...	0	0	0	0	0	0	...
All-Star Game totals (2 years)			0	0	0	0	0	0	1	...	0	0	0	0	0	0	...

RECORD AS MANAGER

BACKGROUND: Spring training instructor, Montreal Expos (1976). ... Coach, Expos (1979-80, 1984 and October 8, 1991-May 22, 1992).

HONORS: Named Florida State League Manager of the Year (1990). ... Named N.L. Manager of the Year by THE SPORTING NEWS (1994). ... Named N.L. Manager of the Year by Baseball Writers' Association of America (1994).

		REGULAR SEASON				POSTSEASON							
						Playoff		Champ. Series		World Series		All-Star Game	
Year	Team (League)	W	L	Pct.	Pos.	W	L	W	L	W	L	W	L
1977	West Palm Beach (Florida State)	77	55	.583	1st (S)	1	2	—	—	—	—	—	—
1978	Memphis (Southern)................................	71	73	.493	2nd (W)	—	—	—	—	—	—	—	—
1981	Denver (American Association)................	76	60	.559	2nd (W)	4	0	—	—	—	—	—	—
1982	Wichita (American Association)................	70	67	.511	2nd (W)	—	—	—	—	—	—	—	—
1983	Wichita (American Association)................	65	71	.478	3rd (W)	—	—	—	—	—	—	—	—
1985	Indianapolis (American Association)	61	81	.430	4th (E)	—	—	—	—	—	—	—	—
1986	West Palm Beach (Florida State)	80	55	.593	1st (S)	3	3	—	—	—	—	—	—

| | | REGULAR SEASON | | | | POSTSEASON | | | | | | | |
| | | | | | | Playoff | | Champ. Series | | World Series | | All-Star Game | |
Year — Team (League)	W	L	Pct.	Pos.		W	L	W	L	W	L	W	L
1987— West Palm Beach (Florida State)	75	63	.543	2nd (S)		—	—	—	—	—	—	—	—
1988— West Palm Beach (Florida State)	41	27	.603	2nd (E)		—	—	—	—	—	—	—	—
— (Second half)	30	36	.455	3rd (E)		2	2	—	—	—	—	—	—
1989— West Palm Beach (Florida State)	39	31	.557	T2nd (E)		—	—	—	—	—	—	—	—
— (Second half)	35	33	.515	2nd (E)		—	—	—	—	—	—	—	—
1990— West Palm Beach (Florida State)	49	19	.721	1st (E)		—	—	—	—	—	—	—	—
— (Second half)	43	21	.672	1st (E)		3	3	—	—	—	—	—	—
1991— West Palm Beach (Florida State)	33	31	.516	4th (E)		—	—	—	—	—	—	—	—
— (Second half)	39	28	.582	2nd (E)		6	1	—	—	—	—	—	—
1992— Montreal (N.L.)	70	55	.560	2nd (E)		—	—	—	—	—	—	—	—
1993— Montreal (N.L.)	94	68	.580	2nd (E)		—	—	—	—	—	—	—	—
1994— Montreal (N.L.)	74	40	.649			—	—	—	—	—	—	—	—
1995— Montreal (N.L.)	66	78	.458	5th (E)		—	—	—	—	—	—	1	0
1996— Montreal (N.L.)	88	74	.543	2nd (E)		—	—	—	—	—	—	—	—
1997— Montreal (N.L.)	78	84	.481	4th (E)		—	—	—	—	—	—	—	—
1998— Montreal (N.L.)	65	97	.401	4th (E)		—	—	—	—	—	—	—	—
Major league totals (7 years)	535	496	.519			—	—	—	—	—	—	1	0

NOTES:
1977—Lost to St. Petersburg in semifinals.
1978—Memphis tied one game.
1981—Defeated Omaha in league championship.
1986—Defeated Winter Haven, two games to none, in semifinals; lost to St. Petersburg, three games to one, in league championship.
1988—Defeated Vero Beach, two games to none, in first round; lost to Osceola, two games to none, in semifinals.
1990—Defeated Lakeland, two games to one, in semifinals; lost to Vero Beach, two games to one, in league championship.
1991—Defeated Vero Beach, two games to one, in first round; defeated Lakeland, two games to none, in semifinals; defeated Clearwater, two games to none, in league championship.
1992—Replaced Montreal manager Tom Runnells with club in fourth place and record of 17-20 (May 22).
1994—Montreal was in first place in N.L. East at time of season-ending strike (August 12).

BAKER, DUSTY — GIANTS

PERSONAL: Born June 15, 1949, in Riverside, Calif. ... 6-2/200. ... Batted right, threw right. ... Full name: Johnnie B. Baker Jr.
HIGH SCHOOL: Del Campo (Fair Oaks, Calif.).
COLLEGE: American River College (Calif.).
TRANSACTIONS/CAREER NOTES: Selected by Atlanta Braves organization in 26th round of free-agent draft (June 6, 1967). ... On West Palm Beach restricted list (April 5-June 13, 1968). ... On Atlanta military list (January 24-April 3, 1969 and June 17-July 3, 1972). ... Traded by Braves with 1B/3B Ed Goodson to Los Angeles Dodgers for OF Jimmy Wynn, 2B Lee Lacy, 1B/OF Tom Paciorek and IF Jerry Royster (November 17, 1975). ... Released on waivers by Dodgers (February 10, 1984); San Francisco Giants claim rejected (February 16, 1984). ... Granted free agency (February 21, 1984). ... Signed by Giants (April 1, 1984). ... On restricted list (April 2-11, 1984). ... Traded by Giants to Oakland Athletics for P Ed Puikunas and C Dan Winters (March 24, 1985). ... Granted free agency (November 10, 1986).
RECORDS: Shares major league records for most plate appearances, most at-bats and most times faced pitcher as batsman in one inning—3 (September 20, 1972, second inning); and most stolen bases in one inning—3 (June 27, 1984, third inning).
HONORS: Named outfielder on THE SPORTING NEWS N.L. All-Star team (1980). ... Named outfielder on THE SPORTING NEWS N.L. Silver Slugger team (1980-81). ... Won N.L. Gold Glove as outfielder (1981).
STATISTICAL NOTES: Led N.L. outfielders with 407 total chances in 1973. ... Career major league grand slams: 4.

| | | | | | | BATTING | | | | | | | | | FIELDING | | | |
Year — Team (League)	Pos.	G	AB	R	H	2B	3B	HR	RBI	Avg.	BB	SO	SB	PO	A	E	Avg.
1967— Austin (Texas)	OF	9	39	6	9	1	0	0	1	.231	2	7	0	17	0	1	.944
1968— W.Palm Beach (FSL)	OF	6	21	2	4	0	0	0	2	.190	1	4	0	6	2	0	1.000
— Greenwood (W. Car.)	OF	52	199	45	68	11	3	6	39	.342	23	39	6	82	1	3	.965
— Atlanta (N.L.)	OF	6	5	0	2	0	0	0	0	.400	0	1	0	0	0	0	...
1969— Shreveport (Texas)	OF	73	265	40	68	5	1	9	31	.257	36	41	2	135	10	3	.980
— Richmond (Int'l)	OF-3B	25	89	7	22	4	0	0	8	.247	11	22	3	40	9	4	.925
— Atlanta (N.L.)	OF	3	7	0	0	0	0	0	0	.000	0	3	0	2	0	0	1.000
1970— Richmond (Int'l)	OF	118	461	97	150	29	3	11	51	.325	53	45	10	236	10	7	.972
— Atlanta (N.L.)	OF	13	24	3	7	0	0	0	4	.292	2	4	0	11	1	3	.800
1971— Richmond (Int'l)	OF-3B	80	341	62	106	23	2	11	41	.311	25	37	10	136	13	4	.974
— Atlanta (N.L.)	OF	29	62	2	14	2	0	0	4	.226	1	14	0	29	1	0	1.000
1972— Atlanta (N.L.)	OF	127	446	62	143	27	2	17	76	.321	45	68	4	344	8	4	.989
1973— Atlanta (N.L.)	OF	159	604	101	174	29	4	21	99	.288	67	72	24	*390	10	7	.983
1974— Atlanta (N.L.)	OF	149	574	80	147	35	0	20	69	.256	71	87	18	359	10	7	.981
1975— Atlanta (N.L.)	OF	142	494	63	129	18	2	19	72	.261	67	57	12	287	10	3	.990
1976— Los Angeles (N.L.)■	OF	112	384	36	93	13	0	4	39	.242	31	54	2	254	3	1	.996
1977— Los Angeles (N.L.)	OF	153	533	86	155	26	1	30	86	.291	58	89	2	227	8	3	.987
1978— Los Angeles (N.L.)	OF	149	522	62	137	24	1	11	66	.262	47	66	12	250	13	4	.985
1979— Los Angeles (N.L.)	OF	151	554	86	152	29	1	23	88	.274	56	70	11	289	14	3	.990
1980— Los Angeles (N.L.)	OF	153	579	80	170	26	4	29	97	.294	43	66	12	308	5	3	.991
1981— Los Angeles (N.L.)	OF	103	400	48	128	17	3	9	49	.320	29	43	10	181	8	2	.990
1982— Los Angeles (N.L.)	OF	147	570	80	171	19	1	23	88	.300	56	62	17	226	7	6	.975
1983— Los Angeles (N.L.)	OF	149	531	71	138	25	1	15	73	.260	72	59	7	249	4	5	.981
1984— San Fran. (N.L.)■	OF	100	243	31	71	7	2	3	32	.292	40	27	4	112	1	3	.974
1985— Oakland (A.L.)■	1B-OF-DH	111	343	48	92	15	1	14	52	.268	50	47	2	465	29	5	.990
1986— Oakland (A.L.)	OF-DH-1B	83	242	25	58	8	0	4	19	.240	27	37	0	90	4	0	1.000
American League totals (2 years)		194	585	73	150	23	1	18	71	.256	77	84	2	555	33	5	.992
National League totals (17 years)		1845	6532	891	1831	297	22	224	942	.280	685	842	135	3518	103	54	.985
Major league totals (19 years)		2039	7117	964	1981	320	23	242	1013	.278	762	926	137	4073	136	59	.986

DIVISION SERIES RECORD

Year Team (League)	Pos.	G	AB	R	H	2B	3B	HR	RBI	Avg.	BB	SO	SB	PO	A	E	Avg.
1981— Los Angeles (N.L.)	OF	5	18	2	3	1	0	0	1	.167	2	0	0	12	0	0	1.000

CHAMPIONSHIP SERIES RECORD

RECORDS: Shares single-game record for most grand slams—1 (October 5, 1977). ... Shares single-inning record for most runs batted in—4 (October 5, 1977, fourth inning). ... Shares N.L. single-game record for most hits—4 (October 7, 1978).
NOTES: Named N.L. Championship Series Most Valuable Player (1977).

Year Team (League)	Pos.	G	AB	R	H	2B	3B	HR	RBI	Avg.	BB	SO	SB	PO	A	E	Avg.
1977— Los Angeles (N.L.)	OF	4	14	4	5	1	0	2	8	.357	2	3	0	3	0	0	1.000
1978— Los Angeles (N.L.)	OF	4	15	1	7	2	0	0	1	.467	3	0	0	5	0	0	1.000
1981— Los Angeles (N.L.)	OF	5	19	3	6	1	0	0	3	.316	1	0	0	10	0	1	.909
1983— Los Angeles (N.L.)	OF	4	14	4	5	1	0	1	1	.357	2	0	0	9	0	0	1.000
Championship series totals (4 years)		17	62	12	23	5	0	3	13	.371	8	3	0	27	0	1	.964

WORLD SERIES RECORD

NOTES: Member of World Series championship team (1981).

Year Team (League)	Pos.	G	AB	R	H	2B	3B	HR	RBI	Avg.	BB	SO	SB	PO	A	E	Avg.
1977— Los Angeles (N.L.)	OF	6	24	4	7	0	0	1	5	.292	0	2	0	11	0	1	.917
1978— Los Angeles (N.L.)	OF	6	21	2	5	0	0	1	1	.238	1	3	0	12	0	0	1.000
1981— Los Angeles (N.L.)	OF	6	24	3	4	0	0	0	1	.167	1	6	0	13	0	0	1.000
World Series totals (3 years)		18	69	9	16	0	0	2	7	.232	2	11	0	36	0	1	.973

ALL-STAR GAME RECORD

Year League	Pos.	AB	R	H	2B	3B	HR	RBI	Avg.	BB	SO	SB	PO	A	E	Avg.
1981— National	OF	2	0	1	0	0	0	0	.500	0	0	0	2	0	0	1.000
1982— National	OF	2	0	0	0	0	0	0	.000	0	0	0	0	0	0	...
All-Star Game totals (2 years)		4	0	1	0	0	0	0	.250	0	0	0	2	0	0	1.000

RECORD AS MANAGER

BACKGROUND: Coach, San Francisco Giants (1988-92). ... Manager, Scottsdale Scorpions, Arizona Fall League (1992, record: 20-22, second place/Northern Division).
HONORS: Named N.L. Manager of the Year by Baseball Writers' Association of America (1993). ... Coach, N.L. All-Star team (1994 and 1997). ... Named N.L. Manager of the Year by The Sporting News (1997).

	REGULAR SEASON				POSTSEASON						
						Playoff		Champ. Series		World Series		All-Star Game
Year Team (League)	W	L	Pct.	Pos.	W	L	W	L	W	L	W L
1993— San Francisco (N.L.)	103	59	.636	2nd (W)	—	—	—	—	—	—	— —
1994— San Francisco (N.L.)	55	60	.478		—	—	—	—	—	—	— —
1995— San Francisco (N.L.)	67	77	.465	4th (W)	—	—	—	—	—	—	— —
1996— San Francisco (N.L.)	68	94	.420	4th (W)	—	—	—	—	—	—	— —
1997— San Francisco (N.L.)	90	72	.556	1st (W)	0	3	—	—	—	—	— —
1998— San Francisco (N.L.)	89	74	.546	2nd (W)	—	—	—	—	—	—	— —
Major league totals (5 years)	472	436	.520		0	3					

NOTES:
1994—San Francisco was in second place in N.L. West at time of season-ending strike (August 12).
1997—Lost to Florida in N.L. divisional playoff.

BOCHY, BRUCE   PADRES

PERSONAL: Born April 16, 1955, in Landes de Boussac, France. ... 6-4/225. ... Batted right, threw right. ... Full name: Bruce Douglas Bochy. ... Brother of Joe Bochy, catcher, Minnesota Twins organization (1969-72). ... Name pronounced BO-chee.
HIGH SCHOOL: Melbourne (Fla.).
JUNIOR COLLEGE: Brevard Community College (Fla.).
COLLEGE: Florida State.
TRANSACTIONS/CAREER NOTES: Selected by Chicago White Sox organization in eighth round of free-agent draft (January 9, 1975); did not sign. ... Selected by Houston Astros organization in secondary phase of free-agent draft (June 4, 1975). ... Traded by Astros to New York Mets organization for two players to be named later (February 11, 1981); Astros acquired IF Randy Rodgers and C Stan Hough to complete deal (April 3, 1981). ... Released by Mets (January 21, 1983). ... Signed by Las Vegas, San Diego Padres organization (February 23, 1983). ... On disabled list (April 13-May 6, 1987). ... Granted free agency (November 9, 1987).
STATISTICAL NOTES: Tied for Florida State League lead with 12 passed balls in 1977.

Year Team (League)	Pos.	G	AB	R	H	2B	3B	HR	RBI	Avg.	BB	SO	SB	PO	A	E	Avg.
1975— Covington (Appal.)	C	37	145	31	49	9	0	4	34	.338	11	18	0	231	36	4	.985
1976— Columbus (Sou.)	C	69	230	9	53	6	0	0	16	.230	14	30	0	266	45	6	.981
—Dubuque (Midwest)....	C-1B	30	103	9	25	4	0	1	8	.243	12	11	1	165	25	5	.974
1977— Cocoa (Fla. St.)	C	128	430	40	109	18	2	3	35	.253	35	50	0	*492	67	12	.979
1978— Columbus (Sou.)	C	79	261	25	70	10	2	7	34	.268	13	30	0	419	49	7	.985
—Houston (N.L.)	C	54	154	8	41	8	0	3	15	.266	11	35	0	268	35	8	.974
1979— Houston (N.L.)	C	56	129	11	28	4	0	1	6	.217	17	25	0	198	29	7	.970
1980— Houston (N.L.)	C-1B	22	22	0	4	1	0	0	0	.182	0	0	0	19	1	0	1.000
1981— Tidewater (Int'l)■.......	C	85	269	23	61	11	2	8	38	.227	22	47	0	253	35	3	.990

MAJOR LEAGUE MANAGERS *(vertical left margin)*

Year Team (League)	Pos.	G	AB	R	H	2B	3B	HR	RBI	Avg.	BB	SO	SB	PO	A	E	Avg.
1982—Tidewater (Int'l).........	C	81	251	32	57	11	0	15	52	.227	19	47	2	427	57	5	.990
—New York (N.L.)..........	C-1B	17	49	4	15	4	0	2	8	.306	4	6	0	92	8	4	.962
1983—Las Vegas (PCL)■.....	C	42	145	28	44	8	1	11	33	.303	15	25	3	157	21	3	.983
—San Diego (N.L.)	C	23	42	2	9	1	1	0	3	.214	0	9	0	51	5	0	1.000
1984—Las Vegas (PCL)	C	34	121	18	32	7	0	7	22	.264	17	13	0	189	17	2	.990
—San Diego (N.L.)	C	37	92	10	21	5	1	4	15	.228	3	21	0	147	12	2	.988
1985—San Diego (N.L.)	C	48	112	16	30	2	0	6	13	.268	6	30	0	148	11	2	.988
1986—San Diego (N.L.)	C	63	127	16	32	9	0	8	22	.252	14	23	1	202	22	2	.991
1987—San Diego (N.L.)	C	38	75	8	12	3	0	2	11	.160	11	21	0	95	7	4	.962
1988—Las Vegas (PCL)	C	53	147	17	34	5	0	5	13	.231	17	28	0	207	19	3	.987
Major league totals (9 years)		358	802	75	192	37	2	26	93	.239	66	170	1	1220	130	29	.979

CHAMPIONSHIP SERIES RECORD

Year Team (League)	Pos.	G	AB	R	H	2B	3B	HR	RBI	Avg.	BB	SO	SB	PO	A	E	Avg.
1980—Houston (N.L.)	C	1	1	0	0	0	0	0	0	.000	0	0	0	5	1	0	1.000

WORLD SERIES RECORD

Year Team (League)	Pos.	G	AB	R	H	2B	3B	HR	RBI	Avg.	BB	SO	SB	PO	A	E	Avg.
1984—San Diego (N.L.)	PH	1	1	0	1	0	0	0	0	1.000	0	0	0	...	...	...	...

RECORD AS MANAGER

BACKGROUND: Player/coach, Las Vegas, San Diego Padres organization (1988). ... Coach, Padres (1993-94).

HONORS: Named N.L. Manager of the Year by The Sporting News (1996 and 1998). ... Named N.L. Manager of the Year by Baseball Writers' Association of America (1996).

| | | REGULAR SEASON | | | POSTSEASON | | | | | | |
| | | | | | | | Champ. Series | | World Series | | All-Star Game | |
Year Team (League)	W	L	Pct.	Pos.	Playoff W	L	W	L	W	L	W	L
1989— Spokane (Northwest)	41	34	.547	1st (N)	2	1	—	—	—	—	—	—
1990— Riverside (California)	35	36	.493	4th (S)	—	—	—	—	—	—	—	—
—(Second half)	29	42	.408	5th (S)	—	—	—	—	—	—	—	—
1991— High Desert (California)	31	37	.456	3rd (S)	—	—	—	—	—	—	—	—
—(Second half)	42	26	.618	1st (S)	6	2	—	—	—	—	—	—
1992— Wichita (Texas)	39	29	.574	1st (W)	—	—	—	—	—	—	—	—
—(Second half)	31	37	.456	4th (W)	6	1	—	—	—	—	—	—
1995— San Diego (N.L.)	70	74	.486	3rd (W)	—	—	—	—	—	—	—	—
1996— San Diego (N.L.)	91	71	.562	1st (W)	0	3	—	—	—	—	—	—
1997— San Diego (N.L.)	76	86	.469	4th (W)	—	—	—	—	—	—	—	—
1998— San Diego (N.L.)	98	64	.605	1sr (W)	3	1	4	2	0	4	—	—
Major league totals (4 years)...........................	335	295	.532		3	4	4	2	0	4	—	—

NOTES:
1989—Defeated Southern Oregon in league championship.
1991—Defeated Bakersfield, three games to none, in semifinals; defeated Stockton, three games to two, in league championship.
1992—Defeated El Paso, two games to one, in semifinals; defeated Shreveport, four games to none, in league championship.
1996—Lost to St. Louis in N.L. divisional playoff.
1998—Defeated Houston in N.L. divisional playoff; defeated Atlanta in N.L. Championship Series; lost to New York Yankees in World Series.

BOLES, JOHN — MARLINS

PERSONAL: Born August 19, 1948, in Chicago.
COLLEGE: Lewis University, then St. Xavier.

RECORD AS MANAGER

BACKGROUND: Head coach, St. Xavier University (1973-79). ... Head coach, University of Louisville (1980-81). ... Director of player development, Kansas City Royals (July 26, 1986-1989). ... Minor league coordinator, Montreal Expos (1990). ... Director of player development, Expos (1991). ... Director of player development, Florida Marlins (November 1, 1991-July 28, 1995). ... Vice president of player development, Marlins (July 28, 1995-present).

HONORS: Named Gulf Coast League Manager of the Year (1982).

| | | REGULAR SEASON | | | POSTSEASON | | | | | | |
| | | | | | | | Champ. Series | | World Series | | All-Star Game | |
Year Team (League)	W	L	Pct.	Pos.	Playoff W	L	W	L	W	L	W	L
1981— Gulf Coast White Sox (GCL)	41	23	.641	2nd	—	—	—	—	—	—	—	—
1982— Gulf Coast White Sox (GCL)	40	23	.635	2nd	—	—	—	—	—	—	—	—
1983—Appleton (Midwest)	87	50	.635	1st (N)	5	2	—	—	—	—	—	—
1984—Glens Falls (Eastern)	75	63	.543	2nd	1	3	—	—	—	—	—	—
1985—Buffalo (American Association)	66	76	.465	3rd (E)	—	—	—	—	—	—	—	—
1986—Omaha (American Association)	40	36	.526		—	—	—	—	—	—	—	—
1996—Florida (N.L.)...	40	35	.540	3rd (E)	—	—	—	—	—	—	—	—

NOTES:
1983—Defeated Waterloo, two games to one, in league semifinals; defeated Springfield, three games to one, to win league championship.
1984—Glens Falls tied one game; lost to Waterbury in league semifinals.
1986—Replaced as Omaha manager by Frank Funk (June 25).
1996—Replaced Florida manager Rene Lachemann with club in fourth place and record of 40-47 (July 8).

PERSONAL: Born May 27, 1949, in Midland, Mich. ... 5-8/160. ... Batted left, threw right. ... Full name: Terry Lee Collins.

HIGH SCHOOL: Midland (Mich.).

COLLEGE: Eastern Michigan (bachelor of science degree).

TRANSACTIONS/CAREER NOTES: Selected by Pittsburgh Pirates organization in 19th round of free-agent draft (June 8, 1971). ... Released by Pirates organization (January 7, 1974). ... Signed by Los Angeles Dodgers organization (January 14, 1974). ... On disabled list (July 2-August 6, 1976). ... Released by Dodgers organization (February 28, 1978). ... Signed by Dodgers organization as player (May 14, 1978). ... On disabled list (June 26-July 6, 1978). ... Signed as player/coach for Albuquerque Dukes for 1979. ... On temporarily inactive list (entire 1979 season). ... Released by Dodgers organization (December 7, 1979). ... Re-signed by Dodgers organization as coach (January 30, 1980); became player/coach for Dodgers organization (May 18, 1980). ... On disabled list (May 29-July 1 and July 12-August 17, 1980). ... Released by Dodgers organization (September 18, 1980). ... Re-signed by Dodgers organization as player/manager (August 17, 1984). ... Released as player by Dodgers organization (September 28, 1984).

STATISTICAL NOTES: Led New York-Pennsylvania League shortstops with 310 total chances and 37 double plays in 1971.

								BATTING							FIELDING		
Year Team (League)	Pos.	G	AB	R	H	2B	3B	HR	RBI	Avg.	BB	SO	SB	PO	A	E	Avg.
1971— Niagara Falls (NYP)	SS	70	265	51	81	12	3	1	26	.306	36	35	12	*112	*179	19	*.939
1972— Salem (Carolina)	2B	126	459	77	116	17	7	1	41	.253	70	75	8	*254	333	*25	.959
1973— Sherbrooke (East.) ..	2-0-3-P-S	114	324	52	76	9	0	0	20	.235	59	54	7	177	206	12	.970
1974— Waterbury (Eastern)■	2B-SS	86	230	28	46	3	2	1	23	.200	46	42	2	144	243	11	.972
1975— Waterbury (Eastern)	SS	4	9	2	1	0	0	0	1	.111	3	2	0	3	9	2	.857
— Albuquerque (PCL).....	2B-SS-3B	64	153	24	48	5	4	0	10	.314	18	19	2	87	53	11	.927
1976— Albuquerque (PCL).....	3B-OF-SS	67	174	23	42	4	5	2	24	.241	19	21	6	46	64	3	.973
1977— Albuquerque (PCL).....	2-3-S-P	54	158	27	39	6	3	0	15	.247	32	21	2	64	113	9	.952
1978— Albuquerque (PCL) ..2-3-S-P-O-1		72	217	29	60	9	4	1	22	.276	21	20	4	115	162	12	.958
1979—									Did not play.							
1980— Albuquerque (PCL).....	DH	11	14	1	2	0	0	0	1	.143	3	4	1	. . .	. . .	. . .
1981—									Did not play.							
1982—									Did not play.							
1983—									Did not play.							
1984— Albuquerque (PCL).....	SS-2B	3	6	1	1	0	0	0	0	.167	0	0	0	5	3	0	1.000

RECORD AS PITCHER

Year Team (League)	W	L	Pct.	ERA	G	GS	CG	ShO	Sv.	IP	H	R	ER	BB	SO
1973— Sherbrooke (Eastern)	0	0	. . .	2.25	3	0	0	0	2	4	3	1	1	3	0
1977— Albuquerque (PCL)............	0	0	. . .	0.00	1	0	0	0	0	2	2	0	0	0	1
1978— Albuquerque (PCL)............	0	0	. . .	0.00	2	0	0	0	1	3	1	0	0	1	1

RECORD AS MANAGER

BACKGROUND: Player/coach, Waterbury, Dodgers organization (1975). ... Player/coach, Albuquerque, Dodgers organization (1977-80). ... Coach, Pittsburgh Pirates (November 26, 1991-November 17, 1993).

HONORS: Named Minor League Manager of the Year by THE SPORTING NEWS (1987). ... Named Pacific Coast League Manager of the Year (1988).

				REGULAR SEASON				POSTSEASON						
						Playoff		Champ. Series		World Series		All-Star Game	
Year Team (League)	W	L	Pct.	Pos.	W	L	W	L	W	L	W	L		
1981— Lodi (California)	30	40	.429	7th	—	—	—	—	—	—	—	—		
— (Second half)	43	27	.614	T2nd	5	2	—	—	—	—	—	—		
1982— Vero Beach (Florida State)	38	31	.551	2nd (S)	—	—	—	—	—	—	—	—		
— (Second half)	42	22	.656	1st (S)	1	2	—	—	—	—	—	—		
1983— San Antonio (Texas)	33	34	.493	3rd (W)	—	—	—	—	—	—	—	—		
— (Second half)	3	4	.429		—	—	—	—	—	—	—	—		
— Albuquerque (PCL), second half	42	26	.618	1st (S)	3	5	—	—	—	—	—	—		
1984— Albuquerque (Pacific Coast)	36	36	.500	5th (S)	—	—	—	—	—	—	—	—		
— (Second half)	26	45	.366	5th (S)	—	—	—	—	—	—	—	—		
1985— Albuquerque (Pacific Coast)	36	35	.507	4th (S)	—	—	—	—	—	—	—	—		
— (Second half)	31	41	.431	4th (S)	—	—	—	—	—	—	—	—		
1986— Albuquerque (Pacific Coast)	28	43	.394	5th (S)	—	—	—	—	—	—	—	—		
— (Second half)	26	45	.366	5th (S)	—	—	—	—	—	—	—	—		
1987— Albuquerque (Pacific Coast)	43	27	.614	1st (S)	—	—	—	—	—	—	—	—		
— (Second half)	34	38	.472	4th (S)	6	1	—	—	—	—	—	—		
1988— Albuquerque (Pacific Coast)	38	33	.535	2nd (S)	—	—	—	—	—	—	—	—		
— (Second half)	48	23	.676	1st (S)	0	3	—	—	—	—	—	—		
1989— Buffalo (American Association)	80	62	.563	2nd (E)	—	—	—	—	—	—	—	—		
1990— Buffalo (American Association)	85	62	.578	2nd (E)	—	—	—	—	—	—	—	—		
1991— Buffalo (American Association)	81	62	.566	1st (E)	2	3	—	—	—	—	—	—		
1994— Houston (N.L.)	66	49	.574		—	—	—	—	—	—	—	—		
1995— Houston (N.L.)	76	68	.528	2nd (C)	—	—	—	—	—	—	—	—		
1996— Houston (N.L.)	82	80	.506	2nd (C)	—	—	—	—	—	—	—	—		
1997— Anaheim (A.L.)	84	78	.519	2nd (W)	—	—	—	—	—	—	—	—		
1998— Anaheim (A.L.)	85	77	.525	2nd (W)	—	—	—	—	—	—	—	—		
American League totals (2 year)......................	169	155	.522		—	—	—	—	—	—	—	—		
National League totals (3 years)......................	224	197	.532		—	—	—	—	—	—	—	—		
Major league totals (5 years)...........................	393	352	.528		—	—	—	—	—	—	—	—		

NOTES:
1981—Defeated Reno, two games to one, in semifinals; defeated Visalia, three games to two, in league championship.
1982—Lost to Fort Lauderdale in playoffs.
1983—Replaced Albuquerque manager Del Crandall (June 29). Defeated Las Vegas, three games to two, in playoffs; lost to Portland, three games to none, in league championship.
1987—Defeated Las Vegas, three games to none, in playoffs; defeated Calgary, three games to one, in league championship.
1988—Lost to Las Vegas in playoffs.
1991—Lost to Denver in league championship.
1994—Houston was in second place in N.L. Central at time of season-ending strike (August 12).
1998—On suspended list (June 9-16).

PERSONAL: Born May 21, 1941, in Tulsa, Okla. ... 6-0/185. ... Batted right, threw right. ... Full name: Robert Joe Cox.

HIGH SCHOOL: Selma (Calif.).

JUNIOR COLLEGE: Reedley Junior College (Calif.).

TRANSACTIONS/CAREER NOTES: Signed by Los Angeles Dodgers organization (1959). ... Selected by Chicago Cubs organization from Dodgers organization in Rule 5 minor league draft (November 30, 1964). ... Acquired by Atlanta Braves organization (1966). ... On Austin disabled list (May 8-18 and May 30-June 9, 1966). ... On disabled list (May 1-June 12, 1967). ... Traded by Braves to New York Yankees for C Bob Tillman and P Dale Roberts (December 7, 1967); Roberts later was transferred to Richmond. ... On disabled list (May 28-June 18, 1970). ... Released by Yankees organization (September 22, 1970). ... Signed by Fort Lauderdale, Yankees organization (July 17, 1971). ... Released as player by Fort Lauderdale (August 28, 1971).

STATISTICAL NOTES: Led Alabama-Florida League shortstops with 71 double plays in 1961. ... Led Pacific Coast League third basemen with .954 fielding percentage in 1965.

| | | | | | | | BATTING | | | | | | | FIELDING | | |
Year Team (League)	Pos.	G	AB	R	H	2B	3B	HR	RBI	Avg.	BB	SO	SB	PO	A	E	Avg.
1960— Reno (California)	2B	125	440	99	112	20	5	13	75	.255	95	129	28	282	*385	*39	.945
1961— Salem (Northwest)	2B	14	44	3	9	2	0	0	2	.205	0	14	0	25	25	2	.962
— Panama City (Al.-Fla.)	2B	92	335	66	102	27	4	17	73	.304	48	72	17	220	247	8	*.983
1962— Salem (Northwest)	3B-2B	*141	514	83	143	26	7	16	82	.278	63	119	7	174	296	28	.944
1963— Albuquerque (Texas)	3B	17	53	5	15	2	0	2	5	.283	3	12	1	8	27	1	.972
— Great Falls (Pio.)	3B	109	407	103	137	*31	4	19	85	.337	73	84	7	82	211	21	*.933
1964— Albuquerque (Texas)	2B	138	523	98	152	29	13	16	91	.291	52	84	8	*322	*415	*28	.963
1965— Salt Lake (PCL)■	3B-2B	136	473	58	125	32	1	12	55	.264	35	96	1	133	337	22	†.955
1966— Tacoma (PCL)	3B-2B	10	34	2	4	1	0	0	4	.118	6	9	0	23	15	0	1.000
— Austin (Texas)■	2B-3B	92	339	35	77	11	1	7	30	.227	25	55	7	140	216	12	.967
1967— Richmond (Int'l)	3B-1B	99	350	52	104	17	4	14	51	.297	34	73	3	84	136	8	.965
1968— New York (A.L.)■	3B	135	437	33	100	15	1	7	41	.229	41	85	3	98	279	17	.957
1969— New York (A.L.)	3B-2B	85	191	17	41	7	1	2	17	.215	34	41	0	50	147	11	.947
1970— Syracuse (Int'l)	3B-SS-2B	90	251	34	55	15	0	9	30	.219	49	40	0	86	163	13	.950
1971— Fort Lauder. (FSL)	2B-P	4	9	1	1	0	0	0	0	.111	1	0	0	4	5	0	1.000
Major league totals (2 years)		220	628	50	141	22	2	9	58	.225	75	126	3	148	426	28	.953

RECORD AS PITCHER

Year Team (League)	W	L	Pct.	ERA	G	GS	CG	ShO	Sv.	IP	H	R	ER	BB	SO
1971— Fort Lauderdale (FSL)	0	1	.000	5.40	3	0	0	0	0	10	15	9	6	5	4

RECORD AS MANAGER

BACKGROUND: Minor league instructor, New York Yankees (October 28, 1970-March 24, 1971). ... Player/manager, Fort Lauderdale, Yankees organization (1971). ... Coach, Yankees (1977).

HONORS: Named Major League Manager of the Year by THE SPORTING NEWS (1985). ... Named A.L. Manager of the Year by Baseball Writers' Association of America (1985). ... Named N.L. Manager of the Year by THE SPORTING NEWS (1991 and 1993). ... Named N.L. Manager of the Year by the Baseball Writers' Association of America (1991).

| | REGULAR SEASON | | | | POSTSEASON | | | | | | | |
| | | | | | Playoff | | Champ. Series | | World Series | | All-Star Game | |
Year Team (League)	W	L	Pct.	Pos.	W	L	W	L	W	L	W	L
1971— Fort Lauderdale (Florida State)	71	70	.504	4th (E)	—	—	—	—	—	—	—	—
1972— West Haven (Eastern)	84	56	.600	1st (E)	3	0	—	—	—	—	—	—
1973— Syracuse (International)	76	70	.521	3rd (A)	—	—	—	—	—	—	—	—
1974— Syracuse (International)	74	70	.514	2nd (N)	—	—	—	—	—	—	—	—
1975— Syracuse (International)	72	64	.529	3rd	—	—	—	—	—	—	—	—
1976— Syracuse (International)	82	57	.590	2nd	6	1	—	—	—	—	—	—
1978— Atlanta (N.L.)	69	93	.426	6th (W)	—	—	—	—	—	—	—	—
1979— Atlanta (N.L.)	66	94	.413	6th (W)	—	—	—	—	—	—	—	—
1980— Atlanta (N.L.)	81	80	.503	4th (W)	—	—	—	—	—	—	—	—
1981— Atlanta (N.L.)	25	29	.463	4th (W)	—	—	—	—	—	—	—	—
— (Second half)	25	27	.481	5th (W)	—	—	—	—	—	—	—	—
1982— Toronto (A.L.)	78	84	.481	T6th (E)	—	—	—	—	—	—	—	—
1983— Toronto (A.L.)	89	73	.549	4th (E)	—	—	—	—	—	—	—	—
1984— Toronto (A.L.)	89	73	.549	2nd (E)	—	—	—	—	—	—	—	—
1985— Toronto (A.L.)	99	62	.615	1st (E)	—	—	3	4	—	—	—	—
1990— Atlanta (N.L.)	40	57	.412	6th (W)	—	—	—	—	—	—	—	—
1991— Atlanta (N.L.)	94	68	.580	1st (W)	—	—	4	3	3	4	—	—
1992— Atlanta (N.L.)	98	64	.605	1st (W)	—	—	4	3	2	4	0	1
1993— Atlanta (N.L.)	104	58	.642	1st (W)	—	—	2	4	—	—	0	1
1994— Atlanta (N.L.)	68	46	.596		—	—	—	—	—	—	—	—
1995— Atlanta (N.L.)	90	54	.625	1st (E)	3	1	4	0	4	2	—	—
1996— Atlanta (N.L.)	96	66	.593	1st (E)	3	0	4	3	2	4	1	0
1997— Atlanta (N.L.)	101	61	.623	1st (E)	3	0	2	4	—	—	0	1
1998— Atlanta (N.L.)	106	56	.654	1st (E)	3	0	2	4	—	—	—	—
American League totals (4 years)	355	292	.549		—	—	3	4	—	—	—	—
National League totals (13 years)	1063	853	.555		12	1	22	21	11	14	1	3
Major league totals (17 years)	1418	1145	.553		12	1	25	25	11	14	1	3

NOTES:

1972—Defeated Three Rivers in playoff.

1976—Defeated Memphis, three games to none, in playoffs; defeated Richmond, three games to one, in league championship.

1985—Lost to Kansas City in A.L. Championship Series.

1990—Replaced Atlanta manager Russ Nixon with club in sixth place and record of 25-40 (June 22).

1991—Defeated Pittsburgh in N.L. Championship Series; lost to Minnesota in World Series.

1992—Defeated Pittsburgh in N.L. Championship Series; lost to Toronto in World Series.

1993—Lost to Philadelphia in N.L. Championship Series.

MAJOR LEAGUE MANAGERS

1994—Atlanta was in second place in N.L. East at time of season-ending strike (August 12).
1995—Defeated Colorado in N.L. divisional playoff; defeated Cincinnati in N.L. Championship Series; defeated Cleveland in World Series.
1996—Defeated Los Angeles in N.L. divisional playoff; defeated St. Louis in N.L. Championship Series; lost to New York Yankees in World Series.
1997—Defeated Houston in N.L. divisional playoff; lost to Florida in N.L. Championship Series.
1998—Defeated Chicago Cubs in N.L. divisional playoff; lost to San Diego in N.L. Championship Series.

DIERKER, LARRY — ASTROS

PERSONAL: Born September 22, 1946, in Hollywood, Calif. ... 6-4/205. ... Threw right, batted right. ... Full name: Lawrence Edward Dierker. ... Brother of Richard Dierker, pitcher, Baltimore Orioles organization (1972-75). ... Name pronounced DUR-ker.
COLLEGE: UC Santa Barbara, then Houston.
TRANSACTIONS/CAREER NOTES: Signed as free agent by Houston Astros organization (1964). ... Served in military (June 25, 1967-remainder of season). ... On disabled list (March 21-May 22 and June 16-July 12, 1973). ... Traded by Astros with IF Jerry DaVanon to St. Louis Cardinals for C/OF Joe Ferguson and OF Bobby Detherage (November 23, 1976). ... On disabled list (March 23-May 19 and July 23, 1977-remainder of season). ... Released by Cardinals (March 28, 1978).
STATISTICAL NOTES: Led N.L. with 20 wild pitches in 1968. ... Pitched 6-0 no-hit victory against Montreal (July 9, 1976).
MISCELLANEOUS: Holds Houston Astros franchise all-time records for most innings pitched (2,296) and most shutouts (25). ... Television and radio color analyst, Astros (1979-1996).

Year	Team (League)	W	L	Pct.	ERA	G	GS	CG	ShO	Sv.	IP	H	R	ER	BB	SO
1964—	Cocoa (Cocoa Rookie)	2	3	.400	3.23	9	9	0			39	21	19	14	18	61
	—Houston (N.L.)	0	1	.000	2.00	3	1	0	0	0	9	7	4	2	3	5
1965—	Houston (N.L.)	7	8	.467	3.49	26	19	1	0	0	147	135	69	57	37	109
1966—	Houston (N.L.)	10	8	.556	3.18	29	28	8	2	0	187	173	73	66	45	108
1967—	Houston (N.L.)	6	5	.545	3.36	15	15	4	0	0	99	95	44	37	25	68
1968—	Houston (N.L.)	12	15	.444	3.31	32	32	10	1	0	234	206	95	86	89	161
1969—	Houston (N.L.)	20	13	.606	2.33	39	37	20	4	0	305	240	97	79	72	232
1970—	Houston (N.L.)	16	12	.571	3.87	37	36	17	2	1	270	263	124	116	82	191
1971—	Houston (N.L.)	12	6	.667	2.72	24	23	6	2	0	159	150	50	48	33	91
1972—	Houston (N.L.)	15	8	.652	3.39	31	31	12	5	0	215	209	87	81	51	115
1973—	Houston (N.L.)	1	1	.500	4.33	14	3	0	0	0	27	27	14	13	13	18
1974—	Houston (N.L.)	11	10	.524	2.89	33	33	7	3	0	224	189	76	72	82	150
1975—	Houston (N.L.)	14	16	.467	4.00	34	34	14	2	0	232	225	109	103	91	127
1976—	Houston (N.L.)	13	14	.481	3.69	28	28	7	4	0	188	171	85	77	72	112
1977—	St. Louis (N.L.)■	2	6	.250	4.62	11	9	0	0	0	39	40	21	20	16	6
Major league totals (14 years)		**139**	**123**	**.531**	**3.30**	**356**	**329**	**106**	**25**	**1**	**2335**	**2130**	**948**	**857**	**711**	**1493**

ALL-STAR GAME RECORD

Year	League	W	L	Pct.	ERA	GS	CG	ShO	Sv.	IP	H	R	ER	BB	SO
1969—	National	0	0	. . .	0.00	0	0	0	0	1/3	1	0	0	0	0
1971—	National					Selected, did not play—injured.									

RECORD AS MANAGER

HONORS: Named N.L. Manager of the Year by Baseball Writers' Association of America (1998).

		REGULAR SEASON				POSTSEASON							
						Playoff		Champ. Series		World Series		All-Star Game	
Year	Team (League)	W	L	Pct.	Pos.	W	L	W	L	W	L	W	L
1997—	Houston (N.L.)	84	78	.519	1st (C)	0	3	—	—	—	—	—	—
1998—	Houston (N.L.)	102	60	.630	1st (C)	1	3	—	—	—	—	—	—
Major league totals (2 years)		**186**	**138**	**.574**		**1**	**6**						

NOTES:
1997—Lost to Atlanta in N.L. divisional playoff.
1998—Lost to San Diego in N.L. divisional playoff.

FRANCONA, TERRY — PHILLIES

PERSONAL: Born April 22, 1959, in New Brighton, Pa. ... 6-1/175. ... Batted left, threw left. ... Full name: Terry Jon Francona. ... Son of Tito Francona, major league outfielder/first baseman with nine teams (1956-70).
HIGH SCHOOL: New Brighton (Pa.).
COLLEGE: Arizona.
TRANSACTIONS/CAREER NOTES: Selected by Chicago Cubs organization in second round of free-agent draft (June 7, 1977); did not sign. ... Selected by Montreal Expos organization in first round (22nd pick overall) of free-agent draft (June 3, 1980); pick received as compensation for New York Yankees signing free-agent P Rudy May. ... On disabled list (June 17-September 27, 1982 and June 15-September 5, 1984). ... Released by Expos (April 1, 1986). ... Signed by Chicago Cubs organization (May 2, 1986). ... Granted free agency (October 18, 1986). ... Signed by Cincinnati Reds (March 23, 1987). ... Granted free agency (November 12, 1987). ... Signed by Colorado Springs, Cleveland Indians organization (February 28, 1988). ... Granted free agency (November 4, 1988). ... Signed by Milwaukee Brewers (March 30, 1989). ... Granted free agency (November 13, 1989). ... Re-signed by Brewers (December 12, 1989). ... Released by Brewers (April 27, 1990). ... Signed by Louisville, St. Louis Cardinals organization (May 5, 1990). ... Released by Cardinals organization (April 2, 1991).
HONORS: Named Golden Spikes Award winner by USA Baseball (1980). ... Named College Player of the Year by THE SPORTING NEWS (1980). ... Named outfielder on THE SPORTING NEWS college All-America team (1980).

					BATTING									FIELDING		
Year	Team (League)	Pos.	G	AB	R	H	2B	3B	HR	RBI	Avg.	BB	SO	SB	PO	A	E	Avg.
1980—	Memphis (Southern)	OF	60	210	20	63	13	2	1	23	.300	10	20	1	59	4	4	.940
1981—	Memphis (Southern)	OF-1B	41	161	20	56	8	1	0	18	.348	7	18	0	102	7	5	.956
	—Denver (A.A.)	OF	93	355	53	125	17	*9	1	58	.352	16	22	7	158	7	3	.982
	—Montreal (N.L.)	OF-1B	34	95	11	26	0	1	1	8	.274	5	6	1	41	5	0	1.000
1982—	Montreal (N.L.)	OF-1B	46	131	14	42	3	0	0	9	.321	8	11	2	65	0	3	.956
1983—	Montreal (N.L.)	OF-1B	120	230	21	59	11	1	3	22	.257	6	20	1	172	10	3	.984
1984—	Montreal (N.L.)	1B-OF	58	214	18	74	19	2	1	18	.346	5	12	0	431	50	3	.994
1985—	Montreal (N.L.)	1B-OF-3B	107	281	19	75	15	1	2	31	.267	12	12	5	431	40	6	.987

Year Team (League)	Pos.	G	AB	R	H	2B	3B	HR	RBI	Avg.	BB	SO	SB	PO	A	E	Avg.
1986—Chicago (N.L.)■........	OF-1B	86	124	13	31	3	0	2	8	.250	6	8	0	123	7	0	1.000
—Iowa (Am. Assoc.)......	1B-OF	17	60	7	15	3	2	0	8	.250	4	5	1	82	3	1	.988
1987—Cincinnati (N.L.)■.....	1B-OF	102	207	16	47	5	0	3	12	.227	10	12	2	377	45	2	.995
1988—Colo. Spr. (PCL)	OF-1B	68	235	29	76	15	5	0	32	.323	13	18	0	115	11	3	.977
—Cleveland (A.L.).........	DH-1B-OF	62	212	24	66	8	0	1	12	.311	5	18	0	47	5	1	.981
1989—Milwaukee (A.L.)■.....	1-DH-O-P	90	233	26	54	10	1	3	23	.232	8	20	2	339	26	4	.989
1990—Milwaukee (A.L.)	1B	3	4	1	0	0	0	0	0	.000	0	0	0	6	0	0	1.000
—Louisville (A.A.)■......	OF-1B-P	86	285	29	75	9	3	6	30	.263	12	23	1	126	7	2	.985
American League totals (3 years)		155	449	51	120	18	1	4	35	.267	13	38	2	392	31	5	.988
National League totals (7 years)		553	1282	112	354	56	5	12	108	.276	52	81	10	1640	157	17	.991
Major league totals (10 years)		708	1731	163	474	74	6	16	143	.274	65	119	12	2032	188	22	.990

DIVISION SERIES RECORD

Year Team (League)	Pos.	G	AB	R	H	2B	3B	HR	RBI	Avg.	BB	SO	SB	PO	A	E	Avg.
1981—Montreal (N.L.)..........	OF	5	12	0	4	0	0	0	0	.333	2	2	2	8	0	0	1.000

CHAMPIONSHIP SERIES RECORD

Year Team (League)	Pos.	G	AB	R	H	2B	3B	HR	RBI	Avg.	BB	SO	SB	PO	A	E	Avg.
1981—Montreal (N.L.)..........	PH-OF	2	1	0	0	0	0	0	0	.000	0	1	0	0	0	0	...

RECORD AS PITCHER

Year Team (League)	W	L	Pct.	ERA	G	GS	CG	ShO	Sv.	IP	H	R	ER	BB	SO
1989—Milwaukee (A.L.)	0	0	...	0.00	1	0	0	0	0	1	0	0	0	0	1
1990—Louisville (A.A.)	0	0	...	1.17	5	0	0	0	0	7 2/3	4	1	1	2	6
Major league totals (1 year)........	0	0	...	0.00	1	0	0	0	0	1	0	0	0	0	1

RECORD AS MANAGER

BACKGROUND: Manager, Scottsdale Scorpions, Arizona Fall League (1994, record: 26-25, second place/Northern Division). ... Coach, Detroit Tigers (1996).

HONORS: Named Southern League Manager of the Year (1993).

Year Team (League)	REGULAR SEASON				POSTSEASON						All-Star Game	
					Playoff		Champ. Series		World Series			
	W	L	Pct.	Pos.	W	L	W	L	W	L	W	L
1992—South Bend (Midwest)	35	33	.515	3rd (N)	—	—	—	—	—	—	—	—
—(Second half)	38	31	.551	2nd (N)	—	—	—	—	—	—	—	—
1993—Birmingham (Southern)	35	36	.493	2nd (W)	—	—	—	—	—	—	—	—
—(Second half)	43	28	.606	1st (W)	6	1	—	—	—	—	—	—
1994—Birmingham (Southern)	31	38	.449	4th (W)	—	—	—	—	—	—	—	—
—(Second half)	34	36	.486	5th (W)	—	—	—	—	—	—	—	—
1995—Birmingham (Southern)	33	39	.458	4th (W)	—	—	—	—	—	—	—	—
—(Second half)	47	25	.653	2nd (W)	—	—	—	—	—	—	—	—
1997—Philadelphia (N.L.)	68	94	.420	5th (E)	—	—	—	—	—	—	—	—
1998—Philadelphia (N.L.)	75	87	.463	3rd (E)	—	—	—	—	—	—	—	—
Major league totals (2 years)...........................	143	181	.441		—	—	—	—	—	—	—	—

NOTES:

1992—South Bend tied one game in first half of season.

1993—Defeated Nashville, three games to none, in first round; defeated Knoxville, three games to one, in league championship.

GARNER, PHIL — BREWERS

PERSONAL: Born April 30, 1949, in Jefferson City, Tenn. ... 5-10/177. ... Batted right, threw right. ... Full name: Philip Mason Garner.

HIGH SCHOOL: Beardon (Knoxville, Tenn.).

COLLEGE: Tennessee (degree in general business, 1973).

TRANSACTIONS/CAREER NOTES: Selected by Montreal Expos organization in eighth round of free-agent draft (June 4, 1970); did not sign. ... Selected by Oakland Athletics organization in secondary phase of free-agent draft (January 13, 1971). ... Traded by A's with IF Tommy Helms and P Chris Batton to Pittsburgh Pirates for P Doc Medich, P Dave Giusti, P Rick Langford, P Doug Bair, OF Mitchell Page and OF Tony Armas (March 15, 1977). ... On Pittsburgh disabled list (April 2-23, 1981). ... Traded by Pirates to Houston Astros for 2B Johnny Ray and two players to be named later (August 31, 1981); Pirates organization acquired OF Kevin Houston and P Randy Niemann to complete deal (September 9, 1981). ... Granted free agency (November 12, 1986). ... Re-signed by Astros (January 6, 1987). ... Traded by Astros to Los Angeles Dodgers for a player to be named later (June 19, 1987); Astros organization acquired P Jeff Edwards to complete deal (June 26, 1987). ... Granted free agency (November 9, 1987). ... Signed by San Francisco Giants (January 28, 1988). ... On San Francisco disabled list (April 13-September 2, 1988); included rehabilitation assignment to Phoenix (August 5-24). ... Granted free agency (November 3, 1988).

RECORDS: Shares major league record for most grand slams in two consecutive games—2 (September 14-15, 1978).

STATISTICAL NOTES: Led Pacific Coast League third basemen with 104 putouts, 261 assists, 35 errors, 400 total chances and 23 double plays in 1973. ... Led A.L. second basemen with 26 errors in 1975. ... Led A.L. second basemen with 865 total chances in 1976. ... Led N.L. second basemen with 499 assists, 21 errors, 869 total chances and 116 double plays in 1980. ... Career major league grand slams: 3.

Year Team (League)	Pos.	G	AB	R	H	2B	3B	HR	RBI	Avg.	BB	SO	SB	PO	A	E	Avg.
1971—Burlington (Midw.)	3B	116	439	73	122	22	4	11	70	.278	49	73	8	*122	203	29	.918
1972—Birmingham. (Sou.)	3B	71	264	45	74	10	6	12	40	.280	27	43	3	74	116	13	.936
—Iowa (Am. Assoc.)......	3B	70	247	33	60	18	4	9	22	.243	30	73	7	50	140	10	.950
1973—Tucson (PCL)	3B-2B	138	516	87	149	23	12	14	73	.289	72	90	3	†107	†270	†35	.915
—Oakland (A.L.)	3B	9	5	0	0	0	0	0	0	.000	0	3	0	2	3	0	1.000
1974—Tucson (PCL)	3B-SS	96	388	78	128	29	10	11	51	.330	53	58	8	92	182	15	.948
—Oakland (A.L.)	3B-SS-2B	30	28	4	5	1	0	0	1	.179	1	5	1	11	24	1	.972
1975—Oakland (A.L.)	2B-SS	•160	488	46	120	21	5	6	54	.246	30	65	4	355	427	†26	.968

Year — Team (League)	Pos.	G	AB	R	H	2B	3B	HR	RBI	Avg.	BB	SO	SB	PO	A	E	Avg.
1976— Oakland (A.L.)	2B	159	555	54	145	29	12	8	74	.261	36	71	35	378	*465	22	.975
1977— Pittsburgh (N.L.)■.....	3B-2B-SS	153	585	99	152	35	10	17	77	.260	55	65	32	223	351	17	.971
1978— Pittsburgh (N.L.)	3B-2B-SS	154	528	66	138	25	9	10	66	.261	66	71	27	258	389	28	.959
1979— Pittsburgh (N.L.)	3B-2B-SS	150	549	76	161	32	8	11	59	.293	55	74	17	234	396	22	.966
1980— Pittsburgh (N.L.)	2B-SS	151	548	62	142	27	6	5	58	.259	46	53	32	349	†500	†21	.976
1981— Pittsburgh (N.L.)	2B	56	181	22	46	6	2	1	20	.254	21	21	4	121	148	9	.968
— Houston (N.L.)■	2B	31	113	13	27	3	1	0	6	.239	15	11	6	62	102	3	.982
1982— Houston (N.L.)	2B-3B	155	588	65	161	33	8	13	83	.274	40	92	24	285	464	17	.978
1983— Houston (N.L.)	3B	154	567	76	135	24	2	14	79	.238	63	84	18	100	311	24	.945
1984— Houston (N.L.)	3B-2B	128	374	60	104	17	6	4	45	.278	43	63	3	136	251	12	.970
1985— Houston (N.L.)	3B-2B	135	463	65	124	23	10	6	51	.268	34	72	4	101	229	21	.940
1986— Houston (N.L.)	3B-2B	107	313	43	83	14	3	9	41	.265	30	45	12	66	152	23	.905
1987— Houston (N.L.)	SS-2B	43	112	15	25	5	0	3	15	.223	8	20	1	28	55	2	.976
— Los Angeles (N.L.)■..	3B-2B-SS	70	126	14	24	4	0	2	8	.190	20	24	5	37	89	11	.920
1988— San Fran. (N.L.)■......	3B	15	13	0	2	0	0	0	1	.154	1	3	0	0	0	0	...
— Phoenix (PCL)	2B-3B	17	45	5	12	2	1	1	5	.267	4	4	0	12	22	0	1.000
American League totals (4 years)		358	1076	104	270	51	17	14	129	.251	67	144	40	746	919	49	.971
National League totals (12 years)		1502	5060	676	1324	248	65	95	609	.262	497	698	185	2000	3437	210	.963
Major league totals (16 years)		1860	6136	780	1594	299	82	109	738	.260	564	842	225	2746	4356	259	.965

DIVISION SERIES RECORD

Year — Team (League)	Pos.	G	AB	R	H	2B	3B	HR	RBI	Avg.	BB	SO	SB	PO	A	E	Avg.
1981— Houston (N.L.)	2B	5	18	1	2	0	0	0	0	.111	3	3	0	6	8	1	.933

CHAMPIONSHIP SERIES RECORD

Year — Team (League)	Pos.	G	AB	R	H	2B	3B	HR	RBI	Avg.	BB	SO	SB	PO	A	E	Avg.
1975— Oakland (A.L.)	2B	3	5	0	0	0	0	0	0	.000	0	1	0	7	4	1	.917
1979— Pittsburgh (N.L.)	2B-SS	3	12	4	5	0	1	1	1	.417	1	0	0	8	9	0	1.000
1986— Houston (N.L.)	3B	3	9	1	2	1	0	0	2	.222	1	2	0	1	9	0	1.000
Championship series totals (3 years)		9	26	5	7	1	1	1	3	.269	2	3	0	16	22	1	.974

WORLD SERIES RECORD

RECORDS: Shares single-series record for collecting one or more hits in each game (1979).
NOTES: Member of World Series championship team (1979).

Year — Team (League)	Pos.	G	AB	R	H	2B	3B	HR	RBI	Avg.	BB	SO	SB	PO	A	E	Avg.
1979— Pittsburgh (N.L.)	2B	7	24	4	12	4	0	0	5	.500	3	1	0	21	23	2	.957

ALL-STAR GAME RECORD

Year — League	Pos.	AB	R	H	2B	3B	HR	RBI	Avg.	BB	SO	SB	PO	A	E	Avg.
1976— American	2B	1	0	0	0	0	0	0	.000	0	1	0	1	1	0	1.000
1980— National	2B	2	1	1	0	0	0	0	.500	1	1	1	1	3	0	1.000
1981— National	2B	0	0	0	0	0	0	0	...	0	0	0	0	0	0	...
All-Star Game totals (3 years)		3	1	1	0	0	0	0	.333	1	2	1	2	4	0	1.000

RECORD AS MANAGER

BACKGROUND: Coach, Houston Astros (1989-91).

	REGULAR SEASON				POSTSEASON							
					Playoff		Champ. Series		World Series		All-Star Game	
Year — Team (League)	W	L	Pct.	Pos.	W	L	W	L	W	L	W	L
1992— Milwaukee (A.L.)..................................	92	70	.568	2nd (E)	—	—	—	—	—	—	—	—
1993— Milwaukee (A.L.)..................................	69	93	.426	7th (E)	—	—	—	—	—	—	—	—
1994— Milwaukee (A.L.)..................................	53	62	.461		—	—	—	—	—	—	—	—
1995— Milwaukee (A.L.)..................................	65	79	.451	4th (C)	—	—	—	—	—	—	—	—
1996— Milwaukee (A.L.)..................................	80	82	.494	3rd (C)	—	—	—	—	—	—	—	—
1997— Milwaukee (A.L.)..................................	78	83	.484	3rd (C)	—	—	—	—	—	—	—	—
1998— Milwaukee (N.L.)..................................	74	88	.457	5th (C)	—	—	—	—	—	—	—	—
American League totals (6 years)....................	437	469	.482		—	—	—	—	—	—	—	—
National League totals (1 year).....................	74	88	.457		—	—	—	—	—	—	—	—
Major league totals (7 years)........................	511	557	.478		—	—	—	—	—	—	—	—

NOTES:
1993—On suspended list (September 24-27).
1994—Milwaukee was in fifth place in A.L. Central at time of season-ending strike (August 12).
1995—On suspended list (July 27-31).

HARGROVE, MIKE — INDIANS

PERSONAL: Born October 26, 1949, in Perryton, Texas. ... 6-0/195. ... Batted left, threw left. ... Full name: Dudley Michael Hargrove.
HIGH SCHOOL: Perryton (Texas).
COLLEGE: Northwestern State, Okla. (degree in physical education and social sciences).
TRANSACTIONS/CAREER NOTES: Selected by Texas Rangers organization in 25th round of free-agent draft (June 6, 1972). ... Traded by Rangers with 3B Kurt Bevacqua and C Bill Fahey to San Diego Padres for OF Oscar Gamble, C Dave Roberts and cash (October 25, 1978). ... Traded by Padres to Cleveland Indians for OF Paul Dade (June 14, 1979). ... Granted free agency (November 12, 1985).
HONORS: Named Western Carolinas League Player of the Year (1973). ... Named A.L. Rookie Player of the Year by THE SPORTING NEWS (1974). ... Named A.L. Rookie of the Year by Baseball Writers' Association of America (1974).

STATISTICAL NOTES: Led New York-Pennsylvania League first basemen with 58 double plays in 1972. ... Led Western Carolinas League with 247 total bases in 1973. ... Led Western Carolinas League first basemen with 118 double plays in 1973. ... Had 23-game hitting streak (April 16-May 15, 1980). ... Led A.L. first basemen with 1,489 total chances in 1980. ... Led A.L. with .432 on-base percentage in 1981. ... Career major league grand slams: 1.

Year Team (League)	Pos.	G	AB	R	H	2B	3B	HR	RBI	Avg.	BB	SO	SB	PO	A	E	Avg.
1972— Geneva (NY-Penn)	1B	•70	243	38	65	8	0	4	37	.267	52	44	3	*537	•40	10	*.983
1973— Gastonia (W. Car.)	1B	•130	456	88	*160	*35	8	12	82	*.351	68	47	10	*1121	•77	14	*.988
1974— Texas (A.L.)	1B-DH-OF	131	415	57	134	18	6	4	66	.323	49	42	0	638	72	9	.987
1975— Texas (A.L.)	OF-1B-DH	145	519	82	157	22	2	11	62	.303	79	66	4	513	45	13	.977
1976— Texas (A.L.)	1B	151	541	80	155	30	1	7	58	.287	*97	64	2	1222	110	*21	.984
1977— Texas (A.L.)	1B	153	525	98	160	28	4	18	69	.305	103	59	2	1393	100	11	.993
1978— Texas (A.L.)	1B-DH	146	494	63	124	24	1	7	40	.251	*107	47	2	1221	*116	*17	.987
1979— San Diego (N.L.)■	1B	52	125	15	24	5	0	0	8	.192	25	15	0	323	17	5	.986
— Cleveland (A.L.)■	OF-1B-DH	100	338	60	110	21	4	10	56	.325	63	40	2	356	16	2	.995
1980— Cleveland (A.L.)	1B	160	589	86	179	22	2	11	85	.304	111	36	4	*1391	88	10	.993
1981— Cleveland (A.L.)	1B-DH	94	322	43	102	21	0	2	49	.317	60	16	5	766	76	•9	.989
1982— Cleveland (A.L.)	1B-DH	160	591	67	160	26	1	4	65	.271	101	58	2	1293	*123	5	.996
1983— Cleveland (A.L.)	1B-DH	134	469	57	134	21	4	3	57	.286	78	40	0	1098	115	7	.994
1984— Cleveland (A.L.)	1B	133	352	44	94	14	2	2	44	.267	53	38	0	790	83	8	.991
1985— Cleveland (A.L.)	1B-DH-OF	107	284	31	81	14	1	1	27	.285	39	29	1	599	66	6	.991
American League totals (12 years)		1614	5439	768	1590	261	28	80	678	.292	940	535	24	11280	1010	118	.990
National League totals (1 year)		52	125	15	24	5	0	0	8	.192	25	15	0	323	17	5	.986
Major league totals (12 years)		1666	5564	783	1614	266	28	80	686	.290	965	550	24	11603	1027	123	.990

ALL-STAR GAME RECORD

Year League	Pos.	AB	R	H	2B	3B	HR	RBI	Avg.	BB	SO	SB	PO	A	E	Avg.
1975— American	PH	1	0	0	0	0	0	0	.000	0	0	0	...	...	...	...

RECORD AS MANAGER

BACKGROUND: Minor league coach, Cleveland Indians organization (1986). ... Coach, Indians (1990-July 6, 1991).

HONORS: Named Carolina League Manager of the Year (1987). ... Named Pacific Coast League Manager of the Year (1989). ... Named A.L. Manager of the Year by THE SPORTING NEWS (1995).

						REGULAR SEASON		POSTSEASON							
								Playoff		Champ. Series		World Series		All-Star Game	
Year Team (League)		W	L	Pct.	Pos.			W	L	W	L	W	L	W	L
1987— Kinston (Carolina)		33	37	.471	T3rd (S)			—	—	—	—	—	—	—	—
— (Second half)		42	28	.600	1st (S)			3	3	—	—	—	—	—	—
1988— Williamsport (Eastern)		66	73	.475	6th			—	—	—	—	—	—	—	—
1989— Colorado Springs (Pacific Coast)		44	26	.629	1st (S)			—	—	—	—	—	—	—	—
— (Second half)		34	38	.472	3rd (S)			2	3	—	—	—	—	—	—
1991— Cleveland (A.L.)		32	53	.376	7th (E)			—	—	—	—	—	—	—	—
1992— Cleveland (A.L.)		76	86	.469	T4th (E)			—	—	—	—	—	—	—	—
1993— Cleveland (A.L.)		76	86	.469	6th (E)			—	—	—	—	—	—	—	—
1994— Cleveland (A.L.)		66	47	.584											
1995— Cleveland (A.L.)		100	44	.694	1st (C)			3	0	4	2	2	4	—	—
1996— Cleveland (A.L.)		99	62	.615	1st (C)			1	3	—	—	—	—	0	1
1997— Cleveland (A.L.)		86	75	.534	1st (C)			3	2	4	2	3	4	—	—
1998— Cleveland (A.L.)		89	73	.549	1st (C)			3	1	2	4	—	—	1	0
Major league totals (8 years)		624	526	.543				10	6	10	8	5	8	1	1

NOTES:
1987—Defeated Winston-Salem, two games to none, in playoffs; lost to Salem, three games to one, in league championship.
1989—Lost to Albuquerque in playoffs.
1991—Replaced Cleveland manager John McNamara with club in seventh place and record of 25-52 (July 6).
1994—Cleveland was in second place in A.L. Central at time of season-ending strike (August 12).
1995—Defeated Boston in A.L. divisional playoff; defeated Seattle in A.L. Championship Series; lost to Atlanta in World Series.
1996—Lost to Baltimore in A.L. divisional playoff.
1997—Defeated New York in A.L. divisional playoff; defeated Baltimore in A.L. Championship Series; lost to Florida in World Series.
1998—Defeated Boston in A.L. divisional playoff; lost to New York Yankees in A.L. Championship Series.

HOWE, ART — ATHLETICS

PERSONAL: Born December 15, 1946, in Pittsburgh. ... 6-1/185. ... Batted right, threw right. ... Full name: Arthur Henry Howe Jr.

HIGH SCHOOL: Shaler (Glenshaw, Pa.).

COLLEGE: Wyoming (bachelor of science degree in business administration, 1969).

TRANSACTIONS/CAREER NOTES: Signed as free agent by Pittsburgh Pirates organization (June, 1971). ... On disabled list (August 17-September 2, 1972 and April 13-May 6, 1973). ... Traded by Pirates to Houston Astros (January 6, 1976), completing deal in which Astros traded 2B Tommy Helms to Pirates for a player to be named later (December 12, 1975). ... On disabled list (May 12-June 19, 1982 and March 27, 1983-entire season). ... Granted free agency (November 7, 1983). ... Signed by St. Louis Cardinals (March 21, 1984). ... Released by Cardinals (April 22, 1985).

STATISTICAL NOTES: Tied for Carolina League lead in putouts by third baseman with 95 in 1971. ... Led International League third basemen with 22 errors and 24 double plays in 1972. ... Had 23-game hitting streak (May 1-24, 1981). ... Career major league grand slams: 1.

Year Team (League)	Pos.	G	AB	R	H	2B	3B	HR	RBI	Avg.	BB	SO	SB	PO	A	E	Avg.
1971— Salem (Carolina)	3B-SS	114	382	77	133	27	7	12	79	*.348	82	74	11	‡110	221	21	.940
1972— Char., W.Va. (Int'l)	3B-2B-SS	109	365	68	99	21	3	14	53	.271	63	69	8	105	248	†24	.936
1973— Char., W.Va. (Int'l)	3B-2B-SS	119	372	50	85	20	1	8	44	.228	54	70	6	141	229	21	.946

Year	Team (League)	Pos.	G	AB	R	H	2B	3B	HR	RBI	Avg.	BB	SO	SB	PO	A	E	Avg.
							BATTING									FIELDING		
1974—Char., W.Va. (Int'l)	3B	60	207	26	70	17	4	8	36	.338	31	27	4	35	90	9	.933
—Pittsburgh (N.L.)	3B-SS	29	74	10	18	4	1	1	5	.243	9	13	0	11	49	4	.938
1975—Char., W.Va. (Int'l)	3B-2B	11	42	4	15	1	3	0	3	.357	2	4	0	15	23	1	.974
—Pittsburgh (N.L.)	3B-SS	63	146	13	25	9	0	1	10	.171	15	15	1	19	89	7	.939
1976—Memphis (Int'l)■	3B-1B	74	259	50	92	21	3	12	59	.355	34	31	1	93	120	14	.938
—Houston (N.L.)	3B-2B	21	29	0	4	1	0	0	0	.138	6	6	0	17	16	1	.971
1977—Houston (N.L.)	2B-3B-SS	125	413	44	109	23	7	8	58	.264	41	60	0	213	333	8	.986
1978—Houston (N.L.)	2B-3B-1B	119	420	46	123	33	3	7	55	.293	34	41	2	240	302	13	.977
1979—Houston (N.L.)	2B-3B-1B	118	355	32	88	15	2	6	33	.248	36	37	3	188	261	7	.985
1980—Houston (N.L.)	1-3-2-S	110	321	34	91	12	5	10	46	.283	34	29	1	598	86	10	.986
1981—Houston (N.L.)	3B-1B	103	361	43	107	22	4	3	36	.296	41	23	1	67	206	9	.968
1982—Houston (N.L.)	3B-1B	110	365	29	87	15	1	5	38	.238	41	45	2	344	174	7	.987
1983—									Did not play.								
1984—St. Louis (N.L.)■	3-1-2-S	89	139	17	30	5	0	2	12	.216	18	18	0	71	80	3	.981
1985—St. Louis (N.L.)	1B-3B	4	3	0	0	0	0	0	0	.000	0	0	0	5	1	0	1.000
Major league totals (11 years)		891	2626	268	682	139	23	43	293	.260	275	287	10	1773	1597	69	.980

DIVISION SERIES RECORD

Year	Team (League)	Pos.	G	AB	R	H	2B	3B	HR	RBI	Avg.	BB	SO	SB	PO	A	E	Avg.
							BATTING									FIELDING		
1981—Houston (N.L.)	3B	5	17	1	4	0	0	1	1	.235	2	1	0	6	9	0	1.000

CHAMPIONSHIP SERIES RECORD

Year	Team (League)	Pos.	G	AB	R	H	2B	3B	HR	RBI	Avg.	BB	SO	SB	PO	A	E	Avg.
							BATTING									FIELDING		
1974—Pittsburgh (N.L.)	PH	1	1	0	0	0	0	0	0	.000	0	0	0	...	...	...	....
1980—Houston (N.L.)	1B-PH	5	15	0	3	1	1	0	2	.200	2	2	0	29	3	0	1.000
Championship series totals (2 years)		6	16	0	3	1	1	0	2	.188	2	2	0	29	3	0	1.000

RECORD AS MANAGER

BACKGROUND: Coach, Texas Rangers (May 21, 1985-88). ... Scout, Los Angeles Dodgers organization (1994). ... Coach, Colorado Rockies (1995).

Year	Team (League)	W	L	Pct.	Pos.	Playoff W	L	Champ. Series W	L	World Series W	L	All-Star Game W	L
		REGULAR SEASON				POSTSEASON							
1989—Houston (N.L.)	86	76	.531	3rd (W)	—	—	—	—	—	—	—	—
1990—Houston (N.L.)	75	87	.463	T4th (W)	—	—	—	—	—	—	—	—
1991—Houston (N.L.)	65	97	.401	6th (W)	—	—	—	—	—	—	—	—
1992—Houston (N.L.)	81	81	.500	4th (W)	—	—	—	—	—	—	—	—
1993—Houston (N.L.)	85	77	.525	3rd (W)	—	—	—	—	—	—	—	—
1996—Oakland (A.L.)	78	84	.481	3rd (W)	—	—	—	—	—	—	—	—
1997—Oakland (A.L.)	65	97	.401	4th (W)	—	—	—	—	—	—	—	—
1998—Oakland (A.L.)	74	88	.457	4th (W)	—	—	—	—	—	—	—	—
National League totals (5 years)	392	418	.484		—	—	—	—	—	—	—	—
American League totals (3 years)	217	269	.447		—	—	—	—	—	—	—	—
Major league totals (8 years)	609	687	.470		—	—	—	—	—	—	—	—

JOHNSON, DAVEY   DODGERS

PERSONAL: Born January 30, 1943, in Orlando. ... 6-1/182. ... Bats right, throws right. ... Full name: David Allen Johnson.

HIGH SCHOOL: Alamo Heights (San Antonio).

COLLEGE: Texas A&M; then Trinity University, Texas (degree in mathematics); then Johns Hopkins.

TRANSACTIONS/CAREER NOTES: Signed as free agent by Baltimore Orioles organization (June 2, 1962). ... On Rochester disabled list (August 7-September 1, 1965). ... Traded by Orioles with P Pat Dobson, P Roric Harrison and C Johnny Oates to Atlanta Braves for C Earl Williams and IF Taylor Duncan (November 30, 1972). ... Released by Braves (April 11, 1975). ... Signed by Yomiuri Giants of Japan Central League (1975). ... Released by Yomiuri (January 21, 1977). ... Signed by Philadelphia Phillies (February 3, 1977). ... On disabled list (June 15-July 1, 1977). ... Traded by Phillies to Chicago Cubs for P Larry Anderson (August 6, 1978). ... Released by Cubs (October 17, 1978). ... Served as player/manager with Miami of Inter-American League (1979). ... Granted free agency when league folded (June 30, 1979).

RECORDS: Shares major league single-season records for most home runs by second baseman—42 (1973, also had one home run as pinch hitter); fewest triples (150 or more games)—0 (1973); and most grand slams by pinch hitter—2 (1978).

HONORS: Won A.L. Gold Glove at second base (1969-71). ... Named second baseman on THE SPORTING NEWS A.L. All-Star team (1970). ... Named N.L. Comeback Player of the Year by THE SPORTING NEWS (1973). ... Named second baseman on THE SPORTING NEWS N.L. All-Star team (1973).

STATISTICAL NOTES: Led California League shortstops with 63 double plays in 1962. ... Led A.L. second basemen with 19 errors in 1966. ... Tied for A.L. lead in putouts by second baseman with 379 in 1970. ... Tied for A.L. lead with eight sacrifice flies in 1967. ... Led A.L. second basemen with 103 double plays in 1971. ... Led N.L. second basemen with 877 total chances and tied for lead with 106 double plays in 1973. ... Career major league grand slams: 5.

Year	Team (League)	Pos.	G	AB	R	H	2B	3B	HR	RBI	Avg.	BB	SO	SB	PO	A	E	Avg.
							BATTING									FIELDING		
1962—Stockton (California)	SS	97	343	58	106	18	•12	10	63	.309	43	61	8	135	307	40	*.917
1963—Elmira (Eastern)	SS-2B	63	233	47	76	11	6	13	42	.326	29	42	12	115	155	12	.957
—Rochester (Int'l)	2B-OF	63	211	31	52	9	3	6	22	.246	25	39	4	141	138	11	.962
1964—Rochester (Int'l)	2B-SS	•155	590	87	156	29	14	19	73	.264	71	95	7	326	445	39	.952
1965—Baltimore (A.L.)	3B-2B-SS	20	47	5	8	3	0	0	1	.170	5	6	3	11	37	3	.941
—Rochester (Int'l)	SS	52	193	29	58	9	3	4	22	.301	16	34	4	96	161	10	.963
1966—Baltimore (A.L.)	2B-SS	131	501	47	129	20	3	7	56	.257	31	64	4	294	357	†20	.970
1967—Baltimore (A.L.)	2B-3B	148	510	62	126	30	3	10	64	.247	59	82	4	344	351	14	.980
1968—Baltimore (A.L.)	2B-SS	145	504	50	122	24	4	9	56	.242	44	80	7	294	370	15	.978
1969—Baltimore (A.L.)	2B-SS	142	511	52	143	34	1	7	57	.280	57	52	3	358	370	12	.984
1970—Baltimore (A.L.)	2B-SS	149	530	68	149	27	1	10	53	.281	66	68	2	‡382	391	8	.990

Year	Team (League)	Pos.	G	AB	R	H	2B	3B	HR	RBI	Avg.	BB	SO	SB	PO	A	E	Avg.
1971—	Baltimore (A.L.).........	2B	142	510	67	144	26	1	18	72	.282	51	55	3	361	367	12	.984
1972—	Baltimore (A.L.).........	2B	118	376	31	83	22	3	5	32	.221	52	68	1	286	307	6	*.990
1973—	Atlanta (N.L.)■..	2B	157	559	84	151	25	0	43	99	.270	81	93	5	383	464	*30	.966
1974—	Atlanta (N.L.).............	1B-2B	136	454	56	114	18	0	15	62	.251	75	59	1	789	231	11	.989
1975—	Atlanta (N.L.).............	PH	1	1	0	1	1	0	0	1	1.000	0	0	0	...	...	...	...
	—Yomiuri (Jp. Cen.)■...	3B-SS	91	289	29	57	7	0	13	38	.197	32	71	1	85	157	11	.957
1976—	Yomiuri (Jp. Cen.)	2B-3B-1B	108	371	48	102	16	2	26	74	.275	55	62	1	226	28	11	.958
1977—	Philadelphia (N.L.)■ ..	1B-2B-3B	78	156	23	50	9	1	8	36	.321	23	20	1	299	31	0	1.000
1978—	Philadelphia (N.L.).......	2B-3B-1B	44	89	14	17	2	0	2	14	.191	10	19	0	56	41	6	.942
	—Chicago (N.L.)■......	3B	12	49	5	15	1	1	2	6	.306	5	9	0	4	22	5	.839
1979—	Miami (In.-Am.)■	1B	10	25	7	6	2	0	1	2	.240	...	...	0	...	...	...	...
American League totals (8 years)			995	3489	382	904	186	16	66	391	.259	365	475	26	2330	2550	90	.982
National League totals (5 years)			428	1308	182	348	56	2	70	218	.266	194	200	7	1531	789	52	.978
Major league totals (13 years)			1423	4797	564	1252	242	18	136	609	.261	559	675	33	3861	3339	142	.981

CHAMPIONSHIP SERIES RECORD

Year	Team (League)	Pos.	G	AB	R	H	2B	3B	HR	RBI	Avg.	BB	SO	SB	PO	A	E	Avg.
1969—	Baltimore (A.L.)..........	2B	3	13	2	3	0	0	0	0	.231	2	1	0	5	11	0	1.000
1970—	Baltimore (A.L.)..........	2B	3	11	4	4	0	0	2	4	.364	1	1	0	11	4	0	1.000
1971—	Baltimore (A.L.)..........	2B	3	10	2	3	2	0	0	0	.300	3	1	0	5	6	1	.917
1977—	Philadelphia (N.L.)......	1B	1	4	0	1	0	0	0	2	.250	0	1	0	8	0	0	1.000
Championship series totals (4 years)			10	38	8	11	2	0	2	6	.289	6	4	0	29	21	1	.980

WORLD SERIES RECORD

Year	Team (League)	Pos.	G	AB	R	H	2B	3B	HR	RBI	Avg.	BB	SO	SB	PO	A	E	Avg.
1966—	Baltimore (A.L.)..........	2B	4	14	1	4	1	0	0	1	.286	0	1	0	12	12	0	1.000
1969—	Baltimore (A.L.)..........	2B	5	16	1	1	0	0	0	0	.063	2	1	0	8	15	0	1.000
1970—	Baltimore (A.L.)..........	2B	5	16	2	5	2	0	0	2	.313	5	2	0	15	9	0	1.000
1971—	Baltimore (A.L.)..........	2B	7	27	1	4	0	0	0	3	.148	0	1	0	18	12	0	1.000
World Series totals (4 years)			21	73	5	14	3	0	0	6	.192	7	5	0	53	48	0	1.000

ALL-STAR GAME RECORD

Year	League	Pos.	AB	R	H	2B	3B	HR	RBI	Avg.	BB	SO	SB	PO	A	E	Avg.
1968—	American	2B	1	0	0	0	0	0	0	.000	0	1	0	1	1	0	1.000
1969—	American							Selected, did not play—injured.									
1970—	American	2B	5	0	1	0	0	0	0	.200	0	1	0	5	1	0	1.000
1973—	National	2B	1	0	0	0	0	0	0	.000	0	0	0	1	1	0	1.000
All-Star Game totals (3 years)			7	0	1	0	0	0	0	.143	0	2	0	7	3	0	1.000

RECORD AS MANAGER

BACKGROUND: Instructor, New York Mets organization (1982). ... Consultant, Cincinnati Reds (December 31, 1992-May 24, 1993).

HONORS: Named A.L. Manager of the Year by The Sporting News (1997). ... Named A.L. Manager of the Year by Baseball Writer's Association of America (1997).

		REGULAR SEASON				POSTSEASON							
						Playoff		Champ. Series		World Series		All-Star Game	
Year	Team (League)	W	L	Pct.	Pos.	W	L	W	L	W	L	W	L
1979—	Miami (Inter-American).............................	43	17	.717	1st	—	—	—	—	—	—	—	—
	—(Second half)	8	4	.667	1st	—	—	—	—	—	—	—	—
1981—	Jackson (Texas)	39	27	.591	1st (E)	—	—	—	—	—	—	—	—
	—(Second half)	29	39	.426	3rd (E)	5	1	—	—	—	—	—	—
1983—	Tidewater (International)	71	68	.511	4th	6	3	—	—	—	—	—	—
1984—	New York (N.L.)	90	72	.556	2nd (E)	—	—	—	—	—	—	—	—
1985—	New York (N.L.)	98	64	.605	2nd (E)	—	—	—	—	—	—	—	—
1986—	New York (N.L.)	108	54	.667	1st (E)	—	—	4	2	4	3	—	—
1987—	New York (N.L.)	92	70	.568	2nd (E)	—	—	—	—	—	—	1	0
1988—	New York (N.L.)	100	60	.625	1st (E)	—	—	3	4	—	—	—	—
1989—	New York (N.L.)	87	75	.537	2nd (E)	—	—	—	—	—	—	—	—
1990—	New York (N.L.)	20	22	.476		—	—	—	—	—	—	—	—
1993—	Cincinnati (N.L.)	53	65	.449	5th (W)	—	—	—	—	—	—	—	—
1994—	Cincinnati (N.L.)	66	48	.579		—	—	—	—	—	—	—	—
1995—	Cincinnati (N.L.)	85	59	.590	1st (C)	3	0	0	4	—	—	—	—
1996—	Baltimore (A.L.)	88	74	.543	2nd (E)	3	1	1	4	—	—	—	—
1997—	Baltimore (A.L.)	98	64	.605	1st (E)	3	1	2	4	—	—	—	—
National League totals (10 years)		799	589	.576		3	0	7	10	4	3	1	0
American League totals (2 years)		186	138	.574		6	2	3	8	—	—	—	—
Major league totals (12 years)		985	727	.575		9	2	10	18	4	3	1	0

NOTES:

1979—Inter-American League folded June 30. Miami finished first in both halves of season and was declared league champion.
1981—Defeated Tulsa, two games to one, in playoffs; defeated San Antonio, three games to none, in league championship.
1983—Defeated Columbus, three games to two, in playoffs; defeated Richmond, three games to one, in league championship.
1986—Defeated Houston in N.L. Championship Series; defeated Boston in World Series.
1988—Lost to Los Angeles in N.L. Championship Series.
1990—Replaced as New York manager by Bud Harrelson, with club in fourth place (May 29).
1993—Replaced Cincinnati manager Tony Perez, with club in fifth place and record of 20-24 (May 24).
1994—Cincinnati was in first place in N.L. Central at time of season-ending strike (August 12).
1995—Defeated Los Angeles in N.L. divisional playoff; lost to Atlanta in N.L. Championship Series.
1996—Defeated Cleveland in A.L. divisional playoff; lost to New York in A.L. Championship Series.
1997—Defeated Seattle in A.L. divisional playoff; lost to Cleveland in A.L. Championship Series.

PERSONAL: Born July 22, 1949, in Grand Forks, N.D. ... 6-3/185. ... Batted left, threw right. ... Full name: Timothy Evald Johnson. ... Brother of Sandy Johnson, former minor league player and manager.
HIGH SCHOOL: Montebello (Calif.).
TRANSACTIONS/CAREER NOTES: Signed as non-drafted free agent by Los Angeles Dodgers organization (August 10, 1967). ... Traded by Dodgers to Milwaukee Brewers for SS Rick Auerbach (April 24, 1973). ... On disabled list (June 24-July 11 and July 28-September 26, 1975). ... On disabled list (July 11-August 2 and August 19-September 15, 1977). ... Traded by Brewers to Toronto Blue Jays for IF Tim Nordbrook (April 28, 1978). ... Released by Blue Jays (November 1, 1979).
STATISTICAL NOTES: Led California League shortstops with 69 double plays and tied for lead in putouts with 231 in 1968.

Year	Team (League)	Pos.	G	AB	R	H	2B	3B	HR	RBI	Avg.	BB	SO	SB	PO	A	E	Avg.
1968	Bakersfield (Calif.)	SS-OF-2B	134	494	57	111	22	2	2	40	.225	37	140	9	‡232	344	41	.934
1969	Albuquerque (Tex.)	SS	92	328	33	81	8	2	1	24	.247	16	73	8	148	287	32	.931
1970	Albuquerque (Tex.)	SS	102	361	45	95	17	8	6	40	.263	24	58	5	177	315	11	*.978
1971	Spokane (PCL)	SS-2B-3B	98	305	38	75	10	1	2	20	.246	39	61	3	141	247	27	.935
1972	El Paso (Texas)	SS	112	409	46	99	11	3	6	35	.242	23	109	6	144	294	35	.926
1973	Albuquerque (PCL)	SS	8	27	2	7	0	0	0	4	.259	3	3	0	9	33	0	1.000
—	Milwaukee (A.L.)■	SS	136	465	39	99	10	2	0	32	.213	29	93	6	*253	381	25	.962
1974	Milwaukee (A.L.)	S-2-0-3	93	245	25	60	7	7	0	25	.245	11	48	4	139	230	9	.976
1975	Milwaukee (A.L.)	2-3-S-1	38	85	6	12	1	0	0	2	.141	6	17	3	38	63	5	.953
1976	Milwaukee (A.L.)	2-3-S-1	105	273	25	75	4	3	0	14	.275	19	32	4	167	238	8	.981
1977	Milwaukee (A.L.)	2-S-3-0	30	33	5	2	1	0	0	2	.061	5	10	1	17	19	1	.973
1978	Milwaukee (A.L.)	SS	3	3	1	0	0	0	0	0	.000	2	0	0	1	0	0	1.000
—	Toronto (A.L.)■	SS-2B	68	79	9	19	2	0	0	3	.241	8	16	0	37	92	2	.985
1979	Toronto (A.L.)	2B-3B-1B	43	86	6	16	2	1	0	6	.186	8	15	0	91	70	7	.958
Major league totals (7 years)			516	1269	116	283	27	13	0	84	.223	88	231	18	743	1093	57	.970

RECORD AS MANAGER

BACKGROUND: Scout, Major League Scouting Bureau (1980-82). ... Scout, Los Angeles Dodgers (1983-86). ... Scout, Montreal Expos (1991-92). ... Coach, Expos (1993-94). ... Coach, Boston Red Sox (1995-96).
HONORS: Named Pioneer League Manager of the Year (1987-88).

		REGULAR SEASON				POSTSEASON							
						Playoff		Champ. Series		World Series		All-Star Game	
Year	Team (League)	W	L	Pct.	Pos.	W	L	W	L	W	L	W	L
1987	Great Falls (Pioneer)	35	34	.507	3rd (N)	—	—	—	—	—	—	—	—
1988	Great Falls (Pioneer)	52	17	.754	1st (N)	3	2	—	—	—	—	—	—
1989	Bakersfield (California)	41	30	.577	1st (S)	—	—	—	—	—	—	—	—
—	(Second half)	41	30	.577	T2nd (S)	6	1	—	—	—	—	—	—
1990	Indianapolis (American Association)	61	85	.418	4th (E)	—	—	—	—	—	—	—	—
1997	Iowa (American Association)	74	69	.517	1st (W)	3	3	—	—	—	—	—	—
1998	Toronto (A.L.)	88	74	.543	3rd (E)	—	—	—	—	—	—	—	—

NOTES:
1988—Defeated Butte in league championship
1989—Defeated San Bernardino, three games to one, in playoffs; defeated Stockton, three games to none, in league championship.
1997—Defeated New Orleans, three games to none; lost to Buffalo, three games to none, in league championship.

PERSONAL: Born August 15, 1950, in Graceville, Minn. ... 5-11/185. ... Batted left, threw left. ... Full name: Jay Thomas Kelly.
HIGH SCHOOL: St. Mary's (South Amboy, N.J.).
JUNIOR COLLEGE: Mesa (Ariz.) Community College.
COLLEGE: Monmouth College (N.J.).
TRANSACTIONS/CAREER NOTES: Selected by Seattle Pilots organization in eighth round of free-agent draft (June 7, 1968). ... Seattle franchise moved to Milwaukee and renamed Brewers (1970). ... On temporarily inactive list (April 16-20, April 25-30 and August 21, 1970-remainder of season). ... On military list (August 27, 1970-February 3, 1971). ... Released by Brewers organization (April 6, 1971). ... Signed by Charlotte, Minnesota Twins organization (April 28, 1971). ... Loaned by Twins organization to Rochester, Baltimore Orioles organization (April 5-September 22, 1976). ... On temporarily inactive list (April 15-19, 1977). ... On disabled list (July 25-August 4, 1977). ... Released by Toledo (December 18, 1978). ... Re-signed by Visalia, Twins organization (January 2, 1979). ... Released by Twins organization (December 2, 1980).
STATISTICAL NOTES: Led Pacific Coast League outfielders with six double plays in 1972.

Year	Team (League)	Pos.	G	AB	R	H	2B	3B	HR	RBI	Avg.	BB	SO	SB	PO	A	E	Avg.
1968	Newark (NY-Penn)	OF	65	218	50	69	11	4	2	10	.317	43	31	*16	*144	*9	3	.981
1969	Clinton (Midwest)	OF	100	269	47	60	10	2	6	35	.223	82	31	10	158	15	4	.977
1970	Jacksonville (Sou.)	OF-1B	93	266	33	64	10	1	8	38	.241	41	37	2	204	19	4	.982
1971	Charlotte (Sou.)■	1B-OF	100	303	50	89	17	0	6	41	.294	59	52	2	508	38	9	.984
1972	Tacoma (PCL)	OF-1B	132	407	76	114	19	2	10	52	.280	70	95	4	282	19	10	.968
1973	Tacoma (PCL)	OF-1B	114	337	67	87	10	2	17	49	.258	89	64	4	200	20	6	.973
1974	Tacoma (PCL)	OF-1B	115	357	68	110	16	0	18	69	.308	78	41	4	514	41	3	.995
1975	Tacoma (PCL)	OF-1B	62	202	38	51	5	0	9	29	.252	47	36	6	185	12	6	.970
—	Minnesota (A.L.)	1B-DH-OF	49	127	11	23	5	0	1	11	.181	15	22	0	360	28	6	.985
1976	Rochester (Int'l)■	OF-1B	127	405	71	117	19	3	18	70	.289	85	71	2	323	28	4	.989
1977	Tacoma (PCL)■	1B-OF-P	113	363	80	99	12	1	12	64	.273	78	61	11	251	15	6	.978
1978	Toledo (Int'l)	OF-1B	119	325	47	74	13	0	10	49	.228	*91	61	2	556	46	5	.992
1979	Visalia (California)■	1B-P	2	0	0	0	0	0	0	0	. . .	1	0	0	3	4	0	1.000
Major league totals (1 year)			49	127	11	23	5	0	1	11	.181	15	22	0	360	28	6	.985

MAJOR LEAGUE MANAGERS

RECORD AS PITCHER

Year — Team (League)	W	L	Pct.	ERA	G	GS	CG	ShO	Sv.	IP	H	R	ER	BB	SO
1977— Tacoma (PCL)	0	0	...	6.00	1	0	0	0	0	3	2	2	2	3	0
1979— Visalia (California)	1	0	1.000	2.25	1	1	0	0	0	8	5	3	2	7	2
1980— Visalia (California)	0	0	...	0.69	2	1	0	0	0	13	12	1	1	6	2

RECORD AS MANAGER

BACKGROUND: Player/manager, Tacoma, Minnesota Twins organization (June 1977-remainder of season). ... Player/coach, Toledo, Twins organization (1978). ... Coach, Twins (1983-September 11, 1986).

HONORS: Named California League Manager of the Year (1979). ... Named California League co-Manager of the Year (1980). ... Named Southern League Manager of the Year (1981). ... Named A.L. Manager of the Year by THE SPORTING NEWS (1991). ... Named A.L. Manager of the Year by Baseball Writers' Association of America (1991).

	REGULAR SEASON				Playoff		Champ. Series		World Series		All-Star Game	
Year — Team (League)	W	L	Pct.	Pos.	W	L	W	L	W	L	W	L
1977— Tacoma (Pacific Coast)	28	26	.519	3rd (W)	—	—	—	—	—	—	—	—
1979— Visalia (California)	44	26	.629	1st (S)	—	—	—	—	—	—	—	—
— (Second half)	42	28	.600	2nd (S)	1	2	—	—	—	—	—	—
1980— Visalia (California)	27	43	.386	4th (S)	—	—	—	—	—	—	—	—
— (Second half)	44	26	.629	1st (S)	2	4	—	—	—	—	—	—
1981— Orlando (Southern)	42	27	.609	1st (E)	—	—	—	—	—	—	—	—
— (Second half)	37	36	.507	3rd (E)	6	2	—	—	—	—	—	—
1982— Orlando (Southern)	31	38	.449	5th (E)	—	—	—	—	—	—	—	—
— (Second half)	43	32	.573	2nd (E)	—	—	—	—	—	—	—	—
1986— Minnesota (A.L.)	12	11	.522	6th (W)	—	—	—	—	—	—	—	—
1987— Minnesota (A.L.)	85	77	.525	1st (W)	—	—	4	1	4	3	—	—
1988— Minnesota (A.L.)	91	71	.562	2nd (W)	—	—	—	—	—	—	1	0
1989— Minnesota (A.L.)	80	82	.494	5th (W)	—	—	—	—	—	—	—	—
1990— Minnesota (A.L.)	74	88	.457	7th (W)	—	—	—	—	—	—	—	—
1991— Minnesota (A.L.)	95	67	.586	1st (W)	—	—	4	1	4	3	—	—
1992— Minnesota (A.L.)	90	72	.556	2nd (W)	—	—	—	—	—	—	1	0
1993— Minnesota (A.L.)	71	91	.438	T5th (W)	—	—	—	—	—	—	—	—
1994— Minnesota (A.L.)	53	60	.469		—	—	—	—	—	—	—	—
1995— Minnesota (A.L.)	56	88	.389	5th (C)	—	—	—	—	—	—	—	—
1996— Minnesota (A.L.)	78	84	.481	4th (C)	—	—	—	—	—	—	—	—
1997— Minnesota (A.L.)	68	94	.420	4th (C)	—	—	—	—	—	—	—	—
1998— Minnesota (A.L.)	70	92	.432	4th (C)	—	—	—	—	—	—	—	—
Major league totals (13 years)	**923**	**977**	**.486**		—	—	**8**	**2**	**8**	**6**	**2**	**0**

NOTES:
1977—Replaced Tacoma manager Del Wilber with record of 40-49 and became player/manager (June).
1979—Lost to San Jose in semifinals.
1980—Defeated Fresno, two games to one, in semifinals; lost to Stockton, three games to none, in league championship.
1981—Defeated Savannah, three games to one, in semifinals; defeated Nashville, three games to one, in league championship.
1986—Replaced Minnesota manager Ray Miller with club in seventh place and record of 59-80 (September 12).
1987—Defeated Detroit in A.L. Championship Series; defeated St. Louis in World Series.
1991—Defeated Toronto in A.L. Championship Series; defeated Atlanta in World Series.
1994—Minnesota was in fourth place in A.L. Central at time of season-ending strike (August 12).

LA RUSSA, TONY — CARDINALS

PERSONAL: Born October 4, 1944, in Tampa. ... 6-0/185. ... Batted right, threw right. ... Full name: Anthony La Russa Jr.

HIGH SCHOOL: Jefferson (Tampa).

COLLEGE: University of Tampa, then South Florida (degree in industrial management), then Florida State (law degree, 1980).

TRANSACTIONS/CAREER NOTES: Signed by Kansas City Athletics organization (June 6, 1962). ... On disabled list (May 9-September 8, 1964; June 3-July 15, 1965; and April 12-May 6 and July 3-September 5, 1967). ... A's franchise moved from Kansas City to Oakland (October 1967). ... Contract sold by A's to Atlanta Braves (August 14, 1971). ... Traded by Braves to Chicago Cubs for P Tom Phoebus (October 20, 1972). ... Contract sold by Cubs to Pittsburgh Pirates organization (March 23, 1974). ... Released by Pirates organization (April 4, 1975). ... Signed by Chicago White Sox organization (April 7, 1975). ... On disabled list (August 8-18, 1976). ... Contract sold by White Sox to St. Louis Cardinals organization (December 13, 1976). ... Released by Cardinals organization (September 29, 1977).

STATISTICAL NOTES: Led International League in being hit by pitch with 11 in 1972.

										BATTING				FIELDING			
Year — Team (League)	Pos.	G	AB	R	H	2B	3B	HR	RBI	Avg.	BB	SO	SB	PO	A	E	Avg.
1962— Daytona Beach (FSL)..	SS	64	225	37	58	7	0	1	32	.258	42	47	11	135	173	38	.890
— Binghamton (Eastern)	SS-2B	12	43	3	8	0	0	0	4	.186	5	9	2	20	27	8	.855
1963— Kansas City (A.L.)	SS-2B	34	44	4	11	1	1	0	1	.250	7	12	0	29	25	2	.964
1964— Lewiston (N'west)	2B-SS	90	329	50	77	22	1	1	25	.234	53	56	10	188	218	18	.958
1965— Birmingham (Sou.)......	2B	75	259	24	50	11	2	1	18	.193	26	37	5	202	161	21	.945
1966— Modesto (California) ..	2B	81	316	67	92	20	1	7	54	.291	44	37	18	201	212	20	.954
— Mobile (Southern)	2B	51	170	20	50	9	4	4	26	.294	23	24	4	117	133	10	.962
1967— Birmingham (Sou.)......	2B	41	139	12	32	6	1	5	22	.230	10	11	3	88	120	5	.977
1968— Oakland (A.L.)	PH	5	3	0	1	0	0	0	0	.333	0	0	0	...	...	...	...
— Vancouver (PCL)	2B	122	455	55	109	16	8	5	29	.240	52	58	4	249	321	14	*.976
1969— Iowa (Am. Assoc.)......	2B	67	235	37	72	11	1	4	27	.306	0	1	5	177	222	15	.964
— Oakland (A.L.)	PH	8	8	0	0	0	0	0	0	.000	42	30	0	...	...	...	...
1970— Iowa (Am. Assoc.)......	2B	22	88	13	22	5	0	2	5	.250	9	14	0	52	59	3	.974
— Oakland (A.L.)	2B	52	106	6	21	4	1	0	6	.198	15	19	0	67	89	5	.969
1971— Iowa (Am. Assoc.)......	2-3-S-O	28	107	21	31	5	1	2	11	.290	10	11	0	70	85	2	.987
— Birmingham (Sou.)	2B-SS-3B	23	8	3	0	0	0	0	0	.000	0	4	0	8	7	2	.882
— Atlanta (N.L.)■......	2B	9	7	1	2	0	0	0	0	.286	1	1	0	8	6	1	.933
1972— Richmond (Int'l)	2B	122	389	68	120	13	2	10	42	.308	72	41	0	305	289	20	.967

Year	Team (League)	Pos.	G	AB	R	H	2B	3B	HR	RBI	Avg.	BB	SO	SB	PO	A	E	Avg.
							BATTING									FIELDING		
1973—	Wichita (A.A.)■	2B-1B-3B	106	392	82	123	16	0	5	75	.314	60	46	10	423	213	26	.961
	—Chicago (N.L.)	PR	1	0	1	0	0	0	0	0	...	0	0	0	...	...	...	...
1974—	Char., W.Va. (Int'l)■	2B	139	457	50	119	17	1	8	35	.260	51	50	4	262	*378	17	.974
1975—	Denver (A.A.)	3-0-S-2	118	354	87	99	23	2	7	46	.280	70	46	13	95	91	10	.949
1976—	Iowa (Am. Assoc.)	3-2-S-1-0-P	107	332	53	86	11	4	4	34	.259	40	43	10	132	160	22	.930
1977—	New Orleans (A.A.)■	2B-3B	50	128	17	24	2	2	3	6	.188	20	21	0	66	87	7	.956
	American League totals (5 years)		122	169	13	33	5	2	0	7	.195	64	65	0	104	121	9	.962
	National League totals (2 years)		10	7	2	2	0	0	0	0	.286	1	1	0	8	6	1	.933
	Major league totals (6 years)		132	176	15	35	5	2	0	7	.199	65	66	0	112	127	10	.960

RECORD AS PITCHER

Year	Team (League)	W	L	Pct.	ERA	G	GS	CG	ShO	Sv.	IP	H	R	ER	BB	SO
1976—	Iowa (Am. Assoc.)	0	0	...	3.00	3	0	0	0	0	3	3	1	1	0	0

RECORD AS MANAGER

BACKGROUND: Coach, St. Louis Cardinals organization (June 20-September 29, 1977). ... Coach, Chicago White Sox (July 3, 1978-remainder of season).

RECORDS: Shares major league single-season record for most clubs managed—2 (1986).

HONORS: Named Major League Manager of the Year by THE SPORTING NEWS (1983). ... Named A.L. Manager of the Year by Baseball Writers' Association of America (1983, 1988 and 1992). ... Named A.L. Manager of the Year by THE SPORTING NEWS (1988 and 1992).

Year	Team (League)	W	L	Pct.	Pos.	Playoff W	L	Champ. Series W	L	World Series W	L	All-Star Game W	L
						REGULAR SEASON		POSTSEASON					
1978—	Knoxville (Southern)	49	21	.700	1st (W)	—	—	—	—	—	—	—	—
	—(Second half)	4	4	.500		—	—	—	—	—	—	—	—
1979—	Iowa (American Association)	54	52	.509		—	—	—	—	—	—	—	—
	—Chicago (A.L.)	27	27	.500	5th (W)	—	—	—	—	—	—	—	—
1980—	Chicago (A.L.)	70	90	.438	5th (W)	—	—	—	—	—	—	—	—
1981—	Chicago (A.L.)	31	22	.585	3rd (W)	—	—	—	—	—	—	—	—
	—(Second half)	23	30	.434	6th (W)	—	—	—	—	—	—	—	—
1982—	Chicago (A.L.)	87	75	.537	3rd (W)	—	—	—	—	—	—	—	—
1983—	Chicago (A.L.)	99	63	.611	1st (W)	—	—	1	3	—	—	—	—
1984—	Chicago (A.L.)	74	88	.457	T5th (W)	—	—	—	—	—	—	—	—
1985—	Chicago (A.L.)	85	77	.525	3rd (W)	—	—	—	—	—	—	—	—
1986—	Chicago (A.L.)	26	38	.406		—	—	—	—	—	—	—	—
	—Oakland (A.L.)	45	34	.570	T3rd (W)	—	—	—	—	—	—	—	—
1987—	Oakland (A.L.)	81	81	.500	3rd (W)	—	—	—	—	—	—	—	—
1988—	Oakland (A.L.)	104	58	.642	1st (W)	—	—	4	0	1	4	—	—
1989—	Oakland (A.L.)	99	63	.611	1st (W)	—	—	4	1	4	0	1	0
1990—	Oakland (A.L.)	103	59	.636	1st (W)	—	—	4	0	0	4	1	0
1991—	Oakland (A.L.)	84	78	.519	4th (W)	—	—	—	—	—	—	1	0
1992—	Oakland (A.L.)	96	66	.593	1st (W)	—	—	2	4	—	—	—	—
1993—	Oakland (A.L.)	68	94	.420	7th (W)	—	—	—	—	—	—	—	—
1994—	Oakland (A.L.)	51	63	.447		—	—	—	—	—	—	—	—
1995—	Oakland (A.L.)	67	77	.465	4th (W)	—	—	—	—	—	—	—	—
1996—	St. Louis (N.L.)	88	74	.543	1st (C)	3	0	3	4	—	—	—	—
1997—	St. Louis (N.L.)	73	89	.451	4th (C)	—	—	—	—	—	—	—	—
1998—	St. Louis (N.L.)	83	79	.512	3rd (C)	—	—	—	—	—	—	—	—
	American League totals (17 years)	1320	1183	.527		—	—	15	8	5	8	3	0
	National League totals (3 years)	244	242	.502		3	0	3	4	—	—	—	—
	Major league totals (20 years)	1564	1425	.523		3	0	18	12	5	8	3	0

NOTES:

1978—Became Chicago White Sox coach and replaced as Knoxville manager by Joe Jones, with club in third place (July 3).

1979—Replaced as Iowa manager by Joe Sparks, with club in second place (August 3); replaced Chicago manager Don Kessinger with club in fifth place and record of 46-60 (August 3).

1983—Lost to Baltimore in A.L. Championship Series.

1986—Replaced as White Sox manager by interim manager Doug Rader, with club in sixth place (June 20); replaced Oakland manager Jackie Moore (record of 29-44) and interim manager Jeff Newman (record of 2-8) with club in seventh place and record of 31-52 (July 7).

1988—Defeated Boston in A.L. Championship Series; lost to Los Angeles in World Series.

1989—Defeated Toronto in A.L. Championship Series; defeated San Francisco in World Series.

1990—Defeated Boston in A.L. Championship Series; lost to Cincinnati in World Series.

1992—Lost to Toronto in A.L. Championship Series.

1993—On suspended list (October 1-remainder of season).

1994—Oakland was in second place in A.L. West at time of season-ending strike (August 12).

1996—Defeated San Diego in N.L. divisional playoff; lost to Atlanta in N.L. Championship Series.

LAMONT, GENE

PIRATES

PERSONAL: Born December 25, 1946, in Rockford, Ill. ... 6-1/190. ... Batted both, threw right. ... Full name: Gene William Lamont.

HIGH SCHOOL: Hiawatha (Kirkland, Ill.).

COLLEGE: Northern Illinois, then Western Illinois.

TRANSACTIONS/CAREER NOTES: Selected by Detroit Tigers organization in first round (13th pick overall) of free-agent draft (June 29, 1965). ... On disabled list (May 18-28, 1966). ... On temporarily inactive list (May 20-25, 1967). ... On military list (May 25, 1967-remainder of season). ... On temporarily inactive list (July 15-31, 1972). ... Traded by Tigers to Atlanta Braves organization for C Bob Didier (May 14, 1973). ... Selected by Tigers from Braves organization in Rule 5 major league draft (December 3, 1973). ... Released by Tigers organization (December 20, 1977).

STATISTICAL NOTES: Led Southern League catchers with nine errors in 1969. ... Led Southern League catchers with 730 putouts, 72 assists, 814 total chances, 9 double plays and 15 passed balls in 1972. ... Led American Association catchers with eight double plays in 1976.

Year Team (League)	Pos.	G	AB	R	H	2B	3B	HR	RBI	Avg.	BB	SO	SB	PO	A	E	Avg.
1965—Syracuse (Int'l)..........	C	5	9	1	1	0	0	1	1	.111	0	6	0	...	...	...	...
—Daytona Beach (FSL)..	C	38	104	9	24	5	1	1	16	.231	13	33	1	222	19	3	.988
1966—States. (W. Caro.).......	C	45	137	14	27	4	2	3	19	.197	21	49	1	283	28	8	.975
—Rocky Mt. (Caro.).......	C	36	102	9	26	4	1	2	9	.255	16	23	0	213	19	5	.979
1967—Rocky Mt. (Caro.).......	C	19	56	4	8	2	0	1	5	.143	8	8	0	107	16	1	.992
1968—Rocky Mt. (Caro.).......	C-OF-3B	101	304	36	76	10	0	4	39	.250	24	60	1	498	72	7	.988
1969—Montgomery (Sou.)....	C-3B	86	268	24	63	15	1	3	29	.235	32	37	0	410	92	†16	.969
1970—Toledo (Int'l).............	C-3B-OF	74	230	27	61	9	1	4	32	.265	19	46	1	313	59	5	.987
—Detroit (A.L.)...........	C	15	44	3	13	3	1	1	4	.295	2	9	0	87	8	0	1.000
1971—Toledo (Int'l).............	C	63	180	17	41	8	1	5	19	.228	19	29	0	321	43	9	.976
—Detroit (A.L.)...........	C	7	15	2	1	0	0	0	1	.067	0	5	0	38	2	2	.952
1972—Montgomery (Sou.)....	C-OF	119	385	47	105	19	1	6	51	.273	64	72	1	†731	†72	12	.985
—Detroit (A.L.)...........	C	1	0	0	0	0	0	0	0	...	0	0	0	1	0	0	1.000
1973—Richmond (Int'l)■...	C-1B	101	275	29	69	11	1	2	25	.251	41	64	0	411	34	3	.993
1974—Detroit (A.L.)■.......	C	60	92	9	20	4	0	3	8	.217	7	19	0	204	21	6	.974
1975—Detroit (A.L.)...........	C	4	8	1	3	1	0	0	1	.375	0	2	1	14	3	1	.944
—Evansville (A.A.)........	C	49	130	15	40	9	0	3	20	.308	20	20	1	211	23	4	.983
1976—Evansville (A.A.)........	C	96	269	23	63	13	0	5	25	.234	36	47	2	467	47	7	.987
1977—Evansville (A.A.)........	C	3	5	0	2	1	0	0	0	.400	1	1	0	4	1	0	1.000
Major league totals (5 years)		87	159	15	37	8	1	4	14	.233	9	35	1	344	34	9	.977

RECORD AS MANAGER

BACKGROUND: Coach, Pittsburgh Pirates (1986-91). ... Scout and adviser to the general manager (July 7, 1995-remainder of season). ... Coach, Pirates (1996).

HONORS: Named Southern League Manager of the Year (1982). ... Named A.L. Manager of the Year by the Baseball Writers' Association of America (1993).

					REGULAR SEASON			POSTSEASON					
							Playoff		Champ. Series		World Series		All-Star Game
Year Team (League)	W	L	Pct.	Pos.			W	L	W	L	W	L	W	L
1978—Fort Myers (Florida State)	38	30	.559	1st (S)			—	—	—	—	—	—	—	—
—(Second half)	33	36	.478	5th (S)			0	1	—	—	—	—	—	—
1979—Fort Myers (Florida State)	38	32	.543	3rd (S)			—	—	—	—	—	—	—	—
—(Second half)	31	37	.456	4th (S)			—	—	—	—	—	—	—	—
1980—Jacksonville (Southern)	31	40	.437	4th (E)			—	—	—	—	—	—	—	—
—(Second half)	32	41	.438	5th (E)			—	—	—	—	—	—	—	—
1981—Jacksonville (Southern)	34	36	.486	4th (E)			—	—	—	—	—	—	—	—
—(Second half)	31	41	.431	4th (E)			—	—	—	—	—	—	—	—
1982—Jacksonville (Southern)	41	31	.569	1st (E)			—	—	—	—	—	—	—	—
—(Second half)	42	30	.583	1st (E)			4	4	—	—	—	—	—	—
1983—Jacksonville (Southern)	36	36	.500	2nd (E)			—	—	—	—	—	—	—	—
—(Second half)	41	32	.562	1st (E)			4	4	—	—	—	—	—	—
1984—Omaha (American Association)	68	86	.442	8th			—	—	—	—	—	—	—	—
1985—Omaha (American Association)	73	69	.514	3rd (W)			—	—	—	—	—	—	—	—
1992—Chicago (A.L.)	86	76	.531	3rd (W)			—	—	—	—	—	—	—	—
1993—Chicago (A.L.)	94	68	.580	1st (W)			—	—	2	4	—	—	—	—
1994—Chicago (A.L.)	67	46	.593				—	—	—	—	—	—	—	—
1995—Chicago (A.L.)	11	20	.355				—	—	—	—	—	—	—	—
1997—Pittsburgh (N.L.)	79	83	.488	2nd (C)			—	—	—	—	—	—	—	—
1998—Pittsburgh (N.L.)	69	93	.426	6th (C)			—	—	—	—	—	—	—	—
American League totals (4 years)	258	210	.551				—	—	2	4	—	—	—	—
National League totals (2 year)	148	176	.457				—	—	—	—	—	—	—	—
Major league totals (6 years)	406	386	.513				—	—	2	4	—	—	—	—

NOTES:
1978—Lost to Miami in Southern Division championship.
1981—Jacksonville tied one game.
1982—Defeated Columbus, three games to one, in Eastern Division championship; lost to Nashville, three games to one, in league championship.
1983—Defeated Savannah, three games to one, in Eastern Division championship; lost to Birmingham, three games to one, in league championship.
1993—Lost to Toronto in A.L. Championship Series.
1994—Chicago was in first place in A.L. Central at time of season-ending strike (August 12).
1995—Replaced as White Sox manager by Terry Bevington, with club in fourth place (June 2).

LEYLAND, JIM   ROCKIES

PERSONAL: Born December 15, 1944, in Toledo, Ohio. ... 5-11/170. ... Batted right, threw right. ... Full name: James Richard Leyland. ... Name pronounced LEE-lund.

HIGH SCHOOL: Perrysburg (Ohio).

TRANSACTIONS/CAREER NOTES: Signed as free agent by Detroit Tigers organization (September 21, 1963). ... On disabled list (June 15-27, 1964). ... Released by Rocky Mount, Tigers organization (March 27, 1971).

Year Team (League)	Pos.	G	AB	R	H	2B	3B	HR	RBI	Avg.	BB	SO	SB	PO	A	E	Avg.
1964—Lakeland (Fla. St.)	C	52	129	8	25	0	1	0	8	.194	18	33	1	268	17	6	.979
—Cocoa Tigers (CRL)....	C	24	52	2	12	1	0	0	4	.231	13	7	1	122	15	3	.979
1965—Jamestown (NYP)	C-3B-P	82	211	18	50	7	2	1	21	.237	37	44	2	318	36	6	.983
1966—Rocky Mt. (Caro.)......	C	67	173	24	42	6	0	0	16	.243	32	35	0	369	23	1	.997
1967—Montgomery (Sou.)......	C	62	171	11	40	3	0	1	16	.234	16	27	0	350	25	6	.984
1968—Montgomery (Sou.)......	C-3B-SS	81	264	19	51	3	0	1	20	.193	14	54	2	511	43	7	.988
1969—Montgomery (Sou.)......	C	16	39	1	8	0	0	0	1	.205	4	7	0	64	6	3	.959
—Lakeland (Fla. St.)	C-P	60	179	20	43	8	0	1	16	.240	31	17	0	321	28	4	.989
1970—Montgomery (Sou.)......	C	2	3	0	0	0	0	0	0	.000	0	0	0	6	0	1	.857

RECORD AS PITCHER

Year	Team (League)	W	L	Pct.	ERA	G	GS	CG	ShO	Sv.	IP	H	R	ER	BB	SO
1965—Jamestown (NYP)		0	0	...	0.00	1	0	0	0	...	2	2	0	0	0	1
1969—Lakeland (Fla. St.)		0	0	...	9.00	1	0	0	0	0	2	4	2	2	0	1

RECORD AS MANAGER

BACKGROUND: Coach, Detroit Tigers organization (1970-June 5, 1971); served as player/coach (1970). ... Coach, Chicago White Sox (1982-85).
HONORS: Named Florida State League Manager of the Year (1977-78). ... Named American Association Manager of the Year (1979). ... Named N.L. co-Manager of the Year by The Sporting News (1988). ... Named N.L. Manager of the Year by The Sporting News (1990 and 1992). ... Named N.L. Manager of the Year by Baseball Writers' Association of America (1990 and 1992).

		REGULAR SEASON				Playoff		Champ. Series		World Series		All-Star Game	
Year	Team (League)	W	L	Pct.	Pos.	W	L	W	L	W	L	W	L
1971—Bristol (Appalachian)		31	35	.470	3rd (S)	—	—	—	—	—	—	—	—
1972—Clinton (Midwest)		22	41	.349	5th (N)	—	—	—	—	—	—	—	—
—(Second half)		27	36	.429	4th (N)	—	—	—	—	—	—	—	—
1973—Clinton (Midwest)		36	26	.581	2nd (N)	—	—	—	—	—	—	—	—
—(Second half)		37	25	.597	1st (N)	0	2	—	—	—	—	—	—
1974—Montgomery (Southern)		61	76	.445	3rd (W)	—	—	—	—	—	—	—	—
1975—Clinton (Midwest)		29	31	.483	4th (S)	—	—	—	—	—	—	—	—
—(Second half)		38	30	.559	2nd (S)	—	—	—	—	—	—	—	—
1976—Lakeland (Florida State)		74	64	.536	2nd (N)	4	0	—	—	—	—	—	—
1977—Lakeland (Florida State)		85	53	.616	1st (N)	5	1	—	—	—	—	—	—
1978—Lakeland (Florida State)		31	38	.449	4th (N)	—	—	—	—	—	—	—	—
—(Second half)		47	22	.681	1st (N)	2	2	—	—	—	—	—	—
1979—Evansville (American Association)		78	58	.574	1st (E)	4	2	—	—	—	—	—	—
1980—Evansville (American Association)		61	74	.452	2nd (E)	—	—	—	—	—	—	—	—
1981—Evansville (American Association)		73	63	.537	1st (E)	1	3	—	—	—	—	—	—
1986—Pittsburgh (N.L.)		64	98	.395	6th (E)	—	—	—	—	—	—	—	—
1987—Pittsburgh (N.L.)		80	82	.494	T4th (E)	—	—	—	—	—	—	—	—
1988—Pittsburgh (N.L.)		85	75	.525	2nd (E)	—	—	—	—	—	—	—	—
1989—Pittsburgh (N.L.)		74	88	.457	5th (E)	—	—	—	—	—	—	—	—
1990—Pittsburgh (N.L.)		95	67	.586	1st (E)	—	—	2	4	—	—	—	—
1991—Pittsburgh (N.L.)		98	64	.605	1st (E)	—	—	3	4	—	—	—	—
1992—Pittsburgh (N.L.)		96	66	.593	1st (E)	—	—	3	4	—	—	—	—
1993—Pittsburgh (N.L.)		75	87	.463	5th (E)	—	—	—	—	—	—	—	—
1994—Pittsburgh (N.L.)		53	61	.465		—	—	—	—	—	—	—	—
1995—Pittsburgh (N.L.)		58	86	.403	5th (C)	—	—	—	—	—	—	—	—
1996—Pittsburgh (N.L.)		73	89	.451	5th (C)	—	—	—	—	—	—	—	—
1997—Florida (N.L.)		92	70	.568	2nd (E)	3	0	4	2	4	3	—	—
1998—Florida (N.L.)		54	108	.333	5th (E)	—	—	—	—	—	—	0	1
Major league totals (13 years)		**997**	**1041**	**.489**		**3**	**0**	**12**	**14**	**4**	**3**	**0**	**1**

NOTES:
1973—Lost to Wisconsin Rapids in playoff.
1976—Defeated Miami, two games to none, in semifinals; defeated Tampa, two games to none, in league championship.
1977—Defeated Miami, two games to none, in semifinals; defeated St. Petersburg, three games to one, in league championship.
1978—Defeated St. Petersburg, one game to none, in Northern Division championship; lost to Miami, two games to one, in league championship.
1979—Defeated Oklahoma City in league championship.
1981—Lost to Denver in semifinals.
1985—Served as acting manager of Chicago White Sox (record of 1-1), with club in fourth place, while manager Tony La Russa served a suspension (August 10 and 11).
1990—Lost to Cincinnati in N.L. Championship Series.
1991—Lost to Atlanta in N.L. Championship Series.
1992—Lost to Atlanta in N.L. Championship Series.
1993—On suspended list (August 27-September 1).
1994—Pittsburgh was tied for third place in N.L. Central at time of season-ending baseball strike (August 12).
1997—Defeated San Francisco in N.L. divisional playoff; defeated Atlanta in N.L. Championship Series; defeated Cleveland in World Series.

MANUEL, JERRY — WHITE SOX

PERSONAL: Born December 23, 1953, in Hahira, Ga. ... 5-11/180. ... Batted right, threw right.
HIGH SCHOOL: Cordova (Rancho Cordova, Calif.).
TRANSACTIONS/CAREER NOTES: Selected by Detroit Tigers organization in first round (20th pick overall) of free-agent draft (June 6, 1972). ... On disabled list (August 18-September 1, 1978). ... Traded by Tigers to Montreal Expos organization for C Duffy Dyer (March 14, 1980). ... On disabled list (May 2-July 31, and August 15-September 1, 1981). ... Traded by Expos to San Diego Padres organization for P Kim Seaman (May 22, 1982). ... Traded by Padres to Expos organization for a player to be named later (June 8, 1982); Padres acquired P Mike Griffin to complete deal (August 30, 1982). ... Traded by Expos to Chicago Cubs organization for C Butch Benton (February 4, 1983). ... Granted free agency following 1983 season. ... Signed by Chicago White Sox organization (April 8, 1984). ... Granted free agency following 1985 season. ... Signed by Expos organization for 1986 season. ... On disabled list (June 23-July 17 and July 25-August 4, 1986).
STATISTICAL NOTES: Led Appalachian League shortstops with 303 total chances and 29 double plays in 1972. ... Led American Association second basemen with 688 total chances and 81 double plays in 1974. ... Led American Association second basemen with 758 total chances and 108 double plays in 1975. ... Led American Association second basemen with 234 putouts, 363 assists and 611 total chances in 1979. ... Led American Association shortstops with 612 total chances in 1980.

					BATTING									FIELDING			
Year	Team (League)	Pos.	G	AB	R	H	2B	3B	HR	RBI	Avg.	BB	SO	SB	PO	A	E	Avg.
1972—Bristol (Appal.)		SS	67	233	31	56	8	8	4	29	.240	19	61	11	*112	*176	15	*.950
1973—Lakeland (Fla. St.)		SS	117	433	66	109	17	4	2	28	.252	52	98	20	167	349	29	.947
—Toledo (Int'l)		SS	27	72	8	20	0	0	0	2	.278	3	16	2	44	90	4	.971
1974—Evansville (A.A.)		2B	127	384	44	81	5	5	1	24	.211	35	74	3	*315	356	17	.975

Year — Team (League)	Pos.	G	AB	R	H	2B	3B	HR	RBI	Avg.	BB	SO	SB	PO	A	E	Avg.
1975— Evansville (A.A.)	2B	*137	501	63	115	10	4	4	43	.230	44	101	5	*348	*394	16	.979
— Detroit (A.L.)	2B	6	18	0	1	0	0	0	0	.056	0	4	0	11	23	2	.944
1976— Detroit (A.L.)	2B-SS	54	43	4	6	1	0	0	2	.140	3	9	1	40	64	8	.929
— Evansville (A.A.)	2B	11	44	6	8	1	0	1	3	.182	2	9	0	25	29	1	.982
1977— Evansville (A.A.)	2B-SS	110	375	52	102	19	7	1	38	.272	45	55	12	198	304	17	.967
1978— Evansville (A.A.)	2B-SS	114	430	65	113	18	5	7	50	.263	50	83	8	264	321	20	.967
1979— Evansville (A.A.)	2B-SS	130	460	71	116	26	3	9	75	.252	67	67	8	†265	†434	22	.969
1980— Denver (A.A.)■	SS	128	491	105	136	23	2	3	61	.277	81	62	11	*233	*357	22	.964
— Montreal (N.L.)	SS	7	6	0	0	0	0	0	0	.000	0	2	0	5	11	1	.941
1981— Montreal (N.L.)	2B-SS	27	55	10	11	5	0	3	10	.200	6	11	0	37	41	1	.987
1982— Wichita (A.A.)■	S-3-2-O	71	263	31	67	22	0	3	37	.255	15	34	2	99	152	11	.958
— San Diego (N.L.)	2B-3B-SS	2	5	0	1	0	1	0	1	.200	1	0	1	1	1	0	1.000
— Hawaii (PCL)	SS	26	92	8	18	3	1	0	7	.196	11	12	2	41	73	1	.991
1983— Iowa (Am. Assoc.)■ ..	2-O-S-3	85	279	37	74	14	3	3	33	.265	22	46	6	129	143	9	.968
1984— Denver (A.A.)■	SS-2B-OF	109	335	43	98	14	3	4	40	.293	37	32	7	184	262	18	.961
1985—										Did not play.							
1986— Indianapolis (A.A.)■ ..	3B-2B	22	41	4	16	2	0	1	9	.390	2	5	0	5	7	1	.923
American League totals (2 years)		60	61	4	7	1	0	0	2	.115	3	13	1	51	87	10	.932
National League totals (3 years)		36	66	10	12	5	1	3	11	.182	7	13	0	43	53	2	.980
Major league totals (5 years)		96	127	14	19	6	1	3	13	.150	10	26	1	94	140	12	.951

DIVISION SERIES RECORD

Year — Team (League)	Pos.	G	AB	R	H	2B	3B	HR	RBI	Avg.	BB	SO	SB	PO	A	E	Avg.
1981— Montreal (N.L.)..........	2B	5	14	0	1	0	0	0	0	.071	2	5	0	13	19	3	.914

CHAMPIONSHIP SERIES RECORD

Year — Team (League)	Pos.	G	AB	R	H	2B	3B	HR	RBI	Avg.	BB	SO	SB	PO	A	E	Avg.
1981— Montreal (N.L.)..........	PR	1	1	0	0	0	0	0	0	.000	0	0	0	...	...	...	...

RECORD AS MANAGER

BACKGROUND: Scout, Chicago White Sox (1985). ... Player/coach, Indianapolis, American Association (1986). ... Roving infield instructor, Montreal Expos organization (1987). ... Minor league field coordinator, Expos (1988-89). ... Coach, Expos (June 3, 1991-1996). ... Coach, Florida Marlins (1997).
HONORS: Named Southern League co-Manager of the Year (1990).

		REGULAR SEASON			Playoff		Champ. Series		World Series		All-Star Game	
Year — Team (League)	W	L	Pct.	Pos.	W	L	W	L	W	L	W	L
1990— Jacksonville (Southern)	38	33	.535	2nd (E)	—	—	—	—	—	—	—	—
— (Second half)	46	27	.630	1st (E)	1	3	—	—	—	—	—	—
1991— Indianapolis (A.A.)	28	22	.560	—	—	—	—	—	—	—	—	—
1998— Chicago (A.L.)	80	82	.494	2nd (C)	—	—	—	—	—	—	—	—

NOTES:
1990—Lost to Orlando in playoffs.
1991—Replaced as Indianapolis manager by Pat Kelly (June 2).

McKEON, JACK   REDS

PERSONAL: Born November 23, 1930, in South Amboy, N.J. ... 5-8/205. ... Batted right, threw right. ... Full name: John Aloysius McKeon. ... Brother of Bill McKeon, minor league catcher (1952-54 and 1956-57); scout, Kansas City Royals (1969-70); scout, San Diego Padres (1981-87); and father-in-law of Greg Booker, pitcher with San Diego Padres and Minnesota Twins (1983-89).
HIGH SCHOOL: St. Mary's (South Amboy, N.J.).
COLLEGE: Holy Cross, then Seton Hall, then Elon (N.C.) College (degree in physical education and science).
TRANSACTIONS/CAREER NOTES: Released by Pittsburgh Pirates organization (September 28, 1954). ... Played 10 games with Fayetteville, five games with Greensboro and was player/manager with Fayetteville for 44 games during 1955 season. ... Player/manager, Missoula, Pioneer League (1956-58).
STATISTICAL NOTES: Led Carolina catchers with 17 double plays in 1953. ... Led Alabama State League catchers with nine double plays in 1949.

Year — Team (League)	Pos.	G	AB	R	H	2B	3B	HR	RBI	Avg.	BB	SO	SB	PO	A	E	Avg.
1949— Greenville (Alabama St.)	C	116	390	54	98	12	1	1	49	.251	41	34	8	*806	65	13	*.985
1950— York (Inter-State)	C	1	3	...	1	...	...	...	...	.333	...	...	...	...	...	...	...
— Gloverton (Can.-Amer.)	C	72	209	18	45	5	0	0	14	.215	19	28	2	281	30	15	.954
1951—								In military service.									
1952— Hutchinson (W. Assn.).	C	116	358	42	78	10	1	4	40	.218	69	54	0	756	68	11	.987
1953— Burlington (Caro.)	C	140	474	46	86	19	2	6	52	.181	60	110	3	*836	*82	21	.978
1954— Burlington (Caro.)	C	17	30	1	4	0	0	0	2	.133	1	5	0	60	9	0	1.000
— Hutchinson (W. Assn.).	C	46	140	18	29	5	0	1	13	.207	27	31	1	273	33	4	.987
1955— Fay.-Greens. (Caro.) ..	C	59	172	20	29	3	0	1	17	.169	29	28	1	292	20	6	.981
1956— Missoula (Pioneer).....	C-P	113	370	44	63	8	0	0	29	.170	53	62	3	630	78	9	.987
1957— Missoula (Pioneer).....	C-P	102	299	37	65	7	0	4	40	.217	60	44	6	645	55	10	.986
1958— Missoula (Pioneer).....	C-P	108	354	49	93	16	0	8	51	.263	51	55	2	739	64	12	.985
1959— Fox Cities (Three-I)	C	11	20	1	2	0	0	0	1	.100	8	3	0	...	...	...	...

RECORD AS PITCHER

Year — Team (League)	W	L	Pct.	ERA	G	GS	CG	ShO	Sv.	IP	H	R	ER	BB	SO
1956— Missoula (Pioneer)	0	0	...	0.00	8	...	...	...	...	...	...	...	...	...	...
1957— Missoula (Pioneer)	0	0	...	0.00	6	...	...	...	...	...	...	...	...	...	...
1958— Missoula (Pioneer)	0	0	...	0.00	2	...	...	...	...	...	...	...	...	...	...

RECORD AS MANAGER

BACKGROUND: Scout, Minnesota Twins (1965-67). ... Coach, Oakland Athletics (April 7-May 22, 1978). ... Scout/assistant to general manager, San Diego Padres (1980). ... Vice-president of baseball operations, Padres (1981-90). ... Senior adviser/player personnel, Cincinnati Reds (January 6, 1993-July 25, 1997).

Year	Team (League)	W	L	Pct.	Pos.	Playoff W	Playoff L	Champ. Series W	Champ. Series L	World Series W	World Series L	All-Star Game W	All-Star Game L
1955—	Fayetteville (Carolina)	70	67	.511	3rd	—	—	—	—	—	—	—	—
1956—	Missoula (Pioneer)	61	71	.462	7th	—	—	—	—	—	—	—	—
1957—	Missoula (Pioneer)	26	35	.426	6th	—	—	—	—	—	—	—	—
	— (Second half)	36	29	.554	3rd	—	—	—	—	—	—	—	—
1958—	Missoula (Pioneer)	34	29	.540	4th	—	—	—	—	—	—	—	—
	— (Second half)	36	30	.545	3rd	—	—	—	—	—	—	—	—
1959—	Fox Cities (Three-I)	26	39	.400	7th	—	—	—	—	—	—	—	—
	— (Second half)	33	28	.541	4th	—	—	—	—	—	—	—	—
1960—	Wilson (Carolina)	36	34	.514	3rd	—	—	—	—	—	—	—	—
	— (Second half)	37	31	.544	2nd	—	—	—	—	—	—	—	—
1961—	Wilson (Carolina)	41	28	.594	1st	—	—	—	—	—	—	—	—
	— (Second half)	42	28	.600	1st	—	—	—	—	—	—	—	—
1962—	Vancouver (Pacific Coast)	72	79	.477	7th	—	—	—	—	—	—	—	—
1963—	Dallas-Fort Worth (Pacific Coast)	79	79	.500	3rd (S)	—	—	—	—	—	—	—	—
1964—	Atlanta (International)	19	42	.311		—	—	—	—	—	—	—	—
1968—	High Point-Thomasville (Carolina)	69	71	.493	2nd (W)	5	1	—	—	—	—	—	—
1969—	Omaha (American Association)	85	55	.607	1st	—	—	—	—	—	—	—	—
1970—	Omaha (American Association)	73	65	.529	1st (E)	5	5	—	—	—	—	—	—
1971—	Omaha (American Association)	69	70	.496	3rd (E)	—	—	—	—	—	—	—	—
1972—	Omaha (American Association)	71	69	.507	2nd (E)	—	—	—	—	—	—	—	—
1973—	Kansas City (A.L.)	88	74	.543	2nd (W)	—	—	—	—	—	—	—	—
1974—	Kansas City (A.L.)	77	85	.475	5th (W)	—	—	—	—	—	—	—	—
1975—	Kansas City (A.L.)	50	46	.521		—	—	—	—	—	—	—	—
1976—	Richmond (International)	69	71	.493	4th	—	—	—	—	—	—	—	—
1977—	Oakland (A.L.)	26	27	.491		—	—	—	—	—	—	—	—
1978—	Oakland (A.L.)	45	78	.366	4th (W)	—	—	—	—	—	—	—	—
1980—	Denver (American Association)	62	73	.459	3rd	—	—	—	—	—	—	—	—
1988—	San Diego (N.L.)	67	48	.583	3rd (W)	—	—	—	—	—	—	—	—
1989—	San Diego (N.L.)	89	73	.549	2nd (W)	—	—	—	—	—	—	—	—
1990—	San Diego (N.L.)	37	43	.436		—	—	—	—	—	—	—	—
1997—	Cincinnati (N.L.)	33	30	.524	3rd (C)	—	—	—	—	—	—	—	—
1998—	Cincinnati (N.L.)	77	85	.475	4th (C)	—	—	—	—	—	—	—	—
American League totals (5 years)		**286**	**310**	**.480**		—	—	—	—	—	—	—	—
National League totals (5 years)		**303**	**279**	**.521**		—	—	—	—	—	—	—	—
Major league totals (10 years)		**589**	**589**	**.500**		—	—	—	—	—	—	—	—

NOTES:
1955—Replaced Fayetteville manager Aaron Robinson (June 11). Replaced as Fayetteville manager by John Sanford (August 6) because of hand injury with team tied for first place (record is for full season).
1964—Replaced as Atlanta manager by Peter Appleton with club in eighth place (June 21).
1968—Defeated Greensboro, one game to none, in quarterfinals; defeated Lynchburg, two games to none in semifinals; defeated Raleigh-Durham, two games to one, in championship.
1970—Defeated Denver, four games to one, in championship; lost to Syracuse, four games to one, in Junior World Series.
1975—Replaced as Kansas City manager by Whitey Herzog, with club in second place (July 24).
1977—Replaced as Oakland manager by Bobby Winkles, with club tied for fifth place (June 10).
1978—Replaced Oakland manager Bobby Winkles, with club in first place and record of 24-15 (May 23).
1988—Replaced San Diego manager Larry Bowa, with club in fifth place and record of 16-30 (May 28).
1990—Replaced as San Diego manager by Greg Riddoch, with club in fourth place (July 11).
1997—Replaced Cincinnati manager Ray Knight, with club in fourth place and record of 43-56 (July 25).

MILLER, RAY — ORIOLES

PERSONAL: Born April 30, 1945, in Takoma Park, Md. ... 6-3/215. ... Threw right, batted right. ... Full name: Raymond Roger Miller.
HIGH SCHOOL: Suitland (Md.).
TRANSACTIONS/CAREER NOTES: Signed as free agent by San Francisco Giants organization (August 15, 1963). ... Drafted by Cleveland Indians from Giants organization in first-year draft (November 30, 1964). ... On disabled list (June 24-July 8, 1965). ... On disabled list (June 28-July 24, 1966). ... On temporarily inactive list (June 17-July 4, 1967). ... On temporarily inactive list (June 13-July 1, 1968). ... On temporarily inactive list (May 15-18, 1970). ... Traded by Indians organization with C Larry Wallin to Baltimore Orioles organization for P Dale Spier and P Rick Thoms (May 12, 1971).
STATISTICAL NOTES: Pitched eighth-inning 0-0 no-hitter (tie, rain) vs. Statesville (August 3, 1964). ... Led Midwest League with 16 hit batsmen in 1965. ... Led California League with 12 hit batsmen in 1966 and 13 in 1968.
MISCELLANEOUS: Appeared in one game as outfielder (1968).

Year	Team (League)	W	L	Pct.	ERA	G	GS	CG	ShO	Sv.	IP	H	R	ER	BB	SO
1964—	Lexington (West. Carolinas)	9	•11	.450	1.87	36	18	7	*5	...	159	97	64	33	*109	195
1965—	Salinas (Calif.)■	0	1	.000	6.00	3	1	0	0	...	6	3	4	4	8	5
	— Dubuque (Midw.)	7	9	.438	3.76	30	15	7	1	...	122	97	66	51	78	147
1966—	Pawtucket (East.)	0	0	...	9.00	1	0	0	0	...	2	3	2	2	1	2
	— Reno (California)	5	7	.417	6.39	24	11	3	0	...	93	87	75	66	55	94
1967—	Reno (California)	1	3	.250	4.95	34	1	0	0	...	60	50	40	33	41	49
1968—	Reno (California)	16	8	.667	3.22	29	25	16	3	...	193	170	86	69	81	206
1969—	Portland (PCL)	11	5	.688	3.38	45	7	2	0	5	112	107	51	42	56	73
1970—	Wichita (Am. Assoc.)	6	6	.500	3.67	•56	1	0	0	7	98	94	49	40	46	87
1971—	Wichita (Am. Assoc.)	0	1	.000	2.45	8	0	0	0	0	11	12	3	3	5	10
	— Rochester (Int'l)■	3	2	.600	3.16	44	0	0	0	11	57	49	26	20	28	48
1972—	Rochester (Int'l)	7	5	.583	3.21	47	0	0	0	7	73	66	31	26	38	61
1973—	Rochester (Int'l)	1	1	.500	1.38	14	0	0	0	1	26	13	8	4	15	15

RECORD AS MANAGER

BACKGROUND: Player/coach, Rochester, Baltimore Orioles organization (1973). ... Minor league pitching instructor, Orioles organization (1974-77). ... Pitching coach, Texas Rangers (November 21, 1977-1978). ... Pitching coach, Orioles (1978-June 20, 1985 and 1997). ... Pitching coach, Pittsburgh Pirates (1987-1996).

		REGULAR SEASON				POSTSEASON						All-Star	
								Champ.		World			
						Playoff		Series		Series		Game	
Year Team (League)	W	L	Pct.	Pos.	W	L	W	L	W	L	W	L
1985— Minnesota (A.L.)	50	50	.500	4th (W)	—	—	—	—	—	—	—	—
1986— Minnesota (A.L.)	59	80	.424		—	—	—	—	—	—	—	—
1998— Baltimore (A.L.)	79	83	.488	4th (E)	—	—	—	—	—	—	—	—
Major league totals (3 years)	188	213	.469		—	—	—	—	—	—	—	—

NOTES:
1985—Replaced Minnesota manager Billy Gardner, with club in sixth place and record of 27-35 (June 21).
1986—Replaced as Twins manager by Tom Kelly, with club in seventh place (September 12).

MUSER, TONY   ROYALS

PERSONAL: Born August 1, 1947, in Los Angeles. ... 6-2/190. ... Batted left, threw left. ... Full name: Anthony Joseph Muser.
HIGH SCHOOL: Lakewood (Calif.).
JUNIOR COLLEGE: San Diego Mesa.
TRANSACTIONS/CAREER NOTES: Signed as non-drafted free agent by Boston Red Sox organization (1967). ... On military list (beginning of 1968 season-July 15, 1968). ... Traded by Red Sox with P Vicente Romo to Chicago White Sox for P Danny Murphy and C Duane Josephson (March 30, 1971). ... Traded by White Sox to Baltimore Orioles for P Jesse Jefferson (June 15, 1975). ... Released by Orioles (February 21, 1978). ... Signed by Milwaukee Brewers organization (March 20, 1978). ... Released by Brewers (February 12, 1979). ... Played in Japan (1979).

							BATTING							FIELDING		
Year Team (League)	Pos.	G	AB	R	H	2B	3B	HR	RBI	Avg.	BB	SO	SB	PO	A	E	Avg.
1967— Waterloo (Midw.)	1B	68	251	40	71	15	1	6	42	.283	38	42	3	674	28	11	.985
1968— Greenv. (W. Car.)	1B-OF	33	114	13	31	7	0	2	12	.272	18	17	1	223	23	2	.992
— Win.-Salem (Car.)	OF-1B	7	21	1	8	0	0	0	2	.381	1	3	1	13	1	0	1.000
1969— Louisville (Int'l)	1B	120	457	57	129	14	4	7	62	.282	43	53	7	1029	63	15	.986
— Boston (A.L.)	1B	2	9	0	1	0	0	0	1	.111	1	1	0	17	3	0	1.000
1970— Louisville (Int'l)	1B	114	462	66	130	25	7	5	45	.281	38	49	1	1013	45	9	*.992
1971— Indianapolis (A.A.)■	1B	85	310	36	91	10	3	3	31	.294	35	27	0	720	42	6	.992
— Chicago (A.L.)	1B	11	16	2	5	0	1	0	0	.313	1	1	0	23	3	1	.963
1972— Tucson (PCL)	1B	83	318	41	86	17	0	3	40	.270	29	28	3	680	49	12	.984
— Chicago (A.L.)	1B-OF	44	61	6	17	2	2	1	9	.279	2	6	1	135	7	2	.986
1973— Chicago (A.L.)	1B-OF	109	309	38	88	14	3	4	30	.285	33	36	8	681	38	6	.992
1974— Chicago (A.L.)	1B	103	206	16	60	5	1	1	18	.291	6	22	1	419	13	1	.998
1975— Chicago (A.L.)	1B	43	111	11	27	3	0	0	6	.243	7	8	2	263	22	2	.993
— Baltimore (A.L.)■	1B	80	82	11	26	3	0	0	11	.317	8	9	0	213	15	1	.996
1976— Baltimore (A.L.)	1B-OF	136	326	25	74	7	1	1	30	.227	21	34	1	693	63	7	.991
1977— Baltimore (A.L.)	1B-OF	120	118	14	27	6	0	0	7	.229	13	16	1	232	20	3	.988
1978— Spokane (PCL)■	1B-OF	78	283	48	83	13	0	6	38	.293	33	25	2	572	50	4	.994
— Milwaukee (A.L.)	1B	15	30	0	4	1	1	0	5	.133	3	5	0	79	5	1	.988
1979— Seibu (Jp. Pac.)■	...	65	168	...	33	...	...	...	2	10	.196	...	...	...	...	...	...
Major league totals (9 years)		663	1268	123	329	41	9	7	117	.259	95	138	14	2755	189	24	.992

RECORD AS MANAGER

BACKGROUND: Coach, Milwaukee Brewers (1985-89). ... Scout, Brewers (1990). ... Coach, Chicago Cubs (1993-July 8, 1997).

		REGULAR SEASON				POSTSEASON						All-Star	
								Champ.		World			
						Playoff		Series		Series		Game	
Year Team (League)	W	L	Pct.	Pos.	W	L	W	L	W	L	W	L
1980—Stockton (California)	49	21	.700	1st (N)	—	—	—	—	—	—	—	—
—(Second half)	41	30	.577	1st (N)	3	0	—	—	—	—	—	—
1981—El Paso (Texas)	37	31	.544	2nd (W)	—	—	—	—	—	—	—	—
—(Second half)	28	38	.424	4th (W)	—	—	—	—	—	—	—	—
1982—El Paso (Texas)	42	23	.646	1st (W)	—	—	—	—	—	—	—	—
—(Second half)	34	37	.479	2nd (W)	2	3	—	—	—	—	—	—
1983—El Paso (Texas)	35	33	.515	2nd (W)	—	—	—	—	—	—	—	—
—Vancouver(Pacific Coast)	29	41	.414	4th (N)	—	—	—	—	—	—	—	—
1984—Vancouver (Pacific Coast)	32	40	.444	3rd (N)	—	—	—	—	—	—	—	—
—(Second half)	39	31	.557	3rd (N)	—	—	—	—	—	—	—	—
1991—Denver (American Association)	79	65	.549	1st (W)	7	3	—	—	—	—	—	—
1992—Denver (American Association)	73	71	.507	2nd (W)	—	—	—	—	—	—	—	—
1997—Kansas City (A.L.)	31	48	.392	4th (C)	—	—	—	—	—	—	—	—
1998—Kansas City (A.L.)	72	89	.447	3rd (C)	—	—	—	—	—	—	—	—
Major league totals (2 years)	103	137	.429		—	—	—	—	—	—	—	—

NOTES:
1980—Defeated Visalia in league championship.
1982—Defeated Midland, two games to one, in playoffs; lost to Tulsa, three games to none, in league championship.
1983—Replaced Vancouver manager Dick Phillips (June 22).
1991—Defeated Buffalo, three games to two, in league championship; defeated Columbus (International League), four games to one, in Class AAA Alliance championship.
1997—Replaced Kansas City manager Bob Boone with club in fourth place and record of 36-46 (July 9).
1998—On suspended list (June 9-17).

PERSONAL: Born January 21, 1946, in Sylva, N.C. ... 5-11/185. ... Batted left, threw right. ... Full name: Johnny Lane Oates.
HIGH SCHOOL: Prince George (Va.).
COLLEGE: Virginia Tech (bachelor of science degree in health and physical education).
TRANSACTIONS/CAREER NOTES: Selected by Chicago White Sox organization in second round of free-agent draft (June 1966); did not sign. ... Selected by Baltimore Orioles organization in secondary phase of free-agent draft (January 28, 1967). ... On military list (April 21-August 22, 1970). ... Traded by Orioles with P Pat Dobson, P Roric Harrison and 2B Dave Johnson to Atlanta Braves for C Earl Williams and IF Taylor Duncan (November 30, 1972). ... On disabled list (July 17-September 2, 1973). ... Traded by Braves with 1B Dick Allen to Philadelphia Phillies for C Jim Essian, OF Barry Bonnell and cash (May 7, 1975). ... On disabled list (April 14-June 1, 1976). ... Traded by Phillies with P Quency Hill to Los Angeles Dodgers for IF Ted Sizemore (December 20, 1976). ... Released by Dodgers (March 27, 1980). ... Signed by New York Yankees (April 4, 1980). ... Granted free agency (November 13, 1980). ... Re-signed by Yankees organization (January 23, 1981). ... On Columbus disabled list (August 3-25, 1981). ... Released by Yankees organization (October 27, 1981).
STATISTICAL NOTES: Led International League catchers with 727 total chances in 1971. ... Led N.L. with 15 passed balls in 1974. ... Tied for N.L. lead in double plays by catcher with 10 in 1975.

						BATTING								FIELDING		
Year	Team (League)	Pos.	G	AB	R	H	2B	3B	HR	RBI	Avg.	BB	SO	SB	PO	A	E	Avg.
1967—	Bluefield (Appal.)........	C	5	12	5	5	1	0	1	4	.417	2	0	0	23	5	0	1.000
—	Miami (Fla. St.)	C-OF	48	156	22	45	5	2	3	19	.288	24	13	2	271	37	8	.975
1968—	Miami (Fla. St.)	C-OF	70	194	24	51	9	3	0	23	.263	33	14	2	384	42	3	.993
1969—	Dall./Fort W. (Tex.)	C	66	191	24	55	12	2	1	18	.288	20	9	0	253	42	4	.987
1970—	Rochester (Int'l).........	C	9	16	1	6	1	0	0	4	.375	4	2	0	24	2	0	1.000
—	Baltimore (A.L.)..........	C	5	18	2	5	0	1	0	2	.278	2	0	0	30	1	2	.939
1971—	Rochester (Int'l).........	C	114	346	49	96	16	3	7	44	.277	49	31	10	*648	*73	6	.992
1972—	Baltimore (A.L.)..........	C	85	253	20	66	12	1	4	21	.261	28	31	5	391	31	2	*.995
1973—	Atlanta (N.L.)■..........	C	93	322	27	80	6	0	4	27	.248	22	31	1	409	57	9	.981
1974—	Atlanta (N.L.)...........	C	100	291	22	65	10	0	1	21	.223	23	24	2	434	55	4	.992
1975—	Atlanta (N.L.)...........	C	8	18	0	4	1	0	0	0	.222	1	4	0	21	1	0	1.000
—	Philadelphia (N.L.)■.	C	90	269	28	77	14	0	1	25	.286	33	29	1	429	44	5	.990
1976—	Philadelphia (N.L.)......	C	37	99	10	25	2	0	0	8	.253	8	12	0	155	15	1	.994
1977—	Los Angeles (N.L.)■..	C	60	156	18	42	4	0	3	11	.269	11	11	1	258	37	4	.987
1978—	Los Angeles (N.L.)	C	40	75	5	23	1	0	0	6	.307	5	3	0	77	10	4	.956
1979—	Los Angeles (N.L.)	C	26	46	4	6	2	0	0	2	.130	4	1	0	64	13	2	.975
1980—	New York (A.L.)■.......	C	39	64	6	12	3	0	1	3	.188	2	3	1	99	10	1	.991
1981—	New York (A.L.)	C	10	26	4	5	1	0	0	0	.192	2	0	0	49	3	2	.963
American League totals (4 years)			139	361	32	88	16	2	5	26	.244	34	34	6	569	45	7	.989
National League totals (7 years)			454	1276	114	322	40	0	9	100	.252	107	115	5	1847	232	29	.986
Major league totals (11 years)			593	1637	146	410	56	2	14	126	.250	141	149	11	2416	277	36	.987

CHAMPIONSHIP SERIES RECORD

						BATTING								FIELDING		
Year	Team (League)	Pos.	G	AB	R	H	2B	3B	HR	RBI	Avg.	BB	SO	SB	PO	A	E	Avg.
1976—	Philadelphia (N.L.)......	C	1	1	0	0	0	0	0	0	.000	0	0	0	1	0	0	1.000

WORLD SERIES RECORD

						BATTING								FIELDING		
Year	Team (League)	Pos.	G	AB	R	H	2B	3B	HR	RBI	Avg.	BB	SO	SB	PO	A	E	Avg.
1977—	Los Angeles (N.L.)	C	1	1	0	0	0	0	0	0	.000	0	0	0	1	0	0	1.000
1978—	Los Angeles (N.L.)	C	1	1	0	1	0	0	0	0	1.000	1	0	0	3	1	0	1.000
World Series totals (2 years)			2	2	0	1	0	0	0	0	.500	1	0	0	4	1	0	1.000

RECORD AS MANAGER

BACKGROUND: Coach, Columbus, New York Yankees organization (July 30, 1981-remainder of season). ... Coach, Chicago Cubs (1984-87). ... Coach, Baltimore Orioles (1989-May 23, 1991).
HONORS: Named International League Manager of the Year (1988). ... Coach, A.L. All-Star team (1993, 1995 and 1997). ... Named A.L. Manager of the Year by The Sporting News (1993 and 1996). ... Named co-A.L. Manager of the Year by Baseball Writers' Association of America (1996).

	REGULAR SEASON				POSTSEASON							
					Playoff		Champ. Series		World Series		All-Star Game	
Year	Team (League)	W	L	Pct.	Pos.	W	L	W	L	W	L	W	L
1982—	Nashville (Southern)	32	38	.457	4th (W)	—	—	—	—	—	—	—	—
	(Second half)	45	29	.608	1st (W)	6	2	—	—	—	—	—	—
1983—	Columbus (International)	83	57	.593	1st	2	3	—	—	—	—	—	—
1988—	Rochester (International)	77	64	.546	1st (W)	5	5	—	—	—	—	—	—
1991—	Baltimore (A.L.)	54	71	.432	6th (E)	—	—	—	—	—	—	—	—
1992—	Baltimore (A.L.)	89	73	.549	3rd (E)	—	—	—	—	—	—	—	—
1993—	Baltimore (A.L.)	85	77	.525	T3rd (E)	—	—	—	—	—	—	—	—
1994—	Baltimore (A.L.)	63	49	.563		—	—	—	—	—	—	—	—
1995—	Texas (A.L.)	74	70	.514	3rd (W)	—	—	—	—	—	—	—	—
1996—	Texas (A.L.)	90	72	.556	1st (W)	1	3	—	—	—	—	—	—
1997—	Texas (A.L.)	77	85	.475	3rd (W)	—	—	—	—	—	—	—	—
1998—	Texas (A.L.)	88	74	.543	1st (W)	0	3	—	—	—	—	—	—
Major league totals (8 years)		620	571	.521		1	6						

NOTES:
1982—Defeated Knoxville, three games to one, in playoffs; defeated Jacksonville, three games to one, in league championship.
1983—Lost to Tidewater in playoffs.
1988—Defeated Tidewater, three games to one, in league championship; lost to Indianapolis (American Association), four games to two, in Class AAA-Alliance championship.
1991—Replaced Baltimore manager Frank Robinson with club in seventh place and record of 13-24 (May 23).
1994—Baltimore was in second place in A.L. East at time of season ending strike (August 12).
1996—Lost to New York Yankees in A.L. divisional playoff.
1998—Lost to New York Yankees in A.L. divisional playoff.

MAJOR LEAGUE MANAGERS

PARRISH, LARRY   TIGERS

PERSONAL: Born November 10, 1953, in Winter Haven, Fla. ... 6-3/220. ... Bats right, throws right. ... Full name: Larry Alton Parrish.
HIGH SCHOOL: Haines City (Fla.).
JUNIOR COLLEGE: Seminole (Fla.) Junior College.
TRANSACTIONS/CAREER NOTES: Signed as free agent by Montreal Expos organization (May 21, 1972). ... On disabled list (June 2-June 30, 1980). ... Traded with 1B Dave Hostetler to Texas Rangers for 1B/OF Al Oliver (March 31, 1982). ... On disabled list (July 6-September 1, 1985). ... On disabled list (May 20-June 18, 1986). ... Released by Rangers (July 9, 1988). ... Signed by Boston Red Sox (July 16, 1988). ... Released by Red Sox (October 26, 1988). ... Played in Japan (1989-90).
HONORS: Named Florida State League Most Valuable Player (1973).
STATISTICAL NOTES: Tied for National League lead in double plays by third basemen with 35 in 1976. ... Led Eastern League third basemen in double plays with 32 in 1974. ... Led Florida State League in sacrifice flies with 9 in 1973. ... Led Florida State League third basemen in putouts with 95 and assists with 285 in 1973.

							BATTING								FIELDING		
Year Team (League)	Pos.	G	AB	R	H	2B	3B	HR	RBI	Avg.	BB	SO	SB	PO	A	E	Avg.
1972—W.P. Beach (FSL)........	OF	2	4	0	1	0	0	0	0	.250	0	1	0	2	0	0	1.000
—Jamestown (NYP)■...	OF	62	223	32	58	4	3	4	28	.260	22	51	5	69	3	3	.960
1973—W.P. Beach (FSL)........	3B-OF	138	481	82	141	14	6	16	81	.293	46	71	12	100	292	32	.925
1974—Que. City (East.)	3B	119	437	61	124	14	2	13	77	.284	50	86	6	108	277	31	.925
—Montreal (N.L.)..........	3B	25	69	9	14	5	0	0	4	.203	6	19	0	20	51	1	.986
1975—Montreal (N.L.)..........	3B-SS-2B	145	532	50	146	32	5	10	65	.274	28	74	4	105	291	35	.919
1976—Montreal (N.L.)..........	3B	154	543	65	126	28	5	11	61	.232	41	91	2	122	310	25	.945
1977—Montreal (N.L.)..........	3B	123	402	50	99	19	2	11	46	.246	37	71	2	81	225	21	.936
1978—Montreal (N.L.)..........	3B	144	520	68	144	39	4	15	70	.277	32	103	2	122	288	23	.947
1979—Montreal (N.L.)..........	3B	153	544	83	167	39	2	30	82	.307	41	101	5	119	290	23	.947
1980—Montreal (N.L.)..........	3B	126	452	55	115	27	3	15	72	.254	36	80	5	106	231	18	.949
1981—Montreal (N.L.)..........	3B	97	349	41	85	19	3	8	44	.244	28	73	0	91	141	16	.935
1982—Texas (A.L.)■............	OF-3B	128	440	59	116	15	0	17	62	.264	30	84	5	190	12	8	.962
1983—Texas (A.L.)	OF	145	555	76	151	26	4	26	88	.272	46	91	0	215	11	9	.962
1984—Texas (A.L.)	OF-3B	156	613	72	175	42	1	22	101	.285	42	116	2	155	35	4	.979
1985—Texas (A.L.)	OF-3B	94	346	44	86	11	1	17	51	.249	33	77	0	111	7	1	.992
1986—Texas (A.L.)	3B	129	464	67	128	22	1	28	94	.276	52	114	3	23	35	'4	.935
1987—Texas (A.L.)	OF-3B	152	557	79	149	22	1	32	100	.268	49	154	3	19	26	4	.918
1988—Texas (A.L.)	DH	68	248	22	47	9	1	7	26	.190	22	79	1	...	...	...	...
—Boston (A.L.)■..........	1B	52	158	10	41	5	0	7	26	.259	8	32	0	221	25	3	.988
1989—Yakult (Jp. Cen.)■.....	3B	130	493	...	132	...	...	42	103	.268	...	...	...	...	...	...	...
1990—Hanshin (Jp.Cen.)■...	3B	105	381	...	95	...	...	28	80	.249	...	...	...	...	...	...	...
American League totals (7 years)		924	3381	429	893	152	9	156	548	.264	282	747	14	934	151	33	.970
National League totals (8 years)		967	3411	421	896	208	24	100	444	.263	1249	612	40	766	1827	162	.941
Major league totals (15 years)		1891	6792	850	1789	360	33	256	992	.263	1531	1359	54	1700	1978	195	.950

RECORD AS MANAGER

BACKGROUND: Roving hitting instructor, Detroit Tigers (February-May 2 1994 and 1995-June 21, 1996). ... Bench coach, Detroit Tigers (November 14, 1996-September 1, 1998).

	——— REGULAR SEASON ———				——— POSTSEASON ———							
					Playoff		Champ. Series		World Series		All-Star Game	
Year Team (League)	W	L	Pct.	Pos.	W	L	W	L	W	L	W	L
1992—Niagara Falls (New York-Penn)..................	39	39	.500	3rd (St)	—	—	—	—	—	—	—	—
1993—Niagara Falls (New York-Penn)..................	47	31	.603	2nd (St)	3	0	—	—	—	—	—	—
1994—Toledo (International)................................	56	62	.475	5th (W)	—	—	—	—	—	—	—	—
1996—Jacksonville (Southern)(Second half).......	36	31	.537	1st (E)	6	3	—	—	—	—	—	—
1998—Detroit (A.L.)...	13	12	.520	5th (C)	—	—	—	—	—	—	—	—

NOTES:
1993—Defeated St. Catharines in one-game semifinal playoff; defeated Pittsfield, two games to none, to win league championship.
1994—Replaced Joe Sparks as Toledo manager (May 2).
1996—Replaced Bill Plummer as Jacksonville manager (June 21); defeated Carolina, three games to two, in league semifinals; defeated Chattanooga, three games to one, to win league championship.
1998—Replaced Detroit manager Buddy Bell on an interim basis, with club in fifth place and record of 52-85 (September 1); named full-time manager (October 15).

PINIELLA, LOU   MARINERS

PERSONAL: Born August 28, 1943, in Tampa. ... 6-2/199. ... Batted right, threw right. ... Full name: Louis Victor Piniella. ... Cousin of Dave Magadan, third baseman/first baseman, San Diego Padres. ... Name pronounced pin-ELL-uh.
HIGH SCHOOL: Jesuit (Tampa).
COLLEGE: Tampa.
TRANSACTIONS/CAREER NOTES: Signed as free agent by Cleveland Indians organization (June 9, 1962). ... Selected by Washington Senators organization from Jacksonville, Indians organization, in Rule 5 major league draft (November 26, 1962). ... On military list (March 9-July 20, 1964). ... Traded by Senators organization to Baltimore Orioles organization (August 4, 1964), completing deal in which Orioles traded P Lester (Buster) Narum to Senators for cash and a player to be named later (March 31, 1964). ... On suspended list (June 27-29, 1965). ... Traded by Orioles organization to Indians organization for C Camilo Carreon (March 10, 1966). ... On temporarily inactive list (May 19-22, 1967). ... On disabled list (May 22-June 6, 1968). ... On temporarily inactive list (June 6-25, 1968). ... Selected by Seattle Pilots in expansion draft (October 15, 1968). ... Traded by Pilots to Kansas City Royals for OF Steve Whitaker and P John Gelnar (April 1, 1969). ... On military list (August 7-22, 1969). ... On disabled list (May 5-June 8, 1971). ... Traded by Royals with P Ken Wright to New York Yankees for P Lindy McDaniel (December 7, 1973). ... On disabled list (June 17-July 6, 1975; August 23-September 7, 1981; and March 30-April 22, 1983). ... Placed on voluntarily retired list (June 17, 1984).
RECORDS: Shares major league record for most assists by outfielder in one inning—2 (May 27, 1974, third inning).

HONORS: Named A.L. Rookie of the Year by Baseball Writers' Association of America (1969).
STATISTICAL NOTES: Led A.L. in grounding into double plays with 25 in 1972. ... Career major league grand slams: 1.

Year	Team (League)	Pos.	G	AB	R	H	2B	3B	HR	RBI	Avg.	BB	SO	SB	PO	A	E	Avg.
1962—	Selma (Ala.-Fla.)........	OF	70	278	40	75	10	5	8	44	.270	10	57	4	94	6	9	.917
1963—	Peninsula (Caro.)■....	OF	143	548	71	170	29	4	16	77	.310	34	70	8	271	*23	8	.974
1964—	Aberdeen (North.)	OF	20	74	8	20	8	3	0	12	.270	6	9	1	37	1	1	.974
	— Baltimore (A.L.)■......	PH	4	1	0	0	0	0	0	0	.000	0	0	0	...	...	...	...
1965—	Elmira (Eastern)	OF	126	490	64	122	29	6	11	64	.249	22	57	5	176	5	7	.963
1966—	Portland (PCL)■	OF	133	457	47	132	22	3	7	52	.289	20	52	6	177	11	11	.945
1967—	Portland (PCL)	OF	113	396	46	122	20	1	8	56	.308	23	47	2	199	7	6	.972
1968—	Portland (PCL)	OF	88	331	49	105	15	3	13	62	.317	19	31	0	167	6	7	.961
	— Cleveland (A.L.)	OF	6	5	1	0	0	0	0	1	.000	0	0	1	1	0	0	1.000
1969—	Kansas City (A.L.)■...	OF	135	493	43	139	21	6	11	68	.282	33	56	2	278	13	7	.977
1970—	Kansas City (A.L.)	OF-1B	144	542	54	163	24	5	11	88	.301	35	42	3	250	6	4	.985
1971—	Kansas City (A.L.)	OF	126	448	43	125	21	5	3	51	.279	21	43	5	201	6	3	.986
1972—	Kansas City (A.L.)	OF	151	574	65	179	*33	4	11	72	.312	34	59	7	275	8	7	.976
1973—	Kansas City (A.L.)	OF-DH	144	513	53	128	28	1	9	69	.250	30	65	5	196	9	3	.986
1974—	New York (A.L.)■....	OF-DH-1B	140	518	71	158	26	0	9	70	.305	32	58	1	270	16	3	.990
1975—	New York (A.L.)	OF-DH	74	199	7	39	4	1	0	22	.196	16	22	0	65	5	1	.986
1976—	New York (A.L.)	OF-DH	100	327	36	92	16	6	3	38	.281	18	34	0	199	10	4	.981
1977—	New York (A.L.)	OF-DH-1B	103	339	47	112	19	3	12	45	.330	20	31	2	86	3	2	.978
1978—	New York (A.L.)	OF-DH	130	472	67	148	34	5	6	69	.314	34	36	3	213	4	7	.969
1979—	New York (A.L.)	OF-DH	130	461	49	137	22	2	11	69	.297	17	31	3	204	13	4	.982
1980—	New York (A.L.)	OF-DH	116	321	39	92	18	0	2	27	.287	29	20	0	157	8	5	.971
1981—	New York (A.L.)	OF-DH	60	159	16	44	9	0	5	18	.277	13	9	0	69	2	1	.986
1982—	New York (A.L.)	DH-OF	102	261	33	80	17	1	6	37	.307	18	18	0	68	2	0	1.000
1983—	New York (A.L.)	OF-DH	53	148	19	43	9	1	2	16	.291	11	12	1	67	4	3	.959
1984—	New York (A.L.)	OF-DH	29	86	8	26	4	1	1	6	.302	7	5	0	40	3	0	1.000
Major league totals (18 years)			1747	5867	651	1705	305	41	102	766	.291	368	541	33	2639	112	54	.981

DIVISION SERIES RECORD

Year	Team (League)	Pos.	G	AB	R	H	2B	3B	HR	RBI	Avg.	BB	SO	SB	PO	A	E	Avg.
1981—	New York (A.L.)..........	DH-PH	4	10	1	2	1	0	1	3	.200	0	0	0	...	...	...	...

CHAMPIONSHIP SERIES RECORD

Year	Team (League)	Pos.	G	AB	R	H	2B	3B	HR	RBI	Avg.	BB	SO	SB	PO	A	E	Avg.
1976—	New York (A.L.)..........	DH-PH	4	11	1	3	1	0	0	0	.273	0	1	0	...	...	...	...
1977—	New York (A.L.)..........	OF-DH	5	21	1	7	3	0	0	2	.333	0	1	0	9	1	0	1.000
1978—	New York (A.L.)..........	OF	4	17	2	4	0	0	0	0	.235	0	3	0	13	0	0	1.000
1980—	New York (A.L.)..........	OF	2	5	1	1	0	0	1	1	.200	2	1	0	5	0	0	1.000
1981—	New York (A.L.)..........	PH-DH-OF	3	5	2	3	0	0	1	3	.600	0	0	0	0	0	0	...
Championship series totals (5 years)			18	59	7	18	4	0	2	6	.305	2	6	0	27	1	0	1.000

WORLD SERIES RECORD

RECORDS: Shares single-series record for collecting one or more hits in each game (1978).
NOTES: Member of World Series championship team (1977-1978).

Year	Team (League)	Pos.	G	AB	R	H	2B	3B	HR	RBI	Avg.	BB	SO	SB	PO	A	E	Avg.
1976—	New York (A.L.)..........	DH-OF-PH	4	9	1	3	1	0	0	0	.333	0	0	0	1	0	0	1.000
1977—	New York (A.L.)..........	OF	6	22	1	6	0	0	0	3	.273	0	3	0	16	1	1	.944
1978—	New York (A.L.)..........	OF	6	25	3	7	0	0	0	4	.280	0	0	1	14	1	0	1.000
1981—	New York (A.L.)..........	OF-PH	6	16	2	7	1	0	0	3	.438	0	1	1	7	0	0	1.000
World Series totals (4 years)			22	72	7	23	2	0	0	10	.319	0	4	2	38	2	1	.976

ALL-STAR GAME RECORD

Year	League	Pos.	AB	R	H	2B	3B	HR	RBI	Avg.	BB	SO	SB	PO	A	E	Avg.
1972—	American	PH	1	0	0	0	0	0	0	.000	0	0	0	...	...	...	...

RECORD AS MANAGER

BACKGROUND: Coach, New York Yankees (June 25, 1984-85). ... Vice-president/general manager, Yankees (beginning of 1988 season-June 22, 1988). ... Special adviser, Yankees (1989).
HONORS: Named A.L. Manager of the Year by Baseball Writers' Association of America (1995).

Year	Team (League)	W	L	Pct.	Pos.	Playoff W	Playoff L	Champ. Series W	Champ. Series L	World Series W	World Series L	All-Star Game W	All-Star Game L
1986—	New York (A.L.)	90	72	.556	2nd (E)	—	—	—	—	—	—	—	—
1987—	New York (A.L.)	89	73	.549	4th (E)	—	—	—	—	—	—	—	—
1988—	New York (A.L.)	45	48	.484	5th (E)	—	—	—	—	—	—	—	—
1990—	Cincinnati (N.L.)	91	71	.562	1st (W)	—	—	4	2	4	0	—	—
1991—	Cincinnati (N.L.)	74	88	.457	5th (W)	—	—	—	—	—	—	0	1
1992—	Cincinnati (N.L.)	90	72	.556	2nd (W)	—	—	—	—	—	—	—	—
1993—	Seattle (A.L.)	82	80	.506	4th (W)	—	—	—	—	—	—	—	—
1994—	Seattle (A.L.)	49	63	.438		—	—	—	—	—	—	—	—
1995—	Seattle (A.L.)	79	66	.545	1st (W)	3	2	2	4	—	—	—	—
1996—	Seattle (A.L.)	85	76	.528	2nd (W)	—	—	—	—	—	—	—	—
1997—	Seattle (A.L.)	90	72	.556	1st (W)	1	3	—	—	—	—	—	—
1998—	Seattle (A.L.)	76	85	.472	3rd (W)	—	—	—	—	—	—	—	—
American League totals (9 years)		685	635	.519		4	5	2	4	—	—	—	—
National League totals (3 years)		255	231	.525		—	—	4	2	4	0	0	1
Major league totals (12 years)		940	866	.520		4	5	6	6	4	0	0	1

NOTES:
1988—Replaced New York manager Billy Martin, with club in second place and record of 40-28 (June 23).
1990—Defeated Pittsburgh in N.L. Championship Series; defeated Oakland in World Series.
1994—Seattle was in third place in A.L. West at time of season-ending strike (August 12).
1995—Defeated New York in A.L. divisional playoff; lost to Cleveland in A.L. Championship Series.
1997—Lost to Baltimore in A.L. divisional playoff.

RIGGLEMAN, JIM — CUBS

PERSONAL: Born December 9, 1952, in Fort Dix, N.J. ... 5-11/175. ... Batted right, threw right. ... Full name: James David Riggleman.
HIGH SCHOOL: Richard Montgomery (Rockville, Md.).
COLLEGE: Frostburg (Md.) State (degree in physical education).
TRANSACTIONS/CAREER NOTES: Selected by Los Angeles Dodgers organization in fourth round of free-agent draft (June 5, 1974). ... Traded by Dodgers organization to St. Louis Cardinals organization for C Sergio Robles (July 19, 1976). ... On Springfield disabled list (April 14-July 3, 1978). ... Released by Arkansas to become coach (May 25, 1981).
STATISTICAL NOTES: Led Eastern League third basemen with 30 double plays in 1975.

														BATTING				FIELDING	
Year	Team (League)	Pos.	G	AB	R	H	2B	3B	HR	RBI	Avg.	BB	SO	SB	PO	A	E	Avg.
1974— Waterbury (Eastern) ...		2B-3B	80	252	29	67	13	1	8	41	.266	25	56	1	159	175	20	.944
1975— Waterbury (Eastern) ...		3B	129	439	61	113	14	7	11	57	.257	54	86	14	109	267	53	.876
1976— Waterbury (Eastern) ...		OF-3B	84	287	38	75	14	2	6	39	.261	31	47	4	99	29	18	.877
—Arkansas (Texas)■...		3B-OF-1B	47	154	29	46	9	1	5	25	.299	19	13	1	38	73	10	.917
1977— Arkansas (Texas)		3B	27	93	10	26	7	2	0	11	.280	16	9	6	25	48	5	.936
—New Orleans (A.A.)		3B-OF-SS	103	346	52	83	16	0	17	52	.240	34	65	10	88	149	24	.908
1978— Arkansas (Texas)		3B-OF	59	174	34	51	8	1	4	34	.293	43	39	2	29	60	14	.864
1979— Arkansas (Texas)		3B-OF-1B	46	110	17	30	9	0	1	23	.273	13	23	5	34	22	4	.933
—Springfield (A.A.)		3B-OF-1B	35	93	9	22	4	0	2	9	.237	5	26	3	47	4	6	.895
1980— Arkansas (Texas)		3B-OF	127	431	84	127	29	7	21	90	.295	60	67	28	123	243	26	.934
1981— Arkansas (Texas)		OF-3B	37	133	17	32	7	1	1	15	.241	16	29	3	56	22	5	.940

RECORD AS MANAGER

BACKGROUND: Coach, Arkansas, St. Louis Cardinals organization, (May 25, 1981-remainder of season). ... Coach, Louisville, Cardinals organization (April 13-May 31, 1982). ... Director of player development, Cardinals (June 21, 1988-remainder of season). ... Coach, Cardinals (1989-90).

				REGULAR SEASON			POSTSEASON						
						Playoff		Champ. Series		World Series		All-Star Game	
Year	Team (League)	W	L	Pct.	Pos.	W	L	W	L	W	L	W	L
1982— St. Petersburg (Florida State)		8	4	.667	2nd	—	—	—	—	—	—	—	—
—(Second half)		35	30	.538	2nd	—	—	—	—	—	—	—	—
1983— St. Petersburg (Florida State)		33	35	.485	T3rd	—	—	—	—	—	—	—	—
—(Second half)		37	29	.561	2nd	—	—	—	—	—	—	—	—
1984— St. Petersburg (Florida State)		39	38	.506	3rd	—	—	—	—	—	—	—	—
—(Second half)		32	35	.478	3rd	—	—	—	—	—	—	—	—
1985— Arkansas (Texas)		33	30	.524	1st (E)	—	—	—	—	—	—	—	—
—(Second half)		31	40	.437	4th (E)	0	2	—	—	—	—	—	—
1986— Arkansas (Texas)		35	28	.556	3rd (E)	—	—	—	—	—	—	—	—
—(Second half)		32	39	.451	3rd (E)	—	—	—	—	—	—	—	—
1987— Arkansas (Texas)		36	29	.554	2nd (E)	—	—	—	—	—	—	—	—
—(Second half)		36	34	.514	3rd (E)	—	—	—	—	—	—	—	—
1988— Arkansas (Texas)		30	37	.448	3rd (E)	—	—	—	—	—	—	—	—
—(Second half)		2	1	.667		—	—	—	—	—	—	—	—
1991— Las Vegas (Pacific Coast)		36	34	.514	4th (S)	—	—	—	—	—	—	—	—
—(Second half)		29	41	.414	5th (S)	—	—	—	—	—	—	—	—
1992— Las Vegas (Pacific Coast)		41	31	.569	1st (S)	—	—	—	—	—	—	—	—
—(Second half)		33	39	.458	3rd (S)	2	3	—	—	—	—	—	—
—San Diego (N.L.)		4	8	.333	3rd (W)	—	—	—	—	—	—	—	—
1993— San Diego (N.L.)		61	101	.377	7th (W)	—	—	—	—	—	—	—	—
1994— San Diego (N.L.)		47	70	.402		—	—	—	—	—	—	—	—
1995— Chicago (N.L.)		73	71	.507	3rd (C)	—	—	—	—	—	—	—	—
1996— Chicago (N.L.)		76	86	.469	4th (C)	—	—	—	—	—	—	—	—
1997— Chicago (N.L.)		68	94	.420	5th (C)	—	—	—	—	—	—	—	—
1998— Chicago (N.L.)		90	73	.552	2nd (C)	0	3	—	—	—	—	—	—
Major league totals (7 years)		**419**	**503**	**.454**		**0**	**3**	**—**	**—**	**—**	**—**	**—**	**—**

NOTES:
1982—Replaced St. Petersburg manager Nick Leyva with club in fourth place and record of 26-30 (June 4).
1985—Lost to Jackson in semifinals.
1988—Replaced as Arkansas manager by Darold Knowles (June 21).
1992—Lost to Colorado Springs in semifinals. Replaced San Diego manager Greg Riddoch with club in third place and record of 78-72 (September 23).
1994—San Diego was in fourth place in N.L. West at time of season-ending baseball strike (August 12).
1998—Lost to Atlanta in N.L. divisional playoff.

ROTHSCHILD, LARRY — DEVIL RAYS

PERSONAL: Born March 12, 1954, in Chicago. ... 6-2/185. ... Threw right, batted right. ... Full name: Lawrence Lee Rothschild.
HIGH SCHOOL: Homewood-Flossmoor (Flossmoor, Ill.).
COLLEGE: Bradley, then Florida State.
TRANSACTIONS/CAREER NOTES: Signed as non-drafted free agent by Cincinnati Reds organization (June 10, 1975). ... Loaned to San Diego Padres organization (May 11, 1978). ... Returned to Reds organization (July 18, 1978). ... Selected by Detroit Tigers from Reds organization

in major league draft (December 8, 1980). ... Sold to Las Vegas, Pacific Coast League (February 25, 1983). ... On disabled list (April 10-May 4, 1983). ... Sold to Denver, American Association (December 18, 1983). ... Sold to Iowa, American Association (October 15, 1984).

Year	Team (League)	W	L	Pct.	ERA	G	GS	CG	ShO	Sv.	IP	H	R	ER	BB	SO
1975—	Billings (Pioneer)	0	2	.000	7.88	6	0	0	0	1	8	14	11	7	7	12
—	Eugene (Northwest)	3	0	1.000	2.73	21	0	0	0	•6	33	17	11	10	21	36
1976—	Three Rivers (East.)	11	3	*.786	2.05	30	12	10	5	5	123	96	33	28	29	75
1977—	Indianapolis (A.A.)	4	4	.500	4.21	29	14	2	1	1	92	93	51	43	34	43
1978—	Nashville (Southern)	0	0	. . .	4.50	5	0	0	0	1	12	14	7	6	4	9
—	Amarillo (Texas)■	5	5	.500	4.17	12	12	5	1	0	82	83	42	38	21	57
—	Indianapolis (A.A.)■	4	0	1.000	2.20	8	6	2	0	0	45	31	15	11	19	38
1979—	Indianapolis (A.A.)	1	6	.143	5.27	33	10	0	0	6	82	85	52	48	56	68
1980—	Indianapolis (A.A.)	8	7	.533	4.22	33	14	1	0	1	113	111	60	53	44	74
1981—	Evansville (A.A.)■	8	5	.615	3.27	56	0	0	0	15	77	62	32	28	29	81
—	Detroit (A.L.)	0	0	. . .	1.50	5	0	0	0	0	6	4	1	1	6	1
1982—	Evansville (A.A.)	6	4	.600	3.65	45	0	0	0	10	69	73	34	28	30	45
—	Detroit (A.L.)	0	0	. . .	13.50	2	0	0	0	0	2⅔	4	4	4	2	0
1983—	Las Vegas (PCL)■	9	2	.818	5.09	38	0	0	0	2	74½	88	43	42	34	39
1984—	Denver (Am. Assoc.)■	6	3	.667	4.02	31	9	1	1	2	109¾	109	58	49	51	71
1985—	Iowa (Am. Assoc.)■	1	5	.167	5.32	40	3	0	0	0	89¾	101	58	53	34	58
Major league totals (2 years)		0	0	. . .	5.19	7	0	0	0	0	8⅔	8	5	5	8	1

RECORD AS MANAGER

BACKGROUND: Coach, Cincinnati Reds organization (1986-89). ... Coach, Reds (1990-May 24, 1993). ... Coach, Atlanta Braves organization (1994). ... Coach, Florida Marlins (1995-97).

			REGULAR SEASON				POSTSEASON					
								Champ. Series		World Series		All-Star Game
						Playoff						
Year	Team (League)	W	L	Pct.	Pos.	W	L	W	L	W	L	W	L
1998—	Tampa Bay (A.L.)	63	99	.389	5th (E)	—	—	—	—	—	—	—	—

SHOWALTER, BUCK — DIAMONDBACKS

PERSONAL: Born May 23, 1956, in DeFuniak Springs, Fla. ... 5-9/195. ... Batted left, threw left. ... Full name: William Nathaniel Showalter III.
JUNIOR COLLEGE: Chipola Junior College (Fla.).
COLLEGE: Mississippi State.
TRANSACTIONS/CAREER NOTES: Selected by New York Yankees organization in fifth round of free-agent draft (June 7, 1977). ... On disabled list (July 1-11 and July 19-August 4, 1981).
STATISTICAL NOTES: Led Southern League first basemen with 1,281 putouts in 1982.

					BATTING										FIELDING		
Year	Team (League)	Pos.	G	AB	R	H	2B	3B	HR	RBI	Avg.	BB	SO	SB	PO	A	E	Avg.
1977—	Fort Lauderdale (FSL)	OF	56	196	32	71	8	1	1	25	.362	36	13	4	96	2	2	.980
1978—	West Haven (East.)	OF	123	429	52	124	13	2	3	46	.289	55	34	19	192	•15	7	.967
1979—	West Haven (East.)	1B-OF	129	469	71	131	7	3	6	51	.279	36	30	8	575	52	7	.989
1980—	Nashville (Southern)	OF-1B	142	550	84	*178	19	3	1	82	.324	53	23	6	71	2	1	.986
1981—	Columbus (Int'l)	OF	14	37	6	7	1	0	1	3	.189	3	0	0	11	0	1	.917
—	Nashville (Southern)	OF-1B	90	307	46	81	17	6	0	38	.264	46	16	3	201	14	7	.968
1982—	Nashville (Southern)	1B-OF	132	517	66	*152	29	3	3	46	.294	61	42	2	†1282	51	13	.990
1983—	Nashville (Southern)	1B-OF-P	89	297	35	82	13	4	1	37	.276	39	22	1	127	6	2	.985
—	Columbus (Int'l)	1B-P	18	63	9	15	3	0	1	8	.238	7	3	1	139	14	1	.994

RECORD AS PITCHER

Year	Team (League)	W	L	Pct.	ERA	G	GS	CG	ShO	Sv.	IP	H	R	ER	BB	SO
1983—	Nashville (Southern)	0	0	. . .	9.00	1	0	0	0	0	1	2	1	1	0	1
—	Columbus (Int'l)	0	0	. . .	0.00	1	0	0	0	0	2	0	0	0	0	2

RECORD AS MANAGER

BACKGROUND: Minor league coach, New York Yankees organization (1984). ... Coach, Yankees (1990-91). ... Manager/scout, Arizona Diamondbacks (1996-97).
HONORS: Named New-York-Pennsylvania League Manager of the Year (1985). ... Named Eastern League Manager of the Year (1989). ... Coach, A.L. All-Star team (1992). ... Named A.L. Manager of the Year by THE SPORTING NEWS (1994). ... Named A.L. Manager of the Year by Baseball Writers' Association of America (1994).

			REGULAR SEASON				POSTSEASON					
								Champ. Series		World Series		All-Star Game
						Playoff						
Year	Team (League)	W	L	Pct.	Pos.	W	L	W	L	W	L	W	L
1985—	Oneonta (New York-Pennsylvania)	55	23	.705	1st (N)	3	0	—	—	—	—	—	—
1986—	Oneonta (New York-Pennsylvania)	59	18	.766	1st (Y)	0	1	—	—	—	—	—	—
1987—	Fort Lauderdale (Florida State)	85	53	.616	1st (S)	5	1	—	—	—	—	—	—
1988—	Fort Lauderdale (Florida State)	39	29	.574	3rd (E)	—	—	—	—	—	—	—	—
—	(Second half)	30	36	.455	T3rd (E)	—	—	—	—	—	—	—	—
1989—	Albany/Colonie (Eastern)	92	48	.657	1st	6	2	—	—	—	—	—	—
1992—	New York (A.L.)	76	86	.469	T4th (E)	—	—	—	—	—	—	—	—
1993—	New York (A.L.)	88	74	.543	2nd (E)	—	—	—	—	—	—	—	—
1994—	New York (A.L.)	70	43	.619	6th (E)	—	—	—	—	—	—	—	—
1995—	New York (A.L.)	79	65	.549	2nd (E)	2	3	—	—	—	—	—	—
1998—	Arizona (N.L.)	65	97	.401	5th (E)	—	—	—	—	—	—	—	—
American League totals (4 years)		313	268	.539		2	3	—	—	—	—	—	—
National League totals (1 year)		65	97	.401		—	—	—	—	—	—	—	—
Major league totals (5 years)		378	365	.509		2	3	—	—	—	—	—	—

NOTES:
1985—Defeated Geneva in one-game semifinal playoff; defeated Auburn, two games to none, in league championship.
1986—Lost to Newark in playoffs.
1987—Defeated Lakeland, two games to none, in playoffs; defeated Osceola, three games to one, in league championship.
1989—Defeated Reading, three games to one, in playoffs; defeated Harrisburg, three games to one, in league championship.
1994—New York was in first place in A.L. East at time of season-ending strike (August 12).
1995—Lost to Seattle in A.L. divisional playoff. Named Arizona Diamondbacks manager (November 15).

TORRE, JOE   YANKEES

PERSONAL: Born July 18, 1940, in Brooklyn, N.Y. ... 6-1/210. ... Batted right, threw right. ... Full name: Joseph Paul Torre. ... Brother of Frank Torre, first baseman with Milwaukee Braves (1956-60) and Philadelphia Phillies (1962-63). ... Name pronounced TORE-ee.
HIGH SCHOOL: St. Francis Prep (Brooklyn, N.Y.).
TRANSACTIONS/CAREER NOTES: Signed by Jacksonville, Milwaukee Braves organization (August 24, 1959). ... On military list (September 30, 1962-March 26, 1963). ... Braves franchise moved from Milwaukee to Atlanta (1966). ... On disabled list (April 18-May 9, 1968). ... Traded by Braves to St. Louis Cardinals for 1B Orlando Cepeda (March 17, 1969). ... Traded by Cardinals to New York Mets for P Tommy Moore and P Ray Sadecki (October 13, 1974). ... Released as player by Mets (June 18, 1977).
RECORDS: Shares major league single-game record for most times grounded into double play—4 (July 21, 1975).
HONORS: Named catcher on THE SPORTING NEWS N.L. All-Star team (1964-66). ... Won N.L. Gold Glove at catcher (1965). ... Named Major League Player of the Year by THE SPORTING NEWS (1971). ... Named N.L. Player of the Year by THE SPORTING NEWS (1971). ... Named third baseman on THE SPORTING NEWS N.L. All-Star team (1971). ... Named N.L. Most Valuable Player by Baseball Writers' Association of America (1971).
STATISTICAL NOTES: Led N.L. catchers with .995 fielding percentage in 1964 and .996 in 1968. ... Led N.L. in grounding into double plays with 26 in 1964, 22 in 1965, 22 in 1967 and 21 in 1968. ... Led N.L. catchers with 12 double plays in 1967. ... Led N.L. with 352 total bases in 1971. ... Hit for the cycle (June 27, 1973). ... Led N.L. first basemen with 102 assists and 144 double plays in 1974. ... Career major league grand slams: 3.

							BATTING							FIELDING		
Year	Team (League)	Pos.	G	AB	R	H	2B	3B	HR	RBI	Avg.	BB	SO	SB	PO	A	E	Avg.
1960—	Eau Claire (North.)	C	117	369	63	127	23	3	16	74	*.344	70	45	7	636	64	9	.987
	— Milwaukee (N.L.)........	PH	2	2	0	1	0	0	0	0	.500	0	1	0	...	...	...	...
1961—	Louisville (A.A.).........	C	27	111	18	38	8	2	3	24	.342	6	9	0	185	14	2	.990
	— Milwaukee (N.L.)........	C	113	406	40	113	21	4	10	42	.278	28	60	3	494	50	10	.982
1962—	Milwaukee (N.L.)........	C	80	220	23	62	8	1	5	26	.282	24	24	1	325	39	5	.986
1963—	Milwaukee (N.L.)........	C-1B-OF	142	501	57	147	19	4	14	71	.293	42	79	1	919	76	6	.994
1964—	Milwaukee (N.L.)........	C-1B	154	601	87	193	36	5	20	109	.321	36	67	4	1081	94	7	†.994
1965—	Milwaukee (N.L.)........	C-1B	148	523	68	152	21	1	27	80	.291	61	79	0	1022	73	8	.993
1966—	Atlanta (N.L.).............	C-1B	148	546	83	172	20	3	36	101	.315	60	61	0	874	87	12	.988
1967—	Atlanta (N.L.).............	C-1B	135	477	67	132	18	1	20	68	.277	75	49	2	785	81	8	.991
1968—	Atlanta (N.L.).............	C-1B	115	424	45	115	11	2	10	55	.271	34	72	1	733	48	2	†.997
1969—	St. Louis (N.L.)■	1B-C	159	602	72	174	29	6	18	101	.289	66	85	0	1360	91	7	.995
1970—	St. Louis (N.L.)........	C-3B-1B	•161	624	89	203	27	9	21	100	.325	70	91	2	651	162	13	.984
1971—	St. Louis (N.L.)........	3B	161	634	97	*230	34	8	24	*137	.363	63	70	4	*136	271	•21	.951
1972—	St. Louis (N.L.)........	3B-1B	149	544	71	157	26	6	11	81	.289	54	74	3	336	198	15	.973
1973—	St. Louis (N.L.)........	1B-3B	141	519	67	149	17	2	13	69	.287	65	78	2	881	128	12	.988
1974—	St. Louis (N.L.)........	1B-3B	147	529	59	149	28	1	11	70	.282	69	68	1	1173	†121	14	.989
1975—	New York (N.L.)■	3B-1B	114	361	33	89	16	3	6	35	.247	35	55	0	172	157	15	.956
1976—	New York (N.L.)........	1B-3B	114	310	36	95	10	3	5	31	.306	21	35	1	593	52	7	.989
1977—	New York (N.L.).........	1B-3B	26	51	2	9	3	0	1	9	.176	2	10	0	83	3	1	.989
	Major league totals (18 years)		2209	7874	996	2342	344	59	252	1185	.297	805	1058	25	11618	1731	163	.988

ALL-STAR GAME RECORD

						BATTING							FIELDING		
Year	League	Pos.	AB	R	H	2B	3B	HR	RBI	Avg.	BB	SO	SB	PO	A	E	Avg.
1963—	National.....................						Did not play.										
1964—	National.....................	C	2	0	0	0	0	0	0	.000	0	0	0	5	0	0	1.000
1965—	National.....................	C	4	1	1	0	0	1	2	.250	0	0	0	5	1	0	1.000
1966—	National.....................	C	3	0	0	0	0	0	0	.000	0	1	0	5	0	0	1.000
1967—	National.....................	C	2	0	0	0	0	0	0	.000	0	0	0	4	1	0	1.000
1970—	National.....................	PH	1	0	0	0	0	0	0	.000	0	0	0	...	...	...	...
1971—	National.....................	3B	3	0	0	0	0	0	0	.000	0	1	0	1	0	0	1.000
1972—	National.....................	3B	3	0	0	0	0	0	0	.000	0	1	0	1	2	0	1.000
1973—	National.....................	1B-3B	3	0	0	0	0	0	0	.000	0	0	0	5	0	0	1.000
	All-Star Game totals (8 years)		21	1	1	0	0	1	2	.048	0	3	0	26	4	0	1.000

RECORD AS MANAGER

BACKGROUND: Player/manager, New York Mets (May 31-June 18, 1977).
HONORS: Named Sportsman of the Year by THE SPORTING NEWS (1996). ... Named co-A.L. Manager of the Year by Baseball Writers' Association of America (1996). ... Named A.L. Manager of the Year by The Sporting News (1998). ... Named A.L. Manager of the Year by Baseball Writers' Association of America (1998).

		REGULAR SEASON				POSTSEASON						All-Star	
						Playoff		Champ. Series		World Series		Game	
Year	Team (League)	W	L	Pct.	Pos.	W	L	W	L	W	L	W	L
1977—	New York (N.L.)	49	68	.419	6th (E)	—	—	—	—	—	—	—	—
1978—	New York (N.L.)	66	96	.407	6th (E)	—	—	—	—	—	—	—	—
1979—	New York (N.L.)	63	99	.389	6th (E)	—	—	—	—	—	—	—	—
1980—	New York (N.L.)	67	95	.414	5th (E)	—	—	—	—	—	—	—	—
1981—	New York (N.L.)	17	34	.333	5th (E)	—	—	—	—	—	—	—	—
	(Second half)	24	28	.462	4th (E)	—	—	—	—	—	—	—	—
1982—	Atlanta (N.L.)	89	73	.549	1st (W)	—	—	0	3	—	—	—	—
1983—	Atlanta (N.L.)	88	74	.543	2nd (W)	—	—	—	—	—	—	—	—
1984—	Atlanta (N.L.)	80	82	.494	T2nd (W)	—	—	—	—	—	—	—	—

MAJOR LEAGUE MANAGERS

| | | REGULAR SEASON | | | | POSTSEASON | | | | | | | | |
| | | | | | | Playoff | | Champ. Series | | World Series | | All-Star Game | |
Year	Team (League)	W	L	Pct.	Pos.	W	L	W	L	W	L	W	L
1990	St. Louis (N.L.)	24	34	.414	6th (E)	—	—	—	—	—	—	—	—
1991	St. Louis (N.L.)	84	78	.519	2nd (E)	—	—	—	—	—	—	—	—
1992	St. Louis (N.L.)	83	79	.512	3rd (E)	—	—	—	—	—	—	—	—
1993	St. Louis (N.L.)	87	75	.537	3rd (E)	—	—	—	—	—	—	—	—
1994	St. Louis (N.L.)	53	61	.465		—	—	—	—	—	—	—	—
1995	St. Louis (N.L.)	20	27	.426	4th (C)	—	—	—	—	—	—	—	—
1996	New York (A.L.)	92	70	.568	1st (E)	3	1	4	1	4	2	—	—
1997	New York (A.L.)	96	66	.593	2nd (E)	2	3	—	—	—	—	1	0
1998	New York (A.L.)	114	48	.704	1st (E)	3	0	4	2	4	0	—	—
American League totals (3 years)		302	184	.621		8	4	8	3	8	2	1	0
National League totals (14 years)		894	1003	.471		—	—	0	3	—	—	—	—
Major league totals (17 years)		1196	1187	.502		8	4	8	6	8	2	1	0

NOTES:
1977—Replaced New York manager Joe Frazier with club in sixth place and record of 15-30 (May 31); served as player/manager (May 31-June 18, when released as player).
1982—Lost to St. Louis in N.L. Championship Series.
1990—Replaced St. Louis manager Whitey Herzog (33-47) and interim manager Red Schoendienst (13-11) with club in sixth place and record of 46-58 (August 1).
1994—St. Louis was tied for third place in N.L. Central at time of season-ending strike (August 12).
1995—Replaced as Cardinals manager by interim manager Mike Jorgensen, with club in fourth place (June 16).
1996—Defeated Texas in A.L. divisional playoff; defeated Baltimore in A.L. Championship Series; defeated Atlanta in World Series.
1997—Lost to Cleveland in A.L. divisional playoff.
1998—Defeated Texas in A.L. divisional playoff; defeated Cleveland in A.L. Championship Series; defeated San Diego in World Series.

VALENTINE, BOBBY — METS

PERSONAL: Born May 13, 1950, in Stamford, Conn. ... 5-10/185. ... Batted right, threw right. ... Full name: Robert John Valentine. ... Son-in-law of Ralph Branca, pitcher with Brooklyn Dodgers (1944-53 and 1956), Detroit Tigers (1953-54), New York Yankees (1955).
HIGH SCHOOL: Rippowan (Stamford, Conn.).
COLLEGE: Arizona State, then Southern California.
TRANSACTIONS/CAREER NOTES: Selected by Los Angeles Dodgers organization in first round (fifth pick overall) of free-agent draft (June 7, 1968). ... Traded by Dodgers with IF Billy Grabarkewitz, OF Frank Robinson, P Bill Singer and P Mike Strahler to California Angels for P Andy Messersmith and 3B Ken McMullen (November 28, 1972). ... On disabled list (May 17, 1973-remainder of season and May 29-June 13, 1974). ... Loaned by Angels to Charleston, Pittsburgh Pirates organization (April 4-June 20, 1975). ... Traded by Angels with a player to be named later to San Diego Padres for P Gary Ross (September 17, 1975); Padres acquired IF Rudy Meoli to complete deal (November 4, 1975). ... Traded by Padres with P Paul Siebert to New York Mets for IF/OF Dave Kingman (June 15, 1977). ... Released by Mets (March 26, 1979). ... Signed by Seattle Mariners (April 10, 1979). ... Granted free agency (November 1, 1979).
HONORS: Named Pacific Coast League Player of the Year (1970).
STATISTICAL NOTES: Led Pioneer League outfielders with 107 putouts and tied for lead with eight assists in 1968. ... Led Pacific Coast League shortstops with 38 errors in 1969. ... Led Pacific Coast League with 324 total bases, with 10 sacrifice flies and in double plays by shortstop with 106 in 1970. ... Led Pacific Coast League shortstops with 217 putouts and 54 errors in 1970.

| | | | | | | | | BATTING | | | | | | | | FIELDING | | | |
Year	Team (League)	Pos.	G	AB	R	H	2B	3B	HR	RBI	Avg.	BB	SO	SB	PO	A	E	Avg.
1968—	Ogden (Pioneer)	OF-SS	62	224	*62	63	14	4	6	26	.281	39	27	*20	†111	‡10	6	.953
1969—	Spokane (PCL)	SS-OF	111	402	61	104	19	5	3	35	.259	32	57	34	166	254	†38	.917
	—Los Angeles (N.L.)	PR	5	0	3	0	0	0	0	0		0	0	0	...	...	...	...
1970—	Spokane (PCL)	SS-2B	•146	*621	*122	*211	*39	*16	14	80	*.340	47	51	29	†217	474	†54	.928
1971—	Spokane (PCL)	SS	7	30	7	10	2	0	1	2	.333	3	6	3	13	18	3	.912
	—Los Angeles (N.L.)	S-3-2-DH	101	281	32	70	10	2	1	25	.249	15	20	5	123	176	16	.949
1972—	Los Angeles (N.L.)	2-3-O-S	119	391	42	107	11	2	3	32	.274	27	33	5	178	245	23	.948
1973—	California (A.L.)	SS-OF	32	126	12	38	5	2	1	13	.302	5	9	6	63	75	6	.958
1974—	California (A.L.)	O-S-3-DH	117	371	39	97	10	3	3	39	.261	25	25	8	160	116	17	.942
1975—	Char., W.Va. (Int'l)■	3B	56	175	27	41	4	0	1	17	.234	30	16	8	44	74	6	.952
	—Salt Lake (PCL)■	1-0-3-2	46	147	29	45	6	1	0	17	.306	31	15	13	92	14	3	.972
	—California (A.L.)	DH-1-3-O	26	57	5	16	2	0	0	5	.281	4	3	0	27	1	2	.933
	—San Diego (N.L.)■	OF	7	15	1	2	0	0	1	1	.133	4	0	1	4	0	0	1.000
1976—	Hawaii (PCL)	1-0-3-S	120	395	67	120	23	2	13	89	.304	47	32	9	578	47	4	.994
	—San Diego (N.L.)■	OF-1B	15	49	3	18	4	0	0	4	.367	6	2	0	55	6	0	1.000
1977—	San Diego (N.L.)	...	44	67	5	12	3	0	1	10	.179	7	10	0	...	...	...	...
	—New York (N.L.)■	...	42	83	8	11	1	0	1	3	.133	6	9	0	...	...	...	...
1978—	New York (N.L.)	2B-3B	69	160	17	43	7	0	1	18	.269	19	18	1	78	109	6	.969
1979—	Seattle (A.L.)■	S-O-2-3-C-DH	62	98	9	27	6	0	0	7	.276	22	5	1	32	38	2	.972
American League totals (4 years)			237	652	65	178	23	5	4	64	.273	56	42	15	282	230	27	.950
National League totals (7 years)			488	1196	124	286	40	4	10	106	.239	97	111	12	...	...	...	...
Major league totals (10 years)			725	1848	189	464	63	9	14	170	.251	153	153	27	...	...	...	...

RECORD AS MANAGER
BACKGROUND: Scout and minor league instructor, San Diego Padres (1981). ... Minor league instructor, New York Mets (1982). ... Coach, Mets (1983-May 15, 1985). ... Coach, Cincinnati Reds (1993).

| | | REGULAR SEASON | | | | POSTSEASON | | | | | | | | |
| | | | | | | Playoff | | Champ. Series | | World Series | | All-Star Game | |
Year	Team (League)	W	L	Pct.	Pos.	W	L	W	L	W	L	W	L
1985—	Texas (A.L.)	53	76	.411	7th (W)	—	—	—	—	—	—	—	—
1986—	Texas (A.L.)	87	75	.537	2nd (W)	—	—	—	—	—	—	—	—

– 655 –

		— REGULAR SEASON —				— POSTSEASON —							
						Playoff		Champ. Series		World Series		All-Star Game	
Year	Team (League)	W	L	Pct.	Pos.	W	L	W	L	W	L	W	L
1987— Texas (A.L.)		75	87	.463	T6th (W)	—	—	—	—	—	—	—	—
1988— Texas (A.L.)		70	91	.435	6th (W)	—	—	—	—	—	—	—	—
1989— Texas (A.L.)		83	79	.512	4th (W)	—	—	—	—	—	—	—	—
1990— Texas (A.L.)		83	79	.512	3rd (W)	—	—	—	—	—	—	—	—
1991— Texas (A.L.)		85	77	.525	3rd (W)	—	—	—	—	—	—	—	—
1992— Texas (A.L.)		45	41	.523		—	—	—	—	—	—	—	—
1994— Norfolk (Int'l)		67	75	.472	4th (W)	—	—	—	—	—	—	—	—
1995— Chiba Lotte (Jp. Cen.)		69	58	.543	2nd (P)	—	—	—	—	—	—	—	—
1996— Norfolk (Int'l)		76	57	.571		—	—	—	—	—	—	—	—
— New York (N.L.)		12	19	.387	4th (E)	—	—	—	—	—	—	—	—
1997— New York (N.L.)		88	74	.543	3rd (E)	—	—	—	—	—	—	—	—
1998— New York (N.L.)		88	74	.543	2nd (E)	—	—	—	—	—	—	—	—
American League totals (8 years)		581	605	.490		—	—	—	—	—	—	—	—
National League totals (3 years)		188	167	.530		—	—	—	—	—	—	—	—
Major league totals (11 years)		769	772	.499		—	—	—	—	—	—	—	—

NOTES:
1985—Replaced Texas manager Doug Rader with club in seventh place and record of 9-23 (May 16).
1992—Replaced as Texas manager by Toby Harrah with club in third place (July 9).
1995—Chiba Lotte tied three games.
1996—Replaced New York manager Dallas Green with club in fourth place and record of 59-72 (August 26).

WILLIAMS, JIMY — RED SOX

PERSONAL: Born October 4, 1943, in Santa Maria, Calif. ... 5-11/170. ... Batted right, threw right. ... Full name: James Francis Williams.
COLLEGE: Fresno State College (bachelor of science degree in agribusiness).
TRANSACTIONS/CAREER NOTES: Selected by St. Louis Cardinals organization from Toronto, Boston Red Sox organization (November 29, 1965). ... In military service (July 24, 1966-remainder of season). ... Traded by Cardinals with C Pat Corrales to Cincinnati Reds for C John Edwards (February 8, 1968). ... Selected by Montreal Expos in expansion draft (October 14, 1968). ... On disabled list (May 13-30 and June 24-September 2, 1969). ... On suspended list (June 7-16, 1971). ... Sold to New York Mets organization (June 16, 1971). ... On temporary inactive list (August 12-16, 1971). ... On disabled list (May 15-July 17 and July 29-August 20, 1975).

						— BATTING —									— FIELDING —			
Year	Team (League)	Pos.	G	AB	R	H	2B	3B	HR	RBI	Avg.	BB	SO	SB	PO	A	E	Avg.
1965— Waterloo (Midwest)....		SS	115	435	64	125	19	3	2	31	.287	41	74	10	173	*312	26	*.949
1966— St. Louis (N.L.)...........		SS-2B	13	11	1	3	0	0	0	1	.273	1	5	0	2	5	0	1.000
1967— Arkansas (Texas)........		SS	28	101	8	21	1	1	0	8	.208	9	14	0	49	80	2	.985
— Tulsa (PCL)		SS	61	164	18	37	2	0	1	21	.226	18	33	4	87	156	26	.903
— St. Louis (N.L.)...........		SS	1	2	0	0	0	0	0	0	.000	0	1	0	6	1	0	1.000
1968— Indianapolis (PCL)■ ..		SS-2B	120	403	38	91	19	5	2	34	.226	20	59	5	198	323	27	.951
1969— Vancouver (PCL)■....		3B-OF-SS	35	66	7	17	1	1	0	9	.258	4	8	1	17	23	2	.952
1970— Winnipeg (Int'l)		SS-2B-3B	109	361	49	83	15	0	3	18	.230	34	48	5	178	244	30	.934
1971— Winn.-Tide. (Int'l)■....		SS-3B-2B	105	327	40	84	7	4	5	31	.257	38	46	7	120	219	22	.939
1972—						Did not play.												
1973—						Did not play.												
1974—						Did not play.												
1975— El Paso (Texas)..........		DH	6	17	3	2	0	0	0	2	.118	2	2	0	...	...	...	...
Major league totals (2 years)			14	13	1	3	0	0	0	1	.231	0	0	0	8	6	0	1.000

RECORD AS MANAGER

BACKGROUND: Coach, Toronto Blue Jays (1980-85). ... Minor league instructor, Atlanta Braves (October 4, 1989-June 25, 1990). ... Coach, Braves (1990-96).
HONORS: Named Pacific Coast League Manager of the Year (1976 and 1979).

		— REGULAR SEASON —				— POSTSEASON —							
						Playoff		Champ. Series		World Series		All-Star Game	
Year	Team (League)	W	L	Pct.	Pos.	W	L	W	L	W	L	W	L
1974— Quad Cities (Midwest)		33	26	.559	1st (S)	—	—	—	—	—	—	—	—
— (Second half)		32	32	.500	3rd (S)	1	2	—	—	—	—	—	—
1975— El Paso (Texas)		62	71	.466	3rd (W)	—	—	—	—	—	—	—	—
1976— Salt Lake City (Pacific Coast)		90	54	.625	1st (E)	2	3	—	—	—	—	—	—
1977— Salt Lake City (Pacific Coast)		74	65	.532	2nd (E)	—	—	—	—	—	—	—	—
1978— Springfield (American Association)		70	66	.515	3rd (E)	—	—	—	—	—	—	—	—
1979— Salt Lake City (Pacific Coast)		34	40	.447	4th (S)	—	—	—	—	—	—	—	—
— (Second half)		46	28	.622	1st (S)	5	0	—	—	—	—	—	—
1986— Toronto (A.L.)		86	76	.531	4th (E)	—	—	—	—	—	—	—	—
1987— Toronto (A.L.)		96	66	.593	2nd (E)	—	—	—	—	—	—	—	—
1988— Toronto (A.L.)		87	75	.537	T3rd (E)	—	—	—	—	—	—	—	—
1989— Toronto (A.L.)		12	24	.333		—	—	—	—	—	—	—	—
1997— Boston (A.L.)		78	84	.481	4th (E)	—	—	—	—	—	—	—	—
1998— Boston (A.L.)		92	70	.568	2nd (E)	1	3	—	—	—	—	—	—
Major league totals (6 years)		451	395	.532		1	3	—	—	—	—	—	—

NOTES:
1974—Lost to Danville in playoffs.
1976—Lost to Hawaii in championship playoff.
1979—Defeated Albuquerque, two games to none, in playoff; defeated Hawaii, three games to none, in championship playoff.
1989—Replaced as Toronto manager by Cito Gaston, with club tied for sixth place (May 15).
1998—Lost to Cleveland in A.L. divisional playoff.

BRETT, GEORGE   3B/1B

PERSONAL: Born May 15, 1953, in Glen Dale, W.Va. ... 6-0/205. ... Batted left, threw right. ... Full name: George Howard Brett. ... Brother of Ken Brett, pitcher with 10 major league teams (1967 and 1969-81); brother of John Brett, minor league infielder (1968); and brother of Bob Brett, minor league outfielder (1972).

HIGH SCHOOL: El Segundo (Calif.).

JUNIOR COLLEGE: Longview Community College (Mo.), then El Camino College (Calif.).

TRANSACTIONS/CAREER NOTES: Selected by Kansas City Royals organization in second round of free-agent draft (June 8, 1971). ... On disabled list (April 29-May 11, 1972; May 4-19 and July 27-August 14, 1978; June 11-July 10, 1980; June 8-29, 1983; April 1-May 18, 1984; April 20-May 13 and May 16-June 12, 1987; April 30-June 10, 1989; and April 26-May 24, 1991). ... Placed on voluntarily retired list (October 4, 1993).

RECORDS: Holds major league single-season record for most consecutive games with three or more hits—6 (May 8-13, 1976). ... Shares major league record for most home runs in month of October—4 (1985). ... Holds A.L. career record for most intentional bases on balls received—229. ... Holds A.L. record for most seasons with 10 or more intentional bases on balls received—11.

HONORS: Named third baseman on THE SPORTING NEWS A.L. All-Star team (1976, 1979 and 1980). ... Named Man of the Year by THE SPORTING NEWS (1980). ... Named Major League Player of the Year by THE SPORTING NEWS (1980). ... Named A.L. Player of the Year by THE SPORTING NEWS (1980). ... Named third baseman on THE SPORTING NEWS Silver Slugger team (1980 and 1985). ... Named A.L. Most Valuable Player by Baseball Writers' Association of America (1980). ... Won A.L. Gold Glove at third base (1985). ... Named first baseman on THE SPORTING NEWS A.L. All-Star team (1988). ... Named first baseman on THE SPORTING NEWS A.L. Silver Slugger team (1988).

STATISTICAL NOTES: Led California League with eight sacrifice hits in 1972. ... Led California League third basemen with 172 assists and 30 errors in 1972. ... Tied for A.L. lead in errors by third baseman with 26 in 1975. ... Led A.L. with 298 total bases in 1976. ... Led A.L. third basemen with 140 putouts in 1976. ... Led A.L. third basemen with 373 assists, 30 errors and 532 total chances in 1979. ... Hit three home runs in one game (July 22, 1979 and April 20, 1983). ... Had 30-game hitting streak (July 18-August 19, 1980). ... Led A.L. with .461 on-base percentage in 1980. ... Led A.L. with .664 slugging percentage in 1980, .563 in 1983 and .585 in 1985. ... Led A.L. third basemen with 33 double plays in 1985. ... Led A.L. with 31 intentional bases on balls received in 1985 and 18 in 1986. ... Hit for the cycle (May 28, 1979 and July 25, 1990). ... Career major league grand slams: 2.

MISCELLANEOUS: Holds Kansas City Royals records for most runs (1,583), most hits (3,154), most doubles (665), most triples (137), most home runs (317), most runs batted in (1,595) and highest batting average (.305).

Year Team (League)	Pos.	G	AB	R	H	2B	3B	HR	RBI	Avg.	BB	SO	SB	PO	A	E	Avg.
1971— Billings (Pioneer)........	SS-3B	68	258	44	75	8	5	5	44	.291	32	38	3	87	140	28	.890
1972— San Jose (Calif.).........	3B-SS-2B	117	431	66	118	13	5	10	68	.274	53	53	2	101	†213	†30	.913
1973— Omaha (A.A.).............	3B-OF	117	405	66	115	16	4	8	64	.284	48	45	3	92	219	26	.923
— Kansas City (A.L.)........	3B	13	40	2	5	2	0	0	0	.125	0	5	0	9	28	1	.974
1974— Omaha (A.A.).............	3B	16	64	9	17	2	0	2	14	.266	6	1	1	8	31	4	.907
— Kansas City (A.L.)........	3B-SS	133	457	49	129	21	5	2	47	.282	21	38	8	102	279	21	.948
1975— Kansas City (A.L.)......	3B-SS	159	*634	84	*195	35	•13	11	89	.308	46	49	13	132	356	‡26	.949
1976— Kansas City (A.L.)......	3B-SS	159	*645	94	*215	34	*14	7	67	*.333	49	36	21	†146	350	26	.950
1977— Kansas City (A.L.)......	3B-DH-SS	139	564	105	176	32	13	22	88	.312	55	24	14	115	325	21	.954
1978— Kansas City (A.L.)......	3B-SS	128	510	79	150	*45	8	9	62	.294	39	35	23	104	289	16	.961
1979— Kansas City (A.L.)......	3B-1B-DH	154	645	119	*212	42	*20	23	107	.329	51	36	17	176	†378	†31	.947
1980— Kansas City (A.L.)......	3B-1B	117	449	87	175	33	9	24	118	*.390	58	22	15	107	256	17	.955
1981— Kansas City (A.L.)......	3B	89	347	42	109	27	7	6	43	.314	27	23	14	74	170	14	.946
1982— Kansas City (A.L.)......	3-1-O-DH	144	552	101	166	32	9	21	82	.301	71	51	6	130	295	17	.962
1983— Kansas City (A.L.)......	3B	123	464	90	144	38	2	25	93	.310	57	39	0	210	192	25	.941
1984— Kansas City (A.L.)......	3B	104	377	42	107	21	3	13	69	.284	38	37	0	59	201	14	.949
1985— Kansas City (A.L.)......	3B-DH	155	550	108	184	38	5	30	112	.335	103	49	9	107	*339	15	.967
1986— Kansas City (A.L.)......	3B-DH-SS	124	441	70	128	28	4	16	73	.290	80	45	1	97	218	16	.952
1987— Kansas City (A.L.)......	1B-DH-3B	115	427	71	124	18	2	22	78	.290	72	47	6	805	69	9	.990
1988— Kansas City (A.L.)......	1B-DH-SS	157	589	90	180	42	3	24	103	.306	82	51	14	1126	70	10	.992
1989— Kansas City (A.L.)......	1B-DH-OF	124	457	67	129	26	3	12	80	.282	59	47	14	898	80	2	.998
1990— Kansas City (A.L.)......	1-DH-O-3	142	544	82	179	•45	7	14	87	*.329	56	63	9	880	67	7	.993
1991— Kansas City (A.L.)......	1B	131	505	77	129	40	2	10	61	.255	58	75	2	87	5	1	.989
1992— Kansas City (A.L.)......	DH-1B-3B	152	592	55	169	35	5	7	61	.285	35	69	8	139	17	3	.981
1993— Kansas City (A.L.)......	DH	145	560	69	149	31	3	19	75	.266	39	67	7	...	...	...	...
Major league totals (21 years)		2707	10349	1583	3154	665	137	317	1595	.305	1096	908	201	5503	3984	292	.970

DIVISION SERIES RECORD

Year Team (League)	Pos.	G	AB	R	H	2B	3B	HR	RBI	Avg.	BB	SO	SB	PO	A	E	Avg.
1981— Kansas City (A.L.)	3B	3	12	0	2	0	0	0	0	.167	0	0	0	1	6	1	.875

CHAMPIONSHIP SERIES RECORD

RECORDS: Holds career records for highest slugging average (50 or more at-bats)—.728; most runs—22; most triples—4; most home runs—9; most total bases—75; and most long hits—18. ... Holds A.L. single-game record for most total bases—12 (October 6, 1978). ... Shares career record for most game-winning RBIs—3. ... Shares single-series records for most triples—2 (1977); and game-winning RBIs—2 (1985). ... Shares single-game records for most runs—3 (October 11, 1985); and most home runs—3 (October 6, 1978). ... Holds A.L. single-series record for highest slugging average—1.056 (1978). ... Shares A.L. single-series record for most home runs—3 (1978 and 1985). ... Shares A.L. single-game record for most long hits—3 (October 6, 1978 and October 11, 1985).

NOTES: Named A.L. Championship Series Most Valuable Player (1985).

Year Team (League)	Pos.	G	AB	R	H	2B	3B	HR	RBI	Avg.	BB	SO	SB	PO	A	E	Avg.
1976— Kansas City (A.L.)	3B	5	18	4	8	1	1	1	5	.444	2	1	0	3	7	3	.769
1977— Kansas City (A.L.)	3B	5	20	2	6	0	2	0	2	.300	1	0	0	5	12	2	.895
1978— Kansas City (A.L.)	3B	4	18	7	7	1	1	3	3	.389	0	1	0	3	8	1	.917
1980— Kansas City (A.L.)	3B	3	11	3	3	1	0	2	4	.273	1	0	0	2	7	0	1.000

Year Team (League)	Pos.	G	AB	R	H	2B	3B	HR	RBI	Avg.	BB	SO	SB	PO	A	E	Avg.
1984— Kansas City (A.L.)	3B	3	13	0	3	0	0	0	0	.231	0	2	0	2	7	0	1.000
1985— Kansas City (A.L.)	3B	7	23	6	8	2	0	3	5	.348	7	5	0	7	8	2	.882
Championship series totals (6 years)		27	103	22	35	5	4	9	19	.340	11	9	0	22	49	8	.899

WORLD SERIES RECORD

NOTES: Member of World Series championship team (1985).

Year Team (League)	Pos.	G	AB	R	H	2B	3B	HR	RBI	Avg.	BB	SO	SB	PO	A	E	Avg.
1980— Kansas City (A.L.)	3B	6	24	3	9	2	1	1	3	.375	2	4	1	4	17	1	.955
1985— Kansas City (A.L.)	3B	7	27	5	10	1	0	0	1	.370	4	7	0	10	19	1	.967
World Series totals (2 years)		13	51	8	19	3	1	1	4	.373	6	11	1	14	36	2	.962

ALL-STAR GAME RECORD

RECORDS: Holds career record for most sacrifice flies—3.

NOTES: Named to A.L. All-Star team for 1986 game; replaced by Brook Jacoby due to injury. ... Named to A.L. All-Star team for 1987 game; replaced by Kevin Seitzer due to injury.

Year League	Pos.	AB	R	H	2B	3B	HR	RBI	Avg.	BB	SO	SB	PO	A	E	Avg.
1976— American	3B	2	0	0	0	0	0	0	.000	1	0	0	0	1	0	1.000
1977— American	3B	2	0	0	0	0	0	0	.000	1	0	0	2	1	0	1.000
1978— American	3B	3	1	2	1	0	0	2	.667	0	0	1	0	2	0	1.000
1979— American	3B	3	1	0	0	0	0	0	.000	0	0	0	1	2	0	1.000
1980— American					Selected, did not play—injured.											
1981— American	3B	3	0	0	0	0	0	0	.000	0	2	0	0	1	0	1.000
1982— American	3B	2	0	2	0	0	0	0	1.000	0	0	0	0	0	0	. . .
1983— American	3B	4	2	2	1	1	0	1	.500	0	0	0	1	5	0	1.000
1984— American	3B	3	1	1	0	0	0	1	.333	0	1	0	3	0	0	1.000
1985— American	3B	1	0	0	0	0	0	1	.000	1	0	0	2	1	0	1.000
1986— American					Selected, did not play—injured.											
1987— American					Selected, did not play—injured.											
1988— American	PH	1	0	0	0	0	0	0	.000	0	0	0	. . .	. . .	. . .	
All-Star Game totals (10 years)		24	5	7	2	1	1	5	.292	3	3	1	9	13	0	1.000

RYAN, NOLAN　　　　　P

PERSONAL: Born January 31, 1947, in Refugio, Texas. ... 6-2/212. ... Threw right, batted right. ... Full name: Lynn Nolan Ryan Jr.

HIGH SCHOOL: Alvin (Texas).

JUNIOR COLLEGE: Alvin (Texas) Junior College.

TRANSACTIONS/CAREER NOTES: Selected by New York Mets organization in eighth round of free-agent draft (June, 1965). ... On military list (January 3-May 13, 1967). ... On Jacksonville disabled list (July 16-August 30, 1967). ... On disabled list (July 30-August 30, 1968; and May 12-June 8, 1969). ... On military list (August 11-September 1, 1969). ... Traded by Mets with P Don Rose, OF Leroy Stanton and C Francisco Estrada to California Angels for IF Jim Fregosi (December 10, 1971). ... On disabled list (June 14-July 5, 1978). ... Granted free agency (November 1, 1979). ... Signed by Houston Astros (November 19, 1979). ... On disabled list (March 25-April 17 and May 3-June 6, 1983; June 2-17 and June 18-July 3, 1984; June 1-24 and July 28-August 12, 1986). ... Granted free agency (November 4, 1988). ... Signed by Texas Rangers (December 7, 1988). ... On disabled list (May 18-June 6, 1990; May 14-29 and July 29-August 19, 1991; April 7-30, 1992; April 15-May 7, May 8-July 19 and August 22-September 12, 1993). ... Placed on voluntarily retired list (October 14, 1993).

RECORDS: Holds major league career records for most seasons played and most seasons pitched—27; most consecutive seasons pitched—26 (1968-93); most bases on balls allowed—2,795; most strikeouts—5,714; most grand slams allowed—10; most seasons leading league in bases on balls allowed—8; most seasons with 300 or more strikeouts—6; most seasons with 200 or more strikeouts—15; most seasons with 100 or more strikeouts—24; most consecutive seasons with 300 or more strikeouts—3 (1972-74); most consecutive seasons with 100 or more strikeouts—23 (1970-92); most games with 15 or more strikeouts—26; most games with 10 or more strikeouts—215; most no-hit games—7; most low-hit (no-hit and one-hit) games—19; and most wild pitches—277. ... Holds major league single-season records for most games with 10 or more strikeouts—23 (1973); and most strikeouts (since 1900)—383 (1973). ... Holds major league records for most strikeouts in three consecutive games—47 (August 12 [19], 16 [9]and 20 [19], 1974, 27 1/3 innings); and most strikeouts by losing pitcher in an extra-inning game—19 (August 20, 1974, 11 innings). ... Holds modern major league record for most consecutive starting assignments—595 (July 30, 1974 through 1993). ... Shares major league single-season record for most no-hit games—2 (1973); and most clubs shut out—8 (1972). ... Shares major league record for striking out side on nine pitches (April 19, 1968, third inning and July 9, 1972, second inning). ... Holds A.L. career records for most games with 10 or more strikeouts—148; most games 15 or more strikeouts—23; most no-hit games—6; and most low-hit (no-hit and one-hit) games—15. ... Shares A.L. career records for most seasons leading league in errors by pitcher—4; and most seasons with 200 or more strikeouts—10. ... Shares A.L. single-season record for most low-hit (no-hit and one-hit) games—3 (1973). ... Shares A.L. record for most strikeouts in two consecutive games—32 (August 7 [13] and 12 [19], 1974). ... Shares A.L. single-game record for most consecutive strikeouts—8 (July 9, 1972 and July 15, 1973).

HONORS: Named Western Carolinas League Pitcher of the Year (1966). ... Named A.L. Pitcher of the Year by THE SPORTING NEWS (1977). ... Named righthanded pitcher on THE SPORTING NEWS A.L. All-Star team (1977). ... Named Man of the Year by THE SPORTING NEWS (1990).

STATISTICAL NOTES: Tied for Appalachian League lead with eight hit batsmen in 1965. ... Led A.L. with 18 wild pitches in 1972, 21 in 1977, 13 in 1978 and 19 in 1989. ... Pitched 3-0 no-hit victory against Kansas City (May 15, 1973). ... Pitched 6-0 no-hit victory against Detroit (July 15, 1973). ... Pitched 5-0 one-hit, complete-game victory against New York (August 29, 1973). ... Pitched 5-0 one-hit, complete-game victory against Texas (June 27, 1974). ... Struck out 17 batters in one game (July 15, 1973; August 18, 1976). ... Struck out 16 batters in one game (September 27, 1973; June 9, 1979; September 9, 1987; April 26, 1990; May 1, 1991). ... Struck out 15 batters in one game (April 30, September 11 and September 28, 1974; June 19, 1976; May 6, 1977; April 24, 1978; April 12, 1989; August 17, 1990). ... Struck out 19 batters in one game (June 14, August 12 and August 20, 1974; June 8, 1977). ... Pitched 4-0 no-hit victory against Minnesota (September 28, 1974). ... Pitched 1-0 no-hit victory against Baltimore (June 1, 1975). ... Struck out 18 batters in one game (September 10, 1976). ... Pitched 7-0 one-hit, complete-game victory against Seattle (April 15, 1977). ... Pitched 5-0 one-hit, complete-game victory against Cleveland (May 5, 1978). ... Pitched 6-1 one-hit, complete-game victory against New York (July 13, 1979). ... Pitched 5-0 no-hit victory against Los Angeles (September 26, 1981). ... Pitched 3-0 one-hit, complete-game victory against San Diego (August 11, 1982). ... Pitched 1-0 one-hit, complete-game victory against San Diego (August 3, 1983). ... Led N.L. with 16 wild pitches in 1981 and 15 in 1986. ... Led N.L. with eight hit batsmen in 1982. ... Tied for N.L. lead with 14 sacrifice hits in 1985. ... Pitched 4-1 one-hit, complete-game victory against Toronto (April 23, 1989).

... Pitched 6-1 one-hit, complete-game victory against Seattle (June 3, 1989). ... Pitched 1-0 one-hit, complete-game victory against Chicago (April 26, 1990). ... Pitched 5-0 no-hit victory against Oakland (June 11, 1990). ... Pitched 3-0 no-hit victory against Toronto (May 1, 1991).
MISCELLANEOUS: Holds California Angels all-time record for most strikeouts (2,416).

Year	Team (League)	W	L	Pct.	ERA	G	GS	CG	ShO	Sv.	IP	H	R	ER	BB	SO
1965—	Marion (Appal.)	3	6	.333	4.38	13	12	2	1	0	78	61	47	38	56	115
1966—	Greenville (W. Caro.)	*17	2	.895	2.51	29	*28	9	5	0	183	109	59	51	*127	*272
	— Williamsport (Eastern)	0	2	.000	0.95	3	3	0	0	0	19	9	6	2	12	35
	— New York (N.L.)	0	1	.000	15.00	2	1	0	0	0	3	5	5	5	3	6
1967—	Winter Haven (FSL)	0	0	...	2.25	1	1	0	0	0	4	1	1	1	2	5
	— Jacksonville (Int'l)	1	0	1.000	0.00	3	0	0	0	0	7	3	1	0	3	18
1968—	New York (N.L.)..................	6	9	.400	3.09	21	18	3	0	0	134	93	50	46	75	133
1969—	New York (N.L.)..................	6	3	.667	3.54	25	10	2	0	1	89	60	38	35	53	92
1970—	New York (N.L.)..................	7	11	.389	3.41	27	19	5	2	1	132	86	59	50	97	125
1971—	New York (N.L.)..................	10	14	.417	3.97	30	26	3	0	0	152	125	78	67	116	137
1972—	California (A.L.)■..............	19	16	.543	2.28	39	39	20	*9	0	284	166	80	72	*157	*329
1973—	California (A.L.)..................	21	16	.568	2.87	41	39	26	4	1	326	238	113	104	*162	*383
1974—	California (A.L.)..................	22	16	.579	2.89	42	41	26	3	0	*333	221	127	107	*202	*367
1975—	California (A.L.)..................	14	12	.538	3.45	28	28	10	5	0	198	152	90	76	132	186
1976—	California (A.L.)..................	17	*18	.486	3.36	39	39	21	*7	0	284	193	117	106	*183	*327
1977—	California (A.L.)..................	19	16	.543	2.77	37	37	•22	4	0	299	198	110	92	*204	*341
1978—	California (A.L.)..................	10	13	.435	3.71	31	31	14	3	0	235	183	106	97	*148	*260
1979—	California (A.L.)..................	16	14	.533	3.59	34	34	17	•5	0	223	169	104	89	114	*223
1980—	Houston (N.L.)■..............	11	10	.524	3.35	35	35	4	2	0	234	205	100	87	*98	200
1981—	Houston (N.L.)	11	5	.688	*1.69	21	21	5	3	0	149	99	34	28	68	140
1982—	Houston (N.L.)	16	12	.571	3.16	35	35	10	3	0	250 1/3	196	100	88	*109	245
1983—	Houston (N.L.)	14	9	.609	2.98	29	29	5	2	0	196 1/3	134	74	65	101	183
1984—	Houston (N.L.)	12	11	.522	3.04	30	30	5	2	0	183 2/3	143	78	62	69	197
1985—	Houston (N.L.)	10	12	.455	3.80	35	35	4	0	0	232	205	108	98	95	209
1986—	Houston (N.L.)	12	8	.600	3.34	30	30	1	0	0	178	119	72	66	82	194
1987—	Houston (N.L.)	8	16	.333	*2.76	34	34	0	0	0	211 2/3	154	75	65	87	*270
1988—	Houston (N.L.)	12	11	.522	3.52	33	33	4	1	0	220	186	98	86	87	*228
1989—	Texas (A.L.)■..............	16	10	.615	3.20	32	32	6	2	0	239 1/3	162	96	85	98	*301
1990—	Texas (A.L.)	13	9	.591	3.44	30	30	5	2	0	204	137	86	78	74	*232
1991—	Texas (A.L.)	12	6	.667	2.91	27	27	2	2	0	173	102	58	56	72	203
1992—	Texas (A.L.)	5	9	.357	3.72	27	27	2	0	0	157 1/3	138	75	65	69	157
1993—	Texas (A.L.)	5	5	.500	4.88	13	13	0	0	0	66 1/3	54	47	36	40	46
A.L. totals (13 years)		189	160	.542	3.17	420	417	171	46	1	3022	2113	1209	1063	1655	3355
N.L. totals (14 years)		135	132	.506	3.23	387	356	51	15	2	2365	1810	969	848	1140	2359
Major league totals (27 years)		324	292	.526	3.19	807	773	222	61	3	5387	3923	2178	1911	2795	5714

DIVISION SERIES RECORD

Year	Team (League)	W	L	Pct.	ERA	G	GS	CG	ShO	Sv.	IP	H	R	ER	BB	SO
1981—	Houston (N.L.)	1	1	.500	1.80	2	2	1	0	0	15	6	4	3	3	14

CHAMPIONSHIP SERIES RECORD

RECORDS: Holds A.L. single-game record for most consecutive strikeouts from start of game—4 (October 3, 1979).

Year	Team (League)	W	L	Pct.	ERA	G	GS	CG	ShO	Sv.	IP	H	R	ER	BB	SO
1969—	New York (N.L.)..................	1	0	1.000	2.57	1	0	0	0	0	7	3	2	2	2	7
1979—	California (A.L.)..................	0	0	...	1.29	1	1	0	0	0	7	4	3	1	3	8
1980—	Houston (N.L.)	0	0	...	5.40	2	0	0	0	0	13 1/3	16	8	8	3	14
1986—	Houston (N.L.)	0	1	.000	3.86	2	2	0	0	0	14	9	6	6	1	17
Champ. series totals (4 years)		1	1	.500	3.70	6	5	0	0	0	41 1/3	32	19	17	9	46

WORLD SERIES RECORD

Year	Team (League)	W	L	Pct.	ERA	G	GS	CG	ShO	Sv.	IP	H	R	ER	BB	SO
1969—	New York (N.L.)..................	0	0	...	0.00	1	0	0	0	1	2 1/3	1	0	0	2	3

ALL-STAR GAME RECORD

NOTES: Named to A.L. All-Star team to replace Frank Tanana for 1977 game; declined.

Year	League	W	L	Pct.	ERA	GS	CG	ShO	Sv.	IP	H	R	ER	BB	SO
1972—	American						Did not play.								
1973—	American	0	0	...	9.00	0	0	0	0	2	2	2	2	2	2
1975—	American						Did not play.								
1977—	American					Selected, did not play—declined.									
1979—	American	0	0	...	13.50	1	0	0	0	2	5	3	3	1	2
1981—	National	0	0	...	0.00	0	0	0	0	1	0	0	0	0	1
1985—	National	0	0	...	0.00	0	0	0	0	3	2	0	0	2	2
1989—	American	1	0	1.000	0.00	0	0	0	0	2	1	0	0	0	3
All-Star totals (5 years)		1	0	1.000	4.50	1	0	0	0	10	10	5	5	5	10

YOUNT, ROBIN   SS/OF

PERSONAL: Born September 16, 1955, in Danville, Ill. ... 6-0/180. ... Batted right, threw right. ... Full name: Robin R. Yount. ... Brother of Larry Yount, pitcher with Houston Astros (1971).
HIGH SCHOOL: Taft (Woodland Hills, Calif.).
TRANSACTIONS/CAREER NOTES: Selected by Milwaukee Brewers organization in first round (third pick overall) of free-agent draft (June 5, 1973). ... On disabled list (March 28-May 3, 1989). ... Granted free agency (November 13, 1989). ... Re-signed by Brewers (December 19, 1989). ... On disabled list (July 6-30, 1991). ... Granted free agency (November 8, 1992). ... Re-signed by Brewers (January 7, 1993). ... On disabled list (April 27-May 14, 1993). ... Granted free agency (November 4, 1993). ... Placed on voluntarily retired list (February 11, 1994).
RECORDS: Holds A.L. career record for most sacrifice flies—123.

HONORS: Named shortstop on THE SPORTING NEWS A.L. All-Star team (1978,1980 and 1982). ... Named shortstop on THE SPORTING NEWS A.L. Silver Slugger team (1980 and 1982). ... Named Major League Player of the Year by THE SPORTING NEWS (1982). ... Named A.L. Player of the Year by THE SPORTING NEWS (1982). ... Won A.L. Gold Glove at shortstop (1982). ... Named A.L. Most Valuable Player by Baseball Writers' Association of America (1982 and 1989). ... Named outfielder on THE SPORTING NEWS A.L. All-Star team (1989). ... Named outfielder on THE SPORTING NEWS A.L. Silver Slugger team (1989).

STATISTICAL NOTES: Led A.L. shortstops with 831 total chances and 104 double plays and tied for lead with 290 putouts in 1976. ... Led A.L. with 367 total bases and .578 slugging percentage in 1982. ... Led A.L. outfielders with .997 fielding percentage in 1986. ... Hit for the cycle (June 12, 1988). ... Career major league grand slams: 3.

MISCELLANEOUS: Holds Milwaukee Brewers all-time records for most runs (1,632), hits (3,142), doubles (583), triples (126), home runs (251) and runs batted in (1,406).

								BATTING						FIELDING			
Year	Team (League)	Pos.	G	AB	R	H	2B	3B	HR	RBI	Avg.	BB	SO	SB	PO	A	E	Avg.
1973—Newark (NY-Penn)	SS	64	242	29	69	15	3	3	25	.285	31	26	8	43	85	18	.877
1974—Milwaukee (A.L.)	SS	107	344	48	86	14	5	3	26	.250	12	46	7	148	327	19	.962
1975—Milwaukee (A.L.)	SS	147	558	67	149	28	2	8	52	.267	33	69	12	273	402	*44	.939
1976—Milwaukee (A.L.)	SS-OF	•161	638	59	161	19	3	2	54	.252	38	69	16	‡290	510	31	.963
1977—Milwaukee (A.L.)	SS	154	605	66	174	34	4	4	49	.288	41	80	16	256	449	29	.960
1978—Milwaukee (A.L.)	SS	127	502	66	147	23	9	9	71	.293	24	43	16	246	453	30	.959
1979—Milwaukee (A.L.)	SS	149	577	72	154	26	5	8	51	.267	35	52	11	267	517	25	.969
1980—Milwaukee (A.L.)	SS-DH	143	611	121	179	*49	10	23	87	.293	26	67	20	239	455	28	.961
1981—Milwaukee (A.L.)	SS-DH	96	377	50	103	15	5	10	49	.273	22	37	4	161	370	8	*.985
1982—Milwaukee (A.L.)	SS-DH	156	635	129	*210	•46	12	29	114	.331	54	63	14	253	*489	24	.969
1983—Milwaukee (A.L.)	SS-DH	149	578	102	178	42	*10	17	80	.308	72	58	12	256	420	19	.973
1984—Milwaukee (A.L.)	SS-DH	160	624	105	186	27	7	16	80	.298	67	67	14	199	402	18	.971
1985—Milwaukee (A.L.)	OF-DH-1B	122	466	76	129	26	3	15	68	.277	49	56	10	267	5	8	.971
1986—Milwaukee (A.L.)	OF-DH-1B	140	522	82	163	31	7	9	46	.312	62	73	14	365	9	2	†.995
1987—Milwaukee (A.L.)	OF-DH	158	635	99	198	25	9	21	103	.312	76	94	19	380	5	5	.987
1988—Milwaukee (A.L.)	OF-DH	*162	621	92	190	38	•11	13	91	.306	63	63	22	444	12	2	.996
1989—Milwaukee (A.L.)	OF-DH	160	614	101	195	38	9	21	103	.318	63	71	19	361	8	7	.981
1990—Milwaukee (A.L.)	OF-DH	158	587	98	145	17	5	17	77	.247	78	89	15	*422	3	4	.991
1991—Milwaukee (A.L.)	OF-DH	130	503	66	131	20	4	10	77	.260	54	79	6	315	1	2	.994
1992—Milwaukee (A.L.)	OF-DH	150	557	71	147	40	3	8	77	.264	53	81	15	371	6	2	.995
1993—Milwaukee (A.L.)	OF-1B-DH	127	454	62	117	25	3	8	51	.258	44	93	9	342	7	1	.997
Major league totals (20 years)		2856	11008	1632	3142	583	126	251	1406	.285	966	1350	271	5855	4850	308	.972

DIVISION SERIES RECORD

RECORDS: Shares career record for most triples—1.

								BATTING						FIELDING			
Year	Team (League)	Pos.	G	AB	R	H	2B	3B	HR	RBI	Avg.	BB	SO	SB	PO	A	E	Avg.
1981—Milwaukee (A.L.)	SS	5	19	4	6	0	1	0	1	.316	2	2	1	6	16	1	.957

CHAMPIONSHIP SERIES RECORD

								BATTING						FIELDING			
Year	Team (League)	Pos.	G	AB	R	H	2B	3B	HR	RBI	Avg.	BB	SO	SB	PO	A	E	Avg.
1982—Milwaukee (A.L.)	SS	5	16	1	4	0	0	0	0	.250	5	0	0	11	12	1	.958

WORLD SERIES RECORD

RECORDS: Shares single-game record for most at-bats (nine-inning game)—6 (October 12, 1982).

								BATTING						FIELDING			
Year	Team (League)	Pos.	G	AB	R	H	2B	3B	HR	RBI	Avg.	BB	SO	SB	PO	A	E	Avg.
1982—Milwaukee (A.L.)	SS	7	29	6	12	3	0	1	6	.414	2	2	0	20	19	3	.929

ALL-STAR GAME RECORD

							BATTING						FIELDING			
Year	League	Pos.	AB	R	H	2B	3B	HR	RBI	Avg.	BB	SO	SB	PO	A	E	Avg.
1980—American	SS	2	0	0	0	0	0	0	.000	0	0	0	3	2	0	1.000
1982—American	SS	3	0	0	0	0	0	0	.000	0	1	0	0	2	0	1.000
1983—American	SS	2	1	0	0	0	0	1	.000	1	1	0	0	1	0	1.000
All-Star Game totals (3 years)		7	1	0	0	0	0	1	.000	1	2	0	3	5	0	1.000

1998 STATISTICAL LEADERS

AMERICAN LEAGUE

BATTING

BATTING AVERAGE

.339 Bernie Williams, N.Y.
.337 Mo Vaughn, Bos.
.328 Albert Belle, Chi.
.327 Eric Davis, Bal.
.324 Derek Jeter, N.Y.

ON-BASE AVERAGE

.429 Edgar Martinez, Sea.
.422 Bernie Williams, N.Y.
.413 Jim Thome, Cle.
.410 Tim Salmon, Ana.
.403 Jose Offerman, K.C.

SLUGGING AVERAGE

.655 Albert Belle, Chi.
.630 Juan Gonzalez, Tex.
.611 Ken Griffey Jr., Sea.
.599 Manny Ramirez, Cle.
.592 Carlos Delgado, Tor.

HOME RUNS

56 Ken Griffey Jr., Sea.
49 Albert Belle, Chi.
46 Jose Canseco, Tor.
45 Juan Gonzalez, Tex.
45 Manny Ramirez, Cle.

RBIs

157 Juan Gonzalez, Tex.
152 Albert Belle, Chi.
146 Ken Griffey Jr., Sea.
145 Manny Ramirez, Cle.
124 Alex Rodriguez, Sea.

RUNS

127 Derek Jeter, N.Y.
126 Ray Durham, Chi.
123 Alex Rodriguez, Sea.
120 Ken Griffey Jr., Sea.
117 Chuck Knoblauch, N.Y.

HITS

213 Alex Rodriguez, Sea.
205 Mo Vaughn, Bos.
203 Derek Jeter, N.Y.
200 Albert Belle, Chi.
195 N. Garciaparra, Bos.

TOTAL BASES

399 Albert Belle, Chi.
387 Ken Griffey Jr., Sea.
384 Alex Rodriguez, Sea.
382 Juan Gonzalez, Tex.
360 Mo Vaughn, Bos.

STOLEN BASES

66 R. Henderson, Oak.
54 Kenny Lofton, Cle.
51 Shannon Stewart, Tor.
46 Alex Rodriguez, Sea.
45 Jose Offerman, K.C.

DOUBLES

50 Juan Gonzalez, Tex.
48 Albert Belle, Chi.
46 Edgar Martinez, Sea.
44 John Valentin, Bos.
43 Carlos Delgado, Tor.

TRIPLES

13 Jose Offerman, K.C.
10 Johnny Damon, K.C.
9 Randy Winn, T.B.
8 Ray Durham, Chi.
8 N. Garciaparra, Bos.
8 Derek Jeter, N.Y.
8 Troy O'Leary, Bos.

PITCHING

VICTORIES

20 Roger Clemens, Tor.
20 David Cone, N.Y.
20 Rick Helling, Tex.
19 Pedro Martinez, Bos.
19 Aaron Sele, Tex.

EARNED RUN AVERAGE

2.65 Roger Clemens, Tor.
2.89 Pedro Martinez, Bos.
3.17 Kenny Rogers, Oak.
3.39 Chuck Finley, Ana.
3.49 David Wells, N.Y.
3.49 Mike Mussina, Bal.

SAVES

46 Tom Gordon, Bos.
42 Troy Percival, Ana.
42 John Wetteland, Tex.
40 Mike Jackson, Cle.
38 Rick Aguilera, Min.

STRIKEOUTS

271 Roger Clemens, Tor.
251 Pedro Martinez, Bos.
213 Randy Johnson, Sea.
212 Chuck Finley, Ana.
209 David Cone, N.Y.

OPPONENTS BATTING AVERAGE

.198 Roger Clemens, Tor.
.217 Pedro Martinez, Bos.

.233 Hideki Irabu, N.Y.
.237 David Cone, N.Y.
.239 David Wells, N.Y.

GAMES

88 Sean Runyan, Det.
82 Paul Quantrill, Tor.
81 G. Swindell, Min.-Bos.
79 Eddie Guardado, Min.
78 Dan Plesac, Tor.

INNINGS PITCHED

251⅓ Scott Erickson, Bal.
238⅔ Kenny Rogers, Oak.
234⅔ Roger Clemens, Tor.
234⅓ Jamie Moyer, Sea.
234 Tim Belcher, K.C.

COMPLETE GAMES

11 Scott Erickson, Bal.
8 David Wells, N.Y.
7 Jeff Fassero, Sea.
7 Kenny Rogers, Oak.
6 Bartolo Colon, Cle.
6 Randy Johnson, Sea.

SHUTOUTS

5 David Wells, N.Y.
3 Roger Clemens, Tor.
3 Brian Moehler, Det.
3 Jamie Moyer, Sea.
2 Eight pitchers tied.

WINNING PERCENTAGE
(15 decisions)

.818 David Wells, N.Y.
.769 Roger Clemens, Tor.
.750 O. Hernandez, N.Y.
.741 David Cone, N.Y.
.741 Rick Helling, Tex.

STATISTICAL LEADERS

STATISTICAL LEADERS

BATTING

BATTING AVERAGE
.363 Larry Walker, Col.
.354 John Olerud, N.Y.
.331 Dante Bichette, Col.
.328 M. Piazza, L.A.-Fla.-N.Y.
.327 Jason Kendall, Pit.

ON-BASE AVERAGE
.470 Mark McGwire, Stl.
.447 John Olerud, N.Y.
.445 Larry Walker, Col.
.438 Barry Bonds, S.F.
.428 G. Sheffield, Fla.-L.A.

SLUGGING AVERAGE
.752 Mark McGwire, Stl.
.647 Sammy Sosa, Chi.
.630 Larry Walker, Col.
.609 Barry Bonds, S.F.
.597 Greg Vaughn, S.D.

HOME RUNS
70 Mark McGwire, Stl.
66 Sammy Sosa, Chi.
50 Greg Vaughn, S.D.
46 Vinny Castilla, Col.
44 Andres Galarraga, Atl.

RBIs
158 Sammy Sosa, Chi.
147 Mark McGwire, Stl.
144 Vinny Castilla, Col.
128 Jeff Kent, S.F.
125 Jeromy Burnitz, Mil.

RUNS
134 Sammy Sosa, Chi.
130 Mark McGwire, Stl.
124 Jeff Bagwell, Hou.
123 Craig Biggio, Hou.
123 Chipper Jones, Atl.

HITS
219 Dante Bichette, Col.
210 Craig Biggio, Hou.
206 Vinny Castilla, Col.
202 V. Guerrero, Mon.
198 Derek Bell, Hou.
198 Sammy Sosa, Chi.
198 Fernando Vina, Mil.

TOTAL BASES
416 Sammy Sosa, Chi.
383 Mark McGwire, Stl.
380 Vinny Castilla, Col.
367 V. Guerrero, Mon.
342 Greg Vaughn, S.D.

STOLEN BASES
58 Tony Womack, Pit.
50 Craig Biggio, Hou.
42 Eric Young, Hou.
41 Edgar Renteria, Fla.
28 Barry Bonds, S.F.

DOUBLES
51 Craig Biggio, Hou.
48 Dante Bichette, Col.
48 Dmitri Young, Cin.
46 Larry Walker, Col.
45 Cliff Floyd, Fla.
45 Scott Rolen, Phil.

TRIPLES
12 David Dellucci, Ariz.
10 Barry Larkin, Cin.
9 Wilton Guerrero, L.A.
9 Neifi Perez, Col.
8 Delino DeShields, Stl.
8 Karim Garcia, Ariz.
8 Andruw Jones, Atl.

PITCHING

VICTORIES
20 Tom Glavine, Atl.
19 S. Reynolds, Hou.
19 Kevin Tapani, Chi.
18 Kevin Brown, S.D.
18 Greg Maddux, Atl.

EARNED RUN AVERAGE
2.22 Greg Maddux, Atl.
2.38 Kevin Brown, S.D.
2.47 Al Leiter, N.Y.
2.47 Tom Glavine, Atl.
2.88 Omar Daal, Ariz.

SAVES
53 Trevor Hoffman, S.D.
51 Rod Beck, Chi.
48 Jeff Shaw, Cin.-L.A.
40 Robb Nen, S.F.
38 John Franco, N.Y.

STRIKEOUTS
300 Curt Schilling, Phil.
257 Kevin Brown, S.D.
233 Kerry Wood, Chi.
209 Shane Reynolds, Hou.
204 Greg Maddux, Atl.

OPPONENTS BATTING AVERAGE
.196 Kerry Wood, Chi.
.216 Al Leiter, N.Y.
.220 Greg Maddux, Atl.
.228 Pete Harnisch, Cin.
.231 John Smoltz, Atl.

GAMES
81 Rod Beck, Chi.
78 Steve Kline, Mon.
78 Chuck McElroy, Col.
78 Robb Nen, S.F.
77 Anthony Telford, Mon.

INNINGS PITCHED
268 ⅔ Curt Schilling, Phil.
257 Kevin Brown, S.D.
251 Greg Maddux, Atl.
241 C. Perez, Mon.-L.A.
234 ⅓ L. Hernandez, Fla.

COMPLETE GAMES
15 Curt Schilling, Phil.
9 Livan Hernandez, Fla.
9 Greg Maddux, Atl.
7 Kevin Brown, S.D.
7 C. Perez, Mon.-L.A.

SHUTOUTS
5 Greg Maddux, Atl.
4 Randy Johnson, Hou.
3 Kevin Brown, S.D.
3 Tom Glavine, Atl.
2 Nine pitchers tied

WINNING PERCENTAGE
(15 decisions)
.850 John Smoltz, Atl.
.769 Tom Glavine, Atl.
.739 Al Leiter, N.Y.
.720 Kevin Brown, S.D.
.704 S. Reynolds, Hou.

DOUBLE HEADER
2 for the price of one

It's the best double header of the season

If you and a friend sign up for The Sporting News Fantasy Baseball Challenge before March 1, both of you play for $39.95. That's 2 for the price of 1, a savings of 50% off the regular registration price. And what makes this 2 for 1 offer even better, is that it's now easier to create your own league with 24 of your friends. So call them up. You'll battle head to head each week, and when it's all over, you'll have something to brag about all winter. Oh yeah, you could walk away with the $25,000 grand prize.

Play now for only $39.95*!

*If registered by March 1, 1999

You know you're going to play, so sign up now and save

CALL 1-800-789-8980

ask for Chris or visit us at

games.sportingnews.com.mlb

Customer Service Hours: M-S 8 am - 10 pm CST

Baseball's Legendary Players...

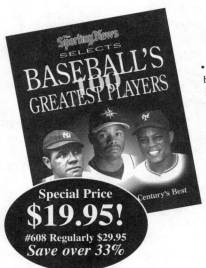

The Sporting News Selects
Baseball's 100 Greatest Players

Foreword by Willie Mays

- A subjective and provocative ranking from 1 to 100 of the best players. Mantle... McGwire... Ruth... Ryan... Feller... Fingers. They're all here, along with 94 others, captured in vintage photographs doing what put them among baseball's greats. Feel the speed of Jackie Robinson, the power of Hank Aaron, the finesse of Ozzie Smith.
  - Large 9" x 11¼" size, hardbound with dust jacket.
  - 224 pages with over 300 beautiful color and historic black and white photos.

" ... guaranteed to help propel the game's great debates in to the next milennium."
—Newsweek, October 19, 1998

Special Price
$19.95!
#608 Regularly $29.95
Save over 33%

...And a Legendary Season

Celebrating 70:
Mark McGwire's Historic Season

Foreword by Hall of Fame broadcaster Jack Buck

- Relive, remember and celebrate the power of baseball's new single-season home run king. Accounts of every home run, from No. 1 to No. 70.
- Exclusive arrangement between The Sporting News and the St. Louis Post-Dispatch.
- Large 9" x 11¼" size, hardbound with dust jacket.
- 184 pages with over 200 exclusive color photographs, including game action, home run celebrations and the duel with Sammy Sosa.

Special Price
$21.95!
#621 Regularly $29.95
Save over 25%

For Fastest Service Call Now to Order Toll Free
1-800-825-8508 Dept. RG9